BASEBALL REGISTER

2001 EDITION

D1541968

Editors/Baseball Register
JEFF PAUR
DAVID WALTON

Contributing Editor/Baseball Register
JOHN DUXBURY

Copyright ©2001 by The Sporting News, a division of Vulcan Print Media, Inc.,
10176 Corporate Square Drive, Suite 200, St. Louis, MO 63132-2924. All rights reserved. Printed in the U.S.A.

ISBN: 0-89204-645-7

10 9 8 7 6 5 4 3 2 1

CONTENTS

EXPLANATION OF FOOTNOTES AND ABBREVIATIONS

Note for statistical comparisons: Player strikes forced the cancellation of games in the 1972 season (10 days missed), the 1981 season (50 days missed), the 1994 season (52 days missed) and the 1995 season (18 games missed).

Positions are listed in descending order of games played; because of limited space, pinch-hitter and pinch-runner are listed in the regular-season section only if a player did not play a defensive position.

*   Led league. For fielding statistics, the player led the league at the position shown.

•   Tied for league lead. For fielding statistics, the player tied for the league lead at the position shown.

†   Led league, but number indicated is total figure for two or more positions. Actual league-leading figure for a position is mentioned in "Statistical Notes" section.

‡   Tied for league lead, but number indicated is total figure for two or more positions. Actual league-tying figure for a position is mentioned in "Statistical Notes" section.

§   Led or tied for league lead, but total figure is divided between two different teams. Actual league-leading or league-tying figure is mentioned in "Statistical Notes" section.

■   Indicates a player's movement from one major league organization to another major league organization or to an independent minor league organization.

. . .   Statistic unavailable, inapplicable, unofficial or mathematically impossible to calculate.

—   Manager statistic inapplicable.

LEAGUES: A.A., Am. Assoc.—American Association. **A.L.**—American. **App., Appal.**—Appalachian. **Ar., Ariz.**—Arizona. **Cal., Calif.**—California. **Car., Caro.**—Carolina. **CRL**—Cocoa Rookie. **DSL**—Dominican Summer. **East.**—Eastern. **Evan.**—Evangeline. **Fla. St., Florida St.**, **FSL**—Florida State. **GCL**—Gulf Coast. **GSL**—Gulf States. **In.-Am.**—Inter-American. **Int'l.**—International. **J.P., Jap. Pac., Jp. Pac.**—Japan Pacific. **Jp. Cen., Jp. Cn.**—Japan Central. **Mex.**—Mexican. **Mex. Cen.**—Mexican Center. **Mid., Midw.**—Midwest. **Miss.-O.V.**—Mississippi-Ohio Valley. **N.C. St.**—North Carolina State. **N.L.**—National. **North.**—Northern. **N'west**—Northwest. **NYP, NY-Penn**—New York-Pennsylvania. **Pac. Coast, PCL**—Pacific Coast. **Pio.**—Pioneer. **S. Atl., SAL**—South Atlantic. **Soph.**—Sophomore. **Sou., South.**—Southern. **Taiw.**—Taiwan. **Tex.**—Texas. **W. Car., W. Caro.**—Western Carolinas.

TEAMS: Aguas.—Aguascalientes. **Alb./Colon.**—Albany/Colonie. **Ariz.**—Arizona. **Ariz. D-backs**—Arizona League Diamondbacks. **Belling.**—Bellingham. **Birm.**—Birmingham. **Brevard Co.**—Brevard County. **Cant./Akr.**—Canton/Akron. **Ced. Rap.**—Cedar Rapids. **Cent. Ore.**—Central Oregon. **Central Vall.**—Central Valley. **Char., Charl.**—Charleston. **Chatt.**—Chattanooga. **Chiba Lot.**—Chiba Lotte. **Ciu. Juarez**—Ciudad Juarez. **Colo. Spr., Colo. Springs**—Colorado Springs. **Dall./Fort W.**—Dallas/Fort Worth. **Day. Beach.**—Daytona Beach. **Dm., Dom.**—Dominican. **Dom. B. Jays**—Dominican Blue Jays. **Elizabeth.**—Elizabethton. **Estadio Quis.**—Estadio Quisqueya. **Eve.**—Everett. **Fort Lauder.**—Fort Lauderdale. **Fukuoka**—Fukuoka Daiei. **GC**—Gulf Coast. **GC Astros-Or.**—Gulf Coast Astros-Orange. **GC Royals-Bl.**—Gulf Coast Royals-Blue. **GC Whi. Sox**—Gulf Coast White Sox. **Grays Har.**—Grays Harbor. **Greens.**—Greensboro. **Greenw.**—Greenwood. **Guana.**—Guanajuato. **H.P.-Thomas.**—High Point-Thomasville. **Hunting.**—Huntington. **Jacksonv.**—Jacksonville. **Johns. City**—Johnson City. **Kane Co.**—Kane County. **Lake Charl.**—Lake Charles. **Matt.**—Mattoon. **M.C., Mex. City**—Mexico City. **Med. Hat**—Medicine Hat. **Monc.**—Monclova. **Niag. F., Niag. Falls**—Niagara Falls. **Okla. City**—Oklahoma City. **Pan. City**—Panama City. **Phoe.**—Phoenix. **Pomp. Beach.**—Pompano Beach. **Pres. Lions**—President Lions. **Prin. Will., Prin. William**—Prince William. **Ral./Dur.**—Raleigh/Durham. **Rancho Cuca.**—Rancho Cucamonga. **Rocky Mount.**—Rocky Mountain. **Salt.**—Saltillo. **San. Dom., San. Domingo**—Santo Domingo. **San Bern.**—San Bernardino. **San Fran.**—San Francisco. **Schen.**—Schenectady. **Scran./W.B.**—Scranton/Wilkes-Barre. **S.C.**—South Carolina. **S.F. de Mac.**—San Francisco de Macoris. **San Luis Pot.**—San Luis Potosi. **S. Oregon**—Southern Oregon. **Spartan.**—Spartanburg. **St. Cath., St. Cathar.**—St. Catharines. **St. Peters.**—St. Petersburg. **States.**—Statesville. **Stock.**—Stockton. **T.-C.**—Tri-Cities. **Vanc.**—Vancouver. **Vent. Co.**—Ventura County. **W. Mich.**—West Michigan. **Win.-Salem, Winst.-Salem**—Winston-Salem. **Wis. Rap., Wis. Rapids**—Wisconsin Rapids. **W.P. Beach**—West Palm Beach. **W.Va.**—West Virginia. **Yuc.**—Yucatan.

STATISTICS: A—assists. **AB**—at-bats. **Avg.**—average. **BB**—bases on balls. **CG**—complete games. **E**—errors. **ER**—earned runs. **ERA**—earned-run average. **G**—games. **GIDP**—grounded into double plays. **GS**—games started. **H**—hits. **HR**—home runs. **IP**—innings pitched. **L**—losses. **Pct.**—winning percentage. **PO**—putouts. **Pos.**—position. **R**—runs. **RBI**—runs batted in. **SB**—stolen bases. **ShO**—shutouts. **SO**—strikeouts. **Sv.**—saves. **W**—wins. **2B**—doubles. **3B**—triples.

PLAYERS

ABBOTT, JEFF — OF — MARLINS

PERSONAL: Born August 17, 1972, in Atlanta. ... 6-2/200. ... Bats right, throws left. ... Full name: Jeffrey William Abbott.
HIGH SCHOOL: Dunwoody (Ga.).
COLLEGE: Kentucky.
TRANSACTIONS/CAREER NOTES: Selected by Chicago White Sox organization in 32nd round of free-agent draft (June 3, 1993); did not sign. ... Selected by White Sox organization in fourth round of free-agent draft (June 2, 1994). ... On Charlotte disabled list (May 30-June 28 and August 1-10, 1999). ... Traded by White Sox to Florida Marlins for OF Julio Ramirez (December 10, 2000).

Year Team (League)	Pos.	G	AB	R	H	2B	3B	HR	RBI	Avg.	BB	SO	SB	PO	A	E	Avg.
1994—Sarasota (GCL)..........	OF	4	15	4	7	1	0	1	3	.467	4	0	2	4	0	0	1.000
—Hickory (S.Atl.)..........	OF	63	224	47	88	16	6	6	48	.393	38	33	2	106	0	2	.981
1995—Prince William (Caro.)	OF	70	264	41	92	16	0	4	47	.348	26	25	7	88	3	4	.958
—Birmingham (Sou.).....	OF	55	197	25	63	11	1	3	28	.320	19	20	1	55	1	2	.966
1996—Nashville (A.A.)	OF-DH	113	440	64	143	27	1	14	60	.325	32	50	12	186	5	2	.990
1997—Nashville (A.A.)	OF-DH	118	465	*88	152	35	3	11	63	.327	41	52	12	237	6	0	*1.000
—Chicago (A.L.)	OF-DH	19	38	8	10	1	0	1	2	.263	0	6	0	15	0	0	1.000
1998—Chicago (A.L.)	OF-DH	89	244	33	68	14	1	12	41	.279	9	28	3	132	0	4	.971
1999—Chicago (A.L.)	OF	17	57	5	9	0	0	2	6	.158	5	12	1	25	0	1	.962
—Charlotte (I.L.)	OF	67	277	42	88	24	1	9	37	.318	16	27	2	136	4	3	.979
2000—Chicago (A.L.)	OF-DH	80	215	31	59	15	1	3	29	.274	21	38	2	101	2	2	.981
Major League totals (4 years)		205	554	77	146	30	2	18	78	.264	35	84	6	273	2	7	.975

DIVISION SERIES RECORD

Year Team (League)	Pos.	G	AB	R	H	2B	3B	HR	RBI	Avg.	BB	SO	SB	PO	A	E	Avg.
2000—Chicago (A.L.)	PH-OF	1	1	0	0	0	0	0	0	.000	0	0	0	1	0	0	1.000

ABBOTT, KURT — IF — BRAVES

PERSONAL: Born June 2, 1969, in Zanesville, Ohio. ... 6-0/200. ... Bats right, throws right. ... Full name: Kurt Thomas Abbott.
HIGH SCHOOL: Dixie Hollins (St. Petersburg, Fla.).
JUNIOR COLLEGE: St. Petersburg (Fla.) Junior College.
TRANSACTIONS/CAREER NOTES: Selected by Oakland Athletics organization in 15th round of free-agent draft (June 5, 1989). ... On Modesto disabled list (May 26-June 6, 1991). ... Traded by A's to Florida Marlins for OF Kerwin Moore (December 20, 1993). ... On Florida disabled list (April 19-May 6, 1995); included rehabilitation assignment to Charlotte (April 30-May 6). ... On Florida disabled list (May 6-21, 1996); included rehabilitation assignment to Charlotte (May 16-20). ... Traded by Marlins to A's for P Eric Ludwick (December 19, 1997). ... On Oakland disabled list (March 22-April 16, 1998); included rehabilitation assignment to Edmonton (April 7-16). ... Traded by A's to Colorado Rockies for a player to be named later and cash (June 9, 1998); A's acquired P Ara Petrosian to complete deal (June 16, 1998). ... On disabled list (May 23-June 7 and July 23-August 7, 1999). ... Granted free agency (November 1, 1999). ... Signed by New York Mets organization (January 26, 2000). ... On New York disabled list (July 3-27, 2000); included rehabilitation assignment to Norfolk (July 25-27). ... Granted free agency (November 3, 2000). ... Signed by Atlanta Braves organization (December 13, 2000).
STATISTICAL NOTES: Led Arizona League shortstops with .922 fielding percentage in 1989. ... Led Southern League shortstops with 87 double plays in 1992. ... Career major league grand slams: 3.

Year Team (League)	Pos.	G	AB	R	H	2B	3B	HR	RBI	Avg.	BB	SO	SB	PO	A	E	Avg.
1989—Ariz. Athletics (Ariz.) ..	SS-2B-3B	36	155	27	42	5	3	0	25	.271	8	40	0	59	90	10	†.937
—S. Oregon (N'West)....	SS	5	10	2	1	0	0	0	1	.100	0	3	1	6	7	1	.929
1990—Madison (Midw.).........	SS-2B-3B	104	362	38	84	18	0	0	28	.232	47	74	21	180	268	40	.918
1991—Modesto (Calif.)	SS	58	216	36	55	8	2	3	25	.255	29	55	6	78	130	9	.959
—Huntsville (Sou.)	SS	53	182	18	46	6	1	0	11	.253	17	39	6	89	164	13	.951
1992—Huntsville (Sou.)	SS	124	452	64	115	14	5	9	52	.254	31	75	16	196	342	29	*.949
—Tacoma (PCL)	SS	11	39	2	6	1	0	0	1	.154	4	9	1	21	32	4	.930
1993—Tacoma (PCL)	SS-DH	133	480	75	153	36	11	12	79	.319	33	123	19	*210	367	30	.951
—Oakland (A.L.)	OF-SS-2B	20	61	11	15	1	0	3	9	.246	3	20	2	36	13	2	.961
1994—Florida (N.L.)■..........	SS	101	345	41	86	17	3	9	33	.249	16	98	3	162	260	15	.966
1995—Charlotte (I.L.)............	SS	5	18	3	5	0	0	1	3	.278	1	3	1	5	15	2	.909
—Florida (N.L.).............	SS	120	420	60	107	18	7	17	60	.255	36	110	4	149	290	19	.959
1996—Florida (N.L.)	SS-3B-2B	109	320	37	81	18	7	8	33	.253	22	99	3	123	205	12	.965
—Charlotte (I.L.)	SS-2B-3B	18	69	20	26	10	1	5	11	.377	7	18	2	31	60	2	.978
1997—Florida (N.L.)..............2-O-S-3-DH	94	252	35	69	18	2	6	30	.274	14	68	3	126	136	8	.970
1998—Edmonton (PCL)■....	SS-DH	7	25	5	10	2	0	2	4	.400	6	8	0	9	13	4	.846
—Oakland (A.L.)...........SS-OF-DH-3B	35	123	17	33	7	1	2	9	.268	10	34	2	46	70	11	.913
—Colorado (N.L.)■......O-2-S-3-DH	42	71	9	18	6	0	3	15	.254	2	19	0	32	24	1	.982
1999—Colorado (N.L......2B-1B-OF-SS	96	286	41	78	17	2	8	41	.273	16	69	3	188	151	4	.988
2000—New York (N.L.)■....SS-2B-3B-OF	79	157	22	34	7	1	6	12	.217	14	51	1	74	105	7	.962
—Norfolk (I.L.)	SS	2	4	1	1	0	0	0	0	.250	0	0	0	1	2	0	1.000
American League totals (2 years)		55	184	28	48	8	1	5	18	.261	13	54	4	82	83	13	.927
National League totals (7 years)		641	1851	245	473	101	22	57	224	.256	120	514	17	854	1171	66	.968
Major League totals (8 years)		696	2035	273	521	109	23	62	242	.256	133	568	21	936	1254	79	.965

DIVISION SERIES RECORD

Year Team (League)	Pos.	G	AB	R	H	2B	3B	HR	RBI	Avg.	BB	SO	SB	PO	A	E	Avg.
1997—Florida (N.L.)	2B-PH	3	8	0	2	0	0	0	0	.250	0	0	0	3	6	0	1.000
2000—New York (N.L.).........	SS	1	2	0	0	0	0	0	0	.000	0	1	0	0	0	0	...
Division series totals (2 years)		4	10	0	2	0	0	0	0	.200	0	1	0	3	6	0	1.000

CHAMPIONSHIP SERIES RECORD

Year	Team (League)	Pos.	G	AB	R	H	2B	3B	HR	RBI	Avg.	BB	SO	SB	PO	A	E	Avg.
1997—	Florida (N.L.)	2B	2	8	0	3	1	0	0	0	.375	0	2	0	4	1	0	1.000
2000—	New York (N.L.)	PR-SS	2	3	0	0	0	0	0	0	.000	0	2	0	1	0	1	.500
Championship series totals (2 years)			4	11	0	3	1	0	0	0	.273	0	4	0	5	1	1	.857

WORLD SERIES RECORD

NOTES: Member of World Series championship team (1997).

Year	Team (League)	Pos.	G	AB	R	H	2B	3B	HR	RBI	Avg.	BB	SO	SB	PO	A	E	Avg.
1997—	Florida (N.L.)	DH-PH	3	3	0	0	0	0	0	0	.000	0	1	0	...	...	...	...
2000—	New York (N.L.)	SS-PH	5	8	0	2	1	0	0	0	.250	1	3	0	3	5	0	1.000
World Series totals (2 years)			8	11	0	2	1	0	0	0	.182	1	4	0	3	5	0	1.000

ABBOTT, PAUL — P — MARINERS

PERSONAL: Born September 15, 1967, in Van Nuys, Calif. ... 6-3/195. ... Throws right, bats right. ... Full name: Paul David Abbott.

HIGH SCHOOL: Sunny Hills (Fullerton, Calif.).

TRANSACTIONS/CAREER NOTES: Selected by Minnesota Twins organization in third round of free-agent draft (June 3, 1985). ... On Minnesota disabled list (March 28-June 5 and August 14-September 1, 1992). ... Released by Twins (March 2, 1993). ... Signed by Cleveland Indians organization (March 27, 1993). ... On Charlotte disabled list (April 8-May 6, 1993). ... Granted free agency (October 15, 1993). ... Signed by Kansas City Royals organization (November 21, 1993). ... On disabled list (March 18-May 25 and June 16-30, 1994). ... Released by Royals (June 30, 1994). ... Signed by Chicago Cubs organization (March 17, 1995). ... Granted free agency (October 16, 1995). ... Signed by San Diego Padres organization (November 29, 1995). ... Granted free agency (October 15, 1996). ... Signed by Seattle Mariners organization (January 10, 1997). ... On Tacoma disabled list (May 23-July 14, 1997). ... On Orlando disabled list (April 2-August 21, 1998; included rehabilitation assignment to Arizona League Mariners (August 19-21). ... Released by Mariners (December 14, 1998). ... Re-signed by Mariners (January 21, 1999). ... On New Haven disabled list (April 9-June 12, 1999).

STATISTICAL NOTES: Pitched 3-0 no-hit victory against Palm Springs (June 26, 1988, seven innings).

Year	League	W	L	Pct.	ERA	G	GS	CG	ShO	Sv.	IP	H	R	ER	BB	SO
1985—	Elizabethton (Appl.)	1	5	.167	6.94	10	10	1	0	0	35	33	32	27	32	34
1986—	Kenosha (Midw.)	6	10	.375	4.50	25	15	1	0	0	98	102	62	49	73	73
1987—	Kenosha (Midw.)	13	6	.684	3.65	26	25	1	0	0	145 1/3	102	76	59	103	138
1988—	Visalia (Calif.)	11	9	.550	4.18	28	•28	4	2	0	172 1/3	141	95	80	*143	*205
1989—	Orlando (Sou.)	9	3	.750	4.37	17	17	1	0	0	90 2/3	71	48	44	48	102
1990—	Portland (PCL)	5	14	.263	4.56	23	23	4	1	0	128 1/3	110	75	65	82	129
	— Minnesota (A.L.)	0	5	.000	5.97	7	7	0	0	0	34 2/3	37	24	23	28	25
1991—	Portland (PCL)	2	3	.400	3.89	8	8	1	1	0	44	44	36	19	19	40
	— Minnesota (A.L.)	3	1	.750	4.75	15	3	0	0	0	47 1/3	38	27	25	36	43
1992—	Portland (PCL)	4	1	.800	2.33	7	7	0	0	0	46 1/3	30	13	12	31	46
	— Minnesota (A.L.)	0	0	...	3.27	6	0	0	0	0	11	12	4	4	5	13
1993—	Canton/Akron (East.)■	4	5	.444	4.06	13	12	1	0	0	75 1/3	72	34	34	28	86
	— Cleveland (A.L.)	0	1	.000	6.38	5	5	0	0	0	18 1/3	19	15	13	11	7
	— Charlotte (I.L.)	0	1	.000	6.63	4	4	0	0	0	19	25	16	14	7	12
1994—	Omaha (A.A.)■	4	1	.800	4.87	15	10	0	0	0	57 1/3	57	32	31	45	48
1995—	Iowa (A.A.)■	7	7	.500	3.67	46	11	0	0	0	115 1/3	104	50	47	64	*127
1996—	Las Vegas (PCL)■	4	2	.667	4.18	28	0	0	0	7	28	27	14	13	12	37
1997—	Tacoma (PCL)■	8	4	.667	4.13	17	14	3	0	0	93 2/3	80	48	43	29	117
	— Arizona Mariners (Ariz.)	0	0	...	0.93	3	3	0	0	0	9 2/3	0	2	1	7	13
1998—	Arizona Mariners (Ariz.)	0	0	...	0.00	1	0	0	0	0	3	1	0	0	0	6
	— Tacoma (PCL)	1	0	1.000	1.20	3	3	0	0	0	15	9	2	2	5	20
	— Seattle (A.L.)	3	1	.750	4.01	4	4	0	0	0	24 2/3	24	11	11	10	22
1999—	Tacoma (PCL)	1	1	.500	6.43	2	2	0	0	0	14	21	11	10	4	10
	— Seattle (A.L.)	6	2	.750	3.10	25	7	0	0	0	72 2/3	50	31	25	32	68
2000—	Seattle (A.L.)	9	7	.563	4.22	35	27	0	0	0	179	164	89	84	80	100
Major League totals (7 years)		21	17	.553	4.29	97	53	0	0	0	387 2/3	344	201	185	202	278

DIVISION SERIES RECORD

Year	League	W	L	Pct.	ERA	G	GS	CG	ShO	Sv.	IP	H	R	ER	BB	SO
2000—	Seattle (A.L.)	1	0	1.000	1.59	1	1	0	0	0	5 2/3	5	2	1	3	1

CHAMPIONSHIP SERIES RECORD

Year	League	W	L	Pct.	ERA	G	GS	CG	ShO	Sv.	IP	H	R	ER	BB	SO
2000—	Seattle (A.L.)	0	1	.000	5.40	1	1	0	0	0	5	3	3	3	3	3

ABERNATHY, BRENT — 2B — DEVIL RAYS

PERSONAL: Born September 23, 1977, in Atlanta. ... 6-1/185. ... Bats right, throws right. ... Full name: Michael Brent Abernathy.

HIGH SCHOOL: Lovett School (Atlanta).

TRANSACTIONS/CAREER NOTES: Selected by Toronto Blue Jays organization in second round of free-agent draft (June 4, 1996); pick received as part of compensation from Florida Marlins for signing of Type B free agent OF Devon White. ... On Syracuse disabled list (June 21-28, 2000). ... Traded by Blue Jays with player to be named later to Tampa Bay Devil Rays for P Steve Trachsel and P Mark Guthrie (July 31, 2000).

STATISTICAL NOTES: Led Florida State League second basemen with 669 total chances in 1999.

MISCELLANEOUS: Member of 2000 U.S. Olympic baseball team.

Year	Team (League)	Pos.	G	AB	R	H	2B	3B	HR	RBI	Avg.	BB	SO	SB	PO	A	E	Avg.
1997—	Hagerstown (S.Atl.)	2B	99	379	69	117	27	2	1	26	.309	30	32	22	178	258	12	.973
1998—	Dunedin (FSL)	2B	124	485	85	169	36	1	3	65	.348	44	38	35	240	338	16	.973
1999—	Knoxville (Sou.)	2B	136	*577	108	*168	42	1	13	62	.291	55	47	34	*292	*361	16	.976
2000—	Syracuse (I.L.)	2B	92	358	47	106	21	2	4	35	.296	36	32	14	146	258	11	.973
	— Durham (I.L.)■	2B	27	91	14	24	6	0	1	15	.264	11	11	9	53	55	3	.973

ABREU, BOBBY   OF   PHILLIES

A

PERSONAL: Born March 11, 1974, in Aragua, Venezuela. ... 6-0/197. ... Bats left, throws right. ... Full name: Bob Kelly Abreu. ... Name pronounced uh-BRAY-yew.

TRANSACTIONS/CAREER NOTES: Signed as non-drafted free agent by Houston Astros organization (August 21, 1990). ... On Houston disabled list (May 25-July 1, 1997); included rehabilitation assignments to Jackson (June 23-26) and New Orleans (June 27-July 1). ... Selected by Tampa Bay Devil Rays in first round (sixth pick overall) of expansion draft (November 18, 1997). ... Traded by Devil Rays to Philadelphia Phillies for SS Kevin Stocker (November 18, 1997).

STATISTICAL NOTES: Led Gulf Coast League outfielders with 11 assists in 1991. ... Led Texas League with .530 slugging percentage in 1994. ... Led Pacific Coast League outfielders with 18 assists in 1995. ... Led Pacific Coast League in caught stealing with 18 in 1996. ... Career major league grand slams: 2.

Year	Team (League)	Pos.	G	AB	R	H	2B	3B	HR	RBI	Avg.	BB	SO	SB	PO	A	E	Avg.
1991—	GC Astros (GCL)	OF-SS	56	183	21	55	7	3	0	20	.301	17	27	10	70	†13	5	.943
1992—	Asheville (S.Atl.).........	OF	135	480	81	140	21	4	8	48	.292	63	79	15	167	15	11	.943
1993—	Osceola (FSL)...........	OF	129	474	62	134	21	17	5	55	.283	51	90	10	179	18	8	.961
1994—	Jackson (Texas)	OF	118	400	61	121	25	9	16	73	.303	42	81	12	113	3	4	.967
1995—	Tucson (PCL)	OF-2B	114	415	72	126	24	*17	10	75	.304	67	120	16	207	†18	7	.970
1996—	Tucson (PCL)	OF-DH	132	484	86	138	14	*16	13	68	.285	83	111	24	202	15	7	.969
	—Houston (N.L.)	OF	15	22	1	5	1	0	0	1	.227	2	3	0	6	0	0	1.000
1997—	Houston (N.L.)	OF	59	188	22	47	10	2	3	26	.250	21	48	7	84	4	2	.978
	—Jackson (Texas)	OF	3	12	2	2	1	0	0	0	.167	1	5	0	1	0	0	1.000
	—New Orleans (A.A.).....	OF	47	194	25	52	9	4	2	22	.268	21	49	7	99	4	1	.990
1998—	Philadelphia (N.L.)■ ..	OF	151	497	68	155	29	6	17	74	.312	84	133	19	272	17	8	.973
1999—	Philadelphia (N.L.)......	OF-DH	152	546	118	183	35	•11	20	93	.335	109	113	27	260	8	3	.989
2000—	Philadelphia (N.L.)......	OF	154	576	103	182	42	10	25	79	.316	100	116	28	337	13	4	.989
Major League totals (5 years)			531	1829	312	572	117	29	65	273	.313	316	413	81	959	42	17	.983

DIVISION SERIES RECORD

Year	Team (League)	Pos.	G	AB	R	H	2B	3B	HR	RBI	Avg.	BB	SO	SB	PO	A	E	Avg.
1997—	Houston (N.L.)	PH	3	3	0	1	0	0	0	0	.333	0	2	1	...	...	...	...

ABREU, WINSTON   P   BRAVES

PERSONAL: Born April 5, 1977, in Cotui, Dominican Republic. ... 6-2/155. ... Throws right, bats right. ... Full name: Winston Leonardo Abreu.
HIGH SCHOOL: Cotiu (Dominican Republic).
TRANSACTIONS/CAREER NOTES: Signed as non-drafted free agent by Atlanta Braves organization (July 2, 1993). ... On disabled list (April 21, 1997-entire season). ... On Greenville disabled list (April 13-July 5, 2000).

Year	League	W	L	Pct.	ERA	G	GS	CG	ShO	Sv.	IP	H	R	ER	BB	SO
1994—	Gulf Coast Braves (GCL)	0	*8	.000	4.08	13	11	0	0	0	57 1/3	57	35	26	24	53
1995—	Danville (Appl.).................	6	3	.667	2.31	13	13	1	0	0	74	54	29	19	13	90
1996—	Macon (S.Atl.).................	4	3	.571	3.00	12	12	0	0	0	60	51	29	20	25	60
1997—									Did not play.							
1998—	Eugene (N'West)	0	4	.000	6.35	17	10	0	0	0	45 1/3	39	36	32	31	52
1999—	Macon (S.Atl.).................	7	2	.778	1.69	14	14	0	0	0	69 1/3	41	17	13	26	95
	—Myrtle Beach (Caro.)	3	2	.600	3.28	13	12	0	0	0	68 2/3	53	26	25	41	76
2000—	Greenville (Sou.)	0	1	.000	2.25	1	1	0	0	0	4	4	1	1	3	5
	—Gulf Coast Braves (GCL)	0	0	...	3.00	2	2	0	0	0	3	2	1	1	2	2
	—Macon (S.Atl.)..................	2	1	.667	1.88	11	1	0	0	3	28 2/3	11	6	6	6	48
	—Richmond (I.L.)................	0	1	.000	7.00	3	0	0	0	0	9	7	8	7	10	5

ACEVEDO, JUAN   P   BREWERS

PERSONAL: Born May 5, 1970, in Juarez, Mexico. ... 6-2/228. ... Throws right, bats right. ... Full name: Juan Carlos Lara Acevedo. ... Name pronounced ah-sah-VAY-doh.
HIGH SCHOOL: Dundee-Crown (Carpentersville, Ill.).
JUNIOR COLLEGE: Parkland College (Ill.).
TRANSACTIONS/CAREER NOTES: Selected by Colorado Rockies organization in 14th round of free-agent draft (June 1, 1992). ... Traded by Rockies with P Arnold Gooch to New York Mets for P Bret Saberhagen and a player to be named later (July 31, 1995); Rockies acquired P David Swanson to complete deal (August 4, 1995). ... On New York disabled list (March 26-May 9, 1996); included rehabilitation assignment to Norfolk (April 10-May 9). ... Traded by Mets to St. Louis Cardinals for P Rigo Beltran (March 29, 1998). ... On St. Louis disabled list (July 18-August 16, 1998); included rehabilitation assignment to Memphis (August 6-16). ... Traded by Cardinals with two players to be named later to Milwaukee Brewers for 2B Fernando Vina (December 20, 1999); Brewers acquired P Matt Parker and C Eliezer Alfonzo to complete deal (June 13, 2000). ... On Milwaukee disabled list (April 7-30, 2000); included rehabilitation assignment to Indianapolis (April 25-29).
HONORS: Named Eastern League Pitcher of the Year (1994).
STATISTICAL NOTES: Tied for Eastern League lead with four balks in 1994. ... Tied for International League lead with four balks in 1997.

Year	League	W	L	Pct.	ERA	G	GS	CG	ShO	Sv.	IP	H	R	ER	BB	SO
1992—	Bend (N'West)...................	0	0	...	13.50	1	0	0	0	0	2	4	3	3	1	3
	—Visalia (Calif.)	3	4	.429	5.43	12	12	1	0	0	64 2/3	75	46	39	33	37
1993—	Central Valley (Calif.).........	9	8	.529	4.40	27	20	1	0	0	118 2/3	119	68	58	58	107
1994—	New Haven (East.).............	*17	6	.739	*2.37	26	26	5	2	0	174 2/3	142	56	46	38	161
1995—	Colorado (N.L.)	4	6	.400	6.44	17	11	0	0	0	65 2/3	82	53	47	20	40
	—Colorado Springs (PCL)	1	1	.500	6.14	3	3	0	0	0	14 2/3	18	11	10	7	7
	—Norfolk (I.L.)■	0	0	...	0.00	2	2	0	0	0	3	0	0	0	1	2
1996—	Norfolk (I.L.)	4	8	.333	5.96	19	19	2	1	0	102 2/3	116	70	68	53	83

Year League	W	L	Pct.	ERA	G	GS	CG	ShO	Sv.	IP	H	R	ER	BB	SO
1997—Norfolk (I.L.)	6	6	.500	3.86	18	18	1	0	0	116²/₃	111	55	50	34	99
—New York (N.L.)	3	1	.750	3.59	25	2	0	0	0	47²/₃	52	24	19	22	33
1998—St. Louis (N.L.)■	8	3	.727	2.56	50	9	0	0	15	98¹/₃	83	30	28	29	56
—Memphis (PCL)	0	0	...	0.00	2	2	0	0	0	8²/₃	5	0	0	1	6
1999—St. Louis (N.L.)	6	8	.429	5.89	50	12	0	0	4	102¹/₃	115	71	67	48	52
2000—Milwaukee (N.L.)■	3	7	.300	3.81	62	0	0	0	0	82²/₃	77	38	35	31	51
—Indianapolis (I.L.)	0	0	...	0.00	2	2	0	0	0	4	3	0	0	0	4
Major League totals (5 years)	24	25	.490	4.45	204	34	0	0	19	396²/₃	409	216	196	150	232

ADAMS, TERRY — P — DODGERS

PERSONAL: Born March 6, 1973, in Mobile, Ala. ... 6-3/215. ... Throws right, bats right. ... Full name: Terry Wayne Adams.
HIGH SCHOOL: Mary G. Montgomery (Semmes, Ala.).
TRANSACTIONS/CAREER NOTES: Selected by Chicago Cubs organization in fourth round of free-agent draft (June 3, 1991). ... On disabled list (June 21-September 21, 1993). ... On Chicago disabled list (March 26-May 8 and June 19-July 4, 1999); included rehabilitation assignments to West Tenn (April 30-May 4) and Iowa (May 6-8). ... Traded by Cubs with P Chad Ricketts and a player to be named later to Los Angeles Dodgers for P Ismael Valdes and 2B Eric Young (December 12, 1999); Dodgers acquired P Brian Stephenson to complete deal (December 16, 1999).

Year League	W	L	Pct.	ERA	G	GS	CG	ShO	Sv.	IP	H	R	ER	BB	SO
1991—Huntington (Appl.)	0	*9	.000	5.77	14	13	0	0	0	57²/₃	67	*56	37	62	52
1992—Peoria (Midw.)	7	12	.368	4.41	25	25	3	1	0	157	144	95	77	86	96
1993—Daytona (FSL)	3	5	.375	4.97	13	13	0	0	0	70²/₃	78	47	39	43	35
1994—Daytona (FSL)	9	10	.474	4.38	39	7	0	0	7	84¹/₃	87	47	41	46	64
1995—Orlando (Sou.)	2	3	.400	1.43	37	0	0	0	19	37²/₃	23	9	6	16	26
—Iowa (A.A.)	0	0	...	0.00	7	0	0	0	5	6¹/₃	3	0	0	2	10
—Chicago (N.L.)	1	1	.500	6.50	18	0	0	0	1	18	22	15	13	10	15
1996—Chicago (N.L.)	3	6	.333	2.94	69	0	0	0	4	101	84	36	33	49	78
1997—Chicago (N.L.)	2	9	.182	4.62	74	0	0	0	18	74	91	43	38	40	64
1998—Chicago (N.L.)	7	7	.500	4.33	63	0	0	0	1	72²/₃	72	39	35	41	73
—Iowa (PCL)	0	0	...	0.00	3	0	0	0	0	4	1	1	0	3	5
1999—West Tenn (Sou.)	0	0	...	16.88	2	1	0	0	0	2²/₃	5	6	5	2	2
—Chicago (N.L.)	6	3	.667	4.02	52	0	0	0	13	65	60	33	29	28	57
2000—Los Angeles (N.L.)■	6	9	.400	3.52	66	0	0	0	2	84¹/₃	80	42	33	39	56
Major League totals (6 years)	25	35	.417	3.93	342	0	0	0	39	415	409	208	181	207	343

AGBAYANI, BENNY — OF — METS

PERSONAL: Born December 28, 1971, in Honolulu, Hawaii. ... 6-0/225. ... Bats right, throws right. ... Full name: Benny Peter Agbayani Jr.
HIGH SCHOOL: St. Louis (Honolulu).
COLLEGE: Oregon Tech, then Hawaii Pacific.
TRANSACTIONS/CAREER NOTES: Selected by California Angels organization in 25th round of free-agent draft (June 1, 1992); did not sign. ... Selected by New York Mets organization in 30th round of free-agent draft (June 3, 1993). ... On Norfolk disabled list (May 10-June 6, 1998).
STATISTICAL NOTES: Tied for International League lead in caught stealing with 14 in 1997. ... Career major league grand slams: 1.

Year Team (League)	Pos.	G	AB	R	H	2B	3B	HR	RBI	Avg.	BB	SO	SB	PO	A	E	Avg.
1993—Pittsfield (NY-Penn)	OF	51	167	26	42	6	3	2	22	.251	20	43	7	62	1	2	.969
1994—St. Lucie (FSL)	OF	119	411	72	115	13	5	5	63	.280	58	67	8	143	6	1	.993
1995—Binghamton (East.)	OF	88	295	38	81	11	2	1	26	.275	39	51	12	100	3	3	.972
—St. Lucie (FSL)	OF	44	155	24	48	9	3	2	29	.310	26	27	8	37	1	2	.950
1996—Binghamton (East.)	OF	21	53	7	9	1	0	2	8	.170	11	13	1	19	1	1	.952
—Norfolk (I.L.)	OF-1B	99	331	43	92	13	9	7	56	.278	30	57	14	172	8	2	.989
1997—Norfolk (I.L.)	OF	127	468	90	145	24	2	11	51	.310	67	106	29	207	12	5	.978
1998—Norfolk (I.L.)	OF-1B	90	322	43	91	20	5	11	53	.283	50	58	16	151	4	4	.975
—New York (N.L.)	OF	11	15	1	2	0	0	0	0	.133	1	5	0	6	0	0	1.000
1999—Norfolk (I.L.)	OF-1B-DH	28	101	21	36	8	1	8	32	.356	16	19	5	113	6	2	.983
—New York (N.L.)	OF-DH	101	276	42	79	18	3	14	42	.286	32	60	6	121	2	2	.984
2000—New York (N.L.)	OF-DH	119	350	59	101	19	1	15	60	.289	54	68	5	155	3	4	.975
Major League totals (3 years)		231	641	102	182	37	4	29	102	.284	87	133	11	282	5	6	.980

DIVISION SERIES RECORD

Year Team (League)	Pos.	G	AB	R	H	2B	3B	HR	RBI	Avg.	BB	SO	SB	PO	A	E	Avg.
1999—New York (N.L.)	OF-PH	4	10	1	3	1	0	0	1	.300	0	3	0	5	0	0	1.000
2000—New York (N.L.)	OF	4	15	1	5	1	0	1	1	.333	3	3	0	10	0	0	1.000
Division series totals (2 years)		8	25	2	8	2	0	1	2	.320	3	6	0	15	0	0	1.000

CHAMPIONSHIP SERIES RECORD

Year Team (League)	Pos.	G	AB	R	H	2B	3B	HR	RBI	Avg.	BB	SO	SB	PO	A	E	Avg.
1999—New York (N.L.)	OF-PH	4	7	2	1	0	0	0	0	.143	4	2	1	4	0	0	1.000
2000—New York (N.L.)	OF	5	17	0	6	2	0	0	3	.353	4	0	0	11	0	1	.917
Championship series totals (2 years)		9	24	2	7	2	0	0	3	.292	8	2	1	15	0	1	.938

WORLD SERIES RECORD

Year Team (League)	Pos.	G	AB	R	H	2B	3B	HR	RBI	Avg.	BB	SO	SB	PO	A	E	Avg.
2000—New York (N.L.)	OF	5	18	2	5	2	0	0	2	.278	3	6	0	9	0	0	1.000

PERSONAL: Born December 31, 1961, in San Gabriel, Calif. ... 6-5/210. ... Throws right, bats right. ... Full name: Richard Warren Aguilera. ... Name pronounced AG-yuh-LAIR-uh.

HIGH SCHOOL: Edgewood (West Covina, Calif.).

COLLEGE: Brigham Young.

TRANSACTIONS/CAREER NOTES: Selected by St. Louis Cardinals organization in 37th round of free-agent draft (June 3, 1980); did not sign. ... Selected by New York Mets organization in third round of free-agent draft (June 6, 1983). ... On New York disabled list (September 3-15, 1985). ... On New York disabled list (May 23-August 24, 1987); included rehabilitation assignment to Tidewater (August 10-24). ... On New York disabled list (April 19-June 19 and July 12-September 7, 1988); included rehabilitation assignments to St. Lucie (June 7-14) and Tidewater (June 15-19). ... Traded by Mets with P David West and three players to be named later to Minnesota Twins for P Frank Viola (July 31, 1989); Twins acquired P Kevin Tapani and P Tim Drummond (August 1, 1989), and Twins acquired P Jack Savage to complete deal (October 16, 1989). ... Traded by Twins to Boston Red Sox for P Frank Rodriguez and a player to be named later (July 6, 1995); Twins acquired OF J.J. Johnson to complete deal (October 11, 1995). ... Granted free agency (October 31, 1995). ... Signed by Twins (December 11, 1995). ... On Minnesota disabled list (March 24-June 11 and September 7, 1996-remainder of season); included rehabilitation assignment to Fort Myers (May 31-June 11). ... Traded by Twins to Boston Red Sox for P Frank Rodriguez and a player to be named later (July 6, 1995); Twins acquired OF J.J. Johnson to complete deal (October 11, 1995). ... Traded by Twins to Chicago Cubs for P Kyle Lohse and P Jason Ryan (May 21, 1999). ... On Chicago disabled list (August 1-25, 1999). ... On disabled list (September 18, 2000-remainder of season). ... Granted free agency (October 30, 2000).

MISCELLANEOUS: Holds Minnesota Twins all-time records for most saves (254) and most games pitched (490). ... Made an out in only appearance as pinch hitter with New York (1989).

Year League	W	L	Pct.	ERA	G	GS	CG	ShO	Sv.	IP	H	R	ER	BB	SO
1983—Little Falls (NY-Penn)	5	6	.455	3.72	16	15	4	•2	0	104	*109	55	43	26	84
1984—Lynchburg (Caro.)	8	3	.727	2.34	13	13	6	•3	0	88 1/3	72	29	23	28	101
—Jackson (Texas)	4	4	.500	4.57	11	11	2	1	0	67	68	37	34	19	71
1985—Tidewater (I.L.)	6	4	.600	2.51	11	11	2	1	0	79	64	24	22	17	55
—New York (N.L.)	10	7	.588	3.24	21	19	2	0	0	122 1/3	118	49	44	37	74
1986—New York (N.L.)	10	7	.588	3.88	28	20	2	0	0	141 2/3	145	70	61	36	104
1987—New York (N.L.)	11	3	.786	3.60	18	17	1	0	0	115	124	53	46	33	77
—Tidewater (I.L.)	1	1	.500	0.69	3	3	0	0	0	13	8	2	1	1	10
1988—New York (N.L.)	0	4	.000	6.93	11	3	0	0	0	24 2/3	29	20	19	10	16
—St. Lucie (FSL)	0	0	...	1.29	2	2	0	0	0	7	8	1	1	1	5
—Tidewater (I.L.)	0	0	...	1.50	1	1	0	0	0	6	6	1	1	1	4
1989—New York (N.L.)	6	6	.500	2.34	36	0	0	0	7	69 1/3	59	19	18	21	80
—Minnesota (A.L.)■	3	5	.375	3.21	11	11	3	0	0	75 2/3	71	32	27	17	57
1990—Minnesota (A.L.)	5	3	.625	2.76	56	0	0	0	32	65 1/3	55	27	20	19	61
1991—Minnesota (A.L.)	4	5	.444	2.35	63	0	0	0	42	69	44	20	18	30	61
1992—Minnesota (A.L.)	2	6	.250	2.84	64	0	0	0	41	66 2/3	60	28	21	17	52
1993—Minnesota (A.L.)	4	3	.571	3.11	65	0	0	0	34	72 1/3	60	25	25	14	59
1994—Minnesota (A.L.)	1	4	.200	3.63	44	0	0	0	23	44 2/3	57	23	18	10	46
1995—Minnesota (A.L.)	1	1	.500	2.52	22	0	0	0	12	25	20	7	7	6	29
—Boston (A.L.)■	2	2	.500	2.67	30	0	0	0	20	30 1/3	26	9	9	7	23
1996—Fort Myers (FSL)■	2	0	1.000	3.75	2	2	0	0	0	12	13	5	5	1	12
—Minnesota (A.L.)	8	6	.571	5.42	19	19	2	0	0	111 1/3	124	69	67	27	83
1997—Minnesota (A.L.)	5	4	.556	3.82	61	0	0	0	26	68 1/3	65	29	29	22	68
1998—Minnesota (A.L.)	4	9	.308	4.24	68	0	0	0	38	74 1/3	75	35	35	15	57
1999—Minnesota (A.L.)	3	1	.750	1.27	17	0	0	0	6	21 1/3	10	3	3	2	13
—Chicago (N.L.)■	6	3	.667	3.69	44	0	0	0	8	46 1/3	44	22	19	10	32
2000—Chicago (N.L.)	1	2	.333	4.91	54	0	0	0	29	47 2/3	47	28	26	18	38
A.L. totals (11 years)	42	49	.462	3.46	521	30	5	0	274	725 2/3	669	307	279	186	612
N.L. totals (7 years)	44	32	.579	3.70	212	59	5	0	44	567	566	261	233	165	421
Major League totals (16 years)	86	81	.515	3.56	733	89	10	0	318	1292 2/3	1235	568	512	351	1033

DIVISION SERIES RECORD

Year League	W	L	Pct.	ERA	G	GS	CG	ShO	Sv.	IP	H	R	ER	BB	SO
1995—Boston (A.L.)	0	0	...	13.50	1	0	0	0	0	2/3	3	1	1	0	1

CHAMPIONSHIP SERIES RECORD

Year League	W	L	Pct.	ERA	G	GS	CG	ShO	Sv.	IP	H	R	ER	BB	SO
1986—New York (N.L.)	0	0	...	0.00	2	0	0	0	0	5	2	1	0	2	2
1988—New York (N.L.)	0	0	...	1.29	3	0	0	0	0	7	3	1	1	2	4
1991—Minnesota (A.L.)	0	0	...	0.00	3	0	0	0	3	3 1/3	1	0	0	0	3
Champ. series totals (3 years)	0	0	...	0.59	8	0	0	0	3	15 1/3	6	2	1	4	9

WORLD SERIES RECORD

NOTES: Flied out in only appearance as pinch-hitter (1991). ... Member of World Series championship team (1986 and 1991).

Year League	W	L	Pct.	ERA	G	GS	CG	ShO	Sv.	IP	H	R	ER	BB	SO
1986—New York (N.L.)	1	0	1.000	12.00	2	0	0	0	0	3	8	4	4	1	4
1991—Minnesota (A.L.)	1	1	.500	1.80	4	0	0	0	2	5	6	1	1	1	3
World Series totals (2 years)	2	1	.667	5.63	6	0	0	0	2	8	14	5	5	2	7

ALL-STAR GAME RECORD

Year League	W	L	Pct.	ERA	GS	CG	ShO	Sv.	IP	H	R	ER	BB	SO
1991—American (A.L.)	0	0	...	0.00	1	0	0	0	1 1/3	2	0	0	0	3
1992—American	0	0	...	13.50	0	0	0	0	2/3	1	1	1	0	0
1993—American	0	0	...	0.00	0	0	0	0	1	2	0	0	0	2
All-Star Game totals (3 years)	0	0	...	3.00	0	0	0	0	3	5	1	1	0	5

PERSONAL: Born December 10, 1969, in San Francisco. ... 6-3/195. ... Throws right, bats right. ... Full name: Patrick Howard Ahearne.
COLLEGE: Pepperdine.

TRANSACTIONS/CAREER NOTES: Selected by Detroit Tigers organization in seventh round of free-agent draft (June 1, 1992). ... Traded by Tigers to New York Mets for SS Steve Lackey (March 24, 1996). ... Released by Mets (May 9, 1996). ... Signed by Duluth-Superior, Northern League (June 1996). ... Contract purchased by Los Angeles Dodgers organization from Duluth-Superior (June 5, 1996). ... Released by Dodgers (January 9, 1998). ... Signed by New York Yankees organization (March 18, 1998). ... Released by Yankees (April 3, 1998). ... Signed by Bridgeport, Atlantic League (August 1998). ... Contract sold by Bridgeport to Seattle Mariners organization (June 10, 1999). ... On Tacoma disabled list (April 6-13, 2000). ... Granted free agency (October 18, 2000). ... Signed by Florida Marlins organization (November 21, 2000).

Year	League	W	L	Pct.	ERA	G	GS	CG	ShO	Sv.	IP	H	R	ER	BB	SO
1992—	Lakeland (FSL)	0	0	...	1.93	1	1	0	0	0	4²/₃	4	2	1	0	4
1993—	Lakeland (FSL)	6	15	.286	4.46	25	24	2	0	0	147¹/₃	160	87	73	48	51
1994—	Trenton (East.)	7	5	.583	3.98	30	13	2	0	0	108²/₃	126	55	48	25	57
1995—	Toledo (I.L.)	7	9	.438	4.70	25	23	1	1	0	139²/₃	165	83	73	37	54
—Detroit (A.L.)		0	2	.000	11.70	4	3	0	0	0	10	20	13	13	5	4
1996—	Norfolk (I.L.)■	1	2	.333	4.62	5	4	0	0	0	25¹/₃	26	14	13	9	14
—Duluth-Superior (Nor.)■		0	0	...	...	1	1	0	0	0	4	10	6	6	1	1
—San Antonio (Texas)■		2	4	.333	5.76	8	8	0	0	0	45¹/₃	59	34	29	18	21
—Vero Beach (FSL)		3	2	.600	2.11	6	6	1	1	0	47	38	16	11	5	26
1997—	Albuquerque (PCL)	2	4	.333	4.90	20	8	0	0	0	60²/₃	82	43	33	20	44
—San Antonio (Texas)		4	5	.444	4.50	14	14	3	0	0	84	109	48	42	13	45
1998—	Bridgeport (Atl.)■	2	2	.500	2.57	5	5	0	0	0	28	29	12	8	5	16
1999—	Bridgeport (Atl.)	6	0	1.000	2.53	7	7	1	1	0	46¹/₃	35	17	13	14	43
—New Haven (East.)■		8	3	.727	*2.61	17	17	4	2	0	124	114	41	36	27	80
2000—	Tacoma (PCL)	*13	8	.619	3.86	29	26	1	0	0	168	190	92	72	53	92
Major League totals (1 year)		0	2	.000	11.70	4	3	0	0	0	10	20	13	13	5	4

ALCANTARA, ISRAEL — 1B/OF

PERSONAL: Born May 6, 1973, in Bani, Dominican Republic. ... 6-2/180. ... Bats right, throws right. ... Full name: Israel Crisostomo Alcantara.

TRANSACTIONS/CAREER NOTES: Signed as non-drafted free agent by Montreal Expos organization (July 2, 1990). ... On Harrisburg disabled list (June 24-August 16, 1996). ... Granted free agency (October 15, 1997). ... Signed by Tampa Bay Devil Rays organization (December 16, 1997). ... On Durham disabled list (April 9-May 9, 1998). ... Granted free agency (October 15, 1998). ... Signed by Boston Red Sox organization (December 14, 1998). ... Granted free agency (October 15, 1999). ... Re-signed by Red Sox organization (January 4, 2000). ... On Boston disabled list (August 14-September 1, 2000); included rehabilitation assignment to Pawtucket (August 19-September 1). ... Granted free agency (December 21, 2000).

STATISTICAL NOTES: Led Gulf Coast League with four intentional bases on balls received in 1992. ... Led Midwest League third basemen with 371 total chances in 1993.

Year	Team (League)	Pos.	G	AB	R	H	2B	3B	HR	RBI	Avg.	BB	SO	SB	PO	A	E	Avg.
						BATTING									FIELDING			
1991—	Dom. Expos (DSL)		68	239	42	68	9	2	•13	51	.285	32	41	8	...	...	...	...
1992—	GC Expos (GCL)	3B-2B-SS	59	*224	29	62	14	2	3	37	.277	17	35	6	55	137	14	.932
1993—	Burlington (Midw.)	3B	126	470	65	115	26	3	18	73	.245	20	125	6	*98	216	*57	.846
1994—	W.P. Beach (FSL)	3B	125	471	65	134	26	4	15	69	.285	26	130	9	97	199	*32	.902
1995—	Harrisburg (East.)	3B-DH	71	237	25	50	12	2	10	29	.211	21	81	1	48	118	20	.892
—W.P. Beach (FSL)	3B-DH-OF		39	134	16	37	7	2	3	22	.276	9	35	3	34	58	9	.911
1996—	Harrisburg (East.)	3B-DH	62	218	26	46	5	0	8	19	.211	14	62	1	33	133	16	.912
—GC Expos (GCL)	3B-DH		7	30	4	9	2	0	2	10	.300	3	6	0	7	15	3	.880
—W.P. Beach (FSL)	3B-DH		15	61	11	19	2	0	4	14	.311	3	13	0	11	24	4	.897
1997—	Harrisburg (East.)	3B-1B-DH-OF	89	301	48	85	9	2	27	68	.282	29	84	4	254	80	19	.946
1998—	St. Pete. (FSL)■	3B-OF-DH	38	141	21	47	5	0	10	26	.333	21	29	1	35	44	8	.908
—Reading (East.)	DH-1B-3B-OF	53	203	36	63	12	2	15	44	.310	17	37	0	152	23	7	.962
—Orlando (Sou.)	DH-1B-OF-3B	15	55	8	13	4	0	3	18	.236	7	15	0	22	4	1	.963
1999—	Trenton (East.)■	OF-DH-1B	77	293	48	86	26	0	20	60	.294	27	78	4	185	10	2	.990
—Pawtucket (I.L.)	OF-DH-1B	24	81	13	22	3	0	9	23	.272	9	29	0	62	2	0	1.000
2000—	Pawtucket (I.L.)	OF-1B	78	299	60	92	17	1	29	76	.308	25	84	2	121	7	8	.941
—Boston (A.L.)	DH-OF-1B	21	45	9	13	1	0	4	7	.289	3	7	0	17	0	1	.944
Major League totals (1 year)			21	45	9	13	1	0	4	7	.289	3	7	0	17	0	1	.944

ALDRED, SCOTT — P — INDIANS

PERSONAL: Born June 12, 1968, in Flint, Mich. ... 6-4/220. ... Throws left, bats left. ... Full name: Scott Phillip Aldred.

HIGH SCHOOL: Hill McCloy (Montrose, Mich.).

TRANSACTIONS/CAREER NOTES: Selected by Detroit Tigers organization in 16th round of free-agent draft (June 2, 1986). ... Selected by Colorado Rockies in first round (15th pick overall) of expansion draft (November 17, 1992). ... Claimed on waivers by Montreal Expos (April 29, 1993). ... On Montreal disabled list (May 15-September 11, 1993). ... Released by Expos (September 11, 1993). ... Missed entire 1994 season with injury. ... Signed by Detroit Tigers organization (February 19, 1995). ... Claimed on waivers by Minnesota Twins (May 28, 1996). ... On Salt Lake disabled list (August 7-September 19, 1997). ... Granted free agency (October 8, 1997). ... Signed by Tampa Bay Devil Rays (December 19, 1997). ... Traded by Devil Rays to Philadelphia Phillies (July 23, 1999), completing deal in which Phillies traded P Marty Barnett to Devil Rays for a player to be named later (July 20, 1999). ... On disabled list (July 2, 2000-remainder of season). ... Granted free agency (October 14, 2000). ... Signed by Cleveland Indians organization (December 20, 2000).

Year	League	W	L	Pct.	ERA	G	GS	CG	ShO	Sv.	IP	H	R	ER	BB	SO
1987—	Fayetteville (S.Atl.)	4	9	.308	3.60	21	20	0	0	0	110	101	56	44	69	91
1988—	Lakeland (FSL)	8	7	.533	3.56	25	25	1	1	0	131¹/₃	122	61	52	72	102
1989—	London (East.)	10	6	.625	3.84	20	20	3	1	0	122	98	55	52	59	97
1990—	Toledo (I.L.)	6	15	.286	4.90	29	*29	2	0	0	158	145	93	86	81	133
—Detroit (A.L.)		1	2	.333	3.77	4	3	0	0	0	14¹/₃	13	6	6	10	7
1991—	Toledo (I.L.)	8	8	.500	3.92	22	20	2	0	1	135¹/₃	127	65	59	72	95
—Detroit (A.L.)		2	4	.333	5.18	11	11	1	0	0	57¹/₃	58	37	33	30	35
1992—	Detroit (A.L.)	3	8	.273	6.78	16	13	0	0	0	65	80	51	49	33	34
—Toledo (I.L.)		4	6	.400	5.13	16	13	3	0	0	86	92	57	49	47	81
1993—	Colorado (N.L.)■	0	0	...	10.80	5	0	0	0	0	6²/₃	10	10	8	9	5
—Montreal (N.L.)■		1	0	1.000	6.75	3	0	0	0	0	5¹/₃	9	4	4	1	4

Year	League	W	L	Pct.	ERA	G	GS	CG	ShO	Sv.	IP	H	R	ER	BB	SO
1994—	....							Did not play.								
1995—Lakeland (FSL)■	....	4	2	.667	3.19	13	7	0	0	2	67²/₃	57	25	24	19	64
—Jacksonville (Sou.)	....	1	0	1.000	0.00	2	2	0	0	0	12	9	0	0	1	11
1996—Detroit (A.L.)	....	0	4	.000	9.35	11	8	0	0	0	43¹/₃	60	52	45	26	36
—Minnesota (A.L.)■	....	6	5	.545	5.09	25	17	0	0	0	122	134	73	69	42	75
1997—Minnesota (A.L.)	....	2	10	.167	7.68	17	15	0	0	0	77¹/₃	102	66	66	28	33
—Salt Lake (PCL)	....	3	3	.500	7.03	7	7	0	0	0	39²/₃	56	39	31	16	23
1998—Durham (I.L.)■	....	2	4	.333	5.35	7	7	0	0	0	35¹/₃	44	26	21	14	19
—Tampa Bay (A.L.)	....	0	0	...	3.73	48	0	0	0	0	31¹/₃	33	13	13	12	21
1999—Tampa Bay (A.L.)	....	3	2	.600	5.18	37	0	0	0	0	24¹/₃	26	15	14	14	22
—Philadelphia (N.L.)■	....	1	1	.500	3.90	29	0	0	0	1	32¹/₃	33	15	14	15	19
2000—Philadelphia (N.L.)	....	1	3	.250	5.75	23	0	0	0	0	20¹/₃	23	14	13	10	21
A.L. totals (7 years)	....	17	35	.327	6.10	169	67	1	0	0	435	506	313	295	195	263
N.L. totals (3 years)	....	3	4	.429	5.43	60	0	0	0	1	64²/₃	75	43	39	35	49
Major League totals (9 years)	....	20	39	.339	6.02	229	67	1	0	1	499²/₃	581	356	334	230	312

ALEXANDER, MANNY — IF

PERSONAL: Born March 20, 1971, in San Pedro de Macoris, Dominican Republic ... 5-10/180. ... Bats right, throws right. ... Full name: Manuel DeJesus Alexander.

TRANSACTIONS/CAREER NOTES: Signed as non-drafted free agent by Baltimore Orioles organization (February 4, 1988). ... On disabled list (April 26-July 23, 1990). ... On Rochester disabled list (May 9-19 and June 9-17, 1993). ... On Baltimore disabled list (March 25-May 2, 1995). ... Traded by Orioles with IF Scott McLain to New York Mets for P Hector Ramirez (March 22, 1997). ... On New York disabled list (June 13-July 10 and August 1-11, 1997). ... Traded by Mets to Chicago Cubs (August 14, 1997), as part of deal in which Mets traded OF Lance Johnson and two players to be named later to Cubs for OF Brian McRae, P Mel Rojas and P Turk Wendell (August 8, 1997); Mets traded P Mark Clark to Cubs to complete deal (August 11, 1997). ... Traded by Cubs to Boston Red Sox for OF Damon Buford (December 10, 1999). ... On disabled list (September 29, 2000-remainder of season). ... Granted free agency (November 1, 2000).

STATISTICAL NOTES: Led Appalachian League shortstops with 349 total chances in 1989. ... Led Carolina League shortstops with 651 total chances and 93 double plays in 1991. ... Career major league grand slams: 1.

							— BATTING —						— FIELDING —			
Year	Team (League)	Pos.	G	AB	R	H	2B	3B	HR	RBI	Avg.	BB	SO	SB	PO	A	E	Avg.
1988—						Dominican Summer League statistics unavailable.												
1989—Bluefield (Appl.)	....	SS	65	*274	49	*85	13	2	2	34	.310	20	49	19	*140	177	*32	.908
1990—Wausau (Midw.)	....	SS	44	152	16	27	3	1	0	11	.178	12	41	8	66	99	11	.938
1991—Hagerstown (East.)	......	SS	3	9	3	3	1	0	0	2	.333	1	3	0	5	4	0	1.000
—Frederick (Caro.)	....	SS	134	548	•81	*143	17	3	3	42	.261	44	68	47	*226	*393	32	*.951
1992—Hagerstown (East.)	......	SS	127	499	69	129	23	8	2	41	.259	25	62	43	216	253	36	.929
—Rochester (I.L.)	....	SS	6	24	3	7	1	0	0	3	.292	1	3	2	12	25	1	.974
—Baltimore (A.L.)	....	SS	4	5	1	1	0	0	0	0	.200	0	3	0	3	3	0	1.000
1993—Rochester (I.L.)	....	SS	120	471	55	115	23	8	6	51	.244	22	60	19	184	335	18	*.966
—Baltimore (A.L.)	....	PR-DH	3	0	1	0	0	0	0	0	...	0	0	0	...	...	...	...
1994—Rochester (I.L.)	....	SS-SS-3B-DH	111	426	63	106	23	6	6	39	.249	16	67	30	219	291	33	.939
1995—Baltimore (A.L.)	.........2B-SS-3B-DH	94	242	35	57	9	1	3	23	.236	20	30	11	139	170	10	.969
1996—Baltimore (A.L.)	.........S-2-3-O-DH-P	54	68	6	7	0	0	0	4	.103	3	27	3	26	47	5	.936
1997—New York (N.L.)■	2B-SS-3B	54	149	26	37	9	3	2	15	.248	9	38	11	59	130	4	.979
—St. Lucie (FSL)	....	SS	1	4	0	1	0	0	0	0	.250	0	1	0	1	4	0	1.000
—Chicago (N.L.)■	....	SS-2B	33	99	11	29	3	1	1	7	.293	8	16	2	38	91	7	.949
1998—Chicago (N.L.)	...........S-2-3-DH-O	108	264	34	60	10	1	5	25	.227	18	66	4	89	140	7	.970
1999—Chicago (N.L.)	...........SS-3B-2B-OF	90	177	17	48	11	2	0	15	.271	10	38	4	56	88	7	.954
2000—Boston (A.L.)■	....	3-S-2-DH	101	194	30	41	4	3	4	19	.211	13	41	2	60	119	7	.962
American League totals (5 years)			256	509	73	106	13	4	7	46	.208	36	101	16	228	339	22	.963
National League totals (3 years)			285	689	88	174	33	7	8	62	.253	45	158	21	242	449	25	.965
Major League totals (8 years)			541	1198	161	280	46	11	15	108	.234	81	259	37	470	788	47	.964

DIVISION SERIES RECORD

							— BATTING —						— FIELDING —			
Year	Team (League)	Pos.	G	AB	R	H	2B	3B	HR	RBI	Avg.	BB	SO	SB	PO	A	E	Avg.
1996—Baltimore (A.L.)	....	DH-PR	3	0	2	0	0	0	0	0	...	0	0	0	...	...	...	...
1998—Chicago (N.L.)	....	SS-PH	2	5	0	0	0	0	0	0	.000	0	1	0	2	2	0	1.000
Division series totals (2 years)			5	5	2	0	0	0	0	0	.000	0	1	0	2	2	0	1.000

RECORD AS PITCHER

Year	League	W	L	Pct.	ERA	G	GS	CG	ShO	Sv.	IP	H	R	ER	BB	SO
1996—Baltimore (A.L.)	....	0	0	...	67.50	1	0	0	0	0	²/₃	1	5	5	4	0

ALFONSECA, ANTONIO — P — MARLINS

PERSONAL: Born April 16, 1972, in La Romana, Dominican Republic. ... 6-5/235. ... Throws right, bats right.

TRANSACTIONS/CAREER NOTES: Signed as non-drafted free agent by Montreal Expos organization (July 3, 1989). ... Selected by Edmonton, Florida Marlins organization, from Harrisburg, Expos organization in Rule 5 minor league draft (December 13, 1993). ... On Portland disabled list (May 15-June 15, 1995). ... On Charlotte disabled list (July 12-September 3, 1996). ... On disabled list (May 14-31, 1998).

HONORS: Named N.L. Fireman of the Year by THE SPORTING NEWS (2000).

Year	League	W	L	Pct.	ERA	G	GS	CG	ShO	Sv.	IP	H	R	ER	BB	SO
1990—Dom. Expos (DSL)	....	3	5	.375	3.60	13	13	1	0	0	60	60	29	24	32	19
1991—Gulf Coast Expos (GCL)	.....	3	3	.500	3.88	11	10	0	0	0	51	46	33	22	25	38
1992—Gulf Coast Expos (GCL)	.....	3	4	.429	3.68	12	10	1	1	0	66	55	31	27	35	62
1993—Jamestown (NY-Penn)	....	2	2	.500	6.15	15	4	0	0	1	33²/₃	31	26	23	22	29

Year League	W	L	Pct.	ERA	G	GS	CG	ShO	Sv.	IP	H	R	ER	BB	SO
1994— Kane County (Midw.)■	6	5	.545	4.07	32	9	0	0	0	86 1/3	78	41	39	21	74
1995— Portland (East.)	9	3	.750	3.64	19	17	1	0	0	96 1/3	81	43	39	42	75
1996— Charlotte (I.L.)	4	4	.500	5.53	14	13	0	0	1	71 2/3	86	47	44	22	51
1997— Charlotte (I.L.)	7	2	.778	4.32	46	0	0	0	7	58 1/3	58	34	28	20	45
— Florida (N.L.)	1	3	.250	4.91	17	0	0	0	0	25 2/3	36	16	14	10	19
1998— Florida (N.L.)	4	6	.400	4.08	58	0	0	0	8	70 2/3	75	36	32	33	46
1999— Florida (N.L.)	4	5	.444	3.24	73	0	0	0	21	77 2/3	79	28	28	29	46
2000— Florida (N.L.)	5	6	.455	4.24	68	0	0	0	*45	70	82	35	33	24	47
Major League totals (4 years)	14	20	.412	3.95	216	0	0	0	74	244	272	115	107	96	158

DIVISION SERIES RECORD

Year League	W	L	Pct.	ERA	G	GS	CG	ShO	Sv.	IP	H	R	ER	BB	SO
1997— Florida (N.L.)							Did not play.								

CHAMPIONSHIP SERIES RECORD

Year League	W	L	Pct.	ERA	G	GS	CG	ShO	Sv.	IP	H	R	ER	BB	SO
1997— Florida (N.L.)							Did not play.								

WORLD SERIES RECORD

NOTES: Member of World Series championship team (1997).

Year League	W	L	Pct.	ERA	G	GS	CG	ShO	Sv.	IP	H	R	ER	BB	SO
1997— Florida (N.L.)	0	0	...	0.00	3	0	0	0	0	6 1/3	6	0	0	1	5

ALFONZO, EDGARDO   2B   METS

PERSONAL: Born November 8, 1973, in St. Teresa, Venezuela. ... 5-11/187. ... Bats right, throws right. ... Full name: Edgardo Antonio Alfonzo. ... Brother of Roberto Alfonzo, second baseman with New York Mets organization (1993-94).

HIGH SCHOOL: Cecilio Acosto (Venezuela).

TRANSACTIONS/CAREER NOTES: Signed as non-drafted free agent by New York Mets organization (February 19, 1991). ... On disabled list (August 11, 1995-remainder of season; and May 4-19, 1998).

RECORDS: Shares major league single-game records for most runs scored—6 (August 30, 1999); and most double plays by third basemen—4 (May 14, 1997).

HONORS: Named second baseman on THE SPORTING NEWS N.L. All-Star team (1999). ... Named second baseman on THE SPORTING NEWS N.L. Silver Slugger team (1999).

STATISTICAL NOTES: Led New York-Pennsylvania League shortstops with 389 total chances and 39 double plays in 1992. ... Had 20-game hitting streak (June 10-July 10, 1997). ... Hit three home runs in one game (August 30, 1999). ... Collected six hits in one game (August 30, 1999). ... Career major league grand slams: 1.

							BATTING							FIELDING		
Year Team (League)	Pos.	G	AB	R	H	2B	3B	HR	RBI	Avg.	BB	SO	SB	PO	A	E	Avg.
1991— GC Mets (GCL)	2B-SS-3B	54	175	29	58	8	4	0	27	.331	34	12	6	99	108	9	.958
1992— St. Lucie (FSL)	2B	4	5	0	0	0	0	0	0	.000	0	0	0	1	3	0	1.000
— Pittsfield (NY-Penn)	SS	74	*298	44	*106	13	5	1	44	*.356	18	31	7	*126	*237	*26	.933
1993— St. Lucie (FSL)	SS	128	494	75	145	18	3	11	86	.294	57	51	26	183	425	29	.954
1994— Binghamton (East.)	SS-2B-1B	127	498	89	146	34	2	15	75	.293	64	55	14	206	408	27	.958
1995— New York (N.L.)	3B-2B-SS	101	335	26	93	13	5	4	41	.278	12	37	1	81	171	7	.973
1996— New York (N.L.)	2B-3B-SS	123	368	36	96	15	2	4	40	.261	25	56	2	146	246	11	.973
1997— New York (N.L.)	3B-SS-2B	151	518	84	163	27	2	10	72	.315	63	56	11	98	290	12	.970
1998— New York (N.L.)	3B-SS	144	557	94	155	28	2	17	78	.278	65	77	8	117	248	9	.976
1999— New York (N.L.)	2B	158	628	123	191	41	1	27	108	.304	85	85	9	298	409	5	*.993
2000— New York (N.L.)	2B-DH	150	544	109	176	40	2	25	94	.324	95	70	3	316	362	10	.985
Major League totals (6 years)		827	2950	472	874	164	14	87	433	.296	345	381	34	1056	1726	54	.981

DIVISION SERIES RECORD

RECORDS: Shares N.L. single-series record for most runs scored—6 (1999). ... Shares single-game records for most home runs—2; most grand slams—1; and most runs batted in—5 (October 5, 1999). ... Shares single-inning record for most runs batted in—4 (October 5, 1999, ninth inning).

							BATTING							FIELDING		
Year Team (League)	Pos.	G	AB	R	H	2B	3B	HR	RBI	Avg.	BB	SO	SB	PO	A	E	Avg.
1999— New York (N.L.)	2B	4	16	6	4	1	0	3	6	.250	3	2	0	5	11	0	1.000
2000— New York (N.L.)	2B	4	18	1	5	2	0	1	5	.278	1	2	0	6	7	0	1.000
Division series totals (2 years)		8	34	7	9	3	0	4	11	.265	4	4	0	11	18	0	1.000

CHAMPIONSHIP SERIES RECORD

							BATTING							FIELDING		
Year Team (League)	Pos.	G	AB	R	H	2B	3B	HR	RBI	Avg.	BB	SO	SB	PO	A	E	Avg.
1999— New York (N.L.)	2B	6	27	2	6	4	0	0	1	.222	1	9	0	15	18	1	.971
2000— New York (N.L.)	2B	5	18	5	8	1	1	0	4	.444	4	1	0	3	10	0	1.000
Championship series totals (2 years)		11	45	7	14	5	1	0	5	.311	5	10	0	18	28	1	.979

WORLD SERIES RECORD

							BATTING							FIELDING		
Year Team (League)	Pos.	G	AB	R	H	2B	3B	HR	RBI	Avg.	BB	SO	SB	PO	A	E	Avg.
2000— New York (N.L.)	2B	5	21	1	3	0	0	0	1	.143	1	5	0	7	19	0	1.000

ALL-STAR GAME RECORD

						BATTING							FIELDING		
Year League	Pos.	AB	R	H	2B	3B	HR	RBI	Avg.	BB	SO	SB	PO	A	E	Avg.
2000— National	2B	2	0	0	0	0	0	0	.000	0	1	0	0	1	0	1.000

ALICEA, LUIS — 2B — ROYALS

A

PERSONAL: Born July 29, 1965, in Santurce, Puerto Rico. ... 5-9/176. ... Bats both, throws right. ... Full name: Luis Rene Alicea. ... Brother of Ed Alicea, minor league infielder with Atlanta Braves (1988-93), Colorado Rockies (1993) and New York Mets (1995).. ... Name pronounced AH-la-SAY-uh.

HIGH SCHOOL: Liceo Castro (Rio Piedras, Puerto Rico).

COLLEGE: Florida State.

TRANSACTIONS/CAREER NOTES: Selected by St. Louis Cardinals organization in first round (23rd pick overall) of free-agent draft (June 2, 1986). ... On St. Petersburg disabled list (April 6-June 4, 1990). ... On Louisville disabled list (April 25-May 25, 1991). ... On St. Louis disabled list (June 1-July 6, 1992); included rehabilitation assignment to Louisville (July 2-6). ... Traded by Cardinals to Boston Red Sox for P Nate Minchey and OF Jeff McNeely (December 7, 1994). ... Claimed on waivers by Cardinals (March 19, 1996). ... Granted free agency (October 31, 1996). ... Signed by Anaheim Angels organization (January 20, 1997). ... Granted free agency (October 30, 1997). ... Signed by Texas Rangers (December 9, 1997). ... Granted free agency (October 28, 1999). ... Re-signed by Rangers (December 7, 1999). ... Granted free agency (October 31, 2000). ... Signed by Kansas City Royals (January 26, 2001).

HONORS: Named second baseman on THE SPORTING NEWS college All-America team (1986).

STATISTICAL NOTES: Switch-hit home runs in one game (July 28, 1995). ... Led A.L. second basemen with 699 total chances and 103 double plays in 1995. ... Career major league grand slams: 1.

Year Team (League)	Pos.	G	AB	R	H	2B	3B	HR	RBI	Avg.	BB	SO	SB	PO	A	E	Avg.
1986— Erie (NY-Penn)	2B	47	163	40	46	6	1	3	18	.282	37	20	27	94	163	12	.955
— Arkansas (Texas)........	2B-SS	25	68	8	16	3	0	0	3	.235	5	11	0	39	63	4	.962
1987— Arkansas (Texas)........	2B	101	337	57	91	14	3	4	47	.270	49	28	13	184	251	11	*.975
— Louisville (A.A.)	2B	29	105	18	32	10	2	2	20	.305	9	9	4	69	81	4	.974
1988— Louisville (A.A.)	2B-SS-OF	49	191	21	53	11	6	1	21	.277	11	21	8	116	165	0	1.000
— St. Louis (N.L.)	2B	93	297	20	63	10	4	1	24	.212	25	32	1	206	240	14	.970
1989— Louisville (A.A.)	2B	124	412	53	102	20	3	8	48	.248	59	55	13	240	310	16	.972
1990— St. Petersburg (FSL) ..	2B	29	95	14	22	1	4	0	12	.232	20	14	9	20	23	0	1.000
— Arkansas (Texas)	2B	14	49	11	14	3	1	0	4	.286	7	8	2	24	34	4	.935
— Louisville (A.A.)	3B	25	92	10	32	6	3	0	10	.348	5	12	0	14	39	6	.898
1991— Louisville (A.A.)	2B	31	112	26	44	6	3	4	16	.393	14	8	5	68	95	5	.970
— St. Louis (N.L.)	2B-3B-SS	56	68	5	13	3	0	0	0	.191	8	19	0	19	23	0	1.000
1992— Louisville (A.A.)	2B-SS	20	71	11	20	8	0	0	6	.282	16	6	0	44	52	4	.960
— St. Louis (N.L.)	2B-SS	85	265	26	65	9	11	2	32	.245	27	40	2	136	233	7	.981
1993— St. Louis (N.L.)	2B-OF-3B	115	362	50	101	19	3	3	46	.279	47	54	11	210	281	11	.978
1994— St. Louis (N.L.)	2B-OF	88	205	32	57	12	5	5	29	.278	30	38	4	126	149	4	.986
1995— Boston (A.L.)■..........	2B	132	419	64	113	20	3	6	44	.270	63	61	13	254	429	16	.977
1996— St. Louis (N.L.)■	2B	129	380	54	98	26	3	5	42	.258	52	78	11	241	288	*24	.957
1997— Anaheim (A.L.)■	2B-3B-DH	128	388	59	98	16	7	5	37	.253	69	65	22	223	287	12	.977
1998— Texas (A.L.)■..........	2-3-DH-O	101	259	51	71	15	3	6	33	.274	37	40	4	97	143	9	.964
1999— Texas (A.L.) 2B-3B-DH-OF	68	164	33	33	10	0	3	17	.201	28	32	2	66	100	5	.971
2000— Texas (A.L.)	2-3-DH-S	139	540	85	159	25	8	6	63	.294	59	75	1	253	328	18	.970
American League totals (5 years)		568	1770	292	474	86	21	26	194	.268	256	273	42	893	1287	60	.973
National League totals (6 years)		566	1577	187	397	79	26	16	173	.252	189	261	29	938	1214	60	.973
Major League totals (11 years)		1134	3347	479	871	165	47	42	367	.260	445	534	71	1831	2501	120	.973

DIVISION SERIES RECORD

Year Team (League)	Pos.	G	AB	R	H	2B	3B	HR	RBI	Avg.	BB	SO	SB	PO	A	E	Avg.
1995— Boston (A.L.).............	2B	3	10	1	6	1	0	1	1	.600	2	2	1	6	11	1	.944
1996— St. Louis (N.L.).............	2B	3	11	1	2	2	0	0	0	.182	1	4	0	2	5	1	.875
1998— Texas (A.L.).............	PH-DH	1	1	0	0	0	0	0	0	.000	0	0	0	...	...	...	...
1999— Texas (A.L.)									Did not play.								
Division series totals (3 years)		7	22	2	8	3	0	1	1	.364	3	6	1	8	16	2	.923

CHAMPIONSHIP SERIES RECORD

Year Team (League)	Pos.	G	AB	R	H	2B	3B	HR	RBI	Avg.	BB	SO	SB	PO	A	E	Avg.
1996— St. Louis (N.L.)..........	2B-PH	5	8	0	0	0	0	0	0	.000	2	1	0	5	7	1	.923

ALLEN, CHAD — OF — TWINS

PERSONAL: Born February 6, 1975, in Dallas. ... 6-1/195. ... Bats right, throws right. ... Full name: John Chad Allen.

HIGH SCHOOL: Duncanville (Texas).

COLLEGE: Texas A&M.

TRANSACTIONS/CAREER NOTES: Selected by Cincinnati Reds organization in 38th round of free-agent draft (June 3, 1993); did not sign. ... Selected by Minnesota Twins organization in fourth round of free-agent draft (June 4, 1996). ... On Salt Lake disabled list (April 11-22, 2000).

MISCELLANEOUS: Member of 1996 U.S. Olympic baseball team.

Year Team (League)	Pos.	G	AB	R	H	2B	3B	HR	RBI	Avg.	BB	SO	SB	PO	A	E	Avg.
1996— Fort Wayne (Midw.).....	OF	7	21	2	9	0	0	0	2	.429	3	2	1	4	1	0	1.000
1997— Fort Myers (FSL)	OF	105	401	66	124	18	4	3	45	.309	40	51	27	206	10	5	.977
— New Britain (East.)	OF	30	115	20	29	9	1	4	18	.252	9	21	2	35	1	1	.973
1998— New Britain (East.)	OF	137	504	70	132	31	7	8	82	.262	51	78	21	185	11	4	.980
1999— Minnesota (A.L.)	OF-DH	137	481	69	133	21	3	10	46	.277	37	89	14	267	9	7	.975
2000— Salt Lake (PCL)	OF	96	389	71	121	21	5	9	67	.311	31	72	10	146	2	1	.993
— Minnesota (A.L.)	OF	15	50	2	15	3	0	0	7	.300	3	14	0	26	2	0	1.000
Major League totals (2 years)		152	531	71	148	24	3	10	53	.279	40	103	14	293	11	7	.977

ALLEN, DUSTY — 1B/OF — TIGERS

PERSONAL: Born August 9, 1972, in Oklahoma City. ... 6-4/215. ... Bats right, throws right. ... Full name: Dustin R. Allen.
HIGH SCHOOL: Edmond (Okla.).
COLLEGE: Stanford.
TRANSACTIONS/CAREER NOTES: Selected by San Diego Padres organization in 30th round of free-agent draft (June 1, 1995). ... On Las Vegas disabled list (April 6-13, 2000). ... Traded by Padres to Detroit Tigers for 3B Gabe Alvarez (July 17, 2000).

Year	Team (League)	Pos.	G	AB	R	H	2B	3B	HR	RBI	Avg.	BB	SO	SB	PO	A	E	Avg.
1995—	Idaho Falls (Pio.)	OF-1B	29	104	21	34	7	0	4	24	.327	21	19	1	51	2	0	1.000
	Clinton (Midw.)	1B-OF	36	139	25	37	12	1	5	31	.266	12	29	1	171	13	9	.953
1996—	Clinton (Midw.)	1B-OF	77	243	46	65	10	3	10	46	.267	67	59	4	652	44	7	.990
	Rancho Cuca. (Calif.)	1B-OF	55	208	41	62	15	1	10	45	.298	38	65	3	348	26	6	.984
1997—	Mobile (Sou.)	1B-OF	131	475	85	120	28	4	17	75	.253	81	116	1	651	54	15	.979
1998—	Mobile (Sou.)	OF-1B	42	154	30	39	10	4	6	42	.253	32	26	1	84	3	3	.967
	Las Vegas (PCL)	OF-1B	87	292	42	78	21	1	16	45	.267	31	80	0	344	22	4	.989
1999—	Las Vegas (PCL)	1B-OF	128	454	68	124	30	3	18	89	.273	79	143	3	586	41	11	.983
2000—	Las Vegas (PCL)	OF-1B	67	222	52	69	14	4	14	55	.311	58	50	3	113	4	4	.967
	San Diego (N.L.)	OF-DH-1B	9	12	0	0	0	0	0	0	.000	2	5	0	2	0	0	1.000
	Toledo (I.L.)■	OF-1B	25	90	9	20	5	0	2	12	.222	5	27	0	84	6	0	1.000
	Detroit (A.L.)	1B-3B-OF	18	16	5	7	2	0	2	2	.438	2	7	0	47	1	0	1.000
American League totals (1 year)			18	16	5	7	2	0	2	2	.438	2	7	0	47	1	0	1.000
National League totals (1 year)			9	12	0	0	0	0	0	0	.000	2	5	0	2	0	0	1.000
Major League totals (1 year)			27	28	5	7	2	0	2	2	.250	4	12	0	49	1	0	1.000

ALMANZA, ARMANDO — P — MARLINS

PERSONAL: Born October 26, 1972, in El Paso, Texas. ... 6-3/205. ... Throws left, bats left.
HIGH SCHOOL: Bel Air (El Paso, Texas).
JUNIOR COLLEGE: New Mexico Junior College.
TRANSACTIONS/CAREER NOTES: Selected by St. Louis Cardinals organization in 21st round of free-agent draft (June 3, 1993). ... On Madison disabled list (April 8, 1994-entire season). ... On Madison reserved list (November 4-December 14, 1994). ... On Memphis disabled list (July 10-21, 1998). ... Traded by Cardinals with P Braden Looper and SS Pablo Ozuna to Florida Marlins for SS Edgar Renteria (December 14, 1998). ... On Calgary disabled list (May 10-June 2, 1999).
STATISTICAL NOTES: Tied for Arizona League lead with 14 wild pitches in 1993.

Year	League	W	L	Pct.	ERA	G	GS	CG	ShO	Sv.	IP	H	R	ER	BB	SO
1993—	Arizona Cardinals (Ariz.)	4	1	.800	3.21	20	4	0	0	0	42	38	19	15	14	56
	Johnson City (Appl.)	1	1	.500	4.15	3	3	0	0	0	4 1/3	6	2	2	3	4
1994—	Madison (Midw.)							Did not play.								
1995—	Savannah (S.Atl.)	3	9	.250	3.92	20	20	0	0	0	108	108	62	47	40	72
1996—	Peoria (Midw.)	8	6	.571	2.76	52	1	0	0	0	62	50	27	19	32	67
1997—	Prince William (Caro.)	2	3	.400	1.67	•58	0	0	0	*36	64 2/3	38	18	12	32	83
1998—	Arkansas (Texas)	4	1	.800	3.31	28	0	0	0	8	32 2/3	27	13	12	18	46
	Memphis (PCL)	3	1	.750	3.03	31	0	0	0	1	35 2/3	35	18	12	19	45
1999—	Calgary (PCL)■	2	2	.500	10.90	15	0	0	0	0	17 1/3	29	27	21	18	20
	Portland (East.)	0	1	.000	3.97	10	0	0	0	3	11 1/3	5	5	5	4	20
	Florida (N.L.)	0	1	.000	1.72	14	0	0	0	0	15 2/3	8	4	3	9	20
2000—	Florida (N.L.)	4	2	.667	4.86	67	0	0	0	0	46 1/3	38	27	25	43	46
Major League totals (2 years)		4	3	.571	4.06	81	0	0	0	0	62	46	31	28	52	66

ALMANZAR, CARLOS — P — PADRES

PERSONAL: Born November 6, 1973, in Santiago, Dominican Republic. ... 6-2/200. ... Throws right, bats right. ... Full name: Carlos Manuel Almanzar.
TRANSACTIONS/CAREER NOTES: Signed as non-drafted free agent by Toronto Blue Jays organization (December 10, 1990). ... On Knoxville disabled list (May 27-June 3, 1997). ... Traded by Blue Jays with P Woody Williams and OF Peter Tucci to San Diego Padres for P Joey Hamilton (December 13, 1998). ... On San Diego disabled list (April 24-May 27, 1999); included rehabilitation assignment to Las Vegas (May 22-27).

Year	League	W	L	Pct.	ERA	G	GS	CG	ShO	Sv.	IP	H	R	ER	BB	SO
1991—	Dom. Blue Jays (DSL)	3	1	.750	2.83	6	6	1	0	0	35	36	17	11	11	20
1992—	Dom. Blue Jays (DSL)	10	0	1.000	2.01	13	11	2	1	1	67	45	26	15	31	60
1993—	Dom. Blue Jays (DSL)	5	2	.714	3.38	16	9	0	0	2	69 1/3	60	35	26	32	59
1994—	Medicine Hat (Pio.)	7	4	.636	2.87	14	14	0	0	0	84 2/3	82	38	27	19	77
1995—	Knoxville (Sou.)	3	12	.200	3.99	35	19	0	0	2	126 1/3	144	77	56	32	93
1996—	Knoxville (Sou.)	7	8	.467	4.85	54	0	0	0	9	94 2/3	106	58	51	33	105
1997—	Knoxville (Sou.)	1	1	.500	4.91	21	0	0	0	8	25 2/3	30	14	14	5	25
	Syracuse (I.L.)	5	1	.833	1.41	32	0	0	0	3	51	30	9	8	8	47
	Toronto (A.L.)	0	1	.000	2.70	4	0	0	0	0	3 1/3	1	1	1	1	4
1998—	Toronto (A.L.)	2	2	.500	5.34	25	0	0	0	0	28 2/3	34	18	17	8	20
	Syracuse (I.L.)	3	6	.333	2.31	30	0	0	0	10	50 2/3	44	21	13	13	53
1999—	San Diego (N.L.)■	0	0	...	7.47	28	0	0	0	0	37 1/3	48	32	31	15	30
	Las Vegas (PCL)	1	3	.250	9.53	11	3	0	0	0	22 2/3	32	25	24	8	18
2000—	San Diego (N.L.)	4	5	.444	4.39	62	0	0	0	0	69 2/3	73	35	34	25	56
	Las Vegas (PCL)	0	0	...	4.50	4	0	0	0	0	6	9	4	3	0	7
A.L. totals (2 years)		2	3	.400	5.06	29	0	0	0	0	32	35	19	18	9	24
N.L. totals (2 years)		4	5	.444	5.47	90	0	0	0	0	107	121	67	65	40	86
Major League totals (4 years)		6	8	.429	5.37	119	0	0	0	0	139	156	86	83	49	110

PERSONAL: Born October 17, 1975, in Santo Domingo, Dominican Republic. ... 6-2/190. ... Throws right, bats right. ... Full name: Hector Radhames Almonte.

HIGH SCHOOL: Liceo Jose Marti (Santo Domingo, Dominican Republic).

TRANSACTIONS/CAREER NOTES: Signed as non-drafted free agent by Florida Marlins organization (February 9, 1993). ... On Calgary disabled list (May 19-August 2, 2000).

Year League	W	L	Pct.	ERA	G	GS	CG	ShO	Sv.	IP	H	R	ER	BB	SO
1993—Dom. Marlins (DSL)	1	6	.143	4.79	13	7	1	0	1	56 $\frac{1}{3}$	59	39	30	29	20
1994—Dom. Marlins (DSL)	3	5	.375	4.34	20	4	0	0	0	58	68	40	28	26	26
1995—Dom. Marlins (DSL)	1	2	.333	4.26	20	1	0	0	9	31 $\frac{2}{3}$	28	17	15	11	27
1996—Dom. Marlins (DSL)	0	0	...	0.00	2	0	0	0	0	1 $\frac{2}{3}$	0	0	0	1	2
1997—GC Marlins (GCL)	2	0	1.000	0.76	8	0	0	0	3	23 $\frac{2}{3}$	12	3	2	6	25
—Kane County (Midw.)	0	1	.000	3.86	8	1	0	0	1	14	11	6	6	6	10
1998—Kane County (Midw.)	1	5	.167	3.95	43	0	0	0	21	43 $\frac{1}{3}$	51	22	19	19	51
1999—Portland (East.)	1	4	.200	2.84	47	0	0	0	23	44 $\frac{1}{3}$	42	14	14	26	42
—Florida (N.L.)	0	2	.000	4.20	15	0	0	0	0	15	20	7	7	6	8
2000—Calgary (PCL)	0	4	.000	11.17	18	0	0	0	3	19 $\frac{1}{3}$	36	24	24	9	16
—Brevard County (FSL)	1	1	.500	2.35	8	2	0	0	0	15 $\frac{1}{3}$	11	6	4	5	16
—Portland (East.)	0	1	.000	3.60	4	0	0	0	3	5	5	2	2	4	6
—Gulf Coast Marlins (GCL)	0	0	...	4.50	1	1	0	0	0	2	3	1	1	1	2
Major League totals (1 year)	0	2	.000	4.20	15	0	0	0	0	15	20	7	7	6	8

PERSONAL: Born February 5, 1968, in Ponce, Puerto Rico. ... 6-0/185. ... Bats both, throws right. ... Full name: Roberto Velazquez Alomar. Son of Sandy Alomar Sr., major league infielder with six teams (1964-78) and coach, Chicago Cubs; and brother of Sandy Alomar Jr., catcher, Chicago White Sox.

TRANSACTIONS/CAREER NOTES: Signed as non-drafted free agent by San Diego Padres organization (February 16, 1985). ... Traded by Padres with OF Joe Carter to Toronto Blue Jays for 1B Fred McGriff and SS Tony Fernandez (December 5, 1990). ... On suspended list (May 23-24, 1995). ... Granted free agency (October 30, 1995). ... Signed by Baltimore Orioles (December 21, 1995). ... On suspended list (April 1-7, 1997). ... On disabled list (July 30-August 26, 1997; and July 19-August 4, 1998). ... Granted free agency (October 26, 1998). ... Signed by Cleveland Indians (December 1, 1998).

RECORDS: Holds major league single-season record for most runs by switch-hitter—138 (1999). ... Holds A.L. career records for highest fielding percentage by second basemen—.986; and most consecutive errorless games by second baseman—104 (June 21, 1994 through July 3, 1995). ... Holds A.L. single-season record for fewest double plays by second baseman (150 or more games)—66 (1992). ... Shares A.L. single-season records for most games with switch-hit home runs—2 (1996); and fewest errors by second baseman (150 or more games)—5 (1992).

HONORS: Won A.L. Gold Glove at second base (1991-96, 1998, 1999 and 2000). ... Named second baseman on THE SPORTING NEWS A.L. All-Star team (1992, 1996, 1998, 1999 and 2000). ... Named second baseman on THE SPORTING NEWS A.L. Silver Slugger team (1992, 1996, 1999 and 2000).

STATISTICAL NOTES: Led South Atlantic League second basemen with 35 errors in 1985. ... Led Texas League shortstops with 167 putouts and 34 errors in 1987. ... Led N.L. with 17 sacrifice hits in 1989. ... Led N.L. second basemen with 17 errors in 1990. ... Switch-hit home runs in one game four times (May 10, 1991; May 3, 1995; July 25 and August 14, 1996). ... Had 22-game hitting streak (May 12-June 8, 1996). ... Hit three home runs in one game (April 26, 1997). ... Led A.L. with 13 sacrifice flies in 1999. ... Had 17-game hitting streak (May 5-25, 2000). ... Had 18-game hitting streak (September 17-October 1, 2000). ... Career major league grand slams: 6.

MISCELLANEOUS: Holds Toronto Blue Jays all-time record for highest career batting average (.307).

							BATTING								FIELDING		
Year Team (League)	Pos.	G	AB	R	H	2B	3B	HR	RBI	Avg.	BB	SO	SB	PO	A	E	Avg.
1985—Char., S.C. (SAL)	2B-SS	*137	*546	89	160	14	3	0	54	.293	61	73	36	298	339	†36	.947
1986—Reno (Calif.)	2B	90	356	53	123	16	4	4	49	*.346	32	38	14	198	265	18	.963
1987—Wichita (Texas)	SS-2B	130	536	88	171	41	4	12	68	.319	49	74	43	†188	309	†36	.932
1988—Las Vegas (PCL)	2B	9	37	5	10	1	0	2	14	.270	1	4	3	22	29	1	.981
—San Diego (N.L.)	2B	143	545	84	145	24	6	9	41	.266	47	83	24	319	459	16	.980
1989—San Diego (N.L.)	2B	158	623	82	184	27	1	7	56	.295	53	76	42	341	472	*28	.967
1990—San Diego (N.L.)	2B-SS	147	586	80	168	27	5	6	60	.287	48	72	24	316	404	†19	.974
1991—Toronto (A.L.)■	2B	161	637	88	188	41	11	9	69	.295	57	86	53	333	447	15	.981
1992—Toronto (A.L.)	2B-DH	152	571	105	177	27	8	8	76	.310	87	52	49	287	378	5	.993
1993—Toronto (A.L.)	2B	153	589	109	192	35	6	17	93	.326	80	67	55	254	439	14	.980
1994—Toronto (A.L.)	2B	107	392	78	120	25	4	8	38	.306	51	41	19	176	275	4	.991
1995—Toronto (A.L.)	2B	130	517	71	155	24	7	13	66	.300	47	45	30	*272	267	4	*.993
1996—Baltimore (A.L.)■	2B-DH	153	588	132	193	43	4	22	94	.328	90	65	17	279	445	11	.985
1997—Baltimore (A.L.)	2B-DH	112	412	64	137	23	2	14	60	.333	40	43	9	202	301	6	.988
1998—Baltimore (A.L.)	2B-DH	147	588	86	166	36	1	14	56	.282	59	70	18	251	*449	11	.985
1999—Cleveland (A.L.)■	2B-DH	159	563	*138	182	40	3	24	120	.323	99	96	37	270	466	6	*.992
2000—Cleveland (A.L.)	2B	155	610	111	189	40	2	19	89	.310	64	82	39	293	*437	15	.980
American League totals (10 years)		1429	5467	982	1699	334	48	148	761	.311	674	647	326	2617	3904	91	.986
National League totals (3 years)		448	1754	246	497	78	12	22	157	.283	148	231	90	976	1335	63	.973
Major League totals (13 years)		1877	7221	1228	2196	412	60	170	918	.304	822	878	416	3593	5239	154	.983

DIVISION SERIES RECORD

RECORDS: Shares single-series record for most doubles—4 (1999).

							BATTING								FIELDING		
Year Team (League)	Pos.	G	AB	R	H	2B	3B	HR	RBI	Avg.	BB	SO	SB	PO	A	E	Avg.
1996—Baltimore (A.L.)	2B	4	17	2	5	0	0	1	4	.294	2	3	0	10	6	0	1.000
1997—Baltimore (A.L.)	2B-PH	4	10	1	3	2	0	0	2	.300	1	1	0	3	6	0	1.000
1999—Cleveland (A.L.)	2B	5	19	4	7	4	0	0	3	.368	2	3	2	13	14	1	.964
Division series totals (3 years)		13	46	7	15	6	0	1	9	.326	5	7	2	26	26	1	.981

CHAMPIONSHIP SERIES RECORD

RECORDS: Shares career record for most times grounded into double play—5.

NOTES: Named Most Valuable Player (1992).

Year Team (League)	Pos.	G	AB	R	H	2B	3B	HR	RBI	Avg.	BB	SO	SB	PO	A	E	Avg.
							BATTING							**FIELDING**			
1991—Toronto (A.L.)............	2B	5	19	3	9	0	0	0	4	.474	2	3	2	14	9	0	1.000
1992—Toronto (A.L.)............	2B	6	26	4	11	1	0	2	4	.423	2	1	5	16	15	0	1.000
1993—Toronto (A.L.)............	2B	6	24	3	7	1	0	0	4	.292	4	3	4	14	19	0	1.000
1996—Baltimore (A.L.).........	2B	5	23	2	5	2	0	0	1	.217	0	4	0	15	26	2	.953
1997—Baltimore (A.L.).........	2B	6	22	2	4	0	0	1	2	.182	7	3	0	10	17	2	.931
Championship series totals (5 years)		28	114	14	36	4	0	3	15	.316	15	14	11	69	86	4	.975

WORLD SERIES RECORD

RECORDS: Shares record for most at-bats in one inning—2 (October 20, 1993, eighth inning).

NOTES: Member of World Series championship team (1992 and 1993).

Year Team (League)	Pos.	G	AB	R	H	2B	3B	HR	RBI	Avg.	BB	SO	SB	PO	A	E	Avg.
							BATTING							**FIELDING**			
1992—Toronto (A.L.)............	2B	6	24	3	5	1	0	0	0	.208	3	3	3	5	12	0	1.000
1993—Toronto (A.L.)............	2B	6	25	5	12	2	1	0	6	.480	2	3	4	9	21	2	.938
World Series totals (2 years)		12	49	8	17	3	1	0	6	.347	5	6	7	14	33	2	.959

ALL-STAR GAME RECORD

RECORDS: Shares single-game record for most stolen bases—2 (July 14, 1992).

NOTES: Named Most Valuable Player (1998).

Year League	Pos.	AB	R	H	2B	3B	HR	RBI	Avg.	BB	SO	SB	PO	A	E	Avg.
						BATTING							**FIELDING**			
1990—National.....................	2B	1	0	0	0	0	0	0	.000	0	0	0	1	2	0	1.000
1991—American....................	2B	4	0	0	0	0	0	0	.000	0	0	0	2	5	0	1.000
1992—American....................	2B	3	1	1	0	0	0	0	.333	0	0	2	0	1	0	1.000
1993—American....................	2B	3	1	1	0	0	1	1	.333	0	0	0	0	0	0	...
1994—American....................	2B	3	1	1	0	0	0	0	.333	0	0	1	0	0	0	...
1995—American....................	PR-2B	1	0	0	0	0	0	0	.000	0	0	1	0	0	0	...
1996—American....................	2B	3	0	1	0	0	0	0	.333	0	0	0	0	3	0	1.000
1997—American....................	2B	2	0	0	0	0	0	0	.000	0	0	0	1	5	0	1.000
1998—American....................	2B	4	2	3	0	0	1	1	.750	1	0	1	3	2	0	1.000
1999—American....................	2B	2	0	0	0	0	0	1	.000	0	0	0	2	2	1	.800
2000—American....................	2B	2	0	0	0	0	0	0	.000	0	0	0	3	1	0	1.000
All-Star Game totals (11 years)		28	5	7	0	0	2	3	.250	1	1	5	12	21	1	.971

ALOMAR, SANDY   C   WHITE SOX

PERSONAL: Born June 18, 1966, in Salinas, Puerto Rico. ... 6-5/220. ... Bats right, throws right. ... Full name: Santos Velazquez Alomar Jr. ... Son of Sandy Alomar Sr., major league infielder with six teams (1964-78) and coach, Chicago Cubs; and brother of Roberto Alomar, second baseman, Cleveland Indians.

HIGH SCHOOL: Luis Munoz Rivera (Salinas, Puerto Rico).

TRANSACTIONS/CAREER NOTES: Signed as non-drafted free agent by San Diego Padres organization (October 21, 1983). ... Traded by Padres with OF Chris James and 3B Carlos Baerga to Cleveland Indians for OF Joe Carter (December 6, 1989). ... On Cleveland disabled list (May 15-June 17 and July 29, 1991-remainder of season); included rehabilitation assignments to Colorado Springs (June 8-17 and August 9-12). ... On disabled list (May 2-18, 1992). ... On suspended list (July 29-August 2, 1992). ... On Cleveland disabled list (May 1-August 7, 1993); included rehabilitation assignment to Charlotte, S.C. (July 22-August 7). ... On disabled list (April 24-May 11, 1994). ... On Cleveland disabled list (April 19-June 29, 1995); included rehabilitation assignment to Canton/Akron (June 22-29). ... On Cleveland disabled list (May 11-September 6, 1999); included rehabilitation assignments to Akron (July 5-19 and September 3-6) and Buffalo (August 10-27). ... On disabled list (April 19-May 8, 2000). ... Granted free agency (October 27, 2000). ... Signed by Chicago White Sox (December 18, 2000).

RECORDS: Shares major league single-game record for most doubles—4 (June 6, 1997).

HONORS: Named Minor League co-Player of the Year by THE SPORTING NEWS (1988). ... Named Pacific Coast League Player of the Year (1988 and 1989). ... Named Minor League Player of the Year by THE SPORTING NEWS (1989). ... Named A.L. Rookie Player of the Year by THE SPORTING NEWS (1990). ... Won A.L. Gold Glove at catcher (1990). ... Named A.L. Rookie of the Year by Baseball Writers' Association of America (1990).

STATISTICAL NOTES: Led Northwest League catchers with .985 fielding percentage and 421 putouts in 1984. ... Led Pacific Coast League catchers with 14 errors in 1988. ... Led Pacific Coast League catchers with 573 putouts in 1988 and 702 in 1989. ... Led Pacific Coast League catchers with 633 total chances in 1988 and 761 in 1989. ... Had 30-game hitting streak (May 25-July 6, 1997). ... Career major league grand slams: 2.

MISCELLANEOUS: Batted as switch hitter (1984-86).

Year Team (League)	Pos.	G	AB	R	H	2B	3B	HR	RBI	Avg.	BB	SO	SB	PO	A	E	Avg.
							BATTING							**FIELDING**			
1984—Spokane (N'West)	C-1B	59	219	13	47	5	0	0	21	.215	13	20	3	†465	51	8	†.985
1985—Char., S.C. (SAL)	C-OF	100	352	38	73	7	0	3	43	.207	31	30	3	779	75	18	.979
1986—Beaumont (Texas)	C	100	346	36	83	15	1	4	27	.240	15	35	2	505	60	*18	.969
1987—Wichita (Texas)	C	103	375	50	115	19	1	8	65	.307	21	37	1	*606	50	*15	.978
1988—Las Vegas (PCL)	C-OF	93	337	59	100	9	5	16	71	.297	28	35	1	†574	46	†14	.978
—San Diego (N.L.)	PH	1	1	0	0	0	0	0	0	.000	0	1	0	...	...	...	...
1989—Las Vegas (PCL)	C-OF	131	*523	88	160	33	8	13	101	.306	42	58	3	†706	47	12	.984
—San Diego (N.L.)	C	7	19	1	4	1	0	1	6	.211	3	3	0	33	1	0	1.000
1990—Cleveland (A.L.)■.........	C	132	445	60	129	26	2	9	66	.290	25	46	4	686	46	*14	.981
1991—Cleveland (A.L.).........	C-DH	51	184	10	40	9	0	0	7	.217	8	24	0	280	19	4	.987
—Colo. Springs (PCL) ..	C	12	35	5	14	2	0	1	10	.400	5	0	0	5	0	1	.833
1992—Cleveland (A.L.).........	C-DH	89	299	22	75	16	0	2	26	.251	13	32	3	477	39	2	.996
1993—Cleveland (A.L.).........	C	64	215	24	58	7	1	6	32	.270	11	28	3	342	25	6	.984
—Charlotte (I.L.)...........	C	12	44	8	16	5	0	1	8	.364	5	8	0	20	1	0	1.000
1994—Cleveland (A.L.).........	C	80	292	44	84	15	1	14	43	.288	25	31	8	453	41	2	.996

Year Team (League)	Pos.	G	AB	R	H	2B	3B	HR	RBI	Avg.	BB	SO	SB	PO	A	E	Avg.
1995—Canton/Akron (East.)..	C-DH	6	15	3	6	1	0	0	1	.400	1	1	0	23	0	1	.958
—Cleveland (A.L.)	C	66	203	32	61	6	0	10	35	.300	7	26	3	364	22	2	.995
1996—Cleveland (A.L.)	C-1B	127	418	53	110	23	0	11	50	.263	19	42	1	724	48	9	.988
1997—Cleveland (A.L.)	C-DH	125	451	63	146	37	0	21	83	.324	19	48	0	743	40	*12	.985
1998—Cleveland (A.L.)	C-DH	117	409	45	96	26	2	6	44	.235	18	45	0	712	42	6	.992
1999—Cleveland (A.L.)	C-DH	37	137	19	42	13	0	6	25	.307	4	23	0	257	10	7	.974
—Akron (East.)	DH-C	10	29	8	9	0	0	1	6	.310	3	2	1	12	1	1	.929
—Buffalo (I.L.)	C-DH	10	33	9	9	2	1	2	10	.273	6	3	0	35	0	3	.921
2000—Cleveland (A.L.)	C-DH	97	356	44	103	16	2	7	42	.289	16	41	2	661	42	8	.989
American League totals (11 years)		985	3409	416	944	194	8	92	453	.277	165	386	24	5699	374	72	.988
National League totals (2 years)		8	20	1	4	1	0	1	6	.200	3	4	0	33	1	0	1.000
Major League totals (13 years)		993	3429	417	948	195	8	93	459	.276	168	390	24	5732	375	72	.988

DIVISION SERIES RECORD

Year Team (League)	Pos.	G	AB	R	H	2B	3B	HR	RBI	Avg.	BB	SO	SB	PO	A	E	Avg.
1995—Cleveland (A.L.)	C	3	11	1	2	1	0	0	1	.182	0	1	0	22	1	0	1.000
1996—Cleveland (A.L.)	C	4	16	0	2	0	0	0	3	.125	0	2	0	40	4	1	.978
1997—Cleveland (A.L.)	C	5	19	4	6	1	0	2	5	.316	0	2	0	28	1	1	.967
1998—Cleveland (A.L.)	C	4	13	2	3	3	0	0	2	.231	1	4	0	29	0	1	.967
1999—Cleveland (A.L.)	C	5	14	1	2	0	0	0	1	.143	2	6	0	33	1	1	.971
Division series totals (5 years)		21	73	8	15	5	0	2	12	.205	3	15	0	152	7	4	.975

CHAMPIONSHIP SERIES RECORD

Year Team (League)	Pos.	G	AB	R	H	2B	3B	HR	RBI	Avg.	BB	SO	SB	PO	A	E	Avg.
1995—Cleveland (A.L.)	C	5	15	0	4	1	1	0	1	.267	1	1	0	30	3	1	.971
1997—Cleveland (A.L.)	C	6	24	3	3	0	0	1	4	.125	1	3	0	49	1	0	1.000
1998—Cleveland (A.L.)	C	5	16	1	1	0	0	0	0	.063	0	2	0	29	1	2	.938
Championship series totals (3 years)		16	55	4	8	1	1	1	5	.145	2	6	0	108	5	3	.974

WORLD SERIES RECORD

Year Team (League)	Pos.	G	AB	R	H	2B	3B	HR	RBI	Avg.	BB	SO	SB	PO	A	E	Avg.
1995—Cleveland (A.L.)	C	5	15	0	3	2	0	0	1	.200	0	2	0	28	0	0	1.000
1997—Cleveland (A.L.)	C	7	30	5	11	1	0	2	10	.367	2	3	0	49	3	0	1.000
World Series totals (2 years)		12	45	5	14	3	0	2	11	.311	2	5	0	77	3	0	1.000

ALL-STAR GAME RECORD

NOTES: Named Most Valuable Player (1997).

Year League	Pos.	AB	R	H	2B	3B	HR	RBI	Avg.	BB	SO	SB	PO	A	E	Avg.
1990—American	C	3	1	2	0	0	0	0	.667	0	0	0	3	0	0	1.000
1991—American	C	2	0	0	0	0	0	0	.000	0	0	0	2	0	0	1.000
1992—American	C	3	0	1	0	0	0	0	.333	0	0	0	3	0	0	1.000
1996—American	PH-C	2	0	0	0	0	0	0	.000	0	0	0	1	0	0	1.000
1997—American	C	1	1	1	0	0	1	2	1.000	0	0	0	4	0	0	1.000
1998—American	C	1	0	1	0	0	0	1	1.000	0	0	0	5	0	0	1.000
All-Star Game totals (6 years)		12	2	5	0	0	1	3	.417	0	0	0	18	0	0	1.000

ALOU, MOISES — OF — ASTROS

PERSONAL: Born July 3, 1966, in Atlanta. ... 6-3/195. ... Bats right, throws right. ... Full name: Moises Rojas Alou. ... Son of Felipe Alou, manager, Montreal Expos; nephew of Jesus Alou, major league outfielder with four teams (1963-75 and 1978-79); nephew of Matty Alou, major league outfielder with six teams (1960-74); and cousin of Mel Rojas, pitcher with five major league teams (1990-99). ... Name pronounced moy-SEZZ ah-LOO.

HIGH SCHOOL: C.E.E. (Santo Domingo, Dominican Republic).

JUNIOR COLLEGE: Canada College (Calif.).

TRANSACTIONS/CAREER NOTES: Selected by Pittsburgh Pirates organization in first round (second pick overall) of free-agent draft (January 14, 1986). ... Traded by Pirates to Montreal Expos (August 16, 1990), completing deal in which Expos traded P Zane Smith to Pirates for P Scott Ruskin, SS Willie Greene and a player to be named later (August 8, 1990). ... On Montreal disabled list (March 19, 1991-entire season; July 7-27, 1992; September 18, 1993-remainder of season; August 18-September 5, 1995 and September 11, 1995-remainder of season). ... On disabled list (July 8-23, 1996). ... On suspended list (August 23-27, 1996). ... Granted free agency (December 7, 1996). ... Signed by Florida Marlins (December 12, 1996). ... Traded by Marlins to Houston Astros for P Oscar Henriquez, P Manuel Barrios and a player to be named later (November 11, 1997). ... Marlins acquired P Mark Johnson to complete deal (December 16, 1997). ... On disabled list (April 3, 1999-entire season). ... On disabled list (April 27-May 14, 2000).

HONORS: Named outfielder on THE SPORTING NEWS N.L. All-Star team (1994 and 1998). ... Named outfielder on THE SPORTING NEWS N.L. Silver Slugger team (1994 and 1998).

STATISTICAL NOTES: Led American Association outfielders with seven double plays in 1990. ... Led N.L. in grounding into double plays with 21 in 2000. ... Career major league grand slams: 2.

Year Team (League)	Pos.	G	AB	R	H	2B	3B	HR	RBI	Avg.	BB	SO	SB	PO	A	E	Avg.
1986—Watertown (NY-Penn)	OF	69	254	30	60	9	*8	6	35	.236	22	72	14	134	6	7	.952
1987—Macon (S.Atl.)	OF	4	8	1	1	0	0	0	0	.125	2	4	0	6	0	0	1.000
—Watertown (NY-Penn)	OF	39	117	20	25	6	2	4	8	.214	16	36	6	43	1	2	.957
1988—Augusta (S.Atl.)	OF	105	358	58	112	23	5	7	62	.313	51	84	24	220	10	9	.962
1989—Salem (Caro.)	OF	86	321	50	97	29	2	14	53	.302	35	69	12	166	12	10	.947
—Harrisburg (East.)	OF	54	205	36	60	5	2	3	19	.293	17	38	8	89	1	2	.978

Year Team (League)	Pos.	G	AB	R	H	2B	3B	HR	RBI	Avg.	BB	SO	SB	PO	A	E	Avg.
1990—Harrisburg (East.)	OF	36	132	19	39	12	2	3	22	.295	16	21	7	93	2	1	.990
—Buffalo (A.A.)	OF	75	271	38	74	4	6	5	31	.273	30	43	9	169	10	8	.957
—Pittsburgh (N.L.)	OF	2	5	0	1	0	0	0	0	.200	0	0	0	3	0	0	1.000
—Indianapolis (A.A.)■	OF	15	55	6	12	1	0	0	6	.218	3	7	4	27	2	0	1.000
—Montreal (N.L.)	OF	14	15	4	3	0	1	0	0	.200	0	3	0	6	1	0	1.000
1991—Montreal (N.L.)							Did not play.										
1992—Montreal (N.L.)	OF	115	341	53	96	28	2	9	56	.282	25	46	16	170	6	4	.978
1993—Montreal (N.L.)	OF	136	482	70	138	29	6	18	85	.286	38	53	17	254	11	4	.985
1994—Montreal (N.L.)	OF	107	422	81	143	31	5	22	78	.339	42	63	7	201	4	3	.986
1995—Montreal (N.L.)	OF	93	344	48	94	22	0	14	58	.273	29	56	4	147	5	3	.981
1996—Montreal (N.L.)	OF	143	540	87	152	28	2	21	96	.281	49	83	9	259	8	3	.989
1997—Florida (N.L.)■	OF	150	538	88	157	29	5	23	115	.292	70	85	9	248	4	3	.988
1998—Houston (N.L.)■	OF-DH	159	584	104	182	34	5	38	124	.312	84	87	11	232	11	5	.980
1999—Houston (N.L.)							Did not play.										
2000—Houston (N.L.)	OF-DH	126	454	82	161	28	2	30	114	.355	52	45	3	191	5	6	.970
Major League totals (9 years)		1045	3725	617	1127	229	28	175	726	.303	389	521	76	1711	55	31	.983

DIVISION SERIES RECORD

Year Team (League)	Pos.	G	AB	R	H	2B	3B	HR	RBI	Avg.	BB	SO	SB	PO	A	E	Avg.
1997—Florida (N.L.)	OF	3	14	1	3	1	0	0	1	.214	0	3	0	5	0	0	1.000
1998—Houston (N.L.)	OF	4	16	0	3	0	0	0	0	.188	0	2	0	4	0	0	1.000
Division series totals (2 years)		7	30	1	6	1	0	0	1	.200	0	5	0	9	0	0	1.000

CHAMPIONSHIP SERIES RECORD

Year Team (League)	Pos.	G	AB	R	H	2B	3B	HR	RBI	Avg.	BB	SO	SB	PO	A	E	Avg.
1997—Florida (N.L.)	OF-PH	5	15	0	1	1	0	0	5	.067	1	3	0	3	0	0	1.000

WORLD SERIES RECORD

NOTES: Member of World Series championship team (1997).

Year Team (League)	Pos.	G	AB	R	H	2B	3B	HR	RBI	Avg.	BB	SO	SB	PO	A	E	Avg.
1997—Florida (N.L.)	OF	7	28	6	9	2	0	3	9	.321	3	6	1	11	0	0	1.000

ALL-STAR GAME RECORD

Year League	Pos.	AB	R	H	2B	3B	HR	RBI	Avg.	BB	SO	SB	PO	A	E	Avg.
1994—National	OF	1	0	1	1	0	0	1	1.000	0	0	0	0	0	0	...
1997—National	OF	2	0	1	0	0	0	0	.500	0	0	0	1	0	0	1.000
1998—National	OF	3	1	1	0	0	0	0	.333	0	0	2	0	0	0	...
All-Star Game totals (3 years)		6	1	3	1	0	0	1	.500	0	2	0	1	0	0	1.000

ALVAREZ, CLEMENTE   C   PHILLIES

PERSONAL: Born May 18, 1968, in Anzoategul, Venezuela. ... 5-11/180. ... Bats right, throws right. ... Full name: Clemente Rafael Alvarez.
TRANSACTIONS/CAREER NOTES: Signed as non-drafted free agent by Chicago White Sox organization (December 18, 1986). ... Granted free agency (October 17, 1994). ... Signed by Montreal Expos organization (March 11, 1995). ... Granted free agency (October 16, 1995). ... Signed by White Sox organization (April 18, 1997). ... Granted free agency (October 17, 1997). ... Signed by Philadelphia Phillies organization (March 19, 1999). ... On Reading disabled list (May 21-June 7, 1999; May 11-June 2, 2000). ... On Scranton/Wilkes-Barre disabled list (June 26-July 26 and July 31-August 12, 2000).

Year Team (League)	Pos.	G	AB	R	H	2B	3B	HR	RBI	Avg.	BB	SO	SB	PO	A	E	Avg.
1987—GC White Sox (GCL)	C	25	55	8	10	1	0	0	4	.182	7	8	1	103	16	2	.983
1988—South Bend (Midw.)	C	15	41	0	3	0	0	0	1	.073	3	19	0	90	5	0	1.000
—Utica (NY-Penn)	C	53	132	15	31	5	1	0	14	.235	11	36	5	302	43	3	.991
1989—South Bend (Midw.)	C	86	230	22	51	15	0	0	22	.222	16	59	4	529	60	8	.987
1990—Sarasota (FSL)	C-3B-OF	37	119	9	19	4	1	1	9	.160	8	24	0	221	30	6	.977
—South Bend (Midw.)	C-1B	48	127	14	30	5	0	2	12	.236	20	38	2	323	47	4	.989
1991—Sarasota (FSL)	C	71	194	14	40	10	2	1	22	.206	20	41	3	408	77	5	.990
1992—Birmingham (Sou.)	C	57	169	7	24	8	0	1	10	.142	10	52	1	353	57	0	1.000
1993—Birmingham (Sou.)	C	35	111	8	25	4	0	1	8	.225	11	28	0	277	27	2	.993
—GC White Sox (GCL)	C	2	5	0	0	0	0	0	0	.000	1	2	0	4	0	0	1.000
—Nashville (A.A.)	C	11	29	1	6	0	0	0	2	.207	1	4	0	75	0	1	1.000
1994—Nashville (A.A.)	C	87	223	18	48	8	1	3	14	.215	17	48	0	555	46	1	*.998
1995—Ottawa (I.L.)■	C	50	143	15	33	7	0	4	20	.231	10	34	0	292	26	4	.988
1996—....................								Did not play.									
1997—Win.-Salem (Caro.)■	C	2	4	0	1	0	0	0	1	.250	0	2	0	8	1	1	.900
—Birmingham (Sou.)	C	79	242	29	49	10	1	3	23	.202	27	49	0	500	49	1	*.998
1998—....................								Did not play.									
1999—Scranton/W.B. (I.L.)■	C	9	28	4	7	4	0	0	6	.250	3	9	0	59	6	0	1.000
—Reading (East.)	C	48	142	12	25	5	1	2	12	.176	11	38	1	326	24	3	.992
2000—Reading (East.)	C	9	18	2	4	1	0	0	5	.222	3	3	0	40	4	0	1.000
—Clearwater (FSL)	C	12	41	1	11	0	0	0	1	.268	2	7	0	55	9	0	1.000
—Scranton/W.B. (I.L.)	C	5	11	0	0	0	0	0	0	.000	0	2	0	19	0	1	1.000
—Philadelphia (N.L.)	C	2	5	1	1	0	0	0	0	.200	0	1	0	10	0	0	1.000
Major League totals (1 year)		2	5	1	1	0	0	0	0	.200	0	1	0	10	0	0	1.000

PERSONAL: Born March 6, 1974, in Navojoa, Sonora, Mexico. ... 6-1/205. ... Bats right, throws right. ... Full name: Gabriel De Jesus Alvarez.
HIGH SCHOOL: Bishop Amat (La Puente, Calif.).
COLLEGE: Southern California.
TRANSACTIONS/CAREER NOTES: Selected by San Diego Padres organization in second round of free-agent draft (June 1, 1995). ... Selected by Arizona Diamondbacks in first round (fifth pick overall) of expansion draft (November 18, 1997). ... Traded by Diamondbacks with 3B Joe Randa and P Matt Drews to Detroit Tigers for 3B Travis Fryman (November 18, 1997). ... Traded by Tigers to San Diego Padres for 1B/OF Dusty Allen (July 17, 2000).
STATISTICAL NOTES: Led Southern League third basemen with 32 errors in 1997. ... Led Southern League in grounding into double plays with 21 in 1997. ... Career major league grand slams: 1.

							BATTING								FIELDING			
Year Team (League)	Pos.	G	AB	R	H	2B	3B	HR	RBI	Avg.	BB	SO	SB	PO	A	E	Avg.
1995— Rancho Cuca. (Calif.) .	SS-3B	59	212	41	73	17	2	6	36	.344	29	30	1	52	132	22	.893
— Memphis (Sou.)	2B-SS	2	9	0	5	1	0	0	4	.556	1	1	0	0	6	1	.857
1996— Memphis (Sou.)	3B-SS	104	368	58	91	23	1	8	40	.247	64	87	2	62	161	31	.878
1997— Mobile (Sou.)	3B-SS	114	427	71	128	28	2	14	78	.300	51	64	1	70	209	†33	.894
1998— Toledo (I.L.)■	3B	67	249	37	68	15	1	20	58	.273	30	60	3	38	142	15	.923
— Detroit (A.L.)	3B-DH	58	199	16	46	11	0	5	29	.231	18	65	1	38	93	19	.873
1999— Toledo (I.L.)	3-O-DH-S	110	410	70	117	24	0	21	67	.285	57	80	1	87	165	26	.906
— Detroit (A.L.)	DH-OF-3B	22	53	5	11	3	0	2	4	.208	3	9	0	3	1	0	1.000
2000— Toledo (I.L.)	1B-3B	69	241	37	50	11	2	8	35	.207	47	53	0	262	35	13	.958
— Detroit (A.L.)	DH	1	1	0	0	0	0	0	0	.000	2	1	0	...	...	...	...
— Las Vegas (PCL)■	1B-OF	43	141	33	43	11	0	9	26	.305	33	44	2	258	19	5	.982
— San Diego (N.L.)	3B-OF	11	13	1	2	1	0	0	0	.154	1	1	0	0	1	0	1.000
American League totals (3 years)		81	253	21	57	14	0	7	33	.225	23	75	1	41	94	19	.877
National League totals (1 year)		11	13	1	2	1	0	0	0	.154	1	1	0	0	1	0	1.000
Major League totals (3 years)		92	266	22	59	15	0	7	33	.222	24	76	1	41	95	19	.877

PERSONAL: Born August 9, 1973, in Coral Gables, Fla. ... 6-0/175. ... Throws left, bats left. ... Full name: Juan M. Alvarez.
HIGH SCHOOL: Coral Gables (Fla.).
COLLEGE: St. Thomas.
TRANSACTIONS/CAREER NOTES: Signed as non-drafted free agent by California Angels organization (July 25, 1995). ... Angels franchise renamed Anaheim Angels for 1997 season.

Year League	W	L	Pct.	ERA	G	GS	CG	ShO	Sv.	IP	H	R	ER	BB	SO
1995— Boise (N'West)	0	0	...	0.77	9	0	0	0	0	11 2/3	12	1	1	2	11
1996— Cedar Rapids (Midw.)	1	2	.333	3.40	40	0	0	0	3	53	50	25	20	30	53
1997— Lake Elsinore (Calif.)	4	2	.667	1.40	27	0	0	0	3	51 1/3	33	9	8	13	46
— Midland (Texas)	4	1	.800	8.27	24	0	0	0	0	37	63	42	34	22	27
1998— Midland (Texas)	3	4	.429	4.30	40	0	0	0	12	46	40	26	22	21	41
— Vancouver (PCL)	1	1	.500	5.02	18	0	0	0	0	14 1/3	14	9	8	8	12
1999— Erie (East.)	1	2	.333	2.05	23	0	0	0	4	30 2/3	20	14	7	6	22
— Edmonton (PCL)	0	3	.000	3.49	27	0	0	0	0	28 1/3	30	13	11	8	25
— Anaheim (A.L.)	0	1	.000	3.00	8	0	0	0	0	3	1	1	1	4	4
2000— Edmonton (PCL)	3	1	.750	2.82	44	0	0	0	0	38 1/3	30	12	12	19	27
— Anaheim (A.L.)	0	0	...	13.50	11	0	0	0	0	6	14	9	9	7	2
Major League totals (2 years)	0	1	.000	10.00	19	0	0	0	0	9	15	10	10	11	6

PERSONAL: Born March 24, 1970, in Maracaibo, Venezuela. ... 6-1/245. ... Throws left, bats left. ... Full name: Wilson Eduardo Alvarez.
TRANSACTIONS/CAREER NOTES: Signed as non-drafted free agent by Texas Rangers organization (September 23, 1986). ... Traded by Rangers with IF Scott Fletcher and OF Sammy Sosa to Chicago White Sox for OF Harold Baines and IF Fred Manrique (July 29, 1989). ... Traded by White Sox with P Danny Darwin and P Roberto Hernandez to San Francisco Giants for SS Michael Caruso, OF Brian Manning, P Lorenzo Barcelo, P Keith Foulke, P Bobby Howry and P Ken Vining (July 31, 1997). ... Granted free agency (November 1, 1997). ... Signed by Tampa Bay Devil Rays (December 3, 1997). ... On Tampa Bay disabled list (May 21-July 6, 1998); included rehabilitation assignments to Gulf Coast Devil Rays (June 26-29), St. Petersburg (June 30-July 4) and Durham (July 5-6). ... On disabled list (April 12-29 and July 24-August 8, 1999). ... On Tampa Bay disabled list (March 25, 2000-entire season); included rehabilitation assignment to St. Petersburg (April 15).
RECORDS: Shares major league single-inning record for most strikeouts—4 (July 21, 1997, seventh inning).
STATISTICAL NOTES: Tied for Gulf Coast League lead with six home runs allowed in 1987. ... Pitched 7-0 no-hit victory for Chicago against Baltimore (August 11, 1991).

Year League	W	L	Pct.	ERA	G	GS	CG	ShO	Sv.	IP	H	R	ER	BB	SO
1987— Gastonia (S.Atl.)	1	5	.167	6.47	8	6	0	0	0	32	39	24	23	23	19
— GC Rangers (GCL)	2	5	.286	5.24	10	10	0	0	0	44 2/3	41	29	26	21	46
1988— Gastonia (S.Atl.)	4	11	.267	2.98	23	23	1	0	0	127	113	63	42	49	134
— Oklahoma City (A.A.)	1	1	.500	3.78	5	3	0	0	0	16 2/3	17	8	7	6	9
1989— Charlotte (FSL)	7	4	.636	2.11	13	13	3	2	0	81	68	29	19	21	51
— Tulsa (Texas)	2	2	.500	2.06	7	7	1	1	0	48	40	14	11	16	29
— Texas (A.L.)	0	1	.000	...	1	1	0	0	0	3	3	3	3	2	0
— Birmingham (Sou.)■	2	1	.667	3.03	6	6	0	0	0	35 2/3	32	12	12	16	18
1990— Birmingham (Sou.)	5	1	.833	4.27	7	7	1	0	0	46 1/3	44	24	22	25	36
— Vancouver (PCL)	7	7	.500	6.00	17	15	1	0	0	75	91	54	50	51	35
1991— Birmingham (Sou.)	10	6	.625	1.83	23	23	3	2	0	152 1/3	109	46	31	74	165
— Chicago (A.L.)	3	2	.600	3.51	10	9	2	1	0	56 1/3	47	26	22	29	32
1992— Chicago (A.L.)	5	3	.625	5.20	34	9	0	0	1	100 1/3	103	64	58	65	66
1993— Chicago (A.L.)	15	8	.652	2.95	31	31	1	1	0	207 2/3	168	78	68	*122	155
— Nashville (A.A.)	0	1	.000	2.84	1	1	0	0	0	6 1/3	7	7	2	2	8

Year League	W	L	Pct.	ERA	G	GS	CG	ShO	Sv.	IP	H	R	ER	BB	SO
1994—Chicago (A.L.)	12	8	.600	3.45	24	24	2	1	0	161 2/3	147	72	62	62	108
1995—Chicago (A.L.)	8	11	.421	4.32	29	29	3	0	0	175	171	96	84	93	118
1996—Chicago (A.L.)	15	10	.600	4.22	35	35	0	0	0	217 1/3	216	106	102	97	181
1997—Chicago (A.L.)	9	8	.529	3.03	22	22	2	1	0	145 2/3	126	61	49	55	110
—San Francisco (N.L.)■	4	3	.571	4.48	11	11	0	0	0	66 1/3	54	36	33	36	69
1998—Tampa Bay (A.L.)■	6	14	.300	4.73	25	25	0	0	0	142 2/3	130	78	75	68	107
—GC Devil Rays (GCL)	0	0	...	0.00	1	1	0	0	0	3	2	0	0	1	4
—St. Petersburg (FSL)	0	1	.000	27.00	1	1	0	0	0	1 2/3	5	5	5	2	2
—Durham (I.L.)	0	0	...	3.86	1	1	0	0	0	4 2/3	4	2	2	2	6
1999—Tampa Bay (A.L.)	9	9	.500	4.22	28	28	1	0	0	160	159	92	75	79	128
2000—St. Petersburg (FSL)	0	0	...	0.00	1	1	0	0	0	4	0	0	0	0	2
A.L. totals (10 years)	82	74	.526	3.94	239	213	11	4	1	1366 2/3	1270	676	598	672	1005
N.L. totals (1 year)	4	3	.571	4.48	11	11	0	0	0	66 1/3	54	36	33	36	69
Major League totals (10 years)	86	77	.528	3.96	250	224	11	4	1	1433	1324	712	631	708	1074

DIVISION SERIES RECORD

Year League	W	L	Pct.	ERA	G	GS	CG	ShO	Sv.	IP	H	R	ER	BB	SO
1997—San Francisco (N.L.)	0	1	.000	6.00	1	1	0	0	0	6	6	4	4	4	4

CHAMPIONSHIP SERIES RECORD

Year League	W	L	Pct.	ERA	G	GS	CG	ShO	Sv.	IP	H	R	ER	BB	SO
1993—Chicago (A.L.)	1	0	1.000	1.00	1	1	1	0	0	9	7	1	1	2	6

ALL-STAR GAME RECORD

Year League	W	L	Pct.	ERA	GS	CG	ShO	Sv.	IP	H	R	ER	BB	SO
1994—American	0	0	...	0.00	0	0	0	0	1	0	0	0	0	0

AMARAL, RICH — OF

PERSONAL: Born April 1, 1962, in Visalia, Calif. ... 6-0/175. ... Bats right, throws right. ... Full name: Richard Louis Amaral. ... Name pronounced AM-ar-all.

HIGH SCHOOL: Estancia (Costa Mesa, Calif.).

JUNIOR COLLEGE: Orange Coast College (Calif.).

COLLEGE: UCLA.

TRANSACTIONS/CAREER NOTES: Selected by Chicago Cubs organization in second round of free-agent draft (June 6, 1983). ... Selected by Chicago White Sox organization from Cubs organization in Rule 5 minor league draft (December 6, 1988). ... Granted free agency (October 15, 1990). ... Signed by Seattle Mariners organization (November 25, 1990). ... On Seattle disabled list (May 29-July 17, 1991); included rehabilitation assignment to Calgary (July 11-17). ... On disabled list (August 1-16, 1993). ... On disabled list (March 28-April 14 and September 9, 1998-remainder of season). ... Granted free agency (October 26, 1998). ... Signed by Baltimore Orioles (December 21, 1998). ... On Baltimore disabled list (June 15-July 28, 2000). ... Released by Orioles (July 28, 2000). ... Signed by Atlanta Braves (August 25, 2000). ... Granted free agency (October 18, 2000).

HONORS: Named second baseman on THE SPORTING NEWS college All-America team (1983).

STATISTICAL NOTES: Tied for New York-Pennsylvania League lead in double plays by second baseman with 39 in 1984. ... Tied for Carolina League lead in errors by second baseman with 25 in 1985. ... Led Pacific Coast League with .433 on-base percentage in 1991.

							BATTING							FIELDING		
Year Team (League)	Pos.	G	AB	R	H	2B	3B	HR	RBI	Avg.	BB	SO	SB	PO	A	E	Avg.
1983—Geneva (NY-Penn)	2B-3B-SS	67	269	63	68	17	3	1	24	.253	45	47	22	135	205	14	.960
1984—Quad Cities (Midw.)	2B-SS	34	119	21	25	1	0	0	7	.210	24	29	12	62	73	6	.957
1985—Win.-Salem (Caro.)	2B-3B	124	428	62	116	15	5	3	36	.271	59	68	26	228	318	‡27	.953
1986—Pittsfield (East.)	2B	114	355	43	89	12	0	0	24	.251	39	65	25	228	266	14	.972
1987—Pittsfield (East.)	2B-1B	104	315	45	80	8	5	0	28	.254	43	50	28	242	274	18	.966
1988—Pittsfield (East.)	2-3-1-S-O	122	422	66	117	15	4	4	47	.277	56	53	54	288	262	19	.967
1989—Birmingham (Sou.)■	2B-SS-3B	122	432	*90	123	15	6	4	48	.285	88	66	57	198	256	23	.952
1990—Vancouver (PCL)	S-3-2-O-1	130	462	87	139	*39	5	4	56	.301	88	68	20	154	260	15	.965
1991—Calgary (PCL)■	SS-2B	86	347	79	120	26	2	3	36	*.346	53	37	30	148	284	15	.966
—Seattle (A.L.)	2-3-S-DH-1	14	16	2	1	0	0	0	0	.063	1	5	0	13	16	2	.935
1992—Calgary (PCL)	SS-2B-OF	106	403	79	128	21	8	0	21	.318	67	69	*53	192	329	22	.959
—Seattle (A.L.)	S-3-O-1-2	35	100	9	24	3	0	1	7	.240	5	16	4	33	68	3	.971
1993—Seattle (A.L.)	2-3-S-DH-1	110	373	53	108	24	1	1	44	.290	33	54	19	180	270	10	.978
—Calgary (PCL)	2B-OF	77	228	37	60	10	2	4	18	.263	24	28	5	107	118	15	.938
1994—Seattle (A.L.)	2-O-S-DH-1	77	228	37	60	10	2	4	18	.263	24	28	5	107	118	15	.938
—Calgary (PCL)	2B-OF	56	13	18	7	0	0	0	12	.321	4	6	2	28	35	3	.955
1995—Seattle (A.L.)	OF-DH	90	238	45	67	14	2	2	19	.282	21	33	21	121	6	1	.992
1996—Seattle (A.L.)	O-2-1-DH-3	118	312	69	91	11	3	1	29	.292	47	55	25	195	24	0	1.000
1997—Seattle (A.L.)	O-2-1-DH-3-S	89	190	34	54	5	0	1	21	.284	10	34	12	103	29	3	.978
1998—Seattle (A.L.)	O-2-1-DH-3	73	134	25	37	6	0	1	4	.276	13	24	11	90	14	0	1.000
1999—Baltimore (A.L.)■	O-DH-1-2-3	91	137	21	38	8	1	0	11	.277	15	20	9	70	2	0	1.000
2000—Baltimore (A.L.)	OF-DH-1B	30	60	10	13	1	1	0	6	.217	7	8	6	50	5	0	1.000
—Richmond (I.L.)■	OF	7	22	3	3	1	0	0	0	.136	4	6	0	11	0	0	1.000
Major League totals (10 years)		727	1788	305	493	82	10	11	159	.276	176	277	112	962	552	34	.978

DIVISION SERIES RECORD

							BATTING							FIELDING		
Year Team (League)	Pos.	G	AB	R	H	2B	3B	HR	RBI	Avg.	BB	SO	SB	PO	A	E	Avg.
1995—Seattle (A.L.)								Did not play.									
1997—Seattle (A.L.)	1B-PH	2	4	2	2	0	0	0	0	.500	0	1	0	7	2	0	1.000

CHAMPIONSHIP SERIES RECORD

							BATTING							FIELDING		
Year Team (League)	Pos.	G	AB	R	H	2B	3B	HR	RBI	Avg.	BB	SO	SB	PO	A	E	Avg.
1995—Seattle (A.L.)	PH	2	2	0	0	0	0	0	0	.000	0	1	0	...	...	...	...

A

PERSONAL: Born January 18, 1964, in Silver Spring, Md. ... 6-1/202. ... Bats left, throws left. ... Full name: Brady Kevin Anderson.
HIGH SCHOOL: Carlsbad (Calif.).
COLLEGE: UC Irvine.
TRANSACTIONS/CAREER NOTES: Selected by Boston Red Sox organization in 10th round of free-agent draft (June 3, 1985). ... Traded by Red Sox with P Curt Schilling to Baltimore Orioles for P Mike Boddicker (July 29, 1988). ... On Baltimore disabled list (June 8-July 20, 1990); included rehabilitation assignments to Hagerstown (July 5-12) and Frederick (July 13-17). ... On Baltimore disabled list (May 28-June 14, 1991) and June 23-July 8, 1993). ... Granted free agency (October 27, 1997). ... Re-signed by Orioles (December 7, 1997). ... On disabled list (April 20-May 8, 1998).
RECORDS: Holds major league single-season record for most home runs leading off game—12 (1996). ... Shares major league single-inning record for most times hit by pitch—2 (May 23, 1999, first inning).
STATISTICAL NOTES: Led A.L. outfielders with six double plays in 1992. ... Led A.L. in being hit by pitch with 22 in 1996, 19 in 1997 and 24 in 1999. ... Career major league grand slams: 3.
MISCELLANEOUS: Holds Baltimore Orioles all-time record for stolen bases (295).

							BATTING								FIELDING		
Year Team (League)	Pos.	G	AB	R	H	2B	3B	HR	RBI	Avg.	BB	SO	SB	PO	A	E	Avg.
1985— Elmira (NY-Penn)	OF	71	215	36	55	7	•6	5	21	.256	*67	32	13	119	5	3	.976
1986— Winter Haven (FSL)....	OF	126	417	86	133	19	11	12	87	.319	*107	47	44	280	5	1	*.997
1987— New Britain (East.)	OF	52	170	30	50	4	3	6	35	.294	45	24	7	127	2	2	.985
— Pawtucket (I.L.)	OF	23	79	18	30	4	0	2	8	.380	16	8	2	48	1	0	1.000
1988— Boston (A.L.)	OF	41	148	14	34	5	3	0	12	.230	15	35	4	87	3	1	.989
— Pawtucket (I.L.)	OF	49	167	27	48	6	1	4	19	.287	26	33	8	115	4	2	.983
— Baltimore (A.L.)■......	OF	53	177	17	35	8	1	1	9	.198	8	40	6	156	1	3	.981
1989— Baltimore (A.L.)	OF-DH	94	266	44	55	12	2	4	16	.207	43	45	16	191	3	3	.985
— Rochester (I.L.)	OF	21	70	14	14	1	2	1	8	.200	12	13	2	1	0	0	1.000
1990— Baltimore (A.L.)	OF-DH	89	234	24	54	5	2	3	24	.231	31	46	15	149	3	2	.987
— Hagerstown (East.)	OF	9	34	8	13	0	2	1	5	.382	5	5	2	8	1	0	1.000
— Frederick (Caro.)	OF	2	7	2	3	1	0	0	3	.429	1	1	0	1	0	0	1.000
1991— Baltimore (A.L.)	OF-DH	113	256	40	59	12	3	2	27	.230	38	44	12	150	3	3	.981
— Rochester (I.L.)	OF	7	26	5	10	3	0	0	2	.385	7	4	4	19	1	0	1.000
1992— Baltimore (A.L.)	OF	159	623	100	169	28	10	21	80	.271	98	98	53	382	10	8	.980
1993— Baltimore (A.L.)	OF-DH	142	560	87	147	36	8	13	66	.263	82	99	24	296	7	2	.993
1994— Baltimore (A.L.)	OF	111	453	78	119	25	5	12	48	.263	57	75	31	247	4	1	.996
1995— Baltimore (A.L.)	OF	143	554	108	145	33	10	16	64	.262	87	111	26	268	1	3	.989
1996— Baltimore (A.L.)	OF-DH	149	579	117	172	37	5	50	110	.297	76	106	21	341	10	3	.992
1997— Baltimore (A.L.)	OF-DH	151	590	97	170	39	7	18	73	.288	84	105	18	276	2	3	.989
1998— Baltimore (A.L.)	OF-DH	133	479	84	113	28	3	18	51	.236	75	78	21	269	1	4	.985
1999— Baltimore (A.L.)	OF-DH	150	564	109	159	28	5	24	81	.282	96	105	36	308	3	1	.997
2000— Baltimore (A.L.)	OF-DH	141	506	89	130	26	0	19	50	.257	92	103	16	301	1	1	.997
Major League totals (13 years)		1669	5989	1008	1561	322	64	201	711	.261	882	1090	299	3421	52	38	.989

NOTES: Hit home run in first at-bat (October 1, 1996).

DIVISION SERIES RECORD

							BATTING								FIELDING		
Year Team (League)	Pos.	G	AB	R	H	2B	3B	HR	RBI	Avg.	BB	SO	SB	PO	A	E	Avg.
1996— Baltimore (A.L.)	OF	4	17	3	5	0	0	2	4	.294	2	3	0	7	0	0	1.000
1997— Baltimore (A.L.)	OF	4	17	3	6	1	0	1	4	.353	1	4	1	6	0	0	1.000
Division series totals (2 years)		8	34	6	11	1	0	3	8	.324	3	7	1	13	0	0	1.000

CHAMPIONSHIP SERIES RECORD

							BATTING								FIELDING		
Year Team (League)	Pos.	G	AB	R	H	2B	3B	HR	RBI	Avg.	BB	SO	SB	PO	A	E	Avg.
1996— Baltimore (A.L.)	OF	5	21	5	4	1	0	1	1	.190	3	5	0	8	0	0	1.000
1997— Baltimore (A.L.)	OF	6	25	5	9	2	0	2	3	.360	4	4	2	13	0	1	.929
Championship series totals (2 years)		11	46	10	13	3	0	3	4	.283	7	9	2	21	0	1	.955

ALL-STAR GAME RECORD

						BATTING							FIELDING		
Year League	Pos.	AB	R	H	2B	3B	HR	RBI	Avg.	BB	SO	SB	PO	A	E	Avg.
1992— American	OF	3	0	0	0	0	0	0	.000	0	0	0	1	0	0	1.000
1996— American	OF	2	0	0	0	0	0	0	.000	0	0	0	0	0	0	...
1997— American	OF	4	0	2	1	0	0	0	.500	0	0	0	1	0	0	1.000
All-Star Game totals (3 years)		9	0	2	1	0	0	0	.222	0	0	0	2	0	0	1.000

ANDERSON, BRIAN   P   DIAMONDBACKS

PERSONAL: Born April 26, 1972, in Geneva, Ohio. ... 6-1/183. ... Throws left, bats both. ... Full name: Brian James Anderson.
HIGH SCHOOL: Geneva (Ohio).
COLLEGE: Wright State.
TRANSACTIONS/CAREER NOTES: Selected by California Angels organization in first round (third pick overall) of free-agent draft (June 3, 1993). ... On California disabled list (May 7-June 7, 1994); included rehabilitation assignment to Lake Elsinore (May 27-June 7). ... On California disabled list (May 6-June 20, 1995); included rehabilitation assignment to Lake Elsinore (June 4-20). ... Traded by Angels to Cleveland Indians for P Jason Grimsley and P Pep Harris (February 15, 1996). ... On Cleveland disabled list (July 5-August 12, 1997); included rehabilitation assignment to Buffalo (August 3-13). ... Selected by Arizona Diamondbacks in first round (second pick overall) of expansion draft (November 18, 1997).
RECORDS: Shares major league single-inning record for most home runs allowed—4 (September 5, 1995, second inning).
HONORS: Named A.L. Rookie Pitcher of the Year by THE SPORTING NEWS (1994).

STATISTICAL NOTES: Tied for A.L. lead with five balks in 1994 and three in 1995. ... Tied for American Association lead with three balks in 1996. ... Led N.L. with six balks and tied for lead with 39 home runs allowed in 1998.

MISCELLANEOUS: Scored one run in three appearances as pinch runner (1998). ... Scored a run in only appearance as pinch runner (1999). ... Walked and grounded into fielder's choice in two appearances as pinch hitter and scored one run in two appearances as pinch runner (2000).

Year League	W	L	Pct.	ERA	G	GS	CG	ShO	Sv.	IP	H	R	ER	BB	SO
1993—Midland (Texas)	0	1	.000	3.38	2	2	0	0	0	10 $^2/_3$	16	5	4	0	9
—Vancouver (PCL)	0	1	.000	12.38	2	2	0	0	0	8	13	12	11	6	2
—California (A.L.)	0	0	...	3.97	4	1	0	0	0	11 $^1/_3$	11	5	5	2	4
1994—California (A.L.)	7	5	.583	5.22	18	18	0	0	0	101 $^2/_3$	120	63	59	27	47
—Lake Elsinore (Calif.)	0	1	.000	3.00	2	2	0	0	0	12	6	4	4	0	9
1995—California (A.L.)	6	8	.429	5.87	18	17	1	0	0	99 $^2/_3$	110	66	65	30	45
—Lake Elsinore (Calif.)	1	1	.500	1.93	3	3	0	0	0	14	10	3	3	1	13
1996—Buffalo (A.A.)■	11	5	.688	3.59	19	19	2	0	0	128	125	57	51	28	85
—Cleveland (A.L.)	3	1	.750	4.91	10	9	0	0	0	51 $^1/_3$	58	29	28	14	21
1997—Buffalo (A.A.)	7	1	.875	3.05	15	15	1	1	0	85 $^2/_3$	78	33	29	15	60
—Cleveland (A.L.)	4	2	.667	4.69	8	8	0	0	0	48	55	28	25	11	22
1998—Arizona (N.L.)■	12	13	.480	4.33	32	32	2	1	0	208	221	109	100	24	95
1999—Arizona (N.L.)	8	2	.800	4.57	31	19	2	1	1	130	144	69	66	28	75
—Tucson (PCL)	0	1	.000	5.40	2	2	0	0	0	6 $^2/_3$	9	5	4	1	8
2000—Arizona (N.L.)	11	7	.611	4.05	33	32	2	0	0	213 $^1/_3$	226	101	96	39	104
A.L. totals (5 years)	20	16	.556	5.25	58	53	1	0	0	312	354	191	182	84	139
N.L. totals (3 years)	31	22	.585	4.28	96	83	6	2	1	551 $^1/_3$	591	279	262	91	274
Major League totals (8 years)	51	38	.573	4.63	154	136	7	2	1	863 $^1/_3$	945	470	444	175	413

DIVISION SERIES RECORD

Year League	W	L	Pct.	ERA	G	GS	CG	ShO	Sv.	IP	H	R	ER	BB	SO
1999—Arizona (N.L.)	0	0	...	2.57	1	1	0	0	0	7	7	2	2	0	4

CHAMPIONSHIP SERIES RECORD

Year League	W	L	Pct.	ERA	G	GS	CG	ShO	Sv.	IP	H	R	ER	BB	SO
1997—Cleveland (A.L.)	1	0	1.000	1.42	3	0	0	0	0	6 $^1/_3$	1	1	1	3	7

WORLD SERIES RECORD

Year League	W	L	Pct.	ERA	G	GS	CG	ShO	Sv.	IP	H	R	ER	BB	SO
1997—Cleveland (A.L.)	0	0	...	2.45	3	0	0	0	1	3 $^2/_3$	2	1	1	0	2

ANDERSON, GARRET — OF — ANGELS

PERSONAL: Born June 30, 1972, in Los Angeles. ... 6-3/220. ... Bats left, throws left. ... Full name: Garret Joseph Anderson.
HIGH SCHOOL: John F. Kennedy (Granada Hills, Calif.).
TRANSACTIONS/CAREER NOTES: Selected by California Angels organization in fourth round of free-agent draft (June 4, 1990). ... Angels franchise renamed Anaheim Angels for 1997 season.
HONORS: Named A.L. Rookie Player of the Year by THE SPORTING NEWS (1995).
STATISTICAL NOTES: Collected six hits in one game (September 27, 1996). ... Had 28-game hitting streak (June 28-July 31, 1998). ... Had 16-game hitting streak (July 6-25, 1999). ... Had 17-game hitting streak (August 30-September 17, 1999). ... Career major league grand slams: 4.

Year Team (League)	Pos.	G	AB	R	H	2B	3B	HR	RBI	Avg.	BB	SO	SB	PO	A	E	Avg.
1990—Arizona Angels (Ariz.)	OF	32	127	5	27	2	0	0	14	.213	2	24	3	53	2	2	.965
—Boise (N'West)	OF	25	83	11	21	3	1	1	8	.253	4	18	0	38	0	2	.950
1991—Quad City (Midw.)	OF	105	392	40	102	22	2	2	42	.260	20	89	5	158	7	10	.943
1992—Palm Springs (Calif.)	OF	81	322	46	104	15	2	1	62	.323	21	61	1	137	4	6	.959
—Midland (Texas)	OF	39	146	16	40	5	0	2	19	.274	9	30	2	62	6	1	.986
1993—Vancouver (PCL)	OF-1B	124	467	57	137	34	4	4	71	.293	31	95	3	198	13	2	.991
1994—Vancouver (PCL)	OF-DH-1B	123	505	75	162	42	6	12	102	.321	28	93	3	196	10	2	.990
—California (A.L.)	OF	5	13	0	5	0	0	0	1	.385	0	2	0	10	0	0	1.000
1995—California (A.L.)	OF-DH	106	374	50	120	19	1	16	69	.321	19	65	6	213	7	5	.978
—Vancouver (PCL)	OF-DH	14	61	9	19	7	0	0	12	.311	5	14	0	22	0	1	.957
1996—California (A.L.)	OF-DH	150	607	79	173	33	2	12	72	.285	27	84	7	316	5	7	.979
1997—Anaheim (A.L.)	OF-DH	154	624	76	189	36	3	8	92	.303	30	70	10	343	14	3	.992
1998—Anaheim (A.L.)	OF	156	622	62	183	41	7	15	79	.294	29	80	8	326	11	6	.983
1999—Anaheim (A.L.)	OF	157	620	88	188	36	2	21	80	.303	34	81	3	*406	7	3	.993
2000—Anaheim (A.L.)	OF-DH-1B	159	647	92	185	40	3	35	117	.286	24	87	7	380	5	4	.990
Major League totals (7 years)		887	3507	447	1043	205	18	107	510	.297	163	469	41	1994	49	28	.986

ANDERSON, JIMMY — P — PIRATES

PERSONAL: Born January 22, 1976, in Portsmouth, Va. ... 6-1/207. ... Throws left, bats left. ... Full name: James Drew Anderson Jr.
HIGH SCHOOL: Western Branch (Chesapeake, Va.).
TRANSACTIONS/CAREER NOTES: Selected by Pittsburgh Pirates organization in ninth round of free-agent draft (June 2, 1994). ... On disabled list (July 5-12, 1998).

Year League	W	L	Pct.	ERA	G	GS	CG	ShO	Sv.	IP	H	R	ER	BB	SO
1994—GC Pirates (GCL)	5	1	.833	1.60	10	10	0	0	0	56 $^1/_3$	35	21	10	27	66
1995—Augusta (S.Atl.)	4	2	.667	1.53	14	14	0	0	0	76 $^2/_3$	51	15	13	31	75
—Lynchburg (Caro.)	1	5	.167	4.13	10	9	0	0	0	52 $^1/_3$	56	29	24	21	32
1996—Lynchburg (Caro.)	5	3	.625	1.93	11	11	1	1	0	65 $^1/_3$	51	25	14	21	56
—Carolina (Sou.)	8	5	.615	3.34	17	16	0	0	0	97	92	40	36	44	79
1997—Carolina (Sou.)	2	1	.667	1.46	4	4	0	0	0	24 $^2/_3$	16	6	4	9	23
—Calgary (PCL)	7	6	.538	5.68	21	21	0	0	0	103	124	78	65	64	71

Year League	W	L	Pct.	ERA	G	GS	CG	ShO	Sv.	IP	H	R	ER	BB	SO
1998—Nashville (PCL)	9	10	.474	5.02	35	17	0	0	0	123 2/3	144	87	69	72	63
1999—Nashville (PCL)	11	2	*.846	3.84	21	21	1	0	0	133 2/3	153	67	57	41	93
—Pittsburgh (N.L.)	2	1	.667	3.99	13	4	0	0	0	29 1/3	25	15	13	16	13
2000—Nashville (PCL)	0	0	...	4.15	2	2	0	0	0	13	18	6	6	4	7
—Pittsburgh (N.L.)	5	11	.313	5.25	27	26	1	0	0	144	169	94	84	58	73
—Altoona (East.)	1	0	1.000	0.00	1	1	1	0	0	9	7	1	0	1	6
Major League totals (2 years)	7	12	.368	5.04	40	30	1	0	0	173 1/3	194	109	97	74	86

ANDERSON, MARLON — 2B — PHILLIES

PERSONAL: Born January 6, 1974, in Montgomery, Ala. ... 5-11/198. ... Bats left, throws right. ... Full name: Marlon Ordell Anderson.
HIGH SCHOOL: Prattville (Ala.).
COLLEGE: South Alabama.
TRANSACTIONS/CAREER NOTES: Selected by Philadelphia Phillies organization in second round of free-agent draft (June 1, 1995); choice received from St. Louis Cardinals as part of compensation for Cardinals signing Type A free-agent P Danny Jackson.
STATISTICAL NOTES: Led New York-Pennsylvania League second basemen with 398 total chances and 67 double plays in 1995. ... Led Eastern League with 748 total chances in 1997. ... Hit home run in first major league at-bat (September 8, 1998). ... Led International League second basemen with 681 total chances in 1998.

Year Team (League)	Pos.	G	AB	R	H	2B	3B	HR	RBI	Avg.	BB	SO	SB	PO	A	E	Avg.
1995—Batavia (NY-Penn)	2B	74	*312	52	92	13	4	3	40	.295	15	20	22	*153	*231	14	*.965
1996—Clearwater (FSL)	2B	60	257	37	70	10	3	2	22	.272	14	18	26	142	221	16	.958
—Reading (East.)	2B	75	314	38	86	14	3	3	28	.274	26	44	17	166	239	18	.957
1997—Reading (East.)	2B	137	*553	88	147	18	6	10	62	.266	42	77	27	*323	*396	*29	.961
1998—Scranton/W.B. (I.L.)	2B	136	575	104	*176	32	*14	16	86	.306	28	77	24	262	391	*28	.959
—Philadelphia (N.L.)	2B	17	43	4	14	3	0	1	4	.326	1	6	2	14	30	1	.978
1999—Philadelphia (N.L.)	2B	129	452	48	114	26	4	5	54	.252	24	61	13	234	284	11	.979
2000—Scranton/W.B. (I.L.)	2B-SS	103	397	57	121	18	8	8	53	.305	39	43	24	167	269	•14	.969
—Philadelphia (N.L.)	2B	41	162	10	37	8	1	1	15	.228	12	22	2	87	100	2	.989
Major League totals (3 years)		187	657	62	165	37	5	7	73	.251	37	89	17	335	414	14	.982

ANDERSON, MATT — P — TIGERS

PERSONAL: Born August 17, 1976, in Louisville, Ky. ... 6-4/200. ... Throws right, bats right. ... Full name: Matthew Jason Anderson.
HIGH SCHOOL: St. Xavier (Louisville, Ky.).
COLLEGE: Rice.
TRANSACTIONS/CAREER NOTES: Selected by Detroit Tigers organization in first round (first pick overall) of free-agent draft (June 3, 1997).

Year League	W	L	Pct.	ERA	G	GS	CG	ShO	Sv.	IP	H	R	ER	BB	SO
1998—Lakeland (FSL)	1	0	1.000	0.69	17	0	0	0	3	26	18	4	2	8	34
—Jacksonville (Sou.)	1	0	1.000	0.60	13	0	0	0	10	15	7	1	1	5	11
—Detroit (A.L.)	5	1	.833	3.27	42	0	0	0	0	44	38	16	16	31	44
1999—Detroit (A.L.)	2	1	.667	5.68	37	0	0	0	0	38	33	27	24	35	32
—Toledo (I.L.)	0	4	.000	6.39	24	4	0	0	5	38	32	27	27	31	35
2000—Detroit (A.L.)	3	2	.600	4.72	69	0	0	0	1	74 1/3	61	44	39	45	71
Major League totals (3 years)	10	4	.714	4.55	148	0	0	0	1	156 1/3	132	87	79	111	147

ANDREWS, CLAYTON — P — REDS

PERSONAL: Born May 15, 1978, in Dunedin, Fla. ... 6-0/175. ... Throws left, bats right. ... Full name: Clayton John Andrews.
HIGH SCHOOL: Seminole (Largo, Fla.).
TRANSACTIONS/CAREER NOTES: Selected by Toronto Blue Jays organization in third round of free-agent draft (June 4, 1996); pick received as compensation for Florida Marlins signing Type B free agent Devon White. ... Traded by Blue Jays with P Leo Estrella to Cincinnati Reds for P Steve Parris (November 22, 2000).
HONORS: Named South Atlantic League Most Valuable Pitcher (1998).

Year League	W	L	Pct.	ERA	G	GS	CG	ShO	Sv.	IP	H	R	ER	BB	SO
1996—Medicine Hat (Pio.)	2	4	.333	7.36	8	4	0	0	0	25 2/3	37	23	21	10	14
1997—Hagerstown (S.Atl.)	7	7	.500	4.55	28	15	0	0	0	114 2/3	120	70	58	47	112
1998—Hagerstown (S.Atl.)	10	7	.588	*2.28	27	26	2	1	0	162	112	59	41	46	193
1999—Knoxville (Sou.)	10	8	.556	3.93	25	25	0	0	0	132 2/3	143	85	58	69	93
—Syracuse (I.L.)	0	1	.000	7.80	3	3	0	0	0	15	10	14	13	13	9
2000—Syracuse (I.L.)	8	7	.533	4.82	19	18	0	0	0	102 2/3	114	56	55	42	59
—Toronto (A.L.)	1	2	.333	10.02	8	2	0	0	0	20 2/3	34	23	23	9	12
Major League totals (1 year)	1	2	.333	10.02	8	2	0	0	0	20 2/3	34	23	23	9	12

ANDREWS, SHANE — 3B — CARDINALS

PERSONAL: Born August 28, 1971, in Dallas. ... 6-1/220. ... Bats right, throws right. ... Full name: Darrell Shane Andrews.
HIGH SCHOOL: Carlsbad (N.M.) Senior.
TRANSACTIONS/CAREER NOTES: Selected by Montreal Expos organization in first round (11th pick overall) of free-agent draft (June 4, 1990). ... On disabled list (August 3-11, 1993). ... On Montreal disabled list (May 1, 1997-remainder of season); included rehabilitation assignments to Ottawa (May 14-18) and West Palm Beach (July 26-August 10). ... On Montreal disabled list (May 11-June 1, 1999); included rehabilitation assignment to Ottawa (May 30-June 1). ... Released by Expos (September 7, 1999). ... Signed by Chicago Cubs (September 10, 1999). ... On Chicago disabled list (May 15-August 25, 2000); included rehabilitation assignment to Iowa (August 7-25). ... Granted free agency (October 31, 2000). ... Signed by St. Louis Cardinals organization (January 5, 2001).

STATISTICAL NOTES: Led South Atlantic League third basemen with 98 putouts in 1992. ... Led International League third basemen with 436 total chances in 1994. ... Career major league grand slams: 3.

Year Team (League)	Pos.	G	AB	R	H	2B	3B	HR	RBI	Avg.	BB	SO	SB	PO	A	E	Avg.
1990—GC Expos (GCL)	3B	56	190	31	46	7	1	3	24	.242	29	46	11	42	105	17	.896
1991—Sumter (S.Atl.)	3B	105	356	46	74	16	7	11	49	.208	65	132	5	71	205	29	.905
1992—Albany (S.Atl.)	3B-1B	136	453	76	104	18	1	*25	87	.230	*107	*174	8	†125	212	26	.928
1993—Harrisburg (East.)	3B-SS	124	442	77	115	29	2	18	70	.260	64	118	10	74	217	23	.927
1994—Ottawa (I.L.)	3B-DH	137	460	79	117	25	2	16	85	.254	80	126	6	84	*320	*32	.927
1995—Montreal (N.L.)	3B-1B	84	220	27	47	10	1	8	31	.214	17	68	1	182	97	7	.976
1996—Montreal (N.L.)	3B	127	375	43	85	15	2	19	64	.227	35	119	3	64	256	15	.955
1997—Montreal (N.L.)	3B	18	64	10	13	3	0	4	9	.203	3	20	0	11	40	6	.895
—Ottawa (I.L.)	3B	3	12	3	3	0	0	1	1	.250	1	0	0	2	4	0	1.000
—W.P. Beach (FSL)	DH-3B	5	17	2	3	2	0	1	5	.176	2	7	0	2	9	1	.917
1998—Montreal (N.L.)	3B	150	492	48	117	30	1	25	69	.238	58	137	1	95	322	20	.954
1999—Montreal (N.L.)	3B-1B-DH	98	281	28	51	8	0	11	37	.181	43	88	1	159	134	14	.954
—Ottawa (I.L.)	3B	2	8	1	2	0	0	1	4	.250	0	2	0	1	2	0	1.000
—Chicago (N.L.)■	3B-1B	19	67	13	17	4	0	5	14	.254	7	21	0	8	34	2	.955
2000—Chicago (N.L.)	3B-1B	66	192	25	44	5	0	14	39	.229	27	59	1	59	101	12	.930
—Iowa (PCL)	3B	15	38	5	7	3	0	2	7	.184	7	10	0	2	20	0	1.000
Major League totals (6 years)		562	1691	194	374	75	4	86	263	.221	190	512	7	578	984	76	.954

ANKIEL, RICK — P — CARDINALS

PERSONAL: Born July 19, 1979, in Fort Pierce, Fla. ... 6-1/210. ... Throws left, bats left. ... Full name: Richard Alexander Ankiel.

HIGH SCHOOL: Port St. Lucie (Fla.).

TRANSACTIONS/CAREER NOTES: Selected by St. Louis Cardinals organization in second round of free-agent draft (June 3, 1997).

HONORS: Named Carolina League Pitcher of the Year (1998). ... Named Minor League Player of the Year by THE SPORTING NEWS (1999). ... Named N.L. Rookie Pitcher of the Year by THE SPORTING NEWS (2000).

STATISTICAL NOTES: Led N.L. pitchers with seven errors in 2000.

MISCELLANEOUS: Appeared in one game as pinch runner (2000). ... Struck out three times in three appearances as pinch hitter (2000).

Year League	W	L	Pct.	ERA	G	GS	CG	ShO	Sv.	IP	H	R	ER	BB	SO
1998—Peoria (Midw.)..................	3	0	1.000	2.06	7	7	0	0	0	35	15	8	8	12	41
—Prince William (Caro.)........	9	6	.600	2.79	21	21	1	0	0	126	91	46	39	38	181
1999—Arkansas (Texas)...............	6	0	1.000	0.91	8	8	1	1	0	49 1/3	25	6	5	16	75
—Memphis (PCL).................	7	3	.700	3.16	16	16	0	0	0	88 1/3	73	37	31	46	119
—St. Louis (N.L.).................	0	1	.000	3.27	9	5	0	0	1	33	26	12	12	14	39
2000—St. Louis (N.L.).................	11	7	.611	3.50	31	30	0	0	0	175	137	80	68	90	194
Major League totals (2 years)	11	8	.579	3.46	40	35	0	0	1	208	163	92	80	104	233

DIVISION SERIES RECORD

Year League	W	L	Pct.	ERA	G	GS	CG	ShO	Sv.	IP	H	R	ER	BB	SO
2000—St. Louis (N.L.).................	0	0	...	13.50	1	1	0	0	0	2 2/3	4	4	4	6	3

CHAMPIONSHIP SERIES RECORD

RECORDS: Shares career record for most wild pitches—4. ... Shares single-inning record for most wild pitches—2 (October 12, 2000, first inning and October 16, 2000, seventh inning).

Year League	W	L	Pct.	ERA	G	GS	CG	ShO	Sv.	IP	H	R	ER	BB	SO
2000—St. Louis (N.L.).................	0	0	...	20.25	2	1	0	0	0	1 1/3	1	3	3	5	2

APPIER, KEVIN — P — METS

PERSONAL: Born December 6, 1967, in Lancaster, Calif. ... 6-2/200. ... Throws right, bats right. ... Full name: Robert Kevin Appier. ... Name pronounced APE-ee-er.

HIGH SCHOOL: Antelope Valley (Lancaster, Calif.).

JUNIOR COLLEGE: Antelope Valley College (Calif.).

COLLEGE: Fresno State.

TRANSACTIONS/CAREER NOTES: Selected by Kansas City Royals organization in first round (ninth pick overall) of free-agent draft (June 2, 1987). ... On disabled list (July 26-August 12, 1995). ... On Kansas City disabled list (March 20-September 1, 1998); included rehabilitation assignments to Gulf Coast Royals (July 16-21), Lansing (July 22-26), Wichita (July 27-30) and Omaha (July 31-August 27). ... Traded by Royals to Oakland Athletics for P Blake Stein, P Jeff D'Amico, and P Brad Rigby (July 31, 1999). ... On disabled list (April 25-May 13, 2000). ... Granted free agency (October 31, 2000). ... Signed by New York Mets (December 11, 2000).

RECORDS: Shares major league record for most strikeouts in one inning—4 (September 3, 1996, fourth inning).

HONORS: Named A.L. Rookie Pitcher of the Year by THE SPORTING NEWS (1990).

STATISTICAL NOTES: Pitched 4-0 one-hit, complete-game victory for Kansas City against Detroit (July 7, 1990). ... Pitched 1-0 one-hit, complete-game loss against Texas (July 27, 1993). ... Tied for A.L. lead with 14 wild pitches in 1997.

MISCELLANEOUS: Holds Kansas City Royals all-time record for strikeouts (1,451).

Year League	W	L	Pct.	ERA	G	GS	CG	ShO	Sv.	IP	H	R	ER	BB	SO
1987—Eugene (N'West)	5	2	.714	3.04	15	•15	0	0	0	77	81	43	26	29	72
1988—Baseball City (FSL)	10	9	.526	2.75	24	24	1	0	0	147 1/3	134	58	45	39	112
—Memphis (Sou.)	2	0	1.000	1.83	3	3	0	0	0	19 2/3	11	5	4	7	18
1989—Omaha (A.A.)...................	8	8	.500	3.95	22	22	3	2	0	139	141	70	61	42	109
—Kansas City (A.L.)	1	4	.200	9.14	6	5	0	0	0	21 2/3	34	22	22	12	10
1990—Omaha (A.A.)...................	2	0	1.000	1.50	3	3	0	0	0	18	15	3	3	2	17
—Kansas City (A.L.)	12	8	.600	2.76	32	24	3	3	0	185 2/3	179	67	57	54	127
1991—Kansas City (A.L.)	13	10	.565	3.42	34	31	6	3	0	207 2/3	205	97	79	61	158
1992—Kansas City (A.L.)	15	8	.652	2.46	30	30	3	0	0	208 1/3	167	59	57	68	150
1993—Kansas City (A.L.)	18	8	.692	*2.56	34	34	5	1	0	238 2/3	183	74	68	81	186
1994—Kansas City (A.L.)	7	6	.538	3.83	23	23	1	0	0	155	137	68	66	63	145

Year League	W	L	Pct.	ERA	G	GS	CG	ShO	Sv.	IP	H	R	ER	BB	SO
1995—Kansas City (A.L.)	15	10	.600	3.89	31	31	4	1	0	201 1/3	163	90	87	80	185
1996—Kansas City (A.L.)	14	11	.560	3.62	32	32	5	1	0	211 1/3	192	87	85	75	207
1997—Kansas City (A.L.)	9	13	.409	3.40	34	34	4	1	0	235 2/3	215	96	89	74	196
1998—Gulf Coast Royals (GCL)	0	1	.000	2.70	1	1	0	0	0	3 1/3	3	3	1	1	2
—Lansing (Midw.)	0	0	...	2.25	1	1	0	0	0	4	4	1	1	0	5
—Wichita (Texas)	0	1	.000	6.00	1	1	0	0	0	6	8	4	4	2	1
—Omaha (PCL)....................	3	2	.600	7.03	6	6	0	0	0	32	41	25	25	12	22
—Kansas City (A.L.)	1	2	.333	7.80	3	3	0	0	0	15	21	13	13	5	9
1999—Kansas City (A.L.)	9	9	.500	4.87	22	22	1	0	0	140 1/3	153	81	76	51	78
—Oakland (A.L.)■	7	5	.583	5.77	12	12	0	0	0	68 2/3	77	50	44	33	53
2000—Oakland (A.L.)	15	11	.577	4.52	31	31	1	1	0	195 1/3	200	109	98	*102	129
Major League totals (12 years)	136	105	.564	3.63	324	312	33	11	0	2084 2/3	1926	913	841	759	1633

DIVISION SERIES RECORD

Year League	W	L	Pct.	ERA	G	GS	CG	ShO	Sv.	IP	H	R	ER	BB	SO
2000—Oakland (A.L.)	0	1	.000	3.48	2	1	0	0	0	10 1/3	10	4	4	6	13

ALL-STAR GAME RECORD

Year League	W	L	Pct.	ERA	GS	CG	ShO	Sv.	IP	H	R	ER	BB	SO
1995—American	0	0	...	0.00	0	0	0	0	2	0	0	0	0	1

ARDOIN, DANNY — C — TWINS

PERSONAL: Born July 8, 1974, in Mamou, La. ... 6-0/218. ... Bats right, throws right. ... Full name: Daniel Wayne Ardoin.
HIGH SCHOOL: Sacred Heart (Ville Platte, La.).
COLLEGE: McNeese State.
TRANSACTIONS/CAREER NOTES: Selected by Oakland Athletics organization in fifth round of free-agent draft (June 1, 1995). ... On disabled list (July 27-August 4, 1998). ... On Sacramento disabled list (June 9-26, 2000). ... Traded by A's to Minnesota Twins for 1B/OF Mario Valdez (July 31, 2000).
STATISTICAL NOTES: Led Northwest League catchers with 477 total chances in 1995. ... Led Pacific Coast League catchers with nine double plays in 1999.

						BATTING								FIELDING		
Year Team (League)	Pos.	G	AB	R	H	2B	3B	HR	RBI	Avg.	BB	SO	SB	PO	A	E	Avg.
1995—S. Oregon (N.W.)........	C	58	175	28	41	9	1	2	23	.234	31	50	2	*402	*61	*14	.971
1996—Modesto (Calif.)	C-3B-1B	91	317	55	83	13	3	6	34	.262	47	81	5	577	62	21	.968
1997—Visalia (Calif.)	C-1B-3B-OF	43	145	16	34	7	1	3	19	.234	21	39	0	331	38	5	.987
—Huntsville (Sou.)	C-3B	57	208	26	48	10	1	4	23	.231	17	38	2	302	45	10	.972
1998—Huntsville (Sou.)	C-OF-1B	109	363	67	90	21	0	16	62	.248	62	87	8	560	87	12	.982
1999—Vancouver (PCL)	C-DH-3B-1B	109	336	53	85	13	2	8	46	.253	50	78	3	538	76	10	.984
2000—Sacramento (PCL)	C-1B-3B	67	234	42	65	16	1	6	34	.278	34	72	6	371	24	8	.980
—Modesto (Calif.)	C	4	10	1	3	1	0	0	2	.300	0	4	0	23	1	1	.960
—Salt Lake (PCL)■	C	3	9	1	2	0	0	0		.222	3	4	0	22	2	0	1.000
—Minnesota (A.L.)	C	15	32	4	4	1	0	1	5	.125	8	10	0	80	8	1	.989
Major League totals (1 year)		15	32	4	4	1	0	1	5	.125	8	10	0	80	8	1	.989

ARIAS, ALEX — SS — PADRES

PERSONAL: Born November 20, 1967, in New York. ... 6-3/202. ... Bats right, throws right. ... Full name: Alejandro Arias. ... Name pronounced air-REE-ahs.
HIGH SCHOOL: George Washington (New York).
TRANSACTIONS/CAREER NOTES: Selected by Chicago Cubs organization in third round of free-agent draft (June 2, 1987). ... Traded by Cubs with 3B Gary Scott to Florida Marlins for P Greg Hibbard (November 17, 1992). ... On disabled list (June 14-July 2, 1997). ... Released by Marlins (December 12, 1997). ... Signed by Philadelphia Phillies (December 26, 1997). ... Granted free agency (October 30, 2000). ... Signed by San Diego Padres (December 13, 2000).
STATISTICAL NOTES: Led Midwest League shortstops with 655 total chances and 83 double plays in 1989. ... Led Southern League shortstops with 583 total chances and 81 double plays in 1991.

						BATTING								FIELDING		
Year Team (League)	Pos.	G	AB	R	H	2B	3B	HR	RBI	Avg.	BB	SO	SB	PO	A	E	Avg.
1987—Wytheville (Appl.)......	SS-3B	61	233	41	69	7	0	0	24	.296	27	29	16	77	141	16	.932
1988—Char., W.Va. (SAL)	SS-3B-2B	127	472	57	122	12	1	0	33	.258	54	44	41	184	396	32	.948
1989—Peoria (Midw.)...........	SS	*136	506	74	140	10	*11	0	64	.277	49	67	31	*210	*408	37	.944
1990—Charlotte (Sou.)........	SS	119	419	55	103	16	3	4	38	.246	42	53	12	171	284	*42	.915
1991—Charlotte (Sou.)........	SS	134	488	69	134	26	0	4	47	.275	47	42	23	*203	*351	29	*.950
1992—Iowa (A.A.)	SS-2B	106	409	52	114	23	3	5	40	.279	44	27	14	183	290	14	.971
—Chicago (N.L.)..........	SS	32	99	14	29	6	0	0	7	.293	11	13	0	43	74	4	.967
1993—Florida (N.L.)■.........	2B-3B-SS	96	249	27	67	5	1	2	20	.269	27	18	1	94	144	6	.975
1994—Florida (N.L.)	SS-3B	59	113	4	27	5	0	0	15	.239	9	19	0	37	51	2	.978
1995—Florida (N.L.)	SS-3B-2B	94	216	22	58	9	2	3	26	.269	22	20	1	57	127	9	.953
1996—Florida (N.L.)	3-S-1-2	100	224	27	62	11	2	3	26	.277	17	28	2	48	127	7	.962
1997—Florida (N.L.)	3B-SS	74	93	13	23	2	0	1	11	.247	12	12	0	26	38	2	.970
1998—Philadelphia (N.L.)■ ...	SS-3B-2B	56	133	17	39	8	0	1	16	.293	13	18	2	43	88	2	.985
1999—Philadelphia (N.L.)......	SS-3B-2B	118	347	43	105	20	1	4	48	.303	36	31	2	120	208	4	.988
2000—Philadelphia (N.L.)......	SS-3B-2B	70	155	17	29	9	0	2	15	.187	16	28	1	45	98	5	.966
Major League totals (9 years)		699	1629	184	439	75	6	16	184	.269	163	187	9	513	955	41	.973

DIVISION SERIES RECORD

						BATTING								FIELDING		
Year Team (League)	Pos.	G	AB	R	H	2B	3B	HR	RBI	Avg.	BB	SO	SB	PO	A	E	Avg.
1997—Florida (N.L.).............	PH	1	1	0	1	0	0	0	1	1.000	0	0	0	...	...	...	...

Year	Team (League)	Pos.	G	AB	R	H	2B	3B	HR	RBI	Avg.	BB	SO	SB	PO	A	E	Avg.
											BATTING						FIELDING	
1997—	Florida (N.L.)	3B-PH	3	1	0	1	0	0	0	0	1.000	0	0	0	0	0	0	...

WORLD SERIES RECORD

NOTES: Member of World Series championship team (1997).

Year	Team (League)	Pos.	G	AB	R	H	2B	3B	HR	RBI	Avg.	BB	SO	SB	PO	A	E	Avg.
											BATTING						FIELDING	
1997—	Florida (N.L.)	3B-PR	2	1	1	0	0	0	0	0	.000	0	0	0	0	0	0	...

ARMAS, TONY — P — EXPOS

PERSONAL: Born April 29, 1978, in Puerto Piritu, Venezuela. ... 6-4/205. ... Throws right, bats right. ... Full name: Antonio Jose Armas Jr. ... Son of Tony Armas, outfielder with four major league teams (1976-89).
TRANSACTIONS/CAREER NOTES: Signed as non-drafted free agent by New York Yankees organization (August 16, 1994). ... Traded by Yankees with a player to be named later to Boston Red Sox for C Mike Stanley and SS Randy Brown (August 13, 1997); Red Sox acquired P Jim Mecir to complete deal (September 29, 1997). ... Traded by Red Sox to Montreal Expos (December 18, 1997), completing deal in which Red Sox traded P Carl Pavano and a player to be named later to Expos for P Pedro Martinez (November 18, 1997). ... On Montreal disabled list (April 1-28 and July 19-September 6, 2000); included rehabilitation assignments to Jupiter (April 22-28) and Ottawa (August 27-September 4).

Year	League	W	L	Pct.	ERA	G	GS	CG	ShO	Sv.	IP	H	R	ER	BB	SO
1995—	Gulf Coast Yankees (GCL)..	0	1	.000	0.64	5	4	0	0	0	14	12	9	1	6	13
1996—	Oneonta (NY-Penn)	1	1	.500	5.74	3	3	0	0	0	15 $^2/_3$	14	12	10	11	14
	Gulf Coast Yankees (GCL)..	4	1	.800	3.15	8	7	0	0	1	45 $^2/_3$	41	18	16	13	45
1997—	Greensboro (S.Atl.)	5	2	.714	1.05	9	9	2	1	0	51 $^2/_3$	36	13	6	13	64
	Tampa (FSL)	3	1	.750	3.33	9	9	0	0	0	46	43	23	17	16	26
	Sarasota (FSL)■	2	1	.667	6.62	3	3	0	0	0	17 $^2/_3$	18	13	13	12	9
1998—	Jupiter (FSL)■	12	8	.600	2.88	27	27	1	1	0	153 $^1/_3$	140	63	49	59	136
1999—	Harrisburg (East.)	9	7	.563	2.89	24	24	2	1	0	149 $^2/_3$	123	62	48	55	106
	Montreal (N.L.)	0	1	.000	1.50	1	1	0	0	0	6	8	4	1	2	2
2000—	Jupiter (FSL)	0	0	...	0.00	1	1	0	0	0	4 $^2/_3$	4	0	0	0	8
	Ottawa (I.L.)	1	2	.333	3.79	4	4	0	0	0	19	22	11	8	4	12
	Montreal (N.L.)	7	9	.438	4.36	17	17	0	0	0	95	74	49	46	50	59
Major League totals (2 years)		**7**	**10**	**.412**	**4.19**	**18**	**18**	**0**	**0**	**0**	**101**	**82**	**53**	**47**	**52**	**61**

ARNOLD, JAMIE — P

PERSONAL: Born March 24, 1974, in Dearborn, Mich. ... 6-2/188. ... Throws right, bats right. ... Full name: James Lee Arnold.
HIGH SCHOOL: Osceola (Kissimmee, Fla.).
TRANSACTIONS/CAREER NOTES: Selected by Atlanta Braves organization in first-round (21st pick overall) of free-agent draft (June 1, 1992). ... Granted free agency (October 16, 1998). ... Signed by Los Angeles Dodgers organization (January 6, 1999). ... On Albuquerque disabled list (April 6-13, 2000). ... Traded by Dodgers with OF Jorge Piedra and cash to Chicago Cubs for P Ismael Valdes (July 26, 2000). ... Granted free agency (December 21, 2000).

Year	League	W	L	Pct.	ERA	G	GS	CG	ShO	Sv.	IP	H	R	ER	BB	SO
1992—	Gulf Coast Braves (GCL)	0	1	.000	4.05	7	5	0	0	0	20	16	12	9	6	22
1993—	Macon (S.Atl.)	8	9	.471	3.12	27	27	1	0	0	164 $^1/_3$	142	67	57	56	124
1994—	Durham (Caro.)	7	7	.500	4.66	25	25	0	0	0	145	144	96	75	79	91
1995—	Greenville (Sou.)	1	5	.167	6.35	10	10	0	0	0	56 $^2/_3$	76	42	40	25	19
	Durham (Caro.)	4	8	.333	3.94	15	14	1	0	0	80	86	42	35	21	44
1996—	Greenville (Sou.)	7	7	.500	4.92	23	23	2	0	0	128	149	79	70	44	64
1997—	Gulf Coast Braves (GCL)	1	0	1.000	2.84	5	5	0	0	0	19	13	6	6	6	21
	Durham (Caro.)	2	2	.500	5.92	5	5	0	0	0	24 $^1/_3$	25	21	16	13	21
	Greenville (Sou.)	0	1	.000	11.57	1	1	0	0	0	4 $^2/_3$	10	6	6	2	3
1998—	Greenville (Sou.)	1	4	.200	4.43	32	6	0	0	1	83 $^1/_3$	93	51	41	46	48
	Richmond (I.L.)	1	0	1.000	9.58	9	2	0	0	1	20 $^2/_3$	30	22	22	17	10
1999—	Albuquerque (PCL)■	0	2	.000	5.59	7	2	0	0	0	19 $^1/_3$	28	14	12	7	13
	Los Angeles (N.L.)	2	4	.333	5.48	36	3	0	0	1	69	81	50	42	34	26
2000—	Los Angeles (N.L.)	0	0	...	4.05	2	0	0	0	0	6 $^2/_3$	4	3	3	5	3
	Albuquerque (PCL)	4	7	.364	5.07	20	13	0	0	0	92 $^1/_3$	94	62	52	54	47
	Iowa (PCL)■	2	1	.667	4.58	3	3	0	0	0	17 $^2/_3$	22	10	9	10	10
	Chicago (N.L.)	0	3	.000	6.61	12	4	0	0	1	32 $^2/_3$	34	28	24	19	13
Major League totals (2 years)		**2**	**7**	**.222**	**5.73**	**50**	**7**	**0**	**0**	**2**	**108 $^1/_3$**	**119**	**81**	**69**	**58**	**42**

ARROJO, ROLANDO — P — RED SOX

PERSONAL: Born July 18, 1968, in Havana, Cuba. ... 6-4/220. ... Throws right, bats right. ... Full name: Luis Rolando Arrojo.
TRANSACTIONS/CAREER NOTES: Signed as non-drafted free agent by Tampa Bay Devil Rays organization (April 21, 1997). ... On disabled list (September 21, 1998-remainder of season). ... On Tampa Bay disabled list (May 25-July 15, 1999); included rehabilitation assignment to St. Petersburg (July 2-15). ... Traded by Devil Rays with IF Aaron Ledesma to Colorado Rockies for 3B Vinny Castilla (December 13, 1999). ... On Colorado disabled list (April 21-May 6, 2000). ... Traded by Rockies with P Rick Croushore, 2B Mike Lansing and cash to Boston Red Sox for P Brian Rose, P John Wasdin, P Jeff Taglienti and 2B Jeff Frye (July 27, 2000).
HONORS: Named A.L. Rookie Pitcher of the Year by THE SPORTING NEWS (1998).
STATISTICAL NOTES: Led A.L. with 19 hit batsmen in 1998.
MISCELLANEOUS: Member of Cuban national baseball team (1986-96). ... Holds Tampa Bay Devil Rays all-time record for most strikeouts (259). ... Shares Tampa Bay Devil Rays all-time records for most wins (21) and shutouts (2).

Year	League	W	L	Pct.	ERA	G	GS	CG	ShO	Sv.	IP	H	R	ER	BB	SO
1997—	St. Petersburg (FSL)	5	6	.455	3.43	16	16	4	1	0	89 1/3	73	40	34	13	73
1998—	Tampa Bay (A.L.)................	14	12	.538	3.56	32	32	2	2	0	202	195	84	80	65	152
1999—	Tampa Bay (A.L.)................	7	12	.368	5.18	24	24	2	0	0	140 2/3	162	84	81	60	107
	— St. Petersburg (FSL)	0	1	.000	4.50	2	2	0	0	0	10	11	6	5	1	10
2000—	Colorado (N.L.)■	5	9	.357	6.04	19	19	0	0	0	101 1/3	120	77	68	46	80
	— Boston (A.L.)■................	5	2	.714	5.05	13	13	0	0	0	71 1/3	67	41	40	22	44
A.L. totals (3 years)		26	26	.500	4.37	69	69	4	2	0	414	424	209	201	147	303
N.L. totals (1 year)		5	9	.357	6.04	19	19	0	0	0	101 1/3	120	77	68	46	80
Major League totals (3 years)		31	35	.470	4.70	88	88	4	2	0	515 1/3	544	286	269	193	383

ALL-STAR GAME RECORD

Year	League	W	L	Pct.	ERA	GS	CG	ShO	Sv.	IP	H	R	ER	BB	SO
1998—	American	0	0	...	0.00	0	0	0	0	1	2	0	0	0	1

ARROYO, BRONSON   P   PIRATES

PERSONAL: Born February 24, 1977, in Key West, Fla. ... 6-5/180. ... Throws right, bats right. ... Full name: Bronson Anthony Arroyo.

HIGH SCHOOL: Hernando (Fla.).

TRANSACTIONS/CAREER NOTES: Selected by Pittsburgh Pirates organization in third round of free-agent draft (June 1, 1995). ... On suspended list (May 29-June 1, 1996). ... On Carolina disabled list (May 18-June 7 and June 18-July 4, 1998).

MISCELLANEOUS: Appeared in one game as pinch runner and grounded out in only appearance as pinch hitter (2000).

Year	League	W	L	Pct.	ERA	G	GS	CG	ShO	Sv.	IP	H	R	ER	BB	SO
1995—	GC Pirates (GCL)...............	5	4	.556	4.26	13	9	0	0	0	61 1/3	72	39	29	9	48
1996—	Augusta (S.Atl.).................	8	6	.571	3.52	26	26	0	0	0	135 2/3	123	64	53	36	107
1997—	Lynchburg (Caro.)	•12	4	.750	3.31	24	24	3	1	0	160 1/3	154	69	59	33	121
1998—	Carolina (Sou.)	9	8	.529	5.46	23	22	1	0	0	127	158	91	77	51	90
1999—	Altoona (East.)	•15	4	.789	3.65	25	25	2	1	0	153	167	73	62	58	100
	— Nashville (PCL)	0	4	.000	10.38	3	3	0	0	0	13	22	15	15	10	11
2000—	Nashville (PCL)	8	2	.800	3.65	13	13	1	0	0	88 2/3	82	43	36	25	52
	— Pittsburgh (N.L.)	2	6	.250	6.40	20	12	0	0	0	71 2/3	88	61	51	36	50
	— Lynchburg (Caro.)	0	0	...	3.86	1	1	0	0	0	7	8	3	3	2	3
Major League totals (1 year)		2	6	.250	6.40	20	12	0	0	0	71 2/3	88	61	51	36	50

ASHBY, ANDY   P   DODGERS

PERSONAL: Born July 11, 1967, in Kansas City, Mo. ... 6-1/202. ... Throws right, bats right. ... Full name: Andrew Jason Ashby.

HIGH SCHOOL: Park Hill (Kansas City, Mo.).

JUNIOR COLLEGE: Crowder College (Mo.).

TRANSACTIONS/CAREER NOTES: Signed as non-drafted free agent by Philadelphia Phillies organization (May 4, 1986). ... On Spartanburg disabled list (April 7-July 10, 1988). ... On Spartanburg disabled list (April 6-26, 1989). ... On Philadelphia disabled list (April 27-August 11, 1992); included rehabilitation assignments to Scranton/Wilkes-Barre (July 8-August 2 and August 6-10). ... Selected by Colorado Rockies in first round (25th pick overall) of expansion draft (November 17, 1992). ... Traded by Rockies to San Diego Padres (July 27, 1993), completing deal in which Padres traded P Bruce Hurst and P Greg W. Harris to Rockies for C Brad Ausmus, P Doug Bochtler and a player to be named later (July 26, 1993). ... On disabled list (June 6-22, June 29-July 15 and July 27-September 1, 1996; May 20-June 15, 1997; and June 7-24, 1999). ... Traded by Padres to Phillies for P Carlton Loewer, P Steve Montgomery and P Adam Eaton (November 10, 1999). ... On Philadelphia disabled list (June 12-27, 2000). ... Traded by Phillies to Atlanta Braves for P Bruce Chen and P Jimmy Osting (July 12, 2000). ... Granted free agency (November 1, 2000). ... Signed by Los Angeles Dodgers (December 6, 2000).

RECORDS: Shares major league record by striking out side on nine pitches (June 15, 1991, fourth inning).

MISCELLANEOUS: Had sacrifice hit in only appearance as pinch-hitter (1996). ... Appeared in one game as pinch runner (1997). ... Appeared in one game as pinch runner (2000).

Year	League	W	L	Pct.	ERA	G	GS	CG	ShO	Sv.	IP	H	R	ER	BB	SO
1986—	Bend (N'West)....................	1	2	.333	4.95	16	6	0	0	2	60	56	40	33	34	45
1987—	Spartanburg (S.Atl.)	4	6	.400	5.60	13	13	1	0	0	64 1/3	73	45	40	38	52
	— Utica (NY-Penn)	3	7	.300	4.05	13	13	0	0	0	60	56	38	27	36	51
1988—	Spartanburg (S.Atl.)	1	1	.500	2.70	3	3	0	0	0	16 2/3	13	7	5	7	16
	— Batavia (NY-Penn)	3	1	.750	1.61	6	6	2	1	0	44 2/3	25	11	8	16	32
1989—	Spartanburg (S.Atl.)	5	9	.357	2.87	17	17	3	1	0	106 2/3	95	48	34	49	100
	— Clearwater (FSL)	1	4	.200	1.24	6	6	2	1	0	43 2/3	28	9	6	21	44
1990—	Reading (East.).................	10	7	.588	3.42	23	23	4	1	0	139 2/3	134	65	53	48	93
1991—	Scranton/W.B. (I.L.)	11	11	.500	3.46	26	26	•6	•3	0	161 1/3	144	78	62	60	113
	— Philadelphia (N.L.)............	1	5	.167	6.00	8	8	0	0	0	42	41	28	28	19	26
1992—	Philadelphia (N.L.)	1	3	.250	7.54	10	8	0	0	0	37	42	31	31	21	24
	— Scranton/W.B. (I.L.)	0	3	.000	3.00	7	7	1	0	0	33	23	13	11	14	18
1993—	Colorado (N.L.)■	0	4	.000	8.50	20	9	0	0	1	54	89	54	51	32	33
	— Colorado Springs (PCL)	4	2	.667	4.10	7	6	1	0	0	41 2/3	45	25	19	12	35
	— San Diego (N.L.)■	3	6	.333	5.48	12	12	0	0	0	69	79	46	42	24	44
1994—	San Diego (N.L.)	6	11	.353	3.40	24	24	4	0	0	164 1/3	145	75	62	43	121
1995—	San Diego (N.L.)	12	10	.545	2.94	31	•31	2	2	0	192 2/3	180	79	63	62	150
1996—	San Diego (N.L.)	9	5	.643	3.23	24	24	1	0	0	150 2/3	147	60	54	34	85
1997—	San Diego (N.L.)	9	11	.450	4.13	30	30	2	0	0	200 2/3	207	108	92	49	144
1998—	San Diego (N.L.)	17	9	.654	3.34	33	33	5	1	0	226 2/3	223	90	84	58	151
1999—	San Diego (N.L.)	14	10	.583	3.80	31	31	4	*3	0	206	204	95	87	54	132
2000—	Philadelphia (N.L.)■	4	7	.364	5.68	16	16	1	0	0	101 1/3	113	75	64	38	51
	— Atlanta (N.L.)■................	8	6	.571	4.13	15	15	2	1	0	98	103	49	45	23	55
Major League totals (10 years)		84	87	.491	4.10	254	241	21	7	1	1542 1/3	1573	790	703	457	1016

DIVISION SERIES RECORD

Year League	W	L	Pct.	ERA	G	GS	CG	ShO	Sv.	IP	H	R	ER	BB	SO
1996— San Diego (N.L.)	0	0	...	6.75	1	1	0	0	0	5 1/3	7	4	4	1	5
1998— San Diego (N.L.)	0	0	...	6.75	1	1	0	0	0	4	6	3	3	1	4
2000— Atlanta (N.L.)	0	0	...	2.45	2	0	0	0	0	3 2/3	1	1	1	3	5
Division series totals (3 years)	0	0	...	5.54	4	2	0	0	0	13	14	8	8	5	14

CHAMPIONSHIP SERIES RECORD

Year League	W	L	Pct.	ERA	G	GS	CG	ShO	Sv.	IP	H	R	ER	BB	SO
1998— San Diego (N.L.)	0	0	...	2.08	2	2	0	0	0	13	14	3	3	2	5

WORLD SERIES RECORD

Year League	W	L	Pct.	ERA	G	GS	CG	ShO	Sv.	IP	H	R	ER	BB	SO
1998— San Diego (N.L.)	0	1	.000	13.50	1	1	0	0	0	2 2/3	10	7	4	1	1

ALL-STAR GAME RECORD

Year League	W	L	Pct.	ERA	GS	CG	ShO	Sv.	IP	H	R	ER	BB	SO
1998— National	0	0	...	9.00	0	0	0	0	1	1	1	1	1	0
1999— National	0	0	...	0.00	0	0	0	0	1/3	0	0	0	0	0
All-Star Game totals (2 years)	0	0	...	6.75	0	0	0	0	1 1/3	1	1	1	1	0

ASTACIO, PEDRO — P — ROCKIES

PERSONAL: Born November 28, 1969, in Hato Mayor, Dominican Republic. ... 6-2/210. ... Throws right, bats right. ... Full name: Pedro Julio Astacio. ... Name pronounced ah-STA-see-oh.

HIGH SCHOOL: Pilar Rondon (Dominican Republic).

TRANSACTIONS/CAREER NOTES: Signed as non-drafted free agent by Los Angeles Dodgers organization (November 21, 1987). ... On Albuquerque disabled list (April 26-May 21, 1992). ... Traded by Dodgers to Colorado Rockies for 2B Eric Young (August 19, 1997).

STATISTICAL NOTES: Led N.L. with nine balks in 1993. ... Led N.L. with 17 hit batsmen and tied for lead with 39 home runs allowed in 1998. ... Led N.L. with 38 home runs allowed in 1999.

MISCELLANEOUS: Holds Colorado Rockies all-time record for most wins (47), innings pitched (686 1/3) and complete games (10). ... Struck out in both appearances as pinch hitter and appeared in one game as pinch runner (1999).

Year League	W	L	Pct.	ERA	G	GS	CG	ShO	Sv.	IP	H	R	ER	BB	SO
1989— Gulf Coast Dodgers (GCL)	7	3	.700	3.17	12	12	1	•1	0	76 2/3	77	30	27	12	52
1990— Vero Beach (FSL)	1	5	.167	6.32	8	8	0	0	0	47	54	39	33	23	41
— Yakima (N'West)	2	0	1.000	1.74	3	3	0	0	0	20 2/3	9	8	4	4	22
— Bakersfield (Calif.)	5	2	.714	2.77	10	7	1	0	0	52	46	22	16	15	34
1991— Vero Beach (FSL)	5	3	.625	1.67	9	9	3	1	0	59 1/3	44	19	11	8	45
— San Antonio (Texas)	4	11	.267	4.78	19	19	2	1	0	113	142	67	60	39	62
1992— Albuquerque (PCL)	6	6	.500	5.47	24	15	1	0	0	98 2/3	115	68	60	44	66
— Los Angeles (N.L.)	5	5	.500	1.98	11	11	4	4	0	82	80	23	18	20	43
1993— Los Angeles (N.L.)	14	9	.609	3.57	31	31	3	2	0	186 1/3	165	80	74	68	122
1994— Los Angeles (N.L.)	6	8	.429	4.29	23	23	3	1	0	149	142	77	71	47	108
1995— Los Angeles (N.L.)	7	8	.467	4.24	48	11	1	1	0	104	103	53	49	29	80
1996— Los Angeles (N.L.)	9	8	.529	3.44	35	32	0	0	0	211 2/3	207	86	81	67	130
1997— Los Angeles (N.L.)	7	9	.438	4.10	26	24	2	1	0	153 2/3	151	75	70	47	115
— Colorado (N.L.)■	5	1	.833	4.25	7	7	0	0	0	48 2/3	49	23	23	14	51
1998— Colorado (N.L.)	13	14	.481	6.23	35	34	0	0	0	209 1/3	245	*160	*145	74	170
1999— Colorado (N.L.)	17	11	.607	5.04	34	34	7	0	0	232	258	140	130	75	210
2000— Colorado (N.L.)	12	9	.571	5.27	32	32	3	0	0	196 1/3	217	119	115	77	193
Major League totals (9 years)	95	82	.537	4.44	282	239	23	9	0	1573	1617	836	776	518	1222

DIVISION SERIES RECORD

Year League	W	L	Pct.	ERA	G	GS	CG	ShO	Sv.	IP	H	R	ER	BB	SO
1995— Los Angeles (N.L.)	0	0	...	0.00	3	0	0	0	0	3 1/3	1	0	0	0	5
1996— Los Angeles (N.L.)	0	0	...	0.00	1	0	0	0	0	1 2/3	0	0	0	0	1
Division series totals (2 years)	0	0	...	0.00	4	0	0	0	0	5	1	0	0	0	6

ATCHLEY, JUSTIN — P — REDS

PERSONAL: Born September 5, 1973, in Sedro Woolley, Wash. ... 6-3/215. ... Throws left, bats left. ... Full name: Justin Scott Atchley.

HIGH SCHOOL: Sedro Woolley (Wash.).

JUNIOR COLLEGE: Walla Walla (Wash.) Community College.

COLLEGE: Texas A&M.

TRANSACTIONS/CAREER NOTES: Selected by San Diego Padres organization in 15th round of free-agent draft (June 3, 1991); did not sign. ... Selected by Atlanta Braves organization in sixth round of free-agent draft (June 1, 1992); did not sign. ... Selected by Cincinnati Reds organization in 12th round of free-agent draft (June 1, 1995). ... On Indianapolis disabled list (April 2, 1998-entire season; August 11-24, 1999). ... On Chattanooga disabled list (May 7-17, 1999). ... On Louisville disabled list (May 5-14, 2000). ... Released by Reds (January 9, 2001). ... Re-signed by Reds organization (January 12, 2001).

Year League	W	L	Pct.	ERA	G	GS	CG	ShO	Sv.	IP	H	R	ER	BB	SO
1995— Billings (Pio.)	*10	0	*1.000	3.51	13	13	0	0	0	77	91	33	30	20	65
1996— Charleston, W.Va. (S.Atl.)	3	3	.500	3.46	17	16	0	0	1	91	98	42	35	23	78
— Winston-Salem (Caro.)	3	3	.500	5.09	12	12	0	0	0	69	74	48	39	16	50
1997— Chattanooga (Sou.)	4	2	.667	4.70	13	13	1	0	0	67	75	45	35	14	48
1998— Indianapolis (I.L.)						Did not play.									
1999— Chattanooga (Sou.)	4	9	.308	3.42	17	17	0	0	0	97 1/3	114	48	37	22	70
— Indianapolis (I.L.)	2	1	.667	5.40	5	4	0	0	1	23 1/3	39	14	14	2	6
2000— Louisville (I.L.)	8	6	.571	5.89	30	19	0	0	1	122 1/3	168	83	80	26	69

PERSONAL: Born September 2, 1971, in Brooklyn, N.Y. ... 6-1/185. ... Bats right, throws right. ... Full name: Richard Santo Aurilia. ... Name pronounced uh-REEL-yuh.
HIGH SCHOOL: Xaverian (Brooklyn, N.Y.).
COLLEGE: St. John's.
TRANSACTIONS/CAREER NOTES: Selected by Texas Rangers organization in 24th round of free-agent draft (June 1, 1992). ... On disabled list (April 9-16, 1993). ... Traded by Rangers with IF/OF Desi Wilson to San Francisco Giants for P John Burkett (December 24, 1994). ... On San Francisco disabled list (September 24, 1996-remainder of season). ... On disabled list (July 4-20, 1998).
STATISTICAL NOTES: Led Texas League shortstops with 635 total chances and tied for lead with 82 double plays in 1994. ... Career major league grand slams: 1.

Year Team (League)	Pos.	G	AB	R	H	2B	3B	HR	RBI	Avg.	BB	SO	SB	PO	A	E	Avg.
1992— Butte (Pio.)	SS	59	202	37	68	11	3	3	30	.337	42	18	13	78	154	14	*.943
1993— Charlotte (FSL)	SS	122	440	80	136	16	5	5	56	.309	75	57	15	200	445	24	.964
1994— Tulsa (Texas)	SS	129	458	67	107	18	6	12	57	.234	53	74	10	*237	374	24	*.962
1995— Shreveport (Texas)■	SS	64	226	29	74	17	1	4	42	.327	27	26	10	122	237	14	.962
— Phoenix (PCL)	SS	71	258	42	72	12	0	5	34	.279	35	29	2	104	246	9	.975
— San Francisco (N.L.)	SS	9	19	4	9	3	0	2	4	.474	1	2	1	8	16	0	1.000
1996— Phoenix (PCL)	SS-2B	7	30	9	13	7	0	0	4	.433	2	3	1	10	25	1	.972
— San Francisco (N.L.)	SS-2B	105	318	27	76	7	1	3	26	.239	25	52	4	142	246	10	.975
1997— San Francisco (N.L.)	SS	46	102	16	28	8	0	5	19	.275	8	15	1	47	91	3	.979
— Phoenix (PCL)	SS	8	34	9	10	2	0	1	5	.294	5	4	2	14	22	0	1.000
1998— San Francisco (N.L.)	SS	122	413	54	110	27	2	9	49	.266	31	62	3	154	313	10	.979
1999— San Francisco (N.L.)	SS	152	558	68	157	23	1	22	80	.281	43	71	2	218	411	*28	.957
2000— San Francisco (N.L.)	SS	141	509	67	138	24	2	20	79	.271	54	90	1	218	403	21	.967
Major League totals (6 years)		575	1919	236	518	92	6	61	257	.270	162	292	12	787	1480	72	.969

DIVISION SERIES RECORD

Year Team (League)	Pos.	G	AB	R	H	2B	3B	HR	RBI	Avg.	BB	SO	SB	PO	A	E	Avg.
2000— San Francisco (N.L.)	SS	4	15	0	2	1	0	0	0	.133	0	3	0	10	11	1	.955

PERSONAL: Born April 14, 1969, in New Haven, Conn. ... 5-11/195. ... Bats right, throws right. ... Full name: Bradley David Ausmus.
HIGH SCHOOL: Cheshire (Conn.).
COLLEGE: Dartmouth.
TRANSACTIONS/CAREER NOTES: Selected by New York Yankees organization in 47th round of free-agent draft (June 2, 1987). ... Selected by Colorado Rockies in third round (54th pick overall) of expansion draft (November 17, 1992). ... Traded by Rockies with P Doug Bochtler and a player to be named later to San Diego Padres for P Bruce Hurst and P Greg W. Harris (July 26, 1993); Padres acquired P Andy Ashby to complete deal (July 27, 1993). ... Traded by Padres with SS Andujar Cedeno and P Russ Spear to Detroit Tigers for C John Flaherty and SS Chris Gomez (June 18, 1996). ... On Detroit suspended list (September 4-5, 1996). ... Traded by Tigers with P Jose Lima, P C.J. Nitkowski, P Trever Miller and IF Daryle Ward to Houston Astros for OF Brian L. Hunter, IF Orlando Miller, P Doug Brocail, P Todd Jones and cash (December 10, 1996). ... Traded by Astros with P C.J. Nitkowski to Tigers for C Paul Bako, P Dean Crow, P Mark Persails, P Brian Powell and 3B Carlos Villalobos (January 14, 1999). ... Traded by Tigers with P Doug Brocail and P Nelson Cruz to Astros for C Mitch Meluskey, P Chris Holt and OF Roger Cedeno (December 11, 2000).
RECORDS: Holds A.L. single-season records for fewest assists by catcher for leader (150 or more games)—68 (2000); and for fewest passed balls (150 or more games)—3 (2000).
STATISTICAL NOTES: Led Gulf Coast League catchers with 434 total chances in 1988. ... Led International League catchers with 666 putouts and 738 total chances in 1992. ... Led N.L. catchers with 683 putouts and 749 total chances in 1994. ... Led N.L. catchers with 14 double plays in 1995. ... Tied for N.L. lead in assists by catcher with 63 in 1995. ... Led A.L. catchers with 898 putouts, 68 assists and 974 total chances in 2000. ... Career major league grand slams: 1.

Year Team (League)	Pos.	G	AB	R	H	2B	3B	HR	RBI	Avg.	BB	SO	SB	PO	A	E	Avg.
1988— Oneonta (NY-Penn)	C	2	4	0	1	0	0	0	0	.250	0	2	0	0	0	0	...
— Sarasota (FSL)	C	43	133	22	34	2	0	0	15	.256	11	25	5	*378	*47	9	.979
1989— Oneonta (NY-Penn)	C-3B	52	165	29	43	6	0	1	18	.261	22	28	6	401	43	7	.984
1990— Prince William (Caro.)	C	107	364	46	86	12	2	0	27	.236	32	73	2	662	84	5	*.993
1991— Prince William (Caro.)	C	63	230	28	70	14	3	2	30	.304	24	37	17	419	54	5	.990
— Alb./Colonie (East.)	C	67	229	36	61	9	2	1	29	.266	27	36	14	470	56	4	.992
1992— Alb./Colonie (East.)	C	5	18	0	3	0	1	0	1	.167	2	3	2	30	2	1	.970
— Columbus (I.L.)	C-OF	111	364	48	88	14	3	2	35	.242	40	56	19	†666	63	9	.988
1993— Colo. Springs (PCL)■	C-DH-OF	76	241	31	65	10	4	2	33	.270	27	41	10	393	57	6	.987
— San Diego (N.L.)■	C	49	160	18	41	8	1	5	12	.256	6	28	2	272	34	8	.975
1994— San Diego (N.L.)	C-1B	101	327	45	82	12	1	7	24	.251	30	63	5	†686	59	7	.991
1995— San Diego (N.L.)	C-1B	103	328	44	96	16	4	5	34	.293	31	56	16	656	†63	6	.992
1996— San Diego (N.L.)	C	50	149	16	27	4	0	1	13	.181	13	27	1	300	22	6	.982
— Detroit (A.L.)■	C	75	226	30	56	12	0	4	22	.248	26	45	3	452	35	4	.992
1997— Houston (N.L.)■	C	130	425	45	113	25	1	4	44	.266	38	78	14	807	73	7	.992
1998— Houston (N.L.)	C	128	412	62	111	10	4	6	45	.269	53	60	10	850	58	7	.992
1999— Detroit (A.L.)■	C	127	458	62	126	25	6	9	54	.275	51	71	12	754	56	2	*.998
2000— Detroit (A.L.)	C-1B-2B-3B	150	523	75	139	25	3	7	51	.266	69	79	11	†900	†68	8	.992
American League totals (3 years)		352	1207	167	321	62	9	20	127	.266	146	195	26	2106	159	14	.994
National League totals (6 years)		561	1801	230	470	75	11	28	172	.261	171	312	48	3571	309	41	.990
Major League totals (8 years)		913	3008	397	791	137	20	48	299	.263	317	507	74	5677	468	55	.991

DIVISION SERIES RECORD

Year	Team (League)	Pos.	G	AB	R	H	2B	3B	HR	RBI	Avg.	BB	SO	SB	PO	A	E	Avg.
1997—	Houston (N.L.)	C	2	5	1	2	1	0	0	2	.400	0	1	0	13	0	0	1.000
1998—	Houston (N.L.)	C	4	9	0	2	0	0	0	0	.222	0	4	0	28	1	0	1.000
Division series totals (2 years)			6	14	1	4	1	0	0	2	.286	0	5	0	41	1	0	1.000

ALL-STAR GAME RECORD

Year	League	Pos.	AB	R	H	2B	3B	HR	RBI	Avg.	BB	SO	SB	PO	A	E	Avg.
1999—	American	C	1	0	0	0	0	0	0	.000	0	0	0	2	1	0	1.000

AVEN, BRUCE — OF — DODGERS

PERSONAL: Born March 4, 1972, in Orange, Texas. ... 5-9/180. ... Bats right, throws right. ... Full name: David Bruce Aven.
HIGH SCHOOL: West Orange-Stark (Orange, Texas).
COLLEGE: Lamar.
TRANSACTIONS/CAREER NOTES: Selected by Cleveland Indians organization in 30th round of free-agent draft (June 2, 1994). ... On Buffalo disabled list (April 9-17, April 23-May 23 and May 27, 1998-remainder of season). ... Claimed on waivers by Florida Marlins (October 20, 1998). ... Traded by Marlins to Pittsburgh Pirates for OF Brant Brown (December 13, 1999). ... On Pittsburgh disabled list (June 30-July 18, 2000); included rehabilitation assignment to Nashville (July 14-18). ... Traded by Pirates to Los Angeles Dodgers for a player to be named later (August 6, 2000).
STATISTICAL NOTES: Led Eastern League outfielders with 289 total chances in 1996. ... Tied for American Association lead in being hit by pitch with 11 in 1997. ... Career major league grand slams: 2.

Year	Team (League)	Pos.	G	AB	R	H	2B	3B	HR	RBI	Avg.	BB	SO	SB	PO	A	E	Avg.
1994—	Watertown (NY-Penn)	OF	61	220	49	73	14	5	5	33	.332	20	45	12	88	6	1	.989
1995—	Kinston (Caro.)	OF	130	479	70	125	23	5	23	69	.261	41	109	15	158	11	3	.983
1996—	Canton/Akron (East.)..	OF	131	481	91	143	31	4	23	79	.297	43	101	22	280	3	6	.979
	— Buffalo (A.A.)	OF	3	9	5	6	0	0	1	2	.667	1	1	0	7	0	0	1.000
1997—	Buffalo (A.A.)	OF-DH	121	432	69	124	27	3	17	77	.287	50	99	10	219	3	2	.991
	— Cleveland (A.L.)	OF	13	19	4	4	1	0	0	2	.211	1	5	0	15	1	0	1.000
1998—	Buffalo (I.L.)	DH	5	15	4	3	1	0	1	1	.200	6	5	3	0	0	0	...
1999—	Florida (N.L.)■..........	OF-DH	137	381	57	110	19	2	12	70	.289	44	82	3	181	4	3	.984
2000—	Pittsburgh (N.L.)■	OF	72	148	18	37	11	0	5	25	.250	5	31	2	49	0	1	.980
	— Nashville (PCL)	OF	3	10	1	3	1	0	0	3	.300	1	3	0	6	0	0	1.000
	— Albuquerque (PCL)■..	OF	9	32	7	9	1	0	0	3	.281	6	6	0	11	1	0	1.000
	— Los Angeles (N.L.)	OF	9	20	2	5	0	0	2	4	.250	3	8	0	12	0	0	1.000
American League totals (1 year)			13	19	4	4	1	0	0	2	.211	1	5	0	15	1	0	1.000
National League totals (2 years)			218	549	77	152	30	2	19	99	.277	52	121	5	242	4	4	.984
Major League totals (3 years)			231	568	81	156	31	2	19	101	.275	53	126	5	257	5	4	.985

AYBAR, MANNY — P — MARLINS

PERSONAL: Born November 28, 1969, in Bani, Dominican Republic. ... 6-1/177. ... Throws right, bats right. ... Full name: Manuel Antonio Aybar. ... Name pronounced I-bar.
TRANSACTIONS/CAREER NOTES: Signed as non-drafted free agent by St. Louis Cardinals organization (October 21, 1991). ... Traded by Cardinals with P Jose Jimenez, P Rick Croushore and IF Brent Butler to Colorado Rockies for P Darryl Kile, P Dave Veres and P Luther Hackman (November 16, 1999). ... Traded by Rockies to Cincinnati Reds for P Gabe White (April 7, 2000). ... On Cincinnati disabled list (July 2-24, 2000); included rehabilitation assignment to Louisville (July 8-23). ... Traded by Reds to Florida Marlins for P Jorge Cordova (July 26, 2000).
MISCELLANEOUS: Appeared in two games as pinch runner (1999).

Year	League	W	L	Pct.	ERA	G	GS	CG	ShO	Sv.	IP	H	R	ER	BB	SO
1992—	Dominican Cardinals (DSL)	1	0	1.000	0.00	55	0	0	0	0	3	1	0	0	3	1
1993—	Dominican Cardinals (DSL)	4	4	.500	3.15	13	11	1	0	0	71 1/3	54	33	25	33	66
1994—	Arizona Cardinals (Ariz.).....	6	1	.857	2.12	13	13	1	0	0	72 1/3	69	25	17	9	79
1995—	Savannah (S.Atl.)	3	8	.273	3.04	18	18	2	1	0	112 2/3	82	46	38	36	99
	— St. Petersburg (FSL)	2	5	.286	3.35	9	9	0	0	0	48 1/3	42	27	18	16	43
1996—	Arkansas (Texas)	8	6	.571	3.05	20	20	0	0	0	121	120	53	41	34	83
	— Louisville (A.A.)	2	2	.500	3.23	5	5	0	0	0	30 2/3	26	12	11	7	25
1997—	Louisville (A.A.)	5	8	.385	3.48	22	22	3	•2	0	137	131	60	53	45	114
	— St. Louis (N.L.)................	2	4	.333	4.24	12	12	0	0	0	68	66	33	32	29	41
1998—	St. Louis (N.L.)................	6	6	.500	5.98	20	14	0	0	0	81 1/3	90	58	54	42	57
	— Memphis (PCL)	10	0	1.000	2.60	13	13	0	0	0	83	62	24	24	17	63
1999—	St. Louis (N.L.)................	4	5	.444	5.47	65	1	0	0	3	97	104	67	59	36	74
2000—	Colorado (N.L.)■	0	1	.000	16.20	1	0	0	0	0	1 2/3	5	3	3	0	0
	— Cincinnati (N.L.)■	1	1	.500	4.83	32	0	0	0	0	50 1/3	51	31	27	22	31
	— Louisville (I.L.)	0	2	.000	13.50	3	2	0	0	0	6 2/3	10	10	10	10	1
	— Florida (N.L.)■................	1	0	1.000	2.63	21	0	0	0	0	27 1/3	18	8	8	13	14
Major League totals (4 years)		14	17	.452	5.06	151	27	0	0	3	325 2/3	334	200	183	142	217

RECORD AS POSITION PLAYER

Year	Team (League)	Pos.	G	AB	R	H	2B	3B	HR	RBI	Avg.	BB	SO	SB	PO	A	E	Avg.
1992—	Dom. Cardinals (DSL)	IF	55	153	18	31	5	0	1	11	.203	10	27	2	53	131	19	.906

PERSONAL: Born September 10, 1977, in Pinar del Rio, Cuba. ... 6-3/225. ... Throws right, bats right.
TRANSACTIONS/CAREER NOTES: Signed as non-drafted free agent by Cleveland Indians organization (November 5, 1999). ... On Buffalo disabled list (June 19-July 4, 2000).

Year League	W	L	Pct.	ERA	G	GS	CG	ShO	Sv.	IP	H	R	ER	BB	SO
2000—Kinston (Caro.)	2	2	.500	4.71	9	9	0	0	0	49 2/3	45	29	26	20	56
—Akron (East.)	4	9	.308	3.68	18	18	0	0	0	102 2/3	98	46	42	32	77

B

PERSONAL: Born May 27, 1968, in Boston. ... 6-0/195. ... Bats right, throws right. ... Full name: Jeffrey Robert Bagwell.
HIGH SCHOOL: Xavier (Middletown, Conn.).
COLLEGE: Hartford.
TRANSACTIONS/CAREER NOTES: Selected by Boston Red Sox organization in fourth round of free-agent draft (June 5, 1989). ... Traded by Red Sox to Houston Astros for P Larry Andersen (August 31, 1990). ... On Houston disabled list (July 31-September 1, 1995); included rehabilitation assignment to Jackson (August 28-September 1). ... On disabled list (May 13-28, 1998).
RECORDS: Shares major league single-season record for most times hitting three or more home runs in a game—2 (1999). ... Shares major league single-game records for most doubles—4 (June 14, 1996); and most bases on balls—6 (August 20, 1999, 16 innings). ... Shares major league single-inning record for most home runs—2 (June 24, 1994, sixth inning). ... Shares N.L. career record for most major league ballparks, one or more home runs (since 1900)—22.
HONORS: Named Eastern League Most Valuable Player (1990). ... Named N.L. Rookie Player of the Year by The Sporting News (1991). ... Named N.L. Rookie of the Year by Baseball Writers' Association of America (1991). ... Named Major League Player of the Year by The Sporting News (1994). ... Named first baseman on The Sporting News N.L. All-Star team (1994, 1996, 1997 and 1999). ... Won N.L. Gold Glove at first base (1994). ... Named first baseman on The Sporting News N.L. Silver Slugger team (1994, 1997 and 1999). ... Named N.L. Most Valuable Player by Baseball Writers' Association of America (1994).
STATISTICAL NOTES: Led Eastern League with 220 total bases and 12 intentional bases on balls received in 1990. ... Led N.L. in being hit by pitch with 13 in 1991. ... Led N.L. with 13 sacrifice flies in 1992. ... Hit three home runs in one game (June 24, 1994; and April 21 and June 9, 1999). ... Led N.L. with .750 slugging percentage in 1994. ... Led N.L. first basemen with 120 assists in 1994. ... Tied for N.L. lead in errors by first basemen with nine and double plays by first basemen with 94 in 1994. ... Had 18-game hitting streak (August 2-20, 2000). ... Career major league grand slams: 3.
MISCELLANEOUS: Holds Houston Astros all-time record for most home runs (310), runs batted in (1,093) and highest career batting average (.305).

						BATTING								FIELDING			
Year Team (League)	Pos.	G	AB	R	H	2B	3B	HR	RBI	Avg.	BB	SO	SB	PO	A	E	Avg.
1989—GC Red Sox (GCL)	3B-2B	5	19	3	6	1	0	0	3	.316	3	0	0	2	12	2	.875
—Winter Haven (FSL)	3B-2B-1B	64	210	27	65	13	2	2	19	.310	22	25	1	53	109	12	.931
1990—New Britain (East.)	3B	136	481	63	*160	•34	7	4	61	.333	73	57	5	93	267	34	.914
1991—Houston (N.L.)■	1B	156	554	79	163	26	4	15	82	.294	75	116	7	1270	106	12	.991
1992—Houston (N.L.)	1B	•162	586	87	160	34	6	18	96	.273	84	97	10	1334	133	7	.995
1993—Houston (N.L.)	1B	142	535	76	171	37	4	20	88	.320	62	73	13	1200	113	9	.993
1994—Houston (N.L.)	1B-OF	110	400	*104	147	32	2	39	*116	.368	65	65	15	923	†121	‡9	.991
1995—Houston (N.L.)	1B	114	448	88	130	29	0	21	87	.290	79	102	12	1004	*129	7	.994
—Jackson (Texas)	1B-DH	4	12	0	2	0	0	0	0	.167	3	2	0	24	6	0	1.000
1996—Houston (N.L.)	1B	*162	568	111	179	*48	2	31	120	.315	135	114	21	1336	*136	*16	.989
1997—Houston (N.L.)	1B-DH	*162	566	109	162	40	2	43	135	.286	127	122	31	1404	*137	11	.993
1998—Houston (N.L.)	1B	147	540	124	164	33	1	34	111	.304	109	90	19	1239	128	7	.995
1999—Houston (N.L.)	1B	•162	562	*143	171	35	0	42	126	.304	*149	127	30	1336	106	8	.994
2000—Houston (N.L.)	1B-DH	159	590	*152	183	37	1	47	132	.310	107	116	9	1264	116	9	.994
Major League totals (10 years)		1476	5349	1073	1630	351	22	310	1093	.305	992	1022	167	12310	1225	95	.993

DIVISION SERIES RECORD

						BATTING								FIELDING			
Year Team (League)	Pos.	G	AB	R	H	2B	3B	HR	RBI	Avg.	BB	SO	SB	PO	A	E	Avg.
1997—Houston (N.L.)	1B	3	12	0	1	0	0	0	0	.083	1	5	0	17	6	2	.920
1998—Houston (N.L.)	1B	4	14	0	2	0	0	0	4	.143	1	6	0	31	4	0	1.000
1999—Houston (N.L.)	1B	4	13	3	2	0	0	0	0	.154	5	4	0	36	3	0	1.000
Division series totals (3 years)		11	39	3	5	0	0	0	4	.128	7	15	0	84	13	2	.980

ALL-STAR GAME RECORD

					BATTING								FIELDING			
Year League	Pos.	AB	R	H	2B	3B	HR	RBI	Avg.	BB	SO	SB	PO	A	E	Avg.
1994—National	PH-1B	4	1	2	0	0	0	0	.500	0	1	0	3	2	0	1.000
1996—National	1B	2	0	0	0	0	0	0	.000	0	1	0	5	0	0	1.000
1997—National	1B	3	0	0	0	0	0	0	.000	0	0	0	8	1	0	1.000
1999—National	DH	3	0	1	0	0	0	0	.333	0	2	0	...	...	...	...
All-Star Game totals (4 years)		12	1	3	0	0	0	0	.250	0	4	0	16	3	0	1.000

PERSONAL: Born March 15, 1959, in St. Michaels, Md. ... 6-2/195. ... Bats left, throws left. ... Full name: Harold Dougleas Baines.
HIGH SCHOOL: St. Michaels (Easton, Md.).
TRANSACTIONS/CAREER NOTES: Selected by Chicago White Sox organization in first round (first pick overall) of free-agent draft (June 7, 1977). ... On disabled list (April 7-May 8, 1987). ... Traded by White Sox with IF Fred Manrique to Texas Rangers for SS Scott Fletcher, OF Sammy Sosa and P Wilson Alvarez (July 29, 1989). ... Traded by Rangers to Oakland Athletics for two players to be named later (August 29, 1990); Rangers acquired P Joe Bitker and P Scott Chiamparino to complete deal (September 4, 1990). ... Granted free agency (October 27, 1992); accepted arbitration. ... Traded by A's to Baltimore Orioles for P Bobby Chouinard and P Allen Plaster (January 14, 1993). ... On Baltimore disabled list (May 5-27, 1993); included rehabilitation assignment to Bowie (May 25-27). ... Granted free agency (November 1, 1993). ...

Re-signed by Orioles (December 2, 1993). ... Granted free agency (October 20, 1994). ... Re-signed by Orioles (December 23, 1994). ... Granted free agency (November 6, 1995). ... Signed by White Sox (December 11, 1995). ... Granted free agency (November 18, 1996). ... Re-signed by White Sox (January 10, 1997). ... Traded by White Sox to Orioles for a player to be named later (July 29, 1997); White Sox acquired SS Juan Bautista to complete deal (August 18, 1997). ... Granted free agency (October 29, 1997). ... Re-signed by Orioles (December 19, 1997). ... On disabled list (July 11-August 4, 1998). ... Traded by Orioles to Cleveland Indians for P Juan Aracena and a player to named later (August 27, 1999); Orioles acquired P Jimmy Hamilton to complete deal (August 31, 1999). ... Granted free agency (October 29, 1999). ... Signed by Orioles (December 9, 1999). ... Traded by Orioles with C Charles Johnson to White Sox for C Brook Fordyce, P Miguel Felix, P Juan Figueroa and P Jason Lakman (July 29, 2000). ... Granted free agency (November 3, 2000). ... Re-signed by White Sox organization (January 8, 2001).

RECORDS: Shares major league single-game record for most plate appearances—12 (May 8, finished May 9, 1984, 25 innings). ... Shares A.L. record for longest errorless game by outfielder—25 innings (May 8, finished May 9, 1984). ... Shares A.L. single-game record for most innings by outfielder—25 (May 8, finished May 9, 1984).

HONORS: Named outfielder on THE SPORTING NEWS A.L. All-Star team (1985). ... Named designated hitter on THE SPORTING NEWS A.L. All-Star team (1988-89). ... Named designated hitter on THE SPORTING NEWS A.L. Silver Slugger team (1989).

STATISTICAL NOTES: Tied for American Association lead in double plays by outfielder with four in 1979. ... Hit three home runs in one game (July 7, 1982; September 17, 1984 and May 7, 1991). ... Led A.L. with 22 game-winning RBIs in 1983. ... Led A.L. with .541 slugging percentage in 1984. ... Career major league grand slams: 13.

Year	Team (League)	Pos.	G	AB	R	H	2B	3B	HR	RBI	Avg.	BB	SO	SB	PO	A	E	Avg.
1977—	Appleton (Midw.)........	OF	69	222	37	58	11	2	5	29	.261	36	62	2	94	10	7	.937
1978—	Knoxville (Sou.).........	OF-1B	137	502	70	138	16	6	13	72	.275	43	91	3	291	22	13	.960
1979—	Iowa (A.A.)	OF	125	466	87	139	25	8	22	87	.298	33	80	5	222	•16	11	.956
1980—	Chicago (A.L.)	OF-DH	141	491	55	125	23	6	13	49	.255	19	65	2	229	6	9	.963
1981—	Chicago (A.L.)	OF-DH	82	280	42	80	11	7	10	41	.286	12	41	6	120	10	2	.985
1982—	Chicago (A.L.)	OF	161	608	89	165	29	8	25	105	.271	49	95	10	326	10	7	.980
1983—	Chicago (A.L.)	OF	156	596	76	167	33	2	20	99	.280	49	85	7	312	10	9	.973
1984—	Chicago (A.L.)	OF	147	569	72	173	28	10	29	94	.304	54	75	1	307	8	6	.981
1985—	Chicago (A.L.)	OF-DH	160	640	86	198	29	3	22	113	.309	42	89	1	318	8	2	.994
1986—	Chicago (A.L.)	OF-DH	145	570	72	169	29	2	21	88	.296	38	89	2	295	15	5	.984
1987—	Chicago (A.L.)	DH-OF	132	505	59	148	26	4	20	93	.293	46	82	0	13	0	0	1.000
1988—	Chicago (A.L.)	DH-OF	158	599	55	166	39	1	13	81	.277	67	109	0	14	1	2	.882
1989—	Chicago (A.L.)	DH-OF	70	333	55	107	20	1	13	56	.321	60	52	0	52	0	1	.981
	— Texas (A.L.)■..........	DH-OF	46	172	18	49	9	0	3	16	.285	13	27	0	2	0	1	.667
1990—	Texas (A.L.)	DH	103	321	41	93	10	1	13	44	.290	47	63	0	...	...	...	...
	— Oakland (A.L.)■........	DH-OF	32	94	11	25	5	0	3	21	.266	20	17	0	5	0	1	.833
1991—	Oakland (A.L.)	DH-OF	141	488	76	144	25	1	20	90	.295	72	67	0	11	1	1	.923
1992—	Oakland (A.L.)	DH-OF	140	478	58	121	18	0	16	76	.253	59	61	1	27	0	1	.964
1993—	Baltimore (A.L.)■.......	DH	118	416	64	130	22	0	20	78	.313	57	52	0	...	...	...	...
	— Bowie (East.)...........	DH	2	6	0	0	0	0	0	0	.000	1	1	0	...	...	...	...
1994—	Baltimore (A.L.)..........	DH	94	326	44	96	12	1	16	54	.294	30	49	0	...	...	...	...
1995—	Baltimore (A.L.)..........	DH	127	385	60	115	19	1	24	63	.299	70	45	0	...	...	...	...
1996—	Chicago (A.L.)■.........	DH	143	495	80	154	29	0	22	95	.311	73	62	3	...	...	...	...
1997—	Chicago (A.L.)	DH-OF	93	318	40	97	18	0	12	52	.305	41	47	0	0	0	0	...
	— Baltimore (A.L.)■......	DH	44	134	15	39	5	0	4	15	.291	14	15	0	...	...	...	...
1998—	Baltimore (A.L.)..........	DH	104	293	40	88	17	0	9	57	.300	32	40	0	...	...	...	...
1999—	Baltimore (A.L.)..........	DH	107	345	57	111	16	1	24	81	.322	43	38	1	...	...	...	...
	— Cleveland (A.L.)■......	DH	28	85	5	23	2	0	1	22	.271	11	10	0	...	...	...	...
2000—	Baltimore (A.L.)■........	DH	72	222	24	59	8	0	10	30	.266	29	39	0	0	0	0	...
	— Chicago (A.L.)■........	DH	24	61	2	13	5	0	1	9	.213	7	11	0	0	0	0	...
Major League totals (21 years)			2768	9824	1296	2855	487	49	384	1622	.291	1054	1425	34	2031	69	47	.978

DIVISION SERIES RECORD

NOTES: Hit home run in first at-bat (October 2, 1997).

Year	Team (League)	Pos.	G	AB	R	H	2B	3B	HR	RBI	Avg.	BB	SO	SB	PO	A	E	Avg.
1997—	Baltimore (A.L.)..........	DH-PH	2	5	2	2	0	0	1	1	.400	1	0	0	...	...	...	...
1999—	Cleveland (A.L.)..........	DH	4	14	1	5	0	0	1	4	.357	2	1	0	...	...	...	...
2000—	Chicago (A.L.)	PH-DH	2	4	1	1	1	0	0	0	.250	0	1	0	...	...	...	...
Division series totals (3 years)			8	23	4	8	1	0	2	5	.348	3	2	0	...	...	...	...

CHAMPIONSHIP SERIES RECORD

Year	Team (League)	Pos.	G	AB	R	H	2B	3B	HR	RBI	Avg.	BB	SO	SB	PO	A	E	Avg.
1983—	Chicago (A.L.)	OF	4	16	0	2	0	0	0	0	.125	1	3	0	5	1	0	1.000
1990—	Oakland (A.L.)	DH	4	14	2	5	1	0	0	3	.357	2	1	1	...	...	...	...
1992—	Oakland (A.L.)	DH	6	25	6	11	2	0	1	4	.440	0	3	0	...	...	...	...
1997—	Baltimore (A.L.)	DH	6	17	1	6	0	0	1	2	.353	2	1	0	...	...	...	...
Championship series totals (4 years)			20	72	9	24	3	0	2	9	.333	5	8	1	5	1	0	1.000

WORLD SERIES RECORD

Year	Team (League)	Pos.	G	AB	R	H	2B	3B	HR	RBI	Avg.	BB	SO	SB	PO	A	E	Avg.
1990—	Oakland (A.L.)	DH-PH	3	7	1	1	0	0	1	2	.143	1	2	0	...	...	...	...

ALL-STAR GAME RECORD

Year	League	Pos.	AB	R	H	2B	3B	HR	RBI	Avg.	BB	SO	SB	PO	A	E	Avg.
1985—	American	PH	1	0	1	0	0	0	0	1.000	0	0	0	...	...	...	...
1986—	American	PH	1	0	0	0	0	0	0	.000	0	0	0	...	...	...	...
1987—	American	PH	1	0	0	0	0	0	0	.000	0	0	0	...	...	...	...
1989—	American	PH	3	1	1	0	0	0	1	.333	0	1	0	...	...	...	...
1991—	American	PH-DH	1	0	1	0	0	0	0	1.000	0	0	0	...	...	...	...
1999—	American	PH-DH	1	0	1	0	0	0	0	1.000	0	0	0	...	...	...	...
All-Star Game totals (6 years)			8	1	3	0	0	0	2	.375	0	1	0	...	...	...	...

PERSONAL: Born June 20, 1972, in Lafayette, La. ... 6-2/205. ... Bats left, throws right. ... Full name: Gabor Paul Bako.
HIGH SCHOOL: Lafayette (La.).
COLLEGE: Southwestern Louisiana.
TRANSACTIONS/CAREER NOTES: Selected by Cincinnati Reds organization in fifth round of free-agent draft (June 3, 1993). ... Traded by Reds with P Donne Wall to Detroit Tigers for OF Melvin Nieves (November 11, 1997). ... Traded by Tigers with P Dean Crow, P Mark Persails, P Brian Powell and 3B Carlos Villalobos to Houston Astros for C Brad Ausmus and P C.J. Nitkowski (January 14, 1999). ... Traded by Astros to Florida Marlins for a player to be named to later (April 11, 2000); Astros acquired cash to complete deal (October 10, 2000). ... Claimed on waivers by Atlanta Braves (July 21, 2000).
STATISTICAL NOTES: Tied for Carolina League lead with 15 passed balls in 1995. ... Led Southern League catchers with 791 total chances in 1996. ... Tied for American Association lead in double plays with 10 and passed balls with nine by a catcher in 1997.

Year	Team (League)	Pos.	G	AB	R	H	2B	3B	HR	RBI	Avg.	BB	SO	SB	PO	A	E	Avg.
1993—Billings (Pio.)		C-1B	57	194	34	61	11	0	4	30	.314	22	37	5	323	45	6	.984
1994—Win.-Salem (Caro.)		C	90	289	29	59	9	1	3	26	.204	35	81	2	570	73	15	.977
1995—Win.-Salem (Caro.)		C	82	249	29	71	11	2	7	27	.285	42	66	3	478	49	6	.989
1996—Chattanooga (Sou.)		C	110	360	53	106	27	0	8	48	.294	48	93	1	*694	*84	13	.984
1997—Indianapolis (A.A.)		C	104	321	34	78	14	1	8	43	.243	34	81	0	622	64	6	.991
1998—Toledo (I.L.)■		C	13	48	5	14	3	1	1	6	.292	1	13	0	75	5	1	.988
—Detroit (A.L.)		C	96	305	23	83	12	1	3	30	.272	23	82	1	493	45	6	.989
1999—New Orleans (PCL)■		C	12	47	2	9	3	1	1	4	.191	1	11	0	58	4	1	.984
—Houston (N.L.)		C	73	215	16	55	14	1	2	17	.256	26	57	1	461	35	6	.988
2000—Houston (N.L.)		C	1	2	0	0	0	0	0	0	.000	0	1	0	2	1	0	1.000
—Florida (N.L.)■		C	56	161	10	39	6	1	0	14	.242	22	48	0	318	21	3	.991
—Atlanta (N.L.)■		C-1B	24	58	8	11	4	0	2	6	.190	5	15	0	118	9	1	.992
American League totals (1 year)			96	305	23	83	12	1	3	30	.272	23	82	1	493	45	6	.989
National League totals (2 years)			154	436	34	105	24	2	4	37	.241	53	121	1	899	66	10	.990
Major League totals (3 years)			250	741	57	188	36	3	7	67	.254	76	203	2	1392	111	16	.989

DIVISION SERIES RECORD

Year	Team (League)	Pos.	G	AB	R	H	2B	3B	HR	RBI	Avg.	BB	SO	SB	PO	A	E	Avg.
2000—Atlanta (N.L.)		C	2	1	0	0	0	0	0	0	.000	0	1	0	4	0	1	.800

PERSONAL: Born July 15, 1971, in Southern Pines, N.C. ... 6-3/210. ... Throws right, bats right. ... Full name: James Baldwin Jr.
HIGH SCHOOL: Pinecrest (Southern Pines, N.C.).
TRANSACTIONS/CAREER NOTES: Selected by Chicago White Sox organization in fourth round of free-agent draft (June 4, 1990). ... On disabled list (August 3-19, 1994).
RECORDS: Shares A.L. single-game record for most hit batsmen (nine innings)—4 (August 17, 2000).
HONORS: Named A.L. Rookie Pitcher of the Year by THE SPORTING NEWS (1996).
STATISTICAL NOTES: Led American Association with 27 home runs allowed and tied for lead with three balks in 1995.. ... Tied for American Association lead with three balks in 1995. ... Tied for A.L. lead with 14 wild pitches and three balks in 1997.

Year	League	W	L	Pct.	ERA	G	GS	CG	ShO	Sv.	IP	H	R	ER	BB	SO
1990—GC White Sox (GCL)		1	6	.143	4.10	9	7	0	0	0	37 1/3	32	29	17	18	32
1991—GC White Sox (GCL)		3	1	.750	2.12	6	6	0	0	0	34	16	8	8	16	48
—Utica (NY-Penn)		1	4	.200	5.30	7	7	1	0	0	37 1/3	40	26	22	27	23
1992—South Bend (Midw.)		9	5	.643	2.42	21	21	1	1	0	137 2/3	118	53	37	45	137
—Sarasota (FSL)		1	2	.333	2.87	6	6	1	0	0	37 2/3	31	13	12	7	39
1993—Birmingham (Sou.)		8	5	.615	*2.25	17	17	•4	0	0	120	94	48	30	43	107
—Nashville (A.A.)		5	4	.556	2.61	10	10	1	0	0	69	43	21	20	36	61
1994—Nashville (A.A.)		12	6	.667	3.72	26	26	2	0	0	162	144	75	67	83	*156
1995—Chicago (A.L.)		0	1	.000	12.89	6	4	0	0	0	14 2/3	32	22	21	9	10
—Nashville (A.A.)		5	9	.357	5.85	18	18	0	0	0	95 1/3	120	76	62	44	89
1996—Nashville (A.A.)		1	1	.500	0.64	2	2	1	0	0	14	5	1	1	4	15
—Chicago (A.L.)		11	6	.647	4.42	28	28	0	0	0	169	168	88	83	57	127
1997—Chicago (A.L.)		12	•15	.444	5.26	32	32	1	0	0	200	205	128	117	83	140
1998—Chicago (A.L.)		13	6	.684	5.32	37	24	1	0	0	159	176	103	94	60	108
1999—Chicago (A.L.)		12	13	.480	5.10	35	33	1	0	0	199 1/3	219	119	113	81	123
2000—Chicago (A.L.)		14	7	.667	4.65	29	28	2	1	0	178	185	96	92	59	116
Major League totals (6 years)		62	48	.564	5.09	167	149	5	1	0	920	985	556	520	349	624

DIVISION SERIES RECORD

Year	League	W	L	Pct.	ERA	G	GS	CG	ShO	Sv.	IP	H	R	ER	BB	SO
2000—Chicago (A.L.)		0	0	...	1.50	1	1	0	0	0	6	3	1	1	3	2

ALL-STAR GAME RECORD

Year	League	W	L	Pct.	ERA	GS	CG	ShO	Sv.	IP	H	R	ER	BB	SO
2000—American		1	0	1.000	9.00	0	0	0	0	1	2	1	1	0	1

PERSONAL: Born May 22, 1974, in Cheverly, Md. ... 6-4/205. ... Throws left, bats left. ... Full name: John Robert Bale.
HIGH SCHOOL: Crestview (Fla.).
JUNIOR COLLEGE: Jefferson Davis Community College (Ala.).
COLLEGE: Southern Mississippi.

TRANSACTIONS/CAREER NOTES: Selected by St. Louis Cardinals organization in 12th round of free-agent draft (June 2, 1994); did not sign. ... Selected by Toronto Blue Jays organization in fifth round of free-agent draft (June 4, 1996). ... On Syracuse disabled list (May 4-19 and June 29-July 20, 2000). ... Traded by Blue Jays to Baltimore Orioles for C Jayson Werth (December 11, 2000).

Year	League	W	L	Pct.	ERA	G	GS	CG	ShO	Sv.	IP	H	R	ER	BB	SO
1996—	St. Catharines (NY-Penn) ...	3	2	.600	4.86	8	8	0	0	0	33 1/3	39	21	18	11	35
1997—	Hagerstown (S.Atl.)..........	7	7	.500	4.30	25	25	0	0	0	140 1/3	130	83	67	63	155
1998—	Dunedin (FSL)...................	4	5	.444	4.64	24	9	0	0	4	66	68	39	34	23	78
	—Knoxville (Sou.)..............	0	0	...	6.75	3	0	0	0	0	1 1/3	1	1	1	0	0
1999—	Knoxville (Sou.).................	2	2	.500	3.75	33	4	0	0	1	62 1/3	64	32	26	16	91
	—Syracuse (I.L.)...............	0	3	.000	3.97	6	4	0	0	0	22 2/3	16	14	10	10	10
	—Toronto (A.L.).................	0	0	...	13.50	1	0	0	0	0	2	2	3	3	2	4
2000—	Syracuse (I.L.).................	3	4	.429	3.19	21	12	0	0	0	79	68	35	28	41	70
	—Toronto (A.L.).................	0	0	...	14.73	2	0	0	0	0	3 2/3	5	7	6	3	6
Major League totals (2 years)......		0	0	...	14.29	3	0	0	0	0	5 2/3	7	10	9	5	10

BARAJAS, ROD   C   DIAMONDBACKS

B

PERSONAL: Born September 5, 1975, in Ontario, Calif. ... 6-2/220. ... Bats right, throws right. ... Full name: Rodrigo Richard Barajas.
HIGH SCHOOL: Sante Fe Springs (Calif.).
JUNIOR COLLEGE: Cerritos.
TRANSACTIONS/CAREER NOTES: Signed as non-drafted free agent by Arizona Diamondbacks organization (January 23, 1996). ... Loaned by Diamondbacks to Visalia, Oakland Athletics organization (April 5-June 16, 1996).
STATISTICAL NOTES: Led Pioneer League catchers with .992 fielding percentage in 1996. ... Led Texas League catchers with 787 putouts, 95 assists, 14 errors and 896 total chances in 1999. ... Tied Pacific Coast League lead with 11 sacrifice flies in 2000. ... Led Pacific Coast League catchers with 69 assists in 2000. ... Tied for Pacific Coast League lead with 11 errors by catchers in 2000.

							BATTING								FIELDING		
Year	Team (League)	Pos.	G	AB	R	H	2B	3B	HR	RBI	Avg.	BB	SO	SB	PO	A	E	Avg.
1996—	Visalia (Calif.)■........	C	27	74	6	12	3	0	0	8	.162	7	21	0	83	14	0	1.000
	—Lethbridge (Pio.)■.....	C-1B	51	175	47	59	9	3	10	50	.337	12	24	2	301	43	5	†.986
1997—	High Desert (Calif.).....	C-1B	57	199	24	53	11	0	7	30	.266	8	41	0	374	38	3	.993
1998—	High Desert (Calif.).....	C	113	442	67	134	26	0	23	81	.303	25	81	1	749	85	14	.983
1999—	El Paso (Texas).........	C-DH-1B	127	510	77	162	41	2	14	95	.318	24	73	2	†827	†97	†14	.985
	—Arizona (N.L.)...........	C	5	16	3	4	1	0	1	3	.250	1	1	0	30	1	0	1.000
2000—	Tucson (PCL)	C-1B-3B	110	416	43	94	25	0	13	75	.226	14	65	4	623	80	‡14	.980
	—Arizona (N.L.)...........	C	5	13	1	3	0	0	1	3	.231	0	4	0	23	0	0	1.000
Major League totals (2 years)			10	29	4	7	1	0	2	6	.241	1	5	0	53	1	0	1.000

BARCELO, LORENZO   P   WHITE SOX

PERSONAL: Born August 10, 1977, in San Pedro de Macoris, Dominican Republic. ... 6-4/220. ... Throws right, bats right. ... Full name: Lorenzo A. Barcelo. ... Brother of Orger Barcelo, player in Atlanta Braves organization (1990).
HIGH SCHOOL: Sanatonio (San Pedro de Macoris, Dominican Republic).
TRANSACTIONS/CAREER NOTES: Signed as non-drafted free agent by San Francisco Giants organization (May 23, 1994). ... Traded by Giants with SS Mike Caruso, OF Brian Manning, P Keith Foulke, P Bob Howry and P Ken Vining by Giants to Chicago White Sox for P Wilson Alvarez, P Danny Darwin and P Roberto Hernandez (July 31, 1997). ... On Birmingham disabled list (April 2, 1998-entire season); included rehabilitation assignment to Arizona League White Sox (June 29-July 9). ... On Birmingham disabled list (April 8-August 13, 1999); included rehabilitation assignment to Burlington (August 11-13).
STATISTICAL NOTES: Led Midwest League with 16 home runs allowed in 1996.

Year	League	W	L	Pct.	ERA	G	GS	CG	ShO	Sv.	IP	H	R	ER	BB	SO
1995—	Bellingham (N'West)	3	2	.600	3.45	12	11	0	0	0	47	43	23	18	19	34
1996—	Bellingham (N'West)	12	10	.545	3.54	26	26	1	0	0	152 2/3	138	70	60	46	139
1997—	San Jose (Calif.).............	5	4	.556	3.94	16	16	1	1	0	89	91	45	39	30	89
	—Shreveport (Texas)...........	2	0	1.000	4.02	5	5	0	0	0	31 1/3	30	19	14	8	20
	—Birmingham (Sou.)■.........	2	1	.667	4.86	6	6	0	0	0	33 1/3	36	20	18	9	29
1998—	Arizona White Sox (Ariz.)....	0	1	.000	1.50	3	3	0	0	0	6	6	1	1	0	9
1999—	Arizona White Sox (Ariz.)...	2	1	.667	1.69	9	9	0	0	0	42 2/3	36	14	8	6	57
	—Burlington (Midw.)............	1	0	1.000	3.60	1	1	0	0	0	5	3	2	2	0	6
	—Birmingham (Sou.)...........	0	1	.000	3.60	4	4	0	0	0	20	14	8	8	6	14
2000—	Charlotte (I.L.)..................	5	6	.455	4.26	17	17	0	0	0	99 1/3	114	53	47	17	62
	—Chicago (A.L.)	4	2	.667	3.69	22	1	0	0	0	39	34	17	16	9	26
Major League totals (1 year)........		4	2	.667	3.69	22	1	0	0	0	39	34	17	16	9	26

DIVISION SERIES RECORD

Year	League	W	L	Pct.	ERA	G	GS	CG	ShO	Sv.	IP	H	R	ER	BB	SO
2000—	Chicago (A.L.)	0	0	...	0.00	1	0	0	0	0	1 2/3	0	0	0	1	0

BARKER, GLEN   OF   ASTROS

PERSONAL: Born May 10, 1971, in Albany, N.Y. ... 5-10/180. ... Bats right, throws right. ... Full name: Glen F. Barker.
HIGH SCHOOL: Albany (N.Y.).
COLLEGE: The College of St. Rose (N.Y.).
TRANSACTIONS/CAREER NOTES: Selected by Detroit Tigers organization in 11th round of free-agent draft (June 3, 1993). ... Selected by Houston Astros from Tigers organization in Rule 5 major league draft (December 14, 1998). ... On disabled list (August 24-September 8, 1999). ... On New Orleans disabled list (May 16-26, 2000).
STATISTICAL NOTES: Led Southern League outfielders in total chances with 323 in 1998.

Year Team (League)	Pos.	G	AB	R	H	2B	3B	HR	RBI	Avg.	BB	SO	SB	PO	A	E	Avg.
1993—Niagara Falls (NY-P)...	OF	72	253	49	55	11	4	5	23	.217	24	71	*37	148	3	1	*.993
1994—Fayetteville (S.Atl.).....	OF	74	267	38	61	13	5	1	30	.228	33	79	41	144	6	3	.980
—Lakeland (FSL)......	OF	28	104	10	19	5	1	2	6	.183	4	34	5	71	4	2	.974
1995—Jacksonville (Sou.).....	OF	133	507	74	121	26	4	10	49	.239	33	*143	39	284	9	8	.973
1996—Jacksonville (Sou.).....	OF	43	120	9	19	2	1	0	8	.158	8	36	6	91	2	2	.979
—Fayetteville (S.Atl.).....	OF	37	132	23	38	1	0	1	9	.288	16	34	20	91	3	1	.989
—Toledo (I.L.)...............	OF	24	80	13	20	2	1	0	2	.250	9	25	6	51	3	1	.982
1997—Toledo (I.L.)...............	OF	21	47	9	9	1	0	1	3	.191	5	15	6	24	1	0	1.000
—Lakeland (FSL).....	OF	13	57	9	18	4	0	1	11	.316	4	17	7	34	0	0	1.000
—Jacksonville (Sou.).....	OF	69	257	47	72	8	4	6	29	.280	29	72	17	154	6	2	.988
1998—Jacksonville (Sou.).....	OF	110	453	95	127	29	6	6	54	.280	57	120	31	*307	16	0	*1.000
1999—Houston (N.L.)■........	OF-DH	81	73	23	21	2	0	1	11	.288	11	19	17	50	2	1	.981
2000—Houston (N.L.).....	OF	84	67	18	15	2	1	2	6	.224	7	23	9	64	1	1	.985
—New Orleans (PCL).....	OF	26	107	15	29	5	0	2	10	.271	10	12	11	63	2	2	.970
Major League totals (2 years)		165	140	41	36	4	1	3	17	.257	18	42	26	114	3	2	.983

DIVISION SERIES RECORD

Year Team (League)	Pos.	G	AB	R	H	2B	3B	HR	RBI	Avg.	BB	SO	SB	PO	A	E	Avg.
1999—Houston (N.L.)	OF-PR	2	3	1	0	0	0	0	0	.000	0	2	1	1	0	0	1.000

BARKER, KEVIN — 1B — BREWERS

PERSONAL: Born July 26, 1975, in Bristol, Va. ... 6-3/205. ... Bats right, throws right. ... Full name: Kevin S. Barker.
HIGH SCHOOL: Virginia (Bristol, Va.).
COLLEGE: Virginia Tech.
TRANSACTIONS/CAREER NOTES: Selected by Milwaukee Brewers organization in third round of free-agent draft (June 4, 1996).

Year Team (League)	Pos.	G	AB	R	H	2B	3B	HR	RBI	Avg.	BB	SO	SB	PO	A	E	Avg.
1996— Ogden (Pio.)...............	1B	71	281	61	89	19	4	9	56	.317	46	54	0	572	*44	11	.982
1997— El Paso (Texas)..........	1B	65	238	37	66	15	6	10	63	.277	28	40	3	455	30	9	.982
—Stockton (Calif.)	1B	70	267	47	81	20	5	13	45	.303	25	60	4	476	31	6	.988
1998— El Paso (Texas)..........	1B	20	85	14	26	6	0	5	14	.306	3	21	2	198	16	1	.995
—Louisville (I.L.)	1B-OF	124	463	59	128	26	4	23	96	.276	36	97	2	957	*73	9	.991
1999— Louisville (I.L.)	1B-OF	121	442	89	123	27	5	23	87	.278	59	94	2	1036	88	10	.991
—Milwaukee (N.L.)........	1B	38	117	13	33	3	0	3	23	.282	9	19	1	254	18	1	.996
2000— Milwaukee (N.L.)........	1B	40	100	14	22	5	0	2	9	.220	20	21	1	250	15	2	.993
—Indianapolis (I.L.).......	1B	85	286	41	56	10	1	11	44	.196	52	76	0	605	57	3	.995
Major League totals (2 years)		78	217	27	55	8	0	5	32	.253	29	40	2	504	33	3	.994

BARNES, JOHN — OF — TWINS

PERSONAL: Born April 24, 1976, in San Diego. ... 6-2/205. ... Bats right, throws right. ... Full name: John Delbert Barnes.
HIGH SCHOOL: Granite Hills (El Cajon, Calif.).
JUNIOR COLLEGE: Grossmont College (Calif.).
TRANSACTIONS/CAREER NOTES: Selected by Boston Red Sox oraganization in fourth round of free-agent draft (June 4, 1996). ... Traded by Red Sox with P Joe Thomas and P Matt Kinney to Minnesota Twins for P Greg Swindell and 1B Orlando Merced (July 31, 1998). ... On New Britain disabled list (August 23-September 3, 1998).

Year Team (League)	Pos.	G	AB	R	H	2B	3B	HR	RBI	Avg.	BB	SO	SB	PO	A	E	Avg.
1996— GC Red Sox (GCL)	OF	30	101	9	28	4	0	1	17	.277	5	17	4	39	3	1	.977
1997— Michigan (Midw.)	OF	130	490	80	149	19	5	6	73	.304	65	42	19	213	8	6	.974
1998— Trenton (East.)	OF	100	380	53	104	18	0	14	36	.274	40	47	3	134	6	3	.979
—New Britain (East.)■..	OF	20	71	9	19	4	1	0	6	.268	9	9	1	39	2	0	1.000
1999— New Britain (East.)	OF	129	452	62	119	21	1	13	58	.263	49	40	10	247	12	4	.985
2000— Salt Lake (PCL)	OF	119	441	107	161	37	6	13	87	.365	57	48	7	244	8	6	.977
—Minnesota (A.L.)	OF	11	37	5	13	4	0	0	2	.351	2	6	0	28	2	0	1.000
Major League totals (1 year)		11	37	5	13	4	0	0	2	.351	2	6	0	28	2	0	1.000

BARNES, LARRY — 1B — ANGELS

PERSONAL: Born July 23, 1974, in Bakersfield, Calif. ... 6-1/195. ... Bats left, throws left. ... Full name: Larry Richard Barnes Jr.
HIGH SCHOOL: Bakersfield (Calif.).
JUNIOR COLLEGE: Bakersfield (Calif.) College.
COLLEGE: Fresno State.
TRANSACTIONS/CAREER NOTES: Selected by Florida Marlins organization in 69th round of free-agent draft (June 3, 1993); did not sign. ... Signed as non-drafted free agent by California Angels organization (June 6, 1995). ... Angels franchise renamed Anaheim Angels for 1997 season. ... On Erie disabled list (September 1, 1999-remainder of season). ... On Edmonton disabled list (July 26-August 9, 2000).
HONORS: Named Midwest League Most Valuable Player (1996).
STATISTICAL NOTES: Led Arizona League first basemen with 49 double plays in 1995. ... Led Midwest League with 282 total bases and .577 slugging percentage in 1996. ... Tied for Midwest League lead with 80 assists by first baseman in 1996. ... Led California League first basemen with .993 fielding percentage in 1997. ... Led Eastern League with 16 sacrifice flies and seven intentional bases on balls received in 1999.

			BATTING										FIELDING		
Year	Team (League)	Pos.	G	AB	R	H	2B	3B	HR	RBI	Avg.	BB	SO	SB	PO	A	E	Avg.
1995	Arizona Angels (Ariz.)	1B	•56	197	•42	61	8	3	3	•37	.310	27	42	12	*494	19	7	.987
1996	Cedar Rapids (Midw.)	1B-DH-OF-C	131	489	84	155	•36	5	*27	*112	.317	58	101	9	1062	‡81	11	.990
1997	Lake Elsinore (Calif.)	1B-OF	115	446	68	128	32	2	13	71	.287	43	84	3	1048	87	8	†.993
1998	Lake Elsinore (Calif.)	1B	51	183	32	45	11	2	7	33	.246	22	49	2	451	17	6	.987
	— Midland (Texas)	1B-DH-OF	69	245	29	67	16	4	6	35	.273	28	54	4	534	37	7	.988
1999	Erie (East.)	1B-DH	130	497	73	142	25	9	20	100	.286	49	99	14	1047	87	9	.992
2000	Edmonton (PCL)	1B-OF	103	397	56	102	22	11	7	54	.257	48	81	3	779	51	3	.996

BARRETT, MICHAEL — 3B/C — EXPOS

PERSONAL: Born October 22, 1976, in Atlanta. ... 6-2/200. ... Bats right, throws right. ... Full name: Michael Patrick Barrett.
HIGH SCHOOL: Pace Academy (Atlanta).
TRANSACTIONS/CAREER NOTES: Selected by Montreal Expos organization in first round (28th pick overall) of free-agent draft (June 1, 1995). ... On Montreal disabled list (June 24-July 11, 1999); included rehabilitation assignment to Ottawa (July 9-10).

			BATTING										FIELDING		
Year	Team (League)	Pos.	G	AB	R	H	2B	3B	HR	RBI	Avg.	BB	SO	SB	PO	A	E	Avg.
1995	GC Expos (GCL)	SS-3B	50	183	22	57	13	4	0	19	.311	15	19	7	65	143	25	.893
	— Vermont (NY-Penn)	SS	3	10	0	1	0	0	0	1	.100	1	1	0	1	3	0	1.000
1996	Delmarva (S.Atl.)	C-DH-3B	129	474	57	113	29	4	4	62	.238	18	42	5	607	74	15	.978
1997	W.P. Beach (FSL)	C-DH	119	423	52	120	30	0	8	61	.284	36	49	7	629	78	13	.982
1998	Harrisburg (East.)	C-3B-DH	120	453	78	145	32	2	19	87	.320	27	43	7	517	113	12	.981
	— Montreal (N.L.)	C-3B	8	23	3	7	2	0	1	2	.304	3	6	0	22	9	3	.912
1999	Montreal (N.L.)	3B-C-SS	126	433	53	127	32	3	8	52	.293	32	39	0	374	130	14	.973
	— Ottawa (I.L.)	3B	2	7	1	3	0	0	0	2	.429	1	0	0	0	4	1	.800
2000	Montreal (N.L.)	3B-C	89	271	28	58	15	1	1	22	.214	23	35	0	186	95	15	.949
Major League totals (3 years)			223	727	84	192	49	4	10	76	.264	58	80	0	582	234	32	.962

BARRIOS, MANUEL — P — METS

PERSONAL: Born September 21, 1974, in Cabecea, Panama. ... 6-0/185. ... Throws right, bats right. ... Full name: Manuel Antonio Barrios.
TRANSACTIONS/CAREER NOTES: Signed as non-drafted free agent by Houston Astros organization (March 2, 1993). ... On suspended list (September 4-8, 1998). ... Traded by Astros with P Oscar Henriquez and a player to be named later to Florida Marlins for OF Moises Alou (November 11, 1997); Marlins acquired P Mark Johnson to complete deal (December 16, 1997). ... Traded by Marlins with OF Gary Sheffield, 3B Bobby Bonilla, C Charles Johnson and OF Jim Eisenreich to Los Angeles Dodgers for C Mike Piazza and 3B Todd Zeile (May 15, 1998). ... Claimed on waivers by Florida Marlins (August 10, 1998). ... Traded by Marlins to Cincinnati Reds for C Guillermo Garcia (December 2, 1998). ... Claimed on waivers by Philadelphia Phillies (October 22, 1999). ... On Scranton/Wilkes-Barre disabled list (August 5-12, 2000). ... Granted free agency (October 18, 2000). ... Signed by New York Mets organization (November 17, 2000).

Year	League	W	L	Pct.	ERA	G	GS	CG	ShO	Sv.	IP	H	R	ER	BB	SO
1993	Dom. Astros (DSL)	6	1	.857	4.64	13	12	2	0	0	77²/₃	77	57	40	23	59
1994	Quad City (Midw.)	0	6	.000	5.95	43	0	0	0	4	65	73	44	43	23	63
1995	Quad City (Midw.)	1	5	.167	2.25	50	0	0	0	23	52	44	16	13	17	55
1996	Jackson (Texas)	6	4	.600	2.37	60	0	0	0	23	68¹/₃	60	29	18	29	69
1997	New Orleans (A.A.)	4	8	.333	3.27	57	0	0	0	0	82²/₃	70	32	30	34	77
	— Houston (N.L.)	0	0	...	12.00	2	0	0	0	0	3	6	4	4	3	3
1998	Charlotte (I.L.)■	2	0	1.000	3.70	18	1	0	0	0	24¹/₃	19	10	10	9	22
	— Florida (N.L.)	0	0	...	3.38	2	0	0	0	0	2²/₃	4	1	1	2	1
	— Albuquerque (PCL)■	1	3	.250	6.00	20	2	0	0	0	36	47	25	24	15	33
	— Los Angeles (N.L.)	0	0	...	0.00	1	0	0	0	0	1	0	0	0	2	0
1999	Indianapolis (I.L.)■	2	7	.222	5.28	49	8	0	0	0	90¹/₃	94	60	53	35	73
2000	Scranton/W.B. (I.L.)■	6	5	.545	4.92	47	0	0	0	4	64	71	35	35	31	60
Major League totals (2 years)		0	0	...	6.75	5	0	0	0	0	6²/₃	10	5	5	7	4

BARTEE, KIMERA — OF — ANGELS

PERSONAL: Born July 21, 1972, in Omaha, Neb. ... 6-0/200. ... Bats right, throws right. ... Full name: Kimera Anotchi Bartee.
HIGH SCHOOL: Central (Omaha, Neb.).
COLLEGE: Creighton.
TRANSACTIONS/CAREER NOTES: Selected by Baltimore Orioles organization in 14th round of free-agent draft (June 3, 1993). ... On Bowie disabled list (June 8-August 8, 1995). ... Traded by Orioles to Minnesota Twins (September 18, 1995), completing deal in which Orioles acquired P Scott Erickson from Twins for P Scott Klingenbeck and a player to be named later (July 7, 1995). ... Selected by Orioles from Twins organization in Rule 5 major league draft (December 4, 1995). ... Claimed on waivers by Detroit Tigers (March 13, 1996). ... Traded by Tigers to Cincinnati Reds for a player to be named later or cash (December 12, 1999). ... On Louisville disabled list (July 27-August 3, 2000). ... Released by Reds (December 1, 2000). ... Signed by Anaheim Angels (December 11, 2000).
STATISTICAL NOTES: Led International League outfielders with 341 total chances in 1997.
MISCELLANEOUS: Batted as switch-hitter (1993-98).

			BATTING										FIELDING		
Year	Team (League)	Pos.	G	AB	R	H	2B	3B	HR	RBI	Avg.	BB	SO	SB	PO	A	E	Avg.
1993	Bluefield (Appl.)	OF	66	264	59	65	15	2	4	37	.246	44	66	*27	124	5	4	.970
1994	Frederick (Caro.)	OF	130	514	97	150	22	4	10	57	.292	56	117	44	*304	7	6	.981
1995	GC Orioles (GCL)	OF	5	21	5	5	0	0	1	3	.238	3	2	1	15	0	0	1.000
	— Bowie (East.)	OF	53	218	45	62	9	1	3	19	.284	23	45	22	155	4	6	.964
	— Rochester (I.L.)	OF	15	52	5	8	2	1	0	3	.154	0	16	0	37	2	0	1.000
1996	Detroit (A.L.)■	OF-DH	110	217	32	55	6	1	1	14	.253	17	77	20	217	1	2	.991
1997	Toledo (I.L.)	OF	136	501	67	109	13	7	3	33	.218	52	*154	*33	*336	4	1	.997
	— Detroit (A.L.)	OF-DH	12	5	4	1	0	0	0	0	.200	2	2	3	3	0	0	1.000

B

Year Team (League)	Pos.	G	AB	R	H	2B	3B	HR	RBI	Avg.	BB	SO	SB	PO	A	E	Avg.
1998—Detroit (A.L.)	OF-DH	57	98	20	19	5	1	3	15	.194	6	35	9	51	3	2	.964
—Toledo (I.L.)	OF-DH	51	215	24	53	10	0	2	13	.247	16	42	6	124	6	0	1.000
1999—Toledo (I.L.)	OF	104	416	64	119	13	8	12	43	.286	38	76	21	239	5	1	*.996
—Detroit (A.L.)	OF-DH	41	77	11	15	1	3	0	3	.195	9	20	3	67	0	1	.985
2000—Louisville (I.L.)■	OF	119	453	69	135	19	4	8	48	.298	48	64	28	263	3	2	.993
—Cincinnati (N.L.)	OF	11	4	2	0	0	0	0	0	.000	0	2	1	1	0	0	1.000
American League totals (4 years)		220	397	67	90	12	5	4	32	.227	34	134	35	338	4	5	.986
National League totals (1 year)		11	4	2	0	0	0	0	0	.000	0	2	1	1	0	0	1.000
Major League totals (5 years)		231	401	69	90	12	5	4	32	.224	34	136	36	339	4	5	.986

BATISTA, MIGUEL — P — DIAMONDBACKS

PERSONAL: Born February 19, 1971, in Santo Domingo, Dominican Republic. ... 6-0/190. ... Throws right, bats right. ... Full name: Miguel Jerez Decartes Batista.

HIGH SCHOOL: Nuevo Horizondes (San Pedro de Macoris, Dominican Republic).

TRANSACTIONS/CAREER NOTES: Signed as non-drafted free agent by Montreal Expos organization (February 29, 1988). ... Selected by Pittsburgh Pirates organization from Expos organization in Rule 5 major league draft (December 9, 1991). ... Returned to Expos organization (April 23, 1992). ... On disabled list (April 14-30 and May 7, 1994-remainder of season). ... Released by Expos (November 18, 1994). ... Signed by Florida Marlins organization (December 9, 1994). ... Claimed on waivers by Chicago Cubs (December 17, 1996). ... Traded by Cubs to Expos for OF Henry Rodriguez (December 12, 1997). ... On Montreal disabled list (July 16-August 10, 1999; included rehabilitation assignment to Ottawa (July 30-August 8). ... Traded by Expos to Kansas City Royals for P Brad Rigby (April 25, 2000). ... Granted free agency (October 2, 2000). ... Signed by Arizona Diamondbacks organization (November 3, 2000).

Year League	W	L	Pct.	ERA	G	GS	CG	ShO	Sv.	IP	H	R	ER	BB	SO
1988—				Dominican Summer League statistics unavailable.											
1989—Dom. Expos (DSL)	1	7	.125	4.24	13	11	0	0	0	68	56	46	32	50	60
1990—Gulf Coast Expos (GCL)	4	3	.571	2.06	9	6	0	0	0	39 1/3	33	16	9	17	21
—Rockford (Midw.)	0	1	.000	8.76	3	2	0	0	0	12 1/3	16	13	12	5	7
1991—Rockford (Midw.)	11	5	.688	4.04	23	23	2	1	0	133 2/3	126	74	60	57	90
1992—Pittsburgh (N.L.)■	0	0	...	9.00	1	0	0	0	0	2	4	2	2	3	1
—West Palm Beach (FSL)■	7	7	.500	3.79	24	24	1	0	0	135 1/3	130	69	57	54	92
1993—Harrisburg (East.)	13	5	.722	4.34	26	26	0	0	0	141	139	79	68	86	91
1994—Harrisburg (East.)	0	1	.000	2.38	3	3	0	0	0	11 1/3	8	3	3	9	5
1995—Charlotte (I.L.)■	6	12	.333	4.80	34	18	0	0	0	116 1/3	118	79	62	60	58
1996—Charlotte (I.L.)	4	3	.571	5.38	47	2	0	0	4	77	93	57	46	39	56
—Florida (N.L.)	0	0	...	5.56	9	0	0	0	0	11 1/3	9	8	7	7	6
1997—Iowa (A.A.)■	9	4	.692	4.20	31	14	2	•2	0	122	117	60	57	38	95
—Chicago (N.L.)	0	5	.000	5.70	11	6	0	0	0	36 1/3	36	24	23	24	27
1998—Montreal (N.L.)■	3	5	.375	3.80	56	13	0	0	0	135	141	66	57	65	92
1999—Ottawa (I.L.)	0	1	.000	2.25	3	3	0	0	0	8	3	2	2	4	7
—Montreal (N.L.)	8	7	.533	4.88	39	17	2	1	1	134 2/3	146	88	73	58	95
2000—Montreal (N.L.)	0	1	.000	14.04	4	0	0	0	0	8 1/3	19	14	13	3	7
—Kansas City (A.L.)■	2	6	.250	7.74	14	9	0	0	0	57	66	54	49	34	30
—Omaha (PCL)	2	2	.500	6.04	18	1	0	0	3	28 1/3	35	20	19	7	27
A.L. totals (1 year)	2	6	.250	7.74	14	9	0	0	0	57	66	54	49	34	30
N.L. totals (6 years)	11	18	.379	4.81	120	36	2	1	1	327 2/3	355	202	175	160	228
Major League totals (6 years)	13	24	.351	5.24	134	45	2	1	1	384 2/3	421	256	224	194	258

BATISTA, TONY — 3B — BLUE JAYS

PERSONAL: Born December 9, 1973, in Puerto Plata, Dominican Republic. ... 6-0/185. ... Bats right, throws right. ... Full name: Leocadio Francisco Batista.

TRANSACTIONS/CAREER NOTES: Signed as non-drafted free agent by Oakland Athletics organization (February 8, 1991). ... On Tacoma disabled list (July 29, 1993-remainder of season). ... On Oakland disabled list (August 27-September 12, 1997); included rehabilitation assignment to Edmonton (September 11-12). ... Selected by Arizona Diamondbacks in first round (27th pick overall) of expansion draft (November 18, 1997). ... Traded by Diamondbacks with P John Frascatore to Toronto Blue Jays for P Dan Plesac (June 12, 1999).

STATISTICAL NOTES: Led California League shortstops with .950 fielding percentage in 1994. ... Had 17-game hitting streak (July 30-August 16, 1999). ... Led A.L. third basemen with 35 double plays in 2000. ... Career major league grand slams: 3.

Year Team (League)	Pos.	G	AB	R	H	2B	3B	HR	RBI	Avg.	BB	SO	SB	PO	A	E	Avg.
1992—Ariz. Athletics (Ariz.)	2B-SS-OF	45	167	32	41	6	2	0	22	.246	15	29	1	67	124	8	.960
1993—Ariz. Athletics (Ariz.)	3B-2B-SS	24	104	21	34	6	2	2	17	.327	6	14	6	34	54	3	.967
—Tacoma (PCL)	OF	4	12	1	2	1	0	0	1	.167	1	4	0	6	9	0	1.000
1994—Modesto (Calif.)	SS-2B	119	466	91	131	26	3	17	68	.281	54	108	7	182	372	30	†.949
1995—Huntsville (Sou.)	SS-2B	120	419	55	107	23	1	16	61	.255	29	98	7	168	371	29	.949
1996—Edmonton (PCL)	SS	57	205	33	66	17	4	8	40	.322	15	30	2	75	213	8	.973
—Oakland (A.L.)	2-3-DH-S	74	238	38	71	10	2	6	25	.298	19	49	7	96	191	5	.983
1997—Oakland (A.L.)	S-3-DH-2	68	188	22	38	10	1	4	18	.202	14	31	2	96	174	8	.971
—Edmonton (PCL)	SS-DH	33	124	25	39	10	1	3	21	.315	17	18	2	40	78	6	.952
1998—Arizona (N.L.)■	2B-SS-3B	106	293	46	80	16	1	18	41	.273	18	52	1	123	205	6	.982
1999—Arizona (N.L.)	SS	44	144	16	37	5	0	5	21	.257	16	17	2	60	130	4	.979
—Toronto (A.L.)■	SS	98	375	61	107	25	1	26	79	.285	22	79	2	165	308	12	.975
2000—Toronto (A.L.)	3B	154	620	96	163	32	2	41	114	.263	35	121	5	120	318	17	.963
American League totals (4 years)		394	1421	217	379	77	6	77	236	.267	90	280	16	477	991	42	.972
National League totals (2 years)		150	437	62	117	21	1	23	62	.268	34	69	3	183	335	10	.981
Major League totals (5 years)		544	1858	279	496	98	7	100	298	.267	124	349	19	660	1326	52	.974

Year	League	Pos.	AB	R	H	2B	3B		HR	RBI	Avg.		BB	SO	SB		PO	A	E	Avg.
								BATTING								FIELDING				
2000	American	PH-3B	1	0	0	0	0		0	0	.000		0	1	0		0	0	0	...

BAUGHMAN, JUSTIN — 2B — ANGELS

PERSONAL: Born August 1, 1974, in Mountain View, Calif. ... 5-11/180. ... Bats right, throws right. ... Full name: Justin Reis Baughman.
HIGH SCHOOL: Bellarmine Prep (San Jose, Calif.).
COLLEGE: Lewis & Clark (Ore.).
TRANSACTIONS/CAREER NOTES: Selected by California Angels organization in fifth round of free-agent draft (June 1, 1995). ... Angels franchise renamed Anaheim Angels for 1997 season. ... On disabled list (March 24, 1999-entire season). ... On Edmonton disabled list (August 4-11, 2000).
STATISTICAL NOTES: Led Midwest League with 15 sacrifice hits in 1996. ... Led Midwest League shortstops with 595 total chances in 1996. ... Led California League shortstops with 674 total chances in 1997.

B

Year	Team (League)	Pos.	G	AB	R	H	2B	3B	HR	RBI	Avg.	BB	SO	SB	PO	A	E	Avg.
									BATTING							FIELDING		
1995	Boise (N'West)	SS	58	215	26	50	4	3	1	20	.233	18	38	19	68	157	21	.915
1996	Cedar Rapids (Midw.)	SS	127	464	78	115	17	8	5	48	.248	45	78	•50	*201	360	34	.943
1997	Lake Elsinore (Calif.)	SS	134	478	71	131	14	3	2	48	.274	40	79	*68	*239	*403	32	.953
1998	Vancouver (PCL)	2B-SS	54	222	35	66	10	4	0	15	.297	13	28	26	136	166	6	.981
—	Anaheim (A.L.)	2B-SS-DH	63	196	24	50	9	1	1	20	.255	6	36	10	106	155	8	.970
1999	Anaheim (A.L.)								Did not play.									
2000	Erie (East.)	2B-SS	31	126	15	36	2	2	1	6	.286	8	20	11	57	92	4	.974
—	Edmonton (PCL)	SS-2B	80	303	44	71	7	2	1	35	.234	30	41	28	117	222	16	.955
—	Anaheim (A.L.)	2B-SS-DH	16	22	4	5	2	0	0	0	.227	1	2	3	12	17	1	.967
Major League totals (2 years)			79	218	28	55	11	1	1	20	.252	7	38	13	118	172	9	.970

BAUTISTA, DANNY — OF — DIAMONDBACKS

PERSONAL: Born May 24, 1972, in Santo Domingo, Dominican Republic. ... 5-11/170. ... Bats right, throws right. ... Full name: Daniel Bautista. ... Stepson of Jesus de la Rosa, outfielder with Houston Astros (1974). ... Name pronounced bough-TEES-tuh.
TRANSACTIONS/CAREER NOTES: Signed as non-drafted free agent by Detroit Tigers organization (June 24, 1989). ... On disabled list (May 24-July 10, 1991). ... On Toledo disabled list (June 8-July 31, 1994). ... Traded by Tigers to Atlanta Braves for OF Anton French (May 31, 1996). ... On Atlanta disabled list (June 28, 1996-remainder of season). ... On Atlanta disabled list (March 23-April 23, 1997); included rehabilitation assignment to Richmond (April 18-23). ... On Atlanta disabled list (April 17-May 7 and August 25-September 17, 1998); included rehabilitation assignment to Greenville (May 5-7). ... Released by Braves (April 2, 1999). ... Signed by Florida Marlins organization (April 8, 1999). ... On Calgary disabled list (June 1-8, 1999). ... Traded by Marlins to Arizona Diamondbacks for IF Andy Fox (June 10, 2000).
RECORDS: Shares major league single-game record for most strikeouts (nine-inning game)—5 (May 28, 1995).
STATISTICAL NOTES: Had 15-game hitting streak (August 13-September 1, 2000).

Year	Team (League)	Pos.	G	AB	R	H	2B	3B	HR	RBI	Avg.	BB	SO	SB	PO	A	E	Avg.
									BATTING							FIELDING		
1989						Dominican Summer League statistics unavailable.												
1990	Bristol (Appl.)	OF	27	95	9	26	3	0	2	12	.274	8	21	2	43	2	0	1.000
1991	Fayetteville (S.Atl.)	OF	69	234	21	45	6	4	1	30	.192	21	65	7	137	6	4	.973
1992	Fayetteville (S.Atl.)	OF	121	453	59	122	22	0	5	52	.269	29	76	18	210	17	6	.974
1993	London (East.)	OF-DH	117	424	55	121	21	1	6	48	.285	32	69	28	256	13	3	.989
—	Detroit (A.L.)	OF-DH	17	61	6	19	3	0	1	9	.311	1	10	3	38	2	0	1.000
1994	Detroit (A.L.)	OF-DH	31	99	12	23	4	1	4	15	.232	3	18	1	66	0	0	1.000
—	Toledo (I.L.)	OF	27	98	7	25	7	0	2	14	.255	6	23	2	54	1	1	.982
1995	Detroit (A.L.)	OF	89	271	28	55	9	0	7	27	.203	12	68	4	164	3	2	.988
—	Toledo (I.L.)	OF	18	58	6	14	3	0	0	4	.241	1	10	1	32	1	2	.943
1996	Detroit (A.L.)	OF-DH	25	64	12	16	2	0	2	8	.250	9	15	1	38	0	1	.974
—	Atlanta (N.L.)■	OF	17	20	1	3	0	0	1	1	.150	2	5	0	10	0	0	1.000
1997	Richmond (I.L.)	OF-DH	46	170	28	48	10	3	2	28	.282	19	30	1	104	4	0	1.000
—	Atlanta (N.L.)	OF	64	103	14	25	3	2	3	9	.243	5	24	2	59	1	1	.984
1998	Atlanta (N.L.)	OF-DH	82	144	17	36	11	0	3	17	.250	7	21	1	47	0	2	.959
—	Greenville (Sou.)	OF	2	6	1	2	0	0	1	2	.333	1	1	0	6	0	0	1.000
1999	Calgary (PCL)■	OF-DH	38	135	25	43	8	1	8	28	.319	11	18	3	90	5	3	.969
—	Florida (N.L.)	OF	70	205	32	59	10	1	5	24	.288	4	30	3	140	3	3	.979
2000	Florida (N.L.)	OF	44	89	9	17	4	0	4	12	.191	5	20	1	46	2	1	.980
—	Arizona (N.L.)■	OF	87	262	45	83	16	7	7	47	.317	20	30	5	142	6	2	.987
American League totals (4 years)			162	495	58	113	18	1	14	59	.228	25	111	9	306	5	3	.990
National League totals (5 years)			364	823	118	223	44	10	22	110	.271	43	130	12	444	12	9	.981
Major League totals (8 years)			526	1318	176	336	62	11	36	169	.255	68	241	21	750	17	12	.985

DIVISION SERIES RECORD

Year	Team (League)	Pos.	G	AB	R	H	2B	3B	HR	RBI	Avg.	BB	SO	SB	PO	A	E	Avg.
									BATTING							FIELDING		
1997	Atlanta (N.L.)	OF	3	3	0	1	0	0	0	2	.333	0	1	0	0	0	0	...
1998	Atlanta (N.L.)	OF	2	2	0	1	1	0	0	0	.500	0	0	0	2	0	0	1.000
Division series totals (2 years)			5	5	0	2	1	0	0	2	.400	0	1	0	2	0	0	1.000

CHAMPIONSHIP SERIES RECORD

Year	Team (League)	Pos.	G	AB	R	H	2B	3B	HR	RBI	Avg.	BB	SO	SB	PO	A	E	Avg.
									BATTING							FIELDING		
1997	Atlanta (N.L.)	OF	2	4	0	1	0	0	0	0	.250	0	0	0	4	0	0	1.000
1998	Atlanta (N.L.)	PR-OF	5	5	0	0	0	0	0	0	.000	0	1	0	2	0	1	.667
Championship series totals (2 years)			7	9	0	1	0	0	0	0	.111	0	1	0	6	0	1	.857

PERSONAL: Born August 3, 1968, in Burbank, Calif. ... 6-1/235. ... Throws right, bats right. ... Full name: Rodney Roy Beck.
HIGH SCHOOL: Grant (Van Nuys, Calif.).
TRANSACTIONS/CAREER NOTES: Selected by Oakland Athletics organization in 13th round of free-agent draft (June 2, 1986). ... Traded by A's to San Francisco Giants for P Charlie Corbell (March 23, 1988). ... On disabled list (April 6-30, 1994). ... Granted free agency (October 27, 1997). ... Signed by Chicago Cubs (January 15, 1998). ... On Chicago disabled list (May 17-July 21, 1999); included rehabiltation assignment to Iowa (July 17-21). ... Traded by Cubs to Boston Red Sox for P Mark Guthrie and a player to named later (August 31, 1999); Cubs acquired 3B Cole Liniak to complete deal (September 1, 1999). ... On Boston disabled list (March 18-June 13 and July 3-22, 2000); included rehabili-tation assignment to Pawtucket (June 2-13).
MISCELLANEOUS: Holds San Francisco Giants franchise all-time record for most saves (199).

Year League	W	L	Pct.	ERA	G	GS	CG	ShO	Sv.	IP	H	R	ER	BB	SO
1986— Medford (N'West)	1	3	.250	5.23	13	6	0	0	1	32²/₃	47	25	19	11	21
1987— Medford (N'West)	5	8	.385	5.18	17	12	2	0	0	92	106	74	53	26	69
1988— Clinton (Midw.)■	12	7	.632	3.00	28	23	5	1	0	177	177	68	59	27	123
1989— San Jose (Calif.)	11	2	*.846	2.40	13	13	4	0	0	97¹/₃	91	29	26	26	88
— Shreveport (Texas)	7	3	.700	3.55	16	14	4	1	0	99	108	45	39	16	74
1990— Shreveport (Texas)	10	3	.769	2.23	14	14	2	1	0	93	85	26	23	17	71
— Phoenix (PCL)	4	7	.364	4.93	12	12	2	0	0	76²/₃	100	51	42	18	43
1991— Phoenix (PCL)	4	3	.571	2.02	23	5	3	0	6	71¹/₃	56	18	16	13	35
— San Francisco (N.L.)	1	1	.500	3.78	31	0	0	0	1	52¹/₃	53	22	22	13	38
1992— San Francisco (N.L.)	3	3	.500	1.76	65	0	0	0	17	92	62	20	18	15	87
1993— San Francisco (N.L.)	3	1	.750	2.16	76	0	0	0	48	79¹/₃	57	20	19	13	86
1994— San Francisco (N.L.)	2	4	.333	2.77	48	0	0	0	28	48²/₃	49	17	15	13	39
1995— San Francisco (N.L.)	5	6	.455	4.45	60	0	0	0	33	58²/₃	60	31	29	21	42
1996— San Francisco (N.L.)	0	9	.000	3.34	63	0	0	0	35	62	56	23	23	10	48
1997— San Francisco (N.L.)	7	4	.636	3.47	73	0	0	0	37	70	67	31	27	8	53
1998— Chicago (N.L.)■	3	4	.429	3.02	*81	0	0	0	51	80¹/₃	86	33	27	20	81
1999— Chicago (N.L.)	2	4	.333	7.80	31	0	0	0	7	30	41	26	26	13	13
— Iowa (PCL)	0	0	...	0.00	2	0	0	0	0	2	1	0	0	0	2
— Boston (A.L.)■	0	1	.000	1.93	12	0	0	0	3	14	9	3	3	5	12
2000— Pawtucket (I.L.)	1	0	1.000	0.00	3	0	0	0	0	6	4	0	0	0	7
— Boston (A.L.)	3	0	1.000	3.10	34	0	0	0	0	40²/₃	34	15	14	12	35
A.L. totals (2 years)	3	1	.750	2.80	46	0	0	0	3	54²/₃	43	18	17	17	47
N.L. totals (9 years)	26	36	.419	3.23	528	0	0	0	257	573¹/₃	531	223	206	126	487
Major League totals (10 years)	29	37	.439	3.20	574	0	0	0	260	628	574	241	223	143	534

DIVISION SERIES RECORD

Year League	W	L	Pct.	ERA	G	GS	CG	ShO	Sv.	IP	H	R	ER	BB	SO
1997— San Francisco (N.L.)	0	0	...	0.00	1	0	0	0	0	1¹/₃	1	0	0	0	1
1998— Chicago (N.L.)	0	0	...	16.20	1	0	0	0	0	1²/₃	5	3	3	2	1
1999— Boston (A.L.)	0	0	...	0.00	2	0	0	0	0	2	2	0	0	0	2
Division series totals (3 years)	0	0	...	5.40	4	0	0	0	0	5	8	3	3	2	4

CHAMPIONSHIP SERIES RECORD

Year League	W	L	Pct.	ERA	G	GS	CG	ShO	Sv.	IP	H	R	ER	BB	SO
1999— Boston (A.L.)	0	1	.000	27.00	2	0	0	0	0	²/₃	2	2	2	0	1

ALL-STAR GAME RECORD

Year League	W	L	Pct.	ERA	GS	CG	ShO	Sv.	IP	H	R	ER	BB	SO
1993— National	0	0	...	9.00	0	0	0	0	1	2	1	1	0	1
1994— National	0	0	...	0.00	0	0	0	0	1²/₃	1	0	0	0	1
1997— National							Did not play.							
All-Star Game totals (2 years)	0	0	...	3.38	0	0	0	0	2²/₃	3	1	1	0	2

PERSONAL: Born February 1, 1972, in Aurora, Ill. ... 5-10/193. ... Bats left, throws left. ... Full name: Richard Goodhard Becker.
HIGH SCHOOL: Aurora (Ill.) West.
TRANSACTIONS/CAREER NOTES: Selected by Minnesota Twins organization in third round of free-agent draft (June 4, 1990). ... On Minnesota disabled list (September 13, 1993-remainder of season; and April 29-May 17, 1994). ... Traded by Twins to New York Mets for OF Alex Ochoa (December 12, 1997). ... Claimed on waivers by Baltimore Orioles (June 16, 1998). ... Released by Orioles (December 9, 1998). ... Signed by Milwaukee Brewers (January 11, 1999). ... Traded by Brewers to Oakland Athletics for a player to be named later (August 17, 1999); Brewers acquired P Carl Dale to complete deal (August 20, 1999). ... Granted free agency (December 21, 1999). ... Re-signed by A's (December 30, 1999). ... Released by A's (May 5, 2000). ... Signed by Detroit Tigers (May 10, 2000). ... Granted free agency (October 30, 2000).
STATISTICAL NOTES: Led Appalachian League with .448 on-base percentage in 1990. ... Led Midwest League with 215 total bases in 1991. ... Led California League outfielders with 355 total chances in 1992. ... Led A.L. outfielders in double plays with five in 1995, nine in 1996 and five in 2000. ... Led A.L. outfielders with 412 total chances in 1996.

						BATTING								FIELDING		
Year Team (League)	Pos.	G	AB	R	H	2B	3B	HR	RBI	Avg.	BB	SO	SB	PO	A	E	Avg.
1990— Elizabethton (Appl.)	OF	56	194	54	56	5	1	6	24	.289	*53	54	18	87	2	9	.908
1991— Kenosha (Midw.)	OF	130	494	100	132	*38	3	13	53	.267	72	108	19	270	19	11	.963
1992— Visalia (Calif.)	OF	*136	506	*118	160	37	2	15	82	.316	*114	122	29	*332	17	6	.983
1993— Nashville (Sou.)	OF	138	516	•93	148	25	7	15	66	.287	94	117	29	303	5	6	.981
— Minnesota (A.L.)	OF	3	7	3	2	2	0	0	0	.286	5	4	1	7	0	1	.875
1994— Minnesota (A.L.)	OF-DH	28	98	12	26	3	0	1	8	.265	13	25	6	87	2	1	.989
— Salt Lake (PCL)	OF	71	282	64	89	21	3	2	38	.316	40	56	7	189	8	3	.985
1995— Salt Lake (PCL)	OF	36	123	26	38	7	0	6	28	.309	26	24	6	108	5	1	.991
— Minnesota (A.L.)	OF	106	392	45	93	15	1	2	33	.237	34	95	8	275	12	4	.986
1996— Minnesota (A.L.)	OF	148	525	92	153	31	4	12	71	.291	68	118	19	*391	18	3	.993
1997— Minnesota (A.L.)	OF	132	443	61	117	22	3	10	45	.264	62	130	17	319	5	5	.985

Year Team (League)	Pos.	G	AB	R	H	2B	3B	HR	RBI	Avg.	BB	SO	SB	PO	A	E	Avg.
1998— New York (N.L.)■	OF	49	100	15	19	4	2	3	10	.190	21	42	3	56	4	1	.984
— Baltimore (A.L.)■......	OF-DH	79	113	22	23	1	0	3	11	.204	22	34	2	59	1	1	.984
1999— Milwaukee (N.L.)■....	OF-DH	89	139	15	35	5	2	5	16	.252	33	38	5	62	3	2	.970
— Oakland (A.L.)■........	OF-DH	40	125	21	33	3	0	1	10	.264	25	43	3	66	4	1	.986
2000— Oakland (A.L.)	OF-DH	23	47	11	11	2	0	1	5	.234	11	17	1	35	2	2	.949
— Detroit (A.L.)■..........	OF-DH	92	238	48	58	12	0	7	34	.244	56	70	1	127	3	6	.956
American League totals (8 years)		651	1988	315	516	91	8	37	217	.260	296	536	58	1366	47	24	.983
National League totals (2 years)		138	239	30	54	9	4	8	26	.226	54	80	8	118	7	3	.977
Major League totals (8 years)		789	2227	345	570	100	12	45	243	.256	350	616	66	1484	54	27	.983

BECKETT, JOSH   P   MARLINS

B

PERSONAL: Born May 15, 1980, in Spring, Texas. ... 6-4/190. ... Throws right, bats right. ... Full name: Joshua Patrick Beckett.
HIGH SCHOOL: Spring (Texas).
TRANSACTIONS/CAREER NOTES: Selected by Florida Marlins organization in first round (second pick overall) of free-agent draft (June 2, 1999). ... On Brevard County disabled list (April 17-May 30 and August 16-September 11, 2000).

Year League	W	L	Pct.	ERA	G	GS	CG	ShO	Sv.	IP	H	R	ER	BB	SO
2000— Kane County (Midw.).........	2	3	.400	2.12	13	12	0	0	0	59 1/3	45	18	14	15	61

BEIRNE, KEVIN   P   BLUE JAYS

PERSONAL: Born January 1, 1974, in Houston. ... 6-4/210. ... Throws right, bats left. ... Full name: Kevin P. Beirne. ... Son of Jim Beirne, wide receiver/tight end with Houston Oilers (1968-73, 1975 and 1976) and San Diego Chargers (1974).
HIGH SCHOOL: McCollough (The Woodlands, Texas).
COLLEGE: Texas A&M.
TRANSACTIONS/CAREER NOTES: Selected by Cincinnati Reds organization in 43rd round of free-agent draft (June 2, 1992); did not sign. ... Selected by Chicago White Sox organization in 11th round of free-agent draft (June 1, 1995). ... On Charlotte disabled list (May 6-14 and August 6, 1999-remainder of season). ... Traded by White Sox with P Mike Sirotka, OF Brian Simmons and P Mike Williams to Toronto Blue Jays for P David Wells and P Matt DeWitt (January 14, 2001).

Year League	W	L	Pct.	ERA	G	GS	CG	ShO	Sv.	IP	H	R	ER	BB	SO
1995— GC White Sox (GCL)	0	0	...	2.45	2	0	0	0	2	3 2/3	2	2	1	1	3
— Bristol (Appl.)....................	1	0	1.000	0.00	9	0	0	0	2	9	4	0	0	4	12
— Hickory (S.Atl.).................	0	0	...	4.50	3	0	0	0	1	4	7	2	2	0	4
1996— South Bend (Midw.)	4	11	.267	4.15	26	25	1	0	0	145 1/3	153	85	67	60	110
1997— Winston-Salem (Caro.).......	4	4	.500	3.05	13	13	1	0	0	82 2/3	66	38	28	28	75
— Birmingham (Sou.)............	6	4	.600	4.92	13	12	0	0	0	75	76	51	41	41	49
1998— Birmingham (Sou.)..........	13	9	.591	3.44	26	26	2	1	0	167 1/3	142	77	64	87	153
— Calgary (PCL)....................	0	0	...	4.50	2	2	0	0	0	8	12	5	4	4	6
1999— Charlotte (I.L.)...............	5	5	.500	5.42	20	20	0	0	0	113	134	75	68	36	63
2000— Charlotte (I.L.)...............	1	2	.333	3.51	7	7	0	0	0	33 1/3	39	13	13	7	28
— Chicago (A.L.)....................	1	3	.250	6.70	29	1	0	0	0	49 2/3	50	41	37	20	41
Major League totals (1 year)........	1	3	.250	6.70	29	1	0	0	0	49 2/3	50	41	37	20	41

BELCHER, TIM   P   ANGELS

PERSONAL: Born October 19, 1961, in Sparta, Ohio. ... 6-3/235. ... Throws right, bats right. ... Full name: Timothy Wayne Belcher.
HIGH SCHOOL: Highland (Sparta, Ohio).
COLLEGE: Mt. Vernon (Ohio) Nazarene.
TRANSACTIONS/CAREER NOTES: Selected by Minnesota Twins organization in first round (first pick overall) of free-agent draft (June 6, 1983); did not sign. ... Selected by New York Yankees organization in secondary phase of free-agent draft (January 17, 1984); did not sign. ... Selected by Oakland Athletics organization in player compensation pool draft (February 8, 1984); A's received compensation for Baltimore Orioles signing Type A free-agent P Tom Underwood (February 7, 1984). ... On disabled list (April 10-May 4 and May 5-July 23, 1986). ... Traded by A's to Los Angeles Dodgers (September 3, 1987), completing deal in which Dodgers traded P Rick Honeycutt to A's for a player to be named later (August 29, 1987). ... On disabled list (August 17, 1990-remainder of season). ... Traded by Dodgers with P John Wetteland to Cincinnati Reds for OF Eric Davis and P Kip Gross (November 27, 1991). ... Traded by Reds to Chicago White Sox for P Johnny Ruffin and P Jeff Pierce (July 31, 1993). ... Granted free agency (October 26, 1993). ... Signed by Detroit Tigers (February 7, 1994). ... Granted free agency (October 20, 1994). ... Signed by Reds organization (May 3, 1995). ... Traded by Reds to Seattle Mariners for P Roger Salkeld (May 15, 1995). ... Granted free agency (October 31, 1995). ... Signed by Kansas City Royals (January 31, 1996). ... Granted free agency (October 26, 1998). ... Signed by Anaheim Angels (December 23, 1998). ... On disabled list (June 27-August 7, 1999). ... On Anaheim disabled list (March 25-June 17 and July 3-September 7, 2000); included rehabilitation assignments to Lake Elsinore (April 15-23 and August 27-31), Edmonton (April 24-May 8 and June 5-17) and Erie (September 1-7). ... On suspended list (September 22-24, 2000). ... Granted free agency (November 1, 2000). ... Re-signed by Angels organization (December 7, 2000).
HONORS: Named righthanded pitcher on THE SPORTING NEWS college All-America team (1983). ... Named N.L. Rookie Pitcher of the Year by THE SPORTING NEWS (1988).
STATISTICAL NOTES: Pitched 6-0 one-hit, complete-game victory against Pittsburgh (July 21, 1990). ... Pitched 4-0 one-hit, complete-game victory for Cincinnati against Atlanta (May 26, 1993). ... Led A.L. with 37 home runs allowed in 1998.

Year League	W	L	Pct.	ERA	G	GS	CG	ShO	Sv.	IP	H	R	ER	BB	SO
1984— Madison (Midw.)	9	4	.692	3.57	16	16	3	1	0	98 1/3	80	45	39	48	111
— Albany/Colonie (East.)........	3	4	.429	3.33	10	10	2	0	0	54	37	30	20	41	40
1985— Huntsville (Sou.)	11	10	.524	4.69	29	26	3	1	0	149 2/3	145	99	78	99	90
1986— Huntsville (Sou.)	2	5	.286	6.57	9	9	0	0	0	37	50	28	27	22	25
1987— Tacoma (PCL)	9	11	.450	4.42	29	28	2	1	0	163	143	89	80	*133	136
— Los Angeles (N.L.)■..........	4	2	.667	2.38	6	5	0	0	0	34	30	11	9	7	23
1988— Los Angeles (N.L.)	12	6	.667	2.91	36	27	4	1	4	179 2/3	143	65	58	51	152
1989— Los Angeles (N.L.)	15	12	.556	2.82	39	30	•10	*8	1	230	182	81	72	80	200
1990— Los Angeles (N.L.)	9	9	.500	4.00	24	24	5	2	0	153	136	76	68	48	102

– 39 –

Year League	W	L	Pct.	ERA	G	GS	CG	ShO	Sv.	IP	H	R	ER	BB	SO
1991— Los Angeles (N.L.)	10	9	.526	2.62	33	33	2	1	0	209 1/3	189	76	61	75	156
1992— Cincinnati (N.L.)■	15	14	.517	3.91	35	34	2	1	0	227 2/3	201	*104	*99	80	149
1993— Cincinnati (N.L.)	9	6	.600	4.47	22	22	4	2	0	137	134	72	68	47	101
— Chicago (A.L.)■	3	5	.375	4.40	12	11	1	1	0	71 2/3	64	36	35	27	34
1994— Detroit (A.L.)■	7	*15	.318	5.89	25	•25	3	0	0	162	192	*124	106	78	76
1995— Indianapolis (A.A.)■	0	0	...	1.80	2	2	0	0	0	10	6	2	2	1	8
— Seattle (A.L.)	10	12	.455	4.52	28	28	1	0	0	179 1/3	188	101	90	88	96
1996— Kansas City (A.L.)■	15	11	.577	3.92	35	35	4	1	0	238 2/3	262	117	104	68	113
1997— Kansas City (A.L.)	13	12	.520	5.02	32	32	3	1	0	213 1/3	242	128	119	70	113
1998— Kansas City (A.L.)	14	14	.500	4.27	34	34	2	0	0	234	247	127	111	73	130
1999— Anaheim (A.L.)■	6	8	.429	6.73	24	24	0	0	0	132 1/3	168	104	99	46	52
2000— Lake Elsinore (Calif.)	1	0	1.000	3.21	3	3	0	0	0	14	6	5	5	2	16
— Edmonton (PCL)	1	1	.500	3.86	3	3	0	0	0	14	12	7	6	7	6
— Anaheim (A.L.)	4	5	.444	6.86	9	9	1	0	0	40 2/3	45	31	31	22	22
— Erie (East.)	1	0	1.000	0.00	1	1	0	0	0	7	4	0	0	0	6
A.L. totals (8 years)	72	82	.468	4.92	199	198	15	3	0	1272	1408	768	695	472	636
N.L. totals (7 years)	74	58	.561	3.34	195	175	27	15	5	1170 2/3	1015	485	435	388	883
Major League totals (14 years)	146	140	.510	4.16	394	373	42	18	5	2442 2/3	2423	1253	1130	860	1519

DIVISION SERIES RECORD

Year League	W	L	Pct.	ERA	G	GS	CG	ShO	Sv.	IP	H	R	ER	BB	SO
1995— Seattle (A.L.)	0	1	.000	6.23	2	0	0	0	0	4 1/3	4	3	3	5	0

CHAMPIONSHIP SERIES RECORD

Year League	W	L	Pct.	ERA	G	GS	CG	ShO	Sv.	IP	H	R	ER	BB	SO
1988— Los Angeles (N.L.)	2	0	1.000	4.11	2	2	0	0	0	15 1/3	12	7	7	4	16
1993— Chicago (A.L.)	1	0	1.000	2.45	1	0	0	0	0	3 2/3	3	1	1	3	1
1995— Seattle (A.L.)	0	1	.000	6.35	1	1	0	0	0	5 2/3	9	4	4	2	1
Champ. series totals (3 years)	3	1	.750	4.38	4	3	0	0	0	24 2/3	24	12	12	9	18

WORLD SERIES RECORD

NOTES: Member of World Series championship team (1988).

Year League	W	L	Pct.	ERA	G	GS	CG	ShO	Sv.	IP	H	R	ER	BB	SO
1988— Los Angeles (N.L.)	1	0	1.000	6.23	2	2	0	0	0	8 2/3	10	7	6	6	10

BELINDA, STAN   P

PERSONAL: Born August 6, 1966, in Huntingdon, Pa. ... 6-3/215. ... Throws right, bats right. ... Full name: Stanley Peter Belinda.

HIGH SCHOOL: State College (Pa.).

JUNIOR COLLEGE: Allegany Community College (Md.).

TRANSACTIONS/CAREER NOTES: Selected by Pittsburgh Pirates organization in 10th round of free-agent draft (June 2, 1986). ... On Gulf Coast Pirates disabled list (June 21-30, 1986). ... Traded by Pirates to Kansas City Royals for P Jon Lieber and P Dan Miceli (July 31, 1993). ... Granted free agency (December 23, 1994). ... Signed by Boston Red Sox (April 9, 1995). ... On Boston disabled list (April 21-May 6, 1995); included rehabilitation assignment to Sarasota (May 4-5). ... On Boston disabled list (March 19-April 6, May 30-July 26 and August 20, 1996-remainder of season); included rehabilitation assignments to Sarasota (June 6-9) and Pawtucket (July 14-25). ... Granted free agency (October 14, 1996). ... Signed by Cincinnati Reds (December 21, 1996). ... On disabled list (June 3-July 9 and August 11, 1998-remainder of season). ... On Cincinnati disabled list (March 24-June 25, 1999); included rehabilitation assignment to Indianapolis (June 3-24). ... Traded by Reds with OF Jeffrey Hammonds to Colorado Rockies for OF Dante Bichette and cash (October 30, 1999). ... Released by Rockies (July 25, 2000). ... Signed by Atlanta Braves (July 29, 2000). ... Released by Braves (September 12, 2000).

Year League	W	L	Pct.	ERA	G	GS	CG	ShO	Sv.	IP	H	R	ER	BB	SO
1986— Watertown (NY-Penn)	0	0	...	3.38	5	0	0	0	2	8	5	3	3	2	5
— Gulf Coast Pirates (GCL)	3	2	.600	2.66	17	0	0	0	7	20 1/3	23	12	6	2	17
1987— Macon (S.Atl.)	6	4	.600	2.09	50	0	0	0	16	82	59	26	19	27	75
1988— Salem (Caro.)	6	4	.600	2.76	53	0	0	0	14	71 2/3	54	33	22	32	63
1989— Harrisburg (East.)	1	4	.200	2.33	32	0	0	0	13	38 2/3	32	13	10	25	33
— Buffalo (A.A.)	2	2	.500	0.95	19	0	0	0	9	28 1/3	13	5	3	13	28
— Pittsburgh (N.L.)	0	1	.000	6.10	8	0	0	0	0	10 1/3	13	8	7	2	10
1990— Buffalo (A.A.)	3	1	.750	1.90	15	0	0	0	5	23 2/3	20	8	5	8	25
— Pittsburgh (N.L.)	3	4	.429	3.55	55	0	0	0	8	58 1/3	48	23	23	29	55
1991— Pittsburgh (N.L.)	7	5	.583	3.45	60	0	0	0	16	78 1/3	50	30	30	35	71
1992— Pittsburgh (N.L.)	6	4	.600	3.15	59	0	0	0	18	71 1/3	58	26	25	29	57
1993— Pittsburgh (N.L.)	3	1	.750	3.61	40	0	0	0	19	42 1/3	35	18	17	11	30
— Kansas City (A.L.)■	1	1	.500	4.28	23	0	0	0	0	27 1/3	30	13	13	6	25
1994— Kansas City (A.L.)	2	2	.500	5.14	37	0	0	0	1	49	47	36	28	24	37
1995— Sarasota (FSL)■	0	0	...	4.50	1	1	0	0	0	2	2	1	1	0	2
— Boston (A.L.)	8	1	.889	3.10	63	0	0	0	10	69 2/3	51	25	24	28	57
1996— Boston (A.L.)	2	1	.667	6.59	31	0	0	0	2	28 2/3	31	22	21	20	18
— Sarasota (FSL)	0	1	.000	45.00	1	1	0	0	0	1	6	5	5	1	1
— Pawtucket (I.L.)	1	0	1.000	0.00	6	0	0	0	0	7 2/3	2	2	0	2	7
1997— Cincinnati (N.L.)■	1	5	.167	3.71	84	0	0	0	1	99 1/3	84	42	41	33	114
1998— Cincinnati (N.L.)	4	8	.333	3.23	40	0	0	0	1	61 1/3	46	23	22	28	57
1999— Indianapolis (I.L.)	2	0	1.000	2.38	10	0	0	0	0	11 1/3	7	3	3	6	10
— Cincinnati (N.L.)	3	1	.750	5.27	29	0	0	0	2	42 2/3	42	26	25	18	40
2000— Colorado (N.L.)■	1	3	.250	7.07	46	0	0	0	1	35 2/3	39	32	28	17	40
— Atlanta (N.L.)■	0	0	...	9.82	10	0	0	0	0	11	16	12	12	5	11
A.L. totals (4 years)	13	5	.722	4.43	154	0	0	0	13	174 2/3	159	96	86	78	137
N.L. totals (9 years)	28	32	.467	4.05	431	0	0	0	66	510 2/3	431	240	230	207	485
Major League totals (12 years)	41	37	.526	4.15	585	0	0	0	79	685 1/3	590	336	316	285	622

DIVISION SERIES RECORD

Year League	W	L	Pct.	ERA	G	GS	CG	ShO	Sv.	IP	H	R	ER	BB	SO
1995— Boston (A.L.)	0	0	...	0.00	1	0	0	0	0	1/3	0	0	0	0	0

Year League	W	L	Pct.	ERA	G	GS	CG	ShO	Sv.	IP	H	R	ER	BB	SO
1990— Pittsburgh (N.L.)	0	0	...	2.45	3	0	0	0	0	3 2/3	3	1	1	0	4
1991— Pittsburgh (N.L.)	1	0	1.000	0.00	3	0	0	0	0	5	0	0	0	3	4
1992— Pittsburgh (N.L.)	0	0	...	0.00	2	0	0	0	0	1 2/3	2	0	0	1	2
Champ. series totals (3 years)	1	0	1.000	0.87	8	0	0	0	0	10 1/3	5	1	1	4	10

BELITZ, TODD   P   ATHLETICS

B

PERSONAL: Born October 23, 1975, in Des Moines, Iowa. ... 6-3/200. ... Throws left, bats left. ... Full name: Todd Stephen Belitz.
HIGH SCHOOL: Edison (Huntington Beach, Calif.).
COLLEGE: Washington State.
TRANSACTIONS/CAREER NOTES: Selected by Kansas City Royals organization in eighth round of free-agent draft (June 2, 1994); did not sign. ... Selected by Tampa Bay Devil Rays organization in fourth round of free-agent draft (June 3, 1997). ... Traded by Devil Rays with P Jim Mecir to Oakland Athletics for P Jesus Colome and a player to be named later (July 28, 2000).

Year League	W	L	Pct.	ERA	G	GS	CG	ShO	Sv.	IP	H	R	ER	BB	SO
1997— Hudson Valley (NY-Penn)...	4	5	.444	3.53	15	15	0	0	0	74	65	41	29	18	78
1998— Charleston, S.C. (S.Atl.)	6	4	.600	2.42	21	21	0	0	0	130	99	44	35	48	123
— St. Petersburg (FSL)	2	2	.500	5.04	7	7	0	0	0	44 2/3	39	28	25	14	40
1999— Orlando (Sou.)	9	9	.500	5.77	28	•28	0	0	0	160 2/3	169	*114	*103	65	118
2000— Durham (I.L.)	1	1	.500	3.83	43	0	0	0	2	47	33	24	20	28	46
— Sacramento (PCL)■..........	0	1	.000	4.38	12	0	0	0	1	12 1/3	12	6	6	5	10
— Oakland (A.L.)	0	0	...	2.70	5	0	0	0	0	3 1/3	4	2	1	4	3
Major League totals (1 year)........	0	0	...	2.70	5	0	0	0	0	3 1/3	4	2	1	4	3

BELL, DAVID   IF   MARINERS

PERSONAL: Born September 14, 1972, in Cincinnati. ... 5-10/190. ... Bats right, throws right. ... Full name: David Michael Bell. ... Son of Buddy Bell, major league third baseman with four teams (1972-89) and manager, Colorado Rockies; brother of Mike Bell, third baseman with Cincinnati Reds (2000); and grandson of Gus Bell, major league outfielder with four teams (1950-64).
HIGH SCHOOL: Moeller (Cincinnati).
TRANSACTIONS/CAREER NOTES: Selected by Cleveland Indians organization in seventh round of free-agent draft (June 4, 1990). ... Traded by Indians with C Pepe McNeal and P Rick Heiserman to St. Louis Cardinals for P Ken Hill (July 27, 1995). ... On St. Louis disabled list (April 29-June 30, 1997); included rehabilitation assignments to Arkansas (June 10-19) and Louisville (June 20-26). ... Claimed on waivers by Indians (April 14, 1998). ... Traded by Indians to Seattle Mariners for 2B Joey Cora (August 31, 1998).
STATISTICAL NOTES: Led South Atlantic League in grounding into double plays with 22 in 1991. ... Led South Atlantic League third basemen with 389 total chances in 1991. ... Led Eastern League third basemen with 32 double plays in 1993. ... Led International League third basemen with .950 fielding percentage in 1994. ... Led A.L. second baseman with 313 putouts and 118 double plays in 1999.

Year Team (League)	Pos.	G	AB	R	H	2B	3B	HR	RBI	Avg.	BB	SO	SB	PO	A	E	Avg.
								BATTING							FIELDING		
1990— GC Indians (GCL)	3B	30	111	18	29	5	1	0	13	.261	10	8	1	29	50	7	.919
— Burlington (Appl.)........	3B	12	42	4	7	1	1	0	2	.167	2	5	2	8	27	3	.921
1991— Columbus (S.Atl.)........	3B	136	491	47	113	24	1	5	63	.230	37	50	3	90	*268	31	.920
1992— Kinston (Caro.)...........	3B	123	464	52	117	17	2	6	47	.252	54	66	2	83	264	20	.946
1993— Canton/Akron (East.)..	3B-2B-SS	129	483	69	141	20	2	9	60	.292	43	54	3	117	283	21	.950
1994— Charlotte (I.L.)...........	3B-SS-2B	134	481	66	141	17	4	18	88	.293	41	54	2	109	326	20	†.956
1995— Buffalo (A.A.)..............	3B-SS-2B	70	254	34	69	11	1	8	34	.272	22	37	0	46	172	11	.952
— Cleveland (A.L.)............	3B	2	2	0	0	0	0	0	0	.000	0	0	0	0	2	0	1.000
— Louisville (A.A.)■......	2B	18	76	9	21	3	1	1	9	.276	2	10	4	39	54	1	.989
— St. Louis (N.L.)...........	2B-3B	39	144	13	36	7	2	2	19	.250	4	25	1	77	108	7	.964
1996— St. Louis (N.L.)..........	3B-2B-SS	62	145	12	31	6	0	1	9	.214	10	22	1	45	113	5	.969
— Louisville (A.A.)...........	2B-3B-SS	42	136	9	24	5	1	0	7	.176	7	15	1	66	114	5	.973
1997— St. Louis (N.L.)..........	3B-2B-SS	66	142	9	30	7	2	1	12	.211	10	28	1	55	95	8	.949
— Arkansas (Texas).........	3B-2B	9	32	3	7	2	0	1	3	.219	2	2	1	3	15	1	.947
— Louisville (A.A.).........2B-3B-DH-SS		6	22	3	5	0	0	1	4	.227	0	6	0	6	10	1	.941
1998— St. Louis (N.L.)..........	3B-2B	4	9	0	2	1	0	0	0	.222	0	3	0	1	4	0	1.000
— Cleveland (A.L.)■........	2-3-1-S	107	340	37	89	21	2	10	41	.262	22	54	0	201	306	9	.983
— Seattle (A.L.)■.........2B-1B-3B-OF		21	80	11	26	8	0	0	8	.325	5	8	0	61	46	1	.991
1999— Seattle (A.L.)	2B-1B-SS	157	597	92	160	31	2	21	78	.268	58	90	7	†329	427	17	.978
2000— Seattle (A.L.)	3-2-1-DH-SS	133	454	57	112	24	2	11	47	.247	42	66	2	139	253	15	.963
American League totals (4 years)		420	1473	197	387	84	6	42	174	.263	127	218	9	730	1034	42	.977
National League totals (4 years)		171	440	34	99	21	4	4	40	.225	24	78	3	178	320	20	.961
Major League totals (6 years)		591	1913	231	486	105	10	46	214	.254	151	296	12	908	1354	62	.973

DIVISION SERIES RECORD

Year Team (League)	Pos.	G	AB	R	H	2B	3B	HR	RBI	Avg.	BB	SO	SB	PO	A	E	Avg.
								BATTING							FIELDING		
2000— Seattle (A.L.)	3B	3	11	0	4	1	0	0	1	.364	2	2	0	2	4	0	1.000

CHAMPIONSHIP SERIES RECORD

Year Team (League)	Pos.	G	AB	R	H	2B	3B	HR	RBI	Avg.	BB	SO	SB	PO	A	E	Avg.
								BATTING							FIELDING		
2000— Seattle (A.L.)	3B	5	18	0	4	0	0	0	0	.222	0	0	0	5	9	0	1.000

BELL, DEREK   OF   PIRATES

PERSONAL: Born December 11, 1968, in Tampa. ... 6-2/215. ... Bats right, throws right. ... Full name: Derek Nathaniel Bell.
HIGH SCHOOL: King (Tampa).

TRANSACTIONS/CAREER NOTES: Selected by Toronto Blue Jays organization in second round of free-agent draft (June 2, 1987). ... On Knoxville disabled list (July 30, 1988-remainder of season; June 13-21 and July 2-12, 1990). ... On Toronto disabled list (April 9-May 8, 1992); included rehabilitation assignment to Dunedin (April 27-May 4). ... Traded by Blue Jays with OF Stoney Briggs to San Diego Padres for OF Darrin Jackson (March 30, 1993). ... On suspended list (July 9-12, 1993 and July 9-17, 1994). ... Traded by Padres with OF Phil Plantier, P Pedro Martinez, P Doug Brocail, IF Craig Shipley and SS Ricky Gutierrez to Houston Astros for 3B Ken Caminiti, OF Steve Finley, SS Andujar Cedeno, 1B Robert Petagine, P Brian Williams and a player to be named later (December 28, 1994); Padres acquired P Sean Fesh to complete deal (May 1, 1995). ... On Houston disabled list (May 14-June 13, 1997); included rehabilitation assignment to New Orleans (June 6-13). ... On disabled list (August 17-September 1, 1999). ... Traded by Astros with P Mike Hampton to New York Mets for OF Roger Cedeno, P Octavio Dotel and P Kyle Kessel (December 23, 1999). ... Granted free agency (October 31, 2000). ... Signed by Pittsburgh Pirates (December 10, 2000).

HONORS: Named International League Most Valuable Player (1991).

STATISTICAL NOTES: Led International League with 243 total bases in 1991. ... Led International League outfielders with seven double plays in 1991. ... Tied for N.L. lead with 10 sacrifice flies in 1998. ... Career major league grand slams: 1.

								— BATTING —							— FIELDING —		
Year	Team (League)	Pos.	G	AB	R	H	2B	3B	HR	RBI	Avg.	BB	SO	SB	PO	A	E	Avg.
1987—St. Catharines (NY-P) .		OF	74	273	46	72	11	3	10	42	.264	18	60	12	126	6	2	.985
1988—Knoxville (Sou.)		OF	14	52	5	13	3	1	0	4	.250	1	14	2	18	2	2	.909
—Myrtle Beach (S.Atl.) ..		OF	91	352	55	121	29	5	12	60	*.344	15	67	18	148	12	10	.941
1989—Knoxville (Sou.)		OF	136	513	72	124	22	6	16	75	.242	26	92	15	216	12	9	.962
1990—Syracuse (I.L.)		OF	109	402	57	105	13	5	7	56	.261	23	75	21	220	9	5	.979
1991—Syracuse (I.L.)		OF	119	457	*89	*158	22	•12	13	*93	*.346	57	69	27	278	*15	*16	.948
—Toronto (A.L.)		OF	18	28	5	4	0	0	0	1	.143	6	5	3	16	0	2	.889
1992—Toronto (A.L.)		OF-DH	61	161	23	39	6	3	2	15	.242	15	34	7	105	4	0	1.000
—Dunedin (FSL)		OF	7	25	7	6	2	0	0	4	.240	4	4	3	13	0	2	.867
1993—San Diego (N.L.)■		OF-3B	150	542	73	142	19	1	21	72	.262	23	122	26	334	37	17	.956
1994—San Diego (N.L.)		OF	108	434	54	135	20	0	14	54	.311	29	88	24	247	3	10	.962
1995—Houston (N.L.)■		OF	112	452	63	151	21	2	8	86	.334	33	71	27	201	10	8	.963
1996—Houston (N.L.)		OF	158	627	84	165	40	3	17	113	.263	40	123	29	283	16	7	.977
1997—Houston (N.L.)		OF-DH	129	493	67	136	29	3	15	71	.276	40	94	15	226	5	8	.967
—New Orleans (A.A.)		OF	5	13	0	2	0	0	0	1	.154	1	1	1	10	0	0	1.000
1998—Houston (N.L.)		OF	156	630	111	198	41	2	22	108	.314	51	126	13	281	8	8	.973
1999—Houston (N.L.)		OF	128	509	61	120	22	0	12	66	.236	50	129	18	192	4	3	.985
2000—New York (N.L.)■		OF-P	144	546	87	145	31	1	18	69	.266	65	125	8	252	5	3	.988
American League totals (2 years)			79	189	28	43	6	3	2	16	.228	21	39	10	121	4	2	.984
National League totals (8 years)			1085	4233	600	1192	223	12	127	639	.282	331	878	160	2016	88	64	.970
Major League totals (10 years)			1164	4422	628	1235	229	15	129	655	.279	352	917	170	2137	92	66	.971

DIVISION SERIES RECORD

								— BATTING —							— FIELDING —		
Year	Team (League)	Pos.	G	AB	R	H	2B	3B	HR	RBI	Avg.	BB	SO	SB	PO	A	E	Avg.
1997—Houston (N.L.)		OF	3	13	0	0	0	0	0	0	.000	0	3	0	3	0	0	1.000
1998—Houston (N.L.)		OF	4	16	1	2	0	0	1	1	.125	0	7	0	5	0	0	1.000
1999—Houston (N.L.)		OF-PH	2	3	0	1	0	0	0	0	.333	0	0	0	1	0	0	1.000
2000—New York (N.L.)		OF	1	1	0	0	0	0	0	0	.000	0	0	0	0	0	0	...
Division series totals (4 years)			10	33	1	3	0	0	1	1	.091	0	10	0	9	0	0	1.000

CHAMPIONSHIP SERIES RECORD

								— BATTING —							— FIELDING —		
Year	Team (League)	Pos.	G	AB	R	H	2B	3B	HR	RBI	Avg.	BB	SO	SB	PO	A	E	Avg.
1992—Toronto (A.L.)		PR-OF	2	0	1	0	0	0	0	0	...	1	0	0	1	0	0	1.000

WORLD SERIES RECORD

NOTES: Member of World Series championship team (1992).

								— BATTING —							— FIELDING —		
Year	Team (League)	Pos.	G	AB	R	H	2B	3B	HR	RBI	Avg.	BB	SO	SB	PO	A	E	Avg.
1992—Toronto (A.L.)		PH	2	1	1	0	0	0	0	0	.000	1	0	0	...	...	...	...

RECORD AS PITCHER

Year	League	W	L	Pct.	ERA	G	GS	CG	ShO	Sv.	IP	H	R	ER	BB	SO
2000—New York (N.L.)		0	0	...	36.00	1	0	0	0	0	1	3	5	4	3	0

BELL, JAY — 2B — DIAMONDBACKS

PERSONAL: Born December 11, 1965, in Eglin AFB, Fla. ... 6-0/184. ... Bats right, throws right. ... Full name: Jay Stuart Bell.

HIGH SCHOOL: Tate (Gonzalez, Fla.).

TRANSACTIONS/CAREER NOTES: Selected by Minnesota Twins organization in first round (eighth pick overall) of free-agent draft (June 4, 1984). ... Traded by Twins with P Curt Wardle, OF Jim Weaver and a player to be named later to Cleveland Indians for P Bert Blyleven (August 1, 1985); Indians acquired P Rich Yett to complete deal (September 17, 1985). ... Traded by Indians to Pittsburgh Pirates for SS Felix Fermin (March 25, 1989). ... Traded by Pirates with 1B/3B Jeff King to Kansas City Royals for 3B Joe Randa, P Jeff Granger, P Jeff Martin and P Jeff Wallace (December 13, 1996). ... Granted free agency (November 4, 1997). ... Signed by Arizona Diamondbacks (November 17, 1997).

HONORS: Named shortstop on The Sporting News N.L. All-Star team (1993). ... Won N.L. Gold Glove at shortstop (1993). ... Named shortstop on The Sporting News N.L. Silver Slugger team (1993).

STATISTICAL NOTES: Led Appalachian League shortstops with 352 total chances and 43 double plays in 1984. ... Led California League shortstops with 84 double plays in 1985. ... Hit home run in first major league at-bat on first pitch (September 29, 1986). ... Led Eastern League shortstops with 613 total chances in 1986. ... Led American Association shortstops with 198 putouts, 322 assists, 30 errors and 550 total chances in 1987. ... Led N.L. with 39 sacrifice hits in 1990 and 30 in 1991. ... Had 22-game hitting streak (August 24-September 17, 1992). ... Led N.L. shortstops with 741 total chances in 1990, 754 in 1991, 816 in 1992, 794 in 1993 and 547 in 1994.. ... Led N.L. shortstops with 94 double plays in 1992. ... Led N.L. second basemen with 22 errors in 1999. ... Career major league grand slams: 5.

MISCELLANEOUS: Holds Arizona Diamondbacks all-time records for most hits (459) runs (298), doubles (91) and home runs (76).

Year	Team (League)	Pos.	G	AB	R	H	2B	3B	HR	RBI	Avg.	BB	SO	SB	PO	A	E	Avg.
							BATTING									FIELDING		
1984—	Elizabethton (Appl.)....	SS	66	245	43	54	12	1	6	30	.220	42	50	4	*109	*218	25	.929
1985—	Visalia (Calif.)........	SS	106	376	56	106	16	6	9	59	.282	41	73	10	176	330	53	.905
—	Waterbury (East.)■....	SS	29	114	13	34	11	2	1	14	.298	9	16	3	41	79	6	.952
1986—	Waterbury (East.).......	SS	138	494	86	137	28	4	7	74	.277	87	65	10	197	*371	*45	.927
—	Cleveland (A.L.).........	2B-DH	5	14	3	5	2	0	1	4	.357	2	3	0	1	6	2	.778
1987—	Buffalo (A.A.).............	SS-2B	110	362	71	94	15	4	17	60	.260	70	84	6	†201	†325	†30	.946
—	Cleveland (A.L.).........	SS	38	125	14	27	9	1	2	13	.216	8	31	2	67	93	9	.947
1988—	Cleveland (A.L.).........	SS-DH	73	211	23	46	5	1	2	21	.218	21	53	4	103	170	10	.965
—	Colo. Springs (PCL)...	SS	49	181	35	50	12	2	7	24	.276	26	27	3	87	171	18	.935
1989—	Pittsburgh (N.L.)■.....	SS	78	271	33	70	13	3	2	27	.258	19	47	5	109	197	10	.968
—	Buffalo (A.A.).............	SS-3B	86	298	49	85	15	3	10	54	.285	38	55	12	110	223	16	.954
1990—	Pittsburgh (N.L.)........	SS	159	583	93	148	28	7	7	52	.254	65	109	10	*260	459	22	.970
1991—	Pittsburgh (N.L.)........	SS	157	608	96	164	32	8	16	67	.270	52	99	10	239	*491	*24	.968
1992—	Pittsburgh (N.L.)........	SS	159	632	87	167	36	6	9	55	.264	55	103	7	*268	*526	22	.973
1993—	Pittsburgh (N.L.)........	SS	154	604	102	187	32	9	9	51	.310	77	122	16	*256	*527	11	*.986
1994—	Pittsburgh (N.L.)........	SS	110	424	68	117	35	4	9	45	.276	49	82	2	152	*380	15	.973
1995—	Pittsburgh (N.L.)........	SS-3B	138	530	79	139	28	4	13	55	.262	55	110	2	206	415	14	.978
1996—	Pittsburgh (N.L.)........	SS	151	527	65	132	29	3	13	71	.250	54	108	6	215	*478	10	*.986
1997—	Kansas City (A.L.)■...	SS-3B	153	573	89	167	28	3	21	92	.291	71	101	10	229	450	10	.985
1998—	Arizona (N.L.)■.........	SS	155	549	79	138	29	5	20	67	.251	81	129	3	224	437	19	.972
1999—	Arizona (N.L.)...........	2B-DH-SS	151	589	132	170	32	6	38	112	.289	82	132	7	320	340	†22	.968
2000—	Arizona (N.L.)............	2B-DH	149	565	87	151	30	6	18	68	.267	70	88	7	290	345	8	.988
	American League totals (4 years)		269	923	129	245	44	5	26	130	.265	102	188	16	400	719	31	.973
	National League totals (11 years)		1561	5882	921	1583	324	61	164	670	.269	659	1129	75	2539	4595	177	.976
	Major League totals (15 years)		1830	6805	1050	1828	368	66	180	800	.269	761	1317	91	2939	5314	208	.975

DIVISION SERIES RECORD

Year	Team (League)	Pos.	G	AB	R	H	2B	3B	HR	RBI	Avg.	BB	SO	SB	PO	A	E	Avg.
							BATTING									FIELDING		
1999—	Arizona (N.L.).............	2B	4	14	3	4	1	0	0	3	.286	1	0	0	8	11	1	.950

RECORDS: Shares single-series record for most singles—9 (1991).

CHAMPIONSHIP SERIES RECORD

Year	Team (League)	Pos.	G	AB	R	H	2B	3B	HR	RBI	Avg.	BB	SO	SB	PO	A	E	Avg.
							BATTING									FIELDING		
1990—	Pittsburgh (N.L.)........	SS	6	20	3	5	1	0	1	1	.250	4	3	0	4	22	1	.963
1991—	Pittsburgh (N.L.)........	SS	7	29	2	12	2	0	1	1	.414	0	10	0	13	19	1	.970
1992—	Pittsburgh (N.L.)........	SS	7	29	3	5	2	0	1	4	.172	3	4	0	6	8	1	.933
	Championship series totals (3 years)		20	78	8	22	5	0	3	6	.282	7	17	0	23	49	3	.960

ALL-STAR GAME RECORD

Year	League	Pos.	AB	R	H	2B	3B	HR	RBI	Avg.	BB	SO	SB	PO	A	E	Avg.
						BATTING									FIELDING		
1993—	National....................	2B	1	0	0	0	0	0	0	.000	0	0	0	1	1	0	1.000
1999—	National....................	2B	1	0	0	0	0	0	0	.000	1	1	0	0	1	0	1.000
	All-Star Game totals (2 years)		2	0	0	0	0	0	0	.000	1	1	0	1	2	0	1.000

BELL, MIKE   3B

PERSONAL: Born December 7, 1974, in Cincinnati. ... 6-2/210. ... Bats right, throws right. ... Full name: Michael John Bell. ... Son of Buddy Bell, major league third baseman with four teams (1972-89); and manager, Colorado Rockies; brother of David Bell, infielder, Seattle Mariners; and grandson of Gus Bell, major league outfielder with four teams (1950-64).
HIGH SCHOOL: Moeller (Cincinnati).
TRANSACTIONS/CAREER NOTES: Selected by Texas Rangers organization in supplemental round ("sandwich pick" between first and second round, 30th pick overall); pick received as part of compensation for Chicago Cubs signing Type A free-agent Jose Guzman. ... Traded by Rangers to Anaheim Angels for P Matt Perisho (October 31, 1997). ... Selected by Arizona Diamondbacks in second round (55th pick overall) of expansion draft (November 18, 1997). ... Traded by Diamondbacks to New York Mets organization for P Joe Lisio (February 10, 1998). ... On Norfolk disabled list (May 28, 1999-remainder of season). ... Granted free agency (October 15, 1999). ... Signed by Cincinnati Reds organization (November 2, 1999). ... Granted free agency (October 18, 2000).
STATISTICAL NOTES: Led Gulf Coast League with 107 total bases in 1993. ... Led Gulf Coast League third basemen with 144 assists and 191 total chances in 1993. ... Led South Atlantic League third basemen with 51 errors in 1994. ... Led Texas League third basemen with 392 total chances and tied for lead with 28 double plays in 1996.

Year	Team (League)	Pos.	G	AB	R	H	2B	3B	HR	RBI	Avg.	BB	SO	SB	PO	A	E	Avg.
							BATTING									FIELDING		
1993—	GC Rangers (GCL)......	3B-2B	*60	•230	48	*73	13	6	3	34	.317	27	23	9	36	†145	12	.938
1994—	Char., S.C. (SAL)........	3B-2B	120	475	58	125	22	6	6	58	.263	47	76	16	96	213	†53	.854
1995—	Charlotte (FSL)..........	3B	129	470	49	122	20	1	5	52	.260	48	72	9	91	280	*35	.914
1996—	Tulsa (Texas)............	3B	128	484	62	129	31	3	16	59	.267	42	75	3	*90	*277	25	*.936
1997—	Oklahoma City (A.A.)..2B-3B-DH-1B		93	328	35	77	18	2	5	38	.235	29	78	4	128	190	20	.941
—	Tulsa (Texas)............	3B	33	123	17	35	11	0	8	23	.285	15	28	0	28	55	9	.902
1998—	Norfolk (I.L.)■........	3B-1B	17	44	6	8	1	0	2	8	.182	8	7	0	2	16	9	.667
—	St. Lucie (FSL)	2B-OF-3B	18	63	11	22	5	2	1	14	.349	8	10	2	29	34	5	.926
—	Binghamton (East.) ...2B-3B-DH-OF		78	275	47	73	14	1	14	56	.265	35	50	3	100	136	12	.952
1999—	Norfolk (I.L.)...........	2B-1B-DH	39	135	11	37	11	1	1	25	.274	9	23	4	137	47	6	.968
2000—	Louisville (I.L.)■........	3B	115	429	70	115	29	2	22	78	.268	45	76	0	68	*228	23	.928
—	Cincinnati (N.L.)........	3B	19	27	5	6	0	0	2	4	.222	4	7	0	2	16	2	.900
	Major League totals (1 year)		19	27	5	6	0	0	2	4	.222	4	7	0	2	16	2	.900

BELL, ROB   P   REDS

PERSONAL: Born January 17, 1977, in Newburgh, N.Y. ... 6-5/225. ... Throws right, bats right. ... Full name: Robert Allen Bell.
HIGH SCHOOL: Marlboro (N.Y.) Central.
TRANSACTIONS/CAREER NOTES: Selected by Atlanta Braves organization in third round of free-agent draft (June 1, 1995). ... Traded by Braves with OF Michael Tucker and P Denny Neagle to Cincinnati Reds for 2B Bret Boone and P Mike Remlinger (November 10, 1998). ... On Chattanooga disabled list (April 20-July 20, 1999).

Year League	W	L	Pct.	ERA	G	GS	CG	ShO	Sv.	IP	H	R	ER	BB	SO
1995—Gulf Coast Braves (GCL)	1	6	.143	6.88	10	8	0	0	0	34	38	29	26	14	33
1996—Eugene (N'West)	5	6	.455	5.11	16	•16	0	0	0	81	89	49	46	29	74
1997—Macon (S.Atl.)	•14	7	.667	3.68	27	27	1	0	0	146 2/3	144	72	60	41	140
1998—Danville (Caro.)	7	9	.438	3.28	28	28	2	0	0	*178 1/3	169	79	65	46	*197
1999—Chattanooga (Sou.)■	3	6	.333	3.13	12	12	2	1	0	72	75	30	25	17	68
—Gulf Coast Reds (GCL)	0	0	...	1.13	2	2	0	0	0	8	3	1	1	0	11
2000—Cincinnati (N.L.)	7	8	.467	5.00	26	26	1	0	0	140 1/3	130	84	78	73	112
—Louisville (I.L.)	4	0	1.000	3.73	6	6	0	0	0	41	35	18	17	13	47
Major League totals (1 year)	7	8	.467	5.00	26	26	1	0	0	140 1/3	130	84	78	73	112

BELLE, ALBERT   OF   ORIOLES

PERSONAL: Born August 25, 1966, in Shreveport, La. ... 6-2/225. ... Bats right, throws right. ... Full name: Albert Jojuan Belle. ... Formerly known as Joey Belle.
HIGH SCHOOL: Huntington (Shreveport, La.).
COLLEGE: Louisiana State.
TRANSACTIONS/CAREER NOTES: Selected by Cleveland Indians organization in second round of free-agent draft (June 2, 1987). ... On suspended list (July 12-18, 1991; August 4-8, 1992; June 4-7, 1993; August 1-7, 1994; and June 21-22, 1996). ... Granted free agency (October 28, 1996). ... Signed by Chicago White Sox (November 19, 1996). ... Granted free agency (October 27, 1998). ... Signed by Baltimore Orioles (December 1, 1998).
RECORDS: Shares major league records for fewest double plays by outfielder (150 or more games)—0 (1996 and 1997); and most home runs in two consecutive games—5 (September 18 [2] and 19 [3], 1995). ... Shares major league single-game record for most doubles—4 (August 29, 1999; and September 23, 1999). ... Shares A.L. single-season record for fewest errors by outfielder who led league in errors—8 (1998).
HONORS: Named outfielder on THE SPORTING NEWS A.L. All-Star team (1993-96 and 1998). ... Named outfielder on THE SPORTING NEWS A.L. Silver Slugger team (1993-96 and 1998). ... Named Major League Player of the Year by THE SPORTING NEWS (1995).
STATISTICAL NOTES: Hit three home runs in one game (September 4, 1992; September 19, 1995; and July 25, 1999). ... Led A.L. with 14 sacrifice flies in 1993. ... Led A.L. outfielders with seven double plays in 1993. ... Led A.L. in total bases with 294 in 1994 and 377 in 1995. ... Led A.L. with .690 slugging percentage in 1995. ... Led A.L. in grounding into double plays with 24 in 1995. ... Had 21-game hitting streak (April 27-May 21, 1996). ... Had 27-game hitting streak (May 3-June 1, 1997). ... Led A.L. in grounding into double plays with 26 in 1997. ... Led A.L. with 399 total bases, 15 sacrifice flies and .655 slugging percentage in 1998. ... Had 15-game hitting streak (September 1-17, 1999). ... Career major league grand slams: 13.
MISCELLANEOUS: Holds Cleveland Indians all-time record for most home runs (242).

Year Team (League)	Pos.	G	AB	R	H	2B	3B	HR	RBI	Avg.	BB	SO	SB	PO	A	E	Avg.
1987—Kinston (Caro.)	OF	10	37	5	12	2	0	3	9	.324	8	16	0	5	0	0	1.000
1988—Kinston (Caro.)	OF	41	153	21	46	16	0	8	39	.301	18	45	2	43	5	5	.906
—Waterloo (Midw.)	OF	9	28	2	7	1	0	1	2	.250	1	9	0	11	1	0	1.000
1989—Canton/Akron (East.)	OF	89	312	48	88	20	0	20	69	.282	32	82	8	136	4	3	.979
—Cleveland (A.L.)	OF-DH	62	218	22	49	8	4	7	37	.225	12	55	2	92	3	2	.979
1990—Cleveland (A.L.)	DH-OF	9	23	1	4	0	0	1	3	.174	1	6	0	0	0	0	...
—Colo. Springs (PCL)	OF	24	96	16	33	3	1	5	19	.344	5	16	4	31	0	2	.939
—Canton/Akron (East.)	DH	9	32	4	8	1	0	0	3	.250	3	7	0	...	...	...	...
1991—Cleveland (A.L.)	OF-DH	123	461	60	130	31	2	28	95	.282	25	99	3	170	8	•9	.952
—Colo. Springs (PCL)	OF	16	61	9	20	3	2	2	16	.328	2	8	1	19	1	1	.952
1992—Cleveland (A.L.)	DH-OF	153	585	81	152	23	1	34	112	.260	52	128	8	94	1	3	.969
1993—Cleveland (A.L.)	OF-DH	159	594	93	172	36	3	38	*129	.290	76	96	23	338	16	5	.986
1994—Cleveland (A.L.)	OF-DH	106	412	90	147	35	2	36	101	.357	58	71	9	205	8	6	.973
1995—Cleveland (A.L.)	OF-DH	143	546	•121	173	•52	1	*50	•126	.317	73	80	5	304	7	6	.981
1996—Cleveland (A.L.)	OF-DH	158	602	124	187	38	3	48	*148	.311	99	87	11	309	11	10	.970
1997—Chicago (A.L.)■	OF-DH	161	634	90	174	45	1	30	116	.274	53	105	4	351	1	10	.972
1998—Chicago (A.L.)	OF-DH	163	609	113	200	48	2	49	152	.328	81	84	6	316	11	8	.970
1999—Baltimore (A.L.)■	OF-DH	161	610	108	181	36	1	37	117	.297	101	82	17	252	•17	4	.985
2000—Baltimore (A.L.)	OF-DH	141	559	71	157	37	1	23	103	.281	52	68	0	211	8	3	.986
Major League totals (12 years)		1539	5853	974	1726	389	21	381	1239	.295	683	961	88	2642	91	66	.976

DIVISION SERIES RECORD

Year Team (League)	Pos.	G	AB	R	H	2B	3B	HR	RBI	Avg.	BB	SO	SB	PO	A	E	Avg.
1995—Cleveland (A.L.)	OF	3	11	3	3	1	0	1	3	.273	4	3	0	7	0	1	.875
1996—Cleveland (A.L.)	OF	4	15	2	3	0	0	2	6	.200	4	2	1	11	1	0	1.000
Division series totals (2 years)		7	26	5	6	1	0	3	9	.231	8	5	1	18	1	1	.950

CHAMPIONSHIP SERIES RECORD

Year Team (League)	Pos.	G	AB	R	H	2B	3B	HR	RBI	Avg.	BB	SO	SB	PO	A	E	Avg.
1995—Cleveland (A.L.)	OF	5	18	1	4	1	0	1	1	.222	3	5	0	4	0	2	.667

WORLD SERIES RECORD

Year Team (League)	Pos.	G	AB	R	H	2B	3B	HR	RBI	Avg.	BB	SO	SB	PO	A	E	Avg.
1995—Cleveland (A.L.)	OF	6	17	4	4	0	0	2	4	.235	7	5	0	10	0	1	.909

Year	League	Pos.	AB	R	H	2B	3B	HR	RBI	Avg.	BB	SO	SB	PO	A	E	Avg.
										BATTING					FIELDING		
1993—American	PH-DH	1	2	1	0	0	0	1	1.000	1	0	0	...	...	...	...
1994—American	OF	2	0	0	0	0	0	0	.000	0	0	0	1	0	0	1.000
1995—American	OF	3	0	0	0	0	0	0	.000	0	1	0	1	0	0	1.000
1996—American	OF	4	0	0	0	0	0	0	.000	0	3	0	1	0	0	1.000
1997—American								Did not play.								
All-Star Game totals (4 years)		10	2	1	0	0	0	1	.100	1	4	0	3	0	0	1.000

BELLHORN, MARK — 3B — ATHLETICS

PERSONAL: Born August 23, 1974, in Boston. ... 6-1/190. ... Bats both, throws right. ... Full name: Mark Christian Bellhorn.
HIGH SCHOOL: Oviedo (Fla.).
COLLEGE: Auburn.
TRANSACTIONS/CAREER NOTES: Selected by Oakland Athletics organization in second round of free agent draft (June 1, 1995). ... On Vancouver disabled list (April 8-July 29, 1999). ... On Sacramento disabled list (May 12-24, 2000).
STATISTICAL NOTES: Tied for Arizona League lead with two intentional bases on balls received in 1999.

Year	Team (League)	Pos.	G	AB	R	H	2B	3B	HR	RBI	Avg.	BB	SO	SB	PO	A	E	Avg.
									BATTING						FIELDING			
1995—Modesto (Calif.)	SS	56	229	35	59	12	0	6	31	.258	27	52	5	94	172	21	.927
1996—Huntsville (Sou.)	IF	131	468	84	117	24	5	10	71	.250	73	124	19	208	344	32	.945
1997—Edmonton (PCL)	2B-SS-3B-DH	70	241	54	79	18	3	11	46	.328	64	59	6	105	187	13	.957
—Oakland (A.L.)	3B-2B-DH-SS	68	224	33	51	9	1	6	19	.228	32	70	7	72	123	9	.956
1998—Edmonton (PCL)	3-2-DH-S-1	87	309	57	77	20	4	10	44	.249	62	90	6	95	205	11	.965
—Oakland (A.L.)	3B-DH-SS-2B	11	12	1	1	1	0	0	1	.083	3	4	2	3	7	0	1.000
1999—Ariz. Athletics (Ariz.)	2B-DH	12	43	11	10	3	0	0	5	.233	11	9	0	22	17	0	1.000
—Midland (Texas)	2B	17	57	12	17	3	0	2	8	.298	11	13	1	30	41	2	.973
2000—Sacramento (PCL)	3B-2B-SS-1B	117	436	*111	116	17	11	24	73	.266	*94	121	20	111	216	15	.956
—Oakland (A.L.)	2B-3B-SS	9	13	2	2	0	0	0	0	.154	2	6	0	0	5	0	1.000
Major League totals (3 years)		88	249	36	54	10	1	6	20	.217	37	80	9	75	135	9	.959

BELLIARD, RON — 2B — BREWERS

PERSONAL: Born July 4, 1976, in Bronx, N.Y. ... 5-8/180. ... Bats right, throws right. ... Full name: Ronald Belliard. ... Name pronounced BELL-ee-ard.
HIGH SCHOOL: Central (Miami).
TRANSACTIONS/CAREER NOTES: Selected by Milwaukee Brewers organization in eighth round of free-agent draft (June 2, 1994).
STATISTICAL NOTES: Led Midwest League second basemen with 25 errors in 1995. ... Led Pacific Coast League second basemen with 229 putouts, 358 assists, 24 errors and 611 total chances and tied for league lead with 92 double plays in 1997. ... Led International League second basemen with 401 assists and 98 double plays in 1998. ... Led N.L. second basemen with 793 total chances and 130 double plays in 2000.

Year	Team (League)	Pos.	G	AB	R	H	2B	3B	HR	RBI	Avg.	BB	SO	SB	PO	A	E	Avg.
									BATTING						FIELDING			
1994—Ariz. Brewers (Ariz.)	2B-3B-SS	39	143	32	42	7	3	0	27	.294	14	25	7	54	119	12	.935
1995—Beloit (Midw.)	2B-3B	130	461	76	137	28	5	13	76	.297	36	67	16	221	346	†26	.956
1996—El Paso (Texas)	2B-DH	109	416	73	116	20	8	3	57	.279	60	51	26	246	314	16	.972
1997—Tucson (PCL)	2B-SS	118	443	80	125	35	4	4	55	.282	61	69	10	†233	†369	†26	.959
1998—Louisville (I.L.)	2B-SS	133	507	*114	163	36	7	14	73	.321	69	77	33	231	†408	14	.979
—Milwaukee (N.L.)	2B	8	5	1	1	0	0	0	0	.200	0	0	0	0	0	0	...
1999—Louisville (I.L.)	2B	29	108	14	26	4	0	1	8	.241	14	13	12	51	66	3	.975
—Milwaukee (N.L.)	2B-3B-SS	124	457	60	135	29	4	8	58	.295	64	59	4	250	333	13	.978
2000—Milwaukee (N.L.)	2B	152	571	83	150	30	9	8	54	.263	82	84	7	*336	437	*19	.976
Major League totals (3 years)		284	1033	144	286	59	13	16	112	.277	146	143	11	586	770	32	.977

BELLINGER, CLAY — OF/IF — YANKEES

PERSONAL: Born November 18, 1968, in Oneonta, N.Y. ... 6-3/215. ... Bats right, throws right. ... Full name: Clayton Daniel Bellinger.
HIGH SCHOOL: Oneonta (N.Y.).
COLLEGE: Rollins.
TRANSACTIONS/CAREER NOTES: Selected by San Francisco Giants organization in second round of free-agent draft (June 5, 1989). ... Granted free agency (October 16, 1995). ... Signed by Baltimore Orioles organization (November 22, 1995). ... Granted free agency (October 15, 1996). ... Signed by New York Yankees organization (November 4, 1996).

Year	Team (League)	Pos.	G	AB	R	H	2B	3B	HR	RBI	Avg.	BB	SO	SB	PO	A	E	Avg.
									BATTING						FIELDING			
1989—Everett (N'West)	SS	51	185	29	37	8	1	4	16	.200	19	47	3	57	110	24	.874
1990—Clinton (Midw.)	SS-3B	109	383	52	83	17	4	10	48	.217	27	102	13	144	229	29	.928
1991—San Jose (Calif.)	SS	105	368	65	95	29	2	8	62	.258	53	88	13	157	297	32	.934
1992—Shreveport (Texas)	SS	126	433	45	90	18	3	13	50	.208	36	82	7	183	346	*41	.928
1993—Phoenix (PCL)	3B-SS-1B	122	407	50	104	20	3	6	49	.256	38	81	7	123	272	28	.934
1994—Phoenix (PCL)	3-2-DH-3-2-C	106	337	48	90	15	1	7	50	.267	18	56	6	248	140	8	.980
1995—Phoenix (PCL)	S-3-0-2-1-C	97	277	34	76	16	1	2	32	.274	27	52	3	116	145	8	.970
1996—Rochester (I.L.)■	SS-1B-2B	125	459	68	138	34	4	15	78	.301	33	90	8	445	228	22	.968
1997—Columbus (I.L.)■	2B-S	111	416	55	114	31	3	12	59	.274	34	74	10	187	137	15	.956
1998—Columbus (I.L.)	1-S-3-2-0-C	115	397	35	89	20	2	9	40	.224	35	79	6	342	185	14	.974
1999—New York (A.L.)	3-1-D-0-2-S	32	45	12	9	2	0	1	2	.200	1	10	1	23	18	0	1.000
—Columbus (I.L.)	3-S-0-2-1	40	141	19	33	10	1	2	14	.234	13	32	6	68	89	2	.987
2000—New York (A.L.)	0-2-3-1-S	98	184	33	38	8	2	6	21	.207	17	48	5	127	87	5	.977
—Columbus (I.L.)	1B-OF-SS-C	8	28	3	9	2	0	2	2	.321	2	5	1	38	3	1	.976
Major League totals (2 years)		130	229	45	47	10	2	7	23	.205	18	58	6	150	105	5	.981

DIVISION SERIES RECORD

Year	Team (League)	Pos.	G	AB	R	H	2B	3B	HR	RBI	Avg.	BB	SO	SB	PO	A	E	Avg.
1999—	New York (A.L.)	PR-DH	1	0	0	0	0	0	0	0	...	0	0	0	...	...	...	...
2000—	New York (A.L.)	OF	2	1	0	1	1	0	0	1	1.000	0	0	0	0	0	0	...
	Division series totals (2 years)		3	1	0	1	1	0	0	1	1.000	0	0	0	0	0	0	...

CHAMPIONSHIP SERIES RECORD

Year	Team (League)	Pos.	G	AB	R	H	2B	3B	HR	RBI	Avg.	BB	SO	SB	PO	A	E	Avg.
1999—	New York (A.L.)	PH-SS-PR-DH	3	1	0	0	0	0	0	0	.000	0	1	0	0	1	0	1.000
2000—	New York (A.L.)	OF-PR	5	1	0	0	0	0	0	0	.000	0	1	0	1	0	0	1.000
	Championship series totals (2 years)		8	2	0	0	0	0	0	0	.000	0	2	0	1	1	0	1.000

WORLD SERIES RECORD

NOTES: Member of World Series championship team (1999 and 2000).

Year	Team (League)	Pos.	G	AB	R	H	2B	3B	HR	RBI	Avg.	BB	SO	SB	PO	A	E	Avg.
1999—	New York (A.L.)							Did not play.										
2000—	New York (A.L.)	PR-OF	4	0	0	0	0	0	0	0	...	0	0	0	2	0	0	1.000

RECORD AS PITCHER

Year	League	W	L	Pct.	ERA	G	GS	CG	ShO	Sv.	IP	H	R	ER	BB	SO
1994—	Phoenix (PCL)	0	0	...	9.00	2	0	0	0	0	2	6	2	2	0	0
1998—	Columbus (I.L.)	0	0	...	0.00	1	0	0	0	0	$1/3$	1	0	0	1	0

BELTRAN, CARLOS — OF — ROYALS

PERSONAL: Born April 24, 1977, in Manati, Puerto Rico. ... 6-1/190. ... Bats both, throws right. ... Full name: Carlos Ivan Beltran.
HIGH SCHOOL: Fernando Callejas (Manati, Puerto Rico).
TRANSACTIONS/CAREER NOTES: Selected by Kansas City Royals organization in second round of free-agent draft (June 1, 1995). ... On Kansas City disabled list (July 4-September 4, 2000); included rehabilitation assignments to Gulf Coast Royals (August 21-24), Wilmington (August 25-30) and Omaha (August 31-September 4).
HONORS: Named A.L. Rookie Player of the Year by THE SPORTING NEWS (1999). ... Named A.L. Rookie of the Year by Baseball Writers' Association of America (1999).
STATISTICAL NOTES: Led A.L. outfielders with 423 total chances in 1999. ... Switch-hit home runs in one game (June 29, 2000).

Year	Team (League)	Pos.	G	AB	R	H	2B	3B	HR	RBI	Avg.	BB	SO	SB	PO	A	E	Avg.
1995—	GC Royals (GCL)	OF	52	180	29	50	9	0	0	23	.278	13	30	5	79	6	2	.977
1996—	Lansing (Midw.)	OF	11	42	3	6	2	0	0	0	.143	1	11	1	28	2	2	.938
	— Spokane (N'West)	OF	59	215	29	58	8	3	7	29	.270	31	65	10	99	6	7	.938
1997—	Wilmington (Caro.)	OF	120	419	57	96	15	4	11	46	.229	46	96	17	236	7	8	.968
1998—	Wilmington (Caro.)	OF	52	192	32	53	14	0	5	32	.276	25	39	11	109	4	2	.983
	— Wichita (Texas)	OF	47	182	50	64	13	3	14	44	.352	23	30	7	93	2	4	.960
	— Kansas City (A.L.)	OF	14	58	12	16	5	3	0	7	.276	3	12	3	44	0	1	.978
1999—	Kansas City (A.L.)	OF-DH	156	663	112	194	27	7	22	108	.293	46	123	27	395	16	*12	.972
2000—	Kansas City (A.L.)	OF-DH	98	372	49	92	15	4	7	44	.247	35	69	13	231	5	6	.975
	— GC Royals (GCL)		1	4	3	2	1	0	1	1	.500	1	0	0	0	0	0	...
	— Wilmington (Caro.)	OF	3	13	2	4	0	1	2	6	.308	0	5	0	2	0	0	1.000
	— Omaha (PCL)	OF	5	18	4	6	1	0	2	2	.333	3	3	1	6	0	0	1.000
	Major League totals (3 years)		268	1093	173	302	47	14	29	159	.276	84	204	43	670	21	19	.973

BELTRAN, RIGO — P — PHILLIES

PERSONAL: Born November 13, 1969, in Tijuana, Mexico. ... 5-11/200. ... Throws left, bats left. ... Full name: Rigoberto Beltran.
HIGH SCHOOL: Point Loma (San Diego).
COLLEGE: Wyoming.
TRANSACTIONS/CAREER NOTES: Selected by St. Louis Cardinals organization in 26th round of free-agent draft (June 3, 1991). ... Traded by Cardinals to New York Mets for P Juan Acevedo (March 29, 1998). ... Traded by Mets with OF Brian McRae and OF Thomas Johnson to Colorado Rockies for OF Darryl Hamilton and P Chuck McElroy (July 31, 1999). ... Granted free agency (October 18, 2000). ... Signed by Philadelphia Phillies organization (December 20, 2000).
STATISTICAL NOTES: Led New York-Pennsylvania League with 12 balks in 1991. ... Led American Association with 18 wild pitches in 1994.
MISCELLANEOUS: Grounded out in only appearance as pinch hitter with Colorado (1999).

Year	League	W	L	Pct.	ERA	G	GS	CG	ShO	Sv.	IP	H	R	ER	BB	SO
1991—	Hamilton (NY-Penn)	5	2	.714	2.63	21	4	0	0	0	48	41	17	14	19	69
1992—	Savannah (S.Atl.)	6	1	.857	2.17	13	13	2	1	0	83	38	20	20	40	106
	— St. Petersburg (FSL)	0	0	...	0.00	2	2	0	0	0	8	6	0	0	2	3
1993—	Arkansas (Texas)	5	5	.500	3.25	18	16	0	0	0	$88 2/3$	74	39	32	38	82
1994—	Arkansas (Texas)	4	0	1.000	0.64	4	4	1	1	0	28	12	2	2	3	21
	— Louisville (A.A.)	11	11	.500	5.07	23	23	1	0	0	$138 1/3$	147	82	78	68	87
1995—	Louisville (A.A.)	8	9	.471	5.21	24	24	0	0	0	$129 2/3$	156	81	75	34	92
1996—	Louisville (A.A.)	8	6	.571	4.35	38	16	3	1	0	$130 1/3$	132	67	63	24	132
1997—	Louisville (A.A.)	5	2	.714	2.32	9	8	1	0	0	$54 1/3$	45	17	14	21	46
	— St. Louis (N.L.)	1	2	.333	3.48	35	4	0	0	1	$54 1/3$	47	25	21	17	50
1998—	Norfolk (I.L.)■	6	5	.545	4.29	36	11	0	0	1	$94 1/3$	104	51	45	40	98
	— New York (N.L.)	0	0	...	3.38	7	0	0	0	0	8	6	3	3	4	5
1999—	Norfolk (I.L.)	2	1	.667	1.61	21	0	0	0	0	$22 1/3$	16	5	4	12	27
	— New York (N.L.)	1	1	.500	3.48	21	0	0	0	0	31	30	15	12	12	35
	— Colorado Springs (PCL)■	1	0	1.000	2.25	6	0	0	0	0	8	12	3	2	5	12
	— Colorado (N.L.)	0	0	...	7.36	12	0	0	0	0	11	20	9	9	7	15
2000—	Colorado Springs (PCL)	6	10	.375	5.90	25	21	1	1	0	125	132	85	82	63	95
	— Colorado (N.L.)	0	0	...	40.50	1	1	0	0	0	$1 1/3$	6	6	6	3	1
	Major League totals (4 years)	2	3	.400	4.34	76	5	0	0	1	$105 2/3$	109	58	51	43	106

PERSONAL: Born April 7, 1979, in Santo Domingo, Dominican Republic. ... 5-11/170. ... Bats right, throws right. ... Full name: Adrian Perez Beltre. ... Name pronounced bell-TREE.

HIGH SCHOOL: Liceo Maximo Gomez (Santo Domingo, Dominican Republic).

TRANSACTIONS/CAREER NOTES: Signed as non-drafted free agent by Los Angeles Dodgers (July 7, 1994). ... On San Bernardino disabled list (June 25-July 2, 1996). ... On Albuquerque disabled list (April 23-May 1 and May 12-19, 1998). ... On disabled list (May 28-June 17, 2000).

HONORS: Named Florida State League Most Valuable Player (1997).

STATISTICAL NOTES: Led Florida State League with .561 slugging percentage and 12 intentional bases on balls in 1997. ... Led Florida State League third basemen with 26 double plays in 1997. ... Led N.L. third basemen with 116 putouts and 412 total chances in 2000. ... Career major league grand slams: 2.

								BATTING							FIELDING		
Year Team (League)	Pos.	G	AB	R	H	2B	3B	HR	RBI	Avg.	BB	SO	SB	PO	A	E	Avg.
1995— Dom. Dodgers (DSL) .	3B	62	218	56	67	15	3	8	40	.307	54	26	2	187	31	19	.920
1996— Savannah (S.Atl.)	3B-2B	68	244	48	75	14	3	16	59	.307	35	46	4	55	143	19	.912
— San Bern. (Calif.)........	3B-DH	63	238	40	62	13	1	10	40	.261	19	44	3	32	110	7	.953
1997— Vero Beach (FSL).......	3B-OF	123	435	95	138	24	2	*26	*104	.317	67	66	25	83	231	37	.895
1998— San Antonio (Texas)...	3B-DH	64	246	49	79	21	2	13	56	.321	39	37	20	41	130	17	.910
— Los Angeles (N.L.)	3B-SS	77	195	18	42	9	0	7	22	.215	14	37	3	32	131	13	.926
1999— Los Angeles (N.L.)	3B	152	538	84	148	27	5	15	67	.275	61	105	18	121	274	•29	.932
2000— Los Angeles (N.L.)	3B-SS	138	510	71	148	30	2	20	85	.290	56	80	12	117	273	23	.944
Major League totals (3 years)		367	1243	173	338	66	7	42	174	.272	131	222	33	270	678	65	.936

PERSONAL: Born January 20, 1970, in Bluefields, Nicaragua. ... 5-9/185. ... Bats left, throws left. ... Full name: Marvin Larry Benard. ... Name pronounced buh-NARD.

HIGH SCHOOL: Bell (Bell Gardens, Calif.).

JUNIOR COLLEGE: Los Angeles Harbor College.

COLLEGE: Lewis-Clark State (Idaho).

TRANSACTIONS/CAREER NOTES: Selected by Philadelphia Phillies organization in 20th round of free-agent draft (June 4, 1990); did not sign. ... Selected by San Francisco Giants organization in 50th round of free-agent draft (June 1, 1992). ... On disabled list (April 17-28, 1993).

STATISTICAL NOTES: Tied for Texas League lead in grounding into double plays with 15 in 1994. ... Led Texas League outfielders with five double plays in 1994.

								BATTING							FIELDING		
Year Team (League)	Pos.	G	AB	R	H	2B	3B	HR	RBI	Avg.	BB	SO	SB	PO	A	E	Avg.
1992— Everett (N'West)........	OF	64	161	31	38	10	2	1	17	.236	24	39	17	90	8	3	.970
1993— Clinton (Midw.)	OF	112	349	84	105	14	2	5	50	.301	56	66	42	179	10	5	.974
1994— Shreveport (Texas).....	OF	125	454	66	143	32	3	4	48	.315	31	58	24	259	17	*12	.958
1995— Phoenix (PCL)	OF-DH	111	378	70	115	14	6	6	32	.304	50	66	10	183	5	8	.959
— San Francisco (N.L.) ...	OF	13	34	5	13	2	0	1	4	.382	1	7	1	19	0	0	1.000
1996— Phoenix (PCL)	OF	4	19	2	7	0	0	0	4	.368	2	2	1	10	0	0	1.000
— San Francisco (N.L.) ...	OF	135	488	89	121	17	4	5	27	.248	59	84	25	309	7	5	.984
1997— Phoenix (PCL)	OF-DH	84	114	13	26	4	0	1	13	.228	13	29	3	27	2	1	.967
— San Francisco (N.L.) ..	OF	17	60	14	20	5	0	0	5	.333	11	9	4	26	2	1	.966
1998— San Francisco (N.L.) ..	OF-DH	121	286	41	92	21	1	3	36	.322	34	39	11	109	1	2	.982
1999— San Francisco (N.L.) ..	OF	149	562	100	163	36	5	16	64	.290	55	97	27	323	5	4	.988
2000— San Francisco (N.L.) ..	OF	149	560	102	147	27	6	12	55	.263	63	97	22	323	11	1	.997
Major League totals (6 years)		651	2044	350	562	107	16	38	199	.275	225	353	89	1110	26	13	.989

DIVISION SERIES RECORD

								BATTING							FIELDING		
Year Team (League)	Pos.	G	AB	R	H	2B	3B	HR	RBI	Avg.	BB	SO	SB	PO	A	E	Avg.
1997— San Francisco (N.L.) ..	PH	2	2	0	0	0	0	0	0	.000	0	1	0	...	...	...	...
2000— San Francisco (N.L.) ..	OF-PH	4	14	0	1	0	0	0	1	.071	1	7	0	12	0	0	1.000
Division series totals (2 years)		6	16	0	1	0	0	0	1	.063	1	8	0	12	0	0	1.000

PERSONAL: Born January 21, 1972, in Evansville, Ind. ... 6-5/235. ... Throws right, bats right. ... Full name: Alan Paul Benes. ... Brother of Andy Benes, pitcher, St. Louis Cardinals; and brother of Adam Benes, pitcher, Cardinals organization. ... Name pronounced BEN-es.

HIGH SCHOOL: Lake Forest (Ill.).

COLLEGE: Creighton.

TRANSACTIONS/CAREER NOTES: Selected by San Diego Padres organization in 49th round of free-agent draft (June 4, 1990); did not sign. ... Selected by St. Louis Cardinals organization in first round (16th pick overall) of free-agent draft (June 3, 1993). ... On Louisville disabled list (May 3-August 9, 1995). ... On disabled list (July 31, 1997-remainder of season; and March 22, 1998-entire season). ... On St. Louis disabled list (March 26-September 5, 1999); included rehabilitation assignments to Arkansas (August 5-10 and August 26-30), Potomac (August 11-15 and August 31-September 3) and Memphis (August 16-25 and September 4-5).

HONORS: Named N.L. Rookie Pitcher of the Year by THE SPORTING NEWS (1996).

Year League	W	L	Pct.	ERA	G	GS	CG	ShO	Sv.	IP	H	R	ER	BB	SO
1993— Glens Falls (NY-Penn)	0	4	.000	3.65	7	7	0	0	0	37	39	20	15	14	29
1994— Savannah (S.Atl.)	2	0	1.000	1.48	4	4	0	0	0	24 1/3	21	5	4	7	24
— St. Petersburg (FSL)	7	1	.875	1.61	11	11	0	0	0	78 1/3	55	18	14	15	69
— Arkansas (Texas).............	7	2	.778	2.98	13	13	1	0	0	87 2/3	58	38	29	26	75
— Louisville (A.A.)................	1	0	1.000	2.93	2	2	1	0	0	15 1/3	10	5	5	4	16
1995— Louisville (A.A.)................	4	2	.667	2.41	11	11	2	1	0	56	37	16	15	14	54
— St. Louis (N.L.).................	1	2	.333	8.44	3	3	0	0	0	16	24	15	15	4	20

Year League	W	L	Pct.	ERA	G	GS	CG	ShO	Sv.	IP	H	R	ER	BB	SO
1996— St. Louis (N.L.).................	13	10	.565	4.90	34	32	3	1	0	191	192	120	104	87	131
1997— St. Louis (N.L.).................	9	9	.500	2.89	23	23	2	0	0	161²/₃	128	60	52	68	160
1998— St. Louis (N.L.).................							Did not play.								
1999— Arkansas (Texas)..............	0	0	...	6.23	2	2	0	0	0	4¹/₃	6	3	3	1	0
— Potomac (Caro.)................	0	0	...	1.80	2	2	0	0	0	5	1	1	1	4	2
— Memphis (PCL)................	0	1	.000	3.18	3	3	0	0	0	5²/₃	8	3	2	2	3
— St. Louis (N.L.)................	0	0	...	0.00	2	0	0	0	0	2	2	0	0	0	2
2000— Memphis (PCL)................	1	2	.333	5.95	9	8	0	0	0	39¹/₃	45	31	26	21	26
— St. Louis (N.L.)................	2	2	.500	5.67	30	0	0	0	0	46	54	33	29	23	26
Major League totals (5 years).......	25	23	.521	4.32	92	58	5	1	0	416²/₃	400	228	200	182	339

CHAMPIONSHIP SERIES RECORD

Year League	W	L	Pct.	ERA	G	GS	CG	ShO	Sv.	IP	H	R	ER	BB	SO
1996— St. Louis (N.L.).................	0	1	.000	2.84	2	1	0	0	0	6¹/₃	3	2	2	3	5

B

BENES, ANDY — P — CARDINALS

PERSONAL: Born August 20, 1967, in Evansville, Ind. ... 6-6/245. ... Throws right, bats right. ... Full name: Andrew Charles Benes. ... Brother of Alan Benes, pitcher, St. Louis Cardinals; and brother of Adam Benes, pitcher, Cardinals organization. ... Name pronounced BEN-es.
HIGH SCHOOL: Central (Evansville, Ind.).
COLLEGE: Evansville.
TRANSACTIONS/CAREER NOTES: Selected by San Diego Padres organization in first round (first pick overall) of free-agent draft (June 1, 1988). ... On suspended list (September 28, 1993-remainder of season). ... Traded by Padres with a player to be named later to Seattle Mariners for P Ron Villone and OF Marc Newfield (July 31, 1995); Mariners acquired P Greg Keagle to complete deal (September 16, 1995). ... Granted free agency (October 31, 1995). ... Signed by St. Louis Cardinals (December 23, 1995). ... On St. Louis disabled list (March 23-April 28, 1997); included rehabilitation assignments to Prince William (April 11), Louisville (April 16) and Arkansas (April 22). ... Granted free agency (October 29, 1997). ... Signed by Arizona Diamondbacks (February 3, 1998). ... Granted free agency (October 29, 1999). ... Signed by Cardinals (January 7, 2000). ... On disabled list (August 15-September 3, 2000).
RECORDS: Holds major league single-season record for fewest hits allowed for leader in most hits allowed—230 (1992). ... Shares major league record for most home runs allowed in one inning—4 (July 23, 2000, second inning).
HONORS: Named N.L. Rookie Pitcher of the Year by THE SPORTING NEWS (1989). ... Named Texas League Pitcher of the Year (1989).
STATISTICAL NOTES: Tied for N.L. lead with five balks in 1990. ... Pitched 7-0 one-hit, complete-game victory against New York (July 3, 1994).
MISCELLANEOUS: Holds San Diego Padres all-time record for most strikeouts (1,036). ... Member of 1988 U.S. Olympic baseball team (1988). ... Made an out in only appearance as pinch hitter (1998).

Year League	W	L	Pct.	ERA	G	GS	CG	ShO	Sv.	IP	H	R	ER	BB	SO
1989— Wichita (Texas)	8	4	.667	2.16	16	16	5	*3	0	108¹/₃	79	32	26	39	115
— Las Vegas (PCL)	2	1	.667	8.10	5	5	0	0	0	26²/₃	41	29	24	12	29
— San Diego (N.L.)	6	3	.667	3.51	10	10	0	0	0	66²/₃	51	28	26	31	66
1990— San Diego (N.L.)	10	11	.476	3.60	32	31	2	0	0	192¹/₃	177	87	77	69	140
1991— San Diego (N.L.)	15	11	.577	3.03	33	33	4	1	0	223	194	76	75	59	167
1992— San Diego (N.L.)	13	14	.481	3.35	34	34	2	2	0	231¹/₃	*230	90	86	61	169
1993— San Diego (N.L.)	15	15	.500	3.78	34	34	4	2	0	230²/₃	200	111	97	86	179
1994— San Diego (N.L.)	6	*14	.300	3.86	25	25	2	2	0	172¹/₃	155	82	74	51	*189
1995— San Diego (N.L.)	4	7	.364	4.17	19	19	1	1	0	118²/₃	121	65	55	45	126
— Seattle (A.L.)■..............	7	2	.778	5.86	12	12	0	0	0	63	72	42	41	33	45
1996— St. Louis (N.L.)■..............	18	10	.643	3.83	36	34	3	1	1	230¹/₃	215	107	98	77	160
1997— Prince William (Caro.)........	0	0	...	0.00	1	1	0	0	0	5	3	1	0	1	9
— Louisville (A.A.)..............	0	0	...	1.80	1	1	0	0	0	5	3	1	1	1	5
— Arkansas (Texas)..............	1	0	1.000	1.29	1	1	0	0	0	7	2	1	1	2	6
— St. Louis (N.L.)..............	10	7	.588	3.10	26	26	0	0	0	177	149	64	61	61	175
1998— Arizona (N.L.)■..............	14	13	.519	3.97	34	34	1	0	0	231¹/₃	221	111	102	74	164
1999— Arizona (N.L.)..............	13	12	.520	4.81	33	32	0	0	0	198¹/₃	216	117	106	82	141
2000— St. Louis (N.L.)..............	12	9	.571	4.88	30	27	1	0	0	166	174	95	90	68	137
A.L. totals (1 year)	7	2	.778	5.86	12	12	0	0	0	63	72	42	41	33	45
N.L. totals (12 years)	136	126	.519	3.81	346	339	20	9	1	2238	2103	1033	947	764	1813
Major League totals (12 years).....	143	128	.528	3.86	358	351	20	9	1	2301	2175	1075	988	797	1858

DIVISION SERIES RECORD

Year League	W	L	Pct.	ERA	G	GS	CG	ShO	Sv.	IP	H	R	ER	BB	SO
1995— Seattle (A.L.)	0	0	...	5.40	2	2	0	0	0	11²/₃	10	7	7	9	8
1996— St. Louis (N.L.)....................	0	0	...	5.14	1	1	0	0	0	7	6	4	4	1	9
2000— St. Louis (N.L.)....................							Did not play.								
Division series totals (2 years)	0	0	...	5.30	3	3	0	0	0	18²/₃	16	11	11	10	17

CHAMPIONSHIP SERIES RECORD

RECORDS: Shares N.L. single-series record for most hits allowed—19 (1996).

Year League	W	L	Pct.	ERA	G	GS	CG	ShO	Sv.	IP	H	R	ER	BB	SO
1995— Seattle (A.L.)	0	1	.000	23.14	1	1	0	0	0	2¹/₃	6	6	6	2	3
1996— St. Louis (N.L.)....................	0	0	...	5.28	3	2	0	0	0	15¹/₃	19	9	9	3	9
2000— St. Louis (N.L.)....................	1	0	1.000	2.25	1	1	0	0	0	8	6	2	2	3	5
Champ. series totals (3 years)	1	1	.500	5.96	5	4	0	0	0	25²/₃	31	17	17	8	17

ALL-STAR GAME RECORD

Year League	W	L	Pct.	ERA	GS	CG	ShO	Sv.	IP	H	R	ER	BB	SO
1993— National	0	0	...	4.50	0	0	0	0	2	2	1	1	0	2

BENITEZ, ARMANDO — P — METS

PERSONAL: Born November 3, 1972, in Ramon Santana, Dominican Republic. ... 6-4/229. ... Throws right, bats right.

TRANSACTIONS/CAREER NOTES: Signed as non-drafted free agent by Baltimore Orioles organization (April 1, 1990). ... On Baltimore disabled list (April 20-August 26, 1996); included rehabilitation assignments to Bowie (May 17-19) and Gulf Coast Orioles (August 13-26). ... On suspended list (May 20-28, 1998). ... Traded by Orioles to New York Mets for C Charles Johnson (December 1, 1998).

Year League	W	L	Pct.	ERA	G	GS	CG	ShO	Sv.	IP	H	R	ER	BB	SO
1990—															
						Dominican Summer League statistics unavailable.									
1991—Gulf Coast Orioles (GCL)....	3	2	.600	2.72	14	3	0	0	0	36 1/3	35	16	11	11	33
1992—Bluefield (Appl.)	1	2	.333	4.31	25	0	0	0	5	31 1/3	35	31	15	23	37
1993—Albany (S.Atl.)	5	1	.833	1.52	40	0	0	0	14	53 1/3	31	10	9	19	83
—Frederick (Caro.)	3	0	1.000	0.66	12	0	0	0	4	13 2/3	7	1	1	4	29
1994—Bowie (East.)	8	4	.667	3.14	53	0	0	0	16	71 2/3	41	29	25	39	106
—Baltimore (A.L.)	0	0	...	0.90	3	0	0	0	0	10	8	1	1	4	14
1995—Baltimore (A.L.)..................	1	5	.167	5.66	44	0	0	0	2	47 2/3	37	33	30	37	56
—Rochester (I.L.)	2	2	.500	1.25	17	0	0	0	8	21 2/3	10	4	3	7	37
1996—Baltimore (A.L.)	1	0	1.000	3.77	18	0	0	0	4	14 1/3	7	6	6	6	20
—Bowie (East.)	0	0	...	4.50	4	4	0	0	0	6	7	3	3	0	8
—Gulf Coast Orioles (GCL)....	1	0	1.000	0.00	1	0	0	0	0	2	1	0	0	0	5
—Rochester (I.L.)	0	0	...	2.25	2	0	0	0	0	4	3	1	1	1	5
1997—Baltimore (A.L.)	4	5	.444	2.45	71	0	0	0	9	73 1/3	49	22	20	43	106
1998—Baltimore (A.L.)	5	6	.455	3.82	71	0	0	0	22	68 1/3	48	29	29	39	87
1999—New York (N.L.)■	4	3	.571	1.85	77	0	0	0	22	78	40	17	16	41	128
2000—New York (N.L.).................	4	4	.500	2.61	76	0	0	0	41	76	39	24	22	38	106
A.L. totals (5 years)	11	16	.407	3.62	207	0	0	0	37	213 2/3	149	91	86	129	283
N.L. totals (2 years)	8	7	.533	2.22	153	0	0	0	63	154	79	41	38	79	234
Major League totals (7 years)	19	23	.452	3.04	360	0	0	0	100	367 2/3	228	132	124	208	517

DIVISION SERIES RECORD

Year League	W	L	Pct.	ERA	G	GS	CG	ShO	Sv.	IP	H	R	ER	BB	SO
1996—Baltimore (A.L.)..................	2	0	1.000	2.25	3	0	0	0	0	4	1	1	1	2	6
1997—Baltimore (A.L.)..................	0	0	...	3.00	3	0	0	0	0	3	3	1	1	2	4
1999—New York (N.L.).................	0	0	...	0.00	2	0	0	0	0	2 1/3	2	0	0	1	2
2000—New York (N.L.).................	1	0	1.000	6.00	2	0	0	0	0	3	4	2	2	1	3
Division series totals (4 years)	3	0	1.000	2.92	10	0	0	0	0	12 1/3	10	4	4	6	15

CHAMPIONSHIP SERIES RECORD

Year League	W	L	Pct.	ERA	G	GS	CG	ShO	Sv.	IP	H	R	ER	BB	SO
1996—Baltimore (A.L.)..................	0	0	...	7.71	3	0	0	0	1	2 1/3	3	2	2	4	2
1997—Baltimore (A.L.)..................	0	2	.000	12.00	4	0	0	0	0	3	3	4	4	4	6
1999—New York (N.L.).................	0	0	...	1.35	5	0	0	0	1	6 2/3	3	1	1	2	9
2000—New York (N.L.).................	0	0	...	0.00	3	0	0	0	1	3	3	2	0	2	2
Champ. series totals (4 years)	0	2	.000	4.20	15	0	0	0	3	15	12	9	7	12	19

WORLD SERIES RECORD

Year League	W	L	Pct.	ERA	G	GS	CG	ShO	Sv.	IP	H	R	ER	BB	SO
2000—New York (N.L.).................	0	0	...	3.00	3	0	0	0	1	3	3	1	1	2	2

BENJAMIN, MIKE   IF   PIRATES

PERSONAL: Born November 22, 1965, in Euclid, Ohio. ... 6-0/172. ... Bats right, throws right. ... Full name: Michael Paul Benjamin.
HIGH SCHOOL: Bellflower (Calif.).
JUNIOR COLLEGE: Cerritos College (Calif.).
COLLEGE: Arizona State.
TRANSACTIONS/CAREER NOTES: Selected by Minnesota Twins organization in seventh round of free-agent draft (January 9, 1985); did not sign. ... Selected by San Francisco Giants organization in third round of free-agent draft (June 2, 1987). ... On San Francisco disabled list (March 31-June 5, 1992); included rehabilitation assignment to Phoenix (April 20-May 10). ... On San Francisco disabled list (July 8-August 6, 1993); included rehabilitation assignment to San Jose (August 4-6). ... Traded by Giants to Philadelphia Phillies for P Jeff Juden and OF/1B Tommy Eason (October 6, 1995). ... On Philadelphia disabled list (March 23-April 26 and July 20, 1996-remainder of season); included rehabilitation assignments to Clearwater (April 8-17) and Scranton/Wilkes-Barre (April 21-26). ... Granted free agency (October 8, 1996). ... Signed by Boston Red Sox organization (January 31, 1997). ... Granted free agency (October 27, 1997). ... Re-signed by Red Sox (November 21, 1997). ... Granted free agency (October 26, 1998). ... Signed by Pittsburgh Pirates (November 17, 1998). ... On disabled list (July 24-August 11, 1999).
RECORDS: Holds modern major league record for most hits in three consecutive games—14 (June 11 [4], 13 [4] and 14 [6], 1995).
STATISTICAL NOTES: Led Pacific Coast League shortstops with 626 total chances in 1990. ... Collected six hits in one game (June 14, 1995).

Year Team (League)	Pos.	G	AB	R	H	2B	3B	HR	RBI	Avg.	BB	SO	SB	PO	A	E	Avg.
1987—Fresno (Calif.)............	SS	64	212	25	51	6	4	6	24	.241	24	71	6	89	188	21	.930
1988—Shreveport (Texas).....	SS	89	309	48	73	19	5	6	37	.236	22	63	14	134	248	11	.972
—Phoenix (PCL)..........	SS	37	106	13	18	4	1	0	6	.170	13	32	2	41	74	4	.966
1989—Phoenix (PCL)..........	SS-2B	113	363	44	94	17	6	3	36	.259	18	82	10	149	332	15	.970
—San Francisco (N.L.) ..	SS	14	6	6	1	0	0	0	0	.167	0	1	0	4	4	0	1.000
1990—Phoenix (PCL)..........	SS	118	419	61	105	21	7	5	39	.251	25	89	13	*216	*386	24	.962
—San Francisco (N.L.) ..	SS	22	56	7	12	3	1	2	3	.214	3	10	1	29	53	1	.988
1991—San Francisco (N.L.) ..	SS-3B	54	106	12	13	3	0	2	8	.123	7	26	3	64	123	3	.984
—Phoenix (PCL)..........	SS	64	226	34	46	13	2	6	31	.204	20	67	3	109	252	9	.976
1992—San Francisco (N.L.) ..	SS-3B	40	75	4	13	2	1	1	3	.173	4	15	1	34	71	1	.991
—Phoenix (PCL)..........	SS-2B	31	108	15	33	10	2	0	17	.306	3	18	4	51	92	2	.986
1993—San Francisco (N.L.) ..	SS-2B-3B	63	146	22	29	7	0	4	16	.199	9	23	0	74	133	5	.976
—San Jose (Calif.)........	SS-2B	2	8	1	0	0	0	0	0	.000	1	0	0	1	5	0	1.000
1994—San Francisco (N.L.) ..	SS-2B-3B	38	62	9	16	5	1	1	9	.258	5	16	5	33	70	3	.972
1995—San Francisco (N.L.) ..	3B-SS-2B	68	186	19	41	6	0	3	12	.220	8	51	11	51	121	4	.977
1996—Clearwater (FSL)■	SS	8	23	3	4	1	0	0	0	.174	3	4	1	9	20	2	.935
—Scranton/W.B. (I.L.) ..	SS	4	13	2	5	2	0	0	4	.385	3	0	0	3	12	0	1.000
—Philadelphia (N.L.)......	SS-2B	35	103	13	23	5	1	4	13	.223	12	21	3	38	87	6	.954

Year	Team (League)	Pos.	G	AB	R	H	2B	3B	HR	RBI	Avg.	BB	SO	SB	PO	A	E	Avg.
1997—Pawtucket (I.L.)■	......SS-DH-3B-2B		33	105	12	26	4	1	4	12	.248	8	20	4	46	86	5	.964
—Boston (A.L.)	.............3-S-2-1-DH-P		49	116	12	27	9	1	0	7	.233	4	27	2	50	81	6	.956
1998—Boston (A.L.)	............2-S-3-1-DH		124	349	46	95	23	0	4	39	.272	15	73	3	233	275	3	.994
1999—Pittsburgh (N.L.)■	..... SS-2B-3B		110	368	42	91	26	7	1	37	.247	20	90	10	162	334	8	.984
2000—Pittsburgh (N.L.)	........3B-SS-2B-1B		93	233	28	63	18	2	2	19	.270	12	45	5	104	206	4	.987
American League totals (2 years)			173	465	58	122	32	1	4	46	.262	19	100	5	283	356	9	.986
National League totals (10 years)			537	1341	162	302	75	13	20	120	.225	80	298	39	593	1202	35	.981
Major League totals (12 years)			710	1806	220	424	107	14	24	166	.235	99	398	44	876	1558	44	.982

DIVISION SERIES RECORD

Year	Team (League)	Pos.	G	AB	R	H	2B	3B	HR	RBI	Avg.	BB	SO	SB	PO	A	E	Avg.
1998—Boston (A.L.)	....	2B-1B	4	11	1	1	0	0	0	0	.091	1	3	0	13	9	0	1.000

RECORD AS PITCHER

Year	League	W	L	Pct.	ERA	G	GS	CG	ShO	Sv.	IP	H	R	ER	BB	SO
1997—Boston (A.L.)	....	0	0	...	0.00	1	0	0	0	0	1	0	0	0	0	0

BENNETT, GARY — C — PHILLIES

PERSONAL: Born April 17, 1972, in Waukegan, Ill. ... 6-0/208. ... Bats right, throws right. ... Full name: Gary David Bennett Jr.
HIGH SCHOOL: Waukegan East (Ill.).
TRANSACTIONS/CAREER NOTES: Selected by Philadelphia Phillies organization in 11th round of free-agent draft (June 4, 1990). ... On Clearwater disabled list (September 5-15, 1993). ... Granted free agency (October 8, 1996). ... Signed by Boston Red Sox organization (February 10, 1997). ... Granted free agency (October 15, 1997). ... Signed by Phillies organization (December 27, 1997). ... On Scranton/Wilkes-Barre disabled list (June 23-July 4, 2000).
STATISTICAL NOTES: Led Eastern League with 22 passed balls in 1994. ... Led Eastern League catchers with 13 double plays in 1995.

Year	Team (League)	Pos.	G	AB	R	H	2B	3B	HR	RBI	Avg.	BB	SO	SB	PO	A	E	Avg.
1990—Martinsville (Appl.)	.....	C	16	52	3	14	2	1	0	10	.269	4	15	0	80	3	3	.965
1991—Martinsville (Appl.)	.....	C	41	136	15	32	7	0	1	16	.235	17	26	0	291	34	2	.994
1992—Batavia (NY-Penn)	.....	C	47	146	22	30	2	0	0	12	.205	15	27	2	292	42	2	*.994
1993—Spartanburg (S.Atl.)	...	C	42	126	18	32	4	1	0	15	.254	12	22	0	199	35	2	.992
—Clearwater (FSL)	....	C	17	55	5	18	0	0	1	6	.327	3	10	0	70	12	0	1.000
1994—Clearwater (FSL)	....	C	19	55	6	13	3	0	0	10	.236	8	6	0	101	10	1	.991
— Reading (East.)	....	C	63	208	13	48	9	0	3	22	.231	14	26	0	376	64	2	.995
1995—Reading (East.)	....	C-DH	86	271	27	64	11	0	4	40	.236	22	36	0	551	65	4	.994
—Scranton/W.B. (I.L.)	...	C	7	20	1	3	0	0	0	1	.150	2	2	0	38	4	0	1.000
—Philadelphia (N.L.)	......	PH	1	1	0	0	0	0	0	0	.000	0	1	0	...	...	...	...
1996—Scranton/W.B. (I.L.)	...	C	91	286	37	71	15	1	8	37	.248	24	43	1	517	61	7	.988
—Philadelphia (N.L.)	......	C	6	16	0	4	0	0	0	1	.250	2	6	0	35	5	0	1.000
1997—Pawtucket (I.L.)■	......	C-1B	71	224	16	48	7	1	4	22	.214	18	39	1	528	36	8	.986
1998—Scranton/W.B. (I.L.)■		C-DH-1B	86	282	33	72	18	0	10	40	.255	25	41	0	425	35	1	.998
—Philadelphia (N.L.)	......	C	9	31	4	9	0	0	0	3	.290	5	5	0	50	2	0	1.000
1999—Philadelphia (N.L.)	......	C	36	88	7	24	4	0	1	21	.273	4	11	0	129	6	4	.971
2000—Scranton/W.B. (I.L.)	.....	C	92	317	47	97	24	0	12	52	.306	40	44	1	483	34	2	*.996
—Philadelphia (N.L.)	......	C	31	74	8	18	5	0	2	5	.243	13	15	0	173	11	1	.995
Major League totals (5 years)			83	210	19	55	9	0	3	30	.262	24	38	0	387	24	5	.988

BENOIT, JOAQUIN — P — RANGERS

PERSONAL: Born July 26, 1979, in Santiago, Dominican Republic. ... 6-3/160. ... Throws right, bats right. ... Full name: Joaquin Antonio Benoit.
TRANSACTIONS/CAREER NOTES: Signed as non-drafted free agent by Texas Rangers organization (May 20, 1996). ... On Tulsa disabled list (May 2-June 21, 2000).

Year	League	W	L	Pct.	ERA	G	GS	CG	ShO	Sv.	IP	H	R	ER	BB	SO
1996—Dominican Rangers (DSL)	.	6	5	.545	2.28	14	13	2	1	0	75	63	26	19	23	63
1997—Gulf Coast Rangers (GCL)	..	3	3	.500	2.05	10	10	1	0	0	44	40	14	10	11	38
1998—Savannah (S.Atl.)	....	4	3	.571	3.83	15	1	0	0	0	80	79	41	34	18	68
1999—Charlotte (FSL)	....	7	4	.636	5.31	22	22	0	0	0	105	117	67	62	50	83
2000—Tulsa (Texas)	....	4	4	.500	3.83	16	16	0	0	0	$82\frac{1}{3}$	73	40	35	30	72

BENSON, KRIS — P — PIRATES

PERSONAL: Born November 7, 1974, in Superior, Wis. ... 6-4/200. ... Throws right, bats right. ... Full name: Kristen James Benson.
HIGH SCHOOL: Spayberry (Marietta, Ga.).
COLLEGE: Clemson.
TRANSACTIONS/CAREER NOTES: Selected by Pittsburgh Pirates organization in first round (first pick overall) of free-agent draft (June 2, 1996).
STATISTICAL NOTES: Tied for N.L. lead in double plays by a pitcher with six in 1999.
MISCELLANEOUS: Member of 1996 U.S. Olympic baseball team.

Year	League	W	L	Pct.	ERA	G	GS	CG	ShO	Sv.	IP	H	R	ER	BB	SO
1997—Lynchburg (Caro.)	....	5	2	.714	2.58	10	10	0	0	0	$59\frac{1}{3}$	49	20	17	13	72
—Carolina (Sou.)	....	3	5	.375	4.98	14	14	0	0	0	$68\frac{2}{3}$	81	49	38	32	66
1998—Nashville (PCL)	....	8	10	.444	5.37	28	28	1	1	0	156	162	102	93	50	129
1999—Pittsburgh (N.L.)	....	11	14	.440	4.07	31	31	2	0	0	$196\frac{2}{3}$	184	105	89	83	139
2000—Pittsburgh (N.L.)	....	10	12	.455	3.85	32	32	2	1	0	$217\frac{2}{3}$	206	104	93	86	184
Major League totals (2 years)	....	21	26	.447	3.95	63	63	4	1	0	$414\frac{1}{3}$	390	209	182	169	323

PERSONAL: Born May 26, 1971, in Cambridge, Mass. ... 6-3/215. ... Throws right, bats right. ... Full name: Jason Phillip Bere. ... Name pronounced burr-AY.
HIGH SCHOOL: Wilmington (Mass.).
JUNIOR COLLEGE: Middlesex Community College (Mass.).
TRANSACTIONS/CAREER NOTES: Selected by Chicago White Sox organization in 36th round of free-agent draft (June 4, 1990). ... On Chicago disabled list (August 5-20, 1995); included rehabilitation assignment to South Bend (August 13-18). ... On Chicago disabled list (April 22-September 3 and September 14, 1996-remainder of season); included rehabilitation assignments to Nashville (May 14-19 and August 27-28), Gulf Coast White Sox (August 5-10), Hickory (August 10-16) and Birmingham (August 16-27). ... On Chicago disabled list (March 31-August 19, 1997); included rehabilitation assignments to Gulf Coast White Sox (July 2-7), Hickory (July 12), Birmingham (July 17-22) and Nashville (July 29-August 14). ... Released by White Sox (July 16, 1998). ... Signed by Cincinnati Reds organization (July 21, 1998). ... On Cincinnati disabled list (June 16-August 4, 1999); included rehabilitation assignment to Indianapolis (July 11-August 4). ... Released by Reds (August 4, 1999). ... Signed by Milwaukee Brewers organization (August 12, 1999). ... Granted free agency (November 1, 1999). ... Re-signed by Brewers (November 19, 1999). ... Traded by Brewers with P Bob Wickman and P Steve Woodard to Cleveland Indians for 1B/OF Richie Sexson, P Paul Rigdon, P Kane Davis and a player to be named later (July 28, 2000); Brewers acquired 2B Marcos Scutaro to complete deal (August 30). ... Granted free agency (October 31, 2000). ... Signed by Chicago Cubs (December 18, 2000).

Year	League	W	L	Pct.	ERA	G	GS	CG	ShO	Sv.	IP	H	R	ER	BB	SO
1990—	GC White Sox (GCL)	0	4	.000	2.37	16	2	0	0	1	38	26	19	10	19	41
1991—	South Bend (Midw.)	9	12	.429	2.87	27	27	2	1	0	163	116	66	52	*100	158
1992—	Sarasota (FSL)	7	2	.778	2.41	18	18	1	1	0	116	84	35	31	34	106
	—Birmingham (Sou.)	4	4	.500	3.00	8	8	4	2	0	54	44	22	18	20	45
	—Vancouver (PCL)	0	0	...	0.00	1	0	0	0	0	1	2	0	0	0	2
1993—	Nashville (A.A.)	5	1	.833	2.37	8	8	0	0	0	49 1/3	36	19	13	25	52
	—Chicago (A.L.)	12	5	.706	3.47	24	24	1	0	0	142 2/3	109	60	55	81	129
1994—	Chicago (A.L.)	12	2	*.857	3.81	24	24	0	0	0	141 2/3	119	65	60	80	127
1995—	Chicago (A.L.)	8	•15	.348	7.19	27	27	1	0	0	137 2/3	151	120	110	106	110
	—Nashville (A.A.)	1	0	1.000	3.38	1	1	0	0	0	5 1/3	6	2	2	2	7
1996—	Chicago (A.L.)	0	1	.000	10.26	5	5	0	0	0	16 2/3	26	19	19	18	19
	—Nashville (A.A.)	0	0	...	1.42	3	3	0	0	0	12 2/3	9	2	2	4	15
	—GC White Sox (GCL)	0	1	.000	6.00	1	1	0	0	0	3	3	2	2	1	3
	—Hickory (S.Atl.)	1	0	1.000	0.00	1	1	0	0	0	5	3	0	0	0	5
	—Birmingham (Sou.)	0	0	...	4.15	1	1	0	0	0	4 1/3	4	2	2	4	5
1997—	GC White Sox (GCL)	0	0	...	0.00	2	2	0	0	0	5	2	0	0	0	5
	—Hickory (S.Atl.)	0	0	...	6.00	1	1	0	0	0	3	4	2	2	0	2
	—Birmingham (Sou.)	0	1	.000	7.71	2	2	0	0	0	7	8	7	6	2	7
	—Nashville (A.A.)	1	1	.500	5.59	4	4	0	0	0	19 1/3	23	13	12	7	13
	—Chicago (A.L.)	4	2	.667	4.71	6	6	0	0	0	28 2/3	20	15	15	17	21
1998—	Chicago (A.L.)	3	7	.300	6.45	18	15	0	0	0	83 2/3	98	71	60	58	53
	—Cincinnati (N.L.)■	3	2	.600	4.12	9	7	0	0	0	43 2/3	39	20	20	20	31
1999—	Cincinnati (N.L.)	3	0	1.000	6.85	12	10	0	0	0	43 1/3	56	37	33	40	28
	—Indianapolis (I.L.)	0	2	.000	10.19	5	4	0	0	0	17 2/3	25	20	20	19	8
	—Louisville (I.L.)■	2	1	.667	2.08	5	5	0	0	0	26	21	8	6	8	27
	—Milwaukee (N.L.)	2	0	1.000	4.63	5	4	0	0	0	23 1/3	23	15	12	10	19
2000—	Milwaukee (N.L.)	6	7	.462	4.93	20	20	0	0	0	115	115	66	63	63	98
	—Cleveland (A.L.)■	6	3	.667	6.63	11	11	0	0	0	54 1/3	65	41	40	26	44
A.L. totals (7 years)		45	35	.563	5.34	115	112	2	0	0	605 1/3	588	391	359	386	503
N.L. totals (3 years)		14	9	.609	5.11	46	41	0	0	0	225 1/3	233	138	128	133	176
Major League totals (8 years)		59	44	.573	5.28	161	153	2	0	0	830 2/3	821	529	487	519	679

CHAMPIONSHIP SERIES RECORD

Year	League	W	L	Pct.	ERA	G	GS	CG	ShO	Sv.	IP	H	R	ER	BB	SO
1993—	Chicago (A.L.)	0	0	...	11.57	1	1	0	0	0	2 1/3	5	3	3	2	3

ALL-STAR GAME RECORD

Year	League	W	L	Pct.	ERA	GS	CG	ShO	Sv.	IP	H	R	ER	BB	SO
1994—	American	0	1	.000	...	0	0	0	0	2	1	1	1	0	0

PERSONAL: Born September 3, 1970, in Roseville, Calif. ... 5-11/185. ... Bats right, throws right. ... Full name: David Scott Berg.
HIGH SCHOOL: Roseville (Calif.).
JUNIOR COLLEGE: Sacramento City College.
COLLEGE: Miami (Fla.).
TRANSACTIONS/CAREER NOTES: Selected by California Angels organization in 32nd round of free-agent draft (June 4, 1990); did not sign. ... Selected by Florida Marlins organization in 38th round of free-agent draft (June 3, 1993). ... On Florida disabled list (April 2-25, 2000); included rehabilitation assignment to Brevard County (April 22-25).
STATISTICAL NOTES: Led New York-Penn League third basemen with 158 assists in 1993. ... Led Midwest League third basemen with .948 fielding percentage in 1994.

Year	Team (League)	Pos.	G	AB	R	H	2B	3B	HR	RBI	Avg.	BB	SO	SB	PO	A	E	Avg.
											BATTING					FIELDING		
1993—	Elmira (NY-Penn)	3B-2B-OF	75	281	37	74	13	1	4	28	.263	34	37	7	55	†193	20	.925
1994—	Kane County (Midw.)	3B-2B	121	437	80	117	27	8	9	53	.268	54	80	8	73	236	17	†.948
1995—	Brevard County (FSL)	SS-3B-2B	114	382	71	114	18	1	3	39	.298	68	61	9	157	348	26	.951
1996—	Portland (East.)	SS-3B	109	414	64	125	28	5	9	73	.302	42	60	17	143	358	26	.951
1997—	Charlotte (I.L.)	SS-2B-3B	117	424	76	125	26	6	9	47	.295	55	71	16	136	324	22	.954
1998—	Florida (N.L.)	2B-3B-SS	81	182	18	57	11	0	2	21	.313	26	46	3	90	130	7	.969
1999—	Florida (N.L.)	S-2-3-O	109	304	42	87	18	1	3	25	.286	27	59	2	103	195	8	.974
2000—	Brevard County (FSL)	2B-3B-SS	3	11	2	3	0	0	0	2	.273	1	3	0	6	7	0	1.000
	—Florida (N.L.)	SS-3B-2B	82	210	23	53	14	1	1	21	.252	25	46	3	71	142	8	.964
Major League totals (3 years)			272	696	83	197	43	2	6	67	.283	78	151	8	264	467	23	.969

BERGERON, PETER — OF — EXPOS

PERSONAL: Born November 9, 1977, in Greenfield, Mass. ... 6-0/185. ... Bats left, throws right. ... Full name: Peter Francis Bergeron.
HIGH SCHOOL: Greenfield (Mass.).
TRANSACTIONS/CAREER NOTES: Selected by Los Angeles Dodgers organization in fourth round of free-agent draft (June 4, 1996). ... Traded by Dodgers with 2B Wilton Guerrero, P Ted Lilly and 1B Jonathan Tucker to Montreal Expos for P Carlos Perez, SS Mark Grudzielanek and OF Hiram Bocachica (July 31, 1998).
STATISTICAL NOTES: Led Texas League outfielders with five double plays in 1998.

											BATTING						FIELDING		
Year — Team (League)	Pos.	G	AB	R	H	2B	3B	HR	RBI	Avg.	BB	SO	SB	PO	A	E	Avg.		
1996—Yakima (N'West)	OF	61	232	36	59	5	3	5	21	.254	28	59	13	99	3	1	*.990		
1997—Savannah (S.Atl.)	OF	131	492	89	138	18	5	5	36	.280	67	110	32	240	8	4	.984		
—San Bern. (Calif.)	OF	2	8	1	2	0	0	1	.250	0	2	2	5	1	0	1.000		
1998—San Antonio (Texas) ...	OF	109	416	81	132	17	8	8	54	.317	61	69	33	228	17	2	*.992		
—Harrisburg (East.)■	OF	34	134	22	33	8	4	0	9	.246	17	26	8	67	5	0	1.000		
1999—Harrisburg (East.)	OF-DH	42	162	29	53	14	2	4	18	.327	24	29	9	72	1	1	.986		
—Ottawa (I.L.)	OF-DH	58	194	36	61	12	3	3	20	.314	23	40	14	64	8	2	.973		
—Montreal (N.L.)	OF	16	45	12	11	2	0	0	1	.244	9	5	0	27	2	1	.967		
2000—Montreal (N.L.)	OF	148	518	80	127	25	7	5	31	.245	58	100	11	303	*16	5	.985		
Major League totals (2 years)		164	563	92	138	27	7	5	32	.245	67	105	11	330	18	6	.983		

BERGMAN, SEAN — P — DEVIL RAYS

PERSONAL: Born April 11, 1970, in Joliet, Ill. ... 6-4/225. ... Throws right, bats right. ... Full name: Sean Frederick Bergman.
HIGH SCHOOL: Joliet (Ill.) Catholic Academy.
COLLEGE: Southern Illinois-Carbondale.
TRANSACTIONS/CAREER NOTES: Selected by Detroit Tigers organization in fourth round of free-agent draft (June 3, 1991). ... On Detroit disabled list (June 26-July 17, 1995); included rehabilitation assignment to Toledo (July 10-17). ... Traded by Tigers with P Cade Gaspar and OF Todd Steverson to San Diego Padres for P Richie Lewis, OF Melvin Nieves and C Raul Casanova (March 22, 1996). ... Traded by Padres to Houston Astros for OF James Mouton (January 14, 1998). ... On Houston disabled list (June 27-August 6, 1999); included rehabilitation assignment to New Orleans (July 25-August 1). ... Released by Astros (August 31, 1999). ... Signed by Atlanta Braves (September 5, 1999). ... Claimed on waivers by Minnesota Twins (October 12, 1999). ... Released by Twins (June 22, 2000). ... Signed by Florida Marlins organization (June 26, 2000). ... Granted free agency (October 18, 2000). ... Signed by Tampa Bay Devil Rays organization (November 22, 2000).
MISCELLANEOUS: Fouled out in only appearance as pinch hitter and appeared in one game as pinch runner (1996).

Year — League	W	L	Pct.	ERA	G	GS	CG	ShO	Sv.	IP	H	R	ER	BB	SO
1991—Niagara Falls (NY-Penn)	5	7	.417	4.46	15	15	0	0	0	84²/₃	87	57	42	42	77
1992—Lakeland (FSL)	5	2	.714	2.49	13	13	0	0	0	83	61	28	23	14	67
—London (East.)	4	7	.364	4.28	14	14	1	0	0	88¹/₃	85	52	42	45	59
1993—Toledo (I.L.)	8	9	.471	4.38	19	19	3	0	0	117	124	62	57	53	91
—Detroit (A.L.)	1	4	.200	5.67	9	6	1	0	0	39²/₃	47	29	25	23	19
1994—Toledo (I.L.)	11	8	.579	3.72	25	25	2	0	0	154²/₃	147	77	64	53	145
—Detroit (A.L.)	2	1	.667	5.60	3	3	0	0	0	17²/₃	22	11	11	7	12
1995—Detroit (A.L.)	7	10	.412	5.12	28	28	1	1	0	135¹/₃	169	95	77	67	86
—Toledo (I.L.)	0	1	.000	6.00	1	1	0	0	0	3	4	2	2	0	4
1996—San Diego (N.L.)■	6	8	.429	4.37	41	14	0	0	0	113¹/₃	119	63	55	33	85
1997—San Diego (N.L.)	2	4	.333	6.09	44	9	0	0	0	99	126	72	67	38	74
1998—Houston (N.L.)■	12	9	.571	3.72	31	27	1	0	0	172	183	81	71	42	100
1999—Houston (N.L.)	4	6	.400	5.36	19	16	2	1	0	99	130	60	59	26	38
—New Orleans (PCL)	0	1	.000	9.95	3	1	0	0	0	6¹/₃	9	8	7	2	2
—Atlanta (N.L.)■.................	1	0	1.000	2.84	6	0	0	0	0	6¹/₃	5	2	2	3	6
2000—Minnesota (A.L.)■	4	5	.444	9.66	15	14	0	0	0	68	111	76	73	33	35
—Calgary (PCL)■.................	4	3	.571	5.73	13	13	0	0	0	81²/₃	107	55	52	23	48
A.L. totals (4 years)	14	20	.412	6.42	55	51	2	1	0	260²/₃	349	211	186	130	152
N.L. totals (4 years)	25	27	.481	4.67	141	66	3	1	0	489²/₃	563	278	254	142	303
Major League totals (8 years)	39	47	.453	5.28	196	117	5	2	0	750¹/₃	912	489	440	272	455

DIVISION SERIES RECORD

Year — League	W	L	Pct.	ERA	G	GS	CG	ShO	Sv.	IP	H	R	ER	BB	SO
1998—Houston (N.L.)							Did not play.								

BERKMAN, LANCE — OF — ASTROS

PERSONAL: Born February 10, 1976, in Waco, Texas. ... 6-1/205. ... Bats both, throws left. ... Full name: William Lance Berkman.
HIGH SCHOOL: Canyon (New Braunfels, Texas).
COLLEGE: Rice.
TRANSACTIONS/CAREER NOTES: Selected by Houston Astros organization in first round (16th pick overall) of free-agent draft (June 3, 1997). ... On New Orleans disabled list (April 13-May 14, 1999).
HONORS: Named first baseman on THE SPORTING NEWS college All-America first team (1997).
STATISTICAL NOTES: Led Texas League with 10 intentional bases on balls in 1998.

											BATTING						FIELDING		
Year — Team (League)	Pos.	G	AB	R	H	2B	3B	HR	RBI	Avg.	BB	SO	SB	PO	A	E	Avg.		
1997—Kissimmee (FSL)........	OF-DH	53	184	31	54	10	0	12	35	.293	37	38	2	70	2	0	1.000		
1998—Jackson (Texas)	OF-DH	122	425	82	130	34	0	24	89	.306	85	82	6	183	9	4	.980		
—New Orleans (PCL).....	OF	17	59	14	16	4	0	6	13	.271	12	16	0	30	0	0	1.000		
1999—New Orleans (PCL).....	OF-1B-DH	64	226	42	73	20	0	8	49	.323	39	47	7	135	6	4	.972		
—Houston (N.L.)	OF-1B	34	93	10	22	2	0	4	15	.237	12	21	5	43	0	2	.956		
2000—New Orleans (PCL).....	OF-1B	31	112	18	37	4	2	6	27	.330	31	20	4	103	7	2	.982		
—Houston (N.L.)	OF-1B	114	353	76	105	28	1	21	67	.297	56	73	6	176	7	6	.968		
Major League totals (2 years)		148	446	86	127	30	1	25	82	.285	68	94	11	219	7	8	.966		

BERNERO, ADAM   P   TIGERS

PERSONAL: Born November 28, 1976, in San Jose, Calif. ... 6-4/205. ... Throws right, bats right. ... Full name: Adam G. Bernero.
HIGH SCHOOL: John F. Kennedy (Sacramento, Calif.).
COLLEGE: Armstrong Atlantic State (Ga.).
TRANSACTIONS/CAREER NOTES: Signed as non-drafted free agent by Detroit Tigers organization (May 21, 1999). ... On Jacksonville disabled list (April 10-28, 2000).

Year League	W	L	Pct.	ERA	G	GS	CG	ShO	Sv.	IP	H	R	ER	BB	SO
1999— West Michigan (Midw.)	8	4	.667	2.54	15	15	2	1	0	95²/₃	75	36	27	23	80
2000— Jacksonville (Sou.)	2	5	.286	2.79	10	10	0	0	0	61¹/₃	54	26	19	24	46
— Toledo (I.L.)	3	1	.750	2.47	7	7	1	1	0	47¹/₃	34	16	13	10	37
— Detroit (A.L.)	0	1	.000	4.19	12	4	0	0	0	34¹/₃	33	18	16	13	20
Major League totals (1 year)	0	1	.000	4.19	12	4	0	0	0	34¹/₃	33	18	16	13	20

BERROA, GERONIMO   OF/DH

PERSONAL: Born March 18, 1965, in Santo Domingo, Dominican Republic. ... 6-0/210. ... Bats right, throws right. ... Full name: Geronimo Emiliano Berroa. ... Name pronounced her-ON-i-mo bur-OH-uh.
TRANSACTIONS/CAREER NOTES: Signed as non-drafted free agent by Toronto Blue Jays organization (September 4, 1983). ... Selected by Atlanta Braves from Blue Jays organization in Rule 5 major league draft (December 5, 1988). ... Released by Braves (February 1, 1991). ... Signed by Seattle Mariners organization (February 27, 1991). ... Contract sold by Mariners to Cleveland Indians organization (March 28, 1991). ... Granted free agency (October 15, 1991). ... Signed by Cincinnati Reds organization (October 31, 1991). ... Released by Reds (November 20, 1992). ... Signed by Florida Marlins (December 9, 1992). ... Granted free agency (October 15, 1993). ... Signed by Oakland Athletics organization (January 20, 1994). ... On disabled list (August 2, 1994-remainder of season). ... Traded by A's to Baltimore Orioles for P Jimmy Haynes and a player to be named later (June 27, 1997); A's acquired P Mark Seaver to complete deal (September 2, 1997). ... Granted free agency (December 21, 1997). ... Signed by Cleveland Indians (January 29, 1998). ... On Cleveland disabled list (May 3-June 3, 1998). ... Traded by Indians to Detroit Tigers for P Tim Worrell and OF Dave Roberts (June 24, 1998). ... Granted free agency (October 23, 1998). ... Signed by Blue Jays organization (December 14, 1998). ... On Toronto disabled list (May 2-June 15 and June 29-August 30, 1999; included rehabilitation assignments to Syracuse (May 20-27 and June 5-13) and Dunedin (August 25-30). ... Released by Blue Jays (August 30, 1999). ... Signed by Los Angeles Dodgers organization (February 1, 2000). ... On disabled list (June 3, 2000-remainder of season). ... Granted free agency (October 14, 2000).
RECORDS: Shares major league single-season record for most games with three home runs—2 (1996).
STATISTICAL NOTES: Led Southern League with 297 total bases in 1987. ... Led International League in being hit by pitch with 10 and tied for lead in sacrifice flies with eight in 1988. ... Led International League in grounding into double plays with 17 in 1990. ... Hit three home runs in one game (May 22 and August 12, 1996). ... Career major league grand slams: 2.

Year Team (League)	Pos.	G	AB	R	H	2B	3B	HR	RBI	Avg.	BB	SO	SB	PO	A	E	Avg.
1984— GC Blue Jays (GCL)	OF-1B	62	235	31	59	16	1	3	34	.251	12	34	2	104	2	5	.955
1985— Kinston (Caro.)	OF	19	43	4	8	0	0	1	4	.186	4	10	0	13	1	1	.933
— Medicine Hat (Pio.)	OF	54	201	39	69	*22	2	6	45	.343	18	40	7	58	3	3	.953
— Florence (S.Atl.)	OF	19	66	7	21	2	0	3	20	.318	6	13	0	24	0	2	.923
1986— Ventura (Calif.)	OF	128	459	76	137	22	5	21	73	.298	38	92	12	194	9	14	.935
— Knoxville (Sou.)	OF	1	4	0	0	0	0	0	0	.000	0	1	0	2	0	0	1.000
1987— Knoxville (Sou.)	OF	134	523	87	150	33	3	36	108	.287	46	104	2	236	6	•15	.942
1988— Syracuse (I.L.)	OF	131	470	55	122	•29	1	8	64	.260	38	88	7	243	12	5	.981
1989— Atlanta (N.L.)■	OF	81	136	7	36	4	0	2	9	.265	7	32	0	67	1	2	.971
1990— Richmond (I.L.)	OF	135	499	56	134	17	2	12	80	.269	34	89	4	200	10	7	.968
— Atlanta (N.L.)	OF	7	4	0	0	0	0	0	0	.000	1	1	0	1	0	0	1.000
1991— Colo. Springs (PCL)■	OF	125	478	81	154	31	7	18	91	.322	35	88	2	151	14	5	.971
1992— Nashville (A.A.)■	OF	112	461	73	151	33	2	22	88	.328	32	69	8	194	16	5	.977
— Cincinnati (N.L.)	OF	13	15	2	4	1	0	0	0	.267	2	1	0	2	1	0	1.000
1993— Edmonton (PCL)	OF-1B	90	327	64	107	33	4	16	68	.327	36	71	1	210	10	7	.969
— Florida (N.L.)	OF	14	34	3	4	1	0	0	0	.118	2	7	0	9	1	2	.833
1994— Oakland (A.L.)■	DH-OF-1B	96	340	55	104	18	2	13	65	.306	41	62	7	131	5	1	.993
1995— Oakland (A.L.)	DH-OF	141	546	87	152	22	3	22	88	.278	63	98	7	129	5	4	.971
1996— Oakland (A.L.)	DH-OF	153	586	101	170	32	1	36	106	.290	47	122	0	91	6	2	.980
1997— Oakland (A.L.)	OF-DH	73	261	40	81	12	0	16	42	.310	36	58	3	71	1	1	.986
— Baltimore (A.L.)■	DH-OF	83	300	48	78	13	0	10	48	.260	40	62	1	70	1	3	.959
1998— Cleveland (A.L.)■	OF-DH	20	65	6	13	3	1	0	3	.200	7	17	1	27	1	0	1.000
— Detroit (A.L.)■	DH-OF	52	126	17	30	4	1	1	10	.238	17	27	0	4	0	0	1.000
1999— Toronto (A.L.)■	DH-OF	22	62	11	12	3	0	1	6	.194	9	15	0	4	0	0	1.000
— Syracuse (I.L.)	DH-OF	10	33	7	9	0	0	3	8	.273	8	5	0	15	1	1	.941
— Dunedin (FSL)	OF-DH	4	5	1	1	1	0	0	2	.200	2	1	0	1	0	1	.500
2000— Los Angeles (N.L.)■	OF-1B	24	31	2	8	0	1	0	5	.258	4	8	0	18	2	1	.952
American League totals (6 years)		640	2286	365	640	107	8	99	368	.280	260	461	19	527	19	11	.980
National League totals (5 years)		139	220	14	52	6	1	2	14	.236	16	49	0	97	5	5	.953
Major League totals (11 years)		779	2506	379	692	113	9	101	382	.276	276	510	19	624	24	16	.976

DIVISION SERIES RECORD

Year Team (League)	Pos.	G	AB	R	H	2B	3B	HR	RBI	Avg.	BB	SO	SB	PO	A	E	Avg.
1997— Baltimore (A.L.)	DH-OF	4	13	4	5	1	0	2	2	.385	2	2	0	0	0	0	...

CHAMPIONSHIP SERIES RECORD

Year Team (League)	Pos.	G	AB	R	H	2B	3B	HR	RBI	Avg.	BB	SO	SB	PO	A	E	Avg.
1997— Baltimore (A.L.)	OF-DH	6	21	1	6	2	0	0	3	.286	0	3	0	9	0	0	1.000

B

PERSONAL: Born March 22, 1966, in Santa Monica, Calif. ... 5-11/200. ... Bats right, throws right. ... Full name: Sean Robert Berry.
HIGH SCHOOL: West Torrance (Torrance, Calif.).
COLLEGE: UCLA.
TRANSACTIONS/CAREER NOTES: Selected by Boston Red Sox organization in fourth round of free-agent draft (June 4, 1984); did not sign. ... Selected by Kansas City Royals organization in secondary phase of free-agent draft (January 14, 1986). ... On disabled list (April 16-May 3, 1987). ... Traded by Royals with P Archie Corbin to Montreal Expos for P Bill Sampen and P Chris Haney (August 29, 1992). ... Traded by Expos to Houston Astros for P Dave Veres and C Raul Chavez (December 20, 1995). ... On Houston disabled list (April 7-22 and August 23-September 7, 1997); including rehabilitation assignment to New Orleans (April 18-22). ... Granted free agency (December 21, 1997). ... Re-signed by Astros (January 13, 1998). ... Granted free agency (October 26, 1998). ... Signed by Milwaukee Brewers (December 10, 1998). ... Released by Brewers (June 21, 2000). ... Signed by Red Sox organization (July 23, 2000). ... Released by Red Sox (August 10, 2000). ... Signed by Cleveland Indians organization (August 24, 2000). ... Granted free agency (October 18, 2000).
STATISTICAL NOTES: Led Northwest League third basemen with 11 double plays in 1986. ... Career major league grand slams: 3.

							BATTING							FIELDING		
Year	Team (League)	Pos.	G	AB	R	H	2B	3B	HR	RBI	Avg.	BB	SO	SB	PO	A	E	Avg.
1986—	Eugene (N'West)	3B	65	238	53	76	20	2	5	44	.319	44	72	10	*63	96	21	.883
1987—	Fort Myers (FSL)	3B	66	205	26	52	7	2	2	30	.254	46	65	5	39	101	23	.859
1988—	Baseball City (FSL)	3B-SS-OF	94	304	34	71	6	4	4	30	.234	31	62	24	84	161	28	.897
1989—	Baseball City (FSL)	3-O-2-S	116	399	67	106	19	7	4	44	.266	44	68	37	100	199	24	.926
1990—	Memphis (Sou.)	3B	135	487	73	142	25	4	14	77	.292	44	89	18	79	238	27	.922
	— Kansas City (A.L.)	3B	8	23	2	5	1	1	0	4	.217	2	5	0	7	10	1	.944
1991—	Omaha (A.A.)	3B-SS-2B	103	368	62	97	21	9	11	54	.264	48	70	8	75	206	20	.934
	— Kansas City (A.L.)	3B	31	60	5	8	3	0	0	1	.133	5	23	0	13	52	2	.970
1992—	Omaha (A.A.)	3B	122	439	61	126	22	2	21	77	.287	39	87	6	86	239	21	*.939
	— Montreal (N.L.)■	3B	24	57	5	19	1	0	1	4	.333	1	11	2	10	19	4	.879
1993—	Montreal (N.L.)	3B	122	299	50	78	15	2	14	49	.261	41	70	12	66	153	15	.936
1994—	Montreal (N.L.)	3B	103	320	43	89	19	2	11	41	.278	32	50	14	66	147	14	.938
1995—	Montreal (N.L.)	3B-1B	103	314	38	100	22	1	14	55	.318	25	53	3	76	165	12	.953
1996—	Houston (N.L.)■	3B	132	431	55	121	38	1	17	95	.281	23	58	12	67	194	22	.922
1997—	New Orleans (A.A.)	3B	3	9	1	3	0	0	0	0	.333	3	3	0	0	6	0	1.000
	— Houston (N.L.)	3B-DH	96	301	37	77	24	1	8	43	.256	25	53	1	47	140	16	.921
1998—	Houston (N.L.)	3B-DH	102	299	48	94	17	1	13	52	.314	31	50	3	55	150	10	.953
1999—	Milwaukee (N.L.)■	1B	106	259	26	59	11	1	2	23	.228	17	50	0	438	27	5	.989
2000—	Milwaukee (N.L.)	3B	32	46	1	7	2	0	1	2	.152	4	13	0	3	4	0	1.000
	— Boston (A.L.)■	3B	1	4	0	0	0	0	0	0	.000	0	2	0	0	0	0	...
	— Sarasota (FSL)		1	4	0	1	0	0	0	0	.250	0	2	0	0	0	0	...
	— Pawtucket (I.L.)	3B	16	57	12	21	3	0	2	4	.368	6	17	0	5	9	1	.933
	— Buffalo (I.L.)■	3B	13	48	2	13	0	0	0	8	.271	4	3	1	8	17	3	.893
American League totals (3 years)			40	87	7	13	4	1	0	5	.149	7	30	0	20	62	3	.965
National League totals (9 years)			820	2326	303	644	149	9	81	364	.277	199	408	47	828	999	98	.949
Major League totals (11 years)			860	2413	310	657	153	10	81	369	.272	206	438	47	848	1061	101	.950

DIVISION SERIES RECORD

							BATTING							FIELDING		
Year	Team (League)	Pos.	G	AB	R	H	2B	3B	HR	RBI	Avg.	BB	SO	SB	PO	A	E	Avg.
1997—	Houston (N.L.)	PH	1	0	0	0	0	0	0	0	.000	0	0	0	...	...	...	...
1998—	Houston (N.L.)	3B	1	2	0	0	0	0	0	0	.000	0	1	0	0	2	1	.667
Division series totals (2 years)			2	3	0	0	0	0	0	0	.000	0	1	0	0	2	1	.667

PERSONAL: Born November 18, 1963, in West Palm Beach, Fla. ... 6-2/235. ... Bats right, throws right. ... Full name: Alphonse Dante Bichette. ... Name pronounced bih-SHETT.
HIGH SCHOOL: Jupiter (Fla.).
JUNIOR COLLEGE: Palm Beach Community College (Fla.).
TRANSACTIONS/CAREER NOTES: Selected by California Angels organization in 17th round of free-agent draft (June 4, 1984). ... Traded by Angels to Milwaukee Brewers for DH Dave Parker (March 14, 1991). ... Traded by Brewers to Colorado Rockies for OF Kevin Reimer (November 17, 1992). ... Traded by Rockies with cash to Cincinnati Reds for OF Jeffrey Hammonds and P Stan Belinda (October 30, 1999). ... Traded by Reds to Boston Red Sox for P Chris Reitsma and P John Curtice (August 31, 2000).
HONORS: Named outfielder on THE SPORTING NEWS N.L. All-Star team (1995). ... Named outfielder on THE SPORTING NEWS N.L. Silver Slugger team (1995).
STATISTICAL NOTES: Led A.L. outfielders with seven double plays in 1991. ... Led N.L. outfielders with four double plays in 1994. ... Led N.L. with .620 slugging percentage and 359 total bases in 1995. ... Had 23-game hitting streak (May 22-June 18, 1995). ... Tied for N.L. lead with 10 sacrifice flies in 1996. ... Hit for the cycle (June 10, 1998). ... Tied for N.L. lead with six double plays by outfielder in 1998. ... Tied for N.L. lead with 10 sacrifice flies in 1999. ... Had 17-game hitting streak (June 30-July 23, 2000). ... Career major league grand slams: 8.
MISCELLANEOUS: Holds Colorado Rockies all-time records for most runs (665), hits (1,278), doubles (270) and runs batted in (826).

							BATTING							FIELDING		
Year	Team (League)	Pos.	G	AB	R	H	2B	3B	HR	RBI	Avg.	BB	SO	SB	PO	A	E	Avg.
1984—	Salem (N'West)	OF-1B-3B	64	250	27	58	9	2	4	30	.232	6	53	6	224	24	11	.958
1985—	Quad Cities (Midw.)	1B-OF-C	137	547	58	145	28	4	11	78	.265	25	89	25	300	21	15	.955
1986—	Palm Springs (Calif.)	OF-3B	68	290	39	79	15	0	10	73	.272	21	53	2	78	68	11	.930
	— Midland (Texas)	OF-3B	62	243	43	69	16	2	12	36	.284	18	50	3	131	30	11	.936
1987—	Edmonton (PCL)	OF-3B	92	360	54	108	20	3	13	50	.300	26	68	3	169	21	9	.955
1988—	Edmonton (PCL)	OF	132	509	64	136	29	•10	14	81	.267	25	78	7	218	*22	*15	.941
	— California (A.L.)	OF	21	46	1	12	2	0	0	8	.261	0	7	0	44	2	1	.979
1989—	California (A.L.)	OF-DH	48	138	13	29	7	0	3	15	.210	6	24	3	95	6	1	.990
	— Edmonton (PCL)	OF	61	226	39	55	11	2	11	40	.243	24	39	4	92	9	1	.990
1990—	California (A.L.)	OF	109	349	40	89	15	1	15	53	.255	16	79	5	183	12	7	.965

							BATTING										FIELDING		
Year Team (League)	Pos.	G	AB	R	H	2B	3B	HR	RBI	Avg.	BB	SO	SB	PO	A	E	Avg.
1991—Milwaukee (A.L.)■	OF-3B	134	445	53	106	18	3	15	59	.238	22	107	14	270	14	7	.976
1992—Milwaukee (A.L.)	OF-DH	112	387	37	111	27	2	5	41	.287	16	74	18	188	6	2	.990
1993—Colorado (N.L.)■	OF	141	538	93	167	43	5	21	89	.310	28	99	14	308	14	9	.973
1994—Colorado (N.L.)	OF	*116	*484	74	147	33	2	27	95	.304	19	70	21	211	10	2	.991
1995—Colorado (N.L.)	OF	139	579	102	•197	38	2	*40	*128	.340	22	96	13	208	9	3	.986
1996—Colorado (N.L.)	OF	159	633	114	198	39	3	31	141	.313	45	105	31	255	5	9	.967
1997—Colorado (N.L.)	OF-DH	151	561	81	173	31	2	26	118	.308	30	90	6	225	4	3	.987
1998—Colorado (N.L.)	OF-DH	161	662	97	*219	48	2	22	122	.331	28	76	14	289	14	11	.965
1999—Colorado (N.L.)	OF-DH	151	593	104	177	38	2	34	133	.298	54	84	6	238	17	13	.951
2000—Cincinnati (N.L.)■	OF	125	461	67	136	27	2	16	76	.295	41	69	5	235	11	8	.969
—Boston (A.L.)■	DH	30	114	13	33	5	0	7	14	.289	8	22	0	...	...	...	...
American League totals (6 years)		454	1479	157	380	74	6	45	190	.257	68	313	40	780	40	18	.979
National League totals (8 years)		1143	4511	732	1414	297	20	217	902	.313	267	689	110	1969	84	58	.973
Major League totals (13 years)		1597	5990	889	1794	371	26	262	1092	.299	335	1002	150	2749	124	76	.974

DIVISION SERIES RECORD

RECORDS: Shares N.L. single-series record for most runs scored—6 (1995).

							BATTING										FIELDING		
Year Team (League)	Pos.	G	AB	R	H	2B	3B	HR	RBI	Avg.	BB	SO	SB	PO	A	E	Avg.
1995—Colorado (N.L.)	OF	4	17	6	10	3	0	1	3	.588	1	3	0	9	0	0	1.000

ALL-STAR GAME RECORD

						BATTING									FIELDING		
Year League	Pos.	AB	R	H	2B	3B	HR	RBI	Avg.	BB	SO	SB	PO	A	E	Avg.
1994—National	PH	1	0	1	0	0	0	0	1.000	0	0	0	...	...	...	...
1995—National	OF	1	0	0	0	0	0	0	.000	0	1	0	2	0	0	1.000
1996—National	OF	3	1	1	1	0	0	0	.333	0	1	0	0	0	0	...
1998—National	OF	2	0	0	0	0	0	0	.000	0	1	0	1	0	0	1.000
All-Star Game totals (4 years)		7	1	2	1	0	0	0	.286	0	3	0	3	0	0	1.000

BIERBROLDT, NICK — P — DIAMONDBACKS

PERSONAL: Born May 16, 1978, in Tarzana, Calif. ... 6-5/185. ... Throws left, bats left. ... Full name: Nicholas Raymond Bierbroldt.
HIGH SCHOOL: Millikan (Long Beach, Calif.).
TRANSACTIONS/CAREER NOTES: Selected by Arizona Diamondbacks organization in first round (30th pick overall) of free-agent draft (June 4, 1996). ... On Tucson disabled list (May 4-July 8 and July 23-28, 2000).

Year League	W	L	Pct.	ERA	G	GS	CG	ShO	Sv.	IP	H	R	ER	BB	SO
1996—Ariz. Diamondbacks (Ariz.).	1	1	.500	1.66	8	8	0	0	0	38	25	9	7	13	46
—Lethbridge (Pio.)	2	0	1.000	0.50	3	3	0	0	0	18	12	4	1	5	23
1997—South Bend (Midw.)	2	4	.333	4.04	15	15	0	0	0	75²/₃	77	43	34	37	64
1998—High Desert (Calif.)............	8	7	.533	3.40	24	23	1	0	0	129²/₃	122	66	49	64	88
1999—El Paso (Texas)..................	5	6	.455	4.62	14	14	2	1	0	76	78	45	39	37	55
—Tucson (PCL)	1	4	.200	7.27	11	11	0	0	0	43¹/₃	57	42	35	30	43
2000—Tucson (PCL)	2	1	.667	4.82	4	3	0	0	0	18²/₃	13	10	10	14	11
—Ariz. Diamondbacks (Ariz.).	0	0	...	4.50	4	3	0	0	0	8	4	4	4	5	10
—El Paso (Texas)..................	1	3	.250	7.13	7	7	0	0	0	35¹/₃	37	30	28	24	36

BIGGIO, CRAIG — 2B — ASTROS

PERSONAL: Born December 14, 1965, in Smithtown, N.Y. ... 5-11/180. ... Bats right, throws right. ... Full name: Craig Alan Biggio. ... Name pronounced BEE-jee-oh.
HIGH SCHOOL: Kings Park (N.Y.).
COLLEGE: Seton Hall.
TRANSACTIONS/CAREER NOTES: Selected by Houston Astros organization in first round (22nd pick overall) of free-agent draft (June 2, 1987). ... Granted free agency (October 31, 1995). ... Re-signed by Astros (December 14, 1995). ... On disabled list (August 2, 2000-remainder of season).
RECORDS: Shares N.L. record for most years leading league in games by second baseman—7.
HONORS: Named catcher on THE SPORTING NEWS college All-America team (1987). ... Named catcher on THE SPORTING NEWS N.L. Silver Slugger team (1989). ... Named second baseman on THE SPORTING NEWS N.L. All-Star team (1994-95 and 1997-98). ... Won N.L. Gold Glove at second base (1994-97). ... Named second baseman on THE SPORTING NEWS N.L. Silver Slugger team (1994-95 and 1997-98).
STATISTICAL NOTES: Led N.L. catchers with 889 putouts, 963 total chances and 13 passed balls in 1991. ... Led N.L. in being hit by pitch with 22 in 1995, 27 in 1996 and 34 in 1997. ... Led N.L. second basemen in total chances with 728 in 1995, 811 in 1996 and 863 in 1997. ... Led N.L. second basemen with 359 putouts, 430 assists, 801 total chances and 117 double plays in 1999. ... Had 16-game hitting streak (April 5-26, 2000). ... Career major league grand slams: 2.
MISCELLANEOUS: Holds Houston Astros all-time record for most runs (1,187), hits (1,969) and doubles (402).

							BATTING										FIELDING		
Year Team (League)	Pos.	G	AB	R	H	2B	3B	HR	RBI	Avg.	BB	SO	SB	PO	A	E	Avg.
1987—Asheville (S.Atl.).........	C-OF	64	216	59	81	17	2	9	49	.375	39	33	31	378	46	2	.995
1988—Tucson (PCL)	C-OF	77	281	60	90	21	4	3	41	.320	40	39	19	318	33	6	.983
—Houston (N.L.)	C	50	123	14	26	6	1	3	5	.211	7	29	6	292	28	3	.991
1989—Houston (N.L.)	C-OF	134	443	64	114	21	2	13	60	.257	49	64	21	742	56	9	.989
1990—Houston (N.L.)	C-OF	150	555	53	153	24	2	4	42	.276	53	79	25	657	60	13	.982
1991—Houston (N.L.)	C-2B-OF	149	546	79	161	23	4	4	46	.295	53	71	19	†894	73	11	.989
1992—Houston (N.L.)	2B	•162	613	96	170	32	3	6	39	.277	94	95	38	*344	413	12	.984
1993—Houston (N.L.)	2B	155	610	98	175	41	5	21	64	.287	77	93	15	306	*447	14	.982
1994—Houston (N.L.)	2B	114	437	88	139	*44	5	6	56	.318	62	58	*39	•225	*338	7	.988
1995—Houston (N.L.)	2B	141	553	*123	167	30	2	22	77	.302	80	85	33	299	*419	10	.986

Year Team (League)	Pos.	G	AB	R	H	2B	3B	HR	RBI	Avg.	BB	SO	SB	PO	A	E	Avg.
								BATTING								FIELDING	
1996—Houston (N.L.)	2B	•162	605	113	174	24	4	15	75	.288	75	72	25	*361	*440	10	.988
1997—Houston (N.L.)	2B-DH	•162	619	*146	191	37	8	22	81	.309	84	107	47	*341	*504	18	.979
1998—Houston (N.L.)	2B-DH	160	646	123	210	*51	2	20	88	.325	64	113	50	318	431	15	.980
1999—Houston (N.L.)	2B-OF-DH	160	639	123	188	*56	0	16	73	.294	88	107	28	†365	†431	12	.985
2000—Houston (N.L.)	2B	101	377	67	101	13	5	8	35	.268	61	73	12	181	280	6	.987
Major League totals (13 years)		1800	6766	1187	1969	402	43	160	741	.291	847	1046	358	5325	3920	140	.985

DIVISION SERIES RECORD

Year Team (League)	Pos.	G	AB	R	H	2B	3B	HR	RBI	Avg.	BB	SO	SB	PO	A	E	Avg.
								BATTING								FIELDING	
1997—Houston (N.L.)	2B	3	12	0	1	0	0	0	0	.083	1	0	0	4	8	1	.923
1998—Houston (N.L.)	2B	4	11	3	2	1	0	0	1	.182	4	4	0	9	10	1	.950
1999—Houston (N.L.)	2B	4	19	1	2	0	0	0	0	.105	1	5	0	14	10	0	1.000
Division series totals (3 years)		11	42	4	5	1	0	0	1	.119	6	9	0	27	28	2	.965

ALL-STAR GAME RECORD

Year League	Pos.	AB	R	H	2B	3B	HR	RBI	Avg.	BB	SO	SB	PO	A	E	Avg.
							BATTING								FIELDING	
1991—National	C	1	0	0	0	0	0	0	.000	0	0	0	2	0	1	.667
1992—National	2B	2	0	0	0	0	0	0	.000	0	0	0	0	2	0	1.000
1994—National	2B	1	1	0	0	0	0	0	.000	0	0	0	2	1	0	1.000
1995—National	2B	2	1	1	0	0	1	1	.500	0	0	0	2	1	0	1.000
1996—National	2B	3	0	0	0	0	0	1	.000	0	1	0	1	1	0	1.000
1997—National	2B	3	0	0	0	0	0	0	.000	0	1	0	0	4	0	1.000
1998—National	2B	3	0	0	0	0	0	0	.000	0	3	0	2	4	0	1.000
All-Star Game totals (7 years)		15	2	1	0	0	1	2	.067	0	5	0	9	13	1	.957

BILLINGSLEY, BRENT — P — EXPOS

PERSONAL: Born April 19, 1975, in Downey, Calif. ... 6-2/200. ... Throws left, bats left. ... Full name: Brent Aaron Billingsley.
HIGH SCHOOL: Chino (Calif.).
COLLEGE: East Carolina, then Cal State Fullerton.
TRANSACTIONS/CAREER NOTES: Selected by Florida Marlins organization in fifth round of free-agent draft (June 2, 1996). ... On Calgary disabled list (July 16-30, 1999). ... Claimed on waivers by Montreal Expos (November 18, 1999). ... On Ottawa disabled list (May 10-June 9 and August 24-September 19, 2000).
STATISTICAL NOTES: Tied for Eastern League lead with 24 home runs allowed in 1998.

Year League	W	L	Pct.	ERA	G	GS	CG	ShO	Sv.	IP	H	R	ER	BB	SO
1996—Utica (NY-Penn)	4	5	.444	4.01	15	•15	0	0	0	89 2/3	83	46	40	28	82
1997—Kane County (Midw.)	14	7	.667	3.01	26	26	3	1	0	170 2/3	146	67	57	50	175
1998—Portland (East.)	6	13	.316	3.74	28	28	0	0	0	171	172	90	71	70	*183
1999—Calgary (PCL)	2	9	.182	5.55	21	21	0	0	0	116 2/3	133	81	72	48	79
—Florida (N.L.)	0	0	...	16.43	8	0	0	0	0	7 2/3	11	14	14	10	3
2000—Ottawa (I.L.)■	8	9	.471	5.66	20	20	0	0	0	103 1/3	118	73	65	46	76
Major League totals (1 year)	0	0	...	16.43	8	0	0	0	0	7 2/3	11	14	14	10	3

BLAIR, WILLIE — P

PERSONAL: Born December 18, 1965, in Paintsville, Ky. ... 6-1/185. ... Throws right, bats right. ... Full name: William Allen Blair.
HIGH SCHOOL: Johnson Central (Paintsville, Ky.).
COLLEGE: Morehead State.
TRANSACTIONS/CAREER NOTES: Selected by Toronto Blue Jays organization in 11th round of free-agent draft (June 2, 1986). ... Traded by Blue Jays to Cleveland Indians for P Alex Sanchez (November 6, 1990). ... Traded by Indians with C Eddie Taubensee to Houston Astros for OF Kenny Lofton and IF Dave Rohde (December 10, 1991). ... Selected by Colorado Rockies in first round (21st pick overall) of expansion draft (November 17, 1992). ... Granted free agency (December 20, 1994). ... Signed by San Diego Padres organization (April 10, 1995). ... Granted free agency (December 21, 1995). ... Re-signed by Padres (December 27, 1995). ... Traded by Padres with C Brian Johnson to Detroit Tigers for P Joey Eischen and P Cam Smith (December 17, 1996). ... On Detroit disabled list (May 5-June 3, 1997); included rehabilitation assignment to West Michigan (May 23-June 3). ... Granted free agency (October 27, 1997). ... Signed by Arizona Diamondbacks (December 6, 1997). ... Traded by Diamondbacks with C Jorge Fabregas and a player to be named later to New York Mets for OF Bernard Gilkey, P Nelson Figueroa and cash (July 31, 1998; Mets received cash to complete deal (September 3, 1998). ... Traded by Mets to Tigers for 3B Joe Randa (December 4, 1998). ... Granted free agency (November 3, 2000).
STATISTICAL NOTES: Combined with starter Pat Hentgen and Enrique Burgos in 2-1 no-hit victory for Dunedin against Osceola (May 10, 1988).

Year League	W	L	Pct.	ERA	G	GS	CG	ShO	Sv.	IP	H	R	ER	BB	SO
1986—St. Catharines (NY-Penn) ...	5	0	1.000	1.68	21	0	0	0	*12	53 2/3	32	10	10	20	55
1987—Dunedin (FSL)	2	9	.182	4.43	50	0	0	0	13	85 1/3	99	51	42	29	72
1988—Dunedin (FSL)	2	0	1.000	2.70	4	0	0	0	0	6 2/3	5	2	2	4	5
—Knoxville (Sou.)	5	5	.500	3.62	34	9	0	0	3	102	94	49	41	35	76
1989—Syracuse (I.L.)	5	6	.455	3.97	19	17	3	1	0	106 2/3	94	55	47	38	76
1990—Toronto (A.L.)	3	5	.375	4.06	27	6	0	0	0	68 2/3	66	33	31	28	43
—Syracuse (I.L.)	0	2	.000	4.74	3	3	1	0	0	19	20	13	10	8	6
1991—Colorado Springs (PCL)■..	9	6	.600	4.99	26	15	0	0	4	113 2/3	130	74	63	30	57
—Cleveland (A.L.)	2	3	.400	6.75	11	5	0	0	0	36	58	27	27	10	13
1992—Tucson (PCL)■	4	4	.500	2.39	21	2	1	0	2	52 2/3	50	20	14	12	35
—Houston (N.L.)	5	7	.417	4.00	29	8	0	0	0	78 2/3	74	47	35	25	48
1993—Colorado (N.L.)■	6	10	.375	4.75	46	18	1	0	0	146	184	90	77	42	84
1994—Colorado (N.L.)	0	5	.000	5.79	47	1	0	0	3	77 2/3	98	57	50	39	68
1995—San Diego (N.L.)■	7	5	.583	4.34	40	12	0	0	0	114	112	60	55	45	83
1996—San Diego (N.L.)	2	6	.250	4.60	60	0	0	0	1	88	80	52	45	29	67

Year League	W	L	Pct.	ERA	G	GS	CG	ShO	Sv.	IP	H	R	ER	BB	SO
1997— Detroit (A.L.)■.................	16	8	.667	4.17	29	27	2	0	0	175	186	85	81	46	90
— West Michigan (Midw.)......	0	0	...	0.00	1	1	0	0	0	5	1	0	0	0	7
— Toledo (I.L.).....................	0	0	...	0.00	1	1	0	0	0	7	1	1	0	2	4
1998— Arizona (N.L.)■.............	4	15	.211	5.34	23	23	0	0	0	146⅔	165	91	87	51	71
— New York (N.L.)■.............	1	1	.500	3.14	11	2	0	0	0	28⅔	23	10	10	10	21
1999— Detroit (A.L.)■.............	3	11	.214	6.85	39	16	0	0	0	134	169	107	102	44	82
2000— Detroit (A.L.).............	10	6	.625	4.88	47	17	0	0	0	156⅔	185	89	85	35	74
A.L. totals (5 years)......................	34	33	.507	5.14	153	71	2	0	0	570⅓	664	341	326	163	302
N.L. totals (6 years)......................	25	49	.338	4.75	256	64	1	0	4	679⅔	736	407	359	241	442
Major League totals (11 years).....	59	82	.418	4.93	409	135	3	0	4	1250	1400	748	685	404	744

DIVISION SERIES RECORD

Year League	W	L	Pct.	ERA	G	GS	CG	ShO	Sv.	IP	H	R	ER	BB	SO
1996— San Diego (N.L.)	0	0	...	0.00	1	0	0	0	0	2	1	0	0	2	3

BLAKE, CASEY — 3B — TWINS

PERSONAL: Born August 23, 1973, in Des Moines, Iowa. ... 6-2/200. ... Bats right, throws right. ... Full name: William Casey Blake.
HIGH SCHOOL: Indianola (Iowa).
COLLEGE: Wichita State.
TRANSACTIONS/CAREER NOTES: Selected by Philadelphia Phillies organization in 11th round of free-agent draft (June 1, 1992); did not sign. ... Selected by New York Yankees organization in 45th round of free-agent draft (June 1, 1995); did not sign. ... Selected by Toronto Blue Jays organization in seventh round of free-agent draft (June 4, 1996). ... Claimed on waivers by Minnesota Twins (May 23, 2000). ... On Salt Lake disabled list (June 28-July 7, 2000).
STATISTICAL NOTES: Led Florida State League third basemen with 98 putouts and 39 errors in 1997. ... Led International League third basemen with .967 fielding percentage in 1999. ... Tied for International League lead with 94 putouts by third basemen in 1999.

							BATTING							FIELDING			
Year Team (League)	Pos.	G	AB	R	H	2B	3B	HR	RBI	Avg.	BB	SO	SB	PO	A	E	Avg.
1996— Hagerstown (S.Atl.)....	3B-1B-OF	48	172	29	43	13	1	2	18	.250	11	40	5	33	83	12	.906
1997— Dunedin (FSL)...........	3B-SS	129	449	56	107	21	0	7	39	.238	48	91	19	†98	235	†39	.895
1998— Dunedin (FSL)...........	3B	88	340	62	119	28	3	11	65	*.350	30	81	9	64	183	16	.939
— Knoxville (Sou.)...........	3B	45	172	41	64	15	4	7	38	.372	22	25	10	27	89	11	.913
1999— Syracuse (I.L.)...........	3B-DH-SS	110	387	69	95	16	2	22	75	.245	61	82	9	‡94	169	10	†.963
— Toronto (A.L.)...........	3B	14	39	6	10	2	0	1	1	.256	2	7	0	12	23	0	1.000
— St. Catharines (NY-P).	3B	1	3	0	2	0	0	0	0	.667	1	0	0	1	3	0	1.000
2000— Syracuse (I.L.)...........	3B-SS	30	106	10	23	6	1	2	7	.217	8	23	0	24	42	2	.971
— Salt Lake (PCL)■......	3B-SS-1B	80	293	59	93	22	2	12	52	.317	39	59	7	49	150	14	.934
— Minnesota (A.L.).......	3B-DH-1B	7	16	1	3	2	0	0	1	.188	3	7	0	7	5	0	1.000
Major League totals (2 years)		21	55	7	13	4	0	1	2	.236	5	14	0	19	28	0	1.000

BLANCO, HENRY — C — BREWERS

PERSONAL: Born August 29, 1971, in Caracas, Venezuela. ... 5-11/170. ... Bats right, throws right. ... Full name: Henry Ramon Blanco.
HIGH SCHOOL: Antonio Jose de Sucre (Venezuela).
TRANSACTIONS/CAREER NOTES: Signed as non-drafted free agent by Los Angeles Dodgers organization (November 12, 1989). ... On disabled list (June 16-25, 1993). ... On Los Angeles disabled list (March 22-July 29, 1998); included rehabilitation assignment to San Bernardino (May 19-27). ... Granted free agency (October 15, 1998). ... Signed by Colorado Rockies organization (December 18, 1998). ... Traded by Rockies with P Jamey Wright to Milwaukee Brewers as part of three-way deal in which Rockies received 3B Jeff Cirillo, P Scott Karl and cash from Brewers, Oakland Athletics received P Justin Miller and cash from Rockies and Brewers received P Jimmy Haynes from Athletics (December 13, 1999). ... On Milwaukee disabled list (April 14-May 2, 2000); included rehabilitation assignment to Indianapolis (April 30-May 2).
STATISTICAL NOTES: Led Pioneer League third basemen with .947 fielding percentage and 10 double plays in 1991. ... Led California League third basemen with 345 total chances and 34 double plays in 1992. ... Led Texas League third basemen with .944 fielding percentage, 92 putouts and 270 total chances in 1993. ... Led Texas League catchers with 13 errors and 17 passed balls in 1996. ... Led Pacific Coast League catchers with 64 assists and 11 double plays in 1997. ... Career major league grand slams: 1.

							BATTING							FIELDING			
Year Team (League)	Pos.	G	AB	R	H	2B	3B	HR	RBI	Avg.	BB	SO	SB	PO	A	E	Avg.
1990— GC Dodgers (GCL)	3B	60	178	23	39	8	0	1	19	.219	26	41	7	*48	129	11	.941
1991— Vero Beach (FSL)	3B-SS	5	7	0	1	0	0	0	0	.143	2	0	0	6	4	0	1.000
— Great Falls (Pio.)	3B-1B	62	216	35	55	7	1	5	28	.255	27	39	3	93	99	8	†.960
1992— Bakersfield (Calif.)	3B	124	401	42	94	21	2	5	52	.234	51	91	10	*95	*236	14	*.959
1993— San Antonio (Texas) ..	3B-1B-SS	117	374	33	73	19	1	10	42	.195	29	80	1	†150	150	16	†.952
1994— San Antonio (Texas) ..	3B-1B-P	*132	405	36	93	23	2	6	38	.230	53	67	6	77	178	21	.924
1995— San Antonio (Texas) ..	3B-C	88	302	37	77	18	4	12	48	.255	29	52	1	81	210	11	.964
— Albuquerque (PCL)	3B-1B-OF	29	97	11	22	4	1	2	13	.227	10	23	0	115	47	2	.988
1996— San Antonio (Texas) ..	C-3B	92	307	39	82	14	1	5	40	.267	28	38	2	532	65	†13	.979
— Albuquerque (PCL).....	C	2	6	1	1	0	0	0	0	.167	0	3	0	11	1	0	1.000
1997— Albuquerque (PCL).....C-1B-DH-OF		91	294	38	92	20	1	6	47	.313	37	63	7	607	†68	3	.996
— Los Angeles (N.L.)	1B-3B	3	5	1	2	0	0	1	1	.400	0	1	0	5	0	0	1.000
1998— San Bern. (Calif.)	C-DH	7	19	5	6	1	0	2	3	.316	4	6	1	17	3	0	1.000
— Albuquerque (PCL).....	C-DH	48	134	19	36	11	0	4	23	.269	22	27	2	243	20	4	.985
1999— Colo. Springs (PCL)■	C	15	57	8	19	4	0	3	12	.333	1	12	0	87	12	1	.990
— Colorado (N.L.)	C-OF	88	263	30	61	12	3	6	28	.232	34	38	1	562	58	5	.992
2000— Milwaukee (N.L.)■.....	C	93	284	29	67	24	0	7	31	.236	36	60	0	506	58	5	.991
— Indianapolis (I.L.).......	DH	1	3	1	1	0	0	0	0	.333	1	0	0	...	...	...	...
Major League totals (3 years)		184	552	60	130	36	3	14	60	.236	70	99	1	1073	116	10	.992

RECORD AS PITCHER

Year League	W	L	Pct.	ERA	G	GS	CG	ShO	Sv.	IP	H	R	ER	BB	SO
1994— San Antonio (Texas)	0	0	...	9.00	1	0	0	0	0	1	3	1	1	0	1

BLANK, MATT — P — EXPOS

PERSONAL: Born April 5, 1976, in Texarkana, Texas. ... 6-2/195. ... Throws left, bats left. ... Full name: Clarence Matt Blank.
HIGH SCHOOL: James W. Martin (Arlington, Texas).
COLLEGE: Texas A&M.
TRANSACTIONS/CAREER NOTES: Selected by New York Yankees organization in 37th round of free-agent draft (June 2, 1994); did not sign. ... Selected by Florida Marlins organization in 40th round of free-agent draft (June 3, 1995); did not sign. ... Selected by Montreal Expos organization in 11th round of free-agent draft (June 3, 1997). ... On disabled list (May 19, 2000-remainder of season).

Year League	W	L	Pct.	ERA	G	GS	CG	ShO	Sv.	IP	H	R	ER	BB	SO
1997— Vermont (NY-Penn)	6	4	.600	*1.69	16	15	2	0	0	95 2/3	74	26	18	14	84
1998— Cape Fear (S.Atl.)	9	2	.818	2.61	21	21	2	2	0	134 2/3	121	45	39	24	114
— Jupiter (FSL)	5	1	.833	2.34	8	6	0	0	0	42 1/3	33	14	11	10	26
1999— Jupiter (FSL)	9	5	.643	2.40	14	14	3	1	0	90	64	26	24	19	66
— Harrisburg (East.)	6	3	.667	3.92	15	14	0	0	0	85	94	41	37	26	42
2000— Montreal (N.L.)	0	1	.000	5.14	13	0	0	0	0	14	12	8	8	5	4
Major League totals (1 year)	0	1	.000	5.14	13	0	0	0	0	14	12	8	8	5	4

BLUM, GEOFF — 3B/SS — EXPOS

PERSONAL: Born April 26, 1973, in Redwood City, Calif. ... 6-3/195. ... Bats both, throws right. ... Full name: Geoffery Edward Blum.
HIGH SCHOOL: Chino (Calif.).
COLLEGE: California.
TRANSACTIONS/CAREER NOTES: Selected by Montreal Expos organization in seventh round of free-agent draft (June 2, 1994). ... On Ottawa disabled list (May 21-June 15, 1999).

Year Team (League)	Pos.	G	AB	R	H	2B	3B	HR	RBI	Avg.	BB	SO	SB	PO	A	E	Avg.
1994— Vermont (NY-Penn)	SS	63	241	48	83	15	1	3	38	.344	33	21	5	87	185	15	.948
1995— W.P. Beach (FSL)	2B-SS-3B	125	457	54	120	20	2	1	62	.263	34	61	6	166	298	18	.963
1996— Harrisburg (East.)	2-S-1-O	120	396	47	95	22	2	1	41	.240	59	51	6	259	281	9	.984
1997— Ottawa (I.L.)	2B-SS-3B	118	407	59	101	21	2	3	35	.248	52	73	14	223	305	17	.969
1998— Ottawa (I.L.)	2B	8	23	1	4	0	0	0	1	.174	3	6	0	18	12	0	1.000
— GC Expos (GCL)	2B	5	18	0	3	1	1	0	1	.167	1	4	0	4	12	0	1.000
— Jupiter (FSL)	2B-3B-SS	17	58	13	16	6	0	0	5	.276	13	14	1	31	51	2	.976
— Harrisburg (East.)	SS-3B-2B-1B	39	139	25	43	12	3	6	21	.309	17	24	2	48	94	2	.986
1999— Ottawa (I.L.)	S-1-2-3-DH	77	268	43	71	14	1	10	37	.265	37	39	6	154	179	12	.965
— Montreal (N.L.)	SS-2B	45	133	21	32	7	2	8	18	.241	17	25	1	47	84	10	.929
2000— Montreal (N.L.)	3B-SS-2B-1B	124	343	40	97	20	2	11	45	.283	26	60	1	122	210	9	.974
Major League totals (2 years)		169	476	61	129	27	4	19	63	.271	43	85	2	169	294	19	.961

BOCACHICA, HIRAM — 2B — DODGERS

PERSONAL: Born March 4, 1976, in Ponce, Puerto Rico. ... 5-11/165. ... Bats right, throws right. ... Full name: Hiram Colon Bocachica.
HIGH SCHOOL: Rexville (Bayamon, Puerto Rico).
TRANSACTIONS/CAREER NOTES: Selected by Montreal Expos organization in first round (21st pick overall) of free-agent draft (June 2, 1994). ... On West Palm Beach disabled list (May 16-July 12, 1996). ... On Harrisburg suspended list (June 15-18, 1997). ... On Harrisburg disabled list (June 18-25, 1997). ... Traded by Expos with P Carlos Perez and SS Mark Grudzielanek to Los Angeles Dodgers for 2B Wilton Guerrero, P Ted Lilly, OF Peter Bergeron and 1B Jonathan Tucker (July 31, 1998). ... On San Antonio suspended list (August 16-19, 1999). ... On Albuquerque disabled list (May 23-June 2, 2000).
STATISTICAL NOTES: Led South Atlantic League shortstops with 58 errors in 1995. ... Led Texas League in being hit by pitch with 13 in 1999. ... Tied for Texas League lead with 77 double plays by second basemen in 1999. ... Led Pacific Coast League second basemen with 99 double plays in 2000.

Year Team (League)	Pos.	G	AB	R	H	2B	3B	HR	RBI	Avg.	BB	SO	SB	PO	A	E	Avg.
1994— GC Expos (GCL)	SS	43	168	31	47	9	0	5	16	.280	15	42	11	72	126	*23	.896
1995— Albany (S.Atl.)	SS-2B	96	380	65	108	20	10	2	30	.284	52	78	47	165	265	†58	.881
1996— W.P. Beach (FSL)	DH-SS	71	267	50	90	17	5	2	26	.337	34	47	21	37	83	24	.833
— GC Expos (GCL)	DH	9	32	11	8	3	0	0	2	.250	5	3	2	...	...	...	...
1997— Harrisburg (East.)	SS-2B-DH	119	443	82	123	19	3	11	35	.278	41	98	29	135	186	32	.909
1998— Harrisburg (East.)	OF-DH	80	296	39	78	18	4	4	27	.264	21	61	20	171	4	10	.946
— Ottawa (I.L.)	OF	12	41	5	8	3	1	0	5	.195	6	14	2	23	1	0	1.000
— Albuquerque (PCL)■	OF	26	101	16	24	7	1	4	16	.238	13	24	5	80	2	2	.976
1999— San Antonio (Texas)	2B-DH	123	477	84	139	22	10	11	60	.291	60	71	30	227	313	*31	.919
2000— Albuquerque (PCL)	2B	124	482	99	155	38	4	23	84	.322	40	100	10	273	326	23	.963
— Los Angeles (N.L.)	2B	8	10	2	3	0	0	0	0	.300	0	2	0	3	9	0	1.000
Major League totals (1 year)		8	10	2	3	0	0	0	0	.300	0	2	0	3	9	0	1.000

BOCHTLER, DOUG — P

PERSONAL: Born July 5, 1970, in West Palm Beach, Fla. ... 6-3/200. ... Throws right, bats right. ... Full name: Douglas Eugene Bochtler. ... Name pronounced BOCK-ler.
HIGH SCHOOL: John I. Leonard (Lake Worth, Fla.).
JUNIOR COLLEGE: Indian River Community College (Fla.).
TRANSACTIONS/CAREER NOTES: Selected by Montreal Expos organization in ninth round of free-agent draft (June 5, 1989). ... On disabled list (June 18-September 6, 1992). ... Selected by Colorado Rockies in second round (32nd pick overall) of expansion draft (November 17, 1992). ... On Colorado Springs disabled list (April 18-26, 1993). ... Traded by Rockies with C Brad Ausmus and a player to be named later to San Diego Padres for P Bruce Hurst and P Greg W. Harris (July 26, 1993); Padres acquired P Andy Ashby to complete deal (July 27, 1993). ... On disabled list (June 16-24 and August 24, 1994-remainder of season). ... On disabled list (July 2-17, 1995). ... Traded by Padres with P Jorge Velandia to Oakland Athletics for P Don Wengert and IF David Newhan (November 26, 1997). ... Traded by A's to Detroit Tigers for cash (March 25, 1998). ... Claimed on waivers by Los Angeles Dodgers (October 6, 1998). ... Released by Dodgers (January 11, 1999). ... Signed by Toronto Blue Jays organization (April 1, 1999). ... Traded by Blue Jays to Dodgers for cash (May 19, 1999). ... On Albuquerque disabled

list (September 3, 1999-remainder of season). ... Granted free agency (October 4, 1999). ... Signed by Kansas City Royals organization (December 10, 1999). ... On Omaha disabled list (August 7, 2000-remainder of season). ... Granted free agency (October 2, 2000).

Year League	W	L	Pct.	ERA	G	GS	CG	ShO	Sv.	IP	H	R	ER	BB	SO
1989— Gulf Coast Expos (GCL)	2	2	.500	3.21	9	9	1	0	0	47 2/3	46	22	17	20	45
1990— Rockford (Midw.)	9	12	.429	3.50	25	25	1	1	0	139	142	82	54	54	109
1991— West Palm Beach (FSL)	•12	9	.571	2.92	26	24	7	2	0	160 1/3	148	63	52	55	109
1992— Harrisburg (East.)..............	6	5	.545	2.32	13	13	2	1	0	77 2/3	50	25	20	36	89
1993— Colorado Springs (PCL)■..	1	4	.200	6.93	12	11	0	0	0	50 2/3	71	41	39	26	38
— Central Valley (Calif.).........	3	1	.750	3.40	8	8	0	0	0	47 2/3	40	23	18	28	43
— Las Vegas (PCL)■	0	5	.000	5.22	7	7	1	0	0	39 2/3	52	26	23	11	30
1994— Las Vegas (PCL)	3	7	.300	5.20	22	20	2	1	0	100 1/3	116	67	58	48	86
1995— Las Vegas (PCL)	2	3	.400	4.25	18	2	0	0	1	36	31	18	17	26	32
— San Diego (N.L.)	4	4	.500	3.57	34	0	0	0	1	45 1/3	38	18	18	19	45
1996— San Diego (N.L.)	2	4	.333	3.02	63	0	0	0	3	65 2/3	45	25	22	39	68
1997— San Diego (N.L.)	3	6	.333	4.77	54	0	0	0	2	60 1/3	51	35	32	50	46
1998— Detroit (A.L.)■................	0	2	.000	6.15	51	0	0	0	0	67 1/3	73	48	46	42	45
1999— Syracuse (I.L.)■	4	0	1.000	2.63	14	0	0	0	0	27 1/3	18	9	8	10	28
— Los Angeles (N.L.)■	0	0	...	5.54	12	0	0	0	0	13	11	8	8	6	7
— Albuquerque (PCL)	3	4	.429	3.18	18	0	0	0	3	22 2/3	16	9	8	11	25
2000— Omaha (PCL)■	2	1	.667	4.02	27	0	0	0	2	40 1/3	37	19	18	28	28
— Kansas City (A.L.)	0	2	.000	6.48	6	0	0	0	0	8 1/3	13	6	6	10	4
A.L. totals (2 years)	0	4	.000	6.19	57	0	0	0	0	75 2/3	86	54	52	52	49
N.L. totals (4 years)	9	14	.391	3.91	163	0	0	0	6	184 1/3	145	86	80	114	166
Major League totals (6 years).......	9	18	.333	4.57	220	0	0	0	6	260	231	140	132	166	215

DIVISION SERIES RECORD

Year League	W	L	Pct.	ERA	G	GS	CG	ShO	Sv.	IP	H	R	ER	BB	SO
1996— San Diego (N.L.)	0	1	.000	27.00	1	0	0	0	0	1/3	0	1	1	3	0

BOEHRINGER, BRIAN   P   YANKEES

PERSONAL: Born January 8, 1970, in St. Louis. ... 6-2/190. ... Throws right, bats both. ... Full name: Brian Edward Boehringer. ... Name pronounced BO-ring-er.
HIGH SCHOOL: Northwest (House Springs, Mo.).
JUNIOR COLLEGE: St. Louis Community College at Meramec.
COLLEGE: UNLV.
TRANSACTIONS/CAREER NOTES: Selected by Houston Astros organization in 10th round of free-agent draft (June 4, 1990); did not sign. ... Selected by Chicago White Sox organization in fourth round of free-agent draft (June 3, 1991). ... On Utica disabled list (June 29-August 25, 1991). ... On disabled list (June 24-August 25, 1992). ... Traded by White Sox to New York Yankees for P Paul Assenmacher (March 21, 1994). ... On New York disabled list (May 27-August 19, 1997); included rehabilitation assignments to Gulf Coast Yankees (August 10-12) and Tampa (August 13-19). ... Selected by Tampa Bay Devil Rays in second round (30th pick overall) of expansion draft (November 18, 1997). ... Traded by Devil Rays with SS Andy Sheets to San Diego Padres for C John Flaherty (November 18, 1997). ... On disabled list (August 14, 1999-remainder of season). ... On San Diego disabled list (April 21-May 24 and July 4, 2000-remainder of season); included rehabilitation assignment to Rancho Cucamonga (May 17-24). ... Granted free agency (October 25, 2000). ... Signed by Yankees organization (December 14, 2000).
STATISTICAL NOTES: Tied for Eastern League lead with four balks in 1994. ... Led International League with 11 hit batsmen in 1996.

Year League	W	L	Pct.	ERA	G	GS	CG	ShO	Sv.	IP	H	R	ER	BB	SO
1991— GC White Sox (GCL)	1	1	.500	6.57	5	1	0	0	0	12 1/3	14	9	9	5	10
— Utica (NY-Penn)	1	1	.500	2.37	4	4	0	0	0	19	14	8	5	8	19
1992— South Bend (Midw.)	6	7	.462	4.38	15	15	2	0	0	86 1/3	87	52	42	40	59
1993— Sarasota (FSL)	10	4	.714	2.80	18	17	3	0	0	119	103	47	37	51	92
— Birmingham (Sou.)...............	2	1	.667	3.54	7	7	1	0	0	40 2/3	41	20	16	14	29
1994— Albany/Colonie (East.)■....	10	11	.476	3.62	27	27	5	1	0	171 2/3	165	85	69	57	145
1995— New York (A.L.)................	0	3	.000	13.75	7	3	0	0	0	17 2/3	24	27	27	22	10
— Columbus (I.L.).................	8	6	.571	2.77	17	17	3	0	0	104	101	39	32	31	58
1996— Columbus (I.L.).................	11	7	.611	4.00	25	25	3	1	0	153	155	79	68	56	132
— New York (A.L.).................	2	4	.333	5.44	15	3	0	0	0	46 1/3	46	28	28	21	37
1997— New York (A.L.)................	3	2	.600	2.63	34	0	0	0	0	48	39	16	14	32	53
— Gulf Coast Yankees (GCL)..	0	0	...	0.00	1	1	0	0	0	2	1	0	0	0	2
— Tampa (FSL)......................	0	1	.000	5.00	3	3	0	0	0	9	9	5	5	5	8
1998— San Diego (N.L.)■............	5	2	.714	4.36	56	1	0	0	0	76 1/3	75	38	37	45	67
1999— San Diego (N.L.)	6	5	.545	3.24	33	11	0	0	0	94 1/3	90	38	34	35	64
2000— San Diego (N.L.)	0	3	.000	5.74	7	3	0	0	0	15 2/3	18	15	10	10	9
— Rancho Cuca. (Calif.)	0	2	.000	5.40	4	2	0	0	0	5	8	3	3	1	5
A.L. totals (3 years)	5	9	.357	5.54	56	6	0	0	0	112	109	71	69	75	100
N.L. totals (3 years)	11	10	.524	3.91	96	15	0	0	0	186 1/3	190	91	81	90	140
Major League totals (6 years)	16	19	.457	4.53	152	21	0	0	0	298 1/3	299	162	150	165	240

DIVISION SERIES RECORD

Year League	W	L	Pct.	ERA	G	GS	CG	ShO	Sv.	IP	H	R	ER	BB	SO
1996— New York (A.L.)................	1	0	1.000	6.75	2	0	0	0	0	1 1/3	3	2	1	2	0
1997— New York (A.L.)................	0	0	...	0.00	1	0	0	0	0	1 2/3	1	0	0	1	2
1998— San Diego (N.L.)							Did not play.								
Division series totals (2 years)	1	0	1.000	3.00	3	0	0	0	0	3	4	2	1	3	2

CHAMPIONSHIP SERIES RECORD

Year League	W	L	Pct.	ERA	G	GS	CG	ShO	Sv.	IP	H	R	ER	BB	SO
1998— San Diego (N.L.)	0	0	...	0.00	3	0	0	0	0	3	3	0	0	1	1

WORLD SERIES RECORD

NOTES: Member of World Series championship team (1996).

Year League	W	L	Pct.	ERA	G	GS	CG	ShO	Sv.	IP	H	R	ER	BB	SO
1996— New York (A.L.)................	0	0	...	5.40	2	0	0	0	0	5	5	5	3	0	5
1998— San Diego (N.L.)	0	0	...	9.00	2	0	0	0	0	2	4	2	2	2	3
World Series totals (2 years)	0	0	...	6.43	4	0	0	0	0	7	9	7	5	2	8

BOGAR, TIM   IF   DODGERS

PERSONAL: Born October 28, 1966, in Indianapolis. ... 6-2/198. ... Bats right, throws right. ... Full name: Timothy Paul Bogar.
HIGH SCHOOL: Buffalo Grove (Ill.).
COLLEGE: Eastern Illinois.
TRANSACTIONS/CAREER NOTES: Selected by New York Mets organization in eighth round of free-agent draft (June 2, 1987). ... On disabled list (June 14, 1990-remainder of season). ... On disabled list (August 16-September 1, 1993). ... On New York disabled list (May 6-June 9, 1994); included rehabilitation assignment to Norfolk (June 4-9). ... Traded by Mets to Houston Astros for IF Luis Lopez (March 31, 1997). ... On disabled list (September 5, 1997-remainder of season). ... Granted free agency (October 23, 1998). ... Re-signed by Astros (December 7, 1998). ... Granted free agency (October 30, 2000). ... Signed by Los Angeles Dodgers organization (January 17, 2001).
MISCELLANEOUS: Played all nine positions in one game for Tidewater (September 4, 1991).

Year	Team (League)	Pos.	G	AB	R	H	2B	3B	HR	RBI	Avg.	BB	SO	SB	PO	A	E	Avg.
1987—Little Falls (NY-Penn) .		SS-2B	58	205	31	48	9	0	0	23	.234	18	39	2	79	194	24	.919
1988—Columbia (S.Atl.)........		2B-SS	45	142	19	40	4	2	3	21	.282	22	29	5	89	120	8	.963
—St. Lucie (FSL)		2B-SS-3B	76	236	34	65	7	1	2	30	.275	34	57	9	141	214	19	.949
1989—Jackson (Texas)		SS	112	406	44	108	13	5	4	45	.266	41	57	8	185	351	29	.949
1990—Tidewater (I.L.)..........		SS	33	117	10	19	2	0	0	4	.162	8	22	1	57	89	10	.936
1991—Williamsport (East.) ...3B-2B-1B-SS			63	243	33	61	12	2	2	25	.251	20	44	13	100	137	8	.967
—Tidewater (I.L.)..........S-2-3-C-1-O-P			65	218	23	56	11	0	1	23	.257	20	35	1	111	183	11	.964
1992—Tidewater (I.L.)..........		2-S-3-P-1	129	481	54	134	32	1	5	38	.279	14	65	7	211	327	15	.973
1993—New York (N.L.)........		SS-3B-2B	78	205	19	50	13	0	3	25	.244	14	29	0	105	217	9	.973
1994—New York (N.L.).........		3-1-S-2-O	50	52	5	8	0	0	2	5	.154	4	11	1	77	38	1	.991
—Norfolk (I.L.).............		3B-2B	5	19	0	2	0	0	0	1	.105	1	4	0	5	11	0	1.000
1995—New York (N.L.)........		S-3-1-2-O	78	145	17	42	7	0	1	21	.290	9	25	1	82	100	6	.968
1996—New York (N.L.)........1B-3B-SS-2B			91	89	17	19	4	0	0	6	.213	8	20	1	104	61	1	.994
1997—Houston (N.L.)■		SS-3B-1B	97	241	30	60	14	4	4	30	.249	24	42	4	110	229	6	.983
1998—Houston (N.L.)........SS-2B-3B-DH			79	156	12	24	4	1	1	8	.154	9	36	2	63	147	3	.986
1999—Houston (N.L.).........		SS-3B-2B	107	309	44	74	16	2	4	31	.239	38	52	3	130	277	9	.978
2000—Houston (N.L.) SS-P-2B-3B			110	304	32	63	9	2	7	33	.207	35	56	1	121	245	12	.968
Major League totals (8 years)			690	1501	176	340	67	9	22	159	.227	141	271	13	792	1314	47	.978

DIVISION SERIES RECORD

Year	Team (League)	Pos.	G	AB	R	H	2B	3B	HR	RBI	Avg.	BB	SO	SB	PO	A	E	Avg.
1999—Houston (N.L.)		PH-SS	2	4	0	3	1	0	0	1	.750	1	0	0	4	4	0	1.000

RECORD AS PITCHER

Year	League	W	L	Pct.	ERA	G	GS	CG	ShO	Sv.	IP	H	R	ER	BB	SO
1991—Tidewater (I.L.).................		0	0	...	27.00	1	0	0	0	0	1/3	0	1	1	0	1
1992—Tidewater (I.L.).................		0	0	...	12.00	3	0	0	0	0	3	4	4	4	3	1
2000—Houston (N.L.).................		0	0	...	4.50	2	0	0	0	0	2	2	1	1	1	1

BOHANON, BRIAN   P   ROCKIES

PERSONAL: Born August 1, 1968, in Denton, Texas. ... 6-2/240. ... Throws left, bats left. ... Full name: Brian Edward Bohanon Jr.
HIGH SCHOOL: North Shore (Houston).
TRANSACTIONS/CAREER NOTES: Selected by Texas Rangers organization in first round (19th pick overall) of free-agent draft (June 2, 1987). ... On disabled list (April 17, 1988-remainder of season). ... On Charlotte disabled list (April 7-May 2, 1989). ... On Texas disabled list (April 7-July 1, 1991); included rehabilitation assignments to Charlotte (June 1-10), Tulsa (June 10-23) and Oklahoma City (June 23-30). ... On Tulsa disabled list (April 28-May 13, 1992). ... On Texas disabled list (June 9-30, 1993); included rehabilitation assignment to Oklahoma City (June 21-30). ... Granted free agency (December 23, 1994). ... Signed by Detroit Tigers organization (March 6, 1995). ... Released by Tigers (October 13, 1995). ... Signed by Toronto Blue Jays organization (February 20, 1996). ... Granted free agency (October 3, 1996). ... Signed by New York Mets organization (December 18, 1996). ... Traded by Mets to Los Angeles Dodgers for P Greg McMichael and cash (July 10, 1998). ... Granted free agency (October 27, 1998). ... Signed by Colorado Rockies (November 9, 1998).
MISCELLANEOUS: Singled and struck out once in two appearances as pinch hitter (1997). ... Grounded out in only appearance as pinch hitter (1999). ... Grounded out in only appearance as pinch hitter (2000).

Year	League	W	L	Pct.	ERA	G	GS	CG	ShO	Sv.	IP	H	R	ER	BB	SO
1987—Gulf Coast Rangers (GCL)..		0	2	.000	4.71	5	4	0	0	0	21	15	13	11	5	21
1988—Charlotte (FSL).................		0	1	.000	5.40	2	2	0	0	0	6 2/3	6	4	4	5	9
1989—Charlotte (FSL).................		0	3	.000	1.81	11	7	0	0	1	54 2/3	40	16	11	20	33
—Tulsa (Texas)		5	0	1.000	2.20	11	11	1	1	0	73 2/3	59	20	18	27	44
1990—Texas (A.L.).................		0	3	.000	6.62	11	6	0	0	0	34	40	30	25	18	15
—Oklahoma City (A.A.).........		1	2	.333	3.66	14	4	0	0	1	32	35	16	13	8	22
1991—Charlotte (FSL).................		1	0	1.000	3.86	2	2	0	0	0	11 2/3	6	5	5	4	7
—Tulsa (Texas)		0	1	.000	2.31	2	2	0	0	0	11 2/3	9	8	3	11	6
—Oklahoma City (A.A.).........		0	4	.000	2.91	7	7	0	0	0	46 1/3	49	19	15	15	37
—Texas (A.L.)		4	3	.571	4.84	11	11	1	0	0	61 1/3	66	35	33	23	34
1992—Oklahoma City (A.A.).........		4	2	.667	2.73	9	9	3	0	0	56	53	21	17	15	24
—Texas (A.L.)		1	1	.500	6.31	18	7	0	0	0	45 2/3	57	38	32	25	29
—Tulsa (Texas)		2	1	.667	1.27	6	6	1	0	0	28 1/3	25	7	4	9	25
1993—Texas (A.L.)		4	4	.500	4.76	36	8	0	0	0	92 2/3	107	54	49	46	45
—Oklahoma City (A.A.).........		0	1	.000	6.43	2	2	0	0	0	7	7	6	5	3	7
1994—Oklahoma City (A.A.).........		5	10	.333	4.12	15	15	2	1	0	98 1/3	106	56	45	33	88
—Texas (A.L.)		2	2	.500	7.23	11	5	0	0	0	37 1/3	51	31	30	8	26
1995—Detroit (A.L.)■.................		1	1	.500	5.54	52	10	0	0	1	105 2/3	121	68	65	41	63
1996—Toronto (A.L.)■.................		0	1	.000	7.77	20	0	0	0	1	22	27	19	19	19	17
—Syracuse (I.L.)....................		4	3	.571	3.86	31	0	0	0	0	58 1/3	56	29	25	17	32
1997—Norfolk (I.L.)■.................		9	3	.750	2.63	15	14	4	2	0	96	88	37	28	32	84
—New York (N.L.)..................		6	4	.600	3.82	19	14	0	0	0	94 1/3	95	49	40	34	66
1998—New York (N.L.)..................		2	4	.333	3.15	25	4	0	0	0	54 1/3	47	21	19	21	39
—Los Angeles (N.L.)■		5	7	.417	2.40	14	14	2	0	0	97 1/3	74	35	26	36	72

Year League	W	L	Pct.	ERA	G	GS	CG	ShO	Sv.	IP	H	R	ER	BB	SO
1999— Colorado (N.L.)■	12	12	.500	6.20	33	33	3	1	0	197 1/3	236	146	136	92	120
2000— Colorado (N.L.)	12	10	.545	4.68	34	26	2	1	0	177	181	101	92	79	98
A.L. totals (7 years)	12	15	.444	5.71	159	47	1	0	2	398 2/3	469	275	253	180	229
N.L. totals (4 years)	37	37	.500	4.54	125	91	7	2	0	620 1/3	633	352	313	262	395
Major League totals (11 years).....	49	52	.485	5.00	284	138	8	2	2	1019	1102	627	566	442	624

BONDS, BARRY   OF   GIANTS

PERSONAL: Born July 24, 1964, in Riverside, Calif. ... 6-2/210. ... Bats left, throws left. ... Full name: Barry Lamar Bonds. ... Son of Bobby Bonds, outfielder with eight major league teams (1968-81); and coach with Cleveland Indians (1984-87) and San Francisco Giants (1993-96).

HIGH SCHOOL: Serra (San Mateo, Calif.).

COLLEGE: Arizona State.

TRANSACTIONS/CAREER NOTES: Selected by San Francisco Giants organization in second round of free-agent draft (June 7, 1982); did not sign. ... Selected by Pittsburgh Pirates organization in first round (sixth pick overall) of free-agent draft (June 3, 1985). ... On disabled list (June 15-July 4, 1992). ... Granted free agency (October 26, 1992). ... Signed by Giants (December 8, 1992). ... On suspended list (August 14-16, 1998). ... On disabled list (April 18-June 9, 1999).

RECORDS: Holds major league career record for most intentional bases on balls—320. ... Shares major league record for most seasons and consecutive seasons leading league in intentional bases on balls received—7 (1992-98). ... Shares major league single-season record for fewest assists by outfielder who led league in assists—14 (1990). ... Holds N.L. career record for most consecutive years leading league in bases on balls—4 (1994-97). ... Shares major league record for fewest double plays by outfielder (150 or more games)—0 (1997 and 1998). ... Shares N.L. single-season record for most consecutive times reached base safely—15 (August 31 [1], September 1 [5], 2 [4], 4 [5], 1998 [5 singles, 2 doubles, 2 home runs, 6 bases on balls]. ... Shares N.L. single-season record for fewest assists by outfielder (150 or more games)—2 (1998).

HONORS: Named outfielder on THE SPORTING NEWS college All-America team (1985). ... Named Major League Player of the Year by THE SPORTING NEWS (1990). ... Named N.L. Player of the Year by THE SPORTING NEWS (1990 and 1991). ... Named outfielder on THE SPORTING NEWS N.L. All-Star team (1990-94, 1996-97 and 2000). ... Won N.L. Gold Glove as outfielder (1990-94 and 1996-98). ... Named outfielder on THE SPORTING NEWS N.L. Silver Slugger team (1990-94, 1996, 1997 and 2000). ... Named N.L. Most Valuable Player by Baseball Writers' Association of America (1990 and 1992-93).

STATISTICAL NOTES: Led N.L. with .565 slugging percentage in 1990, .624 in 1992 and .677 in 1993. ... Led N.L. with 32 intentional bases on balls received in 1992, 43 in 1993, 18 in 1994, 22 in 1995, 30 in 1996, 34 in 1997 and 29 in 1998. ... Led N.L. with .456 on-base percentage in 1992, .458 in 1993 and .431 in 1995. ... Led N.L. with 365 total bases in 1993. ... Hit three home runs in one game (August 2, 1994). ... Tied N.L. outfielders for lead in double plays with four in 2000. ... Career major league grand slams: 8.

Year Team (League)	Pos.	G	AB	R	H	2B	3B	HR	RBI	Avg.	BB	SO	SB	PO	A	E	Avg.
1985— Prince Will. (Caro.).....	OF	71	254	49	76	16	4	13	37	.299	37	52	15	202	4	5	.976
1986— Hawaii (PCL)	OF	44	148	30	46	7	2	7	37	.311	33	31	16	109	4	2	.983
— Pittsburgh (N.L.)	OF	113	413	72	92	26	3	16	48	.223	65	102	36	280	9	5	.983
1987— Pittsburgh (N.L.)	OF	150	551	99	144	34	9	25	59	.261	54	88	32	330	15	5	.986
1988— Pittsburgh (N.L.)	OF	144	538	97	152	30	5	24	58	.283	72	82	17	292	5	6	.980
1989— Pittsburgh (N.L.)	OF	159	580	96	144	34	6	19	58	.248	93	93	32	365	14	6	.984
1990— Pittsburgh (N.L.)	OF	151	519	104	156	32	3	33	114	.301	93	83	52	338	•14	6	.983
1991— Pittsburgh (N.L.)	OF	153	510	95	149	28	5	25	116	.292	107	73	43	321	13	3	.991
1992— Pittsburgh (N.L.)	OF	140	473	*109	147	36	5	34	103	.311	*127	69	39	310	4	3	.991
1993— San Fran. (N.L.)■......	OF	159	539	129	181	38	4	*46	*123	.336	126	79	29	310	7	5	.984
1994— San Francisco (N.L.) ..	OF	112	391	89	122	18	1	37	81	.312	*74	43	29	198	10	3	.986
1995— San Francisco (N.L.) ..	OF	•144	506	109	149	30	7	33	104	.294	*120	83	31	279	12	6	.980
1996— San Francisco (N.L.) ..	OF	158	517	122	159	27	3	42	129	.308	*151	76	40	286	10	6	.980
1997— San Francisco (N.L.) ..	OF	159	532	123	155	26	5	40	101	.291	*145	87	37	289	10	5	.984
1998— San Francisco (N.L.) ..	OF	156	552	120	167	44	7	37	122	.303	130	92	28	301	2	5	.984
1999— San Francisco (N.L.) ..	OF-DH	102	355	91	93	20	2	34	83	.262	73	62	15	177	4	3	.984
2000— San Francisco (N.L.) ..	OF	143	480	129	147	28	4	49	106	.306	*117	77	11	255	8	3	.989
Major League totals (15 years)		2143	7456	1584	2157	451	69	494	1405	.289	1547	1189	471	4331	137	70	.985

DIVISION SERIES RECORD

Year Team (League)	Pos.	G	AB	R	H	2B	3B	HR	RBI	Avg.	BB	SO	SB	PO	A	E	Avg.
1997— San Francisco (N.L.) ..	OF	3	12	0	3	2	0	0	2	.250	0	3	1	6	0	0	1.000
2000— San Francisco (N.L.) ..	OF	4	17	2	3	1	1	0	1	.176	3	4	1	10	0	0	1.000
Division series totals (2 years)		7	29	2	6	3	1	0	3	.207	3	7	2	16	0	0	1.000

CHAMPIONSHIP SERIES RECORD

RECORDS: Shares single-inning record for most hits—2 (October 13, 1992, second inning).

Year Team (League)	Pos.	G	AB	R	H	2B	3B	HR	RBI	Avg.	BB	SO	SB	PO	A	E	Avg.
1990— Pittsburgh (N.L.)	OF	6	18	4	3	0	0	0	1	.167	6	5	2	13	0	0	1.000
1991— Pittsburgh (N.L.)	OF	7	27	1	4	1	0	0	0	.148	2	4	3	14	1	1	.938
1992— Pittsburgh (N.L.)	OF	7	23	5	6	1	0	1	2	.261	6	4	1	17	0	0	1.000
Championship series totals (3 years)		20	68	10	13	2	0	1	3	.191	14	13	6	44	1	1	.978

ALL-STAR GAME RECORD

Year League	Pos.	AB	R	H	2B	3B	HR	RBI	Avg.	BB	SO	SB	PO	A	E	Avg.
1990— National	OF	1	0	0	0	0	0	0	.000	1	0	0	2	0	0	1.000
1992— National	OF	3	1	1	1	0	0	0	.333	0	0	0	2	0	0	1.000
1993— National	OF	3	2	2	2	0	0	0	.667	0	0	0	1	0	0	1.000
1994— National	OF	3	0	0	0	0	0	1	.000	0	2	0	1	0	0	1.000
1995— National	OF	3	0	0	0	0	0	0	.000	0	1	0	0	0	0	...
1996— National	OF	3	0	1	0	0	0	0	.333	0	0	0	2	0	0	1.000
1997— National	OF	2	0	0	0	0	0	0	.000	1	1	1	2	0	0	1.000
1998— National	OF	2	1	1	0	0	1	3	.500	1	0	0	1	0	0	1.000
2000— National						Selected, did not play—injured.										
All-Star Game totals (8 years)		20	4	5	3	0	1	4	.250	3	4	1	11	0	0	1.000

PERSONAL: Born April 7, 1969, in Salinas, Puerto Rico. ... 6-0/202. ... Throws right, bats right. ... Full name: Ricardo Bones. ... Name pronounced Bone-ess.

HIGH SCHOOL: Guayama (Puerto Rico).

TRANSACTIONS/CAREER NOTES: Signed as non-drafted free agent by San Diego Padres organization (May 13, 1986). ... Traded by Padres with SS Jose Valentin and OF Matt Mieske to Milwaukee Brewers for 3B Gary Sheffield and P Geoff Kellogg (March 27, 1992). ... Traded by Brewers with a player to be named later to New York Yankees as compensation for injured status of OF/IF Pat Listach (August 29, 1996); Yankees acquired IF Gabby Martinez to complete deal (November 5, 1996). ... Granted free agency (October 25, 1996). ... Signed by Cincinnati Reds (December 10, 1996). ... Released by Reds (May 6, 1997). ... Signed by Brewers organization (May 12, 1997). ... Traded by Brewers to Kansas City Royals organization for cash (June 26, 1997). ... Granted free agency (November 5, 1997). ... Signed by Minnesota Twins organization (January 6, 1998). ... Released by Twins (May 22, 1998). ... Signed by Royals organization (May 26, 1998). ... Granted free agency (October 29, 1998). ... Signed by Baltimore Orioles (December 21, 1998). ... On Baltimore disabled list (July 2-17, 1999). ... Released by Orioles (August 20, 1999). ... Signed by Florida Marlins organization (December 22, 1999). ... On disabled list (May 6-21, 2000). ... Granted free agency (November 1, 2000). ... Re-signed by Marlins (November 9, 2000).

STATISTICAL NOTES: Led Texas League with 22 home runs allowed in 1989.

MISCELLANEOUS: Appeared in one game as outfielder with no chances (1993). ... Appeared in one game as pinch runner with Kansas City (1997). ... Scored a run in only appearance as pinch runner (1999).

Year	League	W	L	Pct.	ERA	G	GS	CG	ShO	Sv.	IP	H	R	ER	BB	SO
1986—	Spokane (N'West)	1	3	.250	5.59	18	9	0	0	0	58	63	44	36	29	46
1987—	Charleston, S.C. (S.Atl.)	12	5	.706	3.65	26	26	4	1	0	170$^{1}/_{3}$	*183	81	69	45	130
1988—	Riverside (Calif.)	15	6	.714	3.64	25	25	5	2	0	175$^{1}/_{3}$	162	80	71	64	129
1989—	Wichita (Texas)	10	9	.526	5.74	24	24	2	0	0	136$^{1}/_{3}$	162	103	87	47	88
1990—	Wichita (Texas)	6	4	.600	3.48	21	21	2	1	0	137	138	66	53	45	96
	— Las Vegas (PCL)	2	1	.667	3.47	5	5	0	0	0	36$^{1}/_{3}$	45	17	14	10	25
1991—	Las Vegas (PCL)	8	6	.571	4.22	23	23	1	0	0	136$^{1}/_{3}$	155	90	64	43	95
	— San Diego (N.L.)	4	6	.400	4.83	11	11	0	0	0	54	57	33	29	18	31
1992—	Milwaukee (A.L.)■	9	10	.474	4.57	31	28	0	0	0	163$^{1}/_{3}$	169	90	83	48	65
1993—	Milwaukee (A.L.)	11	11	.500	4.86	32	31	3	0	0	203$^{2}/_{3}$	222	122	110	63	63
1994—	Milwaukee (A.L.)	10	9	.526	3.43	24	24	4	1	0	170$^{2}/_{3}$	166	76	65	45	57
1995—	Milwaukee (A.L.)	10	12	.455	4.63	32	31	3	0	0	200$^{1}/_{3}$	218	108	103	83	77
1996—	Milwaukee (A.L.)	7	14	.333	5.83	32	23	0	0	0	145	170	104	94	62	59
	— New York (A.L.)■■	0	0	...	14.14	4	1	0	0	0	7	14	11	11	6	4
1997—	Cincinnati (N.L.)■■	0	1	.000	10.19	9	2	0	0	0	17$^{2}/_{3}$	31	22	20	11	8
	— Tucson (PCL)■	5	0	1.000	2.79	8	7	0	0	0	42	40	18	13	8	22
	— Kansas City (A.L.)■	4	7	.364	5.97	21	11	1	0	0	78$^{1}/_{3}$	102	59	52	25	36
1998—	Salt Lake (PCL)■■	5	1	.833	3.42	8	8	0	0	0	47$^{1}/_{3}$	41	20	18	19	41
	— Omaha (PCL)■	1	2	.333	8.59	3	3	0	0	0	14$^{2}/_{3}$	19	16	14	10	8
	— Kansas City (A.L.)	2	2	.500	3.04	32	0	0	0	1	53$^{1}/_{3}$	49	18	18	24	38
1999—	Baltimore (A.L.)■■	0	3	.000	5.98	30	2	0	0	0	43$^{2}/_{3}$	59	29	29	19	26
2000—	Florida (N.L.)■	2	3	.400	4.54	56	0	0	0	0	77$^{1}/_{3}$	94	43	39	27	59
A.L. totals (8 years)		53	68	.438	4.77	238	151	11	1	1	1065$^{1}/_{3}$	1169	617	565	375	425
N.L. totals (3 years)		6	10	.375	5.32	76	13	0	0	0	149	182	98	88	56	98
Major League totals (10 years)		59	78	.431	4.84	314	164	11	1	1	1214$^{1}/_{3}$	1351	715	653	431	523

ALL-STAR GAME RECORD

Year	League	W	L	Pct.	ERA	GS	CG	ShO	Sv.	IP	H	R	ER	BB	SO
1994—	American						Did not play.								

PERSONAL: Born February 23, 1963, in New York. ... 6-3/240. ... Bats both, throws right. ... Full name: Roberto Martin Antonio Bonilla. ... Name pronounced bo-NEE-yah.

HIGH SCHOOL: Lehman (Bronx, N.Y.).

COLLEGE: New York Technical College.

TRANSACTIONS/CAREER NOTES: Signed as non-drafted free agent by Pittsburgh Pirates organization (July 11, 1981). ... On Pittsburgh disabled list (March 25-July 19, 1985). ... Selected by Chicago White Sox from Pirates organization in Rule 5 major league draft (December 10, 1985). ... Traded by White Sox to Pittsburgh Pirates for P Jose DeLeon (July 23, 1986). ... Granted free agency (October 28, 1991). ... Signed by New York Mets (December 2, 1991). ... On suspended list (July 27-28, 1992). ... On disabled list (August 3-19, 1992). ... Traded by Mets with a player to be named later to Baltimore Orioles for OF Alex Ochoa and OF Damon Buford (July 28, 1995); Orioles acquired P Jimmy Williams to complete deal (August 17, 1995). ... Granted free agency (November 18, 1996). ... Signed by Florida Marlins (November 22, 1996). ... On Florida disabled list (March 22-April 12, 1998). ... Traded by Marlins with OF Gary Sheffield, C Charles Johnson, OF Jim Eisenreich and P Manuel Barrios to Los Angeles Dodgers for C Mike Piazza and 3B Todd Zeile (May 15, 1998). ... On Los Angeles disabled list (June 18-July 3 and July 15-August 5, 1998). ... Traded by Dodgers to Mets for P Mel Rojas (November 11, 1998). ... On New York disabled list (May 11-31 and July 3-September 1, 1999; included rehabilitation assignment to Norfolk (August 27-September 1). ... Released by Mets (January 3, 2000). ... Signed by Atlanta Braves organization (January 28, 2000). ... Granted free agency (October 31, 2000). ... Signed by St. Louis Cardinals (January 5, 2001).

RECORDS: Holds N.L. career record for most home runs by switch-hitter—242. ... Shares major league record for most doubles in one inning—2 (July 21, 1995, eighth inning). ... Shares A.L. single-season record for most sacrifice flies—17 (1996).

HONORS: Named third baseman on THE SPORTING NEWS N.L. All-Star team (1988). ... Named third baseman on THE SPORTING NEWS N.L. Silver Slugger team (1988). ... Named outfielder on THE SPORTING NEWS N.L. All-Star team (1990 and 1991). ... Named outfielder on THE SPORTING NEWS N.L. Silver Slugger team (1990 and 1991).

STATISTICAL NOTES: Led Eastern League outfielders with 15 errors in 1984. ... Switch-hit home runs in one game six times (July 3, 1987; April 6, 1988; April 23 and June 10, 1993; May 4, 1994; and May 12, 1995). ... Led N.L. third basemen with 489 total chances in 1988. ... Led N.L. third basemen with 35 errors in 1989. ... Led N.L. third basemen with 31 double plays in 1989. ... Led N.L. with 15 sacrifice flies in 1990. ... Had 20-game hitting streak (September 10-October 1, 1995). ... Led A.L. with 17 sacrifice flies in 1996. ... Career major league grand slams: 8.

Year	Team (League)	Pos.	G	AB	R	H	2B	3B	HR	RBI	Avg.	BB	SO	SB	PO	A	E	Avg.
									BATTING							FIELDING		
1981—	GC Pirates (GCL).......	1B-C-3B	22	69	6	15	5	0	0	7	.217	7	17	2	124	23	5	.967
1982—	GC Pirates (GCL).......	1B	47	167	20	38	3	0	5	26	.228	11	20	2	318	36	*14	.962
1983—	Alexandria (Caro.)......	OF-1B	•136	504	88	129	19	7	11	59	.256	78	105	28	259	12	15	.948
1984—	Nashua (East.).........	OF-1B	136	484	74	128	19	5	11	71	.264	44	89	15	312	8	†15	.955
1985—	Prince Will. (Caro.).....	1B-3B	39	130	15	34	4	1	3	11	.262	16	29	1	180	9	2	.990
1986—	Chicago (A.L.)■.......	OF-1B	75	234	27	63	10	2	2	26	.269	33	49	4	361	22	2	.995
—	Pittsburgh (N.L.)■......	OF-1B	63	192	28	46	6	2	1	17	.240	29	39	4	90	16	3	.972
1987—	Pittsburgh (N.L.).......	3B-OF-1B	141	466	58	140	33	3	15	77	.300	39	64	3	142	139	16	.946
1988—	Pittsburgh (N.L.).......	3B	159	584	87	160	32	7	24	100	.274	85	82	3	121	*336	*32	.935
1989—	Pittsburgh (N.L.).......	3B-1B-OF	•163	616	96	173	37	10	24	86	.281	76	93	8	190	334	†35	.937
1990—	Pittsburgh (N.L.).......	OF-3B-1B	160	625	112	175	39	7	32	120	.280	45	103	4	315	35	15	.959
1991—	Pittsburgh (N.L.).......	OF-3B-1B	157	577	102	174	*44	6	18	100	.302	90	67	2	247	144	15	.963
1992—	New York (N.L.)■.....	OF-1B	128	438	62	109	23	0	19	70	.249	66	73	4	277	9	4	.986
1993—	New York (N.L.).......	OF-3B-1B	139	502	81	133	21	3	34	87	.265	72	96	3	238	112	17	.954
1994—	New York (N.L.)........	3B	108	403	60	117	24	1	20	67	.290	55	101	1	78	215	*18	.942
1995—	New York (N.L.).......	3B-OF-1B	80	317	49	103	25	4	18	53	.325	31	48	0	164	80	14	.946
—	Baltimore (A.L.)■.......	OF-3B	61	237	47	79	12	4	10	46	.333	23	31	0	80	48	5	.962
1996—	Baltimore (A.L.).........	OF-DH-1B-3B	159	595	107	171	27	5	28	116	.287	75	85	1	214	12	6	.974
1997—	Florida (N.L.)■.........	3B-DH-1B	153	562	77	167	39	3	17	96	.297	73	94	6	107	225	22	.938
1998—	Florida (N.L.).........	3B	28	97	11	27	5	0	4	15	.278	12	22	0	18	41	5	.922
—	Los Angeles (N.L.)■..	3B-OF	72	236	28	56	6	1	7	30	.237	29	37	1	56	84	13	.915
1999—	New York (N.L.)■.....	OF-1B-DH	60	119	12	19	5	0	4	18	.160	19	16	0	59	4	2	.969
—	Norfolk (I.L.)..........	DH	3	13	1	3	0	0	0	1	.231	0	1	0	0	0	0	...
2000—	Atlanta (N.L.)■.........	OF-DH-3B	114	239	23	61	13	3	5	28	.255	37	51	0	51	1	4	.929
American League totals (3 years)			295	1066	181	313	49	11	40	188	.294	131	165	5	655	82	13	.983
National League totals (14 years)			1725	5973	886	1660	352	50	242	964	.278	758	986	39	2153	1775	215	.948
Major League totals (15 years)			2020	7039	1067	1973	401	61	282	1152	.280	889	1151	44	2808	1857	228	.953

DIVISION SERIES RECORD

Year	Team (League)	Pos.	G	AB	R	H	2B	3B	HR	RBI	Avg.	BB	SO	SB	PO	A	E	Avg.
									BATTING							FIELDING		
1996—	Baltimore (A.L.).........	OF	4	15	4	3	0	0	2	5	.200	4	6	0	9	0	1	.900
1997—	Florida (N.L.).............	3B	3	12	1	4	0	0	1	3	.333	2	1	0	3	5	0	1.000
1999—	New York (N.L.).........	PH	2	1	1	0	0	0	0	0	.000	1	0	0	0	0	0	...
2000—	Atlanta (N.L.).............	PH-OF	3	2	0	0	0	0	0	0	.000	2	0	0	0	0	0	...
Division series totals (4 years)			12	30	6	7	0	0	3	8	.233	9	7	0	12	5	1	.944

CHAMPIONSHIP SERIES RECORD

RECORDS: Shares single-game record for most strikeouts—4 (October 10, 1996).

Year	Team (League)	Pos.	G	AB	R	H	2B	3B	HR	RBI	Avg.	BB	SO	SB	PO	A	E	Avg.
									BATTING							FIELDING		
1990—	Pittsburgh (N.L.)........	OF-3B	6	21	0	4	1	0	0	1	.190	3	1	0	4	5	1	.900
1991—	Pittsburgh (N.L.)........	OF	7	23	2	7	2	0	0	1	.304	6	2	0	12	1	0	1.000
1996—	Baltimore (A.L.).........	OF	5	20	1	1	0	0	1	2	.050	1	4	0	11	0	0	1.000
1997—	Florida (N.L.).............	3B	6	23	3	6	1	0	0	4	.261	1	6	0	5	13	0	1.000
1999—	New York (N.L.)..........	PH	3	3	0	1	0	0	0	0	.333	0	2	0	0	0	0	...
Championship series totals (5 years)			27	90	6	19	4	0	1	8	.211	11	15	0	32	19	1	.981

WORLD SERIES RECORD

NOTES: Member of World Series championship team (1997).

Year	Team (League)	Pos.	G	AB	R	H	2B	3B	HR	RBI	Avg.	BB	SO	SB	PO	A	E	Avg.
									BATTING							FIELDING		
1997—	Florida (N.L.).............	3B	7	29	5	6	1	0	1	3	.207	3	5	0	3	20	2	.920

ALL-STAR GAME RECORD

Year	League	Pos.	AB	R	H	2B	3B	HR	RBI	Avg.	BB	SO	SB	PO	A	E	Avg.
									BATTING						FIELDING		
1988—	National..................	3B	4	0	0	0	0	0	0	.000	0	0	0	0	2	0	1.000
1989—	National..................	PH-DH	2	0	2	0	0	0	0	1.000	0	0	0	...	...	...	...
1990—	National..................	1B	1	0	0	0	0	0	0	.000	0	0	0	1	0	0	1.000
1991—	National..................	DH	4	0	2	0	0	0	1	.500	0	1	0	...	...	...	...
1993—	National..................	OF	1	0	1	0	0	0	0	1.000	0	0	0	2	0	0	1.000
1995—	National..................	3B	1	0	0	0	0	0	0	.000	0	1	0	0	0	0	...
All-Star Game totals (6 years)			13	0	5	0	0	0	1	.385	0	2	0	3	2	0	1.000

BOONE, AARON   3B   REDS

PERSONAL: Born March 9, 1973, in La Mesa, Calif. ... 6-2/200. ... Bats right, throws right. ... Full name: Aaron John Boone. ... Son of Bob Boone, manager, Cincinnati Reds; and catcher with three major league teams (1972-90); brother of Bret Boone, second baseman, Seattle Mariners; grandson of Ray Boone, major league infielder with six teams (1948-60); and nephew of Rodney Boone, minor league catcher/out-fielder (1972-75).

HIGH SCHOOL: Villa Park (Calif.).

COLLEGE: Southern California.

TRANSACTIONS/CAREER NOTES: Selected by California Angels organization in 43rd round of free-agent draft (June 3, 1991); did not sign. ... Selected by Cincinnati Reds organization in third round of free-agent draft (June 2, 1994). ... On disabled list (July 10, 2000-remainder of season).

STATISTICAL NOTES: Led Pioneer League third basemen with 46 putouts, 156 assists, 220 total chances and 13 double plays in 1994. ... Led Southern League third basemen with 101 putouts, 347 total chances and 28 double plays in 1996. ... Led American Association third base-men with 76 putouts, 241 assists, 336 total chances and 27 double plays in 1997. ... Career major league grand slams: 1.

Year	Team (League)	Pos.	G	AB	R	H	2B	3B	HR	RBI	Avg.	BB	SO	SB	PO	A	E	Avg.
1994—	Billings (Pio.)	3B-1B	67	256	48	70	15	5	7	55	.273	36	35	6	†60	†158	18	.924
1995—	Chattanooga (Sou.)	3B	23	66	6	15	3	0	0	3	.227	5	12	2	14	28	6	.875
	—Win.-Salem (Caro.)	3B	108	395	61	103	19	1	14	50	.261	43	77	11	59	*272	21	*.940
1996—	Chattanooga (Sou.)	3B-SS-DH	136	*548	86	158	*44	7	17	95	.288	38	77	21	†123	257	22	.945
1997—	Indianapolis (A.A.)	3B-SS-2B	131	476	79	138	30	4	22	75	.290	40	81	12	†112	†269	24	.941
	—Cincinnati (N.L.)	3B-2B	16	49	5	12	1	0	0	5	.245	2	5	1	11	22	3	.917
1998—	Cincinnati (N.L.)	3B-2B-SS	58	181	24	51	13	2	2	28	.282	15	36	6	37	97	8	.944
	—Indianapolis (I.L.)	3B-2B-SS	87	332	56	80	18	1	7	38	.241	31	71	17	72	243	19	.943
1999—	Cincinnati (N.L.)	3B-SS	139	472	56	132	26	5	14	72	.280	30	79	17	87	258	15	.958
	—Indianapolis (I.L.)	3B-2B-SS	11	41	6	14	2	1	0	7	.341	3	4	2	11	29	3	.930
2000—	Cincinnati (N.L.)	3B-SS	84	291	44	83	18	0	12	43	.285	24	52	6	63	157	8	.965
	Major League totals (4 years)		297	993	129	278	58	7	28	148	.280	71	172	30	198	534	34	.956

B — BOONE, BRET — 2B — MARINERS

PERSONAL: Born April 6, 1969, in El Cajon, Calif. ... 5-10/180. ... Bats right, throws right. ... Full name: Bret Robert Boone. ... Son of Bob Boone, manager, Cincinnati Reds; and catcher with three major league teams (1972-90); brother of Aaron Boone, third baseman, Cincinnati Reds; grandson of Ray Boone, major league infielder with six teams (1948-60); and nephew of Rodney Boone, minor league catcher/outfielder (1972-75).

HIGH SCHOOL: El Dorado (Yorba Linda, Calif.).

COLLEGE: Southern California.

TRANSACTIONS/CAREER NOTES: Selected by Minnesota Twins organization in 28th round of free-agent draft (June 2, 1987); did not sign. ... Selected by Seattle Mariners organization in fifth round of free-agent draft (June 4, 1990). ... Traded by Mariners with P Erik Hanson to Cincinnati Reds for P Bobby Ayala and C Dan Wilson (November 2, 1993). ... On disabled list (April 1-16, 1996). ... Traded by Reds with P Mike Remlinger to Atlanta Braves for P Denny Neagle, OF Michael Tucker and P Rob Bell (November 10, 1998). ... Traded by Braves with OF/1B Ryan Klesko and P Jason Shiell to San Diego Padres for 2B Quilvio Veras, 1B Wally Joyner and OF Reggie Sanders (December 22, 1999). ... On disabled list (August 27, 2000-remainder of season). ... Granted free agency (October 31, 2000). ... Signed by Mariners (December 22, 2000).

RECORDS: Holds major league single-season record for highest fielding percentage by second baseman (100 or more games)—.997 (1997).

HONORS: Won N.L. Gold Glove at second base (1998).

STATISTICAL NOTES: Tied for Southern League lead in grounding into double plays with 21 in 1991. ... Led Southern League second basemen with 288 putouts in 1991. ... Led Pacific Coast League second basemen with 90 double plays in 1992. ... Led N.L. second basemen with 106 double plays in 1995. ... Hit three home runs in one game (September 20, 1998 and June 23, 2000). ... Career major league grand slams: 2.

Year	Team (League)	Pos.	G	AB	R	H	2B	3B	HR	RBI	Avg.	BB	SO	SB	PO	A	E	Avg.
1990—	Peninsula (Caro.)	2B	74	255	42	68	13	2	8	38	.267	47	57	5	154	216	19	.951
1991—	Jacksonville (Sou.)	2B-3B	•139	475	64	121	18	1	19	75	.255	72	123	9	†300	369	21	.970
1992—	Calgary (PCL)	2B-SS	118	439	73	138	26	5	13	73	.314	60	88	17	268	366	10	.984
	—Seattle (A.L.)	2B-3B	33	129	15	25	4	0	4	15	.194	4	34	1	72	96	6	.966
1993—	Calgary (PCL)	2B	71	274	48	91	18	3	8	56	.332	28	58	3	146	180	8	.976
	—Seattle (A.L.)	2B-DH	76	271	31	68	12	2	12	38	.251	17	52	2	140	177	3	.991
1994—	Cincinnati (N.L.)■	2B-3B	108	381	59	122	25	2	12	68	.320	24	74	3	191	269	12	.975
1995—	Cincinnati (N.L.)	2B	138	513	63	137	34	2	15	68	.267	41	84	5	*311	362	4	*.994
1996—	Cincinnati (N.L.)	2B	142	520	56	121	21	3	12	69	.233	31	100	3	315	381	6	*.991
1997—	Cincinnati (N.L.)	2B	139	443	40	99	25	1	7	46	.223	45	101	5	271	334	2	*.997
	—Indianapolis (A.A.)	2B	3	7	1	2	1	0	0	1	.286	2	2	1	6	10	0	1.000
1998—	Cincinnati (N.L.)	2B	157	583	76	155	38	1	24	95	.266	48	104	6	329	416	9	.988
1999—	Atlanta (N.L.)■	2B	152	608	102	153	38	1	20	63	.252	47	112	14	270	424	13	.982
2000—	San Diego (N.L.)■	2B	127	463	61	116	18	2	19	74	.251	50	97	8	292	334	15	.977
	American League totals (2 years)		109	400	46	93	16	2	16	53	.233	21	86	3	212	273	9	.982
	National League totals (7 years)		963	3511	457	903	199	12	109	483	.257	286	672	44	1979	2520	61	.987
	Major League totals (9 years)		1072	3911	503	996	215	14	125	536	.255	307	758	47	2191	2793	70	.986

DIVISION SERIES RECORD

RECORDS: Holds N.L. career record for highest batting average (20 or more at-bats)—.414. ... Shares N.L. single-game record for most at-bats—6 (October 8, 1999).

Year	Team (League)	Pos.	G	AB	R	H	2B	3B	HR	RBI	Avg.	BB	SO	SB	PO	A	E	Avg.
1995—	Cincinnati (N.L.)	2B	3	10	4	3	1	0	1	1	.300	1	3	1	7	5	0	1.000
1999—	Atlanta (N.L.)	2B	4	19	3	9	1	0	0	1	.474	0	4	1	11	15	0	1.000
	Division series totals (2 years)		7	29	7	12	2	0	1	2	.414	1	7	2	18	20	0	1.000

CHAMPIONSHIP SERIES RECORD

Year	Team (League)	Pos.	G	AB	R	H	2B	3B	HR	RBI	Avg.	BB	SO	SB	PO	A	E	Avg.
1995—	Cincinnati (N.L.)	2B	4	14	1	3	0	0	0	0	.214	1	2	0	9	13	0	1.000
1999—	Atlanta (N.L.)	2B	6	22	2	4	1	0	0	1	.182	1	7	2	5	14	0	1.000
	Championship series totals (2 years)		10	36	3	7	1	0	0	1	.194	2	9	2	14	27	0	1.000

WORLD SERIES RECORD

Year	Team (League)	Pos.	G	AB	R	H	2B	3B	HR	RBI	Avg.	BB	SO	SB	PO	A	E	Avg.
1999—	Atlanta (N.L.)	2B-PH	4	13	1	7	4	0	0	3	.538	1	3	0	4	9	0	1.000

ALL-STAR GAME RECORD

Year	League	Pos.	AB	R	H	2B	3B	HR	RBI	Avg.	BB	SO	SB	PO	A	E	Avg.
1998—	National								Did not play.								

BORBON, PEDRO   P   BLUE JAYS

PERSONAL: Born November 15, 1967, in Mao, Dominican Republic. ... 6-1/205. ... Throws left, bats left. ... Full name: Pedro Felix Borbon Jr. ... Son of Pedro Borbon, pitcher with four major league teams (1969-80). ... Name pronounced bor-BONE.
HIGH SCHOOL: DeWitt Clinton (Sioux, N.J.).
JUNIOR COLLEGE: Ranger (Texas) Junior College.
TRANSACTIONS/CAREER NOTES: Selected by Milwaukee Brewers organization in 35th round of free-agent draft (June 3, 1985); did not sign. ... Selected by Los Angeles Dodgers organization in secondary phase of free-agent draft (January 14, 1986); did not sign. ... Signed as non-drafted free agent by Chicago White Sox organization (June 4, 1988). ... Released by White Sox (April 1, 1989). ... Signed by Atlanta Braves organization (August 25, 1989). ... On Atlanta disabled list (April 8-26 and August 23, 1996-remainder of season); included rehabilitation assignment to Greenville (April 23-26). ... On disabled list (March 30, 1997-entire season). ... On Atlanta disabled list (March 29, 1998-entire season); included rehabilitation assignments to Macon (June 4-7), Greenville (June 9-July 5 and July 9-14) and Richmond (July 16-August 31 and September 1-8). ... Granted free agency (October 1, 1998). ... Signed by Dodgers organization (December 30, 1998). ... Traded by Dodgers with OF Raul Mondesi to Toronto Blue Jays for OF Shawn Green and 2B Jorge Nunez (November 8, 1999).
STATISTICAL NOTES: Led Gulf Coast League with 14 balks in 1988.

Year	League	W	L	Pct.	ERA	G	GS	CG	ShO	Sv.	IP	H	R	ER	BB	SO
1988—	GC White Sox (GCL)	5	3	.625	2.41	16	11	1	1	1	74 2/3	52	28	20	17	67
1989—									Did not play.							
1990—	Burlington (Midw.)■	11	3	.786	1.47	14	14	6	2	0	97 2/3	73	25	16	23	76
	— Durham (Caro.)	4	5	.444	5.43	11	11	0	0	0	61 1/3	73	40	37	16	37
1991—	Durham (Caro.)	4	3	.571	2.27	37	6	1	0	5	91	85	40	23	35	79
	— Greenville (Sou.)	0	1	.000	2.79	4	4	0	0	0	29	23	12	9	10	22
1992—	Greenville (Sou.)	8	2	.800	3.06	39	10	0	0	3	94	73	36	32	42	79
	— Atlanta (N.L.)	0	1	.000	6.75	2	0	0	0	0	1 1/3	2	1	1	1	1
1993—	Richmond (I.L.)	5	5	.500	4.23	52	0	0	0	1	76 2/3	71	40	36	42	95
	— Atlanta (N.L.)	0	0	...	21.60	3	0	0	0	0	1 2/3	3	4	4	3	2
1994—	Richmond (I.L.)	3	4	.429	2.79	59	0	0	0	4	80 2/3	66	29	25	41	82
1995—	Atlanta (N.L.)	2	2	.500	3.09	41	0	0	0	2	32	29	12	11	17	33
1996—	Atlanta (N.L.)	3	0	1.000	2.75	43	0	0	0	1	36	26	12	11	7	31
	— Greenville (Sou.)	0	0	...	0.00	1	0	0	0	0	1	0	0	0	0	0
1997—	Atlanta (N.L.)								Did not play.							
1998—	Macon (S.Atl.)	0	0	...	9.00	3	0	0	0	0	3	4	3	3	1	3
	— Greenville (Sou.)	0	2	.000	4.74	16	0	0	0	0	19	21	14	10	14	10
	— Richmond (I.L.)	0	1	.000	5.70	20	0	0	0	0	23 2/3	29	17	15	8	15
1999—	Los Angeles (N.L.)■	4	3	.571	4.09	70	0	0	0	1	50 2/3	39	23	23	29	33
2000—	Toronto (A.L.)■	1	1	.500	6.48	59	0	0	0	1	41 2/3	45	37	30	38	29
A.L. totals (1 year)		1	1	.500	6.48	59	0	0	0	1	41 2/3	45	37	30	38	29
N.L. totals (5 years)		9	6	.600	3.70	159	0	0	0	4	121 2/3	99	52	50	57	100
Major League totals (6 years)		10	7	.588	4.41	218	0	0	0	5	163 1/3	144	89	80	95	129

DIVISION SERIES RECORD

Year	League	W	L	Pct.	ERA	G	GS	CG	ShO	Sv.	IP	H	R	ER	BB	SO
1995—	Atlanta (N.L.)	0	0	...	0.00	1	0	0	0	0	1	1	0	0	0	3

CHAMPIONSHIP SERIES RECORD

Year	League	W	L	Pct.	ERA	G	GS	CG	ShO	Sv.	IP	H	R	ER	BB	SO
1995—	Atlanta (N.L.)								Did not play.							

WORLD SERIES RECORD

NOTES: Member of World Series championship team (1995).

Year	League	W	L	Pct.	ERA	G	GS	CG	ShO	Sv.	IP	H	R	ER	BB	SO
1995—	Atlanta (N.L.)	0	0	...	0.00	1	0	0	0	1	1	0	0	0	0	2

BORDICK, MIKE   SS   ORIOLES

PERSONAL: Born July 21, 1965, in Marquette, Mich. ... 5-11/175. ... Bats right, throws right. ... Full name: Michael Todd Bordick.
HIGH SCHOOL: Hampden (Maine) Academy.
COLLEGE: Maine.
TRANSACTIONS/CAREER NOTES: Signed as non-drafted free agent by Oakland Athletics organization (July 10, 1986). ... On Tacoma disabled list (April 14-May 13, 1991). ... On Oakland disabled list (May 8-27, 1995); included rehabilitation assignment to Modesto (May 23-26). ... Granted free agency (December 7, 1996). ... Signed by Baltimore Orioles (December 13, 1996). ... Traded by Orioles to New York Mets for OF Melvin Mora, 3B Mike Kinkade, P Lesli Brea and P Pat Gorman (July 28, 2000). ... Granted free agency (October 27, 2000). ... Signed by Orioles (December 20, 2000).
RECORDS: Shares major league career record for highest fielding percentage by shortstop (1,000 or more games)—.981.
STATISTICAL NOTES: Led Pacific Coast League shortstops with .972 fielding percentage and 82 double plays in 1990. ... Led A.L. shortstops with 280 putouts and tied for lead with 108 double plays in 1993. ... Led A.L. with 15 sacrifice hits in 1998. ... Led A.L. shortstops with 797 total chances and 132 double plays in 1999. ... Career major league grand slams: 1.

Year	Team (League)	Pos.	G	AB	R	H	2B	3B	HR	RBI	Avg.	BB	SO	SB	PO	A	E	Avg.
1986—	Medford (N'West)	SS	46	187	30	48	3	1	0	19	.257	40	21	6	68	143	18	.921
1987—	Modesto (Calif.)	SS	133	497	73	133	17	0	3	75	.268	87	92	8	216	305	17	*.968
1988—	Huntsville (Sou.)	2B-SS-3B	132	481	48	130	13	2	0	28	.270	87	50	7	260	406	24	.965
1989—	Tacoma (PCL)	2B-SS-3B	136	487	55	117	17	1	1	43	.240	58	51	4	261	431	33	.954
1990—	Oakland (A.L.)	3B-SS-2B	25	14	0	1	0	0	0	0	.071	1	4	0	9	8	0	1.000
	— Tacoma (PCL)	SS-2B	111	348	49	79	16	1	2	30	.227	46	40	3	210	366	16	†.973
1991—	Tacoma (PCL)	SS	26	81	15	22	4	1	2	14	.272	17	10	0	35	79	3	.974
	— Oakland (A.L.)	SS-2B-3B	90	235	21	56	5	1	0	21	.238	14	37	3	146	213	11	.970
1992—	Oakland (A.L.)	2B-SS	154	504	62	151	19	4	3	48	.300	40	59	12	311	449	16	.979
1993—	Oakland (A.L.)	SS-2B	159	546	60	136	21	2	3	48	.249	60	58	10	†285	420	13	.982
1994—	Oakland (A.L.)	SS-2B	114	391	38	99	18	4	2	37	.253	38	44	7	187	320	14	.973

Year Team (League)	Pos.	G	AB	R	H	2B	3B	HR	RBI	Avg.	BB	SO	SB	PO	A	E	Avg.
									BATTING					FIELDING			
1995— Oakland (A.L.)............	SS-DH	126	428	46	113	13	6	8	44	.264	35	48	11	*245	338	10	.983
— Modesto (Calif.)	SS	1	2	0	0	0	0	0	0	.000	0	0	0	2	1	0	1.000
1996— Oakland (A.L.)	SS	155	525	46	126	18	4	5	54	.240	52	59	5	265	*476	16	.979
1997— Baltimore (A.L.)■.......	SS	153	509	55	120	19	1	7	46	.236	33	66	0	224	424	13	.980
1998— Baltimore (A.L.).........	SS	151	465	59	121	29	1	13	51	.260	39	65	6	236	*446	7	.990
1999— Baltimore (A.L.).........	SS	160	631	93	175	35	7	10	77	.277	54	102	14	277	*511	9	* .989
2000— Baltimore (A.L.).........	SS	100	391	70	116	22	1	16	59	.297	34	71	6	161	258	9	.979
— New York (N.L.)■	SS	56	192	18	50	8	0	4	21	.260	15	28	3	71	140	7	.968
American League totals (11 years)		1387	4639	550	1214	199	25	67	485	.262	400	613	74	2346	3863	118	.981
National League totals (1 year)		56	192	18	50	8	0	4	21	.260	15	28	3	71	140	7	.968
Major League totals (11 years)		1443	4831	568	1264	207	25	71	506	.262	415	641	77	2417	4003	125	.981

DIVISION SERIES RECORD

Year Team (League)	Pos.	G	AB	R	H	2B	3B	HR	RBI	Avg.	BB	SO	SB	PO	A	E	Avg.
									BATTING					FIELDING			
1997— Baltimore (A.L.).........	SS	4	10	4	4	1	0	0	4	.400	4	2	0	4	15	0	1.000
2000— New York (N.L.).........	SS	4	12	3	2	0	0	0	0	.167	3	4	0	7	10	0	1.000
Division series totals (2 years)		8	22	7	6	1	0	0	4	.273	7	6	0	11	25	0	1.000

CHAMPIONSHIP SERIES RECORD

Year Team (League)	Pos.	G	AB	R	H	2B	3B	HR	RBI	Avg.	BB	SO	SB	PO	A	E	Avg.
									BATTING					FIELDING			
1990— Oakland (A.L.)								Did not play.									
1992— Oakland (A.L.)	SS-2B	6	19	1	1	0	0	0	0	.053	1	2	1	15	14	0	1.000
1997— Baltimore (A.L.).........	SS	6	19	0	3	1	0	0	2	.158	0	6	0	5	14	0	1.000
2000— New York (N.L.).........	SS	5	13	2	1	0	0	0	0	.077	3	1	0	10	11	0	1.000
Championship series totals (3 years)		17	51	3	5	1	0	0	2	.098	4	9	1	30	39	0	1.000

WORLD SERIES RECORD

Year Team (League)	Pos.	G	AB	R	H	2B	3B	HR	RBI	Avg.	BB	SO	SB	PO	A	E	Avg.
									BATTING					FIELDING			
1990— Oakland (A.L.)	SS-PR	3	0	0	0	0	0	0	0	...	0	0	0	0	2	0	1.000
2000— New York (N.L.).........	SS	4	8	0	1	0	0	0	0	.125	0	3	0	4	7	1	.917
World Series totals (2 years)		7	8	0	1	0	0	0	0	.125	0	3	0	4	9	1	.929

ALL-STAR GAME RECORD

Year League	Pos.	AB	R	H	2B	3B	HR	RBI	Avg.	BB	SO	SB	PO	A	E	Avg.
									BATTING					FIELDING		
2000— American	PH	1	0	0	0	0	0	0	.000	0	0	0	...	...	...	...

BORKOWSKI, DAVE — P — TIGERS

PERSONAL: Born February 7, 1977, in Detroit, Mich. ... 6-1/200. ... Throws right, bats right. ... Full name: David Richard Borkowski.
HIGH SCHOOL: Sterling Heights (Mich.).
TRANSACTIONS/CAREER NOTES: Selected by Detroit Tigers organization in 11th round of free-agent draft (June 1, 1995). ... On Toledo disabled list (May 30-August 28, 2000).
STATISTICAL NOTES: Pitched 6-0 no-hit victory against Kane County (April 20, 1997). ... Led Southern League with 25 home runs allowed in 1998.

Year League	W	L	Pct.	ERA	G	GS	CG	ShO	Sv.	IP	H	R	ER	BB	SO
1995— Gulf Coast Tigers (GCL)	3	2	.600	2.96	10	10	1	0	0	51 2/3	45	24	17	8	36
— Lakeland (FSL)	1	0	1.000	0.00	1	1	0	0	0	5	2	0	0	1	3
1996— Fayetteville (S.Atl.)	10	10	.500	3.33	27	27	5	0	0	178 1/3	158	85	66	54	117
1997— West Michigan (Midw.)	•15	3	•.833	3.46	25	25	4	2	0	164	143	79	63	31	104
1998— Jacksonville (Sou.)	*16	7	.696	4.63	28	28	3	1	0	178 2/3	204	99	92	54	97
1999— Toledo (I.L.)......................	6	8	.429	3.50	19	19	3	0	0	126	119	59	49	43	94
— Detroit (A.L.)	2	6	.250	6.10	17	12	0	0	0	76 2/3	86	58	52	40	50
2000— Toledo (I.L.)......................	3	1	.750	4.40	8	8	0	0	0	47	44	27	23	14	29
— Detroit (A.L.)	0	1	.000	21.94	2	1	0	0	0	5 1/3	11	13	13	7	1
— Gulf Coast Tigers (GCL)	0	0	...	2.25	3	3	0	0	0	8	7	3	2	0	6
— Lakeland (FSL)	0	1	.000	8.59	2	2	0	0	0	7 1/3	11	7	7	4	5
Major League totals (2 years)	2	7	.222	7.13	19	13	0	0	0	82	97	71	65	47	51

BOTTALICO, RICKY — P — PHILLIES

PERSONAL: Born August 26, 1969, in New Britain, Conn. ... 6-1/215. ... Throws right, bats left. ... Full name: Richard Paul Bottalico. ... Name pronounced ba-TAL-e-koh.
HIGH SCHOOL: South Catholic (Hartford, Conn.).
COLLEGE: Florida Southern, then Central Connecticut State.
TRANSACTIONS/CAREER NOTES: Signed as non-drafted free agent by Philadelphia Phillies organization (July 21, 1991). ... On Philadelphia disabled list (April 24-July 1, 1998); included rehabilitation assignment to Scranton/Wilkes-Barre (June 6-July 1). ... On suspended list (August 25-28, 1998). ... Traded by Phillies with P Garrett Stephenson to St. Louis Cardinals for OF Ron Gant, P Jeff Brantley and P Cliff Politte (November 19, 1998). ... Granted free agency (December 21, 1999). ... Signed by Kansas City Royals (January 27, 2000). ... Granted free agency (November 4, 2000). ... Signed by Phillies (December 15, 2000).
STATISTICAL NOTES: Pitched two innings, combining with starter Craig Holman (two innings), Gregory Brown (two innings) and Toby Borland (one inning) in seven-inning, 2-0 no-hit victory for Reading against New Britain (September 4, 1993, first game).

Year	League	W	L	Pct.	ERA	G	GS	CG	ShO	Sv.	IP	H	R	ER	BB	SO
1991—Martinsville (Appl.)		3	2	.600	4.09	7	6	2	•1	0	33	32	20	15	13	38
—Spartanburg (S.Atl.)		2	0	1.000	0.00	2	2	0	0	0	15	4	0	0	2	11
1992—Spartanburg (S.Atl.)		5	10	.333	2.41	42	11	1	0	13	119²/₃	94	41	32	56	118
1993—Clearwater (FSL)		1	0	1.000	2.75	13	0	0	0	4	19²/₃	19	6	6	5	19
—Reading (East.)		3	3	.500	2.25	49	0	0	0	20	72	63	22	18	26	65
1994—Scranton/W.B. (I.L.)		3	1	.750	8.87	19	0	0	0	3	22¹/₃	32	27	22	22	22
—Reading (East.)		2	2	.500	2.53	38	0	0	0	22	42²/₃	29	13	12	10	51
—Philadelphia (N.L.)		0	0	...	0.00	3	0	0	0	0	3	3	0	0	1	3
1995—Philadelphia (N.L.)		5	3	.625	2.46	62	0	0	0	1	87²/₃	50	25	24	42	87
1996—Philadelphia (N.L.)		4	5	.444	3.19	61	0	0	0	34	67²/₃	47	24	24	23	74
1997—Philadelphia (N.L.)		2	5	.286	3.65	69	0	0	0	34	74	68	31	30	42	89
1998—Philadelphia (N.L.)		1	5	.167	6.44	39	0	0	0	6	43¹/₃	54	31	31	25	27
—Scranton/W.B. (I.L.)		0	1	.000	2.92	10	5	0	0	1	12¹/₃	8	4	4	9	4
1999—St. Louis (N.L.)■		3	7	.300	4.91	68	0	0	0	20	73¹/₃	83	45	40	49	66
2000—Kansas City (A.L.)■		9	6	.600	4.83	62	0	0	0	16	72²/₃	65	40	39	41	56
A.L. totals (1 year)		9	6	.600	4.83	62	0	0	0	16	72²/₃	65	40	39	41	56
N.L. totals (6 years)		15	25	.375	3.84	302	0	0	0	95	349	305	156	149	182	346
Major League totals (7 years)		24	31	.436	4.01	364	0	0	0	111	421²/₃	370	196	188	223	402

ALL-STAR GAME RECORD

Year	League	W	L	Pct.	ERA	GS	CG	ShO	Sv.	IP	H	R	ER	BB	SO
1996—National		0	0	...	0.00	0	0	0	0	1	0	0	0	0	1

BOTTENFIELD, KENT — P — ASTROS

PERSONAL: Born November 14, 1968, in Portland, Ore. ... 6-3/240. ... Throws right, bats right. ... Full name: Kent Dennis Bottenfield. ... Twin brother of Keven Bottenfield, minor league catcher/infielder (1986-87).

HIGH SCHOOL: James Madison (Portland, Ore.).

TRANSACTIONS/CAREER NOTES: Selected by Montreal Expos organization in fourth round of free-agent draft (June 2, 1986). ... Traded by Expos to Colorado Rockies for P Butch Henry (July 16, 1993). ... On Colorado disabled list (March 25-May 9, 1994); included rehabilitation assignment to Colorado Springs (April 10-May 9). ... Granted free agency (June 27, 1994). ... Signed by San Francisco Giants organization (June 29, 1994). ... Released by Giants (November 8, 1994). ... Signed by Detroit Tigers organization (April 3, 1995). ... Granted free agency (October 16, 1995). ... Signed by Chicago Cubs organization (March 9, 1996). ... Granted free agency (December 21, 1997). ... Signed by St. Louis Cardinals (January 8, 1998). ... Traded by Cardinals with 2B/SS Adam Kennedy to Anaheim Angels for OF Jim Edmonds (March 23, 2000). ... On Anaheim disabled list (June 8-24, 2000). ... Traded by Angels to Philadelphia Phillies for OF Ron Gant (July 30, 2000). ... Granted free agency (October 30, 2000). ... Signed by Houston Astros (January 3, 2001).

Year	League	W	L	Pct.	ERA	G	GS	CG	ShO	Sv.	IP	H	R	ER	BB	SO
1986—Gulf Coast Expos (GCL)		5	6	.455	3.27	13	13	2	0	0	74¹/₃	73	•42	27	30	41
1987—Burlington (Midw.)		9	13	.409	4.53	27	27	6	3	0	161	175	98	81	42	103
1988—West Palm Beach (FSL)		10	8	.556	3.33	27	27	9	4	0	181	165	80	67	47	120
1989—Jacksonville (Sou.)		3	*17	.150	5.26	25	25	1	0	0	138²/₃	137	101	81	73	91
1990—Jacksonville (Sou.)		12	10	.545	3.41	29	28	2	1	0	169	158	72	64	67	121
1991—Indianapolis (A.A.)		8	15	.348	4.06	29	27	•5	2	0	166¹/₃	155	97	75	61	108
1992—Indianapolis (A.A.)		•12	8	.600	3.43	25	23	3	1	0	152¹/₃	139	64	58	58	111
—Montreal (N.L.)		1	2	.333	2.23	10	4	0	0	1	32¹/₃	26	9	8	11	14
1993—Montreal (N.L.)		2	5	.286	4.12	23	11	0	0	0	83	93	49	38	33	33
—Colorado (N.L.)■		3	5	.375	6.10	14	14	1	0	0	76²/₃	86	53	52	38	30
1994—Colorado Springs (PCL)		1	2	.333	4.94	5	4	1	0	0	31	35	19	17	11	17
—Colorado (N.L.)		3	1	.750	5.84	15	1	0	0	1	24²/₃	28	16	16	10	15
—Phoenix (PCL)■		2	1	.667	2.57	8	5	1	1	0	35	30	13	10	11	11
—San Francisco (N.L.)		0	0	...	10.80	1	0	0	0	0	1²/₃	5	2	2	0	0
1995—Toledo (I.L.)■		5	11	.313	4.54	27	19	2	1	1	136²/₃	148	80	69	55	68
1996—Iowa (A.A.)■		1	2	.333	2.19	28	0	0	0	18	24²/₃	19	9	6	8	14
—Chicago (N.L.)		3	5	.375	2.63	48	0	0	0	1	61²/₃	59	25	18	19	33
1997—Chicago (N.L.)		2	3	.400	3.86	64	0	0	0	2	84	82	39	36	35	74
1998—St. Louis (N.L.)■		4	6	.400	4.44	44	17	0	0	4	133²/₃	128	72	66	57	98
1999—St. Louis (N.L.)		18	7	.720	3.97	31	31	0	0	0	190¹/₃	197	91	84	89	124
2000—Anaheim (A.L.)■		7	8	.467	5.71	21	21	0	0	0	127²/₃	144	82	81	56	75
—Philadelphia (N.L.)■		1	2	.333	4.50	8	8	1	1	0	44	41	24	22	21	31
A.L. totals (1 year)		7	8	.467	5.71	21	21	0	0	0	127²/₃	144	82	81	56	75
N.L. totals (8 years)		37	36	.507	4.20	258	86	2	1	9	732	745	380	342	313	452
Major League totals (8 years)		44	44	.500	4.43	279	107	2	1	9	859²/₃	889	462	423	369	527

ALL-STAR GAME RECORD

Year	League	W	L	Pct.	ERA	GS	CG	ShO	Sv.	IP	H	R	ER	BB	SO
1999—National		0	0	...	18.00	0	0	0	0	1	1	2	2	1	2

BOWIE, MICAH — P

PERSONAL: Born November 10, 1974, in Webster, Texas. ... 6-4/210. ... Throws left, bats left. ... Full name: Micah Andrew Bowie. ... Name pronounced bu-ee.

HIGH SCHOOL: Kingwood (Texas).

TRANSACTIONS/CAREER NOTES: Signed as non-drafted free agent by Atlanta Braves organization (July 15, 1993). ... On Durham disabled list (July 4, 1996-remainder of season). ... On Richmond disabled list (May 18-June 10, 1999). ... Traded by Braves with P Ruben Quevado and a player to be named later to Chicago Cubs for P Terry Mulholland and SS Jose Hernandez (July 31, 1999); Cubs acquired P Joey Nation to complete deal (August 24, 1999). ... Released by Cubs (November 27, 2000).

Year	League	W	L	Pct.	ERA	G	GS	CG	ShO	Sv.	IP	H	R	ER	BB	SO
1994—Gulf Coast Braves (GCL)		0	3	.000	3.03	6	5	0	0	0	29²/₃	27	14	10	5	35
—Danville (Appl.)		3	1	.750	3.58	7	5	0	0	0	32²/₃	28	16	13	13	38
1995—Macon (S.Atl.)		4	1	.800	2.28	5	5	0	0	0	27²/₃	9	8	7	11	36
—Durham (Caro.)		4	11	.267	3.66	23	13	0	0	0	66¹/₃	55	29	27	33	65

Year League	W	L	Pct.	ERA	G	GS	CG	ShO	Sv.	IP	H	R	ER	BB	SO
1996—Durham (Caro.)	3	6	.333	3.66	14	13	0	0	0	66⅓	55	29	27	33	65
1997—Durham (Caro.)	2	2	.500	3.66	9	6	0	0	0	39⅓	29	16	16	27	44
—Greenville (Sou.)	3	2	.600	3.50	8	7	0	0	0	43⅔	34	19	17	26	41
1998—Greenville (Sou.)	11	6	.647	3.48	30	•29	1	0	0	163	132	73	63	64	160
1999—Richmond (I.L.)	4	4	.500	2.96	13	13	0	0	0	73	65	24	24	14	82
—Atlanta (N.L.)	0	1	.000	13.50	3	0	0	0	0	4	8	6	6	4	2
—Chicago (N.L.)■	2	6	.250	9.96	11	11	0	0	0	47	73	54	52	30	39
2000—Iowa (PCL)	1	7	.125	7.94	9	9	0	0	0	45⅓	59	44	40	31	35
—West Tenn (Sou.)	7	6	.538	3.45	18	18	1	1	0	117⅓	91	47	45	48	106
Major League totals (1 year)	2	7	.222	10.24	14	11	0	0	0	51	81	60	58	34	41

BOYD, JASON   P   PHILLIES

PERSONAL: Born February 23, 1973, in St. Clair, Ill. ... 6-3/173. ... Throws right, bats right. ... Full name: Jason Pernell Boyd.
HIGH SCHOOL: Edwardsville (Ill.).
JUNIOR COLLEGE: John A. Logan College (Ill.).
TRANSACTIONS/CAREER NOTES: Selected by Philadelphia Phillies organization in eighth round of free-agent draft (June 2, 1994). ... Selected by Arizona Diamondbacks in first round (23rd pick overall) of expansion draft (November 18, 1997). ... On disabled list (May 22, 1998-remainder of season). ... Traded by Diamondbacks to Pittsburgh Pirates (August 25, 1999), completing deal in which Pirates traded 2B Tony Womack to Diamondbacks for OF Paul Weichard and a player to named later (February 26, 1999). ... Claimed on waivers by Milwaukee Brewers (March 29, 2000). ... Claimed on waivers by Philadelphia Phillies (March 31, 2000). ... On Philadelphia disabled list (March 25-May 4 and June 15-August 15, 2000; included rehabilitation assignments to Clearwater (April 7-15 and July 28-31) and Scranton (April 16-19, April 26-May 2 and August 1-15).

Year League	W	L	Pct.	ERA	G	GS	CG	ShO	Sv.	IP	H	R	ER	BB	SO
1994—Martinsville (Appl.)	3	7	.300	4.17	14	13	1	0	0	69	65	46	32	32	45
1995—Piedmont (S.Atl.)	6	8	.429	3.58	26	24	1	0	0	151	151	77	60	44	129
1996—Clearwater (FSL)	11	8	.579	3.90	26	26	2	0	0	161⅔	160	75	70	49	120
1997—Reading (East.)	10	6	.625	4.82	48	7	0	0	0	115⅔	113	65	62	64	98
1998—Tucson (PCL)■	2	2	.500	6.23	15	0	0	0	0	21⅔	28	22	15	14	13
1999—Tucson (PCL)	6	5	.545	4.52	44	0	0	0	5	75⅔	76	42	38	27	60
—Nashville (PCL)■	0	0	...	0.00	5	0	0	0	0	4⅔	2	0	0	0	2
—Pittsburgh (N.L.)	0	0	...	3.38	4	0	0	0	0	5⅓	5	2	2	2	4
2000—Clearwater (FSL)	1	0	1.000	2.38	6	3	0	0	0	11⅓	11	4	3	4	12
—Scranton/W.B. (I.L.)	1	0	1.000	1.72	11	2	0	0	0	15⅔	8	3	3	14	10
—Philadelphia (N.L.)	0	1	.000	6.55	30	0	0	0	0	34⅓	39	28	25	24	32
Major League totals (2 years)	0	1	.000	6.13	34	0	0	0	0	39⅔	44	30	27	26	36

BRADFORD, CHAD   P   ATHLETICS

PERSONAL: Born September 14, 1974, in Jackson, Miss. ... 6-5/205. ... Throws right, bats right. ... Full name: Chadwick Lee Bradford.
HIGH SCHOOL: Byram (Jackson, Miss.).
JUNIOR COLLEGE: Hinds Community College (Miss.).
COLLEGE: Southern Mississippi.
TRANSACTIONS/CAREER NOTES: Selected by Chicago White Sox organization in 13th round of free-agent draft (June 4, 1996). ... On Charlotte disabled list (June 28-July 5, 2000). ... Traded by White Sox to Oakland Athletics for a player to be named later (December 7, 2000); Athletics acquired C Miguel Olivo to complete deal (December 13, 2000).

Year League	W	L	Pct.	ERA	G	GS	CG	ShO	Sv.	IP	H	R	ER	BB	SO
1996—Hickory (S.Atl.)	0	2	.000	0.90	28	0	0	0	18	30	21	7	3	7	27
1997—Winston-Salem (Caro.)	3	7	.300	3.95	46	0	0	0	15	54⅔	51	30	24	25	43
1998—Birmingham (Sou.)	1	1	.500	2.60	10	0	0	0	1	17⅓	13	6	5	8	14
—Calgary (PCL)	4	1	.800	1.94	29	0	0	0	0	51	50	12	11	11	27
—Chicago (A.L.)	2	1	.667	3.23	29	0	0	0	1	30⅔	27	16	11	7	11
1999—Charlotte (I.L.)	9	3	.750	1.94	47	0	0	0	5	74⅓	63	19	16	15	56
—Chicago (A.L.)	0	0	...	19.64	3	0	0	0	0	3⅔	9	8	8	5	0
2000—Charlotte (I.L.)	2	4	.333	1.51	55	0	0	0	10	53⅔	38	18	9	12	42
—Chicago (A.L.)	1	0	1.000	1.98	12	0	0	0	0	13⅔	13	4	3	1	9
Major League totals (3 years)	3	1	.750	4.13	44	0	0	0	1	48	49	28	22	13	20

DIVISION SERIES RECORD

Year League	W	L	Pct.	ERA	G	GS	CG	ShO	Sv.	IP	H	R	ER	BB	SO
2000—Chicago (A.L.)	0	0	...	0.00	1	0	0	0	0	⅔	2	0	0	0	0

BRADLEY, MILTON   OF   EXPOS

PERSONAL: Born April 15, 1978, in Harbor City, Fla. ... 6-0/180. ... Bats both, throws right. ... Full name: Milton Obelle Bradley.
HIGH SCHOOL: Polytechnic (Long Beach, Calif.).
TRANSACTIONS/CAREER NOTES: Selected by Montreal Expos organization in second round of free-agent draft (June 4, 1996). ... On Harrisburg disabled list (June 14-25, 1999).

Year Team (League)	Pos.	G	AB	R	H	2B	3B	HR	RBI	Avg.	BB	SO	SB	PO	A	E	Avg.
							BATTING								FIELDING		
1996—GC Expos (GCL)	OF	32	112	18	27	7	1	1	12	.241	13	15	7	54	2	3	.949
1997—Vermont (NY-Penn)	OF	50	200	29	60	7	5	3	30	.300	17	34	7	113	3	4	.967
—GC Expos (GCL)	OF	9	25	6	5	2	0	1	2	.200	4	4	2	15	0	1	.938
1998—Cape Fear (S.Atl.)	OF	75	281	54	85	21	4	6	50	.302	23	57	13	87	5	3	.968
—Jupiter (FSL)	OF	67	261	55	75	14	1	5	34	.287	30	42	17	138	8	1	.993
1999—Harrisburg (East.)	OF-DH	87	346	62	114	22	5	10	50	.329	33	61	14	166	3	5	.971
2000—Ottawa (I.L.)	OF	88	342	58	104	20	1	6	29	.304	45	56	10	216	7	3	.987
—Montreal (N.L.)	OF	42	154	20	34	8	1	2	15	.221	14	32	2	88	6	2	.979
Major League totals (1 year)		42	154	20	34	8	1	2	15	.221	14	32	2	88	6	2	.979

BRADLEY, RYAN P YANKEES

PERSONAL: Born October 26, 1975, in Covina, Calif. ... 6-4/226. ... Throws right, bats right. ... Full name: Ryan James Bradley.
HIGH SCHOOL: Ayala (Chino, Calif.).
COLLEGE: Arizona State.
TRANSACTIONS/CAREER NOTES: Selected by Kansas City Royals in 14th round of free-agent draft (June 2, 1994); did not sign. ... Selected by New York Yankees organization in supplemental round ("sandwich" pick between first and second round; 40th pick overall) of free-agent draft (June 3, 1997); pick received as compensation for Texas Rangers signing Type A free-agent P John Wetteland. ... On Columbus disabled list (July 3-15, 1999).
STATISTICAL NOTES: Pitched 8-0 no-hit victory for Tampa against Lakeland (June 22, 1998). ... Led International League with 23 wild pitches in 1999. ... Tied for International League lead with 28 home runs allowed in 1999. ... Tied for International League lead with 12 wild pitches in 2000.

Year	League	W	L	Pct.	ERA	G	GS	CG	ShO	Sv.	IP	H	R	ER	BB	SO
1997—	Oneonta (NY-Penn)	3	1	.750	1.35	14	0	0	0	1	26²/₃	22	5	4	5	22
1998—	Tampa (FSL)	7	4	.636	2.38	32	11	1	1	7	94²/₃	59	29	25	30	112
—	Norwich (East.)	2	0	1.000	1.44	3	3	1	1	0	25	8	4	4	8	25
—	Columbus (I.L.)	0	1	.000	6.19	3	3	0	0	0	16	15	13	11	13	12
—	New York (A.L.)	2	1	.667	5.68	5	1	0	0	0	12²/₃	12	9	8	9	13
1999—	Columbus (I.L.)	5	12	.294	6.21	29	24	1	0	0	145	163	112	100	73	118
2000—	Columbus (I.L.)	5	1	.833	5.82	49	0	0	0	0	72²/₃	82	52	47	52	54
Major League totals (1 year)		2	1	.667	5.68	5	1	0	0	0	12²/₃	12	9	8	9	13

B

BRAGG, DARREN OF METS

PERSONAL: Born September 7, 1969, in Waterbury, Conn. ... 5-9/180. ... Bats left, throws right. ... Full name: Darren William Bragg.
HIGH SCHOOL: Taft (Watertown, Conn.).
COLLEGE: Georgia Tech.
TRANSACTIONS/CAREER NOTES: Selected by Seattle Mariners organization in 22nd round of free-agent draft (June 30, 1991). ... Traded by Mariners to Boston Red Sox for P Jamie Moyer (July 30, 1996). ... Granted free agency (December 21, 1998). ... Signed by St. Louis Cardinals (January 12, 1999). ... On disabled list (August 3, 1999-remainder of season). ... Released by Cardinals (December 16, 1999). ... Signed by Colorado Rockies (February 1, 2000). ... Released by Rockies (July 24, 2000). ... Signed by New York Mets organization (January 9, 2001).
STATISTICAL NOTES: Led Carolina League in caught stealing with 19 in 1992. ... Led Pacific Coast League outfielders with 344 total chances and five double plays in 1994. ... Career major league grand slams: 2.

Year	Team (League)	Pos.	G	AB	R	H	2B	3B	HR	RBI	Avg.	BB	SO	SB	PO	A	E	Avg.
								BATTING								FIELDING		
1991—	Peninsula (Caro.)	OF-2B	69	237	42	53	14	0	3	29	.224	66	72	21	167	9	4	.978
1992—	Peninsula (Caro.)	OF	135	428	*83	117	29	5	9	58	.273	*105	76	44	262	11	4	.986
1993—	Jacksonville (Sou.)	OF-P	131	451	74	119	26	3	11	46	.264	81	82	19	306	14	10	.970
1994—	Calgary (PCL)	OF	126	500	112	175	33	6	17	85	.350	68	72	28	317	20	7	.980
—	Seattle (A.L.)	DH-OF	8	19	4	3	1	0	0	2	.158	2	5	0	1	0	0	1.000
1995—	Seattle (A.L.)	OF-DH	52	145	20	34	5	1	3	12	.234	18	37	9	83	7	1	.989
—	Tacoma (PCL)	OF-DH	53	212	24	65	13	3	4	31	.307	23	39	10	115	7	4	.968
1996—	Seattle (A.L.)	OF	69	195	36	53	12	1	7	25	.272	33	35	8	118	7	1	.992
—	Tacoma (PCL)	OF	20	71	17	20	8	0	3	8	.282	14	14	1	32	2	0	1.000
—	Boston (A.L.)■	OF	58	222	38	56	14	1	3	22	.252	36	39	6	136	5	2	.986
1997—	Boston (A.L.)	OF-3B	153	513	65	132	35	2	9	57	.257	61	102	10	364	11	5	.987
1998—	Boston (A.L.)	OF-DH	129	409	51	114	29	3	8	57	.279	42	99	5	218	6	1	*.996
1999—	St. Louis (N.L.)■	OF	93	273	38	71	12	1	6	26	.260	44	67	3	155	7	3	.982
2000—	Colorado (N.L.)■	OF	71	149	16	33	7	1	3	21	.221	17	41	4	53	0	0	1.000
American League totals (5 years)			469	1503	214	392	96	8	30	175	.261	192	317	38	920	36	10	.990
National League totals (2 years)			164	422	54	104	19	2	9	47	.246	61	108	7	208	7	3	.986
Major League totals (7 years)			633	1925	268	496	115	10	39	222	.258	253	425	45	1128	43	13	.989

DIVISION SERIES RECORD

Year	Team (League)	Pos.	G	AB	R	H	2B	3B	HR	RBI	Avg.	BB	SO	SB	PO	A	E	Avg.
								BATTING								FIELDING		
1998—	Boston (A.L.)	OF	3	12	0	1	0	0	0	0	.083	0	5	0	4	0	0	1.000

RECORD AS PITCHER

Year	League	W	L	Pct.	ERA	G	GS	CG	ShO	Sv.	IP	H	R	ER	BB	SO
1993—	Jacksonville (Sou.)	0	0	...	9.00	1	0	0	0	0	1	3	1	1	0	0

BRAMMER, J.D. P INDIANS

PERSONAL: Born January 30, 1975, in West Logan, W.Va. ... 6-4/235. ... Throws right, bats right. ... Full name: John David Brammer.
HIGH SCHOOL: Logan (W.Va.).
COLLEGE: Stanford.
TRANSACTIONS/CAREER NOTES: Selected by Cleveland Indians organization in fourth round of free-agent draft (June 4, 1996). ... On Kinston disabled list (May 20-July 15, 1998). ... On Buffalo disabled list (June 9-19 and July 11-18, 2000).

Year	League	W	L	Pct.	ERA	G	GS	CG	ShO	Sv.	IP	H	R	ER	BB	SO
1996—	Watertown (NY-Penn)	5	0	1.000	3.55	17	0	0	0	1	38	27	22	15	28	49
1997—	Columbia (S.Atl.)	6	10	.375	7.02	28	23	0	0	1	116²/₃	132	102	*91	50	105
1998—	Kinston (Caro.)	3	2	.600	1.33	15	0	0	0	2	27	15	6	4	8	33
—	Akron (East.)	1	0	1.000	5.23	11	0	0	0	3	20²/₃	21	12	12	10	23
1999—	Akron (East.)	3	2	.600	4.76	47	0	0	0	8	75²/₃	53	44	40	60	69
2000—	Akron (East.)	2	1	.667	1.16	16	0	0	0	1	23¹/₃	12	4	3	6	20
—	Buffalo (I.L.)	2	0	1.000	4.79	25	0	0	0	0	35²/₃	38	21	19	17	28

PERSONAL: Born January 26, 1967, in Waynesboro, Miss. ... 6-0/180. ... Bats left, throws right. ... Full name: Jeffery Glenn Branson.
HIGH SCHOOL: Southern Choctaw (Silas, Ala.).
COLLEGE: Livingston (Ala.) University.
TRANSACTIONS/CAREER NOTES: Selected by Cincinnati Reds organization in second round of free-agent draft (June 1, 1988). ... Traded by Reds with P John Smiley to Cleveland Indians for P Danny Graves, P Jim Crowell, P Scott Winchester and IF Damian Jackson (July 31, 1997). ... On Cleveland disabled list (August 2-September 1, 1998); included rehabilitation assignment to Buffalo (August 21-September 1). ... Granted free agency (October 23, 1998). ... Signed by Reds organization (November 17, 1998). ... Granted free agency (October 15, 1999). ... Signed by Los Angeles Dodgers organization (December 27, 1999). ... Granted free agency (October 16, 2000). ... Re-signed by Dodgers organization (December 18, 2000).
STATISTICAL NOTES: Led International League shortstops with .974 fielding percentage and 81 double plays in 1999.
MISCELLANEOUS: Member of 1988 U.S. Olympic baseball team.

Year	Team (League)	Pos.	G	AB	R	H	2B	3B	HR	RBI	Avg.	BB	SO	SB	PO	A	E	Avg.
1989—	Cedar Rapids (Midw.)	SS	127	469	70	132	28	1	10	68	.281	41	90	5	172	394	33	.945
1990—	Cedar Rapids (Midw.)	SS	62	239	37	60	13	4	6	24	.251	24	44	11	96	152	7	.973
—	Chattanooga (Sou.)	2B-SS	63	233	19	49	9	1	2	29	.210	13	48	3	122	151	13	.955
1991—	Chattanooga (Sou.)	SS-2B	88	304	35	80	13	3	2	28	.263	31	51	3	126	212	12	.966
—	Nashville (A.A.)	SS-2B-OF	43	145	10	35	4	1	0	11	.241	8	31	5	61	93	8	.951
1992—	Nashville (A.A.)	SS-3B-2B-OF	36	123	18	40	6	3	4	12	.325	9	19	0	59	76	5	.964
—	Cincinnati (N.L.)	2B-3B-SS	72	115	12	34	7	1	0	15	.296	5	16	0	46	63	7	.940
1993—	Cincinnati (N.L.)	SS-2B-3B-1B	125	381	40	92	15	1	3	22	.241	19	73	4	185	260	11	.976
1994—	Cincinnati (N.L.)	2B-3B-SS-1B	58	109	18	31	4	1	6	16	.284	5	16	0	39	52	1	.989
1995—	Cincinnati (N.L.)	3B-SS-2B-1B	122	331	43	86	18	2	12	45	.260	44	69	2	84	245	9	.973
1996—	Cincinnati (N.L.)	3B-SS-2B	129	311	34	76	16	4	9	37	.244	31	67	2	97	201	14	.955
1997—	Indianapolis (A.A.)	SS-3B	15	57	7	12	3	0	1	4	.211	6	10	0	18	32	1	.980
—	Cincinnati (N.L.)	3B-2B-SS	65	98	9	15	3	1	1	5	.153	7	23	1	35	56	4	.958
—	Cleveland (A.L.)■.....	2B-3B-SS-DH	29	72	5	19	4	0	2	7	.264	7	17	0	23	60	1	.988
1998—	Cleveland (A.L.).........	2B-3B-1B-SS	63	100	6	20	4	1	1	9	.200	3	21	0	49	55	5	.954
—	Buffalo (I.L.)	3B-2B	12	46	5	12	4	1	0	2	.261	5	9	0	20	29	0	1.000
1999—	Indianapolis (I.L.)■.....	S-3-2-DH-1	124	430	57	109	18	2	7	56	.253	46	86	2	182	360	15	†.973
2000—	Albuquerque (PCL)■..	3B-SS-1B	108	332	45	96	23	2	5	41	.289	27	71	6	86	227	8	.975
—	Los Angeles (N.L.)	SS-2B-3B	18	17	3	4	1	0	0	0	.235	1	6	0	8	13	1	.955
American League totals (2 years)			92	172	11	39	8	1	3	16	.227	10	38	0	72	115	6	.969
National League totals (7 years)			589	1362	159	338	64	10	31	140	.248	112	270	9	494	890	47	.967
Major League totals (8 years)			681	1534	170	377	72	11	34	156	.246	122	308	9	566	1005	53	.967

DIVISION SERIES RECORD

Year	Team (League)	Pos.	G	AB	R	H	2B	3B	HR	RBI	Avg.	BB	SO	SB	PO	A	E	Avg.
1995—	Cincinnati (N.L.)	3B	3	7	0	2	1	0	0	2	.286	2	0	0	1	8	0	1.000
1998—	Cleveland (A.L.)										Did not play.							

CHAMPIONSHIP SERIES RECORD

Year	Team (League)	Pos.	G	AB	R	H	2B	3B	HR	RBI	Avg.	BB	SO	SB	PO	A	E	Avg.
1995—	Cincinnati (N.L.)	3B-PH	4	9	2	1	1	0	0	0	.111	0	2	1	1	3	0	1.000
1997—	Cleveland (A.L.)	DH	1	2	0	0	0	0	0	0	.000	0	2	0	...	...	...	...
1998—	Cleveland (A.L.)	PH	1	1	0	0	0	0	0	0	.000	0	0	0	...	...	...	...
Championship series totals (3 years)			6	12	2	1	1	0	0	0	.083	0	4	1	1	3	0	1.000

WORLD SERIES RECORD

Year	Team (League)	Pos.	G	AB	R	H	2B	3B	HR	RBI	Avg.	BB	SO	SB	PO	A	E	Avg.
1997—	Cleveland (A.L.)	PH	1	1	0	0	0	0	0	0	.000	0	1	0	...	...	...	...

PERSONAL: Born September 5, 1963, in Florence, Ala. ... 5-10/197. ... Throws right, bats right. ... Full name: Jeffrey Hoke Brantley.
HIGH SCHOOL: W.A. Berry (Florence, Ala.).
COLLEGE: Mississippi State.
TRANSACTIONS/CAREER NOTES: Selected by Montreal Expos organization in 13th round of free-agent draft (June 4, 1984); did not sign. ... Selected by San Francisco Giants organization in sixth round of free-agent draft (June 3, 1985). ... Granted free agency (December 20, 1993). ... Signed by Cincinnati Reds (January 4, 1994). ... Granted free agency (October 17, 1994). ... Re-signed by Reds (October 28, 1994). ... On disabled list (March 19-April 6, 1996). ... On disabled list (March 27-April 15 and May 20, 1997-remainder of season). ... Traded by Reds to St. Louis Cardinals for 1B Dmitri Young (November 10, 1997). ... On St. Louis disabled list (March 23-April 9, 1998); included rehabilitation assignment to Arkansas (April 5-9). ... Traded by Cardinals with OF Ron Gant and P Cliff Politte to Philadelphia Phillies for P Ricky Bottalico and P Garrett Stephenson (November 19, 1998). ... On disabled list (April 29-May 16 and May 24, 1999-remainder of season). ... Granted free agency (November 1, 1999). ... Re-signed by Phillies (December 7, 1999). ... On Philadelphia disabled list (March 25-May 4, 2000); included rehabilitation assignments to Clearwater (April 6-15) and Scranton (April 16-23 and May 2-4). ... Granted free agency (October 31, 2000). ... Signed by Texas Rangers organization (January 12, 2001).
STATISTICAL NOTES: Tied for Pacific Coast League lead with 11 hit batsmen in 1987.
MISCELLANEOUS: Appeared in one game as pinch runner with San Francisco (1989).

Year	League	W	L	Pct.	ERA	G	GS	CG	ShO	Sv.	IP	H	R	ER	BB	SO
1985—	Fresno (Calif.)	8	2	.800	3.33	14	13	3	0	0	94 2/3	83	39	35	37	85
1986—	Shreveport (Texas)	8	10	.444	3.48	26	26	•8	3	0	165 2/3	139	78	64	68	125
1987—	Shreveport (Texas)	0	1	.000	3.09	2	2	0	0	0	11 2/3	12	7	4	4	7
—	Phoenix (PCL)	6	11	.353	4.65	29	28	2	0	0	170 1/3	187	110	88	82	111
1988—	Phoenix (PCL)	9	5	.643	4.33	27	19	1	0	0	122 2/3	130	65	59	39	83
—	San Francisco (N.L.)	0	1	.000	5.66	9	1	0	0	1	20 2/3	22	13	13	6	11

Year League	W	L	Pct.	ERA	G	GS	CG	ShO	Sv.	IP	H	R	ER	BB	SO
1989—San Francisco (N.L.)	7	1	.875	4.07	59	1	0	0	0	97 1/3	101	50	44	37	69
—Phoenix (PCL)....................	1	1	.500	1.26	7	0	0	0	3	14 1/3	6	2	2	6	20
1990—San Francisco (N.L.)	5	3	.625	1.56	55	0	0	0	19	86 2/3	77	18	15	33	61
1991—San Francisco (N.L.)	5	2	.714	2.45	67	0	0	0	15	95 1/3	78	27	26	52	81
1992—San Francisco (N.L.)	7	7	.500	2.95	56	4	0	0	7	91 2/3	67	32	30	45	86
1993—San Francisco (N.L.)	5	6	.455	4.28	53	12	0	0	0	113 2/3	112	60	54	46	76
1994—Cincinnati (N.L.)■	6	6	.500	2.48	50	0	0	0	15	65 1/3	46	20	18	28	63
1995—Cincinnati (N.L.)	3	2	.600	2.82	56	0	0	0	28	70 1/3	53	22	22	20	62
1996—Cincinnati (N.L.)	1	2	.333	2.41	66	0	0	0	•44	71	54	21	19	28	76
1997—Cincinnati (N.L.)	1	1	.500	3.86	13	0	0	0	1	11 2/3	9	5	5	7	16
1998—Arkansas (Texas)■..............	0	0	...	0.00	2	0	0	0	0	1 2/3	0	0	0	1	3
—St. Louis (N.L.).....................	0	5	.000	4.44	48	0	0	0	14	50 2/3	40	26	25	18	48
1999—Philadelphia (N.L.)■............	1	2	.333	5.19	10	0	0	0	5	8 2/3	5	6	5	8	11
2000—Philadelphia (N.L.)..............	2	7	.222	5.86	55	0	0	0	23	55 1/3	64	36	36	29	57
—Clearwater (FSL)	2	0	1.000	3.00	5	1	0	0	0	6	5	2	2	3	5
—Scranton/W.B. (I.L.)	0	0	...	3.60	5	1	0	0	0	5	3	2	2	1	4
Major League totals (13 years).....	43	45	.489	3.35	597	18	0	0	172	838 1/3	728	336	312	357	717

DIVISION SERIES RECORD

Year League	W	L	Pct.	ERA	G	GS	CG	ShO	Sv.	IP	H	R	ER	BB	SO
1995—Cincinnati (N.L.)	0	0	...	6.00	3	0	0	0	1	3	5	2	2	0	2

CHAMPIONSHIP SERIES RECORD

Year League	W	L	Pct.	ERA	G	GS	CG	ShO	Sv.	IP	H	R	ER	BB	SO
1989—San Francisco (N.L.)	0	0	...	0.00	3	0	0	0	0	5	1	0	0	2	3
1995—Cincinnati (N.L.)	0	0	...	0.00	2	0	0	0	0	2 2/3	0	0	0	2	1
Champ. series totals (2 years)	0	0	...	0.00	5	0	0	0	0	7 2/3	1	0	0	4	4

WORLD SERIES RECORD

Year League	W	L	Pct.	ERA	G	GS	CG	ShO	Sv.	IP	H	R	ER	BB	SO
1989—San Francisco (N.L.)	0	0	...	4.15	3	0	0	0	0	4 1/3	5	2	2	3	1

ALL-STAR GAME RECORD

Year League	W	L	Pct.	ERA	GS	CG	ShO	Sv.	IP	H	R	ER	BB	SO
1990—National.............................	0	1	.000	54.00	0	0	0	0	1/3	2	2	2	0	0

B

BRANYAN, RUSSELL — 3B — INDIANS

PERSONAL: Born December 19, 1975, in Warner Robins, Ga. ... 6-3/195. ... Bats left, throws right. ... Full name: Russell Oles Branyan.
HIGH SCHOOL: Stratford Academy (Warner Robins, Ga.).
TRANSACTIONS/CAREER NOTES: Selected by Cleveland Indians organization in seventh round of free-agent draft (June 2, 1994). ... On Akron disabled list (April 23-May 11 and May 16-August 15, 1998).
HONORS: Named Appalachian League Most Valuable Player (1996).
STATISTICAL NOTES: Led Appalachian League with .575 slugging percentage in 1996. ... Led Appalachian League third basemen with 24 double plays in 1996. ... Career major league grand slams: 1.

						BATTING								FIELDING			
Year Team (League)	Pos.	G	AB	R	H	2B	3B	HR	RBI	Avg.	BB	SO	SB	PO	A	E	Avg.
1994—Burlington (Appl.).......	3B	55	171	21	36	10	0	5	13	.211	25	64	4	32	88	21	.851
1995—Columbus (S.Atl.).......	3B	76	277	46	71	8	6	19	55	.256	27	120	1	34	120	26	.856
1996—Columbus (S.Atl.).......	3B-DH	130	482	102	129	20	4	*40	*106	.268	62	166	7	82	256	44	.885
1997—Kinston (Caro.)...........	3B-DH	83	297	59	86	26	2	27	75	.290	52	94	3	64	118	21	.897
—Akron (East.)	3B-DH	41	137	26	32	4	0	12	30	.234	28	56	0	31	98	11	.921
1998—Akron (East.)	3B-DH	43	163	35	48	11	3	16	46	.294	35	58	1	24	72	7	.932
—Cleveland (A.L.)	3B	1	4	0	0	0	0	0	0	.000	0	2	0	0	1	0	1.000
1999—Buffalo (I.L.)	3B-DH	109	395	51	82	11	1	30	67	.208	52	*187	8	63	205	23	.921
—Cleveland (A.L.)	3B-DH	11	38	4	8	2	0	1	6	.211	3	19	0	6	18	1	.960
2000—Buffalo (I.L.)	3B-OF	64	229	46	56	9	2	21	60	.245	28	93	1	75	70	9	.942
—Cleveland (A.L.).........	OF-DH-3B	67	193	32	46	7	2	16	38	.238	22	76	0	59	3	3	.954
Major League totals (3 years)		79	235	36	54	9	2	17	44	.230	25	97	0	65	22	4	.956

BREA, LESLIE — P — ORIOLES

PERSONAL: Born October 12, 1978, in San Pedro de Macoris, Dominican Republic. ... 5-11/170. ... Throws right, bats right. ... Full name: Leslie Guillermo Brea.
HIGH SCHOOL: Santo Domingo (San Pedro de Macoris, Dominican Republic).
TRANSACTIONS/CAREER NOTES: Signed as non-drafted free agent by Seattle Mariners organization (January 20, 1996). ... Traded by Mariners to New York Mets for OF Butch Huskey (December 14, 1998). ... Traded by Mets with OF Melvin Mora, 3B Mike Kinkade and P Pat Gorman to Baltimore Orioles for SS Mike Bordick (July 28, 2000).

Year League	W	L	Pct.	ERA	G	GS	CG	ShO	Sv.	IP	H	R	ER	BB	SO
1996—Arizona Mariners (Ariz.) ...	1	0	1.000	5.06	7	0	0	0	0	10 2/3	7	10	6	6	12
1997—Lancaster (Calif.)	0	0	...	13.50	1	0	0	0	0	2	5	5	3	1	1
—Everett (N'West)................	2	4	.333	7.99	23	0	0	0	3	32 2/3	34	29	29	29	49
1998—Wisconsin (Midw.)...........	3	4	.429	2.76	49	0	0	0	12	58 2/3	47	26	18	40	86
1999—St. Lucie (FSL)■..............	1	7	.125	3.73	32	18	0	0	3	120 2/3	95	64	50	68	136
2000—Norfolk (I.L.)	0	0	...	0.00	1	1	0	0	0	5	4	2	0	4	4
—Binghamton (East.)	5	8	.385	4.24	19	18	0	0	0	93 1/3	85	53	44	61	86
—Bowie (East.)■....................	1	1	.500	4.26	2	2	0	0	0	12 2/3	12	6	6	9	3
—Baltimore (A.L.)...................	0	1	.000	11.00	6	1	0	0	0	9	12	11	11	10	5
—Rochester (I.L.)...................	1	2	.333	6.05	4	4	0	0	0	19 1/3	27	18	13	8	13
Major League totals (1 year)........	0	1	.000	11.00	6	1	0	0	0	9	12	11	11	10	5

BREWINGTON, JAMIE   P

PERSONAL: Born September 28, 1971, in Greenville, N.C. ... 6-4/190. ... Throws right, bats right. ... Full name: Jamie Chancellor Brewington.
HIGH SCHOOL: J. H. Rose (Greenville, N.C.).
COLLEGE: Virginia Commonwealth.
TRANSACTIONS/CAREER NOTES: Selected by San Francisco Giants organization in 10th round of free-agent draft (June 1, 1992). ... On San Jose temporarily inactive list (April 7-May 3, 1994). ... Traded by Giants to Kansas City Royals for a player to be named later (November 26, 1996). ... Traded by Royals to Milwaukee Brewers for P Jasan Grimsley (July 29, 1997). ... On Louisville disabled list (April 9-25, 1998). ... Released by Brewers (April 25, 1998). ... Signed by Cleveland Indians organization (February 3, 1999). ... Released by Indians (October 20, 2000).
MISCELLANEOUS: Appeared in one game as pinch runner with San Francisco (1995).

Year League	W	L	Pct.	ERA	G	GS	CG	ShO	Sv.	IP	H	R	ER	BB	SO
1992— Everett (N'West)	5	2	.714	4.33	15	11	1	•1	0	68²/₃	65	40	33	47	63
1993— Clinton (Midw.)	13	5	.722	4.78	25	25	1	0	0	133²/₃	126	78	71	61	111
1994— San Jose (Calif.)	7	3	.700	3.20	13	13	0	0	0	76	61	38	27	25	65
— Clinton (Midw.)	2	4	.333	4.92	10	10	0	0	0	53	46	29	29	24	62
1995— Shreveport (Texas)	8	3	.727	3.06	16	16	1	1	0	88¹/₃	72	39	30	55	74
— San Francisco (N.L.)	6	4	.600	4.54	13	13	0	0	0	75¹/₃	68	38	38	45	45
1996— Phoenix (PCL)	6	9	.400	7.02	35	17	0	0	1	110¹/₃	130	93	86	72	75
1997— Omaha (A.A.)■	2	2	.500	8.31	7	4	0	0	0	21²/₃	21	21	20	13	20
— Wichita (Texas)	2	5	.286	6.71	10	10	0	0	0	51	68	43	38	28	31
— Tucson (PCL)■	1	3	.250	10.18	6	5	0	0	0	20¹/₃	33	26	23	17	13
1998—						Did not play.									
1999— Kinston (Caro.)■■	1	10	.091	3.87	36	5	0	0	4	81¹/₃	74	42	35	37	81
2000— Buffalo (I.L.)	1	0	1.000	3.04	17	0	0	0	0	23²/₃	19	8	8	12	25
— Cleveland (A.L.)	3	0	1.000	5.36	26	0	0	0	0	45¹/₃	56	28	27	19	34
A.L. totals (1 year)	3	0	1.000	5.36	26	0	0	0	0	45¹/₃	56	28	27	19	34
N.L. totals (1 year)	6	4	.600	4.54	13	13	0	0	0	75¹/₃	68	38	38	45	45
Major League totals (2 years)	9	4	.692	4.85	39	13	0	0	0	120²/₃	124	66	65	64	79

BROCAIL, DOUG   P   ASTROS

PERSONAL: Born May 16, 1967, in Clearfield, Pa. ... 6-5/235. ... Throws right, bats left. ... Full name: Douglas Keith Brocail.
HIGH SCHOOL: Lamar (Colo.).
JUNIOR COLLEGE: Lamar (Colo.) Community College.
TRANSACTIONS/CAREER NOTES: Selected by San Diego Padres organization in first round (12th pick overall) of free-agent draft (January 14, 1986). ... On Las Vegas disabled list (May 5-12, 1993). ... On San Diego disabled list (April 2-June 28, 1994); included rehabilitation assignments to Wichita (May 26-June 3) and Las Vegas (June 3-23). ... Traded by Padres with OF Phil Plantier, OF Derek Bell, P Pedro Martinez, IF Craig Shipley and SS Ricky Gutierrez to Houston Astros for 3B Ken Caminiti, OF Steve Finley, SS Andujar Cedeno, 1B Robert Petagine, P Brian Williams and a player to be named later (December 28, 1994); Padres acquired P Sean Fesh to complete deal (May 1, 1995). ... On Houston disabled list (May 11-August 15, 1996); included rehabilitation assignments to Jackson (May 27-June 4) and Tucson (July 29-August 15). ... Traded by Astros with OF Brian L. Hunter, IF Orlando Miller, P Todd Jones and cash to Detroit Tigers for C Brad Ausmus, P Jose Lima, P C.J. Nitkowski, P Trever Miller and IF Daryle Ward (December 10, 1996). ... On suspended list (June 10-13, 1998). ... On disabled list (August 9-24, 1998). ... On suspended list (April 28-May 1, 2000). ... On disabled list (August 14-September 1 and September 29, 2000-remainder of season). ... Traded by Tigers with C Brad Ausmus and P Nelson Cruz to Astros for C Mitch Meluskey, P Chris Holt and OF Roger Cedeno (December 11, 2000).
MISCELLANEOUS: Appeared in six games as pinch runner with San Diego (1993). ... Appeared in two games as pinch runner with San Diego (1994). ... Appeared in one game as pinch runner with Houston (1995). ... Appeared in two games as pinch runner with Houston (1996).

Year League	W	L	Pct.	ERA	G	GS	CG	ShO	Sv.	IP	H	R	ER	BB	SO
1986— Spokane (N'West)	5	4	.556	3.81	16	•15	0	0	0	85	85	52	36	53	77
1987— Charleston, S.C. (S.Atl.)	2	6	.250	4.09	19	18	0	0	0	92¹/₃	94	51	42	28	68
1988— Charleston, S.C. (S.Atl.)	8	6	.571	2.69	22	13	5	0	2	107	107	40	32	25	107
1989— Wichita (Texas)	5	9	.357	5.21	23	22	1	1	0	134²/₃	158	88	78	50	95
1990— Wichita (Texas)	2	2	.500	4.33	12	9	0	0	0	52	53	30	25	24	27
1991— Wichita (Texas)	10	7	.588	3.87	34	16	3	•3	6	146¹/₃	147	77	63	43	108
1992— Las Vegas (PCL)	10	10	.500	3.97	29	25	4	0	0	172¹/₃	187	82	76	63	103
— San Diego (N.L.)	0	0	...	6.43	3	3	0	0	0	14	17	10	10	5	15
1993— Las Vegas (PCL)	4	2	.667	3.68	10	8	0	0	1	51¹/₃	51	26	21	14	32
— San Diego (N.L.)	4	13	.235	4.56	24	24	0	0	0	128¹/₃	143	75	65	42	70
1994— Wichita (Texas)	0	0	...	0.00	2	0	0	0	0	4	3	1	0	1	2
— Las Vegas (PCL)	0	0	...	7.11	7	3	0	0	0	12²/₃	21	12	10	2	8
— San Diego (N.L.)	0	0	...	5.82	12	0	0	0	0	17	21	13	11	5	11
1995— Houston (N.L.)■	6	4	.600	4.19	36	7	0	0	1	77¹/₃	87	40	36	22	39
— Tucson (PCL)	1	0	1.000	3.86	3	3	0	0	0	16¹/₃	18	9	7	4	16
1996— Houston (N.L.)	1	5	.167	4.58	23	4	0	0	0	53	58	31	27	23	34
— Jackson (Texas)	0	0	...	0.00	2	2	0	0	0	4	1	0	0	1	5
— Tucson (PCL)	0	1	.000	7.36	5	1	0	0	0	7¹/₃	12	6	6	1	4
1997— Detroit (A.L.)■	3	4	.429	3.23	61	4	0	0	2	78	74	31	28	36	60
1998— Detroit (A.L.)	5	2	.714	2.73	60	0	0	0	0	62²/₃	47	23	19	18	55
1999— Detroit (A.L.)	4	4	.500	2.52	70	0	0	0	2	82	60	23	23	25	78
2000— Detroit (A.L.)	5	4	.556	4.09	49	0	0	0	0	50²/₃	57	25	23	14	41
A.L. totals (4 years)	17	14	.548	3.06	240	4	0	0	4	273¹/₃	238	102	93	93	234
N.L. totals (5 years)	11	22	.333	4.63	98	38	0	0	1	289²/₃	326	169	149	97	169
Major League totals (9 years)	28	36	.438	3.87	338	42	0	0	5	563	564	271	242	190	403

BROCK, CHRIS   P   PHILLIES

PERSONAL: Born February 5, 1970, in Orlando. ... 6-0/185. ... Throws right, bats right. ... Full name: Terrence Christopher Brock.
HIGH SCHOOL: Lyman (Longwood, Fla.).

COLLEGE: Florida State.
TRANSACTIONS/CAREER NOTES: Selected by Atlanta Braves organization in 12th round of free-agent draft (June 1, 1992). ... On disabled list (July 26, 1995-remainder of season). ... Granted free agency (October 15, 1997). ... Signed by San Francisco Giants organization (December 20, 1997). ... On disabled list (July 24, 1999-remainder of season). ... Traded by Giants to Philadelphia Phillies for C Bobby Estalella (December 12, 1999).

Year League	W	L	Pct.	ERA	G	GS	CG	ShO	Sv.	IP	H	R	ER	BB	SO
1992— Idaho Falls (Pio.)...............	6	4	.600	2.31	15	15	1	0	0	78	61	27	20	48	72
1993— Macon (S.Atl.)..................	7	5	.583	2.70	14	14	1	0	0	80	61	37	24	33	92
— Durham (Caro.)................	5	2	.714	2.51	12	12	1	0	0	79	63	28	22	35	67
1994— Greenville (Sou.).............	7	6	.538	3.74	25	23	2	2	0	137 1/3	128	68	57	47	94
1995— Richmond (I.L.)...............	2	8	.200	5.40	22	9	0	0	0	60	68	37	36	27	43
1996— Richmond (I.L.)...............	10	11	.476	4.67	26	25	3	0	0	150 1/3	137	95	78	61	112
1997— Richmond (I.L.)...............	10	6	.625	3.34	20	19	0	0	0	118 2/3	97	50	44	51	83
— Atlanta (N.L.).................	0	0	...	5.58	7	6	0	0	0	30 2/3	34	23	19	19	16
1998— Fresno (PCL)■	11	3	.786	3.29	17	17	2	0	0	115	111	47	42	33	112
— San Francisco (N.L.)	0	0	...	3.90	13	0	0	0	0	27 2/3	31	13	12	7	19
1999— San Francisco (N.L.)	6	8	.429	5.48	19	19	0	0	0	106 2/3	124	69	65	41	76
2000— Philadelphia (N.L.)■	7	8	.467	4.34	63	5	0	0	1	93 1/3	85	48	45	41	69
Major League totals (4 years)	**13**	**16**	**.448**	**4.91**	**102**	**30**	**0**	**0**	**1**	**258 1/3**	**274**	**153**	**141**	**108**	**180**

BROCK, TARRIK — OF — B

PERSONAL: Born December 25, 1973, in Goleta, Calif. ... 6-2/185. ... Bats left, throws left. ... Full name: Tarrik Jumaan Brock. ... Name pronounced TAR-rik.
HIGH SCHOOL: Hawthorne (Calif.).
TRANSACTIONS/CAREER NOTES: Selected by Detroit Tigers organization in second round of free-agent draft (June 3, 1991). ... Selected by Seattle Mariners organization from Tigers organization in Rule 5 minor league draft (December 9, 1996). ... Released by Mariners (January 26, 1999). ... Signed by Colorado Rockies organization (April 8, 1999). ... Traded by Rockies to Chicago Cubs for OF John Cotton and LHP Kevin Rawitzer (March 28, 1999). ... On Iowa disabled list (June 30-July 8, 2000). ... Granted free agency (October 18, 2000).
STATISTICAL NOTES: Led Southern League outfielders with .997 fielding percentage in 1999.

Year Team (League)	Pos.	G	AB	R	H	2B	3B	HR	RBI	Avg.	BB	SO	SB	PO	A	E	Avg.
1991— Bristol (Appl.)............	OF	55	177	26	47	7	3	1	13	.266	22	42	14	49	0	6	.891
1992— Fayetteville (S.Atl.)	OF	100	271	35	59	5	4	0	17	.218	31	69	15	160	9	4	.977
1993— Fayetteville (S.Atl.)	OF	116	427	60	92	8	4	3	47	.215	54	108	25	178	12	10	.950
1994— Lakeland (FSL)	OF	86	331	43	77	17	14	2	32	.233	38	89	15	168	7	3	.983
— Trenton (East.)	OF	34	115	12	16	1	4	2	11	.139	13	43	3	52	0	1	.981
1995— Toledo (I.L.).............	OF	9	31	4	6	1	0	0	0	.194	2	17	2	12	1	1	.929
— Jacksonville (Sou.).....	OF	9	26	4	3	0	0	0	2	.115	3	14	2	12	1	1	.929
— Lakeland (FSL)	OF	28	91	12	19	3	0	0	5	.209	12	32	5	56	1	2	.966
— Visalia (Calif.)	OF	45	138	21	31	5	2	1	15	.225	17	52	11	90	4	5	.949
1996— Lakeland (FSL)	OF	53	212	42	59	11	4	5	27	.278	17	61	9	89	5	3	.969
— Jacksonville (Sou.).....	OF	37	102	14	13	2	0	0	6	.127	10	36	3	48	5	4	.930
— Fayetteville (S.Atl.)	OF	32	119	21	35	5	2	1	11	.294	14	31	4	49	1	2	.962
1997— Lancaster (Calif.)■.....	OF	132	402	88	108	21	12	7	47	.269	78	106	40	225	11	5	.979
1998— Orlando (Sou.)	OF	111	372	76	103	28	7	15	65	.277	59	110	17	173	11	2	.989
— Tacoma (PCL)	OF	24	94	14	23	2	3	1	14	.245	9	28	5	59	1	0	1.000
1999— Carolina (Sou.)■........	OF	66	218	40	54	10	1	7	23	.248	39	67	7	138	2	0	§1.000
— West Tenn (Sou.)■	OF	54	189	29	41	10	4	1	9	.217	33	60	9	136	6	1	§.993
2000— Iowa (PCL)	OF	104	388	60	102	19	5	12	47	.263	43	109	15	262	7	3	.989
— Chicago (N.L.)...........	OF	13	12	1	2	0	0	0	0	.167	4	4	1	8	0	1	.889
Major League totals (1 year)		**13**	**12**	**1**	**2**	**0**	**0**	**0**	**0**	**.167**	**4**	**4**	**1**	**8**	**0**	**1**	**.889**

BROGNA, RICO — 1B — BRAVES

PERSONAL: Born April 18, 1970, in Turners Falls, Mass. ... 6-2/203. ... Bats left, throws left. ... Full name: Rico Joseph Brogna. ... Name pronounced BRONE-yah.
HIGH SCHOOL: Watertown (Conn.).
TRANSACTIONS/CAREER NOTES: Selected by Detroit Tigers organization in first round (26th pick overall) of free-agent draft (June 1, 1988). ... On Toledo disabled list (May 25-June 2, 1991). ... Traded by Tigers to New York Mets for 1B Alan Zinter (March 31, 1994). ... On disabled list (June 20, 1996-remainder of season). ... Traded by Mets to Philadelphia Phillies for P Ricardo Jordan and P Toby Borland (November 27, 1996). ... On Philadelphia disabled list (May 11-July 20, 2000); included rehabilitation assignment to Clearwater (July 12-20). ... Claimed on waivers by Boston Red Sox (August 3, 2000). ... Granted free agency (November 1, 2000). ... Signed by Atlanta Braves (December 13, 2000).
STATISTICAL NOTES: Led Eastern League first basemen with 1,261 total chances and 117 double plays in 1990. ... Tied for N.L. lead with 10 sacrifice flies in 1998. ... Career major league grand slams: 3.

Year Team (League)	Pos.	G	AB	R	H	2B	3B	HR	RBI	Avg.	BB	SO	SB	PO	A	E	Avg.
1988— Bristol (Appl.)............	1B-OF	60	209	37	53	11	2	7	33	.254	25	42	3	319	26	6	.983
1989— Lakeland (FSL)	1B	128	459	47	108	20	7	5	51	.235	38	82	2	1098	83	13	.989
1990— London (East.)	1B	137	488	70	128	21	3	*21	•77	.262	50	100	1	*1155	*93	13	.990
1991— Toledo (I.L.).............	1B	41	132	13	29	6	1	2	13	.220	4	26	2	311	37	5	.986
— London (East.)	1B-OF	77	293	40	80	13	1	13	51	.273	25	59	0	368	46	6	.986
1992— Toledo (I.L.).............	1B	121	387	45	101	19	4	10	58	.261	31	85	1	896	76	9	.991
— Detroit (A.L.)............	1B-DH	9	26	3	5	1	0	1	3	.192	3	5	0	48	6	1	.982
1993— Toledo (I.L.).............	1B-DH	129	483	55	132	30	3	11	59	.273	31	94	7	937	97	8	.992
1994— Norfolk (I.L.)■...........	1B	67	258	33	63	14	5	12	37	.244	15	62	1	583	47	3	.995
— New York (N.L.).........	1B	39	131	16	46	11	2	7	20	.351	6	29	1	307	28	1	.997
1995— New York (N.L.)..........	1B	134	495	72	143	27	2	22	76	.289	39	111	0	1111	93	3	*.998
1996— New York (N.L.)..........	1B	55	188	18	48	10	1	7	30	.255	19	50	0	440	31	2	.996

Year Team (League)	Pos.	G	AB	R	H	2B	3B	HR	RBI	Avg.	BB	SO	SB	PO	A	E	Avg.
1997—Philadelphia (N.L.)■ ..	1B	148	543	68	137	36	1	20	81	.252	33	116	12	1053	119	7	.994
1998—Philadelphia (N.L.)......	1B	153	565	77	150	36	3	20	104	.265	49	125	7	1238	141	5	.996
1999—Philadelphia (N.L.)......	1B	157	619	90	172	29	4	24	102	.278	54	132	8	1240	123	7	.995
2000—Philadelphia (N.L.)......	1B	38	129	12	32	14	0	1	13	.248	7	28	1	248	17	1	.996
—Clearwater (FSL)	1B	7	32	2	7	1	0	0	2	.219	1	4	0	72	6	0	1.000
—Boston (A.L.)■..........	1B-DH	43	56	8	11	3	0	1	8	.196	3	13	0	165	9	3	.983
American League totals (2 years)		52	82	11	16	4	0	2	11	.195	6	18	0	213	15	4	.983
National League totals (7 years)		724	2670	353	728	163	13	101	426	.273	207	591	29	5637	552	26	.996
Major League totals (8 years)		776	2752	364	744	167	13	103	437	.270	213	609	29	5850	567	30	.995

BROSIUS, SCOTT — 3B — YANKEES

B

PERSONAL: Born August 15, 1966, in Hillsboro, Ore. ... 6-1/202. ... Bats right, throws right. ... Full name: Scott David Brosius. ... Name pronounced BRO-shus.

HIGH SCHOOL: Rex Putnam (Milwaukie, Ore.).

COLLEGE: Linfield College (Ore.).

TRANSACTIONS/CAREER NOTES: Selected by Oakland Athletics organization in 20th round of free-agent draft (June 2, 1987). ... On Tacoma disabled list (April 17-May 29, 1991). ... On Oakland disabled list (April 18-May 12, 1992); included rehabilitation assignment to Tacoma (May 6-12). ... On Oakland disabled list (July 13-August 3, 1992); included rehabilitation assignment to Tacoma (July 27-August 3). ... On Tacoma disabled list (July 28-August 5, 1993). ... On disabled list (June 8-26, 1994). ... On Oakland disabled list (May 5-June 25, 1996); included rehabilitation assignment to Edmonton (June 22-25). ... On Oakland disabled list (August 7-29, 1997); included rehabilitation assignment to Modesto (August 27-29). ... Traded by A's to New York Yankees (November 18, 1997), completing deal in which Yankees traded P Kenny Rogers and cash to A's for a player to be named later (November 7, 1997). ... Granted free agency (October 27, 1998). ... Re-signed by Yankees (November 10, 1998). ... On New York disabled list (April 14-29, 1999); included rehabilitation assignment to Tampa (April 27). ... On New York disabled list (April 5-25, 2000); included rehabilitation assignment to Tampa (April 22-25).

RECORDS: Shares major league record for most double plays by third basemen—4 (July 6, 2000).

HONORS: Named third baseman on THE SPORTING NEWS A.L. All-Star team (1998). ... Won A.L. Gold Glove at third base (1999).

STATISTICAL NOTES: Led Northwest League with seven sacrifice flies in 1987. ... Led Southern League with 274 total bases in 1990. ... Tied for Pacific Coast League lead in double plays by third baseman with 24 in 1992. ... Career major league grand slams: 3.

Year Team (League)	Pos.	G	AB	R	H	2B	3B	HR	RBI	Avg.	BB	SO	SB	PO	A	E	Avg.
1987—Medford (N'West) ...	3-S-2-1-P	65	255	34	73	18	1	3	49	.286	26	36	5	123	148	38	.877
1988—Madison (Midw.)......	S-3-O-1	132	504	82	153	28	2	9	58	.304	56	67	13	151	305	61	.882
1989—Huntsville (Sou.) ...	2-3-S-1	128	461	68	125	22	2	7	60	.271	58	62	4	225	316	34	.941
1990—Huntsville (Sou.) ...	SS-2B-3B	•142	547	94	*162	*39	2	23	88	.296	81	81	12	253	419	41	.942
—Tacoma (PCL)	2B	3	7	2	1	0	0	0	0	.143	1	3	0	3	5	0	1.000
1991—Tacoma (PCL)	3B-SS-2B	65	245	28	70	16	3	8	31	.286	18	29	4	49	168	14	.939
—Oakland (A.L.) 2B-OF-3B-DH		36	68	9	16	5	0	2	4	.235	3	11	3	31	16	0	1.000
1992—Oakland (A.L.) O-3-1-DH-S		38	87	13	19	2	0	4	13	.218	3	13	3	68	15	1	.988
—Tacoma (PCL)	3B-OF	63	236	29	56	13	0	9	31	.237	23	44	8	50	167	10	.956
1993—Oakland (A.L.) O-1-3-S-DH		70	213	26	53	10	1	6	25	.249	14	37	6	173	29	2	.990
—Tacoma (PCL)	3-0-2-1-S	56	209	38	62	13	2	8	41	.297	21	50	8	101	109	13	.942
1994—Oakland (A.L.)	3B-OF-1B	96	324	31	77	14	1	14	49	.238	24	57	2	82	157	13	.948
1995—Oakland (A.L.) 3-0-1-2-S-D		123	389	69	102	19	2	17	46	.262	41	67	4	208	121	15	.956
1996—Oakland (A.L.)	3B-1B-OF	114	428	73	130	25	0	22	71	.304	59	85	7	128	234	10	.973
—Edmonton (PCL)	3B	3	8	5	5	1	0	0	0	.625	3	1	0	0	4	2	.667
1997—Oakland (A.L.)	3B-SS-OF	129	479	59	97	20	1	11	41	.203	34	102	9	142	246	10	.975
—Modesto (Calif.)	3B	2	3	1	1	0	0	0	1	.333	1	0	0	1	1	1	.667
1998—New York (A.L.)■.....	3B-1B-OF	152	530	86	159	34	0	19	98	.300	52	97	11	114	294	22	.949
1999—New York (A.L.).......	3B-DH	133	473	64	117	26	1	17	71	.247	39	74	9	87	239	13	*.962
—Tampa (FSL)	3B	1	3	0	1	0	0	0	0	.333	0	0	0	2	0	0	1.000
2000—New York (A.L.)...........	3-1-O-D	135	470	57	108	20	0	16	64	.230	45	73	0	104	231	11	.968
—Tampa (FSL)	3B	2	4	0	1	0	0	0	0	.250	1	0	0	2	2	0	1.000
Major League totals (10 years)		1026	3461	487	878	175	6	128	482	.254	314	616	54	1137	1582	97	.966

DIVISION SERIES RECORD

Year Team (League)	Pos.	G	AB	R	H	2B	3B	HR	RBI	Avg.	BB	SO	SB	PO	A	E	Avg.
1998—New York (A.L.)..........	3B	3	10	1	4	0	0	1	3	.400	0	3	0	2	6	0	1.000
1999—New York (A.L.)..........	3B	3	10	0	1	1	0	0	1	.100	0	0	0	2	3	0	1.000
2000—New York (A.L.)..........	3B	5	17	0	3	1	0	0	1	.176	1	4	0	5	8	0	1.000
Division series totals (3 years)		11	37	1	8	2	0	1	5	.216	1	7	0	9	17	0	1.000

CHAMPIONSHIP SERIES RECORD

Year Team (League)	Pos.	G	AB	R	H	2B	3B	HR	RBI	Avg.	BB	SO	SB	PO	A	E	Avg.
1998—New York (A.L.)■.......	3B	6	20	2	6	1	0	1	6	.300	4	4	0	4	10	1	.933
1999—New York (A.L.)..........	3B	5	18	3	4	0	1	2	3	.222	1	4	0	5	4	0	1.000
2000—New York (A.L.)..........	3B	6	18	2	4	0	0	0	0	.222	2	3	0	4	7	1	.917
Championship series totals (3 years)		17	56	7	14	1	1	3	9	.250	7	11	0	13	21	2	.944

WORLD SERIES RECORD

RECORDS: Shares record for most home runs in two consecutive innings—2 (October 20, 1998, seventh and eighth innings). ... Shares single-inning record for most at-bats—2 (October 17, 1998).

NOTES: Named Most Valuable Player (1998). ... Member of World Series championship team (1998, 1999 and 2000).

Year Team (League)	Pos.	G	AB	R	H	2B	3B	HR	RBI	Avg.	BB	SO	SB	PO	A	E	Avg.
1998—New York (A.L.)..........	3B	4	17	3	8	0	0	2	6	.471	0	4	0	3	6	0	1.000
1999—New York (A.L.)..........	3B	4	16	2	6	1	0	0	1	.375	0	5	0	8	7	0	1.000
2000—New York (A.L.)..........	3B	5	13	2	4	0	0	1	3	.308	2	2	0	1	9	0	1.000
World Series totals (3 years)		13	46	7	18	1	0	3	10	.391	2	11	0	12	22	0	1.000

ALL-STAR GAME RECORD

							BATTING								FIELDING		
Year	League	Pos.	AB	R	H	2B	3B	HR	RBI	Avg.	BB	SO	SB	PO	A	E	Avg.
1998— American		3B	2	1	1	0	0	0	0	.500	0	1	1	0	0	1	.000

RECORD AS PITCHER

Year	League	W	L	Pct.	ERA	G	GS	CG	ShO	Sv.	IP	H	R	ER	BB	SO
1987— Medford (N'West)		0	0	...	0.00	1	0	0	0	0	2	0	0	0	0	1

BROWER, JIM   P   REDS

PERSONAL: Born December 29, 1972, in Edina, Minn. ... 6-2/205. ... Throws right, bats right. ... Full name: James Robert Brower.
HIGH SCHOOL: Minnetonka (Minn.).
COLLEGE: Minnesota.
TRANSACTIONS/CAREER NOTES: Selected by Texas Rangers organization in sixth round of free-agent draft (June 2, 1994). ... Released by Rangers organization (April 15, 1998). ... Signed by Cleveland Indians organization (April 18, 1998). ... Granted free agency (October 16, 1998). ... Re-signed by Indians organization (January 4, 1999). ... Traded by Indians with P Robert Pugmire to Cincinnati Reds for C Eddie Taubensee (November 16, 2000).

Year	League	W	L	Pct.	ERA	G	GS	CG	ShO	Sv.	IP	H	R	ER	BB	SO
1994— Hudson Valley (NY-Penn)		2	1	.667	3.20	4	4	1	0	0	19²/₃	14	10	7	6	15
— Charleston, S.C. (S.Atl.)		7	3	.700	1.72	12	12	3	2	0	78²/₃	52	18	15	26	84
1995— Charlotte (FSL)		7	10	.412	3.89	27	27	2	1	0	173²/₃	170	93	75	62	110
1996— Charlotte (FSL)		9	8	.529	3.79	23	21	2	0	0	145	148	67	61	40	86
— Tulsa (Texas)		3	2	.600	3.78	5	5	1	1	0	33¹/₃	35	16	14	10	16
1997— Tulsa (Texas)		5	12	.294	5.21	23	23	1	0	0	140	156	99	81	42	103
— Oklahoma City (A.A.)		2	1	.667	7.23	4	3	0	0	0	18²/₃	30	17	15	8	7
1998— Akron (East.)■		13	5	.722	3.01	23	23	2	2	0	155²/₃	142	60	52	38	91
1999— Buffalo (I.L.)		11	11	.500	4.72	27	27	0	0	0	160	164	101	84	59	76
— Cleveland (A.L.)		3	1	.750	4.56	9	2	0	0	0	25²/₃	27	13	13	10	18
2000— Buffalo (I.L.)		9	4	.692	3.11	16	15	1	0	0	101¹/₃	99	41	35	24	68
— Cleveland (A.L.)		2	3	.400	6.24	17	11	0	0	0	62	80	45	43	31	32
Major League totals (2 years)		**5**	**4**	**.556**	**5.75**	**26**	**13**	**0**	**0**	**0**	**87²/₃**	**107**	**58**	**56**	**41**	**50**

BROWN, ADRIAN   OF   PIRATES

PERSONAL: Born February 7, 1974, in McComb, Miss. ... 6-0/185. ... Bats both, throws right. ... Full name: Adrian Demond Brown.
HIGH SCHOOL: McComb (Miss.).
TRANSACTIONS/CAREER NOTES: Selected by Pittsburgh Pirates organization in 48th round of free-agent draft (June 1, 1992). ... On Pittsburgh disabled list (June 13-July 4 and July 6-August 7, 2000); included rehabilitation assignments to Altoona (July 2-4) and Nashville (July 30-August 7).

								BATTING						FIELDING		
Year	Team (League)	Pos.	G	AB	R	H	2B	3B	HR	RBI	Avg.	BB	SO	SB	PO	A	E	Avg.
1992— GC Pirates (GCL)		OF-1B	39	121	11	31	2	2	0	12	.256	0	12	8	60	4	1	.985
1993— Lethbridge (Pio.)		OF	69	282	47	75	12	*9	3	27	.266	17	34	22	119	4	1	*.992
1994— Augusta (S.Atl.)		OF	79	308	41	80	17	1	1	18	.260	14	38	19	121	6	2	.984
1995— Lynchburg (Caro.)		OF	54	215	30	52	5	2	1	14	.242	12	20	11	110	6	2	.983
— Augusta (S.Atl.)		OF	76	287	64	86	15	4	4	31	.300	33	23	25	124	8	7	.950
1996— Lynchburg (Caro.)		OF	52	215	39	69	9	3	4	25	.321	14	24	18	99	4	2	.981
— Carolina (Sou.)		OF	84	341	48	101	11	3	3	25	.296	25	40	27	185	5	2	.990
1997— Carolina (Sou.)		OF	37	145	29	44	4	4	2	15	.303	18	12	9	63	2	3	.956
— Pittsburgh (N.L.)		OF	48	147	17	28	6	0	1	10	.190	13	18	8	74	3	1	.987
— Calgary (PCL)		OF	62	248	53	79	10	1	1	19	.319	27	38	20	130	3	1	.993
1998— Nashville (PCL)		OF	85	311	58	90	12	5	3	27	.289	28	38	25	204	7	5	.977
— Pittsburgh (N.L.)		OF	41	152	20	43	4	1	0	5	.283	9	18	4	83	3	2	.977
1999— Pittsburgh (N.L.)		OF	116	226	34	61	5	2	4	17	.270	33	39	5	111	3	4	.966
— Nashville (PCL)		OF	17	56	10	18	3	1	0	4	.321	11	8	6	31	0	1	.969
2000— Pittsburgh (N.L.)		OF	104	308	64	97	18	3	4	28	.315	29	34	13	154	7	4	.976
— Altoona (East.)		OF	2	5	1	0	0	0	0	0	.000	3	1	0	3	1	0	1.000
— Nashville (PCL)		OF	8	26	3	6	1	0	0	2	.231	2	4	3	11	1	0	1.000
Major League totals (4 years)			**309**	**833**	**135**	**229**	**33**	**6**	**9**	**60**	**.275**	**84**	**109**	**30**	**422**	**16**	**11**	**.976**

BROWN, BRANT   IF/OF   BREWERS

PERSONAL: Born June 22, 1971, in Porterville, Calif. ... 6-3/220. ... Bats left, throws left. ... Full name: Brant Michael Brown.
HIGH SCHOOL: Monache (Porterville, Calif.).
COLLEGE: Fresno State.
TRANSACTIONS/CAREER NOTES: Selected by Chicago Cubs organization in third round of free-agent draft (June 1, 1992). ... On Daytona disabled list (April 10-25, 1993). ... On Iowa disabled list (July 22-August 11, 1996). ... On Chicago disabled list (June 26-July 25, 1998); included rehabilitation assignment to Iowa (July 22-25). ... Traded by Cubs to Pittsburgh Pirates for P Jon Lieber (December 14, 1998). ... Traded by Pirates to Florida Marlins for OF Bruce Aven (December 13, 1999). ... Traded by Marlins to Texas Rangers for P Chuck Smith (June 9, 2000). ... Traded by Rangers to Cubs for OF Dave Martinez (June 9, 2000). ... Granted free agency (October 10, 2000). ... Signed by Milwaukee Brewers organization (January 11, 2001).
STATISTICAL NOTES: Hit three home runs in one game (June 18, 1998).

								BATTING						FIELDING		
Year	Team (League)	Pos.	G	AB	R	H	2B	3B	HR	RBI	Avg.	BB	SO	SB	PO	A	E	Avg.
1992— Peoria (Midw.)		1B	70	248	28	68	14	0	3	27	.274	24	49	3	582	39	6	.990
1993— Daytona (FSL)		1B	75	266	26	91	8	7	3	33	.342	11	38	8	643	55	5	.993
— Orlando (Sou.)		1B	28	111	17	35	11	3	4	23	.315	6	19	2	237	27	3	.989

Year Team (League)	Pos.	G	AB	R	H	2B	3B	HR	RBI	Avg.	BB	SO	SB	PO	A	E	Avg.
1994— Orlando (Sou.)	1B-OF	127	470	54	127	30	6	5	37	.270	37	86	11	1031	80	12	.989
1995— Orlando (Sou.)	1B-OF-DH	121	446	67	121	27	4	6	53	.271	39	77	8	931	92	10	.990
1996— Iowa (A.A.)	1B	94	342	48	104	25	3	10	43	.304	19	65	6	762	66	8	.990
— Chicago (N.L.)	1B	29	69	11	21	1	0	5	9	.304	2	17	3	126	17	0	1.000
1997— Chicago (N.L.)	OF-1B	46	137	15	32	7	1	5	15	.234	7	28	2	121	7	2	.985
— Iowa (A.A.)	OF-1B-DH	71	256	51	77	19	3	16	51	.301	31	44	6	202	13	4	.982
1998— Chicago (N.L.)	OF-1B	124	347	56	101	17	7	14	48	.291	30	95	4	212	3	7	.968
— Iowa (PCL)	OF-1B	3	11	1	4	0	0	0	0	.364	0	6	0	5	0	0	1.000
1999— Pittsburgh (N.L.)■	OF-1B-DH	130	341	49	79	20	3	16	58	.232	22	114	3	187	7	3	.985
2000— Florida (N.L.)■	OF-1B	41	73	4	14	6	0	2	6	.192	3	33	1	42	3	1	.978
— Chicago (N.L.)■	OF-1B	54	89	7	14	1	0	3	10	.157	10	29	2	58	3	1	.984
Major League totals (5 years)		424	1056	142	261	52	11	45	146	.247	74	316	15	746	40	14	.983

DIVISION SERIES RECORD

						BATTING								FIELDING			
Year Team (League)	Pos.	G	AB	R	H	2B	3B	HR	RBI	Avg.	BB	SO	SB	PO	A	E	Avg.
1998— Chicago (N.L.)	PH	1	1	0	0	0	0	0	0	.000	0	0	0	...	...	...	...

BROWN, DEE — OF — ROYALS

PERSONAL: Born March 27, 1978, in Bronx, N.Y. ... 6-0/215. ... Bats left, throws right. ... Full name: Dermal Bram Brown.
HIGH SCHOOL: Marlboro (N.Y.) Central.
TRANSACTIONS/CAREER NOTES: Selected by Kansas City Royals organization in first round (14th pick overall) of free-agent draft (June 2, 1996).
HONORS: Named Northwest League Most Valuable Player in 1997.
STATISTICAL NOTES: Led Northwest League with 168 total bases and .564 slugging percentage in 1997. ... Tied for Carolina League lead with five intentional bases on balls received in 1998. ... Tied for Carolina League lead with six intentional bases on balls received in 1999.

						BATTING								FIELDING			
Year Team (League)	Pos.	G	AB	R	H	2B	3B	HR	RBI	Avg.	BB	SO	SB	PO	A	E	Avg.
1996— GC Royals (GCL)	DH	7	20	1	1	1	0	0	1	.050	0	6	0	...	...	...	...
1997— Spokane (N'West)	OF	73	298	67	97	20	6	13	*73	.326	38	65	17	80	2	7	.921
1998— Wilmington (Caro.)......	OF	128	442	64	114	30	2	10	58	.258	53	115	26	124	5	13	.908
— Kansas City (A.L.)	DH-OF	5	3	2	0	0	0	0	0	.000	0	1	0	1	0	0	1.000
1999— Wilmington (Caro.).....	OF-DH	61	221	49	68	10	2	13	46	.308	44	56	20	91	4	2	.979
— Wichita (Texas)	OF	65	235	58	83	14	3	12	56	.353	35	41	10	110	4	5	.958
— Kansas City (A.L.)	OF-DH	12	25	1	2	0	0	0	0	.080	2	7	0	12	1	1	.929
2000— Omaha (PCL)..............	OF	125	479	76	129	25	6	23	70	.269	37	112	20	193	6	7	.966
— Kansas City (A.L.)	OF	15	25	4	4	1	0	0	4	.160	3	9	0	12	0	0	1.000
Major League totals (3 years)		32	53	7	6	1	0	0	4	.113	5	17	0	25	1	1	.963

BROWN, EMIL — OF — PIRATES

PERSONAL: Born December 29, 1974, in Chicago. ... 6-2/193. ... Bats right, throws right. ... Full name: Emil Quincy Brown. ... Name pronounced E-meal.
HIGH SCHOOL: Harlan (Chicago).
JUNIOR COLLEGE: Indian River Community College (Fla.).
TRANSACTIONS/CAREER NOTES: Selected by Oakland Athletics organization in sixth round of free-agent draft (June 2, 1994). ... On Modesto disabled list (April 10-July 1, 1996). ... On Modesto suspended list (August 29-September 2, 1996). ... Selected by Pittsburgh Pirates organization from A's organization in Rule 5 major league draft (December 9, 1996). ... On Nashville disabled list (April 24-May 2, 1999). ... On Pittsburgh disabled list (June 19-July 4, 2000); included rehabilitation assignment to Nashville (June 30-July 4).
STATISTICAL NOTES: Led Midwest League outfielders with four double plays in 1995.

						BATTING								FIELDING			
Year Team (League)	Pos.	G	AB	R	H	2B	3B	HR	RBI	Avg.	BB	SO	SB	PO	A	E	Avg.
1994— Ariz. Athletics (Ariz.) ..	OF	32	86	13	19	1	1	3	12	.221	13	12	5	43	3	1	.979
1995— W. Michigan (Midw.)..	OF	124	459	63	115	17	3	3	67	.251	52	77	35	165	12	8	.957
1996— Modesto (Calif.)	OF	57	211	50	64	10	1	10	47	.303	32	51	13	97	5	4	.962
— Scottsdale (Ariz.)........	OF	4	15	5	4	3	0	0	2	.267	3	2	1	3	1	0	1.000
1997— Pittsburgh (N.L.)■	OF	66	95	16	17	2	1	2	6	.179	10	32	5	53	2	3	.948
1998— Carolina (Sou.)	OF-DH	123	466	89	154	31	2	14	67	.330	50	71	24	199	10	6	.972
— Pittsburgh (N.L.)	OF	13	39	2	10	1	0	0	3	.256	1	11	0	21	2	0	1.000
1999— Nashville (PCL)	OF-DH	110	430	97	132	20	5	18	60	.307	35	80	16	173	10	*10	.948
— Pittsburgh (N.L.)	OF	6	14	0	2	1	0	0	0	.143	0	3	0	8	0	0	1.000
2000— Nashville (PCL)	OF	70	237	44	74	20	1	5	25	.312	40	44	26	127	9	3	.978
— Pittsburgh (N.L.)	OF	50	119	13	26	5	0	3	16	.218	11	34	3	54	3	0	1.000
Major League totals (4 years)		135	267	31	55	9	1	5	25	.206	22	80	8	136	7	3	.979

BROWN, KEVIN — P — DODGERS

PERSONAL: Born March 14, 1965, in McIntyre, Ga. ... 6-4/200. ... Throws right, bats right. ... Full name: James Kevin Brown.
HIGH SCHOOL: Wilkinson County (Irwinton, Ga.).
COLLEGE: Georgia Tech.
TRANSACTIONS/CAREER NOTES: Selected by Texas Rangers organization in first round (fourth pick overall) of free-agent draft (June 2, 1986). ... On disabled list (August 14-29, 1990 and March 27-April 11, 1993). ... Granted free agency (October 15, 1994). ... Signed by Baltimore Orioles (April 9, 1995). ... On disabled list (June 23-July 17, 1995). ... Granted free agency (November 3, 1995). ... Signed by Florida

Marlins (December 22, 1995). ... On disabled list (May 13-28, 1996). ... Traded by Marlins to San Diego Padres for P Rafael Medina, P Steve Hoff and 1B Derrek Lee (December 15, 1997). ... Granted free agency (October 26, 1998). ... Signed by Los Angeles Dodgers (December 12, 1998). ... On disabled list (April 9-25, 2000).

RECORDS: Holds modern N.L. single-season record for most putouts by pitcher—41 (2000).

HONORS: Named righthanded pitcher on THE SPORTING NEWS college All-America team (1986). ... Named N.L. Pitcher of the Year by THE SPORTING NEWS (1998). ... Named righthanded pitcher on THE SPORTING NEWS N.L. All-Star team (1998).

STATISTICAL NOTES: Tied for A.L. lead with 13 hit batsmen in 1991. ... Tied for N.L. lead with 16 hit batsmen in 1996. ... Pitched 9-0 no-hit victory against San Francisco (June 10, 1997). ... Pitched 5-1 one-hit, complete-game victory against Los Angeles (July 16, 1997). ... Led N.L. with 14 hit batsmen in 1997. ... Pitched 4-0 one-hit, complete-game victory against Milwaukee (August 16, 1998). ... Led N.L. pitchers with 41 putouts and 93 total chances in 1999. ... Tied for N.L. lead in errors by a pitcher with six in 1999. ... Led N.L. pitchers with 35 putouts in 2000.

MISCELLANEOUS: Made an out in only appearance as pinch hitter (1990). ... Appeared in one game as pinch runner (1993). ... Appeared in two games as pinch runner (1996). ... Holds Florida Marlins all-time records for most shutouts (5) and complete games (11).

Year League	W	L	Pct.	ERA	G	GS	CG	ShO	Sv.	IP	H	R	ER	BB	SO
1986— Gulf Coast Rangers (GCL)..	0	0	...	6.00	3	0	0	0	0	6	7	4	4	2	1
— Tulsa (Texas)	0	0	...	4.50	3	2	0	0	0	10	9	7	5	5	10
— Texas (A.L.)	1	0	1.000	3.60	1	1	0	0	0	5	6	2	2	0	4
1987— Tulsa (Texas)	1	4	.200	7.29	8	8	0	0	0	42	53	36	34	18	26
— Oklahoma City (A.A.)	0	5	.000	10.73	5	5	0	0	0	24 1/3	32	32	29	17	9
— Charlotte (FSL)	0	2	.000	2.72	6	6	1	0	0	36 1/3	33	14	11	17	21
1988— Tulsa (Texas)	12	10	.545	3.51	26	26	5	0	0	174 1/3	174	94	68	61	118
— Texas (A.L.)	1	1	.500	4.24	4	4	1	0	0	23 1/3	33	15	11	8	12
1989— Texas (A.L.)	12	9	.571	3.35	28	28	7	0	0	191	167	81	71	70	104
1990— Texas (A.L.)	12	10	.545	3.60	26	26	6	2	0	180	175	84	72	60	88
1991— Texas (A.L.)	9	12	.429	4.40	33	33	0	0	0	210 2/3	233	116	103	90	96
1992— Texas (A.L.)	•21	11	.656	3.32	35	35	11	1	0	*265 2/3	*262	117	98	76	173
1993— Texas (A.L.)	15	12	.556	3.59	34	34	12	3	0	233	228	105	93	74	142
1994— Texas (A.L.)	7	9	.438	4.82	26	•25	3	0	0	170	*218	109	91	50	123
1995— Baltimore (A.L.)■	10	9	.526	3.60	26	26	3	1	0	172 1/3	155	73	69	48	117
1996— Florida (N.L.)■	17	11	.607	*1.89	32	32	5	*3	0	233	187	60	49	33	159
1997— Florida (N.L.)	16	8	.667	2.69	33	33	6	2	0	237 1/3	214	77	71	66	205
1998— San Diego (N.L.)■	18	7	.720	2.38	36	•35	7	3	0	257	225	77	68	49	257
1999— Los Angeles (N.L.)■	18	9	.667	3.00	35	•35	5	1	0	252 1/3	210	99	84	59	221
2000— Los Angeles (N.L.)	13	6	.684	*2.58	33	33	5	1	0	230	181	76	66	47	216
A.L. totals (9 years)	88	73	.547	3.78	213	212	43	7	0	1451	1477	702	610	476	859
N.L. totals (5 years)	82	41	.667	2.51	169	168	28	10	0	1209 2/3	1017	389	338	254	1058
Major League totals (14 years)	170	114	.599	3.21	382	380	71	17	0	2660 2/3	2494	1091	948	730	1917

DIVISION SERIES RECORD

RECORDS: Holds career record for most hit batsmen—3.

Year League	W	L	Pct.	ERA	G	GS	CG	ShO	Sv.	IP	H	R	ER	BB	SO
1997— Florida (N.L.)	0	0	...	1.29	1	1	0	0	0	7	4	1	1	0	5
1998— San Diego (N.L.)	1	0	1.000	0.61	2	2	0	0	0	14 2/3	5	1	1	7	21
Division series totals (2 years)	1	0	1.000	0.83	3	3	0	0	0	21 2/3	9	2	2	7	26

CHAMPIONSHIP SERIES RECORD

RECORDS: Shares single-game record for most hits allowed—11 (October 14, 1997).

Year League	W	L	Pct.	ERA	G	GS	CG	ShO	Sv.	IP	H	R	ER	BB	SO
1997— Florida (N.L.)	2	0	1.000	4.20	2	2	1	0	0	15	16	7	7	5	11
1998— San Diego (N.L.)	1	1	.500	2.61	2	1	1	1	0	10 1/3	5	3	3	4	12
Champ. series totals (2 years)	3	1	.750	3.55	4	3	2	1	0	25 1/3	21	10	10	9	23

WORLD SERIES RECORD

NOTES: Member of World Series championship team (1997).

Year League	W	L	Pct.	ERA	G	GS	CG	ShO	Sv.	IP	H	R	ER	BB	SO
1997— Florida (N.L.)	0	2	.000	8.18	2	2	0	0	0	11	15	10	10	5	6
1998— San Diego (N.L.)	0	1	.000	4.40	2	2	0	0	0	14 1/3	14	7	7	6	13
World Series totals (2 years)	0	3	.000	6.04	4	4	0	0	0	25 1/3	29	17	17	11	19

ALL-STAR GAME RECORD

Year League	W	L	Pct.	ERA	GS	CG	ShO	Sv.	IP	H	R	ER	BB	SO
1992— American	1	0	1.000	0.00	1	0	0	0	1	0	0	0	0	1
1996— National	0	0	...	0.00	0	0	0	0	1	0	0	0	0	0
1997— National	0	0	...	0.00	0	0	0	0	1	1	0	0	0	0
1998— National	0	0	...	0.00	0	0	0	0	2/3	0	0	0	0	1
2000— National	0	0	...	9.00	0	0	0	0	1	1	1	1	3	0
All-Star Game totals (5 years)	1	0	1.000	1.93	1	0	0	0	4 2/3	2	1	1	3	2

BROWN, KEVIN — C — BREWERS

PERSONAL: Born April 21, 1973, in Valparaiso, Ind. ... 6-2/215. ... Bats right, throws right. ... Full name: Kevin Lee Brown.

HIGH SCHOOL: Pike Central (Petersburg, Ind.).

COLLEGE: Southern Indiana.

TRANSACTIONS/CAREER NOTES: Selected by Texas Rangers organization in second round of free-agent draft (June 2, 1994). ... Traded by Rangers to Toronto Blue Jays for P Tim Crabtree (March 14, 1998). ... On Toronto disabled list (June 13-30, 1998; included rehabilitation assignment to Syracuse (June 28-30). ... On Syracuse disabled list (April 25-May 5, 2000). ... Traded by Blue Jays to Milwaukee Brewers for OF Alvin Morrow (July 25, 2000).

STATISTICAL NOTES: Led American Association catchers with .991 fielding percentage and tied for the league lead in double plays with 10 in 1997.

							BATTING								FIELDING		
Year Team (League)	Pos.	G	AB	R	H	2B	3B	HR	RBI	Avg.	BB	SO	SB	PO	A	E	Avg.
1994—Hudson Valley (NY-P).	C	68	233	33	57	*19	1	6	32	.245	23	•86	0	316	34	7	.980
1995—Charlotte (FSL)..........	C-1B	107	355	48	94	25	1	11	57	.265	50	96	2	535	60	9	.985
—Oklahoma City (A.A.)..	C	3	10	1	4	1	0	0	0	.400	2	4	0	6	0	2	.750
1996—Tulsa (Texas)..........	C-DH-1B	128	460	77	121	27	1	26	86	.263	73	*150	0	594	69	13	.981
—Texas (A.L.)...............	C-DH	3	4	1	0	0	0	0	1	.000	2	2	0	11	1	0	1.000
1997—Oklahoma City (A.A.)..	C-1B-DH	116	403	56	97	18	2	19	50	.241	38	111	2	640	62	5	†.993
—Texas (A.L.)...............	C	4	5	1	2	0	0	1	1	.400	0	0	0	9	0	1	.900
1998—Toronto (A.L.)■........	C	52	110	17	29	7	1	2	15	.264	9	31	0	261	19	2	.993
—Syracuse (I.L.)...........	C	2	8	2	5	2	0	0	0	.625	1	2	0	7	1	0	1.000
1999—Syracuse (I.L.)..........	C-DH	88	295	39	76	18	2	13	51	.258	21	79	0	575	42	*13	.979
—Toronto (A.L.)............	C	2	9	1	4	2	0	0	1	.444	0	3	0	10	1	0	1.000
2000—Syracuse (I.L.)..........	C	51	179	26	60	15	1	7	29	.335	8	46	0	280	32	3	.990
—Indianapolis (I.L.)■...	C	23	82	5	20	5	0	1	6	.244	6	24	0	129	14	0	1.000
—Milwaukee (N.L.).......	C	5	17	3	4	3	0	0	1	.235	1	5	0	20	2	1	.957
American League totals (4 years)		61	128	20	35	9	1	3	18	.273	11	36	0	291	21	3	.990
National League totals (1 year)		5	17	3	4	3	0	0	1	.235	1	5	0	20	2	1	.957
Major League totals (5 years)		66	145	23	39	12	1	3	19	.269	12	41	0	311	23	4	.988

BROWN, ROOSEVELT   OF   CUBS

PERSONAL: Born August 3, 1975, in Vicksburg, Miss. ... 5-11/195. ... Bats left, throws right. ... Full name: Roosevelt Lawayne Brown. ... Cousin of Ellis Burks, outfielder, Cleveland Indians; cousin of Michael Carter, former Cubs minor league outfielder.
HIGH SCHOOL: Vicksburg (Miss.).
TRANSACTIONS/CAREER NOTES: Selected by Atlanta Braves organization in 20th round of free-agent draft (June 3, 1993). ... Traded by Braves to Florida Marlins for 3B Terry Pendleton (August 13, 1996). ... Selected by Chicago Cubs organization from Marlins organization in Rule 5 minor league draft (December 15, 1997).
STATISTICAL NOTES: Career major league grand slams: 1.

							BATTING								FIELDING		
Year Team (League)	Pos.	G	AB	R	H	2B	3B	HR	RBI	Avg.	BB	SO	SB	PO	A	E	Avg.
1993—GC Braves (GCL).......	OF	26	80	4	9	1	2	0	5	.113	2	9	2	18	4	4	.846
1994—Idaho Falls (Pio.)........	OF	48	160	28	53	8	1	3	22	.331	17	15	8	63	3	1	.985
1995—Eugene (N'West)	OF	57	165	28	51	12	4	7	32	.309	13	30	6	45	3	8	.857
1996—Macon (S.Atl.)..........	OF	113	413	61	115	27	0	19	64	.278	33	60	21	154	6	12	.930
—Kane Co. (Midw.)■..	OF	11	40	1	6	2	0	0	3	.150	1	10	0	13	1	1	.933
1997—Kane County (Midw.)..	OF	61	211	29	50	7	1	4	30	.237	22	52	5	75	5	6	.930
—Brevard County (FSL).	OF	33	114	8	28	7	1	1	12	.246	7	31	0	44	5	1	.980
1998—Daytona (FSL)■........	OF	68	244	49	84	15	5	9	43	.344	23	46	3	106	4	2	.982
—West Tenn (Sou.)	OF	42	160	20	42	11	0	6	24	.263	13	30	3	61	4	3	.956
1999—West Tenn (Sou.)	DH	1	3	0	1	1	0	0	2	.333	0	0	0	...	...	...	...
—Chicago (N.L.)............	OF	34	125	12	37	12	0	3	12	.296	14	29	6	52	5	1	.983
—Iowa (PCL)...............	OF	33	64	6	14	6	1	1	10	.219	2	14	1	20	1	1	.955
2000—Chicago (N.L.)...........	OF-DH	74	268	50	96	25	2	22	79	.358	19	54	3	107	11	5	.959
—Chicago (N.L.)............	OF	45	91	11	32	8	0	3	14	.352	4	22	0	38	1	0	1.000
—Iowa (PCL)...............	OF	100	363	67	112	32	0	12	55	.309	37	60	10	159	6	10	.943
Major League totals (2 years)		78	155	17	46	14	1	4	24	.297	6	36	1	58	2	1	.984

BROWNSON, MARK   P

PERSONAL: Born June 17, 1975, in Lake Worth, Fla. ... 6-2/185. ... Throws right, bats left. ... Full name: Mark Phillip Brownson.
HIGH SCHOOL: Wellington (West Palm Beach, Fla.).
JUNIOR COLLEGE: Palm Beach Community College (Fla.).
TRANSACTIONS/CAREER NOTES: Selected by Colorado Rockies organization in 30th round of free-agent draft (June 3, 1993). ... On Colorado Springs disabled list (August 11-September 8, 1998; and August 21-September 9, 1999). ... Claimed on waivers by Philadelphia Phillies (November 18, 1999). ... Released by Phillies (November 29, 2000).
STATISTICAL NOTES: Led Eastern league with 14 hit batsmen in 1997. ... Pitched shutout in first major league game (July 21, 1998).

Year League	W	L	Pct.	ERA	G	GS	CG	ShO	Sv.	IP	H	R	ER	BB	SO
1994—Arizona Rockies (Ariz.).......	4	1	.800	1.66	19	4	0	0	3	54 1/3	48	18	10	6	72
1995—Asheville (S.Atl.)................	6	7	.462	4.01	23	12	0	0	1	98 2/3	106	52	44	29	94
—New Haven (East.)............	0	0	...	1.50	1	1	0	0	0	6	4	2	1	1	4
1996—New Haven (East.).............	8	13	.381	3.50	37	19	1	0	3	144	141	73	56	43	155
—Salem (Caro.)..................	2	1	.667	4.02	9	1	0	0	1	15 2/3	16	8	7	10	9
1997—New Haven (East.)............	10	9	.526	4.19	29	29	2	0	0	184 2/3	172	101	86	55	170
1998—Colorado Springs (PCL)	6	8	.429	5.34	21	21	3	0	0	124 2/3	131	85	74	37	82
—Colorado (N.L.)...............	1	0	1.000	4.72	2	2	1	1	0	13 1/3	16	7	7	2	8
1999—Colorado Springs (PCL)	6	6	.500	6.20	17	16	2	0	0	103	120	75	71	24	81
—Colorado (N.L.)...............	0	2	.000	7.89	7	7	0	0	0	29 2/3	42	26	26	8	21
2000—Scranton/W.B. (I.L.)■	10	8	.556	4.55	31	20	4	0	0	132 2/3	134	70	67	36	104
—Philadelphia (N.L.).............	1	0	1.000	7.20	2	0	0	0	0	5	7	4	4	3	2
Major League totals (3 years).......	2	2	.500	6.94	11	9	1	1	0	48	65	37	37	13	32

BRUNETTE, JUSTIN   P   CARDINALS

PERSONAL: Born October 7, 1975, in Los Alamitos, Calif. ... 6-1/200. ... Throws left, bats left. ... Full name: Justin Thomas Brunette.
HIGH SCHOOL: Ocean View (Huntington Beach, Calif.).
COLLEGE: San Diego State.

TRANSACTIONS/CAREER NOTES: Selected by St. Louis Cardinals organization in 20th round of free-agent draft (June 3, 1997). ... On New Jersey disabled list (June 16, 1998-entire season). ... On Memphis disabled list (May 24-July 7 and July 29-August 10, 2000).

Year League	W	L	Pct.	ERA	G	GS	CG	ShO	Sv.	IP	H	R	ER	BB	SO
1997—New Jersey (NY-Penn)	1	0	1.000	7.94	6	0	0	0	0	5²/₃	13	6	5	0	6
1998—New Jersey (NY-Penn)							Did not play.								
1999—Peoria (Midw.)	3	1	.750	1.81	38	0	0	0	2	44²/₃	34	9	9	16	44
—Arkansas (Texas)	1	2	.333	1.96	18	0	0	0	0	18¹/₃	21	12	4	7	23
2000—Arkansas (Texas)	0	0	...	3.00	3	0	0	0	0	3	5	4	1	0	1
—St. Louis (N.L.)	0	0	...	5.79	4	0	0	0	0	4²/₃	8	3	3	5	2
—Memphis (PCL)	1	2	.333	6.15	30	0	0	0	0	33²/₃	42	27	23	14	27
Major League totals (1 year)	0	0	...	5.79	4	0	0	0	0	4²/₃	8	3	3	5	2

BRUSKE, JIM   P   B

PERSONAL: Born October 7, 1964, in East St. Louis, Ill. ... 6-1/185. ... Throws right, bats right. ... Full name: James Scott Bruske. ... Name pronounced BREW-ski.

HIGH SCHOOL: Palmdale (Calif.).

JUNIOR COLLEGE: Antelope Valley (Calif.).

COLLEGE: Loyola Marymount.

TRANSACTIONS/CAREER NOTES: Selected by San Diego Padres organization in seventh round of free-agent draft (January 9, 1985); did not sign. ... Selected by Seattle Mariners organization in third round of secondary phase of free-agent draft (January 3, 1985); did not sign. ... Selected by Cleveland Indians organization in first round (sixth player selected) of secondary phase of free-agent draft (June 2, 1986). ... On Canton/Akron disabled list (May 8-25, 1991). ... On Colorado Springs disabled list (May 7-June 9, 1992). ... Released by Indians (June 9, 1992). ... Signed by Houston Astros organization (June 22, 1992). ... On disabled list (May 7-30 and June 9-October 12, 1994). ... Granted free agency (October 15, 1994). ... Signed by Los Angeles Dodgers organization (January 18, 1995). ... On Albuquerque disabled list (May 3-11, 1995). ... Granted free agency (October 16, 1995). ... Re-signed by Dodgers organization (November 12, 1995). ... On Albuquerque disabled list (May 25-June 20, 1996). ... Granted free agency (October 15, 1996). ... Signed by Padres (December 3, 1996). ... On disabled list (August 6-25, 1997). ... Claimed on waivers by Dodgers (October 6, 1997). ... Traded by Dodgers to Padres for P Widd Workman (July 23, 1998). ... Traded by Padres with P Brad Kaufman to New York Yankees for OF Shea Morenz and P Ray Ricken (August 23, 1998). ... Released by Yankees (March 31, 1999). ... Signed by Milwaukee Brewers organization (February 19, 2000). ... On Milwaukee disabled list (May 13-July 27, 2000); included rehabilitation assignment to Indianapolis (June 20-July 7 and July 15-27). ... On Indianapolis disabled list (August 24-31, 2000). ... Granted free agency (October 12, 2000).

MISCELLANEOUS: Played outfield (1986-88). ... Struck out in only appearance as pinch hitter with San Diego (1997).

Year League	W	L	Pct.	ERA	G	GS	CG	ShO	Sv.	IP	H	R	ER	BB	SO
1986—Batavia (NY-Penn)	0	0	...	18.00	1	0	0	0	0	1	1	2	2	3	3
1989—Canton/Akron (East.)	0	0	...	13.50	51	0	0	0	0	2	3	3	3	2	1
1990—Canton/Akron (East.)	9	3	.750	3.28	32	13	3	2	0	118	118	53	43	42	62
1991—Canton/Akron (East.)	5	2	.714	3.47	17	11	0	0	1	80¹/₃	73	36	31	27	35
—Colorado Springs (PCL)	4	0	1.000	2.45	7	1	0	0	2	25²/₃	19	9	7	8	13
1992—Colorado Springs (PCL)	2	0	1.000	4.58	7	0	0	0	10	17²/₃	24	11	9	6	8
—Jackson (Texas)■	4	3	.571	2.63	13	9	1	0	0	61²/₃	54	23	18	14	48
1993—Jackson (Texas)	9	5	.643	2.31	15	15	1	0	0	97¹/₃	86	34	25	22	83
—Tucson (PCL)	4	2	.667	3.78	12	9	0	0	1	66²/₃	77	36	28	18	42
1994—Tucson (PCL)	3	1	.750	4.15	7	7	0	0	0	39	47	22	18	8	25
1995—Los Angeles (N.L.)■	0	0	...	4.50	9	0	0	0	1	10	12	7	5	4	5
—Albuquerque (PCL)	7	5	.583	4.11	43	6	0	0	4	114	128	54	52	41	99
1996—Albuquerque (PCL)	5	2	.714	4.06	36	0	0	0	4	62	63	34	28	21	51
—Los Angeles (N.L.)	0	0	...	5.68	11	0	0	0	0	12²/₃	17	8	8	3	12
1997—Las Vegas (PCL)■	5	4	.556	4.90	16	9	0	0	0	68	73	41	37	22	67
—San Diego (N.L.)	4	1	.800	3.63	28	0	0	0	0	44²/₃	37	22	18	25	32
1998—Los Angeles (N.L.)■	3	0	1.000	3.48	35	0	0	0	1	44	47	18	17	19	31
—San Diego (N.L.)	0	0	...	3.86	4	0	0	0	0	7	10	4	3	4	4
—Las Vegas (PCL)	0	1	.000	6.00	5	0	0	0	1	6	8	4	4	1	2
—Columbus (I.L.)■	0	0	...	1.17	4	0	0	0	1	7²/₃	7	1	1	2	9
—New York (A.L.)	1	0	1.000	3.00	3	1	0	0	0	9	9	3	3	1	3
1999—							Did not play.								
2000—Milwaukee (N.L.)■	1	0	1.000	6.48	15	0	0	0	0	16²/₃	22	15	12	12	8
—Indianapolis (I.L.)	2	4	.333	9.28	19	2	0	0	1	32	47	36	33	14	22
A.L. totals (1 year)	1	0	1.000	3.00	3	1	0	0	0	9	9	3	3	1	3
N.L. totals (5 years)	8	1	.889	4.20	102	0	0	0	2	135	145	74	63	67	92
Major League totals (5 years)	9	1	.900	4.13	105	1	0	0	2	144	154	77	66	68	95

RECORD AS POSITION PLAYER

Year Team (League)	Pos.	G	AB	R	H	2B	3B	HR	RBI	Avg.	BB	SO	SB	PO	A	E	Avg.
1986—Batavia (NY-Penn)	OF-P	56	181	23	44	2	2	3	14	.243	21	50	7	85	4	5	.947
1987—Kinston (Caro.)	OF	123	439	62	102	16	3	7	61	.232	65	118	17	188	7	10	.951
1988—Williamston (East.)	OF	135	443	49	105	12	3	1	44	.237	45	*138	16	238	11	4	.984
1989—Kinston (Caro.)	OF	63	217	29	63	12	1	5	36	.290	34	44	13	114	2	2	.983
—Canton/Akron (East.)	OF-P-SS	51	134	17	32	5	0	1	7	.239	19	28	3	75	4	0	1.000

BUCHANAN, BRIAN   OF   TWINS

PERSONAL: Born July 21, 1973, in Miami. ... 6-4/230. ... Bats right, throws right. ... Full name: Brian James Buchanan.

HIGH SCHOOL: Fairfax (Va.).

COLLEGE: Virginia.

TRANSACTIONS/CAREER NOTES: Selected by New York Yankees organization in first round (24th pick overall) of free-agent draft (June 2, 1994). ... On disabled list (April 29, 1995-remainder of season). ... Traded by Yankees with P Eric Milton, P Danny Mota, SS Cristian Guzman and cash to Minnesota Twins for 2B Chuck Knoblauch (February 6, 1998). ... On Salt Lake disabled list (July 18-27 and July 29-August 9, 1999).

STATISTICAL NOTES: Tied for Pacific Coast League lead with three double plays by outfielder in 1998. ... Tied Pacific Coast League lead with 11 sacrifice flies in 2000.

| | | | | | | | BATTING | | | | | | | | FIELDING | | |
Year Team (League)	Pos.	G	AB	R	H	2B	3B	HR	RBI	Avg.	BB	SO	SB	PO	A	E	Avg.
1994—Oneonta (NY-Penn)	OF	50	177	28	40	9	2	4	26	.226	24	53	5	87	2	0	1.000
1995—Greensboro (S.Atl.)	OF	23	96	19	29	3	0	3	12	.302	9	17	7	31	1	1	.970
1996—Tampa (FSL)	OF	131	526	65	137	22	4	10	58	.260	37	108	23	178	11	6	.969
1997—Norwich (East.)	OF	116	470	75	145	25	2	10	69	.309	32	85	11	192	11	8	.962
—Columbus (I.L.)	OF	18	61	8	17	1	0	4	7	.279	4	11	2	17	1	1	.947
1998—Salt Lake (PCL)■	OF	133	500	74	139	29	3	17	82	.278	36	90	14	244	6	8	.969
1999—Salt Lake (PCL)	OF-DH	107	391	67	116	24	1	10	60	.297	28	85	11	184	9	4	.980
2000—Salt Lake (PCL)	OF-1B	95	364	82	108	20	1	27	103	.297	41	75	5	184	11	4	.980
—Minnesota (A.L.)	OF-DH	30	82	10	19	3	0	1	8	.232	8	22	0	34	1	0	1.000
Major League totals (1 year)		30	82	10	19	3	0	1	8	.232	8	22	0	34	1	0	1.000

B

BUDDIE, MIKE   P   BREWERS

PERSONAL: Born December 12, 1970, in Berea, Ohio. ... 6-3/215. ... Throws right, bats right. ... Full name: Michael Joseph Buddie.
HIGH SCHOOL: St. Ignatius (Cleveland).
COLLEGE: Wake Forest.
TRANSACTIONS/CAREER NOTES: Selected by New York Yankees organization in fourth round of free-agent draft (June 1, 1992). ... Released by Yankees (June 9, 2000). ... Signed by Milwaukee Brewers organization (June 12, 2000).

Year League	W	L	Pct.	ERA	G	GS	CG	ShO	Sv.	IP	H	R	ER	BB	SO
1992—Oneonta (NY-Penn)	1	4	.200	3.88	13	13	1	0	0	67 1/3	69	36	29	34	87
1993—Greensboro (S.Atl.)	13	10	.565	4.87	27	26	0	0	0	155 1/3	138	104	84	89	143
1994—Tampa (FSL)	12	5	.706	4.01	25	24	2	0	0	150 1/3	143	75	67	66	113
1995—Norwich (East.)	10	12	.455	4.81	29	27	2	0	1	149 2/3	155	*102	80	81	106
1996—Norwich (East.)	7	•12	.368	4.45	29	26	4	0	0	159 2/3	176	101	79	71	103
1997—Norwich (East.)	0	0	...	0.00	1	0	0	0	0	1	0	0	0	0	3
—Columbus (I.L.)	6	6	.500	2.64	53	0	0	0	13	75	85	24	22	25	67
1998—New York (A.L.)	4	1	.800	5.62	24	2	0	0	0	41 2/3	46	29	26	13	20
—Columbus (I.L.)	5	0	1.000	2.74	26	0	0	0	4	42 2/3	35	15	13	15	30
1999—Columbus (I.L.)	9	2	.818	2.86	49	2	0	0	0	78 2/3	80	30	25	22	68
—New York (A.L.)	0	0	...	4.50	2	0	0	0	0	2	3	1	1	0	1
2000—Columbus (I.L.)	1	3	.250	7.50	6	6	0	0	0	30	34	30	25	20	16
—Indianapolis (I.L.)■	7	2	.778	2.62	30	0	0	0	2	58 1/3	40	20	17	29	39
—Milwaukee (N.L.)	0	0	...	4.50	5	0	0	0	0	6	8	3	3	1	5
A.L. totals (2 years)	4	1	.800	5.56	26	2	0	0	0	43 2/3	49	30	27	13	21
N.L. totals (1 year)	0	0	...	4.50	5	0	0	0	0	6	8	3	3	1	5
Major League totals (3 years)	4	1	.800	5.44	31	2	0	0	0	49 2/3	57	33	30	14	26

BUEHRLE, MARK   P   WHITE SOX

PERSONAL: Born March 23, 1979, in St. Charles, Mo. ... 6-2/200. ... Throws left, bats left. ... Full name: Mark A. Buehrle.
HIGH SCHOOL: Francis Howell North (St. Charles, Mo.).
JUNIOR COLLEGE: Jefferson College (Mo.).
TRANSACTIONS/CAREER NOTES: Selected by Chicago White Sox organization in 38th round of free-agent draft (June 2, 1998).
HONORS: Named Southern League Most Outstanding Pitcher (2000).

Year League	W	L	Pct.	ERA	G	GS	CG	ShO	Sv.	IP	H	R	ER	BB	SO
1999—Burlington (Midw.)	7	4	.636	4.10	20	14	1	1	3	98 2/3	105	49	45	16	91
2000—Birmingham (Sou.).............	8	4	.667	2.28	16	16	1	1	0	118 2/3	95	37	30	17	68
—Chicago (A.L.)	4	1	.800	4.21	28	3	0	0	0	51 1/3	55	27	24	19	37
Major League totals (1 year)	4	1	.800	4.21	28	3	0	0	0	51 1/3	55	27	24	19	37

DIVISION SERIES RECORD

Year League	W	L	Pct.	ERA	G	GS	CG	ShO	Sv.	IP	H	R	ER	BB	SO
2000—Chicago (A.L.)	0	0	...	0.00	1	0	0	0	0	1/3	2	0	0	0	1

BUFORD, DAMON   OF   CUBS

PERSONAL: Born June 12, 1970, in Baltimore. ... 5-10/180. ... Bats right, throws right. ... Full name: Damon Jackson Buford. ... Son of Don Buford, outfielder with Chicago White Sox (1963-67) and Baltimore Orioles (1968); and brother of Don Buford Jr., minor league infielder (1987-89).
HIGH SCHOOL: Birmingham (Calif.).
COLLEGE: Southern California.
TRANSACTIONS/CAREER NOTES: Selected by Baltimore Orioles organization in 10th round of free-agent draft (June 4, 1990). ... Traded by Orioles with OF Alex Ochoa to New York Mets for 3B/OF Bobby Bonilla and a player to be named later (July 28, 1995); Orioles acquired P Jimmy Williams to complete deal (August 17, 1995). ... Traded by Mets to Texas Rangers for OF Terrell Lowery (January 25, 1996). ... Traded by Rangers with C Jim Leyritz to Boston Red Sox for P Aaron Sele, P Mark Brandenburg and C Bill Haselman (November 6, 1997). ... On disabled list (May 18-June 3 and August 27-September 11, 1998; and August 5-23, 1999). ... Traded by Red Sox to Chicago Cubs for IF Manny Alexander (December 11, 1999).
STATISTICAL NOTES: Led Eastern League outfielders with 279 total chances in 1992. ... Led International League outfielders with 347 total chances in 1994. ... Career major league grand slams: 3.

| | | | | | | | BATTING | | | | | | | | FIELDING | | |
Year Team (League)	Pos.	G	AB	R	H	2B	3B	HR	RBI	Avg.	BB	SO	SB	PO	A	E	Avg.
1990—Wausau (Midw.)	OF	41	160	31	48	7	2	1	14	.300	21	32	15	89	2	2	.978
1991—Frederick (Caro.)	OF	133	505	71	138	25	6	8	54	.273	51	92	50	293	7	5	.984
1992—Hagerstown (East.)......	OF	101	373	53	89	17	3	1	30	.239	42	62	41	*264	13	2	.993
—Rochester (I.L.)	OF	45	155	29	44	10	2	1	12	.284	14	23	23	100	1	3	.971

Year	Team (League)	Pos.	G	AB	R	H	2B	3B	HR	RBI	Avg.	BB	SO	SB	PO	A	E	Avg.
								BATTING								FIELDING		
1993—	Rochester (I.L.)	OF	27	116	24	33	6	1	1	4	.284	7	16	10	73	3	3	.962
—	Baltimore (A.L.)	OF-DH	53	79	18	18	5	0	2	9	.228	9	19	2	61	2	1	.984
1994—	Baltimore (A.L.)	DH-OF	4	2	2	1	0	0	0	0	.500	0	1	0	0	0	0	...
—	Rochester (I.L.)	OF-DH	111	452	*89	122	21	4	16	66	.270	35	81	31	*339	4	4	.988
1995—	Baltimore (A.L.)	OF	24	32	6	2	0	0	0	2	.063	6	7	3	40	0	0	1.000
—	Rochester (I.L.)	OF	46	188	40	58	12	3	4	18	.309	17	26	17	115	2	2	.983
—	New York (N.L.)■	OF	44	136	24	32	5	0	4	12	.235	19	28	7	67	2	2	.972
1996—	Texas (A.L.)■	OF-DH	90	145	30	41	9	0	6	20	.283	15	34	8	93	3	0	1.000
1997—	Texas (A.L.)	OF-DH	122	366	49	82	18	0	8	39	.224	30	83	18	282	7	3	.990
1998—	Boston (A.L.)■	O-DH-2-3	86	216	37	61	14	4	10	42	.282	22	43	5	134	4	0	1.000
1999—	Boston (A.L.)	OF	91	297	39	72	15	2	6	38	.242	21	74	9	189	6	3	.985
2000—	Chicago (N.L.)■	OF	150	495	64	124	18	3	15	48	.251	47	118	4	336	4	5	.986
American League totals (7 years)			470	1137	181	277	61	6	32	150	.244	103	261	45	799	22	7	.992
National League totals (2 years)			194	631	88	156	23	3	19	60	.247	66	146	11	403	6	7	.983
Major League totals (8 years)			664	1768	269	433	84	9	51	210	.245	169	407	56	1202	28	14	.989

DIVISION SERIES RECORD

Year	Team (League)	Pos.	G	AB	R	H	2B	3B	HR	RBI	Avg.	BB	SO	SB	PO	A	E	Avg.
								BATTING								FIELDING		
1996—	Texas (A.L.)	PR	2	0	0	0	0	0	0	0	...	0	0	0	0	0	0	...
1998—	Boston (A.L.)	PR-OF-PH-DH	3	1	2	0	0	0	0	0	.000	0	0	0	1	0	0	1.000
1999—	Boston (A.L.)	OF	1	3	0	0	0	0	0	0	.000	0	1	0	3	0	0	1.000
Division series totals (3 years)			6	4	2	0	0	0	0	0	.000	0	1	0	4	0	0	1.000

CHAMPIONSHIP SERIES RECORD

Year	Team (League)	Pos.	G	AB	R	H	2B	3B	HR	RBI	Avg.	BB	SO	SB	PO	A	E	Avg.
								BATTING								FIELDING		
1999—	Boston (A.L.)	PR-OF-PH	4	5	1	2	0	0	0	0	.400	0	2	1	4	0	0	1.000

BUHNER, JAY   OF/DH   MARINERS

PERSONAL: Born August 13, 1964, in Louisville, Ky. ... 6-3/210. ... Bats right, throws right. ... Full name: Jay Campbell Buhner. ... Brother of Shawn Buhner, infielder, Mariners organization. ... Name pronounced BYOO-ner.

HIGH SCHOOL: Clear Creek (League City, Texas).

JUNIOR COLLEGE: McLennan Community College (Texas).

TRANSACTIONS/CAREER NOTES: Selected by Atlanta Braves organization in ninth round of free-agent draft (June 6, 1983); did not sign. ... Selected by Pittsburgh Pirates organization in secondary phase of free-agent draft (January 17, 1984). ... Traded by Pirates organization with IF Dale Berra and P Alfonso Pulido to New York Yankees for OF Steve Kemp, IF Tim Foli and cash (December 20, 1984). ... On disabled list (April 11-July 28, 1986). ... Traded by Yankees with P Rich Balabon and a player to be named later to Seattle Mariners for DH Ken Phelps (July 21, 1988); Mariners acquired P Troy Evers to complete deal (October 12, 1988). ... On Seattle disabled list (June 29-August 19, 1989); included rehabilitation assignment to Calgary (August 16-19). ... On Seattle disabled list (March 31-June 1, 1990); included rehabilitation assignment to Calgary (May 18-June 1). ... On Seattle disabled list (June 17-August 23, 1990). ... Granted free agency (October 28, 1994). ... Re-signed by Mariners (December 21, 1994). ... On disabled list (June 6-22, 1995). ... On Seattle disabled list (April 7-June 11 and September 8, 1998-remainder of season); included rehabilitation assignment to Tacoma (June 9-11). ... On disabled list (May 19-July 15, 1999). ... Granted free agency (November 11, 1999). ... Re-signed by Mariners (December 6, 1999). ... On disabled list (August 17-September 1, 2000). ... On suspended list (August 25-28, 2000). ... Granted free agency (November 10, 2000). ... Re-signed by Mariners (December 7, 2000).

RECORDS: Shares major league records for most strikeouts in two consecutive nine-inning games—8 (August 23-24, 1990); and most strikeouts in three consecutive nine-inning games—10 (August 23-25, 1990).

HONORS: Won A.L. Gold Glove as outfielder (1996).

STATISTICAL NOTES: Tied for International League lead in double plays by outfielder with six in 1987. ... Hit for the cycle (June 23, 1993). ... Career major league grand slams: 10.

Year	Team (League)	Pos.	G	AB	R	H	2B	3B	HR	RBI	Avg.	BB	SO	SB	PO	A	E	Avg.
								BATTING								FIELDING		
1984—	Watertown (NY-Penn)	OF	65	229	43	74	16	3	9	•58	.323	42	58	3	106	8	1	.991
1985—	Fort Laud. (FSL)■	OF	117	409	65	121	18	10	11	76	.296	65	76	6	235	12	7	.972
1986—	Fort Laud. (FSL)	OF	36	139	24	42	9	1	7	31	.302	15	30	1	84	7	3	.968
1987—	Columbus (I.L.)	OF	134	502	83	140	23	1	*31	85	.279	55	124	4	275	*20	6	.980
—	New York (A.L.)	OF	7	22	0	5	2	0	0	1	.227	1	6	0	11	1	0	1.000
1988—	Columbus (I.L.)	OF	38	129	26	33	5	0	8	18	.256	19	33	1	83	3	1	.989
—	New York (A.L.)	OF	25	69	8	13	0	0	3	13	.188	3	25	0	52	2	2	.964
—	Seattle (A.L.)■	OF	60	192	28	43	13	1	10	25	.224	25	68	1	134	7	1	.993
1989—	Calgary (PCL)	OF	56	196	43	61	12	1	11	45	.311	44	56	4	97	8	2	.981
—	Seattle (A.L.)	OF	58	204	27	56	15	1	9	33	.275	19	55	1	106	6	4	.966
1990—	Calgary (PCL)	OF	13	34	6	7	1	0	2	5	.206	7	11	0	14	1	0	1.000
—	Seattle (A.L.)	OF-DH	51	163	16	45	12	0	7	33	.276	17	50	2	55	1	2	.966
1991—	Seattle (A.L.)	OF	137	406	64	99	14	4	27	77	.244	53	117	0	244	15	5	.981
1992—	Seattle (A.L.)	OF	152	543	69	132	16	3	25	79	.243	71	146	0	314	14	2	.994
1993—	Seattle (A.L.)	OF-DH	158	563	91	153	28	3	27	98	.272	100	144	2	263	8	6	.978
1994—	Seattle (A.L.)	OF-DH	101	358	74	100	23	4	21	68	.279	66	63	0	178	11	2	.990
1995—	Seattle (A.L.)	OF-DH	126	470	86	123	23	0	40	121	.262	60	120	0	180	5	2	.989
1996—	Seattle (A.L.)	OF-DH	150	564	107	153	29	0	44	138	.271	84	*159	0	251	9	3	.989
1997—	Seattle (A.L.)	OF-DH	157	540	104	131	18	2	40	109	.243	119	*175	0	295	5	1	*.997
1998—	Seattle (A.L.)	OF-DH	72	244	33	59	7	1	15	45	.242	38	71	0	127	5	2	.985
—	Tacoma (PCL)	DH-OF	2	4	2	2	2	0	0	2	.500	2	2	0	0	0	0	...
1999—	Seattle (A.L.)	OF-1B	87	266	37	59	11	0	14	38	.222	69	100	0	136	7	1	.993
2000—	Seattle (A.L.)	OF-DH	112	364	50	92	20	0	26	82	.253	59	98	0	176	4	0	1.000
Major League totals (14 years)			1453	4968	794	1263	231	19	308	960	.254	784	1397	6	2522	100	33	.988

B

DIVISION SERIES RECORD

							BATTING												FIELDING		
Year Team (League)	Pos.	G	AB	R	H	2B	3B	HR	RBI	Avg.	BB	SO	SB		PO	A	E	Avg.
1995— Seattle (A.L.)	OF	5	24	2	11	1	0	1	3	.458	2	4	0		11	1	0	1.000
1997— Seattle (A.L.)	OF	4	13	2	3	0	0	2	2	.231	3	6	0		5	1	0	1.000
2000— Seattle (A.L.)	OF	2	5	1	1	0	0	1	1	.200	2	0	0		4	0	0	1.000
Division series totals (3 years)		11	42	5	15	1	0	4	6	.357	7	10	0		20	2	0	1.000

RECORDS: Shares A.L. single-series record for most strikeouts—8 (1995).

CHAMPIONSHIP SERIES RECORD

							BATTING												FIELDING		
Year Team (League)	Pos.	G	AB	R	H	2B	3B	HR	RBI	Avg.	BB	SO	SB		PO	A	E	Avg.
1995— Seattle (A.L.)	OF	6	23	5	7	2	0	3	5	.304	2	8	0		15	0	1	.938
2000— Seattle (A.L.)	OF-PH	4	11	0	2	0	0	0	0	.182	1	6	0		4	0	0	1.000
Championship series totals (2 years)		10	34	5	9	2	0	3	5	.265	3	14	0		19	0	1	.950

ALL-STAR GAME RECORD

						BATTING										FIELDING		
Year League	Pos.	AB	R	H	2B	3B	HR	RBI	Avg.	BB	SO	SB		PO	A	E	Avg.
1996— American	OF	2	0	0	0	0	0	0	.000	0	0	0		1	0	0	1.000

BULLINGER, KIRK　　　　　　P

PERSONAL: Born October 28, 1969, in New Orleans. ... 6-2/170. ... Throws right, bats right. ... Full name: Kirk Matthew Bullinger. ... Brother of Jim Bullinger, pitcher with Chicago Cubs (1992-96), Montreal Expos (1997) and Seattle Mariners (1998).
HIGH SCHOOL: Archbishop Rummel (Metairie, La.).
COLLEGE: Southeastern Louisiana.
TRANSACTIONS/CAREER NOTES: Selected by St. Louis Cardinals in 32nd round of free-agent draft (June 1, 1992). ... Traded by Cardinals with OF DaRond Stovall and P Bryan Eversgerd to Montreal Expos for P Ken Hill (April 5, 1995). ... On Ottawa disabled list (April 9-July 3, 1998); included rehabilitation assignment to Gulf Coast Expos (June 26-July 3). ... Granted free agency (October 15, 1998). ... Signed by Boston Red Sox organization (December 14, 1998). ... On Pawtucket disabled list (August 6-18, 1999). ... Granted free agency (October 4, 1999). ... Signed by Philadelphia Phillies organization (January 29, 2000). ... On Philadelphia disabled list (April 11-June 20, 2000); included rehabilitation assignments to Reading (May 6-8 and May 13-18) and Gulf Coast Phillies (June 19-20). ... Granted free agency (October 2, 2000).

Year League	W	L	Pct.	ERA	G	GS	CG	ShO	Sv.	IP	H	R	ER	BB	SO
1992— Hamilton (NY-Penn)	2	2	.500	1.11	35	0	0	0	2	48 2/3	24	7	6	15	61
1993— Springfield (Midw.)	1	3	.250	2.28	50	0	0	0	*33	51 1/3	26	19	13	21	72
1994— St. Petersburg (FSL)	2	0	1.000	1.17	39	0	0	0	6	53 2/3	37	16	7	20	50
1995— Harrisburg (East.)■..........	5	3	.625	2.42	56	0	0	0	7	67	61	22	18	25	42
1996— Ottawa (I.L.)	2	1	.667	3.52	10	0	0	0	0	15 1/3	10	6	6	9	9
— Harrisburg (East.)..............	3	4	.429	1.97	47	0	0	0	22	45 2/3	46	16	10	18	29
1997— Harrisburg (East.)	3	0	1.000	2.67	21	0	0	0	6	27	22	9	8	6	21
— West Palm Beach (FSL)	2	0	1.000	0.00	2	0	0	0	0	3 2/3	3	0	0	0	7
— Ottawa (I.L.)	3	4	.429	1.71	22	0	0	0	5	31 2/3	17	7	6	10	15
1998— Gulf Coast Expos (GCL)	0	0	...	0.00	2	2	0	0	0	4	2	0	0	0	7
— Jupiter (FSL)	0	0	...	5.40	8	0	0	0	0	10	9	7	6	2	12
— Ottawa (I.L.)	0	0	...	1.06	13	0	0	0	3	17	16	2	2	6	7
— Montreal (N.L.)	1	0	1.000	9.00	8	0	0	0	0	7	14	8	7	0	2
1999— Trenton (East.)■..............	1	1	.500	0.53	17	0	0	0	10	17	6	2	1	5	16
— Pawtucket (I.L.)..................	0	2	.000	2.39	35	0	0	0	15	37 2/3	37	14	10	13	27
— Boston (A.L.)	0	0	...	4.50	4	0	0	0	0	2	2	1	1	2	0
2000— Philadelphia (N.L.)■..........	0	0	...	5.40	3	0	0	0	0	3 1/3	4	2	2	0	4
— Scranton/W.B. (I.L.)	0	1	.000	0.72	26	0	0	0	12	25	19	4	2	10	16
— Reading (East.)..................	0	0	...	0.00	2	1	0	0	0	3	3	0	0	1	1
— Gulf Coast Phillies (GCL)....	0	0	...	0.00	1	1	0	0	0	1	0	0	0	0	1
A.L. totals (1 year)	0	0	...	4.50	4	0	0	0	0	2	2	1	1	2	0
N.L. totals (2 years)	1	0	1.000	7.84	11	0	0	0	0	10 1/3	18	10	9	0	6
Major League totals (3 years)	1	0	1.000	7.30	15	0	0	0	0	12 1/3	20	11	10	2	6

BURBA, DAVE　　　　　　P　　　　　　INDIANS

PERSONAL: Born July 7, 1966, in Dayton, Ohio. ... 6-4/240. ... Throws right, bats right. ... Full name: David Allen Burba. ... Nephew of Ray Hathaway, pitcher with Brooklyn Dodgers (1945).
HIGH SCHOOL: Kenton Ridge (Springfield, Ohio).
COLLEGE: Ohio State.
TRANSACTIONS/CAREER NOTES: Selected by Seattle Mariners organization in second round of free-agent draft (June 2, 1987). ... Traded by Mariners with P Bill Swift and P Mike Jackson to San Francisco Giants for OF Kevin Mitchell and P Mike Remlinger (December 11, 1991). ... Traded by Giants with OF Darren Lewis and P Mark Portugal to Cincinnati Reds for OF Deion Sanders, P John Roper, P Ricky Pickett, P Scott Service and IF Dave McCarty (July 21, 1995). ... On disabled list (August 7-27, 1997). ... Traded by Reds to Cleveland Indians for 1B Sean Casey (March 30, 1998).

Year League	W	L	Pct.	ERA	G	GS	CG	ShO	Sv.	IP	H	R	ER	BB	SO
1987— Bellingham (N'West)	3	1	.750	1.93	5	5	0	0	0	23 1/3	20	10	5	3	24
— Salinas (Calif.)	1	6	.143	4.61	9	9	0	0	0	54 2/3	53	31	28	29	46
1988— San Bernardino (Calif.).......	5	7	.417	2.68	20	20	0	0	0	114	106	41	34	54	102
1989— Williamsport (East.)	11	7	.611	3.16	25	25	5	1	0	156 2/3	138	69	55	55	89
1990— Calgary (PCL).....................	10	6	.625	4.67	31	18	1	0	2	113 2/3	124	64	59	45	72
— Seattle (A.L.)	0	0	...	4.50	6	0	0	0	0	8	8	6	4	2	4
1991— Calgary (PCL).....................	6	4	.600	3.53	23	9	0	0	4	71 1/3	82	35	28	27	42
— Seattle (A.L.)	2	2	.500	3.68	22	2	0	0	1	36 2/3	34	16	15	14	16
1992— San Francisco (N.L.)■	2	7	.222	4.97	23	11	0	0	0	70 2/3	80	43	39	31	47

Year	League	W	L	Pct.	ERA	G	GS	CG	ShO	Sv.	IP	H	R	ER	BB	SO
—	Phoenix (PCL)	5	5	.500	4.72	13	13	0	0	0	74 1/3	86	40	39	24	44
1993—	San Francisco (N.L.)	10	3	.769	4.25	54	5	0	0	0	95 1/3	95	49	45	37	88
1994—	San Francisco (N.L.)	3	6	.333	4.38	57	0	0	0	0	74	59	39	36	45	84
1995—	San Francisco (N.L.)	4	2	.667	4.98	37	0	0	0	0	43 1/3	38	26	24	25	46
—	Cincinnati (N.L.)■	6	2	.750	3.27	15	9	1	1	0	63 1/3	52	24	23	26	50
1996—	Cincinnati (N.L.)	11	13	.458	3.83	34	33	0	0	0	195	179	96	83	97	148
1997—	Cincinnati (N.L.)	11	10	.524	4.72	30	27	2	0	0	160	157	88	84	73	131
1998—	Cleveland (A.L.)■	15	10	.600	4.11	32	31	0	0	0	203 2/3	210	100	93	69	132
1999—	Cleveland (A.L.)	15	9	.625	4.25	34	34	1	0	0	220	211	113	104	96	174
2000—	Cleveland (A.L.)	16	6	.727	4.47	32	32	0	0	0	191 1/3	199	99	95	91	180
A.L. totals (5 years)		48	27	.640	4.24	126	99	1	0	1	659 2/3	662	334	311	272	506
N.L. totals (6 years)		47	43	.522	4.28	250	85	3	1	0	701 2/3	660	365	334	334	594
Major League totals (11 years)		95	70	.576	4.26	376	184	4	1	1	1361 1/3	1322	699	645	606	1100

DIVISION SERIES RECORD

Year	League	W	L	Pct.	ERA	G	GS	CG	ShO	Sv.	IP	H	R	ER	BB	SO
1995—	Cincinnati (N.L.)	1	0	1.000	0.00	1	0	0	0	0	1	2	0	0	1	0
1998—	Cleveland (A.L.)	1	0	1.000	5.06	1	0	0	0	0	5 1/3	4	3	3	2	4
1999—	Cleveland (A.L.)	0	0	...	0.00	1	1	0	0	0	4	1	0	0	1	0
Division series totals (3 years)		2	0	1.000	2.61	3	1	0	0	0	10 1/3	7	3	3	4	4

CHAMPIONSHIP SERIES RECORD

Year	League	W	L	Pct.	ERA	G	GS	CG	ShO	Sv.	IP	H	R	ER	BB	SO
1995—	Cincinnati (N.L.)	0	0	...	0.00	2	0	0	0	0	3 2/3	3	0	0	4	0
1998—	Cleveland (A.L.)	1	0	1.000	3.00	3	0	0	0	0	6	3	4	2	5	8
Champ. series totals (2 years)		1	0	1.000	1.86	5	0	0	0	0	9 2/3	6	4	2	9	8

BURKETT, JOHN　　　　P

PERSONAL: Born November 28, 1964, in New Brighton, Pa. ... 6-3/215. ... Throws right, bats right. ... Full name: John David Burkett. ... Name pronounced bur-KETT.

HIGH SCHOOL: Beaver (Pa.).

TRANSACTIONS/CAREER NOTES: Selected by San Francisco Giants organization in sixth round of free-agent draft (June 6, 1983). ... Traded by Giants to Texas Rangers for IF Rich Aurilia and OF Desi Wilson (December 22, 1994). ... Granted free agency (April 7, 1995). ... Signed by Florida Marlins (April 9, 1995). ... Traded by Marlins to Texas Rangers for P Ryan Dempster and a player to be named later (August 8, 1996); Marlins acquired P Rick Helling to complete deal (September 3, 1996). ... On Texas disabled list (August 6-31, 1997); included rehabilitation assignment to Oklahoma City (August 26). ... On Texas disabled list (April 21-May 9, 1999); included rehabilitation assignment to Tulsa (May 1-9). ... Granted free agency (November 1, 1999). ... Signed by Tampa Bay Devil Rays organization (January 17, 2000). ... Released by Devil Rays (March 29, 2000). ... Signed by Atlanta Braves (April 2, 2000). ... Granted free agency (October 31, 2000).

STATISTICAL NOTES: Led N.L. 10 hit batsmen in 1991.

MISCELLANEOUS: Had sacrifice hit in only appearance as pinch hitter (1995).

Year	League	W	L	Pct.	ERA	G	GS	CG	ShO	Sv.	IP	H	R	ER	BB	SO
1983—	Great Falls (Pio.)	2	6	.250	6.26	13	9	0	0	0	50 1/3	73	44	35	30	38
1984—	Clinton (Midw.)	7	6	.538	4.33	20	20	2	0	0	126 2/3	128	81	61	38	83
1985—	Fresno (Calif.)	7	4	.636	2.87	20	20	1	1	0	109 2/3	98	43	35	46	72
1986—	Fresno (Calif.)	0	3	.000	5.47	4	4	0	0	0	24 2/3	34	19	15	8	14
—	Shreveport (Texas)	10	6	.625	2.66	22	21	4	2	0	128 2/3	99	46	38	42	73
1987—	Shreveport (Texas)	•14	8	.636	3.34	27	27	6	1	0	*177 2/3	181	75	66	53	126
—	San Francisco (N.L.)	0	0	...	4.50	3	0	0	0	0	6	7	4	3	3	5
1988—	Phoenix (PCL)	5	11	.313	5.21	21	21	0	0	0	114	141	79	66	49	74
—	Shreveport (Texas)	5	1	.833	2.13	7	7	2	1	0	50 2/3	33	15	12	18	34
1989—	Phoenix (PCL)	10	11	.476	5.05	28	•28	0	1	0	167 2/3	197	111	94	59	105
1990—	Phoenix (PCL)	2	1	.667	2.74	3	3	2	1	0	23	18	8	7	3	9
—	San Francisco (N.L.)	14	7	.667	3.79	33	32	2	0	1	204	201	92	86	61	118
1991—	San Francisco (N.L.)	12	11	.522	4.18	36	34	3	1	0	206 2/3	223	103	96	60	131
1992—	San Francisco (N.L.)	13	9	.591	3.84	32	32	3	1	0	189 2/3	194	96	81	45	107
1993—	San Francisco (N.L.)	•22	7	.759	3.65	34	34	2	1	0	231 2/3	224	100	94	40	145
1994—	San Francisco (N.L.)	6	8	.429	3.62	25	25	0	0	0	159 1/3	176	72	64	36	85
1995—	Florida (N.L.)■	14	14	.500	4.30	30	30	4	0	0	188 1/3	208	95	90	57	126
1996—	Florida (N.L.)	6	10	.375	4.32	24	24	1	0	0	154	154	84	74	42	108
—	Texas (A.L.)■	5	2	.714	4.06	10	10	1	1	0	68 2/3	75	33	31	16	47
1997—	Texas (A.L.)	9	12	.429	4.56	30	30	2	0	0	189 1/3	240	106	96	30	139
—	Oklahoma City (A.A.)	1	0	1.000	3.60	1	1	0	0	0	5	6	2	2	2	3
1998—	Texas (A.L.)	9	13	.409	5.68	32	32	0	0	0	195	230	131	*123	46	131
1999—	Texas (A.L.)	9	8	.529	5.62	30	25	0	0	0	147 1/3	184	95	92	46	96
—	Tulsa (Texas)	0	1	.000	2.70	2	2	0	0	0	6 2/3	7	5	2	3	3
2000—	Atlanta (N.L.)■	10	6	.625	4.89	31	22	0	0	0	134 1/3	162	79	73	51	110
A.L. totals (4 years)		32	35	.478	5.13	102	97	3	1	0	600 1/3	729	365	342	138	413
N.L. totals (9 years)		97	72	.574	4.04	248	233	15	3	1	1474	1549	725	661	395	935
Major League totals (12 years)		129	107	.547	4.35	350	330	18	4	1	2074 1/3	2278	1090	1003	533	1348

DIVISION SERIES RECORD

Year	League	W	L	Pct.	ERA	G	GS	CG	ShO	Sv.	IP	H	R	ER	BB	SO
1996—	Texas (A.L.)	1	0	1.000	2.00	1	1	1	0	0	9	10	2	2	1	7
1998—	Texas (A.L.)							Did not play.								
1999—	Texas (A.L.)							Did not play.								
2000—	Atlanta (N.L.)	0	0	...	6.75	1	0	0	0	0	1 1/3	1	1	1	0	0
Division series totals (2 years)		1	0	1.000	2.61	2	1	1	0	0	10 1/3	11	3	3	1	7

ALL-STAR GAME RECORD

Year	League	W	L	Pct.	ERA	GS	CG	ShO	Sv.	IP	H	R	ER	BB	SO
1993—	National	0	1	.000	40.50	0	0	0	0	2/3	4	3	3	0	1

PERSONAL: Born January 29, 1972, in St. Louis. ... 5-11/225. ... Bats both, throws left.
HIGH SCHOOL: Hazelwood West (Hazelwood, Mo.).
COLLEGE: Texas State, then Central Missouri State.
TRANSACTIONS/CAREER NOTES: Signed by Richmond, Frontier League (1995). ... Contract sold by Richmond to Boston Red Sox organization (October 21, 1998).
HONORS: Named Frontier League Most Valuable Player (1996, 1997 and 1998).

											BATTING				FIELDING		
Year	Team (League)	Pos.	G	AB	R	H	2B	3B	HR	RBI	Avg.	BB	SO	SB	PO	A	E	Avg.
1995— Richmond (Fron.).......		1B	70	282	58	*93	*28	1	9	*70	.330	41	24	16	...	...	...	
1996— Richmond (Fron.).......		1B	74	266	60	95	*27	1	17	64	.357	49	24	22	...	...	...	
1997— Richmond (Fron.).......		1B	80	285	*76	92	22	0	*24	74	.323	73	47	8	...	...	...	
1998— Richmond (Fron.).......		1B	80	280	*97	113	16	1	*36	*98	*.404	85	38	13	...	...	...	
1999— Sarasota (FSL)■........		1B	68	245	56	89	18	0	23	67	.363	37	33	5	488	32	4	.992
— Trenton (East.)........		1B	66	239	40	55	14	1	12	41	.230	31	43	3	215	7	3	.987
2000— Pawtucket (I.L.)..........		1B-OF	105	353	59	90	17	1	23	77	.255	69	89	0	508	46	4	.993
— Boston (A.L.)..............		DH-1B-OF	25	73	16	21	3	0	4	18	.288	17	25	0	26	1	1	.964
Major League totals (1 year)			25	73	16	21	3	0	4	18	.288	17	25	0	26	1	1	.964

PERSONAL: Born September 11, 1964, in Vicksburg, Miss. ... 6-2/205. ... Bats right, throws right. ... Full name: Ellis Rena Burks. ... Cousin of Roosevelt Brown, outfielder, Chicago Cubs.
HIGH SCHOOL: Everman (Texas).
JUNIOR COLLEGE: Ranger (Texas) Junior College.
TRANSACTIONS/CAREER NOTES: Selected by Boston Red Sox organization in first round (20th pick overall) of free-agent draft (January 11, 1983). ... On disabled list (March 26-April 12, 1988). ... On Boston disabled list (June 15-August 1, 1989); included rehabilitation assignment to Pawtucket (July 26-August 1). ... On disabled list (June 25, 1992-remainder of season). ... Granted free agency (December 19, 1992). ... Signed by Chicago White Sox (January 4, 1993). ... Granted free agency (October 27, 1993). ... Signed by Colorado Rockies (November 30, 1993). ... On Colorado disabled list (May 18-July 31, 1994); included rehabilitation assignment to Colorado Springs (July 18-20). ... On Colorado disabled list (April 17-May 5, 1995); included rehabilitation assignment to Colorado Springs (April 25-May 5). ... On disabled list (June 28-July 29, 1997). ... Traded by Rockies to San Francisco Giants for OF Darryl Hamilton, P James Stoops and a player to be named later (July 31, 1998); Rockies acquired P Jason Brester to complete deal (August 17, 1998). ... Granted free agency (November 2, 1998). ... Re-signed by Giants (November 13, 1998). ... On disabled list (June 9-26, 1999; and May 9-24, 2000). ... Granted free agency (October 30, 2000). ... Signed by Cleveland Indians (November 19, 2000).
RECORDS: Shares major league single-inning record for most home runs—2 (August 27, 1990, fourth inning).
HONORS: Named outfielder on THE SPORTING NEWS A.L. All-Star team (1990). ... Named outfielder on THE SPORTING NEWS A.L. Silver Slugger team (1990). ... Won A.L. Gold Glove as outfielder (1990). ... Named outfielder on THE SPORTING NEWS N.L. All-Star team (1996). ... Named outfielder on THE SPORTING NEWS N.L. Silver Slugger team (1996).
STATISTICAL NOTES: Tied for Florida State League lead in double plays by outfielder with six in 1984. ... Led N.L. with 392 total bases and .639 slugging percentage in 1996. ... Career major league grand slams: 10.

											BATTING				FIELDING		
Year	Team (League)	Pos.	G	AB	R	H	2B	3B	HR	RBI	Avg.	BB	SO	SB	PO	A	E	Avg.
1983— Elmira (NY-Penn)		OF	53	174	30	42	9	0	2	23	.241	17	43	9	89	5	2	.979
1984— Winter Haven (FSL)....		OF	112	375	52	96	15	4	6	43	.256	42	68	29	196	12	5	.977
1985— New Britain (East.)		OF	133	476	66	121	25	7	10	61	.254	42	85	17	306	9	8	.975
1986— New Britain (East.)		OF	124	462	70	126	20	3	14	55	.273	44	75	31	318	5	5	.985
1987— Pawtucket (I.L.).........		OF	11	40	11	9	3	1	3	6	.225	7	7	1	25	0	0	1.000
— Boston (A.L.).............		OF-DH	133	558	94	152	30	2	20	59	.272	41	98	27	320	15	4	.988
1988— Boston (A.L.).............		OF-DH	144	540	93	159	37	5	18	92	.294	62	89	25	370	9	9	.977
1989— Boston (A.L.).............		OF-DH	97	399	73	121	19	6	12	61	.303	36	52	21	245	7	6	.977
— Pawtucket (I.L.).........		OF	5	21	4	3	1	0	0	0	.143	2	3	0	16	0	0	1.000
1990— Boston (A.L.).............		OF-DH	152	588	89	174	33	8	21	89	.296	48	82	9	324	7	2	.994
1991— Boston (A.L.).............		OF-DH	130	474	56	119	33	3	14	56	.251	39	81	6	283	2	2	.993
1992— Boston (A.L.).............		OF-DH	66	235	35	60	8	3	8	30	.255	25	48	5	120	3	2	.984
1993— Chicago (A.L.)■........		OF	146	499	75	137	24	4	17	74	.275	60	97	6	313	6	6	.982
1994— Colorado (N.L.)■		OF	42	149	33	48	8	3	13	24	.322	16	39	3	79	2	3	.964
— Colo. Springs (PCL) ...		OF	2	8	4	4	1	0	1	2	.500	2	1	0	5	0	0	1.000
1995— Colo. Springs (PCL) ..		OF-DH	8	29	9	9	2	1	2	6	.310	4	8	0	16	0	0	1.000
— Colorado (N.L.)		OF	103	278	41	74	10	6	14	49	.266	39	72	7	158	3	5	.970
1996— Colorado (N.L.)		OF	156	613	*142	211	45	8	40	128	.344	61	114	32	279	6	5	.983
1997— Colorado (N.L.)		OF	119	424	91	123	19	2	32	82	.290	47	75	7	207	6	4	.982
1998— Colorado (N.L.)		OF	100	357	54	102	22	5	16	54	.286	39	80	3	187	5	5	.975
— San Fran. (N.L.)■......		OF	42	147	22	45	6	1	5	22	.306	19	31	8	89	1	1	.989
1999— San Francisco (N.L.) ..		OF-DH	120	390	73	110	19	0	31	96	.282	69	86	7	210	3	2	.991
2000— San Francisco (N.L.) ..		OF-DH	122	393	74	135	21	5	24	96	.344	56	49	5	215	4	4	.982
American League totals (7 years)			868	3293	515	922	184	31	110	461	.280	311	547	99	1975	49	31	.985
National League totals (7 years)			804	2751	530	848	150	30	175	551	.308	346	546	72	1424	30	29	.980
Major League totals (14 years)			1672	6044	1045	1770	334	61	285	1012	.293	657	1093	171	3399	79	60	.983

DIVISION SERIES RECORD

											BATTING				FIELDING		
Year	Team (League)	Pos.	G	AB	R	H	2B	3B	HR	RBI	Avg.	BB	SO	SB	PO	A	E	Avg.
1995— Colorado (N.L.)		OF	2	6	1	2	1	0	0	2	.333	0	1	0	4	0	1	.800
2000— San Francisco (N.L.) ..		OF	4	13	2	3	1	0	1	4	.231	4	2	0	12	0	0	1.000
Division series totals (2 years)			6	19	3	5	2	0	1	6	.263	4	3	0	16	0	1	.941

CHAMPIONSHIP SERIES RECORD

Year	Team (League)	Pos.	G	AB	R	H	2B	3B	HR	RBI	Avg.	BB	SO	SB	PO	A	E	Avg.
								BATTING								FIELDING		
1988—	Boston (A.L.).............	OF	4	17	2	4	1	0	0	1	.235	0	3	0	10	0	0	1.000
1990—	Boston (A.L.).............	OF	4	15	1	4	2	0	0	0	.267	1	1	1	9	1	0	1.000
1993—	Chicago (A.L.)	OF	6	23	4	7	1	0	1	3	.304	3	5	0	15	0	0	1.000
Championship series totals (3 years)			14	55	7	15	4	0	1	4	.273	4	9	1	34	1	0	1.000

ALL-STAR GAME RECORD

NOTES: Named to A.L. All-Star team for 1990 game; replaced by Brook Jacoby due to injury.

Year	League	Pos.	AB	R	H	2B	3B	HR	RBI	Avg.	BB	SO	SB	PO	A	E	Avg.
								BATTING							FIELDING		
1990—	American						Selected, did not play—injured.										
1996—	National	OF	2	0	1	0	1	0	0	.500	0	1	0	1	0	0	1.000

B

BURNETT, A.J.　　　　P　　　　MARLINS

PERSONAL: Born January 3, 1977, in North Little Rock, Ark. ... 6-5/205. ... Throws right, bats right. ... Full name: Allen James Burnett.
HIGH SCHOOL: Central Arkansas Christian (North Little Rock, Ark.).
TRANSACTIONS/CAREER NOTES: Selected by New York Mets organization in eighth round of free-agent draft (June 1, 1995). ... Traded by Mets with P Jesus Sanchez and OF Robert Stratton to Florida Marlins for P Al Leiter and 2B Ralph Milliard (February 6, 1998). ... On Florida disabled list (March 17-July 20, 2000); included rehabilitation assignments to Brevard County (July 4-14) and Calgary (July 15-20).
STATISTICAL NOTES: Tied for Appalachian League lead in wild pitches with 16 in 1996.

Year	League	W	L	Pct.	ERA	G	GS	CG	ShO	Sv.	IP	H	R	ER	BB	SO
1995—	Gulf Coast Mets (GCL)	2	3	.400	4.28	9	8	1	0	0	33²/₃	27	16	16	23	26
1996—	Kingsport (Appl.)................	4	0	1.000	3.88	12	12	0	0	0	58	31	26	25	54	68
1997—	Gulf Coast Mets (GCL)	0	1	.000	3.18	3	2	0	0	0	11¹/₃	8	8	4	8	15
	Pittsfield (NY-Penn)	3	1	.750	4.70	20	9	0	0	0	44	28	26	23	35	48
1998—	Kane County (Midw.)■........	10	4	.714	1.97	20	20	0	0	0	119	74	27	26	45	186
1999—	Portland (East.)	6	12	.333	5.52	26	23	0	0	0	120²/₃	132	91	74	71	121
	Florida (N.L.)	4	2	.667	3.48	7	7	0	0	0	41¹/₃	37	23	16	25	33
2000—	Brevard County (FSL).........	0	0	...	3.68	2	2	0	0	0	7¹/₃	4	3	3	6	6
	Calgary (PCL)....................	0	0	...	0.00	1	1	0	0	0	5	0	0	0	3	6
	Florida (N.L.)	3	7	.300	4.79	13	13	0	0	0	82²/₃	80	46	44	44	57
Major League totals (2 years)		7	9	.438	4.35	20	20	0	0	0	124	117	69	60	69	90

BURNITZ, JEROMY　　　　OF　　　　BREWERS

PERSONAL: Born April 15, 1969, in Westminster, Calif. ... 6-0/205. ... Bats left, throws right. ... Full name: Jeromy Neal Burnitz.
HIGH SCHOOL: Conroe (Texas).
COLLEGE: Oklahoma State.
TRANSACTIONS/CAREER NOTES: Selected by Milwaukee Brewers organization in 24th round of free-agent draft (June 2, 1987); did not sign. ... Selected by New York Mets organization in first round (17th pick overall) of free-agent draft (June 4, 1990). ... On disabled list (August 23-September 18, 1992). ... On Norfolk suspended list (August 11-13, 1994). ... Traded by Mets with P Joe Roa to Cleveland Indians for P Paul Byrd, P Jerry DiPoto, P Dave Mlicki and a player to be named later (November 18, 1994); Mets acquired 2B Jesus Azuaje to complete deal (December 6, 1994). ... Traded by Indians to Milwaukee Brewers for 3B/1B Kevin Seitzer (August 31, 1996). ... On disabled list (July 18-August 20, 1999).
RECORDS: Shares A.L. record for most home runs by pinch-hitter in consecutive at-bats—2 (August 2 and 3, 1997).
STATISTICAL NOTES: Led New York-Pennsylvania League with .444 on-base percentage and tied for lead with six intentional bases on balls received in 1990. ... Led American Association with .503 slugging percentage in 1995. ... Led American Association with eight intentional bases on balls received in 1995. ... Career major league grand slams: 5.

Year	Team (League)	Pos.	G	AB	R	H	2B	3B	HR	RBI	Avg.	BB	SO	SB	PO	A	E	Avg.
									BATTING								FIELDING		
1990—	Pittsfield (NY-Penn)....	OF	51	173	37	52	6	5	6	22	.301	45	39	12	79	2	0	1.000
	St. Lucie (FSL)	OF	11	32	6	5	1	0	0	3	.156	7	12	1	18	1	0	1.000
1991—	Williamsport (East.) ...	OF	135	457	80	103	16	•10	*31	•85	.225	*104	127	31	237	13	•11	.958
1992—	Tidewater (I.L.)	OF	121	445	56	108	21	3	8	40	.243	33	84	30	222	11	8	.967
1993—	Norfolk (I.L.)	OF	65	255	33	58	15	3	8	44	.227	25	53	10	133	9	1	.993
	New York (N.L.)	OF	86	263	49	64	10	6	13	38	.243	38	66	3	165	6	4	.977
1994—	New York (N.L.)	OF	45	143	26	34	4	0	3	15	.238	23	45	1	63	1	2	.970
	Norfolk (I.L.)	OF-DH	85	314	58	75	15	5	14	49	.239	49	82	18	170	13	4	.979
1995—	Buffalo (A.A.)■	OF	128	443	72	126	26	7	19	*85	.284	50	83	13	241	12	5	.981
	Cleveland (A.L.)	OF-DH	9	7	4	4	1	0	0	0	.571	0	0	0	10	0	0	1.000
1996—	Cleveland (A.L.)	OF-DH	71	128	30	36	10	0	7	26	.281	25	31	2	44	0	0	1.000
	Milwaukee (A.L.)■	OF	23	72	8	17	4	0	2	14	.236	8	16	2	38	1	1	.975
1997—	Milwaukee (A.L.)	OF	153	494	85	139	37	8	27	85	.281	75	111	20	256	13	7	.975
1998—	Milwaukee (N.L.)	OF	161	609	92	160	28	1	38	125	.263	70	158	7	306	10	9	.972
1999—	Milwaukee (N.L.)	OF-DH	130	467	87	126	33	2	33	103	.270	91	124	7	262	8	5	.982
2000—	Milwaukee (N.L.)	OF-DH	161	564	91	131	29	2	31	98	.232	99	121	6	317	12	7	.979
American League totals (3 years)			256	701	127	196	52	8	36	125	.280	108	158	24	348	14	8	.978
National League totals (5 years)			583	2046	345	515	104	11	118	379	.252	321	514	24	1113	37	27	.977
Major League totals (8 years)			839	2747	472	711	156	19	154	504	.259	429	672	48	1461	51	35	.977

ALL-STAR GAME RECORD

Year	League	Pos.	AB	R	H	2B	3B	HR	RBI	Avg.	BB	SO	SB	PO	A	E	Avg.
								BATTING							FIELDING		
1999—	National	OF	2	1	1	1	0	0	0	.500	0	0	0	0	0	0	...

BURRELL, PAT — OF/1B — PHILLIES

PERSONAL: Born October 10, 1976, in Eureka Springs, Ark. ... 6-4/225. ... Bats right, throws right. ... Name pronounced BURL.
HIGH SCHOOL: Bellarmine Prep (San Jose, Calif.).
COLLEGE: Miami (Fla.).
TRANSACTIONS/CAREER NOTES: Selected by Boston Red Sox organization in 43rd round of free-agent draft (June 1, 1995); did not sign. ... Selected by Philadelphia Phillies organization in first round (first pick overall) of free-agent draft (June 2, 1998).
STATISTICAL NOTES: Career major league grand slams: 2.

Year Team (League)	Pos.	G	AB	R	H	2B	3B	HR	RBI	Avg.	BB	SO	SB	PO	A	E	Avg.
1998— Clearwater (FSL)	1B	37	132	29	40	7	1	7	30	.303	27	22	2	202	13	1	.995
1999— Reading (East.)...........	1B-OF-DH	117	417	84	139	28	6	28	90	.333	79	103	3	715	56	12	.985
— Scranton/W.B. (I.L.) ...	1B-OF	10	33	4	5	0	0	1	4	.152	4	8	0	62	1	0	1.000
2000— Scranton/W.B. (I.L.) ...	OF-1B	40	143	31	42	15	1	4	25	.294	32	36	1	135	16	2	.987
— Philadelphia (N.L.)......	1B-OF-DH	111	408	57	106	27	1	18	79	.260	63	139	0	533	28	8	.986
Major League totals (1 year)		111	408	57	106	27	1	18	79	.260	63	139	0	533	28	8	.986

B

BUSH, HOMER — 2B — BLUE JAYS

PERSONAL: Born November 12, 1972, in East St. Louis, Ill. ... 5-10/180. ... Bats right, throws right. ... Full name: Homer Giles Bush.
HIGH SCHOOL: East St. Louis (Ill.).
COLLEGE: Southern Illinois-Edwardsville.
TRANSACTIONS/CAREER NOTES: Selected by San Diego Padres organization in seventh round of free-agent draft (June 3, 1991). ... On Rancho Cucamonga disabled list (April 27-May 4 and May 9-26, 1994). ... On disabled list (May 20, 1996-remainder of season). ... Traded by Padres with rights to P Hideki Irabu, OF Gordon Amerson and player to be named later to New York Yankees for OF Ruben Rivera, P Rafael Medina and cash (April 22, 1997); Yankees acquired OF Vernon Maxwell to complete deal (June 9, 1997). ... Traded by Yankees with P David Wells and P Graeme Lloyd to Toronto Blue Jays for P Roger Clemens (February 18, 1999). ... On Toronto disabled list (April 11-May 14, 1999); included rehabilitation assignment to Dunedin (May 9-14). ... On disabled list (May 22-June 6 and July 31, 2000-remainder of season).

Year Team (League)	Pos.	G	AB	R	H	2B	3B	HR	RBI	Avg.	BB	SO	SB	PO	A	E	Avg.
1991— Arizona Padres (Ariz.)	3B	32	127	16	41	3	2	0	16	.323	4	33	11	25	60	10	.895
1992— Char., S.C. (SAL)	2B	108	367	37	86	10	5	0	18	.234	13	85	14	199	287	*34	.935
1993— Waterloo (Midw.)	2B	130	472	63	*152	19	3	5	51	.322	19	87	39	215	289	38	.930
1994— Rancho Cuca. (Calif.) .	2B	39	161	37	54	10	3	0	16	.335	9	29	9	69	102	7	.961
— Wichita (Texas)	2B	59	245	35	73	11	4	3	14	.298	10	39	20	101	135	8	.967
1995— Memphis (Sou.)	2B-DH	108	432	53	121	12	5	5	37	.280	15	83	34	235	268	16	.969
1996— Las Vegas (PCL)	2B-DH	32	116	24	42	11	1	2	3	.362	3	33	3	67	88	5	.969
1997— Las Vegas (PCL)	2B-DH	38	155	25	43	10	1	3	14	.277	7	40	5	73	103	4	.978
— Columbus (I.L.)■.......	2B	74	275	36	68	10	3	2	26	.247	25	56	12	153	253	9	.978
— New York (A.L.)...........	2B-DH	10	11	2	4	0	0	0	3	.364	0	0	0	8	13	2	.913
1998— New York (A.L.)...........	2-DH-3-S	45	71	17	27	3	0	1	5	.380	5	19	6	38	38	2	.974
1999— Toronto (A.L.)■...........	2B-SS	128	485	69	155	26	4	5	55	.320	21	82	32	246	404	16	.976
— Dunedin (FSL)	2B-DH	4	14	3	5	2	0	0	0	.357	1	1	1	7	7	0	1.000
2000— Toronto (A.L.)...........	2B	76	297	38	64	8	0	1	18	.215	18	60	9	165	246	6	.986
Major League totals (4 years)		259	864	126	250	37	4	7	81	.289	44	161	47	457	701	26	.978

DIVISION SERIES RECORD

Year Team (League)	Pos.	G	AB	R	H	2B	3B	HR	RBI	Avg.	BB	SO	SB	PO	A	E	Avg.
1998— New York (A.L.)..........	PR-DH	1	0	0	0	0	0	0	0	...	0	0	1	...	...	...	...

CHAMPIONSHIP SERIES RECORD

Year Team (League)	Pos.	G	AB	R	H	2B	3B	HR	RBI	Avg.	BB	SO	SB	PO	A	E	Avg.
1998— New York (A.L.)..........	PR-DH	2	0	1	0	0	0	0	0	...	0	0	1	...	...	...	...

WORLD SERIES RECORD

NOTES: Member of World Series championship team (1998).

Year Team (League)	Pos.	G	AB	R	H	2B	3B	HR	RBI	Avg.	BB	SO	SB	PO	A	E	Avg.
1998— New York (A.L.)..........	PR-DH	2	0	0	0	0	0	0	0	...	0	0	0	...	...	...	...

BUTLER, BRENT — 2B/SS — ROCKIES

PERSONAL: Born February 11, 1978, in Laurinburg, N.C. ... 6-0/180. ... Bats right, throws right. ... Full name: Justin Brent Butler.
HIGH SCHOOL: Scotland County (Laurinburg, N.C.).
TRANSACTIONS/CAREER NOTES: Selected by St. Louis Cardinals organization in third round of free-agent draft (June 2, 1996). ... On Prince William disabled list (June 21-June 28, 1998). ... Traded by Cardinals with P Jose Jimenez, P Manny Aybar and P Rick Croushore to Colorado Rockies for P Darryl Kile, P Dave Veres and P Luther Hackman (November 16, 1999). ... On Colorado Springs disabled list (August 29-September 12, 2000).

Year Team (League)	Pos.	G	AB	R	H	2B	3B	HR	RBI	Avg.	BB	SO	SB	PO	A	E	Avg.
1996— Johnson City (Appl.) ..	SS	62	248	45	85	21	1	8	50	.343	25	29	8	81	127	12	*.945
1997— Peoria (Midw.)............	SS	129	480	81	147	37	2	15	71	.306	63	69	6	*220	345	35	.942
1998— Prince Will. (Caro.).....	S-3-DH-2	126	475	63	136	27	2	11	76	.286	39	74	3	152	349	29	.945
1999— Arkansas (Texas)	SS-3B-2B	•139	528	68	142	21	1	13	54	.269	26	47	0	183	333	17	.968
2000— Colo. Springs (PCL)■	2B-SS	122	438	73	128	35	1	8	54	.292	44	46	1	222	311	16	.971

BYRD, PAUL — P — PHILLIES

PERSONAL: Born December 3, 1970, in Louisville, Ky. ... 6-1/184. ... Throws right, bats right. ... Full name: Paul Gregory Byrd.
HIGH SCHOOL: St. Xavier (Louisville, Ky.).
COLLEGE: Louisiana State.
TRANSACTIONS/CAREER NOTES: Selected by Cincinnati Reds organization in 13th round of free-agent draft (June 1, 1988); did not sign. ... Selected by Cleveland Indians organization in fourth round of free-agent draft (June 3, 1991). ... On disabled list (August 12, 1992-remainder of season). ... On disabled list (May 23-July 24, 1993). ... Traded by Indians organization with P Dave Mlicki, P Jerry DiPoto and a player to be named later to New York Mets organization for OF Jeromy Burnitz and P Joe Roa (November 18, 1994); Mets acquired 2B Jesus Azuaje to complete deal (December 6, 1994). ... On Norfolk disabled list (June 1-19, 1995). ... On New York disabled list (March 22-June 9, 1996); included rehabilitation assignment to Norfolk (May 27-June 9). ... Traded by Mets with a player to be named later to Atlanta Braves for P Greg McMichael (November 25, 1996); Braves acquired P Andy Zwirchitz to complete deal (May 25, 1997). ... On Richmond disabled list (June 3-July 2, 1998). ... Claimed on waivers by Philadelphia Phillies (August 14, 1998). ... On Philadelphia disabled list (July 27, 2000-remainder of season). ... Granted free agency (October 12, 2000). ... Re-signed by Phillies (January 29, 2001).
STATISTICAL NOTES: Led Carolina League with seven balks in 1991. ... Led N.L. with 17 hit batsmen in 1999. ... Tied for N.L. lead in errors by a pitcher with six in 1999.

Year	League	W	L	Pct.	ERA	G	GS	CG	ShO	Sv.	IP	H	R	ER	BB	SO
1991—	Kinston (Caro.)	4	3	.571	3.16	14	11	0	0	0	$62^{2}/_{3}$	40	27	22	36	62
1992—	Canton/Akron (East.)	14	6	.700	3.01	24	24	4	0	0	$152^{1}/_{3}$	122	68	51	75	118
1993—	Charlotte (I.L.)	7	4	.636	3.89	14	14	1	1	0	81	80	43	35	30	54
	— Canton/Akron (East.)	0	0	...	3.60	2	1	0	0	0	10	7	4	4	3	8
1994—	Canton/Akron (East.)	5	9	.357	3.81	21	20	4	1	0	$139^{1}/_{3}$	135	70	59	52	106
	— Charlotte (FSL)	2	2	.500	3.93	9	4	0	0	1	$36^{2}/_{3}$	33	19	16	11	15
1995—	Norfolk (I.L.)■	3	5	.375	2.79	22	10	1	0	6	87	71	29	27	21	61
	— New York (N.L.)	2	0	1.000	2.05	17	0	0	0	0	22	18	6	5	7	26
1996—	New York (N.L.)	1	2	.333	4.24	38	0	0	0	0	$46^{2}/_{3}$	48	22	22	21	31
	— Norfolk (I.L.)	2	0	1.000	3.52	5	0	0	0	1	$7^{2}/_{3}$	4	3	3	4	8
1997—	Atlanta (N.L.)■	4	4	.500	5.26	31	4	0	0	0	53	47	34	31	28	37
	— Richmond (I.L.)	2	1	.667	3.18	3	3	0	0	0	17	14	6	6	1	14
1998—	Richmond (I.L.)	5	5	.500	3.69	17	17	2	0	0	$102^{1}/_{3}$	92	44	42	36	84
	— Atlanta (N.L.)	0	0	...	13.50	1	0	0	0	0	2	4	3	3	1	1
	— Philadelphia (N.L.)■	5	2	.714	2.29	8	8	2	1	0	55	41	16	14	17	38
1999—	Philadelphia (N.L.)	15	11	.577	4.60	32	32	1	0	0	$199^{2}/_{3}$	205	119	102	70	106
2000—	Philadelphia (N.L.)	2	9	.182	6.51	17	15	0	0	0	83	89	67	60	35	53
	— Scranton/W.B. (I.L.)	2	0	1.000	1.73	3	3	2	0	0	26	20	6	5	6	10
Major League totals (6 years)		29	28	.509	4.62	144	59	3	1	0	$461^{1}/_{3}$	452	267	237	179	292

ALL-STAR GAME RECORD

Year	League	W	L	Pct.	ERA	GS	CG	ShO	Sv.	IP	H	R	ER	BB	SO
1999—	National							Selected, did not play.							

BYRDAK, TIM — P — INDIANS

PERSONAL: Born October 31, 1973, in Oak Lawn, Ill. ... 5-11/180. ... Throws left, bats left. ... Full name: Timothy Christopher Byrdak. ... Name pronounced BIRD-ek.
HIGH SCHOOL: Oak Forest (Ill.).
JUNIOR COLLEGE: South Suburban College (Ill.).
COLLEGE: Rice.
TRANSACTIONS/CAREER NOTES: Selected by Kansas City Royals organization in fifth round of free-agent draft (June 2, 1994). ... On disabled list (June 27-August 19, 1996). ... On Omaha disabled list (April 3-June 9, 1997). ... Granted free agency (December 21, 2000). ... Signed by Cleveland Indians organization (December 23, 2000).

Year	League	W	L	Pct.	ERA	G	GS	CG	ShO	Sv.	IP	H	R	ER	BB	SO
1994—	Eugene (N'West)	4	5	.444	3.07	15	15	0	0	0	$73^{1}/_{3}$	60	33	25	20	77
1995—	Wilmington (Caro.)	11	5	.688	2.16	27	26	0	0	0	$166^{1}/_{3}$	118	46	40	45	127
1996—	Wichita (Texas)	5	7	.417	6.91	15	15	0	0	0	$84^{2}/_{3}$	112	73	65	44	47
1997—	Wilmington (Caro.)	4	3	.571	3.51	22	2	0	0	3	41	34	17	16	12	47
1998—	Wichita (Texas)	3	5	.375	4.15	34	0	0	0	2	52	58	29	24	28	37
	— Omaha (PCL)	2	1	.667	2.45	26	0	0	0	1	$36^{2}/_{3}$	31	13	10	20	32
	— Kansas City (A.L.)	0	0	...	5.40	3	0	0	0	0	$1^{2}/_{3}$	5	1	1	0	1
1999—	Omaha (PCL)	3	1	.750	1.81	33	0	0	0	4	$49^{2}/_{3}$	39	19	10	28	51
	— Kansas City (A.L.)	0	3	.000	7.66	33	0	0	0	1	$24^{2}/_{3}$	32	24	21	20	17
2000—	Omaha (PCL)	6	2	.750	4.44	34	1	0	0	4	$52^{2}/_{3}$	59	27	26	29	47
	— Kansas City (A.L.)	0	1	.000	11.37	12	0	0	0	0	$6^{1}/_{3}$	11	8	8	4	8
	— Wichita (Texas)	0	0	...	5.40	4	0	0	0	0	$6^{2}/_{3}$	9	4	4	3	1
Major League totals (3 years)		0	4	.000	8.27	48	0	0	0	1	$32^{2}/_{3}$	48	33	30	24	26

BYRNES, ERIC — OF — ATHLETICS

PERSONAL: Born February 16, 1976, in Redwood City, Calif. ... 6-2/205. ... Bats right, throws right. ... Full name: Eric James Byrnes.
HIGH SCHOOL: St. Francis (Mountain View, Calif.).
COLLEGE: UCLA.
TRANSACTIONS/CAREER NOTES: Selected by Oakland Athletics organization in eighth round of free-agent draft (June 2, 1998).

Year	Team (League)	Pos.	G	AB	R	H	2B	3B	HR	RBI	Avg.	BB	SO	SB	PO	A	E	Avg.
							BATTING								FIELDING			
1998—	S. Oregon (N.W.)	OF	42	169	36	53	10	2	7	31	.314	16	16	6	67	2	1	.986
	— Visalia (Calif.)	OF	29	108	26	46	9	2	4	21	.426	18	15	11	56	4	3	.952
1999—	Modesto (Calif.)	OF	96	365	86	123	28	1	6	66	.337	58	37	28	133	10	6	.960
	— Midland (Texas)	OF	43	164	25	39	14	0	1	22	.238	17	32	6	59	1	5	.923
2000—	Midland (Texas)	OF	67	259	49	78	25	2	5	37	.301	43	38	21	114	5	2	.983
	— Sacramento (PCL)	OF	67	243	55	81	23	1	9	47	.333	31	30	12	94	3	2	.980
	— Oakland (A.L.)	OF-DH	10	10	5	3	0	0	0	0	.300	0	1	2	4	0	0	1.000
Major League totals (1 year)			10	10	5	3	0	0	0	0	.300	0	1	2	4	0	0	1.000

CABRERA, ALEX · 1B

PERSONAL: Born December 24, 1971, in Caripitos, Venezuela. ... 6-2/215. ... Bats right, throws right. ... Full name: Alexander Alberto Cabrera.

TRANSACTIONS/CAREER NOTES: Signed as non-drafted free agent by Chicago Cubs organization (May 5, 1991). ... Released by Cubs (December 16, 1996). ... Signed by Mexico City Tigres, Mexican League (1997). ... Signed by Tampa Bay Devil Rays organization (November 14, 1997). ... Loaned by Devil Rays organization to Mexico City Tigres (March 16-September 21, 1998). ... Granted free agency (October 16, 1998). ... Signed by China Trust, Chinese Professional Baseball League (1999). ... Released by China Trust (1999). ... Signed by Arizona Diamondbacks organization (December 14, 1999). ... On Arizona disabled list (July 2-17, 2000). ... Contract sold by Diamondbacks to Seibu Lions of Japan Pacific League (December 7, 2000).

STATISTICAL NOTES: Led Mexican League first basemen with 1,103 putouts, 88 assists, 1,198 total chances and 144 double plays in 1998. ... Hit home run in first major league at-bat (June 26, 2000).

										BATTING					FIELDING			
Year	Team (League)	Pos.	G	AB	R	H	2B	3B	HR	RBI	Avg.	BB	SO	SB	PO	A	E	Avg.
1991—	Dom. Cubs (DSL)		49	193	35	58	8	3	3	32	.301	11	30	4	...	...	...	...
1992—	Arizona Cubs (Ariz.)	1B-OF-3B	41	135	18	28	4	0	1	19	.207	9	48	1	202	25	11	.954
1993—	Geneva (NY-Penn)	OF-1B	53	167	29	41	5	0	5	27	.246	9	49	4	158	13	9	.950
1994—	Peoria (Midw.)	1B-OF	121	432	57	120	25	1	24	73	.278	19	92	2	306	24	10	.971
1995—	Daytona (FSL)	1B	54	214	26	63	14	0	2	35	.294	9	36	2	335	16	4	.989
1996—	Bakersfield (Calif.)	OF-1B	89	345	45	97	18	1	15	53	.281	14	80	0	364	32	6	.985
1997—	M.C. Tigers (Mex.)■	1B-OF	104	395	52	124	28	5	23	84	.314	17	60	6	604	38	4	.994
1998—	M.C. Tigers (Mex.)	1B-OF	116	451	83	143	26	7	21	83	.317	53	77	4	†1105	†88	7	.994
1999—	China Trust (Taiwan)■		...	302	63	98	23	0	18	64	.325	...	...	...	...	...	...	...
2000—	El Paso (Texas)■	1B-OF	53	212	56	81	19	2	*35	82	.382	25	52	3	480	39	4	.992
—	Tucson (PCL)	1B-OF-3B	21	78	18	22	5	1	4	12	.282	5	19	0	78	3	0	1.000
—	Arizona (N.L.)	1B-OF	31	80	10	21	2	1	5	14	.263	4	21	0	122	7	1	.992
—	Ariz. D'backs (Ariz.)	OF	2	5	0	1	0	0	0	0	.200	0	1	0	1	0	0	1.000
Major League totals (1 year)			31	80	10	21	2	1	5	14	.263	4	21	0	122	7	1	.992

CABRERA, JOLBERT · IF/OF · INDIANS

PERSONAL: Born December 8, 1972, in Cartagena, Colombia. ... 6-0/177. ... Bats right, throws right. ... Full name: Jolbert Alexis Cabrera. ... Brother of Orlando Cabrera, shortstop, Montreal Expos.

HIGH SCHOOL: Confenalco (Cartagena, Colombia).

TRANSACTIONS/CAREER NOTES: Signed as non-drafted free agent by Montreal Expos organization (July 3, 1990). ... Granted free agency (October 17, 1997). ... Signed by Cleveland Indians organization (January 19, 1998).

STATISTICAL NOTES: Led International League in caught stealing with 15 in 1998.

										BATTING					FIELDING			
Year	Team (League)	Pos.	G	AB	R	H	2B	3B	HR	RBI	Avg.	BB	SO	SB	PO	A	E	Avg.
1990—	Dom. Expos (DSL)	SS	29	115	31	36	3	2	0	12	.313	14	10	14	...	...	...	...
1991—	Sumter (S.Atl.)	SS	101	324	33	66	4	0	1	20	.204	19	62	10	141	256	28	.934
1992—	Albany (S.Atl.)	SS	118	377	44	86	9	2	0	23	.228	34	77	22	169	277	35	.927
1993—	Burlington (Midw.)	SS	128	507	62	129	24	2	0	38	.254	39	93	31	•173	300	*36	.929
1994—	W.P. Beach (FSL)	SS	83	266	32	54	4	0	0	13	.203	14	48	7	136	228	26	.933
—	San Bern. (Calif.)	SS	30	109	14	27	5	1	0	11	.248	14	24	2	51	82	7	.950
—	Harrisburg (East.)	SS	3	2	0	0	0	0	0	0	.000	0	1	0	0	1	0	1.000
1995—	W.P. Beach (FSL)	SS-2B-3B	103	357	62	102	23	2	1	25	.286	38	61	19	148	294	29	.938
—	Harrisburg (East.)	SS	9	35	4	10	2	0	0	1	.286	1	3	3	11	18	2	.935
1996—	Harrisburg (East.)	SS-OF-3B	107	354	40	85	18	2	3	29	.240	23	63	10	179	306	25	.951
1997—	Harrisburg (East.)	2B-SS-OF	48	171	28	43	9	0	2	11	.251	28	28	5	98	76	9	.951
—	Ottawa (I.L.)	3B-2B-SS-OF	68	191	28	54	10	4	0	12	.283	11	31	15	51	127	7	.962
1998—	Cleveland (A.L.)■	SS	1	2	0	0	0	0	0	0	.000	0	1	0	2	2	0	1.000
—	Buffalo (I.L.)	SS-OF-2B	129	494	94	157	24	1	10	45	.318	68	71	25	235	352	27	.956
1999—	Cleveland (A.L.)	OF-2B-DH	30	37	6	7	1	0	0	0	.189	1	8	3	26	4	1	.968
—	Buffalo (I.L.)	OF-SS-2B-3B	71	279	44	74	13	4	0	27	.265	26	43	20	153	82	6	.975
2000—	Buffalo (I.L.)	OF-SS-2B	20	74	18	25	6	1	3	11	.338	5	8	2	44	25	0	1.000
—	Cleveland (A.L.)	O-2-S-DH	100	175	27	44	3	1	2	15	.251	8	15	6	109	39	1	.993
Major League totals (3 years)			131	214	33	51	4	1	2	15	.238	9	24	9	137	45	2	.989

CABRERA, JOSE · P · ASTROS

PERSONAL: Born March 24, 1972, in Santiago, Dominican Republic. ... 6-0/180. ... Throws right, bats right. ... Full name: Jose Alberto Cabrera.

TRANSACTIONS/CAREER NOTES: Signed as non-drafted free agent by Cleveland Indians organization (October 12, 1990). ... On disabled list (May 11-28, 1993). ... On Canton disabled list (April 25-May 24, 1995). ... On Buffalo disabled list (April 4-13 and 17-25, 1997). ... Traded by Indians to Houston Astros for P Alvin Morman (May 10, 1997). ... On Houston disabled list (April 5, 1998-remainder of season); included rehabilitation assignment to New Orleans (July 4-20).

Year	League	W	L	Pct.	ERA	G	GS	CG	ShO	Sv.	IP	H	R	ER	BB	SO
1991—	Dom. Indians (DSL)	6	4	.600	3.07	16	12	1	0	0	73 1/3	64	32	25	17	40
1992—	Burlington (Appl.)	•8	3	.727	1.75	13	13	1	0	0	92 1/3	74	27	18	18	79
1993—	Columbus (S.Atl.)	11	6	.647	2.67	26	26	1	0	0	155 1/3	122	54	46	53	105
1994—	Kinston (Caro.)	4	13	.235	4.44	24	24	0	0	0	133 2/3	134	84	66	43	110
1995—	Canton/Akron (East.)	1	1	.500	1.02	4	3	0	0	0	17 2/3	7	2	2	8	19
—	Bakersfield (Calif.)	2	2	.500	3.92	7	7	0	0	0	41 1/3	40	25	18	21	40
1996—	Canton/Akron (East.)	4	3	.571	5.63	15	7	0	0	0	62 1/3	78	45	39	17	40
1997—	Buffalo (A.A.)	3	0	1.000	1.20	5	0	0	0	0	15	8	2	2	7	11
—	New Orleans (A.A.)■	2	2	.500	2.54	31	0	0	0	0	46	31	13	13	13	48
—	Houston (N.L.)	0	0	...	1.17	12	0	0	0	0	15 1/3	6	2	2	6	18

C

Year	League	W	L	Pct.	ERA	G	GS	CG	ShO	Sv.	IP	H	R	ER	BB	SO
1998—	Houston (N.L.)	0	0	...	8.31	3	0	0	0	0	4 1/3	7	4	4	1	1
—	New Orleans (PCL)............	0	0	...	5.40	5	0	0	0	1	5	2	3	3	1	6
1999—	New Orleans (PCL)............	3	1	.750	2.82	31	0	0	0	7	51	34	18	16	12	41
—	Houston (N.L.)	4	0	1.000	2.15	26	0	0	0	0	29 1/3	21	7	7	9	28
2000—	Houston (N.L.)	2	3	.400	5.92	52	0	0	0	2	59 1/3	74	40	39	17	41
—	New Orleans (PCL)............	0	1	.000	2.93	12	0	0	0	4	15 1/3	15	6	5	5	12
Major League totals (4 years)		6	3	.667	4.32	93	0	0	0	2	108 1/3	108	53	52	33	88

DIVISION SERIES RECORD

Year	League	W	L	Pct.	ERA	G	GS	CG	ShO	Sv.	IP	H	R	ER	BB	SO
1999—	Houston (N.L.)	0	0	...	0.00	1	0	0	0	0	2	2	0	0	0	6

CABRERA, ORLANDO — SS — EXPOS

PERSONAL: Born November 2, 1974, in Cartagena, Columbia. ... 5-10/175. ... Bats right, throws right. ... Full name: Orlando Luis Cabrera. ... Brother of Jolbert Cabrera, infielder/outfielder, Cleveland Indians.

TRANSACTIONS/CAREER NOTES: Signed as non-drafted free agent by Montreal Expos organization (June 1, 1993). ... On disabled list (August 9, 1999-remainder of season). ... On Montreal disabled list (July 15-August 15, 2000); included rehabilitation assignment to Ottawa (August 12-15).

							BATTING								FIELDING		
Year	Team (League)	Pos.	G	AB	R	H	2B	3B	HR	RBI	Avg.	BB	SO	SB	PO	A	E	Avg.
1993—	Dom. Expos (DSL)	IF	38	122	24	42	6	1	1	17	.344	18	11	14	86	76	3	.982
1994—	GC Expos (GCL)	2B-SS-OF	22	73	13	23	4	1	0	11	.315	5	8	6	22	42	4	.941
1995—	Vermont (NY-Penn) ...	2B-SS	65	248	37	70	12	5	3	33	.282	16	28	15	135	189	17	.950
1996—	Delmarva (S.Atl.)	SS-2B	134	512	86	129	28	4	14	65	.252	54	63	51	205	344	27	.953
1997—	W.P. Beach (FSL)........	SS-DH-2B	69	279	56	77	19	2	5	26	.276	27	33	32	92	162	20	.927
—	Harrisburg (East.).......	SS-2B	35	133	34	41	13	2	5	20	.308	15	18	7	57	83	5	.966
—	Ottawa (I.L.)	SS-2B	31	122	17	32	5	2	2	14	.262	7	16	8	45	94	3	.979
—	Montreal (N.L.)..........	SS-2B	16	18	4	4	0	0	0	2	.222	1	3	1	11	15	1	.963
1998—	Ottawa (I.L.)	SS-2B	66	272	31	63	9	4	3	26	.232	28	27	19	122	190	12	.963
—	Montreal (N.L.)..........	SS-2B	79	261	44	73	16	5	3	22	.280	18	27	6	122	196	7	.978
1999—	Montreal (N.L.)..........	SS	104	382	48	97	23	5	8	39	.254	18	38	2	186	289	10	.979
2000—	Montreal (N.L.)..........	SS-2B	125	422	47	100	25	1	13	55	.237	25	28	4	167	338	10	.981
—	Ottawa (I.L.)	SS	2	6	1	4	0	0	0	0	.667	1	0	1	3	7	0	1.000
Major League totals (4 years)			324	1083	143	274	64	11	24	118	.253	62	96	13	486	838	28	.979

CACERES, WILMY — SS/2B — ANGELS

PERSONAL: Born October 2, 1978, in Santo Domingo, Dominican Republic. ... 6-0/165. ... Bats both, throws right. ... Full name: Wilmy Antonio Caceres.

TRANSACTIONS/CAREER NOTES: Signed as non-drafted free agent by Cincinnati Reds organization (December 5, 1996). ... Traded by Reds to Anaheim Angels for P Seth Etherton (December 10, 2000).

							BATTING								FIELDING		
Year	Team (League)	Pos.	G	AB	R	H	2B	3B	HR	RBI	Avg.	BB	SO	SB	PO	A	E	Avg.
1997—	Billings (Pio.)	2B-SS	15	38	10	10	2	0	0	9	.263	2	3	1	22	30	6	.897
1998—	Char., W.Va. (SAL)......	SS	103	394	48	102	12	7	0	27	.259	18	62	24	167	303	39	.923
—	Burlington (Midw.)	SS	35	150	23	44	8	0	1	14	.293	4	24	7	40	92	9	.936
1999—	Clinton (Midw.)	SS	117	476	77	124	18	5	1	30	.261	30	65	52	179	340	*42	.925
—	GC Reds (GCL)..........	2B-SS	2	9	2	3	0	0	0	0	.333	0	1	0	3	4	0	1.000
2000—	Chattanooga (Sou.)	SS-2B	130	534	69	143	23	4	2	33	.268	37	71	36	256	454	27	.963

CAIRNCROSS, CAMERON — P — INDIANS

PERSONAL: Born May 11, 1972, in Cairns, Australia. ... 6-0/195. ... Throws left, bats left.

HIGH SCHOOL: Smithfield (Cairns, Australia).

TRANSACTIONS/CAREER NOTES: Signed as non-drafted free agent by San Diego Padres organization (November 11, 1990). ... On disabled list (April 6, 1995-entire season; April 4, 1996-entire season). ... Granted free agency (October 17, 1997). ... Signed by Cleveland Indians organization (March 27, 1999). ... On Buffalo disabled list (June 8-August 9 and August 20-27, 1999).

Year	League	W	L	Pct.	ERA	G	GS	CG	ShO	Sv.	IP	H	R	ER	BB	SO
1991—	Charleston, S.C. (S.Atl.) ...	8	5	.615	3.56	24	24	2	0	0	131 1/3	111	72	52	74	102
1992—	Waterloo (Midw.)	8	8	.500	3.61	24	24	1	1	0	137	127	68	55	61	138
1993—	Rancho Cuca. (Calif.)	10	11	.476	5.12	29	26	0	0	0	154 2/3	182	112	88	81	122
1994—	Rancho Cuca. (Calif.)	3	1	.750	4.41	29	0	0	0	3	34 2/3	26	19	17	14	40
—	Las Vegas (PCL)	0	1	.000	4.26	4	0	0	0	0	6 1/3	8	3	3	6	4
—	Wichita (Texas)	2	3	.400	3.65	31	0	0	0	3	37	37	19	15	15	33
1995—										Did not play.						
1996—										Did not play.						
1997—	Rancho Cuca. (Calif.)	1	3	.250	5.63	40	0	0	0	1	64	81	46	40	15	70
1998—										Did not play.						
1999—	Kinston (Caro.)■.............	2	0	1.000	0.00	6	0	0	0	2	9 2/3	5	1	0	4	11
—	Buffalo (I.L.)	0	3	.000	5.21	19	0	0	0	0	19	22	13	11	6	13
2000—	Akron (East.)	1	0	1.000	1.52	28	0	0	0	4	29 2/3	22	5	5	6	23
—	Cleveland (A.L.)...............	1	0	1.000	3.86	15	0	0	0	0	9 1/3	11	4	4	3	8
—	Buffalo (I.L.)	0	1	.000	2.25	15	0	0	0	1	8	11	2	2	4	11
Major League totals (1 year)		1	0	1.000	3.86	15	0	0	0	0	9 1/3	11	4	4	3	8

PERSONAL: Born May 4, 1974, in Anaco, Venezuela. ... 6-1/200. ... Bats right, throws right. ... Full name: Miguel Jesus Cairo. ... Name pronounced KI-ro.

HIGH SCHOOL: Escuela Anaco (Anaco, Venezuela).

TRANSACTIONS/CAREER NOTES: Signed as non-drafted free agent by Los Angeles Dodgers organization (September 20, 1990). ... Traded by Dodgers with 3B Willis Otanez to Seattle Mariners for 3B Mike Blowers (November 29, 1995). ... Traded by Mariners with P Bill Risley to Toronto Blue Jays for P Edwin Hurtado and P Paul Menhart (December 18, 1995). ... Traded by Blue Jays to Chicago Cubs for P Jason Stevenson (November 20, 1996). ... Selected by Tampa Bay Devil Rays in first round (eighth pick overall) of expansion draft (November 18, 1997). ... On Tampa Bay disabled list (April 24-May 17 and July 26-August 11, 1999); included rehabilitation assignments to Orlando (May 14-17) and St. Petersburg (August 7-11). ... Released by Devil Rays (November 27, 2000).

STATISTICAL NOTES: Led California League in caught stealing with 23 in 1994. ... Led International League second basemen with 64 double plays in 1996. ... Led American Association in caught stealing with 15 in 1997.

MISCELLANEOUS: Holds Tampa Bay Devil Rays all-time record for most stolen bases (69).

Year	Team (League)	Pos.	G	AB	R	H	2B	3B	HR	RBI	Avg.	BB	SO	SB	PO	A	E	Avg.
1991—	Dom. Dodgers (DSL) .	IF	57	203	16	45	5	1	0	17	.222	0	17	8	...	...	...	...
1992—	Vero Beach (FSL)	2B-3B	36	125	7	28	0	0	0	7	.224	11	12	5	69	76	10	.935
—	GC Dodgers (GCL)	SS-3B	21	76	10	23	5	2	0	9	.303	2	6	1	26	56	4	.953
1993—	Vero Beach (FSL)	2B-SS-3B	90	346	50	109	10	1	1	23	.315	28	22	23	172	244	18	.959
1994—	Bakersfield (Calif.)	2B-SS	133	533	76	155	23	4	2	48	.291	34	37	44	268	376	28	.958
1995—	San Antonio (Texas)...	2B-SS-DH	107	435	53	121	20	1	1	41	.278	26	31	33	210	316	23	.958
1996—	Syracuse (I.L.)■	2B-3B-SS	120	465	71	129	14	4	3	48	.277	26	44	27	193	295	23	.955
—	Toronto (A.L.).............	2B	9	27	5	6	2	0	0	1	.222	2	9	0	22	18	0	1.000
1997—	Iowa (A.A.)■	2B-SS	135	*569	82	159	35	4	5	46	.279	24	54	*40	248	386	20	.969
—	Chicago (N.L.)............	2B-SS	16	29	7	7	1	0	0	1	.241	2	3	0	16	18	0	1.000
1998—	Tampa Bay (A.L.)■....	2B-DH	150	515	49	138	26	5	5	46	.268	24	44	19	278	429	16	.978
1999—	Tampa Bay (A.L.)........	2B-DH	120	465	61	137	15	5	3	36	.295	24	46	22	251	377	9	.986
—	Orlando (Sou.)	2B	3	13	1	5	2	0	0	1	.385	0	1	0	2	7	0	1.000
—	St. Petersburg (FSL) ..	2B	3	13	2	5	0	0	0	0	.385	1	2	1	8	15	1	.958
2000—	Tampa Bay (A.L.)........	2B-DH	119	375	49	98	18	2	1	34	.261	29	34	28	218	302	9	.983
American League totals (4 years)			398	1382	164	379	61	12	9	117	.274	79	133	69	769	1126	34	.982
National League totals (1 year)			16	29	7	7	1	0	0	1	.241	2	3	0	16	18	0	1.000
Major League totals (5 years)			414	1411	171	386	62	12	9	118	.274	81	136	69	785	1144	34	.983

PERSONAL: Born January 8, 1973, in La Grange, Ga. ... 6-6/190. ... Bats right, throws right. ... Full name: Michael Terrance Cameron.

HIGH SCHOOL: La Grange (Ga.).

TRANSACTIONS/CAREER NOTES: Selected by Chicago White Sox organization in 18th round of free-agent draft (June 3, 1991). ... Traded by White Sox to Cincinnati Reds for 1B/3B Paul Konerko (November 11, 1998). ... Traded by Reds with P Brett Tomko, IF Antonio Perez and P Jake Meyer to Seattle Mariners for OF Ken Griffey Jr. (February 10, 2000).

STATISTICAL NOTES: Tied for Carolina League lead in double plays by outfielder with four in 1994. ... Led Southern League with .600 slugging percentage and tied for lead in caught stealing with 15 in 1996. ... Led Southern League outfielders with 264 total chances in 1996. ... Career major league grand slams: 1.

Year	Team (League)	Pos.	G	AB	R	H	2B	3B	HR	RBI	Avg.	BB	SO	SB	PO	A	E	Avg.
1991—	GC White Sox (GCL) ..	OF	44	136	20	30	3	0	0	11	.221	17	29	13	55	3	3	.951
1992—	Utica (NY-Penn)	OF	26	87	15	24	1	4	2	12	.276	11	26	3	60	3	0	1.000
—	South Bend (Midw.) ...	OF	35	114	19	26	8	1	1	9	.228	10	37	2	67	0	3	.957
1993—	South Bend (Midw.) ...	OF	122	411	52	98	14	5	0	30	.238	27	101	19	248	13	4	.985
1994—	Prince William (Caro.)	OF	131	468	86	116	15	*17	6	48	.248	60	101	22	275	10	6	.979
1995—	Birmingham (Sou.).....	OF	107	350	64	87	20	5	11	60	.249	54	104	21	250	7	4	.985
—	Chicago (A.L.)	OF	28	38	4	7	2	0	1	2	.184	3	15	0	33	1	0	1.000
1996—	Birmingham (Sou.).....	OF-DH	123	473	*120	142	34	12	28	77	.300	71	117	*39	*249	8	7	.973
—	Chicago (A.L.)	OF-DH	11	11	1	1	0	0	0	0	.091	1	3	0	7	0	0	1.000
1997—	Nashville (A.A.)	OF-DH	30	120	21	33	7	3	6	17	.275	18	31	4	63	3	1	.985
—	Chicago (A.L.)	OF-DH	116	379	63	98	18	3	14	55	.259	55	105	23	334	5	5	.985
1998—	Chicago (A.L.)	OF	141	396	53	83	16	5	8	43	.210	37	101	27	313	6	4	.988
1999—	Cincinnati (N.L.)■......	OF	146	542	93	139	34	9	21	66	.256	80	145	38	372	7	8	.979
2000—	Seattle (A.L.)■	OF	155	543	96	145	28	4	19	78	.267	78	133	24	399	5	6	.985
American League totals (5 years)			451	1367	217	334	64	12	42	178	.244	174	357	74	1086	17	15	.987
National League totals (1 year)			146	542	93	139	34	9	21	66	.256	80	145	38	372	7	8	.979
Major League totals (6 years)			597	1909	310	473	98	21	63	244	.248	254	502	112	1458	24	23	.985

DIVISION SERIES RECORD

Year	Team (League)	Pos.	G	AB	R	H	2B	3B	HR	RBI	Avg.	BB	SO	SB	PO	A	E	Avg.
2000—	Seattle (A.L.)	OF	3	12	2	3	0	0	0	2	.250	0	0	1	12	0	0	1.000

CHAMPIONSHIP SERIES RECORD

Year	Team (League)	Pos.	G	AB	R	H	2B	3B	HR	RBI	Avg.	BB	SO	SB	PO	A	E	Avg.
2000—	Seattle (A.L.)	OF	6	18	3	2	0	0	0	1	.111	2	7	1	16	0	0	1.000

PERSONAL: Born April 21, 1963, in Hanford, Calif. ... 6-0/200. ... Bats both, throws right. ... Full name: Kenneth Gene Caminiti. ... Name pronounced CAM-uh-NET-ee.

HIGH SCHOOL: Leigh (San Jose, Calif.).

COLLEGE: San Jose State.

TRANSACTIONS/CAREER NOTES: Selected by Houston Astros organization in third round of free-agent draft (June 4, 1984). ... On disabled list (April 19-May 11, 1992). ... Traded by Astros with OF Steve Finley, SS Andujar Cedeno, 1B Robert Petagine, P Brian Williams and a player to be named later to San Diego Padres for OF Phil Plantier, OF Derek Bell, P Pedro Martinez, P Doug Brocail, IF Craig Shipley and SS Ricky Gutierrez (December 28, 1994); Padres acquired P Sean Fesh to complete deal (May 1, 1995). ... On disabled list (May 12-27, 1997; and May 2-23, 1998). ... Granted free agency (October 23, 1998). ... Signed by Astros (November 17, 1998). ... On Houston disabled list (May 22-August 16, 1999); included rehabilitation assignment to New Orleans (August 9-16). ... On disabled list (June 16, 2000-remainder of season). ... Granted free agency (October 30, 2000). ... Signed by Texas Rangers (December 10, 2000).

RECORDS: Holds major league record for most consecutive games with switch-hit home runs—2 (September 16-17, 1995). ... Holds major league single-season record for most games with switch-hit home runs—4 (1996). ... Shares major league single-season record for most runs batted in by switch hitter—130 (1996). ... Holds N.L. career record for most games with switch-hit home runs—10. ... Holds N.L. record for most home runs by switch hitter in two consecutive seasons—66 (1995-96 and 1996-97).

HONORS: Named third baseman on THE SPORTING NEWS college All-America team (1984). ... Won N.L. Gold Glove at third base (1995-97). ... Named third baseman on THE SPORTING NEWS N.L. All-Star team (1996). ... Named third baseman on THE SPORTING NEWS N.L. Silver Slugger team (1996). ... Named N.L. Most Valuable Player by Baseball Writers' Association of America (1996).

STATISTICAL NOTES: Led Southern League third basemen with 34 double plays in 1986. ... Led Pacific Coast League third basemen with 382 total chances and 25 double plays in 1988. ... Switch-hit home runs in one game ten times (July 3, 1994; September 16, September 17 and September 19, 1995; August 1, August 21, August 28 and September 11, 1996; July 12, 1998; and August 20, 1999). ... Led N.L. third basemen with 424 total chances and 28 double plays in 1995. ... Tied for N.L. lead with 10 sacrifice flies in 1996. ... Hit three home runs in one game (July 12, 1998). ... Career major league grand slams: 6.

Year Team (League)	Pos.	G	AB	R	H	2B	3B	HR	RBI	Avg.	BB	SO	SB	PO	A	E	Avg.
1985— Osceola (FSL)	3B	126	468	83	133	26	9	4	73	.284	51	54	14	53	193	20	.925
1986— Columbus (Sou.)	3B	137	513	82	154	29	3	12	81	.300	56	79	5	105	*299	33	.924
1987— Columbus (Sou.)	3B	95	375	66	122	25	2	15	69	.325	25	58	11	55	205	21	.925
— Houston (N.L.)	3B	63	203	10	50	7	1	3	23	.246	12	44	0	50	98	8	.949
1988— Tucson (PCL)	3B	109	416	54	113	24	7	5	66	.272	29	54	13	*105	*250	27	.929
— Houston (N.L.)	3B	30	83	5	15	2	0	1	7	.181	5	18	0	12	43	3	.948
1989— Houston (N.L.)	3B	161	585	71	149	31	3	10	72	.255	51	93	4	126	335	22	.954
1990— Houston (N.L.)	3B	153	541	52	131	20	2	4	51	.242	48	97	9	118	243	21	.945
1991— Houston (N.L.)	3B	152	574	65	145	30	3	13	80	.253	46	85	4	129	293	23	.948
1992— Houston (N.L.)	3B	135	506	68	149	31	2	13	62	.294	44	68	10	102	210	11	.966
1993— Houston (N.L.)	3B	143	543	75	142	31	0	13	75	.262	49	88	8	123	246	24	.942
1994— Houston (N.L.)	3B	111	406	63	115	28	2	18	75	.283	43	71	4	79	200	9	.969
1995— San Diego (N.L.)■	3B	143	526	74	159	33	0	26	94	.302	69	94	12	102	*295	*27	.936
1996— San Diego (N.L.)	3B	146	546	109	178	37	2	40	130	.326	78	99	11	103	310	20	.954
1997— San Diego (N.L.)	3B	137	486	92	141	28	0	26	90	.290	80	118	11	90	291	24	.941
1998— San Diego (N.L.)	3B	131	452	87	114	29	0	29	82	.252	71	108	6	77	207	*21	.931
1999— Houston (N.L.)■	3B	78	273	45	78	11	1	13	56	.286	46	58	6	52	139	14	.932
— New Orleans (PCL)	3B	6	20	6	7	4	0	0	3	.350	2	1	0	2	5	3	.700
2000— Houston (N.L.)	3B	59	208	42	63	13	0	15	45	.303	42	37	3	37	81	11	.915
Major League totals (14 years)		1642	5932	858	1629	331	16	224	942	.275	684	1078	88	1200	3009	238	.946

DIVISION SERIES RECORD

RECORDS: Holds N.L. career records for highest slugging average (20 or more at-bats)—.756; and home runs—6. ... Shares single-game record for most home runs—2 (October 5, 1996). ... Shares N.L. single-game record for most at-bats—6 (October 8, 1999).

Year Team (League)	Pos.	G	AB	R	H	2B	3B	HR	RBI	Avg.	BB	SO	SB	PO	A	E	Avg.
1996— San Diego (N.L.)	3B	3	10	3	3	0	0	3	3	.300	3	5	0	0	5	3	.625
1998— San Diego (N.L.)	3B	4	14	2	2	0	0	0	0	.143	1	3	0	2	5	1	.875
1999— Houston (N.L.)	3B	4	17	3	8	0	0	3	8	.471	2	1	0	1	10	0	1.000
Division series totals (3 years)		11	41	8	13	0	0	6	11	.317	6	9	0	3	20	4	.852

CHAMPIONSHIP SERIES RECORD

RECORDS: Shares single-game record for most bases on balls received—4 (October 8, 1998).

Year Team (League)	Pos.	G	AB	R	H	2B	3B	HR	RBI	Avg.	BB	SO	SB	PO	A	E	Avg.
1998— San Diego (N.L.)	3B	6	22	3	6	0	0	2	4	.273	5	4	0	5	10	0	1.000

WORLD SERIES RECORD

Year Team (League)	Pos.	G	AB	R	H	2B	3B	HR	RBI	Avg.	BB	SO	SB	PO	A	E	Avg.
1998— San Diego (N.L.)	3B	4	14	1	2	1	0	0	1	.143	2	7	0	2	2	2	.667

ALL-STAR GAME RECORD

Year League	Pos.	AB	R	H	2B	3B	HR	RBI	Avg.	BB	SO	SB	PO	A	E	Avg.
1994— National	3B	1	0	0	0	0	0	0	.000	0	0	0	0	0	0	...
1996— National	3B	2	1	1	0	0	1	1	.500	0	1	0	0	0	1	.000
1997— National	3B	2	0	0	0	0	0	0	.000	0	0	0	0	0	0	...
All-Star Game totals (3 years)		5	1	1	0	0	1	1	.200	0	1	0	0	0	1	.000

CAMMACK, ERIC   P   METS

PERSONAL: Born August 14, 1975, in Nederland, Texas. ... 6-1/180. ... Throws right, bats right. ... Full name: Eric Wade Cammack.

HIGH SCHOOL: Nederland (Texas).

COLLEGE: Lamar.

TRANSACTIONS/CAREER NOTES: Selected by New York Mets organization in 13th round of free-agent draft (June 3, 1997).

Year League	W	L	Pct.	ERA	G	GS	CG	ShO	Sv.	IP	H	R	ER	BB	SO
1997—Pittsfield (NY-Penn)	0	1	.000	0.86	23	0	0	0	8	31 1/3	9	4	3	14	32
1998—Capital City (S.Atl.)	4	0	1.000	2.81	25	0	0	0	8	32	17	13	10	13	49
—St. Lucie (FSL)	3	2	.600	2.02	29	0	0	0	11	35 2/3	22	12	8	14	53
1999—Binghamton (East.)	4	2	.667	2.38	45	0	0	0	15	56 2/3	28	17	15	38	83
—Norfolk (I.L.)	0	0	...	3.12	9	0	0	0	4	8 2/3	7	3	3	1	17
2000—Norfolk (I.L.)	6	2	.750	1.70	47	0	0	0	9	63 2/3	38	14	12	31	67
—New York (N.L.)	0	0	...	6.30	8	0	0	0	0	10	7	7	7	10	9
Major League totals (1 year)	0	0	...	6.30	8	0	0	0	0	10	7	7	7	10	9

CANIZARO, JAY   2B   GIANTS

PERSONAL: Born July 4, 1973, in Orange, Texas. ... 5-9/178. ... Bats right, throws right. ... Full name: Jason Kyle Canizaro.

HIGH SCHOOL: West Orange-Stark (Orange, Texas).

JUNIOR COLLEGE: Blinn College (Texas).

COLLEGE: Oklahoma State.

TRANSACTIONS/CAREER NOTES: Selected by San Francisco Giants organization in fourth round of free-agent draft (June 3, 1993). ... On Fresno disabled list (July 10-August 15, 1999). ... Released by Giants (April 3, 2000). ... Signed by Minnesota Twins organization (April 4, 2000).

STATISTICAL NOTES: Led Arizona League second basemen with 33 double plays in 1993. ... Led Texas League second basemen with 19 errors in 1995. ... Career major league grand slams: 2.

							BATTING								FIELDING		
Year Team (League)	Pos.	G	AB	R	H	2B	3B	HR	RBI	Avg.	BB	SO	SB	PO	A	E	Avg.
1993—Arizona Giants (Ariz.)	2B-SS	49	180	34	47	10	•6	3	*41	.261	22	40	12	102	106	10	.954
1994—San Jose (Calif.)	2-S-3-O	126	464	77	117	16	2	15	69	.252	46	98	12	262	362	30	.954
1995—Shreveport (Texas)	2B-SS	126	440	83	129	25	7	12	60	.293	58	98	16	254	333	†23	.962
1996—Phoenix (PCL)	2-S-3-DH	102	363	50	95	21	2	7	64	.262	46	77	14	194	308	14	.973
—San Francisco (N.L.)	2B-SS	43	120	11	24	4	1	2	8	.200	9	38	0	64	91	6	.963
1997—Phoenix (PCL)	2B-3B	23	81	12	16	7	0	2	12	.198	9	24	2	32	46	2	.975
—Shreveport (Texas)	2-S-3-DH	50	176	36	45	9	0	11	38	.256	26	44	2	80	124	6	.971
1998—Shreveport (Texas)	2B	83	281	47	63	7	1	12	32	.224	53	46	5	145	255	10	.976
—Fresno (PCL)	2-DH-O-S	45	106	23	24	6	2	6	14	.226	17	23	0	49	64	2	.983
1999—Fresno (PCL)	2B-SS-3B	105	364	76	102	20	2	26	78	.280	49	79	16	184	268	15	.968
—San Francisco (N.L.)	2B	12	18	5	8	2	0	1	9	.444	1	2	1	2	5	0	1.000
2000—Salt Lake (PCL)■	2B-SS-3B	27	101	21	36	9	2	6	32	.356	17	17	4	42	89	7	.949
—Minnesota (A.L.)	2B-DH	102	346	43	93	21	1	7	40	.269	24	57	4	120	199	6	.982
American League totals (1 year)		102	346	43	93	21	1	7	40	.269	24	57	4	120	199	6	.982
National League totals (2 years)		55	138	16	32	6	1	3	17	.232	10	40	1	66	96	6	.964
Major League totals (3 years)		157	484	59	125	27	2	10	57	.258	34	97	5	186	295	12	.976

CANSECO, JOSE   DH/OF   ANGELS

PERSONAL: Born July 2, 1964, in Havana, Cuba. ... 6-4/240. ... Bats right, throws right. ... Full name: Jose Canseco Jr. ... Identical twin brother of Ozzie Canseco, outfielder with Oakland Athletics (1990) and St. Louis Cardinals (1992). ... Name pronounced can-SAY-co.

HIGH SCHOOL: Miami Coral Park Senior.

TRANSACTIONS/CAREER NOTES: Selected by Oakland Athletics organization in 15th round of free-agent draft (June 7, 1982). ... On Huntsville disabled list (May 14-June 3, 1985). ... On Oakland disabled list (March 23-July 13, 1989); included rehabilitation assignments to Huntsville (May 6 and June 28-July 13). ... On disabled list (June 8-23, 1990 and July 1-16, 1992). ... Traded by A's to Texas Rangers for OF Ruben Sierra, P Jeff Russell, P Bobby Witt and cash (August 31, 1992). ... On disabled list (June 24, 1993-remainder of season). ... Traded by Rangers to Boston Red Sox for OF Otis Nixon and 3B Luis Ortiz (December 9, 1994). ... On Boston disabled list (May 15-June 20, 1995); included rehabilitation assignment to Pawtucket (June 18-20). ... Granted free agency (October 30, 1995). ... Re-signed by Red Sox (December 6, 1995). ... On Boston disabled list (April 24-May 9 and July 26-September 17, 1996); included rehabilitation assignment to Pawtucket (May 7-9). ... Traded by Red Sox to A's for P John Wasdin and cash (January 27, 1997). ... On disabled list (August 1-20 and August 27, 1997-remainder of season). ... Granted free agency (October 31, 1997). ... Signed by Toronto Blue Jays (February 4, 1998). ... Granted free agency (October 22, 1998). ... Signed by Tampa Bay Devil Rays (December 11, 1998). ... On disabled list (July 10-August 20, 1999). ... On Tampa Bay disabled list (May 25-July 18, 2000). ... Claimed on waivers by New York Yankees (August 7, 2000). ... Granted free agency (November 10, 2000). ... Signed by Anaheim Angels organization (January 26, 2001).

RECORDS: Shares major league record for most strikeouts in two consecutive games—8 (July 14 [3] and 16 [5], 1997). ... Shares major league single-game record for most strikeouts (nine-inning game)—5 (July 16, 1997). ... Shares major league record for most consecutive bases on balls received—7 (August 4-5, 1992).

HONORS: Named Minor League Player of the Year by THE SPORTING NEWS (1985). ... Named Southern League Most Valuable Player (1985). ... Named A.L. Rookie Player of the Year by THE SPORTING NEWS (1986). ... Named A.L. Rookie of the Year by Baseball Writers' Association of America (1986). ... Named A.L. Player of the Year by THE SPORTING NEWS (1988). ... Named outfielder on THE SPORTING NEWS A.L. All-Star team (1988 and 1990-91). ... Named outfielder on THE SPORTING NEWS A.L. Silver Slugger team (1988 and 1990-91). ... Named A.L. Most Valuable Player by Baseball Writers' Association of America (1988). ... Named designated hitter on THE SPORTING NEWS A.L. Silver Slugger team (1998).

STATISTICAL NOTES: Led California League outfielders with eight double plays in 1984. ... Hit three home runs in one game (July 3, 1988 and June 13, 1994). ... Led A.L. with .569 slugging percentage in 1988. ... Led A.L. in grounding into double plays with 20 in 1994. ... Career major league grand slams: 6.

							BATTING								FIELDING		
Year Team (League)	Pos.	G	AB	R	H	2B	3B	HR	RBI	Avg.	BB	SO	SB	PO	A	E	Avg.
1982—Miami (FSL)	3B	6	9	0	1	0	0	0	0	.111	1	3	0	3	1	1	.800
—Idaho Falls (Pio.)	3B-OF	28	57	13	15	3	0	2	7	.263	9	13	3	6	17	3	.885
1983—Madison (Midw.)	OF	34	88	8	14	4	0	3	10	.159	10	36	2	23	2	1	.962
—Medford (N'West)	OF	59	197	34	53	15	2	11	40	.269	30	*78	6	46	5	5	.911
1984—Modesto (Calif.)	OF	116	410	61	113	21	2	15	73	.276	74	127	10	216	17	9	.963
1985—Huntsville (Sou.)	OF	58	211	47	67	10	2	25	80	.318	30	55	6	117	9	7	.947
—Tacoma (PCL)	OF	60	233	41	81	16	1	11	47	.348	40	66	5	81	7	2	.978
—Oakland (A.L.)	OF	29	96	16	29	3	0	5	13	.302	4	31	1	56	2	3	.951
1986—Oakland (A.L.)	OF-DH	157	600	85	144	29	1	33	117	.240	65	175	15	319	4	•14	.958
1987—Oakland (A.L.)	OF-DH	159	630	81	162	35	3	31	113	.257	50	157	15	263	12	7	.975
1988—Oakland (A.L.)	OF-DH	158	610	120	187	34	0	*42	*124	.307	78	128	40	304	11	7	.978

Year	Team (League)	Pos.	G	AB	R	H	2B	3B	HR	RBI	Avg.	BB	SO	SB	PO	A	E	Avg.
1989—	Huntsville (Sou.)	OF	9	29	2	6	0	0	0	3	.207	5	11	1	9	0	0	1.000
—Oakland (A.L.)		OF-DH	65	227	40	61	9	1	17	57	.269	23	69	6	119	5	3	.976
1990—	Oakland (A.L.)	OF-DH	131	481	83	132	14	2	37	101	.274	72	158	19	182	7	1	.995
1991—	Oakland (A.L.)	OF-DH	154	572	115	152	32	1	•44	122	.266	78	152	26	245	5	•9	.965
1992—	Oakland (A.L.)	OF-DH	97	366	66	90	11	0	22	72	.246	48	104	5	163	5	2	.988
—Texas (A.L.)■		OF-DH	22	73	8	17	4	0	4	15	.233	15	24	1	32	0	1	.970
1993—	Texas (A.L.)	OF-DH-P	60	231	30	59	14	1	10	46	.255	16	62	6	94	4	3	.970
1994—	Texas (A.L.)	DH	111	429	88	121	19	2	31	90	.282	69	114	15	...	...	...	...
1995—	Boston (A.L.)■	DH-OF	102	396	64	121	25	1	24	81	.306	42	93	4	1	0	0	1.000
—Pawtucket (I.L.)		DH	2	6	1	1	0	0	0	1	.167	1	5	0	...	...	...	...
1996—	Boston (A.L.)	DH-OF	96	360	68	104	22	1	28	82	.289	63	82	3	17	1	0	1.000
—Pawtucket (I.L.)		DH	2	5	0	1	0	0	0	0	.200	0	3	0	...	...	...	...
1997—	Boston (A.L.)■	DH-OF	108	388	56	91	19	0	23	74	.235	51	122	8	74	2	5	.938
1998—	Toronto (A.L.)■	DH-OF	151	583	98	138	26	0	46	107	.237	65	*159	29	117	4	5	.960
1999—	Tampa Bay (A.L.)■	DH-OF	113	430	75	120	18	1	34	95	.279	58	135	3	7	1	0	1.000
2000—	Tampa Bay (A.L.)	DH	61	218	31	56	15	0	9	30	.257	41	65	2	...	...	...	...
—New York (A.L.)■		DH-OF	37	111	16	27	3	0	6	19	.243	23	37	0	9	0	2	.818
Major League totals (16 years)			1811	6801	1140	1811	332	14	446	1358	.266	861	1867	198	2002	63	62	.971

DIVISION SERIES RECORD

Year	Team (League)	Pos.	G	AB	R	H	2B	3B	HR	RBI	Avg.	BB	SO	SB	PO	A	E	Avg.
1995—	Boston (A.L.)	DH-OF	3	13	0	0	0	0	0	0	.000	2	2	0	4	0	0	1.000
2000—	New York (A.L.)								Did not play.									

CHAMPIONSHIP SERIES RECORD

Year	Team (League)	Pos.	G	AB	R	H	2B	3B	HR	RBI	Avg.	BB	SO	SB	PO	A	E	Avg.
1988—	Oakland (A.L.)	OF	4	16	4	5	1	0	3	4	.313	1	2	1	6	0	0	1.000
1989—	Oakland (A.L.)	OF-PH	5	17	1	5	0	0	1	3	.294	3	7	0	6	1	1	.875
1990—	Oakland (A.L.)	OF	4	11	3	2	0	0	1	1	.182	5	5	2	14	0	0	1.000
2000—	New York (A.L.)								Did not play.									
Championship series totals (3 years)			13	44	8	12	1	0	4	8	.273	9	14	3	26	1	1	.964

WORLD SERIES RECORD

RECORDS: Shares single-game record for most grand slams—1 (October 15, 1988). ... Shares single-inning record for most runs batted in—4 (October 15, 1988, second inning).

NOTES: Hit home run in first at-bat (October 15, 1988). ... Member of World Series championship team (1989 and 2000).

Year	Team (League)	Pos.	G	AB	R	H	2B	3B	HR	RBI	Avg.	BB	SO	SB	PO	A	E	Avg.
1988—	Oakland (A.L.)	OF	5	19	1	1	0	0	1	5	.053	2	4	1	8	0	0	1.000
1989—	Oakland (A.L.)	OF	4	14	5	5	0	0	1	3	.357	4	3	1	6	0	0	1.000
1990—	Oakland (A.L.)	OF-PH-DH	4	12	1	1	0	0	1	2	.083	2	3	0	4	0	0	1.000
2000—	New York (A.L.)	PH	1	1	0	0	0	0	0	0	.000	0	1	0	...	...	...	...
World Series totals (4 years)			14	46	7	7	0	0	3	10	.152	8	11	2	18	0	0	1.000

ALL-STAR GAME RECORD

Year	League	Pos.	AB	R	H	2B	3B	HR	RBI	Avg.	BB	SO	SB	PO	A	E	Avg.
1986—	American								Did not play.								
1988—	American	OF	4	0	0	0	0	0	0	.000	0	1	0	3	0	0	1.000
1989—	American							Selected, did not play—injured.									
1990—	American	OF	4	0	0	0	0	0	0	.000	1	1	1	1	0	0	1.000
1992—	American							Selected, did not play—injured.									
1999—	American							Selected, did not play—injured.									
All-Star Game totals (2 years)			8	0	0	0	0	0	0	.000	1	2	1	4	0	0	1.000

RECORD AS PITCHER

Year	League	W	L	Pct.	ERA	G	GS	CG	ShO	Sv.	IP	H	R	ER	BB	SO
1993—	Texas (A.L.)	0	0	...	27.00	1	0	0	0	0	1	2	3	3	3	0

CARDONA, JAVIER — C — TIGERS

PERSONAL: Born September 15, 1975, in Santurce, Puerto Rico. ... 6-1/185. ... Bats right, throws right. ... Full name: Javier Peterson Cardona.
HIGH SCHOOL: Jose Alegria (Barrio Maguayo, Puerto Rico).
JUNIOR COLLEGE: Lake Land Community College (Ill.).
TRANSACTIONS/CAREER NOTES: Selected by Detroit Tigers organization in 19th round of free-agent draft (June 3, 1993); did not sign. ... Selected by Tigers organization in 23rd round of free-agent draft (June 4, 1994).
STATISTICAL NOTES: Led Southern League with .569 slugging percentage in 1999.

Year	Team (League)	Pos.	G	AB	R	H	2B	3B	HR	RBI	Avg.	BB	SO	SB	PO	A	E	Avg.
1994—	Jamestown (NY-P)	C	19	46	6	12	2	0	0	5	.261	7	9	0	89	17	4	.964
1995—	Fayetteville (S.Atl.)	C	51	165	18	34	8	0	3	19	.206	13	30	1	339	48	4	.990
1996—	Fayetteville (S.Atl.)	C	97	348	42	98	21	0	4	28	.282	28	53	1	677	112	15	.981
1997—	Lakeland (FSL)	C	85	284	28	82	15	0	7	38	.289	25	51	1	498	75	12	.979
1998—	Jacksonville (Sou.)	C	46	163	31	54	16	1	4	40	.331	15	29	0	208	33	6	.976
—Toledo (I.L.)		C	47	162	12	31	4	0	5	16	.191	9	32	0	262	31	5	.983
1999—	Jacksonville (Sou.)	C	108	418	84	129	31	0	*26	92	.309	46	69	4	565	58	11	.983
2000—	Toledo (I.L.)	C	56	218	29	60	10	0	11	43	.275	15	33	0	317	25	5	.986
—Detroit (A.L.)		C	26	40	1	7	1	0	1	2	.175	0	9	0	66	7	2	.973
Major League totals (1 year)			26	40	1	7	1	0	1	2	.175	0	9	0	66	7	2	.973

C

CARLYLE, BUDDY — P

PERSONAL: Born December 21, 1977, in Omaha, Neb. ... 6-3/175. ... Throws right, bats left. ... Full name: Earl L. Carlyle III.
HIGH SCHOOL: Bellevue (Neb.) East.
TRANSACTIONS/CAREER NOTES: Selected by Cincinnati Reds organization in second round of free-agent draft (June 4, 1996). ... Traded by Reds to San Diego Padres for P Marc Kroon (April 8, 1998). ... Contract sold by Padres to Hanshin Tigers of Japan Central League (November 3, 2000).
STATISTICAL NOTES: Pitched 2-0 no-hit victory against Asheville (May 4, 1997, first game).

Year League	W	L	Pct.	ERA	G	GS	CG	ShO	Sv.	IP	H	R	ER	BB	SO
1996—Princeton (Appl.)	2	4	.333	4.66	10	9	1	0	0	46 1/3	47	33	24	16	42
1997—Charleston, W.Va. (S.Atl.)	•14	5	.737	2.77	23	23	4	1	0	143	130	51	44	27	111
1998—Chattanooga (Sou.)	0	1	.000	5.40	1	1	0	0	0	5	6	3	3	0	3
—Mobile (Sou.)■	14	6	.700	3.38	27	27	2	1	0	183 2/3	179	77	69	46	97
1999—Las Vegas (PCL)	11	8	.579	4.89	25	25	0	0	0	160	180	99	87	42	138
—San Diego (N.L.)	1	3	.250	5.97	7	7	0	0	0	37 2/3	36	28	25	17	29
2000—Las Vegas (PCL)	8	6	.571	4.29	27	27	1	0	0	151	165	93	72	44	127
—San Diego (N.L.)	0	0	...	21.00	4	0	0	0	0	3	6	7	7	3	2
Major League totals (2 years)	1	3	.250	7.08	11	7	0	0	0	40 2/3	42	35	32	20	31

CARPENTER, BUBBA — OF — METS

C

PERSONAL: Born July 23, 1968, in Dallas. ... 6-1/205. ... Bats left, throws left. ... Full name: Charles Sydney Carpenter.
HIGH SCHOOL: West Fork (Ark.).
COLLEGE: Arkansas.
TRANSACTIONS/CAREER NOTES: Signed as non-drafted free agent by New York Yankees organization (May 23, 1991). ... Granted free agency (October 17, 1997). ... Re-signed by Yankees organization (March 3, 1998). ... Granted free agency (October 16, 1998). ... Re-signed by Yankees organization (December 16, 1998). ... Granted free agency (October 15, 1999). ... Signed by Colorado Rockies organization (December 1, 1999). ... On Colorado Springs disabled list (April 28-May 10, 2000). ... Released by Rockies (July 28, 2000). ... Signed by New York Mets organization (December 8, 2000).

Year Team (League)	Pos.	G	AB	R	H	2B	3B	HR	RBI	Avg.	BB	SO	SB	PO	A	E	Avg.
1991—Prince Will. (Caro.)	OF	69	236	33	66	10	3	6	34	.280	40	50	4	98	7	4	.963
1992—Albany (East.)	OF	60	221	24	51	11	5	4	31	.231	25	41	2	91	5	3	.970
—Prince Will. (Caro.)	OF	68	240	41	76	15	2	5	41	.317	35	44	4	100	7	4	.964
1993—Columbus (I.L.)	OF	70	199	29	53	9	0	5	17	.266	29	35	2	91	3	3	.969
—Albany (East.)	OF	14	53	8	17	4	0	2	14	.321	7	4	2	15	1	1	.941
1994—Columbus (I.L.)	OF-1B	7	15	0	4	0	0	0	2	.267	0	7	0	13	1	0	1.000
—Albany (East.)	OF-1B	116	378	47	109	14	1	13	51	.288	58	65	9	310	14	9	.973
1995—Columbus (I.L.)	OF-1B	116	374	57	92	12	3	11	49	.246	40	70	13	231	5	4	.983
1996—Columbus (I.L.)	OF	132	466	55	114	23	3	7	48	.245	48	80	10	225	8	3	.987
1997—Columbus (I.L.)	OF	85	271	47	76	12	4	6	39	.280	48	46	4	164	6	1	.994
1998—Columbus (I.L.)	OF-1B	63	198	28	45	14	2	7	24	.227	36	48	3	56	3	1	.983
—GC Yankees (GCL)	OF	5	17	3	4	0	2	1	7	.235	2	2	0	2	0	0	1.000
1999—Columbus (I.L.)	OF	101	325	78	92	20	2	22	81	.283	75	68	7	197	7	4	.981
2000—Colo. Springs (PCL)■	OF	53	157	23	35	7	2	4	19	.223	33	37	3	103	2	3	.972
—Colorado (N.L.)	OF-DH	15	27	4	6	0	0	3	5	.222	4	13	0	3	0	0	1.000
Major League totals (1 year)		15	27	4	6	0	0	3	5	.222	4	13	0	3	0	0	1.000

CARPENTER, CHRIS — P — BLUE JAYS

PERSONAL: Born April 27, 1975, in Exeter, N.H. ... 6-6/225. ... Throws right, bats right. ... Full name: Christopher John Carpenter.
HIGH SCHOOL: Trinity (Manchester, N.H.).
TRANSACTIONS/CAREER NOTES: Selected by Toronto Blue Jays organization in first round (15th pick overall) of free-agent draft (June 3, 1993). ... On Toronto disabled list (June 3-28, 1999); included rehabilitation assignment to St. Catharines (June 23-28).

Year League	W	L	Pct.	ERA	G	GS	CG	ShO	Sv.	IP	H	R	ER	BB	SO
1994—Medicine Hat (Pio.)	6	3	.667	2.76	15	15	0	0	0	84 2/3	76	40	26	39	80
1995—Dunedin (FSL)	3	5	.375	2.17	15	15	0	0	0	99 1/3	83	29	24	50	56
—Knoxville (Sou.)	3	7	.300	5.18	12	12	0	0	0	64 1/3	71	47	37	31	53
1996—Knoxville (Sou.)	7	9	.438	3.94	28	28	1	0	0	171 1/3	161	94	75	91	150
1997—Syracuse (I.L.)	4	9	.308	4.50	19	19	3	2	0	120	113	64	60	53	97
—Toronto (A.L.)	3	7	.300	5.09	14	13	1	1	0	81 1/3	108	55	46	37	55
1998—Toronto (A.L.)	12	7	.632	4.37	33	24	1	1	0	175	177	97	85	61	136
1999—Toronto (A.L.)	9	8	.529	4.38	24	24	4	1	0	150	177	81	73	48	106
—St. Catharines (NY-Penn)	0	0	...	4.50	1	1	0	0	0	4	5	2	2	1	6
2000—Toronto (A.L.)	10	12	.455	6.26	34	27	2	0	0	175 1/3	204	*130	*122	83	113
Major League totals (4 years)	34	34	.500	5.04	105	88	8	3	0	581 2/3	666	363	326	229	410

CARRARA, GIOVANNI — P — DODGERS

PERSONAL: Born March 4, 1968, in Edo Anzuategni, Venezuela. ... 6-2/210. ... Throws right, bats right.
TRANSACTIONS/CAREER NOTES: Signed as non-drafted free agent by Toronto Blue Jays organization (January 23, 1990). ... Claimed on waivers by Cincinnati Reds (July 3, 1996). ... Granted free agency (October 15, 1996). ... Signed by Baltimore Orioles organization (November 12, 1996). ... Released by Orioles (May 14, 1997). ... Signed by Reds organization (May 17, 1997). ... Granted free agency (September 11, 1997). ... Played for Seibu Lions of Japan Pacific League (1998). ... Signed by Reds organization (December 23, 1998). ... Granted free agency (October 15, 1999). ... Signed by Colorado Rockies organization (December 1, 1999). ... On Colorado Springs disabled list (May 29-June 21, 2000). ... On Colorado disabled list (August 3-September 4, 2000); included rehabilitation assignment to Colorado Springs (August 29-September 4). ... Granted free agency (October 4, 2000). ... Signed by Los Angeles Dodgers organization (January 4, 2001).

Year	League	W	L	Pct.	ERA	G	GS	CG	ShO	Sv.	IP	H	R	ER	BB	SO
1990— Dom. Dodgers (DSL)		8	2	.800	2.62	15	14	4	0	0	86	88	31	25	28	55
1991— St. Catharines (NY-Penn) ...		5	2	.714	1.71	15	13	2	•2	0	89²/₃	66	26	17	21	83
1992— Dunedin (FSL)		0	1	.000	4.63	5	4	0	0	0	23¹/₃	22	13	12	11	16
— Myrtle Beach (S.Atl.)		11	7	.611	3.14	22	16	1	1	0	100¹/₃	86	40	35	36	100
1993— Dunedin (FSL)		6	11	.353	3.45	27	24	1	0	0	140²/₃	136	69	54	59	108
1994— Knoxville (Sou.)		13	7	.650	3.89	26	26	1	0	0	164¹/₃	158	85	71	59	96
1995— Syracuse (I.L.)		7	7	.500	3.96	21	21	0	0	0	131²/₃	116	72	58	56	81
— Toronto (A.L.)		2	4	.333	7.21	12	7	1	0	0	48²/₃	64	46	39	25	27
1996— Syracuse (I.L.)		4	4	.500	3.58	9	6	1	0	0	37²/₃	37	16	15	12	28
— Toronto (A.L.)		0	1	.000	11.40	11	0	0	0	0	15	23	19	19	12	10
— Indianapolis (A.A.)■		4	0	1.000	0.76	9	6	1	1	1	47²/₃	25	6	4	9	45
— Cincinnati (N.L.)		1	0	1.000	5.87	8	5	0	0	0	23	31	17	15	13	13
1997— Rochester (I.L.)■		4	2	.667	4.44	8	8	1	0	0	46²/₃	45	23	23	16	48
— Indianapolis (A.A.)■		12	5	.706	3.51	19	18	2	0	0	120²/₃	111	50	47	51	105
— Cincinnati (N.L.)		0	1	.000	7.84	2	2	0	0	0	10¹/₃	14	9	9	6	5
1998— Seibu (Jap. Pac.)■		1	2	.333	1.11	33	0	0	0	1	73	68	...	...	40	50
1999— Indianapolis (I.L.)■		12	7	.632	•3.47	39	21	2	1	0	158	144	68	61	58	114
2000— Colorado Springs (PCL)■ ..		7	2	.778	3.26	18	15	0	0	0	96²/₃	89	39	35	30	89
— Colorado (N.L.)		0	1	.000	12.82	8	0	0	0	0	13¹/₃	21	19	19	11	15
A.L. totals (2 years)		2	5	.286	8.20	23	7	1	0	0	63²/₃	87	65	58	37	37
N.L. totals (3 years)		1	2	.333	8.29	18	7	0	0	0	46²/₃	66	45	43	30	33
Major League totals (4 years)		3	7	.300	8.24	41	14	1	0	0	110¹/₃	153	110	101	67	70

CARRASCO, HECTOR — P

PERSONAL: Born October 22, 1969, in San Pedro de Macoris, Dominican Republic. ... 6-2/220. ... Throws right, bats right. ... Full name: Hector Pacheco Pipo Carrasco. ... Name pronounced kuh-ROSS-ko.

HIGH SCHOOL: Liceo Mattias Mella (San Pedro de Macoris, Dominican Republic).

TRANSACTIONS/CAREER NOTES: Signed as non-drafted free agent by New York Mets organization (March 20, 1988). ... Released by Mets (January 6, 1992). ... Signed by Houston Astros organization (January 21, 1992). ... Traded by Astros with P Brian Griffiths to Florida Marlins for P Tom Edens (November 17, 1992). ... Traded by Marlins to Cincinnati Reds (September 10, 1993), completing deal in which Reds traded P Chris Hammond to Marlins for 3B Gary Scott and a player to be named later (March 27, 1993). ... On disabled list (May 12-June 1, 1994). ... Traded by Reds with P Scott Service to Kansas City Royals for OF Jon Nunnally and IF/OF Chris Stynes (July 15, 1997). ... Selected by Arizona Diamondbacks in second round (49th pick overall) of expansion draft (November 18, 1997). ... Claimed on waivers by Minnesota Twins (April 3, 1998). ... On Minnesota disabled list (April 3-June 25, 1999); included rehabilitation assignments to Fort Myers (June 16-17) and Salt Lake (June 18-25). ... Traded by Twins to Boston Red Sox for OF Lew Ford (September 10, 2000). ... Granted free agency (November 1, 2000).

Year	League	W	L	Pct.	ERA	G	GS	CG	ShO	Sv.	IP	H	R	ER	BB	SO
1988— Gulf Coast Mets (GCL)		0	2	.000	4.17	14	2	0	0	0	36²/₃	37	29	17	13	21
1989— Kingsport (Appl.)		1	6	.143	5.74	12	10	0	0	0	53¹/₃	69	49	34	34	55
1990— Kingsport (Appl.)		0	0	...	4.05	3	1	0	0	0	6²/₃	8	3	3	1	5
1991— Pittsfield (NY-Penn)		0	1	.000	5.40	12	1	0	0	1	23¹/₃	25	17	14	21	20
1992— Asheville (S.Atl.)■		5	5	.500	2.99	49	0	0	0	8	78¹/₃	66	30	26	47	67
1993— Kane County (Midw.)■.......		6	12	.333	4.11	28	*28	0	0	0	149	153	90	68	76	127
1994— Cincinnati (N.L.)■		5	6	.455	2.24	45	0	0	0	6	56¹/₃	42	17	14	30	41
1995— Cincinnati (N.L.)		2	7	.222	4.12	64	0	0	0	5	87¹/₃	86	45	40	46	64
1996— Cincinnati (N.L.)		4	3	.571	3.75	56	0	0	0	0	74¹/₃	58	37	31	45	59
— Indianapolis (A.A.)		0	1	.000	2.14	13	2	0	0	0	21	18	7	5	13	17
1997— Indianapolis (A.A.)		0	0	...	6.23	3	0	0	0	1	4¹/₃	5	3	3	3	4
— Cincinnati (N.L.)		1	2	.333	3.68	38	0	0	0	0	51¹/₃	51	25	21	25	46
— Kansas City (A.L.)■		1	6	.143	5.45	28	0	0	0	0	34²/₃	29	21	21	16	30
1998— Minnesota (A.L.)■		4	2	.667	4.38	63	0	0	0	1	61²/₃	75	30	30	31	46
1999— Fort Myers (FSL)		0	0	...	4.50	1	1	0	0	0	2	2	1	1	1	1
— Salt Lake (PCL)		1	0	1.000	0.00	3	0	0	0	1	4¹/₃	3	0	0	1	3
— Minnesota (A.L.)		2	3	.400	4.96	39	0	0	0	1	49	48	29	27	18	35
2000— Minnesota (A.L.)		4	3	.571	4.25	61	0	0	0	1	72	75	38	34	33	57
— Boston (A.L.)■		1	1	.500	9.45	8	1	0	0	0	6²/₃	15	8	7	5	7
A.L. totals (4 years)		12	15	.444	4.78	199	1	0	0	3	224	242	126	119	103	175
N.L. totals (4 years)		12	18	.400	3.54	203	0	0	0	11	269¹/₃	237	124	106	146	210
Major League totals (7 years)		24	33	.421	4.10	402	1	0	0	14	493¹/₃	479	250	225	249	385

CHAMPIONSHIP SERIES RECORD

Year	League	W	L	Pct.	ERA	G	GS	CG	ShO	Sv.	IP	H	R	ER	BB	SO
1995— Cincinnati (N.L.)		0	0	...	0.00	1	0	0	0	0	1¹/₃	1	0	0	0	3

CARUSO, MIKE — SS

PERSONAL: Born May 27, 1977, in Queens, N.Y. ... 6-1/175. ... Bats left, throws right. ... Full name: Michael J. Caruso.

HIGH SCHOOL: Stoneman Douglas (Parkland, Fla.).

TRANSACTIONS/CAREER NOTES: Selected by San Francisco Giants organization in second round of free-agent draft (June 2, 1996). ... Traded by Giants with P Keith Foulke, P Lorenzo Barcelo, P Bobby Howry, P Ken Vining and OF Brian Manning to Chicago White Sox for P Danny Darwin, P Wilson Alvarez and P Roberto Hernandez (July 31, 1997). ... On Charlotte disabled list (August 1-9, 2000). ... On Chicago disabled list (August 10, 2000-remainder of season). ... Claimed on waivers by Seattle Mariners (December 14, 2000). ... Granted free agency (December 21, 2000).

STATISTICAL NOTES: Tied for A.L. lead in caught stealing with 14 in 1999.

Year	Team (League)	Pos.	G	AB	R	H	2B	3B	HR	RBI	Avg.	BB	SO	SB	PO	A	E	Avg.
1996—	Bellingham (N'West)..	SS-3B	73	312	48	91	13	1	2	24	.292	16	23	24	107	231	40	.894
1997—	San Jose (Calif.)........	SS-DH	108	441	76	147	24	11	2	50	.333	38	19	11	168	300	33	.934
	—Win.-Salem (Caro.)■.	SS-DH	28	119	12	27	3	2	0	14	.227	4	8	3	44	67	7	.941
1998—	Chicago (A.L.)	SS	133	523	81	160	17	6	5	55	.306	14	38	22	216	378	*35	.944
1999—	Chicago (A.L.)	SS-DH	136	529	60	132	11	4	2	35	.250	20	36	12	183	348	24	.957
2000—	Charlotte (I.L.)..........	SS-2B	88	309	38	76	11	5	0	26	.246	22	23	5	130	256	16	.960
Major League totals (2 years)			269	1052	141	292	28	10	7	90	.278	34	74	34	399	726	59	.950

CASANOVA, RAUL — C — BREWERS

PERSONAL: Born August 23, 1972, in Humacao, Puerto Rico. ... 6-0/195. ... Bats both, throws right.
HIGH SCHOOL: Ponce (Puerto Rico).
TRANSACTIONS/CAREER NOTES: Selected by New York Mets organization in eighth round of free-agent draft (June 4, 1990). ... Traded by Mets to San Diego Padres (December 7, 1992), completing deal in which Padres traded SS Tony Fernandez to Mets for P Wally Whitehurst, OF D.J. Dozier and a player to be named later (October 26, 1992). ... Traded by Padres with P Richie Lewis and OF Melvin Nieves to Detroit Tigers for P Sean Bergman, P Cade Gaspar and OF Todd Steverson (March 22, 1996). ... On Detroit disabled list (June 19-August 13, 1996); included rehabilitation assignments to Jacksonville (July 31-August 9) and Toledo (August 9-13). ... On Detroit disabled list (April 25-May 28 and July 21, 1998-remainder of season); included rehabilitation assignments to Toledo (May 8-27 and July 30-August 3). ... On Detroit disabled list (March 31-July 12, 1999); included rehabilitation assignments to the Gulf Coast Tigers (June 24-28), Lakeland (June 29-July 4) and Toledo (July 5-July 12). ... Granted free agency (October 15, 1999). ... Signed by Colorado Rockies organization (December 15, 1999). ... Released by Rockies (March 24, 2000). ... Signed by Milwaukee Brewers organization (March 25, 2000).
STATISTICAL NOTES: Switch-hit home runs in one game (June 6, 1996). ... Career major league grand slams: 2.

Year	Team (League)	Pos.	G	AB	R	H	2B	3B	HR	RBI	Avg.	BB	SO	SB	PO	A	E	Avg.
1990—	GC Mets (GCL)..........	C	23	65	4	5	0	0	0	1	.077	4	16	0	141	20	8	.953
1991—	GC Mets (GCL)..........	C	32	111	19	27	4	2	0	9	.243	12	22	3	211	24	5	.979
	—Kingsport (Appl.)........	C	5	18	0	1	0	0	0	0	.056	1	10	0	35	4	1	.975
1992—	Columbia (S.Atl.).......	C	5	18	2	3	0	0	0	1	.167	1	4	0	29	1	0	1.000
	—Kingsport (Appl.)........	C	42	137	25	37	9	1	4	27	.270	26	25	3	286	34	6	.982
1993—	Waterloo (Midw.)■■...	C-3B	76	227	32	58	12	0	6	30	.256	21	46	0	361	50	10	.976
1994—	Rancho Cuca. (Calif.) .	C	123	471	83	*160	27	2	23	120	*.340	43	97	1	593	55	14	.979
1995—	Memphis (Sou.)	C-DH	89	306	42	83	18	0	12	44	.271	25	51	4	531	55	*12	.980
1996—	Toledo (I.L.)■..........	C-DH	49	161	23	44	11	0	8	28	.273	20	24	0	234	15	2	.992
	—Detroit (A.L.)	C-DH	25	85	6	16	1	0	4	9	.188	6	18	0	123	12	3	.978
	—Jacksonville (Sou.).....	DH-C	8	30	5	10	2	0	4	9	.333	2	7	0	21	1	0	1.000
1997—	Toledo (I.L.)............	C	12	41	1	8	0	0	1	3	.195	3	8	0	77	8	2	.977
	—Detroit (A.L.)	C-DH	101	304	27	74	10	1	5	24	.243	26	48	1	543	38	9	.985
1998—	Detroit (A.L.)	C	16	42	4	6	2	0	1	3	.143	5	10	0	81	6	3	.967
	—Toledo (I.L.)..............	C-DH	50	171	17	44	8	0	7	26	.257	22	28	0	295	35	9	.973
1999—	GC Tigers (GCL)	C	2	5	1	4	0	0	1	1	.800	0	0	0	7	0	0	1.000
	—Lakeland (FSL)	C-DH	4	12	3	6	2	0	1	6	.500	0	1	0	14	2	0	1.000
	—Toledo (I.L.)..............	C-DH	44	160	21	33	9	0	6	23	.206	7	28	0	173	21	3	.985
2000—	Indianapolis (I.L.)■....	C	20	73	10	21	2	0	5	12	.288	7	10	0	120	15	2	.985
	—Milwaukee (N.L.)	C-DH	86	231	20	57	13	3	6	36	.247	26	48	1	358	28	4	.990
American League totals (3 years)			142	431	37	96	13	1	10	36	.223	37	76	1	747	56	15	.982
National League totals (1 year)			86	231	20	57	13	3	6	36	.247	26	48	1	358	28	4	.990
Major League totals (4 years)			228	662	57	153	26	4	16	72	.231	63	124	2	1105	84	19	.984

CASEY, SEAN — 1B — REDS

PERSONAL: Born July 2, 1974, in Willingsboro, N.J. ... 6-4/225. ... Bats left, throws right. ... Full name: Sean Thomas Casey.
HIGH SCHOOL: Upper St. Clair (Pittsburgh).
COLLEGE: Richmond.
TRANSACTIONS/CAREER NOTES: Selected by Cleveland Indians organization in second round of free-agent draft (June 1, 1995). ... On disabled list (July 23-September 23, 1996). ... On Akron disabled list (April 4-June 8, 1997). ... Traded by Indians to Cincinnati Reds for P Dave Burba (March 30, 1998). ... On Cincinnati disabled list (April 2-May 5, 1998); included rehabilitation assignment to Indianapolis (April 30-May 5). ... On disabled list (April 2-19, 2000).
RECORDS: Shares major league single-game record for most times reached base (nine-inning game)—7 (May 19, 1999).
STATISTICAL NOTES: Led Carolina League with .544 slugging percentage in 1996. ... Had 21-game hitting streak (July 4-30, 2000).

Year	Team (League)	Pos.	G	AB	R	H	2B	3B	HR	RBI	Avg.	BB	SO	SB	PO	A	E	Avg.
1995—	Watertown (NY-P)	1B	55	207	26	68	18	0	2	37	.329	18	21	3	510	24	8	.985
1996—	Kinston (Caro.)..........	1B-DH	92	344	62	114	31	3	12	57	*.331	36	47	1	632	15	6	.991
1997—	Akron (East.)	1B-DH	62	241	38	93	19	1	10	66	.386	23	34	0	405	22	5	.988
	—Buffalo (A.A.).............	DH-1B	20	72	12	26	7	0	5	18	.361	9	11	0	17	1	0	1.000
1998—	Cincinnati (N.L.)■......	1B	96	302	44	82	21	1	7	52	.272	43	45	1	643	36	4	.994
	—Indianapolis (I.L.).......	1B-DH	27	95	14	31	8	1	1	13	.326	14	10	0	205	10	2	.991
1999—	Cincinnati (N.L.)	1B-DH	151	594	103	197	42	3	25	99	.332	61	88	0	1189	55	6	.995
2000—	Cincinnati (N.L.)	1B	133	480	69	151	33	2	20	85	.315	52	80	1	1064	60	6	.995
Major League totals (3 years)			380	1376	216	430	96	6	52	236	.313	156	213	2	2896	151	16	.995

ALL-STAR GAME RECORD

Year	League	Pos.	AB	R	H	2B	3B	HR	RBI	Avg.	BB	SO	SB	PO	A	E	Avg.
1999—	National....................	1B	1	0	0	0	0	0	0	.000	0	0	0	4	0	0	1.000

CASIMIRO, CARLOS — 2B

PERSONAL: Born November 8, 1976, in San Pedro de Macoris, Dominican Republic. ... 5-11/179. ... Bats right, throws right. ... Full name: Carlos Rafael Casimiro.

TRANSACTIONS/CAREER NOTES: Signed as non-drafted free agent by Baltimore Orioles organization (April 15, 1994). ... On Bowie disabled list (April 7-21, 2000). ... Released by Orioles (November 1, 2000).

STATISTICAL NOTES: Led Eastern League second basemen with 281 putouts and 631 total chances. ... Tied for Eastern League lead with 87 double plays by second baseman in 1999.

Year Team (League)	Pos.	G	AB	R	H	2B	3B	HR	RBI	Avg.	BB	SO	SB	PO	A	E	Avg.
1994—Dom. Orioles (DSL)....	IF	41	157	27	30	6	1	3	22	.191	28	41	14	64	76	19	.881
1995—GC Orioles (GCL)....	2B-SS	32	107	14	27	4	2	2	11	.252	10	22	1	48	81	13	.908
1996—Bluefield (Appl.)	2B-3B	62	239	51	66	16	0	10	33	.276	20	52	22	103	131	13	.947
1997—Delmarva (S.Atl.)........	2B	122	457	54	111	21	8	9	51	.243	26	108	20	204	287	21	.959
1998—Frederick (Caro.)	2B-3B-SS	131	478	44	113	23	9	15	61	.236	25	98	10	243	352	23	.963
1999—Bowie (East.)	2B-DH-3B	139	526	73	116	23	1	18	64	.221	39	101	7	†281	333	20	.968
2000—Bowie (East.)	3B	87	290	44	76	12	2	6	32	.262	23	66	2	68	158	30	.883
— Baltimore (A.L.)	DH	2	8	0	1	1	0	0	3	.125	0	2	0	0	0	0	...
— Rochester (I.L.)	2B-3B	24	81	9	18	4	0	4	10	.222	4	16	0	29	50	4	.952
Major League totals (1 year)		2	8	0	1	1	0	0	3	.125	0	2	0	0	0	0	...

CASTILLA, VINNY — 3B — DEVIL RAYS

PERSONAL: Born July 4, 1967, in Oaxaca, Mexico. ... 6-1/205. ... Bats right, throws right. ... Full name: Vinicio Soria Castilla. ... Name pronounced kass-TEE-uh.

HIGH SCHOOL: Instituto Carlos Gracida (Oaxaca, Mexico).

COLLEGE: Benito Suarez.

TRANSACTIONS/CAREER NOTES: Signed as non-drafted free agent by Saltillo of Mexican League (1987). ... Contract sold by Saltillo to Atlanta Braves organization (March 19, 1990). ... Selected by Colorado Rockies in second round (40th pick overall) of expansion draft (November 17, 1992). ... On disabled list (May 20-June 4, 1993). ... Traded by Rockies to Tampa Bay Devil Rays for P Rolando Arrojo and IF Aaron Ledesma (December 13, 1999). ... On Tampa Bay disabled list (March 25-April 11, June 14-July 3 and July 30-September 4, 2000); included rehabilitation assignment to Durham (July 1-3).

HONORS: Named third baseman on THE SPORTING NEWS N.L. All-Star team (1995 and 1997-98). ... Named third baseman on THE SPORTING NEWS N.L. Silver Slugger team (1995 and 1997-98).

STATISTICAL NOTES: Led International League shortstops with 550 total chances and 72 double plays in 1992. ... Led N.L. third basemen with 506 total chances and 43 double plays in 1996. ... Had 22-game hitting streak (August 9-September 1, 1997). ... Led N.L. third basemen with 41 double plays in 1997. ... Hit three home runs in one game (June 5, 1999). ... Career major league grand slams: 2.

MISCELLANEOUS: Holds Colorado Rockies all-time record for most home runs (203).

Year Team (League)	Pos.	G	AB	R	H	2B	3B	HR	RBI	Avg.	BB	SO	SB	PO	A	E	Avg.
1987—Saltillo (Mex.)............	3B	13	27	0	5	2	0	0	1	.185	0	5	0	10	31	1	.976
1988—Salt.-Monc. (Mex.)■ ..	SS	50	124	22	30	2	2	5	18	.242	8	29	1	53	105	13	.924
1989—Saltillo (Mex.)■	SS-3B	128	462	70	142	25	13	10	58	.307	33	70	11	224	427	34	.950
1990—Sumter (S.Atl.)■........	SS	93	339	47	91	15	2	9	53	.268	28	54	2	139	320	23	.952
— Greenville (Sou.)	SS	46	170	20	40	5	1	4	16	.235	13	23	4	71	167	7	.971
1991—Greenville (Sou.)	SS	66	259	34	70	17	3	7	44	.270	9	35	0	86	221	11	.965
— Richmond (I.L.)	SS	67	240	25	54	7	4	7	36	.225	14	32	1	93	208	12	.962
— Atlanta (N.L.)..............	SS	12	5	1	1	0	0	0	0	.200	0	2	0	6	6	0	1.000
1992—Richmond (I.L.)	SS	127	449	49	113	29	1	7	44	.252	21	68	1	162	357	*31	.944
— Atlanta (N.L.)..............	SS-3B	9	16	1	4	1	0	0	1	.250	1	4	0	2	12	1	.933
1993—Colorado (N.L.)■	SS	105	337	36	86	9	7	9	30	.255	13	45	2	141	282	11	.975
1994—Colorado (N.L.) SS-2B-3B-1B		52	130	16	43	11	1	3	18	.331	7	23	2	67	78	2	.986
— Colo. Springs (PCL) ..	3B-2B-SS	22	78	13	19	6	1	1	11	.244	7	11	0	20	60	3	.964
1995—Colorado (N.L.)	3B-SS	139	527	82	163	34	2	32	90	.309	30	87	2	86	264	15	.959
1996—Colorado (N.L.)	3B	160	629	97	191	34	0	40	113	.304	35	88	7	97	*389	20	.960
1997—Colorado (N.L.)	3B	159	612	94	186	25	2	40	113	.304	44	108	2	112	*323	21	.954
1998—Colorado (N.L.)	3B-SS	•162	645	108	206	28	4	46	144	.319	40	89	5	110	316	13	.970
1999—Colorado (N.L.)	3B	158	615	83	169	24	1	33	102	.275	53	75	2	96	298	19	.954
2000—Tampa Bay (A.L.)■.....	3B	85	331	22	73	9	1	6	42	.221	14	41	1	50	185	8	.967
— Durham (I.L.)	3B	2	8	1	3	1	0	1	3	.375	0	1	0	0	2	0	1.000
American League totals (1 year)		85	331	22	73	9	1	6	42	.221	14	41	1	50	185	8	.967
National League totals (9 years)		956	3516	518	1049	166	17	203	611	.298	223	521	22	717	1968	102	.963
Major League totals (10 years)		1041	3847	540	1122	175	18	209	653	.292	237	562	23	767	2153	110	.964

DIVISION SERIES RECORD

Year Team (League)	Pos.	G	AB	R	H	2B	3B	HR	RBI	Avg.	BB	SO	SB	PO	A	E	Avg.
1995—Colorado (N.L.)	3B	4	15	3	7	1	0	3	6	.467	0	1	0	3	13	1	.941

ALL-STAR GAME RECORD

Year League	Pos.	AB	R	H	2B	3B	HR	RBI	Avg.	BB	SO	SB	PO	A	E	Avg.
1995—National	3B	2	0	0	0	0	0	0	.000	0	1	0	0	0	0	...
1998—National	3B	2	0	0	0	0	0	0	.000	0	0	0	0	2	0	1.000
All-Star Game totals (2 years)		4	0	0	0	0	0	0	.000	0	1	0	0	2	0	1.000

CASTILLO, ALBERTO — C — BLUE JAYS

PERSONAL: Born February 10, 1970, in San Juan de la Maguana, Dominican Republic. ... 6-0/185. ... Bats right, throws right. ... Full name: Alberto Terrero Castillo.

HIGH SCHOOL: Mercedes Maria Mateo (Dominican Republic).

TRANSACTIONS/CAREER NOTES: Signed as non-drafted free agent by New York Mets organization (April 15, 1987). ... On disabled list (July 3, 1992-remainder of season; and June 1-July 13, 1994). ... On suspended list (August 27-29, 1994). ... Granted free agency (October 15, 1998). ... Signed by Philadelphia Phillies organization (November 5, 1998). ... Selected by St. Louis Cardinals from Phillies organization in Rule 5 major league draft (December 14, 1998). ... Traded by Cardinals with P Lance Painter and P Matt DeWitt to Toronto Blue Jays for P Pat Hentgen and P Paul Spoljaric (November 11, 1999).

STATISTICAL NOTES: Led International League catchers with 827 total chances and nine double plays in 1996.

							BATTING								FIELDING			
Year Team (League)	Pos.	G	AB	R	H	2B	3B	HR	RBI	Avg.	BB	SO	SB	PO	A	E	Avg.
1987— Kingsport (Appl.)	C	7	9	1	1	0	0	0	0	.111	5	3	1	21	4	0	1.000
1988— GC Mets (GCL)	C	22	68	7	18	4	0	0	10	.265	4	4	2	126	13	1	.993
— Kingsport (Appl.)	C	24	75	7	22	3	0	1	14	.293	15	14	0	161	18	5	.973
1989— Kingsport (Appl.)	C-1B	27	74	15	19	4	0	3	12	.257	11	14	2	140	19	1	.994
— Pittsfield (NY-Penn)	C	34	123	13	29	8	0	1	13	.236	7	26	2	186	26	2	.991
— St. Lucie (FSL)		1	0	0	0	0	0	0	0	...	0	0	0	0	0	0	...
1990— Columbia (S.Atl.)	C	30	103	8	24	4	3	1	14	.233	10	21	1	187	22	5	.977
— Pittsfield (NY-Penn)	C-OF-1B	58	187	19	41	8	1	4	24	.219	26	35	3	378	61	9	.980
1991— Columbia (S.Atl.)	C	90	267	35	74	20	3	3	47	.277	43	44	6	*734	86	15	.982
1992— St. Lucie (FSL)	C	60	162	11	33	6	0	3	17	.204	16	37	0	317	40	12	.967
1993— St. Lucie (FSL)	C	105	333	37	86	21	0	5	42	.258	28	46	0	*604	80	12	.983
1994— Binghamton (East.)	C-1B	90	315	33	78	14	0	7	42	.248	41	46	1	643	54	6	.991
1995— Norfolk (I.L.)	C-DH	69	217	23	58	13	1	4	31	.267	26	32	2	469	44	7	.987
— New York (N.L.)	C	13	29	2	3	0	0	0	0	.103	3	9	1	66	9	2	.974
1996— New York (N.L.)	C	6	11	1	4	0	0	0	0	.364	0	4	0	23	0	0	1.000
— Norfolk (I.L.)	C	113	341	34	71	12	1	11	39	.208	39	67	2	*747	*72	8	.990
1997— New York (N.L.)	C	35	59	3	12	1	0	0	7	.203	9	16	0	142	8	2	.987
— Norfolk (I.L.)	C-OF	34	83	4	18	1	0	1	8	.217	17	16	1	197	16	7	.968
1998— New York (N.L.)	C-DH	38	83	13	17	4	0	2	7	.205	9	17	0	193	15	4	.990
— Norfolk (I.L.)	C-OF	21	49	4	9	2	0	1	6	.184	11	12	0	110	6	1	.991
1999— St. Louis (N.L.)■	C	93	255	21	67	8	0	4	31	.263	24	48	0	514	38	5	.991
2000— Toronto (A.L.)■	C	66	185	14	39	7	0	1	16	.211	21	36	0	372	31	3	.993
American League totals (1 year)		66	185	14	39	7	0	1	16	.211	21	36	0	372	31	3	.993
National League totals (5 years)		185	437	40	103	13	0	6	45	.236	45	94	1	938	70	11	.989
Major League totals (6 years)		251	622	54	142	20	0	7	61	.228	66	130	1	1310	101	14	.990

CASTILLO, FRANK — P — RED SOX

PERSONAL: Born April 1, 1969, in El Paso, Texas. ... 6-1/200. ... Throws right, bats right. ... Full name: Frank Anthony Castillo.

HIGH SCHOOL: Eastwood (El Paso, Texas).

TRANSACTIONS/CAREER NOTES: Selected by Chicago Cubs organization in sixth round of free-agent draft (June 2, 1987). ... On disabled list (April 1-July 23, 1988). ... On Iowa disabled list (April 12-June 6, 1991). ... On Chicago disabled list (August 11-27, 1991). ... On suspended list (September 20-24, 1993). ... On Chicago disabled list (March 20-May 12, 1994; included rehabilitation assignments to Daytona (April 24), Orlando (April 25-May 2) and Iowa (May 2-10). ... On Iowa disabled list (June 21-July 1, 1994). ... Traded by Cubs to Colorado Rockies for P Matt Pool (July 15, 1997). ... Granted free agency (October 30, 1997). ... Signed by Detroit Tigers (December 11, 1997). ... On Detroit disabled list (March 24-April 28, 1998; included rehabilitation assignment to Lakeland (April 18-28). ... Granted free agency (October 27, 1998). ... Signed by Arizona Diamondbacks organization (January 12, 1999). ... Released by Diamondbacks (March 27, 1999). ... Signed by Pittsburgh Pirates organization (April 20, 1999). ... Granted free agency (October 15, 1999). ... Signed by Toronto Blue Jays organization (December 21, 1999). ... On disabled list (August 14-September 16, 2000). ... Granted free agency (October 31, 2000). ... Signed by Boston Red Sox (December 7, 2000).

HONORS: Named Appalachian League Player of the Year (1987).

STATISTICAL NOTES: Pitched 4-0 no-hit victory against Huntsville (July 13, 1990, first game). ... Pitched 7-0 one-hit, complete-game victory against St. Louis (September 25, 1995).

Year League	W	L	Pct.	ERA	G	GS	CG	ShO	Sv.	IP	H	R	ER	BB	SO
1987— Wytheville (Appl.)	*10	1	*.909	2.29	12	12	•5	0	0	90 1/3	86	31	23	21	83
— Geneva (NY-Penn)	1	0	1.000	0.00	1	1	0	0	0	6	3	1	0	1	6
1988— Peoria (Midw.)	6	1	.857	0.71	9	8	2	2	0	51	25	5	4	10	58
1989— Winston-Salem (Caro.)	9	6	.600	2.51	18	18	8	1	0	129 1/3	118	42	36	24	114
— Charlotte (Sou.)	3	4	.429	3.84	10	10	4	0	0	68	73	35	29	12	43
1990— Charlotte (Sou.)	6	6	.500	3.88	18	18	4	1	0	111 1/3	113	54	48	27	112
1991— Iowa (A.A.)	3	1	.750	2.52	4	4	1	1	0	25	20	7	7	7	20
— Chicago (N.L.)	6	7	.462	4.35	18	18	4	0	0	111 2/3	107	56	54	33	73
1992— Chicago (N.L.)	10	11	.476	3.46	33	33	0	0	0	205 1/3	179	91	79	63	135
1993— Chicago (N.L.)	5	8	.385	4.84	29	25	2	0	0	141 1/3	162	83	76	39	84
1994— Daytona (FSL)	0	1	.000	4.50	1	1	0	0	0	4	7	3	2	0	1
— Orlando (Sou.)	1	0	1.000	1.29	1	1	0	0	0	7	4	2	1	1	2
— Iowa (A.A.)	4	2	.667	3.27	11	11	0	0	0	66	57	30	24	10	64
— Chicago (N.L.)	2	1	.667	4.30	4	4	1	0	0	23	25	13	11	5	19
1995— Chicago (N.L.)	11	10	.524	3.21	29	29	2	2	0	188	179	75	67	52	135
1996— Chicago (N.L.)	7	•16	.304	5.28	33	33	1	1	0	182 1/3	209	112	107	46	139
1997— Chicago (N.L.)	6	9	.400	5.42	20	19	0	0	0	98	113	64	59	44	67
— Colorado (N.L.)■	6	3	.667	5.42	14	14	0	0	0	86 1/3	107	57	52	25	59
1998— Lakeland (FSL)■	1	0	1.000	0.00	1	1	0	0	0	5	2	0	0	0	4
— Detroit (A.L.)	3	9	.250	6.83	27	19	0	0	1	116	150	91	88	44	81
1999— Nashville (PCL)■	7	5	.583	4.68	19	19	0	0	0	119 1/3	139	72	62	32	90
2000— Toronto (A.L.)■	10	5	.667	3.59	25	24	0	0	0	138	112	58	55	56	104
A.L. totals (2 years)	13	14	.481	5.07	52	43	0	0	1	254	262	149	143	100	185
N.L. totals (7 years)	53	65	.449	4.39	180	175	10	3	0	1036	1081	551	505	307	711
Major League totals (9 years)	66	79	.455	4.52	232	218	10	3	1	1290	1343	700	648	407	896

CASTILLO, LUIS   2B   MARLINS

PERSONAL: Born September 12, 1975, in San Pedro de Macoris, Dominican Republic. ... 5-11/175. ... Bats both, throws right. ... Full name: Luis Antonio Donato Castillo.

HIGH SCHOOL: Colegio San Benito Abad (San Pedro de Macoris, Dominican Republic).

TRANSACTIONS/CAREER NOTES: Signed as non-drafted free agent by Florida Marlins organization (August 19, 1992). ... On Kane County disabled list (July 20-September 11, 1995). ... On Florida disabled list (May 7-22, 1997). ... On Florida disabled list (April 16-May 5, 2000); included rehabilitation assignment to Calgary (April 28-May 5).

STATISTICAL NOTES: Led Gulf Coast League in caught stealing with 12 in 1994. ... Led Gulf Coast League second basemen with 142 putouts, 318 total chances, 40 double plays and .972 fielding percentage in 1994. ... Led Eastern League in caught stealing with 28 in 1996. ... Led Eastern League second basemen with 557 total chances and 87 double plays in 1996. ... Led International League in caught stealing with 15 in 1998. ... Had 22-game hitting streak (August 9-September 3, 1999). ... Had 19-game hitting streak (July 3-28, 2000). ... Led N.L. in caught stealing with 22 in 2000.

MISCELLANEOUS: Holds Florida Marlins all-time record for stolen bases (148).

									BATTING						FIELDING		
Year	Team (League)	Pos.	G	AB	R	H	2B	3B	HR	RBI	Avg.	BB	SO	SB	PO	A	E	Avg.
1993— Dom. Marlins (DSL) ...		IF	69	266	48	75	7	1	4	31	.282	36	22	21	151	180	20	.943
1994— GC Marlins (GCL)		2B-SS	57	216	49	57	8	0	0	16	.264	37	36	31	†144	170	9	†.972
1995— Kane County (Midw.)...		2B	89	340	71	111	4	4	0	23	.326	55	50	41	193	241	17	.962
1996— Portland (East.)		2B	109	420	83	133	15	7	1	35	.317	66	68	*51	217	*326	14	*.975
— Florida (N.L.)		2B	41	164	26	43	2	1	1	8	.262	14	46	17	99	118	3	.986
1997— Florida (N.L.)		2B	75	263	27	63	8	0	0	8	.240	27	53	16	129	177	9	.971
— Charlotte (I.L.)		2B	37	130	25	46	5	0	0	5	.354	16	22	8	66	97	5	.970
1998— Charlotte (I.L.)...........		2B	100	381	74	109	11	2	0	15	.286	75	68	41	232	281	16	.970
— Florida (N.L.)		2B	44	153	21	31	3	2	1	10	.203	22	33	3	117	113	7	.970
1999— Florida (N.L.)		2B	128	487	76	147	23	4	0	28	.302	67	85	50	257	343	15	.976
2000— Florida (N.L.)		2B	136	539	101	180	17	3	2	17	.334	78	86	*62	282	365	11	.983
— Calgary (PCL)............		2B	4	13	4	4	1	1	0	0	.308	4	2	1	7	10	1	.944
Major League totals (5 years)			424	1606	251	464	53	10	4	71	.289	208	303	148	884	1116	45	.978

CASTRO, JUAN   IF   REDS

PERSONAL: Born June 20, 1972, in Los Mochis, Mexico. ... 5-10/187. ... Bats right, throws right. ... Full name: Juan Gabriel Castro.

HIGH SCHOOL: CBTIS 43 (Los Mochis, Mexico).

TRANSACTIONS/CAREER NOTES: Signed as non-drafted free agent by Los Angeles Dodgers organization (June 13, 1991). ... On Los Angeles disabled list (June 5-August 1, 1997). ... Traded by Dodgers to Cincinnati Reds for a player to be named later and cash (April 1, 2000); Dodgers acquired P Kenny Lutz to complete deal (June 8, 2000).

STATISTICAL NOTES: Tied for Texas League lead in double plays by shortstop with 82 in 1994.

									BATTING						FIELDING		
Year	Team (League)	Pos.	G	AB	R	H	2B	3B	HR	RBI	Avg.	BB	SO	SB	PO	A	E	Avg.
1991— Great Falls (Pio.)		SS-2B	60	217	36	60	4	2	1	27	.276	33	31	7	90	155	21	.921
1992— Bakersfield (Calif.)		SS	113	446	56	116	15	4	4	42	.260	37	64	14	180	309	38	.928
1993— San Antonio (Texas) ...		SS-2B	118	424	55	117	23	8	7	41	.276	30	40	12	169	314	28	.945
1994— San Antonio (Texas) ...		SS	123	445	55	128	25	4	4	44	.288	31	66	4	187	377	29	.951
1995— Albuquerque (PCL)......		SS-2B	104	341	51	91	18	4	3	43	.267	20	42	4	152	344	14	.973
— Los Angeles (N.L.)		3B-SS	11	4	0	1	0	0	0	0	.250	1	1	0	3	7	0	1.000
1996— Albuquerque (PCL)......		3B-SS-2B	17	56	12	21	4	2	1	8	.375	6	7	1	17	33	2	.962
— Los Angeles (N.L.)		S-3-2-0	70	132	16	26	5	3	0	5	.197	10	27	1	54	84	3	.979
1997— Albuquerque (PCL)......		SS-2B	27	101	11	31	5	2	2	11	.307	4	20	1	33	83	9	.928
— Los Angeles (N.L.)		SS-2B-3B	40	75	3	11	3	1	0	4	.147	7	20	0	36	65	1	.990
1998— Los Angeles (N.L.)		SS-2B-3B	89	220	25	43	7	0	2	14	.195	15	37	0	95	182	10	.965
1999— Albuquerque (PCL)......		S-3-2-DH	116	423	52	116	25	4	7	51	.274	34	70	2	126	286	19	.956
— Los Angeles (N.L.)		2B-SS	2	1	0	0	0	0	0	0	.000	0	1	0	1	4	0	1.000
2000— Louisville (I.L.)■.........		SS-2B-3B	19	60	9	19	5	1	2	10	.317	12	12	0	28	58	4	.956
— Cincinnati (N.L.)		SS-2B-3B	82	224	20	54	12	2	4	23	.241	14	33	0	102	165	2	.993
Major League totals (6 years)			294	656	64	135	27	6	6	46	.206	47	119	1	291	507	16	.980

DIVISION SERIES RECORD

									BATTING						FIELDING		
Year	Team (League)	Pos.	G	AB	R	H	2B	3B	HR	RBI	Avg.	BB	SO	SB	PO	A	E	Avg.
1996— Los Angeles (N.L.)		2B	2	5	0	1	1	0	0	1	.200	1	1	0	4	3	0	1.000

CASTRO, NELSON   SS   GIANTS

PERSONAL: Born June 4, 1976, in Monte Cristi, Dominican Republic. ... 5-10/190. ... Bats right, throws right. ... Full name: Nelson Daniel Castro Reynoso.

TRANSACTIONS/CAREER NOTES: Signed as non-drafted free agent by California Angels organization (January 14, 1994). ... Angels franchise renamed Anaheim Angels for 1997 season. ... Claimed on waivers by San Francisco Giants (October 13, 1999).

STATISTICAL NOTES: Led Arizona League shortstops with 297 total chances and 32 double plays in 1997. ... Led Northwest League shortstops with 323 total chances in 1997. ... Led California League shortstops with 591 total chances and 71 double plays in 1998. ... Led California League shortstops with 74 double plays in 1999.

									BATTING						FIELDING		
Year	Team (League)	Pos.	G	AB	R	H	2B	3B	HR	RBI	Avg.	BB	SO	SB	PO	A	E	Avg.
1995— Arizona Angels (Ariz.).		SS	55	190	34	37	1	2	0	22	.195	27	50	15	*106	*173	18	.939
1996— Boise (N'West)		PH	1	1	0	0	0	0	0	0	.000	0	0	0	...	...	...	...
— Arizona Angels (Ariz.).		SS	53	222	31	38	4	3	3	14	.171	32	42	25	75	164	14	.945
1997— Boise (N'West)		SS	69	293	74	86	16	1	7	37	.294	38	53	26	80	218	25	*.923
1998— Lake Elsinore (Calif.) ..		SS	131	470	73	110	16	4	4	41	.234	40	101	36	•185	*372	34	.942
1999— Lake Elsinore (Calif.) ..		SS	125	444	68	111	16	12	1	50	.250	36	75	*53	210	*370	23	*.962
2000— Bakersfield (Calif.)■...		SS	53	218	38	62	14	3	5	41	.284	20	40	27	97	145	12	.953
— Fresno (PCL)..............		SS	67	244	27	62	7	2	5	20	.254	14	51	10	78	201	23	.924

CASTRO, RAMON   C   MARLINS

PERSONAL: Born March 1, 1976, in Vega Baja, Puerto Rico. ... 6-3/225. ... Bats right, throws right. ... Full name: Ramon Abraham Castro.
HIGH SCHOOL: Lino P. Rivera (Vega Baja, Puerto Rico).
TRANSACTIONS/CAREER NOTES: Selected by Houston Astros organization in first round (17th pick overall) of free-agent draft (June 2, 1994). ... On Jackson disabled list (April 27-May 15, 1998). ... Traded by Astros to Florida Marlins for P Jay Powell and C Scott Makarewicz (July 6, 1998). ... On Calgary disabled list (April 20-May 5, 2000).

								BATTING									FIELDING			
Year	Team (League)	Pos.	G	AB	R	H	2B	3B	HR	RBI	Avg.	BB	SO	SB	PO	A	E	Avg.
1994—	GC Astros (GCL)	C	37	123	17	34	7	0	3	14	.276	17	14	5	210	24	4	.983
1995—	Kissimmee (FSL)	C	36	120	6	25	5	0	8	8	.208	6	21	0	184	18	7	.967
—	Auburn (NY-Penn)	C	63	224	40	67	17	0	9	49	.299	24	27	0	297	46	2	.994
1996—	Quad City (Midw.)	C	96	314	38	78	15	0	7	43	.248	31	61	2	660	82	10	.987
1997—	Kissimmee (FSL)	C	115	410	53	115	22	1	8	65	.280	53	73	1	630	88	6	*.992
1998—	Jackson (Texas)	C	48	168	27	43	6	0	8	25	.256	13	31	0	329	40	10	.974
—	Portland (East.)■	C	31	88	9	22	3	0	3	11	.250	8	21	0	82	5	5	.946
1999—	Calgary (PCL)	C-DH	97	349	43	90	22	0	15	61	.258	24	64	0	552	67	7	.989
—	Florida (N.L.)	C	24	67	4	12	4	0	2	4	.179	10	14	0	105	17	1	.992
2000—	Calgary (PCL)	C	67	218	44	73	22	0	14	45	.335	16	38	0	360	32	4	.990
—	Florida (N.L.)	C	50	138	10	33	4	0	2	14	.239	16	36	0	274	24	6	.980
Major League totals (2 years)			74	205	14	45	8	0	4	18	.220	26	50	0	379	41	7	.984

CATALANOTTO, FRANK   IF   RANGERS

PERSONAL: Born April 27, 1974, in Smithtown, N.Y. ... 6-0/195. ... Bats left, throws right. ... Full name: Frank John Catalanotto.
HIGH SCHOOL: Smithtown (N.Y.) East.
COLLEGE: C.W. Post (Brookville, N.Y.).
TRANSACTIONS/CAREER NOTES: Selected by Detroit Tigers organization in 10th round of free-agent draft (June 1, 1992). ... Selected by Oakland Athletics from Tigers organization in Rule 5 major league draft (December 9, 1996). ... Returned to Tigers organization (March 21, 1997). ... On Toledo disabled list (June 18-25, 1998). ... Traded by Tigers with P Justin Thompson, P Francisco Cordero, OF Gabe Kapler, C Bill Haselman and P Alan Webb to Texas Rangers for OF Juan Gonzalez, P Danny Patterson and C Gregg Zaun (November 2, 1999). ... On Texas disabled list (April 22-May 15, 2000); included rehabilitation assignment to Oklahoma (May 12-15).
STATISTICAL NOTES: Led Southern League second basemen with 681 total chances and 95 double plays in 1995. ... Led Southern League second basemen with 689 total chances and 99 double plays in 1996. ... Led International League second basemen with .984 fielding percentage in 1997. ... Career major league grand slams: 1.

								BATTING									FIELDING			
Year	Team (League)	Pos.	G	AB	R	H	2B	3B	HR	RBI	Avg.	BB	SO	SB	PO	A	E	Avg.
1992—	Bristol (Appl.)	2B	21	50	6	10	2	0	0	4	.200	8	8	0	8	6	2	.875
1993—	Bristol (Appl.)	2B	55	199	37	61	9	5	3	22	.307	15	19	3	96	128	10	.957
1994—	Fayetteville (S.Atl.)	2B	119	458	72	149	24	8	3	56	.325	37	54	4	244	304	15	.973
1995—	Jacksonville (Sou.)	2B	134	491	66	111	19	5	8	48	.226	49	56	13	252	*411	18	*.974
1996—	Jacksonville (Sou.)	2B	132	497	105	148	34	6	17	67	.298	74	69	15	246	*421	•22	.968
1997—	Toledo (I.L.)	2-3-O-DH	134	500	75	150	32	3	16	68	.300	47	80	12	168	351	18	†.966
—	Detroit (A.L.)	2B-DH	13	26	2	8	2	0	0	3	.308	3	7	0	7	9	0	1.000
1998—	Detroit (A.L.)	2-DH-1-3	89	213	23	60	13	2	6	25	.282	12	39	3	162	51	3	.986
—	Toledo (I.L.)	1B-2B-DH	28	105	20	35	6	3	4	28	.333	14	21	0	131	43	2	.989
1999—	Detroit (A.L.)	1-2-3-DH	100	286	41	79	19	0	11	35	.276	15	49	3	252	98	5	.986
2000—	Texas (A.L.)■	2-DH-1-O	103	282	55	82	13	2	10	42	.291	33	36	6	169	110	9	.969
—	Oklahoma (PCL)	OF-2B	3	11	2	3	0	0	0	1	.273	0	4	0	0	1	0	1.000
Major League totals (4 years)			305	807	121	229	47	4	27	105	.284	63	131	12	590	268	17	.981

CEDENO, ROGER   OF   TIGERS

PERSONAL: Born August 16, 1974, in Valencia, Venezuela. ... 6-1/205. ... Bats both, throws right. ... Full name: Roger Leandro Cedeno.
TRANSACTIONS/CAREER NOTES: Signed as non-drafted free agent by Los Angeles Dodgers organization (March 28, 1991). ... On disabled list (June 27-July 14, 1994). ... On Los Angeles disabled list (March 25-April 17 and August 25, 1997-remainder of season); included rehabilitation assignment to Albuquerque (April 17-21). ... On Los Angeles disabled list (March 22-April 24, 1998); included rehabilitation assignment to Vero Beach (April 16-24). ... Traded by Dodgers with C Charles Johnson to New York Mets for C Todd Hundley and P Arnold Gooch (December 1, 1998). ... Traded by Mets with P Octavio Dotel and P Kyle Kessel to Houston Astros for P Mike Hampton and OF Derek Bell (December 23, 1999). ... On Houston disabled list (May 26-August 18, 2000); included rehabilitation assignment to New Orleans (August 10-18). ... Traded by Astros with C Mitch Meluskey and P Chris Holt to Detroit Tigers for C Brad Ausmus, P Doug Brocail and P Nelson Cruz (December 11, 2000).
STATISTICAL NOTES: Tied for Pioneer League lead with three intentional bases on balls received in 1992. ... Led Texas League in caught stealing with 20 in 1993. ... Led Pacific Coast League in caught stealing with 18 in 1995.

								BATTING									FIELDING			
Year	Team (League)	Pos.	G	AB	R	H	2B	3B	HR	RBI	Avg.	BB	SO	SB	PO	A	E	Avg.
1991—	Dom. Dodgers (DSL)	OF	58	209	25	50	1	1	0	7	.239	0	0	26	...	...	...	...
1992—	Great Falls (Pio.)	OF	69	256	60	81	6	5	2	27	.316	51	53	*40	113	6	8	.937
1993—	San Antonio (Texas)	OF	122	465	70	134	12	8	4	30	.288	45	90	28	213	6	9	.961
—	Albuquerque (PCL)	OF	6	18	1	4	1	1	0	4	.222	3	3	0	12	0	1	.923
1994—	Albuquerque (PCL)	OF	104	383	84	123	18	5	4	49	.321	51	57	30	194	7	8	.962
1995—	Albuquerque (PCL)	OF-DH	99	367	67	112	19	9	2	44	.305	53	56	23	189	3	3	.985
—	Los Angeles (N.L.)	OF	40	42	4	10	2	0	0	3	.238	3	10	1	43	0	1	.977
1996—	Los Angeles (N.L.)	OF	86	211	26	52	11	1	2	18	.246	24	47	5	117	2	2	.983
—	Albuquerque (PCL)	OF	33	125	16	28	2	3	1	10	.224	15	22	6	71	2	0	1.000
1997—	Los Angeles (N.L.)	OF	80	194	31	53	10	2	3	17	.273	25	44	9	148	1	2	.987
—	Albuquerque (PCL)	OF	29	113	21	40	4	4	2	9	.354	22	16	5	53	1	2	.964
1998—	Vero Beach (FSL)	OF	6	21	5	9	0	1	1	6	.429	5	5	1	14	0	1	.933
—	Los Angeles (N.L.)	OF	105	240	33	58	11	1	2	17	.242	27	57	8	86	4	2	.978

						BATTING										FIELDING		
Year	Team (League)	Pos.	G	AB	R	H	2B	3B	HR	RBI	Avg.	BB	SO	SB	PO	A	E	Avg.
1999— New York (N.L.)■	OF-2B	155	453	90	142	23	4	4	36	.313	60	100	66	256	9	3	.989
2000— Houston (N.L.)■	OF	74	259	54	73	2	5	6	26	.282	43	47	25	135	1	3	.978
— New Orleans (PCL)....	OF	6	20	2	7	0	1	0	3	.350	2	5	1	6	0	0	1.000
Major League totals (6 years)		540	1399	238	388	59	13	17	117	.277	182	305	114	785	17	13	.984

DIVISION SERIES RECORD

						BATTING										FIELDING		
Year	Team (League)	Pos.	G	AB	R	H	2B	3B	HR	RBI	Avg.	BB	SO	SB	PO	A	E	Avg.
1999— New York (N.L.).........	OF-PH	4	7	1	2	0	0	0	2	.286	1	1	1	4	0	0	1.000

CHAMPIONSHIP SERIES RECORD

						BATTING										FIELDING		
Year	Team (League)	Pos.	G	AB	R	H	2B	3B	HR	RBI	Avg.	BB	SO	SB	PO	A	E	Avg.
1999— New York (N.L.).........	OF-PR	5	12	2	6	1	0	0	1	.500	0	1	2	12	0	0	1.000

CHACON, SHAWN   P   ROCKIES

PERSONAL: Born December 23, 1977, in Anchorage, Alaska. ... 6-3/212. ... Throws right, bats right. ... Full name: Shawn A. Chacon.
HIGH SCHOOL: Greeley (Colo.) Central.
TRANSACTIONS/CAREER NOTES: Selected by Colorado Rockies organization in third round of free-agent draft (June 4, 1996).

Year	League	W	L	Pct.	ERA	G	GS	CG	ShO	Sv.	IP	H	R	ER	BB	SO
1996— Arizona Rockies (Ariz.).......	1	2	.333	*1.60	11	11	1	0	0	56 1/3	46	17	10	15	64
— Portland (N'West)	0	2	.000	6.86	4	4	0	0	0	19 2/3	24	18	15	9	17
1997— Asheville (S.Atl.).................	11	7	.611	3.89	28	27	1	0	0	162	155	80	70	63	149
1998— Salem (Caro.)...................	0	4	.000	5.30	12	12	0	0	0	56	53	35	33	31	54
1999— Salem (Caro.)	5	5	.500	4.13	12	12	0	0	0	72	69	44	33	34	66
2000— Carolina (Sou.)	10	10	.500	3.16	27	27	4	*3	0	173 2/3	151	71	61	*85	*172

CHARLES, FRANK   C   ASTROS

PERSONAL: Born February 23, 1969, in Fontana, Calif. ... 6-4/210. ... Bats right, throws right. ... Full name: Franklin Scott Charles.
HIGH SCHOOL: Montclair Prep (Van Nuys, Calif.).
COLLEGE: Pepperdine, then Cal State-Fullerton.
TRANSACTIONS/CAREER NOTES: Selected by San Francisco Giants organization in 17th round of free-agent draft (June 3, 1991). ... Released by Giants (March 29, 1993). ... Signed by St. Paul, Northern League (1993). ... Contract purchased by Texas Rangers organization from St. Paul (March 1, 1994). ... Granted free agency (October 17, 1997). ... Signed by San Francisco Giants organization (March 19, 1998). ... Granted free agency (October 16, 1998). ... Signed by San Diego Padres organization (December 18, 1998). ... Granted free agency (October 15, 1999). ... Signed by Houston Astros organization (January 21, 2000).
STATISTICAL NOTES: Tied for Northern League lead in double plays by catcher with seven in 1993. ... Led Texas League first baseman with 1,200 total chances, 19 errors and 117 double plays in 1995.

						BATTING										FIELDING		
Year	Team (League)	Pos.	G	AB	R	H	2B	3B	HR	RBI	Avg.	BB	SO	SB	PO	A	E	Avg.
1991— Everett (N'West)	C-1B	62	239	31	76	17	1	9	49	.318	21	55	1	398	45	12	.974
1992— Clinton (Midw.)	C	2	5	1	0	0	0	0	0	.000	0	3	0	14	0	0	1.000
— San Jose (Calif.).........	C-1B	87	286	27	83	16	1	0	34	.290	11	61	4	387	33	12	.972
1993— St. Paul (Nor.)■	C	58	216	27	59	13	0	2	37	.273	11	33	5	380	*48	7	.984
1994— Charlotte (FSL)■..........	C-1B	79	254	23	67	17	1	2	33	.264	16	52	2	505	48	12	.979
1995— Tulsa (Texas)	1B-C	126	479	51	121	24	3	13	72	.253	22	92	1	1108	73	†19	.984
1996— Oklahoma City (A.A.)..	C-1B	35	113	10	21	7	2	1	8	.186	4	29	0	188	14	7	.967
— Tulsa (Texas)	C-1B-P	41	147	18	39	6	0	5	15	.265	10	28	2	42	2	0	1.000
1997— Tulsa (Texas) C-1B-3B-OF	95	335	38	77	18	2	9	49	.230	24	81	2	395	51	11	.976
1998— Shreveport (Texas)■..	C-1B	108	411	49	118	39	1	12	66	.287	18	93	0	789	69	14	.984
— Fresno (PCL).............	C	4	10	2	5	0	0	1	1	.500	1	2	0	24	2	1	.963
1999— Las Vegas (PCL) C-1B-3B-OF	80	272	25	67	19	2	2	28	.246	10	61	2	360	42	10	.976
2000— New Orleans (PCL)■...	C-1B-3B	84	284	29	74	10	3	5	37	.261	21	62	1	455	57	13	.975
— Houston (N.L.)...........	C	4	7	1	3	1	0	0	2	.429	0	2	0	7	2	0	1.000
Major League totals (1 year)		4	7	1	3	1	0	0	2	.429	0	2	0	7	2	0	1.000

RECORD AS PITCHER

Year	League	W	L	Pct.	ERA	G	GS	CG	ShO	Sv.	IP	H	R	ER	BB	SO
1996— Tulsa (Texas)	0	0	...	9.00	0	0	0	0	0	1	1	1	1	0	0

CHARLTON, NORM   P   MARINERS

PERSONAL: Born January 6, 1963, in Fort Polk, La. ... 6-3/205. ... Throws left, bats both. ... Full name: Norman Wood Charlton III.
HIGH SCHOOL: James Madison (San Antonio).
COLLEGE: Rice.
TRANSACTIONS/CAREER NOTES: Selected by Montreal Expos organization in supplemental round ("sandwich pick" between first and second round, 28th pick overall) of free-agent draft (June 4, 1984); pick received as compensation for San Francisco Giants signing Type B free-agent 2B Manny Trillo. ... Traded by Expos with a player to be named later to Cincinnati Reds for IF Wayne Krenchicki (March 31, 1986); Reds acquired 2B Tim Barker to complete deal (April 2, 1986). ... On Cincinnati disabled list (April 6-June 26, 1987); included rehabilitation assignment to Nashville (June 9-26). ... On disabled list (May 26-June 11 and June 17-July 19, 1991). ... On suspended list (September 29 and October 4-6, 1991). ... Traded by Reds to Seattle Mariners for OF Kevin Mitchell (November 17, 1992). ... On suspended list (July 9-16, 1993). ... On disabled list (July 21-August 5 and August 8, 1993-remainder of season). ... Granted free agency (November 18, 1993). ... Signed by Philadelphia Phillies organization (February 3, 1994). ... On disabled list (March 31, 1994-entire season). ... Granted free agency (October 28, 1994). ... Re-signed by Phillies organization (December 22, 1994). ... Released by Phillies (July 10, 1995). ... Signed by Mariners (July 14,

1995). ... Granted free agency (November 7, 1997). ... Signed by Baltimore Orioles organization (December 15, 1997). ... Released by Orioles (July 28, 1998). ... Signed by Atlanta Braves organization (August 5, 1998). ... Granted free agency (October 27, 1998). ... Signed by Tampa Bay Devil Rays organization (January 20, 1999). ... On Durham disabled list (April 8-17, 1999). ... Granted free agency (November 2, 1999). ... Re-signed by Devil Rays organization (January 7, 2000). ... Released by Devil Rays (March 31, 2000). ... Signed by Reds organization (April 9, 2000). ... Released by Reds (April 28, 2000). ... Signed by Mariners organization (December 19, 2000).

STATISTICAL NOTES: Led American Association with 13 wild pitches in 1988.

MISCELLANEOUS: Appeared in one game as pinch runner (1990). ... Appeared in two games as pinch runner (1991).

Year League	W	L	Pct.	ERA	G	GS	CG	ShO	Sv.	IP	H	R	ER	BB	SO
1984— West Palm Beach (FSL)	1	4	.200	4.58	8	8	0	0	0	39 1/3	51	27	20	22	27
1985— West Palm Beach (FSL)	7	10	.412	4.57	24	23	5	2	0	128	135	79	65	79	71
1986— Vermont (East.)■.............	10	6	.625	2.83	22	22	6	1	0	136 2/3	109	55	43	74	96
1987— Nashville (A.A.)	2	8	.200	4.30	18	17	3	1	0	98 1/3	97	57	47	44	74
1988— Nashville (A.A.)	11	10	.524	3.02	27	27	8	1	0	182	149	69	61	56	*161
— Cincinnati (N.L.)	4	5	.444	3.96	10	10	0	0	0	61 1/3	60	27	27	20	39
1989— Cincinnati (N.L.)	8	3	.727	2.93	69	0	0	0	0	95 1/3	67	38	31	40	98
1990— Cincinnati (N.L.)	12	9	.571	2.74	56	16	1	1	2	154 1/3	131	53	47	70	117
1991— Cincinnati (N.L.)	3	5	.375	2.91	39	11	0	0	1	108 1/3	92	37	35	34	77
1992— Cincinnati (N.L.)	4	2	.667	2.99	64	0	0	0	26	81 1/3	79	39	27	26	90
1993— Seattle (A.L.)■................	1	3	.250	2.34	34	0	0	0	18	34 2/3	22	12	9	17	48
1994— Philadelphia (N.L.)							Did not play.								
1995— Philadelphia (N.L.)■	2	5	.286	7.36	25	0	0	0	0	22	23	19	18	15	12
— Seattle (A.L.)■	2	1	.667	1.51	30	0	0	0	14	47 2/3	23	12	8	16	58
1996— Seattle (A.L.)	4	7	.364	4.04	70	0	0	0	20	75 2/3	68	37	34	38	73
1997— Seattle (A.L.)	3	8	.273	7.27	71	0	0	0	14	69 1/3	89	59	56	47	55
1998— Baltimore (A.L.)■..............	2	1	.667	6.94	36	0	0	0	0	35	46	27	27	25	41
— Richmond (I.L.)■...............	0	0	...	0.00	2	0	0	0	0	2	2	0	0	0	1
— Atlanta (N.L.)	0	0	...	1.38	13	0	0	0	1	13	7	2	2	8	6
1999— Durham (I.L.)■	3	2	.600	3.69	18	0	0	0	1	31 2/3	27	13	13	10	29
— Tampa Bay (A.L.)..............	2	3	.400	4.44	42	0	0	0	0	50 2/3	49	29	25	36	45
2000— Louisville (I.L.)■	0	0	...	0.00	4	0	0	0	1	2 2/3	0	0	0	2	5
— Cincinnati (N.L.)	0	0	...	27.00	2	0	0	0	0	3	6	9	9	6	1
A.L. totals (6 years)	14	23	.378	4.57	283	0	0	0	66	313	297	176	159	179	320
N.L. totals (8 years)	33	29	.532	3.27	278	37	1	1	30	538 2/3	465	224	196	219	440
Major League totals (12 years)	47	52	.475	3.75	561	37	1	1	96	851 2/3	762	400	355	398	760

DIVISION SERIES RECORD

Year League	W	L	Pct.	ERA	G	GS	CG	ShO	Sv.	IP	H	R	ER	BB	SO
1995— Seattle (A.L.)	1	0	1.000	2.45	4	0	0	0	1	7 1/3	4	2	2	3	9
1997— Seattle (A.L.)	0	0	...	0.00	2	0	0	0	0	2 1/3	2	0	0	0	1
Division series totals (2 years)	1	0	1.000	1.86	6	0	0	0	1	9 2/3	6	2	2	3	10

CHAMPIONSHIP SERIES RECORD

Year League	W	L	Pct.	ERA	G	GS	CG	ShO	Sv.	IP	H	R	ER	BB	SO
1990— Cincinnati (N.L.)	1	1	.500	1.80	4	0	0	0	0	5	4	2	1	3	3
1995— Seattle (A.L.)	1	0	1.000	0.00	3	0	0	0	1	6	1	0	0	1	5
Champ. series totals (2 years)	2	1	.667	0.82	7	0	0	0	1	11	5	2	1	4	8

WORLD SERIES RECORD

NOTES: Member of World Series championship team (1990).

Year League	W	L	Pct.	ERA	G	GS	CG	ShO	Sv.	IP	H	R	ER	BB	SO
1990— Cincinnati (N.L.)	0	0	...	0.00	1	0	0	0	0	1	1	0	0	0	0

ALL-STAR GAME RECORD

Year League	W	L	Pct.	ERA	GS	CG	ShO	Sv.	IP	H	R	ER	BB	SO
1992— National	0	0	...	0.00	0	0	0	0	1	0	0	0	0	1

CHAVEZ, ERIC — 3B — ATHLETICS

PERSONAL: Born December 7, 1977, in Los Angeles. ... 6-0/204. ... Bats left, throws right. ... Full name: Eric Cesar Chavez.
HIGH SCHOOL: Mount Carmel (San Diego).
TRANSACTIONS/CAREER NOTES: Selected by Oakland Athletics organization in first round (10th pick overall) of free-agent draft (June 2, 1996). ... On Oakland disabled list (August 21-September 19, 1999); included rehabilitation assignment to Vancouver (September 14-19).
STATISTICAL NOTES: Had 15-game hitting streak (May 27-June 18, 2000). ... Hit for the cycle (June 21, 2000). ... Career major league grand slams: 2.

Year Team (League)	Pos.	G	AB	R	H	2B	3B	HR	RBI	Avg.	BB	SO	SB	PO	A	E	Avg.
							BATTING								FIELDING		
1997— Visalia (Calif.).............	3B-DH	134	520	67	141	30	3	18	100	.271	37	91	13	84	268	*32	.917
1998— Huntsville (Sou.)	3B-DH	88	335	66	110	27	1	22	86	.328	42	61	12	54	146	14	.935
— Edmonton (PCL)	3B-DH	47	194	38	63	18	0	11	40	.325	12	32	2	34	66	7	.935
— Oakland (A.L.)	3B	16	45	6	14	4	1	0	6	.311	3	5	1	11	21	0	1.000
1999— Oakland (A.L.)	3B-DH-SS	115	356	47	88	21	2	13	50	.247	46	56	1	69	155	9	.961
2000— Oakland (A.L.)	3B-SS-DH	153	501	89	139	23	4	26	86	.277	62	94	2	92	256	18	.951
Major League totals (3 years)		284	902	142	241	48	7	39	142	.267	111	155	4	172	432	27	.957

DIVISION SERIES RECORD

Year Team (League)	Pos.	G	AB	R	H	2B	3B	HR	RBI	Avg.	BB	SO	SB	PO	A	E	Avg.
							BATTING								FIELDING		
2000— Oakland (A.L.)	3B	5	21	4	7	3	0	0	4	.333	0	5	0	4	8	0	1.000

CHAVEZ, RAUL — C — ASTROS

PERSONAL: Born March 18, 1973, in Valencia, Venezuela. ... 5-11/210. ... Bats right, throws right. ... Full name: Raul Alexander Chavez.
TRANSACTIONS/CAREER NOTES: Signed as non-drafted free agent by Houston Astros organization (January 10, 1990). ... Traded by Astros with P Dave Veres to Montreal Expos for 3B Sean Berry (December 20, 1995). ... Traded by Expos to Seattle Mariners for OF Robert Perez (May 8, 1998). ... Granted free agency (October 15, 1999). ... Signed by Astros organization (January 5, 2000).
STATISTICAL NOTES: Tied for International League lead in double plays by catcher with nine in 1997. ... Led Pacific Coast League catchers with 12 double plays in 1998. ... Led Pacific Coast League catchers with 74 assists in 1999.

Year	Team (League)	Pos.	G	AB	R	H	2B	3B	HR	RBI	Avg.	BB	SO	SB	PO	A	E	Avg.
1990—	GC Astros (GCL)	SS-2B-3B	48	155	23	50	8	1	0	23	.323	7	12	5	67	119	9	.954
1991—	Burlington (Midw.)	SS-3B	114	420	54	108	17	0	3	41	.257	25	65	1	144	293	41	.914
1992—	Asheville (S.Atl.)	C	95	348	37	99	22	1	2	40	.284	16	39	1	456	77	13	.976
1993—	Osceola (FSL)	C	58	197	13	45	5	1	0	16	.228	8	19	1	303	62	5	.986
1994—	Jackson (Texas)	C	89	251	17	55	7	0	1	22	.219	17	41	1	*563	64	9	.986
1995—	Tucson (PCL)	C	32	103	14	27	5	0	0	10	.262	8	13	0	203	39	5	.980
—	Jackson (Texas)	C	58	188	16	54	8	0	4	25	.287	8	17	0	316	52	5	.987
1996—	Ottawa (I.L.)■	C	60	198	15	49	10	0	2	24	.247	11	31	0	363	50	4	.990
—	Montreal (N.L.)	C	4	5	1	1	0	0	0	0	.200	1	1	1	14	0	0	1.000
1997—	Ottawa (I.L.)	C-DH	92	310	31	76	17	0	4	46	.245	18	42	1	593	*77	*15	.978
—	Montreal (N.L.)	C	13	26	0	7	0	0	0	2	.269	0	5	1	47	8	0	1.000
1998—	Ottawa (I.L.)	C	11	31	2	7	0	0	0	1	.226	5	5	0	71	15	0	1.000
—	Tacoma (PCL)■	C-DH	76	233	27	52	6	0	4	34	.223	22	41	1	523	*70	6	.990
—	Seattle (A.L.)	C	1	1	0	0	0	0	0	0	.000	0	0	0	3	0	0	1.000
1999—	Tacoma (PCL)	C-D-1-2-3-S	102	354	39	95	20	1	3	40	.268	28	63	1	669	†82	10	.987
2000—	New Orleans (PCL)■	C	99	303	31	74	13	0	2	36	.244	34	44	3	571	52	8	.987
—	Houston (N.L.)	C	14	43	3	11	2	0	1	5	.256	3	6	0	67	6	1	.986
American League totals (1 year)			1	1	0	0	0	0	0	0	.000	0	0	0	3	0	0	1.000
National League totals (3 years)			31	74	4	19	2	0	1	7	.257	4	12	2	128	14	1	.993
Major League totals (4 years)			32	75	4	19	2	0	1	7	.253	4	12	2	131	14	1	.993

CHEN, BRUCE — P — PHILLIES

PERSONAL: Born June 19, 1977, in Panama City, Panama. ... 6-2/210. ... Throws left, bats left. ... Full name: Bruce Kastulo Chen.
HIGH SCHOOL: Instituto Panamericano (Panama).
TRANSACTIONS/CAREER NOTES: Signed as non-drafted free agent by Atlanta Braves organization (July 1, 1993). ... Traded by Braves with P Jimmy Osting to Philadelphia Phillies for P Andy Ashby (July 12, 2000).
HONORS: Named Southern League Most Outstanding Pitcher (1998).

Year	League	W	L	Pct.	ERA	G	GS	CG	ShO	Sv.	IP	H	R	ER	BB	SO
1994—	Gulf Coast Braves (GCL)	1	4	.200	3.80	9	7	0	0	1	42 2/3	42	21	18	3	26
1995—	Danville (Appl.)	4	4	.500	3.97	14	13	1	0	0	70 1/3	78	42	31	19	56
1996—	Eugene (N'West)	4	1	.800	2.27	11	8	0	0	0	35 2/3	23	13	9	14	55
1997—	Macon (S.Atl.)	12	7	.632	3.51	28	28	1	1	0	146 1/3	120	67	57	44	182
1998—	Greenville (Sou.)	13	7	.650	3.29	24	23	1	0	0	139 1/3	106	57	51	48	164
—	Richmond (I.L.)	2	1	.667	1.88	4	4	0	0	0	24	17	5	5	19	29
—	Atlanta (N.L.)	2	0	1.000	3.98	4	4	0	0	0	20 1/3	23	9	9	9	17
1999—	Richmond (I.L.)	6	3	.667	3.81	14	14	0	0	0	78	73	36	33	26	90
—	Atlanta (N.L.)	2	2	.500	5.47	16	7	0	0	0	51	38	32	31	27	45
2000—	Atlanta (N.L.)	4	0	1.000	2.50	22	0	0	0	0	39 2/3	35	15	11	19	32
—	Richmond (I.L.)	1	0	1.000	0.00	1	1	0	0	0	6	5	0	0	1	6
—	Philadelphia (N.L.)■	3	4	.429	3.63	15	15	0	0	0	94 1/3	81	39	38	27	80
Major League totals (3 years)		11	6	.647	3.90	57	26	0	0	0	205 1/3	177	95	89	82	174

DIVISION SERIES RECORD

Year	League	W	L	Pct.	ERA	G	GS	CG	ShO	Sv.	IP	H	R	ER	BB	SO
1999—	Atlanta (N.L.)							Did not play.								

CHAMPIONSHIP SERIES RECORD

Year	League	W	L	Pct.	ERA	G	GS	CG	ShO	Sv.	IP	H	R	ER	BB	SO
1999—	Atlanta (N.L.)							Did not play.								

WORLD SERIES RECORD

Year	League	W	L	Pct.	ERA	G	GS	CG	ShO	Sv.	IP	H	R	ER	BB	SO
1999—	Atlanta (N.L.)							Did not play.								

CHIARAMONTE, GIUSEPPE — C — GIANTS

PERSONAL: Born February 19, 1976, in Santa Cruz, Calif. ... 6-0/200. ... Bats right, throws right. ... Full name: Giuseppe Cario Chiaramonte.
HIGH SCHOOL: Soquel (Calif.).
COLLEGE: Fresno State.
TRANSACTIONS/CAREER NOTES: Selected by San Francisco Giants organization in fifth round of free-agent draft (June 3, 1997).
STATISTICAL NOTES: Led California League with 12 sacrifice flies in 1998.

Year	Team (League)	Pos.	G	AB	R	H	2B	3B	HR	RBI	Avg.	BB	SO	SB	PO	A	E	Avg.
1997—	San Jose (Calif.)	C	64	223	29	51	11	1	12	44	.229	25	58	0	476	59	4	.993
1998—	San Jose (Calif.)	C	129	502	87	137	33	3	22	87	.273	47	139	5	826	71	9	*.990
1999—	Shreveport (Texas)	C	114	400	54	98	20	2	19	74	.245	40	88	4	550	40	8	.987
2000—	Fresno (PCL)	C	122	443	70	113	30	6	24	79	.255	47	81	2	*726	44	8	.990

PERSONAL: Born August 16, 1975, in Jun Ju City, Korea. ... 6-3/220. ... Throws right, bats right.
COLLEGE: Won Kwang (South Korea).
TRANSACTIONS/CAREER NOTES: Signed as non-drafted free agent by Boston Red Sox organization (March 30, 1998). ... On Boston disabled list (March 18-April 27, 2000); included rehabilitation assignment to Sarasota (April 20-27).
MISCELLANEOUS: Member of 1996 South Korean Olympic team.

Year League	W	L	Pct.	ERA	G	GS	CG	ShO	Sv.	IP	H	R	ER	BB	SO
1998— Sarasota (FSL)	3	1	.750	3.09	5	5	0	0	0	32	33	14	11	5	30
— Trenton (East.)	5	2	.714	2.19	13	13	1	1	0	74	59	21	18	19	62
— Boston (A.L.)	0	3	.000	8.20	4	4	0	0	0	18 $2/3$	28	17	17	3	15
1999— Pawtucket (I.L.)	9	3	.750	3.45	17	17	4	0	0	109 $2/3$	99	46	42	29	80
— Boston (A.L.)	2	3	.400	5.72	9	7	0	0	0	39 $1/3$	45	26	25	8	16
2000— Sarasota (FSL)	1	1	.500	2.40	3	3	0	0	0	15	13	5	4	0	15
— Trenton (East.)	3	5	.375	5.83	10	10	0	0	0	58 $2/3$	76	45	38	8	32
— Pawtucket (I.L.)	4	3	.571	4.65	13	9	1	0	0	71 $2/3$	77	37	37	13	37
Major League totals (2 years)	2	6	.250	6.52	13	11	0	0	0	58	73	43	42	11	31

C

PERSONAL: Born September 5, 1975, in San Antonio. ... 6-3/180. ... Throws left, bats left. ... Full name: Randy Doyle Choate.
HIGH SCHOOL: Winston Churchill (San Antonio).
COLLEGE: Florida State.
TRANSACTIONS/CAREER NOTES: Selected by New York Yankees organization in fifth round of free-agent draft (June 3, 1997).

Year League	W	L	Pct.	ERA	G	GS	CG	ShO	Sv.	IP	H	R	ER	BB	SO
1997— Oneonta (NY-Penn)	5	1	.833	1.73	10	10	0	0	0	62 $1/3$	49	12	12	12	61
1998— Tampa (FSL)	1	8	.111	5.27	13	13	0	0	0	70	83	57	41	22	55
— Greensboro (S.Atl.)	1	5	.167	3.00	8	8	1	0	0	39	46	21	13	7	32
1999— Tampa (FSL)	2	2	.500	4.50	47	0	0	0	0	50	51	25	25	24	62
2000— Columbus (I.L.)	2	0	1.000	2.04	33	0	0	0	1	35 $1/3$	34	8	8	14	37
— New York (A.L.)	0	1	.000	4.76	22	0	0	0	0	17	14	10	9	8	12
Major League totals (1 year)	0	1	.000	4.76	22	0	0	0	0	17	14	10	9	8	12

DIVISION SERIES RECORD

Year League	W	L	Pct.	ERA	G	GS	CG	ShO	Sv.	IP	H	R	ER	BB	SO
2000— New York (A.L.)	0	0	...	6.75	1	0	0	0	0	1 $1/3$	0	1	1	1	1

CHAMPIONSHIP SERIES RECORD

Year League	W	L	Pct.	ERA	G	GS	CG	ShO	Sv.	IP	H	R	ER	BB	SO
2000— New York (A.L.)	0	0	...	0.00	1	0	0	0	0	$1/3$	0	0	0	0	1

WORLD SERIES RECORD

NOTES: Member of World Series championship team (2000).

Year League	W	L	Pct.	ERA	G	GS	CG	ShO	Sv.	IP	H	R	ER	BB	SO
2000— New York (A.L.)							Did not play.								

PERSONAL: Born May 1, 1972, in Manilla, The Phillipines. ... 6-1/190. ... Throws right, bats right. ... Full name: Robert William Chouinard.
HIGH SCHOOL: Forest Grove (Ore.).
TRANSACTIONS/CAREER NOTES: Selected by Baltimore Orioles organization in fifth round of free-agent draft (June 4, 1990). ... Traded by Orioles with P Allen Plaster to Oakland Athletics for OF Harold Baines (January 14, 1993). ... Granted free agency (October 15, 1997). ... Signed by Milwaukee Brewers organization (October 31, 1997). ... Claimed on waivers by Arizona Diamondbacks (June 1, 1998). ... On Arizona disabled list (August 22-September 8, 1998); included rehabilitation assignment to Tucson (September 6-8). ... On Tucson disabled list (June 20-28, 1999). ... Released by Diamondbacks (February 2, 2000). ... Signed by Colorado Rockies (June 17, 2000).

Year League	W	L	Pct.	ERA	G	GS	CG	ShO	Sv.	IP	H	R	ER	BB	SO
1990— Bluefield (Appl.)	2	5	.286	3.70	10	10	2	1	0	56	61	34	23	14	30
1991— Kane County (Midw.)	2	4	.333	4.64	6	6	0	0	0	33	45	24	17	5	17
— Bluefield (Appl.)	5	1	.833	3.48	6	6	0	0	0	33 $2/3$	44	19	13	11	31
1992— Kane County (Midw.)	10	14	.417	*2.08	26	26	*9	•2	0	181 $2/3$	151	60	42	38	112
1993— Modesto (Calif.)■	8	10	.444	4.26	24	24	1	0	0	145 $2/3$	154	75	69	56	82
1994— Modesto (Calif.)	12	5	.706	2.59	29	20	0	0	3	145 $2/3$	147	53	42	32	74
1995— Huntsville (Sou.)	14	8	.636	3.62	29	*29	1	1	0	166 $2/3$	155	81	67	50	106
1996— Edmonton (PCL)	10	2	.833	2.77	15	15	0	0	0	84 $1/3$	70	32	26	24	45
— Oakland (A.L.)	4	2	.667	6.10	13	11	0	0	0	59	75	44	40	32	32
1997— Edmonton (PCL)	6	6	.500	6.03	25	21	1	0	0	100	129	80	67	26	58
1998— Louisville (I.L.)■	2	1	.667	4.93	7	7	0	0	0	42	52	31	23	15	33
— Milwaukee (N.L.)	0	0	...	3.00	1	0	0	0	0	3	5	1	1	0	1
— Tucson (PCL)■	0	0	...	4.26	4	0	0	0	1	6 $1/3$	6	3	3	0	6
— Arizona (N.L.)	0	2	.000	4.23	26	2	0	0	0	38 $1/3$	41	23	18	11	26
1999— Tucson (PCL)	4	1	.800	4.06	12	9	0	0	0	62	70	33	28	13	63
— Arizona (N.L.)	5	2	.714	2.68	32	0	0	0	1	40 $1/3$	31	16	12	12	23
2000— Colorado Springs (PCL)■	0	0	...	3.63	9	0	0	0	1	17 $1/3$	18	10	7	3	12
— Colorado (N.L.)	2	2	.500	3.86	31	0	0	0	0	32 $2/3$	35	17	14	9	23
A.L. totals (1 year)	4	2	.667	6.10	13	11	0	0	0	59	75	44	40	32	32
N.L. totals (3 years)	7	6	.538	3.54	90	2	0	0	1	114 $1/3$	112	57	45	32	73
Major League totals (4 years)	11	8	.579	4.41	103	13	0	0	1	173 $1/3$	187	98	85	64	105

DIVISION SERIES RECORD

Year League	W	L	Pct.	ERA	G	GS	CG	ShO	Sv.	IP	H	R	ER	BB	SO
1999— Arizona (N.L.)	0	0	...	4.50	2	0	0	0	0	2	3	1	1	0	1

CHRISTENSEN, McKAY   OF   WHITE SOX

PERSONAL: Born August 14, 1975, in Upland, Calif. ... 5-11/180. ... Bats left, throws left. ... Full name: McKay A. Christensen.
HIGH SCHOOL: Clovis West (Fresno, Calif.).
TRANSACTIONS/CAREER NOTES: Selected by California Angels organization in first round (sixth pick overall) of free-agent draft (June 2, 1994). ... Traded by Angels with P Andrew Lorraine, P Bill Simas and P John Snyder to Chicago White Sox for P Jim Abbott and P Tim Fortugno (July 27, 1995). ... On disabled list (April 10-28 and June 2-17, 1998). ... On Birmingham disabled list (July 13-August 1, 1999). ... On Charlotte disabled list (August 2-26, 2000).
STATISTICAL NOTES: Tied for Carolina League lead with three double plays by outfielder in 1998.

						BATTING								FIELDING		
Year Team (League)	Pos.	G	AB	R	H	2B	3B	HR	RBI	Avg.	BB	SO	SB	PO	A	E	Avg.
1996— GC White Sox (GCL) ..	OF	35	133	17	35	7	5	1	16	.263	10	23	10	54	2	1	.982
—Hickory (S.Atl.)..........	OF	6	11	0	0	0	0	0	0	.000	1	4	0	4	0	0	1.000
1997—Hickory (S.Atl.)..........	OF	127	503	95	141	12	*12	5	47	.280	52	81	28	*280	5	9	.969
1998—Wins.-Salem (Caro.)...	OF	95	361	69	103	17	6	4	32	.285	53	54	20	199	6	4	.981
1999—Chicago (A.L.)	OF	28	53	10	12	1	0	1	6	.226	4	7	2	50	0	3	.943
—Birmingham (Sou.).....	OF	75	293	53	85	8	6	3	28	.290	31	46	18	190	2	2	.990
—Charlotte (I.L.)............	OF	1	4	0	1	0	0	0	0	.250	0	0	1	2	0	0	1.000
2000—Chicago (A.L.)	OF	32	19	4	2	0	0	0	1	.105	2	6	1	20	1	0	1.000
—Charlotte (I.L.)............	OF	90	337	49	89	13	2	6	29	.264	32	51	28	184	3	7	.964
Major League totals (2 years)		60	72	14	14	1	0	1	7	.194	6	13	3	70	1	3	.959

DIVISION SERIES RECORD

						BATTING								FIELDING		
Year Team (League)	Pos.	G	AB	R	H	2B	3B	HR	RBI	Avg.	BB	SO	SB	PO	A	E	Avg.
2000—Chicago (A.L.)	OF	1	0	0	0	0	0	0	0	...	0	0	0	0	0	0	...

CHRISTENSON, RYAN   OF   ATHLETICS

PERSONAL: Born March 28, 1974, in Redlands, Calif. ... 6-0/210. ... Bats right, throws right. ... Full name: Ryan Alan Christenson.
HIGH SCHOOL: Apple Valley (Calif.).
COLLEGE: Pepperdine.
TRANSACTIONS/CAREER NOTES: Selected by Oakland Athletics organization in 10th round of free-agent draft (June 1, 1995).

						BATTING								FIELDING		
Year Team (League)	Pos.	G	AB	R	H	2B	3B	HR	RBI	Avg.	BB	SO	SB	PO	A	E	Avg.
1995—S. Oregon (N.W.)........	OF	49	158	14	30	4	1	1	16	.190	22	33	5	84	3	2	.978
1996—S. Oregon (N.W.)........	OF	36	136	31	39	11	0	5	21	.287	19	21	8	78	5	4	.954
—W. Mich. (Midw.)........	OF-3B	33	122	21	38	2	2	2	18	.311	13	22	2	64	1	3	.956
1997—Visalia (Calif.)	OF	83	308	69	90	18	8	13	54	.292	70	72	20	164	4	3	.982
—Huntsville (Sou.)	OF	29	120	39	44	9	3	2	18	.367	24	23	5	81	1	1	.988
—Edmonton (PCL)	OF	16	49	12	14	2	2	2	5	.286	11	11	2	42	1	0	1.000
1998—Edmonton (PCL)	OF	22	88	17	23	6	1	1	7	.261	15	24	4	56	2	0	1.000
—Oakland (A.L.)	OF	117	370	56	95	22	2	5	40	.257	36	106	5	284	7	5	.983
1999—Oakland (A.L.)	OF-DH	106	268	41	56	12	1	4	24	.209	38	58	7	213	3	7	.969
—Vancouver (PCL)	OF	33	128	30	44	8	1	1	16	.344	22	21	7	88	1	2	.978
2000—Oakland (A.L.)	OF	121	129	31	32	2	2	4	18	.248	19	33	1	95	2	5	.951
Major League totals (3 years)		344	767	128	183	36	5	13	82	.239	93	197	13	592	12	17	.973

DIVISION SERIES RECORD

						BATTING								FIELDING		
Year Team (League)	Pos.	G	AB	R	H	2B	3B	HR	RBI	Avg.	BB	SO	SB	PO	A	E	Avg.
2000—Oakland (A.L.)	OF-PR	2	2	0	1	0	0	0	1	.500	0	1	0	2	0	0	1.000

CHRISTIANSEN, JASON   P   CARDINALS

PERSONAL: Born September 21, 1969, in Omaha, Neb. ... 6-5/241. ... Throws left, bats right. ... Full name: Jason Samuel Christiansen.
HIGH SCHOOL: Elkhorn (Neb.).
JUNIOR COLLEGE: Iowa Western College.
COLLEGE: Cameron (Okla.).
TRANSACTIONS/CAREER NOTES: Signed as non-drafted free agent by Pittsburgh Pirates organization (July 5, 1991). ... On Calgary disabled list (August 12-September 5, 1996). ... On Pittsburgh disabled list (March 31-June 19, 1997). ... On Pittsburgh disabled list (May 7-28, July 29-August 21 and August 24-September 23, 1999); included rehabilitation assignments to Altoona (May 22-28) and Nashville (August 16-21). ... Traded by Pirates to St. Louis Cardinals for SS Jack Wilson (July 30, 2000).

Year League	W	L	Pct.	ERA	G	GS	CG	ShO	Sv.	IP	H	R	ER	BB	SO
1991—Gulf Coast Pirates (GCL)	1	0	1.000	0.00	6	0	0	0	1	8	4	0	0	1	8
—Welland (NY-Penn).............	0	1	.000	2.53	8	1	0	0	0	21 1/3	15	9	6	12	17
1992—Augusta (S.Atl.).................	1	0	1.000	1.80	10	0	0	0	2	20	12	4	4	8	21
—Salem (Caro.)..................	3	1	.750	3.24	38	0	0	0	2	50	47	20	18	22	59
1993—Salem (Caro.)..................	1	1	.500	3.15	57	0	0	0	4	71 1/3	48	30	25	24	70
—Carolina (Sou.)	0	0	...	0.00	2	0	0	0	0	2 2/3	3	0	0	1	2
1994—Carolina (Sou.).................	2	1	.667	2.09	28	0	0	0	2	38 2/3	30	10	9	14	43
—Buffalo (A.A.)..................	3	1	.750	2.41	33	0	0	0	0	33 2/3	19	9	9	16	39
1995—Pittsburgh (N.L.)...............	1	3	.250	4.15	63	0	0	0	0	56 1/3	49	28	26	34	53
1996—Calgary (PCL)...................	1	0	1.000	3.27	2	2	0	0	0	11	9	4	4	1	10
—Pittsburgh (N.L.)...............	3	3	.500	6.70	33	0	0	0	0	44 1/3	56	34	33	19	38
1997—Pittsburgh (N.L.)...............	3	0	1.000	2.94	39	0	0	0	0	33 2/3	37	11	11	17	37
—Carolina (Sou.)	0	1	.000	4.20	8	1	0	0	1	15	17	7	7	5	25
1998—Pittsburgh (N.L.)	3	3	.500	2.51	60	0	0	0	6	64 2/3	51	22	18	27	71

C

Year League	W	L	Pct.	ERA	G	GS	CG	ShO	Sv.	IP	H	R	ER	BB	SO
1999— Pittsburgh (N.L.)	2	3	.400	4.06	39	0	0	0	3	37 2/3	26	17	17	22	35
— Altoona (East.)	0	0	...	0.00	2	1	0	0	0	3	1	0	0	1	2
— Nashville (PCL)	0	0	...	0.00	2	0	0	0	0	2	0	0	0	0	1
2000— Pittsburgh (N.L.)	2	8	.200	4.97	44	0	0	0	1	38	28	22	21	25	41
— St. Louis (N.L.)■	1	0	1.000	5.40	21	0	0	0	0	10	13	7	6	2	12
Major League totals (6 years)	15	20	.429	4.17	299	0	0	0	10	284 2/3	260	141	132	146	287

DIVISION SERIES RECORD

Year League	W	L	Pct.	ERA	G	GS	CG	ShO	Sv.	IP	H	R	ER	BB	SO
2000— St. Louis (N.L.)	0	0	...	0.00	1	0	0	0	0	1/3	0	0	0	0	0

CHAMPIONSHIP SERIES RECORD

Year League	W	L	Pct.	ERA	G	GS	CG	ShO	Sv.	IP	H	R	ER	BB	SO
2000— St. Louis (N.L.)	0	0	...	0.00	2	0	0	0	0	2	0	0	0	0	1

CHRISTMAN, TIM — P — ROCKIES

PERSONAL: Born March 31, 1975, in Oneonta, N.Y. ... 6-0/195. ... Throws left, bats left. ... Full name: Timothy A. Christman.
HIGH SCHOOL: Oneonta (N.Y.).
COLLEGE: Siena.
TRANSACTIONS/CAREER NOTES: Selected by Colorado Rockies organization in 11th round of free-agent draft (June 4, 1996). ... On disabled list (April 10, 1998-entire season). ... On Salem disabled list (April 8-23, 1999). ... On Carolina disabled list (May 5-September 12, 2000).

Year League	W	L	Pct.	ERA	G	GS	CG	ShO	Sv.	IP	H	R	ER	BB	SO
1996— Portland (N'West)	1	2	.333	4.28	21	0	0	0	0	40	30	23	19	23	56
1997— Asheville (S.Atl.)	7	3	.700	3.41	29	0	0	0	3	63 1/3	55	32	24	18	87
1998—								Did not play.							
1999— Salem (Caro.)	1	2	.333	2.42	38	0	0	0	2	48 1/3	38	18	13	12	64
2000— Carolina (Sou.)	0	0	...	2.53	8	0	0	0	0	10 2/3	6	3	3	7	13

CIRILLO, JEFF — 3B — ROCKIES

PERSONAL: Born September 23, 1969, in Pasadena, Calif. ... 6-1/195. ... Bats right, throws right. ... Full name: Jeffrey Howard Cirillo.
HIGH SCHOOL: Providence (Burbank, Calif.).
COLLEGE: Southern California.
TRANSACTIONS/CAREER NOTES: Selected by Chicago Cubs organization in 37th round of free-agent draft (June 2, 1987); did not sign. ... Selected by Milwaukee Brewers organization in 11th round of free-agent draft (June 3, 1991). ... On New Orleans disabled list (July 22-August 6, 1993). ... Traded by Brewers with P Scott Karl and cash to Colorado Rockies as part of three-way deal in which Brewers received P Jamey Wright and C Henry Blanco from Rockies, Oakland Athletics received P Justin Miller and cash from Rockies and Brewers received P Jimmy Haynes from Athletics (December 13, 1999).
RECORDS: Shares N.L. single-season record for most double plays by third baseman—45 (1998).
STATISTICAL NOTES: Led Pioneer League in grounding into double plays with 11 in 1991. ... Led Pioneer League third basemen with 60 putouts, 104 assists and 179 total chances in 1991. ... Tied for Midwest League lead with six intentional bases on balls received in 1992. ... Led A.L. third basemen with 463 total chances and 29 double plays in 1997. ... Led N.L. in grounding into double plays with 26 in 1998. ... Led N.L. third basemen with 340 assists and 45 double plays in 1998. ... Led N.L. third basemen in double plays with 35 in 1999 and 41 in 2000. ... Had 15-game hitting streak (April 21-May 9, 2000). ... Hit three home runs in one game (June 28, 2000). ... Career major league grand slams: 1.
MISCELLANEOUS: Holds Milwaukee Brewers all-time record for highest career batting average (.307).

Year Team (League)	Pos.	G	AB	R	H	2B	3B	HR	RBI	Avg.	BB	SO	SB	PO	A	E	Avg.
1991— Helena (Pio.)	3B-OF	•70	286	60	100	16	2	10	51	.350	31	28	3	†71	†104	15	.921
1992— Stockton (Calif.)	3B	7	27	2	6	1	0	0	5	.222	2	0	0	7	10	0	1.000
— Beloit (Midw.)	3B-2B	126	444	65	135	27	3	9	71	.304	84	85	21	115	309	26	.942
1993— El Paso (Texas)	2B-3B	67	249	53	85	16	2	9	41	.341	26	37	2	83	142	9	.962
— New Orleans (A.A.)	3-2-S-DH	58	215	31	63	13	2	3	32	.293	29	33	2	46	145	5	.974
1994— New Orleans (A.A.)	3-2-DH-S	61	236	45	73	18	2	10	46	.309	28	39	4	67	139	8	.963
— Milwaukee (A.L.)	3B-2B	39	126	17	30	9	0	3	12	.238	11	16	0	23	60	3	.965
1995— Milwaukee (A.L.)	3-2-1-S	125	328	57	91	19	4	9	39	.277	47	42	7	113	230	15	.958
1996— Milwaukee (A.L.)	3-DH-1-2	158	566	101	184	46	5	15	83	.325	58	69	4	112	242	18	.952
1997— Milwaukee (A.L.)	3B-DH	154	580	74	167	46	2	10	82	.288	60	74	4	•126	*320	17	.963
1998— Milwaukee (N.L.)	3B-1B	156	604	97	194	31	1	14	68	.321	79	88	10	149	†353	11	.979
1999— Milwaukee (N.L.)	3B	157	607	98	198	35	1	15	88	.326	75	83	7	*124	312	15	.967
2000— Colorado (N.L.)■	3B	157	598	111	195	53	2	11	115	.326	67	72	3	92	*303	15	.963
American League totals (4 years)		476	1600	249	472	120	11	37	216	.295	176	201	15	374	852	53	.959
National League totals (3 years)		470	1809	306	587	119	4	40	271	.324	221	243	20	365	968	41	.970
Major League totals (7 years)		946	3409	555	1059	239	15	77	487	.311	397	444	35	739	1820	94	.965

ALL-STAR GAME RECORD

Year League	Pos.	AB	R	H	2B	3B	HR	RBI	Avg.	BB	SO	SB	PO	A	E	Avg.
1997— American	3B	1	0	0	0	0	0	0	.000	0	1	0	0	0	0	...
2000— National	3B	1	0	0	0	0	0	0	.000	0	0	0	2	1	0	1.000
All-Star Game totals (2 years)		2	0	0	0	0	0	0	.000	0	1	0	2	1	0	1.000

CLAPINSKI, CHRIS — IF

PERSONAL: Born August 20, 1971, in Buffalo, N.Y. ... 6-0/175. ... Bats both, throws right. ... Full name: Christopher Alan Clapinski. ... Name pronounced clap-in-SKEE.

HIGH SCHOOL: Palm Desert (Calif.).
COLLEGE: California.
TRANSACTIONS/CAREER NOTES: Signed as non-drafted free agent by Florida Marlins organization (June 10, 1992). ... Granted free agency (October 16, 1998). ... Re-signed by Marlins organization (December 21, 1998). ... Granted free agency (October 5, 2000).
STATISTICAL NOTES: Led Gulf Coast League second basemen with 40 double plays and 333 total chances in 1992.

Year	Team (League)	Pos.	G	AB	R	H	2B	3B	HR	RBI	Avg.	BB	SO	SB	PO	A	E	Avg.
											BATTING					FIELDING		
1992—	GC Marlins (GCL)	2B	59	212	36	51	8	1	1	15	.241	49	42	5	*156	*167	10	.970
1993—	Kane County (Midw.)	2B-3B	82	214	22	45	12	1	0	27	.210	31	55	3	121	152	16	.945
1994—	Brevard County (FSL)	2B-3B-OF	65	157	33	45	12	3	1	13	.287	23	28	3	47	106	5	.968
1995—	Portland (East.)	3-2-S-1-O	87	208	32	49	9	3	4	30	.236	28	44	5	80	117	4	.980
1996—	Portland (East.)	SS	23	73	15	19	7	0	3	11	.260	13	13	3	29	68	2	.980
—	Charlotte (I.L.)	S-3-2-O	105	362	74	103	20	1	10	39	.285	47	54	13	143	265	16	.962
1997—	Charlotte (I.L.)	2-S-3-O	110	340	62	89	24	2	12	52	.262	48	64	14	148	234	12	.970
1998—	Charlotte (I.L.)	O-3-S-2	100	312	53	84	18	1	9	35	.269	39	53	11	106	162	9	.968
—	Brevard County (FSL)	2B-SS-3B	5	14	1	1	0	1	0	4	.071	7	2	0	2	8	1	.909
1999—	Calgary (PCL)	2B	81	267	51	86	21	6	8	35	.322	30	53	5	101	136	7	.971
—	Florida (N.L.)	3-S-O-2	36	56	6	13	1	2	0	2	.232	9	12	1	17	23	3	.930
2000—	Florida (N.L.)	2B-3B-OF-SS	34	49	12	15	4	1	1	7	.306	5	7	0	28	33	4	.938
—	Calgary (PCL)	SS-2B-3B-OF	62	214	41	60	10	3	6	24	.280	33	36	3	84	135	6	.973
—	Brevard County (FSL)	2B-SS-OF	4	17	4	6	0	0	1	1	.353	0	2	0	7	6	0	1.000
Major League totals (2 years)			70	105	18	28	5	3	1	9	.267	14	19	1	45	56	7	.935

RECORD AS PITCHER

Year	League	W	L	Pct.	ERA	G	GS	CG	ShO	Sv.	IP	H	R	ER	BB	SO
1996—	Charlotte (I.L.)	0	0	...	4.50	1	0	0	0	0	2	1	1	1	0	2

CLARK, BRADY — OF — REDS

PERSONAL: Born April 18, 1973, in Portland, Ore. ... 6-2/195. ... Bats right, throws right. ... Full name: Brady William Clark.
HIGH SCHOOL: Sunset (Beaverton, Ore.).
COLLEGE: San Diego.
TRANSACTIONS/CAREER NOTES: Signed as non-drafted free agent by Cincinnati Reds organization (January 13, 1996). ... Released by Reds (April 10, 1996). ... Re-signed by Reds organization (February 15, 1997).
HONORS: Named Southern League Most Valuable Player (1999).
STATISTICAL NOTES: Led Midwest League outfielders with 278 total chances in 1997. ... Led Southern League with 261 total bases in 1999. ... Tied for International League lead with nine sacrifice flies in 2000. ... Tied for International League outfielders lead with 298 putouts and four double plays in 2000.

Year	Team (League)	Pos.	G	AB	R	H	2B	3B	HR	RBI	Avg.	BB	SO	SB	PO	A	E	Avg.
											BATTING					FIELDING		
1997—	Burlington (Midw.)	OF	126	459	108	149	29	7	11	63	.325	76	71	31	*265	9	4	.986
1998—	Chattanooga (Sou.)	OF	64	222	41	60	13	1	2	16	.270	31	34	12	149	3	1	.993
1999—	Chattanooga (Sou.)	OF-3B	*138	506	103	165	37	4	17	75	.326	89	58	25	255	10	5	.981
2000—	Louisville (I.L.)	OF	132	487	90	148	*41	6	16	79	.304	72	51	12	*298	10	6	.981
—	Cincinnati (N.L.)	OF	11	11	1	3	1	0	0	2	.273	0	2	0	6	0	0	1.000
Major League totals (1 year)			11	11	1	3	1	0	0	2	.273	0	2	0	6	0	0	1.000

CLARK, MARK — P

PERSONAL: Born May 12, 1968, in Bath, Ill. ... 6-5/235. ... Throws right, bats right. ... Full name: Mark Willard Clark.
HIGH SCHOOL: Balyki (Bath, Ill.).
JUNIOR COLLEGE: Lincoln Land Community College (Ill.).
TRANSACTIONS/CAREER NOTES: Selected by St. Louis Cardinals organization in ninth round of free-agent draft (June 1, 1988). ... On Arkansas disabled list (April 12-May 8, 1991). ... Traded by Cardinals with SS Juan Andujar to Cleveland Indians for OF Mark Whiten (March 31, 1993). ... On Cleveland disabled list (July 17-September 9, 1993 and July 21, 1994-remainder of season). ... Traded by Indians to New York Mets for P Reid Cornelius and OF Ryan Thompson (March 31, 1996). ... Traded by Mets to Chicago Cubs (August 11, 1997), as part of deal in which Mets traded OF Lance Johnson and two players to be named later to Cubs for OF Brian McRae, P Mel Rojas and P Turk Wendell (August 8, 1997); Mets traded IF Manny Alexander to Cubs to complete deal (August 14, 1997). ... Granted free agency (October 28, 1998). ... Signed by Texas Rangers (December 10, 1998). ... On Texas disabled list (June 20, 1999-remainder of season); included rehabilitation assignments to Savannah (August 29-31) and Charlotte (September 1-7). ... Released by Rangers (July 3, 2000).

Year	League	W	L	Pct.	ERA	G	GS	CG	ShO	Sv.	IP	H	R	ER	BB	SO
1988—	Hamilton (NY-Penn)	6	7	.462	3.05	15	15	2	0	0	94 1/3	88	39	32	32	60
1989—	Savannah (S.Atl.)	•14	9	.609	2.44	27	27	4	2	0	173 2/3	143	61	47	52	132
1990—	St. Petersburg (FSL)	3	2	.600	3.05	10	10	1	1	0	62	63	33	21	14	58
—	Arkansas (Texas)	5	11	.313	3.82	19	19	*5	0	0	115 1/3	111	56	49	37	87
1991—	Arkansas (Texas)	5	5	.500	4.00	15	15	4	1	0	92 1/3	99	50	41	30	76
—	Louisville (A.A.)	3	2	.600	2.98	7	6	1	1	0	45 1/3	43	17	15	15	29
—	St. Louis (N.L.)	1	1	.500	4.03	7	2	0	0	0	22 1/3	17	10	10	11	13
1992—	Louisville (A.A.)	4	4	.500	2.80	9	9	4	*3	0	61	56	20	19	15	38
—	St. Louis (N.L.)	3	10	.231	4.45	20	20	1	1	0	113 1/3	117	59	56	36	44
1993—	Cleveland (A.L.)■	7	5	.583	4.28	26	15	1	0	0	109 1/3	119	55	52	25	57
—	Charlotte (I.L.)	1	0	1.000	2.08	2	2	0	0	0	13	9	5	3	2	12
1994—	Cleveland (A.L.)	11	3	.786	3.82	20	20	4	1	0	127 1/3	133	61	54	40	60
1995—	Cleveland (A.L.)	9	7	.563	5.27	22	21	2	0	0	124 2/3	143	77	73	42	68
—	Buffalo (A.A.)	4	0	1.000	3.57	5	5	0	0	0	35 1/3	39	14	14	10	17
1996—	New York (N.L.)■	14	11	.560	3.43	32	32	2	0	0	212 1/3	217	98	81	48	142
1997—	New York (N.L.)	8	7	.533	4.25	23	22	1	0	0	142	158	74	67	47	72
—	Chicago (N.L.)■	6	1	.857	2.86	9	9	2	0	0	63	55	22	20	12	51
1998—	Chicago (N.L.)	9	14	.391	4.84	33	33	2	1	0	213 2/3	236	116	115	48	161

C

Year League	W	L	Pct.	ERA	G	GS	CG	ShO	Sv.	IP	H	R	ER	BB	SO
1999— Texas (A.L.)■	3	7	.300	8.60	15	15	0	0	0	74 1/3	103	73	71	34	44
— Savannah (S.Atl.)	0	0	...	0.00	1	1	0	0	0	4	2	0	0	1	1
— Charlotte (FSL)	0	0	...	1.29	2	2	0	0	0	7	5	1	1	1	2
2000— Texas (A.L.)	3	5	.375	7.98	12	8	0	0	0	44	66	42	39	24	16
A.L. totals (5 years)	33	27	.550	5.42	95	79	7	1	0	479 2/3	564	308	289	165	245
N.L. totals (5 years)	41	44	.482	4.10	124	118	8	2	0	766 2/3	800	379	349	202	483
Major League totals (10 years)	74	71	.510	4.61	219	197	15	3	0	1246 1/3	1364	687	638	367	728

DIVISION SERIES RECORD

Year League	W	L	Pct.	ERA	G	GS	CG	ShO	Sv.	IP	H	R	ER	BB	SO
1998— Chicago (N.L.)	0	1	.000	3.00	1	1	0	0	0	6	7	4	2	1	4

CLARK, TONY — IF — TIGERS

PERSONAL: Born June 15, 1972, in Newton, Kan. ... 6-7/245. ... Bats both, throws right. ... Full name: Anthony Christopher Clark.

HIGH SCHOOL: Valhalla (El Cajon, Calif.), then Christian (El Cajon, Calif.).

COLLEGE: Arizona (did not play baseball), then San Diego State.

TRANSACTIONS/CAREER NOTES: Selected by Detroit Tigers organization in first round (second pick overall) of free-agent draft (June 4, 1990). ... On Niagara Falls temporarily inactive list (June 17, 1991-remainder of season and August 17, 1992-remainder of season). ... On disabled list (August 24, 1993-remainder of season). ... On Detroit disabled list (May 26-June 10, 1999); included rehabilitation assignment to Toledo (June 8-10). ... On Detroit disabled list (May 13-June 12, July 15-September 1 and September 19, 2000-remainder of season); included rehabilitation assignments to Toledo (June 9-12 and August 28-September 1).

RECORDS: Holds A.L. single-season record for most games with switch-hit home runs—3 (1998).

STATISTICAL NOTES: Switch-hit home runs in one game six times (April 5, 1997; June 17, July 26 and August 1, 1998; and July 18 and July 25, 1999). ... Led A.L. first basemen with 1,533 total chances in 1997. ... Had 19-game hitting streak (July 10-August 1, 1999). ... Career major league grand slams: 1.

							BATTING							FIELDING		
Year Team (League)	Pos.	G	AB	R	H	2B	3B	HR	RBI	Avg.	BB	SO	SB	PO	A	E	Avg.
1990— Bristol (Appl.)	OF	25	73	2	12	2	0	1	8	.164	6	28	0	23	3	0	1.000
1991— Niagara Falls (NY-P)						Did not play.											
1992— Niagara Falls (NY-P)	OF	27	85	12	26	9	0	5	17	.306	9	34	1	18	1	0	1.000
1993— Lakeland (FSL)	OF	36	117	14	31	4	1	1	22	.265	18	32	0	34	0	2	.944
1994— Trenton (East.)	DH-1B	107	394	50	110	25	0	21	86	.279	40	113	0	505	48	•13	.977
— Toledo (I.L.)	1B-DH	25	92	10	24	4	0	2	13	.261	12	25	2	144	12	0	1.000
1995— Toledo (I.L.)	1B-DH	110	405	50	98	17	2	14	63	.242	52	*129	0	615	51	*13	.981
— Detroit (A.L.)	1B	27	101	10	24	5	1	3	11	.238	8	30	0	253	18	4	.985
1996— Toledo (I.L.)	1B-DH	55	194	42	58	7	1	14	36	.299	31	58	1	400	28	3	.993
— Detroit (A.L.)	1B-DH	100	376	56	94	14	0	27	72	.250	29	127	0	766	54	6	.993
1997— Detroit (A.L.)	1B-DH	159	580	105	160	28	3	32	117	.276	93	144	1	*1423	100	10	.993
1998— Detroit (A.L.)	1B-DH	157	602	84	175	37	0	34	103	.291	63	128	3	1265	102	13	.991
1999— Detroit (A.L.)	1B-DH	143	536	74	150	29	0	31	99	.280	64	133	2	1126	85	10	.992
— Toledo (I.L.)	1B	1	3	0	0	0	0	0	0	.000	1	1	0	10	1	0	1.000
2000— Detroit (A.L.)	1B-DH	60	208	32	57	14	0	13	37	.274	24	51	0	488	45	4	.993
— Toledo (I.L.)	1B	6	22	1	2	1	0	1	2	.091	1	1	0	40	3	0	1.000
Major League totals (6 years)		646	2403	361	660	127	4	140	439	.275	281	613	6	5321	404	47	.992

CLARK, WILL — 1B

PERSONAL: Born March 13, 1964, in New Orleans. ... 6-1/200. ... Bats left, throws left. ... Full name: William Nuschler Clark Jr.

HIGH SCHOOL: Jesuit (New Orleans).

COLLEGE: Mississippi State.

TRANSACTIONS/CAREER NOTES: Selected by Kansas City Royals organization in fourth round of free-agent draft (June 7, 1982); did not sign. ... Selected by San Francisco Giants organization in first round (second pick overall) of free-agent draft (June 3, 1985). ... On San Francisco disabled list (June 4-July 24, 1986); included rehabilitation assignment to Phoenix (July 7-24). ... On disabled list (August 26-September 10, 1993). ... Granted free agency (October 25, 1993). ... Signed by Texas Rangers (November 22, 1993). ... On Texas disabled list (June 8-23, June 30-July 15 and July 17-August 4, 1996); included rehabilitation assignment to Tulsa (August 1-4). ... On disabled list (March 28-April 18 and August 25, 1997-remainder of season). ... Granted free agency (November 5, 1998). ... Signed by Baltimore Orioles (December 7, 1998). ... On disabled list (April 19-May 25, August 14, 1999-remainder of season; and May 3-18, 2000). ... Traded by Orioles with cash to St. Louis Cardinals for 3B Jose Leon (July 31, 2000). ... Announced retirement (November 2, 2000).

HONORS: Named designated hitter on THE SPORTING NEWS college All-America team (1984). ... Named Golden Spikes Award winner by USA Baseball (1985). ... Named first baseman on THE SPORTING NEWS college All-America team (1985). ... Named first baseman on THE SPORTING NEWS N.L. All-Star team (1988-89 and 1991). ... Named first baseman on THE SPORTING NEWS N.L. Silver Slugger team (1989 and 1991). ... Won N.L. Gold Glove at first base (1991).

STATISTICAL NOTES: Led N.L. first basemen with 130 double plays in 1987, 126 in 1988, 118 in 1990, 115 in 1991 and 130 in 1992. ... Led N.L. with 27 intentional bases on balls received in 1988. ... Led N.L. first basemen with 1,608 total chances in 1988, 1,566 in 1989 and 1,587 in 1990. ... Led N.L. with .536 slugging percentage and tied for lead with 303 total bases in 1991. ... Led A.L. first basemen with 1,051 total chances in 1994. ... Had 16-game hitting streak (August 22-September 7, 1998). ... Career major league grand slams: 5.

MISCELLANEOUS: Member of 1984 U.S. Olympic baseball team. ... Hit home run in first minor league at-bat (June 21, 1985) and first major league at-bat (April 8, 1986); both were on the first swing.

							BATTING							FIELDING		
Year Team (League)	Pos.	G	AB	R	H	2B	3B	HR	RBI	Avg.	BB	SO	SB	PO	A	E	Avg.
1985— Fresno (Calif.)	1B-OF	65	217	41	67	14	0	10	48	.309	62	46	11	523	51	6	.990
1986— San Francisco (N.L.)	1B	111	408	66	117	27	2	11	41	.287	34	76	4	942	72	11	.989
— Phoenix (PCL)	DH	6	20	3	5	0	0	0	1	.250	4	2	1	...	...	...	...
1987— San Francisco (N.L.)	1B	150	529	89	163	29	5	35	91	.308	49	98	5	1253	103	13	.991
1988— San Francisco (N.L.)	1B	*162	575	102	162	31	6	29	*109	.282	*100	129	9	*1492	104	12	.993
1989— San Francisco (N.L.)	1B	159	588	•104	196	38	9	23	111	.333	74	103	8	*1445	111	10	.994
1990— San Francisco (N.L.)	1B	154	600	91	177	25	5	19	95	.295	62	97	8	*1456	119	12	.992

Year	Team (League)	Pos.	G	AB	R	H	2B	3B	HR	RBI	Avg.	BB	SO	SB	PO	A	E	Avg.
							BATTING								FIELDING			
1991—	San Francisco (N.L.) ..	1B	148	565	84	170	32	7	29	116	.301	51	91	4	1273	110	4	*.997
1992—	San Francisco (N.L.) ..	1B	144	513	69	154	40	1	16	73	.300	73	82	12	1275	105	10	.993
1993—	San Francisco (N.L.) ..	1B	132	491	82	139	27	2	14	73	.283	63	68	2	1078	88	14	.988
1994—	Texas (A.L.)■............	1B-DH	110	389	73	128	24	2	13	80	.329	71	59	5	968	73	•10	.990
1995—	Texas (A.L.)................	1B-DH	123	454	85	137	27	3	16	92	.302	68	50	0	1076	88	7	.994
1996—	Texas (A.L.)................	1B	117	436	69	124	25	1	13	72	.284	64	67	2	956	73	4	.996
—	Tulsa (Texas)	1B	3	9	3	2	0	0	0	0	.222	2	0	0	21	3	0	1.000
1997—	Texas (A.L.)................	1B-DH	110	393	56	128	29	1	12	51	.326	49	62	0	880	62	4	.996
1998—	Texas (A.L.)................	1B-DH	149	554	98	169	41	1	23	102	.305	72	97	1	1079	73	13	.989
1999—	Baltimore (A.L.)■.......	1B-DH	77	251	40	76	15	0	10	29	.303	38	42	2	575	42	3	.995
2000—	Baltimore (A.L.)........	1B-DH	79	256	49	77	15	1	9	28	.301	47	45	4	583	44	6	.991
—	St. Louis (N.L.)■	1B	51	171	29	59	15	1	12	42	.345	22	24	1	364	27	3	.992
American League totals (7 years)			765	2733	470	839	176	9	96	454	.307	409	422	14	6117	455	47	.993
National League totals (9 years)			1211	4440	716	1337	264	38	188	751	.301	528	768	53	10578	839	89	.992
Major League totals (15 years)			1976	7173	1186	2176	440	47	284	1205	.303	937	1190	67	16695	1294	136	.992

DIVISION SERIES RECORD

Year	Team (League)	Pos.	G	AB	R	H	2B	3B	HR	RBI	Avg.	BB	SO	SB	PO	A	E	Avg.
							BATTING								FIELDING			
1996—	Texas (A.L.)	1B	4	16	1	2	0	0	0	0	.125	4	2	0	35	4	0	1.000
1998—	Texas (A.L.)	1B	3	11	0	1	0	0	0	0	.091	1	2	0	21	2	0	1.000
2000—	St. Louis (N.L.)...........	1B	3	12	3	3	0	0	1	4	.250	1	3	0	26	2	0	1.000
Division series totals (3 years)			10	39	4	6	0	0	1	4	.154	6	7	0	82	8	0	1.000

C

CHAMPIONSHIP SERIES RECORD

RECORDS: Holds career records for highest batting average (50 or more at-bats)—.468; and highest slugging average (50 or more at-bats)—.806. ... Shares career record for most doubles—7. ... Holds single-series record for most hits—13. ... Shares single-series record for most total bases—24 (1989). ... Shares N.L. career record for most long hits—12. ... Holds single-game record for most runs batted in—6 (October 4, 1989). ... Shares single-series record for most runs—8 (1989). ... Shares single-game records for most runs—4; and most grand slams—1 (October 4, 1989). ... Shares single-inning record for most runs batted in—4 (October 4, 1989, fourth inning). ... Shares N.L. single-series record for most consecutive hits—5 (1989). ... Shares N.L. single-game record for most hits—4 (October 4, 1989).

NOTES: Named N.L. Championship Series Most Valuable Player (1989).

Year	Team (League)	Pos.	G	AB	R	H	2B	3B	HR	RBI	Avg.	BB	SO	SB	PO	A	E	Avg.
							BATTING								FIELDING			
1987—	San Francisco (N.L.) ..	1B	7	25	3	9	2	0	1	3	.360	3	6	1	63	7	1	.986
1989—	San Francisco (N.L.) ..	1B	5	20	8	13	3	1	2	8	.650	2	2	0	43	6	0	1.000
2000—	St. Louis (N.L.)...........	1B	5	17	3	7	2	0	1	1	.412	2	1	0	38	4	2	.955
Championship series totals (3 years)			17	62	14	29	7	1	4	12	.468	7	9	1	144	17	3	.982

WORLD SERIES RECORD

Year	Team (League)	Pos.	G	AB	R	H	2B	3B	HR	RBI	Avg.	BB	SO	SB	PO	A	E	Avg.
							BATTING								FIELDING			
1989—	San Francisco (N.L.) ..	1B	4	16	2	4	1	0	0	0	.250	1	3	0	40	2	0	1.000

ALL-STAR GAME RECORD

Year	League	Pos.	AB	R	H	2B	3B	HR	RBI	Avg.	BB	SO	SB	PO	A	E	Avg.
						BATTING							FIELDING			
1988—	National	1B	2	0	0	0	0	0	0	.000	0	0	0	4	1	0	1.000
1989—	National	1B	2	0	0	0	0	0	0	.000	0	1	0	5	0	0	1.000
1990—	National	1B	3	0	1	0	0	0	0	.333	0	0	0	6	0	0	1.000
1991—	National	1B	2	0	1	0	0	0	0	.500	1	0	0	2	0	0	1.000
1992—	National	PH-1B	2	1	1	0	0	1	3	.500	0	1	0	1	0	0	1.000
1994—	American	1B	2	0	2	0	0	0	0	1.000	0	0	1	7	0	0	1.000
All-Star Game totals (6 years)			13	1	5	0	0	1	3	.385	1	2	1	25	1	0	1.000

CLAYTON, ROYCE   SS   WHITE SOX

PERSONAL: Born January 2, 1970, in Burbank, Calif. ... 6-0/183. ... Bats right, throws right. ... Full name: Royce Spencer Clayton.

HIGH SCHOOL: St. Bernard (Playa del Ray, Calif.).

TRANSACTIONS/CAREER NOTES: Selected by San Francisco Giants organization in first round (15th pick overall) of free-agent draft (June 1, 1988); pick received as compensation for Cincinnati Reds signing Type B free-agent OF Eddie Milner. ... Traded by Giants with a player to be named later to St. Louis Cardinals for P Allen Watson, P Rich DeLucia and P Doug Creek (December 14, 1995); Cardinals acquired 2B Chris Wimmer to complete deal (January 16, 1996). ... On St. Louis disabled list (June 24-July 9, 1998). ... Traded by Cardinals with P Todd Stottlemyre to Texas Rangers for P Darren Oliver, 3B Fernando Tatis and a player to be named later (July 31, 1998); Cardinals acquired OF Mark Little to complete deal (August 9, 1998). ... Granted free agency (October 23, 1998). ... Re-signed by Rangers (December 2, 1998). ... On Texas disabled list (May 1-21, 1999); included rehabilitation assignment to Oklahoma (May 18-21). ... Traded by Rangers to Chicago White Sox for P Aaron Myette and P Brian Schmack (December 14, 2000).

STATISTICAL NOTES: Led Texas League shortstops with 80 double plays in 1991. ... Led N.L. shortstops with 103 double plays in 1993. ... Led N.L. shortstops with 654 total chances in 1995. ... Career major league grand slams: 1.

Year	Team (League)	Pos.	G	AB	R	H	2B	3B	HR	RBI	Avg.	BB	SO	SB	PO	A	E	Avg.
							BATTING								FIELDING			
1988—	Everett (N'West).........	SS	60	212	35	55	4	0	3	29	.259	27	54	10	75	166	35	.873
1989—	Clinton (Midw.)...........	SS	104	385	39	91	13	3	0	24	.236	39	101	28	182	332	31	.943
—	San Jose (Calif.).........	SS	28	92	5	11	2	0	0	4	.120	13	27	10	53	71	8	.939
1990—	San Jose (Calif.).........	SS	123	460	80	123	15	10	7	71	.267	68	98	33	*202	358	37	.938
1991—	Shreveport (Texas).....	SS	126	485	84	136	22	8	5	68	.280	61	104	36	174	379	29	.950
—	San Francisco (N.L.) ..	SS	9	26	0	3	1	0	0	2	.115	1	6	0	16	6	3	.880
1992—	San Francisco (N.L.) ..	SS-3B	98	321	31	72	7	4	4	24	.224	26	63	8	142	257	11	.973
—	Phoenix (PCL)...........	SS	48	192	30	46	8	2	3	18	.240	17	25	15	81	150	7	.971

Year Team (League)	Pos.	G	AB	R	H	2B	3B	HR	RBI	Avg.	BB	SO	SB	PO	A	E	Avg.
1993—San Francisco (N.L.) ..	SS	153	549	54	155	21	5	6	70	.282	38	91	11	251	449	27	.963
1994—San Francisco (N.L.) ..	SS	108	385	38	91	14	6	3	30	.236	30	74	23	177	330	14	.973
1995—San Francisco (N.L.) ..	SS	138	509	56	124	29	3	5	58	.244	38	109	24	*223	•411	20	.969
1996—St. Louis (N.L.)■	SS	129	491	64	136	20	4	6	35	.277	33	89	33	171	347	15	.972
1997—St. Louis (N.L.)..........	SS	154	576	75	153	39	5	9	61	.266	33	109	40	228	*452	19	.973
1998—St. Louis (N.L.)..........	SS	90	355	59	83	19	1	4	29	.234	40	51	19	140	286	13	.970
—Texas (A.L.)■............	SS	52	186	30	53	12	1	5	24	.285	13	32	5	88	152	7	.972
1999—Texas (A.L.)...............	SS	133	465	69	134	21	5	14	52	.288	39	100	8	204	406	*25	.961
—Oklahoma (PCL)........	SS	2	7	1	1	0	0	0	1	.143	3	3	0	4	7	0	1.000
2000—Texas (A.L.)	SS	148	513	70	124	21	5	14	54	.242	42	92	11	*265	411	16	.977
American League totals (3 years)		333	1164	169	311	54	11	33	130	.267	94	224	24	557	969	48	.970
National League totals (8 years)		879	3212	377	817	150	28	37	309	.254	239	592	148	1348	2538	122	.970
Major League totals (10 years)		1212	4376	546	1128	204	39	70	439	.258	333	816	172	1905	3507	170	.970

DIVISION SERIES RECORD

Year Team (League)	Pos.	G	AB	R	H	2B	3B	HR	RBI	Avg.	BB	SO	SB	PO	A	E	Avg.
1996—St. Louis (N.L.)..........	SS	2	6	1	2	0	0	0	0	.333	3	1	0	4	5	0	1.000
1998—Texas (A.L.)	SS	3	9	0	2	0	0	0	0	.222	0	4	0	5	8	1	.929
1999—Texas (A.L.)	SS	3	10	0	0	0	0	0	0	.000	0	1	0	4	10	0	1.000
Division series totals (3 years)		8	25	1	4	0	0	0	0	.160	3	6	0	13	23	1	.973

CHAMPIONSHIP SERIES RECORD

Year Team (League)	Pos.	G	AB	R	H	2B	3B	HR	RBI	Avg.	BB	SO	SB	PO	A	E	Avg.
1996—St. Louis (N.L.)..........	SS	5	20	4	7	0	0	0	1	.350	1	4	1	5	16	2	.913

ALL-STAR GAME RECORD

Year League	Pos.	AB	R	H	2B	3B	HR	RBI	Avg.	BB	SO	SB	PO	A	E	Avg.
1997—National	SS	1	0	0	0	0	0	0	.000	0	1	0	0	1	0	1.000

CLEMENS, ROGER   P   YANKEES

PERSONAL: Born August 4, 1962, in Dayton, Ohio. ... 6-4/238. ... Throws right, bats right. ... Full name: William Roger Clemens.
HIGH SCHOOL: Spring Woods (Houston).
JUNIOR COLLEGE: San Jacinto (North) College (Texas).
COLLEGE: Texas.
TRANSACTIONS/CAREER NOTES: Selected by New York Mets organization in 12th round of free-agent draft (June 8, 1981); did not sign. ... Selected by Boston Red Sox organization in first round (19th pick overall) of free-agent draft (June 6, 1983). ... On disabled list (July 8-August 3 and August 21, 1985-remainder of season). ... On suspended list (April 26-May 3, 1991). ... On Boston disabled list (June 19-July 16, 1993); included rehabilitation assignment to Pawtucket (July 11-16). ... On Boston disabled list (April 16-June 2, 1995); included rehabilitation assignments to Sarasota (May 25-28) and Pawtucket (May 28-June 2). ... Granted free agency (November 5, 1996). ... Signed by Toronto Blue Jays (December 13, 1996). ... Traded by Blue Jays to New York Yankees for P David Wells, P Graeme Lloyd and 2B Homer Bush (February 18, 1999). ... On disabled list (April 28-May 21, 1999; and June 15-July 2, 2000).
RECORDS: Shares major league single-game record for most strikeouts (nine-inning game)—20 (April 29, 1986 and September 18, 1996). ... Shares major league record for most strikeouts by pitcher in one inning—3 (June 27, 1992, sixth inning). ... Holds A.L. record for most consecutive games won—20 (June 3, 1998-June 1, 1999). ... Shares A.L. records for most consecutive seasons with 200 or more strikeouts—7 (1986-92); most seasons with 200 or more strikeouts—10; and most consecutive seasons with 100 or more strikeouts—15 (1986-2000). ... Shares A.L. single-game record for most consecutive strikeouts—8 (April 29, 1986).
HONORS: Named Major League Player of the Year by The Sporting News (1986). ... Named A.L. Pitcher of the Year by The Sporting News (1986, 1991, 1997 and 1998). ... Named righthanded pitcher on The Sporting News A.L. All-Star team (1986-87, 1991 and 1997). ... Named A.L. Most Valuable Player by Baseball Writers' Association of America (1986). ... Named A.L. Cy Young Award winner by Baseball Writers' Association of America (1986, 1987, 1991, 1997 and 1998).
STATISTICAL NOTES: Struck out 15 batters in one game (August 21, 1984; July 9, 1988; August 15 and September 21, 1998). ... Struck out 20 batters in one game (April 29, 1986 and September 18, 1996). ... Struck out 16 batters in one game (May 9 and July 15, 1988 and July 12, 1997). ... Pitched 6-0 one-hit, complete-game victory against Cleveland (September 10, 1988). ... Led A.L. with 14 hit batsmen in 1995. ... Struck out 18 batters in one game (August 25, 1998).
MISCELLANEOUS: Singled in only appearance as pinch hitter (1996).

Year League	W	L	Pct.	ERA	G	GS	CG	ShO	Sv.	IP	H	R	ER	BB	SO
1983—Winter Haven (FSL)............	3	1	.750	1.24	4	4	3	1	0	29	22	4	4	0	36
—New Britain (East.)	4	1	.800	1.38	7	7	1	1	0	52	31	8	8	12	59
1984—Pawtucket (I.L.).................	2	3	.400	1.93	7	6	3	1	0	46²/₃	39	12	10	14	50
—Boston (A.L.)....................	9	4	.692	4.32	21	20	5	1	0	133¹/₃	146	67	64	29	126
1985—Boston (A.L.).................	7	5	.583	3.29	15	15	3	1	0	98¹/₃	83	38	36	37	74
1986—Boston (A.L.).................	*24	4	*.857	*2.48	33	33	10	1	0	254	179	77	70	67	238
1987—Boston (A.L.).................	•20	9	.690	2.97	36	36	*18	*7	0	281²/₃	248	100	93	83	256
1988—Boston (A.L.).................	18	12	.600	2.93	35	35	•14	*8	0	264	217	93	86	62	*291
1989—Boston (A.L.).................	17	11	.607	3.13	35	35	8	3	0	253¹/₃	215	101	88	93	230
1990—Boston (A.L.).................	21	6	.778	*1.93	31	31	7	•4	0	228¹/₃	193	59	49	54	209
1991—Boston (A.L.).................	18	10	.643	*2.62	35	•35	13	*4	0	*271¹/₃	219	93	79	65	*241
1992—Boston (A.L.).................	18	11	.621	*2.41	32	32	11	*5	0	246²/₃	203	80	66	62	208
1993—Boston (A.L.).................	11	14	.440	4.46	29	29	2	1	0	191²/₃	175	99	95	67	160
—Pawtucket (I.L.)...............	0	0	...	0.00	1	1	0	0	0	3²/₃	1	0	0	4	8
1994—Boston (A.L.)....................	9	7	.563	2.85	24	24	3	1	0	170²/₃	124	62	54	71	168
1995—Sarasota (FSL)	0	0	...	0.00	1	1	0	0	0	4	0	0	0	2	7
—Pawtucket (I.L.)...............	0	0	...	0.00	1	1	0	0	0	5	1	0	0	3	5
—Boston (A.L.).....................	10	5	.667	4.18	23	23	0	0	0	140	141	70	65	60	132
1996—Boston (A.L.).....................	10	13	.435	3.63	34	34	6	2	0	242²/₃	216	106	98	106	*257

Year League	W	L	Pct.	ERA	G	GS	CG	ShO	Sv.	IP	H	R	ER	BB	SO
1997—Toronto (A.L.)■	*21	7	.750	*2.05	34	34	•9	•3	0	•264	204	65	60	68	*292
1998—Toronto (A.L.)	•20	6	.769	*2.65	33	33	5	3	0	234²/₃	169	78	69	88	*271
1999—New York (A.L.)■	14	10	.583	4.60	30	30	1	1	0	187²/₃	185	101	96	90	163
2000—New York (A.L.)	13	8	.619	3.70	32	32	1	0	0	204¹/₃	184	96	84	84	188
Major League totals (17 years)	260	142	.647	3.07	512	511	116	45	0	3666²/₃	3101	1385	1252	1186	3504

DIVISION SERIES RECORD

Year League	W	L	Pct.	ERA	G	GS	CG	ShO	Sv.	IP	H	R	ER	BB	SO
1995—Boston (A.L.)	0	0	...	3.86	1	1	0	0	0	7	5	3	3	1	5
1999—New York (A.L.)	1	0	1.000	0.00	1	1	0	0	0	7	3	0	0	2	2
2000—New York (A.L.)	0	2	.000	8.18	2	2	0	0	0	11	13	10	10	8	10
Division series totals (3 years)	1	2	.333	4.68	4	4	0	0	0	25	21	13	13	11	17

CHAMPIONSHIP SERIES RECORD

RECORDS: Holds single-series record for most hits allowed—22 (1986). ... Shares single-series record for most earned runs allowed—11 (1986). ... Shares single-game records for most earned runs allowed—7 (October 7, 1986); and most consecutive strikeouts—4 (October 6, 1988). ... Holds A.L. single-series record for most innings pitched—22 ²/₃ (1986). ... Shares A.L. single-game record for most runs allowed—8 (October 7, 1986). ... Holds single-game record for fewest hits allowed—1 (October 14, 2000).

Year League	W	L	Pct.	ERA	G	GS	CG	ShO	Sv.	IP	H	R	ER	BB	SO
1986—Boston (A.L.)	1	1	.500	4.37	3	3	0	0	0	22²/₃	22	12	11	7	17
1988—Boston (A.L.)	0	0	...	3.86	1	1	0	0	0	7	6	3	3	0	8
1990—Boston (A.L.)	0	1	.000	3.52	2	2	0	0	0	7²/₃	7	3	3	5	4
1999—New York (A.L.)	0	1	.000	22.50	1	1	0	0	0	2	6	5	5	2	2
2000—New York (A.L.)	1	0	1.000	0.00	1	1	1	1	0	9	1	0	0	2	15
Champ. series totals (5 years)	2	3	.400	4.10	8	8	1	1	0	48¹/₃	42	23	22	16	46

WORLD SERIES RECORD

NOTES: Member of World Series championship team (1999 and 2000).

Year League	W	L	Pct.	ERA	G	GS	CG	ShO	Sv.	IP	H	R	ER	BB	SO
1986—Boston (A.L.)	0	0	...	3.18	2	2	0	0	0	11¹/₃	9	5	4	6	11
1999—New York (A.L.)	1	0	1.000	1.17	1	1	0	0	0	7²/₃	4	1	1	2	4
2000—New York (A.L.)	1	0	1.000	0.00	1	1	0	0	0	8	2	0	0	0	9
World Series totals (3 years)	2	0	1.000	1.67	4	4	0	0	0	27	15	6	5	8	24

ALL-STAR GAME RECORD

NOTES: Named Most Valuable Player (1986).

Year League	W	L	Pct.	ERA	GS	CG	ShO	Sv.	IP	H	R	ER	BB	SO
1986—American	1	0	1.000	0.00	1	0	0	0	3	0	0	0	0	2
1988—American	0	0	...	0.00	0	0	0	0	1	0	0	0	0	1
1990—American				Did not play.										
1991—American	0	0		9.00	0	0	0	0	1	1	1	1	0	0
1992—American	0	0		0.00	0	0	0	0	1	2	0	0	0	0
1997—American	0	0		0.00	0	0	0	0	1	1	0	0	0	0
1998—American	0	0		18.00	0	0	0	0	1	2	2	2	1	1
All-Star Game totals (6 years)	1	0	1.000	3.38	1	0	0	0	8	6	3	3	1	4

CLEMENT, MATT   P   PADRES

PERSONAL: Born August 12, 1974, in McCandless Township, Pa. ... 6-3/195. ... Throws right, bats right. ... Full name: Matthew Paul Clement.
HIGH SCHOOL: Butler (Pa.).
TRANSACTIONS/CAREER NOTES: Selected by San Diego Padres organization in third round of free-agent draft (June 3, 1993).
RECORDS: Shares major league single-season record for most grand slams allowed—4 (2000).
STATISTICAL NOTES: Led Pacific Coast League with 30 hit batsmen in 1998. ... Led N.L. with 23 wild pitches in 2000.

Year League	W	L	Pct.	ERA	G	GS	CG	ShO	Sv.	IP	H	R	ER	BB	SO
1994—Peoria (Ariz.)	•8	5	.615	4.43	13	13	0	0	0	67	65	38	33	17	76
—Spokane (N'West)	1	1	.500	6.14	2	2	0	0	0	7¹/₃	8	7	5	11	4
1995—Rancho Cuca. (Calif.)	3	4	.429	4.24	12	12	0	0	0	57¹/₃	61	37	27	49	33
—Idaho Falls (Pio.)	6	3	.667	4.33	14	14	0	0	0	81	61	53	39	42	65
1996—Clinton (Midw.)	8	3	.727	2.80	16	16	1	•1	0	96¹/₃	66	31	30	52	109
—Rancho Cuca. (Calif.)	4	5	.444	5.59	11	11	0	0	0	56¹/₃	61	40	35	26	75
1997—Rancho Cuca. (Calif.)	6	3	.667	1.60	14	14	2	1	0	101	74	30	18	31	109
—Mobile (Sou.)	6	5	.545	2.56	13	13	1	1	0	88	83	37	25	32	92
1998—Las Vegas (PCL)	10	9	.526	3.98	27	27	1	0	0	171²/₃	157	94	76	85	160
—San Diego (N.L.)	2	0	1.000	4.61	4	2	0	0	0	13²/₃	15	8	7	7	13
1999—San Diego (N.L.)	10	12	.455	4.48	31	31	0	0	0	180²/₃	190	106	90	86	135
2000—San Diego (N.L.)	13	17	.433	5.14	34	34	0	0	0	205	194	131	117	*125	170
Major League totals (3 years)	25	29	.463	4.82	69	67	0	0	0	399¹/₃	399	245	214	218	318

CLONTZ, BRAD   P

PERSONAL: Born April 25, 1971, in Stuart, Va. ... 6-1/203. ... Throws right, bats right. ... Full name: John Bradley Clontz.
HIGH SCHOOL: Patrick County (Stuart, Va.).
COLLEGE: Virginia Tech.
TRANSACTIONS/CAREER NOTES: Selected by Atlanta Braves organization in 10th round of free-agent draft (June 1, 1992). ... Released by Braves (March 30, 1998). ... Signed by Los Angeles Dodgers (April 9, 1998). ... Traded by Dodgers with P Hideo Nomo to New York Mets for P Dave Mlicki and P Greg McMichael (June 4, 1998). ... On New York disabled list (September 11, 1998-remainder of season). ... Granted free agency (October 15, 1998). ... Signed by Boston Red Sox organization (December 14, 1998). ... Released by Red Sox (April 6, 1999). ... Signed by Pittsburgh Pirates organization (April 8, 1999). ... Traded by Pirates to Arizona Diamondbacks for a player to be named later (December 13, 1999); Pirates acquired P Roberto Manzueta to complete deal (December 15, 1999). ... Released by Diamondbacks (March 29, 2000). ...

Signed by Pirates organization (April 6, 2000). ... On Pittsburgh disabled list (May 1, 2000-remainder of season); included rehabilitation assignments to Bradenton (July 21-August 25) and Altoona (August 26-September 4). ... Released by Pirates (October 11, 2000).

HONORS: Named Southern League Outstanding Pitcher (1994).

Year League	W	L	Pct.	ERA	G	GS	CG	ShO	Sv.	IP	H	R	ER	BB	SO
1992—Pulaski (Appl.)..................	0	0	...	1.59	4	0	0	0	1	5²/₃	3	1	1	2	7
— Macon (S.Atl.).................	2	1	.667	3.91	17	0	0	0	2	23	19	14	10	10	18
1993— Durham (Caro.)...............	1	7	.125	2.75	51	0	0	0	10	75¹/₃	69	32	23	26	79
1994— Greenville (Sou.)	1	2	.333	1.20	39	0	0	0	*27	45	32	13	6	10	49
— Richmond (I.L.).................	0	0	...	2.10	24	0	0	0	11	25²/₃	19	6	6	9	21
1995— Atlanta (N.L.)....................	8	1	.889	3.65	59	0	0	0	4	69	71	29	28	22	55
1996— Atlanta (N.L.)....................	6	3	.667	5.69	*81	0	0	0	1	80²/₃	78	53	51	33	49
1997— Atlanta (N.L.)....................	5	1	.833	3.75	51	0	0	0	1	48	52	24	20	18	42
— Richmond (I.L.).................	0	0	...	0.00	16	0	0	0	6	22	10	1	0	2	24
1998— Los Angeles (N.L.)■	2	0	1.000	5.66	18	0	0	0	0	20²/₃	15	13	13	10	14
— Albuquerque (PCL)...........	1	2	.333	7.71	6	0	0	0	0	7	11	10	6	5	12
— New York (N.L.)■	0	0	...	9.00	2	0	0	0	0	3	4	3	3	2	2
— Norfolk (I.L.)..................	2	4	.333	3.43	28	0	0	0	0	42	43	26	16	16	49
1999— Nashville (PCL)■	0	2	.000	3.50	12	0	0	0	7	18	12	8	7	6	23
— Pittsburgh (N.L.)	1	3	.250	2.74	56	0	0	0	2	49¹/₃	49	21	15	24	40
2000— Nashville (PCL)	0	0	...	0.00	4	0	0	0	1	4²/₃	1	0	0	2	5
— Pittsburgh (N.L.)	0	0	...	5.14	5	0	0	0	0	7	7	4	4	11	8
— Altoona (East.)	0	0	...	1.93	4	0	0	0	0	4²/₃	4	2	1	1	4
Major League totals (6 years).......	**22**	**8**	**.733**	**4.34**	**272**	**0**	**0**	**0**	**8**	**277²/₃**	**276**	**147**	**134**	**120**	**210**

DIVISION SERIES RECORD

Year League	W	L	Pct.	ERA	G	GS	CG	ShO	Sv.	IP	H	R	ER	BB	SO
1995— Atlanta (N.L.)....................	0	0	...	0.00	1	0	0	0	0	1¹/₃	0	0	0	0	2
1996— Atlanta (N.L.)....................							Did not play.								

CHAMPIONSHIP SERIES RECORD

Year League	W	L	Pct.	ERA	G	GS	CG	ShO	Sv.	IP	H	R	ER	BB	SO
1995— Atlanta (N.L.)....................	0	0	...	0.00	1	0	0	0	0	¹/₃	1	0	0	0	0
1996— Atlanta (N.L.)....................	0	0	...	0.00	1	0	0	0	0	²/₃	0	0	0	0	0
Champ. series totals (2 years)	**0**	**0**	**...**	**0.00**	**2**	**0**	**0**	**0**	**0**	**1**	**1**	**0**	**0**	**0**	**0**

WORLD SERIES RECORD

NOTES: Member of World Series championship team (1995).

Year League	W	L	Pct.	ERA	G	GS	CG	ShO	Sv.	IP	H	R	ER	BB	SO
1995— Atlanta (N.L.)....................	0	0	...	2.70	2	0	0	0	0	3¹/₃	2	1	1	0	2
1996— Atlanta (N.L.)....................	0	0	...	0.00	3	0	0	0	0	1²/₃	1	0	0	2	2
World Series totals (2 years)	**0**	**0**	**...**	**1.80**	**5**	**0**	**0**	**0**	**0**	**5**	**3**	**1**	**1**	**2**	**4**

COCO, PASQUAL   P   BLUE JAYS

PERSONAL: Born September 24, 1977, in Santo Domingo, Dominican Republic. ... 6-1/185. ... Throws right, bats right. ... Full name: Pasqual Reynoso Coco.
TRANSACTIONS/CAREER NOTES: Signed as non-drafted free agent by Toronto Blue Jays organization (August 10, 1994).
STATISTICAL NOTES: Pitched 3-1 no-hit loss for St. Catharines against Jamestown (August 16, 1998). ... Led Southern League with 17 hit batsmen in 2000.

Year League	W	L	Pct.	ERA	G	GS	CG	ShO	Sv.	IP	H	R	ER	BB	SO
1995— Dom. Blue Jays (DSL)........	7	1	.875	2.78	11	11	0	0	0	58¹/₃	51	30	18	36	38
1996— Dom. Blue Jays (DSL)........	7	2	.778	2.99	17	16	2	2	0	96¹/₃	77	46	32	53	92
1997— St. Catharines (NY-Penn) ...	1	4	.200	4.89	10	8	0	0	0	46	48	32	25	16	44
1998— St. Catharines (NY-Penn) ...	3	7	.300	3.20	15	15	1	0	0	81²/₃	62	52	29	32	84
1999— Hagerstown (S.Atl.)............	11	1	*.917	2.21	14	14	0	0	0	97²/₃	67	29	24	25	83
— Dunedin (FSL)..................	4	6	.400	5.28	13	13	2	0	0	75	79	52	44	33	44
2000— Tennessee (Sou.)	12	7	.632	3.76	27	26	2	0	0	167²/₃	154	83	70	68	142
— Toronto (A.L.)...................	0	0	...	9.00	1	1	0	0	0	4	5	4	4	5	2
Major League totals (1 year)........	**0**	**0**	**...**	**9.00**	**1**	**1**	**0**	**0**	**0**	**4**	**5**	**4**	**4**	**5**	**2**

COFFIE, IVANON   3B   ORIOLES

PERSONAL: Born May 16, 1977, in Curacao, Netherlands Antilles. ... 6-1/192. ... Bats left, throws right. ... Full name: Ivanon Angelino Coffie.
TRANSACTIONS/CAREER NOTES: Signed as non-drafted free agent by Baltimore Orioles organization (July 28, 1995).
STATISTICAL NOTES: Led Gulf Coast League shortstops with .941 fielding percentage in 1996.

Year Team (League)	Pos.	G	AB	R	H	2B	3B	HR	RBI	Avg.	BB	SO	SB	PO	A	E	Avg.
1996— GC Orioles (GCL)........	SS-3B	56	193	29	42	8	4	0	20	.218	23	26	6	81	175	16	†.941
1997— Delmarva (S.Atl.)........	SS-3B	90	305	41	84	14	5	3	48	.275	23	45	19	126	203	19	.945
1998— Frederick (Caro.)........	3B-SS	130	473	62	121	19	2	16	75	.256	48	109	17	126	216	25	.932
1999— Bowie (East.)............	3B-SS	57	195	21	36	9	3	3	23	.185	20	46	2	39	90	8	.942
— Frederick (Caro.)	3B-SS-DH	73	276	35	78	18	4	11	53	.283	28	62	7	51	139	20	.905
2000— Bowie (East.)............	SS-3B	87	341	49	91	21	3	9	44	.267	36	53	1	98	199	19	.940
— Baltimore (A.L.)..........	3B-SS-DH	23	60	6	13	4	1	0	6	.217	5	11	1	13	32	1	.978
— Rochester (I.L.)..........	SS-3B	21	78	4	17	2	1	0	10	.218	2	21	0	19	45	3	.955
Major League totals (1 year)		**23**	**60**	**6**	**13**	**4**	**1**	**0**	**6**	**.217**	**5**	**11**	**1**	**13**	**32**	**1**	**.978**

PERSONAL: Born October 30, 1976, in Covina, Calif. ... 6-4/205. ... Throws right, bats right. ... Full name: David Raymond Coggin.
HIGH SCHOOL: Upland (Calif.).
TRANSACTIONS/CAREER NOTES: Selected by Philadelphia Phillies organization in supplemental round ("sandwich pick" between first and second round, 30th pick overall) of free-agent draft (June 1, 1995). ... On Reading disabled list (April 20-May 25, 1998; and May 14-June 4 and June 26, 1999-remainder of season).
STATISTICAL NOTES: Led Florida State League with 24 wild pitches in 1997.

Year	League	W	L	Pct.	ERA	G	GS	CG	ShO	Sv.	IP	H	R	ER	BB	SO
1995—	Martinsville (Appl.)	5	3	.625	3.00	11	11	0	0	0	48	45	25	16	31	37
1996—	Piedmont (S.Atl.)	9	12	.429	4.31	28	•28	3	3	0	169 1/3	156	87	*81	46	129
1997—	Clearwater (FSL)	11	8	.579	4.70	27	27	3	2	0	155	160	96	81	86	110
1998—	Reading (East.)	4	8	.333	4.14	20	20	0	0	0	108 2/3	106	58	50	62	65
1999—	Reading (East.)	2	5	.286	7.50	9	9	0	0	0	42	55	37	35	20	21
2000—	Clearwater (FSL)	2	2	.500	2.67	6	5	0	0	0	33 2/3	25	11	10	13	26
—	Reading (East.)	2	3	.400	4.93	7	7	0	0	0	42	49	24	23	13	30
—	Scranton/W.B. (I.L.)	3	2	.600	4.34	9	9	0	0	0	45 2/3	35	27	22	33	27
—	Philadelphia (N.L.)	2	0	1.000	5.33	5	5	0	0	0	27	35	20	16	12	17
Major League totals (1 year)		2	0	1.000	5.33	5	5	0	0	0	27	35	20	16	12	17

C

PERSONAL: Born October 22, 1976, in Teaneck, N.J. ... 6-1/185. ... Bats right, throws right. ... Full name: Michael Gus Colangelo.
HIGH SCHOOL: C.D. Hylton (Woodbridge, Va.).
COLLEGE: George Mason.
TRANSACTIONS/CAREER NOTES: Selected by Anaheim Angels organization in 21st round of free-agent draft (June 3, 1997). ... On Anaheim disabled list (June 14, 1999-remainder of season). ... On Anaheim disabled list (March 20, 2000-entire season). ... Claimed on waivers by Arizona Diamondbacks (October 5, 2000). ... Claimed on waivers by San Diego Padres (October 17, 2000).

Year	Team (League)	Pos.	G	AB	R	H	2B	3B	HR	RBI	Avg.	BB	SO	SB	PO	A	E	Avg.
1998—	Cedar Rapids (Midw.)	OF	22	83	13	23	8	0	4	8	.277	12	16	5	14	0	1	.933
—	Lake Elsinore (Calif.)	OF	36	145	33	55	11	3	5	21	.379	13	24	2	78	3	0	1.000
1999—	Erie (East.)	OF-DH	28	109	24	37	10	3	1	13	.339	14	22	3	35	3	2	.950
—	Edmonton (PCL)	OF	26	105	13	38	7	1	0	9	.362	13	18	2	29	3	2	.941
—	Anaheim (A.L.)	OF	1	2	0	1	0	0	0	0	.500	1	0	0	1	1	0	1.000
2000—	Anaheim (A.L.)								Did not play.									
Major League totals (1 year)			1	2	0	1	0	0	0	0	.500	1	0	0	1	1	0	1.000

PERSONAL: Born July 26, 1969, in Fontana, Calif. ... 6-0/205. ... Bats right, throws right. ... Full name: Gregory Joseph Colbrunn.
HIGH SCHOOL: Fontana (Calif.).
TRANSACTIONS/CAREER NOTES: Selected by Montreal Expos organization in sixth round of free-agent draft (June 2, 1987). ... On disabled list (April 10, 1991-entire season). ... On Indianapolis disabled list (April 9-May 5, 1992). ... On Montreal disabled list (August 2-18, 1992); included rehabilitation assignment to Indianapolis (August 13-18). ... On Montreal disabled list (April 5-21, 1993); included rehabilitation assignment to West Palm Beach (April 9-20). ... On Montreal disabled list (July 12, 1993-remainder of season); included rehabilitation assignment to Ottawa (July 27-August 2). ... Claimed on waivers by Florida Marlins (October 7, 1993). ... On Florida disabled list (April 9-May 27, and July 15-30, 1994); included rehabilitation assignments to Brevard County (May 12-18 and July 28-30) and Edmonton (May 18-27). ... On disabled list (July 24-August 8, 1996). ... Granted free agency (December 20, 1996). ... Signed by Minnesota Twins organization (January 24, 1997). ... Traded by Twins to Atlanta Braves for a player to be named later (August 14, 1997); Twins acquired OF Marc Lewis to complete deal (October 1, 1997). ... Granted free agency (October 23, 1997). ... Signed by Colorado Rockies organization (December 23, 1997). ... Traded by Rockies to Braves for P David Cortes, P Mike Porzio and a player to be named later (July 30, 1998); Rockies acquired P Anthony Briggs to complete deal (September 9, 1998). ... Granted free agency (October 23, 1998). ... Signed by Arizona Diamondbacks (November 17, 1998).
STATISTICAL NOTES: Had 21-game hitting streak (May 31-June 23, 1996). ... Career major league grand slams: 2.

Year	Team (League)	Pos.	G	AB	R	H	2B	3B	HR	RBI	Avg.	BB	SO	SB	PO	A	E	Avg.
1988—	Rockford (Midw.)	C	115	417	55	111	18	2	7	46	.266	22	60	5	595	81	15	.978
1989—	W. P. Beach (FSL)	C	59	228	20	54	8	0	0	25	.237	6	29	3	376	49	5	.988
—	Jacksonville (Sou.)	C	55	178	21	49	11	1	3	18	.275	13	33	0	304	34	4	.988
1990—	Jacksonville (Sou.)	C	125	458	57	138	29	1	13	76	.301	38	78	1	698	58	15	.981
1991—									Did not play.									
1992—	Indianapolis (A.A.)	1B	57	216	32	66	19	1	11	48	.306	7	41	1	441	27	4	.992
—	Montreal (N.L.)	1B	52	168	12	45	8	0	2	18	.268	6	34	3	363	29	3	.992
1993—	W. P. Beach (FSL)	1B	8	31	6	12	2	1	1	5	.387	4	1	0	74	5	1	.988
—	Montreal (N.L.)	1B	70	153	15	39	9	0	4	23	.255	6	33	4	372	27	2	.995
—	Ottawa (I.L.)	1B	6	22	4	6	1	0	0	8	.273	1	2	1	50	1	0	1.000
1994—	Florida (N.L.)■	1B	47	155	17	47	10	0	6	31	.303	9	27	1	304	26	4	.988
—	Brevard County (FSL).	DH-1B	7	11	3	6	2	0	1	2	.545	1	0	0	16	1	1	.944
—	Edmonton (PCL)	1B-DH	7	17	2	4	0	0	1	2	.235	0	1	0	28	1	1	.967
1995—	Florida (N.L.)	1B	138	528	70	146	22	1	23	89	.277	22	69	11	1066	90	5	.996
1996—	Florida (N.L.)	1B	141	511	60	146	26	2	16	69	.286	25	76	4	1169	101	6	.995
1997—	Minnesota (A.L.)■	1B-DH	70	217	24	61	14	0	5	26	.281	8	38	1	475	35	6	.988
—	Atlanta (N.L.)■	1B-DH	28	54	3	15	3	0	2	9	.278	2	11	0	54	6	1	.984
1998—	Colorado (N.L.)■	1B-OF-DH-C	62	122	12	38	8	2	2	13	.311	8	23	3	222	21	2	.992
—	Atlanta (N.L.)■	1B-OF	28	44	6	13	3	0	1	10	.295	2	11	1	57	4	0	1.000
1999—	Arizona (N.L.)■	1B-DH-3B	67	135	20	44	5	3	5	24	.326	12	23	1	203	19	1	.996
2000—	Arizona (N.L.)	1B-DH-3B	116	329	48	103	22	1	15	57	.313	43	45	0	649	52	8	.989
American League totals (1 year)			70	217	24	61	14	0	5	26	.281	8	38	1	475	35	6	.988
National League totals (9 years)			749	2199	263	636	116	9	76	343	.289	135	352	28	4459	375	32	.993
Major League totals (9 years)			819	2416	287	697	130	9	81	369	.288	143	390	29	4934	410	38	.993

DIVISION SERIES RECORD

							BATTING									FIELDING		
Year	Team (League)	Pos.	G	AB	R	H	2B	3B	HR	RBI	Avg.	BB	SO	SB	PO	A	E	Avg.
1997—	Atlanta (N.L.).............	PH	1	1	0	1	0	0	0	2	1.000	0	0	0	...	...	...	...
1998—	Atlanta (N.L.).............	PH	2	2	0	0	0	0	0	0	.000	0	0	0	...	...	...	...
1999—	Arizona (N.L.)............	1B	2	5	1	2	1	0	1	2	.400	2	2	0	17	0	0	1.000
	Division series totals (3 years)		5	8	1	3	1	0	1	4	.375	2	2	0	17	0	0	1.000

CHAMPIONSHIP SERIES RECORD

							BATTING									FIELDING		
Year	Team (League)	Pos.	G	AB	R	H	2B	3B	HR	RBI	Avg.	BB	SO	SB	PO	A	E	Avg.
1997—	Atlanta (N.L.).............	PH	3	3	0	2	0	0	0	0	.667	0	0	0	...	...	...	...
1998—	Atlanta (N.L.).............	PH	6	6	0	2	0	0	0	0	.333	0	2	0	...	...	...	...
	Championship series totals (2 years)		9	9	0	4	0	0	0	0	.444	0	2	0	...	...	...	...

COLEMAN, MICHAEL — OF — REDS

PERSONAL: Born August 16, 1975, in Nashville, Tenn. ... 5-11/215. ... Bats right, throws right. ... Full name: Michael D. Coleman.
HIGH SCHOOL: Stratford (Nashville, Tenn.).
TRANSACTIONS/CAREER NOTES: Selected by Boston Red Sox organization in 18th round of free-agent draft (June 2, 1994). ... On Pawtucket disabled list (May 9-June 11, 1998; and April 8-27 and July 3-10, 1999). ... On Pawtucket disabled list (April 29-June 27, 2000). ... On Boston disabled list (June 27, 2000-remainder of season). ... Traded by Red Sox with IF Donnie Sadler to Cincinnati Reds for IF Chris Stynes (November 16, 2000).

							BATTING									FIELDING		
Year	Team (League)	Pos.	G	AB	R	H	2B	3B	HR	RBI	Avg.	BB	SO	SB	PO	A	E	Avg.
1994—	GC Red Sox (GCL)	OF	25	95	15	26	6	1	3	15	.274	10	20	5	32	0	0	1.000
	— Fort Myers (GCL)	OF	25	95	15	26	6	1	3	15	.274	10	20	5	32	0	0	1.000
	— Utica (NY-Penn)	OF	23	65	16	11	2	0	1	3	.169	14	21	11	35	2	2	.949
1995—	Michigan (Midw.)	OF	112	422	70	113	16	2	11	61	.268	40	93	29	251	5	5	.981
1996—	Sarasota (FSL)	OF	110	407	54	100	20	5	1	36	.246	38	86	24	261	9	2	*.993
1997—	Trenton (East.)	OF-DH	102	385	56	116	17	8	14	58	.301	41	89	20	259	6	5	.981
	— Pawtucket (I.L.)..........	OF	28	113	27	36	9	2	7	19	.319	12	27	4	53	2	4	.932
	— Boston (A.L.)............	OF	8	24	2	4	1	0	0	2	.167	0	11	1	16	0	1	.941
1998—	Pawtucket (I.L.)..........	OF-DH	93	340	47	86	13	0	14	37	.253	27	92	12	173	9	4	.978
1999—	Pawtucket (I.L.)..........	OF-DH	115	467	95	125	29	2	30	74	.268	51	128	14	299	2	6	.980
	— Boston (A.L.)............	OF	2	5	1	1	0	0	0	0	.200	1	0	0	0	0	0	...
2000—	Pawtucket (I.L.)..........	OF	18	66	11	17	5	1	6	15	.258	3	23	1	26	1	1	.964
	Major League totals (2 years)		10	29	3	5	1	0	0	2	.172	1	11	1	16	0	1	.941

COLLIER, LOU — IF — BREWERS

PERSONAL: Born August 21, 1973, in Chicago. ... 5-10/182. ... Bats right, throws right. ... Full name: Louis Keith Collier.
HIGH SCHOOL: Vocational (Chicago).
JUNIOR COLLEGE: Kishwaukee Junior College (Ill.), then Triton Community College (Ill.).
TRANSACTIONS/CAREER NOTES: Selected by Pittsburgh Pirates organization in 31st round of free-agent draft (June 1, 1992). ... On Pittsburgh disabled list (May 22-June 7, 1998); included rehabilitation assignment to Lynchburg (June 3-7). ... Claimed on waivers by Milwaukee Brewers (December 18, 1998). ... On Indianapolis disabled list (April 27-July 7, 2000).

							BATTING									FIELDING		
Year	Team (League)	Pos.	G	AB	R	H	2B	3B	HR	RBI	Avg.	BB	SO	SB	PO	A	E	Avg.
1993—	Welland (NY-Penn).....	SS	50	201	35	61	6	2	1	19	.303	12	31	8	74	138	27	.887
1994—	Augusta (S.Atl.)..........	SS	85	318	48	89	17	4	7	40	.280	25	53	32	106	262	34	.915
	— Salem (Caro.)............	SS	43	158	25	42	4	1	6	16	.266	15	29	5	65	129	11	.946
1995—	Lynchburg (Caro.).......	SS	114	399	68	110	19	3	4	38	.276	51	60	31	156	361	35	.937
1996—	Carolina (Sou.)..........	SS-DH	119	443	76	124	20	3	3	49	.280	48	73	29	189	310	30	.943
1997—	Calgary (PCL)..........	SS-2B-DH	112	397	65	131	31	5	1	48	.330	37	47	12	187	315	34	.937
	— Pittsburgh (N.L.)	SS	18	37	3	5	0	0	0	3	.135	1	11	1	9	36	0	1.000
1998—	Pittsburgh (N.L.)	SS	110	334	30	82	13	6	2	34	.246	31	70	2	148	287	18	.960
	— Lynchburg (Caro.)	SS	5	18	4	3	2	0	0	0	.167	2	0	2	5	16	4	.840
1999—	Milwaukee (N.L.)■....SS-OF-3B-2B		74	135	18	35	9	0	2	21	.259	14	32	3	42	56	5	.951
	— Louisville (I.L.)..........	3B-SS-OF	27	91	25	35	10	0	4	11	.385	15	14	6	17	59	3	.962
2000—	Indianapolis (I.L.).......	OF-2B-3B	17	56	7	14	4	1	0	12	.250	11	9	2	31	11	3	.933
	— Huntsville (Sou.)	3B-OF-2B-SS	50	172	29	46	4	2	2	29	.267	30	44	7	35	69	8	.929
	— Milwaukee (N.L.)	OF-3B	14	32	9	7	1	0	1	2	.219	6	4	0	16	2	0	1.000
	Major League totals (4 years)		216	538	60	129	23	6	5	60	.240	52	117	6	215	381	23	.963

COLOME, JESUS — P — DEVIL RAYS

PERSONAL: Born June 2, 1980, in San Pedro de Macoris, Dominican Republic. ... 6-2/170. ... Throws right, bats right. ... Full name: Jesus Colome De La Cruz.
TRANSACTIONS/CAREER NOTES: Signed as non-drafted free agent by Oakland Athletics organization (September 29, 1996). ... Traded by Athletics with player to be named to Tampa Bay Devil Rays for P Jim Mecir and P Todd Belitz (July 28, 2000).

Year	League	W	L	Pct.	ERA	G	GS	CG	ShO	Sv.	IP	H	R	ER	BB	SO
1997—	Dominican Athletics (DSL) .	9	3	.750	2.70	18	7	3	0	0	90	73	33	27	22	55
1998—	Arizona Athletics (Ariz.)......	2	5	.286	3.18	12	11	0	0	0	56²/₃	47	27	20	16	62
1999—	Modesto (Calif.)	8	4	.667	3.36	31	22	0	0	1	128²/₃	125	63	48	60	127
2000—	Midland (Texas).................	9	4	.692	3.59	20	20	0	0	0	110¹/₃	99	62	44	50	95
	— Orlando (Sou.)■	1	2	.333	6.75	3	3	0	0	0	14²/₃	18	12	11	7	9

COLON, BARTOLO — P — INDIANS

PERSONAL: Born May 24, 1975, in Altamira, Dominican Republic. ... 6-0/230. ... Throws right, bats right.
TRANSACTIONS/CAREER NOTES: Signed as non-drafted free agent by Cleveland Indians organization (June 26, 1993). ... On Canton/Akron disabled list (May 30-July 24, 1996). ... On Cleveland disabled list (April 16-May 12, 2000); included rehabilitation assignment to Buffalo (May 7-12).
HONORS: Named Carolina League Pitcher of the Year (1995).
STATISTICAL NOTES: Pitched 4-0 no-hit victory against New Orleans (June 20, 1997). ... Pitched 2-0 one-hit, complete-game victory against New York Yankees (September 18, 2000).

Year League	W	L	Pct.	ERA	G	GS	CG	ShO	Sv.	IP	H	R	ER	BB	SO
1993—Santiago (DSL).................	6	1	.857	2.59	11	10	2	1	1	66	44	24	19	33	48
1994—Burlington (Appl.)..............	7	4	.636	3.14	12	12	0	0	0	66	46	32	23	44	84
1995—Kinston (Caro.)...............	13	3	*.813	1.96	21	21	0	0	0	128²/₃	91	31	28	39	*152
1996—Canton/Akron (East.).......	2	2	.500	1.74	13	12	0	0	0	62	44	17	12	25	56
—Buffalo (A.A.)....................	0	0	...	6.00	8	0	0	0	0	15	16	10	10	8	19
1997—Cleveland (A.L.)................	4	7	.364	5.65	19	17	1	0	0	94	107	66	59	45	66
—Buffalo (A.A.)....................	7	1	.875	2.22	10	10	1	1	0	56²/₃	45	15	14	23	54
1998—Cleveland (A.L.)................	14	9	.609	3.71	31	31	6	2	0	204	205	91	84	79	158
1999—Cleveland (A.L.)................	18	5	.783	3.95	32	32	1	1	0	205	185	97	90	76	161
2000—Cleveland (A.L.)................	15	8	.652	3.88	30	30	2	1	0	188	163	86	81	98	212
—Buffalo (I.L.).....................	1	0	1.000	1.80	1	1	0	0	0	5	6	1	1	0	4
Major League totals (4 years)	51	29	.638	4.09	112	110	10	4	0	691	660	340	314	298	597

DIVISION SERIES RECORD

Year League	W	L	Pct.	ERA	G	GS	CG	ShO	Sv.	IP	H	R	ER	BB	SO
1997—Cleveland (A.L.)................							Did not play.								
1998—Cleveland (A.L.)................	0	0	...	1.59	1	1	0	0	0	5²/₃	5	1	1	4	3
1999—Cleveland (A.L.)................	0	1	.000	9.00	2	2	0	0	0	9	11	9	9	4	12
Division series totals (2 years)	0	1	.000	6.14	3	3	0	0	0	14²/₃	16	10	10	8	15

CHAMPIONSHIP SERIES RECORD

Year League	W	L	Pct.	ERA	G	GS	CG	ShO	Sv.	IP	H	R	ER	BB	SO
1997—Cleveland (A.L.)................							Did not play.								
1998—Cleveland (A.L.)................	1	0	1.000	1.00	1	1	1	0	0	9	4	1	1	4	3

WORLD SERIES RECORD

Year League	W	L	Pct.	ERA	G	GS	CG	ShO	Sv.	IP	H	R	ER	BB	SO
1997—Cleveland (A.L.)................							Did not play.								

ALL-STAR GAME RECORD

Year League	W	L	Pct.	ERA	GS	CG	ShO	Sv.	IP	H	R	ER	BB	SO
1998—American	1	0	1.000	27.00	0	0	0	0	1	2	3	3	1	1

CONE, DAVID — P — RED SOX

PERSONAL: Born January 2, 1963, in Kansas City, Mo. ... 6-1/200. ... Throws right, bats left. ... Full name: David Brian Cone.
HIGH SCHOOL: Rockhurst (Kansas City, Mo.).
TRANSACTIONS/CAREER NOTES: Selected by Kansas City Royals organization in third round of free-agent draft (June 8, 1981). ... On disabled list (April 8, 1983-entire season). ... Traded by Royals with C Chris Jelic to New York Mets for C Ed Hearn, P Rick Anderson and P Mauro Gozzo (March 27, 1987). ... On New York disabled list (May 28-August 14, 1987); included rehabilitation assignment to Tidewater (July 30-August 14). ... Traded by Mets to Toronto Blue Jays for IF Jeff Kent and a player to be named later (August 27, 1992); Mets acquired OF Ryan Thompson to complete deal (September 1, 1992). ... Granted free agency (October 30, 1992). ... Signed by Royals (December 8, 1992). ... Traded by Royals to Blue Jays for P David Sinnes, IF Chris Stynes and IF Tony Medrano (April 6, 1995). ... Traded by Blue Jays to New York Yankees for P Marty Janzen, P Jason Jarvis and P Mike Gordon (July 28, 1995). ... Granted free agency (November 3, 1995). ... Re-signed by Yankees (December 21, 1995). ... On New York disabled list (May 3-September 2, 1996); included rehabilitation assignment to Norwich (August 21-September 1). ... On disabled list (August 18-September 20, 1997). ... Granted free agency (November 5, 1998). ... Re-signed by Yankees (November 11, 1998). ... Granted free agency (November 3, 1999). ... Re-signed by Yankees (December 6, 1999). ... Granted free agency (November 7, 2000). ... Signed by Boston Red Sox (January 11, 2001).
RECORDS: Shares major league record for striking out side on nine pitches (August 30, 1991, seventh inning).
HONORS: Named righthanded pitcher on THE SPORTING NEWS A.L. All-Star team (1994). ... Named A.L. Cy Young Award winner by Baseball Writers' Association of America (1994).
STATISTICAL NOTES: Led Southern League with 27 wild pitches in 1984. ... Pitched 6-0 one-hit, complete-game victory against San Diego (August 29, 1988). ... Tied for N.L. lead with 10 balks in 1988. ... Pitched 1-0 one-hit, complete-game victory against St. Louis (September 20, 1991). ... Struck out 19 batters in one game (October 6, 1991). ... Pitched 4-0 one-hit, complete-game victory against California (May 22, 1994). ... Led A.L. with 229 1/3 innings pitched in 1995. ... Struck out 16 batters in one game (June 23, 1997). ... Tied for A.L. lead with 14 wild pitches in 1997. ... Pitched 6-0 perfect game against Montreal (July 18, 1999).
MISCELLANEOUS: Singled in only appearance as pinch hitter (1990).

Year League	W	L	Pct.	ERA	G	GS	CG	ShO	Sv.	IP	H	R	ER	BB	SO
1981—GC Royals-Blue (GCL)	6	4	.600	2.55	14	12	0	0	0	67	52	24	19	33	45
1982—Charleston, S.C. (S.Atl.)	9	2	.818	2.06	16	16	1	1	0	104²/₃	84	38	24	47	87
—Fort Myers (FSL)................	7	1	.875	2.12	10	9	6	1	0	72¹/₃	56	21	17	25	57
1983—Jacksonville (Sou.)							Did not play.								
1984—Memphis (Sou.)	8	12	.400	4.28	29	29	9	1	0	178²/₃	162	103	85	114	110
1985—Omaha (A.A.)	9	15	.375	4.65	28	27	5	1	0	158²/₃	157	90	82	*93	115
1986—Omaha (A.A.)	8	4	.667	2.79	39	2	2	0	14	71	60	23	22	25	63
—Kansas City (A.L.)	0	0	...	5.56	11	0	0	0	0	22²/₃	29	14	14	13	21
1987—New York (N.L.)■	5	6	.455	3.71	21	13	1	0	1	99¹/₃	87	46	41	44	68
—Tidewater (I.L.).................	0	1	.000	5.73	3	3	0	0	0	11	10	8	7	6	7
1988—New York (N.L.)................	20	3	*.870	2.22	35	28	8	4	0	231¹/₃	178	67	57	80	213
1989—New York (N.L.)................	14	8	.636	3.52	34	33	7	2	0	219²/₃	183	92	86	74	190
1990—New York (N.L.)................	14	10	.583	3.23	31	30	6	2	0	211²/₃	177	84	76	65	*233

Year League	W	L	Pct.	ERA	G	GS	CG	ShO	Sv.	IP	H	R	ER	BB	SO
1991— New York (N.L.).................	14	14	.500	3.29	34	34	5	2	0	232²/₃	204	95	85	73	*241
1992— New York (N.L.).................	13	7	.650	2.88	27	27	7	•5	0	196²/₃	162	75	63	*82	214
— Toronto (A.L.)■............	4	3	.571	2.55	8	7	0	0	0	53	39	16	15	29	47
1993— Kansas City (A.L.)■...........	11	14	.440	3.33	34	34	6	1	0	254	205	102	94	114	191
1994— Kansas City (A.L.).............	16	5	.762	2.94	23	23	4	3	0	171²/₃	130	60	56	54	132
1995— Toronto (A.L.)■................	9	6	.600	3.38	17	17	5	2	0	130¹/₃	113	53	49	41	102
— New York (A.L.)■...........	9	2	.818	3.82	13	13	1	0	0	§99	82	42	42	47	89
1996— New York (A.L.).................	7	2	.778	2.88	11	11	1	0	0	72	50	25	23	34	71
— Norwich (East.).................	0	0	...	0.90	2	2	0	0	0	10	9	3	1	1	13
1997— New York (A.L.).................	12	6	.667	2.82	29	29	1	0	0	195	155	67	61	86	222
1998— New York (A.L.).................	•20	7	.741	3.55	31	31	3	0	0	207²/₃	186	89	82	59	209
1999— New York (A.L.).................	12	9	.571	3.44	31	31	1	1	0	193¹/₃	164	84	74	90	177
2000— New York (A.L.).................	4	14	.222	6.91	30	29	0	0	0	155	192	124	119	82	120
A.L. totals (10 years)	104	68	.605	3.64	238	225	22	7	0	1553²/₃	1345	676	629	649	1381
N.L. totals (6 years)	80	48	.625	3.08	182	165	34	15	1	1191¹/₃	991	459	408	418	1159
Major League totals (15 years)	184	116	.613	3.40	420	390	56	22	1	2745	2336	1135	1037	1067	2540

DIVISION SERIES RECORD

RECORDS: Shares A.L. career record for most games started—5.

Year League	W	L	Pct.	ERA	G	GS	CG	ShO	Sv.	IP	H	R	ER	BB	SO
1995— New York (A.L.).................	1	0	1.000	4.60	2	2	0	0	0	15²/₃	15	8	8	9	14
1996— New York (A.L.).................	0	1	.000	9.00	2	1	0	0	0	6	8	6	6	2	8
1997— New York (A.L.).................	0	0	...	16.20	1	1	0	0	0	3¹/₃	7	6	6	2	2
1998— New York (A.L.).................	1	0	1.000	0.00	1	1	0	0	0	5²/₃	2	0	0	1	6
1999— New York (A.L.).................								Did not play.							
Division series totals (4 years)	2	1	.667	5.87	6	5	0	0	0	30²/₃	32	20	20	14	30

CHAMPIONSHIP SERIES RECORD

Year League	W	L	Pct.	ERA	G	GS	CG	ShO	Sv.	IP	H	R	ER	BB	SO
1988— New York (N.L.).................	1	1	.500	4.50	3	2	1	0	0	12	10	6	6	5	9
1992— Toronto (A.L.)...................	1	1	.500	3.00	2	2	0	0	0	12	11	7	4	5	9
1996— New York (A.L.).................	0	0	...	3.00	1	1	0	0	0	6	5	2	2	5	5
1998— New York (A.L.).................	1	0	1.000	4.15	2	2	0	0	0	13	12	6	6	6	13
1999— New York (A.L.).................	1	0	1.000	2.57	1	1	0	0	0	7	7	2	2	3	9
2000— New York (A.L.).................	0	0	...	0.00	1	0	0	0	0	1	0	0	0	0	0
Champ. series totals (6 years)	4	2	.667	3.53	10	8	1	0	0	51	45	23	20	24	45

WORLD SERIES RECORD

NOTES: Member of World Series championship team (1992, 1996, 1998, 1999 and 2000).

Year League	W	L	Pct.	ERA	G	GS	CG	ShO	Sv.	IP	H	R	ER	BB	SO
1992— Toronto (A.L.)...................	0	0	...	3.48	2	2	0	0	0	10¹/₃	9	5	4	8	8
1996— New York (A.L.).................	1	0	1.000	1.50	1	1	0	0	0	6	4	1	1	4	3
1998— New York (A.L.).................	0	0	...	3.00	1	1	0	0	0	6	2	3	2	3	4
1999— New York (A.L.).................	1	0	1.000	0.00	1	1	0	0	0	7	1	0	0	5	4
2000— New York (A.L.).................	0	0	...	0.00	1	0	0	0	0	¹/₃	0	0	0	0	0
World Series totals (5 years)	2	0	1.000	2.12	6	5	0	0	0	29²/₃	16	9	7	20	19

ALL-STAR GAME RECORD

Year League	W	L	Pct.	ERA	G	GS	CG	ShO	Sv.	IP	H	R	ER	BB	SO
1988— National	0	0	...	0.00	0	0	0	0	0	1	0	0	0	0	1
1992— National	0	0	...	0.00	0	0	0	0	0	1	0	0	0	0	1
1994— American	0	0	...	13.50	0	0	0	0	0	2	4	3	3	0	3
1997— American	0	0	...	0.00	0	0	0	0	0	1	0	0	0	2	0
1999— American	0	0	...	4.50	0	0	0	0	0	2	4	1	1	1	3
All-Star Game totals (5 years)	0	0	...	5.14	0	0	0	0	0	7	8	4	4	3	8

CONINE, JEFF   1B/OF   ORIOLES

PERSONAL: Born June 27, 1966, in Tacoma, Wash. ... 6-1/220. ... Bats right, throws right. ... Full name: Jeffrey Guy Conine.

HIGH SCHOOL: Eisenhower (Rialto, Calif.).

COLLEGE: UCLA.

TRANSACTIONS/CAREER NOTES: Selected by Kansas City Royals organization in 58th round of free-agent draft (June 2, 1987). ... On disabled list (June 28, 1991-remainder of season). ... Selected by Florida Marlins in first round (22nd pick overall) of expansion draft (November 17, 1992). ... Traded by Marlins to Royals for P Blaine Mull (November 20, 1997). ... On Kansas City disabled list (March 25-May 5 and July 27-August 19, 1998); included rehabilitation assignment to Omaha (August 17-19). ... Traded by Royals to Baltimore Orioles for P Chris Fussell (April 2, 1999). ... Granted free agency (November 5, 1999). ... Re-signed by Orioles (December 15, 1999).

RECORDS: Shares major league rookie-season record for most games—162 (1993).

HONORS: Named Southern League Most Valuable Player (1990).

STATISTICAL NOTES: Led Southern League first basemen with 1,164 putouts, 95 assists, 22 errors, 1,281 total chances and 108 double plays in 1990. ... Led N.L. with 12 sacrifice flies in 1995. ... Career major league grand slams: 3.

MISCELLANEOUS: Holds Florida Marlins all-time records for most hits (737), runs batted in (422), doubles (122) and highest career batting average (.291).

Year Team (League)	Pos.	G	AB	R	H	2B	3B	HR	RBI	Avg.	BB	SO	SB	PO	A	E	Avg.
1988— Baseball City (FSL)	1B-3B	118	415	63	113	23	9	10	59	.272	46	77	26	661	51	22	.970
1989— Baseball City (FSL)	1B	113	425	68	116	12	7	14	60	.273	40	91	32	830	65	18	.980
1990— Memphis (Sou.)	1B-3B	137	487	89	156	37	8	15	95	.320	94	88	21 †1164	†95	†22	.983
— Kansas City (A.L.)	1B	9	20	3	5	2	0	0	2	.250	2	5	0	39	4	1	.977
1991— Omaha (A.A.)	1B-OF	51	171	23	44	9	1	3	15	.257	26	39	0	392	41	7	.984
1992— Omaha (A.A.)	1B-OF	110	397	69	120	24	5	20	72	.302	54	67	4	845	60	6	.993
— Kansas City (A.L.)	OF-1B	28	91	10	23	5	2	0	9	.253	8	23	0	75	3	0	1.000

Year Team (League)	Pos.	G	AB	R	H	2B	3B	HR	RBI	Avg.	BB	SO	SB	PO	A	E	Avg.
1993—Florida (N.L.)■	OF-1B	*162	595	75	174	24	3	12	79	.292	52	135	2	403	25	2	.995
1994—Florida (N.L.)	OF-1B	115	451	60	144	27	6	18	82	.319	40	92	1	408	24	6	.986
1995—Florida (N.L.)	OF-1B	133	483	72	146	26	2	25	105	.302	66	94	2	292	18	6	.981
1996—Florida (N.L.)	OF-1B	157	597	84	175	32	2	26	95	.293	62	121	1	478	48	8	.985
1997—Florida (N.L.)	1B-OF	151	405	46	98	13	1	17	61	.242	57	89	2	897	104	8	.992
1998—Kansas City (A.L.)■ ...	OF-1B-DH	93	309	30	79	26	0	8	43	.256	26	68	3	235	7	1	.996
—Omaha (PCL)	DH-OF	2	9	0	0	0	0	0	0	.000	0	3	0	2	0	0	1.000
1999—Baltimore (A.L.)■	1-DH-O-3	139	444	54	129	31	1	13	75	.291	30	40	0	848	53	7	.992
2000—Baltimore (A.L.)..........	3-1-DH-O	119	409	53	116	20	2	13	46	.284	36	53	4	363	108	15	.969
American League totals (5 years)		388	1273	150	352	84	5	34	175	.277	102	189	7	1560	175	24	.986
National League totals (5 years)		718	2531	337	737	122	14	98	422	.291	277	531	8	2478	219	30	.989
Major League totals (10 years)		1106	3804	487	1089	206	19	132	597	.286	379	720	15	4038	394	54	.988

DIVISION SERIES RECORD

Year Team (League)	Pos.	G	AB	R	H	2B	3B	HR	RBI	Avg.	BB	SO	SB	PO	A	E	Avg.
1997—Florida (N.L.)	1B	3	11	3	4	1	0	0	0	.364	1	0	0	24	3	1	.964

CHAMPIONSHIP SERIES RECORD

Year Team (League)	Pos.	G	AB	R	H	2B	3B	HR	RBI	Avg.	BB	SO	SB	PO	A	E	Avg.
1997—Florida (N.L.)	1B	6	18	1	2	0	0	0	1	.111	1	4	0	34	5	0	1.000

WORLD SERIES RECORD

NOTES: Member of World Series championship team (1997).

Year Team (League)	Pos.	G	AB	R	H	2B	3B	HR	RBI	Avg.	BB	SO	SB	PO	A	E	Avg.
1997—Florida (N.L.)	1B-PH	6	13	1	3	0	0	0	2	.231	0	0	0	30	2	0	1.000

ALL-STAR GAME RECORD

NOTES: Hit home run in first at-bat (July 11, 1995). ... Named Most Valuable Player (1995).

Year League	Pos.	AB	R	H	2B	3B	HR	RBI	Avg.	BB	SO	SB	PO	A	E	Avg.
1994—National									Did not play.							
1995—National	PH	1	1	1	0	0	1	1	1.000	0	0	0	...	...	...	...

CONTI, JASON — OF — DIAMONDBACKS

PERSONAL: Born January 27, 1975, in Pittsburgh. ... 5-11/180. ... Bats left, throws right. ... Full name: Stanley Jason Conti.
HIGH SCHOOL: Seneca Valley (Harmony, Pa.).
COLLEGE: Pittsburgh.
TRANSACTIONS/CAREER NOTES: Selected by Arizona Diamondbacks organization in 32nd round of free-agent draft (June 4, 1996). ... Loaned by Diamondbacks to Tulsa, Texas Rangers organization (April 1-September 14, 1998).
STATISTICAL NOTES: Tied for Midwest League lead in double plays by outfielder with six in 1997. ... Led Pacific Coast League outfielders with 303 total chances in 1999.

Year Team (League)	Pos.	G	AB	R	H	2B	3B	HR	RBI	Avg.	BB	SO	SB	PO	A	E	Avg.
1996—Lethbridge (Pio.)	OF	63	226	63	83	15	1	4	49	.367	30	29	30	80	5	4	.955
1997—South Bend (Midw.) ...	OF	117	458	78	142	22	10	3	43	.310	45	99	30	240	13	5	.981
—High Desert (Calif.)	OF	14	59	15	21	5	1	2	8	.356	10	12	1	27	2	5	.853
1998—Tulsa (Texas)■	OF	130	530	*125	167	31	12	15	67	.315	63	96	19	183	*20	5	.976
1999—Tucson (PCL)■	OF	133	520	100	151	23	8	9	57	.290	55	89	22	278	17	8	.974
2000—Tucson (PCL)	OF	93	383	75	117	20	5	11	57	.305	23	57	11	186	6	10	.950
—Arizona (N.L.)	OF	47	91	11	21	4	3	1	15	.231	7	30	3	53	4	1	.983
Major League totals (1 year)		47	91	11	21	4	3	1	15	.231	7	30	3	53	4	1	.983

COOK, DENNIS — P — METS

PERSONAL: Born October 4, 1962, in Lamarque, Texas. ... 6-3/190. ... Throws left, bats left. ... Full name: Dennis Bryan Cook.
HIGH SCHOOL: Dickinson (Texas).
JUNIOR COLLEGE: Angelina College (Texas).
COLLEGE: Texas.
TRANSACTIONS/CAREER NOTES: Selected by San Diego Padres organization in sixth round of free-agent draft (January 11, 1983); did not sign. ... Selected by San Francisco Giants organization in 18th round of free-agent draft (June 3, 1985). ... Traded by Giants with P Terry Mulholland and 3B Charlie Hayes to Philadelphia Phillies for P Steve Bedrosian and a player to be named later (June, 18, 1989); Giants acquired IF Rick Parker to complete deal (August 7, 1989). ... Traded by Phillies to Los Angeles Dodgers for C Darrin Fletcher (September 13, 1990). ... Traded by Dodgers with P Mike Christopher to Cleveland Indians for P Rudy Seanez (December 10, 1991). ... Granted free agency (October 15, 1993). ... Signed by Chicago White Sox organization (January 5, 1994). ... Claimed on waivers by Indians (October 17, 1994). ... Traded by Indians to Texas Rangers for SS Guillermo Mercedes (June 22, 1995). ... Granted free agency (October 29, 1996). ... Signed by Florida Marlins (December 10, 1996). ... On suspended list (July 4-5, 1997). ... Traded by Marlins to New York Mets for OF Fletcher Bates and P Scott Comer (December 18, 1997). ... Granted free agency (October 23, 1998). ... Re-signed by Mets (November 18, 1998).
HONORS: Named Texas League Pitcher of the Year (1987).
STATISTICAL NOTES: Led A.L. with five balks in 1992.
MISCELLANEOUS: Appeared in one game as pinch runner with Philadelphia (1989). ... Singled once and scored once in five games as pinch hitter and appeared in one game as pinch runner with Philadelphia (1990). ... Appeared in one game as pinch runner (1997). ... Singled twice, scored once and had an RBI in two games as pinch hitter (1997).

Year League	W	L	Pct.	ERA	G	GS	CG	ShO	Sv.	IP	H	R	ER	BB	SO
1985— Clinton (Midw.)	5	4	.556	3.36	13	13	1	0	0	83	73	35	31	27	40
1986— Fresno (Calif.)....................	12	7	.632	3.97	27	25	2	1	1	170	141	92	75	100	*173
1987— Shreveport (Texas)............	9	2	.818	2.13	16	16	1	1	0	105²/₃	94	32	25	20	98
— Phoenix (PCL)	2	5	.286	5.23	12	11	1	0	0	62	72	45	36	26	24
1988— Phoenix (PCL)....................	11	9	.550	3.88	26	25	5	1	0	141¹/₃	138	73	61	51	110
— San Francisco (N.L.)	2	1	.667	2.86	4	4	1	1	0	22	9	8	7	11	13
1989— Phoenix (PCL)....................	7	4	.636	3.12	12	12	3	1	0	78	73	29	27	19	85
— San Francisco (N.L.)	1	0	1.000	1.80	2	2	1	0	0	15	13	3	3	5	9
— Philadelphia (N.L.)■........	6	8	.429	3.99	21	16	1	1	0	106	97	56	47	33	58
1990— Philadelphia (N.L.).............	8	3	.727	3.56	42	13	2	1	1	141²/₃	132	61	56	54	58
— Los Angeles (N.L.)■.........	1	1	.500	7.53	5	3	0	0	0	14¹/₃	23	13	12	2	6
1991— Albuquerque (PCL).............	7	3	.700	3.63	14	14	1	0	0	91²/₃	73	46	37	32	84
— Los Angeles (N.L.)	1	0	1.000	0.51	20	1	0	0	0	17²/₃	12	3	1	7	8
— San Antonio (Texas)	1	3	.250	2.49	7	7	1	0	0	50²/₃	43	20	14	10	45
1992— Cleveland (A.L.)■..............	5	7	.417	3.82	32	25	1	0	0	158	156	79	67	50	96
1993— Cleveland (A.L.).................	5	5	.500	5.67	25	6	0	0	0	54	62	36	34	16	34
— Charlotte (I.L.).................	3	2	.600	5.06	12	6	0	0	0	42²/₃	46	26	24	6	40
1994— Chicago (A.L.)■................	3	1	.750	3.55	38	0	0	0	0	33	29	17	13	14	26
1995— Cleveland (A.L.)■..............	0	0	…	6.39	11	0	0	0	0	12²/₃	16	9	9	10	13
— Texas (A.L.)■..................	0	2	.000	4.00	35	1	0	0	2	45	47	23	20	16	40
1996— Texas (A.L.)	5	2	.714	4.09	60	0	0	0	0	70¹/₃	53	34	32	35	64
1997— Florida (N.L.)■.................	1	2	.333	3.90	59	0	0	0	0	62¹/₃	64	28	27	28	63
1998— New York (N.L.)■.............	8	4	.667	2.38	73	0	0	0	1	68	60	21	18	27	79
1999— New York (N.L.)...............	10	5	.667	3.86	71	0	0	0	3	63	50	27	27	27	68
2000— New York (N.L.)...............	6	3	.667	5.34	68	0	0	0	2	59	63	35	35	31	53
A.L. totals (5 years)	18	17	.514	4.22	201	32	1	0	2	373	363	198	175	141	273
N.L. totals (8 years)	44	27	.620	3.69	365	39	5	3	7	569	523	255	233	225	415
Major League totals (13 years)	62	44	.585	3.90	566	71	6	3	9	942	886	453	408	366	688

DIVISION SERIES RECORD

Year League	W	L	Pct.	ERA	G	GS	CG	ShO	Sv.	IP	H	R	ER	BB	SO
1996— Texas (A.L.)	0	0	…	0.00	2	0	0	0	0	1¹/₃	0	0	0	1	0
1997— Florida (N.L.)....................	1	0	1.000	0.00	2	0	0	0	0	3	0	0	0	1	3
1999— New York (N.L.)...............	0	0	…	0.00	1	0	0	0	0	1²/₃	1	0	0	1	1
2000— New York (N.L.)...............	0	0	…	0.00	2	0	0	0	0	1¹/₃	0	0	0	2	1
Division series totals (4 years)	1	0	1.000	0.00	7	0	0	0	0	7¹/₃	1	0	0	5	5

CHAMPIONSHIP SERIES RECORD

Year League	W	L	Pct.	ERA	G	GS	CG	ShO	Sv.	IP	H	R	ER	BB	SO
1997— Florida (N.L.)....................	0	0	…	0.00	2	0	0	0	0	2¹/₃	0	0	0	0	2
1999— New York (N.L.)...............	0	0	…	0.00	3	0	0	0	0	1¹/₃	1	0	0	2	1
2000— New York (N.L.)...............	0	0	…	0.00	1	0	0	0	0	1	1	0	0	0	2
Champ. series totals (3 years)	0	0	…	0.00	6	0	0	0	0	4²/₃	2	0	0	2	5

WORLD SERIES RECORD

NOTES: Member of World Series championship team (1997).

Year League	W	L	Pct.	ERA	G	GS	CG	ShO	Sv.	IP	H	R	ER	BB	SO
1997— Florida (N.L.)....................	1	0	1.000	0.00	3	0	0	0	0	3²/₃	1	0	0	1	5
2000— New York (N.L.)................	0	0	…	0.00	3	0	0	0	0	²/₃	1	0	0	3	1
World Series totals (2 years)	1	0	1.000	0.00	6	0	0	0	0	4¹/₃	2	0	0	4	6

COOMER, RON — 1B — CUBS

PERSONAL: Born November 18, 1966, in Chicago. ... 5-11/206. ... Bats right, throws right. ... Full name: Ronald Bryan Coomer.

HIGH SCHOOL: Lockport (Ill.).

JUNIOR COLLEGE: Taft (Calif.) Junior College.

TRANSACTIONS/CAREER NOTES: Selected by Oakland Athletics organization in 14th round of free-agent draft (June 2, 1987). ... Released by A's (August 1, 1990). ... Signed by Chicago White Sox organization (March 18, 1991). ... On disabled list (June 5-19, 1992). ... On Birmingham disabled list (June 12-21, 1993). ... Traded by White Sox to Los Angeles Dodgers for P Isidro Martinez (December 27, 1993). ... Traded by Dodgers with P Greg Hansell, P Jose Parra and a player to be named later to Minnesota Twins for P Kevin Tapani and P Mark Guthrie (July 31, 1995); Twins acquired OF Chris Latham to complete deal (October 30, 1995). ... Granted free agency (December 21, 2000). ... Signed by Chicago Cubs (January 10, 2001).

STATISTICAL NOTES: Led Southern League with eight sacrifice flies and tied for lead in grounding into double plays with 21 in 1991. ... Led Southern League third basemen with 94 putouts, 396 total chances, 24 double plays and tied for lead with 26 errors in 1991. ... Led Pacific Coast League with 293 total bases in 1994. ... Led Pacific Coast League third basemen with .952 fielding percentage, 399 total chances and 299 assists in 1994. ... Tied for A.L. lead in grounding into double plays with 22 in 1998. ... Career major league grand slams: 1.

						BATTING								FIELDING		
Year Team (League)	Pos.	G	AB	R	H	2B	3B	HR	RBI	Avg.	BB	SO	SB	PO	A	E	Avg.
1987— Medford (N'West)	3B-1B	45	168	23	58	10	2	1	26	.345	19	22	1	54	78	11	.923
1988— Modesto (Calif.)	3B-1B	131	495	67	138	23	2	17	85	.279	60	88	2	78	105	16	.920
1989— Madison (Midw.)	3B-1B	61	216	28	69	15	0	4	28	.319	30	34	0	67	64	6	.956
1990— Huntsville (Sou.)	2B-1B-3B	66	194	22	43	7	0	3	27	.222	21	40	3	200	100	11	.965
1991— Birmingham (Sou.)■.	3B-1B	137	505	*81	129	27	5	13	76	.255	59	78	0	†113	278	‡26	.938
1992— Vancouver (PCL)	3B	86	262	29	62	10	0	9	40	.237	16	36	3	49	115	13	.927
1993— Birmingham (Sou.).....	3B-1B	69	262	44	85	18	0	13	50	.324	15	43	1	43	106	11	.931
— Nashville (A.A.)	3B	59	211	34	66	19	0	13	51	.313	10	29	1	30	107	16	.895
1994— Albuquerque (PCL)■.	3B-DH-2B	127	535	89	181	34	6	22	*123	.338	26	62	4	81	†299	19	†.952
1995— Albuquerque (PCL).....	3B-1B-DH	85	323	54	104	23	2	16	76	.322	18	28	5	335	93	9	.979
— Minnesota (A.L.)■.......	1-3-DH	37	101	15	26	3	1	5	19	.257	9	11	0	138	32	2	.988
1996— Minnesota (A.L.)	1-0-3-DH	95	233	34	69	12	1	12	41	.296	17	24	3	275	42	4	.988
1997— Minnesota (A.L.)	3-1-DH-0	140	523	63	156	30	2	13	85	.298	22	91	4	123	223	11	.969

Year	Team (League)	Pos.	G	AB	R	H	2B	3B	HR	RBI	Avg.	BB	SO	SB	PO	A	E	Avg.
									BATTING							FIELDING		
1998— Minnesota (A.L.)	3-1-DH-O	137	529	54	146	22	1	15	72	.276	18	72	2	428	150	6	.990
1999— Minnesota (A.L.)	1-3-DH-O	127	467	53	123	25	1	16	65	.263	30	69	2	542	148	6	.991
2000— Minnesota (A.L.)	1B-DH-3B	140	544	64	147	29	1	16	82	.270	36	50	5	1023	82	5	.995
Major League totals (6 years)		676	2397	283	667	121	7	77	364	.278	132	317	13	2529	677	34	.990

ALL-STAR GAME RECORD

Year	League	Pos.	AB	R	H	2B	3B	HR	RBI	Avg.	BB	SO	SB	PO	A	E	Avg.
									BATTING					FIELDING			
1999— American	1B	1	0	0	0	0	0	0	.000	0	1	0	4	0	0	1.000

COOPER, BRIAN   P   ANGELS

PERSONAL: Born October 22, 1976, in North Hollywood, Calif. ... 6-1/185. ... Throws right, bats right. ... Full name: Brian John Cooper.
HIGH SCHOOL: Glendora (Calif.).
COLLEGE: Southern California.
TRANSACTIONS/CAREER NOTES: Selected by California Angels organization in fourth round of free-agent draft (June 1, 1995). ... Angels franchise renamed Anaheim Angels for 1997 season.
STATISTICAL NOTES: Led Texas League with 35 home runs allowed in 1998.

Year	League	W	L	Pct.	ERA	G	GS	CG	ShO	Sv.	IP	H	R	ER	BB	SO
1995— Boise (N'West)		3	2	.600	3.92	13	11	0	0	1	62	60	31	27	22	66
1996— Lake Elsinore (Calif.)		7	9	.438	4.21	26	23	1	1	0	162 1/3	177	100	76	39	155
1997— Lake Elsinore (Calif.)		7	3	.700	3.54	17	17	1	0	0	117	111	56	46	27	104
1998— Midland (Texas)		8	10	.444	7.13	32	24	5	0	1	161 2/3	215	138	128	59	141
1999— Erie (East.)		10	5	.667	3.30	22	22	*6	0	0	158	146	61	58	29	143
—Edmonton (PCL)		2	1	.667	3.77	5	5	0	0	0	31	30	17	13	10	32
—Anaheim (A.L.)		1	1	.500	4.88	5	5	0	0	0	27 2/3	23	15	15	18	15
2000— Edmonton (PCL)		3	7	.300	7.23	11	11	1	1	0	61	87	51	49	18	37
—Anaheim (A.L.)		4	8	.333	5.90	15	15	1	1	0	87	105	66	57	35	36
—Lake Elsinore (Calif.)		0	0	...	0.00	1	1	0	0	0	7	4	1	0	2	3
Major League totals (2 years)		5	9	.357	5.65	20	20	1	1	0	114 2/3	128	81	72	53	51

COQUILLETTE, TRACE   2B   CUBS

PERSONAL: Born June 4, 1974, in Carmicheal, Calif. ... 5-11/185. ... Bats right, throws right. ... Full name: Trace Robert Coquillette. ... Name pronounced COE-kill-ette.
HIGH SCHOOL: Casa Roble (Orangevale, Calif.).
JUNIOR COLLEGE: Sacramento City College.
TRANSACTIONS/CAREER NOTES: Selected by Montreal Expos organization in 10th round of free-agent draft (June 3, 1993). ... On West Palm Beach disabled list (June 2-August 1, 1996). ... On Ottawa disabled list (April 14-May 20 and July 3-10, 1999). ... Granted free agency (October 18, 2000). ... Signed by Chicago Cubs organization (December 13, 2000).
STATISTICAL NOTES: Led New York-Pennsylvania League second basemen with 366 total chances in 1994. ... Led International League with a .434 on-base percentage and in being hit by pitch with 24 in 1999.

Year	Team (League)	Pos.	G	AB	R	H	2B	3B	HR	RBI	Avg.	BB	SO	SB	PO	A	E	Avg.
										BATTING							FIELDING		
1993— GC Expos (GCL)	2B	44	159	27	40	4	3	2	11	.252	37	28	16	80	123	•12	.944
—W.P. Beach (FSL)	2B	6	18	2	5	3	0	0	3	.278	2	5	0	8	16	1	.960
1994— Burlington (Midw.)	2B	5	17	2	3	1	0	0	0	.176	1	4	1	6	14	1	.952
—Vermont (NY-Penn)	2B	70	252	54	77	11	5	9	52	.306	23	40	7	125	216	*25	.932
1995— Albany (S.Atl.)	2B	128	458	67	123	27	4	3	57	.269	64	91	17	252	292	14	.975
1996— GC Expos (GCL)	2B-3B	7	25	4	4	1	0	0	0	.160	4	6	1	16	16	1	.970
—W.P. Beach (FSL)	2B-3B	72	266	39	67	17	4	1	27	.252	27	72	9	100	142	22	.917
1997— Harrisburg (East.)	2B-3B	81	293	46	76	17	3	10	51	.259	25	40	9	116	169	16	.947
—W.P. Beach (FSL)	2B-3B-OF	53	188	34	60	18	2	8	33	.319	27	27	8	90	111	7	.966
1998— Harrisburg (East.)	2B-3B	49	187	40	62	10	0	9	23	.332	15	41	10	61	124	7	.964
—Ottawa (I.L.)	2B-3B-OF	74	252	30	64	14	0	7	40	.254	17	38	3	125	140	9	.967
1999— Ottawa (I.L.)	2-3-DH-1	98	334	56	109	32	3	14	55	.326	44	68	10	159	212	16	.959
—Montreal (N.L.)	3B-2B	17	49	2	13	3	0	0	4	.265	4	7	1	13	28	1	.976
2000— Montreal (N.L.)	3B-2B-OF	34	59	6	12	4	0	1	8	.203	7	19	0	5	27	1	.970
—Ottawa (I.L.)	OF-3B-2B	75	267	30	64	19	1	1	27	.240	24	58	0	109	65	11	.941
Major League totals (2 years)		51	108	8	25	7	0	1	12	.231	11	26	1	18	55	2	.973

CORA, ALEX   SS   DODGERS

PERSONAL: Born October 18, 1975, in Caguas, Puerto Rico. ... 6-0/180. ... Bats left, throws right. ... Full name: Jose Alexander Cora. ... Brother of Joey Cora, second baseman with four major league teams (1987-98).
HIGH SCHOOL: Bautista (Caguas, Puerto Rico).
COLLEGE: Miami (Fla.).
TRANSACTIONS/CAREER NOTES: Selected by Los Angeles Dodgers organization in third round of free-agent draft (June 4, 1996). ... On Los Angeles disabled list (March 25-June 27, 1999); included rehabilitation assignment to Albuquerque (June 8-27).
STATISTICAL NOTES: Led Texas League shortstops with 629 total chances and 88 double plays in 1997.

Year	Team (League)	Pos.	G	AB	R	H	2B	3B	HR	RBI	Avg.	BB	SO	SB	PO	A	E	Avg.
										BATTING							FIELDING		
1996— Vero Beach (FSL)	SS-OF	61	214	26	55	5	4	0	26	.257	12	36	5	86	164	16	.940
1997— San Antonio (Texas)	SS	127	448	52	105	20	4	3	48	.234	25	60	12	*197	*412	20	*.968
1998— Albuquerque (PCL)	SS-2B	81	299	42	79	17	5	5	45	.264	15	38	10	126	270	18	.957
—Los Angeles (N.L.)	SS-2B	29	33	1	4	0	1	0	0	.121	2	8	0	26	29	2	.965

C

Year	Team (League)	Pos.	G	AB	R	H	2B	3B	HR	RBI	Avg.	BB	SO	SB	PO	A	E	Avg.
1999—Albuquerque (PCL)	SS-DH-2B	80	302	51	93	11	7	4	37	.308	12	37	9	134	234	12	.968
—Los Angeles (N.L.)	SS-2B	11	30	2	5	1	0	0	3	.167	0	4	0	13	20	2	.943
2000—Albuquerque (PCL)	SS	30	110	18	41	8	3	0	20	.373	7	10	5	74	90	7	.959
—Los Angeles (N.L.)	SS-2B	109	353	39	84	18	6	4	32	.238	26	53	4	163	273	12	.973
Major League totals (3 years)		149	416	42	93	19	7	4	35	.224	28	65	4	202	322	16	.970

CORDERO, FRANCISCO   P   RANGERS

PERSONAL: Born August 11, 1977, in Santo Domingo, Dominican Republic. ... 6-2/200. ... Throws right, bats right. ... Full name: Francisco Javier Cordero.

HIGH SCHOOL: Colegio Luz de Arroyo Hondo (Dominican Republic).

TRANSACTIONS/CAREER NOTES: Signed as non-drafted free agent by Detroit Tigers organization (June 18, 1994). ... On Jamestown disabled list (June 28, 1996-remainder of season). ... On Jacksonville disabled list (May 22-June 18 and June 26, 1998-remainder of season). ... Traded by Tigers with P Justin Thompson, OF Gabe Kapler, C Bill Haselman, 2B Frank Catalanotto and P Alan Webb to Texas Rangers for OF Juan Gonzalez, P Danny Patterson and C Gregg Zaun (November 2, 1999).

HONORS: Named Southern League Most Outstanding Pitcher (1999).

Year	League	W	L	Pct.	ERA	G	GS	CG	ShO	Sv.	IP	H	R	ER	BB	SO
1994—Dominican Tigers (DSL)	4	3	.571	3.90	12	12	0	0	0	60	65	47	26	27	36
1995—Fayetteville (S.Atl.)	0	3	.000	6.30	4	4	0	0	0	20	26	16	14	12	19
—Jamestown (NY-Penn)	4	7	.364	5.22	15	14	0	0	0	88	96	62	51	37	54
1996—Fayetteville (S.Atl.)	0	0	...	2.57	2	1	0	0	0	7	2	2	2	6	7
—Jamestown (NY-Penn)	0	0	...	0.82	2	2	0	0	0	11	5	1	1	2	10
1997—West Michigan (Midw.)	6	1	.857	0.99	50	0	0	0	*35	54 1/3	36	13	6	15	67
1998—Jacksonville (Sou.)	1	1	.500	4.86	17	0	0	0	8	16 2/3	19	12	9	9	18
—Lakeland (FSL)	0	0	...	0.00	1	0	0	0	0	16 2/3	1	0	0	0	0
1999—Jacksonville (Sou.)	4	1	.800	1.38	47	0	0	0	*27	52 1/3	35	9	8	22	58
—Detroit (A.L.)	2	2	.500	3.32	20	0	0	0	0	19	19	7	7	18	19
2000—Texas (A.L.)■	1	2	.333	5.35	56	0	0	0	0	77 1/3	87	51	46	48	49
—Oklahoma (PCL)	0	0	...	4.15	3	0	0	0	1	4 1/3	7	3	2	3	5
Major League totals (2 years)	3	4	.429	4.95	76	0	0	0	0	96 1/3	106	58	53	66	68

CORDERO, WIL   OF   INDIANS

PERSONAL: Born October 3, 1971, in Mayaguez, Puerto Rico. ... 6-2/200. ... Bats right, throws right. ... Full name: Wilfredo Nieva Cordero. ... Name pronounced cor-DARE-oh.

HIGH SCHOOL: Centro de Servicios Education de Mayaguez (Puerto Rico).

TRANSACTIONS/CAREER NOTES: Signed as non-drafted free agent by Montreal Expos organization (May 24, 1988). ... On Indianapolis disabled list (August 1, 1991-remainder of season; and May 12-June 11 and July 7-20, 1992). ... Traded by Expos with P Bryan Eversgerd to Boston Red Sox for P Rheal Cormier, 1B Ryan McGuire and P Shayne Bennett (January 10, 1996). ... On Boston disabled list (May 21-August 12, 1996); included rehabilitation assignments to Gulf Coast Red Sox (July 23-27) and Pawtucket (July 27-August 6). ... Released by Red Sox (September 28, 1997). ... Signed by Chicago White Sox (March 23, 1998). ... Granted free agency (November 3, 1998). ... Signed by Cleveland Indians (February 3, 1999). ... On Cleveland disabled list (June 9-September 8, 1999); included rehabilitation assignment to Akron (September 3-8). ... Granted free agency (October 29, 1999). ... Signed by Pittsburgh Pirates (December 14, 1999). ... Traded by Pirates to Indians for OF Alex Ramirez and IF Enrique Wilson (July 28, 2000). ... On suspended list (September 19-23, 2000).

HONORS: Named shortstop on THE SPORTING NEWS N.L. Silver Slugger team (1994).

STATISTICAL NOTES: Had 15-game hitting streak (April 29-May 23, 2000). ... Career major league grand slams: 2.

Year	Team (League)	Pos.	G	AB	R	H	2B	3B	HR	RBI	Avg.	BB	SO	SB	PO	A	E	Avg.
1988—Jamestown (NY-P)	SS	52	190	18	49	3	0	2	22	.258	15	44	3	82	159	31	.886
1989—W.P. Beach (FSL)	SS	78	289	37	80	12	2	6	29	.277	33	58	2	121	224	29	.922
—Jacksonville (Sou.)	SS	39	121	9	26	6	1	3	17	.215	12	33	1	62	93	7	.957
1990—Jacksonville (Sou.)	SS	131	444	63	104	18	4	7	40	.234	56	122	9	179	349	41	.928
1991—Indianapolis (A.A.)	SS	98	360	48	94	16	4	11	52	.261	26	89	9	157	287	27	.943
1992—Indianapolis (A.A.)	SS	52	204	32	64	11	1	6	27	.314	24	54	6	75	146	12	.948
—Montreal (N.L.)	SS-2B	45	126	17	38	4	1	2	8	.302	9	31	0	51	92	8	.947
1993—Montreal (N.L.)	SS-3B	138	475	56	118	32	2	10	58	.248	34	60	12	163	373	36	.937
1994—Montreal (N.L.)	SS	110	415	65	122	30	3	15	63	.294	41	62	16	124	316	22	.952
1995—Montreal (N.L.)	SS-OF	131	514	64	147	35	2	10	49	.286	36	88	9	168	281	22	.953
1996—Boston (A.L.)■	2B-DH-1B	59	198	29	57	14	0	3	37	.288	11	31	2	82	110	10	.950
—GC Red Sox (GCL)	DH-2B	3	10	1	3	0	0	1	3	.300	0	2	0	1	1	0	1.000
—Pawtucket (I.L.)	2B-DH	4	10	2	3	1	0	1	2	.300	2	3	0	2	6	0	1.000
1997—Boston (A.L.)	OF-2B-DH	140	570	82	160	26	3	18	72	.281	31	122	1	248	11	2	.992
1998—Birmingham (Sou.)■	1B-DH	11	35	6	10	2	0	2	11	.286	7	3	0	81	9	1	.989
—Chicago (A.L.)	1B-OF	96	341	58	91	18	2	13	49	.267	22	66	2	713	66	7	.991
1999—Cleveland (A.L.)■	OF-DH	54	194	35	58	15	0	8	32	.299	15	37	2	51	0	1	.981
—Akron (East.)	OF-DH	3	11	2	4	2	0	0	0	.364	0	3	0	0	0	0	...
2000—Pittsburgh (N.L.)■	OF-DH	89	348	46	98	24	3	16	51	.282	25	58	1	110	3	2	.983
—Cleveland (A.L.)■	OF	38	148	18	39	11	2	0	17	.264	7	18	0	79	2	0	1.000
American League totals (5 years)		387	1451	222	405	84	7	42	207	.279	86	274	7	1173	189	20	.986
National League totals (5 years)		513	1878	248	523	125	11	53	229	.278	145	299	38	616	1065	90	.949
Major League totals (9 years)		900	3329	470	928	209	18	95	436	.279	231	573	45	1789	1254	110	.965

DIVISION SERIES RECORD

Year	Team (League)	Pos.	G	AB	R	H	2B	3B	HR	RBI	Avg.	BB	SO	SB	PO	A	E	Avg.
1999—Cleveland (A.L.)	PH-DH-OF	3	9	3	5	0	0	1	2	.556	1	2	0	3	0	0	1.000

Year	League	Pos.	AB	R	H	2B	3B	HR	RBI	Avg.	BB	SO	SB	PO	A	E	Avg.
								BATTING							FIELDING		
1994— National	SS	2	0	0	0	0	0	0	.000	0	0	0	1	1	0	1.000

CORDOVA, FRANCISCO — P — PIRATES

PERSONAL: Born April 26, 1972, in Veracruz, Mexico. ... 6-1/197. ... Throws right, bats right.
TRANSACTIONS/CAREER NOTES: Signed as non-drafted free agent by Pittsburgh Pirates organization (January 18, 1996). ... On Pittsburgh disabled list (April 11-May 19, 1999); included rehabilitation assignments to Nashville (April 28-29 and May 14-15) and Altoona (May 3-4 and May 8-13). ... On disabled list (May 12-20, July 5-29 and August 11, 2000-remainder of season).
STATISTICAL NOTES: Pitched nine innings, combining with Ricardo Rincon (one inning) in 3-0 no-hit victory against Houston (July 12, 1997).

Year	League	W	L	Pct.	ERA	G	GS	CG	ShO	Sv.	IP	H	R	ER	BB	SO
1992— M.C. Red Devils (Mex.)	3	0	1.000	5.79	16	1	0	0	0	28	28	19	18	14	15
1993— M.C. Red Devils (Mex.)	9	2	.818	3.23	43	4	1	0	4	106	96	44	38	47	71
1994— M.C. Red Devils (Mex.)	15	4	.789	2.33	41	15	6	3	8	150 1/3	122	43	39	43	104
1995— M.C. Red Devils (Mex.)	13	0	*1.000	3.10	27	20	1	0	4	125	131	52	43	42	88
1996— Pittsburgh (N.L.)■	4	7	.364	4.09	59	6	0	0	12	99	103	49	45	20	95
1997— Pittsburgh (N.L.)	11	8	.579	3.63	29	29	2	2	0	178 2/3	175	80	72	49	121
1998— Pittsburgh (N.L.)	13	14	.481	3.31	33	33	3	2	0	220 1/3	204	91	81	69	157
1999— Pittsburgh (N.L.)	8	10	.444	4.43	27	27	2	0	0	160 2/3	166	83	79	59	98
— Nashville (PCL)	2	0	1.000	0.75	2	2	0	0	0	12	10	2	1	1	7
— Altoona (East.)	1	1	.500	4.66	2	2	0	0	0	9 2/3	13	8	5	4	12
2000— Pittsburgh (N.L.)	6	8	.429	5.21	18	17	0	0	0	95	107	63	55	38	66
Major League totals (5 years)	42	47	.472	3.96	166	112	7	4	12	753 2/3	755	366	332	235	537

CORDOVA, MARTY — OF — INDIANS

PERSONAL: Born July 10, 1969, in Las Vegas. ... 6-0/206. ... Bats right, throws right. ... Full name: Martin Keevin Cordova.
HIGH SCHOOL: Bishop Gorman (Las Vegas).
JUNIOR COLLEGE: Orange Coast College (Calif.).
COLLEGE: UNLV.
TRANSACTIONS/CAREER NOTES: Selected by San Diego Padres organization in eighth round of free-agent draft (June 2, 1987); did not sign. ... Selected by Minnesota Twins organization in 10th round of free-agent draft (June 5, 1989). ... On Visalia disabled list (April 12-May 20, 1991). ... On Salt Lake disabled list (April 17-May 11, 1994). ... On Minnesota disabled list (April 11-May 26, 1997); included rehabilitation assignment to Salt Lake (May 20-26). ... On disabled list (April 27-May 12, 1998). ... Granted free agency (October 7, 1999). ... Signed by Boston Red Sox organization (January 19, 2000). ... Released by Red Sox (March 26, 2000). ... Signed by Toronto Blue Jays organization (March 27, 2000). ... Granted free agency (October 4, 2000). ... Signed by Cleveland Indians organization (December 20, 2000).
HONORS: Named California League Most Valuable Player (1992). ... Named A.L. Rookie of the Year by Baseball Writers' Association of America (1995).
STATISTICAL NOTES: Led California League with 302 total bases and .589 slugging percentage and tied for lead in grounding into double plays with 20 in 1992. ... Had 23-game hitting streak (June 5-29, 1996). ... Career major league grand slams: 1.

Year	Team (League)	Pos.	G	AB	R	H	2B	3B	HR	RBI	Avg.	BB	SO	SB	PO	A	E	Avg.
							BATTING									FIELDING		
1989— Elizabethton (Appl.)	OF-3B	38	148	32	42	2	3	8	29	.284	14	29	2	6	9	4	.789
1990— Kenosha (Midw.)	OF	81	269	35	58	7	5	7	25	.216	28	73	6	87	5	5	.948
1991— Visalia (Calif.)	OF	71	189	31	40	6	1	7	19	.212	17	46	2	58	2	5	.923
1992— Visalia (Calif.)	OF	134	513	103	175	31	6	*28	*131	.341	76	99	13	173	10	3	.984
1993— Nashville (Sou.)	OF	138	508	83	127	30	5	19	77	.250	64	*153	10	209	7	2	*.991
1994— Salt Lake (PCL)	OF-DH	103	385	69	138	25	4	19	66	.358	39	63	17	187	13	8	.962
1995— Minnesota (A.L.)	OF	137	512	81	142	27	4	24	84	.277	52	111	20	345	12	5	.986
1996— Minnesota (A.L.)	OF	145	569	97	176	46	1	16	111	.309	53	96	11	328	9	3	.991
1997— Minnesota (A.L.)	OF-DH	103	378	44	93	18	4	15	51	.246	30	92	5	217	12	2	.991
— Salt Lake (PCL)	DH-OF	6	24	5	9	4	0	1	4	.375	2	3	1	3	0	1	.750
1998— Minnesota (A.L.)	OF-DH	119	438	52	111	20	2	10	69	.253	50	103	3	257	5	6	.978
1999— Minnesota (A.L.)	DH-OF	124	425	62	121	28	3	14	70	.285	48	96	13	38	0	3	.927
2000— Toronto (A.L.)■	OF-DH	62	200	23	49	7	0	4	18	.245	18	35	3	55	1	1	.982
Major League totals (6 years)		690	2522	359	692	146	14	83	403	.274	251	533	55	1240	39	20	.985

COREY, BRYAN — P — PADRES

PERSONAL: Born October 21, 1973, in Thousand Oaks, Calif. ... 6-0/170. ... Throws right, bats right. ... Full name: Bryan Scott Corey.
HIGH SCHOOL: Thousand Oaks (Calif.).
JUNIOR COLLEGE: Los Angeles Pierce Junior College.
TRANSACTIONS/CAREER NOTES: Selected by Detroit Tigers organization in 12th round of free-agent draft (June 3, 1993). ... Selected by Arizona Diamondbacks in third round (63rd pick overall) of expansion draft (November 18, 1997). ... Claimed on waivers by Tigers (December 4, 1998). ... Granted free agency (October 15, 1999). ... Signed by Oakland Athletics organization (December 3, 1999). ... Granted free agency (October 18, 2000). ... Signed by San Diego Padres organization (November 20, 2000).
MISCELLANEOUS: Played infield (1993-94).

Year	League	W	L	Pct.	ERA	G	GS	CG	ShO	Sv.	IP	H	R	ER	BB	SO
1995— Jamestown (NY-Penn)	2	2	.500	3.86	29	0	0	0	10	28	21	14	12	12	41
1996— Fayetteville (S.Atl.)	6	4	.600	1.21	60	0	0	0	34	82	50	19	11	17	101
1997— Jacksonville (Sou.)	3	8	.273	4.76	52	0	0	0	9	68	74	42	36	21	37
1998— Tucson (PCL)■	4	6	.400	5.44	39	10	0	0	2	87 2/3	116	61	53	24	50
— Arizona (N.L.)	0	0	...	9.00	3	0	0	0	0	4	6	4	4	2	1
1999— Toledo (I.L.)■	5	2	.714	2.86	48	0	0	0	4	69 1/3	63	27	22	34	36
2000— Sacramento (PCL)■	8	3	.727	4.24	47	6	0	0	4	85	88	43	40	29	55
Major League totals (1 year)	0	0	...	9.00	3	0	0	0	0	4	6	4	4	2	1

C

Year	Team (League)	Pos.	G	AB	R	H	2B	3B	HR	RBI	Avg.	BB	SO	SB	PO	A	E	Avg.
							BATTING									FIELDING		
1993— Bristol (Appl.).............		SS-2B	39	95	14	10	3	0	0	3	.105	26	35	2	53	80	10	.930
1994— Jamestown (NY-P)		2B-SS-3B	41	85	14	13	1	1	0	3	.153	13	27	2	38	64	10	.911

CORMIER, RHEAL — P — PHILLIES

PERSONAL: Born April 23, 1967, in Moncton, New Brunswick. ... 5-10/187. ... Throws left, bats left. ... Full name: Rheal Paul Cormier. ... Name pronounced ree-AL COR-mee-AY.

HIGH SCHOOL: Polyvalente Louis J. Robichaud.

JUNIOR COLLEGE: Community College of Rhode Island.

TRANSACTIONS/CAREER NOTES: Selected by St. Louis Cardinals organization in sixth round of free-agent draft (June 6, 1988). ... On Louisville disabled list (April 10-29, 1991). ... On disabled list (August 12-September 7, 1993). ... On St. Louis disabled list (April 28-May 13 and May 21-August 3, 1994); included rehabilitation assignments to Arkansas (July 7-18) and Louisville (July 18-30). ... Traded by Cardinals with OF Mark Whiten to Boston Red Sox for 3B Scott Cooper, P Cory Bailey and a player to be named later (April 8, 1995). ... Traded by Red Sox with 1B Ryan McGuire and P Shayne Bennett to Montreal Expos for SS Wil Cordero and P Bryan Eversgerd (Jauary 10, 1996). ... On disabled list (August 26-September 10, 1996). ... Granted free agency (October 30, 1997). ... Signed by Cleveland Indians organization (December 18, 1997). ... On Buffalo disabled list (April 9-June 2, 1998). ... On Akron disabled list (June 18, 1998-remainder of season). ... Granted free agency (October 15, 1998). ... Signed by Red Sox organization (January 5, 1999). ... On suspended list (May 7-10, 1999). ... Granted free agency (November 1, 2000). ... Signed by Philadelphia Phillies (November 29, 2000).

MISCELLANEOUS: Member of 1988 Canadian Olympic baseball team.

Year League	W	L	Pct.	ERA	G	GS	CG	ShO	Sv.	IP	H	R	ER	BB	SO
1989— St. Petersburg (FSL)	12	7	.632	2.23	26	26	4	1	0	169²/₃	141	63	42	33	122
1990— Arkansas (Texas)...............	5	•12	.294	5.04	22	21	3	1	0	121¹/₃	133	81	68	30	102
— Louisville (A.A.)..................	1	1	.500	2.25	4	4	0	0	0	24	18	8	6	3	9
1991— Louisville (A.A.)..................	7	9	.438	4.23	21	21	3	*3	0	127²/₃	140	64	60	31	74
— St. Louis (N.L.)..................	4	5	.444	4.12	11	10	2	0	0	67²/₃	74	35	31	8	38
1992— Louisville (A.A.)..................	0	1	.000	6.75	1	1	0	0	0	4	8	4	3	0	1
— St. Louis (N.L.)..................	10	10	.500	3.68	31	30	3	0	0	186	194	83	76	33	117
1993— St. Louis (N.L.)..................	7	6	.538	4.33	38	21	1	0	0	145¹/₃	163	80	70	27	75
1994— St. Louis (N.L.)..................	3	2	.600	5.45	7	7	0	0	0	39²/₃	40	24	24	7	26
— Arkansas (Texas)...............	1	0	1.000	1.93	2	2	0	0	0	9¹/₃	9	2	2	0	11
— Louisville (A.A.)..................	1	2	.333	4.50	3	3	1	0	0	22	21	11	11	8	13
1995— Boston (A.L.)■...............	7	5	.583	4.07	48	12	0	0	0	115	131	60	52	31	69
1996— Montreal (N.L.)■...............	7	10	.412	4.17	33	27	1	1	0	159²/₃	165	80	74	41	100
1997— Montreal (N.L.)...............	0	1	.000	33.75	1	1	0	0	0	1¹/₃	4	5	5	1	0
1998— Akron (East.)■...............	0	0	...	6.52	3	3	0	0	0	9²/₃	15	7	7	2	6
1999— Boston (A.L.)■...............	2	0	1.000	3.69	60	0	0	0	0	63¹/₃	61	34	26	18	39
2000— Boston (A.L.)...............	3	3	.500	4.61	64	0	0	0	0	68¹/₃	74	40	35	17	43
A.L. totals (3 years)	12	8	.600	4.12	172	12	0	0	0	246²/₃	266	134	113	66	151
N.L. totals (6 years)	31	34	.477	4.20	121	96	7	1	0	599²/₃	640	307	280	117	356
Major League totals (9 years)	43	42	.506	4.18	293	108	7	1	0	846¹/₃	906	441	393	183	507

DIVISION SERIES RECORD

Year League	W	L	Pct.	ERA	G	GS	CG	ShO	Sv.	IP	H	R	ER	BB	SO
1995— Boston (A.L.)......................	0	0	...	13.50	2	0	0	0	0	²/₃	2	1	1	1	2
1999— Boston (A.L.)......................	0	0	...	0.00	2	0	0	0	0	4	2	0	0	1	4
Division series totals (2 years)	0	0	...	1.93	4	0	0	0	0	4²/₃	4	1	1	2	6

CHAMPIONSHIP SERIES RECORD

Year League	W	L	Pct.	ERA	G	GS	CG	ShO	Sv.	IP	H	R	ER	BB	SO
1999— Boston (A.L.)......................	0	0	...	0.00	4	0	0	0	0	3²/₃	3	0	0	3	4

CORNELIUS, REID — P — MARLINS

PERSONAL: Born June 2, 1970, in Thomasville, Ala. ... 6-0/200. ... Throws right, bats right. ... Full name: Jonathan Reid Cornelius.

HIGH SCHOOL: Thomasville (Alabaster, Ala.).

TRANSACTIONS/CAREER NOTES: Selected by Montreal Expos organization in 11th round of free-agent draft (June 1, 1988). ... On West Palm Beach disabled list (May 27-August 2, 1990 and May 20-June 3, 1991). ... On Harrisburg disabled list (August 6, 1991-remainder of season and April 27-September 6, 1992). ... On disabled list (July 12-28, 1994). ... Traded by Expos to New York Mets for 1B/OF David Segui (June 8, 1995). ... Traded by Mets with OF Ryan Thompson to Cleveland Indians for P Mark Clark (March 31, 1996). ... On disabled list (April 16-28 and June 26-July 28, 1996). ... Granted free agency (October 15, 1996). ... Signed by Florida Marlins organization (March 31, 1997). ... Granted free agency (October 17, 1997). ... Signed by Arizona Diamondbacks organization (November 24, 1997). ... Traded by Diamondbacks to Marlins for a player to be named later (July 24, 1998; Diamondbacks acquired OF Walt White to complete deal (October 29, 1998). ... Granted free agency (October 16, 1998). ... Signed by Anaheim Angels organization (November 18, 1998). ... Released by Angels (March 20, 1999). ... Signed by Marlins organization (April 9, 1999).

STATISTICAL NOTES: Led Pacific Coast League pitchers with 19 putouts and 47 total chances in 1999. ... Led N.L. with five balks in 2000.

MISCELLANEOUS: Fouled out in only appearance as pinch hitter (2000).

Year League	W	L	Pct.	ERA	G	GS	CG	ShO	Sv.	IP	H	R	ER	BB	SO
1989— Rockford (Midw.)...............	5	6	.455	4.27	17	17	0	0	0	84¹/₃	71	58	40	63	66
1990— West Palm Beach (FSL)	2	3	.400	3.38	11	11	0	0	0	56	54	25	21	25	47
1991— West Palm Beach (FSL)	8	3	.727	2.39	17	17	0	0	0	109¹/₃	79	31	29	43	81
— Harrisburg (East.)...............	2	1	.667	2.89	3	3	1	1	0	18²/₃	15	6	6	7	12
1992— Harrisburg (East.)...............	1	0	1.000	3.13	4	4	0	0	0	23	11	8	8	8	17
1993— Harrisburg (East.)...............	10	7	.588	4.17	27	27	1	0	0	157²/₃	146	95	73	82	119
1994— Ottawa (I.L.)...............	9	8	.529	4.38	25	24	1	0	0	148	149	89	72	75	87
1995— Montreal (N.L.)...............	0	0	...	8.00	8	0	0	0	0	9	11	8	8	5	4
— Ottawa (I.L.)...............	1	1	.500	6.75	4	3	0	0	0	10²/₃	16	12	8	5	7
— Norfolk (I.L.)■...............	7	0	1.000	0.90	10	10	1	0	0	70¹/₃	57	10	7	19	43
— New York (N.L.)...............	3	7	.300	5.15	10	10	0	0	0	57²/₃	64	36	33	25	35

Year League	W	L	Pct.	ERA	G	GS	CG	ShO	Sv.	IP	H	R	ER	BB	SO
1996— Buffalo (A.A.)■	5	7	.417	5.60	20	18	0	0	0	90	101	64	56	49	62
1997— Portland (East.)■	5	0	1.000	2.73	6	6	0	0	0	33	32	11	10	17	24
— Charlotte (I.L.)	12	5	.706	5.10	22	22	1	0	0	130$^2/_3$	134	82	74	43	80
1998— Tucson (PCL)■	4	7	.364	5.94	19	16	0	0	0	94	108	70	62	26	65
— Charlotte (I.L.)■	3	2	.600	4.01	8	8	1	1	0	49$^1/_3$	50	25	22	13	31
1999— Calgary (PCL)	10	6	.625	4.49	27	27	2	1	0	172$^1/_3$	184	96	86	68	135
— Florida (N.L.)	1	0	1.000	3.26	5	2	0	0	0	19$^1/_3$	16	7	7	5	12
2000— Calgary (PCL)	2	2	.500	4.57	8	8	0	0	0	43$^1/_3$	45	23	22	18	22
— Florida (N.L.)	4	10	.286	4.82	22	21	0	0	0	125	135	74	67	50	50
Major League totals (3 years)	8	17	.320	4.91	45	33	0	0	0	211	226	125	115	85	101

COTA, HUMBERTO — C — PIRATES

PERSONAL: Born February 7, 1979, in San Luis Rio Colorado, Mexico. ... 6-0/175. ... Bats right, throws right. ... Full name: Humberto Figueroa Cota.
HIGH SCHOOL: Preparatoria Abierta.
TRANSACTIONS/CAREER NOTES: Signed as non-drafted free agent by Atlanta Braves organization (December 22, 1995). ... Loaned by Braves organization to Mexico City Tigers (June 23-September 23, 1996). ... Released by Braves (January 27, 1997). ... Signed by Tampa Bay Devil Rays organization (May 22, 1997). ... Traded by Devil Rays with C Joe Oliver to Pittsburgh Pirates for OF Jose Guillen and P Jeff Sparks (July 23, 1999).
STATISTICAL NOTES: Tied for Gulf Coast League lead in double plays by catcher with four in 1997. ... Led Eastern League catchers with 15 passed balls in 2000.

Year Team (League)	Pos.	G	AB	R	H	2B	3B	HR	RBI	Avg.	BB	SO	SB	PO	A	E	Avg.
1997— Hudson Valley (NY-P).	C	3	9	0	2	0	0	0	2	.222	0	1	0	29	0	0	1.000
— GC Devil Rays (GCL)..	C	44	133	14	32	6	1	2	20	.241	17	27	3	294	26	5	.985
1998— Princeton (Appl.)	C	67	245	48	76	13	4	15	61	.310	32	59	4	*382	48	•12	.973
1999— Char., S.C. (SAL)	C-1B	85	336	42	94	21	1	9	61	.280	20	51	1	443	61	7	.986
— Hickory (S.Atl.)■	C	37	133	28	36	11	2	2	20	.271	21	20	3	235	22	2	.992
2000— Altoona (East.)	C-1B	112	429	49	112	20	1	8	44	.261	21	80	6	572	51	*17	.973

COUNSELL, CRAIG — 2B — DIAMONDBACKS

PERSONAL: Born August 21, 1970, in South Bend, Ind. ... 6-0/175. ... Bats left, throws right. ... Full name: Craig John Counsell. ... Son of John Counsell, outfielder in Minnesota Twins organization (1964-68).
HIGH SCHOOL: Whitefish Bay (Milwaukee).
COLLEGE: Notre Dame. (degree in accounting).
TRANSACTIONS/CAREER NOTES: Selected by Colorado Rockies organization in 11th round of free-agent draft (June 1, 1992). ... On disabled list (April 7-May 13, July 30-August 6 and August 7-27, 1994). ... On disabled list (May 1-July 15 and July 18-September 3, 1996). ... Traded by Rockies to Florida Marlins for P Mark Hutton (July 27, 1997). ... On disabled list (August 4, 1998-remainder of season). ... Traded by Marlins to Los Angeles Dodgers for a player to be named later (June 15, 1999); Marlins acquired P Ryan Moskau to complete deal (July 15, 1999). ... Released by Dodgers (March 15, 2000). ... Signed by Arizona Diamondbacks organization (March 20, 2000).
STATISTICAL NOTES: Led California League shortstops with 621 total chances in 1993. ... Led Pacific Coast League shortstops with 598 total chances and 86 double plays in 1995. ... Career major league grand slams: 2.

Year Team (League)	Pos.	G	AB	R	H	2B	3B	HR	RBI	Avg.	BB	SO	SB	PO	A	E	Avg.
1992— Bend (N'West)	2B-SS	18	61	11	15	6	1	0	8	.246	9	10	1	23	36	2	.967
1993— Central Valley (Calif.)..	SS	131	471	79	132	26	3	5	59	.280	95	68	14	*233	353	35	.944
1994— New Haven (East.)	SS-2B	83	300	47	84	20	1	5	37	.280	37	32	4	122	242	27	.931
1995— Colo. Springs (PCL)	SS	118	399	60	112	22	6	5	53	.281	34	47	10	182	386	30	.950
— Colorado (N.L.)	SS	3	1	0	0	0	0	0	0	.000	1	0	0	1	1	0	1.000
1996— Colo. Springs (PCL)	2B-3B-SS	25	75	17	18	3	0	2	10	.240	24	7	4	35	64	4	.961
1997— Colo. Springs (PCL)	2B-SS	96	376	77	126	31	6	5	63	.335	45	38	12	213	260	9	.981
— Colorado (N.L.)	PR	1	0	0	0	0	0	0	0	...	0	0	0	...	...	...	...
— Florida (N.L.)■	2B	51	164	20	49	9	2	1	16	.299	18	17	1	124	149	3	.989
1998— Florida (N.L.)	2B	107	335	43	84	19	5	4	40	.251	51	47	3	237	299	5	.991
1999— Florida (N.L.)	2B	37	66	4	10	1	0	0	2	.152	5	10	0	20	29	1	.980
— Los Angeles (N.L.)■ ..	2B-SS	50	108	20	28	6	0	0	9	.259	9	14	1	54	86	1	.993
2000— Tucson (PCL)■	2B-3B-SS	50	198	45	69	14	3	3	27	.348	22	20	4	77	133	4	.981
— Arizona (N.L.)	2B-3B-SS	67	152	23	48	8	1	2	11	.316	20	18	3	38	95	6	.957
Major League totals (5 years)		316	826	110	219	43	8	7	78	.265	104	106	8	474	659	16	.986

DIVISION SERIES RECORD

Year Team (League)	Pos.	G	AB	R	H	2B	3B	HR	RBI	Avg.	BB	SO	SB	PO	A	E	Avg.
1997— Florida (N.L.)	2B	3	5	0	2	1	0	0	1	.400	1	0	0	5	2	1	.875

CHAMPIONSHIP SERIES RECORD

Year Team (League)	Pos.	G	AB	R	H	2B	3B	HR	RBI	Avg.	BB	SO	SB	PO	A	E	Avg.
1997— Florida (N.L.)	2B-PH	5	14	0	6	0	0	0	2	.429	3	3	0	7	9	1	.941

WORLD SERIES RECORD

NOTES: Member of World Series championship team (1997).

Year Team (League)	Pos.	G	AB	R	H	2B	3B	HR	RBI	Avg.	BB	SO	SB	PO	A	E	Avg.
1997— Florida (N.L.)	2B	7	22	4	4	1	0	0	2	.182	6	5	1	18	15	1	.971

COX, STEVE — 1B — DEVIL RAYS

PERSONAL: Born October 31, 1974, in Delano, Calif. ... 6-4/222. ... Bats left, throws left. ... Full name: Charles Steven Cox.
HIGH SCHOOL: Monache (Porterville, Calif.).
TRANSACTIONS/CAREER NOTES: Selected by Oakland Athletics organization in fifth round of free-agent draft (June 1, 1992). ... On disabled list (July 23, 1993-remainder of season). ... Selected by Tampa Bay Devil Rays in second round (46th pick overall) of expansion draft (November 18, 1997). ... On Durham disabled list (April 12-26, 1998). ... Re-signed by Devil Rays (November 19, 1998).
HONORS: Named International League Most Valuable Player (1999).
STATISTICAL NOTES: Led California League with 10 sacrifice flies in 1995. ... Tied for Pacific Coast League lead with nine sacrifice flies in 1997. ... Led International League first basemen with 1,079 total chances in 1998. ... Led International League with 314 total bases, a .588 slugging percentage and 11 intentional bases on balls received in 1999. ... Led International League first basemen with 1,203 total chances and 121 double plays in 1999. ... Career major league grand slams: 1.

Year Team (League)	Pos.	G	AB	R	H	2B	3B	HR	RBI	Avg.	BB	SO	SB	PO	A	E	Avg.
1992— Scottsdale (Ariz.)........	1B	52	184	30	43	4	1	1	35	.234	27	51	2	407	28	11	.975
1993— S. Oregon (N.W.)........	1B	15	57	10	18	4	1	2	16	.316	5	15	0	104	11	2	.983
1994— W. Mich. (Midw.).......	1B-OF	99	311	37	75	19	2	6	32	.241	41	95	2	727	49	10	.987
1995— Modesto (Calif.)	1B	132	483	95	144	29	3	*30	*110	.298	84	88	5	991	77	17	.984
1996— Huntsville (Sou.).......	1B-DH	104	381	59	107	21	1	12	61	.281	51	65	2	909	72	15	.985
1997— Edmonton (PCL)	1B-DH	131	467	84	128	34	1	15	93	.274	*88	90	1	1043	70	*10	.991
1998— Durham (I.L.)■....	1B-OF-DH	119	430	64	109	23	2	13	67	.253	56	100	3	*1011	62	7	.994
1999— Durham (I.L.)	1B-DH	134	534	*107	*182	*49	4	25	*127	*.341	67	74	3	*1125	73	5	.996
— Tampa Bay (A.L.).......	1B-OF	6	19	0	4	1	0	0	0	.211	0	2	0	20	1	0	1.000
2000— Tampa Bay (A.L.).......	OF-1B-DH	116	318	44	90	19	1	11	35	.283	46	47	1	267	13	8	.972
Major League totals (2 years)		122	337	44	94	20	1	11	35	.279	46	49	1	287	14	8	.974

CRABTREE, TIM — P — RANGERS

PERSONAL: Born October 13, 1969, in Jackson, Mich. ... 6-4/220. ... Throws right, bats right. ... Full name: Timothy Lyle Crabtree.
HIGH SCHOOL: Grass Lake (Mich.).
COLLEGE: Michigan State.
TRANSACTIONS/CAREER NOTES: Selected by Toronto Blue Jays organization in second round of free-agent draft (June 1, 1992). ... On disabled list (August 16-September 6, 1996). ... On Toronto disabled list (June 4-August 3, 1997); included rehabilitation assignments to St. Catharines (July 22-24) and Syracuse (July 27-August 4). ... Traded by Blue Jays to Texas Rangers for C Kevin Brown (March 14, 1998).

Year League	W	L	Pct.	ERA	G	GS	CG	ShO	Sv.	IP	H	R	ER	BB	SO
1992— St. Catharines (NY-Penn) ...	6	3	.667	1.57	12	12	2	0	0	69	45	19	12	22	47
— Knoxville (Sou.)................	0	2	.000	0.95	3	3	1	0	0	19	14	8	2	4	13
1993— Knoxville (Sou.).................	9	14	.391	4.08	27	27	2	2	0	158 2/3	178	93	72	59	67
1994— Syracuse (I.L.).................	2	6	.250	4.17	51	9	0	0	2	108	125	58	50	49	58
1995— Syracuse (I.L.).................	0	2	.000	5.40	26	0	0	0	5	31 2/3	38	25	19	12	22
— Toronto (A.L.)...................	0	2	.000	3.09	31	0	0	0	0	32	30	16	11	13	21
1996— Toronto (A.L.)...................	5	3	.625	2.54	53	0	0	0	1	67 1/3	59	26	19	22	57
1997— Toronto (A.L.)...................	3	3	.500	7.08	37	0	0	0	2	40 2/3	65	32	32	17	26
— St. Catharines (NY-Penn) ...	0	0	...	3.00	2	1	0	0	0	3	3	2	1	0	3
— Syracuse (I.L.)................	0	0	...	9.82	3	0	0	0	1	3 2/3	7	4	4	1	3
1998— Texas (A.L.)■....	6	1	.857	3.59	64	0	0	0	0	85 1/3	86	40	34	35	60
1999— Texas (A.L.)	5	1	.833	3.46	68	0	0	0	0	65	71	26	25	18	54
2000— Texas (A.L.)	2	7	.222	5.15	68	0	0	0	2	80 1/3	86	52	46	31	54
Major League totals (6 years)........	21	17	.553	4.05	321	0	0	0	5	370 2/3	397	192	167	136	272

DIVISION SERIES RECORD

Year League	W	L	Pct.	ERA	G	GS	CG	ShO	Sv.	IP	H	R	ER	BB	SO
1998— Texas (A.L.)	0	0	...	0.00	2	0	0	0	0	4	1	0	0	0	2
1999— Texas (A.L.)	0	0	...	5.40	2	0	0	0	0	1 2/3	1	2	1	1	1
Division series totals (2 years)	0	0	...	1.59	4	0	0	0	0	5 2/3	2	2	1	1	3

CRAWFORD, PAXTON — P — RED SOX

PERSONAL: Born August 4, 1977, in Little Rock, Ark. ... 6-3/205. ... Throws right, bats right. ... Full name: Paxton Keith Crawford. ... Nickname: Pack.
HIGH SCHOOL: Carlsbad (N.M.).
TRANSACTIONS/CAREER NOTES: Selected by Boston Red Sox organization in ninth round of free-agent draft (June 1, 1995). ... On Pawtucket disabled list (July 20-August 19, 2000).
STATISTICAL NOTES: Pitched 3-0 no-hit victory for Pawtucket against Ottawa (July 18, 2000; first game).

Year League	W	L	Pct.	ERA	G	GS	CG	ShO	Sv.	IP	H	R	ER	BB	SO
1995— Gulf Coast Red Sox (GCL)..	2	4	.333	2.74	12	7	1	0	2	46	38	17	14	12	44
1996— Michigan (Midw.)	6	11	.353	3.58	22	22	1	0	0	128 1/3	120	62	51	42	105
1997— Sarasota (FSL)	4	8	.333	4.55	12	11	2	1	0	65 1/3	69	42	33	27	56
1998— Trenton (East.)	6	5	.545	4.17	22	20	1	0	0	108	104	53	50	39	82
1999— Trenton (East.)	7	8	.467	4.08	28	•28	1	1	0	163 1/3	151	81	74	59	111
2000— Trenton (East.)	2	3	.400	3.10	9	9	0	0	0	52 1/3	50	20	18	6	54
— Pawtucket (I.L.).................	7	4	.636	4.55	12	11	1	1	0	61 1/3	47	32	31	22	47
— Boston (A.L.).....................	2	1	.667	3.41	7	4	0	0	0	29	25	15	11	13	17
Major League totals (1 year)........	2	1	.667	3.41	7	4	0	0	0	29	25	15	11	13	17

CREDE, JOE　　　　　3B　　　　　WHITE SOX

PERSONAL: Born April 26, 1978, in Jefferson City, Mo. ... 6-3/195. ... Bats right, throws right. ... Full name: Joseph Crede.
HIGH SCHOOL: Fatima (Westphalia, Mo.).
TRANSACTIONS/CAREER NOTES: Selected by Chicago White Sox organization in fifth round of free-agent draft (June 2, 1996). ... On Birmingham disabled list (July 2, 1999-remainder of season).
HONORS: Named Carolina League Most Valuable Player (1998). ... Named Southern League Most Valuable Player (2000).
STATISTICAL NOTES: Led Gulf Coast League third basemen with 175 total chances in 1996. ... Led Carolina League with 253 total bases and 11 sacrifice flies in 1998. ... Led Carolina League third basemen with 420 total chances in 1998. ... Led Southern League with 261 total bases in 2000. ... Led Southern League in grounding into double plays with 18 in 2000. ... Led Southern League third basemen with 328 total chances in 2000.

							BATTING								FIELDING		
Year　Team (League)	Pos.	G	AB	R	H	2B	3B	HR	RBI	Avg.	BB	SO	SB	PO	A	E	Avg.
1996— GC White Sox (GCL) ..	3B	56	221	30	66	17	1	4	32	.299	9	41	1	*42	*108	*25	.857
1997— Hickory (S.Atl.)..........	3B	113	402	45	109	25	0	5	62	.271	24	83	3	84	232	33	.905
1998— Win.-Salem (Caro.)	3B	*137	492	•92	155	32	3	20	*88	*.315	53	98	9	*100	*290	*30	.929
1999— Birmingham (Sou.)......	3B-DH	74	291	37	73	14	1	4	42	.251	22	47	2	68	133	20	.910
2000— Birmingham (Sou.)......	3B	138	533	84	*163	35	0	21	94	.306	56	111	3	91	218	19	.942
— Chicago (A.L.)...........	3B-DH	7	14	2	5	1	0	0	3	.357	0	3	0	5	9	1	.933
Major League totals (1 year)		7	14	2	5	1	0	0	3	.357	0	3	0	5	9	1	.933

CREEK, DOUG　　　　　P　　　　　DEVIL RAYS

C

PERSONAL: Born March 1, 1969, in Winchester, Va. ... 6-0/200. ... Throws left, bats left. ... Full name: Paul Douglas Creek.
HIGH SCHOOL: Martinsburg (W.Va.).
COLLEGE: Georgia Tech.
TRANSACTIONS/CAREER NOTES: Selected by California Angels organization in fifth round of free-agent draft (June 4, 1990); did not sign. ... Selected by St. Louis Cardinals organization in seventh round of free-agent draft (June 3, 1991). ... On Arkansas disabled list (April 10-May 21, 1992; July 25-August 1, 1993; and June 25-July 10, 1994). ... Traded by Cardinals with P Allen Watson and P Rich DeLucia to San Francisco Giants for SS Royce Clayton and a player to be named later (December 14, 1995); Cardinals acquired 2B Chris Wimmer to complete deal (January 16, 1996). ... Contract purchased by Chicago White Sox from Giants organization (November 7, 1997). ... Contract sold by White Sox to Hanshin Tigers of Japan Central League (December 4, 1997). ... Signed by Chicago Cubs organization (January 29, 1999). ... Released by Cubs (September 13, 1999). ... Signed by Tampa Bay Devil Rays organization (February 1, 2000). ... On Durham disabled list (April 6-25, 2000).
STATISTICAL NOTES: Tied for Pacific Coast League lead with 12 hit batsmen in 1999.

Year　League	W	L	Pct.	ERA	G	GS	CG	ShO	Sv.	IP	H	R	ER	BB	SO
1991— Hamilton (NY-Penn)	3	2	.600	5.12	9	5	0	0	1	38²/₃	39	22	22	18	45
— Savannah (S.Atl.)	2	1	.667	4.45	5	5	0	0	0	28¹/₃	24	14	14	17	32
1992— Springfield (Midw.)	4	1	.800	2.58	6	6	0	0	0	38¹/₃	32	11	11	13	43
— St. Petersburg (FSL)	5	4	.556	2.82	13	13	0	0	0	73¹/₃	57	31	23	37	63
1993— Louisville (A.A.).................	0	0	...	3.21	2	2	0	0	0	14	10	5	5	9	9
— Arkansas (Texas)..............	11	10	.524	4.02	25	25	1	1	0	147²/₃	142	75	66	48	128
1994— Louisville (A.A.).................	1	4	.200	8.54	7	7	0	0	0	26¹/₃	37	26	25	23	16
— Arkansas (Texas)..............	3	10	.231	4.40	17	17	1	0	0	92	96	54	45	36	65
1995— Louisville (A.A.).................	3	2	.600	3.23	26	0	0	0	0	30²/₃	20	12	11	21	29
— Arkansas (Texas)..............	4	2	.667	2.88	26	0	0	0	1	34¹/₃	24	12	11	16	50
— St. Louis (N.L.).................	0	0	...	0.00	6	0	0	0	0	6²/₃	2	0	0	3	10
1996— San Francisco (N.L.)■	0	2	.000	6.52	63	0	0	0	0	48¹/₃	45	41	35	32	38
1997— Phoenix (PCL)	8	6	.571	4.93	25	23	2	1	0	129²/₃	140	76	71	66	*137
— San Francisco (N.L.)	1	2	.333	6.75	3	3	0	0	0	13¹/₃	12	12	10	14	14
1998— Hanshin (Jap. Pac.)■........	0	4	.000	3.14	...	...	...	...	0	28²/₃	...	...	...	...	24
1999— Iowa (PCL)■	7	3	.700	3.79	25	20	0	0	1	130²/₃	116	66	55	62	140
— Chicago (N.L.)	0	0	...	10.50	3	0	0	0	0	6	6	7	7	8	6
2000— Durham (I.L.)■	0	0	...	1.96	10	1	0	0	0	18¹/₃	10	5	4	14	22
— Tampa Bay (A.L.)...............	1	3	.250	4.60	45	0	0	0	1	60²/₃	49	33	31	39	73
A.L. totals (1 year)	1	3	.250	4.60	45	0	0	0	1	60²/₃	49	33	31	39	73
N.L. totals (4 years)	1	4	.200	6.30	75	3	0	0	0	74¹/₃	65	60	52	57	68
Major League totals (5 years).......	2	7	.222	5.53	120	3	0	0	1	135	114	93	83	96	141

CRESPO, FELIPE　　　　　IF/OF　　　　　GIANTS

PERSONAL: Born March 5, 1973, in Rio Piedras, Puerto Rico. ... 5-11/200. ... Bats both, throws right. ... Full name: Felipe Javier Clauso Crespo.
HIGH SCHOOL: Notre Dame (Caguas, Puerto Rico).
TRANSACTIONS/CAREER NOTES: Selected by Toronto Blue Jays organization in third round of free-agent draft (June 4, 1990). ... On disabled list (May 26-July 2, 1995). ... On Toronto disabled list (April 1-24, 1996); included rehabilitation assignment to Dunedin (April 12-24). ... Released by Blue Jays (March 17, 1999). ... Signed by San Francisco Giants organization (April 27, 1999). ... Granted free agency (October 15, 1999). ... Re-signed by Giants organization (October 29, 1999).
STATISTICAL NOTES: Led Southern League third basemen with 127 putouts and 42 errors in 1994. ... Led Pacific Coast League with a .616 slugging percentage and a .447 on-base percentage in 1999.

							BATTING								FIELDING		
Year　Team (League)	Pos.	G	AB	R	H	2B	3B	HR	RBI	Avg.	BB	SO	SB	PO	A	E	Avg.
1991— Medicine Hat (Pio.)	2B	49	184	40	57	11	4	4	31	.310	25	31	6	*97	133	*23	.909
1992— Myrtle Beach (S.Atl.) ...	2B-3B	81	263	43	74	14	3	1	29	.281	58	38	7	161	149	22	.934
1993— Dunedin (FSL)	2B	96	345	51	103	16	8	6	39	.299	47	40	18	198	269	25	.949
1994— Knoxville (Sou.)..........	3B-2B	129	502	74	135	30	4	8	49	.269	57	95	20	†127	270	†42	.904
1995— Syracuse (I.L.)...........	2B-DH	88	347	56	102	20	5	13	41	.294	41	56	12	160	220	*25	.938

Year Team (League)	Pos.	G	AB	R	H	2B	3B	HR	RBI	Avg.	BB	SO	SB	PO	A	E	Avg.
										BATTING					FIELDING		
1996— Dunedin (FSL)...........	2B	9	34	3	11	1	0	2	6	.324	2	3	1	18	18	2	.947
—Toronto (A.L.).............	2B-3B-1B	22	49	6	9	4	0	0	4	.184	12	13	1	34	38	1	.986
—Syracuse (I.L.)............	2-0-3-1	98	355	53	100	25	0	8	58	.282	56	39	10	220	143	19	.950
1997— Toronto (A.L.)............	3B-DH-2B	12	28	3	8	0	1	1	5	.286	2	4	0	9	9	1	.947
—Syracuse (I.L.)............O-2-1-DH-3		80	290	53	75	12	0	12	26	.259	46	38	7	247	103	12	.967
1998— Toronto (A.L.).............O-2-DH-3-1		66	130	11	34	8	1	1	15	.262	15	27	4	67	17	4	.955
1999— Fresno (PCL)■.........1-O-2-D-3-S		112	385	98	128	27	5	24	84	.332	78	73	17	620	77	13	.982
2000— San Francisco (N.L.) ..	O-1-2-D	89	131	17	38	6	1	4	29	.290	10	23	3	57	4	1	.984
American League totals (3 years)		100	207	20	51	12	2	2	24	.246	29	44	5	110	64	6	.967
National League totals (1 year)		89	131	17	38	6	1	4	29	.290	10	23	3	57	4	1	.984
Major League totals (4 years)		189	338	37	89	18	3	6	53	.263	39	67	8	167	68	7	.971

DIVISION SERIES RECORD

Year Team (League)	Pos.	G	AB	R	H	2B	3B	HR	RBI	Avg.	BB	SO	SB	PO	A	E	Avg.
										BATTING					FIELDING		
2000— San Francisco (N.L.) ..	PH	4	4	0	1	0	0	0	0	.250	0	0	0	...	...	...	...

CRESSEND, JACK   P   TWINS

PERSONAL: Born May 13, 1975, in New Orleans. ... 6-1/185. ... Throws right, bats right. ... Full name: John Baptiste Cressend III.
HIGH SCHOOL: Mandeville (La.).
COLLEGE: Tulane.
TRANSACTIONS/CAREER NOTES: Signed as non-drafted free agent by Boston Red Sox organization (July 24, 1996). ... Claimed on waivers by Minnesota Twins (April 22, 1999).

Year League	W	L	Pct.	ERA	G	GS	CG	ShO	Sv.	IP	H	R	ER	BB	SO
1996— Lowell (NY-Penn)	3	2	.600	2.36	9	8	0	0	0	45 2/3	37	15	12	17	57
1997— Sarasota (FSL)	8	11	.421	3.80	28	25	2	1	0	165 2/3	163	98	70	56	149
1998— Trenton (East.)	10	11	.476	4.34	29	•29	1	1	0	149 1/3	168	86	72	55	130
1999— Trenton (East.)	1	0	1.000	7.20	3	3	0	0	0	15	19	12	12	7	11
—New Britain (East.)■...........	7	10	.412	4.34	25	24	2	2	0	145	152	79	70	50	125
2000— Salt Lake (PCL)	4	4	.500	3.44	54	1	0	0	8	86 1/3	87	40	33	39	87
—Minnesota (A.L.)	0	0	...	5.27	11	0	0	0	0	13 2/3	20	8	8	6	6
Major League totals (1 year)........	0	0	...	5.27	11	0	0	0	0	13 2/3	20	8	8	6	6

CROMER, D.T.   1B/OF   REDS

PERSONAL: Born March 19, 1971, in Lake City, S.C. ... 6-2/190. ... Bats left, throws left. ... Full name: David Thomas Cromer. ... Son of Roy Cromer, former scout with St. Louis Cardinals and minor league pitcher/second baseman (1960-63); brother of Brandon Cromer, minor league shortstop (1992-2000); brother of Tripp Cromer, infielder with St. Louis Cardinals (1993-95), Los Angeles Dodgers (1997-99) and Houston Astros (2000); and brother of Burke Cromer, pitcher, Atlanta Braves organization (1992-93).
HIGH SCHOOL: Lexington (S.C.).
COLLEGE: South Carolina.
TRANSACTIONS/CAREER NOTES: Selected by Oakland Athletics organization in 11th round of free-agent draft (June 1, 1992). ... Granted free agency (October 15, 1998). ... Signed by Cincinnati Reds organization (December 15, 1998).
HONORS: Named California League Most Valuable Player (1996).
STATISTICAL NOTES: Led California League with 316 total bases and .626 slugging percentage in 1996. ... Led Southern League first basemen with 1,167 putouts, 18 errors, 1,285 total chances and 129 double plays in 1997. ... Led Pacific Coast League first basemen with 1,015 putouts, 89 assists, 1,117 total chances and 113 double plays in 1998.

Year Team (League)	Pos.	G	AB	R	H	2B	3B	HR	RBI	Avg.	BB	SO	SB	PO	A	E	Avg.
										BATTING					FIELDING		
1992— S. Oregon (N.W.)........	OF	50	168	17	35	7	0	4	26	.208	13	34	4	61	6	5	.931
1993— Madison (Midw.)........	OF-1B-DH	98	321	37	84	20	4	4	41	.262	22	72	8	233	8	7	.972
1994— W. Mich. (Midw.)........	OF-1B	102	349	50	89	20	5	10	58	.255	33	76	11	328	28	10	.973
1995— Modesto (Calif.)	OF-1B	108	378	59	98	18	5	14	52	.259	36	66	5	160	16	8	.957
1996— Modesto (Calif.)	1B-OF-DH	124	505	100	*166	40	10	30	130	.329	32	67	20	549	67	14	.978
1997— Huntsville (Sou.)	1B-DH-OF	134	545	100	*176	*40	6	15	121	.323	60	102	12	†1169	101	†18	.986
1998— Edmonton (PCL)	1B-DH-OF	125	504	75	148	30	3	16	85	.294	32	93	12	†1018	†89	15	.987
1999— Indianapolis (I.L.)■.....	OF-1B-DH	136	535	83	166	37	4	30	107	.310	44	98	4	507	38	9	.984
2000— Cincinnati (N.L.)	1B	35	47	7	16	4	0	2	8	.340	1	14	0	50	3	2	.964
—Louisville (I.L.)	1B-OF	106	415	58	112	26	3	14	67	.270	33	84	6	461	49	10	.981
Major League totals (1 year)		35	47	7	16	4	0	2	8	.340	1	14	0	50	3	2	.964

CROMER, TRIPP   IF

PERSONAL: Born November 21, 1967, in Lake City, S.C. ... 6-2/165. ... Bats right, throws right. ... Full name: Roy Bunyan Cromer III. ... Son of Roy Cromer, former scout with St. Louis Cardinals and minor league pitcher/second baseman (1960-63); brother of Brandon Cromer, minor league shortstop (1992-2000); brother of D.T. Cromer, first baseman/outfielder, Cincinnati Reds organization; and brother of Burke Cromer, pitcher, Atlanta Braves organization (1992-93).
HIGH SCHOOL: Lake City (S.C.).
COLLEGE: South Carolina.
TRANSACTIONS/CAREER NOTES: Selected by St. Louis Cardinals organization in third round of free-agent draft (June 5, 1989). ... On Arkansas disabled list (May 14-26, 1992). ... On Louisville disabled list (April 30-May 28 and July 5-August 3, 1993). ... On disabled list (May 20-27, 1996). ... Claimed on waivers by Los Angeles Dodgers (October 10, 1996). ... On disabled list (July 31, 1997-remainder of season). ... On Los Angeles disabled list (March 12-July 17 and July 31-September 1, 1998; included rehabilitation assignment to Albuquerque (June 16-26 and July 9-17) and San Bernardino (August 27-September 1). ... On Los Angeles disabled list (July 5-September 1, 1999); included

rehabilitation assignments to Albuquerque (July 21-27) and San Bernardino (August 27-September 1). ... Granted free agency (November 24, 1999). ... Signed by Houston Astros organization (December 21, 1999). ... On Houston disabled list (August 25, 2000-remainder of season). ... Granted free agency (October 12, 2000).

							BATTING								FIELDING		
Year Team (League)	Pos.	G	AB	R	H	2B	3B	HR	RBI	Avg.	BB	SO	SB	PO	A	E	Avg.
1989— Hamilton (NY-Penn) ...	SS	35	137	18	36	6	3	0	6	.263	17	30	4	66	85	11	.932
1990— St. Petersburg (FSL) ..	SS	121	408	53	88	12	5	5	38	.216	46	78	7	202	334	32	.944
1991— St. Petersburg (FSL) ..	SS	43	137	11	28	3	1	0	10	.204	9	17	0	79	134	3	.986
— Arkansas (Texas).......	SS	73	227	28	52	12	1	1	18	.229	15	37	0	117	198	10	.969
1992— Arkansas (Texas).......	SS	110	339	30	81	16	6	7	29	.239	22	82	4	135	315	18	*.962
— Louisville (A.A.).........	SS	6	25	5	5	1	1	1	7	.200	1	6	0	13	20	0	1.000
1993— Louisville (A.A.).........	SS	85	309	39	85	8	4	11	33	.275	15	60	1	123	253	12	.969
— St. Louis (N.L.)..........	SS	10	23	1	2	0	0	0	0	.087	1	6	0	13	18	3	.912
1994— Louisville (A.A.).........	SS	124	419	53	115	23	9	9	50	.274	33	85	5	165	370	12	*.978
— St. Louis (N.L.)..........	SS	2	0	1	0	0	0	0	0	...	0	0	0	0	0	1	.000
1995— St. Louis (N.L.)..........	SS-2B	105	345	36	78	19	0	5	18	.226	14	66	0	126	292	17	.961
1996— Louisville (A.A.).........	SS-2B	80	244	28	55	4	4	4	25	.225	22	47	3	124	238	5	.986
1997— Albuquerque (PCL)■..	SS	43	140	25	45	8	6	5	24	.321	14	34	4	65	106	6	.966
— Los Angeles (N.L.)	2B-SS-3B	28	86	8	25	3	0	4	20	.291	6	16	0	47	61	3	.973
1998— Albuquerque (PCL)......	SS-DH	12	30	3	10	1	0	2	5	.333	1	5	0	3	17	1	.952
— Los Angeles (N.L.)	PH	6	6	1	1	0	0	1	1	.167	0	2	0	...	...	...	...
— San Bern. (Calif.)........	2B-DH	4	15	3	6	1	0	2	6	.400	0	2	0	2	8	0	1.000
1999— Los Angeles (N.L.)	2-S-3-O-1	33	52	5	10	0	0	2	8	.192	5	10	0	21	36	0	1.000
— Albuquerque (PCL)......	2B-1B-SS	5	15	1	4	2	0	0	1	.267	1	3	0	17	11	0	1.000
— San Bern. (Calif.)........	1B-2B-3B-SS	4	18	3	9	3	0	1	8	.500	0	3	0	9	8	0	1.000
2000— New Orleans (PCL)■...	2-3-S-1	66	224	21	48	7	3	4	24	.214	17	47	1	112	131	7	.972
— Houston (N.L.)	3B-2B-SS	9	8	2	1	0	0	0	0	.125	1	1	0	0	2	1	.667
Major League totals (7 years)		193	520	54	117	22	0	12	47	.225	27	101	0	207	409	25	.961

CROUSHORE, RICK   P   RED SOX

PERSONAL: Born August 7, 1970, in Lakehurst, N.J. ... 6-4/210. ... Throws right, bats right. ... Full name: Richard Steven Croushore.
HIGH SCHOOL: Mount Vernon (Texas).
JUNIOR COLLEGE: Hutchinson (Kan.) Community College.
COLLEGE: James Madison.
TRANSACTIONS/CAREER NOTES: Signed as non-drafted free agent by St. Louis Cardinals organization (June 12, 1993). ... On disabled list (April 6-June 19, 1995). ... On Memphis disabled list (April 15-22, 1999). ... Traded by Cardinals with P Jose Jimenez, P Manny Aybar and SS Brent Butler to Colorado Rockies for P Darryl Kile, P Dave Veres and P Luther Hackman (November 16, 1999). ... Traded by Rockies with P Rolando Arrojo, 2B Mike Lansing and cash to Boston Red Sox for P Brian Rose, P John Wasdin, P Jeff Taglienti and 2B Jeff Frye (July 27, 2000).

Year League	W	L	Pct.	ERA	G	GS	CG	ShO	Sv.	IP	H	R	ER	BB	SO
1993— Glens Falls (NY-Penn)	4	1	.800	3.05	31	0	0	0	1	41 1/3	38	16	14	22	36
1994— Madison (Midw.)...............	6	6	.500	4.10	•62	0	0	0	0	94 1/3	90	49	43	46	103
1995— St. Petersburg (FSL)	6	4	.600	3.51	12	11	0	0	0	59	44	25	23	32	57
1996— Arkansas (Texas)...............	5	10	.333	4.92	34	17	2	0	3	108	113	75	59	51	85
1997— Arkansas (Texas)...............	7	5	.583	4.18	17	16	1	0	0	92 2/3	111	52	43	37	67
— Louisville (A.A.).................	1	2	.333	2.47	14	6	0	0	1	43 2/3	37	14	12	13	41
1998— Memphis (PCL)................	0	3	.000	4.71	23	0	0	0	2	28 2/3	21	16	15	9	40
— St. Louis (N.L.).................	0	3	.000	4.97	41	0	0	0	8	54 1/3	44	31	30	29	47
1999— Memphis (PCL)................	1	0	1.000	6.75	7	0	0	0	4	6 2/3	8	5	5	6	11
— St. Louis (N.L.).................	3	7	.300	4.14	59	0	0	0	3	71 2/3	68	42	33	43	88
2000— Colorado Springs (PCL)■...	2	4	.333	7.36	33	2	0	0	0	36 2/3	40	31	30	32	30
— Colorado (N.L.)..............	2	0	1.000	8.74	6	0	0	0	0	11 1/3	15	11	11	6	11
— Pawtucket (I.L.)■..............	0	1	.000	3.43	11	0	0	0	0	21	16	8	8	10	23
— Boston (A.L.)......................	0	1	.000	5.79	5	0	0	0	0	4 2/3	4	3	3	5	3
A.L. totals (1 year)	0	1	.000	5.79	5	0	0	0	0	4 2/3	4	3	3	5	3
N.L. totals (3 years)	5	10	.333	4.85	106	0	0	0	11	137 1/3	127	84	74	78	146
Major League totals (3 years)	5	11	.313	4.88	111	0	0	0	11	142	131	87	77	83	149

CRUZ, DEIVI   IF   TIGERS

PERSONAL: Born November 6, 1975, in Nizao de Bani, Dominican Republic. ... 6-0/184. ... Bats right, throws right. ... Full name: Deivi Garcia Cruz.
HIGH SCHOOL: Liceo Aliro Paulino Nizao (Dominican Republic).
TRANSACTIONS/CAREER NOTES: Signed as non-drafted free agent by San Francisco Giants organization (April 23, 1993). ... Selected by Los Angeles Dodgers organization from Giants organization in Rule 5 major league draft (December 9, 1996). ... Traded by Dodgers with OF Juan Hernaiz to Detroit Tigers for 2B Jeff Berblinger (December 9, 1996). ... On Detroit disabled list (March 20-April 27, 1998; included rehabilitation assignments to Lakeland (April 21-23) and Toledo (April 24-27).
STATISTICAL NOTES: Led Northwest League third basemen with 47 putouts and .941 fielding percentage in 1995. ... Led Midwest League shortstops with 427 assists and .980 fielding percentage in 1996. ... Career major league grand slams: 1.

							BATTING								FIELDING		
Year Team (League)	Pos.	G	AB	R	H	2B	3B	HR	RBI	Avg.	BB	SO	SB	PO	A	E	Avg.
1993— Arizona Giants (Ariz.) .	3B-SS-1B	28	82	8	28	3	0	0	15	.341	4	5	3	17	52	2	.972
1994— Arizona Giants (Ariz.) .	SS-3B	18	53	10	16	8	0	0	5	.302	5	3	0	11	37	1	.980
1995— Burlington (Midw.)	3B-2B-SS	16	58	2	8	1	0	1	9	.138	4	7	1	20	42	2	.969
— Bellingham (N'West) ..	3B-2B	62	223	32	66	17	0	3	28	.296	19	21	6	†55	124	10	†.947
1996— Burlington (Midw.)	SS-3B	127	517	72	152	27	2	9	64	.294	35	49	12	159	†444	13	†.979
1997— Detroit (A.L.)■	SS	147	436	35	105	26	2	2	40	.241	14	55	3	192	420	13	.979

Year Team (League)	Pos.	G	AB	R	H	2B	3B	HR	RBI	Avg.	BB	SO	SB	PO	A	E	Avg.
						BATTING								FIELDING			
1998—Lakeland (FSL)	SS	2	9	0	0	0	0	0	1	.000	0	1	0	1	2	0	1.000
— Toledo (I.L.)...............	SS	2	9	1	1	1	0	0	2	.111	2	3	0	2	7	0	1.000
— Detroit (A.L.)...........	SS	135	454	52	118	22	3	5	45	.260	13	55	3	196	445	11	.983
1999—Detroit (A.L.)	SS	155	518	64	147	35	0	13	58	.284	12	57	1	230	453	12	.983
2000—Detroit (A.L.)	SS	156	583	68	176	46	5	10	82	.302	13	43	1	222	482	13	.982
Major League totals (4 years)		593	1991	219	546	129	8	30	225	.274	52	210	8	840	1800	49	.982

CRUZ, IVAN — 1B

PERSONAL: Born May 3, 1968, in Fajardo, Puerto Rico. ... 6-2/219. ... Bats left, throws left. ... Full name: Luis Ivan Cruz.
HIGH SCHOOL: Colegio Santiago Apostal (Fajardo, Puerto Rico).
COLLEGE: Jacksonville.
TRANSACTIONS/CAREER NOTES: Selected by Detroit Tigers organization in 28th round of free-agent draft (June 5, 1989). ... Granted free agency (October 16, 1995). ... Signed by New York Yankees organization (November 27, 1996). ... Granted free agency (October 3, 1998). ... Signed by Pittsburgh Pirates organization (December 22, 1998). ... On Pittsburgh disabled list (July 4, 1999-remainder of season); included rehabilitation assignments to Altoona (July 23-25) and Nashville (July 26-August 9). ... Granted free agency (October 2, 2000).
STATISTICAL NOTES: Tied for Florida State League lead in double plays by first baseman with 75 in 1990. ... Led Southern League with .564 slugging percentage in 1995. ... Tied for Southern League lead in intentional bases on balls received with 15 in 1995. ... Led International League first basemen with 1,127 total chances and 88 double plays in 1996.

Year Team (League)	Pos.	G	AB	R	H	2B	3B	HR	RBI	Avg.	BB	SO	SB	PO	A	E	Avg.
						BATTING								FIELDING			
1989—Niagara Falls (NY-P) ...	1B	64	226	43	62	11	2	7	40	.274	27	29	2	439	30	5	.989
1990—Lakeland (FSL)	1B	118	414	61	118	23	2	11	73	.285	49	71	8	938	44	11	.989
1991—London (East.)	1B	121	443	46	110	21	0	9	47	.248	36	73	3	845	49	12	.987
— Toledo (I.L.)...............	1B	8	29	2	4	0	0	1	4	.138	2	12	0	70	7	0	1.000
1992—London (East.)	1B	134	*524	71	143	25	1	14	*104	.273	37	102	1	549	35	8	.986
1993—Toledo (I.L.)...............	1B	115	402	44	91	18	4	13	50	.226	30	85	1	268	27	2	.993
1994—Toledo (I.L.)...............	1B-DH	97	303	36	75	11	2	15	43	.248	28	83	1	411	37	6	.987
1995—Toledo (I.L.)...............	1B-DH	11	36	5	7	2	0	0	3	.194	6	9	0	89	6	3	.969
— Jacksonville (Sou.).....	1B-DH	108	397	65	112	17	1	*31	93	.282	60	94	0	795	60	7	.992
1996—Columbus (I.L.)■.......	1B-DH	130	446	84	115	26	0	28	96	.258	48	99	2	*1028	*94	5	*.996
1997—Columbus (I.L.)	1B-DH	116	417	69	125	35	1	24	95	.300	65	78	4	974	83	8	.992
— New York (A.L.)	DH-1B-OF	11	20	0	5	1	0	0	3	.250	2	4	0	8	0	0	1.000
1998—Columbus (I.L.)	1B-DH-OF	56	204	34	54	10	0	13	36	.265	29	44	0	503	39	5	.991
— GC Yankees (GCL)......	1B-DH	5	10	2	6	3	0	1	5	.600	3	3	0	18	0	0	1.000
1999—Nashville (PCL)■.......	1B-DH	75	273	57	89	20	1	25	81	.326	21	56	0	571	37	4	.993
— Pittsburgh (N.L.)	1B-OF	5	10	3	4	0	0	1	2	.400	0	2	0	13	1	0	1.000
— Altoona (East.)	DH	3	13	1	2	1	0	0	3	.154	1	8	0	0	0	0	...
2000—Nashville (PCL)	1B	36	121	15	38	11	0	7	28	.314	15	26	0	232	25	2	.992
— Pittsburgh (N.L.)	1B	8	11	0	1	0	0	0	0	.091	0	8	0	6	0	0	1.000
American League totals (1 year)		11	20	0	5	1	0	0	3	.250	2	4	0	8	0	0	1.000
National League totals (2 years)		13	21	3	5	0	0	1	2	.238	0	10	0	19	1	0	1.000
Major League totals (3 years)		24	41	3	10	1	0	1	5	.244	2	14	0	27	1	0	1.000

CRUZ, JACOB — OF — INDIANS

PERSONAL: Born January 28, 1973, in Oxnard, Calif. ... 6-0/215. ... Bats left, throws left.
HIGH SCHOOL: Channel Islands (Oxnard, Calif.).
COLLEGE: Arizona State.
TRANSACTIONS/CAREER NOTES: Selected by California Angels organization in 45th round of free-agent draft (June 3, 1991); did not sign. ... Selected by San Francisco Giants organization in supplemental round ("sandwich pick" between first and second round; 32nd pick overall) of free-agent draft (June 2, 1994); pick received as part of compensation for Texas Rangers signing Type A free agent 1B Will Clark. ... Traded by Giants with P Steve Reed to Cleveland Indians for P Jose Mesa, IF Shawon Dunston and P Alvin Morman (July 24, 1998). ... On Cleveland disabled list (March 30-April 29 and August 3, 1999-remainder of season); included rehabilitation assignment to Buffalo (April 18-29). ... On disabled list (April 30, 2000-remainder of season).
STATISTICAL NOTES: Led Pacific Coast League with 11 sacrifice flies in 1996. ... Led Pacific Coast League with .434 on-base percentage and tied for league lead with nine intentional bases on balls in 1997.

Year Team (League)	Pos.	G	AB	R	H	2B	3B	HR	RBI	Avg.	BB	SO	SB	PO	A	E	Avg.
						BATTING								FIELDING			
1994—San Jose (Calif.).........	OF	31	118	14	29	7	0	0	12	.246	9	22	0	42	2	2	.957
1995—Shreveport (Texas).....	OF	127	458	88	136	33	1	13	77	.297	57	72	9	235	16	1	*.996
1996—Phoenix (PCL)	OF-DH	121	435	60	124	26	4	7	75	.285	62	77	5	249	11	3	.989
— San Francisco (N.L.) ..	OF	33	77	10	18	3	0	3	10	.234	12	24	0	41	1	1	.977
1997—Phoenix (PCL)	OF-DH	127	493	97	178	*45	3	12	95	*.361	64	64	18	239	*16	8	.970
— San Francisco (N.L.) ..	OF	16	25	3	4	1	0	0	3	.160	3	4	0	12	2	1	.933
1998—Fresno (PCL)	OF-DH	89	342	60	102	17	3	18	62	.298	46	57	12	152	5	6	.963
— San Francisco (N.L.) ..	PH	3	3	0	0	0	0	0	0	.000	0	2	0	0	0	0	...
— Buffalo (I.L.)■...........	OF	43	169	32	56	8	2	13	36	.331	13	26	2	70	5	4	.949
— Cleveland (A.L.).........	PH	1	1	0	0	0	0	0	0	.000	0	1	0	0	0	0	...
1999—Buffalo (I.L.).............	OF-DH	54	202	29	55	7	2	7	31	.272	21	39	4	77	5	4	.953
— Cleveland (A.L.).........	OF-DH	32	88	14	29	5	1	3	17	.330	5	13	0	48	0	0	1.000
2000—Cleveland (A.L.).........	OF-DH	11	29	3	7	3	0	0	5	.241	5	4	1	16	1	0	1.000
American League totals (3 years)		44	118	17	36	8	1	3	22	.305	10	18	1	64	1	0	1.000
National League totals (3 years)		52	105	13	22	4	0	3	13	.210	15	30	0	53	3	2	.966
Major League totals (5 years)		96	223	30	58	12	1	6	35	.260	25	48	1	117	4	2	.984

CRUZ, JOSE   OF   BLUE JAYS

PERSONAL: Born April 19, 1974, in Arroyo, Puerto Rico. ... 6-0/200. ... Bats both, throws right. ... Full name: Jose Cruz Jr. ... Son of Jose Cruz Sr., outfielder with St. Louis Cardinals (1970-1974), Houston Astros (1975-1987) and New York Yankees (1988); nephew of Hector Cruz, outfielder/third baseman with four major league teams (1973, 1975-82); and nephew of Tommy Cruz, outfielder with St. Louis Cardinals (1973), Chicago White Sox (1977) and Nippon Ham Fighters of Japan League (1980-85).
HIGH SCHOOL: Bellaire (Houston).
COLLEGE: Rice.
TRANSACTIONS/CAREER NOTES: Selected by Atlanta Braves organization in 15th round of free-agent draft (June 1, 1992); did not sign. ... Selected by Seattle Mariners organization in first round (third pick overall) of free-agent draft (June 1, 1995). ... Traded by Mariners to Toronto Blue Jays for P Mike Timlin and P Paul Spoljaric (July 31, 1997). ... On Toronto disabled list (June 24-July 9, 1999); included rehabilitation assignment to Syracuse (July 5-9).
STATISTICAL NOTES: Switch-hit home runs in one game (August 24, 1997). ... Had 18-game hitting streak (August 5-24, 1998). ... Led A.L. outfielders with 417 total chances in 2000.

							BATTING								FIELDING		
Year	Team (League)	Pos.	G	AB	R	H	2B	3B	HR	RBI	Avg.	BB	SO	SB	PO	A	E	Avg.
1995—	Everett (N'West)	OF	3	11	6	5	0	0	0	2	.455	3	3	1	7	0	0	1.000
	— Riverside (Calif.)	OF	35	144	34	37	7	1	7	29	.257	24	50	3	70	4	3	.961
1996—	Lancaster (Calif.)	OF-DH	53	203	38	66	17	1	6	43	.325	39	33	7	62	7	1	.986
	— Port City (Sou.)	OF-DH	47	181	39	51	10	2	3	31	.282	27	38	5	90	6	1	.990
	— Tacoma (PCL)	OF	22	76	15	18	1	2	6	15	.237	18	12	1	36	4	0	1.000
1997—	Tacoma (PCL)	OF-DH	50	190	33	51	16	2	6	30	.268	34	44	3	70	3	0	1.000
	— Seattle (A.L.)	OF	49	183	28	49	12	1	12	34	.268	13	45	1	83	1	3	.966
	— Toronto (A.L.)■...........	OF	55	212	31	49	7	0	14	34	.231	28	72	6	98	3	2	.981
1998—	Toronto (A.L.)	OF	105	352	55	89	14	3	11	42	.253	57	99	11	247	7	4	.984
	— Syracuse (I.L.)	OF	40	141	29	42	14	1	7	23	.298	32	32	8	99	7	1	.991
1999—	Toronto (A.L.)	OF	106	349	63	84	19	3	14	45	.241	64	91	14	277	8	3	.990
	— Syracuse (I.L.)	OF-DH	31	103	17	19	3	1	3	14	.184	28	20	5	75	2	0	1.000
2000—	Toronto (A.L.)	OF	•162	603	91	146	32	5	31	76	.242	71	129	15	405	9	3	.993
Major League totals (4 years)			477	1699	268	417	84	12	82	231	.245	233	436	47	1110	28	15	.987

CRUZ, NELSON   P   ASTROS

PERSONAL: Born September 13, 1972, in Puerta Plata, Dominican Republic. ... 6-1/185. ... Throws right, bats right. ... Cousin of Jose Roman, pitcher with Cleveland Indians (1984-86).
HIGH SCHOOL: Liceo Jose Castellanos (Puerto Plata, Dominican Republic).
TRANSACTIONS/CAREER NOTES: Signed as non-drafted free agent by Montreal Expos organization (July 5, 1989). ... Released by Expos (March 27, 1992). ... Signed by Chicago White Sox organization (December 10, 1994). ... Granted free agency (October 15, 1998). ... Signed by Detroit Tigers (November 19, 1998). ... On Toledo disabled list (May 7-24, 2000). ... Traded by Tigers with C Brad Ausmus and P Doug Brocail to Houston Astros for C Mitch Meluskey, P Chris Holt and OF Roger Cedeno (December 11, 2000).

Year	League	W	L	Pct.	ERA	G	GS	CG	ShO	Sv.	IP	H	R	ER	BB	SO
1990—	Dom. Expos (DSL)	9	2	.818	2.62	16	16	0	0	0	103	105	49	30	42	83
1991—	Gulf Coast Expos (GCL)	2	4	.333	2.40	12	8	1	•1	0	48 2/3	40	18	13	19	34
1992—	....						Out of organized baseball.									
1993—	....						Out of organized baseball.									
1994—	....						Out of organized baseball.									
1995—	Bristol (Appl.)■.................	0	0	...	9.00	1	0	0	0	0	1	2	1	1	0	0
	— Hickory (S.Atl.).................	2	7	.222	2.70	44	0	0	0	9	66 2/3	65	31	20	15	68
	— Prince William (Caro.).......	2	1	.667	0.47	9	0	0	0	1	19 1/3	12	1	1	6	15
1996—	Birmingham (Sou.).............	6	6	.500	3.20	37	18	2	1	1	149	150	65	53	41	142
1997—	Nashville (A.A.)	11	7	.611	5.11	21	20	1	0	0	123 1/3	139	75	70	31	93
	— Chicago (A.L.)	0	2	.000	6.49	19	0	0	0	0	26 1/3	29	19	19	9	23
1998—	Calgary (PCL)	10	6	.625	5.33	35	18	2	1	0	126 2/3	159	85	75	40	101
1999—	Toledo (I.L.)■...................	7	1	.875	2.73	10	10	4	•2	0	62 2/3	47	20	19	21	41
	— Detroit (A.L.)	2	5	.286	5.67	29	6	0	0	0	66 2/3	74	44	42	23	46
2000—	Toledo (I.L.).....................	2	4	.333	4.82	11	10	0	0	0	52 1/3	54	37	28	17	39
	— Detroit (A.L.)	5	2	.714	3.07	27	0	0	0	0	41	39	14	14	13	34
Major League totals (3 years)		7	9	.438	5.04	75	6	0	0	0	134	142	77	75	45	103

CUBILLAN, DARWIN   P   BLUE JAYS

PERSONAL: Born November 15, 1974, in Bobure, Venezuela. ... 6-2/170. ... Throws right, bats right. ... Full name: Darwin Harrikson Salom Cubillan.
TRANSACTIONS/CAREER NOTES: Signed as non-drafted free agent by New York Yankees organization (June 28, 1993). ... On disabled list (April 4, 1996-entire season). ... Granted free agency (October 15, 1999). ... Signed by Toronto Blue Jays organization (November 12, 1999). ... Traded by Blue Jays with 2B/SS Mike Young to Texas Rangers for P Esteban Loaiza (July 19, 2000).

Year	League	W	L	Pct.	ERA	G	GS	CG	ShO	Sv.	IP	H	R	ER	BB	SO
1993—	Dominican Yankees (DSL)..	0	2	.000	9.45	4	2	0	0	0	6 2/3	8	9	7	14	3
1994—	Gulf Coast Yankees (GCL)..	4	2	.667	2.35	13	8	1	1	0	57 1/3	45	16	15	16	48
	— Greensboro (S.Atl.)	0	0	...	18.00	1	0	0	0	0	2	6	5	4	2	1
1995—	Greensboro (S.Atl.)	5	5	.500	3.62	22	14	1	1	0	97	86	50	39	38	78
1996—	....						Did not play.									
1997—	Gulf Coast Yankees (GCL)..	0	0	...	0.00	1	0	0	0	0	1 2/3	1	0	0	1	2
1998—	Tampa (FSL).....................	9	2	.818	4.71	45	1	0	0	1	65	79	45	34	36	70
1999—	Tampa (FSL).....................	7	4	.636	2.51	55	0	0	0	3	75 1/3	57	27	21	32	76
2000—	Syracuse (I.L.)■	3	1	.750	0.55	24	0	0	0	6	32 2/3	14	2	2	13	41
	— Toronto (A.L.)...................	1	0	1.000	8.04	7	0	0	0	0	15 2/3	20	14	14	11	14
	— Oklahoma (PCL)■.............	0	0	...	1.08	8	0	0	0	2	16 2/3	9	2	2	4	12
	— Texas (A.L.)	0	0	...	10.70	13	0	0	0	0	17 2/3	32	22	21	14	13
Major League totals (1 year)		1	0	1.000	9.45	20	0	0	0	0	33 1/3	52	36	35	25	27

C

PERSONAL: Born October 14, 1971, in St. Croix, Virgin Islands. ... 6-0/195. ... Bats left, throws right. ... Full name: Midre Almeric Cummings.
HIGH SCHOOL: Miami Edison Senior.
TRANSACTIONS/CAREER NOTES: Selected by Minnesota Twins organization in supplemental round ("sandwich pick" between first and second round, 29th pick overall) of free-agent draft (June 4, 1990); pick received as part of compensation for Boston Red Sox signing Type A free-agent P Jeff Reardon. ... Traded by Twins with P Denny Neagle to Pittsburgh Pirates for P John Smiley (March 17, 1992). ... On Buffalo disabled list (April 21-June 6, 1994). ... On Calgary disabled list (June 17-July 1, 1995). ... Claimed on waivers by Philadelphia Phillies (July 8, 1997). ... Released by Phillies (February 24, 1998). ... Signed by Cincinnati Reds organization (February 27, 1998). ... Claimed on waivers by Boston Red Sox (March 19, 1998). ... On disabled list (July 29-September 7, 1998). ... Released by Red Sox (March 30, 1999). ... Signed by Twins organization (May 14, 1999). ... Traded by Twins to Red Sox for IF Hector De Los Santos (August 31, 2000). ... Granted free agency (October 13, 2000). ... Signed by Arizona Diamondbacks (December 15, 2000).
MISCELLANEOUS: Batted as switch-hitter (1990-92).

Year	Team (League)	Pos.	G	AB	R	H	2B	3B	HR	RBI	Avg.	BB	SO	SB	PO	A	E	Avg.
1990— GC Twins (GCL)		OF	47	177	28	56	3	4	5	28	.316	13	32	14	73	2	6	.926
1991— Kenosha (Midw.)		OF	106	382	59	123	20	4	4	54	*.322	22	66	28	166	6	•13	.930
1992— Salem (Caro.)■		OF	113	420	55	128	20	5	14	75	.305	35	67	23	151	10	6	.964
1993— Carolina (Sou.)		OF	63	237	33	70	17	2	6	26	.295	14	23	5	99	7	4	.964
— Buffalo (A.A.)		OF	60	232	36	64	12	1	9	21	.276	22	45	5	90	1	2	.978
— Pittsburgh (N.L.)		OF	13	36	5	4	1	0	0	3	.111	4	9	0	21	0	0	1.000
1994— Buffalo (A.A.)		OF	49	183	23	57	12	4	2	22	.311	13	26	5	117	2	0	1.000
— Pittsburgh (N.L.)		OF	24	86	11	21	4	0	1	12	.244	4	18	0	49	1	2	.962
1995— Pittsburgh (N.L.)		OF	59	152	13	37	7	1	2	15	.243	13	30	1	79	2	1	.988
— Calgary (PCL)		OF	45	159	19	44	9	1	1	16	.277	6	27	1	96	4	6	.943
1996— Calgary (PCL)		OF-DH	97	368	60	112	24	3	8	56	.304	21	60	6	176	9	5	.974
— Pittsburgh (N.L.)		OF	24	85	11	19	3	1	3	7	.224	0	16	0	49	0	1	.980
1997— Pittsburgh (N.L.)		OF	52	106	11	20	6	2	3	8	.189	8	26	0	37	1	0	1.000
— Philadelphia (N.L.)■..		OF	63	208	24	63	16	4	1	23	.303	23	30	2	113	1	1	.991
1998— Boston (A.L.)■		DH-OF	67	120	20	34	8	0	5	15	.283	17	19	3	16	0	1	.941
1999— New Britain (East.)■..		OF	24	93	28	35	7	0	2	15	.376	17	14	3	50	2	0	1.000
— Salt Lake (PCL)		OF-DH	69	261	50	84	19	4	13	68	.322	23	43	4	101	3	5	.954
— Minnesota (A.L.)		OF-DH	16	38	1	10	0	0	1	9	.263	3	7	2	5	0	0	1.000
2000— Minnesota (A.L.)		OF-DH	77	181	28	50	10	0	4	22	.276	11	25	0	58	4	0	1.000
— Boston (A.L.)		OF-DH	21	25	1	7	0	0	0	2	.280	6	3	0	7	0	0	1.000
American League totals (3 years)			181	364	50	101	18	0	10	48	.277	37	54	5	86	4	1	.989
National League totals (5 years)			235	673	75	164	37	8	10	68	.244	52	129	3	348	5	5	.986
Major League totals (8 years)			416	1037	125	265	55	8	20	116	.256	89	183	8	434	9	6	.987

DIVISION SERIES RECORD
RECORDS: Shares A.L. career record for most games by pinch-hitter—3.

Year	Team (League)	Pos.	G	AB	R	H	2B	3B	HR	RBI	Avg.	BB	SO	SB	PO	A	E	Avg.
1998— Boston (A.L.)		PH	3	3	0	0	0	0	0	0	.000	0	0	0	...	...	...	...

PERSONAL: Born April 24, 1974, in Suffern, N.Y. ... 6-2/200. ... Throws right, bats right. ... Full name: William Joseph Cunnane.
HIGH SCHOOL: Clarkstown North (New City, N.Y.).
TRANSACTIONS/CAREER NOTES: Signed as non-drafted free agent by Florida Marlins organization (August 18, 1992). ... On Portland disabled list (August 7-23, 1996). ... Selected by San Diego Padres from Marlins organization in Rule 5 major league draft (December 9, 1996). ... On San Diego disabled list (March 29-June 21, 1998); included rehabilitation assignment to Las Vegas (June 9-21). ... Traded by Padres to Milwaukee Brewers for OF Chad Green (December 20, 2000), completing deal in which Brewers traded SS Santiago Perez and a player to be named later or cash to San Deigo Padres for P Brandon Kolb (December 1, 2000).
MISCELLANEOUS: Appeared in one game as pinch runner (1997).

Year	League	W	L	Pct.	ERA	G	GS	CG	ShO	Sv.	IP	H	R	ER	BB	SO
1993— Gulf Coast Marlins (GCL) ...		3	3	.500	2.70	16	9	0	0	2	66 2/3	75	32	20	8	64
1994— Kane County (Midw.)		11	3	.786	*1.43	32	16	5	*4	1	138 2/3	110	27	22	23	106
1995— Portland (East.)		9	2	*.818	3.67	21	21	1	1	0	117 2/3	120	48	48	34	83
1996— Portland (East.)		10	12	.455	3.74	25	25	4	0	0	151 2/3	156	73	63	30	101
1997— San Diego (N.L.)■		6	3	.667	5.81	54	8	0	0	0	91 1/3	114	69	59	49	79
1998— Las Vegas (PCL)		1	2	.333	5.25	33	0	0	0	4	36	45	26	21	19	30
— San Diego (N.L.)		0	0	...	6.00	3	0	0	0	0	3	4	2	2	1	1
1999— Las Vegas (PCL)		2	1	.667	0.98	28	0	0	0	11	36 2/3	30	5	4	16	54
— San Diego (N.L.)		2	1	.667	5.23	24	0	0	0	0	31	34	19	18	12	22
2000— San Diego (N.L.)		1	1	.500	4.23	27	3	0	0	0	38 1/3	35	21	18	21	34
— Las Vegas (PCL)		7	4	.636	3.98	17	17	1	1	0	97 1/3	96	46	43	26	97
Major League totals (4 years)		9	5	.643	5.33	108	11	0	0	0	163 2/3	187	111	97	83	136

PERSONAL: Born November 6, 1968, in Marion, Ind. ... 5-10/185. ... Bats right, throws right. ... Full name: Chad David Curtis.
HIGH SCHOOL: Benson (Ariz.) Union.
JUNIOR COLLEGE: Yavapai College (Ariz.), then Cochise County Community College (Ariz.).
COLLEGE: Grand Canyon (Ariz.).
TRANSACTIONS/CAREER NOTES: Selected by California Angels organization in 45th round of free-agent draft (June 5, 1989). ... On disabled list (June 5-20, 1991). ... On suspended list (June 8-12, 1993). ... Traded by Angels to Detroit Tigers for OF/3B Tony Phillips (April 12, 1995). ... Traded by Tigers to Los Angeles Dodgers for P Joey Eischen and P John Cummings (July 31, 1996). ... Granted free agency (October 15,

1996). ... Signed by Cleveland Indians (December 18, 1996). ... On Cleveland disabled list (May 14-June 9, 1997). ... Traded by Indians to New York Yankees for P David Weathers (June 9, 1997); on disabled list when acquired by Yankees and activated on June 11. ... Traded by Yankees to Texas Rangers for P Brandon Knight and P Sam Marsonek (December 13, 1999).

STATISTICAL NOTES: Led Midwest League with 223 total bases in 1990. ... Tied for A.L. lead in caught stealing with 24 in 1993. ... Led A.L. outfielders with 448 total chances and tied for lead with nine errors in 1993. ... Led A.L. outfielders with 345 total chances in 1994. ... Career major league grand slams: 1.

Year Team (League)	Pos.	G	AB	R	H	2B	3B	HR	RBI	Avg.	BB	SO	SB	PO	A	E	Avg.
1989— Arizona Angels (Ariz.).	2B-OF	32	122	30	37	4	4	3	20	.303	14	20	17	62	58	6	.952
— Quad City (Midw.)	OF	23	78	7	19	3	0	2	11	.244	6	17	7	34	1	1	.972
1990— Quad City (Midw.)	2B-OF	135	*492	87	*151	28	1	14	65	.307	57	76	64	216	221	26	.944
1991— Edmonton (PCL)	3B-2B-OF	115	431	81	136	28	7	9	61	.316	51	56	46	124	220	25	.932
1992— California (A.L.)	OF-DH	139	441	59	114	16	2	10	46	.259	51	71	43	250	*16	6	.978
1993— California (A.L.)	OF-2B	152	583	94	166	25	3	6	59	.285	70	89	48	426	13	‡9	.980
1994— California (A.L.)	OF	114	453	67	116	23	4	11	50	.256	37	69	25	*332	9	4	.988
1995— Detroit (A.L.)■	OF	144	586	96	157	29	3	21	67	.268	70	93	27	362	5	3	.992
1996— Detroit (A.L.)	OF	104	400	65	105	20	1	10	37	.263	53	73	16	243	6	9	.965
— Los Angeles (N.L.)■..	OF	43	104	20	22	5	0	2	9	.212	17	15	2	62	2	1	.985
1997— Cleveland (A.L.)■	OF	22	29	8	6	1	0	3	5	.207	7	10	0	20	0	0	1.000
— Akron (East.)	OF	4	18	5	7	1	0	3	6	.389	0	3	0	5	2	0	1.000
— New York (A.L.)■	OF	93	320	51	93	21	1	12	50	.291	36	49	12	168	6	4	.978
1998— New York (A.L.)	OF-DH	151	456	79	111	21	1	10	56	.243	75	80	21	306	8	5	.984
1999— New York (A.L.)	OF-DH	96	195	37	51	6	0	5	24	.262	43	35	8	98	2	1	.990
2000— Texas (A.L.)■	OF-DH	108	335	48	91	25	1	8	48	.272	37	71	3	135	4	5	.965
American League totals (9 years)		1123	3798	604	1010	187	16	96	442	.266	479	640	203	2340	69	46	.981
National League totals (1 year)		43	104	20	22	5	0	2	9	.212	17	15	2	62	2	1	.985
Major League totals (9 years)		1166	3902	624	1032	192	16	98	451	.264	496	655	205	2402	71	47	.981

DIVISION SERIES RECORD

Year Team (League)	Pos.	G	AB	R	H	2B	3B	HR	RBI	Avg.	BB	SO	SB	PO	A	E	Avg.
1996— Los Angeles (N.L.)	OF	1	2	0	0	0	0	0	0	.000	1	1	0	2	0	0	1.000
1997— New York (A.L.)	OF-PR	4	6	0	1	0	0	0	0	.167	3	1	0	4	0	0	1.000
1998— New York (A.L.)	OF	3	3	1	2	1	0	0	0	.667	1	1	1	3	0	0	1.000
1999— New York (A.L.)	OF-PR	3	3	1	0	0	0	0	0	.000	0	0	0	0	0	0	...
Division series totals (4 years)		11	14	2	3	1	0	0	0	.214	5	3	1	9	0	0	1.000

CHAMPIONSHIP SERIES RECORD

Year Team (League)	Pos.	G	AB	R	H	2B	3B	HR	RBI	Avg.	BB	SO	SB	PO	A	E	Avg.
1998— New York (A.L.)	OF	2	4	0	0	0	0	0	0	.000	1	2	0	1	0	0	1.000
1999— New York (A.L.)	OF-PR-DH	3	6	1	0	0	0	0	0	.000	0	2	1	0	0	0	...
Championship series totals (2 years)		5	10	1	0	0	0	0	0	.000	1	4	1	1	0	0	1.000

WORLD SERIES RECORD

NOTES: Member of World Series championship team (1998 and 1999).

Year Team (League)	Pos.	G	AB	R	H	2B	3B	HR	RBI	Avg.	BB	SO	SB	PO	A	E	Avg.
1998— New York (A.L.)								Did not play.									
1999— New York (A.L.)	PR-OF-PH	3	6	3	2	0	0	2	2	.333	0	0	0	5	0	0	1.000

D'AMICO, JEFF   P   BREWERS

PERSONAL: Born December 27, 1975, in St. Petersburg, Fla. ... 6-7/250. ... Throws right, bats right. ... Full name: Jeffrey Charles D'Amico.

HIGH SCHOOL: Northeast (St. Petersburg, Fla.).

TRANSACTIONS/CAREER NOTES: Selected by Milwaukee Brewers organization in first round (23rd pick overall) of free-agent draft (June 3, 1993). ... On disabled list (June 24, 1994-entire season). ... On Milwaukee disabled list (July 28-September 2, 1997; and January 14, 1998-entire season). ... On Milwaukee disabled list (March 29-September 25, 1999); included rehabilitation assignments to Beloit (July 6-15), Huntsville (July 16-21) and Louisville (August 12-25). ... On Milwaukee disabled list (June 6-30, 2000).

Year League	W	L	Pct.	ERA	G	GS	CG	ShO	Sv.	IP	H	R	ER	BB	SO
1994— Arizona Brewers (Ariz.)							Did not play.								
1995— Beloit (Midw.)	13	3	*.813	2.39	21	20	3	1	0	132	102	40	35	31	119
1996— El Paso (Texas)	5	4	.556	3.19	13	13	3	0	0	96	89	42	34	13	76
— Milwaukee (A.L.)	6	6	.500	5.44	17	17	0	0	0	86	88	53	52	31	53
1997— Milwaukee (A.L.)	9	7	.563	4.71	23	23	1	1	0	135 2/3	139	81	71	43	94
— Beloit (Midw.)	0	0	...	0.00	1	1	0	0	0	3	0	0	0	1	7
1998— Milwaukee (A.L.)							Did not play.								
1999— Beloit (Midw.)	1	0	1.000	0.00	2	2	0	0	0	8	7	0	0	1	6
— Huntsville (Sou.)	0	0	...	36.00	1	1	0	0	0	2	6	8	8	1	2
— Louisville (I.L.)	0	0	...	13.50	1	1	0	0	0	3 1/3	6	5	5	2	1
— Milwaukee (N.L.)	0	0	...	0.00	1	0	0	0	0	1	1	0	0	0	1
2000— Indianapolis (I.L.)	1	1	.500	3.16	6	6	0	0	0	31 1/3	25	11	11	11	20
— Milwaukee (N.L.)	12	7	.632	2.66	23	23	1	1	0	162 1/3	143	55	48	46	101
A.L. totals (2 years)	15	13	.536	4.99	40	40	1	1	0	221 2/3	227	134	123	74	147
N.L. totals (2 years)	12	7	.632	2.64	24	23	1	1	0	163 1/3	144	55	48	46	102
Major League totals (4 years)	27	20	.574	4.00	64	63	2	2	0	385	371	189	171	120	249

C
D

PERSONAL: Born November 9, 1974, in Inglewood, Calif. ... 6-3/200. ... Throws right, bats right. ... Full name: Jeffrey Michael D'Amico.
HIGH SCHOOL: Redmond (Wash.).
TRANSACTIONS/CAREER NOTES: Selected by Oakland Athletics organization in second round of free-agent draft (June 3, 1993). ... On West Michigan disabled list (April 22-September 19, 1994). ... On Huntsville disabled list (June 25-July 10, 1998); included rehabilitation assignment to Arizona League Athletics (June 27-July 7). ... Traded by A's with P Blake Stein and P Brad Rigby to Kansas City Royals for P Kevin Appier (July 31, 1999). ... On Omaha disabled list (May 12-24 and August 22-September 12, 2000). ... Granted free agency (December 21, 2000).
STATISTICAL NOTES: Led Southern League with five balks in 1998.
MISCELLANEOUS: Played infield (1993-96).

Year	League	W	L	Pct.	ERA	G	GS	CG	ShO	Sv.	IP	H	R	ER	BB	SO
1996—	Modesto (Calif.)	0	0	...	18.00	1	0	0	0	0	1	3	3	2	1	0
—Arizona Athletics (Ariz.)		3	0	1.000	1.42	8	0	0	0	0	19	14	3	3	2	15
1997—	Modesto (Calif.)	7	3	.700	3.80	20	13	0	0	1	97	115	57	41	34	89
—Edmonton (PCL)		1	2	.333	8.22	10	7	0	0	1	30 $^2/_3$	42	29	28	6	19
1998—	Huntsville (Sou.)	5	5	.500	7.67	24	8	0	0	0	61	77	57	52	34	46
—Arizona Athletics (Ariz.)		0	0	...	3.86	4	1	0	0	0	9 $^1/_3$	6	4	4	1	8
1999—	Midland (Texas)	1	2	.333	4.96	32	0	0	0	3	45 $^1/_3$	53	31	25	16	38
—Vancouver (PCL)		2	2	.500	2.65	14	0	0	0	3	17	16	6	5	10	10
—Omaha (PCL)■		1	3	.250	4.34	12	0	0	0	2	18 $^2/_3$	29	13	9	3	12
2000—	Omaha (PCL)	3	3	.500	3.83	16	16	1	0	0	91 $^2/_3$	87	39	39	26	66
—Kansas City (A.L.)		0	1	.000	9.22	7	1	0	0	0	13 $^2/_3$	19	14	14	15	9
Major League totals (1 year)		0	1	.000	9.22	7	1	0	0	0	13 $^2/_3$	19	14	14	15	9

RECORD AS POSITION PLAYER

Year	Team (League)	Pos.	G	AB	R	H	2B	3B	HR	RBI	Avg.	BB	SO	SB	PO	A	E	Avg.
1993—	S. Oregon (N.W.)	SS-3B	33	114	12	30	9	0	3	15	.263	9	25	2	43	67	14	.887
1994—	W. Mich. (Midw.)	SS	9	36	5	10	3	0	0	3	.278	4	7	2	14	25	1	.975
1995—	W. Mich. (Midw.)	SS-3B	125	434	56	98	24	1	7	55	.226	56	94	8	120	304	37	.920
1996—	Modesto (Calif.)	3B-2B-SS	47	172	28	46	7	1	4	21	.267	19	31	3	36	101	19	.878

PERSONAL: Born March 1, 1972, in Maracaibo, Venezuela. ... 6-3/195. ... Throws left, bats left. ... Full name: Omar Jose Cordaro Daal.
HIGH SCHOOL: Valencia (Venezuela) Superior.
TRANSACTIONS/CAREER NOTES: Signed as non-drafted free agent by Los Angeles Dodgers organization (August 24, 1990). ... Traded by Dodgers to Montreal Expos for P Rick Clelland (December 14, 1995). ... Claimed on waivers by Toronto Blue Jays (July 25, 1997). ... Selected by Arizona Diamondbacks in second round (31st pick overall) of expansion draft (November 18, 1997). ... On Arizona disabled list (June 22-July 11, 1998); included rehabilitation assignment to Tucson (July 9-11). ... Traded by Diamondbacks to Philadelphia Phillies for P Curt Schilling (July 26, 2000).

Year	League	W	L	Pct.	ERA	G	GS	CG	ShO	Sv.	IP	H	R	ER	BB	SO
1990—	Dom. Dodgers (DSL)	3	6	.333	1.18	17	13	6	0	2	91 $^2/_3$	61	29	12	29	91
1991—	Dom. Dodgers (DSL)	7	2	.778	1.16	13	13	0	0	0	93	30	17	12	32	81
1992—	Albuquerque (PCL)	0	2	.000	7.84	12	0	0	0	0	10 $^1/_3$	14	9	9	11	9
—San Antonio (Texas)		2	6	.250	5.02	35	5	0	0	5	57 $^1/_3$	60	39	32	33	52
1993—	Albuquerque (PCL)	1	1	.500	3.38	6	0	0	0	2	5 $^1/_3$	5	2	2	3	2
—Los Angeles (N.L.)		2	3	.400	5.09	47	0	0	0	0	35 $^1/_3$	36	20	20	21	19
1994—	Albuquerque (PCL)	4	2	.667	5.19	11	5	0	0	1	34 $^2/_3$	38	20	20	16	28
—Los Angeles (N.L.)		0	0	...	3.29	24	0	0	0	0	13 $^2/_3$	12	5	5	5	9
1995—	Albuquerque (PCL)	2	3	.400	4.05	17	9	0	0	1	53 $^1/_3$	56	28	24	26	46
—Los Angeles (N.L.)		4	0	1.000	7.20	28	0	0	0	0	20	29	16	16	15	11
1996—	Montreal (N.L.)■	4	5	.444	4.02	64	6	0	0	0	87 $^1/_3$	74	40	39	37	82
1997—	Montreal (N.L.)	1	2	.333	9.79	33	0	0	0	1	30 $^1/_3$	48	35	33	15	16
—Ottawa (I.L.)		0	1	.000	5.63	2	2	0	0	0	8	10	6	5	1	9
—Toronto (A.L.)■		1	1	.500	4.00	9	3	0	0	0	27	34	13	12	6	28
1998—	Arizona (N.L.)■	8	12	.400	2.88	33	23	3	1	0	162 $^2/_3$	146	60	52	51	132
—Tucson (PCL)		0	0	...	3.00	1	1	0	0	0	3	3	2	1	1	4
1999—	Arizona (N.L.)	16	9	.640	3.65	32	32	2	1	0	214 $^2/_3$	188	92	87	79	148
2000—	Arizona (N.L.)	2	10	.167	7.22	20	16	0	0	0	96	127	88	77	42	45
—Philadelphia (N.L.)■		2	§9	.182	4.69	12	12	0	0	0	71	81	40	37	30	51
A.L. totals (1 year)		1	1	.500	4.00	9	3	0	0	0	27	34	13	12	6	28
N.L. totals (8 years)		39	50	.438	4.51	293	89	5	2	1	731	741	396	366	295	513
Major League totals (8 years)		40	51	.440	4.49	302	92	5	2	1	758	775	409	378	301	541

DIVISION SERIES RECORD

Year	League	W	L	Pct.	ERA	G	GS	CG	ShO	Sv.	IP	H	R	ER	BB	SO
1999—	Arizona (N.L.)	0	1	.000	6.75	1	1	0	0	0	4	6	3	3	3	4

PERSONAL: Born November 5, 1973, in Fort Riley, Kan. ... 6-2/190. ... Bats left, throws left. ... Full name: Johnny David Damon.
HIGH SCHOOL: Dr. Phillips (Orlando).
TRANSACTIONS/CAREER NOTES: Selected by Kansas City Royals organization in supplemental round ("sandwich pick" between first and second round, 35th pick overall) of free-agent draft (June 1, 1992); pick received as part of compensation for San Diego Padres signing Type A free-agent IF Kurt Stillwell. ... On suspended list (September 5-7, 1997). ... Traded by Royals with IF Mark Ellis and a player to be named later to Oakland Athletics as part of three-way deal in which Royals received P Roberto Hernandez from Tampa Bay Devil Rays, Athletics

received P Cory Lidle from Devil Rays, Royals received C A.J. Hinch, IF Angel Berroa and cash from Athletics and Devil Rays received OF Ben Grieve and a player to be named later or cash from Athletics (January 8, 2001).
RECORDS: Shares major league single-game record for most doubles—4 (July 18, 2000). ... Shares A.L. record for most hits in four consecutive games—15 (July 18-21, 2000).
HONORS: Named Texas League Player of the Year (1995).
STATISTICAL NOTES: Led Gulf Coast League with 109 total bases in 1992. ... Led Midwest League outfielders with five double plays in 1993. ... Led Texas League with .434 on-base percentage in 1995. ... Led Texas League with .534 slugging percentage in 1995. ... Led Texas League with 13 intentional bases on balls received in 1995. ... Had 16-game hitting streak (April 27-May 12, 1999). ... Had 16-game hitting streak (August 5-21, 2000). ... Career major league grand slams: 3.

Year	Team (League)	Pos.	G	AB	R	H	2B	3B	HR	RBI	Avg.	BB	SO	SB	PO	A	E	Avg.
							BATTING								FIELDING			
1992— GC Royals (GCL)	OF	50	192	*58	67	12	*9	4	24	*.349	31	21	33	77	7	1	.988
— Baseball City (FSL)	OF	1	1	0	0	0	0	0	0	.000	0	0	0	0	0	0	...
1993— Rockford (Midw.)	OF	127	511	82	148	25	*13	5	50	.290	52	83	59	240	14	6	.977
1994— Wilmington (Caro.)	OF	119	472	96	149	25	13	6	75	.316	62	55	44	273	9	3	.989
1995— Wichita (Texas)	OF-DH	111	423	83	145	15	9	16	54	.343	67	35	26	296	11	5	.984
— Kansas City (A.L.)	OF	47	188	32	53	11	5	3	23	.282	12	22	7	110	0	1	.991
1996— Kansas City (A.L.)	OF-DH	145	517	61	140	22	5	6	50	.271	31	64	25	350	5	6	.983
1997— Kansas City (A.L.)	OF-DH	146	472	70	130	12	8	8	48	.275	42	70	16	322	5	4	.988
1998— Kansas City (A.L.)	OF	161	642	104	178	30	10	18	66	.277	58	84	26	372	10	4	.990
1999— Kansas City (A.L.)	OF-DH	145	583	101	179	39	9	14	77	.307	67	50	36	301	8	4	.987
2000— Kansas City (A.L.)	OF-DH	159	655	*136	214	42	10	16	88	.327	65	60	*46	334	6	5	.986
Major League totals (6 years)		803	3057	504	894	156	47	65	352	.292	275	350	156	1789	34	24	.987

DARENSBOURG, VIC   P   MARLINS

PERSONAL: Born November 13, 1970, in Los Angeles. ... 5-10/165. ... Throws left, bats left. ... Full name: Victor Anthony Darensbourg.
HIGH SCHOOL: Westchester (Los Angeles).
COLLEGE: Lewis and Clark (Ore.).
TRANSACTIONS/CAREER NOTES: Signed as non-drafted free agent by Florida Marlins organization (June 11, 1992). ... On disabled list entire 1995 season. ... On Portland disabled list (April 4-15, 1996). ... On Charlotte disabled list (April 25-June 21 and July 29-September 6, 1997).

Year	League	W	L	Pct.	ERA	G	GS	CG	ShO	Sv.	IP	H	R	ER	BB	SO
1992— Gulf Coast Marlins (GCL)	2	1	.667	0.64	8	4	0	0	2	42	28	5	3	11	37
1993— Kane County (Midw.)	9	1	.900	2.14	46	0	0	0	16	71 1/3	58	17	17	28	89
— High Desert (Calif.)	0	0	...	0.00	1	0	0	0	0	1	0	0	0	0	1
1994— Portland (East.)	10	7	.588	3.81	35	21	1	1	4	149	146	76	63	60	103
1995— Florida (N.L.)	Did not play.															
1995—	Did not play.															
1996— Brevard County (FSL)	0	0	...	0.00	2	0	0	0	0	3	1	0	0	1	5
— Charlotte (I.L.)	1	5	.167	3.69	47	0	0	0	7	63 1/3	61	30	26	32	66
1997— Charlotte (I.L.)	4	2	.667	4.38	27	0	0	0	2	24 2/3	22	12	12	15	21
1998— Florida (N.L.)	0	7	.000	3.68	59	0	0	0	1	71	52	29	29	30	74
1999— Florida (N.L.)	0	1	.000	8.83	56	0	0	0	0	34 2/3	50	36	34	21	16
— Calgary (PCL)	0	0	...	4.63	9	0	0	0	1	11 2/3	13	6	6	0	12
2000— Florida (N.L.)	5	3	.625	4.06	56	0	0	0	0	62	61	32	28	28	59
Major League totals (3 years)	5	11	.313	4.88	171	0	0	0	1	167 2/3	163	97	91	79	149

DARR, MIKE   OF   PADRES

PERSONAL: Born March 21, 1976, in Corona, Calif. ... 6-3/205. ... Bats left, throws right. ... Full name: Michael Curtis Darr.
HIGH SCHOOL: Corona (Calif.).
TRANSACTIONS/CAREER NOTES: Selected by Detroit Tigers organization in second round of free-agent draft (June 2, 1994). ... On disabled list (April 4-May 28, 1996). ... Traded by Tigers with P Mike Skrmetta to San Diego Padres for 2B Jody Reed (March 22, 1997). ... On Las Vegas disabled list (April 25-May 7, 1999).

Year	Team (League)	Pos.	G	AB	R	H	2B	3B	HR	RBI	Avg.	BB	SO	SB	PO	A	E	Avg.
							BATTING								FIELDING			
1994— Bristol (Appl.)	OF	44	149	23	41	6	0	1	18	.275	23	22	4	59	4	4	.940
1995— Fayetteville (S.Atl.)	OF	112	395	58	114	21	2	5	66	.289	58	88	5	123	15	9	.939
1996— Lakeland (FSL)	OF	85	311	26	77	14	7	0	38	.248	28	64	7	128	8	3	.978
1997— Rancho Cuca. (Calif.)■	OF	134	521	104	179	32	11	15	94	.344	57	90	23	176	12	8	.959
1998— Mobile (Sou.)	OF	132	523	105	162	41	4	6	90	.310	62	79	28	261	13	6	.979
1999— Las Vegas (PCL)	OF-DH	100	383	57	114	34	0	10	62	.298	50	103	10	172	11	2	.989
— San Diego (N.L.)	OF	25	48	6	13	1	0	2	3	.271	5	18	2	28	0	0	1.000
2000— Las Vegas (PCL)	OF	91	366	79	126	23	5	9	65	.344	44	55	13	205	6	5	.977
— San Diego (N.L.)	OF	58	205	21	55	14	4	1	30	.268	23	45	9	124	7	0	1.000
Major League totals (2 years)		83	253	27	68	15	4	3	33	.269	28	63	11	152	7	0	1.000

DAUBACH, BRIAN   1B/DH   RED SOX

PERSONAL: Born February 11, 1972, in Belleville, Ill. ... 6-1/201. ... Bats left, throws right. ... Full name: Brian Michael Daubach.
HIGH SCHOOL: Belleville (Ill.) West.
TRANSACTIONS/CAREER NOTES: Selected by New York Mets organization in 17th round of free-agent draft (June 4, 1990). ... Granted free agency (October 15, 1996). ... Signed by Florida Marlins organization (November 7, 1996). ... Granted free agency (October 17, 1997). ... Re-signed by Marlins organization (January 6, 1998). ... Released by Marlins (November 19, 1998). ... Signed by Boston Red Sox organization (December 18, 1998).
STATISTICAL NOTES: Tied for Appalachian League lead in intentional bases on balls received with five in 1991. ... Led Appalachian League first basemen with 623 total chances and 41 double plays in 1991. ... Tied for Florida State League lead in double plays by first basemen with

D

127 in 1994. ... Led Eastern League first basemen with 111 double plays and .992 fielding percentage and tied for lead with 98 assists in 1995. ... Led Eastern League first basemen with 115 assists in 1996. ... Led International League with 10 sacrifice flies in 1997. ... Led International League with 315 total bases, .634 slugging percentage and nine intentional bases on balls received and tied for lead in being hit by pitch with 15 in 1998.

Year	Team (League)	Pos.	G	AB	R	H	2B	3B	HR	RBI	Avg.	BB	SO	SB	PO	A	E	Avg.
1990—	GC Mets (GCL)	1B	45	152	26	41	8	4	1	19	.270	22	41	2	274	16	7	.976
	—Charlotte (I.L.)	OF-1B	140	497	102	157	45	4	35	124	.316	80	114	9	262	28	3	.990
1991—	Kingsport (Appl.)	1B	65	218	30	53	9	1	7	42	.243	33	64	1	*562	*52	9	.986
1992—	Pittsfield (NY-Penn)	1B	72	260	26	63	15	2	2	40	.242	30	61	4	609	•44	12	.982
1993—	Capital City (S.Atl.)	1B-OF	102	379	50	106	19	3	7	72	.280	52	84	6	393	43	5	.989
1994—	St. Lucie (FSL)	1B	129	450	52	123	30	2	6	74	.273	58	120	14	1172	*115	12	.991
1995—	Binghamton (East.)	1B-3B	135	469	61	115	25	2	10	72	.245	51	104	6	1137	98	10	†.992
	—Norfolk (I.L.)	1B	2	7	0	0	0	0	0	0	.000	1	0	0	21	3	0	1.000
1996—	Binghamton (East.)	1B-3B	122	436	80	129	24	1	22	96	.296	74	103	7	1108	†115	11	.991
	—Norfolk (I.L.)	1B	17	54	7	11	2	0	0	6	.204	6	14	1	72	3	0	1.000
1997—	Charlotte (I.L.)■	1B	136	461	66	128	40	2	21	93	.278	65	126	1	870	62	8	.991
1998—	Charlotte (I.L.)	OF-1B	140	497	102	157	*45	4	*35	*124	.316	80	114	9	362	28	3	.992
	—Florida (N.L.)	1B	10	15	0	3	1	0	0	3	.200	1	5	0	23	1	0	1.000
1999—	Boston (A.L.)■	1-DH-O-3	110	381	61	112	33	3	21	73	.294	36	92	0	420	35	8	.983
	—Pawtucket (I.L.)	DH-1B-OF	9	31	4	9	2	0	1	6	.290	6	8	0	31	2	1	.971
2000—	Boston (A.L.)	1-DH-O-3	142	495	55	123	32	2	21	76	.248	44	130	1	662	52	3	.996
American League totals (2 years)			252	876	116	235	65	5	42	149	.268	80	222	1	1082	87	11	.991
National League totals (1 year)			10	15	0	3	1	0	0	3	.200	1	5	0	23	1	0	1.000
Major League totals (3 years)			262	891	116	238	66	5	42	152	.267	81	227	1	1105	88	11	.991

DIVISION SERIES RECORD

RECORDS: Holds single-game record for most at-bats with no hits—6 (October 10, 1999). ... Shares single-game record for most at-bats (nine-inning game)—6 (October 10, 1999).

Year	Team (League)	Pos.	G	AB	R	H	2B	3B	HR	RBI	Avg.	BB	SO	SB	PO	A	E	Avg.
1999—	Boston (A.L.)	DH-PH-1B	4	16	3	4	2	0	1	3	.250	0	7	0	1	0	0	1.000

CHAMPIONSHIP SERIES RECORD

Year	Team (League)	Pos.	G	AB	R	H	2B	3B	HR	RBI	Avg.	BB	SO	SB	PO	A	E	Avg.
1999—	Boston (A.L.)	DH-1B-PH	5	17	2	3	1	0	1	3	.176	1	4	0	0	0	0	...

DAVEY, TOM   P   PADRES

PERSONAL: Born September 11, 1973, in Garden City, Mich. ... 6-7/230. ... Throws right, bats right. ... Full name: Thomas Joseph Davey.
HIGH SCHOOL: Plymouth Salem (Canton, Mich.).
JUNIOR COLLEGE: Henry Ford Community College (Mich.).
TRANSACTIONS/CAREER NOTES: Selected by Toronto Blue Jays organization in fifth round of free-agent draft (June 2, 1994). ... Selected by Baltimore Orioles organization from Blue Jays organization in Rule 5 major league draft (December 9, 1996). ... Returned to Blue Jays organization (March 20, 1997). ... Traded by Blue Jays with P Steve Sinclair to Seattle Mariners for 1B David Segui (July 28, 1999). ... Traded by Mariners with OF/3B John Mabry to San Diego Padres for OF Al Martin (July 31, 2000).

Year	League	W	L	Pct.	ERA	G	GS	CG	ShO	Sv.	IP	H	R	ER	BB	SO
1994—	Medicine Hat (Pio.)	2	•8	.200	5.12	14	14	0	0	0	65	76	59	37	*59	35
1995—	St. Catharines (NY-Penn)	4	3	.571	3.32	7	7	0	0	0	38	27	19	14	21	29
	—Hagerstown (S.Atl.)	4	1	.800	3.38	8	8	0	0	0	37 1/3	29	23	14	31	25
1996—	Hagerstown (S.Atl.)	10	9	.526	3.87	26	26	2	1	0	155 2/3	132	76	67	91	98
1997—	Dunedin (FSL)	1	3	.250	4.31	7	6	0	0	0	39 2/3	44	21	19	15	36
	—Knoxville (Sou.)	6	7	.462	5.83	20	16	0	0	0	92 2/3	108	65	60	50	72
1998—	Knoxville (Sou.)	5	3	.625	3.87	48	9	0	0	16	76 2/3	70	35	33	52	78
1999—	Toronto (A.L.)	1	1	.500	4.70	29	0	0	0	1	44	40	28	23	26	42
	—Syracuse (I.L.)	1	2	.333	3.48	6	6	0	0	0	33 2/3	30	15	13	19	20
	—Seattle (A.L.)■	1	0	1.000	4.71	16	0	0	0	0	21	22	13	11	14	17
2000—	Tacoma (PCL)	8	6	.571	4.61	28	12	0	0	2	93 2/3	104	59	48	37	77
	—Las Vegas (PCL)■	1	2	.333	4.02	13	0	0	0	0	15 2/3	27	13	7	7	17
	—San Diego (N.L.)	2	1	.667	0.71	11	0	0	0	0	12 2/3	12	1	1	2	6
A.L. totals (1 year)		2	1	.667	4.71	45	0	0	0	1	65	62	41	34	40	59
N.L. totals (1 year)		2	1	.667	0.71	11	0	0	0	0	12 2/3	12	1	1	2	6
Major League totals (2 years)		4	2	.667	4.06	56	0	0	0	1	77 2/3	74	42	35	42	65

DAVIS, BEN   C   PADRES

PERSONAL: Born March 10, 1977, in Chester, Pa. ... 6-4/215. ... Bats both, throws right. ... Full name: Matthew Benjamin Davis.
HIGH SCHOOL: Malvern (Pa.) Prep.
TRANSACTIONS/CAREER NOTES: Selected by San Diego Padres organization in first round (second pick overall) of free-agent draft (June 3, 1995). ... On San Diego disabled list (August 13-September 1, 2000).
STATISTICAL NOTES: Led Southern League catchers with 1,002 total chances in 1998.

Year	Team (League)	Pos.	G	AB	R	H	2B	3B	HR	RBI	Avg.	BB	SO	SB	PO	A	E	Avg.
1995—	Idaho Falls (Pio.)	C	52	197	36	55	8	3	5	46	.279	17	36	0	*362	44	6	.985
1996—	Rancho Cuca. (Calif.)	C-DH	98	353	35	71	10	1	6	41	.201	31	89	1	642	51	9	.987
1997—	Rancho Cuca. (Calif.)	C-DH-1B	122	474	67	132	30	1	17	76	.278	28	107	3	993	103	14	.987
1998—	Mobile (Sou.)	C-DH	116	433	65	124	29	2	14	75	.286	42	60	4	*920	76	6	.994
	—San Diego (N.L.)	C	1	1	0	0	0	0	0	0	.000	0	0	0	2	0	0	1.000
1999—	Las Vegas (PCL)	C	58	201	27	62	18	1	7	44	.308	24	41	4	454	32	4	.992
	—San Diego (N.L.)	C	76	266	29	65	14	1	5	30	.244	25	70	2	471	29	7	.986

D

Year Team (League)	Pos.	G	AB	R	H	2B	3B	HR	RBI	Avg.	BB	SO	SB	PO	A	E	Avg.
2000—Las Vegas (PCL)	C	59	221	38	58	16	1	7	40	.262	38	43	5	441	37	7	.986
— San Diego (N.L.)	C-DH	43	130	12	29	6	0	3	14	.223	14	35	1	236	17	1	.996
Major League totals (3 years)		120	397	41	94	20	1	8	44	.237	39	105	3	709	46	8	.990

DAVIS, DOUG — P — RANGERS

PERSONAL: Born September 21, 1975, in Sacramento. ... 6-3/190. ... Throws left, bats right. ... Full name: Douglas P. Davis.
HIGH SCHOOL: Northgate (Walnut Creek, Calif.).
JUNIOR COLLEGE: City College of San Francisco.
TRANSACTIONS/CAREER NOTES: Selected by Texas Rangers organization in 10th round of free-agent draft (June 4, 1996).

Year League	W	L	Pct.	ERA	G	GS	CG	ShO	Sv.	IP	H	R	ER	BB	SO
1996—Gulf Coast Rangers (GCL)..	3	1	.750	1.90	8	7	0	0	0	42 2/3	28	13	9	26	49
1997—Gulf Coast Rangers (GCL)..	3	1	.750	1.71	4	4	0	0	0	21	14	5	4	15	27
—Charlotte (FSL)	5	3	.625	3.10	9	8	1	0	0	49 1/3	29	19	17	33	52
1998—Charlotte (FSL)	11	7	.611	3.24	27	27	1	1	0	155 1/3	129	69	56	74	*173
1999—Tulsa (Texas)	4	4	.500	2.42	12	12	1	0	0	74 1/3	65	26	20	25	79
—Oklahoma (PCL)	7	0	1.000	3.00	13	11	0	0	0	78	77	27	26	31	74
—Texas (A.L.)	0	0	...	33.75	2	0	0	0	0	2 2/3	12	10	10	0	3
2000—Texas (A.L.)	7	6	.538	5.38	30	13	1	0	0	98 2/3	109	61	59	58	66
—Oklahoma (PCL)	8	3	.727	2.84	12	12	2	0	0	69 2/3	62	32	22	34	53
Major League totals (2 years)	7	6	.538	6.13	32	13	1	0	0	101 1/3	121	71	69	58	69

DAVIS, ERIC — OF — GIANTS

PERSONAL: Born May 29, 1962, in Los Angeles. ... 6-3/200. ... Bats right, throws right. ... Full name: Eric Keith Davis.
HIGH SCHOOL: Fremont (Los Angeles).
TRANSACTIONS/CAREER NOTES: Selected by Cincinnati Reds organization in eighth round of free-agent draft (June 3, 1980). ... On Cincinnati disabled list (August 16-September 1, 1984; May 3-18, 1989; April 25-May 19, 1990; June 12-27 and July 31-August 26, 1991). ... Traded by Reds with P Kip Gross to Los Angeles Dodgers for P Tim Belcher and P John Wetteland (November 27, 1991). ... On disabled list (May 23-June 19 and August 2-25, 1992). ... Granted free agency (November 3, 1992). ... Re-signed by Dodgers (December 1, 1992). ... Traded by Dodgers to Detroit Tigers for a player to be named later (August 31, 1993); Dodgers acquired P John DeSilva to complete deal (September 7, 1993). ... Granted free agency (October 28, 1993). ... Re-signed by Tigers (November 1, 1993). ... On disabled list (May 23-July 19 and July 27, 1994-remainder of season). ... Granted free agency (October 20, 1994). ... On retired list (October 20, 1994-January 2, 1996). ... Signed by Reds organization (January 2, 1996). ... On disabled list (May 26-June 10, 1996). ... Granted free agency (October 28, 1996). ... Signed by Baltimore Orioles (December 19, 1996). ... On disabled list (May 26-September 15, 1997). ... Granted free agency (October 27, 1998). ... Signed by St. Louis Cardinals (November 19, 1998). ... On disabled list (June 28, 1999-remainder of season). ... Granted free agency (November 2, 2000). ... Signed by San Francisco Giants (December 20, 2000).
RECORDS: Shares major league records for most grand slams in two consecutive games—2 (May 4 and 5, 1996); and most strikeouts in two consecutive games—9 (April 24 [4] and 25 [5], 1987, 21 innings). ... Shares major league single-month record for most grand slams—3 (May 1987). ... Holds N.L. career record for highest stolen-base percentage (300 or more attempts)—.861. ... Shares major league record for most grand slams in two consecutive games—2 (August 13 and 14, 1991).
HONORS: Named outfielder on THE SPORTING NEWS N.L. All-Star team (1987 and 1989). ... Named outfielder on THE SPORTING NEWS N.L. Silver Slugger team (1987 and 1989). ... Won N.L. Gold Glove as outfielder (1987-89). ... Named N.L. Comeback Player of the Year by THE SPORTING NEWS (1996).
STATISTICAL NOTES: Hit three home runs in one game (September 10, 1986 and May 3, 1987). ... Led N.L. outfielders with 394 total chances in 1987. ... Led N.L. with 21 game-winning RBIs in 1988. ... Hit for the cycle (June 2, 1989). ... Had 30-game hitting streak (July 12-August 15, 1998). ... Career major league grand slams: 11.

Year Team (League)	Pos.	G	AB	R	H	2B	3B	HR	RBI	Avg.	BB	SO	SB	PO	A	E	Avg.
1980—Eugene (N'West)	SS-2B-OF	33	73	12	16	1	0	1	11	.219	14	26	10	29	36	11	.855
1981—Eugene (N'West)	OF	62	214	*67	69	10	4	11	39	.322	57	59	*40	94	11	4	.963
1982—Cedar Rapids (Midw.)	OF	111	434	80	120	20	5	15	56	.276	51	103	53	239	9	9	.965
1983—Waterbury (East.)	OF	89	293	56	85	13	1	15	43	.290	65	75	39	214	8	2	.991
— Indianapolis (A.A.)	OF	19	77	18	23	4	0	7	19	.299	8	22	9	61	1	1	.984
1984—Wichita (A.A.)	OF	52	194	42	61	9	5	14	34	.314	25	55	27	110	5	5	.958
— Cincinnati (N.L.)	OF	57	174	33	39	10	1	10	30	.224	24	48	10	125	4	1	.992
1985—Cincinnati (N.L.)	OF	56	122	26	30	3	3	8	18	.246	7	39	16	75	3	1	.987
— Denver (A.A.)	OF	64	206	48	57	10	2	15	38	.277	29	67	35	94	5	3	.971
1986—Cincinnati (N.L.)	OF	132	415	97	115	15	3	27	71	.277	68	100	80	274	2	7	.975
1987—Cincinnati (N.L.)	OF	129	474	120	139	23	4	37	100	.293	84	134	50	*380	10	4	.990
1988—Cincinnati (N.L.)	OF	135	472	81	129	18	3	26	93	.273	65	124	35	300	2	6	.981
1989—Cincinnati (N.L.)	OF	131	462	74	130	14	2	34	101	.281	68	116	21	298	2	5	.984
1990—Cincinnati (N.L.)	OF	127	453	84	118	26	2	24	86	.260	60	100	21	257	11	2	.993
1991—Cincinnati (N.L.)	OF	89	285	39	67	10	0	11	33	.235	48	92	14	190	5	3	.985
1992—Los Angeles (N.L.)■..	OF	76	267	21	61	8	1	5	32	.228	36	71	19	123	0	5	.961
1993—Los Angeles (N.L.)	OF	108	376	57	88	17	0	14	53	.234	41	88	33	221	7	2	.991
— Detroit (A.L.)■..........	OF-DH	23	75	14	19	1	1	6	15	.253	14	18	2	52	0	1	.981
1994—Detroit (A.L.)	OF	37	120	19	22	4	0	3	13	.183	18	45	5	85	1	1	.989
1995—						Did not play-retired.											
1996—Cincinnati (N.L.)■.......	OF-1B	129	415	81	119	20	0	26	83	.287	70	121	23	279	3	3	.989
1997—Baltimore (A.L.)■.......	OF-DH	42	158	29	48	11	0	8	25	.304	14	47	6	39	0	1	.975
1998—Baltimore (A.L.)	OF-DH	131	452	81	148	29	1	28	89	.327	44	108	7	119	4	1	.992
1999—St. Louis (N.L.)■	OF-DH	58	191	27	49	9	2	5	30	.257	30	49	5	93	4	0	1.000
2000—St. Louis (N.L.)	OF-DH	92	254	38	77	14	0	6	40	.303	36	60	1	120	1	4	.968
American League totals (4 years)		233	805	143	237	45	2	45	142	.294	90	218	20	295	5	4	.987
National League totals (13 years)		1319	4360	778	1161	187	21	233	770	.266	637	1142	328	2735	54	43	.985
Major League totals (16 years)		1552	5165	921	1398	232	23	278	912	.271	727	1360	348	3030	59	47	.985

DIVISION SERIES RECORD

						BATTING								FIELDING			
Year	Team (League)	Pos.	G	AB	R	H	2B	3B	HR	RBI	Avg.	BB	SO	SB	PO	A	E	Avg.
1997— Baltimore (A.L.).........	OF	3	9	0	2	0	0	0	2	.222	0	5	0	1	0	0	1.000
2000— St. Louis (N.L.).........	OF-PH	2	4	0	0	0	0	0	1	.000	0	2	0	0	0	0	...
Division series totals (2 years)		5	13	0	2	0	0	0	3	.154	0	7	0	1	0	0	1.000

CHAMPIONSHIP SERIES RECORD

						BATTING								FIELDING			
Year	Team (League)	Pos.	G	AB	R	H	2B	3B	HR	RBI	Avg.	BB	SO	SB	PO	A	E	Avg.
1990— Cincinnati (N.L.)	OF	6	23	2	4	1	0	0	2	.174	1	9	0	12	1	0	1.000
1997— Baltimore (A.L.).........	OF-DH	6	13	1	2	0	0	1	1	.154	1	3	0	3	0	0	1.000
2000— St. Louis (N.L.).........	OF-PH	4	10	1	2	1	0	0	1	.200	0	2	0	5	0	0	1.000
Championship series totals (3 years)		16	46	4	8	2	0	1	4	.174	2	14	0	20	1	0	1.000

WORLD SERIES RECORD

NOTES: Hit home run in first at-bat (October 16, 1990). ... Member of World Series championship team (1990).

						BATTING								FIELDING			
Year	Team (League)	Pos.	G	AB	R	H	2B	3B	HR	RBI	Avg.	BB	SO	SB	PO	A	E	Avg.
1990— Cincinnati (N.L.)	OF	4	14	3	4	0	0	1	5	.286	0	0	0	4	0	0	1.000

ALL-STAR GAME RECORD

					BATTING								FIELDING			
Year	League	Pos.	AB	R	H	2B	3B	HR	RBI	Avg.	BB	SO	SB	PO	A	E	Avg.
1987— National	OF	3	0	0	0	0	0	0	.000	0	1	0	1	0	0	1.000
1989— National	OF	2	0	0	0	0	0	0	.000	1	0	1	1	0	0	1.000
All-Star Game totals (2 years)		5	0	0	0	0	0	0	.000	1	1	1	2	0	0	1.000

DAVIS, KANE   P   BREWERS

PERSONAL: Born June 25, 1975, in Ripley, W.Va. ... 6-3/194. ... Throws right, bats right. ... Full name: Kane Thomas Davis.
HIGH SCHOOL: Spencer (W.Va.).
TRANSACTIONS/CAREER NOTES: Selected by Pittsburgh Pirates organization in 13th round of free-agent draft (June 3, 1993). ... On Pittsburgh disabled list (March 22-May 1, 1998). ... On Carolina disabled list (May 17-June 6, 1998). ... On Nashville disabled list (August 25-September 2, 1999). ... Granted free agency (October 15, 1999). ... Signed by Cleveland Indians organization (December 22, 1999). ... On Buffalo disabled list (April 7-24, 2000). ... Traded by Indians with P Paul Rigdon, 1B/OF Richie Sexson and a player to be named later to Milwaukee Brewers for P Bob Wickman, P Steve Woodard and P Jason Bere (July 28, 2000); Brewers acquired 2B Marcos Scutaro to complete deal (August 30, 2000).

Year	League	W	L	Pct.	ERA	G	GS	CG	ShO	Sv.	IP	H	R	ER	BB	SO
1993— Gulf Coast Pirates (GCL)	0	4	.000	7.07	11	4	0	0	0	28	34	30	22	19	24
1994— Welland (NY-Penn)	5	5	.500	2.65	15	•15	0	0	0	98 1/3	90	36	29	32	74
1995— Augusta (S.Atl.)	12	6	.667	3.75	26	25	1	0	0	139 1/3	136	73	58	43	78
1996— Lynchburg (Caro.)	11	9	.550	4.29	26	26	3	1	0	157 1/3	160	84	75	56	116
1997— Carolina (Sou.)	0	3	.000	3.77	6	6	0	0	0	28 2/3	22	17	12	16	23
1998— Augusta (S.Atl.)	0	0	...	6.00	2	2	0	0	0	9	8	6	6	3	6
— Carolina (Sou.)	1	11	.083	9.24	18	16	0	0	0	74	102	84	76	38	39
1999— Altoona (East.)	4	6	.400	3.78	16	16	0	0	0	95 1/3	97	51	40	41	53
— Nashville (PCL)	3	2	.600	6.75	12	9	0	0	0	49 1/3	65	38	37	17	31
2000— Akron (East.)■	0	1	.000	2.70	5	5	0	0	0	20	17	7	6	5	13
— Buffalo (I.L.)	2	0	1.000	4.20	6	4	0	0	0	30	30	16	14	12	19
— Cleveland (A.L.)	0	3	.000	14.73	5	2	0	0	0	11	20	21	18	8	2
— Milwaukee (N.L.)■	0	0	...	6.75	3	0	0	0	0	4	7	3	3	5	2
— Indianapolis (I.L.)	1	1	.500	3.54	4	4	0	0	0	20 1/3	19	8	8	7	12
A.L. totals (1 year)	0	3	.000	14.73	5	2	0	0	0	11	20	21	18	8	2
N.L. totals (1 year)	0	0	...	6.75	3	0	0	0	0	4	7	3	3	5	2
Major League totals (1 year)	0	3	.000	12.60	8	2	0	0	0	15	27	24	21	13	4

DAVIS, RUSS   3B   GIANTS

PERSONAL: Born September 13, 1969, in Birmingham, Ala. ... 6-0/195. ... Bats right, throws right. ... Full name: Russell Stewart Davis.
HIGH SCHOOL: Hueytown (Ala.).
JUNIOR COLLEGE: Shelton State Junior College (Ala.).
TRANSACTIONS/CAREER NOTES: Selected by New York Yankees organization in 29th round of free-agent draft (June 1, 1988). ... On disabled list (July 13-August 1, 1993). ... On Columbus disabled list (April 7-15 and August 26, 1994-remainder of season). ... Traded by Yankees with P Sterling Hitchcock to Seattle Mariners for 1B Tino Martinez, P Jeff Nelson and P Jim Mecir (December 7, 1995). ... On disabled list (June 8, 1996-remainder of season; and August 25-September 26, 1997). ... Granted free agency (December 21, 1999). ... Signed by San Francisco Giants organization (January 24, 2000).
HONORS: Named Eastern League Most Valuable Player (1992).
STATISTICAL NOTES: Tied for New York-Pennsylvania League lead with 11 double plays by third baseman in 1989. ... Led Carolina League third basemen with 336 total chances and 18 double plays in 1990. ... Tied for Eastern League lead with .917 fielding percentage, 83 putouts, 205 assists, 26 errors and 314 total chances by third basemen in 1991. ... Led Eastern League with 237 total bases and .483 slugging percentage in 1992. ... Led International League third basemen with 25 errors in 1993. ... Led A.L. third basemen with 32 errors in 1998. ... Career major league grand slams: 1.

						BATTING								FIELDING			
Year	Team (League)	Pos.	G	AB	R	H	2B	3B	HR	RBI	Avg.	BB	SO	SB	PO	A	E	Avg.
1988— GC Yankees (GCL)	2B-3B	58	213	33	49	11	3	2	30	.230	16	39	6	64	105	15	.918
1989— Fort Lauderdale (FSL) ...	3B-2B	48	147	8	27	5	1	2	22	.184	11	38	3	32	72	17	.860
— Oneonta (NY-Penn)	3B	65	236	33	68	7	5	7	42	.288	19	44	3	27	87	17	.870
1990— Prince William (Caro.)	3B	137	510	55	127	*37	3	16	71	.249	37	136	3	*68	*244	24	.929

Year	Team (League)	Pos.	G	AB	R	H	2B	3B	HR	RBI	Avg.	BB	SO	SB	PO	A	E	Avg.
1991—	Alb./Colonie (East.)	3B-2B	135	473	57	103	23	3	8	58	.218	50	102	3	‡83	‡206	‡26	‡.917
1992—	Alb./Colonie (East.)	3B	132	491	77	140	23	4	22	71	.285	49	93	3	78	185	23	.920
1993—	Columbus (I.L.)	3B-SS	113	424	63	108	24	1	26	83	.255	40	118	1	85	245	†26	.927
1994—	Columbus (I.L.)	3B-DH-1B	117	416	76	115	30	2	25	69	.276	62	93	3	86	250	23	.936
	—New York (A.L.)	3B	4	14	0	2	0	0	0	1	.143	0	4	0	2	6	0	1.000
1995—	Columbus (I.L.)	3B-1B	20	76	12	19	4	1	2	15	.250	17	23	0	17	31	7	.873
	—New York (A.L.)	3B-DH-1B	40	98	14	27	5	2	2	12	.276	10	26	0	16	45	2	.968
1996—	Seattle (A.L.)■	3B	51	167	24	39	9	0	5	18	.234	17	50	2	31	67	7	.933
1997—	Seattle (A.L.)	3B-DH	119	420	57	114	29	1	20	63	.271	27	100	6	56	219	18	.939
1998—	Seattle (A.L.)	3B-OF	141	502	68	130	30	1	20	82	.259	34	134	4	56	254	†34	.901
1999—	Seattle (A.L.)	3B-SS	124	432	55	106	17	1	21	59	.245	32	111	3	71	207	12	.959
2000—	San Fran. (N.L.)■	3B-1B-DH	80	180	27	47	5	0	9	24	.261	9	29	0	37	43	6	.930
American League totals (6 years)			479	1633	218	418	90	5	68	235	.256	120	425	15	232	798	73	.934
National League totals (1 year)			80	180	27	47	5	0	9	24	.261	9	29	0	37	43	6	.930
Major League totals (7 years)			559	1813	245	465	95	5	77	259	.256	129	454	15	269	841	79	.934

DIVISION SERIES RECORD

Year	Team (League)	Pos.	G	AB	R	H	2B	3B	HR	RBI	Avg.	BB	SO	SB	PO	A	E	Avg.
1995—	New York (A.L.)	3B	2	5	0	1	0	0	0	0	.200	0	2	0	0	1	0	1.000
2000—	San Francisco (N.L.) ..	PH	2	2	0	0	0	0	0	0	.000	0	1	0	...	...	...	...
Division series totals (2 years)			4	7	0	1	0	0	0	0	.143	0	3	0	0	1	0	1.000

DAWKINS, GOOKIE — SS — REDS

PERSONAL: Born May 12, 1979, in Newberry, S.C. ... 6-1/180. ... Bats right, throws right. ... Full name: Travis Sentell Dawkins. ... Nickname: Gookie.

HIGH SCHOOL: Newberry (S.C.).

TRANSACTIONS/CAREER NOTES: Selected by Cincinnati Reds organization in second round of free-agent draft (June 3, 1997). ... On Louisville disabled list (August 1-8, 2000).

STATISTICAL NOTES: Led Pioneer League shortstops with 368 total chances in 1997.

Year	Team (League)	Pos.	G	AB	R	H	2B	3B	HR	RBI	Avg.	BB	SO	SB	PO	A	E	Avg.
1997—	Billings (Pio.)	SS	70	253	47	61	5	0	4	37	.241	30	38	16	*118	*216	34	.908
1998—	Burlington (Midw.)	SS	102	367	52	97	7	6	1	30	.264	37	60	37	149	298	36	.925
1999—	Rockford (Midw.)	SS	76	305	56	83	10	6	8	32	.272	35	38	38	120	206	17	.950
	—Chattanooga (Sou.)	SS	32	129	24	47	7	0	2	13	.364	14	17	15	52	89	3	.979
	—Cincinnati (N.L.)	SS	7	7	1	1	0	0	0	0	.143	0	4	0	2	4	0	1.000
2000—	Cincinnati (N.L.)	SS	14	41	5	9	2	0	0	3	.220	2	7	0	21	34	2	.965
	—Chattanooga (Sou.)	SS-2B	95	368	54	85	20	6	6	31	.231	40	71	22	185	290	19	.962
Major League totals (2 years)			21	48	6	10	2	0	0	3	.208	2	11	0	23	38	2	.968

DE LA ROSA, TOMAS — SS — EXPOS

PERSONAL: Born January 28, 1978, in La Victoria, Dominican Republic. ... 5-10/165. ... Bats right, throws right. ... Full name: Tomas Agramonte De La Rosa.

HIGH SCHOOL: Licey Padre Garcia (La Victoria, Dominican Republic).

TRANSACTIONS/CAREER NOTES: Signed as non-drafted free agent by Montreal Expos organization (July 12, 1995).

STATISTICAL NOTES: Led Gulf Coast League shortstops with 301 total chances in 1996. ... Led Eastern League shortstops with 83 double plays in 1999.

Year	Team (League)	Pos.	G	AB	R	H	2B	3B	HR	RBI	Avg.	BB	SO	SB	PO	A	E	Avg.
1996—	GC Expos (GCL)	SS	54	187	35	47	7	1	0	21	.251	22	25	8	86	*189	26	.914
	—Vermont (NY-Penn)	SS	3	8	1	2	0	0	0	1	.250	0	3	0	1	4	1	.833
1997—	W.P. Beach (FSL)	SS	4	9	1	2	0	0	0	0	.222	2	3	2	5	6	1	.917
	—Vermont (NY-Penn)	SS	69	271	46	72	14	6	2	40	.266	32	47	19	85	201	21	.932
1998—	Jupiter (FSL)	SS	117	390	56	98	22	1	3	43	.251	37	61	27	*208	382	30	.952
1999—	Harrisburg (East.)	SS-DH	135	467	70	122	22	3	6	43	.261	42	64	28	219	381	34	.946
2000—	Ottawa (I.L.)	SS	103	340	27	69	10	1	1	36	.203	31	43	10	156	270	16	.964
	—Montreal (N.L.)	SS-DH	32	66	7	19	3	1	2	9	.288	7	11	2	39	58	2	.980
Major League totals (1 year)			32	66	7	19	3	1	2	9	.288	7	11	2	39	58	2	.980

DE LOS SANTOS, LUIS — P — YANKEES

PERSONAL: Born November 1, 1977, in Santo Domingo, Dominican Republic. ... 6-2/187. ... Throws right, bats right.

TRANSACTIONS/CAREER NOTES: Signed as non-drafted free agent by New York Yankees organization (February 11, 1995). ... On Norwich disabled list (April 23-May 22, 1998). ... On Columbus disabled list (May 6-July 5 and August 5-September 14, 1999). ... On New York disabled list (September 16, 1999-remainder of season). ... On New York disabled list (April 2, 2000-entire season); included rehabilitation assignment to Gulf Coast Yankees (June 24-July 13).

STATISTICAL NOTES: Pitched 4-0 no-hit victory against Batavia (July 28, 1996).

Year	League	W	L	Pct.	ERA	G	GS	CG	ShO	Sv.	IP	H	R	ER	BB	SO
1995—	Dominican Yankees (DSL)..						Statistics unavailable.									
	—Tampa (FSL)	0	0	...	0.00	2	0	0	0	0	5	5	2	0	2	6
1996—	Oneonta (NY-Penn)	4	4	.500	3.72	10	10	3	2	0	58	44	28	24	21	62
	—Greensboro (S.Atl.)	4	1	.800	4.83	7	6	0	0	0	$31^2/_3$	39	17	17	11	21

Year League	W	L	Pct.	ERA	G	GS	CG	ShO	Sv.	IP	H	R	ER	BB	SO
1997—Greensboro (S.Atl.)	5	6	.455	3.05	14	14	1	0	0	88 2/3	91	45	30	13	62
—Tampa (FSL)	5	0	1.000	2.34	10	10	0	0	0	61 2/3	49	19	16	8	39
—Norwich (East.)	1	1	.500	2.52	4	4	0	0	0	25	23	9	7	7	15
1998—Norwich (East.)	2	6	.250	4.90	13	13	2	0	0	79	97	49	43	23	51
—Tampa (FSL)	4	2	.667	4.18	10	10	1	0	0	66 2/3	69	40	31	11	33
1999—Columbus (I.L.)	6	3	.667	4.77	12	12	0	0	0	66	81	42	35	24	45
—Gulf Coast Yankees (GCL)	0	0	...	0.00	2	2	0	0	0	8	5	0	0	0	7
2000—Gulf Coast Yankees (GCL)	2	0	1.000	3.00	4	3	0	0	0	15	15	5	5	6	19

DE LOS SANTOS, VALERIO　　　P　　　BREWERS

PERSONAL: Born October 6, 1975, in Las Matas, Dominican Republic. ... 6-2/180. ... Throws left, bats left. ... Full name: Valerio Lorenzo De Los Santos.

TRANSACTIONS/CAREER NOTES: Signed as non-drafted free agent by Milwaukee Brewers organization (January 26, 1993). ... On El Paso disabled list (April 27-May 4, 1998). ... On Milwaukee disabled list (April 29-September 23, 1999).

Year League	W	L	Pct.	ERA	G	GS	CG	ShO	Sv.	IP	H	R	ER	BB	SO
1993—Dom. Brewers (DSL)	1	7	.125	6.50	19	6	1	0	0	63 2/3	91	57	46	37	39
1994—Dom. Brewers (DSL)	7	6	.538	3.69	17	•16	1	1	0	90 1/3	90	52	37	35	50
1995—Arizona Brewers (Ariz.)	4	6	.400	2.20	14	12	0	0	0	82	81	34	20	12	57
1996—Beloit (Midw.)	10	8	.556	3.55	33	23	5	1	4	164 2/3	164	83	65	59	137
1997—El Paso (Texas)	6	10	.375	5.75	26	16	1	0	2	114 1/3	146	83	73	38	61
1998—El Paso (Texas)	6	2	.750	3.91	42	4	0	0	10	66 2/3	81	34	29	25	62
—Milwaukee (N.L.)	0	0	...	2.91	13	0	0	0	0	21 2/3	11	7	7	2	18
—Louisville (I.L.)	0	0	...	3.60	5	0	0	0	0	5	4	2	2	0	0
1999—Milwaukee (N.L.)	0	1	.000	6.48	7	0	0	0	0	8 1/3	12	6	6	7	5
2000—Milwaukee (N.L.)	2	3	.400	5.13	66	2	0	0	0	73 2/3	72	43	42	33	70
Major League totals (3 years)	2	4	.333	4.77	86	2	0	0	0	103 2/3	95	56	55	42	93

DeHAAN, KORY　　　OF　　　PADRES

PERSONAL: Born July 16, 1976, in Pella, Iowa. ... 6-2/187. ... Bats left, throws right. ... Full name: Korwin Jay DeHaan.
HIGH SCHOOL: Pella (Iowa) Christian.
COLLEGE: Morningside College (Iowa).
TRANSACTIONS/CAREER NOTES: Selected by Pittsburgh Pirates organization in seventh round of free-agent draft (June 3, 1997). ... Selected by San Diego Padres from Pirates organization in Rule 5 major league draft (December 13, 1999). ... On San Diego disabled list (April 1-24, 2000); included rehabilitation assignments to Rancho Cucamonga (April 11-15) and Las Vegas (April 16-24).

Year Team (League)	Pos.	G	AB	R	H	2B	3B	HR	RBI	Avg.	BB	SO	SB	PO	A	E	Avg.
1997—Erie (NY-Penn)	OF	58	205	43	49	8	6	1	18	.239	38	43	14	105	0	1	.991
1998—Augusta (S.Atl.)	OF	132	475	85	149	*39	8	8	75	.314	69	114	33	244	7	4	.984
1999—Lynchburg (Caro.)	OF	78	295	55	96	19	5	7	42	.325	36	63	32	164	2	4	.976
—Altoona (East.)	OF	47	190	26	51	13	2	3	24	.268	11	46	14	88	1	1	.989
2000—Rancho Cuca. (Calif.)■	OF	4	14	2	3	1	0	1	1	.214	1	4	0	4	0	0	1.000
—Las Vegas (PCL)	OF	10	41	7	12	4	0	0	3	.293	2	11	3	37	0	0	1.000
—San Diego (N.L.)	OF-DH	90	103	19	21	7	0	2	13	.204	5	39	4	50	3	0	1.000
Major League totals (1 year)		90	103	19	21	7	0	2	13	.204	5	39	4	50	3	0	1.000

DeJEAN, MIKE　　　P　　　ROCKIES

PERSONAL: Born September 28, 1970, in Baton Rouge, La. ... 6-2/212. ... Throws right, bats right. ... Full name: Michael Dwain DeJean.
HIGH SCHOOL: Walker (La.).
JUNIOR COLLEGE: Mississippi Delta Community College.
COLLEGE: Livingston (La.).
TRANSACTIONS/CAREER NOTES: Selected by New York Yankees organization in 24th round of free-agent draft (June 1, 1992). ... On disabled list (June 4-July 21 and July 26, 1993-remainder of season). ... Traded by Yankees with a player to be named later to Colorado Rockies for C Joe Girardi (November 20, 1995). ... Rockies acquired P Steve Shoemaker to complete deal (December 6, 1995). ... On Colorado disabled list (July 18-August 8, 1997); included rehabilitation assignment to New Haven (July 30-August 8). ... On disabled list (September 2, 1998-remainder of season). ... On Colorado disabled list (August 14-September 1, 1999); included rehabilitation assignment to Colorado Springs (August 30-September 1). ... On Colorado disabled list (March 29-April 28 and July 25-August 15, 2000); included rehabilitation assignments to Colorado Springs (April 6-28 and August 10-13).

Year League	W	L	Pct.	ERA	G	GS	CG	ShO	Sv.	IP	H	R	ER	BB	SO
1992—Oneonta (NY-Penn)	0	0	...	0.44	20	0	0	0	16	20 2/3	12	3	1	3	20
1993—Greensboro (S.Atl.)	2	3	.400	5.00	20	0	0	0	9	18	22	12	10	8	16
1994—Tampa (FSL)	0	2	.000	2.38	34	0	0	0	16	34	39	15	9	13	22
—Albany (East.)	0	2	.000	4.38	16	0	0	0	4	24 2/3	22	14	12	15	13
1995—Norwich (East.)	5	5	.500	2.99	59	0	0	0	20	78 1/3	58	29	26	34	57
1996—Colorado Springs (PCL)■	0	2	.000	5.13	30	0	0	0	1	40 1/3	52	24	23	21	31
—New Haven (East.)	0	0	...	3.22	16	0	0	0	11	22 1/3	20	9	8	12	12
1997—Colorado Springs (PCL)	0	1	.000	5.40	10	0	0	0	4	10	17	6	6	7	9
—Colorado (N.L.)	5	0	1.000	3.99	55	0	0	0	2	67 2/3	74	34	30	24	38
—New Haven (East.)	0	1	.000	6.00	2	0	0	0	0	3	3	2	2	2	2
1998—Colorado (N.L.)	3	1	.750	3.03	59	1	0	0	2	74 1/3	78	29	25	24	27
1999—Colorado (N.L.)	2	4	.333	8.41	56	0	0	0	0	61	83	61	57	32	31
—Colorado Springs (PCL)	0	0	...	0.00	1	0	0	0	0	1	1	0	0	0	0
2000—Colorado Springs (PCL)	1	1	.500	2.51	12	0	0	0	5	14 1/3	15	4	4	4	12
—Colorado (N.L.)	4	4	.500	4.89	54	0	0	0	4	53 1/3	54	31	29	30	34
Major League totals (4 years)	14	9	.609	4.95	224	1	0	0	4	256 1/3	289	155	141	110	130

PERSONAL: Born June 22, 1972, in Sonora, Mexico. ... 6-1/160. ... Throws right, bats right. ... Full name: Miguel Alfonso Del Toro.
HIGH SCHOOL: Cobash (San Ignacio, Mexico).
TRANSACTIONS/CAREER NOTES: Signed as non-drafted free agent by Pittsburgh Pirates organization (April 3, 1992). ... Granted free agency (October 16, 1998). ... Signed by San Francisco Giants organization (November 20, 1998). ... Released by Giants (December 15, 2000).

Year	League	W	L	Pct.	ERA	G	GS	CG	ShO	Sv.	IP	H	R	ER	BB	SO
1992—Gulf Coast Pirates (GCL)		2	5	.286	3.43	10	1	1	0	1	60 1/3	64	30	23	21	42
1993—M.C. Red Devils (Mex.)■...		0	0	...	7.94	5	0	0	0	0	5 2/3	7	7	5	5	2
1994—M.C. Red Devils (Mex.)		0	0	...	6.97	12	0	0	0	0	10 1/3	14	8	8	8	8
1995—M.C. Red Devils (Mex.)		5	4	.556	2.25	37	0	0	0	16	68	54	23	17	43	49
1996—Reynosa (Mex.)		1	1	.500	4.11	32	0	0	0	7	46	45	27	21	36	29
1997—M.C. Red Devils (Mex.)		0	0	...	3.75	26	0	0	0	0	36	21	18	15	32	30
1998—M.C. Red Devils (Mex.)		9	4	.692	3.82	39	10	0	0	5	92	81	41	39	44	56
1999—San Francisco (N.L.)■		0	0	...	4.18	14	0	0	0	0	23 2/3	24	11	11	11	20
—Fresno (PCL)		4	2	.667	4.42	40	0	0	0	0	71 1/3	76	41	35	29	71
2000—Fresno (PCL)		6	6	.500	6.01	21	20	0	0	0	112 1/3	117	82	75	42	98
—San Francisco (N.L.)		2	0	1.000	5.19	9	1	0	0	0	17 1/3	17	10	10	6	16
Major League totals (2 years)		2	0	1.000	4.61	23	1	0	0	0	41	41	21	21	17	36

DIVISION SERIES RECORD

Year	League	W	L	Pct.	ERA	G	GS	CG	ShO	Sv.	IP	H	R	ER	BB	SO
2000—San Francisco (N.L.)		0	0	...	0.00	1	0	0	0	0	1	1	0	0	0	2

PERSONAL: Born June 25, 1972, in Aguadilla, Puerto Rico. ... 6-3/225. ... Bats left, throws right. ... Full name: Carlos Juan Delgado.
HIGH SCHOOL: Jose de Diego (Aguadilla, Puerto Rico).
TRANSACTIONS/CAREER NOTES: Signed as non-drafted free agent by Toronto Blue Jays organization (October 9, 1988). ... On Toronto disabled list (March 15-April 24, 1998); included rehabilitation assignments to Dunedin (April 17-19) and Syracuse (April 20-24).
HONORS: Named Florida State League Most Valuable Player (1992). ... Named Southern League Most Valuable Player (1993). ... Named first baseman on THE SPORTING NEWS A.L. Silver Slugger team (1999 and 2000). ... Named Major League Player of the Year by THE SPORTING NEWS (2000). ... Named first baseman on THE SPORTING NEWS A.L. All-Star team (2000).
STATISTICAL NOTES: Led New York-Pennsylvania League catchers with 540 total chances and six double plays in 1990. ... Led South Atlantic League with 29 passed balls in 1991. ... Led Florida State League with 281 total bases, .579 slugging percentage, .402 on-base percentage and 11 intentional bases on balls received in 1992. ... Led Florida State League catchers with 784 total chances in 1992. ... Led Southern League with .524 slugging percentage, .430 on-base percentage and 18 intentional bases on balls received in 1993. ... Led Southern League catchers with 800 total chances in 1993. ... Led International League with .610 slugging percentage in 1995. ... Led International League with seven intentional bases on balls received in 1995. ... Had 19-game hitting streak (May 21-June 9, 1998). ... Hit three home runs in one game (August 4, 1998 and August 6, 1999). ... Led A.L. first baseman with 134 double plays in 1999. ... Had 22-game hitting streak (June 4-29, 2000). ... Led A.L. first baseman with 1,511 total chances and 157 double plays in 2000. ... Led A.L. with 378 total bases in 2000. ... Tied for A.L. lead in being hit by pitch with 15 in 2000. ... Career major league grand slams: 7.

								BATTING							FIELDING		
Year	Team (League)	Pos.	G	AB	R	H	2B	3B	HR	RBI	Avg.	BB	SO	SB	PO	A	E	Avg.
1989—St. Cath. (NY-P)		C	31	89	9	16	5	0	0	11	.180	23	39	0	63	13	2	.974
1990—St. Cath. (NY-P)		C	67	228	30	64	13	0	6	39	.281	35	65	2	*471	*62	7	.987
1991—Myrtle Beach (S.Atl.) ..		C	132	441	72	126	18	2	18	70	.286	75	97	9	679	*100	19	.976
—Syracuse (I.L.)		C	1	3	0	0	0	0	0	0	.000	0	2	0	5	0	0	1.000
1992—Dunedin (FSL)		C	133	485	83	*157	*30	2	*30	*100	.324	59	91	2	*684	89	11	.986
1993—Knoxville (Sou.)		C	140	468	91	142	28	0	*25	*102	.303	*102	98	10	*683	*103	*14	.983
—Toronto (A.L.)		DH-C	2	1	0	0	0	0	0	0	.000	1	0	0	2	0	0	1.000
1994—Toronto (A.L.)		OF-C	43	130	17	28	2	0	9	24	.215	25	46	1	56	2	2	.967
—Syracuse (I.L.)		DH-C-1B	85	307	52	98	11	0	19	58	.319	42	58	1	235	25	7	.974
1995—Toronto (A.L.)		OF-DH-1B	37	91	7	15	3	0	3	11	.165	6	26	0	54	2	0	1.000
—Syracuse (I.L.)		1B-OF	91	333	59	106	23	4	22	74	.318	45	78	4	724	49	4	.995
1996—Toronto (A.L.)		DH-1B	138	488	68	132	28	2	25	92	.270	58	139	0	221	13	4	.983
1997—Toronto (A.L.)		1B-DH	153	519	79	136	42	3	30	91	.262	64	133	0	962	67	12	.988
1998—Dunedin (FSL)		DH-1B	4	16	4	5	1	0	2	7	.313	2	4	0	13	0	0	1.000
—Syracuse (I.L.)		1B	2	7	4	4	2	0	1	6	.571	2	0	0	22	2	0	1.000
—Toronto (A.L.)		1B-DH	142	530	94	155	43	1	38	115	.292	73	139	3	1165	87	10	.992
1999—Toronto (A.L.)		1B-DH	152	573	113	156	39	0	44	134	.272	86	141	1	*1306	84	*14	.990
2000—Toronto (A.L.)		1B	•162	569	115	196	*57	1	41	137	.344	123	104	0	*1416	82	13	.991
Major League totals (8 years)			829	2901	493	818	214	7	190	604	.282	436	728	5	5182	337	55	.990

ALL-STAR GAME RECORD

						BATTING							FIELDING		
Year	League	Pos.	AB	R	H	2B	3B	HR	RBI	Avg.	BB	SO	SB	PO	A	E	Avg.
2000—American		1B	1	0	1	1	0	0	0	1.000	0	0	0	4	0	0	1.000

PERSONAL: Born July 15, 1975, in San Cristobal, Dominican Republic. ... 5-11/165. ... Bats both, throws right. ... Full name: Wilson Duran Delgado.
TRANSACTIONS/CAREER NOTES: Signed as non-drafted free agent by Seattle Mariners organization (October 29, 1992). ... Traded by Mariners with P Shawn Estes to San Francisco Giants for P Salomon Torres (May 21, 1995). ... Traded by Giants to New York Yankees for SS Juan Melo (March 23, 2000). ... Traded by Yankees to Kansas City Royals for SS Nick Ortiz (August 11, 2000).
STATISTICAL NOTES: Led Pacific Coast League shortstops with 197 putouts, 547 total chances and 86 double plays in 1997.

Year	Team (League)	Pos.	G	AB	R	H	2B	3B	HR	RBI	Avg.	BB	SO	SB	PO	A	E	Avg.
1993—Dom. Mariners (DSL).		IF	60	171	19	50	8	0	0	26	.292	34	25	5	96	148	16	.938
1994—Ariz. Mariners (Ariz.) ..		SS-2B	39	149	30	56	5	4	0	10	*.376	15	24	13	58	114	10	.945
1995—Wisconsin (Midw.)		SS	19	70	13	17	3	0	0	7	.243	3	15	3	29	65	6	.940
—Burlington (Midw.)■..		SS	93	365	52	113	20	3	5	37	.310	32	57	9	127	285	19	.956
1996—San Jose (Calif.)		SS	121	462	59	124	19	6	2	54	.268	48	89	8	192	343	24	.957
—Phoenix (PCL)...........		SS	12	43	1	6	0	1	0	1	.140	3	7	0	30	47	2	.975
—San Francisco (N.L.) ..		SS	6	22	3	8	0	0	0	2	.364	1	5	1	12	12	1	.960
1997—San Francisco (N.L.) ..		2B-SS	8	7	1	1	1	0	0	0	.143	0	2	0	2	3	0	1.000
—Phoenix (PCL)...........		SS-2B	119	416	47	120	22	4	9	59	.288	24	70	9	†208	347	18	.969
1998—Fresno (PCL)		SS	127	512	87	142	22	2	12	63	.277	52	92	9	205	373	23	.962
—San Francisco (N.L.) ..		SS	10	12	1	2	1	0	0	1	.167	1	3	0	3	6	0	1.000
1999—Fresno (PCL)		SS-DH-2B	57	213	28	64	10	3	1	33	.300	18	35	4	86	166	15	.944
—San Francisco (N.L.) ..		SS-2B	35	71	7	18	2	1	0	3	.254	5	9	1	39	42	5	.942
2000—New York (A.L.)■........		2B-SS-3B	31	45	6	11	1	0	1	4	.244	5	9	1	23	37	3	.952
—Kansas City (A.L.)■ ...		2B-SS-3B	33	83	15	22	1	0	0	7	.265	6	17	1	38	97	1	.993
American League totals (1 year)			64	128	21	33	2	0	1	11	.258	11	26	2	61	134	4	.980
National League totals (4 years)			59	112	12	29	4	1	0	6	.259	7	19	2	56	63	6	.952
Major League totals (5 years)			123	240	33	62	6	1	1	17	.258	18	45	4	117	197	10	.969

DELLAERO, JASON   SS   WHITE SOX

PERSONAL: Born December 17, 1976, in Mount Kisco, N.Y. ... 6-2/195. ... Bats both, throws right. ... Full name: Jason Christopher Dellaero.
HIGH SCHOOL: Brewster (N.Y.).
COLLEGE: South Florida.
TRANSACTIONS/CAREER NOTES: Selected by New York Mets organization in 17th round of free-agent draft (June 2, 1994); did not sign. ... Selected by Chicago White Sox organization in first round (15th pick overall) of free-agent draft (June 3, 1997).

Year	Team (League)	Pos.	G	AB	R	H	2B	3B	HR	RBI	Avg.	BB	SO	SB	PO	A	E	Avg.
1997—GC White Sox (GCL) ..		SS	5	15	1	3	2	0	0	1	.200	1	2	0	5	6	2	.846
—Hickory (S.Atl.)...........		SS	55	191	37	53	10	3	6	29	.277	17	49	3	79	150	14	.942
1998—Win.-Salem (Caro.)		SS	121	428	45	89	23	3	10	49	.208	25	147	12	183	306	*46	.914
1999—Win.-Salem (Caro.)		SS	54	184	22	41	13	0	2	19	.223	18	59	9	89	170	19	.932
—Birmingham (Sou.).......		SS-DH	81	272	40	73	13	3	10	44	.268	14	76	6	138	227	20	.948
—Chicago (A.L.)..............		SS	11	33	1	3	0	0	0	2	.091	1	13	0	16	28	4	.917
2000—Birmingham (Sou.).....		SS	122	438	36	81	18	1	7	42	.185	20	142	9	201	347	25	.956
Major League totals (1 year)			11	33	1	3	0	0	0	2	.091	1	13	0	16	28	4	.917

DELLUCCI, DAVID   OF   DIAMONDBACKS

PERSONAL: Born October 31, 1973, in Baton Rouge, La. ... 5-10/180. ... Bats left, throws left. ... Full name: David Michael Dellucci. ... Name pronounced duh-LOO-chee.
HIGH SCHOOL: Catholic (Baton Rouge, La.).
COLLEGE: Mississippi.
TRANSACTIONS/CAREER NOTES: Selected by Baltimore Orioles organization in 10th round of free agent draft (June 1, 1995). ... Selected by Arizona Diamondbacks in second round (45th pick overall) of expansion draft (November 18, 1997). ... On disabled list (July 25, 1999-remainder of season). ... On Tucson disabled list (May 8-July 26, 2000).

Year	Team (League)	Pos.	G	AB	R	H	2B	3B	HR	RBI	Avg.	BB	SO	SB	PO	A	E	Avg.
1995—Frederick (Caro.)		OF	28	96	16	27	3	0	1	10	.281	12	10	1	26	2	1	.966
—Bluefield (Appl.)		OF	20	69	11	23	5	1	2	12	.333	6	7	3	11	0	2	.846
1996—Frederick (Caro.)		OF	59	185	33	60	11	1	4	28	.324	38	34	5	100	4	3	.972
—Bowie (East.)..............		OF	66	251	27	73	14	1	2	33	.291	28	56	2	134	5	3	.979
1997—Bowie (East.)..............		OF-DH	107	385	71	126	29	3	20	55	.327	58	69	11	162	2	1	.994
—Baltimore (A.L.)..........		OF-DH	17	27	3	6	1	0	1	3	.222	4	7	0	20	1	0	1.000
1998—Tucson (PCL)■		OF	17	72	17	22	4	3	1	11	.306	5	8	4	38	0	0	1.000
—Arizona (N.L.)..............		OF	124	416	43	108	19	*12	5	51	.260	33	103	3	230	3	3	.987
1999—Arizona (N.L.).............		OF-DH	63	109	27	43	7	1	1	15	.394	11	24	2	37	1	0	1.000
2000—Arizona (N.L.).............		OF	34	50	2	15	3	0	0	2	.300	4	9	0	15	0	0	1.000
—Tucson (PCL)		OF	33	122	16	28	6	3	3	17	.230	13	15	4	55	1	2	.966
—Ariz. D'backs (Ariz.)....		OF	2	6	0	2	1	0	0	2	.333	0	1	0	0	0	0	...
—South Bend (Midw.) ...		OF	2	5	3	1	1	0	0	1	.200	2	0	0	1	0	0	1.000
American League totals (1 year)			17	27	3	6	1	0	1	3	.222	4	7	0	20	1	0	1.000
National League totals (3 years)			221	575	72	166	29	13	6	68	.289	48	136	5	282	4	3	.990
Major League totals (4 years)			238	602	75	172	30	13	7	71	.286	52	143	5	302	5	3	.990

DEMPSTER, RYAN   P   MARLINS

PERSONAL: Born May 3, 1977, in Sechelt, B.C. ... 6-1/201. ... Throws right, bats right. ... Full name: Ryan Scott Dempster.
HIGH SCHOOL: Elphinstone (Gibsons, B.C.).
TRANSACTIONS/CAREER NOTES: Selected by Texas Rangers organization in third round of free-agent draft (June 1, 1995). ... Traded by Rangers with a player to be named later to Florida Marlins for P John Burkett (August 8, 1996); Marlins acquired P Rick Helling to complete deal (September 3, 1996).
STATISTICAL NOTES: Pitched 3-0 one-hit, complete-game victory against New York Mets (May 7, 2000).
MISCELLANEOUS: Appeared in one game as pinch runner (1999).

Year	League	W	L	Pct.	ERA	G	GS	CG	ShO	Sv.	IP	H	R	ER	BB	SO
1995—	Gulf Coast Rangers (GCL)..	3	1	.750	2.36	8	6	1	0	0	34 $1/3$	34	21	9	17	37
	— Hudson Valley (NY-Penn)...	1	0	1.000	3.18	1	1	0	0	0	5 $2/3$	7	2	2	1	6
1996—	Charleston, S.C. (S.Atl.)	7	11	.389	3.30	23	23	2	0	0	144 $1/3$	120	71	53	58	141
	— Kane County (Midw.)■......	2	1	.667	2.73	4	4	1	1	0	26 $1/3$	18	10	8	18	16
1997—	Brevard County (FSL).........	10	9	.526	4.90	28	26	2	1	0	165 $1/3$	190	100	*90	46	131
1998—	Portland (East.)..................	4	3	.571	3.22	7	7	0	0	0	44 $2/3$	34	20	16	15	33
	— Florida (N.L.).....................	1	5	.167	7.08	14	11	0	0	0	54 $2/3$	72	47	43	38	35
	— Charlotte (I.L.).....................	3	1	.750	3.27	5	5	1	0	0	33	33	14	12	12	24
1999—	Calgary (PCL)...................	1	1	.500	4.99	5	5	0	0	0	30 $2/3$	30	17	17	10	29
	— Florida (N.L.).....................	7	8	.467	4.71	25	25	0	0	0	147	146	77	77	93	126
2000—	Florida (N.L.)...................	14	10	.583	3.66	33	33	2	1	0	226 $1/3$	210	102	92	97	209
	Major League totals (3 years)......	22	23	.489	4.46	72	69	2	1	0	428	428	226	212	228	370

ALL-STAR GAME RECORD

Year	League	W	L	Pct.	ERA	GS	CG	ShO	Sv.	IP	H	R	ER	BB	SO
2000—	National.............................							Did not play.							

DePAULA, SEAN — P — INDIANS

PERSONAL: Born November 7, 1973, in Newton, Mass. ... 6-4/215. ... Throws right, bats right. ... Full name: Sean Michael DePaula.
HIGH SCHOOL: Pinkerton Academy (Derry, N.H.), then Cushing Academy (Ashburnham, Mass.).
COLLEGE: Wake Forest.
TRANSACTIONS/CAREER NOTES: Selected by Boston Red Sox organization in eighth round of free-agent draft (June 3, 1993); did not sign. ... Selected by Cleveland Indians organization in ninth round of free-agent draft (June 4, 1996). ... On Cleveland disabled list (May 28-July 9 and September 8, 2000-remainder of season); included rehabilitation assignment to Akron (June 24-July 9). ... On Buffalo disabled list (August 2-September 6, 2000).

Year	League	W	L	Pct.	ERA	G	GS	CG	ShO	Sv.	IP	H	R	ER	BB	SO
1996—	Burlington (Appl.)...............	4	2	.667	3.82	23	0	0	0	1	35 $1/3$	31	16	15	13	42
	— Watertown (NY-Penn)	0	0	...	0.00	1	0	0	0	0	2	0	0	0	0	5
1997—	Columbus (S.Atl.)..............	4	5	.444	5.20	29	1	0	0	0	71	71	56	41	43	75
	— Watertown (NY-Penn)	1	1	.500	2.84	9	0	0	0	0	19	21	6	6	8	17
1998—	Kinston (Caro.)..................	3	2	.600	2.36	28	1	0	0	1	49 $2/3$	50	20	13	18	59
	— Akron (East.).....................	1	1	.500	4.76	8	1	0	0	0	17	16	10	9	15	17
1999—	Kinston (Caro.)..................	4	2	.667	2.28	23	0	0	0	7	51 $1/3$	36	17	13	17	75
	— Akron (East.).....................	1	0	1.000	3.54	14	0	0	0	0	28	20	11	11	17	31
	— Buffalo (I.L.)......................	0	0	...	0.00	5	0	0	0	2	5	0	0	0	3	7
	— Cleveland (A.L.).................	0	0	...	4.63	11	0	0	0	0	11 $2/3$	8	6	6	3	18
2000—	Buffalo (I.L.)......................	1	0	1.000	5.54	9	0	0	0	1	13	16	10	8	7	11
	— Cleveland (A.L.).................	0	0	...	5.94	13	0	0	0	0	16 $2/3$	20	11	11	14	16
	— Akron (East.).....................	0	0	...	1.80	4	0	0	0	0	5	1	1	1	2	4
	Major League totals (2 years).......	0	0	...	5.40	24	0	0	0	0	28 $1/3$	28	17	17	17	34

DIVISION SERIES RECORD

Year	League	W	L	Pct.	ERA	G	GS	CG	ShO	Sv.	IP	H	R	ER	BB	SO
1999—	Cleveland (A.L.).................	0	0	...	1.80	3	0	0	0	0	5	2	1	1	3	5

DeROSA, MARK — SS — BRAVES

PERSONAL: Born February 2, 1975, in Passaic, N.J. ... 6-1/195. ... Bats right, throws right. ... Full name: Mark Thomas DeRosa.
HIGH SCHOOL: Bergen Catholic (Oradell, N.J.).
COLLEGE: Pennsylvania.
TRANSACTIONS/CAREER NOTES: Selected by Atlanta Braves organization in seventh round of free-agent draft (June 4, 1996).

							BATTING								FIELDING		
Year	Team (League)	Pos.	G	AB	R	H	2B	3B	HR	RBI	Avg.	BB	SO	SB	PO	A	E	Avg.
---	---	---	---	---	---	---	---	---	---	---	---	---	---	---	---	---	---	---
1996—	Eugene (N'West)	SS	70	255	43	66	13	1	2	28	.259	38	48	3	82	196	24	.921
1997—	Durham (Caro.)	SS	92	346	51	93	11	3	8	37	.269	25	73	6	136	245	21	.948
1998—	Greenville (Sou.)	SS	125	461	67	123	26	2	8	49	.267	60	57	7	195	338	20	*.964
	— Atlanta (N.L.).............	SS	5	3	2	1	0	0	0	0	.333	0	1	0	1	1	0	1.000
1999—	Richmond (I.L.)...........	SS-DH	105	364	41	99	16	2	1	40	.272	21	49	7	139	249	20	.951
	— Atlanta (N.L.).............	SS	7	8	0	0	0	0	0	0	.000	0	2	0	2	2	0	1.000
2000—	Richmond (I.L.)..........	SS-2B-3B	101	370	62	108	22	3	3	35	.292	38	36	13	146	287	19	.958
	— Atlanta (N.L.).............	SS	22	13	9	4	1	0	0	3	.308	2	1	0	6	7	0	1.000
	Major League totals (3 years)		34	24	11	5	1	0	0	3	.208	2	4	0	9	10	0	1.000

DeSHIELDS, DELINO — 2B — ORIOLES

PERSONAL: Born January 15, 1969, in Seaford, Del. ... 6-1/175. ... Bats left, throws right. ... Full name: Delino Lamont DeShields. ... Name pronounced duh-LINE-oh.
HIGH SCHOOL: Seaford (Del.).
COLLEGE: Villanova.
TRANSACTIONS/CAREER NOTES: Selected by Montreal Expos organization in first round (12th pick overall) of free-agent draft (June 2, 1987). ... On disabled list (June 16-July 12, 1990 and August 12-September 11, 1993). ... Traded by Expos to Los Angeles Dodgers for P Pedro J. Martinez (November 19, 1993). ... On disabled list (May 26-June 20, 1994). ... Granted free agency (October 29, 1996). ... Signed by St. Louis Cardinals (November 20, 1996). ... On St. Louis disabled list (July 5-August 10, 1998); included rehabilitation assignment to Arkansas (August 5-10). ... Granted free agency (October 23, 1998). ... Signed by Baltimore Orioles (December 7, 1998). ... On Baltimore disabled list (March 25-April 11, June 21-July 23 and October 1, 1999-remainder of season); included rehabilitation assignments to Bowie (April 9-11 and July 20-22), Delmarva (July 15-16) and Frederick (July 17-19).

RECORDS: Shares modern N.L. record for most hits in first major league game—4 (April 9, 1990). ... Shares major league single-game record for most strikeouts (nine-inning game)—5 (September 17, 1991, second game).

STATISTICAL NOTES: Led Gulf Coast League shortstops with 22 errors in 1987. ... Had 21-game hitting streak (June 28-July 21, 1993). ... Had 18-game hitting streak (May 30-June 20, 1998). ... Career major league grand slams: 1.

Year Team (League)	Pos.	G	AB	R	H	2B	3B	HR	RBI	Avg.	BB	SO	SB	PO	A	E	Avg.
1987— GC Expos (GCL)	SS-3B	31	111	17	24	5	2	1	4	.216	21	30	16	47	90	†22	.862
—Jamestown (NY-P)	SS	34	96	16	21	1	2	1	5	.219	24	28	14	25	57	21	.796
1988— Rockford (Midw.)	SS	129	460	97	116	26	6	12	46	.252	95	110	59	173	344	42	.925
1989— Jacksonville (Sou.)	SS	93	307	55	83	10	6	3	35	.270	76	80	37	127	218	34	.910
—Indianapolis (A.A.)	SS	47	181	29	47	8	4	2	14	.260	16	53	16	73	101	13	.930
1990— Montreal (N.L.)	2B	129	499	69	144	28	6	4	45	.289	66	96	42	236	371	12	.981
1991— Montreal (N.L.)	2B	151	563	83	134	15	4	10	51	.238	95	*151	56	285	405	*27	.962
1992— Montreal (N.L.)	2B	135	530	82	155	19	8	7	56	.292	54	108	46	251	360	15	.976
1993— Montreal (N.L.)	2B	123	481	75	142	17	7	2	29	.295	72	64	43	243	381	11	.983
1994— Los Angeles (N.L.)■ ..	2B-SS	89	320	51	80	11	3	2	33	.250	54	53	27	156	282	7	.984
1995— Los Angeles (N.L.)	2B	127	425	66	109	18	3	8	37	.256	63	83	39	204	330	•11	.980
1996— Los Angeles (N.L.)	2B	154	581	75	130	12	8	5	41	.224	53	124	48	274	400	17	.975
1997— St. Louis (N.L.)■	2B	150	572	92	169	26	*14	11	58	.295	55	72	55	272	398	19	.972
1998— St. Louis (N.L.)	2B-1B	117	420	74	122	21	8	7	44	.290	56	61	26	247	273	9	.983
—Arkansas (Texas)	2B-DH	4	13	1	2	0	0	0	0	.154	2	6	0	6	5	0	1.000
1999— Bowie (East.)■	2B-DH	4	15	2	4	1	0	0	0	.267	3	2	0	5	5	0	1.000
—Baltimore (A.L.)	2B	96	330	46	87	11	2	6	34	.264	37	52	11	178	249	10	.977
—Delmarva (S.Atl.)	2B	2	7	1	2	0	0	1	2	.286	1	1	0	4	5	0	1.000
—Frederick (Caro.)	2B	2	8	1	1	0	0	1	2	.125	0	1	0	5	5	0	1.000
2000— Baltimore (A.L.)	2B-OF-DH	151	561	84	166	43	5	10	86	.296	69	82	37	247	257	13	.975
American League totals (2 years)		247	891	130	253	54	7	16	120	.284	106	134	48	425	506	23	.976
National League totals (9 years)		1175	4391	667	1185	167	61	56	394	.270	568	812	382	2168	3200	128	.977
Major League totals (11 years)		1422	5282	797	1438	221	68	72	514	.272	674	946	430	2593	3706	151	.977

DIVISION SERIES RECORD

Year Team (League)	Pos.	G	AB	R	H	2B	3B	HR	RBI	Avg.	BB	SO	SB	PO	A	E	Avg.
1995— Los Angeles (N.L.)	2B	3	12	1	3	0	0	0	0	.250	1	3	0	8	7	0	1.000
1996— Los Angeles (N.L.)	2B	2	4	0	0	0	0	0	0	.000	0	1	0	3	2	0	1.000
Division series totals (2 years)		5	16	1	3	0	0	0	0	.188	1	4	0	11	9	0	1.000

DESSENS, ELMER   P   REDS

PERSONAL: Born January 13, 1972, in Hermosillo, Mexico. ... 6-0/187. ... Throws right, bats right. ... Full name: Elmer Dessens Jusaino. ... Name pronounced DAH-cenz.

HIGH SCHOOL: Carrera Technica (Hermosillo, Mexico).

TRANSACTIONS/CAREER NOTES: Signed as non-drafted free agent by Pittsburgh Pirates organization (January 27, 1993). ... Loaned by Pirates organization to Mexico City Red Devils of Mexican League for 1993 and 1994 seasons; returned to Pirates organization for 1995 season. ... Loaned by Pirates organization to Red Devils (May 7, 1996). ... Returned to Pirates organization (June 21, 1996). ... On Pittsburgh disabled list (July 31-September 10, 1996); included rehabilitation assignment to Carolina (August 16-September 10). ... Loaned by Pirates to Red Devils (March 27-September 5, 1997). ... On Pittsburgh disabled list (April 8-24, 1998); included rehabilitation assignment to Nashville (April 21-24). ... Released by Pirates (March 31, 1999). ... Played for Yomiuri Giants of Japan Central League (1999). ... Signed by Cincinnati Reds (December 15, 1999).

Year League	W	L	Pct.	ERA	G	GS	CG	ShO	Sv.	IP	H	R	ER	BB	SO
1993— M.C. Red Devils (Mex.)	3	1	.750	2.35	14	0	0	0	2	30²/₃	31	8	8	5	16
1994— M.C. Red Devils (Mex.)	11	4	.733	2.04	37	15	4	1	3	127²/₃	121	37	29	32	51
1995— Carolina (Sou.)■	*15	8	.652	*2.49	27	27	1	0	0	152	170	62	42	21	68
1996— Calgary (PCL)	2	2	.500	3.15	6	6	0	0	0	34¹/₃	40	14	12	15	15
—M.C. Red Devils (Mex.)■ ..	7	0	1.000	1.26	7	7	1	0	0	50	44	12	7	10	17
—Pittsburgh (N.L.)■	0	2	.000	8.28	15	3	0	0	0	25	40	23	23	4	13
—Carolina (Sou.)	0	1	.000	5.40	5	1	0	0	0	11²/₃	15	8	7	4	7
1997— M.C. Red Devils (Mex.)■ ...	•16	5	.762	3.56	26	25	3	1	0	159¹/₃	156	73	63	51	61
—Pittsburgh (N.L.)■	0	0	...	0.00	3	0	0	0	0	3¹/₃	2	0	0	0	2
1998— Pittsburgh (N.L.)	2	6	.250	5.67	43	5	0	0	0	74²/₃	90	50	47	25	43
—Nashville (PCL)	3	1	.750	3.30	6	5	0	0	0	30	32	12	11	6	13
1999— Yomiuri (Jap. Cen.)■	0	1	.000	3.86	8	0	0	0	0	16¹/₃	24	7	7	4	6
2000— Louisville (I.L.)■	2	0	1.000	3.18	4	4	0	0	0	22²/₃	24	10	8	7	14
—Cincinnati (N.L.)	11	5	.688	4.28	40	16	0	0	1	147¹/₃	170	73	70	43	80
Major League totals (4 years)	13	13	.500	5.03	101	24	1	0	1	250¹/₃	302	146	140	72	143

DeWITT, MATT   P   WHITE SOX

PERSONAL: Born September 4, 1977, in San Bernardino, Calif. ... 6-3/210. ... Throws right, bats right. ... Full name: Matthew Brian DeWitt.

HIGH SCHOOL: Valley (Las Vegas).

TRANSACTIONS/CAREER NOTES: Selected by St. Louis Cardinals organization in 10th round of free-agent draft (June 1, 1995). ... Traded by Cardinals with P Lance Painter and C Alberto Castillo to Toronto Blue Jays for P Pat Hentgen and P Paul Spoljaric (November 11, 1999). ... On Toronto disabled list (August 23, 2000-remainder of season). ... Traded by Blue Jays with P David Wells to Chicago White Sox for P Mike Sirotka, P Kevin Beirne, OF Brian Simmons and P Mike Williams (January 14, 2001).

STATISTICAL NOTES: Led Appalachian League pitchers with 17 home runs allowed in 1996.

Year League	W	L	Pct.	ERA	G	GS	CG	ShO	Sv.	IP	H	R	ER	BB	SO
1995— Johnson City (Appl.)	2	6	.250	7.04	13	12	0	0	0	62²/₃	84	56	*49	32	45
1996— Johnson City (Appl.)	5	5	.500	5.42	14	*14	0	0	0	*79²/₃	66	53	48	26	58
1997— Peoria (Midw.)	9	9	.500	4.09	27	•27	1	0	0	158¹/₃	152	84	72	57	121

Year	League	W	L	Pct.	ERA	G	GS	CG	ShO	Sv.	IP	H	R	ER	BB	SO
1998—	Prince William (Caro.)	6	9	.400	3.64	24	24	1	0	0	148 1/3	132	65	60	18	118
1999—	Arkansas (Texas)	9	8	.529	4.43	26	26	0	0	0	148 1/3	153	87	73	59	107
2000—	Syracuse (I.L.)■	4	5	.444	4.87	31	7	0	0	15	64 2/3	78	42	35	25	41
	—Toronto (A.L.)	1	0	1.000	8.56	8	0	0	0	0	13 2/3	20	13	13	9	6
Major League totals (1 year)		1	0	1.000	8.56	8	0	0	0	0	13 2/3	20	13	13	9	6

DIAZ, EINAR — C — INDIANS

PERSONAL: Born December 28, 1972, in Chiniqui, Panama. ... 5-10/185. ... Bats right, throws right. ... Full name: Einar Antonio Diaz.
TRANSACTIONS/CAREER NOTES: Signed as non-drafted free agent by Cleveland Indians organization (October 5, 1990).
STATISTICAL NOTES: Led Appalachian League third basemen with 125 assists and .959 fielding percentage in 1992. ... Led Appalachian League catchers with 54 assists and nine errors in 1993. ... Led South Atlantic League in grounding into double plays with 18 in 1994. ... Led South Atlantic League catchers with 966 total chances, 845 putouts, 112 assists and tied for lead with eight double plays in 1994. ... Led Carolina League catchers with 107 assists and .992 fielding percentage in 1995. ... Led Eastern League catchers with 15 errors in 1996. ... Led American Association catchers with 18 errors in 1997. ... Led International League catchers with 873 total chances in 1998.

							BATTING								FIELDING		
Year	Team (League)	Pos.	G	AB	R	H	2B	3B	HR	RBI	Avg.	BB	SO	SB	PO	A	E	Avg.
1991—	Dom. Indians (DSL)		62	239	35	67	6	3	1	29	.280	14	5	10	...	...	...	...
1992—	Burlington (Appl.)	3B-SS	52	178	19	37	3	0	1	14	.208	20	9	2	27	†137	7	†.959
1993—	Burlington (Appl.)	C-3B	60	231	40	69	15	3	5	33	.299	8	7	7	315	†55	†10	.974
	—Columbus (S.Atl.)	C	1	5	0	0	0	0	0	0	.000	0	1	0	3	1	0	1.000
1994—	Columbus (S.Atl.)	C-3B	120	491	67	137	23	2	16	71	.279	17	34	4	†848	†134	9	.991
1995—	Kinston (Caro.)	C-3B-DH	104	373	46	98	21	0	6	43	.263	12	29	3	676	†111	7	†.991
1996—	Canton/Akron (East.)	C-3B	104	395	47	111	26	2	3	35	.281	12	22	3	765	88	†15	.983
	—Cleveland (A.L.)	C	4	1	0	0	0	0	0	0	.000	0	0	0	4	0	0	1.000
1997—	Buffalo (A.A.)	C-3B	109	336	40	86	18	2	3	31	.256	18	34	2	653	67	†19	.974
	—Cleveland (A.L.)	C	5	7	1	1	1	0	0	1	.143	0	2	0	18	3	1	.955
1998—	Cleveland (A.L.)	C	17	48	8	11	1	0	2	9	.229	3	2	0	101	9	3	.973
	—Buffalo (I.L.)	C	115	415	62	130	21	3	8	63	.313	21	33	3	*791	*70	*12	.986
1999—	Cleveland (A.L.)	C	119	392	43	110	21	1	3	32	.281	23	41	11	751	81	10	.988
2000—	Cleveland (A.L.)	C-3B	75	250	29	68	14	2	4	25	.272	11	29	4	579	48	4	.994
Major League totals (5 years)			220	698	81	190	37	3	9	67	.272	37	74	15	1453	141	18	.989

DIVISION SERIES RECORD

							BATTING								FIELDING		
Year	Team (League)	Pos.	G	AB	R	H	2B	3B	HR	RBI	Avg.	BB	SO	SB	PO	A	E	Avg.
1998—	Cleveland (A.L.)							Did not play.										
1999—	Cleveland (A.L.)	C-PH	2	1	0	0	0	0	0	0	.000	0	0	0	3	0	0	1.000

CHAMPIONSHIP SERIES RECORD

							BATTING								FIELDING		
Year	Team (League)	Pos.	G	AB	R	H	2B	3B	HR	RBI	Avg.	BB	SO	SB	PO	A	E	Avg.
1998—	Cleveland (A.L.)	C	4	4	0	0	0	0	0	0	.000	0	1	0	13	3	0	1.000

DICKSON, JASON — P — BLUE JAYS

PERSONAL: Born March 30, 1973, in London, Ont. ... 6-0/195. ... Throws right, bats left. ... Full name: Jason Royce Dickson.
HIGH SCHOOL: James M. Hill (Chatham, New Brunswick).
JUNIOR COLLEGE: Northeastern Oklahoma A&M.
TRANSACTIONS/CAREER NOTES: Selected by California Angels organization in sixth round of free-agent draft (June 2, 1994). ... Angels franchise renamed Anaheim Angels for 1997 season. ... On disabled list (April 4, 1999-entire season). ... On Anaheim disabled list (April 29-May 14 and May 20, 2000-remainder of season); included rehabilitation assignment to Edmonton (June 11-16). ... Granted free agency (October 6, 2000). ... Signed by Toronto Blue Jays organization (November 13, 2000).
HONORS: Named A.L. Rookie Pitcher of the Year by THE SPORTING NEWS (1997).

Year	League	W	L	Pct.	ERA	G	GS	CG	ShO	Sv.	IP	H	R	ER	BB	SO
1994—	Boise (N'West)	3	1	.750	3.86	9	7	0	0	1	44 1/3	40	22	19	18	37
1995—	Cedar Rapids (Midw.)	14	6	.700	2.86	25	25	*9	1	0	173	151	71	55	45	134
1996—	Midland (Texas)	5	2	.714	3.58	8	8	3	1	0	55 1/3	55	27	22	10	40
	—Vancouver (PCL)	7	11	.389	3.80	18	18	*7	0	0	130 1/3	134	73	55	40	70
	—California (A.L.)	1	4	.200	4.57	7	7	0	0	0	43 1/3	52	22	22	18	20
1997—	Anaheim (A.L.)■	13	9	.591	4.29	33	32	2	1	0	203 2/3	236	111	97	56	115
1998—	Anaheim (A.L.)	10	10	.500	6.05	27	18	0	0	0	122	147	89	82	41	61
	—Vancouver (PCL)	2	1	.667	1.78	4	4	0	0	0	25 1/3	26	5	5	4	18
1999—	Anaheim (A.L.)							Did not play.								
2000—	Anaheim (A.L.)	2	2	.500	6.11	6	6	0	0	0	28	39	20	19	7	18
	—Edmonton (PCL)	0	2	.000	10.13	2	2	0	0	0	8	13	9	9	4	4
Major League totals (4 years)		26	25	.510	4.99	73	63	2	1	0	397	474	242	220	122	214

ALL-STAR GAME RECORD

Year	League	W	L	Pct.	ERA	GS	CG	ShO	Sv.	IP	H	R	ER	BB	SO
1997—	American						Did not play.								

DIFELICE, MIKE — C — DEVIL RAYS

PERSONAL: Born May 28, 1969, in Philadelphia. ... 6-2/205. ... Bats right, throws right. ... Full name: Michael William Difelice. ... Name pronounced DEE-fah-lease.
HIGH SCHOOL: Bearden (Knoxville, Tenn.).
COLLEGE: Tennessee.

TRANSACTIONS/CAREER NOTES: Selected by St. Louis Cardinals organization in 11th round of free-agent draft (June 3, 1991). ... Selected by Tampa Bay Devil Rays in first round (20th pick overall) of expansion draft (November 18, 1997).
RECORDS: Shares major league single-season record for fewest double plays by catcher for leader—8 (1998).
STATISTICAL NOTES: Tied for N.L. lead in passed balls with 12 in 1997. ... Tied for A.L. lead in double plays by catcher with eight in 1998.

							BATTING								FIELDING		
Year Team (League)	Pos.	G	AB	R	H	2B	3B	HR	RBI	Avg.	BB	SO	SB	PO	A	E	Avg.
1991—Hamilton (NY-Penn)...	C	43	157	10	33	5	0	4	15	.210	9	40	1	297	40	9	.974
1992—Hamilton (NY-Penn)...	C-1B	18	58	11	20	3	0	2	9	.345	4	7	2	135	19	5	.969
—St. Petersburg (FSL)..	C	17	53	0	12	3	0	0	4	.226	3	11	0	73	11	2	.977
1993—Springfield (Midw.) ...	C	8	20	5	7	1	0	0	3	.350	2	3	0	52	9	0	1.000
—St. Petersburg (FSL)..	C	30	97	5	22	2	0	0	8	.227	11	13	1	165	23	7	.964
1994—Arkansas (Texas).......	C	71	200	19	50	11	2	2	15	.250	12	48	0	419	40	6	.987
1995—Arkansas (Texas).......	C	62	176	14	47	10	1	1	24	.267	23	29	0	327	48	6	.984
—Louisville (A.A.).........	C	21	63	8	17	4	0	0	3	.270	5	11	1	111	10	2	.984
1996—Louisville (A.A.).........	C	79	246	25	70	13	0	9	33	.285	20	43	0	455	48	8	.984
—St. Louis (N.L.)...........	C	4	7	0	2	1	0	0	2	.286	0	1	0	15	1	0	1.000
1997—Arkansas (Texas).......	C	1	3	0	1	1	0	0	0	.333	1	0	0	6	2	0	1.000
—St. Louis (N.L.)...........	C-1B	93	260	16	62	10	1	4	30	.238	19	61	1	587	64	6	.991
—Louisville (A.A.).........	C	1	4	1	1	0	0	1	1	.250	0	1	0	3	1	0	1.000
1998—Tampa Bay (A.L.)■.....	C	84	248	17	57	12	3	3	23	.230	15	56	0	483	52	4	.993
1999—Tampa Bay (A.L.).......	C	51	179	21	55	11	0	6	27	.307	8	23	0	344	28	5	.987
2000—Tampa Bay (A.L.).......	C	60	204	23	49	13	1	6	19	.240	12	40	0	351	35	8	.980
American League totals (3 years)		195	631	61	161	36	4	15	69	.255	35	119	0	1178	115	17	.987
National League totals (2 years)		97	267	16	64	11	1	4	32	.240	19	62	1	602	65	6	.991
Major League totals (5 years)		292	898	77	225	47	5	19	101	.251	54	181	1	1780	180	23	.988

DINGMAN, CRAIG — P — YANKEES

PERSONAL: Born March 12, 1974, in Wichita, Kan. ... 6-4/215. ... Throws right, bats right. ... Full name: Craig Allen Dingman.
HIGH SCHOOL: North (Wichita, Kan.).
JUNIOR COLLEGE: Hutchinson (Kan.) Community College.
TRANSACTIONS/CAREER NOTES: Selected by New York Yankees organization in 36th round of free-agent draft (June 3, 1993). ... On disabled list (June 19, 1995-entire season).

Year League	W	L	Pct.	ERA	G	GS	CG	ShO	Sv.	IP	H	R	ER	BB	SO
1994—GC Yankees (GCL).............	0	5	.000	3.38	17	1	0	0	1	32	27	17	12	10	51
1995—							Did not play.								
1996—Oneonta (NY-Penn)..........	0	2	.000	2.04	20	0	0	0	9	35 1/3	17	11	8	9	52
1997—Greensboro (S.Atl.)...........	2	0	1.000	1.91	30	0	0	0	19	33	19	7	7	12	41
—Tampa (FSL).....................	0	4	.000	5.24	19	0	0	0	6	22 1/3	15	14	13	14	26
1998—Tampa (FSL)......................	5	4	.556	2.93	50	0	0	0	7	70 2/3	48	29	23	39	95
1999—Norwich (East.).................	8	6	.571	1.57	55	0	0	0	9	74 1/3	56	16	13	12	90
2000—Columbus (I.L.).................	6	1	.857	3.05	47	2	0	0	1	73 2/3	60	31	25	20	65
—New York (A.L.)...................	0	0	...	6.55	10	0	0	0	0	11	18	8	8	3	8
Major League totals (1 year)........	0	0	...	6.55	10	0	0	0	0	11	18	8	8	3	8

DIPOTO, JERRY — P — ROCKIES

PERSONAL: Born May 24, 1968, in Jersey City, N.J. ... 6-2/205. ... Throws right, bats right. ... Full name: Gerard Peter Dipoto III.
HIGH SCHOOL: Toms River (N.J.).
COLLEGE: Virginia Commonwealth.
TRANSACTIONS/CAREER NOTES: Selected by Cleveland Indians organization in third round of free-agent draft (June 5, 1989). ... On Cleveland disabled list (March 25-June 12, 1994); included rehabilitation assignment to Charlotte (May 10-June 8). ... Traded by Indians with P Paul Byrd, P Dave Mlicki and a player to be named later to New York Mets for OF Jeromy Burnitz and P Joe Roa (November 18, 1994); Mets acquired 2B Jesus Azuaje to complete deal (December 6, 1994). ... Traded by Mets to Colorado Rockies for P Armando Reynoso (November 27, 1996). ... Granted free agency (November 3, 1999). ... Re-signed by Rockies (November 17, 1999). ... On Colorado disabled list (March 25-April 15 and April 26-September 1, 2000); included rehabilitation assignments to Colorado Springs (April 6-15 and August 24-September 1).
STATISTICAL NOTES: Led Eastern League with 15 wild pitches and tied for lead with three balks in 1991.

Year League	W	L	Pct.	ERA	G	GS	CG	ShO	Sv.	IP	H	R	ER	BB	SO
1989—Watertown (NY-Penn)	6	5	.545	3.61	14	14	1	0	0	87 1/3	75	42	35	39	98
1990—Kinston (Caro.)..................	11	4	.733	3.78	24	24	1	0	0	145 1/3	129	75	61	77	143
—Canton/Akron (East.)........	1	0	1.000	2.57	3	2	0	0	0	14	11	5	4	4	12
1991—Canton/Akron (East.)........	6	11	.353	3.81	28	26	2	0	0	156	143	83	66	74	97
1992—Colorado Springs (PCL)	9	9	.500	4.94	50	9	0	0	2	122	148	78	67	66	62
1993—Charlotte (I.L.)..................	6	3	.667	1.93	34	0	0	0	12	46 2/3	34	10	10	13	44
—Cleveland (A.L.)..............	4	4	.500	2.40	46	0	0	0	11	56 1/3	57	21	15	30	41
1994—Charlotte (I.L.)..................	3	2	.600	3.15	25	2	0	0	9	34 1/3	37	13	12	12	26
—Cleveland (A.L.)..............	0	0	...	8.04	7	0	0	0	0	15 2/3	26	14	14	10	9
1995—New York (N.L.)■...........	4	6	.400	3.78	58	0	0	0	2	78 2/3	77	41	33	29	49
1996—New York (N.L.).............	7	2	.778	4.19	57	0	0	0	0	77 1/3	91	44	36	45	52
1997—Colorado (N.L.)■............	5	3	.625	4.70	74	0	0	0	16	95 2/3	108	56	50	33	74
1998—Colorado (N.L.).............	3	4	.429	3.53	68	0	0	0	19	71 1/3	61	31	28	25	49
1999—Colorado (N.L.).............	4	5	.444	4.26	63	0	0	0	1	86 2/3	91	44	41	44	69
2000—Colorado Springs (PCL)	1	0	1.000	2.00	9	0	0	0	0	9	6	2	2	3	12
—Colorado (N.L.)..............	0	0	...	3.95	17	0	0	0	0	13 2/3	16	6	6	5	9
A.L. totals (2 years)	4	4	.500	3.63	53	0	0	0	11	72	83	35	29	40	50
N.L. totals (6 years)	23	20	.535	4.12	337	0	0	0	38	423 1/3	444	222	194	181	302
Major League totals (8 years)	27	24	.529	4.05	390	0	0	0	49	495 1/3	527	257	223	221	352

DiSARCINA, GARY   SS   ANGELS

PERSONAL: Born November 19, 1967, in Malden, Mass. ... 6-2/195. ... Bats right, throws right. ... Full name: Gary Thomas DiSarcina. ... Brother of Glenn DiSarcina, shortstop in Chicago White Sox organization (1991-96). ... Name pronounced DEE-sar-SEE-na.

HIGH SCHOOL: Billerica (Mass.) Memorial.

COLLEGE: Massachusetts.

TRANSACTIONS/CAREER NOTES: Selected by California Angels organization in sixth round of free-agent draft (June 1, 1988). ... On disabled list (August 27, 1993-remainder of season and August 4-September 17, 1995). ... Angels franchise renamed Anaheim Angels for 1997 season. ... On Anaheim disabled list (March 24-June 22, 1999); included rehabilitation assignments to Lake Elsinore (June 10-14) and Erie (June 15-22). ... On disabled list (April 11-24 and May 9, 2000-remainder of season). ... Granted free agency (November 3, 2000). ... Re-signed by Angels organization (December 6, 2000).

RECORDS: Holds A.L. single-season record for fewest putouts by shortstop (150 or more games)—212 (1996).

STATISTICAL NOTES: Led Pacific Coast League shortstops with .968 fielding percentage and 419 assists in 1991. ... Led A.L. shortstops with 761 total chances in 1992. ... Led A.L. shortstops with 103 double plays in 1998.

						BATTING									FIELDING		
Year Team (League)	Pos.	G	AB	R	H	2B	3B	HR	RBI	Avg.	BB	SO	SB	PO	A	E	Avg.
1988—Bend (N'West)	SS	71	295	40	90	11	•5	2	39	.305	27	34	7	104	*237	27	.927
1989—Midland (Texas)	SS	126	441	65	126	18	7	4	54	.286	24	54	11	206	*411	30	*.954
—California (A.L.)	SS	2	0	0	0	0	0	0	0	...	0	0	0	0	0	0	...
1990—Edmonton (PCL)	SS	97	330	46	70	12	2	4	37	.212	25	46	5	165	289	24	.950
—California (A.L.)	SS-2B	18	57	8	8	1	1	0	0	.140	3	10	1	17	57	4	.949
1991—Edmonton (PCL)	SS-2B	119	390	61	121	21	4	4	58	.310	29	32	16	191	†425	20	†.969
—California (A.L.)	SS-2B-3B	18	57	5	12	2	0	0	3	.211	3	4	0	29	45	4	.949
1992—California (A.L.)	SS	157	518	48	128	19	0	3	42	.247	20	50	9	250	*486	•25	.967
1993—California (A.L.)	SS	126	416	44	99	20	1	3	45	.238	15	38	5	193	362	14	.975
1994—California (A.L.)	SS	112	389	53	101	14	2	3	33	.260	18	28	3	159	*358	9	.983
1995—California (A.L.)	SS	99	362	61	111	28	6	5	41	.307	20	25	7	146	275	6	.986
1996—California (A.L.)	SS	150	536	62	137	26	4	5	48	.256	21	36	2	212	460	20	.971
1997—Anaheim (A.L.)	SS	154	549	52	135	28	2	4	47	.246	17	29	7	227	421	15	.977
1998—Anaheim (A.L.)	SS	157	551	73	158	39	3	3	56	.287	21	51	11	253	437	14	.980
1999—Lake Elsinore (Calif.)	SS-DH	4	12	0	1	0	0	0	0	.083	1	0	0	1	5	1	.857
—Erie (East.)	SS	5	20	1	6	0	0	0	2	.300	0	4	0	5	12	0	1.000
—Anaheim (A.L.)	SS	81	271	32	62	7	1	1	29	.229	15	32	2	138	249	15	.963
2000—Anaheim (A.L.)	SS	12	38	6	15	2	0	1	11	.395	1	3	0	24	47	5	.934
Major League totals (12 years)		1086	3744	444	966	186	20	28	355	.258	154	306	47	1648	3197	131	.974

ALL-STAR GAME RECORD

				BATTING									FIELDING		
Year League	Pos.	AB	R	H	2B	3B	HR	RBI	Avg.	BB	SO	SB	PO	A	E	Avg.
1995—American	PR-SS	1	0	0	0	0	0	0	.000	0	0	0	0	0	0	...

DONNELS, CHRIS   IF   DODGERS

PERSONAL: Born April 21, 1966, in Los Angeles. ... 6-0/185. ... Bats left, throws right. ... Full name: Chris Barton Donnels. ... Name pronounced DON-uls.

HIGH SCHOOL: South Torrance (Calif.).

COLLEGE: Loyola Marymount.

TRANSACTIONS/CAREER NOTES: Selected by New York Mets organization in first round (24th pick overall) of free-agent draft (June 2, 1987). ... On Tidewater disabled list (June 20-28, 1991). ... Selected by Florida Marlins in third round (67th pick overall) of expansion draft (November 17, 1992). ... Claimed on waivers by Houston Astros (December 18, 1992). ... On Houston disabled list (April 23-May 12, 1995); included rehabilitation assignment to Jackson (May 8-12). ... Traded by Astros to Boston Red Sox for a player to be named later (June 10, 1995). ... Released by Red Sox (October 26, 1995). ... Traded to Kintetsu Buffaloes of Japan Pacific League for cash (October 27, 1996). ... Re-signed by Red Sox (December 20, 1996). ... Released by Red Sox (March 26, 1997). ... Played with Orix Blue Wave of Japan Pacific League (1997-99). ... Signed by Los Angeles Dodgers organization (February 8, 2000). ... On Los Angeles disabled list (August 2-September 1, 2000); included rehabilitation assignment to Albuquerque (August 12-31).

HONORS: Named Florida State League Most Valuable Player (1989).

STATISTICAL NOTES: Led Florida State League with .510 slugging percentage and 15 intentional bases on balls received in 1989. ... Led Florida State League third basemen with 93 putouts, 202 assists and 320 total chances in 1989. ... Led Texas League third basemen with 79 putouts, 242 assists, 31 errors, 352 total chances and 24 double plays in 1990. ... Led Pacific Coast League with .660 slugging percentage in 2000.

						BATTING									FIELDING		
Year Team (League)	Pos.	G	AB	R	H	2B	3B	HR	RBI	Avg.	BB	SO	SB	PO	A	E	Avg.
1987—Kingsport (Appl.)	3B	26	86	18	26	4	0	3	16	.302	17	17	4	16	44	5	.909
—Columbia (S.Atl.)	3B	41	136	20	35	7	0	2	17	.257	24	27	3	32	86	10	.922
1988—St. Lucie (FSL)	3B	65	198	25	43	14	2	3	22	.217	32	53	4	40	116	15	.912
—Columbia (S.Atl.)	3B	42	133	19	32	6	0	2	13	.241	30	25	5	29	84	7	.942
1989—St. Lucie (FSL)	3B-1B	117	386	70	121	23	1	17	*78	.313	83	65	18	†242	†209	28	.942
1990—Jackson (Texas)	3B-1B-2B	130	419	66	114	24	0	12	63	.272	*111	81	11	†95	†244	†32	.914
1991—Tidewater (I.L.)	3B-2B	84	287	45	87	19	2	8	56	.303	62	56	1	88	189	14	.952
—New York (N.L.)	1B-3B	37	89	7	20	2	0	0	5	.225	14	19	1	131	34	2	.988
1992—Tidewater (I.L.)	3B-1B-2B	81	279	35	84	15	3	5	32	.301	58	45	12	160	156	16	.952
—New York (N.L.)	3B-2B	45	121	8	21	4	0	0	6	.174	17	25	1	34	77	5	.957
1993—Houston (N.L.)■	3B-1B-2B	88	179	18	46	14	2	2	24	.257	19	33	2	169	54	8	.965
1994—Houston (N.L.)	3B-1B-2B	54	86	12	23	5	0	3	5	.267	13	18	1	42	28	0	1.000
1995—Jackson (Texas)	3B	4	12	1	2	1	0	0	1	.167	4	4	0	6	7	1	.929
—Houston (N.L.)	3B-2B	19	30	4	9	0	0	2	2	.300	3	6	0	3	7	2	.833
—Boston (A.L.)■■	3B-1B-2B	40	91	13	23	2	2	2	11	.253	9	18	0	54	41	4	.960
—Pawtucket (I.L.)	3B-DH	4	15	1	6	0	0	1	4	.400	1	3	0	2	3	1	.833
1996—Kintetsu (Jap. Pac.)■		108	324	50	91	20	2	20	53	.281	54	86	3	...	...	...	...

D

Year Team (League)	Pos.	G	AB	R	H	2B	3B	HR	RBI	Avg.	BB	SO	SB	PO	A	E	Avg.
1997—Orix (Jap. Pac.)■		112	384	...	116	...	...	17	67	.302	...	...	...	...	...	...	...
1998—Orix (Jap. Pac.)		44	140	...	37	...	...	5	22	.264	...	...	...	...	...	...	...
1999—Orix (Jap. Pac.)					Did not play—injured.												
2000—Albuquerque (PCL)■..1B-3B-2B-C		105	332	79	109	27	1	27	84	.328	66	52	6	513	79	9	.985
—Los Angeles (N.L.) OF-1B-3B-2B		27	34	8	10	3	0	4	9	.294	6	7	0	29	1	1	.968
American League totals (1 year)		40	91	13	23	2	2	2	11	.253	9	18	0	54	41	4	.960
National League totals (6 years)		270	539	57	129	28	2	9	51	.239	72	108	5	408	201	18	.971
Major League totals (6 years)		310	630	70	152	30	4	11	62	.241	81	126	5	462	242	22	.970

DOTEL, OCTAVIO — P — ASTROS

PERSONAL: Born November 25, 1975, in Santo Domingo, Dominican Republic. ... 6-0/175. ... Throws right, bats right. ... Full name: Octavio Eduardo Dotel. ... Brother of Angel Dotel, third baseman in Los Angeles Dodgers organization (1991-93).
HIGH SCHOOL: Liceo Eansino Afuera (Dominican Republic).
TRANSACTIONS/CAREER NOTES: Signed as non-drafted free agent by New York Mets organization (March 20, 1993). ... On disabled list (July 18-August 16, 1996). ... On Binghamton disabled list (June 3-24, 1997). ... On Norfolk disabled list (May 7-17, 1999). ... Traded by Mets with OF Roger Cedeno and P Kyle Kessel to Houston Astros for P Mike Hampton and OF Derek Bell (December 23, 1999).

Year League	W	L	Pct.	ERA	G	GS	CG	ShO	Sv.	IP	H	R	ER	BB	SO
1993—Dom. Mets (DSL)	6	2	.750	4.10	...	11	0	0	0	59 1/3	46	30	27	38	48
1994—Dom. Mets (DSL)	5	0	1.000	4.32	15	14	1	0	0	81 1/3	84	53	39	31	95
1995—Gulf Coast Mets (GCL)	•7	4	.636	2.18	13	12	2	0	0	•74 1/3	48	23	18	17	*86
—St. Lucie (FSL)	1	0	1.000	5.63	3	0	0	0	0	8	10	5	5	4	9
1996—Columbia (S.Atl.)	11	3	.786	3.59	22	19	0	0	0	115 1/3	89	49	46	49	142
1997—St. Lucie (FSL)	5	2	.714	2.52	9	8	1	1	0	50	44	18	14	23	39
—Binghamton (East.)	3	4	.429	5.98	12	12	0	0	0	55 2/3	66	50	37	38	40
—Gulf Coast Mets (GCL)	0	0	...	0.96	3	2	0	0	1	9 1/3	9	1	1	2	7
1998—Binghamton (East.)	4	2	.667	1.97	10	10	2	1	0	68 2/3	41	19	15	24	82
—Norfolk (I.L.)	8	6	.571	3.45	17	16	1	0	0	99	82	47	38	43	118
1999—Norfolk (I.L.)	5	2	.714	3.84	13	13	1	0	0	70 1/3	52	33	30	34	90
—New York (N.L.)...................	8	3	.727	5.38	19	14	0	0	0	85 1/3	69	52	51	49	85
2000—Houston (N.L.)■	3	7	.300	5.40	50	16	0	0	16	125	127	80	75	61	142
Major League totals (2 years).......	11	10	.524	5.39	69	30	0	0	16	210 1/3	196	132	126	110	227

DIVISION SERIES RECORD

Year League	W	L	Pct.	ERA	G	GS	CG	ShO	Sv.	IP	H	R	ER	BB	SO
1999—New York (N.L.).................	0	0	...	54.00	1	0	0	0	0	1/3	1	2	2	2	0

CHAMPIONSHIP SERIES RECORD

Year League	W	L	Pct.	ERA	G	GS	CG	ShO	Sv.	IP	H	R	ER	BB	SO
1999—New York (N.L.).................	1	0	1.000	3.00	1	0	0	0	0	3	4	1	1	2	5

D

DOWNS, SCOTT — P — EXPOS

PERSONAL: Born March 17, 1976, in Louisville, Ky. ... 6-2/190. ... Throws left, bats left. ... Full name: Scott Jeremy Downs.
HIGH SCHOOL: Pleasure Ridge Park (Louisville, Ky.).
COLLEGE: Kentucky.
TRANSACTIONS/CAREER NOTES: Selected by Chicago Cubs organization in third round of free-agent draft (June 3, 1997). ... Traded by Cubs to Minnesota Twins (November 3, 1998), completing deal in which Twins traded P Mike Morgan to Cubs for cash and a player to be named later (August 25, 1998). ... Traded by Twins with P Rick Aguilera to Cubs for P Kyle Lohse and P Jason Ryan (May 21, 1999). ... Traded by Cubs to Montreal Expos for OF Rondell White (July 31, 2000). ... On Montreal disabled list (August 9, 2000-remainder of season).

Year League	W	L	Pct.	ERA	G	GS	CG	ShO	Sv.	IP	H	R	ER	BB	SO
1997—Williamsport (NY-Penn)	0	2	.000	2.74	5	5	0	0	0	23	15	11	7	7	28
—Rockford (Midw.)	3	0	1.000	1.25	5	5	0	0	0	36	17	5	5	8	43
1998—Daytona (FSL)	8	9	.471	3.90	27	27	2	0	0	161 2/3	179	83	70	55	117
1999—New Britain (East.)■	0	0	...	8.69	6	3	0	0	0	19 2/3	33	21	19	10	22
—Fort Myers (Fla.)	0	1	.000	0.00	2	2	0	0	0	9 2/3	7	3	0	6	9
—Daytona (FSL)■	5	0	1.000	1.88	7	7	1	1	0	48	41	12	10	11	41
—West Tenn (Sou.)	8	1	.889	1.35	13	12	1	0	0	80	56	13	12	28	101
2000—Chicago (N.L.)	4	3	.571	5.17	18	18	0	0	0	94	117	59	54	37	63
—Montreal (N.L.)■...............	0	0	...	9.00	1	1	0	0	0	3	5	3	3	3	0
Major League totals (1 year)........	4	3	.571	5.29	19	19	0	0	0	97	122	62	57	40	63

DRANSFELDT, KELLY — SS — RANGERS

PERSONAL: Born April 16, 1975, in Joliet, Ill. ... 6-2/195. ... Bats right, throws right. ... Full name: Kelly Daniel Dransfeldt.
HIGH SCHOOL: Morris (Ill.).
COLLEGE: Michigan.
TRANSACTIONS/CAREER NOTES: Selected by Texas Rangers organization in fourth round of free-agent draft (June 4, 1996). ... On Oklahoma disabled list (June 29-July 7, 1999).
STATISTICAL NOTES: Led New York-Pennsylvania League shortstops with 391 total chances in 1996. ... Led Florida State League shortstops with 227 putouts and 85 double plays in 1997. ... Led Pacific Coast League shortstops with 86 double plays in 2000.

Year Team (League)	Pos.	G	AB	R	H	2B	3B	HR	RBI	Avg.	BB	SO	SB	PO	A	E	Avg.
1996—Hudson Valley (NY-P).	SS	75	284	42	67	17	1	7	29	.236	27	76	13	*117	*253	*21	.946
1997—Charlotte (FSL)..........	SS-3B	135	466	64	106	20	7	6	58	.227	42	115	25	†227	369	36	.943
1998—Charlotte (FSL)..........	SS	67	245	46	79	17	0	18	76	.322	29	67	7	100	205	19	.941
—Tulsa (Texas)	SS	58	226	43	57	15	4	9	36	.252	18	79	8	81	184	14	.950

Year	Team (League)	Pos.	G	AB	R	H	2B	3B	HR	RBI	Avg.	BB	SO	SB	PO	A	E	Avg.
1999—	Oklahoma (PCL)	SS-2B-DH	102	359	55	85	21	2	10	44	.237	24	108	6	162	297	19	.960
—	Texas (A.L.)	SS	16	53	3	10	1	0	1	5	.189	3	12	0	31	54	3	.966
2000—	Oklahoma (PCL)	SS	117	441	60	109	22	3	8	42	.247	38	123	10	208	345	22	.962
—	Texas (A.L.)	SS-2B	16	26	2	3	2	0	0	2	.115	1	14	0	13	29	0	1.000
Major League totals (2 years)			32	79	5	13	3	0	1	7	.165	4	26	0	44	83	3	.977

DREIFORT, DARREN — P — DODGERS

PERSONAL: Born May 3, 1972, in Wichita, Kan. ... 6-2/211. ... Throws right, bats right. ... Full name: Darren John Dreifort. ... Name pronounced DRY-fert.
HIGH SCHOOL: Wichita (Kan.) Heights.
COLLEGE: Wichita State.
TRANSACTIONS/CAREER NOTES: Selected by New York Mets organization in 11th round of free-agent draft (June 4, 1990); did not sign. ... Selected by Los Angeles Dodgers organization in first round (second pick overall) of free-agent draft (June 3, 1993). ... On San Antonio disabled list (July 7-28, 1994). ... On Albuquerque disabled list (August 27, 1994-remainder of season). ... On disabled list (April 23, 1995-entire season). ... On Los Angeles disabled list (March 25-May 16, 1996); included rehabilitation assignment to Albuquerque (April 18-May 15). ... On Los Angeles disabled list (May 12-June 17, 1997); included rehabilitation assignment to Albuquerque (June 11-17). ... Granted free agency (October 30, 2000). ... Re-signed by Dodgers (December 11, 2000).
HONORS: Named righthanded pitcher on The Sporting News college All-America team (1992-93). ... Named Golden Spikes Award winner by USA Baseball (1993).
STATISTICAL NOTES: Tied for N.L. lead with four balks in 1999.
MISCELLANEOUS: Member of 1992 U.S. Olympic baseball team. ... Singled with an RBI in one game as pinch hitter with Los Angeles (1994). ... Made an out in only appearance as pinch hitter with Los Angeles (1996). ... Received a base on balls in only appearance as pinch hitter (1998).

Year	League	W	L	Pct.	ERA	G	GS	CG	ShO	Sv.	IP	H	R	ER	BB	SO
1994—	Los Angeles (N.L.)	0	5	.000	6.21	27	0	0	0	6	29	45	21	20	15	22
—	San Antonio (Texas)	3	1	.750	2.80	8	8	0	0	0	35 1/3	36	14	11	13	32
—	Albuquerque (PCL)	1	0	1.000	5.68	1	1	0	0	0	6 1/3	8	4	4	3	3
1995—	Los Angeles (N.L.)							Did not play.								
1996—	Albuquerque (PCL)	5	6	.455	4.17	18	18	0	0	0	86 1/3	88	49	40	52	75
—	Los Angeles (N.L.)	1	4	.200	4.94	19	0	0	0	0	23 2/3	23	13	13	12	24
1997—	Los Angeles (N.L.)	5	2	.714	2.86	48	0	0	0	4	63	45	21	20	34	63
—	Albuquerque (PCL)	0	0	...	1.59	2	2	0	0	0	5 2/3	2	1	1	1	3
1998—	Los Angeles (N.L.)	8	12	.400	4.00	32	26	1	1	0	180	171	84	80	57	168
1999—	Los Angeles (N.L.)	13	13	.500	4.79	30	29	1	1	0	178 2/3	177	105	95	76	140
2000—	Los Angeles (N.L.)	12	9	.571	4.16	32	32	1	1	0	192 2/3	175	105	89	87	164
Major League totals (6 years)		39	45	.464	4.28	188	87	3	3	10	667	636	349	317	281	581

DIVISION SERIES RECORD

Year	League	W	L	Pct.	ERA	G	GS	CG	ShO	Sv.	IP	H	R	ER	BB	SO
1996—	Los Angeles (N.L.)	0	0	...	0.00	1	0	0	0	0	2/3	0	0	0	0	0

DREW, J.D. — OF — CARDINALS

PERSONAL: Born November 20, 1975, in Valdosta, Ga. ... 6-1/195. ... Bats left, throws right. ... Full name: David Jonathan Drew. ... Brother of Tim Drew, pitcher, Cleveland Indians organization.
HIGH SCHOOL: Lowndes County (Hahira, Ga.).
COLLEGE: Florida State.
TRANSACTIONS/CAREER NOTES: Selected by San Francisco Giants organization in 20th round of free-agent draft (June 2, 1994); did not sign. ... Selected by Philadelphia Phillies organization in first round (second pick overall) of free-agent draft (June 3, 1997); did not sign. ... Selected by St. Louis Cardinals organization in first round (fifth pick overall) of free-agent draft (June 2, 1998). ... On Arkansas disabled list (July 21-August 6, 1998). ... On St. Louis disabled list (May 16-June 17, 1999); included rehabilitation assignment to Memphis (May 28-June 17). ... On disabled list (July 8-27, 2000).
HONORS: Named Golden Spikes Award winner by USA Baseball (1997). ... Named college Player of the Year by The Sporting News (1997). ... Named outfielder on The Sporting News college All-America team (1997).
STATISTICAL NOTES: Led N.L. outfielders with six double plays in 1999. ... Career major league grand slams: 1.

Year	Team (League)	Pos.	G	AB	R	H	2B	3B	HR	RBI	Avg.	BB	SO	SB	PO	A	E	Avg.
1997—	St. Paul (Nor.)	OF	44	170	51	58	6	1	18	50	.341	30	40	5	...	...	...	...
1998—	St. Paul (Nor.)	OF	30	114	27	44	11	2	9	33	.386	21	32	8	...	...	...	...
—	Arkansas (Texas)■	OF	19	67	18	22	3	1	5	11	.328	13	15	2	46	2	1	.980
—	Memphis (PCL)	OF	26	79	15	25	8	1	2	13	.316	22	18	1	54	3	2	.966
—	St. Louis (N.L.)	OF	14	36	9	15	3	1	5	13	.417	4	10	0	19	1	0	1.000
1999—	St. Louis (N.L.)	OF	104	368	72	89	16	6	13	39	.242	50	77	19	235	9	7	.972
—	Memphis (PCL)	OF	25	87	11	26	5	1	2	15	.299	8	20	6	44	2	0	1.000
2000—	St. Louis (N.L.)	OF	135	407	73	120	17	2	18	57	.295	67	99	17	248	6	6	.966
Major League totals (3 years)			253	811	154	224	36	9	36	109	.276	121	186	36	502	16	16	.970

DIVISION SERIES RECORD

Year	Team (League)	Pos.	G	AB	R	H	2B	3B	HR	RBI	Avg.	BB	SO	SB	PO	A	E	Avg.
2000—	St. Louis (N.L.)	OF	2	6	1	1	0	0	0	0	.167	2	1	2	2	0	0	1.000

CHAMPIONSHIP SERIES RECORD

Year	Team (League)	Pos.	G	AB	R	H	2B	3B	HR	RBI	Avg.	BB	SO	SB	PO	A	E	Avg.
2000—	St. Louis (N.L.)	OF-PH	5	12	2	4	1	0	0	1	.333	0	3	0	7	0	0	1.000

D

DREW, TIM — P — INDIANS

PERSONAL: Born August 31, 1978, in Valdosta, Ga. ... 6-1/195. ... Throws right, bats right. ... Full name: Timothy Andrew Drew. ... Brother of J.D. Drew, outfielder, St. Louis Cardinals.
HIGH SCHOOL: Lowndes County (Hahira, Ga.).
TRANSACTIONS/CAREER NOTES: Selected by Cleveland Indians organization in first round (28th pick overall) of free-agent draft (June 3, 1997).

Year League	W	L	Pct.	ERA	G	GS	CG	ShO	Sv.	IP	H	R	ER	BB	SO
1997—Burlington (Appl.)	0	1	.000	6.17	4	4	0	0	0	11²/₃	16	15	8	4	14
—Watertown (NY-Penn)	0	0	...	1.93	1	1	0	0	0	4²/₃	4	1	1	3	9
1998—Columbus (S.Atl.)	4	3	.571	3.79	13	13	0	0	0	71¹/₃	68	43	30	26	64
—Kinston (Caro.)	3	8	.273	5.20	15	15	0	0	0	90	105	58	52	31	67
1999—Kinston (Caro.)	13	5	*.722	3.73	28	*28	2	0	0	169	154	79	70	60	125
2000—Akron (East.)	3	2	.600	2.42	9	9	0	0	0	52	41	19	14	15	22
—Cleveland (A.L.)	1	0	1.000	10.00	3	3	0	0	0	9	17	12	10	8	5
—Buffalo (I.L.)	7	8	.467	5.87	16	16	2	0	0	95	122	69	62	31	53
Major League totals (1 year)	1	0	1.000	10.00	3	3	0	0	0	9	17	12	10	8	5

DuBOSE, ERIC — P — TIGERS

PERSONAL: Born May 15, 1976, in Bradenton, Fla. ... 6-3/215. ... Throws left, bats left. ... Full name: Eric Ladell DuBose.
HIGH SCHOOL: Patrician Academy (Butler, Ala.).
COLLEGE: Mississippi State.
TRANSACTIONS/CAREER NOTES: Selected by Oakland Athletics organization in first round (21st pick overall) of free-agent draft (June 3, 1997); pick received as compensation for Baltimore Orioles signing SS Mike Bordick. ... On Midland disabled list (June 18-July 23, 1999). ... On Midland disabled list (April 14-June 13, 2000). ... Claimed on waivers by Cleveland Indians (September 8, 2000). ... Claimed on waivers by Detroit Tigers (September 22, 2000).

Year League	W	L	Pct.	ERA	G	GS	CG	ShO	Sv.	IP	H	R	ER	BB	SO
1997—Southern Oregon (N'West).	1	0	1.000	0.00	3	1	0	0	0	10	5	0	0	6	15
—Visalia (Calif.)	1	3	.250	7.04	10	9	0	0	0	38¹/₃	43	37	30	28	39
1998—Visalia (Calif.)	6	1	.857	3.38	17	10	0	0	1	72	56	34	27	25	85
—Huntsville (Sou.)	7	6	.538	2.70	14	14	1	1	0	83¹/₃	86	37	25	34	66
1999—Midland (Texas)	4	2	.667	5.49	21	14	0	0	1	77	89	57	47	44	68
2000—Midland (Texas)	5	1	.833	4.13	18	0	0	0	1	28¹/₃	25	16	13	18	20
—Visalia (Calif.)	0	1	.000	1.69	5	0	0	0	1	10²/₃	8	2	2	5	12

DUCEY, ROB — OF — PHILLIES

PERSONAL: Born May 24, 1965, in Toronto. ... 6-2/183. ... Bats left, throws right. ... Full name: Robert Thomas Ducey.
HIGH SCHOOL: Glenview Park (Toronto).
JUNIOR COLLEGE: Seminole Community College (Fla.).
TRANSACTIONS/CAREER NOTES: Signed as non-drafted free agent by Toronto Blue Jays organization (May 16, 1984). ... On Toronto disabled list (June 9-September 2, 1989); included rehabilitation assignments to Syracuse (July 5-14 and August 24-September 2). ... Traded by Blue Jays with C Greg Myers to California Angels for P Mark Eichhorn (July 30, 1992). ... Released by Angels (November 19, 1992). ... Signed by Texas Rangers organization (December 18, 1992). ... On Oklahoma City disabled list (April 21-May 16, 1993). ... Contract purchased by Nippon Ham Fighters of Japan Pacific League from Rangers (October 14, 1994). ... Signed by Seattle Mariners organization (January 22, 1997). ... On Seattle disabled list (August 3-21, 1997). ... On disabled list (March 27-April 20, 1998). ... Granted free agency (December 21, 1998). ... Signed by Philadelphia Phillies (December 22, 1998). ... Traded by Phillies to Blue Jays for a player to be named later (July 26, 2000); Phillies acquired P John Sneed to complete deal (July 31, 2000). ... Traded by Blue Jays to Phillies (August 7, 2000), completing deal in which Phillies traded 2B Mickey Morandini to Blue Jays for a player to be named later (August 6, 2000).
STATISTICAL NOTES: Tied for Southern League lead in double plays by outfielder with six in 1986. ... Tied for International League lead in double plays by outfielder with four in 1990.

Year Team (League)	Pos.	G	AB	R	H	2B	3B	HR	RBI	Avg.	BB	SO	SB	PO	A	E	Avg.
1984—Medicine Hat (Pio.)	OF-1B	63	235	49	71	10	3	12	49	.302	41	61	13	185	11	6	.970
1985—Florence (S.Atl.)	OF-1B	134	529	78	133	22	2	13	86	.251	49	103	12	228	8	9	.963
1986—Ventura (Calif.)	OF-1B	47	178	36	60	11	3	12	38	.337	21	24	17	97	3	2	.980
—Knoxville (Sou.)	OF	88	344	49	106	22	3	11	58	.308	29	59	7	186	10	6	.970
1987—Syracuse (I.L.)	OF	100	359	62	102	14	•10	10	60	.284	61	89	8	171	13	6	.968
—Toronto (A.L.)	OF-DH	34	48	12	9	1	0	1	6	.188	8	10	2	31	0	0	1.000
1988—Syracuse (I.L.)	OF	90	317	40	81	14	4	7	42	.256	43	81	7	233	6	4	.984
—Toronto (A.L.)	OF-DH	27	54	15	17	4	1	0	6	.315	5	7	1	35	1	0	1.000
1989—Toronto (A.L.)	OF-DH	41	76	5	16	4	0	0	7	.211	9	25	2	56	3	0	1.000
—Syracuse (I.L.)	OF	10	29	0	3	0	1	0	3	.103	10	13	0	14	0	1	.933
1990—Syracuse (I.L.)	OF	127	438	53	117	32	7	7	47	.267	60	87	13	262	13	13	.955
—Toronto (A.L.)	OF	19	53	7	16	5	0	0	7	.302	7	15	1	37	0	0	1.000
1991—Syracuse (I.L.)	OF	72	266	53	78	10	3	8	40	.293	51	58	5	120	1	0	1.000
—Toronto (A.L.)	OF-DH	39	68	8	16	2	2	1	4	.235	6	26	2	32	1	4	.892
1992—Toronto (A.L.)	OF-DH	23	21	3	1	1	0	0	0	.048	0	10	0	11	0	0	1.000
—California (A.L.)■	OF-DH	31	59	4	14	3	0	0	2	.237	5	12	2	32	2	2	.944
1993—Okla. City (A.A.)■	OF	105	389	68	118	17	•10	17	56	.303	46	97	17	244	8	7	.973
—Texas (A.L.)	OF	27	85	15	24	6	3	2	9	.282	10	17	2	51	1	0	1.000
1994—Oklahoma City (A.A.).	OF-DH	115	403	69	108	27	9	17	65	.268	75	91	9	221	9	4	.983
—Texas (A.L.)	OF	11	29	1	5	1	0	0	1	.172	2	1	0	15	0	2	.882
1995—Nippon (Jap. Pac.)■ ..		117	425	61	106	19	4	25	61	.249	54	103	7	...	...	...	...
1996—Nippon (Jap. Pac.) ...	OF	120	427	68	105	17	5	26	59	.246	86	90	3	...	...	...	...
1997—Tacoma (PCL)■	OF	23	74	8	24	8	0	0	11	.324	8	15	0	44	3	3	.940
—Seattle (A.L.)	OF	76	143	25	41	15	2	5	10	.287	6	31	3	66	3	1	.986

Year Team (League)	Pos.	G	AB	R	H	2B	3B	HR	RBI	Avg.	BB	SO	SB	PO	A	E	Avg.
						BATTING								FIELDING			
1998—Seattle (A.L.)	OF	97	217	30	52	18	2	5	23	.240	23	61	4	127	4	4	.970
1999—Philadelphia (N.L.)■ ..	OF-DH	104	188	29	49	10	2	8	33	.261	38	57	2	89	1	0	1.000
2000—Philadelphia (N.L.)......	OF-DH	112	152	24	30	4	1	6	25	.197	29	47	1	44	1	3	.938
—Toronto (A.L.)■.........	OF	5	13	2	2	1	0	0	1	.154	2	2	0	8	0	1	.889
American League totals (11 years)		430	866	127	213	61	10	14	76	.246	83	217	19	501	15	14	.974
National League totals (2 years)		216	340	53	79	14	3	14	58	.232	67	104	3	133	2	3	.978
Major League totals (12 years)		646	1206	180	292	75	13	28	134	.242	150	321	22	634	17	17	.975

DIVISION SERIES RECORD

Year Team (League)	Pos.	G	AB	R	H	2B	3B	HR	RBI	Avg.	BB	SO	SB	PO	A	E	Avg.
						BATTING								FIELDING			
1997—Seattle (A.L.)	PH-OF	2	4	0	2	0	0	0	1	.500	0	0	0	0	0	0	...

CHAMPIONSHIP SERIES RECORD

Year Team (League)	Pos.	G	AB	R	H	2B	3B	HR	RBI	Avg.	BB	SO	SB	PO	A	E	Avg.
						BATTING								FIELDING			
1989—Toronto (A.L.).............								Did not play.									
1991—Toronto (A.L.).............	PR-OF	1	1	0	0	0	0	0	0	.000	0	0	0	0	0	0	...

DUCKWORTH, BRANDON　　　P　　　PHILLIES

PERSONAL: Born January 23, 1976, in Salt Lake City, Utah. ... 6-2/185. ... Throws right, bats both. ... Full name: Brandon J. Duckworth.
HIGH SCHOOL: Kearns (Utah).
JUNIOR COLLEGE: College of Southern Idaho.
COLLEGE: Cal State Fullerton.
TRANSACTIONS/CAREER NOTES: Selected by Toronto Blue Jays organization in 30th round of free-agent draft (June 1, 1995); did not sign. ... Selected by Arizona Diamondbacks organization in 61st round of free-agent draft (June 4, 1996); did not sign. ... Signed by Philadelphia Phillies organization as non-drafted free agent (August 13, 1997).

Year League	W	L	Pct.	ERA	G	GS	CG	ShO	Sv.	IP	H	R	ER	BB	SO
1998—Piedmont (S.Atl.)...............	9	8	.529	2.80	21	21	•5	•3	0	147 2/3	116	58	46	24	119
—Clearwater (FSL)	6	2	.750	3.74	9	9	1	1	0	53	64	25	22	22	46
1999—Clearwater (FSL)	11	5	.688	4.84	27	17	0	0	1	132	164	84	71	40	101
2000—Reading (East.).................	13	7	.650	3.16	27	27	1	0	0	165	145	70	58	52	178

DUNCAN, COURTNEY　　　P　　　CUBS

PERSONAL: Born October 9, 1974, in Mobile, Ala. ... 6-0/180. ... Throws right, bats left. ... Full name: Courtney Demond Duncan.
HIGH SCHOOL: Daphne (Ala.).
COLLEGE: Grambling State.
TRANSACTIONS/CAREER NOTES: Selected by Chicago Cubs organization in 20th round of free-agent draft (June 2, 1996). ... On West Tenn disabled list (June 10-24, 1999).

Year League	W	L	Pct.	ERA	G	GS	CG	ShO	Sv.	IP	H	R	ER	BB	SO
1996—Williamsport (NY-Penn)	*11	1	*.917	2.19	15	•15	1	0	0	90 1/3	58	28	22	34	91
1997—Daytona (FSL)	8	4	.667	*1.63	19	19	1	0	0	121 2/3	90	35	22	35	120
—Orlando (Sou.)	2	2	.500	3.40	8	8	0	0	0	45	37	28	17	29	45
1998—West Tenn (Sou.)	7	9	.438	4.26	29	•29	0	0	0	162 2/3	141	89	77	*108	157
1999—West Tenn (Sou.)	1	7	.125	7.13	11	8	0	0	0	41 2/3	44	42	33	42	42
—Daytona (FSL)	4	5	.444	5.54	15	11	1	1	1	65	70	60	40	34	48
2000—West Tenn (Sou.)	5	4	.556	3.07	61	0	0	0	25	73 1/3	57	32	25	33	72

DUNN, ADAM　　　OF　　　REDS

PERSONAL: Born November 9, 1979, in Houston. ... 6-6/235. ... Bats left, throws right. ... Full name: Adam Troy Dunn.
HIGH SCHOOL: New Caney (Texas).
COLLEGE: Texas.
TRANSACTIONS/CAREER NOTES: Selected by Cincinnati Reds organization in second round of free-agent draft (June 2, 1998). ... On Clinton disabled list (June 8-25, 2000).

Year Team (League)	Pos.	G	AB	R	H	2B	3B	HR	RBI	Avg.	BB	SO	SB	PO	A	E	Avg.
						BATTING								FIELDING			
1998—Billings (Pio.)	OF	34	125	26	36	3	1	4	13	.288	22	33	4	35	2	6	.860
1999—Rockford (Midw.)	OF	93	313	62	96	16	2	11	44	.307	46	64	21	85	5	8	.918
2000—Dayton (Midw.)	OF	122	420	101	118	29	1	16	79	.281	100	101	24	197	10	9	.958

DUNSTON, SHAWON　　　OF/IF　　　GIANTS

PERSONAL: Born March 21, 1963, in Brooklyn, N.Y. ... 6-1/180. ... Bats right, throws right. ... Full name: Shawon Donnell Dunston.
HIGH SCHOOL: Thomas Jefferson (Brooklyn, N.Y.).
TRANSACTIONS/CAREER NOTES: Selected by Chicago Cubs organization in first round (first pick overall) of free-agent draft (June 7, 1982). ... On disabled list (May 31-June 10, 1983). ... On Chicago disabled list (June 16-August 21, 1987); included rehabilitation assignment to Iowa (August 14-21). ... On disabled list (May 5, 1992-remainder of season and March 27-September 1, 1993). ... On suspended list (September 8-12, 1995). ... Granted free agency (October 31, 1995). ... Signed by San Francisco Giants (January 9, 1996). ... On disabled list (April 24-May 13 and August 5-October 1, 1996). ... Granted free agency (November 18, 1996). ... Signed by Cubs (December 7, 1996). ... On Chicago disabled list (June 9-24, 1997). ... Traded by Cubs to Pittsburgh Pirates for a player to be named later (August 31, 1997). ... Granted free agency (October 28, 1997). ... Signed by Cleveland Indians (February 16, 1998). ... Traded by Indians with P Jose Mesa and P Alvin Morman

to Giants for P Steve Reed and OF Jacob Cruz (July 23, 1998). ... Granted free agency (October 23, 1998). ... Signed by St. Louis Cardinals (February 16, 1999). ... On suspended list (June 17-20, 1999). ... On St. Louis disabled list (June 23-July 9, 1999). ... Traded by Cardinals to New York Mets for IF Craig Paquette (July 31, 1999). ... Granted free agency (October 29, 1999). ... Signed by Cardinals organization (February 3, 2000). ... Granted free agency (October 27, 2000). ... Signed by Giants (December 8, 2000).

RECORDS: Shares modern major league single-game record for most triples—3 (July 28, 1990).

HONORS: Named shortstop on THE SPORTING NEWS N.L. All-Star team (1989).

STATISTICAL NOTES: Led N.L. shortstops with 817 total chances and tied for lead in double plays with 96 in 1986. ... Career major league grand slams: 5.

Year Team (League)	Pos.	G	AB	R	H	2B	3B	HR	RBI	Avg.	BB	SO	SB	PO	A	E	Avg.
										BATTING					FIELDING		
1982— GC Cubs (GCL)..........	SS-3B	53	190	27	61	11	0	2	28	.321	11	22	32	61	129	24	.888
1983— Quad Cities (Midw.).....	SS	117	455	65	141	17	8	4	62	.310	7	51	58	172	326	47	.914
1984— Midland (Texas)..........	SS	73	298	44	98	13	3	3	34	.329	11	38	11	164	203	32	.920
— Iowa (A.A.)	SS	61	210	25	49	11	1	7	27	.233	4	40	9	90	165	26	.907
1985— Chicago (N.L.)..........	SS	74	250	40	65	12	4	4	18	.260	19	42	11	144	248	17	.958
— Iowa (A.A.)	SS	73	272	24	73	9	6	2	28	.268	5	48	17	138	176	12	.963
1986— Chicago (N.L.)..........	SS	150	581	66	145	37	3	17	68	.250	21	114	13	*320	*465	*32	.961
1987— Chicago (N.L.)..........	SS	95	346	40	85	18	3	5	22	.246	10	68	12	160	271	14	.969
— Iowa (A.A.)	SS	5	19	1	8	1	0	0	2	.421	0	3	1	6	12	1	.947
1988— Chicago (N.L.)..........	SS	155	575	69	143	23	6	9	56	.249	16	108	30	*257	455	20	.973
1989— Chicago (N.L.)..........	SS	138	471	52	131	20	6	9	60	.278	30	86	19	213	379	17	.972
1990— Chicago (N.L.)..........	SS	146	545	73	143	22	8	17	66	.262	15	87	25	255	392	20	.970
1991— Chicago (N.L.)..........	SS	142	492	59	128	22	7	12	50	.260	23	64	21	*261	383	21	.968
1992— Chicago (N.L.)..........	SS	18	73	8	23	3	1	0	2	.315	3	13	2	28	42	1	.986
1993— Chicago (N.L.)..........	SS	7	10	3	4	2	0	0	2	.400	0	1	0	5	0	0	1.000
1994— Chicago (N.L.)..........	SS	88	331	38	92	19	0	11	35	.278	16	48	3	121	218	12	.966
1995— Chicago (N.L.)..........	SS	127	477	58	141	30	6	14	69	.296	10	75	10	187	336	17	.969
1996— San Fran. (N.L.)■......	SS	82	287	27	86	12	2	5	25	.300	13	40	8	116	217	15	.957
1997— Chicago (N.L.)■......	SS-OF	114	419	57	119	18	4	9	41	.284	8	64	29	179	227	12	.971
— Pittsburgh (N.L.)■......	SS	18	71	14	28	4	1	5	16	.394	0	11	3	28	55	3	.965
1998— Cleveland (A.L.)■......	2-S-O-D	62	156	26	37	11	3	3	12	.237	6	18	9	63	76	4	.972
— San Fran. (N.L.)■......	SS-OF-2B	36	51	10	9	2	0	3	8	.176	0	10	0	20	5	2	.926
1999— St. Louis (N.L.)■......	O-1-S-3-D	62	150	23	46	5	2	5	25	.307	2	23	6	78	23	2	.981
— New York (N.L.)■......	OF-3B	42	93	12	32	6	1	0	16	.344	0	16	4	44	2	1	.979
2000— St. Louis (N.L.)■......	O-S-1-3-D	98	216	28	54	11	2	12	43	.250	6	47	3	110	10	2	.984
American League totals (1 year)		62	156	26	37	11	3	3	12	.237	6	18	9	63	76	4	.972
National League totals (16 years)		1592	5438	677	1474	266	56	137	622	.271	192	917	199	2526	3728	208	.968
Major League totals (16 years)		1654	5594	703	1511	277	59	140	634	.270	198	935	208	2589	3804	212	.968

DIVISION SERIES RECORD

Year Team (League)	Pos.	G	AB	R	H	2B	3B	HR	RBI	Avg.	BB	SO	SB	PO	A	E	Avg.
										BATTING					FIELDING		
1999— New York (N.L.)..........	OF-PH-PR	4	6	0	1	0	0	0	0	.167	0	1	0	7	0	0	1.000
2000— St. Louis (N.L.)..........	PH	1	1	0	1	0	0	0	0	1.000	0	0	0	...	...	...	...
Division series totals (2 years)		5	7	0	2	0	0	0	0	.286	0	1	0	7	0	0	1.000

CHAMPIONSHIP SERIES RECORD

Year Team (League)	Pos.	G	AB	R	H	2B	3B	HR	RBI	Avg.	BB	SO	SB	PO	A	E	Avg.
										BATTING					FIELDING		
1989— Chicago (N.L.)..........	SS	5	19	2	6	0	0	0	0	.316	1	1	1	10	14	1	.960
1999— New York (N.L.)..........	PH-OF	5	7	2	1	0	0	0	0	.143	0	2	1	0	0	0	...
2000— St. Louis (N.L.)..........	PH-OF	4	6	1	2	1	0	0	0	.333	0	0	0	1	0	0	1.000
Championship series totals (3 years)		14	32	5	9	1	0	0	0	.281	1	3	2	11	14	1	.962

ALL-STAR GAME RECORD

Year League	Pos.	AB	R	H	2B	3B	HR	RBI	Avg.	BB	SO	SB	PO	A	E	Avg.
						BATTING							FIELDING			
1988— National								Did not play.								
1990— National	SS	2	0	0	0	0	0	0	.000	0	0	0	0	0	0	...

DUNWOODY, TODD   OF   CUBS

PERSONAL: Born April 11, 1975, in Lafayette, Ind. ... 6-1/205. ... Bats left, throws left. ... Full name: Todd Franklin Dunwoody.

HIGH SCHOOL: West Lafayette (Ind.) Harrison.

TRANSACTIONS/CAREER NOTES: Selected by Florida Marlins organization in seventh round of free-agent draft (June 3, 1993). ... On Charlotte disabled list (April 11-18, 1998). ... Traded by Marlins to Kansas City Royals for IF Sean McNally (December 15, 1999). ... On Kansas City disabled list (March 24-June 3, 2000); included rehabilitation assignments to Omaha (May 13-20 and June 1-3). ... Granted free agency (December 21, 2000). ... Signed by Chicago Cubs organization (January 9, 2001).

STATISTICAL NOTES: Led Eastern League with 267 total bases in 1996.

Year Team (League)	Pos.	G	AB	R	H	2B	3B	HR	RBI	Avg.	BB	SO	SB	PO	A	E	Avg.
										BATTING					FIELDING		
1993— GC Marlins (GCL).......	OF	31	109	13	21	2	2	0	7	.193	7	28	5	45	1	1	.979
1994— GC Marlins (GCL).......	OF	46	169	32	44	6	6	1	25	.260	21	28	11	91	1	1	.989
— Kane County (Midw.)..	OF	15	45	7	5	0	0	1	1	.111	5	17	1	21	2	0	1.000
1995— Kane County (Midw.)..	OF	132	494	89	140	20	8	14	89	.283	52	105	39	284	6	5	.983
1996— Portland (East.).........	OF	138	*552	88	153	30	6	24	93	.277	45	*149	24	254	2	1	*.996
1997— Charlotte (I.L.)...........	OF-DH	107	401	74	105	16	7	23	62	.262	39	129	25	231	5	2	.992
— Florida (N.L.).............	OF	19	50	7	13	2	2	2	7	.260	7	21	2	26	0	2	.929
1998— Charlotte (I.L.)...........	OF	28	102	20	31	6	3	6	22	.304	12	28	4	76	2	1	.987
— Florida (N.L.).............	OF	116	434	53	109	27	7	5	28	.251	21	113	5	273	9	3	.989

Year	Team (League)	Pos.	G	AB	R	H	2B	3B	HR	RBI	Avg.	BB	SO	SB	PO	A	E	Avg.
1999—	Florida (N.L.)	OF	64	186	20	41	6	3	2	20	.220	12	41	3	102	3	2	.981
	— Calgary (PCL)	OF-DH	65	246	35	67	16	7	9	36	.272	10	56	7	159	10	4	.977
2000—	Omaha (PCL)■	OF	9	31	5	10	1	0	1	5	.323	4	8	1	11	0	0	1.000
	— Kansas City (A.L.)	OF-DH	61	178	12	37	9	0	1	23	.208	8	42	3	81	0	2	.976
American League totals (1 year)			61	178	12	37	9	0	1	23	.208	8	42	3	81	0	2	.976
National League totals (3 years)			199	670	80	163	35	12	9	55	.243	40	175	10	401	12	7	.983
Major League totals (4 years)			260	848	92	200	44	12	10	78	.236	48	217	13	482	12	9	.982

DURAZO, ERUBIEL — 1B — DIAMONDBACKS

PERSONAL: Born January 23, 1974, in Hermosillo, Mexico. ... 6-3/225. ... Bats left, throws left. ... Full name: Erubiel Durazo Cardenas.
HIGH SCHOOL: Amphitheater (Tucson, Ariz.).
JUNIOR COLLEGE: Pima Community College (Ariz.).
TRANSACTIONS/CAREER NOTES: Signed by Monterrey, Mexican League (1997). ... Contract sold by Monterrey to Arizona Diamondbacks organization (December 16, 1998). ... On Arizona disabled list (May 30-June 24, June 27-July 13 and August 20, 2000-remainder of season); included rehabilitation assignments to Tuscon (June 20-24 and July 8-9) and Arizona League Diamondbacks (July 9-13).
STATISTICAL NOTES: Led Southern League with a .569 slugging percentage in 1999.

Year	Team (League)	Pos.	G	AB	R	H	2B	3B	HR	RBI	Avg.	BB	SO	SB	PO	A	E	Avg.
1997—	Monterrey (Mex.)	1B-OF	110	358	47	101	21	10	8	61	.282	52	43	3	480	48	3	.994
1998—	Monterrey (Mex.)	OF-1B	119	420	84	147	32	2	19	98	.350	99	71	4	219	15	0	1.000
1999—	El Paso (Texas)■	1B	64	226	53	91	18	3	14	55	.403	44	37	2	523	36	10	.982
	— Tucson (PCL)	1B-DH	30	118	27	48	7	0	10	28	.407	14	18	1	241	20	1	.996
	— Arizona (N.L.)	1B	52	155	31	51	4	2	11	30	.329	26	43	1	324	20	0	1.000
2000—	Arizona (N.L.)	1B	67	196	35	52	11	0	8	33	.265	34	43	1	422	23	5	.989
Major League totals (2 years)			119	351	66	103	15	2	19	63	.293	60	86	2	746	43	5	.994

DIVISION SERIES RECORD

Year	Team (League)	Pos.	G	AB	R	H	2B	3B	HR	RBI	Avg.	BB	SO	SB	PO	A	E	Avg.
1999—	Arizona (N.L.)	1B	2	7	1	1	0	0	1	1	.143	1	0	0	15	1	0	1.000

DURBIN, CHAD — P — ROYALS

D

PERSONAL: Born December 3, 1977, in Spring Valley, Ill. ... 6-2/200. ... Throws right, bats right. ... Full name: Chad Griffin Durbin.
HIGH SCHOOL: Woodlawn (Shreveport, La.).
TRANSACTIONS/CAREER NOTES: Selected by Kansas City Royals organization in third round of free-agent draft (June 4, 1996).

Year	League	W	L	Pct.	ERA	G	GS	CG	ShO	Sv.	IP	H	R	ER	BB	SO
1996—	Gulf Coast Royals (GCL) ..	3	2	.600	4.26	11	8	1	1	0	44 $1/3$	34	22	21	25	43
1997—	Lansing (Midw.)	5	8	.385	4.79	26	26	0	0	0	144 $2/3$	157	85	77	53	116
1998—	Wilmington (Caro.)	10	7	.588	2.93	26	26	0	0	0	147 $2/3$	126	57	48	59	162
1999—	Wichita (Texas)	8	10	.444	4.64	28	27	1	1	0	157	154	88	81	49	122
	— Kansas City (A.L.)	0	0	...	0.00	1	0	0	0	0	2 $1/3$	1	0	0	1	3
2000—	Kansas City (A.L.)	2	5	.286	8.21	16	16	0	0	0	72 $1/3$	91	71	66	43	37
	— Omaha (PCL)	4	4	.500	4.46	12	12	0	0	0	72 $2/3$	75	37	36	22	53
Major League totals (2 years)		2	5	.286	7.96	17	16	0	0	0	74 $2/3$	92	71	66	44	40

DURHAM, RAY — 2B — WHITE SOX

PERSONAL: Born November 30, 1971, in Charlotte. ... 5-8/180. ... Bats both, throws right.
HIGH SCHOOL: Harding (Charlotte).
TRANSACTIONS/CAREER NOTES: Selected by Chicago White Sox organization in fifth round of free-agent draft (June 4, 1990). ... On Utica suspended list (April 1-May 22, 1992). ... On Sarasota disabled list (June 16-July 9, 1992).
RECORDS: Holds major league single-season record for fewest putouts by second baseman (150 or more games)—236 (1996).
STATISTICAL NOTES: Led Southern League in caught stealing with 25 in 1993. ... Led Southern League second basemen with 541 total chances in 1993. ... Led American Association with 261 total bases in 1994. ... Led American Association second basemen with 701 total chances and 92 double plays in 1994. ... Led A.L. second basemen with 738 total chances and 128 double plays in 1998. ... Led A.L. second basemen with 126 double plays in 2000. ... Career major league grand slams: 3.

Year	Team (League)	Pos.	G	AB	R	H	2B	3B	HR	RBI	Avg.	BB	SO	SB	PO	A	E	Avg.
1990—	GC White Sox (GCL) ..	2B-SS	35	116	18	32	3	3	0	13	.276	15	36	23	61	85	15	.907
1991—	Utica (NY-Penn)	2B	39	142	29	36	2	7	0	17	.254	25	44	12	54	101	12	.928
	— GC White Sox (GCL) ..	2B	6	23	3	7	1	0	0	4	.304	3	5	5	18	15	0	1.000
1992—	Sarasota (FSL)	2B	57	202	37	55	6	3	0	7	.272	32	36	28	66	107	10	.945
	— GC White Sox (GCL) ..	2B	5	13	3	7	2	0	0	2	.538	3	1	1	4	3	0	1.000
1993—	Birmingham (Sou.).....	2B	137	528	83	143	22	*10	3	37	.271	42	100	39	227	284	*30	.945
1994—	Nashville (A.A.)	2B	133	527	89	156	33	•12	16	66	.296	46	91	34	*254	*429	*19	*.973
1995—	Chicago (A.L.)	2B-DH	125	471	68	121	27	6	7	51	.257	31	83	18	245	298	15	.973
1996—	Chicago (A.L.)	2B-DH	156	557	79	153	33	5	10	65	.275	58	95	30	236	423	11	.984
1997—	Chicago (A.L.)	2B-DH	155	634	106	172	27	5	11	53	.271	61	96	33	270	395	*18	.974
1998—	Chicago (A.L.)	2B	158	635	126	181	35	8	19	67	.285	73	105	36	282	438	18	.976
1999—	Chicago (A.L.)	2B-DH	153	612	109	181	30	8	13	60	.296	73	105	34	305	412	19	.974
2000—	Chicago (A.L.)	2B	151	614	121	172	35	9	17	75	.280	75	105	25	299	419	15	.980
Major League totals (6 years)			898	3523	609	980	187	41	77	371	.278	371	589	176	1637	2385	96	.977

Year Team (League)	Pos.	G	AB	R	H	2B	3B	HR	RBI	Avg.	BB	SO	SB	PO	A	E	Avg.
2000—Chicago (A.L.)	2B	3	10	2	2	1	0	1	1	.200	3	3	0	10	6	0	1.000

(header spanning: BATTING / FIELDING)

ALL-STAR GAME RECORD

Year League	Pos.	AB	R	H	2B	3B	HR	RBI	Avg.	BB	SO	SB	PO	A	E	Avg.
1998—American	2B	1	1	1	0	0	0	1	1.000	0	0	0	0	0	0	...
2000—American	2B	2	1	1	0	0	0	0	.500	0	0	0	1	3	0	1.000
All-Star Game totals (2 years)		3	2	2	0	0	0	1	.667	0	0	0	1	3	0	1.000

DURRINGTON, TRENT — 2B

PERSONAL: Born August 27, 1975, in Sydney, Australia. ... 5-10/188. ... Bats right, throws right. ... Full name: Trent John Durrington.
HIGH SCHOOL: The Southport School (Australia).
TRANSACTIONS/CAREER NOTES: Signed as non-drafted free agent by California Angels organization (April 22, 1994). ... Angels franchise renamed Anaheim Angels for 1997 season. ... On Edmonton disabled list (May 25-August 29, 2000).

Year Team (League)	Pos.	G	AB	R	H	2B	3B	HR	RBI	Avg.	BB	SO	SB	PO	A	E	Avg.
1994—Arizona Angels (Ariz.).	SS-2B	16	52	13	14	3	0	1	2	.269	11	16	5	18	31	5	.907
1995—Boise (N'West)	2B-SS	50	140	23	24	4	1	3	19	.171	17	35	2	70	119	8	.959
1996—Cedar Rapids (Midw.)	2B	25	76	12	19	1	0	0	4	.250	33	20	15	46	48	3	.969
—Boise (N'West)	2B-3B-SS	40	154	38	43	7	2	0	14	.279	31	32	24	87	122	12	.946
1997—Lake Elsinore (Calif.)..	2B-OF-3B	123	409	80	101	21	3	3	36	.247	51	90	52	222	311	17	.969
1998—Midland (Texas)..........	2-0-3-S	112	351	62	79	10	1	1	30	.225	50	74	24	191	241	13	.971
1999—Erie (East.)	2B	107	396	84	114	26	1	3	34	.288	52	66	59	212	312	14	.974
—Anaheim (A.L.)	2B-DH	43	122	14	22	2	0	0	2	.180	9	28	4	73	98	6	.966
2000—Edmonton (PCL)	2B-SS	28	105	19	23	4	1	3	14	.219	16	25	8	59	85	2	.986
—Anaheim (A.L.)	2B	4	3	0	0	0	0	0	0	.000	0	0	0	1	2	0	1.000
Major League totals (2 years)		47	125	14	22	2	0	0	2	.176	9	28	4	74	100	6	.967

D — DUVALL, MIKE — P — DEVIL RAYS

PERSONAL: Born October 11, 1974, in Warrenton, Va. ... 6-0/200. ... Throws left, bats right. ... Full name: Michael Alan Duvall.
HIGH SCHOOL: Fauquier (Warrenton, Va.).
JUNIOR COLLEGE: Potomac State College (W.Va.).
TRANSACTIONS/CAREER NOTES: Selected by Florida Marlins organization in 19th round of free-agent draft (June 1, 1995). ... Selected by Tampa Bay Devil Rays in second round (32nd pick overall) of expansion draft (November 18, 1997). ... On Durham disabled list (April 9-May 13, 1998). ... On Tampa Bay disabled list (June 9-July 6, 1999). ... On Durham disabled list (April 6-20 and August 19-September 1, 2000).

Year League	W	L	Pct.	ERA	G	GS	CG	ShO	Sv.	IP	H	R	ER	BB	SO
1995—Gulf Coast Marlins (GCL) ...	5	0	1.000	2.22	16	1	0	0	1	28 1/3	15	8	7	12	34
1996—Kane County (Midw.)..........	4	1	.800	2.06	41	0	0	0	8	48	43	20	11	21	46
1997—Brevard County (FSL)........	1	0	1.000	0.73	11	0	0	0	6	12 1/3	7	1	1	3	9
—Portland (East.)................	4	6	.400	1.84	45	0	0	0	18	68 1/3	63	20	14	20	49
1998—St. Petersburg (FSL)■	0	0	...	2.70	2	0	0	0	0	3 1/3	4	1	1	2	3
—Durham (I.L.)................	5	3	.625	3.22	32	9	1	0	0	72 2/3	74	31	26	32	55
—Tampa Bay (A.L.)................	0	0	...	6.75	3	0	0	0	0	4	4	3	3	2	1
1999—Tampa Bay (A.L.)................	1	1	.500	4.05	40	0	0	0	0	40	46	21	18	27	18
—Durham (I.L.)................	2	2	.500	5.40	19	1	0	0	2	30	32	20	18	12	27
2000—Durham (I.L.)................	6	2	.750	4.59	30	8	0	0	0	80 1/3	85	47	41	44	49
—Tampa Bay (A.L.)................	0	0	...	7.71	2	0	0	0	0	2 1/3	5	2	2	1	0
Major League totals (3 years)	1	1	.500	4.47	45	0	0	0	0	46 1/3	55	26	23	30	19

DYE, JERMAINE — OF — ROYALS

PERSONAL: Born January 28, 1974, in Vacaville, Calif. ... 6-5/220. ... Bats right, throws right. ... Full name: Jermaine Trevell Dye.
HIGH SCHOOL: Will C. Wood (Vacaville, Calif.).
JUNIOR COLLEGE: Cosumnes River (Calif.) College.
TRANSACTIONS/CAREER NOTES: Selected by Atlanta Braves organization in 17th round of free-agent draft (June 3, 1993). ... On disabled list (July 13-August 9, 1995). ... Traded by Braves with P Jamie Walker to Kansas City Royals for OF Michael Tucker and IF Keith Lockhart (March 27, 1997). ... On Kansas City disabled list (April 17-May 3, 1997; included rehabilitation assignment to Omaha (May 1-3). ... On Kansas City disabled list (July 10-August 13, 1997); included rehabilitation assignment to Omaha (July 27-August 13). ... On Kansas City disabled list (March 23-May 8 and September 1, 1998-remainder of season); included rehabilitation assignment to Omaha (April 21-May 8).
HONORS: Won A.L. Gold Glove as outfielder (2000).
STATISTICAL NOTES: Led South Atlantic League outfielders with six double plays in 1994. ... Led A.L. outfielders with six double plays in 1999. ... Career major league grand slams: 3.
MISCELLANEOUS: Hit home run in first major league at-bat (May 17, 1996).

Year Team (League)	Pos.	G	AB	R	H	2B	3B	HR	RBI	Avg.	BB	SO	SB	PO	A	E	Avg.
1993—GC Braves (GCL)	OF-3B	31	124	17	43	14	0	0	27	.347	5	13	5	46	9	3	.948
—Danville (Appl.)..........	OF	25	94	6	26	6	1	2	12	.277	8	10	19	51	1	2	.963
1994—Macon (S.Atl.)............	OF	135	506	73	151	*41	1	15	98	.298	33	82	19	263	*22	9	.969
1995—Greenville (Sou.)	OF	104	403	50	115	26	4	15	71	.285	27	74	4	234	*22	5	.981
1996—Richmond (I.L.).........	OF	36	142	25	33	7	1	6	19	.232	5	25	3	83	2	4	.955
—Atlanta (N.L.)..............	OF	98	292	32	82	16	0	12	37	.281	8	67	1	150	2	8	.950

Year	Team (League)	Pos.	G	AB	R	H	2B	3B	HR	RBI	Avg.	BB	SO	SB	PO	A	E	Avg.
								BATTING								FIELDING		
1997— Kansas City (A.L.)■ ...		OF	75	263	26	62	14	0	7	22	.236	17	51	2	164	7	6	.966
— Omaha (A.A.)		OF-DH	39	144	21	44	6	0	10	25	.306	9	25	0	41	2	0	1.000
1998— Omaha (PCL)		OF-1B-DH	41	157	29	47	6	0	12	35	.299	19	29	7	119	4	1	.992
— Kansas City (A.L.)		OF	60	214	24	50	5	1	5	23	.234	11	46	2	152	4	2	.987
1999— Kansas City (A.L.)		OF-DH	158	608	96	179	44	8	27	119	.294	58	119	2	362	•17	6	.984
2000— Kansas City (A.L.)		OF-DH	157	601	107	193	41	2	33	118	.321	69	99	0	277	11	7	.976
American League totals (4 years)			450	1686	253	484	104	11	72	282	.287	155	315	6	955	39	21	.979
National League totals (1 year)			98	292	32	82	16	0	12	37	.281	8	67	1	150	2	8	.950
Major League totals (5 years)			548	1978	285	566	120	11	84	319	.286	163	382	7	1105	41	29	.975

DIVISION SERIES RECORD

Year	Team (League)	Pos.	G	AB	R	H	2B	3B	HR	RBI	Avg.	BB	SO	SB	PO	A	E	Avg.
1996— Atlanta (N.L.)		OF	3	11	1	2	0	0	1	1	.182	0	6	1	11	1	0	1.000

RECORDS: Shares N.L. single-game record for most at-bats—6 (October 14, 1996).

CHAMPIONSHIP SERIES RECORD

Year	Team (League)	Pos.	G	AB	R	H	2B	3B	HR	RBI	Avg.	BB	SO	SB	PO	A	E	Avg.
1996— Atlanta (N.L.)		OF	7	28	2	6	1	0	0	4	.214	1	7	0	14	0	0	1.000

WORLD SERIES RECORD

Year	Team (League)	Pos.	G	AB	R	H	2B	3B	HR	RBI	Avg.	BB	SO	SB	PO	A	E	Avg.
1996— Atlanta (N.L.)		OF	5	17	0	2	0	0	0	1	.118	1	1	0	15	0	1	.938

ALL-STAR GAME RECORD

Year	League	Pos.	AB	R	H	2B	3B	HR	RBI	Avg.	BB	SO	SB	PO	A	E	Avg.
2000— American		RF	2	1	0	0	0	0	0	.000	1	1	0	1	0	0	1.000

EASLEY, DAMION — 2B — TIGERS

PERSONAL: Born November 11, 1969, in New York. ... 5-11/185. ... Bats right, throws right. ... Full name: Jacinto Damion Easley.
HIGH SCHOOL: Lakewood (Calif.).
JUNIOR COLLEGE: Long Beach (Calif.) City College.
COLLEGE: Long Beach State.
TRANSACTIONS/CAREER NOTES: Selected by California Angels organization in 30th round of free-agent draft (June 1, 1988). ... On disabled list (June 19-July 4 and July 28, 1993-remainder of season; and May 30-June 17, 1994). ... On California disabled list (April 1-May 10, 1996); included rehabilitation assignment to Vancouver (April 30-May 10). ... Traded by Angels to Detroit Tigers for P Greg Gohr (July 31, 1996). ... On Detroit disabled list (April 10-25 and May 9-June 2, 2000); included rehabilitation assignments to Toledo (April 24-25 and May 29-June 2).
RECORDS: Holds major league single-season record for fewest putouts by second baseman for leader—285 (1998). ... Shares major league single-game record for most times hit by pitch—3 (May 31, 1999).
HONORS: Named second baseman on THE SPORTING NEWS A.L. Silver Slugger team (1998).
STATISTICAL NOTES: Led A.L. second basemen with 285 putouts and .985 fielding percentage in 1998. ... Had 19-game hitting streaks (May 10-30 and July 3-23, 1998). ... Career major league grand slams: 1.

Year	Team (League)	Pos.	G	AB	R	H	2B	3B	HR	RBI	Avg.	BB	SO	SB	PO	A	E	Avg.
1989— Bend (N'West)		2B	36	131	34	39	5	1	4	21	.298	25	21	9	49	89	22	.863
1990— Quad City (Midw.)		SS	103	365	59	100	19	3	10	56	.274	41	60	25	136	206	41	.893
1991— Midland (Texas)		SS	127	452	73	115	24	5	6	57	.254	58	67	23	186	388	*47	.924
1992— Edmonton (PCL)		SS-3B	108	429	61	124	18	3	3	44	.289	31	44	26	152	342	30	.943
— California (A.L.)		3B-SS	47	151	14	39	5	0	1	12	.258	8	26	9	30	102	5	.964
1993— California (A.L.)		2B-3B-DH	73	230	33	72	13	2	2	22	.313	28	35	6	111	157	6	.978
1994— California (A.L.)		3B-2B	88	316	41	68	16	1	6	30	.215	29	48	4	122	178	7	.977
1995— California (A.L.)		2B-SS	114	357	35	77	14	2	4	35	.216	32	47	5	186	276	10	.979
1996— Vancouver (PCL)		SS-2B-3B	12	48	13	15	2	1	2	8	.313	9	6	4	20	26	2	.958
— Midland (Texas)		3B-SS	4	14	1	6	2	0	0	2	.429	0	0	1	5	12	1	.944
— California (A.L.)		S-2-3-DH-O	28	45	4	7	1	0	2	7	.156	6	12	0	23	39	3	.954
— Detroit (A.L.)■		2-S-3-DH	21	67	10	23	1	0	2	10	.343	4	13	3	22	47	3	.958
1997— Detroit (A.L.)		2B-SS-DH	151	527	97	139	37	3	22	72	.264	68	102	28	244	405	12	.982
1998— Detroit (A.L.)		2B-SS-DH	153	594	84	161	38	2	27	100	.271	39	112	15	†312	480	12	†.985
1999— Detroit (A.L.)		2B-SS	151	549	83	146	30	1	20	65	.266	51	124	11	318	445	8	.990
2000— Detroit (A.L.)		2B	126	464	76	120	27	2	14	58	.259	55	79	13	198	411	6	*.990
— Toledo (I.L.)		2B	4	13	3	3	1	0	1	4	.231	4	2	0	5	9	0	1.000
Major League totals (9 years)			952	3300	477	852	182	13	100	411	.258	320	598	94	1566	2541	72	.983

ALL-STAR GAME RECORD

Year	League	Pos.	AB	R	H	2B	3B	HR	RBI	Avg.	BB	SO	SB	PO	A	E	Avg.
1998— American		PH	1	1	1	0	0	0	0	1.000	0	0	0	0	0	0	...

EATON, ADAM — P — PHILLIES

PERSONAL: Born November 23, 1977, in Seattle. ... 6-2/190. ... Throws right, bats right. ... Full name: Adam Thomas Eaton.
HIGH SCHOOL: Snohomish (Wash.).
TRANSACTIONS/CAREER NOTES: Selected by Philadelphia Phillies organization in first round (11th pick overall) of free-agent draft (June 4, 1996). ... Traded by Phillies with P Carlton Loewer and P Steve Montgomery to San Diego Padres for P Andy Ashby (November 10, 1999).

STATISTICAL NOTES: Pitched 1-0 no-hit loss for Reading against Norwich (June 22, 1999).
MISCELLANEOUS: Appeared in one game as pinch runner (2000).

Year League	W	L	Pct.	ERA	G	GS	CG	ShO	Sv.	IP	H	R	ER	BB	SO
1997— Piedmont (S.Atl.)................	5	6	.455	4.16	14	14	0	0	0	71 1/3	81	38	33	30	57
1998— Clearwater (FSL)	9	8	.529	4.44	24	23	1	0	0	131 2/3	152	68	65	47	89
1999— Clearwater (FSL)	5	5	.500	3.91	13	13	0	0	0	69	81	39	30	24	50
— Reading (East.).................	5	4	.556	2.92	12	12	2	0	0	77	60	30	25	28	67
— Scranton/W.B. (I.L.)	1	1	.500	3.00	3	3	0	0	0	21	17	10	7	6	10
2000— Mobile (Sou.)■	4	1	.800	2.68	10	10	1	1	0	57	47	20	17	18	58
— San Diego (N.L.)	7	4	.636	4.13	22	22	0	0	0	135	134	63	62	61	90
Major League totals (1 year)........	7	4	.636	4.13	22	22	0	0	0	135	134	63	62	61	90

EBERT, DERRIN   P   DEVIL RAYS

PERSONAL: Born August 21, 1976, in Anaheim, Calif. ... 6-3/200. ... Throws left, bats right. ... Full name: Derrin Lee Ebert.
HIGH SCHOOL: Hesperia (Calif.).
JUNIOR COLLEGE: Victor Valley Community College (Calif.).
COLLEGE: Cal State Fullerton.
TRANSACTIONS/CAREER NOTES: Selected by Atlanta Braves organization in 18th round of free-agent draft (June 2, 1994). ... Granted free agency (October 18, 2000). ... Signed by Tampa Bay Devil Rays organization (November 9, 2000).
STATISTICAL NOTES: Pitched 6-0 seven-inning no-hit victory against Gulf Coast Marlins (August 12, 1994).

Year League	W	L	Pct.	ERA	G	GS	CG	ShO	Sv.	IP	H	R	ER	BB	SO
1994— Gulf Coast Braves (GCL)	1	3	.250	2.93	10	7	1	1	0	43	40	18	14	8	25
1995— Macon (S.Atl.)	*14	5	.737	3.31	28	28	0	0	0	*182	*184	87	67	46	124
1996— Durham (Caro.)	12	9	.571	4.00	27	27	2	0	0	166 1/3	189	102	74	37	99
1997— Greenville (Sou.)	11	8	.579	4.10	27	25	0	0	0	175 2/3	191	95	80	48	101
1998— Richmond (I.L.)	9	9	.500	4.51	29	29	0	0	0	163 2/3	195	94	82	49	88
1999— Atlanta (N.L.).....................	0	1	.000	5.63	5	0	0	0	1	8	9	5	5	5	4
— Richmond (I.L.).................	8	7	.533	4.30	25	24	2	1	0	150 2/3	173	79	72	44	82
2000— Richmond (I.L.).................	5	9	.357	4.78	32	23	0	0	0	150 2/3	192	94	80	44	91
Major League totals (1 year)........	0	1	.000	5.63	5	0	0	0	1	8	9	5	5	5	4

ECHEVARRIA, ANGEL   OF   BREWERS

PERSONAL: Born May 25, 1971, in Bridgeport, Conn. ... 6-3/226. ... Bats right, throws right. ... Full name: Angel Santos Echevarria.
HIGH SCHOOL: Bassick (Bridgeport, Conn.).
COLLEGE: Rutgers.
TRANSACTIONS/CAREER NOTES: Selected by Colorado Rockies organization in 17th round of free-agent draft (June 1, 1992). ... On Colorado disabled list (April 29-June 4 and July 29-August 16, 1997). ... Claimed on waivers by Milwaukee Brewers (July 19, 2000).

							BATTING							FIELDING		
Year Team (League)	Pos.	G	AB	R	H	2B	3B	HR	RBI	Avg.	BB	SO	SB	PO	A	E	Avg.
1992— Bend (N'West)...........	OF	57	205	24	46	4	1	5	30	.224	19	54	8	65	7	0	1.000
1993— Central Valley (Calif.)..	OF	104	358	45	97	16	2	6	52	.271	44	74	6	141	8	6	.961
1994— Central Valley (Calif.)..	OF	50	192	25	58	8	1	6	35	.302	9	25	2	52	3	1	.982
— New Haven (East.)......	OF	58	205	25	52	6	0	6	32	.254	15	46	2	91	5	2	.980
1995— New Haven (East.)......	OF	124	453	78	136	30	1	21	*100	.300	56	93	8	202	*20	5	.978
1996— Colo. Springs (PCL) ...	OF-DH	110	415	67	140	19	2	16	74	.337	38	81	4	168	8	4	.978
— Colorado (N.L.)	OF	26	21	2	6	0	0	0	6	.286	2	5	0	1	0	0	1.000
1997— Colo. Springs (PCL) ...	OF-DH-1B	77	295	59	95	24	0	13	80	.322	28	47	6	135	9	1	.993
— Colorado (N.L.)	OF	15	20	4	5	2	0	0	0	.250	2	5	0	4	1	0	1.000
1998— Colo. Springs (PCL) ...	1B-OF-DH	85	301	50	98	21	2	15	60	.326	14	47	0	408	28	7	.984
— Colorado (N.L.)	1B-OF	19	29	7	11	3	0	1	9	.379	2	3	0	23	2	0	1.000
1999— Colorado (N.L.)	OF-1B	102	191	28	56	7	0	11	35	.293	17	34	1	122	7	1	.992
2000— Colo. Springs (PCL) ...	OF-1B	74	284	46	95	23	2	7	50	.335	26	44	1	196	13	4	.981
— Colorado (N.L.)	1B-OF	10	9	0	1	0	0	0	2	.111	0	2	0	3	0	0	1.000
— Milwaukee (N.L.)■....	1B-OF	31	42	3	9	2	0	1	4	.214	7	9	0	29	4	0	1.000
Major League totals (5 years)		203	312	44	88	14	0	13	56	.282	30	58	1	182	14	1	.995

ECKSTEIN, DAVID   2B   ANGELS

PERSONAL: Born January 20, 1975, in Sanford, Fla. ... 5-8/165. ... Bats right, throws right. ... Full name: David Mark Eckstein.
HIGH SCHOOL: Seminole (Sanford, Fla.).
COLLEGE: Florida.
TRANSACTIONS/CAREER NOTES: Selected by Boston Red Sox organization in 19th round of free-agent draft (June 3, 1997). ... Claimed on waivers by Anaheim Angels (August 16, 2000).
STATISTICAL NOTES: Tied for New York-Pennsylvania League lead in sacrifice hits with eight in 1997. ... Led Florida State League in being hit by pitch with 22 in 1998. ... Led Florida State League second basemen in fielding percentage with .989 in 1998. ... Tied for Eastern League lead with 87 double plays by second baseman in 1999. ... Led International League in being hit by pitch with 20 in 2000. ... Led International League with .992 fielding percentage in 2000.

							BATTING							FIELDING		
Year Team (League)	Pos.	G	AB	R	H	2B	3B	HR	RBI	Avg.	BB	SO	SB	PO	A	E	Avg.
1997— Lowell (NY-Penn)	2B	68	249	43	75	11	4	4	39	.301	33	29	21	139	166	9	*.971
1998— Sarasota (FSL)	2B-SS	135	503	99	154	29	4	3	58	.306	87	51	45	214	368	8	†.986
1999— Trenton (East.)	2B-DH	131	483	109	151	22	5	6	52	.313	89	48	32	232	359	9	.985
2000— Pawtucket (I.L.)...........	2B-SS	119	422	77	104	20	0	1	31	.246	60	45	11	183	324	4	.992
— Edmonton (PCL)■	2B	15	52	17	18	8	0	3	8	.346	9	1	5	27	28	0	1.000

PERSONAL: Born June 27, 1970, in Fullerton, Calif. ... 6-1/212. ... Bats left, throws left. ... Full name: James Patrick Edmonds. ... Name pronounced ED-muns.

HIGH SCHOOL: Diamond Bar (Calif.).

TRANSACTIONS/CAREER NOTES: Selected by California Angels organization in seventh round of free-agent draft (June 1, 1988). ... On disabled list (June 19-September 2, 1989; April 10-May 7 and May 23, 1991-remainder of season). ... On Vancouver disabled list (June 29-July 19, 1993). ... On California disabled list (May 26-June 10 and June 12-July 18, 1996); included rehabilitation assignment to Lake Elsinore (July 13-18). ... Angels franchise renamed Anaheim Angels for 1997 season. ... On disabled list (August 1-16, 1997). ... On Anaheim disabled list (March 30-August 2, 1999): included rehabilitation assignment to Lake Elsinore (July 26-August 2). ... Traded by Angels to St. Louis Cardinals for 2B/SS Adam Kennedy and P Kent Bottenfield (March 23, 2000).

RECORDS: Holds N.L. single-season record for most strikeouts by lefthander—167 (2000).

HONORS: Named outfielder on THE SPORTING NEWS A.L. All-Star team (1995). ... Won A.L. Gold Glove as outfielder (1997-98). ... Won N.L. Gold Glove as outfielder (2000).

STATISTICAL NOTES: Had 23-game hitting streak (June 4-29, 1995). ... Career major league grand slams: 2.

								BATTING							FIELDING		
Year Team (League)	Pos.	G	AB	R	H	2B	3B	HR	RBI	Avg.	BB	SO	SB	PO	A	E	Avg.
1988— Bend (N'West)	OF	35	122	23	27	4	0	0	13	.221	20	44	4	59	1	1	.984
1989— Quad City (Midw.)	OF	31	92	11	24	4	0	1	4	.261	7	34	1	47	2	3	.942
1990— Palm Springs (Calif.)..	OF	91	314	36	92	18	6	3	56	.293	27	75	5	199	9	10	.954
1991— Palm Springs (Calif.)..	OF-1B-P	60	187	28	55	15	1	2	27	.294	40	57	2	97	6	0	1.000
1992— Midland (Texas).........	OF	70	246	42	77	15	2	8	32	.313	41	83	3	139	6	5	.967
— Edmonton (PCL)	OF	50	194	37	58	15	2	6	36	.299	14	55	3	79	5	1	.988
1993— Vancouver (PCL)	OF	95	356	59	112	28	4	9	74	.315	41	81	6	167	4	3	.983
— California (A.L.)..........	OF	18	61	5	15	4	1	0	4	.246	2	16	0	47	4	1	.981
1994— California (A.L.)..........	OF-1B	94	289	35	79	13	1	5	37	.273	30	72	4	301	20	3	.991
1995— California (A.L.)..........	OF	141	558	120	162	30	4	33	107	.290	51	130	1	401	8	1	.998
1996— California (A.L.)..........	OF-DH	114	431	73	131	28	3	27	66	.304	46	101	4	280	6	1	.997
— Lake Elsinore (Calif.)..	OF-DH	5	15	4	6	2	0	1	4	.400	1	1	0	5	0	0	1.000
1997— Anaheim (A.L.)..........	OF-1B-DH	133	502	82	146	27	0	26	80	.291	60	80	5	395	16	5	.988
1998— Anaheim (A.L.)..........	OF	154	599	115	184	42	1	25	91	.307	57	114	7	392	10	5	.988
1999— Lake Elsinore (Calif.)..	DH	5	19	4	8	2	0	0	3	.421	4	2	2	0	0	0	...
— Anaheim (A.L.)..........	OF-DH-1B	55	204	34	51	17	2	5	23	.250	28	45	5	138	5	1	.993
2000— St. Louis (N.L.)■	OF-1B	152	525	129	155	25	0	42	108	.295	103	167	10	392	14	4	.990
American League totals (7 years)		709	2644	464	768	161	12	121	408	.290	274	558	26	1954	69	17	.992
National League totals (1 year)		152	525	129	155	25	0	42	108	.295	103	167	10	392	14	4	.990
Major League totals (8 years)		861	3169	593	923	186	12	163	516	.291	377	725	36	2346	83	21	.991

DIVISION SERIES RECORD

RECORDS: Holds N.L. career record for most doubles—4.

								BATTING							FIELDING		
Year Team (League)	Pos.	G	AB	R	H	2B	3B	HR	RBI	Avg.	BB	SO	SB	PO	A	E	Avg.
2000— St. Louis (N.L.)..........	OF	3	14	5	8	4	0	2	7	.571	1	2	1	7	0	0	1.000

CHAMPIONSHIP SERIES RECORD

								BATTING							FIELDING		
Year Team (League)	Pos.	G	AB	R	H	2B	3B	HR	RBI	Avg.	BB	SO	SB	PO	A	E	Avg.
2000— St. Louis (N.L.)..........	OF	5	22	1	5	1	0	1	5	.227	1	9	0	13	1	1	.933

ALL-STAR GAME RECORD

						BATTING							FIELDING		
Year League	Pos.	AB	R	H	2B	3B	HR	RBI	Avg.	BB	SO	SB	PO	A	E	Avg.
1995— American	PH-OF	1	0	0	0	0	0	0	.000	0	1	0	0	0	0	...
2000— National	OF	2	0	1	0	0	0	0	.500	0	0	0	3	0	0	1.000
All-Star Game totals (2 years)		3	0	1	0	0	0	0	.333	0	1	0	3	0	0	1.000

RECORD AS PITCHER

Year League	W	L	Pct.	ERA	G	GS	CG	ShO	Sv.	IP	H	R	ER	BB	SO
1991— Palm Springs (Calif.)..........	0	0	...	0.00	1	0	0	0	0	2	1	0	0	3	2

PERSONAL: Born July 5, 1966, in Dade City, Fla. ... 6-3/208. ... Throws right, bats right. ... Full name: David William Eiland. ... Name pronounced EYE-land.

HIGH SCHOOL: Zephyrhills (Fla.).

COLLEGE: South Florida, then Florida.

TRANSACTIONS/CAREER NOTES: Selected by New York Yankees organization in seventh round of free-agent draft (June 2, 1987). ... On New York disabled list (May 28-July 12, 1991); included rehabilitation assignment to Columbus (June 16-July 12). ... Released by Yankees (January 19, 1992). ... Signed by San Diego Padres organization (January 27, 1992). ... On San Diego disabled list (May 4-June 26, 1992); included rehabilitation assignment to Las Vegas (May 27-June 25). ... On San Diego disabled list (July 5-August 26, 1992); included rehabilitation assignment to Las Vegas (July 28-August 26). ... Granted free agency (December 7, 1992). ... Re-signed by Padres organization (February 28, 1993). ... Granted free agency (May 27, 1993). ... Signed by Cleveland Indians organization (May 29, 1993). ... Traded by Indians to Texas Rangers for P Gerald Alexander and P Allan Anderson (August 4, 1993). ... Granted free agency (October 15, 1993). ... Signed by Yankees organization (March 12, 1994). ... Granted free agency (October 3, 1995). ... Signed by St. Louis Cardinals organization (December 6, 1995). ... On Louisville temporarily inactive list (April 10-18, 1996). ... On Louisville disabled list (May 14-22 and June 3-15, 1996). ... Released by Cardinals (June 15, 1996). ... Signed by Yankees organization (June 18, 1996). ... Granted free agency (October 15, 1996). ... Signed by Yankees organization (December 23, 1996). ... On Columbus disabled list (May 14-25, 1997). ... Granted free agency (October 15, 1997). ... Signed by Tampa Bay Devil Rays (December 19, 1997). ... Granted free agency (October 15, 1998). ... Re-signed by Devil Rays (November 28, 1998). ... On Tampa Bay disabled list (June 8-23 and August 27-September 11, 1999); included rehabilitation assignments to Durham (September 6-8). ... On Tampa Bay disabled list (May 24-August 9, 2000); included rehabilitation assignments to Orlando (June 28-July 6) and Durham (July 8-16 and July 30-August 9). ... On suspended list (September 24-26, 2000). ... Granted free agency (October 12, 2000). ... Signed by Oakland Athletics organization (December 6, 2000).

HONORS: Named International League Most Valuable Pitcher (1990).

STATISTICAL NOTES: Hit home run in first major league at-bat (April 10, 1992).

Year	League	W	L	Pct.	ERA	G	GS	CG	ShO	Sv.	IP	H	R	ER	BB	SO
1987—	Oneonta (NY-Penn)	4	0	1.000	1.84	5	5	0	0	0	29 1/3	20	6	6	3	16
	— Fort Lauderdale (FSL)	5	3	.625	1.88	8	8	4	1	0	62 1/3	57	17	13	8	28
1988—	Albany/Colonie (East.).......	9	5	.643	2.56	18	18	•7	2	0	119 1/3	95	39	34	22	66
	— Columbus (I.L.)	1	1	.500	2.59	4	4	0	0	0	24 1/3	25	8	7	6	13
	— New York (A.L.)	0	0	...	6.39	3	3	0	0	0	12 2/3	15	9	9	4	7
1989—	Columbus (I.L.)	9	4	.692	3.76	18	18	2	0	0	103	107	47	43	21	45
	— New York (A.L.)	1	3	.250	5.77	6	6	0	0	0	34 1/3	44	25	22	13	11
1990—	Columbus (I.L.)	*16	5	.762	2.87	27	26	*11	•3	0	175 1/3	155	63	56	32	96
	— New York (A.L.)	2	1	.667	3.56	5	5	0	0	0	30 1/3	31	14	12	5	16
1991—	New York (A.L.)	2	5	.286	5.33	18	13	0	0	0	72 2/3	87	51	43	23	18
	— Columbus (I.L.)	6	1	.857	2.40	9	9	2	0	0	60	54	22	16	7	18
1992—	San Diego (N.L.)■............	0	2	.000	5.67	7	7	0	0	0	27	33	21	17	5	10
	— Las Vegas (PCL)	4	5	.444	5.23	14	14	0	0	0	63 2/3	78	43	37	11	31
1993—	San Diego (N.L.)	0	3	.000	5.21	10	9	0	0	0	48 1/3	58	33	28	17	14
	— Charlotte (I.L.)■..............	1	3	.250	5.30	8	8	0	0	0	35 2/3	42	22	21	12	13
	— Oklahoma City (A.A.)■.......	3	1	.750	4.29	7	7	1	0	0	35 2/3	39	18	17	9	15
1994—	Columbus (I.L.)■............	9	6	.600	3.58	26	26	0	0	0	140 2/3	141	72	56	33	84
1995—	Columbus (I.L.)■............	8	7	.533	3.14	19	18	1	1	0	109	109	44	38	22	62
	— New York (A.L.)	1	1	.500	6.30	4	1	0	0	0	10	16	10	7	3	6
1996—	Louisville (A.A.)■............	0	1	.000	5.55	8	6	0	0	0	24 1/3	27	17	15	8	17
	— Columbus (I.L.)■............	8	4	.667	2.92	15	15	3	0	0	92 1/3	77	37	30	13	76
1997—	Columbus (I.L.)	4	2	.667	6.64	13	11	0	0	0	61 1/3	80	47	46	14	43
	— Gulf Coast Yankees (GCL)..	0	1	.000	9.00	2	1	0	0	0	7	12	8	7	0	5
	— Tampa (FSL)......................	1	0	1.000	3.75	3	3	0	0	0	12	11	5	5	0	11
1998—	Durham (I.L.)■	13	5	.722	2.99	28	28	2	1	0	171 2/3	177	70	57	27	112
	— Tampa Bay (A.L.)...............	0	1	.000	20.25	1	1	0	0	0	2 2/3	6	6	6	3	1
1999—	Durham (I.L.)	5	3	.625	3.36	10	10	0	0	0	59	60	26	22	9	46
	— Tampa Bay (A.L.)...............	4	8	.333	5.60	21	15	0	0	0	80 1/3	98	59	50	27	53
2000—	Tampa Bay (A.L.)...............	2	3	.400	7.24	17	10	0	0	0	54 2/3	77	46	44	18	17
	— Orlando (Sou.)	1	0	1.000	1.59	2	2	0	0	0	11 1/3	7	3	2	1	8
	— Durham (I.L.)	2	1	.667	4.63	4	4	0	0	0	23 1/3	31	13	12	3	10
A.L. totals (8 years)		12	22	.353	5.84	75	54	0	0	0	297 2/3	374	220	193	96	129
N.L. totals (2 years)		0	5	.000	5.38	17	16	0	0	0	75 1/3	91	54	45	22	24
Major League totals (10 years)		12	27	.308	5.74	92	70	0	0	0	373	465	274	238	118	153

EINERTSON, DARRELL   P   YANKEES

PERSONAL: Born September 4, 1972, in Rhinelander, Wis. ... 6-2/196. ... Throws right, bats right. ... Full name: Darrell Lee Einertson.
HIGH SCHOOL: Urbandale (Iowa).
JUNIOR COLLEGE: Indian Hills Community College (Iowa).
COLLEGE: Cameron, then Iowa Wesleyan.
TRANSACTIONS/CAREER NOTES: Selected by New York Yankees organization in 11th round of free-agent draft (June 1, 1995). ... On Norwich disabled list (May 22-August 31, 1998). ... On New York disabled list (August 31, 1998-remainder of season). ... On New York disabled list (March 26-July 19, 1999); included rehabilitation assignments to Gulf Coast Yankees (June 19-23), Tampa (June 25-30) and Norwich (July 1-18). ... On New York disabled list (September 5, 2000-remainder of season).

Year	League	W	L	Pct.	ERA	G	GS	CG	ShO	Sv.	IP	H	R	ER	BB	SO
1995—	Oneonta (NY-Penn)	0	4	.000	1.88	25	0	0	0	0	38 1/3	32	20	8	15	35
1996—	Greensboro (S.Atl.)	3	9	.250	2.70	48	0	0	0	0	70	69	29	21	19	48
1997—	Tampa (FSL)......................	5	4	.556	2.15	45	0	0	0	6	71	63	24	17	19	55
1998—	Norwich (East.)	3	1	.750	1.02	17	0	0	0	0	35 1/3	23	7	4	10	33
1999—	Gulf Coast Yankees (GCL)..	0	1	.000	0.00	1	0	0	0	0	2	3	3	0	1	4
	— Tampa (FSL)	0	0	...	1.93	2	1	0	0	0	4 2/3	1	1	1	1	3
	— Norwich (East.)	2	2	.500	4.97	21	0	0	0	0	29	39	23	16	10	16
2000—	Columbus (I.L.)	5	3	.625	3.24	26	0	0	0	1	33 1/3	31	19	12	18	20
	— New York (A.L.)	0	0	...	3.55	11	0	0	0	0	12 2/3	16	9	5	4	3
Major League totals (1 year)		0	0	...	3.55	11	0	0	0	0	12 2/3	16	9	5	4	3

ELARTON, SCOTT   P   ASTROS

PERSONAL: Born February 23, 1976, in Lamar, Colo. ... 6-7/240. ... Throws right, bats right. ... Full name: Vincent Scott Elarton.
HIGH SCHOOL: Lamar (Colo.).
TRANSACTIONS/CAREER NOTES: Selected by Houston Astros organization in first round (25th pick overall) of free-agent draft (June 2, 1994). ... On Houston disabled list (March 29-April 23, 2000); included rehabilitation assignments to New Orleans (April 6-11) and Round Rock (April 18).
MISCELLANEOUS: Appeared in one game as outfielder with no chances (1999).

Year	League	W	L	Pct.	ERA	G	GS	CG	ShO	Sv.	IP	H	R	ER	BB	SO
1994—	Gulf Coast Astros (GCL).....	4	0	1.000	0.00	5	5	0	0	0	28	9	0	0	5	28
	— Quad City (Midw.)	4	1	.800	3.29	9	9	0	0	0	54 2/3	42	23	20	18	42
1995—	Quad City (Midw.)	13	7	.650	4.45	26	26	0	0	0	149 2/3	149	86	74	71	112
1996—	Kissimmee (FSL)...............	12	7	.632	2.92	27	27	3	1	0	172 1/3	154	67	56	54	130
1997—	Jackson (Texas)	7	4	.636	3.24	20	20	2	0	0	133 1/3	103	57	48	47	141
	— New Orleans (A.A.)...........	4	4	.500	5.33	9	9	0	0	0	54	51	36	32	17	50
1998—	New Orleans (PCL)............	9	4	.692	4.01	14	14	2	1	0	92	71	42	41	41	100
	— Houston (N.L.)	2	1	.667	3.32	28	2	0	0	2	57	40	21	21	20	56

Year League	W	L	Pct.	ERA	G	GS	CG	ShO	Sv.	IP	H	R	ER	BB	SO
1999— Houston (N.L.)	9	5	.643	3.48	42	15	0	0	1	124	111	55	48	43	121
2000— New Orleans (PCL)	1	0	1.000	0.75	2	2	0	0	0	12	3	1	1	4	12
— Round Rock (Texas)	1	0	1.000	2.84	1	1	0	0	0	6 1/3	7	2	2	0	7
— Houston (N.L.)	17	7	.708	4.81	30	30	2	0	0	192 2/3	198	117	103	84	131
Major League totals (3 years)	28	13	.683	4.14	100	47	2	0	3	373 2/3	349	193	172	147	308

DIVISION SERIES RECORD

Year League	W	L	Pct.	ERA	G	GS	CG	ShO	Sv.	IP	H	R	ER	BB	SO
1998— Houston (N.L.)	0	1	.000	4.50	1	0	0	0	0	2	1	1	1	1	3
1999— Houston (N.L.)	0	0	...	3.86	2	0	0	0	0	2 1/3	4	1	1	1	3
Division series totals (2 years)	0	1	.000	4.15	3	0	0	0	0	4 1/3	5	2	2	2	6

ELDER, DAVID P RANGERS

PERSONAL: Born September 23, 1975, in Atlanta. ... 6-0/180. ... Throws right, bats right. ... Full name: David Matthew Elder.
HIGH SCHOOL: Booker T. Washington (Pensacola, Fla.).
COLLEGE: Georgia Tech.
TRANSACTIONS/CAREER NOTES: Selected by Texas Rangers organization in fourth round of free-agent draft (June 3, 1997). ... On Pulaski disabled list (April 7, 1998-entire season). ... On Charlotte disabled list (May 8-19, 1999).

Year League	W	L	Pct.	ERA	G	GS	CG	ShO	Sv.	IP	H	R	ER	BB	SO
1997— Pulaski (Appl.)	2	2	.500	1.95	20	0	0	0	6	32 1/3	18	8	7	12	57
1998— Pulaski (Appl.)							Did not play.								
1999— Charlotte (FSL)	4	2	.667	2.84	24	1	0	0	4	44 1/3	33	15	14	25	42
— Tulsa (Texas)	1	0	1.000	8.10	3	0	0	0	0	6 2/3	8	7	6	6	7
2000— Tulsa (Texas)	7	6	.538	4.94	33	21	0	0	3	116 2/3	121	80	64	*88	104

ELDRED, CAL P WHITE SOX

PERSONAL: Born November 24, 1967, in Cedar Rapids, Iowa. ... 6-4/237. ... Throws right, bats right. ... Full name: Calvin John Eldred.
HIGH SCHOOL: Urbana (Iowa) Community.
COLLEGE: Iowa.
TRANSACTIONS/CAREER NOTES: Selected by Milwaukee Brewers organization in first round (17th pick overall) of free-agent draft (June 5, 1989). ... On disabled list (May 15, 1995-remainder of season). ... On Milwaukee disabled list (March 29-July 14, 1996); included rehabilitation assignment to New Orleans (June 10-July 9). ... On disabled list (July 26, 1998-remainder of season). ... On Milwaukee disabled list (March 29-April 20 and July 2-August 15, 1999); included rehabilitation assignments to Huntsville (April 8-17) and Louisville (April 18-20 and July 31-August 15). ... Traded by Brewers with SS Jose Valentin to Chicago White Sox for P Jaime Navarro and P John Snyder (January 12, 2000). ... On Chicago disabled list (July 15-September 27, 2000); included rehabilitation assignment to Charlotte (August 29-September 22). ... Granted free agency (November 8, 2000). ... Re-signed by White Sox (December 7, 2000).
RECORDS: Shares N.L. single-inning record for most consecutive home runs allowed—3 (August 22, 1999, first inning).
HONORS: Named A.L. Rookie Pitcher of the Year by THE SPORTING NEWS (1992).
STATISTICAL NOTES: Led American Association with 12 hit batsmen in 1991.
MISCELLANEOUS: Appeared in one game as pinch runner (1998). ... Scored one run in three appearances as pinch runner (1999).

Year League	W	L	Pct.	ERA	G	GS	CG	ShO	Sv.	IP	H	R	ER	BB	SO
1989— Beloit (Midw.)	2	1	.667	2.30	5	5	0	0	0	31 1/3	23	10	8	11	32
1990— Stockton (Calif.)	4	2	.667	1.62	7	7	3	1	0	50	31	12	9	19	75
— El Paso (Texas)	5	4	.556	4.49	19	19	0	0	0	110 1/3	126	61	55	47	93
1991— Denver (A.A.)	13	9	.591	3.75	29	*29	3	1	0	*185	161	82	77	84	*168
— Milwaukee (A.L.)	2	0	1.000	4.50	3	3	0	0	0	16	20	9	8	6	10
1992— Denver (A.A.)	10	6	.625	3.00	19	19	4	1	0	141	122	49	47	42	99
— Milwaukee (A.L.)	11	2	.846	1.79	14	14	2	1	0	100 1/3	76	21	20	23	62
1993— Milwaukee (A.L.)	16	16	.500	4.01	36	•36	8	1	0	*258	232	120	115	91	180
1994— Milwaukee (A.L.)	11	11	.500	4.68	25	•25	6	0	0	179	158	96	93	84	98
1995— Milwaukee (A.L.)	1	1	.500	3.42	4	4	0	0	0	23 2/3	24	10	9	10	18
1996— New Orleans (A.A.)	2	2	.500	3.34	6	6	0	0	0	32 1/3	24	12	12	17	30
— Milwaukee (A.L.)	4	4	.500	4.46	15	15	0	0	0	84 2/3	82	43	42	38	50
1997— Milwaukee (A.L.)	13	•15	.464	4.99	34	34	1	1	0	202	207	118	112	89	122
1998— Milwaukee (N.L.)	4	8	.333	4.80	23	23	0	0	0	133	157	82	71	61	86
1999— Huntsville (Sou.)	0	1	.000	7.50	2	2	1	0	0	12	13	10	10	3	16
— Louisville (I.L.)	0	1	.000	5.30	4	4	0	0	0	18 2/3	19	12	11	10	21
— Milwaukee (N.L.)	2	8	.200	7.79	20	15	0	0	0	82	101	75	71	46	60
2000— Chicago (A.L.)■	10	2	.833	4.58	20	20	2	1	0	112	103	61	57	59	97
— Charlotte (I.L.)	0	1	.000	7.20	2	2	0	0	0	5	4	4	4	0	1
A.L. totals (8 years)	68	51	.571	4.21	151	151	19	4	0	975 2/3	902	478	456	400	637
N.L. totals (2 years)	6	16	.273	5.94	43	38	0	0	0	215	258	157	142	107	146
Major League totals (10 years)	74	67	.525	4.52	194	189	19	4	0	1190 2/3	1160	635	598	507	783

ELSTER, KEVIN SS

PERSONAL: Born August 3, 1964, in San Pedro, Calif. ... 6-2/205. ... Bats right, throws right. ... Full name: Kevin Daniel Elster.
HIGH SCHOOL: Marina (Huntington Beach, Calif.).
JUNIOR COLLEGE: Golden West College (Calif.).
TRANSACTIONS/CAREER NOTES: Selected by New York Mets organization in second round of free-agent draft (January 17, 1984). ... On Jackson disabled list (August 11, 1985-remainder of season). ... On disabled list (August 4, 1990-remainder of season; May 6-21, 1991; and April 13, 1992-remainder of season). ... Granted free agency (December 19, 1992). ... Signed by Los Angeles Dodgers organization (January 12, 1993). ... On Albuquerque disabled list (April 8-May 2, 1993). ... Released by Dodgers (May 17, 1993). ... Signed by Florida Marlins organization (May 22, 1993). ... Released by Marlins organization (June 4, 1993). ... Signed by San Diego Padres organization (December 17, 1993). ... Released by Padres organization (March 21, 1994). ... Signed by New York Yankees organization (May 1, 1994). ... On Columbus

E

temporarily inactive list (May 1-June 1, 1994). ... On New York disabled list (July 7, 1994-remainder of season); included rehabilitation assignment to Albany (August 1-20). ... Released by Yankees (June 8, 1995). ... Signed by Kansas City Royals organization (June 29, 1995). ... Released by Royals organization (July 3, 1995). ... Signed by Philadelphia Phillies organization (July 7, 1995). ... Granted free agency (October 5, 1995). ... Signed by Texas Rangers organization (January 16, 1996). ... Granted free agency (October 31, 1996). ... Signed by Pittsburgh Pirates (December 20, 1996). ... On disabled list (May 17, 1997-remainder of season). ... Granted free agency (October 28, 1997). ... Signed by Rangers (December 8, 1997). ... On Texas disabled list (June 2-17, 1998). ... Released by Rangers (July 31, 1998). ... Signed by Dodgers organization (January 14, 2000). ... On disabled list (May 4-21 and August 23-September 5, 2000). ... Granted free agency (October 15, 2000).

RECORDS: Holds major league single-season record for fewest putouts by shortstop who led league in putouts—235 (1989).

HONORS: Named A.L. Comeback Player of the Year by The Sporting News (1996).

STATISTICAL NOTES: Led New York-Pennsylvania League shortstops with 358 total chances and 45 double plays in 1984. ... Led Texas League shortstops with 589 total chances and 83 double plays in 1986. ... Hit three home runs in one game (April 11, 2000). ... Career major league grand slams: 3.

Year Team (League)	Pos.	G	AB	R	H	2B	3B	HR	RBI	Avg.	BB	SO	SB	PO	A	E	Avg.
										BATTING					FIELDING		
1984— Little Falls (NY-Penn) .	SS	71	257	35	66	7	3	3	35	.257	35	41	13	*128	214	16	*.955
1985— Lynchburg (Caro.)	SS	59	224	41	66	9	0	7	26	.295	33	21	8	82	195	16	.945
— Jackson (Texas)	SS	59	214	30	55	13	0	2	22	.257	19	29	2	107	220	10	.970
1986— Jackson (Texas)	SS	127	435	69	117	19	3	2	52	.269	61	46	6	*196	*365	28	*.952
— New York (N.L.)..........	SS	19	30	3	5	1	0	0	0	.167	3	8	0	16	35	2	.962
1987— Tidewater (I.L.)..........	SS	134	*549	83	*170	33	7	8	74	.310	35	62	7	219	419	21	.968
— New York (N.L.)..........	SS	5	10	1	4	2	0	0	1	.400	0	1	0	4	6	1	.909
1988— New York (N.L.)..........	SS	149	406	41	87	11	1	9	37	.214	35	47	2	196	345	13	.977
1989— New York (N.L.)..........	SS	151	458	52	106	25	2	10	55	.231	34	77	4	*235	374	15	.976
1990— New York (N.L.)..........	SS	92	314	36	65	20	1	9	45	.207	30	54	2	159	251	17	.960
1991— New York (N.L.)..........	SS	115	348	33	84	16	2	6	36	.241	40	53	2	149	299	14	.970
1992— New York (N.L.)..........	SS	6	18	0	4	0	0	0	0	.222	0	2	0	8	10	0	1.000
1993— San Antonio (Texas)■	SS	10	39	5	11	2	1	0	7	.282	4	4	0	14	31	4	.918
1994— Tampa (FSL)■...........	2B-3B	3	11	2	2	1	0	0	2	.182	2	2	0	4	7	1	.917
— Alb./Colonie (East.)	SS-3B-2B	41	135	19	33	7	0	2	21	.244	21	16	2	64	112	7	.962
— New York (A.L.)..........	SS	7	20	0	0	0	0	0	0	.000	1	6	0	5	27	0	1.000
1995— New York (A.L.)..........	SS-2B	10	17	1	2	1	0	0	0	.118	1	5	0	10	14	0	1.000
— Omaha (A.A.)■............	SS	11	42	5	10	4	0	0	6	.238	5	8	0	22	30	0	1.000
— Scranton/W.B. (I.L.)■	SS	5	17	2	5	3	0	0	2	.294	2	3	0	6	12	1	.947
— Philadelphia (N.L.)......	SS-1B-3B	26	53	10	11	4	1	1	9	.208	7	14	0	37	38	1	.987
1996— Texas (A.L.)■............	SS	157	515	79	130	32	2	24	99	.252	52	138	4	*285	441	14	.981
1997— Pittsburgh (N.L.)■	SS	39	138	14	31	6	2	7	25	.225	21	39	0	54	123	1	.994
1998— Texas (A.L.)■...........	SS	84	297	33	69	10	1	8	37	.232	33	66	0	107	257	9	.976
1999—									Did not play.								
2000— Los Angeles (N.L.)■ ..	SS-3B-1B	80	220	29	50	8	0	14	32	.227	38	52	0	66	149	14	.939
American League totals (4 years)		258	849	113	201	43	3	32	136	.237	87	215	4	407	739	23	.980
National League totals (10 years)		682	1995	219	447	93	9	56	240	.224	208	347	10	924	1630	78	.970
Major League totals (13 years)		940	2844	332	648	136	12	88	376	.228	295	562	14	1331	2369	101	.973

DIVISION SERIES RECORD

Year Team (League)	Pos.	G	AB	R	H	2B	3B	HR	RBI	Avg.	BB	SO	SB	PO	A	E	Avg.
										BATTING					FIELDING		
1996— Texas (A.L.)	SS	4	12	2	4	2	0	0	0	.333	3	2	1	6	7	1	.929

CHAMPIONSHIP SERIES RECORD

Year Team (League)	Pos.	G	AB	R	H	2B	3B	HR	RBI	Avg.	BB	SO	SB	PO	A	E	Avg.
										BATTING					FIELDING		
1986— New York (N.L.)..........	SS-PR	4	3	0	0	0	0	0	0	.000	0	1	0	2	3	0	1.000
1988— New York (N.L.)..........	SS-PR	5	8	1	2	1	0	0	1	.250	3	0	0	7	7	2	.875
Championship series totals (2 years)		9	11	1	2	1	0	0	1	.182	3	1	0	9	10	2	.905

NOTES: Member of World Series championship team (1986).

WORLD SERIES RECORD

Year Team (League)	Pos.	G	AB	R	H	2B	3B	HR	RBI	Avg.	BB	SO	SB	PO	A	E	Avg.
										BATTING					FIELDING		
1986— New York (N.L.)..........	SS	1	1	0	0	0	0	0	0	.000	0	0	0	3	3	1	.857

EMBREE, ALAN   P   GIANTS

PERSONAL: Born January 23, 1970, in Vancouver, Wash. ... 6-2/190. ... Throws left, bats left. ... Full name: Alan Duane Embree.

HIGH SCHOOL: Prairie (Vancouver, Wash.).

TRANSACTIONS/CAREER NOTES: Selected by Cleveland Indians organization in fifth round of free-agent draft (June 5, 1989). ... On Cleveland disabled list (April 1-June 2 and June 2, 1993-remainder of season); included rehabilitation assignment to Canton/Akron (June 2-15). ... On Cleveland disabled list (August 1-September 7, 1996); included rehabilitation assignment to Buffalo (August 6-September 4). ... Traded by Indians with OF Kenny Lofton to Atlanta Braves for OF Marquis Grissom and OF Dave Justice (March 25, 1997). ... Traded by Braves to Arizona Diamondbacks for P Russ Springer (June 23, 1998). ... Traded by Diamondbacks to San Francisco Giants for OF Dante Powell (November 10, 1998).

Year League	W	L	Pct.	ERA	G	GS	CG	ShO	Sv.	IP	H	R	ER	BB	SO
1990— Burlington (Appl.)...............	4	4	.500	2.64	15	•15	0	0	0	81 2/3	87	36	24	30	58
1991— Columbus (S.Atl.)...............	10	8	.556	3.59	27	26	3	1	0	155 1/3	126	80	62	77	137
1992— Kinston (Caro.)...................	10	5	.667	3.30	15	15	1	0	0	101	89	48	37	32	115
— Canton/Akron (East.)	7	2	.778	2.28	12	12	0	0	0	79	61	24	20	28	56
— Cleveland (A.L.)..................	0	2	.000	7.00	4	4	0	0	0	18	19	14	14	8	12
1993— Canton/Akron (East.)	0	0	...	3.38	1	1	0	0	0	5 1/3	3	2	2	3	4
1994— Canton/Akron (East.)	9	•16	.360	5.50	30	27	2	1	0	157	183	106	96	64	81
1995— Buffalo (A.A.)....................	3	4	.429	0.89	30	0	0	0	5	40 2/3	31	10	4	19	56
— Cleveland (A.L.)..................	3	2	.600	5.11	23	0	0	0	1	24 2/3	23	16	14	16	23

Year League	W	L	Pct.	ERA	G	GS	CG	ShO	Sv.	IP	H	R	ER	BB	SO
1996— Cleveland (A.L.)	1	1	.500	6.39	24	0	0	0	0	31	30	26	22	21	33
— Buffalo (A.A.)	4	1	.800	3.93	20	0	0	0	5	34 1/3	26	16	15	14	46
1997— Atlanta (N.L.)■	3	1	.750	2.54	66	0	0	0	0	46	36	13	13	20	45
1998— Atlanta (N.L.)	1	0	1.000	4.34	20	0	0	0	0	18 2/3	23	14	9	10	19
— Arizona (N.L.)■	3	2	.600	4.11	35	0	0	0	1	35	33	18	16	13	24
1999— San Francisco (N.L.)■	3	2	.600	3.38	68	0	0	0	0	58 2/3	42	22	22	26	53
2000— San Francisco (N.L.)	3	5	.375	4.95	63	0	0	0	2	60	62	34	33	25	49
A.L. totals (3 years)	4	5	.444	6.11	51	4	0	0	1	73 2/3	72	56	50	45	68
N.L. totals (4 years)	13	10	.565	3.83	252	0	0	0	3	218 1/3	196	101	93	94	190
Major League totals (7 years)	17	15	.531	4.41	303	4	0	0	4	292	268	157	143	139	258

DIVISION SERIES RECORD

Year League	W	L	Pct.	ERA	G	GS	CG	ShO	Sv.	IP	H	R	ER	BB	SO
1996— Cleveland (A.L.)	0	0	...	9.00	3	0	0	0	0	1	0	1	1	0	1
2000— San Francisco (N.L.)	0	0	...	0.00	2	0	0	0	0	1 2/3	0	0	0	0	0
Division series totals (2 years)	0	0	...	3.38	5	0	0	0	0	2 2/3	0	1	1	0	1

CHAMPIONSHIP SERIES RECORD

Year League	W	L	Pct.	ERA	G	GS	CG	ShO	Sv.	IP	H	R	ER	BB	SO
1995— Cleveland (A.L.)	0	0	...	0.00	1	0	0	0	0	1/3	0	0	0	0	1
1997— Atlanta (N.L.)	0	0	...	0.00	1	0	0	0	0	1	0	0	0	1	1
Champ. series totals (2 years)	0	0	...	0.00	2	0	0	0	0	1 1/3	0	0	0	1	2

WORLD SERIES RECORD

Year League	W	L	Pct.	ERA	G	GS	CG	ShO	Sv.	IP	H	R	ER	BB	SO
1995— Cleveland (A.L.)	0	0	...	2.70	4	0	0	0	0	3 1/3	2	1	1	2	2

ENCARNACION, JUAN   OF   TIGERS

PERSONAL: Born March 8, 1976, in Las Matas de Faran, Dominican Republic. ... 6-3/187. ... Bats right, throws right. ... Full name: Juan DeDios Encarnacion. ... Name pronounced en-car-nah-CION.

HIGH SCHOOL: Liceo Mercedes Maria Mateo (Las Matas de Faran, Dominican Republic).

TRANSACTIONS/CAREER NOTES: Signed as non-drafted free agent by Detroit Tigers organization (December 27, 1992). ... On Detroit disabled list (March 20-April 29, 1998); included rehabilitation assignment to Lakeland (April 24-29). ... On suspended list (May 27-29, 2000).

STATISTICAL NOTES: Led Southern League in being hit by pitch with 12 in 1997. ... Tied for International League lead in double plays by outfielder with three in 1998. ... Had 19-game hitting streak (April 16-May 7, 2000). ... Career major league grand slams: 1.

							BATTING						FIELDING		
Year Team (League)	Pos.	G	AB	R	H	2B	3B	HR	RBI	Avg.	BB	SO	SB	PO	A	E	Avg.
1993— Dom. Tigers (DSL)	OF	72	251	36	63	13	4	13	49	.251	15	65	6	110	13	17	.879
1994— Bristol (Appl.)	OF	54	197	16	49	7	1	4	31	.249	13	54	9	83	*9	3	.968
— Fayetteville (S.Atl.)	OF	24	83	6	16	1	1	1	4	.193	8	36	1	22	1	2	.920
— Lakeland (FSL)	OF	3	6	1	2	0	0	0	0	.333	0	3	0	0	0	0	...
1995— Fayetteville (S.Atl.)	OF	124	457	62	129	31	7	16	72	.282	30	113	30	143	10	7	.956
1996— Lakeland (FSL)	OF	131	499	54	120	31	2	15	58	.240	24	104	11	233	12	6	.976
1997— Jacksonville (Sou.)	OF-DH	131	493	91	159	31	4	26	90	.323	43	86	17	208	12	3	.987
— Detroit (A.L.)	OF	11	33	3	7	1	1	1	5	.212	3	12	3	22	0	0	1.000
1998— Lakeland (FSL)	OF	4	16	4	4	0	1	0	4	.250	2	4	4	7	1	0	1.000
— Toledo (I.L.)	OF-DH	92	356	55	102	17	3	8	41	.287	29	85	24	168	10	5	.973
— Detroit (A.L.)	OF-DH	40	164	30	54	9	4	7	21	.329	7	31	7	60	4	1	.985
1999— Detroit (A.L.)	OF	132	509	62	130	30	6	19	74	.255	14	113	33	264	10	9	.968
2000— Detroit (A.L.)	OF	141	547	75	158	25	6	14	72	.289	29	90	16	363	3	5	.987
Major League totals (4 years)		324	1253	170	349	65	17	41	172	.279	53	246	59	709	17	15	.980

ENCARNACION, MARIO   OF   ATHLETICS

PERSONAL: Born September 24, 1977, in Bani, Dominican Republic. ... 6-2/205. ... Bats right, throws right. ... Full name: Mario Gonzalez Encarnacion.

TRANSACTIONS/CAREER NOTES: Signed as non-drafted free agent by Oakland Athletics organization (July 11, 1994). ... On Sacramento disabled list (May 25-July 7, 2000).

							BATTING						FIELDING		
Year Team (League)	Pos.	G	AB	R	H	2B	3B	HR	RBI	Avg.	BB	SO	SB	PO	A	E	Avg.
1995— Dom. Athletics (DSL)	OF	64	229	56	79	11	5	8	44	.345	40	36	17	112	9	7	.945
1996— W. Michigan (Midw.)	OF	118	401	55	92	14	3	7	43	.229	49	131	23	192	13	11	.949
1997— Modesto (Calif.)	OF	111	364	70	108	17	9	18	78	.297	42	121	14	145	7	12	.927
1998— Huntsville (Sou.)	OF	110	357	70	97	15	2	15	61	.272	60	123	11	181	8	6	.969
1999— Midland (Texas)	OF-DH	94	353	69	109	21	4	18	71	.309	47	86	9	126	6	9	.936
— Vancouver (PCL)	OF-DH	39	145	18	35	5	0	3	17	.241	6	44	5	91	6	4	.960
2000— Sacramento (PCL)	OF	81	301	51	81	16	3	13	61	.269	36	95	15	165	10	5	.972
— Modesto (Calif.)	OF	5	15	1	3	0	0	0	1	.200	1	4	0	11	2	0	1.000

ENDERS, TREVOR   P   DEVIL RAYS

PERSONAL: Born December 22, 1974, in Milwaukee. ... 6-0/215. ... Throws left, bats left. ... Full name: Trevor Hale Enders.

HIGH SCHOOL: James E. Taylor (Katy, Texas).

COLLEGE: Houston Baptist.

TRANSACTIONS/CAREER NOTES: Signed as non-drafted free agent by Tampa Bay Devil Rays organization (July 7, 1996).

Year	League	W	L	Pct.	ERA	G	GS	CG	ShO	Sv.	IP	H	R	ER	BB	SO
1996—	Butte (Pio.)	0	1	.000	4.88	19	0	0	0	1	27²/₃	34	22	15	13	24
1997—	Charleston, S.C. (S.Atl.)	4	3	.571	1.88	44	0	0	0	2	67	55	18	14	17	73
1998—	St. Petersburg (FSL)	10	1	.909	2.23	51	0	0	0	1	68²/₃	48	20	17	15	61
1999—	Orlando (Sou.)	8	2	.800	3.30	60	0	0	0	1	95¹/₃	86	37	35	33	63
2000—	Orlando (Sou.)	6	3	.667	3.22	29	5	0	0	0	67	63	26	24	11	41
—	Durham (I.L.)	0	1	.000	2.70	15	0	0	0	0	26²/₃	22	8	8	6	16
—	Tampa Bay (A.L.)	0	1	.000	10.61	9	0	0	0	0	9¹/₃	14	13	11	5	5
Major League totals (1 year)		0	1	.000	10.61	9	0	0	0	0	9¹/₃	14	13	11	5	5

ENSBERG, MORGAN   3B   ASTROS

PERSONAL: Born August 26, 1975, in Redondo Beach, Calif. ... 6-2/210. ... Bats right, throws right. ... Full name: Morgan P. Ensberg.
HIGH SCHOOL: Redondo Union (Redondo Beach, Calif.).
COLLEGE: Southern California.
TRANSACTIONS/CAREER NOTES: Selected by Houston Astros organization in ninth round of free-agent draft (June 2, 1998).
STATISTICAL NOTES: Led New York-Pennsylvania League third baseman with .926 fielding percentage in 1998. ... Led Texas League with 415 total chances in 2000.

							BATTING								FIELDING		
Year	Team (League)	Pos.	G	AB	R	H	2B	3B	HR	RBI	Avg.	BB	SO	SB	PO	A	E	Avg.
1998—	Auburn (NY-Penn)	3B-SS	59	196	39	45	10	1	5	31	.230	46	51	15	39	101	11	†.927
1999—	Kissimmee (FSL)	3B-SS-1B	123	427	72	102	25	2	15	69	.239	68	90	17	73	243	15	.900
2000—	Round Rock (Texas)	3B	137	483	95	145	34	0	28	90	.300	92	107	9	•84	*307	24	.942
—	Houston (N.L.)	3B	4	7	0	2	0	0	0	0	.286	0	1	0	1	1	1	.667
Major League totals (1 year)			4	7	0	2	0	0	0	0	.286	0	1	0	1	1	1	.667

ERDOS, TODD   P   PADRES

PERSONAL: Born November 21, 1973, in Washington, Pa. ... 6-1/204. ... Throws right, bats right. ... Full name: Todd Michael Erdos. ... Name pronounced er-DOHS.
HIGH SCHOOL: Meadville (Pa.).
TRANSACTIONS/CAREER NOTES: Selected by San Diego Padres organization in ninth round of free-agent draft (June 1, 1992). ... On Arizona Padres disabled list (June 4, 1994-remainder of season). ... Selected by Arizona Diamondbacks in second round (41st pick overall) of expansion draft (November 18, 1997). ... Traded by Diamondbacks with P Marty Janzen to New York Yankees for IF Andy Fox (March 8, 1998). ... On Columbus disabled list (July 24, 1998-remainder of season). ... Claimed on waivers by Padres (July 12, 2000).
STATISTICAL NOTES: Led Northwest League with 13 home runs allowed in 1993.

Year	League	W	L	Pct.	ERA	G	GS	CG	ShO	Sv.	IP	H	R	ER	BB	SO
1992—	Arizona Padres (Ariz.)	3	4	.429	2.65	12	9	1	0	0	57²/₃	36	28	17	18	61
—	Spokane (N'West)	1	0	1.000	0.69	2	2	0	0	0	13	9	2	1	5	11
1993—	Spokane (N'West)	5	6	.455	3.19	16	15	0	0	0	90¹/₃	73	39	32	•53	64
—	Waterloo (Midw.)	1	9	.100	8.31	11	11	0	0	0	47²/₃	64	51	44	31	27
1994—	Arizona Padres (Ariz.)				Did not play.											
1995—	Idaho Falls (Pio.)	5	3	.625	3.48	32	0	0	0	0	41¹/₃	34	19	16	30	48
1996—	Rancho Cuca. (Calif.)	3	3	.500	3.74	55	0	0	0	17	67¹/₃	63	33	28	37	82
1997—	Mobile (Sou.)	1	4	.200	3.36	55	0	0	0	27	59	45	22	22	22	49
—	San Diego (N.L.)	2	0	1.000	5.27	11	0	0	0	0	13²/₃	17	9	8	4	13
1998—	Columbus (I.L.)■	3	2	.600	4.62	39	0	0	0	16	48²/₃	52	27	25	20	50
—	New York (A.L.)	0	0	...	9.00	2	0	0	0	0	2	5	2	2	1	0
1999—	Columbus (I.L.)	3	2	.600	6.56	27	8	0	0	0	59	70	47	43	25	53
—	New York (A.L.)	0	0	...	3.86	4	0	0	0	0	7	5	4	3	4	4
2000—	Columbus (I.L.)	0	0	...	5.04	14	0	0	0	1	25	31	14	14	11	18
—	San Diego (N.L.)■	0	0	...	6.67	22	0	0	0	1	29²/₃	32	24	22	17	16
A.L. totals (3 years)		0	0	...	5.03	20	0	0	0	1	34	41	20	19	16	22
N.L. totals (2 years)		2	0	1.000	6.23	33	0	0	0	1	43¹/₃	49	33	30	21	29
Major League totals (4 years)		2	0	1.000	5.70	53	0	0	0	2	77¹/₃	90	53	49	37	51

ERICKSON, SCOTT   P   ORIOLES

PERSONAL: Born February 2, 1968, in Long Beach, Calif. ... 6-4/230. ... Throws right, bats right. ... Full name: Scott Gavin Erickson.
HIGH SCHOOL: Homestead (Cupertino, Calif.).
JUNIOR COLLEGE: San Jose City College.
COLLEGE: Arizona.
TRANSACTIONS/CAREER NOTES: Selected by New York Mets organization in 36th round of free-agent draft (June 2, 1986); did not sign. ... Selected by Houston Astros organization in 34th round of free-agent draft (June 2, 1987); did not sign. ... Selected by Toronto Blue Jays organization in 44th round of free-agent draft (June 1, 1988); did not sign. ... Selected by Minnesota Twins organization in fourth round of free-agent draft (June 5, 1989). ... On disabled list (June 30-July 15, 1991; April 3-18, 1993 and May 15-31, 1994). ... Traded by Twins to Baltimore Orioles for P Scott Klingenbeck and a player to be named later (July 7, 1995); Twins acquired OF Kimera Bartee to complete deal (September 18, 1995). ... On Baltimore disabled list (March 28-May 4 and July 28, 2000-remainder of season); included rehabilitation assignments to Frederick (April 25) and Bowie (April 30).
RECORDS: Holds A.L. single-season record for fewest innings pitched for league leader—251¹/₃ (1998).
STATISTICAL NOTES: Pitched 5-0 one-hit, complete-game victory against Boston (July 24, 1992, first game). ... Pitched 6-0 no-hit victory against Milwaukee (April 27, 1994). ... Tied for A.L. lead with nine hit batsmen in 1994. ... Led A.L. pitchers with 24 putouts and 68 total chances in 1999.
MISCELLANEOUS: Appeared in one game as pinch runner (2000).

Year	League	W	L	Pct.	ERA	G	GS	CG	ShO	Sv.	IP	H	R	ER	BB	SO
1989—	Visalia (Calif.)	3	4	.429	2.97	12	12	2	0	0	78²/₃	79	29	26	22	59
1990—	Orlando (Sou.)	8	3	.727	3.03	15	15	3	1	0	101	75	38	34	24	69
—	Minnesota (A.L.)	8	4	.667	2.87	19	17	1	0	0	113	108	49	36	51	53
1991—	Minnesota (A.L.)	•20	8	.714	3.18	32	32	5	3	0	204	189	80	72	71	108
1992—	Minnesota (A.L.)	13	12	.520	3.40	32	32	5	3	0	212	197	86	80	83	101
1993—	Minnesota (A.L.)	8	*19	.296	5.19	34	34	1	0	0	218²/₃	*266	*138	126	71	116
1994—	Minnesota (A.L.)	8	11	.421	5.44	23	23	2	1	0	144	173	95	87	59	104
1995—	Minnesota (A.L.)	4	6	.400	5.95	15	15	0	0	0	87²/₃	102	61	58	32	45
—	Baltimore (A.L.)■	9	4	.692	3.89	17	16	7	2	0	108²/₃	111	47	47	35	61
1996—	Baltimore (A.L.)	13	12	.520	5.02	34	34	6	0	0	222¹/₃	262	137	124	66	100
1997—	Baltimore (A.L.)	16	7	.696	3.69	34	33	3	2	0	221²/₃	218	100	91	61	131
1998—	Baltimore (A.L.)	16	13	.552	4.01	36	*36	*11	2	0	*251¹/₃	*284	125	112	69	186
1999—	Baltimore (A.L.)	15	12	.556	4.81	34	34	6	*3	0	230¹/₃	244	127	123	*99	106
2000—	Frederick (Caro.)	0	0	...	2.70	1	1	0	0	0	6²/₃	3	2	2	1	5
—	Bowie (East.)	0	0	...	0.00	1	1	0	0	0	7	4	0	0	0	5
—	Baltimore (A.L.)	5	8	.385	7.87	16	16	1	0	0	92²/₃	127	81	81	48	41
Major League totals (11 years)		**135**	**116**	**.538**	**4.43**	**326**	**322**	**48**	**16**	**0**	**2106¹/₃**	**2281**	**1126**	**1037**	**745**	**1152**

DIVISION SERIES RECORD

Year	League	W	L	Pct.	ERA	G	GS	CG	ShO	Sv.	IP	H	R	ER	BB	SO
1996—	Baltimore (A.L.)	0	0	...	4.05	1	1	0	0	0	6²/₃	6	3	3	2	6
1997—	Baltimore (A.L.)	1	0	1.000	4.05	1	1	0	0	0	6²/₃	7	3	3	2	6
Division series totals (2 years)		**1**	**0**	**1.000**	**4.05**	**2**	**2**	**0**	**0**	**0**	**13¹/₃**	**13**	**6**	**6**	**4**	**12**

CHAMPIONSHIP SERIES RECORD

RECORDS: Shares A.L. record for most runs allowed in one inning—6 (October 13, 1996, third inning). ... Holds record for most home runs allowed in one inning—3 (October 13, 1996, third inning).

Year	League	W	L	Pct.	ERA	G	GS	CG	ShO	Sv.	IP	H	R	ER	BB	SO
1991—	Minnesota (A.L.)	0	0	...	4.50	1	1	0	0	0	4	3	2	2	5	2
1996—	Baltimore (A.L.)	0	1	.000	2.38	2	2	0	0	0	11¹/₃	14	9	3	4	8
1997—	Baltimore (A.L.)	1	0	1.000	4.26	2	2	0	0	0	12²/₃	15	7	6	1	6
Champ. series totals (3 years)		**1**	**1**	**.500**	**3.54**	**5**	**5**	**0**	**0**	**0**	**28**	**32**	**18**	**11**	**10**	**16**

WORLD SERIES RECORD

NOTES: Member of World Series championship team (1991).

Year	League	W	L	Pct.	ERA	G	GS	CG	ShO	Sv.	IP	H	R	ER	BB	SO
1991—	Minnesota (A.L.)	0	0	...	5.06	2	2	0	0	0	10²/₃	10	7	6	4	5

ERSTAD, DARIN   OF   ANGELS

PERSONAL: Born June 4, 1974, in Jamestown, N.D. ... 6-2/212. ... Bats left, throws left. ... Full name: Darin Charles Erstad.
HIGH SCHOOL: Jamestown (N.D.).
COLLEGE: Nebraska.
TRANSACTIONS/CAREER NOTES: Selected by New York Mets organization in 13th round of free-agent draft (June 1, 1992); did not sign. ... Selected by California Angels organization in first round (first pick overall) of free-agent draft (June 1, 1995). ... Angels franchise renamed Anaheim Angels for 1997 season. ... On disabled list (August 4-19, 1998; and August 11-26, 1999).
HONORS: Won A.L. Gold Glove as outfielder (2000). ... Named outfielder on The Sporting News A.L. All-Star team (2000). ... Named outfielder on The Sporting News A.L. Silver Slugger team (2000).
STATISTICAL NOTES: Had 15-game hitting streak (April 1-18, 1998). ... Career major league grand slams: 1.

						BATTING							FIELDING		
Year	Team (League)	Pos.	G	AB	R	H	2B	3B	HR	RBI	Avg.	BB	SO	SB	PO	A	E	Avg.
1995—	Arizona Angels (Ariz.)	OF	4	18	2	10	1	0	0	1	.556	1	1	1	3	0	0	1.000
—	Lake Elsinore (Calif.)	OF	25	113	24	41	7	2	5	24	.363	6	22	3	65	2	1	.985
1996—	Vancouver (PCL)	OF-1B-DH	85	351	63	107	22	5	6	41	.305	44	53	11	184	10	1	.995
—	California (A.L.)	OF	57	208	34	59	5	1	4	20	.284	17	29	3	121	2	3	.976
1997—	Anaheim (A.L.)	1B-DH-OF	139	539	99	161	34	4	16	77	.299	51	86	23	1003	64	11	.990
1998—	Anaheim (A.L.)	OF-1B-DH	133	537	84	159	39	3	19	82	.296	43	77	20	580	43	3	.995
1999—	Anaheim (A.L.)	1B-OF-DH	142	585	84	148	22	5	13	53	.253	47	101	13	854	48	1	.999
2000—	Anaheim (A.L.)	OF-DH-1B	157	*676	121	*240	39	6	25	100	.355	64	82	28	355	9	3	.992
Major League totals (5 years)			**628**	**2545**	**422**	**767**	**139**	**19**	**77**	**332**	**.301**	**222**	**375**	**87**	**2913**	**166**	**21**	**.993**

ALL-STAR GAME RECORD

				BATTING							FIELDING		
Year	League	Pos.	AB	R	H	2B	3B	HR	RBI	Avg.	BB	SO	SB	PO	A	E	Avg.
1998—	American	OF	2	1	0	0	0	0	0	.000	0	0	0	3	0	0	1.000
2000—	American	LF	2	0	0	0	0	0	1	.000	0	0	0	0	0	0	...
All-Star Game totals (2 years)			**4**	**1**	**0**	**0**	**0**	**0**	**1**	**.000**	**0**	**0**	**0**	**3**	**0**	**0**	**1.000**

ESCOBAR, ALEX   OF   METS

PERSONAL: Born September 6, 1978, in Valencia, Venezuela. ... 6-1/180. ... Bats right, throws right. ... Full name: Alexander Jose Escobar.
HIGH SCHOOL: El Santuario (Valencia, Venezuela).
TRANSACTIONS/CAREER NOTES: Signed as non-drafted free agent by New York Mets organization (July 1, 1995). ... On St. Lucie disabled list (April 14-June 21 and July 8, 1999-remainder of season).

						BATTING							FIELDING		
Year	Team (League)	Pos.	G	AB	R	H	2B	3B	HR	RBI	Avg.	BB	SO	SB	PO	A	E	Avg.
1996—	GC Mets (GCL)	OF-SS	24	75	15	27	4	0	0	10	.360	4	9	0	42	2	3	.936
1997—	Little Falls (NY-Penn)	OF	10	36	6	7	3	0	0	3	.194	3	8	1	19	0	2	.905
—	GC Mets (GCL)	OF	26	73	12	18	4	1	1	11	.247	10	17	0	26	2	1	.966
1998—	Capital City (S.Atl.)	OF	112	416	90	129	23	5	27	91	.310	54	133	49	186	5	12	.941
1999—	GC Mets (GCL)	DH-OF	2	8	1	3	2	0	0	1	.375	1	2	0	1	0	0	1.000
—	St. Lucie (FSL)	OF	1	3	1	2	0	0	1	3	.667	1	1	1	2	0	0	1.000
2000—	Binghamton (East.)	OF	122	437	79	126	25	7	16	67	.288	57	114	24	276	10	5	.983

E

ESCOBAR, KELVIM — P — BLUE JAYS

PERSONAL: Born April 11, 1976, in La Guaria, Venezuela. ... 6-1/210. ... Throws right, bats right. ... Full name: Kelvim Jose Bolivar Escobar.
TRANSACTIONS/CAREER NOTES: Signed as non-drafted free agent by Toronto Blue Jays organization (July 9, 1992). ... On Toronto disabled list (April 16-May 6, 1998); included rehabilitation assignment to Syracuse (May 2-6).

Year League	W	L	Pct.	ERA	G	GS	CG	ShO	Sv.	IP	H	R	ER	BB	SO
1993—Dom. Blue Jays (DSL)	2	1	.667	4.13	8	7	0	0	0	32⅔	34	17	15	25	31
1994—GC Blue Jays (GCL)	4	4	.500	2.35	11	10	1	0	1	65	56	23	17	18	64
1995—Dom. Blue Jays (DSL)	0	1	.000	1.72	3	2	0	0	0	15⅔	14	3	3	5	20
—Medicine Hat (Pio.)	3	3	.500	5.71	14	14	1	•1	0	69⅓	66	47	44	33	75
1996—Dunedin (FSL)	9	5	.643	2.69	18	18	1	0	0	110⅓	101	44	33	33	113
—Knoxville (Sou.)	3	4	.429	5.33	10	10	0	0	0	54	61	36	32	24	44
1997—Knoxville (Sou.)	2	1	.667	3.70	5	5	1	0	0	24⅓	20	13	10	16	31
—Dunedin (FSL)	0	1	.000	3.75	3	2	0	0	0	12	16	9	5	3	16
—Toronto (A.L.)	3	2	.600	2.90	27	0	0	0	14	31	28	12	10	19	36
1998—Toronto (A.L.)	7	3	.700	3.73	22	10	0	0	0	79⅔	72	37	33	35	72
—Syracuse (I.L.)	2	2	.500	3.77	13	10	0	0	1	59⅔	51	26	25	24	64
1999—Toronto (A.L.)	14	11	.560	5.69	33	30	1	0	0	174	203	118	110	81	129
2000—Toronto (A.L.)	10	15	.400	5.35	43	24	3	1	2	180	186	118	107	85	142
Major League totals (4 years)	34	31	.523	5.04	125	64	4	1	16	464⅔	489	285	260	220	379

ESTALELLA, BOBBY — C — GIANTS

PERSONAL: Born August 23, 1974, in Hialeah, Fla. ... 6-1/205. ... Bats right, throws right. ... Full name: Robert M. Estalella. ... Grandson of Bobby Estalella, outfielder with Washington Senators (1935-36, 1939 and 1942), St. Louis Browns (1941), and Philadelphia Athletics (1943-45 and 1949).
HIGH SCHOOL: Cooper City (Fla.).
JUNIOR COLLEGE: Miami-Dade (South) Community College.
TRANSACTIONS/CAREER NOTES: Selected by Philadelphia Phillies organization in 23rd round of free-agent draft (June 1, 1992). ... On Philadelphia disabled list (March 27-April 29, 1999); included rehabilitation assignments to Clearwater (April 9-17) and to Scraton/Wilkes-Barre (April 19-29). ... Traded by Phillies to San Francisco Giants for P Chris Brock (December 12, 1999).
STATISTICAL NOTES: Tied for South Atlantic League lead in double plays by catcher with eight in 1994. ... Led Florida State League catchers with 864 total chances in 1995. ... Led International League with 928 total chances and tied for league lead in double plays by catcher with nine in 1997. ... Hit three home runs in one game (September 4, 1997). ... Led International League catchers with 10 double plays in 1999. ... Led N.L. catchers with 14 double plays in 2000. ... Career major league grand slams: 2.

Year Team (League)	Pos.	G	AB	R	H	2B	3B	HR	RBI	Avg.	BB	SO	SB	PO	A	E	Avg.
1993—Martinsville (Appl.)	C	35	122	14	36	11	0	3	19	.295	14	24	0	210	25	6	.975
—Clearwater (FSL)	C	11	35	4	8	0	0	0	4	.229	2	3	0	47	8	0	1.000
1994—Spartanburg (S.Atl.)	C	86	299	34	65	19	1	9	41	.217	31	85	0	592	87	10	.985
—Clearwater (FSL)	C	13	46	3	12	1	0	2	9	.261	3	17	0	92	5	1	.990
1995—Clearwater (FSL)	C	117	404	61	105	24	1	15	58	.260	56	76	0	*771	82	11	.987
—Reading (East.)	C	10	34	5	8	1	0	2	9	.235	4	7	0	60	9	1	.986
1996—Reading (East.)	C	111	365	48	89	14	2	23	72	.244	67	104	2	775	84	14	.984
—Scranton/W.B. (I.L.)	C	11	36	7	9	3	0	3	8	.250	5	10	0	55	6	2	.968
—Philadelphia (N.L.)	C	7	17	5	6	0	0	2	4	.353	1	6	1	24	1	0	1.000
1997—Scranton/W.B. (I.L.)	C-DH	123	433	63	101	32	0	16	65	.233	56	109	3	*844	71	13	.986
—Philadelphia (N.L.)	C	13	29	9	10	1	0	4	9	.345	7	7	0	49	3	0	1.000
1998—Scranton/W.B. (I.L.)	C-DH	76	242	49	68	14	1	17	49	.281	66	49	0	469	25	5	.990
—Philadelphia (N.L.)	C	47	165	16	31	6	1	8	20	.188	13	49	0	321	12	4	.988
1999—Clearwater (FSL)	C-DH	8	26	3	11	3	0	1	8	.423	3	3	0	37	4	1	.976
—Scranton/W.B. (I.L.)	C-DH	110	386	58	89	23	2	15	62	.231	55	100	4	652	43	5	.993
—Philadelphia (N.L.)	C	9	18	2	3	0	0	0	1	.167	4	7	0	38	2	1	.976
2000—San Fran. (N.L.)■	C	106	299	45	70	22	3	14	53	.234	57	92	3	654	49	5	.993
Major League totals (5 years)		182	528	77	120	29	4	28	87	.227	82	161	4	1086	67	10	.991

DIVISION SERIES RECORD

Year Team (League)	Pos.	G	AB	R	H	2B	3B	HR	RBI	Avg.	BB	SO	SB	PO	A	E	Avg.
2000—San Francisco (N.L.)	C	4	12	1	1	0	0	0	1	.083	0	2	0	25	2	0	1.000

ESTES, SHAWN — P — GIANTS

PERSONAL: Born February 18, 1973, in San Francisco. ... 6-2/195. ... Throws left, bats right. ... Full name: Aaron Shawn Estes. ... Name pronounced EST-us.
HIGH SCHOOL: Douglas (Minden, Nev.).
TRANSACTIONS/CAREER NOTES: Selected by Seattle Mariners organization in first round (11th pick overall) of free-agent draft (June 3, 1991). ... On Appleton disabled list (April 8-July 19 and July 25-August 15, 1994). ... Traded by Mariners with IF Wilson Delgado to San Francisco Giants for P Salomon Torres (May 21, 1995). ... On disabled list (March 23-April 6, 1997). ... On San Francisco disabled list (July 11-September 4, 1998); included rehabilitation assignments to Bakersfield (August 26-29) and Fresno (August 30-September 4). ... On San Francisco disabled list (March 29-April 17, 2000); included rehabilitation assignments to Fresno (April 7-12) and San Jose (April 13-17).
STATISTICAL NOTES: Tied for N.L. lead with 15 wild pitches in 1999. ... Career major league grand slams: 1. ... Led N.L. pitchers with seven double plays in 2000.
MISCELLANEOUS: Appeared in four games as pinch runner with San Francisco (1996). ... Appeared in four games as pinch runner (1997). ... Scored two runs in two games as pinch runner with San Francisco (1998). ... Struck out in both appearances as pinch hitter and scored two runs in eight appearances as pinch runner (1999). ... Appeared in two games as pinch runner (2000).

Year	League	W	L	Pct.	ERA	G	GS	CG	ShO	Sv.	IP	H	R	ER	BB	SO
1991— Bellingham (N'West)		1	3	.250	6.88	9	9	0	0	0	34	27	33	26	55	35
1992— Bellingham (N'West)		3	3	.500	4.32	15	15	0	0	0	77	84	55	37	45	77
1993— Appleton (Midw.)		5	9	.357	7.24	19	18	0	0	0	83 1/3	108	85	67	52	65
1994— Appleton (Midw.)		0	2	.000	4.58	5	4	0	0	0	19 2/3	19	13	10	17	28
— Arizona Mariners (Ariz.)		0	3	.000	3.15	5	5	0	0	0	20	16	9	7	6	31
1995— Wisconsin (Midw.)		0	0	...	0.90	2	2	0	0	0	10	5	1	1	5	11
— Burlington (Midw.)■........		0	0	...	4.11	4	4	0	0	0	15 1/3	13	8	7	12	22
— San Jose (Calif.)		5	2	.714	2.17	9	8	0	0	0	49 2/3	32	13	12	17	61
— Shreveport (Texas)		2	0	1.000	2.01	4	4	0	0	0	22 1/3	14	5	5	10	18
— San Francisco (N.L.)		0	3	.000	6.75	3	3	0	0	0	17 1/3	16	14	13	5	14
1996— Phoenix (PCL)		9	3	.750	3.43	18	18	0	0	0	110 1/3	92	43	42	38	95
— San Francisco (N.L.)		3	5	.375	3.60	11	11	0	0	0	70	63	30	28	39	60
1997— San Francisco (N.L.)		19	5	.792	3.18	32	32	3	2	0	201	162	80	71	*100	181
1998— San Francisco (N.L.)		7	12	.368	5.06	25	25	1	1	0	149 1/3	150	89	84	80	136
— Bakersfield (Calif.)		0	0	...	0.00	1	1	0	0	0	4 1/3	3	0	0	1	5
— Fresno (PCL)		1	0	1.000	1.80	1	1	0	0	0	5	3	1	1	3	6
1999— San Francisco (N.L.)		11	11	.500	4.92	32	32	1	1	0	203	209	121	111	112	159
2000— Fresno (PCL)		0	1	.000	9.00	1	1	0	0	0	3	5	9	3	2	2
— San Jose (Calif.)		1	0	1.000	0.00	1	1	0	0	0	7	2	0	0	1	11
— San Francisco (N.L.)		15	6	.714	4.26	30	30	4	2	0	190 1/3	194	99	90	108	136
Major League totals (6 years)		55	42	.567	4.30	133	133	9	6	0	831	794	433	397	444	686

DIVISION SERIES RECORD

Year	League	W	L	Pct.	ERA	G	GS	CG	ShO	Sv.	IP	H	R	ER	BB	SO
1997— San Francisco (N.L.)		0	0	...	15.00	1	1	0	0	0	3	5	5	5	4	3
2000— San Francisco (N.L.)		0	0	...	6.00	1	1	0	0	0	3	3	2	2	3	3
Division series totals (2 years)		0	0	...	10.50	2	2	0	0	0	6	8	7	7	7	6

ALL-STAR GAME RECORD

Year	League	W	L	Pct.	ERA	GS	CG	ShO	Sv.	IP	H	R	ER	BB	SO
1997— National		0	1	.000	18.00	0	0	0	0	1	1	2	2	1	1

ESTRADA, HORACIO   P   BREWERS

PERSONAL: Born October 19, 1975, in San Joaquin, Venezuela. ... 6-0/160. ... Throws left, bats left. ... Full name: Horacio Jimenez Estrada.
HIGH SCHOOL: Domingo Segado (San Joaquin, Venezuela).
TRANSACTIONS/CAREER NOTES: Signed as non-drafted free agent by Milwaukee Brewers organization (July 3, 1992). ... On Louisville disabled list (May 28, 1998-remainder of season; and June 9-19, 1999).

Year	League	W	L	Pct.	ERA	G	GS	CG	ShO	Sv.	IP	H	R	ER	BB	SO
1993— Dom. Brewers (DSL)		1	2	.333	4.41	22	3	0	0	0	51	39	33	25	37	60
1994— Dom. Brewers (DSL)		3	4	.429	2.67	26	2	0	0	7	60 2/3	41	27	18	46	52
1995— Arizona Brewers (Ariz.)		0	1	.000	3.71	8	1	0	0	2	17	13	9	7	8	21
— Helena (Pio.)		1	2	.333	5.40	13	0	0	0	0	30	27	21	18	24	30
1996— Beloit (Midw.)		2	1	.667	1.23	17	0	0	0	1	29 1/3	21	8	4	11	34
— Stockton (Calif.)		1	3	.250	4.59	29	0	0	0	3	51	43	29	26	21	62
1997— El Paso (Texas)		8	10	.444	4.74	29	23	1	0	1	153 2/3	174	93	81	70	127
1998— El Paso (Texas)		5	0	1.000	4.53	8	8	0	0	0	49 2/3	50	27	25	21	37
— Louisville (I.L.)		0	0	...	3.00	2	2	0	0	0	12	10	4	4	5	4
1999— Louisville (I.L.)		6	6	.500	5.67	25	24	1	0	0	131 2/3	128	87	83	65	112
— Milwaukee (N.L.)		0	0	...	7.36	4	0	0	0	0	7 1/3	10	6	6	4	5
2000— Indianapolis (I.L.)		*14	4	.778	3.33	25	25	3	•2	0	159 1/3	149	63	59	45	103
— Milwaukee (N.L.)		3	0	1.000	6.29	7	4	0	0	0	24 1/3	30	18	17	20	13
Major League totals (2 years)		3	0	1.000	6.54	11	4	0	0	0	31 2/3	40	24	23	24	18

ESTRADA, JOHNNY   C   PHILLIES

PERSONAL: Born June 27, 1976, in Hayward, Calif. ... 5-11/210. ... Bats both, throws right. ... Full name: Johnny P. Estrada III.
HIGH SCHOOL: Roosevelt (Fresno, Calif.).
JUNIOR COLLEGE: Fresno (Calif.) City College, then College of the Sequoias (Calif.).
TRANSACTIONS/CAREER NOTES: Selected by Houston Astros organization in 71st round of free-agent draft (June 2, 1994); did not sign. ... Selected by Phiadelphia Phillies organization in 17th round of free-agent draft (June 3, 1997).
STATISTICAL NOTES: Led New York-Pennsylvania League catchers with 391 putouts, 434 total chances and 1.000 fielding percentage in 1997. ... Tied for South Atlantic League lead in double plays by catcher with six in 1998.

Year	Team (League)	Pos.	G	AB	R	H	2B	3B	HR	RBI	Avg.	BB	SO	SB	PO	A	E	Avg.
						BATTING									FIELDING			
1997— Batavia (NY-Penn)		C-1B	58	223	28	70	17	2	6	43	.314	9	15	0	•403	44	0	•1.000
1998— Piedmont (S.Atl.)		C	77	303	33	94	14	2	7	44	.310	6	19	0	523	63	6	.990
— Clearwater (FSL)		C	37	117	8	26	8	0	0	13	.222	5	7	0	200	32	5	.979
1999— Clearwater (FSL)		C	98	346	35	96	15	0	9	52	.277	14	26	1	417	54	5	.989
2000— Reading (East.)		C	95	356	42	105	18	0	12	42	.295	10	20	1	603	64	7	.990

ESTRELLA, LEO   P   REDS

PERSONAL: Born February 20, 1975, in Puerto Plata, Dominican Republic. ... 6-1/185. ... Throws right, bats right. ... Full name: Leoncio Ramirez Estrella.
HIGH SCHOOL: Liceo Padre Las Casas (Puerto Plata, Dominican Republic).

E

TRANSACTIONS/CAREER NOTES: Signed as non-drafted free agent by New York Mets organization (October 12, 1993). ... On Capital City disabled list (April 10-24, 1998). ... Traded by Mets to Toronto Blue Jays for IF/OF Tony Phillips (July 31, 1998). ... Traded by Blue Jays with P Clayton Andrews to Cincinnati Reds for P Steve Parris (November 22, 2000).

STATISTICAL NOTES: Pitched 3-0 no-hit victory for Tennessee against Orlando (May 27, 2000; six innings). ... Pitched 5-0 no-hit victory for Syracuse against Indianapolis (June 17, 2000; first game).

Year League	W	L	Pct.	ERA	G	GS	CG	ShO	Sv.	IP	H	R	ER	BB	SO
1994— Dom. Mets (DSL)	5	0	1.000	3.47	30	0	0	0	3	36 1/3	33	28	14	32	20
1995— Dom. Mets (DSL)	2	4	.333	5.44	12	8	0	0	0	43	61	37	26	13	32
1996— Kingsport (Appl.)	6	3	.667	3.88	15	7	1	0	0	58	54	32	25	24	52
1997— Pittsfield (NY-Penn)	7	6	.538	3.03	15	15	0	0	0	92	91	48	31	27	55
1998— Columbia (S.Atl.)	10	8	.556	3.93	20	20	3	0	0	119	120	66	52	23	97
— Hagerstown (S.Atl.)■	1	3	.250	4.50	5	5	0	0	0	30	34	19	15	13	27
1999— Dunedin (FSL)	14	7	.667	3.21	27	24	2	2	0	168	166	74	60	47	116
2000— Tennessee (Sou.)	5	5	.500	3.67	13	13	3	2	0	76	68	36	31	30	63
— Syracuse (I.L.)	5	4	.556	4.01	15	15	3	1	0	89 2/3	68	42	40	40	48
— Toronto (A.L.)	0	0	...	5.79	2	0	0	0	0	4 2/3	9	3	3	0	3
Major League totals (1 year)	0	0	...	5.79	2	0	0	0	0	4 2/3	9	3	3	0	3

ETHERTON, SETH   P   REDS

PERSONAL: Born October 17, 1976, in Laguna Beach, Calif. ... 6-1/200. ... Throws right, bats right. ... Full name: Seth Michael Etherton.
HIGH SCHOOL: Dana Hills (Dana Point, Calif.).
COLLEGE: Southern California.
TRANSACTIONS/CAREER NOTES: Selected by St. Louis Cardinals organization in ninth-round of free-agent draft (June 3, 1997); did not sign. ... Selected by Anaheim Angels organization in first round (18th pick overall) of free-agent draft (June 2, 1998). ... On Anaheim disabled list (August 5, 2000-remainder of season). ... Traded by Angels to Cincinnati Reds for SS Wilmy Caceres (December 10, 2000).

Year League	W	L	Pct.	ERA	G	GS	CG	ShO	Sv.	IP	H	R	ER	BB	SO
1998— Midland (Texas)	1	5	.167	6.14	9	7	1	0	0	48 1/3	57	36	33	12	35
1999— Erie (East.)	10	10	.500	3.27	24	24	4	1	0	167 2/3	153	72	61	43	153
— Edmonton (PCL)	0	2	.000	5.48	4	4	0	0	0	21 1/3	25	13	13	6	19
2000— Edmonton (PCL)	3	2	.600	4.01	9	9	0	0	0	58 1/3	60	30	26	19	50
— Anaheim (A.L.)	5	1	.833	5.52	11	11	0	0	0	60 1/3	68	38	37	22	32
Major League totals (1 year)	5	1	.833	5.52	11	11	0	0	0	60 1/3	68	38	37	22	32

EUSEBIO, TONY   C   ASTROS

PERSONAL: Born April 27, 1967, in San Jose de Los Llames, Dominican Republic. ... 6-2/210. ... Bats right, throws right. ... Full name: Raul Antonio Eusebio. ... Name pronounced you-SAY-bee-o.
HIGH SCHOOL: San Rafael (Dominican Republic).
TRANSACTIONS/CAREER NOTES: Signed as non-drafted free agent by Houston Astros organization (May 30, 1985). ... On disabled list (August 5, 1990-remainder of season; April 16-23, 1992; and August 24, 1993-remainder of season). ... On Houston disabled list (May 8-June 17 and June 22-August 7, 1996); included rehabilitation assignments to Tucson (June 10-17 and July 29-August 7). ... On disabled list (July 30-August 15, 1999). ... Granted free agency (October 28, 1999). ... Re-signed by Astros (December 2, 1999).
STATISTICAL NOTES: Tied for Southern League lead in double plays by catcher with eight in 1989. ... Led Texas League catchers with .9963 fielding percentage and 12 double plays in 1992. ... Had 24-game hitting streak (July 9-August 28, 2000). ... Career major league grand slams: 2.

Year Team (League)	Pos.	G	AB	R	H	2B	3B	HR	RBI	Avg.	BB	SO	SB	PO	A	E	Avg.
1985— GC Astros (GCL)	C	1	1	0	0	0	0	0	0	.000	0	0	0	4	0	0	1.000
1985—					Dominican Summer League statistics unavailable.												
1986—					Dominican Summer League statistics unavailable.												
1987— GC Astros (GCL)	C-1B	42	125	26	26	1	2	1	15	.208	18	19	8	204	24	4	.983
1988— Osceola (FSL)	C-OF	118	392	45	96	6	3	0	40	.245	40	69	19	611	66	8	.988
1989— Columbus (Sou.)	C	65	203	20	38	6	1	0	18	.187	38	47	7	355	46	7	.983
— Osceola (FSL)	C	52	175	22	50	6	3	0	30	.286	19	27	5	290	40	5	.985
1990— Columbus (Sou.)	C	92	318	36	90	18	0	4	37	.283	21	80	6	558	69	4	*.994
1991— Jackson (Texas)	C	66	222	27	58	8	3	2	31	.261	25	54	3	424	48	7	.985
— Tucson (PCL)	C	5	20	5	8	1	0	0	2	.400	3	3	1	40	1	0	1.000
— Houston (N.L.)	C	10	19	4	2	1	0	0	0	.105	6	8	0	49	4	1	.981
1992— Jackson (Texas)	C	94	339	33	104	9	3	5	44	.307	25	58	1	493	51	2	*.996
1993— Tucson (PCL)	C	78	281	39	91	20	1	1	43	.324	22	40	1	450	46	3	.994
1994— Houston (N.L.)	C	55	159	18	47	9	1	5	30	.296	8	33	0	263	24	2	.993
1995— Houston (N.L.)	C	113	368	46	110	21	1	6	58	.299	31	59	0	645	49	5	.993
1996— Houston (N.L.)	C	58	152	15	41	7	2	1	19	.270	18	20	0	255	24	1	.996
— Tucson (PCL)	C-DH	15	53	8	22	4	0	0	14	.415	2	7	0	45	1	0	1.000
1997— Houston (N.L.)	C	60	164	12	45	2	0	1	18	.274	19	27	0	297	16	4	.987
1998— Houston (N.L.)	C	66	182	13	46	6	1	1	36	.253	18	31	1	352	19	3	.992
1999— Houston (N.L.)	C	103	323	31	88	15	0	4	33	.272	40	67	0	652	37	4	.994
2000— Houston (N.L.)	C	74	218	24	61	18	0	7	33	.280	25	45	0	411	17	5	.988
Major League totals (8 years)		539	1585	163	440	79	5	25	227	.278	165	290	1	2924	190	25	.992

DIVISION SERIES RECORD

Year Team (League)	Pos.	G	AB	R	H	2B	3B	HR	RBI	Avg.	BB	SO	SB	PO	A	E	Avg.
1997— Houston (N.L.)	C	1	3	1	2	0	0	0	0	.667	0	1	1	6	1	0	1.000
1998— Houston (N.L.)	C	1	3	0	1	1	0	0	0	.333	0	2	0	6	0	0	1.000
1999— Houston (N.L.)	C	4	15	2	4	0	0	1	3	.267	1	2	0	34	3	1	.974
Division series totals (3 years)		6	21	3	7	1	0	1	3	.333	1	5	1	46	4	1	.980

EVANS, TOM — 3B — TIGERS

PERSONAL: Born July 9, 1974, in Kirkland, Wash. ... 6-1/200. ... Bats right, throws right. ... Full name: Thomas John Evans.
HIGH SCHOOL: Juanita (Kirkland, Wash.).
TRANSACTIONS/CAREER NOTES: Selected by Toronto Blue Jays organization in fourth round of free-agent draft (June 1, 1992). ... On disabled list (April 7-May 17, 1994). ... On Toronto disabled list (September 14-28, 1997). ... On Syracuse disabled list (July 29-August 11, 1998). ... Claimed on waivers by Texas Rangers (April 2, 1999). ... On Oklahoma disabled list (September 3-10, 1999). ... Granted free agency (October 15, 1999). ... Re-signed by Rangers organization (December 16, 1999). ... On disabled list (May 15, 2000-remainder of season). ... Granted free agency (October 14, 2000). ... Signed by Detroit Tigers organization (January 18, 2001).
STATISTICAL NOTES: Led Florida State League third basemen with 435 total chances in 1995. ... Led Southern League with .453 on-base percentage in 1996. ... Led International league third basemen with 337 total chances and 27 double plays in 1997. ... Led Pacific Coast League third baseman with 266 assists and 365 total chances in 1999.

							BATTING								FIELDING			
Year	Team (League)	Pos.	G	AB	R	H	2B	3B	HR	RBI	Avg.	BB	SO	SB	PO	A	E	Avg.
1992— Medicine Hat (Pio.)		3B	52	166	17	36	3	0	1	21	.217	33	29	4	53	115	20	.894
1993— Hagerstown (S.Atl.)		3B-1B-SS	119	389	47	100	25	1	7	54	.257	53	92	9	92	181	27	.910
1994— Hagerstown (S.Atl.)		3B	95	322	52	88	16	2	13	48	.273	51	80	2	60	196	36	.877
1995— Dunedin (FSL)		3B	130	444	63	124	29	3	9	66	.279	51	80	7	*92	*309	34	.922
1996— Knoxville (Sou.)..........		3B-DH-1B	120	394	87	111	27	1	17	65	.282	*115	113	4	52	146	12	.943
1997— Dunedin (FSL)		DH-3B	15	42	8	11	2	0	2	4	.262	11	10	0	6	12	2	.900
— Syracuse (I.L.)............		3B-DH	107	376	60	99	17	1	15	65	.263	53	104	1	*83	*242	12	*.964
— Toronto (A.L.)............		3B	12	38	7	11	2	0	1	2	.289	2	10	0	9	24	3	.917
1998— Syracuse (I.L.)............		3B-DH	109	400	57	120	32	1	15	55	.300	50	74	11	89	208	14	.955
— Toronto (A.L.)............		3B	7	10	0	0	0	0	0	0	.000	1	2	0	5	3	1	.889
1999— Oklahoma (PCL)■.....		3B-DH-1B	128	439	84	123	35	3	12	68	.280	66	100	5	82	*266	18	.951
2000— Texas (A.L.)		3B-DH-1B	23	54	10	15	4	0	0	5	.278	10	13	0	13	40	5	.914
Major League totals (3 years)			42	102	17	26	6	0	1	7	.255	13	25	0	27	67	9	.913

EVERETT, ADAM — SS — ASTROS

PERSONAL: Born February 2, 1977, in Austell, Ga. ... 6-0/156. ... Bats right, throws right.
HIGH SCHOOL: Harrison (Kennesaw, Ga.).
COLLEGE: North Carolina State, then South Carolina.
TRANSACTIONS/CAREER NOTES: Selected by Boston Red Sox organization in first round (12th pick overall) of free-agent draft (June 2, 1998). ... Traded by Red Sox with P Greg Miller to Houston Astros for OF Carl Everett (December 14, 1999).

							BATTING								FIELDING			
Year	Team (League)	Pos.	G	AB	R	H	2B	3B	HR	RBI	Avg.	BB	SO	SB	PO	A	E	Avg.
1998— Lowell (NY-Penn)		SS	21	71	11	21	6	2	0	9	.296	11	13	2	34	67	9	.918
1999— Trenton (East.)		SS	98	338	56	89	11	0	10	44	.263	41	64	21	150	273	18	.959
2000— New Orleans (PCL)■..		SS	126	453	82	111	25	2	5	37	.245	75	100	13	172	*410	25	.959

EVERETT, CARL — OF — RED SOX

E

PERSONAL: Born June 3, 1971, in Tampa. ... 6-0/215. ... Bats both, throws right. ... Full name: Carl Edward Everett.
HIGH SCHOOL: Hillsborough (Tampa).
TRANSACTIONS/CAREER NOTES: Selected by New York Yankees organization in first round (10th pick overall) of free-agent draft (June 4, 1990). ... On Fort Lauderdale disabled list (July 7-August 15, 1992). ... Selected by Florida Marlins in second round (27th pick overall) of expansion draft (November 17, 1992). ... On High Desert disabled list (April 8-13, 1993). ... On Florida disabled list (July 23-August 10, 1994). ... On Edmonton suspended list (August 29, 1994-remainder of season). ... Traded by Marlins to New York Mets for 2B Quilvio Veras (November 29, 1994). ... On disabled list (April 12-27, 1996). ... Traded by Mets to Houston Astros for P John Hudek (December 22, 1997). ... On disabled list (July 16-August 6, 1999). ... Traded by Astros to Boston Red Sox for SS Adam Everett and P Greg Miller (December 14, 1999). ... On suspended list (July 24-August 5, 2000).
STATISTICAL NOTES: Led South Atlantic League in being hit by pitch with 23 in 1991. ... Switch-hit home runs in one game five times (April 20, 1997, first game; April 24, 1998; August 7, 1999; April 11 and August 25, 2000). ... Career major league grand slams: 5.

							BATTING								FIELDING			
Year	Team (League)	Pos.	G	AB	R	H	2B	3B	HR	RBI	Avg.	BB	SO	SB	PO	A	E	Avg.
1990— GC Yankees (GCL)		OF	48	185	28	48	8	5	1	14	.259	15	38	15	64	5	5	.932
1991— Greensboro (S.Atl.)		OF	123	468	96	127	18	0	4	40	.271	57	122	28	250	14	7	.974
1992— Fort Laud. (FSL)		OF	46	183	30	42	8	2	2	9	.230	12	40	11	111	5	3	.975
— Prince Will. (Caro.).....		OF	6	22	7	7	0	0	4	9	.318	5	7	1	12	1	0	1.000
1993— High Desert (Calif.)■..		OF	59	253	48	73	12	6	10	52	.289	22	73	24	124	6	2	.985
— Florida (N.L.)		OF	11	19	0	2	0	0	0	0	.105	1	9	1	6	0	1	.857
— Edmonton (PCL)		OF-DH	35	136	28	42	13	4	6	16	.309	19	45	12	69	12	2	.976
1994— Edmonton (PCL)		OF-DH	78	321	63	108	17	2	11	47	.336	19	65	16	167	11	2	.989
— Florida (N.L.)		OF	16	51	7	11	1	0	2	6	.216	3	15	4	28	2	0	1.000
1995— New York (N.L.)■		OF	79	289	48	75	13	1	12	54	.260	39	67	2	148	9	3	.981
— Norfolk (I.L.)		OF-DH-SS	67	260	52	78	16	4	6	35	.300	20	47	12	133	7	0	1.000
1996— New York (N.L.)..........		OF	101	192	29	46	8	1	1	16	.240	21	53	6	96	4	7	.935
1997— New York (N.L.)..........		OF	142	443	58	110	28	3	14	57	.248	32	102	17	226	8	7	.971
1998— Houston (N.L.)■..........		OF	133	467	72	138	34	4	15	76	.296	44	102	14	296	12	4	.987
1999— Houston (N.L.)		OF-DH	123	464	86	151	33	3	25	108	.325	50	94	27	256	11	6	.978
2000— Boston (A.L.)■..........		OF-DH	137	496	82	149	32	4	34	108	.300	52	113	11	276	11	6	.980
American League totals (1 year)			137	496	82	149	32	4	34	108	.300	52	113	11	276	11	6	.980
National League totals (7 years)			605	1925	300	533	117	12	69	317	.277	190	442	71	1056	46	28	.975
Major League totals (8 years)			742	2421	382	682	149	16	103	425	.282	242	555	82	1332	57	34	.976

DIVISION SERIES RECORD

Year Team (League)	Pos.	G	AB	R	H	2B	3B	HR	RBI	Avg.	BB	SO	SB	PO	A	E	Avg.
1998— Houston (N.L.)	OF-PH	4	13	1	2	0	0	0	0	.154	0	4	0	8	0	0	1.000
1999— Houston (N.L.)	OF	4	15	2	2	0	0	0	1	.133	2	8	1	8	0	0	1.000
Division series totals (2 years)		8	28	3	4	0	0	0	1	.143	2	12	1	16	0	0	1.000

ALL-STAR GAME RECORD

Year League	Pos.	AB	R	H	2B	3B	HR	RBI	Avg.	BB	SO	SB	PO	A	E	Avg.
2000— American	OF	2	0	0	0	0	0	1	.000	1	0	0	1	0	0	1.000

EYRE, SCOTT   P   BLUE JAYS

PERSONAL: Born May 30, 1972, in Inglewood, Calif. ... 6-1/200. ... Throws left, bats left. ... Full name: Scott Alan Eyre.

HIGH SCHOOL: Cyprus (Magna, Utah).

JUNIOR COLLEGE: College of Southern Idaho.

TRANSACTIONS/CAREER NOTES: Selected by Texas Rangers organization in ninth round of free-agent draft (June 3, 1991). ... Traded by Rangers to Chicago White Sox for SS Esteban Beltre (March 28, 1994). ... On disabled list (April 8-27, 1994). ... On Prince William disabled list (April 6-September 7, 1995). ... On Charlotte disabled list (June 2-13, 1999). ... On Chicago disabled list (August 31-September 26, 1999); included rehabilitation assignment to Charlotte (September 8-26). ... Traded by White Sox to Toronto Blue Jays for P Gary Glover (November 7, 2000).

HONORS: Named Southern League Most Outstanding Pitcher (1997).

Year League	W	L	Pct.	ERA	G	GS	CG	ShO	Sv.	IP	H	R	ER	BB	SO
1992— Butte (Pio.)......................	7	3	.700	2.90	15	14	2	1	0	80²/₃	71	30	26	39	94
1993— Charleston, S.C. (S.Atl.)	11	7	.611	3.45	26	26	0	0	0	143²/₃	115	74	55	59	154
1994— South Bend (Midw.)■........	8	4	.667	3.47	19	18	2	0	0	111²/₃	108	56	43	37	111
1995— GC White Sox (GCL)	0	2	.000	2.30	9	9	0	0	0	27¹/₃	16	7	7	12	40
1996— Birmingham (Sou.).............	12	7	.632	4.38	27	27	0	0	0	158¹/₃	170	90	77	79	137
1997— Birmingham (Sou.).............	•13	5	.722	3.84	22	22	0	0	0	126²/₃	110	61	54	55	127
— Chicago (A.L.)	4	4	.500	5.04	11	11	0	0	0	60²/₃	62	36	34	31	36
1998— Chicago (A.L.)	3	8	.273	5.38	33	17	0	0	0	107	114	78	64	64	73
1999— Charlotte (I.L.)	6	4	.600	3.82	12	11	0	0	0	68¹/₃	75	32	29	23	63
— Chicago (A.L.)	1	1	.500	7.56	21	0	0	0	0	25	38	22	21	15	17
2000— Chicago (A.L.)	1	1	.500	6.63	13	1	0	0	0	19	29	15	14	12	16
— Charlotte (I.L.)	3	2	.600	3.00	47	0	0	0	12	48	33	18	16	20	46
Major League totals (4 years).......	9	14	.391	5.66	78	29	0	0	0	211²/₃	243	151	133	122	142

FABREGAS, JORGE   C   ANGELS

PERSONAL: Born March 13, 1970, in Miami. ... 6-3/215. ... Bats left, throws right. ... Name pronounced FAB-ruh-gas.

HIGH SCHOOL: Christopher Columbus (Miami).

COLLEGE: Miami (Fla.).

TRANSACTIONS/CAREER NOTES: Selected by Cleveland Indians organization in 11th round of free-agent draft (June 1, 1988); did not sign. ... Selected by California Angels organization in supplemental round ("sandwich pick" between first and second round, 34th pick overall) of free-agent draft (June 3, 1991); pick received as part of compensation for Minnesota Twins signing Type A free-agent OF/DH Chili Davis. ... On disabled list (April 12-May 4 and July 28-September 5, 1992). ... Angels franchise renamed Anaheim Angels for 1997 season. ... Traded by Angels with P Chuck McElroy to Chicago White Sox for OF Tony Phillips and C Chad Kreuter (May 18, 1997). ... Selected by Arizona Diamondbacks in first round (seventh pick overall) of expansion draft (November 18, 1997). ... On Arizona disabled list (May 31-June 30, 1998); included rehabilitation assignment to Tucson (June 22-30). ... Traded by Diamondbacks with P Willie Blair and cash considerations to New York Mets for OF Bernard Gilkey, P Nelson Figueroa and cash (July 31, 1998); Mets received cash to complete deal (September 3, 1998). ... Traded by Mets to Florida Marlins for P Oscar Henriquez (November 20, 1998). ... Released by Marlins (August 26, 1999). ... Signed by Atlanta Braves (August 31, 1999). ... Released by Braves (November 5, 1999). ... Signed by Kansas City Royals organization (January 12, 2000). ... On Kansas City disabled list (July 19-September 1, 2000); included rehabilitation assignment to Omaha (July 31-August 9 and August 24-September 1). ... Granted free agency (November 1, 2000). ... Signed by Angels (November 20, 2000).

STATISTICAL NOTES: Led Texas League with 17 passed balls in 1993. ... Career major league grand slams: 1.

Year Team (League)	Pos.	G	AB	R	H	2B	3B	HR	RBI	Avg.	BB	SO	SB	PO	A	E	Avg.
1992— Palm Springs (Calif.)..	C	70	258	35	73	13	0	0	40	.283	30	27	0	436	63	*17	.967
1993— Midland (Texas).........	C	113	409	63	118	26	3	6	56	.289	31	60	1	620	99	•11	.985
— Vancouver (PCL)	C	4	13	1	3	1	0	0	1	.231	1	3	0	30	3	0	1.000
1994— Vancouver (PCL)	C-DH	66	211	17	47	6	1	1	24	.223	12	25	1	365	41	4	.990
— California (A.L.)	C	43	127	12	36	3	0	0	16	.283	7	18	2	217	16	3	.987
1995— California (A.L.)	C	73	227	24	56	10	0	1	22	.247	17	28	0	391	36	6	.986
— Vancouver (PCL)	C	21	73	9	18	3	0	4	10	.247	9	12	0	112	12	4	.969
1996— California (A.L.)	C-DH	90	254	18	73	6	0	2	26	.287	17	27	0	502	46	6	.989
— Vancouver (PCL)	DH-C-1B	10	37	4	11	3	0	0	5	.297	4	4	0	27	2	0	1.000
1997— Anaheim (A.L.)	C	21	38	2	3	1	0	0	3	.079	3	3	0	81	5	1	.989
— Chicago (A.L.)■........	C-1B	100	322	31	90	10	1	7	48	.280	11	43	1	520	46	7	.988
1998— Arizona (N.L.)■.........	C	50	151	8	30	4	0	1	15	.199	13	26	0	228	30	1	.996
— Tucson (PCL)	C-DH	6	20	2	5	1	0	0	3	.250	3	1	0	28	3	0	1.000
— New York (N.L.)■.......	C	20	32	3	6	0	0	1	5	.188	1	6	0	62	6	2	.971
1999— Florida (N.L.)■..........	C	82	223	20	46	10	2	3	21	.206	26	27	0	404	52	5	.989
— Atlanta (N.L.)■..........	C-1B	8	8	0	0	0	0	0	0	.000	0	0	0	21	1	0	1.000
2000— Omaha (PCL)■.........	C-1B	37	129	8	32	5	1	1	18	.248	12	9	1	183	20	3	.985
— Kansas City (A.L.)	C-DH	43	142	13	40	4	0	3	17	.282	8	11	1	219	21	2	.992
American League totals (5 years)		370	1110	100	298	34	1	13	132	.268	63	130	4	1930	170	25	.988
National League totals (2 years)		158	414	31	82	14	2	5	41	.198	40	59	0	715	89	8	.990
Major League totals (7 years)		528	1524	131	380	48	3	18	173	.249	103	189	4	2645	259	33	.989

E

F

DIVISION SERIES RECORD

Year	Team (League)	Pos.	G	AB	R	H	2B	3B	HR	RBI	Avg.	BB	SO	SB	PO	A	E	Avg.
									BATTING						FIELDING			
1999— Atlanta (N.L.)..............									Did not play.									

CHAMPIONSHIP SERIES RECORD

Year	Team (League)	Pos.	G	AB	R	H	2B	3B	HR	RBI	Avg.	BB	SO	SB	PO	A	E	Avg.
1999— Atlanta (N.L.)..............		PH	2	2	0	0	0	0	0	0	.000	0	1	0	...	...	...	...

WORLD SERIES RECORD

Year	Team (League)	Pos.	G	AB	R	H	2B	3B	HR	RBI	Avg.	BB	SO	SB	PO	A	E	Avg.
1999— Atlanta (N.L.)..............		PH	1	1	0	0	0	0	0	0	.000	0	1	0	...	...	...	...

FAGGETT, ETHAN   OF   PADRES

PERSONAL: Born August 21, 1974, in Fort Worth, Texas. ... 6-0/190. ... Bats left, throws left. ... Full name: Ethan Mershon Faggett.
HIGH SCHOOL: Dunbar (Fort Worth, Texas).
TRANSACTIONS/CAREER NOTES: Selected by Boston Red Sox organization in 33rd round of free agent draft (June 1, 1992). ... Traded by Red Sox with C Jim Leyritz to San Diego Padres for P Carlos Reyes, P Dario Veras and C Mandy Romero (June 21, 1998). ... Granted free agency (October 18, 2000). ... Re-signed by Padres organization (November 20, 2000).

									BATTING						FIELDING			
Year	Team (League)	Pos.	G	AB	R	H	2B	3B	HR	RBI	Avg.	BB	SO	SB	PO	A	E	Avg.
1992— GC Red Sox (GCL)		OF	34	103	9	18	1	1	1	9	.175	10	37	1	31	4	2	.946
1993— GC Red Sox (GCL)		OF	23	58	4	10	2	1	0	2	.172	10	15	5	19	0	1	.950
1994— GC Red Sox (GCL)		OF	41	117	14	34	2	2	1	17	.291	12	33	10	49	3	5	.912
1995— Michigan (Midw.)		OF	115	399	56	97	11	7	8	47	.243	37	112	23	168	5	6	.966
1996— Sarasota (FSL)		OF	110	408	48	112	12	8	4	35	.275	35	118	24	171	6	8	.957
1997— Sarasota (FSL)		OF	114	410	56	120	19	9	3	46	.293	43	87	23	184	9	11	.946
— Trenton (East.)		OF	17	56	10	16	2	0	2	8	.286	8	17	2	19	0	1	.950
1998— Sarasota (FSL)		OF	62	233	42	65	12	1	4	25	.279	25	55	13	98	6	3	.972
— Mobile (Sou.)■..........		OF	54	162	22	40	2	1	3	25	.247	16	40	7	66	2	5	.932
1999— Mobile (Sou.)		OF	128	527	82	128	18	*11	6	43	.243	53	126	*63	293	11	9	.971
2000— Mobile (Sou.)		OF	97	370	55	89	20	4	2	23	.241	42	84	12	173	1	3	.983
— Las Vegas (PCL)		OF	34	137	21	38	7	2	6	15	.277	16	31	7	70	1	0	1.000

FARNSWORTH, KYLE   P   CUBS

PERSONAL: Born April 14, 1976, in Wichita, Kan. ... 6-4/215. ... Throws right, bats right. ... Full name: Kyle Lynn Farnsworth.
HIGH SCHOOL: Milton (Alpharetta, Ga.).
JUNIOR COLLEGE: Abraham Baldwin Agricultural College (Ga.).
TRANSACTIONS/CAREER NOTES: Selected by Chicago Cubs organization in 47th round of free-agent draft (June 2, 1994).
RECORDS: Shares N.L. single-inning record for most consecutive home runs allowed—3 (April 6, 2000, third inning).

Year	League	W	L	Pct.	ERA	G	GS	CG	ShO	Sv.	IP	H	R	ER	BB	SO
1995— Gulf Coast Cubs (GCL)		3	2	.600	0.87	16	0	0	0	1	31	22	8	3	11	18
1996— Rockford (Midw.)		9	6	.600	3.70	20	20	1	0	0	112	122	62	46	35	82
1997— Daytona (FSL)		10	10	.500	4.09	27	27	2	0	0	156 1/3	178	91	71	47	105
1998— West Tenn (Sou.)		8	2	.800	2.77	13	13	0	0	0	81 1/3	70	32	25	21	73
— Iowa (PCL)		5	9	.357	6.93	18	18	0	0	0	102 2/3	129	88	79	36	79
1999— Iowa (PCL)		2	5	.500	3.20	6	6	0	0	0	39 1/3	38	16	14	9	29
— Chicago (N.L.)..................		5	9	.357	5.05	27	21	1	1	0	130	140	80	73	52	70
2000— Chicago (N.L.)..................		2	9	.182	6.43	46	5	0	0	1	77	90	58	55	50	74
— Iowa (PCL)		0	2	.000	3.20	22	0	0	0	9	25 1/3	24	10	9	18	22
Major League totals (2 years)		7	18	.280	5.57	73	26	1	1	1	207	230	138	128	102	144

FASANO, SAL   C   ATHLETICS

PERSONAL: Born August 10, 1971, in Chicago. ... 6-2/230. ... Bats right, throws right. ... Full name: Salvatore Frank Fasano.
HIGH SCHOOL: Hoffman Estates (Ill.).
COLLEGE: Evansville.
TRANSACTIONS/CAREER NOTES: Selected by Kansas City Royals organization in 37th round of free-agent draft (June 3, 1993). ... On Kansas City disabled list (April 20-May 9 and August 30, 1998-remainder of season); included rehabilitation assignment to Omaha (May 5-9). ... On Omaha disabled list (August 1-26, 1999). ... Traded by Royals to Oakland Athletics for cash (March 30, 2000).
STATISTICAL NOTES: Led Northwest League catchers with seven double plays in 1993. ... Led Pacific Coast League in being hit by pitch with 26 in 1999. ... Tied for Pacific Coast League lead with 12 errors by catcher in 1999. ... Career major league grand slams: 1.

									BATTING						FIELDING			
Year	Team (League)	Pos.	G	AB	R	H	2B	3B	HR	RBI	Avg.	BB	SO	SB	PO	A	E	Avg.
1993— Eugene (N'West)		C	49	176	25	47	11	1	10	36	.267	19	49	4	276	38	1	.997
1994— Rockford (Midw.)		C-1B	97	345	61	97	16	1	25	81	.281	33	66	8	527	86	12	.981
— Wilmington (Caro.)......		C-1B	23	90	15	29	7	0	7	32	.322	13	24	0	80	9	4	.957
1995— Wilmington (Caro.)......		C-1B	23	88	12	20	2	1	2	7	.227	5	16	0	132	12	0	1.000
— Wichita (Texas)		C-1B	87	317	60	92	19	2	20	66	.290	27	61	3	589	64	14	.979
1996— Kansas City (A.L.)		C	51	143	20	29	2	0	6	19	.203	14	25	1	291	14	5	.984
— Omaha (A.A.)..............		C-1B-3B	29	104	12	24	4	0	4	15	.231	6	21	0	198	21	4	.982
1997— Omaha (A.A.)..............		C-DH	49	152	17	25	7	0	4	14	.164	12	53	0	296	34	4	.988
— Kansas City (A.L.)		C-DH	13	38	4	8	2	0	1	1	.211	1	12	0	53	3	1	.982
— Wichita (Texas)		C-1B	40	131	27	31	5	0	13	27	.237	20	35	0	232	21	4	.984

F

Year	Team (League)	Pos.	G	AB	R	H	2B	3B	HR	RBI	Avg.	BB	SO	SB	PO	A	E	Avg.
								BATTING								FIELDING		
1998—Kansas City (A.L.)		C-1B-3B	74	216	21	49	10	0	8	31	.227	10	56	1	437	25	2	.996
— Omaha (PCL).............		C	4	14	1	3	1	0	1	2	.214	1	4	0	26	1	0	1.000
1999—Omaha (PCL).............		C-DH-1B	88	280	63	77	15	0	21	49	.275	42	69	4	582	51	‡12	.981
— Kansas City (A.L.)		C	23	60	11	14	2	0	5	16	.233	7	17	0	143	8	0	1.000
2000—Oakland (A.L.)■		C	52	126	21	27	6	0	7	19	.214	14	47	0	231	22	5	.981
Major League totals (5 years)			213	583	77	127	22	0	27	86	.218	46	157	2	1155	72	13	.990

DIVISION SERIES RECORD

Year	Team (League)	Pos.	G	AB	R	H	2B	3B	HR	RBI	Avg.	BB	SO	SB	PO	A	E	Avg.
								BATTING								FIELDING		
2000—Oakland (A.L.)		C	1	0	0	0	0	0	0	0	...	0	0	0	1	0	0	1.000

FASSERO, JEFF — P — CUBS

PERSONAL: Born January 5, 1963, in Springfield, Ill. ... 6-1/195. ... Throws left, bats left. ... Full name: Jeffrey Joseph Fassero. ... Name pronounced fuh-SAIR-oh.
HIGH SCHOOL: Griffin (Springfield, Ill.).
JUNIOR COLLEGE: Lincoln Land Community College (Ill.).
COLLEGE: Mississippi.
TRANSACTIONS/CAREER NOTES: Selected by St. Louis Cardinals organization in 22nd round of free-agent draft (June 4, 1984). ... Selected by Chicago White Sox organization from Cardinals organization in Rule 5 minor league draft (December 5, 1989). ... Released by White Sox (April 3, 1990). ... Signed by Cleveland Indians organization (April 9, 1990). ... Granted free agency (October 15, 1990). ... Signed by Montreal Expos organization (January 3, 1991). ... On disabled list (July 24-August 11, 1994). ... Traded by Expos with P Alex Pacheco to Seattle Mariners for C Chris Widger, P Trey Moore and P Matt Wagner (October 29, 1996). ... On disabled list (March 22-April 12, 1998). ... Traded by Mariners to Texas Rangers for a player to named later (August 27, 1999); Mariners acquired OF Adrian Myers to complete deal (September 22, 1999). ... Granted free agency (October 28, 1999). ... Signed by Boston Red Sox (December 22, 1999). ... On disabled list (June 19-July 5, 2000). ... Granted free agency (November 1, 2000). ... Signed by Chicago Cubs (December 8, 2000).
STATISTICAL NOTES: Pitched 5-0 no-hit victory for Arkansas against Jackson (June 12, 1989).

Year	League	W	L	Pct.	ERA	G	GS	CG	ShO	Sv.	IP	H	R	ER	BB	SO
1984—Johnson City (Appl.)		4	7	.364	4.59	13	11	2	0	1	66²/₃	65	42	34	39	59
1985—Springfield (Midw.)		4	8	.333	4.01	29	15	1	0	1	119	125	78	53	45	65
1986—St. Petersburg (FSL)		13	7	.650	2.45	26	•26	6	1	0	*176	156	63	48	56	112
1987—Arkansas (Texas)..............		10	7	.588	4.10	28	27	2	1	0	151¹/₃	168	90	69	67	118
1988—Arkansas (Texas)..............		5	5	.500	3.58	70	1	0	0	17	78	97	48	31	41	72
1989—Louisville (A.A.).................		3	10	.231	5.22	22	19	0	0	0	112	136	79	65	47	73
—Arkansas (Texas)		4	1	.800	1.64	6	6	2	1	0	44	32	11	8	12	38
1990—Canton/Akron (East.)■.......		5	4	.556	2.80	*61	0	0	0	6	64¹/₃	66	24	20	24	61
1991—Indianapolis (A.A.)■		3	0	1.000	1.47	18	0	0	0	4	18¹/₃	11	3	3	7	12
—Montreal (N.L.)....................		2	5	.286	2.44	51	0	0	0	8	55¹/₃	39	17	15	17	42
1992—Montreal (N.L.).................		8	7	.533	2.84	70	0	0	0	1	85²/₃	81	35	27	34	63
1993—Montreal (N.L.).................		12	5	.706	2.29	56	15	1	0	1	149²/₃	119	50	38	54	140
1994—Montreal (N.L.).................		8	6	.571	2.99	21	21	1	0	0	138²/₃	119	54	46	40	119
1995—Montreal (N.L.).................		13	14	.481	4.33	30	30	1	0	0	189	207	102	91	74	164
1996—Montreal (N.L.).................		15	11	.577	3.30	34	34	5	1	0	231²/₃	217	95	85	55	222
1997—Seattle (A.L.)■.................		16	9	.640	3.61	35	•35	2	1	0	234¹/₃	226	108	94	84	189
1998—Seattle (A.L.).................		13	12	.520	3.97	32	32	7	0	0	224²/₃	223	115	99	66	176
1999—Seattle (A.L.).................		4	14	.222	7.38	30	24	0	0	0	139	188	123	114	73	101
—Texas (A.L.)■.................		1	0	1.000	5.71	7	3	0	0	0	17¹/₃	20	12	11	10	13
2000—Boston (A.L.)■.................		8	8	.500	4.78	38	23	0	0	0	130	153	72	69	50	97
A.L. totals (4 years)		42	43	.494	4.67	142	117	9	1	0	745¹/₃	810	430	387	283	576
N.L. totals (6 years)		58	48	.547	3.20	262	100	8	1	10	850	782	353	302	274	750
Major League totals (10 years)		100	91	.524	3.89	404	217	17	2	10	1595¹/₃	1592	783	689	557	1326

DIVISION SERIES RECORD

Year	League	W	L	Pct.	ERA	G	GS	CG	ShO	Sv.	IP	H	R	ER	BB	SO
1997—Seattle (A.L.)		1	0	1.000	1.13	1	1	0	0	0	8	3	1	1	4	3
1999—Texas (A.L.)		0	0	...	9.00	1	0	0	0	0	1	2	1	1	1	1
Division series totals (2 years)		1	0	1.000	2.00	2	1	0	0	0	9	5	2	2	5	4

FEBLES, CARLOS — 2B — ROYALS

PERSONAL: Born May 24, 1976, in El Seybo, Dominican Republic. ... 5-11/185. ... Bats right, throws right. ... Full name: Carlos Manuel Febles.
HIGH SCHOOL: Sagrado Corazon de Jesus (Dominican Republic).
TRANSACTIONS/CAREER NOTES: Signed as non-drafted free agent by Kansas City Royals (November 2, 1993). ... On disabled list (August 24-September 17, 1999). ... On Kansas City disabled list (June 5-July 18 and August 14-September 2, 2000); included rehabilitation assignments to Gulf Coast Royals (June 29-30), Wichita (July 1-4) and Omaha (July 10-18).
STATISTICAL NOTES: Led Gulf Coast League second basemen with 230 total chances and 39 double plays in 1995. ... Led Carolina League with 590 total chances and 85 double plays in 1997. ... Led Texas League with .441 on-base percentage in 1998. ... Had 15-game hitting streak (April 6-21, 2000).

Year	Team (League)	Pos.	G	AB	R	H	2B	3B	HR	RBI	Avg.	BB	SO	SB	PO	A	E	Avg.
								BATTING								FIELDING		
1994—Dom. Royals (DSL)		2B	56	184	38	61	9	3	2	37	.332	38	27	12	113	113	16	.934
1995—GC Royals (GCL)........		2B	54	188	40	53	13	5	3	20	.282	26	30	16	*117	101	12	.948
1996—Lansing (Midw.).........		2B-SS	102	363	84	107	23	5	5	43	.295	66	64	30	206	292	19	.963
1997—Wilmington (Caro.)......		2B	122	438	78	104	27	6	3	29	.237	51	95	49	212	*355	*23	.961
1998—Wichita (Texas)		2B	126	432	110	141	28	9	14	52	.326	80	70	*51	248	334	19	.968
—Kansas City (A.L.)		2B	11	25	5	10	1	2	0	2	.400	4	7	2	16	18	0	1.000
1999—Kansas City (A.L.)		2B	123	453	71	116	22	9	10	53	.256	47	91	20	272	375	14	.979

– 168 –

Year Team (League)	Pos.	G	AB	R	H	2B	3B	HR	RBI	Avg.	BB	SO	SB	PO	A	E	Avg.
2000— Kansas City (A.L.)	2B	100	339	59	87	12	1	2	29	.257	36	48	17	165	285	10	.978
— GC Royals (GCL)	2B	1	3	0	1	1	0	0	0	.333	1	0	1	0	1	0	1.000
— Wichita (Texas)	2B	4	15	2	2	0	0	0	1	.133	2	4	2	5	13	0	1.000
— Omaha (PCL).............	2B	11	42	6	9	4	0	1	5	.214	7	10	3	27	31	1	.983
Major League totals (3 years)		234	817	135	213	35	12	12	84	.261	87	146	39	453	678	24	.979

FELIZ, PEDRO — 3B — GIANTS

PERSONAL: Born April 27, 1977, in Azua, Dominican Republic. ... 6-1/195. ... Bats right, throws right.
HIGH SCHOOL: Augustine de Chequer (Dominican Republic).
TRANSACTIONS/CAREER NOTES: Signed as non-drafted free agent by San Francisco Giants organization (February 7, 1994).
STATISTICAL NOTES: Led California League third basemen with 457 total chances and 39 double plays in 1997. ... Led Texas League third basemen with 21 double plays in 1998. ... Led Texas League in grounding into double plays with 18 in 1999. ... Led Texas League third baseman with 407 total chances in 1999. ... Led Pacific Coast League third basemen with 287 assists, 24 errors and 394 total chances in 2000.

Year Team (League)	Pos.	G	AB	R	H	2B	3B	HR	RBI	Avg.	BB	SO	SB	PO	A	E	Avg.
1994— Arizona Giants (Ariz.) .	3B	38	119	7	23	0	0	0	3	.193	2	20	2	19	82	5	.953
1995— Bellingham (N'West) ..	3B-1B	43	113	14	31	2	1	0	16	.274	7	33	1	30	37	2	.971
1996— Bellingham (N'West) ..	3B-1B	93	321	36	85	12	2	5	36	.265	18	65	5	66	186	17	.937
1997— Bakersfield (Calif.)......	3B	135	515	59	140	25	4	14	56	.272	23	90	5	*112	*322	23	*.950
1998— Shreveport (Texas)	3B	100	364	39	96	23	2	12	50	.264	9	62	0	*71	204	22	*.926
— Fresno (PCL)	3B	3	7	1	3	1	0	1	3	.429	1	0	0	0	2	0	1.000
1999— Shreveport (Texas)	3B	131	491	52	124	24	6	13	77	.253	19	90	4	76	*304	27	.934
2000— Fresno (PCL)	3B-SS	128	503	85	150	34	2	33	105	.298	30	94	1	84	†288	†24	.939
— San Francisco (N.L.) ..	3B	8	7	1	2	0	0	0	0	.286	0	1	0	0	0	0	...
Major League totals (1 year)		8	7	1	2	0	0	0	0	.286	0	1	0	0	0	0	...

FERNANDEZ, ALEX — P — MARLINS

PERSONAL: Born August 13, 1969, in Miami Beach, Fla. ... 6-1/225. ... Throws right, bats right. ... Full name: Alexander Fernandez.
HIGH SCHOOL: Pace (Miami).
JUNIOR COLLEGE: Miami-Dade (South) Community College.
COLLEGE: Miami (Fla.).
TRANSACTIONS/CAREER NOTES: Selected by Milwaukee Brewers organization in first round (24th pick overall) of free-agent draft (June 1, 1988); did not sign. ... Selected by Chicago White Sox organization in first round (fourth pick overall) of free-agent draft (June 4, 1990). ... Granted free agency (December 7, 1996). ... Signed by Florida Marlins (December 9, 1996). ... On disabled list (March 21, 1998-entire season; April 12-27, May 2-18 and September 7, 1999-remainder of season; and May 19, 2000-remainder of season).
HONORS: Named Golden Spikes Award winner by USA Baseball (1990).
STATISTICAL NOTES: Pitched 7-0 one-hit, complete-game victory for Chicago against Milwaukee (May 4, 1992). ... Pitched 1-0 one-hit, complete-game victory against Chicago (April 10, 1997).
MISCELLANEOUS: Had a sacrifice hit in only appearance as pinch hitter (1997). ... Flied out in only appearance as pinch hitter (1999). ... Struck out in only appearance as pinch hitter (2000).

Year League	W	L	Pct.	ERA	G	GS	CG	ShO	Sv.	IP	H	R	ER	BB	SO
1990— GC White Sox (GCL)	1	0	1.000	3.60	2	2	0	0	0	10	11	4	4	1	16
— Sarasota (FSL)	1	1	.500	1.84	2	2	0	0	0	14 2/3	8	4	3	3	23
— Birmingham (Sou.)............	3	0	1.000	1.08	4	4	0	0	0	25	20	7	3	6	27
— Chicago (A.L.)	5	5	.500	3.80	13	13	3	0	0	87 2/3	89	40	37	34	61
1991— Chicago (A.L.)	9	13	.409	4.51	34	32	2	0	0	191 2/3	186	100	96	88	145
1992— Chicago (A.L.)	8	11	.421	4.27	29	29	4	2	0	187 2/3	199	100	89	50	95
— Vancouver (PCL)	2	1	.667	0.94	4	3	2	1	0	28 2/3	15	8	3	6	27
1993— Chicago (A.L.)	18	9	.667	3.13	34	34	3	1	0	247 1/3	221	95	86	67	169
1994— Chicago (A.L.)	11	7	.611	3.86	24	24	4	3	0	170 1/3	163	83	73	50	122
1995— Chicago (A.L.)	12	8	.600	3.80	30	30	5	2	0	203 2/3	200	98	86	65	159
1996— Chicago (A.L.)	16	10	.615	3.45	35	35	6	1	0	258	248	110	99	72	200
1997— Florida (N.L.)■	17	12	.586	3.59	32	32	5	1	0	220 2/3	193	93	88	69	183
1998— Florida (N.L.)							Did not play.								
1999— Florida (N.L.)	7	8	.467	3.38	24	24	1	0	0	141	135	60	53	41	91
2000— Florida (N.L.)	4	4	.500	4.13	8	8	0	0	0	52 1/3	59	25	24	16	27
A.L. totals (7 years)	79	63	.556	3.78	199	197	27	9	0	1346 1/3	1306	626	566	426	951
N.L. totals (3 years)	28	24	.538	3.59	64	64	6	1	0	414	387	178	165	126	301
Major League totals (10 years)	107	87	.552	3.74	263	261	33	10	0	1760 1/3	1693	804	731	552	1252

DIVISION SERIES RECORD

Year League	W	L	Pct.	ERA	G	GS	CG	ShO	Sv.	IP	H	R	ER	BB	SO
1997— Florida (N.L.)	1	0	1.000	2.57	1	1	0	0	0	7	7	2	2	0	5

CHAMPIONSHIP SERIES RECORD

Year League	W	L	Pct.	ERA	G	GS	CG	ShO	Sv.	IP	H	R	ER	BB	SO
1993— Chicago (A.L.)	0	2	.000	1.80	2	2	0	0	0	15	15	6	3	6	10
1997— Florida (N.L.)	0	1	.000	16.88	1	1	0	0	0	2 2/3	6	5	5	1	3
Champ. series totals (2 years)	0	3	.000	4.08	3	3	0	0	0	17 2/3	21	11	8	7	13

WORLD SERIES RECORD

NOTES: Member of World Series championship team (1997); inactive due to injury.

Year League	W	L	Pct.	ERA	G	GS	CG	ShO	Sv.	IP	H	R	ER	BB	SO
1997— Florida (N.L.)							Did not play.								

F

FERNANDEZ, OSVALDO   P   REDS

PERSONAL: Born November 4, 1968, in Holguin, Cuba. ... 6-2/193. ... Throws right, bats right.
HIGH SCHOOL: Universidad de Holguin (Holguin, Cuba).
TRANSACTIONS/CAREER NOTES: Signed as non-drafted free agent by San Francisco Giants organization (January 16, 1996). ... On San Francisco disabled list (May 20-June 19 and June 26-September 28, 1997); included rehabilitation assignment to Phoenix (June 11-20). ... On disabled list (March 22, 1998-entire season). ... Granted free agency (December 21, 1998). ... Re-signed by Giants organization (January 4, 1999). ... On Fresno disabled list (April 8-August 1, 1999). ... On San Jose disabled list (August 25, 1999-remainder of season). ... Granted free agency (October 15, 1999). ... Signed by Cincinnati Reds organization (February 15, 2000). ... On Cincinnati disabled list (July 7-September 1, 2000); inlcuded rehabilitation assignment to Louisville (August 5-September 1).
MISCELLANEOUS: Appeared in three games as pinch runner (1996). ... Appeared in one game as pinch runner with San Francisco (1997).

Year League	W	L	Pct.	ERA	G	GS	CG	ShO	Sv.	IP	H	R	ER	BB	SO
1996— San Francisco (N.L.)	7	13	.350	4.61	30	28	2	0	0	171²/₃	193	95	88	57	106
1997— San Francisco (N.L.)	3	4	.429	4.95	11	11	0	0	0	56¹/₃	74	39	31	15	31
— Phoenix (PCL)	0	0	...	3.00	2	2	0	0	0	12	10	5	4	3	4
1998— San Francisco (N.L.)							Did not play.								
1999— San Jose (Calif.)	0	1	.000	6.00	4	4	0	0	0	9	6	6	6	2	5
2000— Chattanooga (Sou.)■........	0	0	...	12.71	1	1	0	0	0	5²/₃	11	9	8	3	1
— Louisville (I.L.)	6	1	.857	4.13	10	10	0	0	0	56²/₃	57	27	26	19	44
— Cincinnati (N.L.)	4	3	.571	3.62	15	14	1	0	0	79²/₃	69	33	32	31	36
Major League totals (3 years)	14	20	.412	4.42	56	53	3	0	0	307²/₃	336	167	151	103	173

FETTERS, MIKE   P   DODGERS

PERSONAL: Born December 19, 1964, in Van Nuys, Calif. ... 6-4/226. ... Throws right, bats right. ... Full name: Michael Lee Fetters.
HIGH SCHOOL: Iolani (Honolulu, Hawaii).
COLLEGE: Pepperdine.
TRANSACTIONS/CAREER NOTES: Selected by Los Angeles Dodgers organization in 22nd round of free-agent draft (June 6, 1983); did not sign. ... Selected by California Angels organization in supplemental round ("sandwich pick" between first and second round, 27th pick overall) of free-agent draft (June 2, 1986); pick received as compensation for Baltimore Orioles signing Type A free-agent OF/IF Juan Beniquez. ... Traded by Angels with P Glenn Carter to Milwaukee Brewers for P Chuck Crim (December 10, 1991). ... On disabled list (May 3-19, 1992 and May 25-June 9, 1995). ... On Milwaukee disabled list (April 4-May 5, 1997); included rehabilitation assignment to Tucson (April 30-May 5). ... Traded by Brewers with P Ben McDonald and P Ron Villone to Cleveland Indians for OF Marquis Grissom and P Jeff Juden (December 8, 1997). ... Traded by Indians to Oakland Athletics for P Steve Karsay (December 8, 1997). ... On Oakland disabled list (April 6-26, 1998). ... Traded by A's to Angels for a player to be named later and cash (August 10, 1998). ... Granted free agency (October 26, 1998). ... Signed by Baltimore Orioles organization (February 4, 1999). ... On Baltimore disabled list (June 7-September 1, 1999); included rehabilitation assignment to Rochester (August 23-31). ... Granted free agency (November 1, 1999). ... Signed by Dodgers organization (December 15, 1999). ... On disabled list (May 4-26, 2000).

Year League	W	L	Pct.	ERA	G	GS	CG	ShO	Sv.	IP	H	R	ER	BB	SO
1986— Salem (N'West)	4	2	.667	3.38	12	12	1	0	0	72	60	39	27	51	72
1987— Palm Springs (Calif.)	9	7	.563	3.57	19	19	2	0	0	116	106	62	46	73	105
1988— Midland (Texas)................	8	8	.500	5.92	20	20	2	0	0	114	116	78	75	67	101
— Edmonton (PCL)	2	0	1.000	1.93	2	2	1	0	0	14	8	3	3	10	11
1989— Edmonton (PCL)	12	8	.600	3.80	26	26	•6	2	0	168	160	80	71	72	*144
— California (A.L.)	0	0	...	8.10	1	0	0	0	0	3¹/₃	5	4	3	1	4
1990— Edmonton (PCL)	1	1	.500	0.99	5	5	1	1	0	27¹/₃	22	9	3	13	26
— California (A.L.)	1	1	.500	4.12	26	2	0	0	1	67²/₃	77	33	31	20	35
1991— Edmonton (PCL)	2	7	.222	4.87	11	11	1	0	0	61	65	39	33	26	43
— California (A.L.)	2	5	.286	4.84	19	4	0	0	0	44²/₃	53	29	24	28	24
1992— Milwaukee (A.L.)■............	5	1	.833	1.87	50	0	0	0	2	62²/₃	38	15	13	24	43
1993— Milwaukee (A.L.)	3	3	.500	3.34	45	0	0	0	0	59¹/₃	59	29	22	22	23
1994— Milwaukee (A.L.)	1	4	.200	2.54	42	0	0	0	17	46	41	16	13	27	31
1995— Milwaukee (A.L.)	0	3	.000	3.38	40	0	0	0	22	34²/₃	40	16	13	20	33
1996— Milwaukee (A.L.)	3	3	.500	3.38	61	0	0	0	32	61¹/₃	65	28	23	26	53
1997— Milwaukee (A.L.)	1	5	.167	3.45	51	0	0	0	6	70¹/₃	62	30	27	33	62
— Tucson (PCL)	0	0	...	10.80	2	0	0	0	0	1²/₃	1	2	2	1	0
1998— Oakland (A.L.)■..............	1	6	.143	3.99	48	0	0	0	5	47¹/₃	48	26	21	21	34
— Anaheim (A.L.)■..............	1	2	.333	5.56	12	0	0	0	0	11¹/₃	14	8	7	4	9
1999— Baltimore (A.L.)■............	1	0	1.000	5.81	27	0	0	0	0	31	35	23	20	22	22
— Rochester (I.L.)	0	0	...	0.00	4	0	0	0	0	3²/₃	0	0	0	2	6
2000— Los Angeles (N.L.)■	6	2	.750	3.24	51	0	0	0	5	50	35	18	18	25	40
A.L. totals (11 years)	19	33	.365	3.62	422	6	0	0	85	539²/₃	537	257	217	248	373
N.L. totals (1 year)........................	6	2	.750	3.24	51	0	0	0	5	50	35	18	18	25	40
Major League totals (12 years)	25	35	.417	3.59	473	6	0	0	90	589²/₃	572	275	235	273	413

FICK, ROBERT   C/1B   TIGERS

PERSONAL: Born March 15, 1974, in Torrance, Calif. ... 6-1/189. ... Bats left, throws right. ... Full name: Robert Charles John Fick. ... Brother of Chris Fick, former outfielder/first baseman in St. Louis Cardinals and Arizona Diamondacks organizations; and brother of Chuck Fick, St. Louis Cardinals scout and former catcher in Montreal Expos and Oakland Athletics organization.
HIGH SCHOOL: Newbury Park (Calif.).
JUNIOR COLLEGE: Ventura (Calif.) College.
COLLEGE: Cal State Northridge.
TRANSACTIONS/CAREER NOTES: Selected by Oakland Athletics organization in 45th round of free-agent draft (June 1, 1992); did not sign. ... Selected by Detroit Tigers organization in 43rd round of free-agent draft (June 1, 1995); did not sign. ... Selected by Tigers organization in fifth round of free-agent draft (June 4, 1996). ... On Detroit disabled list (March 31-September 7, 1999); included rehabilitation assignments to Gulf Coast Tigers (August 18-20), West Michigan (August 21-23) and Toledo (August 24-September 6). ... On suspended list (May 23-26, 2000). ... On Detroit disabled list (July 6-September 1, 2000); included rehabilitation assignment to Toledo (August 13-September 1).

F

HONORS: Named Midwest League Most Valuable Player (1996).
STATISTICAL NOTES: Led Midwest League with 262 total bases and .566 slugging percentage in 1997. ... Career major league grand slams: 1.

Year	Team (League)	Pos.	G	AB	R	H	2B	3B	HR	RBI	Avg.	BB	SO	SB	PO	A	E	Avg.
								BATTING							FIELDING			
1996—Jamestown (NY-P)	C	43	133	18	33	6	0	1	14	.248	12	25	3	155	13	3	.982
1997—W. Michigan (Midw.)..	1B-C-3B	122	463	100	*158	*50	3	16	90	*.341	75	74	13	1043	68	12	.989
1998—Jacksonville (Sou.)....	C-1B-OF	130	515	101	164	47	6	18	114	.318	71	83	8	540	45	9	.985
—Detroit (A.L.)	C-DH-1B	7	22	6	8	1	0	3	7	.364	2	7	1	27	1	1	.966
1999—GC Tigers (GCL)	DH-C-1B	3	9	2	3	1	0	0	2	.333	2	0	1	13	5	0	1.000
—W. Michigan (Midw.) ..	DH-C-1B	3	11	2	3	0	0	0	0	.273	2	0	1	18	3	2	.913
—Toledo (I.L.)................	1B-C-DH-3B	14	48	11	15	0	1	2	8	.313	8	5	1	77	8	5	.944
—Detroit (A.L.)	DH-C	15	41	6	9	0	0	3	10	.220	7	6	1	24	1	0	1.000
2000—Detroit (A.L.)..........	1B-C-DH	66	163	18	41	7	2	3	22	.252	22	39	2	272	21	5	.983
—Toledo (I.L.)...............	1B	17	68	5	10	5	0	1	7	.147	6	13	1	53	4	0	1.000
Major League totals (3 years)		88	226	30	58	8	2	9	39	.257	31	52	4	323	23	6	.983

FIGGA, MIKE C CARDINALS

PERSONAL: Born July 31, 1970, in Tampa. ... 6-0/200. ... Bats right, throws right. ... Full name: Michael Anthony Figga.
HIGH SCHOOL: Leto (Tampa), then Central Florida (Ocala).
JUNIOR COLLEGE: Central Florida Community College.
TRANSACTIONS/CAREER NOTES: Selected by New York Yankees organization in 44th round of free-agent draft (June 5, 1989). ... On disabled list (August 31, 1996-remainder of season). ... On Columbus disabled list (July 29-August 12, 1998). ... Claimed on waivers by Baltimore Orioles (June 3, 1999). ... Claimed on waivers by Tampa Bay Devil Rays (November 18, 1999). ... Granted free agency (December 21, 1999). ... Re-signed by Devil Rays (December 22, 1999). ... Released by Devil Rays (March 29, 2000). ... Signed by Boston Red Sox organization (April 25, 2000). ... Released by Red Sox (June 6, 2000). ... Signed by Los Angeles Dodgers organization (June 16, 2000). ... Granted free agency (October 18, 2000). ... Signed by St. Louis Cardinals organization (November 15, 2000).
STATISTICAL NOTES: Led Gulf Coast League catchers with 296 total chances in 1990. ... Led International League catchers with 15 double plays in 1998.

Year	Team (League)	Pos.	G	AB	R	H	2B	3B	HR	RBI	Avg.	BB	SO	SB	PO	A	E	Avg.
								BATTING							FIELDING			
1990—GC Yankees (GCL)......	C	40	123	19	35	1	1	2	18	.285	17	33	4	*270	19	7	.976
1991—Prince Will. (Caro.).....	C	55	174	15	34	6	0	3	17	.195	19	51	2	278	33	5	.984
1992—Fort Laud. (FSL)........	C	80	249	12	44	13	0	1	15	.177	13	78	3	568	71	12	.982
—Prince Will. (Caro.).....	C	3	10	0	2	1	0	0	0	.200	2	3	1	27	1	0	1.000
1993—San Bern. (Calif.)........	C	83	308	48	82	17	1	25	71	.266	17	84	2	491	70	12	.979
—Alb./Colonie (East.)	C	6	22	3	5	0	0	2	2	.227	2	9	1	31	2	1	.971
1994—Tampa (FSL)..............	C	111	420	48	116	17	5	15	75	.276	22	94	3	703	79	10	.987
—Alb./Colonie (East.)	C	1	2	1	1	1	0	0	0	.500	0	1	0	5	0	0	1.000
1995—Norwich (East.)..........	C	109	399	59	108	22	4	13	61	.271	43	90	1	640	92	11	.985
—Columbus (I.L.)..........	C	8	25	2	7	1	0	1	3	.280	3	5	0	29	4	0	1.000
1996—Columbus (I.L.)..........	C	4	11	3	3	1	0	0	0	.273	1	3	0	17	2	0	1.000
1997—Columbus (I.L.)..........	C-DH	110	390	48	95	14	4	12	54	.244	18	104	3	706	62	11	.986
—New York (A.L.).........	DH-C	2	4	0	0	0	0	0	0	.000	0	3	0	6	0	0	1.000
1998—Columbus (I.L.)..........	C-DH-1B	123	461	57	129	30	3	26	95	.280	35	109	2	733	63	10	.988
—New York (A.L.).........	C	1	4	1	1	0	0	0	0	.250	0	1	0	3	1	0	1.000
1999—New York (A.L.).........	C	2	0	0	0	0	0	0	0	...	0	0	0	3	0	0	1.000
—Baltimore (A.L.)■......	C	41	86	12	19	4	0	1	5	.221	2	27	0	168	12	5	.973
2000—Pawtucket (I.L.)■.......	C	2	8	0	0	0	0	0	0	.000	1	2	0	14	1	0	1.000
—Trenton (East.)	C	8	27	1	5	0	0	1	2	.185	2	8	0	32	2	1	.971
—Albuquerque (PCL)■..	C-1B-OF	15	35	10	13	4	0	0	8	.371	2	12	0	55	2	0	1.000
—San Antonio (Texas)..	C-1B-OF	43	148	16	35	5	0	8	21	.236	12	37	0	167	16	5	.973
Major League totals (3 years)		46	94	13	20	4	0	1	5	.213	2	31	0	180	13	5	.975

FIGUEROA, NELSON P PHILLIES

PERSONAL: Born May 18, 1974, in Brooklyn, N.Y. ... 6-1/155. ... Throws right, bats both. ... Full name: Nelson Walter Figueroa Jr.
HIGH SCHOOL: Abraham Lincoln (Brooklyn, N.Y.).
COLLEGE: Brandeis (Mass.).
TRANSACTIONS/CAREER NOTES: Selected by New York Mets organization in 30th round of free-agent draft (June 1, 1995). ... Traded by Mets with OF Bernard Gilkey and cash to Arizona Diamondbacks for P Willie Blair, C Jorge Fabregas and cash considerations (July 31, 1998); Mets received cash to complete deal (September 3, 1998). ... On Tucson disabled list (June 12-23 and July 6-30, 1999). ... Traded by Diamondbacks with OF Travis Lee, P Omar Daal and P Vicente Padilla to Philadelphia Phillies for P Curt Schilling (July 26, 2000).
HONORS: Named South Atlantic League Most Outstanding Pitcher (1996).

Year	League	W	L	Pct.	ERA	G	GS	CG	ShO	Sv.	IP	H	R	ER	BB	SO
1995—Kingsport (Appl.).............		7	3	.700	3.07	12	12	2	*2	0	76 1/3	57	31	26	22	79
1996—Columbia (S.Atl.).............		14	7	.667	*2.04	26	25	*8	4	0	*185 1/3	119	55	42	58	*200
1997—Binghamton (East.)		5	11	.313	4.34	33	22	0	0	0	143	137	76	69	68	116
1998—Binghamton (East.)		12	3	.800	4.66	21	21	3	2	0	123 2/3	133	73	64	44	116
—Tucson (PCL)■...............		2	2	.500	3.70	7	7	0	0	0	41 1/3	46	22	17	16	29
1999—Tucson (PCL)		11	6	.647	3.94	24	21	1	1	0	128	128	59	56	41	106
—Ariz. Diamondbacks (Ariz.)..		0	1	.000	0.00	1	1	0	0	0	3	3	1	0	0	2
2000—Tucson (PCL)		9	4	.692	2.81	17	16	1	0	0	112	101	41	35	28	78
—Arizona (N.L.)..................		0	1	.000	7.47	3	3	0	0	0	15 2/3	17	13	13	5	7
—Scranton/W.B. (I.L.)■......		4	3	.571	3.78	8	8	1	0	0	50	50	28	21	11	35
Major League totals (1 year)........		0	1	.000	7.47	3	3	0	0	0	15 2/3	17	13	13	5	7

F

FINLEY, CHUCK   P   INDIANS

PERSONAL: Born November 26, 1962, in Monroe, La. ... 6-6/225. ... Throws left, bats left. ... Full name: Charles Edward Finley.
HIGH SCHOOL: West Monroe (La.).
COLLEGE: Northeast Louisiana.
TRANSACTIONS/CAREER NOTES: Selected by California Angels organization in 15th round of free-agent draft (June 4, 1984); did not sign. ... Selected by Angels organization in secondary phase of free-agent draft (January 9, 1985). ... On disabled list (August 22-September 15, 1989 and April 6-22, 1992). ... Granted free agency (November 7, 1995). ... Re-signed by Angels (January 4, 1996). ... Angels franchise renamed Anaheim Angels for 1997 season. ... On Anaheim disabled list (March 23-April 15 and August 20, 1997-remainder of season); included rehabilitation assignment to Lake Elsinore (April 5-10). ... Granted free agency (November 2, 1999). ... Signed by Cleveland Indians (December 16, 1999).
RECORDS: Shares major league single-inning record for most strikeouts—4 (May 12, 1999, third inning; August 15, 1999, first inning; and April 16, 2000, third inning).
HONORS: Named lefthanded pitcher on THE SPORTING NEWS A.L. All-Star team (1989-90).
STATISTICAL NOTES: Pitched 5-0 one-hit, complete-game victory against Boston (May 26, 1989). ... Struck out 15 batters in one game (June 24, 1989 and May 23, 1995). ... Led A.L. with 17 wild pitches in 1996 and 15 wild pitches in 1999.
MISCELLANEOUS: Holds Anaheim Angels all-time records for most wins (165), innings pitched (2,675) and games pitched (436).

Year	League	W	L	Pct.	ERA	G	GS	CG	ShO	Sv.	IP	H	R	ER	BB	SO
1985—	Salem (N'West)	3	1	.750	4.66	18	0	0	0	5	29	34	21	15	10	32
1986—	Quad Cities (Midw.)	1	0	1.000	0.00	10	0	0	0	6	12	4	0	0	3	16
—	California (A.L.)	3	1	.750	3.30	25	0	0	0	0	46 1/3	40	17	17	23	37
1987—	California (A.L.)	2	7	.222	4.67	35	3	0	0	0	90 2/3	102	54	47	43	63
1988—	California (A.L.)	9	15	.375	4.17	31	31	2	0	0	194 1/3	191	95	90	82	111
1989—	California (A.L.)	16	9	.640	2.57	29	29	9	1	0	199 2/3	171	64	57	82	156
1990—	California (A.L.)	18	9	.667	2.40	32	32	7	2	0	236	210	77	63	81	177
1991—	California (A.L.)	18	9	.667	3.80	34	34	4	2	0	227 1/3	205	102	96	101	171
1992—	California (A.L.)	7	12	.368	3.96	31	31	4	1	0	204 1/3	212	99	90	98	124
1993—	California (A.L.)	16	14	.533	3.15	35	35	*13	2	0	251 1/3	243	108	88	82	187
1994—	California (A.L.)	10	10	.500	4.32	25	*25	7	2	0	*183 1/3	178	95	88	71	148
1995—	California (A.L.)	15	12	.556	4.21	32	32	2	1	0	203	192	106	95	93	195
1996—	California (A.L.)	15	16	.484	4.16	35	35	4	1	0	238	241	124	110	94	215
1997—	Lake Elsinore (Calif.)	0	0	...	2.00	2	2	0	0	0	9	5	3	2	4	12
—	Anaheim (A.L.)	13	6	.684	4.23	25	25	3	1	0	164	152	79	77	65	155
1998—	Anaheim (A.L.)	11	9	.550	3.39	34	34	1	1	0	223 1/3	210	97	84	109	212
1999—	Anaheim (A.L.)	12	11	.522	4.43	33	33	1	0	0	213 1/3	197	117	105	94	200
2000—	Cleveland (A.L.)■	16	11	.593	4.17	34	34	3	0	0	218	211	108	101	101	189
Major League totals (15 years)		181	151	.545	3.76	470	413	60	14	0	2893	2755	1342	1208	1219	2340

CHAMPIONSHIP SERIES RECORD

Year	League	W	L	Pct.	ERA	G	GS	CG	ShO	Sv.	IP	H	R	ER	BB	SO
1986—	California (A.L.)	0	0	...	0.00	3	0	0	0	0	2	1	0	0	0	1

ALL-STAR GAME RECORD

Year	League	W	L	Pct.	ERA	GS	CG	ShO	Sv.	IP	H	R	ER	BB	SO
1989—	American				Did not play.										
1990—	American	0	0	...	0.00	0	0	0	0	1	0	0	0	1	1
1995—	American				Did not play.										
1996—	American	0	0	...	4.50	0	0	0	0	2	3	1	1	0	4
2000—	American				Did not play.										
All-Star Game totals (2 years)		0	0	...	3.00	0	0	0	0	3	3	1	1	1	5

FINLEY, STEVE   OF   DIAMONDBACKS

PERSONAL: Born March 12, 1965, in Union City, Tenn. ... 6-2/180. ... Bats left, throws left. ... Full name: Steven Allen Finley.
HIGH SCHOOL: Paducah (Ky.) Tilghman.
COLLEGE: Southern Illinois.
TRANSACTIONS/CAREER NOTES: Selected by Atlanta Braves organization in 11th round of free-agent draft (June 2, 1986); did not sign. ... Selected by Baltimore Orioles organization in 13th round of free-agent draft (June 2, 1987). ... On Baltimore disabled list (April 4-22, 1989). ... On Baltimore disabled list (July 29-September 1, 1989); included rehabilitation assignment to Hagerstown (August 21-23). ... Traded by Orioles with P Pete Harnisch and P Curt Schilling to Houston Astros for 1B Glenn Davis (January 10, 1991). ... On disabled list (April 25-May 14, 1993). ... On Houston disabled list (June 13-July 3, 1994); included rehabilitation assignment to Jackson (June 28-July 3). ... Traded by Astros with 3B Ken Caminiti, SS Andujar Cedeno, 1B Roberto Petagine, P Brian Williams and a player to be named later to San Diego Padres for OF Phil Plantier, OF Derek Bell, P Pedro Martinez, P Doug Brocail, IF Craig Shipley and SS Ricky Gutierrez (December 28, 1994); Padres acquired P Sean Fesh to complete deal (May 1, 1995). ... On San Diego disabled list (April 20-May 6, 1997); included rehabilitation assignment to Rancho Cucamonga (April 25-May 6). ... Granted free agency (October 26, 1998). ... Signed by Arizona Diamondbacks (December 18, 1998).
RECORDS: Shares major league single-season records for most games with three home runs—2 (1997); and fewest double plays by outfielder (150 or more games)—0 (1999).
HONORS: Won N.L. Gold Glove as outfielder (1995, 1996, 1999 and 2000).
STATISTICAL NOTES: Led International League outfielders with 315 total chances in 1988. ... Had 21-game hitting streak (June 20-July 14, 1996). ... Hit three home runs in one game (May 19 and June 23, 1997; and September 8, 1999). ... Tied for N.L. lead with six double plays by outfielder in 1998. ... Career major league grand slams: 7.

Year	Team (League)	Pos.	G	AB	R	H	2B	3B	HR	RBI	Avg.	BB	SO	SB	PO	A	E	Avg.
1987—	Newark (NY-Penn)	OF	54	222	40	65	13	2	3	33	.293	22	24	26	122	7	4	.970
—	Hagerstown (Caro.)	OF	15	65	9	22	3	2	1	5	.338	1	6	7	32	3	0	1.000
1988—	Hagerstown (Caro.)	OF	8	28	2	6	2	0	0	3	.214	4	3	4	17	0	0	1.000
—	Charlotte (Sou.)	OF	10	40	7	12	4	2	1	6	.300	4	3	2	14	0	0	1.000
—	Rochester (I.L.)	OF	120	456	61	*143	19	7	5	54	*.314	28	55	20	*289	14	*12	.962

– 172 –

Year	Team (League)	Pos.	G	AB	R	H	2B	3B	HR	RBI	Avg.	BB	SO	SB	PO	A	E	Avg.
1989—	Baltimore (A.L.)..........	OF-DH	81	217	35	54	5	2	2	25	.249	15	30	17	144	1	2	.986
—	Rochester (I.L.)............	OF	7	25	2	4	0	0	0	2	.160	1	5	3	17	2	0	1.000
—	Hagerstown (East.).......	OF	11	48	11	20	3	1	0	7	.417	4	3	4	35	2	3	.925
1990—	Baltimore (A.L.)..........	OF-DH	142	464	46	119	16	4	3	37	.256	32	53	22	298	4	7	.977
1991—	Houston (N.L.)■........	OF	159	596	84	170	28	10	8	54	.285	42	65	34	323	13	5	.985
1992—	Houston (N.L.)	OF	•162	607	84	177	29	13	5	55	.292	58	63	44	417	8	3	.993
1993—	Houston (N.L.)	OF	142	545	69	145	15	*13	8	44	.266	28	65	19	329	12	4	.988
1994—	Houston (N.L.)	OF	94	373	64	103	16	5	11	33	.276	28	52	13	214	9	4	.982
—	Jackson (Texas)	OF-DH	5	13	3	4	0	0	0	0	.308	4	0	1	6	0	0	1.000
1995—	San Diego (N.L.)■	OF	139	562	104	167	23	8	10	44	.297	59	62	36	291	8	7	.977
1996—	San Diego (N.L.)	OF	161	655	126	195	45	9	30	95	.298	56	87	22	385	7	7	.982
1997—	San Diego (N.L.)	OF	143	560	101	146	26	5	28	92	.261	43	92	15	338	10	4	.989
—	Rancho Cuca. (Calif.) .	DH-OF	4	14	3	4	0	0	2	3	.286	3	2	1	0	0	0	...
—	Mobile (Sou.)	DH	1	4	1	2	0	0	1	2	.500	1	2	0	...	...	...	...
1998—	San Diego (N.L.)	OF	159	619	92	154	40	6	14	67	.249	45	103	12	351	12	7	.981
1999—	Arizona (N.L.)■.........	OF-DH	156	590	100	156	32	10	34	103	.264	63	94	8	397	5	2	.995
2000—	Arizona (N.L.)■.........	OF-DH	152	539	100	151	27	5	35	96	.280	65	87	12	342	10	3	.992
American League totals (2 years)			223	681	81	173	21	6	5	62	.254	47	83	39	442	5	9	.980
National League totals (10 years)			1467	5646	924	1564	281	84	183	683	.277	487	770	215	3387	94	46	.987
Major League totals (12 years)			1690	6327	1005	1737	302	90	188	745	.275	534	853	254	3829	99	55	.986

RECORDS: Shares N.L. single-game record for most runs batted in—5 (October 6, 1999).

DIVISION SERIES RECORD

Year	Team (League)	Pos.	G	AB	R	H	2B	3B	HR	RBI	Avg.	BB	SO	SB	PO	A	E	Avg.
1996—	San Diego (N.L.)	OF	3	12	0	1	0	0	0	1	.083	0	4	1	10	0	0	1.000
1998—	San Diego (N.L.)	OF-PR	4	10	2	1	1	0	0	1	.100	1	4	0	6	0	0	1.000
1999—	Arizona (N.L.).............	OF	4	13	0	5	1	0	0	5	.385	3	1	0	10	0	0	1.000
Division series totals (3 years)			11	35	2	7	2	0	0	7	.200	4	9	1	26	0	0	1.000

CHAMPIONSHIP SERIES RECORD

Year	Team (League)	Pos.	G	AB	R	H	2B	3B	HR	RBI	Avg.	BB	SO	SB	PO	A	E	Avg.
1998—	San Diego (N.L.)	OF	6	21	3	7	1	0	0	2	.333	6	2	1	15	0	0	1.000

WORLD SERIES RECORD

Year	Team (League)	Pos.	G	AB	R	H	2B	3B	HR	RBI	Avg.	BB	SO	SB	PO	A	E	Avg.
1998—	San Diego (N.L.)	OF	3	12	0	1	1	0	0	0	.083	0	2	1	9	1	0	1.000

ALL-STAR GAME RECORD

Year	League	Pos.	AB	R	H	2B	3B	HR	RBI	Avg.	BB	SO	SB	PO	A	E	Avg.
1997—	National	OF	1	0	0	0	0	0	0	.000	0	1	0	1	0	0	1.000
2000—	National	OF	1	0	1	0	0	0	1	1.000	0	0	0	0	0	0	...
All-Star Game totals (2 years)			2	0	1	0	0	0	1	.500	0	1	0	1	0	0	1.000

FIORE, TONY   P   DEVIL RAYS

PERSONAL: Born October 12, 1971, in Oak Park, Ill. ... 6-4/210. ... Throws right, bats right. ... Full name: Anthony James Fiore.
HIGH SCHOOL: Holy Cross (River Grove, Ill.).
JUNIOR COLLEGE: Triton College (Ill.).
TRANSACTIONS/CAREER NOTES: Selected by Philadelphia Phillies organization in 28th round of free-agent draft (June 1, 1992). ... On disabled list (April 2-20, 1995). ... Granted free agency (October 15, 1998). ... Re-signed by Phillies organization (November 28, 1998). ... Released by Phillies (May 19, 1999). ... Signed by Minnesota Twins organization (June 3, 1999). ... Granted free agency (October 15, 1999). ... Signed by Tampa Bay Devil Rays organization (January 14, 1999). ... On suspended list (September 22-24, 2000).

Year	League	W	L	Pct.	ERA	G	GS	CG	ShO	Sv.	IP	H	R	ER	BB	SO
1992—	Martinsville (Appl.).............	2	3	.400	4.18	17	2	0	0	0	32 1/3	32	20	15	31	30
1993—	Batavia (NY-Penn).............	2	•8	.200	3.05	16	•16	1	0	0	97 1/3	82	51	33	40	55
1994—	Spartanburg (S.Atl.)...........	12	13	.480	4.10	28	•28	*9	1	0	166 2/3	162	94	76	77	113
1995—	Clearwater (FSL)	6	2	.750	3.71	24	10	0	0	0	70 1/3	70	41	29	44	45
1996—	Clearwater (FSL)	8	4	.667	3.16	22	22	3	1	0	128	102	61	45	56	80
—	Reading (East.)..................	1	2	.333	4.35	5	5	0	0	0	31	32	21	15	18	19
1997—	Reading (East.)..................	8	3	.727	3.01	9	16	0	0	0	104 2/3	89	47	35	40	64
—	Scranton/W.B. (I.L.)	3	5	.375	3.86	9	9	1	0	0	60 2/3	60	34	26	26	56
1999—	Scranton/W.B. (I.L.)	0	0		6.64	13	0	0	0	0	20 1/3	28	19	15	15	13
—	Salt Lake (PCL)■..............	2	1	.667	3.47	40	0	0	0	19	46 2/3	45	21	18	26	38
2000—	Durham (I.L.)■.................	8	5	.615	2.28	53	1	0	0	8	75	62	22	19	38	39
—	Tampa Bay (A.L.)...............	1	1	.500	8.40	11	0	0	0	0	15	21	16	14	9	8
Major League totals (1 year)........		1	1	.500	8.40	11	0	0	0	0	15	21	16	14	9	8

FLAHERTY, JOHN   C   DEVIL RAYS

PERSONAL: Born October 21, 1967, in New York. ... 6-1/200. ... Bats right, throws right. ... Full name: John Timothy Flaherty.
HIGH SCHOOL: St. Joseph's Regional (Montvale, N.J.).
COLLEGE: George Washington.
TRANSACTIONS/CAREER NOTES: Selected by Boston Red Sox organization in 25th round of free-agent draft (June 1, 1988). ... Traded by Red Sox to Detroit Tigers for C Rich Rowland (April 1, 1994). ... Traded by Tigers with SS Chris Gomez to San Diego Padres for C Brad

Ausmus, SS Andujar Cedeno and P Russ Spear (June 18, 1996). ... Traded by Padres to Tampa Bay Devil Rays for P Brian Boehringer and IF Andy Sheets (November 18, 1997). ... On Tampa Bay disabled list (May 26-June 20, 1998); included rehabilitation assignment to Durham (June 14-20).

STATISTICAL NOTES: Tied for Florida State League lead with 19 passed balls in 1989. ... Had 27-game hitting streak (June 21-July 27, 1996). ... Career major league grand slams: 1.

Year Team (League)	Pos.	G	AB	R	H	2B	3B	HR	RBI	Avg.	BB	SO	SB	PO	A	E	Avg.
1988—Elmira (NY-Penn)	C	46	162	17	38	3	0	3	16	.235	12	23	2	235	39	7	.975
1989—Winter Haven (FSL)	C-1B	95	334	31	87	14	2	4	28	.260	20	44	1	369	60	9	.979
1990—Pawtucket (I.L.)	C-3B	99	317	35	72	18	0	4	32	.227	24	43	1	509	59	10	.983
—Lynchburg (Caro.)	C	1	4	0	0	0	0	0	1	.000	0	1	0	3	2	0	1.000
1991—New Britain (East.)	C	67	225	27	65	9	0	3	18	.289	31	22	0	337	46	9	.977
—Pawtucket (I.L.)	C	45	156	18	29	7	0	3	13	.186	15	14	0	270	18	•9	.970
1992—Boston (A.L.)	C	35	66	3	13	2	0	0	2	.197	3	7	0	102	7	2	.982
—Pawtucket (I.L.)	C	31	104	11	26	3	0	0	7	.250	5	8	0	158	17	4	.978
1993—Pawtucket (I.L.)	C	105	365	29	99	22	0	6	35	.271	26	41	0	626	78	10	.986
—Boston (A.L.)	C	13	25	3	3	2	0	0	2	.120	2	6	0	35	9	0	1.000
1994—Toledo (I.L.)■	C-DH	44	151	20	39	10	2	7	17	.258	6	21	3	286	24	2	.994
—Detroit (A.L.)	C-DH	34	40	2	6	1	0	0	4	.150	1	11	0	78	9	0	1.000
1995—Detroit (A.L.)	C	112	354	39	86	22	1	11	40	.243	18	47	0	569	33	*11	.982
1996—Detroit (A.L.)	C	47	152	18	38	12	0	4	23	.250	8	25	1	243	13	5	.981
—San Diego (N.L.)■	C	72	264	22	80	12	0	9	41	.303	9	36	2	471	29	5	.990
1997—San Diego (N.L.)	C	129	439	38	120	21	1	9	46	.273	33	62	4	753	65	11	.987
1998—Tampa Bay (A.L.)■	C	91	304	21	63	11	0	3	24	.207	22	46	0	542	45	4	.993
—Durham (I.L.)	DH-C	6	23	1	3	1	0	0	2	.130	1	5	0	23	4	0	1.000
1999—Tampa Bay (A.L.)	C-DH	117	446	53	124	19	0	14	71	.278	19	64	0	726	*87	6	.993
2000—Tampa Bay (A.L.)	C	109	394	36	103	15	0	10	39	.261	20	57	0	611	51	5	.993
American League totals (8 years)		558	1781	175	436	84	1	42	205	.245	93	263	1	2906	254	33	.990
National League totals (2 years)		201	703	60	200	33	1	18	87	.284	42	98	6	1224	94	16	.988
Major League totals (9 years)		759	2484	235	636	117	2	60	292	.256	135	361	7	4130	348	49	.989

DIVISION SERIES RECORD

Year Team (League)	Pos.	G	AB	R	H	2B	3B	HR	RBI	Avg.	BB	SO	SB	PO	A	E	Avg.
1996—San Diego (N.L.)	C	2	4	0	0	0	0	0	0	.000	0	1	0	9	0	0	1.000

FLETCHER, DARRIN   C   BLUE JAYS

PERSONAL: Born October 3, 1966, in Elmhurst, Ill. ... 6-2/205. ... Bats left, throws right. ... Full name: Darrin Glen Fletcher. ... Son of Tom Fletcher, pitcher with Detroit Tigers (1962); and grandson of Glen Fletcher, pitcher in Philadelphia Phillies organization (1938-48).
HIGH SCHOOL: Oakwood (Ill.).
COLLEGE: Illinois.
TRANSACTIONS/CAREER NOTES: Selected by Los Angeles Dodgers organization in sixth round of free-agent draft (June 2, 1987). ... Traded by Dodgers to Philadelphia Phillies for P Dennis Cook (September 13, 1990). ... Traded by Phillies with cash to Montreal Expos for P Barry Jones (December 9, 1991). ... On Montreal disabled list (May 12-June 15, 1992); included rehabilitation assignment to Indianapolis (May 31-June 14). ... On disabled list (June 18-July 3, 1997). ... Granted free agency (October 27, 1997). ... Signed by Toronto Blue Jays (November 26, 1997). ... On disabled list (May 30-June 14, 1998). ... On Toronto disabled list (May 1-June 1, 1999); included rehabilitation assignment to Syracuse (May 24-27). ... On disabled list (June 11-July 4, 2000).
STATISTICAL NOTES: Tied for Texas League lead in double plays by catcher with nine in 1988. ... Led Pacific Coast League catchers with 787 total chances in 1990. ... Led N.L. with 12 sacrifice flies in 1994. ... Hit three home runs in one game (August 27, 2000). ... Career major league grand slams: 6.

Year Team (League)	Pos.	G	AB	R	H	2B	3B	HR	RBI	Avg.	BB	SO	SB	PO	A	E	Avg.
1987—Vero Beach (FSL)	C	43	124	13	33	7	0	0	15	.266	22	12	0	212	35	3	.988
1988—San Antonio (Texas)	C	89	279	19	58	8	0	1	20	.208	17	42	2	529	64	5	*.992
1989—Albuquerque (PCL)	C	100	315	34	86	16	1	5	44	.273	30	38	1	632	63	9	.987
—Los Angeles (N.L.)	C	5	8	1	4	0	0	1	2	.500	1	0	0	16	1	0	1.000
1990—Albuquerque (PCL)	C	105	350	58	102	23	1	13	65	.291	40	37	1	*715	64	8	.990
—Los Angeles (N.L.)	C	2	1	0	0	0	0	0	0	.000	0	1	0	0	0	0	...
—Philadelphia (N.L.)■	C	9	22	3	3	1	0	0	1	.136	1	5	0	30	3	0	1.000
1991—Scranton/W.B. (I.L.)	C-1B	90	306	39	87	13	1	8	50	.284	23	29	1	491	44	5	.991
—Philadelphia (N.L.)	C	46	136	5	31	8	0	1	12	.228	5	15	0	242	22	2	.992
1992—Montreal (N.L.)■	C	83	222	13	54	10	2	2	26	.243	14	28	0	360	33	2	.995
—Indianapolis (A.A.)	C	13	51	2	13	2	0	1	9	.255	2	10	0	65	7	1	.986
1993—Montreal (N.L.)	C	133	396	33	101	20	1	9	60	.255	34	40	0	620	41	8	.988
1994—Montreal (N.L.)	C	94	285	28	74	18	1	10	57	.260	25	23	0	479	20	2	.996
1995—Montreal (N.L.)	C	110	350	42	100	21	1	11	45	.286	32	23	0	613	44	4	.994
1996—Montreal (N.L.)	C	127	394	41	105	22	0	12	57	.266	27	42	0	721	30	6	.992
1997—Montreal (N.L.)	C	96	310	39	86	20	1	17	55	.277	17	35	1	606	26	4	.994
1998—Toronto (A.L.)■	C-DH	124	407	37	115	23	1	9	52	.283	25	39	0	832	51	8	.997
1999—Toronto (A.L.)	C	115	412	48	120	26	0	18	80	.291	26	47	0	638	42	2	.997
—Syracuse (I.L.)	C-DH	4	15	0	4	0	0	0	2	.267	1	1	0	18	5	0	1.000
2000—Toronto (A.L.)	C	122	416	43	133	19	1	20	58	.320	20	45	1	621	39	4	.993
American League totals (3 years)		361	1235	128	368	68	2	47	190	.298	71	131	1	2091	132	14	.994
National League totals (9 years)		705	2124	205	558	120	6	63	315	.263	156	212	1	3687	220	28	.993
Major League totals (12 years)		1066	3359	333	926	188	8	110	505	.276	227	343	2	5778	352	42	.993

ALL-STAR GAME RECORD

Year League	Pos.	AB	R	H	2B	3B	HR	RBI	Avg.	BB	SO	SB	PO	A	E	Avg.
1994—National	C	0	0	0	0	0	0	0	...	0	0	0	3	0	0	1.000

PERSONAL: Born May 21, 1970, in Charleston, S.C. ... 5-11/192. ... Throws right, bats right. ... Full name: Bryce Bettencourt Florie.
HIGH SCHOOL: Hanahan (Charleston, S.C.).
COLLEGE: Trident Technical College (S.C.).
TRANSACTIONS/CAREER NOTES: Selected by San Diego Padres organization in fifth round of free-agent draft (June 1, 1988). ... Traded by Padres with P Ron Villone and OF Marc Newfield to Milwaukee Brewers for OF Greg Vaughn and a player to be named later (July 31, 1996); Padres acquired OF Gerald Parent to complete deal (September 16, 1996). ... On disabled list (August 31-September 8, 1997). ... Traded by Brewers with a player to be named later to Detroit Tigers for P Mike Myers, P Rick Greene and SS Santiago Perez (November 20, 1997). ... On Detroit disabled list (June 23-July 20, 1998); included rehabilitation assignment to Toledo (July 14-20). ... On Detroit disabled list (March 31-May 6, 1999); included rehabilitation assignment to Lakeland (May 1-6). ... Traded by Tigers to Boston Red Sox for P Mike Maroth (July 31, 1999). ... On Boston disabled list (April 9-June 19 and September 10, 2000-remainder of season); included rehabilitation assignments to Sarasota (June 8-12) and Trenton (June 13-19).
STATISTICAL NOTES: Led Texas League with 25 wild pitches in 1993.

Year League	W	L	Pct.	ERA	G	GS	CG	ShO	Sv.	IP	H	R	ER	BB	SO
1988— Arizona Padres (Ariz.)	4	5	.444	7.98	11	6	0	0	0	38 1/3	52	44	34	22	29
1989— Spokane (N'West)	4	5	.444	7.08	14	14	0	0	0	61	79	•66	48	40	50
— Charleston, S.C. (S.Atl.)	1	7	.125	6.95	12	12	0	0	0	44	54	47	34	42	22
1990— Waterloo (Midw.)	4	5	.444	4.39	14	14	1	0	0	65 2/3	60	37	32	37	38
1991— Waterloo (Midw.)	7	6	.538	3.92	23	23	2	0	0	133	119	66	58	79	90
1992— High Desert (Calif.)	9	7	.563	4.12	26	24	0	0	0	137 2/3	99	79	63	*114	106
— Charleston, S.C. (S.Atl.)	0	1	.000	1.80	1	1	0	0	0	5	5	3	1	0	5
1993— Wichita (Texas)	11	8	.579	3.96	27	•27	0	0	0	154 2/3	128	80	68	*100	133
1994— Las Vegas (PCL)	2	5	.286	5.15	50	0	0	0	1	71 2/3	76	47	41	47	67
— San Diego (N.L.)	0	0	...	0.96	9	0	0	0	0	9 1/3	8	1	1	3	8
1995— San Diego (N.L.)	2	2	.500	3.01	47	0	0	0	1	68 2/3	49	30	23	38	68
1996— San Diego (N.L.)	2	2	.500	4.01	39	0	0	0	0	49 1/3	45	24	22	27	51
— Milwaukee (A.L.)■	0	1	.000	6.63	15	0	0	0	0	19	20	16	14	13	12
1997— Milwaukee (A.L.)	4	4	.500	4.32	32	8	0	0	0	75	74	43	36	42	53
1998— Detroit (A.L.)■	8	9	.471	4.80	42	16	0	0	0	133	141	80	71	59	97
— Toledo (I.L.).....................	0	0	...	0.00	1	1	0	0	0	4	0	0	0	0	3
1999— Lakeland (FSL)	0	0	...	0.00	1	1	0	0	0	3	0	0	0	0	7
— Detroit (A.L.)	2	1	.667	4.56	27	3	0	0	0	51 1/3	61	31	26	20	40
— Boston (A.L.)■	2	0	1.000	4.80	14	2	0	0	0	30	33	19	16	15	25
2000— Boston (A.L.)	0	4	.000	4.56	29	0	0	0	1	49 1/3	57	30	25	19	34
— Sarasota (FSL)	0	0	...	0.00	1	1	0	0	0	3	3	1	0	1	2
— Trenton (East.)	0	0	...	0.00	3	1	0	0	0	5	2	0	0	2	11
A.L. totals (5 years)	16	19	.457	4.73	159	29	0	0	1	357 2/3	386	219	188	168	261
N.L. totals (3 years)	4	4	.500	3.25	95	0	0	0	1	127 1/3	102	55	46	68	127
Major League totals (7 years)	20	23	.465	4.34	254	29	0	0	2	485	488	274	234	236	388

DIVISION SERIES RECORD

Year League	W	L	Pct.	ERA	G	GS	CG	ShO	Sv.	IP	H	R	ER	BB	SO
1999— Boston (A.L.)							Did not play.								

CHAMPIONSHIP SERIES RECORD

Year League	W	L	Pct.	ERA	G	GS	CG	ShO	Sv.	IP	H	R	ER	BB	SO
1999— Boston (A.L.)							Did not play.								

PERSONAL: Born December 5, 1972, in Chicago. ... 6-4/240. ... Bats left, throws right. ... Full name: Cornelius Clifford Floyd.
HIGH SCHOOL: Thornwood (South Holland, Ill.).
TRANSACTIONS/CAREER NOTES: Selected by Montreal Expos organization in first round (14th pick overall) of free-agent draft (June 3, 1991). ... On disabled list (May 16-September 11, 1995). ... Traded by Expos to Florida Marlins for OF Joe Orsulak and P Dustin Hermanson (March 26, 1997). ... On Florida disabled list (May 9-24 and June 21-September 1, 1997); included rehabilitation assignment to Charlotte (July 20-September 1). ... On Florida disabled list (March 30-April 27 and June 20-September 7, 1999); included rehabilitation assigment to Calgary (August 28-September 7). ... On disabled list (July 29-August 29, 2000).
HONORS: Named Minor League Player of the Year by THE SPORTING NEWS (1993). ... Named Eastern League Most Valuable Player (1993).
STATISTICAL NOTES: Led South Atlantic League with 261 total bases and nine intentional bases on balls received in 1992. ... Led Eastern League with .600 slugging percentage and 12 intentional bases on balls received in 1993. ... Career major league grand slams: 1.

Year Team (League)	Pos.	G	AB	R	H	2B	3B	HR	RBI	Avg.	BB	SO	SB	PO	A	E	Avg.
1991— GC Expos (GCL)	1B	56	214	35	56	9	3	6	30	.262	19	37	13	451	27	*15	.970
1992— Albany (S.Atl.)	OF-1B	134	516	83	157	24	*16	16	*97	.304	45	75	32	423	29	17	.964
— W.P. Beach (FSL)........	OF	1	4	0	0	0	0	0	1	.000	0	1	0	2	0	0	1.000
1993— Harrisburg (East.).......	1B-OF	101	380	82	125	17	4	•26	*101	.329	54	71	31	564	27	19	.969
— Ottawa (I.L.)	1B	32	125	12	30	2	2	2	18	.240	16	34	2	272	23	5	.983
— Montreal (N.L.)...........	1B	10	31	3	7	0	0	1	2	.226	0	9	0	79	4	0	1.000
1994— Montreal (N.L.)..........	1B-OF	100	334	43	94	19	4	4	41	.281	24	63	10	565	42	6	.990
1995— Montreal (N.L.)..........	1B-OF	29	69	6	9	1	0	1	8	.130	7	22	3	146	12	3	.981
1996— Ottawa (I.L.)	OF-DH-3B	20	76	7	23	3	1	1	8	.303	7	20	2	38	1	2	.951
— Montreal (N.L.)..........	OF-1B	117	227	29	55	15	4	6	26	.242	30	52	7	109	2	5	.957
1997— Florida (N.L.)■..........	OF-1B	61	137	23	32	9	1	6	19	.234	24	33	6	96	5	3	.971
— Charlotte (I.L.)...........	OF-1B	39	131	27	48	10	0	9	33	.366	10	29	7	79	5	1	.988
1998— Florida (N.L.)............	OF-DH	153	588	85	166	45	3	22	90	.282	47	112	27	251	10	7	.974
1999— Florida (N.L.)............	OF-DH	69	251	37	76	19	1	11	49	.303	30	47	5	115	4	6	.952
— Calgary (PCL)	OF	9	31	6	12	1	0	3	8	.387	2	8	0	8	0	0	1.000
2000— Florida (N.L.)............	OF-DH	121	420	75	126	30	0	22	91	.300	50	82	24	168	7	9	.951
Major League totals (8 years)		660	2057	301	565	138	13	73	326	.275	212	420	82	1529	86	39	.976

DIVISION SERIES RECORD

Year Team (League)	Pos.	G	AB	R	H	2B	3B	HR	RBI	Avg.	BB	SO	SB	PO	A	E	Avg.
1997— Florida (N.L.).............								Did not play.									

| | | | | | BATTING | | | | | | | | | FIELDING | | | |

CHAMPIONSHIP SERIES RECORD

Year Team (League)	Pos.	G	AB	R	H	2B	3B	HR	RBI	Avg.	BB	SO	SB	PO	A	E	Avg.
1997— Florida (N.L.).............								Did not play.									

WORLD SERIES RECORD

NOTES: Member of World Series championship team (1997).

Year Team (League)	Pos.	G	AB	R	H	2B	3B	HR	RBI	Avg.	BB	SO	SB	PO	A	E	Avg.
1997— Florida (N.L.).............	PH-DH	4	2	1	0	0	0	0	0	.000	1	1	0	...	...	...	...

FORD, BEN   P

PERSONAL: Born August 15, 1975, in Cedar Rapids, Iowa. ... 6-7/225. ... Throws right, bats right. ... Full name: Benjamin Cooper Ford.
HIGH SCHOOL: George Washington (Cedar Rapids, Iowa).
JUNIOR COLLEGE: Indian Hills Community College (Iowa).
TRANSACTIONS/CAREER NOTES: Selected by New York Yankees organization in 20th round of free-agent draft (June 2, 1994). ... Selected by Arizona Diamondbacks in first round (17th pick overall) of expansion draft (November 18, 1997). ... Traded by Diamondbacks with C Izzy Molina to Yankees for P Darren Holmes and cash (March 30, 1999). ... Traded by Yankees with P Ozwaldo Mairena to Chicago Cubs for OF Glenallen Hill (July 21, 2000). ... Released by Cubs (November 27, 2000).

Year League	W	L	Pct.	ERA	G	GS	CG	ShO	Sv.	IP	H	R	ER	BB	SO
1994—Gulf Coast Yankees (GCL)..	2	2	.500	2.38	18	0	0	0	3	34	27	13	9	8	31
1995—Oneonta (NY-Penn)	5	0	1.000	0.87	29	0	0	0	0	52	39	23	5	16	50
—Greensboro (S.Atl.)	0	0	...	5.14	7	0	0	0	0	7	4	4	4	5	8
1996—Greensboro (S.Atl.)	2	6	.250	4.26	43	0	0	0	2	82 $\frac{1}{3}$	75	48	39	33	84
1997—Tampa (FSL)	4	0	1.000	1.93	32	0	0	0	18	37 $\frac{1}{3}$	27	8	8	14	37
—Norwich (East.)	4	3	.571	4.22	28	0	0	0	1	42 $\frac{2}{3}$	35	28	20	19	38
1998—Tucson (PCL)■	2	5	.286	4.35	48	0	0	0	13	68 $\frac{1}{3}$	68	41	33	33	63
—Arizona (N.L.)	0	0	...	9.90	8	0	0	0	0	10	13	12	11	3	5
1999—Columbus (I.L.)■.............	6	3	.667	4.73	53	0	0	0	3	70 $\frac{1}{3}$	69	42	37	39	40
2000—Columbus (I.L.)	3	0	1.000	3.07	20	2	0	0	0	44	37	15	15	24	41
—New York (A.L.)	0	1	.000	9.00	4	2	0	0	0	11	14	11	11	7	5
—Iowa (PCL)■	1	3	.250	6.63	8	8	0	0	0	36 $\frac{2}{3}$	36	30	27	31	30
A.L. totals (1 year)	0	1	.000	9.00	4	2	0	0	0	11	14	11	11	7	5
N.L. totals (1 year)	0	0	...	9.90	8	0	0	0	0	10	13	12	11	3	5
Major League totals (2 years)	0	1	.000	9.43	12	2	0	0	0	21	27	23	22	10	10

FORDYCE, BROOK   C   ORIOLES

PERSONAL: Born May 7, 1970, in New London, Conn. ... 6-0/190. ... Bats right, throws right. ... Full name: Brook Alexander Fordyce. ... Name pronounced FOR-dice.
HIGH SCHOOL: St. Bernard (Uncasville, Conn.).
TRANSACTIONS/CAREER NOTES: Selected by New York Mets organization in third round of free-agent draft (June 5, 1989). ... On disabled list (June 19-July 2 and July 18-August 30, 1994). ... On suspended list (August 30-September 1, 1994). ... Claimed on waivers by Cleveland Indians (May 15, 1995). ... Granted free agency (October 16, 1995). ... Signed by Cincinnati Reds organization (December 7, 1995). ... On disabled list (July 16-August 5, 1997); included rehabilitation assignment to Indianapolis (July 21-August 5). ... On Cincinnati disabled list (July 13-August 12, 1998); included rehabilitation assignment to Indianapolis (August 4-12). ... Traded by Reds to Chicago White Sox for P Jake Meyer (March 25, 1999). ... On Chicago disabled list (March 25-May 23, 2000); included rehabilitation assignment to Charlotte (May 5-23). ... Traded by White Sox with P Miguel Felix, P Juan Figueroa and P Jason Lakman to Baltimore Orioles for C Charles Johnson and DH Harold Baines (July 29, 2000).
STATISTICAL NOTES: Led Appalachian League catchers with .991 fielding percentage in 1989. ... Led South Atlantic League in slugging percentage with .478 and tied for lead in grounding into double plays with 18 in 1990. ... Led South Atlantic League with 30 passed balls in 1990. ... Led Eastern League catchers with 795 total chances in 1992. ... Led International League catchers with 810 total chances and tied for lead in double plays by catcher with 11 in 1993.

Year Team (League)	Pos.	G	AB	R	H	2B	3B	HR	RBI	Avg.	BB	SO	SB	PO	A	E	Avg.
1989—Kingsport (Appl.)...........	C-OF-3B	69	226	45	74	15	0	9	38	.327	30	26	10	311	28	4	†.988
1990—Columbia (S.Atl.)........	C	104	372	45	117	29	1	10	54	.315	39	42	4	574	63	15	.977
1991—St. Lucie (FSL)	C	115	406	42	97	19	3	7	55	.239	37	50	4	630	87	13	.982
1992—Binghamton (East.)	C	118	425	59	118	30	0	11	61	.278	37	78	1	*713	*79	3	*.996
1993—Norfolk (I.L.)..............	C	116	409	33	106	21	2	2	41	.259	26	62	2	*735	67	8	.990
1994—Norfolk (I.L.)	C-DH	66	229	26	60	13	3	3	32	.262	19	26	1	330	33	7	.981
1995—New York (N.L.).........		4	2	1	1	1	0	0	0	.500	1	0	0	0	0	0	...
—Buffalo (A.A.)■	C	58	176	18	44	13	0	0	9	.250	14	20	1	306	18	3	.991
1996—Indianapolis (A.A.)■..	C-DH-1B	107	374	48	103	20	3	16	64	.275	25	56	2	620	49	4	*.994
—Cincinnati (N.L.)	C	4	7	0	2	1	0	0	1	.286	3	1	0	18	0	0	1.000
1997—Cincinnati (N.L.)	C-DH	47	96	7	20	5	0	1	8	.208	8	15	2	162	12	3	.983
—Indianapolis (A.A.).......	C-DH	12	47	7	11	2	0	2	6	.234	5	6	1	73	8	0	1.000
1998—Cincinnati (N.L.)........	C	57	146	8	37	9	0	3	14	.253	11	28	0	288	20	7	.978
—Indianapolis (I.L.).......	C	6	24	4	6	1	0	2	3	.250	1	2	0	28	4	0	1.000
1999—Chicago (A.L.)■.........	C	105	333	36	99	25	1	9	49	.297	21	48	2	561	30	8	.987
2000—Charlotte (I.L.)............	C	17	67	9	16	5	0	2	12	.239	8	13	0	76	3	0	1.000
—Chicago (A.L.)■	C	6	24	2	6	1	0	2	3	.250	1	2	0	28	4	0	1.000
—Baltimore (A.L.)■.......	C	53	177	23	57	11	0	9	28	.322	11	27	0	313	20	4	.988
American League totals (2 years)		198	635	77	190	43	2	23	98	.299	38	98	2	1125	63	12	.990
National League totals (4 years)		112	251	16	60	16	0	4	23	.239	23	44	2	468	32	10	.980
Major League totals (6 years)		310	886	93	250	59	2	27	121	.282	61	142	4	1593	95	22	.987

FOSTER, KRIS   P   DODGERS

PERSONAL: Born June 30, 1974, in Riverdale, N.J. ... 6-1/200. ... Throws right, bats right. ... Full name: John Kristian Foster.
HIGH SCHOOL: Riverdale (Fort Myers, Fla.).
JUNIOR COLLEGE: Edison Community College (Fla.).
TRANSACTIONS/CAREER NOTES: Selected by Montreal Expos organization in 39th round of free-agent draft (June 1, 1992). ... Traded by Expos to Los Angeles Dodgers for SS Rafael Bournigal (June 10, 1995). ... On Albuquerque disabled list (April 8-20, 1999). ... Granted free agency (October 15, 1999). ... Re-signed by Dodgers (October 22, 1999). ... On Los Angeles disabled list (March 28, 2000-entire season); included rehabilitation assignment to San Bernardino (July 9-September 3).

Year League	W	L	Pct.	ERA	G	GS	CG	ShO	Sv.	IP	H	R	ER	BB	SO
1993— Gulf Coast Expos (GCL)	1	6	.143	3.43	17	3	0	0	1	44 2/3	44	26	17	16	30
1994— Gulf Coast Expos (GCL)	4	2	.667	1.55	18	5	0	0	4	52 1/3	34	21	9	32	65
1995— Yakima (N'West)■	2	3	.400	2.89	15	10	0	0	3	56	38	27	18	38	55
1996— San Bernardino (Calif.)	3	5	.375	3.86	30	8	0	0	2	81 2/3	66	46	35	54	78
1997— Vero Beach (FSL)	6	3	.667	5.32	17	17	2	0	0	89 2/3	97	69	53	44	77
1998— Vero Beach (FSL)	3	5	.375	6.79	24	6	0	0	1	53	59	45	40	27	52
1999— Vero Beach (FSL)	1	1	.500	1.76	8	0	0	0	0	15 1/3	10	5	3	2	15
— San Antonio (Texas)	0	2	.000	3.59	33	0	0	0	4	52 2/3	43	24	21	26	53
2000— San Bernardino (Calif.)	0	0	...	0.77	10	1	0	0	2	11 2/3	7	2	1	1	19

FOULKE, KEITH   P   WHITE SOX

PERSONAL: Born October 19, 1972, in San Diego. ... 6-0/200. ... Throws right, bats right. ... Full name: Keith Charles Foulke.
HIGH SCHOOL: Hargrove (Huffman, Texas).
JUNIOR COLLEGE: Galveston (Texas) College.
COLLEGE: Lewis-Clark State (Idaho).
TRANSACTIONS/CAREER NOTES: Selected by San Francisco Giants organization in ninth round of free-agent draft (June 2, 1994). ... Traded by Giants with SS Mike Caruso, OF Brian Manning, P Lorenzo Barcelo, P Bobby Howry and P Ken Vining to Chicago White Sox for P Wilson Alvarez, P Danny Darwin and P Roberto Hernandez (July 31, 1997). ... On disabled list (August 28, 1998-remainder of season). ... On suspended list (May 5-7, 2000).

Year League	W	L	Pct.	ERA	G	GS	CG	ShO	Sv.	IP	H	R	ER	BB	SO
1994— Everett (N'West)	2	0	1.000	0.93	4	4	0	0	0	19 1/3	17	4	2	3	22
1995— San Jose (Calif.)	13	6	.684	3.50	28	26	2	1	0	177 1/3	166	85	69	32	168
1996— Shreveport (Texas)	12	7	.632	*2.76	27	27	4	2	0	*182 2/3	149	61	56	35	129
1997— Phoenix (PCL)	5	4	.556	4.50	12	12	0	0	0	76	79	38	38	15	54
— San Francisco (N.L.)	1	5	.167	8.26	11	8	0	0	0	44 2/3	60	41	41	18	33
— Nashville (A.A.)■	0	0	...	5.79	1	1	0	0	0	4 2/3	8	3	3	0	4
— Chicago (A.L.)	3	0	1.000	3.45	16	0	0	0	3	28 2/3	28	11	11	5	21
1998— Chicago (A.L.)	3	2	.600	4.13	54	0	0	0	1	65 1/3	51	31	30	20	57
1999— Chicago (A.L.)	3	3	.500	2.22	67	0	0	0	9	105 1/3	72	28	26	21	123
2000— Chicago (A.L.)	3	1	.750	2.97	72	0	0	0	34	88	66	31	29	22	91
A.L. totals (4 years)	12	6	.667	3.01	209	0	0	0	47	287 1/3	217	101	96	68	292
N.L. totals (1 year)	1	5	.167	8.26	11	8	0	0	0	44 2/3	60	41	41	18	33
Major League totals (4 years)	13	11	.542	3.71	220	8	0	0	47	332	277	142	137	86	325

DIVISION SERIES RECORD

Year League	W	L	Pct.	ERA	G	GS	CG	ShO	Sv.	IP	H	R	ER	BB	SO
2000— Chicago (A.L.)	0	1	.000	11.57	2	0	0	0	0	2 1/3	4	3	3	2	2

FOX, ANDY   IF   MARLINS

F

PERSONAL: Born January 12, 1971, in Sacramento. ... 6-4/202. ... Bats left, throws right. ... Full name: Andrew Junipero Fox.
HIGH SCHOOL: Christian Brothers (Sacramento).
TRANSACTIONS/CAREER NOTES: Selected by New York Yankees organization in second round of free-agent draft (June 5, 1989). ... On disabled list (June 11-21, 1991; April 9-22, 1992 and June 10-August 1, 1993). ... On Columbus disabled list (August 5-19, 1997). ... Traded by Yankees to Arizona Diamondbacks for P Marty Janzen and P Todd Erdos (March 8, 1998). ... On disabled list (August 28-September 11, 1999). ... On Arizona disabled list (March 23-April 17, 2000); included rehabilitation assignments to El Paso (April 10-14) and Tucson (April 15-17). ... Traded by Diamondbacks to Florida Marlins for OF Danny Bautista (June 9, 2000).
STATISTICAL NOTES: Led Carolina League third basemen with 96 putouts in 1992. ... Led Eastern League third basemen with 30 errors in 1994. ... Led International League third basemen with 22 double plays in 1995.

							BATTING						FIELDING		
Year Team (League)	Pos.	G	AB	R	H	2B	3B	HR	RBI	Avg.	BB	SO	SB	PO	A	E	Avg.
1989— GC Yankees (GCL)	3B	40	141	26	35	9	2	3	25	.248	31	29	6	37	78	10	.920
1990— Greensboro (S.Atl.)	3B	134	455	68	99	19	4	9	55	.218	92	132	26	93	238	*45	.880
1991— Prince Will. (Caro.)	3B	126	417	60	96	22	2	10	46	.230	81	104	15	85	247	*29	.920
1992— Prince Will. (Caro.)	3B-SS	125	473	75	113	18	3	7	42	.239	54	81	28	†97	304	27	.937
1993— Alb./Colonie (East.)	3B	65	236	44	65	16	1	3	24	.275	32	54	12	59	150	19	.917
1994— Alb./Colonie (East.)	3B-SS-2B	121	472	75	105	20	3	11	43	.222	62	102	22	110	261	†34	.916
1995— Norwich (East.)	SS	44	175	23	36	3	5	5	17	.206	19	36	8	77	127	9	.958
— Columbus (I.L.) 3B-SS-OF-2B		82	302	61	105	16	6	9	37	.348	43	41	22	84	211	9	.970
1996— New York (A.L.) 2-3-S-DH-O		113	189	26	37	4	0	3	13	.196	20	28	11	96	158	12	.955
1997— Columbus (I.L.) 3-2-S-O-DH		95	318	66	87	11	4	6	33	.274	54	64	28	111	218	14	.959
— New York (A.L.) 3-2-DH-S-O		22	31	13	7	1	0	0	1	.226	7	9	2	19	30	1	.980
1998— Arizona (N.L.)■	2-O-3-1	139	502	67	139	21	6	9	44	.277	43	97	14	307	175	8	.984
1999— Arizona (N.L.)	SS-3B	99	274	34	70	12	2	6	33	.255	33	61	4	100	196	14	.955
2000— El Paso (Texas)	3B-SS-OF	4	15	3	6	2	0	0	4	.400	2	2	1	2	3	2	.714
— Tucson (PCL)	2B-3B-SS	3	13	1	3	0	1	0	3	.231	0	1	0	5	6	1	.917
— Arizona (N.L.)	3B-OF-1B	31	86	10	18	4	0	1	10	.209	4	16	2	21	29	2	.962
— Florida (N.L.)■ SS-OF-3B-2B		69	164	19	40	4	2	3	10	.244	18	37	8	51	115	11	.938
American League totals (2 years)		135	220	39	44	5	0	3	14	.200	27	37	13	115	188	13	.959
National League totals (3 years)		338	1026	130	267	41	10	19	97	.260	98	211	28	479	515	35	.966
Major League totals (5 years)		473	1246	169	311	46	10	22	111	.250	125	248	41	594	703	48	.964

DIVISION SERIES RECORD

Year Team (League)	Pos.	G	AB	R	H	2B	3B	HR	RBI	Avg.	BB	SO	SB	PO	A	E	Avg.
1996— New York (A.L.)........	DH-PR	2	0	0	0	0	0	0	0	...	0	0	0	...	...	...	...
1997— New York (A.L.).........	2B-PR	2	0	0	0	0	0	0	0	...	0	0	0	0	0	0	...
1999— Arizona (N.L.)............	SS	1	3	0	0	0	0	0	0	.000	0	1	0	1	2	1	.750
Division series totals (3 years)		5	3	0	0	0	0	0	0	.000	0	1	0	1	2	1	.750

CHAMPIONSHIP SERIES RECORD

Year Team (League)	Pos.	G	AB	R	H	2B	3B	HR	RBI	Avg.	BB	SO	SB	PO	A	E	Avg.
1996— New York (A.L.).........	DH-PR	2	0	0	0	0	0	0	0	...	0	0	0	...	...	...	...

WORLD SERIES RECORD

NOTES: Member of World Series championship team (1996).

Year Team (League)	Pos.	G	AB	R	H	2B	3B	HR	RBI	Avg.	BB	SO	SB	PO	A	E	Avg.
1996— New York (A.L.).........	2B-PR-3B	4	0	1	0	0	0	0	0	...	0	0	0	1	0	0	1.000

FRANCO, JOHN   P   METS

PERSONAL: Born September 17, 1960, in Brooklyn, N.Y. ... 5-10/185. ... Throws left, bats left. ... Full name: John Anthony Franco.
HIGH SCHOOL: Lafayette (Brooklyn, N.Y.).
COLLEGE: St. John's.
TRANSACTIONS/CAREER NOTES: Selected by Los Angeles Dodgers organization in fifth round of free-agent draft (June 8, 1981). ... Traded by Dodgers organization with P Brett Wise to Cincinnati Reds organization for IF Rafael Landestoy (May 9, 1983). ... Traded by Reds with OF Don Brown to New York Mets for P Randy Myers and P Kip Gross (December 6, 1989). ... On disabled list (June 30-August 1 and August 26, 1992-remainder of season; April 17-May 7 and August 3-26, 1993). ... Granted free agency (October 18, 1994). ... Re-signed by Mets (April 5, 1995). ... On New York disabled list (July 3-September 4, 1999; included rehabilitation assignment to Binghamton (September 3-4). ... Granted free agency (October 31, 2000). ... Re-signed by Mets (November 25, 2000).
RECORDS: Holds N.L. career record for most saves—420.
HONORS: Named N.L. Fireman of the Year by THE SPORTING NEWS (1988, 1990 and 1994).
MISCELLANEOUS: Holds Cincinnati Reds all-time record for most saves (148). ... Holds New York Mets all-time record for most saves (272) and games pitched (547).

Year League	W	L	Pct.	ERA	G	GS	CG	ShO	Sv.	IP	H	R	ER	BB	SO
1981— Vero Beach (FSL)	7	4	.636	3.53	13	11	3	0	0	79	78	41	31	41	60
1982— Albuquerque (PCL)	1	2	.333	7.24	5	5	0	0	0	27 1/3	41	22	22	15	24
— San Antonio (Texas)	10	5	.667	4.96	17	17	3	0	0	105 1/3	137	70	58	46	76
1983— Albuquerque (PCL)............	0	0	...	5.40	11	0	0	0	0	15	10	11	9	11	8
— Indianapolis (A.A.)■	6	10	.375	4.85	23	18	2	0	2	115	148	69	62	42	54
1984— Wichita (A.A.)	1	0	1.000	5.79	6	0	0	0	0	9 1/3	8	6	6	4	11
— Cincinnati (N.L.)	6	2	.750	2.61	54	0	0	0	4	79 1/3	74	28	23	36	55
1985— Cincinnati (N.L.)	12	3	.800	2.18	67	0	0	0	12	99	83	27	24	40	61
1986— Cincinnati (N.L.)	6	6	.500	2.94	74	0	0	0	29	101	90	40	33	44	84
1987— Cincinnati (N.L.)	8	5	.615	2.52	68	0	0	0	32	82	76	26	23	27	61
1988— Cincinnati (N.L.)	6	6	.500	1.57	70	0	0	0	*39	86	60	18	15	27	46
1989— Cincinnati (N.L.)	4	8	.333	3.12	60	0	0	0	32	80 2/3	77	35	28	36	60
1990— New York (N.L.)■	5	3	.625	2.53	55	0	0	0	*33	67 2/3	66	22	19	21	56
1991— New York (N.L.)	5	9	.357	2.93	52	0	0	0	30	55 1/3	61	27	18	18	45
1992— New York (N.L.)	6	2	.750	1.64	31	0	0	0	15	33	24	6	6	11	20
1993— New York (N.L.)	4	3	.571	5.20	35	0	0	0	10	36 1/3	46	24	21	19	29
1994— New York (N.L.)	1	4	.200	2.70	47	0	0	0	*30	50	47	20	15	19	42
1995— New York (N.L.)	5	3	.625	2.44	48	0	0	0	29	51 2/3	48	17	14	17	41
1996— New York (N.L.)	4	3	.571	1.83	51	0	0	0	28	54	54	15	11	21	48
1997— New York (N.L.)	5	3	.625	2.55	59	0	0	0	36	60	49	18	17	20	53
1998— New York (N.L.)	0	8	.000	3.62	61	0	0	0	38	64 2/3	66	28	26	29	59
1999— New York (N.L.)	0	2	.000	2.88	46	0	0	0	19	40 2/3	40	14	13	19	41
— Binghamton (East.)	0	0	...	0.00	1	1	0	0	0	1 1/3	0	0	0	0	1
2000— New York (N.L.)	5	4	.556	3.40	62	0	0	0	4	55 2/3	46	24	21	26	56
Major League totals (17 years)	82	74	.526	2.68	940	0	0	0	420	1097	1007	389	327	430	857

DIVISION SERIES RECORD

Year League	W	L	Pct.	ERA	G	GS	CG	ShO	Sv.	IP	H	R	ER	BB	SO
1999— New York (N.L.).................	1	0	1.000	0.00	3	0	0	0	0	3 2/3	1	0	0	0	2
2000— New York (N.L.).................	0	0	...	0.00	2	0	0	0	1	2	1	0	0	0	2
Division series totals (2 years)	1	0	1.000	0.00	5	0	0	0	1	5 2/3	2	0	0	0	4

CHAMPIONSHIP SERIES RECORD

Year League	W	L	Pct.	ERA	G	GS	CG	ShO	Sv.	IP	H	R	ER	BB	SO
1999— New York (N.L.).................	0	0	...	3.38	3	0	0	0	0	2 2/3	3	1	1	1	3
2000— New York (N.L.).................	0	0	...	6.75	3	0	0	0	0	2 2/3	3	2	2	2	2
Champ. series totals (2 years)	0	0	...	5.06	6	0	0	0	0	5 1/3	6	3	3	3	5

WORLD SERIES RECORD

Year League	W	L	Pct.	ERA	G	GS	CG	ShO	Sv.	IP	H	R	ER	BB	SO
2000— New York (N.L.).................	1	0	1.000	0.00	4	0	0	0	0	3 1/3	3	0	0	0	1

ALL-STAR GAME RECORD

Year League	W	L	Pct.	ERA	GS	CG	ShO	Sv.	IP	H	R	ER	BB	SO
1986— National						Did not play.								
1987— National	0	0	...	0.00	0	0	0	0	2/3	0	0	0	0	0
1989— National						Did not play.								
1990— National	0	0	...	0.00	0	0	0	0	1	0	0	0	0	0
1991— National						Did not play.								
All-Star Game totals (2 years)	0	0	...	0.00	0	0	0	0	1 2/3	0	0	0	0	0

FRANCO, MATT — IF/OF

PERSONAL: Born August 19, 1969, in Santa Monica, Calif. ... 6-1/210. ... Bats left, throws right. ... Full name: Matthew Neil Franco. ... Nephew of actor Kurt Russell.

HIGH SCHOOL: Westlake (Calif.).

TRANSACTIONS/CAREER NOTES: Selected by Chicago Cubs organization in seventh round of free-agent draft (June 2, 1987). ... On disabled list (May 6-13, 1994). ... Traded by Cubs to New York Mets organization for a player to be named later (April 8, 1996); Cubs acquired P Chris DeWitt to complete deal (June 11, 1996). ... On Norfolk disabled list (April 8-11, 1996). ... Granted free agency (October 15, 1996). ... Re-signed by Mets organization (November 21, 1996). ... On New York disabled list (June 29-July 14, 1998); included rehabilitation assignment to Norfolk (July 9-14). ... Granted free agency (December 21, 2000).

RECORDS: Holds major league single-season record for most bases on balls by pinch hitter—20 (1999).

STATISTICAL NOTES: Led Midwest League in grounding into double plays with 19 in 1990.

Year	Team (League)	Pos.	G	AB	R	H	2B	3B	HR	RBI	Avg.	BB	SO	SB	PO	A	E	Avg.
1987—	Wytheville (Appl.)	3B-1B-2B	62	202	25	50	10	1	1	21	.248	26	41	4	95	88	23	.888
1988—	Wytheville (Appl.)	3B-1B	20	79	14	31	9	1	0	16	.392	7	5	0	31	24	6	.902
—	Geneva (NY-Penn)	3B-1B	44	164	19	42	2	0	3	21	.256	19	13	2	190	43	14	.943
1989—	Char., W.Va. (SAL)	3-1-0-S	109	377	42	102	16	1	5	48	.271	57	40	2	113	189	22	.932
—	Peoria (Midw.)	3B	16	58	4	13	4	0	0	9	.224	5	5	0	11	32	6	.878
1990—	Peoria (Midw.)	1B-3B	123	443	52	125	*33	2	6	65	.282	43	39	4	810	75	18	.980
1991—	Win.-Salem (Caro.)	1B-3B-SS	104	307	47	66	12	1	4	41	.215	46	42	4	711	53	11	.986
1992—	Charlotte (Sou.)	3B-1B-OF	108	343	35	97	18	3	2	31	.283	26	46	3	248	69	13	.961
1993—	Orlando (Sou.)	1B-3B	68	237	31	75	20	1	7	37	.316	29	30	3	444	40	4	.992
—	Iowa (A.A.)	1-DH-O-2-P	62	199	24	58	17	4	5	29	.291	16	30	4	450	39	2	.996
1994—	Iowa (A.A.)	1-DH-3-O	128	437	63	121	32	4	11	71	.277	52	66	3	976	81	7	.993
1995—	Iowa (A.A.)	3-1-DH-P-C	121	455	51	128	28	5	6	58	.281	37	44	1	283	179	19	.960
—	Chicago (N.L.)	2B-1B-3B	16	17	3	5	1	0	0	1	.294	0	4	0	2	2	0	1.000
1996—	Norfolk (I.L.)■	3B-1B-DH	133	508	74	*164	*40	2	7	81	.323	36	55	5	383	167	22	.962
—	New York (N.L.)	3B-1B	14	31	3	6	1	0	1	2	.194	1	5	0	15	12	3	.900
1997—	Norfolk (I.L.)	OF-DH-1B-3B	7	26	5	7	2	0	0	0	.269	2	2	0	13	4	0	1.000
—	New York (N.L.)	3-1-DH-O	112	163	21	45	5	0	5	21	.276	13	23	1	61	52	4	.966
1998—	New York (N.L.)	3-O-1-DH	103	161	20	44	7	2	1	13	.273	23	26	0	84	23	1	.991
—	Norfolk (I.L.)	3B-OF-1B	5	19	2	7	1	0	0	1	.368	3	1	2	16	4	2	.909
1999—	New York (N.L.)	1-O-3-DH-P	122	132	18	31	5	0	4	21	.235	28	21	0	55	23	1	.987
2000—	New York (N.L.)	1-3-O-DH-2	101	134	9	32	4	0	2	14	.239	21	22	0	100	26	4	.969
—	Norfolk (I.L.)	3B-OF-1B	14	51	3	7	1	0	0	1	.137	3	10	0	11	17	2	.933
Major League totals (6 years)			468	638	74	163	23	2	13	72	.255	86	101	1	317	138	13	.972

DIVISION SERIES RECORD

Year	Team (League)	Pos.	G	AB	R	H	2B	3B	HR	RBI	Avg.	BB	SO	SB	PO	A	E	Avg.
1999—	New York (N.L.)	PH	1	0	0	0	0	0	0	0	...	1	0	0	...	...	...	...
2000—	New York (A.L.)									Did not play.								

CHAMPIONSHIP SERIES RECORD

Year	Team (League)	Pos.	G	AB	R	H	2B	3B	HR	RBI	Avg.	BB	SO	SB	PO	A	E	Avg.
1999—	New York (N.L.)	PH	5	2	1	1	1	0	0	0	.500	1	0	0	...	...	...	...
2000—	New York (N.L.)	PH-1B	2	3	0	0	0	0	0	0	.000	0	1	0	2	0	0	1.000
Championship series totals (2 years)			7	5	1	1	1	0	0	0	.200	1	1	0	2	0	0	1.000

WORLD SERIES RECORD

Year	Team (League)	Pos.	G	AB	R	H	2B	3B	HR	RBI	Avg.	BB	SO	SB	PO	A	E	Avg.
2000—	New York (N.L.)	1B	1	1	0	0	0	0	0	0	.000	0	1	0	1	0	0	1.000

RECORD AS PITCHER

Year	League	W	L	Pct.	ERA	G	GS	CG	ShO	Sv.	IP	H	R	ER	BB	SO
1993—	Iowa (A.A.)	0	0	...	36.00	1	0	0	0	0	1	5	4	4	1	1
1995—	Iowa (A.A.)	0	0	...	0.00	1	0	0	0	0	1	1	0	0	1	1
1999—	New York (N.L.)	0	0	...	13.50	2	0	0	0	0	1 1/3	3	2	2	3	2

FRANK, MIKE — OF — YANKEES

PERSONAL: Born January 14, 1975, in Pomona, Calif. ... 6-2/195. ... Bats left, throws left. ... Full name: Stephen Michael Frank.

HIGH SCHOOL: Escondido (Calif.).

COLLEGE: Santa Clara.

TRANSACTIONS/CAREER NOTES: Selected by Cincinnati Reds organization in seventh round of free-agent draft (June 3, 1997). ... On Cincinnati disabled list (July 27-August 25, 1998). ... Traded by Reds with P Denny Neagle to New York Yankees for 3B Drew Henson, OF Jackson Melian, P Brian Reith and P Ed Yarnall (July 12, 2000).

STATISTICAL NOTES: Tied for Pioneer League lead in intentional bases on balls received with five in 1997.

Year	Team (League)	Pos.	G	AB	R	H	2B	3B	HR	RBI	Avg.	BB	SO	SB	PO	A	E	Avg.
1997—	Billings (Pio.)	OF	69	266	62	100	22	6	10	62	.376	35	24	18	•118	*11	4	.970
1998—	Chattanooga (Sou.)	OF	58	231	43	75	12	4	12	43	.325	19	28	5	127	3	2	.985
—	Indianapolis (I.L.)	OF	22	88	8	30	4	0	0	13	.341	7	9	1	44	2	1	.979
—	Cincinnati (N.L.)	OF	28	89	14	20	6	0	0	7	.225	7	12	0	60	1	0	1.000
1999—	Indianapolis (I.L.)	OF-DH	121	433	73	128	36	7	9	62	.296	36	55	10	220	10	1	.996
2000—	Louisville (I.L.)	OF	62	197	30	54	16	2	6	28	.274	20	26	8	106	4	0	1.000
—	Chattanooga (Sou.)	OF	8	30	6	8	1	2	0	5	.267	1	1	0	9	0	0	1.000
—	Columbus (I.L.)■	OF	45	138	19	33	5	3	2	12	.239	16	13	5	90	4	0	1.000
Major League totals (1 year)			28	89	14	20	6	0	0	7	.225	7	12	0	60	1	0	1.000

FRANKLIN, RYAN P MARINERS

PERSONAL: Born March 5, 1973, in Fort Smith, Ark. ... 6-3/165. ... Throws right, bats right. ... Full name: Ryan Ray Franklin.
HIGH SCHOOL: Spiro (Okla.).
JUNIOR COLLEGE: Seminole (Okla.) State College.
TRANSACTIONS/CAREER NOTES: Selected by Toronto Blue Jays organization in 25th round of free-agent draft (June 3, 1991); did not sign. ... Selected by Seattle Mariners organization in 23rd round of free-agent draft (June 1, 1992).
STATISTICAL NOTES: Led Southern League with 16 hit batsmen in 1996. ... Pitched 6-0 no-hit victory against Carolina (April 21, 1997, first game). ... Led Pacific Coast League with 28 home runs allowed in 2000.

Year — League	W	L	Pct.	ERA	G	GS	CG	ShO	Sv.	IP	H	R	ER	BB	SO
1993— Bellingham (N'West)	5	3	.625	2.92	15	14	1	1	0	74	72	38	24	27	55
1994— Appleton (Midw.)	9	6	.600	3.13	18	18	5	1	0	118	105	60	41	23	102
— Riverside (Calif.)	4	2	.667	3.06	8	8	1	1	0	61 2/3	61	26	21	8	35
— Calgary (PCL)	0	0	...	7.94	1	1	0	0	0	5 2/3	9	6	5	1	2
1995— Port City (Sou.)	6	10	.375	4.32	31	20	1	1	0	146	153	84	70	43	102
1996— Port City (Sou.)	6	12	.333	4.01	28	27	2	0	0	182	186	99	81	37	127
1997— Memphis (Sou.)	4	2	.667	3.03	11	8	2	•2	0	59 1/3	45	22	20	14	49
— Tacoma (PCL)	5	5	.500	4.18	14	14	0	0	0	90 1/3	97	48	42	24	59
1998— Tacoma (PCL)	5	6	.455	4.51	34	16	1	0	1	127 2/3	148	75	64	32	90
1999— Tacoma (PCL)	6	9	.400	4.71	29	19	2	1	2	135 2/3	142	81	71	33	94
— Seattle (A.L.)	0	0	...	4.76	6	0	0	0	0	11 1/3	10	6	6	8	6
2000— Tacoma (PCL)	11	5	.688	3.90	31	22	4	0	0	164	147	85	71	35	142
Major League totals (1 year)	0	0	...	4.76	6	0	0	0	0	11 1/3	10	6	6	8	6

FRANKLIN, WAYNE P ASTROS

PERSONAL: Born March 9, 1974, in Wilmington, Del. ... 6-2/195. ... Throws left, bats left. ... Full name: Gary Wayne Franklin Jr.
HIGH SCHOOL: Northeast (Md.).
COLLEGE: Maryland-Baltimore County.
TRANSACTIONS/CAREER NOTES: Selected by Los Angeles Dodgers organization in 36th round of free-agent draft (June 4, 1996). ... Selected by Houston Astros from Dodgers organization in Rule 5 minor league draft (December 14, 1998).

Year — League	W	L	Pct.	ERA	G	GS	CG	ShO	Sv.	IP	H	R	ER	BB	SO
1996— Yakima (N'West)	1	0	1.000	2.52	20	0	0	0	1	25	32	10	7	12	22
1997— Savannah (S.Atl.)	5	3	.625	3.18	28	7	1	0	2	82	79	41	29	35	58
— San Bernardino (Calif.)	0	0	...	0.00	1	0	0	0	0	2	2	0	0	0	1
1998— Vero Beach (FSL)	9	3	.750	3.53	48	0	0	0	10	86 2/3	81	43	34	26	78
1999— Kissimmee (FSL)■	3	0	1.000	1.53	12	0	0	0	1	17 2/3	11	4	3	6	22
— Jackson (Texas)	3	1	.750	1.61	46	0	0	0	20	50 1/3	31	11	9	16	40
2000— New Orleans (PCL)	3	3	.500	3.63	48	0	0	0	4	44 2/3	51	29	18	19	37
— Houston (N.L.)	0	0	...	5.48	25	0	0	0	0	21 1/3	24	14	13	12	21
Major League totals (1 year)	0	0	...	5.48	25	0	0	0	0	21 1/3	24	14	13	12	21

FRASCATORE, JOHN P BLUE JAYS

PERSONAL: Born February 4, 1970, in Queens, N.Y. ... 6-1/223. ... Throws right, bats right. ... Full name: John Vincent Frascatore. ... Name pronounced FRASS-kuh-TOR-ee.
HIGH SCHOOL: Oceanside (N.Y.).
COLLEGE: C.W. Post (N.Y.).
TRANSACTIONS/CAREER NOTES: Selected by St. Louis Cardinals organization in 24th round of free-agent draft (June 3, 1991). ... Traded by Cardinals to Arizona Diamondbacks for P Clint Sodowsky (March 30, 1999). ... Traded by Diamondbacks with SS Tony Batista to Toronto Blue Jays for P Dan Plesac (June 12, 1999).
RECORDS: Shares N.L. single-inning record for most consecutive home runs allowed—3 (August 26, 1998, ninth inning).

Year — League	W	L	Pct.	ERA	G	GS	CG	ShO	Sv.	IP	H	R	ER	BB	SO
1991— Hamilton (NY-Penn)	2	7	.222	9.20	30	1	0	0	1	30 1/3	44	38	31	22	18
1992— Savannah (S.Atl.)	5	7	.417	3.84	50	0	0	0	23	58 2/3	49	32	25	29	56
1993— Springfield (Midw.)	7	12	.368	3.78	27	26	2	1	0	157 1/3	157	84	66	33	126
1994— Arkansas (Texas)	7	3	.700	3.10	12	12	4	1	0	78 1/3	76	37	27	15	63
— Louisville (A.A.)	8	3	.727	3.39	13	12	2	1	0	85	82	34	32	33	58
— St. Louis (N.L.)	0	1	.000	16.20	1	1	0	0	0	3 1/3	7	6	6	2	2
1995— Louisville (A.A.)	2	8	.200	3.95	28	10	1	0	5	82	89	54	36	34	55
— St. Louis (N.L.)	1	1	.500	4.41	14	4	0	0	0	32 2/3	39	19	16	16	21
1996— Louisville (A.A.)	6	13	.316	5.18	36	21	3	0	0	156 1/3	180	106	90	42	95
1997— St. Louis (N.L.)	5	2	.714	2.47	59	0	0	0	0	80	74	25	22	33	58
1998— St. Louis (N.L.)	3	4	.429	4.14	69	0	0	0	0	95 2/3	95	48	44	36	49
1999— Arizona (N.L.)■	1	4	.200	4.09	26	0	0	0	0	33	31	16	15	12	15
— Toronto (A.L.)■	7	1	.875	3.41	33	0	0	0	1	37	42	16	14	9	22
2000— Toronto (A.L.)	2	4	.333	5.42	60	0	0	0	0	73	87	51	44	33	30
A.L. totals (2 years)	9	5	.643	4.75	93	0	0	0	1	110	129	67	58	42	52
N.L. totals (5 years)	10	12	.455	3.79	169	5	0	0	0	244 2/3	246	114	103	99	145
Major League totals (6 years)	19	17	.528	4.09	262	5	0	0	1	354 2/3	375	181	161	141	197

FREEL, RYAN OF BLUE JAYS

PERSONAL: Born March 8, 1976, in Jacksonville. ... 5-10/175. ... Bats right, throws right. ... Full name: Ryan Paul Freel.
HIGH SCHOOL: Englewood (Jacksonville).
JUNIOR COLLEGE: Tallahassee (Fla.) Community College.

TRANSACTIONS/CAREER NOTES: Selected by St. Louis Cardinals organization in 14th round of free-agent draft (June 2, 1994); did not sign. ... Selected by Toronto Blue Jays organization in 10th round of free-agent draft (June 1, 1995). ... On Dunedin disabled list (July 2-18 and July 23-30, 1997). ... On Syracuse disabled list (May 10, 1999-remainder of season). ... On Tennessee disabled list (April 10-May 3 and May 10-21, 2000).

								BATTING						FIELDING			
Year	Team (League)	Pos.	G	AB	R	H	2B	3B	HR	RBI	Avg.	BB	SO	SB	PO	A	E	Avg.
1995— St. Catharines (NY-P).		2B	65	243	30	68	10	5	3	29	.280	22	49	12	118	181	*19	.940
1996— Knoxville (Sou.)..........		OF-SS-2B	66	252	47	72	17	3	4	36	.286	33	32	18	127	35	3	.982
— Dunedin (FSL).............		2B-3B	104	381	64	97	23	3	4	41	.255	33	76	19	193	276	20	.959
1997— Knoxville (Sou.)..........		SS	33	94	18	19	1	1	0	4	.202	19	13	5	44	92	13	.913
— Dunedin (FSL).............		SS-OF-2B-3B	61	181	42	51	8	2	3	17	.282	46	28	24	88	93	18	.910
1998— Knoxville (Sou.)..........		OF-2B-SS	66	252	47	72	17	3	4	36	.286	33	32	18	127	35	3	.982
— Syracuse (I.L.)............		OF-2B	37	118	19	27	4	0	2	12	.229	26	16	9	57	19	3	.962
1999— Knoxville (Sou.)..........		OF	11	46	9	13	5	1	1	9	.283	8	4	4	23	1	0	1.000
— Syracuse (I.L.)............		OF-SS-DH	20	77	15	23	3	2	1	11	.299	8	13	10	39	2	1	.976
2000— Tennessee (Sou.)		OF-2B	12	44	11	13	3	1	0	8	.295	8	6	2	25	7	0	1.000
— Dunedin (FSL)............		OF	4	18	7	9	1	0	3	6	.500	0	1	0	3	0	0	1.000
— Syracuse (I.L.)............		2B-OF-3B-SS	80	283	62	81	14	5	10	30	.286	35	44	30	101	99	9	.957

FRESE, NATE   SS   CUBS

PERSONAL: Born July 10, 1977, in Cedar Rapids, Iowa. ... 6-3/200. ... Bats right, throws right. ... Full name: Nathan Robert Frese. ... Great-great nephew of Hal Trosky, first basemen with Cleveland Indians (1933-41) and Chicago White Sox (1944 and 1946) and cousin of Hal Trosky Jr., pitcher with Chicago White Sox (1958). ... Name pronounced FREEZE.
HIGH SCHOOL: Benton Community (Van Horne, Iowa).
COLLEGE: Iowa.
TRANSACTIONS/CAREER NOTES: Selected by Chicago Cubs organization in 10th round of free-agent draft (June 2, 1998).

								BATTING						FIELDING			
Year	Team (League)	Pos.	G	AB	R	H	2B	3B	HR	RBI	Avg.	BB	SO	SB	PO	A	E	Avg.
1998— Williamsport (NY-P) ...		SS	54	174	28	38	8	0	2	18	.218	16	38	5	88	163	11	.958
1999— Lansing (Midw.)		SS	107	373	68	99	27	4	4	49	.265	58	67	10	176	371	21	.963
2000— Daytona (FSL)		SS	117	425	70	126	24	5	7	52	.296	64	84	10	139	364	13	*.975

FRIAS, HANLEY   SS   DIAMONDBACKS

PERSONAL: Born December 5, 1973, in Villa Atiagracia, Dominican Republic. ... 6-0/173. ... Bats both, throws right. ... Full name: Hanley Acevedo Frias. ... Name pronounced FREE-us.
TRANSACTIONS/CAREER NOTES: Signed as non-drafted free agent by Texas Rangers organization (July 3, 1990). ... Selected by Arizona Diamondbacks in second round (51st pick overall) of expansion draft (November 18, 1997). ... On Arizona disabled list (March 20-July 14, 1998); included rehabilitation assignment to Tucson (June 9-July 8).
STATISTICAL NOTES: Tied for American Association lead in caught stealing with 15 in 1997. ... Led American Association shortstops with 623 total chances in 1997.

								BATTING						FIELDING			
Year	Team (League)	Pos.	G	AB	R	H	2B	3B	HR	RBI	Avg.	BB	SO	SB	PO	A	E	Avg.
1991— Dom. Rangers (DSL)..	...		63	234	34	58	11	7	0	18	.248	33	34	25	...	...	...	...
1992— GC Rangers (GCL).......	2B-SS		58	205	37	50	9	2	0	28	.244	27	30	28	90	143	11	.955
1993— Char., S.C. (SAL).......	2-0-S-3		132	473	61	109	20	4	4	37	.230	40	108	27	211	249	25	.948
1994— High Desert (Calif.)......	SS		124	452	70	115	17	6	3	59	.254	41	74	37	169	*404	37	.939
1995— Charlotte (FSL)..........	SS		33	120	23	40	6	3	0	14	.333	15	11	8	45	106	11	.932
— Tulsa (Texas)	SS		93	360	44	101	18	4	0	27	.281	45	53	14	137	301	24	.948
1996— Tulsa (Texas)	SS		134	505	73	145	24	12	2	41	.287	30	73	9	197	*417	23	.964
1997— Oklahoma City (A.A.)..	SS-DH		132	484	64	128	17	4	5	46	.264	56	72	35	*176	*414	33	.947
— Texas (A.L.)	SS-2B		14	26	4	5	1	0	0	1	.192	1	4	0	12	13	0	1.000
1998— Tucson (PCL)■	SS-3B-2B		63	253	32	73	10	4	1	21	.289	24	41	16	92	172	12	.957
— Arizona (N.L.).............	2B-3B-SS		15	23	4	3	0	1	1	2	.130	0	5	0	9	10	0	1.000
1999— Arizona (N.L.).............	SS-2B		69	150	27	41	3	2	1	16	.273	29	18	4	46	101	5	.967
— Tucson (PCL)	3B-2B-SS		23	80	15	24	3	0	0	6	.300	7	15	3	23	41	4	.941
2000— Arizona (N.L.).............	SS-2B-3B		75	112	18	23	5	0	2	6	.205	17	18	2	29	59	5	.946
American League totals (1 year)			14	26	4	5	1	0	0	1	.192	1	4	0	12	13	0	1.000
National League totals (3 years)			159	285	49	67	8	3	4	24	.235	46	41	6	84	170	10	.962
Major League totals (4 years)			173	311	53	72	9	3	4	25	.232	47	45	6	96	183	10	.965

DIVISION SERIES RECORD

								BATTING						FIELDING			
Year	Team (League)	Pos.	G	AB	R	H	2B	3B	HR	RBI	Avg.	BB	SO	SB	PO	A	E	Avg.
1999— Arizona (N.L.).............	SS	4	7	0	0	0	0	0	0	.000	0	3	0	4	1	0	1.000

FRYE, JEFF   2B   BLUE JAYS

PERSONAL: Born August 31, 1966, in Oakland. ... 5-9/170. ... Bats right, throws right. ... Full name: Jeffrey Dustin Frye.
HIGH SCHOOL: Panama (Okla.).
JUNIOR COLLEGE: Carl Albert (Poteau, Okla.).
COLLEGE: Southeastern State (Okla.).
TRANSACTIONS/CAREER NOTES: Selected by Texas Rangers organization in 30th round of free-agent draft (June 1, 1988). ... On Texas disabled list (March 27, 1993-entire season; June 9-24, 1994; and June 3-18 and June 21-July 6, 1995). ... Granted free agency (December 21, 1995). ... Re-signed by Rangers organization (March 25, 1996). ... Released by Rangers organization (June 5, 1996). ... Signed by Boston Red Sox (June 5, 1996). ... On disabled list (March 13, 1998-entire season). ... On Boston disabled list (June 16-September 1, 1999); included

F

rehabilitation assignments to Gulf Coast Red Sox (July 31-August 9) and Pawtucket (August 10-18). ... Traded by Red Sox with P Brian Rose, P John Wasdin and P Jeff Taglienti to Colorado Rockies for P Rolando Arrojo, P Rick Croushore, 2B Mike Lansing and cash (July 27, 2000). ... Granted free agency (October 30, 2000). ... Signed by Toronto Blue Jays (December 11, 2000).

STATISTICAL NOTES: Led Pioneer League second basemen with 44 double plays in 1988. ... Tied for American Association lead in being hit by pitch with 11 in 1992.

Year Team (League)	Pos.	G	AB	R	H	2B	3B	HR	RBI	Avg.	BB	SO	SB	PO	A	E	Avg.
1988—Butte (Pio.)................	2B	54	185	47	53	7	1	0	14	.286	35	25	16	96	149	7	.972
1989—Gastonia (S.Atl.).........	2B	125	464	85	145	26	3	1	40	*.313	72	53	33	242	340	14	*.977
1990—Charlotte (FSL).........	2B	131	503	77	137	16	7	0	50	.272	80	66	29	252	350	13	*.979
1991—Tulsa (Texas).............	2B	131	503	92	152	32	11	4	41	.302	71	60	15	262	322	*26	.957
1992—Oklahoma City (A.A.)..	2B	87	337	64	101	26	2	2	28	.300	51	39	11	212	248	7	.985
— Texas (A.L.)...............	2B	67	199	24	51	9	1	1	12	.256	16	27	1	120	196	7	.978
1993—Texas (A.L.)...............								Did not play.									
1994—Oklahoma City (A.A.)..	2B	17	68	7	19	3	0	1	5	.279	6	7	2	28	44	1	.986
— Texas (A.L.)........	2B-DH-3B	57	205	37	67	20	3	0	18	.327	29	23	6	90	136	4	.983
1995—Texas (A.L.)...............	2B	90	313	38	87	15	2	4	29	.278	24	45	3	173	248	11	.975
1996—Oklahoma City (A.A.)..2B-SS-OF-3B		49	181	25	43	10	0	1	18	.238	24	21	10	94	148	8	.968
— Boston (A.L.)■......	2-O-S-DH	105	419	74	120	27	2	4	41	.286	54	57	18	211	317	9	.983
1997—Boston (A.L.).............2-3-O-D-S-1		127	404	56	126	36	2	3	51	.312	27	44	19	227	264	12	.976
1998—Boston (A.L.)								Did not play.									
1999—Boston (A.L.)..............2B-3B-DH-SS		41	114	14	32	3	0	1	12	.281	14	11	2	52	71	4	.969
— GC Red Sox (GCL)	2B-DH	6	20	4	8	1	0	0	1	.400	2	2	0	3	12	0	1.000
— Pawtucket (I.L.).......		3	9	0	3	0	0	0	2	.333	2	1	0	1	11	0	1.000
2000—Boston (A.L.).............2B-OF-DH-3B		69	239	35	69	13	0	1	13	.289	28	38	1	116	124	2	.992
— Colorado (N.L.)■	2B-3B	37	87	14	31	6	0	0	3	.356	8	16	4	37	60	1	.990
American League totals (7 years)		556	1893	278	552	123	10	14	176	.292	192	245	50	989	1356	49	.980
National League totals (1 year)		37	87	14	31	6	0	0	3	.356	8	16	4	37	60	1	.990
Major League totals (7 years)		593	1980	292	583	129	10	14	179	.294	200	261	54	1026	1416	50	.980

FRYMAN, TRAVIS   3B   INDIANS

PERSONAL: Born March 25, 1969, in Lexington, Ky. ... 6-1/195. ... Bats right, throws right. ... Full name: David Travis Fryman.
HIGH SCHOOL: Tate (Gonzalez, Fla.).
TRANSACTIONS/CAREER NOTES: Selected by Detroit Tigers organization in supplemental round ("sandwich pick" between first and second round, 30th pick overall) of free-agent draft (June 2, 1987); pick received as compensation for Philadelphia Phillies signing Type A free-agent C Lance Parrish. ... Traded by Tigers to Arizona Diamondbacks for 3B Joe Randa, P Matt Drews and 3B Gabe Alvarez (November 18, 1997). ... Traded by Diamondbacks with P Tom Martin and cash to Cleveland Indians for 3B Matt Williams (December 1, 1997). ... On Cleveland disabled list (June 6-25 and July 4-September 2, 1999); included rehabilitation assignments to Akron (August 24-30) and Buffalo (August 31-September 2).
RECORDS: Holds A.L. single-season record for fewest putouts by third baseman (150 or more games)—79 (2000).
HONORS: Named shortstop on THE SPORTING NEWS A.L. All-Star team (1992). ... Named shortstop on THE SPORTING NEWS A.L. Silver Slugger team (1992). ... Named third baseman on THE SPORTING NEWS A.L. All-Star team (1993 and 2000). ... Won A.L. Gold Glove as third baseman (2000).
STATISTICAL NOTES: Led Appalachian League shortstops with 313 total chances in 1987. ... Hit for the cycle (July 28, 1993). ... Tied for A.L. lead with 13 sacrifice flies in 1994. ... Led A.L. third basemen with 313 total chances in 1994 and 337 in 1995. ... Led A.L. third basemen with 38 double plays in 1995. ... Led A.L. third basemen with 133 putouts and .979 fielding percentage in 1996. ... Led A.L. third basemen in 2000. ... Career major league grand slams: 4.

Year Team (League)	Pos.	G	AB	R	H	2B	3B	HR	RBI	Avg.	BB	SO	SB	PO	A	E	Avg.
1987—Bristol (Appl.)............	SS	67	248	25	58	9	0	2	20	.234	22	39	6	*103	187	•23	.927
1988—Fayetteville (S.Atl.)	SS-2B	123	411	44	96	17	4	0	47	.234	24	83	16	174	390	32	.946
1989—London (East.)	SS	118	426	52	113	*30	1	9	56	.265	19	78	5	192	346	*27	.952
1990—Toledo (I.L.).............	SS	87	327	38	84	22	2	10	53	.257	17	59	4	128	277	26	.940
— Detroit (A.L.)	3B-SS-DH	66	232	32	69	11	1	9	27	.297	17	51	3	47	145	14	.932
1991—Detroit (A.L.)	3B-SS	149	557	65	144	36	3	21	91	.259	40	149	12	153	354	23	.957
1992—Detroit (A.L.)	SS-3B	161	*659	87	175	31	4	20	96	.266	45	144	8	220	489	22	.970
1993—Detroit (A.L.)	SS-3B-DH	151	607	98	182	37	5	22	97	.300	77	128	9	169	382	23	.960
1994—Detroit (A.L.)	3B	114	*464	66	122	34	5	18	85	.263	45	*128	2	78	*221	14	.955
1995—Detroit (A.L.)	3B	144	567	79	156	21	5	15	81	.275	63	100	4	107	*337	14	.969
1996—Detroit (A.L.)	3B-SS	157	616	90	165	32	3	22	100	.268	57	118	4	149	†354	10	†.981
1997—Detroit (A.L.)	3B	154	595	90	163	27	3	22	102	.274	46	113	16	•126	312	10	*.978
1998—Cleveland (A.L.)■......	3B-SS-DH	146	557	74	160	33	2	28	96	.287	44	125	10	101	242	13	.969
1999—Cleveland (A.L.)	3B	85	322	45	82	16	2	10	48	.255	25	57	2	41	146	6	.969
— Akron (East.)	DH-3B	4	12	4	3	0	0	1	4	.250	2	4	0	0	2	0	1.000
— Buffalo (I.L.).............	3B-DH	3	11	1	2	0	0	1	2	.182	0	3	0	0	3	1	.750
2000—Cleveland (A.L.)..........	3B-DH-1B	155	574	93	184	38	4	22	106	.321	73	111	1	83	276	8	†.978
Major League totals (11 years)		1482	5750	819	1602	316	37	209	929	.279	532	1224	71	1274	3258	157	.967

DIVISION SERIES RECORD

Year Team (League)	Pos.	G	AB	R	H	2B	3B	HR	RBI	Avg.	BB	SO	SB	PO	A	E	Avg.
1998—Cleveland (A.L.)..........	3B	4	13	1	2	1	0	0	0	.154	3	4	1	5	8	0	1.000
1999—Cleveland (A.L.)..........	3B	5	15	2	4	0	0	1	4	.267	3	2	1	0	10	0	1.000
Division series totals (2 years)		9	28	3	6	1	0	1	4	.214	6	6	2	5	18	0	1.000

CHAMPIONSHIP SERIES RECORD

Year Team (League)	Pos.	G	AB	R	H	2B	3B	HR	RBI	Avg.	BB	SO	SB	PO	A	E	Avg.
1998—Cleveland (A.L.)..........	3B	6	23	2	4	0	0	0	0	.174	1	5	1	1	7	1	.889

F

Year League	Pos.	AB	R	H	2B	3B	HR	RBI	Avg.	BB	SO	SB	PO	A	E	Avg.
1992— American	SS	1	1	1	0	0	0	1	1.000	1	0	0	0	3	0	1.000
1993— American	SS	1	0	0	0	0	0	0	.000	0	0	0	1	1	0	1.000
1994— American	PH	1	0	0	0	0	0	0	.000	0	0	0	...	...	...	...
1996— American	PH-3B	1	0	0	0	0	0	0	.000	0	1	0	0	1	0	1.000
2000— American	3B	2	1	1	0	0	0	0	.500	0	1	0	0	0	0	...
All-Star Game totals (5 years)		6	2	2	0	0	0	1	.333	1	2	0	1	5	0	1.000

FUENTES, BRIAN — P — MARINERS

PERSONAL: Born August 9, 1975, in Merced, Calif. ... 6-4/220. ... Throws left, bats left. ... Full name: Brian Christopher Fuentes.
HIGH SCHOOL: Merced (Calif.).
JUNIOR COLLEGE: Merced (Calif.) Junior College.
TRANSACTIONS/CAREER NOTES: Selected by Seattle Mariners organization in 25th round of free-agent draft (June 1, 1995). ... On disabled list (April 2-20, 1998). ... On New Haven disabled list (June 9-August 22, 1999).
STATISTICAL NOTES: Tied for Eastern League lead with 14 wild pitches in 2000.

Year League	W	L	Pct.	ERA	G	GS	CG	ShO	Sv.	IP	H	R	ER	BB	SO
1996— Everett (N'West)	0	1	.000	4.39	13	2	0	0	0	26²/₃	23	14	13	13	26
1997— Wisconsin (Midw.)	6	7	.462	3.56	22	22	0	0	0	118²/₃	84	52	47	59	153
1998— Lancaster (Calif.)	7	7	.500	4.17	24	22	0	0	0	118²/₃	121	73	55	81	137
1999— New Haven (East.)	3	3	.500	4.95	15	14	0	0	0	60	53	36	33	46	66
2000— New Haven (East.)	7	12	.368	4.51	26	26	1	0	0	139²/₃	127	80	70	70	152

FULLMER, BRAD — DH/1B — BLUE JAYS

PERSONAL: Born January 17, 1975, in Chatsworth, Calif. ... 6-0/215. ... Bats left, throws right. ... Full name: Bradley Ryan Fullmer.
HIGH SCHOOL: Montclair Prep (Van Nuys, Calif.).
TRANSACTIONS/CAREER NOTES: Selected by Montreal Expos organization in second round of free-agent draft (June 3, 1993). ... On disabled list (June 20, 1994-entire season). ... Traded by Expos to Toronto Blue Jays as part of three-way deal in which Blue Jays sent 1B/DH David Segui and cash to Texas Rangers and Rangers sent 1B Lee Stevens to Expos (March 16, 2000).
STATISTICAL NOTES: Hit home run in first major league at-bat (September 2, 1997). ... Had 16-game hitting streak (August 7-22, 1999). ... Career major league grand slams: 2.

Year Team (League)	Pos.	G	AB	R	H	2B	3B	HR	RBI	Avg.	BB	SO	SB	PO	A	E	Avg.
1994—						Did not play.											
1995— Albany (S.Atl.)	3B-1B	123	468	69	•151	38	4	8	67	.323	36	33	10	269	66	30	.918
1996— W.P. Beach (FSL)	OF-1B	102	380	52	115	29	1	5	63	.303	32	43	4	197	10	7	.967
— Harrisburg (East.)	OF-1B	24	98	11	27	4	1	4	14	.276	3	8	0	43	1	2	.957
1997— Harrisburg (East.)	1B-OF-DH	94	357	60	111	24	2	19	62	.311	30	25	6	538	41	6	.990
— Ottawa (I.L.)	1B-DH-OF	24	91	13	27	7	0	3	17	.297	3	10	1	173	12	1	.995
— Montreal (N.L.)	1B-OF	19	40	4	12	2	0	3	8	.300	2	7	0	50	7	2	.966
1998— Montreal (N.L.)	1B	140	505	58	138	44	2	13	73	.273	39	70	6	1070	79	*17	.985
1999— Montreal (N.L.)	1B	100	347	38	96	34	2	9	47	.277	22	35	2	700	41	7	.991
— Ottawa (I.L.)	1B-DH	39	142	31	45	9	0	11	32	.317	12	16	2	187	13	2	.990
2000— Toronto (A.L.)■	DH-1B	133	482	76	142	29	1	32	104	.295	30	68	3	2	1	0	1.000
American League totals (1 year)		133	482	76	142	29	1	32	104	.295	30	68	3	2	1	0	1.000
National League totals (3 years)		259	892	100	246	80	4	25	128	.276	63	112	8	1820	127	26	.987
Major League totals (4 years)		392	1374	176	388	109	5	57	232	.282	93	180	11	1822	128	26	.987

FULTZ, AARON — P — GIANTS

PERSONAL: Born September 4, 1973, in Memphis, Tenn. ... 6-0/196. ... Throws left, bats left. ... Full name: Richard Aaron Fultz.
HIGH SCHOOL: Munford (Tenn.).
JUNIOR COLLEGE: North Florida Junior College.
TRANSACTIONS/CAREER NOTES: Selected by San Francisco Giants organization in sixth round of free-agent draft (June 1, 1992). ... Traded by Giants with SS Andres Duncan and P Greg Brummett to Minnesota Twins for P Jim Deshaies (August 28, 1993). ... Released by Twins (April 1, 1996). ... Signed by Giants organization (April 4, 1996). ... Granted free agency (October 16, 1998). ... Re-signed by Giants organization (October 23, 1998).

Year League	W	L	Pct.	ERA	G	GS	CG	ShO	Sv.	IP	H	R	ER	BB	SO
1992— Arizona Giants (Ariz.)	3	2	.600	2.13	14	•14	0	0	0	67²/₃	51	24	16	33	72
1993— Clinton (Midw.)	14	8	.636	3.41	26	25	2	1	0	148	132	63	56	64	144
— Fort Wayne (Midw.)■	0	0	...	9.00	1	1	0	0	0	4	10	4	4	0	3
1994— Fort Myers (FSL)	9	10	.474	4.33	28	28	3	0	0	168¹/₃	193	95	*81	60	132
1995— New Britain (East.)	0	2	.000	6.60	3	3	0	0	0	15	11	12	11	9	12
— Fort Myers (FSL)	3	6	.333	3.25	21	21	2	2	0	122	115	52	44	41	127
1996— San Jose (Calif.)■	9	5	.643	3.96	36	12	0	0	1	104²/₃	101	52	46	54	103
1997— Shreveport (Texas)	6	3	.667	2.83	49	0	0	0	1	70	65	30	22	19	60
1998— Shreveport (Texas)	5	7	.417	3.77	54	0	0	0	15	62	58	40	26	29	61
— Fresno (PCL)	0	0	...	5.06	10	0	0	0	0	16	22	10	9	2	13
1999— Fresno (PCL)	9	8	.529	4.98	37	20	1	0	0	137¹/₃	141	87	76	51	151
2000— San Francisco (N.L.)	5	2	.714	4.67	58	0	0	0	1	69¹/₃	67	38	36	28	62
Major League totals (1 year)	5	2	.714	4.67	58	0	0	0	1	69¹/₃	67	38	36	28	62

DIVISION SERIES RECORD

Year League	W	L	Pct.	ERA	G	GS	CG	ShO	Sv.	IP	H	R	ER	BB	SO
2000— San Francisco (N.L.)	0	1	.000	6.75	1	0	0	0	0	1¹/₃	3	1	1	0	0

F

FURCAL, RAFAEL — SS/2B — BRAVES

PERSONAL: Born August 24, 1980, in Loma De Cabrera, Dominican Republic. ... 5-10/165. ... Bats both, throws right. ... Full name: Rafael Antoni Furcal.
HIGH SCHOOL: Jose Cabrera (Loma De Cabrera, Dominican Republic).
TRANSACTIONS/CAREER NOTES: Signed as non-drafted free agent by Atlanta Braves organization (November 9, 1996). ... On Atlanta disabled list (June 13-29, 2000).
HONORS: Named N.L. Rookie Player of the Year by THE SPORTING NEWS (2000). ... Named N.L. Rookie of the Year by Baseball Writers' Association of America (2000).
STATISTICAL NOTES: Led Gulf Coast League second basemen with 122 putouts and 257 total chances in 1997. ... Led Appalachian League in caught stealing with 15 in 1998. ... Led Appalachian League second basemen with 395 total chances and 51 double plays in 1998. ... Led South Atlantic League in on-base percentage with .417 in 1999.

							BATTING								FIELDING		
Year	Team (League)	Pos.	G	AB	R	H	2B	3B	HR	RBI	Avg.	BB	SO	SB	PO	A	E	Avg.
1997—GC Braves (GCL)		2B-OF	50	190	31	49	5	4	1	9	.258	20	21	15	•122	125	10	.961
1998—Danville (Appl.)		2B	66	268	56	88	15	4	0	23	.328	36	29	*60	•183	198	14	.965
1999—Macon (S.Atl.)		SS	83	335	73	113	15	1	1	29	*.337	41	36	*73	117	192	30	.912
— Myrtle Beach (Caro.)		SS	43	184	32	54	9	3	0	12	.293	14	42	23	48	109	4	.975
2000—Greenville (Sou.)		SS	3	10	1	2	0	0	1	3	.200	1	0	0	0	8	1	.889
— Atlanta (N.L.)		SS-2B	131	455	87	134	20	4	4	37	.295	73	80	40	192	362	24	.958
Major League totals (1 year)			131	455	87	134	20	4	4	37	.295	73	80	40	192	362	24	.958

DIVISION SERIES RECORD

							BATTING								FIELDING		
Year	Team (League)	Pos.	G	AB	R	H	2B	3B	HR	RBI	Avg.	BB	SO	SB	PO	A	E	Avg.
2000—Atlanta (N.L.)		2B-SS	3	11	2	1	0	0	0	0	.091	3	0	1	3	11	1	.933

FUSSELL, CHRIS — P — ROYALS

PERSONAL: Born May 19, 1976, in Oregon, Ohio. ... 6-2/200. ... Throws right, bats right. ... Full name: Christopher Wren Fussell.
HIGH SCHOOL: Clay (Ohio).
TRANSACTIONS/CAREER NOTES: Selected by Baltimore Orioles organization in ninth round of free-agent draft (June 2, 1994). ... On disabled list (July 13, 1996-remainder of season). ... Traded by Orioles to Kansas City Royals for OF/1B Jeff Conine (April 2, 1999). ... On Omaha disabled list (July 21-29, 1999). ... On Kansas City disabled list (June 8-August 8, 2000); included rehabilitation assignment to Gulf Coast Royals (July 10-15) and Omaha (July 16-August 8).

Year	League	W	L	Pct.	ERA	G	GS	CG	ShO	Sv.	IP	H	R	ER	BB	SO
1994—Gulf Coast Orioles (GCL)		2	3	.400	4.15	14	8	0	0	0	56 1/3	53	30	26	24	65
1995—Bluefield (Appl.)		9	1	.900	2.19	12	12	1	1	0	65 2/3	37	18	16	32	98
1996—Frederick (Caro.)		5	2	.714	2.81	15	14	1	1	0	86 1/3	71	36	27	44	94
1997—Bowie (East.)		1	8	.111	7.11	19	18	0	0	0	82 1/3	102	71	65	58	71
— Frederick (Caro.)		3	3	.500	3.96	9	9	1	0	0	50	42	23	22	31	54
1998—Bowie (East.)		3	7	.300	4.26	18	18	0	0	0	93	87	54	44	52	84
— Rochester (I.L.)		5	2	.714	3.99	10	10	0	0	0	58 2/3	50	30	26	28	51
— Baltimore (A.L.)		0	1	.000	8.38	3	2	0	0	0	9 2/3	11	9	9	9	8
1999—Omaha (PCL)■		10	3	.769	3.54	14	13	1	1	0	81 1/3	66	35	32	27	80
— Kansas City (A.L.)		0	5	.000	7.39	17	8	0	0	2	56	72	51	46	36	37
2000—Kansas City (A.L.)		5	3	.625	6.30	20	9	0	0	0	70	76	52	49	44	46
— Omaha (PCL)		1	1	.500	4.98	6	6	0	0	0	21 2/3	22	13	12	12	12
— Gulf Coast Royals (GCL)		0	1	.000	2.45	2	2	0	0	0	3 2/3	6	5	1	2	6
Major League totals (3 years)		5	9	.357	6.90	40	19	0	0	2	135 2/3	159	112	104	89	91

FYHRIE, MICHAEL — P — ANGELS

PERSONAL: Born December 9, 1969, in Westminster, Calif. ... 6-2/203. ... Throws right, bats right. ... Full name: Michael Edwin Fyhrie. ... Name pronounced Feery.
HIGH SCHOOL: Ocean View (Huntington Beach, Calif.).
COLLEGE: UCLA.
TRANSACTIONS/CAREER NOTES: Selected by Kansas City Royals organization in 12th round of free-agent draft (June 3, 1991). ... Traded by Royals to New York Mets for a player to be named later (March 23, 1996). ... Contract sold by Mets to Chiba Lotte of Japan Pacific League (November 25, 1996). ... Re-signed by Mets organization (December 6, 1997). ... On Norfolk disabled list (August 2, 1998-remainder of season). ... Granted free agency (October 15, 1998). ... Signed by Anaheim Angels organization (November 18, 1998). ... On Anaheim disabled list (August 12-September 4, 2000).
HONORS: Named International League Most Valuable Pitcher in 1996.

Year	League	W	L	Pct.	ERA	G	GS	CG	ShO	Sv.	IP	H	R	ER	BB	SO
1991—Eugene (N'West)		2	1	.667	2.52	21	0	0	0	5	39 1/3	42	17	11	19	45
1992—Baseball City (FSL)		7	13	.350	2.50	26	26	0	0	0	162	148	65	45	37	92
1993—Wilmington (Caro.)		3	2	.600	3.68	5	5	0	0	0	29 1/3	32	15	12	8	19
— Memphis (Sou.)		11	4	.733	3.56	22	22	3	0	0	131 1/3	143	59	52	59	59
1994—Omaha (A.A.)		6	5	.545	5.72	18	16	0	0	0	85	100	57	54	33	37
— Memphis (Sou.)		2	5	.286	3.22	11	11	0	0	0	67	67	29	24	17	38
1995—Wichita (Texas)		3	2	.600	3.04	17	9	0	0	1	74	76	31	25	23	41
— Omaha (A.A.)		3	4	.429	4.45	14	11	0	0	0	60 2/3	71	34	30	14	39
1996—Norfolk (I.L.)■		*15	6	.714	3.04	27	27	2	•2	0	169	150	61	57	33	103
— New York (N.L.)		0	1	.000	15.43	2	0	0	0	0	2 1/3	4	4	4	3	0
1997—Chiba Lotte (Jp. Pac.)■		3	4	.429	5.86	8	...	...	...	0	43	54	...	28	15	15
1998—Norfolk (I.L.)■		3	7	.300	6.64	24	17	0	0	0	100 1/3	115	83	74	45	60
1999—Edmonton (PCL)■		9	5	.643	3.47	19	18	0	0	0	114	90	47	44	40	113
— Anaheim (A.L.)		0	4	.000	5.05	16	7	0	0	0	51 2/3	61	32	29	21	26

Year League	W	L	Pct.	ERA	G	GS	CG	ShO	Sv.	IP	H	R	ER	BB	SO
2000— Anaheim (A.L.)	0	0	...	2.39	32	0	0	0	0	52 2/3	54	14	14	15	43
— Edmonton (PCL)	2	1	.667	2.30	9	0	0	0	1	15 2/3	6	4	4	12	9
A.L. totals (2 years)	0	4	.000	3.71	48	7	0	0	0	104 1/3	115	46	43	36	69
N.L. totals (1 year)	0	1	.000	15.43	2	0	0	0	0	2 1/3	4	4	4	3	0
Major League totals (3 years)	0	5	.000	3.97	50	7	0	0	0	106 2/3	119	50	47	39	69

GAETTI, GARY — 3B

PERSONAL: Born August 19, 1958, in Centralia, Ill. ... 6-0/205. ... Bats right, throws right. ... Full name: Gary Joseph Gaetti. ... Name pronounced guy-ETT-ee.
HIGH SCHOOL: Centralia (Ill.).
JUNIOR COLLEGE: Lake Land College (Ill.).
COLLEGE: Northwest Missouri State.
TRANSACTIONS/CAREER NOTES: Selected by St. Louis Cardinals organization in fourth round of free-agent draft (January 10, 1978); did not sign. ... Selected by Chicago White Sox organization in secondary phase of free-agent draft (June 6, 1978); did not sign. ... Selected by Minnesota Twins organization in secondary phase of free-agent draft (June 5, 1979). ... Granted free agency (November 9, 1987). ... Re-signed by Twins (January 7, 1988). ... On disabled list (August 21-September 5, 1988 and August 26-September 13, 1989). ... Granted free agency (December 7, 1990). ... Signed by California Angels (January 23, 1991). ... Released by Angels (June 3, 1993). ... Signed by Kansas City Royals (June 19, 1993). ... Granted free agency (October 25, 1993). ... Re-signed by Royals organization (December 16, 1993). ... On disabled list (July 5-20, 1994). ... Granted free agency (October 28, 1994). ... Re-signed by Royals organization (December 20, 1994). ... Granted free agency (November 3, 1995). ... Signed by Cardinals (December 18, 1995). ... On disabled list (April 28-May 14, 1996). ... Granted free agency (October 27, 1997). ... Re-signed by Cardinals (December 6, 1997). ... Released by Cardinals (August 14, 1998). ... Signed by Chicago Cubs (August 19, 1998). ... Granted free agency (October 23, 1998). ... Re-signed by Cubs (December 7, 1998). ... Released by Cubs (October 15, 1999). ... Signed by Boston Red Sox (April 2, 2000). ... Announced retirement (April 13, 2000).
RECORDS: Shares major league rookie-season record for most sacrifice flies—13 (1982).
HONORS: Won A.L. Gold Glove at third base (1986-89). ... Named third baseman on THE SPORTING NEWS A.L. Silver Slugger team (1995).
STATISTICAL NOTES: Tied for Appalachian League lead in errors by third baseman with 18 in 1979. ... Led Midwest League third basemen with 492 total chances and 35 double plays in 1980. ... Led Southern League third basemen with 122 putouts, 281 assists, 32 errors and 435 total chances in 1981. ... Hit home run in first major-league at-bat (September 20, 1981). ... Led A.L. with 13 sacrifice flies in 1982. ... Led A.L. third basemen with 131 putouts in 1983, 142 in 1984 and 146 in 1985. ... Led A.L. third basemen with 46 double plays in 1983, 36 in 1986 and 1990 and 39 in 1991. ... Led A.L. third basemen with 496 total chances in 1984, 473 in 1986, 438 in 1990 and 481 in 1991. ... Led A.L. third basemen with 334 assists in both 1984 and 1986 and 318 in 1990. ... Tied for A.L. lead in errors by third baseman with 20 in 1984. ... Led A.L. in grounding into double plays with 25 in 1987. ... Led A.L. third basemen with .982 fielding percentage in 1994. ... Led N.L. third basemen in fielding percentage with .978 in 1997 and .983 in 1998. ... Career major league grand slams: 11.

Year Team (League)	Pos.	G	AB	R	H	2B	3B	HR	RBI	Avg.	BB	SO	SB	PO	A	E	Avg.
1979— Elizabethton (Appl.)	3B-SS	66	230	50	59	15	2	14	42	.257	43	40	6	70	134	‡21	.907
1980— Wisconsin (Midw.)	3B	138	503	77	134	27	3	*22	82	.266	67	120	24	*94	*363	•35	.929
1981— Orlando (Sou.)	3B-1B	137	495	92	137	19	2	30	93	.277	58	105	15	†143	†283	†32	.930
— Minnesota (A.L.)	3B-DH	9	26	4	5	0	0	2	3	.192	0	6	0	5	17	0	1.000
1982— Minnesota (A.L.)	3B-SS-DH	145	508	59	117	25	4	25	84	.230	37	107	0	106	291	17	.959
1983— Minnesota (A.L.)	3B-SS-DH	157	584	81	143	30	3	21	78	.245	54	121	7	†131	361	17	.967
1984— Minnesota (A.L.)	3B-OF-SS	•162	588	55	154	29	4	5	65	.262	44	81	11	†163	†335	‡21	.960
1985— Minnesota (A.L.)	3-0-1-DH	160	560	71	138	31	0	20	63	.246	37	89	13	†162	316	18	.964
1986— Minnesota (A.L.)	3-S-O-2	157	596	91	171	34	1	34	108	.287	52	108	14	120	†335	21	.956
1987— Minnesota (A.L.)	3B-DH	154	584	95	150	36	2	31	109	.257	37	92	10	•134	261	11	.973
1988— Minnesota (A.L.)	3B-DH-SS	133	468	66	141	29	2	28	88	.301	36	85	7	105	191	7	.977
1989— Minnesota (A.L.)	3B-DH-1B	130	498	63	125	11	4	19	75	.251	25	87	6	115	253	10	.974
1990— Minnesota (A.L.)	3B	154	577	61	132	27	5	16	85	.229	36	101	6	125	†319	18	.961
1991— California (A.L.)■	3B	152	586	58	144	22	1	18	66	.246	33	104	5	111	*353	17	.965
1992— California (A.L.)	3B-1B-DH	130	456	41	103	13	2	12	48	.226	21	79	3	423	196	22	.966
1993— California (A.L.)	3B-1B-DH	20	50	3	9	2	0	4	4	.180	5	12	1	38	7	1	.978
— Kansas City (A.L.)■ ..	3B-1B-DH	82	281	37	72	18	1	14	46	.256	16	75	0	147	146	6	.980
1994— Kansas City (A.L.)	3B-1B	90	327	53	94	15	3	12	57	.287	19	63	0	99	166	4	†.985
1995— Kansas City (A.L.)	3B-1B-DH	137	514	76	134	27	0	35	96	.261	47	91	3	182	228	16	.962
1996— St. Louis (N.L.)■	3B-1B	141	522	71	143	27	4	23	80	.274	35	97	2	148	231	10	.974
1997— St. Louis (N.L.)	3B-1B-P	148	502	63	126	24	1	17	69	.251	36	88	7	133	250	7	†.982
1998— St. Louis (N.L.)	3-1-P-2-O	91	306	39	81	23	1	11	43	.265	31	39	1	62	153	3	.986
— Chicago (N.L.)■.......	3B	37	128	21	41	11	0	8	27	.320	12	23	0	24	68	2	‡.979
1999— Chicago (N.L.) 3B-1B-P-SS		113	280	22	57	9	1	9	46	.204	21	51	0	74	147	9	.961
2000— Boston (A.L.)■..........	DH	5	10	0	0	0	0	0	1	.000	0	3	0	...	...	...	...
American League totals (16 years)		1977	7213	914	1832	349	32	292	1076	.254	499	1304	86	2166	3775	206	.966
National League totals (4 years)		530	1738	216	448	94	7	68	265	.258	135	298	10	441	849	31	.977
Major League totals (20 years)		2507	8951	1130	2280	443	39	360	1341	.255	634	1602	96	2607	4624	237	.968

DIVISION SERIES RECORD

Year Team (League)	Pos.	G	AB	R	H	2B	3B	HR	RBI	Avg.	BB	SO	SB	PO	A	E	Avg.
1996— St. Louis (N.L.)	3B	3	11	1	1	0	0	1	3	.091	0	3	0	1	3	0	1.000
1998— Chicago (N.L.)	3B	3	11	0	1	0	0	0	0	.091	0	4	0	2	6	1	.889
Division series totals (2 years)		6	22	1	2	0	0	1	3	.091	0	7	0	3	9	1	.923

CHAMPIONSHIP SERIES RECORD

RECORDS: Shares single-game record for most grand slams—1 (October 10, 1996). ... Shares single-inning record for most runs batted in—4 (October 10, 1996, seventh inning).
NOTES: Hit home run in first at-bat (October 7, 1987). ... Named Most Valuable Player (1987).

Year Team (League)	Pos.	G	AB	R	H	2B	3B	HR	RBI	Avg.	BB	SO	SB	PO	A	E	Avg.
1987— Minnesota (A.L.)	3B	5	20	5	6	1	0	2	5	.300	1	3	0	8	7	0	1.000
1996— St. Louis (N.L.)	3B	7	24	1	7	0	0	1	4	.292	1	5	0	4	12	0	1.000
Championship series totals (2 years)		12	44	6	13	1	0	3	9	.295	2	8	0	12	19	0	1.000

F
G

RECORDS: Shares single-inning records for most at-bats—2; and most hits—2 (October 17, 1987, fourth inning).
NOTES: Member of World Series championship team (1987).

Year	Team (League)	Pos.	G	AB	R	H	2B	3B	HR	RBI	Avg.	BB	SO	SB	PO	A	E	Avg.
											BATTING					FIELDING		
1987— Minnesota (A.L.)		3B	7	27	4	7	2	1	1	4	.259	2	5	2	6	15	0	1.000

ALL-STAR GAME RECORD

Year	League	Pos.	AB	R	H	2B	3B	HR	RBI	Avg.	BB	SO	SB	PO	A	E	Avg.
								BATTING							FIELDING		
1988— American		PH	1	0	0	0	0	0	0	.000	0	0	0	...	...	...	...
1989— American		3B	1	0	0	0	0	0	0	.000	0	1	0	1	0	0	1.000
All-Star Game totals (2 years)			2	0	0	0	0	0	0	.000	0	1	0	1	0	0	1.000

RECORD AS PITCHER

Year	League	W	L	Pct.	ERA	G	GS	CG	ShO	Sv.	IP	H	R	ER	BB	SO
1997— St. Louis (N.L.)..................		0	0	...	0.00	1	0	0	0	0	$1/3$	1	0	0	0	0
1998— St. Louis (N.L.)..................		0	0	...	0.00	1	0	0	0	0	1	2	0	0	0	0
1999— Chicago (N.L.)..................		0	0	...	18.00	1	0	0	0	0	1	2	2	2	1	1
Major League totals (3 years).......		0	0	...	7.71	3	0	0	0	0	$2\,1/3$	5	2	2	1	1

GAGNE, ERIC   P   DODGERS

PERSONAL: Born January 7, 1976, in Montreal. ... 6-2/195. ... Throws right, bats right. ... Full name: Eric Serge Gagne.
HIGH SCHOOL: Polyvalente Edouard Montpetit (Montreal).
TRANSACTIONS/CAREER NOTES: Signed as non-drafted free agent by Los Angeles Dodgers organization (July 26, 1995). ... On disabled list entire 1997 season. ... On San Antonio suspended list (April 26-29, 1999).
HONORS: Named Texas League Pitcher of the Year (1999).

Year	League	W	L	Pct.	ERA	G	GS	CG	ShO	Sv.	IP	H	R	ER	BB	SO
1996— Savannah (S.Atl.)		7	6	.538	3.28	23	21	1	1	0	$115\,1/3$	94	48	42	43	131
1997—								Did not play.								
1998— Vero Beach (FSL)		9	7	.563	3.74	25	25	3	1	0	$139\,2/3$	118	69	58	48	144
1999— San Antonio (Texas)		12	4	.750	*2.63	26	26	0	0	0	$167\,2/3$	122	55	49	64	*185
— Los Angeles (N.L.)		1	1	.500	2.10	5	5	0	0	0	30	18	8	7	15	30
2000— Albuquerque (PCL)............		5	1	.833	3.88	9	9	0	0	0	$55\,2/3$	56	30	24	15	59
— Los Angeles (N.L.)		4	6	.400	5.15	20	19	0	0	0	$101\,1/3$	106	62	58	60	79
Major League totals (2 years).......		5	7	.417	4.45	25	24	0	0	0	$131\,1/3$	124	70	65	75	109

GALARRAGA, ANDRES   1B   RANGERS

PERSONAL: Born June 18, 1961, in Caracas, Venezuela. ... 6-3/235. ... Bats right, throws right. ... Full name: Andres Jose Galarraga. ... Name pronounced GAHL-ah-RAH-guh.
HIGH SCHOOL: Enrique Felmi (Caracas, Venezuela).
TRANSACTIONS/CAREER NOTES: Signed as non-drafted free agent by Montreal Expos organization (January 19, 1979). ... On disabled list (July 10-August 19 and August 20-September 4, 1986; and May 26-July 4, 1991). ... Traded by Expos to St. Louis Cardinals for P Ken Hill (November 25, 1991). ... On St. Louis disabled list (April 8-May 22, 1992; included rehabilitation assignment to Louisville (May 13-22). ... Granted free agency (October 27, 1992). ... Signed by Colorado Rockies (November 16, 1992). ... On disabled list (May 10-27 and July 25-August 21, 1993). ... Granted free agency (October 25, 1993). ... Re-signed by Rockies (December 6, 1993). ... On disabled list (July 29, 1994-remainder of season). ... On suspended list (August 3-5, 1997). ... Granted free agency (October 27, 1997). ... Signed by Atlanta Braves (November 20, 1997). ... On suspended list (September 2-5, 1998). ... On Atlanta disabled list (April 3, 1999-entire season). ... On suspended list (September 7-10, 2000). ... Granted free agency (October 30, 2000). ... Signed by Texas Rangers (December 8, 2000).
RECORDS: Shares major league single-inning record for most times hit by pitch—2 (July 12, 1996, seventh inning).
HONORS: Named Southern League Most Valuable Player (1984). ... Named first baseman on THE SPORTING NEWS N.L. Silver Slugger team (1988 and 1996). ... Won N.L. Gold Glove at first base (1989-90). ... Named N.L. Comeback Player of the Year by THE SPORTING NEWS (1993 and 2000).
STATISTICAL NOTES: Led Southern League with 271 total bases, .508 slugging percentage and 10 intentional bases on balls received and tied for lead in being hit by pitch with nine in 1984. ... Led Southern League first basemen with 1,428 total chances and 130 double plays in 1984. ... Led N.L. in being hit by pitch with 10 in 1987 and tied for lead with 13 in 1989. ... Led N.L. with 329 total bases in 1988. ... Hit three home runs in one game (June 25, 1995). ... Collected six hits in one game (July 3, 1995). ... Led N.L. first basemen with 1,432 total chances and 129 double plays in 1995. ... Led N.L. first basemen with 1,528 putouts, 1,658 total chances and 154 double plays in 1996. ... Led N.L. first basemen with 1,590 total chances and 176 double plays in 1997. ... Had 15-game hitting streak (April 23-May 8, 1998). ... Career major league grand slams: 10.

Year	Team (League)	Pos.	G	AB	R	H	2B	3B	HR	RBI	Avg.	BB	SO	SB	PO	A	E	Avg.
									BATTING							FIELDING		
1979— W.P. Beach (FSL)........		1B	7	23	3	3	0	0	0	1	.130	2	11	0	2	1	0	1.000
— Calgary (Pio.)		1B-3B-C	42	112	14	24	3	1	4	16	.214	9	42	1	187	21	5	.977
1980— Calgary (Pio.)		1B-3B-C-OF	59	190	27	50	11	4	4	22	.263	7	55	3	287	52	21	.942
1981— Jamestown (NY-P)		C-1B-OF-3B	47	154	24	40	5	4	6	26	.260	15	44	0	154	15	0	1.000
1982— W.P. Beach (FSL)........		1B-OF	105	338	39	95	20	2	14	51	.281	34	77	2	462	36	9	.982
1983— W.P. Beach (FSL)........		1B-OF-3B	104	401	55	116	18	3	10	66	.289	33	68	7	861	77	13	.986
1984— Jacksonville (Sou.)......		1B	143	533	81	154	28	4	27	87	.289	59	122	2	*1302	*110	16	.989
1985— Indianapolis (A.A.)......		1B-OF	121	439	*75	118	15	8	25	87	.269	45	103	3	930	63	14	.986
— Montreal (N.L.)..........		1B	24	75	9	14	1	0	2	4	.187	3	18	1	173	22	1	.995
1986— Montreal (N.L.)..........		1B	105	321	39	87	13	0	10	42	.271	30	79	6	805	40	4	.995
1987— Montreal (N.L.)..........		1B	147	551	72	168	40	3	13	90	.305	41	127	7	*1300	103	10	.993
1988— Montreal (N.L.)..........		1B	157	609	99	*184	*42	8	29	92	.302	39	*153	13	1464	103	15	.991
1989— Montreal (N.L.)..........		1B	152	572	76	147	30	1	23	85	.257	48	*158	12	1335	91	11	.992
1990— Montreal (N.L.)..........		1B	155	579	65	148	29	0	20	87	.256	40	*169	10	1300	94	10	.993
1991— Montreal (N.L.)..........		1B	107	375	34	82	13	2	9	33	.219	23	86	5	887	80	9	.991

Year	Team (League)	Pos.	G	AB	R	H	2B	3B	HR	RBI	Avg.	BB	SO	SB	PO	A	E	Avg.
1992—	St. Louis (N.L.)■	1B	95	325	38	79	14	2	10	39	.243	11	69	5	777	62	8	.991
	—Louisville (A.A.)	1B	11	34	3	6	0	1	2	3	.176	0	8	1	61	7	2	.971
1993—	Colorado (N.L.)■	1B	120	470	71	174	35	4	22	98	*.370	24	73	2	1018	103	11	.990
1994—	Colorado (N.L.)	1B	103	417	77	133	21	0	31	85	.319	19	93	8	953	65	8	.992
1995—	Colorado (N.L.)	1B	143	554	89	155	29	3	31	106	.280	32	*146	12	*1299	120	*13	.991
1996—	Colorado (N.L.)	1B-3B	159	626	119	190	39	3	*47	*150	.304	40	157	18	†1528	116	14	.992
1997—	Colorado (N.L.)	1B	154	600	120	191	31	3	41	*140	.318	54	141	15	*1458	117	*15	.991
1998—	Atlanta (N.L.)■	1B-DH	153	555	103	169	27	1	44	121	.305	63	146	7	1218	81	11	.992
1999—	Atlanta (N.L.)								Did not play.									
2000—	Atlanta (N.L.)	1B-DH	141	494	67	149	25	1	28	100	.302	36	126	3	1105	61	14	.988
Major League totals (15 years)			1915	7123	1078	2070	389	31	360	1272	.291	503	1741	124	16620	1258	154	.991

DIVISION SERIES RECORD

Year	Team (League)	Pos.	G	AB	R	H	2B	3B	HR	RBI	Avg.	BB	SO	SB	PO	A	E	Avg.
1995—	Colorado (N.L.)	1B	4	18	1	5	1	0	0	2	.278	0	6	0	41	2	0	1.000
1998—	Atlanta (N.L.)	1B	3	12	1	3	0	0	0	0	.250	1	3	0	5	0	0	1.000
2000—	Atlanta (N.L.)	1B	3	10	1	2	1	0	0	1	.200	2	4	0	26	1	0	1.000
Division series totals (3 years)			10	40	3	10	2	0	0	3	.250	3	13	0	72	3	0	1.000

CHAMPIONSHIP SERIES RECORD

RECORDS: Shares single-inning record for most runs batted in—4 (October 11, 1998, seventh inning).

Year	Team (League)	Pos.	G	AB	R	H	2B	3B	HR	RBI	Avg.	BB	SO	SB	PO	A	E	Avg.
1998—	Atlanta (N.L.)	1B	6	21	1	2	0	0	1	4	.095	6	6	0	63	11	4	.949

ALL-STAR GAME RECORD

Year	League	Pos.	AB	R	H	2B	3B	HR	RBI	Avg.	BB	SO	SB	PO	A	E	Avg.
1988—	National	1B	2	0	0	0	0	0	0	.000	0	1	0	6	0	0	1.000
1993—	National	1B	1	0	0	0	0	0	0	.000	0	0	0	0	0	0	...
1997—	National	PH-DH	1	0	0	0	0	0	0	.000	0	1	0	...	...	...	...
1998—	National	1B	2	0	0	0	0	0	0	.000	0	0	0	7	0	0	1.000
2000—	National	1B	2	0	1	0	0	0	0	.500	0	0	0	4	0	0	1.000
All-Star Game totals (5 years)			8	0	1	0	0	0	0	.125	0	2	0	17	0	0	1.000

GANT, RON   OF   ROCKIES

PERSONAL: Born March 2, 1965, in Victoria, Texas. ... 6-0/196. ... Bats right, throws right. ... Full name: Ronald Edwin Gant.

HIGH SCHOOL: Victoria (Texas).

TRANSACTIONS/CAREER NOTES: Selected by Atlanta Braves organization in fourth round of free-agent draft (June 6, 1983). ... On suspended list (July 31, 1991). ... Released by Braves (March 15, 1994). ... Signed by Cincinnati Reds (June 21, 1994). ... On disabled list (June 21, 1994-remainder of season). ... On suspended list (September 11-15, 1995). ... Granted free agency (October 30, 1995). ... Signed by St. Louis Cardinals (December 23, 1995). ... On disabled list (May 11-June 14, 1996). ... On disabled list (June 21-July 11, 1998). ... Traded by Cardinals with P Jeff Brantley and P Cliff Politte to Philadelphia Phillies for P Ricky Bottalico and P Garrett Stephenson (November 19, 1998). ... Traded by Phillies to Anaheim Angels for P Kent Bottenfield (July 30, 2000). ... Granted free agency (October 30, 2000). ... Signed by Colorado Rockies (December 10, 2000).

HONORS: Named outfielder on THE SPORTING NEWS N.L. All-Star team (1991). ... Named outfielder on THE SPORTING NEWS N.L. Silver Slugger team (1991). ... Named N.L. Comeback Player of the Year by THE SPORTING NEWS (1995).

STATISTICAL NOTES: Led South Atlantic League second basemen with 75 double plays in 1984. ... Led Carolina League with 271 total bases in 1986. ... Led Southern League second basemen with 783 total chances and 108 double plays in 1987. ... Led N.L. second basemen with 26 errors in 1988. ... Career major league grand slams: 4.

Year	Team (League)	Pos.	G	AB	R	H	2B	3B	HR	RBI	Avg.	BB	SO	SB	PO	A	E	Avg.
1983—	GC Braves (GCL)	SS	56	193	32	45	2	2	1	14	.233	41	34	4	68	134	22	.902
1984—	Anderson (S.Atl.)	2B	105	359	44	85	14	6	3	38	.237	29	65	13	248	263	31	.943
1985—	Sumter (S.Atl.)	2B-SS-OF	102	305	46	78	14	4	7	37	.256	33	59	19	160	200	10	.973
1986—	Durham (Caro.)	2B	137	512	108	142	31	10	*26	102	.277	78	85	35	240	384	26	.960
1987—	Greenville (Sou.)	2B	140	527	78	130	27	3	14	82	.247	59	91	24	*328	*434	21	*.973
	—Atlanta (N.L.)	2B	21	83	9	22	4	0	2	9	.265	1	11	4	45	59	3	.972
1988—	Richmond (I.L.)	2B	12	45	3	14	2	2	0	4	.311	2	10	1	22	23	5	.900
	—Atlanta (N.L.)	2B-3B	146	563	85	146	28	8	19	60	.259	46	118	19	316	417	†31	.959
1989—	Atlanta (N.L.)	3B-OF	75	260	26	46	8	3	9	25	.177	20	63	9	70	103	17	.911
	—Sumter (S.Atl.)	OF	12	39	13	15	4	1	1	5	.385	11	3	4	19	1	2	.909
	—Richmond (I.L.)	OF-3B	63	225	42	59	13	2	11	27	.262	29	42	6	111	14	5	.962
1990—	Atlanta (N.L.)	OF	152	575	107	174	34	3	32	84	.303	50	86	33	357	7	8	.978
1991—	Atlanta (N.L.)■	OF	154	561	101	141	35	3	32	105	.251	71	104	34	338	7	6	.983
1992—	Atlanta (N.L.)	OF	153	544	74	141	22	6	17	80	.259	45	101	32	277	5	4	.986
1993—	Atlanta (N.L.)	OF	157	606	113	166	27	4	36	117	.274	67	117	26	271	5	*11	.962
1994—	Cincinnati (N.L.)■								Did not play.									
1995—	Cincinnati (N.L.)	OF	119	410	79	113	19	4	29	88	.276	74	108	23	191	7	3	.985
1996—	St. Louis (N.L.)■	OF	122	419	74	103	14	2	30	82	.246	73	98	13	216	4	5	.978
1997—	St. Louis (N.L.)	OF-DH	139	502	68	115	21	4	17	62	.229	58	162	14	247	4	6	.977
1998—	St. Louis (N.L.)	OF	121	383	60	92	17	1	26	67	.240	51	92	8	162	4	5	.971
1999—	Philadelphia (N.L.)■	OF-DH	138	516	107	134	27	5	17	77	.260	85	112	13	260	7	2	.993
2000—	Philadelphia (N.L.)	OF	89	343	54	87	16	2	20	38	.254	36	73	5	175	5	8	.968
	—Anaheim (A.L.)■	OF-DH	34	82	15	19	3	1	6	16	.232	20	18	1	42	1	1	.977
American League totals (1 year)			34	82	15	19	3	1	6	16	.232	20	18	1	42	1	1	.977
National League totals (13 years)			1586	5765	957	1480	272	45	286	894	.257	677	1245	233	2925	633	107	.971
Major League totals (13 years)			1620	5847	972	1499	275	46	292	910	.256	697	1263	234	2967	634	108	.971

DIVISION SERIES RECORD

Year Team (League)	Pos.	G	AB	R	H	2B	3B	HR	RBI	Avg.	BB	SO	SB	PO	A	E	Avg.
1995— Cincinnati (N.L.)........	OF	3	13	3	3	0	0	1	2	.231	0	3	0	8	1	0	1.000
1996— St. Louis (N.L.)..........	OF	3	10	3	4	1	0	1	4	.400	2	0	2	5	0	0	1.000
Division series totals (2 years)		6	23	6	7	1	0	2	6	.304	2	3	2	13	1	0	1.000

CHAMPIONSHIP SERIES RECORD

RECORDS: Shares single-game record for most grand slams—1 (October 7, 1992). ... Shares single-inning records for most runs batted in—4 (October 7, 1992, fifth inning); and most stolen bases—2 (October 10, 1991, third inning). ... Holds N.L. career record for most strikeouts—26. ... Holds N.L. single-series record for most stolen bases—7 (1991). ... Shares N.L. single-game record for most stolen bases—3 (October 10, 1991).

Year Team (League)	Pos.	G	AB	R	H	2B	3B	HR	RBI	Avg.	BB	SO	SB	PO	A	E	Avg.
1991— Atlanta (N.L.)..............	OF	7	27	4	7	1	0	1	3	.259	2	4	7	15	2	0	1.000
1992— Atlanta (N.L.)..............	OF	7	22	5	4	0	0	2	6	.182	4	4	1	16	0	0	1.000
1993— Atlanta (N.L.)..............	OF	6	27	4	5	3	0	0	3	.185	2	9	0	10	1	1	.917
1995— Cincinnati (N.L.)........	OF	4	16	1	3	0	0	0	1	.188	0	3	0	9	0	0	1.000
1996— St. Louis (N.L.)..........	OF	7	25	3	6	1	0	2	4	.240	2	6	0	12	0	0	1.000
Championship series totals (5 years)		31	117	17	25	5	0	5	17	.214	10	26	8	62	3	1	.985

WORLD SERIES RECORD

Year Team (League)	Pos.	G	AB	R	H	2B	3B	HR	RBI	Avg.	BB	SO	SB	PO	A	E	Avg.
1991— Atlanta (N.L.)..............	OF	7	30	3	8	0	1	0	4	.267	2	3	1	19	0	0	1.000
1992— Atlanta (N.L.)..............	OF-PR-PH	4	8	2	1	1	0	0	0	.125	1	2	2	3	1	0	1.000
World Series totals (2 years)		11	38	5	9	1	1	0	4	.237	3	5	3	22	1	0	1.000

ALL-STAR GAME RECORD

Year League	Pos.	AB	R	H	2B	3B	HR	RBI	Avg.	BB	SO	SB	PO	A	E	Avg.
1992— National	PH-OF	2	0	0	0	0	0	0	.000	0	0	0	1	0	0	1.000
1995— National	DH	2	0	0	0	0	0	0	.000	0	1	0	...	...	...	...
All-Star Game totals (2 years)		4	0	0	0	0	0	0	.000	0	1	0	1	0	0	1.000

GARCES, RICHARD   P   RED SOX

PERSONAL: Born May 18, 1971, in Maracay, Venezuela. ... 6-0/215. ... Throws right, bats right. ... Full name: Richard Aron Garces Jr. ... Name pronounced gar-SESS.

HIGH SCHOOL: Jose Felix Rivas (Maracay, Venezuela).

COLLEGE: Venezuela Universidad.

TRANSACTIONS/CAREER NOTES: Signed as non-drafted free agent by Minnesota Twins organization (December 29, 1987). ... On Portland suspended list (May 17-September 16, 1991). ... On Portland disabled list (July 28, 1991-remainder of season). ... Granted free agency (October 15, 1994). ... Signed by Chicago Cubs organization (January 30, 1995). ... Claimed on waivers by Florida Marlins (August 9, 1995). ... Granted free agency (October 16, 1995). ... Signed by Boston Red Sox (April 25, 1996). ... On Boston disabled list (July 25-August 20 and August 24, 1996-remainder of season); included rehabilitation assignment to Pawtucket (August 9-20). ... On Boston disabled list (March 27-April 27 and June 2-23, 1997); included rehabilitation assignments to Pawtucket (April 18-21, April 25-27 and June 12-23). ... On Boston disabled list (April 11-May 7, July 1-17 and August 3, 1998-remainder of season); included rehabilitation assignments to Pawtucket (April 21-May 7 and August 30-September 3) and Gulf Coast Red Sox (August 12-29). ... Released by Red Sox (November 23, 1998). ... Re-signed by Red Sox organization (January 26, 1999). ... On Pawtucket disabled list (April 8-22 and May 15-31, 1999).

Year League	W	L	Pct.	ERA	G	GS	CG	ShO	Sv.	IP	H	R	ER	BB	SO
1988— Elizabethton (Appl.)	5	4	.556	2.29	17	3	1	0	5	59	51	22	15	27	69
1989— Kenosha (Midw.)	9	10	.474	3.41	24	24	4	1	0	142$^{2}/_{3}$	117	70	54	62	84
1990— Visalia (Calif.)	2	2	.500	1.81	47	0	0	0	*28	54$^{2}/_{3}$	33	14	11	16	75
— Orlando (Sou.)	2	1	.667	2.08	15	0	0	0	8	17$^{1}/_{3}$	17	4	4	14	22
— Minnesota (A.L.)	0	0	...	1.59	5	0	0	0	2	5$^{2}/_{3}$	4	2	1	4	1
1991— Portland (PCL)	0	1	.000	4.85	10	0	0	0	3	13	10	7	7	8	13
— Orlando (Sou.)	2	1	.667	3.31	10	0	0	0	0	16$^{1}/_{3}$	12	6	6	14	17
1992— Orlando (Sou.)	3	3	.500	4.54	58	0	0	0	13	73$^{1}/_{3}$	76	46	37	39	72
1993— Portland (PCL)	1	3	.250	8.33	35	7	0	0	0	54	70	55	50	64	48
— Minnesota (A.L.)	0	0	...	0.00	3	0	0	0	0	4	4	2	0	2	3
1994— Nashville (Sou.)	4	5	.444	3.72	40	1	0	0	3	77$^{1}/_{3}$	70	40	32	31	76
1995— Iowa (A.A.)■	0	2	.000	2.86	23	0	0	0	7	28$^{1}/_{3}$	25	10	9	8	36
— Chicago (N.L.)	0	0	...	3.27	7	0	0	0	0	11	11	6	4	3	6
— Florida (N.L.)■	0	2	.000	5.40	11	0	0	0	0	13$^{1}/_{3}$	14	9	8	8	16
1996— Pawtucket (I.L.)■	4	0	1.000	2.30	10	0	0	0	0	15$^{2}/_{3}$	10	4	4	5	13
— Boston (A.L.)	3	2	.600	4.91	37	0	0	0	0	44	42	26	24	33	55
1997— Boston (A.L.)	0	1	.000	4.61	12	0	0	0	0	13$^{2}/_{3}$	14	9	7	9	12
— Pawtucket (I.L.)	2	1	.667	1.45	26	0	0	0	5	31	24	5	5	13	42
1998— Boston (A.L.)	1	1	.500	3.33	30	0	0	0	1	46	36	19	17	27	34
— Pawtucket (I.L.)	0	1	.000	5.40	7	0	0	0	3	8$^{1}/_{3}$	6	5	5	2	10
— Gulf Coast Red Sox (GCL)..	0	0	...	3.27	7	7	0	0	0	11	11	4	4	0	8
1999— Pawtucket (I.L.)	1	0	1.000	3.25	21	0	0	0	0	27$^{2}/_{3}$	24	11	10	10	24
— Boston (A.L.)	5	1	.833	1.55	30	0	0	0	2	40$^{2}/_{3}$	25	9	7	18	33
2000— Boston (A.L.)	8	1	.889	3.25	64	0	0	0	1	74$^{2}/_{3}$	64	28	27	23	69
A.L. totals (7 years)	17	6	.739	3.27	181	0	0	0	6	228$^{2}/_{3}$	189	95	83	116	207
N.L. totals (1 year)	0	2	.000	4.44	18	0	0	0	0	24$^{1}/_{3}$	25	15	12	11	22
Major League totals (8 years)	17	8	.680	3.38	199	0	0	0	6	253	214	110	95	127	229

G

Year	League	W	L	Pct.	ERA	G	GS	CG	ShO	Sv.	IP	H	R	ER	BB	SO

DIVISION SERIES RECORD

Year	League	W	L	Pct.	ERA	G	GS	CG	ShO	Sv.	IP	H	R	ER	BB	SO
1999— Boston (A.L.)......................		1	0	1.000	3.86	2	0	0	0	0	2 1/3	2	1	1	3	2

CHAMPIONSHIP SERIES RECORD

Year	League	W	L	Pct.	ERA	G	GS	CG	ShO	Sv.	IP	H	R	ER	BB	SO
1999— Boston (A.L.)......................		0	0	...	12.00	2	0	0	0	0	3	3	5	4	1	2

GARCIA, AMAURY — 2B — WHITE SOX

PERSONAL: Born May 20, 1975, in Santo Domingo, Dominican Republic. ... 5-10/160. ... Bats right, throws right. ... Full name: Amaury Miguel Garcia.

HIGH SCHOOL: Colegio Discipulos de Jesus (Santo Domingo, Dominican Republic).

TRANSACTIONS/CAREER NOTES: Signed as non-drafted free agent by Florida Marlins organization (December 4, 1992). ... On Calgary disabled list (April 26-May 8, 2000). ... Traded by Marlins to Chicago White Sox for a player to be named later (November 27, 2000); Marlins acquired P Mark Roberts to complete deal (December 11, 2000).

STATISTICAL NOTES: Led Eastern League second basemen with 669 total chances in 1998. ... Led Pacific Coast league second basemen with 90 double plays in 1999. ... Led Pacific Coast League second basemen with 18 errrors in 2000.

									BATTING					FIELDING			
Year	Team (League)	Pos.	G	AB	R	H	2B	3B	HR	RBI	Avg.	BB	SO	SB	PO	A	E	Avg.
1993— Dom. Marlins (DSL)...		IF	64	237	35	67	5	3	4	29	.283	31	41	9	129	112	19	.927
1994— GC Marlins (GCL).......		3B-2B-OF	58	208	46	65	9	3	0	25	.313	33	49	10	44	113	17	.902
1995— Kane County (Midw.)..		3B-2B	26	58	19	14	4	1	1	5	.241	18	12	5	11	31	13	.764
— Elmira (NY-Penn)		2B	62	231	40	63	7	3	0	17	.273	34	50	*41	128	178	18	.944
1996— Kane County (Midw.)..		2B	106	395	65	104	19	7	6	36	.263	62	84	37	219	286	19	.964
1997— Brevard County (FSL).		2B	124	479	77	138	30	2	7	44	.288	49	97	45	246	329	16	.973
1998— Portland (East.)...........		2B	137	544	79	147	19	6	13	62	.270	45	126	23	*287	355	*27	.960
1999— Calgary (PCL).............		2B	119	479	94	152	37	•9	17	53	.317	44	79	17	227	308	16	.971
— Florida (N.L.).............		2B	10	24	6	6	0	1	2	2	.250	3	11	0	15	26	3	.932
2000— Calgary (PCL).............		2B-OF	120	479	83	140	26	3	13	47	.292	41	79	35	241	264	20	.962
Major League totals (1 year)			10	24	6	6	0	1	2	2	.250	3	11	0	15	26	3	.932

GARCIA, FREDDY — P — MARINERS

PERSONAL: Born October 6, 1976, in Caracas, Venezuela. ... 6-4/235. ... Throws right, bats right. ... Full name: Freddy Antonio Garcia.

TRANSACTIONS/CAREER NOTES: Signed as non-drafted free agent by Houston Astros organization (October 21, 1993). ... Traded by Astros with SS Carlos Guillen and a player to be named later to Seattle Mariners for P Randy Johnson (July 31, 1998); Mariners acquired P John Halama to complete deal (October 1, 1998). ... On Seattle disabled list (April 22-July 7, 2000); included rehabilitation assignments to Tacoma (June 15-20) and Everett (June 21-July 7).

STATISTICAL NOTES: Tied for A.L. lead with three balks in 1999.

MISCELLANEOUS: Struck out in only appearance as pinch hitter (1999).

Year	League	W	L	Pct.	ERA	G	GS	CG	ShO	Sv.	IP	H	R	ER	BB	SO
1994— Dom. Astros (DSL)............	4	6	.400	5.29	16	15	0	0	0	85	80	61	50	38	68
1995— Gulf Coast Astros (GCL).....	6	3	.667	4.47	11	11	0	0	0	58 1/3	60	32	29	14	58
1996— Quad City (Midw.)	5	4	.556	3.12	13	13	0	0	0	60 2/3	57	27	21	27	50
1997— Kissimmee (FSL)...............	10	8	.556	2.56	27	27	5	2	0	179	165	63	51	49	131
1998— Jackson (Texas)	6	7	.462	3.24	19	19	2	0	0	119 1/3	94	48	43	58	115
— New Orleans (PCL)............	1	0	1.000	3.14	2	2	0	0	0	14 1/3	14	5	5	1	13
— Tacoma (PCL)■	3	1	.750	3.86	5	5	0	0	0	32 2/3	30	14	14	13	30
1999— Seattle (A.L.).....................	17	8	.680	4.07	33	33	2	1	0	201 1/3	205	96	91	90	170
2000— Seattle (A.L.).....................	9	5	.643	3.91	21	20	0	0	0	124 1/3	112	62	54	64	79
— Tacoma (PCL)	1	0	1.000	2.57	1	1	0	0	0	7	5	2	2	2	11
— Everett (N'West)	0	0	...	4.50	2	2	0	0	0	10	11	5	5	2	15
Major League totals (2 years).......	26	13	.667	4.01	54	53	2	1	0	325 2/3	317	158	145	154	249

DIVISION SERIES RECORD

Year	League	W	L	Pct.	ERA	G	GS	CG	ShO	Sv.	IP	H	R	ER	BB	SO
2000— Seattle (A.L.).....................	0	0	...	10.80	1	1	0	0	0	3 1/3	6	4	4	3	2

CHAMPIONSHIP SERIES RECORD

Year	League	W	L	Pct.	ERA	G	GS	CG	ShO	Sv.	IP	H	R	ER	BB	SO
2000— Seattle (A.L.).....................	2	0	1.000	1.54	2	2	0	0	0	11 2/3	10	2	2	4	11

GARCIA, JESSE — SS/2B — BRAVES

PERSONAL: Born September 24, 1973, in Corpus Christi, Texas. ... 5-10/171. ... Bats right, throws right. ... Full name: Jesus Jesse Garcia Jr.

HIGH SCHOOL: Robstown (Texas).

JUNIOR COLLEGE: Lee College (Texas).

TRANSACTIONS/CAREER NOTES: Selected by Baltimore Orioles organization in 26th round of free-agent draft (June 3, 1993). ... On disabled list (June 19, 1994-remainder of season). ... Granted free agency (December 21, 1998). ... Re-signed by Orioles organization (December 21, 1998). ... On Rochester disabled list (May 25-July 18, 1999). ... Traded by Orioles for Atlanta Braves for IF Steve Sisco (December 18, 2000).

STATISTICAL NOTES: Led California League with 20 sacrifice hits in 1996. ... Led California League second basemen with 263 putouts, 409 assists, .968 fielding percentage, 694 total chances and 81 double plays in 1996; tied for lead in errors with 22. ... Led Eastern League with 24 sacrifice hits in 1997. ... Led Eastern League second basemen with .985 fielding percentage in 1997. ... Tied for International League lead with 16 sacrifice hits in 2000.

G

Year	Team (League)	Pos.	G	AB	R	H	2B	3B	HR	RBI	Avg.	BB	SO	SB	PO	A	E	Avg.
									BATTING						FIELDING			
1993—GC Orioles (GCL)........	2B-SS-3B	48	156	20	37	4	0	0	16	.237	21	32	14	61	136	14	.934
1994—Bluefield (Appl.)					Did not play.												
1995—Frederick (Caro.)	2B	124	365	52	82	11	3	3	27	.225	49	75	5	283	275	28	.952
1996—High Desert (Calif.).....	2B-SS	137	459	94	122	21	5	10	66	.266	57	81	25	†263	†409	†22	†.968
1997—Bowie (East.)..............	2B-SS-3B	*141	437	52	103	18	1	5	42	.236	38	71	7	290	377	13	†.981
1998—Bowie (East.)..............	2B-SS-OF	86	258	46	73	13	1	2	20	.283	34	37	12	133	196	9	.973
—Rochester (I.L.)...........	2B	44	160	20	47	6	4	0	18	.294	7	22	7	102	145	8	.969
1999—Baltimore (A.L.)........SS-2B-3B-DH		17	29	6	6	0	0	2	2	.207	2	3	0	16	22	0	1.000
—Rochester (I.L.)..........	SS-2B	62	220	25	56	10	2	2	23	.255	11	21	9	95	156	15	.944
2000—Baltimore (A.L.).........	2B-SS	14	17	2	1	0	0	0	0	.059	2	2	0	9	22	0	1.000
—Rochester (I.L.).......	SS-2B-3B	106	372	44	90	12	2	1	23	.242	27	60	9	164	299	18	.963
Major League totals (2 years)		31	46	8	7	0	0	2	2	.152	4	5	0	25	44	0	1.000

GARCIA, KARIM — OF — INDIANS

PERSONAL: Born October 29, 1975, in Ciudad Obregon, Mexico. ... 6-0/172. ... Bats left, throws left. ... Full name: Gustavo Garcia.
HIGH SCHOOL: Preparatoria Abierta (Ciudad Obregon, Mexico).
TRANSACTIONS/CAREER NOTES: Signed as non-drafted free agent by Los Angeles Dodgers organization (July 16, 1992). ... On Los Angeles disabled list (September 1, 1997-remainder of season). ... Selected by Arizona Diamondbacks in first round (ninth pick overall) of expansion draft (November 18, 1997). ... Traded by Diamondbacks to Detroit Tigers for OF Luis Gonzalez (December 28, 1998). ... Traded by Tigers to Baltimore Orioles for future considerations (June 12, 2000). ... On suspended list (September 1-4, 2000). ... Released by Orioles (October 17, 2000). ... Signed by Cleveland Indians organization (December 22, 2000).
HONORS: Named Minor League Player of the Year by THE SPORTING NEWS (1995).
STATISTICAL NOTES: Career major league grand slams: 1.

Year	Team (League)	Pos.	G	AB	R	H	2B	3B	HR	RBI	Avg.	BB	SO	SB	PO	A	E	Avg.
									BATTING						FIELDING			
1993—Bakersfield (Calif.)......	OF	123	460	61	111	20	9	19	54	.241	37	109	5	193	12	*13	.940
1994—Vero Beach (FSL)	OF	121	452	72	120	28	10	*21	84	.265	37	112	8	229	12	5	.980
1995—Albuquerque (PCL).....	OF-DH	124	474	88	151	26	10	20	•91	.319	38	102	12	185	7	*14	.932
—Los Angeles (N.L.)	OF	13	20	1	4	0	0	0	0	.200	0	4	0	5	2	0	1.000
1996—Albuquerque (PCL).....	OF-DH	84	327	54	97	17	10	13	58	.297	29	67	6	148	4	13	.921
—San Antonio (Texas)...	OF	35	129	21	32	6	1	5	22	.248	9	38	1	60	6	2	.971
—Los Angeles (N.L.)	OF	1	1	0	0	0	0	0	0	.000	0	1	0	0	0	0	...
1997—Albuquerque (PCL).....	OF-DH	71	262	53	80	17	6	20	66	.305	23	70	11	97	3	5	.952
—Los Angeles (N.L.)	OF	15	39	5	5	0	0	1	8	.128	6	14	0	13	0	0	1.000
1998—Arizona (N.L.)■.........	OF	113	333	39	74	10	8	9	43	.222	18	78	5	191	6	5	.975
—Tucson (PCL)	OF	27	106	21	33	4	2	10	27	.311	15	24	5	67	1	3	.958
1999—Detroit (A.L.)■..........	OF-DH	96	288	38	69	10	3	14	32	.240	20	67	2	152	7	7	.958
2000—Detroit (A.L.)	OF-DH	8	17	1	3	0	0	0	0	.176	0	4	0	8	0	0	1.000
—Toledo (I.L.).............	OF	40	155	31	46	6	2	15	38	.297	11	32	2	82	5	4	.956
—Rochester (I.L.)■......	OF	76	270	38	75	17	1	13	54	.278	34	70	3	121	4	3	.977
—Baltimore (A.L.).........	DH-OF	8	16	0	0	0	0	0	0	.000	0	6	0	2	0	0	1.000
American League totals (2 years)		112	321	39	72	10	3	14	32	.224	20	77	2	162	7	7	.960
National League totals (4 years)		142	393	45	83	10	8	10	51	.211	24	97	5	209	8	5	.977
Major League totals (6 years)		254	714	84	155	20	11	24	83	.217	44	174	7	371	15	12	.970

GARCIA, MIKE — P

PERSONAL: Born May 11, 1968, in Riverside, Calif. ... 6-2/220. ... Throws right, bats right. ... Full name: Michael R. Garcia.
HIGH SCHOOL: John W. North (Riverside, Calif.).
JUNIOR COLLEGE: Riverside (Calif.) Community College.
TRANSACTIONS/CAREER NOTES: Selected by Detroit Tigers organization in 55th round of free-agent draft (June 5, 1989). ... Released by Tigers (May 5, 1993). ... Signed by Rochester, Northern League (1993). ... Signed by Colorado Rockies organization (October 8, 1993). ... Released by Rockies (March 26, 1994). ... Signed by Tabasco, Mexican League (1994). ... Played in Taiwan (1996-98). ... Signed by Pittsburgh Pirates organization (December 23, 1998). ... Released by Pirates (July 20, 2000).

Year	League	W	L	Pct.	ERA	G	GS	CG	ShO	Sv.	IP	H	R	ER	BB	SO
1989—Bristol (Appl.)....................	0	3	.000	4.60	8	0	0	0	0	$15\frac{2}{3}$	17	9	8	4	13
—Niagara Falls (NY-Penn)	5	1	.833	1.56	7	6	1	0	0	$40\frac{1}{3}$	27	12	7	7	39
1990—Fayetteville (S.Atl.)............	12	8	.600	2.55	28	28	6	2	0	$*180\frac{1}{3}$	152	69	51	41	113
1991—Lakeland (FSL)	6	8	.429	3.13	25	24	0	0	0	144	130	63	50	41	109
1992—London (East.)	8	8	.500	3.89	27	20	1	1	0	$136\frac{2}{3}$	149	69	59	35	92
1993—London (East.)	8	4	.667	3.89	42	7	0	0	3	111	103	53	48	37	110
—Rochester (Nor.)■..............	9	2	.818	2.94	16	16	1	0	0	95	89	36	31	27	*100
1994—Tabasco (Mex.)■..............	3	5	.375	2.14	36	4	1	1	15	$71\frac{1}{3}$	57	21	17	25	71
1995—Tabasco (Mex.)..................	2	1	.667	1.94	26	2	1	0	14	$46\frac{1}{3}$	36	10	10	6	30
1996—Weichuan (Taiwan)■..........	4	5	.444	2.09	58	2	0	0	29	$146\frac{1}{3}$	124	44	34	22	183
1997—Weichuan (Taiwan)..........	7	4	.636	1.89	50	1	1	1	20	$104\frac{2}{3}$	87	33	22	21	128
1998—Weichuan (Taiwan)...........	6	7	.462	3.01	48	1	0	0	26	$95\frac{2}{3}$	84	32	32	19	133
1999—M.C. Red Devils (Mex.)■...	0	0	...	0.75	12	0	0	0	8	12	5	1	1	3	20
—Nashville (PCL)■..............	0	2	.000	3.95	23	0	0	0	0	$27\frac{1}{3}$	24	12	12	10	35
—Pittsburgh (N.L.)	1	0	1.000	1.29	7	0	0	0	0	7	2	1	1	3	9
2000—Nashville (PCL)	2	2	.500	3.55	24	0	0	0	0	33	31	17	13	8	31
—Pittsburgh (N.L.)	0	2	.000	11.12	13	0	0	0	0	$11\frac{1}{3}$	21	15	14	7	9
Major League totals (2 years).......	1	2	.333	7.36	20	0	0	0	0	$18\frac{1}{3}$	23	16	15	10	18

G

GARCIAPARRA, NOMAR   SS   RED SOX

PERSONAL: Born July 23, 1973, in Whittier, Calif. ... 6-0/180. ... Bats right, throws right. ... Full name: Anthony Nomar Garciaparra.
HIGH SCHOOL: St. John Bosco (Bellflower, Calif.).
COLLEGE: Georgia Tech.
TRANSACTIONS/CAREER NOTES: Selected by Milwaukee Brewers organization in fifth round of free-agent draft (June 3, 1991); did not sign. ... Selected by Boston Red Sox organization in first round (12th pick overall) of free-agent draft (June 2, 1994). ... On Pawtucket disabled list (April 4-15 and April 19-July 11, 1996). ... On disabled list (May 9-28, 1998; and May 12-27, 2000).
RECORDS: Shares major league single-game record for most grand slams—2 (May 10, 1999). ... Holds A.L. rookie-season record for most consecutive games batted safely—30 (1997).
HONORS: Named A.L. Rookie Player of the Year by THE SPORTING NEWS (1997). ... Named shortstop on THE SPORTING NEWS A.L. All-Star team (1997 and 1999). ... Named shortstop on THE SPORTING NEWS A.L. Silver Slugger team (1997). ... Named A.L. Rookie of the Year by Baseball Writers' Association of America (1997).
STATISTICAL NOTES: Led Eastern League shortstops with 624 total chances in 1994. ... Had 30-game hitting streak (July 26-August 29, 1997). ... Led A.L. shortstops in total chances with 720 and double plays with 113 in 1997. ... Had 16-game hitting streak (April 2-19, 1998). ... Had 24-game hitting streak (June 7-July 3, 1998). ... Had 16-game hitting streak (April 26-May 14, 1999). ... Hit three home runs in one game (May 10, 1999). ... Had 17-game hitting streak (June 13-July 2, 1999). ... Had 20-game hitting streak (September 10-29, 2000). ... Led A.L. with 20 intentional bases on balls received in 2000. ... Career major league grand slams: 3.
MISCELLANEOUS: Member of 1992 U.S. Olympic baseball team.

							BATTING								FIELDING		
Year	Team (League)	Pos.	G	AB	R	H	2B	3B	HR	RBI	Avg.	BB	SO	SB	PO	A	E	Avg.
1994—Sarasota (FSL)	SS	28	105	20	31	8	1	1	16	.295	10	6	5	42	72	3	.974
1995—Trenton (East.)	SS	125	513	77	137	20	8	8	47	.267	50	42	35	205	*396	23	.963
1996—Pawtucket (I.L.)	SS	43	172	40	59	15	2	16	46	.343	14	21	3	63	120	5	.973
—GC Red Sox (GCL)	SS	5	14	4	4	2	1	0	5	.286	1	0	0	7	12	1	.950
—Boston (A.L.)	SS-DH-2B	24	87	11	21	2	3	4	16	.241	4	14	5	37	51	1	.989
1997—Boston (A.L.)	SS	153	*684	122	*209	44	*11	30	98	.306	35	92	22	*249	450	21	.971
1998—Boston (A.L.)	SS	143	604	111	195	37	8	35	122	.323	33	62	12	228	402	25	.962
1999—Boston (A.L.)	SS	135	532	103	190	42	4	27	104	*.357	51	39	14	232	357	17	.972
2000—Boston (A.L.)	SS-DH	140	529	104	197	51	3	21	96	*.372	61	50	5	201	402	18	.971
Major League totals (5 years)		595	2436	451	812	176	29	117	436	.333	184	257	58	947	1662	82	.970

DIVISION SERIES RECORD

RECORDS: Holds career record for highest slugging average (20 or more at-bats)—1.037.

							BATTING								FIELDING		
Year	Team (League)	Pos.	G	AB	R	H	2B	3B	HR	RBI	Avg.	BB	SO	SB	PO	A	E	Avg.
1998—Boston (A.L.)	SS	4	15	4	5	1	0	3	11	.333	2	0	0	3	7	0	1.000
1999—Boston (A.L.)	SS	4	12	6	5	2	0	2	4	.417	3	3	0	5	11	0	1.000
Division series totals (2 years)		8	27	10	10	3	0	5	15	.370	5	3	0	8	18	0	1.000

CHAMPIONSHIP SERIES RECORD

							BATTING								FIELDING		
Year	Team (League)	Pos.	G	AB	R	H	2B	3B	HR	RBI	Avg.	BB	SO	SB	PO	A	E	Avg.
1999—Boston (A.L.)	SS	5	20	2	8	2	0	2	5	.400	2	2	1	7	13	4	.833

ALL-STAR GAME RECORD

						BATTING							FIELDING		
Year	League	Pos.	AB	R	H	2B	3B	HR	RBI	Avg.	BB	SO	SB	PO	A	E	Avg.
1997—American	SS	1	0	0	0	0	0	0	.000	0	0	0	1	0	0	1.000
1999—American	SS	2	0	0	0	0	0	0	.000	0	0	0	0	0	0	...
2000—American	SS	2	1	1	0	0	0	0	.500	0	0	0	2	2	2	.667
All-Star Game totals (3 years)		5	1	1	0	0	0	0	.200	0	0	0	3	2	2	.714

GARDNER, MARK   P   GIANTS

PERSONAL: Born March 1, 1962, in Los Angeles. ... 6-1/220. ... Throws right, bats right. ... Full name: Mark Allan Gardner.
HIGH SCHOOL: Clovis (Calif.).
JUNIOR COLLEGE: Fresno (Calif.) City College.
COLLEGE: Fresno State.
TRANSACTIONS/CAREER NOTES: Selected by California Angels organization in sixth round of free-agent draft (January 11, 1983); did not sign. ... Selected by Cleveland Indians organization in 17th round of free-agent draft (June 4, 1984); did not sign. ... Selected by Montreal Expos organization in eighth round of free-agent draft (June 3, 1985). ... On disabled list (September 20, 1990-remainder of season). ... On Montreal disabled list (April 2-May 14, 1991); included rehabilitation assignment to Indianapolis (April 11-May 8). ... Traded by Expos with P Doug Piatt to Kansas City Royals for C Tim Spehr and P Jeff Shaw (December 9, 1992). ... On Kansas City disabled list (July 7-August 27, 1993); included rehabilitation assignment to Omaha (July 28-August 26). ... Released by Royals (December 8, 1993). ... Signed by Florida Marlins organization (January 6, 1994). ... On Florida disabled list (June 8-26, 1994); included rehabilitation assignment to Brevard County (June 18-22). ... Granted free agency (February 17, 1995). ... Re-signed by Marlins (April 7, 1995). ... Granted free agency (October 16, 1995). ... Re-signed by Marlins organization (December 8, 1995). ... Granted free agency (March 28, 1996). ... Signed by San Francisco Giants (March 29, 1996). ... On San Francisco disabled list (July 3-21, 1996); included rehabilitation assignment to San Jose (July 17-21). ... Granted free agency (October 23, 1998). ... Re-signed by Giants (November 9, 1998). ... On San Francisco disabled list (April 17-May 9, 1999); included rehabilitation assignment to San Jose (April 28-May 9). ... Granted free agency (October 31, 2000). ... Re-signed by Giants (December 7, 2000).
RECORDS: Shares major league single-inning record for most hit batsmen—3 (August 15, 1992, first inning).
HONORS: Named American Association Pitcher of the Year (1989).
STATISTICAL NOTES: Led N.L. with nine hit batsmen in 1990. ... Pitched nine hitless innings against Los Angeles Dodgers, but gave up two hits in 10th inning and lost, 1-0, when reliever Jeff Fassero gave up game-winning hit in 10th (July 26, 1991).
MISCELLANEOUS: Struck out once in two appearances as pinch hitter for Montreal (1991). ... Had two sacrifice hits in three appearances as pinch hitter for San Francisco (1996).

G

Year	League	W	L	Pct.	ERA	G	GS	CG	ShO	Sv.	IP	H	R	ER	BB	SO
1985—	Jamestown (NY-Penn)	0	0	...	2.77	3	3	0	0	0	13	9	4	4	4	16
	West Palm Beach (FSL)	5	4	.556	2.37	10	9	4	0	0	60²/₃	54	24	16	18	44
1986—	Jacksonville (Sou.)..........	10	11	.476	3.84	29	28	3	1	0	168²/₃	144	88	72	90	140
1987—	Indianapolis (A.A.)...........	3	3	.500	5.67	9	9	0	0	0	46	48	32	29	28	41
	Jacksonville (Sou.)..........	4	6	.400	4.19	17	17	1	0	0	101	101	50	47	42	78
1988—	Jacksonville (Sou.)..........	6	3	.667	1.60	15	15	4	2	0	112¹/₃	72	24	20	36	130
	Indianapolis (A.A.)...........	4	2	.667	2.77	13	13	3	1	0	84¹/₃	65	30	26	32	71
1989—	Indianapolis (A.A.)...........	12	4	*.750	2.37	24	23	4	2	0	163¹/₃	122	51	43	59	*175
	Montreal (N.L.).................	0	3	.000	5.13	7	4	0	0	0	26¹/₃	26	16	15	11	21
1990—	Montreal (N.L.).................	7	9	.438	3.42	27	26	3	3	0	152²/₃	129	62	58	61	135
1991—	Indianapolis (A.A.)...........	2	0	1.000	3.48	6	6	0	0	0	31	26	13	12	16	38
	Montreal (N.L.).................	9	11	.450	3.85	27	27	0	0	0	168¹/₃	139	78	72	75	107
1992—	Montreal (N.L.).................	12	10	.545	4.36	33	30	0	0	0	179²/₃	179	91	87	60	132
1993—	Kansas City (A.L.)■	4	6	.400	6.19	17	16	0	0	0	91²/₃	92	65	63	36	54
	Omaha (A.A.)..................	4	2	.667	2.79	8	8	1	0	0	48¹/₃	34	17	15	19	41
1994—	Florida (N.L.)■...............	4	4	.500	4.87	20	14	0	0	0	92¹/₃	97	53	50	30	57
	Edmonton (PCL)	1	0	1.000	0.00	1	1	0	0	0	6	4	0	0	1	11
	Brevard County (FSL)	1	0	1.000	0.00	1	1	0	0	0	5	1	0	0	1	3
1995—	Florida (N.L.)	5	5	.500	4.49	39	11	1	1	1	102¹/₃	109	60	51	43	87
1996—	San Francisco (N.L.)■	12	7	.632	4.42	30	28	4	1	0	179¹/₃	200	105	88	57	145
	San Jose (Calif.)	0	0	...	3.18	1	1	0	0	0	5²/₃	4	2	2	0	7
1997—	San Francisco (N.L.)	12	9	.571	4.29	30	30	2	1	0	180¹/₃	188	92	86	57	136
1998—	San Francisco (N.L.)	13	6	.684	4.33	33	33	4	2	0	212	203	106	102	65	151
1999—	San Francisco (N.L.)	5	11	.313	6.47	29	21	1	0	0	139	142	103	100	57	86
	San Jose (Calif.)	1	0	1.000	4.50	2	2	0	0	0	10	10	5	5	3	13
2000—	San Francisco (N.L.)	11	7	.611	4.05	30	20	0	0	0	149	155	72	67	42	92
A.L. totals (1 year)		4	6	.400	6.19	17	16	0	0	0	91²/₃	92	65	63	36	54
N.L. totals (11 years)		90	82	.523	4.42	305	244	15	8	1	1581¹/₃	1567	838	776	558	1149
Major League totals (12 years)		94	88	.516	4.51	322	260	15	8	1	1673	1659	903	839	594	1203

DIVISION SERIES RECORD

Year	League	W	L	Pct.	ERA	G	GS	CG	ShO	Sv.	IP	H	R	ER	BB	SO
2000—	San Francisco (N.L.)	0	1	.000	8.31	1	1	0	0	0	4¹/₃	4	4	4	2	5

GARIBAY, DANIEL   P   CUBS

PERSONAL: Born February 14, 1973, in Manaidero, Mexico. ... 5-8/155. ... Throws left, bats left.

TRANSACTIONS/CAREER NOTES: Signed as non-drafted free agent by Los Angeles Dodgers organization (April 12, 1992). ... Loaned by Dodgers organization to Mexico City, Mexican League (1993-August 3, 1994). ... Contract sold by Dodgers to Mexico City, Mexican League (September 26, 1994). ... Contract sold by Mexico City, Mexican League to Tampa Bay Devil Rays (October 31, 1997). ... Loaned by Devil Rays organization to Mexico City, Mexican League (March 24-September 21, 1998; and April 1-September 20, 1999). ... Granted free agency (October 15, 1999). ... Signed by Chicago Cubs organization (November 14, 1999).

Year	League	W	L	Pct.	ERA	G	GS	CG	ShO	Sv.	IP	H	R	ER	BB	SO
1992—	Dom. Dodgers (DSL)	2	3	.400	3.38	10	5	1	1	2	32	20	15	12	23	36
1993—	M.C. Tigers (Mex.)■	8	8	.500	5.15	26	26	2	0	0	146²/₃	157	89	84	80	57
1994—	Mexico City Tigers (Mex.) ..	10	6	.625	4.85	26	20	4	0	0	130	147	79	70	86	68
	San Antonio (Texas)■	0	1	.000	121.50	1	0	0	0	0	²/₃	10	10	9	4	0
1995—	M.C. Tigers (Mex.)■	2	0	1.000	6.40	21	5	0	0	0	45	49	32	32	29	26
1996—	Mexico City Tigers (Mex.) ..	2	4	.333	4.98	20	10	0	0	0	59²/₃	64	39	33	32	36
1997—	Mexico City Tigers (Mex.) ..	13	8	.619	3.51	26	26	5	3	0	159	140	70	62	67	95
1998—	Mexico City Tigers (Mex.) ..	10	2	.833	3.37	26	24	2	1	0	155	143	65	58	86	112
1999—	Mexico City Tigers (Mex.) ..	2	5	.286	5.06	16	16	1	0	0	89	91	62	50	56	59
2000—	Iowa (PCL)■	0	0	...	2.08	1	1	0	0	0	4¹/₃	3	1	1	5	2
	Chicago (N.L.)	2	8	.200	6.03	30	8	0	0	0	74²/₃	88	54	50	39	46
Major League totals (1 year)		2	8	.200	6.03	30	8	0	0	0	74²/₃	88	54	50	39	46

GARLAND, JON   P   WHITE SOX

PERSONAL: Born September 27, 1979, in Valencia, Calif. ... 6-6/205. ... Throws right, bats right. ... Full name: Jon Steven Garland.

HIGH SCHOOL: John F. Kennedy (Granada Hills, Calif.).

TRANSACTIONS/CAREER NOTES: Selected by Chicago Cubs organization in first round (10th pick overall) of free-agent draft (June 3, 1997). ... Traded by Cubs to Chicago White Sox for P Matt Karchner (July 29, 1998). ... On Chicago disabled list (August 19-September 3, 2000); included rehabilitation assignment to Birmingham (August 30-September 3).

HONORS: Named International League Most Valuable Pitcher (2000).

Year	League	W	L	Pct.	ERA	G	GS	CG	ShO	Sv.	IP	H	R	ER	BB	SO
1997—	Arizona Cubs (Ariz.)	3	2	.600	2.70	10	7	0	0	0	40	37	14	12	10	39
1998—	Rockford (Midw.)	4	7	.364	5.03	19	19	1	0	0	107¹/₃	124	69	60	45	70
	Hickory (S.Atl.)■	1	4	.200	5.40	5	5	0	0	0	26²/₃	36	20	16	13	19
1999—	Winston-Salem (Caro.).......	5	7	.417	3.33	19	19	2	1	0	119	109	57	44	39	84
	Birmingham (Sou.)...........	3	1	.750	4.38	7	7	0	0	0	39	39	22	19	18	27
2000—	Charlotte (I.L.).................	9	2	.818	2.26	16	16	2	1	0	103²/₃	99	28	26	32	63
	Chicago (A.L.)■	4	8	.333	6.46	15	13	0	0	0	69²/₃	82	55	50	40	42
	Birmingham (Sou.)...........	0	0	...	0.00	1	1	0	0	0	6	4	0	0	1	10
Major League totals (1 year)		4	8	.333	6.46	15	13	0	0	0	69²/₃	82	55	50	40	42

G

GIAMBI, JASON   1B   ATHLETICS

PERSONAL: Born January 8, 1971, in West Covina, Calif. ... 6-3/235. ... Bats left, throws right. ... Full name: Jason Gilbert Giambi. ... Brother of Jeremy Giambi, first baseman/outfielder, Oakland Athletics. ... Name pronounced GEE-om-bee.
HIGH SCHOOL: South Hills (West Covina, Calif.).
COLLEGE: Long Beach State.
TRANSACTIONS/CAREER NOTES: Selected by Milwaukee Brewers organization in 43rd round of free-agent draft (June 5, 1989); did not sign. ... Selected by Oakland Athletics organization in second round of free-agent draft (June 1, 1992). ... On disabled list (July 27-August 28, 1993). ... On Huntsville disabled list (April 7-14, 1994).
HONORS: Named A.L. Most Valuable Player by Baseball Writers' Association of America (2000).
STATISTICAL NOTES: Had 25-game hitting streak (May 12-June 23, 1997). ... Had 17-game hitting streak (July 16-August 2, 1998). ... Had 16-game hitting streak (September 5-24, 1998). ... Had 19-game hitting streak (July 23-August 10, 1999). ... Led A.L. with a .476 on-base percentage in 2000. ... Career major league grand slams: 7.
MISCELLANEOUS: Member of 1992 U.S. Olympic baseball team. ... Holds Oakland Athletics all-time record for highest career batting average (.302).

| | | | | | | | BATTING | | | | | | | FIELDING | |
Year	Team (League)	Pos.	G	AB	R	H	2B	3B	HR	RBI	Avg.	BB	SO	SB	PO	A	E	Avg.
1992—	S. Oregon (N'West)....	3B	13	41	9	13	3	0	3	13	.317	9	6	1	5	20	1	.962
1993—	Modesto (Calif.)	3B	89	313	72	91	16	2	12	60	.291	73	47	2	49	145	19	.911
1994—	Huntsville (Sou.)	3B-1B	56	193	31	43	9	0	6	30	.223	27	31	0	111	77	11	.945
—	Tacoma (PCL)	3B-SS	52	176	28	56	20	0	4	38	.318	25	32	1	39	110	8	.949
1995—	Edmonton (PCL)	3B-DH-1B	55	190	34	65	26	1	3	41	.342	34	26	0	38	98	9	.938
—	Oakland (A.L.)	3B-1B-DH	54	176	27	45	7	0	6	25	.256	28	31	2	194	55	4	.984
1996—	Oakland (A.L.)	1-0-3-DH	140	536	84	156	40	1	20	79	.291	51	95	0	478	117	11	.982
1997—	Oakland (A.L.)	OF-1B-DH	142	519	66	152	41	2	20	81	.293	55	89	0	501	44	7	.987
1998—	Oakland (A.L.)	1B-DH	153	562	92	166	28	0	27	110	.295	81	102	2	1255	73	*14	.990
1999—	Oakland (A.L.)	1B-DH-3B	158	575	115	181	36	1	33	123	.315	105	106	1	1251	45	7	.995
2000—	Oakland (A.L.)	1B-DH	152	510	108	170	29	1	43	137	.333	*137	96	2	1161	59	6	.995
Major League totals (6 years)			799	2878	492	870	181	5	149	555	.302	457	519	7	4840	393	49	.991

DIVISION SERIES RECORD

| | | | | | | | BATTING | | | | | | | FIELDING | |
Year	Team (League)	Pos.	G	AB	R	H	2B	3B	HR	RBI	Avg.	BB	SO	SB	PO	A	E	Avg.
2000—	Oakland (A.L.)	1B	5	14	2	4	0	0	0	1	.286	7	2	1	40	0	1	.976

ALL-STAR GAME RECORD

| | | | | | | BATTING | | | | | | | FIELDING | |
Year	League	Pos.	AB	R	H	2B	3B	HR	RBI	Avg.	BB	SO	SB	PO	A	E	Avg.
2000—	American	1B	2	0	0	0	0	0	0	.000	1	2	0	2	0	...	1.000

GIAMBI, JEREMY   1B/OF   ATHLETICS

PERSONAL: Born September 30, 1974, in San Jose, Calif. ... 6-0/200. ... Bats left, throws left. ... Full name: Jeremy Dean Giambi. ... Brother of Jason Giambi, first baseman, Oakland Athletics.
HIGH SCHOOL: South Hills (West Covina, Calif.).
COLLEGE: Cal State-Fullerton.
TRANSACTIONS/CAREER NOTES: Selected by Kansas City Royals organization in sixth round of free-agent draft (June 4, 1996). ... On Omaha disabled list (July 12-August 2, 1998). ... On Kansas City disabled list (March 27-May 15, 1999); included rehabilitation assignment to Omaha (April 28-May 15). ... Traded by Royals to Oakland Athletics for P Brett Laxton (February 18, 2000). ... On Oakland disabled list (August 22-September 8, 2000); included rehabilitation assignment to Sacramento (September 6-8).
HONORS: Led Northwest League with .440 on-base percentage in 1996. ... Led Pacific Coast League with .469 on-base percentage in 1998.
STATISTICAL NOTES: Career major league grand slams: 1.

| | | | | | | | BATTING | | | | | | | FIELDING | |
Year	Team (League)	Pos.	G	AB	R	H	2B	3B	HR	RBI	Avg.	BB	SO	SB	PO	A	E	Avg.
1996—	Spokane (N'West)	OF	67	231	•58	63	17	0	6	39	.273	*61	32	22	97	3	*11	.901
1997—	Lansing (Midw.)	OF	31	116	33	39	11	1	5	21	.336	23	16	5	30	2	0	1.000
—	Wichita (Texas)	OF-1B	74	268	50	86	15	1	11	52	.321	44	47	4	117	2	3	.975
1998—	Omaha (PCL)	OF-1B	96	325	68	121	21	2	20	66	*.372	57	64	8	113	8	3	.976
—	Kansas City (A.L.)	OF-DH	18	58	6	13	4	0	2	8	.224	11	9	0	14	1	0	1.000
1999—	Kansas City (A.L.)	DH-1B-OF	90	288	34	82	13	1	3	34	.285	40	67	0	213	8	2	.991
—	Omaha (PCL)	OF-1B-DH	35	127	31	44	5	1	12	28	.346	31	30	1	156	9	2	.988
2000—	Oakland (A.L.)■	OF-DH-1B	104	260	42	66	10	2	10	50	.254	32	61	0	136	8	3	.980
—	Sacramento (PCL)	OF-1B	8	31	8	11	2	0	2	8	.355	8	7	1	23	1	1	.960
Major League totals (3 years)			212	606	82	161	27	3	15	92	.266	83	137	0	363	17	5	.987

DIVISION SERIES RECORD

| | | | | | | | BATTING | | | | | | | FIELDING | |
Year	Team (League)	Pos.	G	AB	R	H	2B	3B	HR	RBI	Avg.	BB	SO	SB	PO	A	E	Avg.
2000—	Oakland (A.L.)	DH-OF-PH	4	9	1	3	0	0	0	1	.333	2	2	0	1	0	0	1.000

GIBSON, DERRICK   OF   DEVIL RAYS

PERSONAL: Born February 5, 1975, in Winter Haven, Fla. ... 6-2/244. ... Bats right, throws right. ... Full name: Derrick Lamont Gibson.
HIGH SCHOOL: Haines City (Fla.).
TRANSACTIONS/CAREER NOTES: Selected by Colorado Rockies organization in 13th round of free-agent draft (June 3, 1993). ... Claimed on waivers by Florida Marlins (March 24, 2000). ... On Calgary disabled list (August 5-September 20, 2000). ... Granted free agency (October 18, 2000). ... Signed by Tampa Bay Devil Rays organization (November 9, 2000).
STATISTICAL NOTES: Tied for Pacific Coast League lead with three double plays by outfielder in 1998.

G

Year Team (League)	Pos.	G	AB	R	H	2B	3B	HR	RBI	Avg.	BB	SO	SB	PO	A	E	Avg.
1993—Ariz. Rockies (Ariz.)	OF	34	119	13	18	2	2	0	10	.151	5	55	3	22	1	5	.821
1994—Bend (N'West)	OF	73	284	47	75	19	5	•12	57	.264	29	*102	14	82	*10	9	.911
1995—Asheville (S.Atl.)	OF	135	506	91	148	16	10	•32	*115	.292	29	136	31	190	11	9	.957
1996—New Haven (East.)	OF	122	449	58	115	21	4	15	62	.256	31	125	3	168	10	*13	.932
1997—New Haven (East.)	OF-DH	119	461	91	146	24	2	23	75	.317	36	100	20	188	8	*11	.947
—Colo. Springs (PCL)	OF-DH	21	78	14	33	7	0	3	12	.423	5	9	0	30	0	1	.968
1998—Colo. Springs (PCL)	OF-DH	126	497	84	145	20	3	14	81	.292	35	110	14	211	11	*13	.945
—Colorado (N.L.)	OF	7	21	4	9	1	0	0	2	.429	1	4	0	11	2	1	.929
1999—Colo. Springs (PCL)	OF-DH	110	385	68	106	19	6	17	67	.275	30	82	12	171	5	8	.957
—Colorado (N.L.)	OF	10	28	2	5	1	0	2	6	.179	0	7	0	15	2	1	.944
2000—Calgary (PCL)■	OF	100	340	43	95	12	2	10	43	.279	18	84	13	187	6	4	.980
Major League totals (2 years)		17	49	6	14	2	0	2	8	.286	1	11	0	26	4	2	.938

GIL, BENJI — SS — ANGELS

PERSONAL: Born October 6, 1972, in Tijuana, Mexico. ... 6-2/190. ... Bats right, throws right. ... Full name: Romas Benjamin Gil.
HIGH SCHOOL: Castle Park (Chula Vista, Calif.).
TRANSACTIONS/CAREER NOTES: Selected by Texas Rangers organization in first round (19th pick overall) of free-agent draft (June 3, 1991). ... On Texas disabled list (March 22-May 22, 1996); included rehabilitation assigments to Charlotte (May 2-17) and Oklahoma City (May 17-21). ... Traded by Rangers to Chicago White Sox for P Al Levine and P Larry Thomas (December 19, 1997). ... On Calgary disabled list (August 12-20, 1998). ... Selected by Florida Marlins organization from White Sox organization in Rule 5 minor league draft (December 15, 1998). ... Granted free agency (October 15, 1999). ... Signed by Anaheim Angels organization (February 1, 2000).
STATISTICAL NOTES: Led American Association shortstops with 660 total chances and 85 double plays in 1994. ... Career major league grand slams: 1.

Year Team (League)	Pos.	G	AB	R	H	2B	3B	HR	RBI	Avg.	BB	SO	SB	PO	A	E	Avg.
1991—Butte (Pio.)	SS	32	129	25	37	4	3	2	15	.287	14	36	9	61	88	14	.914
1992—Gastonia (S.Atl.)	SS	132	482	75	132	21	1	9	55	.274	50	106	26	226	384	45	.931
1993—Texas (A.L.)	SS	22	57	3	7	0	0	0	2	.123	5	22	1	27	76	5	.954
—Tulsa (Texas)	SS	101	342	45	94	9	1	17	59	.275	35	89	20	159	285	19	.959
1994—Oklahoma City (A.A.)	SS	*139	487	62	121	20	6	10	55	.248	33	120	14	*222	*401	*37	.944
1995—Texas (A.L.)	SS	130	415	36	91	20	3	9	46	.219	26	147	2	226	409	17	.974
1996—Charlotte (FSL)	SS-DH	11	31	2	8	6	0	1	7	.258	3	7	0	6	21	2	.931
—Oklahoma City (A.A.)	SS	84	292	32	65	15	1	6	28	.223	21	90	4	121	267	21	.949
—Texas (A.L.)	SS	5	5	0	2	0	0	0	1	.400	1	1	0	5	7	1	.923
1997—Texas (A.L.)	SS-DH	110	317	35	71	13	2	5	31	.224	17	96	1	163	328	19	.963
1998—Calgary (PCL)■	SS-DH-OF	128	460	80	114	24	5	14	69	.248	41	90	11	161	319	30	.941
1999—Calgary (PCL)■	SS-OF	116	412	74	115	29	1	17	64	.279	27	101	17	183	304	29	.944
2000—Anaheim (A.L.)■	S-2-DH-1	110	301	28	72	14	1	6	23	.239	30	59	10	164	280	18	.961
Major League totals (5 years)		377	1095	102	243	47	6	20	103	.222	79	325	14	585	1100	60	.966

GILBERT, SHAWN — OF — DODGERS

PERSONAL: Born March 12, 1965, in Camden, N.J. ... 5-9/185. ... Bats right, throws right. ... Full name: Albert Shawn Gilbert Jr.
HIGH SCHOOL: Agua Fria Union (Avondale, Ariz.).
JUNIOR COLLEGE: Golden West College (Calif.).
COLLEGE: Arizona State, then Fresno State.
TRANSACTIONS/CAREER NOTES: Selected by Los Angeles Dodgers organization in 21st round of free-agent draft (June 6, 1983); did not sign. ... Selected by Cincinnati Reds organization in secondary phase of free-agent draft (January 9, 1985); did not sign. ... Selected by Minnesota Twins organization in secondary phase of free-agent draft (June 5, 1985); did not sign. ... Selected by Twins organization in 12th round of free-agent draft (June 2, 1987). ... Claimed on waivers by Chicago White Sox (November 12, 1992). ... Granted free agency (October 15, 1993). ... Signed by Philadelphia Phillies organization (January 5, 1994). ... Granted free agency (October 16, 1995). ... Signed by New York Mets organization (January 30, 1996). ... On New York disabled list (June 16-30, 1997). ... Granted free agency (October 15, 1997). ... Re-signed by Mets organization (December 19, 1997). ... Traded by Mets organization with a player to be named later to St. Louis Cardinals organization for OF Wayne Kirby (June 10, 1998). ... Granted free agency (October 15, 1998). ... Signed by Los Angeles Dodgers organization (February 2, 1999). ... Granted free agency (October 15, 1999). ... Re-signed by Dodgers organization (December 16, 1999). ... On Albuquerque disabled list (April 17-28, 2000). ... Granted free agency (October 2, 2000). ... Re-signed by Dodgers organization (January 4, 2001).
STATISTICAL NOTES: Led Midwest League shortstops with 80 double plays in 1988. ... Led Southern League in caught stealing with 19 in 1991.

Year Team (League)	Pos.	G	AB	R	H	2B	3B	HR	RBI	Avg.	BB	SO	SB	PO	A	E	Avg.
1987—Visalia (Calif.)	SS	82	272	39	61	5	0	5	27	.224	34	59	6	122	214	30	.918
1988—Visalia (Calif.)	SS-2B	14	43	10	16	3	2	0	8	.372	10	7	1	18	34	10	.839
—Kenosha (Midw.)	SS	108	402	80	112	21	2	3	44	.279	63	61	49	151	325	41	.921
1989—Visalia (Calif.)	SS	125	453	52	113	17	1	2	43	.249	54	70	42	204	382	39	.938
1990—Orlando (Sou.)	SS	123	433	68	110	18	2	4	44	.254	61	69	31	157	*361	41	.927
1991—Orlando (Sou.)	OF-SS-2B-3B	138	529	69	136	12	5	3	38	.257	53	71	*43	247	250	20	.961
1992—Portland (PCL)	SS-OF-2B-3B	138	444	60	109	17	2	3	52	.245	36	55	31	214	303	25	.954
1993—Nashville (A.A.)■	3B-OF-SS-2B	104	278	28	63	17	2	0	17	.227	12	41	6	81	123	17	.923
1994—Scranton/W.B. (I.L.)■	SS-OF-2B	*141	*547	81	139	33	4	7	52	.254	66	86	20	215	275	27	.948
1995—Scranton/W.B. (I.L.)	SS-OF-DH-3B	136	536	84	141	26	2	2	42	.263	64	102	16	213	361	28	.953
1996—Norfolk (I.L.)■	3-2-S-O-DH	131	493	76	126	28	1	9	50	.256	46	97	17	174	312	25	.951
1997—Norfolk (I.L.)	SS-OF-2B-3B	78	288	53	76	13	1	8	33	.264	43	64	16	124	134	16	.942
—New York (N.L.)	2B-SS-3B-OF	22	3	3	0	0	1	1	.136	1	8	1	11	8	1	.950
1998—Norfolk (I.L.)	OF-SS-2B-3B	39	133	21	36	8	0	2	12	.271	16	28	7	46	26	2	.973
—New York (N.L.)	3B	3	3	1	0	0	0	0	0	.000	0	1	0	0	0	0	...
—Memphis (PCL)■	3B-OF-2B-SS	62	216	37	58	15	2	7	32	.269	29	53	7	65	106	12	.934
—St. Louis (N.L.)	2B	4	2	0	1	0	0	0	0	.500	0	1	1	1	0	0	1.000

G

– 194 –

Year	Team (League)	Pos.	G	AB	R	H	2B	3B	HR	RBI	Avg.	BB	SO	SB	PO	A	E	Avg.
1999—	Albuquerque (PCL)■..O-3-S-2-D-P		114	421	88	128	35	3	10	52	.304	62	84	25	147	113	7	.974
2000—	Albuquerque (PCL).....SS-OF-2B-1B		86	297	67	99	19	4	14	49	.333	60	69	11	135	223	22	.942
—	Los Angeles (N.L.)	OF	15	20	5	3	1	0	1	3	.150	2	7	0	15	1	1	.941
	Major League totals (3 years)		51	47	9	7	1	0	2	4	.149	3	17	2	27	9	2	.947

RECORD AS PITCHER

Year	League	W	L	Pct.	ERA	G	GS	CG	ShO	Sv.	IP	H	R	ER	BB	SO
1999—	Albuquerque (PCL)............	0	0	...	13.53	1	0	0	0	0	1 1/3	2	2	2	1	0

GILES, BRIAN   OF   PIRATES

PERSONAL: Born January 20, 1971, in El Cajon, Calif. ... 5-10/200. ... Bats left, throws left. ... Full name: Brian Stephen Giles. ... Brother of Marcus Giles, second baseman, Atlanta Braves organization. ... Name pronounced JYLES.
HIGH SCHOOL: Granite Hills (El Cajon, Calif.).
TRANSACTIONS/CAREER NOTES: Selected by Cleveland Indians organization in 17th round of free-agent draft (June 5, 1989). ... On Canton/Akron disabled list (May 15-July 7, 1992). ... On Cleveland disabled list (June 1-July 7, 1998); included rehabilitation assignment to Buffalo (June 23-July 7). ... Traded by Indians to Pittsburgh Pirates for P Ricardo Rincon (November 18, 1998).
STATISTICAL NOTES: Led International League with 10 intentional bases on balls received in 1994. ... Led International League outfielders with five double plays in 1994. ... Career major league grand slams: 3.

Year	Team (League)	Pos.	G	AB	R	H	2B	3B	HR	RBI	Avg.	BB	SO	SB	PO	A	E	Avg.
1989—	Burlington (Appl.).......	OF	36	129	18	40	7	0	0	20	.310	11	19	6	52	3	1	.982
1990—	Watertown (NY-P)......	OF	70	246	44	71	15	2	1	23	.289	48	23	11	108	8	1	.991
1991—	Kinston (Caro.)..........	OF	125	394	71	122	14	0	4	47	.310	68	70	19	187	10	5	.975
1992—	Canton/Akron (East.)..	OF	23	74	6	16	4	0	0	3	.216	10	10	3	45	0	0	1.000
—	Kinston (Caro.)..........	OF	42	140	28	37	5	1	3	18	.264	30	21	3	74	3	1	.987
1993—	Canton/Akron (East.)..	OF	123	425	64	139	17	6	6	64	.327	57	43	18	186	3	5	.974
1994—	Charlotte (I.L.)..........	OF	128	434	74	136	18	3	16	58	.313	55	61	8	242	12	4	.984
1995—	Buffalo (A.A.).............	OF-DH	123	413	67	128	18	•8	15	67	.310	54	40	7	248	4	5	.981
—	Cleveland (A.L.)..........	OF-DH	6	9	6	5	0	0	1	3	.556	0	1	0	2	1	0	1.000
1996—	Buffalo (A.A.).............	OF	83	318	65	100	17	6	20	64	.314	42	29	1	132	5	2	.986
—	Cleveland (A.L.)..........	DH-OF	51	121	26	43	14	1	5	27	.355	19	13	3	26	0	0	1.000
1997—	Cleveland (A.L.)..........	OF-DH	130	377	62	101	15	3	17	61	.268	63	50	13	201	7	6	.972
1998—	Cleveland (A.L.)..........	OF-DH	112	350	56	94	19	0	16	66	.269	73	75	10	213	7	5	.978
—	Buffalo (I.L.)..............	OF-DH	13	46	5	11	2	0	2	7	.239	6	8	0	18	0	1	.947
1999—	Pittsburgh (N.L.)■......	OF-DH	141	521	109	164	33	3	39	115	.315	95	80	6	294	8	3	.990
2000—	Pittsburgh (N.L.)	OF	156	559	111	176	37	7	35	123	.315	114	69	6	316	14	6	.982
	American League totals (4 years)		299	857	150	243	48	4	39	157	.284	155	139	26	442	15	11	.976
	National League totals (2 years)		297	1080	220	340	70	10	74	238	.315	209	149	12	610	22	9	.986
	Major League totals (6 years)		596	1937	370	583	118	14	113	395	.301	364	288	38	1052	37	20	.982

DIVISION SERIES RECORD

Year	Team (League)	Pos.	G	AB	R	H	2B	3B	HR	RBI	Avg.	BB	SO	SB	PO	A	E	Avg.
1996—	Cleveland (A.L.).........	PH	1	1	0	0	0	0	0	0	.000	0	1	0	...	...	...	...
1997—	Cleveland (A.L.).........	OF	3	7	0	1	0	0	0	0	.143	0	1	0	4	1	0	1.000
1998—	Cleveland (A.L.).........	OF-DH	3	10	1	2	1	0	0	0	.200	1	4	0	4	0	0	1.000
	Division series totals (3 years)		7	18	1	3	1	0	0	0	.167	1	6	0	8	1	0	1.000

CHAMPIONSHIP SERIES RECORD

Year	Team (League)	Pos.	G	AB	R	H	2B	3B	HR	RBI	Avg.	BB	SO	SB	PO	A	E	Avg.
1997—	Cleveland (A.L.)..........	OF	6	16	1	3	3	0	0	0	.188	2	6	0	9	0	0	1.000
1998—	Cleveland (A.L.)..........	OF-PH	4	12	0	1	0	0	0	0	.083	1	3	0	7	0	1	.875
	Championship series totals (2 years)		10	28	1	4	3	0	0	0	.143	3	9	0	16	0	1	.941

WORLD SERIES RECORD

Year	Team (League)	Pos.	G	AB	R	H	2B	3B	HR	RBI	Avg.	BB	SO	SB	PO	A	E	Avg.
1997—	Cleveland (A.L.)..........	PH-OF	5	4	1	2	1	0	0	2	.500	4	1	0	2	0	0	1.000

ALL-STAR GAME RECORD

Year	League	Pos.	AB	R	H	2B	3B	HR	RBI	Avg.	BB	SO	SB	PO	A	E	Avg.
2000—	National	OF	2	0	0	0	0	0	0	.000	0	0	0	0	0	0	...

GILES, MARCUS   2B   BRAVES   G

PERSONAL: Born May 18, 1978, in San Diego, Calif. ... 5-8/180. ... Bats right, throws right. ... Full name: Marcus William Giles. ... Brother of Brian Giles, outfielder, Pittsburgh Pirates. ... Name pronounced JYLES.
HIGH SCHOOL: Granite Hills (Calif.).
JUNIOR COLLEGE: Grossmont (Calif.).
TRANSACTIONS/CAREER NOTES: Selected by Atlanta Braves organization in 53rd round of free-agent draft (June 4, 1996).
HONORS: Named South Atlantic League Most Valuable Player (1998). ... Named Carolina League Most Valuable Player (1999).
STATISTICAL NOTES: Led South Atlantic League with 321 total bases and .636 slugging percentage in 1998. ... Led Southern League second basemen with 655 total chances and 70 double plays in 2000.

Year	Team (League)	Pos.	G	AB	R	H	2B	3B	HR	RBI	Avg.	BB	SO	SB	PO	A	E	Avg.
1997—	Danville (Appl.)..........	2B	55	207	53	72	13	3	8	45	.348	32	47	5	86	92	7	.962
1998—	Macon (S.Atl.)...........	2B	135	505	*111	166	38	3	*37	*108	.329	*85	103	12	229	294	25	.954
1999—	Myrtle Beach (Caro.)..		126	497	80	*162	*40	7	13	73	*.326	54	89	9	222	291	8	*.985
2000—	Greenville (Sou.)	2B	132	458	73	133	28	2	17	62	.290	72	71	25	*304	*333	18	*.973

PERSONAL: Born September 24, 1966, in St. Louis. ... 6-0/198. ... Bats right, throws right. ... Full name: Otis Bernard Gilkey.
HIGH SCHOOL: University City (Mo.).
TRANSACTIONS/CAREER NOTES: Signed as non-drafted free agent by St. Louis Cardinals organization (August 22, 1984). ... On disabled list (April 10-25, 1986 and May 29, 1987-remainder of season). ... On St. Louis disabled list (June 14-July 11, 1991 and April 29-May 14, 1993). ... On suspended list (July 8-9, 1994). ... Granted free agency (April 7, 1995). ... Re-signed by Cardinals (April 8, 1995). ... On St. Louis disabled list (June 28-July 17, 1995); included rehabilitation assignment to Louisville (July 15-17). ... Traded to New York Mets for P Eric Ludwick, P Erik Hiljus and OF Yudith Ozorio (January 22, 1996). ... On New York disabled list (April 27-May 12, 1998). ... Traded by Mets with P Nelson Figueroa and cash to Arizona Diamondbacks for P Willie Blair, C Jorge Fabregas and a player to be named later (July 31, 1998); Mets received cash to complete deal (September 3, 1998). ... Released by Diamondbacks (June 27, 2000). ... Signed by Boston Red Sox (July 4, 2000). ... Granted free agency (November 1, 2000). ... Signed by Cardinals organization (January 5, 2001).
STATISTICAL NOTES: Led New York-Pennsylvania League outfielders with 185 total chances in 1985. ... Led Texas League in caught stealing with 22 in 1989. ... Led American Association in caught stealing with 33 in 1990. ... Led N.L. outfielders with 19 assists in 1993. ... Tied for N.L. lead in double plays by outfielder with four in 1995. ... Tied for N.L. lead with 12 sacrifice flies in 1997.

Year	Team (League)	Pos.	G	AB	R	H	2B	3B	HR	RBI	Avg.	BB	SO	SB	PO	A	E	Avg.
1985—	Erie (NY-Penn)	OF	•77	*294	57	60	9	1	7	27	.204	55	57	34	*164	*13	*8	.957
1986—	Savannah (S.Atl.)	OF	105	374	64	88	15	4	6	36	.235	84	57	32	220	7	5	.978
1987—	Springfield (Midw.)	OF	46	162	30	37	5	0	0	9	.228	39	28	18	79	5	4	.955
1988—	Springfield (Midw.)	OF	125	491	84	120	18	7	6	36	.244	65	54	54	165	10	6	.967
1989—	Arkansas (Texas)	OF	131	500	*104	139	25	3	6	57	.278	70	54	*53	236	*22	9	.966
1990—	Louisville (A.A.)	OF	132	499	83	147	26	8	3	46	.295	*75	49	45	236	18	•11	.958
—	St. Louis (N.L.)	OF	18	64	11	19	5	2	1	3	.297	8	5	6	47	2	2	.961
1991—	St. Louis (N.L.)	OF	81	268	28	58	7	2	5	20	.216	39	33	14	164	6	1	.994
—	Louisville (A.A.)	OF	11	41	5	6	2	0	0	2	.146	6	10	1	33	1	0	1.000
1992—	St. Louis (N.L.)	OF	131	384	56	116	19	4	7	43	.302	39	52	18	217	9	5	.978
1993—	St. Louis (N.L.)	OF-1B	137	557	99	170	40	5	16	70	.305	56	66	15	251	†20	8	.971
1994—	St. Louis (N.L.)	OF	105	380	52	96	22	1	6	45	.253	39	65	15	168	9	3	.983
1995—	St. Louis (N.L.)	OF	121	480	73	143	33	4	17	69	.298	42	70	12	206	10	3	.986
—	Louisville (A.A.)	OF	2	6	3	2	1	0	1	1	.333	1	0	0	2	0	0	1.000
1996—	New York (N.L.)■	OF	153	571	108	181	44	3	30	117	.317	73	125	17	309	*18	6	.982
1997—	New York (N.L.)	OF-DH	145	518	85	129	31	1	18	78	.249	70	111	7	251	*17	3	.989
1998—	New York (N.L.)	OF	82	264	33	60	15	0	4	28	.227	32	66	5	121	9	1	.992
—	Arizona (N.L.)■	OF	29	101	8	25	0	0	1	5	.248	11	14	4	49	3	1	.981
1999—	Arizona (N.L.)	OF	94	204	28	60	16	1	8	39	.294	29	42	2	90	3	3	.969
2000—	Arizona (N.L.)	OF	38	73	6	8	1	0	2	6	.110	7	16	0	29	1	0	1.000
—	Boston (A.L.)■	OF-DH	36	91	11	21	5	1	1	9	.231	10	12	0	36	1	0	1.000
American League totals (1 year)			36	91	11	21	5	1	1	9	.231	10	12	0	36	1	0	1.000
National League totals (11 years)			1134	3864	587	1065	233	23	115	523	.276	445	665	115	1902	107	36	.982
Major League totals (11 years)			1170	3955	598	1086	238	24	116	532	.275	455	677	115	1938	108	36	.983

DIVISION SERIES RECORD

Year	Team (League)	Pos.	G	AB	R	H	2B	3B	HR	RBI	Avg.	BB	SO	SB	PO	A	E	Avg.
1999—	Arizona (N.L.)	OF	2	6	0	0	0	0	0	0	.000	0	0	0	5	0	0	1.000

PERSONAL: Born May 5, 1976, in Norwalk, Conn. ... 5-10/190. ... Bats right, throws right. ... Full name: Keith Michael Ginter.
HIGH SCHOOL: Fullerton Union (Fullerton, Calif.).
JUNIOR COLLEGE: Cypress (Calif.) College.
COLLEGE: Texas Tech.
TRANSACTIONS/CAREER NOTES: Selected by Houston Astros organization in 10th round of free-agent draft (June 2, 1998).
HONORS: Named Texas League Most Valuable Player (2000).
STATISTICAL NOTES: Led Texas League with .457 on-base percentage and in being hit by pitch with 24 in 2000.

Year	Team (League)	Pos.	G	AB	R	H	2B	3B	HR	RBI	Avg.	BB	SO	SB	PO	A	E	Avg.
1998—	Auburn (NY-Penn)	2B	71	241	•55	76	22	1	8	41	.315	*60	68	10	93	178	8	*.971
1999—	Kissimmee (FSL)	2B	103	376	66	99	15	4	13	46	.263	61	90	9	209	281	21	.959
—	Jackson (Texas)	2B	9	34	9	13	1	0	1	6	.382	4	6	0	19	24	2	.956
2000—	Round Rock (Texas)	2B	125	462	108	154	30	3	26	92	.333	82	127	24	255	*338	17	.972
—	Houston (N.L.)	2B	5	8	3	2	0	0	1	3	.250	1	3	0	4	5	0	1.000
Major League totals (1 year)			5	8	3	2	0	0	1	3	.250	1	3	0	4	5	0	1.000

G

PERSONAL: Born December 24, 1977, in Lexington, Ky. ... 6-1/215. ... Throws right, bats right. ... Full name: Matthew Shane Ginter.
HIGH SCHOOL: George Rogers Clark (Winchester, Ky.).
COLLEGE: Mississippi State.
TRANSACTIONS/CAREER NOTES: Selected by New York Yankees organization in 17th round of free-agent draft (June 4, 1996); did not sign. ... Selected by Chicago White Sox organization in first round (22nd pick overall) of free-agent draft (June 2, 1999); pick received from New York Mets as compensation for signing Type A free agent 3B Robin Ventura.

Year	League	W	L	Pct.	ERA	G	GS	CG	ShO	Sv.	IP	H	R	ER	BB	SO
1999—	Arizona White Sox (Ariz.)	1	0	1.000	3.24	3	0	0	0	1	8 1/3	5	4	3	3	10
—	Burlington (Midw.)	4	2	.667	4.05	9	9	0	0	0	40	38	20	18	19	29
2000—	Birmingham (Sou.)	11	8	.579	2.25	27	26	0	0	0	179 2/3	153	72	45	60	126
—	Chicago (A.L.)	1	0	1.000	13.50	7	0	0	0	0	9 1/3	18	14	14	7	6
Major League totals (1 year)		1	0	1.000	13.50	7	0	0	0	0	9 1/3	18	14	14	7	6

PERSONAL: Born December 16, 1972, in Orange, Calif. ... 6-2/180. ... Bats right, throws right. ... Full name: Charles Wells Gipson Jr.
HIGH SCHOOL: Loara (Anaheim, Calif.).
JUNIOR COLLEGE: Cypress (Calif.) College.
TRANSACTIONS/CAREER NOTES: Selected by Seattle Mariners organization in 63rd round of free-agent draft (June 3, 1991). ... On disabled list (May 4-19, 1993). ... On Seattle disabled list (July 11-September 1, 1999); included rehabilitation assignments to New Haven (August 14-21) and Everett (August 22-September 1).
STATISTICAL NOTES: Led Midwest League in being hit by pitch with 27 in 1993. ... Tied for Southern League lead in double plays by outfielder with four in 1995. ... Tied for Southern League lead in caught stealing with 15 in 1996.

Year	Team (League)	Pos.	G	AB	R	H	2B	3B	HR	RBI	Avg.	BB	SO	SB	PO	A	E	Avg.
1992—Ariz. Mariners (Ariz.)..	SS	39	124	30	29	2	0	0	14	.234	13	19	11	49	114	•23	.876
1993—Appleton (Midw.)........	2B-OF-SS	109	348	53	89	13	1	0	20	.256	61	76	21	192	201	28	.933
1994—Riverside (Calif.).........	OF	128	481	*102	141	12	3	1	41	.293	76	67	34	293	14	9	.972
1995—Port City (Sou.)..........	OF-2B	112	391	36	87	11	2	0	29	.223	30	66	10	235	19	6	.977
1996—Port City (Sou.)..........	OF-SS	119	407	54	109	12	3	1	30	.268	41	62	15	210	162	15	.961
1997—Memphis (Sou.).......SS-3B-2B-OF		88	320	56	79	9	4	1	28	.247	34	71	31	143	211	23	.939
—Tacoma (PCL) 3B-OF-2B-SS		11	35	5	11	2	0	0	5	.314	4	3	0	15	16	3	.912
1998—Seattle (A.L.)	OF-3B-DH	44	51	11	12	1	0	0	2	.235	5	9	2	40	5	2	.957
—Tacoma (PCL) OF-SS-2B-3B		75	278	39	67	16	2	0	11	.241	27	50	14	142	88	11	.954
1999—Seattle (A.L.) O-3-DH-2-S		55	80	16	18	5	2	0	9	.225	6	13	3	35	52	3	.967
—Tacoma (PCL) S-O-3-2-DH		47	174	26	52	6	3	0	21	.299	14	24	18	76	65	9	.940
—New Haven (East.).....2-DH-3-S-O		5	18	2	0	1	0	0	0	.000	3	2	1	10	7	1	.944
—Everett (N'West)	SS	1	2	0	1	0	1	0	1	.500	2	0	1	0	4	0	1.000
2000—Seattle (A.L.) OF-3B-SS-DH		59	29	7	9	1	1	0	3	.310	4	9	2	23	12	0	1.000
—Tacoma (PCL) OF-3B-SS-2B		67	214	27	53	6	6	1	22	.248	31	38	16	119	80	6	.971
Major League totals (3 years)		158	160	34	39	7	3	0	14	.244	15	31	7	98	69	5	.971

CHAMPIONSHIP SERIES RECORD

Year	Team (League)	Pos.	G	AB	R	H	2B	3B	HR	RBI	Avg.	BB	SO	SB	PO	A	E	Avg.
2000—Seattle (A.L.)	OF	2	0	0	0	0	0	0	0	...	0	0	0	0	0	0	...

PERSONAL: Born October 14, 1964, in Peoria, Ill. ... 5-11/200. ... Bats right, throws right. ... Full name: Joseph Elliott Girardi. ... Name pronounced jeh-RAR-dee.
HIGH SCHOOL: Spalding Institute (Peoria, Ill.).
COLLEGE: Northwestern.
TRANSACTIONS/CAREER NOTES: Selected by Chicago Cubs organization in fifth round of free-agent draft (June 2, 1986). ... On disabled list (August 27, 1986-remainder of season and August 7, 1988-remainder of season). ... On Chicago disabled list (April 17-August 6, 1991); included rehabilitation assignment to Iowa (July 23-August 6). ... Selected by Colorado Rockies in first round (19th pick overall) of expansion draft (November 17, 1992). ... On Colorado disabled list (June 5-August 11, 1993); included rehabilitation assignment to Colorado Springs (August 1-11). ... On disabled list (July 11-26, 1994). ... Traded by Rockies to New York Yankees for P Mike DeJean and a player to be named later (November 20, 1995); Rockies acquired P Steve Shoemaker to complete deal (December 6, 1995). ... Granted free agency (November 5, 1996). ... Re-signed by Yankees (December 3, 1996). ... Granted free agency (November 5, 1999). ... Signed by Cubs (December 15, 1999).
STATISTICAL NOTES: Led Carolina League catchers with 661 total chances and tied for lead with 17 passed balls in 1987. ... Led Eastern League catchers with .992 fielding percentage, 448 putouts, 76 assists and 528 total chances and tied for lead with five double plays in 1988. ... Tied for N.L. lead with 16 passed balls in 1990.

Year	Team (League)	Pos.	G	AB	R	H	2B	3B	HR	RBI	Avg.	BB	SO	SB	PO	A	E	Avg.
1986—Peoria (Midw.)............	C	68	230	36	71	13	1	3	28	.309	17	36	6	405	34	5	.989
1987—Win.-Salem (Caro.)	C	99	364	51	102	9	8	8	46	.280	33	64	9	*569	*74	18	.973
1988—Pittsfield (East.).........	C-OF	104	357	44	97	14	1	7	41	.272	29	51	7	†460	†76	6	†.989
1989—Chicago (N.L.)...........	C	59	157	15	39	10	0	1	14	.248	11	26	2	332	28	7	.981
—Iowa (A.A.)................	C	32	110	12	27	4	2	2	11	.245	5	19	3	172	21	1	.995
1990—Chicago (N.L.)...........	C	133	419	36	113	24	2	1	38	.270	17	50	8	653	61	11	.985
1991—Chicago (N.L.)...........	C	21	47	3	9	2	0	0	6	.191	6	6	0	95	11	3	.972
—Iowa (A.A.)................	C	12	36	3	8	1	0	0	4	.222	4	8	2	62	5	3	.957
1992—Chicago (N.L.)...........	C	91	270	19	73	3	1	1	12	.270	19	38	0	369	51	4	.991
1993—Colorado (N.L.)■........	C	86	310	35	90	14	5	3	31	.290	24	41	6	478	46	6	.989
—Colo. Springs (PCL) ...	C	8	31	6	15	1	1	1	6	.484	0	3	1	40	3	1	.977
1994—Colorado (N.L.)..........	C	93	330	47	91	9	4	4	34	.276	21	48	3	549	56	5	.992
1995—Colorado (N.L.)..........	C	125	462	63	121	17	2	8	55	.262	29	76	3	730	60	10	.988
1996—New York (A.L.)■........	C-DH	124	422	55	124	22	3	2	45	.294	30	55	13	803	46	3	.996
1997—New York (A.L.).........	C	112	398	38	105	23	1	1	50	.264	26	53	2	829	55	5	.994
1998—New York (A.L.).........	C	78	254	31	70	11	4	3	31	.276	14	38	2	541	38	3	.995
1999—New York (A.L.).........	C	65	209	23	50	16	1	2	27	.239	10	26	3	452	34	8	.984
2000—Chicago (N.L.)■.........	C	106	363	47	101	15	1	6	40	.278	32	61	1	706	43	5	.993
American League totals (4 years)		379	1283	147	349	72	9	8	153	.272	80	172	20	2625	173	19	.993
National League totals (8 years)		714	2358	265	637	94	15	24	230	.270	159	346	23	3912	356	51	.988
Major League totals (12 years)		1093	3641	412	986	166	24	32	383	.271	239	518	43	6537	529	70	.990

DIVISION SERIES RECORD

Year	Team (League)	Pos.	G	AB	R	H	2B	3B	HR	RBI	Avg.	BB	SO	SB	PO	A	E	Avg.
1995—Colorado (N.L.)	C	4	16	0	2	0	0	0	0	.125	0	2	0	25	3	1	.966
1996—New York (A.L.).........	C-PR	4	9	1	2	0	0	0	0	.222	4	1	0	28	1	1	.967
1997—New York (A.L.).........	C	5	15	2	2	0	0	0	0	.133	1	3	0	21	2	0	1.000
1998—New York (A.L.).........	C	2	7	0	3	0	0	0	0	.429	0	1	0	19	1	0	1.000
1999—New York (A.L.).........	C	2	6	0	0	0	0	0	0	.000	0	1	0	12	0	0	1.000
Division series totals (5 years)		17	53	3	9	0	0	0	0	.170	5	8	0	105	7	1	.991

G

CHAMPIONSHIP SERIES RECORD

Year Team (League)	Pos.	G	AB	R	H	2B	3B	HR	RBI	Avg.	BB	SO	SB	PO	A	E	Avg.
1989— Chicago (N.L.)............	C	4	10	1	1	0	0	0	0	.100	1	2	0	20	0	0	1.000
1996— New York (A.L.).........	C-PH	4	12	1	3	0	1	0	0	.250	1	3	0	22	0	0	1.000
1998— New York (A.L.).........	C	3	8	2	2	0	0	0	0	.250	1	0	0	22	1	0	1.000
1999— New York (A.L.).........	C	3	8	0	2	0	0	0	0	.250	0	2	0	20	1	0	1.000
Championship series totals (4 years)		14	38	4	8	0	1	0	0	.211	3	7	0	84	2	0	1.000

WORLD SERIES RECORD

NOTES: Member of World Series championship team (1996, 1998 and 1999).

Year Team (League)	Pos.	G	AB	R	H	2B	3B	HR	RBI	Avg.	BB	SO	SB	PO	A	E	Avg.
1996— New York (A.L.).........	C	4	10	1	2	0	1	0	1	.200	1	2	0	23	4	0	1.000
1998— New York (A.L.).........	C	2	6	0	0	0	0	0	0	.000	0	2	0	9	2	0	1.000
1999— New York (A.L.).........	C	2	7	1	2	0	0	0	0	.286	0	1	0	9	2	0	1.000
World Series totals (3 years)		8	23	2	4	0	1	0	1	.174	1	5	0	41	8	0	1.000

ALL-STAR GAME RECORD

Year League	Pos.	AB	R	H	2B	3B	HR	RBI	Avg.	BB	SO	SB	PO	A	E	Avg.
2000— National.....................								Did not play.								

GISSELL, CHRIS   P   CUBS

PERSONAL: Born January 4, 1978, in Tacoma, Wash. ... 6-5/200. ... Throws right, bats right. ... Full name: Christopher Odell Gissell. ... Name pronounced gihs-ZELL.
HIGH SCHOOL: Hudson's Bay (Vancouver, Wash.).
TRANSACTIONS/CAREER NOTES: Selected by Chicago Cubs organization in fourth round of free-draft (June 4, 1996). ... On West Tenn disabled list (July 29, 1999-remainder of season). ... On West Tennessee disabled list (April 6-May 13 and July 15-August 8, 2000).

Year League	W	L	Pct.	ERA	G	GS	CG	ShO	Sv.	IP	H	R	ER	BB	SO
1996— Gulf Coast Cubs (GCL).......	4	2	.667	2.35	11	10	0	0	0	61 $1/3$	54	23	16	8	64
1997— Rockford (Midw.)	6	11	.353	4.45	26	24	3	1	0	143 $2/3$	155	89	71	62	105
1998— Rockford (Midw.)	3	0	1.000	0.80	5	5	0	0	0	33 $2/3$	27	8	3	15	23
—Daytona (FSL)	7	6	.538	4.17	22	21	1	0	0	136	149	80	63	38	123
—West Tenn (Sou.)	0	1	.000	13.50	1	1	0	0	0	4	5	7	6	4	4
1999— West Tenn (Sou.)	3	8	.273	5.99	20	18	0	0	0	97 $2/3$	121	76	65	62	57
2000— West Tenn (Sou.)	7	5	.583	3.10	16	16	0	0	0	93	80	39	32	41	65

GLANVILLE, DOUG   OF   PHILLIES

PERSONAL: Born August 25, 1970, in Hackensack, N.J. ... 6-2/172. ... Bats right, throws right. ... Full name: Douglas Metunwa Glanville.
HIGH SCHOOL: Teaneck (N.J.).
COLLEGE: Pennsylvania.
TRANSACTIONS/CAREER NOTES: Selected by Chicago Cubs organization in first round (12th pick overall) of free-agent draft (June 3, 1991). ... Traded by Cubs to Philadelphia Phillies for 2B Mickey Morandini (December 23, 1997).
STATISTICAL NOTES: Led Carolina League outfielders with 312 total chances in 1992. ... Led Southern League in caught stealing with 20 in 1994. ... Led Southern League outfielders with 339 total chances in 1994. ... Had 18-game hitting streak (May 1-20, 1998). ... Had 17-game hitting streak (May 30-June 17, 1998). ... Tied N.L. outfielders for lead in double plays with four in 2000.

Year Team (League)	Pos.	G	AB	R	H	2B	3B	HR	RBI	Avg.	BB	SO	SB	PO	A	E	Avg.
1991— Geneva (NY-Penn)......	OF	36	152	29	46	8	0	2	12	.303	11	25	17	77	4	0	1.000
1992— Win.-Salem (Caro.)	OF	120	485	72	125	18	4	4	36	.258	40	78	32	*293	12	7	.978
1993— Daytona (FSL)	OF	61	239	47	70	10	1	2	21	.293	28	24	18	123	11	7	.950
—Orlando (Sou.)	OF	73	296	42	78	14	4	9	40	.264	12	41	15	168	8	5	.972
1994— Orlando (Sou.)	OF	130	483	53	127	22	2	5	52	.263	24	49	26	*322	14	3	.991
1995— Iowa (A.A.)	OF-DH	112	419	48	113	16	2	4	37	.270	16	64	13	209	9	4	.982
1996— Iowa (A.A.)	OF-DH	90	373	53	115	23	3	3	34	.308	12	35	15	217	6	3	.987
—Chicago (N.L.)	OF	49	83	10	20	5	1	1	10	.241	3	11	2	35	1	1	.973
1997— Chicago (N.L.)	OF	146	474	79	142	22	5	4	35	.300	24	46	19	247	12	3	.989
1998— Philadelphia (N.L.)■ ..	OF	158	*678	106	189	28	7	8	49	.279	42	89	23	360	14	2	.995
1999— Philadelphia (N.L.)......	OF	150	628	101	204	38	6	11	73	.325	48	82	34	385	13	8	.980
2000— Philadelphia (N.L.)......	OF	154	637	89	175	27	6	8	52	.275	31	76	31	380	9	4	.990
Major League totals (5 years)		657	2500	385	730	120	25	32	219	.292	148	304	109	1407	49	18	.988

GLAUBER, KEITH   P   REDS

PERSONAL: Born January 18, 1972, in Brooklyn, N.Y. ... 6-2/190. ... Throws right, bats right. ... Full name: Keith H. Glauber.
HIGH SCHOOL: Marlboro (N.J.).
COLLEGE: Montclair (N.J.) State.
TRANSACTIONS/CAREER NOTES: Selected by St. Louis Cardinals organization in 42nd round of free-agent draft (June 2, 1994). ... Selected by Cincinnati Reds from Cardinals organization in Rule 5 major league draft (December 15, 1997). ... On Cincinnati disabled list (March 12-September 1, 1998); included rehabilitation assignments to Burlington (June 19-July 16), Chattanooga (August 1-10) and Indianapolis (August 10-September 1). ... Granted free agency (December 21, 1998). ... Re-signed by Reds organization (March 23, 1999). ... On Indianapolis disabled list (July 20, 1999-remainder of season). ... Granted free agency (October 15, 1999). ... Re-signed by Reds (November 13, 1999).

G

Year League	W	L	Pct.	ERA	G	GS	CG	ShO	Sv.	IP	H	R	ER	BB	SO
1994—New Jersey (NY-Penn)	4	6	.400	4.19	17	10	0	0	0	68²/₃	67	36	32	26	51
1995—Savannah (S.Atl.)	2	1	.667	3.73	40	0	0	0	0	62²/₃	50	29	26	36	62
1996—Peoria (Midw.)	3	3	.500	3.09	54	0	0	0	0	64	54	31	22	26	80
1997—Arkansas (Texas)	5	7	.417	2.75	50	0	0	0	3	59	48	22	18	25	53
—Louisville (A.A.)	1	3	.250	5.17	15	0	0	0	5	15²/₃	18	14	9	4	14
1998—Burlington (Midw.)■	0	1	.000	3.86	7	1	0	0	0	14	13	9	6	6	13
—Chattanooga (Sou.)	1	1	.500	4.00	2	2	0	0	0	9	3	4	4	6	5
—Indianapolis (I.L.)	1	3	.250	9.00	4	4	0	0	0	16	20	17	16	14	15
—Cincinnati (N.L.)	0	0	...	2.35	3	0	0	0	0	7²/₃	6	2	2	1	4
1999—Chattanooga (Sou.)	5	0	1.000	1.98	7	7	0	0	0	50	42	12	11	8	26
—Indianapolis (I.L.)	3	3	.500	5.82	12	12	1	1	0	68	84	49	44	20	51
2000—Chattanooga (Sou.)	0	4	.000	3.51	32	0	0	0	2	41	42	19	16	12	27
—Louisville (I.L.)	1	2	.333	1.52	18	0	0	0	4	29²/₃	26	5	5	6	15
—Cincinnati (N.L.)	0	0	...	3.68	4	0	0	0	0	7¹/₃	5	3	3	2	4
Major League totals (2 years)	0	0	...	3.00	7	0	0	0	0	15	11	5	5	3	8

GLAUS, TROY 3B ANGELS

PERSONAL: Born August 3, 1976, in Tarzana, Calif. ... 6-5/229. ... Bats right, throws right. ... Full name: Troy Edward Glaus. ... Name pronounced GLOSS.
HIGH SCHOOL: Carlsbad (Calif.).
COLLEGE: UCLA.
TRANSACTIONS/CAREER NOTES: Selected by San Diego Padres organization in second round of free-agent draft (June 2, 1994); did not sign. ... Selected by Anaheim Angels organization in first round (third pick overall) of free-agent draft (June 3, 1997).
RECORDS: Hold A.L. single-season record for most home runs by third baseman—46 (2000).
HONORS: Named third baseman on THE SPORTING NEWS A.L. Silver Slugger team (2000).
STATISTICAL NOTES: Led A.L. third basemen with 349 assists, 33 errors and 493 total chances in 2000. ... Career major league grand slams: 1.
MISCELLANEOUS: Member of 1996 U.S. Olympic baseball team.

							BATTING								FIELDING		
Year Team (League)	Pos.	G	AB	R	H	2B	3B	HR	RBI	Avg.	BB	SO	SB	PO	A	E	Avg.
1998—Midland (Texas)	3B	50	188	51	58	11	2	19	51	.309	39	41	4	34	101	11	.925
—Vancouver (PCL)	3B	59	219	33	67	16	0	16	42	.306	21	55	3	46	131	13	.932
—Anaheim (A.L.)	3B	48	165	19	36	9	0	1	23	.218	15	51	1	27	85	7	.941
1999—Anaheim (A.L.)	3B-DH	154	551	85	132	29	0	29	79	.240	71	143	5	114	277	19	.954
2000—Anaheim (A.L.)	3B-SS-DH	159	563	120	160	37	1	*47	102	.284	112	163	14	112	†353	†33	.934
Major League totals (3 years)		361	1279	224	328	75	1	77	204	.256	198	357	20	253	715	59	.943

ALL-STAR GAME RECORD

						BATTING						FIELDING		
Year League	Pos.	AB	R	H	2B	3B	HR	RBI	Avg.	BB	SO	SB	PO	A	E	Avg.
2000—American	3B	1	0	0	0	0	0	0	.000	0	0	0	2	0	0	1.000

GLAVINE, TOM P BRAVES

PERSONAL: Born March 25, 1966, in Concord, Mass. ... 6-0/185. ... Throws left, bats left. ... Full name: Thomas Michael Glavine. ... Brother of Mike Glavine, first baseman, Atlanta Braves organization. ... Name pronounced GLAV-in.
HIGH SCHOOL: Billerica (Mass.).
TRANSACTIONS/CAREER NOTES: Selected by Atlanta Braves organization in second round of free-agent draft (June 4, 1984).
HONORS: Named N.L. Pitcher of the Year by THE SPORTING NEWS (1991 and 2000). ... Named lefthanded pitcher on THE SPORTING NEWS N.L. All-Star team (1991-92, 1998 and 2000). ... Named pitcher on THE SPORTING NEWS N.L. Silver Slugger team (1991, 1995, 1996 and 1998). ... Named N.L. Cy Young Award winner by Baseball Writers' Association of America (1991 and 1998).
STATISTICAL NOTES: Led Gulf Coast League with 12 wild pitches in 1984. ... Led N.L. pitchers with 59 assists in 1999. ... Tied for N.L. lead in double plays by a pitcher with six in 1999.
MISCELLANEOUS: Selected by Los Angeles Kings in fourth round (69th pick overall) of NHL entry draft (June 9, 1984). ... Appeared in eight games as pinch runner (1988). ... Appeared in one game as pinch runner (1989). ... Appeared in one game as pinch runner (1990). ... Received a base on balls and scored once in one game as pinch hitter and appeared in one game as pinch runner (1991). ... Singled and struck out in two appearances as pinch hitter (1992). ... Struck out in only appearance as pinch hitter (1994). ... Singled and struck out in three appearances as pinch hitter (1996). ... Had a sacrifice hit in only appearance as pinch hitter (1999). ... Grounded out twice in two appearances as pinch hitter (2000).

Year League	W	L	Pct.	ERA	G	GS	CG	ShO	Sv.	IP	H	R	ER	BB	SO
1984—Gulf Coast Braves (GCL)	2	3	.400	3.34	8	7	0	0	0	32¹/₃	29	17	12	13	34
1985—Sumter (S.Atl.)	9	6	.600	*2.35	26	26	2	1	0	168²/₃	114	58	44	73	174
1986—Greenville (Sou.)	11	6	.647	3.41	22	22	2	1	0	145¹/₃	129	62	55	70	114
—Richmond (I.L.)	1	5	.167	5.63	7	7	1	1	0	40	40	29	25	27	12
1987—Richmond (I.L.)	6	12	.333	3.35	22	22	4	1	0	150¹/₃	142	70	56	56	91
—Atlanta (N.L.)	2	4	.333	5.54	9	9	0	0	0	50¹/₃	55	34	31	33	20
1988—Atlanta (N.L.)	7	*17	.292	4.56	34	34	1	0	0	195¹/₃	201	111	99	63	84
1989—Atlanta (N.L.)	14	8	.636	3.68	29	29	6	4	0	186	172	88	76	40	90
1990—Atlanta (N.L.)	10	12	.455	4.28	33	33	1	0	0	214¹/₃	232	111	102	78	129
1991—Atlanta (N.L.)	•20	11	.645	2.55	34	34	•9	1	0	246²/₃	201	83	70	69	192
1992—Atlanta (N.L.)	•20	8	.714	2.76	33	33	7	•5	0	225	197	81	69	70	129
1993—Atlanta (N.L.)	•22	6	.786	3.20	36	•36	4	2	0	239¹/₃	236	91	85	90	120
1994—Atlanta (N.L.)	13	9	.591	3.97	25	25	2	0	0	165¹/₃	173	76	73	70	140
1995—Atlanta (N.L.)	16	7	.696	3.08	29	29	3	1	0	198²/₃	182	76	68	66	127
1996—Atlanta (N.L.)	15	10	.600	2.98	36	*36	1	0	0	235¹/₃	222	91	78	85	181
1997—Atlanta (N.L.)	14	7	.667	2.96	33	33	5	2	0	240	197	86	79	79	152
1998—Atlanta (N.L.)	*20	6	.769	2.47	33	33	4	3	0	229¹/₃	202	67	63	74	157
1999—Atlanta (N.L.)	14	11	.560	4.12	35	•35	2	0	0	234	*259	115	107	83	138
2000—Atlanta (N.L.)	*21	9	.700	3.40	35	•35	4	2	0	241	222	101	91	65	152
Major League totals (14 years)	208	125	.625	3.39	434	434	49	20	0	2900²/₃	2751	1211	1091	965	1811

G

DIVISION SERIES RECORD

RECORDS: Holds N.L. career record for most bases on balls allowed—14.

Year League	W	L	Pct.	ERA	G	GS	CG	ShO	Sv.	IP	H	R	ER	BB	SO
1995— Atlanta (N.L.)	0	0	...	2.57	1	1	0	0	0	7	5	3	2	1	3
1996— Atlanta (N.L.)	1	0	1.000	1.35	1	1	0	0	0	6²/₃	5	1	1	3	7
1997— Atlanta (N.L.)	1	0	1.000	4.50	1	1	0	0	0	6	5	3	3	5	4
1998— Atlanta (N.L.)	0	0	...	1.29	1	1	0	0	0	7	3	1	1	1	8
1999— Atlanta (N.L.)	0	0	...	3.00	1	1	0	0	0	6	5	2	2	3	6
2000— Atlanta (N.L.)	0	1	.000	27.00	1	1	0	0	0	2¹/₃	6	7	7	1	2
Division series totals (6 years)	2	1	.667	4.11	6	6	0	0	0	35	29	17	16	14	30

CHAMPIONSHIP SERIES RECORD

RECORDS: Holds career records for most losses—8; earned runs allowed—32; and hit batsmen—5. ... Holds single-inning records for most runs allowed—8 (October 13, 1992, second inning); and most earned runs allowed—7 (October 13, 1992, second inning). ... Shares career records for most games started—13; and hits allowed—81. ... Shares single-game record for most earned runs allowed—7 (October 13, 1992 and October 14, 1997). ... Shares single-inning record for most hits allowed—6 (October 13, 1992, second inning). ... Shares N.L. career record for most series with one team—8 (Atlanta, 1991-93 and 1995-99). ... Shares N.L. single-series record for most hit batsmen—2 (1992).

NOTES: Received a base on balls in only appearance as pinch hitter (1998).

Year League	W	L	Pct.	ERA	G	GS	CG	ShO	Sv.	IP	H	R	ER	BB	SO
1991— Atlanta (N.L.)	0	2	.000	3.21	2	2	0	0	0	14	12	5	5	6	11
1992— Atlanta (N.L.)	0	2	.000	12.27	2	2	0	0	0	7¹/₃	13	11	10	3	2
1993— Atlanta (N.L.)	1	0	1.000	2.57	1	1	0	0	0	7	6	2	2	0	5
1995— Atlanta (N.L.)	0	0	...	1.29	1	1	0	0	0	7	7	1	1	2	5
1996— Atlanta (N.L.)	1	1	.500	2.08	2	2	0	0	0	13	10	3	3	0	9
1997— Atlanta (N.L.)	1	1	.500	5.40	2	2	0	0	0	13¹/₃	13	8	8	11	9
1998— Atlanta (N.L.)	0	2	.000	2.31	2	2	0	0	0	11²/₃	13	6	3	9	8
1999— Atlanta (N.L.)	1	0	1.000	0.00	1	1	0	0	0	7	7	0	0	1	8
Champ. series totals (8 years)	4	8	.333	3.59	13	13	0	0	0	80¹/₃	81	36	32	32	57

WORLD SERIES RECORD

RECORDS: Shares single-inning records for most bases on balls allowed—4 (October 24, 1991, sixth inning); and most consecutive bases on balls allowed—3 (October 24, 1991, sixth inning).

NOTES: Named Most Valuable Player (1995). ... Member of World Series championship team (1995).

Year League	W	L	Pct.	ERA	G	GS	CG	ShO	Sv.	IP	H	R	ER	BB	SO
1991— Atlanta (N.L.)	1	1	.500	2.70	2	2	1	0	0	13¹/₃	8	6	4	7	8
1992— Atlanta (N.L.)	1	1	.500	1.59	2	2	2	0	0	17	10	3	3	4	8
1995— Atlanta (N.L.)	2	0	1.000	1.29	2	2	0	0	0	14	4	2	2	6	11
1996— Atlanta (N.L.)	0	1	.000	1.29	1	1	0	0	0	7	4	2	1	3	8
1999— Atlanta (N.L.)	0	0	...	5.14	1	1	0	0	0	7	7	5	4	0	3
World Series totals (5 years)	4	3	.571	2.16	8	8	3	0	0	58¹/₃	33	18	14	20	38

ALL-STAR GAME RECORD

RECORDS: Holds single-game record for most hits allowed—9 (July 14, 1992). ... Holds single-inning record for most hits allowed—7 (July 14, 1992, first inning).

Year League	W	L	Pct.	ERA	GS	CG	ShO	Sv.	IP	H	R	ER	BB	SO
1991— National	0	0	...	0.00	1	0	0	0	2	1	0	0	1	3
1992— National	0	1	.000	27.00	1	0	0	0	1²/₃	9	5	5	0	2
1993— National						Did not play.								
1996— National	0	0	...	0.00	0	0	0	0	1	0	0	0	0	1
1997— National						Did not play.								
1998— National	0	0	...	27.00	0	0	0	0	1¹/₃	5	4	4	3	0
2000— National	0	0	...	0.00	0	0	0	0	1	0	0	0	0	1
All-Star Game totals (5 years)	0	1	.000	11.57	2	0	0	0	7	15	9	9	4	7

GLOAD, ROSS — 1B/OF — CUBS

PERSONAL: Born April 5, 1976, in Brooklyn, N.Y. ... 6-0/185. ... Bats left, throws left. ... Full name: Ross Peter Gload.
HIGH SCHOOL: East Hampton (N.Y.).
COLLEGE: South Florida.
TRANSACTIONS/CAREER NOTES: Selected by Florida Marlins organization in 13th round of free-agent draft (June 3, 1997).... Traded by Marlins with P David Noyce to Chicago Cubs for OF Henry Rodriguez (July 31, 2000).
STATISTICAL NOTES: Led New York Pennsylvania League first basemen with 599 total chances in 1997.

						BATTING								FIELDING			
Year Team (League)	Pos.	G	AB	R	H	2B	3B	HR	RBI	Avg.	BB	SO	SB	PO	A	E	Avg.
1997— Utica (NY-Penn)	1B	68	245	28	64	15	2	3	43	.261	28	57	1	*546	37	*16	.973
1998— Kane County (Midw.)	1B	132	501	77	157	*41	3	12	92	.313	58	84	7	1160	69	14	.989
1999— Brevard County (FSL)	1B	133	490	80	146	26	3	10	74	.298	53	76	3	1200	83	9	.993
2000— Portland (East.)	OF-1B	100	401	60	114	28	4	16	65	.284	29	53	4	462	30	7	.986
— Iowa (PCL)■	OF	28	104	24	42	10	2	14	39	.404	9	13	1	42	2	4	.917
— Chicago (N.L.)	OF-1B	18	31	4	6	0	1	1	3	.194	3	10	0	15	0	0	1.000
Major League totals (1 year)		18	31	4	6	0	1	1	3	.194	3	10	0	0	0	0	...

GLOVER, GARY — P — WHITE SOX

PERSONAL: Born December 3, 1976, in Cleveland. ... 6-5/205. ... Throws right, bats right. ... Full name: John Gary Glover II.
HIGH SCHOOL: Deland (Fla.).
TRANSACTIONS/CAREER NOTES: Selected by Toronto Blue Jays organization in 15th round of free-agent draft (June 2, 1994). ... On disabled list (August 10-September 8, 1994). ... Traded by Blue Jays to Chicago White Sox for P Scott Eyre (November 7, 2000).

Year League	W	L	Pct.	ERA	G	GS	CG	ShO	Sv.	IP	H	R	ER	BB	SO
1994—Gulf Coast Blue Jays (GCL)	0	0	...	47.25	2	0	0	0	0	1⅓	4	8	7	4	2
1995—Gulf Coast Blue Jays (GCL)	3	7	.300	4.91	12	10	2	0	0	62⅓	62	48	34	26	46
1996—Medicine Hat (Pio.)	3	*12	.200	7.75	15	•15	*2	0	0	83⅔	*119	*94	72	29	54
1997—Hagerstown (S.Atl.)	6	*17	.261	3.73	28	28	3	0	0	173⅔	165	94	72	58	155
1998—Knoxville (Sou.)	0	5	.000	6.75	8	8	0	0	0	37⅓	41	36	28	28	14
— Dunedin (FSL)	7	6	.538	4.28	19	18	0	0	0	109⅓	117	66	52	36	88
1999—Knoxville (Sou.)	8	2	.800	3.56	13	13	1	0	0	86	70	39	34	27	77
— Syracuse (I.L.)	4	6	.400	5.19	14	14	0	0	0	76⅓	93	50	44	35	57
— Toronto (A.L.)	0	0	...	0.00	1	0	0	0	0	1	0	0	0	1	0
2000—Sycaruse (I.L.)	9	9	.500	5.02	27	27	1	0	0	166⅔	181	104	93	62	119
Major League totals (1 year)	0	0	...	0.00	1	0	0	0	0	1	0	0	0	1	0

GLYNN, RYAN — P — RANGERS

PERSONAL: Born November 1, 1974, in Portsmouth, Va. ... 6-3/195. ... Throws right, bats right. ... Full name: Ryan David Glynn.
HIGH SCHOOL: Churchland (Portsmouth, Va.).
COLLEGE: Virginia Military Institute.
TRANSACTIONS/CAREER NOTES: Selected by Texas Rangers organization in fourth round of free-agent draft (June 1, 1995). ... On Texas disabled list (July 2-17 and August 15-29, 2000); included rehabilitation assignment to Oklahoma (August 24-29).

Year League	W	L	Pct.	ERA	G	GS	CG	ShO	Sv.	IP	H	R	ER	BB	SO
1995—Hudson Valley (NY-Penn)	3	3	.500	4.70	9	8	0	0	0	44	56	27	23	16	21
1996—Charleston, S.C. (S.Atl.)	8	7	.533	4.54	19	19	2	1	0	121	118	70	61	59	72
1997—Charlotte (FSL)	8	7	.533	4.97	23	22	5	1	1	134	148	81	74	44	96
— Tulsa (Texas)	1	1	.500	3.38	3	3	0	0	0	21⅓	21	9	8	10	18
1998—Tulsa (Texas)	9	6	.600	3.44	26	24	4	1	0	157	140	66	60	64	111
1999—Oklahoma (PCL)	6	2	.750	3.39	16	16	2	1	0	90⅓	81	46	34	36	55
— Texas (A.L.)	2	4	.333	7.24	13	10	0	0	0	54⅔	71	46	44	35	39
2000—Oklahoma (PCL)	4	2	.667	3.55	15	14	2	2	0	83⅔	72	36	33	33	66
— Texas (A.L.)	5	7	.417	5.58	16	16	0	0	0	88⅔	107	65	55	41	33
Major League totals (2 years)	7	11	.389	6.22	29	26	0	0	0	143⅓	178	111	99	76	72

GOMES, WAYNE — P — PHILLIES

PERSONAL: Born January 15, 1973, in Hampton, Va. ... 6-2/227. ... Throws right, bats right. ... Full name: Wayne Maurice Gomes.
HIGH SCHOOL: Phoebus (Hampton, Va.).
COLLEGE: Old Dominion.
TRANSACTIONS/CAREER NOTES: Selected by Philadelphia Phillies organization in first round (fourth pick overall) of free-agent draft (June 3, 1993). ... On disabled list (May 12-June 23, 1995). ... On Philadelphia disabled list (July 7-August 8, 2000); included rehabilitation assignment to Scranton/Wilkes-Barre (August 1-8).
STATISTICAL NOTES: Led Florida State League with 27 wild pitches in 1994. ... Tied for Eastern League lead with six balks in 1995.

Year League	W	L	Pct.	ERA	G	GS	CG	ShO	Sv.	IP	H	R	ER	BB	SO
1993—Batavia (NY-Penn)	1	0	1.000	1.23	5	0	0	0	0	7⅓	1	1	1	8	11
— Clearwater (FSL)	0	0	...	1.17	9	0	0	0	4	7⅔	4	1	1	9	13
1994—Clearwater (FSL)	6	8	.429	4.74	23	21	1	1	0	104⅓	85	63	55	82	102
1995—Reading (East.)	7	4	.636	3.96	22	22	1	1	0	104⅔	89	54	46	70	102
1996—Reading (East.)	0	4	.000	4.48	*67	0	0	0	24	64⅓	53	35	32	48	79
1997—Scranton/W.B. (I.L.)	3	1	.750	2.37	26	0	0	0	7	38	31	11	10	24	36
— Philadelphia (N.L.)	5	1	.833	5.27	37	0	0	0	0	42⅔	45	26	25	24	24
1998—Philadelphia (N.L.)	9	6	.600	4.24	71	0	0	0	1	93⅓	94	48	44	35	86
1999—Philadelphia (N.L.)	5	5	.500	4.26	73	0	0	0	19	74	70	38	35	56	58
2000—Philadelphia (N.L.)	4	6	.400	4.40	65	0	0	0	7	73⅔	72	41	36	35	49
— Scranton/W.B. (I.L.)	0	0	...	2.25	3	0	0	0	0	4	3	1	1	1	1
Major League totals (4 years)	23	18	.561	4.44	246	0	0	0	27	283⅔	281	153	140	150	217

GOMEZ, CHRIS — SS — PADRES

PERSONAL: Born June 16, 1971, in Los Angeles. ... 6-1/195. ... Bats right, throws right. ... Full name: Christopher Cory Gomez.
HIGH SCHOOL: Lakewood (Calif.).
COLLEGE: Loyola Marymount, then Long Beach State.
TRANSACTIONS/CAREER NOTES: Selected by California Angels organization in 37th round of free-agent draft (June 5, 1989); did not sign. ... Selected by Detroit Tigers organization in third round of free-agent draft (June 1, 1992). ... Traded by Tigers with C John Flaherty to San Diego Padres for C Brad Ausmus, SS Andujar Cedeno and P Russ Spear (June 18, 1996). ... On San Diego disabled list (June 2-July 31, 1999); included rehabilitation assignment to Las Vegas (July 15-30). ... On disabled list (June 22, 2000-remainder of season).

Year Team (League)	Pos.	G	AB	R	H	2B	3B	HR	RBI	Avg.	BB	SO	SB	PO	A	E	Avg.
1992—London (East.)	SS	64	220	20	59	13	2	1	19	.268	20	34	1	100	174	14	.951
1993—Toledo (I.L.)	SS	87	277	29	68	12	2	0	20	.245	23	37	6	133	261	16	.961
— Detroit (A.L.)	SS-2B-DH	46	128	11	32	7	1	0	11	.250	9	17	2	69	118	5	.974
1994—Detroit (A.L.)	SS-2B	84	296	32	76	19	0	8	53	.257	33	64	5	140	210	8	.978
1995—Detroit (A.L.)	SS-2B-DH	123	431	49	96	20	2	11	50	.223	41	96	4	210	361	15	.974
1996—Detroit (A.L.)	SS	48	128	21	31	5	0	1	16	.242	18	20	1	77	114	6	.970
— San Diego (N.L.)■	SS	89	328	32	86	16	1	3	29	.262	39	64	2	124	261	13	.967
1997—San Diego (N.L.)	SS	150	522	62	132	19	2	5	54	.253	53	114	5	226	433	15	.978
1998—San Diego (N.L.)	SS	145	449	55	120	32	3	4	39	.267	51	87	1	180	397	12	*.980
1999—San Diego (N.L.)	SS	76	234	20	59	8	1	1	15	.252	27	49	1	101	195	12	.961
— Las Vegas (PCL)	SS	10	27	3	9	1	0	0	4	.333	2	6	0	8	20	2	.933
2000—San Diego (N.L.)	SS-2B	33	54	4	12	0	0	0	3	.222	7	5	0	27	43	5	.933
American League totals (4 years)		301	983	113	235	51	3	20	130	.239	101	197	12	496	803	34	.974
National League totals (5 years)		493	1587	173	409	75	7	13	140	.258	177	319	9	658	1329	57	.972
Major League totals (8 years)		794	2570	286	644	126	10	33	270	.251	278	516	21	1154	2132	91	.973

G

DIVISION SERIES RECORD

Year Team (League)	Pos.	G	AB	R	H	2B	3B	HR	RBI	Avg.	BB	SO	SB	PO	A	E	Avg.
1996—San Diego (N.L.)	SS	3	12	0	2	0	0	0	1	.167	0	4	0	8	5	0	1.000
1998—San Diego (N.L.)	SS	4	11	1	3	0	0	0	0	.273	4	1	0	6	9	1	.938
Division series totals (2 years)		7	23	1	5	0	0	0	1	.217	4	5	0	14	14	1	.966

CHAMPIONSHIP SERIES RECORD

Year Team (League)	Pos.	G	AB	R	H	2B	3B	HR	RBI	Avg.	BB	SO	SB	PO	A	E	Avg.
1998—San Diego (N.L.)	SS	6	20	2	3	1	0	0	0	.150	2	5	0	5	14	1	.950

WORLD SERIES RECORD

Year Team (League)	Pos.	G	AB	R	H	2B	3B	HR	RBI	Avg.	BB	SO	SB	PO	A	E	Avg.
1998—San Diego (N.L.)	SS	4	11	2	4	0	1	0	0	.364	1	1	0	5	9	0	1.000

GONZALEZ, ALEX   SS   BLUE JAYS

PERSONAL: Born April 8, 1973, in Miami. ... 6-0/200. ... Bats right, throws right. ... Full name: Alexander Scott Gonzalez.
HIGH SCHOOL: Miami Killian.
TRANSACTIONS/CAREER NOTES: Selected by Toronto Blue Jays organization in 14th round of free-agent draft (June 3, 1991). ... On Toronto disabled list (April 29-May 27, 1994); included rehabilitation assignment to Syracuse (May 14-27). ... On disabled list (August 13-September 14, 1997; and May 17, 1999-remainder of season). ... On Toronto disabled list (July 7-22, 2000); included rehabilitation assignment to Syracuse (July 21). ... Granted free agency (October 30, 2000). ... Re-signed by Blue Jays (December 10, 2000).
RECORDS: Shares major league single-game record for most strikeouts—6 (September 9, 1998, 13 innings). ... Shares A.L. record for most assists by shortstop (nine-inning game)—13 (1996).
STATISTICAL NOTES: Led Gulf Coast League shortstops with 247 total chances in 1991. ... Led Southern League with 253 total bases in 1993. ... Led Southern League shortstops with 682 total chances and 92 double plays in 1993. ... Led International League shortstops with 542 total chances in 1994. ... Led A.L. shortstops with 765 total chances and 122 double plays in 1996. ... Had 15-game hitting streak (August 2-18, 2000). ... Led A.L. with 16 sacrifice hits in 2000.

Year Team (League)	Pos.	G	AB	R	H	2B	3B	HR	RBI	Avg.	BB	SO	SB	PO	A	E	Avg.
1991—GC Blue Jays (GCL)....	SS	53	191	29	40	5	4	0	10	.209	12	41	7	66	*160	21	.915
1992—Myrtle Beach (S.Atl.)..	SS	134	535	83	145	22	9	10	62	.271	38	119	26	*248	*406	48	.932
1993—Knoxville (S.Atl.)	SS	*142	561	*93	162	29	7	16	69	.289	39	110	38	*224	*428	30	*.956
1994—Toronto (A.L.).............	SS	15	53	7	8	3	1	0	1	.151	4	17	3	18	49	6	.918
—Syracuse (I.L.)............	SS-DH	110	437	69	124	22	4	12	57	.284	53	92	23	*163	*348	*31	.943
1995—Toronto (A.L.).............	SS-3B-DH	111	367	51	89	19	4	10	42	.243	44	114	4	164	227	19	.954
1996—Toronto (A.L.).............	SS	147	527	64	124	30	5	14	64	.235	45	127	16	279	465	21	.973
1997—Toronto (A.L.).............	SS	126	426	46	102	23	2	12	35	.239	34	94	15	209	341	8	*.986
1998—Toronto (A.L.).............	SS	158	568	70	136	28	1	13	51	.239	28	121	21	259	427	17	.976
1999—Toronto (A.L.).............	SS-DH	38	154	22	45	13	0	2	12	.292	16	23	4	69	132	4	.980
2000—Toronto (A.L.).............	SS	141	527	68	133	31	2	15	69	.252	43	113	4	213	407	16	.975
—Syracuse (I.L.)............	SS	1	5	0	0	0	0	0	0	.000	0	2	0	2	3	0	1.000
Major League totals (7 years)		736	2622	328	637	147	15	66	274	.243	214	609	67	1211	2048	91	.973

GONZALEZ, ALEX   SS   MARLINS

PERSONAL: Born February 15, 1977, in Cagua, Venezuela. ... 6-0/170. ... Bats right, throws right. ... Full name: Alexander Gonzalez.
HIGH SCHOOL: Liceo Ramon Bastidas (Venezuela).
TRANSACTIONS/CAREER NOTES: Signed as non-drafted free agent by Florida Marlins organization (April 18, 1994). ... On Kane County disabled list (April 5-August 17, 1996). ... On Portland disabled list (September 7, 1996-remainder of season). ... On Florida disabled list (July 28-September 1, 2000); included rehabilitation assignment to Brevard County (August 26-31).

Year Team (League)	Pos.	G	AB	R	H	2B	3B	HR	RBI	Avg.	BB	SO	SB	PO	A	E	Avg.
1994—Dom. Marlins (DSL)...	SS	54	239	30	54	7	3	3	31	.226	15	36	4	140	222	34	.914
1995—GC Marlins (GCL)	SS	53	187	30	55	7	4	2	30	.294	19	27	11	65	168	17	.932
—Brevard County (FSL).	SS	17	59	6	12	2	1	0	8	.203	1	14	1	26	51	8	.906
1996—Portland (East.)	SS	11	34	4	8	0	1	0	1	.235	2	10	0	17	38	7	.887
—Kane County (Midw.)..	SS	4	10	2	2	0	0	0	0	.200	2	4	0	2	10	0	1.000
—GC Marlins (GCL)	SS	10	41	6	16	3	0	0	6	.390	2	4	1	14	30	5	.898
1997—Portland (East.)	SS	133	449	69	114	16	4	19	65	.254	27	83	4	192	423	*37	.943
1998—Charlotte (I.L.)............	SS	108	422	71	117	20	10	10	51	.277	28	80	4	161	322	20	.960
—Florida (N.L.)	SS	25	86	11	13	2	0	3	7	.151	9	30	0	29	58	2	.978
1999—Florida (N.L.)	SS	136	560	81	155	28	8	14	59	.277	15	113	3	237	339	27	.955
2000—Florida (N.L.)	SS	109	385	35	77	17	4	7	42	.200	13	77	7	139	288	19	.957
—Brevard County (FSL).	SS	4	17	1	2	0	0	0	2	.118	1	3	1	8	11	0	1.000
Major League totals (3 years)		270	1031	127	245	47	12	24	108	.238	37	220	10	405	685	48	.958

ALL-STAR GAME RECORD

Year League	Pos.	AB	R	H	2B	3B	HR	RBI	Avg.	BB	SO	SB	PO	A	E	Avg.
1999—National	PH-SS	1	0	0	0	0	0	0	.000	0	0	0	1	0	0	1.000

G

GONZALEZ, DICKY   P   METS

PERSONAL: Born October 21, 1978, in Bayamon, Puerto Rico. ... 5-11/170. ... Throws right, bats right. ... Full name: Dicky Angel Gonzalez.
HIGH SCHOOL: Puig (Puerto Rico).
TRANSACTIONS/CAREER NOTES: Selected by New York Mets organization in 16th round of free-agent draft (June 4, 1996).

Year	League	W	L	Pct.	ERA	G	GS	CG	ShO	Sv.	IP	H	R	ER	BB	SO
1996—	Gulf Coast Mets (GCL)	4	2	.667	2.66	11	8	2	1	0	47⅓	50	19	14	3	51
	—Little Falls (NY-Penn)	1	0	1.000	1.80	1	1	0	0	0	5	4	2	1	0	7
1997—	Capital City (S.Atl.)	1	4	.200	4.94	10	7	1	0	0	47⅓	50	28	26	15	49
	—Little Falls (NY-Penn)	3	6	.333	4.36	12	12	1	0	0	66	70	38	32	10	76
1998—	St. Lucie (FSL)	2	1	.667	3.09	8	8	0	0	0	46⅔	46	22	16	13	23
	—Capital City (S.Atl.)	10	3	.769	3.31	18	18	1	0	0	111⅓	104	57	41	14	107
1999—	St. Lucie (FSL)	14	9	.609	2.83	25	25	3	0	0	168⅔	156	66	53	30	143
	—Norfolk (I.L.)	0	1	.000	2.70	1	1	0	0	0	6⅔	5	2	2	1	3
2000—	Binghamton (East.)	13	5	.722	3.84	26	25	2	1	0	147⅔	130	75	63	36	138

GONZALEZ, JEREMI   P   CUBS

PERSONAL: Born January 8, 1975, in Maracaibo, Venezuela. ... 6-2/215. ... Throws right, bats right. ... Full name: Geremis Segundo Acosta Gonzalez.
HIGH SCHOOL: Colegro La Chinita (Maracaibo, Venezuela).
TRANSACTIONS/CAREER NOTES: Signed as non-drafted free agent by Chicago Cubs organization (October 21, 1991). ... On disabled list (July 6-August 10, 1996). ... On disabled list (July 25, 1998-remainder of season). ... On Chicago disabled list (April 1, 1999-entire season); included rehabilitation assignments to Dayton (April 16-22), West Tenn (April 26-May 8) and Iowa (May 12-18 and May 29-31). ... On Chicago disabled list (March 28, 2000-remainder of season); included rehabilitation assignments to Arizona Cubs (July 19-August 7) and Lansing (August 7-18).
STATISTICAL NOTES: Led Arizona League with 10 hit batsmen in 1992.
MISCELLANEOUS: Appeared in one game as pinch runner (1998).

Year	League	W	L	Pct.	ERA	G	GS	CG	ShO	Sv.	IP	H	R	ER	BB	SO
1992—	Arizona Cubs (Ariz.)	0	5	.000	7.80	14	7	0	0	0	45	65	59	39	22	39
1993—	Huntington (Appl.)	3	9	.250	6.25	12	12	1	0	0	67⅔	82	59	47	38	42
1994—	Peoria (Midw.)	1	7	.125	5.55	13	13	1	0	0	71⅓	86	53	44	32	39
	—Williamsport (NY-Penn)	4	6	.400	4.24	16	12	1	1	1	80⅔	83	46	38	29	64
1995—	Rockford (Midw.)	4	4	.500	5.10	12	12	1	0	0	65⅓	63	43	37	28	36
	—Daytona (FSL)	5	1	.833	1.22	19	2	0	0	4	44⅓	34	15	6	13	30
1996—	Orlando (Sou.)	6	3	.667	3.34	17	14	0	0	0	97	95	39	36	28	85
1997—	Iowa (A.A.)	2	2	.500	3.48	10	10	1	1	0	62	47	27	24	21	58
	—Chicago (N.L.)	11	9	.550	4.25	23	23	1	1	0	144	126	73	68	69	93
1998—	Chicago (N.L.)	7	7	.500	5.32	20	20	1	1	0	110	124	72	65	41	70
1999—	Daytona (FSL)	0	0	...	0.00	2	2	0	0	0	4⅔	2	0	0	0	4
	—West Tenn (Sou.)	0	0	...	1.74	3	3	0	0	0	10⅓	7	2	2	9	12
	—Iowa (PCL)	0	1	.000	4.50	3	3	0	0	0	10	10	8	5	6	10
2000—	Arizona Cubs (Ariz.)	0	1	.000	2.70	4	4	0	0	0	10	8	3	3	2	15
	—Lansing (Midw.)	0	0	...	0.00	1	1	0	0	0	⅔	0	0	0	0	2
Major League totals (2 years)		18	16	.529	4.71	43	43	2	2	0	254	250	145	133	110	163

GONZALEZ, JUAN   OF   INDIANS

PERSONAL: Born October 16, 1969, in Vega Baja, Puerto Rico. ... 6-3/220. ... Bats right, throws right. ... Full name: Juan Alberto Vazquez Gonzalez.
HIGH SCHOOL: Vega Baja (Puerto Rico).
TRANSACTIONS/CAREER NOTES: Signed as non-drafted free agent by Texas Rangers organization (May 30, 1986). ... On disabled list (April 27-June 17, 1988; March 30-April 26, 1991; April 16-June 1 and July 27-August 16, 1995; May 8-June 1, 1996; and March 24-May 2, 1997). ... Traded by Rangers with P Danny Patterson and C Gregg Zaun to Detroit Tigers for P Justin Thompson, P Francisco Cordero, OF Gabe Kapler, C Bill Haselman, 2B Frank Catalanotto and P Alan Webb (November 2, 1999). ... On disabled list (July 8-26, 2000). ... Granted free agency (November 1, 2000). ... Signed by Cleveland Indians (January 9, 2001).
RECORDS: Shares major league single-game record for most sacrifice flies—3 (July 3, 1999). ... Holds A.L. single-season record for most major league ballparks, one or more home runs—16 (1999).
HONORS: Named American Association Most Valuable Player (1990). ... Named outfielder on THE SPORTING NEWS A.L. Silver Slugger team (1992-93 and 1996-98). ... Named outfielder on THE SPORTING NEWS A.L. All-Star team (1993, 1996 and 1998). ... Named A.L. Most Valuable Player by Baseball Writers' Association of America (1996 and 1998).
STATISTICAL NOTES: Led Texas League with 254 total bases in 1989. ... Led American Association with 252 total bases in 1990. ... Hit three home runs in one game (June 7, 1992; August 28, 1993; and September 24, 1999). ... Led A.L. with .632 slugging percentage in 1993. ... Had 21-game hitting streaks (June 25-July 19 and August 8-31, 1996). ... Had 20-game hitting streak (August 20-September 9, 1998). ... Career major league grand slams: 5.
MISCELLANEOUS: Holds Texas Rangers all-time records for most runs (791), hits (1,421), doubles (282), most home runs (340) and runs batted in (1,075).

						BATTING								FIELDING			
Year	Team (League)	Pos.	G	AB	R	H	2B	3B	HR	RBI	Avg.	BB	SO	SB	PO	A	E	Avg.
1986—	GC Rangers (GCL)	OF	60	*233	24	56	4	1	0	36	.240	21	57	7	89	6	•6	.941
1987—	Gastonia (S.Atl.)	OF	127	509	69	135	21	2	14	74	.265	30	92	9	234	10	12	.953
1988—	Charlotte (FSL)	OF	77	277	25	71	14	3	8	43	.256	25	64	5	139	5	4	.973
1989—	Tulsa (Texas)	OF	133	502	73	147	30	7	21	85	.293	31	98	1	292	15	9	.972
	—Texas (A.L.)	OF	24	60	6	9	3	0	1	7	.150	6	17	0	53	0	2	.964
1990—	Oklahoma City (A.A.)	OF	128	496	78	128	29	4	*29	*101	.258	32	109	2	220	7	8	.966
	—Texas (A.L.)	OF-DH	25	90	11	26	7	1	4	12	.289	2	18	0	33	0	0	1.000
1991—	Texas (A.L.)	OF-DH	142	545	78	144	34	1	27	102	.264	42	118	4	310	6	6	.981
1992—	Texas (A.L.)	OF-DH	155	584	77	152	24	2	*43	109	.260	35	143	0	379	6	10	.975
1993—	Texas (A.L.)	OF-DH	140	536	105	166	33	1	*46	118	.310	37	99	4	265	5	4	.985

Year	Team (League)	Pos.	G	AB	R	H	2B	3B	HR	RBI	Avg.	BB	SO	SB	PO	A	E	Avg.
								BATTING								FIELDING		
1994— Texas (A.L.)		OF	107	422	57	116	18	4	19	85	.275	30	66	6	223	9	2	.991
1995— Texas (A.L.)		DH-OF	90	352	57	104	20	2	27	82	.295	17	66	0	6	1	0	1.000
1996— Texas (A.L.)		OF-DH	134	541	89	170	33	2	47	144	.314	45	82	2	163	6	2	.988
1997— Texas (A.L.)		DH-OF	133	533	87	158	24	3	42	131	.296	33	107	0	128	6	4	.971
1998— Texas (A.L.)		OF-DH	154	606	110	193	*50	2	45	*157	.318	46	126	2	213	8	4	.982
1999— Texas (A.L.)		OF-DH	144	562	114	183	36	1	39	128	.326	51	105	3	223	7	4	.983
2000— Detroit (A.L.)■		OF-DH	115	461	69	133	30	2	22	67	.289	32	84	1	118	2	1	.992
Major League totals (12 years)			1363	5292	860	1554	312	21	362	1142	.294	376	1031	22	2114	59	39	.982

DIVISION SERIES RECORD

RECORDS: Shares single-series record for most home runs—5 (1996). ... Shares single-game record for most home runs—2 (October 2, 1996).

NOTES: Shares postseason single-series record for most home runs—5 (1996).

Year	Team (League)	Pos.	G	AB	R	H	2B	3B	HR	RBI	Avg.	BB	SO	SB	PO	A	E	Avg.
								BATTING								FIELDING		
1996— Texas (A.L.)		OF	4	16	5	7	0	0	5	9	.438	4	2	0	8	0	0	1.000
1998— Texas (A.L.)		OF	3	12	1	1	1	0	0	0	.083	0	3	0	8	0	0	1.000
1999— Texas (A.L.)		OF	3	11	1	2	0	0	1	1	.182	1	3	0	5	0	0	1.000
Division series totals (3 years)			10	39	7	10	1	0	6	10	.256	5	8	0	21	0	0	1.000

ALL-STAR GAME RECORD

Year	League	Pos.	AB	R	H	2B	3B	HR	RBI	Avg.	BB	SO	SB	PO	A	E	Avg.
							BATTING								FIELDING		
1993— American		OF	1	0	0	0	0	0	0	.000	1	1	0	1	0	0	1.000
1998— American		OF	3	0	0	0	0	0	1	.000	0	1	0	0	0	0	
All-Star Game totals (2 years)			4	0	0	0	0	0	1	.000	1	2	0	1	0	0	1.000

GONZALEZ, LARIEL   P

PERSONAL: Born May 25, 1976, in San Cristobal, Dominican Republic. ... 6-4/228. ... Throws right, bats right. ... Full name: Lariel Alfonso Gonzalez.

HIGH SCHOOL: Americo Tolentino.

TRANSACTIONS/CAREER NOTES: Signed as non-drafted free agent by Colorado Rockies organization (May 19, 1993). ... On Colorado Springs disabled list (April 14-May 17, 1999). ... Traded by Rockies with P Bobby M. Jones to New York Mets for P Masato Yoshii (January 14, 2000). ... Granted free agency (December 21, 2000).

STATISTICAL NOTES: Tied for Northwest League lead with five balks in 1995.

Year	League	W	L	Pct.	ERA	G	GS	CG	ShO	Sv.	IP	H	R	ER	BB	SO
1993— DSL Rockies (DSL)		0	4	.000	9.38	14	7	0	0	1	24	32	34	25	46	17
1994— Arizona Rockies (Ariz.)		3	2	.600	4.71	16	1	0	0	0	28 2/3	28	24	15	21	23
1995— Portland (N'West)		3	4	.429	4.06	15	11	0	0	2	57 2/3	44	31	26	43	48
1996— Asheville (S.Atl.)		1	1	.500	3.60	35	0	0	0	4	45	37	21	18	37	53
1997— Salem (Caro.)		5	0	1.000	2.53	44	0	0	0	8	57	42	19	16	23	79
1998— New Haven (East.)		0	4	.000	4.19	58	0	0	0	22	58	46	30	27	40	63
— Colorado (N.L.)		0	0	...	0.00	1	0	0	0	0	1	0	0	0	0	0
1999— Colo. Springs (PCL)		0	1	.000	10.13	11	0	0	0	0	13 1/3	18	16	15	12	9
— Carolina (Sou.)		2	1	.667	5.29	30	0	0	0	14	34	39	27	20	22	41
2000— Norfolk (I.L.)■		5	5	.500	4.18	52	0	0	0	5	66 2/3	68	33	31	38	61
Major League totals (1 year)		0	0	...	0.00	1	0	0	0	0	1	0	0	0	0	0

GONZALEZ, LUIS   OF   DIAMONDBACKS

PERSONAL: Born September 2, 1967, in Tampa. ... 6-2/190. ... Bats left, throws right. ... Full name: Luis Emilio Gonzalez.

HIGH SCHOOL: Jefferson (Tampa).

COLLEGE: South Alabama.

TRANSACTIONS/CAREER NOTES: Selected by Houston Astros organization in fourth round of free-agent draft (June 1, 1988). ... On disabled list (May 26-July 5, 1989 and August 29-September 13, 1991). ... On Houston disabled list (July 21-August 5, 1992). ... Traded by Astros with C Scott Servais to Chicago Cubs for C Rick Wilkins (June 28, 1995). ... Granted free agency (December 7, 1996). ... Signed by Astros (December 19, 1996). ... Granted free agency (October 28, 1997). ... Signed by Detroit Tigers (December 9, 1997). ... Traded by Tigers to Arizona Diamondbacks for OF Karim Garcia (December 28, 1998).

STATISTICAL NOTES: Tied for Southern League lead with 12 sacrifice flies and nine intentional bases on balls received in 1990. ... Led N.L. with 10 sacrifice flies in 1993. ... Had 23-game hitting streak (May 26-June 20, 1997). ... Had 30-game hitting streak (April 11-May 18, 1999). ... Had 16-game hitting streak (August 16-September 1, 1999). ... Hit for the cycle (July 5, 2000). ... Career major league grand slams: 1.

MISCELLANEOUS: Holds Arizona Diamondbacks all-time record for highest career batting average (.323).

Year	Team (League)	Pos.	G	AB	R	H	2B	3B	HR	RBI	Avg.	BB	SO	SB	PO	A	E	Avg.
								BATTING								FIELDING		
1988— Asheville (S.Atl.)		3B	31	115	13	29	7	1	2	14	.252	12	17	2	19	62	6	.931
— Auburn (NY-Penn)		3B-SS-1B	39	157	32	49	10	3	5	27	.312	12	19	2	37	83	13	.902
1989— Osceola (FSL)		DH	86	287	46	82	16	7	6	38	.286	37	49	2	...	...	...	...
1990— Columbus (Sou.)		1B-3B	138	495	86	131	30	6	•24	89	.265	54	100	27	1039	88	23	.980
— Houston (N.L.)		3B-1B	12	21	1	4	2	0	0	0	.190	2	5	0	22	10	0	1.000
1991— Houston (N.L.)		OF	137	473	51	120	28	9	13	69	.254	40	101	10	294	6	5	.984
1992— Houston (N.L.)		OF	122	387	40	94	19	3	10	55	.243	24	52	7	261	5	2	.993
— Tucson (PCL)		OF	13	44	11	19	4	2	1	9	.432	5	7	4	26	0	1	.963
1993— Houston (N.L.)		OF	154	540	82	162	34	3	15	72	.300	47	83	20	347	10	8	.978
1994— Houston (N.L.)		OF	112	392	57	107	29	4	8	67	.273	49	57	15	228	5	2	.991
1995— Houston (N.L.)		OF	56	209	35	54	10	4	6	35	.258	18	30	1	94	2	2	.980
— Chicago (N.L.)■		OF	77	262	34	76	19	4	7	34	.290	39	33	5	172	5	4	.978

							BATTING									FIELDING		
Year Team (League)	Pos.	G	AB	R	H	2B	3B	HR	RBI	Avg.	BB	SO	SB	PO	A	E	Avg.
1996— Chicago (N.L.)............	OF-1B	146	483	70	131	30	4	15	79	.271	61	49	9	244	7	3	.988
1997— Houston (N.L.)■.......	OF-1B	152	550	78	142	31	2	10	68	.258	71	67	10	266	10	5	.982
1998— Detroit (A.L.)■...........	OF-DH	154	547	84	146	35	5	23	71	.267	57	62	12	232	8	3	.988
1999— Arizona (N.L.)■...........	OF-DH	153	614	112	*206	45	4	26	111	.336	66	63	9	271	10	5	.983
2000— Arizona (N.L.)............	OF	•162	618	106	192	47	2	31	114	.311	78	85	2	293	4	3	.990
American League totals (1 year)		154	547	84	146	35	5	23	71	.267	57	62	12	232	8	3	.988
National League totals (10 years)		1283	4549	666	1288	294	39	141	704	.283	495	625	88	2492	74	39	.985
Major League totals (11 years)		1437	5096	750	1434	329	44	164	775	.281	552	687	100	2724	82	42	.985

DIVISION SERIES RECORD

							BATTING									FIELDING		
Year Team (League)	Pos.	G	AB	R	H	2B	3B	HR	RBI	Avg.	BB	SO	SB	PO	A	E	Avg.
1997— Houston (N.L.)	OF	3	12	0	4	0	0	0	0	.333	0	1	0	13	1	1	.933
1999— Arizona (N.L.)	OF	4	10	3	2	1	0	1	2	.200	5	1	0	6	0	0	1.000
Division series totals (2 years)		7	22	3	6	1	0	1	2	.273	5	2	0	19	1	1	.952

ALL-STAR GAME RECORD

					BATTING									FIELDING		
Year League	Pos.	AB	R	H	2B	3B	HR	RBI	Avg.	BB	SO	SB	PO	A	E	Avg.
1999— National	OF	2	0	1	1	0	0	0	.500	0	0	0	0	0	0	...

GONZALEZ, WIKI — C — PADRES

PERSONAL: Born May 17, 1974, in Aragua, Venezuela. ... 5-11/203. ... Bats right, throws right. ... Full name: Wiklenman Vicente Gonzalez.

TRANSACTIONS/CAREER NOTES: Signed as non-drafted free agent by Pittsburgh Pirates organization (February 12, 1992). ... Selected by San Diego Padres organization from Pirates organization in Rule 5 minor league draft (December 9, 1996). ... Granted free agency (October 16, 1998). ... Re-signed by Padres organization (October 23, 1998). ... On Mobile disabled list (May 24-June 6, 1999).

							BATTING									FIELDING		
Year Team (League)	Pos.	G	AB	R	H	2B	3B	HR	RBI	Avg.	BB	SO	SB	PO	A	E	Avg.
1992— Dom. Pirates (DSL)....	C	63	190	20	48	6	1	3	33	.253	22	12	4	244	42	9	.969
1993— Dom. Pirates (DSL)....	C-IF	69	244	47	73	10	3	7	47	.299	40	15	24	506	48	8	.986
1994— GC Pirates (GCL).......	C-1B	41	143	25	48	8	2	4	26	.336	13	13	2	259	37	12	.961
1995— Augusta (S.Atl.).........	C	84	278	41	67	17	0	3	36	.241	26	32	5	345	43	6	.985
1996— Augusta (S.Atl.).........	C	118	419	52	106	21	3	4	62	.253	58	41	4	810	115	*23	.976
1997— Rancho Cuca. (Calif.)■	C	33	110	18	33	9	1	5	26	.300	7	25	1	117	17	2	.985
— Mobile (Sou.)	C	47	143	15	39	7	1	4	25	.273	10	12	1	250	24	3	.989
1998— Rancho Cuca. (Calif.) .	C	75	292	51	84	24	2	10	59	.288	26	54	0	346	56	3	.993
— Mobile (Sou.)	C	22	67	20	26	9	0	4	26	.388	14	4	0	65	7	0	1.000
1999— Mobile (Sou.)	C-DH	61	225	38	76	16	2	10	49	.338	29	28	0	329	43	7	.982
— Las Vegas (PCL)	C-DH	24	92	13	25	6	0	6	12	.272	5	10	0	175	10	3	.984
— San Diego (N.L.)	C	30	83	7	21	2	1	3	12	.253	1	8	0	109	15	1	.992
2000— San Diego (N.L.)	C	95	284	25	66	15	1	5	30	.232	30	31	1	525	42	5	.991
Major League totals (2 years)		125	367	32	87	17	2	8	42	.237	31	39	1	634	57	6	.991

GOODEN, DWIGHT — P — YANKEES

PERSONAL: Born November 16, 1964, in Tampa. ... 6-3/210. ... Throws right, bats right. ... Full name: Dwight Eugene Gooden. ... Uncle of Gary Sheffield, outfielder, Los Angeles Dodgers.

HIGH SCHOOL: Hillsborough (Tampa).

TRANSACTIONS/CAREER NOTES: Selected by New York Mets organization in first round (fifth pick overall) of free-agent draft (June 7, 1982). ... On New York disabled list (April 1-June 5, 1987); included rehabilitation assignment to Tidewater (May 12-17 and May 21-June 1). ... On disabled list (July 2-September 2, 1989; August 24, 1991-remainder of season and July 18-August 8, 1992). ... On suspended list (September 2-7, 1993). ... On New York disabled list (April 22-June 9, 1994); included rehabilitation assignments to Norfolk (May 30-June 4) and Binghamton (June 4-9). ... On suspended list (June 28, 1994-remainder of season). ... Granted free agency (October 24, 1994). ... On suspended list (November 4, 1994-entire 1995 season). ... Signed by New York Yankees (February 20, 1996). ... On New York disabled list (April 11-June 15, 1997); included rehabilitation assignment to Norwich (May 18-June 2). ... Granted free agency (November 1, 1997). ... Signed by Cleveland Indians (December 8, 1997). ... On Cleveland disabled list (March 22-May 20, 1998); included rehabilitation assignment to Buffalo (May 3-20). ... On Cleveland disabled list (August 3-31, 1999); included rehabilitation assignments to Akron (August 19-23) and Buffalo (August 24-31). ... Granted free agency (November 4, 1999). ... Signed by Houston Astros organization (January 6, 2000). ... Traded by Astros to Tampa Bay Devil Rays for cash (April 13, 2000). ... Released by Devil Rays (May 25, 2000). ... Signed by Yankees organization (June 11, 2000). ... On Columbus disabled list (June 24-July 8, 2000); included rehabilitation assignment to Gulf Coast Yankees (July 7-8). ... Granted free agency (November 10, 2000). ... Re-signed by Yankees organization (December 7, 2000).

RECORDS: Holds major league rookie-season record for most strikeouts—276 (1984). ... Holds N.L. record for most strikeouts in three consecutive games—43 (September 7 [11], 12 [16] and 17 [16], 1984).

HONORS: Named Carolina League Pitcher of the Year (1983). ... Named N.L. Rookie Pitcher of the Year by THE SPORTING NEWS (1984). ... Named N.L. Rookie of the Year by Baseball Writers' Association of America (1984). ... Named N.L. Pitcher of the Year by THE SPORTING NEWS (1985). ... Named righthanded pitcher on THE SPORTING NEWS N.L. All-Star team (1985). ... Named N.L. Cy Young Award winner by Baseball Writers' Association of America (1985). ... Named pitcher on THE SPORTING NEWS N.L. Silver Slugger team (1992).

STATISTICAL NOTES: Pitched 10-0 one-hit, complete-game victory against Chicago (September 7, 1984). ... Struck out 16 batters in one game (September 12 and September 17, 1984; August 20, 1985). ... Tied for N.L. lead with seven balks in 1984. ... Struck out 15 batters in one game (May 11, 1990). ... Pitched 2-0 no-hit victory against Seattle (May 14, 1996).

MISCELLANEOUS: Appeared in one game as pinch runner (1990). ... Singled and made an out in two appearances as pinch hitter (1992). ... Tripled with an RBI in only appearance as pinch hitter (1993).

G

Year League	W	L	Pct.	ERA	G	GS	CG	ShO	Sv.	IP	H	R	ER	BB	SO
1982—Kingsport (Appl.)	5	4	.556	2.47	9	9	4	2	0	65 2/3	53	34	18	25	66
— Little Falls (NY-Penn)	0	1	.000	4.15	2	2	0	0	0	13	11	6	6	3	18
1983—Lynchburg (Caro.)	*19	4	.826	*2.50	27	27	10	*6	0	191	121	58	53	*112	*300
1984—New York (N.L.)	17	9	.654	2.60	31	31	7	3	0	218	161	72	63	73	276
1985—New York (N.L.)	*24	4	.857	*1.53	35	35	*16	8	0	*276 2/3	198	51	47	69	*268
1986—New York (N.L.)	17	6	.739	2.84	33	33	12	2	0	250	197	92	79	80	200
1987—Tidewater (I.L.)	3	0	1.000	2.05	4	4	1	0	0	22	20	7	5	9	24
— Lynchburg (Caro.)	0	0	...	0.00	1	1	0	0	0	4	2	0	0	2	3
— New York (N.L.)	15	7	.682	3.21	25	25	7	3	0	179 2/3	162	68	64	53	148
1988—New York (N.L.)	18	9	.667	3.19	34	34	10	3	0	248 1/3	242	98	88	57	175
1989—New York (N.L.)	9	4	.692	2.89	19	17	0	0	1	118 1/3	93	42	38	47	101
1990—New York (N.L.)	19	7	.731	3.83	34	34	2	1	0	232 2/3	229	106	99	70	223
1991—New York (N.L.)	13	7	.650	3.60	27	27	3	1	0	190	180	86	76	56	150
1992—New York (N.L.)	10	13	.435	3.67	31	31	3	0	0	206	197	93	84	70	145
1993—New York (N.L.)	12	15	.444	3.45	29	29	7	2	0	208 2/3	188	89	80	61	149
1994—New York (N.L.)	3	4	.429	6.31	7	7	0	0	0	41 1/3	46	32	29	15	40
— Norfolk (I.L.)	0	0	...	0.00	1	1	0	0	0	3	0	0	0	1	4
— Binghamton (East.)	1	0	1.000	0.00	1	1	0	0	0	5	2	0	0	1	4
1995—							Out of organized baseball.								
1996—New York (A.L.)■	11	7	.611	5.01	29	29	1	1	0	170 2/3	169	101	95	88	126
1997—New York (A.L.)	9	5	.643	4.91	20	19	0	0	0	106 1/3	116	61	58	53	66
— Norwich (East.)	3	0	1.000	3.00	3	3	0	0	0	18	13	6	6	5	14
— Columbus (I.L.)	1	1	.500	3.75	2	2	0	0	0	12	7	5	5	4	10
1998—Buffalo (I.L.)■	1	2	.333	9.00	4	4	0	0	0	16	23	16	16	7	18
— Cleveland (A.L.)	8	6	.571	3.76	23	23	0	0	0	134	135	59	56	51	83
1999—Cleveland (A.L.)	3	4	.429	6.26	26	22	0	0	0	115	127	90	80	67	88
— Akron (East.)	0	0	...	3.00	1	1	0	0	0	3	3	2	1	1	2
— Buffalo (I.L.)	0	1	.000	2.45	1	1	0	0	0	3 2/3	6	1	1	3	3
2000—Houston (N.L.)■	0	0	...	9.00	1	1	0	0	0	4	6	4	4	3	1
— Tampa Bay (A.L.)■	2	3	.400	6.63	8	8	0	0	0	36 2/3	47	32	27	20	23
— GC Yankees (GCL)■	0	0	...	0.00	2	2	0	0	0	8	3	0	0	1	12
— New York (A.L.)	4	2	.667	3.36	18	5	0	0	2	64 1/3	66	28	24	21	31
A.L. totals (5 years)	37	27	.578	4.88	124	106	1	1	2	627	660	371	340	300	417
N.L. totals (12 years)	157	85	.649	3.11	306	304	67	23	1	2173 2/3	1904	827	751	654	1876
Major League totals (16 years)	194	112	.634	3.51	430	410	68	24	3	2800 2/3	2564	1198	1091	954	2293

DIVISION SERIES RECORD

Year League	W	L	Pct.	ERA	G	GS	CG	ShO	Sv.	IP	H	R	ER	BB	SO
1997—New York (A.L.)	0	0	...	1.59	1	1	0	0	0	5 2/3	5	1	1	3	5
1998—Cleveland (A.L.)	0	0	...	54.00	1	1	0	0	0	1/3	1	2	2	2	1
1999—Cleveland (A.L.)							Did not play.								
2000—New York (A.L.)	0	0	...	21.60	1	0	0	0	0	1 2/3	4	4	4	1	1
Division series totals (3 years)	0	0	...	8.22	3	2	0	0	0	7 2/3	10	7	7	6	7

CHAMPIONSHIP SERIES RECORD

RECORDS: Holds single-series record for most strikeouts—20 (1988). ... Shares N.L. single-game record for most innings pitched—10 (October 14, 1986).

Year League	W	L	Pct.	ERA	G	GS	CG	ShO	Sv.	IP	H	R	ER	BB	SO
1986—New York (N.L.)	0	1	.000	1.06	2	2	0	0	0	17	16	2	2	5	9
1988—New York (N.L.)	0	0	...	2.95	3	2	0	0	0	18 1/3	10	6	6	8	20
1998—Cleveland (A.L.)	0	1	.000	5.79	1	1	0	0	0	4 2/3	3	3	3	3	3
2000—New York (A.L.)	0	0	...	0.00	1	0	0	0	0	2 1/3	1	0	0	0	1
Champ. series totals (4 years)	0	2	.000	2.34	7	5	0	0	0	42 1/3	30	11	11	16	33

WORLD SERIES RECORD

NOTES: Member of World Series championship team (1986 and 2000). ... Member of World Series championship team (1996); inactive.

Year League	W	L	Pct.	ERA	G	GS	CG	ShO	Sv.	IP	H	R	ER	BB	SO
1986—New York (N.L.)	0	2	.000	8.00	2	2	0	0	0	9	17	10	8	4	9
2000—New York (A.L.)							Did not play.								

ALL-STAR GAME RECORD

RECORDS: Holds career record for most balks—2. ... Shares career record for most games lost—2.

Year League	W	L	Pct.	ERA	GS	CG	ShO	Sv.	IP	H	R	ER	BB	SO
1984—National	0	0	...	0.00	0	0	0	0	2	1	0	0	0	3
1985—National						Did not play.								
1986—National	0	1	.000	6.00	1	0	0	0	3	3	2	2	0	2
1988—National	0	1	.000	3.00	1	0	0	0	3	3	1	1	1	1
All-Star Game totals (3 years)	0	2	.000	3.38	2	0	0	0	8	7	3	3	1	6

G

GOODWIN, TOM — OF — DODGERS

PERSONAL: Born July 27, 1968, in Fresno, Calif. ... 6-1/175. ... Bats left, throws right. ... Full name: Thomas Jones Goodwin.

HIGH SCHOOL: Central (Fresno, Calif.).

COLLEGE: Fresno State.

TRANSACTIONS/CAREER NOTES: Selected by Pittsburgh Pirates organization in sixth round of free-agent draft (June 2, 1986); did not sign. ... Selected by Los Angeles Dodgers organization in first round (22nd pick overall) of free-agent draft (June 5, 1989). ... Claimed on waivers by Kansas City Royals (January 6, 1994). ... Traded by Royals to Texas Rangers for 3B Dean Palmer (July 25, 1997). ... On Texas disabled list (June 11-27 and June 28-August 6, 1999); included rehabilitation assignment to Charlotte (August 2-6). ... Granted free agency (October 28, 1999). ... Signed by Colorado Rockies (December 9, 1999). ... Traded by Rockies with cash to Dodgers for OF Todd Hollandsworth, OF Kevin Gibbs and P Randey Dorame (July 31, 2000).

HONORS: Named outfielder on THE SPORTING NEWS college All-America team (1989).

STATISTICAL NOTES: Tied for Pacific Coast League lead in caught stealing with 23 in 1991. ... Led American Association in caught stealing with 20 in 1994. ... Led A.L. in sacrifice hits with 14 in 1995 and 21 in 1996. ... Led A.L. in caught stealing with 22 in 1996 and 20 in 1998. ... Career major league grand slams: 1.
MISCELLANEOUS: Member of 1988 U.S. Olympic baseball team.

						BATTING									FIELDING		
Year Team (League)	Pos.	G	AB	R	H	2B	3B	HR	RBI	Avg.	BB	SO	SB	PO	A	E	Avg.
1989— Great Falls (Pio.)	OF	63	240	*55	74	12	3	2	33	.308	28	30	*60	67	3	1	.986
1990— San Antonio (Texas) ...	OF	102	428	76	119	15	4	0	28	.278	38	72	*60	264	7	3	*.989
— Bakersfield (Calif.)	OF	32	134	24	39	6	2	0	13	.291	11	22	22	55	2	0	1.000
1991— Albuquerque (PCL)	OF	132	509	84	139	19	4	1	45	.273	59	83	48	284	6	3	.990
— Los Angeles (N.L.)	OF	16	7	3	1	0	0	0	0	.143	0	0	1	8	0	0	1.000
1992— Albuquerque (PCL)	OF	82	319	48	96	10	4	2	28	.301	37	47	27	184	5	1	.995
— Los Angeles (N.L.)	OF	57	73	15	17	1	1	0	3	.233	6	10	7	43	0	0	1.000
1993— Los Angeles (N.L.)	OF	30	17	6	5	1	0	0	1	.294	1	4	1	8	0	0	1.000
— Albuquerque (PCL)	OF	85	289	48	75	5	5	1	28	.260	30	51	21	145	1	2	.986
1994— Kansas City (A.L.)■ ...	DH-OF	2	2	0	0	0	0	0	0	.000	0	1	0	1	0	0	1.000
— Omaha (A.A.)	OF	113	429	67	132	17	7	2	34	.308	23	60	*50	276	3	2	.993
1995— Kansas City (A.L.)	OF-DH	133	480	72	138	16	3	4	28	.288	38	72	50	292	6	3	.990
1996— Kansas City (A.L.)	OF-DH	143	524	80	148	14	4	1	35	.282	39	79	66	303	7	5	.984
1997— Kansas City (A.L.)	OF	97	367	51	100	13	4	2	22	.272	19	51	34	232	3	1	.996
— Texas (A.L.)■............	OF	53	207	39	49	13	2	0	17	.237	25	37	16	138	3	2	.986
1998— Texas (A.L.)	OF-DH	154	520	102	151	13	3	2	33	.290	73	90	38	370	5	3	.992
1999— Texas (A.L.)	OF	109	405	63	105	12	6	3	33	.259	40	61	39	258	4	3	.989
— Charlotte (FSL)	OF	3	11	2	4	1	0	0	0	.364	1	4	0	8	0	0	1.000
2000— Colorado (N.L.)■	OF	91	317	65	86	8	8	5	47	.271	50	76	39	208	3	3	.986
— Los Angeles (N.L.)■ ..	OF	56	211	29	53	3	1	1	11	.251	18	41	16	138	2	0	1.000
American League totals (6 years)		691	2505	407	691	81	22	12	168	.276	234	391	243	1594	28	17	.990
National League totals (4 years)		250	625	118	162	13	10	6	62	.259	75	131	64	405	5	3	.993
Major League totals (10 years)		941	3130	525	853	94	32	18	230	.273	309	522	307	1999	33	20	.990

DIVISION SERIES RECORD

						BATTING									FIELDING		
Year Team (League)	Pos.	G	AB	R	H	2B	3B	HR	RBI	Avg.	BB	SO	SB	PO	A	E	Avg.
1998— Texas (A.L.)	OF	2	4	0	1	0	0	0	0	.250	0	1	0	1	0	0	1.000
1999— Texas (A.L.)	OF	3	7	0	1	0	0	0	0	.143	0	1	0	6	0	0	1.000
Division series totals (2 years)		5	11	0	2	0	0	0	0	.182	0	2	0	7	0	0	1.000

GRABOWSKI, JASON   3B   RANGERS

PERSONAL: Born May 24, 1976, in New Haven, Conn. ... 6-3/200. ... Bats left, throws right. ... Full name: Jason William Grabowski.
HIGH SCHOOL: The Morgan School (Clinton, Conn.).
COLLEGE: Connecticut.
TRANSACTIONS/CAREER NOTES: Selected by New York Yankees organization in 17th round of free-agent draft (June 2, 1994); did not sign. ... Selected by Texas Rangers organization in second round of free-agent draft (June 3, 1997).

						BATTING									FIELDING		
Year Team (League)	Pos.	G	AB	R	H	2B	3B	HR	RBI	Avg.	BB	SO	SB	PO	A	E	Avg.
1997— Pulaski (Appl.)	C	50	174	36	51	14	0	4	24	.293	40	32	6	386	40	8	.982
1998— Savannah (S.Atl.)	C-1B	104	352	63	95	13	6	14	52	.270	57	93	16	573	50	6	.990
1999— Charlotte (FSL)	3B-1B	123	434	68	136	31	6	12	87	.313	65	66	13	100	199	27	.917
— Tulsa (Texas)	DH	2	6	1	1	0	0	0	0	.167	2	2	0	...	...	...	...
2000— Tulsa (Texas)	3B	135	493	93	135	33	5	19	90	.274	88	106	8	•84	270	*40	.898

GRACE, MARK   1B   DIAMONDBACKS

PERSONAL: Born June 28, 1964, in Winston-Salem, N.C. ... 6-2/200. ... Bats left, throws left. ... Full name: Mark Eugene Grace.
HIGH SCHOOL: Tustin (Calif.).
JUNIOR COLLEGE: Saddleback Community College (Calif.).
COLLEGE: San Diego State.
TRANSACTIONS/CAREER NOTES: Selected by Minnesota Twins organization in 15th round of free-agent draft (January 17, 1984); did not sign. ... Selected by Chicago Cubs organization in 24th round of free-agent draft (June 3, 1985). ... On disabled list (June 5-23, 1989). ... Granted free agency (October 15, 1994). ... Re-signed by Cubs (April 7, 1995). ... Granted free agency (November 3, 1995). ... Re-signed by Cubs (December 19, 1995). ... On disabled list (June 11-28, 1996; and April 4-19, 1997). ... On disabled list (May 11-31, 2000). ... Granted free agency (October 30, 2000). ... Signed by Arizona Diamondbacks (December 8, 2000).
RECORDS: Holds major league single-season record for fewest double plays by first baseman (150 or more games)—82 (1998). ... Shares major league record for most assists by first baseman in one inning—3 (May 23, 1990, fourth inning). ... Holds N.L. single-season record for most assists by first baseman—180 (1990).
HONORS: Named Eastern League Most Valuable Player (1987). ... Named N.L. Rookie Player of the Year by THE SPORTING NEWS (1988). ... Won N.L. Gold Glove at first base (1992-93 and 1995-96).
STATISTICAL NOTES: Led Midwest League first basemen with 103 double plays in 1986. ... Led Eastern League with .545 slugging percentage in 1987. ... Led N.L. first basemen with 1,695 total chances in 1991, 1,725 in 1992 and 1,573 in 1993. ... Tied for N.L. lead in grounding into double plays with 25 in 1993. ... Led N.L. first basemen with 134 double plays in 1993. ... Hit for the cycle (May 9, 1993). ... Tied for N.L. lead with 10 sacrifice flies in 1999. ... Career major league grand slams: 2.

						BATTING									FIELDING		
Year Team (League)	Pos.	G	AB	R	H	2B	3B	HR	RBI	Avg.	BB	SO	SB	PO	A	E	Avg.
1986— Peoria (Midw.)	1B-OF	126	465	81	159	30	4	15	95	*.342	60	28	6	1050	69	13	.989
1987— Pittsfield (East.)	1B	123	453	81	151	29	8	17	*101	.333	48	24	5	1054	*96	6	*.995
1988— Iowa (A.A.)	1B	21	67	11	17	4	0	0	14	.254	13	4	1	189	20	1	.995
— Chicago (N.L.)	1B	134	486	65	144	23	4	7	57	.296	60	43	3	1182	87	•17	.987

G

Year	Team (League)	Pos.	G	AB	R	H	2B	3B	HR	RBI	Avg.	BB	SO	SB	PO	A	E	Avg.
								BATTING								FIELDING		
1989—	Chicago (N.L.)	1B	142	510	74	160	28	3	13	79	.314	80	42	14	1230	126	6	.996
1990—	Chicago (N.L.)	1B	157	589	72	182	32	1	9	82	.309	59	54	15	1324	*180	12	.992
1991—	Chicago (N.L.)	1B	160	*619	87	169	28	5	8	58	.273	70	53	3	*1520	*167	8	.995
1992—	Chicago (N.L.)	1B	158	603	72	185	37	5	9	79	.307	72	36	6	*1580	*141	4	.998
1993—	Chicago (N.L.)	1B	155	594	86	193	39	4	14	98	.325	71	32	8	*1456	112	5	.997
1994—	Chicago (N.L.)	1B	106	403	55	120	23	3	6	44	.298	48	41	0	925	78	7	.993
1995—	Chicago (N.L.)	1B	143	552	97	180	*51	3	16	92	.326	65	46	6	1211	114	7	.995
1996—	Chicago (N.L.)	1B	142	547	88	181	39	1	9	75	.331	62	41	2	1259	107	4	.997
1997—	Chicago (N.L.)	1B	151	555	87	177	32	5	13	78	.319	88	45	2	1202	120	6	.995
1998—	Chicago (N.L.)	1B	158	595	92	184	39	3	17	89	.309	93	56	4	1279	122	8	.994
1999—	Chicago (N.L.)	1B	161	593	107	183	44	5	16	91	.309	83	44	3	1335	93	8	.994
2000—	Chicago (N.L.)	1B	143	510	75	143	41	1	11	82	.280	95	28	1	1098	103	4	*.997
Major League totals (13 years)			1910	7156	1057	2201	456	43	148	1004	.308	946	561	67	16601	1550	96	.995

DIVISION SERIES RECORD

Year	Team (League)	Pos.	G	AB	R	H	2B	3B	HR	RBI	Avg.	BB	SO	SB	PO	A	E	Avg.
								BATTING								FIELDING		
1998—	Chicago (N.L.)	1B	3	12	0	1	0	0	0	1	.083	0	2	0	20	2	0	1.000

CHAMPIONSHIP SERIES RECORD

NOTES: Hit home run in first at-bat (October 4, 1989).

Year	Team (League)	Pos.	G	AB	R	H	2B	3B	HR	RBI	Avg.	BB	SO	SB	PO	A	E	Avg.
								BATTING								FIELDING		
1989—	Chicago (N.L.)	1B	5	17	3	11	3	1	1	8	.647	4	1	1	44	3	0	1.000

ALL-STAR GAME RECORD

Year	League	Pos.	AB	R	H	2B	3B	HR	RBI	Avg.	BB	SO	SB	PO	A	E	Avg.
							BATTING								FIELDING		
1993—	National	DH	3	0	0	0	0	0	0	.000	0	0	0	...	...	...	...
1995—	National	1B	0	0	0	0	0	0	0	...	0	0	0	1	0	0	1.000
1997—	National	1B	1	0	0	0	0	0	0	.000	0	0	0	1	0	0	1.000
All-Star Game totals (3 years)			4	0	0	0	0	0	0	.000	0	0	0	2	0	0	1.000

GRAFFANINO, TONY — SS/2B — WHITE SOX

PERSONAL: Born June 6, 1972, in Amityville, N.Y. ... 6-1/195. ... Bats right, throws right. ... Full name: Anthony Joseph Graffanino. ... Name pronounced GRAF-uh-NEE-noh.

HIGH SCHOOL: East Islip (Islip Terrace, N.Y.).

TRANSACTIONS/CAREER NOTES: Selected by Atlanta Braves organization in 10th round of free-agent draft (June 4, 1990). ... On disabled list (July 3, 1995-remainder of season). ... Released by Braves (April 2, 1999). ... Signed by Tampa Bay Devil Rays organization (April 9, 1999). ... Traded by Devil Rays to Chicago White Sox for P Tanyon Sturtze (May 31, 2000).

STATISTICAL NOTES: Led Pioneer League shortstops with 41 double plays in 1991. ... Led Carolina League second basemen with .968 fielding percentage in 1993. ... Led International League second basemen with 441 total chances in 1996. ... Career major league grand slams: 1.

Year	Team (League)	Pos.	G	AB	R	H	2B	3B	HR	RBI	Avg.	BB	SO	SB	PO	A	E	Avg.
								BATTING								FIELDING		
1990—	Pulaski (Appl.)	SS	42	131	23	27	5	1	0	11	.206	26	17	6	60	105	24	.873
1991—	Idaho Falls (Pio.)	SS	66	274	53	95	16	4	4	56	.347	27	37	19	112	187	*29	.912
1992—	Macon (S.Atl.)	2B	112	400	50	96	15	5	10	31	.240	50	84	9	178	239	17	.961
1993—	Durham (Caro.) ...	2B-DH-SS	123	459	78	126	30	5	15	69	.275	45	78	24	186	263	15	†.968
1994—	Greenville (Sou.) ...	2B-DH	124	440	66	132	28	3	7	52	.300	50	53	29	254	326	14	.976
1995—	Richmond (I.L.)	2B	50	179	20	34	6	0	4	17	.190	15	49	2	102	127	4	.983
1996—	Richmond (I.L.)	2B	96	353	57	100	29	2	7	33	.283	34	72	11	*215	216	10	.977
—	Atlanta (N.L.)	2B	22	46	7	8	1	1	0	2	.174	4	13	0	24	39	2	.969
1997—	Atlanta (N.L.) ...	2B-3B-SS-1B	104	186	33	48	9	1	8	20	.258	26	46	6	90	180	5	.982
1998—	Atlanta (N.L.) ...	2B-SS-3B	105	289	32	61	14	1	5	22	.211	24	68	1	139	227	11	.971
1999—	Durham (I.L.) ■	2B-DH-3B	87	345	66	108	25	6	9	58	.313	37	46	16	182	233	1	.998
—	Tampa Bay (A.L.) ...	2B-SS-DH-3B	39	130	20	41	9	4	2	19	.315	9	22	3	66	114	5	.973
2000—	Tampa Bay (A.L.) ...	2B-3B-SS	13	20	8	6	1	0	0	1	.300	1	2	0	14	19	0	1.000
—	Durham (I.L.)	SS-2B-1B-3B	10	35	9	10	3	0	2	6	.286	7	8	2	13	27	0	1.000
—	Chicago (A.L.) ■	SS-2B-3B-DH	57	148	25	40	5	1	2	16	.270	21	25	7	61	122	6	.968
American League totals (2 years)			109	298	53	87	15	5	4	36	.292	31	49	10	141	255	11	.973
National League totals (3 years)			231	521	72	117	24	3	13	44	.225	54	127	7	253	446	18	.975
Major League totals (5 years)			340	819	125	204	39	8	17	80	.249	85	176	17	394	701	29	.974

DIVISION SERIES RECORD

Year	Team (League)	Pos.	G	AB	R	H	2B	3B	HR	RBI	Avg.	BB	SO	SB	PO	A	E	Avg.
								BATTING								FIELDING		
1997—	Atlanta (N.L.)	2B	3	3	0	0	0	0	0	0	.000	2	1	0	1	6	0	1.000
1998—	Atlanta (N.L.)	PH	1	0	0	0	0	0	0	0	...	0	0	0	...	...	...	...
2000—	Chicago (A.L.)	PR-3B	1	0	0	0	0	0	0	0	...	0	0	0	0	1	0	1.000
Division series totals (3 years)			5	3	0	0	0	0	0	0	.000	2	1	0	1	7	0	1.000

CHAMPIONSHIP SERIES RECORD

Year	Team (League)	Pos.	G	AB	R	H	2B	3B	HR	RBI	Avg.	BB	SO	SB	PO	A	E	Avg.
								BATTING								FIELDING		
1997—	Atlanta (N.L.)	2B	3	8	1	2	1	0	0	0	.250	0	3	0	4	2	0	1.000
1998—	Atlanta (N.L.)	PH-2B	4	3	2	1	1	0	0	1	.333	2	1	0	2	5	0	1.000
Championship series totals (2 years)			7	11	3	3	2	0	0	1	.273	2	4	0	6	7	0	1.000

G

PERSONAL: Born August 7, 1973, in Saigon, Vietnam. ... 5-11/185. ... Throws right, bats right. ... Full name: Daniel Peter Graves.
HIGH SCHOOL: Brandon (Fla.).
COLLEGE: Miami (Fla.).
TRANSACTIONS/CAREER NOTES: Selected by Cleveland Indians organization in fourth round of free-agent draft (June 2, 1994). ... Traded by Indians with P Jim Crowell, P Scott Winchester and IF Damian Jackson to Cincinnati Reds for P John Smiley and IF Jeff Branson (July 31, 1997).

Year League	W	L	Pct.	ERA	G	GS	CG	ShO	Sv.	IP	H	R	ER	BB	SO
1995—Kinston (Caro.)	3	1	.750	0.82	38	0	0	0	21	44	30	11	4	12	46
—Canton/Akron (East.)	1	0	1.000	0.00	17	0	0	0	10	23 $\frac{1}{3}$	10	1	0	2	11
—Buffalo (A.A.)	0	0	...	3.00	3	0	0	0	0	3	5	4	1	1	2
1996—Buffalo (A.A.)	4	3	.571	1.48	43	0	0	0	19	79	57	14	13	24	46
—Cleveland (A.L.)	2	0	1.000	4.55	15	0	0	0	0	29 $\frac{2}{3}$	29	18	15	10	22
1997—Buffalo (A.A.)	2	3	.400	4.19	19	3	0	0	2	43	45	21	20	11	21
—Cleveland (A.L.)	0	0	...	4.76	5	0	0	0	0	11 $\frac{1}{3}$	15	8	6	9	4
—Indianapolis (A.A.)■	1	0	1.000	3.09	11	0	0	0	5	11 $\frac{2}{3}$	7	4	4	5	5
—Cincinnati (N.L.)	0	0	...	6.14	10	0	0	0	0	14 $\frac{2}{3}$	26	14	10	11	7
1998—Indianapolis (I.L.)	1	0	1.000	1.93	13	0	0	0	0	14	15	3	3	3	11
—Cincinnati (N.L.)	2	1	.667	3.32	62	0	0	0	8	81 $\frac{1}{3}$	76	31	30	28	44
1999—Cincinnati (N.L.)	8	7	.533	3.08	75	0	0	0	27	111	90	42	38	49	69
2000—Cincinnati (N.L.)	10	5	.667	2.56	66	0	0	0	30	91 $\frac{1}{3}$	81	31	26	42	53
A.L. totals (2 years)	2	0	1.000	4.61	20	0	0	0	0	41	44	26	21	19	26
N.L. totals (4 years)	20	13	.606	3.14	213	0	0	0	65	298 $\frac{1}{3}$	273	118	104	130	173
Major League totals (5 years)	22	13	.629	3.32	233	0	0	0	65	339 $\frac{1}{3}$	317	144	125	149	199

ALL-STAR GAME RECORD

Year League	W	L	Pct.	ERA	GS	CG	ShO	Sv.	IP	H	R	ER	BB	SO
2000—National	0	0	...	0.00	0	0	0	0	1	1	0	0	0	1

PERSONAL: Born December 29, 1964, in Johnstown, Pa. ... 5-7/155. ... Bats right, throws right. ... Full name: Craig Allen Grebeck. ... Brother of Brian Grebeck, infielder with California Angels and Houston Astros organizations (1990-97). ... Name pronounced GRAY-bek.
HIGH SCHOOL: Lakewood (Calif.).
COLLEGE: Cal State Dominguez Hills.
TRANSACTIONS/CAREER NOTES: Signed as non-drafted free agent by Chicago White Sox organization (August 13, 1986). ... On disabled list (August 9, 1992-remainder of season). ... On Chicago disabled list (May 21-June 30, 1994); included rehabilitation assignment at Nashville (June 23-30). ... Granted free agency (December 21, 1995). ... Signed by Florida Marlins organization (December 22, 1995). ... On disabled list (July 4-August 13, 1996). ... Granted free agency (October 31, 1996). ... Signed by Anaheim Angels (December 6, 1996). ... Granted free agency (October 9, 1997). ... Signed by Toronto Blue Jays organization (November 27, 1997). ... On Toronto disabled list (April 20-May 5, 1998). ... Granted free agency (October 23, 1998). ... Re-signed by Blue Jays (October 27, 1998). ... On Toronto disabled list (April 11-May 14 and August 5, 1998-remainder of season); included rehabilitation assignment to Syracuse (May 10-14). ... Granted free agency (November 1, 2000). ... Signed by Boston Red Sox organization (January 19, 2001).
STATISTICAL NOTES: Led Southern League in grounding into double plays with 15 in 1989. ... Career major league grand slams: 1.

Year Team (League)	Pos.	G	AB	R	H	2B	3B	HR	RBI	Avg.	BB	SO	SB	PO	A	E	Avg.
1987—Peninsula (Caro.)	SS-3B	104	378	63	106	22	3	15	67	.280	37	62	3	137	278	16	.963
1988—Birmingham (Sou.)	2B	133	450	57	126	21	1	9	53	.280	65	72	5	238	368	19	.970
1989—Birmingham (Sou.)	SS-3B-2B	•143	•533	85	*153	25	4	5	80	.287	63	77	14	234	364	28	.955
1990—Chicago (A.L.)	3B-SS-2B	59	119	7	20	3	1	1	9	.168	8	24	0	36	98	3	.978
—Vancouver (PCL)	SS-3B-2B	12	41	8	8	0	0	1	3	.195	6	7	1	28	26	1	.982
1991—Chicago (A.L.)	3B-2B-SS	107	224	37	63	16	3	6	31	.281	38	40	1	104	183	10	.966
1992—Chicago (A.L.)	SS-3B-OF	88	287	24	77	21	2	3	35	.268	30	34	0	112	283	8	.980
1993—Chicago (A.L.)	SS-2B-3B	72	190	25	43	5	0	1	12	.226	26	26	1	91	185	5	.982
1994—Chicago (A.L.)	2B-SS	35	97	17	30	5	0	0	5	.309	12	5	0	44	65	2	.982
—Nashville (A.A.)	SS	5	15	3	6	2	0	0	4	.400	1	2	0	5	12	1	.944
1995—Chicago (A.L.)	SS-3B-2B	53	154	19	40	12	0	1	18	.260	21	23	0	76	127	7	.967
1996—Florida (N.L.)■	2B-SS-3B	50	95	8	20	1	0	1	9	.211	4	14	0	67	66	2	.985
1997—Anaheim (A.L.)■	2-S-3-O-DH	63	126	12	34	9	0	1	6	.270	18	11	0	68	88	2	.987
1998—Toronto (A.L.)■	2B-SS-3B	102	301	33	77	17	2	2	27	.256	29	42	2	151	269	11	.974
—Syracuse (I.L.)	2B	1	3	0	1	0	0	0	0	.333	0	0	0	2	6	0	1.000
1999—Toronto (A.L.)	2B-DH-SS-3B	34	113	18	41	7	0	0	10	.363	15	13	0	42	45	5	.946
—Syracuse (I.L.)	2B-SS	4	16	3	4	1	0	1	2	.250	1	1	0	9	10	2	.905
2000—Toronto (A.L.)	2B-SS	66	241	38	71	19	0	3	23	.295	25	33	0	110	193	9	.971
American League totals (10 years)		679	1852	230	496	114	8	18	176	.268	222	251	4	834	1536	62	.975
National League totals (1 year)		50	95	8	20	1	0	1	9	.211	4	14	0	67	66	2	.985
Major League totals (11 years)		729	1947	238	516	115	8	19	185	.265	226	265	4	901	1602	64	.975

CHAMPIONSHIP SERIES RECORD

Year Team (League)	Pos.	G	AB	R	H	2B	3B	HR	RBI	Avg.	BB	SO	SB	PO	A	E	Avg.
1993—Chicago (A.L.)	PH-3B	1	1	0	1	0	0	0	0	1.000	0	0	0	0	0	0	...

G

PERSONAL: Born June 28, 1975, in Dunkirk, N.Y. ... 5-10/180. ... Bats both, throws right. ... Full name: Chad Elton Green.
HIGH SCHOOL: Mentor (Ohio).
COLLEGE: Kentucky.

TRANSACTIONS/CAREER NOTES: Selected by Kansas City Royals organization in ninth round of free-agent draft (June 3, 1993); did not sign. ... Selected by Milwaukee Brewers organization in first round (eighth pick overall) of free-agent draft (June 4, 1996). ... On Stockton disabled list (April 2-May 8 and June 24-July 18, 1998). ... On El Paso disabled list (July 27-August 10, 1998). ... Traded by Brewers to San Diego Padres for P Wil Cunnane (December 20, 2000), completing deal in which Brewers traded SS Santiago Perez and a player to be named later or cash to San Deigo Padres for P Brandon Kolb (December 1, 2000).

STATISTICAL NOTES: Led California League outfielders with 311 total chances in 1997. ... Led Southern League outfielders with six double plays in 2000.

MISCELLANEOUS: Member of 1996 U.S. Olympic baseball team.

Year	Team (League)	Pos.	G	AB	R	H	2B	3B	HR	RBI	Avg.	BB	SO	SB	PO	A	E	Avg.
1996—	Ogden (Pio.)	OF	21	81	22	29	4	1	3	8	.358	15	23	12	53	3	0	1.000
1997—	Stockton (Calif.)	OF	127	513	78	128	26	14	2	43	.250	37	138	37	*291	11	9	.971
1998—	Stockton (Calif.)	OF	40	151	30	52	13	2	0	17	.344	12	22	22	61	6	0	1.000
	— El Paso (Texas)	PH	7	6	0	0	0	0	0	0	.000	1	3	0	0	0	0	...
1999—	Huntsville (Sou.)	OF	116	422	56	104	22	3	10	46	.246	46	109	28	240	6	4	.984
2000—	Huntsville (Sou.)	OF	85	317	44	74	22	2	3	27	.233	29	85	19	204	9	4	.982
	— Indianapolis (I.L.)	OF	43	123	18	25	8	2	3	10	.203	10	36	6	86	2	3	.967

GREEN, JASON   P

PERSONAL: Born June 5, 1975, in Port Hope, Ont. ... 6-1/205. ... Throws right, bats right. ... Full name: David Jason Green.
HIGH SCHOOL: District High School (Port Hope, Ont.).
JUNIOR COLLEGE: Chipola Junior College (Fla.).
TRANSACTIONS/CAREER NOTES: Selected by Houston Astros organization in 30th round of free-agent draft (June 3, 1993). ... On disabled list (July 1-September 11, 1996). ... On Jackson disabled list (May 1-28, 1999). ... Claimed on waivers by Colorado Rockies (October 13, 2000). ... Released by Rockies (November 20, 2000).

Year	League	W	L	Pct.	ERA	G	GS	CG	ShO	Sv.	IP	H	R	ER	BB	SO
1994—	Gulf Coast Astros (GCL)	2	1	.667	2.74	18	0	0	0	1	23	16	11	7	16	12
1995—	Auburn (NY-Penn)	8	2	.800	3.81	14	14	2	•1	0	82 2/3	82	48	35	29	48
1996—	Auburn (NY-Penn)	0	0	...	0.00	2	2	0	0	0	6	4	1	0	1	2
1997—	Kissimmee (FSL)	0	3	.000	5.19	8	0	0	0	0	8 2/3	11	12	5	10	3
	— Quad City (Midw.)	7	12	.368	4.58	23	22	1	0	0	125 2/3	126	79	64	53	96
1998—	Kissimmee (FSL)	2	5	.286	3.34	51	3	0	0	14	67 1/3	64	34	25	32	67
1999—	Jackson (Texas)	3	3	.500	3.40	33	0	0	0	10	42 1/3	41	20	16	20	50
2000—	Round Rock (Texas)	8	2	.800	1.98	31	0	0	0	15	41	38	10	9	11	54
	— New Orleans (PCL)	2	1	.667	2.08	10	0	0	0	1	13	10	3	3	4	12
	— Houston (N.L.)	1	1	.500	6.62	14	0	0	0	0	17 2/3	15	16	13	20	19
Major League totals (1 year)		1	1	.500	6.62	14	0	0	0	0	17 2/3	15	16	13	20	19

GREEN, SCARBOROUGH   OF   CUBS

PERSONAL: Born June 9, 1974, in Creve Coeur, Mo. ... 5-10/170. ... Bats both, throws right. ... Full name: Bertrum Scarborough Green.
HIGH SCHOOL: Lafayette (Ballwin, Mo.).
JUNIOR COLLEGE: St. Louis Community College at Meramec.
TRANSACTIONS/CAREER NOTES: Selected by St. Louis Cardinals organization in 10th round of free-agent draft (June 1, 1992). ... Claimed on waivers by Texas Rangers organization (September 8, 1998). ... Released by Rangers (November 17, 2000). ... Signed by Chicago Cubs organization (December 13, 2000).
STATISTICAL NOTES: Tied for Texas League lead with four intentional bases on balls in 1997.

Year	Team (League)	Pos.	G	AB	R	H	2B	3B	HR	RBI	Avg.	BB	SO	SB	PO	A	E	Avg.
1993—	Ariz. Cardinals (Ariz.)	SS	33	95	16	21	3	1	0	11	.221	7	17	3	35	87	14	.897
1994—	Johnson City (Appl.)	SS-OF	54	199	32	48	5	0	0	11	.241	25	61	22	58	140	22	.900
1995—	Savannah (S.Atl.)	SS	132	429	48	98	7	6	1	25	.228	55	101	26	*205	358	51	.917
1996—	St. Petersburg (FSL)	OF	36	140	26	41	4	1	1	11	.293	21	22	13	90	4	2	.979
	— Arkansas (Texas)	OF	92	300	45	60	6	3	3	24	.200	38	58	21	194	7	2	.990
1997—	Arkansas (Texas)	OF	76	251	45	77	14	4	2	29	.307	36	48	11	170	8	1	.994
	— Louisville (A.A.)	OF	52	209	26	53	11	2	3	13	.254	22	55	10	138	7	1	.993
	— St. Louis (N.L.)	OF	20	31	5	3	0	0	0	1	.097	2	5	0	19	1	1	.952
1998—	Memphis (PCL)	OF	26	81	11	16	5	0	0	2	.198	8	22	1	48	1	0	1.000
	— Arkansas (Texas)	OF	18	75	16	27	2	1	2	9	.360	6	12	9	44	1	0	1.000
1999—	Texas (A.L.)■	OF-DH	18	13	4	4	0	0	0	0	.308	1	2	0	6	0	0	1.000
	— Oklahoma (PCL)	OF	104	359	68	89	16	6	3	29	.248	34	86	26	219	13	6	.975
2000—	Oklahoma (PCL)	OF	27	99	20	31	6	0	1	10	.313	22	24	14	62	3	1	.985
	— Texas (A.L.)	OF-DH	79	124	21	29	1	1	0	9	.234	10	26	10	102	8	0	1.000
American League totals (2 years)			97	137	25	33	1	1	0	9	.241	11	28	10	108	8	0	1.000
National League totals (1 year)			20	31	5	3	0	0	0	1	.097	2	5	0	19	1	1	.952
Major League totals (3 years)			117	168	30	36	1	1	0	10	.214	13	33	10	127	9	1	.993

G

GREEN, SHAWN   OF   DODGERS

PERSONAL: Born November 10, 1972, in Des Plaines, Ill. ... 6-4/200. ... Bats left, throws left. ... Full name: Shawn David Green.
HIGH SCHOOL: Tustin (Calif.).
TRANSACTIONS/CAREER NOTES: Selected by Toronto Blue Jays organization in first round (16th pick overall) of free-agent draft (June 3, 1991); pick received as compensation for San Francisco Giants signing Type A free-agent P Bud Black. ... On disabled list (June 30-July 23, 1992). ... On Knoxville disabled list (June 11-July 24, 1993). ... Traded by Blue Jays with 2B Jorge Nunez to Los Angeles Dodgers for OF Raul Mondesi and P Pedro Borbon (November 8, 1999).

HONORS: Won A.L. Gold Glove as outfielder (1999). ... Named outfielder on THE SPORTING NEWS A.L. All-Star team (1999). ... Named outfielder on THE SPORTING NEWS A.L. Silver Slugger team (1999).

STATISTICAL NOTES: Tied for Florida State League lead with eight sacrifice flies in 1992. ... Had 28-game hitting streak (June 29-July 31, 1999). ... Led A.L. with 361 total bases in 1999. ... Career major league grand slams: 2.

Year Team (League)	Pos.	G	AB	R	H	2B	3B	HR	RBI	Avg.	BB	SO	SB	PO	A	E	Avg.
1992—Dunedin (FSL)	OF	114	417	44	114	21	3	1	49	.273	28	66	22	182	3	5	.974
1993—Knoxville (Sou.)	OF	99	360	40	102	14	2	4	34	.283	26	72	4	172	3	8	.956
—Toronto (A.L.)	OF-DH	3	6	0	0	0	0	0	0	.000	0	1	0	1	0	0	1.000
1994—Syracuse (I.L.)	OF-DH	109	433	82	149	27	3	13	61	*.344	40	54	19	220	5	1	*.996
—Toronto (A.L.)	OF	14	33	1	3	1	0	0	1	.091	1	8	1	12	2	0	1.000
1995—Toronto (A.L.)	OF	121	379	52	109	31	4	15	54	.288	20	68	1	207	9	6	.973
1996—Toronto (A.L.)	OF-DH	132	422	52	118	32	3	11	45	.280	33	75	5	254	10	2	.992
1997—Toronto (A.L.)	OF-DH	135	429	57	123	22	4	16	53	.287	36	99	14	173	6	3	.984
1998—Toronto (A.L.)	OF	158	630	106	175	33	4	35	100	.278	50	142	35	311	14	7	.979
1999—Toronto (A.L.)	OF	153	614	134	190	*45	0	42	123	.309	66	117	20	340	5	1	.997
2000—Los Angeles (N.L.)■..	OF	•162	610	98	164	44	4	24	99	.269	90	121	24	280	9	6	.980
American League totals (7 years)		716	2513	402	718	164	15	119	376	.286	206	510	76	1298	46	19	.986
National League totals (1 year)		162	610	98	164	44	4	24	99	.269	90	121	24	280	9	6	.980
Major League totals (8 years)		878	3123	500	882	208	19	143	475	.282	296	631	100	1578	55	25	.985

ALL-STAR GAME RECORD

Year League	Pos.	AB	R	H	2B	3B	HR	RBI	Avg.	BB	SO	SB	PO	A	E	Avg.
1999—American	OF	1	0	1	0	0	0	0	1.000	0	0	0	0	0	0	...

GREENE, CHARLIE — C — PADRES

PERSONAL: Born January 23, 1971, in Miami. ... 6-2/170. ... Bats right, throws right. ... Full name: Charles Patrick Greene.

HIGH SCHOOL: Miami Killian.

JUNIOR COLLEGE: Miami-Dade (South) Community College.

TRANSACTIONS/CAREER NOTES: Selected by San Diego Padres organization in 19th round of free-agent draft (June 3, 1991). ... Selected by New York Mets organization from Padres organization in Rule 5 minor league draft (December 13, 1993). ... Claimed on waivers by Baltimore Orioles (September 11, 1997). ... Claimed on waivers by Milwaukee Brewers (December 5, 1998). ... Granted free agency (October 11, 1999). ... Signed by Toronto Blue Jays organization (Novemeber 10, 1999). ... Granted free agency (October 18, 2000). ... Signed by Padres organization (November 20, 2000).

STATISTICAL NOTES: Tied for Midwest League lead in double plays by catcher with 11 in 1993.

Year Team (League)	Pos.	G	AB	R	H	2B	3B	HR	RBI	Avg.	BB	SO	SB	PO	A	E	Avg.
1991—Arizona Padres (Ariz.)	C-1B-3B	49	183	27	52	15	1	5	38	.284	16	26	6	334	30	3	.992
1992—Char., S.C. (S.Atl.)	C-3B	98	298	22	55	9	1	1	24	.185	11	60	1	561	119	14	.980
1993—Waterloo (Midw.)	C-1B-3B-SS	84	213	19	38	8	0	2	20	.178	13	33	0	460	96	16	.972
1994—St. Lucie (FSL)■	C	69	224	23	57	4	0	0	21	.254	9	31	0	380	65	13	.972
—Binghamton (East.)	C	30	106	13	18	4	0	0	2	.170	6	18	0	190	30	3	.987
1995—Binghamton (East.)	C	100	346	26	82	13	0	2	34	.237	15	47	2	670	54	4	*.995
—Norfolk (I.L.)	C	27	88	6	17	3	0	0	4	.193	3	28	0	157	25	0	1.000
1996—Binghamton (East.)	C	100	336	35	82	17	0	2	27	.244	17	52	2	550	75	3	.995
—New York (N.L.)	C	2	1	0	0	0	0	0	0	.000	0	0	0	1	0	0	1.000
1997—Norfolk (I.L.)	C	76	238	27	49	7	0	8	28	.206	9	54	1	475	49	8	.985
—Baltimore (A.L.)■	C	5	2	0	0	0	0	0	1	.000	0	1	0	4	0	0	1.000
1998—Rochester (I.L.)	C	77	250	23	53	10	0	4	28	.212	9	54	1	517	55	7	.988
—Baltimore (A.L.)	C	13	21	1	4	1	0	0	0	.190	0	8	0	58	4	0	1.000
1999—Louisville (I.L.)■	C	56	161	16	34	8	0	4	15	.211	7	26	0	306	27	2	.994
—Milwaukee (N.L.)	C	32	42	4	8	1	0	0	1	.190	5	11	0	104	8	1	.991
2000—Syracuse (I.L.)■	C	77	267	23	60	12	0	5	26	.225	17	46	1	468	41	9	.983
—Toronto (A.L.)	C	3	9	0	1	0	0	0	0	.111	0	5	0	13	0	0	1.000
American League totals (3 years)		21	32	1	5	1	0	0	1	.156	0	14	0	75	4	0	1.000
National League totals (2 years)		34	43	4	8	1	0	0	1	.186	5	11	0	105	8	1	.991
Major League totals (5 years)		55	75	5	13	2	0	0	2	.173	5	25	0	180	12	1	.995

GREENE, TODD — OF/DH — BLUE JAYS

G

PERSONAL: Born May 8, 1971, in Augusta, Ga. ... 5-10/208. ... Bats right, throws right. ... Full name: Todd Anthony Greene.

HIGH SCHOOL: Evans (Ga.).

COLLEGE: Georgia Southern.

TRANSACTIONS/CAREER NOTES: Selected by Atlanta Braves organization in 27th round of free-agent draft (June 5, 1989); did not sign. ... Selected by California Angels organization in 12th round of free-agent draft (June 3, 1993). ... On Vancouver disabled list (April 11-May 25, 1996). ... Angels franchise renamed Anaheim Angels for 1997 season. ... On Anaheim disabled list (August 20, 1997-remainder of season). ... On Anaheim disabled list (March 19-August 5, 1998); included rehabilitation assignments to Lake Elsinore (April 14-May 16, May 21 and May 27-31) and Vancouver (May 17-20, May 22-26, June 1-2 and July 17-August 5). ... On suspended list (May 13-16, 1999). ... Released by Angels (March 29, 2000). ... Signed by Toronto Blue Jays organization (April 10, 2000). ... On Toronto disabled list (June 7-23, 2000); included rehabilitation assignment to Dunedin (June 20-22).

HONORS: Named California League Most Valuable Player (1994).

STATISTICAL NOTES: Led California League with 306 total bases, 12 intentional bases on balls received and .584 slugging percentage in 1994. ... Led California League catchers with 15 errors, 13 double plays and 44 passed balls in 1994. ... Career major league grand slams: 1.

Year	Team (League)	Pos.	G	AB	R	H	2B	3B	HR	RBI	Avg.	BB	SO	SB	PO	A	E	Avg.
1993—	Boise (N'West)	OF	•76	*305	55	82	15	3	*15	*71	.269	34	44	4	136	4	3	.979
1994—	Lake Elsinore (Calif.)..	C-OF-1B	133	524	98	158	*39	2	*35	*124	.302	64	96	10	624	90	†15	.979
1995—	Midland (Texas)	C-DH-1B	82	318	59	104	19	1	26	57	.327	17	55	3	314	44	3	.992
	— Vancouver (PCL)	C-DH	43	168	28	42	3	1	14	35	.250	11	36	1	175	17	1	.995
1996—	Vancouver (PCL)	C-DH	60	223	27	68	18	0	5	33	.305	16	36	0	219	37	3	.988
	— California (A.L.)	C-DH	29	79	9	15	1	0	2	9	.190	4	11	2	119	19	0	1.000
1997—	Anaheim (A.L.)	C-DH	34	124	24	36	6	0	9	24	.290	7	25	2	153	7	0	1.000
	— Vancouver (PCL) C-DH-1B-OF		64	260	51	92	22	0	25	75	.354	20	31	5	331	43	3	.992
1998—	Lake Elsinore (Calif.) ..	DH-1B	12	44	9	10	2	0	1	6	.227	4	7	1	9	1	2	.833
	— Vancouver (PCL) DH-1B-C-OF		30	108	16	30	12	0	7	20	.278	12	17	1	97	7	1	.990
	— Anaheim (A.L.)	OF-DH-1B	29	71	3	18	4	0	1	7	.254	2	20	0	28	1	0	1.000
1999—	Anaheim (A.L.)	DH-OF-C	97	321	36	78	20	0	14	42	.243	12	63	1	91	8	2	.980
	— Edmonton (PCL)	OF-DH	19	74	10	18	6	0	5	14	.243	0	12	0	23	0	0	1.000
2000—	Syracuse (I.L.)■	OF-C	24	91	14	27	3	0	7	14	.297	6	16	1	31	1	1	.970
	— Toronto (A.L.)	DH-C-OF	34	85	11	20	2	0	5	10	.235	5	18	0	2	0	0	1.000
	— Dunedin (FSL)	OF	5	20	2	4	1	0	1	4	.200	2	4	0	4	0	0	1.000
Major League totals (5 years)			223	680	83	167	33	0	31	92	.246	30	137	5	393	35	2	.995

GREENE, WILLIE   3B/OF

PERSONAL: Born September 23, 1971, in Milledgeville, Ga. ... 5-11/190. ... Bats left, throws right. ... Full name: Willie Louis Greene.

HIGH SCHOOL: Jones County (Gray, Ga.).

TRANSACTIONS/CAREER NOTES: Selected by Pittsburgh Pirates organization in first round (18th pick overall) of free-agent draft (June 5, 1989). ... Traded by Pirates with P Scott Ruskin and a player to be named later to Montreal Expos for P Zane Smith (August 8, 1990); Expos acquired OF Moises Alou to complete deal (August 16, 1990). ... Traded by Expos with OF Dave Martinez and P Scott Ruskin to Cincinnati Reds for P John Wetteland and P Bill Risley (December 11, 1991). ... On Cincinnati disabled list (August 21, 1993-remainder of season). ... On Indianapolis disabled list (June 7-19, 1995). ... On disabled list (June 27-July 12, 1996). ... Traded by Reds to Baltimore Orioles for OF Jeffrey Hammonds (August 10, 1998). ... Granted free agency (December 21, 1998). ... Signed by Toronto Blue Jays (January 19, 1999). ... Granted free agency (October 15, 1999). ... Signed by Chicago Cubs (January 19, 2000). ... On Chicago disabled list (March 23-April 26, 2000); included rehabilitation assignment to Iowa (April 19-26). ... Granted free agency (October 11, 2000).

STATISTICAL NOTES: Led Florida State League third basemen with 31 errors in 1991. ... Led Southern League third basemen with 24 double plays in 1992. ... Led American Association third basemen with 23 errors in 1993. ... Hit three home runs in one game (September 24, 1996). ... Career major league grand slams: 3.

Year	Team (League)	Pos.	G	AB	R	H	2B	3B	HR	RBI	Avg.	BB	SO	SB	PO	A	E	Avg.
1989—	Princeton (Appl.)........	SS	39	136	22	44	6	4	2	24	.324	9	29	4	33	69	19	.843
	— GC Pirates (GCL)........	SS	23	86	17	24	3	3	5	11	.279	9	6	4	25	49	3	.961
1990—	Augusta (S.Atl.)..........	SS-2B	86	291	59	75	12	4	11	47	.258	61	58	7	117	209	34	.906
	— Salem (Caro.)............	SS	17	60	9	11	1	1	3	9	.183	7	18	0	22	43	2	.970
	— Rockford (Midw.)■......	SS	11	35	4	14	3	0	0	2	.400	6	7	2	14	37	4	.927
1991—	W.P. Beach (FSL)........	3B-SS	99	322	46	70	9	3	12	43	.217	50	93	10	72	184	†32	.889
1992—	Cedar Rap. (Midw.)■..	3B	34	120	26	34	8	2	12	40	.283	18	27	3	13	60	8	.901
	— Chattanooga (Sou.)....	3B	96	349	47	97	19	2	15	66	.278	46	90	9	*77	174	14	*.947
	— Cincinnati (N.L.)	3B	29	93	10	25	5	2	2	13	.269	10	23	0	15	40	3	.948
1993—	Indianapolis (A.A.)......	3B-SS	98	341	62	91	19	0	22	58	.267	51	83	2	77	171	†23	.915
	— Cincinnati (N.L.)	SS-3B	15	50	7	8	1	1	2	5	.160	2	19	0	19	37	1	.982
1994—	Cincinnati (N.L.)	3B-OF	16	37	5	8	2	0	0	3	.216	6	14	0	2	21	1	.958
	— Indianapolis (A.A.)......	3B-SS-DH	114	435	77	124	24	1	23	80	.285	56	88	8	93	249	17	.953
1995—	Cincinnati (N.L.)	3B	8	19	1	2	0	0	0	0	.105	3	7	0	1	13	0	1.000
	— Indianapolis (A.A.).........3B-SS-DH-OF		91	325	57	79	12	2	19	45	.243	38	67	3	60	160	12	.948
1996—	Cincinnati (N.L.)	3-0-1-S-2	115	287	48	70	5	5	19	63	.244	36	88	0	57	149	16	.928
1997—	Cincinnati (N.L.)	3-0-1-S	151	495	62	125	22	1	26	91	.253	78	111	6	176	175	17	.954
1998—	Cincinnati (N.L.)	3-0-S-DH	111	356	57	96	18	1	14	49	.270	56	80	6	92	132	13	.945
	— Baltimore (A.L.)■........	OF-DH	24	40	8	6	1	0	1	5	.150	13	10	1	15	1	1	.941
1999—	Toronto (A.L.)■........	DH-3B-OF	81	226	22	46	7	0	12	41	.204	20	56	0	7	7	1	.933
	— Syracuse (I.L.)............	OF	14	52	12	17	1	0	5	11	.327	6	14	0	24	2	0	1.000
2000—	Iowa (PCL)■	3B-1B	6	17	4	5	2	0	1	4	.294	3	5	1	13	2	1	.938
	— Chicago (N.L.)............	3B	105	299	34	60	15	2	10	37	.201	36	69	4	46	158	7	.967
American League totals (2 years)			105	266	30	52	8	0	13	46	.195	33	66	1	22	8	2	.938
National League totals (8 years)			550	1636	224	394	68	12	73	261	.241	227	411	16	408	725	58	.951
Major League totals (9 years)			655	1902	254	446	76	12	86	307	.234	260	477	17	430	733	60	.951

GREER, RUSTY   OF   RANGERS

PERSONAL: Born January 21, 1969, in Fort Rucker, Ala. ... 6-0/195. ... Bats left, throws left. ... Full name: Thurman Clyde Greer III.

HIGH SCHOOL: Albertville (Ala.).

COLLEGE: Montevallo (Ala.).

TRANSACTIONS/CAREER NOTES: Selected by Texas Rangers organization in 10th round of free-agent draft (June 4, 1990). ... On disabled list (July 31-August 22, 1992). ... On Texas disabled list (April 15-May 27, 2000); included rehabilitation assignment to Tulsa (May 15-27).

RECORDS: Shares major league record for fewest double plays by outfielder (150 or more games)—0 (1997 and 1998).

STATISTICAL NOTES: Led Florida State League with .395 on-base percentage in 1991. ... Career major league grand slams: 6.

Year	Team (League)	Pos.	G	AB	R	H	2B	3B	HR	RBI	Avg.	BB	SO	SB	PO	A	E	Avg.
1990—	Butte (Pio.)................	OF	62	226	48	78	12	6	10	50	.345	41	23	9	84	5	*8	.918
1991—	Charlotte (FSL)..........	OF-1B	111	388	52	114	25	1	5	48	.294	66	48	12	213	15	7	.970
	— Tulsa (Texas)	OF	20	64	12	19	3	2	3	12	.297	17	6	2	34	0	0	1.000
1992—	Tulsa (Texas)	1B-OF	106	359	47	96	22	4	5	37	.267	60	63	2	814	50	11	.987

G

Year	Team (League)	Pos.	G	AB	R	H	2B	3B	HR	RBI	Avg.	BB	SO	SB	PO	A	E	Avg.
						BATTING										FIELDING		
1993—	Tulsa (Texas)	1B	129	474	76	138	25	6	15	59	.291	53	79	10	1055	93	8	.993
—	Oklahoma City (A.A.)..	OF	8	27	6	6	2	0	1	4	.222	6	7	0	16	0	0	1.000
1994—	Oklahoma City (A.A.)..	OF-DH-1B	31	111	18	35	12	1	3	13	.315	18	24	1	52	3	3	.948
—	Texas (A.L.)	OF-1B	80	277	36	87	16	1	10	46	.314	46	46	0	216	4	6	.973
1995—	Texas (A.L.)	OF-1B	131	417	58	113	21	2	13	61	.271	55	66	3	240	9	6	.976
1996—	Texas (A.L.)	OF-DH-1B	139	542	96	180	41	6	18	100	.332	62	86	9	304	6	5	.984
1997—	Texas (A.L.)	OF-DH	157	601	112	193	42	3	26	87	.321	83	87	9	318	9	*12	.965
1998—	Texas (A.L.)	OF	155	598	107	183	31	5	16	108	.306	80	93	2	304	6	3	.990
1999—	Texas (A.L.)	OF-DH	147	556	107	167	41	3	20	101	.300	96	67	2	286	5	5	.983
2000—	Texas (A.L.)	OF-DH	105	394	65	117	34	3	8	65	.297	51	61	4	194	3	3	.985
—	Tulsa (Texas)	OF	2	7	0	1	0	0	0	1	.143	1	3	0	2	1	0	1.000
Major League totals (7 years)			914	3385	581	1040	226	23	111	568	.307	473	506	29	1862	40	40	.979

DIVISION SERIES RECORD

Year	Team (League)	Pos.	G	AB	R	H	2B	3B	HR	RBI	Avg.	BB	SO	SB	PO	A	E	Avg.
						BATTING										FIELDING		
1996—	Texas (A.L.)	OF	4	16	2	2	0	0	0	0	.125	3	3	0	12	0	0	1.000
1998—	Texas (A.L.)	OF	3	11	0	1	0	0	0	0	.091	1	2	0	4	1	0	1.000
1999—	Texas (A.L.)	OF	3	9	0	1	0	0	0	0	.111	3	1	0	9	0	0	1.000
Division series totals (3 years)			10	36	2	4	0	0	0	0	.111	7	6	0	25	1	0	1.000

GREISINGER, SETH   P   TIGERS

PERSONAL: Born July 29, 1975, in Kansas City, Kan. ... 6-3/200. ... Throws right, bats right. ... Full name: Seth Adam Greisinger.

HIGH SCHOOL: McLean (Va.).

COLLEGE: Virginia.

TRANSACTIONS/CAREER NOTES: Selected by Cleveland Indians organization in seventh round of free-agent draft (June 3, 1993); did not sign. ... Selected by Detroit Tigers organization in first round (sixth pick overall) of free-agent draft (June 4, 1996). ... On Detroit disabled list (March 26, 1999-entire season); included rehabilitation assignments to Lakeland (May 12-25) and Toledo (June 1-30). ... On disabled list (March 13, 2000-entire season).

STATISTICAL NOTES: Led Southern League in home runs allowed with 29 in 1997.

MISCELLANEOUS: Member of 1996 U.S. Olympic baseball team.

Year	League	W	L	Pct.	ERA	G	GS	CG	ShO	Sv.	IP	H	R	ER	BB	SO
1997—	Jacksonville (Sou.).............	10	6	.625	5.20	28	*28	1	0	0	159 1/3	194	103	92	53	105
1998—	Toledo (I.L.)	3	4	.429	2.91	10	10	0	0	0	58 2/3	50	21	19	22	37
—	Detroit (A.L.)	6	9	.400	5.12	21	21	0	0	0	130	142	79	74	48	66
1999—	Lakeland (FSL)	0	0	...	3.86	1	1	0	0	0	4 2/3	2	2	2	1	2
—	Toledo (I.L.)	0	1	.000	5.87	2	2	0	0	0	7 2/3	9	5	5	3	4
2000—	Detroit (A.L.)							Did not play.								
Major League totals (1 year)........		6	9	.400	5.12	21	21	0	0	0	130	142	79	74	48	66

GRIEVE, BEN   OF   DEVIL RAYS

PERSONAL: Born May 4, 1976, in Arlington, Texas. ... 6-4/230. ... Bats left, throws right. ... Full name: Benjamin Grieve. ... Son of Tom Grieve, outfielder with four major league teams (1970-79); first father/son combination to be selected in first round of free-agent draft.

HIGH SCHOOL: James W. Martin (Arlington, Texas).

TRANSACTIONS/CAREER NOTES: Selected by Oakland Athletics organization in first round (second pick overall) of free-agent draft (June 2, 1994). ... Traded to A's with a player to be named later or cash to Tampa Bay Devil Rays as part of three-way trade in which Kansas City Royals received P Roberto Hernandez from Devil Rays, A's received P Cory Lidle from Devil Rays, A's received OF Johnny Damon, IF Mark Ellis and a player to be named later from Royals and Royals received C A.J. Hinch, IF Angel Berroa and cash from A's (January 8, 2001).

RECORDS: Shares major league record for fewest double plays by outfielder (150 or more games)—0 (1998).

HONORS: Named Minor League Player of the Year by THE SPORTING NEWS (1997). ... Named Southern League Most Valuable Player (1997). ... Named A.L. Rookie Player of the Year by THE SPORTING NEWS (1998). ... Named A.L. Rookie of the Year by Baseball Writers' Association of America (1998).

STATISTICAL NOTES: Tied for Northwest League lead with seven intentional bases on balls received in 1994. ... Led Southern League with .455 on-base percentage in 1997. ... Led A.L. in grounding into double plays with 32 in 2000. ... Career major league grand slams: 3.

Year	Team (League)	Pos.	G	AB	R	H	2B	3B	HR	RBI	Avg.	BB	SO	SB	PO	A	E	Avg.
						BATTING										FIELDING		
1994—	S. Oregon (N'West)....	OF	72	252	44	83	13	0	7	50	.329	51	48	2	133	8	6	.959
1995—	W. Mich. (Midw.)........	OF	102	371	53	97	16	1	4	62	.261	60	75	11	125	6	8	.942
—	Modesto (Calif.)	OF	28	107	17	28	5	0	2	14	.262	14	15	2	37	2	2	.951
1996—	Modesto (Calif.)	OF-DH	72	281	61	100	20	1	11	51	.356	38	52	8	104	5	5	.956
—	Huntsville (Sou.)	OF-DH	63	232	34	55	8	1	8	32	.237	35	53	0	79	2	4	.953
1997—	Huntsville (Sou.)	OF-DH	100	372	100	122	29	2	24	108	.328	81	75	5	193	6	•8	.961
—	Edmonton (PCL)	OF	27	108	27	46	11	1	7	28	.426	12	16	0	51	2	2	.964
—	Oakland (A.L.)	OF	24	93	12	29	6	0	3	24	.312	13	25	0	39	1	0	1.000
1998—	Oakland (A.L.)	OF-DH	155	583	94	168	41	2	18	89	.288	85	123	2	262	7	2	.993
1999—	Oakland (A.L.)	OF-DH	148	486	80	129	21	0	28	86	.265	63	108	4	232	6	3	.988
2000—	Oakland (A.L.)	OF-DH	158	594	92	166	40	1	27	104	.279	73	130	3	237	6	3	.988
Major League totals (4 years)			485	1756	278	492	108	3	76	303	.280	234	386	9	770	20	8	.990

DIVISION SERIES RECORD

Year	Team (League)	Pos.	G	AB	R	H	2B	3B	HR	RBI	Avg.	BB	SO	SB	PO	A	E	Avg.
						BATTING										FIELDING		
2000—	Oakland (A.L.)	OF	5	17	1	2	0	0	0	2	.118	3	7	0	7	0	0	1.000

ALL-STAR GAME RECORD

Year	League	Pos.	AB	R	H	2B	3B	HR	RBI	Avg.	BB	SO	SB	PO	A	E	Avg.
					BATTING										FIELDING		
1998—	American	PH	0	0	0	0	0	0	0	...	1	0	0	...	...	...	...

G

PERSONAL: Born November 21, 1969, in Donora, Pa. ... 6-3/205. ... Bats left, throws left. ... Full name: George Kenneth Griffey Jr. ... Son of Ken Griffey Sr., bench coach, Cincinnati Reds, and major league outfielder with four teams (1973-91); and brother of Craig Griffey, outfielder in Seattle Mariners and Cincinnati Reds organizations (1991-97).

HIGH SCHOOL: Moeller (Cincinnati).

TRANSACTIONS/CAREER NOTES: Selected by Seattle Mariners organization in first round (first pick overall) of free-agent draft (June 2, 1987). ... On San Bernardino disabled list (June 9-August 15, 1988). ... On disabled list (July 24-August 20, 1989; June 9-25, 1992; and June 20-July 13, 1996). ... On Seattle disabled list (May 27-August 15, 1995); included rehabilitation assignment to Tacoma (August 13-15). ... Traded by Mariners to Cincinnati Reds for P Brett Tomko, OF Mike Cameron, IF Antonio Perez and P Jake Meyer (February 10, 2000).

RECORDS: Shares major league record for most consecutive games with one or more home runs—8 (July 20 through July 28, 1993). ... Holds A.L. single-season record for most major league ballparks, one or more home runs—16 (1998). ... Shares A.L. career record for most major league ballparks, one or more home runs (since 1900)—24.

HONORS: Won A.L. Gold Glove as outfielder (1990-99). ... Named outfielder on THE SPORTING NEWS A.L. All-Star team (1991, 1993-94 and 1996-99). ... Named outfielder on THE SPORTING NEWS A.L. Silver Slugger team (1991, 1993-94 and 1996-99). ... Named Major League Player of the Year by THE SPORTING NEWS (1997). ... Named A.L. Most Valuable Player by Baseball Writers' Association of America (1997).

STATISTICAL NOTES: Led A.L. outfielders with six double plays in 1989. ... Led A.L. with 359 total bases in 1993 and 393 in 1997. ... Hit three home runs in one game (May 24, 1996 and April 25, 1997). ... Led A.L. with 23 intentional bases on balls received in 1997. ... Led A.L. in slugging percentage with .646 in 1997. ... Led A.L. outfielders with 409 putouts and 425 total chances in 1998. ... Had 16-game hitting streak (May 10-28, 1999). ... Tied for A.L. lead with 17 intentional bases on balls received in 1999. ... Career major league grand slams: 14.

MISCELLANEOUS: Holds Seattle Mariners franchise all-time record for most runs (1,063), hits (1,742), home runs (398) and runs batted in (1,152).

Year Team (League)	Pos.	G	AB	R	H	2B	3B	HR	RBI	Avg.	BB	SO	SB	PO	A	E	Avg.
1987—Bellingham (N'West) ..	OF	54	182	43	57	9	1	14	40	.313	44	42	13	117	4	1	*.992
1988—San Bern. (Calif.)........	OF	58	219	50	74	13	3	11	42	.338	34	39	32	145	3	2	.987
—Vermont (East.)..........	OF	17	61	10	17	5	1	2	10	.279	5	12	4	40	2	1	.977
1989—Seattle (A.L.)	OF-DH	127	455	61	120	23	0	16	61	.264	44	83	16	302	12	•10	.969
1990—Seattle (A.L.)	OF	155	597	91	179	28	7	22	80	.300	63	81	16	330	8	7	.980
1991—Seattle (A.L.)	OF-DH	154	548	76	179	42	1	22	100	.327	71	82	18	360	15	4	.989
1992—Seattle (A.L.)	OF-DH	142	565	83	174	39	4	27	103	.308	44	67	10	359	8	1	.997
1993—Seattle (A.L.)	OF-DH-1B	156	582	113	180	38	3	45	109	.309	96	91	17	317	8	3	.991
1994—Seattle (A.L.)	OF-DH	111	433	94	140	24	4	*40	90	.323	56	73	11	225	12	4	.983
1995—Seattle (A.L.)	OF-DH	72	260	52	67	7	0	17	42	.258	52	53	4	190	5	2	.990
—Tacoma (PCL)	DH	1	3	0	0	0	0	0	0	.000	0	1	0	...	...	...	...
1996—Seattle (A.L.)	OF-DH	140	545	125	165	26	2	49	140	.303	78	104	16	375	10	4	.990
1997—Seattle (A.L.)	OF-DH	157	608	*125	185	34	3	*56	*147	.304	76	121	15	388	9	6	.985
1998—Seattle (A.L.)	OF-DH-1B	161	633	120	180	33	3	*56	146	.284	76	121	20	†409	11	5	.988
1999—Seattle (A.L.)	OF-DH	160	606	123	173	26	3	*48	134	.285	91	108	24	387	10	9	.978
2000—Cincinnati (N.L.)■......	OF	145	520	100	141	22	3	40	118	.271	94	117	6	375	9	5	.987
American League totals (11 years)		1535	5832	1063	1742	320	30	398	1152	.299	747	984	167	3642	108	55	.986
National League totals (1 year)		145	520	100	141	22	3	40	118	.271	94	117	6	375	9	5	.987
Major League totals (12 years)		1680	6352	1163	1883	342	33	438	1270	.296	841	1101	173	4017	117	60	.986

DIVISION SERIES RECORD

RECORDS: Holds single-series record for most runs scored—9 (1995). ... Shares single-game record for most home runs—2 (October 3, 1995). ... Shares single-series record for most home runs—5 (1996).

NOTES: Shares postseason single-series record for most home runs—5 (1995).

Year Team (League)	Pos.	G	AB	R	H	2B	3B	HR	RBI	Avg.	BB	SO	SB	PO	A	E	Avg.
1995—Seattle (A.L.)	OF	5	23	9	9	0	0	5	7	.391	2	4	1	15	1	0	1.000
1997—Seattle (A.L.)	OF	4	15	0	2	0	0	0	2	.133	1	3	2	12	1	0	1.000
Division series totals (2 years)		9	38	9	11	0	0	5	9	.289	3	7	3	27	2	0	1.000

CHAMPIONSHIP SERIES RECORD

Year Team (League)	Pos.	G	AB	R	H	2B	3B	HR	RBI	Avg.	BB	SO	SB	PO	A	E	Avg.
1995—Seattle (A.L.)	OF	6	21	2	7	2	0	1	2	.333	4	4	2	13	0	1	.929

ALL-STAR GAME RECORD

NOTES: Named Most Valuable Player (1992).

Year League	Pos.	AB	R	H	2B	3B	HR	RBI	Avg.	BB	SO	SB	PO	A	E	Avg.
1990—American....................	OF	2	0	0	0	0	0	0	.000	1	0	0	2	0	0	1.000
1991—American....................	OF	3	0	2	0	0	0	0	.667	0	0	0	2	0	0	1.000
1992—American....................	OF	3	2	3	1	0	1	2	1.000	0	0	0	1	0	0	1.000
1993—American....................	OF	3	1	1	0	0	0	1	.333	0	1	0	2	0	0	1.000
1994—American....................	OF	3	0	2	1	0	0	1	.667	0	0	0	2	0	0	1.000
1995—American....................					Selected, did not play—injured.											
1996—American....................					Selected, did not play—injured.											
1997—American....................	OF	4	0	0	0	0	0	0	.000	0	2	0	0	0	0	...
1998—American....................	OF	3	1	2	0	0	0	1	.667	1	0	1	0	0	1	.000
1999—American....................	OF	2	0	0	0	0	0	0	.000	0	1	0	0	0	0	...
2000—National....................					Selected, did not play—injured.											
All-Star Game totals (8 years)		23	4	10	2	0	1	5	.435	2	4	1	9	0	1	.900

G

GRILLI, JASON　　　　　　　　　P　　　　　　　　　MARLINS

PERSONAL: Born November 11, 1976, in Royal Oak, Mich. ... 6-4/185. ... Throws right, bats right. ... Full name: Jason Michael Grilli. ... Son of Steve Grilli, pitcher with Detroit Tigers (1975-77) and Toronto Blue Jays (1979).
HIGH SCHOOL: C.W. Baker (Baldwinsville, N.Y.).
COLLEGE: Seton Hall.
TRANSACTIONS/CAREER NOTES: Selected by San Francisco Giants organization in first round (fourth pick overall) of free-agent draft (June 3, 1997). ... Traded by Giants with P Nathan Bump to Florida Marlins for P Livan Hernandez (July 24, 1999). ... On Calgary disabled list (May 23-September 5, 2000).

Year	League	W	L	Pct.	ERA	G	GS	CG	ShO	Sv.	IP	H	R	ER	BB	SO
1998—	Shreveport (Texas)	7	10	.412	3.79	21	21	3	0	0	123 1/3	113	60	52	37	100
—	Fresno (PCL)	2	3	.400	5.14	8	8	0	0	0	42	49	30	24	18	37
1999—	Fresno (PCL)	7	5	.583	5.54	19	19	1	0	0	100 2/3	124	69	62	39	76
—	Calgary (PCL)■	1	5	.167	7.68	8	8	0	0	0	41	56	48	35	23	27
2000—	Calgary (PCL)	1	4	.200	7.19	8	8	0	0	0	41 1/3	58	37	33	23	21
—	Florida (N.L.)	1	0	1.000	5.40	1	1	0	0	0	6 2/3	11	4	4	2	3
Major League totals (1 year)		1	0	1.000	5.40	1	1	0	0	0	6 2/3	11	4	4	2	3

GRIMSLEY, JASON　　　　　　　　　P

PERSONAL: Born August 7, 1967, in Cleveland, Texas. ... 6-3/205. ... Throws right, bats right. ... Full name: Jason Alan Grimsley.
HIGH SCHOOL: Tarkington (Cleveland, Texas).
TRANSACTIONS/CAREER NOTES: Selected by Philadelphia Phillies organization in 10th round of free-agent draft (June 3, 1985). ... On Clearwater disabled list (April 8-May 10, 1988). ... On Philadelphia disabled list (June 6-August 22, 1991); included rehabilitation assignments to Scranton/Wilkes-Barre (June 15-30 and August 7-21). ... Traded by Phillies to Houston Astros for P Curt Schilling (April 2, 1992). ... On disabled list (May 14-June 14, 1992). ... Released by Astros (March 30, 1993). ... Signed by Cleveland Indians organization (April 7, 1993). ... On Charlotte disabled list (April 15-26, 1993). ... Traded by Indians with P Pep Harris to California Angels for P Brian Anderson (February 15, 1996). ... Granted free agency (October 8, 1996). ... Signed by Detroit Tigers organization (January 17, 1997). ... Released by Tigers (March 20, 1997). ... Signed by Milwaukee Brewers (April 3, 1997). ... Traded by Brewers to Kansas City Royals for P Jamie Brewington (July 29, 1997). ... Granted free agency (October 15, 1997). ... Signed by Indians organization (January 8, 1998). ... Granted free agency (October 15, 1998). ... Signed by New York Yankees organization (January 26, 1999). ... On suspended list (August 11-15, 1999). ... Released by Yankees (November 20, 2000).
STATISTICAL NOTES: Led New York-Pennsylvania League with 11 hit batsmen and 18 wild pitches in 1986. ... Pitched 3-0 no-hit victory for Reading against Harrisburg (May 3, 1989, first game). ... Led International League with 18 wild pitches in 1990. ... Tied for A.L. lead with 13 hit batsmen in 1996. ... Led Pacific Coast League with 20 wild pitches in 1997.
MISCELLANEOUS: Appeared in one game as pinch runner with Philadelphia (1990).

Year	League	W	L	Pct.	ERA	G	GS	CG	ShO	Sv.	IP	H	R	ER	BB	SO
1985—	Bend (N'West)	0	1	.000	13.50	6	1	0	0	0	11 1/3	12	21	17	25	10
1986—	Utica (NY-Penn)	1	•10	.091	6.40	14	14	3	0	0	64 2/3	63	61	46	*77	45
1987—	Spartanburg (S.Atl.)	7	4	.636	3.16	23	9	3	0	0	88 1/3	59	48	31	54	98
1988—	Clearwater (FSL)	4	7	.364	3.73	16	15	2	0	0	101 1/3	80	48	42	37	90
—	Reading (East.)	1	3	.250	7.17	5	4	0	0	0	21 1/3	20	19	17	13	14
1989—	Reading (East.)	11	8	.579	2.98	26	26	8	2	0	172	121	65	57	*109	134
—	Philadelphia (N.L.)	1	3	.250	5.89	4	4	0	0	0	18 1/3	19	13	12	19	7
1990—	Scranton/W.B. (I.L.)	8	5	.615	3.93	22	22	0	0	0	128 1/3	111	68	56	78	99
—	Philadelphia (N.L.)	3	2	.600	3.30	11	11	0	0	0	57 1/3	47	21	21	43	41
1991—	Philadelphia (N.L.)	1	7	.125	4.87	12	12	0	0	0	61	54	34	33	41	42
—	Scranton/W.B. (I.L.)	2	3	.400	4.35	9	9	0	0	0	51 2/3	48	28	25	37	43
1992—	Tucson (PCL)■	8	7	.533	5.05	26	20	0	0	0	124 2/3	152	79	70	55	90
1993—	Charlotte (I.L.)■	6	6	.500	3.39	28	19	3	1	0	135 1/3	138	64	51	49	102
—	Cleveland (A.L.)	3	4	.429	5.31	10	6	0	0	0	42 1/3	52	26	25	20	27
1994—	Charlotte (I.L.)	7	0	1.000	3.42	10	10	2	0	0	71	58	36	27	17	60
—	Cleveland (A.L.)	5	2	.714	4.57	14	13	1	0	0	82 2/3	91	47	42	34	59
1995—	Cleveland (A.L.)	0	0	...	6.09	15	2	0	0	1	34	37	24	23	32	25
—	Buffalo (A.A.)	5	3	.625	2.91	10	10	2	0	0	68	61	26	22	19	40
1996—	Vancouver (PCL)■	2	0	1.000	1.20	2	2	1	0	0	15	8	2	2	3	11
—	California (A.L.)	5	7	.417	6.84	35	20	2	1	0	130 1/3	150	110	99	74	82
1997—	Tucson (PCL)■	5	10	.333	5.70	36	10	0	0	4	85 1/3	96	70	54	43	65
—	Omaha (A.A.)■	1	5	.167	6.68	7	6	0	0	0	31	36	26	23	29	22
1998—	Buffalo (I.L.)■	6	3	.667	3.76	52	0	0	0	0	88 2/3	76	40	37	57	68
1999—	New York (A.L.)■	7	2	.778	3.60	55	0	0	0	1	75	66	39	30	40	49
2000—	New York (A.L.)	3	2	.600	5.04	63	4	0	0	1	96 1/3	100	58	54	42	53
A.L. totals (6 years)		23	17	.575	5.33	192	45	3	1	3	460 2/3	496	304	273	242	295
N.L. totals (3 years)		5	12	.294	4.35	27	27	0	0	0	136 2/3	120	68	66	103	90
Major League totals (9 years)		28	29	.491	5.11	219	72	3	1	3	597 1/3	616	372	339	345	385

DIVISION SERIES RECORD

Year	League	W	L	Pct.	ERA	G	GS	CG	ShO	Sv.	IP	H	R	ER	BB	SO
1999—	New York (A.L.)							Did not play.								
2000—	New York (A.L.)							Did not play.								

CHAMPIONSHIP SERIES RECORD

Year	League	W	L	Pct.	ERA	G	GS	CG	ShO	Sv.	IP	H	R	ER	BB	SO
1999—	New York (A.L.)							Did not play.								
2000—	New York (A.L.)	0	0	...	0.00	2	0	0	0	0	1	2	0	0	3	1

WORLD SERIES RECORD

NOTES: Member of World Series championship team (1999 and 2000).

Year	League	W	L	Pct.	ERA	G	GS	CG	ShO	Sv.	IP	H	R	ER	BB	SO
1999—	New York (A.L.)	0	0	...	0.00	1	0	0	0	0	2 1/3	2	0	0	2	0
2000—	New York (A.L.)							Did not play.								

G

PERSONAL: Born April 17, 1967, in Atlanta. ... 5-11/188. ... Bats right, throws right. ... Full name: Marquis Deon Grissom. ... Brother of Antonio Grissom, outfielder in Philadelphia Phillies (1990-91) and Montreal Expos organizations (1992-94). ... Name pronounced mar-KEESE.

HIGH SCHOOL: Lakeshore (College Park, Ga.).

COLLEGE: Florida A&M.

TRANSACTIONS/CAREER NOTES: Selected by Montreal Expos organization in third round of free-agent draft (June 1, 1988). ... On Montreal disabled list (May 29-June 30, 1990); included rehabilitation assignment to Indianapolis (June 25-30). ... Traded by Expos to Atlanta Braves for OF Roberto Kelly, OF Tony Tarasco and P Esteban Yan (April 6, 1995). ... Traded by Braves with OF Dave Justice to Cleveland Indians for OF Kenny Lofton and P Alan Embree (March 25, 1997). ... On disabled list (April 22-May 5, 1997). ... Traded by Indians with P Jeff Juden to Milwaukee Brewers for P Ben McDonald, P Mike Fetters and P Ron Villone (December 8, 1997).

HONORS: Won N.L. Gold Glove as outfielder (1993-96).

STATISTICAL NOTES: Led New York-Pennsylvania League with 146 total bases in 1988. ... Led N.L. outfielders with 333 total chances in 1994. ... Had 28-game hitting streak (July 25-August 24, 1996). ... Career major league grand slams: 3.

Year Team (League)	Pos.	G	AB	R	H	2B	3B	HR	RBI	Avg.	BB	SO	SB	PO	A	E	Avg.
1988— Jamestown (NY-P)	OF	74	*291	*69	94	14	7	8	39	.323	35	39	23	123	•11	3	.978
1989— Jacksonville (Sou.)	OF	78	278	43	83	15	4	3	31	.299	24	31	24	141	7	3	.980
— Indianapolis (A.A.)	OF	49	187	28	52	10	4	2	21	.278	14	23	16	106	5	0	1.000
— Montreal (N.L.)	OF	26	74	16	19	2	0	1	2	.257	12	21	1	32	1	2	.943
1990— Montreal (N.L.)	OF	98	288	42	74	14	2	3	29	.257	27	40	22	165	5	2	.988
— Indianapolis (A.A.)	OF	5	22	3	4	0	0	2	3	.182	0	5	1	16	0	0	1.000
1991— Montreal (N.L.)	OF	148	558	73	149	23	9	6	39	.267	34	89	*76	350	•15	6	.984
1992— Montreal (N.L.)	OF	159	*653	99	180	39	6	14	66	.276	42	81	*78	401	7	7	.983
1993— Montreal (N.L.)	OF	157	630	104	188	27	2	19	95	.298	52	76	53	416	8	7	.984
1994— Montreal (N.L.)	OF	110	475	96	137	25	4	11	45	.288	41	66	36	*321	7	5	.985
1995— Atlanta (N.L.)■.........	OF	139	551	80	142	23	3	12	42	.258	47	61	29	309	9	2	.994
1996— Atlanta (N.L.)	OF	158	671	106	207	32	10	23	74	.308	41	73	28	338	10	1	.997
1997— Cleveland (A.L.)■......	OF	144	558	74	146	27	6	12	66	.262	43	89	22	356	7	3	.992
1998— Milwaukee (N.L.)■......	OF	142	542	57	147	28	1	10	60	.271	24	78	13	317	8	3	.991
1999— Milwaukee (N.L.)	OF	154	603	92	161	27	1	20	83	.267	49	109	24	374	1	5	.987
2000— Milwaukee (N.L.)	OF	146	595	67	145	18	2	14	62	.244	39	99	20	352	3	3	.992
American League totals (1 year)		144	558	74	146	27	6	12	66	.262	43	89	22	356	7	3	.992
National League totals (11 years)		1437	5640	832	1549	258	40	133	597	.275	408	793	380	3375	74	43	.988
Major League totals (12 years)		1581	6198	906	1695	285	46	145	663	.273	451	882	402	3731	81	46	.988

DIVISION SERIES RECORD

RECORDS: Holds single-game record for most hits—5 (October 7, 1995). ... Holds N.L. single-series record for most hits—11 (1995). ... Shares single-game records for most at-bats (nine-inning game)—6 (October 4, 1995); and most home runs—2 (October 4, 1995). ... Shares career record for most triples—1.

Year Team (League)	Pos.	G	AB	R	H	2B	3B	HR	RBI	Avg.	BB	SO	SB	PO	A	E	Avg.
1995— Atlanta (N.L.)	OF	4	21	5	11	2	0	3	4	.524	0	3	2	9	0	0	1.000
1996— Atlanta (N.L.)	OF	3	12	2	1	0	0	0	0	.083	1	2	1	4	0	1	.800
1997— Cleveland (A.L.)	OF	5	17	3	4	0	1	0	0	.235	1	2	0	14	0	0	1.000
Division series totals (3 years)		12	50	10	16	2	1	3	4	.320	2	7	3	27	0	1	.964

CHAMPIONSHIP SERIES RECORD

RECORDS: Holds single-series record for most at-bats—35 (1996). ... Shares single-game record for most strikeouts—4 (October 11 [12 innings] and 15 [11 innings], 1997). ... Shares N.L. single-game record for most at-bats—6 (October 14 and 17, 1996).

NOTES: Named A.L. Championship Series Most Valuable Player (1997).

Year Team (League)	Pos.	G	AB	R	H	2B	3B	HR	RBI	Avg.	BB	SO	SB	PO	A	E	Avg.
1995— Atlanta (N.L.)	OF	4	19	2	5	0	1	0	0	.263	1	4	0	8	0	1	.889
1996— Atlanta (N.L.)	OF	7	35	7	10	1	0	1	3	.286	0	8	2	17	0	1	.944
1997— Cleveland (A.L.)	OF	6	23	2	6	0	0	1	4	.261	1	9	3	13	1	0	1.000
Championship series totals (3 years)		17	77	11	21	1	1	2	7	.273	2	21	5	38	1	2	.951

WORLD SERIES RECORD

NOTES: Member of World Series championship team (1995).

Year Team (League)	Pos.	G	AB	R	H	2B	3B	HR	RBI	Avg.	BB	SO	SB	PO	A	E	Avg.
1995— Atlanta (N.L.)	OF	6	25	3	9	1	0	0	1	.360	1	3	3	13	0	0	1.000
1996— Atlanta (N.L.)	OF	6	27	4	12	2	1	0	5	.444	1	2	1	7	0	1	.875
1997— Cleveland (A.L.)	OF	7	25	5	9	1	0	0	2	.360	4	4	0	19	0	1	.950
World Series totals (3 years)		19	77	12	30	4	1	0	8	.390	6	9	4	39	0	2	.951

ALL-STAR GAME RECORD

Year League	Pos.	AB	R	H	2B	3B	HR	RBI	Avg.	BB	SO	SB	PO	A	E	Avg.
1993— National	OF	3	0	0	0	0	0	0	.000	0	1	0	1	0	0	1.000
1994— National	OF	1	1	1	0	0	1	1	1.000	1	0	0	2	1	0	1.000
All-Star Game totals (2 years)		4	1	1	0	0	1	1	.250	1	1	0	3	1	0	1.000

GROOM, BUDDY   P   ORIOLES

PERSONAL: Born July 10, 1965, in Dallas. ... 6-2/207. ... Throws left, bats left. ... Full name: Wedsel Gary Groom Jr.

HIGH SCHOOL: Red Oak (Texas).

COLLEGE: Mary Hardin-Baylor (Texas).

G

TRANSACTIONS/CAREER NOTES: Selected by Chicago White Sox organization in 12th round of free-agent draft (June 2, 1987). ... Selected by Detroit Tigers organization from White Sox organization in Rule 5 minor league draft (December 3, 1990). ... Traded by Tigers to Florida Marlins for a player to be named later (August 7, 1995); Tigers acquired P Mike Myers to complete deal (August 9, 1995). ... Granted free agency (October 16, 1995). ... Signed by Oakland Athletics organization (November 27, 1995). ... Granted free agency (November 1, 1999). ... Signed by Baltimore Orioles (December 21, 1999).

Year League	W	L	Pct.	ERA	G	GS	CG	ShO	Sv.	IP	H	R	ER	BB	SO
1987— GC White Sox (GCL)	1	0	1.000	0.75	4	1	0	0	1	12	12	1	1	2	8
— Daytona Beach (FSL).........	7	2	.778	3.59	11	10	2	0	0	67 2/3	60	30	27	33	29
1988— Tampa (FSL)......	13	10	.565	2.54	27	27	8	0	0	*195	181	69	55	51	118
1989— Birmingham (Sou.).......	13	8	.619	4.52	26	26	3	1	0	167 1/3	172	101	84	78	94
1990— Birmingham (Sou.)...........	6	8	.429	5.07	20	20	0	0	0	115 1/3	135	81	65	48	66
1991— Toledo (I.L.)■..................	2	5	.286	4.32	24	6	0	0	1	75	75	39	36	25	49
— London (East.)	7	1	.875	3.48	11	7	0	0	0	51 2/3	51	?0	20	12	39
1992— Toledo (I.L.)...........	7	7	.500	2.80	16	16	1	0	0	109 1/3	102	41	34	23	71
— Detroit (A.L.)	0	5	.000	5.82	12	7	0	0	1	38 2/3	48	28	25	22	15
1993— Toledo (I.L.)...........	9	3	.750	2.74	16	15	0	0	0	102	98	34	31	30	78
— Detroit (A.L.)	0	2	.000	6.14	19	3	0	0	0	36 2/3	48	25	25	13	15
1994— Toledo (I.L.)...........	0	0	....	2.25	5	0	0	0	0	4	2	1	1	0	6
— Detroit (A.L.)	0	1	.000	3.94	40	0	0	0	1	32	31	14	14	13	27
1995— Detroit (A.L.)	1	3	.250	7.52	23	4	0	0	1	40 2/3	55	35	34	26	23
— Toledo (I.L.)...........	2	3	.400	1.91	6	5	1	0	0	33	31	14	7	4	24
— Florida (N.L.)■	1	2	.333	7.20	14	0	0	0	0	15	26	12	12	6	12
1996— Oakland (A.L.)■	5	0	1.000	3.84	72	1	0	0	2	77 1/3	85	37	33	34	57
1997— Oakland (A.L.)	2	2	.500	5.15	78	0	0	0	3	64 2/3	75	38	37	24	45
1998— Oakland (A.L.)	3	1	.750	4.24	75	0	0	0	0	57 1/3	62	30	27	20	36
1999— Oakland (A.L.)	3	2	.600	5.09	•76	0	0	0	0	46	48	29	26	18	32
2000— Baltimore (A.L.)■..............	6	3	.667	4.85	70	0	0	0	4	59 1/3	63	37	32	21	44
A.L. totals (9 years)	20	19	.513	5.03	465	15	0	0	12	452 2/3	515	273	253	191	294
N.L. totals (1 year)......................	1	2	.333	7.20	14	0	0	0	0	15	26	12	12	6	12
Major League totals (9 years)......	21	21	.500	5.10	479	15	0	0	12	467 2/3	541	285	265	197	306

GROSS, KIP   P

PERSONAL: Born August 24, 1964, in Scottsbluff, Neb. ... 6-2/195. ... Throws right, bats right. ... Full name: Kip Lee Gross.
HIGH SCHOOL: Gering (Neb.).
COLLEGE: Murray State, then Nebraska.
TRANSACTIONS/CAREER NOTES: Selected by St. Louis Cardinals organization in third round of free-agent draft (January 9, 1985); did not sign. ... Selected by New York Mets organization in fourth round of free-agent draft (June 2, 1986). ... Traded by Mets with P Randy Myers to Cincinnati Reds for P John Franco and OF Don Brown (December 6, 1989). ... Traded by Reds with OF Eric Davis to Los Angeles Dodgers for P Tim Belcher and P John Wetteland (November 27, 1991). ... On Albuquerque disabled list (August 5-12, 1993). ... On Albuquerque temporarily inactive list (May 5-10, 1994). ... Contract sold by Dodgers to Nippon Ham of Japan of Pacific League (May 10, 1994). ... Signed by Boston Red Sox (January 5, 1999). ... On Boston disabled list (May 17-June 4, 1999); included rehabilitation assignment to Pawtucket (May 25-June 1). ... Granted free agency (October 4, 1999). ... Signed by Houston Astros organization (February 1, 2000). ... Granted free agency (October 5, 2000).

Year League	W	L	Pct.	ERA	G	GS	CG	ShO	Sv.	IP	H	R	ER	BB	SO
1987— Lynchburg (Caro.)	7	4	.636	2.72	16	15	2	0	0	89 1/3	92	37	27	22	39
1988— St. Lucie (FSL)......	13	9	.591	2.62	28	27	7	3	0	178 1/3	153	72	52	53	124
1989— Jackson (Texas)	6	5	.545	2.49	16	16	4	0	0	112	96	47	31	13	60
— Tidewater (I.L.)	4	4	.500	3.97	12	12	0	0	0	70 1/3	72	33	31	17	39
1990— Nashville (A.A.)■	12	7	.632	3.33	40	11	2	1	3	127	113	54	47	47	62
— Cincinnati (N.L.)	0	0	...	4.26	5	0	0	0	0	6 1/3	6	3	3	2	3
1991— Nashville (A.A.)	5	3	.625	2.08	14	6	1	1	0	47 2/3	39	13	11	16	28
— Cincinnati (N.L.)	6	4	.600	3.47	29	9	1	0	0	85 2/3	93	43	33	40	40
1992— Albuquerque (PCL)■	6	5	.545	3.51	31	14	2	0	8	107 2/3	96	48	42	36	58
— Los Angeles (N.L.)	1	1	.500	4.18	16	1	0	0	0	23 2/3	32	14	11	10	14
1993— Albuquerque (PCL)	13	7	.650	4.05	59	7	0	0	13	124 1/3	115	58	56	41	96
— Los Angeles (N.L.)	0	0	...	0.60	10	0	0	0	0	15	13	1	1	4	12
1994— Albuquerque (PCL)	1	1	.500	5.06	10	0	0	0	1	16	14	9	9	6	11
— Nippon Ham (Jap. Pac.)■..	6	12	.333	4.29	25	...	...	...	0	149	...	...	71	56	62
1995— Nippon Ham (Jap. Pac.).....	16	13	.552	3.04	31	...	...	...	0	231	...	...	78	59	114
1996— Nippon Ham (Jap. Pac.).....	17	9	.654	3.62	28	...	...	...	0	193 2/3	...	...	78	53	79
1997— Nippon Ham (Jap. Pac.).....	13	11	.542	3.63	33	...	...	...	0	233 1/3	...	...	94	69	98
1998— Nippon Ham (Jap. Pac.).....	3	4	.429	3.96	7	7	1	0	0	36 1/3	30	18	16	15	11
1999— Boston (A.L.)■	0	2	.000	7.82	11	1	0	0	0	12 2/3	15	11	11	8	9
— Pawtucket (I.L.)	1	0	1.000	5.40	10	2	0	0	0	21 2/3	24	14	13	12	16
2000— New Orleans (PCL)■..	8	7	.533	3.94	25	25	2	0	0	157 2/3	156	80	69	44	94
— Houston (N.L.)	0	1	.000	10.38	2	1	0	0	0	4 1/3	9	8	5	2	3
A.L. totals (1 year)	0	2	.000	7.82	11	1	0	0	0	12 2/3	15	11	11	8	9
N.L. totals (5 years)......................	7	6	.538	3.53	62	11	1	0	0	135	153	69	53	58	72
Major League totals (6 years)......	7	8	.467	3.90	73	12	1	0	0	147 2/3	168	80	64	66	81

G

GRUDZIELANEK, MARK   SS   DODGERS

PERSONAL: Born June 30, 1970, in Milwaukee. ... 6-1/185. ... Bats right, throws right. ... Full name: Mark James Grudzielanek. ... Name pronounced gress-UH-lawn-ick.
HIGH SCHOOL: J.M. Hanks (El Paso, Texas).
JUNIOR COLLEGE: Trinidad (Colo.) State Junior College.
COLLEGE: Oklahoma State.

TRANSACTIONS/CAREER NOTES: Selected by New York Mets organization in 17th round of free-agent draft (June 5, 1989); did not sign. ... Selected by Montreal Expos organization in 11th round of free-agent draft (June 3, 1991). ... On disabled list (July 13-August 9, 1993 and May 12-19, 1994). ... Traded by Expos with P Carlos Perez and OF Hiram Bocachica to Los Angeles Dodgers for 2B Wilton Guerrero, P Ted Lilly, OF Peter Bergeron and 1B Jonathan Tucker (July 31, 1998). ... On Los Angeles disabled list (June 3-July 6, 1999); included rehabilitation assignment to San Bernadino (July 2-6).
RECORDS: Holds major league single-season record for fewest chances accepted by shortstop who led league in chances accepted—683 (1997). ... Shares major league single-season record for fewest putouts by shortstop (150 or more games)—180 (1996).
HONORS: Named Eastern League Most Valuable Player (1994).
STATISTICAL NOTES: Led Eastern League shortstops with .959 fielding percentage in 1994. ... Led N.L. shortstops with 715 total chances and 99 double plays in 1997. ... Led N.L. shortstops with 33 errors in 1998.

Year	Team (League)	Pos.	G	AB	R	H	2B	3B	HR	RBI	Avg.	BB	SO	SB	PO	A	E	Avg.
1991—Jamestown (NY-P)		SS	72	275	44	72	9	3	2	32	.262	18	43	14	112	206	23	.933
1992—Rockford (Midw.)		SS	128	496	64	122	12	5	5	54	.246	22	59	25	173	290	41	.919
1993—W.P. Beach (FSL)		2B-SS-OF-3B	86	300	41	80	11	6	1	34	.267	14	42	17	105	135	13	.949
1994—Harrisburg (East.)		SS-3B	122	488	92	157	•37	3	11	66	.322	43	66	32	178	344	23	†.958
1995—Montreal (N.L.)		SS-3B-2B	78	269	27	66	12	2	1	20	.245	14	47	8	94	198	10	.967
—Ottawa (I.L.)		SS	49	181	26	54	9	1	1	22	.298	10	17	12	58	156	14	.939
1996—Montreal (N.L.)		SS	153	657	99	201	34	4	6	49	.306	26	83	33	180	453	27	.959
1997—Montreal (N.L.)		SS	156	*649	76	177	•54	3	4	51	.273	23	76	25	237	446	*32	.955
1998—Montreal (N.L.)		SS	105	396	51	109	15	1	8	41	.275	21	50	11	152	283	23	.950
—Los Angeles (N.L.)■		SS	51	193	11	51	6	0	2	21	.264	5	23	7	78	172	§10	.962
1999—Los Angeles (N.L.)		SS	123	488	72	159	23	5	7	46	.326	31	65	6	171	306	13	.973
—San Bern. (Calif.)		SS	4	16	2	4	0	0	0	0	.250	0	1	0	1	11	0	1.000
2000—Los Angeles (N.L.)		2B-SS	148	617	101	172	35	6	7	49	.279	45	81	12	288	416	17	.976
Major League totals (6 years)			814	3269	437	935	179	21	35	277	.286	165	425	102	1200	2274	132	.963

ALL-STAR GAME RECORD

Year	League	Pos.	AB	R	H	2B	3B	HR	RBI	Avg.	BB	SO	SB	PO	A	E	Avg.
1996—National		3B	1	0	0	0	0	0	0	.000	0	0	0	0	0	0	...

GUARDADO, EDDIE — P — TWINS

PERSONAL: Born October 2, 1970, in Stockton, Calif. ... 6-0/194. ... Throws left, bats right. ... Full name: Edward Adrian Guardado. ... Name pronounced gwar-DAH-doh.
HIGH SCHOOL: Franklin (Stockton, Calif.).
JUNIOR COLLEGE: San Joaquin Delta College (Calif.).
TRANSACTIONS/CAREER NOTES: Selected by Minnesota Twins organization in 21st round of free-agent draft (June 4, 1990). ... On Minnesota disabled list (May 22-June 28, 1999); included rehabilitation assignment to New Britain (June 22-28).
STATISTICAL NOTES: Pitched 5-0 no-hit victory against Pulaski (August 26, 1991).

Year	League	W	L	Pct.	ERA	G	GS	CG	ShO	Sv.	IP	H	R	ER	BB	SO
1991—Elizabethton (Appl.)		8	4	.667	1.86	14	13	3	•1	0	92	67	30	19	31	*106
1992—Kenosha (Midw.)		5	10	.333	4.37	18	18	2	1	0	101	106	57	49	30	103
—Visalia (Calif.)		7	0	1.000	1.64	7	7	1	1	0	49 1/3	47	13	9	10	39
1993—Nashville (Sou.)		4	0	1.000	1.24	10	10	2	2	0	65 1/3	53	10	9	10	57
—Minnesota (A.L.)		3	8	.273	6.18	19	16	0	0	0	94 2/3	123	68	65	36	46
1994—Salt Lake (PCL)		12	7	.632	4.83	24	24	2	0	0	151	171	90	81	51	87
—Minnesota (A.L.)		0	2	.000	8.47	4	4	0	0	0	17	26	16	16	4	8
1995—Minnesota (A.L.)		4	9	.308	5.12	51	5	0	0	2	91 1/3	99	54	52	45	71
1996—Minnesota (A.L.)		6	5	.545	5.25	•83	0	0	0	0	73 2/3	61	45	43	33	74
1997—Minnesota (A.L.)		0	4	.000	3.91	69	0	0	0	1	46	45	23	20	17	54
1998—Minnesota (A.L.)		3	1	.750	4.52	79	0	0	0	0	65 2/3	66	34	33	28	53
1999—Minnesota (A.L.)		2	5	.286	4.50	63	0	0	0	2	48	37	24	24	25	50
—New Britain (East.)		0	0	...	1.93	3	0	0	0	0	4 2/3	3	1	1	0	5
2000—Minnesota (A.L.)		7	4	.636	3.94	70	0	0	0	9	61 2/3	55	27	27	25	52
Major League totals (8 years)		25	38	.397	5.06	438	25	0	0	18	498	512	291	280	213	408

GUERRERO, VLADIMIR — OF — EXPOS

PERSONAL: Born February 9, 1976, in Nizao Bani, Dominican Republican ... 6-3/205. ... Bats right, throws right. ... Full name: Vladimir Alvino Guerrero. ... Brother of Wilton Guerrero, outfielder/second baseman, Cincinnati Reds.
TRANSACTIONS/CAREER NOTES: Signed as non-drafted free agent by Montreal Expos organization (March 1, 1993). ... On Montreal disabled list (March 30-May 2, June 5-21 and July 12-27, 1997); included rehabilitation assignment to West Palm Beach (April 29-May 2).
HONORS: Named Eastern League Most Valuable Player (1996). ... Named Minor League Player of the Year by THE SPORTING NEWS (1996). ... Named outfielder on THE SPORTING NEWS N.L. All-Star team (1999 and 2000). ... Named outfielder on THE SPORTING NEWS N.L. Silver Slugger team (1999 and 2000).
STATISTICAL NOTES: Tied for South Atlantic League lead in double plays by outfielder with four in 1995. ... Led Eastern League with .438 on-base percentage and 13 intentional bases on balls received in 1996. ... Had 31-game hitting streak (July 27-August 26, 1999). ... Led N.L. with 23 intentional bases on balls received in 2000.

Year	Team (League)	Pos.	G	AB	R	H	2B	3B	HR	RBI	Avg.	BB	SO	SB	PO	A	E	Avg.
1993—Dom. Expos (DSL)		OF-IF-P	34	105	19	35	4	0	1	14	.333	8	13	4	75	7	5	.943
1994—Dom. Expos (DSL)		OF	25	92	34	39	11	0	12	35	.424	21	6	5	38	6	2	.957
—GC Expos (GCL)		OF	37	137	24	43	13	3	5	25	.314	11	18	0	64	9	1	.986
1995—Albany (S.Atl.)		OF	110	421	77	140	21	10	16	63	*.333	30	45	12	207	15	11	.953
1996—W.P. Beach (FSL)		OF	20	80	16	29	8	0	5	18	.363	3	10	2	28	5	3	.917
—Harrisburg (East.)		OF	118	417	84	150	32	8	19	78	*.360	51	42	17	184	13	8	.961
—Montreal (N.L.)		OF	9	27	2	5	0	0	1	1	.185	0	3	0	11	0	0	1.000
1997—W.P. Beach (FSL)		OF	3	10	0	4	2	0	0	2	.400	1	0	1	4	1	0	1.000
—Montreal (N.L.)		OF	90	325	44	98	22	2	11	40	.302	19	39	3	148	10	*12	.929

G

Year— Team (League)	Pos.	G	AB	R	H	2B	3B	HR	RBI	Avg.	BB	SO	SB	PO	A	E	Avg.
1998— Montreal (N.L.)..........	OF	159	623	108	202	37	7	38	109	.324	42	95	11	323	9	*17	.951
1999— Montreal (N.L.)..........	OF	160	610	102	193	37	5	42	131	.316	55	62	14	332	15	*19	.948
2000— Montreal (N.L.)..........	OF-DH	154	571	101	197	28	11	44	123	.345	58	74	9	299	12	•10	.969
Major League totals (5 years)		572	2156	357	695	124	25	136	404	.322	174	273	37	1113	46	58	.952

ALL-STAR GAME RECORD

Year League	Pos.	AB	R	H	2B	3B	HR	RBI	Avg.	BB	SO	SB	PO	A	E	Avg.
1999— National.....................	OF	1	0	0	0	0	0	0	.000	0	0	0	1	0	0	1.000
2000— National.....................	OF	2	0	1	0	0	0	0	.500	0	0	0	1	0	0	1.000
All-Star Game totals (2 years)		3	0	1	0	0	0	0	.333	0	0	0	2	0	0	1.000

RECORD AS PITCHER

Year League	W	L	Pct.	ERA	G	GS	CG	ShO	Sv.	IP	H	R	ER	BB	SO
1993— Dom. Expos (DSL)	0	0	...	2.25	3	0	0	0	0	8	10	3	2	4	6

GUERRERO, WILTON — OF/2B — REDS

PERSONAL: Born October 24, 1974, in Don Gregorio, Dominican Republic. ... 6-0/175. ... Bats both, throws right. ... Full name: Wilton Alvaro Guerrero. ... Brother of Vladimir Guerrero, outfielder, Montreal Expos.

HIGH SCHOOL: Escuela Primaria Don Gregorio (Dominican Republic).

TRANSACTIONS/CAREER NOTES: Signed as non-drafted free agent by Los Angeles Dodgers organization (October 8, 1991). ... On Albuquerque disabled list (June 26-July 5 and July 26-August 23, 1996). ... On suspended list (June 2-9, 1997). ... Traded by Dodgers with P Ted Lilly, OF Peter Bergeron and 1B Jonathan Tucker to Montreal Expos for P Carlos Perez, SS Mark Grudzielanek and OF Hiram Bocachica (July 31, 1998). ... Granted free agency (December 21, 2000). ... Signed by Cincinnati Reds (January 9, 2001).

STATISTICAL NOTES: Led Florida State League in caught stealing with 20 in 1994. ... Led Texas League in caught stealing with 22 in 1995. ... Career major league grand slams: 1.

Year— Team (League)	Pos.	G	AB	R	H	2B	3B	HR	RBI	Avg.	BB	SO	SB	PO	A	E	Avg.
1992— Dom. Dodgers (DSL) .	SS	61	225	52	87	7	4	0	38	.387	34	21	15	104	215	21	.938
1993— Great Falls (Pio.)	SS	66	256	44	76	5	1	0	21	.297	24	33	20	76	184	21	.925
— Dom. Dodgers (DSL) .	SS	8	31	6	11	0	1	0	4	.355	4	3	2	15	18	1	.971
1994— Vero Beach (FSL) ...	SS	110	402	55	118	11	4	1	32	.294	29	71	23	111	292	17	.960
1995— San Antonio (Texas) ...	SS	95	382	53	133	13	6	0	26	*.348	26	63	21	121	263	19	.953
— Albuquerque (PCL).....	SS-OF	14	49	10	16	1	1	0	2	.327	1	7	2	13	39	9	.852
1996— Albuquerque (PCL).....	2B-SS	98	425	79	146	17	12	2	38	.344	26	48	26	183	306	19	.963
— Los Angeles (N.L.)	OF	5	2	1	0	0	0	0	0	.000	0	2	0	0	0	0	...
1997— Los Angeles (N.L.)	2B-SS	111	357	39	104	10	9	4	32	.291	8	52	6	148	231	4	.990
— Albuquerque (PCL).....	SS-2B	10	45	9	18	0	1	0	5	.400	2	3	3	16	38	5	.915
1998— Los Angeles (N.L.)	2B-SS-OF	64	180	21	51	4	3	0	7	.283	4	33	5	71	91	7	.959
— Albuquerque (PCL).....	2B-OF-DH	30	121	15	36	3	2	1	10	.298	9	12	11	55	49	1	.990
— Montreal (N.L.)■........	2B	52	222	29	63	10	6	2	20	.284	10	30	3	103	130	6	.975
1999— Montreal (N.L.)...........	2B-OF-DH	132	315	42	92	15	7	2	31	.292	13	38	7	86	98	12	.939
2000— Montreal (N.L.)...........	OF-DH-2B	127	288	30	77	7	2	2	23	.267	19	41	8	115	4	4	.967
Major League totals (5 years)		491	1364	162	387	46	27	10	113	.284	54	196	29	523	554	33	.970

GUILLEN, CARLOS — 2B — MARINERS

PERSONAL: Born September 30, 1975, in Maracay, Venezuela. ... 6-1/180. ... Bats both, throws right. ... Full name: Carlos Alfonso Guillen.

TRANSACTIONS/CAREER NOTES: Signed as non-drafted free agent by Houston Astros organization (September 19, 1992). ... On disabled list (June 1-September 12, 1994). ... On disabled list (May 21, 1996-entire season). ... Traded by Astros with P Freddy Garcia and a player to be named later to Seattle Mariners for P Randy Johnson (July 31, 1998); Mariners acquired P John Halama to complete deal (October 1, 1998). ... On disabled list (April 7, 1999-remainder of season). ... On disabled list (April 13-28, 2000); included rehabilitation assignment to Tacoma (April 22-28).

STATISTICAL NOTES: Career major league grand slams: 1.

Year Team (League)	Pos.	G	AB	R	H	2B	3B	HR	RBI	Avg.	BB	SO	SB	PO	A	E	Avg.
1993— Dom. Astros (DSL).....	IF	18	56	12	14	4	2	0	8	.250	8	12	0	37	6	2	.956
1994—							Did not play.										
1995— GC Astros (GCL)		30	105	17	31	4	2	2	15	.295	9	17	17	...	...	...	...
1996— Quad City (Midw.)	SS	29	112	23	37	7	1	3	17	.330	16	25	13	47	71	9	.929
1997— Jackson (Texas)	SS-DH	115	390	47	99	16	1	10	39	.254	38	78	6	169	313	35	.932
— New Orleans (A.A.).......	SS	3	13	3	4	1	0	0	0	.308	0	4	0	5	6	0	1.000
1998— New Orleans (PCL).....	SS	100	374	67	109	18	4	12	51	.291	31	61	3	145	287	26	.943
— Tacoma (PCL)■	2B	24	92	8	21	1	1	1	4	.228	9	17	1	49	63	2	.982
— Seattle (A.L.)	2B	10	39	9	13	1	1	0	5	.333	3	9	2	15	29	0	1.000
1999— Seattle (A.L.)	SS-2B	5	19	2	3	0	0	1	3	.158	1	6	0	12	15	1	.964
2000— Seattle (A.L.)	3B-SS	90	288	45	74	15	2	7	42	.257	28	53	1	85	160	21	.921
— Tacoma (PCL)	3B-SS	24	87	19	26	4	1	2	11	.299	12	17	4	27	48	6	.926
Major League totals (3 years)		105	346	56	90	16	3	8	50	.260	32	68	3	112	204	22	.935

DIVISION SERIES RECORD

Year Team (League)	Pos.	G	AB	R	H	2B	3B	HR	RBI	Avg.	BB	SO	SB	PO	A	E	Avg.
2000— Seattle (A.L.)	PH	1	1	0	1	0	0	0	1	1.000	0	0	0	...	...	...	...

CHAMPIONSHIP SERIES RECORD

Year Team (League)	Pos.	G	AB	R	H	2B	3B	HR	RBI	Avg.	BB	SO	SB	PO	A	E	Avg.
2000— Seattle (A.L.)	3B	2	5	1	1	0	0	1	2	.200	2	2	0	1	3	0	1.000

G

PERSONAL: Born May 17, 1976, in San Cristobal, Dominican Republic. ... 5-11/195. ... Bats right, throws right. ... Full name: Jose Manuel Guillen.

TRANSACTIONS/CAREER NOTES: Signed as non-drafted free agent by Pittsburgh Pirates organization (August 19, 1992). ... Traded by Pirates with P Jeff Sparks to Tampa Bay Devil Rays for C Joe Oliver and C Humberto Cota (July 23, 1999). ... On Durham disabled list (July 23-30, 1999). ... On Tampa Bay disabled list (March 28-April 12, 2000).

RECORDS: Shares major league single-inning record for most doubles—2 (May 16, 1999, fourth inning; and May 28, 2000, eighth inning).

HONORS: Named Carolina League Most Valuable Player (1996).

STATISTICAL NOTES: Led Carolina League with 263 total bases and grounding into double plays with 16 in 1996. ... Led Carolina League outfielders with six double plays in 1996. ... Career major league grand slams: 2.

Year Team (League)	Pos.	G	AB	R	H	2B	3B	HR	RBI	Avg.	BB	SO	SB	PO	A	E	Avg.
1993—Dom. Pirates (DSL)....	OF	63	234	39	53	3	4	11	41	.226	21	55	10	112	12	7	.947
1994—GC Pirates (GCL).......	OF	30	110	17	29	4	1	4	11	.264	7	15	2	59	5	2	.970
1995—Erie (NY-Penn)	OF	66	258	41	81	17	1	*12	46	.314	10	44	1	107	10	13	.900
—Augusta (S.Atl.)..........	OF	10	34	6	8	1	1	2	6	.235	2	9	0	5	0	0	1.000
1996—Lynchburg (Caro.).......	OF-DH	136	*528	78	*170	30	0	•21	94	.322	20	73	24	224	16	*13	.949
1997—Pittsburgh (N.L.)	OF	143	498	58	133	20	5	14	70	.267	17	88	1	226	9	9	.963
1998—Pittsburgh (N.L.)	OF	153	573	60	153	38	2	14	84	.267	21	100	3	283	16	10	.968
1999—Pittsburgh (N.L.)	OF	40	120	18	32	6	0	1	18	.267	10	21	1	58	1	3	.952
—Nashville (PCL)........	OF-DH	35	132	28	44	10	0	5	22	.333	8	21	0	57	5	4	.939
—Durham (I.L.)■.........	OF	9	34	8	13	1	0	3	12	.382	7	7	0	19	1	0	1.000
—Tampa Bay (A.L.).......	OF	47	168	24	41	10	0	2	13	.244	10	36	0	80	5	3	.966
2000—Durham (I.L.).........	OF	19	78	20	33	8	2	9	31	.423	8	11	0	29	2	3	.912
—Tampa Bay (A.L.).......	OF	105	316	40	80	16	5	10	41	.253	18	65	3	169	7	4	.978
American League totals (2 years)		152	484	64	121	26	5	12	54	.250	28	101	3	249	12	7	.974
National League totals (3 years)		336	1191	136	318	64	7	29	172	.267	48	209	5	567	26	22	.964
Major League totals (4 years)		488	1675	200	439	90	12	41	226	.262	76	310	8	816	38	29	.967

PERSONAL: Born January 20, 1964, in Ocumare del Tuy, Miranda, Venezuela. ... 5-11/165. ... Bats left, throws right. ... Full name: Oswaldo Jose Barrios Guillen.

TRANSACTIONS/CAREER NOTES: Signed as non-drafted free agent by San Diego Padres organization (December 17, 1980). ... Traded by Padres with P Tim Lollar, P Bill Long and 3B Luis Salazar to Chicago White Sox for P LaMarr Hoyt, P Kevin Kristan and P Todd Simmons (December 6, 1984). ... On disabled list (April 22, 1992-remainder of season). ... Granted free agency (October 31, 1997). ... Signed by Baltimore Orioles organization (January 29, 1998). ... Released by Orioles (May 1, 1998). ... Signed by Atlanta Braves (May 6, 1998). ... Granted free agency (November 2, 1998). ... Re-signed by Braves (December 2, 1998). ... Released by Braves (April 5, 2000). ... Signed by Tampa Bay Devil Rays (April 5, 2000). ... Granted free agency (November 9, 2000). ... Re-signed by Devil Rays organization (December 6, 2000).

RECORDS: Holds major league single-season record for fewest bases on balls received (150 or more games)—10 (1996). ... Holds A.L. single-season record for fewest putouts by shortstop (150 or more games)—220 (1985).

HONORS: Named A.L. Rookie Player of the Year by The Sporting News (1985). ... Named A.L. Rookie of the Year by Baseball Writers' Association of America (1985). ... Won A.L. Gold Glove at shortstop (1990).

STATISTICAL NOTES: Tied for California League lead with 14 sacrifice hits in 1982. ... Led Pacific Coast League shortstops with 362 assists and 549 total chances in 1984. ... Led A.L. shortstops with 760 total chances in 1987 and 863 in 1988. ... Led A.L. shortstops with 105 double plays in 1987. ... Career major league grand slams: 1.

MISCELLANEOUS: Batted as switch-hitter (1981-84).

Year Team (League)	Pos.	G	AB	R	H	2B	3B	HR	RBI	Avg.	BB	SO	SB	PO	A	E	Avg.
1981—GC Padres (GCL).......	SS-2B	55	189	26	49	4	1	0	16	.259	13	24	8	105	135	15	.941
1982—Reno (Calif.).............	SS	130	528	*103	*183	33	1	2	54	.347	16	53	25	*240	399	41	.940
1983—Beaumont (Texas)	SS	114	427	62	126	20	4	2	48	.295	15	29	7	185	327	*38	.931
1984—Las Vegas (PCL)	SS-2B	122	463	81	137	26	6	5	53	.296	13	40	9	172	†364	17	.969
1985—Chicago (A.L.)■........	SS	150	491	71	134	21	9	1	33	.273	12	36	7	220	382	12	*.980
1986—Chicago (A.L.)...........	SS-DH	159	547	58	137	19	4	2	47	.250	12	52	8	261	459	22	.970
1987—Chicago (A.L.)...........	SS	149	560	64	156	22	7	2	51	.279	22	52	25	266	475	19	.975
1988—Chicago (A.L.)...........	SS	156	566	58	148	16	7	0	39	.261	25	40	25	273	*570	20	.977
1989—Chicago (A.L.)...........	SS	155	597	63	151	20	8	1	54	.253	15	48	36	272	512	22	.973
1990—Chicago (A.L.)...........	SS	160	516	61	144	21	4	1	58	.279	26	37	13	252	474	17	.977
1991—Chicago (A.L.)...........	SS	154	524	52	143	20	3	3	49	.273	11	38	21	249	439	21	.970
1992—Chicago (A.L.)...........	SS	12	40	5	8	4	0	0	7	.200	1	5	1	20	39	0	1.000
1993—Chicago (A.L.)...........	SS	134	457	44	128	23	4	4	50	.280	10	41	5	189	361	16	.972
1994—Chicago (A.L.)...........	SS	100	365	46	105	9	5	1	39	.288	14	35	5	139	237	16	.959
1995—Chicago (A.L.)...........	SS-DH	122	415	50	103	20	3	1	41	.248	13	25	6	167	319	12	.976
1996—Chicago (A.L.)...........	SS-OF	150	499	62	131	24	8	4	45	.263	10	27	6	222	348	11	.981
1997—Chicago (A.L.)...........	SS	142	490	59	120	21	6	4	52	.245	22	24	5	207	348	15	.974
1998—Baltimore (A.L.).........	SS-3B	12	16	2	1	0	0	0	0	.063	1	2	0	3	11	1	.933
—Atlanta (N.L.)■.....SS-2B-1B-3B		83	264	35	73	15	1	1	22	.277	24	25	1	97	166	6	.978
1999—Atlanta (N.L.).............	SS-3B-2B	92	232	21	56	16	0	1	20	.241	15	17	4	58	146	7	.967
2000—Tampa Bay (A.L.)■.....SS-3B-1B-2B		63	107	22	26	4	0	2	12	.243	6	7	1	40	90	5	.963
American League totals (15 years)		1818	6190	717	1635	244	68	26	577	.264	200	469	164	2780	5064	209	.974
National League totals (2 years)		175	496	56	129	31	1	2	42	.260	39	42	5	155	312	13	.973
Major League totals (16 years)		1993	6686	773	1764	275	69	28	619	.264	239	511	169	2935	5376	222	.974

G

DIVISION SERIES RECORD

Year Team (League)	Pos.	G	AB	R	H	2B	3B	HR	RBI	Avg.	BB	SO	SB	PO	A	E	Avg.
										BATTING					FIELDING		
1998— Atlanta (N.L.)...............	PH	1	1	0	0	0	0	0	0	.000	0	0	0	...	...	...	...
1999— Atlanta (N.L.)...............	PH	1	1	0	0	0	0	0	0	.000	0	0	0	...	...	...	...
Division series totals (2 years)		2	2	0	0	0	0	0	0	.000	0	0	0	...	...	...	...

CHAMPIONSHIP SERIES RECORD

Year Team (League)	Pos.	G	AB	R	H	2B	3B	HR	RBI	Avg.	BB	SO	SB	PO	A	E	Avg.
										BATTING					FIELDING		
1993— Chicago (A.L.)............	SS	6	22	4	6	1	0	0	2	.273	0	2	1	12	14	0	1.000
1998— Atlanta (N.L.)...............	PH-SS	4	12	1	5	0	0	0	1	.417	0	1	0	1	6	0	1.000
1999— Atlanta (N.L.)...............	PH-SS	3	3	0	1	0	0	0	1	.333	0	0	0	0	0	—	—
Championship series totals (3 years)		13	37	5	12	1	0	0	4	.324	0	3	1	13	20	0	1.000

WORLD SERIES RECORD

Year Team (League)	Pos.	G	AB	R	H	2B	3B	HR	RBI	Avg.	BB	SO	SB	PO	A	E	Avg.
										BATTING					FIELDING		
1999— Atlanta (N.L.)..............	PH-SS-DH	3	5	0	0	0	0	0	0	.000	0	1	0	4	3	1	.875

ALL-STAR GAME RECORD

NOTES: Named to A.L. All-Star team; replaced by Kurt Stillwell due to injury (1988).

Year League	Pos.	AB	R	H	2B	3B	HR	RBI	Avg.	BB	SO	SB	PO	A	E	Avg.
							BATTING							FIELDING		
1988— American..................						Selected, did not play—injured.										
1990— American..................	SS	2	0	0	0	0	0	0	.000	0	0	0	0	2	0	1.000
1991— American..................	SS	0	0	0	0	0	0	0	...	0	0	0	1	0	0	1.000
All-Star Game totals (2 years)		2	0	0	0	0	0	0	.000	0	0	0	1	2	0	1.000

GUNDERSON, ERIC   P   INDIANS

PERSONAL: Born March 29, 1966, in Portland, Ore. ... 6-0/190. ... Throws left, bats right. ... Full name: Eric Andrew Gunderson.

HIGH SCHOOL: Aloha (Portland, Ore.).

COLLEGE: Portland State.

TRANSACTIONS/CAREER NOTES: Selected by San Francisco Giants organization in second round of free-agent draft (June 2, 1987). ... Released by Giants (March 31, 1992). ... Signed by Seattle Mariners organization (April 10, 1992). ... On Jacksonville disabled list (April 10-17, 1992). ... On Seattle suspended list (September 30-October 4, 1992). ... Released by Mariners (April 29, 1993). ... Signed by New York Mets organization (June 10, 1993). ... Granted free agency (October 15, 1993). ... Signed by San Diego Padres organization (December 24, 1993). ... Released by Padres (April 2, 1994). ... Signed by Mets organization (May 5, 1994). ... Claimed on waivers by Mariners (August 4, 1995). ... Claimed on waivers by Boston Red Sox (August 10, 1995). ... Granted free agency (October 7, 1996). ... Signed by Texas Rangers organization (January 24, 1997). ... On disabled list (August 26-September 7, 1997). ... On Texas disabled list (May 8, 1999-remainder of season); included rehabilitation assignment to Oklahoma (June 9-July 8). ... Released by Rangers (October 28, 1999). ... Re-signed by Rangers organization (February 16, 2000). ... Signed by Toronto Blue Jays organization (February 16, 2000). ... Traded by Blue Jays to Giants for a player to be named later (July 26, 2000). ... Granted free agency (October 18, 2000). ... Signed by Cleveland Indians organization (December 20, 2000).

STATISTICAL NOTES: Led California League with 17 hit batsmen in 1988.

Year League	W	L	Pct.	ERA	G	GS	CG	ShO	Sv.	IP	H	R	ER	BB	SO
1987— Everett (N'West)................	8	4	.667	2.46	15	•15	*5	•3	0	98²/₃	80	34	27	34	*99
1988— San Jose (Calif.)................	12	5	.706	2.65	20	20	5	•4	0	149¹/₃	131	56	44	52	151
— Shreveport (Texas)............	1	2	.333	5.15	7	6	0	0	0	36²/₃	45	25	21	13	28
1989— Shreveport (Texas)............	8	2	*.800	2.72	11	11	2	1	0	72²/₃	68	24	22	23	61
— Phoenix (PCL).................	2	4	.333	5.04	14	14	2	1	0	85²/₃	93	51	48	36	56
1990— San Francisco (N.L.)	1	2	.333	5.49	7	4	0	0	0	19²/₃	24	14	12	11	14
— Phoenix (PCL).................	5	7	.417	8.23	16	16	0	0	0	82	137	87	75	46	41
— Shreveport (Texas)............	2	2	.500	3.25	8	8	1	1	0	52²/₃	51	24	19	17	44
1991— San Francisco (N.L.)	0	0	...	5.40	2	0	0	0	1	3¹/₃	6	4	2	1	2
— Phoenix (PCL).................	7	6	.538	6.14	40	14	0	0	3	107	153	85	73	44	53
1992— Jacksonville (Sou.)■........	2	0	1.000	2.31	15	0	0	0	2	23¹/₃	18	10	6	7	23
— Calgary (PCL).................	0	2	.000	6.02	27	1	0	0	5	52¹/₃	57	37	35	31	50
— Seattle (A.L.).................	2	1	.667	8.68	9	0	0	0	0	9¹/₃	12	12	9	5	2
1993— Calgary (PCL).................	0	1	.000	18.90	5	0	0	0	0	6²/₃	14	15	14	8	3
— Binghamton (East.)■........	2	1	.667	5.24	20	1	0	0	1	22¹/₃	20	14	13	14	26
— Norfolk (I.L.).................	3	2	.600	3.71	6	5	1	0	0	34	41	16	14	9	26
1994— St. Lucie (FSL)...............	1	0	1.000	0.00	3	0	0	0	1	4²/₃	4	0	0	0	6
— Norfolk (I.L.).................	3	1	.750	3.68	19	2	1	1	1	36²/₃	25	16	15	17	31
— New York (N.L.)...............	0	0	...	0.00	14	0	0	0	0	9	5	0	0	4	4
1995— New York (N.L.)...............	1	1	.500	3.70	30	0	0	0	0	24¹/₃	25	10	10	8	19
— Boston (A.L.)■...............	2	1	.667	5.11	19	0	0	0	0	12¹/₃	13	7	7	9	9
1996— Pawtucket (I.L.)...............	2	1	.667	3.48	26	1	0	0	2	33²/₃	38	15	13	9	34
— Boston (A.L.).................	0	1	.000	8.31	26	0	0	0	0	17¹/₃	21	17	16	8	7
1997— Texas (A.L.)■...............	2	1	.667	3.26	60	0	0	0	1	49²/₃	45	19	18	15	31
1998— Texas (A.L.).................	0	3	.000	5.19	68	1	0	0	0	67²/₃	88	43	39	19	41
1999— Texas (A.L.).................	0	0	...	7.20	11	0	0	0	0	10	20	8	8	2	6
— Oklahoma (PCL).................	0	1	.000	8.10	5	0	0	0	1	6²/₃	11	6	6	1	3
2000— Syracuse (I.L.)■	0	3	.000	2.67	33	0	0	0	2	27	26	12	8	11	17
— Toronto (A.L.).................	0	1	.000	7.11	6	0	0	0	0	6¹/₃	15	6	5	2	2
— Fresno (PCL)■...............	2	1	.667	5.01	13	0	0	0	2	23¹/₃	34	18	13	7	14
A.L. totals (7 years)	6	8	.429	5.32	201	1	0	0	1	172²/₃	214	112	102	60	98
N.L. totals (4 years)	2	3	.400	3.83	53	4	0	0	1	56¹/₃	60	28	24	24	39
Major League totals (10 years)	8	11	.421	4.95	254	5	0	0	2	229	274	140	126	84	137

G

GUTHRIE, MARK — P — ATHLETICS

PERSONAL: Born September 22, 1965, in Buffalo. ... 6-4/215. ... Throws left, bats right. ... Full name: Mark Andrew Guthrie.
HIGH SCHOOL: Venice (Fla.).
COLLEGE: Louisiana State.
TRANSACTIONS/CAREER NOTES: Selected by St. Louis Cardinals organization in fourth round of free-agent draft (June 2, 1986); did not sign. ... Selected by Minnesota Twins organization in seventh round of free-agent draft (June 2, 1987). ... On disabled list (May 29, 1993-remainder of season). ... Traded by Twins with P Kevin Tapani to Los Angeles Dodgers for 1B/3B Ron Coomer, P Greg Hansell, P Jose Parra and a player to be named later (July 31, 1995); Twins acquired OF Chris Latham to complete deal (October 30, 1995). ... Granted free agency (October 29, 1996). ... Re-signed by Dodgers (November 6, 1996). ... Granted free agency (October 26, 1998). ... Signed by Boston Red Sox (December 19, 1998). ... On Boston disabled list (July 5-24, 1999); included rehabilitation assignment to Pawtucket (July 22-23). ... Traded by Red Sox with a player to named later to Chicago Cubs for P Rod Beck (August 31, 1999); Cubs acquired 3B Cole Liniak to complete deal (September 1, 1999). ... Traded by Cubs to Tampa Bay Devil Rays for OF Dave Martinez (May 12, 2000). ... Traded by Devil Rays with P Steve Trachsel to Toronto Blue Jays for 2B Brent Abernathy and a player to be named later (July 31, 2000). ... Granted free agency (October 31, 2000). ... Signed by Oakland Athletics (January 5, 2001).
MISCELLANEOUS: Appeared in one game as pinch runner (1991).

Year League	W	L	Pct.	ERA	G	GS	CG	ShO	Sv.	IP	H	R	ER	BB	SO
1987— Visalia (Calif.)	2	1	.667	4.50	4	1	0	0	0	12	10	7	6	5	9
1988— Visalia (Calif.)	12	9	.571	3.31	25	25	4	1	0	171 1/3	169	81	63	86	182
1989— Orlando (Sou.)	8	3	.727	1.97	14	14	0	0	0	96	75	32	21	38	103
— Portland (PCL)	3	4	.429	3.65	7	7	1	0	0	44 1/3	45	21	18	16	35
— Minnesota (A.L.)	2	4	.333	4.55	13	8	0	0	0	57 1/3	66	32	29	21	38
1990— Minnesota (A.L.)	7	9	.438	3.79	24	21	3	1	0	144 2/3	154	65	61	39	101
— Portland (PCL)	1	3	.250	2.98	9	8	1	0	0	42 1/3	47	19	14	12	39
1991— Minnesota (A.L.)	7	5	.583	4.32	41	12	0	0	2	98	116	52	47	41	72
1992— Minnesota (A.L.)	2	3	.400	2.88	54	0	0	0	5	75	59	27	24	23	76
1993— Minnesota (A.L.)	2	1	.667	4.71	22	0	0	0	0	21	20	11	11	16	15
1994— Minnesota (A.L.)	4	2	.667	6.14	50	2	0	0	1	51 1/3	65	43	35	18	38
1995— Minnesota (A.L.)	5	3	.625	4.46	36	0	0	0	0	42 1/3	47	22	21	16	48
— Los Angeles (N.L.)■	0	2	.000	3.66	24	0	0	0	0	19 2/3	19	11	8	9	19
1996— Los Angeles (N.L.)	2	3	.400	2.22	66	0	0	0	1	73	65	21	18	22	56
1997— Los Angeles (N.L.)	1	4	.200	5.32	62	0	0	0	1	69 1/3	71	44	41	30	42
1998— Los Angeles (N.L.)	2	1	.667	3.50	53	0	0	0	0	54	56	26	21	24	45
1999— Boston (A.L.)■	1	1	.500	5.83	46	0	0	0	2	46 1/3	50	32	30	20	36
— Pawtucket (I.L.)	0	0	...	0.00	1	1	0	0	0	1	0	0	0	0	1
— Chicago (N.L.)■	0	2	.000	3.65	11	0	0	0	0	12 1/3	7	6	5	4	9
2000— Chicago (N.L.)	2	3	.400	4.82	19	0	0	0	0	18 2/3	17	11	10	10	17
— Tampa Bay (A.L.)■	1	1	.500	4.50	34	0	0	0	0	32	33	18	16	18	26
— Toronto (A.L.)■	0	2	.000	4.79	23	0	0	0	0	20 2/3	20	12	11	9	20
A.L. totals (9 years)	31	31	.500	4.36	343	43	3	1	10	588 2/3	630	314	285	221	470
N.L. totals (6 years)	7	15	.318	3.75	235	0	0	0	2	247	235	119	103	99	188
Major League totals (12 years)	38	46	.452	4.18	578	43	3	1	12	835 2/3	865	433	388	320	658

DIVISION SERIES RECORD

Year League	W	L	Pct.	ERA	G	GS	CG	ShO	Sv.	IP	H	R	ER	BB	SO
1995— Los Angeles (N.L.)	0	0	...	6.75	3	0	0	0	0	1 1/3	2	1	1	1	1
1996— Los Angeles (N.L.)	0	0	...	0.00	1	0	0	0	0	1/3	0	0	0	1	1
Division series totals (2 years)	0	0	...	5.40	4	0	0	0	0	1 2/3	2	1	1	2	2

CHAMPIONSHIP SERIES RECORD

Year League	W	L	Pct.	ERA	G	GS	CG	ShO	Sv.	IP	H	R	ER	BB	SO
1991— Minnesota (A.L.)	1	0	1.000	0.00	2	0	0	0	0	2 2/3	0	0	0	0	0

WORLD SERIES RECORD

NOTES: Member of World Series championship team (1991).

Year League	W	L	Pct.	ERA	G	GS	CG	ShO	Sv.	IP	H	R	ER	BB	SO
1991— Minnesota (A.L.)	0	1	.000	2.25	4	0	0	0	0	4	3	1	1	4	3

GUTIERREZ, RICKY — SS — CUBS

PERSONAL: Born May 23, 1970, in Miami. ... 6-1/195. ... Bats right, throws right. ... Full name: Ricardo Gutierrez.
HIGH SCHOOL: American (Hialeah, Fla.).
TRANSACTIONS/CAREER NOTES: Selected by Baltimore Orioles organization in supplemental round ("sandwich pick" between first and second round, 28th pick overall) of free-agent draft (June 1, 1988); pick received as compensation for Orioles failing to sign 1987 No. 1 pick P Brad DuVall. ... Traded by Orioles to San Diego Padres (September 4, 1992), completing deal in which Padres traded P Craig Lefferts to Orioles for P Erik Schullstrom and a player to be named later (August 31, 1992). ... Traded by Padres with OF Phil Plantier, OF Derek Bell, P Pedro Martinez, P Doug Brocail and IF Craig Shipley to Houston Astros for 3B Ken Caminiti, OF Steve Finley, SS Andujar Cedeno, 1B Robert Petagine, P Brian Williams and a player to be named later (December 28, 1994); Padres acquired P Sean Fesh to complete deal (May 1, 1995). ... On Houston disabled list (March 31-May 6, 1997); included rehabilitation assignment to New Orleans (April 29-May 6). ... On Houston disabled list (April 28-June 7 and July 10-August 9, 1999); included rehabilitation assignments to Jackson (June 3-7) and New Orleans (August 5-9). ... Granted free agency (October 28, 1999). ... Signed by Chicago Cubs (December 20, 1999). ... On Chicago disabled list (May 25-June 23, 2000); included rehabilitation assignment to Daytona (June 19-23).
STATISTICAL NOTES: Led Appalachian League shortstops with 309 total chances in 1988. ... Led N.L. with 16 sacrifice bunts in 2000.

			BATTING											FIELDING			
Year Team (League)	Pos.	G	AB	R	H	2B	3B	HR	RBI	Avg.	BB	SO	SB	PO	A	E	Avg.
1988— Bluefield (Appl.)	SS	62	208	35	51	8	2	2	19	.245	44	40	5	*100	175	34	.890
1989— Frederick (Caro.)	SS	127	456	48	106	16	2	3	41	.232	39	89	15	190	372	34	*.943
1990— Frederick (Caro.)	SS	112	425	54	117	16	4	1	46	.275	38	59	12	192	286	26	.948
— Hagerstown (East.)	SS	20	64	4	15	0	1	0	6	.234	3	8	2	31	36	4	.944
1991— Hagerstown (East.)	SS	84	292	47	69	6	4	0	30	.236	57	52	11	158	196	22	.941
— Rochester (I.L.)	SS-3B	49	157	23	48	5	3	0	15	.306	24	27	4	61	129	8	.960

							BATTING								FIELDING		
Year	Team (League)	Pos.	G	AB	R	H	2B	3B	HR	RBI	Avg.	BB	SO	SB	PO	A	E	Avg.
1992—	Rochester (I.L.)	2B-SS	125	431	54	109	9	3	0	41	.253	53	77	14	251	283	15	.973
—	Las Vegas (PCL)■	SS	3	6	0	1	0	0	0	1	.167	1	3	0	1	8	0	1.000
1993—	Las Vegas (PCL)	2B-SS	5	24	4	10	4	0	0	4	.417	0	4	4	11	14	2	.926
—	San Diego (N.L.)	SS-2B-OF-3B	133	438	76	110	10	5	5	26	.251	50	97	4	194	305	14	.973
1994—	San Diego (N.L.)	SS-2B	90	275	27	66	11	2	1	28	.240	32	54	2	93	202	22	.931
1995—	Houston (N.L.)■	SS-3B	52	156	22	43	6	0	0	12	.276	10	33	5	64	108	8	.956
—	Tucson (PCL)	SS-DH	64	236	46	71	12	4	1	26	.301	28	28	9	91	167	6	.977
1996—	Houston (N.L.)	SS-3B-2B	89	218	28	62	8	1	1	15	.284	23	42	6	86	149	12	.951
1997—	New Orleans (A.A.)	SS	7	27	2	5	1	0	0	4	.185	2	4	0	12	21	1	.971
—	Houston (N.L.)	SS-3B-2B	102	303	33	79	14	4	3	34	.261	21	50	5	104	191	8	.974
1998—	Houston (N.L.)	SS	141	491	55	128	24	3	2	46	.261	54	84	13	215	404	15	.976
1999—	Houston (N.L.)	SS-3B	85	268	33	70	7	5	1	25	.261	37	45	2	102	203	9	.971
—	Jackson (Texas)	SS-DH	4	12	4	4	1	0	0	1	.333	4	3	0	2	5	0	1.000
—	New Orleans (PCL)	SS	4	14	0	3	0	0	0	1	.214	2	3	0	10	11	3	.875
2000—	Chicago (N.L.)■	SS	125	449	73	124	19	2	11	56	.276	66	58	8	190	290	7	*.986
—	Daytona (FSL)	SS	4	10	0	4	1	0	0	1	.400	2	2	1	2	6	3	.727
Major League totals (8 years)			817	2598	347	682	99	22	24	242	.263	293	463	45	1048	1852	95	.968

DIVISION SERIES RECORD

							BATTING								FIELDING		
Year	Team (League)	Pos.	G	AB	R	H	2B	3B	HR	RBI	Avg.	BB	SO	SB	PO	A	E	Avg.
1997—	Houston (N.L.)	SS	3	8	0	1	0	0	0	0	.125	2	1	0	5	5	0	1.000
1998—	Houston (N.L.)	SS	4	10	1	3	0	0	0	0	.300	3	7	1	7	13	0	1.000
1999—	Houston (N.L.)	SS	3	10	0	0	0	0	0	0	.000	2	5	0	4	16	1	.952
Division series totals (3 years)			10	28	1	4	0	0	0	0	.143	7	13	1	16	34	1	.980

GUZMAN, CRISTIAN   SS   TWINS

PERSONAL: Born March 21, 1978, in Santo Domingo, Dominican Republic. ... 6-0/195. ... Bats both, throws right. ... Full name: Cristian Antonio Guzman.

TRANSACTIONS/CAREER NOTES: Signed as non-drafted free agent by New York Yankees organization (August 24, 1994). ... Traded by Yankees with P Eric Milton, P Danny Mota, OF Brian Buchanan and cash to Minnesota Twins for 2B Chuck Knoblauch (February 6, 1998). ... On disabled list (May 27-June 11, 1999). ... On suspended list (September 10-13, 1999).

STATISTICAL NOTES: Led South Atlantic League shortstops with 68 double plays in 1997. ... Led Eastern League with 17 sacrifice hits in 1998. ... Led Eastern League shortstops with 95 double plays in 1998.

							BATTING								FIELDING		
Year	Team (League)	Pos.	G	AB	R	H	2B	3B	HR	RBI	Avg.	BB	SO	SB	PO	A	E	Avg.
1995—	Dom. Yankees (DSL)	SS	46	160	24	43	6	5	3	20	.269	12	23	11	159	29	13	.935
1996—	GC Yankees (GCL)	SS	42	170	37	50	8	2	1	21	.294	10	31	7	55	106	20	.890
1997—	Tampa (FSL)	SS	4	14	4	4	0	0	0	1	.286	1	1	0	6	10	2	.889
—	Greensboro (S.Atl.)	SS	124	495	68	135	21	4	4	52	.273	17	105	23	173	364	37	.936
1998—	New Britain (East.)■	SS	•140	566	68	157	29	5	1	40	.277	21	111	23	211	*426	*32	.952
1999—	Minnesota (A.L.)	SS	131	420	47	95	12	3	1	26	.226	22	90	9	196	363	24	.959
2000—	Minnesota (A.L.)	SS-DH	156	631	89	156	25	*20	8	54	.247	46	101	28	228	413	22	.967
Major League totals (2 years)			287	1051	136	251	37	23	9	80	.239	68	191	37	424	776	46	.963

GUZMAN, DOMINGO   P   PADRES

PERSONAL: Born April 5, 1975, in San Cristobal, Dominican Republic. ... 6-0/210. ... Throws right, bats right. ... Full name: Domingo Serrano Guzman.

TRANSACTIONS/CAREER NOTES: Signed as non-drafted free agent by San Diego Padres organization (June 15, 1993). ... On Clinton suspended list (May 15-18, 1997). ... On Rancho Cucamonga disabled list (April 2-May 26, 1998). ... On Mobile disabled list (August 7-27, 1998; and April 28-May 27, 1999). ... Granted free agency (October 18, 2000). ... Re-signed by Padres organization (November 20, 2000).

STATISTICAL NOTES: Pitched 6-0 no-hit victory vs. Butte (August 15, 1996).

Year	League	W	L	Pct.	ERA	G	GS	CG	ShO	Sv.	IP	H	R	ER	BB	SO
1994—	Arizona Padres (Ariz.)	•8	4	.667	4.11	13	13	0	0	0	70	65	39	32	25	55
1995—	Idaho Falls (Pio.)	2	1	.667	6.66	27	0	0	0	•11	$25\frac{2}{3}$	25	22	19	25	33
1996—	Idaho Falls (Pio.)	4	2	.667	4.13	15	10	1	•1	0	$65\frac{1}{3}$	52	41	30	29	75
—	Clinton (Midw.)	0	5	.000	12.63	6	5	0	0	0	$20\frac{2}{3}$	32	33	29	19	18
1997—	Clinton (Midw.)	4	5	.444	3.19	12	12	5	0	0	79	66	36	28	25	91
—	Rancho Cuca. (Calif.)	3	2	.600	5.45	6	6	0	0	0	38	42	23	23	16	39
1998—	Rancho Cuca. (Calif.)	1	1	.500	3.74	4	4	0	0	0	$21\frac{2}{3}$	22	11	9	6	16
—	Mobile (Sou.)	5	2	.714	4.50	12	8	0	0	1	48	51	34	24	26	39
1999—	Mobile (Sou.)	1	2	.333	5.47	41	0	0	0	6	51	60	33	31	25	38
—	San Diego (N.L.)	0	1	.000	21.60	7	0	0	0	0	5	13	12	12	3	4
2000—	Mobile (Sou.)	0	0	...	2.08	14	1	0	0	0	$17\frac{1}{3}$	13	8	4	11	14
—	Las Vegas (PCL)	3	5	.375	5.97	43	3	0	0	1	$63\frac{1}{3}$	56	47	42	35	54
—	San Diego (N.L.)	0	0	...	9.00	1	0	0	0	0	1	1	1	1	1	0
Major League totals (2 years)		0	1	.000	19.50	8	0	0	0	0	6	14	13	13	4	4

GUZMAN, ELPIDIO   OF   ANGELS

PERSONAL: Born February 24, 1979, in Santo Domingo, Dominican Republic. ... 6-0/165. ... Bats left, throws left.

HIGH SCHOOL: Carl Morgan (Santo Domingo, Dominican Republic).

TRANSACTIONS/CAREER NOTES: Signed as non-drafted free agent by California Angels organization (October 15, 1995). ... Angels franchise renamed Anaheim Angels for 1997 season.

STATISTICAL NOTES: Led Pioneer League outfielders with 147 total chances in 1998. ... Led California League with 11 sacrifice flies in 2000.

G

							BATTING								FIELDING		
Year Team (League)	Pos.	G	AB	R	H	2B	3B	HR	RBI	Avg.	BB	SO	SB	PO	A	E	Avg.
1996— Dom. Angels (DSL)	OF	42	116	11	27	6	0	0	13	.233	19	17	11	76	2	6	.929
1997— Butte (Pio.)	OF	17	43	12	13	2	1	3	13	.302	5	5	3	21	2	1	.958
1998— Butte (Pio.)	OF	69	299	70	99	16	5	9	61	.331	24	44	40	*136	6	5	.966
1999— Cedar Rapids (Midw.)	OF	130	526	74	144	26	13	4	48	.274	41	84	52	256	9	13	.953
2000— Lake Elsinore (Calif.) ..	OF	135	532	96	150	20	16	9	72	.282	61	116	53	297	15	*14	.957

GUZMAN, GERALDO · P · DIAMONDBACKS

PERSONAL: Born November 28, 1973, in Teoares, Dominican Republic. ... 6-2/180. ... Throws right, bats right.

TRANSACTIONS/CAREER NOTES: Signed as non-drafted free agent by Montreal Expos organization (September 27, 1989). ... Released by Expos (October 14, 1992). ... Out of organized baseball (1993-98). ... Played with China Trust, Taiwan (1999). ... Signed by Arizona Diamondbacks organization (November 12, 1999).

Year League	W	L	Pct.	ERA	G	GS	CG	ShO	Sv.	IP	H	R	ER	BB	SO
1990— Dom. Expos (DSL)	2	1	.667	2.98	8	7	0	0	0	45 1/3	45	22	15	10	16
1991— Dom. Expos (DSL)	5	5	.500	3.00	15	15	3	1	0	75	72	40	25	26	38
1992— Dom. Expos (DSL)							Statistics unavailable.								
1999— China Trust (Taiwan)■	0	0	...	2.08	9	...	...	...	1	13	15	...	3	3	6
2000— Tucson (PCL)■	4	1	.800	1.42	6	6	1	1	0	38	23	7	6	10	44
— Arizona (N.L.)	5	4	.556	5.37	13	10	0	0	0	60 1/3	66	36	36	22	52
— El Paso (Texas)	3	3	.500	3.75	17	7	0	0	3	50 1/3	47	23	21	22	53
Major League totals (1 year)	5	4	.556	5.37	13	10	0	0	0	60 1/3	66	36	36	22	52

GUZMAN, JUAN · P · DEVIL RAYS

PERSONAL: Born October 28, 1966, in Santo Domingo, Dominican Republic. ... 5-11/195. ... Throws right, bats right. ... Full name: Juan Andres Correa Guzman.

HIGH SCHOOL: Liceo Las Americas (Dominican Republic).

TRANSACTIONS/CAREER NOTES: Signed as non-drafted free agent by Los Angeles Dodgers organization (March 16, 1985). ... Traded by Dodgers to Toronto Blue Jays for IF Mike Sharperson (September 22, 1987). ... On Toronto disabled list (August 4-29, 1992); included rehabilitation assignment to Syracuse (August 24-25). ... On Toronto disabled list (May 16-June 5 and August 10-29, 1995); included rehabilitation assignment to Syracuse (August 25-26). ... On Toronto disabled list (May 23-June 7, 1996; May 29-June 26 and July 16-September 28, 1997). ... Traded by Blue Jays to Baltimore Orioles for P Nerio Rodriguez and OF Shannon Carter (July 31, 1998). ... Traded by Orioles to Cincinnati Reds for P B.J. Ryan and P Jacobo Sequea (July 31, 1999). ... Granted free agency (October 29, 1999). ... Signed by Tampa Bay Devil Rays (January 8, 2000). ... On Tampa Bay disabled list (April 8, 2000-remainder of season); included rehabilitation assignments to St. Petersburg (May 30-June 4), Orlando (June 4-9) and Durham (June 10-16).

RECORDS: Holds A.L. single-season record for most wild pitches—26 (1993).

HONORS: Named A.L. Rookie Pitcher of the Year by THE SPORTING NEWS (1991).

STATISTICAL NOTES: Led Gulf Coast League with 15 wild pitches in 1985. ... Led Florida State League with 16 wild pitches in 1986. ... Led Southern League with 21 wild pitches in 1990. ... Led A.L. with 26 wild pitches in 1993 and tied for lead with 13 in 1994. ... Tied for A.L. lead with 16 losses in 1998.

Year League	W	L	Pct.	ERA	G	GS	CG	ShO	Sv.	IP	H	R	ER	BB	SO
1985— Gulf Coast Dodgers (GCL)..	5	1	.833	3.86	21	3	0	0	4	42	39	26	18	25	43
1986— Vero Beach (FSL)	10	9	.526	3.49	20	24	3	0	0	131 1/3	114	69	51	90	96
1987— Bakersfield (Calif.)	5	6	.455	4.75	22	21	0	0	0	110	106	71	58	84	113
1988— Knoxville (Sou.)■	4	5	.444	2.36	46	2	0	0	6	84	52	29	22	61	90
1989— Syracuse (I.L.)	1	1	.500	3.98	14	0	0	0	0	20 1/3	13	9	9	30	28
— Knoxville (Sou.)	1	4	.200	6.23	22	8	0	0	0	47 2/3	34	36	33	60	50
1990— Knoxville (Sou.)	11	9	.550	4.24	37	21	2	0	1	157	145	84	74	80	138
1991— Syracuse (I.L.)	4	5	.444	4.03	12	11	0	0	0	67	46	39	30	42	67
— Toronto (A.L.)	10	3	.769	2.99	23	23	1	0	0	138 2/3	98	53	46	66	123
1992— Toronto (A.L.)	16	5	.762	2.64	28	28	1	0	0	180 2/3	135	56	53	72	165
— Syracuse (I.L.)	0	0	...	6.00	1	1	0	0	0	3	6	2	2	1	3
1993— Toronto (A.L.)	14	3	*.824	3.99	33	33	2	1	0	221	211	107	98	110	194
1994— Toronto (A.L.)	12	11	.522	5.68	25	•25	2	0	0	147 1/3	165	102	93	76	124
1995— Toronto (A.L.)	4	14	.222	6.32	24	24	3	0	0	135 1/3	151	101	95	73	94
— Syracuse (I.L.)	0	0	...	0.00	1	1	0	0	0	5	1	0	0	3	5
1996— Toronto (A.L.)	11	8	.579	*2.93	27	27	4	1	0	187 2/3	158	68	61	53	165
1997— Toronto (A.L.)	3	6	.333	4.95	13	13	0	0	0	60	48	42	33	31	52
— Dunedin (FSL)	0	0	...	0.00	2	2	0	0	0	4	3	0	0	1	3
1998— Toronto (A.L.)	6	12	.333	4.41	22	22	2	0	0	145	133	83	71	65	113
— Baltimore (A.L.)■	4	§4	.500	4.23	11	11	0	0	0	66	60	34	31	33	55
1999— Baltimore (A.L.)	5	9	.357	4.18	21	21	1	1	0	122 2/3	124	63	57	65	95
— Cincinnati (N.L.)■	6	3	.667	3.03	12	12	1	0	0	77 1/3	70	33	26	21	60
2000— Tampa Bay (A.L.)■	0	1	.000	43.20	1	1	0	0	0	1 2/3	7	8	8	2	3
— St. Petersburg (FSL)	1	0	1.000	0.00	1	1	0	0	0	5	4	0	0	2	6
— Orlando (Sou.)	0	1	.000	8.44	1	1	0	0	0	5 1/3	6	6	5	3	5
— Durham (I.L.)	0	2	.000	5.59	2	2	0	0	0	9 2/3	13	6	6	1	7
A.L. totals (10 years)	85	76	.528	4.14	228	228	16	3	0	1406	1290	717	646	646	1183
N.L. totals (1 year)	6	3	.667	3.03	12	12	1	0	0	77 1/3	70	33	26	21	60
Major League totals (10 years)	91	79	.535	4.08	240	240	17	3	0	1483 1/3	1360	750	672	667	1243

CHAMPIONSHIP SERIES RECORD

RECORDS: Shares career record for most wild pitches—4. ... Shares single-inning record for most wild pitches—2 (October 5, 1993, first inning).

Year League	W	L	Pct.	ERA	G	GS	CG	ShO	Sv.	IP	H	R	ER	BB	SO
1991— Toronto (A.L.)	1	0	1.000	3.18	1	1	0	0	0	5 2/3	4	2	2	4	2
1992— Toronto (A.L.)	2	0	1.000	2.08	2	2	0	0	0	13	12	3	3	5	11
1993— Toronto (A.L.)	2	0	1.000	2.08	2	2	0	0	0	13	8	4	3	9	9
Champ. series totals (3 years)	5	0	1.000	2.27	5	5	0	0	0	31 2/3	24	9	8	18	22

G

NOTES: Member of World Series championship team (1992 and 1993).

Year	League	W	L	Pct.	ERA	G	GS	CG	ShO	Sv.	IP	H	R	ER	BB	SO
1992— Toronto (A.L.)		0	0	...	1.13	1	1	0	0	0	8	8	2	1	1	7
1993— Toronto (A.L.)		0	1	.000	3.75	2	2	0	0	0	12	10	6	5	8	12
World Series totals (2 years)		0	1	.000	2.70	3	3	0	0	0	20	18	8	6	9	19

ALL-STAR GAME RECORD

Year	League	W	L	Pct.	ERA	GS	CG	ShO	Sv.	IP	H	R	ER	BB	SO
1992— American		0	0	...	0.00	0	0	0	0	1	2	0	0	1	2

GWYNN, TONY   OF   PADRES

PERSONAL: Born May 9, 1960, in Los Angeles. ... 5-11/225. ... Bats left, throws left. ... Full name: Anthony Keith Gwynn. ... Brother of Chris Gwynn, outfielder with Los Angeles Dodgers (1987-91 and 1994-95), Kansas City Royals (1992-93) and San Diego Padres (1996) and current scout, Padres.

HIGH SCHOOL: Long Beach (Calif.) Polytechnic.

COLLEGE: San Diego State.

TRANSACTIONS/CAREER NOTES: Selected by San Diego Padres organization in third round of free-agent draft (June 8, 1981). ... On San Diego disabled list (August 26-September 10, 1982). ... On San Diego disabled list (March 26-June 21, 1983); included rehabilitation to Las Vegas (May 31-June 20). ... On disabled list (May 8-29, 1988; July 2-August 6, 1996; and August 13-September 1, 1998). ... On disabled list (May 22-June 12 and June 20-July 19, 1999; April 29-May 15 and June 24, 2000-remainder of season). ... Granted free agency (October 31, 2000). ... Re-signed by Padres (December 7, 2000).

RECORDS: Holds N.L. career records for most years leading league in singles—7 (1984, 1986, 1987, 1989, 1994, 1995 and 1997). ... Holds N.L. single-season record for lowest batting average by leader—.313 (1988). ... Shares N.L. career records for most consecutive years batting .300 or over (50 or more games) since 1900—17; most years batting .300 or over (50 or more games)—17; and most years leading league in hits—7. ... Shares N.L. single-season record for most times collecting five or more hits in one game—4 (1993). ... Shares N.L. career record for most years leading league in batting average—8.

HONORS: Named Northwest League Most Valuable Player (1981). ... Named outfielder on THE SPORTING NEWS N.L. All-Star team (1984, 1986-87, 1989, 1994 and 1997). ... Named outfielder on THE SPORTING NEWS N.L. Silver Slugger team (1984, 1986-87, 1989, 1994-95 and 1997). ... Won N.L. Gold Glove as outfielder (1986-87 and 1989-91).

STATISTICAL NOTES: Had 25-game hitting streak (August 21-September 18, 1983). ... Led N.L. with .410 on-base percentage in 1984. ... Led N.L. outfielders with 360 total chances in 1986. ... Collected six hits in one game (August 4, 1993, 12 innings). ... Led N.L. in grounding into double plays with 20 in 1994. ... Had 20-game hitting streak (May 20-June 10, 1997). ... Tied for N.L. lead with 12 sacrifice flies in 1997. ... Had 16-game hitting streak (September 5-21, 1999). ... Career major league grand slams: 3.

MISCELLANEOUS: Holds San Diego Padres all-time records for most runs (1,378), hits (3,108), doubles (534), triples (84), runs batted in (1,121), stolen bases (318) and highest career batting average (.338). ... Selected by San Diego Clippers in 10th round (210th pick overall) of 1981 NBA draft (June 9, 1981).

							BATTING							FIELDING		
Year	Team (League)	Pos.	G	AB	R	H	2B	3B	HR	RBI	Avg.	BB	SO	SB	PO	A	E	Avg.
1981— Walla Walla (N'West)..		OF	42	178	46	59	12	1	12	37	*.331	23	21	17	76	2	3	.963
— Amarillo (Texas)		OF	23	91	22	42	8	2	4	19	.462	5	7	5	41	1	0	1.000
1982— Hawaii (PCL)		OF	93	366	65	120	23	2	5	46	.328	18	18	14	208	11	4	.982
— San Diego (N.L.)		OF	54	190	33	55	12	2	1	17	.289	14	16	8	110	1	1	.991
1983— Las Vegas (PCL)		OF	17	73	15	25	6	0	0	7	.342	6	5	3	23	2	3	.893
— San Diego (N.L.)		OF	86	304	34	94	12	2	1	37	.309	23	21	7	163	9	1	.994
1984— San Diego (N.L.)		OF	158	606	88	*213	21	10	5	71	*.351	59	23	33	345	11	4	.989
1985— San Diego (N.L.)		OF	154	622	90	197	29	5	6	46	.317	45	33	14	337	14	4	.989
1986— San Diego (N.L.)		OF	160	*642	•107	*211	33	7	14	59	.329	52	35	37	*337	19	4	.989
1987— San Diego (N.L.)		OF	157	589	119	*218	36	13	7	54	*.370	82	35	56	298	13	6	.981
1988— San Diego (N.L.)		OF	133	521	64	163	22	5	7	70	*.313	51	40	26	264	8	5	.982
1989— San Diego (N.L.)		OF	158	604	82	*203	27	7	4	62	*.336	56	30	40	353	13	6	.984
1990— San Diego (N.L.)		OF	141	573	79	177	29	10	4	72	.309	44	23	17	327	11	5	.985
1991— San Diego (N.L.)		OF	134	530	69	168	27	11	4	62	.317	34	19	8	291	8	3	.990
1992— San Diego (N.L.)		OF	128	520	77	165	27	3	6	41	.317	46	16	3	270	9	5	.982
1993— San Diego (N.L.)		OF	122	489	70	175	41	3	7	59	.358	36	19	14	244	8	5	.981
1994— San Diego (N.L.)		OF	110	419	79	*165	35	1	12	64	*.394	48	19	5	191	6	3	.985
1995— San Diego (N.L.)		OF	135	535	82	•197	33	1	9	90	*.368	35	15	17	245	8	2	.992
1996— San Diego (N.L.)		OF	116	451	67	159	27	2	3	50	*.353	39	17	11	182	2	2	.989
1997— San Diego (N.L.)		OF-DH	149	592	97	*220	49	2	17	119	*.372	43	28	12	218	8	4	.983
1998— San Diego (N.L.)		OF-DH	127	461	65	148	35	0	16	69	.321	35	18	3	142	5	1	.993
1999— San Diego (N.L.)		OF-DH	111	411	59	139	27	0	10	62	.338	29	14	7	147	4	1	.993
2000— San Diego (N.L.)		OF-DH	36	127	17	41	12	0	1	17	.323	9	4	0	31	1	0	1.000
Major League totals (19 years)			2369	9186	1378	3108	534	84	134	1121	.338	780	425	318	4495	158	62	.987

DIVISION SERIES RECORD

							BATTING							FIELDING		
Year	Team (League)	Pos.	G	AB	R	H	2B	3B	HR	RBI	Avg.	BB	SO	SB	PO	A	E	Avg.
1996— San Diego (N.L.)		OF	3	13	0	4	1	0	0	1	.308	0	2	1	2	0	0	1.000
1998— San Diego (N.L.)		OF	4	15	1	3	2	0	0	2	.200	0	2	0	4	1	0	1.000
Division series totals (2 years)			7	28	1	7	3	0	0	3	.250	0	4	1	6	1	0	1.000

CHAMPIONSHIP SERIES RECORD

							BATTING							FIELDING		
Year	Team (League)	Pos.	G	AB	R	H	2B	3B	HR	RBI	Avg.	BB	SO	SB	PO	A	E	Avg.
1984— San Diego (N.L.)		OF	5	19	6	7	3	0	0	3	.368	1	2	0	9	0	0	1.000
1998— San Diego (N.L.)		OF	6	26	1	6	1	0	0	2	.231	1	2	0	5	0	0	1.000
Championship series totals (2 years)			11	45	7	13	4	0	0	5	.289	2	4	0	14	0	0	1.000

G

Year	Team (League)	Pos.	G	AB	R	H	2B	3B	HR	RBI	Avg.	BB	SO	SB	PO	A	E	Avg.
							BATTING									FIELDING		
1984—	San Diego (N.L.)	OF	5	19	1	5	0	0	0	0	.263	3	2	1	12	1	1	.929
1998—	San Diego (N.L.)	OF	4	16	2	8	0	0	1	3	.500	1	0	0	6	0	0	1.000
World Series totals (2 years)			9	35	3	13	0	0	1	3	.371	4	2	1	18	1	1	.950

ALL-STAR GAME RECORD

RECORDS: Shares single-game record for most at-bats in nine-inning game—5 (July 12, 1994).
NOTES: Named to All-Star team for 1996 game; replaced by Henry Rodriguez due to injury.

Year	League	Pos.	AB	R	H	2B	3B	HR	RBI	Avg.	BB	SO	SB	PO	A	E	Avg.
						BATTING									FIELDING		
1984—	National	OF	3	0	1	0	0	0	0	.333	0	0	0	0	0	0	...
1985—	National	OF	1	0	0	0	0	0	0	.000	0	0	0	1	0	0	1.000
1986—	National	OF	3	0	0	0	0	0	0	.000	0	0	0	1	0	0	1.000
1987—	National	PH	1	0	0	0	0	0	0	.000	0	0	0	...	...	...	...
1989—	National	OF	2	1	1	0	0	0	0	.500	1	1	1	2	0	0	1.000
1990—	National	PH	0	0	0	0	0	0	0	...	1	0	0	...	...	...	...
1991—	National	OF	4	1	2	0	0	0	0	.500	0	0	0	6	0	0	1.000
1992—	National	OF	2	0	0	0	0	0	0	.000	1	0	0	0	2	0	1.000
1993—	National	OF	1	0	0	0	0	0	0	.000	0	0	0	0	0	0	...
1994—	National	OF	5	2	2	1	0	0	2	.400	0	0	0	2	0	0	1.000
1995—	National	OF	2	0	0	0	0	0	0	.000	0	0	0	1	0	0	1.000
1996—	National						Selected, did not play—injured.											
1997—	National	DH	3	0	0	0	0	0	0	.000	0	0	0	0	0	0	...
1998—	National	OF	2	0	1	0	0	0	0	.500	0	0	0	0	0	0	...
1999—	National						Selected, did not play—injured.											
All-Star Game totals (13 years)			29	4	7	1	0	0	4	.241	3	1	1	13	2	0	1.000

HAAS, CHRIS — 3B/1B — CARDINALS

PERSONAL: Born October 15, 1976, in Paducah, Ky. ... 6-1/205. ... Bats left, throws right. ... Full name: Christopher Mark Haas.
HIGH SCHOOL: St. Mary's (Paducah, Ky.).
TRANSACTIONS/CAREER NOTES: Selected by St. Louis Cardinals organization in supplemental round ("sandwich pick" between first and second round, 29th pick overall) of free-agent draft (June 1, 1995); pick received as part of compensation for Philadelphia Phillies signing Type A free-agent 1B Gregg Jefferies (June 1, 1995). ... On Memphis disabled list (July 2-16, 1999). ... On Memphis disabled list (April 6-29 and June 17-24, 2000).
STATISTICAL NOTES: Led Appalachian League third basemen with 187 total chances in 1995.

Year	Team (League)	Pos.	G	AB	R	H	2B	3B	HR	RBI	Avg.	BB	SO	SB	PO	A	E	Avg.
								BATTING									FIELDING		
1995—	Johnson City (Appl.) ..	3B	•67	242	43	65	15	3	7	50	.269	*52	93	1	51	*116	20	.893
1996—	Peoria (Midw.)...........	3B	124	421	56	101	19	1	11	65	.240	64	169	3	75	241	42	.883
1997—	Peoria (Midw.)...........	3B	36	115	23	36	11	0	5	22	.313	22	38	3	16	52	6	.919
—	Prince William (Caro.)	3B	100	361	58	86	10	2	14	54	.238	42	144	1	89	183	19	*.935
1998—	Arkansas (Texas).......	3B-1B	132	445	75	122	27	4	20	83	.274	73	129	1	146	211	22	.942
1999—	Memphis (PCL)	3B-1B-DH	114	397	63	91	19	2	18	73	.229	66	155	4	312	180	12	.976
2000—	Memphis (PCL)	1B-3B-OF	23	56	7	12	1	0	1	9	.214	9	11	0	82	6	2	.978
—	Arkansas (Texas).......	3B-1B	82	291	52	79	14	2	17	59	.271	40	84	0	144	126	13	.954

HACKMAN, LUTHER — P — CARDINALS

PERSONAL: Born October 10, 1974, in Columbus, Miss. ... 6-4/195. ... Throws right, bats right. ... Full name: Luther Gean Hackman.
HIGH SCHOOL: Columbus (Miss.).
TRANSACTIONS/CAREER NOTES: Selected by Colorado Rockies organization in sixth round of free-agent draft (June 2, 1994). ... On disabled list (June 1-July 10, 1996). ... Traded by Rockies with P Darryl Kile and P Dave Veres to St. Louis Cardinals for P Jose Jimenez, P Manny Aybar, P Rick Croushore and SS Brent Butler (November 16, 1999). ... On Memphis disabled list (June 3-July 4, 2000).

Year	League	W	L	Pct.	ERA	G	GS	CG	ShO	Sv.	IP	H	R	ER	BB	SO
1994—	Arizona Rockies (Ariz.).......	1	3	.250	2.10	12	12	0	0	0	55²/₃	50	21	13	16	43
1995—	Asheville (S.Atl.)..............	11	11	.500	4.64	28	28	2	0	0	165	162	*95	*85	65	108
1996—	Carolina (Sou.)	5	7	.417	4.24	21	21	1	0	0	110¹/₃	93	60	52	69	83
1997—	New Haven (East.)...........	0	6	.000	7.82	10	10	0	0	0	50²/₃	58	49	44	34	34
—	Salem (Caro.)	1	4	.200	5.80	15	15	2	0	0	80²/₃	99	60	52	37	59
1998—	New Haven (East.)...........	3	12	.200	5.44	28	23	1	0	0	139	169	•102	84	54	90
1999—	Carolina (Sou.)	4	3	.571	4.04	11	10	0	0	0	62¹/₃	53	33	28	28	50
—	Colorado Springs (PCL)....	7	6	.538	3.74	15	15	1	1	0	101	106	49	42	44	43
—	Colorado (N.L.)	1	2	.333	10.69	5	3	0	0	0	16	26	19	19	12	10
2000—	Memphis (PCL)■...............	8	9	.471	4.74	21	21	0	0	0	119²/₃	134	71	63	36	66
—	St. Louis (N.L.)...............	0	0	...	10.13	1	0	0	0	0	2²/₃	4	3	3	4	0
Major League totals (2 years)		1	2	.333	10.61	6	3	0	0	0	18²/₃	30	22	22	16	10

G

H

HAIRSTON, JERRY — 2B/SS — ORIOLES

PERSONAL: Born May 29, 1976, in Des Moines, Iowa. ... 5-10/175. ... Bats right, throws right. ... Full name: Jerry W. Hairston Jr. ... Grandson of Sam Hairston, catcher with Chicago White Sox (1951) and Cincinnati and Indianapolis of Negro American League (1945-49); son of Jerry Hairston, outfielder with Chicago White Sox (1973-77 and 1981-89) and Pittsburgh Pirates (1977); nephew of John Hairston, catcher/outfielder with Chicago Cubs (1969); and nephew of Sam Hairston Jr., former minor league player in Chicago White Sox organization (1966 and 1969).
HIGH SCHOOL: Naperville (Ill.) North.
COLLEGE: Southern Illinois-Carbondale.

TRANSACTIONS/CAREER NOTES: Selected by Baltimore Orioles organization in 11th round of free-agent draft (June 3, 1997). ... On Rochester disabled list (May 16-July 4, 2000).
STATISTICAL NOTES: Tied for Appalachian League lead in caught stealing with nine in 1997.

Year	Team (League)	Pos.	G	AB	R	H	2B	3B	HR	RBI	Avg.	BB	SO	SB	PO	A	E	Avg.
																FIELDING		
1997—Bluefield (Appl.)		SS	59	221	44	73	13	4	2	36	.330	21	29	13	84	174	14	*.949
1998—Frederick (Caro.)		SS-2B	80	293	56	83	22	3	5	33	.283	28	32	13	116	281	24	.943
— Bowie (East.) ■............		2B-SS	55	221	42	72	12	3	5	37	.326	20	25	6	109	135	5	.980
— Baltimore (A.L.)..........		2B	6	7	2	0	0	0	0	0	.000	0	1	0	4	2	2	.750
1999—Rochester (I.L.)		2B-SS	107	413	65	120	24	5	7	48	.291	30	50	19	206	277	16	.968
— Baltimore (A.L.)..........		2B	50	175	26	47	12	1	4	17	.269	11	24	9	115	154	0	1.000
2000—Baltimore (A.L.)..........		2B	49	180	27	46	5	0	5	19	.256	21	22	8	101	156	5	.981
— Rochester (I.L.)		2B-SS	58	201	43	59	15	1	4	21	.294	29	32	6	136	149	11	.963
— GC Orioles (GCL)		2B	4	10	3	3	2	0	0	3	.300	3	2	4	5	5	0	1.000
— Frederick (Caro.)		2B	2	8	1	3	2	0	0	1	.375	1	0	0	2	7	0	1.000
Major League totals (3 years)			105	362	55	93	17	1	9	36	.257	32	47	17	220	312	7	.987

HALAMA, JOHN   P   MARINERS

PERSONAL: Born February 22, 1972, in Brooklyn, N.Y. ... 6-5/210. ... Throws left, bats left. ... Full name: John Thadeuz Halama. ... Name pronounced ha-LA-ma.
HIGH SCHOOL: Bishop Ford (Brooklyn, N.Y.).
COLLEGE: St. Francis (N.Y.).
TRANSACTIONS/CAREER NOTES: Selected by Houston Astros organization in 23rd round of free-agent draft (June 3, 1994). ... On New Orleans disabled list (July 2-August 6, 1998). ... Traded by Astros to Seattle Mariners (October 1, 1998), completing deal in which Mariners traded P Randy Johnson to Astros for SS Carlos Guillen, P Freddy Garcia and a player to be named later (July 31, 1998).

Year	League	W	L	Pct.	ERA	G	GS	CG	ShO	Sv.	IP	H	R	ER	BB	SO
1994—Auburn (NY-Penn)............	4	1	.800	1.29	6	3	0	0	1	28	18	5	4	5	27
— Quad City (Midw.)	3	4	.429	4.56	9	9	1	1	0	51 1/3	63	31	26	18	37
1995—Quad City (Midw.)	1	2	.333	2.02	55	0	0	0	2	62 1/3	48	16	14	22	56
1996—Jackson (Texas)	9	10	.474	3.21	27	27	0	0	0	162 2/3	151	77	58	59	110
1997—New Orleans (A.A.)...........	13	3	*.813	2.58	26	24	1	0	0	171	150	57	49	32	126
1998—Houston (N.L.)	1	1	.500	5.85	6	6	0	0	0	32 1/3	37	21	21	13	21
— New Orleans (PCL)............	12	3	.800	3.20	17	17	4	1	0	121	118	48	43	16	86
1999—Seattle (A.L.)■....................	11	10	.524	4.22	38	24	1	1	0	179	193	88	84	56	105
2000—Seattle (A.L.)	14	9	.609	5.08	30	30	1	1	0	166 2/3	206	108	94	56	87
A.L. totals (2 years)	25	19	.568	4.63	68	54	2	2	0	345 2/3	399	196	178	112	192
N.L. totals (1 year)	1	1	.500	5.85	6	6	0	0	0	32 1/3	37	21	21	13	21
Major League totals (3 years).......	26	20	.565	4.74	74	60	2	2	0	378	436	217	199	125	213

CHAMPIONSHIP SERIES RECORD

Year	League	W	L	Pct.	ERA	G	GS	CG	ShO	Sv.	IP	H	R	ER	BB	SO
2000—Seattle (A.L.)	0	0	...	2.89	2	2	0	0	0	9 1/3	10	3	3	5	3

HALL, TOBY   C   DEVIL RAYS

PERSONAL: Born October 21, 1975, in Tacoma, Wash. ... 6-3/205. ... Bats right, throws right. ... Full name: Toby Jason Hall.
HIGH SCHOOL: El Dorado (Placentia, Calif.).
COLLEGE: UNLV.
TRANSACTIONS/CAREER NOTES: Selected by Tampa Bay Devil Rays organization in ninth round of free-agent draft (June 3, 1997).

Year	Team (League)	Pos.	G	AB	R	H	2B	3B	HR	RBI	Avg.	BB	SO	SB	PO	A	E	Avg.
																FIELDING		
1997—Hudson Valley (NY-P.)		C	55	200	25	50	3	0	1	27	.250	13	33	0	243	21	3	.989
1998—Char., S.C. (SAL)........		C	105	377	59	121	25	1	6	50	.321	39	32	3	749	84	18	.979
1999—Orlando (Sou.)		C	46	173	20	44	7	0	9	34	.254	4	10	1	261	27	4	.986
— St. Petersburg (FSL) ..		C	56	212	24	63	13	1	4	36	.297	17	9	0	173	27	4	.980
2000—Orlando (Sou.)		C	68	271	37	93	14	0	9	50	.343	17	24	3	395	33	7	.984
— Durham (I.L.)		C	47	184	21	56	15	0	7	35	.304	3	19	0	249	22	2	.993
— Tampa Bay (A.L.)........		C	4	12	1	2	0	0	1	1	.167	1	0	0	19	2	0	1.000
Major League totals (1 year)			4	12	1	2	0	0	1	1	.167	1	0	0	19	2	0	1.000

HALLADAY, ROY   P   BLUE JAYS

PERSONAL: Born May 14, 1977, in Denver. ... 6-6/225. ... Throws right, bats right. ... Full name: Harry Leroy Halladay III.
HIGH SCHOOL: Arvada (Colo.) West.
TRANSACTIONS/CAREER NOTES: Selected by Toronto Blue Jays organization in first round (17th pick overall) of free-agent draft (June 1, 1995). ... On Syracuse disabled list (May 15-June 17, 1998).
STATISTICAL NOTES: Pitched 2-1 one-hit, complete-game victory against Detroit (September 27, 1998).

Year	League	W	L	Pct.	ERA	G	GS	CG	ShO	Sv.	IP	H	R	ER	BB	SO
1995—GC Blue Jays (GCL)...........	3	5	.375	3.40	10	8	0	0	0	50 1/3	35	25	19	16	48
1996—Dunedin (FSL)	15	7	.682	2.73	27	27	2	•2	0	164 2/3	158	75	50	46	109
1997—Knoxville (Sou.)	2	3	.400	5.40	7	7	0	0	0	36 2/3	46	26	22	11	30
— Syracuse (I.L.)...................	7	10	.412	4.58	22	22	2	2	0	125 2/3	132	74	64	53	64
1998—Syracuse (I.L.)...................	9	5	.643	3.79	21	21	1	1	0	116 1/3	107	52	49	53	71
— Toronto (A.L.)...................	1	0	1.000	1.93	2	2	1	0	0	14	9	4	3	2	13
1999—Toronto (A.L.)...................	8	7	.533	3.92	36	18	1	1	1	149 1/3	156	76	65	79	82
2000—Toronto (A.L.)...................	4	7	.364	10.64	19	13	0	0	0	67 2/3	107	87	80	42	44
— Syracuse (I.L.)...................	2	3	.400	5.50	11	11	3	0	0	73 2/3	85	46	45	21	38
Major League totals (3 years).......	13	14	.481	5.77	57	33	2	1	1	231	272	167	148	123	139

H

PERSONAL: Born November 8, 1969, in La Plata, Md. ... 6-0/180. ... Bats right, throws right. ... Full name: Shane David Halter.
HIGH SCHOOL: Hooks (Texas).
JUNIOR COLLEGE: Seminole (Okla.) Junior College.
COLLEGE: Texas.
TRANSACTIONS/CAREER NOTES: Selected by Cincinnati Reds organization in 16th round of free-agent draft (June 4, 1990); did not sign. ... Selected by Kansas City Royals organization in fifth round of free-agent draft (June 3, 1991). ... Traded by Royals to New York Mets for OF Jonathan Guzman (March 23, 1999). ... Claimed on waivers by Detroit Tigers (March 13, 2000).
STATISTICAL NOTES: Led Midwest League shortstops with 64 double plays in 1992. ... Led American Association with 19 sacrifice hits in 1995. ... Led International League with 17 sacrifice hits and in caught stealing with 18 in 1999.

Year Team (League)	Pos.	G	AB	R	H	2B	3B	HR	RBI	Avg.	BB	SO	SB	PO	A	E	Avg.
1991— Eugene (N'West)	SS	64	236	41	55	9	1	1	18	.233	49	60	12	*118	154	21	.928
1992— Appleton (Midw.)........	SS	80	313	50	83	22	3	3	33	.265	41	54	21	150	227	16	.959
— Baseball City (FSL)	SS	44	117	11	28	1	0	1	14	.239	24	31	5	70	115	6	.969
1993— Wilmington (Caro.).....	SS	54	211	44	63	8	5	5	32	.299	27	55	5	84	146	15	.939
— Memphis (Sou.)	SS	81	306	50	79	7	0	4	20	.258	30	74	4	142	229	16	.959
1994— Memphis (Sou.)	SS	129	494	61	111	23	1	6	35	.225	39	102	10	177	369	29	.950
1995— Omaha (A.A.)............	SS-2B	124	392	42	90	19	3	8	39	.230	40	97	2	225	355	19	.968
1996— Omaha (A.A.)............	O-3-S-2-P	93	299	43	77	24	0	3	33	.258	31	49	7	130	75	13	.940
— Charlotte (I.L.)............	O-2-DH-3-1	16	41	3	12	1	0	0	4	.293	2	8	0	15	10	1	.962
1997— Omaha (A.A.)............	3B-OF-2B-SS	14	49	10	13	1	1	2	9	.265	6	10	0	22	14	2	.947
— Kansas City (A.L.)	O-2-3-S-DH	74	123	16	34	5	1	2	10	.276	10	28	4	63	40	1	.990
1998— Kansas City (A.L.)	S-O-3-2-P-1	86	204	17	45	12	0	2	13	.221	12	38	2	91	177	10	.964
— Omaha (PCL)............	S-1-2-3-O	22	97	15	30	6	1	1	13	.309	6	15	4	64	46	3	.973
1999— Norfolk (I.L.)■.........	S-O-2-3-C	127	474	77	130	22	3	6	35	.274	60	90	19	187	239	20	.955
— New York (N.L.)..........	OF-SS	7	0	0	0	0	0	0	0	...	0	0	0	0	0	0	...
2000— Detroit (A.L.)■.........	IF-OF-C-P	105	238	26	62	12	2	3	27	.261	14	49	5	245	125	8	.979
American League totals (3 years)		265	565	59	141	29	3	7	50	.250	36	115	11	399	342	19	.975
National League totals (1 year)		7	0	0	0	0	0	0	0	...	0	0	0	0	0	0	...
Major League totals (4 years)		272	565	59	141	29	3	7	50	.250	36	115	11	399	342	19	.975

RECORD AS PITCHER

Year League	W	L	Pct.	ERA	G	GS	CG	ShO	Sv.	IP	H	R	ER	BB	SO
1998— Kansas City (A.L.)	0	0	...	0.00	1	0	0	0	0	1	1	0	0	0	0
2000— Detroit (A.L.)	0	0	...	0.00	1	0	0	0	0	0	0	0	0	1	0
Major League totals (2 years).......	0	0	...	0.00	2	0	0	0	0	1	1	0	0	1	0

PERSONAL: Born December 3, 1964, in Baton Rouge, La. ... 6-1/192. ... Bats left, throws right. ... Full name: Darryl Quinn Hamilton.
HIGH SCHOOL: University (Baton Rouge, La.).
COLLEGE: Nicholls State (La.).
TRANSACTIONS/CAREER NOTES: Selected by Milwaukee Brewers organization in 11th round of free-agent draft (June 2, 1986). ... On disabled list (May 22-June 15, 1991; May 6-24, 1992; May 2-17, 1993; May 11-26 and June 10, 1994-remainder of season). ... Granted free agency (November 1, 1995). ... Signed by Texas Rangers (December 14, 1995). ... Granted free agency (November 18, 1996). ... Signed by San Francisco Giants (January 10, 1997). ... On San Francisco disabled list (April 18-May 8, 1997; included rehabilitation assignment to Phoenix (May 5-8). ... Traded by Giants with P James Stoops and a player to be named later to Colorado Rockies for OF Ellis Burks (July 31, 1998); Rockies acquired P Jason Brester to complete deal (August 17, 1998). ... Granted free agency (October 23, 1998). ... Re-signed by Rockies (November 9, 1998). ... Traded by Rockies with P Chuck McElroy to New York Mets for OF Brian McRae, P Rigo Beltran and OF Thomas Johnson (July 31, 1999). ... On New York disabled list (April 7-August 10, 2000); included rehabilitation assignments to St. Lucie (June 28-29) and Norfolk (July 29-August 9).
RECORDS: Shares major league career record for highest fielding average by outfielder (1,000 or more games)—.995.
STATISTICAL NOTES: Led California League with nine intentional bases on balls received in 1987. ... Led N.L. outfielders with .997 fielding percentage in 1998. ... Led N.L. outfielders with 1.000 fielding percentage in 1998. ... Career major league grand slams: 3.

Year Team (League)	Pos.	G	AB	R	H	2B	3B	HR	RBI	Avg.	BB	SO	SB	PO	A	E	Avg.
1986— Helena (Pio.)	OF	65	248	*72	•97	12	•6	0	35	*.391	51	18	34	132	9	0	*1.000
1987— Stockton (Calif.)	OF	125	494	102	162	17	6	8	61	.328	74	59	42	221	8	1	*.996
1988— Denver (A.A.)............	OF	72	277	55	90	11	4	0	32	.325	39	28	28	160	2	2	.988
— Milwaukee (A.L.)	OF-DH	44	103	14	19	4	0	1	11	.184	12	9	7	75	1	0	1.000
1989— Denver (A.A.)............	OF	129	497	72	142	24	4	2	40	.286	42	58	20	263	11	0	*1.000
1990— Milwaukee (A.L.)	OF-DH	89	156	27	46	5	0	1	18	.295	9	12	10	120	1	1	.992
1991— Milwaukee (A.L.)	OF	122	405	64	126	15	6	1	57	.311	33	38	16	234	3	1	.996
1992— Milwaukee (A.L.)	OF	128	470	67	140	19	7	5	62	.298	45	42	41	279	10	0	*1.000
1993— Milwaukee (A.L.)	OF-DH	135	520	74	161	21	1	9	48	.310	45	62	21	340	10	3	.992
1994— Milwaukee (A.L.)	OF-DH	36	141	23	37	10	1	1	13	.262	15	17	3	60	2	0	1.000
1995— Milwaukee (A.L.)	OF-DH	112	398	54	108	20	6	5	44	.271	47	35	11	262	4	3	.989
1996— Texas (A.L.)■..........	OF	148	627	94	184	29	4	6	51	.293	54	66	15	387	2	0	•1.000
1997— San Fran. (N.L.)■......	OF	125	460	78	124	23	3	5	43	.270	61	61	15	243	1	5	.980
— Phoenix (PCL)...........	OF	3	14	1	4	1	0	1	2	.286	0	2	0	6	0	0	1.000
1998— San Francisco (N.L.) ..	OF	97	367	65	108	19	2	1	26	.294	59	53	9	194	4	0	1.000
— Colorado (N.L.)■.......	OF	51	194	30	65	9	1	5	25	.335	23	20	4	103	1	1	§.990
1999— Colorado (N.L.)	OF	91	337	63	102	11	3	4	24	.303	38	21	4	205	1	0	1.000
— New York (N.L.)■.......	OF	55	168	19	57	8	1	5	21	.339	19	18	2	100	2	0	§1.000
2000— New York (N.L.)	OF	43	105	20	29	4	1	1	6	.276	14	20	2	41	1	0	1.000
— St. Lucie (FSL)	OF	1	3	0	1	0	0	0	0	.333	1	0	0	0	0	0	...
— Norfolk (I.L.)	OF	10	40	3	9	0	0	1	4	.225	6	5	0	18	1	0	1.000
American League totals (8 years)		814	2820	417	821	123	25	29	304	.291	260	281	124	1757	33	8	.996
National League totals (4 years)		462	1631	275	485	74	11	21	145	.297	214	193	36	886	10	6	.993
Major League totals (12 years)		1276	4451	692	1306	197	36	50	449	.293	474	474	160	2643	43	14	.995

H

DIVISION SERIES RECORD

Year	Team (League)	Pos.	G	AB	R	H	2B	3B	HR	RBI	Avg.	BB	SO	SB	PO	A	E	Avg.
1996—	Texas (A.L.)	OF	4	19	0	3	0	0	0	0	.158	0	2	0	16	1	0	1.000
1997—	San Francisco (N.L.)	OF	2	5	1	0	0	0	0	0	.000	0	1	0	3	0	0	1.000
1999—	New York (N.L.)	OF-PH	4	8	0	1	0	0	0	2	.125	2	0	0	9	0	0	1.000
2000—	New York (N.L.)	OF-PH	3	4	1	2	1	0	0	0	.500	1	1	0	0	0	0	...
Division series totals (4 years)			13	36	2	6	1	0	0	2	.167	3	4	0	28	1	0	1.000

CHAMPIONSHIP SERIES RECORD

Year	Team (League)	Pos.	G	AB	R	H	2B	3B	HR	RBI	Avg.	BB	SO	SB	PO	A	E	Avg.
1999—	New York (N.L.)	OF	5	17	0	6	1	0	0	2	.353	0	4	0	8	0	0	1.000
2000—	New York (N.L.)	PH	3	2	0	0	0	0	0	0	.000	0	0	0	...	...	...	...
Championship series totals (2 years)			8	19	0	6	1	0	0	2	.316	0	4	0	8	0	0	1.000

WORLD SERIES RECORD

Year	Team (League)	Pos.	G	AB	R	H	2B	3B	HR	RBI	Avg.	BB	SO	SB	PO	A	E	Avg.
2000—	New York (N.L.)	PH	4	3	0	0	0	0	0	0	.000	0	2	0	...	...	...	...

HAMILTON, JOEY   P   BLUE JAYS

PERSONAL: Born September 9, 1970, in Statesboro, Ga. ... 6-4/230. ... Throws right, bats right. ... Full name: Johns Joseph Hamilton.
HIGH SCHOOL: Statesboro (Ga.).
COLLEGE: Georgia Southern.
TRANSACTIONS/CAREER NOTES: Selected by Baltimore Orioles organization in 28th round of free-agent draft (June 1, 1988); did not sign. ... Selected by San Diego Padres organization in first round (eighth pick overall) of free-agent draft (June 3, 1991). ... On Rancho Cucamonga disabled list (April 5-20, 1993). ... On disabled list (April 24-May 17, 1997). ... Traded by Padres to Toronto Blue Jays for P Woody Williams, P Carlos Almanzar and OF Peter Tucci (December 13, 1998). ... On Toronto disabled list (April 14-May 24, 1999); included rehabilitation assignment to Syracuse (May 10-24). ... On Toronto disabled list (March 21-August 19, 2000); included rehabilitation assignment to Syracuse (July 17-August 15).
HONORS: Named righthanded pitcher on THE SPORTING NEWS college All-America second team (1990).
MISCELLANEOUS: Made an out in only appearance as pinch hitter (1998).

Year	League	W	L	Pct.	ERA	G	GS	CG	ShO	Sv.	IP	H	R	ER	BB	SO
1992—	Charleston, S.C. (S.Atl.)	2	2	.500	3.38	7	7	0	0	0	34 2/3	37	24	13	4	35
—	High Desert (Calif.)	4	3	.571	2.74	9	8	0	0	0	49 1/3	46	20	15	18	43
—	Wichita (Texas)	3	0	1.000	2.86	6	6	0	0	0	34 2/3	33	12	11	11	26
1993—	Rancho Cuca. (Calif.)	1	0	1.000	4.09	2	2	0	0	0	11	11	5	5	2	6
—	Wichita (Texas)	4	9	.308	3.97	15	15	0	0	0	90 2/3	101	55	40	36	20
—	Las Vegas (PCL)	3	2	.600	4.40	8	8	0	0	0	47	49	25	23	22	33
1994—	Las Vegas (PCL)	3	5	.375	2.73	9	9	1	1	0	59 1/3	69	25	18	22	32
—	San Diego (N.L.)	9	6	.600	2.98	16	16	1	1	0	108 2/3	98	40	36	29	61
1995—	San Diego (N.L.)	6	9	.400	3.08	31	30	2	2	0	204 1/3	189	89	70	56	123
1996—	San Diego (N.L.)	15	9	.625	4.17	34	33	3	1	0	211 2/3	206	100	98	83	184
1997—	San Diego (N.L.)	12	7	.632	4.25	31	29	1	0	0	192 2/3	199	100	91	69	124
1998—	San Diego (N.L.)	13	13	.500	4.27	34	34	0	0	0	217 1/3	220	113	103	*106	147
1999—	Toronto (A.L.)■	7	8	.467	6.52	22	18	0	0	0	98	118	73	71	39	56
—	Syracuse (I.L.)	0	1	.000	5.11	3	3	0	0	0	12 1/3	15	8	7	5	9
2000—	Syracuse (I.L.)	3	2	.600	3.66	6	6	1	0	0	39 1/3	41	18	16	12	17
—	Toronto (A.L.)	2	1	.667	3.55	6	6	0	0	0	33	28	13	13	12	15
A.L. totals (2 years)		9	9	.500	5.77	28	24	0	0	0	131	146	86	84	51	71
N.L. totals (5 years)		55	44	.556	3.83	146	142	7	4	0	934 2/3	912	442	398	343	639
Major League totals (7 years)		64	53	.547	4.07	174	166	7	4	0	1065 2/3	1058	528	482	394	710

DIVISION SERIES RECORD

Year	League	W	L	Pct.	ERA	G	GS	CG	ShO	Sv.	IP	H	R	ER	BB	SO
1996—	San Diego (N.L.)	0	1	.000	4.50	1	1	0	0	0	6	5	3	3	0	6
1998—	San Diego (N.L.)	0	0	...	0.00	2	0	0	0	0	3 1/3	1	0	0	2	3
Division series totals (2 years)		0	1	.000	2.89	3	1	0	0	0	9 1/3	6	3	3	2	9

CHAMPIONSHIP SERIES RECORD

Year	League	W	L	Pct.	ERA	G	GS	CG	ShO	Sv.	IP	H	R	ER	BB	SO
1998—	San Diego (N.L.)	0	1	.000	4.91	2	1	0	0	0	7 1/3	7	4	4	3	6

WORLD SERIES RECORD

Year	League	W	L	Pct.	ERA	G	GS	CG	ShO	Sv.	IP	H	R	ER	BB	SO
1998—	San Diego (N.L.)	0	0	...	0.00	1	0	0	0	0	1	0	0	0	1	1

HAMMONDS, JEFFREY   OF   BREWERS

PERSONAL: Born March 5, 1971, in Scotch Plains, N.J. ... 6-0/200. ... Bats right, throws right. ... Full name: Jeffrey Bryan Hammonds. ... Brother of Reggie Hammonds, outfielder with Pittsburgh Pirates organization (1984-86).
HIGH SCHOOL: Scotch Plains (N.J.)-Fanwood.
COLLEGE: Stanford.
TRANSACTIONS/CAREER NOTES: Selected by Toronto Blue Jays organization in ninth round of free-agent draft (June 5, 1989); did not sign. ... Selected by Baltimore Orioles organization in first round (fourth pick overall) of free-agent draft (June 1, 1992). ... On Hagerstown temporarily inactive list (August 6-September 14, 1992). ... On Rochester disabled list (May 17-28, 1993). ... On Baltimore disabled list (August 8-September 1 and September 28, 1993-remainder of season); included rehabilitation assignment to Bowie (August 28-September 1). ... On Baltimore disabled list (May 4-June 16, 1994; July 18-September 3, 1995; and August 17-September 22, 1996). ... On Baltimore disabled list

H

(June 3-July 11, 1998); included rehabilitation assignment to Bowie (July 9-11). ... Traded by Orioles to Cincinnati Reds for 3B/OF Willie Greene (August 10, 1998). ... Traded by Reds with P Stan Belinda to Colorado Rockies for OF Dante Bichette and cash (October 30, 1999). ... On disabled list (April 4-22, 2000). ... Granted free agency (October 27, 2000). ... Signed by Milwaukee Brewers (December 22, 2000).

HONORS: Named outfielder on The Sporting News college All-America team (1990 and 1992).

STATISTICAL NOTES: Hit three home runs in one game (May 19, 1999). ... Had 18-game hitting streak (May 29-June 21, 2000). ... Career major league grand slams: 2.

MISCELLANEOUS: Member of 1992 U.S. Olympic baseball team.

								BATTING								FIELDING		
Year Team (League)	Pos.	G	AB	R	H	2B	3B	HR	RBI	Avg.	BB	SO	SB	PO	A	E	Avg.
1992— Hagerstown (East.)								Did not play.									
1993— Bowie (East.).............	OF	24	92	13	26	3	0	3	10	.283	9	18	4	48	2	0	1.000
— Rochester (I.L.).........	OF	36	151	25	47	9	1	5	23	.311	5	27	6	72	1	0	1.000
— Baltimore (A.L.).........	OF-DH	33	105	10	32	8	0	3	19	.305	2	16	4	47	2	2	.961
1994— Baltimore (A.L.).........	OF	68	250	45	74	18	2	8	31	.296	17	39	5	147	5	6	.962
1995— Baltimore (A.L.).........	OF-DH	57	178	18	43	9	1	4	23	.242	9	30	4	88	1	1	.989
— Bowie (East.).............	OF-DH	9	31	7	12	3	1	1	11	.387	10	7	3	12	0	1	.923
1996— Baltimore (A.L.).........	OF-DH	71	248	38	56	10	1	9	27	.226	23	53	3	145	3	3	.980
— Rochester (I.L.).........	OF-DH	34	125	24	34	4	2	3	19	.272	19	19	3	75	1	1	.987
1997— Baltimore (A.L.).........	OF-DH	118	397	71	105	19	3	21	55	.264	32	73	15	240	4	5	.980
1998— Baltimore (A.L.).........	OF-DH	63	171	36	46	12	1	6	28	.269	26	38	7	94	2	2	.980
— Bowie (East.).............	OF	3	6	4	2	0	0	0	0	.333	2	2	3	3	0	0	1.000
— Cincinnati (N.L.)■.....	OF	26	86	14	26	4	1	0	11	.302	13	18	1	64	3	1	.985
1999— Cincinnati (N.L.)	OF	123	262	43	73	13	0	17	41	.279	27	64	3	157	5	0	1.000
2000— Colorado (N.L.)■	OF	122	454	94	152	24	2	20	106	.335	44	83	14	207	8	2	.991
American League totals (6 years)		410	1349	218	356	76	8	51	183	.264	109	249	38	761	17	19	.976
National League totals (3 years)		271	802	151	251	41	3	37	158	.313	84	165	18	428	16	3	.993
Major League totals (8 years)		681	2151	369	607	117	11	88	341	.282	193	414	56	1189	33	22	.982

DIVISION SERIES RECORD

								BATTING								FIELDING		
Year Team (League)	Pos.	G	AB	R	H	2B	3B	HR	RBI	Avg.	BB	SO	SB	PO	A	E	Avg.
1997— Baltimore (A.L.)..........	OF-PR	4	10	3	1	1	0	0	2	.100	2	2	1	8	1	0	1.000

CHAMPIONSHIP SERIES RECORD

								BATTING								FIELDING		
Year Team (League)	Pos.	G	AB	R	H	2B	3B	HR	RBI	Avg.	BB	SO	SB	PO	A	E	Avg.
1997— Baltimore (A.L.)..........	PH-OF-PR	5	3	0	0	0	0	0	0	.000	1	2	1	2	0	0	1.000

ALL-STAR GAME RECORD

						BATTING							FIELDING		
Year League	Pos.	AB	R	H	2B	3B	HR	RBI	Avg.	BB	SO	SB	PO	A	E	Avg.
2000— National	PH	1	0	0	0	0	0	0	.000	0	0	0	...	...	...	...

HAMPTON, MIKE   P   ROCKIES

PERSONAL: Born September 9, 1972, in Brooksville, Fla. ... 5-10/180. ... Throws left, bats right. ... Full name: Michael William Hampton.

HIGH SCHOOL: Crystal River (Fla.).

TRANSACTIONS/CAREER NOTES: Selected by Seattle Mariners organization in sixth round of free-agent draft (June 4, 1990). ... Traded by Mariners with OF Mike Felder to Houston Astros for OF Eric Anthony (December 10, 1993). ... On disabled list (May 15-June 13, 1995; June 16-July 4, 1998). ... Traded by Astros with OF Derek Bell to New York Mets for OF Roger Cedeno, P Octavio Dotel and P Kyle Kessel (December 23, 1999). ... Granted free agency (November 4, 2000). ... Signed by Colorado Rockies (December 9, 2000).

HONORS: Named N.L. Pitcher of the Year by The Sporting News (1999). ... Named lefthanded pitcher on The Sporting News N.L. All-Star team (1999). ... Named pitcher on The Sporting News N.L. Silver Slugger team (1999 and 2000).

STATISTICAL NOTES: Led Arizona League with 10 wild pitches in 1990. ... Pitched 6-0 no-hit victory for San Bernardino against Visalia (May 31, 1991).

MISCELLANEOUS: Appeared in two games as pinch runner (1996). ... Scored run in only appearance as pinch runner (2000). ... Struck out in only appearance as pinch hitter (2000).

Year League	W	L	Pct.	ERA	G	GS	CG	ShO	Sv.	IP	H	R	ER	BB	SO
1990— Arizona Mariners (Ariz.)	•7	2	.778	2.66	14	•13	0	0	0	64¹/₃	52	32	19	40	59
1991— San Bernardino (Calif.).......	1	7	.125	5.25	18	15	1	1	0	73²/₃	71	58	43	47	57
— Bellingham (N'West)	5	2	.714	1.58	9	9	0	0	0	57	32	15	10	26	65
1992— San Bernardino (Calif.).......	13	8	.619	3.12	25	25	6	•2	0	170	163	75	59	66	132
— Jacksonville (Sou.)............	0	1	.000	4.35	2	2	1	0	0	10¹/₃	13	5	5	1	6
1993— Seattle (A.L.)	1	3	.250	9.53	13	3	0	0	1	17	28	20	18	17	8
— Jacksonville (Sou.)............	6	4	.600	3.71	15	14	1	0	0	87¹/₃	71	43	36	33	84
1994— Houston (N.L.)■...............	2	1	.667	3.70	44	0	0	0	0	41²/₃	46	19	17	16	24
1995— Houston (N.L.)	9	8	.529	3.35	24	24	0	0	0	150²/₃	141	73	56	49	115
1996— Houston (N.L.)	10	10	.500	3.59	27	27	2	1	0	160¹/₃	175	79	64	49	101
1997— Houston (N.L.)	15	10	.600	3.83	34	34	7	2	0	223	217	105	95	77	139
1998— Houston (N.L.)	11	7	.611	3.36	32	32	1	1	0	211²/₃	227	92	79	81	137
1999— Houston (N.L.)	*22	4	*.846	2.90	34	34	3	2	0	239	206	86	77	101	177
2000— New York (N.L.)■	15	10	.600	3.14	33	33	3	1	0	217²/₃	194	89	76	99	151
A.L. totals (1 year)	1	3	.250	9.53	13	3	0	0	1	17	28	20	18	17	8
N.L. totals (7 years)	84	50	.627	3.36	228	184	16	7	0	1243²/₃	1206	543	464	472	844
Major League totals (8 years)	85	53	.616	3.44	241	187	16	7	1	1260²/₃	1234	563	482	489	852

DIVISION SERIES RECORD

Year League	W	L	Pct.	ERA	G	GS	CG	ShO	Sv.	IP	H	R	ER	BB	SO
1997— Houston (N.L.)	0	1	.000	11.57	1	1	0	0	0	4²/₃	2	6	6	8	2
1998— Houston (N.L.)	0	0	...	1.50	1	1	0	0	0	6	2	1	1	1	2
1999— Houston (N.L.)	0	0	...	3.86	1	1	0	0	0	7	6	3	3	1	9
2000— New York (N.L.)	0	1	.000	8.44	1	1	0	0	0	5¹/₃	6	5	5	3	2
Division series totals (4 years)	0	2	.000	5.87	4	4	0	0	0	23	16	15	15	13	15

CHAMPIONSHIP SERIES RECORD

NOTES: Named Most Valuable Player (2000).

Year	League	W	L	Pct.	ERA	G	GS	CG	ShO	Sv.	IP	H	R	ER	BB	SO
2000—	New York (N.L.)	2	0	1.000	0.00	2	2	1	1	0	16	9	0	0	4	12

WORLD SERIES RECORD

Year	League	W	L	Pct.	ERA	G	GS	CG	ShO	Sv.	IP	H	R	ER	BB	SO
2000—	New York (N.L.)	0	1	.000	6.00	1	1	0	0	0	6	8	4	4	5	4

ALL-STAR GAME RECORD

Year	League	W	L	Pct.	ERA	GS	CG	ShO	Sv.	IP	H	R	ER	BB	SO
1999—	National	0	0	...	0.00	0	0	0	0	$2/_3$	0	0	0	0	0

HANEY, CHRIS   P

PERSONAL: Born November 16, 1968, in Baltimore. ... 6-3/210. ... Throws left, bats left. ... Full name: Christopher Deane Haney. ... Son of Larry Haney, catcher with five major league teams (1966-70 and 1972-78), and coach, Milwaukee Brewers (1978-91).
HIGH SCHOOL: Orange County (Va.).
COLLEGE: UNC Charlotte.
TRANSACTIONS/CAREER NOTES: Selected by Milwaukee Brewers organization in 25th round of free-agent draft (June 2, 1987); did not sign. ... Selected by Montreal Expos organization in second round of free-agent draft (June 4, 1990). ... On Indianapolis disabled list (June 17-25, 1992). ... Traded by Expos with P Bill Sampen to Kansas City Royals for 3B Sean Berry and P Archie Corbin (August 29, 1992). ... On disabled list (July 13, 1995-remainder of season). ... On Kansas City disabled list (April 15-June 17 and June 27-September 3, 1997); included rehabilitation assignments to Omaha (May 31-June 13) and Wichita (August 25-29). ... On Kansas City disabled list (June 8-24, 1998); included rehabilitation assignment to Gulf Coast Royals (June 22). ... Contract sold by Royals to Chicago Cubs (September 12, 1998). ... Granted free agency (October 27, 1998). ... Signed by Los Angeles Dodgers organization (January 22, 1999). ... Released by Dodgers (April 1, 1999). ... Signed by Cleveland Indians organzation (April 6, 1999). ... On Buffalo disabled list (May 3-June 11, 1999). ... Granted free agency (October 28, 1999). ... Re-signed by Indians organization (January 8, 2000). ... On Buffalo disabled list (April 6-June 22, 2000). ... Released by Indians (October 6, 2000).
MISCELLANEOUS: Appeared in one game as pinch runner with Montreal (1992).

Year	League	W	L	Pct.	ERA	G	GS	CG	ShO	Sv.	IP	H	R	ER	BB	SO
1990—	Jamestown (NY-Penn)	3	0	1.000	0.96	6	5	0	0	1	28	17	3	3	10	26
—	Rockford (Midw.)	2	4	.333	2.21	8	8	3	0	0	53	40	15	13	6	45
—	Jacksonville (Sou.)	1	0	1.000	0.00	1	1	0	0	0	6	6	0	0	3	6
1991—	Harrisburg (East.)	5	3	.625	2.16	12	12	3	0	0	$83^1/_3$	65	21	20	31	68
—	Montreal (N.L.)	3	7	.300	4.04	16	16	0	0	0	$84^2/_3$	94	49	38	43	51
—	Indianapolis (A.A.)	1	1	.500	4.35	2	2	0	0	0	$10^1/_3$	14	10	5	6	8
1992—	Montreal (N.L.)	2	3	.400	5.45	9	6	1	1	0	38	40	25	23	10	27
—	Indianapolis (A.A.)	5	2	.714	5.14	15	15	0	0	0	84	88	50	48	42	61
—	Kansas City (A.L.)■	2	3	.400	3.86	7	7	1	1	0	42	35	18	18	16	27
1993—	Omaha (A.A.)	6	1	.857	2.27	8	7	2	0	0	$47^2/_3$	43	13	12	14	32
—	Kansas City (A.L.)	9	9	.500	6.02	23	23	1	1	0	124	141	87	83	53	65
1994—	Kansas City (A.L.)	2	2	.500	7.31	6	6	0	0	0	$28^1/_3$	36	25	23	11	18
—	Omaha (A.A.)	8	7	.533	5.25	18	18	1	0	0	$104^2/_3$	125	77	61	37	78
1995—	Kansas City (A.L.)	3	4	.429	3.65	16	13	1	0	0	$81^1/_3$	78	35	33	33	31
1996—	Kansas City (A.L.)	10	14	.417	4.70	35	35	4	1	0	228	*267	136	119	51	115
1997—	Kansas City (A.L.)	1	2	.333	4.38	8	3	0	0	0	$24^2/_3$	29	16	12	5	16
—	Omaha (A.A.)	1	0	1.000	3.79	4	3	0	0	0	19	16	12	8	6	7
—	Wichita (Texas)	0	1	.000	2.70	2	2	0	0	0	$6^2/_3$	5	3	2	0	2
1998—	Kansas City (A.L.)	6	6	.500	7.03	33	12	0	0	0	$97^1/_3$	125	78	76	36	51
—	Gulf Coast Royals (GCL)	0	1	.000	0.00	1	1	0	0	0	$2^1/_3$	2	2	0	0	1
—	Chicago (N.L.)■	0	0	...	7.20	5	0	0	0	0	5	3	4	4	1	4
1999—	Buffalo (I.L.)■	2	5	.286	3.22	13	10	0	0	0	$58^2/_3$	50	25	21	22	37
—	Cleveland (A.L.)	0	2	.000	4.69	13	4	0	0	0	$40^1/_3$	43	22	21	16	22
2000—	Buffalo (I.L.)	8	3	.727	2.44	15	13	1	1	0	$92^1/_3$	87	27	25	17	70
—	Cleveland (A.L.)	0	0	...	9.00	1	0	0	0	0	1	1	1	1	1	0
A.L. totals (9 years)		33	42	.440	5.21	142	103	7	3	0	667	755	418	386	222	345
N.L. totals (3 years)		5	10	.333	4.58	30	22	1	1	0	$127^2/_3$	137	78	65	54	82
Major League totals (10 years)		38	52	.422	5.11	172	125	8	4	0	$794^2/_3$	892	496	451	276	427

HANSEN, DAVE   3B   DODGERS

PERSONAL: Born November 24, 1968, in Long Beach, Calif. ... 6-0/195. ... Bats left, throws right. ... Full name: David Andrew Hansen.
HIGH SCHOOL: Rowland (Long Beach, Calif.).
TRANSACTIONS/CAREER NOTES: Selected by Los Angeles Dodgers organization in second round of free-agent draft (June 2, 1986). ... On disabled list (May 9-28, 1994). ... Granted free agency (November 27, 1996). ... Signed by Chicago Cubs organization (January 22, 1997). ... Granted free agency (October 27, 1997). ... Signed by Hanshin Tigers of Japan Central League (November 7, 1997). ... Signed by Dodgers (January 11, 1999).
RECORDS: Holds major league single-season record for most home runs by pinch-hitter—7 (2000).
STATISTICAL NOTES: Led California League third basemen with 45 errors in 1987. ... Led Florida State League with 210 total bases and tied for lead with nine sacrifice flies in 1988. ... Led Florida State League third basemen with 383 total chances and 24 double plays in 1988. ... Led Pacific Coast League third basemen with .926 fielding percentage, 254 assists, 349 total chances and 25 double plays in 1990. ... Career major league grand slams: 1.

Year	Team (League)	Pos.	G	AB	R	H	2B	3B	HR	RBI	Avg.	BB	SO	SB	PO	A	E	Avg.
1986—	Great Falls (Pio.)	OF-3B-C-2B	61	204	39	61	7	3	1	36	.299	27	28	9	54	10	7	.901
1987—	Bakersfield (Calif.)	3B-OF	132	432	68	113	22	1	3	38	.262	65	61	4	79	198	†45	.860
1988—	Vero Beach (FSL)	3B	135	512	68	*149	•28	6	7	*81	.291	56	46	2	*102	*263	18	*.953
1989—	San Antonio (Texas)	3B	121	464	72	138	21	4	6	52	.297	50	44	3	*92	208	16	*.949
—	Albuquerque (PCL)	3B	6	30	6	8	1	0	2	10	.267	2	3	0	3	8	3	.786

								BATTING								FIELDING		
Year	Team (League)	Pos.	G	AB	R	H	2B	3B	HR	RBI	Avg.	BB	SO	SB	PO	A	E	Avg.
1990— Albuquerque (PCL).....		3B-OF-SS	135	487	90	154	20	3	11	92	.316	*90	54	9	71	†255	26	†.926
— Los Angeles (N.L.)		3B	5	7	0	1	0	0	0	1	.143	0	0	0	0	1	1	.500
1991— Albuquerque (PCL).....		3B-SS	68	254	42	77	11	1	5	40	.303	49	33	4	43	125	6	.966
— Los Angeles (N.L.)		3B-SS	53	56	3	15	4	0	1	5	.268	2	12	1	5	19	0	1.000
1992— Los Angeles (N.L.)		3B	132	341	30	73	11	0	6	22	.214	34	49	0	61	183	8	*.968
1993— Los Angeles (N.L.)		3B	84	105	13	38	3	0	4	30	.362	21	13	0	11	27	3	.927
1994— Los Angeles (N.L.)		3B	40	44	3	15	3	0	0	5	.341	5	5	0	0	6	1	.857
1995— Los Angeles (N.L.)		3B	100	181	19	52	10	0	1	14	.287	28	28	0	27	70	7	.933
1996— Los Angeles (N.L.)		3B-1B	80	104	7	23	1	0	0	6	.221	11	22	0	60	23	1	.988
1997— Chicago (N.L.)■........		3B-1B-2B	90	151	19	47	8	2	3	21	.311	31	32	1	45	47	7	.929
1998— Hanshin (Jp. Cen.)■ ..			121	400	42	101	13	1	11	55	.253	42	89	0	...	...	...	...
1999— Los Angeles (N.L.)■ ..		1-3-DH-O	100	107	14	27	8	1	2	17	.252	26	20	0	58	17	3	.962
2000— Los Angeles (N.L.)		1-3-DH-O	102	121	18	35	6	2	8	26	.289	26	32	0	51	22	2	.973
Major League totals (10 years)			786	1217	126	326	54	5	25	147	.268	184	213	2	318	415	33	.957

DIVISION SERIES RECORD

								BATTING								FIELDING		
Year	Team (League)	Pos.	G	AB	R	H	2B	3B	HR	RBI	Avg.	BB	SO	SB	PO	A	E	Avg.
1995— Los Angeles (N.L.)		PH	3	3	0	2	0	0	0	0	.667	0	0	0	...	...	...	...
1996— Los Angeles (N.L.)		PH-3B	2	2	0	0	0	0	0	0	.000	0	0	0	1	0	0	1.000
Division series totals (2 years)			5	5	0	2	0	0	0	0	.400	0	0	0	1	0	0	1.000

HARNISCH, PETE — P — REDS

PERSONAL: Born September 23, 1966, in Huntington, N.Y. ... 6-0/228. ... Throws right, bats right. ... Full name: Peter Thomas Harnisch.

HIGH SCHOOL: Commack (N.Y.).

COLLEGE: Fordham.

TRANSACTIONS/CAREER NOTES: Selected by Baltimore Orioles organization in supplemental round ("sandwich pick" between first and second round, 27th pick overall) of free-agent draft (June 2, 1987); pick received as compensation for Cleveland Indians signing Type A free-agent C Rick Dempsey. ... Traded by Orioles with P Curt Schilling and OF Steve Finley to Houston Astros for 1B Glenn Davis (January 10, 1991). ... On suspended list (July 7-9, 1992). ... On Houston disabled list (May 23-June 30, 1994); included rehabilitation assignment to Tucson (June 25-26). ... Traded by Astros to New York Mets for two players to be named later (November 28, 1994; Astros acquired P Andy Beckerman (December 6, 1994) and P Juan Castillo (April 12, 1995) to complete deal. ... Granted free agency (December 23, 1994). ... Re-signed by Mets (April 7, 1995). ... On disabled list (August 2, 1995-remainder of season). ... On New York disabled list (March 26-April 14, 1996); included rehabilitation assignment to St. Lucie (March 30-April 14). ... On New York suspended list (May 22-31, 1996). ... On New York disabled list (April 2-August 5, 1997); included rehabilitation assignments to Gulf Coast Mets (July 7-10), St. Lucie (July 11-19) and Norfolk (July 20-August 5). ... Traded by Mets to Milwaukee Brewers for OF Donny Moore (August 31, 1997). ... Granted free agency (October 27, 1997). ... Signed by Cincinnati Reds (January 21, 1998). ... On Cincinnati disabled list (May 5-June 29, 2000); included rehabilitation assignment to Louisville (June 25-29).

RECORDS: Shares major league record for striking out side on nine pitches (September 6, 1991, seventh inning). ... Shares N.L. record for most consecutive home runs allowed in one inning—4 (July 23, 1996, first inning).

STATISTICAL NOTES: Pitched 4-0 one-hit, complete-game victory against Chicago (July 10, 1993). ... Pitched 3-0 one-hit, complete-game victory against San Diego (September 17, 1993).

MISCELLANEOUS: Appeared in one game as pinch runner with Houston (1994). ... Appeared in one game as pinch runner with New York (1996). ... Appeared in two games as pinch runner (2000).

Year	League	W	L	Pct.	ERA	G	GS	CG	ShO	Sv.	IP	H	R	ER	BB	SO
1987— Bluefield (Appl.)		3	1	.750	2.56	9	9	0	0	0	52 1/3	38	19	15	26	64
— Hagerstown (Caro.)		1	2	.333	2.25	4	4	0	0	0	20	17	7	5	14	18
1988— Charlotte (Sou.)		7	6	.538	2.58	20	20	4	2	0	132 1/3	113	55	38	52	141
— Rochester (I.L.)		4	1	.800	2.16	7	7	3	2	0	58 1/3	44	16	14	14	43
— Baltimore (A.L.)		0	2	.000	5.54	2	2	0	0	0	13	13	8	8	9	10
1989— Baltimore (A.L.)		5	9	.357	4.62	18	17	2	0	0	103 1/3	97	55	53	64	70
— Rochester (I.L.)		5	5	.500	2.58	12	12	3	1	0	87 1/3	60	27	25	35	59
1990— Baltimore (A.L.)		11	11	.500	4.34	31	31	3	0	0	188 2/3	189	96	91	86	122
1991— Houston (N.L.)■		12	9	.571	2.70	33	33	4	2	0	216 2/3	169	71	65	83	172
1992— Houston (N.L.)		9	10	.474	3.70	34	34	0	0	0	206 2/3	182	92	85	64	164
1993— Houston (N.L.)		16	9	.640	2.98	33	33	5	*4	0	217 2/3	171	84	72	79	185
1994— Houston (N.L.)		8	5	.615	5.40	17	17	1	0	0	95	100	59	57	39	62
— Tucson (PCL)		0	0	...	0.00	1	1	0	0	0	5	2	0	0	1	1
1995— New York (N.L.)■		2	8	.200	3.68	18	18	0	0	0	110	111	55	45	24	82
1996— St. Lucie (FSL)		1	0	1.000	2.77	2	2	0	0	0	13	11	4	4	0	12
— New York (N.L.)		8	12	.400	4.21	31	31	2	1	0	194 2/3	195	103	91	61	114
1997— Gulf Coast Mets (GCL)		0	0	...	12.00	1	1	0	0	0	3	7	4	4	0	5
— St. Lucie (FSL)		1	0	1.000	3.00	2	2	0	0	0	12	5	5	4	4	7
— Norfolk (I.L.)		1	1	.500	5.40	3	3	0	0	0	16 2/3	16	12	10	10	16
— New York (N.L.)		0	1	.000	8.06	6	5	0	0	0	25 2/3	35	24	23	11	12
— Milwaukee (A.L.)■		1	1	.500	5.14	4	3	0	0	0	14	13	9	8	12	10
1998— Cincinnati (N.L.)■		14	7	.667	3.14	32	32	2	1	0	209	176	79	73	64	157
1999— Cincinnati (N.L.)		16	10	.615	3.68	33	33	2	2	0	198 1/3	190	86	81	57	120
2000— Cincinnati (N.L.)		8	6	.571	4.74	22	22	3	1	0	131	133	76	69	46	71
— Louisville (I.L.)		0	0	...	3.18	1	1	0	0	0	5 2/3	6	2	2	2	6
A.L. totals (4 years)		17	23	.425	4.51	55	53	5	0	0	319	312	168	160	171	212
N.L. totals (10 years)		93	77	.547	3.71	259	258	19	11	0	1604 2/3	1462	729	661	528	1139
Major League totals (13 years)		110	100	.524	3.84	314	311	24	11	0	1923 2/3	1774	897	821	699	1351

ALL-STAR GAME RECORD

Year	League	W	L	Pct.	ERA	GS	CG	ShO	Sv.	IP	H	R	ER	BB	SO
1991— National		0	0	...	0.00	0	0	0	0	1	2	0	0	0	1

H

PERSONAL: Born May 21, 1976, in Harrisonburg, Va. ... 6-4/195. ... Throws right, bats left. ... Full name: Travis Boyd Harper.
HIGH SCHOOL: Circleville (W.Va.).
COLLEGE: James Madison.
TRANSACTIONS/CAREER NOTES: Selected by New York Mets organization in 14th round of free-agent draft (June 2, 1994); did not sign. ... Selected by Boston Red Sox organization in third round of free-agent draft (June 3, 1997). ... Contract with Red Sox voided due to pre-existing injury (October 29, 1997). ... Signed by Tampa Bay Devil Rays organization (June 29, 1998).

Year League	W	L	Pct.	ERA	G	GS	CG	ShO	Sv.	IP	H	R	ER	BB	SO
1998—Hudson Valley (NY-Penn)...	6	2	.750	1.92	13	10	0	0	0	56 $^1/_3$	38	14	12	20	81
1999—St. Petersburg (FSL)	5	4	.556	3.43	14	14	14	0	0	81 $^1/_3$	82	36	31	23	79
— Orlando (Sou.)	6	3	.667	5.38	14	14	1	1	0	72	73	45	43	26	68
2000— Orlando (Sou.)	3	1	.750	2.63	9	9	0	0	0	51 $^1/_3$	49	19	15	11	33
— Durham (I.L.)	7	4	.636	4.24	17	17	0	0	0	104	98	53	49	26	48
— Tampa Bay (A.L.)...............	1	2	.333	4.78	6	5	1	1	0	32	30	17	17	15	14
Major League totals (1 year)........	1	2	.333	4.78	6	5	1	1	0	32	30	17	17	15	14

PERSONAL: Born October 28, 1964, in Miami. ... 5-10/220. ... Bats left, throws right. ... Full name: Leonard Anthony Harris.
HIGH SCHOOL: Jackson (Miami).
JUNIOR COLLEGE: Miami-Dade (North) Community College.
TRANSACTIONS/CAREER NOTES: Selected by Cincinnati Reds organization in fifth round of free-agent draft (June 6, 1983). ... Loaned by Reds organization to Glens Falls, Detroit Tigers organization (May 6-28, 1988). ... Traded by Reds with OF Kal Daniels to Los Angeles Dodgers for P Tim Leary and SS Mariano Duncan (July 18, 1989). ... Granted free agency (October 8, 1993). ... Signed by Reds (December 1, 1993). ... Granted free agency (October 31, 1996). ... Re-signed by Reds (November 13, 1996). ... Traded by Reds to New York Mets for P John Hudek (July 3, 1998). ... Granted free agency (October 27, 1998). ... Signed by Colorado Rockies (November 9, 1998). ... Traded by Rockies to Arizona Diamondbacks for IF Belvani Martinez (August 31, 1999). ... Traded by Diamondbacks to Mets for P Bill Pulsipher (June 2, 2000).
STATISTICAL NOTES: Led Florida State League third basemen with 34 double plays in 1985. ... Led Eastern League third basemen with 116 putouts, 28 errors and 360 total chances in 1986. ... Led American Association in caught stealing with 22 in 1988. ... Led American Association second basemen with 23 errors in 1988. ... Career major league grand slams: 3.

Year Team (League)	Pos.	G	AB	R	H	2B	3B	HR	RBI	Avg.	BB	SO	SB	PO	A	E	Avg.
1983—Billings (Pio.)	3B	56	224	37	63	8	1	1	26	.281	13	35	7	34	95	22	.854
1984—Cedar Rapids (Midw.)	3B	132	468	52	115	15	3	6	53	.246	42	59	31	111	204	*34	.903
1985—Tampa (FSL)..............	3B	132	499	66	129	11	8	3	51	.259	37	57	15	89	*277	*35	.913
1986—Vermont (East.)	3B-SS	119	450	68	114	17	2	10	52	.253	29	38	36	†119	220	†28	.924
1987—Nashville (A.A.)	SS-3B	120	403	45	100	12	3	2	31	.248	27	43	30	124	210	34	.908
1988—Nashville (A.A.)■......	2B-SS-3B	107	422	46	117	20	2	0	35	.277	22	36	*45	203	247	†25	.947
— Glens Falls (East.)■....	2B	17	65	9	22	5	1	1	7	.338	9	6	6	40	49	5	.947
— Cincinnati (N.L.)■........	3B-2B	16	43	7	16	1	0	0	8	.372	5	4	4	14	33	1	.979
1989—Cincinnati (N.L.)........	2B-SS-3B	61	188	17	42	4	0	2	11	.223	9	20	10	92	134	13	.946
— Nashville (A.A.)	2B	8	34	6	9	2	0	3	6	.265	0	5	0	23	20	0	1.000
— Los Angeles (N.L.)■....	..OF-2B-3B-SS	54	147	19	37	6	1	1	15	.252	11	13	4	55	34	2	.978
1990—Los Angeles (N.L.) 3B-2B-OF-SS		137	431	61	131	16	4	2	29	.304	29	31	15	140	205	11	.969
1991—Los Angeles (N.L.) 3B-2B-SS-OF		145	429	59	123	16	1	3	38	.287	37	32	12	125	250	20	.949
1992—Los Angeles (N.L.) 2B-3B-OF-SS		135	347	28	94	11	0	0	30	.271	24	24	19	199	248	27	.943
1993—Los Angeles (N.L.) 2B-3B-SS-OF		107	160	20	38	6	1	2	11	.238	15	15	3	61	99	3	.982
1994—Cincinnati (N.L.)........3B-1B-OF-2B		66	100	13	31	3	1	0	14	.310	5	13	7	27	29	6	.903
1995—Cincinnati (N.L.)........3B-1B-OF-2B		101	197	32	41	8	3	2	16	.208	14	20	10	147	68	4	.982
1996—Cincinnati (N.L.)........OF-3B-1B-2B		125	302	33	86	17	2	5	32	.285	21	31	14	199	66	6	.978
1997—Cincinnati (N.L.)........OF-2B-3B-1B		120	238	32	65	13	1	3	28	.273	18	18	4	120	57	3	.983
1998—Cincinnati (N.L.)	OF-DH-P	57	122	12	36	8	0	0	10	.295	8	9	1	37	2	3	.929
— New York (N.L.)■.......OF-3B-2B-1B		75	168	18	39	7	0	6	17	.232	9	12	5	84	14	2	.980
1999—Colorado (N.L.)■........	2-O-DH-3	91	158	15	47	12	0	0	13	.297	6	6	1	60	53	9	.926
— Arizona (N.L.)■..........	3B-OF	19	29	2	11	1	0	1	7	.379	0	1	1	6	5	0	1.000
2000—Arizona (N.L.)	3B-OF	36	85	9	16	1	1	1	13	.188	3	5	5	11	29	4	.909
— New York (N.L.)■.......3-O-1-2-DH		76	138	22	42	6	3	3	13	.304	17	17	8	67	36	11	.904
Major League totals (13 years)		1421	3282	399	895	136	18	31	305	.273	231	271	123	1444	1362	125	.957

DIVISION SERIES RECORD

Year Team (League)	Pos.	G	AB	R	H	2B	3B	HR	RBI	Avg.	BB	SO	SB	PO	A	E	Avg.
1999—Arizona (N.L.)	PH-3B	2	2	0	0	0	0	0	0	.000	0	0	0	0	0	0	...
2000—New York (N.L.).........	PH	2	2	1	0	0	0	0	0	.000	0	0	1				...
Division series totals (2 years)		4	4	1	0	0	0	0	0	.000	0	0	1	0	0	0	...

CHAMPIONSHIP SERIES RECORD

Year Team (League)	Pos.	G	AB	R	H	2B	3B	HR	RBI	Avg.	BB	SO	SB	PO	A	E	Avg.
1995—Cincinnati (N.L.)	PH	3	2	0	2	0	0	0	1	1.000	0	0	1	...	...	...	...
2000—New York (N.L.)..........	PH	2	1	0	0	0	0	0	0	.000	0	1	0	...	...	...	...
Championship series totals (2 years)		5	3	0	2	0	0	0	1	.667	0	1	1	...	...	...	...

WORLD SERIES RECORD

Year Team (League)	Pos.	G	AB	R	H	2B	3B	HR	RBI	Avg.	BB	SO	SB	PO	A	E	Avg.
2000—New York (N.L.)..........	DH-PH	3	4	1	0	0	0	0	0	.000	1	1	0	...	...	...	...

RECORD AS PITCHER

Year League	W	L	Pct.	ERA	G	GS	CG	ShO	Sv.	IP	H	R	ER	BB	SO
1998—Cincinnati (N.L.)................	0	0	...	0.00	1	0	0	0	0	1	0	0	0	0	1

H

PERSONAL: Born September 16, 1976, in Selmer, Tenn. ... 5-9/180. ... Throws right, bats right. ... Full name: Chad Ashley Harville.
HIGH SCHOOL: Hardin County (Savannah, Tenn.).
COLLEGE: Memphis.
TRANSACTIONS/CAREER NOTES: Selected by Oakland Athletics organization in second round of free-agent draft (June 3, 1997).

Year League	W	L	Pct.	ERA	G	GS	CG	ShO	Sv.	IP	H	R	ER	BB	SO
1997— Southern Oregon (N'West).	1	0	1.000	0.00	3	0	0	0	0	5	3	0	0	3	6
—Visalia (Calif.)	0	0	...	5.79	14	0	0	0	0	18²/₃	25	14	12	13	24
1998— Visalia (Calif.)	4	3	.571	3.00	24	7	0	0	4	69	59	25	23	31	76
—Huntsville (Sou.)	0	0	...	2.45	12	0	0	0	8	14²/₃	6	4	4	13	24
1999— Midland (Texas)	2	0	1.000	2.01	17	0	0	0	7	22¹/₃	13	6	5	9	35
—Vancouver (PCL)	1	0	1.000	1.75	22	0	0	0	11	25²/₃	24	5	5	11	36
—Oakland (A.L.)	0	2	.000	6.91	15	0	0	0	0	14¹/₃	18	11	11	10	15
2000—Sacramento (PCL)	5	3	.625	4.50	53	0	0	0	9	64	53	35	32	35	77
Major League totals (1 year)	0	2	.000	6.91	15	0	0	0	0	14¹/₃	18	11	11	10	15

PERSONAL: Born August 1, 1968, in Kobe, Japan ... 5-11/178. ... Throws right, bats right. ... Name pronounced SHE-geh-TOE-she HAH-seh-GAH-wah.
COLLEGE: Ritsumeikan University (Kyoto, Japan).
TRANSACTIONS/CAREER NOTES: Played for Orix Blue Wave of Japan Pacific League (1991-96). ... Signed as non-drafted free agent by Anaheim Angels (January 9, 1997).

Year League	W	L	Pct.	ERA	G	GS	CG	ShO	Sv.	IP	H	R	ER	BB	SO
1991— Orix (Jap. Pac.)	12	9	.571	3.55	28	25	11	3	1	185	184	76	73	50	111
1992— Orix (Jap. Pac.)	6	8	.429	3.27	24	19	4	0	1	143¹/₃	138	60	52	51	86
1993— Orix (Jap. Pac.)	12	6	.667	2.71	23	22	9	3	0	159²/₃	146	61	48	48	86
1994— Orix (Jap. Pac.)	11	9	.550	3.11	25	22	8	3	1	156¹/₃	169	61	54	46	86
1995— Orix (Jap. Pac.)	12	7	.632	2.89	24	23	9	4	0	171	167	62	55	51	91
1996— Orix (Jap. Pac.)	4	6	.400	5.34	18	16	2	0	1	87²/₃	109	60	52	40	55
1997— Anaheim (A.L.)■	3	7	.300	3.93	50	7	0	0	0	116²/₃	118	60	51	46	83
1998— Anaheim (A.L.)	8	3	.727	3.14	61	0	0	0	5	97¹/₃	86	37	34	32	73
1999— Anaheim (A.L.)	4	6	.400	4.91	64	1	0	0	2	77	80	45	42	34	44
2000— Anaheim (A.L.)	10	6	.625	3.57	66	0	0	0	9	95²/₃	100	43	38	38	59
Major League totals (4 years)	25	22	.532	3.84	241	8	0	0	16	386²/₃	384	185	165	150	259

PERSONAL: Born May 25, 1966, in Long Branch, N.J. ... 6-3/225. ... Bats right, throws right. ... Full name: William Joseph Haselman.
HIGH SCHOOL: Saratoga (Calif.).
COLLEGE: UCLA.
TRANSACTIONS/CAREER NOTES: Selected by Texas Rangers organization in first round (23rd pick overall) of free-agent draft (June 2, 1987); pick received as compensation for New York Yankees signing Type A free-agent OF Gary Ward. ... On Oklahoma City disabled list (March 28-May 4, 1992). ... Claimed on waivers by Seattle Mariners (May 29, 1992). ... On suspended list (July 22-25, 1993). ... Granted free agency (October 15, 1994). ... Signed by Boston Red Sox (November 7, 1994). ... On Boston disabled list (June 30-August 8, 1997); included rehabilitation assignment to Gulf Coast Red Sox (July 29-August 1) and Trenton (August 1-8). ... Traded by Red Sox with P Aaron Sele and P Mark Brandenburg to Rangers for C Jim Leyritz and OF Damon Buford (November 6, 1997). ... Granted free agency (October 23, 1998). ... Signed by Detroit Tigers (December 14, 1998). ... Traded by Tigers with P Justin Thompson, P Francisco Cordero, OF Gabe Kapler, 2B Frank Catalanotto and P Alan Webb to Rangers for OF Juan Gonzalez, P Danny Patterson and C Gregg Zaun (November 2, 1999).
RECORDS: Holds major league record for most chances accepted in consecutive nine-inning games—37 (April 29 and 30, 1996). ... Shares A.L. single-game record for most chances accepted by catcher (nine-inning game)—20 (September 18, 1996).
STATISTICAL NOTES: Led Texas League with 12 passed balls in 1989. ... Led Texas League catchers with 676 putouts, 90 assists, 20 errors, 786 total chances and 20 passed balls in 1990. ... Led American Association catchers with 673 putouts and 751 total chances in 1991. ... Tied for A.L. lead in passed balls with 17 in 1997. ... Career major league grand slams: 1.

						BATTING								FIELDING		
Year Team (League)	Pos.	G	AB	R	H	2B	3B	HR	RBI	Avg.	BB	SO	SB	PO	A	E	Avg.
1987—Gastonia (S.Atl.)	C	61	235	35	72	13	1	8	33	.306	19	46	1	26	2	2	.933
1988—Charlotte (FSL)	C	122	453	56	111	17	2	10	54	.245	45	99	8	249	30	6	.979
1989—Tulsa (Texas)	C	107	352	38	95	17	2	7	36	.270	40	88	5	508	63	9	.984
1990—Tulsa (Texas)	C-1B-OF-3B	120	430	68	137	39	2	18	80	.319	43	96	3	†722	†93	†20	.976
—Texas (A.L.)	DH-C	7	13	0	2	0	0	0	3	.154	1	5	0	8	0	0	1.000
1991—Oklahoma City (A.A.)	C-OF-1B-3B	126	442	57	113	22	2	9	60	.256	61	89	10	†706	71	11	.986
1992—Oklahoma City (A.A.)	OF-C	17	58	8	14	5	0	1	9	.241	13	12	1	45	7	3	.945
—Calgary (PCL)■	C-OF	88	302	49	77	14	2	19	53	.255	41	89	3	227	23	6	.977
—Seattle (A.L.)	C-OF	8	19	1	5	0	0	0	0	.263	0	7	0	19	2	0	1.000
1993—Seattle (A.L.)	C-DH-OF	58	137	21	35	8	0	5	16	.255	12	19	2	236	17	2	.992
1994—Seattle (A.L.)	C-DH-OF	38	83	11	16	7	1	1	8	.193	3	11	1	157	6	3	.982
—Calgary (PCL)	C-DH	44	163	44	54	10	0	15	46	.331	30	33	1	219	16	5	.979
1995—Boston (A.L.)■	C-DH-1B-3B	64	152	22	37	6	1	5	23	.243	17	30	0	259	16	3	.989
1996—Boston (A.L.)	C-DH-1B	77	237	33	65	13	1	8	34	.274	19	52	4	507	33	3	.994
1997—Boston (A.L.)	C	67	212	22	50	15	0	6	26	.236	15	44	0	373	40	7	.983
—GC Red Sox (GCL)	DH	4	16	2	2	0	0	0	1	.125	0	1	1	0	0	0	...
—Trenton (East.)	C-DH	7	26	3	6	1	0	2	3	.231	2	2	0	30	2	0	1.000
1998—Texas (A.L.)	C-DH	40	105	11	33	6	0	6	17	.314	3	17	0	176	8	1	.995
1999—Detroit (A.L.)■	C-DH	48	143	13	39	8	0	4	14	.273	10	26	2	231	13	1	.996
2000—Texas (A.L.)■	C	62	193	23	53	18	0	6	26	.275	15	36	0	336	20	4	.989
Major League totals (10 years)		469	1294	157	335	81	3	41	167	.259	95	247	9	2302	155	24	.990

DIVISION SERIES RECORD

						BATTING								FIELDING		
Year Team (League)	Pos.	G	AB	R	H	2B	3B	HR	RBI	Avg.	BB	SO	SB	PO	A	E	Avg.
1995—Boston (A.L.)	C	1	2	0	0	0	0	0	0	.000	0	0	0	6	0	0	1.000

H

HATCHER, CHRIS   OF   DEVIL RAYS

PERSONAL: Born January 7, 1969, in Anaheim, Calif. ... 6-3/235. ... Bats right, throws right. ... Full name: Christopher Kenneth Hatcher.
HIGH SCHOOL: Thomas Jefferson (Council Bluffs, Iowa).
COLLEGE: Iowa.
TRANSACTIONS/CAREER NOTES: Selected by Houston Astros organization in third round of free-agent draft (June 4, 1990). ... On disabled list (June 8-July 15, 1992, June 3-July 1, 1993 and April 7-15, 1994). ... Granted free agency (October 15, 1996). ... Signed by Kansas City Royals organization (November 13, 1996). ... Granted free agency (October 15, 1997). ... Re-signed by Royals (February 1998). ... Granted free agency (October 15, 1998). ... Signed by Colorado Rockies organization (December 18, 1998). ... On Colorado Springs disabled list (August 4-20, 1999). ... Granted free agency (October 15, 1999). ... Signed by Chicago Cubs organization (November 22, 1999). ... Traded by Cubs with P Mike Heathcott and SS Brett King to Anaheim Angels for P Brett Hinchcliffe and IF Keith Luuloa (July 28, 2000). ... Granted free agency (October 2, 2000). ... Signed by Tampa Bay Devil Rays organization (November 10, 2000).
HONORS: Named Pacific Coast League Most Valuable Player (1998).
STATISTICAL NOTES: Led Pacific Coast League first basemen with 15 errors in 1995. ... Led Pacific Coast League with 313 total bases in 1998.

												BATTING				FIELDING		
Year	Team (League)	Pos.	G	AB	R	H	2B	3B	HR	RBI	Avg.	BB	SO	SB	PO	A	E	Avg.
1990—	Auburn (NY-Penn)......	OF	72	259	37	64	10	0	9	45	.247	27	86	8	62	5	5	.931
1991—	Burlington (Midw.).....	OF	129	497	69	116	23	5	13	65	.233	46	*180	10	235	10	10	.961
1992—	Osceola (FSL)............	OF	97	367	49	103	19	6	17	68	.281	20	97	11	139	8	5	.967
1993—	Jackson (Texas).........	OF	101	367	45	95	15	3	15	64	.259	11	104	5	78	2	5	.941
1994—	Tucson (PCL)	OF-DH-1B	108	349	55	104	28	4	12	73	.298	19	90	5	150	3	5	.968
1995—	Tucson (PCL)	1B-DH-OF	94	290	59	83	19	2	14	50	.286	42	107	7	599	40	†15	.977
—	Jackson (Texas)	OF-1B-DH	11	39	5	12	1	0	1	3	.308	4	6	0	41	5	2	.958
1996—	Jackson (Texas)	OF-DH	41	156	29	48	9	1	13	36	.308	9	39	2	53	1	3	.947
—	Tucson (PCL)	OF-DH	95	348	53	105	21	4	18	61	.302	14	87	10	122	4	2	.984
1997—	Wichita (Texas)■	OF-DH	11	42	7	11	0	0	5	7	.262	4	16	1	9	0	1	.900
—	Omaha (A.A.).............	OF-DH	68	222	34	51	9	0	11	24	.230	17	68	0	56	2	5	.921
1998—	Omaha (PCL)............OF-DH-1B-P	126	485	84	150	21	2	*46	106	.309	25	125	8	195	7	7	.967
—	Kansas City (A.L.)	OF	8	15	0	1	0	0	0	1	.067	1	7	0	7	0	0	1.000
1999—	Colo. Springs (PCL)■	OF-DH-1B	98	334	63	115	24	2	21	69	.344	23	89	12	163	14	10	.947
2000—	Iowa (PCL)■.............	OF-1B	86	288	46	80	15	1	24	71	.278	26	64	4	137	13	2	.987
—	Edmonton (PCL)■	1B-OF	30	115	19	39	8	4	7	24	.339	8	24	1	58	9	3	.957
Major League totals (1 year)			8	15	0	1	0	0	0	1	.067	1	7	0	7	0	0	1.000

RECORD AS PITCHER

Year	League	W	L	Pct.	ERA	G	GS	CG	ShO	Sv.	IP	H	R	ER	BB	SO
1998—	Omaha (PCL)...................	0	1	.000	9.00	1	0	0	0	0	1	1	1	1	3	0

HATTEBERG, SCOTT   C   RED SOX

PERSONAL: Born December 14, 1969, in Salem, Ore. ... 6-1/205. ... Bats left, throws right. ... Full name: Scott Allen Hatteberg. ... Name pronounced HAT-ee-berg.
HIGH SCHOOL: Eisenhower (Yakima, Wash.).
COLLEGE: Washington State.
TRANSACTIONS/CAREER NOTES: Selected by Philadelphia Phillies organization in 12th round of free-agent draft (June 1, 1988); did not sign. ... Selected by Boston Red Sox organization in supplemental round ("sandwich pick" between first and second round, 43rd pick overall) of free-agent draft (June 3, 1991); pick received as part of compensation for Kansas City signing Type A free-agent P Mike Boddicker. ... On disabled list (July 27-August 3, 1992). ... On Boston disabled list (April 15-May 7 and May 17-August 16, 1999); included rehabilitation assignments to Pawtucket (May 4-7 and August 3-13), Gulf Coast Red Sox (July 24-31) and Sarasota (August 1-2).
STATISTICAL NOTES: Tied for A.L. lead in double plays by catcher with 13 and passed balls with 17 in 1997. ... Career major league grand slams: 1.

												BATTING				FIELDING		
Year	Team (League)	Pos.	G	AB	R	H	2B	3B	HR	RBI	Avg.	BB	SO	SB	PO	A	E	Avg.
1991—	Winter Haven (FSL)....	C	56	191	21	53	7	3	1	25	.277	22	22	1	261	35	5	.983
—	Lynchburg (Caro.)......	C	8	25	4	5	1	0	0	2	.200	7	6	0	35	2	0	1.000
1992—	New Britain (East.)	C	103	297	28	69	13	2	1	30	.232	41	49	1	473	44	11	.979
1993—	New Britain (East.)	C	68	227	35	63	10	2	7	28	.278	42	38	1	410	45	10	.978
—	Pawtucket (I.L.)..........	C	18	53	6	10	0	0	1	2	.189	6	12	0	131	4	5	.964
1994—	New Britain (East.)	C	20	68	6	18	4	1	1	9	.265	7	9	0	125	14	1	.993
—	Pawtucket (I.L.)..........	C	78	238	26	56	14	0	7	19	.235	32	49	2	467	36	7	.986
1995—	Pawtucket (I.L.)..........	C-DH	85	251	36	68	15	1	7	27	.271	40	39	2	446	45	•8	.984
—	Boston (A.L.).............	C	2	2	1	1	0	0	0	0	.500	0	0	0	4	0	0	1.000
1996—	Pawtucket (I.L.)..........	C-DH	90	287	52	77	16	0	12	49	.268	58	66	1	566	42	6	.990
—	Boston (A.L.).............	C	10	11	3	2	1	0	0	0	.182	3	2	0	32	2	0	1.000
1997—	Boston (A.L.).............	C-DH	114	350	46	97	23	1	10	44	.277	40	70	0	574	46	11	.983
1998—	Boston (A.L.).............	C	112	359	46	99	23	1	12	43	.276	43	58	0	664	61	5	.993
1999—	Boston (A.L.).............	C-DH	30	80	12	22	5	0	1	11	.275	18	14	0	128	14	1	.993
—	Pawtucket (I.L.)..........	C-DH	10	34	3	6	2	0	0	4	.176	4	6	0	47	4	0	1.000
—	GC Red Sox (GCL)	C-DH	6	15	4	6	2	0	1	6	.400	7	1	0	37	4	0	1.000
—	Sarasota (FSL)	C	1	1	0	1	0	0	0	1	1.000	0	0	0	3	1	0	1.000
2000—	Boston (A.L.).............	C-DH-3B	92	230	21	61	15	0	8	36	.265	38	39	0	297	16	6	.981
Major League totals (6 years)			360	1032	129	282	67	2	31	134	.273	142	183	0	1699	139	23	.988

DIVISION SERIES RECORD

												BATTING				FIELDING		
Year	Team (League)	Pos.	G	AB	R	H	2B	3B	HR	RBI	Avg.	BB	SO	SB	PO	A	E	Avg.
1998—	Boston (A.L.).............	C	3	9	0	1	0	0	0	0	.111	3	1	0	20	0	0	1.000
1999—	Boston (A.L.).............	C	1	1	1	1	0	0	0	1	1.000	0	0	0	2	0	0	1.000
Division series totals (2 years)			4	10	1	2	0	0	0	1	.200	3	1	0	22	0	0	1.000

CHAMPIONSHIP SERIES RECORD

												BATTING				FIELDING		
Year	Team (League)	Pos.	G	AB	R	H	2B	3B	HR	RBI	Avg.	BB	SO	SB	PO	A	E	Avg.
1999—	Boston (A.L.).............	PH-C	3	1	0	0	0	0	0	0	.000	0	1	0	0	0	0	—

H

PERSONAL: Born December 21, 1972, in Gary, Ind. ... 6-5/204. ... Throws right, bats right.
HIGH SCHOOL: West Side (Gary, Ind.).
TRANSACTIONS/CAREER NOTES: Selected by Minnesota Twins organization in seventh round of free-agent draft (June 3, 1991).
STATISTICAL NOTES: Tied for A.L. lead with three balks in 1997.

Year League	W	L	Pct.	ERA	G	GS	CG	ShO	Sv.	IP	H	R	ER	BB	SO
1991— Gulf Coast Twins (GCL)	4	3	.571	4.75	11	11	0	0	0	55	62	34	29	26	47
1992— Gulf Coast Twins (GCL)	3	2	.600	3.22	6	6	1	0	0	36$\frac{1}{3}$	36	19	13	10	35
— Elizabethton (Appl.)	0	1	.000	3.38	5	5	1	0	0	26$\frac{2}{3}$	21	12	10	11	36
1993— Fort Wayne (Midw.)	•15	5	.750	*2.06	26	23	4	•3	0	157$\frac{1}{3}$	110	53	36	41	*179
1994— Fort Myers (FSL)	4	0	1.000	2.33	6	6	1	1	0	38$\frac{2}{3}$	32	10	10	6	36
— Nashville (Sou.)	9	2	*.818	2.33	11	11	1	0	0	73$\frac{1}{3}$	50	23	19	28	53
— Salt Lake (PCL)	5	4	.556	4.08	12	12	1	0	0	81$\frac{2}{3}$	92	42	37	33	37
1995— Minnesota (A.L.)	2	3	.400	8.67	6	6	1	0	0	27	39	29	26	12	9
— Salt Lake (PCL)	9	7	.563	3.55	22	22	4	1	0	144$\frac{1}{3}$	150	63	57	40	74
1996— Minnesota (A.L.)	1	1	.500	8.20	7	6	0	0	0	26$\frac{1}{3}$	42	24	24	9	24
— Salt Lake (PCL)	9	8	.529	3.92	20	20	4	1	0	137$\frac{2}{3}$	138	66	60	31	99
1997— Salt Lake (PCL)	9	4	.692	5.45	14	13	2	1	0	76	100	53	46	16	53
— Minnesota (A.L.)	6	12	.333	5.84	20	20	0	0	0	103$\frac{1}{3}$	134	71	67	47	58
1998— Minnesota (A.L.)	7	14	.333	5.25	33	33	0	0	0	190$\frac{1}{3}$	227	126	111	61	105
1999— Minnesota (A.L.)	10	14	.417	6.66	33	33	1	0	0	174$\frac{1}{3}$	238	*136	*129	60	103
2000— Minnesota (A.L.)	2	5	.286	3.39	66	0	0	0	14	87$\frac{2}{3}$	85	34	33	32	59
Major League totals (6 years)	28	49	.364	5.76	165	98	2	0	14	609	765	420	390	221	358

PERSONAL: Born May 29, 1965, in Hattiesburg, Miss. ... 6-0/215. ... Bats right, throws right. ... Full name: Charles Dewayne Hayes.
HIGH SCHOOL: Forrest County Agricultural (Brooklyn, Miss.).
TRANSACTIONS/CAREER NOTES: Selected by San Francisco Giants organization in fourth round of free-agent draft (June 6, 1983). ... On disabled list (July 20, 1983-remainder of season). ... Traded by Giants with P Dennis Cook and P Terry Mulholland to Philadelphia Phillies for P Steve Bedrosian and a player to be named later (June 18, 1989); Giants organization acquired IF Rick Parker to complete deal (August 7, 1989). ... Traded by Phillies to New York Yankees (February 19, 1992), completing deal in which Yankees traded P Darrin Chapin to Phillies for a player to be named later (January 8, 1992). ... Selected by Colorado Rockies in first round (third pick overall) of expansion draft (November 17, 1992). ... On suspended list (August 10-13, 1993). ... Granted free agency (December 23, 1994). ... Signed by Phillies (April 6, 1995). ... Granted free agency (November 2, 1995). ... Signed by Pittsburgh Pirates (December 28, 1995). ... Traded by Pirates to Yankees for a player to be named later (August 30, 1996); Pirates acquired P Chris Corn to complete deal (August 31, 1996). ... Traded by Yankees with cash to Giants for OF Chris Singleton and P Alberto Castillo (November 11, 1997). ... On suspended list (July 28-30, 1998). ... On suspended list (April 20-24, 1999). ... On disabled list (July 2-21, 1999). ... Granted free agency (November 1, 1999). ... Signed by New York Mets organization (January 19, 2000). ... Released by Mets (March 20, 2000). ... Signed by Milwaukee Brewers organization (March 22, 2000). ... Granted free agency (October 31, 2000). ... Signed by Houston Astros organization (January 2, 2001).
STATISTICAL NOTES: Led Texas League third basemen with 27 double plays in 1986. ... Led Texas League third basemen with 334 total chances in 1987. ... Led Pacific Coast League in grounding into double plays with 19 in 1988. ... Led N.L. third basemen with 324 assists and tied for lead with 465 total chances in 1990. ... Tied for A.L. lead in double plays by third baseman with 29 in 1992. ... Tied for N.L. lead in grounding into double plays with 25 in 1993. ... Led N.L. in grounding into double plays with 23 in 1995. ... Career major league grand slams: 3.

Year Team (League)	Pos.	G	AB	R	H	2B	3B	HR	RBI	Avg.	BB	SO	PO	A	E	Avg.
1983— Great Falls (Pio.)	3B-OF	34	111	9	29	4	2	0	9	.261	7	26	1	13	32	9	.833
1984— Clinton (Midw.)	3B	116	392	41	96	17	2	2	51	.245	34	110	4	68	216	28	.910
1985— Fresno (Calif.)	3B	131	467	73	132	17	2	4	68	.283	56	95	7	*100	233	18	*.949
1986— Shreveport (Texas)	3B	121	434	52	107	23	2	5	45	.247	28	83	1	89	*259	25	.933
1987— Shreveport (Texas)	3B	128	487	66	148	33	3	14	75	.304	26	76	5	*100	*212	22	*.934
1988— Phoenix (PCL)	OF-3B	131	492	71	151	26	4	7	71	.307	34	91	4	206	100	23	.930
— San Francisco (N.L.)	OF-3B	7	11	0	1	0	0	0	0	.091	0	3	0	5	0	1	1.000
1989— Phoenix (PCL)	3-O-1-S-2	61	229	25	65	15	1	7	27	.284	15	48	5	76	76	8	.950
— San Francisco (N.L.)	3B	3	5	0	1	0	0	0	0	.200	0	1	0	2	1	0	1.000
— Scranton/W.B. (I.L.)■	3B	7	27	4	11	3	1	1	3	.407	0	3	0	8	8	0	1.000
— Philadelphia (N.L.)	3B	84	299	26	77	15	1	8	43	.258	11	49	3	49	173	22	.910
1990— Philadelphia (N.L.)	3B-1B-2B	152	561	56	145	20	0	10	57	.258	28	91	4	151	†329	20	.960
1991— Philadelphia (N.L.)	3B-SS	142	460	34	106	23	1	12	53	.230	16	75	3	88	240	15	.956
1992— New York (A.L.)■	3B-1B	142	509	52	131	19	2	18	66	.257	28	100	3	125	249	13	.966
1993— Colorado (N.L.)■	3B-SS	157	573	89	175	*45	2	25	98	.305	43	82	11	123	292	20	.954
1994— Colorado (N.L.)	3B	113	423	46	122	23	4	10	50	.288	36	71	3	72	216	17	.944
1995— Philadelphia (N.L.)■	3B	141	529	58	146	30	3	11	85	.276	50	88	5	•104	264	14	.963
1996— Pittsburgh (N.L.)■	3B	128	459	51	114	21	2	10	62	.248	36	78	6	66	275	18	.960
— New York (A.L.)■	3B	20	67	7	19	3	0	2	13	.284	1	12	0	14	30	0	1.000
1997— New York (A.L.)	3B-2B	100	353	39	91	16	0	11	53	.258	40	66	3	67	169	13	.948
1998— San Fran. (N.L.)■	3B-1B-DH	111	329	39	94	8	0	12	62	.286	34	61	2	369	101	3	.994
1999— San Fran. (N.L.)	3B-1B-DH-OF	95	264	33	54	9	1	6	48	.205	33	41	3	130	91	7	.969
2000— Milwaukee (N.L.)■	3B-1B-DH	121	370	46	93	17	0	9	46	.251	57	84	1	438	119	7	.988
American League totals (3 years)		262	929	98	241	38	2	31	132	.259	69	178	6	206	448	26	.962
National League totals (11 years)		1254	4283	478	1128	211	14	113	604	.263	344	724	41	1597	2101	143	.963
Major League totals (13 years)		1516	5212	576	1369	249	16	144	736	.263	413	902	47	1803	2549	169	.963

DIVISION SERIES RECORD

Year Team (League)	Pos.	G	AB	R	H	2B	3B	HR	RBI	Avg.	BB	SO	SB	PO	A	E	Avg.
1996— New York (A.L.)	3B-DH	3	5	0	1	0	0	0	1	.200	0	0	0	1	3	0	1.000
1997— New York (A.L.)	3B-2B	5	15	0	5	0	0	0	1	.333	0	2	0	3	9	3	.800
Division series totals (2 years)		8	20	0	6	0	0	0	2	.300	0	2	0	4	12	3	.842

H

Year	Team (League)	Pos.	G	AB	R	H	2B	3B	HR	RBI	Avg.	BB	SO	SB	PO	A	E	Avg.
						BATTING									FIELDING			
1996— New York (A.L.)		PH-3B-DH	4	7	0	1	0	0	0	0	.143	2	2	0	0	3	0	1.000

WORLD SERIES RECORD

NOTES: Member of World Series championship team (1996).

Year	Team (League)	Pos.	G	AB	R	H	2B	3B	HR	RBI	Avg.	BB	SO	SB	PO	A	E	Avg.
						BATTING									FIELDING			
1996— New York (A.L.)		3B-PH-1B	4	16	2	3	0	0	0	1	.188	1	5	0	3	6	0	1.000

HAYNES, JIMMY — P — BREWERS

PERSONAL: Born September 5, 1972, in La Grange, Ga. ... 6-4/203. ... Throws right, bats right. ... Full name: Jimmy Wayne Haynes.
HIGH SCHOOL: Troup (La Grange, Ga.).
TRANSACTIONS/CAREER NOTES: Selected by Baltimore Orioles organization in seventh round of free-agent draft (June 3, 1991). ... Traded by Orioles with a player to be named later to Oakland Athletics for OF Geronimo Berroa (June 27, 1997); A's acquired P Mark Seaver to complete deal (September 2, 1997). ... Traded by Athletics to Milwaukee Brewers as part of three-way deal in which Athletics received P Justin Miller and cash from Colorado Rockies, Brewers received P Jamey Wright and C Henry Blanco from Rockies and Rockies received 3B Jeff Cirillo, P Scott Karl and cash from Brewers (December 13, 1999).
STATISTICAL NOTES: Led A.L. pitchers with five errors in 1999.

Year	League	W	L	Pct.	ERA	G	GS	CG	ShO	Sv.	IP	H	R	ER	BB	SO
1991— Gulf Coast Orioles (GCL)		3	2	.600	1.60	14	8	1	0	2	62	44	27	11	21	67
1992— Kane County (Midw.)		7	11	.389	2.56	24	24	4	0	0	144	131	66	41	45	141
1993— Frederick (Caro.)		12	8	.600	3.03	27	27	2	1	0	172 1/3	139	73	58	61	174
1994— Bowie (East.)		13	8	.619	2.90	25	25	5	1	0	173 2/3	154	67	56	46	*177
— Rochester (I.L.)		1	0	1.000	6.75	3	3	0	0	0	13 1/3	20	12	10	6	14
1995— Rochester (I.L.)		•12	8	.600	3.29	26	25	3	1	0	167	162	77	61	49	*140
— Baltimore (A.L.)		2	1	.667	2.25	4	3	0	0	0	24	11	6	6	12	22
1996— Baltimore (A.L.)		3	6	.333	8.29	26	11	0	0	1	89	122	84	82	58	65
— Rochester (I.L.)		1	1	.500	5.65	5	5	0	0	0	28 2/3	31	19	18	18	24
1997— Rochester (I.L.)		5	4	.556	3.44	16	16	2	1	0	102	89	49	39	55	113
— Edmonton (PCL)■		0	2	.000	4.85	5	5	0	0	0	29 2/3	36	22	16	11	24
— Oakland (A.L.)		3	6	.333	4.42	13	13	0	0	0	73 1/3	74	38	36	40	65
1998— Oakland (A.L.)		11	9	.550	5.09	33	33	1	1	0	194 1/3	229	124	110	88	134
1999— Oakland (A.L.)		7	12	.368	6.34	30	25	0	0	0	142	158	112	100	80	93
2000— Milwaukee (N.L.)■		12	13	.480	5.33	33	33	0	0	0	199 1/3	228	128	118	100	88
A.L. totals (5 years)		26	34	.433	5.75	106	85	1	1	1	522 2/3	594	364	334	278	379
N.L. totals (1 year)		12	13	.480	5.33	33	33	0	0	0	199 1/3	228	128	118	100	88
Major League totals (6 years)		38	47	.447	5.63	139	118	1	1	1	722	822	492	452	378	467

HEAMS, SHANE — P — TIGERS

PERSONAL: Born September 29, 1975, in Toledo, Ohio. ... 6-1/175. ... Throws right, bats right. ... Full name: Shane Timothy Heams.
HIGH SCHOOL: Bedford (Temperance, Mich.).
COLLEGE: Illinois.
TRANSACTIONS/CAREER NOTES: Selected by Seattle Mariners organization in 41st round of free-agent draft (June 2, 1994). ... Announced retirement (March 24, 1998). ... Signed by Detroit Tigers organization (April 23, 1998).
MISCELLANEOUS: Played outfield (1995).

Year	League	W	L	Pct.	ERA	G	GS	CG	ShO	Sv.	IP	H	R	ER	BB	SO
1996— Arizona Mariners (Ariz.)		1	1	.500	2.93	9	0	0	0	2	15 1/3	10	7	5	6	12
1997— Arizona Mariners (Ariz.)		•6	2	*.750	1.70	21	0	0	0	2	37	30	20	7	22	42
1998— Jamestown (NY-Penn)■		2	2	.500	3.99	24	0	0	0	6	47 1/3	43	27	21	16	73
1999— West Michigan (Midw.)		5	4	.556	2.35	51	0	0	0	10	69	41	26	18	39	101
2000— Jacksonville (Sou.)		6	2	.750	2.59	39	0	0	0	5	55 2/3	35	17	16	34	67
— Toledo (I.L.)		0	0	...	11.17	6	0	0	0	0	9 2/3	13	12	12	12	7

RECORD AS POSITION PLAYER

Year	Team (League)	Pos.	G	AB	R	H	2B	3B	HR	RBI	Avg.	BB	SO	SB	PO	A	E	Avg.
						BATTING									FIELDING			
1995— Everett (N'West)		OF	27	61	5	12	4	0	1	4	.197	3	28	2	13	4	2	.895

HELLING, RICK — P — RANGERS

PERSONAL: Born December 15, 1970, in Devils Lake, N.D. ... 6-3/220. ... Throws right, bats right. ... Full name: Ricky Allen Helling.
HIGH SCHOOL: Lakota (Fargo, N.D.), then Shanley (N.D.).
JUNIOR COLLEGE: Kishwaukee College (Ill.).
COLLEGE: North Dakota, then Stanford.
TRANSACTIONS/CAREER NOTES: Selected by New York Mets organization in 50th round of free-agent draft (June 4, 1990); did not sign. ... Selected by Texas Rangers organization in first round (22nd pick overall) of free-agent draft (June 1, 1992). ... Traded by Rangers to Florida Marlins (September 3, 1996), completing deal in which Marlins traded P John Burkett to Rangers for P Ryan Dempster and a player to be named later (August 8, 1996). ... Traded by Marlins to Rangers for P Ed Vosberg (August 12, 1997).
STATISTICAL NOTES: Pitched 4-0 no-hit victory against Nashville (August 13, 1996). ... Led A.L. with 41 home runs allowed in 1999.
MISCELLANEOUS: Member of 1992 U.S. Olympic baseball team.

H

Year League	W	L	Pct.	ERA	G	GS	CG	ShO	Sv.	IP	H	R	ER	BB	SO
1992— Charlotte (FSL)	1	1	.500	2.29	3	3	0	0	0	19²/₃	13	5	5	4	20
1993— Tulsa (Texas)	12	8	.600	3.60	26	26	2	•2	0	177¹/₃	150	76	71	46	*188
— Oklahoma City (A.A.)	1	1	.500	1.64	2	2	1	0	0	11	5	3	2	3	17
1994— Texas (A.L.)	3	2	.600	5.88	9	9	1	1	0	52	62	34	34	18	25
— Oklahoma City (A.A.)	4	12	.250	5.78	20	20	2	0	0	132¹/₃	153	93	85	43	85
1995— Texas (A.L.)	0	2	.000	6.57	3	3	0	0	0	12¹/₃	17	11	9	8	5
— Oklahoma City (A.A.)	4	8	.333	5.33	20	20	3	0	0	109²/₃	132	73	65	41	80
1996— Oklahoma City (A.A.)	12	4	.750	2.96	23	22	2	1	0	140	124	54	46	38	157
— Texas (A.L.)	1	2	.333	7.52	6	2	0	0	0	20¹/₃	23	17	17	9	16
— Florida (N.L.)■	2	1	.667	1.95	5	4	0	0	0	27²/₃	14	6	6	7	26
1997— Florida (N.L.)	2	6	.250	4.38	31	8	0	0	0	76	61	38	37	48	53
— Texas (A.L.)■	3	3	.500	4.58	10	8	0	0	0	55	47	29	28	21	46
1998— Texas (A.L.)	•20	7	.741	4.41	33	33	4	2	0	216¹/₃	209	109	106	78	164
1999— Texas (A.L.)	13	11	.542	4.84	35	*35	3	0	0	219¹/₃	228	127	118	85	131
2000— Texas (A.L.)	16	13	.552	4.48	35	•35	0	0	0	217	212	122	108	99	146
A.L. totals (7 years)	56	40	.583	4.77	131	125	8	3	0	792¹/₃	798	449	420	318	533
N.L. totals (2 years)	4	7	.364	3.73	36	12	0	0	0	103²/₃	75	44	43	55	79
Major League totals (7 years)	60	47	.561	4.65	167	137	8	3	0	896	873	493	463	373	612

DIVISION SERIES RECORD

Year League	W	L	Pct.	ERA	G	GS	CG	ShO	Sv.	IP	H	R	ER	BB	SO
1998— Texas (A.L.)	0	1	.000	4.50	1	1	0	0	0	6	8	3	3	1	9
1999— Texas (A.L.)	0	1	.000	2.84	1	1	0	0	0	6¹/₃	5	2	2	1	8
Division series totals (2 years)	0	2	.000	3.65	2	2	0	0	0	12¹/₃	13	5	5	2	17

HELMS, WES — 3B — BRAVES

PERSONAL: Born May 12, 1976, in Gastonia, N.C. ... 6-4/230. ... Bats right, throws right. ... Full name: Wesley Ray Helms.
HIGH SCHOOL: Ashbrook (Gastonia, N.C.).
TRANSACTIONS/CAREER NOTES: Selected by Atlanta Braves organization in 10th round of free-agent draft (June 2, 1994). ... On Atlanta disabled list (April 3-July 15 and September 5, 1999-remainder of season); included rehabilitation assignment to Gulf Coast Braves (June 22-July 11). ... On Greenville disabled list (August 15-September 4, 1999).
STATISTICAL NOTES: Led South Atlantic League third basemen with 25 double plays in 1995. ... Led International League third basemen with 24 double plays in 1998. ... Led International League third basemen with 341 total chances and 28 double plays in 2000.

							BATTING						FIELDING		
Year Team (League)	Pos.	G	AB	R	H	2B	3B	HR	RBI	Avg.	BB	SO	SB	PO	A	E	Avg.
1994— GC Braves (GCL)	3B	56	184	22	49	15	1	4	29	.266	22	36	6	•47	93	20	.875
1995— Macon (S.Atl.)	3B	136	*539	89	149	32	1	11	85	.276	50	107	2	91	*269	40	.900
1996— Durham (Caro.)	3B	67	258	40	83	19	2	13	54	.322	12	51	1	40	133	15	.920
— Greenville (Sou.)	3B	64	231	24	59	13	2	4	22	.255	13	48	2	50	96	12	.924
1997— Richmond (I.L.)	3B	32	110	11	21	4	0	3	15	.191	10	34	1	18	65	9	.902
— Greenville (Sou.)	3B	86	314	50	93	14	1	11	44	.296	33	50	3	60	147	11	.950
1998— Richmond (I.L.)	3B-DH	125	451	56	124	27	1	13	75	.275	35	103	6	75	220	15	.952
— Atlanta (N.L.)	3B	7	13	2	4	1	0	1	2	.308	0	4	0	1	2	1	.750
1999— GC Braves (GCL)	DH-1B	9	33	1	15	2	0	0	10	.455	5	4	0	27	0	0	1.000
— Greenville (Sou.)	1B	30	113	15	34	6	0	8	26	.301	7	34	1	226	18	4	.984
2000— Richmond (I.L.)	3B	136	539	74	155	27	7	20	88	.288	27	92	0	96	222	23	.933
— Atlanta (N.L.)	3B	6	5	0	1	0	0	0	0	.200	0	2	0	1	4	1	.833
Major League totals (2 years)		13	18	2	5	1	0	1	2	.278	0	6	0	2	6	2	.800

HELTON, TODD — 1B — ROCKIES

PERSONAL: Born August 20, 1973, in Knoxville, Tenn. ... 6-2/206. ... Bats left, throws left. ... Full name: Todd Lynn Helton.
HIGH SCHOOL: Knoxville (Tenn.) Central.
COLLEGE: Tennessee.
TRANSACTIONS/CAREER NOTES: Selected by San Diego Padres organization in second round of free-agent draft (June 1, 1992); did not sign. ... Selected by Colorado Rockies organization in first round (eighth pick overall) of free-agent draft (June 3, 1995). ... On New Haven disabled list (June 15-24, 1996).
HONORS: Named N.L. Rookie Player of the Year by THE SPORTING NEWS (1998). ... Named first baseman on THE SPORTING NEWS N.L. All-Star team (2000). ... Named first baseman on THE SPORTING NEWS N.L. Silver Slugger team (2000).
STATISTICAL NOTES: Led N.L. first basemen in double plays with 156 in 1998, 152 in 1999 and 143 in 2000.. ... Hit for the cycle (June 19, 1999). ... Led N.L. first basemen with 1,482 total chances in 2000. ... Hit three home runs in one game (May 1, 2000). ... Led N.L. with 405 total bases, .463 on base percentage and .698 slugging percentage in 2000.

							BATTING						FIELDING		
Year Team (League)	Pos.	G	AB	R	H	2B	3B	HR	RBI	Avg.	BB	SO	SB	PO	A	E	Avg.
1995— Asheville (S.Atl.)	1B-DH	54	201	24	51	11	1	1	15	.254	25	32	1	388	21	4	.990
1996— New Haven (East.)	1B-DH	93	319	46	106	24	2	7	51	.332	51	37	2	788	61	5	.994
— Colo. Springs (PCL)	1B-OF	21	71	13	25	4	1	2	13	.352	11	12	0	144	17	2	.988
1997— Colo. Springs (PCL)	1B-OF-DH	99	392	87	138	31	2	16	88	.352	61	68	3	622	64	9	.987
— Colorado (N.L.)	OF-1B	35	93	13	26	2	1	5	11	.280	8	11	0	84	12	0	1.000
1998— Colorado (N.L.)	1B	152	530	78	167	37	4	25	97	.315	53	54	3	1164	*146	7	.995
1999— Colorado (N.L.)	1B	159	578	114	185	39	5	35	113	.320	68	77	7	1243	103	9	.993
2000— Colorado (N.L.)	1B	160	580	138	*216	*59	2	42	*147	*.372	103	61	5	*1328	*148	7	.995
Major League totals (4 years)		506	1781	343	594	137	9	107	368	.334	232	203	15	3819	409	23	.995

ALL-STAR GAME RECORD

						BATTING						FIELDING		
Year League	Pos.	AB	R	H	2B	3B	HR	RBI	Avg.	BB	SO	SB	PO	A	E	Avg.
2000— National	PR-1B	2	0	0	0	0	0	0	.000	0	0	0	5	0	0	1.000

PERSONAL: Born December 25, 1958, in Chicago. ... 5-10/190. ... Bats right, throws left. ... Full name: Rickey Henley Henderson.

HIGH SCHOOL: Technical (Oakland).

TRANSACTIONS/CAREER NOTES: Selected by Oakland Athletics organization in fourth round of free-agent draft (June 8, 1976). ... Traded by A's with P Bert Bradley and cash to New York Yankees for OF Stan Javier, P Jay Howell, P Jose Rijo, P Eric Plunk and P Tim Birtsas (December 5, 1984). ... On New York disabled list (March 30-April 22, 1985); included rehabilitation assignment to Fort Lauderdale (April 19-22). ... On disabled list (June 5-29 and July 26-September 1, 1987). ... Traded by Yankees to A's for P Greg Cadaret, P Eric Plunk and OF Luis Polonia (June 21, 1989). ... Granted free agency (November 13, 1989). ... Re-signed by A's (November 28, 1989). ... On disabled list (April 12-27, 1991; May 28-June 17 and June 30-July 16, 1992). ... Traded by A's to Toronto Blue Jays for P Steve Karsay and a player to be named later (July 31, 1993); A's acquired OF Jose Herrera to complete deal (August 6, 1993). ... Granted free agency (October 29, 1993). ... Signed by A's (December 17, 1993). ... On disabled list (May 11-27, 1994). ... Granted free agency (October 30, 1995). ... Signed by San Diego Padres (December 29, 1995). ... On San Diago disabled list (May 9-24, 1997). ... Traded by Padres to Anaheim Angels for P Ryan Hancock, P Stevenson Agosto and a player to be named later (August 13, 1997); Padres acquired 3B George Arias to complete deal (August 19, 1997). ... Granted free agency (October 27, 1997). ... Signed by A's (January 22, 1998). ... Granted free agency (October 26, 1998). ... Signed by New York Mets (December 16, 1998). ... On disabled list (May 3-22, 1999). ... Released by Mets (May 13, 2000). ... Signed by Seattle Mariners (May 19, 2000). ... Granted free agency (November 3, 2000).

RECORDS: Holds major league career records for most stolen bases—1,370; most times caught stealing—326; and most home runs leading off game—78. ... Holds major league single-season records for most stolen bases—130 (1982); and most times caught stealing—42 (1982). ... Holds major league record for most seasons leading league in stolen bases—12; and most years with 50 or more stolen bases—13. ... Holds A.L. career records for most stolen bases—1,262; most home runs leading off game—72; and most times caught stealing—291. ... Holds A.L. record for most consecutive years with 50 or more stolen bases—7 (1980-86). ... Shares A.L. single-season record for fewest times caught stealing (50 or more stolen bases)—8 (1993). ... Shares A.L. record for most stolen bases in two consecutive games—7 (July 3 [4], 15 innings, and 4 [3], 1983).

HONORS: Named outfielder on THE SPORTING NEWS A.L. All-Star team (1981, 1985 and 1990). ... Named outfielder on THE SPORTING NEWS A.L. Silver Slugger team (1981, 1985 and 1990). ... Won A.L. Gold Glove as outfielder (1981). ... Won THE SPORTING NEWS Silver Shoe Award (1982). ... Won THE SPORTING NEWS Golden Shoe Award (1983). ... Named A.L. Most Valuable Player by Baseball Writers' Association of America (1990). ... Named N.L. Comeback Player of the Year by THE SPORTING NEWS (1999).

STATISTICAL NOTES: Led California League in caught stealing with 22 in 1977. ... Led Eastern League in caught stealing with 28 in 1978. ... Led Eastern League outfielders with four double plays in 1978. ... Led A.L. in caught stealing with 26 in 1980, 22 in 1981, 42 in 1983, 19 in 1983 and tied for lead with 18 in 1986. ... Led A.L. outfielders with 341 total chances in 1981. ... Tied for A.L. lead in double plays by outfielder with five in 1988. ... Led A.L. with 77 stolen bases and 126 bases on balls in 1989. ... Tied for A.L. lead with 113 runs scored in 1989. ... Led A.L. with .439 on-base percentage in 1990. ... Career major league grand slams: 3.

MISCELLANEOUS: Holds Oakland Athletics franchise all-time records for most runs (1,270) and most stolen bases (867). ... Holds New York Yankees all-time record for most stolen bases (326).

Year	Team (League)	Pos.	G	AB	R	H	2B	3B	HR	RBI	Avg.	BB	SO	SB	PO	A	E	Avg.
1976—	Boise (N'West)	OF	46	140	34	47	13	2	3	23	.336	33	32	29	99	3	*12	.895
1977—	Modesto (Calif.)	OF	134	481	120	166	18	4	11	69	.345	104	67	*95	278	15	*20	.936
1978—	Jersey City (East.)	OF	133	455	81	141	14	4	0	34	.310	83	67	*81	305	•15	7	.979
1979—	Ogden (PCL)	OF	71	259	66	80	11	8	3	26	.309	53	41	44	149	6	6	.963
—	Oakland (A.L.)	OF	89	351	49	96	13	3	1	26	.274	34	39	33	215	5	6	.973
1980—	Oakland (A.L.)	OF-DH	158	591	111	179	22	4	9	53	.303	117	54	*100	407	15	7	.984
1981—	Oakland (A.L.)	OF	108	423	*89	*135	18	7	6	35	.319	64	68	*56	*327	7	7	.979
1982—	Oakland (A.L.)	OF-DH	149	536	119	143	24	4	10	51	.267	*116	94	*130	379	2	9	.977
1983—	Oakland (A.L.)	OF-DH	145	513	105	150	25	7	9	48	.292	*103	80	*108	349	9	3	.992
1984—	Oakland (A.L.)	OF	142	502	113	147	27	4	16	58	.293	86	81	*66	341	7	11	.969
1985—	Fort Laud. (FSL)■	OF	3	6	5	1	0	1	0	3	.167	5	2	1	6	0	0	1.000
—	New York (A.L.)	OF-DH	143	547	*146	172	28	5	24	72	.314	99	65	*80	439	7	9	.980
1986—	New York (A.L.)	OF-DH	153	608	*130	160	31	5	28	74	.263	89	81	*87	426	4	6	.986
1987—	New York (A.L.)	OF-DH	95	358	78	104	17	3	17	37	.291	80	52	41	189	3	4	.980
1988—	New York (A.L.)	OF-DH	140	554	118	169	30	2	6	50	.305	82	54	*93	320	7	12	.965
1989—	New York (A.L.)	OF	65	235	41	58	13	1	3	22	.247	56	29	25	144	3	1	.993
—	Oakland (A.L.)■	OF-DH	85	306	§72	90	13	2	9	35	.294	§70	39	§52	191	3	3	.985
1990—	Oakland (A.L.)	OF-DH	136	489	*119	159	33	3	28	61	.325	97	60	*65	289	5	5	.983
1991—	Oakland (A.L.)	OF-DH	134	470	105	126	17	1	18	57	.268	98	73	*58	249	10	8	.970
1992—	Oakland (A.L.)	OF-DH	117	396	77	112	18	3	15	46	.283	95	56	48	231	9	4	.984
1993—	Oakland (A.L.)	OF-DH	90	318	77	104	19	1	17	47	.327	85	46	31	182	5	5	.974
—	Toronto (A.L.)■	OF	44	163	37	35	3	1	4	12	.215	35	19	22	76	1	2	.975
1994—	Oakland (A.L.)	OF-DH	87	296	66	77	13	0	6	20	.260	72	45	22	166	4	4	.977
1995—	Oakland (A.L.)	OF-DH	112	407	67	122	31	1	9	54	.300	72	66	32	162	5	2	.988
1996—	San Diego (N.L.)■	OF	148	465	110	112	17	2	9	29	.241	125	90	37	228	3	6	.975
1997—	San Diego (N.L.)	OF-DH	88	288	63	79	11	0	6	27	.274	71	62	29	160	4	7	.959
—	Anaheim (A.L.)■	DH-OF	32	115	21	21	3	0	2	7	.183	26	23	16	26	0	0	1.000
1998—	Oakland (A.L.)	OF	152	542	101	128	16	1	14	57	.236	*118	114	*66	327	3	4	.988
1999—	New York (N.L.)	OF-DH	121	438	89	138	30	0	12	42	.315	82	82	37	168	0	2	.988
2000—	New York (N.L.)	OF	31	96	17	21	1	0	0	2	.219	25	20	5	35	0	2	.946
—	Seattle (A.L.)■	OF-DH	92	324	58	77	13	2	4	30	.238	63	55	31	181	0	3	.984
American League totals (20 years)			2468	9044	1899	2564	427	60	255	952	.284	1757	1293	1262	5616	114	115	.980
National League totals (4 years)			388	1287	279	350	59	2	27	100	.272	303	254	108	591	7	17	.972
Major League totals (22 years)			2856	10331	2178	2914	486	62	282	1052	.282	2060	1547	1370	6207	121	132	.980

DIVISION SERIES RECORD

RECORDS: Shares career record for most stolen bases—9.

Year	Team (League)	Pos.	G	AB	R	H	2B	3B	HR	RBI	Avg.	BB	SO	SB	PO	A	E	Avg.
1981—	Oakland (A.L.)	OF	3	11	3	2	0	0	0	0	.182	2	0	2	8	0	0	1.000
1996—	San Diego (N.L.)	OF	3	12	2	4	0	0	1	1	.333	2	3	0	4	0	0	1.000
1999—	New York (N.L.)	OF	4	15	5	6	0	0	0	1	.400	3	1	6	7	1	0	1.000
2000—	Seattle (A.L.)	OF-PR	3	5	3	2	0	0	0	0	.400	1	0	1	2	0	0	1.000
Division series totals (4 years)			13	43	13	14	0	0	1	2	.326	8	4	9	21	1	0	1.000

H

CHAMPIONSHIP SERIES RECORD

RECORDS: Holds career records for most stolen bases—17; and most runs scored—22. ... Holds single-series record for most stolen bases—8 (1989). ... Holds single-game record for most stolen bases—4 (October 4, 1989). ... Shares career record for most doubles—7. ... Shares single inning records for most at-bats in—2; most hits in—2; most singles in—2 (October 6, 1990, ninth inning); and most stolen bases in—2 (October 4, 1989, fourth and seventh innings). ... Shares single-series record for most runs—8 (1989). ... Shares A.L. career record for most bases on balls received—19. ... Shares A.L. single-game record for most at-bats—6 (October 5, 1993).

NOTES: Named Most Valuable Player (1989).

									BATTING						FIELDING		
Year	Team (League)	Pos.	G	AB	R	H	2B	3B	HR	RBI	Avg.	BB	SO	SB	PO	A	E	Avg.
1981— Oakland (A.L.)		OF	3	11	0	4	2	1	0	1	.364	1	2	2	6	0	1	.857
1989— Oakland (A.L.)		OF	5	15	8	6	1	1	2	5	.400	7	0	8	13	0	1	.929
1990— Oakland (A.L.)		OF	4	17	1	5	0	0	0	3	.294	1	2	2	10	0	0	1.000
1992— Oakland (A.L.)		OF	6	23	5	6	0	0	0	1	.261	4	4	2	15	0	3	.833
1993— Toronto (A.L.)		OF	6	25	4	3	2	0	0	0	.120	4	5	2	9	0	1	.900
1999— New York (N.L.)		OF	6	23	2	4	1	0	0	1	.174	0	5	1	7	2	1	.900
2000— Seattle (A.L.)		OF	3	9	2	2	1	0	0	1	.222	2	2	0	2	0	0	1.000
Championship series totals (7 years)			33	123	22	30	7	2	2	12	.244	19	20	17	62	2	7	.901

WORLD SERIES RECORD

RECORDS: Shares single-game record for most at-bats—6 (October 28, 1989).

NOTES: Member of World Series championship team (1989 and 1993).

									BATTING						FIELDING		
Year	Team (League)	Pos.	G	AB	R	H	2B	3B	HR	RBI	Avg.	BB	SO	SB	PO	A	E	Avg.
1989— Oakland (A.L.)		OF	4	19	4	9	1	2	1	3	.474	2	2	3	9	0	0	1.000
1990— Oakland (A.L.)		OF	4	15	2	5	2	0	1	1	.333	3	4	3	12	1	0	1.000
1993— Toronto (A.L.)		OF	6	22	6	5	2	0	0	2	.227	5	2	1	8	0	0	1.000
World Series totals (3 years)			14	56	12	19	5	2	2	6	.339	10	8	7	29	1	0	1.000

ALL-STAR GAME RECORD

RECORDS: Shares single-game record for most singles—3 (July 13, 1982).

								BATTING						FIELDING		
Year	League	Pos.	AB	R	H	2B	3B	HR	RBI	Avg.	BB	SO	SB	PO	A	E	Avg.
1980— American		OF	1	0	0	0	0	0	0	.000	0	1	0	0	0	0	...
1982— American		OF	4	1	3	0	0	0	0	.750	0	0	1	3	0	1	.750
1983— American		OF	1	0	0	0	0	0	1	.000	0	0	0	0	0	0	...
1984— American		OF	2	0	0	0	0	0	0	.000	0	0	0	0	0	0	...
1985— American		OF	3	1	1	0	0	0	0	.333	0	1	1	1	0	0	1.000
1986— American		OF	3	0	0	0	0	0	0	.000	0	1	0	2	0	0	1.000
1987— American		OF	3	0	1	0	0	0	0	.333	0	0	0	0	0	0	...
1988— American		OF	2	0	1	0	0	0	0	.500	1	0	0	1	0	0	1.000
1990— American		OF	3	0	0	0	0	0	0	.000	0	1	0	2	0	0	1.000
1991— American		OF	2	1	1	0	0	0	0	.500	0	0	0	0	0	0	...
All-Star Game totals (10 years)			24	3	7	0	0	0	1	.292	1	4	2	9	0	1	.900

HENLEY, BOB   C   EXPOS

PERSONAL: Born January 30, 1973, in Mobile, Ala. ... 6-2/205. ... Bats right, throws right. ... Full name: Robert Clifton Henley.
HIGH SCHOOL: Mobile County (Grand Bay, Ala.).
JUNIOR COLLEGE: Okaloosa-Walton Community College (Fla.).
TRANSACTIONS/CAREER NOTES: Selected by Montreal Expos organization in 26th round of free-agent draft (June 13, 1991). ... On disabled list (June 18-August 31, 1992). ... On disabled list (July 20-30 and July 31, 1997-remainder of season). ... On Montreal disabled list (March 30-May 5, 1998); included rehabilitation assignment to Jupiter (April 21-May 5). ... On Ottawa disabled list (May 27-June 19, 1998). ... On Monteal disabled list (March 31, 1999-entire season); included rehabilitation assignment to Gulf Coast Expos (July 3-4). ... On disabled list (April 1, 2000-entire season).
STATISTICAL NOTES: Led South Atlantic League catchers with nine double plays in 1995. ... Tied for Eastern League lead with 11 double plays by catcher in 1996.

									BATTING						FIELDING		
Year	Team (League)	Pos.	G	AB	R	H	2B	3B	HR	RBI	Avg.	BB	SO	SB	PO	A	E	Avg.
1992— GC Expos (GCL)							Did not play.											
1993— Jamestown (NY-P)		C	60	206	25	53	10	4	7	29	.257	20	60	0	143	36	4	.978
1994— Burlington (Midw.)		C-1B	98	346	72	104	20	1	20	67	.301	49	91	1	322	64	11	.972
1995— Albany (S.Atl.)		C	102	335	45	94	20	1	3	46	.281	83	57	1	684	*111	•14	.983
1996— Harrisburg (East.)		C	103	289	33	66	12	1	3	27	.228	70	78	1	565	*92	9	.986
1997— Harrisburg (East.)		C-DH	79	280	41	85	19	0	12	49	.304	32	40	5	574	77	3	*.995
1998— Jupiter (FSL)		C-DH	13	50	10	17	3	0	2	14	.340	5	5	1	63	8	1	.986
— Ottawa (I.L.)		C-DH	37	126	13	31	6	1	4	20	.246	12	34	1	176	22	2	.990
— Montreal (N.L.)		C	41	115	16	35	8	1	3	18	.304	11	26	3	189	14	1	.995
1999— GC Expos (GCL)		DH-C	2	4	0	1	0	0	0	1	.250	1	1	0	3	0	1	.750
2000— Montreal (N.L.)							Did not play.											
Major League totals (1 year)			41	115	16	35	8	1	3	18	.304	11	26	3	189	14	1	.995

HENRY, DOUG   P   ROYALS

H

PERSONAL: Born December 10, 1963, in Sacramento. ... 6-4/205. ... Throws right, bats right. ... Full name: Richard Douglas Henry.
HIGH SCHOOL: Tennyson (Hayward, Calif.).
COLLEGE: Arizona State.
TRANSACTIONS/CAREER NOTES: Selected by New York Mets organization in 16th round of free-agent draft (June 7, 1982); did not sign. ... Selected by Milwaukee Brewers organization in eighth round of free-agent draft (June 3, 1985). ... On El Paso disabled list (April 5-June 5 and

June 18-August 9, 1989). ... On Milwaukee disabled list (March 25-April 26, 1994); included rehabilitation assignments to El Paso (April 8-22) and New Orleans (April 22-26). ... Traded by Brewers to New York Mets for two players to be named later (November 30, 1994); Brewers acquired C Javier Gonzales (December 6, 1994) and IF Fernando Vina (December 22, 1994) to complete deal. ... Released by Mets (November 25, 1996). ... Signed by San Francisco Giants (January 8, 1997). ... Granted free agency (October 27, 1997). ... Signed by Houston Astros (November 26, 1997). ... On Houston disabled list (May 10-July 15, 1999); included rehabilitation assignments to New Orleans (July 4-12) and Jackson (July 13-15). ... Granted free agency (November 1, 1999). ... Re-signed by Astros (December 3, 1999). ... Traded by Astros to San Francisco Giants for P Scott Linebrink (July 30, 2000). ... Granted free agency (October 31, 2000). ... Signed by Kansas City Royals (December 11, 2000).

STATISTICAL NOTES: Combined with Michael Ignasiak in 6-3 no-hit victory for Stockton against San Jose (April 15, 1990, first game).

Year League	W	L	Pct.	ERA	G	GS	CG	ShO	Sv.	IP	H	R	ER	BB	SO
1986— Beloit (Midw.)	7	8	.467	4.65	27	24	4	1	1	143 1/3	153	95	74	56	115
1987— Beloit (Midw.)	8	9	.471	4.88	31	15	1	0	2	132 2/3	145	83	72	51	106
1988— Stockton (Calif.)	7	1	.875	1.78	23	1	1	0	7	70 2/3	46	19	14	31	71
— El Paso (Texas)	4	0	1.000	3.15	14	3	3	1	0	45 2/3	33	16	16	19	50
1989— Stockton (Calif.)	0	1	.000	0.00	4	3	0	0	0	11	9	4	0	3	9
— El Paso (Texas)	0	0	...	13.50	1	1	0	0	0	2	3	3	3	3	2
1990— Stockton (Calif.)	1	0	1.000	1.13	4	0	0	0	1	8	4	1	1	3	13
— El Paso (Texas)	1	0	1.000	2.93	15	0	0	0	9	30 2/3	31	13	10	11	25
— Denver (A.A.)	2	3	.400	4.44	27	0	0	0	8	50 2/3	46	26	25	27	54
1991— Denver (A.A.)	3	2	.600	2.18	32	0	0	0	14	57 2/3	47	16	14	20	47
— Milwaukee (A.L.)	2	1	.667	1.00	32	0	0	0	15	36	16	4	4	14	28
1992— Milwaukee (A.L.)	1	4	.200	4.02	68	0	0	0	29	65	64	34	29	24	52
1993— Milwaukee (A.L.)	4	4	.500	5.56	54	0	0	0	17	55	67	37	34	25	38
1994— El Paso (Texas)	1	0	1.000	5.40	6	0	0	0	3	8 1/3	7	5	5	2	10
— New Orleans (A.A.)	1	0	1.000	1.84	10	0	0	0	3	14 2/3	5	3	3	10	10
— Milwaukee (A.L.)	2	3	.400	4.60	25	0	0	0	0	31 1/3	32	17	16	23	20
1995— New York (N.L.)■	3	6	.333	2.96	51	0	0	0	4	67	48	23	22	25	62
1996— New York (N.L.)	2	8	.200	4.68	58	0	0	0	9	75	82	48	39	36	58
1997— San Francisco (N.L.)■	4	5	.444	4.71	75	0	0	0	3	70 2/3	70	45	37	41	69
1998— Houston (N.L.)■	8	2	.800	3.04	59	0	0	0	2	71	55	25	24	35	59
1999— Houston (N.L.)	2	3	.400	4.65	35	0	0	0	2	40 2/3	45	24	21	24	36
— New Orleans (PCL)	0	0	...	4.50	3	3	0	0	0	4	4	2	2	3	3
— Jackson (Texas)	0	1	.000	4.50	2	1	0	0	0	2	2	1	1	1	3
2000— Houston (N.L.)	1	3	.250	4.42	45	0	0	0	1	53	39	26	26	28	46
— San Francisco (N.L.)■	3	1	.750	2.49	27	0	0	0	0	25 1/3	18	10	7	21	16
A.L. totals (4 years)	9	12	.429	3.99	179	0	0	0	61	187 1/3	179	92	83	86	138
N.L. totals (6 years)	23	28	.451	3.93	350	0	0	0	21	402 2/3	357	201	176	210	346
Major League totals (10 years)	32	40	.444	3.95	529	0	0	0	82	590	536	293	259	296	484

DIVISION SERIES RECORD

RECORDS: Shares N.L. record for most games pitched—8.

Year League	W	L	Pct.	ERA	G	GS	CG	ShO	Sv.	IP	H	R	ER	BB	SO
1997— San Francisco (N.L.)	0	0	...	0.00	1	0	0	0	0	2	1	0	0	3	2
1998— Houston (N.L.)	0	0	...	5.40	2	0	0	0	0	1 2/3	2	1	1	0	1
1999— Houston (N.L.)	0	0	...	0.00	2	0	0	0	0	3 2/3	1	0	0	3	2
2000— San Francisco (N.L.)	0	0	...	2.25	3	0	0	0	0	4	1	1	1	3	1
Division series totals (4 years)	0	0	...	1.59	8	0	0	0	0	11 1/3	5	2	2	9	6

HENTGEN, PAT   P   ORIOLES

PERSONAL: Born November 13, 1968, in Detroit. ... 6-2/195. ... Throws right, bats right. ... Full name: Patrick George Hentgen.

HIGH SCHOOL: Fraser (Mich.).

TRANSACTIONS/CAREER NOTES: Selected by Toronto Blue Jays organization in fifth round of free-agent draft (June 2, 1986). ... On Toronto disabled list (August 13-September 29, 1992); included rehabilitation assignment to Syracuse (September 1-8). ... Traded by Blue Jays with P Paul Spoljaric to St. Louis Cardinals for P Lance Painter, C Alberto Castillo and P Matt DeWitt (November 11, 1999). ... Granted free agency (October 31, 2000). ... Signed by Baltimore Orioles (December 19, 2000).

HONORS: Named A.L. Pitcher of the Year by THE SPORTING NEWS (1996). ... Named righthanded pitcher on THE SPORTING NEWS A.L. All-Star team (1996). ... Named A.L. Cy Young Award winner by Baseball Writers' Association of America (1996).

STATISTICAL NOTES: Combined with relievers Willie Blair and Enrique Burgos in 2-1 no-hit victory against Osceola (May 10, 1988).

Year League	W	L	Pct.	ERA	G	GS	CG	ShO	Sv.	IP	H	R	ER	BB	SO
1986— St. Catharines (NY-Penn)	0	4	.000	4.50	13	11	0	0	1	40	38	27	20	30	30
1987— Myrtle Beach (S.Atl.)	11	5	.688	2.35	32	*31	2	2	0	*188	145	62	49	60	131
1988— Dunedin (FSL)	3	12	.200	3.45	31	*30	0	0	0	151 1/3	139	80	58	65	125
1989— Dunedin (FSL)	9	8	.529	2.68	29	28	0	0	0	151 1/3	123	53	45	71	148
1990— Knoxville (Sou.)	9	5	.643	3.05	28	26	0	0	0	153 1/3	121	57	52	68	142
1991— Syracuse (I.L.)	8	9	.471	4.47	31	•28	1	0	0	171	146	91	85	*90	*155
— Toronto (A.L.)	0	0	...	2.45	3	1	0	0	0	7 1/3	5	2	2	3	3
1992— Toronto (A.L.)	5	2	.714	5.36	28	2	0	0	0	50 1/3	49	30	30	32	39
— Syracuse (I.L.)	1	2	.333	2.66	4	4	0	0	0	20 1/3	15	6	6	8	17
1993— Toronto (A.L.)	19	9	.679	3.87	34	32	3	0	0	216 1/3	215	103	93	74	122
1994— Toronto (A.L.)	13	8	.619	3.40	24	24	6	3	0	174 2/3	158	74	66	59	147
1995— Toronto (A.L.)	10	14	.417	5.11	30	30	2	0	0	200 2/3	*236	*129	*114	90	135
1996— Toronto (A.L.)	20	10	.667	3.22	35	35	*10	•3	0	*265 2/3	238	105	95	94	177
1997— Toronto (A.L.)	15	10	.600	3.68	35	•35	•9	•3	0	•264	253	116	108	71	160
1998— Toronto (A.L.)	12	11	.522	5.17	29	29	0	0	0	177 2/3	208	109	102	69	94
1999— Toronto (A.L.)	11	12	.478	4.79	34	34	1	0	0	199	225	115	106	65	118
2000— St. Louis (N.L.)■	15	12	.556	4.72	33	33	1	1	0	194 1/3	202	107	102	89	118
A.L. totals (9 years)	105	76	.580	4.14	252	222	31	9	0	1555 2/3	1587	783	716	557	995
N.L. totals (1 year)	15	12	.556	4.72	33	33	1	1	0	194 1/3	202	107	102	89	118
Major League totals (10 years)	120	88	.577	4.21	285	255	32	10	0	1750	1789	890	818	646	1113

H

DIVISION SERIES RECORD

Year League	W	L	Pct.	ERA	G	GS	CG	ShO	Sv.	IP	H	R	ER	BB	SO
2000— St. Louis (N.L.)							Did not play.								

CHAMPIONSHIP SERIES RECORD

Year League	W	L	Pct.	ERA	G	GS	CG	ShO	Sv.	IP	H	R	ER	BB	SO
1993— Toronto (A.L.)	0	1	.000	18.00	1	1	0	0	0	3	9	6	6	2	3
2000— St. Louis (N.L.)	0	1	.000	14.73	1	1	0	0	0	$3^2/_3$	7	6	6	5	2
Champ. series totals (2 years)	0	2	.000	16.20	2	2	0	0	0	$6^2/_3$	16	12	12	7	5

NOTES: Member of World Series championship team (1993).

WORLD SERIES RECORD

Year League	W	L	Pct.	ERA	G	GS	CG	ShO	Sv.	IP	H	R	ER	BB	SO
1993— Toronto (A.L.)	1	0	1.000	1.50	1	1	0	0	0	6	5	1	1	3	6

ALL-STAR GAME RECORD

Year League	W	L	Pct.	ERA	GS	CG	ShO	Sv.	IP	H	R	ER	BB	SO
1993— American							Did not play.							
1994— American	0	0	...	0.00	0	0	0	0	1	1	0	0	0	0
1997— American	0	0	...	0.00	0	0	0	0	1	0	0	0	0	0
All-Star Game totals (2 years)	0	0	...	0.00	0	0	0	0	2	1	0	0	0	0

HEREDIA, FELIX   P   CUBS

PERSONAL: Born June 18, 1976, in Barahona, Dominican Republic. ... 6-0/180. ... Throws left, bats left. ... Full name: Felix Perez Heredia. ... Name pronounced heh-RAY-dee-ah.

HIGH SCHOOL: Escuela Dominical (Barahona, Dominican Republic).

TRANSACTIONS/CAREER NOTES: Signed as non-drafted free agent by Florida Marlins organization (November 22, 1992). ... Traded by Marlins with P Steve Hoff to Chicago Cubs for 3B Kevin Orie, P Todd Noel and P Justin Speier (July 31, 1998).

Year League	W	L	Pct.	ERA	G	GS	CG	ShO	Sv.	IP	H	R	ER	BB	SO
1993— Gulf Coast Marlins (GCL)	5	1	.833	2.47	12	•12	0	0	0	62	50	18	17	11	53
1994— Kane County (Midw.)	4	5	.444	5.69	24	8	1	0	3	68	86	55	43	14	65
1995— Brevard County (FSL)	6	4	.600	3.57	34	8	0	0	1	$95^2/_3$	101	52	38	36	76
1996— Portland (East.)	8	1	.889	1.50	55	0	0	0	5	60	48	11	10	15	42
— Florida (N.L.)	1	1	.500	4.32	21	0	0	0	0	$16^2/_3$	21	8	8	10	10
1997— Florida (N.L.)	5	3	.625	4.29	56	0	0	0	0	$56^2/_3$	53	30	27	30	54
1998— Florida (N.L.)	0	3	.000	5.49	41	2	0	0	2	41	38	30	25	32	38
— Chicago (N.L.)■	3	0	1.000	4.08	30	0	0	0	0	$17^2/_3$	19	9	8	6	16
1999— Chicago (N.L.)	3	1	.750	4.85	69	0	0	0	1	52	56	35	28	25	50
2000— Chicago (N.L.)	7	3	.700	4.76	74	0	0	0	2	$58^2/_3$	46	31	31	33	52
Major League totals (5 years)	19	11	.633	4.71	291	2	0	0	5	$242^2/_3$	233	143	127	136	220

DIVISION SERIES RECORD

Year League	W	L	Pct.	ERA	G	GS	CG	ShO	Sv.	IP	H	R	ER	BB	SO
1997— Florida (N.L.)							Did not play.								
1998— Chicago (N.L.)	0	0	...	54.00	1	0	0	0	0	$^1/_3$	0	2	2	2	0

CHAMPIONSHIP SERIES RECORD

Year League	W	L	Pct.	ERA	G	GS	CG	ShO	Sv.	IP	H	R	ER	BB	SO
1997— Florida (N.L.)	0	0	...	5.40	2	0	0	0	0	$3^1/_3$	3	2	2	2	4

WORLD SERIES RECORD

NOTES: Member of World Series championship team (1997).

Year League	W	L	Pct.	ERA	G	GS	CG	ShO	Sv.	IP	H	R	ER	BB	SO
1997— Florida (N.L.)	0	0	...	0.00	4	0	0	0	0	$5^1/_3$	2	0	0	1	5

HEREDIA, GIL   P   ATHLETICS

PERSONAL: Born October 26, 1965, in Nogales, Ariz. ... 6-1/221. ... Throws right, bats right. ... Full name: Gilbert Heredia. ... Name pronounced err-AY-dee-uh.

HIGH SCHOOL: Nogales (Ariz.).

JUNIOR COLLEGE: Pima Community College (Ariz.).

COLLEGE: Arizona.

TRANSACTIONS/CAREER NOTES: Selected by Pittsburgh Pirates organization in first round (16th pick overall) of free-agent draft (January 17, 1984); did not sign. ... Selected by Baltimore Orioles organization in sixth round of free-agent draft (January 9, 1985); did not sign. ... Selected by San Francisco Giants organization in ninth round of free-agent draft (June 2, 1987). ... Loaned by Giants organization to San Luis Potosi of Mexican League (1989). ... Claimed on waivers by Montreal Expos (August 18, 1992). ... Granted free agency (December 21, 1995). ... Signed by Texas Rangers organization (January 5, 1996). ... Released by Rangers (November 13, 1996). ... Signed by Expos organization (January 13, 1997). ... Traded by Expos to Chicago Cubs for 2B Saul Bustos and OF David Jefferson (June 23, 1997). ... Granted free agency (October 15, 1997). ... Signed by Oakland Athletics organization (December 16, 1997).

Year League	W	L	Pct.	ERA	G	GS	CG	ShO	Sv.	IP	H	R	ER	BB	SO
1987— Everett (N'West)	2	0	1.000	3.60	3	3	1	0	0	20	24	8	8	1	14
— Fresno (Calif.)	5	3	.625	2.90	11	11	5	2	0	$80^2/_3$	62	28	26	23	60
1988— San Jose (Calif.)	13	12	.520	3.49	27	27	9	0	0	*$206^1/_3$	•216	107	80	46	121
1989— Shreveport (Texas)	1	0	1.000	2.55	7	2	1	0	0	$24^2/_3$	28	10	7	4	8
— San Luis Potosi (Mex.)■	14	9	.609	2.99	24	24	15	3	0	$180^2/_3$	183	73	60	35	125
1990— Phoenix (PCL)■	9	7	.563	4.10	29	19	0	0	1	147	159	81	67	37	75
1991— Phoenix (PCL)	9	11	.450	*2.82	33	15	•5	1	1	$140^1/_3$	155	60	44	28	75
— San Francisco (N.L.)	0	2	.000	3.82	7	4	0	0	0	33	27	14	14	7	13
1992— Phoenix (PCL)	5	5	.500	2.01	22	7	1	1	1	$80^2/_3$	83	30	18	13	37
— San Francisco (N.L.)	2	3	.400	5.40	13	4	0	0	0	30	32	20	18	16	15
— Indianapolis (A.A.)■	2	0	1.000	1.02	3	3	0	0	0	$17^2/_3$	18	2	2	3	10
— Montreal (N.L.)	0	0	...	1.84	7	1	0	0	0	$14^2/_3$	12	3	3	4	7

H

Year League	W	L	Pct.	ERA	G	GS	CG	ShO	Sv.	IP	H	R	ER	BB	SO
1993— Ottawa (I.L.)	8	4	.667	2.98	16	16	1	0	0	102 2/3	97	46	34	26	66
— Montreal (N.L.)	4	2	.667	3.92	20	9	1	0	2	57 1/3	66	28	25	14	40
1994— Montreal (N.L.)	6	3	.667	3.46	39	3	0	0	1	75 1/3	85	34	29	13	62
1995— Montreal (N.L.)	5	6	.455	4.31	40	18	0	0	1	119	137	60	57	21	74
1996— Texas (A.L.)■	2	5	.286	5.89	44	0	0	0	1	73 1/3	91	50	48	14	43
— Oklahoma City (A.A.)	0	0	...	1.86	6	0	0	0	0	9 2/3	11	3	2	0	4
1997— Ottawa (I.L.)■	0	4	.000	4.70	28	0	0	0	0	44	50	29	23	9	41
— Iowa (A.A.)■	4	2	.667	3.86	31	1	0	0	1	46 2/3	54	22	20	9	30
1998— Edmonton (PCL)■	10	8	.556	3.67	29	19	6	1	1	144 2/3	154	69	59	18	99
— Oakland (A.L.)	3	3	.500	2.74	8	6	0	0	0	42 2/3	43	14	13	3	27
1999— Oakland (A.L.)	13	8	.619	4.81	33	33	1	0	0	200 1/3	228	119	107	34	117
2000— Oakland (A.L.)	15	11	.577	4.12	32	32	2	0	0	198 2/3	214	106	91	66	101
A.L. totals (4 years)	33	27	.550	4.53	117	71	3	0	1	515	576	289	259	117	288
N.L. totals (5 years)	17	16	.515	3.99	126	39	1	0	3	329 1/3	359	159	146	75	211
Major League totals (9 years)	50	43	.538	4.32	243	110	4	0	4	844 1/3	935	448	405	192	499

DIVISION SERIES RECORD

Year League	W	L	Pct.	ERA	G	GS	CG	ShO	Sv.	IP	H	R	ER	BB	SO
2000— Oakland (A.L.)	1	1	.500	12.79	2	2	0	0	0	6 1/3	11	9	9	3	3

HERGES, MATT P DODGERS

PERSONAL: Born April 1, 1970, in Champaign, Ill. ... 6-0/200. ... Throws right, bats left. ... Full name: Matthew Tyler Herges.
HIGH SCHOOL: Centennial (Champaign, Ill.).
COLLEGE: Illinois State.
TRANSACTIONS/CAREER NOTES: Signed as non-drafted free agent by Los Angeles Dodgers organization (June 13, 1992). ... Granted free agency (October 15, 1998). ... Re-signed by Dodgers organization (January 1, 1999).

Year League	W	L	Pct.	ERA	G	GS	CG	ShO	Sv.	IP	H	R	ER	BB	SO
1992— Yakima (N'West)	2	3	.400	3.22	27	0	0	0	9	44 2/3	33	21	16	24	57
1993— Bakersfield (Calif.)	2	6	.250	3.69	51	0	0	0	2	90 1/3	70	49	37	56	84
1994— Vero Beach (FSL)	8	9	.471	3.32	48	3	1	0	3	111	115	45	41	33	61
1995— San Antonio (Texas)	0	3	.000	4.88	19	0	0	0	8	27 2/3	34	16	15	16	18
— San Bernardino (Calif.)	5	2	.714	3.66	22	2	0	0	1	51 2/3	58	29	21	15	35
1996— San Antonio (Texas)	3	2	.600	2.71	30	6	0	0	3	83	83	38	25	28	45
— Albuquerque (PCL)	4	1	.800	2.60	10	4	2	1	0	34 2/3	33	11	10	14	15
1997— Albuquerque (PCL)	0	8	.000	8.89	31	12	0	0	0	85	120	92	84	46	61
— San Antonio (Texas)	0	1	.000	8.80	4	3	0	0	0	15 1/3	22	15	15	10	12
1998— Albuquerque (PCL)	3	5	.375	5.71	34	8	0	0	0	88 1/3	115	64	56	37	75
— San Antonio (Texas)	0	0	...	0.00	3	0	0	0	0	6	3	0	0	2	3
1999— Albuquerque (PCL)	8	3	.727	4.73	21	21	2	0	0	131 1/3	135	82	69	47	88
— Los Angeles (N.L.)	0	2	.000	4.07	17	0	0	0	0	24 1/3	24	13	11	8	18
2000— Los Angeles (N.L.)	11	3	.786	3.17	59	4	0	0	1	110 2/3	100	43	39	40	75
Major League totals (2 years)	11	5	.688	3.33	76	4	0	0	1	135	124	56	50	48	93

HERMANSEN, CHAD OF PIRATES

PERSONAL: Born September 10, 1977, in Salt Lake City. ... 6-2/185. ... Bats right, throws right. ... Full name: Chad B. Hermansen.
HIGH SCHOOL: Green Valley (Henderson, Nev.).
TRANSACTIONS/CAREER NOTES: Selected by Pittsburgh Pirates organization in first round (10th pick overall) of free-agent draft (June 1, 1995).
STATISTICAL NOTES: Tied for Southern League lead in errors by outfielder with eight in 1997.

Year Team (League)	Pos.	G	AB	R	H	2B	3B	HR	RBI	Avg.	BB	SO	SB	PO	A	E	Avg.
1995— GC Pirates (GCL)	SS	24	92	14	28	10	1	3	17	.304	9	19	0	20	56	10	.884
— GC Pirates (GCL)	SS	24	92	14	28	10	1	3	17	.304	9	19	0	20	56	10	.884
— Erie (NY-Penn)	SS	44	165	30	45	8	3	6	25	.273	18	39	4	52	104	30	.839
1996— Augusta (S.Atl.)	SS-DH	62	226	41	57	11	3	14	41	.252	38	65	11	71	135	25	.892
— Lynchburg (Caro.)	SS-DH	66	251	40	69	11	3	10	46	.275	29	56	5	75	168	28	.897
1997— Carolina (Sou.)	O-S-2-DH	129	487	87	134	31	4	20	70	.275	69	*136	18	194	125	‡39	.891
1998— Nashville (PCL)	OF-2B	126	458	81	118	26	5	28	78	.258	50	152	21	208	21	14	.942
1999— Nashville (PCL)	OF-DH	125	496	89	134	27	3	32	97	.270	35	119	19	258	9	3	.989
— Pittsburgh (N.L.)	OF	19	60	5	14	3	0	1	1	.233	7	19	2	29	0	0	1.000
2000— Pittsburgh (N.L.)	OF	33	108	12	20	4	1	2	8	.185	6	37	0	44	2	1	.979
— Nashville (PCL)	OF	78	294	47	66	12	1	11	38	.224	25	89	16	156	2	4	.975
Major League totals (2 years)		52	168	17	34	7	1	3	9	.202	13	56	2	73	2	1	.987

HERMANSON, DUSTIN P CARDINALS

PERSONAL: Born December 21, 1972, in Springfield, Ohio. ... 6-2/200. ... Throws right, bats right. ... Full name: Dustin Michael Hermanson.
HIGH SCHOOL: Kenton Ridge (Springfield, Ohio).
COLLEGE: Kent.
TRANSACTIONS/CAREER NOTES: Selected by Pittsburgh Pirates organization in 39th round of free-agent draft (June 3, 1991); did not sign. ... Selected by San Diego Padres organization in first round (third pick overall) of free-agent draft (June 2, 1994). ... Traded by Padres to Florida Marlins for 2B Quilvio Veras (November 21, 1996). ... Traded by Marlins with OF Joe Orsulak to Montreal Expos for OF/1B Cliff Floyd (March 26, 1997). ... On disabled list (May 15-30, 1998). ... Traded by Expos with P Steve Kline to St. Louis Cardinals for 3B Fernando Tatis and P Britt Reames (December 14, 2000).
STATISTICAL NOTES: Hit home run in first major league at-bat (April 16, 1997).

H

Year League	W	L	Pct.	ERA	G	GS	CG	ShO	Sv.	IP	H	R	ER	BB	SO
1994— Wichita (Texas)	1	0	1.000	0.43	16	0	0	0	8	21	13	1	1	6	30
— Las Vegas (PCL)	0	0	...	6.14	7	0	0	0	3	7 1/3	6	5	5	5	6
1995— Las Vegas (PCL)	0	1	.000	3.50	31	0	0	0	11	36	35	23	14	29	42
— San Diego (N.L.)	3	1	.750	6.82	26	0	0	0	0	31 2/3	35	26	24	22	19
1996— Las Vegas (PCL)	1	4	.200	3.13	42	0	0	0	21	46	41	20	16	27	54
— San Diego (N.L.)	1	0	1.000	8.56	8	0	0	0	0	13 2/3	18	15	13	4	11
1997— Montreal (N.L.)■..............	8	8	.500	3.69	32	28	1	1	0	158 1/3	134	68	65	66	136
1998— Montreal (N.L.)..................	14	11	.560	3.13	32	30	1	0	0	187	163	80	65	56	154
1999— Montreal (N.L.)..................	9	14	.391	4.20	34	34	0	0	0	216 1/3	225	110	101	69	145
2000— Montreal (N.L.)..................	12	14	.462	4.77	38	30	2	1	4	198	226	128	105	75	94
Major League totals (6 years)	47	48	.495	4.17	170	122	4	2	4	805	801	427	373	292	559

HERNANDEZ, ALEX — OF — PIRATES

PERSONAL: Born May 28, 1977, in San Juan, Puerto Rico. ... 6-4/186. ... Bats left, throws left. ... Full name: Alexander Vargas Hernandez.
TRANSACTIONS/CAREER NOTES: Selected by Pittsburgh Pirates organization in fourth round of free-agent draft (June 1, 1995).

								BATTING						FIELDING		
Year Team (League)	Pos.	G	AB	R	H	2B	3B	HR	RBI	Avg.	BB	SO	SB	PO	A	E	Avg.
1995— GC Pirates (GCL)........	OF-1B	49	186	24	50	5	3	1	17	.269	17	33	4	148	7	5	.969
1996— Erie (NY-Penn)	OF-1B	61	225	38	65	13	4	4	30	.289	20	47	7	305	19	7	.979
1997— Lynchburg (Caro.)	OF	131	520	75	151	37	4	5	68	.290	27	140	13	212	*15	9	.962
1998— Carolina (Sou.)	OF	115	452	62	117	22	7	8	48	.259	41	81	11	217	15	11	.955
1999— Altoona (East.)	OF-DH-1B	126	475	76	122	26	3	15	63	.257	54	110	11	249	15	5	.981
2000— Altoona (East.)	1B-OF	50	199	28	67	16	1	4	34	.337	13	42	1	140	7	2	.987
— Nashville (PCL)	OF-1B	76	276	29	76	17	2	8	37	.275	11	60	6	436	26	4	.991
— Pittsburgh (N.L.)	1B-OF	20	60	4	12	3	0	1	5	.200	0	13	1	127	4	1	.992
Major League totals (1 year)		20	60	4	12	3	0	1	5	.200	0	13	1	127	4	1	.992

HERNANDEZ, CARLOS — C — CARDINALS

PERSONAL: Born May 24, 1967, in San Felix, Bolivar, Venezuela. ... 5-10/215. ... Bats right, throws right. ... Full name: Carlos Alberto Hernandez.
HIGH SCHOOL: Escula Tecnica Industrial (San Felix, Bolivar, Venezuela).
TRANSACTIONS/CAREER NOTES: Signed as non-drafted free agent by Los Angeles Dodgers organization (October 10, 1984). ... On Albuquerque disabled list (May 27-June 20, 1990). ... On disabled list (April 4-22, 1994). ... On Los Angeles disabled list (May 17-June 14, 1996); included rehabilitation assignment to Albuquerque (June 5-14). ... Granted free agency (October 15, 1996). ... Signed by San Diego Padres organization (December 2, 1996). ... On San Diego disabled list (July 13-August 15, 1997); included rehabilitation assignments to Rancho Cucamonga (August 9-10) and Las Vegas (August 11-15). ... Granted free agency (October 31, 1997). ... Re-signed by Padres (November 12, 1997). ... Granted free agency (October 23, 1998). ... Re-signed by Padres (December 2, 1998). ... On disabled list (March 29, 1999-entire season). ... On disabled list (April 7-22 and July 6-28, 2000). ... Traded by Padres with IF/OF Nate Tebbs to St. Louis Cardinals for P Heathcliff Slocumb and OF Ben Johnson (July 31, 2000).
STATISTICAL NOTES: Tied for Gulf Coast League lead in double plays by catcher with three in 1986. ... Led Texas League catchers with 737 total chances in 1989. ... Led Pacific Coast League catchers with 684 total chances in 1991.

								BATTING						FIELDING		
Year Team (League)	Pos.	G	AB	R	H	2B	3B	HR	RBI	Avg.	BB	SO	SB	PO	A	E	Avg.
1985— GC Dodgers (GCL)	3B-1B	22	49	3	12	1	0	0	0	.245	3	8	0	48	16	2	.970
1986— GC Dodgers (GCL)	C-3B	57	205	19	64	7	0	1	31	.312	5	18	1	217	36	10	.962
1987— Bakersfield (Calif.)	C	48	162	22	37	6	1	3	22	.228	14	23	8	181	26	8	.963
1988— Bakersfield (Calif.)	C	92	333	37	103	15	2	5	52	.309	16	39	3	480	88	14	.976
— Albuquerque (PCL).....	C	3	8	0	1	0	0	0	1	.125	0	0	0	11	0	1	.917
1989— San Antonio (Texas)...	C	99	370	37	111	16	3	8	41	.300	12	46	2	*629	*90	*18	.976
— Albuquerque (PCL).....	C	4	14	1	3	0	0	0	1	.214	2	1	0	23	3	3	.897
1990— Albuquerque (PCL).....	C	52	143	11	45	8	1	0	16	.315	8	25	2	207	31	8	.967
— Los Angeles (N.L.)	C	10	20	2	4	1	0	0	1	.200	0	2	0	37	2	0	1.000
1991— Albuquerque (PCL).....	C	95	345	60	119	24	2	8	44	.345	24	36	5	*592	*77	*15	.978
— Los Angeles (N.L.)	C-3B	15	14	1	3	1	0	0	1	.214	0	5	1	24	4	1	.966
1992— Los Angeles (N.L.)	C	69	173	11	45	4	0	3	17	.260	11	21	0	295	37	7	.979
1993— Los Angeles (N.L.)	C	50	99	6	25	5	0	2	7	.253	2	11	0	181	15	7	.966
1994— Los Angeles (N.L.)	C	32	64	6	14	2	0	2	6	.219	1	14	0	104	13	0	1.000
1995— Los Angeles (N.L.)	C	45	94	3	14	1	0	2	8	.149	7	25	0	210	25	4	.983
1996— Los Angeles (N.L.)	C	13	14	1	4	0	0	0	0	.286	2	2	0	31	1	0	1.000
— Albuquerque (PCL).....C-DH-1B-3B		66	233	19	56	11	0	5	30	.240	11	49	5	331	38	9	.976
1997— San Diego (N.L.)■......	C-1B	50	134	15	42	7	1	3	14	.313	3	27	0	239	29	3	.989
— Rancho Cuca. (Calif.) .	C	1	4	0	1	0	0	0	0	.250	0	1	0	11	1	0	1.000
— Las Vegas (PCL)	C	3	10	1	4	0	0	1	5	.400	1	3	0	15	2	0	1.000
1998— San Diego (N.L.)	C-1B	129	390	34	102	15	0	9	52	.262	16	54	1	795	53	7	.992
1999— San Diego (N.L.)								Did not play.									
2000— San Diego (N.L.)	C-1B	58	191	16	48	11	0	2	25	.251	16	26	1	345	33	5	.987
— St. Louis (N.L.)■	C	17	51	7	14	4	0	1	10	.275	5	9	1	96	9	4	.963
Major League totals (10 years)		488	1244	102	315	51	1	24	141	.253	63	196	5	2357	221	38	.985

DIVISION SERIES RECORD

								BATTING						FIELDING		
Year Team (League)	Pos.	G	AB	R	H	2B	3B	HR	RBI	Avg.	BB	SO	SB	PO	A	E	Avg.
1998— San Diego (N.L.)	C	4	12	0	5	0	0	0	0	.417	0	0	0	34	6	0	1.000
2000— St. Louis (N.L.)..........	C	3	11	3	3	0	0	1	1	.273	1	2	0	20	4	0	1.000
Division series totals (2 years)		7	23	3	8	0	0	1	1	.348	1	2	0	54	10	0	1.000

H

Year Team (League)	Pos.	G	AB	R	H	2B	3B	HR	RBI	Avg.	BB	SO	SB	PO	A	E	Avg.
1998— San Diego (N.L.)	C	6	18	2	6	1	0	0	0	.333	1	5	0	36	4	0	1.000
2000— St. Louis (N.L.)	C	5	16	3	4	0	0	0	1	.250	1	1	0	15	2	1	.944
Championship series totals (2 years)		11	34	5	10	1	0	0	1	.294	2	6	0	51	6	1	.983

WORLD SERIES RECORD

Year Team (League)	Pos.	G	AB	R	H	2B	3B	HR	RBI	Avg.	BB	SO	SB	PO	A	E	Avg.
1998— San Diego (N.L.)	C-PH	4	10	0	2	0	0	0	0	.200	0	3	0	18	1	0	1.000

HERNANDEZ, CARLOS — SS/2B

PERSONAL: Born December 12, 1975, in Caracas, Venezuela. ... 5-9/175. ... Bats right, throws right. ... Full name: Carlos Eduardo Hernandez.
TRANSACTIONS/CAREER NOTES: Signed as non-drafted free agent by Houston Astros organization (July 2, 1992). ... On disabled list (August 1, 1997-remainder of season). ... Traded by Astros to Seattle Mariners for C Carlos Maldonado (March 21, 2000). ... On Tacoma disabled list (April 11-19, July 3-August 18 and August 21-30, 2000). ... On Seattle disabled list (August 31, 2000-remainder of season). ... Granted free agency (October 18, 2000).
STATISTICAL NOTES: Tied for Midwest League lead in double plays by second baseman with 79 in 1996. ... Led Pacific Coast League second basemen with .983 fielding percentage in 1998.

Year Team (League)	Pos.	G	AB	R	H	2B	3B	HR	RBI	Avg.	BB	SO	SB	PO	A	E	Avg.
1993— Dom. Astros (DSL)	IF	67	245	52	75	13	4	1	36	.306	27	29	36	181	134	21	.938
1994— GC Astros (GCL)	2B-SS	51	192	45	62	10	1	0	23	.323	19	22	25	89	149	8	.967
1995— Quad City (Midw.)	2B-SS	126	470	74	122	19	6	4	40	.260	39	68	*58	188	349	21	.962
1996— Quad City (Midw.)	2B-SS	112	456	67	123	15	7	5	49	.270	27	71	41	238	336	19	.968
1997— Jackson (Texas)	2B	91	363	62	106	12	1	4	33	.292	33	59	17	187	269	8	.983
1998— New Orleans (PCL)	2B-SS	134	494	64	147	23	2	1	54	.298	21	81	29	249	359	13	†.979
1999— New Orleans (PCL)	SS-2B	94	355	56	104	14	0	0	43	.293	27	65	22	145	292	15	.967
— Houston (N.L.)	2B-SS	16	14	4	2	0	0	0	1	.143	0	0	3	7	11	1	.947
2000— Tacoma (PCL)■	2B-SS-3B	62	210	21	50	10	1	0	15	.238	15	38	9	120	136	12	.955
— Seattle (A.L.)	3B	2	1	0	0	0	0	0	0	.000	0	1	0	1	0	0	1.000
American League totals (1 year)		2	1	0	0	0	0	0	0	.000	0	1	0	1	0	0	1.000
National League totals (1 year)		16	14	4	2	0	0	0	1	.143	0	0	3	7	11	1	.947
Major League totals (2 years)		18	15	4	2	0	0	0	1	.133	0	1	3	8	11	1	.950

HERNANDEZ, JOSE — IF — BREWERS

PERSONAL: Born July 14, 1969, in Vega Alta, Puerto Rico. ... 6-1/180. ... Bats right, throws right. ... Full name: Jose Antonio Hernandez.
HIGH SCHOOL: Maestro Ladi (Vega Alta, Puerto Rico).
COLLEGE: Interamerican (Puerto Rico).
TRANSACTIONS/CAREER NOTES: Signed as non-drafted free agent by Texas Rangers organization (January 13, 1987). ... Claimed on waivers by Cleveland Indians (April 3, 1992). ... Traded by Indians to Chicago Cubs for P Heathcliff Slocumb (June 1, 1993). ... Traded by Cubs with P Terry Mulholland to Atlanta Braves for P Micah Bowie, P Ruben Quevado and a player to be named later (July 31, 1999); Cubs acquired P Joey Nation to complete deal (August 24, 1999). ... Granted free agency (November 5, 1999). ... Signed by Milwaukee Brewers (December 16, 1999). ... On Milwaukee disabled list (August 10-September 1, 2000); included rehabilitation assignment to Indianapolis (August 29-31).
STATISTICAL NOTES: Led Gulf Coast League third basemen with .950 fielding percentage, 47 putouts and 11 double plays in 1988. ... Led Florida State League shortstops with .959 fielding percentage in 1990. ... Career major league grand slams: 3.

Year Team (League)	Pos.	G	AB	R	H	2B	3B	HR	RBI	Avg.	BB	SO	SB	PO	A	E	Avg.
1987— GC Rangers (GCL)	SS	24	52	5	9	1	1	0	2	.173	9	25	2	30	38	5	.932
1988— GC Rangers (GCL)	3-2-S-1-O	55	162	19	26	7	1	1	13	.160	12	36	4	†68	115	8	†.958
1989— Gastonia (S.Atl.)	3B-SS-2B-OF	91	215	35	47	7	6	1	16	.219	33	67	9	101	169	17	.941
1990— Charlotte (FSL)	SS-OF	121	388	43	99	14	7	1	44	.255	50	122	11	192	372	25	†.958
1991— Tulsa (Texas)	SS	91	301	36	72	17	4	1	20	.239	26	75	4	151	300	15	*.968
— Oklahoma City (A.A.) ..	SS	14	46	6	14	1	1	1	3	.304	4	10	0	32	43	3	.962
— Texas (A.L.)	SS-3B	45	98	8	18	2	1	0	4	.184	3	31	0	49	111	4	.976
1992— Cant./Akron (East.)■ ..	SS	130	404	56	103	16	4	3	46	.255	37	108	7	*226	320	*40	.932
— Cleveland (A.L.)	SS	3	4	0	0	0	0	0	0	.000	0	2	0	3	3	1	.857
1993— Canton/Akron (East.) ..	SS-3B	45	150	19	30	6	0	2	17	.200	10	39	9	75	135	7	.968
— Orlando (Sou.)■	SS	71	263	42	80	8	3	8	33	.304	20	60	8	136	205	14	.961
— Iowa (A.A.)	SS	6	24	3	6	1	0	0	3	.250	0	2	0	14	26	1	.976
1994— Chicago (N.L.) 3B-SS-2B-OF		56	132	18	32	2	3	1	9	.242	8	29	2	46	86	4	.971
1995— Chicago (N.L.)	SS-2B-3B	93	245	37	60	11	4	13	40	.245	·13	69	1	113	189	9	.971
1996— Chicago (N.L.) SS-3B-2B-OF		131	331	52	80	14	1	10	41	.242	24	97	4	148	248	20	.952
1997— Chicago (N.L.) 3-S-2-O-D-1		121	183	33	50	8	5	7	26	.273	14	42	2	79	91	8	.955
1998— Chicago (N.L.)	3-O-S-1-2	149	488	76	124	23	7	23	75	.254	40	140	4	193	226	13	.970
1999— Chicago (N.L.)	SS-OF-1B	99	342	57	93	12	2	15	43	.272	40	101	7	140	249	11	.973
— Atlanta (N.L.)■	SS-1B-OF	48	166	22	42	8	0	4	19	.253	12	44	4	54	114	6	.966
2000— Milwaukee (N.L.)■	3B-SS-OF	124	446	51	109	22	1	11	59	.244	41	125	3	141	258	19	.955
— Indianapolis (I.L.)	3B	2	9	2	3	0	0	2	3	.333	1	3	0	0	2	0	1.000
American League totals (2 years)		48	102	8	18	2	1	0	4	.176	3	33	0	52	114	5	.971
National League totals (7 years)		821	2333	346	590	100	23	84	312	.253	192	647	27	914	1461	90	.963
Major League totals (9 years)		869	2435	354	608	102	24	84	316	.250	195	680	27	966	1575	95	.964

H

DIVISION SERIES RECORD

Year	Team (League)	Pos.	G	AB	R	H	2B	3B	HR	RBI	Avg.	BB	SO	SB	PO	A	E	Avg.
1998—	Chicago (N.L.)............	SS	2	7	1	2	0	0	0	0	.286	0	2	0	5	1	2	.750
1999—	Atlanta (N.L.)............	SS	4	11	1	1	0	0	0	0	.091	1	3	1	6	9	1	.938
	Division series totals (2 years)		6	18	2	3	0	0	0	0	.167	1	5	1	11	10	3	.875

CHAMPIONSHIP SERIES RECORD

Year	Team (League)	Pos.	G	AB	R	H	2B	3B	HR	RBI	Avg.	BB	SO	SB	PO	A	E	Avg.
1999—	Atlanta (N.L.).............	PH	2	2	0	1	0	0	0	2	.500	0	1	0	...	...	...	...

WORLD SERIES RECORD

Year	Team (League)	Pos.	G	AB	R	H	2B	3B	HR	RBI	Avg.	BB	SO	SB	PO	A	E	Avg.
1999—	Atlanta (N.L.).............	PH-SS-DH	2	5	0	1	1	0	0	2	.200	0	2	1	1	0	0	1.000

HERNANDEZ, LIVAN   P   GIANTS

PERSONAL: Born February 20, 1975, in Villa Clara, Cuba. ... 6-2/222. ... Throws right, bats right. ... Full name: Eisler Hernandez. ... Half-brother of Orlando Hernandez, pitcher, New York Yankees. ... Name pronounced lee-VAHN.
TRANSACTIONS/CAREER NOTES: Signed as non-drafted free agent by Florida Marlins orgaization (January 13, 1996). ... Traded by Marlins to San Francisco Giants for P Jason Grilli and P Nathan Bump (July 24, 1999).
STATISTICAL NOTES: Led International League with four balks in 1996. ... Led N.L. pitchers with a 1.000 fielding percentage in 2000.
MISCELLANEOUS: Member of Cuban national baseball team (1994-95). ... Struck out once in two appearances as pinch hitter (1998). ... Struck out in only appearance as pinch hitter with Giants (1999). ... Struck out in only appearance as pinch hitter (2000).

Year	League	W	L	Pct.	ERA	G	GS	CG	ShO	Sv.	IP	H	R	ER	BB	SO
1996—	Charlotte (I.L.)...................	2	4	.333	5.14	10	10	0	0	0	49	61	32	28	34	45
	—Florida (N.L.).....................	0	0	...	0.00	1	0	0	0	0	3	3	0	0	2	2
1997—	Portland (East.)	0	0	...	2.25	1	1	0	0	0	4	2	1	1	7	2
	—Charlotte (I.L.)	5	3	.625	3.98	14	14	0	0	0	81 1/3	76	39	36	38	58
	—Florida (N.L.)	9	3	.750	3.18	17	17	0	0	0	96 1/3	81	39	34	38	72
1998—	Florida (N.L.).....................	10	12	.455	4.72	33	33	9	0	0	234 1/3	*265	133	123	104	162
1999—	Florida (N.L.).....................	5	9	.357	4.76	20	20	2	0	0	136	161	78	72	55	97
	—San Francisco (N.L.)■	3	3	.500	4.38	10	10	0	0	0	63 2/3	66	32	31	21	47
2000—	San Francisco (N.L.)	17	11	.607	3.75	33	33	5	2	0	240	*254	114	100	73	165
Major League totals (5 years)		44	38	.537	4.19	114	113	16	2	0	773 1/3	830	396	360	293	545

DIVISION SERIES RECORD

Year	League	W	L	Pct.	ERA	G	GS	CG	ShO	Sv.	IP	H	R	ER	BB	SO
1997—	Florida (N.L.)	0	0	...	2.25	1	0	0	0	0	4	3	1	1	0	3
2000—	San Francisco (N.L.)	1	0	1.000	1.17	1	1	0	0	0	7 2/3	5	1	1	5	5
	Division series totals (2 years)	1	0	1.000	1.54	2	1	0	0	0	11 2/3	8	2	2	5	8

CHAMPIONSHIP SERIES RECORD

NOTES: Named N.L. Championship Series Most Valuable Player (1997).

Year	League	W	L	Pct.	ERA	G	GS	CG	ShO	Sv.	IP	H	R	ER	BB	SO
1997—	Florida (N.L.)	2	0	1.000	0.84	2	1	1	0	0	10 2/3	5	1	1	2	16

WORLD SERIES RECORD

NOTES: Named Most Valuable Player (1997). ... Member of World Series championship team (1997).

Year	League	W	L	Pct.	ERA	G	GS	CG	ShO	Sv.	IP	H	R	ER	BB	SO
1997—	Florida (N.L.)	2	0	1.000	5.27	2	2	0	0	0	13 2/3	15	9	8	10	7

HERNANDEZ, ORLANDO   P   YANKEES

PERSONAL: Born October 11, 1965, in Villa Clara, Cuba. ... 6-2/220. ... Throws right, bats right. ... Full name: Orlando P. Hernandez. ... Nickname: El Duque. ... Half-brother of Livan Hernandez, pitcher, San Francisco Giants.
TRANSACTIONS/CAREER NOTES: Signed as non-drafted free agent by New York Yankees (March 23, 1998). ... On New York disabled list (July 18-August 6, 2000); included rehabilitation assignment to Tampa (August 1-3).
MISCELLANEOUS: Member of Cuban national baseball team.

Year	League	W	L	Pct.	ERA	G	GS	CG	ShO	Sv.	IP	H	R	ER	BB	SO
1998—	Tampa (FSL).....................	1	1	.500	1.00	2	2	0	0	0	9	3	2	1	3	15
	—Columbus (I.L.).................	6	0	1.000	3.83	7	7	0	0	0	42 1/3	41	19	18	17	59
	—New York (A.L.).................	12	4	.750	3.13	21	21	3	1	0	141	113	53	49	52	131
1999—	New York (A.L.).................	17	9	.654	4.12	33	33	2	1	0	214 1/3	187	108	98	87	157
2000—	New York (A.L.).................	12	13	.480	4.51	29	29	3	0	0	195 2/3	186	104	98	51	141
	—Tampa (FSL).....................	0	0	...	0.00	1	0	0	0	0	4	1	0	0	1	5
Major League totals (3 years)		41	26	.612	4.00	83	83	8	2	0	551	486	265	245	190	429

DIVISION SERIES RECORD

Year	League	W	L	Pct.	ERA	G	GS	CG	ShO	Sv.	IP	H	R	ER	BB	SO
1998—	New York (A.L.)							Did not play.								
1999—	New York (A.L.)	1	0	1.000	0.00	1	1	0	0	0	8	2	0	0	6	4
2000—	New York (A.L.)	1	0	1.000	2.45	2	1	0	0	0	7 1/3	5	2	2	5	5
	Division series totals (2 years)	2	0	1.000	1.17	3	2	0	0	0	15 1/3	7	2	2	11	9

CHAMPIONSHIP SERIES RECORD

NOTES: Named A.L. Championship Series Most Valuable Player (1999).

Year	League	W	L	Pct.	ERA	G	GS	CG	ShO	Sv.	IP	H	R	ER	BB	SO
1998—	New York (A.L.)	1	0	1.000	0.00	1	1	0	0	0	7	3	0	0	2	6
1999—	New York (A.L.)	1	0	1.000	1.80	2	2	0	0	0	15	12	4	3	6	13
2000—	New York (A.L.)	2	0	1.000	4.20	2	2	0	0	0	15	13	7	7	8	14
Champ. series totals (3 years)		4	0	1.000	2.43	5	5	0	0	0	37	28	11	10	16	33

H

WORLD SERIES RECORD

NOTES: Member of World Series championship team (1998, 1999 and 2000).

Year League	W	L	Pct.	ERA	G	GS	CG	ShO	Sv.	IP	H	R	ER	BB	SO
1998— New York (A.L.)................	1	0	1.000	1.29	1	1	0	0	0	7	6	1	1	3	7
1999— New York (A.L.)................	1	0	1.000	1.29	1	1	0	0	0	7	1	1	1	2	10
2000— New York (A.L.)................	0	1	.000	4.91	1	1	0	0	0	7 1/3	9	4	4	3	12
World Series totals (3 years)	2	1	.667	2.53	3	3	0	0	0	21 1/3	16	6	6	8	29

HERNANDEZ, RAMON   C   ATHLETICS

PERSONAL: Born May 20, 1976, in Caracas, Venezuela. ... 6-0/227. ... Bats right, throws right. ... Full name: Ramon Jose Marin Hernandez.

TRANSACTIONS/CAREER NOTES: Signed as non-drafted free agent by Oakland Athletics organization (February 18, 1994). ... On Oakland disabled list (July 26-August 27, 1999); included rehabilitation assignment to Vancouver (August 13-27).

HONORS: Named Arizona League Most Valuable Player (1995).

STATISTICAL NOTES: Led Arizona League catchers with a .982 fielding percentage in 1995. ... Led Midwest League catchers with 877 putouts and 981 totals chances and tied for lead with 20 errors in 1996. ... Led California League with .427 on-base percentage in 1997. ... Led California League catchers with 16 errors in 1997. ... Led Southern League in being hit by pitch with 19 in 1998.

							BATTING								FIELDING		
Year Team (League)	Pos.	G	AB	R	H	2B	3B	HR	RBI	Avg.	BB	SO	SB	PO	A	E	Avg.
1994— Dom. Athletics (DSL) .	C	42	134	24	33	2	0	2	18	.246	18	10	1	182	28	2	.991
1995— Ariz. Athletics (Ariz.) ..	C-1B-3B	48	143	37	52	9	6	4	37	.364	39	16	6	358	61	12	†.972
1996— W. Mich. (Midw.)........	C-DH-1B	123	447	62	114	26	2	12	68	.255	69	62	2	†917	85	‡20	.980
1997— Visalia (Calif.)	C-DH-1B	86	332	57	120	21	2	15	85	*.361	35	47	2	577	80	†16	.976
— Huntsville (Sou.) C-DH-1B-3B		44	161	27	31	3	0	4	24	.193	18	23	0	274	27	1	.997
1998— Huntsville (Sou.)	DH-C-1B	127	479	83	142	24	1	15	98	.296	57	61	4	524	42	11	.981
1999— Vancouver (PCL) C-DH-3B-1B		77	291	38	76	11	3	13	55	.261	23	37	1	339	40	5	.987
— Oakland (A.L.)	C	40	136	13	38	7	0	3	21	.279	18	11	1	274	19	6	.980
2000— Oakland (A.L.)	C	143	419	52	101	19	0	14	62	.241	38	64	1	764	43	*13	.984
Major League totals (2 years)		183	555	65	139	26	0	17	83	.250	56	75	2	1038	62	19	.983

DIVISION SERIES RECORD

							BATTING								FIELDING		
Year Team (League)	Pos.	G	AB	R	H	2B	3B	HR	RBI	Avg.	BB	SO	SB	PO	A	E	Avg.
2000— Oakland (A.L.)	C	5	16	3	6	2	0	0	3	.375	0	3	0	34	3	1	.974

HERNANDEZ, ROBERTO   P   ROYALS

PERSONAL: Born November 11, 1964, in Santurce, Puerto Rico. ... 6-4/250. ... Throws right, bats right. ... Full name: Roberto Manuel Hernandez.

HIGH SCHOOL: New Hampton (N.H.) Prep.

COLLEGE: South Carolina-Aiken.

TRANSACTIONS/CAREER NOTES: Selected by California Angels organization in first round (16th pick overall) of free-agent draft (June 2, 1986); pick received as compensation for Baltimore Orioles signing Type A free-agent OF/IF Juan Beniquez. ... On disabled list (May 6-21 and June 4-August 14, 1987). ... Traded by Angels with OF Mark Doran to Chicago White Sox organization for OF Mark Davis (August 2, 1989). ... On Vancouver disabled list (May 17-August 10, 1991). ... Traded by White Sox with P Wilson Alvarez and P Danny Darwin to San Francisco Giants for SS Mike Caruso, OF Brian Manning, P Lorenzo Barcelo, P Keith Foulke and P Bobby Howry and P Ken Vining (July 31, 1997). ... Granted free agency (October 30, 1997). ... Signed by Tampa Bay Devil Rays (November 18, 1997). ... Traded by Devil Rays to Kansas City Royals as part of three-way deal in which Devil Rays received OF Ben Grieve and a player to be named later or cash from the Oakland Athletics, Athletics received P Cory Lidle from Devil Rays, Athletics received OF Johnny Damon, IF Mark Ellis and a player to be named later from Royals and Royals received C A.J. Hinch, IF Angel Berroa and cash from Athletics (January 8, 2001).

MISCELLANEOUS: Holds Tampa Bay Devil Rays all-time record for most games pitched (207) and saves (101).

Year League	W	L	Pct.	ERA	G	GS	CG	ShO	Sv.	IP	H	R	ER	BB	SO
1986— Salem (N'West)	2	2	.500	4.58	10	10	0	0	0	55	57	37	28	42	38
1987— Quad City (Midw.)	2	3	.400	6.86	7	6	0	0	1	21	24	21	16	12	21
1988— Quad City (Midw.)	9	10	.474	3.17	24	24	6	1	0	164 2/3	157	70	58	48	114
— Midland (Texas)	0	2	.000	6.57	3	3	0	0	0	12 1/3	16	13	9	8	7
1989— Midland (Texas)	2	7	.222	6.89	12	12	0	0	0	64	94	57	49	30	42
— Palm Springs (Calif.)	1	4	.200	4.64	7	7	0	0	0	42 2/3	49	27	22	16	33
— South Bend (Midw.)■........	1	1	.500	3.33	4	4	0	0	0	24 1/3	19	9	9	7	17
1990— Birmingham (Sou.)..........	8	5	.615	3.67	17	17	1	0	0	108	103	57	44	43	62
— Vancouver (PCL)	3	5	.375	2.84	11	11	3	1	0	79 1/3	73	33	25	26	49
1991— Birmingham (Sou.)..........	2	1	.667	1.99	4	4	0	0	0	22 2/3	11	5	5	6	25
— Vancouver (PCL)	4	1	.800	3.22	7	7	0	0	0	44 2/3	41	17	16	23	40
— GC White Sox (GCL)	0	0	...	0.00	1	1	0	0	0	6	2	0	0	0	7
— Chicago (A.L.)	1	0	1.000	7.80	9	3	0	0	0	15	18	15	13	7	6
1992— Chicago (A.L.)	7	3	.700	1.65	43	0	0	0	12	71	45	15	13	20	68
— Vancouver (PCL)	3	3	.500	2.61	9	0	0	0	2	20 2/3	13	9	6	11	23
1993— Chicago (A.L.)	3	4	.429	2.29	70	0	0	0	38	78 2/3	66	21	20	20	71
1994— Chicago (A.L.)	4	4	.500	4.91	45	0	0	0	14	47 2/3	44	26	26	19	50
1995— Chicago (A.L.)	3	7	.300	3.92	60	0	0	0	32	59 2/3	63	30	26	28	84
1996— Chicago (A.L.)	6	5	.545	1.91	72	0	0	0	38	84 2/3	65	21	18	38	85
1997— Chicago (A.L.)	5	1	.833	2.44	46	0	0	0	27	48	38	15	13	24	47
— San Francisco (N.L.)■............	5	2	.714	2.48	28	0	0	0	4	32 2/3	29	9	9	14	35
1998— Tampa Bay (A.L.)■............	2	6	.250	4.04	67	0	0	0	26	71 1/3	55	33	32	41	55
1999— Tampa Bay (A.L.)................	2	3	.400	3.07	72	0	0	0	43	73 1/3	68	27	25	33	69
2000— Tampa Bay (A.L.)................	4	7	.364	3.19	68	0	0	0	32	73 1/3	76	33	26	23	61
A.L. totals (10 years)	37	40	.481	3.06	552	3	0	0	262	622 2/3	538	239	212	253	596
N.L. totals (1 year)	5	2	.714	2.48	28	0	0	0	4	32 2/3	29	9	9	14	35
Major League totals (10 years)	42	42	.500	3.04	580	3	0	0	266	655 1/3	567	248	221	267	631

H

DIVISION SERIES RECORD

Year League	W	L	Pct.	ERA	G	GS	CG	ShO	Sv.	IP	H	R	ER	BB	SO
1997— San Francisco (N.L.)	0	1	.000	20.25	3	0	0	0	0	1 1/3	5	3	3	3	1

CHAMPIONSHIP SERIES RECORD

Year League	W	L	Pct.	ERA	G	GS	CG	ShO	Sv.	IP	H	R	ER	BB	SO
1993— Chicago (A.L.)	0	0	...	0.00	4	0	0	0	1	4	4	0	0	0	1

ALL-STAR GAME RECORD

Year League	W	L	Pct.	ERA	GS	CG	ShO	Sv.	IP	H	R	ER	BB	SO
1996— American	0	0	...	0.00	0	0	0	0	1	1	0	0	0	0
1999— American	0	0	...	0.00	0	0	0	0	1	0	0	0	0	0
All-Star Game totals (2 years)	0	0	...	0.00	0	0	0	0	2	1	0	0	0	0

HERSHISER, OREL — P

PERSONAL: Born September 16, 1958, in Buffalo. ... 6-3/195. ... Throws right, bats right. ... Full name: Orel Leonard Hershiser IV. ... Brother of Gordie Hershiser, minor league pitcher (1987-88). ... Name pronounced her-SHY-zer.

HIGH SCHOOL: Cherry Hill (N.J.) East.

COLLEGE: Bowling Green State.

TRANSACTIONS/CAREER NOTES: Selected by Los Angeles Dodgers organization in 17th round of free-agent draft (June 5, 1979). ... On disabled list (April 27, 1990-remainder of season). ... On Los Angeles disabled list (March 31-May 29, 1991); included rehabilitation assignments to Bakersfield (May 8-13 and May 18-24), Albuquerque (May 13-18) and San Antonio (May 24-29). ... Granted free agency (November 1, 1991). ... Re-signed by Dodgers (December 3, 1991). ... Granted free agency (October 17, 1994). ... Signed by Cleveland Indians (April 8, 1995). ... On disabled list (June 22-July 7, 1995 and July 29-August 13, 1997). ... Granted free agency (October 29, 1997). ... Signed by San Francisco Giants (December 9, 1997). ... Granted free agency (November 2, 1998). ... Signed by Indians organization (February 20, 1999). ... Released by Indians (March 25, 1999). ... Signed by New York Mets (March 25, 1999). ... Granted free agency (November 1, 1999). ... Signed by Dodgers (December 5, 1999). ... Released by Dodgers (June 27, 2000).

RECORDS: Holds major league single-season record for most consecutive scoreless innings—59 (August 30, sixth inning through September 28, 10th inning, 1988). ... Shares major league single-season record for fewest games lost for leader—15 (1992). ... Shares N.L. single-season record for fewest games lost by pitcher who led league in games lost—15 (1989 and 1992). ... Shares N.L. record for most shutouts in one month—5 (September 1988). ... Shares N.L. single-game record for most hit batsmen (nine innings)—4 (April 19, 2000).

HONORS: Named Major League Player of the Year by THE SPORTING NEWS (1988). ... Named N.L. Pitcher of the Year by THE SPORTING NEWS (1988). ... Named righthanded pitcher on THE SPORTING NEWS N.L. All-Star team (1988). ... Won N.L. Gold Glove at pitcher (1988). ... Named N.L. Cy Young Award winner by Baseball Writers' Association of America (1988). ... Named pitcher on THE SPORTING NEWS N.L. Silver Slugger team (1993).

STATISTICAL NOTES: Pitched 2-0 one-hit, complete-game victory against San Diego (April 26, 1985). ... Pitched 6-0 one-hit, complete-game victory against Pittsburgh (July 23, 1985). ... Tied for N.L. lead with 19 sacrifice hits in 1988. ... Tied for N.L. lead with 13 intentional bases on balls issued in 1993.

MISCELLANEOUS: Had sacrifice hit in only appearance as pinch hitter (1988). ... Singled once in two appearances as pinch hitter (1992). ... Started one game at third base but was replaced before first plate appearance and never played in field (1993).

Year League	W	L	Pct.	ERA	G	GS	CG	ShO	Sv.	IP	H	R	ER	BB	SO
1979— Clinton (Midw.)	4	0	1.000	2.09	15	4	1	0	2	43	33	15	10	17	33
1980— San Antonio (Texas)	5	9	.357	3.55	49	3	1	0	14	109	120	59	43	59	75
1981— San Antonio (Texas)	7	6	.538	4.68	42	4	3	0	*15	102	94	54	53	50	95
1982— Albuquerque (PCL)	9	6	.600	3.71	47	7	2	0	4	123 2/3	121	73	51	63	93
1983— Albuquerque (PCL)	10	8	.556	4.09	49	10	6	0	16	134 1/3	132	73	61	57	95
— Los Angeles (N.L.)	0	0	...	3.38	8	0	0	0	1	8	7	6	3	6	5
1984— Los Angeles (N.L.)	11	8	.579	2.66	45	20	8	•4	2	189 2/3	160	65	56	50	150
1985— Los Angeles (N.L.)	19	3	*.864	2.03	36	34	9	5	0	239 2/3	179	72	54	68	157
1986— Los Angeles (N.L.)	14	14	.500	3.85	35	35	8	1	0	231 1/3	213	112	99	86	153
1987— Los Angeles (N.L.)	16	16	.500	3.06	37	35	10	1	1	*264 2/3	247	105	90	74	190
1988— Los Angeles (N.L.)	•23	8	.742	2.26	35	34	•15	*8	1	*267	208	73	67	73	178
1989— Los Angeles (N.L.)	15	•15	.500	2.31	35	33	8	4	0	*256 2/3	226	75	66	77	178
1990— Los Angeles (N.L.)	1	1	.500	4.26	4	4	0	0	0	25 1/3	26	12	12	4	16
1991— Bakersfield (Calif.)	2	0	1.000	0.82	2	2	0	0	0	11	5	2	1	1	6
— Albuquerque (PCL)	0	0	...	0.00	1	1	0	0	0	5	5	0	0	0	5
— San Antonio (Texas)	0	1	.000	2.57	1	1	0	0	0	7	11	3	2	1	5
— Los Angeles (N.L.)	7	2	.778	3.46	21	21	0	0	0	112	112	43	43	32	73
1992— Los Angeles (N.L.)	10	•15	.400	3.67	33	33	1	0	0	210 2/3	209	101	86	69	130
1993— Los Angeles (N.L.)	12	14	.462	3.59	33	33	5	1	0	215 2/3	201	106	86	72	141
1994— Los Angeles (N.L.)	6	6	.500	3.79	21	21	1	0	0	135 1/3	146	67	57	42	72
1995— Cleveland (A.L.)■.............	16	6	.727	3.87	26	26	1	1	0	167 1/3	151	76	72	51	111
1996— Cleveland (A.L.)	15	9	.625	4.24	33	33	1	0	0	206	238	115	97	58	125
1997— Cleveland (A.L.)	14	6	.700	4.47	32	32	1	0	0	195 1/3	199	105	97	69	107
1998— San Francisco (N.L.)■	11	10	.524	4.41	34	34	0	0	0	202	200	105	99	85	126
1999— New York (N.L.)■	13	12	.520	4.58	32	32	0	0	0	179	175	92	91	77	89
2000— Los Angeles (N.L.)■...........	1	5	.167	13.14	10	6	0	0	0	24 2/3	42	36	36	14	13
— San Bernardino (Calif.).......	1	0	1.000	3.06	3	3	0	0	0	17 2/3	18	7	6	5	8
A.L. totals (3 years)	45	21	.682	4.21	91	91	3	1	0	568 2/3	588	296	266	178	343
N.L. totals (15 years)	159	129	.552	3.32	419	375	65	24	5	2561 2/3	2351	1070	945	829	1671
Major League totals (18 years)	204	150	.576	3.48	510	466	68	25	5	3130 1/3	2939	1366	1211	1007	2014

DIVISION SERIES RECORD

Year League	W	L	Pct.	ERA	G	GS	CG	ShO	Sv.	IP	H	R	ER	BB	SO
1995— Cleveland (A.L.).................	1	0	1.000	0.00	1	1	0	0	0	7 1/3	3	0	0	2	7
1996— Cleveland (A.L.).................	0	0	...	5.40	1	1	0	0	0	5	7	4	3	3	3
1997— Cleveland (A.L.).................	0	0	...	3.97	2	2	0	0	0	11 1/3	14	5	5	2	4
1999— New York (N.L.).................	0	0	...	0.00	1	0	0	0	0	1	0	0	0	0	1
Division series totals (4 years)	1	0	1.000	2.92	5	4	0	0	0	24 2/3	24	9	8	7	15

H

CHAMPIONSHIP SERIES RECORD

RECORDS: Holds career record for lowest earned-run average (30 or more innings)—1.52. ... Holds single-series record for most innings pitched—24 2/3 (1988). ... Holds N.L. single-game record for most hit batsmen—2 (October 12, 1988). ... Shares N.L. career record for most complete games—2. ... Shares N.L. single-series record for most hit batsmen—2 (1988).

NOTES: Named N.L. Championship Series Most Valuable Player (1988). ... Named A.L. Championship Series Most Valuable Player (1995).

Year League	W	L	Pct.	ERA	G	GS	CG	ShO	Sv.	IP	H	R	ER	BB	SO
1983— Los Angeles (N.L.)							Did not play.								
1985— Los Angeles (N.L.)	1	0	1.000	3.52	2	2	1	0	0	15 1/3	17	6	6	6	5
1988— Los Angeles (N.L.)	1	0	1.000	1.09	4	3	1	1	1	24 2/3	18	5	3	7	15
1995— Cleveland (A.L.)	2	0	1.000	1.29	2	2	0	0	0	14	9	3	2	3	15
1997— Cleveland (A.L.)	0	0	...	0.00	1	1	0	0	0	7	4	0	0	1	7
1999— New York (N.L.)	0	0	...	0.00	2	0	0	0	0	4 1/3	1	0	0	3	5
Champ. series totals (5 years)	4	0	1.000	1.52	11	8	2	1	1	65 1/3	49	14	11	20	47

WORLD SERIES RECORD

RECORDS: Shares single-game record for most earned runs allowed—7 (October 18, 1997).

NOTES: Named Most Valuable Player (1988). ... Member of World Series championship team (1988).

Year League	W	L	Pct.	ERA	G	GS	CG	ShO	Sv.	IP	H	R	ER	BB	SO
1988— Los Angeles (N.L.)	2	0	1.000	1.00	2	2	2	1	0	18	7	2	2	6	17
1995— Cleveland (A.L.)	1	1	.500	2.57	2	2	0	0	0	14	8	5	4	4	13
1997— Cleveland (A.L.)	0	2	.000	11.70	2	2	0	0	0	10	15	13	13	6	5
World Series totals (3 years)	3	3	.500	4.07	6	6	2	1	0	42	30	20	19	16	35

ALL-STAR GAME RECORD

Year League	W	L	Pct.	ERA	GS	CG	ShO	Sv.	IP	H	R	ER	BB	SO
1987— National	0	0	...	0.00	0	0	0	0	2	1	0	0	1	0
1988— National	0	0	...	0.00	0	0	0	0	1	0	0	0	0	0
1989— National							Did not play.							
All-Star Game totals (2 years)	0	0	...	0.00	0	0	0	0	3	1	0	0	1	0

HIDALGO, RICHARD   OF   ASTROS

PERSONAL: Born July 2, 1975, in Caracas, Venezuela. ... 6-3/190. ... Bats right, throws right. ... Full name: Richard Jose Hidalgo.

TRANSACTIONS/CAREER NOTES: Signed as non-drafted free agent by Houston Astros organization (July 2, 1991). ... On Houston disabled list (May 30-July 21, 1998); included rehabilitation assignment to New Orleans (July 11-21). ... On disabled list (August 9, 1999-remainder of season).

RECORDS: Shares major league single-game record for most times hit by pitch—3 (April 19, 2000).

STATISTICAL NOTES: Led Texas League in grounding into double plays with 24 in 1996. ... Had 15-game hitting streak (August 28-September 13, 2000). ... Career major league grand slams: 1.

						BATTING								FIELDING		
Year Team (League)	Pos.	G	AB	R	H	2B	3B	HR	RBI	Avg.	BB	SO	SB	PO	A	E	Avg.
1992— GC Astros (GCL)	OF	51	184	20	57	7	3	1	27	.310	13	27	14	67	6	0	1.000
1993— Asheville (S.Atl.)	OF	111	403	49	109	23	3	10	55	.270	30	76	21	197	*30	6	.974
1994— Quad City (Midw.)	OF	124	476	68	139	*47	6	12	76	.292	23	80	12	202	*23	11	.953
1995— Jackson (Texas)	OF	133	489	59	130	28	6	14	59	.266	32	76	8	238	14	5	.981
1996— Jackson (Texas)	OF-DH	130	513	66	151	34	2	14	78	.294	29	55	11	302	14	6	.981
1997— New Orleans (A.A.)	OF-DH	134	526	74	147	*37	5	11	78	.279	35	57	6	261	*15	9	.968
— Houston (N.L.)	OF	19	62	8	19	5	0	2	6	.306	4	18	1	28	0	0	1.000
1998— Houston (N.L.)	OF	74	211	31	64	15	0	7	35	.303	17	37	3	131	3	3	.978
— New Orleans (PCL)	OF	10	24	0	4	2	0	0	1	.167	3	2	0	17	0	0	1.000
1999— Houston (N.L.)	OF	108	383	49	87	25	2	15	56	.227	56	73	8	214	15	2	.991
2000— Houston (N.L.)	OF	153	558	118	175	42	3	44	122	.314	56	110	13	425	7	7	.984
Major League totals (4 years)		354	1214	206	345	87	5	68	219	.284	133	238	25	798	25	12	.986

DIVISION SERIES RECORD

						BATTING								FIELDING		
Year Team (League)	Pos.	G	AB	R	H	2B	3B	HR	RBI	Avg.	BB	SO	SB	PO	A	E	Avg.
1997— Houston (N.L.)	OF	2	5	1	0	0	0	0	0	.000	1	2	0	5	0	0	1.000
1998— Houston (N.L.)	OF	1	4	0	1	0	0	0	0	.250	0	1	0	1	0	0	1.000
1999— Houston (N.L.)						Did not play.											
Division series totals (2 years)		3	9	1	1	0	0	0	0	.111	1	3	0	6	0	0	1.000

HIGGINSON, BOBBY   OF   TIGERS

PERSONAL: Born August 18, 1970, in Philadelphia. ... 5-11/195. ... Bats left, throws right. ... Full name: Robert Leigh Higginson.

HIGH SCHOOL: Frankford (Philadelphia).

COLLEGE: Temple.

TRANSACTIONS/CAREER NOTES: Selected by Detroit Tigers organization in 12th round of free-agent draft (June 1, 1992). ... On Detroit disabled list (May 11-June 7, 1996); included rehabilitation assignment to Toledo (June 4-7). ... On disabled list (June 15-26, 1997). ... On suspended list (September 26, 1997). ... On disabled list (July 24-August 24, 1999). ... On suspended list (May 10-16, 2000).

RECORDS: Shares major league record for most consecutive home runs—4 (June 30 [3], July 1 [1], 1997).

STATISTICAL NOTES: Hit three home runs in one game (June 30, 1997 and June 24, 2000). ... Tied for A.L. lead in double plays by outfielder with five in 1997. ... Career major league grand slams: 4.

						BATTING								FIELDING		
Year Team (League)	Pos.	G	AB	R	H	2B	3B	HR	RBI	Avg.	BB	SO	SB	PO	A	E	Avg.
1992— Niagara Falls (NY-P)	OF	70	232	35	68	17	4	2	37	.293	33	47	12	109	5	2	.983
1993— Lakeland (FSL)	OF	61	223	42	67	11	7	3	25	.300	40	31	8	88	7	2	.979
— London (East.)	OF	63	224	25	69	15	4	4	35	.308	19	37	3	100	11	2	.982
1994— Toledo (I.L.)	OF	137	476	81	131	28	3	23	67	.275	46	99	16	282	10	8	.973

Year Team (League)	Pos.	G	AB	R	H	2B	3B	HR	RBI	Avg.	BB	SO	SB	PO	A	E	Avg.
						BATTING									**FIELDING**		
1995— Detroit (A.L.)	OF-DH	131	410	61	92	17	5	14	43	.224	62	107	6	247	*13	4	.985
1996— Detroit (A.L.)	OF-DH	130	440	75	141	35	0	26	81	.320	65	66	6	227	9	9	.963
— Toledo (I.L.)	OF	3	13	4	4	0	1	0	1	.308	3	0	0	3	0	0	1.000
1997— Detroit (A.L.)	OF-DH	146	546	94	163	30	5	27	101	.299	70	85	12	287	*20	9	.972
1998— Detroit (A.L.)	OF-DH	157	612	92	174	37	4	25	85	.284	63	101	3	303	18	6	.982
1999— Detroit (A.L.)	OF-DH	107	377	51	90	18	0	12	46	.239	64	66	4	175	2	3	.983
2000— Detroit (A.L.)	OF-DH	154	597	104	179	44	4	30	102	.300	74	99	15	307	*19	7	.979
Major League totals (6 years)		825	2982	477	839	181	18	134	458	.281	398	524	46	1546	81	38	.977

HILJUS, ERIK   P   ATHLETICS

PERSONAL: Born December 25, 1972, in Panorama City, Calif. ... 6-5/230. ... Throws right, bats right. ... Full name: Erik Kristian Hiljus.
HIGH SCHOOL: Canyon (Anaheim).
TRANSACTIONS/CAREER NOTES: Selected by New York Mets organization in fourth round of free-agent draft (June 3, 1991). ... Traded by Mets with P Eric Ludwick and OF Yudith Ozono to St. Louis Cardinals for OF Bernard Gilkey (January 23, 1996). ... On disabled list (April 4-July 14, 1996). ... On disabled list (April 3-August 20, 1997). ... Released by Cardinals (August 20, 1997). ... Signed by Detroit Tigers organization (March 9, 1998). ... On Toledo disabled list (April 8-19, 1999). ... Released by Tigers (November 27, 2000). ... Signed by Oakland Athletics organization (December 6, 2000).

Year League	W	L	Pct.	ERA	G	GS	CG	ShO	Sv.	IP	H	R	ER	BB	SO
1991— GC Mets (GCL)	2	3	.400	4.26	9	9	1	•1	0	38	31	27	18	37	38
1992— Little Falls (NY-Penn)	3	6	.333	5.09	12	11	0	0	0	70²/₃	66	49	40	40	63
1993— Capital City (S.Atl.)	7	10	.412	4.32	27	27	1	0	0	145²/₃	114	76	70	*111	157
1994— St. Lucie (FSL)	11	10	.524	3.98	26	26	3	1	0	160²/₃	159	85	71	*90	140
1995— St. Lucie (FSL)	8	4	.667	2.99	17	17	0	0	0	111¹/₃	85	46	37	50	98
— Binghamton (East.)	2	4	.333	5.86	10	10	0	0	0	55¹/₃	60	38	36	32	40
1996— Arkansas (Texas)■	3	5	.375	6.11	10	10	0	0	0	45²/₃	62	37	31	30	21
1997—							Did not play.								
1998— Jacksonville (Sou.)■	2	3	.400	3.70	42	0	0	0	2	65²/₃	49	31	27	35	85
1999— Lakeland (FSL)	0	0	...	2.25	3	0	0	0	0	4	4	1	1	0	9
— Jacksonville (Sou.)	1	0	1.000	1.04	10	0	0	0	0	17¹/₃	5	4	2	5	28
— Toledo (I.L.)	2	3	.400	4.40	33	0	0	0	5	59¹/₃	49	31	29	16	73
— Detroit (A.L.)	0	0	...	5.19	6	0	0	0	0	8²/₃	7	5	5	5	1
2000— Toledo (I.L.)	5	3	.625	3.44	46	0	0	0	2	70²/₃	67	33	27	20	81
— Detroit (A.L.)	0	0	...	7.36	3	0	0	0	0	3²/₃	5	3	3	1	2
Major League totals (2 years)	0	0	...	5.84	9	0	0	0	0	12¹/₃	12	8	8	6	3

HILL, GLENALLEN   OF   YANKEES

PERSONAL: Born March 22, 1965, in Santa Cruz, Calif. ... 6-3/230. ... Bats right, throws right.
HIGH SCHOOL: Santa Cruz (Calif.).
TRANSACTIONS/CAREER NOTES: Selected by Toronto Blue Jays organization in ninth round of free-agent draft (June 6, 1983). ... On disabled list (July 6-21, 1990). ... Traded by Blue Jays with P Denis Boucher, OF Mark Whiten and a player to be named later to Cleveland Indians for P Tom Candiotti and OF Turner Ward (June 27, 1991). Indians acquired cash to complete deal (October 15, 1991). ... On Cleveland disabled list (September 8, 1991-remainder of season). ... On Cleveland disabled list (April 23-May 22, 1992); included rehabilitation assignment to Canton/Akron (May 18-22). ... Traded by Indians to Chicago Cubs for OF Candy Maldonado (August 19, 1993). ... Granted free agency (October 27, 1993). ... Re-signed by Cubs (November 24, 1993). ... Granted free agency (April 7, 1995). ... Signed by San Francisco Giants (April 9, 1995). ... On San Francisco disabled list (May 27-August 5, 1996); included rehabilitation assignment to Phoenix (July 29-August 5). ... Granted free agency (October 29, 1997). ... Signed by Seattle Mariners organization (January 8, 1998). ... Claimed on waivers by Cubs (July 6, 1998). ... Granted free agency (October 23, 1998). ... Re-signed by Cubs (December 7, 1998). ... On disabled list (May 8-23, 1999). ... On disabled list (March 23-April 7, 2000). ... Traded by Cubs to New York Yankees for P Ben Ford and P Ozwaldo Mairena (July 21, 2000).
STATISTICAL NOTES: Led Southern League with 287 total bases and tied for lead with 13 sacrifice flies in 1986. ... Led International League with 279 total bases and .578 slugging percentage in 1989. ... Career major league grand slams: 5.

Year Team (League)	Pos.	G	AB	R	H	2B	3B	HR	RBI	Avg.	BB	SO	SB	PO	A	E	Avg.
						BATTING									**FIELDING**		
1983— Medicine Hat (Pio.)	OF	46	133	34	63	3	4	6	27	.474	17	49	4	63	3	6	.917
1984— Florence (S.Atl.)	OF	129	440	75	105	19	5	16	64	.239	63	*150	30	281	9	16	.948
1985— Kinston (Caro.)	OF	131	466	57	98	13	0	20	56	.210	57	*211	42	234	12	13	.950
1986— Knoxville (Sou.)	OF	141	*570	87	159	23	6	*31	96	.279	39	*153	18	230	9	*21	.919
1987— Syracuse (I.L.)	OF	*137	536	65	126	25	6	16	77	.235	25	*152	22	176	10	10	.949
1988— Syracuse (I.L.)	OF	51	172	21	40	7	0	4	19	.233	15	59	7	101	2	1	.990
— Knoxville (Sou.)	OF	79	269	37	71	13	2	12	38	.264	28	75	10	130	6	5	.965
1989— Syracuse (I.L.)	OF	125	483	*86	*155	31	*15	*21	72	.321	34	107	21	242	3	*7	.972
— Toronto (A.L.)	OF-DH	19	52	4	15	0	0	1	7	.288	3	12	2	27	0	1	.964
1990— Toronto (A.L.)	OF-DH	84	260	47	60	11	3	12	32	.231	18	62	8	115	4	2	.983
1991— Toronto (A.L.)	DH-OF	35	99	14	25	5	2	3	11	.253	7	24	2	29	0	1	.967
— Cleveland (A.L.)■	OF	37	122	15	32	3	0	5	14	.262	16	30	4	89	0	2	.978
1992— Cleveland (A.L.)	OF-DH	102	369	38	89	16	1	18	49	.241	20	73	9	126	5	6	.956
— Canton/Akron (East.)..	OF	3	9	1	1	1	0	0	1	.111	3	4	0	4	0	1	.800
1993— Cleveland (A.L.)	OF-DH	66	174	19	39	7	2	5	25	.224	11	50	7	62	1	4	.940
— Chicago (N.L.)■	OF	31	87	14	30	7	0	10	22	.345	6	21	1	42	2	2	.957
1994— Chicago (N.L.)	OF	89	269	48	80	12	1	10	38	.297	29	57	19	149	0	2	.987
1995— San Fran. (N.L.)■	OF	132	497	71	131	29	4	24	86	.264	39	98	25	226	10	10	.959
1996— San Francisco (N.L.) ..	OF	98	379	56	106	26	0	19	67	.280	33	95	6	160	6	7	.960
— Phoenix (PCL)	OF	5	17	4	6	1	0	2	2	.353	0	3	1	8	0	0	1.000
1997— San Francisco (N.L.) ..	OF-DH	128	398	47	104	28	4	11	64	.261	19	87	7	158	2	9	.947
1998— Seattle (A.L.)■	OF	74	259	37	75	20	2	12	33	.290	14	45	1	107	2	4	.965
— Chicago (N.L.)■	OF	48	131	26	46	5	0	8	23	.351	14	34	0	59	3	1	.984

Year	Team (League)	Pos.	G	AB	R	H	2B	3B	HR	RBI	Avg.	BB	SO	SB	PO	A	E	Avg.
							BATTING									FIELDING		
1999—	Chicago (N.L.)	OF-DH	99	253	43	76	9	1	20	55	.300	22	61	5	81	3	4	.955
2000—	Chicago (N.L.)	OF-DH	64	168	23	44	4	1	11	29	.262	10	43	0	39	3	2	.955
—	New York (A.L.)■	DH-OF	40	132	22	44	5	0	16	29	.333	9	33	0	19	0	0	1.000
	American League totals (7 years)		457	1467	196	379	67	10	72	200	.258	98	329	33	574	12	20	.967
	National League totals (8 years)		689	2182	328	617	120	11	113	384	.283	172	496	63	914	29	37	.962
	Major League totals (12 years)		1146	3649	524	996	187	21	185	584	.273	270	825	96	1488	41	57	.964

DIVISION SERIES RECORD

Year	Team (League)	Pos.	G	AB	R	H	2B	3B	HR	RBI	Avg.	BB	SO	SB	PO	A	E	Avg.
							BATTING									FIELDING		
1997—	San Francisco (N.L.) ..	OF-PH	3	7	0	0	0	0	0	0	.000	2	2	0	2	0	0	1.000
1998—	Chicago (N.L.)	OF	1	3	0	1	0	0	0	0	.333	1	2	1	3	0	0	1.000
2000—	New York (A.L.)	PH-DH	4	12	1	1	0	0	0	2	.083	1	5	0	...	...	...	...
	Division series totals (3 years)		8	22	1	2	0	0	0	2	.091	4	9	1	5	0	0	1.000

CHAMPIONSHIP SERIES RECORD

Year	Team (League)	Pos.	G	AB	R	H	2B	3B	HR	RBI	Avg.	BB	SO	SB	PO	A	E	Avg.
							BATTING									FIELDING		
2000—	New York (A.L.)	PH	2	2	0	0	0	0	0	0	.000	0	2	0	...	...	...	...

WORLD SERIES RECORD

NOTES: Member of World Series championship team (2000).

Year	Team (League)	Pos.	G	AB	R	H	2B	3B	HR	RBI	Avg.	BB	SO	SB	PO	A	E	Avg.
							BATTING									FIELDING		
2000—	New York (A.L.)	PH-OF	3	3	0	0	0	0	0	0	.000	0	0	0	0	0	0	...

HILL, KEN P

PERSONAL: Born December 14, 1965, in Lynn, Mass. ... 6-2/215. ... Throws right, bats right. ... Full name: Kenneth Wade Hill.

HIGH SCHOOL: Classical (Lynn, Mass.).

COLLEGE: North Adams (Mass.) State.

TRANSACTIONS/CAREER NOTES: Signed as non-drafted free agent by Detroit Tigers organization (February 14, 1985). ... Traded by Tigers with a player to be named later to St. Louis Cardinals for C Mike Heath (August 10, 1986); Cardinals acquired 1B Mike Laga to complete deal (September 2, 1986). ... On St. Louis disabled list (March 26-May 9, 1988). ... On St. Louis disabled list (August 11-September 1, 1991); included rehabilitation assignment to Louisville (August 29-30). ... Traded by Cardinals to Montreal Expos for 1B Andres Galarraga (November 25, 1991). ... On Montreal disabled list (June 26-July 17, 1993); included rehabilitation assignment to Ottawa (July 12-15). ... Traded by Expos to Cardinals for P Brian Eversgerd, P Kirk Bullinger and OF Darond Stovall (April 5, 1995). ... Traded by Cardinals to Cleveland Indians for 3B/2B David Bell, P Rick Heiserman and C Pepe McNeal (July 27, 1995). ... Granted free agency (November 1, 1995). ... Signed by Texas Rangers (December 22, 1995). ... Traded by Rangers to Anaheim Angels for C Jim Leyritz and a player to be named later (July 29, 1997); Rangers acquired IF Rob Sasser to complete deal (October 31, 1997). ... On disabled list (May 1-24, 1997); included rehabilitation assignment to Tulsa (May 20-24). ... Granted free agency (November 7, 1997). ... Re-signed by Angels (November 15, 1997). ... On Anaheim disabled list (June 11-August 28, 1998); included rehabilitation assignments to Cedar Rapids (August 9-17) and Lake Elsinore (August 18-24). ... On disabled list (July 1-19 and August 15-September 1, 1999). ... On Anaheim disabled list (May 10-June 28, 2000); included rehabilitation assignments to Lake Elsinore (June 10-15) and Edmonton (June 16-22). ... Released by Angels (August 7, 2000). ... Signed by Chicago White Sox organization (August 18, 2000). ... Released by White Sox (August 29, 2000).

RECORDS: Shares N.L. single-season record for fewest games lost by pitcher who led league in games lost—15 (1989).

STATISTICAL NOTES: Pitched 6-0 one-hit, complete-game victory against New York (June 8, 1992). ... Led N.L. with 16 sacrifice hits in 1994. ... Pitched 11-0 one-hit, complete-game victory against Detroit (May 3, 1996). ... Led A.L. with four balks in 1996. ... Led A.L. with 95 bases on balls in 1997.

MISCELLANEOUS: Made an out in only appearance as pinch hitter with Montreal (1993). ... Had sacrifice hit in only appearance as pinch hitter (1994).

Year	League	W	L	Pct.	ERA	G	GS	CG	ShO	Sv.	IP	H	R	ER	BB	SO
1985—	Gastonia (S.Atl.)	3	6	.333	4.96	15	12	0	0	0	69	60	51	38	57	48
1986—	Gastonia (S.Atl.)	9	5	.643	2.79	22	16	1	0	0	122²/₃	95	51	38	80	86
—	Glens Falls (East.)	0	1	.000	5.14	1	1	0	0	0	7	4	4	4	6	4
—	Arkansas (Texas)■	1	2	.333	4.50	3	3	1	0	0	18	18	10	9	7	9
1987—	Arkansas (Texas)	3	5	.375	5.20	18	8	0	0	2	53²/₃	60	33	31	30	48
—	St. Petersburg (FSL)	1	3	.250	4.17	18	4	0	0	2	41	38	19	19	17	32
1988—	St. Louis (N.L.)	0	1	.000	5.14	4	1	0	0	0	14	16	9	8	6	6
—	Arkansas (Texas)	9	9	.500	4.92	22	22	3	1	0	115¹/₃	129	76	63	50	107
1989—	Louisville (A.A.)	0	2	.000	3.50	3	3	0	0	0	18	13	8	7	10	18
—	St. Louis (N.L.)■	7	•15	.318	3.80	33	33	2	1	0	196²/₃	186	92	83	*99	112
1990—	St. Louis (N.L.)	5	6	.455	5.49	17	14	1	0	0	78²/₃	79	49	48	33	58
—	Louisville (A.A.)	6	1	.857	1.79	12	12	2	1	0	85¹/₃	47	20	17	27	104
1991—	St. Louis (N.L.)	11	10	.524	3.57	30	30	0	0	0	181¹/₃	147	76	72	67	121
—	Louisville (A.A.)	0	0	...	0.00	1	1	0	0	0	1	0	0	0	0	2
1992—	Montreal (N.L.)■	16	9	.640	2.68	33	33	3	3	0	218	187	76	65	75	150
1993—	Montreal (N.L.)	9	7	.563	3.23	28	28	2	0	0	183²/₃	163	84	66	74	90
—	Ottawa (I.L.)	0	0	...	0.00	1	1	0	0	0	4	1	0	0	1	0
1994—	Montreal (N.L.)	•16	5	.762	3.32	23	23	2	1	0	154²/₃	145	61	57	44	85
1995—	St. Louis (N.L.)■	6	7	.462	5.06	18	18	0	0	0	110¹/₃	125	71	62	45	50
—	Cleveland (A.L.)■	4	1	.800	3.98	12	11	1	0	0	74²/₃	77	36	33	32	48
1996—	Texas (A.L.)■	16	10	.615	3.63	35	35	7	•3	0	250²/₃	250	110	101	95	170
1997—	Texas (A.L.)	5	8	.385	5.19	19	19	0	0	0	111	129	69	64	56	68
—	Tulsa (Texas)	0	0	...	0.00	1	1	0	0	0	5	2	0	0	1	3
—	Anaheim (A.L.)■	4	4	.500	3.65	12	12	1	0	0	79	65	34	32	§39	38
1998—	Anaheim (A.L.)	9	6	.600	4.98	19	19	0	0	0	103	123	60	57	47	57
—	Cedar Rapids (Midw.)	0	0	...	1.23	2	2	0	0	0	7¹/₃	7	1	1	1	6
—	Lake Elsinore (Calif.)	0	0	...	6.75	1	1	0	0	0	4	5	4	3	5	2

H

Year League	W	L	Pct.	ERA	G	GS	CG	ShO	Sv.	IP	H	R	ER	BB	SO
1999— Anaheim (A.L.)	4	11	.267	4.77	26	22	0	0	0	128 1/3	129	72	68	76	76
2000— Anaheim (A.L.)	5	7	.417	6.52	16	16	0	0	0	78 2/3	102	59	57	53	50
— Lake Elsinore (Calif.)	0	0	...	0.00	1	1	0	0	0	4	5	2	0	1	3
— Edmonton (PCL)	0	0	...	6.52	2	2	0	0	0	9 2/3	14	8	7	8	5
— Charlotte (I.L.)■	0	0	...	4.50	1	1	0	0	0	4	6	2	2	0	7
— Chicago (A.L.)	0	1	.000	24.00	2	1	0	0	0	3	5	8	8	6	0
A.L. totals (6 years)	47	48	.495	4.56	141	135	9	3	0	828 1/3	880	448	420	404	507
N.L. totals (8 years)	70	60	.538	3.65	186	180	10	5	0	1137 1/3	1048	518	461	443	672
Major League totals (13 years)	117	108	.520	4.03	327	315	19	8	0	1965 2/3	1928	966	881	847	1179

DIVISION SERIES RECORD

Year League	W	L	Pct.	ERA	G	GS	CG	ShO	Sv.	IP	H	R	ER	BB	SO
1995— Cleveland (A.L.)	1	0	1.000	0.00	1	0	0	0	0	1 1/3	1	0	0	0	2
1996— Texas (A.L.)	0	0	...	4.50	1	1	0	0	0	6	5	3	3	3	1
Division series totals (2 years)	1	0	1.000	3.68	2	1	0	0	0	7 1/3	6	3	3	3	3

CHAMPIONSHIP SERIES RECORD

Year League	W	L	Pct.	ERA	G	GS	CG	ShO	Sv.	IP	H	R	ER	BB	SO
1995— Cleveland (A.L.)	1	0	1.000	0.00	1	1	0	0	0	7	5	0	0	3	6

WORLD SERIES RECORD

Year League	W	L	Pct.	ERA	G	GS	CG	ShO	Sv.	IP	H	R	ER	BB	SO
1995— Cleveland (A.L.)	0	1	.000	4.26	2	1	0	0	0	6 1/3	7	3	3	4	1

ALL-STAR GAME RECORD

Year League	W	L	Pct.	ERA	GS	CG	ShO	Sv.	IP	H	R	ER	BB	SO
1994— National	0	0	...	0.00	0	0	0	0	2	0	0	0	1	0

HINCH, A.J.　　　　　　　　　C　　　　　　　　　ROYALS

PERSONAL: Born May 15, 1974, in Waverly, Iowa. ... 6-1/207. ... Bats right, throws right. ... Full name: Andrew Jay Hinch.
HIGH SCHOOL: Midwest City (Okla.).
COLLEGE: Stanford.
TRANSACTIONS/CAREER NOTES: Selected by Chicago White Sox organization in second round of free-agent draft (June 2, 1992); did not sign. ... Selected by Minnesota Twins organization in third round of free-agent draft (June 1, 1995); did not sign. ... Selected by Oakland Athletics organization in third round of free-agent draft (June 4, 1996). ... On Modesto suspended list (June 7-9, 1997). ... Traded by A's with IF Angel Berroa and cash to Kansas City Royals as part of three-way deal in which Royals received P Roberto Hernandez from Tampa Bay Devil Rays, A's received P Cory Lidle from Devil Rays, A's received OF Johnny Damon, IF Mark Ellis and a player to be named later from Royals and Devil Rays received OF Ben Grieve and a player to be named later or cash from A's (January 8, 2001).
RECORDS: Shares major league single-season record for fewest double plays by catcher for leader—8 (1998).
STATISTICAL NOTES: Led California League catchers with .996 fielding percentage in 1997. ... Tied for A.L. lead in double plays by catcher with eight in 1998. ... Led Pacific Coast League catchers with .994 fielding percentage in 2000. ... Career major league grand slams: 1.
MISCELLANEOUS: Member of 1996 U.S. Olympic baseball team.

Year Team (League)	Pos.	G	AB	R	H	2B	3B	HR	RBI	Avg.	BB	SO	SB	PO	A	E	Avg.
1997— Modesto (Calif.)	C-DH-1B	95	333	70	103	25	3	20	73	.309	42	68	8	622	66	3	†.996
— Edmonton (PCL)	C-DH-OF	39	125	23	47	7	0	4	24	.376	20	13	2	201	7	3	.986
1998— Oakland (A.L.)	C	120	337	34	78	10	0	9	35	.231	30	89	3	602	47	•9	.986
1999— Oakland (A.L.)	C	76	205	26	44	4	1	7	24	.215	11	41	6	368	26	5	.987
— Vancouver (PCL)	C-DH	15	61	9	23	3	0	2	7	.377	3	12	1	83	3	1	.989
2000— Sacramento (PCL)	C-1B	109	417	65	111	23	2	6	47	.266	45	67	5	586	47	4	.994
— Oakland (A.L.)	C-DH	6	8	1	2	0	0	0	0	.250	1	1	0	9	0	1	.900
Major League totals (3 years)		202	550	61	124	14	1	16	59	.225	42	131	9	979	73	15	.986

HINCHLIFFE, BRETT　　　　　　　　　P　　　　　　　　　METS

PERSONAL: Born July 21, 1974, in Detroit. ... 6-5/190. ... Throws right, bats right.
HIGH SCHOOL: Bishop Gallagher (Harper Woods, Mich.).
TRANSACTIONS/CAREER NOTES: Selected by Seattle Mariners organization in 16th round of free-agent draft (June 1, 1992). ... On suspended list (April 21-25, 1999). ... Released by Mariners (January 3, 2000). ... Signed by Anaheim Angels organization (January 19, 2000). ... Traded by Angels with IF Keith Luuloa to Chicago Cubs for OF Chris Hatcher, P Mike Heathcott and SS Brett King (July 28, 2000). ... Granted free agency (October 18, 2000). ... Signed by New York Mets organization (December 5, 2000).
STATISTICAL NOTES: Pitched 12-0 no-hit victory against Cedar Rapids (June 28, 1994).

Year League	W	L	Pct.	ERA	G	GS	CG	ShO	Sv.	IP	H	R	ER	BB	SO
1992— Arizona Mariners (Ariz.)	5	4	.556	2.31	*24	0	0	0	3	35	42	17	9	9	26
1993— Arizona Mariners (Ariz.)	0	4	.000	5.08	10	9	0	0	0	44 1/3	55	32	25	5	29
1994— Appleton (Midw.)	11	7	.611	3.21	27	27	3	1	0	173 2/3	140	79	62	50	160
1995— Riverside (Calif.)	3	8	.273	6.61	15	15	0	0	0	77 2/3	110	69	57	35	68
1996— Lancaster (Calif.)	11	10	.524	4.24	27	26	0	0	0	163 1/3	179	105	77	64	146
1997— Memphis (Sou.)	10	10	.500	4.45	24	24	*5	1	0	145 2/3	159	81	72	45	107
1998— Lancaster (Calif.)	1	1	.500	1.59	3	3	0	0	0	17	8	5	3	5	14
— Tacoma (PCL)	10	8	.556	4.00	25	25	2	1	0	159 2/3	132	80	71	88	100
1999— Seattle (A.L.)	0	4	.000	8.80	11	4	0	0	0	30 2/3	41	31	30	21	14
— Tacoma (PCL)	9	7	.563	5.15	21	21	3	0	0	131	141	78	75	44	107
2000— Edmonton (PCL)■	2	3	.400	3.80	27	3	0	0	2	64	63	29	27	24	30
— Anaheim (A.L.)	0	0	...	5.40	2	0	0	0	0	1 2/3	1	1	1	1	0
— Iowa (PCL)■	2	0	1.000	2.81	7	4	1	1	0	32	32	10	10	8	22
Major League totals (2 years)	0	4	.000	8.63	13	4	0	0	0	32 1/3	42	32	31	22	14

H

HINSKE, ERIC — 3B/1B — CUBS

PERSONAL: Born August 5, 1977, in Neenah, Wisc. ... 6-2/225. ... Bats left, throws right. ... Full name: Eric Scott Hinske. ... Name pronounced hin-SKEE.
HIGH SCHOOL: Menasha (Wisc.).
COLLEGE: Arkansas.
TRANSACTIONS/CAREER NOTES: Selected by Chicago Cubs organization in 17th round of free-agent draft (June 2, 1998).
STATISTICAL NOTES: Led New York-Pennsylvania League first basemen with 612 total chances in 1998.

Year Team (League)	Pos.	G	AB	R	H	2B	3B	HR	RBI	Avg.	BB	SO	SB	PO	A	E	Avg.
1998— Williamsport (NY-P) ...	1B	68	248	46	74	20	0	9	57	.298	35	61	19	*561	*49	2	*.997
— Rockford (Midw.)	1B	6	20	8	9	4	0	1	4	.450	5	6	1	15	0	0	1.000
1999— Daytona (FSL)	3B-1B-OF	130	445	76	132	28	6	19	79	.297	62	90	16	458	140	22	.965
— Iowa (PCL)	1B-3B	4	15	3	4	0	1	1	2	.267	1	4	0	17	3	1	.952
2000— West Tenn (Sou.)	3B-1B-OF	131	436	76	113	21	9	20	73	.259	78	133	14	112	194	28	.916

HITCHCOCK, STERLING — P — PADRES

PERSONAL: Born April 29, 1971, in Fayetteville, N.C. ... 6-0/205. ... Throws left, bats left. ... Full name: Sterling Alex Hitchcock.
HIGH SCHOOL: Armwood (Seffner, Fla.).
TRANSACTIONS/CAREER NOTES: Selected by New York Yankees organization in ninth round of free-agent draft (June 5, 1989). ... On disabled list (June 26-August 14, 1991). ... On Columbus disabled list (May 23-July 21, 1993). ... Traded by Yankees with 3B Russ Davis to Seattle Mariners for 1B Tino Martinez, P Jeff Nelson and P Jim Mecir (December 7, 1995). ... Traded by Mariners to San Diego Padres for P Scott Sanders (December 6, 1996). ... On disabled list (June 6-July 3, 1997). ... On disabled list (May 27, 2000-remainder of season).
STATISTICAL NOTES: Pitched 1-0 no-hit victory against Sumter (July 16, 1990). ... Struck out 15 batters in one game (August 29, 1998). ... Tied for N.L. lead with 15 wild pitches in 1999.

Year League	W	L	Pct.	ERA	G	GS	CG	ShO	Sv.	IP	H	R	ER	BB	SO
1989— Gulf Coast Yankees (GCL)..	*9	1	.900	1.64	13	•13	0	0	0	76 2/3	48	16	14	27	*98
1990— Greensboro (S.Atl.)	12	12	.500	2.91	27	27	6	*5	0	173 1/3	122	68	56	60	*171
1991— Prince William (Caro.).......	7	7	.500	2.64	19	19	2	0	0	119 1/3	111	49	35	26	101
1992— Albany/Colonie (East.)........	6	9	.400	2.58	24	24	2	0	0	146 2/3	116	51	42	42	*155
— New York (A.L.).................	0	2	.000	8.31	3	3	0	0	0	13	23	12	12	6	6
1993— Columbus (I.L.)..............	3	5	.375	4.81	16	16	0	0	0	76 2/3	80	43	41	28	85
— New York (A.L.).................	1	2	.333	4.65	6	6	0	0	0	31	32	18	16	14	26
1994— New York (A.L.).................	4	1	.800	4.20	23	5	1	0	2	49 1/3	48	24	23	29	37
— Columbus (I.L.)..............	3	4	.429	4.32	10	9	1	0	0	50	53	30	24	18	47
— Albany/Colonie (East.)........	1	0	1.000	1.80	1	1	0	0	0	5	4	1	1	0	7
1995— New York (A.L.)..............	11	10	.524	4.70	27	27	4	1	0	168 1/3	155	91	88	68	121
1996— Seattle (A.L.)■.............	13	9	.591	5.35	35	35	0	0	0	196 2/3	245	131	117	73	132
1997— San Diego (N.L.)■	10	11	.476	5.20	32	28	1	0	0	161	172	102	93	55	106
1998— San Diego (N.L.)	9	7	.563	3.93	39	27	2	1	1	176 1/3	169	83	77	48	158
1999— San Diego (N.L.)	12	14	.462	4.11	33	33	1	0	0	205 2/3	202	99	94	76	194
2000— San Diego (N.L.)	1	6	.143	4.93	11	11	0	0	0	65 2/3	69	38	36	26	61
A.L. totals (5 years)	29	24	.547	5.03	94	76	5	1	2	458 1/3	503	276	256	190	322
N.L. totals (4 years)	32	38	.457	4.44	115	99	4	1	1	608 2/3	612	322	300	205	519
Major League totals (9 years).......	61	62	.496	4.69	209	175	9	2	3	1067	1115	598	556	395	841

DIVISION SERIES RECORD

Year League	W	L	Pct.	ERA	G	GS	CG	ShO	Sv.	IP	H	R	ER	BB	SO
1995— New York (A.L.)	0	0	...	5.40	2	0	0	0	0	1 2/3	2	2	1	2	1
1998— San Diego (N.L.)	1	0	1.000	1.50	1	1	0	0	0	6	3	1	1	0	11
Division series totals (2 years)	1	0	1.000	2.35	3	1	0	0	0	7 2/3	5	3	2	2	12

CHAMPIONSHIP SERIES RECORD

RECORDS: Shares single-inning record for most wild pitches—2 (October 14, 1998, second inning).
NOTES: Named N.L. Championship Series Most Valuable Player (1998).

Year League	W	L	Pct.	ERA	G	GS	CG	ShO	Sv.	IP	H	R	ER	BB	SO
1998— San Diego (N.L.)	2	0	1.000	0.90	2	2	0	0	0	10	5	1	1	8	14

WORLD SERIES RECORD

Year League	W	L	Pct.	ERA	G	GS	CG	ShO	Sv.	IP	H	R	ER	BB	SO
1998— San Diego (N.L.)	0	0	...	1.50	1	1	0	0	0	6	7	2	1	1	7

HOCKING, DENNY — IF — TWINS

PERSONAL: Born April 2, 1970, in Torrance, Calif. ... 5-10/183. ... Bats both, throws right. ... Full name: Dennis Lee Hocking.
HIGH SCHOOL: West Torrance (Calif.).
COLLEGE: El Camino College (Calif.).
TRANSACTIONS/CAREER NOTES: Selected by Minnesota Twins organization in 52nd round of free-agent draft (June 5, 1989). ... On Nashville disabled list (April 8-29, 1993). ... On Minnesota disabled list (March 22-April 30, May 30-June 29 and July 31-September 8, 1996); included rehabilitation assignments to Salt Lake (April 4-30, June 21-29 and August 24-September 8).
STATISTICAL NOTES: Led California League shortstops with 721 total chances in 1992. ... Led Pacific Coast League shortstops with .966 fielding percentage and 390 assists in 1995. ... Career major league grand slams: 1.

Year Team (League)	Pos.	G	AB	R	H	2B	3B	HR	RBI	Avg.	BB	SO	SB	PO	A	E	Avg.
1990— Elizabethton (Appl.)....	SS-2B-3B	54	201	45	59	6	2	6	30	.294	40	26	14	77	179	20	.928
1991— Kenosha (Midw.)........	SS	125	432	72	110	17	8	2	36	.255	77	69	22	193	308	42	.923
1992— Visalia (Calif.)	SS	135	*550	117	*182	34	9	7	81	.331	72	77	38	214	*469	38	.947

H

								BATTING								FIELDING		
Year	Team (League)	Pos.	G	AB	R	H	2B	3B	HR	RBI	Avg.	BB	SO	SB	PO	A	E	Avg.
1993—	Nashville (Sou.)	SS-DH-2B	107	409	54	109	9	4	8	50	.267	34	66	15	144	300	30	.937
—	Minnesota (A.L.)	SS-2B	15	36	7	5	1	0	0	0	.139	6	8	1	19	23	1	.977
1994—	Salt Lake (PCL)	SS	112	394	61	110	14	6	5	57	.279	28	57	13	143	342	26	.949
—	Minnesota (A.L.)	SS	11	31	3	10	3	0	0	2	.323	0	4	2	11	27	0	1.000
1995—	Salt Lake (PCL)	SS-DH-2B	117	397	51	112	24	2	8	75	.282	25	41	12	173	†393	20	†.966
—	Minnesota (A.L.)	SS	9	25	4	5	0	2	0	3	.200	2	2	1	13	20	1	.971
1996—	Minnesota (A.L.)	O-S-2-DH-1	49	127	16	25	6	0	1	10	.197	8	24	3	67	9	1	.987
—	Salt Lake (PCL)	S-O-D-1-2-3	37	130	18	36	6	2	3	22	.277	10	17	2	51	69	3	.976
1997—	Minnesota (A.L.)	S-3-O-2-D-1	115	253	28	65	12	4	2	25	.257	18	51	3	124	146	4	.985
1998—	Minnesota (A.L.)	2-S-O-3-D-1	110	198	32	40	6	1	3	15	.202	16	44	2	118	102	4	.982
1999—	Minnesota (A.L.)	S-2-O-3-1	136	386	47	103	18	2	7	41	.267	22	54	11	193	190	3	.992
2000—	Minnesota (A.L.)	O-2-3-S-1-D	134	373	52	111	24	4	4	47	.298	48	77	7	183	143	5	.985
Major League totals (8 years)			579	1429	189	364	70	13	17	143	.255	120	264	30	728	660	19	.986

HODGES, KEVIN — P — MARINERS

PERSONAL: Born June 24, 1973, in Houston. ... 6-4/200. ... Throws right, bats right. ... Full name: Kevin Jon Hodges.
HIGH SCHOOL: Klein Oak (Spring, Texas).
TRANSACTIONS/CAREER NOTES: Selected by Kansas City Royals organization in eighth round of free-agent draft (June 3, 1991). ... Granted free agency (October 17, 1997). ... Signed by Houston Astros organization (March 31, 1998). ... Traded by Astros to Seattle Mariners for OF Matt Mieske (June 20, 1999).

Year	League	W	L	Pct.	ERA	G	GS	CG	ShO	Sv.	IP	H	R	ER	BB	SO
1991—	Gulf Coast Royals (GCL)	1	2	.333	4.30	9	3	0	0	0	23	22	14	11	11	13
1992—	Gulf Coast Royals (GCL)	5	3	.625	4.71	11	9	0	0	0	49²/₃	60	30	26	25	24
1993—	Gulf Coast Royals (GCL)	7	2	.778	2.03	12	10	0	0	0	71	52	25	16	25	40
—	Wilmington (Caro.)	1	1	.500	0.00	3	0	0	0	0	4²/₃	2	0	0	3	1
1994—	Rockford (Midw.)	9	6	.600	3.38	24	17	2	1	3	114¹/₃	96	53	43	35	83
1995—	Wilmington (Caro.)	2	3	.400	4.53	12	10	0	0	0	53²/₃	53	31	27	25	27
1996—	Lansing (Midw.)	1	2	.333	4.66	9	9	0	0	0	48¹/₃	47	32	25	19	23
1997—	Wilmington (Caro.)	8	11	.421	4.48	28	20	0	0	1	124²/₃	150	78	62	44	63
1998—	Jackson (Texas)■	4	5	.444	3.61	29	15	0	0	0	107¹/₃	108	55	43	38	70
1999—	Jackson (Texas)	1	4	.200	2.94	8	8	0	0	0	49	48	22	16	16	21
—	New Orleans (PCL)	1	3	.250	7.24	5	5	0	0	0	27¹/₃	34	23	22	11	16
—	Tacoma (PCL)■	3	3	.500	3.25	14	12	0	0	1	83	88	31	30	27	42
2000—	Tacoma (PCL)	4	3	.571	2.76	30	11	2	1	3	98	87	32	30	21	73
—	Seattle (A.L.)	0	0	...	5.19	13	0	0	0	0	17¹/₃	18	10	10	12	7
Major League totals (1 year)		0	0	...	5.19	13	0	0	0	0	17¹/₃	18	10	10	12	7

HOFFMAN, TREVOR — P — PADRES

PERSONAL: Born October 13, 1967, in Bellflower, Calif. ... 6-0/215. ... Throws right, bats right. ... Full name: Trevor William Hoffman. ... Brother of Glenn Hoffman, assistant coach, Los Angeles Dodgers; and infielder with Boston Red Sox (1980-87), Los Angeles Dodgers (1987) and California Angels (1989).
HIGH SCHOOL: Savanna (Anaheim).
JUNIOR COLLEGE: Cypress (Calif.) College.
COLLEGE: Arizona.
TRANSACTIONS/CAREER NOTES: Selected by Cincinnati Reds organization in 11th round of free-agent draft (June 5, 1989). ... Selected by Florida Marlins in first round (eighth pick overall) of expansion draft (November 17, 1992). ... Traded by Marlins with P Jose Martinez and P Andres Berumen to San Diego Padres for 3B Gary Sheffield and P Rich Rodriguez (June 24, 1993).
RECORDS: Shares N.L. single-season record for most saves—53 (1998).
HONORS: Named N.L. Fireman of the Year by THE SPORTING NEWS (1996 and 1998).
STATISTICAL NOTES: Tied for N.L. lead with 13 intentional bases on balls issued in 1993.
MISCELLANEOUS: Holds San Diego Padres all-time record for most games pitched (481) and saves (269).

Year	League	W	L	Pct.	ERA	G	GS	CG	ShO	Sv.	IP	H	R	ER	BB	SO
1991—	Cedar Rapids (Midw.)	1	1	.500	1.87	27	0	0	0	12	33²/₃	22	8	7	13	52
—	Chattanooga (Sou.)	1	0	1.000	1.93	14	0	0	0	8	14	10	4	3	7	23
1992—	Chattanooga (Sou.)	3	0	1.000	1.52	6	6	0	0	0	29²/₃	22	6	5	11	31
—	Nashville (A.A.)	4	6	.400	4.27	42	5	0	0	6	65¹/₃	57	32	31	32	63
1993—	Florida (N.L.)■	2	2	.500	3.28	28	0	0	0	2	35²/₃	24	13	13	19	26
—	San Diego (N.L.)■	2	4	.333	4.31	39	0	0	0	3	54¹/₃	56	30	26	20	53
1994—	San Diego (N.L.)	4	4	.500	2.57	47	0	0	0	20	56	39	16	16	20	68
1995—	San Diego (N.L.)	7	4	.636	3.88	55	0	0	0	31	53¹/₃	48	25	23	14	52
1996—	San Diego (N.L.)	9	5	.643	2.25	70	0	0	0	42	88	50	23	22	31	111
1997—	San Diego (N.L.)	6	4	.600	2.66	70	0	0	0	37	81¹/₃	59	25	24	24	111
1998—	San Diego (N.L.)	4	2	.667	1.48	66	0	0	0	*53	73	41	12	12	21	86
1999—	San Diego (N.L.)	2	3	.400	2.14	64	0	0	0	40	67¹/₃	48	23	16	15	73
2000—	San Diego (N.L.)	4	7	.364	2.99	70	0	0	0	43	72¹/₃	61	29	24	11	85
Major League totals (8 years)		40	35	.533	2.72	509	0	0	0	271	581¹/₃	426	196	176	175	665

DIVISION SERIES RECORD

Year	League	W	L	Pct.	ERA	G	GS	CG	ShO	Sv.	IP	H	R	ER	BB	SO
1996—	San Diego (N.L.)	0	1	.000	10.80	2	0	0	0	0	1²/₃	3	2	2	1	2
1998—	San Diego (N.L.)	0	0	...	0.00	4	0	0	0	2	3	3	1	0	1	4
Division series totals (2 years)		0	1	.000	3.86	6	0	0	0	2	4²/₃	6	3	2	2	6

CHAMPIONSHIP SERIES RECORD

Year	League	W	L	Pct.	ERA	G	GS	CG	ShO	Sv.	IP	H	R	ER	BB	SO
1998—	San Diego (N.L.)	1	0	1.000	2.08	3	0	0	0	1	4¹/₃	2	1	1	2	7

H

WORLD SERIES RECORD

Year	League	W	L	Pct.	ERA	G	GS	CG	ShO	Sv.	IP	H	R	ER	BB	SO
1998—San Diego (N.L.)		0	1	.000	9.00	1	0	0	0	0	2	2	2	2	1	0

ALL-STAR GAME RECORD

Year	League	W	L	Pct.	ERA	GS	CG	ShO	Sv.	IP	H	R	ER	BB	SO
1998—National	0	0	...	9.00	0	0	0	0	1	1	1	1	0	1
1999—National	0	0	...	0.00	0	0	0	0	1/3	0	0	0	0	1
2000—National	0	0	...	27.00	0	0	0	0	1	3	3	3	0	2
All-Star Game totals (3 years)	0	0	...	15.43	0	0	0	0	2 1/3	4	4	4	0	4

RECORD AS POSITION PLAYER

						BATTING								FIELDING		
Year	Team (League)	Pos.	G	AB	R	H	2B	3B	HR	RBI	Avg.	BB	SO	SB	PO	A	E	Avg.
1989—Billings (Pio.)	SS	61	201	22	50	5	0	1	20	.249	19	40	1	*116	140	•25	.911
1990—Char., W.Va. (SAL)......	SS-3B	103	278	41	59	10	1	2	23	.212	38	53	3	114	209	30	.915

HOLBERT, RAY   IF   DEVIL RAYS

PERSONAL: Born September 25, 1970, in Torrance, Calif. ... 6-0/185. ... Bats right, throws right. ... Full name: Ray Arthur Holbert III. ... Brother of Aaron Holbert, minor league shortstop (1990-99).

HIGH SCHOOL: David Starr Jordan (Long Beach, Calif.).

TRANSACTIONS/CAREER NOTES: Selected by San Diego Padres organization in third round of free-agent draft (June 1, 1988). ... On disabled list (July 7-28, 1992). ... On San Diego disabled list (July 30, 1995-remainder of season). ... Traded by Padres to Houston Astros for P Pedro A. Martinez (October 10, 1995). ... Granted free agency (October 15, 1996). ... Signed by Detroit Tigers organization (December 15, 1996). ... Granted free agency (October 15, 1997). ... Signed by Atlanta Braves organization (January 13, 1998). ... Released by Braves (May 13, 1998). ... Signed by Montreal Expos organization (May 18, 1998). ... Granted free agency (October 15, 1998). ... Signed by Kansas City Royals organization (December 17, 1998). ... On Omaha disabled list (May 8-July 4, 1999); included rehabilitation assignment to Gulf Coast Royals (June 29-July 4). ... Granted free agency (October 2, 2000). ... Signed by Tampa Bay Devil Rays organization (November 22, 2000).

STATISTICAL NOTES: Led Arizona League shortstops with .927 fielding percentage and 132 assists in 1988. ... Led Midwest League shortstops with 642 total chances and 75 double plays in 1990. ... Led Texas League with nine sacrifice flies in 1993. ... Led Pacific Coast League with 10 sacrifice hits in 1994. ... Led Pacific Coast League shortstops with 34 errors in 1994. ... Led International League shortstops with 183 putouts in 1997. ... Career major league grand slams: 1.

						BATTING								FIELDING		
Year	Team (League)	Pos.	G	AB	R	H	2B	3B	HR	RBI	Avg.	BB	SO	SB	PO	A	E	Avg.
1988—Ariz. Padres (Ariz.)	SS-3B	49	170	38	44	1	0	3	19	.259	38	32	20	59	†137	15	†.929
1989—Waterloo (Midw.)	SS-3B	117	354	37	55	7	1	0	20	.155	41	99	13	205	303	32	.941
1990—Waterloo (Midw.)	SS	133	411	51	84	10	1	3	39	.204	51	117	16	*233	*378	31	.952
1991—High Desert (Calif.)	SS	122	386	76	102	14	2	4	51	.264	56	83	19	196	331	*37	.934
1992—Wichita (Texas)	SS	95	304	46	86	7	3	2	23	.283	42	68	26	150	217	17	.956
1993—Wichita (Texas)	SS	112	388	56	101	13	5	5	48	.260	54	87	30	155	267	30	.934
1994—Las Vegas (PCL)	SS-OF	118	426	68	128	21	5	8	52	.300	50	99	27	157	333	†34	.935
—San Diego (N.L.)	SS	5	5	1	1	0	0	0	0	.200	0	4	0	0	0	0	...
1995—San Diego (N.L.)	SS-2B-OF	63	73	11	13	2	1	2	5	.178	8	20	4	27	58	5	.944
—Las Vegas (PCL)	2B	9	26	3	3	1	0	0	3	.115	5	10	1	9	26	1	.972
1996—Tucson (PCL)■............	SS	28	97	13	24	3	2	0	10	.247	7	19	4	37	65	9	.919
1997—Toledo (I.L.)■............	SS-3B	109	372	43	90	18	7	7	37	.242	32	109	16	†187	302	25	.951
1998—Richmond (I.L.)■.......	SS	1	1	1	0	0	0	0	0	.000	2	1	0	2	3	1	.833
—Atlanta (N.L.).............	SS	8	15	2	2	0	0	0	1	.133	2	4	0	6	14	1	.952
—Ottawa (I.L.)■............	SS-3B-2B	86	266	38	82	17	4	2	25	.308	29	66	10	133	207	11	.969
—Montreal (N.L.)...........	2B	2	5	0	0	0	0	0	0	.000	0	1	0	2	3	0	1.000
1999—Omaha (PCL)■	SS-2B	33	128	26	38	4	0	4	12	.297	12	35	13	51	72	4	.969
—GC Royals (GCL)	SS-DH	5	16	5	3	2	0	0	1	.188	1	4	1	7	7	0	1.000
—Kansas City (A.L.)	SS-2B-3B	34	100	14	28	3	0	0	5	.280	8	20	7	45	76	2	.984
2000—Omaha (PCL)...........	SS-2B-3B	94	338	41	86	12	1	2	40	.254	35	49	14	108	227	21	.941
—Kansas City (A.L.)	2B-3B-SS	3	4	0	1	0	0	0	0	.250	0	2	0	4	2	0	1.000
American League totals (2 years)		37	104	14	29	3	0	0	5	.279	8	22	7	49	78	2	.984
National League totals (3 years)		78	98	14	16	2	1	2	6	.163	10	29	4	35	75	6	.948
Major League totals (5 years)		115	202	28	45	5	1	2	11	.223	18	51	11	84	153	8	.967

HOLLANDSWORTH, TODD   OF   ROCKIES

PERSONAL: Born April 20, 1973, in Dayton, Ohio. ... 6-2/215. ... Bats left, throws left. ... Full name: Todd Mathew Hollandsworth.

HIGH SCHOOL: Newport (Bellevue, Wash.).

TRANSACTIONS/CAREER NOTES: Selected by Los Angeles Dodgers organization in third round of free-agent draft (June 3, 1991); pick received as part of compensation for Kansas City Royals signing Type B free-agent OF/DH Kirk Gibson. ... On Los Angeles disabled list (May 3-July 7 and August 9-September 12, 1995); included rehabilitation assignments to San Bernardino (June 6-7) and Albuquerque (June 27-July 7). ... On Los Angeles disabled list (August 2-16 and August 17-September 6, 1997); included rehabilitation assignment to San Bernardino (August 15-17). ... On disabled list (June 5, 1998-remainder of season). ... On Los Angeles disabled list (April 3-23 and June 4-19, 1999); included rehabilitation assignments to San Bernardino (April 20-23 and June 18-19). ... Traded by Dodgers with OF Kevin Gibbs and P Randey Dorame to Colorado Rockies for OF Tom Goodwin and cash (July 31, 2000). ... Granted free agency (October 27, 2000). ... Re-signed by Rockies (November 16, 2000).

HONORS: Named N.L. Rookie of the Year by Baseball Writers' Association of America (1996).

STATISTICAL NOTES: Career major league grand slams: 1.

						BATTING								FIELDING		
Year	Team (League)	Pos.	G	AB	R	H	2B	3B	HR	RBI	Avg.	BB	SO	SB	PO	A	E	Avg.
1991—Yakima (N'West)	OF	56	203	34	48	5	1	8	33	.236	27	57	11	106	1	7	.939
1992—Bakersfield (Calif.)......	OF	119	430	70	111	23	5	13	58	.258	50	113	27	230	8	6	.975
1993—San Antonio (Texas)...	OF	126	474	57	119	24	9	17	63	.251	29	101	24	246	13	12	.956

H

Year	Team (League)	Pos.	G	AB	R	H	2B	3B	HR	RBI	Avg.	BB	SO	SB	PO	A	E	Avg.
											BATTING					FIELDING		
1994—	Albuquerque (PCL)	OF	132	505	80	144	31	5	19	91	.285	46	96	15	237	5	13	.949
1995—	Los Angeles (N.L.)	OF	41	103	16	24	2	0	5	13	.233	10	29	2	60	1	4	.938
	San Bern. (Calif.)	OF	1	2	0	1	0	0	0	0	.500	0	1	0	0	0	0	...
	Albuquerque (PCL)	OF	10	38	9	9	2	0	2	4	.237	6	8	1	19	3	0	1.000
1996—	Los Angeles (N.L.)	OF	149	478	64	139	26	4	12	59	.291	41	93	21	217	7	5	.978
1997—	Los Angeles (N.L.)	OF	106	296	39	73	20	2	4	31	.247	17	60	5	185	2	3	.984
	Albuquerque (PCL)	OF	13	56	13	24	4	3	1	14	.429	4	4	2	32	1	0	1.000
	San Bern. (Calif.)	OF	2	8	1	2	0	1	0	2	.250	1	2	0	2	1	0	1.000
1998—	Los Angeles (N.L.)	OF	55	175	23	47	6	4	3	20	.269	9	42	4	87	1	4	.957
1999—	San Bern. (Calif.)	OF	4	13	3	5	2	0	0	3	.385	2	4	0	3	1	0	1.000
	Los Angeles (N.L.)	OF-1B	92	261	39	74	12	2	9	32	.284	24	61	5	211	11	3	.987
2000—	Los Angeles (N.L.)	OF	81	261	42	61	12	0	8	24	.234	30	61	11	143	6	2	.987
	Colorado (N.L.)■	OF	56	167	39	54	8	0	11	23	.323	11	38	7	74	6	1	.988
Major League totals (6 years)			580	1741	262	472	86	12	52	202	.271	142	384	55	977	34	22	.979

DIVISION SERIES RECORD

Year	Team (League)	Pos.	G	AB	R	H	2B	3B	HR	RBI	Avg.	BB	SO	SB	PO	A	E	Avg.
											BATTING					FIELDING		
1995—	Los Angeles (N.L.)	OF-PH	2	2	0	0	0	0	0	0	.000	0	0	0	0	0	0	...
1996—	Los Angeles (N.L.)	OF	3	12	1	4	3	0	0	1	.333	0	3	0	4	0	0	1.000
Division series totals (2 years)			5	14	1	4	3	0	0	1	.286	0	3	0	4	0	0	1.000

HOLMES, DARREN   P

PERSONAL: Born April 25, 1966, in Asheville, N.C. ... 6-0/202. ... Throws right, bats right. ... Full name: Darren Lee Holmes.

HIGH SCHOOL: T.C. Roberson (Asheville, N.C.).

TRANSACTIONS/CAREER NOTES: Selected by Los Angeles Dodgers organization in 16th round of free-agent draft (June 4, 1984). ... On disabled list (June 5, 1986-remainder of season). ... Loaned by Dodgers organization to San Luis Potosi of the Mexican League (1988). ... Traded by Dodgers to Milwaukee Brewers for C Bert Heffernan (December 20, 1990). ... On Milwaukee disabled list (July 3-18, 1991); included rehabilitation assignment to Beloit (July 13-18). ... Selected by Colorado Rockies in first round (fifth pick overall) of expansion draft (November 17, 1992). ... On Colorado disabled list (May 30-June 24 and July 21-August 11, 1994); included rehabilitation assignments to Asheville (June 14-19) and Colorado Springs (June 20). ... On disabled list (April 30-May 15, 1997). ... Granted free agency (October 27, 1997). ... Signed by New York Yankees (December 22, 1997). ... On New York disabled list (July 30-September 4, 1998); included rehabilitation assignment to Tampa (August 31-September 4). ... Traded by Yankees with cash to Arizona Diamondbacks for C Izzy Molina and P Ben Ford (March 30, 1999). ... On Arizona disabled list (June 24-July 15 and July 18-August 11, 1999); included rehabilitation assignments to Arizona League Diamondbacks (August 3-8) and Tucson (August 9-11). ... Released by Diamondbacks (April 28, 2000). ... Signed by St. Louis Cardinals organization (May 4, 2000). ... Traded by Cardinals to Baltimore Orioles for future considerations (June 28, 2000). ... Released by Orioles (July 19, 2000). ... Signed by Diamondbacks organization (August 11, 2000). ... Granted free agency (October 13, 2000).

Year	League	W	L	Pct.	ERA	G	GS	CG	ShO	Sv.	IP	H	R	ER	BB	SO
1984—	Great Falls (Pio.)	2	5	.286	6.65	18	6	1	0	0	44 2/3	53	41	33	30	29
1985—	Vero Beach (FSL)	4	3	.571	3.11	33	0	0	0	2	63 2/3	57	31	22	35	46
1986—	Vero Beach (FSL)	3	6	.333	2.92	11	10	0	0	0	64 2/3	55	30	21	39	59
1987—	Vero Beach (FSL)	6	4	.600	4.52	19	19	1	0	0	99 2/3	111	60	50	53	46
1988—	San Luis Potosi (Mex.)■	9	9	.500	4.64	23	23	7	1	0	139 2/3	151	88	72	92	110
	Albuquerque (PCL)■	0	1	.000	5.06	2	1	0	0	0	5 1/3	6	3	3	1	1
1989—	San Antonio (Texas)	5	8	.385	3.83	17	16	3	2	1	110 1/3	102	59	47	44	81
	Albuquerque (PCL)	1	4	.200	7.45	9	8	0	0	0	38 2/3	50	32	32	18	31
1990—	Albuquerque (PCL)	12	2	*.857	3.11	56	0	0	0	13	92 2/3	78	34	32	39	99
	Los Angeles (N.L.)	0	1	.000	5.19	14	0	0	0	0	17 1/3	15	10	10	11	19
1991—	Denver (A.A.)■	0	0	...	9.00	1	0	0	0	0	1	1	1	1	2	2
	Milwaukee (A.L.)	1	4	.200	4.72	40	0	0	0	3	76 1/3	90	43	40	27	59
	Beloit (Midw.)	0	0	...	0.00	2	0	0	0	2	2	0	0	0	0	3
1992—	Denver (A.A.)	0	0	...	1.38	12	0	0	0	7	13	7	2	2	1	12
	Milwaukee (A.L.)	4	4	.500	2.55	41	0	0	0	6	42 1/3	35	12	12	11	31
1993—	Colorado (N.L.)■	3	3	.500	4.05	62	0	0	0	25	66 2/3	56	31	30	20	60
	Colo. Springs (PCL)	1	0	1.000	0.00	3	2	0	0	0	8 2/3	1	1	0	1	9
1994—	Colorado (N.L.)	0	3	.000	6.35	29	0	0	0	3	28 1/3	35	25	20	24	33
	Colo. Springs (PCL)	0	1	.000	8.22	4	2	0	0	0	7 2/3	11	7	7	3	12
	Asheville (S.Atl.)	0	0	...	0.00	2	1	0	0	0	3	1	0	0	0	7
1995—	Colorado (N.L.)	6	1	.857	3.24	68	0	0	0	14	66 2/3	59	26	24	28	61
1996—	Colorado (N.L.)	5	4	.556	3.97	62	0	0	0	1	77	78	41	34	28	73
1997—	Colorado (N.L.)	9	2	.818	5.34	42	6	0	0	3	89 1/3	113	58	53	36	70
1998—	New York (A.L.)■	0	3	.000	3.33	34	0	0	0	2	51 1/3	53	19	19	14	31
	Tampa (FSL)	0	0	...	4.50	2	1	0	0	0	2	4	2	1	0	6
1999—	Arizona (N.L.)■	4	3	.571	3.70	44	0	0	0	0	48 2/3	50	21	20	25	35
	Ariz. Diamondbacks (Ariz.)	0	0	...	0.00	2	2	0	0	0	2 2/3	1	0	0	0	4
	Tucson (PCL)	0	0	...	0.00	1	1	0	0	0	1	0	0	0	1	0
2000—	Arizona (N.L.)	0	0	...	8.53	8	0	0	0	0	6 1/3	12	6	6	1	5
	Tucson (PCL)	1	0	.500	2.08	3	0	0	0	1	4 1/3	4	1	1	4	2
	St. Louis (N.L.)■	0	1	.000	9.72	5	0	0	0	0	8 1/3	12	9	9	3	5
	Memphis (PCL)	0	0	...	2.45	9	0	0	0	0	14 2/3	10	4	4	3	8
	Baltimore (A.L.)■	0	0	...	25.07	5	0	0	0	0	4 2/3	13	13	13	5	6
A.L. totals (4 years)		5	11	.313	4.33	120	0	0	0	11	174 2/3	191	87	84	57	127
N.L. totals (8 years)		27	18	.600	4.54	334	6	0	0	47	408 2/3	430	227	206	176	361
Major League totals (11 years)		32	29	.525	4.47	454	6	0	0	58	583 1/3	621	314	290	233	488

DIVISION SERIES RECORD

Year	League	W	L	Pct.	ERA	G	GS	CG	ShO	Sv.	IP	H	R	ER	BB	SO
1995—	Colorado (N.L.)	1	0	1.000	0.00	3	0	0	0	0	1 2/3	6	2	0	9	2
1998—	New York (A.L.)							Did not play.								
1999—	Arizona (N.L.)	0	0	...	27.00	1	0	0	0	0	1 1/3	1	4	4	3	0
Division series totals (2 years)		1	0	1.000	12.00	4	0	0	0	0	3	7	6	4	12	2

CHAMPIONSHIP SERIES RECORD

Year League	W	L	Pct.	ERA	G	GS	CG	ShO	Sv.	IP	H	R	ER	BB	SO
1998— New York (A.L.).................							Did not play.								

WORLD SERIES RECORD

NOTES: Member of World Series championship team (1998).

Year League	W	L	Pct.	ERA	G	GS	CG	ShO	Sv.	IP	H	R	ER	BB	SO
1998— New York (A.L.).................							Did not play.								

HOLT, CHRIS   P   TIGERS

PERSONAL: Born September 18, 1971, in Dallas. ... 6-4/205. ... Throws right, bats right. ... Full name: Christopher Michael Holt.
HIGH SCHOOL: Skyline (Dallas).
JUNIOR COLLEGE: Navarro College (Texas).
TRANSACTIONS/CAREER NOTES: Selected by Houston Astros organization in third round of free-agent draft (June 1, 1992). ... On Houston disabled list (March 30, 1998-entire season); included rehabilitation assignment to Kissimmee (April 25-26). ... Traded by Astros with C Mitch Meluskey and OF Roger Cedeno to Detroit Tigers for C Brad Ausmus, P Doug Brocail and P Nelson Cruz (December 11, 2000).
STATISTICAL NOTES: Pitched 7-0 one-hit, complete-game victory against Milwaukee (April 28, 2000).

Year League	W	L	Pct.	ERA	G	GS	CG	ShO	Sv.	IP	H	R	ER	BB	SO
1992— Auburn (NY-Penn).............	2	5	.286	4.45	14	14	0	0	0	83	75	48	41	24	81
1993— Quad City (Midw.)	11	10	.524	2.27	26	26	*10	•3	0	*186 1/3	162	70	47	54	176
1994— Jackson (Texas)	10	9	.526	3.45	26	25	5	•2	0	167	169	78	64	22	111
1995— Jackson (Texas)	2	2	.500	1.67	5	5	1	1	0	32 1/3	27	8	6	5	24
— Tucson (PCL)	5	8	.385	4.10	20	19	0	0	0	118 2/3	155	65	54	32	69
1996— Tucson (PCL)	9	6	.600	3.62	28	27	4	1	0	*186 1/3	208	87	75	38	137
— Houston (N.L.)	0	1	.000	5.79	4	0	0	0	0	4 2/3	5	3	3	3	0
1997— Houston (N.L.)	8	12	.400	3.52	33	32	0	0	0	209 2/3	211	98	82	61	95
1998— Kissimmee (FSL)	0	1	.000	9.00	1	1	0	0	0	4	6	4	4	4	1
1999— Houston (N.L.)	5	13	.278	4.66	32	26	0	0	1	164	193	92	85	57	115
2000— Houston (N.L.)	8	16	.333	5.35	34	32	3	1	0	207	247	131	123	75	136
Major League totals (4 years).......	21	42	.333	4.51	103	90	3	1	1	585 1/3	656	324	293	196	346

DIVISION SERIES RECORD

Year League	W	L	Pct.	ERA	G	GS	CG	ShO	Sv.	IP	H	R	ER	BB	SO
1999— Houston (N.L.)	0	0	...	...	1	0	0	0	0	3	3	3	3	0	0

HOLTZ, MIKE   P   ANGELS

PERSONAL: Born October 10, 1972, in Arlington, Va. ... 5-9/188. ... Throws left, bats left. ... Full name: Michael James Holtz.
HIGH SCHOOL: Central Cambria (Ebensburg, Pa.).
COLLEGE: Clemson.
TRANSACTIONS/CAREER NOTES: Selected by California Angels organization in 17th round of free-agent draft (June 2, 1994). ... Angels franchise renamed Anaheim Angels for 1997 season. ... On suspended list (June 18-20, 1998). ... On Anaheim disabled list (August 25-September 10, 1999).

Year League	W	L	Pct.	ERA	G	GS	CG	ShO	Sv.	IP	H	R	ER	BB	SO
1994— Boise (N'West)	0	0	...	0.51	22	0	0	0	11	35	22	4	2	11	59
1995— Lake Elsinore (Calif.)	4	4	.500	2.29	*56	0	0	0	3	82 2/3	70	26	21	23	101
1996— Midland (Texas)................	1	2	.333	4.17	33	0	0	0	2	41	52	34	19	9	41
— California (A.L.)	3	3	.500	2.45	30	0	0	0	0	29 1/3	21	11	8	19	31
1997— Anaheim (A.L.)	3	4	.429	3.32	66	0	0	0	2	43 1/3	38	21	16	15	40
1998— Anaheim (A.L.)	2	2	.500	4.75	53	0	0	0	1	30 1/3	38	16	16	15	29
— Vancouver (PCL)	0	0	...	1.74	10	0	0	0	2	10 1/3	10	4	2	6	18
1999— Anaheim (A.L.)	2	3	.400	8.06	28	0	0	0	0	22 1/3	26	20	20	15	17
— Edmonton (PCL)	2	1	.667	2.30	20	0	0	0	1	27 1/3	20	7	7	11	39
2000— Edmonton (PCL)	0	1	.000	10.80	6	0	0	0	0	5	5	6	6	1	1
— Anaheim (A.L.)	3	3	.500	5.05	61	0	0	0	0	41	37	26	23	18	40
Major League totals (5 years).......	13	15	.464	4.49	238	0	0	0	3	166 1/3	160	94	83	82	157

HOLZEMER, MARK   P   PHILLIES

PERSONAL: Born August 20, 1969, in Littleton, Colo. ... 6-0/165. ... Throws left, bats left. ... Full name: Mark Harold Holzemer. ... Name pronounced HOLE-zeh-mer.
HIGH SCHOOL: J.K. Mullen (Denver).
JUNIOR COLLEGE: Seminole (Okla.) Junior College.
TRANSACTIONS/CAREER NOTES: Selected by California Angels organization in fourth round of free-agent draft (June 2, 1987). ... On Midland disabled list (July 2-September 18, 1990; April 12-May 25 and June 7-26, 1991). ... On California disabled list (June 10-September 1, 1996); included rehabilitation assignment to Lake Elsinore (August 16-September 1). ... Granted free agency (October 15, 1996). ... Signed by Seattle Mariners organization (December 11, 1996). ... Granted free agency (October 16, 1997). ... Signed by Oakland Athletics organization (December 9, 1997). ... Released by Athletics (March 31, 1999). ... Signed by Colorado Rockies organization (May 10, 1999). ... Granted free agency (October 15, 1999). ... Signed by Philadelphia Phillies organization (November 15, 1999). ... On Philadelphia disabled list (July 3-18, 2000); included rehabilitation assignment to Reading (July 3-18).
STATISTICAL NOTES: Led Pacific Coast League with 15 wild pitches in 1994.

Year League	W	L	Pct.	ERA	G	GS	CG	ShO	Sv.	IP	H	R	ER	BB	SO
1988— Bend (N'West)..................	4	6	.400	5.24	13	13	1	1	0	68 2/3	59	51	40	47	72
1989— Quad City (Midw.)	12	7	.632	3.36	25	25	3	1	0	139 1/3	122	68	52	64	131
1990— Midland (Texas)................	1	7	.125	5.26	15	15	1	0	0	77	92	55	45	41	54
1991— Midland (Texas)................	0	0	...	1.42	2	2	0	0	0	6 1/3	3	2	1	5	7
— Palm Springs (Calif.)	0	4	.000	2.86	6	6	0	0	0	22	15	14	7	16	19

– 257 –

H

Year League	W	L	Pct.	ERA	G	GS	CG	ShO	Sv.	IP	H	R	ER	BB	SO
1992— Palm Springs (Calif.)	3	2	.600	3.00	5	5	2	0	0	30	23	10	10	13	32
— Midland (Texas).................	2	5	.286	3.83	7	7	2	0	0	44²/₃	45	22	19	13	36
— Edmonton (PCL).............	5	7	.417	6.67	17	16	4	0	0	89	114	69	66	55	49
1993— Vancouver (PCL)	9	6	.600	4.82	24	23	2	0	0	145²/₃	158	94	78	70	80
— California (A.L.)	0	3	.000	8.87	5	4	0	0	0	23¹/₃	34	24	23	13	10
1994— Vancouver (PCL)	5	10	.333	6.60	29	17	0	0	0	117¹/₃	144	93	86	58	77
1995— Vancouver (PCL)	3	2	.600	2.47	28	4	0	0	2	54²/₃	45	18	15	24	35
— California (A.L.)	0	1	.000	5.40	12	0	0	0	0	8¹/₃	11	6	5	7	5
1996— California (A.L.)	1	0	1.000	8.76	25	0	0	0	0	24²/₃	35	28	24	8	20
— Lake Elsinore (Calif.)	0	1	.000	2.38	9	3	0	0	0	11¹/₃	10	3	3	4	10
1997— Tacoma (PCL)■	1	0	1.000	2.20	37	0	0	0	13	41	32	10	10	10	38
— Seattle (A.L.)	0	0	...	6.00	14	0	0	0	1	9	9	6	6	8	7
1998— Edmonton (PCL)■	1	1	.500	3.23	30	0	0	0	6	39	41	15	14	11	27
— Oakland (A.L.)	1	0	1.000	5.59	13	0	0	0	0	9²/₃	13	6	6	3	3
1999— Colorado Springs (PCL)■..	3	2	.600	5.69	41	1	0	0	1	55¹/₃	77	39	35	24	49
2000— Scranton/W.B. (I.L.)■	3	2	.600	3.63	24	3	0	0	2	44²/₃	40	19	18	16	35
— Philadelphia (N.L.).............	0	1	.000	7.71	25	0	0	0	0	25²/₃	36	23	22	8	19
— Reading (East.)..................	0	0	...	0.00	3	1	0	0	0	2²/₃	0	0	0	2	1
A.L. totals (5 years)	2	4	.333	7.68	69	4	0	0	1	75	102	70	64	39	45
N.L. totals (1 year)......................	0	1	.000	7.71	25	0	0	0	0	25²/₃	36	23	22	8	19
Major League totals (6 years).......	2	5	.286	7.69	94	4	0	0	1	100²/₃	138	93	86	47	64

HOUSE, CRAIG   P   ROCKIES

PERSONAL: Born July 8, 1977, in Nash AFB, Okinawa, Japan. ... 6-2/210. ... Throws right, bats right. ... Full name: Craig Michael House.
HIGH SCHOOL: Christian Brothers (Memphis, Tenn.).
COLLEGE: Memphis.
TRANSACTIONS/CAREER NOTES: Selected by Colorado Rockies organization in 12th round of free-agent draft (June 2, 1999).

Year League	W	L	Pct.	ERA	G	GS	CG	ShO	Sv.	IP	H	R	ER	BB	SO
1999— Portland (N'West)	2	1	.667	2.08	26	0	0	0	11	34²/₃	28	14	8	14	58
2000— Salem (Caro.)....................	2	0	1.000	2.25	13	0	0	0	8	16	7	4	4	10	24
— Carolina (Sou.)..................	0	2	.000	3.80	18	0	0	0	9	21¹/₃	14	11	9	15	28
— Colorado Springs (PCL)	0	0	...	3.24	8	0	0	0	4	8¹/₃	6	4	3	2	8
— Colorado (N.L.)	1	1	.500	7.24	16	0	0	0	0	13²/₃	13	11	11	17	8
Major League totals (1 year).........	1	1	.500	7.24	16	0	0	0	0	13²/₃	13	11	11	17	8

HOUSTON, TYLER   C   BREWERS

PERSONAL: Born January 17, 1971, in Long Beach, Calif. ... 6-1/210. ... Bats left, throws right. ... Full name: Tyler Sam Houston.
HIGH SCHOOL: Valley (Las Vegas).
TRANSACTIONS/CAREER NOTES: Selected by Atlanta Braves organization in first round (second pick overall) of free-agent draft (June 5, 1989). ... On Greenville disabled list (June 25-July 5, 1993). ... Traded by Braves to Chicago Cubs for P Ismael Villegas (June 27, 1996). ... On Chicago disabled list (May 3-19, 1997; included rehabilitation assignment to Iowa (May 14-19, 1997). ... On Chicago disabled list (June 11-July 11, 1997; included rehabilitation assignment to Rockford (July 9-11). ... On suspended list (September 16, 1997). ... On disabled list (May 26-June 24, 1998). ... Traded by Cubs to Cleveland Indians for P Richard Negrette (August 31, 1999). ... Granted free agency (December 21, 1999). ... Signed by Milwaukee Brewers (January 17, 2000). ... On disabled list (May 19-June 2, 2000).
STATISTICAL NOTES: Led Pioneer League with 14 passed balls in 1989. ... Hit three home runs in one game (July 9, 2000).

Year Team (League)	Pos.	G	AB	R	H	2B	3B	HR	RBI	Avg.	BB	SO	SB	PO	A	E	Avg.
1989— Idaho Falls (Pio.).........	C	50	176	30	43	11	0	4	24	.244	25	41	4	148	15	5	.970
1990— Sumter (S.Atl.)	C	117	442	58	93	14	3	13	56	.210	49	101	6	498	55	*18	.968
1991— Macon (S.Atl.)	C	107	351	41	81	16	3	8	47	.231	39	70	10	591	75	10	.985
1992— Durham (Caro.)	C-3B-1B	117	402	39	91	17	1	7	38	.226	20	89	5	493	65	15	.974
1993— Greenville (Sou.)	C-OF	84	262	27	73	14	1	5	33	.279	13	50	5	410	34	9	.980
— Richmond (I.L.)...........	C-DH	13	36	4	5	1	1	1	3	.139	1	8	0	69	2	3	.959
1994— Richmond (I.L.)..........1B-C-DH-OF		97	312	33	76	15	2	4	33	.244	16	44	3	619	54	7	.990
1995— Richmond (I.L.)..........1-C-O-3-DH		103	349	41	89	10	3	12	42	.255	18	62	3	579	69	11	.983
1996— Atlanta (N.L.)	1B-OF-3B	33	27	3	6	2	1	1	8	.222	1	9	0	16	1	0	1.000
— Chicago (N.L.)■.....C-3B-2B-1B		46	115	18	39	7	0	2	19	.339	8	18	3	139	25	3	.982
1997— Chicago (N.L.)	C-3-1-2-S	72	196	15	51	10	0	2	28	.260	9	35	1	280	37	5	.984
— Iowa (A.A.)	3B-DH-C	6	23	0	5	2	0	0	4	.217	0	2	0	6	9	2	.882
— Rockford (Midw.)	C-3B	2	6	1	3	1	0	0	1	.500	0	0	0	5	0	0	1.000
1998— Chicago (N.L.)	C-3B-1B	95	255	26	65	7	1	9	33	.255	13	53	2	451	36	5	.990
1999— Chicago (N.L.) 3B-C-1B-OF		100	249	26	58	9	1	9	27	.233	28	67	1	109	89	17	.921
— Cleveland (A.L.)■......	3B-C	13	27	2	4	1	0	1	3	.148	3	11	0	7	11	0	1.000
2000— Milwaukee (N.L.)■......	1B-3B-C	101	284	30	71	15	0	18	43	.250	17	72	2	399	80	13	.974
American League totals (1 year)		13	27	2	4	1	0	1	3	.148	3	11	0	7	11	0	1.000
National League totals (5 years)		447	1126	118	290	50	3	41	158	.258	76	254	9	1394	268	43	.975
Major League totals (5 years)		460	1153	120	294	51	3	42	161	.255	79	265	9	1401	279	43	.975

DIVISION SERIES RECORD

Year Team (League)	Pos.	G	AB	R	H	2B	3B	HR	RBI	Avg.	BB	SO	SB	PO	A	E	Avg.
1998— Chicago (N.L.)	C	3	6	1	1	0	0	1	1	.167	0	3	0	13	0	0	1.000
1999— Cleveland (A.L.)								Did not play.									

H

PERSONAL: Born December 11, 1964, in Middletown, Ohio. ... 6-2/205. ... Bats both, throws right. ... Full name: Thomas Sylvester Howard.
HIGH SCHOOL: Valley View (Germantown, Ohio).
COLLEGE: Ball State.
TRANSACTIONS/CAREER NOTES: Selected by San Diego Padres organization in first round (11th pick overall) of free-agent draft (June 2, 1986). ... On disabled list (June 5-July 17, 1989). ... Traded by Padres to Cleveland Indians for SS Jason Hardtke and a player to be named later (April 14, 1992); Padres acquired C Christopher Maffett to complete deal (July 10, 1992). ... Traded by Indians to Cincinnati Reds (August 20, 1993), completing deal in which Reds traded 1B Randy Milligan to Indians for a player to be named later (August 17, 1993). ... On Cincinnati disabled list (March 23-April 20, 1996); included rehabilitation assignments to Chattanooga (April 11-19) and Indianapolis (April 19-20). ... Released by Reds (November 18, 1996). ... Signed by Houston Astros (December 4, 1996). ... Granted free agency (October 28, 1997). ... Signed by Los Angeles Dodgers organization (January 7, 1998). ... Released by Dodgers (June 29, 1998). ... Signed by St. Louis Cardinals organization (December 31, 1998). ... Granted free agency (November 4, 1999). ... Re-signed by Cardinals (December 22, 1999). ... Granted free agency (November 2, 2000). ... Signed by Pittsburgh Pirates organization (January 9, 2001).
HONORS: Named outfielder on THE SPORTING NEWS college All-America team (1986).
STATISTICAL NOTES: Career major league grand slams: 1.

Year	Team (League)	Pos.	G	AB	R	H	2B	3B	HR	RBI	Avg.	BB	SO	SB	PO	A	E	Avg.
1986—	Spokane (N'West)	OF	13	55	16	23	3	3	2	17	.418	3	9	2	24	3	0	1.000
—	Reno (Calif.)	OF	61	223	35	57	7	3	10	39	.256	34	49	10	104	5	6	.948
1987—	Wichita (Texas)	OF	113	401	72	133	27	4	14	60	.332	36	72	26	226	6	6	.975
1988—	Wichita (Texas)	OF	29	103	15	31	9	2	0	16	.301	13	14	6	51	2	2	.964
—	Las Vegas (PCL)	OF	44	167	29	42	9	1	0	15	.251	12	31	3	74	3	2	.975
1989—	Las Vegas (PCL)	OF	80	303	45	91	18	3	3	31	.300	30	56	22	178	7	2	.989
1990—	Las Vegas (PCL)	OF	89	341	58	112	26	8	5	51	.328	44	63	27	159	6	2	.988
—	San Diego (N.L.)	OF	20	44	4	12	2	0	0	0	.273	0	11	0	19	0	1	.950
1991—	San Diego (N.L.)	OF	106	281	30	70	12	3	4	22	.249	24	57	10	182	4	1	.995
—	Las Vegas (PCL)	OF	25	94	22	29	3	1	2	16	.309	10	16	11	54	2	2	.966
1992—	San Diego (N.L.)	PH	5	3	1	1	0	0	0	0	.333	0	0	0	...	...	...	...
—	Cleveland (A.L.)■......	OF-DH	117	358	36	99	15	2	2	32	.277	17	60	15	185	5	2	.990
1993—	Cleveland (A.L.)	OF-DH	74	178	26	42	7	0	3	23	.236	12	42	5	81	3	2	.977
—	Cincinnati (N.L.)■......	OF	38	141	22	39	8	3	4	13	.277	12	21	5	73	4	1	.987
1994—	Cincinnati (N.L.)	OF	83	178	24	47	11	0	5	24	.264	10	30	4	80	2	3	.965
1995—	Cincinnati (N.L.)	OF	113	281	42	85	15	2	3	26	.302	20	37	17	127	2	2	.985
1996—	Cincinnati (N.L.)	OF	121	360	50	98	19	10	6	42	.272	17	51	6	160	7	3	.982
—	Chattanooga (Sou.)	OF-DH	8	30	4	10	1	0	1	2	.333	2	7	1	8	0	0	1.000
—	Indianapolis (A.A.)	OF	1	6	2	2	0	0	1	2	.333	0	0	0	3	0	0	1.000
1997—	Houston (N.L.)■.........	OF	107	255	24	63	16	1	3	22	.247	26	48	1	107	5	0	1.000
1998—	Los Angeles (N.L.)■..	OF-DH	47	76	9	14	4	0	2	4	.184	3	15	1	33	2	0	1.000
1999—	Memphis (PCL)■.......	OF	35	119	24	43	10	2	2	21	.361	13	21	1	54	2	1	.982
—	St. Louis (N.L.)..........	OF-DH	98	195	16	57	10	0	6	28	.292	17	26	1	77	0	1	.987
2000—	St. Louis (N.L.)..........	OF-DH-1B	86	133	13	28	4	1	6	28	.211	7	34	1	27	1	1	.966
—	Memphis (PCL)	OF	17	34	7	9	2	0	0	5	.265	7	6	0	19	0	2	.905
American League totals (2 years)			191	536	62	141	22	2	5	55	.263	29	102	20	266	8	4	.986
National League totals (11 years)			824	1947	235	514	101	20	39	209	.264	136	330	46	885	27	13	.986
Major League totals (11 years)			1015	2483	297	655	123	22	44	264	.264	165	432	66	1151	35	17	.986

DIVISION SERIES RECORD

Year	Team (League)	Pos.	G	AB	R	H	2B	3B	HR	RBI	Avg.	BB	SO	SB	PO	A	E	Avg.
1995—	Cincinnati (N.L.)	OF	3	10	0	1	1	0	0	0	.100	0	2	0	5	0	0	1.000
1997—	Houston (N.L.)	PH	2	1	0	0	0	0	0	0	.000	1	1	0	...	...	...	...
Division series totals (2 years)			5	11	0	1	1	0	0	0	.091	1	3	0	5	0	0	1.000

CHAMPIONSHIP SERIES RECORD

Year	Team (League)	Pos.	G	AB	R	H	2B	3B	HR	RBI	Avg.	BB	SO	SB	PO	A	E	Avg.
1995—	Cincinnati (N.L.)	PH-OF	4	8	0	2	1	0	0	1	.250	2	0	0	2	0	0	1.000

PERSONAL: Born August 4, 1973, in Phoenix. ... 6-5/215. ... Throws right, bats left. ... Full name: Bobby Dean Howry.
HIGH SCHOOL: Deer Valley (Phoenix).
JUNIOR COLLEGE: Yavapai College (Ariz.).
COLLEGE: McNeese State.
TRANSACTIONS/CAREER NOTES: Selected by San Francisco Giants organization in fifth round of free-agent draft (June 2, 1994). ... Traded by Giants with SS Mike Caruso, OF Brian Manning, P Keith Foulke, P Lorenzo Barcelo and P Ken Vining to Chicago White Sox for P Wilson Alvarez, P Danny Darwin and P Roberto Hernandez (July 31, 1997). ... On suspended list (April 28-May 30, 2000).

Year	League	W	L	Pct.	ERA	G	GS	CG	ShO	Sv.	IP	H	R	ER	BB	SO
1994—	Everett (N'West)	0	4	.000	4.74	5	5	0	0	0	19	29	15	10	10	16
—	Clinton (Midw.)	1	3	.250	4.20	9	8	0	0	0	49 1/3	61	29	23	16	22
1995—	San Jose (Calif.)	12	10	.545	3.54	27	25	1	0	0	165 1/3	171	79	65	54	107
1996—	Shreveport (Texas)	12	10	.545	4.65	27	27	0	0	0	156 2/3	163	90	81	56	57
1997—	Shreveport (Texas)	6	3	.667	4.91	48	0	0	0	*22	55	58	35	30	21	43
—	Birmingham (Sou.)■	0	0	...	2.84	12	0	0	0	0	12 2/3	16	4	4	3	3
1998—	Calgary (PCL)	1	2	.333	3.41	23	0	0	0	5	31 2/3	25	12	12	10	22
—	Chicago (A.L.)	0	3	.000	3.15	44	0	0	0	9	54 1/3	37	20	19	19	51
1999—	Chicago (A.L.)	5	3	.625	3.59	69	0	0	0	28	67 2/3	58	34	27	38	80
2000—	Chicago (A.L.)	2	4	.333	3.17	65	0	0	0	7	71	54	26	25	29	60
Major League totals (3 years)		7	10	.412	3.31	178	0	0	0	44	193	149	80	71	86	191

DIVISION SERIES RECORD

Year	League	W	L	Pct.	ERA	G	GS	CG	ShO	Sv.	IP	H	R	ER	BB	SO
2000—	Chicago (A.L.)	0	0	...	3.38	2	0	0	0	0	2 2/3	2	1	1	2	4

H

PERSONAL: Born February 16, 1971, in Lynchburg, Va. ... 6-1/205. ... Bats right, throws right. ... Full name: Michael Wayne Hubbard.
HIGH SCHOOL: Amherst (Va.) County.
COLLEGE: James Madison.
TRANSACTIONS/CAREER NOTES: Selected by Chicago Cubs organization in eighth round of free-agent draft (June 1, 1992). ... Claimed on waivers by Montreal Expos (March 30, 1998). ... Granted free agency (September 29, 1998). ... Signed by Texas Rangers organization (December 2, 1998). ... Granted free agency (October 15, 1999). ... Signed by Cincinnati Reds organization (December 16, 1999). ... On Louisville disabled list (April 19-28, 2000). ... Released by Reds (May 8, 2000). ... Sigend by Atlanta Braves organization (May 10, 2000). ... Granted free agency (October 17, 2000). ... Signed by Rangers organization (November 6, 2000).
STATISTICAL NOTES: Led Pacific League catchers with a .994 fielding percentage in 1999.

									BATTING						FIELDING		
Year	Team (League)	Pos.	G	AB	R	H	2B	3B	HR	RBI	Avg.	BB	SO	SB	PO	A	E	Avg.
1992— Geneva (NY-Penn)		C	50	183	25	44	4	4	3	25	.240	7	29	6	325	27	5	.986
1993— Daytona (FSL)		C-2B	68	245	25	72	10	3	1	20	.294	18	41	10	354	66	9	.979
1994— Orlando (Sou.)		C-3B-1B	104	357	52	102	13	3	11	39	.286	29	58	7	498	78	12	.980
1995— Iowa (A.A.)		C-DH-3B	75	254	28	66	6	3	5	23	.260	26	60	6	447	34	9	.982
— Chicago (N.L.)		C	15	23	2	4	0	0	0	1	.174	2	2	0	33	0	1	.971
1996— Iowa (A.A.)		C-3B-DH-OF	67	232	38	68	12	0	7	33	.293	10	56	2	372	27	5	.988
— Chicago (N.L.)		C	21	38	1	4	0	0	1	4	.105	0	15	0	53	3	0	1.000
1997— Iowa (A.A.)		C-DH-OF	50	186	24	52	15	1	6	26	.280	11	23	2	310	22	2	.994
— Chicago (N.L.)		C-3B	29	64	4	13	0	0	1	2	.203	2	21	0	120	8	1	.992
1998— Montreal (N.L.)■		C-2B	32	55	3	8	1	0	1	3	.145	0	17	0	83	4	0	1.000
— Ottawa (I.L.)		C	20	70	9	16	5	0	0	8	.229	3	13	0	121	8	1	.992
1999— Oklahoma (PCL)■		C-DH-1B-OF	110	392	48	111	19	0	9	49	.283	25	70	4	682	47	4	†.995
2000— Louisville (I.L.)■		C	8	8	1	3	1	0	0	0	.375	1	4	0	14	0	0	1.000
— Richmond (I.L.)■		C-1B	70	224	33	66	8	1	6	31	.295	22	24	4	349	20	5	.987
— Atlanta (N.L.)		C	2	1	0	0	0	0	0	0	.000	0	1	0	3	0	0	1.000
Major League totals (5 years)			99	181	10	29	1	0	3	10	.160	4	56	0	292	15	2	.994

PERSONAL: Born May 11, 1966, in Chicago. ... 5-9/203. ... Bats right, throws right. ... Full name: Trenidad Aviel Hubbard. ... Cousin of Joe Cribbs, running back with Buffalo Bills (1980-83 and 1985).
HIGH SCHOOL: South Shore (Chicago).
COLLEGE: Southern (La.).
TRANSACTIONS/CAREER NOTES: Selected by Houston Astros organization in 12th round of free-agent draft (June 2, 1986). ... Granted free agency (October 15, 1992). ... Signed by Colorado Rockies organization (October 30, 1992). ... On disabled list (June 15-24, 1993). ... Granted free agency (October 15, 1993). ... Re-signed by Rockies organization (December 3, 1993). ... Granted free agency (October 15, 1994). ... Re-signed by Rockies organization (November 14, 1994). ... Claimed on waivers by San Francisco Giants (August 21, 1996). ... On San Francisco disabled list (September 13, 1996-remainder of season). ... Traded by Giants to Cleveland Indians for P Joe Roa (December 16, 1996), completing deal in which Indians traded IF Jeff Kent, IF Jose Vizcaino, P Julian Tavarez and a player to be named later to Giants for 3B Matt Williams and a player to be named later (November 13, 1996). ... Granted free agency (October 8, 1997). ... Signed by Los Angeles Dodgers (December 3, 1997). ... On Los Angeles disabled list (May 14-June 22, 1998); included rehabilitation assignment to Albuquerque (June 9-22). ... Granted free agency (January 19, 2000). ... Signed by Atlanta Braves organization (January 20, 2000). ... Traded by Braves with P Luis Rivera and C Fernando Rivera to Baltimore Orioles for OF B.J. Surhoff and P Gabe Molina (July 31, 2000). ... Released by Orioles (October 5, 2000).
STATISTICAL NOTES: Led Texas League second basemen with 296 putouts, 653 total chances and 81 double plays in 1991. ... Tied for Pacific Coast League lead in caught stealing with 18 in 1993. ... Led Pacific Coast League with .416 on-base percentage in 1995.
MISCELLANEOUS: Batted lefthanded on occasion though not a switch hitter (1986-91).

									BATTING						FIELDING		
Year	Team (League)	Pos.	G	AB	R	H	2B	3B	HR	RBI	Avg.	BB	SO	SB	PO	A	E	Avg.
1986— Auburn (NY-Penn)		2B-OF	70	242	42	75	12	1	1	32	.310	28	42	35	131	110	18	.931
1987— Asheville (S.Atl.)		2-O-C-3-P	101	284	39	67	8	1	1	35	.236	28	42	28	124	108	14	.943
1988— Osceola (FSL)		2-C-O-3-1	130	446	68	116	15	11	3	65	.260	61	72	44	261	150	12	.972
1989— Columbus (Sou.)		2B-C-OF-3B	104	348	55	92	7	8	3	37	.264	43	53	28	321	122	15	.967
— Tucson (PCL)		OF-3B	21	50	3	11	2	0	0	2	.220	1	10	3	20	9	1	.967
1990— Columbus (Sou.)		2B-OF-C-3B	95	335	39	84	14	4	4	35	.251	32	51	17	216	116	11	.968
— Tucson (PCL)		2B-3B-C	12	27	5	6	2	2	0	2	.222	3	6	1	20	22	3	.933
1991— Jackson (Texas)		2B-OF-1B-P	126	455	78	135	21	3	2	41	.297	65	81	39	†299	338	21	.968
— Tucson (PCL)		2B	2	4	0	0	0	0	0	0	.000	0	0	0	1	2	0	1.000
1992— Tucson (PCL)		2B-3B	115	420	69	130	16	4	2	33	.310	45	68	34	238	353	18	.970
1993— Colo. Springs (PCL)■		O-2-3-DH-S	117	439	83	138	24	8	7	56	.314	47	57	33	208	29	6	.975
1994— Colo. Springs (PCL)		OF	79	320	78	116	22	5	8	38	.363	44	40	28	183	5	7	.964
— Colorado (N.L.)		OF	18	25	3	7	1	1	1	3	.280	3	4	0	4	0	0	1.000
1995— Colo. Springs (PCL)		OF	123	480	*102	163	29	7	12	66	.340	61	59	*37	285	11	6	.980
— Colorado (N.L.)		OF	24	58	13	18	4	0	3	9	.310	8	6	2	16	1	0	1.000
1996— Colorado (N.L.)		OF	45	60	12	13	5	1	1	12	.217	9	22	2	32	0	0	1.000
— Colo. Springs (PCL)		OF-2B-3B-C	50	188	41	59	15	5	6	16	.314	28	14	6	89	55	4	.973
— San Fran. (N.L.)		OF	10	29	3	6	0	1	1	2	.207	2	5	0	19	1	0	1.000
1997— Buffalo (A.A.)■		OF-3B-DH	103	375	71	117	22	1	16	60	.312	57	52	26	236	26	2	.992
— Cleveland (A.L.)		OF	7	12	3	3	1	0	0	0	.250	1	3	2	3	0	0	1.000
1998— Los Angeles (N.L.)■		OF-3B	94	208	29	62	9	1	7	18	.298	18	46	9	110	3	1	.991
— Albuquerque (PCL)		OF-DH	11	30	6	9	0	0	3	5	.300	5	5	2	13	1	0	1.000
1999— Albuquerque (PCL)		OF-DH	32	123	24	41	8	2	5	24	.333	16	27	16	72	2	2	.974
— Los Angeles (N.L.)		OF-C-2B	82	105	23	33	5	0	1	13	.314	13	24	4	50	1	1	.981
2000— Atlanta (N.L.)■		OF	60	81	15	15	2	1	1	6	.185	11	20	2	39	1	0	1.000
— Baltimore (A.L.)■		OF-DH	31	27	3	5	0	1	0	0	.185	0	3	2	12	1	1	.929
American League totals (2 years)			38	39	6	8	1	1	0	0	.205	1	6	4	15	1	1	.941
National League totals (6 years)			333	566	98	154	26	5	15	63	.272	64	127	19	270	7	2	.993
Major League totals (7 years)			371	605	104	162	27	6	15	63	.268	65	133	23	285	8	3	.990

H

DIVISION SERIES RECORD

Year	Team (League)	Pos.	G	AB	R	H	2B	3B	HR	RBI	Avg.	BB	SO	SB	PO	A	E	Avg.
						BATTING										FIELDING		
1995— Colorado (N.L.)	PH	3	2	0	0	0	0	0	0	.000	0	0	0	...	...	...	...

RECORD AS PITCHER

Year	League	W	L	Pct.	ERA	G	GS	CG	ShO	Sv.	IP	H	R	ER	BB	SO
1987— Asheville (S.Atl.)................	0	0	...	0.00	1	0	0	0	0	1	1	0	0	1	0
1991— Jackson (Texas)	0	0	...	0.00	1	0	0	0	0	1	0	0	0	2	0

HUCKABY, KEN   C   DIAMONDBACKS

PERSONAL: Born January 27, 1971, in San Leandro, Calif. ... 6-1/205. ... Bats right, throws right. ... Full name: Kenneth Paul Huckaby.
HIGH SCHOOL: Manteca (Calif.).
JUNIOR COLLEGE: San Joaquin Delta (Calif.).
TRANSACTIONS/CAREER NOTES: Selected by Los Angeles Dodgers organization in second round of free-agent draft (June 3, 1991). ... On disabled list (May 26-June 5 and July 2-21, 1992). ... On San Antonio disabled list (May 4-13, 1994). ... Granted free agency (October 15, 1997). ... Signed by Seattle Mariners organization (December 3, 1997). ... On Tacoma disabled list (April 7-May 3, 1998). ... Released by Mariners (June 13, 1998). ... Signed by New York Yankees organization (June 28, 1998). ... Granted free agency (October 16, 1998). ... Signed by Arizona Diamondbacks organization (January 22, 1999). ... Granted free agency (October 15, 1999). ... Re-signed by Diamondbacks organization (November 15, 1999). ... Granted free agency (October 18, 2000). ... Re-signed by Diamondbacks organization (November 2, 2000).
STATISTICAL NOTES: Led Florida State League catchers with 14 double plays in 1993. ... Led Pacific Coast League catchers with 592 total chances in 1995. ... Led Pacific Coast League catchers with 11 double plays in 1996. ... Led Pacific Coast League catchers with 695 putouts and 756 total chances in 1999.

Year	Team (League)	Pos.	G	AB	R	H	2B	3B	HR	RBI	Avg.	BB	SO	SB	PO	A	E	Avg.
							BATTING									FIELDING		
1991— Great Falls (Pio.)	C	57	213	39	55	16	0	3	37	.258	17	38	3	456	48	*12	.977
1992— Vero Beach (FSL)	C	73	261	14	63	9	0	0	21	.241	7	42	1	442	56	9	.982
1993— San Antonio (Texas) ...	C	28	82	4	18	1	0	0	5	.220	2	7	0	149	29	4	.978
— Vero Beach (FSL)	C	79	281	22	75	14	1	4	41	.267	11	35	2	481	*99	12	.980
1994— San Antonio (Texas) ...	C	11	41	3	11	1	0	1	9	.268	1	1	1	73	8	6	.931
— Bakersfield (Calif.)	C	77	270	29	81	18	1	2	30	.300	10	37	2	591	93	10	.986
1995— Albuquerque (PCL).....	C-1B	89	278	30	90	16	2	1	40	.324	12	26	3	518	61	16	.973
1996— Albuquerque (PCL).....	C	103	287	37	79	16	2	3	41	.275	17	35	0	557	63	6	.990
1997— Albuquerque (PCL).....	C-DH	69	201	14	40	5	1	0	18	.199	9	36	1	359	25	10	.975
1998— Tacoma (PCL)■.........	C-1B	16	49	4	11	2	0	0	1	.224	5	6	0	91	4	0	1.000
— Columbus (I.L.)■.........	C	36	101	13	21	3	1	1	10	.208	11	14	0	201	21	5	.978
1999— Tucson (PCL)■ C-3B-DH-1B	107	355	44	107	20	1	2	42	.301	13	33	0	†706	55	10	.987
2000— Tucson (PCL) C-3B-OF-1B	76	243	31	67	14	1	4	33	.276	10	30	2	382	51	8	.982

HUDSON, TIM   P   ATHLETICS

PERSONAL: Born July 14, 1975, in Columbus, Ga. ... 6-0/160. ... Throws right, bats right. ... Full name: Timothy Adam Hudson.
HIGH SCHOOL: Glenwood (Phenix City, Ala.).
COLLEGE: Auburn.
TRANSACTIONS/CAREER NOTES: Selected by Oakland Athletics organization in sixth-round of free-agent draft (June 3, 1997).
HONORS: Named A.L. Rookie Pitcher of the Year by THE SPORTING NEWS (1999).
STATISTICAL NOTES: Pitched 3-0 one-hit, complete-game victory against Chicago White Sox (August 28, 2000).
MISCELLANEOUS: Appeared in three games as pinch runner (1999). ... Appeared in one game as pinch runner (2000).

Year	League	W	L	Pct.	ERA	G	GS	CG	ShO	Sv.	IP	H	R	ER	BB	SO
1997— Southern Oregon (N'West).	3	1	.750	2.51	8	4	0	0	0	28 2/3	12	8	8	15	37
1998— Modesto (Calif.)	4	0	1.000	1.67	8	5	0	0	0	37 2/3	19	10	7	18	48
— Huntsville (Sou.)	10	9	.526	4.54	22	22	2	0	0	134 2/3	136	84	68	71	104
1999— Midland (Texas).................	3	0	1.000	0.50	3	3	0	0	0	18	9	1	1	3	18
— Vancouver (PCL)	4	0	1.000	2.20	8	8	0	0	0	49	38	16	12	21	61
— Oakland (A.L.)	11	2	.846	3.23	21	21	1	0	0	136 1/3	121	56	49	62	132
2000— Oakland (A.L.)	•20	6	*.769	4.14	32	32	2	2	0	202 1/3	169	100	93	82	169
Major League totals (2 years)	31	8	.795	3.77	53	53	3	2	0	338 2/3	290	156	142	144	301

DIVISION SERIES RECORD

Year	League	W	L	Pct.	ERA	G	GS	CG	ShO	Sv.	IP	H	R	ER	BB	SO
2000— Oakland (A.L.)	0	1	.000	3.38	1	1	1	0	0	8	6	4	3	4	5

ALL-STAR GAME RECORD

Year	League	W	L	Pct.	ERA	GS	CG	ShO	Sv.	IP	H	R	ER	BB	SO
2000— American	0	0	...	0.00	0	0	0	0	1	0	0	0	0	1

HUFF, AUBREY   3B   DEVIL RAYS

PERSONAL: Born December 20, 1976, in Marion, Ohio. ... 6-4/220. ... Bats left, throws right. ... Full name: Aubrey L. Huff.
HIGH SCHOOL: Brewer (Fort Worth, Texas).
JUNIOR COLLEGE: Vernon Regional (Texas).
COLLEGE: Miami (Fla.).
TRANSACTIONS/CAREER NOTES: Selected by Tampa Bay Devil Rays organization in fifth round of free-agent draft (June 2, 1998).
STATISTICAL NOTES: Led Southern League third baseman with 395 total chances in 1999.

Year	Team (League)	Pos.	G	AB	R	H	2B	3B	HR	RBI	Avg.	BB	SO	SB	PO	A	E	Avg.
							BATTING									FIELDING		
1998— Char., S.C. (SAL)	3B	69	265	38	85	19	1	13	54	.321	242	40	3	47	133	8	.957
1999— Orlando (Sou.)	3B	133	491	85	148	40	3	22	78	.301	64	77	2	93	273	29	.927
2000— Durham (I.L.)	3B-1B	108	408	73	129	36	3	20	76	.316	51	72	2	60	166	21	.915
— Tampa Bay (A.L.)........	3B	39	122	12	35	7	0	4	14	.287	5	18	0	24	53	5	.939
Major League totals (1 year)	39	122	12	35	7	0	4	14	.287	5	18	0	24	53	5	.939

H

HUNDLEY, TODD   C   CUBS

PERSONAL: Born May 27, 1969, in Martinsville, Va. ... 5-11/199. ... Bats both, throws right. ... Full name: Todd Randolph Hundley. ... Son of Randy Hundley, catcher with four major league teams (1964-77).

HIGH SCHOOL: William Fremd (Palatine, Ill.).

COLLEGE: William Rainey Harper College (Ill.).

TRANSACTIONS/CAREER NOTES: Selected by New York Mets organization in second round of free-agent draft (June 2, 1987); pick received as compensation for Baltimore Orioles signing Type B free-agent 3B/1B Ray Knight. ... On Tidewater disabled list (June 29-July 6, 1991). ... On disabled list (July 23, 1995-remainder of season). ... On New York disabled list (March 21-July 11 and August 28-September 12, 1998); included rehabilitation assignments to St. Lucie (June 24-July 6 and July 9), Gulf Coast Mets (July 7-8) and Norfolk (July 10-11 and August 31-September 8). ... Traded by Mets with P Arnold Gooch to Los Angeles Dodgers for C Charles Johnson and OF Roger Cedeno (December 1, 1998). ... On suspended list (July 22-24, 1999). ... On Los Angeles disabled list (May 31-June 26 and July 9-27, 2000); included rehabilitation assignment to Albuquerque (June 23-26). ... Granted free agency (October 27, 2000). ... Signed by Chicago Cubs (December 13, 2000).

RECORDS: Holds major league single-season record for most home runs by catcher—41 (1996). ... Holds N.L. single-season record for most strikeouts by switch hitter—146 (1996).

STATISTICAL NOTES: Led South Atlantic League in intentional bases on balls received with 10 and in grounding into double plays with 20 in 1989. ... Led South Atlantic League catchers with 826 putouts and 930 total chances in 1989. ... Tied for International League lead in errors by catcher with nine and double plays with 12 in 1991. ... Switch-hit home runs in one game five times (June 18, 1994; May 18; June 10, 1996; May 5 and July 20, 1997). ... Career major league grand slams: 7.

								BATTING							FIELDING		
Year Team (League)	Pos.	G	AB	R	H	2B	3B	HR	RBI	Avg.	BB	SO	SB	PO	A	E	Avg.
1987— Little Falls (NY-Penn) .	C	34	103	12	15	4	0	1	10	.146	12	27	0	181	25	7	.967
1988— Little Falls (NY-Penn) .	C	52	176	23	33	8	0	2	18	.188	16	31	1	345	54	8	.980
— St. Lucie (FSL)	C	1	1	0	0	0	0	0	0	.000	2	1	0	4	0	1	.800
1989— Columbia (S.Atl.)	C-OF	125	439	67	118	23	4	11	66	.269	54	67	6	†829	91	13	.986
1990— Jackson (Texas)	C-3B	81	279	27	74	12	2	1	35	.265	34	44	5	474	63	9	.984
— New York (N.L.)	C	36	67	8	14	6	0	0	2	.209	6	18	0	162	8	2	.988
1991— Tidewater (I.L.)	C-1B	125	454	62	124	24	4	14	66	.273	51	95	1	585	63	‡9	.986
— New York (N.L.)	C	21	60	5	8	0	1	1	7	.133	6	14	0	85	11	0	1.000
1992— New York (N.L.)	C	123	358	32	75	17	0	7	32	.209	19	76	3	700	48	3	.996
1993— New York (N.L.)	C	130	417	40	95	17	2	11	53	.228	23	62	1	592	63	8	.988
1994— New York (N.L.)	C	91	291	45	69	10	1	16	42	.237	25	73	2	448	28	5	.990
1995— New York (N.L.)	C	90	275	39	77	11	0	15	51	.280	42	64	1	488	29	7	.987
1996— New York (N.L.)	C	153	540	85	140	32	1	41	112	.259	79	146	1	911	72	8	.992
1997— New York (N.L.)	C	132	417	78	114	21	2	30	86	.273	83	116	2	678	54	10	.987
1998— St. Lucie (FSL)	OF-DH	12	42	4	9	2	0	1	6	.214	12	8	0	17	1	2	.900
— GC Mets (GCL)	OF	1	2	0	0	0	0	0	0	.000	2	1	0	2	0	0	1.000
— Norfolk (I.L.)	OF-DH-C	10	30	9	13	1	0	4	15	.433	14	10	0	22	2	1	.960
— New York (N.L.)	OF-C	53	124	8	20	4	0	3	12	.161	16	55	1	60	4	5	.928
1999— Los Angeles (N.L.)■..	C	115	376	49	78	14	0	24	55	.207	44	113	3	681	51	*16	.979
2000— Los Angeles (N.L.)	C-DH	90	299	49	85	16	0	24	70	.284	45	69	0	554	38	*13	.979
— Albuquerque (PCL)	C	3	9	2	5	0	0	1	5	.556	1	0	0	15	0	0	1.000
Major League totals (11 years)		1034	3224	438	775	148	7	172	522	.240	388	806	14	5359	406	77	.987

ALL-STAR GAME RECORD

						BATTING								FIELDING		
Year League	Pos.	AB	R	H	2B	3B	HR	RBI	Avg.	BB	SO	SB	PO	A	E	Avg.
1996— National	C	1	0	0	0	0	0	0	.000	0	0	0	1	0	0	1.000
1997— National							Did not play.									

HUNTER, BRIAN L.   OF   PHILLIES

PERSONAL: Born March 5, 1971, in Portland, Ore. ... 6-3/180. ... Bats right, throws right. ... Full name: Brian Lee Hunter.

HIGH SCHOOL: Fort Vancouver (Vancouver, Wash.).

TRANSACTIONS/CAREER NOTES: Selected by Houston Astros organization in second round of free-agent draft (June 5, 1989); pick received as part of compensation for Texas Rangers signing Type A free-agent P Nolan Ryan. ... On Houston disabled list (July 5-23, 1995); included rehabilitation assignment to Jackson (July 21-23). ... On Houston disabled list (June 29-July 27, 1996); included rehabilitation assignment to Tucson (July 23-27). ... Traded by Astros with IF Orlando Miller, P Doug Brocail, P Todd Jones and cash to Detroit Tigers for C Brad Ausmus, P Jose Lima, P C.J. Nitkowski, P Trever Miller and IF Daryle Ward (December 10, 1996). ... Traded by Tigers to Seattle Mariners for two players to be named later (April 29, 1999); Tigers acquired P Andrew Vanhekken (June 27, 1999) and OF Jerry Amador (August 26, 1999) to complete deal. ... On Seattle disabled list (July 12-27, 1999). ... Released by Mariners (March 27, 2000). ... Signed by Colorado Rockies (March 31, 2000). ... Traded by Rockies from Cincinnati Reds for P Robert Averette (August 6, 2000). ... On suspended list (August 14-17, 2000). ... Released by Reds (November 27, 2000). ... Signed by Philadelphia Phillies (January 10, 2001).

RECORDS: Holds major league record for most at-bats with no hits in doubleheader (more than 18 innings)—13 (June 20, 1998, 26 innings). ... Shares major league single season record for fewest double plays by outfielder (150 or more games)—0 (1997).

STATISTICAL NOTES: Tied for American Association lead with 249 total bases in 1997. ... Led A.L. in caught stealing with 18 in 1997. ... Led A.L. outfielders with 420 total chances in 1997. ... Led A.L. with 44 stolen bases in 1999. ... Career major league grand slams: 1.

								BATTING							FIELDING		
Year Team (League)	Pos.	G	AB	R	H	2B	3B	HR	RBI	Avg.	BB	SO	SB	PO	A	E	Avg.
1989— GC Astros (GCL)	OF	51	206	15	35	2	0	0	13	.170	7	42	12	95	4	2	.980
1990— Asheville (S.Atl.)	OF	127	444	84	111	14	6	0	16	.250	60	72	45	219	13	11	.955
1991— Osceola (FSL)	OF	118	392	51	94	15	3	1	30	.240	45	75	32	250	7	9	.966
1992— Osceola (FSL)	OF	131	489	62	146	18	9	1	62	.299	31	76	39	295	10	9	.971
1993— Jackson (Texas)	OF-DH	133	523	84	154	22	5	10	52	.294	34	85	*35	276	9	*14	.953
1994— Tucson (PCL)	OF-DH	128	513	*113	*191	28	9	10	51	*.372	52	52	*49	244	14	5	.981
— Houston (N.L.)	OF	6	24	2	6	1	0	0	0	.250	1	6	2	14	1	1	.938
1995— Tucson (PCL)	OF	38	155	28	51	5	1	1	16	.329	17	13	11	91	1	0	1.000
— Houston (N.L.)	OF	78	321	52	97	14	5	2	28	.302	21	52	24	182	8	9	.955
— Jackson (Texas)	OF	2	6	1	3	0	0	0	0	.500	1	0	0	5	0	0	1.000
1996— Houston (N.L.)	OF	132	526	74	145	27	2	5	35	.276	17	92	35	279	11	•12	.960
— Tucson (PCL)	OF	3	14	3	5	0	1	0	1	.357	0	2	3	8	0	0	1.000

H

Year Team (League)	Pos.	G	AB	R	H	2B	3B	HR	RBI	Avg.	BB	SO	SB	PO	A	E	Avg.
1997— Detroit (A.L.)■	OF	•162	658	112	177	29	7	4	45	.269	66	121	*74	*408	8	4	.990
1998— Detroit (A.L.)	OF	142	595	67	151	29	3	4	36	.254	36	94	42	386	11	5	.988
1999— Detroit (A.L.)	OF	18	55	8	13	2	1	0	0	.236	5	11	0	49	1	0	1.000
—Seattle (A.L.)■	OF	121	484	71	112	11	5	4	34	.231	32	80	§44	252	14	4	.985
2000— Colorado (N.L.)■	OF	72	200	36	55	4	1	1	13	.275	21	31	15	103	3	2	.981
—Cincinnati (N.L.)■	OF	32	40	11	9	1	0	0	1	.225	6	9	5	30	4	1	.971
American League totals (3 years)		443	1792	258	453	71	16	12	115	.253	139	306	160	1095	34	13	.989
National League totals (4 years)		320	1111	175	312	47	8	8	77	.281	66	190	81	608	27	25	.962
Major League totals (7 years)		763	2903	433	765	118	24	20	192	.264	205	496	241	1703	61	38	.979

HUNTER, BRIAN   1B   PHILLIES

PERSONAL: Born March 4, 1968, in El Toro, Calif. ... 6-0/225. ... Bats right, throws left. ... Full name: Brian Ronald Hunter.
HIGH SCHOOL: Paramount (Calif.).
JUNIOR COLLEGE: Cerritos College (Calif.).
TRANSACTIONS/CAREER NOTES: Selected by Atlanta Braves organization in eighth round of free-agent draft (June 2, 1987). ... On Atlanta disabled list (April 18-May 18, 1993). ... Traded by Braves to Pittsburgh Pirates for a player to be named later (November 17, 1993); Braves acquired SS Jose Delgado to complete deal (June 6, 1994). ... Traded by Pirates to Cincinnati Reds for a player to be named later (July 27, 1994); Pirates acquired OF Micah Franklin to complete deal (October 13, 1994). ... On Cincinnati disabled list (June 19-July 24 and August 14-September 1, 1995); included rehabilitation assignment to Indianapolis (August 22-31). ... Released by Reds (March 8, 1996). ... Signed by Seattle Mariners (May 4, 1996). ... Granted free agency (October 8, 1996). ... Signed by Reds organization (January 14, 1997). ... Granted free agency (October 15, 1997). ... Signed by St. Louis Cardinals (March 30, 1998). ... Released by Cardinals (August 2, 1998). ... Signed by Chicago White Sox organization (August 14, 1998). ... On Calgary disabled list (August 25-September 2, 1998). ... Granted free agency (October 15, 1998). ... Signed by Braves organization (February 23, 1999). ... Granted free agency (November 9, 1999). ... Re-signed by Braves organization (December 7, 1999). ... Claimed on waivers by Philadelphia Phillies (April 21, 2000). ... Granted free agency (October 31, 2000). ... Re-signed by Phillies (November 30, 2000).
STATISTICAL NOTES: Led Appalachian League first basemen with 43 double plays in 1987. ... Led Midwest League first basemen with 21 errors in 1988. ... Tied for Southern League lead with nine sacrifice flies in 1989. ... Career major league grand slams: 3.

Year Team (League)	Pos.	G	AB	R	H	2B	3B	HR	RBI	Avg.	BB	SO	SB	PO	A	E	Avg.
1987— Pulaski (Appl.)............	1B-OF	65	251	38	58	10	2	8	30	.231	18	47	3	498	29	11	.980
1988— Burlington (Midw.)....	1B-OF	117	417	58	108	17	0	•22	71	.259	45	90	7	987	69	†22	.980
—Durham (Caro.)	OF-1B	13	49	13	17	3	0	3	9	.347	7	8	2	52	6	0	1.000
1989— Greenville (Sou.)	OF-1B	124	451	57	114	19	2	19	82	.253	33	62	5	248	15	4	.985
1990— Richmond (I.L.)	OF-1B	43	137	13	27	4	0	5	16	.197	18	37	2	126	5	3	.978
—Greenville (Sou.)	OF-1B	88	320	45	77	13	1	14	55	.241	43	62	6	189	19	8	.963
1991— Richmond (I.L.).........	OF	48	181	28	47	7	0	10	30	.260	11	24	3	121	4	4	.969
—Atlanta (N.L.)	1B-OF	97	271	32	68	16	1	12	50	.251	17	48	0	624	46	8	.988
1992— Atlanta (N.L.)	1B-OF	102	238	34	57	13	2	14	41	.239	21	50	1	542	50	4	.993
1993— Atlanta (N.L.)	1B-OF	37	80	4	11	3	1	0	8	.138	2	15	0	168	13	1	.995
—Richmond (I.L.).........	1B-OF	30	99	16	24	7	0	6	26	.242	10	21	4	174	15	0	1.000
1994— Pittsburgh (N.L.)■	1B-OF	76	233	28	53	15	1	11	47	.227	15	55	0	496	37	5	.991
—Cincinnati (N.L.)■	OF-1B	9	23	6	7	1	0	4	10	.304	2	1	0	20	1	0	1.000
1995— Cincinnati (N.L.)	1B-OF	40	79	9	17	6	0	1	9	.215	11	21	2	171	13	3	.984
—Indianapolis (A.A.)	OF-1B	9	36	7	13	5	0	4	11	.361	6	11	0	42	2	1	.978
1996— Tacoma (PCL)■	OF-1B-DH	25	92	19	32	6	1	7	24	.348	9	11	1	45	5	1	.980
—Seattle (A.L.)■	1B-OF-DH	75	198	21	53	10	0	7	28	.268	15	43	0	280	10	5	.983
1997— Indianapolis (A.A.)■ ..	1B-OF-DH	139	506	74	142	36	4	21	85	.281	42	76	9	734	56	9	.989
1998— St. Louis (N.L.)■	1B-OF-DH	62	112	11	23	9	1	4	13	.205	7	23	1	66	3	3	.958
—Calgary (PCL)■.........	OF-1B	11	31	1	3	1	0	0	6	.097	2	9	0	26	2	0	1.000
1999— Atlanta (N.L.)■	1B-OF	114	181	28	45	12	1	6	30	.249	31	40	0	435	36	4	.992
2000— Richmond (I.L.).........	1B	2	8	2	1	0	0	1	1	.125	1	1	1	16	1	0	1.000
—Atlanta (N.L.)	PH	2	2	1	1	0	0	1	1	.500	0	0	0	0	0	0	...
—Philadelphia (N.L.)■ ..	1B-OF-DH	85	138	13	29	5	0	7	22	.210	20	39	0	167	16	1	.995
American League totals (1 year)		75	198	21	53	10	0	7	28	.268	15	43	0	280	10	5	.983
National League totals (8 years)		624	1357	166	311	80	7	60	231	.229	126	292	4	2689	215	29	.990
Major League totals (9 years)		699	1555	187	364	90	7	67	259	.234	141	335	4	2969	225	34	.989

DIVISION SERIES RECORD

Year Team (League)	Pos.	G	AB	R	H	2B	3B	HR	RBI	Avg.	BB	SO	SB	PO	A	E	Avg.
1999— Atlanta (N.L.).............	1B	3	4	0	0	0	0	0	0	.000	1	3	0	11	1	0	1.000

CHAMPIONSHIP SERIES RECORD

Year Team (League)	Pos.	G	AB	R	H	2B	3B	HR	RBI	Avg.	BB	SO	SB	PO	A	E	Avg.
1991— Atlanta (N.L.).............	1B	5	18	2	6	2	0	1	4	.333	0	2	0	30	4	0	1.000
1992— Atlanta (N.L.).............	1B-PH	3	5	1	1	0	0	0	0	.200	0	1	0	7	0	0	1.000
1999— Atlanta (N.L.).............	1B-PH	6	10	1	1	0	0	0	2	.100	5	2	1	31	2	1	.971
Championship series totals (3 years)		14	33	4	8	2	0	1	6	.242	5	5	1	68	6	1	.987

WORLD SERIES RECORD

RECORDS: Shares single-inning record for most errors by first baseman—2 (October 23, 1999, eighth inning).

Year Team (League)	Pos.	G	AB	R	H	2B	3B	HR	RBI	Avg.	BB	SO	SB	PO	A	E	Avg.
1991— Atlanta (N.L.).............	OF-1B-PH	7	21	2	4	1	0	1	3	.190	0	2	0	6	1	0	1.000
1992— Atlanta (N.L.).............	1B-PH-PR	4	5	0	1	0	0	0	2	.200	0	1	0	14	1	0	1.000
1999— Atlanta (N.L.).............	1B	2	4	0	1	0	0	0	0	.250	0	1	0	9	2	2	.846
World Series totals (3 years)		13	30	2	6	1	0	1	5	.200	0	4	0	29	4	2	.943

H

HUNTER, TORII   OF   TWINS

PERSONAL: Born July 18, 1975, in Pine Bluff, Ark. ... 6-2/205. ... Bats right, throws right. ... Full name: Torii Kedar Hunter. ... Name pronounced TORE-ee.

HIGH SCHOOL: Pine Bluff (Ark.).

TRANSACTIONS/CAREER NOTES: Selected by Minnesota Twins organization in first round (20th pick overall) of free-agent draft (June 3, 1993); pick recieved as part of compensation for Cincinnati Reds signing Type A free-agent P John Smiley. ... On New Britain disabled list (April 4-May 10, 1996). ... On Salt Lake disabled list (July 28-August 11, 1998).

STATISTICAL NOTES: Led Florida State League outfielders with seven double plays in 1995. ... Tied for Eastern League lead for double plays by an outfielder with four in 1997. ... Career major league grand slams: 1.

Year	Team (League)	Pos.	G	AB	R	H	2B	3B	HR	RBI	Avg.	BB	SO	SB	PO	A	E	Avg.
1993—	GC Twins (GCL).........	OF	28	100	6	19	3	0	0	8	.190	4	23	4	50	1	•6	.895
1994—	Fort Wayne (Midw.).....	OF	91	335	57	98	17	1	10	50	.293	25	80	8	224	12	7	.971
1995—	Fort Myers (FSL)........	OF	113	391	64	96	15	2	7	36	.246	38	77	7	242	15	7	.973
1996—	New Britain (East.)	OF	99	342	49	90	20	3	7	33	.263	28	60	7	207	11	4	.982
—	Fort Myers (FSL)	OF	4	16	1	3	0	0	0	1	.188	2	5	1	9	0	0	1.000
1997—	New Britain (East.)	OF-DH	127	471	57	109	22	2	8	56	.231	47	94	8	252	7	7	.974
—	Minnesota (A.L.)	PR	1	0	0	0	0	0	0	0	...	0	0	0	...	...	...	...
1998—	New Britain (East.)	OF	82	308	42	87	24	3	6	32	.282	19	64	11	168	8	2	.989
—	Minnesota (A.L.)	OF	6	17	0	4	1	0	0	2	.235	2	6	0	8	0	0	1.000
—	Salt Lake (PCL)	OF-DH	26	92	15	31	7	0	4	20	.337	1	13	2	55	1	2	.966
1999—	Minnesota (A.L.)	OF	135	384	52	98	17	2	9	35	.255	26	72	10	284	7	1	.997
2000—	Minnesota (A.L.)	OF	99	336	44	94	14	7	5	44	.280	18	68	4	270	12	3	.989
Major League totals (4 years)			241	737	96	196	32	9	14	81	.266	46	146	14	562	19	4	.993

HUSKEY, BUTCH   OF/1B   INDIANS

PERSONAL: Born November 10, 1971, in Anadarko, Okla. ... 6-3/244. ... Bats right, throws right. ... Full name: Robert Leon Huskey.

HIGH SCHOOL: Lawton (Okla.).

TRANSACTIONS/CAREER NOTES: Selected by New York Mets organization in seventh round of free-agent draft (June 5, 1989). ... On New York disabled list (August 3-September 1, 1998); included rehabilitation assignment to Norfolk (August 21-23). ... Traded by Mets to Seattle Mariners for P Lesli Brea (December 14, 1998). ... Traded by Mariners to Boston Red Sox for P Robert Ramsay (July 26, 1999). ... Granted free agency (December 21, 1999). ... Signed by Minnesota Twins organization (January 27, 2000). ... Traded by Twins with 2B Todd Walker to Colorado Rockies for 2B Todd Sears and cash (July 16, 2000). ... Granted free agency (December 21, 2000). ... Signed by Cleveland Indians organization (January 26, 2001).

HONORS: Named International League Most Valuable Player (1995).

STATISTICAL NOTES: Led Gulf Coast League third basemen with 50 putouts and 23 errors in 1989. ... Led Appalachian League third basemen with 217 total chances and tied for lead with 11 double plays in 1990. ... Led South Atlantic League with 256 total bases in 1991. ... Led South Atlantic League third basemen with 21 double plays in 1991. ... Led Florida State League third basemen with 456 total chances and 28 double plays in 1992. ... Led Eastern League third basemen with 101 putouts, 297 assists, 34 errors and 432 total chances in 1993. ... Led International League third basemen with 31 double plays in 1994. ... Had 20-game hitting streak (August 22-September 13, 1997). ... Career major league grand slams: 2.

Year	Team (League)	Pos.	G	AB	R	H	2B	3B	HR	RBI	Avg.	BB	SO	SB	PO	A	E	Avg.
1989—	GC Mets (GCL)..........	3B-1B	54	190	27	50	14	2	6	34	.263	14	36	4	†73	106	†23	.886
1990—	Kingsport (Appl.)........	3B	*72	*279	39	75	13	0	14	53	.269	24	74	7	45	*150	•22	.899
1991—	Columbia (S.Atl.)........	3B	134	492	88	141	27	5	*26	*99	.287	54	89	22	*102	218	31	.912
1992—	St. Lucie (FSL).........	3B	134	493	65	125	17	1	18	75	.254	33	74	7	*108	*310	*38	.917
1993—	Binghamton (East.)	3B-SS-DH	*139	*526	72	132	23	1	25	98	.251	48	102	11	†101	†297	†34	.921
—	New York (N.L.)..........	3B	13	41	2	6	1	0	0	3	.146	1	13	0	9	27	3	.923
1994—	Norfolk (I.L.)	3B-DH	127	474	59	108	23	3	10	57	.228	37	88	16	*95	297	25	.940
1995—	Norfolk (I.L.)	3-0-1-DH	109	394	66	112	18	1	*28	87	.284	39	88	8	248	132	13	.967
—	New York (N.L.)..........	3B-OF	28	90	8	17	1	0	3	11	.189	10	16	1	16	60	6	.927
1996—	New York (N.L.)..........	1B-OF-3B	118	414	43	115	16	2	15	60	.278	27	77	1	638	54	15	.979
1997—	New York (N.L.)..........	O-1-3-DH	142	471	61	135	26	2	24	81	.287	25	84	8	377	38	15	.965
1998—	New York (N.L.)..........	OF-DH	113	369	43	93	18	0	13	59	.252	26	66	7	166	8	4	.978
—	Norfolk (I.L.)	DH	2	8	0	2	0	0	0	3	.250	0	1	0	0	0	0	...
1999—	Seattle (A.L.)■.....OF-1B-DH-3B		74	262	44	76	9	0	15	49	.290	27	45	3	177	4	1	.995
—	Boston (A.L.)■......	DH-OF-3B	45	124	18	33	6	0	7	28	.266	7	20	0	5	2	0	1.000
2000—	Minnesota (A.L.)■	DH-OF-1B	64	215	22	48	13	0	5	27	.223	25	49	0	98	7	3	.972
—	Salt Lake (PCL)	3B	2	9	2	3	0	0	2	5	.333	1	2	0	1	3	0	1.000
—	Colorado (N.L.)■	OF-1B	45	92	18	32	8	0	4	18	.348	16	14	1	60	2	0	1.000
American League totals (2 years)			183	601	84	157	28	0	27	104	.261	59	114	3	280	13	4	.987
National League totals (6 years)			459	1477	175	398	70	4	59	232	.269	105	270	18	1266	189	43	.971
Major League totals (7 years)			642	2078	259	555	98	4	86	336	.267	164	384	21	1546	202	47	.974

DIVISION SERIES RECORD

Year	Team (League)	Pos.	G	AB	R	H	2B	3B	HR	RBI	Avg.	BB	SO	SB	PO	A	E	Avg.
1999—	Boston (A.L.)..............	DH	2	5	0	1	0	0	0	0	.200	0	1	0	...	...	...	...

CHAMPIONSHIP SERIES RECORD

Year	Team (League)	Pos.	G	AB	R	H	2B	3B	HR	RBI	Avg.	BB	SO	SB	PO	A	E	Avg.
1999—	Boston (A.L.)..............	PH-DH	4	5	1	1	1	0	0	0	.200	1	1	0	...	...	...	...

PERSONAL: Born August 15, 1964, in Scottsdale, Ariz. ... 6-3/180. ... Bats left, throws right. ... Full name: Jeffrey Kent Huson. ... Name pronounced YOO-son.
HIGH SCHOOL: Mingus Union (Cottonwood, Ariz.).
JUNIOR COLLEGE: Glendale (Ariz.) Community College.
COLLEGE: Wyoming.
TRANSACTIONS/CAREER NOTES: Signed as non-drafted free agent by Montreal Expos organization (August 18, 1985). ... Traded by Expos to Texas Rangers for P Drew Hall (April 2, 1990). ... On Texas disabled list (August 8-31, 1991); included rehabilitation assignment to Oklahoma City (August 29-31). ... On Texas disabled list (March 27-May 27, June 5-July 15, and July 24-August 23, 1993); included rehabilitation assignments to Oklahoma City (May 24-27, July 10-15 and July 31-August 19). ... On Texas disabled list (March 25-June 6, 1994); included rehabilitation assignment to Oklahoma City (May 17-June 5). ... Released by Rangers (November 30, 1994). ... Signed by Rochester, Baltimore Orioles organization (December 31, 1994). ... On Baltimore disabled list (May 18-July 15, 1996); including rehabilitation assignment to Frederick (June 27-July 15). ... Released by Orioles (August 13, 1996). ... Signed by Colorado Rockies organization (August 19, 1996). ... Traded by Rockies to Milwaukee Brewers for a player to be named later (April 23, 1997). ... Granted free agency (October 28, 1997). ... Signed by Rockies organization (November 18, 1997). ... Selected by Seattle Mariners from Rockies organization in Rule 5 major league draft (December 15, 1997). ... Released by Mariners (July 8, 1998). ... Signed by Arizona Diamondbacks organization (August 7, 1998). ... Granted free agency (October 15, 1998). ... Signed by Anaheim Angels organization (November 18, 1998). ... Granted free agency (November 1, 1999). ... Signed by Chicago Cubs organization (January 14, 2000). ... Granted free agency (October 31, 2000).

Year	Team (League)	Pos.	G	AB	R	H	2B	3B	HR	RBI	Avg.	BB	SO	SB	PO	A	E	Avg.
								BATTING								FIELDING		
1986—	Burlington (Midw.)	SS-3B-2B	133	457	85	132	19	1	16	72	.289	76	68	32	183	324	37	.932
—	Jacksonville (Sou.).....	3B	1	4	0	0	0	0	0	0	.000	0	0	0	0	1	0	1.000
1987—	W.P. Beach (FSL)........	SS-OF-2B	131	455	54	130	15	4	1	53	.286	50	30	33	234	347	34	.945
1988—	Jacksonville (Sou.).......	S-2-O-3	128	471	72	117	18	1	0	34	.248	59	45	*56	217	285	26	.951
—	Montreal (N.L.)...........	SS-2B-3B-OF	20	42	7	13	2	0	0	3	.310	4	3	2	18	41	4	.937
1989—	Indianapolis (A.A.).......	SS-OF-2B	102	378	70	115	17	4	3	35	.304	50	26	30	172	214	17	.958
—	Montreal (N.L.)...........	SS-2B-3B	32	74	1	12	5	0	0	2	.162	6	6	3	40	65	8	.929
1990—	Texas (A.L.)■............	SS-3B-2B	145	396	57	95	12	2	0	28	.240	46	54	12	183	304	19	.962
1991—	Texas (A.L.).............	SS-2B-3B	119	268	36	57	8	3	2	26	.213	39	32	8	143	269	15	.965
—	Oklahoma City (A.A.)..	SS	2	6	0	3	1	0	0	2	.500	0	1	0	5	3	0	1.000
1992—	Texas (A.L.).............	S-2-O-DH	123	318	49	83	14	3	4	24	.261	41	43	18	178	250	9	.979
1993—	Oklahoma City (A.A.)..3B-SS-2B-OF		24	76	11	22	5	0	1	10	.289	13	10	1	39	52	3	.968
—	Texas (A.L.)..............SS-2B-DH-3B		23	45	3	6	1	1	0	2	.133	0	10	0	25	42	6	.918
1994—	Oklahoma City (A.A.)..2-3-O-DH-S		83	302	47	91	20	2	1	27	.301	30	32	18	140	165	7	.978
1995—	Rochester (I.L.)■........	SS-2B	60	223	28	56	9	0	3	21	.251	26	29	16	110	203	7	.978
—	Baltimore (A.L.)..........3B-2B-DH-SS		66	161	24	40	4	2	1	19	.248	15	20	5	59	89	1	.993
1996—	Baltimore (A.L.).........	2B-3B-DF	17	28	5	9	1	0	0	2	.321	1	3	0	20	17	1	.974
—	Rochester (I.L.).........	OF	2	8	0	2	0	0	0	1	.250	0	2	0	4	0	0	1.000
—	Frederick (Caro.)	OF	4	16	4	7	2	0	1	1	.438	2	0	0	6	0	0	1.000
—	Bowie (East.)..........	OF-3B	3	13	3	5	2	0	0	0	.385	1	0	0	4	4	0	1.000
—	Colo. Springs (PCL)■	2B-SS	14	61	10	18	4	0	0	8	.295	3	1	6	36	42	1	.987
1997—	Colo. Springs (PCL) ...	3B-2B	9	20	3	7	3	0	1	5	.350	2	2	0	5	8	0	1.000
—	Milwaukee (A.L.)■.....2-1-O-DH-3		84	143	12	29	3	0	0	11	.203	5	15	3	109	52	1	.994
1998—	Seattle (A.L.)■.........2-3-1-DH-S-O		31	49	8	8	1	0	1	4	.163	5	6	1	31	14	2	.957
—	Tucson (PCL)■ SS-2B-3B-OF		27	82	7	25	4	1	1	12	.305	5	14	0	39	54	6	.939
1999—	Anaheim (A.L.)■.......2-S-3-1-D-O		97	225	21	59	7	1	0	18	.262	16	27	10	104	147	5	.980
2000—	Chicago (N.L.)■.......3B-2B-SS-1B		70	130	19	28	7	1	0	11	.215	13	9	2	53	70	3	.976
American League totals (9 years)			705	1633	215	386	51	12	8	134	.236	168	210	57	852	1184	59	.972
National League totals (3 years)			122	246	27	53	14	1	0	16	.215	23	18	7	111	176	15	.950
Major League totals (12 years)			827	1879	242	439	65	13	8	150	.234	191	228	64	963	1360	74	.969

PERSONAL: Born February 21, 1977, in Del Mar, Calif. ... 6-5/230. ... Throws right, bats right. ... Full name: Chad Martin Hutchinson. ... Son of Lloyd Hutchinson, outfielder in Philadelphia Phillies organization (1969-72).
HIGH SCHOOL: Torrey Pines (Encinitas, Calif.).
COLLEGE: Stanford.
TRANSACTIONS/CAREER NOTES: Selected by Atlanta Braves organization in first round (26th overall) of free-agent draft (June 1, 1995); did not sign. ... Selected by St. Louis Cardinals organization in second round of free-agent draft (June 2, 1998). ... On Arkansas disabled list (June 12-August 24, 2000).
STATISTICAL NOTES: Led Texas League with 20 wild pitches in 1999.

Year	League	W	L	Pct.	ERA	G	GS	CG	ShO	Sv.	IP	H	R	ER	BB	SO
1998—	New Jersey (NY-Penn)	0	1	.000	3.52	3	3	0	0	0	15 1/3	15	7	6	4	20
—	Prince William (Caro.)	2	0	1.000	2.79	5	5	0	0	0	29	20	12	9	11	31
1999—	Arkansas (Texas)...............	7	11	.389	4.72	25	25	0	0	0	141	127	79	74	*85	150
—	Memphis (PCL).................	2	0	1.000	2.19	2	2	0	0	0	12 1/3	4	3	3	8	16
2000—	Memphis (PCL).................	0	1	.000	25.92	5	4	0	0	0	8 1/3	10	24	24	27	9
—	Arkansas (Texas)...............	2	3	.400	3.38	11	11	1	1	0	48	40	21	18	27	54

PERSONAL: Born December 6, 1971, in San Jose, Calif. ... 6-2/220. ... Bats right, throws right. ... Full name: Adam Davis Hyzdu. ... Name pronounced HIZE-doo.
HIGH SCHOOL: Moeller (Cincinnati).
COLLEGE: Xavier.

TRANSACTIONS/CAREER NOTES: Selected by San Francisco Giants organization in first round (15th pick overall) of free-agent draft (June 4, 1990); pick received as compensation for Houston Astros signing Type B free-agent IF Ken Oberkfell. ... Selected by Cincinnati Reds from Giants organization in Rule 5 major league draft (December 13, 1993). ... Released by Reds (March 23, 1996). ... Signed by Boston Red Sox organization (April 26, 1996). ... Signed by Arizona Diamondbacks organization (January 2, 1998). ... On Tucson disabled list (June 30-August 23, 1998). ... Granted free agency (October 15, 1998). ... Signed by Pittsburgh Pirates organization (May 10, 1999). ... Granted free agency (October 15, 1999). ... Re-signed by Pirates organization (October 30, 1999). ... Granted free agency (October 18, 2000). ... Re-signed by Pirates organization (October 24, 2000).

HONORS: Named Eastern League Most Valuable Player (2000).

STATISTICAL NOTES: Led Eastern League with .618 slugging percentage in 1996. ... Led Eastern League with 285 total bases in 2000. ... Tied for Eastern League lead with seven intentional bases on balls received in 2000.

Year	Team (League)	Pos.	G	AB	R	H	2B	3B	HR	RBI	Avg.	BB	SO	SB	PO	A	E	Avg.
1990—	Everett (N'West)	OF	69	253	31	62	16	1	6	34	.245	28	78	2	128	2	5	.963
1991—	Clinton (Midw.)	OF	124	410	47	96	13	5	5	50	.234	64	131	4	185	8	9	.955
1992—	San Jose (Calif.)	OF	128	457	60	127	25	5	9	60	.278	55	134	10	193	8	5	.976
1993—	San Jose (Calif.)	OF	44	165	35	48	11	3	13	38	.291	29	53	1	72	5	3	.963
	— Shreveport (Texas)	OF	86	302	30	61	17	0	6	25	.202	20	82	0	136	8	4	.973
1994—	Chattanooga (Sou.)■	OF-DH-1B	38	133	17	35	10	0	3	9	.263	8	21	0	70	4	4	.949
	— Indianapolis (A.A.)	OF	12	25	3	3	2	0	0	3	.120	1	5	0	10	1	1	.917
	— Win.-Salem (Caro.)	OF-DH	55	210	30	58	11	1	15	39	.276	18	33	1	67	2	4	.945
1995—	Chattanooga (Sou.)	OF	102	312	55	82	14	1	13	48	.263	45	56	3	182	4	1	*.995
1996—	Trenton (East.)■	OF-DH-C	109	374	71	126	24	3	25	80	.337	56	75	1	135	9	3	.980
1997—	Pawtucket (I.L.)	OF-DH	119	413	77	114	21	1	23	84	.276	72	113	10	170	10	4	.978
1998—	Tucson (PCL)■	OF-DH-P	34	100	21	34	7	1	4	14	.340	15	23	0	38	0	1	.974
1999—	Pawtucket (I.L.)■	OF-DH	12	35	4	8	0	0	1	6	.229	4	13	0	10	0	0	1.000
	— Altoona (East.)■	OF-1B-3B-DH	91	345	64	109	26	2	24	78	.316	40	62	8	275	27	11	.965
	— Nashville (PCL)	OF	14	44	6	11	1	0	5	13	.250	4	11	0	26	1	0	1.000
2000—	Altoona (East.)	OF-1B	*142	514	*96	149	39	2	*31	*106	.290	94	102	3	269	9	1	.996
	— Pittsburgh (N.L.)	OF	12	18	2	7	2	0	1	4	.389	0	4	0	5	0	0	1.000
Major League totals (1 year)			12	18	2	7	2	0	1	4	.389	0	4	0	5	0	0	1.000

RECORD AS PITCHER

Year	League	W	L	Pct.	ERA	G	GS	CG	ShO	Sv.	IP	H	R	ER	BB	SO
1998—	Tucson (PCL)	0	0	...	0.00	1	0	0	0	0	1	0	0	0	0	1

IBANEZ, RAUL — OF

PERSONAL: Born June 2, 1972, in Manhattan, N.Y. ... 6-2/200. ... Bats left, throws right. ... Full name: Raul Javier Ibanez.
HIGH SCHOOL: Sunset (Miami).
JUNIOR COLLEGE: Miami-Dade (South) Community College.
TRANSACTIONS/CAREER NOTES: Selected by Seattle Mariners organization in 36th round of free-agent draft (June 1, 1992). ... On disabled list (June 4-July 16, 1994). ... On Seattle disabled list (March 30-June 29, 1998); included rehabilitation assignment to Tacoma (May 30-June 28). ... On Tacoma disabled list (July 7-14, 1998). ... On Seattle disabled list (May 18-June 3, 1999); included rehabilitation assignment to Tacoma (May 26-June 3). ... On Seattle disabled list (August 7-22, 2000); included rehabilitation assignment to Tacoma (August 11-22). ... Granted free agency (December 21, 2000).

STATISTICAL NOTES: Led California League with .612 slugging percentage in 1995. ... Led California League with 25 passed balls in 1995. ... Career major league grand slams: 1.

Year	Team (League)	Pos.	G	AB	R	H	2B	3B	HR	RBI	Avg.	BB	SO	SB	PO	A	E	Avg.
1992—	Ariz. Mariners (Ariz.)	1B-C-OF	33	120	25	37	8	2	1	16	.308	9	18	1	51	3	4	.931
1993—	Appleton (Midw.)	1B-C-OF	52	157	26	43	9	0	5	21	.274	24	31	0	98	2	2	.980
	— Bellingham (N'West)	C	43	134	16	38	5	2	0	15	.284	21	23	0	137	15	1	.993
1994—	Appleton (Midw.)	C-1B-OF	91	327	55	102	30	3	7	59	.312	32	37	10	304	28	10	.971
1995—	Riverside (Calif.)	C-1B	95	361	59	120	23	9	20	108	.332	41	49	4	465	54	12	.977
1996—	Tacoma (PCL)	OF-1B-DH	111	405	59	115	20	3	11	47	.284	44	56	7	201	12	11	.951
	— Port City (Sou.)	OF-DH-C-1B	19	76	12	28	8	1	1	13	.368	8	7	3	36	2	4	.905
	— Seattle (A.L.)	DH	4	5	0	0	0	0	0	0	.000	0	1	0	0	0	0	...
1997—	Tacoma (PCL)	OF	111	438	84	133	30	5	15	84	.304	32	75	7	192	12	5	.976
	— Seattle (A.L.)	OF-DH	11	26	3	4	0	1	1	4	.154	0	6	0	9	0	0	1.000
1998—	Tacoma (PCL)	OF-DH	52	190	24	41	8	1	6	25	.216	24	47	1	78	2	1	.988
	— Seattle (A.L.)	OF-1B-DH	37	98	12	25	7	1	2	12	.255	5	22	0	105	7	1	.991
1999—	Seattle (A.L.)	OF-1B-DH-C	87	209	23	54	7	0	9	27	.258	17	32	5	234	8	3	.988
	— Tacoma (PCL)	OF-DH-1B	8	31	6	11	1	0	3	5	.355	1	7	1	13	0	0	1.000
2000—	Seattle (A.L.)	OF-DH-1B	92	140	21	32	8	0	2	15	.229	14	25	2	99	1	2	.980
	— Tacoma (PCL)	OF	10	40	3	10	4	0	0	6	.250	1	3	0	9	0	0	1.000
Major League totals (5 years)			231	478	59	115	22	2	14	58	.241	36	86	7	447	16	6	.987

DIVISION SERIES RECORD

Year	Team (League)	Pos.	G	AB	R	H	2B	3B	HR	RBI	Avg.	BB	SO	SB	PO	A	E	Avg.
2000—	Seattle (A.L.)	PR-OF	3	8	2	3	0	0	0	0	.375	0	0	0	4	0	0	1.000

CHAMPIONSHIP SERIES RECORD

Year	Team (League)	Pos.	G	AB	R	H	2B	3B	HR	RBI	Avg.	BB	SO	SB	PO	A	E	Avg.
2000—	Seattle (A.L.)	OF-PH	6	9	0	0	0	0	0	0	.000	0	2	0	6	0	0	1.000

IRABU, HIDEKI — P — EXPOS

PERSONAL: Born May 5, 1969, in Hyogo, Japan. ... 6-4/240. ... Throws right, bats right.
HIGH SCHOOL: Jinsei.

TRANSACTIONS/CAREER NOTES: Rights acquired by San Diego Padres from Chiba Lotte Marines of Japan Pacific League (January 13, 1997). ... Rights traded by Padres with 2B Homer Bush, OF Gordon Amerson and a player to be named later to New York Yankees for OF Ruben Rivera, P Rafael Medina and cash (April 22, 1997); Padres traded OF Vernon Maxwell to Yankees to complete deal (June 9, 1997). ... Signed by Yankees (May 29, 1997). ... Traded by Yankees to Montreal Expos for P Jake Westbrook and two players to be named (December 22, 1999); Yankees acquired P Ted Lilly (March 17, 2000) and P Christian Parker (March 22, 2000) to complete deal. ... On Montreal disabled list (May 27-July 26 and July 28, 2000-remainder of season); included rehabilitation assignments to Jupiter (July 8-18) and Ottawa (July 19-20).

STATISTICAL NOTES: Tied for A.L. lead with three balks in 1997.

Year League	W	L	Pct.	ERA	G	GS	CG	ShO	Sv.	IP	H	R	ER	BB	SO
1988— Lotte Orions (Jap. Pac.)	2	5	.286	3.89	14	6	...	...	1	39 1/3	30	19	17	15	21
1989— Lotte Orions (Jap. Pac.)	0	2	.000	3.53	33	2	...	...	9	51	37	20	20	27	50
1990— Lotte Orions (Jap. Pac.)	8	5	.615	3.78	34	7	...	...	0	123 2/3	110	56	52	72	102
1991— Lotte Orions (Jap. Pac.)	3	8	.273	6.88	24	14	...	...	0	100 2/3	110	78	77	70	78
1992— Chiba Lotte (Jap. Pac.)	0	5	.000	3.86	28	4	...	...	0	77	38	33	33	37	55
1993— Chiba Lotte (Jap. Pac.)	8	7	.533	3.10	32	8	...	...	1	142 1/3	125	59	49	58	160
1994— Chiba Lotte (Jap. Pac.)	*15	10	.600	3.04	27	20	...	...	0	207 1/3	170	77	70	94	239
1995— Chiba Lotte (Jap. Pac.)	11	11	.500	*2.53	28	18	...	...	0	203	158	70	57	72	239
1996— Chiba Lotte (Jap. Pac.)	12	6	.667	*2.40	23	20	3	...	0	157 1/3	108	57	42	59	167
1997— Tampa (FSL)■	1	0	1.000	0.00	2	2	0	0	0	9	4	0	0	0	12
— Norwich (East.)	1	1	.500	4.50	2	2	0	0	0	10	13	5	5	0	9
— Columbus (I.L.)	2	0	1.000	1.67	4	4	1	1	0	27	19	7	5	5	28
— New York (A.L.)	5	4	.556	7.09	13	9	0	0	0	53 1/3	69	47	42	20	56
1998— New York (A.L.)	13	9	.591	4.06	29	28	2	1	0	173	148	79	78	76	126
1999— New York (A.L.)	11	7	.611	4.84	32	27	2	1	0	169 1/3	180	98	91	46	133
2000— Montreal (N.L.)■	2	5	.286	7.24	11	11	0	0	0	54 2/3	77	45	44	14	42
— Jupiter (FSL)	1	0	1.000	1.04	2	2	0	0	0	8 2/3	7	1	1	1	9
— Ottawa (I.L.)	0	1	.000	3.18	1	1	0	0	0	5 2/3	5	2	2	2	6
A.L. totals (3 years)	29	20	.592	4.80	74	64	4	2	0	395 2/3	397	224	211	142	315
N.L. totals (1 year)	2	5	.286	7.24	11	11	0	0	0	54 2/3	77	45	44	14	42
Major League totals (4 years)	31	25	.554	5.10	85	75	4	2	0	450 1/3	474	269	255	156	357

DIVISION SERIES RECORD

Year League	W	L	Pct.	ERA	G	GS	CG	ShO	Sv.	IP	H	R	ER	BB	SO
1998— New York (A.L.)				Did not play.											
1999— New York (A.L.)				Did not play.											

CHAMPIONSHIP SERIES RECORD

Year League	W	L	Pct.	ERA	G	GS	CG	ShO	Sv.	IP	H	R	ER	BB	SO
1998— New York (A.L.)				Did not play.											
1999— New York (A.L.)	0	0	...	13.50	1	0	0	0	0	4 2/3	13	8	7	0	3

WORLD SERIES RECORD

NOTES: Member of World Series championship team (1998 and 1999).

Year League	W	L	Pct.	ERA	G	GS	CG	ShO	Sv.	IP	H	R	ER	BB	SO
1998— New York (A.L.)				Did not play.											
1999— New York (A.L.)				Did not play.											

IRELAND, ERIC   P   ATHLETICS

PERSONAL: Born March 11, 1977, in Long Beach, Calif. ... 6-1/170. ... Throws right, bats right. ... Full name: Eric Wayne Ireland.
HIGH SCHOOL: Robert A. Millikan (Long Beach, Calif.).
TRANSACTIONS/CAREER NOTES: Selected by Houston Astros organization in second round of free-agent draft (June 1, 1995). ... Claimed on waivers by Chicago Cubs (November 20, 2000). ... Traded by Cubs to Oakland Athletics for OF Matt Stairs (November 20, 2000).
STATISTICAL NOTES: Pitched 5-0 no-hit victory for Kissimmee against St. Petersburg (June 23, 1999). ... Tied for Florida State League lead in putouts with 15 and total chances by pitcher with 47 and led Florida State League pitchers with eight errors in 1999. ... Led Texas League with 21 putouts in 2000.

Year League	W	L	Pct.	ERA	G	GS	CG	ShO	Sv.	IP	H	R	ER	BB	SO
1996— Gulf Coast Astros (GCL)	3	4	.429	4.70	12	11	0	0	0	53 2/3	54	33	28	23	43
1997— Auburn (NY-Penn)	5	7	.417	3.70	16	16	2	0	0	*107	*111	55	44	21	79
1998— Quad City (Midw.)	14	9	.609	2.88	29	•28	•6	•2	0	*206	172	80	66	71	191
1999— Kissimmee (FSL)	10	7	.588	*2.06	24	24	•5	2	0	*170 1/3	145	59	39	30	133
— Jackson (Texas)	0	1	.000	4.30	3	3	0	0	0	14 2/3	19	9	7	2	15
2000— Round Rock (Texas)	11	9	.550	3.41	29	•29	2	2	0	179 2/3	171	84	68	64	123

ISRINGHAUSEN, JASON   P   ATHLETICS

PERSONAL: Born September 7, 1972, in Brighton, Ill. ... 6-3/210. ... Throws right, bats right. ... Full name: Jason Derik Isringhausen. ... Name pronounced IS-ring-how-zin.
HIGH SCHOOL: Southwestern (Brighton, Ill.).
JUNIOR COLLEGE: Lewis & Clark Community College (Ill.).
TRANSACTIONS/CAREER NOTES: Selected by New York Mets organization in 44th round of free-agent draft (June 3, 1991). ... On disabled list (August 13-September 1, 1996). ... On disabled list (March 24-August 27, 1997); included rehabilitation assignment to Norfolk (April 6-11 and August 22-27), Gulf Coast Mets (August 6-11) and St. Lucie (August 11-22). ... On disabled list (March 21, 1998-entire season). ... Traded by Mets with P Greg McMichael to Oakland Athletics for P Billy Taylor (July 31, 1999).
HONORS: Named International League Most Valuable Pitcher (1995).

Year League	W	L	Pct.	ERA	G	GS	CG	ShO	Sv.	IP	H	R	ER	BB	SO
1992— Gulf Coast Mets (GCL)	2	4	.333	4.34	6	6	0	0	0	29	26	19	14	17	25
— Kingsport (Appl.)	4	1	.800	3.25	7	6	1	1	0	36	32	22	13	12	24
1993— Pittsfield (NY-Penn)	7	4	.636	3.29	15	15	2	0	0	90 1/3	68	45	33	28	*104
1994— St. Lucie (FSL)	6	4	.600	2.23	14	14	•6	•3	0	101	76	31	25	27	59
— Binghamton (East.)	5	4	.556	3.02	14	14	2	0	0	92 1/3	78	35	31	23	69

Year	League	W	L	Pct.	ERA	G	GS	CG	ShO	Sv.	IP	H	R	ER	BB	SO
1995—	Binghamton (East.)	2	1	.667	2.85	6	6	1	0	0	41	26	15	13	12	59
—	Norfolk (I.L.)	9	1	*.900	1.55	12	12	3	*3	0	87	64	17	15	24	75
—	New York (N.L.)	9	2	.818	2.81	14	14	1	0	0	93	88	29	29	31	55
1996—	New York (N.L.)	6	14	.300	4.77	27	27	2	1	0	171²/₃	190	103	91	73	114
1997—	Norfolk (I.L.)	0	2	.000	4.05	3	3	0	0	0	20	20	10	9	8	17
—	Gulf Coast Mets (GCL)	1	0	1.000	1.93	1	0	0	0	0	4²/₃	2	1	1	1	7
—	St. Lucie (FSL)	1	0	1.000	0.00	2	2	0	0	0	12	8	1	0	5	15
—	New York (N.L.)	2	2	.500	7.58	6	6	0	0	0	29²/₃	40	27	25	22	25
1998—	New York (N.L.)							Did not play.								
1999—	Norfolk (I.L.)	3	1	.750	2.29	12	8	0	0	0	51	33	18	13	20	51
—	New York (N.L.)	1	3	.250	6.41	13	5	0	0	1	39¹/₃	43	29	28	22	31
—	Oakland (A.L.)■	0	1	.000	2.13	20	0	0	0	8	25¹/₃	21	6	6	12	20
2000—	Oakland (A.L.)	6	4	.600	3.78	66	0	0	0	33	69	67	34	29	32	57
A.L. totals (2 years)		6	5	.545	3.34	86	0	0	0	41	94¹/₃	88	40	35	44	77
N.L. totals (4 years)		18	21	.462	4.67	60	52	3	1	1	333²/₃	361	188	173	148	225
Major League totals (5 years)		24	26	.480	4.37	146	52	3	1	42	428	449	228	208	192	302

DIVISION SERIES RECORD

Year	League	W	L	Pct.	ERA	G	GS	CG	ShO	Sv.	IP	H	R	ER	BB	SO
2000—	Oakland (A.L.)	0	0	...	0.00	2	0	0	0	1	2	1	0	0	0	3

ALL-STAR GAME RECORD

Year	League	W	L	Pct.	ERA	GS	CG	ShO	Sv.	IP	H	R	ER	BB	SO
2000—	American	0	0	...	9.00	0	0	0	0	1	2	1	1	1	0

JACKSON, DAMIAN — SS — PADRES

PERSONAL: Born August 6, 1973, in Los Angeles. ... 5-11/185. ... Bats right, throws right. ... Full name: Damian Jacques Jackson.
HIGH SCHOOL: Ygnacio Valley (Concord, Calif.).
JUNIOR COLLEGE: Laney (Calif.).
TRANSACTIONS/CAREER NOTES: Selected by Cleveland Indians organization in 44th round of free-agent draft (June 3, 1991). ... Traded by Indians with P Danny Graves, P Jim Crowell and P Scott Winchester to Cincinnati Reds for P John Smiley and IF Jeff Branson (July 31, 1997). ... Traded by Reds with OF Reggie Sanders and P Josh Harris to San Diego Padres for OF Greg Vaughn and OF/1B Mark Sweeney (February 2, 1999).
STATISTICAL NOTES: Led Appalachian League shortstops with 342 total chances and 45 double plays in 1992. ... Led Eastern League shortstops with 241 putouts, 446 assists, 54 errors, 741 total chances and 85 double plays in 1994. ... Led Eastern League in caught stealing with 22 in 1995. ... Tied for Eastern League lead in double plays by shortstop with 80 in 1995. ... Led American Association shortstops with 635 total chances and 84 double plays in 1996. ... Led International League shortstops with 227 putouts, 434 assists, 44 errors, 705 total chances and 101 double plays in 1998.

						BATTING								FIELDING		
Year	Team (League)	Pos.	G	AB	R	H	2B	3B	HR	RBI	Avg.	BB	SO	SB	PO	A	E	Avg.
1992—	Burlington (Appl.)	SS	62	226	32	56	12	1	0	23	.248	32	31	29	*102	*217	23	.933
1993—	Columbus (S.Atl.)	SS	108	350	70	94	19	3	6	45	.269	41	61	26	191	324	52	.908
1994—	Canton/Akron (East.)	SS-OF	138	531	85	143	29	5	5	60	.269	60	121	37	†241	†446	†54	.927
1995—	Canton/Akron (East.)	SS	131	484	67	120	20	2	3	34	.248	65	103	40	*220	337	*36	.939
1996—	Buffalo (A.A.)	SS	133	452	77	116	15	1	12	49	.257	48	78	24	*203	*403	29	.954
—	Cleveland (A.L.)	SS	5	10	2	3	2	0	0	1	.300	1	4	0	3	13	0	1.000
1997—	Buffalo (A.A.)	SS-2B-OF	73	266	51	78	12	0	4	13	.293	37	45	20	128	246	23	.942
—	Cleveland (A.L.)	SS-2B	8	9	2	1	0	0	0	0	.111	0	1	1	7	7	0	1.000
—	Indianapolis (A.A.)■	2B-SS	19	71	12	19	6	1	0	7	.268	10	17	4	36	55	5	.948
—	Cincinnati (N.L.)	SS-2B	12	27	6	6	2	1	1	2	.222	4	7	1	12	21	1	.971
1998—	Indianapolis (I.L.)	SS-OF	131	517	102	135	36	10	6	49	.261	62	125	25	†230	†435	†44	.938
—	Cincinnati (N.L.)	SS-OF	13	38	4	12	5	0	0	7	.316	4	6	2	20	21	1	.976
1999—	San Diego (N.L.)■	SS-2B-OF	133	388	56	87	20	2	9	39	.224	53	105	34	174	303	26	.948
2000—	San Diego (N.L.)	SS-2B-OF	138	470	68	120	27	6	6	37	.255	62	108	28	234	362	25	.960
American League totals (2 years)			13	19	4	4	2	0	0	1	.211	1	5	1	10	20	0	1.000
National League totals (4 years)			296	923	134	225	54	9	16	85	.244	125	224	65	440	707	53	.956
Major League totals (5 years)			309	942	138	229	56	9	16	86	.243	126	229	66	450	727	53	.957

JACKSON, MIKE — P — ASTROS

PERSONAL: Born December 22, 1964, in Houston. ... 6-2/225. ... Throws right, bats right. ... Full name: Michael Ray Jackson.
HIGH SCHOOL: Forest Brook (Houston).
JUNIOR COLLEGE: Hill Junior College (Texas).
TRANSACTIONS/CAREER NOTES: Selected by Philadelphia Phillies organization in 29th round of free-agent draft (June 6, 1983); did not sign. ... Selected by Phillies organization in secondary phase of free-agent draft (January 17, 1984). ... On Philadelphia disabled list (August 6-21, 1987). ... Traded by Phillies with OF Glenn Wilson and OF Dave Brundage to Seattle Mariners for OF Phil Bradley and P Tim Fortugno (December 9, 1987). ... Traded by Mariners with P Bill Swift and P Dave Burba to San Francisco Giants for OF Kevin Mitchell and P Mike Remlinger (December 11, 1991). ... On disabled list (July 24-August 9, 1993; June 17-July 2 and July 7, 1994-remainder of season). ... Granted free agency (October 17, 1994). ... Signed by Cincinnati Reds (April 8, 1995). ... On Cincinnati disabled list (April 20-June 5, 1995); included rehabilitation assignments to Chattanooga (May 21-30) and Indianapolis (May 30-June 5). ... Granted free agency (November 3, 1995). ... Signed by Mariners (February 2, 1996). ... Granted free agency (October 30, 1996). ... Signed by Cleveland Indians (December 12, 1996). ... Granted free agency (October 28, 1999). ... Signed by Phillies (December 7, 1999). ... On disabled list (March 31, 2000-remainder of season). ... Granted free agency (October 14, 2000). ... Signed by Houston Astros (December 14, 2000).
STATISTICAL NOTES: Led Carolina League with seven balks in 1985. ... Tied for N.L. lead with eight balks in 1987. ... Tied for A.L. lead with three balks in 1998.
MISCELLANEOUS: Holds Seattle Mariners all-time record for most games pitched (335).

Year League	W	L	Pct.	ERA	G	GS	CG	ShO	Sv.	IP	H	R	ER	BB	SO
1984— Spartanburg (S.Atl.)	7	2	.778	2.68	14	0	0	0	0	80 2/3	53	35	24	50	77
1985— Peninsula (Caro.)	7	9	.438	4.60	31	18	0	0	1	125 1/3	127	71	64	53	96
1986— Reading (East.)	2	3	.400	1.66	30	0	0	0	6	43 1/3	25	9	8	22	42
— Portland (PCL)	3	1	.750	3.18	17	0	0	0	3	22 2/3	18	8	8	13	23
— Philadelphia (N.L.)	0	0	...	3.38	9	0	0	0	0	13 1/3	12	5	5	4	3
1987— Philadelphia (N.L.)	3	10	.231	4.20	55	7	0	0	1	109 1/3	88	55	51	56	93
— Maine (I.L.)	1	0	1.000	0.82	2	2	0	0	0	11	9	2	1	5	13
1988— Seattle (A.L.)■	6	5	.545	2.63	62	0	0	0	4	99 1/3	74	37	29	43	76
1989— Seattle (A.L.)	4	6	.400	3.17	65	0	0	0	7	99 1/3	81	43	35	54	94
1990— Seattle (A.L.)	5	7	.417	4.54	63	0	0	0	3	77 1/3	64	42	39	44	69
1991— Seattle (A.L.)	7	7	.500	3.25	72	0	0	0	14	88 2/3	64	35	32	34	74
1992— San Francisco (N.L.)■	6	6	.500	3.73	67	0	0	0	2	82	76	35	34	33	80
1993— San Francisco (N.L.)	6	6	.500	3.03	*81	0	0	0	1	77 1/3	58	28	26	24	70
1994— San Francisco (N.L.)	3	2	.600	1.49	36	0	0	0	4	42 1/3	23	8	7	11	51
1995— Chattanooga (Sou.)■	0	0	...	0.00	3	2	0	0	0	3	2	0	0	0	2
— Indianapolis (A.A.)	0	0	...	0.00	2	1	0	0	0	2	0	0	0	0	1
— Cincinnati (N.L.)	6	1	.857	2.39	40	0	0	0	2	49	38	13	13	19	41
1996— Seattle (A.L.)	1	1	.500	3.63	73	0	0	0	6	72	61	32	29	24	70
1997— Cleveland (A.L.)■	2	5	.286	3.24	71	0	0	0	15	75	59	33	27	29	74
1998— Cleveland (A.L.)	1	1	.500	1.55	69	0	0	0	40	64	43	11	11	13	55
1999— Cleveland (A.L.)	3	4	.429	4.06	72	0	0	0	39	68 2/3	60	32	31	26	55
2000— Philadelphia (N.L.)■							Did not play.								
A.L. totals (8 years)	29	36	.446	3.25	547	0	0	0	128	644 1/3	506	265	233	267	567
N.L. totals (6 years)	24	25	.490	3.28	288	7	0	0	10	373 1/3	295	144	136	147	338
Major League totals (14 years)	53	61	.465	3.26	835	7	0	0	138	1017 2/3	801	409	369	414	905

NOTES: Shares A.L. single-series record for most saves—3.

DIVISION SERIES RECORD

Year League	W	L	Pct.	ERA	G	GS	CG	ShO	Sv.	IP	H	R	ER	BB	SO
1995— Cincinnati (N.L.)	0	0	...	0.00	3	0	0	0	0	3 2/3	4	0	0	0	1
1997— Cleveland (A.L.)	1	0	1.000	0.00	4	0	0	0	0	4 1/3	3	0	0	1	5
1998— Cleveland (A.L.)	0	0	...	4.50	3	0	0	0	3	4	3	2	2	1	1
1999— Cleveland (A.L.)	0	0	...	4.50	2	0	0	0	0	2	2	1	1	1	1
Division series totals (4 years)	1	0	1.000	1.93	12	0	0	0	3	14	12	3	3	3	8

CHAMPIONSHIP SERIES RECORD

Year League	W	L	Pct.	ERA	G	GS	CG	ShO	Sv.	IP	H	R	ER	BB	SO
1995— Cincinnati (N.L.)	0	1	.000	23.14	3	0	0	0	0	2 1/3	5	6	6	4	1
1997— Cleveland (A.L.)	0	0	...	0.00	5	0	0	0	0	4 1/3	1	0	0	1	7
1998— Cleveland (A.L.)	0	0	...	0.00	1	0	0	0	1	1	0	0	0	0	2
Champ. series totals (3 years)	0	1	.000	7.04	9	0	0	0	1	7 2/3	6	6	6	5	10

WORLD SERIES RECORD

Year League	W	L	Pct.	ERA	G	GS	CG	ShO	Sv.	IP	H	R	ER	BB	SO
1997— Cleveland (A.L.)	0	0	...	1.93	4	0	0	0	0	4 2/3	5	1	1	3	4

JACOBS, DWAYNE · P · DEVIL RAYS

PERSONAL: Born July 17, 1976, in Jacksonville. ... 6-10/225. ... Throws right, bats right. ... Full name: Dwayne Allen Jacobs.
HIGH SCHOOL: First Coast (Jacksonville).
TRANSACTIONS/CAREER NOTES: Selected by Atlanta Braves organization in 24th round of free-agent draft (June 2, 1994). ... On restricted list (June 12, 1995-remainder of season). ... On disabled list (April 22-May 11, 1996). ... Claimed on waivers by Chicago White Sox (November 19, 1998). ... On Winston-Salem disabled list (July 12-24, 1999). ... Claimed on waivers by Los Angeles Dodgers (September 10, 1999). ... On Vero Beach disabled list (April 6-May 19, 2000). ... On San Bernardino disabled list (July 21-August 10 and September 10-30, 2000). ... Granted free agency (October 18, 2000). ... Signed by Tampa Bay Devil Rays organization (November 22, 2000).
STATISTICAL NOTES: Led Carolina League with 19 wild pitches in 1998. ... Led Carolina League with 28 wild pitches in 1999.

Year League	W	L	Pct.	ERA	G	GS	CG	ShO	Sv.	IP	H	R	ER	BB	SO
1994— Gulf Coast Braves (GCL)	1	2	.333	8.16	12	1	0	0	0	28 2/3	35	29	26	19	14
1995—							Did not play.								
1996— Macon (S.Atl.)	2	7	.222	6.80	26	15	0	0	0	82	85	82	62	76	76
1997— Durham (Caro.)	4	8	.333	5.01	25	24	1	1	0	116 2/3	112	78	65	85	115
1998— Danville (Caro.)	5	10	.333	4.99	31	19	0	0	0	110	92	71	61	*89	112
1999— Winston-Salem (Caro.)■	1	3	.250	5.03	46	1	0	0	4	59	33	38	33	79	76
2000— San Bernardino (Calif.)■	3	2	.600	4.03	21	0	0	0	4	29	23	14	13	30	41

JACQUEZ, TOM · P · PHILLIES

PERSONAL: Born December 29, 1975, in Stockton, Calif. ... 6-2/195. ... Throws left, bats left. ... Full name: Thomas Patrick Jacquez.
HIGH SCHOOL: Lincoln (Stockton, Calif.).
COLLEGE: UCLA.
TRANSACTIONS/CAREER NOTES: Selected by Philadelphia Phillies organization in sixth round of free-agent draft (June 3, 1997).

Year League	W	L	Pct.	ERA	G	GS	CG	ShO	Sv.	IP	H	R	ER	BB	SO
1997— Batavia (NY-Penn)	2	1	.667	2.42	4	4	0	0	0	22 1/3	20	6	6	2	20
— Piedmont (S.Atl.)	2	4	.333	4.63	8	8	0	0	0	44 2/3	45	29	23	13	26
1998— Clearwater (FSL)	9	11	.450	4.30	29	28	2	1	0	169 2/3	*215	102	81	31	108
1999— Reading (East.)	6	5	.545	5.28	38	14	0	0	1	122 2/3	149	84	72	32	68
— Scranton/W.B. (I.L.)	0	1	.000	2.45	3	0	0	0	0	3 2/3	4	1	1	0	4
2000— Reading (East.)	0	3	.000	2.96	13	0	0	0	3	27 1/3	26	11	9	9	21
— Scranton/W.B. (I.L.)	5	1	.833	1.98	35	1	0	0	1	54 2/3	53	15	12	20	34
— Philadelphia (N.L.)	0	0	...	11.05	9	0	0	0	1	7 1/3	10	9	9	3	6
Major League totals (1 year)	0	0	...	11.05	9	0	0	0	1	7 1/3	10	9	9	3	6

PERSONAL: Born May 27, 1966, in Portland, Ore. ... 6-1/217. ... Bats right, throws right. ... Full name: John Emil Jaha. ... Name pronounced JAH-ha.

HIGH SCHOOL: David Douglas (Portland, Ore.).

TRANSACTIONS/CAREER NOTES: Selected by Milwaukee Brewers organization in 14th round of free-agent draft (June 4, 1984). ... On disabled list (April 6-August 1, 1990 and May 21-June 6, 1995). ... On Milwaukee disabled list (June 24-July 27, 1995); included rehabilitation assignments to Beloit (July 16-20) and New Orleans (July 20-27). ... On disabled list (June 3, 1997-remainder of season). ... On Milwaukee disabled list (April 23-June 7 and August 16-September 1, 1998); included rehabilitation assignment to Beloit (June 4-8). ... Granted free agency (October 26, 1998). ... Signed by Oakland Athletics organization (February 17, 1999). ... On Oakland disabled list (April 24-June 3 and July 9, 2000-remainder of season); included rehabilitation assignment to Sacramento (May 28-31) and Modesto (June 1-3).

RECORDS: Shares major league single-game record for most strikeouts (nine-inning game)—5 (April 20, 2000).

HONORS: Named Texas League Most Valuable Player (1991). ... Named A.L. Comeback Player of the Year by The Sporting News (1999).

STATISTICAL NOTES: Led Northwest League with 144 total bases and tied for lead with four intentional bases on balls received in 1986. ... Led Texas League with 301 total bases, .619 slugging percentage and .438 on-base percentage in 1991. ... Led Texas League first basemen with 81 assists in 1991. ... Career major league grand slams: 7.

									BATTING						FIELDING			
Year	Team (League)	Pos.	G	AB	R	H	2B	3B	HR	RBI	Avg.	BB	SO	SB	PO	A	E	Avg.
1985—Helena (Pio.)		3B	24	68	13	18	3	0	2	14	.265	14	23	4	9	32	1	.976
1986—Tri-Cities (N'West)		1B-3B	•73	258	65	82	13	2	*15	67	.318	*70	75	9	352	101	18	.962
1987—Beloit (Midw.)		3B-1B-SS	122	376	68	101	22	0	7	47	.269	102	86	10	493	113	18	.971
1988—Stockton (Calif.)		1B	99	302	58	77	14	6	8	54	.255	69	85	10	793	60	5	*.994
1989—Stockton (Calif.)		1B-3B	140	479	83	140	26	5	25	91	.292	*112	115	8	1081	62	8	.993
1990—Stockton (Calif.)		DH	26	84	12	22	5	0	4	19	.262	18	25	0	...	...	...	...
1991—El Paso (Texas)		1B-3B	130	486	*121	167	38	3	*30	*134	.344	78	101	12	883	†87	10	.990
1992—Denver (A.A.)		1B	79	274	61	88	18	2	18	69	.321	50	60	6	654	50	7	.990
—Milwaukee (A.L.)		1B-DH-OF	47	133	17	30	3	1	2	10	.226	12	30	10	286	22	0	1.000
1993—Milwaukee (A.L.)		1B-3B-2B	153	515	78	136	21	0	19	70	.264	51	109	13	1187	128	10	.992
1994—Milwaukee (A.L.)		1B-DH	84	291	45	70	14	0	12	39	.241	32	75	3	660	47	8	.989
—New Orleans (A.A.)		1B-DH	18	62	8	25	7	1	2	16	.403	12	8	2	122	14	1	.993
1995—Milwaukee (A.L.)		1B-DH	88	316	59	99	20	2	20	65	.313	36	66	2	649	60	2	.997
—Beloit (Midw.)		DH	1	4	1	0	0	0	0	0	.000	0	1	0	0	0	0	...
—New Orleans (A.A.)		DH-1B	3	10	2	4	1	0	1	3	.400	2	1	0	9	2	0	1.000
1996—Milwaukee (A.L.)		1B-DH	148	543	108	163	28	1	34	118	.300	85	118	3	676	58	6	.992
1997—Milwaukee (A.L.)		1B-DH	46	162	25	40	7	0	11	26	.247	25	40	1	220	14	2	.992
1998—Milwaukee (N.L.)		1B-DH	73	216	29	45	6	1	7	38	.208	49	66	1	441	23	3	.994
—Beloit (Midw.)		DH	2	4	1	0	0	0	0	0	.000	2	2	0	...	...	...	...
1999—Oakland (A.L.)■		DH-1B	142	457	93	126	23	0	35	111	.276	101	129	2	42	4	0	1.000
2000—Oakland (A.L.)		DH	33	97	14	17	1	0	1	5	.175	33	38	1	...	...	...	...
—Sacramento (PCL)		DH	3	9	0	4	1	0	0	2	.444	4	2	0	...	...	...	...
—Modesto (Calif.)		DH	2	1	0	0	0	0	0	0	.000	2	1	0	...	...	...	...
American League totals (8 years)			741	2514	439	681	117	4	134	444	.271	375	605	35	3720	333	28	.993
National League totals (1 year)			73	216	29	45	6	1	7	38	.208	49	66	1	441	23	3	.994
Major League totals (9 years)			814	2730	468	726	123	5	141	482	.266	424	671	36	4161	356	31	.993

ALL-STAR GAME RECORD

							BATTING						FIELDING		
Year	League	Pos.	AB	R	H	2B	3B	HR	RBI	Avg.	BB	SO	SB	PO	A	E	Avg.
1999—American	PH-DH	1	0	0	0	0	0	0	.000	0	1	0	...	...	...	...

PERSONAL: Born August 15, 1967, in Fort Walton Beach, Fla. ... 6-3/205. ... Throws right, bats right. ... Full name: Michael Elmo James.

HIGH SCHOOL: Fort Walton Beach (Fla.).

JUNIOR COLLEGE: Lurleen B. Wallace State Junior College (Ala.).

TRANSACTIONS/CAREER NOTES: Selected by Los Angeles Dodgers organization in 43rd round of free-agent draft (June 2, 1987). ... On Albuquerque disabled list (July 12-August 26, 1992). ... On Vero Beach disabled list (July 2-9, 1993). ... Traded by Dodgers to California Angels for OF Reggie Williams (October 26, 1993). ... On California disabled list (May 11-June 1, 1995); included rehabilitation assignment to Lake Elsinore (May 25-June 1). ... Angels franchise renamed Anaheim Angels for 1997 season. ... On disabled list (July 3-27, 1997; and May 5, 1998-remainder of season). ... On Anaheim disabled list (March 24-September 7, 1999); included rehabilitation assignment to Lake Elsinore (July 31-September 3). ... Released by Angels (September 7, 1999). ... Signed by St. Louis Cardinals organization (October 15, 1999). ... On St. Louis disabled list (May 26-June 20, 2000); included rehabilitation assignment to Memphis (June 18-20).

MISCELLANEOUS: Scored run in only appearance as pinch runner (2000).

Year	League	W	L	Pct.	ERA	G	GS	CG	ShO	Sv.	IP	H	R	ER	BB	SO
1988—Great Falls (Pio.)	7	1	*.875	3.76	14	12	0	0	0	67	61	36	28	41	59
1989—Bakersfield (Calif.)	11	8	.579	3.78	27	27	1	1	0	159 2/3	144	82	67	78	127
1990—San Antonio (Texas)	11	4	.733	3.32	26	26	3	0	0	157	144	73	58	78	97
1991—Albuquerque (PCL)	1	3	.250	6.60	13	8	0	0	0	45	51	36	33	30	39
—San Antonio (Texas)	9	5	.643	4.53	15	15	2	1	0	89 1/3	88	54	45	51	74
1992—Albuquerque (PCL)	2	1	.667	5.59	18	6	0	0	1	46 2/3	55	35	29	22	33
—San Antonio (Texas)	2	1	.667	2.67	8	8	0	0	0	54	39	16	16	20	52
1993—Albuquerque (PCL)	1	0	1.000	7.47	16	0	0	0	2	31 1/3	38	28	26	19	32
—Vero Beach (FSL)	2	3	.400	4.92	30	1	0	0	5	60 1/3	54	37	33	33	60
1994—Vancouver (PCL)■	5	3	.625	5.22	37	10	0	0	8	91 1/3	101	56	53	34	66
1995—California (A.L.)	3	0	1.000	3.88	46	0	0	0	1	55 2/3	49	27	24	26	36
—Lake Elsinore (Calif.)	0	0	...	9.53	5	1	0	0	0	5 2/3	9	6	6	3	8
1996—California (A.L.)	5	5	.500	2.67	69	0	0	0	1	81	62	27	24	42	65
1997—Anaheim (A.L.)	5	5	.500	4.31	58	0	0	0	7	62 2/3	69	32	30	28	57
1998—Anaheim (A.L.)	0	0	...	1.93	11	0	0	0	0	14	10	3	3	7	12

Year League	W	L	Pct.	ERA	G	GS	CG	ShO	Sv.	IP	H	R	ER	BB	SO
1999— Lake Elsinore (Calif.)	0	0	...	5.79	3	3	0	0	0	9⅓	12	6	6	0	6
— Edmonton (PCL)	1	2	.333	8.64	8	1	0	0	0	8⅓	16	14	8	2	3
2000— Memphis (PCL)■	2	1	.667	0.93	8	0	0	0	1	9⅔	6	3	1	4	8
— St. Louis (N.L.)	2	2	.500	3.16	51	0	0	0	2	51⅓	40	22	18	24	41
A.L. totals (4 years)	13	10	.565	3.42	184	0	0	0	9	213⅓	190	89	81	103	170
N.L. totals (1 year)	2	2	.500	3.16	51	0	0	0	2	51⅓	40	22	18	24	41
Major League totals (5 years)	15	12	.556	3.37	235	0	0	0	11	264⅔	230	111	99	127	211

DIVISION SERIES RECORD

Year League	W	L	Pct.	ERA	G	GS	CG	ShO	Sv.	IP	H	R	ER	BB	SO
2000— St. Louis (N.L.)	1	0	1.000	0.00	2	0	0	0	0	4⅓	1	0	0	1	1

CHAMPIONSHIP SERIES RECORD

Year League	W	L	Pct.	ERA	G	GS	CG	ShO	Sv.	IP	H	R	ER	BB	SO
2000— St. Louis (N.L.)	0	0	...	15.43	4	0	0	0	0	2⅓	5	4	4	1	0

JARVIS, KEVIN — P — PADRES

PERSONAL: Born August 1, 1969, in Lexington, Ky. ... 6-2/200. ... Throws right, bats left. ... Full name: Kevin Thomas Jarvis.

HIGH SCHOOL: Tates Creek (Lexington, Ky.).

COLLEGE: Wake Forest.

TRANSACTIONS/CAREER NOTES: Selected by Cincinnati Reds organization in 21st round of free-agent draft (June 3, 1991). ... Claimed on waivers by Detroit Tigers (May 2, 1997). ... Claimed on waivers by Minnesota Twins (May 9, 1997). ... Claimed on waivers by Tigers (June 17, 1997). ... On Detroit disabled list (June 25-July 14, 1997); included rehabilitation assignment to Toledo (July 4-14). ... Released by Tigers (December 12, 1997). ... Signed by Chunichi Dragons of the Japan Central League (January 23, 1998). ... Signed by Reds organization (August 27, 1998). ... Released by Reds (September 9, 1998). ... Signed by Oakland Athletics organization (January 4, 1999). ... On Oakland disabled list (April 19-June 4, 1999); included rehabilitation assignment to Modesto (May 28-June 4). ... Granted free agency (October 8, 1999). ... Signed by Colorado Rockies organization (December 1, 1999). ... On Colorado disabled list (July 28-September 1, 2000); included rehabilitation assignment to Colorado Springs (August 12-September 1). ... Granted free agency (December 21, 2000). ... Signed by San Diego Padres (January 5, 2001).

MISCELLANEOUS: Appeared in one game as pinch runner (2000).

Year League	W	L	Pct.	ERA	G	GS	CG	ShO	Sv.	IP	H	R	ER	BB	SO
1991— Princeton (Appl.)	5	6	.455	2.42	13	13	4	•1	0	85⅔	73	34	23	29	79
1992— Cedar Rapids (Midw.)	0	0	...	0.00	1	0	0	0	0	1	1	0	0	0	0
— Charleston, W.Va. (S.Atl.)	6	8	.429	3.11	28	18	2	1	0	133	123	59	46	37	131
1993— Winston-Salem (Caro.)	8	7	.533	3.41	21	20	2	1	0	145	133	68	55	48	101
— Chattanooga (Sou.)	3	1	.750	1.69	7	3	2	0	0	37⅓	26	7	7	11	18
1994— Cincinnati (N.L.)	1	1	.500	7.13	6	3	0	0	0	17⅔	22	14	14	5	10
— Indianapolis (A.A.)	10	2	•.833	3.54	21	20	2	0	0	132⅓	136	55	52	34	90
1995— Indianapolis (A.A.)	4	2	.667	4.45	10	10	2	1	0	60⅔	62	33	30	18	37
— Cincinnati (N.L.)	3	4	.429	5.70	19	11	1	1	0	79	91	56	50	32	33
1996— Indianapolis (A.A.)	4	3	.571	5.06	8	8	0	0	0	42⅔	45	27	24	12	32
— Cincinnati (N.L.)	8	9	.471	5.98	24	20	2	1	0	120⅓	152	93	80	43	63
1997— Cincinnati (N.L.)	0	1	.000	10.13	9	0	0	0	1	13⅓	21	16	15	7	12
— Toledo (I.L.)■	0	1	.000	6.75	2	2	0	0	0	8	7	6	6	4	5
— Minnesota (A.L.)■	0	0	...	12.46	6	2	0	0	0	13	23	18	18	8	9
— Detroit (A.L.)■	0	3	.000	5.40	17	3	0	0	0	41⅔	55	28	25	14	27
1998— Chunichi (Jap. Cen.)■	1	2	.333	4.41	4	...	...	...	0	16⅓	16	18	8	5	7
— Indianapolis (I.L.)■	1	0	1.000	9.00	2	2	0	0	0	7	10	7	7	1	5
1999— Vancouver (PCL)■	10	2	.833	3.41	17	16	2	1	0	103	110	47	39	26	64
— Oakland (A.L.)	0	1	.000	11.57	4	1	0	0	0	14	28	19	18	6	11
— Modesto (Calif.)	0	0	...	1.29	2	2	0	0	0	7	4	1	1	1	10
2000— Colorado Springs (PCL)■	3	2	.600	0.69	7	7	0	0	0	39	18	6	3	13	18
— Colorado (N.L.)	3	4	.429	5.95	24	19	0	0	0	115	138	83	76	33	60
A.L. totals (2 years)	0	4	.000	8.00	27	6	0	0	0	68⅔	106	65	61	28	47
N.L. totals (5 years)	15	19	.441	6.12	82	53	3	2	1	345⅓	424	262	235	120	178
Major League totals (6 years)	15	23	.395	6.43	109	59	3	2	1	414	530	327	296	148	225

JAVIER, STAN — OF — MARINERS

PERSONAL: Born January 9, 1964, in San Francisco de Macoris, Dominican Republic. ... 6-0/200. ... Bats both, throws right. ... Full name: Stanley Julian Javier. ... Son of Julian Javier, infielder with St. Louis Cardinals (1960-71) and Cincinnati Reds (1972). ... Name pronounced HA-vee-AIR.

HIGH SCHOOL: La Altagracia (San Francisco de Macoris, Dominican Republic).

TRANSACTIONS/CAREER NOTES: Signed as non-drafted free agent by St. Louis Cardinals organization (March 26, 1981). ... Traded by Cardinals with SS Bobby Meacham to New York Yankees for OF Bob Helsom, P Marty Mason and P Steve Fincher (December 14, 1982). ... Traded by Yankees with P Jay Howell, P Jose Rijo, P Eric Plunk and P Tim Birtsas to Oakland Athletics for OF Rickey Henderson, P Bert Bradley and cash (December 5, 1984). ... On Oakland disabled list (August 3-September 1, 1987); included rehabilitation assignment to Tacoma (August 20-September 1). ... On disabled list (August 18-September 2, 1988; and July 7-24, 1989). ... Traded by A's to Los Angeles Dodgers for 2B Willie Randolph (May 13, 1990). ... Traded by Dodgers to Philadelphia Phillies for P Steve Searcy and a player to be named later (July 2, 1992); Dodgers acquired IF Julio Peguero to complete deal (July 28, 1992). ... Granted free agency (October 27, 1992). ... Signed by California Angels organization (January 15, 1993). ... Granted free agency (October 29, 1993). ... Signed by A's (December 7, 1993). ... Granted free agency (November 2, 1995). ... Signed by San Francisco Giants (December 8, 1995). ... On San Francisco disabled list (April 13-29 and July 17, 1996-remainder of season); included rehabilitation assignment to San Jose (April 26-29). ... On restricted list (April 13-18, 1997). ... Granted free agency (October 28, 1997). ... Re-signed by Giants (November 26, 1997). ... Traded by Giants to Houstson Astros for P Joe Messman (August 31, 1999). ... Granted free agency (October 28, 1999). ... Signed by Seattle Mariners (December 20, 1999).

STATISTICAL NOTES: Led A.L. outfielders with 1.000 fielding percentage in 1995.

Year Team (League)	Pos.	G	AB	R	H	2B	3B	HR	RBI	Avg.	BB	SO	SB	PO	A	E	Avg.
1981— Johnson City (Appl.) ..	OF	53	144	30	36	5	4	3	19	.250	40	33	2	53	2	3	.948
1982— Johnson City (Appl.) ..	OF	57	185	45	51	3	•4	8	36	.276	42	55	11	94	8	4	.962
1983— Greensboro (S.Atl.)■ .	OF	129	489	109	152	*34	6	12	77	.311	75	95	33	250	10	15	.945
1984— New York (A.L.).........	OF	7	7	1	1	0	0	0	0	.143	0	1	0	3	0	0	1.000
— Nashville (Sou.).........	OF	76	262	40	76	17	4	7	38	.290	39	57	17	202	4	7	.967
— Columbus (I.L.).........	OF	32	99	12	22	3	1	0	7	.222	12	26	1	77	4	2	.976
1985— Huntsville (Sou.)■	OF	140	486	105	138	22	8	9	64	.284	*112	92	61	363	8	7	.981
1986— Tacoma (PCL)	OF-1B	69	248	50	81	16	2	4	51	.327	47	46	18	172	9	6	.968
— Oakland (A.L.)	OF-DH	59	114	13	23	8	0	0	8	.202	16	27	8	118	1	0	1.000
1987— Oakland (A.L.)	OF-1B-DH	81	151	22	28	3	1	2	9	.185	19	33	3	149	5	3	.981
— Tacoma (PCL)	OF-1B	15	51	6	11	2	0	0	2	.216	4	12	3	26	0	2	.929
1988— Oakland (A.L.)	OF-1B-DH	125	397	49	102	13	3	2	35	.257	32	63	20	274	7	5	.983
1989— Oakland (A.L.)	OF-2B-1B	112	310	42	77	12	3	1	28	.248	31	45	12	221	8	2	.991
1990— Oakland (A.L.)	OF-DH	19	33	4	8	0	2	0	3	.242	3	6	0	19	0	0	1.000
— Los Angeles (N.L.)■..	OF	104	276	56	84	9	4	3	24	.304	37	44	15	204	2	0	1.000
1991— Los Angeles (N.L.)	OF-1B	121	176	21	36	5	3	1	11	.205	16	36	7	90	4	3	.969
1992— Los Angeles (N.L.)	OF	56	58	6	11	3	0	1	5	.190	6	11	1	17	0	0	1.000
— Philadelphia (N.L.)■ .	OF	74	276	36	72	14	1	0	24	.261	31	43	17	212	7	3	.986
1993— California (A.L.)■......OF-1B-2B-DH		92	237	33	69	10	4	3	28	.291	27	33	12	167	4	4	.977
1994— Oakland (A.L.)■	OF-1B-3B	109	419	75	114	23	0	10	44	.272	49	76	24	274	4	4	.986
1995— Oakland (A.L.)	OF-3B	130	442	81	123	20	2	8	56	.278	49	63	36	332	3	0	†1.000
1996— San Fran. (N.L.)■.......	OF	71	274	44	74	25	0	2	22	.270	25	51	14	180	2	3	.984
— San Jose (Calif.)..........	OF-DH	3	5	1	2	0	0	0	1	.400	1	1	0	1	0	0	1.000
1997— San Francisco (N.L.) ..	OF-1B	142	440	69	126	16	4	8	50	.286	56	70	25	279	2	7	.976
1998— San Francisco (N.L.) ..	OF	135	417	63	121	13	5	4	49	.290	65	63	21	217	0	3	.986
1999— San Francisco (N.L.) ..	OF-DH	112	333	49	92	15	1	3	30	.276	29	55	13	158	4	4	.976
— Houston (N.L.)■	OF	20	64	12	21	4	1	0	4	.328	9	8	3	31	1	0	1.000
2000— Seattle (A.L.)■...........	OF-DH-1B	105	342	61	94	18	5	5	40	.275	42	64	4	161	7	1	.994
American League totals (10 years)		839	2452	381	639	107	20	31	251	.261	268	411	119	1718	39	19	.989
National League totals (7 years)		835	2314	356	637	104	19	22	219	.275	274	381	116	1388	22	23	.984
Major League totals (16 years)		1674	4766	737	1276	211	39	53	470	.268	542	792	235	3106	61	42	.987

DIVISION SERIES RECORD

Year Team (League)	Pos.	G	AB	R	H	2B	3B	HR	RBI	Avg.	BB	SO	SB	PO	A	E	Avg.
1997— San Francisco (N.L.) ..	OF	3	12	2	5	1	0	0	1	.417	0	2	1	11	0	0	1.000
1999— Houston (N.L.)	PH-OF	4	11	1	3	0	0	0	0	.273	1	1	0	4	0	0	1.000
2000— Seattle (A.L.)	PH-OF	3	6	0	1	0	0	0	1	.167	0	3	0	4	0	0	1.000
Division series totals (3 years)		10	29	3	9	1	0	0	2	.310	1	6	1	19	0	0	1.000

CHAMPIONSHIP SERIES RECORD

Year Team (League)	Pos.	G	AB	R	H	2B	3B	HR	RBI	Avg.	BB	SO	SB	PO	A	E	Avg.
1988— Oakland (A.L.)	OF-PR	2	4	0	2	0	0	0	1	.500	1	0	0	5	0	0	1.000
1989— Oakland (A.L.)	OF	1	2	0	0	0	0	0	0	.000	0	1	0	1	0	0	1.000
2000— Seattle (A.L.)	OF-PH	4	14	0	1	0	0	0	1	.071	0	4	0	4	0	0	1.000
Championship series totals (3 years)		7	20	0	3	0	0	0	2	.150	1	5	0	10	0	0	1.000

WORLD SERIES RECORD

NOTES: Member of World Series championship team (1989).

Year Team (League)	Pos.	G	AB	R	H	2B	3B	HR	RBI	Avg.	BB	SO	SB	PO	A	E	Avg.
1988— Oakland (A.L.)	PR-OF	3	4	0	2	0	0	0	2	.500	0	1	0	1	0	0	1.000
1989— Oakland (A.L.)	OF	1	0	0	0	0	0	0	0	...	0	0	0	0	0	0	...
World Series totals (2 years)		4	4	0	2	0	0	0	2	.500	0	1	0	1	0	0	1.000

JEFFERIES, GREGG   OF

PERSONAL: Born August 1, 1967, in Burlingame, Calif. ... 5-10/185. ... Bats both, throws right. ... Full name: Gregory Scott Jefferies.
HIGH SCHOOL: Serra (San Mateo, Calif.).
TRANSACTIONS/CAREER NOTES: Selected by New York Mets organization in first round (20th pick overall) of free-agent draft (June 3, 1985). ... On disabled list (April 27-May 13, 1991). ... Traded by Mets with OF Kevin McReynolds and 2B Keith Miller to Kansas City Royals for P Bret Saberhagen and IF Bill Pecota (December 11, 1991). ... Traded by Royals with OF Ed Gerald to St. Louis Cardinals for OF Felix Jose and IF/OF Craig Wilson (February 12, 1993). ... Granted free agency (October 18, 1994). ... Signed by Philadelphia Phillies (December 14, 1994). ... On disabled list (June 17-July 2, 1995). ... On Philadelphia disabled list (April 5-June 4, 1996); included rehabilitation assignment to Scranton/Wilkes-Barre (May 30-June 4). ... On disabled list (August 18-September 2, 1997). ... Traded by Phillies to Anaheim Angels for a player to be named later (August 28, 1998); Phillies acquired P Doug Nickle to complete deal (September 9, 1998). ... Granted free agency (October 26, 1998). ... Signed by Detroit Tigers (December 28, 1998). ... On Detroit disabled list (June 21-July 6, August 3-20 and August 22-September 6, 1999); included rehabilitation assignment to Toledo (July 2-6). ... On disabled list (May 30, 2000-remainder of season). ... Granted free agency (October 31, 2000). ... Announced retirement (December 15, 2000).
HONORS: Named Appalachian League Player of the Year (1985). ... Named Carolina League Most Valuable Player (1986). ... Named Texas League Most Valuable Player (1987).
STATISTICAL NOTES: Led Carolina League with .549 slugging percentage in 1986. ... Led Texas League with 18 intentional bases on balls received in 1987. ... Tied for International League lead with 10 intentional bases on balls received in 1988. ... Led International League third basemen with 240 assists in 1988. ... Led A.L. third basemen with 26 errors in 1992. ... Tied for N.L. lead with 94 double plays by first basemen in 1994Ö Hit for the cycle (August 25, 1995). ... Had 15-game hitting streak (August 20-September 5, 1998). ... Career major league grand slams: 2.

						BATTING										FIELDING		
Year	Team (League)	Pos.	G	AB	R	H	2B	3B	HR	RBI	Avg.	BB	SO	SB	PO	A	E	Avg.
1985—	Kingsport (Appl.)........	SS-2B	47	166	27	57	18	2	3	29	.343	14	16	21	78	130	21	.908
—	Columbia (S.Atl.)........	2B-SS	20	64	7	18	2	2	1	12	.281	4	4	7	28	26	2	.964
1986—	Columbia (S.Atl.)........	SS	25	112	29	38	6	1	5	24	.339	9	10	13	36	83	7	.944
—	Lynchburg (Caro.)......	SS	95	390	66	138	25	9	11	80	*.354	33	29	43	138	273	20	.954
—	Jackson (Texas).........	SS-3B	5	19	1	8	1	1	0	7	.421	2	2	1	7	9	1	.941
1987—	Jackson (Texas).........	SS-3B	134	510	81	187	*48	5	20	101	.367	49	43	26	167	388	35	.941
—	New York (N.L.)...........	PH	6	6	0	3	1	0	0	2	.500	0	0	0	...	...	...	...
1988—	Tidewater (I.L.)...........3B-SS-2B-OF		132	504	62	142	28	4	7	61	.282	32	35	32	110	†330	27	.942
—	New York (N.L.)..........	3B-2B	29	109	19	35	8	2	6	17	.321	8	10	5	33	46	2	.975
1989—	New York (N.L.)..........	2B-3B	141	508	72	131	28	2	12	56	.258	39	46	21	242	280	14	.974
1990—	New York (N.L.)..........	2B-3B	153	604	96	171	*40	3	15	68	.283	46	40	11	242	341	16	.973
1991—	New York (N.L.)..........	2B-3B	136	486	59	132	19	2	9	62	.272	47	38	26	170	271	17	.963
1992—	Kansas City (A.L.)■ ...	3B-DH-2B	152	604	66	172	36	3	10	75	.285	43	29	19	96	304	†26	.939
1993—	St. Louis (N.L.)■	1B-2B	142	544	89	186	24	3	16	83	.342	62	32	46	1281	77	9	.993
1994—	St. Louis (N.L.)...........	1B	103	397	52	129	27	1	12	55	.325	45	26	12	889	53	7	.993
1995—	Philadelphia (N.L.)■ ...	1B-OF	114	480	69	147	31	2	11	56	.306	35	26	9	579	36	3	.995
1996—	Philadelphia (N.L.)......	1B-OF	104	404	59	118	17	3	7	51	.292	36	21	20	522	39	1	.998
—	Scranton/W.B. (I.L.)...	1B-DH	4	17	1	2	0	1	0	0	.118	1	3	0	22	3	1	.962
1997—	Philadelphia (N.L.)......	OF	130	476	68	122	25	3	11	48	.256	53	27	12	211	5	3	.986
1998—	Philadelphia (N.L.)......	OF	125	483	65	142	22	3	8	48	.294	29	27	11	168	7	1	.994
—	Anaheim (A.L.)■........	OF-1B	19	72	7	25	6	0	1	10	.347	0	5	1	48	2	0	1.000
1999—	Detroit (A.L.)■ DH-1B-2B-OF		70	205	22	41	8	0	6	18	.200	13	11	3	21	5	0	1.000
—	Toledo (I.L.)..............	DH	2	8	0	2	0	0	0	0	.250	0	2	0	...	...	...	...
2000—	Detroit (A.L.)...........	1-2-3-D-O	41	142	18	39	8	0	2	14	.275	16	10	0	188	52	1	.996
American League totals (4 years)			282	1023	113	277	58	3	19	117	.271	72	55	23	353	363	27	.964
National League totals (11 years)			1183	4497	648	1316	242	24	107	546	.293	400	293	173	4337	1155	73	.987
Major League totals (14 years)			1465	5520	761	1593	300	27	126	663	.289	472	348	196	4690	1518	100	.984

CHAMPIONSHIP SERIES RECORD

						BATTING										FIELDING		
Year	Team (League)	Pos.	G	AB	R	H	2B	3B	HR	RBI	Avg.	BB	SO	SB	PO	A	E	Avg.
1988—	New York (N.L.)..........	3B	7	27	2	9	2	0	0	1	.333	4	0	0	5	8	1	.929

ALL-STAR GAME RECORD

					BATTING									FIELDING		
Year	League	Pos.	AB	R	H	2B	3B	HR	RBI	Avg.	BB	SO	SB	PO	A	E	Avg.
1993—	National	PH-DH	1	0	0	0	0	0	0	.000	0	1	0	...	...	...	...
1994—	National	1B	1	2	1	1	0	0	0	1.000	0	0	0	6	0	0	1.000
All-Star Game totals (2 years)			2	2	1	1	0	0	0	.500	0	1	0	6	0	0	1.000

JENKINS, GEOFF — OF — BREWERS

PERSONAL: Born July 21, 1974, in Olympia, Wash. ... 6-1/204. ... Bats left, throws right. ... Full name: Geoffrey Scott Jenkins.
HIGH SCHOOL: Cordova Senior (Rancho Cordova, Calif.).
COLLEGE: Southern California.
TRANSACTIONS/CAREER NOTES: Selected by Milwaukee Brewers organization in first round (ninth pick overall) of free-agent draft (June 1, 1995). ... On El Paso disabled list (May 8-July 23, 1996). ... On disabled list (July 4-August 11, 1997). ... On disabled list (May 7-29, 2000).

						BATTING										FIELDING		
Year	Team (League)	Pos.	G	AB	R	H	2B	3B	HR	RBI	Avg.	BB	SO	SB	PO	A	E	Avg.
1995—	Helena (Pio.)	OF	7	28	2	9	0	1	0	9	.321	3	11	0	15	1	0	1.000
—	Stockton (Calif.)	OF	13	47	13	12	2	0	3	12	.255	10	12	2	14	3	2	.895
—	El Paso (Texas)..........	OF	22	79	12	22	4	2	1	13	.278	8	23	3	41	1	7	.857
1996—	El Paso (Texas)..........	DH	22	77	17	22	5	4	1	11	.286	12	21	1	...	...	...	...
—	Stockton (Calif.)	DH-OF	37	138	27	48	8	4	3	25	.348	20	32	3	2	0	0	1.000
1997—	Tucson (PCL)	OF-SS	93	347	44	82	24	3	10	56	.236	33	87	0	115	7	5	.961
1998—	Louisville (I.L.)	OF	55	215	38	71	10	4	7	52	.330	14	39	1	90	3	2	.979
—	Milwaukee (N.L.)	OF	84	262	33	60	12	1	9	28	.229	20	61	1	115	6	4	.968
1999—	Milwaukee (N.L.)	OF	135	447	70	140	43	3	21	82	.313	35	87	5	250	14	7	.974
2000—	Milwaukee (N.L.)	OF	135	512	100	155	36	4	34	94	.303	33	135	11	263	12	7	.975
Major League totals (3 years)			354	1221	203	355	91	8	64	204	.291	88	283	17	628	32	18	.973

JENSEN, MARCUS — C

PERSONAL: Born December 14, 1972, in Oakland. ... 6-4/204. ... Bats both, throws right. ... Full name: Marcus C. Jensen.
HIGH SCHOOL: Skyline (Oakland).
TRANSACTIONS/CAREER NOTES: Selected by San Francisco Giants organization in supplemental round ("sandwich pick" between first and second round, 33rd pick overall) of free-agent draft (June 4, 1990); pick received as part of compensation for San Diego Padres signing Type A free-agent P Craig Lefferts. ... On disabled list (June 1-14, 1993). ... Traded by Giants to Detroit Tigers for C Brian Johnson (July 16, 1997). ... Granted free agency (July 22, 1997). ... Re-signed by Tigers (July 26, 1997). ... Released by Tigers (March 25, 1998). ... Signed by Milwaukee Brewers organization (April 5, 1998). ... On Louisville disabled list (April 9-21, 1998). ... Released by Brewers (September 29, 1998). ... Signed by St. Louis Cardinals organization (January 13, 1999). ... Granted free agency (October 15, 1999). ... Signed by Minnesota Twins organization (January 4, 2000). ... Granted free agency (October 2, 2000).
STATISTICAL NOTES: Tied for Arizona League lead with three intentional bases on balls received in 1991. ... Led California League catchers with 722 total chances in 1994. ... Led Texas League catchers with 546 total chances in 1995.
MISCELLANEOUS NOTES: Member of 2000 U.S. Olympic baseball team.

Year Team (League)	Pos.	G	AB	R	H	2B	3B	HR	RBI	Avg.	BB	SO	SB	PO	A	E	Avg.
										BATTING					FIELDING		
1990— Everett (N'West).........	C	51	171	21	29	3	0	2	12	.170	24	60	0	191	27	3	.986
1991— Arizona Giants (Ariz.) .	C-1B	48	155	28	44	8	3	2	30	.284	34	22	4	226	29	7	.973
1992— Clinton (Midw.)	C-1B	86	264	35	62	14	0	4	33	.235	54	87	4	493	68	10	.982
1993— Clinton (Midw.)	C	104	324	53	85	24	2	11	56	.262	66	98	1	641	73	7	.990
1994— San Jose (Calif.).........	C-DH	118	418	56	101	18	0	7	47	.242	61	100	1	*627	86	9	.988
1995— Shreveport (Texas).....	C-DH	95	321	55	91	22	8	4	45	.283	41	68	0	*471	70	5	.991
1996— Phoenix (PCL)............	C-DH	120	405	41	107	22	4	5	53	.264	44	95	1	568	65	8	.988
— San Francisco (N.L.) ..	C	9	19	4	4	1	0	0	4	.211	8	7	0	37	5	2	.955
1997— San Francisco (N.L.) ..	C	30	74	5	11	2	0	1	3	.149	7	23	0	106	10	2	.983
— Toledo (I.L.)■............	C-DH	24	80	5	14	5	0	0	9	.175	9	25	0	149	6	1	.994
— Detroit (A.L.)	C	8	11	1	2	0	0	0	1	.182	1	5	0	26	1	1	.964
1998— Louisville (I.L.)■........	C-1B	74	230	29	52	13	0	10	33	.226	33	64	0	444	34	3	.994
— Milwaukee (N.L.)........	C	2	2	0	0	0	0	0	0	.000	0	2	0	1	0	0	1.000
1999— Memphis (PCL)■.........	C-DH	72	237	38	69	19	4	8	44	.291	30	59	0	380	32	2	.995
— St. Louis (N.L.)..........	C	16	34	5	8	5	0	1	1	.235	6	12	0	71	9	1	.988
2000— Minnesota (A.L.)■	C-DH	52	139	16	29	7	1	3	14	.209	24	36	0	261	13	2	.993
— Salt Lake (PCL)	C	15	55	10	16	4	0	1	12	.291	11	10	0	71	4	2	.974
American League totals (2 years)		60	150	17	31	7	1	3	15	.207	25	41	0	287	14	3	.990
National League totals (4 years)		57	129	14	23	8	0	2	8	.178	21	44	0	215	24	5	.980
Major League totals (5 years)		117	279	31	54	15	1	5	23	.194	46	85	0	502	38	8	.985

JENSEN, RYAN　　　　P　　　　GIANTS

PERSONAL: Born September 17, 1975, in Salt Lake City, Utah. ... 6-0/205. ... Throws right, bats right. ... Full name: Larry Ryan Jensen.
HIGH SCHOOL: Cottonwood (Salt Lake City, Utah).
COLLEGE: Southern Utah.
TRANSACTIONS/CAREER NOTES: Selected by San Francisco Giants organization in eighth round of free-agent draft (June 4, 1996). ... On Fresno disabled list (June 21-30, 1999).
STATISTICAL NOTES: Tied for Northwest League lead in home runs allowed with 10 in 1997.

Year League	W	L	Pct.	ERA	G	GS	CG	ShO	Sv.	IP	H	R	ER	BB	SO
1996— Bellingham (N'West)	2	4	.333	4.98	13	11	0	0	0	47	35	30	26	38	31
1997— Bakersfield (Calif.).............	0	0	...	13.50	1	1	0	0	0	1 1/3	3	2	2	0	2
— Salem-Kaizer (N'West)	7	3	.700	5.15	16	•16	0	0	0	80 1/3	87	55	46	32	67
1998— Bakersfield (Calif.).............	11	12	.478	3.37	29	27	0	0	0	168 1/3	162	89	63	61	164
— Fresno (PCL)....................	0	0	...	4.76	2	1	0	0	0	5 2/3	4	5	3	4	6
1999— Fresno (PCL)....................	11	10	.524	5.12	27	27	0	0	0	156 1/3	160	96	89	68	150
2000— Fresno (PCL)....................	5	8	.385	5.79	26	26	1	0	0	135 1/3	167	106	87	63	114

JETER, DEREK　　　　SS　　　　YANKEES

PERSONAL: Born June 26, 1974, in Pequannock, N.J. ... 6-3/195. ... Bats right, throws right. ... Full name: Derek Sanderson Jeter.
HIGH SCHOOL: Central (Kalamazoo, Mich.).
COLLEGE: Michigan.
TRANSACTIONS/CAREER NOTES: Selected by New York Yankees organization in first round (sixth pick overall) of free-agent draft (June 1, 1992). ... On New York disabled list (June 3-19, 1998); included rehabilitation assignment to Columbus (June 18-19). ... On New York disabled list (May 12-27, 2000); included rehabilitation assignment to Tampa (May 26-27).
HONORS: Named Minor League Player of the Year by The Sporting News (1994). ... Named A.L. Rookie Player of the Year by The Sporting News (1996). ... Named A.L. Rookie of the Year by Baseball Writers' Association of America (1996).
STATISTICAL NOTES: Had 15-game hitting streak (May 2-20, 1998). ... Had 16-game hitting streak (May 4-22, 1999).

Year Team (League)	Pos.	G	AB	R	H	2B	3B	HR	RBI	Avg.	BB	SO	SB	PO	A	E	Avg.
										BATTING					FIELDING		
1992— GC Yankees (GCL)......	SS	47	173	19	35	10	0	3	25	.202	19	36	2	67	132	12	.943
— Greensboro (S.Atl.)	SS	11	37	4	9	0	0	1	4	.243	7	16	0	14	25	9	.813
1993— Greensboro (S.Atl.)	SS	128	515	85	152	14	11	5	71	.295	56	95	18	158	292	56	.889
1994— Tampa (FSL)................	SS	69	292	61	96	13	8	0	39	.329	23	30	28	93	204	12	.961
— Alb./Colonie (East.)	SS	34	122	17	46	7	2	2	13	.377	15	16	12	42	105	6	.961
— Columbus (I.L.).........	SS	35	126	25	44	7	1	3	16	.349	20	15	10	54	93	7	.955
1995— Columbus (I.L.).........	SS	123	486	*96	154	27	9	2	45	.317	61	56	20	189	394	*29	.953
— New York (A.L.).........	SS	15	48	5	12	4	1	0	7	.250	3	11	0	17	34	2	.962
1996— New York (A.L.).........	SS	157	582	104	183	25	6	10	78	.314	48	102	14	244	444	22	.969
1997— New York (A.L.).........	SS	159	654	116	190	31	7	10	70	.291	74	125	23	243	*457	18	.975
1998— New York (A.L.).........	SS	149	626	*127	203	25	8	19	84	.324	57	119	30	223	393	9	.986
— Columbus (I.L.).........	SS	1	5	2	2	2	0	0	0	.400	0	2	0	4	3	1	.875
1999— New York (A.L.).........	SS	158	627	134	*219	37	9	24	102	.349	91	116	19	230	391	14	.978
2000— New York (A.L.).........	SS	148	593	119	201	31	4	15	73	.339	68	99	22	237	349	24	.961
— Tampa (FSL)..............	SS	1	3	2	2	1	0	0	0	.667	0	0	0	1	3	0	1.000
Major League totals (6 years)		786	3130	605	1008	153	35	78	414	.322	341	572	108	1194	2068	89	.973

DIVISION SERIES RECORD

Year Team (League)	Pos.	G	AB	R	H	2B	3B	HR	RBI	Avg.	BB	SO	SB	PO	A	E	Avg.
										BATTING					FIELDING		
1996— New York (A.L.).........	SS	4	17	2	7	1	0	0	1	.412	0	2	0	8	10	2	.900
1997— New York (A.L.).........	SS	5	21	6	7	1	0	2	2	.333	3	5	1	12	15	0	1.000
1998— New York (A.L.).........	SS	3	9	0	1	0	0	0	0	.111	2	2	0	4	5	0	1.000
1999— New York (A.L.).........	SS	3	11	3	5	1	1	0	0	.455	2	3	0	5	10	0	1.000
2000— New York (A.L.).........	SS	5	19	1	4	0	0	0	2	.211	2	3	0	6	15	0	1.000
Division series totals (5 years)		20	77	12	24	3	1	2	5	.312	9	15	1	35	55	2	.978

CHAMPIONSHIP SERIES RECORD

							BATTING										FIELDING		
Year	Team (League)	Pos.	G	AB	R	H	2B	3B	HR	RBI	Avg.	BB	SO	SB	PO	A	E	Avg.
1996— New York (A.L.).........		SS	5	24	5	10	2	0	1	1	.417	0	5	2	6	13	0	1.000
1998— New York (A.L.).........		SS	6	25	3	5	1	1	0	2	.200	2	5	3	9	13	0	1.000
1999— New York (A.L.).........		SS	5	20	3	7	1	0	1	3	.350	2	3	0	10	10	2	.909
2000— New York (A.L.).........		SS	6	22	6	7	0	0	2	5	.318	6	7	1	9	16	0	1.000
Championship series totals (4 years)			22	91	17	29	4	1	4	11	.319	10	20	6	34	52	2	.977

WORLD SERIES RECORD

NOTES: Named Most Valuable Player (2000). ... Member of World Series championship team (1996, 1998, 1999 and 2000).

							BATTING										FIELDING		
Year	Team (League)	Pos.	G	AB	R	H	2B	3B	HR	RBI	Avg.	BB	SO	SB	PO	A	E	Avg.
1996— New York (A.L.).........		SS	6	20	5	5	0	0	0	1	.250	4	6	1	15	22	2	.949
1998— New York (A.L.).........		SS	4	17	4	6	0	0	0	1	.353	3	3	0	7	8	0	1.000
1999— New York (A.L.).........		SS	4	17	4	6	1	0	0	1	.353	1	3	3	6	15	0	1.000
2000— New York (A.L.).........		SS	5	22	6	9	2	1	2	2	.409	3	8	0	5	15	0	1.000
World Series totals (4 years)			19	76	19	26	3	1	2	5	.342	11	20	4	33	60	2	.979

ALL-STAR GAME RECORD

NOTES: Named Most Valuable Player (2000).

						BATTING									FIELDING		
Year	League	Pos.	AB	R	H	2B	3B	HR	RBI	Avg.	BB	SO	SB	PO	A	E	Avg.
1998— American..................		SS	1	0	0	0	0	0	0	.000	0	1	0	0	2	0	1.000
1999— American..................		SS	1	0	0	0	0	0	0	.000	0	1	0	1	0	0	1.000
2000— American..................		SS	3	1	3	1	0	0	2	1.000	0	0	0	0	1	0	1.000
All-Star Game totals (3 years)			5	1	3	1	0	0	2	.600	0	2	0	1	3	0	1.000

JIMENEZ, D'ANGELO   SS   YANKEES

PERSONAL: Born December 21, 1977, in Santo Domingo, Dominican Republic. ... 6-0/194. ... Bats both, throws right.

TRANSACTIONS/CAREER NOTES: Signed as non-drafted free agent by New York Yankees organization (August 1, 1994). ... On Columbus disabled list (August 6-19, 1999). ... On New York disabled list (March 23-August 24, 2000); included rehabilitation assignments to Gulf Coast Yankees (July 26-31), Tampa (August 1-14) and Columbus (August 15-24).

STATISTICAL NOTES: Led Gulf Coast League shortstops with 289 total chances in 1995. ... Led South Atlantic League shortstops with 640 total chances in 1996. ... Led International League shortstops with 188 putouts in 1999.

							BATTING										FIELDING		
Year	Team (League)	Pos.	G	AB	R	H	2B	3B	HR	RBI	Avg.	BB	SO	SB	PO	A	E	Avg.
1995— GC Yankees (GCL)......		SS	57	214	41	60	14	*8	2	28	.280	23	31	6	*95	*173	21	.927
1996— Greensboro (S.Atl.)....		SS	138	*537	68	131	25	5	6	48	.244	56	113	15	190	*400	50	.922
1997— Columbus (A.A.)........		SS	2	7	1	1	0	0	0	1	.143	0	1	0	2	8	2	.833
—Tampa (FSL)..............		SS	94	352	52	99	14	6	6	48	.281	50	50	8	147	283	21	.953
1998— Norwich (East.)		SS	40	152	21	41	6	2	2	21	.270	25	26	5	62	119	12	.938
—Columbus (I.L.)..........		SS-2B	91	344	55	88	19	4	8	51	.256	46	67	6	150	302	26	.946
1999— Columbus (I.L.).........		SS-3B-2B	126	526	97	172	32	5	15	88	.327	59	75	26	†202	372	26	.957
—New York (A.L.)........		3B-2B	7	20	3	8	2	0	0	4	.400	3	4	0	3	9	0	1.000
2000— GC Yankees (GCL)......		2B-SS	4	10	2	1	0	0	0	0	.100	5	1	0	7	11	2	.900
—Tampa (FSL)..............		SS-2B	12	41	8	8	1	1	1	2	.195	8	7	0	19	30	7	.875
—Columbus (I.L.)..........		2B-3B-SS	21	73	11	17	3	1	1	5	.233	7	12	2	33	34	4	.944
Major League totals (1 year)			7	20	3	8	2	0	0	4	.400	3	4	0	3	9	0	1.000

JIMENEZ, JOSE   P   ROCKIES

PERSONAL: Born July 7, 1973, in San Pedro de Macoris, Dominican Republic. ... 6-3/190. ... Throws right, bats right. ... Name pronounced he-MEN-ez.

TRANSACTIONS/CAREER NOTES: Signed as non-drafted free agent by St. Louis Cardinals organization (October 21, 1991). ... Traded by Cardinals with P Manny Aybar, P Rick Croushore and SS Brent Butler to Colorado Rockies for P Darryl Kile, P Dave Veres and P Luther Hackman (November 16, 1999).

HONORS: Named Texas League Pitcher of the Year (1998).

STATISTICAL NOTES: Pitched 6-0 no-hit victory for Arkansas against Shreveport (August 27, 1998). ... Pitched 1-0 no-hit victory against Arizona (June 25, 1999).

MISCELLANEOUS: Scored one run in two appearances as pinch runner (1999).

Year	League	W	L	Pct.	ERA	G	GS	CG	ShO	Sv.	IP	H	R	ER	BB	SO
1992— Dom. Cardinals (DSL)		3	2	.600	6.10	18	2	0	0	0	48²/₃	68	43	33	23	21
1993— Dom. Cardinals (DSL)		3	5	.375	3.51	12	12	0	0	0	56¹/₃	61	47	22	35	30
1994— Dom. Cardinals (DSL)		3	9	.250	2.77	19	9	0	0	3	68¹/₃	54	43	21	30	54
1995— Johnson City (Appl.)		5	7	.417	3.49	14	•14	1	1	0	*90¹/₃	81	48	35	25	85
1996— Peoria (Midw.)....................		12	9	.571	2.92	28	27	3	1	0	172¹/₃	158	75	56	53	129
1997— Prince William (Caro.)........		9	7	.563	3.09	24	24	2	0	0	145²/₃	128	73	50	42	81
1998— Arkansas (Texas)...............		15	6	.714	3.11	26	26	1	1	0	179²/₃	156	71	62	68	88
—St. Louis (N.L.).................		3	0	1.000	2.95	4	3	0	0	0	21¹/₃	22	8	7	8	12
1999— St. Louis (N.L.)..................		5	14	.263	5.85	29	28	2	2	0	163	173	114	106	71	113
—Memphis (PCL).................		2	2	.500	3.04	4	4	0	0	0	26²/₃	30	10	9	9	18
2000— Colorado (N.L.)■		5	2	.714	3.18	72	0	0	0	24	70²/₃	63	27	25	28	44
Major League totals (3 years)		13	16	.448	4.87	105	31	2	2	24	255	258	149	138	107	169

PERSONAL: Born January 8, 1968, in Oakland. ... 6-2/210. ... Bats right, throws right. ... Full name: Brian David Johnson.
HIGH SCHOOL: Skyline (Oakland).
COLLEGE: Stanford.
TRANSACTIONS/CAREER NOTES: Selected by Montreal Expos organization in 36th round of free-agent draft (June 2, 1986); did not sign. ... Selected by New York Yankees organization in 16th round of free-agent draft (June 5, 1989). ... Selected by Las Vegas, San Diego Padres organization from Albany/Colonie, Yankees organization, in Rule 5 minor league draft (December 9, 1991). ... On disabled list (April 22-May 16, 1992). ... Traded by Padres with P Willie Blair to Detroit Tigers for P Joey Eischen and P Cam Smith (December 17, 1996). ... Traded by Tigers to San Francisco Giants for C Marcus Jensen (July 16, 1997). ... On San Francisco disabled list (May 4-21 and July 22-August 7, 1998); included rehabilitation assignment to Fresno (July 31-August 7). ... Granted free agency (December 21, 1998). ... Signed by Cincinnati Reds (January 11, 1999). ... On Cincinnati disabled list (June 14-August 1, 1999); included rehabilitation assignment to Indianapolis (July 23-30). ... Released by Reds (October 11, 1999). ... Signed by Kansas City Royals (December 14, 1999). ... Released by Royals (June 30, 2000). ... Signed by St. Louis Cardinals organization (July 11, 2000). ... Released by Cardinals (August 4, 2000). ... Signed by Yankees organization (August 8, 2000). ... Granted free agency (October 18, 2000).
STATISTICAL NOTES: Led South Atlantic League catchers with 752 putouts and 844 total chances in 1990. ... Led Florida State League catchers with 654 putouts in 1991. ... Career major league grand slams: 3.

								BATTING							FIELDING		
Year Team (League)	Pos.	G	AB	R	H	2B	3B	HR	RBI	Avg.	BB	SO	SB	PO	A	E	Avg.
1989— GC Yankees (GCL)	C	17	61	7	22	1	1	0	8	.361	4	5	0	84	14	1	.990
1990— Greensboro (S.Atl.)	C-3B-1B	137	496	58	118	15	0	7	51	.238	57	65	4	†773	91	13	.985
1991— Alb./Colonie (East.)	C-1B	2	8	0	0	0	0	0	0	.000	0	2	0	10	2	0	1.000
— Fort Laud. (FSL)	C-1B-3B	113	394	35	94	19	0	1	44	.239	34	67	4	†738	65	13	.984
1992— Wichita (Texas)■	C-3B	75	245	30	71	20	0	3	26	.290	22	32	3	472	40	3	.994
1993— Las Vegas (PCL)	C-3B-DH-OF	115	416	58	141	35	6	10	71	.339	41	53	0	513	67	9	.985
1994— San Diego (N.L.)	C-1B	36	93	7	23	4	1	3	16	.247	5	21	0	185	15	0	1.000
— Las Vegas (PCL)	C-DH	15	51	6	11	1	0	2	9	.216	8	6	0	61	5	0	1.000
1995— San Diego (N.L.)	C-1B	68	207	20	52	9	0	3	29	.251	11	39	0	403	32	4	.991
1996— San Diego (N.L.)	C-1B-3B	82	243	18	66	13	1	8	35	.272	4	36	0	456	21	5	.990
1997— Detroit (A.L.)■	C-DH	45	139	13	33	6	1	2	18	.237	5	19	1	217	9	3	.987
— Toledo (I.L.)	C-DH	7	21	0	3	2	0	0	1	.143	0	2	0	38	4	0	1.000
— San Fran. (N.L.)■	C-1B	56	179	19	50	7	2	11	27	.279	14	26	0	352	24	2	.995
1998— San Francisco (N.L.)	C-OF	99	308	34	73	8	1	13	34	.237	28	67	0	591	33	4	.994
— Fresno (PCL)	OF	5	19	4	6	1	0	2	3	.316	1	5	0	10	0	0	1.000
1999— Cincinnati (N.L.)■	C	45	117	12	27	7	0	5	18	.231	9	31	0	201	11	1	.995
— Indianapolis (I.L.)	C	6	19	2	4	3	0	0	4	.211	1	3	0	22	2	0	1.000
2000— Kansas City (A.L.)■	C	37	125	9	26	6	0	4	18	.208	4	28	0	221	12	2	.991
— Memphis (PCL)■	C	15	48	6	12	6	0	2	7	.250	4	10	0	78	5	2	.976
— Columbus (I.L.)■	C	18	68	12	13	5	0	1	6	.191	8	9	0	139	8	1	.993
American League totals (2 years)		82	264	22	59	12	1	6	36	.223	9	47	1	438	21	5	.989
National League totals (6 years)		386	1147	110	291	48	5	43	159	.254	71	220	0	2188	136	16	.993
Major League totals (7 years)		468	1411	132	350	60	6	49	195	.248	80	267	1	2626	157	21	.993

DIVISION SERIES RECORD

								BATTING							FIELDING		
Year Team (League)	Pos.	G	AB	R	H	2B	3B	HR	RBI	Avg.	BB	SO	SB	PO	A	E	Avg.
1996— San Diego (N.L.)	C	2	8	2	3	1	0	0	0	.375	0	1	0	15	3	0	1.000
1997— San Francisco (N.L.)	C	3	10	2	1	0	0	1	1	.100	1	4	0	18	0	0	1.000
Division series totals (2 years)		5	18	4	4	1	0	1	1	.222	1	5	0	33	3	0	1.000

PERSONAL: Born July 20, 1971, in Fort Pierce, Fla. ... 6-2/220. ... Bats right, throws right. ... Full name: Charles Edward Johnson Jr. ... Nephew of Fred McGriff, first baseman, Tampa Bay Devil Rays.
HIGH SCHOOL: Westwood (Fort Pierce, Fla.).
COLLEGE: Miami (Fla.).
TRANSACTIONS/CAREER NOTES: Selected by Montreal Expos organization in first round (10th pick overall) of free-agent draft (June 5, 1989); did not sign. ... Selected by Florida Marlins organization in first round (28th pick overall) of free-agent draft (June 1, 1992). ... On Florida disabled list (August 9-September 1, 1995); included rehabilitation assignment to Portland (August 30-September 1). ... On disabled list (July 28-September 1, 1996). ... Traded by Marlins with OF Gary Sheffield, 3B Bobby Bonilla, OF Jim Eisenreich and P Manuel Barrios to Los Angeles Dodgers for C Mike Piazza and 3B Todd Zeile (May 15, 1998). ... Traded by Dodgers with OF Roger Cedeno to New York Mets for C Todd Hundley and P Arnold Gooch; then traded by Mets to Baltimore Orioles for P Armando Benitez (December 1, 1998). ... Traded by Orioles with DH Harold Baines to Chicago White Sox for C Brook Fordyce, P Miguel Felix, P Juan Figueroa and P Jason Lakman (July 29, 2000). ... Granted free agency (October 30, 2000). ... Signed by Marlins (December 18, 2000).
RECORDS: Holds major league career records for most consecutive errorless games by catcher—159 (June 24, 1996-September 28, 1997); and most consecutive chances accepted by catcher without an error—1,294 (June 23, 1996-September 28, 1997). ... Holds major league single-season records for most consecutive errorless games by catcher—123 (April 1 through September 28, 1997); and most chances accepted without an error by catcher—973 (April 1 through September 28, 1997). ... Shares major league single-season records for highest fielding average by catcher (100 or more games)—1.000 (1997); and fewest errors (100 or more games)—0 (1997).
HONORS: Named catcher on THE SPORTING NEWS college All-America team (1992). ... Won N.L. Gold Glove at catcher (1995-98).
STATISTICAL NOTES: Led Midwest League with 230 total bases in 1993. ... Led Midwest League catchers with 1,004 total chances in 1993. ... Led N.L. catchers with 12 double plays in 1996. ... Led A.L. catchers with 14 double plays in 1999.
MISCELLANEOUS: Member of 1992 U.S. Olympic baseball team.

								BATTING							FIELDING		
Year Team (League)	Pos.	G	AB	R	H	2B	3B	HR	RBI	Avg.	BB	SO	SB	PO	A	E	Avg.
1993— Kane County (Midw.)	C	135	488	74	134	29	5	19	*94	.275	62	111	9	*852	*140	12	.988
1994— Portland (East.)	C-DH	132	443	64	117	29	1	*28	80	.264	*74	97	4	713	*84	7	.991
— Florida (N.L.)	C	4	11	5	5	1	0	1	4	.455	1	4	0	18	2	0	1.000
1995— Florida (N.L.)	C	97	315	40	79	15	1	11	39	.251	46	71	0	641	•63	6	.992
— Portland (East.)	C	2	7	0	0	0	0	0	0	.000	1	3	0	21	2	1	.958

Year Team (League)	Pos.	G	AB	R	H	2B	3B	HR	RBI	Avg.	BB	SO	SB	PO	A	E	Avg.
1996— Florida (N.L.)	C	120	386	34	84	13	1	13	37	.218	40	91	1	751	70	4	*.995
1997— Florida (N.L.)	C	124	416	43	104	26	1	19	63	.250	60	109	0	901	73	0	*1.000
1998— Florida (N.L.)	C	31	113	13	25	5	0	7	23	.221	16	30	0	193	10	2	.990
—Los Angeles (N.L.)■	C	102	346	31	75	13	0	12	35	.217	29	99	0	715	50	6	.992
1999— Baltimore (A.L.)■	C	135	426	58	107	19	1	16	54	.251	55	107	0	770	66	5	.994
2000— Baltimore (A.L.)	C-DH	84	286	52	84	16	0	21	55	.294	32	69	2	498	30	3	.994
—Chicago (A.L.)■	C	44	135	24	44	8	0	10	36	.326	20	37	0	224	12	3	.987
American League totals (2 years)		263	847	134	235	43	1	47	145	.277	107	213	2	1492	108	11	.993
National League totals (5 years)		478	1587	166	372	73	3	63	201	.234	192	404	1	3219	268	18	.995
Major League totals (7 years)		741	2434	300	607	116	4	110	346	.249	299	617	3	4711	376	29	.994

DIVISION SERIES RECORD

Year Team (League)	Pos.	G	AB	R	H	2B	3B	HR	RBI	Avg.	BB	SO	SB	PO	A	E	Avg.
1997— Florida (N.L.)	C	3	8	5	2	1	0	1	2	.250	3	2	0	21	3	0	1.000
2000— Chicago (A.L.)	C	3	9	0	3	0	0	0	0	.333	1	1	0	13	2	0	1.000
Division series totals (2 years)		6	17	5	5	1	0	1	2	.294	4	3	0	34	5	0	1.000

CHAMPIONSHIP SERIES RECORD

Year Team (League)	Pos.	G	AB	R	H	2B	3B	HR	RBI	Avg.	BB	SO	SB	PO	A	E	Avg.
1997— Florida (N.L.)	C	6	17	1	2	2	0	0	5	.118	3	8	0	52	3	2	.965

WORLD SERIES RECORD

NOTES: Member of World Series championship team (1997).

Year Team (League)	Pos.	G	AB	R	H	2B	3B	HR	RBI	Avg.	BB	SO	SB	PO	A	E	Avg.
1997— Florida (N.L.)	C	7	28	4	10	0	0	1	3	.357	1	6	0	49	2	0	1.000

ALL-STAR GAME RECORD

Year League	Pos.	AB	R	H	2B	3B	HR	RBI	Avg.	BB	SO	SB	PO	A	E	Avg.
1997— National	C	1	0	0	0	0	0	0	.000	0	1	0	2	0	0	1.000

JOHNSON, JASON — P — ORIOLES

PERSONAL: Born October 27, 1973, in Santa Barbara, Calif. ... 6-6/235. ... Throws right, bats right. ... Full name: Jason Michael Johnson.
HIGH SCHOOL: Conner (Hebron, Ky.).
TRANSACTIONS/CAREER NOTES: Signed as non-drafted free agent by Pittsburgh Pirates organization (July 21, 1992). ... Selected by Tampa Bay Devil Rays in first round (14th pick overall) of expansion draft (November 18, 1997). ... On Tampa Bay disabled list (July 4, 1998-remainder of season). ... Traded by Devil Rays to Baltimore Orioles for OF Danny Clyburn and a player to be named later (March 29, 1999); Devil Rays acquired SS Bolivar Voquez to complete deal (April 22, 1999).

Year League	W	L	Pct.	ERA	G	GS	CG	ShO	Sv.	IP	H	R	ER	BB	SO
1992— Gulf Coast Pirates (GCL)	2	0	1.000	3.68	5	0	0	0	0	7 1/3	6	3	3	6	3
1993— Gulf Coast Pirates (GCL)	1	4	.200	2.33	9	9	0	0	0	54	48	22	14	14	39
—Welland (NY-Penn)	1	5	.167	4.63	6	6	1	0	0	35	33	24	18	9	19
1994— Augusta (S.Atl.)	2	12	.143	4.03	20	19	1	0	0	102 2/3	119	67	46	32	69
1995— Augusta (S.Atl.)	3	5	.375	4.36	11	11	1	0	0	53 2/3	57	32	26	17	42
—Lynchburg (Caro.)	1	2	.333	2.05	5	4	0	0	0	22	23	6	5	5	9
1996— Lynchburg (Caro.)	1	4	.200	6.50	15	5	0	0	0	44 1/3	56	37	32	12	27
—Augusta (S.Atl.)	4	4	.500	3.11	14	14	1	1	0	84	82	40	29	25	83
1997— Lynchburg (Caro.)	8	4	.667	3.71	17	17	0	0	0	99 1/3	98	43	41	30	92
—Carolina (Sou.)	3	3	.500	4.08	9	9	1	0	0	57 1/3	56	31	26	16	63
—Pittsburgh (N.L.)	0	0	...	6.00	3	0	0	0	0	6	10	4	4	1	3
1998— Durham (I.L.)■	1	0	1.000	2.92	2	2	0	0	0	12 1/3	6	4	4	2	14
—Tampa Bay (A.L.)	2	5	.286	5.70	13	13	0	0	0	60	74	38	38	27	36
1999— Rochester (I.L.)■	4	2	.667	3.65	8	8	0	0	0	44 1/3	35	19	18	27	47
—Baltimore (A.L.)	8	7	.533	5.46	22	21	0	0	0	115 1/3	120	74	70	55	71
2000— Rochester (I.L.)	3	1	.750	1.47	8	8	1	1	0	55	32	12	9	21	56
—Baltimore (A.L.)	1	10	.091	7.02	25	13	0	0	0	107 2/3	119	95	84	61	79
A.L. totals (3 years)	11	22	.333	6.11	60	47	0	0	0	283	313	207	192	143	186
N.L. totals (1 year)	0	0	...	6.00	3	0	0	0	0	6	10	4	4	1	3
Major League totals (4 years)	11	22	.333	6.10	63	47	0	0	0	289	323	211	196	144	189

JOHNSON, JONATHAN — P — RANGERS

PERSONAL: Born July 16, 1974, in LaGrange, Ga. ... 6-0/180. ... Throws right, bats right. ... Full name: Jonathan Kent Johnson.
HIGH SCHOOL: Forest (Ocala, Fla.).
COLLEGE: Florida State.
TRANSACTIONS/CAREER NOTES: Selected by Texas Rangers organization in first round (seventh pick overall) of free-agent draft (June 1, 1995). ... On Oklahoma disabled list (May 1-17, 1998; and May 13-July 5, 1999).

Year League	W	L	Pct.	ERA	G	GS	CG	ShO	Sv.	IP	H	R	ER	BB	SO
1995— Charlotte (FSL)	1	5	.167	2.70	8	7	1	0	0	43 1/3	34	14	13	16	25
1996— Tulsa (Texas)	*13	10	.565	3.56	26	25	*6	0	0	174 1/3	176	86	69	41	97
—Oklahoma City (A.A.)	1	0	1.000	0.00	1	1	1	1	0	9	2	0	0	1	6
1997— Oklahoma City (A.A.)	1	8	.111	7.29	13	12	1	0	1	58	83	54	47	29	33
—Tulsa (Texas)	5	4	.556	3.52	10	10	4	0	0	71 2/3	70	35	28	15	47

Year League	W	L	Pct.	ERA	G	GS	CG	ShO	Sv.	IP	H	R	ER	BB	SO
1998—Oklahoma (PCL)	6	6	.500	4.90	19	18	1	0	1	112	109	66	61	32	94
—Charlotte (FSL)	0	2	.000	4.63	3	3	0	0	0	11²/₃	10	6	6	4	11
—Texas (A.L.)	0	0	...	8.31	1	1	0	0	0	4¹/₃	5	4	4	5	3
1999—Oklahoma (PCL)	8	4	.667	6.25	21	8	0	0	2	67²/₃	91	53	47	23	38
—Gulf Coast Rangers (GCL)	0	0	...	1.80	1	1	0	0	0	5	3	1	1	0	5
—Tulsa (Texas)	0	0	...	9.53	1	1	0	0	0	5²/₃	12	6	6	0	4
—Texas (A.L.)	0	0	...	15.00	1	0	0	0	0	3	9	5	5	2	3
2000—Oklahoma (PCL)	4	7	.364	5.08	36	2	0	0	5	56²/₃	55	38	32	26	63
—Texas (A.L.)	1	1	.500	6.21	15	0	0	0	0	29	34	23	20	19	23
Major League totals (3 years)	1	1	.500	7.18	17	1	0	0	0	36¹/₃	48	32	29	26	29

JOHNSON, LANCE — OF

PERSONAL: Born July 6, 1963, in Lincoln Heights, Ohio. ... 5-11/165. ... Bats left, throws left. ... Full name: Kenneth Lance Johnson.
HIGH SCHOOL: Princeton (Cincinnati).
JUNIOR COLLEGE: Triton College (Ill.).
COLLEGE: South Alabama.
TRANSACTIONS/CAREER NOTES: Selected by Pittsburgh Pirates organization in 30th round of free-agent draft (June 8, 1981); did not sign. ... Selected by Seattle Mariners organization in 31st round of free-agent draft (June 7, 1982); did not sign. ... Selected by St. Louis Cardinals organization in sixth round of free-agent draft (June 4, 1984). ... Traded by Cardinals with P Rick Horton and cash to Chicago White Sox for P Jose DeLeon (February 9, 1988). ... Granted free agency (November 8, 1995). ... Signed by New York Mets (December 14, 1995). ... On New York disabled list (May 2-June 16, 1997). ... Traded by Mets with two players to be named later to Chicago Cubs for OF Brian McRae, P Mel Rojas and P Turk Wendell (August 8, 1997); Cubs acquired P Mark Clark (August 11) and IF Manny Alexander (August 14) to complete deal. ... On disabled list (April 28-July 13, 1998). ... On disabled list (June 10-August 21, 1999). ... Released by Cubs (October 6, 1999). ... Signed by Cleveland Indians organization (January 13, 2000). ... Released by Indians (March 30, 2000). ... Signed by New York Yankees organization (April 2, 2000). ... Released by Yankees (June 6, 2000).
RECORDS: Holds major league record for most consecutive years leading league in triples—4 (1991-94). ... Shares A.L. single-game record for most triples—3 (September 23, 1995).
HONORS: Named American Association Most Valuable Player (1987).
STATISTICAL NOTES: Led New York-Pennsylvania League outfielders with 201 total chances in 1984. ... Led Texas League in caught stealing with 15 in 1986. ... Led American Association outfielders with 333 total chances in 1987. ... Led Pacific Coast League outfielders with five double plays in 1988. ... Led Pacific Coast League outfielders with 273 total chances in 1989. ... Led Pacific Coast League in caught stealing with 18 in 1989. ... Led A.L. in caught stealing with 22 in 1990. ... Led N.L. outfielders with 412 total chances in 1996. ... Had 25-game hitting streak (July 16-August 11, 1992). ... Collected six hits in one game (September 23, 1995). ... Career major league grand slams: 1.

Year Team (League)	Pos.	G	AB	R	H	2B	3B	HR	RBI	Avg.	BB	SO	SB	PO	A	E	Avg.
1984—Erie (NY-Penn)	OF	71	283	*63	*96	7	5	1	28	.339	45	20	29	*188	5	8	.960
1985—St. Petersburg (FSL)	OF	129	497	68	134	17	10	2	55	.270	58	39	33	338	16	5	.986
1986—Arkansas (Texas)	OF	127	445	82	128	24	6	2	33	.288	59	57	*49	262	11	7	.975
1987—Louisville (A.A.)	OF	116	477	89	159	21	11	5	50	.333	49	45	42	*319	6	•8	.976
—St. Louis (N.L.)	OF	33	59	4	13	2	1	0	7	.220	4	6	6	27	0	2	.931
1988—Chicago (A.L.)■	OF-DH	33	124	11	23	4	1	0	6	.185	6	11	6	63	1	2	.970
—Vancouver (PCL)	OF	100	411	71	126	12	6	2	36	.307	42	52	49	262	9	5	.982
1989—Vancouver (PCL)	OF	106	408	69	124	11	7	0	28	.304	46	36	33	*261	7	5	.982
—Chicago (A.L.)	OF-DH	50	180	28	54	8	2	0	16	.300	17	24	16	113	0	2	.983
1990—Chicago (A.L.)	OF-DH	151	541	76	154	18	9	1	51	.285	33	45	36	353	5	10	.973
1991—Chicago (A.L.)	OF	159	588	72	161	14	•13	0	49	.274	26	58	26	425	11	2	.995
1992—Chicago (A.L.)	OF	157	567	67	158	15	*12	3	47	.279	34	33	41	433	11	6	.987
1993—Chicago (A.L.)	OF	147	540	75	168	18	*14	0	47	.311	36	33	35	*427	7	•9	.980
1994—Chicago (A.L.)	OF-DH	106	412	56	114	11	*14	3	54	.277	26	23	26	317	1	0	*1.000
1995—Chicago (A.L.)	OF-DH	142	*607	98	*186	18	12	10	57	.306	32	31	40	338	8	3	.991
1996—New York (N.L.)■	OF	160	*682	117	*227	31	*21	9	69	.333	33	40	50	*391	9	•12	.971
1997—New York (N.L.)	OF	72	265	43	82	10	6	1	24	.309	33	21	15	152	4	4	.975
—Chicago (N.L.)■	OF-DH	39	145	17	44	6	2	4	15	.303	9	10	5	79	0	3	.963
1998—Chicago (N.L.)	OF	85	304	51	85	8	4	2	21	.280	26	22	10	154	5	4	.975
1999—Chicago (N.L.)	OF	95	335	46	87	11	6	1	21	.260	37	20	13	235	6	3	.988
2000—New York (A.L.)■	OF-DH	18	30	6	9	1	0	0	2	.300	0	7	2	2	0	0	1.000
American League totals (9 years)		963	3589	489	1027	107	77	17	329	.286	210	265	228	2471	44	34	.987
National League totals (5 years)		484	1790	278	538	68	40	17	157	.301	142	119	99	1038	24	28	.974
Major League totals (14 years)		1447	5379	767	1565	175	117	34	486	.291	352	384	327	3509	68	62	.983

DIVISION SERIES RECORD

Year Team (League)	Pos.	G	AB	R	H	2B	3B	HR	RBI	Avg.	BB	SO	SB	PO	A	E	Avg.
1998—Chicago (N.L.)	OF	3	12	0	2	0	0	0	1	.167	0	1	0	10	0	0	1.000

CHAMPIONSHIP SERIES RECORD

Year Team (League)	Pos.	G	AB	R	H	2B	3B	HR	RBI	Avg.	BB	SO	SB	PO	A	E	Avg.
1987—St. Louis (N.L.)	PR	1	0	1	0	0	0	0	0	...	0	0	1	...	...	...	...
1993—Chicago (A.L.)	OF	6	23	2	5	1	1	1	6	.217	2	1	1	15	0	0	1.000
Championship series totals (2 years)		7	23	3	5	1	1	1	6	.217	2	1	2	15	0	0	1.000

WORLD SERIES RECORD

Year Team (League)	Pos.	G	AB	R	H	2B	3B	HR	RBI	Avg.	BB	SO	SB	PO	A	E	Avg.
1987—St. Louis (N.L.)	PR	1	0	0	0	0	0	0	0	...	0	0	1	...	...	...	...

ALL-STAR GAME RECORD

Year League	Pos.	AB	R	H	2B	3B	HR	RBI	Avg.	BB	SO	SB	PO	A	E	Avg.
1996—National	OF	4	1	3	1	0	0	0	.750	0	0	1	5	0	0	1.000

JOHNSON, MARK — 1B

PERSONAL: Born October 17, 1967, in Worcester, Mass. ... 6-4/230. ... Bats left, throws left. ... Full name: Mark Patrick Johnson.
HIGH SCHOOL: Holy Name (Worcester, Mass.).
COLLEGE: Dartmouth.
TRANSACTIONS/CAREER NOTES: Selected by Pittsburgh Pirates organization in 42nd round of free-agent draft (June 5, 1989); did not sign. ... Selected by Pirates organization in 20th round of free-agent draft (June 4, 1990). ... On Calgary disabled list (August 26-September 8, 1995). ... Claimed on waivers by Cincinnati Reds (August 29, 1997). ... Traded by Reds to Anaheim Angels for a player to be named later (September 11, 1998). ... Released by Angels (December 22, 1998). ... Signed by Hanshin Tigers of Japan Central League (December 22, 1998). ... Signed by New York Mets organization (February 22, 2000). ... Granted free agency (October 18, 2000).
HONORS: Named Southern League Most Valuable Player (1994).
STATISTICAL NOTES: Led Southern League with 11 intentional bases on balls received in 1994. ... Career major league grand slams: 1.

							— BATTING —								— FIELDING —			
Year	Team (League)	Pos.	G	AB	R	H	2B	3B	HR	RBI	Avg.	BB	SO	SB	PO	A	E	Avg.
1990— Welland (NY-Penn)....		1B	5	8	2	4	1	0	0	2	.500	2	0	0	2	1	0	1.000
—Augusta (S.Atl.).........		1B	43	144	12	36	7	0	0	19	.250	24	18	4	240	18	5	.981
1991— Augusta (S.Atl.)......		1B	49	139	23	36	7	4	2	25	.259	29	1	15	319	33	9	.975
—Salem (Caro.)............	1B-OF-3B		37	103	12	26	2	0	2	13	.252	18	25	0	32	28	3	.952
1992— Carolina (Sou.).........		1B	122	383	40	89	16	1	7	45	.232	55	94	16	610	41	8	.988
1993— Carolina (Sou.).........	1B-OF		125	399	48	93	18	4	14	52	.233	66	93	6	500	40	4	.993
1994— Carolina (Sou.).........	1B-OF		111	388	69	107	20	2	*23	85	.276	67	89	6	570	52	6	.990
1995— Pittsburgh (N.L.).......		1B	79	221	32	46	6	1	13	28	.208	37	66	5	527	36	8	.986
—Calgary (PCL)............		1B	9	23	7	7	4	0	2	8	.304	6	4	1	65	5	2	.972
1996— Pittsburgh (N.L.).......	1B-OF		127	343	55	94	24	0	13	47	.274	44	64	6	778	73	6	.993
1997— Pittsburgh (N.L.).......	1B-DH		78	219	30	47	10	0	4	29	.215	43	78	1	542	44	5	.992
—Calgary (PCL)............	1B-DH-OF		34	115	28	39	11	1	6	16	.339	22	28	4	183	25	0	1.000
—Indianapolis (A.A.)■..		1B	3	4	0	0	0	0	0	0	.000	2	2	0	17	2	0	1.000
1998— Indianapolis (I.L.).....	1B-OF-DH		116	357	65	107	33	1	22	75	.300	68	82	2	443	37	5	.990
—Anaheim (A.L.)■........	1B-DH		10	14	1	1	0	0	0	0	.071	0	6	0	13	1	0	1.000
1999— Haushin (Jp. Cen.)■..		IF	125	438	52	95	23	1	20	66	.253	53	78	1	...	...	...	...
2000— Norfolk (I.L.)■..........		1B-OF	94	315	49	85	21	1	17	60	.270	67	54	14	368	33	3	.993
—New York (N.L.)..........	1B-DH-OF		21	22	2	4	0	0	1	6	.182	5	9	0	10	1	0	1.000
American League totals (1 year)			10	14	1	1	0	0	0	0	.071	0	6	0	13	1	0	1.000
National League totals (4 years)			305	805	119	191	40	1	31	110	.237	129	217	12	1857	154	19	.991
Major League totals (5 years)			315	819	120	192	40	1	31	110	.234	129	223	12	1870	155	19	.991

JOHNSON, MARK — C — WHITE SOX

PERSONAL: Born September 12, 1975, in Wheatridge, Colo. ... 6-0/185. ... Bats left, throws right. ... Full name: Mark Landon Johnson.
HIGH SCHOOL: Warner Robins (Ga.).
TRANSACTIONS/CAREER NOTES: Selected by Chicago White Sox organization in first round (26th pick overall) of free-agent draft (June 2, 1994).
STATISTICAL NOTES: Led Carolina League with .420 on-base percentage in 1997. ... Led Carolina League catchers with 1000 total chances and tied for league lead with eight double plays in 1997. ... Led Southern League with .443 on-base percentage in 1998.

							— BATTING —								— FIELDING —			
Year	Team (League)	Pos.	G	AB	R	H	2B	3B	HR	RBI	Avg.	BB	SO	SB	PO	A	E	Avg.
1994— GC White Sox (GCL) ..		C	32	87	10	21	5	0	0	14	.241	14	15	1	182	22	3	.986
1995— Hickory (S.Atl.)..........		C	107	319	31	58	9	0	2	17	.182	59	52	3	*681	67	11	.986
1996— South Bend (Midw.) ...		C	67	214	29	55	14	3	2	27	.257	39	25	3	408	37	9	.980
—Prince Will. (Caro.).....		C	18	58	9	14	3	0	0	3	.241	13	6	0	112	8	1	.992
1997— Win.-Salem (Caro.)		C	120	375	59	95	27	4	4	46	.253	*106	85	4	*899	90	11	*.989
1998— Birmingham (Sou.).....	C-1B		117	382	68	108	17	3	9	59	.283	*105	72	0	723	65	8	.990
—Chicago (A.L.)............		C	7	23	2	2	0	2	0	1	.087	1	8	0	36	2	0	1.000
1999— Chicago (A.L.)............	C-DH		73	207	27	47	11	0	4	16	.227	36	58	3	413	33	3	.993
2000— Chicago (A.L.)............	C-DH		75	213	29	48	11	0	3	23	.225	27	40	3	466	27	4	.992
Major League totals (3 years)			155	443	58	97	22	2	7	40	.219	64	106	6	915	62	7	.993

JOHNSON, MARK — P — TIGERS

PERSONAL: Born May 2, 1975, in Dayton, Ohio. ... 6-3/226. ... Throws right, bats right. ... Full name: Mark J. Johnson.
HIGH SCHOOL: Springboro (Ohio).
COLLEGE: Hawaii.
TRANSACTIONS/CAREER NOTES: Selected by Houston Astros organization in first round (19th pick overall) of free-agent draft (June 4, 1996). ... Traded by Astros to Florida Marlins (December 16, 1997), completing deal in which Marlins traded OF Moises Alou to Astros for P Oscar Henriquez, P Manuel Barrios and a player to be named later (November 11, 1997). ... Traded by Marlins with P Ed Yarnall and P Todd Noel to New York Yankees for 3B Mike Lowell (February 1, 1999). ... Selected by Detroit Tigers from Yankees organization in Rule 5 major league draft (December 13, 1999). ... On Detroit disabled list (May 18-June 24, 2000; included rehabilitation assignment to Toledo (May 22-June 19). ... Released by Tigers (June 28, 2000). ... Re-signed by Tigers organization (June 30, 2000).

Year	League	W	L	Pct.	ERA	G	GS	CG	ShO	Sv.	IP	H	R	ER	BB	SO
1997— Kissimmee (FSL)................		8	9	.471	3.07	26	26	3	1	0	155 1/3	150	67	53	39	127
1998— Portland (East.)■		5	•14	.263	4.62	26	26	2	0	0	142 1/3	147	89	73	60	120
1999— Norwich (East.)................		9	3	.750	3.68	16	15	0	0	0	88	88	51	36	39	52
—Gulf Coast Yankees (GCL) ..		0	0	.000	8.18	3	2	0	0	0	11	15	11	10	5	10
—Tampa (FSL).....................		1	0	1.000	1.50	1	1	0	0	0	6	4	1	1	1	6
2000— Detroit (A.L.)■................		0	1	.000	7.50	9	3	0	0	0	24	25	23	20	16	11
—Toledo (I.L.).....................		2	11	.154	6.57	17	17	1	0	0	100	142	81	73	26	48
Major League totals (1 year).........		0	1	.000	7.50	9	3	0	0	0	24	25	23	20	16	11

JOHNSON, MIKE · P · EXPOS

PERSONAL: Born October 3, 1975, in Edmonton. ... 6-2/170. ... Throws right, bats left. ... Full name: Michael Keith Johnson.
HIGH SCHOOL: Salisbury Composite (Edmonton).
TRANSACTIONS/CAREER NOTES: Selected by Toronto Blue Jays organization in 17th round of free-agent draft (June 3, 1993). ... Selected by San Francisco Giants from Blue Jays in Rule 5 major league draft (December 9, 1996). ... Traded by Giants to Baltimore Orioles for cash considerations (December 9, 1996). ... Traded by Orioles to Montreal Expos for a player to be named later (July 31, 1997); Orioles acquired P Everett Stull to complete deal (October 31, 1997).
STATISTICAL NOTES: Led International League pitchers with six errors in 1999.

Year League	W	L	Pct.	ERA	G	GS	CG	ShO	Sv.	IP	H	R	ER	BB	SO
1993—GC Blue Jays (GCL)	0	2	.000	4.87	16	1	0	0	1	44 1/3	51	40	24	22	31
1994—Medicine Hat (Pio.)	1	3	.250	4.46	9	9	0	0	0	36 1/3	48	31	18	22	43
1995—GC Blue Jays (GCL)	0	2	.000	7.20	3	3	0	0	0	15	20	15	12	8	13
—Medicine Hat (Pio.)	4	1	.800	3.86	19	0	0	0	3	49	46	26	21	25	32
1996—Hagerstown (S.Atl.)	11	8	.579	3.15	29	23	5	3	0	162 2/3	157	74	57	39	155
1997—Baltimore (A.L.)■	0	1	.000	7.94	14	5	0	0	2	39 2/3	52	36	35	16	29
—Montreal (N.L.)■	2	5	.286	5.94	11	11	0	0	0	50	54	34	33	21	28
1998—Harrisburg (East.)	3	2	.600	6.95	7	7	0	0	0	33 2/3	35	27	26	10	38
—Ottawa (I.L.)	4	9	.308	4.29	18	18	1	0	0	109	105	63	52	38	88
—Montreal (N.L.)	0	2	.000	14.73	2	2	0	0	0	7 1/3	16	12	12	2	4
1999—Ottawa (I.L.)	6	12	.333	5.38	28	27	0	0	0	147 1/3	174	105	88	63	120
—Montreal (N.L.)	0	0		8.64	3	1	0	0	0	8 1/3	12	8	8	7	6
2000—Ottawa (I.L.)	2	0	1.000	2.10	5	5	0	0	0	30	14	8	7	14	27
—Montreal (N.L.)	5	6	.455	6.39	41	13	0	0	0	101 1/3	107	73	72	53	70
A.L. totals (1 year)	0	1	.000	7.94	14	5	0	0	2	39 2/3	52	36	35	16	29
N.L. totals (4 years)	7	13	.350	6.74	57	27	0	0	0	167	189	127	125	83	108
Major League totals (4 years)	7	14	.333	6.97	71	32	0	0	2	206 2/3	241	163	160	99	137

JOHNSON, NICK · 1B · YANKEES

PERSONAL: Born September 19, 1978, in Sacramento. ... 6-3/224. ... Bats left, throws left. ... Full name: Nicholas Robert Johnson. ... Nephew of Larry Bowa, manager, Philadelphia Phillies and shortstop with Phillies (1970-81) and Chicago Cubs (1982-85).
HIGH SCHOOL: McClatchy (Sacramento).
TRANSACTIONS/CAREER NOTES: Selected by New York Yankees organization in third round of free-agent draft (June 4, 1996). ... On disabled list (April 2, 2000-entire season).
STATISTICAL NOTES: Led Gulf Coast League with .422 on-base percentage in 1996. ... Led South Atlantic League first basemen with 99 double plays in 1997. ... Led Florida State League with .466 on-base percentage in 1998. ... Led Eastern League with a .525 on-base percentage and in being hit by pitch with 37 in 1999.

Year Team (League)	Pos.	G	AB	R	H	2B	3B	HR	RBI	Avg.	BB	SO	SB	PO	A	E	Avg.
1996—GC Yankees (GCL)	1B	47	157	31	45	11	1	2	33	.287	30	35	0	314	19	3	.991
1997—Greensboro (S.Atl.)	1B	127	433	77	118	23	1	16	75	.273	76	99	16	*1176	59	16	.987
1998—Tampa (FSL)	1B	92	303	69	96	14	1	17	58	.317	68	76	1	785	58	12	.986
1999—Norwich (East.)	1B	132	420	*114	145	33	5	14	87	*.345	*123	88	8	1070	85	*20	.983
2000—New York (A.L.)					Did not play.												

JOHNSON, RANDY · P · DIAMONDBACKS

PERSONAL: Born September 10, 1963, in Walnut Grove, Calif. ... 6-10/230. ... Throws left, bats right. ... Full name: Randall David Johnson.
HIGH SCHOOL: Livermore (Calif.).
COLLEGE: Southern California.
TRANSACTIONS/CAREER NOTES: Selected by Atlanta Braves organization in third round of free-agent draft (June 7, 1982); did not sign. ... Selected by Montreal Expos organization in second round of free-agent draft (June 3, 1985). ... Traded by Expos with P Brian Holman and P Gene Harris to Seattle Mariners for P Mark Langston and a player to be named later (May 25, 1989); Expos acquired P Mike Campbell to complete deal (July 31, 1989). ... On disabled list (June 11-27, 1992). ... On Seattle disabled list (May 15-August 6 and August 27, 1996-remainder of season); included rehabilitation assignment to Everett (August 3-6). ... On suspended list (April 24-27, 1998). ... Traded by Mariners to Houston Astros for SS Carlos Guillen, P Freddy Garcia and a player to be named later (July 31, 1998); Mariners acquired P John Halama to complete deal (October 1, 1998). ... Granted free agency (October 28, 1998). ... Signed by Arizona Diamondbacks (December 10, 1998).
RECORDS: Shares major league single-game record for most strikeouts by lefthander—19 (June 24 and August 8, 1997). ... Shares major league single-season record for fewest complete games for leader—8 (2000). ... Holds N.L. single-season record for most games with 10 or more strikeouts—23 (1999). ... Shares A.L. record for most strikeouts in two consecutive games—32 (August 8 [19] and 15 [13], 1997, 17 innings). ... Shares N.L. record for most strikeouts in three consecutive games—43 (June 25 [14] and 30 [17] and July 5 [12], 1999).
HONORS: Named A.L. Pitcher of the Year by THE SPORTING NEWS (1995). ... Named lefthanded pitcher on THE SPORTING NEWS A.L. All-Star team (1995 and 1997). ... Named A.L. Cy Young Award winner by Baseball Writers' Association of America (1995). ... Named N.L. Cy Young Award winner by Baseball Writers' Association of America (1999 and 2000).
STATISTICAL NOTES: Led American Association with 20 balks in 1988. ... Pitched 2-0 no-hit victory against Detroit (June 2, 1990). ... Pitched 4-0 one-hit, complete-game victory against Oakland (August 14, 1991). ... Struck out 15 batters in one game (September 16, 1992; June 14 and September 16, 1993; June 4 and August 11, 1994; June 24 and September 23, 1995; May 28 and June 8, 1997; April 10, May 24 and July 11, 1998; and April 10, 1999). ... Struck out 18 batters in one game (September 27, 1992). ... Led A.L. with 18 hit batsmen in 1992 and 16 in 1993. ... Pitched 7-0 one-hit, complete-game victory against Oakland (May 16, 1993). ... Struck out 16 batters in one game (July 15, 1995; July 18, 1997; and August 28, 1998). ... Struck out 19 batters in one game (June 24 and August 8, 1997). ... Pitched 3-0 one-hit, complete-game victory against Minnesota (July 16, 1998). ... Struck out 17 batters in one game (June 30, 1999).
MISCELLANEOUS: Holds Seattle Mariners franchise all-time records for most wins (130), lowest earned-run average (3.42), most innings pitched (1,838 1/3), most strikeouts (2,162) and most shutouts (19). ... Appeared in one game as outfielder with no chances (1993). ... Shares Arizona Diamondbacks all-time record for most shutouts (2). ... Holds Arizona Diamondbacks all-time records for most wins (36), strikeouts (711), innings pitched (520 1/3), complete games (20), shutouts (5) and lowest earned-run average (2.56).

Year League	W	L	Pct.	ERA	G	GS	CG	ShO	Sv.	IP	H	R	ER	BB	SO
1985— Jamestown (NY-Penn)	0	3	.000	5.93	8	8	0	0	0	27 1/3	29	22	18	24	21
1986— West Palm Beach (FSL)	8	7	.533	3.16	26	•26	2	1	0	119 2/3	89	49	42	*94	133
1987— Jacksonville (Sou.)...........	11	8	.579	3.73	25	24	0	0	0	140	100	63	58	128	*163
1988— Indianapolis (A.A.)..............	8	7	.533	3.26	20	19	0	0	0	113 1/3	85	52	41	72	111
— Montreal (N.L.)..................	3	0	1.000	2.42	4	4	1	0	0	26	23	8	7	7	25
1989— Montreal (N.L.)................	0	4	.000	6.67	7	6	0	0	0	29 2/3	29	25	22	26	26
— Indianapolis (A.A.).............	1	1	.500	2.00	3	3	0	0	0	18	13	5	4	9	17
— Seattle (A.L.)■................	7	9	.438	4.40	22	22	2	0	0	131	118	75	64	70	104
1990— Seattle (A.L.)................	14	11	.560	3.65	33	33	5	2	0	219 2/3	174	103	89	*120	194
1991— Seattle (A.L.)................	13	10	.565	3.98	33	33	2	1	0	201 1/3	151	96	89	*152	228
1992— Seattle (A.L.)................	12	14	.462	3.77	31	31	6	2	0	210 1/3	154	104	88	*144	*241
1993— Seattle (A.L.)................	19	8	.704	3.24	35	34	10	3	1	255 1/3	185	97	92	99	*308
1994— Seattle (A.L.)................	13	6	.684	3.19	23	23	*9	*4	0	172	132	65	61	72	*204
1995— Seattle (A.L.)................	18	2	*.900	*2.48	30	30	6	3	0	214 1/3	159	65	59	65	*294
1996— Seattle (A.L.)................	5	0	1.000	3.67	14	8	0	0	1	61 1/3	48	27	25	25	85
— Everett (N'West)..............	0	0	...	0.00	1	1	0	0	0	2	0	0	0	0	5
1997— Seattle (A.L.)................	20	4	*.833	2.28	30	29	5	2	0	213	147	60	54	77	291
1998— Seattle (A.L.)................	9	10	.474	4.33	23	23	6	2	0	160	146	90	77	60	213
— Houston (N.L.)■..............	10	1	.909	1.28	11	11	4	4	0	84 1/3	57	12	12	26	116
1999— Arizona (N.L.)■............	17	9	.654	*2.48	35	•35	*12	2	0	*271 2/3	207	86	75	70	*364
2000— Arizona (N.L.)............	19	7	*.731	2.64	35	•35	•8	•3	0	248 2/3	202	89	73	76	*347
A.L. totals (10 years)	130	74	.637	3.42	274	266	51	19	2	1838 1/3	1414	782	698	884	2162
N.L. totals (5 years)	49	21	.700	2.58	92	91	25	9	0	660 1/3	518	220	189	205	878
Major League totals (13 years)	179	95	.653	3.19	366	357	76	28	2	2498 2/3	1932	1002	887	1089	3040

DIVISION SERIES RECORD

RECORDS: Holds career records for most losses—5; and strikeouts—60. ... Holds single-game record for most strikeouts—13 (October 5, 1997). ... Holds A.L. career record for most strikeouts—32.

Year League	W	L	Pct.	ERA	G	GS	CG	ShO	Sv.	IP	H	R	ER	BB	SO
1995— Seattle (A.L.)	2	0	1.000	2.70	2	1	0	0	0	10	5	3	3	6	16
1997— Seattle (A.L.)	0	2	.000	5.54	2	2	1	0	0	13	14	8	8	6	16
1998— Houston (N.L.)	0	2	.000	1.93	2	2	0	0	0	14	12	4	3	2	17
1999— Arizona (N.L.)	0	1	.000	7.56	1	1	0	0	0	8 1/3	8	7	7	3	11
Division series totals (4 years)	2	5	.286	4.17	7	6	1	0	0	45 1/3	39	22	21	17	60

CHAMPIONSHIP SERIES RECORD

Year League	W	L	Pct.	ERA	G	GS	CG	ShO	Sv.	IP	H	R	ER	BB	SO
1995— Seattle (A.L.)	0	1	.000	2.35	2	2	0	0	0	15 1/3	12	6	4	2	13

ALL-STAR GAME RECORD

Year League	W	L	Pct.	ERA	GS	CG	ShO	Sv.	IP	H	R	ER	BB	SO
1990— American							Did not play.							
1993— American	0	0	...	0.00	0	0	0	0	2	0	0	0	0	1
1994— American	0	0	...	9.00	0	0	0	0	1	2	1	1	0	0
1995— American	0	0	...	0.00	1	0	0	0	2	0	0	0	1	3
1997— American	0	0	...	0.00	1	0	0	0	2	0	0	0	1	2
1999— National	0	0	...	0.00	0	0	0	0	1	0	0	0	0	1
2000— National	0	0	...	0.00	1	0	0	0	1	1	0	0	0	1
All-Star Game totals (6 years)	0	0	...	1.00	3	0	0	0	9	3	1	1	2	8

JOHNSON, RUSS   IF   DEVIL RAYS

PERSONAL: Born February 22, 1973, in Baton Rouge, La. ... 5-10/180. ... Bats right, throws right. ... Full name: William Russell Johnson.
HIGH SCHOOL: Denham Springs (La.).
COLLEGE: Louisiana State.
TRANSACTIONS/CAREER NOTES: Selected by Houston Astros organization in supplemental round ("sandwich pick" between first and second round, 30th pick overall) of free-agent draft (June 2, 1994); pick received as part of compensation for San Francisco Giants signing Type A free-agent P Mark Portugal. ... Traded by Astros to Tampa Bay Devil Rays for P Marc Valdes (May 27, 2000).
STATISTICAL NOTES: Led Texas League shortstops with 664 total chances and 87 double plays in 1995. ... Led Pacific Coast League third basemen with .962 fielding percentage in 1998.

Year Team (League)	Pos.	G	AB	R	H	2B	3B	HR	RBI	Avg.	BB	SO	SB	PO	A	E	Avg.
1995— Jackson (Texas)	SS	132	475	65	118	16	2	9	53	.248	50	60	10	182	383	13	.978
1996— Jackson (Texas)	SS	132	496	86	154	24	5	15	74	.310	56	50	9	219	411	34	.949
1997— New Orleans (A.A.)......	3B-SS-DH	122	445	72	123	16	6	4	49	.276	66	78	7	86	269	21	.944
— Houston (N.L.)	3B-2B	21	60	7	18	1	0	2	9	.300	6	14	1	13	24	1	.974
1998— New Orleans (PCL)....	3-2-S-DH	122	453	*95	140	28	2	7	52	.309	*90	64	11	76	235	11	†.966
— Houston (N.L.)	3B	8	13	2	3	1	0	0	0	.231	1	5	1	3	9	0	1.000
1999— New Orleans (PCL)....	2B-SS-OF	22	77	17	27	6	0	1	12	.351	16	13	1	32	60	3	.968
— Houston (N.L.)	3B-2B-SS	83	156	24	44	10	0	5	23	.282	20	31	2	33	88	7	.945
2000— New Orleans (PCL)....	SS-3B-2B	26	45	4	8	0	0	3	3	.178	2	10	1	11	14	1	.962
— Tampa Bay (A.L.)■...	3B-2B-SS	74	185	28	47	8	0	2	17	.254	25	30	4	45	143	5	.974
American League totals (1 year)		74	185	28	47	8	0	2	17	.254	25	30	4	45	143	5	.974
National League totals (4 years)		138	274	37	73	12	0	7	35	.266	29	60	5	60	135	9	.956
Major League totals (4 years)		212	459	65	120	20	0	9	52	.261	54	90	9	105	278	14	.965

DIVISION SERIES RECORD

Year Team (League)	Pos.	G	AB	R	H	2B	3B	HR	RBI	Avg.	BB	SO	SB	PO	A	E	Avg.
1997— Houston (N.L.)	PH	1	1	0	0	0	0	0	0	.000	0	1	0	...	...	...	...
1999— Houston (N.L.)	PH	2	1	0	1	1	0	0	0	1.000	1	0	0	...	...	...	...
Division series totals (2 years)		3	2	0	1	1	0	0	0	.500	1	1	0	...	...	...	...

PERSONAL: Born November 25, 1968, in Liverpool, N.Y. ... 6-3/210. ... Throws right, bats right. ... Full name: John William Johnstone.
HIGH SCHOOL: Bishop Ludden (Syracuse, N.Y.).
JUNIOR COLLEGE: Onondaga Community College (N.Y.).
TRANSACTIONS/CAREER NOTES: Selected by New York Mets organization in 20th round of free-agent draft (June 2, 1987). ... On disabled list (June 24-July 7, 1992). ... Selected by Florida Marlins in second round (31st pick overall) of expansion draft (November 17, 1992). ... On disabled list (May 8, 1995-remainder of season). ... Granted free agency (December 21, 1995). ... Signed by Houston Astros organization (December 28, 1995). ... Granted free agency (September 30, 1996). ... Signed by San Francisco Giants organization (December 17, 1996). ... Claimed on waivers by Oakland Athletics (August 7, 1997). ... Granted free agency (August 31, 1997). ... Signed by Giants organization (September 1, 1997). ... On San Francisco disabled list (July 19-September 2, 2000); included rehabilitation assignments to San Jose (August 15-30), Arizona League Giants (September 1) and Fresno (September 2).

Year League	W	L	Pct.	ERA	G	GS	CG	ShO	Sv.	IP	H	R	ER	BB	SO
1987— Kingsport (Appl.)	1	1	.500	7.45	17	1	0	0	0	29	42	28	24	20	21
1988— Gulf Coast Mets (GCL)	3	4	.429	2.68	12	12	3	0	0	74	65	29	22	25	57
1989— Pittsfield (NY-Penn)	*11	2	.846	2.77	15	15	2	1	0	104	101	47	32	28	60
1990— St. Lucie (FSL)	*15	6	.714	2.24	25	25	*9	3	0	172²/₃	145	53	43	60	120
1991— Williamsport (East.)	7	9	.438	3.97	27	•27	2	0	0	165¹/₃	159	94	73	79	100
1992— Binghamton (East.)	7	7	.500	3.74	24	24	2	0	0	149¹/₃	132	66	62	36	121
1993— Edmonton (PCL)■	4	*15	.211	5.18	30	21	1	0	4	144¹/₃	167	95	83	59	126
— Florida (N.L.)	0	2	.000	5.91	7	0	0	0	0	10²/₃	16	8	7	7	5
1994— Edmonton (PCL)	5	3	.625	4.46	29	0	0	0	4	42¹/₃	46	23	21	9	43
— Florida (N.L.)	1	2	.333	5.91	17	0	0	0	0	21¹/₃	23	20	14	16	23
1995— Florida (N.L.)	0	0	...	3.86	4	0	0	0	0	4²/₃	7	2	2	2	3
1996— Tucson (PCL)■	3	3	.500	3.42	45	1	0	0	5	55¹/₃	59	27	21	22	70
— Houston (N.L.)	1	0	1.000	5.54	9	0	0	0	0	13	17	8	8	5	5
1997— Phoenix (PCL)■	0	3	.000	4.03	38	0	0	0	*24	38	34	17	17	15	30
— San Francisco (N.L.)	0	0	...	3.38	13	0	0	0	0	18²/₃	15	7	7	7	15
1998— San Francisco (N.L.)	6	5	.545	3.07	70	0	0	0	0	88	72	32	30	38	86
1999— San Francisco (N.L.)	4	6	.400	2.60	62	0	0	0	3	65²/₃	48	24	19	20	56
2000— San Francisco (N.L.)	3	4	.429	6.30	47	0	0	0	0	50	64	35	35	13	37
— San Jose (Calif.)	0	0	...	9.00	2	2	0	0	0	2	4	2	2	0	3
— Arizona Giants (Ariz.)	0	0	...	0.00	1	1	0	0	0	1	0	0	0	0	1
— Fresno (PCL)	0	0	...	0.00	1	1	0	0	0	2	0	0	0	1	1
Major League totals (8 years)	15	19	.441	4.04	229	0	0	0	3	272	262	136	122	108	230

PERSONAL: Born April 23, 1977, in Willemstad, Curacao. ... 6-1/210. ... Bats right, throws right. ... Full name: Andruw Rudolf Jones.
HIGH SCHOOL: St. Paulus (Willemstad, Curacao).
TRANSACTIONS/CAREER NOTES: Signed as non-drafted free agent by Atlanta Braves organization (July 1, 1993).
RECORDS: Holds N.L. single-season record for fewest singles (150 or more games)—55 (1997).
HONORS: Named South Atlantic League Most Valuable Player (1995). ... Won N.L. Gold Glove as outfielder (1998, 1999 and 2000).
STATISTICAL NOTES: Led South Atlantic League with nine sacrifice flies in 1995. ... Led South Atlantic League outfielders with 246 total chances and tied for lead with four double plays in 1995. ... Led N.L. outfielders with 435 total chances and tied for lead with six double plays in 1998. ... Led N.L. outfielders in total chances with 515 in 1999 and 449 in 2000. ... Career major league grand slams: 1.

						BATTING								FIELDING		
Year Team (League)	Pos.	G	AB	R	H	2B	3B	HR	RBI	Avg.	BB	SO	SB	PO	A	E	Avg.
1994— GC Braves (GCL)	OF	27	95	22	21	5	1	2	10	.221	16	19	5	90	0	3	.968
— Danville (Appl.)	OF	36	143	20	48	9	2	1	16	.336	9	25	16	81	3	2	.977
1995— Macon (S.Atl.)	OF	•139	537	*104	149	41	5	25	100	.277	70	122	*56	*332	10	4	.988
1996— Durham (Caro.)	OF	66	243	65	76	14	3	17	43	.313	42	54	16	174	9	7	.963
— Greenville (Sou.)	OF	38	157	39	58	10	1	12	37	.369	17	34	12	129	7	1	.993
— Richmond (I.L.)	OF	12	45	11	17	3	1	5	12	.378	1	9	2	34	1	1	.972
— Atlanta (N.L.)	OF	31	106	11	23	7	1	5	13	.217	7	29	3	73	4	2	.975
1997— Atlanta (N.L.)	OF	153	399	60	92	18	1	18	70	.231	56	107	20	287	14	7	.977
1998— Atlanta (N.L.)	OF	159	582	89	158	33	8	31	90	.271	40	129	27	*413	•20	2	.995
1999— Atlanta (N.L.)	OF	•162	592	97	163	35	5	26	84	.275	76	103	24	*492	13	10	.981
2000— Atlanta (N.L.)	OF	161	*656	122	199	36	6	36	104	.303	59	100	21	*438	9	2	.996
Major League totals (5 years)		666	2335	379	635	129	21	116	361	.272	238	468	95	1703	60	23	.987

DIVISION SERIES RECORD

RECORDS: Holds record for most at-bats without a hit—14.

						BATTING								FIELDING		
Year Team (League)	Pos.	G	AB	R	H	2B	3B	HR	RBI	Avg.	BB	SO	SB	PO	A	E	Avg.
1996— Atlanta (N.L.)	OF-PR	3	0	0	0	0	0	0	0	...	1	0	0	2	0	0	1.000
1997— Atlanta (N.L.)	OF	3	5	1	0	0	0	0	1	.000	1	1	0	10	0	0	1.000
1998— Atlanta (N.L.)	OF	3	9	2	0	0	0	0	1	.000	3	2	1	8	0	0	1.000
1999— Atlanta (N.L.)	OF	4	18	1	4	1	0	0	2	.222	1	3	0	12	0	0	1.000
2000— Atlanta (N.L.)	OF	3	9	3	1	0	0	1	1	.111	4	1	0	8	0	0	1.000
Division series totals (5 years)		16	41	7	5	1	0	1	5	.122	10	7	2	40	0	0	1.000

CHAMPIONSHIP SERIES RECORD

						BATTING								FIELDING		
Year Team (League)	Pos.	G	AB	R	H	2B	3B	HR	RBI	Avg.	BB	SO	SB	PO	A	E	Avg.
1996— Atlanta (N.L.)	OF-PR-PH	5	9	3	2	0	0	1	3	.222	3	2	0	5	0	0	1.000
1997— Atlanta (N.L.)	OF-PH	5	9	0	4	0	0	0	1	.444	1	1	0	12	1	0	1.000
1998— Atlanta (N.L.)	OF	6	22	3	6	0	0	1	2	.273	1	4	1	15	0	0	1.000
1999— Atlanta (N.L.)	OF	6	23	5	5	0	0	1	1	.217	4	3	0	17	0	0	1.000
Championship series totals (4 years)		22	63	11	17	0	0	2	7	.270	9	10	1	49	1	0	1.000

WORLD SERIES RECORD

RECORDS: Shares record for most home runs in two consecutive innings—2 (October 20, 1996, second and third innings). ... Shares single-inning record for most putouts by outfielder—3 (October 24, 1999, seventh inning).

NOTES: Hit home runs in first two at-bats (October 20, 1996, second and third innings).

Year Team (League)	Pos.	G	AB	R	H	2B	3B	HR	RBI	Avg.	BB	SO	SB	PO	A	E	Avg.
1996— Atlanta (N.L.)	OF	6	20	4	8	1	0	2	6	.400	3	6	1	7	1	0	1.000
1999— Atlanta (N.L.)	OF	4	13	1	1	0	0	0	0	.077	1	3	0	10	0	0	1.000
World Series totals (2 years)		10	33	5	9	1	0	2	6	.273	4	9	1	17	1	0	1.000

ALL-STAR GAME RECORD

Year League	Pos.	AB	R	H	2B	3B	HR	RBI	Avg.	BB	SO	SB	PO	A	E	Avg.
2000— National	OF	2	0	1	0	0	0	1	.500	0	1	0	2	0	0	1.000

JONES, BOBBY J.　　　P

PERSONAL: Born February 10, 1970, in Fresno, Calif. ... 6-4/225. ... Throws right, bats right. ... Full name: Robert Joseph Jones.
HIGH SCHOOL: Fresno (Calif.).
COLLEGE: Fresno State.
TRANSACTIONS/CAREER NOTES: Selected by New York Mets organization in supplemental round ("sandwich pick" between first and second round, 36th pick overall) of free-agent draft (June 3, 1991); pick received as part of compensation for Los Angeles Dodgers signing Type A free-agent OF Darryl Strawberry. ... On New York disabled list (May 24-September 10, 1999); included rehabilitation assignments to Binghamton (August 7-17 and September 5-10) and Norfolk (August 18-25). ... On New York disabled list (April 17-May 18, 2000); included rehabilitation assignment to Norfolk (May 7-18). ... Granted free agency (November 4, 2000).
HONORS: Named Eastern League Pitcher of the Year (1992).
STATISTICAL NOTES: Led International League with 11 hit batsmen in 1993. ... Led N.L. with 18 sacrifice hits in 1995.

Year League	W	L	Pct.	ERA	G	GS	CG	ShO	Sv.	IP	H	R	ER	BB	SO
1991— Columbia (S.Atl.)	3	1	.750	1.85	5	5	0	0	0	24 1/3	20	5	5	3	35
1992— Binghamton (East.)	12	4	.750	*1.88	24	24	4	*4	0	158	118	40	33	43	143
1993— Norfolk (I.L.)	12	10	.545	3.63	24	24	6	*3	0	166	149	72	67	32	126
— New York (N.L.)	2	4	.333	3.65	9	9	0	0	0	61 2/3	61	35	25	22	35
1994— New York (N.L.)	12	7	.632	3.15	24	24	1	1	0	160	157	75	56	56	80
1995— New York (N.L.)	10	10	.500	4.19	30	30	3	1	0	195 2/3	209	107	91	53	127
1996— New York (N.L.)	12	8	.600	4.42	31	31	3	1	0	195 2/3	219	102	96	46	116
1997— New York (N.L.)	15	9	.625	3.63	30	30	2	1	0	193 1/3	177	88	78	63	125
1998— New York (N.L.)	9	9	.500	4.42	30	30	0	0	0	195 1/3	192	94	88	53	115
1999— New York (N.L.)	3	3	.500	5.61	12	9	0	0	0	59 1/3	69	37	37	11	31
— Binghamton (East.)	1	2	.333	3.86	3	3	0	0	0	11 2/3	11	5	5	5	12
— Norfolk (I.L.)	2	0	1.000	2.45	2	2	0	0	0	11	11	3	3	3	8
2000— New York (N.L.)	11	6	.647	5.06	27	27	1	0	0	154 2/3	171	90	87	49	85
— Norfolk (I.L.)	2	0	1.000	5.32	4	4	0	0	0	23 2/3	31	14	14	4	19
Major League totals (8 years)	74	56	.569	4.13	193	190	10	4	0	1215 2/3	1255	628	558	353	714

DIVISION SERIES RECORD

RECORDS: Shares career record for most shutouts—1.

Year League	W	L	Pct.	ERA	G	GS	CG	ShO	Sv.	IP	H	R	ER	BB	SO
1999— New York (N.L.)							Did not play.								
2000— New York (N.L.)	1	0	1.000	0.00	1	1	1	1	0	9	1	0	0	2	5

CHAMPIONSHIP SERIES RECORD

Year League	W	L	Pct.	ERA	G	GS	CG	ShO	Sv.	IP	H	R	ER	BB	SO
1999— New York (N.L.)							Did not play.								
2000— New York (N.L.)	0	0	...	13.50	1	1	0	0	0	4	6	6	6	0	2

WORLD SERIES RECORD

Year League	W	L	Pct.	ERA	G	GS	CG	ShO	Sv.	IP	H	R	ER	BB	SO
2000— New York (N.L.)	0	1	.000	5.40	1	1	0	0	0	5	4	3	3	3	3

ALL-STAR GAME RECORD

Year League	W	L	Pct.	ERA	GS	CG	ShO	Sv.	IP	H	R	ER	BB	SO
1997— National	0	0	...	0.00	0	0	0	0	1	1	0	0	0	2

JONES, BOBBY M.　　　P　　　METS

PERSONAL: Born April 11, 1972, in Orange, N.J. ... 6-0/178. ... Throws left, bats right. ... Full name: Robert Mitchell Jones.
HIGH SCHOOL: Rutherford (N.J.).
JUNIOR COLLEGE: Chipola Junior College (Fla.).
TRANSACTIONS/CAREER NOTES: Selected by Milwaukee Brewers organization in 44th round of free-agent draft (June 3, 1991). ... Selected by Colorado Rockies organization from Brewers organization in Rule 5 minor league draft (December 5, 1994). ... Traded by Rockies with P Lariel Gonzalez to New York Mets for P Masato Yoshii (January 14, 2000).
STATISTICAL NOTES: Tied for Pacific Coast League lead with 12 hit batsmen in 1997.

Year League	W	L	Pct.	ERA	G	GS	CG	ShO	Sv.	IP	H	R	ER	BB	SO
1992— Helena (Pio.)	5	4	.556	4.36	14	13	1	0	0	76 1/3	93	51	37	23	53
1993— Beloit (Midw.)	10	10	.500	4.11	25	25	4	0	0	144 2/3	159	82	66	65	115
1994— Stockton (Calif.)	6	12	.333	4.21	26	26	2	0	0	147 2/3	131	90	69	64	147
1995— New Haven (East.)■	5	2	.714	2.58	27	8	0	0	3	73 1/3	61	27	21	36	70
— Colorado Springs (PCL)	1	2	.333	7.30	11	8	0	0	0	40 2/3	50	38	33	33	48
1996— Colorado Springs (PCL)	2	8	.200	4.97	57	0	0	0	3	88 2/3	88	54	49	63	78
1997— Colorado Springs (PCL)	7	11	.389	5.14	25	21	0	0	0	133	135	89	76	71	104
— Colorado (N.L.)	1	1	.500	8.38	4	4	0	0	0	19 1/3	30	18	18	12	5

Year League	W	L	Pct.	ERA	G	GS	CG	ShO	Sv.	IP	H	R	ER	BB	SO
1998— Colorado (N.L.)	7	8	.467	5.22	35	20	1	0	0	141 $^1/_3$	153	87	82	66	109
1999— Colorado (N.L.)	6	10	.375	6.33	30	20	0	0	0	112 $^1/_3$	132	91	79	77	74
— Colorado Springs (PCL)	2	1	.667	5.40	3	3	0	0	0	16 $^2/_3$	17	13	10	15	14
2000— Norfolk (I.L.)■	10	8	.556	4.32	22	21	4	1	0	133 $^1/_3$	122	66	64	58	100
— New York (N.L.)	0	1	.000	4.15	11	1	0	0	0	21 $^2/_3$	18	11	10	14	20
Major League totals (4 years)	**14**	**20**	**.412**	**5.77**	**80**	**45**	**1**	**0**	**0**	**294** $^2/_3$	**333**	**207**	**189**	**169**	**208**

JONES, CHIPPER　　　　3B　　　　BRAVES

PERSONAL: Born April 24, 1972, in De Land, Fla. ... 6-4/210. ... Bats both, throws right. ... Full name: Larry Wayne Jones Jr.
HIGH SCHOOL: The Bolles School (Jacksonville).
TRANSACTIONS/CAREER NOTES: Selected by Atlanta Braves organization in first round (first pick overall) of free-agent draft (June 4, 1990). ... On Atlanta disabled list (March 20, 1994-entire season). ... On disabled list (March 22-April 6, 1996).
RECORDS: Holds major league single-season records for fewest putouts by third baseman (150 or more games)—77 (1997); and fewest chances accepted by third baseman (150 or more games)—318. ... Holds N.L. record for most home runs by switch hitter in two consecutive seasons—81 (1999-2000). ... Holds N.L. single-season records for most home runs by switch hitter—45 (1999); most home runs hit at home by switch hitter—25 (1999); highest slugging average by switch hitter—.633 (1999); most bases on balls by switch-hitter—126 (1999); fewest putouts by third baseman (150 or more games)—77 (1997); fewest assists by third baseman (150 or more games)—237 (1999); and fewest chances by third baseman (150 or more games)—318 (1997).. ... Shares major league single-season record for most extra-base hits by switch-hitter—87 (1999). ... Shares N.L. single-season record for fewest double plays by third baseman (150 or more games)—10 (1999).
HONORS: Named N.L. Rookie Player of the Year by THE SPORTING NEWS (1995). ... Named N.L. Most Valuable Player by Baseball Writers' Association of America (1999). ... Named third baseman on THE SPORTING NEWS N.L. All-Star team (1999 and 2000). ... Named third baseman on THE SPORTING NEWS N.L. Silver Slugger team (1999 and 2000).
STATISTICAL NOTES: Led South Atlantic League with 10 sacrifice flies in 1991. ... Led South Atlantic League shortstops with 692 total chances and 71 double plays in 1991. ... Led International League with 268 total bases in 1993. ... Led International League shortstops with 619 total chances in 1993. ... Switch-hit home runs in one game five times (May 1, August 1 and September 21, 1999; and May 14 and July 5, 2000). ... Had 19-game hitting streak (June 1-21, 2000). ... Career major league grand slams: 4.

						BATTING								FIELDING		
Year Team (League)	Pos.	G	AB	R	H	2B	3B	HR	RBI	Avg.	BB	SO	SB	PO	A	E	Avg.
1990— GC Braves (GCL)	SS	44	140	20	32	1	1	1	18	.229	14	25	5	64	140	18	.919
1991— Macon (S.Atl.)	SS	136	473	*104	154	24	11	15	98	.326	69	70	40	*217	*419	56	.919
1992— Durham (Caro.)	SS	70	264	43	73	22	1	4	31	.277	31	34	10	106	200	14	.956
— Greenville (Sou.)	SS	67	266	43	92	17	11	9	42	.346	11	32	14	92	218	18	.945
1993— Richmond (I.L.)	SS	139	536	*97	*174	31	*12	13	89	.325	57	70	23	195	381	*43	.931
— Atlanta (N.L.)	SS	8	3	2	2	1	0	0	0	.667	1	1	0	1	1	0	1.000
1994— Atlanta (N.L.)								Did not play.								
1995— Atlanta (N.L.)	3B-OF	140	524	87	139	22	3	23	86	.265	73	99	8	103	255	25	.935
1996— Atlanta (N.L.)	3B-SS-OF	157	598	114	185	32	5	30	110	.309	87	88	14	103	288	17	.958
1997— Atlanta (N.L.)	3B-OF	157	597	100	176	41	3	21	111	.295	76	88	20	83	241	15	.956
1998— Atlanta (N.L.)	3B	160	601	123	188	29	5	34	107	.313	96	93	16	105	290	12	.971
1999— Atlanta (N.L.)	3B-SS	157	567	116	181	41	1	45	110	.319	126	94	25	88	237	17	.950
2000— Atlanta (N.L.)	3B-SS	156	579	118	180	38	1	36	111	.311	95	64	14	96	305	25	.941
Major League totals (7 years)		935	3469	660	1051	204	18	189	635	.303	554	527	97	579	1617	111	.952

DIVISION SERIES RECORD

RECORDS: Holds career records for most bases on balls—18; and strikeouts—17. ... Holds N.L. career records for most games—20; at-bats—70; runs—15; hits—22; total bases—37; and extra-base hits—7. ... Shares single-game record for most home runs—2 (October 3, 1995).

						BATTING								FIELDING		
Year Team (League)	Pos.	G	AB	R	H	2B	3B	HR	RBI	Avg.	BB	SO	SB	PO	A	E	Avg.
1995— Atlanta (N.L.)	3B	4	18	4	7	2	0	2	4	.389	2	2	0	3	4	0	1.000
1996— Atlanta (N.L.)	3B	3	9	2	2	0	0	1	2	.222	3	4	1	1	3	0	1.000
1997— Atlanta (N.L.)	3B	3	8	3	4	0	0	1	2	.500	3	2	1	2	3	1	.833
1998— Atlanta (N.L.)	3B	3	10	2	2	0	0	0	1	.200	4	3	0	2	2	0	1.000
1999— Atlanta (N.L.)	3B	4	13	2	3	0	0	0	1	.231	5	2	0	3	4	1	.875
2000— Atlanta (N.L.)	3B	3	12	2	4	1	0	0	1	.333	1	4	0	3	5	2	.800
Division series totals (6 years)		20	70	15	22	3	0	4	11	.314	18	17	2	14	21	4	.897

CHAMPIONSHIP SERIES RECORD

RECORDS: Holds N.L. career record for most runs scored—19. ... Shares single-series record for most singles—9 (1996). ... Shares single-game record for most singles—4 (October 9, 1996).

						BATTING								FIELDING		
Year Team (League)	Pos.	G	AB	R	H	2B	3B	HR	RBI	Avg.	BB	SO	SB	PO	A	E	Avg.
1995— Atlanta (N.L.)	3B	4	16	3	7	0	0	1	3	.438	3	1	1	4	13	0	1.000
1996— Atlanta (N.L.)	3B	7	25	6	11	2	0	0	4	.440	3	1	1	5	7	1	.923
1997— Atlanta (N.L.)	3B	6	24	5	7	1	0	2	4	.292	2	3	0	1	8	0	1.000
1998— Atlanta (N.L.)	3B	6	24	2	5	1	0	0	1	.208	4	5	0	1	12	0	1.000
1999— Atlanta (N.L.)	3B	6	19	3	5	2	0	0	1	.263	9	7	3	5	8	2	.867
Championship series totals (5 years)		29	108	19	35	6	0	3	13	.324	21	17	5	16	48	3	.955

WORLD SERIES RECORD

NOTES: Member of World Series championship team (1995).

						BATTING								FIELDING		
Year Team (League)	Pos.	G	AB	R	H	2B	3B	HR	RBI	Avg.	BB	SO	SB	PO	A	E	Avg.
1995— Atlanta (N.L.)	3B	6	21	3	6	3	0	0	1	.286	4	3	0	6	12	1	.947
1996— Atlanta (N.L.)	3B-SS	6	21	3	6	3	0	0	3	.286	4	2	0	4	7	0	1.000
1999— Atlanta (N.L.)	3B	4	13	2	3	0	0	1	2	.231	4	2	0	1	5	0	1.000
World Series totals (3 years)		16	55	8	15	6	0	1	6	.273	12	7	0	11	24	1	.972

Year	League	Pos.	AB	R	H	2B	3B	HR	RBI	Avg.	BB	SO	SB	PO	A	E	Avg.
								BATTING							FIELDING		
1996— National		3B	2	1	1	0	0	0	0	.500	0	0	0	1	1	0	1.000
1997— National		3B	1	0	0	0	0	0	0	.000	0	0	0	0	1	0	1.000
1998— National		3B	2	1	0	0	0	0	0	.000	1	0	0	0	0	0	...
2000— National		3B	3	1	3	0	0	1	1	1.000	0	0	0	1	0	0	1.000
All-Star Game totals (4 years)			8	3	4	0	0	1	1	.500	1	0	0	2	2	0	1.000

JONES, CHRIS — OF

PERSONAL: Born December 16, 1965, in Utica, N.Y. ... 6-2/210. ... Bats right, throws right. ... Full name: Christopher Carlos Jones.
HIGH SCHOOL: Liverpool (N.Y.).
TRANSACTIONS/CAREER NOTES: Selected by Cincinnati Reds organization in third round of free-agent draft (June 4, 1984). ... Released by Reds (December 13, 1991). ... Signed by Houston Astros organization (December 19, 1991). ... Granted free agency (October 16, 1992). ... Signed by Colorado Rockies (October 26, 1992). ... Granted free agency (December 20, 1993). ... Re-signed by Rockies organization (December 22, 1993). ... Granted free agency (October 15, 1994). ... Signed by New York Mets (December 7, 1994). ... Granted free agency (October 15, 1996). ... Signed by San Diego Padres (November 4, 1996). ... On disabled list (May 22-June 10, 1997). ... Granted free agency (October 6, 1997). ... Signed by Arizona Diamondbacks (November 19, 1997). ... Traded by Diamondbacks to San Francisco Giants for P Ricky Pickett (April 27, 1998). ... Released by Giants (October 2, 1998). ... Signed by Padres organization (February 1, 1999). ... Released by Padres (March 29, 1999). ... Signed by Toronto Blue Jays organization (April 5, 1999). ... On Syracuse disabled list (August 4-12 and August 20, 1999-remainder of season). ... Granted free agency (October 15, 1999). ... Signed by Padres organization (February 27, 2000). ... Released by Padres (April 29, 2000). ... Signed by Milwaukee Brewers organization (May 23, 2000). ... Granted free agency (October 3, 2000).

Year	Team (League)	Pos.	G	AB	R	H	2B	3B	HR	RBI	Avg.	BB	SO	SB	PO	A	E	Avg.
									BATTING							FIELDING		
1984— Billings (Pio.)		3B	21	73	8	11	2	0	2	13	.151	2	24	4	6	27	5	.868
1985— Billings (Pio.)		OF	63	240	43	62	12	5	4	33	.258	19	72	13	112	4	*13	.899
1986— Cedar Rapids (Midw.)		OF	128	473	65	117	13	9	20	78	.247	20	126	23	218	15	11	.955
1987— Vermont (East.)		OF	113	383	50	88	11	4	10	39	.230	23	99	13	207	12	8	.965
1988— Chattanooga (Sou.)		OF	116	410	50	111	20	7	4	61	.271	29	102	11	185	15	8	.962
1989— Chattanooga (Sou.)		OF	103	378	47	95	18	2	10	54	.251	23	68	10	197	8	7	.967
— Nashville (A.A.)		OF	21	49	8	8	1	0	2	5	.163	0	16	2	25	0	1	.962
1990— Nashville (A.A.)		OF	134	436	53	114	23	3	10	52	.261	23	86	12	209	17	8	.966
1991— Nashville (A.A.)		OF	73	267	29	65	5	4	9	33	.243	19	65	10	110	5	6	.950
— Cincinnati (N.L.)		OF	52	89	14	26	1	2	2	6	.292	2	31	2	27	1	0	1.000
1992— Houston (N.L.)■		OF	54	63	7	12	2	1	1	4	.190	7	21	3	27	0	2	.931
— Tucson (PCL)		OF	45	170	25	55	9	8	3	28	.324	18	34	7	86	7	2	.979
1993— Colo. Springs (PCL)■		OF	46	168	41	47	5	5	12	40	.280	19	47	8	107	5	3	.974
— Colorado (N.L.)		OF	86	209	29	57	11	4	6	31	.273	10	48	9	114	2	2	.983
1994— Colo. Springs (PCL)		OF	98	386	77	124	22	4	20	75	.321	35	72	12	191	11	*15	.931
— Colorado (N.L.)		OF	21	40	6	12	2	1	0	2	.300	2	14	0	16	0	1	.941
1995— Norfolk (I.L.)■		OF-DH	33	114	20	38	12	1	3	19	.333	11	20	5	62	4	1	.985
— New York (N.L.)		OF-1B	79	182	33	51	6	2	8	31	.280	13	45	2	122	6	2	.985
1996— New York (N.L.)		OF-1B	89	149	22	36	7	0	4	18	.242	12	42	1	83	1	3	.966
1997— San Diego (N.L.)■		OF	92	152	24	37	9	0	7	25	.243	16	45	7	73	4	4	.951
1998— Arizona (N.L.)■		OF	20	31	3	6	1	0	0	3	.194	3	9	0	11	0	0	1.000
— San Fran. (N.L.)■		OF-DH	43	90	14	17	2	1	2	10	.189	8	28	2	31	1	2	.941
— Fresno (PCL)		OF-DH	25	60	11	16	1	3	3	8	.267	6	12	2	17	0	1	.944
1999— Syracuse (I.L.)■		DH-OF	81	279	45	66	12	3	8	40	.237	19	74	11	57	2	1	.983
2000— Las Vegas (PCL)■		OF	13	26	6	7	2	0	1	6	.269	2	9	1	7	1	0	1.000
— Indianapolis (I.L.)■		OF	64	233	32	71	17	6	3	25	.305	12	58	5	120	3	4	.969
— Milwaukee (N.L.)		OF	12	16	3	3	2	0	0	1	.188	1	4	0	6	0	0	1.000
Major League totals (9 years)			548	1021	155	257	43	11	30	131	.252	74	287	26	510	15	16	.970

JONES, DOUG — P

PERSONAL: Born June 24, 1957, in Covina, Calif. ... 6-2/224. ... Throws right, bats right. ... Full name: Douglas Reid Jones.
HIGH SCHOOL: Lebanon (Ind.).
JUNIOR COLLEGE: Central Arizona College.
COLLEGE: Butler.
TRANSACTIONS/CAREER NOTES: Selected by Milwaukee Brewers organization in third round of free-agent draft (January 10, 1978). ... On disabled list (June 20-July 12, 1978). ... On Vancouver disabled list (April 11-September 1, 1983 and April 25-May 30, 1984). ... Granted free agency (October 15, 1984). ... Signed by Cleveland Indians organization (April 3, 1985). ... Granted free agency (December 20, 1991). ... Signed by Houston Astros organization (January 24, 1992). ... Traded by Astros with P Jeff Juden to Philadelphia Phillies for P Mitch Williams (December 2, 1993). ... Granted free agency (October 15, 1994). ... Signed by Baltimore Orioles (April 8, 1995). ... Granted free agency (November 3, 1995). ... Signed by Chicago Cubs (December 28, 1995). ... Released by Cubs (June 15, 1996). ... Signed by Brewers organization (June 28, 1996). ... Granted free agency (November 6, 1996). ... Re-signed by Brewers (December 7, 1996). ... On disabled list (July 16-August 3, 1997). ... Granted free agency (October 27, 1997). ... Re-signed by Brewers (November 18, 1997). ... Traded by Brewers to Indians for P Eric Plunk (July 23, 1998). ... Granted free agency (October 29, 1998). ... Signed by Oakland Athletics (January 11, 1999). ... On disabled list (April 2-April 9, 2000). ... Granted free agency (November 1, 2000).
HONORS: Named N.L. co-Fireman of the Year by THE SPORTING NEWS (1992).
MISCELLANEOUS: Holds Cleveland Indians all-time record for most saves (129).

Year	League	W	L	Pct.	ERA	G	GS	CG	ShO	Sv.	IP	H	R	ER	BB	SO
1978— Newark (NY-Penn)		2	4	.333	5.21	15	3	1	0	2	38	49	30	22	15	27
1979— Burlington (Midw.)		10	10	.500	*1.75	28	20	*16	•3	0	*190	144	63	37	73	115
1980— Stockton (Calif.)		6	2	.750	2.84	11	11	5	1	0	76	63	32	24	31	54
— Vancouver (PCL)		3	2	.600	3.23	8	8	1	1	0	53	52	19	19	15	28
— Holyoke (East.)		5	3	.625	2.90	8	8	4	2	0	62	57	23	20	26	39

Year	League	W	L	Pct.	ERA	G	GS	CG	ShO	Sv.	IP	H	R	ER	BB	SO
1981—	El Paso (Texas)	5	7	.417	5.80	15	15	3	1	0	90	121	67	58	28	62
—	Vancouver (PCL)	5	3	.625	3.04	11	10	2	0	0	80	79	29	27	22	38
1982—	Milwaukee (A.L.)	0	0	...	10.13	4	0	0	0	0	2²/₃	5	3	3	1	1
—	Vancouver (PCL)	5	8	.385	2.97	23	9	4	0	2	106	109	48	35	31	60
1983—	Vancouver (PCL)	0	1	.000	10.29	3	1	0	0	0	7	10	8	8	5	4
1984—	Vancouver (PCL)	1	0	1.000	10.13	3	0	0	0	0	8	9	9	9	3	2
—	El Paso (Texas)	6	8	.429	4.28	16	16	7	0	0	109¹/₃	120	61	52	35	62
1985—	Waterbury (East.)■	9	4	.692	3.65	39	1	0	0	7	116	123	59	47	36	113
1986—	Maine (I.L.)	5	6	.455	*2.09	43	3	0	0	9	116¹/₃	105	35	27	27	98
—	Cleveland (A.L.)	1	0	1.000	2.50	11	0	0	0	1	18	18	5	5	6	12
1987—	Cleveland (A.L.)	6	5	.545	3.15	49	0	0	0	8	91¹/₃	101	45	32	24	87
—	Buffalo (A.A.)	5	2	.714	2.04	23	0	0	0	7	61²/₃	49	18	14	12	61
1988—	Cleveland (A.L.)	3	4	.429	2.27	51	0	0	0	37	83¹/₃	69	26	21	16	72
1989—	Cleveland (A.L.)	7	10	.412	2.34	59	0	0	0	32	80²/₃	76	25	21	13	65
1990—	Cleveland (A.L.)	5	5	.500	2.56	66	0	0	0	43	84¹/₃	66	26	24	22	55
1991—	Cleveland (A.L.)	4	8	.333	5.54	36	4	0	0	7	63¹/₃	87	42	39	17	48
—	Colo. Springs (PCL)	2	2	.500	3.28	17	2	1	1	7	35²/₃	30	14	13	5	29
1992—	Houston (N.L.)■	11	8	.579	1.85	80	0	0	0	36	111²/₃	96	29	23	17	93
1993—	Houston (N.L.)	4	10	.286	4.54	71	0	0	0	26	85¹/₃	102	46	43	21	66
1994—	Philadelphia (N.L.)■	2	4	.333	2.17	47	0	0	0	27	54	55	14	13	6	38
1995—	Baltimore (A.L.)■	0	4	.000	5.01	52	0	0	0	22	46²/₃	55	30	26	16	42
1996—	Chicago (N.L.)■	2	2	.500	5.01	28	0	0	0	2	32¹/₃	41	20	18	7	26
—	New Orleans (A.A.)■	0	3	.000	3.75	13	0	0	0	6	24	28	10	10	6	17
—	Milwaukee (A.L.)	5	0	1.000	3.41	24	0	0	0	1	31²/₃	31	13	12	13	34
1997—	Milwaukee (A.L.)■	6	6	.500	2.02	75	0	0	0	36	80¹/₃	62	20	18	9	82
1998—	Milwaukee (N.L.)	3	4	.429	5.17	46	0	0	0	12	54	65	32	31	11	43
—	Cleveland (A.L.)■	1	2	.333	3.45	23	0	0	0	1	31¹/₃	34	12	12	6	28
1999—	Oakland (A.L.)■	5	5	.500	3.55	70	0	0	0	10	104	106	43	41	24	63
2000—	Oakland (A.L.)	4	2	.667	3.93	54	0	0	0	2	73¹/₃	86	34	32	18	54
A.L. totals (13 years)		47	51	.480	3.25	574	4	0	0	200	791	796	324	286	185	643
N.L. totals (5 years)		22	28	.440	3.42	272	0	0	0	103	337¹/₃	359	141	128	62	266
Major League totals (16 years)		69	79	.466	3.30	846	4	0	0	303	1128¹/₃	1155	465	414	247	909

DIVISION SERIES RECORD

Year	League	W	L	Pct.	ERA	G	GS	CG	ShO	Sv.	IP	H	R	ER	BB	SO
1998—	Cleveland (A.L.)	0	0	...	6.75	1	0	0	0	0	2²/₃	3	2	2	1	1
2000—	Oakland (A.L.)	0	0	...	0.00	2	0	0	0	0	1¹/₃	1	0	0	0	1
Division series totals (2 years)		0	0	...	4.50	3	0	0	0	0	4	4	2	2	1	2

CHAMPIONSHIP SERIES RECORD

Year	League	W	L	Pct.	ERA	G	GS	CG	ShO	Sv.	IP	H	R	ER	BB	SO
1998—	Cleveland (A.L.)				Did not play.											

ALL-STAR GAME RECORD

Year	League	W	L	Pct.	ERA	GS	CG	ShO	Sv.	IP	H	R	ER	BB	SO
1988—	American	0	0	...	0.00	0	0	0	0	²/₃	0	0	0	0	1
1989—	American	0	0	...	0.00	0	0	0	1	1¹/₃	1	0	0	0	0
1990—	American				Did not play.										
1992—	National	0	0	...	27.00	0	0	0	0	1	4	3	3	0	2
1994—	National	1	0	1.000	0.00	0	0	0	0	1	2	0	0	0	2
All-Star Game totals (4 years)		1	0	1.000	6.75	0	0	0	1	4	7	3	3	0	5

JONES, JACQUE   OF   TWINS

PERSONAL: Born April 25, 1975, in San Diego. ... 5-10/176. ... Bats left, throws left. ... Full name: Jacque Dewayne Jones.
HIGH SCHOOL: San Diego High.
COLLEGE: Southern California.
TRANSACTIONS/CAREER NOTES: Selected by Minnesota Twins organization in second round of free-agent draft (June 2, 1996).
MISCELLANEOUS: Member of 1996 U.S. Olympic baseball team.

								BATTING							FIELDING		
Year	Team (League)	Pos.	G	AB	R	H	2B	3B	HR	RBI	Avg.	BB	SO	SB	PO	A	E	Avg.
1996—	Fort Myers (FSL)	OF	1	3	0	2	1	0	0	1	.667	0	0	0	0	0	0	...
1997—	Fort Myers (FSL)	OF	131	539	84	*160	33	6	15	82	.297	33	110	24	313	8	7	.979
1998—	New Britain (East.)	OF-DH	134	518	78	155	39	3	21	85	.299	37	134	18	288	12	10	.968
1999—	Salt Lake (PCL)	OF	52	198	32	59	13	2	4	26	.298	9	36	9	150	2	2	.987
—	Minnesota (A.L.)	OF	95	322	54	93	24	2	9	44	.289	17	63	3	231	9	5	.980
2000—	Minnesota (A.L.)	OF	154	523	66	149	26	5	19	76	.285	26	111	7	334	9	2	.994
Major League totals (2 years)			249	845	120	242	50	7	28	120	.286	43	174	10	565	18	7	.988

JONES, MARCUS   P   ATHLETICS

PERSONAL: Born March 29, 1975, in Bellflower, Calif. ... 6-5/235. ... Throws right, bats right. ... Full name: Marcus Ray Jones.
HIGH SCHOOL: Esperanza (Anaheim).
COLLEGE: Long Beach State.
TRANSACTIONS/CAREER NOTES: Selected by Oakland Athletics organization in third round of free-agent draft (June 3, 1997).

Year	League	W	L	Pct.	ERA	G	GS	CG	ShO	Sv.	IP	H	R	ER	BB	SO
1997—	Southern Oregon (N'West)	3	3	.500	4.50	14	10	0	0	0	56	58	37	28	22	49
1998—	Visalia (Calif.)	7	9	.438	4.67	29	20	0	0	4	131	155	79	68	45	112
—	Edmonton (PCL)	2	0	1.000	2.53	2	2	0	0	0	10²/₃	14	7	3	5	4

Year	League	W	L	Pct.	ERA	G	GS	CG	ShO	Sv.	IP	H	R	ER	BB	SO
1999—	Visalia (Calif.)	6	4	.600	4.45	18	15	0	0	0	91	103	56	45	32	82
—	Vancouver (PCL)	2	1	.667	2.40	3	3	0	0	0	15	23	11	4	5	5
—	Modesto (Calif.)	2	1	.667	2.81	7	5	0	0	0	32	29	18	10	14	36
2000—	Visalia (Calif.)	0	1	.000	6.55	3	2	0	0	0	11	15	8	8	3	11
—	Sacramento (PCL)	6	4	.600	4.35	17	17	0	0	0	101 1/3	108	57	49	36	51
—	Oakland (A.L.)	0	0	...	15.43	1	1	0	0	0	2 1/3	5	4	4	3	1
—	Midland (Texas)	2	0	1.000	2.74	5	5	0	0	0	23	24	8	7	1	12
Major League totals (1 year)		0	0	...	15.43	1	1	0	0	0	2 1/3	5	4	4	3	1

JONES, TERRY — OF — EXPOS

PERSONAL: Born February 15, 1971, in Birmingham, Ala. ... 5-10/165. ... Bats both, throws right. ... Full name: Terry Lee Jones.
HIGH SCHOOL: Pinson Valley (Pinson, Ala.).
JUNIOR COLLEGE: Wallace State Community College (Ala.).
COLLEGE: North Alabama.
TRANSACTIONS/CAREER NOTES: Selected by Colorado Rockies organization in 40th round of free-agent draft (June 3, 1993). ... Traded by Rockies with a player to be named later to Montreal Expos for P Dave Veres and a player to be named later (December 10, 1997). ... On Ottawa disabled list (April 21-May 7, 1999). ... Granted free agency (October 4, 1999). ... Signed by Los Angeles Dodgers organization (October 28, 1999). ... Traded by Dodgers to New York Yankees for a player to be named later (January 6, 2000). ... Claimed on waivers by Expos (March 31, 2000). ... On disabled list (July 18-August 4, 2000).
STATISTICAL NOTES: Led California League outfielders with 342 total chances and tied for lead with four double plays in 1994. ... Led Pacific Coast League outfielders with 311 total chances in 1996.

Year	Team (League)	Pos.	G	AB	R	H	2B	3B	HR	RBI	Avg.	BB	SO	SB	PO	A	E	Avg.
1993—	Bend (N'West)	OF	33	138	21	40	5	4	0	18	.290	12	19	16	57	7	1	.985
—	Central Valley (Calif.)	OF	21	73	16	21	1	0	0	7	.288	10	15	5	36	2	1	.974
1994—	Central Valley (Calif.)	OF	129	*536	94	157	20	1	2	34	.293	42	85	44	*312	*16	14	.959
1995—	New Haven (East.)	OF	124	472	78	127	12	1	1	26	.269	39	104	*51	264	18	*10	.966
1996—	Colo. Springs (PCL)	OF	128	497	75	143	7	4	0	33	.288	37	80	26	281	14	*16	.949
—	Colorado (N.L.)	OF	12	10	6	3	0	0	0	1	.300	0	3	0	5	0	0	1.000
1997—	Colo. Springs (PCL)	OF	92	363	70	98	14	4	1	25	.270	25	49	*36	139	11	1	.993
1998—	Ottawa (I.L.)■	OF	81	278	36	66	3	4	0	21	.237	32	48	35	193	5	4	.980
—	Montreal (N.L.)	OF	60	212	30	46	7	2	1	15	.217	21	46	16	161	4	2	.988
1999—	Ottawa (I.L.)	OF-DH	88	332	49	87	17	2	0	23	.262	24	66	30	172	9	3	.984
—	Montreal (N.L.)	OF	17	63	4	17	1	1	0	3	.270	3	14	1	47	2	0	1.000
2000—	Montreal (N.L.)	OF	108	168	30	42	8	2	0	13	.250	10	32	7	95	4	3	.971
Major League totals (4 years)			197	453	70	108	16	5	1	32	.238	34	95	24	308	10	5	.985

JONES, TODD — P — TIGERS

PERSONAL: Born April 24, 1968, in Marietta, Ga. ... 6-3/230. ... Throws right, bats right. ... Full name: Todd Barton Jones.
HIGH SCHOOL: Osborne (Ga.).
COLLEGE: Jacksonville (Ala.) State.
TRANSACTIONS/CAREER NOTES: Selected by New York Mets organization in 41st round of free-agent draft (June 2, 1986); did not sign. ... Selected by Houston Astros organization in supplemental round ("sandwich pick" between first and second round, 27th pick overall) of free-agent draft (June 5, 1989); pick received as part of compensation for Texas Rangers signing Type A free-agent P Nolan Ryan. ... On suspended list (September 14-16, 1993). ... On Houston disabled list (July 19-August 12 and August 18-September 12, 1996); included rehabilitation assignment to Tucson (August 9-12). ... Traded by Astros with OF Brian Hunter, IF Orlando Miller, P Doug Brocail and cash to Detroit Tigers for C Brad Ausmus, P Jose Lima, P C.J. Nitkowski, P Trever Miller and IF Daryle Ward (December 10, 1996).
HONORS: Named A.L. Fireman of the Year by THE SPORTING NEWS (2000).

Year	League	W	L	Pct.	ERA	G	GS	CG	ShO	Sv.	IP	H	R	ER	BB	SO
1989—	Auburn (NY-Penn)	2	3	.400	5.44	11	9	1	0	0	49 2/3	47	39	30	42	71
1990—	Osceola (FSL)	12	10	.545	3.51	27	•27	1	0	0	151 1/3	124	81	59	*109	106
1991—	Osceola (FSL)	4	4	.500	4.35	14	14	0	0	0	72 1/3	69	38	35	35	51
—	Jackson (Texas)	4	3	.571	4.88	10	10	0	0	0	55 1/3	51	37	30	39	37
1992—	Jackson (Texas)	3	7	.300	3.14	*61	0	0	0	25	66	52	28	23	44	60
—	Tucson (PCL)	0	1	.000	4.50	3	0	0	0	0	4	1	2	2	10	4
1993—	Tucson (PCL)	4	2	.667	4.44	41	0	0	0	12	48 2/3	49	26	24	31	45
—	Houston (N.L.)	1	2	.333	3.13	27	0	0	0	2	37 1/3	28	14	13	15	25
1994—	Houston (N.L.)	5	2	.714	2.72	48	0	0	0	5	72 2/3	52	23	22	26	63
1995—	Houston (N.L.)	6	5	.545	3.07	68	0	0	0	15	99 2/3	89	38	34	52	96
1996—	Houston (N.L.)	6	3	.667	4.40	51	0	0	0	17	57 1/3	61	30	28	32	44
—	Tucson (PCL)	0	0	...	0.00	1	0	0	0	0	2	1	1	0	2	0
1997—	Detroit (A.L.)■	5	4	.556	3.09	68	0	0	0	31	70	60	29	24	35	70
1998—	Detroit (A.L.)	1	4	.200	4.97	65	0	0	0	28	63 1/3	58	38	35	36	57
1999—	Detroit (A.L.)	4	4	.500	3.80	65	0	0	0	30	66 1/3	64	30	28	35	64
2000—	Detroit (A.L.)	2	4	.333	3.52	67	0	0	0	•42	64	67	28	25	25	67
A.L. totals (4 years)		12	16	.429	3.82	265	0	0	0	131	263 2/3	249	125	112	131	258
N.L. totals (4 years)		18	12	.600	3.27	194	0	0	0	39	267	230	105	97	125	228
Major League totals (8 years)		30	28	.517	3.54	459	0	0	0	170	530 2/3	479	230	209	256	486

ALL-STAR GAME RECORD

Year	League	W	L	Pct.	ERA	GS	CG	ShO	Sv.	IP	H	R	ER	BB	SO
2000—	American	0	0	...	0.00	0	0	0	0	1	0	0	0	0	1

PERSONAL: Born March 29, 1967, in Baltimore. ... 6-1/205. ... Bats right, throws right. ... Full name: Brian O'Neal Jordan.

HIGH SCHOOL: Milford (Baltimore).

COLLEGE: Richmond.

TRANSACTIONS/CAREER NOTES: Selected by Cleveland Indians organization in 20th round of free-agent draft (June 3, 1985); did not sign. ... Selected by St. Louis Cardinals organization in supplemental round ("sandwich pick" between first and second round, 30th pick overall) of free-agent draft (June 1, 1988); pick received as part of compensation for New York Yankees signing Type A free-agent 1B/OF Jack Clark. ... On disabled list (May 1-8 and June 3-10, 1991). ... On temporarily inactive (July 3, 1991-remainder of season). ... On St. Louis disabled list (May 23-June 22, 1992); included rehabilitation assignment to Louisville (June 10-22). ... On Louisville disabled list (June 7-14, 1993). ... On disabled list (July 10, 1994-remainder of season; and March 31-April 15, 1996). ... On St. Louis disabled list (May 6-June 13, June 26-August 10 and August 25, 1997-remainder of season); included rehabilitation assignment to Louisville (June 5-13). ... Granted free agency (October 22, 1998). ... Signed by Atlanta Braves (November 23, 1998). ... On disabled list (April 4-19, 2000).

STATISTICAL NOTES: Tied for N.L. lead with six double plays by outfielder in 1998. ... Career major league grand slams: 3.

Year Team (League)	Pos.	G	AB	R	H	2B	3B	HR	RBI	Avg.	BB	SO	SB	PO	A	E	Avg.
1988—Hamilton (NY-Penn) ...	OF	19	71	12	22	3	1	4	12	.310	6	15	3	32	1	1	.971
1989—St. Petersburg (FSL) ..	OF	11	43	7	15	4	1	2	11	.349	0	8	0	22	2	0	1.000
1990—Arkansas (Texas)	OF	16	50	4	8	1	0	0	0	.160	0	11	0	28	0	2	.933
—St. Petersburg (FSL) ..	OF	9	30	3	5	0	1	0	1	.167	2	11	0	23	0	0	1.000
1991—Louisville (A.A.).........	OF	61	212	35	56	11	4	4	24	.264	17	41	10	144	3	2	.987
1992—Louisville (A.A.)	OF	43	155	23	45	3	1	4	16	.290	8	21	13	89	3	1	.989
—St. Louis (N.L.)..........	OF	55	193	17	40	9	4	5	22	.207	10	48	7	101	4	1	.991
1993—St. Louis (N.L.)..........	OF	67	223	33	69	10	6	10	44	.309	12	35	6	140	4	4	.973
—Louisville (A.A.).........	OF	38	144	24	54	13	2	5	35	.375	16	17	9	75	2	0	1.000
1994—St. Louis (N.L.)..........	OF-1B	53	178	14	46	8	2	5	15	.258	16	40	4	105	6	1	.991
1995—St. Louis (N.L.)..........	OF	131	490	83	145	20	4	22	81	.296	22	79	24	267	4	1	.996
1996—St. Louis (N.L.)..........	OF-1B	140	513	82	159	36	1	17	104	.310	29	84	22	310	9	2	.994
1997—St. Louis (N.L.)..........	OF	47	145	17	34	5	0	0	10	.234	10	21	6	82	2	0	1.000
—Louisville (A.A.).........	OF-DH	6	20	1	3	0	0	0	2	.150	1	2	0	6	0	0	1.000
1998—St. Louis (N.L.)..........	OF-DH-3B	150	564	100	178	34	7	25	91	.316	40	66	17	284	12	9	.970
1999—Atlanta (N.L.)■..........	OF	153	576	100	163	28	4	23	115	.283	51	81	13	295	9	3	.990
2000—Atlanta (N.L.).............	OF	133	489	71	129	26	0	17	77	.264	38	80	10	287	7	3	.990
Major League totals (9 years)		929	3371	517	963	176	28	124	559	.286	228	534	109	1871	57	24	.988

DIVISION SERIES RECORD

RECORDS: Holds N.L. career record for most runs batted in—14. ... Shares N.L. single-game record for most runs batted in—5 (October 8, 1999). ... Shares single-inning record for most at-bats—2 (October 9, 1999, sixth inning).

Year Team (League)	Pos.	G	AB	R	H	2B	3B	HR	RBI	Avg.	BB	SO	SB	PO	A	E	Avg.
1996—St. Louis (N.L.)..........	OF	3	12	4	4	0	0	1	3	.333	1	3	1	5	0	0	1.000
1999—Atlanta (N.L.).............	OF	4	17	2	8	1	0	1	7	.471	1	2	0	12	1	0	1.000
2000—Atlanta (N.L.).............	OF	3	11	1	4	1	0	0	4	.364	1	1	0	6	0	0	1.000
Division series totals (3 years)		10	40	7	16	2	0	2	14	.400	3	6	1	23	1	0	1.000

CHAMPIONSHIP SERIES RECORD

Year Team (League)	Pos.	G	AB	R	H	2B	3B	HR	RBI	Avg.	BB	SO	SB	PO	A	E	Avg.
1996—St. Louis (N.L.)..........	OF	7	25	3	6	1	1	1	2	.240	2	3	0	13	0	0	1.000
1999—Atlanta (N.L.).............	OF	6	25	3	5	0	0	2	5	.200	3	5	0	17	0	0	1.000
Championship series totals (2 years)		13	50	6	11	1	1	3	7	.220	5	8	0	30	0	0	1.000

WORLD SERIES RECORD

Year Team (League)	Pos.	G	AB	R	H	2B	3B	HR	RBI	Avg.	BB	SO	SB	PO	A	E	Avg.
1999—Atlanta (N.L.).............	OF	4	13	1	1	0	0	0	1	.077	4	2	0	8	0	1	.889

ALL-STAR GAME RECORD

Year League	Pos.	AB	R	H	2B	3B	HR	RBI	Avg.	BB	SO	SB	PO	A	E	Avg.
1999—National	OF	1	0	1	0	0	0	0	1.000	1	0	0	0	0	0	...

RECORD AS FOOTBALL PLAYER

TRANSACTIONS/CAREER NOTES: Selected by Buffalo Bills in seventh round (173rd pick overall) of 1989 NFL draft. ... Signed by Bills (July 17, 1989). ... Claimed on waivers by Atlanta Falcons (September 5, 1989). ... On injured reserve with ankle injury (September 9-October 22, 1989). ... On developmental squad (October 23-December 2, 1989). ... Granted free agency (February 1, 1992).

PRO STATISTICS: 1989—Recovered two fumbles. 1990—Recovered one fumble. 1991—Credited with two safeties and recovered one fumble.

MISCELLANEOUS: Played safety. ... Named alternate for 1992 Pro Bowl.

		INTERCEPTIONS			SACKS	PUNT RETURNS				KICKOFF RETURNS				TOTAL		
Year Team	G	No.	Yds.	Avg.	TD	No.	No.	Yds.	Avg.	TD	No.	Yds.	Avg.	TD	TD	Pts.	Fum.
1989—Atlanta NFL...............	4	0	0	...	0	0.0	4	34	8.5	0	3	27	9.0	0	0	0	1
1990—Atlanta NFL...............	16	3	14	4.7	0	0.0	2	19	9.5	0	0	0	...	0	0	0	0
1991—Atlanta NFL...............	16	2	3	1.5	0	4.0	14	116	8.3	0	5	100	20.0	0	0	4	0
Pro totals (3 years)	36	5	17	3.4	0	4.0	20	169	8.5	0	8	127	15.9	0	0	4	1

JORDAN, KEVIN   IF

PERSONAL: Born October 9, 1969, in San Francisco. ... 6-1/201. ... Bats right, throws right. ... Full name: Kevin Wayne Jordan.

HIGH SCHOOL: Lowell (San Francisco).

JUNIOR COLLEGE: Canada College (Calif.).

COLLEGE: Nebraska.

TRANSACTIONS/CAREER NOTES: Selected by Los Angeles Dodgers organization in 10th round of free-agent draft (June 5, 1989); did not sign. ... Selected by New York Yankees organization in 20th round of free-agent draft (June 4, 1990). ... Traded by Yankees with P Bobby Munoz and P Ryan Karp to Philadelphia Phillies for P Terry Mulholland and a player to be named later (February 9, 1994); Yankees acquired P Jeff Patterson to complete deal (November 8, 1994). ... On disabled list (May 1-June 20, 1994; and June 17, 1996-remainder of season). ... Granted free agency (December 21, 2000).

STATISTICAL NOTES: Led Eastern League with 234 total bases in 1993. ... Led Eastern League second basemen with 93 double plays in 1993.

Year Team (League)	Pos.	G	AB	R	H	2B	3B	HR	RBI	Avg.	BB	SO	SB	PO	A	E	Avg.
1990— Oneonta (NY-Penn)	2B	73	276	47	92	13	•7	4	54	.333	23	31	19	131	158	8	.973
1991— Fort Lauderdale (FSL)	2B-1B	121	448	61	122	25	5	4	53	.272	37	66	14	182	306	16	.968
1992— Prince William (Caro.)	2B-3B	112	438	67	136	29	8	8	63	.311	27	54	6	192	288	20	.960
1993— Alb./Colonie (East.)	2B	135	513	87	145	*33	4	16	87	.283	41	53	8	261	359	21	.967
1994— Scranton/W.B. (I.L.)■	2B-3B-DH	81	314	44	91	22	1	12	57	.290	29	28	0	160	237	16	.961
1995— Scranton/W.B. (I.L.)	2B-DH	106	410	61	127	29	4	5	60	.310	28	36	3	217	279	12	.976
— Philadelphia (N.L.)	2B-3B	24	54	6	10	1	0	2	6	.185	2	9	0	29	35	1	.985
1996— Philadelphia (N.L.)....	1B-2B-3B	43	131	15	37	10	0	3	12	.282	5	20	2	243	27	0	1.000
1997— Scranton/W.B. (I.L.)	3B-2B	7	30	5	9	2	2	0	2	.300	2	6	2	23	18	1	.976
— Philadelphia (N.L.)......1B-3B-2B-DH		84	177	19	47	8	0	6	30	.266	3	26	0	157	31	6	.969
1998— Philadelphia (N.L.)	1-2-DH-3	112	250	23	69	13	0	2	27	.276	8	30	0	195	77	4	.986
1999— Philadelphia (N.L.)	3B-2B-1B	120	347	36	99	17	3	4	51	.285	24	34	0	151	164	10	.969
2000— Philadelphia (N.L.)	2B-3B-1B	109	337	30	74	16	2	5	36	.220	17	41	0	147	163	7	.978
Major League totals (6 years)		492	1296	129	336	65	5	22	162	.259	59	160	2	922	497	28	.981

JOSE, FELIX   OF

PERSONAL: Born May 8, 1965, in Santo Domingo, Dominican Republic. ... 6-1/220. ... Bats both, throws right. ... Full name: Domingo Felix Jose.

HIGH SCHOOL: Eldo Foreda Reyez de Munoz (Santo Domingo, Dominican Republic).

TRANSACTIONS/CAREER NOTES: Signed as non-drafted free agent by Oakland Athletics organization (January 3, 1984). ... Traded by A's with 3B Stan Royer and P Daryl Green to St. Louis Cardinals for OF Willie McGee (August 29, 1990). ... On St. Louis disabled list (March 28-April 29, 1992); included rehabilitation assignments to Louisville (April 17-22) and St. Petersburg (April 22-29). ... Traded by Cardinals with IF/OF Craig Wilson to Kansas City Royals for 3B Gregg Jefferies and OF Ed Gerald (February 12, 1993). ... On Kansas City disabled list (March 25-April 15, 1994); included rehabilitation assignment to Memphis (April 7-13). ... Granted free agency (December 12, 1994). ... Re-signed by Royals organization (April 19, 1995). ... Released by Royals (May 14, 1995). ... Signed by Chicago Cubs organization (May 24, 1995). ... Released by Cubs (June 1, 1995). ... Signed by Boston Red Sox organization (February 15, 1996). ... On Pawtucket disabled list (April 4-20, 1996). ... Released by Red Sox (May 12, 1996). ... Signed by Toronto Blue Jays organization (May 24, 1996). ... Granted free agency (October 15, 1996). ... Signed by New York Yankees organization (April 2, 2000). ... On New York disabled list (April 30-May 30, 2000); included rehabilitation assignment to Columbus (May 19-29). ... Granted free agency (October 2, 2000).

STATISTICAL NOTES: Career major league grand slams: 2.

Year Team (League)	Pos.	G	AB	R	H	2B	3B	HR	RBI	Avg.	BB	SO	SB	PO	A	E	Avg.
1984— Idaho Falls (Pio.)........	OF	45	152	16	33	6	0	1	18	.217	18	37	5	48	6	1	.982
1985— Madison (Midw.)........	OF	117	409	46	89	13	3	3	33	.218	32	82	6	187	9	12	.942
1986— Modesto (Calif.)	OF	127	516	77	147	22	8	14	77	.285	36	89	14	215	12	14	.942
1987— Huntsville (Sou.)........	OF	91	296	29	67	11	1	5	42	.226	28	61	9	131	7	8	.945
1988— Tacoma (PCL)............	OF	134	508	72	161	29	5	12	83	.317	53	75	16	253	11	8	.971
— Oakland (A.L.)	OF	8	6	2	2	1	0	0	1	.333	0	1	1	8	0	0	1.000
1989— Tacoma (PCL)............	OF	104	387	59	111	26	0	14	63	.287	41	82	11	186	7	*10	.951
— Oakland (A.L.)	OF	20	57	3	11	2	0	0	5	.193	4	13	0	35	2	1	.974
1990— Oakland (A.L.)	OF-DH	101	341	42	90	12	0	8	39	.264	16	65	8	212	5	5	.977
— St. Louis (N.L.)■......	OF	25	85	12	23	4	1	3	13	.271	8	16	4	42	0	0	1.000
1991— St. Louis (N.L.)........	OF	154	568	69	173	40	6	8	77	.305	50	113	20	268	•15	3	.990
1992— Louisville (A.A.)........	OF	2	7	0	1	0	0	0	0	.143	1	0	0	2	0	0	1.000
— St. Petersburg (FSL) ..	OF	6	18	2	8	1	1	0	2	.444	1	2	1	6	0	0	1.000
— St. Louis (N.L.)........	OF	131	509	62	150	22	3	14	75	.295	40	100	28	273	11	6	.979
1993— Kansas City (A.L.)■ ...	OF-DH	149	499	64	126	24	3	6	43	.253	36	95	31	237	6	7	.972
1994— Memphis (Sou.)	OF	6	21	3	7	2	0	0	6	.333	5	6	1	9	0	0	1.000
— Kansas City (A.L.)	OF	99	366	56	111	28	1	11	55	.303	35	75	10	192	7	4	.980
1995— Kansas City (A.L.)	OF	9	30	2	4	1	0	0	1	.133	2	9	0	15	2	0	1.000
— Iowa (A.A.)■............	OF-DH	10	37	2	5	3	0	0	1	.135	1	6	0	12	0	0	1.000
1996— Pawtucket (I.L.)■........	DH-OF	11	32	3	7	3	0	2	5	.219	3	10	0	8	0	1	.889
— Syracuse (I.L.)■	DH-OF	88	327	47	84	14	2	16	61	.257	32	63	3	10	1	1	.923
1997—								Did not play.									
1998— Nashua (Atl.)■..........	OF-DH	98	327	72	112	19	1	26	86	.343	78	55	8	104	11	3	.975
1999—								Did not play.									
2000— New York (A.L.)■........	OF-DH	20	29	4	7	0	0	1	5	.241	2	9	0	13	0	1	.929
— Columbus (I.L.)	OF	59	210	31	65	17	2	11	38	.310	23	60	4	30	2	1	.970
American League totals (7 years)		406	1328	173	351	68	4	26	149	.264	95	267	50	712	22	18	.976
National League totals (3 years)		310	1162	143	346	66	10	25	165	.298	98	229	52	583	26	9	.985
Major League totals (9 years)		716	2490	316	697	134	14	51	314	.280	193	496	102	1295	48	27	.980

ALL-STAR GAME RECORD

Year League	Pos.	AB	R	H	2B	3B	HR	RBI	Avg.	BB	SO	SB	PO	A	E	Avg.
1991— National.....................	OF	2	0	1	0	0	0	0	.500	0	0	0	1	0	0	1.000

JOSEPH, KEVIN — P — GIANTS

PERSONAL: Born August 1, 1976, in Camp Hill, Pa. ... 6-4/200. ... Throws right, bats right. ... Full name: Kevin John Joseph.
HIGH SCHOOL: Trinity Christian (Addison, Texas).
COLLEGE: Rice.
TRANSACTIONS/CAREER NOTES: Selected by San Francisco Giants organization in sixth round of free-agent draft (June 3, 1997). ... On Shreveport disabled list (May 11-June 9, 2000).

Year League	W	L	Pct.	ERA	G	GS	CG	ShO	Sv.	IP	H	R	ER	BB	SO
1997— Salem-Kaizer (N'West)	3	5	.375	5.40	17	6	0	0	1	45	44	35	27	26	45
1998— Bakersfield (Calif.)	0	4	.000	8.14	6	6	0	0	0	21	35	26	19	20	17
— Salem-Kaizer (N'West)	1	1	.500	4.36	23	0	0	0	0	43 1/3	36	25	21	27	37
1999— San Jose (Calif.)	1	2	.333	2.35	20	0	0	0	2	30 2/3	17	9	8	13	30
— Shreveport (Texas)	0	2	.000	1.42	7	0	0	0	0	12 2/3	8	4	2	5	16
2000— Shreveport (Texas)	3	11	.214	5.17	27	16	0	0	1	102 2/3	116	60	59	48	71

JOYNER, WALLY — 1B — ANGELS

PERSONAL: Born June 16, 1962, in Atlanta. ... 6-2/200. ... Bats left, throws left. ... Full name: Wallace Keith Joyner.
HIGH SCHOOL: Redan (Stone Mountain, Ga.).
COLLEGE: Brigham Young.
TRANSACTIONS/CAREER NOTES: Selected by California Angels organization in third round of free-agent draft (June 6, 1983); pick received as compensation for New York Yankees signing free-agent DH Don Baylor. ... On disabled list (July 12, 1990-remainder of season). ... Granted free agency (October 28, 1991). ... Signed by Kansas City Royals (December 9, 1991). ... On disabled list (June 26-July 14, 1994). ... Traded by Royals with P Aaron Dorlarque to San Diego Padres for 2B/OF Bip Roberts and P Bryan Wolff (December 21, 1995). ... On San Diego disabled list (June 3-July 11, 1996); included rehabilitation assignment to Rancho Cucamonga (July 7-11). ... On San Diego disabled list (April 28-May 13, 1997); included rehabilitation assignment to Las Vegas (May 8-12). ... On San Diego disabled list (May 17-June 25, 1999); included rehabilitation assignment to Las Vegas (June 18-25). ... Traded by Padres with 2B Quilvio Veras and OF Reggie Sanders to Atlanta Braves for OF/1B Ryan Klesko, 2B Bret Boone and P Jason Shiell (December 22, 1999). ... Granted free agency (October 30, 2000). ... Signed by Angels organization (January 25, 2001).
RECORDS: Shares major league record for most home runs in month of October—4 (1987).
STATISTICAL NOTES: Tied for Eastern League lead with eight intentional bases on balls received in 1984. ... Led Pacific Coast League first basemen with 1,229 total chances and 121 double plays in 1985. ... Led A.L. with 12 sacrifice flies in 1986. ... Hit three home runs in one game (October 3, 1987). ... Led A.L. first basemen with 1,520 total chances in 1988 and 1,441 in 1991. ... Led A.L. first basemen with 148 double plays in 1988 and 138 in 1992. ... Career major league grand slams: 6.

							BATTING							FIELDING		
Year Team (League)	Pos.	G	AB	R	H	2B	3B	HR	RBI	Avg.	BB	SO	SB	PO	A	E	Avg.
1983— Peoria (Midw.)	1B	54	192	25	63	16	2	3	33	.328	19	25	1	480	45	6	.989
1984— Waterbury (East.)	1B-OF	134	467	81	148	24	7	12	72	.317	67	60	0	906	86	9	.991
1985— Edmonton (PCL)	1B	126	477	68	135	29	5	12	73	.283	60	64	2	*1107	*107	•15	.988
1986— California (A.L.)	1B	154	593	82	172	27	3	22	100	.290	57	58	5	1222	139	15	.989
1987— California (A.L.)	1B	149	564	100	161	33	1	34	117	.285	72	64	8	1276	92	10	.993
1988— California (A.L.)	1B	158	597	81	176	31	2	13	85	.295	55	51	8	*1369	*143	8	.995
1989— California (A.L.)	1B	159	593	78	167	30	2	16	79	.282	46	58	3	*1487	99	4	*.997
1990— California (A.L.)	1B	83	310	35	83	15	0	8	41	.268	41	34	2	727	62	4	.995
1991— California (A.L.)	1B	143	551	79	166	34	3	21	96	.301	52	66	2	*1335	98	8	.994
1992— Kansas City (A.L.)■	1B-DH	149	572	66	154	36	2	9	66	.269	55	50	11	1236	137	10	.993
1993— Kansas City (A.L.)	1B	141	497	83	145	36	3	15	65	.292	66	67	5	1116	145	7	.994
1994— Kansas City (A.L.)	1B-DH	97	363	52	113	20	3	8	57	.311	47	43	3	777	64	8	.991
1995— Kansas City (A.L.)	1B-DH	131	465	69	144	28	0	12	83	.310	69	65	3	1111	118	3	*.998
1996— San Diego (N.L.)	1B	121	433	59	120	29	1	8	65	.277	69	71	5	1059	89	3	*.997
— Rancho Cuca. (Calif.)	1B	3	10	1	3	1	0	0	2	.300	1	1	0	14	2	0	1.000
1997— San Diego (N.L.)	1B	135	455	59	149	29	2	13	83	.327	51	51	3	1027	89	4	*.996
— Las Vegas (PCL)	1B	3	8	1	2	0	0	0	1	.250	0	1	0	16	1	0	1.000
1998— San Diego (N.L.)	1B	131	439	58	131	30	1	12	80	.298	51	44	1	985	81	7	.993
1999— San Diego (N.L.)	1B-DH	110	323	34	80	14	2	5	43	.248	58	54	0	731	66	4	.995
— Las Vegas (PCL)	1B	6	17	4	4	0	0	0	2	.235	3	2	0	38	2	0	1.000
2000— Atlanta (N.L.)■	1B-DH	119	224	24	63	12	0	5	32	.281	31	31	0	353	30	3	.992
American League totals (10 years)		1364	5105	725	1481	290	19	158	789	.290	560	556	50	11656	1097	77	.994
National League totals (5 years)		616	1874	234	543	114	6	43	303	.290	260	251	9	4155	355	21	.995
Major League totals (15 years)		1980	6979	959	2024	404	25	201	1092	.290	820	807	59	15811	1452	98	.994

DIVISION SERIES RECORD

							BATTING							FIELDING		
Year Team (League)	Pos.	G	AB	R	H	2B	3B	HR	RBI	Avg.	BB	SO	SB	PO	A	E	Avg.
1996— San Diego (N.L.)	1B	3	9	0	1	0	0	0	0	.111	0	2	0	12	2	0	1.000
1998— San Diego (N.L.)	1B	4	6	1	1	0	0	1	2	.167	1	2	0	19	1	1	.952
2000— Atlanta (N.L.)	PH	3	3	0	1	1	0	0	0	.333	0	0	0	...	...	0	
Division series totals (3 years)		10	18	1	3	1	0	1	2	.167	1	4	0	31	3	1	.971

CHAMPIONSHIP SERIES RECORD

							BATTING							FIELDING		
Year Team (League)	Pos.	G	AB	R	H	2B	3B	HR	RBI	Avg.	BB	SO	SB	PO	A	E	Avg.
1986— California (A.L.)	1B	3	11	3	5	2	0	1	2	.455	2	0	0	24	1	0	1.000
1998— San Diego (N.L.)	1B	6	16	3	5	0	0	0	2	.313	4	3	0	45	6	0	1.000
Championship series totals (2 years)		9	27	6	10	2	0	1	4	.370	6	3	0	69	7	0	1.000

WORLD SERIES RECORD

							BATTING							FIELDING		
Year Team (League)	Pos.	G	AB	R	H	2B	3B	HR	RBI	Avg.	BB	SO	SB	PO	A	E	Avg.
1998— San Diego (N.L.)	1B	3	8	0	0	0	0	0	0	.000	3	1	0	22	0	0	1.000

ALL-STAR GAME RECORD

						BATTING							FIELDING		
Year League	Pos.	AB	R	H	2B	3B	HR	RBI	Avg.	BB	SO	SB	PO	A	E	Avg.
1986— American	1B	1	0	0	0	0	0	0	.000	0	0	0	3	1	0	1.000

PERSONAL: Born June 30, 1975, in San Diego. ... 6-1/217. ... Throws right, bats right. ... Full name: Michael Galen Judd.
HIGH SCHOOL: Helix (San Diego).
JUNIOR COLLEGE: Grossmont College (Calif.).
TRANSACTIONS/CAREER NOTES: Selected by New York Yankees organization in ninth round of free-agent draft (June 1, 1995). ... Traded by Yankees to Los Angeles Dodgers for P Billy Brewer (June 22, 1996). ... On Albuquerque disabled list (May 3-16, 2000).

Year	League	W	L	Pct.	ERA	G	GS	CG	ShO	Sv.	IP	H	R	ER	BB	SO
1995—	Gulf Coast Yankees (GCL)..	1	1	.500	1.11	21	0	0	0	8	32 $\frac{1}{3}$	18	5	4	6	30
	—Greensboro (S.Atl.)	0	0	...	0.00	1	0	0	0	0	2 $\frac{2}{3}$	2	0	0	0	1
1996—	Greensboro (S.Atl.)	2	2	.500	3.81	29	0	0	0	10	28 $\frac{1}{3}$	22	14	12	8	36
	—Savannah (S.Atl.)■	4	2	.667	2.44	15	8	1	0	3	55 $\frac{1}{3}$	40	21	15	15	62
1997—	Vero Beach (FSL)	6	5	.545	3.53	14	14	1	0	0	86 $\frac{2}{3}$	67	37	34	39	104
	—San Antonio (Texas)	4	2	.667	2.73	12	12	0	0	0	79	69	27	24	33	65
	—Los Angeles (N.L.)	0	0	...	0.00	1	0	0	0	0	2 $\frac{2}{3}$	4	0	0	0	4
1998—	Albuquerque (PCL)	5	7	.417	4.56	17	17	3	1	0	94 $\frac{2}{3}$	98	62	48	44	77
	—Los Angeles (N.L.)	0	0	...	15.09	7	0	0	0	0	11 $\frac{1}{3}$	19	19	19	9	14
1999—	Albuquerque (PCL)	8	7	.533	6.67	21	21	1	0	0	110 $\frac{2}{3}$	132	90	82	47	122
	—Los Angeles (N.L.)	3	1	.750	5.46	7	4	0	0	0	28	30	17	17	12	22
2000—	Albuquerque (PCL)	7	6	.538	4.51	24	23	1	0	0	141 $\frac{2}{3}$	153	86	71	62	92
	—Los Angeles (N.L.)	0	1	.000	15.75	1	1	0	0	0	4	4	7	7	3	5
Major League totals (4 years)		3	2	.600	8.41	16	5	0	0	0	46	57	43	43	24	45

PERSONAL: Born April 14, 1966, in Cincinnati. ... 6-3/200. ... Bats left, throws left. ... Full name: David Christopher Justice.
HIGH SCHOOL: Covington (Ky.) Latin.
COLLEGE: Thomas More College (Ky.).
TRANSACTIONS/CAREER NOTES: Selected by Atlanta Braves organization in fourth round of free-agent draft (June 3, 1985). ... On Atlanta disabled list (June 27-August 20, 1991); included rehabilitation assignment to Macon (August 16-20). ... On disabled list (April 12-27, 1992; June 2-17, 1995 and May 16, 1996-remainder of season). ... Traded by Braves with OF Marquis Grissom to Cleveland Indians for OF Kenny Lofton and P Alan Embree (March 25, 1997). ... On disabled list (June 24-July 10, 1997). ... Traded by Indians to New York Yankees for OF Ricky Ledee and two players to be named later (June 29, 2000); Indians acquired P Jake Westbrook and P Zach Day to complete deal (July 25, 2000).
RECORDS: Holds major league single-season record for fewest errors by outfielder who led league in errors—8 (1992).
HONORS: Named N.L. Rookie Player of the Year by THE SPORTING NEWS (1990). ... Named N.L. Rookie of the Year by Baseball Writers' Association of America (1990). ... Named outfielder on THE SPORTING NEWS N.L. All-Star team (1993). ... Named outfielder on THE SPORTING NEWS N.L. Silver Slugger team (1993). ... Named outfielder on THE SPORTING NEWS A.L. Silver Slugger team (1997). ... Named A.L. Comeback Player of the Year by THE SPORTING NEWS (1997). ... Named outfielder on THE SPORTING NEWS A.L. All-Star team (1997).
STATISTICAL NOTES: Tied for Appalachian League lead with five sacrifice flies in 1985. ... Career major league grand slams: 4.

Year	Team (League)	Pos.	G	AB	R	H	2B	3B	HR	RBI	Avg.	BB	SO	SB	PO	A	E	Avg.
1985—	Pulaski (Appl.)	OF	66	204	39	50	8	0	•10	46	.245	40	30	0	86	2	4	.957
1986—	Sumter (S.Atl.)	OF	61	220	48	66	16	0	10	61	.300	48	28	10	124	7	4	.970
	—Durham (Caro.)	OF-1B	67	229	47	64	9	1	12	44	.279	46	24	2	163	5	1	.994
1987—	Greenville (Sou.)	OF	93	348	38	79	12	4	6	40	.227	53	48	3	199	4	8	.962
1988—	Richmond (I.L.)	OF	70	227	27	46	9	1	8	28	.203	39	55	4	136	5	4	.972
	—Greenville (Sou.)	OF	58	198	34	55	13	1	9	37	.278	37	41	6	100	3	5	.954
1989—	Richmond (I.L.)	OF-1B	115	391	47	102	24	3	12	58	.261	59	66	12	220	15	6	.975
	—Atlanta (N.L.)	OF	16	51	7	12	3	0	1	3	.235	3	9	2	24	0	0	1.000
1990—	Richmond (I.L.)	OF-1B	12	45	7	16	5	1	2	7	.356	7	6	0	23	4	2	.931
	—Atlanta (N.L.)	1B-OF	127	439	76	124	23	2	28	78	.282	64	92	11	604	42	14	.979
1991—	Atlanta (N.L.)	OF	109	396	67	109	25	1	21	87	.275	65	81	8	204	9	7	.968
	—Macon (S.Atl.)	OF	3	10	2	2	0	0	2	5	.200	2	1	0	1	0	0	1.000
1992—	Atlanta (N.L.)	OF	144	484	78	124	19	5	21	72	.256	79	85	2	313	8	*8	.976
1993—	Atlanta (N.L.)	OF	157	585	90	158	15	4	40	120	.270	78	90	3	323	9	5	.985
1994—	Atlanta (N.L.)	OF	104	352	61	110	16	2	19	59	.313	69	45	2	192	6	*11	.947
1995—	Atlanta (N.L.)	OF	120	411	73	104	17	2	24	78	.253	73	68	4	233	8	4	.984
1996—	Atlanta (N.L.)	OF	40	140	23	45	9	0	6	25	.321	21	22	1	88	3	0	1.000
1997—	Cleveland (A.L.)■	OF-DH	139	495	84	163	31	1	33	101	.329	80	79	3	120	3	2	.984
1998—	Cleveland (A.L.)	DH-OF	146	540	94	151	39	2	21	88	.280	76	98	9	37	0	0	1.000
1999—	Cleveland (A.L.)	OF-DH	133	429	75	123	18	0	21	88	.287	94	90	1	161	7	4	.977
2000—	Cleveland (A.L.)	OF-DH	68	249	46	66	14	1	21	58	.265	38	49	1	84	2	2	.977
	—New York (A.L.)■	OF-DH	78	275	43	84	17	0	20	60	.305	39	42	1	127	6	2	.985
American League totals (4 years)			564	1988	342	587	119	4	116	395	.295	327	358	15	529	18	10	.982
National League totals (8 years)			817	2858	475	786	127	16	160	522	.275	452	492	33	1981	85	49	.977
Major League totals (12 years)			1381	4846	817	1373	246	20	276	917	.283	779	850	48	2510	103	59	.978

DIVISION SERIES RECORD

RECORDS: Shares single-series record for most doubles—4 (1998).

Year	Team (League)	Pos.	G	AB	R	H	2B	3B	HR	RBI	Avg.	BB	SO	SB	PO	A	E	Avg.
1995—	Atlanta (N.L.)	OF	4	13	2	3	0	0	0	0	.231	5	2	0	6	0	1	.857
1997—	Cleveland (A.L.)	DH	5	19	3	5	2	0	1	2	.263	2	3	0	0	0	0	...
1998—	Cleveland (A.L.)	DH-OF	4	16	2	5	4	0	1	6	.313	0	1	0	5	1	0	1.000
1999—	Cleveland (A.L.)	OF	3	8	0	0	0	0	0	0	.000	2	2	0	7	2	0	1.000
2000—	New York (A.L.)	OF	5	18	2	4	0	0	1	1	.222	3	4	0	10	0	0	1.000
Division series totals (5 years)			21	74	9	17	6	0	3	10	.230	12	12	0	28	3	1	.969

CHAMPIONSHIP SERIES RECORD

NOTES: Named Most Valuable Player (2000).

Year Team (League)	Pos.	G	AB	R	H	2B	3B	HR	RBI	Avg.	BB	SO	SB	PO	A	E	Avg.
1991— Atlanta (N.L.)............	OF	7	25	4	5	1	0	1	2	.200	3	7	0	17	0	1	.944
1992— Atlanta (N.L.)............	OF	7	25	5	7	1	0	2	6	.280	6	2	0	19	3	0	1.000
1993— Atlanta (N.L.)............	OF	6	21	2	3	1	0	0	4	.143	3	3	0	14	0	1	.933
1995— Atlanta (N.L.)............	OF	3	11	1	3	0	0	0	1	.273	2	1	0	0	0	0	...
1997— Cleveland (A.L.).........	DH	6	21	3	7	1	0	0	0	.333	2	4	0	...	...	...	...
1998— Cleveland (A.L.).........	OF-DH-PH	6	19	2	3	0	0	1	2	.158	3	3	0	3	0	0	1.000
2000— New York (A.L.)..........	OF	6	26	4	6	2	0	2	8	.231	2	7	0	9	0	0	1.000
Championship series totals (7 years)		41	148	21	34	6	0	6	23	.230	21	27	0	62	3	2	.970

WORLD SERIES RECORD

NOTES: Member of World Series championship team (1995 and 2000).

Year Team (League)	Pos.	G	AB	R	H	2B	3B	HR	RBI	Avg.	BB	SO	SB	PO	A	E	Avg.
1991— Atlanta (N.L.)............	OF	7	27	5	7	0	0	2	6	.259	5	5	2	21	1	1	.957
1992— Atlanta (N.L.)............	OF	6	19	4	3	0	0	1	3	.158	6	5	1	15	0	1	.938
1995— Atlanta (N.L.)............	OF	6	20	3	5	1	0	1	5	.250	5	1	0	16	0	0	1.000
1997— Cleveland (A.L.).........	OF-DH	7	27	4	5	0	0	0	4	.185	6	8	0	9	0	0	1.000
2000— New York (A.L.)..........	OF	5	19	1	3	2	0	0	3	.158	3	2	0	8	1	0	1.000
World Series totals (5 years)		31	112	17	23	3	0	4	21	.205	25	21	3	69	2	2	.973

ALL-STAR GAME RECORD

Year League	Pos.	AB	R	H	2B	3B	HR	RBI	Avg.	BB	SO	SB	PO	A	E	Avg.
1993— National	OF	3	0	1	0	0	0	0	.333	0	0	0	1	0	1	.500
1994— National	OF	2	0	0	0	0	0	0	.000	0	0	0	1	0	0	1.000
1997— American....................						Selected, did not play—injured.										
All-Star Game totals (2 years)		5	0	1	0	0	0	0	.200	0	0	0	2	0	1	.667

KALINOWSKI, JOSH   P   ROCKIES

PERSONAL: Born December 12, 1976, in Pasco, Wash. ... 6-2/190. ... Throws left, bats left. ... Full name: Joshua David Kalinowski.

HIGH SCHOOL: Natrona County (Casper, Wyoming).

JUNIOR COLLEGE: Indian Hills Community College (Iowa).

TRANSACTIONS/CAREER NOTES: Selected by Colorado Rockies organization in 37th round of free-agent draft (June 1, 1995); did not sign. ... Selected by Rockies organization in 33rd round of free-agent draft (June 4, 1996). ... On Salem disabled list (May 2-9, 1999). ... On Carolina disabled list (April 28-June 9 and June 16-August 31, 2000). ... On Colorado disabled list (September 1, 2000-remainder of season).

HONORS: Named Carolina League Pitcher of the Year (1999).

STATISTICAL NOTES: Pitches 5-0 no-hit victory for Asheville against Charleston, S.C. (August 28, 1998). ... Led Carolina League pitchers with 34 assists in 1999.

Year League	W	L	Pct.	ERA	G	GS	CG	ShO	Sv.	IP	H	R	ER	BB	SO
1997— Portland (N'West)	0	1	.000	2.41	6	6	0	0	0	18 2/3	15	6	5	10	27
1998— Asheville (S.Atl.).................	12	10	.545	3.92	28	28	3	1	0	172 1/3	159	93	75	65	*215
1999— Salem (Caro.)....................	11	6	.647	*2.11	27	27	1	0	0	162 1/3	119	47	38	71	*176
2000— Carolina (Sou.)	1	3	.250	6.23	6	6	0	0	0	26	30	22	18	12	27

KAMIENIECKI, SCOTT   P

PERSONAL: Born April 19, 1964, in Mt. Clemens, Mich. ... 6-0/200. ... Throws right, bats right. ... Full name: Scott Andrew Kamieniecki. ... Name pronounced KAM-ah-NIK-ee.

HIGH SCHOOL: Redford St. Mary's (Detroit).

COLLEGE: Michigan.

TRANSACTIONS/CAREER NOTES: Selected by Detroit Tigers organization in second round of free-agent draft (June 7, 1982); did not sign. ... Selected by Milwaukee Brewers organization in 23rd round of free-agent draft (June 3, 1985); did not sign. ... Selected by New York Yankees organization in 14th round of free-agent draft (June 2, 1986). ... On New York disabled list (August 3, 1991-remainder of season). ... On New York disabled list (April 2-29, 1992); included rehabilitation assignments to Fort Lauderdale (April 9-17) and Columbus (April 17-29). ... On New York disabled list (May 6-July 15, 1995); included rehabilitation assignments to Tampa (July 5-10) and Columbus (July 10-12). ... On New York disabled list (March 27-April 24 and July 31, 1996-remainder of season); included rehabilitation assignment to Tampa (April 6-24). ... On Columbus disabled list (June 20-July 31, 1996). ... Granted free agency (December 20, 1996). ... Signed by Baltimore Orioles organization (January 22, 1997). ... Granted free agency (October 30, 1997). ... Re-signed by Orioles (December 5, 1997). ... On Baltimore disabled list (May 25-May 12, May 23-July 25 and August 23, 1998-remainder of season); included rehabilitation assignment to Bowie (July 9-25). ... On Baltimore disabled list (March 25-May 8, 1999); included rehabilitation assignments to Bowie (April 25-29) and Frederick (April 30-May 3). ... Granted free agency (November 2, 1999). ... Signed by Cleveland Indians (December 3, 1999). ... Released by Indians (July 4, 2000). ... Signed by Atlanta Braves (July 5, 2000). ... Granted free agency (October 31, 2000).

Year League	W	L	Pct.	ERA	G	GS	CG	ShO	Sv.	IP	H	R	ER	BB	SO
1987— Albany/Colonie (East.)........	1	3	.250	5.35	10	7	0	0	0	37	41	25	22	33	19
— Prince William (Caro.)	9	5	.643	4.17	19	19	1	0	0	112 1/3	91	61	52	78	84
1988— Prince William (Caro.)........	6	7	.462	4.40	15	15	•7	2	0	100 1/3	115	62	49	50	72
— Fort Lauderdale (FSL)	3	6	.333	3.62	12	11	1	1	0	77	71	36	31	40	51
1989— Albany/Colonie (East.)........	10	9	.526	3.70	24	23	6	3	0	151	142	67	62	57	*140
1990— Albany/Colonie (East.)........	10	9	.526	3.20	22	21	3	1	0	132	113	55	47	61	99
1991— Columbus (I.L.)..................	6	3	.667	2.36	11	11	3	1	0	76 1/3	61	25	20	20	58
— New York (A.L.)..................	4	4	.500	3.90	9	9	0	0	0	55 3/4	54	24	24	22	34
1992— Fort Lauderdale (FSL)	1	0	1.000	1.29	1	1	0	0	0	7	8	1	1	0	3
— Columbus (I.L.)..................	1	0	1.000	0.69	2	2	0	0	0	13	6	1	1	4	12
— New York (A.L.)..................	6	14	.300	4.36	28	28	4	0	0	188	193	100	91	74	88

J

K

Year League	W	L	Pct.	ERA	G	GS	CG	ShO	Sv.	IP	H	R	ER	BB	SO
1993— New York (A.L.)	10	7	.588	4.08	30	20	2	0	1	154 1/3	163	73	70	59	72
— Columbus (I.L.)	1	0	1.000	1.50	1	1	0	0	0	6	5	1	1	0	4
1994— New York (A.L.)	8	6	.571	3.76	22	16	1	0	0	117 1/3	115	53	49	59	71
1995— New York (A.L.)	7	6	.538	4.01	17	16	1	0	0	89 2/3	83	43	40	49	43
— Tampa (FSL)	1	0	1.000	1.80	1	1	0	0	0	5	6	2	1	1	2
— Columbus (I.L.)	1	0	1.000	0.00	1	1	0	0	0	6 2/3	2	0	0	1	10
1996— Tampa (FSL)	2	1	.667	1.17	3	3	1	0	0	23	20	6	3	4	17
— New York (A.L.)	1	2	.333	11.12	7	5	0	0	0	22 2/3	36	30	28	19	15
— Columbus (I.L.)	2	1	.667	5.64	5	5	2	0	0	30 1/3	33	21	19	8	27
1997— Baltimore (A.L.)■	10	6	.625	4.01	30	30	0	0	0	179 1/3	179	83	80	67	109
1998— Baltimore (A.L.)	2	6	.250	6.75	12	11	0	0	0	54 2/3	67	41	41	26	25
— Bowie (East.)	1	0	1.000	4.76	3	3	0	0	0	11 1/3	13	6	6	2	5
1999— Bowie (East.)	0	1	.000	3.60	1	1	0	0	0	5	6	2	2	0	1
— Frederick (Caro.)	0	0	...	0.00	1	1	0	0	0	4	0	0	0	1	3
— Baltimore (A.L.)	2	4	.333	4.95	43	3	0	0	2	56 1/3	52	32	31	29	39
— Rochester (I.L.)	1	2	.333	5.09	4	4	0	0	0	23	23	13	13	6	14
2000— Cleveland (A.L.)■	1	3	.250	5.67	26	0	0	0	0	33 1/3	42	22	21	20	29
— Atlanta (N.L.)■	2	1	.667	5.47	26	0	0	0	2	24 2/3	22	18	15	22	17
A.L. totals (10 years)	51	58	.468	4.50	224	138	8	0	3	951	984	501	475	424	525
N.L. totals (1 year)	2	1	.667	5.47	26	0	0	0	2	24 2/3	22	18	15	22	17
Major League totals (10 years)	53	59	.473	4.52	250	138	8	0	5	975 2/3	1006	519	490	446	542

DIVISION SERIES RECORD

Year League	W	L	Pct.	ERA	G	GS	CG	ShO	Sv.	IP	H	R	ER	BB	SO
1995— New York (A.L.)	0	0	...	7.20	1	1	0	0	0	5	9	5	4	4	4
1997— Baltimore (A.L.)						Did not play.									

CHAMPIONSHIP SERIES RECORD

Year League	W	L	Pct.	ERA	G	GS	CG	ShO	Sv.	IP	H	R	ER	BB	SO
1997— Baltimore (A.L.)	1	0	1.000	0.00	2	1	0	0	0	8	4	0	0	2	5

KAPLER, GABE — OF — RANGERS

PERSONAL: Born August 31, 1975, in Hollywood, Calif. ... 6-2/208. ... Bats right, throws right. ... Full name: Gabriel Stefan Kapler.
HIGH SCHOOL: Taft (Woodland Hills, Calif.).
JUNIOR COLLEGE: Moorpark (Calif.) College.
TRANSACTIONS/CAREER NOTES: Selected by Detroit Tigers organization in 57th round of free-agent draft (June 1, 1995). ... Traded by Tigers with P Justin Thompson, P Francisco Cordero, C Bill Haselman, 2B Frank Catalanotto and P Alan Webb to Texas Rangers for OF Juan Gonzalez, P Danny Patterson and C Gregg Zaun (November 2, 1999). ... On Texas disabled list (May 4-June 9, 2000); included rehabilitation assignments to Oklahoma (May 20-24) and Tulsa (June 5-9).
HONORS: Named Minor League Player of the Year by THE SPORTING NEWS (1998). ... Named Southern League Most Valuable Player (1998).
STATISTICAL NOTES: Led South Atlantic League with 280 total bases in 1996. ... Led Florida State League with 262 total bases in 1997. ... Led Southern League with 319 total bases and 11 sacrifice flies in 1998. ... Had 28-game hitting streak (July 17-August 15, 2000).

Year Team (League)	Pos.	G	AB	R	H	2B	3B	HR	RBI	Avg.	BB	SO	SB	PO	A	E	Avg.
								BATTING							FIELDING		
1995— Jamestown (NY-P)	OF	63	236	38	68	19	4	4	34	.288	23	37	1	103	9	9	.926
1996— Fayetteville (S.Atl.)	OF-3B	138	524	81	*157	*45	0	26	99	.300	62	73	14	195	14	7	.968
1997— Lakeland (FSL)	OF	137	519	87	153	*40	6	19	87	.295	54	68	8	252	14	6	.978
1998— Jacksonville (Sou.)	OF-1B	139	547	*113	*176	*47	6	*28	*146	.322	66	93	6	294	12	5	.984
— Detroit (A.L.)	OF-DH	7	25	3	5	0	1	0	0	.200	1	4	2	9	0	0	1.000
1999— Detroit (A.L.)	OF-DH	130	416	60	102	22	4	18	49	.245	42	74	11	302	4	6	.981
— Toledo (I.L.)	OF	14	54	11	17	6	2	3	14	.315	9	10	0	33	0	0	1.000
2000— Texas (A.L.)■	OF	116	444	59	134	32	1	14	66	.302	42	57	8	307	5	*10	.969
— Oklahoma (PCL)	OF	3	9	3	3	0	0	0	0	.333	3	2	0	1	1	0	1.000
— Tulsa (Texas)	OF	3	12	3	7	0	0	1	4	.583	1	2	0	6	0	0	1.000
Major League totals (3 years)		253	885	122	241	54	6	32	115	.272	85	135	21	618	9	16	.975

KARCHNER, MATT — P

PERSONAL: Born June 28, 1967, in Berwick, Pa. ... 6-4/220. ... Throws right, bats right. ... Full name: Matthew Dean Karchner.
HIGH SCHOOL: Berwick (Pa.).
COLLEGE: Bloomsburg (Pa.).
TRANSACTIONS/CAREER NOTES: Selected by Kansas City Royals organization in eighth round of free-agent draft (June 5, 1989). ... On disabled list (August 1-8, 1991). ... Selected by Montreal Expos organization in Rule 5 major league draft (December 9, 1991). ... Returned to Royals (April 4, 1992). ... On disabled list (September 2-18, 1992; and May 10, 1993-remainder of season). ... Selected by Chicago White Sox organization from Royals organization, in Rule 5 minor league draft (December 13, 1993). ... On Chicago disabled list (August 11-September 1, 1996); included rehabilitation assignment to Nashville (August 30-September 1). ... On Chicago disabled list (May 7-23 and June 24-July 9, 1998). ... Traded by White Sox to Chicago Cubs for P Jon Garland (July 29, 1998). ... On Chicago disabled list (April 26-June 24 and July 17, 1999-remainder of season); included rehabilitation assignment to Iowa (May 30-June 7 and June 18-23). ... On Iowa disabled list (August 2-September 5, 2000). ... Released by Cubs (September 5, 2000).

Year League	W	L	Pct.	ERA	G	GS	CG	ShO	Sv.	IP	H	R	ER	BB	SO
1989— Eugene (N'West)	1	1	.500	3.90	8	5	0	0	0	30	30	19	13	8	25
1990— Appleton (Midw.)	2	7	.222	4.82	27	11	1	0	0	71	70	42	38	31	58
1991— Baseball City (FSL)	6	3	.667	1.97	38	0	0	0	5	73	49	28	16	25	65
1992— Memphis (Sou.)	8	8	.500	4.47	33	18	2	0	1	141	161	83	70	35	88
1993— Memphis (Sou.)	3	2	.600	4.20	6	5	0	0	0	30	34	16	14	4	14
1994— Birmingham (Sou.)■	5	2	.714	1.26	39	0	0	0	6	43	36	10	6	14	29
— Nashville (A.A.)	4	2	.667	1.37	17	0	0	0	2	26 1/3	18	5	4	7	19

– 293 –

Year League	W	L	Pct.	ERA	G	GS	CG	ShO	Sv.	IP	H	R	ER	BB	SO
1995— Nashville (A.A.)	3	3	.500	1.45	28	0	0	0	9	37 1/3	39	7	6	10	29
— Chicago (A.L.)	4	2	.667	1.69	31	0	0	0	0	32	33	8	6	12	24
1996— Chicago (A.L.)	7	4	.636	5.76	50	0	0	0	1	59 1/3	61	42	38	41	46
— Nashville (A.A.)	0	0	...	0.00	1	0	0	0	0	2/3	0	0	0	0	0
1997— Nashville (A.A.)	2	1	.667	1.93	13	0	0	0	3	18 2/3	12	5	4	6	11
— Chicago (A.L.)	3	1	.750	2.91	52	0	0	0	15	52 2/3	50	18	17	26	30
1998— Chicago (A.L.)	2	4	.333	5.15	32	0	0	0	11	36 2/3	33	21	21	19	30
— Chicago (N.L.)■	3	1	.750	5.14	29	0	0	0	0	28	30	18	16	14	22
1999— Chicago (N.L.)	1	0	1.000	2.50	16	0	0	0	0	18	16	5	5	9	9
— Iowa (PCL)	0	0	...	6.35	5	1	0	0	0	5 2/3	6	4	4	1	6
2000— Chicago (N.L.)	1	1	.500	6.14	13	0	0	0	0	14 2/3	19	11	10	11	5
— Iowa (PCL)	2	1	.667	4.01	20	1	0	0	2	42 2/3	46	23	19	12	35
A.L. totals (4 years)	16	11	.593	4.08	165	0	0	0	27	180 2/3	177	89	82	98	130
N.L. totals (3 years)	5	2	.714	4.60	58	0	0	0	0	60 2/3	65	34	31	34	36
Major League totals (6 years)	21	13	.618	4.21	223	0	0	0	27	241 1/3	242	123	113	132	166

DIVISION SERIES RECORD

Year League	W	L	Pct.	ERA	G	GS	CG	ShO	Sv.	IP	H	R	ER	BB	SO
1998— Chicago (N.L.)	0	0	...	13.50	1	0	0	0	0	2/3	1	1	1	0	1

KARL, SCOTT   P   PADRES

K

PERSONAL: Born August 9, 1971, in Riverside, Calif. ... 6-2/209. ... Throws left, bats left. ... Full name: Randall Scott Karl.
HIGH SCHOOL: Carlsbad (Calif.).
COLLEGE: Hawaii.
TRANSACTIONS/CAREER NOTES: Selected by Milwaukee Brewers organization in sixth round of free-agent draft (June 1, 1992). ... On New Orleans disabled list (April 27-May 31, 1994). ... Traded by Brewers with 3B Jeff Cirillo and cash to Colorado Rockies as part of three-way deal in which Brewers received P Jamey Wright and C Henry Blanco from Rockies, Oakland Athletics received P Justin Miller and cash from Rockies and Brewers received P Jimmy Haynes from Athletics (December 13, 1999). ... On Colorado disabled list (July 15-August 5, 2000); included rehabilitation assignment to Colorado Springs (July 20-August 1). ... Traded by Rockies with cash to Anaheim Angels for a player to be named later (August 22, 2000). ... Granted free agency (October 6, 2000). ... Signed by San Diego Padres (December 1, 2000).
STATISTICAL NOTES: Tied for Texas League lead with seven balks in 1993.
MISCELLANEOUS: Appeared in one game as pinch runner (1998).

Year League	W	L	Pct.	ERA	G	GS	CG	ShO	Sv.	IP	H	R	ER	BB	SO
1992— Helena (Pio.)	7	0	•1.000	*1.46	9	9	1	1	0	61 2/3	54	13	10	16	57
1993— El Paso (Texas)	13	8	.619	2.45	27	•27	•4	•2	0	*180	172	67	49	35	95
1994— New Orleans (A.A.)	5	5	.500	3.84	15	13	2	0	0	89	92	38	38	33	54
— El Paso (Texas)	5	1	.833	2.96	8	8	3	0	0	54 2/3	44	21	18	15	51
1995— New Orleans (A.A.)	3	4	.429	3.30	8	6	1	1	0	46 1/3	47	18	17	12	29
— Milwaukee (A.L.)	6	7	.462	4.14	25	18	1	0	0	124	141	65	57	50	59
1996— Milwaukee (A.L.)	13	9	.591	4.86	32	32	3	1	0	207 1/3	220	124	112	72	121
1997— Milwaukee (A.L.)	10	13	.435	4.47	32	32	1	0	0	193 1/3	212	103	96	67	119
1998— Milwaukee (N.L.)	10	11	.476	4.40	33	33	0	0	0	192 1/3	219	104	94	66	102
1999— Milwaukee (N.L.)	11	11	.500	4.78	33	33	0	0	0	197 2/3	246	121	105	69	74
2000— Colorado (N.L.)■	2	3	.400	7.68	17	9	0	0	0	65 2/3	95	56	56	33	29
— Colorado Springs (PCL)	0	3	.000	5.66	3	2	0	0	0	20 2/3	21	17	13	4	16
— Lake Elsinore (Calif.)■	1	0	1.000	0.00	1	0	0	0	0	7	5	0	0	1	5
— Anaheim (A.L.)	2	2	.500	6.65	6	4	0	0	0	21 2/3	31	21	16	12	9
A.L. totals (4 years)	31	31	.500	4.63	95	86	5	1	0	546 1/3	604	313	281	201	308
N.L. totals (3 years)	23	25	.479	5.04	83	75	0	0	0	455 2/3	560	281	255	168	205
Major League totals (6 years)	54	56	.491	4.81	178	161	5	1	0	1002	1164	594	536	369	513

KARNUTH, JASON   P   CARDINALS

PERSONAL: Born May 15, 1976, in LaGrange, Ill. ... 6-2/190. ... Throws right, bats right. ... Full name: Jason A. Karnuth.
HIGH SCHOOL: Glenbard South (Glen Ellyn, Ill.).
COLLEGE: Illinois State.
TRANSACTIONS/CAREER NOTES: Selected by St. Louis Cardinals organization in eighth round of free-agent draft (June 3, 1997).

Year League	W	L	Pct.	ERA	G	GS	CG	ShO	Sv.	IP	H	R	ER	BB	SO
1997— New Jersey (NY-Penn)	4	1	.800	1.86	7	7	0	0	0	38 2/3	33	8	8	9	23
— Peoria (Midw.)	0	3	.000	6.65	4	4	0	0	0	23	29	19	17	7	12
1998— Prince William (Caro.)	8	1	.889	1.67	16	15	2	2	0	108	86	26	20	14	53
1999— Arkansas (Texas)	7	11	.389	5.22	26	26	2	0	0	160 1/3	175	105	93	55	71
2000— Arkansas (Texas)	2	3	.400	3.75	8	8	1	0	0	50 1/3	59	30	21	14	31
— Memphis (PCL)	5	4	.556	4.04	16	13	0	0	0	78	89	47	35	27	28

KARROS, ERIC   1B   DODGERS

PERSONAL: Born November 4, 1967, in Hackensack, N.J. ... 6-4/226. ... Bats right, throws right. ... Full name: Eric Peter Karros. ... Name pronounced CARE-ose.
HIGH SCHOOL: Patrick Henry (San Diego).
COLLEGE: UCLA.
TRANSACTIONS/CAREER NOTES: Selected by Los Angeles Dodgers organization in sixth round of free-agent draft (June 1, 1988). ... On Los Angeles disabled list (March 29-April 24, 1998); included rehabilitation assignment to San Bernardino (April 19-25).
RECORDS: Shares major league single-inning record for most home runs—2 (August 22, 2000, sixth inning).

HONORS: Named N.L. Rookie Player of the Year by THE SPORTING NEWS (1992). ... Named N.L. Rookie of the Year by Baseball Writers' Association of America (1992). ... Named first baseman on THE SPORTING NEWS N.L. All-Star team (1995). ... Named first baseman on THE SPORTING NEWS N.L. Silver Slugger team (1995).

STATISTICAL NOTES: Tied for Pioneer League lead in errors by first baseman with 14 in 1988. ... Led California League first basemen with 1,232 putouts, 110 assists and 1,358 total chances in 1989. ... Led Texas League with 282 total bases in 1990. ... Led Texas League first basemen with 1,337 total chances and 129 double plays in 1990. ... Led Pacific Coast League with 269 total bases in 1991. ... Tied for Pacific Coast League lead with eight intentional bases on balls received in 1991. ... Led Pacific Coast League first basemen with 1,095 putouts, 109 assists and 1,215 total chances in 1991. ... Led N.L. in grounding into double plays with 27 in 1996. ... Career major league grand slams: 2.

Year	Team (League)	Pos.	G	AB	R	H	2B	3B	HR	RBI	Avg.	BB	SO	SB	PO	A	E	Avg.
						BATTING									FIELDING			
1988—	Great Falls (Pio.)	1B-3B	66	268	68	98	12	1	12	55	.366	32	35	8	516	31	‡19	.966
1989—	Bakersfield (Calif.)	1B-3B	*142	545	86	*165	*40	1	15	86	.303	63	99	18	†1238	*113	19	.986
1990—	San Antonio (Texas)...	1B	•131	509	91	*179	*45	2	18	78	*.352	57	79	8	*1223	*106	8	*.994
1991—	Albuquerque (PCL).....	1B-3B	132	488	88	154	33	8	22	101	.316	58	80	3	†1095	†109	11	.991
	—Los Angeles (N.L.)	1B	14	14	0	1	1	0	0	1	.071	1	6	0	33	2	0	1.000
1992—	Los Angeles (N.L.)	1B	149	545	63	140	30	1	20	88	.257	37	103	2	1211	126	9	.993
1993—	Los Angeles (N.L.)	1B	158	619	74	153	27	2	23	80	.247	34	82	0	1335	*147	12	.992
1994—	Los Angeles (N.L.)	1B	111	406	51	108	21	1	14	46	.266	29	53	2	896	118	•9	.991
1995—	Los Angeles (N.L.)	1B	143	551	83	164	29	3	32	105	.298	61	115	4	1234	109	7	.995
1996—	Los Angeles (N.L.)	1B	154	608	84	158	29	1	34	111	.260	53	121	8	1314	121	15	.990
1997—	Los Angeles (N.L.)	1B	•162	628	86	167	28	0	31	104	.266	61	116	15	1317	121	11	.992
1998—	San Bern. (Calif.)........	1B	4	15	3	4	1	0	0	1	.267	0	2	0	32	2	0	1.000
	—Los Angeles (N.L.)	1B-DH	139	507	59	150	20	1	23	87	.296	47	93	7	1150	110	12	.991
1999—	Los Angeles (N.L.)	1B	153	578	74	176	40	0	34	112	.304	53	119	8	1291	*126	13	.991
2000—	Los Angeles (N.L.)	1B-DH	155	584	84	146	29	0	31	106	.250	63	122	4	1296	138	7	.995
Major League totals (10 years)			1338	5040	658	1363	254	9	242	840	.270	439	930	50	11077	1118	95	.992

DIVISION SERIES RECORD

RECORDS: Shares single-game record for most home runs—2 (October 4, 1995).

Year	Team (League)	Pos.	G	AB	R	H	2B	3B	HR	RBI	Avg.	BB	SO	SB	PO	A	E	Avg.
						BATTING									FIELDING			
1995—	Los Angeles (N.L.)	1B	3	12	3	6	1	0	2	4	.500	1	0	0	14	0	0	1.000
1996—	Los Angeles (N.L.)	1B	3	9	0	0	0	0	0	0	.000	2	3	0	28	2	0	1.000
Division series totals (2 years)			6	21	3	6	1	0	2	4	.286	3	3	0	42	2	0	1.000

KARSAY, STEVE — P — INDIANS

PERSONAL: Born March 24, 1972, in Flushing, N.Y. ... 6-3/215. ... Throws right, bats right. ... Full name: Stefan Andrew Karsay. ... Name pronounced CAR-say.

HIGH SCHOOL: Christ the King (Queens, N.Y.).

TRANSACTIONS/CAREER NOTES: Selected by Toronto Blue Jays organization in first round (22nd pick overall) of free-agent draft (June 4, 1990). ... On Knoxville disabled list (July 3-16, 1993). ... Traded by Blue Jays with a player to be named later to Oakland Athletics for OF Rickey Henderson (July 31, 1993); A's acquired OF Jose Herrera to complete deal (August 6, 1993). ... On disabled list (April 26, 1994-remainder of season; April 24, 1995-entire season; and August 6, 1997-remainder of season). ... Traded by A's to Cleveland Indians for P Mike Fetters (December 8, 1997). ... On Buffalo disabled list (May 14-25 and June 12-July 15, 1998). ... On Cleveland disabled list (July 2-26 and August 25-September 22, 1999).

MISCELLANEOUS: Appeared in one game as pinch runner (1997).

Year	League	W	L	Pct.	ERA	G	GS	CG	ShO	Sv.	IP	H	R	ER	BB	SO
1990—	St. Catharines (NY-Penn)	1	1	.500	0.79	5	5	0	0	0	22 2/3	11	4	2	12	25
1991—	Myrtle Beach (S.Atl.)	4	9	.308	3.58	20	20	1	0	0	110 2/3	96	58	44	48	100
1992—	Dunedin (FSL)	6	3	.667	2.73	16	16	3	2	0	85 2/3	56	32	26	29	87
1993—	Knoxville (Sou.).................	8	4	.667	3.38	19	18	1	0	0	104	98	42	39	32	100
	—Huntsville (Sou.)■	0	0	...	5.14	2	2	0	0	0	14	13	8	8	3	22
	—Oakland (A.L.)	3	3	.500	4.04	8	8	0	0	0	49	49	23	22	16	33
1994—	Oakland (A.L.)	1	1	.500	2.57	4	4	1	0	0	28	26	8	8	8	15
1995—	Oakland (A.L.)							Did not play.								
1996—	Modesto (Calif.)	0	1	.000	2.65	14	14	0	0	0	34	35	16	10	1	31
1997—	Oakland (A.L.)	3	12	.200	5.77	24	24	0	0	0	132 2/3	166	92	85	47	92
1998—	Buffalo (I.L.)■	6	4	.600	3.76	16	14	0	0	0	79	89	39	33	15	63
	—Cleveland (A.L.)................	0	2	.000	5.92	11	1	0	0	0	24 1/3	31	16	16	6	13
1999—	Cleveland (A.L.).................	10	2	.833	2.97	50	3	0	0	1	78 2/3	71	29	26	30	68
2000—	Cleveland (A.L.).................	5	9	.357	3.76	72	0	0	0	20	76 2/3	79	33	32	25	66
Major League totals (6 years)		22	29	.431	4.37	169	40	1	0	21	389 1/3	422	201	189	132	287

DIVISION SERIES RECORD

Year	League	W	L	Pct.	ERA	G	GS	CG	ShO	Sv.	IP	H	R	ER	BB	SO
1999—	Cleveland (A.L.).................	0	0	...	9.00	2	0	0	0	0	3	5	3	3	1	3

KEISLER, RANDY — P — YANKEES

PERSONAL: Born February 24, 1976, in Richards, Texas. ... 6-3/190. ... Throws left, bats left. ... Full name: Randy Dean Keisler.

HIGH SCHOOL: Navasota (Texas), then Palmer (Texas).

JUNIOR COLLEGE: Navarro College (Texas).

COLLEGE: Louisiana State.

TRANSACTIONS/CAREER NOTES: Selected by Cleveland Indians organization in 40th round of free-agent draft (June 1, 1995); did not sign. ... Selected by Cleveland Indians organization in 57th round of free-agent draft (June 4, 1996); did not sign. ... Selected by New York Yankees organization in second round of free-agent draft (June 2, 1998).

Year	League	W	L	Pct.	ERA	G	GS	CG	ShO	Sv.	IP	H	R	ER	BB	SO
1998— Oneonta (NY-Penn)		1	1	.500	7.45	6	2	0	0	1	9²/₃	14	10	8	7	11
1999— Greensboro (S.Atl.)		1	1	.500	2.38	4	4	0	0	0	22²/₃	12	6	6	10	42
— Tampa (FSL)		10	3	.769	3.30	15	15	1	0	0	90	67	43	33	40	77
— Norwich (East.)		3	4	.429	4.57	8	8	0	0	0	43¹/₃	45	24	22	17	33
2000— Norwich (East.)		6	2	.750	2.60	11	11	1	0	0	72²/₃	63	29	21	34	70
— Columbus (I.L.)		8	3	.727	3.02	17	17	1	1	0	113¹/₃	104	44	38	42	86
— New York (A.L.)		1	0	1.000	11.81	4	1	0	0	0	10²/₃	16	14	14	8	6
Major League totals (1 year)		1	0	1.000	11.81	4	1	0	0	0	10²/₃	16	14	14	8	6

KELLER, KRIS   P   TIGERS

PERSONAL: Born March 1, 1978, in Williamsport, Pa. ... 6-2/225. ... Throws right, bats right. ... Full name: Kristopher Shane Keller.
HIGH SCHOOL: Fletcher (Neptune Beach, Fla.).
TRANSACTIONS/CAREER NOTES: Selected by Detroit Tigers organization in fourth round of free-agent draft (June 4, 1996).

Year	League	W	L	Pct.	ERA	G	GS	CG	ShO	Sv.	IP	H	R	ER	BB	SO
1996— Gulf Coast Tigers (GCL)		1	1	.500	2.38	8	6	0	0	0	34	23	12	9	21	23
1997— Jamestown (NY-Penn)		0	2	.000	8.67	16	0	0	0	0	27	37	33	26	20	18
1998— Jamestown (NY-Penn)		1	3	.250	3.27	27	0	0	0	8	33	29	12	12	16	41
1999— West Michigan (Midw.)		5	3	.625	2.92	49	0	0	0	8	77	63	28	25	36	87
2000— Jacksonville (Sou.)		2	3	.400	2.91	62	0	0	0	*26	68	58	24	22	44	60

K

KELLY, KENNY   OF   DEVIL RAYS

PERSONAL: Born January 26, 1979, in Plant City, Fla. ... 6-2/180. ... Bats right, throws right. ... Full name: Kenneth Alphonso Kelly.
HIGH SCHOOL: Tampa Catholic.
COLLEGE: Miami (Fla.).
TRANSACTIONS/CAREER NOTES: Selected by Tampa Bay Devil Rays organization in second round of free-agent draft (June 3, 1997).
STATISTICAL NOTES: Led Southern League with 21 caught stealing in 2000.

							BATTING							FIELDING		
Year	Team (League)	Pos.	G	AB	R	H	2B	3B	HR	RBI	Avg.	BB	SO	SB	PO	A	E	Avg.
1997— GC Devil Rays (GCL) ..		OF	27	99	21	21	2	1	2	7	.212	11	24	6	43	3	2	.958
1998— Char., S.C. (SAL)		OF	54	218	46	61	7	5	3	17	.280	19	52	19	122	10	5	.964
1999— St. Petersburg (FSL) ..		OF	51	206	39	57	10	4	3	21	.277	18	46	14	121	9	4	.970
2000— Orlando (Sou.)		OF	124	489	73	123	17	8	3	29	.252	59	119	31	286	9	8	.974
— Tampa Bay (A.L.).......		DH	2	1	0	0	0	0	0	0	.000	0	0	0	...	...	...	...
Major League totals (1 year)			2	1	0	0	0	0	0	0	.000	0	0	0	...	...	...	...

KELLY, ROBERTO   OF   ROCKIES

PERSONAL: Born October 1, 1964, in Panama City, Panama. ... 6-2/198. ... Bats right, throws right. ... Full name: Roberto Conrado Kelly.
HIGH SCHOOL: Panama City (Panama).
COLLEGE: Jose Dolores Moscote College (Panama).
TRANSACTIONS/CAREER NOTES: Signed as non-drafted free agent by New York Yankees organization (February 21, 1982). ... On disabled list (July 10-August 23, 1986). ... On New York disabled list (June 29-September 1, 1988; May 26-June 12, 1989; and July 6-August 13, 1991). ... Traded by Yankees to Cincinnati Reds for OF Paul O'Neill and 1B Joe DeBerry (November 3, 1992). ... On disabled list (July 14, 1993-remainder of season). ... Traded by Reds with P Roger Etheridge to Atlanta Braves for OF Deion Sanders (May 29, 1994). ... Traded by Braves with OF Tony Tarasco and P Esteban Yan to Montreal Expos for OF Marquis Grissom (April 6, 1995). ... Traded by Expos with P Joey Eischen to Los Angeles Dodgers for OF Henry Rodriguez and IF Jeff Treadway (May 23, 1995). ... Granted free agency (November 6, 1995). ... Signed by Minnesota Twins (January 29, 1996). ... On disabled list (June 27-July 12, 1996). ... On Minnesota disabled list (March 24-April 16, 1997); included rehabilitation assignment to Fort Myers (April 11-16). ... Traded by Twins to Seattle Mariners for two players to be named later (August 20, 1997); Twins acquired P Joe Mays and P Jeromy Palki to complete deal (October 9, 1997). ... Granted free agency (October 31, 1997). ... Signed by Texas Rangers (December 9, 1997). ... On disabled list (April 27-June 6, 1998). ... Granted free agency (October 28, 1999). ... Signed by Yankees organization (January 26, 2000). ... On disabled list (April 29, 2000-remainder of season). ... Granted free agency (October 30, 2000). ... Signed by Colorado Rockies organization (January 12, 2001).
RECORDS: Holds major league single-season record for most times reaching base on catcher's interference—8 (1992). ... Shares major league single-season record for fewest double plays by outfielder (150 or more games)—0 (1990).
STATISTICAL NOTES: Led International League outfielders with 345 total chances in 1987. ... Led A.L. outfielders with 430 total chances in 1990. ... Career major league grand slams: 2.
MISCELLANEOUS: Batted as switch hitter (1985).

							BATTING							FIELDING		
Year	Team (League)	Pos.	G	AB	R	H	2B	3B	HR	RBI	Avg.	BB	SO	SB	PO	A	E	Avg.
1982— GC Yankees (GCL)		SS-OF	31	86	13	17	1	1	1	18	.198	10	18	3	47	79	19	.869
1983— Oneonta (NY-Penn)		OF-3B	48	167	17	36	1	2	2	17	.216	12	20	12	70	3	5	.936
— Greensboro (S.Atl.)		OF-SS	20	49	6	13	0	0	0	3	.265	3	5	3	30	2	0	1.000
1984— Greensboro (S.Atl.)		OF-1B	111	361	68	86	13	2	1	26	.238	57	49	42	228	5	4	.983
1985— Fort Lauderdale (FSL)		OF	114	417	86	103	4	*13	3	38	.247	58	70	49	187	1	1	.995
1986— Alb./Colonie (East.)		OF	86	299	42	87	11	4	2	43	.291	29	63	10	206	8	7	.968
1987— Columbus (I.L.)		OF	118	471	77	131	19	8	13	62	.278	33	116	*51	*331	4	10	.971
— New York (A.L.).........		OF-DH	23	52	12	14	3	0	1	7	.269	5	15	9	42	0	2	.955
1988— New York (A.L.)		OF-DH	38	77	9	19	4	1	1	7	.247	3	15	5	70	1	1	.986
— Columbus (I.L.)		OF	30	120	25	40	8	1	3	16	.333	6	29	11	51	1	0	1.000
1989— New York (A.L.)		OF	137	441	65	133	18	3	9	48	.302	41	89	35	353	9	6	.984
1990— New York (A.L.)		OF	*162	641	85	183	32	4	15	61	.285	33	148	42	420	5	5	.988
1991— New York (A.L.)		OF	126	486	68	130	22	2	20	69	.267	45	77	32	268	8	4	.986
1992— New York (A.L.)		OF	152	580	81	158	31	2	10	66	.272	41	96	28	389	8	7	.983
1993— Cincinnati (N.L.)■......		OF	78	320	44	102	17	3	9	35	.319	17	43	21	198	3	1	.995

								BATTING							FIELDING		
Year	Team (League)	Pos.	G	AB	R	H	2B	3B	HR	RBI	Avg.	BB	SO	SB	PO	A	E	Avg.
1994— Cincinnati (N.L.)		OF	47	179	29	54	8	0	3	21	.302	11	35	9	118	2	1	.992
— Atlanta (N.L.)■..........		OF	63	255	44	73	15	3	6	24	.286	24	36	10	128	3	2	.985
1995— Montreal (N.L.)■......		OF	24	95	11	26	4	0	1	9	.274	7	14	4	42	1	0	1.000
— Los Angeles (N.L.)■ ..		OF	112	409	47	114	19	2	6	48	.279	15	65	15	183	2	6	.969
1996— Minnesota (A.L.)■		OF-DH	98	322	41	104	17	4	6	47	.323	23	53	10	203	4	2	.990
1997— Fort Myers (FSL)		OF	4	11	2	4	0	0	1	3	.364	4	1	0	6	0	0	1.000
— Minnesota (A.L.)		OF-DH	75	247	39	71	19	2	5	37	.287	17	50	7	101	1	0	1.000
— Seattle (A.L.)■..........		OF-DH	30	121	19	36	7	0	7	22	.298	5	17	2	53	1	0	1.000
1998— Texas (A.L.)■		OF-DH	75	257	48	83	7	3	16	46	.323	8	46	0	155	5	4	.976
1999— Texas (A.L.)		OF	87	290	41	87	17	1	8	37	.300	21	57	6	155	4	3	.981
2000— New York (A.L.)■.......		OF	10	25	4	3	1	0	1	1	.120	1	6	0	18	0	0	1.000
American League totals (11 years)			1013	3539	512	1021	178	22	99	448	.288	243	669	176	2227	46	34	.985
National League totals (3 years)			324	1258	175	369	63	8	25	137	.293	74	193	59	669	11	10	.986
Major League totals (14 years)			1337	4797	687	1390	241	30	124	585	.290	317	862	235	2896	57	44	.985

DIVISION SERIES RECORD

								BATTING							FIELDING		
Year	Team (League)	Pos.	G	AB	R	H	2B	3B	HR	RBI	Avg.	BB	SO	SB	PO	A	E	Avg.
1995— Los Angeles (N.L.)		OF	3	11	0	4	0	0	0	0	.364	1	0	0	8	0	1	.889
1997— Seattle (A.L.)		OF-PH	4	13	1	4	3	0	0	1	.308	0	3	0	4	0	0	1.000
1998— Texas (A.L.)		OF	2	7	0	1	1	0	0	0	.143	0	2	0	3	0	0	1.000
1999— Texas (A.L.)		OF	1	3	0	1	0	0	0	0	.333	0	2	0	1	0	0	1.000
Division series totals (4 years)			10	34	1	10	4	0	0	1	.294	1	7	0	16	0	1	.941

ALL-STAR GAME RECORD

						BATTING							FIELDING		
Year	League	Pos.	AB	R	H	2B	3B	HR	RBI	Avg.	BB	SO	SB	PO	A	E	Avg.
1992— American		OF	2	0	1	1	0	0	2	.500	0	1	0	1	0	0	1.000
1993— National		OF	1	0	0	0	0	0	0	.000	0	1	0	0	1	0	1.000
All-Star Game totals (2 years)			3	0	1	1	0	0	2	.333	0	2	0	1	1	0	1.000

KENDALL, JASON — C — PIRATES

PERSONAL: Born June 26, 1974, in San Diego. ... 6-0/195. ... Bats right, throws right. ... Full name: Jason Daniel Kendall. ... Son of Fred Kendall, coach, Detroit Tigers; and catcher/first baseman with three major league teams (1969-80).
HIGH SCHOOL: Torrance (Calif.).
TRANSACTIONS/CAREER NOTES: Selected by Pittsburgh Pirates organization in first round (23rd pick overall) of free-agent draft (June 1, 1992). ... On suspended list (July 21-23, 1998). ... On disabled list (July 5, 1999-remainder of season).
HONORS: Named Southern League Most Valuable Player (1995). ... Named N.L. Rookie Player of the Year by THE SPORTING NEWS (1996).
STATISTICAL NOTES: Led Gulf Coast League with 13 passed balls in 1992. ... Led Southern League with .414 on-base percentage in 1995. ... Led Southern League catchers with 754 total chances in 1995. ... Led N.L. catchers with 20 double plays in 1997. ... Led N.L. in being hit by pitch with 31 in 1998. ... Led N.L. catchers in total chances with 1,082 in 1998 and 1,081 in 2000. ... Had 16-game hitting streak (May 20-June 7, 1999). ... Led N.L. catchers with 13 double plays in 1999. ... Led N.L. catchers with 11 passed balls in 2000. ... Hit for the cycle (May 19, 2000).

								BATTING							FIELDING		
Year	Team (League)	Pos.	G	AB	R	H	2B	3B	HR	RBI	Avg.	BB	SO	SB	PO	A	E	Avg.
1992— GC Pirates (GCL)........		C	33	111	7	29	2	0	0	10	.261	8	9	2	182	36	5	.978
1993— Augusta (S.Atl.)..........		C	102	366	43	101	17	4	1	40	.276	22	30	8	472	65	20	.964
1994— Salem (Caro.)............		C	101	371	68	118	19	2	7	66	.318	47	21	14	409	33	9	.980
— Carolina (Sou.)..........		C	13	47	6	11	2	0	0	6	.234	2	3	0	54	9	2	.969
1995— Carolina (Sou.)		C	117	429	87	140	26	1	8	71	.326	56	22	10	*692	54	8	.989
1996— Pittsburgh (N.L.)		C	130	414	54	124	23	5	3	42	.300	35	30	5	797	71	*18	.980
1997— Pittsburgh (N.L.)		C	144	486	71	143	36	4	8	49	.294	49	53	18	952	*103	11	.990
1998— Pittsburgh (N.L.)		C	149	535	95	175	36	3	12	75	.327	51	51	26	*1015	58	9	.992
1999— Pittsburgh (N.L.)		C	78	280	61	93	20	3	8	41	.332	38	32	22	505	48	7	.988
2000— Pittsburgh (N.L.)		C	152	579	112	185	33	6	14	58	.320	79	79	22	*990	*81	10	.991
Major League totals (5 years)			653	2294	393	720	148	21	45	265	.314	252	245	93	4259	361	55	.988

ALL-STAR GAME RECORD

						BATTING							FIELDING		
Year	League	Pos.	AB	R	H	2B	3B	HR	RBI	Avg.	BB	SO	SB	PO	A	E	Avg.
1996— National		C	0	0	0	0	0	0	0	...	0	0	0	0	0	0	...
1998— National		PH	1	0	1	0	0	0	0	1.000	0	0	0	...	...	...	...
2000— National		C	2	0	0	0	0	0	0	.000	0	1	0	3	1	0	1.000
All-Star Game totals (3 years)			3	0	1	0	0	0	0	.333	0	1	0	3	1	0	1.000

KENNEDY, ADAM — 2B — ANGELS

PERSONAL: Born January 10, 1976, in Riverside, Calif. ... 6-1/180. ... Bats left, throws right. ... Full name: Adam Thomas Kennedy.
HIGH SCHOOL: J.W. North (Riverside, Calif.).
COLLEGE: Cal State Northridge.
TRANSACTIONS/CAREER NOTES: Selected by St. Louis Cardinals organization in first round (20th pick overall) of free-agent draft (June 3, 1997). ... On Memphis disabled list (June 9-19, 1999). ... Traded by Cardinals with P Kent Bottenfield to Anaheim Angels for OF Jim Edmonds (March 23, 2000).
STATISTICAL NOTES: Led A.L. second basemen with 781 total chances in 2000. ... Career major league grand slams: 1.

Year Team (League)	Pos.	G	AB	R	H	2B	3B	HR	RBI	Avg.	BB	SO	SB	PO	A	E	Avg.
1997—New Jersey (NY-P).....	SS	29	114	20	39	6	3	0	19	.342	13	10	9	41	96	7	.951
—Prince Will. (Caro.).....	SS	35	154	24	48	9	3	1	27	.312	6	17	4	63	92	10	.939
1998—Prince Will. (Caro.).....	2B-SS	17	69	9	18	6	0	0	7	.261	5	12	5	26	49	5	.938
—Arkansas (Texas).........	SS-2B	52	205	35	57	11	2	6	24	.278	8	21	6	91	143	15	.940
—Memphis (PCL).........	SS-2B	74	305	36	93	22	7	4	41	.305	12	42	15	128	225	10	.972
1999—Memphis (PCL).........2-S-O-3-DH		91	367	69	120	22	4	10	63	.327	29	36	20	160	206	18	.953
—St. Louis (N.L.)........	2B	33	102	12	26	10	1	1	16	.255	3	8	0	68	64	4	.971
2000—Anaheim (A.L.)■........	2B	156	598	82	159	33	11	9	72	.266	28	73	22	*337	425	*19	.976
American League totals (1 year)		156	598	82	159	33	11	9	72	.266	28	73	22	337	425	19	.976
National League totals (1 year)		33	102	12	26	10	1	1	16	.255	3	8	0	68	64	4	.971
Major League totals (2 years)		189	700	94	185	43	12	10	88	.264	31	81	22	405	489	23	.975

KENT, JEFF — 2B — GIANTS

PERSONAL: Born March 7, 1968, in Bellflower, Calif. ... 6-1/205. ... Bats right, throws right. ... Full name: Jeffrey Franklin Kent.
HIGH SCHOOL: Edison (Huntington Beach, Calif.).
COLLEGE: California.
TRANSACTIONS/CAREER NOTES: Selected by Toronto Blue Jays organization in 20th round of free-agent draft (June 5, 1989). ... Traded by Blue Jays with a player to be named later to New York Mets for P David Cone (August 27, 1992); Mets acquired OF Ryan Thompson to complete deal (September 1, 1992). ... On disabled list (July 6-21, 1995). ... Traded by New York Mets with IF Jose Vizcaino to Cleveland Indians for 2B Carlos Baerga and IF Alvaro Espinoza (July 29, 1996). ... Traded by Indians with IF Jose Vizcaino, P Julian Tavarez and a player to be named later to San Francisco Giants for 3B Matt Williams and a player to be named later (November 13, 1996); Indians acquired P Joe Roa to Giants for OF Trenidad Hubbard to complete deal (December 16, 1996). ... On suspended list (August 22-25, 1997). ... On disabled list (June 10-July 10, 1998; and August 3-21, 1999).
HONORS: Named second baseman on THE SPORTING NEWS N.L. All-Star team (2000). ... Named second baseman on THE SPORTING NEWS N.L. Silver Slugger team (2000). ... Named N.L. Most Valuable Player by Baseball Writers' Association of America (2000).
STATISTICAL NOTES: Led Florida State League second basemen with 680 total chances and 83 double plays in 1990. ... Led Southern League second basemen with 673 total chances and 96 double plays in 1991. ... Led N.L. second basemen in errors with 18 in 1993 and 20 in 1998. ... Tied for N.L. lead with 10 sacrifice flies in 1998. ... Hit for the cycle (May 3, 1999). ... Career major league grand slams: 9.

Year Team (League)	Pos.	G	AB	R	H	2B	3B	HR	RBI	Avg.	BB	SO	SB	PO	A	E	Avg.
1989—St. Catharines (NY-P).	SS-3B	73	268	34	60	14	1	*13	37	.224	33	81	5	103	178	29	.906
1990—Dunedin (FSL)	2B	132	447	72	124	32	2	16	60	.277	53	98	17	*261	*404	15	.978
1991—Knoxville (Sou.)	2B	•139	445	68	114	*34	1	2	61	.256	80	104	25	249	*395	*29	.957
1992—Toronto (A.L.)	3B-2B-1B	65	192	36	46	13	1	8	35	.240	20	47	2	62	112	11	.941
—New York (N.L.)■	2B-SS-3B	37	113	16	27	8	1	3	15	.239	7	29	0	62	93	3	.981
1993—New York (N.L.)	2B-3B-SS	140	496	65	134	24	0	21	80	.270	30	88	4	261	341	†22	.965
1994—New York (N.L.)	2B	107	415	53	121	24	5	14	68	.292	23	84	1	222	337	•14	.976
1995—New York (N.L.)	2B	125	472	65	131	22	3	20	65	.278	29	89	3	245	354	10	.984
1996—New York (N.L.)	3B	89	335	45	97	20	1	9	39	.290	21	56	4	75	184	21	.925
—Cleveland (A.L.)■.....1B-2B-3B-DH		39	102	16	27	7	0	3	16	.265	10	22	2	125	46	1	.994
1997—San Fran. (N.L.)	2B-1B	155	580	90	145	38	2	29	121	.250	48	133	11	405	429	16	.981
1998—San Francisco (N.L.) ..	2B-1B	137	526	94	156	37	3	31	128	.297	48	110	9	279	404	†20	.972
1999—San Francisco (N.L.) ..	2B-1B	138	511	86	148	40	2	23	101	.290	61	112	13	286	326	10	.984
2000—San Francisco (N.L.) ..	2B-1B	159	587	114	196	41	7	33	125	.334	90	107	12	375	394	12	.985
American League totals (2 years)		104	294	52	73	20	1	11	51	.248	30	69	4	187	158	12	.966
National League totals (9 years)		1087	4035	628	1155	254	24	183	742	.286	357	808	57	2210	2862	128	.975
Major League totals (9 years)		1191	4329	680	1228	274	25	194	793	.284	387	877	61	2397	3020	140	.975

DIVISION SERIES RECORD

RECORDS: Shares single-game record for most home runs—2 (October 3, 1997).

Year Team (League)	Pos.	G	AB	R	H	2B	3B	HR	RBI	Avg.	BB	SO	SB	PO	A	E	Avg.
1996—Cleveland (A.L.).........2B-1B-PR-3B		4	8	2	1	1	0	0	0	.125	0	0	0	3	3	0	1.000
1997—San Francisco (N.L.) ..	2B-1B	3	10	2	3	0	0	2	2	.300	2	1	0	19	7	0	1.000
2000—San Francisco (N.L.) ..	2B-1B	4	16	3	6	1	0	0	1	.375	1	3	1	9	13	0	1.000
Division series totals (3 years)		11	34	7	10	2	0	2	3	.294	3	4	1	31	23	0	1.000

ALL-STAR GAME RECORD

Year League	Pos.	AB	R	H	2B	3B	HR	RBI	Avg.	BB	SO	SB	PO	A	E	Avg.
1999—National	2B	1	0	0	0	0	0	0	.000	1	0	0	1	2	0	1.000
2000—National	2B	2	0	0	0	0	0	0	.000	0	0	0	0	0	0	...
All-Star Game totals (2 years)		3	0	0	0	0	0	0	.000	1	0	0	1	2	0	1.000

KIDA, MASAO — P

PERSONAL: Born September 12, 1968, in Tokyo, Japan. ... 6-3/210. ... Throws right, bats right.
TRANSACTIONS/CAREER NOTES: Played with Yomiuri Giants (1989-97) and Orix Blue Wave (1998) of Japan League. ... Signed as non-drafted free agent by Detroit Tigers (December 16, 1998). ... On Detroit disabled list (June 30-July 28, 1999); included rehabilitation assignment to Toledo (July 14-28). ... Contract sold by Tigers to Orix of Japan Pacific League (June 8, 2000).

Year League	W	L	Pct.	ERA	G	GS	CG	ShO	Sv.	IP	H	R	ER	BB	SO
1988—Miami (FSL)	7	17	.292	3.99	27	27	9	1	0	162 1/3	149	88	72	62	100
1989—Yomiuri (Jap. Cen.)■	2	1	.667	4.62	8	4	1	0	0	37	41	19	19	14	26
1990—Yomiuri (Jap. Cen.)	12	8	.600	2.71	32	17	13	1	0	182 2/3	130	56	55	51	182
1991—Yomiuri (Jap. Cen.)	4	7	.364	6.44	19	5	2	0	1	50 1/3	51	41	36	31	44
1992—Yomiuri (Jap. Cen.)	3	6	.333	4.53	29	11	2	1	0	93 1/3	103	48	47	35	87

K

Year	League	W	L	Pct.	ERA	G	GS	CG	ShO	Sv.	IP	H	R	ER	BB	SO
1993—	Yomiuri (Jap. Cen.)	7	7	.500	3.35	35	17	1	1	2	131²/₃	129	50	49	40	97
1994—	Yomiuri (Jap. Cen.)	6	8	.429	4.93	28	13	1	0	1	87²/₃	86	52	48	37	61
1995—	Yomiuri (Jap. Cen.)	7	9	.438	3.40	40	12	2	0	0	121²/₃	117	49	46	31	97
1996—	Yomiuri (Jap. Cen.)	7	9	.438	3.78	33	16	3	2	2	123²/₃	121	53	52	34	99
1997—	Yomiuri (Jap. Cen.)	2	2	.500	1.99	39	0	0	0	7	49²/₃	47	13	11	22	53
1998—	Orix (Jap. Pac.)■	4	7	.364	4.62	36	13	1	0	16	97¹/₃	97	54	50	36	74
1999—	Detroit (A.L.)■	1	0	1.000	6.26	49	0	0	0	1	64²/₃	73	48	45	30	50
—	Toledo (I.L.)	0	0	...	3.18	3	0	0	0	0	5²/₃	6	2	2	1	4
2000—	Toledo (I.L.)	2	1	.667	2.16	21	0	0	0	7	25	21	6	6	4	26
—	Detroit (A.L.)	0	0	...	10.13	2	0	0	0	0	2²/₃	5	3	3	0	0
Major League totals (2 years)		1	0	1.000	6.42	51	0	0	0	1	67¹/₃	78	51	48	30	50

KIESCHNICK, BROOKS   OF

PERSONAL: Born June 6, 1972, in Robstown, Texas. ... 6-4/230. ... Bats left, throws right. ... Full name: Michael Brooks Kieschnick. ... Name pronounced KEY-shnik.

HIGH SCHOOL: Mary Carroll (Corpus Christi, Texas).

COLLEGE: Texas.

TRANSACTIONS/CAREER NOTES: Selected by Chicago Cubs organization in first round (10th pick overall) of free-agent draft (June 3, 1993). ... Selected by Tampa Bay Devil Rays in third round (64th pick overall) of expansion draft (November 18, 1997). ... On Durham disabled list (April 16-August 2, 1998). ... Loaned by Devil Rays organization to Anaheim Angels organization (May 24-September 20, 1999). ... Granted free agency (October 15, 1999). ... Signed by Cincinnati Reds organization (November 16, 1999). ... Granted free agency (October 3, 2000).

STATISTICAL NOTES: Led American Association with 250 total bases in 1995.

							BATTING								FIELDING			
Year	Team (League)	Pos.	G	AB	R	H	2B	3B	HR	RBI	Avg.	BB	SO	SB	PO	A	E	Avg.
1993—	GC Cubs (GCL)..........	OF	3	9	0	2	1	0	0	0	.222	0	1	0	3	1	0	1.000
—	Daytona (FSL)	OF	6	22	1	4	2	0	0	2	.182	1	4	0	9	1	0	1.000
—	Orlando (Sou.)	OF	25	91	12	31	8	0	2	10	.341	7	19	1	22	1	3	.885
1994—	Orlando (Sou.)	OF-1B-3B	126	468	57	132	25	3	14	55	.282	33	78	3	259	14	6	.978
1995—	Iowa (A.A.)	OF-DH-1B	138	505	61	*149	30	1	*23	73	.295	58	91	2	179	15	2	.990
1996—	Chicago (N.L.)..........	OF	25	29	6	10	2	0	1	6	.345	3	8	0	5	0	1	.833
—	Iowa (A.A.)	1B-OF-DH	117	441	47	114	20	1	18	64	.259	37	108	0	498	28	8	.985
1997—	Iowa (A.A.) 1B-OF-DH-3B		97	360	57	93	21	0	21	66	.258	36	89	0	562	54	8	.987
—	Chicago (N.L.)..........	OF	39	90	9	18	2	0	4	12	.200	12	21	1	39	1	2	.952
1998—	Durham (I.L.)..............	OF-1B	7	23	4	3	1	0	1	2	.130	4	8	0	21	0	1	.955
—	St. Petersburg (FSL) ..	OF-DH	28	105	15	26	6	0	5	18	.248	11	18	0	24	0	3	.889
—	GC Devil Rays (GCL) ..	DH-1B	4	12	4	6	1	0	2	8	.500	1	0	0	11	0	0	1.000
1999—	Durham (I.L.)	DH-OF-P	23	75	6	15	5	0	1	5	.200	5	14	0	15	0	0	1.000
—	Edmonton (PCL)■ DH-1B-OF-3B		77	296	54	93	20	3	23	73	.314	19	60	0	246	26	5	.982
2000—	Louisville (I.L.)■........	OF-1B	113	440	68	122	35	0	25	90	.277	38	107	2	444	35	5	.990
—	Cincinnati (N.L.)	1B	14	12	0	0	0	0	0	0	.000	1	5	0	1	0	0	1.000
Major League totals (3 years)			78	131	15	28	4	0	5	18	.214	16	34	1	45	1	3	.939

RECORD AS PITCHER

Year	League	W	L	Pct.	ERA	G	GS	CG	ShO	Sv.	IP	H	R	ER	BB	SO
1999—	Durham (I.L.)	0	0	...	0.00	1	0	0	0	0	2	1	1	0	1	1

KILE, DARRYL   P   CARDINALS

PERSONAL: Born December 2, 1968, in Garden Grove, Calif. ... 6-5/212. ... Throws right, bats right. ... Full name: Darryl Andrew Kile.

HIGH SCHOOL: Norco Senior (Calif.).

JUNIOR COLLEGE: Chaffey College (Calif.).

TRANSACTIONS/CAREER NOTES: Selected by Houston Astros organization in 30th round of free-agent draft (June 2, 1987). ... On Tucson disabled list (June 25-July 5, 1992). ... Granted free agency (October 28, 1997). ... Signed by Colorado Rockies (December 4, 1997). ... Traded by Rockies with P Dave Veres and P Luther Hackman to St. Louis Cardinals for P Jose Jimenez, P Manny Aybar, P Rick Croushore and SS Brent Butler (November 16, 1999).

RECORDS: Shares modern N.L. record for most hit batsmen (nine-inning game)—4 (June 2, 1996).

STATISTICAL NOTES: Led N.L. with 15 hit batsmen in 1993. ... Pitched 7-1 no-hit victory against New York (September 8, 1993). ... Tied for N.L. lead with 10 wild pitches in 1994. ... Tied for N.L. lead with 16 hit batsmen in 1996.

MISCELLANEOUS: Appeared in two games as pinch runner (1996). ... Had one sacrifice hit in two appearances as pinch hitter and appeared in one game as pinch runner (1998).

Year	League	W	L	Pct.	ERA	G	GS	CG	ShO	Sv.	IP	H	R	ER	BB	SO
1988—	Gulf Coast Astros (GCL).....	5	3	.625	3.17	12	12	0	0	0	59²/₃	48	34	21	33	54
1989—	Columbus (Sou.)................	11	6	.647	2.58	20	20	6	•2	0	125²/₃	74	47	36	68	108
—	Tucson (PCL)	2	1	.667	5.96	6	6	1	1	0	25²/₃	33	20	17	13	18
1990—	Tucson (PCL)	5	10	.333	6.64	26	23	1	0	0	123¹/₃	147	97	91	68	77
1991—	Houston (N.L.)..................	7	11	.389	3.69	37	22	0	0	0	153²/₃	144	81	63	84	100
1992—	Houston (N.L.)..................	5	10	.333	3.95	22	22	2	0	0	125¹/₃	124	61	55	63	90
—	Tucson (PCL)	4	1	.800	3.99	9	9	0	0	0	56¹/₃	50	31	25	32	43
1993—	Houston (N.L.).................	15	8	.652	3.51	32	26	4	2	0	171²/₃	152	73	67	69	141
1994—	Houston (N.L.)..................	9	6	.600	4.57	24	24	0	0	0	147²/₃	153	84	75	*82	105
1995—	Houston (N.L.)..................	4	12	.250	4.96	25	21	0	0	0	127	114	81	70	73	113
—	Tucson (PCL)	2	1	.667	8.51	4	4	0	0	0	24¹/₃	29	23	23	12	15
1996—	Houston (N.L.)..................	12	11	.522	4.19	35	33	4	0	0	219	233	113	102	97	219
1997—	Houston (N.L.)..................	19	7	.731	2.57	34	34	6	4	0	255²/₃	208	87	73	94	205
1998—	Colorado (N.L.)■	13	*17	.433	5.20	36	•35	4	1	0	230¹/₃	257	141	133	96	158
1999—	Colorado (N.L.)■	8	13	.381	6.61	32	32	1	0	0	190²/₃	225	*150	*140	109	116
2000—	St. Louis (N.L.)■	20	9	.690	3.91	34	34	5	1	0	232¹/₃	215	109	101	58	192
Major League totals (10 years)		112	104	.519	4.27	311	283	26	8	0	1853¹/₃	1825	980	879	825	1439

DIVISION SERIES RECORD

Year League	W	L	Pct.	ERA	G	GS	CG	ShO	Sv.	IP	H	R	ER	BB	SO
1997— Houston (N.L.)	0	1	.000	2.57	1	1	0	0	0	7	2	2	2	2	4
2000— St. Louis (N.L.)	1	0	1.000	2.57	1	1	0	0	0	7	4	2	2	2	6
Division series totals (2 years)	1	1	.500	2.57	2	2	0	0	0	14	6	4	4	4	10

CHAMPIONSHIP SERIES RECORD

RECORDS: Shares single-game record for most earned runs allowed—7 (October 15, 2000).

Year League	W	L	Pct.	ERA	G	GS	CG	ShO	Sv.	IP	H	R	ER	BB	SO
2000— St. Louis (N.L.)	0	2	.000	9.00	2	2	0	0	0	10	13	10	10	5	3

ALL-STAR GAME RECORD

Year League	W	L	Pct.	ERA	GS	CG	ShO	Sv.	IP	H	R	ER	BB	SO
1993— National						Did not play.								
1997— National						Did not play.								
2000— National	0	0	...	0.00	0	0	0	0	2	2	0	0	0	0

KIM, BYUNG-HYUN — P — DIAMONDBACKS

PERSONAL: Born January 21, 1979, in Kwangsan-ku Songjunsdon, Korea. ... 5-11/176. ... Throws right, bats right.
HIGH SCHOOL: Kwang-ju (Korea).
TRANSACTIONS/CAREER NOTES: Signed as non-drafted free agent by Arizona Diamondbacks organization (February 19, 1999). ... On Arizona disabled list (July 28-September 7, 2000).
MISCELLANEOUS: Member of Korean National Team (1997-98).

Year League	W	L	Pct.	ERA	G	GS	CG	ShO	Sv.	IP	H	R	ER	BB	SO
1999— El Paso (Texas)	2	0	1.000	2.11	10	0	0	0	0	21 $\frac{1}{3}$	6	5	5	9	32
— Tucson (PCL)	4	0	1.000	2.40	11	3	0	0	1	30	21	9	8	15	40
— Arizona (N.L.)	1	2	.333	4.61	25	0	0	0	1	27 $\frac{1}{3}$	20	15	14	20	31
— Ariz. Diamondbacks (Ariz.)	0	0	...	0.00	1	1	0	0	0	2	1	0	0	1	2
2000— Arizona (N.L.)	6	6	.500	4.46	61	1	0	0	14	70 $\frac{2}{3}$	52	39	35	46	111
— Tucson (PCL)	0	0	...	0.00	2	2	0	0	0	8 $\frac{1}{3}$	1	0	0	4	13
Major League totals (2 years)	7	8	.467	4.50	86	1	0	0	15	98	72	54	49	66	142

KING, RAY — P — BREWERS

PERSONAL: Born January 15, 1974, in Chicago. ... 6-1/230. ... Throws left, bats left. ... Full name: Raymond Keith King.
HIGH SCHOOL: Ripley (Tenn.).
COLLEGE: Lambuth (Tenn.).
TRANSACTIONS/CAREER NOTES: Selected by Cincinnati Red organization in eighth round of free-agent draft (June 1, 1995). ... Loaned by Reds organization to Atlanta Braves organization (March 22-June 11, 1996). ... Traded by Reds to Braves (June 11, 1996), completing deal in which Braves traded OF Mike Kelly to Reds for P Chad Fox and a player to be named later (January 9, 1996). ... Traded by Braves to Chicago Cubs for P Jon Ratliff (January 20, 1998). ... Traded by Cubs to Milwaukee Brewers for P Doug Johnston (April 14, 2000).

Year League	W	L	Pct.	ERA	G	GS	CG	ShO	Sv.	IP	H	R	ER	BB	SO
1995— Billings (Pio.)	3	0	1.000	1.67	28	0	0	0	5	43	31	11	8	15	43
1996— Macon (S.Atl.)■	3	5	.375	2.80	18	10	1	0	0	70 $\frac{2}{3}$	63	34	22	20	63
— Durham (Caro.)	3	6	.333	4.46	14	14	2	0	0	82 $\frac{2}{3}$	104	54	41	15	52
1997— Greenville (Sou.)	5	5	.500	6.85	12	9	0	0	0	65 $\frac{2}{3}$	85	53	50	24	42
— Durham (Caro.)	6	9	.400	5.40	24	6	0	0	3	71 $\frac{2}{3}$	89	54	43	26	60
1998— West Tenn (Sou.)■	1	2	.333	2.43	25	0	0	0	3	29 $\frac{2}{3}$	23	9	8	10	26
— Iowa (PCL)	1	3	.250	5.01	37	0	0	0	2	32 $\frac{1}{3}$	36	20	18	15	26
1999— Iowa (PCL)	4	4	.500	1.88	37	0	0	0	2	43	31	11	9	22	41
— Chicago (N.L.)	0	0	...	5.91	10	0	0	0	0	10 $\frac{2}{3}$	11	8	7	10	5
2000— Iowa (PCL)	1	0	1.000	0.00	1	0	0	0	0	1 $\frac{1}{3}$	1	0	0	0	1
— Indianapolis (I.L.)■	0	3	.000	3.51	29	0	0	0	1	25 $\frac{2}{3}$	26	15	10	12	20
— Milwaukee (N.L.)	3	2	.600	1.26	36	0	0	0	0	28 $\frac{2}{3}$	18	7	4	10	19
Major League totals (2 years)	3	2	.600	2.52	46	0	0	0	0	39 $\frac{1}{3}$	29	15	11	20	24

KINGSALE, GENE — OF — ORIOLES

PERSONAL: Born August 20, 1976, in Oranjestad, Aruba. ... 6-3/194. ... Bats both, throws right. ... Full name: Eugene Humphrey Kingsale.
HIGH SCHOOL: John F. Kennedy Technical School (Oranjestad, Aruba).
TRANSACTIONS/CAREER NOTES: Signed as non-drafted free agent by Baltimore Orioles organization (June 19, 1993). ... On Frederick disabled list (May 29-August 31, 1996). ... On Bowie disabled list (April 8-August 8, 1997). ... On Baltimore disabled list (March 29-August 27, 2000); included rehabilitation assignments Gulf Coast Orioles (August 8-18), Frederick (August 19-25) and Bowie (August 26-27).
STATISTICAL NOTES: Tied for Gulf Coast League lead in double plays by outfielder with two in 1994.

Year Team (League)	Pos.	G	AB	R	H	2B	3B	HR	RBI	Avg.	BB	SO	SB	PO	A	E	Avg.
1994— GC Orioles (GCL)	OF-2B	50	168	26	52	2	3	0	9	.310	18	24	15	100	2	3	.971
1995— Bluefield (Appl.)	OF	47	171	45	54	11	2	0	16	.316	27	31	20	95	3	*11	.899
1996— Frederick (Caro.)	OF	49	166	26	45	6	4	0	9	.271	19	32	23	100	1	4	.962
— Baltimore (A.L.)	OF	3	0	0	0	0	0	0	0	...	0	0	0	2	0	0	1.000
1997— Bowie (East.)	OF	13	46	8	19	6	0	0	4	.413	5	4	5	23	0	1	.958
— GC Orioles (GCL)	OF	6	17	2	5	0	0	0	0	.294	2	2	1	16	0	1	.941
1998— Bowie (East.)	OF	111	427	69	112	11	5	1	34	.262	48	79	29	279	9	6	.980
— Rochester (I.L.)	OF-DH	18	55	3	12	1	1	0	2	.218	4	8	3	38	2	0	1.000
— Baltimore (A.L.)	OF-DH	11	2	1	0	0	0	0	0	.000	0	1	0	2	0	0	1.000
1999— Bowie (East.)	OF	67	268	43	63	11	4	3	23	.235	33	46	13	173	2	4	.978
— Rochester (I.L.)	OF	48	191	31	59	9	0	2	20	.309	13	23	10	118	1	3	.975
— Baltimore (A.L.)	OF-DH	28	85	9	21	2	0	0	7	.247	5	13	1	48	1	1	.980

Year Team (League)	Pos.	G	AB	R	H	2B	3B	HR	RBI	Avg.	BB	SO	SB	PO	A	E	Avg.
2000— GC Orioles (GCL)........	OF	5	16	7	5	0	0	0	4	.313	4	0	2	2	0	0	1.000
—Frederick (Caro.)	OF	6	25	8	11	3	0	1	3	.440	1	6	2	12	0	0	1.000
—Bowie (East.)	OF	3	11	5	4	2	0	1	5	.364	3	0	1	3	0	0	1.000
—Rochester (I.L.)..........	OF	2	10	2	4	1	0	0	1	.400	0	0	1	11	1	0	1.000
—Baltimore (A.L.).........	OF-DH	26	88	13	21	2	1	0	9	.239	2	14	1	60	2	3	.954
Major League totals (4 years)		68	175	23	42	4	1	0	16	.240	7	28	2	112	3	4	.966

KINKADE, MIKE   3B   ORIOLES

PERSONAL: Born May 6, 1973, in Livonia, Mich. ... 6-1/210. ... Bats right, throws right. ... Full name: Michael A. Kinkade.
HIGH SCHOOL: Tigard (Ore.).
COLLEGE: Washington State.
TRANSACTIONS/CAREER NOTES: Selected by Milwaukee Brewers organization in ninth round of free-agent draft (June 1, 1995). ... On Louisville disabled list (April 20-May 14, 1998). ... Traded by Brewers to New York Mets for P Bill Pulsipher (July 31, 1998). ... Traded by Mets with OF Melvin Mora, P Leslie Brea and P Pat Gorman to Baltimore Orioles for SS Mike Bordick (July 28, 2000).
HONORS: Named Texas League Player of the Year (1997).
STATISTICAL NOTES: Led Texas League with .455 on-base percentage and tied for league lead with 275 total bases in 1997. ... Led Eastern League with .434 on-base percentage and .561 slugging percentage in 2000.

Year Team (League)	Pos.	G	AB	R	H	2B	3B	HR	RBI	Avg.	BB	SO	SB	PO	A	E	Avg.
1995—Helena (Pio.)	3B-1B-C	69	266	76	94	19	1	4	39	.353	43	38	26	291	79	10	.974
1996—Beloit (Midw.)..............	3B-C-1B	135	499	105	151	33	4	15	100	.303	47	69	23	148	310	39	.922
1997—El Paso (Texas)..............	3B-DH	125	468	•112	*180	35	12	12	*109	*.385	52	66	17	*79	249	*60	.845
1998—Louisville (I.L.)	3B-1B-DH	80	291	57	90	24	6	7	46	.309	36	52	10	183	120	15	.953
—Norfolk (I.L.)■..........	3B-1B	30	125	12	35	5	0	1	18	.280	3	24	6	32	61	5	.949
—New York (N.L.)..........	3B	3	2	2	0	0	0	0	0	.000	0	0	0	0	0	0	...
1999—New York (N.L.).........OF-3B-C-1B		28	46	3	9	2	1	2	6	.196	3	9	1	18	2	0	1.000
—Norfolk (I.L.).........3-C-1-O-DH		84	312	53	96	20	2	7	49	.308	21	31	7	209	88	10	.967
2000—Binghamton (East.)	C-3B-OF	90	317	66	116	24	3	10	67	.366	35	39	18	516	80	9	.985
—New York (N.L.)	OF	2	2	0	0	0	0	0	0	.000	0	1	0	0	0	0	...
—Bowie (East.)■..........	C-3B	8	27	4	7	1	0	3	5	.259	3	7	0	29	3	0	1.000
—Rochester (I.L.)..........	C-1B-3B	15	55	10	20	5	0	1	10	.364	11	11	0	70	11	4	.953
—Baltimore (A.L.)..........	DH-1B	3	7	0	3	1	0	0	1	.429	0	0	0	1	0	0	1.000
American League totals (1 year)		3	7	0	3	1	0	0	1	.429	0	0	0	1	0	0	1.000
National League totals (3 years)		33	50	5	9	2	1	2	6	.180	3	10	1	18	2	0	1.000
Major League totals (3 years)		36	57	5	12	3	1	2	7	.211	3	10	1	19	2	0	1.000

DIVISION SERIES RECORD

Year Team (League)	Pos.	G	AB	R	H	2B	3B	HR	RBI	Avg.	BB	SO	SB	PO	A	E	Avg.
1999— New York (N.L.)							Did not play.										

CHAMPIONSHIP SERIES RECORD

Year Team (League)	Pos.	G	AB	R	H	2B	3B	HR	RBI	Avg.	BB	SO	SB	PO	A	E	Avg.
1999— New York (N.L.)							Did not play.										

KINNEY, MATT   P   TWINS

PERSONAL: Born December 16, 1976, in Bangor, Maine. ... 6-5/220. ... Throws right, bats right. ... Full name: Matthew John Kinney.
HIGH SCHOOL: Bangor (Maine).
TRANSACTIONS/CAREER NOTES: Selected by Boston Red Sox organization in sixth round of free-agent draft (June 1, 1995). ... Traded by Red Sox with P Joe Thomas and OF John Barnes to Minnesota Twins for P Greg Swindell and 1B Orlando Merced (July 31, 1998). ... On New Britain disabled list (June 7-August 16, 1999).
STATISTICAL NOTES: Led Florida State League with 93 bases on balls and 25 wild pitches in 1998.

Year League	W	L	Pct.	ERA	G	GS	CG	ShO	Sv.	IP	H	R	ER	BB	SO
1995— Gulf Coast Red Sox (GCL)..	1	3	.250	2.93	8	2	0	0	2	27 2/3	29	13	9	10	11
1996— Lowell (NY-Penn)	3	9	.250	2.68	15	•15	0	0	0	87 1/3	68	51	26	44	72
1997— Michigan (Midw.)	8	5	.615	3.53	22	22	2	1	0	117 1/3	93	59	46	78	123
1998— Sarasota (FSL)	9	6	.600	4.01	22	20	2	1	1	121 1/3	109	70	54	*75	96
—Fort Myers (FSL)■..............	3	2	.600	3.13	7	7	0	0	0	37 1/3	31	18	13	§18	39
1999— New Britain (East.)	4	7	.364	7.12	14	13	0	0	0	60 2/3	69	54	48	36	50
—Gulf Coast Twins (GCL)......	0	1	.000	4.76	3	3	0	0	0	5 2/3	6	4	3	3	8
2000— New Britain (East.)	6	1	.857	2.71	15	15	0	0	0	86 1/3	74	31	26	35	93
—Salt Lake (PCL)	5	2	.714	4.25	9	9	0	0	0	55	42	26	26	26	59
—Minnesota (A.L.)	2	2	.500	5.10	8	8	0	0	0	42 1/3	41	26	24	25	24
Major League totals (1 year)........	2	2	.500	5.10	8	8	0	0	0	42 1/3	41	26	24	25	24

KLASSEN, DANNY   SS/2B   DIAMONDBACKS

PERSONAL: Born September 22, 1975, in Learington, Ont. ... 6-0/175. ... Bats right, throws right. ... Full name: Daniel Victor Klassen.
HIGH SCHOOL: John Carroll (Fort Pierce, Fla.).
TRANSACTIONS/CAREER NOTES: Selected by Milwaukee Brewers organization in second round of free-agent draft (June 3, 1993). ... On disabled list (April 7-June 23, 1995 and April 11-22, 1996). ... Selected by Arizona Diamondbacks in second round (37th pick overall) of expansion draft (November 18, 1997). ... On Tucson disabled list (August 13-September 8, 1998; and June 11-August 26, 1999). ... On Arizona disabled list (July 8-September 1, 2000).
STATISTICAL NOTES: Tied for Arizona League lead in intentional bases on balls received with three in 1994.

K

Year	Team (League)	Pos.	G	AB	R	H	2B	3B	HR	RBI	Avg.	BB	SO	SB	PO	A	E	Avg.
1993—Ariz. Brewers (Ariz.) ...		SS	38	117	26	26	5	0	2	20	.222	24	28	14	45	97	12	.922
—Helena (Pio.)		SS	18	45	8	9	1	0	0	3	.200	7	11	2	25	42	7	.905
1994—Beloit (Midw.)		SS	133	458	61	119	20	3	6	54	.260	58	123	28	177	328	40	.927
1995—Beloit (Midw.)		SS-3B	59	218	27	60	15	2	2	25	.275	16	43	12	73	133	18	.920
1996—Stockton (Calif.)		SS	118	432	58	116	22	4	2	46	.269	34	77	14	186	373	*33	.944
1997—El Paso (Texas)		SS	135	519	112	172	30	6	14	81	.331	48	104	16	177	399	*50	.920
1998—Tucson (PCL)■		SS-2B	73	281	47	82	25	2	10	47	.292	19	54	6	128	202	8	.976
—Arizona (N.L.)		2B	29	108	12	21	2	1	3	8	.194	9	33	1	60	74	5	.964
1999—Tucson (PCL)		SS-DH-2B	64	245	38	66	16	3	6	33	.269	20	51	5	87	193	9	.969
—Ariz. D-backs (Ariz.) ...		SS	6	17	2	4	1	0	0	1	.235	1	4	0	4	21	1	.962
—Arizona (N.L.)		PH	1	1	0	1	0	0	0	0	1.000	0	0	0	...	...	...	...
2000—Tucson (PCL)		SS-2B-3B	28	97	25	31	7	2	2	14	.320	19	23	1	42	97	8	.946
—Arizona (N.L.)		3B-SS	29	76	13	18	3	0	2	8	.237	8	24	1	14	42	2	.966
Major League totals (3 years)			59	185	25	40	5	1	5	16	.216	17	57	2	74	116	7	.964

KLESKO, RYAN   1B   PADRES

PERSONAL: Born June 12, 1971, in Westminster, Calif. ... 6-3/220. ... Bats left, throws left. ... Full name: Ryan Anthony Klesko.

HIGH SCHOOL: Westminster (Calif.).

TRANSACTIONS/CAREER NOTES: Selected by Atlanta Braves organization in fifth round of free-agent draft (June 5, 1989). ... On Atlanta disabled list (May 3-18, 1995); included rehabilitation assignment to Greenville (May 13-17). ... Traded by Braves with 2B Bret Boone and P Jason Shiell to San Diego Padres for 2B Quilvio Veras, 1B Wally Joyner and OF Reggie Sanders (December 22, 1999).

HONORS: Named Southern League Most Valuable Player (1991).

STATISTICAL NOTES: Career major league grand slams: 6.

Year	Team (League)	Pos.	G	AB	R	H	2B	3B	HR	RBI	Avg.	BB	SO	SB	PO	A	E	Avg.
1989—GC Braves (GCL)		DH	17	57	14	23	5	4	1	16	.404	6	6	4	...	...	...	...
—Sumter (S.Atl.)		1B	25	90	17	26	6	0	1	12	.289	11	14	1	173	11	4	.979
1990—Sumter (S.Atl.)		1B	63	231	41	85	15	1	10	38	.368	31	30	13	575	43	14	.978
—Durham (Caro.)		1B	77	292	40	80	16	1	7	47	.274	32	53	10	490	34	13	.976
1991—Greenville (Sou.)		1B	126	419	64	122	22	3	14	67	.291	75	60	14	1043	57	*17	.985
1992—Richmond (I.L.)		1B	123	418	63	105	22	2	17	59	.251	41	72	3	947	51	*11	.989
—Atlanta (N.L.)		1B	13	14	0	0	0	0	0	1	.000	0	5	0	25	0	0	1.000
1993—Richmond (I.L.)		1B-OF	98	343	59	94	14	2	22	74	.274	47	69	4	587	45	12	.981
—Atlanta (N.L.)		1B-OF	22	17	3	6	1	0	2	5	.353	3	4	0	8	0	0	1.000
1994—Atlanta (N.L.)		OF-1B	92	245	42	68	13	3	17	47	.278	26	48	1	89	3	7	.929
1995—Atlanta (N.L.)		OF-1B	107	329	48	102	25	2	23	70	.310	47	72	5	131	4	8	.944
—Greenville (Sou.)		DH-OF	4	13	1	3	0	0	1	4	.231	2	1	0	2	0	0	1.000
1996—Atlanta (N.L.)		OF-1B	153	528	90	149	21	4	34	93	.282	68	129	6	204	8	5	.977
1997—Atlanta (N.L.)		OF-1B	143	467	67	122	23	6	24	84	.261	48	130	4	245	6	6	.977
1998—Atlanta (N.L.)		OF-1B	129	427	69	117	29	1	18	70	.274	56	66	5	195	13	2	.990
1999—Atlanta (N.L.)		1B-OF-DH	133	404	55	120	28	2	21	80	.297	53	69	5	554	32	6	.990
2000—San Diego (N.L.)■		1B-OF	145	494	88	140	33	2	26	92	.283	91	81	23	1031	90	9	.992
Major League totals (9 years)			937	2925	462	824	173	20	165	542	.282	392	604	49	2482	156	43	.984

DIVISION SERIES RECORD

RECORDS: Shares career record for most grand slams—1 (September 30, 1998). ... Shares single-inning record for most runs batted in—4 (September 30, 1998).

Year	Team (League)	Pos.	G	AB	R	H	2B	3B	HR	RBI	Avg.	BB	SO	SB	PO	A	E	Avg.
1995—Atlanta (N.L.)		OF	4	15	5	7	1	0	0	1	.467	0	3	0	3	0	0	1.000
1996—Atlanta (N.L.)		OF	3	8	1	1	0	0	1	1	.125	3	4	1	2	0	1	.667
1997—Atlanta (N.L.)		OF	3	8	2	2	1	0	1	1	.250	0	2	0	3	0	1	.750
1998—Atlanta (N.L.)		OF	3	11	1	3	0	0	1	4	.273	0	3	0	5	0	0	1.000
1999—Atlanta (N.L.)		1B-PH	4	12	3	4	0	0	0	1	.333	1	4	0	22	2	0	1.000
Division series totals (5 years)			17	54	12	17	2	0	3	8	.315	4	16	1	35	2	2	.949

CHAMPIONSHIP SERIES RECORD

Year	Team (League)	Pos.	G	AB	R	H	2B	3B	HR	RBI	Avg.	BB	SO	SB	PO	A	E	Avg.
1995—Atlanta (N.L.)		OF-PH	4	7	0	0	0	0	0	0	.000	3	4	0	1	0	0	1.000
1996—Atlanta (N.L.)		OF	6	16	1	4	0	0	1	3	.250	2	6	0	13	0	0	1.000
1997—Atlanta (N.L.)		OF	5	17	2	4	0	0	2	4	.235	2	3	0	5	0	0	1.000
1998—Atlanta (N.L.)		OF-PH	5	12	2	1	0	0	0	1	.083	6	3	0	3	0	1	.750
1999—Atlanta (N.L.)		1B-PH	4	8	1	1	0	0	1	1	.125	2	1	0	27	2	2	.935
Championship series totals (5 years)			24	60	6	10	0	0	4	9	.167	15	17	0	49	2	3	.944

WORLD SERIES RECORD

NOTES: Member of World Series championship team (1995).

Year	Team (League)	Pos.	G	AB	R	H	2B	3B	HR	RBI	Avg.	BB	SO	SB	PO	A	E	Avg.
1995—Atlanta (N.L.)		OF-DH	6	16	4	5	0	0	3	4	.313	3	4	0	1	0	0	1.000
1996—Atlanta (N.L.)		DH-OF-1B-PH	5	10	2	1	0	0	0	1	.100	3	4	0	1	0	1	.500
1999—Atlanta (N.L.)		1B-PH	4	12	0	2	0	0	0	0	.167	0	1	0	21	0	0	1.000
World Series totals (3 years)			15	38	6	8	0	0	3	5	.211	6	9	0	23	0	1	.958

PERSONAL: Born August 22, 1972, in Sunbury, Pa. ... 6-1/215. ... Throws left, bats both. ... Full name: Steven James Kline.
HIGH SCHOOL: Lewisburg (Pa.).
COLLEGE: West Virginia.
TRANSACTIONS/CAREER NOTES: Selected by Cleveland Indians organization in eighth round of free-agent draft (June 3, 1993). ... On disabled list (May 23-August 5, 1995). ... On temporarily inactive list (April 5-20, 1996). ... Traded by Indians to Montreal Expos for P Jeff Juden (July 31, 1997). ... On disabled list (April 11-27, 1999). ... Traded by Expos with P Dustin Hermanson to St. Louis Cardinals for 3B Fernando Tatis and P Britt Reames (December 14, 2000).
RECORDS: Shares major league single-inning record for most strikeouts—4 (August 17, 2000, seventh inning).
STATISTICAL NOTES: Led N.L. pitchers with 41putouts in 1999.

Year League	W	L	Pct.	ERA	G	GS	CG	ShO	Sv.	IP	H	R	ER	BB	SO
1993—Burlington (Appl.)	1	1	.500	4.91	2	1	0	0	0	7⅓	11	4	4	2	4
—Watertown (NY-Penn)	5	4	.556	3.19	13	13	2	1	0	79	77	36	28	12	45
1994—Columbus (S.Atl.)	*18	5	.783	3.01	28	•28	2	1	0	*185⅔	175	67	62	36	*174
1995—Canton/Akron (East.)	2	3	.400	2.42	14	14	0	0	0	89⅓	86	34	24	30	45
1996—Canton/Akron (East.)	8	12	.400	5.46	25	24	0	0	0	146⅔	168	98	89	55	107
1997—Cleveland (A.L.)	3	1	.750	5.81	20	1	0	0	0	26⅓	42	19	17	13	17
—Buffalo (A.A.)	3	3	.500	4.03	20	4	0	0	1	51⅓	53	26	23	13	41
—Montreal (N.L.)■	1	3	.250	6.15	26	0	0	0	0	26⅓	31	18	18	10	20
1998—Ottawa (I.L.)	0	0	...	0.00	2	0	0	0	0	2⅔	1	0	0	0	1
—Montreal (N.L.)	3	6	.333	2.76	78	0	0	0	1	71⅔	62	25	22	41	76
1999—Montreal (N.L.)	7	4	.636	3.75	*82	0	0	0	0	69⅔	56	32	29	33	69
2000—Montreal (N.L.)	1	5	.167	3.50	*83	0	0	0	14	82⅓	88	36	32	27	64
A.L. totals (1 year)	3	1	.750	5.81	20	1	0	0	0	26⅓	42	19	17	13	17
N.L. totals (4 years)	12	18	.400	3.64	269	0	0	0	15	250	237	111	101	111	229
Major League totals (4 years)	15	19	.441	3.84	289	1	0	0	15	276⅓	279	130	118	124	246

PERSONAL: Born October 1, 1975, in Oxnard, Calif. ... 6-0/170. ... Throws right, bats left. ... Full name: Brandon Michael Knight.
HIGH SCHOOL: Buena (Ventura, Calif.).
JUNIOR COLLEGE: Ventura (Calif.) College.
TRANSACTIONS/CAREER NOTES: Selected by Texas Rangers organization in 14th round of free-agent draft (June 1, 1995). ... Traded by Rangers with P Sam Marsonek to New York Yankees for OF Chad Curtis (December 13, 1999). ... Selected by Minnesota Twins from Yankees organization in Rule 5 major league draft (December 11, 2000).
STATISTICAL NOTES: Led International League with 51 total chances and 32 assists in 2000. ... Tied for International League lead with six errors in 2000.

Year League	W	L	Pct.	ERA	G	GS	CG	ShO	Sv.	IP	H	R	ER	BB	SO
1995—Gulf Coast Rangers (GCL)	2	1	.667	5.25	3	2	0	0	0	12	12	7	7	6	11
—Charleston, S.C. (S.Atl.)	4	2	.667	3.13	9	9	0	0	0	54⅔	37	22	19	21	52
1996—Charlotte (FSL)	4	10	.286	5.12	19	17	2	0	0	102	118	65	58	45	74
—Hudson Valley (NY-Penn)	2	2	.500	4.42	9	9	0	0	0	53	59	29	26	21	52
1997—Charlotte (FSL)	7	4	.636	2.23	14	12	3	1	0	92⅔	82	33	23	22	91
—Tulsa (Texas)	6	4	.600	4.50	14	14	2	•1	0	90	83	52	45	35	84
1998—Tulsa (Texas)	6	6	.500	5.11	14	14	0	0	0	86⅓	94	54	49	37	87
—Oklahoma City (PCL)	0	7	.000	9.74	16	12	0	0	0	64⅔	100	75	70	29	52
1999—Oklahoma (PCL)	9	8	.529	4.91	27	26	*5	0	0	163	173	96	89	47	97
2000—Columbus (I.L.)■	10	12	.455	4.44	28	28	*8	1	0	*184⅔	172	105	91	61	138

PERSONAL: Born July 7, 1968, in Houston. ... 5-9/175. ... Bats right, throws right. ... Full name: Edward Charles Knoblauch. ... Son of Ray Knoblauch, minor league pitcher (1947-56); and nephew of Ed Knoblauch, minor league outfielder (1938-42 and 1947-55). ... Name pronounced NOB-lock.
HIGH SCHOOL: Bellaire (Houston).
COLLEGE: Texas A&M.
TRANSACTIONS/CAREER NOTES: Selected by Philadelphia Phillies organization in 18th round of free-agent draft (June 2, 1986); did not sign. ... Selected by Minnesota Twins organization in first round (25th pick overall) of free-agent draft (June 5, 1989). ... Traded by Twins to New York Yankees for P Eric Milton, P Danny Mota, OF Brian Buchanan, SS Cristian Guzman and cash (February 6, 1998). ... On New York disabled list (August 3-September 1, 2000); included rehabilitation assignment to Tampa (August 25-September 1).
HONORS: Named A.L. Rookie Player of the Year by The Sporting News (1991). ... Named A.L. Rookie of the Year by Baseball Writers' Association of America (1991). ... Named second baseman on The Sporting News A.L. All-Star team (1994 and 1997). ... Named second baseman on The Sporting News A.L. Silver Slugger team (1995 and 1997). ... Won A.L. Gold Glove at second base (1997).
STATISTICAL NOTES: Had 20-game hitting streak (September 2-25, 1991). ... Led A.L. second basemen with 424 assists, 101 double plays and 718 total chances in 1997. ... Led A.L. in being hit by pitch with 18 in 1998. ... Career major league grand slams: 3.
MISCELLANEOUS: Holds Minnesota Twins all-time record for most stolen bases (276).

Year Team (League)	Pos.	G	AB	R	H	2B	3B	HR	RBI	Avg.	BB	SO	SB	PO	A	E	Avg.
1989—Kenosha (Midw.)	SS	51	196	29	56	13	1	2	19	.286	32	23	9	60	124	21	.898
—Visalia (Calif.)	SS	18	77	20	28	10	0	0	21	.364	6	11	4	23	52	10	.882
1990—Orlando (Sou.)	2B	118	432	74	125	23	6	2	53	.289	63	31	23	275	300	20	.966
1991—Minnesota (A.L.)	2B	151	565	78	159	24	6	1	50	.281	59	40	25	249	460	18	.975
1992—Minnesota (A.L.)	2B-DH-SS	155	600	104	178	19	6	2	56	.297	88	60	34	306	415	6	.992
1993—Minnesota (A.L.)	2B-SS-OF	153	602	82	167	27	4	2	41	.277	65	44	29	302	431	9	.988
1994—Minnesota (A.L.)	2B-SS	109	445	85	139	*45	3	5	51	.312	41	56	35	191	285	3	.994
1995—Minnesota (A.L.)	2B-SS	136	538	107	179	34	8	11	63	.333	78	95	46	254	400	10	.985

Year	Team (League)	Pos.	G	AB	R	H	2B	3B	HR	RBI	Avg.	BB	SO	SB	PO	A	E	Avg.
								BATTING								**FIELDING**		
1996—Minnesota (A.L.)		2B-DH	153	578	140	197	35	*14	13	72	.341	98	74	45	271	390	8	*.988
1997—Minnesota (A.L.)		2B-DH-SS	156	611	117	178	26	10	9	58	.291	84	84	62	285	†428	12	.983
1998—New York (A.L.)■......		2B-DH	150	603	117	160	25	4	17	64	.265	76	70	31	275	408	13	.981
1999—New York (A.L.).........		2B	150	603	120	176	36	4	18	68	.292	83	57	28	254	425	*26	.963
2000—New York (A.L.).........		2B-DH	102	400	75	113	22	2	5	26	.283	46	45	15	149	190	15	.958
—Tampa (FSL).............		2B	1	1	0	0	0	0	0	0	.000	0	1	0	0	1	0	1.000
Major League totals (10 years)			1415	5545	1025	1646	293	61	83	549	.297	718	625	350	2536	3832	120	.982

DIVISION SERIES RECORD

Year	Team (League)	Pos.	G	AB	R	H	2B	3B	HR	RBI	Avg.	BB	SO	SB	PO	A	E	Avg.
								BATTING								**FIELDING**		
1998—New York (A.L.).........		2B	3	11	0	1	0	0	0	0	.091	0	4	0	4	10	1	.933
1999—New York (A.L.).........		2B	3	12	1	2	0	0	0	0	.167	1	3	0	2	11	1	.929
2000—New York (A.L.).........		DH-PR	3	9	1	3	0	0	0	1	.333	0	2	1	...	...	...	...
Division series totals (3 years)			9	32	2	6	0	0	0	1	.188	1	9	1	6	21	2	.931

CHAMPIONSHIP SERIES RECORD

Year	Team (League)	Pos.	G	AB	R	H	2B	3B	HR	RBI	Avg.	BB	SO	SB	PO	A	E	Avg.
								BATTING								**FIELDING**		
1991—Minnesota (A.L.)		2B	5	20	5	7	2	0	0	3	.350	3	3	2	8	14	0	1.000
1998—New York (A.L.).........		2B	6	25	4	5	1	0	0	0	.200	4	2	0	9	17	0	1.000
1999—New York (A.L.).........		2B	5	18	3	6	1	0	0	1	.333	3	0	1	8	10	1	.947
2000—New York (A.L.).........		DH	6	23	3	6	2	0	0	2	.261	3	4	0	...	...	...	...
Championship series totals (4 years)			22	86	15	24	6	0	0	6	.279	13	9	3	25	41	1	.985

WORLD SERIES RECORD

NOTES: Member of World Series championship team (1991, 1998, 1999 and 2000).

Year	Team (League)	Pos.	G	AB	R	H	2B	3B	HR	RBI	Avg.	BB	SO	SB	PO	A	E	Avg.
								BATTING								**FIELDING**		
1991—Minnesota (A.L.)		2B	7	26	3	8	1	0	0	2	.308	4	2	4	15	14	1	.967
1998—New York (A.L.).........		2B	4	16	3	6	0	0	1	3	.375	3	2	1	7	10	1	.944
1999—New York (A.L.).........		2B	4	16	5	5	1	0	1	3	.313	1	3	1	10	10	0	1.000
2000—New York (A.L.).........		DH-PR	4	10	1	1	0	0	0	1	.100	2	1	0	...	...	...	...
World Series totals (4 years)			19	68	12	20	2	0	2	9	.294	10	8	6	32	34	2	.971

ALL-STAR GAME RECORD

Year	League	Pos.	AB	R	H	2B	3B	HR	RBI	Avg.	BB	SO	SB	PO	A	E	Avg.
							BATTING								**FIELDING**		
1992—American		PH-2B	1	0	0	0	0	0	0	.000	1	0	0	0	0	0	...
1994—American		2B	3	1	0	0	0	0	0	.000	0	2	0	1	2	0	1.000
1996—American		2B	1	0	1	0	0	0	0	1.000	0	0	0	3	1	0	1.000
1997—American		2B	0	0	0	0	0	0	0	...	0	0	0	1	1	0	1.000
All-Star Game totals (4 years)			5	1	1	0	0	0	0	.200	1	2	0	5	4	0	1.000

KNORR, RANDY — C — EXPOS

PERSONAL: Born November 12, 1968, in San Gabriel, Calif. ... 6-2/215. ... Bats right, throws right. ... Full name: Randy Duane Knorr. ... Name pronounced NOR.

HIGH SCHOOL: Baldwin Park (Calif.).

TRANSACTIONS/CAREER NOTES: Selected by Toronto Blue Jays organization in 10th round of free-agent draft (June 2, 1986). ... On disabled list (June 24-July 4, 1986 and May 10, 1989-remainder of season). ... On Syracuse disabled list (May 11-23, 1992). ... On Toronto disabled list (August 20-September 30, 1992). ... On Toronto disabled list (July 1-August 11, 1995); included rehabilitation assignment to Syracuse (July 21-August 9). ... Traded by Blue Jays to Houston Astros for cash (May 17, 1996). ... Granted free agency (December 20, 1996). ... Re-signed by Astros organization (December 23, 1996). ... On Houston disabled list (August 29-September 6, 1997); included rehabilitation assignment to New Orleans (August 29-September 6). ... Granted free agency (October 14, 1997). ... Signed by Florida Marlins organization (December 22, 1997). ... On Charlotte disabled list (April 24-May 22, 1998). ... Granted free agency (September 29, 1998). ... Signed by Astros organization (January 21, 1999). ... Granted free agency (October 15, 1999). ... Signed by Pittsburgh Pirates organization (December 20, 1999). ... Granted free agency (May 6, 2000). ... Signed by Texas Rangers organization (May 11, 2000). ... Granted free agency (October 14, 2000). ... Signed by Montreal Expos organization (November 17, 2000).

STATISTICAL NOTES: Led South Atlantic League catchers with 960 total chances and 25 passed balls in 1988.

Year	Team (League)	Pos.	G	AB	R	H	2B	3B	HR	RBI	Avg.	BB	SO	SB	PO	A	E	Avg.
								BATTING								**FIELDING**		
1986—Medicine Hat (Pio.)		1B	55	215	21	58	13	0	4	52	.270	17	53	0	451	29	10	.980
1987—Myrtle Beach (S.Atl.)..		C-1B-2B	46	129	17	34	4	0	6	21	.264	6	46	0	95	7	1	.990
—Medicine Hat (Pio.)		C	26	106	21	31	7	0	10	24	.292	5	26	0	70	5	4	.949
1988—Myrtle Beach (S.Atl.)..		C	117	364	43	85	13	0	9	42	.234	41	91	0	*870	75	15	.984
1989—Dunedin (FSL)		C	33	122	13	32	6	0	6	23	.262	6	21	0	186	20	2	.990
1990—Knoxville (Sou.).........		C	116	392	51	108	12	1	13	64	.276	31	83	0	599	72	15	.978
1991—Knoxville (Sou.).........		C-1B	24	74	7	13	4	0	0	4	.176	10	18	2	136	16	2	.987
—Syracuse (I.L.)............		C	91	342	29	89	20	0	5	44	.260	23	58	1	477	49	7	.987
—Toronto (A.L.).............		C	3	1	0	0	0	0	0	0	.000	1	1	0	6	1	0	1.000
1992—Syracuse (I.L.)............		C	61	228	27	62	13	1	11	27	.272	17	38	1	220	22	3	.988
—Toronto (A.L.).............		C	8	19	1	5	0	0	1	2	.263	1	5	0	33	3	0	1.000
1993—Toronto (A.L.).............		C	39	101	11	25	3	2	4	20	.248	9	29	0	168	20	0	1.000
1994—Toronto (A.L.).............		C	40	124	20	30	2	0	7	19	.242	10	35	0	247	21	2	.993
1995—Toronto (A.L.).............		C	45	132	18	28	8	0	3	16	.212	11	28	0	243	22	8	.971
—Syracuse (I.L.)............		C-DH	18	67	6	18	5	1	1	6	.269	5	14	0	129	14	3	.979
1996—Syracuse (I.L.)............		C-DH	12	36	1	10	5	0	0	5	.278	5	8	0	53	2	0	1.000
—Houston (N.L.)■		C	37	87	7	17	5	0	1	7	.195	5	18	0	204	14	0	1.000

Year	Team (League)	Pos.	G	AB	R	H	2B	3B	HR	RBI	Avg.	BB	SO	SB	PO	A	E	Avg.
1997—	New Orleans (A.A.).....	C	72	244	22	58	10	0	5	27	.238	22	38	0	502	54	9	.984
—Houston (N.L.)		C-1B	4	8	1	3	0	0	1	1	.375	0	2	0	19	3	0	1.000
1998—	Charlotte (I.L.)■........	C-DH	68	201	30	66	15	0	7	39	.328	34	41	1	349	25	9	.977
—Florida (N.L.).............		C	15	49	4	10	4	1	2	11	.204	1	10	0	82	7	1	.989
1999—	New Orleans (PCL)■..C-1B-DH-OF		77	270	33	95	22	1	11	41	.352	20	41	0	437	40	7	.986
—Houston (N.L.)		C	13	30	2	5	1	0	0	0	.167	1	8	0	54	3	0	1.000
2000—	Nashville (PCL)■	C	13	40	3	6	1	0	1	4	.150	6	11	0	69	9	3	.963
—Oklahoma (PCL)■......		C-1B	70	252	36	64	16	1	6	41	.254	22	50	0	368	34	4	.990
—Texas (A.L.)		C	15	34	5	10	2	0	2	2	.294	0	3	0	64	2	1	.985
American League totals (6 years)			150	411	55	98	15	2	17	59	.238	32	101	0	761	69	11	.987
National League totals (4 years)			69	174	14	35	10	1	4	19	.201	7	38	0	359	27	1	.997
Major League totals (10 years)			219	585	69	133	25	3	21	78	.227	39	139	0	1120	96	12	.990

CHAMPIONSHIP SERIES RECORD

Year	Team (League)	Pos.	G	AB	R	H	2B	3B	HR	RBI	Avg.	BB	SO	SB	PO	A	E	Avg.
1992—	Toronto (A.L.)								Did not play.									
1993—	Toronto (A.L.)								Did not play.									

WORLD SERIES RECORD

NOTES: Member of World Series championship team (1992 and 1993).

Year	Team (League)	Pos.	G	AB	R	H	2B	3B	HR	RBI	Avg.	BB	SO	SB	PO	A	E	Avg.
1992—	Toronto (A.L.)								Did not play.									
1993—	Toronto (A.L.).............	C	1	0	0	0	0	0	0	0	...	0	0	0	3	0	0	1.000

K

KNOTTS, GARY — P — MARLINS

PERSONAL: Born February 12, 1977, in Decatur, Ala. ... 6-4/235. ... Throws right, bats right. ... Full name: Gary E. Knotts.
HIGH SCHOOL: Brewer (Somerville, Ala.).
JUNIOR COLLEGE: Northwest Shoals Community College (Ala.).
TRANSACTIONS/CAREER NOTES: Selected by Florida Marlins organization in 11th round of free agent draft (June 1, 1995). ... Granted free agency (December 21, 1999). ... Re-signed by Marlins organization (December 22, 1999).

Year	League	W	L	Pct.	ERA	G	GS	CG	ShO	Sv.	IP	H	R	ER	BB	SO
1996—	Gulf Coast Marlins (GCL) ...	4	2	.667	2.04	12	9	1	1	0	57 1/3	35	16	13	17	48
1997—	Kane County (Midw.).........	1	5	.167	13.05	7	7	0	0	0	20	33	34	29	17	19
—Utica (NY-Penn)		3	5	.375	3.62	12	12	1	0	0	69 2/3	70	34	28	27	65
1998—	Kane County (Midw.).........	8	8	.500	3.87	27	27	3	0	0	158 1/3	144	84	68	66	148
1999—	Brevard County (FSL)........	9	6	.600	4.60	16	16	3	2	0	94	101	52	48	29	65
—Portland (East.)		6	3	.667	3.75	12	12	1	1	0	81 2/3	79	39	34	33	63
2000—	Portland (East.)	9	8	.529	4.66	27	27	2	0	0	156 1/3	161	102	81	63	113

KOCH, BILLY — P — BLUE JAYS

PERSONAL: Born December 14, 1974, in Rockville Center, N.Y. ... 6-3/205. ... Throws right, bats right. ... Full name: William Christopher Koch.
HIGH SCHOOL: West Babylon (N.Y.).
COLLEGE: Clemson.
TRANSACTIONS/CAREER NOTES: Selected by Toronto Blue Jays organization in first round (fourth pick overall) of free-agent draft (June 4, 1996). ... On disabled list (April 14, 1997-remainder of season).
MISCELLANEOUS: Member of 1996 U.S. Olympic baseball team.

Year	League	W	L	Pct.	ERA	G	GS	CG	ShO	Sv.	IP	H	R	ER	BB	SO
1997—	Dunedin (FSL)...................	0	1	.000	2.49	3	3	0	0	0	21 2/3	27	10	6	3	20
1998—	Dunedin (FSL)	•14	7	.667	3.75	25	25	0	0	0	124 2/3	120	65	52	41	108
—Syracuse (I.L.)..................		0	1	.000	14.29	2	2	0	0	0	5 2/3	9	9	9	5	9
1999—	Syracuse (I.L.)	3	0	1.000	3.86	5	5	0	0	0	25 2/3	27	11	11	10	22
—Toronto (A.L.)....................		0	5	.000	3.39	56	0	0	0	31	63 2/3	55	26	24	30	57
2000—	Toronto (A.L.)....................	9	3	.750	2.63	68	0	0	0	33	78 2/3	78	28	23	18	60
Major League totals (2 years)		9	8	.529	2.97	124	0	0	0	64	142 1/3	133	54	47	48	117

KOHLMEIER, RYAN — P — ORIOLES

PERSONAL: Born June 25, 1977, in Salina, Kan. ... 6-2/195. ... Throws right, bats right. ... Full name: Ryan Lyle Kohlmeier.
HIGH SCHOOL: Chase County (Cottonwood Falls, Kan.).
JUNIOR COLLEGE: Butler County Community College (Kan.).
TRANSACTIONS/CAREER NOTES: Selected by Baltimore Orioles organization in 14th round of free-agent draft (June 14, 1996).

Year	League	W	L	Pct.	ERA	G	GS	CG	ShO	Sv.	IP	H	R	ER	BB	SO
1997—	Delmarva (S.Atl.)...............	2	2	.500	2.65	50	0	0	0	*24	74 2/3	48	22	22	17	99
—Bowie (East.)		0	0	...	0.00	2	0	0	0	1	2 2/3	0	0	0	2	5
1998—	Bowie (East.)......................	4	4	.500	6.12	42	0	0	0	7	50	52	37	34	16	56
—Frederick (Caro.)		1	2	.333	7.45	9	0	0	0	5	9 2/3	10	9	8	3	15
1999—	Bowie (East.)......................	3	7	.300	3.16	55	0	0	0	23	62 2/3	44	23	22	29	78
2000—	Rochester (I.L.)	1	4	.200	2.51	37	0	0	0	10	46 2/3	33	14	13	16	49
—Baltimore (A.L.).................		0	1	.000	2.39	25	0	0	0	13	26 1/3	30	9	7	15	17
Major League totals (1 year)........		0	1	.000	2.39	25	0	0	0	13	26 1/3	30	9	7	15	17

KOLB, BRANDON   P   BREWERS

PERSONAL: Born November 20, 1973, in Oakland. ... 6-1/190. ... Throws right, bats right. ... Full name: Brandon Charles Kolb.
HIGH SCHOOL: Danville (Calif.).
COLLEGE: Texas Tech.
TRANSACTIONS/CAREER NOTES: Selected by San Diego Padres organization in fourth round of free-agent draft (June 1, 1995). ... On Las Vegas disabled list (July 27-August 20, 1999). ... Traded by Padres to Milwaukee Brewers for SS Santiago Perez and a player to be named later or cash (December 1, 2000); Brewers traded OF Chad Green to Padres for P Wil Cunnane to complete deal (December 20, 2000).

Year	League	W	L	Pct.	ERA	G	GS	CG	ShO	Sv.	IP	H	R	ER	BB	SO
1995—	Idaho Falls (Pio.)	2	3	.400	7.04	9	8	0	0	0	38 1/3	42	33	30	29	21
—	Arizona Padres (Ariz.)	1	1	.500	1.17	4	4	1	•1	0	23	13	10	3	13	21
1996—	Clinton (Midw.)	*16	9	.640	3.42	27	27	3	0	0	181 1/3	170	84	69	76	138
1997—	Rancho Cuca. (Calif.)	3	2	.600	3.00	10	10	0	0	0	63	60	29	21	22	49
1998—	Mobile (Sou.)	4	3	.571	4.50	21	6	0	0	1	62	46	33	31	40	58
—	Rancho Cuca. (Calif.)	0	2	.000	3.05	4	4	0	0	0	20 2/3	14	8	7	18	16
1999—	Mobile (Sou.)	0	2	.000	0.79	7	0	0	0	2	11 1/3	8	4	1	4	14
—	Las Vegas (PCL)	2	1	.667	3.94	42	0	0	0	4	61 2/3	72	36	27	29	63
2000—	Las Vegas (PCL)	3	3	.500	4.47	47	0	0	0	16	56 1/3	53	35	28	21	59
—	San Diego (N.L.)	0	1	.000	4.50	11	0	0	0	0	14	16	8	7	11	12
Major League totals (1 year)		0	1	.000	4.50	11	0	0	0	0	14	16	8	7	11	12

KOLB, DANNY   P   RANGERS

PERSONAL: Born March 29, 1975, in Sterling, Ill. ... 6-4/215. ... Throws right, bats right. ... Full name: Daniel Lee Kolb. ... Cousin of Gary Kolb, outfielder with four major league teams (1960-69).
HIGH SCHOOL: Walnut (Ill.).
JUNIOR COLLEGE: Sauk Valley Community College (Ill.).
COLLEGE: Illinois State.
TRANSACTIONS/CAREER NOTES: Selected by Minnesota Twins organization in 17th round of free-agent draft (June 3, 1993); did not sign. ... Selected by Texas Rangers organization in sixth round of free-agent draft (June 3, 1995). ... On Texas disabled list (October 3, 1999-remainder of season). ... On Texas disabled list (May 29, 2000-remainder of season).
STATISTICAL NOTES: Pitched six-inning, 3-0 no-hit victory against Columbus (June 12, 1996). ... Tied for Appalachian League lead with 22 hit batsmen in 1996.

Year	League	W	L	Pct.	ERA	G	GS	CG	ShO	Sv.	IP	H	R	ER	BB	SO
1995—	Gulf Coast Rangers (GCL)	1	7	.125	2.21	12	11	0	0	0	53	38	22	13	28	46
1996—	Charleston, S.C. (S.Atl.)	8	6	.571	2.57	20	20	4	2	0	126	80	50	36	60	127
—	Charlotte (FSL)	2	2	.500	4.26	6	6	0	0	0	38	38	18	18	14	28
—	Tulsa (Texas)	1	0	1.000	0.77	2	2	0	0	0	11 2/3	5	1	1	8	7
1997—	Charlotte (FSL)	4	10	.286	4.87	24	23	3	0	0	133	146	91	72	62	83
—	Tulsa (Texas)	0	2	.000	4.76	2	2	0	0	0	11 1/3	7	7	6	11	6
1998—	Tulsa (Texas)	12	11	.522	4.82	28	28	2	0	0	162 1/3	187	104	87	76	83
—	Oklahoma (PCL)	0	0	...	0.00	1	0	0	0	0	1	1	0	0	1	0
1999—	Tulsa (Texas)	1	2	.333	2.79	7	7	1	1	0	38 2/3	38	16	12	18	32
—	Oklahoma (PCL)	5	3	.625	5.10	11	8	0	0	0	60	74	35	34	27	21
—	Texas (A.L.)	2	1	.667	4.65	16	0	0	0	0	31	33	18	16	15	15
2000—	Oklahoma (PCL)	4	1	.800	0.98	13	0	0	0	4	18 1/3	11	6	2	8	18
—	Texas (A.L.)	0	0	...	67.50	1	0	0	0	0	2/3	5	5	5	2	0
Major League totals (2 years)		2	1	.667	5.97	17	0	0	0	0	31 2/3	38	23	21	17	15

KONERKO, PAUL   1B   WHITE SOX

PERSONAL: Born March 5, 1976, in Providence, R.I. ... 6-3/211. ... Bats right, throws right. ... Full name: Paul Henry Konerko.
HIGH SCHOOL: Chaparral (Scottsdale, Ariz.).
TRANSACTIONS/CAREER NOTES: Selected by Los Angeles Dodgers organization in first round (13th pick overall) of free-agent draft (June 2, 1994). ... Traded by Dodgers with P Dennis Reyes to Cincinnati Reds for P Jeff Shaw (July 4, 1998). ... Traded by Reds to Chicago White Sox for OF Mike Cameron (November 11, 1998).
HONORS: Named Pacific Coast League Most Valuable Player (1997).
STATISTICAL NOTES: Led Northwest League with seven sacrifice flies in 1994. ... Led Pacific Coast League with 300 total bases and .621 slugging percentage in 1997. ... Career major league grand slams: 1.

Year	Team (League)	Pos.	G	AB	R	H	2B	3B	HR	RBI	Avg.	BB	SO	SB	PO	A	E	Avg.
								BATTING								FIELDING		
1994—	Yakima (N'West)	C-DH	67	257	25	74	15	2	6	*58	.288	36	52	1	271	33	5	.984
1995—	San Bern. (Calif.)	C-DH	118	448	7	124	21	1	19	77	.277	59	88	3	676	68	11	.985
1996—	San Antonio (Texas)	1B-DH	133	470	78	141	23	2	29	86	.300	72	85	1	1114	92	14	.989
—	Albuquerque (PCL)	1B	4	14	2	6	0	0	1	2	.429	1	2	0	30	0	0	1.000
1997—	Albuquerque (PCL)	3-1-DH-2	130	483	97	156	31	1	*37	*127	.323	64	61	2	257	216	24	.952
—	Los Angeles (N.L.)	1B-3B	6	7	0	1	0	0	0	0	.143	1	2	0	3	0	0	1.000
1998—	Los Angeles (N.L.)	1B-3B-OF-DH	49	144	14	31	1	0	4	16	.215	10	30	0	187	30	2	.991
—	Albuquerque (PCL)	OF-1B-3B	24	87	16	33	10	0	6	26	.379	11	12	0	61	3	3	.955
—	Cincinnati (N.L.)■	3B-1B-OF	26	73	7	16	3	0	3	13	.219	6	10	0	48	24	0	1.000
—	Indianapolis (I.L.)	3B	39	150	25	49	8	0	8	39	.327	19	18	1	21	68	4	.957
1999—	Chicago (A.L.)■	1B-DH-3B	142	513	71	151	31	4	24	81	.294	45	68	1	740	58	4	.995
2000—	Chicago (A.L.)	1B-DH-3B	143	524	84	156	31	1	21	97	.298	47	72	1	1053	74	11	.990
American League totals (2 years)			285	1037	155	307	62	5	45	178	.296	92	140	2	1793	132	15	.992
National League totals (2 years)			81	224	21	48	4	0	7	29	.214	17	42	0	238	54	2	.993
Major League totals (4 years)			366	1261	176	355	66	5	52	207	.282	109	182	2	2031	186	17	.992

DIVISION SERIES RECORD

Year	Team (League)	Pos.	G	AB	R	H	2B	3B	HR	RBI	Avg.	BB	SO	SB	PO	A	E	Avg.
								BATTING								FIELDING		
2000—	Chicago (A.L.)	1B-PH	3	9	1	0	0	0	0	0	.000	1	1	0	17	1	0	1.000

PERSONAL: Born June 28, 1973, in Anola, Man. ... 6-3/217. ... Bats left, throws right. ... Full name: Cordel Leonard Koskie.
HIGH SCHOOL: Springfield Collegiate (Oakbank, Man.).
JUNIOR COLLEGE: Des Moines (Iowa) Area Community College.
COLLEGE: Manitoba, then Kwantlen (B.C.).
TRANSACTIONS/CAREER NOTES: Selected by Minnesota Twins organization in 26th round of free-agent draft (June 2, 1994). ... On Fort Myers disabled list (May 10-28 and June 25-July 4, 1996).
STATISTICAL NOTES: Tied for Eastern League lead with 10 intentional bases on balls in 1997. ... Career major league grand slams: 1.

								BATTING								FIELDING		
Year	Team (League)	Pos.	G	AB	R	H	2B	3B	HR	RBI	Avg.	BB	SO	SB	PO	A	E	Avg.
1994—Elizabethton (Appl.)		3B	34	107	13	25	2	1	3	10	.234	18	27	0	23	84	8	.930
1995—Fort Wayne (Midw.)		3B	123	462	64	143	37	5	16	78	.310	38	79	2	80	244	36	.900
1996—Fort Myers (FSL)		3B	95	338	43	88	19	4	9	55	.260	40	76	1	62	176	19	.926
1997—New Britain (East.)		3B-DH	131	437	88	125	26	6	23	79	.286	90	106	9	72	234	22	.933
1998—Salt Lake (PCL)		3B-DH	135	505	91	152	32	5	26	105	.301	51	104	15	83	250	23	.935
—Minnesota (A.L.)		3B	11	29	2	4	0	0	1	2	.138	2	10	0	6	10	1	.941
1999—Minnesota (A.L.)		3B-OF-DH	117	342	42	106	21	0	11	58	.310	40	72	4	58	143	8	.962
2000—Minnesota (A.L.)		3B-DH	146	474	79	142	32	4	9	65	.300	77	104	5	96	241	12	.966
Major League totals (3 years)			274	845	123	252	53	4	21	125	.298	119	186	9	160	394	21	.963

PERSONAL: Born December 2, 1975, in Whittier, Calif. ... 6-0/190. ... Bats left, throws left. ... Full name: Mark Steven Kotsay.
HIGH SCHOOL: Santa Fe Springs (Calif.).
COLLEGE: Cal State Fullerton.
TRANSACTIONS/CAREER NOTES: Selected by Florida Marlins organization in first round (ninth pick overall) of free-agent draft (June 4, 1996).
HONORS: Named Golden Spikes Award winner by USA Baseball (1995). ... Named Most Outstanding Player of College World Series (1995).
STATISTICAL NOTES: Tied for Eastern League lead in double plays by outfielder with four in 1997. ... Tied for N.L. lead with 20 assists by outfielder in 1998. ... Led N.L. outfielders with 19 assists in 1999. ... Career major league grand slams: 2.
MISCELLANEOUS: Member of 1996 U.S. Olympic baseball team.

								BATTING								FIELDING		
Year	Team (League)	Pos.	G	AB	R	H	2B	3B	HR	RBI	Avg.	BB	SO	SB	PO	A	E	Avg.
1996—Kane County (Midw.)		OF	17	60	16	17	5	0	2	8	.283	16	8	3	37	2	0	1.000
1997—Portland (East.)		OF-DH	114	438	*103	134	27	2	20	77	.306	75	65	17	230	12	2	*.992
—Florida (N.L.)		OF	14	52	5	10	1	1	0	4	.192	4	7	3	31	2	0	1.000
1998—Florida (N.L.)		OF-1B	154	578	72	161	25	7	11	68	.279	34	61	10	350	‡21	6	.984
1999—Florida (N.L.)		OF-1B	148	495	57	134	23	9	8	50	.271	29	50	7	349	†27	5	.987
2000—Florida (N.L.)		OF-1B	152	530	87	158	31	5	12	57	.298	42	46	19	289	14	3	.990
Major League totals (4 years)			468	1655	221	463	80	22	31	179	.280	109	164	39	1019	64	14	.987

PERSONAL: Born August 26, 1964, in Greenbrae, Calif. ... 6-2/200. ... Bats both, throws right. ... Full name: Chad Michael Kreuter. ... Name pronounced CREW-ter.
HIGH SCHOOL: Redwood (Calif.).
COLLEGE: Pepperdine.
TRANSACTIONS/CAREER NOTES: Selected by Texas Rangers organization in fifth round of free-agent draft (June 3, 1985). ... Granted free agency (October 15, 1991). ... Signed by Detroit Tigers organization (January 2, 1992). ... Granted free agency (December 23, 1994). ... Signed by Seattle Mariners (April 8, 1995). ... On Seattle disabled list (June 19-July 6, 1995). ... On Tacoma disabled list (August 4-25, 1995). ... Granted free agency (October 16, 1995). ... Signed by Chicago White Sox organization (December 11, 1995). ... On disabled list (July 20, 1996-remainder of season). ... Granted free agency (October 14, 1996). ... Re-signed by White Sox organization (January 29, 1997). ... Traded by White Sox with OF Tony Phillips to Anaheim Angels for P Chuck McElroy and C Jorge Fabregas (May 18, 1997). ... Granted free agency (November 7, 1997). ... Signed by White Sox (December 10, 1997). ... Traded by White Sox to Angels for cash considerations (September 18, 1998). ... Granted free agency (October 26, 1998). ... Signed by Kansas City Royals (December 15, 1998). ... Granted free agency (October 29, 1999). ... Signed by Los Angeles Dodgers organization (January 20, 2000).
RECORDS: Shares major league single-game record for most sacrifice flies—3 (July 30, 1994). ... Shares major league record for most hits in one inning in first major league game—2 (September 14, 1988, fifth inning).
STATISTICAL NOTES: Led Carolina League catchers with 21 errors and 17 double plays and tied for lead with 113 assists in 1986. ... Tied for Texas League lead in double plays by catcher with nine in 1988. ... Led A.L. with 21 passed balls in 1989. ... Switch-hit home runs in one game (September 7, 1993). ... Career major league grand slams: 1.
MISCELLANEOUS: Batted righthanded only (1985 and 1990).

								BATTING								FIELDING		
Year	Team (League)	Pos.	G	AB	R	H	2B	3B	HR	RBI	Avg.	BB	SO	SB	PO	A	E	Avg.
1985—Burlington (Midw.)		C	69	199	25	53	9	0	4	26	.266	38	48	3	349	34	8	.980
1986—Salem (Caro.)		C-OF-3B	125	387	55	85	21	2	6	49	.220	67	82	5	613	†115	†21	.972
1987—Charlotte (FSL)		C-OF-3B	85	281	36	61	18	1	9	40	.217	31	32	1	380	54	8	.982
1988—Tulsa (Texas)		C	108	358	46	95	24	6	3	51	.265	55	66	2	603	71	•13	.981
—Texas (A.L.)		C	16	51	3	14	2	1	1	5	.275	7	13	0	93	8	1	.990
1989—Texas (A.L.)		C	87	158	16	24	3	0	5	9	.152	27	40	0	453	26	4	.992
—Oklahoma City (A.A.)		C	26	87	10	22	3	0	0	6	.253	13	11	1	146	14	2	.988
1990—Texas (A.L.)		C	22	22	2	1	1	0	0	2	.045	8	9	0	39	4	1	.977
—Oklahoma City (A.A.)		C	92	291	41	65	17	1	7	35	.223	52	80	0	559	64	10	.984
1991—Texas (A.L.)		C	3	4	0	0	0	0	0	0	.000	0	1	0	5	0	0	1.000
—Oklahoma City (A.A.)		C	24	70	14	19	6	0	1	12	.271	18	16	2	146	23	7	.960
—Tulsa (Texas)		C	42	128	23	30	5	1	2	10	.234	29	23	1	269	27	4	.987

Year	Team (League)	Pos.	G	AB	R	H	2B	3B	HR	RBI	Avg.	BB	SO	SB	PO	A	E	Avg.
1992—Detroit (A.L.)■		C-DH	67	190	22	48	9	0	2	16	.253	20	38	0	271	22	5	.983
1993—Detroit (A.L.)		C-DH-1B	119	374	59	107	23	3	15	51	.286	49	92	2	522	70	7	.988
1994—Detroit (A.L.)		C-1B-OF	65	170	17	38	8	0	1	19	.224	28	36	0	280	22	4	.987
1995—Seattle (A.L.)■		C	26	75	12	17	5	0	1	8	.227	5	22	0	151	12	4	.976
—Tacoma (PCL)		C-DH	15	48	6	14	5	0	1	11	.292	8	11	0	70	10	1	.988
1996—Chicago (A.L.)■		C-1B-DH	46	114	14	25	8	0	3	18	.219	13	29	0	182	12	2	.990
1997—Chicago (A.L.)		C-1B	19	37	6	8	2	1	1	3	.216	8	9	0	59	4	2	.969
—Anaheim (A.L.)■		C-DH	70	218	19	51	7	1	4	18	.234	21	57	0	431	29	3	.994
1998—Chicago (A.L.)		C	93	245	26	62	9	1	2	33	.253	32	45	1	424	35	7	.985
—Anaheim (A.L.)■		C	3	7	1	1	1	0	0	0	.143	1	4	0	14	1	2	.882
1999—Kansas City (A.L.)■		C-DH	107	324	31	73	15	0	5	35	.225	34	65	0	460	44	3	.994
2000—Los Angeles (N.L.)■		C	80	212	32	56	13	0	6	28	.264	54	48	1	483	35	3	.994
American League totals (12 years)			743	1989	228	469	93	7	40	217	.236	253	460	3	3384	289	45	.988
National League totals (1 year)			80	212	32	56	13	0	6	28	.264	54	48	1	483	35	3	.994
Major League totals (13 years)			823	2201	260	525	106	7	46	245	.239	307	508	4	3867	324	48	.989

LAMB, DAVID — SS/2B

PERSONAL: Born June 6, 1975, in West Hills, Cailf. ... 6-2/165. ... Bats both, throws right. ... Full name: David Christian Lamb.
HIGH SCHOOL: Newbury Park (Calif.).
TRANSACTIONS/CAREER NOTES: Selected by Baltimore Orioles organization in second round of free-agent draft (June 3, 1993). ... Selected by Tampa Bay Devil Rays from Orioles organization in Rule 5 major league draft (December 14, 1998). ... On Tampa Bay disabled list (August 14-September 1, 1999); included rehabilitation assignment to Durham (August 24-31). ... Claimed on waivers by New York Mets (February 7, 2000). ... Granted free agency (October 3, 2000).

Year	Team (League)	Pos.	G	AB	R	H	2B	3B	HR	RBI	Avg.	BB	SO	SB	PO	A	E	Avg.
1993—GC Orioles (GCL)		SS	16	56	4	10	1	0	0	6	.179	10	8	2	16	22	3	.927
1994—Albany (S.Atl.)		SS	92	308	37	74	9	2	0	29	.240	32	40	4	118	230	22	.941
1995—Bowie (East.)		SS	1	4	0	1	0	0	0	1	.250	0	1	0	1	3	1	.800
—Frederick (Caro.)		SS-2B	124	436	39	97	14	2	2	34	.222	38	81	6	151	348	24	.954
1996—High Desert (Calif.)		SS	116	460	63	118	24	3	3	55	.257	50	68	5	202	356	18	.969
1997—Frederick (Caro.)		2B-SS-3B	70	249	30	65	21	1	2	39	.261	25	32	3	119	183	9	.971
—Bowie (East.)		SS-3B-2B	73	269	46	89	20	2	4	38	.331	34	35	0	81	159	11	.956
1998—Bowie (East.)		SS	66	241	29	73	10	1	2	25	.303	27	33	1	73	171	14	.946
—Rochester (I.L.)		SS-3B-2B	48	178	24	53	7	1	1	16	.298	17	25	1	69	116	7	.964
1999—Tampa Bay (A.L.)■		SS-2B-DH	55	124	18	28	5	1	1	13	.226	10	18	0	58	100	9	.946
—Durham (I.L.)		SS-2B	7	30	7	7	3	0	0	7	.233	2	4	0	13	23	3	.923
2000—Norfolk (I.L.)■		SS-3B-2B	109	356	45	80	23	1	2	35	.225	40	49	8	138	246	9	.977
—New York (N.L.)		3B-2B-SS	7	5	1	1	0	0	0	0	.200	1	1	0	2	3	0	1.000
American League totals (1 year)			55	124	18	28	5	1	1	13	.226	10	18	0	58	100	9	.946
National League totals (1 year)			7	5	1	1	0	0	0	0	.200	1	1	0	2	3	0	1.000
Major League totals (2 years)			62	129	19	29	5	1	1	13	.225	11	19	0	60	103	9	.948

LAMB, MIKE — 3B — RANGERS

PERSONAL: Born August 9, 1975, in West Covina, Calif. ... 6-1/195. ... Bats left, throws right. ... Full name: Michael Robert Lamb.
HIGH SCHOOL: Bishop Amat (La Puente, Calif.).
COLLEGE: Cal State Fullerton.
TRANSACTIONS/CAREER NOTES: Selected by Texas Rangers organization in seventh round of free-agent draft (June 3, 1997).
STATISTICAL NOTES: Led Florida State League third basemen with 98 putouts, 304 assists, 432 total chances, 19 double plays and .931 fielding percentage in 1998.

Year	Team (League)	Pos.	G	AB	R	H	2B	3B	HR	RBI	Avg.	BB	SO	SB	PO	A	E	Avg.
1997—Pulaski (Appl.)		3B	60	233	59	78	19	3	9	47	.335	31	18	7	38	118	25	.862
1998—Charlotte (FSL)		3B-1B	135	536	83	162	35	3	9	93	.302	45	63	18	†124	†305	31	†.933
1999—Tulsa (Texas)		3B-C	137	*544	98	*176	*51	5	21	100	.324	53	65	4	90	284	28	.930
—Oklahoma (PCL)		3B	2	2	0	1	0	0	0	0	.500	1	0	0	0	0	0	...
2000—Oklahoma (PCL)		3B	14	55	8	14	5	1	2	5	.255	5	6	2	12	17	7	.806
—Texas (A.L.)		3B-DH	138	493	65	137	25	2	6	47	.278	34	60	0	118	230	33	.913
Major League totals (1 year)			138	493	65	137	25	2	6	47	.278	34	60	0	118	230	33	.913

LAMPKIN, TOM — C — MARINERS

PERSONAL: Born March 4, 1964, in Cincinnati. ... 5-11/195. ... Bats left, throws right. ... Full name: Thomas Michael Lampkin.
HIGH SCHOOL: Blanchet (Seattle).
JUNIOR COLLEGE: Edmonds College (Wash.).
COLLEGE: Portland.
TRANSACTIONS/CAREER NOTES: Selected by Cleveland Indians organization in 11th round of free-agent draft (June 2, 1986). ... On disabled list (July 6, 1989-remainder of season). ... Traded by Indians to San Diego Padres for OF Alex Cole (July 11, 1990). ... Traded by Padres to Milwaukee Brewers for cash (March 25, 1993). ... Granted free agency (December 20, 1993). ... Signed by San Francisco Giants organization (January 5, 1994). ... On San Francisco disabled list (March 31-April 24 and August 26, 1996-remainder of season); included rehabilitation assignment to San Jose (April 22-24). ... Traded by Giants to St. Louis Cardinals for a player to be named later or cash (December 19, 1996); Giants acquired P Rene Arocha to complete deal (February 12, 1997). ... Granted free agency (October 23, 1998). ... Signed by Seattle Mariners (December 14, 1998). ... On Seattle disabled list (March 25-April 13 and June 28, 2000-remainder of season); included rehabilitation assignment to Tacoma (April 8-13). ... Granted free agency (October 27, 2000). ... Re-signed by Mariners (December 22, 2000).
STATISTICAL NOTES: Led Pacific Coast League catchers with 11 double plays in 1992. ... Led Pacific Coast League catchers with 595 putouts in 1994. ... Career major league grand slams: 1.

Year Team (League)	Pos.	G	AB	R	H	2B	3B	HR	RBI	Avg.	BB	SO	SB	PO	A	E	Avg.
1986—Batavia (NY-Penn)	C	63	190	24	49	5	1	1	20	.258	31	14	4	323	36	8	.978
1987—Waterloo (Midw.)	C	118	398	49	106	19	2	7	55	.266	34	41	5	689	*100	15	.981
1988—Williamsport (East.) ...	C	80	263	38	71	10	0	3	23	.270	25	20	1	431	60	9	.982
— Colo. Springs (PCL) ...	C	34	107	14	30	5	0	0	7	.280	9	2	0	171	28	5	.975
— Cleveland (A.L.)..........	C	4	4	0	0	0	0	0	0	.000	1	0	0	3	0	0	1.000
1989—Colo. Springs (PCL) ...	C	63	209	26	67	10	3	4	32	.321	10	18	4	305	21	8	.976
1990—Colo. Springs (PCL) ...	C-2B	69	199	32	44	7	5	1	18	.221	19	19	7	312	36	12	.967
— San Diego (N.L.)■......	C	26	63	4	14	0	1	1	4	.222	4	9	0	91	10	3	.971
— Las Vegas (PCL)	C	1	2	0	1	0	0	0	0	.500	0	1	0	3	0	0	1.000
1991—San Diego (N.L.)	C	38	58	4	11	3	1	0	3	.190	3	9	0	49	5	0	1.000
— Las Vegas (PCL)	C-1B-OF	45	164	25	52	11	1	2	29	.317	10	19	2	211	26	6	.975
1992—Las Vegas (PCL)	C	108	340	45	104	17	4	3	48	.306	53	27	15	506	*64	12	.979
— San Diego (N.L.)	C-OF	9	17	3	4	0	0	0	0	.235	6	1	2	30	3	0	1.000
1993—New Orleans (A.A.)■...	C-OF	25	80	18	26	5	0	2	10	.325	18	4	5	152	12	3	.982
— Milwaukee (A.L.)	C-OF-DH	73	162	22	32	8	0	4	25	.198	20	26	7	242	24	6	.978
1994—Phoenix (PCL)■......	C-DH-OF	118	453	76	136	32	8	8	70	.300	42	49	8	†595	59	10	.985
1995—San Francisco (N.L.) ..	C-OF	65	76	8	21	2	0	1	9	.276	9	8	2	62	5	0	1.000
1996—San Jose (Calif.)..........	C	2	7	2	2	0	1	0	2	.286	1	2	0	10	1	0	1.000
— San Francisco (N.L.) ..	C	66	177	26	41	8	0	6	29	.232	20	22	1	342	27	3	.992
1997—St. Louis (N.L.)■.......	C	108	229	28	56	8	1	7	22	.245	28	30	2	413	37	5	.989
1998—St. Louis (N.L.)...........	C-OF-1B	93	216	25	50	12	1	6	28	.231	24	32	3	337	19	5	.986
1999—Seattle (A.L.)■...........	C-DH-OF	76	206	29	60	11	2	9	34	.291	13	32	1	292	27	5	.985
2000—Tacoma (PCL)	C	3	8	1	2	1	0	0	0	.250	3	2	0	12	2	0	1.000
— Seattle (A.L.)	C-DH	36	103	15	26	6	1	7	23	.252	9	17	0	138	13	2	.987
American League totals (4 years)		189	475	66	118	25	3	20	82	.248	43	75	8	675	64	13	.983
National League totals (7 years)		405	836	98	197	33	4	21	95	.236	94	111	10	1324	106	16	.989
Major League totals (11 years)		594	1311	164	315	58	7	41	177	.240	137	186	18	1999	170	29	.987

LANKFORD, RAY   OF   CARDINALS

PERSONAL: Born June 5, 1967, in Los Angeles, Calif. ... 5-11/200. ... Bats left, throws left. ... Full name: Raymond Lewis Lankford. ... Nephew of Carl Nichols, catcher with Baltimore Orioles (1986-88) and Houston Astros (1989-91).
HIGH SCHOOL: Grace Davis (Modesto, Calif.).
JUNIOR COLLEGE: Modesto (Calif.) Junior College.
TRANSACTIONS/CAREER NOTES: Selected by Chicago Cubs organization in third round of free-agent draft (January 14, 1986); did not sign. ... Selected by St. Louis Cardinals organization in third round of free-agent draft (June 2, 1987). ... On disabled list (June 24-July 9, 1993). ... On St. Louis disabled list (March 27-April 22, 1997); included rehabilitation assignment to Prince William (April 14-22). ... On disabled list (March 26-April 24, 1999).
RECORDS: Shares major league single-season record for fewest double plays by outfielder (150 or more games)—0 (1992).
HONORS: Named Texas League Most Valuable Player (1989).
STATISTICAL NOTES: Led Appalachian League outfielders with 155 total chances in 1987. ... Led Appalachian League in caught stealing with 11 in 1987. ... Led Midwest League with 242 total bases in 1988. ... Led Texas League outfielders with 387 total chances in 1989. ... Led American Association outfielders with 352 total chances in 1990. ... Tied for American Association lead with nine intentional bases on balls received in 1990. ... Hit for the cycle (September 15, 1991). ... Led N.L. in caught stealing with 42 in 1992. ... Career major league grand slams: 5.

Year Team (League)	Pos.	G	AB	R	H	2B	3B	HR	RBI	Avg.	BB	SO	SB	PO	A	E	Avg.
1987—Johnson City (Appl.) ..	OF	66	253	45	78	17	4	3	32	.308	19	43	14	*143	7	5	.968
1988—Springfield (Midw.)	OF	135	532	90	151	26	*16	11	66	.284	60	92	33	284	5	7	.976
1989—Arkansas (Texas)........	OF	*134	498	98	*158	28	*12	11	98	.317	65	57	38	*367	9	11	.972
1990—Louisville (A.A.)..........	OF	132	473	61	123	25	8	10	72	.260	72	81	30	*333	8	•11	.969
— St. Louis (N.L.).........	OF	39	126	12	36	10	1	3	12	.286	13	27	8	92	1	1	.989
1991—St. Louis (N.L.)...........	OF	151	566	83	142	23	*15	9	69	.251	41	114	44	367	7	6	.984
1992—St. Louis (N.L.)...........	OF	153	598	87	175	40	6	20	86	.293	72	*147	42	*438	5	2	.996
1993—St. Louis (N.L.)...........	OF	127	407	64	97	17	3	7	45	.238	81	111	14	312	6	7	.978
1994—St. Louis (N.L.)...........	OF	109	416	89	111	25	5	19	57	.267	58	113	11	260	5	6	.978
1995—St. Louis (N.L.)...........	OF	132	483	81	134	35	2	25	82	.277	63	110	24	300	7	3	.990
1996—St. Louis (N.L.)...........	OF	149	545	100	150	36	8	21	86	.275	79	133	35	356	9	1	*.997
1997—Prince Will. (Caro.).....	DH-OF	4	13	3	4	1	0	0	4	.308	4	5	1	6	0	0	1.000
— St. Louis (N.L.)..........	OF	133	465	94	137	36	3	31	98	.295	95	125	21	293	4	9	.971
1998—St. Louis (N.L.)..........	OF-DH	154	533	94	156	37	4	31	105	.293	86	151	26	338	7	5	.986
1999—St. Louis (N.L.)..........	OF-DH	122	422	77	129	32	1	15	63	.306	49	110	14	214	6	3	.987
2000—St. Louis (N.L.)..........	OF-DH	128	392	73	99	16	3	26	65	.253	70	148	5	179	4	5	.973
Major League totals (11 years)		1397	4953	854	1366	307	48	207	768	.276	707	1289	244	3149	61	48	.985

DIVISION SERIES RECORD

Year Team (League)	Pos.	G	AB	R	H	2B	3B	HR	RBI	Avg.	BB	SO	SB	PO	A	E	Avg.
1996—St. Louis (N.L.)..........	OF-PH	1	2	1	1	0	0	0	0	.500	1	0	0	4	0	0	1.000
2000—St. Louis (N.L.)..........	OF	3	10	2	2	1	0	0	3	.200	2	5	0	8	0	0	1.000
Division series totals (2 years)		4	12	3	3	1	0	0	3	.250	3	5	0	12	0	0	1.000

CHAMPIONSHIP SERIES RECORD

Year Team (League)	Pos.	G	AB	R	H	2B	3B	HR	RBI	Avg.	BB	SO	SB	PO	A	E	Avg.
1996—St. Louis (N.L.)..........	OF-PH	5	13	1	0	0	0	0	1	.000	1	4	0	7	0	0	1.000
2000—St. Louis (N.L.)..........	PH-OF	5	12	1	4	1	0	0	1	.333	1	5	0	10	1	0	1.000
Championship series totals (2 years)		10	25	2	4	1	0	0	2	.160	2	9	0	17	1	0	1.000

ALL-STAR GAME RECORD

Year League	Pos.	AB	R	H	2B	3B	HR	RBI	Avg.	BB	SO	SB	PO	A	E	Avg.
1997—National	OF	2	0	0	0	0	0	0	.000	1	1	0	0	0	0	...

PERSONAL: Born April 3, 1968, in Rawlins, Wyo. ... 6-0/195. ... Bats right, throws right. ... Full name: Michael Thomas Lansing.
HIGH SCHOOL: Natrona County (Casper, Wyo.).
COLLEGE: Wichita State.
TRANSACTIONS/CAREER NOTES: Selected by Baltimore Orioles organization in ninth round of free-agent draft (June 5, 1989); did not sign. ... Selected by Miami Miracle, independent, in sixth round of free-agent draft (June 4, 1990). ... On disabled list (April 29-May 9, 1991). ... Contract sold by Miami to Montreal Expos organization (September 18, 1991). ... On disabled list (May 31-June 15, 1995). ... Traded by Expos to Colorado Rockies for P Jake Westbrook, P John Nicholson and OF Mark Hamlin (November 18, 1997). ... On disabled list (May 21, 1999-remainder of season). ... Traded by Rockies with P Rolando Arrojo, P Rick Croushore and cash to Boston Red Sox for P Brian Rose, P John Wasdin, P Jeff Taglienti and 2B Jeff Frye (July 27, 2000).
RECORDS: Shares major league single-inning record for most home runs—2 (May 7, 1997, sixth inning).
STATISTICAL NOTES: Led Eastern League shortstops with 76 double plays in 1992. ... Hit three home runs in one game (September 22, 1998). ... Hit for the cycle (June 18, 2000). ... Career major league grand slams: 2.

							BATTING								FIELDING		
Year Team (League)	Pos.	G	AB	R	H	2B	3B	HR	RBI	Avg.	BB	SO	SB	PO	A	E	Avg.
1990—Miami (FSL)	SS	61	207	20	50	5	2	2	11	.242	29	35	15	104	166	10	.964
1991—Miami (FSL)	SS-2B	104	384	54	110	20	7	6	55	.286	40	75	29	148	273	27	.940
1992—Harrisburg (East.)■	SS	128	483	66	135	20	6	6	54	.280	52	64	46	189	*373	20	*.966
1993—Montreal (N.L.)	3B-SS-2B	141	491	64	141	29	1	3	45	.287	46	56	23	136	336	24	.952
1994—Montreal (N.L.)	2B-3B-SS	106	394	44	105	21	2	5	35	.266	30	37	12	164	283	10	.978
1995—Montreal (N.L.)	2B-SS	127	467	47	119	30	2	10	62	.255	28	65	27	306	373	6	.991
1996—Montreal (N.L.)	2B-SS	159	641	99	183	40	2	11	53	.285	44	85	23	349	395	11	.985
1997—Montreal (N.L.)	2B	144	572	86	161	45	2	20	70	.281	45	92	11	279	395	9	.987
1998—Colorado (N.L.)■	2B-3B	153	584	73	161	39	2	12	66	.276	39	88	10	345	425	10	.987
1999—Colorado (N.L.)	2B	35	145	24	45	9	0	4	15	.310	7	22	2	91	98	2	.990
2000—Colorado (N.L.)	2B	90	365	62	94	14	6	11	47	.258	31	49	8	175	221	7	.983
—Boston (A.L.)■	2B-3B	49	139	10	27	4	0	0	13	.194	7	26	0	73	106	0	1.000
American League totals (1 year)		49	139	10	27	4	0	0	13	.194	7	26	0	73	106	0	1.000
National League totals (8 years)		955	3659	499	1009	227	17	76	393	.276	270	494	116	1845	2526	79	.982
Major League totals (8 years)		1004	3798	509	1036	231	17	76	406	.273	277	520	116	1918	2632	79	.983

L

PERSONAL: Born July 15, 1978, in Santo Domingo, Dominican Republic. ... 6-4/185. ... Throws right, bats right. ... Full name: Nelson Rafael Lara.
HIGH SCHOOL: Colegio San Jose (Santo Domingo, Dominican Republic).
TRANSACTIONS/CAREER NOTES: Signed as non-drafted free agent by Florida Marlins organization (September 15, 1994). ... On Brevard County disabled list (August 7-September 5, 2000).

Year League	W	L	Pct.	ERA	G	GS	CG	ShO	Sv.	IP	H	R	ER	BB	SO
1995—Dom. Marlins (DSL)	0	3	.000	8.10	5	5	0	0	0	20	26	24	18	17	8
—Gulf Coast Marlins (GCL)	1	1	.500	3.74	11	0	0	0	1	21²/₃	21	13	9	11	9
1996—Gulf Coast Marlins (GCL)	1	2	.333	5.59	7	0	0	0	0	9²/₃	6	11	6	12	3
1997—Kane County (Midw.)	1	2	.333	3.99	29	0	0	0	3	38¹/₃	37	20	17	14	43
1998—Brevard County (FSL)	2	5	.286	9.42	19	4	0	0	0	28²/₃	27	36	30	33	32
—Kane County (Midw.)	2	2	.500	6.14	10	4	0	0	0	29¹/₃	29	23	20	23	21
1999—Kane County (Midw.)	3	2	.600	6.06	46	0	0	0	10	52	50	38	35	47	45
2000—Portland (East.)	1	1	.500	8.22	21	0	0	0	1	30²/₃	35	31	28	32	38
—Brevard County (FSL)	0	0	...	9.28	7	0	0	0	0	10²/₃	12	11	11	10	6

PERSONAL: Born June 27, 1974, in Chelan, Wash. ... 6-4/210. ... Throws right, bats right. ... Full name: Andrew Dane Larkin.
HIGH SCHOOL: South Medford (Medford, Ore).
TRANSACTIONS/CAREER NOTES: Selected by Florida Marlins organization in 25th round of free-agent draft (June 1, 1992). ... On disabled list (June 14-August 23, 1995). ... On Portland disabled list (April 4-May 11, 1996). ... On Florida disabled list (May 11-July 17, 1996); included rehabilitation assignment to Brevard County (June 18-July 17). ... On Calgary disabled list (April 8-July 22, 1999). ... Granted free agency (October 15, 1999). ... Signed by Chicago Cubs organization (December 17, 1999). ... Released by Cubs (February 14, 2000). ... Signed by Cincinnati Reds organization (February 16, 2000). ... Claimed on waivers by Kansas City Royals (July 19, 2000). ... Granted free agency (October 10, 2000).
STATISTICAL NOTES: Pitched 6-0 no-hit victory against Welland (July 25, 1993). ... Led New York-Pennsylvania League with 12 hit batsmen in 1993. ... Led Midwest League with 19 hit batsmen in 1994. ... Led International League with 15 hit batsmen in 1997.

Year League	W	L	Pct.	ERA	G	GS	CG	ShO	Sv.	IP	H	R	ER	BB	SO
1992—Gulf Coast Marlins (GCL)	1	2	.333	5.23	14	4	0	0	2	41¹/₃	41	26	24	19	20
1993—Elmira (NY-Penn)	5	7	.417	2.97	14	14	•4	•1	0	88	74	43	29	23	89
1994—Kane County (Midw.)	9	7	.563	2.83	21	21	3	1	0	140	125	53	44	27	125
1995—Portland (East.)	1	2	.333	3.38	9	9	0	0	0	40	29	16	15	11	23
1996—Brevard County (FSL)	0	4	.000	4.23	6	6	0	0	0	27²/₃	34	20	13	7	18
—Portland (East.)	4	1	.800	3.10	8	8	0	0	0	49¹/₃	45	18	17	10	40
—Florida (N.L.)	0	0	...	1.80	1	1	0	0	0	5	3	1	1	4	2
1997—Charlotte (I.L.)	6	11	.353	6.05	28	27	3	0	0	144¹/₃	166	109	97	76	103
1998—Charlotte (I.L.)	4	1	.800	6.37	11	10	0	0	0	53²/₃	55	39	38	32	41
—Florida (N.L.)	3	8	.273	9.64	17	14	0	0	0	74²/₃	101	87	80	55	43
1999—Brevard County (FSL)	0	1	.000	2.40	4	4	0	0	0	15	16	5	4	3	7
—Portland (East.)	1	1	.500	7.11	7	1	0	0	0	12²/₃	16	10	10	4	7
2000—Louisville (I.L.)■	1	0	1.000	2.59	27	0	0	0	4	41²/₃	30	13	12	17	40
—Cincinnati (N.L.)	0	0	...	5.40	3	0	0	0	0	6²/₃	6	4	4	5	7
—Kansas City (A.L.)■	0	3	.000	8.84	18	0	0	0	1	19¹/₃	29	20	19	11	17
A.L. totals (1 year)	0	3	.000	8.84	18	0	0	0	1	19¹/₃	29	20	19	11	17
N.L. totals (3 years)	3	8	.273	8.86	21	15	0	0	0	86¹/₃	110	92	85	64	52
Major League totals (3 years)	3	11	.214	8.86	39	15	0	0	1	105²/₃	139	112	104	75	69

PERSONAL: Born April 28, 1964, in Cincinnati. ... 6-0/185. ... Bats right, throws right. ... Full name: Barry Louis Larkin. ... Brother of Steve Larkin, outfielder/first baseman, Baltimore Orioles organization; and cousin of Nathan Davis, defensive tackle with Atlanta Falcons (1997) and Dallas Cowboys (1998-99).
HIGH SCHOOL: Moeller (Cincinnati).
COLLEGE: Michigan.
TRANSACTIONS/CAREER NOTES: Selected by Cincinnati Reds organization in second round of free-agent draft (June 7, 1982); did not sign. ... Selected by Reds organization in first round (fourth pick overall) of free-agent draft (June 3, 1985). ... On disabled list (April 13-May 2, 1987). ... On Cincinnati disabled list (July 11-September 1, 1989); included rehabilitation assignment to Nashville (August 27-September 1). ... On disabled list (May 18-June 4, 1991; April 19-May 8, 1992; and August 5, 1993-remainder of season). ... On disabled list (June 17-August 2 and September 1, 1997-remainder of season; March 12-April 7, 1998; and April 22-May 16, 2000). ... On disabled list (April 22-May 16, 2000).
RECORDS: Holds major league single-season record for fewest putouts by shortstop for leader—230 (1996). ... Shares major league record for most home runs in two consecutive games—5 (June 27 [2] and 28 [3], 1991).
HONORS: Named shortstop on The Sporting News college All-America team (1985). ... Named American Association Most Valuable Player (1986). ... Named shortstop on The Sporting News N.L. All-Star team (1988-92, 1994-96, 1998 and 1999). ... Named shortstop on The Sporting News N.L. Silver Slugger team (1988-92, 1995-96, 1998 and 1999). ... Won N.L. Gold Glove at shortstop (1994-96). ... Named N.L. Most Valuable Player by Baseball Writers' Association of America (1995).
STATISTICAL NOTES: Led American Association with .525 slugging percentage in 1986. ... Had 21-game hitting streak (September 10-October 2, 1988). ... Tied for N.L. lead in double plays by shortstop with 86 in 1990. ... Hit three home runs in one game (June 28, 1991). ... Had 16-game hitting streak (June 20-July 6, 1999).
MISCELLANEOUS: Member of 1984 U.S. Olympic baseball team.

								BATTING						FIELDING			
Year Team (League)	Pos.	G	AB	R	H	2B	3B	HR	RBI	Avg.	BB	SO	SB	PO	A	E	Avg.
1985—Vermont (East.)	SS	72	255	42	68	13	2	1	31	.267	23	21	12	110	166	17	.942
1986—Denver (A.A.)	SS-2B	103	413	67	136	31	10	10	51	.329	31	43	19	172	287	18	.962
—Cincinnati (N.L.)	SS-2B	41	159	27	45	4	3	3	19	.283	9	21	8	51	125	4	.978
1987—Cincinnati (N.L.)	SS	125	439	64	107	16	2	12	43	.244	36	52	21	168	358	19	.965
1988—Cincinnati (N.L.)	SS	151	588	91	174	32	5	12	56	.296	41	24	40	231	470	•29	.960
1989—Cincinnati (N.L.)	SS	97	325	47	111	14	4	4	36	.342	20	23	10	142	267	10	.976
—Nashville (A.A.)	SS	2	5	2	5	1	0	0	0	1.000	0	0	0	1	3	0	1.000
1990—Cincinnati (N.L.)	SS	158	614	85	185	25	6	7	67	.301	49	49	30	254	*469	17	.977
1991—Cincinnati (N.L.)	SS	123	464	88	140	27	4	20	69	.302	55	64	24	226	372	15	.976
1992—Cincinnati (N.L.)	SS	140	533	76	162	32	6	12	78	.304	63	58	15	233	408	11	.983
1993—Cincinnati (N.L.)	SS	100	384	57	121	20	3	8	51	.315	51	33	14	159	281	16	.965
1994—Cincinnati (N.L.)	SS	110	427	78	119	23	5	9	52	.279	64	58	26	*178	312	10	.980
1995—Cincinnati (N.L.)	SS	131	496	98	158	29	6	15	66	.319	61	49	51	192	341	11	.980
1996—Cincinnati (N.L.)	SS	152	517	117	154	32	4	33	89	.298	96	52	36	*230	426	17	.975
1997—Cincinnati (N.L.)	SS-DH	73	224	34	71	17	3	4	20	.317	47	24	14	77	171	5	.980
1998—Cincinnati (N.L.)	SS	145	538	93	166	34	10	17	72	.309	79	69	26	207	361	12	.979
1999—Cincinnati (N.L.)	SS	161	583	108	171	30	4	12	75	.293	93	57	30	220	401	14	.978
2000—Cincinnati (N.L.)	SS-DH	102	396	71	124	26	5	11	41	.313	48	31	14	153	249	11	.973
Major League totals (15 years)		1809	6687	1134	2008	361	70	179	834	.300	812	664	359	2721	5011	201	.975

DIVISION SERIES RECORD

								BATTING						FIELDING			
Year Team (League)	Pos.	G	AB	R	H	2B	3B	HR	RBI	Avg.	BB	SO	SB	PO	A	E	Avg.
1995—Cincinnati (N.L.)	SS	3	13	2	5	0	0	0	1	.385	1	2	4	3	8	0	1.000

CHAMPIONSHIP SERIES RECORD

								BATTING						FIELDING			
Year Team (League)	Pos.	G	AB	R	H	2B	3B	HR	RBI	Avg.	BB	SO	SB	PO	A	E	Avg.
1990—Cincinnati (N.L.)	SS	6	23	5	6	2	0	0	1	.261	3	1	3	21	15	1	.973
1995—Cincinnati (N.L.)	SS	4	18	1	7	2	1	0	0	.389	1	1	1	10	15	1	.962
Championship series totals (2 years)		10	41	6	13	4	1	0	1	.317	4	2	4	31	30	2	.968

WORLD SERIES RECORD

RECORDS: Shares single-inning record for most at-bats—2 (October 19, 1990, third inning).
NOTES: Member of World Series championship team (1990).

								BATTING						FIELDING			
Year Team (League)	Pos.	G	AB	R	H	2B	3B	HR	RBI	Avg.	BB	SO	SB	PO	A	E	Avg.
1990—Cincinnati (N.L.)	SS	4	17	3	6	1	1	0	1	.353	2	0	0	1	14	0	1.000

ALL-STAR GAME RECORD

						BATTING							FIELDING			
Year League	Pos.	AB	R	H	2B	3B	HR	RBI	Avg.	BB	SO	SB	PO	A	E	Avg.
1988—National	SS	2	0	0	0	0	0	0	.000	0	1	0	0	1	0	1.000
1989—National						Did not play.										
1990—National	PR-SS	0	0	0	0	0	0	0	...	0	0	1	1	2	0	1.000
1991—National	SS	1	0	0	0	0	0	0	.000	0	0	0	0	2	0	1.000
1993—National	SS	2	0	0	0	0	0	1	.000	0	1	0	2	1	0	1.000
1994—National						Selected, did not play—injured.										
1995—National	SS	3	0	0	0	0	0	0	.000	0	0	0	2	3	0	1.000
1996—National	SS	3	1	1	0	0	0	0	.333	0	0	0	0	2	0	1.000
1997—National						Selected, did not play—injured.										
1999—National	SS	3	0	1	0	0	0	1	.333	0	1	0	1	1	0	1.000
2000—National	SS	3	0	0	0	0	0	0	.000	0	0	0	0	2	1	.667
All-Star Game totals (8 years)		17	1	2	0	0	0	2	.118	0	3	1	6	14	1	.952

PERSONAL: Born May 24, 1976, in San Angelo, Texas. ... 6-0/210. ... Bats right, throws right. ... Full name: Brandon John Larson.
HIGH SCHOOL: Holmes (San Antonio, Texas).
JUNIOR COLLEGE: Blinn College (Texas).
COLLEGE: Louisiana State.
TRANSACTIONS/CAREER NOTES: Selected by Pittsburgh Pirates organization in 46th round of free-agent draft (June 2, 1994); did not sign. ... Selected by Pittsburgh Pirates organization in 38th round of free-agent draft (June 1, 1995); did not sign. ... Selected by San Francisco Giants organization in 44th round of free-agent draft (June 4, 1996); did not sign. ... Selected by Cincinnati Reds organization in first round (14th pick overall) of free-agent draft (June 3, 1997). ... On Chattanooga disabled list (July 3-18, 1999).

														BATTING					FIELDING		
Year	Team (League)	Pos.	G	AB	R	H	2B	3B	HR	RBI	Avg.	BB	SO	SB	PO	A	E	Avg.
1997—Chattanooga (Sou.)		SS	11	41	4	11	5	1	0	6	.268	1	10	0	19	22	5	.891
1998—Burlington (Midw.)		3B	18	68	5	15	3	0	2	9	.221	4	16	2	10	52	0	1.000
1999—Rockford (Midw.)		3B	69	250	38	75	18	1	13	52	.300	25	67	12	33	153	18	.912
—Chattanooga (Sou.)		3B	43	172	28	49	10	0	12	42	.285	10	51	4	22	93	15	.885
2000—Chattanooga (Sou.)		3B	111	427	61	116	26	0	20	64	.272	31	122	15	54	212	24	.917
—Louisville (I.L.)		3B	17	63	11	18	7	1	2	4	.286	4	16	0	6	46	4	.929

PERSONAL: Born March 19, 1974, in Houston. ... 5-11/200. ... Bats right, throws right. ... Full name: Michael Jason LaRue.
HIGH SCHOOL: Spring Valley (Spring Branch, Texas).
COLLEGE: Dallas Baptist.
TRANSACTIONS/CAREER NOTES: Selected by Cincinnati Reds organization in fifth round of free-agent draft (June 1, 1995). ... On disabled list (June 30-September 13, 1996).
STATISTICAL NOTES: Tied for Pioneer League lead in being hit by pitch with 12 in 1995. ... Led Pioneer League catchers with seven double plays in 1995. ... Led Southern League with .617 slugging percentage in 1998. ... Tied for Southern League lead with 21 passed balls in 1998.

														BATTING					FIELDING		
Year	Team (League)	Pos.	G	AB	R	H	2B	3B	HR	RBI	Avg.	BB	SO	SB	PO	A	E	Avg.
1995—Billings (Pio.)		C	58	183	35	50	8	1	5	31	.273	16	28	3	346	46	8	.980
1996—Char., W.Va. (SAL)		C-1B	37	123	17	26	8	0	2	14	.211	11	28	3	234	48	6	.979
1997—Char., W.Va. (SAL)		C-1B-3B-OF	132	473	78	149	*50	3	8	81	.315	47	90	14	711	84	19	.977
1998—Chattanooga (Sou.)		C-3B-1B	105	386	71	141	39	8	14	82	*.365	40	60	4	546	90	10	.985
—Indianapolis (I.L.)		C	15	51	5	12	4	0	0	5	.235	4	8	0	83	11	0	1.000
1999—Indianapolis (I.L.)		C-DH	70	263	42	66	12	2	12	37	.251	15	52	0	384	45	7	.984
—Cincinnati (N.L.)		C	36	90	12	19	7	0	3	10	.211	11	32	4	179	15	2	.990
2000—Louisville (I.L.)		C	82	307	54	78	22	1	14	48	.254	22	52	3	445	57	8	.984
—Cincinnati (N.L.)		C	31	98	12	23	3	0	5	12	.235	5	19	0	190	22	2	.991
Major League totals (2 years)			67	188	24	42	10	0	8	22	.223	16	51	4	369	37	4	.990

PERSONAL: Born November 3, 1971, in Gulfport, Miss. ... 5-10/186. ... Bats left, throws right. ... Full name: Matthew Lawton III. ... Brother of Marcus Lawton, outfielder with New York Yankees (1989).
HIGH SCHOOL: Harrison Central (Gulfport, Miss.).
JUNIOR COLLEGE: Gulf Coast Community College (Fla.).
TRANSACTIONS/CAREER NOTES: Selected by Minnesota Twins organization in 12th round of free-agent draft (June 3, 1991). ... On Minnesota disabled list (June 9-July 18, 1999); included rehabilitation assignments to Fort Myers (July 12-16) and Gulf Coast Twins (July 17-18).
STATISTICAL NOTES: Led Florida State League with .407 on-base percentage in 1994. ... Had 16-game hitting streak (April 13-30, 2000). ... Career major league grand slams: 3.

														BATTING					FIELDING		
Year	Team (League)	Pos.	G	AB	R	H	2B	3B	HR	RBI	Avg.	BB	SO	SB	PO	A	E	Avg.
1992—GC Twins (GCL)		2B	53	173	39	45	8	3	2	26	.260	27	27	20	129	142	12	.958
1993—Fort Wayne (Midw.)		OF	111	340	50	97	21	3	9	38	.285	65	42	23	65	6	3	.959
1994—Fort Myers (FSL)		OF	122	446	79	134	30	1	7	51	.300	80	64	42	188	13	6	.971
1995—New Britain (East.)		OF-DH	114	412	75	111	19	5	13	54	.269	56	70	26	221	12	2	*.991
—Minnesota (A.L.)		OF-DH	21	60	11	19	4	1	1	12	.317	7	11	1	34	1	1	.972
1996—Minnesota (A.L.)		OF-DH	79	252	34	65	7	1	6	42	.258	28	28	4	196	4	3	.985
—Salt Lake (PCL)		OF-DH	53	212	40	63	16	1	7	33	.297	26	34	2	88	0	6	.936
1997—Minnesota (A.L.)		OF	142	460	74	114	29	3	14	60	.248	76	81	7	278	9	7	.976
1998—Minnesota (A.L.)		OF	152	557	91	155	36	6	21	77	.278	86	64	16	398	12	4	.990
1999—Minnesota (A.L.)		OF-DH	118	406	58	105	18	0	7	54	.259	57	42	26	213	3	4	.982
—Fort Myers (FSL)		OF	4	14	3	8	1	0	0	2	.571	3	1	1	8	0	0	1.000
—GC Twins (GCL)		OF	1	4	0	1	0	0	0	1	.250	0	2	0	1	0	0	1.000
2000—Minnesota (A.L.)		OF-DH	156	561	84	171	44	2	13	88	.305	91	63	23	278	4	5	.983
Major League totals (6 years)			668	2296	352	629	138	13	62	333	.274	345	289	77	1397	33	24	.983

ALL-STAR GAME RECORD

								BATTING					FIELDING		
Year	League	Pos.	AB	R	H	2B	3B	HR	RBI	Avg.	BB	SO	SB	PO	A	E	Avg.
2000—American		OF	2	1	1	0	0	0	1	.500	0	0	1	0	0	0	...

LAXTON, BRETT — P — ATHLETICS

PERSONAL: Born October 5, 1973, in Stafford, N.J. ... 6-1/210. ... Throws right, bats left. ... Full name: Brett William Laxton. ... Son of Bill Laxton, pitcher with five major league teams (1970-71, 1974 and 1976-77).
HIGH SCHOOL: Audobon (N.J.).
COLLEGE: Louisiana State.
TRANSACTIONS/CAREER NOTES: Selected by San Diego Padres organization in fourth round of free-agent draft (June 1, 1992); did not sign. ... Selected by Oakland Athletics organization in 24th round of free-agent draft (June 4, 1996). ... Traded by A's to Kansas City Royals for 1B/OF Jeremy Giambi (February 18, 2000).

Year	League	W	L	Pct.	ERA	G	GS	CG	ShO	Sv.	IP	H	R	ER	BB	SO
1996—	Southern Oregon (N'West).	0	5	.000	7.71	13	8	0	0	0	32 2/3	39	34	28	26	38
1997—	Visalia (Calif.)	11	5	.688	2.99	29	22	0	0	0	138 2/3	141	62	46	50	121
1998—	Huntsville (Sou.)	11	4	.733	3.40	21	21	0	0	0	129 2/3	109	64	49	79	82
—	Edmonton (PCL)	2	4	.333	6.60	8	8	0	0	0	46 1/3	45	35	34	24	21
1999—	Vancouver (PCL)	13	8	.619	3.46	25	25	3	1	0	161 1/3	158	68	62	49	112
—	Oakland (A.L.)	0	1	.000	7.45	3	2	0	0	0	9 2/3	12	12	8	7	9
2000—	Omaha (PCL)■	5	9	.357	5.32	21	21	0	0	0	108 1/3	118	69	64	61	88
—	Kansas City (A.L.)	0	1	.000	8.10	6	1	0	0	0	16 2/3	23	15	15	10	14
Major League totals (2 years)		0	2	.000	7.86	9	3	0	0	0	26 1/3	35	27	23	17	23

LeCROY, MATT — C — TWINS

PERSONAL: Born December 13, 1975, in Belton, S.C. ... 6-2/225. ... Bats right, throws right. ... Full name: Matthew Hanks LeCroy.
HIGH SCHOOL: Belton-Honea Path (S.C.).
COLLEGE: Clemson.
TRANSACTIONS/CAREER NOTES: Selected by Minnesota Twins organization in supplemental round ("sandwich pick" between first and second round, 50th pick overall) of free-agent draft (June 3, 1997); pick received as compensation for failure to sign 1996 first-round pick Travis Lee. ... On Salt Lake disabled list (September 10, 1999-remainder of season).
MISCELLANEOUS: Member of 1996 U.S. Olympic baseball team.

									BATTING						FIELDING		
Year	Team (League)	Pos.	G	AB	R	H	2B	3B	HR	RBI	Avg.	BB	SO	SB	PO	A	E	Avg.
1998—	Fort Wayne (Midw.)	C	64	225	33	62	17	1	9	40	.276	34	45	0	344	35	1	.997
—	Fort Myers (FSL)	C	51	200	32	61	9	1	12	51	.305	21	35	2	309	28	3	.991
—	Salt Lake (PCL)	C	3	13	2	4	1	0	2	4	.308	0	7	0	6	0	0	1.000
1999—	Fort Myers (FSL)	C	89	333	54	93	20	1	20	69	.279	42	51	0	406	48	8	.983
—	Salt Lake (PCL)	C	29	119	23	36	4	1	10	30	.303	5	22	0	100	6	0	1.000
2000—	Minnesota (A.L.)	C-DH-1B	56	167	18	29	10	0	5	17	.174	17	38	0	330	16	4	.989
—	New Britain (East.)	C	54	195	33	55	12	1	10	38	.282	29	34	0	297	31	10	.970
—	Salt Lake (PCL)	C	16	65	15	20	5	0	5	15	.308	4	11	0	76	3	0	1.000
Major League totals (1 year)			56	167	18	29	10	0	5	17	.174	17	38	0	330	16	4	.989

LEDEE, RICKY — OF — RANGERS

PERSONAL: Born November 22, 1973, in Ponce, Puerto Rico. ... 6-1/200. ... Bats left, throws left. ... Full name: Ricardo Alberto Ledee. ... Name pronounced le-DAY.
HIGH SCHOOL: Colonel Nuestra Sonora de Valvanera (Coano, Puerto Rico).
TRANSACTIONS/CAREER NOTES: Selected by New York Yankees organization in 16th round of free-agent draft (June 3, 1990). ... On Tampa disabled list (April 6-May 27, 1996). ... On Columbus disabled list (May 5-16 and May 22-August 4, 1997; and May 25-June 3, 1999). ... Traded by Yankees with two players to be named later to Cleveland Indians for OF David Justice (June 29, 2000); Indians acquired P Jake Westbrook and P Zach Day to complete deal (July 24, 2000). ... Traded by Indians to Texas Rangers for 1B/DH David Segui (July 28, 2000).
STATISTICAL NOTES: Career major league grand slams: 2.

									BATTING						FIELDING		
Year	Team (League)	Pos.	G	AB	R	H	2B	3B	HR	RBI	Avg.	BB	SO	SB	PO	A	E	Avg.
1990—	GC Yankees (GCL)	OF	19	37	5	4	2	0	0	1	.108	6	18	2	18	1	0	1.000
1991—	GC Yankees (GCL)	OF	47	165	22	44	6	2	0	18	.267	22	40	3	79	6	6	.934
1992—	GC Yankees (GCL)	OF	52	179	25	41	9	2	2	23	.229	24	47	1	62	4	2	.971
1993—	Oneonta (NY-Penn)	OF	52	192	32	49	7	6	8	20	.255	25	46	7	91	6	3	.970
1994—	Greensboro (S.Atl.)	OF	134	484	87	121	23	9	22	71	.250	91	126	10	170	10	5	.973
1995—	Greensboro (S.Atl.)	OF	89	335	65	90	16	6	14	49	.269	51	66	10	160	7	3	.982
1996—	Norwich (East.)	OF	39	137	27	50	11	1	8	37	.365	16	25	2	48	2	1	.980
—	Columbus (I.L.)	OF	96	358	79	101	22	6	21	64	.282	44	95	6	97	3	5	.952
1997—	Columbus (I.L.)	OF-DH	43	170	38	52	12	1	10	39	.306	21	49	4	56	0	2	.966
—	GC Yankees (GCL)	DH-OF	7	21	3	7	1	0	0	2	.333	2	4	0	1	0	0	1.000
1998—	Columbus (I.L.)	OF-DH	96	360	70	102	21	1	19	41	.283	54	108	7	132	1	4	.971
—	New York (A.L.)	OF	42	79	13	19	5	2	1	12	.241	7	29	3	47	4	1	.981
1999—	New York (A.L.)	OF-DH	88	250	45	69	13	5	9	40	.276	28	73	4	143	3	9	.942
—	Columbus (I.L.)	OF	30	115	18	29	7	1	4	15	.252	17	29	4	59	2	3	.953
2000—	New York (A.L.)	OF-DH	62	191	23	46	11	1	7	31	.241	26	39	7	94	1	2	.979
—	Cleveland (A.L.)■	OF	17	63	13	14	2	1	2	8	.222	8	9	0	39	1	0	1.000
—	Texas (A.L.)■	OF	58	213	23	50	6	3	4	38	.235	25	50	6	128	0	3	.977
Major League totals (3 years)			267	796	117	198	37	12	23	129	.249	94	200	20	451	9	15	.968

DIVISION SERIES RECORD

									BATTING						FIELDING		
Year	Team (League)	Pos.	G	AB	R	H	2B	3B	HR	RBI	Avg.	BB	SO	SB	PO	A	E	Avg.
1998—	New York (A.L.)							Did not play.										
1999—	New York (A.L.)	OF	3	11	1	3	2	0	0	2	.273	1	5	0	6	0	0	1.000

RECORDS: Shares single-game record for most grand slams—1 (October 17, 1999). ... Shares single-inning record for most runs batted in—4 (October 17, 1999, ninth inning).

Year	Team (League)	Pos.	G	AB	R	H	2B	3B	HR	RBI	Avg.	BB	SO	SB	PO	A	E	Avg.
											BATTING					FIELDING		
1998—	New York (A.L.).........	PH-OF-PR-DH	3	5	0	0	0	0	0	0	.000	0	0	0	3	0	0	1.000
1999—	New York (A.L.).........	OF-PH-DH	3	8	2	2	0	0	1	4	.250	1	4	0	3	0	1	.750
	Championship series totals (2 years)		6	13	2	2	0	0	1	4	.154	1	4	0	6	0	1	.857

WORLD SERIES RECORD

NOTES: Member of World Series championship team (1998 and 1999).

Year	Team (League)	Pos.	G	AB	R	H	2B	3B	HR	RBI	Avg.	BB	SO	SB	PO	A	E	Avg.
											BATTING					FIELDING		
1998—	New York (A.L.).........	OF-PH	4	10	1	6	3	0	0	4	.600	2	1	0	8	0	0	1.000
1999—	New York (A.L.).........	OF	3	10	0	2	1	0	0	1	.200	1	4	0	1	0	0	1.000
	World Series totals (2 years)		7	20	1	8	4	0	0	5	.400	3	5	0	9	0	0	1.000

LEDESMA, AARON   IF

PERSONAL: Born June 3, 1971, in Union City, Calif. ... 6-2/200. ... Bats right, throws right. ... Full name: Aaron David Ledesma.
HIGH SCHOOL: James Logan (Union City, Calif.).
JUNIOR COLLEGE: Chabot College (Calif.).
TRANSACTIONS/CAREER NOTES: Selected by New York Mets organization in second round of free-agent draft (June 4, 1990). ... On disabled list (April 13-May 24, 1991 and July 19, 1993-remainder of season). ... On suspended list (July 29-31, 1994). ... Traded by Mets to California Angels for OF Kevin Flora (January 18, 1996). ... Granted free agency (October 15, 1996). ... Signed by Baltimore Orioles organization (January 17, 1997). ... Selected by Tampa Bay Devil Rays in third round (62nd pick overall) of expansion draft (November 18, 1997). ... On Tampa Bay disabled list (April 4-May 12, 1999; included rehabilitation assignments to St. Petersburg (May 7-10) and Durham (May 11-12). ... Traded by Devil Rays with P Rolando Arrojo to Colorado Rockies for 3B Vinny Castilla (December 13, 1999). ... Granted free agency (October 2, 2000).
STATISTICAL NOTES: Led Florida State League shortstops with 641 total chances and 79 double plays in 1992. ... Led International League shortstops with 68 double plays in 1994. ... Led Pacific Coast League in grounding into double plays with 18 in 1996.

Year	Team (League)	Pos.	G	AB	R	H	2B	3B	HR	RBI	Avg.	BB	SO	SB	PO	A	E	Avg.
											BATTING					FIELDING		
1990—	Kingsport (Appl.)........	SS	66	243	50	81	11	1	5	38	.333	30	28	27	78	*170	24	.912
1991—	Columbia (S.Atl.)........	SS	33	115	19	39	8	0	1	14	.339	8	16	3	44	64	10	.915
1992—	St. Lucie (FSL)	SS	134	456	51	120	17	2	2	50	.263	46	66	20	185	*411	45	.930
1993—	Binghamton (East.)	SS	66	206	23	55	12	0	5	22	.267	14	43	2	36	65	10	.910
1994—	Norfolk (I.L.).............	SS-DH	119	431	49	118	20	1	3	57	.274	28	41	18	157	347	26	*.951
1995—	Norfolk (I.L.)	3B-1B-SS	56	201	26	60	12	1	0	28	.299	10	22	6	73	94	10	.944
—	New York (N.L.)..........	3B-1B-SS	21	33	4	8	0	0	0	3	.242	6	7	0	5	12	2	.895
1996—	Vancouver (PCL)■.....	SS-3B-3B	109	440	60	134	27	4	1	51	.305	32	59	2	150	261	20	.954
1997—	Rochester (I.L.)■......	SS-DH-1B	85	326	40	106	26	1	3	43	.325	35	48	12	121	185	13	.959
—	Baltimore (A.L.)..........2B-3B-1B-SS		43	88	24	31	5	1	2	11	.352	13	9	1	68	52	3	.976
1998—	Tampa Bay (A.L.)■.....S-2-3-DH-1		95	299	30	97	16	3	0	29	.324	9	51	9	151	227	12	.969
1999—	St. Petersburg (FSL) ..	3B-SS	2	7	0	1	1	0	0	0	.143	1	1	0	3	4	1	.875
—	Durham (I.L.)	2B-SS	2	10	0	1	0	0	0	0	.100	0	1	0	7	10	1	.944
—	Tampa Bay (A.L.).......S-3-2-1-DH		93	294	32	78	15	0	0	30	.265	14	35	1	164	225	10	.975
2000—	Colorado (N.L.)■	3B-1B	32	40	4	9	2	0	0	3	.225	2	9	0	28	6	0	1.000
—	Colo. Springs (PCL) ...	3-2-O-S-1	59	224	31	77	9	1	0	37	.344	17	30	10	102	98	7	.966
	American League totals (3 years)		231	681	86	206	36	4	2	70	.302	36	95	11	383	504	25	.973
	National League totals (2 years)		53	73	8	17	2	0	0	6	.233	8	16	0	33	18	2	.962
	Major League totals (5 years)		284	754	94	223	38	4	2	76	.296	44	111	11	416	522	27	.972

LEE, CARLOS   OF   WHITE SOX

PERSONAL: Born June 20, 1976, in Aguadulce, Panama. ... 6-2/220. ... Bats right, throws right. ... Full name: Carlos Noriel Lee.
TRANSACTIONS/CAREER NOTES: Signed as non-drafted free agent by Chicago White Sox organization (February 8, 1994). ... On suspended list (April 28-May 1, 2000).
STATISTICAL NOTES: Led Southern League in grounding into double plays with 32 in 1998. ... Hit home run in first major league at-bat (May 7, 1999). ... Had 15-game hitting streak (August 23-September 6, 1999). ... Career major league grand slams: 2.

Year	Team (League)	Pos.	G	AB	R	H	2B	3B	HR	RBI	Avg.	BB	SO	SB	PO	A	E	Avg.
											BATTING					FIELDING		
1994—	Sarasota (GCL)..........	3B	29	56	6	7	1	0	0	1	.125	4	8	0	18	29	2	.959
1995—	Hickory (S.Atl.)..........	3B	63	218	18	54	9	1	4	30	.248	8	34	1	30	76	19	.848
—	Bristol (Appl.).............	3B-1B	*67	*269	43	*93	17	1	7	45	.346	8	34	17	84	107	18	.914
1996—	Hickory (S.Atl.)..........	3B-1B	119	480	65	150	23	6	8	70	.313	23	50	18	149	235	32	.923
1997—	Win.-Salem (Caro.)	3B-DH	*139	*546	81	*173	*50	4	17	82	.317	36	65	11	*93	233	34	.906
1998—	Birmingham (Sou.)......	3B-DH	138	*549	77	166	33	2	21	106	.302	39	55	11	*99	223	*35	.902
1999—	Charlotte (I.L.)...........3B-OF-1B-DH		25	94	16	33	5	0	4	20	.351	8	14	2	56	22	4	.951
—	Chicago (A.L.)..........	OF-DH-1B	127	492	66	144	32	2	16	84	.293	13	72	4	225	7	5	.979
2000—	Chicago (A.L.)	OF-DH	152	572	107	172	29	2	24	92	.301	38	94	13	273	10	3	.990
	Major League totals (2 years)		279	1064	173	316	61	4	40	176	.297	51	166	17	498	17	8	.985

DIVISION SERIES RECORD

Year	Team (League)	Pos.	G	AB	R	H	2B	3B	HR	RBI	Avg.	BB	SO	SB	PO	A	E	Avg.
											BATTING					FIELDING		
2000—	Chicago (A.L.)	OF	3	11	0	1	1	0	0	1	.091	0	2	0	6	0	0	1.000

LEE, DAVID   P   YANKEES

PERSONAL: Born March 12, 1973, in Pittsburgh. ... 6-1/202. ... Throws right, bats right. ... Full name: David Emmer Lee.
HIGH SCHOOL: Langley (Pittsburgh).
JUNIOR COLLEGE: Community College of Allegheny County-North Campus (Pa.).
COLLEGE: Mercyhurst College (Pa.).
TRANSACTIONS/CAREER NOTES: Selected by Colorado Rockies organization in 23rd round of free-agent draft (June 1, 1995). ... On Colorado Springs disabled list (July 13-22, 2000). ... Traded by Rockies to New York Yankees for P Jay Tessmer and SS Seth Taylor (January 3, 2001).

Year	League	W	L	Pct.	ERA	G	GS	CG	ShO	Sv.	IP	H	R	ER	BB	SO
1996—	Portland (N'West)	5	1	.833	0.78	17	0	0	0	7	23	13	3	2	16	24
—	Salem (Caro.)	0	2	.000	2.25	8	0	0	0	1	12	14	6	3	6	10
1997—	Asheville (S.Atl.)	4	8	.333	4.08	51	0	0	0	22	53	61	30	24	23	59
1998—	Salem (Caro.)	3	5	.375	3.77	54	0	0	0	25	57 1/3	57	26	24	15	54
1999—	Carolina (Sou.)	0	0	...	1.04	16	0	0	0	10	17 1/3	8	3	2	3	16
—	Colorado (N.L.)	3	2	.600	3.67	36	0	0	0	0	49	43	21	20	29	38
—	Colo. Springs (PCL)	0	0	...	0.00	6	0	0	0	3	5 2/3	0	0	0	1	7
2000—	Colorado (N.L.)	0	0	...	11.12	7	0	0	0	1	5 2/3	10	9	7	6	6
—	Colo. Springs (PCL)	2	3	.400	5.96	47	0	0	0	12	48 1/3	50	38	32	28	44
Major League totals (2 years)		**3**	**2**	**.600**	**4.45**	**43**	**0**	**0**	**0**	**1**	**54 2/3**	**53**	**30**	**27**	**35**	**44**

LEE, DERREK   1B   MARLINS

PERSONAL: Born September 6, 1975, in Sacramento. ... 6-5/225. ... Bats right, throws right. ... Full name: Derrek Leon Lee. ... Son of Leon Lee, infielder in St. Louis Cardinals organization (1969-71) and Lotte Orions (1978-82), Taiyo Whales (1983-85) and Yakult Swallows (1986-87) of Japan League; and nephew of Leron Lee, outfielder with four major league teams (1969-76) and Lotte Orions (1977-87) of Japan League.
HIGH SCHOOL: El Camino (Sacramento).
TRANSACTIONS/CAREER NOTES: Selected by San Diego Padres in first round (14th pick overall) of free-agent draft (June 2, 1994). ... Traded by Padres with P Rafael Medina and P Steve Hoff to Florida Marlins for P Kevin Brown (December 15, 1997).
RECORDS: Shares major league single-inning record for most assists by first baseman—3 (June 2, 1999, second inning).
HONORS: Named Southern League Most Valuable Player (1996).
STATISTICAL NOTES: Led Southern League with 285 total bases in 1996. ... Led Southern League first basemen 1,121 putouts in 1996. ... Led Pacific Coast League first basemen with 1,189 total chances and 108 double plays in 1997. ... Career major league grand slams: 3.

									BATTING							FIELDING		
Year	Team (League)	Pos.	G	AB	R	H	2B	3B	HR	RBI	Avg.	BB	SO	SB	PO	A	E	Avg.
1993—	Ariz. Padres (Ariz.)	1B	15	52	11	17	1	1	2	5	.327	6	7	4	115	14	2	.985
—	Rancho Cuca. (Calif.)	1B-DH	20	73	13	20	5	1	1	10	.274	10	20	0	115	6	5	.960
1994—	Rancho Cuca. (Calif.)	DH-1B	126	442	66	118	19	2	8	53	.267	42	95	18	289	27	4	.988
1995—	Rancho Cuca. (Calif.)	1B	128	502	82	151	25	2	23	95	.301	49	130	14	970	86	*18	.983
—	Memphis (Sou.)	1B	2	9	0	1	0	0	0	1	.111	0	2	0	16	3	0	1.000
1996—	Memphis (Sou.)	1B-DH-3B	134	500	98	140	39	2	34	*104	.280	65	*170	13	†1121	77	11	.991
1997—	Las Vegas (PCL)	1B	125	472	86	153	29	2	13	64	.324	60	116	17	*1069	*111	9	*.992
—	San Diego (N.L.)	1B	22	54	9	14	3	0	1	4	.259	9	24	0	131	13	0	1.000
1998—	Florida (N.L.)■	1B	141	454	62	106	29	1	17	74	.233	47	120	5	950	114	8	.993
1999—	Florida (N.L.)	1B	70	218	21	45	9	1	5	20	.206	17	70	2	463	47	3	.994
—	Calgary (PCL)	1B-DH	89	339	60	96	20	1	19	73	.283	30	90	3	718	68	14	.983
2000—	Florida (N.L.)	1B	158	477	70	134	18	3	28	70	.281	63	123	0	1101	102	8	.993
Major League totals (4 years)			**391**	**1203**	**162**	**299**	**59**	**6**	**51**	**168**	**.249**	**136**	**337**	**7**	**2645**	**276**	**19**	**.994**

LEE, SANG   P   RED SOX

PERSONAL: Born March 11, 1971, in Seoul, Korea. ... 6-1/190. ... Throws left, bats left. ... Full name: Sang-Hoon Lee.
COLLEGE: Korea University.
TRANSACTIONS/CAREER NOTES: Signed as non-drafted free agent by Boston Red Sox organization (December 23, 1999).

Year	League	W	L	Pct.	ERA	G	GS	CG	ShO	Sv.	IP	H	R	ER	BB	SO
1993—	LG Twins (Korean)	9	9	.500	3.75	28	...	7	...	0	151	129	...	63	78	131
1994—	LG Twins (Korean)	18	8	.692	2.46	27	...	8	...	0	190	140	...	52	64	148
1995—	LG Twins (Korean)	20	5	.800	2.01	30	...	12	...	0	228	150	...	51	51	142
1996—	LG Twins (Korean)	3	3	.500	2.55	41	...	0	...	10	99	10	...	28	42	95
1997—	LG Twins (Korean)	10	6	.625	2.12	57	...	0	...	37	85	56	...	20	27	103
1998—	Chunichi (Jap. Cen.)■	1	0	1.000	4.68	11	1	0	0	0	32 2/3	32	17	17	12	33
1999—	Chunichi (Jap. Cen.)	6	5	.545	2.84	36	11	2	0	3	95	75	30	30	30	65
2000—	Pawtucket (I.L.)■	5	2	.714	2.03	45	1	0	0	2	71	51	23	16	24	73
—	Boston (A.L.)	0	0	...	3.09	9	0	0	0	0	11 2/3	11	4	4	5	6
Major League totals (1 year)		**0**	**0**	**...**	**3.09**	**9**	**0**	**0**	**0**	**0**	**11 2/3**	**11**	**4**	**4**	**5**	**6**

LEE, TRAVIS   OF   PHILLIES

PERSONAL: Born May 26, 1975, in San Diego. ... 6-3/214. ... Bats left, throws left. ... Full name: Travis Reynolds Lee.
HIGH SCHOOL: Olympia (Wash.).
COLLEGE: San Diego State.
TRANSACTIONS/CAREER NOTES: Selected by Minnesota Twins organization in first round (second pick overall) of free-agent draft (June 4, 1996). ... Granted free agency (June 19, 1996). ... Signed by Arizona Diamondbacks organization (October 15, 1996). ... Loaned by Diamondbacks organization to Tucson, Milwaukee Brewers organization (June 5, 1997). ... Returned to Diamondbacks (March 30, 1998). ...

On disabled list (July 25-August 9, 1998; and August 16-September 9, 1999). ... On Arizona disabled list (May 25-June 9, 2000); included rehabilitation assignment to El Paso (June 5-9). ... Traded by Diamondbacks with P Vicente Padilla, P Omar Daal and P Nelson Figueroa to Philadelphia Phillies for P Curt Schilling (July 26, 2000).

HONORS: Named Golden Spikes Award winner by USA Baseball (1996).

STATISTICAL NOTES: Led N.L. first basemen with .997 fielding percentage in 1999. ... Career major league grand slams: 2.

MISCELLANEOUS: Member of 1996 U.S. Olympic baseball team.

								BATTING							FIELDING		
Year Team (League)	Pos.	G	AB	R	H	2B	3B	HR	RBI	Avg.	BB	SO	SB	PO	A	E	Avg.
1997— High Desert (Calif.).....	1B-DH	61	226	63	82	18	1	18	63	.363	47	36	5	553	67	1	.998
— Tucson (PCL)■..........	1B-DH-OF	59	227	42	68	16	2	14	46	.300	31	46	2	382	32	3	.993
1998— Arizona (N.L.)■..........	1B	146	562	71	151	20	2	22	72	.269	67	123	8	1269	100	3	.998
1999— Arizona (N.L.)............	1B-OF	120	375	57	89	16	2	9	50	.237	58	50	17	805	62	3	†.997
2000— Arizona (N.L.)............	OF-1B	72	224	34	52	13	0	8	40	.232	25	46	5	227	11	4	.983
— El Paso (Texas)..........	1B-OF	3	10	0	2	0	0	0	0	.200	2	1	0	15	1	0	1.000
— Tucson (PCL)	1B-OF	7	30	4	11	4	0	0	3	.367	1	6	1	44	3	0	1.000
— Philadelphia (N.L.)■ ..	1B-OF	56	180	19	43	11	1	1	14	.239	40	33	3	347	35	0	1.000
Major League totals (3 years)		394	1341	181	335	60	5	40	176	.250	190	252	33	2648	208	10	.997

LEITER, AL   P   METS

PERSONAL: Born October 23, 1965, in Toms River, N.J. ... 6-3/220. ... Throws left, bats left. ... Full name: Alois Terry Leiter. ... Brother of Mark Leiter, pitcher, New York Mets organization; and brother of Kurt Leiter, minor league pitcher (1982-84 and 1986). ... Name pronounced LIE-ter.

HIGH SCHOOL: Central Regional (Bayville, N.J.).

TRANSACTIONS/CAREER NOTES: Selected by New York Yankees organization in second round of free-agent draft (June 4, 1984). ... On New York disabled list (June 22-July 26, 1988); included rehabilitation assignment to Columbus (July 17-25). ... Traded by Yankees to Toronto Blue Jays for OF Jesse Barfield (April 30, 1989). ... On Toronto disabled list (May 11, 1989-remainder of season); included rehabilitation assignment to Dunedin (August 12-29). ... On Syracuse disabled list (May 20-June 13, 1990). ... On Toronto disabled list (April 27, 1991-remainder of season); included rehabilitation assignments to Dunedin (May 20-28 and July 19-August 7). ... On disabled list (April 24-May 9, 1993; and June 9-24, 1994). ... Granted free agency (November 6, 1995). ... Signed by Florida Marlins (December 14, 1995). ... On disabled list (May 1-20 and August 13-29, 1997). ... Traded by Marlins with 2B Ralph Milliard to New York Mets for P Jesus Sanchez, P A.J. Burnett and OF Robert Stratton (February 6, 1998). ... On disabled list (June 27-July 18, 1998).

HONORS: Named lefthanded pitcher on THE SPORTING NEWS N.L. All-Star team (1996).

STATISTICAL NOTES: Tied for A.L. lead with five balks in 1994. ... Led A.L. with 14 wild pitches in 1995. ... Pitched 11-0 no-hit victory against Colorado (May 11, 1996). ... Struck out 15 batters in one game (August 1, 1999).

Year League	W	L	Pct.	ERA	G	GS	CG	ShO	Sv.	IP	H	R	ER	BB	SO
1984— Oneonta (NY-Penn)	3	2	.600	3.63	10	10	0	0	0	57	52	32	23	26	48
1985— Oneonta (NY-Penn)	3	2	.600	2.37	6	6	2	0	0	38	27	14	10	25	34
— Fort Lauderdale (FSL)	1	6	.143	6.48	17	17	1	0	0	82	87	70	59	57	44
1986— Fort Lauderdale (FSL)	4	8	.333	4.05	22	21	1	1	0	117²/₃	96	64	53	90	101
1987— Columbus (I.L.)................	1	4	.200	6.17	5	5	0	0	0	23¹/₃	21	18	16	15	23
— Albany/Colonie (East.).......	3	3	.500	3.35	15	14	2	0	0	78	64	34	29	37	71
— New York (A.L.).................	2	2	.500	6.35	4	4	0	0	0	22²/₃	24	16	16	15	28
1988— New York (A.L.).................	4	4	.500	3.92	14	14	0	0	0	57¹/₃	49	27	25	33	60
— Columbus (I.L.)................	0	2	.000	3.46	4	4	0	0	0	13	5	7	5	14	12
1989— New York (A.L.).................	1	2	.333	6.07	4	4	0	0	0	26²/₃	23	20	18	21	22
— Toronto (A.L.)■.................	0	0	...	4.05	1	1	0	0	0	6²/₃	9	3	3	2	4
— Dunedin (FSL)	0	2	.000	5.63	3	3	0	0	0	8	11	5	5	5	4
1990— Dunedin (FSL)	0	0	...	2.63	6	6	0	0	0	24	18	8	7	12	14
— Syracuse (I.L.).................	3	8	.273	4.62	15	14	1	1	0	78	59	43	40	68	69
— Toronto (A.L.).................	0	0	...	0.00	4	0	0	0	0	6¹/₃	1	0	0	2	5
1991— Toronto (A.L.).................	0	0	...	27.00	3	0	0	0	0	1²/₃	3	5	5	5	1
— Dunedin (FSL)	0	0	...	1.86	4	3	0	0	0	9²/₃	5	2	2	7	5
1992— Syracuse (I.L.).................	8	9	.471	3.86	27	27	2	0	0	163¹/₃	159	82	70	64	108
— Toronto (A.L.).................	0	0	...	9.00	1	0	0	0	0	1	1	1	1	2	0
1993— Toronto (A.L.).................	9	6	.600	4.11	34	12	1	1	2	105	93	52	48	56	66
1994— Toronto (A.L.).................	6	7	.462	5.08	20	20	1	0	0	111²/₃	125	68	63	65	100
1995— Toronto (A.L.).................	11	11	.500	3.64	28	28	2	1	0	183	162	80	74	*108	153
1996— Florida (N.L.)■.................	16	12	.571	2.93	33	33	2	1	0	215¹/₃	153	74	70	*119	200
1997— Florida (N.L.).................	11	9	.550	4.34	27	27	0	0	0	151¹/₃	133	78	73	91	132
1998— New York (N.L.)■............	17	6	.739	2.47	28	28	4	2	0	193	151	55	53	71	174
1999— New York (N.L.)............	13	12	.520	4.23	32	32	1	1	0	213	209	107	100	93	162
2000— New York (N.L.)............	16	8	.667	3.20	31	31	2	1	0	208	176	84	74	76	200
A.L. totals (9 years)	33	32	.508	4.36	113	83	4	2	2	522	490	272	253	309	439
N.L. totals (5 years)	73	47	.608	3.40	151	151	9	5	0	980²/₃	822	398	370	450	868
Major League totals (14 years)	106	79	.573	3.73	264	234	13	7	2	1502²/₃	1312	670	623	759	1307

DIVISION SERIES RECORD

Year League	W	L	Pct.	ERA	G	GS	CG	ShO	Sv.	IP	H	R	ER	BB	SO
1997— Florida (N.L.)■.................	0	0	...	9.00	1	1	0	0	0	4	7	4	4	3	3
1999— New York (N.L.).................	0	0	...	3.52	1	1	0	0	0	7²/₃	3	3	3	3	4
2000— New York (N.L.).................	0	0	...	2.25	1	1	0	0	0	8	5	2	2	3	6
Division series totals (3 years)	0	0	...	4.12	3	3	0	0	0	19²/₃	15	9	9	9	13

CHAMPIONSHIP SERIES RECORD

Year League	W	L	Pct.	ERA	G	GS	CG	ShO	Sv.	IP	H	R	ER	BB	SO
1993— Toronto (A.L.).................	0	0	...	3.38	2	0	0	0	0	2²/₃	4	1	1	2	2
1997— Florida (N.L.).................	0	1	.000	4.32	2	1	0	0	0	8¹/₃	13	4	4	2	6
1999— New York (N.L.).................	0	1	.000	6.43	2	2	0	0	0	7	5	6	5	4	5
2000— New York (N.L.).................	0	0	...	3.86	1	1	0	0	0	7	8	3	3	0	9
Champ. series totals (4 years)	0	2	.000	4.68	7	4	0	0	0	25	30	14	13	8	22

WORLD SERIES RECORD

RECORDS: Shares single-inning record for most bases on balls allowed—4 (October 21, 1997, fourth inning).

NOTES: Member of World Series championship team (1993 and 1997).

Year	League	W	L	Pct.	ERA	G	GS	CG	ShO	Sv.	IP	H	R	ER	BB	SO
1993—	Toronto (A.L.)..................	1	0	1.000	7.71	3	0	0	0	0	7	12	6	6	2	5
1997—	Florida (N.L.)	0	0	...	5.06	2	2	0	0	0	$10^2/_3$	10	9	6	10	10
2000—	New York (N.L.)	0	1	.000	2.87	2	2	0	0	0	$15^2/_3$	12	6	5	6	16
World Series totals (3 years)		1	1	.500	4.59	7	4	0	0	0	$33^1/_3$	34	21	17	18	31

ALL-STAR GAME RECORD

Year	League	W	L	Pct.	ERA	GS	CG	ShO	Sv.	IP	H	R	ER	BB	SO
1996—	National	0	0	...	0.00	0	0	0	0	$^1/_3$	0	0	0	0	0
2000—	National	0	1	.000	9.00	0	0	0	0	1	2	2	1	1	1
All-Star Game totals (2 years)		0	1	.000	6.75	0	0	0	0	$1^1/_3$	2	2	1	1	1

LESHER, BRIAN   OF

PERSONAL: Born March 5, 1971, in Antwerp, Belgium. ... 6-5/216. ... Bats right, throws left. ... Full name: Brian Herbert Lesher.

HIGH SCHOOL: Newark (Del.).

COLLEGE: Delaware.

TRANSACTIONS/CAREER NOTES: Selected by Oakland Athletics organization in 25th round of free-agent draft (June 1, 1992). ... On Oakland disabled list (March 22-May 11, 1998); included rehabilitation assignment to Edmonton (May 2-11). ... On Modesto disabled list (August 5, 1999-remainder of season). ... Granted free agency (October 15, 1999). ... Signed by Seattle Mariners organization (January 14, 2000). ... Released by Mariners (November 16, 2000).

STATISTICAL NOTES: Led Pacific Coast League first basemen with 85 assists in 2000.

Year	Team (League)	Pos.	G	AB	R	H	2B	3B	HR	RBI	Avg.	BB	SO	SB	PO	A	E	Avg.
1992—	S. Oregon (N'West)	OF-1B	46	136	21	26	7	1	3	18	.191	12	35	3	63	3	4	.943
1993—	Madison (Midw.)	OF	119	394	63	108	13	5	5	47	.274	46	102	20	193	9	5	.976
1994—	Modesto (Calif.)	OF-1B	117	393	76	114	21	0	14	68	.290	81	84	11	332	20	11	.970
1995—	Huntsville (Sou.)	OF-1B	127	471	78	123	23	2	19	71	.261	64	110	7	198	7	6	.972
1996—	Edmonton (PCL)	1B-OF-DH	109	414	57	119	29	2	18	75	.287	36	108	6	699	44	9	.988
	— Oakland (A.L.)	OF-1B	26	82	11	19	3	0	5	16	.232	5	17	0	46	2	1	.980
1997—	Edmonton (PCL)	OF-1B-DH	110	415	85	134	27	5	21	78	.323	64	86	14	220	6	6	.974
	— Oakland (A.L.)	OF-DH-1B	46	131	17	30	4	1	4	16	.229	9	30	4	87	5	3	.968
1998—	Edmonton (PCL)	OF-1B-DH	99	360	62	108	31	1	11	60	.300	46	96	3	224	6	5	.979
	— Oakland (A.L.)	OF-1B	7	7	0	1	1	0	0	1	.143	0	3	0	4	2	1	.857
1999—	Vancouver (PCL)	1B-OF-DH	103	387	66	113	29	2	14	64	.292	41	71	8	599	37	4	.994
2000—	Tacoma (PCL)■	1B-OF	132	489	77	141	33	3	25	92	.288	70	104	4	1019	85	6	.995
	— Seattle (A.L.)	1B-DH	5	5	1	4	1	0	3	3	.800	1	0	1	4	1	0	1.000
Major League totals (4 years)			84	225	29	54	9	2	9	36	.240	15	50	5	141	10	5	.968

LESKANIC, CURTIS   P   BREWERS

PERSONAL: Born April 2, 1968, in Homestead, Pa. ... 6-0/186. ... Throws right, bats right. ... Full name: Curtis John Leskanic. ... Name pronounced less-CAN-ik.

HIGH SCHOOL: Steel Valley (Munhall, Pa.).

COLLEGE: Louisiana State.

TRANSACTIONS/CAREER NOTES: Selected by Cleveland Indians organization in eighth round of free-agent draft (June 5, 1989). ... On disabled list (April 23-June 25, 1990). ... Traded by Indians with P Oscar Munoz to Minnesota Twins for 1B Paul Sorrento (March 28, 1992). ... Selected by Colorado Rockies in third round (66th pick overall) of expansion draft (November 17, 1992). ... Loaned by Rockies organization to Wichita, San Diego Padres organization (April 7-May 20, 1993). ... On Colorado disabled list (May 30-June 28, 1996); included rehabilitation assignment to Colorado Springs (June 22-27). ... On Colorado disabled list (March 23-April 12, 1997); included rehabilitation assignment to Salem (April 6-8). ... Traded by Rockies to Milwaukee Brewers for P Mike Myers (November 17, 1999). ... On disabled list (May 17-30, 2000).

MISCELLANEOUS: Had a sacrifice hit in only appearance as pinch hitter (1998). ... Holds Colorado Rockies all-time record for most games pitched (356).

Year	League	W	L	Pct.	ERA	G	GS	CG	ShO	Sv.	IP	H	R	ER	BB	SO
1990—	Kinston (Caro.)	6	5	.545	3.68	14	14	2	0	0	$73^1/_3$	61	34	30	30	71
1991—	Kinston (Caro.)	•15	8	.652	2.79	28	28	0	0	0	$174^1/_3$	143	63	54	91	*163
1992—	Orlando (Sou.)■	9	11	.450	4.30	26	23	3	0	0	$152^2/_3$	158	84	73	64	126
	— Portland (PCL)	1	2	.333	9.98	5	3	0	0	0	$15^1/_3$	16	17	17	8	14
1993—	Wichita (Texas)■	3	2	.600	3.45	7	7	0	0	0	$44^1/_3$	37	20	17	17	42
	— Colorado Springs (PCL)■..	4	3	.571	4.47	9	7	1	1	0	$44^1/_3$	39	24	22	26	38
	— Colorado (N.L.)	1	5	.167	5.37	18	8	0	0	0	57	59	40	34	27	30
1994—	Colorado Springs (PCL)	5	7	.417	3.31	21	21	2	0	0	$130^1/_3$	129	60	48	54	98
	— Colorado (N.L.)	1	1	.500	5.64	8	3	0	0	0	$22^1/_3$	27	14	14	10	17
1995—	Colorado (N.L.)	6	3	.667	3.40	*76	0	0	0	10	98	83	38	37	33	107
1996—	Colorado (N.L.)	7	5	.583	6.23	70	0	0	0	6	$73^2/_3$	82	51	51	38	76
	— Colorado Springs (PCL)	0	0	...	3.00	3	0	0	0	0	3	5	1	1	1	2
1997—	Salem (Caro.)	0	0	...	3.86	2	1	0	0	0	$2^1/_3$	5	2	1	1	3
	— Colorado (N.L.)	4	0	1.000	5.55	55	0	0	0	2	$58^1/_3$	59	36	36	24	53
	— Colorado Springs (PCL)	0	0	...	3.79	10	3	0	0	2	19	11	9	8	18	20
1998—	Colorado (N.L.)	6	4	.600	4.40	66	0	0	0	2	$75^2/_3$	75	37	37	40	55
1999—	Colorado (N.L.)	6	2	.750	5.08	63	0	0	0	0	85	87	54	48	49	77
2000—	Milwaukee (N.L.)■	9	3	.750	2.56	73	0	0	0	12	$77^1/_3$	58	23	22	51	75
Major League totals (8 years)		40	23	.635	4.59	429	11	0	0	32	$547^1/_3$	530	293	279	272	490

DIVISION SERIES RECORD

Year	League	W	L	Pct.	ERA	G	GS	CG	ShO	Sv.	IP	H	R	ER	BB	SO
1995—	Colorado (N.L.)	0	1	.000	6.00	3	0	0	0	0	3	3	2	2	0	4

PERSONAL: Born May 22, 1968, in Park Ridge, Ill. ... 6-3/198. ... Throws right, bats right. ... Full name: Alan Brian Levine.
HIGH SCHOOL: Hoffman Estates (Ill.).
JUNIOR COLLEGE: Harper Junior College (Ill.).
COLLEGE: Southern Illinois-Carbondale.
TRANSACTIONS/CAREER NOTES: Selected by Chicago White Sox in 11th round of free-agent draft (June 3, 1991). ... Traded by White Sox with P Larry Thomas to Texas Rangers for SS Benji Gil (December 19, 1997). ... Claimed on waivers by Anaheim Angels (April 2, 1999). ... On Anaheim disabled list (July 31-August 19, 2000); included rehabilitation assignment to Erie (August 17).

Year League	W	L	Pct.	ERA	G	GS	CG	ShO	Sv.	IP	H	R	ER	BB	SO
1991—Utica (NY-Penn)	6	4	.600	3.18	16	12	2	1	1	85	75	45	30	26	83
1992—South Bend (Midw.)	9	5	.643	2.81	23	23	2	0	0	156 2/3	151	67	49	36	131
—Sarasota (FSL)	0	2	.000	4.02	3	2	0	0	0	15 2/3	17	11	7	5	11
1993—Sarasota (FSL)	11	8	.579	3.68	27	26	5	1	0	161 1/3	169	87	66	50	*129
1994—Birmingham (Sou.)	5	9	.357	3.31	18	18	1	0	0	114 1/3	117	50	42	44	94
—Nashville (A.A.)	0	2	.000	7.88	8	4	0	0	0	24	34	23	21	11	24
1995—Nashville (A.A.)	0	2	.000	5.14	3	3	0	0	0	14	20	10	8	7	14
—Birmingham (Sou.)	4	3	.571	2.34	43	1	0	0	7	73	61	22	19	25	68
1996—Nashville (A.A.)	4	5	.444	3.65	43	0	0	0	12	61 2/3	58	27	25	24	45
—Chicago (A.L.)	0	1	.000	5.40	16	0	0	0	0	18 1/3	22	14	11	7	12
1997—Chicago (A.L.)	2	2	.500	6.91	25	0	0	0	0	27 1/3	35	22	21	16	22
—Nashville (A.A.)	1	1	.500	7.13	26	0	0	0	2	35 1/3	58	32	28	11	29
1998—Oklahoma (PCL)■	1	3	.250	4.72	12	7	0	0	1	53 1/3	51	33	28	17	30
—Texas (A.L.)	0	1	.000	4.50	30	0	0	0	0	58	68	30	29	16	19
1999—Anaheim (A.L.)■	1	1	.500	3.39	50	1	0	0	0	85	76	40	32	29	37
2000—Anaheim (A.L.)	3	4	.429	3.87	51	5	0	0	2	95 1/3	98	44	41	49	42
—Erie (East.)	0	0	...	0.00	1	1	0	0	0	2	3	2	0	0	0
Major League totals (5 years)	6	9	.400	4.25	172	6	0	0	2	284	299	150	134	117	132

PERSONAL: Born April 14, 1968, in Philadelphia. ... 5-9/200. ... Bats left, throws right.
HIGH SCHOOL: Northeast (Philadelphia).
COLLEGE: North Carolina.
TRANSACTIONS/CAREER NOTES: Selected by Philadelphia Phillies organization in 36th round of free-agent draft (June 2, 1986); did not sign. ... Selected by Cleveland Indians organization in fourth round of free-agent draft (June 5, 1989). ... Traded by Indians to Milwaukee Brewers for P Scott Nate and a player to be named later (April 4, 1996); Indians acquired P Jared Camp to complete deal (June 9, 1996). ... On disabled list (May 8, 1998-remainder of season). ... Released by Brewers (September 29, 1998). ... Signed by Tampa Bay Devil Rays organization (December 18, 1998). ... On Durham disabled list (April 8-May 8, 1999). ... Released by Devil Rays (July 28, 1999). ... Signed by Indians (July 30, 1999). ... Granted free agency (October 4, 1999). ... Re-signed by Indians organization (January 13, 2000). ... On Buffalo disabled list (May 4-13, 2000). ... Granted free agency (October 18, 2000). ... Signed by Atlanta Braves organization (November 16, 2000).
STATISTICAL NOTES: Led Eastern League catchers with 733 total chances in 1991.

Year Team (League)	Pos.	G	AB	R	H	2B	3B	HR	RBI	Avg.	BB	SO	SB	PO	A	E	Avg.
1989—Burlington (Appl.)	C	27	93	11	32	4	0	4	16	.344	10	7	1	189	27	2	.991
—Kinston (Caro.)	C	27	87	11	26	6	0	2	11	.299	12	15	1	95	17	2	.982
—Colo. Springs (PCL)	PH	1	1	0	0	0	0	0	0	.000	0	0	0	...	...	...	...
1990—Kinston (Caro.)	C	107	382	63	113	18	3	7	64	.296	64	42	4	517	63	5	.991
1991—Canton/Akron (East.)	C	115	382	31	101	17	3	6	45	.264	40	36	2	*644	*77	12	.984
1992—Colo. Springs (PCL)	C	87	253	39	92	20	1	6	44	.364	37	25	1	375	47	4	.991
—Cleveland (A.L.)	C-DH	28	43	2	12	4	0	1	3	.279	0	5	0	59	5	1	.985
1993—Charlotte (I.L.)	C	47	129	10	32	6	1	2	20	.248	15	12	0	266	22	4	.986
—Cleveland (A.L.)	C	31	63	7	11	2	0	0	4	.175	2	10	0	109	7	1	.991
1994—Charlotte (I.L.)	C-DH	111	375	55	107	20	0	10	59	.285	55	39	2	452	34	4	.992
—Cleveland (A.L.)	PH	1	1	0	1	0	0	0	0	1.000	0	0	0	...	...	...	...
1995—Buffalo (A.A.)	C-DH	66	196	26	61	16	0	4	20	.311	32	11	0	338	20	2	.994
—Cleveland (A.L.)	C	12	18	1	6	2	0	0	3	.333	1	0	0	33	5	0	1.000
1996—Milwaukee (A.L.)■	C-DH	104	233	27	55	6	1	1	21	.236	38	15	0	373	26	1	*.998
1997—Milwaukee (A.L.)	C-DH	99	200	19	57	7	0	1	19	.285	24	17	1	296	19	2	.994
1998—Milwaukee (N.L.)	C	22	37	4	13	0	0	0	4	.351	7	6	1	83	2	0	1.000
1999—Durham (I.L.)■	C-DH	27	94	20	31	5	0	1	8	.330	15	9	0	142	9	0	1.000
—Orlando (Sou.)	C-DH	13	48	6	19	7	0	1	11	.396	6	4	0	52	4	1	.982
—Cleveland (A.L.)■	C	10	26	0	4	0	0	0	3	.154	1	6	0	53	3	0	1.000
2000—Buffalo (I.L.)	C	53	168	17	48	8	0	3	21	.286	17	12	0	286	20	1	.997
American League totals (7 years)		285	584	56	146	21	1	3	53	.250	66	53	1	923	65	5	.995
National League totals (1 year)		22	37	4	13	0	0	0	4	.351	7	6	1	83	2	0	1.000
Major League totals (8 years)		307	621	60	159	21	1	3	57	.256	73	59	2	1006	67	5	.995

(Table columns grouped under **BATTING** through Avg./SB and **FIELDING** for PO, A, E, Avg.)

PERSONAL: Born August 15, 1977, in Fall River, Mass. ... 6-3/230. ... Throws right, bats right. ... Full name: Allen Harry Levrault.
HIGH SCHOOL: Westport (Mass.).
JUNIOR COLLEGE: Community College of Rhode Island.
TRANSACTIONS/CAREER NOTES: Selected by Milwaukee Brewers organization in 13th round of free-agent draft (June 4, 1996). ... On Huntsville disabled list (June 20-July 10 and August 1-17, 1999). ... On Indianapolis disabled list (April 27-May 12 and September 12-19, 2000).
STATISTICAL NOTES: Led Midwest League with 12 balks in 1997.

Year League	W	L	Pct.	ERA	G	GS	CG	ShO	Sv.	IP	H	R	ER	BB	SO
1996—Helena (Pio.)	4	3	.571	5.32	18	11	0	0	1	71	70	43	42	22	68
1997—Beloit (Midw.)	3	10	.231	5.28	24	24	1	0	0	131 1/3	141	89	77	40	112
1998—Stockton (Calif.)	9	3	.750	2.87	16	15	*4	•1	0	97 1/3	76	33	31	27	86
—El Paso (Texas)	1	5	.167	5.89	11	11	0	0	0	62 2/3	77	51	41	17	46
1999—Huntsville (Sou.)	9	2	*.818	3.43	16	16	2	1	0	99 2/3	77	44	38	33	82
—Louisville (I.L.)	1	3	.250	8.65	9	5	0	0	0	34 1/3	48	37	33	16	33
2000—Indianapolis (I.L.)	6	8	.429	4.24	21	18	1	0	0	108 1/3	98	55	51	46	78
—Milwaukee (N.L.)	0	1	.000	4.50	5	1	0	0	0	12	10	7	6	7	9
Major League totals (1 year)	0	1	.000	4.50	5	1	0	0	0	12	10	7	6	7	9

LEWIS, DARREN   OF   RED SOX

PERSONAL: Born August 28, 1967, in Berkeley, Calif. ... 6-0/190. ... Bats right, throws right. ... Full name: Darren Joel Lewis.

HIGH SCHOOL: Moreau (Hayward, Calif.).

JUNIOR COLLEGE: Chabot College (Calif.).

COLLEGE: California.

TRANSACTIONS/CAREER NOTES: Selected by Los Angeles Dodgers organization in sixth round of free-agent draft (January 14, 1986); did not sign. ... Selected by Toronto Blue Jays organization in 45th round of free-agent draft (June 2, 1987); did not sign. ... Selected by Oakland Athletics organization in 18th round of free-agent draft (June 1, 1988). ... Traded by A's with a player to be named later to San Francisco Giants for IF Ernest Riles (December 4, 1990); Giants acquired P Pedro Pena to complete deal (December 17, 1990). ... On disabled list (August 20-September 4, 1993). ... Traded by Giants with P Mark Portugal and P Dave Burba to Cincinnati Reds for OF Deion Sanders, P John Roper, P Ricky Pickett, P Scott Service and IF Dave McCarty (July 21, 1995). ... Released by Reds (December 1, 1995). ... Signed by Chicago White Sox (December 14, 1995). ... Traded by White Sox to Dodgers for a player to be named later (August 27, 1997); White Sox acquired IF Chad Fonville to complete deal (September 2, 1997). ... Granted free agency (October 27, 1997). ... Signed by Boston Red Sox (December 23, 1997). ... Granted free agency (November 3, 1998). ... Re-signed by Red Sox (November 5, 1998). ... On Boston disabled list (July 1-14, 2000); included rehabilitation assignment to Gulf Coast Red Sox (July 11-13).

RECORDS: Holds major league records for most consecutive errorless games by outfielder—392 (August 21, 1990-June 29, 1994); and most consecutive chances accepted without an error by outfielder—938 (August 21, 1990-June 29, 1994). ... Shares major league career record for highest fielding average by outfielder (1,000 or more games)—.995. ... Shares major league record for fewest double plays by outfielder (150 or more games)—0 (1998). ... Holds N.L. records for most consecutive errorless games by outfielder—369 (July 13, 1991-June 29, 1994); and most consecutive chances accepted without an error by outfielder—905 (July 13, 1991-June 29, 1994).

HONORS: Won N.L. Gold Glove as outfielder (1994).

STATISTICAL NOTES: Led California League outfielders with 324 total chances in 1989. ... Career major league grand slams: 1.

							BATTING								FIELDING		
Year Team (League)	Pos.	G	AB	R	H	2B	3B	HR	RBI	Avg.	BB	SO	SB	PO	A	E	Avg.
1988—Ariz. Athletics (Ariz.)	OF	5	15	8	5	3	0	0	4	.333	6	5	4	15	1	0	1.000
—Madison (Midw.)	OF-2B	60	199	38	49	4	1	0	11	.246	46	37	31	195	3	4	.980
1989—Modesto (Calif.)	OF	129	503	74	150	23	5	4	39	.298	59	84	27	*311	8	5	.985
—Huntsville (Sou.)	OF	9	31	7	10	1	1	1	7	.323	2	6	0	16	0	0	1.000
1990—Huntsville (Sou.)	OF	71	284	52	84	11	3	3	23	.296	36	28	21	186	6	0	1.000
—Tacoma (PCL)	OF	60	247	32	72	5	2	2	26	.291	16	35	16	132	9	2	.986
—Oakland (A.L.)	OF-DH	25	35	4	8	0	0	0	1	.229	7	4	2	33	0	0	1.000
1991—Phoenix (PCL)■	OF	81	315	63	107	12	10	2	52	.340	41	36	32	243	5	2	.992
—San Francisco (N.L.)	OF	72	222	41	55	5	3	1	15	.248	36	30	13	159	2	0	1.000
1992—San Francisco (N.L.)	OF	100	320	38	74	8	1	1	18	.231	29	46	28	225	3	0	1.000
—Phoenix (PCL)	OF	42	158	22	36	5	2	0	6	.228	11	15	9	93	2	0	1.000
1993—San Francisco (N.L.)	OF	136	522	84	132	17	7	2	48	.253	30	40	46	344	4	0	•1.000
1994—San Francisco (N.L.)	OF	114	451	70	116	15	•9	4	29	.257	53	50	30	279	5	2	.993
1995—San Francisco (N.L.)	OF	74	309	47	78	10	3	1	16	.252	17	37	21	200	2	1	.995
—Cincinnati (N.L.)■	OF	58	163	19	40	3	0	0	8	.245	17	20	11	121	3	1	.992
1996—Chicago (A.L.)	OF	141	337	55	77	12	2	4	53	.228	45	40	21	287	0	3	.990
1997—Chicago (A.L.)	OF-DH	81	77	15	18	1	0	0	5	.234	11	14	11	90	1	0	1.000
—Los Angeles (N.L.)■	OF	26	77	7	23	3	1	1	10	.299	6	17	3	49	1	1	.980
1998—Boston (A.L.)■	OF-DH	155	585	95	157	25	3	8	63	.268	70	94	29	382	6	3	.992
1999—Boston (A.L.)	OF-DH	135	470	63	113	14	6	2	40	.240	45	52	16	309	4	2	.994
2000—Boston (A.L.)	OF-DH	97	270	44	65	12	0	2	17	.241	22	34	10	152	5	3	.981
—GC Red Sox (GCL)	OF	2	6	0	1	0	0	0	1	.167	1	0	1	2	0	0	1.000
American League totals (6 years)		634	1774	276	438	64	11	16	179	.247	200	238	89	1253	16	11	.991
National League totals (6 years)		580	2064	306	518	61	24	10	144	.251	188	240	152	1377	20	5	.996
Major League totals (11 years)		1214	3838	582	956	125	35	26	323	.249	388	478	241	2630	36	16	.994

DIVISION SERIES RECORD

							BATTING								FIELDING		
Year Team (League)	Pos.	G	AB	R	H	2B	3B	HR	RBI	Avg.	BB	SO	SB	PO	A	E	Avg.
1995—Cincinnati (N.L.)	OF-PH	3	3	0	0	0	0	0	0	.000	0	1	0	3	0	0	1.000
1998—Boston (A.L.)	OF	4	14	4	5	2	0	0	0	.357	1	3	1	10	0	0	1.000
1999—Boston (A.L.)	OF	4	16	5	6	1	0	0	2	.375	0	2	1	7	0	0	1.000
Division series totals (3 years)		11	33	9	11	3	0	0	2	.333	1	6	2	20	0	0	1.000

CHAMPIONSHIP SERIES RECORD

							BATTING								FIELDING		
Year Team (League)	Pos.	G	AB	R	H	2B	3B	HR	RBI	Avg.	BB	SO	SB	PO	A	E	Avg.
1995—Cincinnati (N.L.)	OF-PR	2	1	0	0	0	0	0	0	.000	0	0	0	2	0	0	1.000
1999—Boston (A.L.)	OF	5	17	2	2	1	0	0	1	.118	1	3	1	7	0	1	.875
Championship series totals (2 years)		7	18	2	2	1	0	0	1	.111	1	3	1	9	0	1	.900

PERSONAL: Born May 7, 1976, in Montgomery, Ala. ... 6-5/215. ... Throws right, bats right. ... Full name: Derrick Lamar Lewis.
HIGH SCHOOL: Sidney Lanier (Montgomery, Ala.).
JUNIOR COLLEGE: Central Alabama Community College.
COLLEGE: Florida A&M.
TRANSACTIONS/CAREER NOTES: Selected by Atlanta Braves organization in 20th round of free-agent draft (June 3, 1997). ... On Myrtle Beach disabled list (August 29-September 20, 1999).

Year	League	W	L	Pct.	ERA	G	GS	CG	ShO	Sv.	IP	H	R	ER	BB	SO
1997—	Danville (Appl.)	2	4	.333	6.34	16	9	0	0	0	49²/₃	59	48	35	31	46
1998—	Macon (S.Atl.)	5	6	.455	3.81	23	23	0	0	0	113¹/₃	108	64	48	55	100
1999—	Myrtle Beach (Caro.)	8	4	.667	2.40	24	23	0	0	0	131	100	44	35	*81	102
2000—	Greenville (Sou.)	7	9	.438	3.30	27	27	1	1	0	163²/₃	146	70	60	83	143

LEWIS, MARK   3B/2B

PERSONAL: Born November 30, 1969, in Hamilton, Ohio. ... 6-1/195. ... Bats right, throws right. ... Full name: Mark David Lewis.
HIGH SCHOOL: Hamilton (Ohio).
TRANSACTIONS/CAREER NOTES: Selected by Cleveland Indians organization in first round (second pick overall) of free-agent draft (June 1, 1988). ... On Kinston disabled list (May 29-June 20, 1989). ... Traded by Indians to Cincinnati Reds for IF Tim Costo (December 14, 1994). ... Traded by Reds to Detroit Tigers (November 16, 1995), completing deal in which Tigers traded P David Wells to Reds for P C.J. Nitkowski, P David Tuttle and a player to be named later (July 31, 1995). ... Traded by Tigers to San Francisco Giants for 1B Jesus Ibarra (December 16, 1996). ... On disabled list (March 31-April 12, 1997). ... Granted free agency (December 21, 1997). ... Signed by Philadelphia Phillies (December 23, 1997). ... Granted free agency (October 26, 1998). ... Signed by Reds (December 23, 1998). ... Granted free agency (October 29, 1999). ... Re-signed by Reds (November 18, 1999). ... Claimed on waivers by Baltimore Orioles (April 26, 2000). ... On Baltimore disabled list (July 21-August 5, 2000). ... Granted free agency (November 1, 2000).
STATISTICAL NOTES: Tied for A.L. lead in errors by shortstop with 25 in 1992. ... Tied for International League lead in grounding into double plays with 19 in 1993. ... Led International League shortstops with 81 double plays in 1993. ... Career major league grand slams: 1.

Year	Team (League)	Pos.	G	AB	R	H	2B	3B	HR	RBI	Avg.	BB	SO	SB	PO	A	E	Avg.
1988—	Burlington (Appl.)	SS	61	227	39	60	13	1	7	43	.264	25	44	14	70	*177	23	.915
1989—	Kinston (Caro.)	SS	93	349	50	94	16	3	1	32	.269	34	50	17	130	244	32	.921
	—Canton/Akron (East.)	SS	7	25	4	5	1	0	0	1	.200	1	3	0	15	28	2	.956
1990—	Canton/Akron (East.)	SS	102	390	55	106	19	3	10	60	.272	23	49	8	152	286	31	.934
	—Colo. Springs (PCL)	SS	34	124	16	38	8	1	1	21	.306	9	13	2	52	84	11	.925
1991—	Colo. Springs (PCL)	SS-2B-3B	46	179	29	50	10	3	2	31	.279	18	23	3	65	135	10	.952
	—Cleveland (A.L.)	2B-SS	84	314	29	83	15	1	0	30	.264	15	45	2	129	231	9	.976
1992—	Cleveland (A.L.)	SS-3B	122	413	44	109	21	0	5	30	.264	25	69	4	184	336	‡26	.952
1993—	Charlotte (I.L.)	SS	126	507	93	144	30	4	17	67	.284	34	76	9	168	*403	23	.961
	—Cleveland (A.L.)	SS	14	52	6	13	2	0	1	5	.250	0	7	3	22	31	2	.964
1994—	Cleveland (A.L.)	SS-3B-2B	20	73	6	15	5	0	1	8	.205	2	13	1	17	40	6	.905
	—Charlotte (I.L.)	SS-2B-3B	86	328	56	85	16	1	8	34	.259	35	48	2	117	199	12	.963
1995—	Cincinnati (N.L.)■	3B-2B-SS	81	171	25	58	13	1	3	30	.339	21	33	0	19	107	4	.969
1996—	Detroit (A.L.)■	2B-DH	145	545	69	147	30	3	11	55	.270	42	109	6	264	413	9	.987
1997—	San Fran. (N.L.)	3B-2B-DH	118	341	50	91	14	6	10	42	.267	23	62	3	74	157	14	.943
1998—	Philadelphia (N.L.)■	2B	142	518	52	129	21	2	9	54	.249	48	111	3	276	437	16	.978
1999—	Cincinnati (N.L.)■	3B-2B	88	173	18	44	16	0	6	28	.254	7	24	0	21	55	6	.927
2000—	Cincinnati (N.L.)	3B	11	19	1	2	1	0	0	3	.105	1	3	0	2	8	1	.909
	—Baltimore (A.L.)■	3B-2B-SS-DH	71	163	19	44	17	0	2	21	.270	12	31	7	64	105	10	.944
American League totals (6 years)			456	1560	173	411	90	4	20	149	.263	96	274	23	680	1156	62	.967
National League totals (5 years)			440	1222	146	324	65	9	28	157	.265	100	233	6	392	764	41	.966
Major League totals (10 years)			896	2782	319	735	155	13	48	306	.264	196	507	29	1072	1920	103	.967

DIVISION SERIES RECORD

Year	Team (League)	Pos.	G	AB	R	H	2B	3B	HR	RBI	Avg.	BB	SO	SB	PO	A	E	Avg.
1995—	Cincinnati (N.L.)	3B-PH	2	2	2	1	0	0	1	5	.500	1	0	0	0	0	1	.000
1997—	San Francisco (N.L.)	2B	1	5	0	3	0	0	0	1	.600	0	0	0	1	3	0	1.000
Division series totals (2 years)			3	7	2	4	0	0	1	6	.571	1	0	0	1	3	1	.800

CHAMPIONSHIP SERIES RECORD

Year	Team (League)	Pos.	G	AB	R	H	2B	3B	HR	RBI	Avg.	BB	SO	SB	PO	A	E	Avg.
1995—	Cincinnati (N.L.)	3B	2	4	0	1	0	0	0	0	.250	1	1	0	2	3	0	1.000

LEYRITZ, JIM   IF/DH

PERSONAL: Born December 27, 1963, in Lakewood, Ohio. ... 5-11/220. ... Bats right, throws right. ... Full name: James Joseph Leyritz. ... Name pronounced LAY-rits.
HIGH SCHOOL: Turpin (Cincinnati).
JUNIOR COLLEGE: Middle Georgia College.
COLLEGE: Kentucky.
TRANSACTIONS/CAREER NOTES: Signed as non-drafted free agent by New York Yankees organization (August 24, 1985). ... Traded by Yankees to Anaheim Angels for two players to be named later (December 5, 1996); Yankees acquired 3B Ryan Kane and P Jeremy Blevins to complete deal (December 9, 1996). ... Traded by Angels with a player to be named later to Texas Rangers for P Ken Hill (July 29, 1997); Rangers acquired IF Rob Sasser to complete deal (October 31, 1997). ... Traded by Rangers with OF Damon Buford to Boston Red Sox for P Aaron Sele, P Mark Brandenburg and C Bill Haselman (November 6, 1997). ... Traded by Red Sox with OF Ethan Faggett to San Diego Padres

for P Carlos Reyes, P Dario Veras and C Mandy Romero (June 21, 1998). ... On San Diego disabled list (June 23-July 30, 1999); included rehabilitation assignments to Rancho Cucamonga (July 27-28) and Las Vegas (July 29-30). ... Traded by Padres to Yankees for P Geraldo Padua (July 31, 1999). ... Traded by Yankees to Los Angeles Dodgers for SS Jose Vizcaino (June 20, 2000). ... Granted free agency (November 1, 2000).

STATISTICAL NOTES: Led Florida State League with 25 passed balls in 1987. ... Tied for Eastern League lead in being hit by pitch with nine in 1989. ... Career major league grand slams: 2.

							BATTING								FIELDING		
Year	Team (League)	Pos.	G	AB	R	H	2B	3B	HR	RBI	Avg.	BB	SO	SB	PO	A	E	Avg.
1986— Oneonta (NY-Penn)		C	23	91	12	33	3	1	4	15	.363	5	10	1	170	21	2	.990
— Fort Laud. (FSL)		C	12	34	3	10	1	1	0	1	.294	4	5	0	32	8	1	.976
1987— Fort Laud. (FSL)		C	102	374	48	115	22	0	6	51	.307	38	54	2	458	*76	13	.976
1988— Alb./Colonie (East.)	C-3B-1B	112	382	40	92	18	3	5	50	.241	43	62	3	418	73	6	.988
1989— Alb./Colonie (East.)	C-OF-3B	114	375	53	118	18	2	10	66	*.315	65	51	2	421	41	3	.994
1990— Columbus (I.L.)	3-2-1-O-C	59	204	36	59	11	1	8	32	.289	37	33	4	75	96	13	.929
— New York (A.L.)	3B-OF-C	92	303	28	78	13	1	5	25	.257	27	51	2	117	107	13	.945
1991— New York (A.L.) 3B-C-1B-DH		32	77	8	14	3	0	0	4	.182	13	15	0	38	21	3	.952
— Columbus (I.L.) C-3B-SS-2B		79	270	50	72	24	1	11	48	.267	38	50	1	209	48	5	.981
1992— New York (A.L.) DH-C-O-3-1-2		63	144	17	37	6	0	7	26	.257	14	22	0	96	15	1	.991
1993— New York (A.L.) 1B-OF-DH-C		95	259	43	80	14	0	14	53	.309	37	59	0	333	15	2	.994
1994— New York (A.L.)	C-DH-1B	75	249	47	66	12	0	17	58	.265	35	61	0	282	15	0	1.000
1995— New York (A.L.)	C-1B-DH	77	264	37	71	12	0	7	37	.269	37	73	1	417	24	3	.993
1996— New York (A.L.) C-DH-3-1-O-2		88	265	23	70	10	0	7	40	.264	30	68	2	387	31	6	.986
1997— Anaheim (A.L.)■.......	C-1B-DH	84	294	47	81	7	0	11	50	.276	37	56	1	440	45	2	.996
— Texas (A.L.)■............	C-DH-1B	37	85	11	24	4	0	0	14	.282	23	22	1	116	7	1	.992
1998— Boston (A.L.)■.........	DH-C-1B	52	129	17	37	6	0	8	24	.287	21	34	0	13	0	0	1.000
— San Diego (N.L.)■....C-1B-3B-OF		62	143	17	38	10	0	4	18	.266	21	40	0	276	19	3	.990
1999— San Diego (N.L.)	C-1B-3B	50	134	17	32	5	0	8	21	.239	15	37	0	266	23	3	.990
— Rancho Cuca. (Calif.) .	DH	1	4	0	0	0	0	0	0	.000	0	1	0	0	0	0	...
— Las Vegas (PCL)	1B	2	8	0	0	0	0	0	0	.000	0	5	0	17	1	0	1.000
— New York (A.L.)■......DH-1B-C-3B		31	66	8	15	4	1	0	5	.227	13	17	0	62	10	2	.973
2000— San Diego (N.L.)	C-1B-DH	24	55	2	12	0	0	1	4	.218	7	14	0	15	0	0	1.000
— Los Angeles (N.L.)■..	1B-OF-C	41	60	3	12	1	0	1	8	.200	7	12	0	41	3	0	1.000
American League totals (11 years)		750	2190	288	585	91	2	77	340	.267	294	492	7	2316	290	33	.987
National League totals (3 years)		153	337	37	82	16	0	13	47	.243	43	89	0	583	45	6	.991
Major League totals (11 years)		903	2527	325	667	107	2	90	387	.264	337	581	7	2899	335	39	.988

DIVISION SERIES RECORD

RECORDS: Shares A.L. career record for most games by pinch-hitter—3.

							BATTING								FIELDING		
Year	Team (League)	Pos.	G	AB	R	H	2B	3B	HR	RBI	Avg.	BB	SO	SB	PO	A	E	Avg.
1995— New York (A.L.)..........	C-PH	2	7	1	1	0	0	1	2	.143	0	1	0	13	0	0	1.000
1996— New York (A.L.)..........	C-DH	2	3	0	0	0	0	0	1	1.000	0	1	0	4	0	0	1.000
1998— San Diego (N.L.)	1B-C-PH	4	10	3	4	0	0	3	5	.400	0	2	0	34	0	0	1.000
1999— New York (A.L.)..........	PH-DH	2	2	0	0	0	0	0	1	.000	1	0	0	...	...	...	...
Division series totals (4 years)		10	22	4	5	0	0	4	9	.227	1	4	0	51	0	0	1.000

CHAMPIONSHIP SERIES RECORD

							BATTING								FIELDING		
Year	Team (League)	Pos.	G	AB	R	H	2B	3B	HR	RBI	Avg.	BB	SO	SB	PO	A	E	Avg.
1996— New York (A.L.)..........	C-OF-PH	3	8	1	2	0	0	1	2	.250	1	4	0	11	2	0	1.000
1998— San Diego (N.L.)	PH-1B-C	5	12	1	2	0	0	1	4	.167	0	2	0	24	1	0	1.000
1999— New York (A.L.)							Did not play.										
Championship series totals (2 years)		8	20	2	4	0	0	2	6	.200	1	6	0	35	3	0	1.000

WORLD SERIES RECORD

NOTES: Member of World Series championship team (1996 and 1999).

							BATTING								FIELDING		
Year	Team (League)	Pos.	G	AB	R	H	2B	3B	HR	RBI	Avg.	BB	SO	SB	PO	A	E	Avg.
1996— New York (A.L.)..........	C-PH	4	8	1	3	0	0	1	3	.375	4	2	1	15	0	0	1.000
1998— San Diego (N.L.) DH-PH-1B-C		4	10	0	0	0	0	0	0	.000	1	4	0	19	0	0	1.000
1999— New York (A.L.)..........	PH-DH	2	1	1	1	0	0	1	2	1.000	1	0	0	...	...	...	...
World Series totals (3 years)		10	19	2	4	0	0	2	5	.211	6	6	1	34	0	0	1.000

LIDLE, CORY P ATHLETICS

PERSONAL: Born March 22, 1972, in Hollywood, Calif. ... 5-11/180. ... Throws right, bats right. ... Full name: Cory Fulton Lidle. ... Twin brother of Kevin Lidle, catcher, San Diego Padres organization.

HIGH SCHOOL: South Hills (Covina, Calif.).

TRANSACTIONS/CAREER NOTES: Signed as non-drafted free agent by Minnesota Twins organization (August 25, 1990). ... Released by Twins (April 1, 1993). ... Signed by Pocatello, Pioneer League (May 28, 1993). ... Contract sold by Pocatello to Milwaukee Brewers organization (September 17, 1993). ... Traded by Brewers to New York Mets for C Kelly Stinnett (January 17, 1996). ... Selected by Arizona Diamondbacks in first round (13th pick overall) of expansion draft (November 18, 1997). ... On Arizona disabled list (March 31, 1998-entire season); included rehabilitation assignments to High Desert (April 20-28) and Tucson (September 3-7). ... Claimed on waivers by Tampa Bay Devil Rays (October 7, 1998). ... On Tampa Bay disabled list (March 23-September 18, 1999); included rehabilitation assignments to St. Petersburg (August 20-28) and Durham (August 29-September 18). ... On suspended list (September 5-8, 2000). ... Traded by Devil Rays to Oakland Athletics as part of three-way deal in which Devil Rays received OF Ben Grieve and a player to be named later or cash from Athletics, Kansas City Royals received P Roberto Hernandez from Devil Rays, Athletics received OF Johnny Damon, IF Mark Ellis and a player to be named later from Royals and Royals received C A.J. Hinch, IF Angel Berroa and cash from Athletics (January 8, 2001).

Year League	W	L	Pct.	ERA	G	GS	CG	ShO	Sv.	IP	H	R	ER	BB	SO
1991— Gulf Coast Twins (GCL)	1	1	.500	5.79	4	0	0	0	0	4²/₃	5	3	3	0	5
1992— Elizabethton (Appl.)	2	1	.667	3.71	19	2	0	0	6	43²/₃	40	29	18	21	32
1993— Pocatello (Pio.)■	•8	4	.667	4.13	17	16	3	0	1	106²/₃	104	59	49	54	91
1994— Stockton (Calif.)■	1	2	.333	4.43	25	1	0	0	4	42²/₃	60	32	21	13	38
— Beloit (Midw.)	3	4	.429	2.61	13	9	1	1	0	69	65	24	20	11	62
1995— El Paso (Texas)	5	4	.556	3.36	45	9	0	0	2	109²/₃	126	52	41	36	78
1996— Binghamton (East.)■	14	10	.583	3.31	27	27	•6	1	0	*190¹/₃	186	78	70	49	141
1997— Norfolk (I.L.)	4	2	.667	3.64	7	7	1	0	0	42	46	20	17	10	34
— New York (N.L.)	7	2	.778	3.53	54	2	0	0	2	81²/₃	86	38	32	20	54
1998— High Desert (Calif.)■	0	0	...	0.00	1	1	0	0	0	2²/₃	2	1	0	2	6
— Tucson (PCL)	0	0	...	0.00	1	1	0	0	0	4²/₃	2	0	0	2	2
1999— St. Petersburg (FSL)■	0	0	...	0.00	2	2	0	0	0	5	2	0	0	2	5
— Durham (I.L.)	0	0	...	4.76	3	2	0	0	0	5²/₃	9	3	3	1	6
— Tampa Bay (A.L.)...............	1	0	1.000	7.20	5	1	0	0	0	5	8	4	4	2	4
2000— Durham (I.L.)	6	2	.750	2.52	9	9	0	0	0	50	52	15	14	8	44
— Tampa Bay (A.L.)...............	4	6	.400	5.03	31	11	0	0	0	96²/₃	114	61	54	29	62
A.L. totals (2 years)	5	6	.455	5.13	36	12	0	0	0	101²/₃	122	65	58	31	66
N.L. totals (1 year)	7	2	.778	3.53	54	2	0	0	2	81²/₃	86	38	32	20	54
Major League totals (3 years)	12	8	.600	4.42	90	14	0	0	2	183¹/₃	208	103	90	51	120

LIEBER, JON   P   CUBS

PERSONAL: Born April 2, 1970, in Council Bluffs, Iowa. ... 6-3/225. ... Throws right, bats left. ... Full name: Jonathan Ray Lieber. ... Name pronounced LEE-ber.

HIGH SCHOOL: Abraham Lincoln (Council Bluffs, Iowa.).

JUNIOR COLLEGE: Iowa Western Community College-Council Bluffs.

COLLEGE: South Alabama.

TRANSACTIONS/CAREER NOTES: Selected by Chicago Cubs organization in ninth round of free-agent draft (June 3, 1991); did not sign. ... Selected by Kansas City Royals organization in second round of free-agent draft (June 1, 1992); pick received as part of compensation for New York Yankees signing Type A free-agent OF Danny Tartabull. ... Traded by Royals with P Dan Miceli to Pittsburgh Pirates for P Stan Belinda (July 31, 1993). ... On disabled list (August 21-September 15, 1998). ... Traded by Pirates to Chicago Cubs for OF Brant Brown (December 14, 1998). ... On disabled list (April 21-May 8, 1999).

MISCELLANEOUS: Walked in only appearance as pinch hitter (2000).

Year League	W	L	Pct.	ERA	G	GS	CG	ShO	Sv.	IP	H	R	ER	BB	SO
1992— Eugene (N'West)	3	0	1.000	1.16	5	5	0	0	0	31	26	6	4	2	23
— Baseball City (FSL)..............	3	3	.500	4.65	7	6	0	0	0	31	45	20	16	8	19
1993— Wilmington (Caro.)	9	3	.750	2.67	17	16	2	0	0	114²/₃	125	47	34	9	89
— Memphis (Sou.)	2	1	.667	6.86	4	4	0	0	0	21	32	16	16	6	17
— Carolina (Sou.)■	4	2	.667	3.97	6	6	0	0	0	34	39	15	15	10	28
1994— Carolina (Sou.)	2	0	1.000	1.29	3	3	1	1	0	21	13	4	3	2	21
— Buffalo (A.A.)...................	1	1	.500	1.69	3	3	0	0	0	21¹/₃	16	4	4	1	21
— Pittsburgh (N.L.)	6	7	.462	3.73	17	17	1	0	0	108²/₃	116	62	45	25	71
1995— Pittsburgh (N.L.)	4	7	.364	6.32	21	12	0	0	0	72²/₃	103	56	51	14	45
— Calgary (PCL)	1	5	.167	7.01	14	14	0	0	0	77	122	69	60	19	34
1996— Pittsburgh (N.L.)	9	5	.643	3.99	51	15	0	0	1	142	156	70	63	28	94
1997— Pittsburgh (N.L.)	11	14	.440	4.49	33	32	1	0	0	188¹/₃	193	102	94	51	160
1998— Pittsburgh (N.L.)	8	14	.364	4.11	29	28	2	0	1	171	182	93	78	40	138
1999— Chicago (N.L.)■	10	11	.476	4.07	31	31	3	1	0	203¹/₃	226	107	92	46	186
2000— Chicago (N.L.)	12	11	.522	4.41	35	•35	6	1	0	*251	248	130	123	54	192
Major League totals (7 years)	60	69	.465	4.32	217	170	13	2	2	1137	1224	620	546	258	886

LIEBERTHAL, MIKE   C   PHILLIES

PERSONAL: Born January 18, 1972, in Glendale, Calif. ... 6-0/190. ... Bats right, throws right. ... Full name: Michael Scott Lieberthal. ... Name pronounced LEE-ber-thal.

HIGH SCHOOL: Westlake (Westlake Village, Calif.).

TRANSACTIONS/CAREER NOTES: Selected by Philadelphia Phillies organization in first round (third pick overall) of free-agent draft (June 4, 1990). ... On Scranton/Wilkes-Barre disabled list (August 31, 1992-remainder of season). ... On disabled list (August 22, 1996-remainder of season; July 24-September 2, 1998; July 18-August 4 and September 11, 2000-remainder of season).

HONORS: Won N.L. Gold Glove at catcher (1999).

STATISTICAL NOTES: Tied for N.L. lead with 12 passed balls in 1997. ... Tied for N.L. lead with 11 passed balls in 1999. ... Career major league grand slams: 2.

Year Team (League)	Pos.	G	AB	R	H	2B	3B	HR	RBI	Avg.	BB	SO	SB	PO	A	E	Avg.
1990— Martinsville (Appl.).....	C	49	184	26	42	9	0	4	22	.228	11	40	2	421	*52	5	*.990
1991— Spartanburg (S.Atl.) ...	C	72	243	34	74	17	0	0	31	.305	23	25	1	565	68	10	.984
— Clearwater (FSL)	C	16	52	7	15	2	0	0	7	.288	3	12	0	128	9	1	.993
1992— Reading (East.).........	C	86	309	30	88	16	1	2	37	.285	19	26	4	524	48	7	.988
— Scranton/W.B. (I.L.) ...	C	16	45	4	9	1	0	0	4	.200	2	5	0	86	6	1	.989
1993— Scranton/W.B. (I.L.) ...	C	112	382	35	100	17	0	7	40	.262	24	32	2	659	75	•11	.985
1994— Scranton/W.B. (I.L.) ...	C-DH	84	296	23	69	16	0	1	32	.233	21	29	1	472	50	9	.983
— Philadelphia (N.L.)......	C	24	79	6	21	3	1	1	5	.266	3	5	0	122	4	4	.969
1995— Philadelphia (N.L.)......	C	16	47	1	12	2	0	0	4	.255	5	5	0	95	10	1	.991
— Scranton/W.B. (I.L.) ...	C-DH-3B	85	278	44	78	20	2	6	42	.281	44	26	1	503	46	5	.991
1996— Philadelphia (N.L.)......	C	50	166	21	42	8	0	7	23	.253	10	30	0	284	20	3	.990
1997— Philadelphia (N.L.)......	C-DH	134	455	59	112	27	1	20	77	.246	44	76	3	934	73	12	.988
1998— Philadelphia (N.L.)......	C	86	313	39	80	15	3	8	45	.256	17	44	2	607	41	8	.988
1999— Philadelphia (N.L.)......	C	145	510	84	153	33	1	31	96	.300	44	86	0	881	*62	3	*.997
2000— Philadelphia (N.L.)......	C	108	389	55	108	30	0	15	71	.278	40	53	2	724	40	5	.993
Major League totals (7 years)		563	1959	265	528	118	6	82	321	.270	163	299	7	3647	250	36	.991

ALL-STAR GAME RECORD

					BATTING									FIELDING			
Year	League	Pos.	AB	R	H	2B	3B	HR	RBI	Avg.	BB	SO	SB	PO	A	E	Avg.
1999—	National	C	1	0	0	0	0	0	0	.000	0	0	0	1	0	0	1.000
2000—	National	C	2	1	1	0	0	0	0	.500	0	0	0	4	0	0	1.000
All-Star Game totals (2 years)			3	1	1	0	0	0	0	.333	0	0	0	5	0	0	1.000

LIEFER, JEFF   OF   WHITE SOX

PERSONAL: Born August 17, 1974, in Fontana, CA ... 6-3/195. ... Bats left, throws right. ... Full name: Jeffery David Liefer.
HIGH SCHOOL: Upland (Calif.).
COLLEGE: Long Beach State.
TRANSACTIONS/CAREER NOTES: Selected by Cleveland Indians organization in sixth round of free-agent draft (June 1, 1992); did not sign. ... Selected by Chicago White Sox organization in first round (25th pick overall) of free-agent draft (June 1, 1995). ... On Charlotte disabled list (August 30, 1999-remainder of season). ... On Chicago disabled list (March 25-April 17, 2000).

							BATTING								FIELDING		
Year	Team (League)	Pos.	G	AB	R	H	2B	3B	HR	RBI	Avg.	BB	SO	SB	PO	A	E	Avg.
1996—	South Bend (Midw.) ...	DH-3B	74	277	60	90	14	0	15	58	.325	30	62	6	31	62	23	.802
	— Prince Will. (Caro.) ...	DH	37	147	17	33	6	0	1	13	.224	11	27	0	0	0	0	...
1997—	Birmingham (Sou.)	OF-DH	119	474	67	113	24	9	15	71	.238	38	115	2	166	2	•8	.955
1998—	Birmingham (Sou.)	1B-DH-OF	127	471	84	137	33	6	21	89	.291	60	125	1	763	60	11	.987
	— Calgary (PCL)	OF-1B-DH	8	31	3	8	3	0	1	10	.258	2	12	0	26	3	0	1.000
1999—	Chicago (A.L.)	OF-1B-DH	45	113	8	28	7	1	0	14	.248	8	28	2	124	12	0	1.000
	— Charlotte (I.L.)	1B-OF-3B	46	171	36	58	17	1	9	34	.339	21	26	2	226	24	3	.988
2000—	Chicago (A.L.)	OF-1B	5	11	0	2	0	0	0	0	.182	0	4	0	8	1	1	.900
	— Charlotte (I.L.)	1B-OF-3B	120	445	75	125	29	1	32	91	.281	53	107	2	580	80	9	.987
Major League totals (2 years)			50	124	8	30	7	1	0	14	.242	8	32	2	132	13	1	.993

LIGTENBERG, KERRY   P   BRAVES

PERSONAL: Born May 11, 1971, in Rapid City, S.D. ... 6-2/215. ... Throws right, bats right. ... Full name: Kerry Dale Ligtenberg. ... Name pronounced Light-en-berg.
HIGH SCHOOL: Park (Cottage Grove, Minn.).
COLLEGE: Minnesota-Morris, then Minnesota.
TRANSACTIONS/CAREER NOTES: Signed by Minneapolis, North Central League (1994). ... Contract sold by Minnesota to Seattle Mariners organization (March 28, 1995). ... Released by Mariners (April 2, 1995). ... Signed by Minneapolis, Prairie League (1995). ... Contract sold by Minneapolis to Atlanta Braves organization (January 27, 1996). ... On disabled list (April 3, 1999-entire season).

Year	League	W	L	Pct.	ERA	G	GS	CG	ShO	Sv.	IP	H	R	ER	BB	SO
1994—	Minneapolis (NCL)	5	5	.500	3.31	19	19	2	...	0	114 1/3	103	47	42	44	94
1995—	Minneapolis (PRA)	11	2	.846	2.73	17	15	4	...	0	108 2/3	101	41	33	26	100
1996—	Durham (Caro.)■	7	4	.636	2.41	49	0	0	0	20	59 2/3	58	20	16	16	76
1997—	Greenville (Sou.)	3	1	.750	2.04	31	0	0	0	16	35 1/3	20	8	8	14	43
	— Richmond (I.L.)	0	3	.000	4.32	14	0	0	0	1	25	21	13	12	2	35
	— Atlanta (N.L.)	1	0	1.000	3.00	15	0	0	0	1	15	12	5	5	4	19
1998—	Atlanta (N.L.)	3	2	.600	2.71	75	0	0	0	30	73	51	24	22	24	79
1999—	Atlanta (N.L.)							Did not play.								
2000—	Atlanta (N.L.)	2	3	.400	3.61	59	0	0	0	12	52 1/3	43	21	21	24	51
	— Richmond (I.L.)	0	0	...	0.00	5	0	0	0	1	5 2/3	0	0	0	4	7
Major League totals (3 years)		6	5	.545	3.08	149	0	0	0	43	140 1/3	106	50	48	52	149

DIVISION SERIES RECORD

Year	League	W	L	Pct.	ERA	G	GS	CG	ShO	Sv.	IP	H	R	ER	BB	SO
1998—	Atlanta (N.L.)	0	0	...	0.00	3	0	0	0	0	3 1/3	1	0	0	5	3
2000—	Atlanta (N.L.)	0	0	...	5.40	3	0	0	0	0	1 2/3	0	1	1	1	3
Division series totals (2 years)		0	0	...	1.80	6	0	0	0	0	5	1	1	1	6	6

CHAMPIONSHIP SERIES RECORD

Year	League	W	L	Pct.	ERA	G	GS	CG	ShO	Sv.	IP	H	R	ER	BB	SO
1997—	Atlanta (N.L.)	0	0	...	0.00	2	0	0	0	0	3	1	0	0	0	4
1998—	Atlanta (N.L.)	0	1	.000	7.36	4	0	0	0	0	3 2/3	3	3	3	2	5
Champ. series totals (2 years)		0	1	.000	4.05	6	0	0	0	0	6 2/3	4	3	3	2	9

LILLY, TED   P   YANKEES

PERSONAL: Born January 4, 1976, in Lameta, Calif. ... 6-0/185. ... Throws left, bats left. ... Full name: Theodore Roosevelt Lilly.
HIGH SCHOOL: Yosemite (Oakhurst, Calif.).
JUNIOR COLLEGE: Fresno (Calif.) City College.
TRANSACTIONS/CAREER NOTES: Selected by Los Angeles Dodgers in 23rd round of free-agent draft (June 4, 1996). ... Traded by Dodgers with 2B Wilton Guerrero, OF Peter Bergeron and 1B Jonathan Tucker to Montreal Expos for P Carlos Perez, SS Mark Grudzielanek and IF Hiram Bocachica (July 31, 1998). ... On Ottawa disabled list (June 21, 1999-remainder of season). ... Traded by Expos to New York Yankees (March 17, 2000), as part of deal in which Yankees traded P Hideki Irabu to Expos for P Jake Westbrook and two players to be named later (December 29, 1999); Yankees acquired P Christian Parker to complete deal (March 22, 2000). ... On New York disabled list (April 2-May 23, 2000); included rehabilitation assignments to Tampa (April 27-May 1) and Columbus (May 2-6 and May 20-23).
HONORS: Named California League Pitcher of the Year (1997).
STATISTICAL NOTES: Pitched 8-0 no-hit victory against Lake Elsinore (May 10, 1997).

Year League	W	L	Pct.	ERA	G	GS	CG	ShO	Sv.	IP	H	R	ER	BB	SO
1996— Yakima (N'West)	4	0	1.000	0.84	13	8	0	0	0	53 2/3	25	9	5	14	75
1997— San Bernardino (Calif.)	7	8	.467	*2.81	23	21	2	1	0	134 2/3	116	52	42	32	158
1998— San Antonio (Texas)	8	4	.667	3.30	17	17	0	0	0	111 2/3	114	50	41	37	96
— Albuquerque (PCL)	1	3	.250	4.94	5	5	0	0	0	31	39	20	17	9	25
— Ottawa (I.L.)■	2	2	.500	4.85	7	7	0	0	0	39	45	28	21	19	49
1999— Ottawa (I.L.)	8	5	.615	3.84	16	16	0	0	0	89	81	40	38	23	78
— Montreal (N.L.)	0	1	.000	7.61	9	3	0	0	0	23 2/3	30	20	20	9	28
2000— Tampa (FSL)■	0	0	...	1.35	1	1	0	0	0	6 2/3	5	3	1	1	6
— Columbus (I.L.)	8	11	.421	4.19	22	22	3	1	0	137 1/3	157	77	64	48	127
— New York (A.L.)	0	0	...	5.63	7	0	0	0	0	8	8	6	5	5	11
A.L. totals (1 year)	0	0	...	5.63	7	0	0	0	0	8	8	6	5	5	11
N.L. totals (1 year)	0	1	.000	7.61	9	3	0	0	0	23 2/3	30	20	20	9	28
Major League totals (2 years)	0	1	.000	7.11	16	3	0	0	0	31 2/3	38	26	25	14	39

LIMA, JOSE   P   ASTROS

PERSONAL: Born September 30, 1972, in Santiago, Dominican Republic. ... 6-2/205. ... Throws right, bats right. ... Full name: Jose D. Lima. ... Name pronounced LEE-mah.

HIGH SCHOOL: Escuela Primaria Las Charcas (Santiago, Dominican Replublic).

TRANSACTIONS/CAREER NOTES: Signed as non-drafted free agent by Detroit Tigers organization (July 5, 1989). ... Traded by Tigers with C Brad Ausmus, P C.J. Nitkowski, P Trever Miller and IF Daryle Ward to Houston Astros for OF Brian Hunter, IF Orlando Miller, P Doug Brocail, P Todd Jones and cash (December 10, 1996).

RECORDS: Shares major league record for most home runs allowed in one inning—4 (April 27, 2000, first inning). ... Holds N.L. single-season record for most home runs allowed—48 (2000). ... Shares N.L. single-inning record for most consecutive home runs allowed—3 (September 17, 1999, fourth inning).

HONORS: Named righthanded pitcher on THE SPORTING NEWS N.L. All-Star team (1999).

STATISTICAL NOTES: Led Florida State League with 14 home runs allowed in 1992. ... Led Eastern League with 13 balks in 1993. ... Pitched 3-0 no-hit victory for Toledo against Pawtucket (August 17, 1994). ... Led N.L. with 48 home runs allowed in 2000.

MISCELLANEOUS: Appeared in one game as third baseman with no chances (1999).

Year League	W	L	Pct.	ERA	G	GS	CG	ShO	Sv.	IP	H	R	ER	BB	SO
1990— Bristol (Appl.)	3	8	.273	5.02	14	12	1	0	1	75 1/3	89	49	42	22	64
1991— Lakeland (FSL)	0	1	.000	10.38	4	1	0	0	0	8 2/3	16	10	10	2	5
— Fayetteville (S.Atl.)	1	3	.250	4.97	18	7	0	0	0	58	53	38	32	25	60
1992— Lakeland (FSL)	5	11	.313	3.16	25	25	5	2	0	151	132	57	53	21	137
1993— London (East.)	8	•13	.381	4.07	27	27	2	0	0	177	160	96	80	59	138
1994— Toledo (I.L.)	7	9	.438	3.60	23	22	3	2	0	142 1/3	124	70	57	48	117
— Detroit (A.L.)	0	1	.000	13.50	3	1	0	0	0	6 2/3	11	10	10	3	7
1995— Lakeland (FSL)	3	1	.750	2.57	4	4	0	0	0	21	23	11	6	0	20
— Toledo (I.L.)	5	3	.625	3.01	11	11	1	0	0	74 2/3	69	26	25	14	40
— Detroit (A.L.)	3	9	.250	6.11	15	15	0	0	0	73 2/3	85	52	50	18	37
1996— Toledo (I.L.)	5	4	.556	6.78	12	12	0	0	0	69	93	53	52	12	57
— Detroit (A.L.)	5	6	.455	5.70	39	4	0	0	3	72 2/3	87	48	46	22	59
1997— Houston (N.L.)■	1	6	.143	5.28	52	1	0	0	2	75	79	45	44	16	63
1998— Houston (N.L.)	16	8	.667	3.70	33	33	3	1	0	233 1/3	229	100	96	32	169
1999— Houston (N.L.)	21	10	.677	3.58	35	•35	3	0	0	246 1/3	256	108	98	44	187
2000— Houston (N.L.)	7	16	.304	6.65	33	33	0	0	0	196 1/3	251	*152	*145	68	124
A.L. totals (3 years)	8	16	.333	6.24	57	20	0	0	3	153	183	110	106	43	103
N.L. totals (4 years)	45	40	.529	4.59	153	102	6	1	2	751	815	405	383	160	543
Major League totals (7 years)	53	56	.486	4.87	210	122	6	1	5	904	998	515	489	203	646

DIVISION SERIES RECORD

Year League	W	L	Pct.	ERA	G	GS	CG	ShO	Sv.	IP	H	R	ER	BB	SO
1997— Houston (N.L.)	0	0	...	0.00	1	0	0	0	0	1	0	0	0	1	1
1998— Houston (N.L.)						Did not play.									
1999— Houston (N.L.)	0	1	.000	5.40	1	1	0	0	0	6 2/3	9	4	4	2	4
Division series totals (2 years)	0	1	.000	4.70	2	1	0	0	0	7 2/3	9	4	4	3	5

ALL-STAR GAME RECORD

Year League	W	L	Pct.	ERA	GS	CG	ShO	Sv.	IP	H	R	ER	BB	SO
1999— National	0	0	...	0.00	0	0	0	0	1	1	0	0	0	0

LINCOLN, MIKE   P   TWINS

PERSONAL: Born April 10, 1975, in Carmichael, Calif. ... 6-2/210. ... Throws right, bats right. ... Full name: Michael George Lincoln.

HIGH SCHOOL: Casa Roble (Orangevale, Calif.).

JUNIOR COLLEGE: American River College (Calif.).

COLLEGE: Tennessee.

TRANSACTIONS/CAREER NOTES: Selected by Minnesota Twins organization in 13th round of free-agent draft (June 4, 1996). ... On Minnesota disabled list (July 23, 2000-remainder of season).

Year League	W	L	Pct.	ERA	G	GS	CG	ShO	Sv.	IP	H	R	ER	BB	SO
1996— Fort Myers (FSL)	5	2	.714	4.07	12	11	0	0	0	59 2/3	64	31	27	25	24
1997— Fort Myers (FSL)	13	4	.765	2.28	20	20	1	1	0	134	130	41	34	25	75
1998— New Britain (East.)	*15	7	.682	3.22	26	26	1	0	0	173 1/3	180	80	62	35	109
1999— Minnesota (A.L.)	3	10	.231	6.84	18	15	0	0	0	76 1/3	102	59	58	26	27
— Salt Lake (PCL)	5	2	.714	7.78	9	9	0	0	0	59	82	52	51	21	39
2000— Salt Lake (PCL)	4	1	.800	3.87	12	12	2	1	0	74 1/3	72	35	32	16	37
— Minnesota (A.L.)	0	3	.000	10.89	8	4	0	0	0	20 2/3	36	25	25	13	15
Major League totals (2 years)	3	13	.188	7.70	26	19	0	0	0	97	138	84	83	39	42

LINDSEY, RODNEY   OF   TIGERS

PERSONAL: Born January 28, 1976, in Opelika, Ala. ... 5-8/175. ... Bats right, throws right. ... Full name: Rodney Lee Lindsey.
HIGH SCHOOL: Opelika (Ala.).
TRANSACTIONS/CAREER NOTES: Selected by San Diego Padres organization in 39th round of free-agent draft (June 2, 1994). ... Traded by Padres to Detroit Tigers (June 1, 1998), completing deal in which Tigers traded P Scott Sanders and cash to Padres for player to be named (May 6, 1998). ... On Jacksonville disabled list (May 10-26, 2000).

								BATTING							FIELDING		
Year Team (League)	Pos.	G	AB	R	H	2B	3B	HR	RBI	Avg.	BB	SO	SB	PO	A	E	Avg.
1994— Ariz. Padres (Ariz.)	OF	48	172	29	46	3	0	0	19	.267	11	59	15	58	6	7	.901
1995— Idaho Falls (Pio.)........	OF	35	155	30	41	4	4	0	14	.265	13	37	21	69	6	4	.949
1996— Clinton (Midw.)	OF	23	87	11	14	2	0	0	4	.161	11	30	12	50	0	4	.926
— Idaho Falls (Pio.).......	OF	48	185	45	56	4	6	5	17	.303	23	53	16	73	4	5	.939
1997— Clinton (Midw.)	OF	130	502	80	107	15	8	6	49	.213	62	161	*70	206	8	12	.947
1998— Clinton (Midw.)	OF	40	155	32	42	4	4	4	17	.271	17	54	36	72	2	4	.949
— W. Mich. (Midw.)■....	OF	45	158	37	43	7	4	3	17	.272	22	42	24	79	2	2	.976
1999— Lakeland (FSL)	OF	120	485	81	129	20	8	7	51	.266	25	129	*61	282	7	8	.973
— Jacksonville (Sou.).....	OF	7	27	3	5	1	0	0	2	.185	1	6	0	12	1	1	.929
2000— Jacksonville (Sou.).....	OF	114	393	57	88	11	4	0	20	.224	38	100	46	273	12	8	.973
— Detroit (A.L.)	OF	11	3	6	1	1	0	0	0	.333	0	1	2	2	0	0	1.000
Major League totals (1 year)		11	3	6	1	1	0	0	0	.333	0	1	2	2	0	0	1.000

LINEBRINK, SCOTT   P   ASTROS

PERSONAL: Born August 4, 1976, in Austin, Texas. ... 6-3/185. ... Throws right, bats right. ... Full name: Scott Cameron Linebrink.
HIGH SCHOOL: McNeil (Austin, Texas).
COLLEGE: Concordia, then Southwest Texas State.
TRANSACTIONS/CAREER NOTES: Selected by San Francisco Giants organization in second round of free-agent draft (June 3, 1997). ... On Shreveport disabled list (April 8-July 17, 1999). ... Traded by Giants to Houston Astros for P Doug Henry (July 30, 2000).

Year League	W	L	Pct.	ERA	G	GS	CG	ShO	Sv.	IP	H	R	ER	BB	SO
1997— Salem-Kaizer (N'West)	0	0	...	4.50	3	3	0	0	0	10	7	5	5	6	6
— San Jose (Calif.).................	2	1	.667	3.18	6	6	0	0	0	28 1/3	29	11	10	10	40
1998— Shreveport (Texas)............	10	8	.556	5.02	21	21	0	0	0	113	101	66	63	58	128
1999— Shreveport (Texas)	1	8	.111	6.44	10	10	0	0	0	43 1/3	48	31	31	14	33
2000— Fresno (PCL)	1	4	.200	5.23	28	7	0	0	4	62	54	42	36	12	49
— San Francisco (N.L.)	0	0	...	11.57	3	0	0	0	0	2 1/3	7	3	3	2	0
— Houston (N.L.)■..............	0	0	...	4.66	8	0	0	0	0	9 2/3	11	5	5	6	6
— New Orleans (PCL)............	2	0	1.000	1.80	11	0	0	0	1	15	15	4	3	7	22
Major League totals (1 year)........	0	0	...	6.00	11	0	0	0	0	12	18	8	8	8	6

LINIAK, COLE   3B   CUBS

PERSONAL: Born August 23, 1976, in Encinitas, Calif. ... 6-1/190. ... Bats right, throws right. ... Full name: Cole Edward Liniak. ... Name pronounced lin-ee-AK.
HIGH SCHOOL: San Dieguito (Encinitas, Calif.).
TRANSACTIONS/CAREER NOTES: Selected by Boston Red Sox organization in seventh round of free-agent draft (June 1, 1995). ... On Pawtucket disabled list (May 24-June 17, 1999). ... Traded by Red Sox to Chicago Cubs (September 1, 1999), completing deal in which Cubs traded P Rod Beck to Red Sox for P Mark Guthrie and a player to named later (August 31, 1999).
STATISTICAL NOTES: Led Midwest League third basemen with .967 fielding percentage in 1996. ... Led Pacific Coast League third basemen with 91 putouts in 2000.

								BATTING							FIELDING		
Year Team (League)	Pos.	G	AB	R	H	2B	3B	HR	RBI	Avg.	BB	SO	SB	PO	A	E	Avg.
1995— GC Red Sox (GCL)	3B	23	79	9	21	7	0	1	8	.266	4	8	2	21	53	2	.974
1996— Michigan (Midw.)	3B-2B	121	437	65	115	26	2	3	46	.263	59	59	7	79	248	11	†.967
1997— Sarasota (FSL)	3B	64	217	32	73	16	0	6	42	.336	22	31	1	38	116	18	.895
— Trenton (East.)	3B	53	200	20	56	11	0	2	18	.280	17	29	0	35	82	9	.929
1998— Pawtucket (I.L.)	3B	112	429	65	112	31	1	17	59	.261	39	71	4	86	192	18	.939
— GC Red Sox (GCL)	DH	2	8	1	0	0	0	0	0	.000	0	1	0	...	...	...	...
1999— Pawtucket (I.L.).........	3B-DH	95	348	55	92	25	0	12	42	.264	40	57	0	66	156	14	.941
— Chicago (N.L.)■........	3B	12	29	3	7	2	0	0	2	.241	1	4	0	8	8	0	1.000
2000— Chicago (N.L.)...........		3	3	0	0	0	0	0	0	.000	0	2	0	0	0	0	...
— Iowa (PCL)	3B-2B	123	411	63	97	24	1	19	58	.236	39	77	5	92	197	23	.926
Major League totals (2 years)		15	32	3	7	2	0	0	2	.219	1	6	0	8	8	0	1.000

LIRA, FELIPE   P   EXPOS

PERSONAL: Born April 26, 1972, in Miranda, Venezuela. ... 6-0/170. ... Throws right, bats right. ... Full name: Antonio Felipe Lira.
HIGH SCHOOL: Rafael O. Figueroa (Venezuela).
TRANSACTIONS/CAREER NOTES: Signed as non-drafted free agent by Detroit Tigers organization (February 20, 1990). ... On Lakeland disabled list (April 10-June 10, 1991). ... Traded by Tigers with P Omar Olivares to Seattle Mariners for P Scott Sanders, P Dean Crow and 3B Carlos Villalobos (July 18, 1997). ... Granted free agency (October 15, 1998). ... Re-signed by Tigers organization (November 24, 1998). ... Granted free agency (October 15, 1999). ... Signed by Montreal Expos organization (February 16, 2000). ... Granted free agency (October 10, 2000). ... Re-signed by Expos organization (November 17, 2000).
STATISTICAL NOTES: Pitched seven-inning, 4-0 no-hit victory against Columbus (May 4, 1994). ... Led International League with 16 wild pitches in 1994.
MISCELLANEOUS: Struck out in only appearance as pinch hitter (2000).

Year League	W	L	Pct.	ERA	G	GS	CG	ShO	Sv.	IP	H	R	ER	BB	SO
1990— Bristol (Appl.)	5	5	.500	2.41	13	10	2	1	1	78 1/3	70	26	21	16	71
— Lakeland (FSL)	0	0	...	5.40	1	0	0	0	0	1 2/3	3	1	1	3	4
1991— Fayetteville (S.Atl.)	5	5	.500	4.66	15	13	0	0	1	73 1/3	79	43	38	19	56
1992— Lakeland (FSL)	11	5	.688	2.39	32	8	2	1	1	109	95	36	29	16	84
1993— London (East.)	10	4	.714	3.38	22	22	2	0	0	152	157	63	57	39	122
— Toledo (I.L.)	1	2	.333	4.60	5	5	0	0	0	31 1/3	32	18	16	11	23
1994— Toledo (I.L.)	7	12	.368	4.70	26	26	1	1	0	151 1/3	171	91	79	45	110
1995— Detroit (A.L.)	9	13	.409	4.31	37	22	0	0	1	146 1/3	151	74	70	56	89
1996— Detroit (A.L.)	6	14	.300	5.22	32	32	3	2	0	194 2/3	204	123	113	66	113
1997— Detroit (A.L.)	5	7	.417	5.77	20	15	1	1	0	92	101	61	59	45	64
— Seattle (A.L.)■	0	4	.000	9.16	8	3	0	0	0	18 2/3	31	21	19	10	9
— Everett (N'West)	1	0	1.000	3.60	1	1	0	0	0	5	6	3	2	2	9
— Tacoma (PCL)	2	0	1.000	3.43	3	3	0	0	0	21	21	8	8	5	17
1998— Tacoma (PCL)	6	8	.429	4.26	20	20	2	1	0	129	142	69	61	42	88
— Seattle (A.L.)	1	0	1.000	4.60	7	0	0	0	0	15 2/3	22	10	8	5	16
1999— Detroit (A.L.)■	0	0	...	10.80	2	0	0	0	0	3 1/3	7	5	4	2	3
— Toledo (I.L.)	2	11	.154	6.71	30	17	0	0	1	114	163	97	85	35	70
2000— Ottawa (I.L.)■	0	3	.000	4.95	4	4	0	0	0	20	24	12	11	3	10
— Montreal (N.L.)	5	8	.385	5.40	53	7	0	0	0	101 2/3	129	71	61	36	51
A.L. totals (5 years)	21	38	.356	5.22	106	72	4	3	1	470 2/3	516	294	273	184	294
N.L. totals (1 year)	5	8	.385	5.40	53	7	0	0	0	101 2/3	129	71	61	36	51
Major League totals (6 years)	26	46	.361	5.25	159	79	4	3	1	572 1/3	645	365	334	220	345

LLOYD, GRAEME — P — EXPOS

PERSONAL: Born April 9, 1967, in Geelong, Victoria, Australia. ... 6-7/234. ... Throws left, bats left. ... Full name: Graeme John Lloyd. ... Name pronounced GRAM.
HIGH SCHOOL: Geelong Technical School (Victoria, Australia).
COLLEGE: Geelong Tech.
TRANSACTIONS/CAREER NOTES: Signed as non-drafted free agent by Toronto Blue Jays organization (January 26, 1988). ... On Myrtle Beach disabled list (June 29-September 1, 1989). ... Selected by Philadelphia Phillies from Blue Jays organization in Rule 5 major league draft (December 7, 1992). ... Traded by Phillies to Milwaukee Brewers for P John Trisler (December 8, 1992). ... On disabled list (August 20-September 4, 1993 and July 25-September 10, 1995). ... On suspended list (September 5-9, 1993). ... Traded by Brewers with OF Pat Listach to New York Yankees for OF Gerald Williams and P Bob Wickman (August 23, 1996). ... On disabled list (April 22-May 8, 1998). ... On suspended list (May 25-27, 1998). ... Traded by Yankees with P David Wells and 2B Homer Bush to Toronto Blue Jays for P Roger Clemens (February 18, 1999). ... Granted free agency (October 29, 1999). ... Signed by Montreal Expos (December 20, 1999). ... On disabled list (March 29, 2000-entire season).

Year League	W	L	Pct.	ERA	G	GS	CG	ShO	Sv.	IP	H	R	ER	BB	SO
1988— Myrtle Beach (S.Atl.)	3	2	.600	3.62	41	0	0	0	2	59 2/3	71	33	24	30	43
1989— Dunedin (FSL)	0	0	...	10.13	2	0	0	0	0	2 2/3	6	3	3	1	0
— Myrtle Beach (S.Atl.)	0	0	...	5.40	1	1	0	0	0	5	5	4	3	0	3
1990— Myrtle Beach (S.Atl.)	5	2	.714	2.72	19	6	0	0	6	49 2/3	51	20	15	16	42
1991— Dunedin (FSL)	2	5	.286	2.24	50	0	0	0	24	60 1/3	54	17	15	25	39
— Knoxville (Sou.)	0	0	...	0.00	2	0	0	0	0	1 2/3	1	0	0	1	2
1992— Knoxville (Sou.)	4	8	.333	1.96	49	7	1	0	14	92	79	30	20	25	65
1993— Milwaukee (A.L.)■	3	4	.429	2.83	55	0	0	0	0	63 2/3	64	24	20	13	31
1994— Milwaukee (A.L.)	2	3	.400	5.17	43	0	0	0	3	47	49	28	27	15	31
1995— Milwaukee (A.L.)	0	5	.000	4.50	33	0	0	0	4	32	28	16	16	8	13
1996— Milwaukee (A.L.)	2	4	.333	2.82	52	0	0	0	0	51	49	19	16	17	24
— New York (A.L.)■	0	2	.000	17.47	13	0	0	0	0	5 2/3	12	11	11	5	6
1997— New York (A.L.)	1	1	.500	3.31	46	0	0	0	1	49	55	24	18	20	26
1998— New York (A.L.)	3	0	1.000	1.67	50	0	0	0	0	37 2/3	26	10	7	6	20
1999— Toronto (A.L.)■	5	3	.625	3.63	74	0	0	0	3	72	68	36	29	23	47
2000— Montreal (N.L.)■								Did not play.							
Major League totals (7 years)	16	22	.421	3.62	366	0	0	0	11	358	351	168	144	107	198

DIVISION SERIES RECORD

Year League	W	L	Pct.	ERA	G	GS	CG	ShO	Sv.	IP	H	R	ER	BB	SO
1996— New York (A.L.)	0	0	...	0.00	2	0	0	0	0	1	1	0	0	0	0
1997— New York (A.L.)	0	0	...	0.00	2	0	0	0	0	1 1/3	0	0	0	0	1
1998— New York (A.L.)	0	0	...	0.00	1	0	0	0	0	1/3	0	0	0	0	0
Division series totals (3 years)	0	0	...	0.00	5	0	0	0	0	2 2/3	1	0	0	0	1

CHAMPIONSHIP SERIES RECORD

Year League	W	L	Pct.	ERA	G	GS	CG	ShO	Sv.	IP	H	R	ER	BB	SO
1996— New York (A.L.)	0	0	...	0.00	2	0	0	0	0	1 2/3	0	0	0	0	1
1998— New York (A.L.)	0	0	...	0.00	1	0	0	0	0	2/3	1	0	0	0	0
Champ. series totals (2 years)	0	0	...	0.00	3	0	0	0	0	2 1/3	1	0	0	0	1

WORLD SERIES RECORD

NOTES: Member of World Series championship team (1996 and 1998).

Year League	W	L	Pct.	ERA	G	GS	CG	ShO	Sv.	IP	H	R	ER	BB	SO
1996— New York (A.L.)	1	0	1.000	0.00	4	0	0	0	0	2 2/3	0	0	0	0	4
1998— New York (A.L.)	0	0	...	0.00	1	0	0	0	0	1/3	0	0	0	0	0
World Series totals (2 years)	1	0	1.000	0.00	5	0	0	0	0	3	0	0	0	0	4

LOAIZA, ESTEBAN — P — BLUE JAYS

PERSONAL: Born December 31, 1971, in Tijuana, Mexico. ... 6-3/205. ... Throws right, bats right. ... Full name: Esteban Antonio Veyna Loaiza. ... Name pronounced low-EYE-zah.

HIGH SCHOOL: Mar Vista (Imperial Beach, Calif.).

TRANSACTIONS/CAREER NOTES: Signed as non-drafted free agent by Pittsburgh Pirates organization (March 21, 1991). ... Loaned by Pirates organization to Mexico City Red Devils of Mexican League (May 7-28, 1993). ... On disabled list (April 7-28 and July 7-14, 1994). ... Loaned to Red Devils of Mexican League (June 19-August 14, 1996). ... Traded by Pirates to Texas Rangers for P Todd Van Poppel and 2B Warren Morris (July 17, 1998). ... On Texas disabled list (May 12-July 5, 1999); included rehabilitation assignment to Oklahoma City (June 26-July 5). ... Traded by Rangers to Toronto Blue Jays for P Darwin Cubillan and 2B/SS Mike Young (July 19, 2000).

MISCELLANEOUS: Made an out in only appearance as pinch hitter (1995). ... Had a sacrifice hit in only appearance as pinch hitter (1996).

Year League	W	L	Pct.	ERA	G	GS	CG	ShO	Sv.	IP	H	R	ER	BB	SO
1991— Gulf Coast Pirates (GCL)	5	1	.833	2.26	11	11	1	•1	0	51²/₃	48	17	13	14	41
1992— Augusta (S.Atl.)	10	8	.556	3.89	26	25	3	0	0	143¹/₃	134	72	62	60	123
1993— Salem (Caro.)	6	7	.462	3.39	17	17	3	0	0	109	113	53	41	30	61
— M.C. Red Devils (Mex.)■ ...	1	1	.500	5.18	4	3	0	0	0	24¹/₃	32	18	14	4	15
— Carolina (Sou.)	2	1	.667	3.77	7	7	1	0	0	43	39	18	18	12	40
1994— Carolina (Sou.)	10	5	.667	3.79	24	24	3	0	0	154¹/₃	169	69	65	30	115
1995— Pittsburgh (N.L.)	8	9	.471	5.16	32	•31	1	0	0	172²/₃	205	*115	*99	55	85
1996— Calgary (PCL)	3	4	.429	4.02	12	11	1	1	0	69¹/₃	61	34	31	25	38
— M.C. Red Devils (Mex.)■ ...	2	0	1.000	2.43	5	5	0	0	0	33¹/₃	28	12	9	14	16
— Pittsburgh (N.L.)■	2	3	.400	4.96	10	10	1	1	0	52²/₃	65	32	29	19	32
1997— Pittsburgh (N.L.)	11	11	.500	4.13	33	32	1	0	0	196¹/₃	214	99	90	56	122
1998— Pittsburgh (N.L.)	6	5	.545	4.52	21	14	0	0	0	91²/₃	96	50	46	30	53
— Texas (A.L.)■	3	6	.333	5.90	14	14	1	0	0	79¹/₃	103	57	52	22	55
1999— Texas (A.L.)	9	5	.643	4.56	30	15	0	0	0	120¹/₃	128	65	61	40	77
— Oklahoma (PCL)	0	0	...	0.00	2	2	0	0	0	4¹/₃	3	0	0	3	6
2000— Texas (A.L.)	5	6	.455	5.37	20	17	0	0	1	107¹/₃	133	67	64	31	75
— Toronto (A.L.)■	5	7	.417	3.62	14	14	1	1	0	92	95	45	37	26	62
A.L. totals (3 years)	22	24	.478	4.83	78	60	2	1	1	399	459	234	214	119	269
N.L. totals (4 years)	27	28	.491	4.63	96	87	3	1	0	513¹/₃	580	296	264	160	292
Major League totals (6 years)	49	52	.485	4.72	174	147	5	2	1	912¹/₃	1039	530	478	279	561

DIVISION SERIES RECORD

Year League	W	L	Pct.	ERA	G	GS	CG	ShO	Sv.	IP	H	R	ER	BB	SO
1998— Texas (A.L.)							Did not play.								
1999— Texas (A.L.)	0	1	.000	3.86	1	1	0	0	0	7	5	3	3	1	4

LOCKHART, KEITH 2B BRAVES L

PERSONAL: Born November 10, 1964, in Whittier, Calif. ... 5-10/170. ... Bats left, throws right. ... Full name: Keith Virgil Lockhart.
HIGH SCHOOL: Northview (Covina, Calif.).
JUNIOR COLLEGE: Mount San Antonio College (Calif.).
COLLEGE: Oral Roberts.
TRANSACTIONS/CAREER NOTES: Selected by Cincinnati Reds organization in 11th round of free-agent draft (June 2, 1986). ... Contract sold by Reds organization to Oakland Athletics organization (February 4, 1992). ... Granted free agency (October 15, 1992). ... Signed by St. Louis Cardinals organization (December 12, 1992). ... Granted free agency (October 15, 1993). ... Signed by San Diego Padres organization (January 7, 1994). ... Granted free agency (October 15, 1994). ... Signed by Kansas City Royals organization (November 14, 1994). ... Traded by Royals with OF Michael Tucker to Atlanta Braves for OF Jermaine Dye and P Jamie Walker (March 27, 1997). ... On disabled list (August 6-22, 1997).
STATISTICAL NOTES: Led Midwest League third basemen with 33 double plays in 1987. ... Led Southern League with 11 sacrifice flies in 1988. ... Led American Association second basemen with 631 total chances in 1989. ... Career major league grand slams: 1.

							BATTING							FIELDING			
Year Team (League)	Pos.	G	AB	R	H	2B	3B	HR	RBI	Avg.	BB	SO	SB	PO	A	E	Avg.
1986— Billings (Pio.)	2B-3B	53	202	51	70	11	3	7	31	.347	35	22	4	81	150	17	.931
— Ced. Rap. (Midw.)	2B-3B	13	42	4	8	2	0	0	1	.190	6	6	1	17	15	0	1.000
1987— Ced. Rap. (Midw.)	3B-2B	*140	511	101	160	37	5	23	84	.313	86	70	20	85	292	28	.931
1988— Chattanooga (Sou.)	3B-2B	139	515	74	137	27	3	12	67	.266	61	59	7	102	323	36	.922
1989— Nashville (A.A.)	2B	131	479	77	128	21	6	14	58	.267	61	41	4	*279	*335	17	.973
1990— Nashville (A.A.)	2B-3B-OF	126	431	48	112	25	4	9	63	.260	51	74	8	173	248	9	.979
1991— Nashville (A.A.)	3B-2B-OF	116	411	53	107	25	3	8	36	.260	24	64	3	153	241	13	.968
1992— Tacoma (PCL)■	2B-3B-SS	107	363	44	101	25	3	5	37	.278	29	21	5	199	239	11	.976
1993— Louisville (A.A.)■	2B-3B-OF-1B	132	467	66	140	24	3	13	68	.300	60	43	3	157	239	12	.971
1994— San Diego (N.L.)■ ...3B-2B-SS-OF		27	43	4	9	0	0	2	6	.209	4	10	1	10	21	1	.969
— Las Vegas (PCL) O-S-2-3-P-C		89	331	61	106	15	5	7	43	.320	26	37	3	143	113	10	.962
1995— Omaha (A.A.)	3B-DH	44	148	24	56	7	1	5	19	.378	16	10	1	31	72	8	.928
— Kansas City (A.L.)	2B-3B-DH	94	274	41	88	19	3	6	33	.321	14	21	8	111	178	8	.973
1996— Kansas City (A.L.)	2B-3B-DH	138	433	49	118	33	3	7	55	.273	30	40	11	137	281	13	.970
1997— Atlanta (N.L.)■	2B-3B-DH	96	147	25	41	5	3	6	32	.279	14	17	0	24	48	3	.960
1998— Atlanta (N.L.)	2B-DH-3B	109	366	50	94	21	0	9	37	.257	29	37	2	130	250	6	.984
1999— Atlanta (N.L.)	2B-3B-DH	108	161	20	42	3	1	1	21	.261	19	21	3	27	64	1	.989
2000— Atlanta (N.L.)	2B-3B	113	275	32	73	12	3	2	32	.265	29	31	4	111	204	8	.975
American League totals (2 years)		232	707	90	206	52	6	13	88	.291	44	61	19	248	459	21	.971
National League totals (5 years)		453	992	131	259	41	7	20	128	.261	95	116	10	302	587	19	.979
Major League totals (7 years)		685	1699	221	465	93	13	33	216	.274	139	177	29	550	1046	40	.976

DIVISION SERIES RECORD

							BATTING							FIELDING			
Year Team (League)	Pos.	G	AB	R	H	2B	3B	HR	RBI	Avg.	BB	SO	SB	PO	A	E	Avg.
1997— Atlanta (N.L.)	2B	2	6	0	0	0	0	0	0	.000	0	1	0	1	8	1	.900
1998— Atlanta (N.L.)	2B	3	12	2	4	0	0	0	0	.333	1	0	0	9	9	0	1.000
1999— Atlanta (N.L.)	PH-2B	3	1	0	0	0	0	0	0	.000	0	1	0	0	0	0	...
2000— Atlanta (N.L.)	2B	3	8	0	1	0	0	0	0	.125	0	1	0	4	6	0	1.000
Division series totals (4 years)		11	27	2	5	0	0	0	0	.185	1	3	0	14	23	1	.974

CHAMPIONSHIP SERIES RECORD

						BATTING									FIELDING		
Year	Team (League)	Pos.	G	AB	R	H	2B	3B	HR	RBI	Avg.	BB	SO	SB	PO	A	E	Avg.
1997— Atlanta (N.L.)..............		2B-PH	5	16	4	8	1	1	0	3	.500	1	1	0	14	5	0	1.000
1998— Atlanta (N.L.)..............		2B-PH	6	17	2	4	1	1	0	0	.235	0	4	0	5	12	0	1.000
1999— Atlanta (N.L.)..............		PH-2B	3	5	0	2	0	1	0	1	.400	0	2	0	1	3	0	1.000
Championship series totals (3 years)			14	38	6	14	2	3	0	4	.368	1	7	0	20	20	0	1.000

WORLD SERIES RECORD

						BATTING									FIELDING		
Year	Team (League)	Pos.	G	AB	R	H	2B	3B	HR	RBI	Avg.	BB	SO	SB	PO	A	E	Avg.
1999— Atlanta (N.L.)..............		PH-2B-DH	4	7	1	1	0	0	0	0	.143	2	0	0	1	2	0	1.000

RECORD AS PITCHER

Year	League	W	L	Pct.	ERA	G	GS	CG	ShO	Sv.	IP	H	R	ER	BB	SO
1994— Las Vegas (PCL)		0	0	...	0.00	1	1	0	0	0	1	0	0	0	0	0

LoDUCA, PAUL   C   DODGERS

PERSONAL: Born April 12, 1972, in Brooklyn, N.Y. ... 5-10/185. ... Bats right, throws right. ... Full name: Paul Anthony LoDuca.

HIGH SCHOOL: Apollo (Phoenix).

JUNIOR COLLEGE: Glendale (Ariz.) Community College.

COLLEGE: Arizona State.

TRANSACTIONS/CAREER NOTES: Selected by Los Angeles Dodgers organization in 25th round of free-agent draft (June 3, 1993). ... On Albuquerque disabled list (June 4-July 20, 1999).

STATISTICAL NOTES: Led Florida State League with .400 on-base percentage in 1996. ... Led Florida State League catchers with 17 errors in 1996. ... Led Texas League catchers with .990 fielding percentage, 84 assists and 667 total chances in 1997. ... Led Pacific Coast League in grounding into double plays with 20 in 1998.

						BATTING									FIELDING		
Year	Team (League)	Pos.	G	AB	R	H	2B	3B	HR	RBI	Avg.	BB	SO	SB	PO	A	E	Avg.
1993— Vero Beach (FSL)		C	39	134	17	42	6	0	0	13	.313	13	22	0	209	26	2	.992
1994— Bakersfield (Calif.)		1B-C	123	455	65	144	32	1	6	68	.316	52	49	16	657	59	5	.993
1995— San Antonio (Texas) ...		C-1B-3B	61	199	27	49	8	0	1	8	.246	26	25	5	353	43	11	.973
1996— Vero Beach (FSL)		C-1B-3B	124	439	54	134	22	0	3	66	.305	70	38	8	747	116	†18	.980
1997— San Antonio (Texas) ...		C-1B	105	385	63	126	28	2	7	69	.327	46	27	16	636	†91	7	†.990
1998— Albuquerque (PCL)		C-1B-3B	126	451	69	144	30	3	8	58	.319	59	40	19	742	92	17	.980
—Los Angeles (N.L.)		C	6	14	2	4	1	0	0	1	.286	0	1	0	18	2	0	1.000
1999— Los Angeles (N.L.)		C	36	95	11	22	1	0	3	11	.232	10	9	1	178	21	2	.990
—Albuquerque (PCL)......		C	26	76	17	28	9	0	1	8	.368	10	1	1	162	15	4	.978
2000— Albuquerque (PCL).....		C-O-1-3-2	78	279	47	98	27	3	4	54	.351	33	14	8	364	48	9	.979
—Los Angeles (N.L.)		C-OF-3B	34	65	6	16	2	0	2	8	.246	6	8	0	122	14	1	.993
Major League totals (3 years)			76	174	19	42	4	0	5	20	.241	16	18	1	318	37	3	.992

LOEWER, CARLTON   P   PADRES

PERSONAL: Born September 24, 1973, in Lafayette, La. ... 6-6/211. ... Throws right, bats right. ... Full name: Carlton Edward Loewer.

HIGH SCHOOL: St. Edmund (Eunice, La.).

COLLEGE: Mississippi State.

TRANSACTIONS/CAREER NOTES: Selected by Toronto Blue Jays organization in seventh round of free-agent draft (June 3, 1991); did not sign. ... Selected by Philadelphia Phillies organization in first round (23rd pick overall) of free-agent draft (June 2, 1994). ... On Philadelphia disabled list (June 6-September 6, 1999); included rehabilitation assignments to Gulf Coast League Phillies (August 26-30) and Clearwater (August 31-September 6). ... Traded by Phillies with P Steve Montgomery and P Adam Eaton to San Diego Padres for P Andy Ashby (November 10, 1999). ... On San Diego disabled list (March 28, 2000-remainder of season); included rehabilitation assignments to Las Vegas (May 27-30) and Rancho Cucamonga (May 31-June 12).

STATISTICAL NOTES: Led Eastern League with 24 home runs allowed in 1996.

Year	League	W	L	Pct.	ERA	G	GS	CG	ShO	Sv.	IP	H	R	ER	BB	SO
1995— Clearwater (FSL)		7	5	.583	3.30	20	20	1	0	0	114 2/3	124	59	42	36	83
—Reading (East.)...................		4	1	.800	2.16	8	8	0	0	0	50	42	17	12	31	35
1996— Reading (East.)...................		7	10	.412	5.26	27	27	3	1	0	171	*191	115	100	57	119
1997— Scranton/W.B. (I.L.)		5	13	.278	4.60	29	*29	4	0	0	184	*198	*120	94	50	152
1998— Scranton/W.B. (I.L.)		7	3	.700	2.87	12	12	*5	•2	0	94	89	34	30	22	69
—Philadelphia (N.L.)		7	8	.467	6.09	21	21	1	0	0	122 2/3	154	86	83	39	58
1999— Philadelphia (N.L.).............		2	6	.250	5.12	20	13	2	1	0	89 2/3	100	54	51	26	48
—Gulf Coast Phillies (GCL)....		0	0	...	0.00	1	1	0	0	0	2	2	0	0	0	2
—Clearwater (FSL)		0	2	.000	7.71	3	3	0	0	0	7	10	6	6	1	5
2000— Las Vegas (PCL)■		0	0	...	0.00	1	1	0	0	0	4 2/3	3	0	0	0	4
—Rancho Cuca. (Calif.)		0	0	...	2.57	1	1	0	0	0	7	7	3	2	0	4
Major League totals (2 years).......		9	14	.391	5.68	41	34	3	1	0	212 1/3	254	140	134	65	106

LOFTON, KENNY   OF   INDIANS

PERSONAL: Born May 31, 1967, in East Chicago, Ind. ... 6-0/190. ... Bats left, throws left. ... Full name: Kenneth Lofton.

HIGH SCHOOL: Washington (East Chicago, Ind.).

COLLEGE: Arizona.

TRANSACTIONS/CAREER NOTES: Selected by Houston Astros organization in 17th round of free-agent draft (June 1, 1988). ... Traded by Astros with IF Dave Rohde to Cleveland Indians for P Willie Blair and C Eddie Taubensee (December 10, 1991). ... On disabled list (July 17-August 1, 1995). ... Traded by Indians with P Alan Embree to Atlanta Braves for OF Marquis Grissom and OF Dave Justice (March 25, 1997).

... On disabled list (June 18-July 5 and July 6-28, 1997). ... Granted free agency (October 28, 1997). ... Signed by Indians (December 8, 1997). ... On disabled list (July 28-August 14 and August 17-September 1, 1999; and April 30-May 12, 2000).

RECORDS: Holds A.L. rookie-season record for most stolen bases—66 (1992). ... Shares A.L. single-season record for fewest errors by outfielder who led league in errors—8 (1998). ... Shares A.L. record for most consecutive games scoring one or more runs—18 (26 runs, August 15-September 3, 2000).

HONORS: Won A.L. Gold Glove as outfielder (1993-96).

STATISTICAL NOTES: Tied for Pacific Coast League lead in caught stealing with 23 in 1991. ... Led Pacific Coast League outfielders with 344 total chances in 1991. ... Led N.L. in caught stealing with 20 in 1997. ... Career major league grand slams: 2.

MISCELLANEOUS: Holds Cleveland Indians all-time record for most stolen bases (404).

							BATTING							FIELDING		
Year	Team (League)	Pos.	G	AB	R	H	2B	3B	HR	RBI	Avg.	BB	SO	SB	PO	A	E	Avg.
1988— Auburn (NY-Penn)......	OF	48	187	23	40	6	1	1	14	.214	19	51	26	94	5	4	.961
1989— Auburn (NY-Penn)......	OF	34	110	21	29	3	1	0	8	.264	14	30	26	37	4	8	.837
—Asheville (S.Atl.).........	OF	22	82	14	27	2	0	1	9	.329	12	10	14	38	1	2	.951
1990— Osceola (FSL)............	OF	124	481	98	*159	15	5	2	35	.331	61	77	62	246	13	7	.974
1991— Tucson (PCL)............	OF	130	*545	93	*168	19	*17	2	50	.308	52	95	40	*308	*27	9	.974
—Houston (N.L.)	OF	20	74	9	15	1	0	0	0	.203	5	19	2	41	1	1	.977
1992— Cleveland (A.L.)■......	OF	148	576	96	164	15	8	5	42	.285	68	54	*66	420	14	8	.982
1993— Cleveland (A.L.).........	OF	148	569	116	185	28	8	1	42	.325	81	83	*70	402	11	•9	.979
1994— Cleveland (A.L.).........	OF	112	459	105	*160	32	9	12	57	.349	52	56	*60	276	•13	2	.993
1995— Cleveland (A.L.).........	OF-DH	118	481	93	149	22	*13	7	53	.310	40	49	*54	248	•11	8	.970
1996— Cleveland (A.L.).........	OF	154	*662	132	210	35	4	14	67	.317	61	82	*75	376	13	10	.975
1997— Atlanta (N.L.)■..........	OF	122	493	90	164	20	6	5	48	.333	64	83	27	290	5	5	.983
1998— Cleveland (A.L.)■.......	OF	154	600	101	169	31	6	12	64	.282	87	80	54	339	*19	8	.978
1999— Cleveland (A.L.).........	OF-DH	120	465	110	140	28	6	7	39	.301	79	84	25	255	11	3	.989
2000— Cleveland (A.L.).........	OF-DH	137	543	107	151	23	5	15	73	.278	79	72	30	348	4	4	.989
American League totals (8 years)		1091	4355	860	1328	214	59	73	437	.305	547	560	434	2664	96	52	.982
National League totals (2 years)		142	567	99	179	21	6	5	48	.316	69	102	29	331	6	6	.983
Major League totals (10 years)		1233	4922	959	1507	235	65	78	485	.306	616	662	463	2995	102	58	.982

DIVISION SERIES RECORD

							BATTING							FIELDING		
Year	Team (League)	Pos.	G	AB	R	H	2B	3B	HR	RBI	Avg.	BB	SO	SB	PO	A	E	Avg.
1995— Cleveland (A.L.).........	OF	3	13	1	2	0	0	0	0	.154	1	3	0	9	0	2	.818
1996— Cleveland (A.L.).........	OF	4	18	3	3	0	0	0	1	.167	2	3	5	10	0	0	1.000
1997— Atlanta (N.L.)............	OF	3	13	2	2	1	0	0	0	.154	1	2	0	6	1	0	1.000
1998— Cleveland (A.L.).........	OF	4	16	5	6	1	0	2	4	.375	1	1	2	10	0	0	1.000
1999— Cleveland (A.L.).........	OF	5	16	5	2	1	0	0	1	.125	5	6	2	14	0	1	.933
Division series totals (5 years)		19	76	16	15	3	0	2	6	.197	10	15	9	49	1	3	.943

CHAMPIONSHIP SERIES RECORD

							BATTING							FIELDING		
Year	Team (League)	Pos.	G	AB	R	H	2B	3B	HR	RBI	Avg.	BB	SO	SB	PO	A	E	Avg.
1995— Cleveland (A.L.).........	OF	6	24	4	11	0	2	0	3	.458	4	6	5	15	0	0	1.000
1997— Atlanta (N.L.)............	OF	6	27	3	5	0	1	0	1	.185	1	7	1	9	1	2	.833
1998— Cleveland (A.L.).........	OF	6	27	2	5	1	0	1	3	.185	1	7	1	8	0	1	.889
Championship series totals (3 years)		18	78	9	21	1	3	1	7	.269	6	20	7	32	1	3	.917

WORLD SERIES RECORD

RECORDS: Shares single-inning record for most stolen bases—2 (October 21, 1995).

							BATTING							FIELDING		
Year	Team (League)	Pos.	G	AB	R	H	2B	3B	HR	RBI	Avg.	BB	SO	SB	PO	A	E	Avg.
1995— Cleveland (A.L.).........	OF	6	25	6	5	1	0	0	0	.200	3	1	6	12	0	0	1.000

ALL-STAR GAME RECORD

RECORDS: Shares single-game record for most stolen bases—2 (July 9, 1996).

					BATTING						FIELDING		
Year	League	Pos.	AB	R	H	2B	3B	HR	RBI	Avg.	BB	SO	SB	PO	A	E	Avg.
1994— American..................	OF	2	0	1	0	0	0	2	.500	0	1	1	1	0	0	1.000
1995— American..................	OF	3	0	0	0	0	0	0	.000	0	1	0	0	0	0	...
1996— American..................	OF	3	0	2	0	0	0	0	.667	0	0	2	0	0	0	...
1997— National....................				Selected, did not play—injured.											
1998— American..................	OF	3	0	1	0	0	0	0	.333	1	0	1	2	0	0	1.000
1999— American..................	OF	3	1	1	0	0	0	0	.333	0	1	1	0	0	0	...
All-Star Game totals (5 years)		14	1	5	0	0	0	2	.357	1	3	5	3	0	0	1.000

LOISELLE, RICH   P   PIRATES

PERSONAL: Born January 12, 1972, in Neenah, Wis. ... 6-5/253. ... Throws right, bats right. ... Full name: Richard Frank Loiselle.

HIGH SCHOOL: Lawton (Okla.).

JUNIOR COLLEGE: Odessa (Texas) College.

TRANSACTIONS/CAREER NOTES: Selected by San Diego Padres organization in 38th round of free-agent draft (June 3, 1991). ... Traded by Padres with P Jeff Tabaka to Houston Astros for OF Phil Plantier (July 19, 1995). ... On Tucson disabled list (August 2, 1995-remainder of season). ... Traded by Astros to Pittsburgh Pirates for P Danny Darwin (July 23, 1996). ... On Pittsburgh disabled list (July 20-August 17, 1998); included rehabilitation assignment to Nashville (August 7-16). ... On disabled list (May 8, 1999-remainder of season). ... On Pittsburgh disabled list (April 2-May 22 and June 25-August 3, 2000); included rehabilitation assignments to Altoona (April 26-May 21 and July 22-25), Gulf Coast Pirates (July 18-21) and Nashville (July 25-August 2).

Year League	W	L	Pct.	ERA	G	GS	CG	ShO	Sv.	IP	H	R	ER	BB	SO
1991— Arizona Padres (Ariz.)	2	3	.400	3.52	12	12	0	0	0	61 $1/3$	72	40	24	26	47
1992— Charleston (A.A.)	4	8	.333	3.71	19	19	2	2	0	97	93	51	40	42	64
1993— Waterloo (Midw.)	1	5	.167	3.94	14	10	1	1	0	59 $1/3$	55	28	26	29	47
— Rancho Cuca. (Calif.)	5	8	.385	5.77	14	14	1	0	0	82 $2/3$	109	64	53	34	53
1994— Rancho Cuca. (Calif.)	9	10	.474	3.96	27	27	0	0	0	156 $2/3$	160	83	69	76	120
1995— Memphis (Sou.)	6	3	.667	3.55	13	13	1	0	0	78 $2/3$	82	46	31	33	48
— Las Vegas (PCL)	2	2	.500	7.24	8	7	1	1	0	27 $1/3$	36	27	22	9	16
— Tucson (PCL)■.................	0	0	...	2.61	2	1	0	0	0	10 $1/3$	8	4	3	4	4
1996— Jackson (Texas)	7	4	.636	3.47	16	16	2	0	0	98 $2/3$	107	46	38	27	65
— Tucson (PCL)	2	2	.500	2.43	5	5	1	1	0	33 $1/3$	28	20	9	11	31
— Calgary (PCL)■................	2	2	.500	4.09	8	8	0	0	0	50 $2/3$	64	28	23	16	41
— Pittsburgh (N.L.)	1	0	1.000	3.05	5	3	0	0	0	20 $2/3$	22	8	7	8	9
1997— Pittsburgh (N.L.)	1	5	.167	3.10	72	0	0	0	29	72 $2/3$	76	29	25	24	66
1998— Pittsburgh (N.L.)	2	7	.222	3.44	54	0	0	0	19	55	56	26	21	36	48
— Nashville (PCL)	0	0	...	0.00	4	0	0	0	2	5	3	0	0	0	6
1999— Pittsburgh (N.L.)	3	2	.600	5.28	13	0	0	0	0	15 $1/3$	16	9	9	9	14
2000— Altoona (East.)	0	1	.000	5.27	13	0	0	0	2	13 $2/3$	17	9	8	6	18
— Pittsburgh (N.L.)	2	3	.400	5.10	40	0	0	0	0	42 $1/3$	43	27	24	30	32
— Gulf Coast Pirates (GCL)	0	0	...	0.00	1	1	0	0	0	1	0	0	0	0	2
— Nashville (PCL)	0	0	...	0.00	4	0	0	0	0	4 $2/3$	2	0	0	2	3
Major League totals (5 years)	**9**	**17**	**.346**	**3.76**	**184**	**3**	**0**	**0**	**48**	**206**	**213**	**99**	**86**	**107**	**169**

PERSONAL: Born August 29, 1977, in Melrose, Mass. ... 6-0/195. ... Bats right, throws right. ... Full name: Steven James Lomasney.
HIGH SCHOOL: Peabody (Mass.).
TRANSACTIONS/CAREER NOTES: Selected by Boston Red Sox organization in fifth round of free-agent draft (June 1, 1995). ... On Sarasota disabled list (April 8-17 and June 10-21, 1999).
STATISTICAL NOTES: Led New York-Pennsylvania League catchers with 21 passed balls in 1996.

							BATTING						FIELDING		
Year Team (League)	Pos.	G	AB	R	H	2B	3B	HR	RBI	Avg.	BB	SO	SB	PO	A	E	Avg.
1995— GC Red Sox (GCL)	C	29	92	10	15	6	0	0	7	.163	8	16	2	146	29	5	.972
1996— Lowell (NY-Penn)	C	59	173	26	24	10	0	4	21	.139	42	63	2	402	47	9	.980
1997— Michigan (Midw.)	C	102	324	50	89	27	3	12	51	.275	32	98	3	623	83	12	.983
1998— Sarasota (FSL)	C-1B	122	443	74	106	22	1	22	63	.239	59	145	13	590	79	13	.981
1999— Sarasota (FSL)	C-DH-1B	55	189	35	51	10	0	8	28	.270	26	57	5	284	46	9	.973
— Trenton (East.)	C-DH	47	151	24	37	6	0	12	31	.245	31	44	7	355	33	12	.970
— Boston (A.L.)...............	C	1	2	0	0	0	0	0	0	.000	0	2	0	7	2	0	1.000
2000— Trenton (East.)	C	66	233	30	57	16	1	8	27	.245	24	81	4	418	35	6	.987
— GC Red Sox (GCL)	C	6	15	2	4	2	0	0	1	.267	4	6	0	37	6	2	.956
Major League totals (1 year)		1	2	0	0	0	0	0	0	.000	0	2	0	7	2	0	1.000

PERSONAL: Born September 14, 1975, in Atlanta. ... 6-0/202. ... Bats left, throws right. ... Full name: George Paul Lombard.
HIGH SCHOOL: Lovett (Atlanta).
TRANSACTIONS/CAREER NOTES: Selected by Atlanta Braves organization in second round of free-agent draft (June 2, 1994). ... On disabled list (August 16, 1996-remainder of season). ... On Richmond disabled list (May 29-June 22 and July 2-August 11, 1999).
STATISTICAL NOTES: Tied for South Atlantic League lead in caught stealing with 13 in 1995. ... Led Carolina League outfielders with 284 total chances in 1997. ... Led Southern League with 10 intentional bases on balls in 1998.

							BATTING						FIELDING		
Year Team (League)	Pos.	G	AB	R	H	2B	3B	HR	RBI	Avg.	BB	SO	SB	PO	A	E	Avg.
1994— GC Braves (GCL)	OF	40	129	10	18	2	0	0	5	.140	18	47	10	33	1	2	.944
1995— Eugene (N'West)	OF	68	262	38	66	5	3	5	19	.252	23	91	35	71	5	3	.962
— Macon (S.Atl.)	OF	49	180	32	37	6	1	3	16	.206	27	44	16	44	2	2	.958
1996— Macon (S.Atl.)	OF-DH	116	444	76	109	16	8	15	51	.245	36	122	24	229	2	7	.971
1997— Durham (Caro.)	OF-DH	131	462	65	122	25	7	14	72	.264	66	145	35	*270	5	9	.968
1998— Greenville (Sou.)	OF	122	422	84	130	25	4	22	65	.308	71	140	35	170	8	10	.947
— Atlanta (N.L.)...............	OF	6	6	2	2	0	0	1	1	.333	0	1	1	2	0	0	1.000
1999— Richmond (I.L.)..........	OF-DH	74	233	25	48	11	3	7	29	.206	35	98	21	108	3	3	.974
— Atlanta (N.L.)...............	OF	6	6	1	2	0	0	0	0	.333	1	2	2	4	0	0	1.000
2000— Richmond (I.L.)..........	OF	112	424	72	117	25	7	10	48	.276	55	130	32	202	5	6	.972
— Atlanta (N.L.)...............	OF	27	39	8	4	0	0	0	2	.103	1	14	4	17	1	0	1.000
Major League totals (3 years)		39	51	11	8	0	0	1	3	.157	2	17	7	23	1	0	1.000

PERSONAL: Born February 29, 1976, in Montgomery, Ala. ... 6-1/190. ... Bats left, throws left. ... Full name: Terrence Deon Long.
HIGH SCHOOL: Stanhope Elmore (Millbrook, Ala.).
TRANSACTIONS/CAREER NOTES: Selected by New York Mets organization in first round (20th pick overall) of free-agent draft (June 2, 1994); pick received as compensation for Baltimore Orioles signing Type A free-agent P Sid Fernandez. ... On disabled list (May 15-27, 1996). ... Traded by Mets with P Leo Vasquez to Oakland Athletics for P Kenny Rogers (July 23, 1999).
STATISTICAL NOTES: Had 17-game hitting streak (June 10-29, 2000). ... Career major league grand slams: 1.

Year	Team (League)	Pos.	G	AB	R	H	2B	3B	HR	RBI	Avg.	BB	SO	SB	PO	A	E	Avg.
1994—Kingsport (Appl.)........	OF-1B	60	215	39	50	9	2	12	39	.233	32	52	9	237	5	5	.980
1995—Capital City (S.Atl.).....	OF	55	178	27	35	1	2	2	13	.197	28	43	8	69	5	5	.937
—Pittsfield (NY-Penn)....	OF	51	187	24	48	9	4	4	31	.257	18	36	11	111	3	1	*.991
1996—Columbia (S.Atl.).......	OF-DH	123	473	66	136	26	9	12	78	.288	36	120	32	246	8	5	.981
1997—St. Lucie (FSL)	OF-DH	126	470	52	118	29	7	8	61	.251	40	102	24	235	7	7	.972
1998—Binghamton (East.)	OF-DH	130	455	69	135	20	*10	16	58	.297	62	105	23	218	9	10	.958
1999—Norfolk (I.L.)	OF	78	304	41	99	20	4	7	47	.326	23	41	14	192	8	4	.980
—New York (N.L.)..........		3	3	0	0	0	0	0	0	.000	0	2	0	0	0	0	...
—Vancouver (PCL)■.....	OF-DH	40	154	16	38	6	2	2	21	.247	10	29	7	95	3	4	.961
2000—Sacramento (PCL)......	OF	15	60	11	24	6	0	3	15	.400	4	4	0	28	0	3	.903
—Oakland (A.L.)	OF	138	584	104	168	34	4	18	80	.288	43	77	5	328	2	*10	.971
American League totals (1 year)		138	584	104	168	34	4	18	80	.288	43	77	5	328	2	10	.971
National League totals (1 year)		3	3	0	0	0	0	0	0	.000	0	2	0	0	0	0	...
Major League totals (2 years)		141	587	104	168	34	4	18	80	.286	43	79	5	328	2	10	.971

DIVISION SERIES RECORD

Year	Team (League)	Pos.	G	AB	R	H	2B	3B	HR	RBI	Avg.	BB	SO	SB	PO	A	E	Avg.
2000—Oakland (A.L.)	OF	5	19	2	3	0	0	1	1	.158	3	2	0	11	1	1	.923

LOOPER, BRADEN   P   MARLINS

PERSONAL: Born October 28, 1974, in Weatherford, Okla. ... 6-5/225. ... Throws right, bats right. ... Full name: Braden LaVern Looper. ... Name pronounced BRAY-dun.
HIGH SCHOOL: Mangum (Okla.).
COLLEGE: Wichita State.
TRANSACTIONS/CAREER NOTES: Selected by St. Louis Cardinals organization in first round (third pick overall) of free-agent draft (June 2, 1996). ... On Memphis disabled list (May 6-June 21, 1998). ... Traded by Cardinals with P Armando Almanza and SS Pablo Ozuna to Florida Marlins for SS Edgar Renteria (December 14, 1998).
MISCELLANEOUS: Member of 1996 U.S. Olympic baseball team.

Year	League	W	L	Pct.	ERA	G	GS	CG	ShO	Sv.	IP	H	R	ER	BB	SO
1997—Prince William (Caro.)........		3	6	.333	4.48	12	12	0	0	0	64 1/3	71	38	32	25	58
—Arkansas (Texas)		1	4	.200	5.91	19	0	0	0	5	21 1/3	24	14	14	7	20
1998—St. Louis (N.L.)...............		0	1	.000	5.40	4	0	0	0	0	3 1/3	5	4	2	1	4
—Memphis (PCL)................		2	3	.400	3.10	40	0	0	0	20	40 2/3	43	16	14	13	43
1999—Florida (N.L.)■............		3	3	.500	3.80	72	0	0	0	0	83	96	43	35	31	50
2000—Florida (N.L.)		5	1	.833	4.41	73	0	0	0	2	67 1/3	71	41	33	36	29
Major League totals (3 years).......		8	5	.615	4.10	149	0	0	0	2	153 2/3	172	88	70	68	83

LOPEZ, ALBIE   P   DEVIL RAYS

PERSONAL: Born August 18, 1971, in Mesa, Ariz. ... 6-2/240. ... Throws right, bats right. ... Full name: Albert Anthony Lopez.
HIGH SCHOOL: Westwood (Mesa, Ariz.).
JUNIOR COLLEGE: Mesa (Ariz.) Community College.
TRANSACTIONS/CAREER NOTES: Selected by San Francisco Giants organization in 46th round of free-agent draft (June 5, 1989); did not sign. ... Selected by Seattle Mariners organization in 19th round of free-agent draft (June 4, 1990); did not sign. ... Selected by Cleveland Indians organization in 20th round of free-agent draft (June 3, 1991). ... On Cleveland disabled list (July 2-28 and August 13-September 1, 1997). ... Selected by Tampa Bay Devil Rays in second round (48th pick overall) of expansion draft (November 18, 1997). ... On Tampa Bay disabled list (August 1-26, 1998); included rehabilitation assignments to Durham (August 15-18) and St. Petersburg (August 25-26). ... On Tampa Bay disabled list (May 12-June 20, 1999); included rehabilitation assignment to St. Petersburg (June 14-20).
STATISTICAL NOTES: Led American Association with 10 hit batsmen and tied for lead with three balks in 1996.
MISCELLANEOUS: Holds Tampa Bay Devils Rays all-time record for lowest earned-run average (3.86). ... Tied for Tampa Devil Rays all-time record for most wins (21).

Year	League	W	L	Pct.	ERA	G	GS	CG	ShO	Sv.	IP	H	R	ER	BB	SO
1991—Burlington (Appl.)...............		4	5	.444	3.44	13	13	0	0	0	73 1/3	61	33	28	23	81
1992—Columbus (S.Atl.)...............		7	2	.778	2.88	16	16	1	0	0	97	80	41	31	33	117
—Kinston (Caro.)...............		5	2	.714	3.52	10	10	1	1	0	64	56	28	25	26	44
1993—Canton/Akron (East.)..........		9	4	.692	3.11	16	16	2	0	0	110	79	44	38	47	80
—Cleveland (A.L.)...........		3	1	.750	5.98	9	9	0	0	0	49 2/3	49	34	33	32	25
—Charlotte (I.L.)............		1	0	1.000	2.25	3	2	0	0	0	12	8	3	3	2	7
1994—Charlotte (I.L.)...........		13	8	.813	3.94	22	22	3	0	0	144	136	68	63	42	105
—Cleveland (A.L.)...........		1	2	.333	4.24	4	4	1	1	0	17	20	11	8	6	18
1995—Buffalo (A.A.).................		5	10	.333	4.44	18	18	1	1	0	101 1/3	101	57	50	51	82
—Cleveland (A.L.)...........		0	0	...	3.13	6	2	0	0	0	23	17	8	8	7	22
1996—Buffalo (A.A.).................		10	2	.833	3.87	17	17	2	0	0	104 2/3	90	54	45	40	89
—Cleveland (A.L.)...........		5	4	.556	6.39	13	10	0	0	0	62	80	47	44	22	45
1997—Cleveland (A.L.)...........		3	7	.300	6.93	37	6	0	0	0	76 2/3	101	61	59	40	63
—Buffalo (A.A.).................		1	0	1.000	0.00	7	0	0	0	1	11 1/3	6	0	0	2	13
—Akron (East.)		0	0	...	0.00	1	0	0	0	0	1	2	0	0	0	2
1998—Tampa Bay (A.L.)■..........		7	4	.636	2.60	54	0	0	0	1	79 2/3	73	31	23	32	62
—Durham (I.L.)		0	0	...	0.00	2	0	0	0	0	3	4	0	0	1	2
—St. Petersburg (FSL)		0	1	.000	18.00	1	1	0	0	0	1	2	2	2	0	1
1999—Tampa Bay (A.L.)...........		3	2	.600	4.64	51	0	0	0	1	64	66	40	33	24	37
—St. Petersburg (FSL)		0	0	...	5.40	2	1	0	0	0	3 1/3	7	5	2	0	3
2000—Tampa Bay (A.L.).................		11	13	.458	4.13	45	24	4	1	2	185 1/3	199	95	85	70	96
—Princeton (Appl.)		0	0	...	0.00	1	0	0	0	0	2/3	0	0	0	0	1
Major League totals (8 years).......		33	33	.500	4.73	219	55	5	2	4	557 1/3	605	327	293	233	368

PERSONAL: Born November 5, 1970, in Ponce, Puerto Rico. ... 6-3/200. ... Bats right, throws right. ... Full name: Javier Torres Lopez.
HIGH SCHOOL: Academia Cristo Rey (Urb la Ramble Ponce, Puerto Rico).
TRANSACTIONS/CAREER NOTES: Signed as non-drafted free agent by Atlanta Braves organization (November 6, 1987). ... On Greenville disabled list (July 18-August 2, 1992). ... On Atlanta disabled list (July 6-22, 1997; and June 21-July 15 and July 25, 1999-remainder of season).
HONORS: Named Southern League Most Valuable Player (1992).
STATISTICAL NOTES: Led Midwest League catchers with 11 double plays and 31 passed balls in 1990. ... Led Carolina League catchers with 701 total chances and 14 double plays in 1991. ... Led Southern League catchers with 763 total chances and 19 passed balls in 1992. ... Led International League catchers with 15 passed balls in 1993. ... Tied for N.L. lead with 10 passed balls in 1994. ... Career major league grand slams: 3.

Year	Team (League)	Pos.	G	AB	R	H	2B	3B	HR	RBI	Avg.	BB	SO	SB	PO	A	E	Avg.
1988—	GC Braves (GCL)	C	31	94	8	18	4	0	1	9	.191	3	19	1	131	30	7	.958
1989—	Pulaski (Appl.)	C	51	153	27	40	8	1	3	27	.261	5	35	3	264	26	5	.983
1990—	Burlington (Midw.)	C	116	422	48	112	17	3	11	55	.265	14	84	0	724	79	11	.986
1991—	Durham (Caro.)	C	113	384	43	94	14	2	11	51	.245	25	88	10	*610	85	6	.991
1992—	Greenville (Sou.)	C	115	442	63	142	28	3	16	60	.321	24	47	7	*680	75	8	.990
—	Atlanta (N.L.)	C	9	16	3	6	2	0	0	2	.375	0	1	0	28	2	0	1.000
1993—	Richmond (I.L.)	C-DH	100	380	56	116	23	2	17	74	.305	12	53	1	718	70	10	.987
—	Atlanta (N.L.)	C	8	16	1	6	1	1	1	2	.375	0	2	0	37	2	1	.975
1994—	Atlanta (N.L.)	C	80	277	27	68	9	0	13	35	.245	17	61	0	559	35	3	.995
1995—	Atlanta (N.L.)	C	100	333	37	105	11	4	14	51	.315	14	57	0	625	50	8	.988
1996—	Atlanta (N.L.)	C	138	489	56	138	19	1	23	69	.282	28	84	1	993	*81	6	.994
1997—	Atlanta (N.L.)	C	123	414	52	122	28	1	23	68	.295	40	82	1	792	56	6	.993
1998—	Atlanta (N.L.)	C-DH	133	489	73	139	21	1	34	106	.284	30	85	5	978	68	5	*.995
1999—	Atlanta (N.L.)	C-DH	65	246	34	78	18	1	11	45	.317	20	41	0	413	29	4	.991
2000—	Atlanta (N.L.)	C	134	481	60	138	21	0	24	89	.287	35	80	0	817	62	6	.993
Major League totals (9 years)			790	2761	343	800	130	10	143	467	.290	184	493	7	5242	385	39	.993

DIVISION SERIES RECORD

Year	Team (League)	Pos.	G	AB	R	H	2B	3B	HR	RBI	Avg.	BB	SO	SB	PO	A	E	Avg.
1995—	Atlanta (N.L.)	C	3	9	0	4	0	0	0	3	.444	0	3	0	22	3	0	1.000
1996—	Atlanta (N.L.)	C	2	7	1	2	0	0	1	1	.286	1	0	1	21	1	1	.957
1997—	Atlanta (N.L.)	C	2	7	3	2	2	0	1	1	.286	2	1	0	18	0	0	1.000
1998—	Atlanta (N.L.)	C	2	7	1	2	0	0	1	1	.286	1	1	0	20	3	0	1.000
2000—	Atlanta (N.L.)	PH-C	3	11	0	1	0	0	0	0	.091	0	1	0	15	2	0	1.000
Division series totals (5 years)			12	41	5	11	2	0	2	6	.268	4	6	1	96	9	1	.991

CHAMPIONSHIP SERIES RECORD

RECORDS: Shares career record for most doubles—7. ... Shares single-game record for most runs—4 (October 14, 1996). ... Holds N.L. single-series record for most runs—8 (1996). ... Shares N.L. single-series record for most consecutive hits—5 (1996). ... Holds single-series records for most doubles—5 (1996); and most long hits—7 (1996). ... Shares single-series record for most total bases—24 (1996).
NOTES: Named N.L. Championship Series Most Valuable Player (1996).

Year	Team (League)	Pos.	G	AB	R	H	2B	3B	HR	RBI	Avg.	BB	SO	SB	PO	A	E	Avg.
1992—	Atlanta (N.L.)	C	1	1	0	0	0	0	0	0	.000	0	0	0	2	0	0	1.000
1995—	Atlanta (N.L.)	C	3	14	2	5	1	0	1	3	.357	0	1	0	28	2	0	1.000
1996—	Atlanta (N.L.)	C	7	24	8	13	5	0	2	6	.542	4	1	1	48	3	0	1.000
1997—	Atlanta (N.L.)	C-PH	5	17	0	1	1	0	0	2	.059	1	7	0	40	3	0	1.000
1998—	Atlanta (N.L.)	C-PH	6	20	2	6	0	0	1	1	.300	0	7	0	43	2	1	.978
Championship series totals (5 years)			22	76	12	25	7	0	4	12	.329	5	16	1	161	10	1	.994

WORLD SERIES RECORD

NOTES: Member of World Series championship team (1995).

Year	Team (League)	Pos.	G	AB	R	H	2B	3B	HR	RBI	Avg.	BB	SO	SB	PO	A	E	Avg.
1992—	Atlanta (N.L.)							Did not play.										
1995—	Atlanta (N.L.)	C-PH	6	17	1	3	2	0	1	3	.176	1	1	0	32	4	0	1.000
1996—	Atlanta (N.L.)	C	6	21	3	4	0	0	0	1	.190	3	4	0	41	4	0	1.000
World Series totals (2 years)			12	38	4	7	2	0	1	4	.184	4	5	0	73	8	0	1.000

ALL-STAR GAME RECORD

RECORDS: Hit home run in first at-bat (July 8, 1997).

Year	League	Pos.	AB	R	H	2B	3B	HR	RBI	Avg.	BB	SO	SB	PO	A	E	Avg.
1997—	National	C	1	1	1	0	0	1	1	1.000	0	0	0	4	1	0	1.000
1998—	National	C	1	0	0	0	0	0	0	.000	0	1	0	3	0	0	1.000
All-Star Game totals (2 years)			2	1	1	0	0	1	1	.500	0	1	0	7	1	0	1.000

PERSONAL: Born September 4, 1970, in Cidra, Puerto Rico. ... 5-11/166. ... Bats both, throws right. ... Full name: Luis Manuel Lopez.
HIGH SCHOOL: San Jose (Caguas, Puerto Rico).
TRANSACTIONS/CAREER NOTES: Signed as non-drafted free agent by San Diego Padres organization (September 9, 1987). ... On Las Vegas disabled list (July 3-14, 1994). ... Granted free agency (October 15, 1994). ... Re-signed by Padres (April 20, 1995). ... On disabled list (April 24, 1995-entire season). ... On San Diego disabled list (March 29-April 18 and July 31-September 1, 1996); included rehabilitation assignments to Las Vegas (March 30-April 18 and August 17-September 1). ... Traded by Padres to Houston Astros for P Sean Runyan (March 15, 1997). ... Traded by Astros to New York Mets for IF Tim Bogar (March 31, 1997). ... Traded by Mets to Milwaukee Brewers for P Bill Pulsipher (January 21, 2000).

STATISTICAL NOTES: Led South Atlantic League shortstops with 703 total chances and 78 double plays in 1989. ... Led Pacific Coast League shortstops with 30 errors in 1992. ... Tied for Pacific Coast League lead with 13 sacrifice hits in 1993. ... Career major league grand slams: 1.

Year	Team (League)	Pos.	G	AB	R	H	2B	3B	HR	RBI	Avg.	BB	SO	SB	PO	A	E	Avg.
1988—	Spokane (N'West)	SS	70	312	50	95	13	1	0	35	.304	18	59	14	*118	217	*47	.877
1989—	Char., S.C. (SAL)	SS	127	460	50	102	15	1	1	29	.222	17	85	12	*256	*373	*74	.895
1990—	Riverside (Calif.)	SS	14	46	5	17	3	1	1	4	.370	3	3	4	18	38	6	.903
1991—	Wichita (Texas)	2B-SS	125	452	43	121	17	1	1	41	.268	18	70	6	274	339	26	.959
1992—	Las Vegas (PCL)	SS-OF	120	395	44	92	8	8	1	31	.233	19	65	6	200	358	†30	.949
1993—	Las Vegas (PCL)	SS-2B-DH	131	491	52	150	36	6	6	58	.305	27	62	8	230	380	29	.955
—	San Diego (N.L.)	2B	17	43	1	5	1	0	0	1	.116	0	8	0	23	34	1	.983
1994—	Las Vegas (PCL)	2B	12	49	2	10	2	2	0	6	.204	1	5	0	28	43	2	.973
—	San Diego (N.L.)	SS-2B-3B	77	235	29	65	16	1	2	20	.277	15	39	3	101	174	14	.952
1995—	San Diego (N.L.)						Did not play.											
1996—	Las Vegas (PCL)	2B-SS	18	68	4	14	3	0	1	12	.206	2	15	0	39	43	2	.976
—	San Diego (N.L.)	SS-2B-3B	63	139	10	25	3	0	2	11	.180	9	35	0	57	100	4	.975
1997—	Norfolk (I.L.)■	SS-2B-DH	48	203	32	67	12	1	4	19	.330	9	29	2	79	123	14	.935
—	New York (N.L.)	SS-2B-3B	78	178	19	48	12	1	1	19	.270	12	42	2	79	156	9	.963
1998—	New York (N.L.)	2-S-3-O	117	266	37	67	13	2	2	22	.252	20	60	2	123	144	11	.960
1999—	New York (N.L.)	SS-2B-3B	68	104	11	22	4	0	2	13	.212	12	33	1	34	68	4	.962
2000—	Milwaukee (N.L.)■	SS-2B-3B	78	201	24	53	14	0	6	27	.264	9	35	1	101	146	8	.969
Major League totals (7 years)			498	1166	131	285	83	4	15	113	.244	77	252	9	518	822	51	.963

DIVISION SERIES RECORD

Year	Team (League)	Pos.	G	AB	R	H	2B	3B	HR	RBI	Avg.	BB	SO	SB	PO	A	E	Avg.
1996—	San Diego (N.L.)	PR	1	0	0	0	0	0	0	0	...	0	0	0	...	...	...	...
1999—	New York (N.L.)						Did not play.											

CHAMPIONSHIP SERIES RECORD

Year	Team (League)	Pos.	G	AB	R	H	2B	3B	HR	RBI	Avg.	BB	SO	SB	PO	A	E	Avg.
1999—	New York (N.L.)						Did not play.											

LOPEZ, MENDY   IF   L

PERSONAL: Born October 15, 1974, in Santo Domingo, Dominican Republic. ... 6-2/190. ... Bats right, throws right. ... Full name: Mendy Aude Lopez.

HIGH SCHOOL: Liceo Los Trinitanos (Santo Domingo, Dominican Republic).

TRANSACTIONS/CAREER NOTES: Signed as non-drafted free agent by Kansas City Royals organization (February 26, 1992). ... On Omaha disabled list (May 28-July 7, 1999). ... Released by Royals (December 13, 1999). ... Signed by Florida Marlins organization (January 12, 2000). ... On Calgary disabled list (April 6-June 23, 2000). ... Granted free agency (October 2, 2000).

STATISTICAL NOTES: Led Gulf Coast League shortstops with .971 fielding percentage, 80 putouts, 154 assists, 241 total chances and 39 double plays in 1994. ... Tied for Texas League lead with 28 double plays by third baseman in 1996.

Year	Team (League)	Pos.	G	AB	R	H	2B	3B	HR	RBI	Avg.	BB	SO	SB	PO	A	E	Avg.
1992—	Dom. Royals (DSL)	SS	49	145	22	40	1	0	1	23	.276	22	15	7	81	155	26	.901
1993—	Dom. Royals (DSL)	IF	28	98	15	27	5	2	0	20	.276	11	5	2	52	75	15	.894
1994—	GC Royals (GCL)	SS-3B-2B	59	*235	56	85	*19	3	5	*50	.362	22	27	10	†84	†195	12	†.959
1995—	Wilmington (Caro.)......	3B-SS	130	428	42	116	29	3	2	36	.271	28	73	18	84	335	25	.944
1996—	Wichita (Texas)	3B-SS	93	327	47	92	20	5	6	32	.281	26	67	14	80	265	24	.935
1997—	Omaha (A.A.)	3B	17	52	6	12	2	0	1	6	.231	8	21	0	15	38	6	.898
—	Wichita (Texas)	SS	101	357	56	83	16	3	5	42	.232	36	70	7	193	296	20	.961
1998—	Omaha (PCL)	SS-3B	60	195	18	35	6	1	3	14	.179	18	44	2	71	167	10	.960
—	Kansas City (A.L.)	SS-3B	74	206	18	50	10	2	1	15	.243	12	40	5	102	225	15	.956
1999—	Omaha (PCL)	SS-2B-3B-DH	61	222	41	69	8	0	12	40	.311	18	41	2	98	171	8	.971
—	GC Royals (GCL)	SS-DH	3	5	0	1	1	0	0	2	.200	3	1	0	2	4	0	1.000
—	Kansas City (A.L.)	2B-SS	7	20	2	8	0	1	0	3	.400	0	5	0	11	16	0	1.000
2000—	Calgary (PCL)■	SS-2B-3B	56	225	34	73	20	1	7	29	.324	13	38	1	97	155	12	.955
—	Florida (N.L.)	PH	4	3	0	0	0	0	0	0	.000	1	1	0	...	...	...	...
American League totals (2 years)			81	226	20	58	10	3	1	18	.257	12	45	5	113	241	15	.959
National League totals (1 year)			4	3	0	0	0	0	0	0	.000	1	1	0	0	0	0	...
Major League totals (3 years)			85	229	20	58	10	3	1	18	.253	13	46	5	113	241	15	.959

LOPEZ, RODRIGO   P   PADRES

PERSONAL: Born December 14, 1975, in Mexico City, Mexico. ... 6-1/180. ... Throws right, bats right. ... Full name: Rodrigo Munoz Lopez.

TRANSACTIONS/CAREER NOTES: Signed by Aguila of Mexican League (1994). ... Contract sold by Aguila to San Diego Padres organization (March 17, 1995). ... Loaned by Padres to Mexico City Red Devils of Mexican League (March 13, 1998). ... Returned to Padres organization (August 19, 1998).

Year	League	W	L	Pct.	ERA	G	GS	CG	ShO	Sv.	IP	H	R	ER	BB	SO
1994—	Aguila (Mex.)	0	0	...	4.97	10	0	0	0	0	12 2/3	15	7	7	3	5
1995—	Arizona Padres (Ariz.)■	1	1	.500	5.45	11	7	0	0	1	34 2/3	41	29	21	14	33
1996—	Idaho Falls (Pio.)	4	4	.500	5.70	15	14	0	0	1	71	76	52	45	34	72
1997—	Clinton (Midw.)	6	8	.429	3.18	37	14	2	0	9	121 2/3	103	49	43	42	123
1998—	M.C. Red Devils (Mex.)■ ...	10	6	.625	3.35	26	26	1	0	0	163 2/3	165	73	61	79	95
—	Mobile (Sou.)■	3	0	1.000	1.40	4	4	2	1	0	25 2/3	21	11	4	4	22
1999—	Mobile (Sou.)	10	8	.556	4.41	28	•28	2	1	0	169 1/3	187	91	83	58	138
2000—	Las Vegas (PCL)	8	7	.533	4.69	20	20	1	0	0	109 1/3	123	66	57	45	100
—	San Diego (N.L.)	0	3	.000	8.76	6	6	0	0	0	24 2/3	40	24	24	13	17
Major League totals (1 year)		0	3	.000	8.76	6	6	0	0	0	24 2/3	40	24	24	13	17

PERSONAL: Born August 14, 1971, in Santa Monica, Calif. ... 6-0/180. ... Bats right, throws right. ... Full name: Mark David Loretta.
HIGH SCHOOL: St. Francis (La Canada, Calif.).
COLLEGE: Northwestern.
TRANSACTIONS/CAREER NOTES: Selected by Milwaukee Brewers organization in seventh round of free-agent draft (June 3, 1993). ... On New Orleans suspended list (May 17-20, 1996). ... On Milwaukee disabled list (June 3-August 16, 2000); included rehabilitation assignment to Indianapolis (August 3-16).
STATISTICAL NOTES: Led American Association shortstops with 200 putouts and 591 total chances in 1995.

								BATTING						FIELDING			
Year Team (League)	Pos.	G	AB	R	H	2B	3B	HR	RBI	Avg.	BB	SO	SB	PO	A	E	Avg.
1993—Helena (Pio.)	SS	6	28	5	9	1	0	1	8	.321	1	4	0	11	18	0	1.000
—Stockton (Calif.)	SS-3B	53	201	36	73	4	1	4	31	.363	22	17	8	75	173	15	.943
1994—El Paso (Texas)..........	SS-P	77	302	50	95	13	6	0	38	.315	27	33	8	125	271	11	.973
—New Orleans (A.A.).....	SS-2B	43	138	16	29	7	0	1	14	.210	12	13	2	68	121	11	.945
1995—New Orleans (A.A.).....	S-3-DH-2	127	479	48	137	22	5	7	79	.286	34	47	8	†204	376	25	.959
—Milwaukee (A.L.)	SS-2B-DH	19	50	13	13	3	0	1	3	.260	4	7	1	18	42	1	.984
1996—New Orleans (A.A.).....	SS	19	71	10	18	5	1	0	11	.254	9	8	1	31	60	5	.948
—Milwaukee (A.L.)	2B-3B-SS	73	154	20	43	3	0	1	13	.279	14	15	2	63	116	2	.989
1997—Milwaukee (A.L.) 2-S-1-3-DH		132	418	56	120	17	5	5	47	.287	47	60	5	334	277	15	.976
1998—Milwaukee (N.L.)	1-S-3-2-O	140	434	55	137	29	0	6	54	.316	42	47	9	450	215	6	.991
1999—Milwaukee (N.L.) SS-1B-2B-3B		153	587	93	170	34	5	5	67	.290	52	59	4	625	260	13	.986
2000—Milwaukee (N.L.)	SS-2B	91	352	49	99	21	1	7	40	.281	37	38	0	122	254	2	.995
—Indianapolis (I.L.).......	SS	10	25	6	6	1	0	0	5	.240	2	4	0	4	14	0	1.000
American League totals (3 years)		224	622	89	176	23	5	7	63	.283	65	82	8	415	435	18	.979
National League totals (3 years)		384	1373	197	406	84	6	18	161	.296	131	144	13	1197	729	21	.989
Major League totals (6 years)		608	1995	286	582	107	11	25	224	.292	196	226	21	1612	1164	39	.986

RECORD AS PITCHER

Year League	W	L	Pct.	ERA	G	GS	CG	ShO	Sv.	IP	H	R	ER	BB	SO
1994—El Paso (Texas)..................	0	0	...	...	1	0	0	0	0	0	1	1	1	1	0

PERSONAL: Born August 11, 1972, in Los Angeles. ... 6-3/200. ... Throws left, bats left. ... Full name: Andrew Jason Lorraine.
HIGH SCHOOL: William S. Hart (Newhall, Calif.).
COLLEGE: Stanford.
TRANSACTIONS/CAREER NOTES: Selected by New York Mets organization in 38th round of free-agent draft (June 4, 1990); did not sign. ... Selected by California Angels organization in fourth round of free-agent draft (June 3, 1993). ... Traded by Angels with OF McKay Christensen, P Bill Simas and P John Snyder to Chicago White Sox for P Jim Abbott and P Tim Fortugno (July 27, 1995). ... Traded by White Sox with OF Charles Poe to Oakland Athletics for OF/DH Danny Tartabull (January 22, 1996). ... Released by A's (October 16, 1997). ... Signed by Seattle Mariners organization (October 17, 1997). ... Granted free agency (October 3, 1998). ... Signed by Chicago Cubs organization (November 13, 1998). ... Released by Cubs (May 21, 2000). ... Signed by Cleveland Indians organization (May 22, 2000). ... Granted free agency (October 5, 2000).
MISCELLANEOUS: Scored a run in only appearance as pinch runner (1999).

Year League	W	L	Pct.	ERA	G	GS	CG	ShO	Sv.	IP	H	R	ER	BB	SO
1993—Boise (N'West)	4	1	.800	1.29	6	6	3	1	0	42	33	6	6	6	39
1994—Vancouver (PCL)	12	4	.750	3.42	22	22	•4	•2	0	142	156	63	54	34	90
—California (A.L.)..............	0	2	.000	10.61	4	3	0	0	0	18²/₃	30	23	22	11	10
1995—Vancouver (PCL)	6	6	.500	3.96	18	18	4	1	0	97²/₃	105	49	43	30	51
—Nashville (A.A.)■	4	1	.800	6.00	7	7	0	0	0	39	51	29	26	12	26
—Chicago (A.L.)	0	0	...	3.38	5	0	0	0	0	8	3	3	3	2	5
1996—Edmonton (PCL)■	8	10	.444	5.68	30	25	0	0	0	141	181	95	89	46	73
1997—Edmonton (PCL)	8	6	.571	4.74	23	20	2	2	0	117²/₃	143	72	62	34	75
—Oakland (A.L.)	3	1	.750	6.37	12	6	0	0	0	29²/₃	45	22	21	15	18
1998—Tacoma (PCL)■	7	4	.636	4.82	52	4	0	0	2	80¹/₃	93	44	43	36	70
—Seattle (A.L.)	0	0	...	2.45	4	0	0	0	0	3²/₃	3	1	1	4	0
1999—Iowa (PCL)■	9	8	.529	3.71	22	21	1	0	0	143	149	67	59	34	96
—Chicago (N.L.)	2	5	.286	5.55	11	11	2	1	0	61²/₃	71	42	38	22	40
2000—Chicago (N.L.)	1	2	.333	6.47	8	5	0	0	0	32	36	25	23	18	25
—Buffalo (I.L.)■	8	3	.727	3.47	14	13	0	0	0	90²/₃	97	37	35	24	51
—Cleveland (A.L.)	0	0	...	3.86	10	0	0	0	0	9¹/₃	8	4	4	5	5
A.L. totals (5 years)	3	3	.500	6.62	35	9	0	0	0	69¹/₃	89	53	51	37	38
N.L. totals (2 years)	3	7	.300	5.86	19	16	2	1	0	93²/₃	107	67	61	40	65
Major League totals (6 years).......	6	10	.375	6.18	54	25	2	1	0	163	196	120	112	77	103

PERSONAL: Born June 1, 1973, in Dearborn, Mich. ... 6-6/200. ... Throws right, bats right. ... Full name: Derek Christopher Lowe.
HIGH SCHOOL: Edsel Ford (Dearborn, Mich.).
TRANSACTIONS/CAREER NOTES: Selected by Seattle Mariners organization in eighth round of free-agent draft (June 3, 1991). ... Traded by Mariners with C Jason Varitek to Boston Red Sox for P Heathcliff Slocumb (July 31, 1997).
STATISTICAL NOTES: Led Southern League with seven balks in 1994.
MISCELLANEOUS: Struck out in only appearance as pinch hitter (2000).

Year League	W	L	Pct.	ERA	G	GS	CG	ShO	Sv.	IP	H	R	ER	BB	SO
1991—Arizona Mariners (Ariz.)	5	3	.625	2.41	12	12	0	0	0	71	58	26	19	21	60
1992—Bellingham (N'West)	7	3	.700	2.42	14	13	2	•1	0	85²/₃	69	34	23	22	66
1993—Riverside (Calif.)................	12	9	.571	5.26	27	26	3	2	0	154	189	104	90	60	80

Year	League	W	L	Pct.	ERA	G	GS	CG	ShO	Sv.	IP	H	R	ER	BB	SO
1994—	Jacksonville (Sou.)............	7	10	.412	4.94	26	26	2	0	0	151 1/3	177	92	83	50	75
1995—	Port City (Sou.)	1	6	.143	6.07	10	10	1	0	0	53 1/3	70	41	36	22	30
—	Arizona Mariners (Ariz.) ...	1	0	1.000	0.93	2	2	0	0	0	9 2/3	5	1	1	2	11
1996—	Port City (Sou.)	5	3	.625	3.05	10	10	0	0	0	65	56	27	22	17	33
—	Tacoma (PCL)	6	9	.400	4.54	17	16	1	1	0	105	118	64	53	37	54
1997—	Tacoma (PCL)	3	4	.429	3.45	10	9	1	0	0	57 1/3	53	26	22	20	49
—	Seattle (A.L.)	2	4	.333	6.96	12	9	0	0	0	53	59	43	41	20	39
—	Pawtucket (I.L.)■...............	4	0	1.000	2.37	6	5	0	0	0	30 1/3	23	8	8	11	21
—	Boston (A.L.).....................	0	2	.000	3.38	8	0	0	0	0	16	15	6	6	3	13
1998—	Boston (A.L.).....................	3	9	.250	4.02	63	10	0	0	4	123	126	65	55	42	77
1999—	Boston (A.L.).....................	6	3	.667	2.63	74	0	0	0	15	109 1/3	84	35	32	25	80
2000—	Boston (A.L.).....................	4	4	.500	2.56	74	0	0	0	•42	91 1/3	90	27	26	22	79
Major League totals (4 years)......		**15**	**22**	**.405**	**3.67**	**231**	**19**	**0**	**0**	**61**	**392 2/3**	**374**	**176**	**160**	**112**	**288**

DIVISION SERIES RECORD

Year	League	W	L	Pct.	ERA	G	GS	CG	ShO	Sv.	IP	H	R	ER	BB	SO
1998—	Boston (A.L.).....................	0	0	...	2.08	2	0	0	0	0	4 1/3	3	1	1	2	2
1999—	Boston (A.L.).....................	1	1	.500	4.32	3	0	0	0	0	8 1/3	6	7	4	1	7
Division series totals (2 years)		**1**	**1**	**.500**	**3.55**	**5**	**0**	**0**	**0**	**0**	**12 2/3**	**9**	**8**	**5**	**3**	**9**

CHAMPIONSHIP SERIES RECORD

Year	League	W	L	Pct.	ERA	G	GS	CG	ShO	Sv.	IP	H	R	ER	BB	SO
1999—	Boston (A.L.).....................	0	0	...	1.42	3	0	0	0	0	6 1/3	6	3	1	2	7

ALL-STAR GAME RECORD

Year	League	W	L	Pct.	ERA	GS	CG	ShO	Sv.	IP	H	R	ER	BB	SO
2000—	American	0	0	...	0.00	0	0	0	0	1	0	0	0	0	0

LOWE, SEAN   P   WHITE SOX

PERSONAL: Born March 29, 1971, in Dallas. ... 6-2/205. ... Throws right, bats right. ... Full name: Jonathan Sean Lowe.
HIGH SCHOOL: Mesquite (Texas).
JUNIOR COLLEGE: McLennan Community College (Texas).
COLLEGE: Arizona State.
TRANSACTIONS/CAREER NOTES: Selected by Cincinnati Reds organization in 43rd round of free-agent draft (June 5, 1989); did not sign. ... Selected by Oakland Athletics organization in 43rd round of free-agent draft (June 4, 1990); did not sign. ... Selected by St. Louis Cardinals organization in first round (15th pick overall) of free-agent draft (June 1, 1992). ... On St. Petersburg disabled list (July 19-August 8, 1994). ... On Arkansas disabled list (May 28-June 4, 1996). ... On Louisville disabled list (April 9-18, 1997). ... Traded by Cardinals to Chicago White Sox for P John Ambrose (February 9, 1999). ... On Chicago disabled list (July 29-August 23, 2000); included rehabilitation assignment to Charlotte (August 8-23).
STATISTICAL NOTES: Tied for American Association lead with 10 hit batsmen in 1997.

Year	League	W	L	Pct.	ERA	G	GS	CG	ShO	Sv.	IP	H	R	ER	BB	SO
1992—	Hamilton (NY-Penn)	2	0	1.000	1.61	5	5	0	0	0	28	14	8	5	14	22
1993—	St. Petersburg (FSL)	6	11	.353	4.27	25	25	0	0	0	132 2/3	152	80	63	62	87
1994—	St. Petersburg (FSL)	5	6	.455	3.47	21	21	0	0	0	114	119	51	44	37	92
—	Arkansas (Texas)..............	2	1	.667	1.40	3	3	0	0	0	19 1/3	13	3	3	8	11
1995—	Arkansas (Texas)..............	9	8	.529	4.88	24	24	0	0	0	129	143	84	70	64	77
1996—	Louisville (A.A.)	8	9	.471	4.70	25	18	0	0	0	115	127	72	60	51	76
—	Arkansas (Texas)..............	2	3	.400	6.00	6	6	0	0	0	33	32	24	22	15	25
1997—	Louisville (A.A.)	6	10	.375	4.37	26	23	1	0	1	131 2/3	142	74	64	53	117
—	St. Louis (N.L.)	0	2	.000	9.35	6	4	0	0	0	17 1/3	27	21	18	10	8
1998—	Memphis (PCL)	12	8	.600	3.18	25	21	0	0	0	153	147	57	54	61	114
—	St. Louis (N.L.)	0	3	.000	15.19	4	1	0	0	0	5 1/3	11	9	9	5	2
1999—	Chicago (A.L.)■	4	1	.800	3.67	64	0	0	0	0	95 2/3	90	39	39	46	62
2000—	Chicago (A.L.)	4	1	.800	5.48	50	5	0	0	0	70 2/3	78	47	43	39	53
—	Charlotte (I.L.)	0	0	...	3.00	2	1	0	0	0	3	5	1	1	1	1
A.L. totals (2 years)		**8**	**2**	**.800**	**4.44**	**114**	**5**	**0**	**0**	**0**	**166 1/3**	**168**	**86**	**82**	**85**	**115**
N.L. totals (2 years)		**0**	**5**	**.000**	**10.72**	**10**	**5**	**0**	**0**	**0**	**22 2/3**	**38**	**30**	**27**	**15**	**10**
Major League totals (4 years).......		**8**	**7**	**.533**	**5.19**	**124**	**10**	**0**	**0**	**0**	**189**	**206**	**116**	**109**	**100**	**125**

LOWELL, MIKE   3B   MARLINS

PERSONAL: Born February 24, 1974, in San Juan, Puerto Rico. ... 6-4/205. ... Bats right, throws right. ... Full name: Michael Averett Lowell.
HIGH SCHOOL: Coral Gables (Fla.).
COLLEGE: Florida International.
TRANSACTIONS/CAREER NOTES: Selected by New York Yankees organization in 20th round of free-agent draft (June 1, 1995). ... Traded by Yankees to Florida Marlins for P Ed Yarnall, P Mark Johnson and P Todd Noel (February 1, 1999). ... On Florida disabled list (March 26-May 29, 1999); included rehabilitation assignments to Calgary (April 8-13 and May 6-29). ... On disabled list (May 13-29, 2000).
STATISTICAL NOTES: Led New York-Pennsylvania League third basemen with 271 total chances in 1995. ... Led South Atlantic League third basemen with .926 fielding percentage, 301 putouts and 421 total chances in 1996. ... Tied for International League lead with 20 errors by third baseman in 1998. ... Had 16-game hitting streak (August 18-September 5, 2000). ... Career major league grand slams: 1.

Year	Team (League)	Pos.	G	AB	R	H	2B	3B	HR	RBI	Avg.	BB	SO	SB	PO	A	E	Avg.
1995—	Oneonta (NY-Penn)	3B	72	281	36	73	18	0	1	27	.260	23	34	3	59	188	24	.911
1996—	Greensboro (S.Atl.)	3B-SS	113	433	58	122	33	0	8	64	.282	46	43	10	91	†302	32	.925
—	Tampa (FSL)..............	3B	24	78	8	22	5	0	0	11	.282	3	13	1	22	40	3	.954
1997—	Norwich (East.)	3B-SS	78	285	60	98	17	0	15	47	.344	48	30	2	57	133	15	.927
—	Columbus (I.L.)	3B-SS	57	210	36	58	13	1	15	45	.276	23	34	2	31	73	5	.954

Year	Team (League)	Pos.	G	AB	R	H	2B	3B	HR	RBI	Avg.	BB	SO	SB	PO	A	E	Avg.
1998—	Columbus (I.L.)	3B-1B-SS	126	510	79	155	34	3	26	99	.304	37	85	4	114	283	‡21	.950
—	New York (A.L.)	3B-DH	8	15	1	4	0	0	0	0	.267	0	1	0	2	5	0	1.000
1999—	Calgary (PCL)■	3B	24	83	11	26	3	0	2	9	.313	8	19	0	11	51	4	.939
—	Florida (N.L.)	3B	97	308	32	78	15	0	12	47	.253	26	69	0	59	143	4	.981
2000—	Florida (N.L.)	3B	140	508	73	137	38	0	22	91	.270	54	75	4	102	260	12	.968
American League totals (1 year)			8	15	1	4	0	0	0	0	.267	0	1	0	2	5	0	1.000
National League totals (2 years)			237	816	105	215	53	0	34	138	.263	80	144	4	161	403	16	.972
Major League totals (3 years)			245	831	106	219	53	0	34	138	.264	80	145	4	163	408	16	.973

LOWERY, TERRELL — OF — GIANTS

PERSONAL: Born October 25, 1970, in Oakland. ... 6-3/195. ... Bats right, throws right. ... Full name: Quenton Terrell Lowery. ... Brother of Josh Lowery, minor league shortstop (1989-90).
HIGH SCHOOL: Oakland Technical.
COLLEGE: Loyola Marymount.
TRANSACTIONS/CAREER NOTES: Selected by Texas Rangers organization in second round of free-agent draft (June 3, 1991). ... On Butte disabled list (June 17-27, 1992). ... On restricted list (June 27, 1992-February 5, 1993). ... On Oklahoma City disabled list (April 6-August 24, 1995). ... Traded by Rangers to New York Mets for OF Damon Buford (January 25, 1996). ... Selected by Chicago Cubs from Mets organization in Rule 5 major league draft (December 9, 1996). ... On Iowa disabled list (September 4, 1998-remainder of season). ... Granted free agency (October 15, 1998). ... Signed by Tampa Bay Devil Rays organization (November 19, 1998). ... Granted free agency (October 10, 1999). ... Signed by San Francisco Giants organization (January 13, 2000).
STATISTICAL NOTES: Led Texas League outfielders with 303 total chances in 1994. ... Led American Association with .401 on-base percentage in 1997. ... Career major league grand slams: 1.

Year	Team (League)	Pos.	G	AB	R	H	2B	3B	HR	RBI	Avg.	BB	SO	SB	PO	A	E	Avg.
1991—	Butte (Pio.)	OF	54	214	38	64	10	7	3	33	.299	29	44	23	92	7	6	.943
1992—	Butte (Pio.)								Did not play.									
1993—	Charlotte (FSL)	OF	65	257	46	77	7	9	3	36	.300	46	47	14	156	5	4	.976
—	Tulsa (Texas)	OF	66	258	29	62	5	1	3	14	.240	28	50	10	152	6	2	.988
1994—	Tulsa (Texas)	OF	129	496	89	142	34	8	8	54	.286	59	113	33	*280	16	7	.977
1995—	GC Rangers (GCL)	DH-OF	10	34	10	9	3	1	3	7	.265	6	7	1	7	0	0	1.000
—	Charlotte (FSL)	OF	11	35	4	9	2	2	0	4	.257	6	6	1	18	0	0	1.000
1996—	Norfolk (I.L.)■	OF	62	193	25	45	7	2	4	21	.233	22	44	6	106	4	1	.991
—	Binghamton (East.)	OF-DH	62	211	34	58	13	4	7	32	.275	44	44	5	97	3	3	.971
1997—	Iowa (A.A.)■	OF-DH	110	386	69	116	28	3	17	71	.301	65	97	9	244	8	3	.988
—	Chicago (N.L.)	OF	9	14	2	4	0	0	0	0	.286	3	3	1	7	2	0	1.000
1998—	Iowa (PCL)	OF	65	246	41	73	14	1	12	49	.297	27	63	5	155	5	1	.994
—	Chicago (N.L.)	OF	24	15	2	3	1	0	0	1	.200	3	7	0	13	0	1	.929
1999—	Durham (I.L.)■	OF-DH	71	275	69	92	20	5	15	57	.335	43	62	10	129	3	1	.992
—	Tampa Bay (A.L.)	OF-DH	66	185	25	48	15	1	2	17	.259	19	53	0	97	4	3	.971
2000—	Fresno (PCL)■	OF	84	301	48	60	9	1	16	44	.199	36	88	6	146	2	4	.974
—	San Francisco (N.L.)	OF-DH	24	34	13	15	4	0	1	5	.441	7	8	1	11	0	1	.917
American League totals (1 year)			66	185	25	48	15	1	2	17	.259	19	53	0	97	4	3	.971
National League totals (3 years)			57	63	17	22	5	0	1	6	.349	13	18	2	31	2	2	.943
Major League totals (4 years)			123	248	42	70	20	1	3	23	.282	32	71	2	128	6	5	.964

LUCCA, LOU — IF — CARDINALS

PERSONAL: Born October 13, 1970, in San Francisco. ... 5-11/210. ... Bats right, throws right. ... Full name: Louis Raul Lucca Jr.
HIGH SCHOOL: South San Francisco (Calif.).
JUNIOR COLLEGE: San Jose City.
COLLEGE: Oklahoma State.
TRANSACTIONS/CAREER NOTES: Selected by Florida Marlins organization in 32nd round of free-agent draft (June 1, 1992). ... Granted free agency (October 16, 1998). ... Signed by Philadelphia Phillies organization (November 3, 1998). ... Granted free agency (October 15, 1999). ... Signed by St. Louis Cardinals organization (December 13, 1999).
STATISTICAL NOTES: Led New York-Pennsylvania League third basemen with 255 total chances in 1992. ... Tied for Midwest League lead in double plays by third basemen with 24 in 1993. ... Led Florida State League third basemen with 442 total chances in 1994. ... Led Eastern League third basemen with 23 double plays in 1995. ... Led International League third basemen with 402 total chances and 27 double plays in 1999.

Year	Team (League)	Pos.	G	AB	R	H	2B	3B	HR	RBI	Avg.	BB	SO	SB	PO	A	E	Avg.
1992—	Erie (NY-Penn)	3B	76	263	51	74	16	1	13	44	.281	33	40	6	•56	*175	•24	.906
1993—	Kane County (Midw.)	3B	127	419	52	116	25	2	6	53	.277	60	58	4	82	235	23	*.932
1994—	Brevard County (FSL)	3B	130	441	62	125	29	1	8	76	.283	72	73	3	66	*355	21	*.952
1995—	Portland (East.)	3B	112	388	57	107	28	1	9	64	.276	59	77	4	56	*261	16	*.952
1996—	Charlotte (I.L.)	3B	87	273	26	71	14	1	7	35	.260	11	62	0	38	151	18	.913
1997—	Charlotte (I.L.)	3B	96	292	40	83	22	1	18	51	.284	22	56	5	43	201	14	.946
1998—	Charlotte (I.L.)	3B-OF-SS	112	397	47	115	32	0	11	51	.290	13	75	2	111	155	16	.943
1999—	Scranton/W.B. (I.L.)■	3B	136	533	61	143	33	2	12	70	.268	22	94	4	76	*310	16	.960
2000—	Memphis (PCL)■	3-1-2-S	122	462	70	131	31	2	14	70	.284	32	61	7	96	257	16	.957

LUEBBERS, LARRY — P — REDS

PERSONAL: Born October 11, 1969, in Cincinnati. ... 6-6/210. ... Throws right, bats right. ... Full name: Larry Christopher Luebbers.
HIGH SCHOOL: St. Henry (Erlanger, Ky.).

COLLEGE: Kentucky.
TRANSACTIONS/CAREER NOTES: Selected by Cincinnati Reds organization in eighth round of free-agent draft (June 4, 1990). ... Traded by Reds with P Mike Anderson and C Darron Cox to Chicago Cubs for P Chuck McElroy (December 10, 1993). ... Claimed on waivers by Reds (November 18, 1994). ... Granted free agency (October 15, 1996). ... Signed by Atlanta Braves organization (February 24, 1997). ... Granted free agency (October 15, 1997). ... Signed by St. Louis Cardinals organization (November 24, 1997). ... Granted free agency (October 15, 1998). ... Re-signed by Cardinals organization (November 12, 1998). ... Granted free agency (October 13, 1999). ... Signed by Reds organization (November 16, 1999).
STATISTICAL NOTES: Pitched 5-0 no-hit victory for Louisville against Charlotte (May 14, 2000; first game).

Year	League	W	L	Pct.	ERA	G	GS	CG	ShO	Sv.	IP	H	R	ER	BB	SO
1990—	Billings (Pio.)	5	4	.556	4.48	13	13	1	•1	0	72 1/3	74	46	36	31	48
1991—	Cedar Rapids (Midw.)	8	10	.444	3.12	28	28	3	0	0	184 2/3	177	85	64	64	98
1992—	Cedar Rapids (Midw.)	7	0	1.000	2.62	14	14	1	0	0	82 1/3	71	33	24	33	56
—	Chattanooga (Sou.)	6	5	.545	2.27	14	14	1	0	0	87 1/3	86	34	22	34	56
1993—	Indianapolis (A.A.)	4	7	.364	4.16	15	15	0	0	0	84 1/3	81	45	39	47	51
—	Cincinnati (N.L.)	2	5	.286	4.54	14	14	0	0	0	77 1/3	74	49	39	38	38
1994—	Iowa (A.A.)■	10	12	.455	6.04	27	26	0	0	0	138 2/3	149	100	93	87	90
1995—	Chattanooga (Sou.)■	10	6	.625	4.65	28	21	0	0	0	118	112	71	61	59	87
1996—	Chattanooga (Sou.)	3	5	.375	3.63	11	11	0	0	0	69 1/3	64	32	28	26	38
—	Indianapolis (A.A.)	5	4	.556	3.91	14	11	0	0	0	71 1/3	76	44	31	23	35
1997—	Richmond (I.L.)■	3	*14	.176	5.38	27	26	2	0	0	144	180	101	86	44	91
1998—	Memphis (PCL)■	11	11	.500	4.10	29	29	2	2	0	173 1/3	183	90	79	47	110
1999—	Memphis (PCL)	13	4	.765	4.03	21	19	1	1	0	129 2/3	134	61	58	33	84
—	St. Louis (N.L.)	3	3	.500	5.12	8	8	1	0	0	45 2/3	46	27	26	16	16
2000—	Louisville (I.L.)■	7	6	.538	3.53	18	17	2	1	0	114 2/3	97	50	45	40	69
—	Cincinnati (N.L.)	0	2	.000	6.20	14	1	0	0	1	20 1/3	27	15	14	12	9
Major League totals (3 years)		5	10	.333	4.96	36	23	1	0	1	143 1/3	147	91	79	66	63

LUGO, JULIO   SS   ASTROS

PERSONAL: Born November 16, 1975, in Barahona, Dominican Republic. ... 6-2/165. ... Bats right, throws right. ... Full name: Julio Cesar Lugo.
JUNIOR COLLEGE: Connors State College (Okla.).
TRANSACTIONS/CAREER NOTES: Selected by Houston Astros organization in 43rd round of free-agent draft (June 2, 1994). ... On Jackson disabled list (July 21-29, 1999).
STATISTICAL NOTES: Led Florida State League shortstops with 40 errors in 1997.

						BATTING								FIELDING		
Year	Team (League)	Pos.	G	AB	R	H	2B	3B	HR	RBI	Avg.	BB	SO	SB	PO	A	E	Avg.
1995—	Auburn (NY-Penn)	2B-SS-OF	59	230	36	67	6	3	1	16	.291	26	31	17	85	116	12	.944
1996—	Quad City (Midw.)	SS-2B-3B	101	393	60	116	18	2	10	50	.295	32	75	24	122	289	29	.934
1997—	Kissimmee (FSL)	SS-2B-3B	125	505	89	135	22	*14	7	61	.267	46	99	35	186	433	†41	.938
1998—	Kissimmee (FSL)	SS	128	509	81	154	20	*14	7	62	.303	49	72	51	181	308	42	.921
1999—	Jackson (Texas)	SS-2B-DH	116	445	77	142	24	5	10	42	.319	44	53	25	185	328	29	.946
2000—	Houston (N.L.)	SS-2B-OF	116	420	78	119	22	5	10	40	.283	37	93	22	189	249	17	.963
Major League totals (1 year)			116	420	78	119	22	5	10	40	.283	37	93	22	189	249	17	.963

LUKASIEWICZ, MARK   P   ANGELS

PERSONAL: Born March 8, 1973, in Jersey City, N.J. ... 6-7/240. ... Throws left, bats left. ... Full name: Mark Francis Lukasiewicz.
HIGH SCHOOL: Secaucus (N.J.).
JUNIOR COLLEGE: Brevard Community College.
COLLEGE: Oklahoma State.
TRANSACTIONS/CAREER NOTES: Selected by Toronto Blue Jays organization in supplemental round ("sandwich pick" between first and second round, 41st pick overall) of free-agent draft (June 3, 1993); pick received as partial compensation for New York Yankees signing Type A free agent P Jimmy Key. ... Claimed on waivers by Anaheim Angels (October 10, 2000).

Year	League	W	L	Pct.	ERA	G	GS	CG	ShO	Sv.	IP	H	R	ER	BB	SO
1994—	Hagerstown (S.Atl.)	3	6	.333	4.78	29	17	0	0	0	98	108	70	52	21	84
1995—	Dunedin (FSL)	3	6	.333	5.73	31	13	0	0	1	86 1/3	80	62	55	42	71
1996—	Dunedin (FSL)	2	1	.667	4.60	23	0	0	0	1	31 1/3	28	20	16	22	31
—	Bakersfield (Calif.)	0	2	.000	9.24	7	0	0	0	0	12 2/3	17	14	13	11	9
—	Hagerstown (S.Atl.)	2	0	1.000	2.30	9	1	0	0	0	15 2/3	8	5	4	7	20
1997—	Knoxville (Sou.)	2	0	1.000	3.65	27	0	0	0	7	37	26	17	15	14	43
—	Syracuse (I.L.)	2	3	.400	5.17	30	0	0	0	0	31 1/3	37	22	18	13	31
1998—	Syracuse (I.L.)	2	2	.500	3.40	22	4	0	0	1	47 2/3	38	18	18	24	30
—	Knoxville (Sou.)	0	0	...	1.93	5	0	0	0	1	9 1/3	6	2	2	1	16
—	Dunedin (FSL)	1	1	.500	0.84	9	0	0	0	0	10 2/3	7	2	1	4	8
1999—	Syracuse (I.L.)	4	4	.500	5.34	37	9	1	0	3	97 2/3	109	69	58	40	77
2000—	Syracuse (I.L.)	2	1	.667	3.48	42	0	0	0	0	41 1/3	34	17	16	25	52
—	Tennessee (Sou.)	0	0	...	5.79	3	0	0	0	0	4 2/3	4	3	3	4	6

LUNAR, FERNANDO   C   ORIOLES

PERSONAL: Born May 25, 1977, in Cantanura, Venezuela. ... 6-1/190. ... Bats right, throws right. ... Full name: Fernando Jose Lunar.
HIGH SCHOOL: Liceo Anaco Venezuela (Anzoategui, El Salvador).
TRANSACTIONS/CAREER NOTES: Signed as non-drafted free agent by Atlanta Braves organization (March 15, 1994). ... On disabled list (April 16-24, 1995). ... Traded by Braves with OF Trinidad Hubbard and P Luis Rivera to Baltimore Orioles for OF B.J. Surhoff and P Gabe Molina (July 31, 2000).

STATISTICAL NOTES: Tied for Gulf Coast League lead in double plays by catcher with three in 1994. ... Led South Atlantic League catchers with 11 double plays in 1996. ... Led South Atlantic League with 1,026 total chances in 1997. ... Led Carolina League catchers with nine double plays in 1998. ... Led Southern League catchers with 12 double plays in 1999.

Year Team (League)	Pos.	G	AB	R	H	2B	3B	HR	RBI	Avg.	BB	SO	SB	PO	A	E	Avg.
1994—GC Braves (GCL)	C	33	100	9	24	5	0	2	12	.240	1	13	0	203	32	7	.971
1995—Eugene (N'West)		39	131	13	32	6	0	2	16	.244	9	28	0	...	...	8	.000
—Macon (S.Atl.)	C	39	134	13	24	2	0	0	9	.179	10	38	1	261	35	10	.967
1996—Macon (S.Atl.)	C	104	343	33	63	9	0	7	33	.184	20	65	3	648	112	12	.984
1997—Macon (S.Atl.)	C	105	380	41	99	26	2	7	37	.261	18	42	0	*888	*135	13	.987
1998—Danville (Caro.)	C	91	286	19	63	9	0	3	28	.220	6	52	1	726	103	8	.990
1999—Greenville (Sou.)	C-DH	105	343	33	77	15	1	3	35	.224	12	64	0	611	*88	10	.986
2000—Greenville (Sou.)	C	31	102	6	17	3	0	0	4	.167	8	15	0	228	37	3	.989
—Atlanta (N.L.)	C	22	54	5	10	1	0	0	5	.185	3	15	0	125	12	1	.993
—Bowie (East.)■	C	22	80	12	23	7	1	0	8	.288	6	8	0	165	22	2	.989
—Baltimore (A.L.)	C	9	16	0	2	0	0	0	1	.125	0	4	0	43	2	0	1.000
American League totals (1 year)		9	16	0	2	0	0	0	1	.125	0	4	0	43	2	0	1.000
National League totals (1 year)		22	54	5	10	1	0	0	5	.185	3	15	0	125	12	1	.993
Major League totals (1 year)		31	70	5	12	1	0	0	6	.171	3	19	0	168	14	1	.995

LUULOA, KEITH — IF — PADRES

PERSONAL: Born December 24, 1974, in Honolulu, Hawaii. ... 6-0/185. ... Bats right, throws right. ... Full name: Keith H.M. Luuloa. ... Name pronounced lew-UH-low-uh.
TRANSACTIONS/CAREER NOTES: Selected by California Angels organization in 33rd round of free-agent draft (June 3, 1993). ... Angels franchise renamed Anaheim Angels for 1997 season. ... Traded by Angels with P Brett Hinchcliffe to Chicago Cubs for OF Chris Hatcher, P Mike Heathcott and SS Brett King (July 28, 2000). ... On Iowa disabled list (August 2-September 5, 2000). ... Granted free agency (October 18, 2000). ... Signed by San Diego Padres organization (November 20, 2000).
STATISTICAL NOTES: Led Texas League with 274 total bases and 16 sacrifice flies in 1998.

Year Team (League)	Pos.	G	AB	R	H	2B	3B	HR	RBI	Avg.	BB	SO	SB	PO	A	E	Avg.
1994—Arizona (N.L.)	SS	28	97	14	29	4	1	1	10	.299	8	14	3	26	69	8	.922
1995—Lake Elsinore (Calif.)	SS	102	380	50	100	22	7	5	53	.263	24	47	1	155	290	38	.921
1996—Midland (Texas)	2B-SS	134	531	80	138	24	2	7	44	.260	47	54	4	307	397	35	.953
1997—Midland (Texas)	2B-SS	120	421	67	115	29	5	9	59	.273	36	59	7	240	337	24	.960
1998—Midland (Texas)	2-3-1-O-S	130	479	85	160	*43	10	17	102	.334	75	54	6	342	279	17	.973
—Vancouver (PCL)	2B-3B-SS	8	30	4	10	1	0	0	3	.333	4	3	1	18	22	0	1.000
1999—Edmonton (PCL)	2B-3B-OF-1B	115	396	54	113	23	1	4	46	.285	44	53	7	189	259	18	.961
2000—Edmonton (PCL)	3B-SS-2B-OF	76	270	39	66	17	2	8	44	.244	30	30	2	112	196	15	.954
—Anaheim (A.L.)	SS-2B	6	18	3	6	0	0	0	0	.333	1	1	0	8	12	1	.952
—Iowa (PCL)■	OF-2B	4	16	4	6	1	0	1	4	.375	2	1	1	6	0	0	1.000
American League totals (1 year)		6	18	3	6	0	0	0	0	.333	1	1	0	8	12	1	.952
National League totals (1 year)		28	97	14	29	4	1	1	10	.299	8	14	3	0	0	0	...
Major League totals (2 years)		34	115	17	35	4	1	1	10	.304	9	15	3	8	12	1	.952

MABRY, JOHN — OF/3B — CARDINALS

PERSONAL: Born October 17, 1970, in Wilmington, Del. ... 6-4/210. ... Bats left, throws right. ... Full name: John Steven Mabry. ... Name pronounced MAY-bree.
HIGH SCHOOL: Bohemia Manor (Chesapeake City, Md.).
COLLEGE: West Chester (Pa.) University.
TRANSACTIONS/CAREER NOTES: Selected by St. Louis Cardinals organization in sixth round of free-agent draft (June 3, 1991). ... On disabled list (April 22-30 and May 6-18, 1992). ... On disabled list (August 20-September 24, 1997). ... Granted free agency (December 21, 1998). ... Signed by Seattle Mariners (December 30, 1998). ... On disabled list (August 14, 1999-remainder of season). ... On Seattle disabled list (April 22-May 12, 2000); included rehabilitation assignment to Tacoma (May 8-12). ... Traded by Mariners with P Tom Davey to San Diego Padres for OF Al Martin (July 31, 2000). ... Granted free agency (October 30, 2000). ... Signed by Cardinals organization (January 5, 2001).
STATISTICAL NOTES: Led Texas League in grounding into double plays with 17 in 1993. ... Led Texas League outfielders with six double plays in 1993. ... Hit for the cycle (May 18, 1996). ... Had 20-game hitting streak (May 19-June 9, 1997).

Year Team (League)	Pos.	G	AB	R	H	2B	3B	HR	RBI	Avg.	BB	SO	SB	PO	A	E	Avg.
1991—Hamilton (NY-Penn)	OF	49	187	25	58	11	0	1	31	.310	17	18	9	73	*10	5	.943
—Savannah (S.Atl.)	OF	22	86	10	20	6	1	0	8	.233	7	12	1	36	1	1	.974
1992—Springfield (Midw.)	OF	115	438	63	115	13	6	11	57	.263	24	39	2	171	14	6	.969
1993—Arkansas (Texas)	OF	*136	528	68	153	32	2	16	72	.290	27	68	7	262	15	3	*.989
—Louisville (A.A.)	OF	4	7	0	1	0	0	0	1	.143	0	1	0	3	0	0	1.000
1994—Louisville (A.A.)	OF	122	477	76	125	30	1	15	68	.262	32	67	2	237	4	2	.992
—St. Louis (N.L.)	OF	6	23	2	7	3	0	0	3	.304	2	4	0	16	0	0	1.000
1995—St. Louis (N.L.)	1B-OF	129	388	35	119	21	1	5	41	.307	24	45	0	652	58	4	.994
—Louisville (A.A.)	OF	4	12	0	1	0	0	0	0	.083	0	0	0	8	0	1	.889
1996—St. Louis (N.L.)	1B-OF	151	543	63	161	30	2	13	74	.297	37	84	3	1182	76	8	.994
1997—St. Louis (N.L.)	OF-1B-3B	116	388	40	110	19	0	5	36	.284	39	77	0	455	30	1	.998
1998—St. Louis (N.L.)	OF-3B-1B	142	377	41	94	22	0	9	46	.249	30	76	0	206	64	9	.968
1999—Seattle (A.L.)■	OF-3B-1B-DH	87	262	34	64	14	0	9	33	.244	20	60	2	221	50	10	.964
2000—Seattle (A.L.)	3-0-D-1-P	48	103	18	25	5	0	1	7	.243	10	31	0	37	20	4	.934
—Tacoma (PCL)	1B-3B	4	14	1	3	1	0	0	1	.214	0	4	0	2	2	1	.800
—San Diego (N.L.)■	OF-1B	48	123	17	28	8	0	7	25	.228	5	38	0	57	2	1	.983
American League totals (2 years)		135	365	52	89	19	0	10	40	.244	30	91	2	258	70	14	.959
National League totals (6 years)		592	1842	198	519	103	3	39	225	.282	137	324	3	2568	230	23	.992
Major League totals (7 years)		727	2207	250	608	122	3	49	265	.275	167	415	5	2826	300	37	.988

RECORDS: Shares career record for most triples—1.

								BATTING								FIELDING		
Year	Team (League)	Pos.	G	AB	R	H	2B	3B	HR	RBI	Avg.	BB	SO	SB	PO	A	E	Avg.
1996—St. Louis (N.L.)		1B	3	10	1	3	0	1	0	1	.300	2	1	0	20	1	0	1.000

CHAMPIONSHIP SERIES RECORD

								BATTING								FIELDING		
Year	Team (League)	Pos.	G	AB	R	H	2B	3B	HR	RBI	Avg.	BB	SO	SB	PO	A	E	Avg.
1996—St. Louis (N.L.)		1B-OF	7	23	1	6	0	0	0	0	.261	0	6	0	45	1	0	1.000

RECORD AS PITCHER

Year	League	W	L	Pct.	ERA	G	GS	CG	ShO	Sv.	IP	H	R	ER	BB	SO
2000—San Diego (N.L.)		0	0	...	27.27	1	0	0	0	0	$2/3$	3	2	2	1	0

MACHADO, ROBERT   C   CUBS

PERSONAL: Born June 3, 1973, in Caracas, Venezuela. ... 6-1/205. ... Bats right, throws right. ... Full name: Robert Alexis Machado.
TRANSACTIONS/CAREER NOTES: Signed as non-drafted free agent by Chicago White Sox organization (August 10, 1989). ... Released by White Sox (May 19, 1999). ... Signed by Montreal Expos organization (May 21, 1999). ... Granted free agency (October 15, 1999). ... Signed by Seattle Mariners organization (November 17, 1999). ... Granted free agency (October 2, 2000). ... Signed by Chicago Cubs organization (December 13, 2000).
STATISTICAL NOTES: Led Gulf Coast League catchers with 349 total chances in 1991. ... Tied for Southern League lead in double plays by catcher with 10 in 1996. ... Tied for American Association lead in passed balls with nine in 1997.

								BATTING								FIELDING		
Year	Team (League)	Pos.	G	AB	R	H	2B	3B	HR	RBI	Avg.	BB	SO	SB	PO	A	E	Avg.
1991—GC White Sox (GCL)		C	38	126	11	31	4	1	0	15	.246	6	21	2	*287	*54	4	.977
1992—Utica (NY-Penn)		C	45	161	16	44	13	1	2	20	.273	5	26	1	279	30	12	.963
1993—South Bend (Midw.)		C	75	281	34	86	14	3	2	33	.306	19	59	1	490	66	12	.979
1994—Prince Will. (Caro.)		C	93	312	45	81	17	1	11	47	.260	27	68	0	562	66	*16	.975
1995—Nashville (A.A.)		C	16	49	7	7	3	0	1	5	.143	7	12	0	87	17	3	.972
—Prince Will. (Caro.)		C	83	272	37	69	14	0	6	31	.254	40	47	0	548	78	5	.992
1996—Birmingham (Sou.)		C-DH	87	309	35	74	16	0	6	28	.239	20	56	1	502	67	5	.991
—Chicago (A.L.)		C	4	6	1	4	1	0	0	2	.667	0	0	0	6	0	0	1.000
1997—Nashville (A.A.)		C-DH	84	308	43	83	18	0	8	30	.269	12	61	5	461	49	6	.988
—Chicago (A.L.)		C	10	15	1	3	0	1	0	2	.200	1	6	0	34	3	0	1.000
1998—Calgary (PCL)		C-DH	66	239	31	63	19	0	4	27	.264	20	33	2	409	39	6	.987
—Chicago (A.L.)		C	34	111	14	23	6	0	3	15	.207	7	22	0	189	17	4	.981
1999—Charlotte (I.L.)		C	16	54	4	11	3	0	2	7	.204	4	13	0	111	12	3	.976
—Ottawa (I.L.)■		C-DH	21	75	6	17	5	0	0	3	.227	0	13	0	141	12	3	.981
—Montreal (N.L.)		C	17	22	3	4	1	0	0	0	.182	2	6	0	33	3	0	1.000
2000—Tacoma (PCL)■		C	92	330	41	99	20	0	9	58	.300	28	43	1	491	57	•11	.980
—Seattle (A.L.)		C	8	14	2	3	0	0	1	1	.214	1	4	0	35	2	0	1.000
American League totals (4 years)			56	146	18	33	7	1	4	20	.226	9	32	0	264	22	4	.986
National League totals (1 year)			17	22	3	4	1	0	0	0	.182	2	6	0	33	3	0	1.000
Major League totals (5 years)			73	168	21	37	8	1	4	20	.220	11	38	0	297	25	4	.988

MACIAS, JOSE   2B   TIGERS

PERSONAL: Born January 25, 1974, in Panama City, Panama. ... 5-10/173. ... Bats both, throws right. ... Full name: Jose Prade Macias.
HIGH SCHOOL: Instituto Technologico (Panama City, Panama).
TRANSACTIONS/CAREER NOTES: Signed as non-drafted free agent by Montreal Expos organization (February 14, 1992). ... Selected by Detroit Tigers organization from Expos organization in Rule 5 minor league draft (December 9, 1996).
STATISTICAL NOTES: Led Florida State League second basemen with 255 putouts, 349 assists, 611 total chances and .989 fielding percentage in 1997. ... Tied for International League lead with 16 errors by second baseman in 1999. ... Career major league grand slams: 1.

								BATTING								FIELDING		
Year	Team (League)	Pos.	G	AB	R	H	2B	3B	HR	RBI	Avg.	BB	SO	SB	PO	A	E	Avg.
1992—Dom. Expos (DSL)		OF	61	198	58	58	5	1	2	23	.293	60	11	41	73	41	7	.942
1993—Dom. Expos (DSL)			64	211	60	66	12	1	4	26	.313	59	26	38	100	44	7	.954
1994—GC Expos (GCL)		OF-2B-3B	31	104	23	28	8	2	1	6	.269	14	15	4	39	20	4	.937
1995—Vermont (NY-Penn)		OF-2B-3B	53	176	24	42	4	2	0	9	.239	19	19	11	93	76	9	.949
1996—Delmarva (S.Atl.)		OF-2B-3B	116	369	64	91	13	4	1	33	.247	56	48	38	179	80	8	.970
1997—Lakeland (FSL)■		2B-OF	122	424	54	113	18	2	2	52	.267	52	33	10	†255	†349	7	†.989
1998—Jacksonville (Sou.)		2B	128	511	82	156	28	10	12	71	.305	52	46	6	246	354	14	*.977
1999—Toledo (I.L.)		2B-OF-SS	112	438	44	107	18	8	2	36	.244	36	60	10	218	351	‡18	.969
—Detroit (A.L.)		2B	5	4	2	1	0	0	1	2	.250	0	1	0	1	6	0	1.000
2000—Toledo (I.L.)		OF-SS-2B	33	130	19	30	5	0	0	8	.231	17	17	2	64	30	6	.940
—Detroit (A.L.)		2-3-O-DH-S	73	173	25	44	3	5	2	24	.254	18	24	2	53	116	4	.977
Major League totals (2 years)			78	177	27	45	3	5	3	26	.254	18	25	2	54	122	4	.978

RECORD AS PITCHER

Year	League	W	L	Pct.	ERA	G	GS	CG	ShO	Sv.	IP	H	R	ER	BB	SO
1994—GC Expos (GCL)		0	0	...	0.00	1	0	0	0	0	1	0	0	0	0	0

MADDUX, GREG   P   BRAVES

PERSONAL: Born April 14, 1966, in San Angelo, Texas. ... 6-0/185. ... Throws right, bats right. ... Full name: Gregory Alan Maddux. ... Brother of Mike Maddux, pitcher with nine major league teams (1986-2000).
HIGH SCHOOL: Valley (Las Vegas).

TRANSACTIONS/CAREER NOTES: Selected by Chicago Cubs organization in second round of free-agent draft (June 4, 1984). ... Granted free agency (October 26, 1992). ... Signed by Atlanta Braves (December 9, 1992).

RECORDS: Holds major league career records for most years leading league in putouts by pitcher—7; and most years leading league in chances accepted by pitcher—11. ... Holds major league single-season record for fewest complete games by pitcher for leader—8 (1993). ... Shares major league career records for most years leading league in double plays by pitcher—5; and most years leading league in assists by pitcher—7. ... Shares major league single-season record for fewest complete games for leader—8 (1993). ... Shares major league single-game record for most putouts by pitcher—7 (April 29, 1990). ... Holds major league career record for most putouts by pitcher—403. ... Shares N.L. career record for most years leading league in assists by pitcher—5.

HONORS: Won N.L. Gold Glove at pitcher (1990-2000). ... Named righthanded pitcher on THE SPORTING NEWS N.L. All-Star team (1992-95 and 2000). ... Named N.L. Cy Young Award winner by Baseball Writers' Association of America (1992-95). ... Named N.L. Pitcher of the Year by THE SPORTING NEWS (1993-95).

STATISTICAL NOTES: Led Appalachian League with eight hit batsmen in 1984. ... Led American Association with 12 hit batsmen in 1986. ... Led N.L. with 14 hit batsmen in 1992. ... Pitched 3-1 one-hit, complete-game victory against Houston (May 28, 1995). ... Pitched 2-0 one-hit, complete-game victory against San Diego (April 27, 1997).

MISCELLANEOUS: Appeared in three games as pinch runner (1988). ... Singled and scored and struck out in two appearances as pinch hitter (1991).

Year	League	W	L	Pct.	ERA	G	GS	CG	ShO	Sv.	IP	H	R	ER	BB	SO
1984—	Pikeville (Appl.)	6	2	.750	2.63	14	12	2	•2	0	85²/₃	63	35	25	41	62
1985—	Peoria (Midw.)	13	9	.591	3.19	27	27	6	0	0	186	176	86	66	52	125
1986—	Pittsfield (East.)	4	3	.571	2.73	8	8	4	2	0	62²/₃	49	22	19	15	35
—	Iowa (A.A.)	10	1	*.909	3.02	18	18	5	•2	0	128¹/₃	127	49	43	30	65
—	Chicago (N.L.)	2	4	.333	5.52	6	5	1	0	0	31	44	20	19	11	20
1987—	Chicago (N.L.)	6	14	.300	5.61	30	27	1	1	0	155²/₃	181	111	97	74	101
—	Iowa (A.A.)	3	0	1.000	0.98	4	4	2	•2	0	27²/₃	17	3	3	12	22
1988—	Chicago (N.L.)	18	8	.692	3.18	34	34	9	3	0	249	230	97	88	81	140
1989—	Chicago (N.L.)	19	12	.613	2.95	35	35	7	1	0	238¹/₃	222	90	78	82	135
1990—	Chicago (N.L.)	15	15	.500	3.46	35	•35	8	2	0	237	*242	*116	91	71	144
1991—	Chicago (N.L.)	15	11	.577	3.35	37	*37	7	2	0	*263	232	113	98	66	198
1992—	Chicago (N.L.)	•20	11	.645	2.18	35	•35	9	4	0	*268	201	68	65	70	199
1993—	Atlanta (N.L.)■	20	10	.667	*2.36	36	•36	*8	1	0	*267	228	85	70	52	197
1994—	Atlanta (N.L.)	•16	6	.727	*1.56	25	25	*10	•3	0	*202	150	44	35	31	156
1995—	Atlanta (N.L.)	*19	2	*.905	*1.63	28	28	*10	•3	0	•209²/₃	147	39	38	23	181
1996—	Atlanta (N.L.)	15	11	.577	2.72	35	35	5	1	0	245	225	85	74	28	172
1997—	Atlanta (N.L.)	19	4	*.826	2.20	33	33	5	2	0	232²/₃	200	58	57	20	177
1998—	Atlanta (N.L.)	18	9	.667	*2.22	34	34	9	*5	0	251	201	75	62	45	204
1999—	Atlanta (N.L.)	19	9	.679	3.57	33	33	4	0	0	219¹/₃	258	103	87	37	136
2000—	Atlanta (N.L.)	19	9	.679	3.00	35	•35	6	•3	0	249¹/₃	225	91	83	42	190
Major League totals (15 years)		**240**	**135**	**.640**	**2.83**	**471**	**467**	**99**	**31**	**0**	**3318**	**2986**	**1195**	**1042**	**733**	**2350**

DIVISION SERIES RECORD

RECORDS: Holds career record for most hits allowed—55. ... Shares career records most wins—4; and complete games—1. ... Holds N.L. career records for most wins—4; games started—7; innings pitched—48; runs allowed—21; and earned runs allowed—17. ... Shares N.L. career record for most games pitched—8.

Year	League	W	L	Pct.	ERA	G	GS	CG	ShO	Sv.	IP	H	R	ER	BB	SO
1995—	Atlanta (N.L.)	1	0	1.000	4.50	2	2	0	0	0	14	19	7	7	2	7
1996—	Atlanta (N.L.)	1	0	1.000	0.00	1	1	0	0	0	7	3	2	0	0	7
1997—	Atlanta (N.L.)	1	0	1.000	1.00	1	1	1	0	0	9	7	1	1	1	6
1998—	Atlanta (N.L.)	1	0	1.000	2.57	1	1	0	0	0	7	7	2	2	0	4
1999—	Atlanta (N.L.)	0	1	.000	2.57	2	1	0	0	0	7	10	2	2	5	5
2000—	Atlanta (N.L.)	0	1	.000	11.25	1	1	0	0	0	4	9	7	5	3	2
Division series totals (6 years)		**4**	**2**	**.667**	**3.19**	**8**	**7**	**1**	**0**	**0**	**48**	**55**	**21**	**17**	**11**	**31**

CHAMPIONSHIP SERIES RECORD

RECORDS: Holds career records for most runs allowed—42; and sacrifice hits—6. ... Shares single-series record for most earned runs allowed—11 (1989). ... Holds N.L. single-series record for most runs allowed—12 (1989).

NOTES: Scored in only appearance as pinch runner (1989).

Year	League	W	L	Pct.	ERA	G	GS	CG	ShO	Sv.	IP	H	R	ER	BB	SO
1989—	Chicago (N.L.)	0	1	.000	13.50	2	2	0	0	0	7¹/₃	13	12	11	4	5
1993—	Atlanta (N.L.)	1	1	.500	4.97	2	2	0	0	0	12²/₃	11	8	7	7	11
1995—	Atlanta (N.L.)	1	0	1.000	1.13	1	1	0	0	0	8	7	1	1	2	4
1996—	Atlanta (N.L.)	1	1	.500	2.51	2	2	0	0	0	14¹/₃	15	9	4	3	10
1997—	Atlanta (N.L.)	0	2	.000	1.38	2	2	0	0	0	13	9	7	2	4	16
1998—	Atlanta (N.L.)	0	1	.000	3.00	2	1	0	0	1	6	5	2	2	3	4
1999—	Atlanta (N.L.)	1	0	1.000	1.93	2	2	0	0	0	14	12	3	3	1	7
Champ. series totals (7 years)		**4**	**6**	**.400**	**3.58**	**13**	**12**	**0**	**0**	**1**	**75¹/₃**	**72**	**42**	**30**	**24**	**57**

WORLD SERIES RECORD

NOTES: Member of World Series championship team (1995).

Year	League	W	L	Pct.	ERA	G	GS	CG	ShO	Sv.	IP	H	R	ER	BB	SO
1995—	Atlanta (N.L.)	1	1	.500	2.25	2	2	1	0	0	16	9	6	4	3	8
1996—	Atlanta (N.L.)	1	1	.500	1.72	2	2	0	0	0	15²/₃	14	3	3	1	5
1999—	Atlanta (N.L.)	0	1	.000	2.57	1	1	0	0	0	7	5	4	2	3	5
World Series totals (3 years)		**2**	**3**	**.400**	**2.09**	**5**	**5**	**1**	**0**	**0**	**38²/₃**	**28**	**13**	**9**	**7**	**18**

ALL-STAR GAME RECORD

Year	League	W	L	Pct.	ERA	GS	CG	ShO	Sv.	IP	H	R	ER	BB	SO
1988—	National			—	Did not play.										
1992—	National	0	0	...	6.75	0	0	0	0	1¹/₃	1	1	1	0	0
1994—	National	0	0	...	3.00	1	0	0	0	3	3	1	1	0	2
1995—	National			—	Selected, did not play—injured.										
1996—	National			—	Did not play.										
1997—	National	0	0	...	4.50	1	0	0	0	2	2	1	1	0	0
1998—	National	0	0	...	0.00	1	0	0	0	2	3	0	0	1	1
2000—	National			—	Selected, did not play—injured.										
All-Star Game totals (4 years)		**0**	**0**	**...**	**3.24**	**3**	**0**	**0**	**0**	**8¹/₃**	**9**	**3**	**3**	**1**	**3**

PERSONAL: Born August 27, 1961, in Dayton, Ohio. ... 6-2/185. ... Throws right, bats left. ... Full name: Michael Ausley Maddux. ... Brother of Greg Maddux, pitcher, Atlanta Braves.
HIGH SCHOOL: Rancho (Las Vegas).
COLLEGE: Texas-El Paso.
TRANSACTIONS/CAREER NOTES: Selected by Cincinnati Reds organization in 36th round of free-agent draft (June 5, 1979); did not sign. ... Selected by Philadelphia Phillies organization in fifth round of free-agent draft (June 7, 1982). ... On Philadelphia disabled list (April 21-June 1, 1988); included rehabilitation assignment to Maine (May 13-22). ... Released by Phillies (November 20, 1989). ... Signed by Los Angeles Dodgers (December 21, 1989). ... Granted free agency (October 15, 1990). ... Signed by San Diego Padres (March 30, 1991). ... On disabled list (April 5-26, 1992). ... Traded by Padres to New York Mets for P Roger Mason and P Mike Freitas (December 17, 1992). ... On disabled list (April 27-May 13, 1994). ... Granted free agency (October 18, 1994). ... Signed by Pittsburgh Pirates organization (April 10, 1995). ... Released by Pirates (May 16, 1995). ... Signed by Boston Red Sox (May 30, 1995). ... Granted free agency (November 6, 1995). ... Re-signed by Red Sox (December 15, 1995). ... On Boston disabled list (May 6-August 2, 1996); included rehabilitation assignments to Pawtucket (May 24-25, July 12-16 and July 25-31). ... Granted free agency (November 1, 1996). ... Re-signed by Red Sox (December 7, 1996). ... Released by Red Sox (March 26, 1997). ... Signed by Seattle Mariners organization (April 11, 1997). ... On Seattle disabled list (June 22-July 13, 1997). ... Released by Mariners (July 23, 1997). ... Signed by Padres organization (August 19, 1997). ... Granted free agency (October 15, 1997). ... Signed by Montreal Expos (March 30, 1998). ... On disabled list (April 8-May 1 and June 7-July 9, 1998). ... Granted free agency (September 29, 1998). ... Re-signed by Expos organization (February 2, 1999). ... Released by Expos (April 15, 1999). ... Signed by Dodgers organization (April 24, 1999). ... Granted free agency (October 14, 1999). ... Signed by Houston Astros organization (February 1, 2000). ... On disabled list (May 28-June 22, 2000). ... Released by Astros (July 5, 2000).
MISCELLANEOUS: Appeared in one game as pinch runner with Philadelphia (1988).

Year	League	W	L	Pct.	ERA	G	GS	CG	ShO	Sv.	IP	H	R	ER	BB	SO
1982—	Bend (N'West)	3	6	.333	3.99	11	10	3	0	0	65 1/3	68	35	29	26	59
1983—	Spartanburg (S.Atl.)	4	6	.400	5.44	13	13	3	0	0	84 1/3	98	62	51	47	85
—	Peninsula (Caro.)	8	4	.667	3.62	14	14	6	0	0	99 1/3	92	46	40	35	78
—	Reading (East.)	0	0	...	6.00	1	1	0	0	0	3	4	2	2	1	2
1984—	Reading (East.)	3	•12	.200	5.04	20	19	4	0	0	116	143	82	65	49	77
—	Portland (PCL)	2	4	.333	5.84	8	8	1	0	0	44 2/3	58	32	29	17	22
1985—	Portland (PCL)	9	12	.429	5.31	27	26	6	1	0	166	195	106	98	51	96
1986—	Portland (PCL)	5	2	.714	2.36	12	12	3	0	0	84	70	26	22	22	65
—	Philadelphia (N.L.)	3	7	.300	5.42	16	16	0	0	0	78	88	56	47	34	44
1987—	Maine (I.L.)	6	6	.500	4.35	18	16	3	1	0	103 1/3	116	58	50	26	71
—	Philadelphia (N.L.)	2	0	1.000	2.65	7	2	0	0	0	17	17	5	5	5	15
1988—	Philadelphia (N.L.)	4	3	.571	3.76	25	11	0	0	0	88 2/3	91	41	37	34	59
—	Maine (I.L.)	0	2	.000	4.18	5	3	1	0	0	23 2/3	25	18	11	10	18
1989—	Philadelphia (N.L.)	1	3	.250	5.15	16	4	2	1	1	43 2/3	52	29	25	14	26
—	Scranton/W.B. (I.L.)	7	7	.500	3.66	19	17	3	1	0	123	119	55	50	26	100
1990—	Albuquerque (PCL)■	8	5	.615	4.25	20	19	2	0	0	108	122	59	51	32	85
—	Los Angeles (N.L.)	0	1	.000	6.53	11	2	0	0	0	20 2/3	24	15	15	4	11
1991—	San Diego (N.L.)■	7	2	.778	2.46	64	1	0	0	5	98 2/3	78	30	27	27	57
1992—	San Diego (N.L.)	2	2	.500	2.37	50	1	0	0	5	79 2/3	71	25	21	24	60
1993—	New York (N.L.)■	3	8	.273	3.60	58	0	0	0	5	75	67	34	30	27	57
1994—	New York (N.L.)	2	1	.667	5.11	27	0	0	0	2	44	45	25	25	13	32
1995—	Pittsburgh (N.L.)■	1	0	1.000	9.00	8	0	0	0	0	9	14	9	9	3	4
—	Boston (A.L.)■	4	1	.800	3.61	36	4	0	0	1	89 2/3	86	40	36	15	65
1996—	Boston (A.L.)	3	2	.600	4.48	23	7	0	0	0	64 1/3	76	37	32	27	32
—	Pawtucket (I.L.)	2	0	1.000	3.21	3	3	0	0	0	14	13	5	5	2	9
1997—	Tacoma (PCL)■	0	0	...	0.00	1	1	0	0	0	5	1	0	0	2	5
—	Seattle (A.L.)	1	0	1.000	10.13	6	0	0	0	0	10 2/3	20	12	12	8	7
—	Las Vegas (PCL)■	0	2	.000	5.63	3	3	0	0	0	16	23	11	10	9	13
1998—	Montreal (N.L.)■	3	4	.429	3.72	51	0	0	0	1	55 2/3	50	24	23	15	33
1999—	Montreal (N.L.)	0	0	...	9.00	4	0	0	0	0	5	9	5	5	3	4
—	San Bernardino (Calif.)■	0	0	...	3.00	5	0	0	0	2	9	8	4	3	2	10
—	Los Angeles (N.L.)	1	1	.500	3.29	49	0	0	0	0	54 2/3	54	21	20	19	41
2000—	Houston (N.L.)■	2	2	.500	6.26	21	0	0	0	0	27 1/3	31	20	19	12	17
A.L. totals (3 years)		8	3	.727	4.37	65	11	0	0	1	164 2/3	182	89	80	50	104
N.L. totals (13 years)		31	34	.477	3.98	407	37	2	1	19	697	691	339	308	234	460
Major League totals (15 years)		39	37	.513	4.05	472	48	2	1	20	861 2/3	873	428	388	284	564

DIVISION SERIES RECORD

Year	League	W	L	Pct.	ERA	G	GS	CG	ShO	Sv.	IP	H	R	ER	BB	SO
1995—	Boston (A.L.)	0	0	...	0.00	2	0	0	0	0	3	2	0	0	1	1

MADURO, CALVIN   P

PERSONAL: Born September 5, 1974, in Santa Cruz, Aruba. ... 6-0/180. ... Throws right, bats right. ... Full name: Calvin Gregory Maduro.
HIGH SCHOOL: Tourist Economy School (Santa Cruz, Aruba).
COLLEGE: St. Antonius College (Aruba).
TRANSACTIONS/CAREER NOTES: Signed as non-drafted free agent by Baltimore Orioles organization (September 9, 1991). ... Traded by Orioles with P Garrett Stephenson to Philadelphia Phillies (September 4, 1996), completing deal in which Phillies traded 3B Todd Zeile and OF Pete Incaviglia to Orioles for two players to be named later (August 29, 1996). ... Released by Phillies (November 19, 1998). ... Signed by Orioles organization (February 5, 1999). ... On Baltimore disabled list (May 14-June 20 and June 22, 2000-remainder of season); included rehabilitation assignments to Rochester (June 10-16) and Frederick (June 17). ... Granted free agency (December 21, 2000).
STATISTICAL NOTES: Pitched 5-0 no-hit victory for Bowie against Portland (May 28, 1996, first game).
MISCELLANEOUS: Appeared in one game as pinch runner with Philadelphia (1997).

Year	League	W	L	Pct.	ERA	G	GS	CG	ShO	Sv.	IP	H	R	ER	BB	SO
1992—Gulf Coast Orioles (GCL)....		1	4	.200	2.27	13	•12	1	1	0	71 1/3	56	29	18	26	66
1993—Bluefield (Appl.)		•9	4	.692	3.96	14	•14	*3	0	0	*91	90	46	40	17	*83
1994—Frederick (Caro.)		9	8	.529	4.25	27	26	0	0	0	152 1/3	132	86	72	59	137
1995—Frederick (Caro.)		8	5	.615	2.94	20	20	2	2	0	122 1/3	109	43	40	34	120
— Bowie (East.)......................		0	6	.000	5.09	7	7	0	0	0	35 1/3	39	28	20	27	26
1996—Bowie (East.)......................		9	7	.563	3.26	19	19	4	*3	0	124 1/3	116	50	45	36	87
— Rochester (I.L.).................		3	5	.375	4.74	8	8	0	0	0	43 2/3	49	25	23	18	40
— Philadelphia (N.L.)■.........		0	1	.000	3.52	4	2	0	0	0	15 1/3	13	6	6	3	11
1997—Philadelphia (N.L.)...........		3	7	.300	7.23	15	13	0	0	0	71	83	59	57	41	31
— Scranton/W.B. (I.L.)		6	4	.600	4.99	13	13	2	0	0	79 1/3	71	48	44	57	53
1998—Scranton/W.B. (I.L.)...........		12	9	.571	5.98	28	27	4	1	0	177 2/3	*211	123	118	68	120
1999—Rochester (I.L.)■..............		11	11	.500	3.99	29	•28	2	1	0	169	179	88	75	60	149
2000—Baltimore (A.L.)................		0	0	...	9.64	15	2	0	0	0	23 1/3	29	25	25	16	18
— Rochester (I.L.)		1	0	1.000	0.00	4	1	0	0	0	4	1	1	0	4	6
— Frederick (Caro.)		0	0	...	0.00	1	1	0	0	0	2	1	0	0	0	6
A.L. totals (1 year)		0	0	...	9.64	15	2	0	0	0	23 1/3	29	25	25	16	18
N.L. totals (2 years)		3	8	.273	6.57	19	15	0	0	0	86 1/3	96	65	63	44	42
Major League totals (3 years)		3	8	.273	7.22	34	17	0	0	0	109 2/3	125	90	88	60	60

MAGADAN, DAVE — 3B/1B — PADRES

PERSONAL: Born September 30, 1962, in Tampa. ... 6-4/215. ... Bats left, throws right. ... Full name: David Joseph Magadan. ... Cousin of Lou Piniella, manager, Seattle Mariners, and outfielder/designated hitter with four major league teams (1964 and 1968-84). ... Name pronounced MAG-uh-dun.

HIGH SCHOOL: Jesuit (Tampa).

COLLEGE: Alabama.

TRANSACTIONS/CAREER NOTES: Selected by Boston Red Sox organization in 12th round of free-agent draft (June 3, 1980); did not sign. ... Selected by New York Mets organization in second round of free-agent draft (June 6, 1983). ... On disabled list (August 7-September 10, 1984; March 29-April 17, 1987; May 5-20, 1988; and August 9, 1992-remainder of season). ... Granted free agency (October 27, 1992). ... Signed by Florida Marlins organization (December 8, 1992). ... Traded by Marlins to Seattle Mariners for OF Henry Cotto and P Jeff Darwin (June 27, 1993). ... Traded by Mariners to Marlins for P Jeff Darwin and cash (November 9, 1993). ... On disabled list (March 29-April 13 and July 21, 1994-remainder of season). ... Granted free agency (October 19, 1994). ... Signed by Houston Astros (April 15, 1995). ... Granted free agency (October 30, 1995). ... Signed by Chicago Cubs (December 26, 1995). ... On Chicago disabled list (March 22-April 16 and April 17-May 31, 1996); included rehabilitation assignment to Daytona (May 17-29). ... Granted free agency (November 18, 1996). ... Signed by Oakland Athletics organization (January 23, 1997). ... Granted free agency (October 27, 1997). ... Re-signed by A's (November 12, 1997). ... On disabled list (May 16, 1998-remainder of season). ... Granted free agency (October 29, 1998). ... Signed by San Diego Padres (December 21, 1998). ... On disabled list (April 11-30, 2000). ... Granted free agency (October 27, 2000). ... Re-signed by Padres (January 5, 2001).

HONORS: Named Golden Spikes Award winner by USA Baseball (1983). ... Named designated hitter on THE SPORTING NEWS college All-America team (1983).

STATISTICAL NOTES: Led Carolina League with 10 intentional bases on balls received in 1984. ... Led Texas League third basemen with 87 putouts, 275 assists, 393 total chances and 31 errors in 1985. ... Led International League third basemen with .934 fielding percentage, 283 assists and 31 double plays in 1986. ... Led N.L. first basemen with .998 fielding percentage in 1990.

							BATTING								FIELDING		
Year	Team (League)	Pos.	G	AB	R	H	2B	3B	HR	RBI	Avg.	BB	SO	SB	PO	A	E	Avg.
1983—Columbia (S.Atl.)........		1B	64	220	41	74	13	1	3	32	.336	51	29	2	520	37	7	.988
1984—Lynchburg (Caro.)		1B	112	371	78	130	22	4	0	62	*.350	104	43	2	896	64	16	.984
1985—Jackson (Texas)		3B-1B	134	466	84	144	22	0	0	76	.309	*106	57	0	†106	†276	†31	.925
1986—Tidewater (I.L.)........		3B-1B	133	473	68	147	33	6	1	64	.311	84	45	2	78	†284	25	†.935
— New York (N.L.)........		1B	10	18	3	8	0	0	0	3	.444	3	1	0	48	5	0	1.000
1987—New York (N.L.)........		3B-1B	85	192	21	61	13	1	3	24	.318	22	22	0	88	92	4	.978
1988—New York (N.L.)........		1B-3B	112	314	39	87	15	0	1	35	.277	60	39	0	459	99	10	.982
1989—New York (N.L.)........		1B-3B	127	374	47	107	22	3	4	41	.286	49	37	1	587	89	7	.990
1990—New York (N.L.)........		1B-3B	144	451	74	148	28	6	6	72	.328	74	55	2	837	99	3	†.997
1991—New York (N.L.)........		1B	124	418	58	108	23	0	4	51	.258	83	50	1	1035	90	5	.996
1992—New York (N.L.)........		3B-1B	99	321	33	91	9	1	3	28	.283	56	44	1	54	136	11	.945
1993—Florida (N.L.)■........		3B-1B	66	227	22	65	12	0	4	29	.286	44	30	0	55	122	7	.962
— Seattle (A.L.)■...........	1B-3B-DH	71	228	27	59	11	0	1	21	.259	36	33	2	325	72	5	.988
1994—Florida (N.L.)■........		3B-1B	74	211	30	58	7	0	1	17	.275	39	25	0	127	78	4	.981
1995—Houston (N.L.)■........		3B-1B	127	348	44	109	24	0	2	51	.313	71	56	2	121	163	18	.940
1996—Daytona (FSL)■........		3B-DH	7	20	5	6	1	0	0	3	.300	7	2	0	0	6	1	.857
— Iowa (A.A.)...............		3B	3	9	0	2	1	0	0	1	.222	1	2	0	3	3	0	1.000
— Chicago (N.L.)..........		3B-1B	78	169	23	43	10	0	3	17	.254	29	23	0	75	67	3	.979
1997—Oakland (A.L.)■........	3B-1B-DH	128	271	38	82	10	1	4	30	.303	50	40	1	148	65	5	.977
1998—Oakland (A.L.)........		3B-1B	35	109	12	35	8	0	1	13	.321	13	12	0	48	55	6	.945
1999—San Diego (N.L.)■		3B-1B	116	248	20	68	12	1	2	30	.274	45	34	1	209	85	6	.980
2000—San Diego (N.L.)	3B-1B-DH-SS	95	132	13	36	7	0	2	21	.273	32	23	0	58	41	2	.980
American League totals (3 years)			234	608	77	176	29	1	6	64	.289	99	85	3	521	192	16	.978
National League totals (13 years)			1257	3423	427	989	182	12	35	419	.289	607	441	8	3753	1166	80	.984
Major League totals (15 years)			1491	4031	504	1165	211	13	41	483	.289	706	526	11	4274	1358	96	.983

CHAMPIONSHIP SERIES RECORD

							BATTING								FIELDING		
Year	Team (League)	Pos.	G	AB	R	H	2B	3B	HR	RBI	Avg.	BB	SO	SB	PO	A	E	Avg.
1988— New York (N.L.)...........		PH	3	3	0	0	0	0	0	0	.000	0	2	0	...	...	...	...

MAGEE, WENDELL — OF — TIGERS

PERSONAL: Born August 3, 1972, in Hattiesburg, Miss. ... 6-0/220. ... Bats right, throws right. ... Full name: Wendell Errol Magee Jr.

HIGH SCHOOL: Hattiesburg (Miss.).

JUNIOR COLLEGE: Pearl River Community College (Miss.).
COLLEGE: Samford.
TRANSACTIONS/CAREER NOTES: Selected by Philadelphia Phillies organization in 12th round of free-agent draft (June 2, 1994). ... Traded by Phillies to Detroit Tigers for P Bobby Sismondo (March 10, 2000). ... On Detroit disabled list (May 7-29, 2000); included rehabilitation assignment to Toledo (May 27-29).
STATISTICAL NOTES: Led International League outfielders with 320 total chances in 1998. ... Led International League outfielders with 325 total chances in 1999.

Year Team (League)	Pos.	G	AB	R	H	2B	3B	HR	RBI	Avg.	BB	SO	SB	PO	A	E	Avg.
1994— Batavia (NY-Penn)	OF	63	229	42	64	12	4	2	35	.279	16	24	10	115	7	6	.953
1995— Clearwater (FSL)	OF	96	388	67	137	24	5	6	46	*.353	33	40	7	166	12	5	.973
— Reading (East.)	OF	39	136	17	40	9	1	3	21	.294	21	17	3	65	4	5	.932
1996— Reading (East.)	OF	71	270	38	79	15	5	6	30	.293	24	40	10	101	8	3	.973
— Scranton/W.B. (I.L.)	OF	44	155	31	44	9	2	10	32	.284	21	31	3	92	2	4	.959
— Philadelphia (N.L.)	OF	38	142	9	29	7	0	2	14	.204	9	33	0	88	2	2	.978
1997— Philadelphia (N.L.)	OF	38	115	7	23	4	0	1	9	.200	9	20	1	95	2	4	.960
— Scranton/W.B. (I.L.)	OF	83	294	39	72	20	1	10	39	.245	30	56	4	167	3	3	.983
1998— Scranton/W.B. (I.L.)	OF	126	507	86	147	30	7	24	72	.290	46	102	7	*302	7	•11	.966
— Philadelphia (N.L.)	OF	20	75	9	22	6	1	1	11	.293	7	11	0	31	1	2	.941
1999— Scranton/W.B. (I.L.)	OF	*142	*566	95	160	34	2	20	79	.283	55	124	10	*310	7	*8	.975
— Philadelphia (N.L.)	OF	12	14	4	5	1	0	2	5	.357	1	4	0	5	0	0	1.000
2000— Detroit (A.L.)■	OF-DH	91	186	31	51	4	2	7	31	.274	10	28	1	86	3	0	1.000
— Toledo (I.L.)	OF	2	7	1	4	1	0	0	1	.571	1	1	0	2	0	0	1.000
American League totals (1 year)		91	186	31	51	4	2	7	31	.274	10	28	1	86	3	0	1.000
National League totals (4 years)		108	346	29	79	18	1	6	39	.228	26	68	1	219	5	8	.966
Major League totals (5 years)		199	532	60	130	22	3	13	70	.244	36	96	2	305	8	8	.975

MAGNANTE, MIKE — P — ATHLETICS

PERSONAL: Born June 17, 1965, in Glendale, Calif. ... 6-1/185. ... Throws left, bats left. ... Full name: Michael Anthony Magnante. ... Name pronounced mag-NAN-tee.
HIGH SCHOOL: John Burroughs (Burbank, Calif.).
COLLEGE: UCLA.
TRANSACTIONS/CAREER NOTES: Selected by Kansas City Royals organization in 11th round of free-agent draft (June 1, 1988). ... On disabled list (June 17, 1990-remainder of season; July 2-20, 1992; and July 16-31, 1994). ... On Kansas City disabled list (May 19-June 13, 1996); included rehabilitation assignment to Omaha (June 8-13). ... Released by Royals (October 2, 1996). ... Signed by Houston Astros organization (December 19, 1996). ... On disabled list (May 10-25, 1998). ... Granted free agency (October 23, 1998). ... Signed by Anaheim Angels (January 27, 1999). ... Granted free agency (October 29, 1999). ... Signed by Oakland Athletics (November 19, 1999). ... On Oakland disabled list (May 27-June 27, 2000); included rehabilitation assignments to Sacramento (June 8-14 and June 23-27).
RECORDS: Shares major league record for striking out side on nine pitches (August 22, 1997, ninth inning).

Year League	W	L	Pct.	ERA	G	GS	CG	ShO	Sv.	IP	H	R	ER	BB	SO
1988— Eugene (N'West)	1	1	.500	0.56	3	3	0	0	0	16	10	6	1	2	26
— Appleton (Midw.)	3	2	.600	3.21	9	8	0	0	0	47 2/3	48	20	17	15	40
— Baseball City (FSL)	1	1	.500	4.13	4	4	1	0	0	24	19	12	11	8	19
1989— Memphis (Sou.)	8	9	.471	3.66	26	26	4	1	0	157 1/3	137	70	64	53	118
1990— Omaha (A.A.)	2	5	.286	4.11	13	13	2	0	0	76 2/3	72	39	35	25	56
1991— Omaha (A.A.)	6	1	.857	3.02	10	10	2	0	0	65 2/3	53	23	22	23	50
— Kansas City (A.L.)	0	1	.000	2.45	38	0	0	0	0	55	55	19	15	23	42
1992— Kansas City (A.L.)	4	9	.308	4.94	44	12	0	0	0	89 1/3	115	53	49	35	31
1993— Omaha (A.A.)	2	6	.250	3.67	33	13	0	0	2	105 1/3	97	46	43	29	74
— Kansas City (A.L.)	1	2	.333	4.08	7	6	0	0	0	35 1/3	37	16	16	11	16
1994— Kansas City (A.L.)	2	3	.400	4.60	36	1	0	0	0	47	55	27	24	16	21
1995— Omaha (A.A.)	5	1	.833	2.84	15	8	0	0	0	57	55	23	18	13	38
— Kansas City (A.L.)	1	1	.500	4.23	28	0	0	0	0	44 2/3	45	23	21	16	28
1996— Kansas City (A.L.)	2	2	.500	5.67	38	0	0	0	0	54	58	38	34	24	32
— Omaha (A.A.)	1	0	1.000	0.00	1	0	0	0	0	3	3	1	0	0	6
1997— New Orleans (A.A.)■	2	3	.400	4.50	17	0	0	0	1	24	31	14	12	5	23
— Houston (N.L.)	3	1	.750	2.27	40	0	0	0	1	47 2/3	39	16	12	11	43
1998— Houston (N.L.)	4	7	.364	4.88	48	0	0	0	2	51 2/3	56	28	28	26	39
1999— Anaheim (A.L.)■	5	2	.714	3.38	53	0	0	0	0	69 1/3	68	30	26	29	44
2000— Oakland (A.L.)■	1	1	.500	4.31	55	0	0	0	0	39 2/3	50	22	19	19	17
— Sacramento (PCL)	0	0	...	4.05	5	2	0	0	0	6 2/3	6	3	3	1	4
A.L. totals (8 years)	16	21	.432	4.23	299	19	0	0	0	434 1/3	483	228	204	173	231
N.L. totals (2 years)	7	8	.467	3.62	88	0	0	0	3	99 1/3	95	44	40	37	82
Major League totals (10 years)	23	29	.442	4.11	387	19	0	0	3	533 2/3	578	272	244	210	313

DIVISION SERIES RECORD

Year League	W	L	Pct.	ERA	G	GS	CG	ShO	Sv.	IP	H	R	ER	BB	SO
1997— Houston (N.L.)	0	0	...	4.50	2	0	0	0	0	2	4	3	1	0	2
1998— Houston (N.L.)							Did not play.								
2000— Oakland (A.L.)	0	0	...	0.00	2	0	0	0	0	3	1	0	0	0	2
Division series totals (2 years)	0	0	...	1.80	4	0	0	0	0	5	5	3	1	0	4

MAHAY, RON — P — PADRES

PERSONAL: Born June 28, 1971, in Crestwood, Ill. ... 6-2/190. ... Throws left, bats left. ... Full name: Ronald Matthew Mahay.
HIGH SCHOOL: Alan B. Shepard (Palos Heights, Ill.).
JUNIOR COLLEGE: South Suburban College (Ill.).

TRANSACTIONS/CAREER NOTES: Selected by Boston Red Sox organization in 18th round of free-agent draft (June 3, 1991). ... On disabled list (May 5, 1992-remainder of season). ... On Lynchburg disabled list (August 6-September 9, 1993). ... On disabled list (August 23-September 1, 1994). ... On Pawtucket temporarily inactive list (April 19-25, 1995). ... On Sarasota disabled list (April 4-25, 1996). ... Claimed on waivers by Oakland Athletics (March 30, 1999). ... Traded by Athletics to Florida Marlins for cash (May 11, 2000). ... Granted free agency (October 2, 2000). ... Signed by San Diego Padres organization (November 20, 2000).

MISCELLANEOUS: Played outfield (1991-95). ... Appeared in one game as pinch runner with Oakland (2000).

Year	League	W	L	Pct.	ERA	G	GS	CG	ShO	Sv.	IP	H	R	ER	BB	SO
1996—	Sarasota (FSL)	2	2	.500	3.82	31	4	0	0	2	70 2/3	61	33	30	35	68
	—Trenton (East.)	0	1	.000	29.45	1	1	0	0	0	3 2/3	12	13	12	6	0
1997—	Trenton (East.)	3	3	.500	3.10	17	4	0	0	5	40 2/3	29	16	14	13	47
	—Pawtucket (I.L.)	1	0	1.000	0.00	2	0	0	0	0	4 2/3	3	0	0	1	6
	—Boston (A.L.)	3	0	1.000	2.52	28	0	0	0	0	25	19	7	7	11	22
1998—	Pawtucket (I.L.)	3	1	.750	4.17	23	1	0	0	3	41	37	20	19	19	41
	—Boston (A.L.)	1	1	.500	3.46	29	0	0	0	1	26	26	16	10	15	14
1999—	Oakland (A.L.)■	2	0	1.000	1.86	6	1	0	0	1	19 1/3	8	4	4	3	15
	—Vancouver (PCL)	7	2	.778	4.29	32	15	0	0	0	107	116	57	51	45	73
2000—	Oakland (A.L.)	0	1	.000	9.00	5	2	0	0	0	16	26	18	16	9	5
	—Florida (N.L.)■	1	0	1.000	6.04	18	0	0	0	0	25 1/3	31	17	17	16	27
	—Calgary (PCL)	0	1	.000	4.85	8	0	0	0	0	13	7	7	7	7	15
A.L. totals (5 years)		6	2	.750	3.86	73	3	0	0	2	86 1/3	79	45	37	38	56
N.L. totals (1 year)		1	0	1.000	6.04	18	0	0	0	0	25 1/3	31	17	17	16	27
Major League totals (5 years)		7	2	.778	4.35	91	3	0	0	2	111 2/3	110	62	54	54	83

RECORD AS POSITION PLAYER

Year	Team (League)	Pos.	G	AB	R	H	2B	3B	HR	RBI	Avg.	BB	SO	SB	PO	A	E	Avg.
1991—	GC Red Sox (GCL)	OF	54	187	30	51	6	5	1	29	.273	33	40	2	97	2	3	.971
1992—	Winter Haven (FSL)	OF	19	63	6	16	2	1	0	4	.254	2	19	0	33	2	1	.972
1993—	Lynchburg (Caro.)	OF-C	73	254	28	54	8	1	5	23	.213	11	63	2	174	7	5	.973
	—New Britain (East.)	OF	8	25	2	3	0	0	1	2	.120	1	6	1	15	1	2	.889
1994—	Sarasota (FSL)	OF	105	367	43	102	18	0	4	46	.278	39	67	3	189	16	4	.981
1995—	Pawtucket (I.L.)	OF	11	44	5	14	4	0	0	3	.318	4	9	1	30	2	0	1.000
	—Trenton (East.)	OF	93	310	37	73	12	3	5	28	.235	44	90	5	187	9	6	.970
	—Boston (A.L.)	OF	5	20	3	4	2	0	1	3	.200	1	6	0	9	0	0	1.000
Major League totals (1 year)			5	20	3	4	2	0	1	3	.200	1	6	0	9	0	0	1.000

MAHOMES, PAT — P — RANGERS

PERSONAL: Born August 9, 1970, in Bryan, Texas. ... 6-4/212. ... Throws right, bats right. ... Full name: Patrick Lavon Mahomes. ... Name pronounced muh-HOMES.

HIGH SCHOOL: Lindale (Texas).

TRANSACTIONS/CAREER NOTES: Selected by Minnesota Twins organization in sixth round of free-agent draft (June 1, 1988). ... On disabled list (July 6-23, 1994). ... Traded by Twins to Boston Red Sox for a player to be named later (August 26, 1996); Twins acquired P Brian Looney to complete deal (December 17, 1996). ... Signed by Yokohoma of Japan Central League (1997). ... Signed by New York Mets (December 21, 1998). ... Granted free agency (December 21, 2000). ... Signed by Texas Rangers organization (January 21, 2001).

MISCELLANEOUS: Appeared in one game as pinch runner (1994). ... Struck out in only appearance as pinch hitter and appeared in one game as pinch runner (1999).

Year	League	W	L	Pct.	ERA	G	GS	CG	ShO	Sv.	IP	H	R	ER	BB	SO
1988—	Elizabethton (Appl.)	6	3	.667	3.69	13	13	3	0	0	78	66	45	32	51	93
1989—	Kenosha (Midw.)	13	7	.650	3.28	25	25	3	1	0	156 1/3	120	66	57	•100	167
1990—	Visalia (Calif.)	11	11	.500	3.30	28	*28	5	1	0	•185 1/3	136	77	68	*118	178
1991—	Orlando (Sou.)	8	5	.615	*1.78	18	17	2	0	0	116	77	30	23	57	136
	—Portland (PCL)	3	5	.375	3.44	9	9	2	0	0	55	50	26	21	36	41
1992—	Minnesota (A.L.)	3	4	.429	5.04	14	13	0	0	0	69 2/3	73	41	39	37	44
	—Portland (PCL)	9	5	.643	3.41	17	16	3	*3	1	111	97	43	42	43	87
1993—	Minnesota (A.L.)	1	5	.167	7.71	12	5	0	0	0	37 1/3	47	34	32	16	23
	—Portland (PCL)	11	4	•.733	*3.03	17	16	3	1	0	115 2/3	89	47	39	54	94
1994—	Minnesota (A.L.)	9	5	.643	4.72	21	21	0	0	0	120	121	68	63	62	53
1995—	Minnesota (A.L.)	4	10	.286	6.37	47	7	0	0	3	94 2/3	100	74	67	47	67
1996—	Minnesota (A.L.)	1	4	.200	7.20	20	5	0	0	0	45	63	38	36	27	30
	—Salt Lake (PCL)	3	1	.750	3.74	22	0	0	0	7	33 2/3	32	14	14	12	41
	—Boston (A.L.)■	2	0	1.000	5.84	11	0	0	0	2	12 1/3	9	8	8	6	6
1997—	Boston (A.L.)	1	0	1.000	8.10	10	0	0	0	0	10	15	10	9	10	5
	—Pawtucket (I.L.)	5	1	.833	2.84	18	1	0	0	7	31 2/3	22	11	10	17	40
	—Yokohama (Jap. Cen.)■	3	4	.429	4.82	11	9	0	0	0	52 1/3	54	30	28	25	24
1998—	Yokohama (Jap. Cen.)	0	4	.000	5.98	10	8	0	0	0	43 2/3	61	30	29	29	24
1999—	Norfolk (I.L.)■	4	1	.800	3.49	6	6	0	0	0	38 2/3	38	17	15	12	24
	—New York (N.L.)	8	0	1.000	3.68	39	0	0	0	0	63 2/3	44	26	26	37	51
2000—	New York (N.L.)	5	3	.625	5.46	53	5	0	0	0	94	96	63	57	66	76
A.L. totals (6 years)		21	28	.429	5.88	135	51	0	0	5	389	427	273	254	205	228
N.L. totals (2 years)		13	3	.813	4.74	92	5	0	0	0	157 2/3	140	89	83	103	127
Major League totals (8 years)		34	31	.523	5.55	227	56	0	0	5	546 2/3	568	362	337	308	355

DIVISION SERIES RECORD

Year	League	W	L	Pct.	ERA	G	GS	CG	ShO	Sv.	IP	H	R	ER	BB	SO
1999—	New York (N.L.)	0	0	...	5.40	1	0	0	0	0	1 2/3	3	1	1	0	1
2000—	New York (N.L.)								Did not play.							

CHAMPIONSHIP SERIES RECORD

Year	League	W	L	Pct.	ERA	G	GS	CG	ShO	Sv.	IP	H	R	ER	BB	SO
1999—	New York (N.L.)	0	0	...	1.42	3	0	0	0	0	6 1/3	4	1	1	3	3
2000—	New York (N.L.)								Did not play.							

WORLD SERIES RECORD

Year	League	W	L	Pct.	ERA	G	GS	CG	ShO	Sv.	IP	H	R	ER	BB	SO
2000—	New York (N.L.)								Did not play.							

PERSONAL: Born July 30, 1975, in Chinandega, Nicaragua. ... 5-11/165. ... Throws left, bats left. ... Full name: Oswaldo Antonito Mairena.
COLLEGE: Universidad Unan (Chinandega, Nicaragua).
TRANSACTIONS/CAREER NOTES: Signed as non-drafted free agent by New York Yankees organization (August 2, 1996). ... Traded by Yankees with P Ben Ford to Chicago Cubs for OF Glenallen Hill (July 21, 2000). ... On Iowa disabled list (August 25-September 1, 2000).

Year	League	W	L	Pct.	ERA	G	GS	CG	ShO	Sv.	IP	H	R	ER	BB	SO
1997—	Greensboro (S.Atl.)	6	1	.857	2.54	49	0	0	0	8	60 1/3	43	24	17	16	75
—	Tampa (FSL)....................	0	0	...	4.15	3	0	0	0	0	4 1/3	6	2	2	0	6
1998—	Tampa (FSL)....................	1	5	.167	3.17	52	0	0	0	0	54	53	24	19	23	50
1999—	Norwich (East.)	4	3	.571	2.67	49	0	0	0	2	57 1/3	48	24	17	27	47
2000—	Norwich (East.)	0	4	.000	2.78	35	0	0	0	0	32 1/3	29	16	10	11	30
—	Columbus (I.L.)	1	1	.500	3.00	5	1	0	0	0	9	12	3	3	5	4
—	West Tenn (Sou.)■	0	1	.000	0.00	2	0	0	0	0	2	3	1	0	1	0
—	Iowa (PCL)	1	0	1.000	4.91	11	0	0	0	0	14 2/3	13	9	8	2	4
—	Chicago (N.L.)..................	0	0	...	18.00	2	0	0	0	0	2	7	4	4	2	0
Major League totals (1 year)........		0	0	...	18.00	2	0	0	0	0	2	7	4	4	2	0

PERSONAL: Born November 17, 1974, in Brockton, Mass. ... 6-3/225. ... Throws right, bats right. ... Full name: James Joseph Mann.
HIGH SCHOOL: Holbrook (Mass.).
JUNIOR COLLEGE: Massasoit Community College (Mass.).
TRANSACTIONS/CAREER NOTES: Selected by Toronto Blue Jays organization in 54th round of free-agent draft (June 3, 1993). ... Selected by New York Mets from Blue Jays organization in Rule 5 major league draft (December 13, 1999); Blue Jays acquired IF Jersen Perez as compensation for Mets keeping Mann (March 22, 2000). ... Granted free agency (October 18, 2000). ... Signed by Houston Astros organization (January 3, 2001).

Year	League	W	L	Pct.	ERA	G	GS	CG	ShO	Sv.	IP	H	R	ER	BB	SO
1994—	GC Blue Jays (GCL)...........	3	2	.600	3.74	11	9	0	0	0	53	54	28	22	26	41
1995—	Medicine Hat (Pio.)	5	4	.556	4.29	14	14	1	•1	0	77 2/3	78	47	37	37	66
1996—	St. Catharines (NY-Penn) ...	2	1	.667	3.62	26	0	0	0	17	27 1/3	22	12	11	10	37
1997—	Hagerstown (S.Atl.)...........	0	1	.000	5.06	19	0	0	0	4	26 2/3	35	18	15	11	30
—	Dunedin (FSL)..................	1	0	1.000	6.00	12	0	0	0	0	18	27	12	12	6	13
1998—	Dunedin (FSL)..................	0	2	.000	3.04	51	0	0	0	25	50 1/3	31	19	17	24	59
1999—	Knoxville (Sou.)................	1	2	.333	0.93	6	0	0	0	0	9 2/3	6	2	1	1	12
—	Syracuse (I.L.).................	6	5	.545	4.64	47	0	0	0	5	66	53	35	34	39	72
2000—	Norfolk (I.L.)■	3	4	.429	2.98	49	0	0	0	3	81 2/3	61	27	27	33	74
—	New York (N.L.)................	0	0	...	10.13	2	0	0	0	0	2 2/3	6	3	3	1	0
Major League totals (1 year)........		0	0	...	10.13	2	0	0	0	0	2 2/3	6	3	3	1	0

M

PERSONAL: Born July 7, 1973, in Tampa. ... 6-1/190. ... Throws right, bats right. ... Full name: Matthew Bruce Mantei. ... Name pronounced MAN-tay.
HIGH SCHOOL: River Valley (Three Oaks, Mich.).
TRANSACTIONS/CAREER NOTES: Selected by Seattle Mariners organization in 25th round of free-agent draft (June 3, 1991). ... Selected by Florida Marlins from Mariners organization in Rule 5 major league draft (December 5, 1994). ... On Florida disabled list (April 20-June 18 and July 29-September 1, 1995); included rehabilitation assignments to Portland and Charlotte (May 13-June 18). ... On Florida disabled list (June 19, 1996-remainder of season). ... On Florida disabled list (March 31, 1997-entire season). ... Granted free agency (December 21, 1997). ... Re-signed by Marlins organization (December 21, 1997). ... On Florida disabled list (August 19-September 4, 1998). ... Traded by Marlins to Arizona Diamondbacks for P Vladimir Nunez, P Brad Penny and a player to be named later (July 9, 1999); Marlins acquired OF Abraham Nunez to complete deal (December 13, 1999). ... On Arizona disabled list (April 2-21 and May 5-21, 2000); included rehabilitation assignment to Tuscon (April 14-21).

Year	League	W	L	Pct.	ERA	G	GS	CG	ShO	Sv.	IP	H	R	ER	BB	SO
1991—	Arizona Mariners (Ariz.)	1	4	.200	6.69	17	5	0	0	0	40 1/3	54	40	30	28	29
1992—	Arizona Mariners (Ariz.)	1	1	.500	5.63	3	3	0	0	0	16	18	10	10	5	19
1993—	Bellingham (N'West)	1	1	.500	5.96	26	0	0	0	*12	25 2/3	26	19	17	15	34
1994—	Appleton (Midw.)..............	5	1	.833	2.06	48	0	0	0	26	48	42	14	11	21	70
1995—	Portland (East.)■	1	0	1.000	2.38	8	0	0	0	1	11 1/3	10	3	3	5	15
—	Charlotte (I.L.)..................	0	1	.000	2.57	6	0	0	0	0	7	1	3	2	5	10
—	Florida (N.L.)...................	0	0	...	4.72	12	0	0	0	0	13 1/3	12	8	7	13	15
1996—	Florida (N.L.)...................	1	0	1.000	6.38	14	0	0	0	0	18 1/3	13	13	13	21	25
—	Charlotte (I.L.)..................	0	2	.000	4.70	7	0	0	0	2	7 2/3	6	4	4	7	8
1997—	Brevard County (FSL)........	0	0	...	6.00	4	0	0	0	0	6	4	4	4	6	11
—	Portland (East.)................	1	0	1.000	6.75	5	0	0	0	0	4	1	3	3	8	7
1998—	Charlotte (I.L.).................	1	2	.333	5.51	16	0	0	0	3	16 1/3	11	10	10	18	25
—	Florida (N.L.)...................	3	4	.429	2.96	42	0	0	0	9	54 2/3	38	19	18	23	63
1999—	Florida (N.L.)...................	1	2	.333	2.72	35	0	0	0	10	36 1/3	24	11	11	25	50
—	Arizona (N.L.)■.................	0	1	.000	2.79	30	0	0	0	22	29	20	10	9	19	49
2000—	Tucson (PCL)	0	0	...	2.45	4	2	0	0	0	3 2/3	1	1	1	3	2
—	Arizona (N.L.)..................	1	1	.500	4.57	47	0	0	0	17	45 1/3	31	24	23	35	53
Major League totals (5 years)........		6	9	.400	3.70	180	0	0	0	58	197	138	85	81	136	255

DIVISION SERIES RECORD

Year	League	W	L	Pct.	ERA	G	GS	CG	ShO	Sv.	IP	H	R	ER	BB	SO
1999—	Arizona (N.L.)....................	0	1	.000	4.50	1	0	0	0	0	2	1	1	1	3	1

PERSONAL: Born August 23, 1964, in Bristol, Pa. ... 6-3/210. ... Bats right, throws right. ... Full name: Jeffrey Paul Manto.
HIGH SCHOOL: Bristol (Pa.).
COLLEGE: Temple.
TRANSACTIONS/CAREER NOTES: Selected by New York Yankees organization in 35th round of free-agent draft (June 7, 1982); did not sign. ... Selected by California Angels organization in 14th round of free-agent draft (June 3, 1985). ... On disabled list (July 16, 1986-remainder of season). ... Traded by Angels with P Colin Charland to Cleveland Indians for P Scott Bailes (January 9, 1990). ... Released by Indians (November 27, 1991). ... Signed by Atlanta Braves organization (January 23, 1992). ... On disabled list (May 4-14, 1992). ... Granted free agency (October 15, 1992). ... Signed by Philadelphia Phillies organization (December 16, 1992). ... Granted free agency (October 15, 1993). ... Signed by New York Mets organization (December 16, 1993). ... Traded by Mets to Baltimore Orioles for future considerations (May 19, 1994). ... On Baltimore disabled list (June 26-July 13, 1995); included rehabilitation assignments to Bowie (July 9-10) and Frederick (July 10-13). ... Contract sold by Mets to Yomiuri Giants of Japan Central League (January 25, 1996). ... Released by Giants (April 23, 1996). ... Signed by Boston Red Sox organization (May 7, 1996). ... On Boston disabled list (May 26-June 27, 1996); included rehabilitation assignment to Trenton (June 21-27). ... Traded by Red Sox to Seattle Mariners for IF Arquimedez Pozo (July 23, 1996). ... Claimed on waivers by Red Sox (August 29, 1996). ... Granted free agency (October 8, 1996). ... Signed by Toronto Blue Jays organization (February 17, 1997). ... On Syracuse disabled list (May 26-June 2, 1997). ... Traded by Blue Jays to Indians for OF Ryan Thompson (June 6, 1997). ... Claimed on waivers by Detroit Tigers (April 24, 1998). ... Released by Tigers (June 12, 1998). ... Signed by Indians organization (June 16, 1998). ... Released by Indians (October 15, 1998). ... Re-signed by Indians organization (January 5, 1999). ... Claimed on waivers by Yankees (July 2, 1999). ... Released by Yankees (August 10, 1999). ... Signed by Indians organization (August 13, 1999). ... Granted free agency (October 15, 1999). ... Signed by Colorado Rockies organization (November 3, 1999). ... Granted free agency (April 28, 2000). ... Signed by Indians organization (April 30, 2000). ... Granted free agency (October 18, 2000).
RECORDS: Shares major league record for most consecutive home runs in three games—4 (June 8 [1], 9 [2] and 10 [1], 1995).
HONORS: Named Texas League Most Valuable Player (1988). ... Named International League Most Valuable Player (1994).
STATISTICAL NOTES: Led California League third basemen with 245 assists and 365 total chances in 1987. ... Tied for Texas League lead in errors by third baseman with 32 in 1988. ... Led Texas League in grounding into double plays with 17 in 1988. ... Led Pacific Coast League with .446 on-base percentage in 1990. ... Led Pacific Coast League third basemen with .943 fielding percentage, 265 assists and 22 double plays in 1989. ... Led International League with 12 sacrifice flies in 1992. ... Led International League with .404 on-base percentage, 260 total bases, 31 home runs, 100 RBIs and tied for lead in being hit by pitch with 11 in 1994.

								BATTING							FIELDING		
Year Team (League)	Pos.	G	AB	R	H	2B	3B	HR	RBI	Avg.	BB	SO	SB	PO	A	E	Avg.
1985— Quad Cities (Midw.)....	OF-3B	74	233	34	46	5	2	11	34	.197	40	74	3	87	8	3	.969
1986— Quad Cities (Midw.)....	3B	73	239	31	59	13	0	8	49	.247	37	70	2	48	114	28	.853
1987— Palm Springs (Calif.)..	3B-1B	112	375	61	96	21	4	7	63	.256	102	85	8	93	†246	37	.902
1988— Midland (Texas).........	3B-2B-1B	120	408	88	123	23	3	24	101	.301	62	76	7	82	208	‡32	.901
1989— Edmonton (PCL)	3B-1B	127	408	89	113	25	3	23	67	.277	91	81	4	140	†266	21	†.951
1990— Colo. Springs (PCL)■	3B-1B	96	316	73	94	27	1	18	82	.297	78	65	10	340	131	10	.979
— Cleveland (A.L.)...........	1B-3B	30	76	12	17	5	1	2	14	.224	21	18	0	185	24	2	.991
1991— Cleveland (A.L.).........3B-1B-C-OF		47	128	15	27	7	0	2	13	.211	14	22	2	109	63	8	.956
— Colo. Springs (PCL) ...	3-1-C-S-O	43	153	36	49	16	0	6	36	.320	33	24	1	169	53	11	.953
1992— Richmond (I.L.)■.......	3B-2B-1B	127	450	65	131	24	1	13	68	.291	57	63	1	89	245	23	.936
1993— Scranton/W.B. (I.L.)■	3B-1B-C	106	388	62	112	30	1	17	88	.289	55	58	4	401	134	8	.985
— Philadelphia (N.L.).......	3B-SS	8	18	0	1	0	0	0	0	.056	0	3	0	2	8	0	1.000
1994— Norfolk (I.L.)..........3B-DH-1B-2B		37	115	20	30	6	0	4	17	.261	27	28	1	73	46	4	.967
— Rochester (I.L.)■........	3B-1B-DH	94	329	61	102	25	2	§27	§83	.310	43	47	2	277	102	15	.962
1995— Baltimore (A.L.)■.......	3B-DH-1B	89	254	31	65	9	0	17	38	.256	24	69	0	68	103	6	.966
— Bowie (East.)..............	DH	1	4	1	1	0	0	0	0	.250	0	2	0	0	0	0	...
— Frederick (Caro.).......	DH-3B	2	8	1	3	0	0	1	3	.375	0	1	0	0	2	0	1.000
1996— Yomiuri (Jap. Cen.)■.		10	27	1	3	...	...	0	1	.111	...	...	...	...	...	...	...
— Pawtucket (I.L.)■........	3B-2B	12	45	6	11	5	0	2	6	.244	5	8	1	13	29	2	.955
— Boston (A.L.)............3B-2B-SS-1B		22	48	8	10	3	1	2	6	.208	8	12	0	25	47	4	.947
— Trenton (East.) 3B-DH-2B-SS		6	21	3	6	0	0	0	5	.286	1	5	0	5	5	3	.769
— Seattle (A.L.)■...........	3B-DH-OF	21	54	7	10	3	0	1	4	.185	9	12	0	8	26	1	.971
1997— Syracuse (I.L.)■........DH-3B-OF-1B		40	132	18	27	5	1	3	11	.205	22	30	1	23	19	1	.977
— Buffalo (A.A.)■.........3B-DH-1B-OF		54	187	37	60	11	0	20	54	.321	31	43	0	59	54	6	.950
— Cleveland (A.L.).........	3B-1B-OF	16	30	3	8	3	0	2	7	.267	1	10	0	35	5	0	1.000
1998— Buffalo (I.L.)■.........	3B-1B-2B	15	37	8	8	1	0	2	6	.216	2	10	0	49	8	1	.983
— Detroit (A.L.)■...........	1B-DH-3B	16	30	6	8	2	0	1	3	.267	3	11	1	43	0	1	.977
— Buffalo (I.L.)■...........	1B-DH-3B	62	209	46	65	11	0	23	63	.311	58	48	4	282	35	2	.994
1999— Buffalo (I.L.)...........	1B-DH	66	203	47	60	9	0	23	44	.296	66	47	3	417	22	3	.993
— Cleveland (A.L.).........	3B-1B	12	25	5	5	0	0	1	2	.200	11	11	0	12	16	0	1.000
— New York (A.L.)■.......	1B-3B	6	8	0	1	0	0	0	0	.125	2	4	0	14	1	0	1.000
2000— Colorado (N.L.)■	1B-DH	7	5	2	4	2	0	1	4	.800	2	0	0	1	1	0	1.000
— Buffalo (I.L.)■...........	3B-1B	94	324	39	65	14	1	13	46	.201	51	96	0	81	31	3	.974
American League totals (7 years)		274	690	95	159	33	2	30	93	.230	95	179	3	548	293	23	.973
National League totals (2 years)		15	23	2	5	2	0	1	4	.217	2	3	0	3	9	0	1.000
Major League totals (9 years)		289	713	97	164	35	2	31	97	.230	97	182	3	551	302	23	.974

PERSONAL: Born October 16, 1967, in San Pedro de Macoris, Dominican Republic ... 6-0/205. ... Throws right, bats right. ... Brother of Ravelo Manzanillo, pitcher with Chicago White Sox (1988) and Pittsburgh Pirates (1994-1995). ... Name pronounced hose-EYE-ess MAN-zan-EE-oh...
TRANSACTIONS/CAREER NOTES: Signed as non-drafted free agent by Boston Red Sox organization (January 10, 1983). ... On disabled list (June 8, 1987-remainder of season; and April 8, 1988-entire season). ... Granted free agency (March 24, 1992). ... Signed by Omaha, Kansas City Royals organization (April 3, 1992). ... Granted free agency (October 15, 1992). ... Signed by Milwaukee Brewers (November 20, 1992). ... Traded by Brewers to New York Mets for OF Wayne Housie (June 12, 1993). ... On New York disabled list (July 27, 1994-remainder of season). ... Claimed on waivers by New York Yankees (June 5, 1995). ... On New York disabled list (July 6, 1995-remainder of season). ... Granted free agency (October 16, 1995). ... Played in Taiwan for 1996 season. ... Signed by Seattle Mariners organization (December 21, 1996). ... On Seattle disabled list (April 9-May 6 and May 25-July 1, 1997); included rehabilitation assignments to Memphis (May 1-6) and Tacoma (May 25-July 1). ... Released by Mariners (July 17, 1997). ... Signed by Houston Astros organization (July 27, 1997). ... Granted free

agency (October 15, 1997). ... Signed by Tampa Bay Devil Rays organization (December 18, 1997). ... Released by Devil Rays (July 1, 1998). ... Signed by Mets organization (July 3, 1998). ... Granted free agency (October 15, 1998). ... Re-signed by Mets organization (December 18, 1998). ... On Norfolk disabled list (June 21, 1999-remainder of season). ... Granted free agency (October 4, 1999). ... Signed by Pittsburgh Pirates organization (February 9, 2000).

MISCELLANEOUS: Appeared in one game as pinch runner (1999).

Year	League	W	L	Pct.	ERA	G	GS	CG	ShO	Sv.	IP	H	R	ER	BB	SO
1983—	Elmira (NY-Penn)	1	5	.167	7.98	12	4	0	0	0	38 1/3	52	44	34	20	19
1984—	Elmira (NY-Penn)	2	3	.400	5.26	14	0	0	0	1	25 2/3	27	24	15	26	15
1985—	Greensboro (S.Atl.)	1	1	.500	9.75	7	0	0	0	0	12	12	13	13	18	10
	— Elmira (NY-Penn)	2	4	.333	3.86	19	4	0	0	1	39 2/3	36	19	17	36	43
1986—	Winter Haven (FSL)	13	5	.722	2.27	23	21	3	2	0	142 2/3	110	51	36	81	102
1987—	New Britain (East.)	2	0	1.000	4.50	2	2	0	0	0	10	8	5	5	8	12
1988—	New Britain (East.)							Did not play.								
1989—	New Britain (East.)	9	10	.474	3.66	26	•26	3	1	0	147 2/3	129	78	60	85	93
1990—	New Britain (East.)	4	4	.500	3.41	12	12	2	1	0	74	66	34	28	37	51
	— Pawtucket (I.L.)	4	7	.364	5.55	15	15	5	0	0	82 2/3	75	57	51	45	77
1991—	Pawtucket (I.L.)	5	5	.500	5.61	20	16	0	0	0	102 2/3	109	69	64	53	65
	— New Britain (East.)	2	2	.500	2.90	7	7	0	0	0	49 2/3	37	25	16	28	35
	— Boston (A.L.)	0	0	...	18.00	1	0	0	0	0	1	2	2	2	3	1
1992—	Omaha (A.A.)■	7	10	.412	4.36	26	21	0	0	0	136 1/3	138	76	66	71	114
	— Memphis (Sou.)	0	2	.000	7.36	2	0	0	0	0	7 1/3	6	6	6	6	8
1993—	Milwaukee (A.L.)■	1	1	.500	9.53	10	1	0	0	1	17	22	20	18	10	10
	— New Orleans (A.A.)	0	1	.000	9.00	1	0	0	0	0	1	1	1	1	0	3
	— Norfolk (I.L.)■	1	5	.167	3.11	14	12	2	1	0	84	82	40	29	25	79
	— New York (N.L.)	0	0	...	3.00	6	0	0	0	0	12	8	7	4	9	11
1994—	Norfolk (I.L.)	0	1	.000	4.38	8	0	0	0	3	12 1/3	12	6	6	6	10
	— New York (N.L.)	3	2	.600	2.66	37	0	0	0	2	47 1/3	34	15	14	13	48
1995—	New York (N.L.)	1	2	.333	7.88	12	0	0	0	0	16	18	15	14	6	14
	— New York (A.L.)■	0	0	...	2.08	11	0	0	0	0	17 1/3	19	4	4	9	11
1996—								Statistics unavailable.								
1997—	Seattle (A.L.)■	0	1	.000	5.40	16	0	0	0	0	18 1/3	19	13	11	17	18
	— Memphis (Sou.)	0	0	...	3.00	2	0	0	0	0	3	1	1	1	0	6
	— Tacoma (PCL)	0	0	...	6.43	11	0	0	0	1	14	16	10	10	8	15
	— New Orleans (A.A.)■	0	0	...	4.40	11	0	0	0	0	14 1/3	17	7	7	6	11
1998—	Durham (I.L.)■	7	6	.538	4.64	19	14	0	0	1	85 1/3	93	57	44	30	61
	— Norfolk (I.L.)■	4	4	.500	3.24	13	12	1	0	1	77 2/3	77	35	28	31	72
1999—	New York (N.L.)	0	0	...	5.79	12	0	0	0	0	18 2/3	19	12	12	4	25
2000—	Nashville (PCL)■	0	2	.000	2.70	15	0	0	0	3	23 1/3	19	8	7	6	23
	— Pittsburgh (N.L.)	2	2	.500	3.38	43	0	0	0	0	58 2/3	50	23	22	32	39
A.L. totals (4 years)		1	2	.333	5.87	38	1	0	0	1	53 2/3	62	39	35	39	40
N.L. totals (5 years)		6	6	.500	3.89	110	0	0	0	2	152 2/3	129	72	66	64	137
Major League totals (7 years)		7	8	.467	4.41	148	1	0	0	3	206 1/3	191	111	101	103	177

MARQUIS, JASON   P   BRAVES

M

PERSONAL: Born August 21, 1978, in Manhasset, N.Y. ... 6-1/185. ... Throws right, bats left. ... Full name: Jason Scott Marquis.
HIGH SCHOOL: Tottenville (Staten Island, N.Y.).
TRANSACTIONS/CAREER NOTES: Selected by Atlanta Braves organization as "sandwich" pick between first and second round of free-agent draft (June 4, 1996); pick received as supplemental pick for failure to signed 1995 first-round choice. ... On Greenville disabled list (July 5-31, 1999).

Year	League	W	L	Pct.	ERA	G	GS	CG	ShO	Sv.	IP	H	R	ER	BB	SO
1996—	Danville (Appl.)	1	1	.500	4.63	7	4	0	0	0	23 1/3	30	18	12	7	24
1997—	Macon (S.Atl.)	•14	10	.583	4.38	28	28	0	0	0	141 2/3	156	78	69	55	121
1998—	Danville (Caro.)	2	12	.143	4.87	22	22	1	0	0	114 2/3	120	65	62	41	135
1999—	Myrtle Beach (Caro.)	3	0	1.000	0.28	6	6	0	0	0	32	22	2	1	17	41
	— Greenville (Sou.)	3	4	.429	4.58	12	12	1	0	0	55	52	33	28	29	35
2000—	Greenville (Sou.)	4	2	.667	3.57	11	11	0	0	0	68	68	35	27	23	49
	— Atlanta (N.L.)	1	0	1.000	5.01	15	0	0	0	0	23 1/3	23	16	13	12	17
	— Richmond (I.L.)	0	3	.000	9.00	6	6	0	0	0	20	26	21	20	13	18
Major League totals (1 year)		1	0	1.000	5.01	15	0	0	0	0	23 1/3	23	16	13	12	17

MARRERO, ELI   C   CARDINALS

PERSONAL: Born November 17, 1973, in Havana, Cuba. ... 6-1/180. ... Bats right, throws right. ... Full name: Elieser Marrero.
HIGH SCHOOL: Coral Gables (Fla.).
TRANSACTIONS/CAREER NOTES: Selected by St. Louis Cardinals organization in third round of free-agent draft (June 3, 1993). ... On St. Louis disabled list (March 22-April 13, 1998). ... On St. Louis disabled list (July 2-September 1, 2000); included rehabilitation assignment to Memphis (August 24-September 1).
STATISTICAL NOTES: Led Texas League catchers with 746 total chances in 1996. ... Led American Association catchers with 750 total chances in 1997. ... Career major league grand slams: 1.

Year	Team (League)	Pos.	G	AB	R	H	2B	3B	HR	RBI	Avg.	BB	SO	SB	PO	A	E	Avg.
1993—	Johnson City (Appl.)	C	18	61	10	22	8	0	2	14	.361	12	9	2	154	18	1	.994
1994—	Savannah (S.Atl.)	C	116	421	71	110	16	3	21	79	.261	39	92	5	821	92	•15	.984
1995—	St. Petersburg (FSL)	C	107	383	43	81	16	1	10	55	.211	23	55	9	574	52	10	.984
1996—	Arkansas (Texas)	C-DH	116	374	65	101	17	3	19	65	.270	32	55	9	*676	67	3	*.996
1997—	Louisville (A.A.)	C-DH	112	395	60	108	21	7	20	68	.273	25	53	4	*675	*68	7	.991
	— St. Louis (N.L.)	C	17	45	4	11	2	0	2	7	.244	2	13	4	82	12	3	.969

Year	Team (League)	Pos.	G	AB	R	H	2B	3B	HR	RBI	Avg.	BB	SO	SB	PO	A	E	Avg.
								BATTING								FIELDING		
1998—St. Louis (N.L.).............		C-1B	83	254	28	62	18	1	4	20	.244	28	42	6	427	31	4	.991
—Memphis (PCL)..........		C-DH	32	130	22	31	5	0	7	21	.238	13	23	5	195	17	2	.991
1999—St. Louis (N.L.).............		C-1B	114	317	32	61	13	1	6	34	.192	18	56	11	537	47	7	.988
2000—St. Louis (N.L.).............		C-1B	53	102	21	23	3	1	5	17	.225	9	16	5	212	14	0	1.000
—Memphis (PCL)..........		C	6	15	1	1	0	0	0	0	.067	0	2	0	16	1	0	1.000
Major League totals (4 years)			267	718	85	157	36	3	17	78	.219	57	127	26	1258	104	14	.990

DIVISION SERIES RECORD

Year	Team (League)	Pos.	G	AB	R	H	2B	3B	HR	RBI	Avg.	BB	SO	SB	PO	A	E	Avg.
								BATTING								FIELDING		
2000—St. Louis (N.L.)...........									Did not play.									

CHAMPIONSHIP SERIES RECORD

Year	Team (League)	Pos.	G	AB	R	H	2B	3B	HR	RBI	Avg.	BB	SO	SB	PO	A	E	Avg.
								BATTING								FIELDING		
2000—St. Louis (N.L.)...........		PR-C	4	4	0	0	0	0	0	1	.000	0	1	0	11	0	0	1.000

MARTIN, AL — OF — MARINERS

PERSONAL: Born November 24, 1967, in West Covina, Calif. ... 6-2/214. ... Bats left, throws left. ... Full name: Albert Lee Martin. ... Formerly known as Albert Scales-Martin. ... Nephew of Rod Martin, linebacker with Oakland/Los Angeles Raiders (1977-88).

HIGH SCHOOL: West Covina (Calif.).

COLLEGE: Southern California.

TRANSACTIONS/CAREER NOTES: Selected by Atlanta Braves organization in eighth round of free-agent draft (June 3, 1985). ... Granted free agency (October 15, 1991). ... Signed by Pittsburgh Pirates organization (November 11, 1991). ... On suspended list (September 17-20, 1993). ... On disabled list (July 11, 1994-remainder of season). ... On Pittsburgh disabled list (May 22-June 24, 1997; included rehabilitation assignment to Carolina (June 21-23). ... Traded by Pirates with cash to San Diego Padres for OF John Vander Wal, P Geraldo Padua and P James Sak (February 23, 2000). ... Traded by Padres to Seattle Mariners for OF/3B John Mabry and P Tom Davey (July 31, 2000).

RECORDS: Shares major league record for fewest double plays by outfielder (150 or more games)—0 (1996). ... Holds modern N.L. single-season record for fewest putouts by outfielder (150 or more games)—217 (1996). ... Holds N.L. single-season record for fewest chances accepted by outfielder (150 or more games)—222 (1996).

STATISTICAL NOTES: Led Gulf Coast League first basemen with 15 errors in 1985. ... Led American Association with .557 slugging percentage in 1992. ... Led American Association outfielders with six double plays in 1992. ... Had 20-game hitting streak (June 20-July 11, 1999). ... Had 15-game hitting streak (August 25-September 11, 1999). ... Career major league grand slams: 1.

Year	Team (League)	Pos.	G	AB	R	H	2B	3B	HR	RBI	Avg.	BB	SO	SB	PO	A	E	Avg.
								BATTING								FIELDING		
1985—GC Braves (GCL)........		1B-OF	40	138	16	32	3	0	0	9	.232	19	36	1	246	13	†15	.945
1986—Sumter (S.Atl.)..........		1B	44	156	23	38	5	0	1	24	.244	23	36	6	299	12	8	.975
—Idaho Falls (Pio.).........		OF-1B	63	242	39	80	17	•6	4	44	.331	20	53	11	272	15	8	.973
1987—Sumter (S.Atl.)..........		OF-1B	117	375	59	95	18	5	12	64	.253	44	69	27	137	7	9	.941
1988—Burlington (Midw.)		OF	123	480	69	134	21	3	7	42	.279	30	88	40	224	4	8	.966
1989—Durham (Caro.)........		OF	128	457	*84	124	26	3	9	48	.271	34	107	27	169	7	7	.962
1990—Greenville (Sou.)		OF	133	455	64	110	17	4	11	50	.242	43	102	20	200	8	7	.967
1991—Greenville (Sou.)		OF-1B	86	301	38	73	13	3	7	38	.243	32	84	19	134	7	6	.959
—Richmond (I.L.)........		OF	44	151	20	42	11	1	5	18	.278	7	33	11	73	4	2	.975
1992—Buffalo (A.A.)■........		OF	125	420	85	128	16	*15	20	59	.305	35	93	20	222	10	8	.967
—Pittsburgh (N.L.)........		OF	12	12	1	2	0	1	0	2	.167	0	5	0	6	0	0	1.000
1993—Pittsburgh (N.L.)........		OF	143	480	85	135	26	8	18	64	.281	42	122	16	268	6	7	.975
1994—Pittsburgh (N.L.)........		OF	82	276	48	79	12	4	9	33	.286	34	56	15	129	8	3	.979
1995—Pittsburgh (N.L.)........		OF	124	439	70	124	25	3	13	41	.282	44	92	20	206	8	5	.977
1996—Pittsburgh (N.L.)........		OF	155	630	101	189	40	1	18	72	.300	54	116	38	217	5	8	.965
1997—Pittsburgh (N.L.)........		OF	113	423	64	123	24	7	13	59	.291	45	83	23	125	8	6	.957
—Carolina (Sou.)..........		OF	3	9	0	1	0	0	0	0	.111	0	0	0	2	0	0	1.000
1998—Pittsburgh (N.L.)........		OF-DH	125	440	57	105	15	2	12	47	.239	32	91	20	192	6	3	.985
1999—Pittsburgh (N.L.)........		OF	143	541	97	150	36	8	24	63	.277	49	119	20	196	3	10	.952
2000—San Diego (N.L.)■		OF	93	346	62	106	13	6	11	27	.306	28	54	6	128	4	7	.950
—Seattle (A.L.)■..........		OF-DH	42	134	19	31	2	4	4	9	.231	8	31	4	76	3	3	.963
American League totals (1 year)			42	134	19	31	2	4	4	9	.231	8	31	4	76	3	3	.963
National League totals (9 years)			990	3587	585	1013	191	40	118	408	.282	328	738	158	1467	48	49	.969
Major League totals (9 years)			1032	3721	604	1044	193	44	122	417	.281	336	769	162	1543	51	52	.968

DIVISION SERIES RECORD

Year	Team (League)	Pos.	G	AB	R	H	2B	3B	HR	RBI	Avg.	BB	SO	SB	PO	A	E	Avg.
								BATTING								FIELDING		
2000— Seattle (A.L.)		PH	1	1	0	0	0	0	0	0	.000	0	0	0	...	...	...	...

CHAMPIONSHIP SERIES RECORD

Year	Team (League)	Pos.	G	AB	R	H	2B	3B	HR	RBI	Avg.	BB	SO	SB	PO	A	E	Avg.
								BATTING								FIELDING		
2000— Seattle (A.L.)		OF-PH	4	11	1	2	2	0	0	0	.182	2	3	0	9	0	0	1.000

MARTIN, TOM — P — METS

PERSONAL: Born May 21, 1970, in Charleston, S.C. ... 6-1/200. ... Throws left, bats left. ... Full name: Thomas Edgar Martin.

HIGH SCHOOL: Bay (Panama City, Fla.).

TRANSACTIONS/CAREER NOTES: Selected by Baltimore Orioles organization in sixth round of free-agent draft (June 1, 1988). ... Traded by Orioles with 3B Craig Worthington to San Diego Padres for P Jim Lewis and OF Steve Martin (February 17, 1992). ... Selected by Atlanta Braves organization from Padres organization in Rule 5 minor league draft (December 13, 1993). ... Released by Braves (January 25, 1996). ... Signed by Houston Astros organization (February 21, 1996). ... On disabled list (May 30-June 15, 1997). ... Selected by Arizona Diamondbacks in second round (29th pick overall) of expansion draft (November 18, 1997). ... Traded by Diamondbacks with 3B Travis Fryman and cash to Cleveland Indians for 3B Matt Williams (December 1, 1997). ... On Cleveland disabled list (April 30-May 18 and August 31-September 19, 1998); included rehabilitation assignments to Buffalo (May 13-18 and September 3-19). ... On Cleveland disabled list (April 4-August 9, 1999); included rehabilitation assignment to Akron (July 27-August 9). ... On Cleveland disabled list (June 13-August 4, 2000); included rehabilitation assignment to Buffalo (July 28-August 4). ... Traded by Indians to New York Mets for C Javier Ochoa (January 11, 2001).

Year League	W	L	Pct.	ERA	G	GS	CG	ShO	Sv.	IP	H	R	ER	BB	SO
1989— Bluefield (Appl.)	3	3	.500	4.62	8	8	0	0	0	39	36	28	20	25	31
— Erie (NY-Penn)	0	5	.000	6.64	7	7	0	0	0	40 2/3	42	39	30	25	44
1990— Wausau (Midw.)	2	3	.400	2.47	9	9	0	0	0	40	31	25	11	27	45
1991— Kane County (Midw.)	4	10	.286	3.64	38	10	0	0	6	99	92	50	40	56	106
1992— High Desert (Calif.)■	0	2	.000	9.37	11	0	0	0	0	16 1/3	23	19	17	16	10
— Waterloo (Midw.)	2	6	.250	4.25	39	2	0	0	3	55	62	38	26	22	57
1993— Rancho Cuca. (Calif.)	1	4	.200	5.61	47	1	0	0	0	59 1/3	72	41	37	39	53
1994— Greenville (Sou.)■	5	6	.455	4.62	36	6	0	0	0	74	82	40	38	27	51
1995— Richmond (I.L.)	0	0	...	9.00	7	0	0	0	0	9	10	9	9	10	3
1996— Tucson (PCL)■	0	0	...	0.00	5	0	0	0	0	6	6	0	0	2	1
— Jackson (Texas)	6	2	.750	3.24	57	0	0	0	3	75	71	35	27	42	58
1997— Houston (N.L.)	5	3	.625	2.09	55	0	0	0	2	56	52	13	13	23	36
1998— Cleveland (A.L.)■	1	1	.500	12.89	14	0	0	0	0	14 2/3	29	21	21	12	9
— Buffalo (I.L.)	3	1	.750	6.00	41	0	0	0	0	36	46	25	24	13	35
1999— Akron (East.)	0	0	...	1.00	3	3	0	0	0	9	4	1	1	3	9
— Cleveland (A.L.)	0	1	.000	8.68	6	0	0	0	0	9 1/3	13	9	9	3	8
— Buffalo (I.L.)	1	0	1.000	3.00	5	0	0	0	0	6	5	2	2	1	6
2000— Cleveland (A.L.)	1	0	1.000	4.05	31	0	0	0	0	33 1/3	32	16	15	15	21
— Buffalo (I.L.)	0	1	.000	3.60	9	3	0	0	0	10	12	4	4	1	4
A.L. totals (3 years)	2	2	.500	7.06	51	0	0	0	0	57 1/3	74	46	45	30	38
N.L. totals (1 year)	5	3	.625	2.09	55	0	0	0	2	56	52	13	13	23	36
Major League totals (4 years)	7	5	.583	4.61	106	0	0	0	2	113 1/3	126	59	58	53	74

DIVISION SERIES RECORD

Year League	W	L	Pct.	ERA	G	GS	CG	ShO	Sv.	IP	H	R	ER	BB	SO
1997— Houston (N.L.)	0	0	...	0.00	2	0	0	0	0	2/3	1	1	0	1	0

MARTINEZ, DAVE — OF — BRAVES

PERSONAL: Born September 26, 1964, in Brooklyn, N.Y. ... 5-10/190. ... Bats left, throws left. ... Full name: David Martinez.

HIGH SCHOOL: Lake Howell (Casselberry, Fla.).

JUNIOR COLLEGE: Valencia Community College (Fla.).

TRANSACTIONS/CAREER NOTES: Selected by Texas Rangers organization in 40th round of free-agent draft (June 7, 1982); did not sign. ... Selected by Chicago Cubs organization in secondary phase of free-agent draft (January 11, 1983). ... On disabled list (April 27, 1984-remainder of season). ... Traded by Cubs to Montreal Expos for OF Mitch Webster (July 14, 1988). ... On disqualified list (October 4-5, 1991). ... Traded by Expos with P Scott Ruskin and SS Willie Greene to Cincinnati Reds for P John Wetteland and P Bill Risley (December 11, 1991). ... Granted free agency (October 27, 1992). ... Signed by San Francisco Giants (December 9, 1992). ... On San Francisco disabled list (April 30-June 4, 1993); included rehabilitation assignment to Phoenix (June 1-4). ... Granted free agency (October 14, 1994). ... Signed by Chicago White Sox (April 5, 1995). ... Granted free agency (November 3, 1995). ... Re-signed by White Sox (November 14, 1995). ... Granted free agency (October 27, 1997). ... Signed by Tampa Bay Devil Rays (December 4, 1997). ... On disabled list (July 22, 1998-remainder of season). ... Traded by Devil Rays to Cubs for P Mark Guthrie (May 12, 2000). ... Traded by Cubs to Rangers for IF/OF Brant Brown (June 9, 2000). ... Traded by Rangers to Toronto Blue Jays for a player to be named later (August 4, 2000); Rangers acquired P Peter Munro to complete deal (August 8, 2000). ... Granted free agency (October 31, 2000). ... Signed by Atlanta Braves (December 10, 2000).

RECORDS: Shares major league single-game record for most unassisted double plays by first baseman—2 (June 21, 1997). ... Shares major league record for most clubs played for in one season—4 (2000).

STATISTICAL NOTES: Had 21-game hitting streak (August 6-September 1, 2000). ... Career major league grand slams: 2.

Year Team (League)	Pos.	G	AB	R	H	2B	3B	HR	RBI	Avg.	BB	SO	SB	PO	A	E	Avg.
1983— Quad Cities (Midw.)	OF	44	119	17	29	6	2	0	10	.244	26	30	10	47	8	1	.982
— Geneva (NY-Penn)	OF	64	241	35	63	15	2	5	33	.261	40	52	16	132	6	8	.945
1984— Quad Cities (Midw.)	OF	12	41	6	9	2	2	0	5	.220	9	13	3	13	2	1	.938
1985— Win.-Salem (Caro.)	OF	115	386	52	132	14	4	5	54	*.342	62	35	38	206	11	7	.969
1986— Iowa (A.A.)	OF	83	318	52	92	11	5	5	32	.289	36	34	42	214	7	2	.991
— Chicago (N.L.)	OF	53	108	13	15	1	1	1	7	.139	6	22	4	77	2	1	.988
1987— Chicago (N.L.)	OF	142	459	70	134	18	8	8	36	.292	57	96	16	283	10	6	.980
1988— Chicago (N.L.)	OF	75	256	27	65	10	1	4	34	.254	21	46	7	162	2	5	.970
— Montreal (N.L.)■	OF	63	191	24	49	3	5	2	12	.257	17	48	16	119	2	1	.992
1989— Montreal (N.L.)	OF	126	361	41	99	16	7	3	27	.274	27	57	23	199	7	7	.967
1990— Montreal (N.L.)	OF-P	118	391	60	109	13	5	11	39	.279	24	48	13	257	6	3	.989
1991— Montreal (N.L.)	OF	124	396	47	117	18	5	7	42	.295	20	54	16	213	10	4	.982
1992— Cincinnati (N.L.)■	OF-1B	135	393	47	100	20	5	3	31	.254	42	54	12	382	18	5	.985
1993— San Fran. (N.L.)■	OF	91	241	28	58	12	1	5	27	.241	27	39	6	131	6	1	.993
— Phoenix (PCL)■	OF	3	15	4	7	0	0	0	2	.467	1	1	1	5	1	0	1.000
1994— San Francisco (N.L.)	OF-1B	97	235	23	58	9	3	4	27	.247	21	22	3	256	18	3	.989
1995— Chicago (A.L.)■ OF-1B-DH-P		119	303	49	93	16	4	5	37	.307	32	41	8	392	25	3	.993
1996— Chicago (A.L.)	OF-1B	146	440	85	140	20	8	10	53	.318	52	52	15	368	16	6	.985
1997— Chicago (A.L.)	OF-1B-DH	145	504	78	144	16	6	12	55	.286	55	69	12	485	30	7	.987
1998— Tampa Bay (A.L.)■...	OF-DH-1B	90	309	31	79	11	0	3	20	.256	35	52	8	163	9	1	.994
1999— Tampa Bay (A.L.)	OF	143	514	79	146	25	5	6	66	.284	60	76	13	253	8	4	.985
2000— Tampa Bay (A.L.)	OF	29	104	12	27	4	2	1	12	.260	10	17	1	46	5	0	1.000
— Chicago (N.L.)■	OF-1B	18	54	5	10	1	1	0	1	.185	2	8	1	77	5	1	.988
— Texas (A.L.)■	OF-1B	38	119	14	32	4	1	2	12	.269	14	20	2	93	2	0	1.000
— Toronto (A.L.)■	OF	47	180	29	56	10	1	2	22	.311	24	28	4	101	8	2	.982
American League totals (6 years)		757	2473	377	717	106	27	41	277	.290	282	355	63	1901	103	23	.989
National League totals (10 years)		1042	3085	385	814	121	42	48	283	.264	264	494	117	2156	86	38	.983
Major League totals (15 years)		1799	5558	762	1531	227	69	89	560	.275	546	849	180	4057	189	61	.986

M

Year	League	W	L	Pct.	ERA	G	GS	CG	ShO	Sv.	IP	H	R	ER	BB	SO
1990— Montreal (N.L.)		0	0	...	54.00	1	0	0	0	0	1/3	2	2	2	2	0
1995— Chicago (A.L.)		0	0	...	0.00	1	0	0	0	0	1	0	0	0	2	0
Major League totals (2 years)		0	0	...	13.50	2	0	0	0	0	1 1/3	2	2	2	4	0

MARTINEZ, EDDY — SS — ORIOLES

PERSONAL: Born October 23, 1977, in San Pedro de Macoris, Dominican Republic. ... 6-2/173. ... Bats right, throws right.
TRANSACTIONS/CAREER NOTES: Signed as non-drafted free agent by Baltimore Orioles organization (December 19, 1994). ... On Bowie disabled list (July 19-August 6, 2000).
STATISTICAL NOTES: Led Appalachian League shortstops with 31 double plays in 1995. ... Led Carolina League shortstops with 611 total chances and 80 double plays in 1999.

						BATTING								FIELDING			
Year Team (League)	Pos.	G	AB	R	H	2B	3B	HR	RBI	Avg.	BB	SO	SB	PO	A	E	Avg.
1995— Bluefield (Appl.)	SS	57	185	42	57	11	3	1	35	.308	23	42	5	71	135	22	.904
1996— Frederick (Caro.)	SS	74	244	21	54	4	0	2	25	.221	21	48	13	94	209	19	.941
— Bluefield (Appl.)	SS	37	122	18	27	3	0	1	15	.221	13	29	15	43	80	14	.898
1997— Frederick (Caro.)	SS	54	174	14	42	6	0	1	14	.241	19	43	6	100	112	19	.918
— Bowie (East.)	SS	16	45	3	7	3	0	0	1	.156	6	12	2	17	49	4	.943
— Rochester (I.L.)	SS	12	27	0	2	1	0	0	3	.074	1	8	0	6	25	1	.969
1998— Delmarva (S.Atl.)	SS	113	361	46	95	18	1	2	39	.263	33	66	21	153	319	25	.950
— Bowie (East.)	SS	5	14	1	4	0	0	0	1	.286	1	3	0	5	6	1	.917
1999— Frederick (Caro.)	SS-DH	127	416	68	121	21	1	2	55	.291	52	99	8	*189	386	36	.941
2000— Rochester (I.L.)	SS	13	36	7	8	2	0	0	1	.222	5	7	1	15	29	3	.936
— Frederick (Caro.)	SS	40	152	23	46	10	1	0	15	.303	24	34	7	46	89	9	.938
— Bowie (East.)	SS-2B-3B	41	127	17	32	2	2	1	20	.252	17	21	0	63	103	5	.971

MARTINEZ, EDGAR — DH — MARINERS

PERSONAL: Born January 2, 1963, in New York. ... 5-11/210. ... Bats right, throws right. ... Cousin of Carmelo Martinez, first baseman/outfielder with six major league teams (1983-91).
HIGH SCHOOL: Dorado (Puerto Rico).
COLLEGE: American College (Puerto Rico).
TRANSACTIONS/CAREER NOTES: Signed as non-drafted free agent by Seattle Mariners organization (December 19, 1982). ... On Seattle disabled list (April 4-May 17, June 15-July 21 and August 17, 1993-remainder of season); included rehabilitation assignment to Jacksonville (July 17-21). ... On disabled list (April 16-May 6, 1994; and July 21-August 12, 1996).
RECORDS: Shares A.L. single-game record for most errors by third baseman—4 (May 6, 1990).
HONORS: Named third baseman on The Sporting News A.L. All-Star team (1992). ... Named third baseman on The Sporting News A.L. Silver Slugger team (1992). ... Named designated hitter on The Sporting News A.L. All-Star team (1995 and 1997). ... Named designated hitter on The Sporting News A.L. Silver Slugger team (1995 and 1997).
STATISTICAL NOTES: Led Southern League third basemen with 360 total chances and 34 double plays in 1985. ... Led Southern League with 12 sacrifice flies in 1985. ... Led Southern League third basemen with .960 fielding percentage in 1986. ... Led Pacific Coast League third basemen with 389 total chances and 31 double plays in 1987. ... Led A.L. in on-base percentage with .479 in 1995 and .429 in 1998. ... Hit three home runs in one game (July 6, 1996 and May 18, 1999). ... Led A.L. with a .447 on-base percentage in 1999. ... Career major league grand slams: 8.
MISCELLANEOUS: Holds Seattle Mariners franchise all-time records for most doubles (403) and highest batting average (.320).

						BATTING								FIELDING			
Year Team (League)	Pos.	G	AB	R	H	2B	3B	HR	RBI	Avg.	BB	SO	SB	PO	A	E	Avg.
1983— Bellingham (N'West)	3B	32	104	14	18	1	1	0	5	.173	18	24	1	22	58	6	.930
1984— Wausau (Midw.)	3B	126	433	72	131	32	2	15	66	.303	84	57	1	85	246	25	.930
1985— Chattanooga (Sou.)	3B	111	357	43	92	15	5	3	47	.258	71	30	1	*94	*247	19	*.947
— Calgary (PCL)	3B-2B	20	68	8	24	7	1	0	14	.353	12	7	1	15	44	4	.937
1986— Chattanooga (Sou.)	3B-2B	132	451	71	119	29	5	6	74	.264	89	35	2	94	263	15	†.960
1987— Calgary (PCL)	3B	129	438	75	144	31	1	10	66	.329	82	47	3	*91	*278	20	.949
— Seattle (A.L.)	3B-DH	13	43	6	16	5	2	0	5	.372	2	5	0	13	19	0	1.000
1988— Calgary (PCL)	3B-2B	95	331	63	120	19	4	8	64	*.363	66	40	9	48	185	20	.921
— Seattle (A.L.)	3B	14	32	0	9	4	0	0	5	.281	4	7	0	5	8	1	.929
1989— Seattle (A.L.)	3B	65	171	20	41	5	0	2	20	.240	17	26	2	40	72	6	.949
— Calgary (PCL)	3B-2B	32	113	30	39	11	0	3	23	.345	22	13	2	22	56	12	.867
1990— Seattle (A.L.)	3B-DH	144	487	71	147	27	2	11	49	.302	74	62	1	89	259	*27	.928
1991— Seattle (A.L.)	3B-DH	150	544	98	167	35	1	14	52	.307	84	72	0	84	299	15	.962
1992— Seattle (A.L.)	3B-DH-1B	135	528	100	181	•46	3	18	73	*.343	54	61	14	88	211	17	.946
1993— Seattle (A.L.)	DH-3B	42	135	20	32	7	0	4	13	.237	28	19	0	5	11	2	.889
— Jacksonville (Sou.)	DH	4	14	2	5	0	0	1	3	.357	2	0	0	...	...	...	...
1994— Seattle (A.L.)	3B-DH	89	326	47	93	23	1	13	51	.285	53	42	6	44	128	9	.950
1995— Seattle (A.L.)	DH-3B-1B	•145	511	•121	182	•52	0	29	113	*.356	116	87	4	30	4	2	.944
1996— Seattle (A.L.)	DH-1-3-0	139	499	121	163	52	2	26	103	.327	123	84	3	29	1	1	.968
1997— Seattle (A.L.)	DH-1B-3B	155	542	104	179	35	1	28	108	.330	119	86	2	68	4	1	.986
1998— Seattle (A.L.)	DH-1B	154	556	86	179	46	1	29	102	.322	106	96	1	22	6	0	1.000
1999— Seattle (A.L.)	DH-1B	142	502	86	169	35	1	24	86	.337	97	99	7	29	2	0	1.000
2000— Seattle (A.L.)	DH-1B	153	556	100	180	31	0	37	*145	.324	96	95	3	12	1	0	1.000
Major League totals (14 years)		1540	5432	980	1738	403	14	235	925	.320	973	841	43	558	1025	81	.951

DIVISION SERIES RECORD

RECORDS: Holds career record for highest slugging percentage (20 or more at-bats)—.811. ... Holds single-series record for most hits—12 (1995). ... Shares single-game records for most runs batted in—7; and most home runs—2 (October 7, 1995).
NOTES: Shares postseason single-game record for most RBIs—7 (October 7, 1995).

Year	Team (League)	Pos.	G	AB	R	H	2B	3B	HR	RBI	Avg.	BB	SO	SB	PO	A	E	Avg.
1995—Seattle (A.L.)		DH	5	21	6	12	3	0	2	10	.571	6	2	0	...	...	...	...
1997—Seattle (A.L.)		DH	4	16	2	3	0	0	2	3	.188	0	3	0	...	...	...	...
2000—Seattle (A.L.)		DH	3	11	2	4	1	0	1	2	.364	2	1	0	...	...	...	...
Division series totals (3 years)			12	48	10	19	4	0	5	15	.396	8	6	0	...	...	...	...

CHAMPIONSHIP SERIES RECORD

Year	Team (League)	Pos.	G	AB	R	H	2B	3B	HR	RBI	Avg.	BB	SO	SB	PO	A	E	Avg.
1995—Seattle (A.L.)		DH	6	23	0	2	0	0	0	0	.087	2	5	1	...	...	...	...
2000—Seattle (A.L.)		DH	6	21	2	5	1	0	1	4	.238	3	5	0	...	...	...	...
Championship series totals (2 years)			12	44	2	7	1	0	1	4	.159	5	10	1	...	...	...	...

ALL-STAR GAME RECORD

Year	League	Pos.	AB	R	H	2B	3B	HR	RBI	Avg.	BB	SO	SB	PO	A	E	Avg.
1992—American		PH	1	0	0	0	0	0	0	.000	0	0	0	...	...	...	...
1995—American		DH	3	0	0	0	0	0	0	.000	0	1	0	...	...	...	...
1996—American		PH	1	0	0	0	0	0	0	.000	0	0	0	...	...	...	...
1997—American		DH	2	1	2	0	0	1	1	1.000	0	0	0	...	...	...	...
2000—American		PH	1	0	0	0	0	0	0	.000	0	0	0	...	...	...	...
All-Star Game totals (5 years)			8	1	2	0	0	1	1	.250	0	1	0	...	...	...	...

MARTINEZ, FELIX   SS   DEVIL RAYS

PERSONAL: Born May 18, 1974, in Nagua, Dominican Republic. ... 6-0/180. ... Bats both, throws right. ... Full name: Felix Mata Martinez.
HIGH SCHOOL: Solome Urena (Nagua, Dominican Republic).
TRANSACTIONS/CAREER NOTES: Contract purchased by Kansas City Royals organization from Hiroshima Toyo Carp of Japan Central League (March 5, 1993). ... Suspended four games by American League (June 5, 1998) to be served in 1999 season. ... On suspended list (September 1-6, 1999). ... Claimed on waivers by Philadelphia Phillies (October 6, 1999). ... Claimed on waivers by Tampa Bay Devil Rays (April 5, 2000).
STATISTICAL NOTES: Led Texas League shortstops with 643 total chances in 1995.

Year	Team (League)	Pos.	G	AB	R	H	2B	3B	HR	RBI	Avg.	BB	SO	SB	PO	A	E	Avg.
1993—GC Royals (GCL)	SS-2B-3B	57	165	23	42	5	1	0	12	.255	17	26	22	79	136	30	.878
1994—Wilmington (Caro.)		SS	117	400	65	107	16	4	2	43	.268	30	91	19	177	329	30	.944
1995—Wichita (Texas)		SS	127	426	53	112	15	3	3	30	.263	31	71	*44	*222	371	*50	.922
1996—Omaha (A.A.)		SS	118	395	54	93	13	3	5	35	.235	44	79	18	177	374	*42	.929
1997—Omaha (A.A.)		SS	112	410	55	104	19	4	2	36	.254	29	86	21	175	312	*36	.931
—Kansas City (A.L.)		SS-DH	16	31	3	7	1	1	0	3	.226	6	8	0	17	22	1	.975
1998—Kansas City (A.L.)		SS-2B	34	85	7	11	1	1	0	5	.129	5	21	3	49	80	6	.956
—Omaha (PCL)		SS-DH-2B	51	164	27	41	8	3	2	16	.250	15	40	6	74	135	14	.937
1999—Wichita (Texas)	SS-2B-3B-DH	87	327	57	88	22	2	4	37	.269	37	43	19	141	274	23	.947
—Omaha (PCL)		SS	8	23	2	7	5	0	0	2	.304	2	6	0	8	18	1	.963
—Kansas City (A.L.)		SS-2B	6	7	1	1	0	0	0	0	.143	0	0	0	1	2	0	1.000
2000—Durham (I.L.)■		SS	42	149	17	36	7	2	3	17	.242	7	28	3	66	132	6	.971
—Tampa Bay (A.L.)		SS	106	299	42	64	11	4	2	17	.214	32	68	9	191	368	14	.976
Major League totals (4 years)			162	422	53	83	13	6	2	25	.197	43	97	12	258	472	21	.972

MARTINEZ, PEDRO   P   RED SOX

PERSONAL: Born October 25, 1971, in Manoguayabo, Dominican Republic. ... 5-11/170. ... Throws right, bats right. ... Full name: Pedro Jaime Martinez. ... Brother of Ramon J. Martinez, pitcher, Los Angeles Dodgers; and brother of Jesus Martinez, pitcher in Los Angeles Dodgers (1991-97) and Cincinnati Reds (1998) organizations.
COLLEGE: Ohio Dominican College (Dominican Republic).
TRANSACTIONS/CAREER NOTES: Signed as non-drafted free agent by Los Angeles Dodgers organization (June 18, 1988). ... On Albuquerque disabled list (June 20-July 2 and July 13-August 25, 1992). ... Traded by Dodgers to Montreal Expos for 2B Delino DeShields (November 19, 1993). ... On suspended list (April 1-9, 1997). ... Traded by Expos to Boston Red Sox for P Carl Pavano and a player to be named later (November 18, 1997); Expos acquired P Tony Armas Jr. to complete deal (December 18, 1997). ... On disabled list (July 19-August 3, 1999; and June 29-July 13, 2000).
RECORDS: Shares A.L. record for most strikeouts in two consecutive games—32 (May 6 [17] and 12 [15], 2000, 18 innings).
HONORS: Named Minor League Player of the Year by THE SPORTING NEWS (1991). ... Named N.L. Pitcher of the Year by THE SPORTING NEWS (1997). ... Named righthanded pitcher on THE SPORTING NEWS N.L. All-Star team (1997). ... Named N.L. Cy Young Award winner by Baseball Writers' Association of America (1997). ... Named righthanded pitcher on THE SPORTING NEWS A.L. All-Star team (1998, 1999 and 2000). ... Named A.L. Pitcher of the Year by THE SPORTING NEWS (1999 and 2000). ... Named A.L. Cy Young Award winner by Baseball Writers' Association of America (1999 and 2000).
STATISTICAL NOTES: Led N.L. with 11 hit batsmen in 1994. ... Pitched nine perfect innings against San Diego, before being relieved after yielding leadoff double in 10th inning (June 3, 1995). ... Tied for N.L. lead with 16 sacrifice hits in 1996. ... Pitched 2-0 one-hit, complete-game victory against Cincinnati (July 13, 1997). ... Struck out 15 batters in one game (May 7, May 12, August 24 and September 4, 1999; May 12 and July 23, 2000). ... Struck out 16 batters in one game (June 4, 1999). ... Struck out 17 batters in one game (September 10, 1999; and May 6, 2000). ... Pitched 3-1 one-hit, complete-game victory against New York Yankees (September 10, 1999). ... Pitched 8-0 one-hit, complete-game victory against Tampa Bay (August 29, 2000).

Year	League	W	L	Pct.	ERA	G	GS	CG	ShO	Sv.	IP	H	R	ER	BB	SO
1988—Dom. Dodgers (DSL)		5	1	.833	3.10	8	7	1	0	0	49 1/3	45	25	17	16	28
1989—Dom. Dodgers (DSL)		7	2	.778	2.73	13	7	2	3	1	85 2/3	59	30	26	25	63
1990—Great Falls (Pio.)		8	3	.727	3.62	14	•14	0	0	0	77	74	39	31	40	82
1991—Bakersfield (Calif.)		8	0	1.000	2.05	10	10	0	0	0	61 1/3	41	17	14	19	83
—San Antonio (Texas)		7	5	.583	1.76	12	12	4	•3	0	76 2/3	57	21	15	31	74
—Albuquerque (PCL)		3	3	.500	3.66	6	6	0	0	0	39 1/3	28	17	16	16	35

M

Year League	W	L	Pct.	ERA	G	GS	CG	ShO	Sv.	IP	H	R	ER	BB	SO
1992—Albuquerque (PCL)............	7	6	.538	3.81	20	20	3	1	0	125¹/₃	104	57	53	57	124
— Los Angeles (N.L.)	0	1	.000	2.25	2	1	0	0	0	8	6	2	2	1	8
1993—Albuquerque (PCL)............	0	0	...	3.00	1	1	0	0	0	3	1	1	1	1	4
— Los Angeles (N.L.)	10	5	.667	2.61	65	2	0	0	2	107	76	34	31	57	119
1994—Montreal (N.L.)■................	11	5	.688	3.42	24	23	1	1	1	144²/₃	115	58	55	45	142
1995—Montreal (N.L.)..................	14	10	.583	3.51	30	30	2	2	0	194²/₃	158	79	76	66	174
1996—Montreal (N.L.)..................	13	10	.565	3.70	33	33	4	1	0	216²/₃	189	100	89	70	222
1997—Montreal (N.L.)..................	17	8	.680	*1.90	31	31	*13	4	0	241¹/₃	158	65	51	67	305
1998—Boston (A.L.)■..................	19	7	.731	2.89	33	33	3	2	0	233²/₃	188	82	75	67	251
1999—Boston (A.L.)...................	*23	4	*.852	*2.07	31	29	5	1	0	213¹/₃	160	56	49	37	*313
2000—Boston (A.L.)...................	18	6	.750	1.74	29	29	7	4	0	217	128	44	42	32	*284
A.L. totals (3 years)	60	17	.779	2.25	93	91	15	7	0	664	476	182	166	136	848
N.L. totals (6 years)	65	39	.625	3.00	185	120	20	8	3	912¹/₃	702	338	304	306	970
Major League totals (9 years).......	125	56	.691	2.68	278	211	35	15	3	1576¹/₃	1178	520	470	442	1818

DIVISION SERIES RECORD

Year League	W	L	Pct.	ERA	G	GS	CG	ShO	Sv.	IP	H	R	ER	BB	SO
1998—Boston (A.L.)...................	1	0	1.000	3.86	1	1	0	0	0	7	6	3	3	0	8
1999—Boston (A.L.)...................	1	0	1.000	0.00	2	1	0	0	0	10	3	0	0	4	11
Division series totals (2 years)	2	0	1.000	1.59	3	2	0	0	0	17	9	3	3	4	19

CHAMPIONSHIP SERIES RECORD

Year League	W	L	Pct.	ERA	G	GS	CG	ShO	Sv.	IP	H	R	ER	BB	SO
1999—Boston (A.L.)...................	1	0	1.000	0.00	1	1	0	0	0	7	2	0	0	2	12

ALL-STAR GAME RECORD

RECORDS: Holds record for most consecutive strikeouts from start of game—4 (1999).

NOTES: Named Most Valuable Player (1999).

Year League	W	L	Pct.	ERA	GS	CG	ShO	Sv.	IP	H	R	ER	BB	SO
1996— National	0	0	...	0.00	0	0	0	0	1	2	0	0	0	1
1997— National	0	0	...	0.00	0	0	0	0	1	0	0	0	0	2
1998— American				Did not play.										
1999— American	1	0	1.000	0.00	1	0	0	0	2	0	0	0	0	5
All-Star Game totals (3 years)	1	0	1.000	0.00	1	0	0	0	4	2	0	0	0	8

MARTINEZ, RAMON   2B/SS   GIANTS

PERSONAL: Born October 10, 1972, in Philadelphia. ... 6-1/187. ... Bats right, throws right. ... Full name: Ramon E. Martinez.

HIGH SCHOOL: Escuela Superior Catholica (Bayamon, Puerto Rico).

JUNIOR COLLEGE: Vernon (Texas) Regional Junior College.

TRANSACTIONS/CAREER NOTES: Signed as non-drafted free agent by Kansas City Royals organization (January 15, 1994). ... Traded by Royals to San Francisco Giants (December 9, 1996), completing deal in which Giants traded P Jamie Brewington to Royals for a player to be named later (November 26, 1996). ... On Fresno disabled list (June 10-23, 1999). ... On San Francisco disabled list (August 21-September 5, 1999).

STATISTICAL NOTES: Led Texas League with 18 sacrifice hits and nine sacrifice flies in 1995. ... Led Texas League second basemen with .984 fielding percentage in 1995. ... Led American Association with 13 sacrifice hits in 1996.

Year Team (League)	Pos.	G	AB	R	H	2B	3B	HR	RBI	Avg.	BB	SO	SB	PO	A	E	Avg.
1993— GC Royals (GCL)	2B	37	97	16	23	5	0	0	9	.237	8	6	3	71	108	5	.973
— Wilmington (Caro.)......	2B-SS	24	75	8	19	4	0	0	6	.253	11	9	1	52	72	6	.954
1994— Wilmington (Caro.)......	2B	90	325	40	87	13	2	2	35	.268	35	25	6	176	249	16	.964
— Rockford (Midw.)	2B	6	18	3	5	0	0	0	3	.278	4	2	1	9	12	1	.955
1995— Wichita (Texas)	2B-SS	103	393	58	108	20	2	3	51	.275	42	50	11	186	311	9	†.982
1996— Omaha (A.A.).............	2B	85	320	35	81	12	3	6	41	.253	21	34	3	163	207	12	.969
— Wichita (Texas)	2B	26	93	16	32	4	1	1	8	.344	7	8	4	47	84	6	.956
1997— Shreveport (Texas)■..	SS	105	404	72	129	32	4	5	54	.319	40	48	4	167	370	18	.968
— Phoenix (PCL)	2B-SS	18	57	6	16	2	0	1	7	.281	5	9	1	26	44	3	.959
1998— Fresno (PCL)	2B-SS	98	364	58	114	21	2	14	59	.313	38	42	0	209	280	10	.980
— San Francisco (N.L.) ..	2B	19	19	4	6	1	0	0	0	.316	4	2	0	15	20	0	1.000
1999— San Francisco (N.L.) ..2B-SS-3B-DH		61	144	21	38	6	0	5	19	.264	14	17	1	66	102	6	.966
— Fresno (PCL)	SS-DH-3B	29	114	13	37	7	1	2	17	.325	10	17	2	26	72	5	.951
2000— San Francisco (N.L.) ..SS-2B-1B-3B		88	189	30	57	13	2	6	25	.302	15	22	3	88	108	1	.995
Major League totals (3 years)		168	352	55	101	20	2	11	44	.287	33	41	4	169	230	7	.983

DIVISION SERIES RECORD

Year Team (League)	Pos.	G	AB	R	H	2B	3B	HR	RBI	Avg.	BB	SO	SB	PO	A	E	Avg.
2000— San Francisco (N.L.) ..	2B-SS	2	6	0	2	0	0	0	0	.333	0	2	0	3	7	0	1.000

MARTINEZ, RAMON J.   P   DODGERS

PERSONAL: Born March 22, 1968, in Santo Domingo, Dominican Republic. ... 6-4/184. ... Throws right, bats right. ... Full name: Ramon Jaime Martinez. ... Brother of Pedro Martinez, pitcher, Boston Red Sox; and brother of Jesus Martinez, pitcher with Los Angeles Dodgers (1991-97) and Cincinnati Reds (1998) organizations.

HIGH SCHOOL: Liceo Secundaria Las Americas (Dominican Republic).

TRANSACTIONS/CAREER NOTES: Signed as non-drafted free agent by Los Angeles Dodgers organization (September 1, 1984). ... On suspended list (July 8-12, 1993). ... Granted free agency (November 1, 1995). ... Re-signed by Dodgers (November 16, 1995). ... On Los Angeles disabled list (April 7-May 14, 1996); included rehabilitation assignments to San Antonio (May 4-9) and Vero Beach (May 9-14). ... On Los Angeles disabled list (June 15-August 20, 1997); included rehabilitation assignment to San Bernardino (July 26-August 20). ... On disabled list

(June 19, 1998-remainder of season). ... Granted free agency (November 17, 1998). ... Signed by Boston Red Sox (March 11, 1999). ... On Boston disabled list (April 1-September 2, 1999); included rehabilitation assignments to Lowell (June 21-25), Gulf Coast Red Sox (July 11-August 1), Sarasota (August 2-21) and Pawtucket (August 22-30). ... On Boston disabled list (August 1-September 2, 2000); included rehabilitation assignment to Pawtucket (August 20-September 2). ... Granted free agency (November 1, 2000). ... Signed by Dodgers (January 18, 2001).
STATISTICAL NOTES: Struck out 18 batters in one game (June 4, 1990). ... Pitched 7-0 no-hit victory against Florida (July 14, 1995).
MISCELLANEOUS: Member of 1984 Dominican Republic Olympic baseball team. ... Appeared in one game as pinch runner (1989). ... Appeared in one game as pinch runner (1992). ... Appeared in one game as pinch hitter and appeared in one game as pinch runner with Los Angeles (1996).

Year League	W	L	Pct.	ERA	G	GS	CG	ShO	Sv.	IP	H	R	ER	BB	SO
1985—Gulf Coast Dodgers (GCL)..	4	1	.800	2.59	23	6	0	0	1	59	57	30	17	23	42
1986—Bakersfield (Calif.)	4	8	.333	4.75	20	20	2	1	0	106	119	73	56	63	78
1987—Vero Beach (FSL)	16	5	.762	2.17	25	25	6	1	0	170 1/3	128	45	41	78	148
1988—San Antonio (Texas)	8	4	.667	2.46	14	14	2	1	0	95	79	29	26	34	89
—Albuquerque (PCL)	5	2	.714	2.76	10	10	1	1	0	58 2/3	43	24	18	32	49
—Los Angeles (N.L.)	1	3	.250	3.79	9	6	0	0	0	35 2/3	27	17	15	22	23
1989—Albuquerque (PCL)	10	2	.833	2.79	18	18	2	1	0	113	92	40	35	50	127
—Los Angeles (N.L.)	6	4	.600	3.19	15	15	2	2	0	98 2/3	79	39	35	41	89
1990—Los Angeles (N.L.)	20	6	.769	2.92	33	33	*12	3	0	234 1/3	191	89	76	67	223
1991—Los Angeles (N.L.)	17	13	.567	3.27	33	33	6	4	0	220 1/3	190	89	80	69	150
1992—Los Angeles (N.L.)	8	11	.421	4.00	25	25	1	1	0	150 2/3	141	82	67	69	101
1993—Los Angeles (N.L.)	10	12	.455	3.44	32	32	4	3	0	211 2/3	202	88	81	*104	127
1994—Los Angeles (N.L.)	12	7	.632	3.97	24	24	4	•3	0	170	160	83	75	56	119
1995—Los Angeles (N.L.)	17	7	.708	3.66	30	30	4	2	0	206 1/3	176	95	84	*81	138
1996—San Antonio (Texas)	0	0	...	0.00	1	1	0	0	0	2 2/3	0	0	0	3	1
—Vero Beach (FSL)	1	0	1.000	0.00	1	1	0	0	0	7	5	1	0	0	10
—Los Angeles (N.L.)	15	6	.714	3.42	29	27	2	2	0	168 2/3	153	76	64	86	133
1997—Los Angeles (N.L.)	10	5	.667	3.64	22	22	1	0	0	133 2/3	123	64	54	68	120
—San Bernardino (Calif.)	0	1	.000	1.15	4	4	0	0	0	15 2/3	10	2	2	4	16
1998—Los Angeles (N.L.)	7	3	.700	2.83	15	15	1	0	0	101 2/3	76	41	32	41	91
1999—Lowell (NY-Penn)■	0	0	...	0.00	1	1	0	0	0	2	0	0	0	0	3
—Gulf Coast Red Sox (GCL)..	1	0	1.000	1.38	4	4	0	0	0	13	9	4	2	3	15
—Sarasota (FSL)	1	0	1.000	3.00	3	3	0	0	0	12	11	7	4	7	9
—Pawtucket (I.L.)	0	1	.000	9.00	2	2	0	0	0	9	10	9	9	6	7
—Boston (A.L.)	2	1	.667	3.05	4	4	0	0	0	20 2/3	14	8	7	8	15
2000—Boston (A.L.)	10	8	.556	6.13	27	27	0	0	0	127 2/3	143	94	87	67	89
—Pawtucket (I.L.)	1	0	1.000	2.31	2	2	0	0	0	11 2/3	8	4	3	4	10
A.L. totals (2 years)	12	9	.571	5.70	31	31	0	0	0	148 1/3	157	102	94	75	104
N.L. totals (11 years)	123	77	.615	3.45	267	262	37	20	0	1731 2/3	1518	763	663	704	1314
Major League totals (13 years)	135	86	.611	3.62	298	293	37	20	0	1880	1675	865	757	779	1418

DIVISION SERIES RECORD

Year League	W	L	Pct.	ERA	G	GS	CG	ShO	Sv.	IP	H	R	ER	BB	SO
1995—Los Angeles (N.L.)	0	1	.000	14.54	1	1	0	0	0	4 1/3	10	7	7	2	3
1996—Los Angeles (N.L.)	0	0	...	1.13	1	1	0	0	0	8	3	1	1	3	6
1999—Boston (A.L.)	0	0	...	3.18	1	1	0	0	0	5 2/3	5	2	2	3	6
Division series totals (3 years)	0	1	.000	5.00	3	3	0	0	0	18	18	10	10	8	15

CHAMPIONSHIP SERIES RECORD

Year League	W	L	Pct.	ERA	G	GS	CG	ShO	Sv.	IP	H	R	ER	BB	SO
1999—Boston (A.L.)	0	1	.000	4.05	1	1	0	0	0	6 2/3	6	3	3	3	5

MARTINEZ, SANDY   C   EXPOS

PERSONAL: Born October 3, 1972, in Villa Mella, Dominican Republic. ... 6-2/215. ... Bats left, throws right. ... Full name: Angel Sandy Martinez.
HIGH SCHOOL: Villa Mella (Dominican Republic).
TRANSACTIONS/CAREER NOTES: Signed as non-drafted free agent by Toronto Blue Jays organization (January 10, 1990). ... On disabled list (May 15-June 8, 1993). ... On Toronto disabled list (August 17-September 1, 1996); included rehabilitation assignment to Knoxville (August 26-September 1). ... On Syracuse disabled list (June 14-24, 1997). ... Traded by Blue Jays to Chicago Cubs for a player to be named later (December 11, 1997); Blue Jays acquired P Trevor Schaffer to complete deal (December 19, 1997). ... On suspended list (July 1-3, 1998). ... On Chicago disabled list (May 13-June 10, 1999); included rehabilitation assignment to Iowa (June 5-10). ... Granted free agency (October 15, 1999). ... Signed by Florida Marlins organization (December 6, 1999). ... Granted free agency (October 11, 2000). ... Signed by Montreal Expos organization (November 17, 2000).
RECORDS: Shares major league single-game record for most putouts by catcher (nine-inning game)—20 (May 6, 1998); and most chances accepted by catcher (nine-inning game) since 1900—20 (May 6, 1998).
STATISTICAL NOTES: Led Pioneer League with 24 passed balls in 1992. ... Led Florida State League catchers with 14 errors in 1994.

Year Team (League)	Pos.	G	AB	R	H	2B	3B	HR	RBI	Avg.	BB	SO	SB	PO	A	E	Avg.
					BATTING									FIELDING			
1990—Dom. Blue Jays (DSL)	C	44	145	21	35	2	0	0	10	.241	18	15	1	...	...	...	...
1991—Dunedin (FSL)	C	12	38	3	7	1	0	0	3	.184	7	7	0	82	9	2	.978
—Medicine Hat (Pio.)	C	34	98	8	17	1	0	2	16	.173	12	29	0	141	19	3	.982
1992—Dunedin (FSL)	C	4	15	4	3	1	0	2	4	.200	0	3	0	11	2	1	.929
—Medicine Hat (Pio.)	C-1B-SS	57	206	27	52	15	0	4	39	.252	14	62	0	275	58	5	.985
1993—Hagerstown (S.Atl.)	C-DH	94	338	41	89	16	1	9	46	.263	19	71	1	493	68	14	.976
1994—Dunedin (FSL)	C-DH-1B	122	450	50	117	14	6	7	52	.260	22	79	1	615	79	†14	.980
1995—Knoxville (Sou.)	C-DH	41	144	14	33	8	1	2	22	.229	6	34	0	219	30	5	.980
—Toronto (A.L.)	C	62	191	12	46	12	0	2	25	.241	7	45	0	329	28	5	.986
1996—Toronto (A.L.)	C	76	229	17	52	9	3	3	18	.227	16	58	0	413	33	3	.993
—Knoxville (Sou.)	C-DH	4	16	2	3	0	0	0	0	.188	0	5	0	17	2	1	.950
1997—Syracuse (I.L.)	C-DH	96	322	28	72	12	1	4	29	.224	27	76	7	588	50	9	.986
—Toronto (A.L.)	C	3	2	1	0	0	0	0	0	.000	1	1	0	12	2	1	.933

Year Team (League)	Pos.	G	AB	R	H	2B	3B	HR	RBI	Avg.	BB	SO	SB	PO	A	E	Avg.
1998—Chicago (N.L.)■........	C	45	87	7	23	9	1	0	7	.264	13	21	1	185	7	3	.985
1999—Chicago (N.L.)...........	C	17	30	1	5	0	0	1	1	.167	0	11	0	45	2	2	.959
— Iowa (PCL).................	C	36	125	8	29	6	0	2	18	.232	5	29	1	239	17	1	.996
2000—Florida (N.L.)■.........	C	10	18	1	4	2	0	0	0	.222	0	8	0	43	2	0	1.000
— Calgary (PCL)............	C	86	277	45	83	20	0	15	48	.300	16	57	2	373	38	4	.990
American League totals (3 years)		141	422	30	98	21	3	5	43	.232	24	104	0	754	63	9	.989
National League totals (3 years)		72	135	9	32	11	1	1	8	.237	13	40	1	273	11	5	.983
Major League totals (6 years)		213	557	39	130	32	4	6	51	.233	37	144	1	1027	74	14	.987

DIVISION SERIES RECORD

Year Team (League)	Pos.	G	AB	R	H	2B	3B	HR	RBI	Avg.	BB	SO	SB	PO	A	E	Avg.
1998—Chicago (N.L.)...........	C	1	1	1	1	0	0	0	0	1.000	0	0	0	1	0	0	1.000

MARTINEZ, TINO — 1B — YANKEES

PERSONAL: Born December 7, 1967, in Tampa. ... 6-2/210. ... Bats left, throws right. ... Full name: Constantino Martinez.

HIGH SCHOOL: Tampa Catholic.

COLLEGE: Tampa (Fla.).

TRANSACTIONS/CAREER NOTES: Selected by Boston Red Sox organization in third round of free-agent draft (June 3, 1985); did not sign. ... Selected by Seattle Mariners organization in first round (14th pick overall) of free-agent draft (June 1, 1988). ... On disabled list (August 10, 1993-remainder of season). ... Traded by Mariners with P Jeff Nelson and P Jim Mecir to New York Yankees for P Sterling Hitchcock and 3B Russ Davis (December 7, 1995).

HONORS: Named first baseman on THE SPORTING NEWS college All-America team (1988). ... Named Pacific Coast League Most Valuable Player (1991). ... Named first baseman on THE SPORTING NEWS A.L. All-Star team (1997). ... Named first baseman on THE SPORTING NEWS A.L. Silver Slugger team (1997).

STATISTICAL NOTES: Led Eastern League with 13 intentional bases on balls received in 1989. ... Led Eastern League first basemen with 1,348 total chances and 106 double plays in 1989. ... Tied for Pacific Coast League lead with 11 intentional bases on balls received in 1990. ... Led Pacific Coast League first basemen with .991 fielding percentage, 1,051 putouts, 98 assists, 1,159 total chances and 117 double plays in 1990. ... Led Pacific Coast League first basemen with .992 fielding percentage and 122 double plays in 1991. ... Hit three home runs in one game (April 2, 1997). ... Led A.L. with 13 sacrifice flies in 1997. ... Led A.L. first baseman with 1,410 total chances in 1999. ... Career major league grand slams: 8.

MISCELLANEOUS: Member of 1988 U.S. Olympic baseball team.

Year Team (League)	Pos.	G	AB	R	H	2B	3B	HR	RBI	Avg.	BB	SO	SB	PO	A	E	Avg.
1989—Williamsport (East.)...	1B	*137	*509	51	131	29	2	13	64	.257	59	54	7	*1260	*81	7	*.995
1990—Calgary (PCL)............	1B-3B	128	453	83	145	28	1	17	93	.320	74	37	8	†1051	†98	10	†.991
— Seattle (A.L.)............	1B	24	68	4	15	4	0	0	5	.221	9	9	0	155	12	0	1.000
1991—Calgary (PCL)............	1B-3B	122	442	94	144	34	5	18	86	.326	82	44	3	1078	106	9	†.992
— Seattle (A.L.)............	1B-DH	36	112	11	23	2	0	4	9	.205	11	24	0	249	22	2	.993
1992—Seattle (A.L.)............	1B-DH	136	460	53	118	19	2	16	66	.257	42	77	2	678	58	4	.995
1993—Seattle (A.L.)............	1B-DH	109	408	48	108	25	1	17	60	.265	45	56	0	932	60	3	.997
1994—Seattle (A.L.)............	1B-DH	97	329	42	86	21	0	20	61	.261	29	52	1	705	45	2	.997
1995—Seattle (A.L.)............	1B-DH	141	519	92	152	35	3	31	111	.293	62	91	0	1048	101	8	.993
1996—New York (A.L.)■......	1B-DH	155	595	82	174	28	0	25	117	.292	68	85	2	1238	83	5	*.996
1997—New York (A.L.).........	1B-DH	158	594	96	176	31	2	44	141	.296	75	75	3	1302	105	8	.994
1998—New York (A.L.).........	1B	142	531	92	149	33	1	28	123	.281	61	83	2	1180	93	10	.992
1999—New York (A.L.).........	1B	159	589	95	155	27	2	28	105	.263	69	86	3	1297	*106	7	.995
2000—New York (A.L.).........	1B	155	569	69	147	37	4	16	91	.258	52	74	4	1154	88	7	.994
Major League totals (11 years)		1312	4774	684	1303	262	15	229	889	.273	523	712	17	9938	773	56	.995

DIVISION SERIES RECORD

RECORDS: Holds career records for at-bats—96; hits—30; and doubles—8. ... Shares career record for most games—25. ... Shares single-game record for most at-bats—7 (October 4, 1995).

Year Team (League)	Pos.	G	AB	R	H	2B	3B	HR	RBI	Avg.	BB	SO	SB	PO	A	E	Avg.
1995—Seattle (A.L.)	1B	5	22	4	9	1	0	1	5	.409	3	4	0	39	5	0	1.000
1996—New York (A.L.).........	1B	4	15	3	4	2	0	0	0	.267	4	1	0	33	3	0	1.000
1997—New York (A.L.).........	1B	5	18	1	4	1	0	1	4	.222	2	4	0	48	6	0	1.000
1998—New York (A.L.).........	1B	3	11	1	3	2	0	0	0	.273	0	2	0	27	1	0	1.000
1999—New York (A.L.).........	1B	3	11	2	2	0	0	0	0	.182	2	2	0	29	1	1	.968
2000—New York (A.L.).........	1B	5	19	2	8	2	0	0	4	.421	1	3	0	45	5	1	.980
Division series totals (6 years)		25	96	13	30	8	0	2	13	.313	12	16	0	221	21	2	.992

CHAMPIONSHIP SERIES RECORD

RECORDS: Shares A.L. career record for most times hit by pitch—3.

Year Team (League)	Pos.	G	AB	R	H	2B	3B	HR	RBI	Avg.	BB	SO	SB	PO	A	E	Avg.
1995—Seattle (A.L.)	1B	6	22	1	3	0	0	0	0	.136	3	7	0	45	5	1	.980
1996—New York (A.L.).........	1B	5	22	3	4	1	0	0	0	.182	0	2	0	49	2	0	1.000
1998—New York (A.L.).........	1B	6	19	1	2	1	0	0	1	.105	6	8	2	47	4	1	.981
1999—New York (A.L.).........	1B	5	19	3	5	1	0	1	3	.263	2	4	0	29	5	0	1.000
2000—New York (A.L.).........	1B	6	25	5	8	2	0	1	1	.320	2	4	0	47	6	0	1.000
Championship series totals (5 years)		28	107	13	22	5	0	2	5	.206	13	25	2	217	22	2	.992

WORLD SERIES RECORD

RECORDS: Shares single-game record for most grand slams—1 (October 17, 1998). ... Shares single-inning record for most runs batted in—4 (October 17, 1998, seventh inning).

NOTES: Member of World Series championship team (1996, 1998, 1999 and 2000).

M

Year Team (League)	Pos.	G	AB	R	H	2B	3B	HR	RBI	Avg.	BB	SO	SB	PO	A	E	Avg.
1996— New York (A.L.)..........	1B-PH	6	11	0	1	0	0	0	0	.091	2	5	0	27	0	0	1.000
1998— New York (A.L.)..........	1B	4	13	4	5	0	0	1	4	.385	6	2	0	36	3	0	1.000
1999— New York (A.L.)..........	1B	4	15	3	4	0	0	1	5	.267	2	4	0	41	2	0	1.000
2000— New York (A.L.)..........	1B	5	22	3	8	1	0	0	2	.364	1	4	0	39	4	0	1.000
World Series totals (4 years)		19	61	10	18	1	0	2	11	.295	11	15	0	143	9	0	1.000

ALL-STAR GAME RECORD

Year League	Pos.	AB	R	H	2B	3B	HR	RBI	Avg.	BB	SO	SB	PO	A	E	Avg.
1995— American	PH	1	0	1	0	0	0	0	1.000	0	0	0	...	...	...	...
1997— American	1B	2	0	0	0	0	0	0	.000	0	0	0	10	0	0	1.000
All-Star Game totals (2 years)		3	0	1	0	0	0	0	.333	0	0	0	10	0	0	1.000

MARTINEZ, WILLIE   P   TWINS

PERSONAL: Born January 4, 1978, in Barquisimeto, Venezuela. ... 6-2/180. ... Throws right, bats right. ... Full name: William Jose Martinez.
HIGH SCHOOL: Barquisimeto (Venezuela).
TRANSACTIONS/CAREER NOTES: Signed as non-drafted free agent by Cleveland Indians organization (January 16, 1995). ... On Akron disabled list (May 3-17 and July 11-18, 1998). ... On Cleveland disabled list (September 8, 1999-remainder of season). ... Claimed on waivers by Minnesota Twins (October 24, 2000).
STATISTICAL NOTES: Tied for Eastern League lead with six errors by pitcher in 1999.

Year League	W	L	Pct.	ERA	G	GS	CG	ShO	Sv.	IP	H	R	ER	BB	SO
1995— Burlington (Appl.)..............	0	7	.000	9.45	11	11	0	0	0	40	64	50	42	25	36
1996— Watertown (NY-Penn)	6	5	.545	2.40	14	14	1	1	0	90	79	25	24	21	92
1997— Kinston (Caro.)..................	8	2	.800	3.09	23	23	1	0	0	137	125	61	47	42	120
1998— Akron (East.)	9	7	.563	4.38	26	26	2	1	0	154	169	92	75	44	117
1999— Akron (East.)	9	8	.529	4.09	24	24	0	0	0	147 1/3	163	83	67	45	91
— Buffalo (I.L.)......................	2	2	.500	6.85	4	4	0	0	0	22 1/3	28	17	17	7	12
2000— Buffalo (I.L.)....................	8	5	.615	4.46	28	22	0	0	1	135 1/3	132	72	67	67	95
— Cleveland (A.L.)................	0	0	...	3.00	1	0	0	0	0	3	1	1	1	1	1
Major League totals (1 year)........	0	0	...	3.00	1	0	0	0	0	3	1	1	1	1	1

MASAOKA, ONAN   P   DODGERS

PERSONAL: Born October 27, 1977, in Hilo, Hawaii. ... 6-0/188. ... Throws left, bats right. ... Full name: Onan Kainoa Satoshi Masaoka.
HIGH SCHOOL: Waiakea (Hilo, Hawaii).
TRANSACTIONS/CAREER NOTES: Selected by Los Angeles Dodgers organization in third round of free-agent draft (June 1, 1995).

Year League	W	L	Pct.	ERA	G	GS	CG	ShO	Sv.	IP	H	R	ER	BB	SO
1995— Yakima (N'West)	2	4	.333	3.65	15	7	0	0	3	49 1/3	28	25	20	47	75
1996— Savannah (S.Atl.)	2	5	.286	4.29	13	13	0	0	0	65	55	35	31	35	80
1997— Vero Beach (FSL)	6	8	.429	3.87	28	24	2	1	1	148 2/3	113	72	64	55	132
1998— San Antonio (Texas)	6	6	.500	5.32	27	20	1	1	1	110	114	79	65	63	94
1999— Los Angeles (N.L.)	2	4	.333	4.32	54	0	0	0	1	66 2/3	55	33	32	47	61
2000— Los Angeles (N.L.)	1	1	.500	4.00	29	0	0	0	0	27	23	12	12	15	27
— Albuquerque (PCL)............	3	1	.750	3.86	18	5	0	0	0	37 1/3	31	17	16	36	22
Major League totals (2 years).......	3	5	.375	4.23	83	0	0	0	1	93 2/3	78	45	44	62	88

MATEO, RUBEN   OF   RANGERS

PERSONAL: Born February 10, 1978, in San Cristobal, Dominican Republic. ... 6-0/185. ... Bats right, throws right. ... Full name: Ruben Amaurys Mateo.
HIGH SCHOOL: Liceo Jose Manuel Maria Balance (San Cristobal, Dominican Republic).
TRANSACTIONS/CAREER NOTES: Signed as non-drafted free agent by Texas Rangers organization (October 24, 1994). ... On Tulsa disabled list (April 13-May 13, 1998). ... On Texas disabled list (June 23-July 9 and August 5, 1999-remainder of season); included rehabilitation assignment to Oklahoma (July 6-9). ... On disabled list (June 3, 2000-remainder of season).

Year Team (League)	Pos.	G	AB	R	H	2B	3B	HR	RBI	Avg.	BB	SO	SB	PO	A	E	Avg.
1995— Dom. Rangers (DSL)..	OF	48	176	30	53	9	3	4	42	.301	20	23	1	55	1	1	.982
1996— Char., S.C. (SAL)......	OF-DH	134	496	65	129	30	8	8	58	.260	26	78	30	215	15	7	.970
1997— Charlotte (FSL)..........	OF-DH	99	385	63	121	23	8	12	67	.314	22	55	20	174	10	8	.958
1998— Tulsa (Texas)	OF	107	433	79	134	32	3	18	75	.309	30	56	18	215	11	7	.970
— Charlotte (FSL)	OF	1	4	0	0	0	0	0	1	.000	0	1	0	2	0	0	1.000
1999— Texas (A.L.)	OF-DH	32	122	16	29	9	1	5	18	.238	4	28	3	62	3	0	1.000
— Oklahoma (PCL).........	OF-DH	63	253	53	85	12	0	18	62	.336	14	36	6	128	3	5	.963
2000— Texas (A.L.)	OF	52	206	32	60	11	0	7	19	.291	10	34	6	140	4	3	.980
Major League totals (2 years)		84	328	48	89	20	1	12	37	.271	14	62	9	202	7	3	.986

MATHENY, MIKE   C   CARDINALS

PERSONAL: Born September 22, 1970, in Reynoldsburg, Ohio. ... 6-3/205. ... Bats right, throws right. ... Full name: Michael Scott Matheny.
HIGH SCHOOL: Reynoldsburg (Ohio).
COLLEGE: Michigan.
TRANSACTIONS/CAREER NOTES: Selected by Toronto Blue Jays organization in 31st round of free-agent draft (June 1, 1988); did not sign. ... Selected by Milwaukee Brewers organization in eighth round of free-agent draft (June 3, 1991). ... On Milwaukee suspended list (June 20-

M

23, 1996). ... On Milwaukee disabled list (June 15-July 12, 1998); included rehabilitation assignment to Beloit (July 11-13). ... Granted free agency (December 21, 1998). ... Signed by Blue Jays (December 23, 1998). ... Released by Blue Jays (November 16, 1999). ... Signed by St. Louis Cardinals (December 15, 1999).

HONORS: Won N.L. Gold Glove as catcher (2000).

STATISTICAL NOTES: Led California League catchers with 20 double plays in 1992. ... Led Texas League catchers with 18 double plays in 1993. ... Career major league grand slams: 2.

Year Team (League)	Pos.	G	AB	R	H	2B	3B	HR	RBI	Avg.	BB	SO	SB	PO	A	E	Avg.
1991— Helena (Pio.)	C	64	253	35	72	14	0	2	34	.285	19	52	2	456	68	5	*.991
1992— Stockton (Calif.)	C	106	333	42	73	13	2	6	46	.219	35	81	2	582	114	8	*.989
1993— El Paso (Texas)..........	C	107	339	39	86	21	2	2	28	.254	17	73	1	524	*100	9	.986
1994— Milwaukee (A.L.)	C	28	53	3	12	3	0	1	2	.226	3	13	0	81	8	1	.989
— New Orleans (A.A.).....	C-DH-1B	57	177	20	39	10	1	4	21	.220	16	39	1	345	43	5	.987
1995— New Orleans (A.A.).....	C	6	17	3	6	2	0	3	4	.353	0	5	0	30	4	0	1.000
— Milwaukee (A.L.)	C	80	166	13	41	9	1	0	21	.247	12	28	2	261	18	4	.986
1996— Milwaukee (A.L.)	C-DH	106	313	31	64	15	2	8	46	.204	14	80	3	475	40	8	.985
— New Orleans (A.A.).....	C-DH	20	66	3	15	4	0	1	6	.227	2	17	1	87	6	0	1.000
1997— Milwaukee (A.L.)	C-1B	123	320	29	78	16	1	4	32	.244	17	68	0	697	58	5	.993
1998— Milwaukee (N.L.)	C	108	320	24	76	13	0	6	27	.238	11	63	1	570	45	8	.987
— Beloit (Midw.).............	DH-C	2	8	1	2	1	0	0	2	.250	1	3	0	13	1	0	1.000
1999— Toronto (A.L.)■.........	C	57	163	16	35	6	0	3	17	.215	12	37	0	346	33	2	.995
2000— St. Louis (N.L.)■	C-1B	128	417	43	109	22	1	6	47	.261	32	96	0	815	76	5	.994
American League totals (5 years)		394	1015	92	230	49	4	16	118	.227	58	226	5	1860	157	20	.990
National League totals (2 years)		236	737	67	185	35	1	12	74	.251	43	159	1	1385	121	13	.991
Major League totals (7 years)		630	1752	159	415	84	5	28	192	.237	101	385	6	3245	278	33	.991

DIVISION SERIES RECORD

Year Team (League)	Pos.	G	AB	R	H	2B	3B	HR	RBI	Avg.	BB	SO	SB	PO	A	E	Avg.
2000— St. Louis (N.L.)							Did not play.										

CHAMPIONSHIP SERIES RECORD

Year Team (League)	Pos.	G	AB	R	H	2B	3B	HR	RBI	Avg.	BB	SO	SB	PO	A	E	Avg.
2000— St. Louis (N.L.)							Did not play.										

MATHEWS, T.J. P ATHLETICS

PERSONAL: Born January 19, 1970, in Belleville, Ill. ... 6-1/214. ... Throws right, bats right. ... Full name: Timothy Jay Mathews. ... Son of Nelson Mathews, outfielder with Chicago Cubs (1960-63) and Kansas City Athletics (1964-65).

HIGH SCHOOL: Columbia (Ill.).

JUNIOR COLLEGE: Meremac Community College (Mo.).

COLLEGE: UNLV.

TRANSACTIONS/CAREER NOTES: Selected by St. Louis Cardinals organization in 36th round of free-agent draft (June 1, 1992). ... On Louisville disabled list (May 30-June 6, 1995). ... On suspended list (April 1-7, 1997). ... Traded by Cardinals with P Eric Ludwick and P Blake Stein to Oakland Athletics for 1B Mark McGwire (July 31, 1997). ... On Oakland disabled list (July 1-24, 1999); included rehabilitation assignment to Vancouver (July 21-24). ... On Oakland disabled list (August 11-September 1, 2000); included rehabilitation assignment to Sacramento (August 27-September 1).

STATISTICAL NOTES: Pitched 4-0 no-hit victory against Burlington (August 13, 1993).

Year League	W	L	Pct.	ERA	G	GS	CG	ShO	Sv.	IP	H	R	ER	BB	SO
1992— Hamilton (NY-Penn)	10	1	*.909	2.18	14	14	1	0	0	86²/₃	70	25	21	30	89
1993— Springfield (Midw.)	12	9	.571	2.71	25	25	5	2	0	159¹/₃	121	59	48	29	144
1994— St. Petersburg (FSL)	5	5	.500	2.44	11	11	1	0	0	66¹/₃	52	22	18	23	62
— Arkansas (Texas).............	5	5	.500	3.15	16	16	1	0	0	97	83	37	34	24	93
1995— Louisville (A.A.)................	9	4	.692	2.70	32	7	0	0	1	66²/₃	60	35	20	27	50
— St. Louis (N.L.)..............	1	1	.500	1.52	23	0	0	0	2	29²/₃	21	7	5	11	28
1996— St. Louis (N.L.)................	2	6	.250	3.01	67	0	0	0	6	83²/₃	62	32	28	32	80
1997— St. Louis (N.L.)................	4	4	.500	2.15	40	0	0	0	0	46	41	14	11	18	46
— Oakland (A.L.)■	6	2	.750	4.40	24	0	0	0	3	28²/₃	34	18	14	12	24
1998— Oakland (A.L.)	7	4	.636	4.58	66	0	0	0	1	72²/₃	71	44	37	29	53
1999— Oakland (A.L.)	9	5	.643	3.81	50	0	0	0	3	59	46	28	25	20	42
— Vancouver (PCL)	0	0	...	9.00	1	1	0	0	0	1	1	1	1	0	0
2000— Oakland (A.L.)	2	3	.400	6.03	50	0	0	0	0	59²/₃	73	40	40	25	42
— Sacramento (PCL).............	0	0	...	0.00	3	1	0	0	0	3²/₃	2	1	0	1	5
A.L. totals (4 years)	24	14	.632	4.75	190	0	0	0	7	220	224	130	116	86	161
N.L. totals (3 years)	7	11	.389	2.49	130	0	0	0	8	159¹/₃	124	53	44	61	154
Major League totals (6 years)	31	25	.554	3.80	320	0	0	0	15	379¹/₃	348	183	160	147	315

DIVISION SERIES RECORD

Year League	W	L	Pct.	ERA	G	GS	CG	ShO	Sv.	IP	H	R	ER	BB	SO
1996— St. Louis (N.L.)...................	1	0	1.000	0.00	1	0	0	0	0	1	1	0	0	0	2

CHAMPIONSHIP SERIES RECORD

Year League	W	L	Pct.	ERA	G	GS	CG	ShO	Sv.	IP	H	R	ER	BB	SO
1996— St. Louis (N.L.)...................	0	0	...	0.00	2	0	0	0	0	²/₃	2	0	0	2	2

MATOS, LUIS OF ORIOLES

PERSONAL: Born October 30, 1978, in Bayamon, Puerto Rico. ... 6-0/179. ... Bats right, throws right. ... Full name: Luis D. Matos.

HIGH SCHOOL: Disciple of Christ Academy (Bayamon, Puerto Rico).

TRANSACTIONS/CAREER NOTES: Selected by Baltimore Orioles organization in 10th round of free-agent draft (June 4, 1996).

Year	Team (League)	Pos.	G	AB	R	H	2B	3B	HR	RBI	Avg.	BB	SO	SB	PO	A	E	Avg.
1996—	GC Orioles (GCL)........	OF	43	130	21	38	2	0	0	13	.292	15	18	12	56	3	1	.983
1997—	Delmarva (S.Atl.)........	OF	36	119	10	25	1	2	0	13	.210	9	21	8	66	3	2	.972
	— Bluefield (Appl.)	OF	61	240	37	66	7	3	2	35	.275	20	36	26	125	4	3	.977
1998—	Delmarva (S.Atl.)........	OF	133	503	73	137	26	6	7	32	.272	38	90	42	254	12	10	.964
	— Bowie (East.)..............	OF	5	19	2	5	0	0	1	3	.263	1	1	1	4	1	1	.833
1999—	Frederick (Caro.)	OF-DH	68	273	40	81	15	1	7	41	.297	20	35	27	143	6	2	.987
	— Bowie (East.).............	OF	66	283	41	67	11	1	9	36	.237	15	39	14	152	8	3	.982
2000—	Baltimore (A.L.).........	OF-DH	72	182	21	41	6	3	1	17	.225	12	30	13	168	3	2	.988
Major League totals (1 year)			72	182	21	41	6	3	1	17	.225	12	30	13	168	3	2	.988

MATTHEWS, GARY OF CUBS

PERSONAL: Born August 25, 1974, in San Francisco. ... 6-3/200. ... Bats both, throws right. ... Full name: Gary Nathaniel Matthews Jr. ... Son of Gary Matthews, hitting coach with Toronto Blue Jays (1997-99); and outfielder with five major league teams (1972-87).
HIGH SCHOOL: Granada Hills (Calif.).
JUNIOR COLLEGE: Mission College (Calif.).
TRANSACTIONS/CAREER NOTES: Selected by San Diego Padres organization in 13th round of free-agent draft (June 3, 1993). ... Traded by Padres to Chicago Cubs for P Rodney Myers (March 23, 2000).

Year	Team (League)	Pos.	G	AB	R	H	2B	3B	HR	RBI	Avg.	BB	SO	SB	PO	A	E	Avg.
1994—	Spokane (N'West)	OF-2B	52	191	23	40	6	1	0	18	.209	19	58	3	96	2	4	.961
1995—	Clinton (Midw.)	OF	128	421	57	100	18	4	2	40	.238	68	109	28	245	9	9	.966
1996—	Rancho Cuca. (Calif.) .	OF	123	435	65	118	21	11	7	54	.271	60	102	7	218	7	16	.934
1997—	Rancho Cuca. (Calif.) .	OF	69	268	66	81	15	4	8	40	.302	49	57	10	110	6	5	.959
	— Mobile (Sou.)	OF	28	90	14	22	4	1	2	12	.244	15	29	3	45	3	2	.960
1998—	Mobile (Sou.)	OF	72	254	62	78	15	4	7	51	.307	55	50	11	184	8	1	.995
1999—	Las Vegas (PCL)	OF	121	422	57	108	22	3	9	52	.256	58	104	17	273	7	7	.976
	— San Diego (N.L.)	OF	23	36	4	8	0	0	0	7	.222	9	9	2	22	0	0	1.000
2000—	Iowa (PCL)■	OF	60	211	27	51	11	3	5	22	.242	18	41	6	125	5	4	.970
	— Chicago (N.L.)	OF	80	158	24	30	1	2	4	14	.190	15	28	3	84	3	2	.978
Major League totals (2 years)			103	194	28	38	1	2	4	21	.196	24	37	5	106	3	2	.982

MATTHEWS, MIKE P CARDINALS

PERSONAL: Born October 24, 1973, in Fredericksburg, Va. ... 6-2/175. ... Throws left, bats left. ... Full name: Michael Scott Matthews.
HIGH SCHOOL: Woodbridge Senior (Va.).
JUNIOR COLLEGE: Montgomery-Rockville College (Md.).
TRANSACTIONS/CAREER NOTES: Selected by Cleveland Indians organization in second round of free-agent draft (June 1, 1992). ... On Watertown disabled list (June 17, 1993-entire season). ... On disabled list (June 7-28, 1995). ... On Buffalo disabled list (June 8-July 1, 1998). ... Traded by Indians to Boston Red Sox for IF Jose Olmeda (August 4, 1999). ... Traded by Red Sox with C David Menham to St. Louis Cardinals for P Kent Mercker (August 24, 1999). ... On St. Louis disabled list (July 16, 2000-remainder of season).
STATISTICAL NOTES: Tied for Eastern League lead with four balks in 1997.

Year	League	W	L	Pct.	ERA	G	GS	CG	ShO	Sv.	IP	H	R	ER	BB	SO
1992—	Burlington (Appl.)..............	7	0	•1.000	*1.01	10	10	0	0	0	62 1/3	33	13	7	27	55
	— Watertown (NY-Penn)	1	0	1.000	3.27	2	2	0	0	0	11	10	4	4	8	5
1993—								Did not play.								
1994—	Columbus (S.Atl.)..............	6	8	.429	3.08	23	23	0	0	0	119 2/3	120	53	41	44	99
1995—	Canton/Akron (East.)..........	5	8	.385	5.93	15	15	1	0	0	74 1/3	82	62	49	43	37
1996—	Canton/Akron (East.)..........	9	11	.450	4.66	27	27	3	0	0	162 1/3	178	96	84	74	112
1997—	Buffalo (A.A.)....................	0	2	.000	7.71	5	5	0	0	0	21	32	19	18	10	17
	— Akron (East.)	6	8	.429	3.82	19	19	3	1	0	113	116	62	48	57	69
1998—	Buffalo (I.L.).....................	9	6	.600	4.63	24	23	0	0	0	130 1/3	137	79	67	68	86
1999—	Buffalo (I.L.).....................	1	2	.333	7.59	25	0	0	0	0	21 1/3	23	18	18	18	16
	— Akron (East.)	0	5	.000	8.77	6	6	0	0	0	25 2/3	36	30	25	15	10
	— Trenton (East.)■	0	0	...	4.63	3	3	0	0	0	11 2/3	11	7	6	9	8
	— Arkansas (Texas)■.............	2	0	1.000	0.00	2	2	1	1	0	12	3	0	0	1	10
2000—	Memphis (PCL)	3	1	.750	3.12	9	9	0	0	0	52	33	19	18	32	50
	— St. Louis (N.L.)	0	0	...	11.57	14	0	0	0	0	9 1/3	15	12	12	10	8
Major League totals (1 year)........		0	0	...	11.57	14	0	0	0	0	9 1/3	15	12	12	10	8

MAURER, DAVID P PADRES

PERSONAL: Born February 23, 1975, in Minneapolis. ... 6-2/205. ... Throws left, bats right. ... Full name: David Charles Maurer. ... Brother of Mike Maurer, pitcher, Oakland Athletics organization; son of Thomas Maurer, pitcher in Minnesota Twins organization.
HIGH SCHOOL: Apple Valley (Minn.).
COLLEGE: Oklahoma State.
TRANSACTIONS/CAREER NOTES: Selected by San Diego Padres organization in 11th round of free-agent draft (June 3, 1997). ... Selected by San Francisco Giants from Padres organization in Rule 5 major league draft (December 13, 1999). ... Returned to Padres (March 20, 2000).

Year	League	W	L	Pct.	ERA	G	GS	CG	ShO	Sv.	IP	H	R	ER	BB	SO
1997—	Clinton (Midw.)	0	4	.000	2.88	25	0	0	0	3	34 1/3	24	15	11	15	43
1998—	Rancho Cuca. (Calif.)	5	2	.714	2.70	48	0	0	0	5	83 1/3	56	27	25	46	93
1999—	Mobile (Sou.)	4	4	.500	3.63	54	0	0	0	3	72	59	30	29	26	59
2000—	Mobile (Sou.)	1	2	.333	2.70	24	0	0	0	0	26 2/3	15	8	8	3	28
	— Las Vegas (PCL)	4	1	.800	3.25	35	0	0	0	0	44 1/3	47	19	16	15	44
	— San Diego (N.L.)	1	0	1.000	3.68	14	0	0	0	0	14 2/3	15	8	6	5	13
Major League totals (1 year)........		1	0	1.000	3.68	14	0	0	0	0	14 2/3	15	8	6	5	13

M

MAXWELL, JASON — IF

PERSONAL: Born March 26, 1972, in Lewisburg, Tenn. ... 6-1/180. ... Bats right, throws right. ... Full name: Jason Ramond Maxwell.
HIGH SCHOOL: Marshall County (Lewisburg, Tenn.).
COLLEGE: Middle Tennessee State.
TRANSACTIONS/CAREER NOTES: Selected by Chicago Cubs organization in 74th round of free-agent draft (June 3, 1993). ... Claimed on waivers by Detroit Tigers (March 24, 1999). ... Granted free agency (October 15, 1999). ... Signed by Minnesota Twins organization (November 15, 1999). ... On disabled list (May 9-26, 2000). ... Granted free agency (October 4, 2000).
STATISTICAL NOTES: Led Southern League with nine sacrifice flies in 1997.

Year Team (League)	Pos.	G	AB	R	H	2B	3B	HR	RBI	Avg.	BB	SO	SB	PO	A	E	Avg.
1993— Huntington (Appl.)	SS	61	179	50	52	7	2	7	38	.291	35	39	6	60	140	9	.957
1994— Daytona (FSL)	SS	116	368	71	85	18	2	10	31	.231	55	96	7	167	333	*38	.929
1995— Daytona (FSL)	SS	117	388	66	102	13	3	10	58	.263	63	68	12	181	325	16	*.969
1996— Orlando (Sou.)	S-2-3-D	126	433	64	115	20	1	9	45	.266	56	77	19	188	336	29	.948
1997— Orlando (Sou.)	SS-2B	122	409	87	114	22	6	14	58	.279	82	72	12	176	376	28	.952
1998— Iowa (PCL)	2B-SS-DH	124	483	86	144	40	3	15	60	.298	52	93	8	237	306	16	.971
— Chicago (N.L.)	2B	7	3	2	1	0	0	1	2	.333	0	2	0	0	1	0	1.000
1999— Toledo (I.L.)■..........	S-2-3-1	119	419	60	99	17	2	15	62	.236	53	87	6	191	328	18	.966
2000— Minnesota (A.L.)■......	2-3-D-S-O	64	111	14	27	6	0	1	11	.243	9	32	2	38	95	6	.957
American League totals (1 year)		64	111	14	27	6	0	1	11	.243	9	32	2	38	95	6	.957
National League totals (1 year)		7	3	2	1	0	0	1	2	.333	0	2	0	0	1	0	1.000
Major League totals (2 years)		71	114	16	28	6	0	2	13	.246	9	34	2	38	96	6	.957

MAYNE, BRENT — C — ROCKIES

PERSONAL: Born April 19, 1968, in Loma Linda, Calif. ... 6-1/192. ... Bats left, throws right. ... Full name: Brent Danem Mayne.
HIGH SCHOOL: Costa Mesa (Calif.).
JUNIOR COLLEGE: Orange Coast College (Calif.).
COLLEGE: Cal State Fullerton.
TRANSACTIONS/CAREER NOTES: Selected by Kansas City Royals organization in first round (13th pick overall) of free-agent draft (June 5, 1989). ... On disabled list (July 24, 1989-remainder of season). ... Traded by Royals to New York Mets for OF Al Shirley (December 19, 1995). ... Granted free agency (December 7, 1996). ... Signed by Seattle Mariners organization (January 10, 1997). ... Released by Mariners (March 28, 1997). ... Signed by Oakland Athletics organization (April 8, 1997). ... Granted free agency (October 30, 1997). ... Signed by San Francisco Giants (November 21, 1997). ... Granted free agency (October 28, 1999). ... Signed by Colorado Rockies (December 9, 1999).
STATISTICAL NOTES: Led A.L. catchers with 11 double plays in 1995. ... Career major league grand slams: 2.

Year Team (League)	Pos.	G	AB	R	H	2B	3B	HR	RBI	Avg.	BB	SO	SB	PO	A	E	Avg.
1989— Baseball City (FSL).....	C	7	24	5	13	3	1	0	8	.542	0	3	0	31	2	0	1.000
1990— Memphis (Sou.)	C	115	412	48	110	16	3	2	61	.267	52	51	5	591	61	11	.983
— Kansas City (A.L.)	C	5	13	2	3	0	0	1	.231	3	3	0	29	3	1	.970
1991— Kansas City (A.L.)	C-DH	85	231	22	58	8	0	3	31	.251	23	42	2	425	38	6	.987
1992— Kansas City (A.L.)	C-3B-DH	82	213	16	48	10	0	0	18	.225	11	26	0	281	33	3	.991
1993— Kansas City (A.L.)	C-DH	71	205	22	52	9	1	2	22	.254	18	31	3	356	27	2	.995
1994— Kansas City (A.L.)	C-DH	46	144	19	37	5	1	2	20	.257	14	27	1	246	14	1	.996
1995— Kansas City (A.L.)	C	110	307	23	77	18	1	1	27	.251	25	41	0	540	40	3	.995
1996— New York (N.L.)■........	C	70	99	9	26	6	0	1	6	.263	12	22	0	85	3	0	1.000
1997— Edmonton (PCL)■........	C	2	3	0	0	0	0	0	0	.000	0	1	0	5	0	0	1.000
— Oakland (A.L.)	C	85	256	29	74	12	0	6	22	.289	18	33	1	419	36	2	.996
1998— San Fran. (N.L.)	C	94	275	26	75	15	0	3	32	.273	37	47	2	493	39	5	.991
1999— San Francisco (N.L.) ..	C	117	322	39	97	32	0	2	39	.301	43	65	2	597	47	3	.995
2000— Colorado (N.L.)■	C-P	117	335	36	101	21	0	6	64	.301	47	48	1	582	36	6	.990
American League totals (7 years)		484	1369	133	349	62	3	14	141	.255	112	203	7	2296	191	18	.993
National League totals (4 years)		398	1031	110	299	74	0	12	141	.290	139	182	5	1757	125	14	.993
Major League totals (11 years)		882	2400	243	648	136	3	26	282	.270	251	385	12	4053	316	32	.993

RECORD AS PITCHER

Year League	W	L	Pct.	ERA	G	GS	CG	ShO	Sv.	IP	H	R	ER	BB	SO
2000— Colorado (N.L.)	1	0	1.000	0.00	1	0	0	0	0	1	1	0	0	1	0

MAYS, JOE — P — TWINS

PERSONAL: Born December 10, 1975, in Flint, Mich. ... 6-1/185. ... Throws right, bats both. ... Full name: Joseph E. Mays.
HIGH SCHOOL: Southeast (Bradenton, Fla.).
JUNIOR COLLEGE: Manatee.
TRANSACTIONS/CAREER NOTES: Selected by Seattle Mariners organization in sixth round of free-agent draft (June 2, 1994). ... Traded by Mariners to Minnesota Twins (October 8, 1997), completing deal in which Twins traded OF Roberto Kelly to Mariners for P Jeromy Palki and a player to be named later (August 20, 1997).

Year League	W	L	Pct.	ERA	G	GS	CG	ShO	Sv.	IP	H	R	ER	BB	SO
1995— Arizona Mariners (Ariz.)	2	3	.400	3.25	10	10	0	0	0	44 1/3	41	24	16	18	44
1996— Everett (N'West)	4	4	.500	3.08	13	10	0	0	0	64 1/3	55	33	22	22	56
1997— Wisconsin (Midw.)	9	3	.750	2.09	13	13	1	0	0	81 2/3	62	20	19	23	79
— Lancaster (Calif.)	7	4	.636	4.86	15	15	0	0	0	96 1/3	108	55	52	34	82
1998— Fort Myers (FSL)■............	7	2	.778	3.04	16	15	0	0	0	94 2/3	101	45	32	23	83
— New Britain (East.)	5	3	.625	4.99	11	10	0	0	0	57 2/3	63	40	32	21	45
1999— Minnesota (A.L.)	6	11	.353	4.37	49	20	2	1	0	171	179	92	83	67	115
2000— Minnesota (A.L.)	7	15	.318	5.56	31	28	2	1	0	160 1/3	193	105	99	67	102
— Salt Lake (PCL)	2	0	1.000	1.72	3	3	0	0	0	15 2/3	16	4	3	2	18
Major League totals (2 years)	13	26	.333	4.94	80	48	4	2	0	331 1/3	372	197	182	134	217

McCARTY, DAVE   1B/OF   ROYALS

PERSONAL: Born November 23, 1969, in Houston. ... 6-5/215. ... Bats right, throws left. ... Full name: David Andrew McCarty.
HIGH SCHOOL: Sharpstown (Houston).
COLLEGE: Stanford.
TRANSACTIONS/CAREER NOTES: Selected by Minnesota Twins organization in first round (third pick overall) of free-agent draft (June 3, 1991). ... Traded by Twins to Cincinnati Reds for P John Courtright (June 8, 1995). ... Traded by Reds with OF Deion Sanders, P Ricky Pickett, P Scott Service and P John Roper to San Francisco Giants for OF Darren Lewis, P Mark Portugal and P Dave Burba (July 21, 1995). ... On San Francisco disabled list (June 6-27, 1996); included rehabilitation assignment to Phoenix (June 20-27). ... Traded by Giants to Seattle Mariners for OF Jay Leach and OF Scott Smith (January 30, 1998). ... Granted free agency (September 30, 1998). ... Signed by Detroit Tigers organization (December 18, 1998). ... Granted free agency (October 15, 1999). ... Signed by Oakland Athletics organization (November 23, 1999). ... Traded by A's to Kansas City Royals for cash (March 24, 2000).
STATISTICAL NOTES: Led International League first basemen with 104 assists and .999 fielding percentage in 1999. ... Career major league grand slams: 1.

Year	Team (League)	Pos.	G	AB	R	H	2B	3B	HR	RBI	Avg.	BB	SO	SB	PO	A	E	Avg.
1991—	Visalia (Calif.)	OF	15	50	16	19	3	0	3	8	.380	13	7	3	23	1	0	1.000
—	Orlando (Sou.)	OF	28	88	18	23	4	0	3	11	.261	10	20	0	38	4	1	.977
1992—	Orlando (Sou.)	OF-1B	129	456	75	124	16	2	18	79	.272	55	89	6	357	32	9	.977
—	Portland (PCL)	OF-1B	7	26	7	13	2	0	1	8	.500	5	3	1	40	3	1	.977
1993—	Portland (PCL)	OF-1B	40	143	42	55	11	0	8	31	.385	27	25	5	185	21	2	.990
—	Minnesota (A.L.)	OF-1B-DH	98	350	36	75	15	2	2	21	.214	19	80	2	412	38	8	.983
1994—	Minnesota (A.L.)	1B-OF	44	131	21	34	8	2	1	12	.260	7	32	2	243	28	5	.982
—	Salt Lake (PCL)	OF-1B	55	186	32	47	9	3	3	19	.253	35	34	1	191	16	5	.976
1995—	Minnesota (A.L.)	1B-OF	25	55	10	12	3	1	0	4	.218	4	18	0	130	10	1	.993
—	Indianapolis (A.A.)■	1B	37	140	31	47	10	1	8	32	.336	15	30	0	335	14	2	.994
—	Phoenix (PCL)■	1B-OF-DH	37	151	31	53	19	2	4	19	.351	17	27	1	330	32	2	.995
—	San Francisco (N.L.)	OF-1B	12	20	1	5	1	0	0	2	.250	2	4	1	19	0	1	.950
1996—	San Francisco (N.L.)	1B-OF	91	175	16	38	3	0	6	24	.217	18	43	2	291	18	3	.990
—	Phoenix (PCL)	OF-1B	6	25	4	10	1	1	1	7	.400	2	4	0	29	1	0	1.000
1997—	Phoenix (PCL)	1B-DH-OF	121	434	85	153	27	5	22	92	.353	49	75	9	563	53	3	.995
1998—	Tacoma (PCL)■	OF-1B-DH	108	398	73	126	30	2	11	52	.317	59	85	9	430	32	2	.996
—	Seattle (A.L.)	OF-1B	8	18	1	5	0	0	1	2	.278	5	4	1	21	0	0	1.000
1999—	Toledo (I.L.)■	1B-OF-P-DH	132	466	85	125	24	3	31	77	.268	70	110	6	1001	†106	2	†.998
2000—	Kansas City (A.L.)■	1B-OF-DH	103	270	34	75	14	2	12	53	.278	22	68	0	482	61	5	.991
American League totals (5 years)			278	824	102	201	40	7	16	92	.244	57	202	5	1288	137	19	.987
National League totals (2 years)			103	195	17	43	4	0	6	26	.221	20	47	3	310	18	4	.988
Major League totals (6 years)			381	1019	119	244	44	7	22	118	.239	77	249	8	1598	155	23	.987

RECORD AS PITCHER

Year	League	W	L	Pct.	ERA	G	GS	CG	ShO	Sv.	IP	H	R	ER	BB	SO
1999—	Toledo (I.L.)	0	0	...	4.50	2	0	0	0	0	2	1	1	1	1	0

McCRACKEN, QUINTON   OF   CARDINALS

PERSONAL: Born March 16, 1970, in Wilmington, N.C. ... 5-7/173. ... Bats both, throws right. ... Full name: Quinton Antoine McCracken.
HIGH SCHOOL: South Brunswick (Southport, N.C.).
COLLEGE: Duke.
TRANSACTIONS/CAREER NOTES: Selected by Colorado Rockies organization in 25th round of free-agent draft (June 1, 1992). ... Selected by Tampa Bay Devil Rays in first round (fourth pick overall) of expansion draft (November 18, 1997). ... On disabled list (May 25, 1999-remainder of season). ... Released by Devil Rays (November 27, 2000). ... Signed by St. Louis Cardinals (December 22, 2000).
STATISTICAL NOTES: Led California League with 12 sacrifice hits in 1993. ... Led Eastern League in caught stealing with 19 in 1994. ... Had 18-game hitting streak (August 18-September 9, 1998).

Year	Team (League)	Pos.	G	AB	R	H	2B	3B	HR	RBI	Avg.	BB	SO	SB	PO	A	E	Avg.
1992—	Bend (N'West)	2B-OF	67	232	37	65	13	2	0	27	.280	25	39	18	98	129	17	.930
1993—	Central Valley (Calif.)	OF-2B	127	483	94	141	17	7	2	58	.292	78	90	60	153	75	13	.946
1994—	New Haven (East.)	OF	136	544	94	151	27	4	5	39	.278	48	72	36	273	6	8	.972
1995—	New Haven (East.)	OF-DH	55	221	33	79	11	4	1	26	.357	21	32	26	92	10	3	.971
—	Colo. Springs (PCL)	OF-DH	61	244	55	88	14	6	3	28	.361	23	30	17	104	5	1	.991
—	Colorado (N.L.)	OF	3	1	0	0	0	0	0	0	.000	0	1	0	0	0	0	...
1996—	Colorado (N.L.)	OF	124	283	50	82	13	6	3	40	.290	32	62	17	131	3	6	.957
1997—	Colorado (N.L.)	OF	147	325	69	95	11	1	3	36	.292	42	62	28	195	5	4	.980
1998—	Tampa Bay (A.L.)■	OF	155	614	77	179	38	7	7	59	.292	41	107	19	343	18	3	.992
1999—	Tampa Bay (A.L.)	OF	40	148	20	37	6	1	1	18	.250	14	23	6	80	1	1	.988
2000—	Tampa Bay (A.L.)	OF	15	31	5	4	0	0	0	2	.129	6	4	0	19	0	0	1.000
—	Durham (I.L.)	OF	85	334	54	87	18	2	2	28	.260	34	57	13	161	8	4	.977
American League totals (3 years)			210	793	102	220	44	8	8	79	.277	61	134	25	442	19	4	.991
National League totals (3 years)			274	609	119	177	24	7	6	76	.291	74	125	45	326	8	10	.971
Major League totals (6 years)			484	1402	221	397	68	15	14	155	.283	135	259	70	768	27	14	.983

McDILL, ALLEN   P

PERSONAL: Born August 23, 1971, in Greenville, Miss. ... 6-0/170. ... Throws left, bats left. ... Full name: Allen Gabriel McDill.
HIGH SCHOOL: Lake Hamilton (Ark.).
TRANSACTIONS/CAREER NOTES: Selected by New York Mets organization in 20th round of free-agent draft (June 1, 1992). ... Traded by Mets with P Jason Jacome to Kansas City Royals for P Derek Wallace and a player to be named later (July 21, 1995); Mets acquired P John Carter to complete deal (November 16, 1995). ... Granted free agency (December 21, 1998). ... Re-signed by Royals (January 14, 1999). ... Released

by Royals (March 12, 1999). ... Signed by Texas Rangers organization (March 17, 1999). ... Granted free agency (October 15, 1999). ... Signed by Detroit Tigers organization (December 16, 1999). ... Released by Tigers (June 24, 2000). ... Signed by St. Louis Cardinals organization (June 27, 2000). ... On Memphis disabled list (July 23-30, 2000). ... Granted free agency (October 18, 2000).

Year League	W	L	Pct.	ERA	G	GS	CG	ShO	Sv.	IP	H	R	ER	BB	SO
1992—Gulf Coast Mets (GCL)	3	4	.429	2.70	10	9	0	0	0	53 1/3	36	23	16	15	60
—Kingsport (Appl.)	0	0	...	0.00	1	0	0	0	0	1/3	0	0	0	2	0
1993—Kingsport (Appl.)	5	2	.714	2.19	9	9	0	0	0	53 1/3	52	19	13	14	42
—Pittsfield (NY-Penn)	2	3	.400	5.40	5	5	0	0	0	28 1/3	31	22	17	15	24
1994—Columbia (S.Atl.)	9	6	.600	3.55	19	19	1	0	0	111 2/3	101	52	44	38	102
1995—Binghamton (East.)	3	5	.375	4.56	12	12	1	0	0	73	69	42	37	38	44
—St. Lucie (FSL)	4	2	.667	1.64	7	7	1	1	0	49 1/3	36	11	9	13	28
—Wichita (Texas)■	1	0	1.000	2.11	12	1	0	0	1	21 1/3	16	7	5	5	20
1996—Wichita (Texas)	1	5	.167	5.54	54	0	0	0	11	65	79	43	40	21	62
—Omaha (A.A.)	0	1	.000	54.00	2	0	0	0	0	1/3	3	2	2	1	1
1997—Omaha (A.A.)	5	2	.714	5.88	23	6	0	0	2	64 1/3	80	42	42	26	51
—Kansas City (A.L.)	0	0	...	13.50	3	0	0	0	0	4	3	6	6	8	2
—Wichita (Texas)	0	1	.000	3.12	16	0	0	0	3	17 1/3	18	7	6	7	14
1998—Omaha (PCL)	6	4	.600	2.39	61	0	0	0	4	60 1/3	54	22	16	24	62
—Kansas City (A.L.)	0	0	...	10.50	7	0	0	0	0	6	9	7	7	2	3
1999—Oklahoma (PCL)■	1	3	.250	3.72	42	0	0	0	18	48 1/3	45	22	20	17	46
2000—Toledo (I.L.)■	1	0	1.000	0.96	16	0	0	0	0	18 2/3	21	4	2	7	15
—Detroit (A.L.)	0	0	...	7.20	13	0	0	0	0	10	13	9	8	1	7
—Memphis (PCL)■	0	2	.000	4.38	23	0	0	0	0	24 2/3	24	13	12	17	28
Major League totals (3 years)	0	0	...	9.45	23	0	0	0	0	20	25	22	21	11	12

McDONALD, DONZELL — OF — YANKEES

PERSONAL: Born February 20, 1975, in Long Beach, Calif. ... 5-11/180. ... Bats both, throws right. ... Brother of Darnell McDonald, outfielder, Baltimore Orioles organization.
HIGH SCHOOL: Cherry Creek (Colo.).
JUNIOR COLLEGE: Yavapai College (Ariz.).
TRANSACTIONS/CAREER NOTES: Selected by New York Yankees organization in 22nd round of free-agent draft (June 1, 1995). ... On disabled list (July 3-August 6, 1997). ... On Columbus disabled list (May 10-July 21, 2000).
STATISTICAL NOTES: Led New York-Pennsylvania League outfielders with 179 total chances in 1996. ... Led Eastern League in caught stealing with 22 in 1998. ... Led Eastern League outfielders with 328 total chances in 1998.

Year Team (League)	Pos.	G	AB	R	H	2B	3B	HR	RBI	Avg.	BB	SO	SB	PO	A	E	Avg.
1995—GC Yankees (GCL)	OF	28	110	23	26	5	1	0	9	.236	16	24	11	44	0	3	.936
1996—Oneonta (NY-Penn)	OF	74	282	57	78	8	*10	2	30	.277	43	62	*54	*169	4	6	.966
1997—Tampa (FSL)	OF	77	297	69	88	23	8	3	23	.296	48	75	39	173	3	4	.978
1998—Norwich (East.)	OF	134	495	80	125	20	7	6	36	.253	55	127	35	*312	8	8	.976
—Tampa (FSL)	OF	5	18	6	6	1	2	0	2	.333	2	7	2	14	0	0	1.000
1999—Norwich (East.)	OF-DH	137	533	95	145	19	10	4	33	.272	90	110	54	314	8	9	.973
2000—Columbus (I.L.)	OF	24	77	17	19	4	4	1	6	.247	23	11	12	51	2	0	1.000
—Norwich (East.)	OF	44	170	23	41	7	2	2	10	.241	35	36	13	96	1	2	.980

McDONALD, JASON — OF — BREWERS

PERSONAL: Born March 20, 1972, in Modesto, Calif. ... 5-7/190. ... Bats both, throws right. ... Full name: Jason Adam McDonald.
HIGH SCHOOL: Elk Grove (Calif.) Unified School.
COLLEGE: Houston.
TRANSACTIONS/CAREER NOTES: Selected by Oakland Athletics organization in fourth round of free-agent draft (June 3, 1993). ... On Oakland disabled list (April 19-May 4 and May 24-August 4, 1998); included rehabilitation assignments to Edmonton (April 30-May 4) and Huntsville (July 27-August 4). ... Granted free agency (October 15, 1999). ... Signed by Texas Rangers organization (January 10, 2000). ... On Oklahoma disabled list (June 23-July 25, 2000). ... Granted free agency (October 2, 2000). ... Signed by Milwaukee Brewers organization (January 8, 2001).
STATISTICAL NOTES: Led California League shortstops with 43 errors in 1995. ... Tied for Pacific Coast League lead in being hit by pitch with 15 in 1996. ... Led Pacific Coast League second basemen with 254 putouts, 352 assists, 24 errors, 630 total chances and 75 double plays in 1996.

Year Team (League)	Pos.	G	AB	R	H	2B	3B	HR	RBI	Avg.	BB	SO	SB	PO	A	E	Avg.
1993—S. Oregon (N'West)	2B	35	112	26	33	5	2	0	8	.295	31	17	22	70	77	7	.955
1994—W. Mich. (Midw.)	2B-OF-SS	116	404	67	96	11	*9	2	31	.238	81	87	52	253	167	21	.952
1995—Modesto (Calif.)	SS-OF-2B	133	493	109	129	25	7	6	50	.262	*110	84	*70	247	246	†50	.908
1996—Edmonton (PCL)	2B-OF-DH	137	479	71	114	7	5	8	46	.238	63	82	33	†302	†352	†25	.963
1997—Edmonton (PCL)	OF-DH	79	276	74	73	14	6	4	30	.264	74	58	31	187	10	5	.975
—Oakland (A.L.)	OF	78	236	47	62	11	4	4	14	.263	36	49	13	151	3	5	.969
1998—Oakland (A.L.)	OF-DH	70	175	25	44	9	0	1	16	.251	27	33	10	122	7	6	.956
—Edmonton (PCL)	OF	12	43	12	10	1	1	2	5	.233	15	11	7	37	3	0	1.000
—Huntsville (Sou.)	OF-DH	7	20	9	6	2	0	2	4	.300	8	6	4	10	1	0	1.000
1999—Oakland (A.L.)	OF-DH-2B	100	187	26	39	2	1	3	8	.209	25	48	6	150	3	1	.994
—Vancouver (PCL)	OF-2B	32	129	27	42	9	1	4	18	.326	19	33	8	79	6	1	.988
2000—Oklahoma (PCL)	OF	32	105	13	25	6	1	2	12	.238	14	29	2	71	5	2	.974
—Texas (A.L.)	OF-DH	38	94	15	22	5	0	3	13	.234	17	25	4	75	6	1	.988
—GC Rangers (GCL)	OF	3	10	0	2	0	0	0	0	.200	1	2	0	2	0	0	1.000
—Charlotte (FSL)	OF	5	15	4	5	2	0	0	1	.333	4	5	1	4	0	0	1.000
Major League totals (4 years)		286	692	113	167	27	5	11	51	.241	105	155	33	498	19	13	.975

M

McDONALD, JOHN   SS/2B   INDIANS

PERSONAL: Born September 24, 1974, in New London, Conn. ... 5-11/175. ... Bats right, throws right. ... Full name: John J. McDonald.
HIGH SCHOOL: East Lyme (Conn.).
JUNIOR COLLEGE: Univ. of Connecticut-Avery Point.
COLLEGE: Providence.
TRANSACTIONS/CAREER NOTES: Selected by Cleveland Indians organization in 12th round of free-agent draft (June 4, 1996). ... On Buffalo disabled list (April 27-May 9 and May 10-June 22, 2000).
STATISTICAL NOTES: Led Carolina League shortstops with 647 total chances and 105 double plays in 1997. ... Led Eastern League shortstops with 672 total chances in 1998.

											BATTING				FIELDING			
Year	Team (League)	Pos.	G	AB	R	H	2B	3B	HR	RBI	Avg.	BB	SO	SB	PO	A	E	Avg.
1996—Watertown (NY-Penn)		SS	75	278	48	75	11	0	2	26	.270	32	49	11	85	228	18	.946
1997—Kinston (Caro.)..........		SS	130	541	77	140	27	3	5	53	.259	51	75	6	*209	*413	25	*.961
1998—Akron (East.)		SS	132	514	68	118	18	2	2	43	.230	43	61	17	*242	407	23	.966
1999—Akron (East.)		SS-2B	55	226	31	67	12	0	1	26	.296	19	26	7	102	153	8	.970
—Buffalo (I.L.)...............		SS-3B-2B	66	237	30	75	12	1	0	25	.316	11	23	6	87	194	13	.956
—Cleveland (A.L.).........		2B-SS	18	21	2	7	0	0	0	0	.333	0	3	0	8	21	1	.967
2000—Buffalo (I.L.)..........		SS-2B-3B	75	286	37	77	17	2	1	36	.269	21	29	4	112	202	8	.975
—Mahoning Val. (NY-P)		SS	5	17	0	2	1	0	0	1	.118	2	3	0	2	16	0	1.000
—Cleveland (A.L.).........		SS-2B	9	9	0	4	0	0	0	0	.444	0	1	0	4	8	0	1.000
—Kinston (Caro.)..........		SS	1	3	0	1	0	0	0	0	.333	0	0	0	1	3	0	1.000
Major League totals (2 years)			27	30	2	11	0	0	0	0	.367	0	4	0	12	29	1	.976

McELROY, CHUCK   P   ORIOLES

PERSONAL: Born October 1, 1967, in Port Arthur, Texas. ... 6-0/205. ... Throws left, bats left. ... Full name: Charles Dwayne McElroy. ... Name pronounced MACK-il-roy.
HIGH SCHOOL: Lincoln (Port Arthur, Texas).
TRANSACTIONS/CAREER NOTES: Selected by Philadelphia Phillies organization in eighth round of free-agent draft (June 2, 1986). ... Traded by Phillies with P Bob Scanlan to Chicago Cubs for P Mitch Williams (April 7, 1991). ... Traded by Cubs to Cincinnati Reds for P Larry Luebbers, P Mike Anderson and C Darron Cox (December 10, 1993). ... On disabled list (June 7-23, 1995). ... On Cincinnati disabled list (March 28-April 28, 1996); included rehabilitation assignment to Indianapolis (April 12-28). ... Traded by Reds to California Angels for P Lee Smith (May 27, 1996). ... On California disabled list (August 11-28, 1996). ... Angels franchise renamed Anaheim Angels for 1997 season. ... Traded by Angels with C Jorge Fabregas to Chicago White Sox for OF Tony Phillips and C Chad Kreuter (May 18, 1997). ... Selected by Arizona Diamondbacks in third round (67th pick overall) of expansion draft (November 18, 1997). ... Traded by Diamondbacks to Colorado Rockies for OF Harvey Pulliam (November 18, 1997). ... Traded by Rockies with OF Darryl Hamilton to New York Mets for OF Brian McRae, P Rigo Beltran and OF Thomas Johnson (July 31, 1999). ... Traded by Mets to Baltimore Orioles for P Jesse Orosco (December 10, 1999).
MISCELLANEOUS: Appeared in one game as pinch runner with Chicago (1997). ... Appeared in one game as outfielder with one putout for Mets (1999).

Year	League	W	L	Pct.	ERA	G	GS	CG	ShO	Sv.	IP	H	R	ER	BB	SO
1986—Utica (NY-Penn)		4	6	.400	2.95	14	14	5	1	0	94 2/3	85	40	31	28	91
1987—Spartanburg (S.Atl.)		14	4	.778	3.11	24	21	5	2	0	130 1/3	117	51	45	48	115
—Clearwater (FSL)		1	0	1.000	0.00	2	2	0	0	0	7 1/3	1	1	0	4	7
1988—Reading (East.)...............		9	12	.429	4.50	28	26	4	2	0	160	•173	89	*80	70	92
1989—Reading (East.)		3	1	.750	2.68	32	0	0	0	12	47	39	14	14	14	39
—Scranton/W.B. (I.L.)		1	2	.333	2.93	14	0	0	0	3	15 1/3	13	6	5	11	12
—Philadelphia (N.L.)		0	0	...	1.74	11	0	0	0	0	10 1/3	12	2	2	4	8
1990—Scranton/W.B. (I.L.)		6	8	.429	2.72	57	1	0	0	7	76	62	24	23	34	78
—Philadelphia (N.L.)		0	1	.000	7.71	16	0	0	0	0	14	24	13	12	10	16
1991—Chicago (N.L.)■		6	2	.750	1.95	71	0	0	0	3	101 1/3	73	33	22	57	92
1992—Chicago (N.L.)		4	7	.364	3.55	72	0	0	0	6	83 2/3	73	40	33	51	83
1993—Chicago (N.L.)		2	2	.500	4.56	49	0	0	0	0	47 1/3	51	30	24	25	31
—Iowa (A.A.)		0	1	.000	4.60	9	0	0	0	2	15 2/3	19	10	8	9	13
1994—Cincinnati (N.L.)■............		1	2	.333	2.34	52	0	0	0	5	57 2/3	52	15	15	15	38
1995—Cincinnati (N.L.)		3	4	.429	6.02	44	0	0	0	0	40 1/3	46	29	27	15	27
1996—Indianapolis (A.A.).............		1	1	.500	2.70	5	3	0	0	0	13 1/3	11	4	4	4	10
—Cincinnati (N.L.)		2	0	1.000	6.57	12	0	0	0	0	12 1/3	13	10	9	10	13
—California (A.L.)■		5	1	.833	2.95	40	0	0	0	0	36 2/3	32	12	12	13	32
1997—Anaheim (A.L.)		0	0	...	3.45	13	0	0	0	0	15 2/3	17	7	6	3	18
—Chicago (A.L.)■		1	3	.250	3.94	48	0	0	0	1	59 1/3	56	29	26	19	44
1998—Colorado (N.L.)■		6	4	.600	2.90	78	0	0	0	2	68 1/3	68	23	22	24	61
1999—Colorado (N.L.)		3	1	.750	6.20	41	0	0	0	0	40 2/3	48	29	28	28	37
—New York (N.L.)■		0	0	...	3.38	15	0	0	0	0	13 1/3	12	5	5	8	7
2000—Baltimore (A.L.)■.............		3	0	1.000	4.69	43	2	0	0	0	63 1/3	60	36	33	34	50
A.L. totals (3 years)		9	4	.692	3.96	144	2	0	0	1	175	165	84	77	69	144
N.L. totals (10 years)		27	23	.540	3.66	461	0	0	0	16	489 1/3	472	229	199	247	413
Major League totals (12 years)		36	27	.571	3.74	605	2	0	0	17	664 1/3	637	313	276	316	557

DIVISION SERIES RECORD

Year	League	W	L	Pct.	ERA	G	GS	CG	ShO	Sv.	IP	H	R	ER	BB	SO
1999— New York (N.L.).................								Did not play.								

CHAMPIONSHIP SERIES RECORD

Year	League	W	L	Pct.	ERA	G	GS	CG	ShO	Sv.	IP	H	R	ER	BB	SO
1999— New York (N.L.).................								Did not play.								

M

PERSONAL: Born October 19, 1972, in Bristol, Pa. ... 5-11/170. ... Bats right, throws right. ... Full name: Joseph Earl McEwing.
HIGH SCHOOL: Bishop Egan (Fairless Hills, Pa.).
JUNIOR COLLEGE: County College of Morris (N.J.).
TRANSACTIONS/CAREER NOTES: Selected by St. Louis Cardinals organization in 28th round of free-agent draft (June 1, 1992). ... Traded by Cardinals to New York Mets for P Jesse Orosco (March 18, 2000).
STATISTICAL NOTES: Led Arizona League outfielders with 94 putouts, 11 assists, four double plays, 106 total chances and .991 fielding percentage in 1992. ... Led South Atlantic League with 15 sacrifice hits in 1993. ... Led Texas League outfielders with .993 fielding percentage in 1996. ... Tied for Pacific Coast League lead with three double plays by outfielder in 1998. ... Had 25-game hitting streak (June 8-July 4, 1999).

								BATTING								FIELDING		
Year	Team (League)	Pos.	G	AB	R	H	2B	3B	HR	RBI	Avg.	BB	SO	SB	PO	A	E	Avg.
1992—	Ariz. Cardinals (Ariz.) .	OF-SS	55	211	*55	71	4	2	0	13	.336	24	18	23	†94	†12	1	.991
1993—	Savannah (S.Atl.)	OF	138	511	*94	127	35	1	0	43	.249	89	73	22	262	13	5	.982
1994—	Madison (Midw.)	OF	90	346	58	112	24	2	4	47	.324	32	53	18	184	6	5	.974
—	St. Petersburg (FSL) ..	OF-2B	50	197	22	49	7	0	1	20	.249	19	32	8	105	23	2	.985
1995—	St. Petersburg (FSL) ..	2B-OF	75	281	33	64	13	0	1	23	.228	25	49	2	139	176	15	.955
—	Arkansas (Texas)........	OF-2B	42	121	16	30	4	0	2	12	.248	9	13	3	61	12	0	1.000
1996—	Arkansas (Texas)........	OF-2B	106	216	27	45	7	3	2	14	.208	13	32	2	134	15	2	†.987
1997—	Arkansas (Texas)........	OF-2B-1B-3B	103	263	33	68	6	3	4	35	.259	19	39	2	134	24	2	.988
1998—	Arkansas (Texas)........	OF-SS-P	60	223	45	79	21	4	9	46	.354	21	18	4	130	25	1	.994
—	Memphis (PCL).........	OF-3B-SS-2B	78	329	52	110	30	7	6	46	.334	21	39	11	143	24	3	.982
—	St. Louis (N.L.)...........	2B-OF	10	20	5	4	1	0	0	1	.200	1	3	0	10	10	0	1.000
1999—	St. Louis (N.L.)...........	2-0-3-1-S	152	513	65	141	28	4	9	44	.275	41	87	7	320	246	11	.981
2000—	Norfolk (I.L.)■..........	OF-2B-3B-SS	43	171	28	44	10	2	5	18	.257	16	34	7	77	67	4	.973
—	New York (N.L.)..........	OF-3B-2B-SS	87	153	20	34	14	1	2	19	.222	5	29	3	67	45	5	.957
Major League totals (3 years)			249	686	90	179	43	5	11	64	.261	47	119	10	397	301	16	.978

DIVISION SERIES RECORD

								BATTING								FIELDING		
Year	Team (League)	Pos.	G	AB	R	H	2B	3B	HR	RBI	Avg.	BB	SO	SB	PO	A	E	Avg.
2000—	New York (N.L.)..........	OF-PR-3B	4	1	0	1	0	0	0	0	1.000	0	0	0	0	0	0	...

CHAMPIONSHIP SERIES RECORD

								BATTING								FIELDING		
Year	Team (League)	Pos.	G	AB	R	H	2B	3B	HR	RBI	Avg.	BB	SO	SB	PO	A	E	Avg.
2000—	New York (N.L.)..........	PR-OF-3B	4	0	2	0	0	0	0	0	...	0	0	0	1	0	0	1.000

WORLD SERIES RECORD

								BATTING								FIELDING		
Year	Team (League)	Pos.	G	AB	R	H	2B	3B	HR	RBI	Avg.	BB	SO	SB	PO	A	E	Avg.
2000—	New York (N.L.)..........	OF-PR	3	1	1	0	0	0	0	0	.000	0	0	0	2	0	0	1.000

RECORD AS PITCHER

Year	League	W	L	Pct.	ERA	G	GS	CG	ShO	Sv.	IP	H	R	ER	BB	SO
1997—	Arkansas (Texas)................	0	0	...	27.00	1	0	0	0	0	$\frac{1}{3}$	1	1	1	0	0
1998—	Arkansas (Texas)................	0	0	...	27.00	1	0	0	0	0	1	3	3	3	1	1

M

PERSONAL: Born June 28, 1977, in Malden, Mass. ... 6-5/220. ... Throws right, bats right. ... Full name: Kevin Michael McGlinchy.
HIGH SCHOOL: Malden (Mass.).
JUNIOR COLLEGE: Central Florida Community College.
TRANSACTIONS/CAREER NOTES: Selected by Atlanta Braves organization in fifth round of free-agent draft (June 1, 1995). ... On Atlanta disabled list (April 17-May 13 and May 23-September 9, 2000); included rehabilitation assignments to Greenville (April 30-May 13), Richmond (July 6-20 and August 27-September 5) and Gulf Coast Braves (August 14-26).

Year	League	W	L	Pct.	ERA	G	GS	CG	ShO	Sv.	IP	H	R	ER	BB	SO
1996—	Danville (Appl.)..................	3	2	.600	1.13	13	13	0	0	0	72	52	21	9	11	77
—	Eugene (N'West)	0	0	...	5.40	2	2	0	0	0	$6\frac{2}{3}$	7	5	4	1	5
1997—	Durham (Caro.)	3	7	.300	4.90	26	26	0	0	0	$139\frac{2}{3}$	145	78	76	39	113
1998—	Danville (Caro.)	9	8	.529	2.91	22	22	1	0	0	$142\frac{1}{3}$	122	55	46	29	129
—	Greenville (Sou.)	1	1	.500	5.18	6	6	0	0	0	33	35	19	19	15	20
1999—	Atlanta (N.L.).....................	7	3	.700	2.82	64	0	0	0	0	$70\frac{1}{3}$	66	25	22	30	67
2000—	Atlanta (N.L.).....................	0	0	...	2.16	10	0	0	0	0	$8\frac{1}{3}$	11	4	2	6	9
—	Greenville (Sou.)	0	0	...	0.00	4	0	0	0	0	4	2	1	0	0	7
—	Richmond (I.L.)..................	0	1	.000	3.60	9	0	0	0	1	10	9	4	4	3	7
—	Gulf Coast Braves (GCL)	0	0	...	9.00	4	2	0	0	0	5	12	8	5	1	6
Major League totals (2 years)		7	3	.700	2.75	74	0	0	0	0	$78\frac{2}{3}$	77	29	24	36	76

DIVISION SERIES RECORD

Year	League	W	L	Pct.	ERA	G	GS	CG	ShO	Sv.	IP	H	R	ER	BB	SO
1999—	Atlanta (N.L.).....................	0	0	...	0.00	1	0	0	0	0	$\frac{1}{3}$	0	0	0	0	0

CHAMPIONSHIP SERIES RECORD

Year	League	W	L	Pct.	ERA	G	GS	CG	ShO	Sv.	IP	H	R	ER	BB	SO
1999—	Atlanta (N.L.).....................	0	1	.000	18.00	1	0	0	0	0	1	2	2	2	4	1

WORLD SERIES RECORD

Year	League	W	L	Pct.	ERA	G	GS	CG	ShO	Sv.	IP	H	R	ER	BB	SO
1999—	Atlanta (N.L.).....................	0	0	...	0.00	1	0	0	0	0	2	3	0	0	1	2

PERSONAL: Born October 31, 1963, in Tampa. ... 6-3/215. ... Bats left, throws left. ... Full name: Frederick Stanley McGriff. ... Cousin of Terry McGriff, catcher with four major league teams (1987-90, 1993 and 1994); and uncle of Charles Johnson, catcher, Florida Marlins.

HIGH SCHOOL: Jefferson (Tampa).

TRANSACTIONS/CAREER NOTES: Selected by New York Yankees organization in ninth round of free-agent draft (June 8, 1981). ... Traded by Yankees with OF Dave Collins, P Mike Morgan and cash to Toronto Blue Jays for OF/C Tom Dodd and P Dale Murray (December 9, 1982). ... On disabled list (June 5-August 14, 1985). ... Traded by Blue Jays with SS Tony Fernandez to San Diego Padres for OF Joe Carter and 2B Roberto Alomar (December 5, 1990). ... On suspended list (June 23-26, 1992). ... Traded by Padres to Atlanta Braves for OF Melvin Nieves, P Donnie Elliott and OF Vince Moore (July 18, 1993). ... Granted free agency (November 6, 1995). ... Re-signed by Braves (December 2, 1995). ... Traded by Braves to Tampa Bay Devil Rays for a player to be named later or cash (November 18, 1997); Braves received an undisclosed amount of cash to complete deal (April 1, 1998).

RECORDS: Shares major league career record for most major league ballparks, one or more home runs (since 1900)—37. ... Shares major league record for most grand slams in two consecutive games—2 (August 13 and 14, 1991). ... Shares N.L. single-season record for fewest errors by first baseman who led league in errors—12 (1992).

HONORS: Named first baseman on THE SPORTING NEWS A.L. All-Star team (1989). ... Named first baseman on THE SPORTING NEWS A.L. Silver Slugger team (1989). ... Named first baseman on THE SPORTING NEWS N.L. All-Star team (1992-93). ... Named first baseman on THE SPORTING NEWS N.L. Silver Slugger team (1992-93).

STATISTICAL NOTES: Led International League first basemen with .992 fielding percentage, 1,219 putouts, 85 assists, 1,314 total chances and 108 double plays in 1986. ... Tied for International League lead in intentional bases on balls received with eight and in grounding into double plays with 16 in 1986. ... Led A.L. first basemen with 1,592 total chances and 148 double plays in 1989. ... Led N.L. with 26 intentional base on balls received in 1991. ... Led N.L. first basemen with 1,077 total chances in 1994. ... Led N.L. in grounding into double plays with 22 in 1997. ... Led A.L. first basemen with 140 double plays in 1998. ... Career major league grand slams: 7.

MISCELLANEOUS: Holds Tampa Bay Devil Rays all-time records for most runs (230), hits (481), doubles (81), home runs (78), runs batted in (291) and highest career batting average (.290).

						BATTING								FIELDING			
Year Team (League)	Pos.	G	AB	R	H	2B	3B	HR	RBI	Avg.	BB	SO	SB	PO	A	E	Avg.
1981— GC Yankees (GCL)	1B	29	81	6	12	2	0	0	9	.148	11	20	0	176	8	7	.963
1982— GC Yankees (GCL)	1B	62	217	38	59	11	1	•9	•41	.272	*48	63	6	514	*56	8	.986
1983— Florence (S.Atl.)■	1B	33	119	26	37	3	1	7	26	.311	20	35	3	250	14	6	.978
— Kinston (Caro.)	1B	94	350	53	85	14	1	21	57	.243	55	112	3	784	57	10	.988
1984— Knoxville (Sou.)	1B	56	189	29	47	13	2	9	25	.249	29	55	0	481	45	10	.981
— Syracuse (I.L.)	1B	70	238	28	56	10	1	13	28	.235	26	89	0	644	45	3	.996
1985— Syracuse (I.L.)	1B	51	176	19	40	8	2	5	20	.227	23	53	0	433	37	5	.989
1986— Syracuse (I.L.)	1B-OF	133	468	69	121	23	4	19	74	.259	83	119	0	†1219	†85	10	†.992
— Toronto (A.L.)	DH-1B	3	5	1	1	0	0	0	0	.200	0	2	0	3	0	0	1.000
1987— Toronto (A.L.)	DH-1B	107	295	58	73	16	0	20	43	.247	60	104	3	108	7	2	.983
1988— Toronto (A.L.)	1B	154	536	100	151	35	4	34	82	.282	79	149	6	1344	93	5	*.997
1989— Toronto (A.L.)	1B-DH	161	551	98	148	27	3	*36	92	.269	119	131	7	1460	115	*17	.989
1990— Toronto (A.L.)	1B-DH	153	557	91	167	21	1	35	88	.300	94	108	5	1246	126	6	.996
1991— San Diego (N.L.)■	1B	153	528	84	147	19	1	31	106	.278	105	135	4	1370	87	14	.990
1992— San Diego (N.L.)	1B	152	531	79	152	30	4	*35	104	.286	96	108	8	1219	108	•12	.991
1993— San Diego (N.L.)	1B	83	302	52	83	11	1	18	46	.275	42	55	4	640	47	12	.983
— Atlanta (N.L.)■	1B	68	255	59	79	18	1	19	55	.310	34	51	1	563	45	5	.992
1994— Atlanta (N.L.)	1B	113	424	81	135	25	1	34	94	.318	50	76	7	*1004	66	7	.994
1995— Atlanta (N.L.)	1B	•144	528	85	148	27	1	27	93	.280	65	99	3	1285	96	5	.996
1996— Atlanta (N.L.)	1B	159	617	81	182	37	1	28	107	.295	68	116	7	1416	124	12	.992
1997— Atlanta (N.L.)	1B	152	564	77	156	25	1	22	97	.277	68	112	5	1191	96	13	.990
1998— Tampa Bay (A.L.)■	1B-DH	151	564	73	160	33	0	19	81	.284	79	118	7	1150	81	6	.995
1999— Tampa Bay (A.L.)	1B-DH	144	529	75	164	30	1	32	104	.310	86	107	1	1037	88	13	.989
2000— Tampa Bay (A.L.)	1B-DH	158	566	82	157	18	0	27	106	.277	91	120	2	1300	82	10	.993
American League totals (8 years)		1031	3603	578	1021	180	9	203	596	.283	608	839	31	7648	592	59	.993
National League totals (7 years)		1024	3749	598	1082	192	11	214	702	.289	528	752	39	8688	669	80	.992
Major League totals (15 years)		2055	7352	1176	2103	372	20	417	1298	.286	1136	1591	70	16336	1261	139	.992

DIVISION SERIES RECORD

RECORDS: Holds N.L. single-game record for most runs batted in—5 (October 7, 1995). ... Shares single-game record for most home runs—2 (October 7, 1995).

						BATTING								FIELDING			
Year Team (League)	Pos.	G	AB	R	H	2B	3B	HR	RBI	Avg.	BB	SO	SB	PO	A	E	Avg.
1995—Atlanta (N.L.)	1B	4	18	4	6	0	0	2	6	.333	2	3	0	39	2	0	1.000
1996—Atlanta (N.L.)	1B	3	9	1	3	1	0	1	3	.333	2	1	0	25	3	0	1.000
1997—Atlanta (N.L.)	1B	3	9	4	2	0	0	0	1	.222	3	2	0	27	3	0	1.000
Division series totals (3 years)		10	36	9	11	1	0	3	10	.306	7	6	0	91	8	0	1.000

CHAMPIONSHIP SERIES RECORD

RECORDS: Shares N.L. single-game record for most at-bats—6 (October 14, 1996). ... Shares N.L. single-game record for most runs—4 (October 17, 1996). ... Shares career record for most doubles—7.

						BATTING								FIELDING			
Year Team (League)	Pos.	G	AB	R	H	2B	3B	HR	RBI	Avg.	BB	SO	SB	PO	A	E	Avg.
1989—Toronto (A.L.)	1B	5	21	1	3	0	0	0	3	.143	0	4	0	35	2	1	.974
1993—Atlanta (N.L.)	1B	6	23	6	10	2	0	1	4	.435	4	7	0	49	4	0	1.000
1995—Atlanta (N.L.)	1B	4	16	5	7	4	0	0	0	.438	3	0	0	42	4	0	1.000
1996—Atlanta (N.L.)	1B	7	28	6	7	0	1	2	7	.250	3	5	0	55	2	1	.983
1997—Atlanta (N.L.)	1B	6	21	0	7	1	0	0	4	.333	2	7	0	41	2	1	.977
Championship series totals (5 years)		28	109	18	34	7	1	3	18	.312	12	23	0	222	14	3	.987

WORLD SERIES RECORD

NOTES: Hit home run in first at-bat (October 21, 1995). ... Member of World Series championship team (1995).

M

Year	Team (League)	Pos.	G	AB	R	H	2B	3B	HR	RBI	Avg.	BB	SO	SB	PO	A	E	Avg.
								BATTING									FIELDING	
1995—Atlanta (N.L.).............	1B	6	23	5	6	2	0	2	3	.261	3	7	1	68	2	1	.986
1996—Atlanta (N.L.).............	1B	6	20	4	6	0	0	2	6	.300	6	4	0	62	5	0	1.000
World Series totals (2 years)		12	43	9	12	2	0	4	9	.279	9	11	1	130	7	1	.993

ALL-STAR GAME RECORD

NOTES: Named Most Valuable Player (1994).

Year	League	Pos.	AB	R	H	2B	3B	HR	RBI	Avg.	BB	SO	SB	PO	A	E	Avg.
						BATTING										FIELDING	
1992—National......................	1B	3	0	2	0	0	0	1	.667	0	0	0	7	1	0	1.000
1994—National......................	PH-1B	1	1	1	0	0	1	2	1.000	0	0	0	0	0	0	...
1995—National......................	1B	3	0	0	0	0	0	0	.000	0	2	0	5	0	0	1.000
1996—National......................	1B	2	0	0	0	0	0	0	.000	0	2	0	2	1	0	1.000
2000—American....................	1B	2	0	0	0	0	0	0	.000	0	1	0	5	0	0	1.000
All-Star Game totals (5 years)		11	1	3	0	0	1	3	.273	0	5	0	19	2	0	1.000

McGUIRE, RYAN — 1B — MARLINS

PERSONAL: Born November 23, 1971, in Bellflower, Calif. ... 6-0/215. ... Bats left, throws left. ... Full name: Ryan Byron McGuire.
HIGH SCHOOL: El Camino Real (Woodland Hills, Calif.).
COLLEGE: UCLA.
TRANSACTIONS/CAREER NOTES: Selected by Boston Red Sox organization in third round of free-agent draft (June 3, 1993). ... Traded by Red Sox with P Rheal Cormier and P Shayne Bennett to Montreal Expos for SS Wil Cordero and P Bryan Eversgerd (January 10, 1996). ... Granted free agency (November 19, 1999). ... Signed by New York Mets organization (December 13, 1999). ... Granted free agency (October 3, 2000). ... Signed by Florida Marlins organization (November 3, 2000).
STATISTICAL NOTES: Led Carolina League first basemen with 1,312 total chances in 1994.

Year	Team (League)	Pos.	G	AB	R	H	2B	3B	HR	RBI	Avg.	BB	SO	SB	PO	A	E	Avg.
								BATTING									FIELDING	
1993—Fort Laud. (FSL).........	1B	56	213	23	69	12	2	4	38	.324	27	34	2	513	61	5	.991
1994—Lynchburg (Caro.)......	1B	*137	489	70	133	29	0	10	73	.272	79	77	10	*1165	*129	18	.986
1995—Trenton (East.)...........	1B	109	414	59	138	29	1	7	59	.333	58	51	11	708	55	10	.987
1996—Ottawa (I.L.)■...........	1B-DH-OF	134	451	62	116	21	2	12	60	.257	59	80	11	987	73	8	.993
1997—Ottawa (I.L.)...............	1B	50	184	37	55	11	1	3	15	.299	36	29	5	421	52	2	.996
—Montreal (N.L.)...........	OF-1B-DH	84	199	22	51	15	2	3	17	.256	19	34	1	226	19	3	.988
1998—Montreal (N.L.)..........	1B-OF	130	210	17	39	9	0	1	10	.186	32	55	0	326	26	7	.981
1999—Ottawa (I.L.)...............	1B-OF-DH	53	183	23	46	6	1	4	27	.251	35	37	1	275	15	1	.997
—Montreal (N.L.)...........	1B-OF	88	140	17	31	7	2	2	18	.221	27	33	1	290	38	2	.994
2000—Norfolk (I.L.)■..........	OF-1B	122	392	63	117	23	1	10	62	.298	*87	84	6	394	26	1	.998
—New York (N.L.)..........	OF	1	2	0	0	0	0	0	0	.000	1	0	0	3	0	0	1.000
Major League totals (4 years)		303	551	56	121	31	4	6	45	.220	79	122	2	845	83	12	.987

McGWIRE, MARK — 1B — CARDINALS

PERSONAL: Born October 1, 1963, in Pomona, Calif. ... 6-5/250. ... Bats right, throws right. ... Full name: Mark David McGwire. ... Brother of Dan McGwire, quarterback with Seattle Seahawks (1991-94) and Miami Dolphins (1995).
HIGH SCHOOL: Damien (Claremont, Calif.).
COLLEGE: Southern California.
TRANSACTIONS/CAREER NOTES: Selected by Montreal Expos organization in eighth round of free-agent draft (June 8, 1981); did not sign. ... Selected by Oakland Athletics organization in first round (10th pick overall) of free-agent draft (June 4, 1984). ... On disabled list (April 11-26, 1989 and August 22-September 11, 1992). ... Granted free agency (October 26, 1992). ... Re-signed by A's (December 24, 1992). ... On disabled list (May 14-September 3, 1993; April 30-June 18 and July 27, 1994-remainder of season). ... On suspended list (September 4-8, 1993). ... On disabled list (July 18-August 2 and August 5-26, 1995). ... On disabled list (March 22-April 23, 1996). ... Traded by A's to St. Louis Cardinals for P T.J. Mathews, P Eric Ludwick and P Blake Stein (July 31, 1997). ... On disabled list (July 7-September 8, 2000).
RECORDS: Holds major league career record for most home runs by first baseman—537 (1986-2000). ... Holds major league single-season records for most home runs—70 (1998); and most home runs by first baseman—69 (1998). ... Holds major league records for most home runs in consecutive years—135 (1998-99); most consecutive seasons with 50 or more home runs—4 (1996-99); and fewest singles in season (150 or more games)—53 (1991). ... Holds major league rookie-season records for most home runs—49; and extra bases on long hits—183 (1987). ... Shares major league career record for most major league ballparks, one or more home runs (since 1900)—37. ... Shares major league single-season record for most games with three home runs—2 (1998). ... Shares major league single-inning recor for most home runs—2 (September 22, 1996, fifth inning). ... Shares major league records for most home runs in two consecutive games—5 (June 27 [3] and 28 [2], 1987 and June 10 [2] and 11 [3], 1995); and most home runs in one inning—2 (September 22, 1996, fifth inning); most seasons with 50 or more home runs—4; and most home runs in July—16 (1999). ... Shares modern major league record for most runs in two consecutive games—9 (June 27 and 28, 1987). ... Holds N.L. single-season record for most bases on balls—162 (1998). ... Holds N.L. record for most consecutive seasons with 50 or more home runs—2 (1998-99). ... Holds A.L. rookie-season record for highest slugging percentage—.618 (1987).
HONORS: Named College Player of the Year by THE SPORTING NEWS (1984). ... Named first baseman on THE SPORTING NEWS college All-America team (1984). ... Named A.L. Rookie Player of the Year by THE SPORTING NEWS (1987). ... Named A.L. Rookie of the Year by Baseball Writers' Association of America (1987). ... Won A.L. Gold Glove at first base (1990). ... Named first baseman on THE SPORTING NEWS A.L. All-Star team (1992 and 1996). ... Named first baseman on THE SPORTING NEWS A.L. Silver Slugger team (1992 and 1996). ... Named Sportsman of the Year by THE SPORTING NEWS (1997). ... Named first baseman on THE SPORTING NEWS N.L. All-Star team (1998). ... Named first baseman on THE SPORTING NEWS N.L. Silver Slugger team (1998). ... Named co-Sportsman of the Year by THE SPORTING NEWS (1998).
STATISTICAL NOTES: Led California League third basemen with 239 assists and 354 total chances in 1985. ... Hit three home runs in one game (June 27, 1987; June 11, 1995; April 14 and May 19, 1998; and May 18, 2000). ... Led A.L. in slugging percentage with .618 in 1987, .585 in 1992 and .730 in 1996. ... Led A.L. first basemen with 1,429 total chances in 1990. ... Led A.L. with .467 on-base percentage in 1996. ... Led major leagues with 58 home runs in 1997. ... Led N.L. with .752 slugging percentage and .470 on-base percentage in 1998. ... Led N.L. first basemen with 1,435 total chances in 1998. ... Led N.L. with 21 intentional bases on balls received in 1999. ... Career major league grand slams: 13.
MISCELLANEOUS: Holds Oakland Athletics franchise all-time records for most home runs (363) and runs batted in (941). ... Member of 1984 U.S. Olympic baseball team.

M

Year	Team (League)	Pos.	G	AB	R	H	2B	3B	HR	RBI	Avg.	BB	SO	SB	PO	A	E	Avg.
										BATTING					FIELDING			
1984—	Modesto (Calif.)	1B	16	55	7	11	3	0	1	1	.200	8	21	0	107	6	1	.991
1985—	Modesto (Calif.)	3B-1B	138	489	95	134	23	3	•24	•106	.274	96	108	1	105	†240	33	.913
1986—	Huntsville (Sou.)	3B	55	195	40	59	15	0	10	53	.303	46	45	3	34	124	16	.908
—	Tacoma (PCL)	3B	78	280	42	89	21	5	13	59	.318	42	67	1	53	126	25	.877
—	Oakland (A.L.)	3B	18	53	10	10	1	0	3	9	.189	4	18	0	10	20	6	.833
1987—	Oakland (A.L.)	1B-3B-OF	151	557	97	161	28	4	*49	118	.289	71	131	1	1176	101	13	.990
1988—	Oakland (A.L.)	1B-OF	155	550	87	143	22	1	32	99	.260	76	117	0	1228	88	9	.993
1989—	Oakland (A.L.)	1B-DH	143	490	74	113	17	0	33	95	.231	83	94	1	1170	114	6	.995
1990—	Oakland (A.L.)	1B-DH	156	523	87	123	16	0	39	108	.235	*110	116	2	*1329	95	5	.997
1991—	Oakland (A.L.)	1B	154	483	62	97	22	0	22	75	.201	93	116	2	1191	•101	4	.997
1992—	Oakland (A.L.)	1B	139	467	87	125	22	0	42	104	.268	90	105	0	1118	71	6	.995
1993—	Oakland (A.L.)	1B	27	84	16	28	6	0	9	24	.333	21	19	0	197	14	0	1.000
1994—	Oakland (A.L.)	1B-DH	47	135	26	34	3	0	9	25	.252	37	40	0	307	18	4	.988
1995—	Oakland (A.L.)	1B-DH	104	317	75	87	13	0	39	90	.274	88	77	1	775	64	*12	.986
1996—	Oakland (A.L.)	1B-DH	130	423	104	132	21	0	*52	113	.312	116	112	0	913	60	10	.990
1997—	Oakland (A.L.)	1B	105	366	48	104	24	0	34	81	.284	58	98	1	884	60	6	.994
—	St. Louis (N.L.)■	1B	51	174	38	44	3	0	§24	42	.253	43	61	2	438	34	1	.998
1998—	St. Louis (N.L.)..........	1B	155	509	130	152	21	0	*70	147	.299	*162	155	1	1326	97	12	.992
1999—	St. Louis (N.L.)..........	1B	153	521	118	145	21	1	*65	*147	.278	133	141	0	1180	80	13	.990
2000—	St. Louis (N.L.)..........	1B	89	236	60	72	8	0	32	73	.305	76	78	1	535	23	1	.998
American League totals (12 years)			1329	4448	773	1157	195	5	363	941	.260	847	1043	8	10298	806	81	.993
National League totals (4 years)			448	1440	346	413	53	1	191	409	.287	414	435	4	3479	234	27	.993
Major League totals (15 years)			1777	5888	1119	1570	248	6	554	1350	.267	1261	1478	12	13777	1040	108	.993

DIVISION SERIES RECORD

Year	Team (League)	Pos.	G	AB	R	H	2B	3B	HR	RBI	Avg.	BB	SO	SB	PO	A	E	Avg.
										BATTING					FIELDING			
2000—	St. Louis (N.L.)...........	PH	3	2	1	1	0	0	1	1	.500	1	0	0	...	...	...	...

CHAMPIONSHIP SERIES RECORD

Year	Team (League)	Pos.	G	AB	R	H	2B	3B	HR	RBI	Avg.	BB	SO	SB	PO	A	E	Avg.
										BATTING					FIELDING			
1988—	Oakland (A.L.)	1B	4	15	4	5	0	0	1	3	.333	1	5	0	24	2	0	1.000
1989—	Oakland (A.L.)	1B	5	18	3	7	1	0	1	3	.389	1	4	0	46	1	1	.979
1990—	Oakland (A.L.)	1B	4	13	2	2	0	0	2	2	.154	3	3	0	40	0	0	1.000
1992—	Oakland (A.L.)	1B	6	20	1	3	0	0	1	3	.150	5	4	0	46	2	1	.980
2000—	St. Louis (N.L.)..........	PH	3	2	0	0	0	0	0	0	.000	1	0	0	...	...	...	...
Championship series totals (5 years)			22	68	10	17	1	0	3	11	.250	11	16	0	156	5	2	.988

WORLD SERIES RECORD

NOTES: Member of World Series championship team (1989).

Year	Team (League)	Pos.	G	AB	R	H	2B	3B	HR	RBI	Avg.	BB	SO	SB	PO	A	E	Avg.
										BATTING					FIELDING			
1988—	Oakland (A.L.)	1B	5	17	1	1	0	0	1	1	.059	3	4	0	40	3	0	1.000
1989—	Oakland (A.L.)	1B	4	17	0	5	1	0	0	1	.294	1	3	0	28	2	0	1.000
1990—	Oakland (A.L.)	1B	4	14	1	3	0	0	0	0	.214	2	4	0	42	1	2	.956
World Series totals (3 years)			13	48	2	9	1	0	1	2	.188	6	11	0	110	6	2	.983

ALL-STAR GAME RECORD

NOTES: Named to A.L. All-Star team for 1991 game; replaced by Rafael Palmeiro due to injury.

Year	League	Pos.	AB	R	H	2B	3B	HR	RBI	Avg.	BB	SO	SB	PO	A	E	Avg.
										BATTING					FIELDING		
1987—	American	1B	3	0	0	0	0	0	0	.000	0	0	0	7	0	1	.875
1988—	American	1B	2	0	1	0	0	0	0	.500	0	1	0	8	0	0	1.000
1989—	American	1B	3	0	1	0	0	0	0	.333	0	0	0	5	0	0	1.000
1990—	American	1B	2	0	0	0	0	0	0	.000	0	2	0	7	0	0	1.000
1991—	American						Selected, did not play—injured.										
1992—	American	1B	3	1	1	0	0	0	2	.333	0	0	0	4	0	0	1.000
1995—	American						Selected, did not play—injured.										
1996—	American	1B	1	0	1	0	0	0	0	1.000	0	0	0	2	1	0	1.000
1997—	American	1B	2	0	0	0	0	0	0	.000	0	2	0	4	0	0	1.000
1998—	National	1B	2	1	0	0	0	0	0	.000	1	1	0	6	0	0	1.000
1999—	National	1B	2	0	0	0	0	0	0	.000	1	2	0	3	0	0	1.000
2000—	National						Selected, did not play—injured.										
All-Star Game totals (9 years)			20	2	4	0	0	0	2	.200	2	8	0	46	1	1	.979

McKNIGHT, TONY   P   ASTROS

PERSONAL: Born June 29, 1977, in Texarkana, Ark. ... 6-5/205. ... Throws right, bats right. ... Full name: Tony Mark McKnight.

HIGH SCHOOL: Arkansas (Texarkana, Ark.).

TRANSACTIONS/CAREER NOTES: Selected by Houston Astros organization in first round (22nd pick overall) of free-agent draft (June 1, 1995). ... On disabled list (June 19-July 15, 1996). ... On Jackson disabled list (July 20-August 2, 1999). ... On New Orleans disabled list (April 6-16, 2000).

STATISTICAL NOTES: Led Texas League pitchers with 18 putouts in 1999.

Year	League	W	L	Pct.	ERA	G	GS	CG	ShO	Sv.	IP	H	R	ER	BB	SO
1995—	Gulf Coast Astros (GCL).....	1	1	.500	3.86	3	3	0	0	0	11 2/3	14	5	5	2	8
1996—	Gulf Coast Astros (GCL).....	2	1	.667	6.23	8	5	0	0	0	21 2/3	28	21	15	7	15
1997—	Quad City (Midw.)	4	9	.308	4.68	20	20	0	0	0	115 1/3	116	71	60	55	92
1998—	Kissimmee (FSL)................	11	13	.458	4.67	28	•28	0	0	0	154 1/3	191	101	80	50	104
1999—	Jackson (Texas)	9	9	.500	2.75	24	24	0	0	0	160 1/3	134	60	49	44	118
2000—	Round Rock (Texas)..........	0	2	.000	4.78	6	6	0	0	0	32	39	19	17	10	24
—	New Orleans (PCL)............	4	8	.333	4.56	19	19	0	0	0	118 1/3	129	66	60	36	63
—	Houston (N.L.)	4	1	.800	3.86	6	6	1	0	0	35	35	19	15	9	23
Major League totals (1 year)........		4	1	.800	3.86	6	6	1	0	0	35	35	19	15	9	23

PERSONAL: Born October 4, 1964, in San Diego. ... 5-11/207. ... Bats both, throws right. ... Full name: Mark Tremell McLemore.
HIGH SCHOOL: Morse (San Diego).
TRANSACTIONS/CAREER NOTES: Selected by California Angels organization in ninth round of free-agent draft (June 7, 1982). ... On disabled list (May 15-27, 1985). ... On California disabled list (May 24-August 2, 1988); included rehabilitation assignments to Palm Springs (July 7-21) and Edmonton (July 22-27). ... On California disabled list (May 17-August 17, 1990); included rehabilitation assignments to Edmonton (May 24-June 6) and Palm Springs (August 9-13). ... Traded by Angels to Cleveland Indians (August 17, 1990), completing deal in which Indians traded C Ron Tingley to Angels for a player to be named later (September 6, 1989). ... Released by Indians (December 13, 1990). ... Signed by Houston Astros organization (March 6, 1991). ... On Houston disabled list (May 9-June 25, 1991); included rehabilitation assignments to Tucson (May 24-29) and Jackson (June 14-22). ... Released by Astros (June 25, 1991). ... Signed by Baltimore Orioles organization (July 5, 1991). ... Granted free agency (October 15, 1991). ... Re-signed by Orioles organization (February 5, 1992). ... Granted free agency (December 19, 1992). ... Re-signed by Orioles organization (January 6, 1993). ... Granted free agency (October 18, 1994). ... Signed by Texas Rangers (December 13, 1994). ... Granted free agency (December 7, 1996). ... Re-signed by Rangers (December 13, 1996). ... On Texas disabled list (May 15-June 12 and August 19-September 28, 1997); included rehabilitation assignments to Charlotte (June 7-8) and Oklahoma City (June 9-12). ... On disabled list (June 7-22, 1998). ... Granted free agency (October 29, 1999). ... Signed by Seattle Mariners (December 20, 1999). ... On suspended list (June 20-24, 2000).
STATISTICAL NOTES: Led California League second basemen with 400 assists and 84 double plays in 1984. ... Led Pacific Coast League second basemen with 597 total chances and 95 double plays in 1989. ... Led A.L. second basemen with 473 assists and 798 total chances in 1996. ... Led A.L. in caught stealing with 14 in 2000.

| | | | | | | | | | | BATTING | | | | | | FIELDING | | |
Year	Team (League)	Pos.	G	AB	R	H	2B	3B	HR	RBI	Avg.	BB	SO	SB	PO	A	E	Avg.
1982—	Salem (N'West)	2B-SS	55	165	42	49	6	2	0	25	.297	39	38	14	81	125	11	.949
1983—	Peoria (Midw.)	2B-SS	95	329	42	79	7	3	0	18	.240	53	64	15	170	250	24	.946
1984—	Redwood (Calif.)	2B-SS	134	482	102	142	8	3	0	45	.295	106	75	59	274	†429	25	.966
1985—	Midland (Texas)	2B-SS	117	458	80	124	17	6	2	46	.271	66	59	31	301	339	19	.971
1986—	Midland (Texas)	2B	63	237	54	75	9	1	1	29	.316	48	18	38	155	194	13	.964
	—Edmonton (PCL)	2B	73	286	41	79	13	1	0	23	.276	39	30	29	173	215	7	.982
	—California (A.L.)	2B	5	4	0	0	0	0	0	0	.000	1	2	0	3	10	0	1.000
1987—	California (A.L.)	2B-SS-DH	138	433	61	102	13	3	3	41	.236	48	72	25	293	363	17	.975
1988—	California (A.L.)	2B-3B-DH	77	233	38	56	11	2	2	16	.240	25	25	13	108	178	6	.979
	—Palm Springs (Calif.)	2B	11	44	9	15	3	1	0	6	.341	11	7	7	18	24	1	.977
	—Edmonton (PCL)	2B	12	45	7	12	3	0	0	6	.267	4	4	7	35	33	1	.986
1989—	Edmonton (PCL)	2B	114	430	60	105	13	2	2	34	.244	49	67	26	*264	323	10	*.983
	—California (A.L.)	2B-DH	32	103	12	25	3	1	0	14	.243	7	19	6	55	88	5	.966
1990—	California (A.L.)	2B	20	48	4	7	2	0	0	2	.146	4	9	1	14	15	0	1.000
	—Edmonton (PCL)	2B-SS	9	39	4	10	2	0	0	3	.256	6	10	0	24	32	4	.933
	—Palm Springs (Calif.)	2B	6	22	3	6	0	0	0	2	.273	3	7	0	20	22	0	1.000
	—Colo. Springs (PCL)■	2B-3B-SS	14	54	11	15	2	0	1	7	.278	11	8	5	23	40	2	.969
	—Cleveland (A.L.)	SS-3B-2B	8	12	2	2	0	0	0	0	.167	0	6	0	23	24	4	.922
1991—	Houston (N.L.)■	2B	21	61	6	9	1	0	0	2	.148	6	13	0	25	54	2	.975
	—Tucson (PCL)	2B	4	14	2	5	1	0	0	0	.357	2	1	0	8	6	0	1.000
	—Jackson (Texas)	2B	7	22	6	5	3	0	1	4	.227	6	3	1	27	24	0	1.000
	—Rochester (I.L.)■	2B	57	228	32	64	11	4	1	28	.281	27	29	12	134	166	5	.984
1992—	Baltimore (A.L.)	2B-DH	101	228	40	56	7	2	0	27	.246	21	26	11	126	186	7	.978
1993—	Baltimore (A.L.)	O-2-3-DH	148	581	81	165	27	5	4	72	.284	64	92	21	335	80	6	.986
1994—	Baltimore (A.L.)	2B-OF-DH	104	343	44	88	11	1	3	29	.257	51	50	20	219	269	9	.982
1995—	Texas (A.L.)■	OF-2B-DH	129	467	73	122	20	5	5	41	.261	59	71	21	248	184	4	.991
1996—	Texas (A.L.)	2B-OF	147	517	84	150	23	4	5	46	.290	87	69	27	313	†473	12	.985
1997—	Texas (A.L.)	2B-OF	89	349	47	91	17	2	1	25	.261	40	54	7	148	254	8	.980
	—Charlotte (FSL)	2B	2	7	1	4	1	0	0	3	.571	2	1	1	3	3	0	1.000
	—Oklahoma City (A.A.)	2B-DH	3	10	0	1	0	0	0	1	.100	1	1	1	2	3	0	1.000
1998—	Texas (A.L.)	2B-DH	126	461	79	114	15	1	5	53	.247	89	64	12	249	332	15	.975
1999—	Texas (A.L.)	2B-OF-DH	144	566	105	155	20	7	6	45	.274	83	79	16	276	433	12	.983
2000—	Seattle (A.L.)■	2B-OF	138	481	72	118	23	1	3	46	.245	81	78	30	286	346	8	.988
American League totals (14 years)			1406	4826	742	1251	192	34	37	457	.259	660	716	210	2696	3235	113	.981
National League totals (1 year)			21	61	6	9	1	0	0	2	.148	6	13	0	25	54	2	.975
Major League totals (15 years)			1427	4887	748	1260	193	34	37	459	.258	666	729	210	2721	3289	115	.931

DIVISION SERIES RECORD

| | | | | | | | | | | BATTING | | | | | | FIELDING | | |
Year	Team (League)	Pos.	G	AB	R	H	2B	3B	HR	RBI	Avg.	BB	SO	SB	PO	A	E	Avg.
1996—	Texas (A.L.)	2B	4	15	1	2	0	0	0	2	.133	0	4	0	10	16	0	1.000
1998—	Texas (A.L.)	2B	3	10	0	1	1	0	0	0	.100	2	3	0	4	12	0	1.000
1999—	Texas (A.L.)	2B	3	10	0	1	0	0	0	0	.100	1	3	0	2	9	0	1.000
2000—	Seattle (A.L.)	2B	3	9	1	1	0	0	0	0	.111	2	1	0	6	9	0	1.000
Division series totals (4 years)			13	44	2	5	1	0	0	2	.114	5	11	0	22	46	0	1.000

CHAMPIONSHIP SERIES RECORD

| | | | | | | | | | | BATTING | | | | | | FIELDING | | |
Year	Team (League)	Pos.	G	AB	R	H	2B	3B	HR	RBI	Avg.	BB	SO	SB	PO	A	E	Avg.
2000—	Seattle (A.L.)	2B	5	16	2	4	3	0	0	2	.250	2	1	0	6	18	2	.923

PERSONAL: Born December 1, 1966, in Knoxville, Tenn. ... 6-3/215. ... Throws right, bats right. ... Full name: Gregory Winston McMichael.
HIGH SCHOOL: Webb School of Knoxville (Knoxville, Tenn.).
COLLEGE: Tennessee.
TRANSACTIONS/CAREER NOTES: Selected by Cleveland Indians organization in seventh round of free-agent draft (June 1, 1988). ... Released by Indians (April 4, 1991). ... Signed by Atlanta Braves organization (April 16, 1991). ... Traded by Braves to New York Mets for P Paul Byrd

M

and a player to be named later (November 25, 1996); Braves acquired P Andy Zwirchitz to complete deal (May 25, 1997). ... Traded by Mets with P Dave Mlicki to Los Angeles Dodgers for P Hideo Nomo and P Brad Clontz (June 5, 1998). ... Traded by Dodgers with cash to Mets for P Brian Bohanon (July 10, 1998). ... On New York disabled list (March 21-June 11, 1999); included rehabilitation assignments to Binghamton (May 26-June 1) and Norfolk (June 2-11). ... Traded by Mets with P Jason Isringhausen to Oakland Athletics for P Billy Taylor (July 31, 1999). ... Granted free agency (November 3, 1999). ... Signed by Chicago Cubs organization (February 8, 2000). ... Released by Cubs (March 23, 2000). ... Signed by Braves organization (March 26, 2000). ... On disabled list (May 29, 2000-remainder of season). ... Granted free agency (November 6, 2000).

Year League	W	L	Pct.	ERA	G	GS	CG	ShO	Sv.	IP	H	R	ER	BB	SO
1988— Burlington (Appl.)	2	0	1.000	2.57	3	3	1	1	0	21	17	9	6	4	20
— Kinston (Caro.)	4	2	.667	2.68	11	11	2	0	0	77 1/3	57	31	23	18	35
1989— Canton/Akron (East.)	11	11	.500	3.49	26	•26	8	•5	0	170	164	81	66	64	101
1990— Canton/Akron (East.)	2	3	.400	3.35	13	4	0	0	0	40 1/3	39	17	15	17	19
— Colo. Springs (PCL)	2	3	.400	5.80	12	12	1	1	0	59	72	45	38	30	34
1991— Durham (Caro.)■	5	6	.455	3.62	36	6	0	0	2	79 2/3	83	34	32	29	82
1992— Greenville (Sou.)	4	2	.667	1.36	15	4	0	0	1	46 1/3	37	14	7	13	53
— Richmond (I.L.)	6	5	.545	4.38	19	13	0	0	2	90 1/3	89	52	44	34	86
1993— Atlanta (N.L.)	2	3	.400	2.06	74	0	0	0	19	91 2/3	68	22	21	29	89
1994— Atlanta (N.L.)	4	6	.400	3.84	51	0	0	0	21	58 2/3	66	29	25	19	47
1995— Atlanta (N.L.)	7	2	.778	2.79	67	0	0	0	2	80 2/3	64	27	25	32	74
1996— Atlanta (N.L.)	5	3	.625	3.22	73	0	0	0	2	86 2/3	84	37	31	27	78
1997— New York (N.L.)■	7	10	.412	2.98	73	0	0	0	7	87 1/3	73	34	29	27	81
1998— New York (N.L.)	5	3	.625	4.02	52	0	0	0	1	53 2/3	64	31	24	29	44
— Los Angeles (N.L.)■	0	1	.000	4.40	12	0	0	0	1	14 1/3	17	8	7	6	11
1999— Binghamton (East.)■	0	0	...	0.00	2	2	0	0	0	3	2	1	0	1	5
— Norfolk (I.L.)	0	0	...	2.70	3	1	0	0	0	3 1/3	4	1	1	3	4
— New York (N.L.)	1	1	.500	4.82	19	0	0	0	0	18 2/3	20	10	10	8	18
— Oakland (A.L.)■	0	0	...	5.40	17	0	0	0	0	15	15	9	9	12	3
2000— Atlanta (N.L.)■	0	0	...	4.41	15	0	0	0	0	16 1/3	12	8	8	4	14
A.L. totals (1 year)	0	0	...	5.40	17	0	0	0	0	15	15	9	9	12	3
N.L. totals (8 years)	31	29	.517	3.19	436	0	0	0	53	508 1/3	468	206	180	181	456
Major League totals (8 years)	31	29	.517	3.25	453	0	0	0	53	523 1/3	483	215	189	193	459

DIVISION SERIES RECORD

Year League	W	L	Pct.	ERA	G	GS	CG	ShO	Sv.	IP	H	R	ER	BB	SO
1995— Atlanta (N.L.)	0	0	...	6.75	2	0	0	0	0	1 1/3	1	1	1	2	1
1996— Atlanta (N.L.)	0	0	...	6.75	2	0	0	0	0	1 1/3	1	1	1	1	3
Division series totals (2 years)	0	0	...	6.75	4	0	0	0	0	2 2/3	2	2	2	3	4

CHAMPIONSHIP SERIES RECORD

Year League	W	L	Pct.	ERA	G	GS	CG	ShO	Sv.	IP	H	R	ER	BB	SO
1993— Atlanta (N.L.)	0	1	.000	6.75	4	0	0	0	0	4	7	3	3	2	1
1995— Atlanta (N.L.)	1	0	1.000	0.00	3	0	0	0	1	2 2/3	0	0	0	1	2
1996— Atlanta (N.L.)	0	1	.000	9.00	3	0	0	0	0	2	4	2	2	1	3
Champ. series totals (3 years)	1	2	.333	5.19	10	0	0	0	1	8 2/3	11	5	5	4	6

WORLD SERIES RECORD

NOTES: Member of World Series championship team (1995).

Year League	W	L	Pct.	ERA	G	GS	CG	ShO	Sv.	IP	H	R	ER	BB	SO
1995— Atlanta (N.L.)	0	0	...	2.70	3	0	0	0	0	3 1/3	3	2	1	2	2
1996— Atlanta (N.L.)	0	0	...	27.00	2	0	0	0	0	1	5	3	3	0	1
World Series totals (2 years)	0	0	...	8.31	5	0	0	0	0	4 1/3	8	5	4	2	3

McMILLON, BILLY   OF   TIGERS

M

PERSONAL: Born November 17, 1971, in Otero, N.M. ... 5-11/179. ... Bats left, throws left. ... Full name: William Edward McMillon.
HIGH SCHOOL: Bishopville (S.C.).
COLLEGE: Clemson.
TRANSACTIONS/CAREER NOTES: Selected by Florida Marlins organization in eighth round of free-agent draft (June 3, 1993). ... On Charlotte disabled list (April 20-29, 1997). ... Traded by Marlins to Philadelphia Phillies for OF/1B Darren Daulton (July 21, 1997). ... On Scranton/Wilkes-Barre disabled list (May 20-July 13, 1998). ... Granted free agency (December 21, 1998). ... Re-signed by Phillies organization (January 25, 1999). ... Granted free agency (October 15, 1999). ... Signed by Detroit Tigers organization (January 10, 2000).
STATISTICAL NOTES: Tied for New York-Pennsylvania League lead with four intentional bases on balls received in 1993. ... Tied for Midwest League lead with nine sacrifice flies in 1994. ... Led Eastern League with .423 on-base percentage in 1995. ... Led International League with .418 on-base percentage in 1996. ... Led International League with 10 sacrifice flies in 1999. ... Led International League with .446 on-base percentage in 2000. ... Career major league grand slams: 2.

Year Team (League)	Pos.	G	AB	R	H	2B	3B	HR	RBI	Avg.	BB	SO	SB	PO	A	E	Avg.
1993— Elmira (NY-Penn)	OF	57	226	38	69	14	2	6	35	.305	31	43	5	66	1	5	.931
1994— Kane County (Midw.)	OF	•137	496	88	125	25	3	17	*101	.252	*84	99	7	187	9	7	.966
1995— Portland (East.)	OF	*141	518	92	*162	29	3	14	93	.313	*96	90	15	207	14	4	.982
1996— Charlotte (I.L.)	OF-DH	97	347	72	122	32	2	17	70	*.352	36	76	5	135	10	4	.973
— Florida (N.L.)	OF	28	51	4	11	0	0	0	4	.216	5	14	0	17	0	0	1.000
1997— Charlotte (I.L.)	OF	57	204	34	57	18	0	8	26	.279	32	51	8	84	5	2	.978
— Florida (N.L.)	OF	13	18	0	2	1	0	0	1	.111	0	7	0	4	0	0	1.000
— Scranton/W.B. (I.L.)■	OF	26	92	18	27	8	1	4	21	.293	12	24	2	49	3	0	1.000
— Philadelphia (N.L.)	OF	24	72	10	21	4	1	2	13	.292	6	17	2	42	2	2	.957
1998— Scranton/W.B. (I.L.)	OF-DH	77	267	42	69	16	1	13	38	.258	34	59	6	133	9	2	.986
1999— Scranton/W.B. (I.L.)	OF-DH	132	464	97	141	38	4	16	85	.304	65	79	11	219	11	5	.979
2000— Toledo (I.L.)■	OF	105	380	61	131	30	1	13	50	.345	71	65	3	208	7	6	.973
— Detroit (A.L.)	DH-OF	46	123	20	37	7	1	4	24	.301	19	19	1	27	0	1	.964
American League totals (1 year)		46	123	20	37	7	1	4	24	.301	19	19	1	27	0	1	.964
National League totals (2 years)		65	141	14	34	5	1	2	18	.241	11	38	2	63	2	2	.970
Major League totals (3 years)		111	264	34	71	12	2	6	42	.269	30	57	3	90	2	3	.968

McNEAL, AARON — 1B — ASTROS

PERSONAL: Born April 28, 1978, in Oakland. ... 6-3/230. ... Bats right, throws right. ... Full name: Aaron G. McNeal.
HIGH SCHOOL: Castro Valley (Calif.).
JUNIOR COLLEGE: Chabot College (Calif.).
TRANSACTIONS/CAREER NOTES: Selected by Houston Astros organization in 27th round of free-agent draft (June 1, 1995). ... On Round Rock disabled list (July 25-August 5 and August 28-September 19, 2000).
HONORS: Named Midwest League Most Valuable Player (1999).
STATISTICAL NOTES: Led Gulf Coast League first basemen with 423 total chances in 1996. ... Led Midwest League with 315 total bases in 1999. ... Led Midwest League first basemen with 1,141 total chances in 1999.

Year Team (League)	Pos.	G	AB	R	H	2B	3B	HR	RBI	Avg.	BB	SO	SB	PO	A	E	Avg.
1996— GC Astros (GCL)	1B	55	200	22	50	10	2	2	31	.250	13	52	0	381	*35	7	.983
1997— Auburn (NY-Penn)......	1B	12	40	5	10	3	0	0	3	.250	4	10	1	88	8	2	.980
— GC Astros (GCL).......	1B	46	164	22	48	12	0	3	26	.293	11	28	0	279	16	5	.983
1998— Quad City (Midw.)	1B	112	370	54	105	15	1	14	61	.284	31	112	3	850	69	11	.988
1999— Michigan (Midw.)	1B	133	*536	95	*166	29	3	*38	*131	.310	40	121	7	1013	*111	17	.985
2000— Round Rock (Texas)...	1B	97	361	40	112	20	2	11	69	.310	24	91	0	733	61	9	.989

MEACHAM, RUSTY — P

PERSONAL: Born January 27, 1968, in Stuart, Fla. ... 6-2/175. ... Throws right, bats right. ... Full name: Russell Loren Meacham.
JUNIOR COLLEGE: Indian River Community College (Fla.).
TRANSACTIONS/CAREER NOTES: Selected by Detroit Tigers organization in 33rd round of free-agent draft (June 2, 1987). ... Claimed on waivers by Kansas City Royals (October 23, 1991). ... On Kansas City disabled list (May 1-June 4, 1993); included rehabilitation assignment to Omaha (May 18-June 4). ... On Kansas City disabled list (June 15, 1993-remainder of season). ... Traded by Royals to Seattle Mariners for IF Jose Amado (June 21, 1996). ... Released by Mariners (March 28, 1997). ... Signed by Boston Red Sox organization (May 8, 1997). ... Granted free agency (October 15, 1997). ... Signed by St. Louis Cardinals organization (December 18, 1997). ... Released by Cardinals (July 14, 1998). ... Signed by Pittsburgh Pirates organization (July 25, 1998). ... Granted free agency (October 15, 1998). ... Signed by Cincinnati Reds organization (February 2, 1999). ... On Indianapolis disabled list (April 8-18, 1999). ... Released by Reds (June 4, 1999). ... Signed by Houston Astros organization (June 26, 1999). ... On New Orleans disabled list (June 22-July 18, 2000). ... Granted free agency (October 14, 2000).

Year League	W	L	Pct.	ERA	G	GS	CG	ShO	Sv.	IP	H	R	ER	BB	SO
1988— Fayetteville (S.Atl.)	0	3	.000	6.20	6	5	0	0	0	$24\frac{2}{3}$	37	19	17	6	16
— Bristol (Appl.)..................	•9	1	•.900	*1.43	13	9	2	•2	0	$75\frac{1}{3}$	55	14	12	22	85
1989— Fayetteville (S.Atl.)	10	3	.769	2.29	16	15	2	0	0	102	103	33	26	23	114
— Lakeland (FSL).................	5	4	.556	1.95	11	9	4	2	0	$64\frac{2}{3}$	59	15	14	12	39
1990— London (East.)	*15	9	.625	3.13	26	26	•9	•3	0	178	161	70	62	36	123
1991— Toledo (I.L.).....................	9	7	.563	3.09	26	17	3	1	2	$125\frac{1}{3}$	117	53	43	40	70
— Detroit (A.L.)...................	2	1	.667	5.20	10	4	0	0	0	$27\frac{2}{3}$	35	17	16	11	14
1992— Kansas City (A.L.)■..........	10	4	.714	2.74	64	0	0	0	2	$101\frac{2}{3}$	88	39	31	21	64
1993— Kansas City (A.L.)	2	2	.500	5.57	15	0	0	0	0	21	31	15	13	5	13
— Omaha (A.A.)....................	0	0	...	4.82	7	0	0	0	0	$9\frac{1}{3}$	10	5	5	1	10
1994— Omaha (A.A.)....................	1	1	.500	7.00	8	0	0	0	1	9	9	7	7	3	16
— Kansas City (A.L.)............	3	3	.500	3.73	36	0	0	0	4	$50\frac{2}{3}$	51	23	21	12	36
1995— Kansas City (A.L.)	4	3	.571	4.98	49	0	0	0	2	$59\frac{2}{3}$	72	36	33	19	30
1996— Omaha (A.A.)....................	3	3	.500	4.82	23	4	0	0	2	$52\frac{1}{3}$	56	30	28	18	39
— Seattle (A.L.)■.................	1	1	.500	5.74	15	5	0	0	1	$42\frac{1}{3}$	57	28	27	13	25
— Tacoma (PCL)...................	2	1	.667	2.29	7	2	0	0	2	$19\frac{2}{3}$	13	7	5	5	20
1997— Pawtucket (I.L.)...............	3	3	.500	4.78	28	2	0	0	1	$43\frac{1}{3}$	54	23	23	15	42
1998— Memphis (PCL)■..............	1	2	.333	5.16	38	0	0	0	2	$52\frac{1}{3}$	68	30	30	15	56
— Nashville (PCL)■.............	2	1	.667	3.34	15	2	0	0	3	$29\frac{2}{3}$	35	14	11	8	25
1999— Indianapolis (I.L.)...........	1	3	.250	6.98	16	1	0	0	1	$29\frac{2}{3}$	38	27	23	15	19
— New Orleans (PCL)■...........	3	4	.429	4.94	17	5	0	0	1	$47\frac{1}{3}$	56	26	26	9	47
2000— New Orleans (PCL)...........	4	3	.571	2.20	33	4	0	0	0	$57\frac{1}{3}$	43	16	14	14	56
— Houston (N.L.).................	0	0	...	11.57	5	0	0	0	0	$4\frac{2}{3}$	8	6	6	2	3
A.L. totals (6 years)	22	14	.611	4.19	189	9	0	0	9	303	334	158	141	81	182
N.L. totals (1 year).........................	0	0	...	11.57	5	0	0	0	0	$4\frac{2}{3}$	8	6	6	2	3
Major League totals (7 years)	22	14	.611	4.30	194	9	0	0	9	$307\frac{2}{3}$	342	164	147	83	185

MEADOWS, BRIAN — P — ROYALS

PERSONAL: Born November 21, 1975, in Montgomery, Ala. ... 6-4/220. ... Throws right, bats right. ... Full name: Matthew Brian Meadows.
HIGH SCHOOL: Charles Henderson (Troy, Ala.).
TRANSACTIONS/CAREER NOTES: Selected by Florida Marlins organization in third round of free-agent draft (June 2, 1994); pick received as compensation for Colorado Rockies signing Type B free-agent SS Walt Weiss. ... On disabled list (July 28-August 13, 1998). ... Traded by Marlins to San Diego Padres for P Dan Miceli (November 15, 1999). ... Traded by Padres to Kansas City Royals for P Jay Witasick (July 31, 2000).
RECORDS: Shares major league single-inning record for most putouts by pitcher—3 (June 2, 1998, second inning).

Year League	W	L	Pct.	ERA	G	GS	CG	ShO	Sv.	IP	H	R	ER	BB	SO
1994— Gulf Coast Marlins (GCL) ...	3	0	1.000	1.95	8	7	0	0	0	37	34	9	8	6	33
1995— Kane County (Midw.).........	9	9	.500	4.22	26	26	1	1	0	147	163	90	69	41	103
1996— Portland (East.)	0	1	.000	4.33	4	4	0	0	0	27	26	15	13	4	13
— Brevard County (FSL)........	8	7	.533	3.58	24	23	3	1	0	146	129	73	58	25	69
1997— Portland (East.)	9	7	.563	4.61	29	*29	4	0	0	$175\frac{1}{3}$	204	99	90	48	115
1998— Florida (N.L.)....................	11	13	.458	5.21	31	31	1	0	0	$174\frac{1}{3}$	222	106	101	46	88
1999— Florida (N.L.)...................	11	15	.423	5.60	31	31	0	0	0	$178\frac{1}{3}$	214	117	111	57	72
2000— San Diego (N.L.)■...........	7	8	.467	5.34	22	22	0	0	0	$124\frac{2}{3}$	150	80	74	50	53
— Kansas City (A.L.)■.........	6	2	.750	4.77	11	10	2	0	0	$71\frac{2}{3}$	84	39	38	14	26
A.L. totals (1 year)	6	2	.750	4.77	11	10	2	0	0	$71\frac{2}{3}$	84	39	38	14	26
N.L. totals (3 years)	29	36	.446	5.39	84	84	1	0	0	$477\frac{1}{3}$	586	303	286	153	213
Major League totals (3 years) ...	35	38	.479	5.31	95	94	3	0	0	549	670	342	324	167	239

M

MEARES, PAT · SS · PIRATES

PERSONAL: Born September 6, 1968, in Salina, Kan. ... 6-0/187. ... Bats right, throws right. ... Full name: Patrick James Meares.
HIGH SCHOOL: Sacred Heart (Salina, Kan.).
COLLEGE: Wichita State.
TRANSACTIONS/CAREER NOTES: Selected by Minnesota Twins organization in 15th round of free-agent draft (June 4, 1990). ... On disabled list (June 22-July 7, 1994 and August 11-26, 1997). ... Granted free agency (December 21, 1998). ... Signed by Pittsburgh Pirates (February 20, 1999). ... On Pittsburgh disabled list (April 2-23 and May 12-September 21, 1999); included rehabilitation assignment to Nashville (August 26-September 3).
RECORDS: Holds major league single-season record for fewest assists by shortstop (150 or more games)—344 (1996).
STATISTICAL NOTES: Career major league grand slams: 1.

										BATTING					FIELDING			
Year	Team (League)	Pos.	G	AB	R	H	2B	3B	HR	RBI	Avg.	BB	SO	SB	PO	A	E	Avg.
1990—	Kenosha (Midw.)	3B-2B	52	197	26	47	10	2	4	22	.239	25	45	2	35	94	16	.890
1991—	Visalia (Calif.)	2B-3B-OF	89	360	53	109	21	4	6	44	.303	24	63	15	155	224	26	.936
1992—	Orlando (Sou.)	SS	81	300	42	76	19	0	3	23	.253	11	57	5	91	190	35	.889
1993—	Portland (PCL)	SS	18	54	6	16	5	0	0	3	.296	3	11	0	28	48	5	.938
	— Minnesota (A.L.)	SS	111	346	33	87	14	3	0	33	.251	7	52	4	165	304	19	.961
1994—	Minnesota (A.L.)	SS	80	229	29	61	12	1	2	24	.266	14	50	5	133	209	13	.963
1995—	Minnesota (A.L.)	SS-OF	116	390	57	105	19	4	12	49	.269	15	68	10	187	317	•18	.966
1996—	Minnesota (A.L.)	SS-OF	152	517	66	138	26	7	8	67	.267	17	90	9	257	344	22	.965
1997—	Minnesota (A.L.)	SS	134	439	63	121	23	3	10	60	.276	18	86	7	211	415	20	.969
1998—	Minnesota (A.L.)	SS	149	543	56	141	26	3	9	70	.260	24	86	7	263	412	24	.966
1999—	Pittsburgh (N.L.)■	SS	21	91	15	28	4	0	0	7	.308	9	20	0	26	67	6	.939
	— Nashville (PCL)	SS	5	18	3	3	0	0	0	0	.167	1	3	1	2	6	2	.800
2000—	Minnesota (A.L.)	SS	132	462	55	111	22	2	13	47	.240	36	91	1	191	401	20	.967
American League totals (6 years)			742	2464	304	653	120	21	41	303	.265	95	432	42	1216	2001	116	.965
National League totals (2 years)			153	553	70	139	26	2	13	54	.251	45	111	1	217	468	26	.963
Major League totals (8 years)			895	3017	374	792	146	23	54	357	.263	140	543	43	1433	2469	142	.965

MEARS, CHRIS · P · MARINERS

PERSONAL: Born January 20, 1978, in Ottawa, Ont. ... 6-4/180. ... Throws right, bats right. ... Full name: Christopher Peter Mears.
HIGH SCHOOL: Lord Bing (Vancouver, B.C.).
TRANSACTIONS/CAREER NOTES: Selected by Seattle Mariners organization in fifth round of free agent draft (June 4, 1996). ... On Lancaster disabled list (August 20-29, 1999).

Year	League	W	L	Pct.	ERA	G	GS	CG	ShO	Sv.	IP	H	R	ER	BB	SO
1996—	Arizona Mariners (Ariz.)	1	2	.333	3.60	6	5	0	0	0	25	23	11	10	5	27
1997—	Everett (N'West)	3	5	.375	5.34	12	12	0	0	0	62 1/3	82	47	37	20	47
1998—	Orlando (Sou.)	0	1	.000	9.64	1	1	0	0	0	4 2/3	8	5	5	2	4
	— Everett (N'West)	•9	1	*.900	2.74	15	15	•1	0	0	*98 2/3	86	39	30	33	67
1999—	Wisconsin (Midw.)	10	1	*.909	2.43	13	13	2	1	0	89	76	33	24	16	78
	— Lancaster (Calif.)	3	6	.333	7.08	10	10	0	0	0	54 2/3	71	44	43	18	45

MECHE, GIL · P · MARINERS

PERSONAL: Born September 8, 1978, in Lafayette, La. ... 6-3/200. ... Throws right, bats right. ... Full name: Gilbert Allen Meche.
HIGH SCHOOL: Acadiana (Lafayette, La.).
TRANSACTIONS/CAREER NOTES: Selected by Seattle Mariners organization in first round (22nd pick overall) of free-agent draft (June 4, 1996). ... On Seattle disabled list (May 29-June 13 and July 31, 2000-remainder of season); included rehabilitation assignments to Tacoma (June 7-13), Wisconsin (August 22-27) and Everett (August 27-28).
STATISTICAL NOTES: Pitched 7-0 one-hit, complete-game victory against Kansas City (June 13, 2000).

Year	League	W	L	Pct.	ERA	G	GS	CG	ShO	Sv.	IP	H	R	ER	BB	SO
1996—	Arizona Mariners (Ariz.)	0	1	.000	6.00	2	0	0	0	0	3	4	2	2	1	4
1997—	Everett (N'West)	3	4	.429	3.98	12	12	1	0	0	74 2/3	75	40	33	24	62
	— Wisconsin (Midw.)	0	2	.000	3.00	2	2	0	0	0	12	12	5	4	4	14
1998—	Wisconsin (Midw.)	8	7	.533	3.44	26	0	0	0	0	149	136	77	57	63	168
1999—	New Haven (East.)	3	4	.429	3.05	10	10	0	0	0	59	51	24	20	26	56
	— Tacoma (PCL)	2	4	.500	3.19	6	6	0	0	0	31	31	12	11	13	24
	— Seattle (A.L.)	8	4	.667	4.73	16	15	0	0	0	85 2/3	73	48	45	57	47
2000—	Seattle (A.L.)	4	4	.500	3.78	15	15	1	1	0	85 2/3	75	37	36	40	60
	— Tacoma (PCL)	1	1	.500	3.86	3	3	0	0	0	14	10	7	6	10	15
	— Wisconsin (Midw.)	0	0	...	0.00	1	1	0	0	0	5	1	0	0	2	6
	— Everett (N'West)	0	1	.000	9.00	1	1	0	0	0	1	3	1	1	0	0
Major League totals (2 years)		12	8	.600	4.25	31	30	1	1	0	171 1/3	148	85	81	97	107

MECIR, JIM · P · ATHLETICS

PERSONAL: Born May 16, 1970, in Queens, N.Y. ... 6-1/210. ... Throws right, bats both. ... Full name: James Jason Mecir. ... Name pronounced ma-SEER.
HIGH SCHOOL: Smithtown East (St. James, N.Y.).
COLLEGE: Eckerd (Fla.).
TRANSACTIONS/CAREER NOTES: Selected by Seattle Mariners organization in third round of free-agent draft (June 3, 1991). ... On disabled list (June 25-August 25, 1992). ... Traded by Mariners with 1B Tino Martinez and P Jeff Nelson to New York Yankees for P Sterling Hitchcock and 3B Russ Davis (December 7, 1995). ... Traded by Yankees to Boston Red Sox (September 29, 1997), completing deal in which Yankees traded P Tony Armas Jr. and a player to be named later to Red Sox for C Mike Stanley and IF Randy Brown (August 13, 1997). ... Selected by

Tampa Bay Devil Rays in second round (36th pick overall) of expansion draft (November 18, 1997). ... On disabled list (May 12, 1999-remainder of season). ... On Tampa Bay disabled list (April 27-May 23, 2000). ... Traded by Devil Rays with P Todd Belitz to Oakland Athletics for P Jesus Colome and a player to be named later (July 28, 2000).

STATISTICAL NOTES: Led California League with 15 hit batsmen in 1993.

Year League	W	L	Pct.	ERA	G	GS	CG	ShO	Sv.	IP	H	R	ER	BB	SO
1991— San Bernardino (Calif.).......	3	5	.375	4.22	14	12	0	0	1	70 1/3	72	40	33	37	48
1992— San Bernardino (Calif.).......	4	5	.444	4.67	14	11	0	0	0	61 2/3	72	40	32	26	53
1993— Riverside (Calif.)................	9	11	.450	4.33	26	26	1	0	0	145 1/3	160	89	70	58	85
1994— Jacksonville (Sou.).............	6	5	.545	2.69	46	0	0	0	13	80 1/3	73	28	24	35	53
1995— Tacoma (PCL)	1	4	.200	3.10	40	0	0	0	8	69 2/3	63	29	24	28	46
— Seattle (A.L.)	0	0	...	0.00	2	0	0	0	0	4 2/3	5	1	0	2	3
1996— Columbus (I.L.)■..............	3	3	.500	2.27	33	0	0	0	7	47 2/3	37	14	12	15	52
— New York (A.L.).................	1	1	.500	5.13	26	0	0	0	0	40 1/3	42	24	23	23	38
1997— Columbus (I.L.)	1	1	.500	1.00	24	0	0	0	11	27	14	4	3	6	34
— New York (A.L.).................	0	4	.000	5.88	25	0	0	0	0	33 2/3	36	23	22	10	25
1998— Tampa Bay (A.L.)■............	7	2	.778	3.11	68	0	0	0	0	84	68	30	29	33	77
1999— Tampa Bay (A.L.)...............	0	1	.000	2.61	17	0	0	0	0	20 2/3	15	7	6	14	15
2000— Tampa Bay (A.L.)...............	7	2	.778	3.08	38	0	0	0	1	49 2/3	35	17	17	22	33
— Oakland (A.L.)■	3	1	.750	2.80	25	0	0	0	4	35 1/3	35	14	11	14	37
Major League totals (6 years)......	18	11	.621	3.62	201	0	0	0	5	268 1/3	236	116	108	118	228

DIVISION SERIES RECORD

Year League	W	L	Pct.	ERA	G	GS	CG	ShO	Sv.	IP	H	R	ER	BB	SO
2000— Oakland (A.L.)	0	0	...	0.00	3	0	0	0	0	5 1/3	1	0	0	0	2

MELIAN, JACKSON   OF   REDS

PERSONAL: Born January 7, 1980, in Barcelona, Venezuela. ... 6-2/190. ... Bats right, throws right.

TRANSACTIONS/CAREER NOTES: Signed as non-drafted free agent by New York Yankees organization (July 2, 1996). ... Traded by Yankees with 3B Drew Henson, P Brian Reith and P Ed Yarnall to Cincinnati Reds for P Denny Neagle and OF Mike Frank (July 12, 2000).

STATISTICAL NOTES: Led Gulf Coast League outfielders with 120 total chances in 1997.

Year Team (League)	Pos.	G	AB	R	H	2B	3B	HR	RBI	Avg.	BB	SO	SB	PO	A	E	Avg.
1997— GC Yankees (GCL)......	OF	57	213	32	56	11	2	3	36	.263	20	52	9	*110	7	3	.975
1998— Greensboro (S.Atl.)	OF	135	467	66	119	18	2	8	45	.255	41	120	15	201	13	8	.964
1999— Tampa (FSL)............	OF	128	467	65	132	17	13	6	61	.283	49	98	11	268	7	10	.965
2000— Norwich (East.)	OF	81	290	34	73	8	4	9	38	.252	18	69	17	181	4	9	.954
— Chattanooga (Sou.)■.	OF	2	6	0	1	0	0	0	0	.167	0	0	0	2	0	1	.667

MELO, JUAN   SS   GIANTS

PERSONAL: Born May 11, 1976, in Bani, Dominican Republic. ... 6-1/160. ... Bats both, throws right. ... Full name: Juan Esteban Melo.

HIGH SCHOOL: Colegio Redentol (Bani, Dominican Republic).

TRANSACTIONS/CAREER NOTES: Signed as non-drafted free agent San Diego Padres organization (June 15, 1993). ... On suspended list (July 9-13, 1996). ... On Las Vegas disabled list (April 18-May 26, 1999). ... Traded by Padres to Toronto Blue Jays for P Isabel Giron (July 8, 1999). ... Traded by Blue Jays to Cincinnati Reds for a player to be named later (September 3, 1999); Blue Jays acquired 2B Jaime Goudie to complete trade (September 13, 1999). ... Released by Reds (December 10, 1999). ... Signed by New York Yankees organization (January 14, 2000). ... Traded by Yankees to San Francisco Giants for SS/2B Wilson Delgado (March 23, 2000).

STATISTICAL NOTES: Tied for Midwest League lead in double plays by shortstop with 70 in 1995. ... Led California League shortstops with 613 total chances and 92 double plays in 1996.

Year Team (League)	Pos.	G	AB	R	H	2B	3B	HR	RBI	Avg.	BB	SO	SB	PO	A	E	Avg.
1994— Ariz. Padres (Ariz.)	SS	37	145	20	41	3	3	0	15	.283	10	36	3	46	117	13	.926
— Spokane (N'West)	SS	3	11	4	4	1	0	1	2	.364	1	3	0	2	11	2	.867
1995— Clinton (Midw.)	SS	134	479	65	135	32	1	5	46	.282	33	88	12	183	372	47	.922
1996— Rancho Cuca. (Calif.) .	SS	128	503	75	153	27	6	8	75	.304	22	102	6	*209	*378	26	.958
1997— Mobile (Sou.)	SS	113	456	52	131	22	2	7	67	.287	29	90	7	182	307	28	.946
— Las Vegas (PCL)	SS	12	48	6	13	4	0	1	6	.271	1	10	0	11	33	3	.936
1998— Las Vegas (PCL)	SS	130	467	61	127	26	1	6	47	.272	24	91	9	214	360	21	.965
1999— Las Vegas (PCL)	SS-3B	45	169	17	34	3	2	2	13	.201	7	34	1	70	108	8	.957
— Syracuse (I.L.)■	SS-2B	41	141	21	33	9	1	3	13	.234	10	31	8	72	110	6	.968
— Indianapolis (I.L.)■....	SS	3	9	2	3	0	0	1	3	.333	0	2	1	5	7	0	1.000
2000— Fresno (PCL)■............	SS-2B	123	417	58	123	26	6	12	50	.295	35	89	13	217	315	14	.974
— San Francisco (N.L.) ..	2B	11	13	0	1	0	0	0	1	.077	0	5	0	3	4	0	1.000
Major League totals (1 year)		11	13	0	1	0	0	0	1	.077	0	5	0	3	4	0	1.000

MELUSKEY, MITCH   C   TIGERS

PERSONAL: Born September 18, 1973, in Yakima, Wash. ... 6-0/185. ... Bats both, throws right. ... Full name: Mitchell Wade Meluskey.

HIGH SCHOOL: Eisenhower (Yakima, Wash.).

TRANSACTIONS/CAREER NOTES: Selected by Cleveland Indians organization in 12th round of free-agent draft (June 1, 1992). ... Traded by Indians to Houston Astros for OF Buck McNabb (April 27, 1995). ... On disabled list (April 26, 1999-remainder of season; and July 31-August 18, 2000). ... Traded by Astros with P Chris Holt and OF Roger Cedeno to Detroit Tigers for C Brad Ausmus, P Doug Brocail and P Nelson Cruz (December 11, 2000).

STATISTICAL NOTES: Led South Atlantic catchers with nine double plays in 1993. ... Tied for Texas League lead with four intentional bases on balls in 1997. ... Led Pacific Coast League with 10 intentional bases on balls received in 1998.

Year	Team (League)	Pos.	G	AB	R	H	2B	3B	HR	RBI	Avg.	BB	SO	SB	PO	A	E	Avg.
1992—Burlington (Appl.).......	C	43	126	23	29	7	0	3	16	.230	29	36	3	227	29	4	.985
1993—Columbus (S.Atl.).......	C	101	342	36	84	18	3	3	47	.246	35	69	1	639	87	7	.990
1995—Kinston (Caro.)...........	C	8	29	5	7	5	0	0	2	.241	2	9	0	58	6	1	.985
—Kissimmee (FSL)■.....	C	78	261	23	56	18	1	3	31	.215	27	33	3	443	40	10	.980
1996—Kissimmee (FSL)........	C	74	231	29	77	19	0	1	31	.333	29	26	1	315	27	9	.974
—Jackson (Texas)	C	38	134	18	42	11	0	0	21	.313	18	24	0	207	18	5	.978
1997—Jackson (Texas)	C	73	241	49	82	18	0	14	46	.340	31	39	1	356	43	6	.985
—New Orleans (A.A.).....	C	51	172	22	43	7	0	3	21	.250	25	38	0	323	26	4	.989
1998—New Orleans (PCL)........	C-OF	121	397	76	140	41	0	17	71	.353	85	59	2	702	49	10	.987
—Houston (N.L.)	C	8	8	1	2	1	0	0	0	.250	1	4	0	9	0	1	1.000
1999—Houston (N.L.)	C	10	33	4	7	1	0	1	3	.212	5	6	1	62	6	0	1.000
2000—Houston (N.L.)	C-3B	117	337	47	101	21	0	14	69	.300	55	74	1	623	31	13	.981
Major League totals (3 years)		135	378	52	110	23	0	15	72	.291	61	84	2	694	37	13	.983

MENDOZA, CARLOS   OF

PERSONAL: Born November 14, 1974, in Ciudad Bolivar, Venezuela ... 6-0/165. ... Bats left, throws left. ... Full name: Carlos Ramon Mendoza.
HIGH SCHOOL: Agosto Mendez (Bolivar, Venezuela).
TRANSACTIONS/CAREER NOTES: Signed as non-drafted free agent by New York Mets organization (November 10, 1992). ... On disabled list (May 27-June 9, 1996). ... On Binghamton disabled list (April 17-June 22, 1997). ... Selected by Tampa Bay Devil Rays in second round (52nd pick overall) of expansion draft (November 18, 1997). ... On Durham disabled list (April 9-22 and June 24-July 26, 1998; and July 13-28 and August 11, 1999-remainder of season). ... Granted free agency (October 15, 1999). ... Signed by Mets organization (December 15, 1999). ... Traded by Mets to Colorado Rockies (March 31, 2000); trade arranged as compensation for OF Thomas Johnson who retired following trade to Rockies. ... On Colorado Springs disabled list (June 19-28, 2000). ... Granted free agency (October 18, 2000).
STATISTICAL NOTES: Led Pacific Coast League with .449 on-base percentage in 2000.

Year	Team (League)	Pos.	G	AB	R	H	2B	3B	HR	RBI	Avg.	BB	SO	SB	PO	A	E	Avg.
1993—Dom. Mets (DSL).......	OF	36	96	25	23	1	0	1	14	.240	23	10	7	17	3	1	.952
1994—Dom. Mets (DSL).......	OF	57	197	66	69	11	1	1	25	.350	68	13	15	74	6	3	.964
1995—Kingsport (Appl.)........	OF	51	192	*56	63	9	0	1	24	.328	27	24	28	54	4	3	.951
1996—Columbia (S.Atl.)........	OF-DH	85	304	61	102	10	2	0	37	*.336	57	47	31	54	6	2	.968
1997—Binghamton (East.)	OF-DH	59	228	36	87	12	2	1	13	.382	14	25	14	79	5	1	.988
—Norfolk (I.L.)	OF	10	35	3	5	0	1	0	0	.143	3	4	1	17	0	0	1.000
—New York (N.L.)........	OF	15	12	6	3	0	0	0	1	.250	4	2	0	5	0	0	1.000
1998—St. Peters. (FSL)■......	OF	8	32	6	10	2	0	0	8	.313	4	3	4	20	1	0	1.000
—Durham (I.L.)	OF	51	201	32	54	8	0	0	11	.269	16	29	9	99	5	5	.954
—GC Devil Rays (GCL) ..	OF	6	18	6	8	1	0	0	4	.444	5	3	3	13	0	0	1.000
—Orlando (Sou.)	OF-DH	35	139	27	47	3	3	1	19	.338	19	18	16	53	1	2	.964
1999—Durham (I.L.)	OF-DH	75	266	57	78	8	3	1	25	.293	32	38	9	107	8	2	.983
2000—Colo. Springs (PCL)■	OF	107	359	79	127	16	*14	0	42	.354	60	50	26	159	5	4	.976
—Colorado (N.L.)	OF	13	10	0	1	0	0	0	0	.100	1	4	0	0	0	1	.000
Major League totals (2 years)		28	22	6	4	0	0	0	1	.182	5	6	0	5	0	1	.833

MENDOZA, RAMIRO   P   YANKEES

PERSONAL: Born June 15, 1972, in Los Santos, Panama. ... 6-2/195. ... Throws right, bats right.
TRANSACTIONS/CAREER NOTES: Signed as non-drafted free agent by New York Yankees organization (November 13, 1991). ... On New York disabled list (June 28-July 28 and August 4, 2000-remainder of season); included rehabilitation assignment to Tampa (July 19-27).

Year	League	W	L	Pct.	ERA	G	GS	CG	ShO	Sv.	IP	H	R	ER	BB	SO
1992—Dominican Yankees (DSL)...	10	2	.833	2.13	15	15	5	0	0	109 2/3	93	37	26	28	79
1993—Gulf Coast Yankees (GCL)..	4	5	.444	2.79	15	9	0	0	1	67 2/3	59	26	21	7	61
—Greensboro (S.Atl.)	0	1	.000	2.45	2	0	0	0	0	3 2/3	3	1	1	5	3
1994—Tampa (FSL)......................	12	6	.667	3.01	22	21	1	0	0	134 1/3	133	54	45	35	110
1995—Norwich (East.)	5	6	.455	3.21	19	19	2	1	0	89 2/3	87	39	32	33	68
—Columbus (I.L.)	1	0	1.000	2.57	2	2	0	0	0	14	10	4	4	2	13
1996—Columbus (I.L.)	6	2	.750	2.51	15	15	0	0	0	97	96	30	27	19	61
—New York (A.L.)	4	5	.444	6.79	12	11	0	0	0	53	80	43	40	10	34
1997—Columbus (I.L.)	0	0	...	5.68	1	1	0	0	0	6 1/3	7	6	4	1	4
—New York (A.L.)	8	6	.571	4.24	39	15	0	0	2	133 2/3	157	67	63	28	82
1998—New York (A.L.)	10	2	.833	3.25	41	14	1	1	1	130 1/3	131	50	47	30	56
1999—New York (A.L.)	9	9	.500	4.29	53	6	0	0	3	123 2/3	141	68	59	27	80
2000—New York (A.L.)	7	4	.636	4.25	14	9	1	1	0	65 2/3	66	32	31	20	30
—Tampa (FSL).....................	0	0	.000	7.20	2	2	0	0	0	5	9	4	4	0	7
Major League totals (5 years).......	38	26	.594	4.27	159	55	2	2	6	506 1/3	575	260	240	115	282

DIVISION SERIES RECORD

Year	League	W	L	Pct.	ERA	G	GS	CG	ShO	Sv.	IP	H	R	ER	BB	SO
1997—New York (A.L.)	1	1	.500	2.45	2	0	0	0	0	3 2/3	3	1	1	0	2
1998—New York (A.L.)							Did not play.								
1999—New York (A.L.)							Did not play.								

CHAMPIONSHIP SERIES RECORD

Year	League	W	L	Pct.	ERA	G	GS	CG	ShO	Sv.	IP	H	R	ER	BB	SO
1998—New York (A.L.).................	0	0	...	0.00	2	0	0	0	0	4 1/3	4	0	0	0	1
1999—New York (A.L.).................	0	0	...	0.00	2	0	0	0	1	2 1/3	0	0	0	0	2
Champ. series totals (2 years)	0	0	...	0.00	4	0	0	0	1	6 2/3	4	0	0	0	3

M

WORLD SERIES RECORD

NOTES: Member of World Series championship team (1998 and 1999).

Year	League	W	L	Pct.	ERA	G	GS	CG	ShO	Sv.	IP	H	R	ER	BB	SO
1998—	New York (A.L.)	1	0	1.000	9.00	1	0	0	0	0	1	2	1	1	0	1
1999—	New York (A.L.)	0	0	...	10.80	1	0	0	0	0	$1\frac{2}{3}$	3	2	2	1	0
World Series totals (2 years)		1	0	1.000	10.13	2	0	0	0	0	$2\frac{2}{3}$	5	3	3	1	1

MENECHINO, FRANK   IF   ATHLETICS

PERSONAL: Born January 7, 1971, in Staten Island, N.Y. ... 5-9/175. ... Bats right, throws right.
HIGH SCHOOL: Susan E. Wagner (Staten Island, N.Y.).
JUNIOR COLLEGE: Gulf Coast Community College (Fla.).
COLLEGE: Alabama.
TRANSACTIONS/CAREER NOTES: Selected by Chicago White Sox organization in 45th round of free-agent draft (June 3, 1993). ... Selected by Oakland Athletics organization from White Sox organization in Rule 5 minor league draft (December 15, 1997).
STATISTICAL NOTES: Led Carolina League second basemen with 603 total chances in 1995. ... Led Pacific Coast League with seven intentional bases on balls received in 1999.

									— BATTING —						— FIELDING —		
Year	Team (League)	Pos.	G	AB	R	H	2B	3B	HR	RBI	Avg.	BB	SO	SB	PO	A	E	Avg.
1993—	GC White Sox (GCL) ..	2B	17	45	10	11	4	1	1	9	.244	12	4	3	22	25	1	.979
—	Hickory (S.Atl.)...........	2B	50	178	35	50	6	3	4	19	.281	33	28	11	102	148	6	.977
1994—	South Bend (Midw.) ...	2B	106	379	77	113	21	5	5	48	.298	78	70	15	213	254	10	*.979
1995—	Prince William (Caro.)	2B	137	476	65	124	31	3	6	58	.261	96	75	6	*293	295	15	.975
1996—	Birmingham (Sou.).....	2B	125	415	77	121	25	3	12	62	.292	64	84	7	*273	308	13	.978
1997—	Nashville (A.A.)	2B-3B-OF	37	113	20	26	4	0	4	11	.230	26	31	3	79	86	9	.948
—	Birmingham (Sou.)......	2B-3B	90	318	78	95	28	4	12	60	.299	79	77	7	176	237	11	.974
1998—	Edmonton (PCL)■	2B	106	378	72	105	11	7	10	40	.278	70	75	9	133	192	7	.979
1999—	Vancouver (PCL)	3-S-2-DH	130	501	103	155	31	•9	15	88	.309	73	97	4	152	341	10	.980
—	Oakland (A.L.)	SS-DH-3B	9	9	0	2	0	0	0	0	.222	0	4	0	4	7	0	1.000
2000—	Oakland (A.L.)	2-S-D-3-P	66	145	31	37	9	1	6	26	.255	20	45	1	90	139	6	.974
—	Sacramento (PCL)......	SS-3B	9	38	8	12	2	0	2	2	.316	5	4	1	13	30	0	1.000
Major League totals (2 years)			75	154	31	39	9	1	6	26	.253	20	49	1	94	146	6	.976

DIVISION SERIES RECORD

									— BATTING —						— FIELDING —		
Year	Team (League)	Pos.	G	AB	R	H	2B	3B	HR	RBI	Avg.	BB	SO	SB	PO	A	E	Avg.
2000—	Oakland (A.L.)	2B	1	0	0	0	0	0	0	0	...	0	0	0	2	0	0	1.000

RECORD AS PITCHER

Year	League	W	L	Pct.	ERA	G	GS	CG	ShO	Sv.	IP	H	R	ER	BB	SO
2000—	Oakland (A.L.)	0	0	...	36.00	1	0	0	0	0	1	6	4	4	0	0

MERCADO, HECTOR   P   REDS

PERSONAL: Born April 29, 1974, in Catano, Puerto Rico. ... 6-3/235. ... Throws left, bats left. ... Full name: Hector Luis Mercado.
HIGH SCHOOL: Jose S. Alegria (Dorado, Puerto Rico).
TRANSACTIONS/CAREER NOTES: Selected by Houston Astros organization in 13th round of free-agent draft (June 1, 1992). ... Selected by Florida Marlins organization from Astros organization in Rule 5 minor league draft (December 9, 1996). ... Selected by Philadelphia Phillies from Marlins organization in Rule 5 major league draft (December 15, 1997). ... Traded by Phillies to New York Mets for P Mike Welch (December 15, 1997). ... On New York disabled list (March 21, 1998-entire season). ... On Norfolk disabled list (April 8-18 and April 24, 1999-remainder of season). ... Released by Mets (August 4, 1999). ... Signed by Cincinnati Reds organization (December 16, 1999).

Year	League	W	L	Pct.	ERA	G	GS	CG	ShO	Sv.	IP	H	R	ER	BB	SO
1992—	Gulf Coast Astros (GCL).....	1	2	.333	4.20	13	3	0	0	0	30	22	17	14	25	36
1993—	Gulf Coast Astros (GCL).....	5	4	.556	2.42	11	11	1	1	0	67	49	26	18	29	59
—	Osceola (FSL).....................	1	1	.500	5.19	2	2	0	0	0	$8\frac{2}{3}$	9	7	5	6	5
1994—	Osceola (FSL)....................	6	•13	.316	3.95	25	25	1	1	0	$136\frac{2}{3}$	123	75	60	79	88
1995—	Jackson (Texas)	1	4	.200	7.80	8	7	0	0	0	30	36	33	26	32	20
—	Kissimmee (FSL)................	6	8	.429	3.46	19	17	2	0	0	104	96	50	40	37	75
1996—	Kissimmee (FSL)................	3	5	.375	4.16	56	0	0	0	3	80	78	43	37	48	68
1997—	Portland (East.)■..............	11	3	.786	3.96	31	17	1	1	0	$129\frac{2}{3}$	129	66	57	54	125
—	Charlotte (I.L.)...................	0	1	.000	9.00	1	1	0	0	0	5	5	5	5	5	1
1998—	New York (N.L.)■							Did not play.								
1999—	Norfolk (I.L.)	0	0	...	1.50	2	2	0	0	0	6	3	1	1	1	2
2000—	Cincinnati (N.L.)■..............	0	0	...	4.50	12	0	0	0	0	14	12	7	7	8	13
—	Louisville (I.L.)...................	1	5	.167	3.04	47	5	0	0	2	77	69	26	26	48	67
Major League totals (1 year)........		0	0	...	4.50	12	0	0	0	0	14	12	7	7	8	13

MERCEDES, JOSE   P   ORIOLES

PERSONAL: Born March 5, 1971, in El Seibo, Dominican Republic. ... 6-1/180. ... Throws right, bats right. ... Full name: Jose Miguel Mercedes.
TRANSACTIONS/CAREER NOTES: Signed as non-drafted free agent by Baltimore Orioles organization (August 10, 1989). ... Selected by Milwaukee Brewers from Orioles organization in Rule 5 major league draft (December 13, 1993). ... On Milwaukee disabled list (April 2-May 30, 1994; included rehabilitation assignments to El Paso (April 30-May 14) and New Orleans (May 14-28). ... On disabled list (May 14, 1995-remainder of season). ... On Milwaukee disabled list (May 5, 1998-remainder of season); included rehabilitation assignment to El Paso (June 15-16). ... Released by Brewers (December 16, 1998). ... Signed by San Diego Padres organization (March 19, 1999). ... Released by Padres (June 24, 1999). ... Signed by Florida Marlins organization (June 30, 1999). ... Released by Marlins (July 30, 1999). ... Signed by New York Mets organization (August 6, 1999). ... Granted free agency (October 15, 1999). ... Signed by Orioles organization (January 3, 2000).

Year	League	W	L	Pct.	ERA	G	GS	CG	ShO	Sv.	IP	H	R	ER	BB	SO
1990—		Dominican Summer League statistics unavailable.														
1991—		Dominican Summer League statistics unavailable.														
1992—	Gulf Coast Orioles (GCL)	2	3	.400	1.78	8	5	2	0	0	35 1/3	31	12	7	13	21
—	Kane County (Midw.)	3	2	.600	2.66	8	8	2	•2	0	47 1/3	40	26	14	15	45
1993—	Bowie (East.)	6	8	.429	4.78	26	23	3	0	0	147	170	86	78	65	75
1994—	El Paso (Texas)■	2	0	1.000	4.66	3	0	0	0	0	9 2/3	13	6	5	4	8
—	New Orleans (A.A.)	0	0	...	4.91	3	3	0	0	0	18 1/3	19	10	10	8	7
—	Milwaukee (A.L.)	2	0	1.000	2.32	19	0	0	0	0	31	22	9	8	16	11
1995—	Milwaukee (A.L.)	0	1	.000	9.82	5	0	0	0	0	7 1/3	12	9	8	8	6
1996—	New Orleans (A.A.)	3	7	.300	3.56	25	15	0	0	1	101	109	58	40	28	47
—	Milwaukee (A.L.)	0	2	.000	9.18	11	0	0	0	0	16 2/3	20	18	17	5	6
1997—	Milwaukee (A.L.)	7	10	.412	3.79	29	23	2	1	0	159	146	76	67	53	80
1998—	Milwaukee (N.L.)	2	2	.500	6.75	7	5	0	0	0	32	42	25	24	9	11
—	El Paso (Texas)	0	0	...	10.80	1	1	0	0	0	3 1/3	9	4	4	0	0
1999—	Las Vegas (PCL)■	2	6	.250	4.30	15	14	0	0	0	88	110	57	42	20	57
—	Calgary (PCL)■	1	2	.333	3.12	4	4	0	0	0	26	30	13	9	3	13
—	Norfolk (I.L.)■	2	1	.667	2.53	6	6	0	0	0	32	36	15	9	11	19
2000—	Baltimore (A.L.)■	14	7	.667	4.02	36	20	1	0	0	145 2/3	150	71	65	64	70
A.L. totals (5 years)		23	20	.535	4.13	100	43	3	1	0	359 2/3	350	183	165	146	173
N.L. totals (1 year)		2	2	.500	6.75	7	5	0	0	0	32	42	25	24	9	11
Major League totals (6 years)		25	22	.532	4.34	107	48	3	1	0	391 2/3	392	208	189	155	184

MERCKER, KENT — P — RED SOX

PERSONAL: Born February 1, 1968, in Dublin, Ohio. ... 6-2/200. ... Throws left, bats left. ... Full name: Kent Franklin Mercker.

HIGH SCHOOL: Dublin (Ohio).

TRANSACTIONS/CAREER NOTES: Selected by Atlanta Braves organization in first round (fifth pick overall) of free-agent draft (June 2, 1986). ... On Richmond disabled list (March 30-May 6, 1990). ... On disabled list (August 9-24, 1991). ... Traded by Braves to Baltimore Orioles for P Joe Borowski and P Rachaad Stewart (December 17, 1995). ... Traded by Orioles to Cleveland Indians for 1B Eddie Murray (July 21, 1996). ... Granted free agency (November 4, 1996). ... Signed by Cincinnati Reds (December 10, 1996). ... On disabled list (August 17-September 2, 1997). ... Granted free agency (October 27, 1997). ... Signed by St. Louis Cardinals (December 16, 1997). ... On disabled list (June 14-July 1, 1998). ... Traded by Cardinals to Boston Red Sox for P Mike Matthews and C David Benham (August 24, 1999). ... On Boston disabled list (September 7-23, 1999). ... Granted free agency (November 8, 1999). ... Signed by Anaheim Angels organization (January 26, 2000). ... On Anaheim disabled list (May 12-August 12, 2000); included rehabilitation assignment to Lake Elsinore (August 4-8). ... Granted free agency (November 8, 2000). ... Signed by Red Sox organization (January 5, 2001).

HONORS: Named Carolina League co-Pitcher of the Year (1988).

STATISTICAL NOTES: Pitched six innings, combining with Mark Wohlers (two innings) and Alejandro Pena (one inning) in 1-0 no-hit victory against San Diego (September 11, 1991). ... Pitched 6-0 no-hit victory against Los Angeles (April 8, 1994). ... Career major league grand slams: 1.

MISCELLANEOUS: Had a sacrifice hit and received a base on balls in two games as pinch hitter (1991). ... Appeared in one game as pinch runner (1997). ... Appeared in one game as pinch runner (1998). ... Scored a run in only appearance as pinch runner with Cardinals (1999).

Year	League	W	L	Pct.	ERA	G	GS	CG	ShO	Sv.	IP	H	R	ER	BB	SO
1986—	Gulf Coast Braves (GCL)	4	3	.571	2.47	9	8	0	0	0	47 1/3	37	21	13	16	42
1987—	Durham (Caro.)	0	1	.000	5.40	3	3	0	0	0	11 2/3	11	8	7	6	14
1988—	Durham (Caro.)	11	4	.733	*2.75	19	19	5	0	0	127 2/3	102	44	39	47	159
—	Greenville (Sou.)	3	1	.750	3.35	9	9	0	0	0	48 1/3	36	20	18	26	60
1989—	Richmond (I.L.)	9	12	.429	3.20	27	•27	4	0	0	168 2/3	107	66	60	*95	*144
—	Atlanta (N.L.)	0	0	...	12.46	2	1	0	0	0	4 1/3	8	6	6	6	4
1990—	Richmond (I.L.)	5	4	.556	3.55	12	10	0	0	1	58 1/3	60	30	23	27	69
—	Atlanta (N.L.)	4	7	.364	3.17	36	0	0	0	7	48 1/3	43	22	17	24	39
1991—	Atlanta (N.L.)	5	3	.625	2.58	50	4	0	0	6	73 1/3	56	23	21	35	62
1992—	Atlanta (N.L.)	3	2	.600	3.42	53	0	0	0	6	68 1/3	51	27	26	35	49
1993—	Atlanta (N.L.)	3	1	.750	2.86	43	6	0	0	0	66	52	24	21	36	59
1994—	Atlanta (N.L.)	9	4	.692	3.45	20	17	2	1	0	112 1/3	90	46	43	45	111
1995—	Atlanta (N.L.)	7	8	.467	4.15	29	26	0	0	0	143	140	73	66	61	102
1996—	Baltimore (A.L.)■	3	6	.333	7.76	14	12	0	0	0	58	73	56	50	35	22
—	Buffalo (A.A.)■	0	2	.000	3.94	3	3	0	0	0	16	11	7	7	9	11
—	Cleveland (A.L.)	1	0	1.000	3.09	10	0	0	0	0	11 2/3	10	4	4	3	7
1997—	Cincinnati (N.L.)■	8	11	.421	3.92	28	25	0	0	0	144 2/3	135	65	63	62	75
1998—	St. Louis (N.L.)■	11	11	.500	5.07	30	29	0	0	0	161 2/3	199	99	91	53	72
1999—	St. Louis (N.L.)	6	5	.545	5.12	25	18	0	0	0	103 2/3	125	73	59	51	64
—	Boston (A.L.)■	2	0	1.000	3.51	5	5	0	0	0	25 2/3	23	12	10	13	17
2000—	Anaheim (A.L.)■	1	3	.250	6.52	21	7	0	0	0	48 1/3	57	35	35	29	30
—	Lake Elsinore (Calif.)	0	0	...	0.00	1	1	0	0	0	4	0	0	0	0	3
A.L. totals (3 years)		7	9	.438	6.20	50	24	0	0	0	143 2/3	163	107	99	80	76
N.L. totals (10 years)		56	52	.519	4.02	316	126	2	1	19	925 2/3	899	458	413	408	637
Major League totals (12 years)		63	61	.508	4.31	366	150	2	1	19	1069 1/3	1062	565	512	488	713

DIVISION SERIES RECORD

Year	League	W	L	Pct.	ERA	G	GS	CG	ShO	Sv.	IP	H	R	ER	BB	SO
1995—	Atlanta (N.L.)	0	0	...	0.00	1	0	0	0	0	1/3	0	0	0	0	0
1999—	Boston (A.L.)	0	0	...	10.80	1	1	0	0	0	1 2/3	3	2	2	3	1
Division series totals (2 years)		0	0	...	9.00	2	1	0	0	0	2	3	2	2	3	1

CHAMPIONSHIP SERIES RECORD

Year	League	W	L	Pct.	ERA	G	GS	CG	ShO	Sv.	IP	H	R	ER	BB	SO
1991—	Atlanta (N.L.)	0	1	.000	13.50	1	0	0	0	0	2/3	0	1	1	2	0
1992—	Atlanta (N.L.)	0	0	...	0.00	2	0	0	0	0	3	1	0	0	1	1
1993—	Atlanta (N.L.)	0	0	...	1.80	5	0	0	0	0	5	3	1	1	2	4
1999—	Boston (A.L.)	0	1	.000	4.70	2	2	0	0	0	7 2/3	12	4	4	4	5
Champ. series totals (4 years)		0	2	.000	3.31	10	2	0	0	0	16 1/3	16	6	6	9	10

NOTES: Member of World Series championship team (1995).

Year League	W	L	Pct.	ERA	G	GS	CG	ShO	Sv.	IP	H	R	ER	BB	SO
1991—Atlanta (N.L.)	0	0	...	0.00	2	0	0	0	0	1	0	0	0	0	1
1995—Atlanta (N.L.)	0	0	...	4.50	1	0	0	0	0	2	1	1	1	2	2
World Series totals (2 years)	0	0	...	3.00	3	0	0	0	0	3	1	1	1	2	3

MERLONI, LOU   IF   RED SOX

PERSONAL: Born April 6, 1971, in Framingham, Mass. ... 5-10/195. ... Bats right, throws right. ... Full name: Louis William Merloni.

HIGH SCHOOL: Framingham (Mass.) South.

COLLEGE: Providence.

TRANSACTIONS/CAREER NOTES: Selected by Boston Red Sox organization in 10th round of free-agent draft (June 3, 1993). ... On Boston disabled list (June 29-September 12, 1998); included rehabilitation assignment to Gulf Coast Red Sox (August 8-20).

							BATTING							FIELDING		
Year Team (League)	Pos.	G	AB	R	H	2B	3B	HR	RBI	Avg.	BB	SO	SB	PO	A	E	Avg.
1993—GC Red Sox (GCL)	SS	4	14	4	5	1	0	0	1	.357	1	1	1	7	13	1	.952
—Fort Lauderdale (FSL)	3B-SS	44	156	14	38	1	1	2	21	.244	13	26	1	40	114	8	.951
1994—Sarasota (FSL)	2B-3B-SS	113	419	59	120	16	2	1	63	.286	36	57	5	196	304	18	.965
1995—Trenton (East.)	2B-3B-SS	93	318	42	88	16	1	1	30	.277	39	50	7	166	222	20	.951
1996—GC Red Sox (GCL)	2B	1	4	1	1	0	0	0	1	.250	0	0	0	3	3	0	1.000
—Trenton (East.)	3B-2B-SS-1B	28	95	11	22	6	1	3	16	.232	9	18	0	39	67	8	.930
—Pawtucket (I.L.)	3B-2B-SS	38	115	19	29	6	0	1	12	.252	10	20	0	39	99	8	.945
1997—Trenton (East.)	3B-2B-SS	69	255	49	79	17	4	5	37	.310	30	43	3	68	130	9	.957
—Pawtucket (I.L.)	3B-2B-SS	49	165	24	49	10	0	5	24	.297	15	20	0	61	122	4	.979
1998—Pawtucket (I.L.)	SS-2B-3B	27	88	17	34	3	1	8	22	.386	16	13	2	27	56	2	.976
—Boston (A.L.)	2B-3B-SS	39	96	10	27	6	0	1	15	.281	7	20	1	52	73	5	.962
—GC Red Sox (GCL)	2B	1	1	0	0	0	0	0	0	.000	0	0	0	0	0	0	...
1999—Boston (A.L.)	S-3-2-DH-1-O	43	126	18	32	7	0	1	13	.254	8	16	0	68	88	10	.940
—Pawtucket (I.L.)	S-3-DH-1-2	66	229	45	64	14	1	7	36	.279	30	38	1	79	127	12	.945
2000—Pawtucket (I.L.)	SS-1B-2B-3B	11	39	6	16	2	0	1	5	.410	3	3	0	23	12	4	.897
—Boston (A.L.)	3B	40	128	10	41	11	2	0	18	.320	4	22	1	26	64	7	.928
Major League totals (3 years)		122	350	38	100	24	2	2	46	.286	19	58	2	146	225	22	.944

DIVISION SERIES RECORD

							BATTING							FIELDING		
Year Team (League)	Pos.	G	AB	R	H	2B	3B	HR	RBI	Avg.	BB	SO	SB	PO	A	E	Avg.
1999—Boston (A.L.)	SS-PH	3	6	1	2	0	0	0	1	.333	1	1	0	3	2	1	.833

CHAMPIONSHIP SERIES RECORD

							BATTING							FIELDING		
Year Team (League)	Pos.	G	AB	R	H	2B	3B	HR	RBI	Avg.	BB	SO	SB	PO	A	E	Avg.
1999—Boston (A.L.)	PH	1	0	0	0	0	0	0	0	...	1	0	0	...	...	...	...

M   MESA, JOSE   P   PHILLIES

PERSONAL: Born May 22, 1966, in Azua, Dominican Republic. ... 6-3/225. ... Throws right, bats right. ... Full name: Jose Ramon Mesa.

HIGH SCHOOL: Santa School (Azua, Dominican Republic).

TRANSACTIONS/CAREER NOTES: Signed as non-drafted free agent by Toronto Blue Jays organization (October 31, 1981). ... On Kinston disabled list (August 27, 1984-remainder of season). ... Traded by Blue Jays to Baltimore Orioles (September 4, 1987), completing deal in which Orioles traded P Mike Flanagan to Blue Jays for P Oswald Peraza and a player to be named later (August 31, 1987). ... On Rochester disabled list (April 18-May 16 and June 30, 1988-remainder of season; May 27, 1989-remainder of season; and August 21-September 5, 1991). ... Traded by Orioles to Cleveland Indians for OF Kyle Washington (July 14, 1992). ... On suspended list (April 5-8, 1993). ... Traded by Indians with IF Shawon Dunston and P Alvin Morman to San Francisco Giants for P Steve Reed and OF Jacob Cruz (July 23, 1998). ... Granted free agency (October 23, 1998). ... Signed by Seattle Mariners (November 13, 1998). ... Granted free agency (November 6, 2000). ... Signed by Philadelphia Phillies (November 17, 2000).

HONORS: Named A.L. Fireman of the Year by THE SPORTING NEWS (1995).

STATISTICAL NOTES: Tied for Carolina League lead with nine hit batsmen in 1985.

MISCELLANEOUS: Appeared in one game as pinch runner for Baltimore (1991).

Year League	W	L	Pct.	ERA	G	GS	CG	ShO	Sv.	IP	H	R	ER	BB	SO
1982—GC Blue Jays (GCL)	6	4	.600	2.70	13	12	6	*3	1	83 1/3	58	34	25	20	40
1983—Florence (S.Atl.)	6	12	.333	5.48	28	27	1	0	0	141 1/3	153	*116	86	93	91
1984—Florence (S.Atl.)	4	3	.571	3.76	7	7	0	0	0	38 1/3	38	24	16	25	35
—Kinston (Caro.)	5	2	.714	3.91	10	9	0	0	0	50 2/3	51	23	22	28	24
1985—Kinston (Caro.)	5	10	.333	6.16	30	20	0	0	1	106 2/3	110	89	73	79	71
1986—Ventura County (Calif.)	10	6	.625	3.86	24	24	2	1	0	142 1/3	141	71	61	58	113
—Knoxville (Sou.)	2	2	.500	4.35	9	8	2	1	0	41 1/3	40	32	20	23	30
1987—Knoxville (Sou.)	10	•13	.435	5.21	35	*35	4	2	0	*193 1/3	*206	*131	*112	104	115
—Baltimore (A.L.)■	1	3	.250	6.03	6	5	0	0	0	31 1/3	38	23	21	15	17
1988—Rochester (I.L.)	0	3	.000	8.62	11	2	0	0	0	15 2/3	21	20	15	14	15
1989—Rochester (I.L.)	0	2	.000	5.40	7	1	0	0	0	10	10	6	6	6	3
—Hagerstown (East.)	0	0	...	1.38	3	3	0	0	0	13	9	2	2	4	12
1990—Hagerstown (East.)	5	5	.500	3.42	15	15	3	1	0	79	77	35	30	30	72
—Rochester (I.L.)	1	2	.333	2.42	4	4	0	0	0	26	21	11	7	12	23
—Baltimore (A.L.)	3	2	.600	3.86	7	7	0	0	0	46 2/3	37	20	20	27	24
1991—Baltimore (A.L.)	6	11	.353	5.97	23	23	2	1	0	123 2/3	151	86	82	62	64
—Rochester (I.L.)	3	3	.500	3.86	8	8	1	1	0	51 1/3	37	25	22	30	48
1992—Baltimore (A.L.)	3	8	.273	5.19	13	12	0	0	0	67 2/3	77	41	39	27	22
—Cleveland (A.L.)■	4	4	.500	4.16	15	15	1	1	0	93	92	45	43	43	40
1993—Cleveland (A.L.)	10	12	.455	4.92	34	33	3	0	0	208 2/3	232	122	114	62	118
1994—Cleveland (A.L.)	7	5	.583	3.82	51	0	0	0	2	73	71	33	31	26	63
1995—Cleveland (A.L.)	3	0	1.000	1.13	62	0	0	0	*46	64	49	9	8	17	58

Year League	W	L	Pct.	ERA	G	GS	CG	ShO	Sv.	IP	H	R	ER	BB	SO
1996— Cleveland (A.L.)	2	7	.222	3.73	69	0	0	0	39	72 1/3	69	32	30	28	64
1997— Cleveland (A.L.)	4	4	.500	2.40	66	0	0	0	16	82 1/3	83	28	22	28	69
1998— Cleveland (A.L.)	3	4	.429	5.17	44	0	0	0	1	54	61	36	31	20	35
— San Francisco (N.L.)■	5	3	.625	3.52	32	0	0	0	0	30 2/3	30	14	12	18	28
1999— Seattle (A.L.)■	3	6	.333	4.98	68	0	0	0	33	68 2/3	84	42	38	40	42
2000— Seattle (A.L.)	4	6	.400	5.36	66	0	0	0	1	80 2/3	89	48	48	41	84
A.L. totals (12 years)	53	72	.424	4.45	524	95	6	2	138	1066	1133	565	527	436	700
N.L. totals (1 year)	5	3	.625	3.52	32	0	0	0	0	30 2/3	30	14	12	18	28
Major League totals (12 years)	58	75	.436	4.42	556	95	6	2	138	1096 2/3	1163	579	539	454	728

DIVISION SERIES RECORD

Year League	W	L	Pct.	ERA	G	GS	CG	ShO	Sv.	IP	H	R	ER	BB	SO
1995— Cleveland (A.L.)	0	0	...	0.00	2	0	0	0	0	2	0	0	0	2	0
1996— Cleveland (A.L.)	0	1	.000	3.86	2	0	0	0	0	4 2/3	8	2	2	0	7
1997— Cleveland (A.L.)	0	0	...	2.70	2	0	0	0	1	3 1/3	5	1	1	1	2
2000— Seattle (A.L.)	1	0	1.000	0.00	2	0	0	0	0	2	0	0	0	1	2
Division series totals (4 years)	1	1	.500	2.25	8	0	0	0	1	12	13	3	3	4	11

CHAMPIONSHIP SERIES RECORD

Year League	W	L	Pct.	ERA	G	GS	CG	ShO	Sv.	IP	H	R	ER	BB	SO
1995— Cleveland (A.L.)	0	0	...	2.25	4	0	0	0	1	4	3	1	1	1	1
1997— Cleveland (A.L.)	1	0	1.000	3.38	4	0	0	0	2	5 1/3	5	2	2	3	5
2000— Seattle (A.L.)	0	0	...	12.46	3	0	0	0	0	4 1/3	5	6	6	3	3
Champ. series totals (3 years)	1	0	1.000	5.93	11	0	0	0	3	13 2/3	13	9	9	7	9

WORLD SERIES RECORD

Year League	W	L	Pct.	ERA	G	GS	CG	ShO	Sv.	IP	H	R	ER	BB	SO
1995— Cleveland (A.L.)	1	0	1.000	4.50	2	0	0	0	1	4	5	2	2	1	4
1997— Cleveland (A.L.)	0	0	...	5.40	5	0	0	0	1	5	10	3	3	1	5
World Series totals (2 years)	1	0	1.000	5.00	7	0	0	0	2	9	15	5	5	2	9

ALL-STAR GAME RECORD

Year League	W	L	Pct.	ERA	GS	CG	ShO	Sv.	IP	H	R	ER	BB	SO
1995— American	0	0	...	0.00	0	0	0	0	1	0	0	0	0	1
1996— American							Did not play.							

METCALFE, MIKE — 2B — DEVIL RAYS

PERSONAL: Born January 2, 1973, in Qunatico, Va. ... 5-10/175. ... Bats right, throws right. ... Full name: Michael Henry Metcalfe Jr.
HIGH SCHOOL: Colonial (Orlando).
COLLEGE: Miami (Fla.).
TRANSACTIONS/CAREER NOTES: Selected by Los Angeles Dodgers organization in third round of free-agent draft (June 2, 1994). ... On disabled list (June 17-August 23 and August 27, 1996-remainder of season). ... On San Antonio disabled list (April 23-July 9, 1998). ... On Albuquerque disabled list (July 27-August 28 and September 4-11, 2000). ... Granted free agency (October 18, 2000). ... Signed by Tampa Bay Devil Rays organization (November 22, 2000).
STATISTICAL NOTES: Led Florida State League in caught stealing with 27 in 1995. ... Led California League in caught stealing with 32 in 1997. ... Led Texas League in caught stealing with 21 in 1999.

							BATTING							FIELDING			
Year Team (League)	Pos.	G	AB	R	H	2B	3B	HR	RBI	Avg.	BB	SO	SB	PO	A	E	Avg.
1994— Bakersfield (Calif.)	SS	69	275	44	78	10	0	0	18	.284	28	34	41	98	208	17	.947
1995— San Antonio (Texas)	SS	10	41	10	10	1	0	0	2	.244	7	2	1	14	31	2	.957
— Vero Beach (FSL)	SS	120	435	86	131	13	3	3	35	.301	60	37	*60	153	301	*40	.919
1996— Vero Beach (FSL)	DH	2	5	0	0	0	0	0	0	.000	0	0	0	...	...	...	...
1997— San Bern. (Calif.)	2B	132	519	83	147	28	7	3	47	.283	55	79	67	*228	324	12	*.979
1998— San Antonio (Texas)	2B	57	213	35	60	5	5	3	19	.282	30	24	19	117	151	14	.950
— Los Angeles (N.L.)	2B	4	1	0	0	0	0	0	0	.000	0	1	2	0	0	0	...
1999— San Antonio (Texas)	S-O-D-2	123	461	78	135	25	3	3	57	.293	65	47	*57	169	337	29	.946
2000— San Antonio (Texas)	2B-OF-SS	52	196	42	48	5	3	2	25	.245	30	18	34	117	122	3	.988
— Albuquerque (PCL)	SS-OF-2B	35	149	22	45	6	3	0	21	.302	10	16	9	53	100	7	.956
— Los Angeles (N.L.)	OF-2B	4	12	0	1	0	0	0	0	.083	1	2	0	5	1	0	1.000
Major League totals (2 years)		8	13	0	1	0	0	0	0	.077	1	3	2	5	1	0	1.000

MEYERS, CHAD — 2B/OF — CUBS

PERSONAL: Born August 8, 1975, in Omaha, Neb. ... 6-0/190. ... Bats right, throws right. ... Full name: Chad William Meyers.
HIGH SCHOOL: Daniel J. Gross (Omaha, Neb.).
COLLEGE: Creighton.
TRANSACTIONS/CAREER NOTES: Selected by Chicago Cubs organization in fifth round of free-agent draft (June 4, 1996).
STATISTICAL NOTES: Led New York-Pennsylvania League second basemen with 33 double plays in 1996.

							BATTING							FIELDING			
Year Team (League)	Pos.	G	AB	R	H	2B	3B	HR	RBI	Avg.	BB	SO	SB	PO	A	E	Avg.
1996— Williamsport (NY-P)	2B-OF	67	230	46	56	9	2	2	26	.243	33	39	27	123	136	12	.956
1997— Rockford (Midw.)	2-0-3-S	125	439	89	132	28	4	4	58	.301	74	72	54	205	266	26	.948
1998— Daytona (FSL)	2B-OF	48	186	39	60	8	3	3	25	.323	33	29	23	97	109	13	.941
— West Tenn (Sou.)	2B	77	293	63	79	14	0	0	26	.270	58	43	37	154	173	23	.934
1999— West Tenn (Sou.)	2B	64	238	45	69	19	2	3	29	.290	26	40	22	106	148	9	.966
— Iowa (PCL)	2B-OF	44	175	39	62	13	2	0	16	.354	29	20	17	104	99	4	.981
— Chicago (N.L.)	2B-OF	43	142	17	33	9	0	0	4	.232	9	27	4	76	69	2	.986
2000— Chicago (N.L.)	2B-3B	36	52	8	9	2	0	0	5	.173	3	11	1	11	19	2	.938
— Iowa (PCL)	2B-OF-3B-SS	80	301	54	81	10	0	2	26	.269	43	41	34	171	143	19	.943
Major League totals (2 years)		79	194	25	42	11	0	0	9	.216	12	38	5	87	88	4	.978

M

MEYERS, MIKE   P   CUBS

PERSONAL: Born October 18, 1977, in London, Ont. ... 6-2/210. ... Throws right, bats right. ... Full name: Michael Gregory Meyers.
HIGH SCHOOL: Annadale (Tillsonburg, Ont.).
JUNIOR COLLEGE: Blackhawk College (Ill.).
TRANSACTIONS/CAREER NOTES: Selected by Chicago Cubs organization in 26th round of free-agent draft (June 3, 1997). ... On Iowa disabled list (June 8-16 and July 22-August 17, 2000).

Year League	W	L	Pct.	ERA	G	GS	CG	ShO	Sv.	IP	H	R	ER	BB	SO
1997— Arizona Cubs (Ariz.)	3	1	.750	1.41	12	2	0	0	3	38 1/3	34	15	6	13	45
— Williamsport (NY-Penn)	0	0	...	0.00	1	1	0	0	0	4	3	0	0	1	2
1998— Rockford (Midw.)	7	5	.583	3.36	17	16	0	0	0	85 2/3	75	37	32	32	86
1999— Daytona (FSL)	10	3	.769	1.93	19	17	2	0	0	107 1/3	68	30	23	40	122
— West Tenn (Sou.)	4	0	1.000	1.09	5	5	0	0	0	33	21	5	4	10	51
2000— West Tenn (Sou.)	5	2	.714	2.44	9	9	3	1	0	59	41	18	16	26	51
— Iowa (PCL)	2	6	.250	7.28	13	12	0	0	0	59 1/3	74	51	48	30	44

MICELI, DAN   P   MARLINS

PERSONAL: Born September 9, 1970, in Newark, N.J. ... 6-0/216. ... Throws right, bats right. ... Full name: Daniel Miceli.
HIGH SCHOOL: Dr. Phillips (Orlando).
TRANSACTIONS/CAREER NOTES: Signed as non-drafted free agent by Kansas City Royals organization (March 7, 1990). ... Traded by Royals with P Jon Lieber to Pittsburgh Pirates for P Stan Belinda (July 31, 1993). ... Traded by Pirates to Detroit Tigers for P Clint Sodowsky (November 1, 1996). ... Traded by Tigers with P Donne Wall and 3B Ryan Balfe to San Diego Padres for P Tim Worrell and OF Trey Beamon (November 19, 1997). ... Traded by Padres to Florida Marlins for P Brian Meadows (November 15, 1999). ... On Florida disabled list (May 30-July 19, 2000); included rehabilitation assignments to Gulf Coast Marlins (July 4-8) and Brevard County (July 9-19).

Year League	W	L	Pct.	ERA	G	GS	CG	ShO	Sv.	IP	H	R	ER	BB	SO
1990— Gulf Coast Royals (GCL)	3	4	.429	3.91	*27	0	0	0	4	53	45	27	23	29	48
1991— Eugene (N'West)	0	1	.000	2.14	25	0	0	0	10	33 2/3	18	8	8	18	43
1992— Appleton (Midw.)...............	1	1	.500	1.93	23	0	0	0	9	23 1/3	12	6	5	4	44
— Memphis (Sou.)	3	0	1.000	1.91	32	0	0	0	4	37 2/3	20	10	8	13	46
1993— Memphis (Sou.)	6	4	.600	4.60	40	0	0	0	7	58 2/3	54	30	30	39	68
— Carolina (Sou.)■...............	0	2	.000	5.11	13	0	0	0	10	12 1/3	11	8	7	4	19
— Pittsburgh (N.L.)	0	0	...	5.06	9	0	0	0	0	5 1/3	6	3	3	3	4
1994— Buffalo (A.A.).................	1	1	.500	1.88	19	0	0	0	2	24	15	5	5	6	31
— Pittsburgh (N.L.)	2	1	.667	5.93	28	0	0	0	2	27 1/3	28	19	18	11	27
1995— Pittsburgh (N.L.)	4	4	.500	4.66	58	0	0	0	21	58	61	30	30	28	56
1996— Pittsburgh (N.L.)	2	10	.167	5.78	44	9	0	0	1	85 2/3	99	65	55	45	66
— Carolina (Sou.)	1	0	1.000	1.00	3	0	0	0	1	9	4	1	1	1	17
1997— Detroit (A.L.)■	3	2	.600	5.01	71	0	0	0	3	82 2/3	77	49	46	38	79
1998— San Diego (N.L.)■	10	5	.667	3.22	67	0	0	0	2	72 2/3	64	28	26	27	70
1999— San Diego (N.L.)■	4	5	.444	4.46	66	0	0	0	2	68 2/3	67	39	34	36	59
2000— Florida (N.L.)	6	4	.600	4.25	45	0	0	0	0	48 2/3	45	23	23	18	40
— Gulf Coast Marlins (GCL) ...	0	0	...	0.00	2	2	0	0	0	3	0	0	0	1	3
— Brevard County (FSL)........	1	0	1.000	3.00	5	4	0	0	0	6	3	2	2	0	7
A.L. totals (1 year)	3	2	.600	5.01	71	0	0	0	3	82 2/3	77	49	46	38	79
N.L. totals (7 years)	28	29	.491	4.64	317	9	0	0	28	366 1/3	370	207	189	168	322
Major League totals (8 years)	31	31	.500	4.71	388	9	0	0	31	449	447	256	235	206	401

DIVISION SERIES RECORD

Year League	W	L	Pct.	ERA	G	GS	CG	ShO	Sv.	IP	H	R	ER	BB	SO
1998— San Diego (N.L.)	1	1	.500	2.70	3	0	0	0	0	3 1/3	2	1	1	0	4

CHAMPIONSHIP SERIES RECORD

Year League	W	L	Pct.	ERA	G	GS	CG	ShO	Sv.	IP	H	R	ER	BB	SO
1998— San Diego (N.L.)	0	0	...	13.50	3	0	0	0	0	2/3	4	1	1	0	1

WORLD SERIES RECORD

Year League	W	L	Pct.	ERA	G	GS	CG	ShO	Sv.	IP	H	R	ER	BB	SO
1998— San Diego (N.L.)	0	0	...	0.00	2	0	0	0	0	1 2/3	2	0	0	2	1

MICHAELS, JASON   OF   PHILLIES

PERSONAL: Born May 4, 1976, in Tampa, Fla. ... 6-0/205. ... Bats right, throws right. ... Full name: Jason Drew Michaels.
HIGH SCHOOL: Jesuit (Tampa, Fla.).
JUNIOR COLLEGE: Okaloosa-Walton Community College (Fla.).
COLLEGE: Miami (Fla.).
TRANSACTIONS/CAREER NOTES: Selected by San Diego Padres organization in 49th round of free-agent draft (June 2, 1994); did not sign. ... Selected by Tampa Bay Devil Rays organization in 44th round of free-agent draft (June 4, 1996); did not sign. ... Selected by St. Louis Cardinals organization in 15th round of free-agent draft (June 3, 1997); did not sign. ... Selected by Philadelphia Phillies organization in fourth round of free-agent draft (June 2, 1998).

Year Team (League)	Pos.	G	AB	R	H	2B	3B	HR	RBI	Avg.	BB	SO	SB	PO	A	E	Avg.
													BATTING —		FIELDING —		
1998— Batavia (NY-Penn)	OF	67	235	45	63	14	3	11	49	.268	40	69	4	93	1	5	.949
1999— Clearwater (FSL)	OF	122	451	91	138	31	6	14	65	.306	68	103	10	247	12	1	.996
2000— Reading (East.)...........	OF	113	437	71	129	30	4	10	74	.295	28	87	7	244	8	6	.977

MIDDLEBROOK, JASON — P — PADRES

PERSONAL: Born June 26, 1975, in Jackson, Mich. ... 6-3/215. ... Throws right, bats right. ... Full name: Jason Douglas Middlebrook.
HIGH SCHOOL: Grass Lake (Mich.).
COLLEGE: Stanford.
TRANSACTIONS/CAREER NOTES: Selected by New York Mets organization in 18th round of free-agent draft (June 3, 1993); did not sign. ... Selected by San Diego Padres organization in ninth round of free-agent draft (June 4, 1996). ... On Rancho Cucamonga disabled list (April 8-June 25, 1999). ... On Mobile disabled list (May 8-June 2, 2000). ... Claimed on waivers by Mets (October 5, 2000). ... Claimed on waivers by Padres (November 22, 2000).

Year	League	W	L	Pct.	ERA	G	GS	CG	ShO	Sv.	IP	H	R	ER	BB	SO
1997—	Rancho Cuca. (Calif.)	0	2	.000	4.03	6	6	0	0	0	22 1/3	29	15	10	12	18
—	Clinton (Midw.)	6	4	.600	3.98	14	14	2	1	0	81 1/3	76	46	36	39	86
1998—	Rancho Cuca. (Calif.)	10	12	.455	4.92	28	•28	0	0	0	150	162	99	82	63	132
1999—	Arizona Padres (Ariz.)	1	0	1.000	7.20	1	1	0	0	0	5	9	5	4	1	3
—	Mobile (Sou.)	4	6	.400	8.06	13	13	0	0	0	63 2/3	78	59	57	30	38
2000—	Mobile (Sou.)	5	13	.278	6.15	24	24	0	0	0	120	133	89	82	52	75
—	Las Vegas (PCL)	0	1	.000	216.00	1	1	0	0	0	1/3	8	8	8	0	0

MIENTKIEWICZ, DOUG — 1B — TWINS

PERSONAL: Born June 19, 1974, in Toledo, Ohio. ... 6-2/200. ... Bats left, throws right. ... Full name: Douglas Andrew Mientkiewicz. ... Name pronounced mint-KAY-vich.
HIGH SCHOOL: Westminster Christian (Miami).
COLLEGE: Florida State.
TRANSACTIONS/CAREER NOTES: Selected by Minnesota Twin organization in fifth round of free-agent draft (June 1, 1995).
STATISTICAL NOTES: Led Florida State League first basemen with 1,271 total chances and 113 double plays in 1996. ... Led Eastern League first basemen with .995 fielding percentage in 1997.
MISCELLANEOUS: Member of 2000 Olympic baseball team.

Year	Team (League)	Pos.	G	AB	R	H	2B	3B	HR	RBI	Avg.	BB	SO	SB	PO	A	E	Avg.
1995—	Fort Myers (FSL)	1B	38	110	9	27	6	1	1	15	.245	18	19	2	160	12	1	.994
1996—	Fort Myers (FSL)	1B	133	492	69	143	•36	4	5	79	.291	66	47	12	*1183	85	3	*.998
1997—	New Britain (East.)	1B-OF	132	467	87	119	28	2	15	61	.255	*98	67	21	989	63	5	†.995
1998—	New Britain (East.)	1B-OF	139	502	*96	162	*45	0	16	88	*.323	96	58	11	1171	92	12	.991
—	Minnesota (A.L.)	1B	8	25	1	5	1	0	0	2	.200	4	3	1	61	3	0	1.000
1999—	Minnesota (A.L.)	1B	118	327	34	75	21	3	2	32	.229	43	51	1	882	50	3	*.997
2000—	Salt Lake (PCL)	1B-3B-2B-OF	130	485	96	162	32	3	18	96	.334	61	68	9	786	154	10	.989
—	Minnesota (A.L.)	1B	3	14	0	6	0	0	0	4	.429	1	2	0	22	0	1	1.000
Major League totals (3 years)			129	366	35	86	22	3	2	38	.235	47	54	2	965	53	3	.997

MIESKE, MATT — OF

PERSONAL: Born February 13, 1968, in Midland, Mich. ... 6-0/194. ... Bats right, throws right. ... Full name: Matthew Todd Mieske. ... Name pronounced MEE-skee.
HIGH SCHOOL: Bay City Western (Auburn, Mich.).
COLLEGE: Western Michigan.
TRANSACTIONS/CAREER NOTES: Selected by Oakland Athletics organization in 20th round of free-agent draft (June 5, 1989); did not sign. ... Selected by San Diego Padres organization in 17th round of free-agent draft (June 4, 1990). ... Traded by Padres with P Ricky Bones and SS Jose Valentin to Milwaukee Brewers for 3B Gary Sheffield and P Geoff Kellogg (March 27, 1992). ... On New Orleans disabled list (May 25-June 10 and June 13-July 29, 1993). ... On disabled list (August 9-September 2, 1997). ... Granted free agency (December 21, 1997). ... Signed by Chicago Cubs (December 29, 1997). ... Released by Cubs (December 7, 1998). ... Signed by Seattle Mariners (December 17, 1998). ... Traded by Mariners to Houston Astros for P Kevin Hodges (June 20, 1999). ... On Houston disabled list (March 28-April 13, 2000). ... Released by Astros (August 17, 2000). ... Signed by Arizona Diamondbacks organization (August 24, 2000). ... Granted free agency (October 30, 2000).
HONORS: Named Northwest League Most Valuable Player (1990). ... Named California League Most Valuable Player (1991).
STATISTICAL NOTES: Led Northwest League with 155 total bases in 1990. ... Led Northwest League outfielders with 148 total chances in 1990. ... Led California League with 261 total bases and .456 on-base percentage in 1991. ... Career major league grand slams: 3.

Year	Team (League)	Pos.	G	AB	R	H	2B	3B	HR	RBI	Avg.	BB	SO	SB	PO	A	E	Avg.
1990—	Spokane (N'West)	OF	*76	*291	*59	99	20	0	*12	*63	.340	45	43	26	*134	7	7	.953
1991—	High Desert (Calif.)	OF	•133	492	108	*168	*36	6	15	119	*.341	*94	82	39	258	14	*15	.948
1992—	Denver (A.A.)	OF	134	*524	80	140	29	11	19	77	.267	39	90	13	252	*23	*13	.955
1993—	New Orleans (A.A.)	OF	60	219	36	57	14	2	8	22	.260	27	46	6	114	4	2	.983
—	Milwaukee (A.L.)	OF	23	58	9	14	0	0	3	7	.241	4	14	0	43	1	3	.936
1994—	Milwaukee (A.L.)	OF-DH	84	259	39	67	13	1	10	38	.259	21	62	3	154	7	4	.976
—	New Orleans (A.A.)	OF	2	8	2	2	0	0	1	3	.250	1	1	1	2	0	0	1.000
1995—	Milwaukee (A.L.)	OF-DH	117	267	42	67	13	1	12	48	.251	27	45	2	177	7	4	.979
1996—	Milwaukee (A.L.)	OF	127	374	46	104	24	3	14	64	.278	26	76	1	250	7	1	.996
1997—	Milwaukee (A.L.)	OF-DH	84	253	39	63	15	3	5	21	.249	19	50	1	121	6	5	.962
1998—	Chicago (N.L.)■	OF	77	97	16	29	7	0	1	12	.299	11	17	0	36	1	1	.974
—	Iowa (PCL)	OF-DH	35	106	17	27	5	0	7	19	.255	10	27	0	35	3	2	.950
1999—	Seattle (A.L.)■	OF-DH	24	41	11	15	0	0	4	7	.366	2	9	0	25	1	0	1.000
—	Houston (N.L.)■	OF	54	109	13	31	5	0	5	22	.284	6	22	0	54	1	0	1.000
2000—	Houston (N.L.)	OF	62	81	7	14	1	2	1	5	.173	7	17	0	14	0	1	.933
—	Tucson (PCL)■	OF	6	25	2	6	2	0	1	3	.240	0	7	0	10	0	0	1.000
—	Arizona (N.L.)	OF	11	8	3	2	0	0	1	2	.250	1	1	0	2	0	0	1.000
American League totals (6 years)			459	1252	186	330	65	8	48	185	.264	99	256	7	770	29	17	.979
National League totals (3 years)			204	295	39	76	13	2	8	41	.258	25	57	0	106	2	2	.982
Major League totals (8 years)			663	1547	225	406	78	10	56	226	.262	124	313	7	876	31	19	.979

DIVISION SERIES RECORD

Year	Team (League)	Pos.	G	AB	R	H	2B	3B	HR	RBI	Avg.	BB	SO	SB	PO	A	E	Avg.
1999—	Houston (N.L.)	PH-OF	2	4	1	0	0	0	0	0	.000	1	0	0	0	0	0	...

M

PERSONAL: Born September 24, 1971, in Los Angeles. ... 6-0/210. ... Bats right, throws right. ... Full name: Kevin Charles Millar. ... Nephew of Wayne Nordhagen, outfielder with four major league teams (1976-83). ... Name pronounced mi-LAR.
HIGH SCHOOL: University (Los Angeles).
JUNIOR COLLEGE: Los Angeles Community College.
COLLEGE: Lamar.
TRANSACTIONS/CAREER NOTES: Contract sold by St. Paul, Northern League to Florida Marlins organization (September 20, 1993). ... Granted free agency (December 21, 1997). ... Re-signed by Marlins (December 21, 1997). ... On Florida disabled list (April 19, 1998-remainder of season); included rehabilitation assignment to Charlotte (June 14-29).
HONORS: Named Eastern League Player of the Year (1997).
STATISTICAL NOTES: Led Midwest League with 240 total bases in 1994. ... Led Florida State League with 10 sacrifice flies in 1995. ... Led Florida State League first basemen with 1,320 total chances in 1995. ... Led Eastern League with 309 total bases and .423 on-base percentage and tied for league lead with seven sacrifice flies in 1997. ... Led Eastern League first basemen with 93 assists and 116 double plays in 1997.

Year Team (League)	Pos.	G	AB	R	H	2B	3B	HR	RBI	Avg.	BB	SO	SB	PO	A	E	Avg.
1993—St. Paul (Nor.)	3B-2B	63	227	33	59	11	1	5	30	.260	24	27	2	51	133	18	.911
1994—Kane Co. (Midw.)■	1B	135	477	75	144	35	2	19	93	.302	74	88	3	1010	64	11	.990
1995—Brevard County (FSL)	1B	129	459	53	132	32	2	13	68	.288	70	66	4	*1213	95	12	.991
1996—Portland (East.)	1B-3B	130	472	69	150	32	0	18	86	.318	37	53	6	753	134	15	.983
1997—Portland (East.)	1B-3B	135	511	94	*175	•34	2	32	*131	.342	66	53	2	1146	†121	17	.987
1998—Florida (N.L.)	3B	2	2	1	1	0	0	0	0	.500	1	0	0	2	3	1	.833
—Charlotte (I.L.)	3B-1B	14	46	14	15	3	0	4	15	.326	9	7	1	34	19	4	.930
1999—Calgary (PCL)	OF-3B-1B	36	143	24	43	11	1	7	26	.301	11	19	2	63	9	2	.973
—Florida (N.L.)	1B-3B-OF	105	351	48	100	17	4	9	67	.285	40	64	1	720	53	4	.995
2000—Florida (N.L.)	1B-OF-3B-DH	123	259	36	67	14	3	14	42	.259	36	47	0	269	52	5	.985
Major League totals (3 years)		230	612	85	168	31	7	23	109	.275	77	111	1	991	108	10	.991

PERSONAL: Born October 13, 1969, in La Crosse, Wis. ... 6-2/212. ... Bats right, throws right. ... Full name: Damian Donald Miller.
HIGH SCHOOL: West Salem (Wis.).
COLLEGE: Viterbo (Wis.).
TRANSACTIONS/CAREER NOTES: Selected by Minnesota Twins organization in 20th round of free-agent draft (June 4, 1990). ... Selected by Arizona Diamondbacks in second round (47th pick overall) of expansion draft (November 18, 1997).
RECORDS: Shares major league single-game records for most double plays (nine-inning game)—3 (May 25, 1999); and most double plays started (nine-inning game)—3 (May 25, 1999).
STATISTICAL NOTES: Led Pacific Coast League catchers with .998 fielding percentage in 1995. ... Led Pacific Coast League catchers with 70 assists and 695 total chances in 1996. ... Tied for N.L. lead with 11 passed balls in 1999. ... Career major league grand slams: 3.

Year Team (League)	Pos.	G	AB	R	H	2B	3B	HR	RBI	Avg.	BB	SO	SB	PO	A	E	Avg.
1990—Elizabethton (Appl.)	C	14	45	7	10	1	0	1	6	.222	9	3	1	102	6	2	.982
1991—Kenosha (Midw.)	C-1B-OF	80	267	28	62	11	1	3	34	.232	24	53	3	357	52	4	.990
1992—Kenosha (Midw.)	C	115	377	53	110	27	2	5	56	.292	53	66	6	696	89	9	.989
1993—Fort Myers (FSL)	C	87	325	31	69	12	1	1	26	.212	31	44	6	465	62	8	.985
—Nashville (Sou.)	C	4	13	0	3	0	0	0	0	.231	2	4	0	26	3	0	1.000
1994—Nashville (Sou.)	C	103	328	36	88	10	0	8	35	.268	35	51	4	628	81	8	.989
1995—Salt Lake (PCL)	C-OF	83	295	39	84	23	1	3	41	.285	15	39	2	395	52	1	†.998
1996—Salt Lake (PCL)	C	104	385	54	110	27	1	7	55	.286	25	58	1	619	†70	6	.991
1997—Salt Lake (PCL)	C-DH	85	314	48	106	19	3	11	82	.338	29	62	6	445	35	6	.988
—Minnesota (A.L.)	C-DH	25	66	5	18	1	0	2	13	.273	2	12	0	85	3	0	1.000
1998—Tucson (PCL)■	C	18	63	14	22	7	1	0	11	.349	9	9	0	95	15	3	.973
—Arizona (N.L.)	C-DH-OF-1B	57	168	17	48	14	2	3	14	.286	11	43	1	255	27	4	.986
1999—Arizona (N.L.)	C	86	296	35	80	19	0	11	47	.270	19	78	0	622	61	6	.991
2000—Arizona (N.L.)	C-1B	100	324	43	89	24	0	10	44	.275	36	74	2	683	47	7	.991
American League totals (1 year)		25	66	5	18	1	0	2	13	.273	2	12	0	85	3	0	1.000
National League totals (3 years)		243	788	95	217	57	2	24	105	.275	66	195	3	1560	135	17	.990
Major League totals (4 years)		268	854	100	235	58	2	26	118	.275	68	207	3	1645	138	17	.991

PERSONAL: Born August 27, 1977, in Torrance, Calif. ... 6-2/195. ... Throws right, bats right. ... Full name: Justin M. Miller.
HIGH SCHOOL: Torrance (Calif.).
JUNIOR COLLEGE: Los Angeles Harbor College.
TRANSACTIONS/CAREER NOTES: Selected by San Francisco Giants organization in 34th round of free-agent draft (June 1, 1995); did not sign. ... Selected by Colorado Rockies organization in fifth round of free-agent draft (June 3, 1997). ... On Salem disabled list (May 5-June 18, 1999). ... Traded by Rockies with cash to Oakland Athletics as part of three-way deal in which Brewers received P Jimmy Haynes from Athletics, Rockies received 3B Jeff Cirillo, P Scott Karl and cash from Brewers and Brewers received P Jamey Wright and C Henry Blanco from Rockies (December 13, 1999). ... On Midland disabled list (June 8-17 and June 22-30, 2000).

Year League	W	L	Pct.	ERA	G	GS	CG	ShO	Sv.	IP	H	R	ER	BB	SO
1997—Portland (N'West)	4	2	.667	*2.14	14	11	0	0	0	67 1/3	68	26	16	20	54
1998—Asheville (S.Atl.)	13	8	.619	3.69	27	27	3	1	0	163 1/3	177	89	67	40	142
1999—Salem (Caro.)	1	2	.333	4.14	8	8	0	0	0	37	35	18	17	11	35
2000—Midland (Texas)■	5	4	.556	4.55	18	18	0	0	0	87	74	49	44	41	82
—Sacramento (PCL)	4	1	.800	2.47	9	9	0	0	0	54 2/3	42	18	15	13	34

MILLER, TRAVIS — P — TWINS

PERSONAL: Born November 2, 1972, in Dayton, Ohio. ... 6-3/215. ... Throws left, bats right. ... Full name: Travis Eugene Miller.
HIGH SCHOOL: National Trail (New Paris, Ohio).
COLLEGE: Kent.
TRANSACTIONS/CAREER NOTES: Selected by Minnesota Twins organization in supplemental round ("sandwich pick" between first and second round, 34th pick overall) of free-agent draft (June 2, 1994); pick received as compensation for Twins failing to sign 1993 first-round pick C Jason Varitek. ... On Salt Lake disabled list (April 20-May 3, 1998).

Year League	W	L	Pct.	ERA	G	GS	CG	ShO	Sv.	IP	H	R	ER	BB	SO
1994— Fort Wayne (Midw.)	4	1	.800	2.60	11	9	1	0	0	55 1/3	52	17	16	12	50
— Nashville (Sou.)	0	0	...	2.84	1	1	0	0	0	6 1/3	3	3	2	2	4
1995— New Britain (East.)	7	9	.438	4.37	28	27	1	1	0	162 2/3	*172	93	79	65	151
1996— Minnesota (A.L.)	1	2	.333	9.23	7	7	0	0	0	26 1/3	45	29	27	9	15
— Salt Lake (PCL)	8	10	.444	4.83	27	27	1	0	0	160 1/3	187	97	86	57	*143
1997— Salt Lake (PCL)	10	6	.625	4.73	21	21	0	0	0	125 2/3	140	73	66	57	86
— Minnesota (A.L.)	1	5	.167	7.63	13	7	0	0	0	48 1/3	64	49	41	23	26
1998— Salt Lake (PCL)	3	4	.429	4.84	34	2	0	0	9	57 2/3	60	33	31	31	65
— Minnesota (A.L.)	0	2	.000	3.86	14	0	0	0	0	23 1/3	25	10	10	11	23
1999— Salt Lake (PCL)	1	2	.333	2.50	16	0	0	0	1	18	16	7	5	6	19
— Minnesota (A.L.)	2	2	.500	2.72	52	0	0	0	0	49 2/3	55	19	15	16	40
2000— Minnesota (A.L.)	2	3	.400	3.90	67	0	0	0	1	67	83	35	29	32	62
Major League totals (5 years)	6	14	.300	5.11	153	14	0	0	1	214 2/3	272	142	122	91	166

MILLER, TREVER — P

PERSONAL: Born May 29, 1973, in Louisville, Ky. ... 6-4/195. ... Throws left, bats right. ... Full name: Trever Douglas Miller.
HIGH SCHOOL: Trinity (Louisville, Ky.).
TRANSACTIONS/CAREER NOTES: Selected by Detroit Tigers organization in supplemental round ("sandwich pick" between first and second round, 41st pick overall) of free-agent draft (June 3, 1991); pick received as part of compensation for Atlanta Braves signing Type A free-agent C Mike Heath. ... Traded by Tigers with C Brad Ausmus, P Jose Lima, P C.J. Nitkowski and IF Daryle Ward to Houston Astros for OF Brian Hunter, IF Orlando Miller, P Doug Brocail, P Todd Jones and cash (December 10, 1996). ... On disabled list (August 23-September 7, 1998). ... Traded by Astros to Philadelphia Phillies for P Yorkis Perez (March 29, 2000). ... Claimed on waivers by Los Angeles Dodgers (May 19, 2000). ... On Albuquerque disabled list (August 3-17 and August 31-September 11, 2000). ... Granted free agency (October 18, 2000).
STATISTICAL NOTES: Tied for Appalachian League lead with seven home runs allowed in 1991.

Year League	W	L	Pct.	ERA	G	GS	CG	ShO	Sv.	IP	H	R	ER	BB	SO
1991— Bristol (Appl.)	2	7	.222	5.67	13	13	0	0	0	54	60	44	34	29	46
1992— Bristol (Appl.)	3	•8	.273	4.93	12	12	1	0	0	69 1/3	75	45	38	27	64
1993— Fayetteville (S.Atl.)	8	13	.381	4.19	28	28	2	0	0	161	151	99	75	67	116
1994— Trenton (East.)	7	•16	.304	4.39	26	26	*6	0	0	174 1/3	*198	95	85	51	73
1995— Jacksonville (Sou.)	8	2	.800	2.72	31	16	3	2	0	122 1/3	122	46	37	34	77
1996— Toledo (I.L.)	13	6	.684	4.90	27	27	0	0	0	165 1/3	167	98	90	65	115
— Detroit (A.L.)	0	4	.000	9.18	5	4	0	0	0	16 2/3	28	17	17	9	8
1997— New Orleans (A.A.)■	6	7	.462	3.30	29	27	2	0	0	163 2/3	177	71	60	54	99
1998— Houston (N.L.)	2	0	1.000	3.04	37	1	0	0	1	53 1/3	57	21	18	20	30
1999— Houston (N.L.)	3	2	.600	5.07	47	0	0	0	1	49 2/3	58	29	28	29	37
2000— Philadelphia (N.L.)■	0	0	...	8.36	14	0	0	0	0	14	19	16	13	9	10
— Los Angeles (N.L.)■	0	0	...	23.14	2	0	0	0	0	2 1/3	8	6	6	3	1
— Albuquerque (PCL)	4	2	.667	3.41	12	9	1	1	0	58	60	29	22	20	39
A.L. totals (1 year)	0	4	.000	9.18	5	4	0	0	0	16 2/3	28	17	17	9	8
N.L. totals (3 years)	5	2	.714	4.90	100	1	0	0	2	119 1/3	142	72	65	61	78
Major League totals (4 years)	5	6	.455	5.43	105	5	0	0	2	136	170	89	82	70	86

DIVISION SERIES RECORD

Year League	W	L	Pct.	ERA	G	GS	CG	ShO	Sv.	IP	H	R	ER	BB	SO
1998— Houston (N.L.)	0	0	...	...	1	0	0	0	0	0	0	0	0	1	0
1999— Houston (N.L.)	0	0	...	0.00	2	0	0	0	0	1 1/3	1	0	0	0	2
Division series totals (2 years)	0	0	...	0.00	3	0	0	0	0	1 1/3	1	0	0	1	2

MILLER, WADE — P — ASTROS

PERSONAL: Born September 13, 1976, in Reading, Pa. ... 6-2/185. ... Throws right, bats right. ... Full name: Wade T. Miller.
HIGH SCHOOL: Brandywine Heights (Pa.).
COLLEGE: Alvernia (Pa.) College.
TRANSACTIONS/CAREER NOTES: Selected by Houston Astros organization in 20th round of free-agent draft (June 4, 1996). ... On disabled list (June 1, 1998-remainder of season). ... On New Orleans disabled list (May 16-25, 2000).

Year League	W	L	Pct.	ERA	G	GS	CG	ShO	Sv.	IP	H	R	ER	BB	SO
1996— Auburn (NY-Penn)	1	1	.500	5.00	2	2	0	0	0	9	8	9	5	4	11
— Gulf Coast Astros (GCL)	3	4	.429	3.79	11	10	0	0	0	57	49	26	24	12	53
1997— Quad City (Midw.)	5	3	.625	3.36	10	8	2	0	0	59	45	27	22	10	50
— Kissimmee (FSL)	10	2	.833	1.80	14	14	4	1	0	100	79	28	20	14	76
1998— Jackson (Texas)	5	0	1.000	2.32	10	10	0	0	0	62	49	23	16	27	48
1999— New Orleans (PCL)	11	9	.550	4.38	26	26	2	0	0	162 1/3	156	85	79	64	135
— Houston (N.L.)	0	1	.000	9.58	5	1	0	0	0	10 1/3	17	11	11	5	8
2000— New Orleans (PCL)	4	5	.444	3.67	16	15	0	0	0	105 1/3	95	46	43	38	81
— Houston (N.L.)	6	6	.500	5.14	16	16	2	0	0	105	104	66	60	42	89
Major League totals (2 years)	6	7	.462	5.54	21	17	2	0	0	115 1/3	121	77	71	47	97

M

PERSONAL: Born December 30, 1973, in Willemstad, Curacao. ... 5-11/175. ... Bats right, throws right. ... Full name: Ralph Gregory Milliard.
HIGH SCHOOL: Aamsvdorda Technical School (Soest, The Netherlands).
TRANSACTIONS/CAREER NOTES: Signed as non-drafted free agent by Florida Marlins organization (July 26, 1992). ... On Charlotte disabled list (April 22-May 7, 1997). ... Traded by Marlins with P Al Leiter to New York Mets for P Jesus Sanchez, P A.J. Burnett, and OF Robert Stratton (February 6, 1998). ... Traded by Mets to Cincinnati Reds for P Mark Corey (February 4, 1999). ... On Cincinnati disabled list (March 22-May 17, 1999). ... On Chattanooga disabled list (June 17-24 and July 3, 1999-remainder of season). ... Granted free agency (October 15, 1999). ... Signed by San Diego Padres organization (November 4, 1999). ... On Las Vegas disabled list (August 9-16, 2000). ... Granted free agency (October 18, 2000). ... Signed by Cleveland Indians organization (November 15, 2000).
STATISTICAL NOTES: Led Gulf Coast League second basemen with 111 putouts, 142 assists, 257 total chances and .984 fielding percentage in 1993. ... Led Midwest League second basemen with 659 total chances and 72 double plays in 1994. ... Led International League second basemen with 276 putouts in 1998.

									— BATTING —						— FIELDING —		
Year	Team (League)	Pos.	G	AB	R	H	2B	3B	HR	RBI	Avg.	BB	SO	SB	PO	A	E	Avg.
1993—	GC Marlins (GCL)	2B-3B	53	192	35	45	15	0	0	25	.234	30	17	11	†114	†145	5	.981
1994—	Kane County (Midw.)	2B	133	515	*97	153	34	2	8	67	.297	68	63	10	*248	*390	21	.968
1995—	Portland (East.)	2B	128	464	*104	124	22	3	11	40	.267	85	83	22	*299	357	17	.975
1996—	Portland (East.)	2B	6	20	2	4	0	1	0	2	.200	1	5	1	12	18	0	1.000
—	Charlotte (I.L.)	2B	69	250	47	69	15	2	6	26	.276	38	43	8	154	188	5	.986
—	Florida (N.L.)	2B	24	62	7	10	2	0	0	1	.161	14	16	2	42	65	5	.955
1997—	Charlotte (I.L.)	2B	33	132	19	35	5	1	4	18	.265	9	21	5	71	91	1	.994
—	Florida (N.L.)	2B	8	30	2	6	0	0	0	2	.200	3	3	1	14	32	0	1.000
—	Portland (East.)	2B	19	69	13	19	1	2	0	5	.275	7	8	3	37	53	1	.989
1998—	Norfolk (I.L.)■	2B-SS	127	417	73	108	24	4	15	52	.259	79	59	17	†277	373	13	.980
—	New York (N.L.)	2B-SS	10	1	3	0	0	0	0	0	.000	0	1	0	3	2	1	.833
1999—	Chattanooga (Sou.)■	SS-DH	32	102	19	30	3	1	4	23	.294	20	13	2	44	87	5	.963
2000—	Las Vegas (PCL)■	SS-2B-3B	108	371	61	104	26	3	5	40	.280	63	63	18	171	270	21	.955
	Major League totals (3 years)		42	93	12	16	2	0	0	3	.172	17	20	3	59	99	6	.963

PERSONAL: Born October 18, 1966, in Lakeland, Fla. ... 6-1/195. ... Throws right, bats right. ... Full name: Alan Bernard Mills.
HIGH SCHOOL: Kathleen (Fla.).
JUNIOR COLLEGE: Polk Community College (Fla.).
COLLEGE: Tuskegee.
TRANSACTIONS/CAREER NOTES: Selected by Boston Red Sox organization in first round (13th pick overall) of free-agent draft (January 14, 1986); did not sign. ... Selected by California Angels organization in secondary phase of free-agent draft (June 2, 1986). ... Traded by Angels to New York Yankees (June 22, 1987), completing deal in which Angels traded P Ron Romanick and a player to be named later to Yankees for C Butch Wynegar (December 19, 1986). ... Traded by Yankees to Baltimore Orioles for two players to be named later (February 29, 1992); Yankees acquired P Francisco de la Rosa (February 29, 1992) and P Mark Carper (June 8, 1992) to complete deal. ... On suspended list (June 26-30, 1993). ... On Rochester disabled list (July 4-September 16, 1995). ... On disabled list (March 22-May 12, 1996; and April 10-June 15, 1997). ... On suspended list (May 29-30, 1998). ... Granted free agency (October 23, 1998). ... Signed by Los Angeles Dodgers (December 10, 1998). ... Traded by Dodgers with cash considerations to Orioles for P Al Reyes (June 13, 2000). ... On Baltimore disabled list (August 11-30, 2000); included rehabilitation assignment to Frederick (August 28-30).

Year	League	W	L	Pct.	ERA	G	GS	CG	ShO	Sv.	IP	H	R	ER	BB	SO
1986—	Salem (N'West)	6	6	.500	4.63	14	14	1	0	0	83²/₃	77	58	43	60	50
1987—	Prince William (Caro.)■■■	2	11	.154	6.09	35	8	0	0	1	85²/₃	102	75	58	64	53
1988—	Prince William (Caro.)	3	8	.273	4.13	42	5	0	0	4	93²/₃	93	56	43	43	59
1989—	Prince William (Caro.)	6	1	.857	0.91	26	0	0	0	7	39²/₃	22	5	4	13	44
—	Fort Lauderdale (FSL)	1	4	.200	3.77	22	0	0	0	6	31	40	15	13	9	25
1990—	New York (A.L.)	1	5	.167	4.10	36	0	0	0	0	41²/₃	48	21	19	33	24
—	Columbus (I.L.)	3	3	.500	3.38	17	0	0	0	6	29¹/₃	22	11	11	14	30
1991—	Columbus (I.L.)	7	5	.583	4.43	38	15	0	0	8	113²/₃	109	65	56	75	77
—	New York (A.L.)	1	1	.500	4.41	6	2	0	0	0	16¹/₃	16	9	8	8	11
1992—	Rochester (I.L.)■	0	1	.000	5.40	3	0	0	0	1	5	6	3	3	2	8
—	Baltimore (A.L.)	10	4	.714	2.61	35	3	0	0	2	103¹/₃	78	33	30	54	60
1993—	Baltimore (A.L.)	5	4	.556	3.23	45	0	0	0	4	100¹/₃	80	39	36	51	68
1994—	Baltimore (A.L.)	3	3	.500	5.16	47	0	0	0	2	45¹/₃	43	26	26	24	44
1995—	Baltimore (A.L.)	3	0	1.000	7.43	21	0	0	0	0	23	30	20	19	18	16
—	Rochester (I.L.)	0	1	.000	0.00	1	1	0	0	0	2²/₃	2	6	0	5	2
—	Gulf Coast Orioles (GCL)	0	0	...	0.00	1	1	0	0	0	2	3	0	0	2	1
1996—	Baltimore (A.L.)	3	2	.600	4.28	49	0	0	0	3	54²/₃	40	26	26	35	50
1997—	Baltimore (A.L.)	2	3	.400	4.89	39	0	0	0	0	38²/₃	41	23	21	33	32
1998—	Baltimore (A.L.)	3	4	.429	3.74	72	0	0	0	2	77	55	32	32	50	57
1999—	Los Angeles (N.L.)■	3	4	.429	3.73	68	0	0	0	0	72¹/₃	70	33	30	43	49
2000—	Los Angeles (N.L.)	2	1	.667	4.21	18	0	0	0	1	25²/₃	31	12	12	16	18
—	Baltimore (A.L.)■	2	0	1.000	6.46	23	0	0	0	1	23²/₃	25	17	17	19	18
—	Frederick (Caro.)	0	0	...	4.50	1	1	0	0	0	2	2	1	1	0	1
	A.L. totals (10 years)	33	26	.559	4.02	373	5	0	0	14	524	456	246	234	325	380
	N.L. totals (2 years)	5	5	.500	3.86	86	0	0	0	1	98	101	45	42	59	67
	Major League totals (11 years)	38	31	.551	3.99	459	5	0	0	15	622	557	291	276	384	447

DIVISION SERIES RECORD

Year	League	W	L	Pct.	ERA	G	GS	CG	ShO	Sv.	IP	H	R	ER	BB	SO
1997—	Baltimore (A.L.)	0	0	...	0.00	1	0	0	0	0	1	1	0	0	0	1

CHAMPIONSHIP SERIES RECORD

Year	League	W	L	Pct.	ERA	G	GS	CG	ShO	Sv.	IP	H	R	ER	BB	SO
1996—	Baltimore (A.L.)	0	0	...	3.86	3	0	0	0	0	2¹/₃	3	1	1	1	3
1997—	Baltimore (A.L.)	0	1	.000	2.70	3	0	0	0	0	3¹/₃	1	1	1	2	3
	Champ. series totals (2 years)	0	1	.000	3.18	6	0	0	0	0	5²/₃	4	2	2	3	6

M

PERSONAL: Born December 24, 1974, in Gastonia, N.C. ... 6-4/220. ... Throws right, bats right. ... Full name: Kevin Austin Millwood.
HIGH SCHOOL: Bessemer City (N.C.).
TRANSACTIONS/CAREER NOTES: Selected by Atlanta Braves organization in 11th round of free-agent draft (June 3, 1993).
STATISTICAL NOTES: Pitched 6-0 one-hit, complete-game victory against Pittsburgh (April 14, 1998).

Year	League	W	L	Pct.	ERA	G	GS	CG	ShO	Sv.	IP	H	R	ER	BB	SO
1993—	Gulf Coast Braves (GCL)	3	3	.500	3.06	12	9	0	0	0	50	36	27	17	28	49
1994—	Danville (Appl.)	3	3	.500	3.72	13	5	0	0	1	46	42	25	19	34	56
—	Macon (S.Atl.)	0	5	.000	5.79	12	4	0	0	1	32²/₃	31	31	21	32	24
1995—	Macon (S.Atl.)	5	6	.455	4.63	29	12	0	0	0	103	86	65	53	57	89
1996—	Durham (Caro.)	6	9	.400	4.28	33	20	1	0	1	149¹/₃	138	77	71	58	139
1997—	Greenville (Sou.)	3	5	.375	4.11	11	11	0	0	0	61¹/₃	59	37	28	24	61
—	Richmond (I.L.)	7	0	1.000	1.93	9	9	1	0	0	60²/₃	38	13	13	16	46
—	Atlanta (N.L.)	5	3	.625	4.03	12	8	0	0	0	51¹/₃	55	26	23	21	42
1998—	Atlanta (N.L.)	17	8	.680	4.08	31	29	3	1	0	174¹/₃	175	86	79	56	163
1999—	Atlanta (N.L.)	18	7	.720	2.68	33	33	2	0	0	228	168	80	68	59	205
2000—	Atlanta (N.L.)	10	13	.435	4.66	36	•35	0	0	0	212²/₃	213	115	110	62	168
Major League totals (4 years)		50	31	.617	3.78	112	105	5	1	0	666¹/₃	611	307	280	198	578

DIVISION SERIES RECORD

Year	League	W	L	Pct.	ERA	G	GS	CG	ShO	Sv.	IP	H	R	ER	BB	SO
1999—	Atlanta (N.L.)	1	0	1.000	0.90	2	1	1	0	1	10	1	1	1	0	9
2000—	Atlanta (N.L.)	0	1	.000	7.71	1	1	0	0	0	4²/₃	4	4	4	3	3
Division series totals (2 years)		1	1	.500	3.07	3	2	1	0	1	14²/₃	5	5	5	3	12

CHAMPIONSHIP SERIES RECORD

Year	League	W	L	Pct.	ERA	G	GS	CG	ShO	Sv.	IP	H	R	ER	BB	SO
1999—	Atlanta (N.L.)	1	0	1.000	3.55	2	2	0	0	0	12²/₃	13	6	5	1	9

WORLD SERIES RECORD

Year	League	W	L	Pct.	ERA	G	GS	CG	ShO	Sv.	IP	H	R	ER	BB	SO
1999—	Atlanta (N.L.)	0	1	.000	18.00	1	1	0	0	0	2	8	5	4	2	2

ALL-STAR GAME RECORD

Year	League	W	L	Pct.	ERA	GS	CG	ShO	Sv.	IP	H	R	ER	BB	SO
1999—	National	0	0	...	0.00	0	0	0	0	1	1	0	0	0	1

PERSONAL: Born August 4, 1975, in State College, Pa. ... 6-3/220. ... Throws left, bats left. ... Full name: Eric Robert Milton.
HIGH SCHOOL: Bellefonte (Pa.).
COLLEGE: Maryland.
TRANSACTIONS/CAREER NOTES: Selected by New York Yankees organization in first round (20th pick overall) of free-agent draft (June 2, 1996). ... Traded by Yankees with P Danny Mota, OF Brian Buchanan, SS Cristian Guzman and cash to Minnesota Twins for 2B Chuck Knoblauch (February 6, 1998).
STATISTICAL NOTES: Tied for Eastern League lead with four balks in 1997. ... Pitched 7-0 no-hit victory against Anaheim (September 11, 1999).

Year	League	W	L	Pct.	ERA	G	GS	CG	ShO	Sv.	IP	H	R	ER	BB	SO
1997—	Tampa (FSL)	8	3	.727	3.09	14	14	1	0	0	93¹/₃	78	35	32	14	95
—	Norwich (East.)	6	3	.667	3.13	14	14	1	0	0	77²/₃	59	29	27	36	67
1998—	Minnesota (A.L.)■	8	14	.364	5.64	32	32	1	0	0	172¹/₃	195	113	108	70	107
1999—	Minnesota (A.L.)	7	11	.389	4.49	34	34	5	2	0	206¹/₃	190	111	103	63	163
2000—	Minnesota (A.L.)	13	10	.565	4.86	33	33	0	0	0	200	205	123	108	44	160
Major League totals (3 years)		28	35	.444	4.96	99	99	6	2	0	578²/₃	590	347	319	177	430

PERSONAL: Born January 9, 1975, in Canton, Ohio. ... 6-7/230. ... Bats left, throws left. ... Full name: Damon Reed Minor. ... Brother of Ryan Minor, third baseman, Montreal Expos.
HIGH SCHOOL: Hammon (Okla.).
COLLEGE: Oklahoma.
TRANSACTIONS/CAREER NOTES: Selected by San Francisco Giants organization in 12th round of free-agent draft (June 4, 1996).
STATISTICAL NOTES: Tied for Northwest League lead in intentional bases on balls received with four in 1996. ... Led Northwest League first basemen with 693 total chances in 1996. ... Led California League with eight intentional bases in balls received in 1997. ... Led California League first basemen with 127 double plays and 1,371 total chances in 1997. ... Led Texas League first baseman with 1,273 total chances in 1999. ... Led Pacific Coast League with 1,205 total chances and 115 double plays in 2000.

Year	Team (League)	Pos.	G	AB	R	H	2B	3B	HR	RBI	Avg.	BB	SO	SB	PO	A	E	Avg.
							BATTING								FIELDING			
1996—	Bellingham (N'West) ..	1B	75	269	44	65	11	1	12	55	.242	47	86	0	*650	38	5	.993
1997—	Bakersfield (Calif.)	1B	*140	532	98	154	34	1	31	99	.289	87	143	2	*1261	*88	*22	.984
1998—	Shreveport (Texas)	1B	81	289	39	69	11	1	14	52	.239	30	51	1	641	39	8	.988
—	San Jose (Calif.)	1B	48	176	26	50	10	1	7	36	.284	28	40	0	413	36	6	.987
1999—	Shreveport (Texas)	1B-DH	136	473	76	129	33	4	20	82	.273	80	115	1	*1160	*104	9	*.993
2000—	Fresno (PCL)	1B	133	482	84	140	27	1	30	106	.290	87	97	0	*1134	60	11	.991
—	San Francisco (N.L.) ..	1B-2B	10	9	3	4	0	0	3	6	.444	2	1	0	5	0	0	1.000
Major League totals (1 year)			10	9	3	4	0	0	3	6	.444	2	1	0	5	0	0	1.000

M

PERSONAL: Born January 5, 1974, in Canton, Ohio. ... 6-7/245. ... Bats right, throws right. ... Full name: Ryan Dale Minor. ... Brother of Damon Minor, first baseman, San Francisco Giants organization.
HIGH SCHOOL: Hammon (Okla.).
COLLEGE: Oklahoma.
TRANSACTIONS/CAREER NOTES: Selected by Baltimore Orioles organization in 15th round of free-agent draft (June 1, 1992); did not sign. ... Selected by Orioles organization in 33rd round of free-agent draft (June 4, 1996). ... On Baltimore disabled list (July 5-28, 2000); included rehabilitation assignment to Frederick (July 26-28). ... Traded by Orioles to Montreal Expos for P Jorge Julio (December 22, 2000).
STATISTICAL NOTES: Led Eastern League third basemen with 27 double plays in 1998.
MISCELLANEOUS: Selected by Philadelphia 76ers in second round (32nd pick overall) of 1996 NBA draft. ... Played in Continental Basketball Association with Oklahoma City Calvary (1996-97).

Year Team (League)	Pos.	G	AB	R	H	2B	3B	HR	RBI	Avg.	BB	SO	SB	PO	A	E	Avg.
1996— Bluefield (Appl.)	3B-SS	25	87	14	22	6	0	4	9	.253	7	32	1	13	45	5	.921
1997— Delmarva (S.Atl.)........	3B-1B-DH	134	488	83	150	42	1	24	97	.307	51	102	7	193	209	34	.922
1998— Bowie (East.)	3B-DH	138	521	73	130	20	3	17	71	.250	34	*152	2	89	245	*26	.928
— Baltimore (A.L.)...........	3B-1B-DH	9	14	3	6	1	0	0	1	.429	0	3	0	6	5	1	.917
1999— Rochester (I.L.)...........	3B-1B-DH	101	383	56	98	24	1	21	67	.256	37	119	3	170	148	13	.961
— Baltimore (A.L.)...........	3B-1B	46	124	13	24	7	0	3	10	.194	8	43	1	36	80	5	.959
2000— Rochester (I.L.)...........	3B-1B	68	241	33	71	9	1	14	48	.295	32	57	1	97	112	17	.925
— Baltimore (A.L.)...........	3B-1B	32	84	4	11	1	0	0	3	.131	3	20	0	44	35	4	.952
— Frederick (Caro.).......	3B	2	9	3	3	0	0	0	0	.333	0	4	0	1	1	0	1.000
— GC Orioles (GCL).......	3B	3	13	2	2	1	0	1	4	.154	1	6	0	2	1	1	.750
Major League totals (3 years)		87	222	20	41	9	0	3	14	.185	11	66	1	86	120	10	.954

CBA REGULAR-SEASON RECORD

TRANSACTIONS/CAREER NOTES: Selected by Philadelphia 76ers in second round (32nd pick overall) of 1996 NBA draft. ... Played in Continental Basketball Association with Oklahoma City Calvary (1996-97).

Season Team	G	Min.	FGM	FGA	Pct.	FTM	FTA	Pct.	Reb.	Ast.	Pts.	RPG	APG	PPG
96-97—Oklahoma City	32	892	124	270	.459	38	50	.760	141	62	304	4.4	1.9	9.5

PERSONAL: Born October 18, 1970, in Kingman, Ariz. ... 6-1/218. ... Bats right, throws right. ... Full name: Douglas Anthony Mirabelli. ... Name pronounced mirr-uh-BEL-ee.
HIGH SCHOOL: Valley (Las Vegas).
COLLEGE: Wichita State.
TRANSACTIONS/CAREER NOTES: Selected by Detroit Tigers organization in sixth round of free-agent draft (June 5, 1989); did not sign. ... Selected by San Francisco Giants organization in fifth round of free-agent draft (June 1, 1992). ... On Phoenix disabled list (May 16-23, 1995).
STATISTICAL NOTES: Led Texas League with .419 on-base percentage in 1996. ... Led Pacific Coast League catchers with 680 total chances in 1997.

M

Year Team (League)	Pos.	G	AB	R	H	2B	3B	HR	RBI	Avg.	BB	SO	SB	PO	A	E	Avg.
1992— San Jose (Calif.)........	C	53	177	30	41	11	1	0	21	.232	24	18	1	321	38	10	.973
1993— San Jose (Calif.)........	C	113	371	58	100	19	2	1	48	.270	72	55	0	737	99	9	.989
1994— Shreveport (Texas)	C-1B	85	255	23	56	8	0	4	24	.220	36	48	3	391	51	3	.993
1995— Shreveport (Texas)	C-1B	40	126	14	38	13	0	0	16	.302	20	14	1	193	21	3	.986
— Phoenix (PCL)	C	23	66	3	11	0	1	0	7	.167	12	10	1	115	17	2	.985
1996— Shreveport (Texas)	C-DH-1B	115	380	60	112	23	0	21	70	.295	76	49	0	548	56	7	.989
— Phoenix (PCL)	C	14	47	10	14	7	0	0	7	.298	4	7	0	97	10	2	.982
— San Francisco (N.L.) ..	C	9	18	2	4	1	0	0	1	.222	3	4	0	29	2	0	1.000
1997— Phoenix (PCL)	C-DH	100	332	49	88	23	2	8	48	.265	58	69	1	*629	47	4	.994
— San Francisco (N.L.) ..	C	6	7	0	1	0	0	0	0	.143	1	3	0	16	0	0	1.000
1998— Fresno (PCL)	C-DH	85	265	45	69	12	2	13	53	.260	52	55	2	605	50	3	*.995
— San Francisco (N.L.) ..	C	10	17	2	4	2	0	1	4	.235	2	6	0	34	4	1	.974
1999— Fresno (PCL)	C-1B-DH	86	320	63	100	24	1	14	51	.313	48	56	8	619	73	5	.993
— San Francisco (N.L.) ..	C	33	87	10	22	6	0	1	10	.253	9	25	0	156	11	0	1.000
2000— San Francisco (N.L.) ..	C	82	230	23	53	10	2	6	28	.230	36	57	1	429	38	7	.985
Major League totals (5 years)		140	359	37	84	19	2	8	43	.234	51	95	1	664	55	8	.989

DIVISION SERIES RECORD

Year Team (League)	Pos.	G	AB	R	H	2B	3B	HR	RBI	Avg.	BB	SO	SB	PO	A	E	Avg.
2000— San Francisco (N.L.) ..	C	2	2	0	0	0	0	0	0	.000	1	1	0	6	1	0	1.000

PERSONAL: Born June 8, 1968, in Cleveland. ... 6-4/205. ... Throws right, bats right. ... Full name: David John Mlicki. ... Brother of Doug Mlicki, minor league pitcher (1992-99). ... Name pronounced muh-LICK-ee.
HIGH SCHOOL: Cheyenne Mountain (Colorado Springs, Colo.).
COLLEGE: Oklahoma State.
TRANSACTIONS/CAREER NOTES: Selected by Seattle Mariners organization in 23rd round of free-agent draft (June 5, 1989); did not sign. ... Selected by Cleveland Indians organization in 17th round of free-agent draft (June 4, 1990). ... On Cleveland disabled list (April 4-August 4, 1993); included rehabilitation assignment to Canton/Akron (July 19-August 4). ... Traded by Indians with P Jerry DiPoto, P Paul Byrd and a player to be named later to New York Mets for OF Jeromy Burnitz and P Joe Roa (November 18, 1994); Mets acquired 2B Jesus Azuaje to complete deal (December 6, 1994). ... Traded by Mets with P Greg McMichael to Los Angeles Dodgers for P Hideo Nomo and P Brad Clontz

(June 5, 1998). ... Traded by Dodgers with P Mel Rojas and cash considerations to Detroit Tigers for P Robinson Checo, P Apostol Garcia and P Rick Roberts (April 16, 1999). ... On Detroit disabled list (July 23-September 5, 2000); included rehabilitation assignment to West Michigan (August 25-31) and Toledo (August 31-September 5).
STATISTICAL NOTES: Led International League with 26 home runs allowed in 1994.
MISCELLANEOUS: Struck out in only appearance as pinch hitter (1996). ... Appeared in one game as pinch runner (1997).

Year	League	W	L	Pct.	ERA	G	GS	CG	ShO	Sv.	IP	H	R	ER	BB	SO
1990—	Burlington (Appl.)	3	1	.750	3.50	8	1	0	0	0	18	16	11	7	6	17
	Watertown (NY-Penn)	3	0	1.000	3.38	7	4	0	0	0	32	33	15	12	11	28
1991—	Columbus (S.Atl.)	8	6	.571	4.20	22	19	2	0	0	115²/₃	101	70	54	70	136
1992—	Canton/Akron (East.)	11	9	.550	3.60	27	*27	2	0	0	172²/₃	143	77	69	•80	146
	Cleveland (A.L.)	0	2	.000	4.98	4	4	0	0	0	21²/₃	23	14	12	16	16
1993—	Canton/Akron (East.)	2	1	.667	0.39	6	6	0	0	0	23	15	2	1	8	21
	Cleveland (A.L.)	0	0	...	3.38	3	3	0	0	0	13¹/₃	11	6	5	6	7
1994—	Charlotte (I.L.)	6	10	.375	4.25	28	28	0	0	0	165¹/₃	179	85	78	64	152
1995—	New York (N.L.)■	9	7	.563	4.26	29	25	0	0	0	160²/₃	160	82	76	54	123
1996—	New York (N.L.)	6	7	.462	3.30	51	2	0	0	1	90	95	46	33	33	83
1997—	New York (N.L.)	8	12	.400	4.00	32	32	1	1	0	193²/₃	194	89	86	76	157
1998—	New York (N.L.)	1	4	.200	5.68	10	10	1	0	0	57	68	38	36	25	39
	Los Angeles (N.L.)■■	7	3	.700	4.05	20	20	2	1	0	124¹/₃	120	64	56	38	78
1999—	Los Angeles (N.L.)	0	1	.000	4.91	2	0	0	0	0	7¹/₃	10	4	4	2	1
	Detroit (A.L.)■	14	12	.538	4.60	31	31	2	0	0	191²/₃	209	108	98	70	119
2000—	Detroit (A.L.)	6	11	.353	5.58	24	21	0	0	0	119¹/₃	143	79	74	44	57
	West Michigan (Midw.)	1	0	1.000	0.00	1	1	0	0	0	6	1	0	0	1	6
	Toledo (I.L.)	0	1	.000	7.94	1	1	0	0	0	5²/₃	11	5	5	0	3
A.L. totals (4 years)		20	25	.444	4.92	62	59	2	0	0	346	386	207	189	136	199
N.L. totals (5 years)		31	34	.477	4.14	144	89	4	2	1	633	647	323	291	228	481
Major League totals (8 years)		51	59	.464	4.41	206	148	6	2	1	979	1033	530	480	364	680

MOEHLER, BRIAN — P — TIGERS

PERSONAL: Born December 31, 1971, in Rockingham, N.C. ... 6-3/235. ... Throws right, bats right. ... Full name: Brian Merritt Moehler.
HIGH SCHOOL: Richmond (N.C.) South.
COLLEGE: UNC Greensboro.
TRANSACTIONS/CAREER NOTES: Selected by Detroit Tigers organization in sixth round of free-agent draft (June 3, 1993). ... On disabled list (August 9-22, 1997). ... On suspended list (May 3-13, 1999). ... On Detroit disabled list (April 17-May 19, 2000); included rehabilitation assignment to West Michigan (May 12-19).

Year	League	W	L	Pct.	ERA	G	GS	CG	ShO	Sv.	IP	H	R	ER	BB	SO
1993—	Niagara Falls (NY-Penn)	6	5	.545	3.22	12	11	0	0	0	58²/₃	51	33	21	27	38
1994—	Lakeland (FSL)	12	12	.500	3.01	26	25	5	2	0	164²/₃	153	66	55	65	92
1995—	Jacksonville (Sou.)	8	10	.444	4.82	28	27	0	0	0	162¹/₃	176	94	87	52	89
1996—	Detroit (A.L.)	0	1	.000	4.35	2	2	0	0	0	10¹/₃	11	10	5	8	2
	Jacksonville (Sou.)	15	6	.714	3.48	28	28	1	0	0	173¹/₃	186	80	67	50	120
1997—	Detroit (A.L.)	11	12	.478	4.67	31	31	2	1	0	175¹/₃	198	97	91	61	97
1998—	Detroit (A.L.)	14	13	.519	3.90	33	33	4	3	0	221¹/₃	220	103	96	56	123
1999—	Detroit (A.L.)	10	*16	.385	5.04	32	32	2	2	0	196¹/₃	229	116	110	59	106
2000—	Detroit (A.L.)	12	9	.571	4.50	29	29	2	0	0	178	222	99	89	40	103
	West Michigan (Midw.)	0	1	.000	4.26	1	1	0	0	0	6¹/₃	5	3	3	1	4
Major League totals (5 years)		47	51	.480	4.50	127	127	10	6	0	781¹/₃	880	425	391	224	431

MOELLER, CHAD — C — TWINS

PERSONAL: Born February 18, 1975, in Upland, Calif. ... 6-3/210. ... Bats right, throws right. ... Full name: Chad Edward Moeller.
HIGH SCHOOL: Upland (Calif.).
COLLEGE: Southern California.
TRANSACTIONS/CAREER NOTES: Selected by New York Yankees organization in 25th round of free-agent draft (June 3, 1993); did not sign. ... Selected by Minnesota Twins organization in seventh round of free-agent draft (June 4, 1996). ... On disabled list (July 12, 1996-remainder of season). ... On disabled list (August 12-30, 2000).

							BATTING							FIELDING		
Year	Team (League)	Pos.	G	AB	R	H	2B	3B	HR	RBI	Avg.	BB	SO	SB	PO	A	E	Avg.
1996—	Elizabethton (Appl.)	C	17	59	17	21	4	0	4	13	.356	18	9	1	99	16	1	.991
1997—	Fort Wayne (Midw.)	C	108	384	58	111	18	3	9	39	.289	48	76	11	824	90	*15	.984
1998—	Fort Myers (FSL)	C	66	254	37	83	24	1	6	39	.327	31	37	2	395	36	9	.980
	New Britain (East.)	C	58	187	21	44	10	0	6	23	.235	24	41	2	414	25	6	.987
1999—	New Britain (East.)	C	89	250	29	62	11	3	4	24	.248	21	44	0	548	59	10	.984
2000—	Salt Lake (PCL)	C	47	167	30	48	13	1	5	20	.287	9	45	0	256	25	2	.993
	Minnesota (A.L.)	C	48	128	13	27	3	1	1	9	.211	9	33	1	266	13	6	.979
Major League totals (1 year)			48	128	13	27	3	1	1	9	.211	9	33	1	266	13	6	.979

MOHLER, MIKE — P

PERSONAL: Born July 26, 1968, in Dayton, Ohio. ... 6-2/208. ... Throws left, bats right. ... Full name: Michael Ross Mohler.
HIGH SCHOOL: East Ascension (Gonzales, La.).
COLLEGE: Nicholls State (La.).
TRANSACTIONS/CAREER NOTES: Selected by Oakland Athletics organization in 42nd round of free-agent draft (June 5, 1989). ... On Tacoma disabled list (April 7-May 24, 1994). ... Granted free agency (December 21, 1998). ... Signed by St. Louis Cardinals (January 15, 1999). ... Released by Cardinals (June 5, 2000). ... Signed by Cleveland Indians organization (June 16, 2000). ... Released by Indians (July 1, 2000). ... Signed by A's organization (July 6, 2000). ... Granted free agency (October 18, 2000).
MISCELLANEOUS: Appeared in two games as pinch runner (1997).

Year	League	W	L	Pct.	ERA	G	GS	CG	ShO	Sv.	IP	H	R	ER	BB	SO
1990—	Madison (Midw.)	1	1	.500	3.41	42	2	0	0	1	63 1/3	56	34	24	32	72
1991—	Modesto (Calif.)	9	4	.692	2.86	21	20	1	0	0	122 2/3	106	48	39	45	98
—	Huntsville (Sou.)	4	2	.667	3.57	8	8	0	0	0	53	55	22	21	20	27
1992—	Huntsville (Sou.)	3	8	.273	3.59	44	6	0	0	3	80 1/3	72	41	32	39	56
1993—	Oakland (A.L.)	1	6	.143	5.60	42	9	0	0	0	64 1/3	57	45	40	44	42
1994—	Modesto (Calif.)	1	1	.500	2.76	7	5	0	0	1	29 1/3	21	9	9	6	29
—	Tacoma (PCL)	1	3	.250	3.53	17	11	0	0	0	63 2/3	66	31	25	21	50
—	Oakland (A.L.)	0	1	.000	7.71	1	1	0	0	0	2 1/3	2	3	2	2	4
1995—	Edmonton (PCL)	2	1	.667	2.60	29	0	0	0	5	45	40	16	13	20	28
—	Oakland (A.L.)	1	1	.500	3.04	28	0	0	0	1	23 2/3	16	8	8	18	15
1996—	Oakland (A.L.)	6	3	.667	3.67	72	0	0	0	7	81	79	36	33	41	64
1997—	Oakland (A.L.)	1	10	.091	5.13	62	10	0	0	1	101 2/3	116	65	58	54	66
1998—	Oakland (A.L.)	3	3	.500	5.16	57	0	0	0	1	61	70	38	35	26	42
1999—	St. Louis (N.L.)■	1	1	.500	4.38	48	0	0	0	1	49 1/3	47	26	24	23	31
—	Memphis (PCL)	2	1	.667	3.07	10	0	0	0	1	14 2/3	16	5	5	5	17
2000—	St. Louis (N.L.)	1	1	.500	9.00	22	0	0	0	0	19	26	20	19	15	8
—	Buffalo (I.L.)■	0	0	...	0.00	3	0	0	0	0	6	3	0	0	3	3
—	Cleveland (A.L.)	0	1	.000	9.00	2	0	0	0	0	1	1	1	1	0	2
—	Sacramento (PCL)■	2	0	1.000	6.50	18	0	0	0	1	18	22	13	13	16	14
A.L. totals (7 years)		12	25	.324	4.76	264	20	0	0	9	335	341	196	177	185	235
N.L. totals (2 years)		2	2	.500	5.66	70	0	0	0	1	68 1/3	73	46	43	38	39
Major League totals (8 years)		14	27	.341	4.91	334	20	0	0	10	403 1/3	414	242	220	223	274

MOLINA, BENGIE   C   ANGELS

PERSONAL: Born July 20, 1974, in Rio Pedras, Puerto Rico. ... 5-11/207. ... Bats right, throws right. ... Full name: Benjamin Jose Molina. ... Brother of Jose Molina, catcher with Chicago Cubs (1999).
HIGH SCHOOL: Maestra Ladi (Puerto Rico).
JUNIOR COLLEGE: Arizona Western.
TRANSACTIONS/CAREER NOTES: Signed as non-drafted free agent by California Angels organization (May 23, 1993). ... Angels franchise renamed Anaheim Angels for 1997 season. ... On Vancouver disabled list (May 13-22, 1998). ... On Edmonton disabled list (June 4-14, 1999).
STATISTICAL NOTES: Led Texas League catchers with 703 total chances and nine double plays in 1996. ... Career major league grand slams: 1.

Year	Team (League)	Pos.	G	AB	R	H	2B	3B	HR	RBI	Avg.	BB	SO	SB	PO	A	E	Avg.
1993—	Arizona Angels (Ariz.)	C	27	80	9	21	6	2	0	10	.263	10	4	0	47	2	0	1.000
1994—	Ced. Rap. (Midw.)	C	48	171	14	48	8	0	3	16	.281	8	12	1	349	40	10	.975
1995—	Vancouver (PCL)		2	2	0	0	0	0	0	0	.000	0	1	0	4	0	0	1.000
—	Ced. Rap. (Midw.)	C	39	133	15	39	9	0	4	17	.293	15	11	1	283	32	7	.978
—	Lake Elsinore (Calif.)	C	27	96	21	37	7	2	2	12	.385	8	7	0	195	16	1	.995
1996—	Midland (Texas)	C	108	365	45	100	21	2	8	54	.274	25	25	0	*615	*81	7	.990
1997—	Lake Elsinore (Calif.)	C	36	149	18	42	10	2	4	33	.282	7	9	0	239	36	1	.996
—	Midland (Texas)	C	29	106	18	35	8	0	6	30	.330	10	7	0	74	15	2	.978
1998—	Vancouver (PCL)	C	49	184	13	54	9	1	1	22	.293	5	14	1	316	24	5	.986
—	Midland (Texas)	C	41	154	28	55	8	0	9	39	.357	14	7	0	233	21	3	.988
—	Anaheim (A.L.)	C	2	1	0	0	0	0	0	0	.000	0	0	0	1	0	0	1.000
1999—	Edmonton (PCL)	C-DH	65	241	28	69	16	0	7	41	.286	15	17	1	351	47	3	.993
—	Anaheim (A.L.)	C	31	101	8	26	5	0	1	10	.257	6	6	0	192	19	2	.991
2000—	Anaheim (A.L.)	C-DH	130	473	59	133	20	2	14	71	.281	23	33	1	683	61	7	.991
Major League totals (3 years)			163	575	67	159	25	2	15	81	.277	29	39	1	876	80	9	.991

MOLINA, GABE   P

PERSONAL: Born May 3, 1975, in Denver. ... 6-1/220. ... Throws right, bats right. ... Full name: Cruz Gabriel Molina.
HIGH SCHOOL: John F. Kennedy (Denver).
COLLEGE: Arizona State.
TRANSACTIONS/CAREER NOTES: Selected by Baltimore Orioles organization in 21st round of free-agent draft (June 4, 1996). ... Traded by Orioles with OF B.J. Surhoff to Atlanta Braves for OF Trenidad Hubbard, C Fernando Lunar and P Luis Rivera (July 31, 2000). ... Granted free agency (December 21, 2000).

Year	League	W	L	Pct.	ERA	G	GS	CG	ShO	Sv.	IP	H	R	ER	BB	SO
1996—	Bluefield (Appl.)	4	0	1.000	3.60	23	0	0	0	7	30	29	12	12	13	33
1997—	Delmarva (S.Atl.)	8	6	.571	2.18	46	0	0	0	7	91	59	24	22	32	119
1998—	Bowie (East.)	3	2	.600	3.36	47	0	0	0	24	61 2/3	48	24	23	27	75
1999—	Rochester (I.L.)	2	2	.500	3.14	45	0	0	0	18	57 1/3	45	22	20	23	58
—	Baltimore (A.L.)	1	2	.333	6.65	20	0	0	0	0	23	22	19	17	16	14
2000—	Rochester (I.L.)	1	2	.333	4.94	18	4	0	0	5	27 1/3	30	16	15	10	26
—	Baltimore (A.L.)	0	0	...	9.00	9	0	0	0	0	13	25	14	13	9	8
—	Richmond (I.L.)■	1	0	1.000	3.60	9	0	0	0	3	10	7	5	4	3	9
—	Atlanta (N.L.)	0	0	...	9.00	2	0	0	0	0	2	3	4	2	1	1
A.L. totals (2 years)		1	2	.333	7.50	29	0	0	0	0	36	47	33	30	25	22
N.L. totals (1 year)		0	0	...	9.00	2	0	0	0	0	2	3	4	2	1	1
Major League totals (2 years)		1	2	.333	7.58	31	0	0	0	0	38	50	37	32	26	23

MOLINA, JOSE   C

PERSONAL: Born June 3, 1975, in Bayamon, Puerto Rico. ... 6-1/215. ... Bats right, throws right. ... Full name: Jose Benjamin Molina Matta. ... Brother of Bengie Molina, catcher with Anaheim Angels.
HIGH SCHOOL: Maestro Ladi (Vega Alta, Puerto Rico).

M

TRANSACTIONS/CAREER NOTES: Selected by Chicago Cubs organization in 14th round of free-agent draft (June 3, 1993). ... On Iowa disabled list (July 31-August 10, 1999). ... On Iowa disabled list (August 4-September 5, 2000). ... Released by Cubs (November 27, 2000).
STATISTICAL NOTES: Led Southern League catchers with 108 assists and tied for lead with 21 passed balls in 1998.

Year Team (League)	Pos.	G	AB	R	H	2B	3B	HR	RBI	Avg.	BB	SO	SB	PO	A	E	Avg.
1993—GC Cubs (GCL)..........	C-1B	33	78	5	17	2	0	0	4	.218	12	12	3	143	27	7	.960
—Daytona (FSL)	C	3	7	0	1	0	0	0	1	.143	2	0	0	13	2	0	1.000
1994—Peoria (Midw.)...........	C	78	253	31	58	13	1	1	33	.229	24	61	4	567	79	13	.980
1995—Daytona (FSL)	C	82	233	27	55	9	1	1	19	.236	29	53	1	501	91	8	.987
1996—Rockford (Midw.)	C	96	305	35	69	10	1	2	27	.226	36	71	2	620	98	11	.985
1997—Daytona (FSL)	C	55	179	17	45	9	1	0	23	.251	14	25	4	341	71	8	.981
—Iowa (A.A.)	C	1	3	0	1	0	0	0	0	.333	1	1	0	1	0	0	1.000
—Orlando (Sou.)	C	37	99	10	17	3	0	1	15	.172	12	28	0	237	28	2	.993
1998—West Tenn (Sou.)	C-1B	109	320	33	71	10	1	2	28	.222	32	74	1	740	†108	8	.991
1999—West Tenn (Sou.)	C	14	35	2	6	3	0	0	5	.171	2	14	0	97	13	2	.982
—Iowa (PCL)	C	74	240	24	63	11	1	4	26	.263	20	54	0	488	44	7	.987
—Chicago (N.L.)...........	C	10	19	3	5	1	0	0	1	.263	2	4	0	44	5	0	1.000
2000—Iowa (PCL)	C-1B	76	248	22	58	9	0	1	17	.234	23	61	1	505	67	11	.981
Major League totals (1 year)		10	19	3	5	1	0	0	1	.263	2	4	0	44	5	0	1.000

MONDESI, RAUL   OF   BLUE JAYS

PERSONAL: Born March 12, 1971, in San Cristobal, Dominican Republic. ... 5-11/215. ... Bats right, throws right. ... Name pronounced MON-de-see.
HIGH SCHOOL: Liceo Manuel Maria Valencia (Dominican Republic).
TRANSACTIONS/CAREER NOTES: Signed as non-drafted free agent by Los Angeles Dodgers organization (June 6, 1988). ... On Bakersfield disabled list (May 8-July 5, 1991). ... On Albuquerque disabled list (May 8-16, 1992). ... On San Antonio disabled list (June 2-16, June 24-August 10 and August 24, 1992-remainder of season). ... Traded by Dodgers with P Pedro Borbon to Toronto Blue Jays for OF Shawn Green and 2B Jorge Nunez (November 8, 1999). ... On disabled list (July 22-September 20, 2000).
HONORS: Named N.L. Rookie Player of the Year by THE SPORTING NEWS (1994). ... Named N.L. Rookie of the Year by Baseball Writers' Association of America (1994). ... Won N.L. Gold Glove as outfielder (1995 and 1997).
STATISTICAL NOTES: Career major league grand slams: 2.

Year Team (League)	Pos.	G	AB	R	H	2B	3B	HR	RBI	Avg.	BB	SO	SB	PO	A	E	Avg.
1988—Dom. Dodgers (DSL) .	OF	36	117	21	26	10	1	2	44	.222	23	36	4	...	...	...	...
1989—Dom. Dodgers (DSL) .	OF	46	156	32	43	15	3	2	27	.276	16	26	8	...	...	...	...
1990—Great Falls (Pio.)	OF	44	175	35	53	10	4	8	31	.303	11	30	30	65	4	1	.986
1991—Bakersfield (Calif.)......	OF	28	106	23	30	7	2	3	13	.283	5	21	9	42	5	3	.940
—San Antonio (Texas)...	OF	53	213	32	58	11	5	5	26	.272	8	47	8	101	6	4	.964
—Albuquerque (PCL).....	OF	2	9	3	3	0	1	0	0	.333	0	1	1	0	0	1	1.000
1992—Albuquerque (PCL).....	OF	35	138	23	43	4	7	4	15	.312	9	35	2	89	8	7	.933
—San Antonio (Texas)...	OF	18	68	8	18	2	2	2	14	.265	1	24	3	31	6	1	.974
1993—Albuquerque (PCL).....	OF	110	425	65	119	22	7	12	65	.280	18	85	13	211	10	10	.957
—Los Angeles (N.L.)	OF	42	86	13	25	3	1	4	10	.291	4	16	4	55	3	3	.951
1994—Los Angeles (N.L.)	OF	112	434	63	133	27	8	16	56	.306	16	78	11	206	*16	8	.965
1995—Los Angeles (N.L.)	OF	139	536	91	153	23	6	26	88	.285	33	96	27	282	*16	6	.980
1996—Los Angeles (N.L.)	OF	157	634	98	188	40	7	24	88	.297	32	122	14	337	11	•12	.967
1997—Los Angeles (N.L.)	OF	159	616	95	191	42	5	30	87	.310	44	105	32	338	10	4	.989
1998—Los Angeles (N.L.)	OF	148	580	85	162	26	5	30	90	.279	30	112	16	284	6	6	.980
1999—Los Angeles (N.L.)	OF	159	601	98	152	29	5	33	99	.253	71	134	36	315	7	6	.982
2000—Toronto (A.L.)■.........	OF	96	388	78	105	22	2	24	67	.271	32	73	22	203	5	7	.967
American League totals (1 year)		96	388	78	105	22	2	24	67	.271	32	73	22	203	5	7	.967
National League totals (7 years)		916	3487	543	1004	190	37	163	518	.288	230	663	140	1817	69	45	.977
Major League totals (8 years)		1012	3875	621	1109	212	39	187	585	.286	262	736	162	2020	74	52	.976

DIVISION SERIES RECORD

Year Team (League)	Pos.	G	AB	R	H	2B	3B	HR	RBI	Avg.	BB	SO	SB	PO	A	E	Avg.
1995—Los Angeles (N.L.)	OF	3	9	0	2	0	0	0	1	.222	0	2	0	8	0	0	1.000
1996—Los Angeles (N.L.)	OF	3	11	0	2	2	0	0	1	.182	0	4	0	2	0	0	1.000
Division series totals (2 years)		6	20	0	4	2	0	0	2	.200	0	6	0	10	0	0	1.000

ALL-STAR GAME RECORD

Year League	Pos.	AB	R	H	2B	3B	HR	RBI	Avg.	BB	SO	SB	PO	A	E	Avg.
1995—National....................	OF	1	0	0	0	0	0	0	.000	0	0	0	2	0	0	1.000

MONTGOMERY, RAY   OF   METS

PERSONAL: Born August 8, 1969, in Bronxville, N.Y. ... 6-3/195. ... Bats right, throws right. ... Full name: Raymond James Montgomery.
HIGH SCHOOL: Archbishop Stepinac (White Plains, N.Y.).
COLLEGE: Fordham.
TRANSACTIONS/CAREER NOTES: Selected by Houston Astros organization in 13th round of free-agent draft (June 4, 1990). ... On disabled list (April 10-17 and June 3-July 24, 1992). ... On Houston disabled list (June 18, 1997-remainder of season). ... On Houston disabled list (March 22-April 6, 1998). ... On New Orleans disabled list (July 18-31, 1998). ... Granted free agency (October 15, 1998). ... Signed by Pittsburgh Pirates organization (December 22, 1998). ... On Nashville disabled list (August 15, 1999-remainder of season). ... Released by Pirates (November 24, 1999). ... Re-signed by Pirates organization (January 4, 2000). ... On Nashville disabled list (April 11-25 and May 23-June 14, 2000). ... Granted free agency (October 18, 2000). ... Signed by New York Mets organization (November 17, 2000).

Year Team (League)	Pos.	G	AB	R	H	2B	3B	HR	RBI	Avg.	BB	SO	SB	PO	A	E	Avg.
1990—Auburn (NY-Penn)......	OF-1B	61	193	19	45	8	1	0	13	.233	23	32	12	245	14	8	.970
1991—Burlington (Midw.).....	OF	120	433	60	109	24	3	3	57	.252	37	65	16	249	12	4	.985
1992—Jackson (Texas)........	OF	51	148	13	31	4	1	1	10	.209	7	27	4	76	3	2	.975
1993—Jackson (Texas)........	OF	100	338	50	95	16	3	10	59	.281	36	54	12	151	9	6	.964
—Tucson (PCL)...........	OF	15	50	9	17	3	1	2	6	.340	5	7	1	33	1	0	1.000
1994—Tucson (PCL)...........	OF	103	332	51	85	19	6	7	51	.256	35	54	5	179	11	8	.960
1995—Jackson (Texas)........	OF-1B	35	127	24	38	8	1	10	24	.299	13	13	6	102	10	1	.991
—Tucson (PCL)...........	OF	88	291	48	88	19	0	11	68	.302	24	58	5	182	10	7	.965
1996—Tucson (PCL)...........	OF-DH-1B	100	360	70	110	20	0	22	75	.306	59	54	7	182	8	4	.979
—Houston (N.L.).........	OF	12	14	4	3	1	0	1	4	.214	1	5	0	6	0	0	1.000
1997—Houston (N.L.)........	OF	29	68	8	16	4	1	0	4	.235	5	18	0	25	2	0	1.000
—New Orleans (A.A.).....	OF-DH	20	73	17	21	5	0	6	13	.288	11	15	1	33	0	1	.971
1998—New Orleans (PCL)....	OF-DH	75	272	42	79	18	1	9	45	.290	26	48	4	156	4	4	.976
—Houston (N.L.).........	OF	6	5	2	2	0	0	0	0	.400	0	0	0	1	0	0	1.000
1999—Nashville (PCL)■......	OF-1B	90	272	57	90	23	2	16	52	.331	24	49	5	180	9	6	.969
2000—Nashville (PCL).......	OF	71	228	36	59	10	1	7	29	.259	19	38	3	105	1	3	.972
Major League totals (3 years)		47	87	14	21	5	1	1	8	.241	6	23	0	32	2	0	1.000

MONTGOMERY, STEVE — P — PADRES

PERSONAL: Born December 25, 1970, in Westminster, Calif. ... 6-4/200. ... Throws right, bats right. ... Full name: Steven Lewis Montgomery.
HIGH SCHOOL: Fountain Valley (Calif.).
COLLEGE: Pepperdine.
TRANSACTIONS/CAREER NOTES: Selected by St. Louis Cardinals organization in third round of free-agent draft (June 1, 1992). ... Traded by Cardinals to Oakland Athletics for P Dennis Eckersley (February 13, 1996). ... Claimed on waivers by Cleveland Indians (August 7, 1997). ... Released by Indians (March 30, 1998). ... Signed by Baltimore Orioles organization (April 4, 1998). ... Granted free agency (October 15, 1998). ... Signed by Philadelphia Phillies organization (November 5, 1998). ... On Philadelphia disabled list (August 4-20, 1999); included rehabilitation assignment to Scranton/Wilkes-Barre (August 18-19). ... Traded by Phillies with P Carlton Loewer and P Adam Eaton to San Diego Padres for P Andy Ashby (November 10, 1999). ... On San Diego disabled list (March 25-June 27 and July 18, 2000-remainder of season); included rehabilitation assignments to Rancho Cucamonga (May 30-June 4 and June 18-27).

Year League	W	L	Pct.	ERA	G	GS	CG	ShO	Sv.	IP	H	R	ER	BB	SO
1993—St. Petersburg (FSL).........	2	1	.667	2.66	14	5	0	0	3	40 2/3	33	14	12	9	34
—Arkansas (Texas)..............	3	3	.500	3.94	6	6	0	0	0	32	34	17	14	12	19
1994—Arkansas (Texas)..............	4	5	.444	3.28	50	9	0	0	2	107	97	43	39	33	73
1995—Arkansas (Texas)..............	5	2	.714	3.25	*55	0	0	0	*36	61	52	22	22	22	56
1996—Oakland (A.L.)■................	1	0	1.000	9.22	8	0	0	0	0	13 2/3	18	14	14	13	8
—Edmonton (PCL)	2	0	1.000	2.89	37	0	0	0	1	56	51	19	18	12	40
1997—Edmonton (PCL)	2	1	.667	5.79	30	0	0	0	3	46 2/3	61	30	30	17	38
—Oakland (A.L.)	0	1	.000	9.95	4	0	0	0	0	6 1/3	10	7	7	8	1
—Buffalo (A.A.)■	1	2	.333	5.63	7	0	0	0	1	8	12	6	5	3	5
1998—Rochester (I.L.)■	4	6	.400	4.40	51	4	0	0	8	88	79	50	43	24	66
1999—Scranton/W.B. (I.L.)■	0	0	...	6.23	14	0	0	0	7	13	17	9	9	11	13
—Philadelphia (N.L.)	1	5	.167	3.34	53	0	0	0	3	64 2/3	54	25	24	31	55
2000—San Diego (N.L.)■	0	2	.000	7.94	7	0	0	0	0	5 2/3	6	6	5	4	3
—Rancho Cuca. (Calif.)	0	1	.000	7.50	6	0	0	0	0	6	8	7	5	2	8
—Las Vegas (PCL)	0	1	.000	27.00	1	1	0	0	0	2/3	2	2	2	0	1
A.L. totals (2 years)	1	1	.500	9.45	12	0	0	0	0	20	28	21	21	21	9
N.L. totals (2 years)	1	7	.125	3.71	60	0	0	0	3	70 1/3	60	31	29	35	58
Major League totals (4 years)	2	8	.200	4.98	72	0	0	0	3	90 1/3	88	52	50	56	67

MOORE, TREY — P — BRAVES

PERSONAL: Born October 2, 1972, in Houston. ... 6-0/190. ... Throws left, bats left. ... Full name: Warren Neal Moore III.
HIGH SCHOOL: Keller (Texas).
COLLEGE: Texas A&M.
TRANSACTIONS/CAREER NOTES: Selected by Seattle Mariners organization in second round of free-agent draft (June 2, 1994). ... Traded by Mariners with C Chris Widger and P Matt Wagner to Montreal Expos for P Alex Pacheco and P Jeff Fassero (October 29, 1996). ... On Montreal disabled list (June 7, 1998-remainder of season); included rehabilitation assignment to Ottawa (July 9-20). ... On disabled list (March 31, 1999-entire season). ... On Ottawa disabled list (April 6-May 11 and June 2-22, 2000). ... Claimed on waivers by Atlanta Braves (December 4, 2000).
MISCELLANEOUS: Struck out in only appearance as pinch hitter with Montreal (1998).

Year League	W	L	Pct.	ERA	G	GS	CG	ShO	Sv.	IP	H	R	ER	BB	SO
1994—Bellingham (N'West).........	5	2	.714	2.63	11	10	1	0	0	61 2/3	48	18	18	24	73
1995—Riverside (Calif.)...............	14	6	.700	3.09	24	24	0	0	0	148 1/3	122	65	51	58	134
1996—Port City (Sou.)...............	1	6	.143	7.71	11	11	0	0	0	53 2/3	73	54	46	33	42
—Lancaster (Calif.).........	7	5	.583	4.10	15	15	2	0	0	94 1/3	106	57	43	31	77
1997—Harrisburg (East.)■..........	11	6	.647	4.15	27	27	2	•2	0	162 2/3	152	91	75	66	137
1998—Montreal (N.L.)...............	2	5	.286	5.02	13	11	0	0	0	61	78	37	34	17	35
—Ottawa (I.L.).....................	1	1	.500	5.54	3	3	0	0	0	13	18	8	8	4	8
1999—Montreal (N.L.)...............							Did not play.								
2000—Ottawa (I.L.)...............	3	2	.600	4.17	12	12	1	0	0	58 1/3	56	36	27	18	43
—Montreal (N.L.)...............	1	5	.167	6.62	8	8	0	0	0	35 1/3	55	31	26	21	24
Major League totals (2 years).......	3	10	.231	5.61	21	19	0	0	0	96 1/3	133	68	60	38	59

M

PERSONAL: Born February 2, 1972, in Aqua Negar, Venezuela. ... 5-10/180. ... Bats right, throws right.
HIGH SCHOOL: Libertador (Venezuela).
TRANSACTIONS/CAREER NOTES: Signed as non-drafted free agent by Houston Astros organization (March 30, 1991). ... Granted free agency (October 17, 1997). ... Played in Taiwan (1998). ... Signed by New York Mets organization (July 24, 1998). ... Granted free agency (October 16, 1998). ... Re-signed by Mets organization (February 5, 1999). ... On New York disabled list (May 13-30, 2000); included rehabilitation assignment to Norfolk (May 22-30). ... Traded by Mets with 3B Mike Kinkade, P Leslie Brea and P Pat Gorman to Baltimore Orioles for SS Mike Bordick (July 28, 2000).
STATISTICAL NOTES: Tied for Texas League lead in double plays by outfielder with six in 1995.

											BATTING				FIELDING			
Year	Team (League)	Pos.	G	AB	R	H	2B	3B	HR	RBI	Avg.	BB	SO	SB	PO	A	E	Avg.
1991—Dom. Astros (DSL).....			58	211	38	63	18	1	0	20	.299	19	22	21	...	...	...	...
1992—GC Astros (GCL)	OF-2B-3B		49	144	28	32	3	0	0	8	.222	18	16	16	71	27	4	.961
1993—Asheville (S.Atl.)	2-0-3-S		108	365	66	104	22	2	2	31	.285	36	46	20	135	114	17	.936
1994—Osceola (FSL)	OF-3B		118	425	57	120	29	4	8	46	.282	37	60	24	198	70	15	.947
1995—Jackson (Texas)	OF-3B-2B		123	467	63	139	32	0	3	45	.298	32	57	22	244	16	6	.977
—Tucson (PCL)	OF		2	5	3	3	0	1	0	1	.600	2	0	1	2	0	0	1.000
1996—Jackson (Texas)	OF-2B-SS-3B		70	255	36	73	6	1	5	23	.286	14	23	4	108	56	7	.959
—Tucson (PCL)	3B-OF-2B		62	228	35	64	11	2	3	26	.281	17	27	3	75	70	14	.912
1997—New Orleans (A.A.)	O-3-2-S		119	370	55	95	15	3	2	38	.257	47	52	7	161	80	11	.956
1998—Mercury (Taiwan)■			...	164	34	55	11	2	3	11	.335	...	...	...	...	...	...	...
—St. Lucie (FSL)■	2B-SS-SF		17	55	5	15	0	0	0	8	.273	5	9	1	21	43	1	.985
—Norfolk (I.L.)	3B-OF-2B		11	28	5	5	1	0	0	2	.179	5	7	0	8	6	2	.875
1999—Norfolk (I.L.)	SS-OF-2B-3B		82	304	55	92	17	2	8	36	.303	41	54	18	126	134	16	.942
—New York (N.L.)	OF-2B-3B-SS		66	31	6	5	0	0	0	1	.161	4	7	2	21	7	0	1.000
2000—New York (N.L.)	SS-OF-2B-3B		79	215	35	56	13	2	6	30	.260	18	48	7	89	115	8	.962
—Norfolk (I.L.)	OF-2B-SS		8	27	7	9	2	0	0	7	.333	7	3	2	11	7	0	1.000
—Baltimore (A.L.)■	SS-2B		53	199	25	58	9	3	2	17	.291	17	32	5	80	161	12	.953
American League totals (1 year)			53	199	25	58	9	3	2	17	.291	17	32	5	80	161	12	.953
National League totals (2 years)			145	246	41	61	13	2	6	31	.248	22	55	9	110	122	8	.967
Major League totals (2 years)			198	445	66	119	22	5	8	48	.267	39	87	14	190	283	20	.959

DIVISION SERIES RECORD

											BATTING				FIELDING			
Year	Team (League)	Pos.	G	AB	R	H	2B	3B	HR	RBI	Avg.	BB	SO	SB	PO	A	E	Avg.
1999—New York (N.L.)	OF	3	1	1	0	0	0	0	0	.000		1	0	0	2	1	0	1.000

CHAMPIONSHIP SERIES RECORD

											BATTING				FIELDING			
Year	Team (League)	Pos.	G	AB	R	H	2B	3B	HR	RBI	Avg.	BB	SO	SB	PO	A	E	Avg.
1999—New York (N.L.)	PH-OF	6	14	3	6	0	0	1	2	.429		2	2	2	7	3	0	1.000

RECORD AS PITCHER

Year	League	W	L	Pct.	ERA	G	GS	CG	ShO	Sv.	IP	H	R	ER	BB	SO
1993—Asheville (SAL)		0	0	...	0.00	1	0	0	0	0	$\frac{2}{3}$	1	0	0	0	0
1997—New Orleans (A.A.)		0	0	...	0.00	1	0	0	0	0	1	2	1	1	1	0

PERSONAL: Born April 22, 1966, in Leechburg, Pa. ... 5-11/180. ... Bats left, throws right. ... Full name: Michael Robert Morandini. ... Name pronounced MOR-an-DEEN-ee.
HIGH SCHOOL: Leechburg (Pa.) Area.
COLLEGE: Indiana.
TRANSACTIONS/CAREER NOTES: Selected by Pittsburgh Pirates organization in seventh round of free-agent draft (June 2, 1987); did not sign. ... Selected by Philadelphia Phillies organization in fifth round of free-agent draft (June 1, 1988). ... On disabled list (June 15-30, 1996). ... Traded by Phillies to Chicago Cubs for OF Doug Glanville (December 23, 1997). ... On suspended list (September 23-25, 1999). ... Granted free agency (October 28, 1999). ... Signed by Montreal Expos organization (January 27, 2000). ... Traded by Expos to Phillies for cash (March 28, 2000). ... Traded by Phillies to Toronto Blue Jays for a player to be named later (August 6, 2000); Phillies acquired P Rob Ducey to complete deal (August 7, 2000). ... Granted free agency (October 31, 2000). ... Re-signed by Blue Jays organization (December 6, 2000).
RECORDS: Holds N.L. single-season record for fewest chances accepted by second baseman (150 games or more)—671 (1998).
STATISTICAL NOTES: Led International League second basemen with 271 putouts, 419 assists and 701 total chances in 1990.
MISCELLANEOUS: Member of 1988 U.S. Olympic baseball team. ... Turned unassisted triple play while playing second base (September 20, 1992, sixth inning); ninth player ever to accomplish feat and first ever by second baseman during regular season.

											BATTING				FIELDING			
Year	Team (League)	Pos.	G	AB	R	H	2B	3B	HR	RBI	Avg.	BB	SO	SB	PO	A	E	Avg.
1989—Spartanburg (S.Atl.)	SS	63	231	43	78	19	1	1	30	.338		35	45	18	87	198	10	.966
—Clearwater (FSL)	SS	17	63	14	19	4	1	0	4	.302		7	8	3	20	59	2	.975
—Reading (East.)	SS	48	188	39	66	12	1	5	29	.351		23	32	5	73	137	10	.955
1990—Scranton/W.B. (I.L.)	2B-SS	139	503	76	131	24	*10	1	31	.260		60	90	16	†271	†419	11	.984
—Philadelphia (N.L.)	2B	25	79	9	19	4	0	1	3	.241		6	19	3	37	61	1	.990
1991—Scranton/W.B. (I.L.)	2B	12	46	7	12	4	0	1	9	.261		5	6	2	19	38	1	.983
—Philadelphia (N.L.)	2B	98	325	38	81	11	4	1	20	.249		29	45	13	183	254	6	.986
1992—Philadelphia (N.L.)	2B-SS	127	422	47	112	8	8	3	30	.265		25	64	8	239	336	6	.990
1993—Philadelphia (N.L.)	2B	120	425	57	105	19	9	3	33	.247		34	73	13	208	288	5	.990
1994—Philadelphia (N.L.)	2B	87	274	40	80	16	5	2	26	.292		34	33	10	167	216	6	.985
1995—Philadelphia (N.L.)	2B	127	494	65	140	34	7	6	49	.283		42	80	9	269	336	7	.989
1996—Philadelphia (N.L.)	2B	140	539	64	135	24	6	3	32	.250		49	87	26	286	352	12	.982
1997—Philadelphia (N.L.)	2B-SS	150	553	83	163	40	2	1	39	.295		62	91	16	254	350	6	.990
1998—Chicago (N.L.)■	2B	154	582	93	172	20	4	8	53	.296		72	84	13	267	404	5	*.993

M

Year Team (League)	Pos.	G	AB	R	H	2B	3B	HR	RBI	Avg.	BB	SO	SB	PO	A	E	Avg.
1999—Chicago (N.L.)	2B	144	456	60	110	18	5	4	37	.241	48	61	6	239	319	5	.991
2000—Philadelphia (N.L.)■..	2B	91	302	31	76	13	3	0	22	.252	29	54	5	179	196	5	.987
—Toronto (A.L.)■	2B	35	107	10	29	2	1	0	7	.271	7	23	1	58	92	1	.993
American League totals (1 year)		35	107	10	29	2	1	0	7	.271	7	23	1	58	92	1	.993
National League totals (11 years)		1263	4451	587	1193	207	53	32	344	.268	430	691	122	2328	3112	64	.988
Major League totals (11 years)		1298	4558	597	1222	209	54	32	351	.268	437	714	123	2386	3204	65	.989

DIVISION SERIES RECORD

Year Team (League)	Pos.	G	AB	R	H	2B	3B	HR	RBI	Avg.	BB	SO	SB	PO	A	E	Avg.
1998—Chicago (N.L.)	2B	3	9	1	2	0	0	0	1	.222	3	2	0	5	3	0	1.000

CHAMPIONSHIP SERIES RECORD

Year Team (League)	Pos.	G	AB	R	H	2B	3B	HR	RBI	Avg.	BB	SO	SB	PO	A	E	Avg.
1993—Philadelphia (N.L.)	2B-PH	4	16	1	4	0	1	0	2	.250	0	3	1	8	9	1	.944

WORLD SERIES RECORD

Year Team (League)	Pos.	G	AB	R	H	2B	3B	HR	RBI	Avg.	BB	SO	SB	PO	A	E	Avg.
1993—Philadelphia (N.L.)	PH-2B	3	5	1	1	0	0	0	0	.200	1	2	0	2	0	0	1.000

ALL-STAR GAME RECORD

Year League	Pos.	AB	R	H	2B	3B	HR	RBI	Avg.	BB	SO	SB	PO	A	E	Avg.
1995—National	2B	1	0	0	0	0	0	0	.000	0	1	0	0	1	0	1.000

MORDECAI, MIKE — IF — EXPOS

PERSONAL: Born December 13, 1967, in Birmingham, Ala. ... 5-10/185. ... Bats right, throws right. ... Full name: Michael Howard Mordecai.
HIGH SCHOOL: Hewitt Trussville (Ala.).
COLLEGE: Southern Alabama.
TRANSACTIONS/CAREER NOTES: Selected by Pittsburgh Pirates organization in 33rd round of free-agent draft (June 2, 1986); did not sign. ... Selected by Atlanta Braves organization in sixth round of free-agent draft (June 5, 1989). ... On Atlanta disabled list (April 8-May 11, 1996); included rehabilitation assignment to Richmond (May 8-11). ... Granted free agency (December 21, 1997). ... Signed by Montreal Expos organization (March 27, 1998). ... On Montreal disabled list (June 24-July 24, 1998); included rehabilitation assignments to Jupiter (July 16-19) and Ottawa (July 19-24).

Year Team (League)	Pos.	G	AB	R	H	2B	3B	HR	RBI	Avg.	BB	SO	SB	PO	A	E	Avg.
1989—Burlington (Midw.)	SS-3B	65	241	39	61	11	1	1	22	.253	33	43	12	80	163	21	.920
—Greenville (Sou.)	3B-2B	4	8	0	3	0	0	0	1	.375	1	1	0	4	6	0	1.000
1990—Durham (Caro.)	SS	72	271	42	76	11	7	3	36	.280	42	45	10	111	221	29	.920
1991—Durham (Caro.)	SS	109	397	52	104	15	2	4	42	.262	40	58	30	164	302	27	.945
1992—Greenville (Sou.)	SS	65	222	31	58	13	1	4	31	.261	29	31	9	93	204	11	.964
—Richmond (I.L.)	SS-2B-3B	36	118	12	29	3	0	1	6	.246	5	19	0	48	101	10	.937
1993—Richmond (I.L.)	2-S-3-O-C-1	72	205	29	55	8	1	2	14	.268	14	33	10	98	145	9	.964
1994—Richmond (I.L.)	SS-1B-DH-3B	99	382	67	107	25	1	14	57	.280	35	50	14	117	279	22	.947
—Atlanta (N.L.)	SS	4	4	1	1	0	0	1	3	.250	1	0	0	1	4	0	1.000
1995—Atlanta (N.L.)	2-1-3-S-O	69	75	10	21	6	0	3	11	.280	9	16	0	39	31	0	1.000
1996—Atlanta (N.L.)	2B-3B-SS-1B	66	108	12	26	5	0	2	8	.241	9	24	1	33	52	2	.977
—Richmond (I.L.)	SS	3	11	2	2	0	0	1	2	.182	0	3	0	3	13	0	1.000
1997—Atlanta (N.L.)	3-2-S-1-DH-O	61	81	8	14	2	1	0	3	.173	6	16	0	26	17	0	1.000
—Richmond (I.L.)	2B-3B-DH-SS	31	122	23	38	10	0	3	15	.311	9	17	0	29	61	1	.989
1998—Montreal (N.L.)■	SS-2B-3B-1B	73	119	12	24	4	2	3	10	.202	9	20	1	38	82	5	.960
—Jupiter (FSL)	2B-SS	2	8	0	0	0	0	0	0	.000	1	3	0	4	4	0	1.000
—Ottawa (I.L.)	SS-2B	6	22	2	5	2	0	0	1	.227	3	3	0	9	22	1	.969
1999—Montreal (N.L.)	2-S-3-1	109	226	29	53	10	2	5	25	.235	20	31	2	72	156	7	.970
2000—Montreal (N.L.)	3B-SS-2B-1B	86	169	20	48	16	0	4	16	.284	12	34	2	42	88	8	.942
Major League totals (7 years)		468	782	92	187	43	5	18	76	.239	66	141	6	251	430	22	.969

DIVISION SERIES RECORD

Year Team (League)	Pos.	G	AB	R	H	2B	3B	HR	RBI	Avg.	BB	SO	SB	PO	A	E	Avg.
1995—Atlanta (N.L.)	PH-SS	2	3	1	2	1	0	0	2	.667	0	0	0	1	0	0	1.000
1996—Atlanta (N.L.)							Did not play.										

CHAMPIONSHIP SERIES RECORD

Year Team (League)	Pos.	G	AB	R	H	2B	3B	HR	RBI	Avg.	BB	SO	SB	PO	A	E	Avg.
1995—Atlanta (N.L.)	PH-SS	2	2	0	0	0	0	0	0	.000	0	1	0	0	0	0	...
1996—Atlanta (N.L.)	3B-PH-2B	4	4	1	1	0	0	0	0	.250	0	1	0	1	1	0	1.000
Championship series totals (2 years)		6	6	1	1	0	0	0	0	.167	0	2	0	1	1	0	1.000

WORLD SERIES RECORD

NOTES: Member of World Series championship team (1995).

Year Team (League)	Pos.	G	AB	R	H	2B	3B	HR	RBI	Avg.	BB	SO	SB	PO	A	E	Avg.
1995—Atlanta (N.L.)	SS-DH	3	3	0	1	0	0	0	0	.333	0	1	0	0	6	0	1.000
1996—Atlanta (N.L.)	PH	1	1	0	0	0	0	0	0	.000	0	0	0	...	...	...	...
World Series totals (2 years)		4	4	0	1	0	0	0	0	.250	0	1	0	0	6	0	1.000

PERSONAL: Born April 27, 1977, in Caracas, Venezuela. ... 6-3/200. ... Throws right, bats right. ... Full name: Orber Aquiles Moreno.
HIGH SCHOOL: Luisa Caceres (Venezuela).
TRANSACTIONS/CAREER NOTES: Signed as non-drafted free agent by Kansas City Royals organization (November 10, 1993). ... On Kansas City disabled list (June 10, 1999-remainder of season); included rehabilitation assignment to Gulf Coast Royals (July 26-27). ... On Kansas City disabled list (March 24, 2000-entire season).

Year League	W	L	Pct.	ERA	G	GS	CG	ShO	Sv.	IP	H	R	ER	BB	SO
1994— Dominican Royals (DSL)....	3	3	.500	3.19	16	11	0	0	1	67²/₃	51	33	24	27	44
1995— Gulf Coast Royals (GCL) ...	1	1	.500	2.45	8	3	0	0	0	22	15	9	6	7	21
1996— Gulf Coast Royals (GCL) ...	5	1	.833	1.36	12	7	0	0	1	46¹/₃	37	15	7	10	50
1997— Lansing (Midw.)	4	8	.333	4.81	27	25	0	0	0	138¹/₃	150	83	74	45	128
1998— Wilmington (Caro.).............	3	2	.600	0.82	23	0	0	0	7	33	8	3	3	10	50
— Wichita (Texas)	0	1	.000	2.88	24	0	0	0	7	34¹/₃	28	13	11	12	40
1999— Omaha (PCL).................	3	1	.750	2.10	16	0	0	0	4	25²/₃	17	6	6	4	30
— Kansas City (A.L.)	0	0	...	5.63	7	0	0	0	0	8	4	5	5	6	7
— Gulf Coast Royals (GCL) ...	0	0	...	0.00	1	1	0	0	0	1	0	0	0	0	1
2000— Kansas City (A.L.)							Did not play.								
Major League totals (1 year)........	0	0	...	5.63	7	0	0	0	0	8	4	5	5	6	7

PERSONAL: Born October 8, 1959, in Tulare, Calif. ... 6-2/220. ... Throws right, bats right. ... Full name: Michael Thomas Morgan.
HIGH SCHOOL: Valley (Las Vegas).
TRANSACTIONS/CAREER NOTES: Selected by Oakland Athletics organization in first round (fourth pick overall) of free-agent draft (June 6, 1978). ... On disabled list (May 14-June 27, 1980). ... Traded by A's to New York Yankees for SS Fred Stanley and a player to be named later (November 3, 1980); A's acquired 2B Brian Doyle to complete deal (November 17, 1980). ... On disabled list (April 9-22, 1981). ... Traded by Yankees with OF/1B Dave Collins, 1B Fred McGriff and cash to Toronto Blue Jays for P Dale Murray and OF/C Tom Dodd (December 9, 1982). ... On Toronto disabled list (July 2-August 23, 1983); included rehabilitation assignment to Syracuse (August 1-18). ... Selected by Seattle Mariners from Blue Jays organization in Rule 5 major league draft (December 3, 1984). ... On Seattle disabled list (April 17, 1985-remainder of season); included rehabilitation assignment to Calgary (July 19-22). ... Traded by Mariners to Baltimore Orioles for P Ken Dixon (December 9, 1987). ... On Baltimore disabled list (June 9-July 19, 1988); included rehabilitation assignment to Rochester (June 30-July 17). ... On Baltimore disabled list (August 12, 1988-remainder of season). ... Traded by Orioles to Los Angeles Dodgers for OF Mike Devereaux (March 12, 1989). ... Granted free agency (October 28, 1991). ... Signed by Chicago Cubs (December 3, 1991). ... On disabled list (June 14-29, 1993; May 9-27, June 2-22 and July 28, 1994-remainder of season). ... On Chicago disabled list (April 24-May 25, 1995); included rehabilitation assignment to Orlando (May 15-25). ... Traded by Cubs with 3B/OF Paul Torres and C Francisco Morales to St. Louis Cardinals for 3B Todd Zeile and cash (June 16, 1995). ... On St. Louis disabled list (July 4-24, 1995). ... Granted free agency (November 6, 1995). ... Re-signed by Cardinals (December 7, 1995). ... On St. Louis disabled list (March 22-May 18, 1996); included rehabilitation assignment to St. Petersburg (April 20-May 15). ... Released by Cardinals (August 28, 1996). ... Signed by Cincinnati Reds (September 4, 1996). ... On disabled list (June 8-24, 1997). ... Granted free agency (October 28, 1997). ... Signed by Minnesota Twins (December 16, 1997). ... On Minnesota disabled list (June 27-July 13 and July 15-August 16, 1998). ... Traded by Twins to Cubs for cash and a player to be named later (August 25, 1998); Twins acquired P Scott Downs to complete deal (November 3, 1998). ... Granted free agency (October 30, 1998). ... Signed by Texas Rangers organization (January 26, 1999). ... On disabled list (May 25-June 9, 1999). ... Granted free agency (November 8, 1999). ... Signed by Arizona Diamondbacks organization (January 14, 2000).
RECORDS: Holds major league record for most clubs played and pitched for in career (since 1900)—12.

Year League	W	L	Pct.	ERA	G	GS	CG	ShO	Sv.	IP	H	R	ER	BB	SO
1978— Oakland (A.L.)	0	3	.000	7.50	3	3	1	0	0	12	19	12	10	8	0
— Vancouver (PCL)	5	6	.455	5.58	14	14	5	1	0	92	109	67	57	54	31
1979— Ogden (PCL)	5	5	.500	3.48	13	13	6	0	0	101	93	48	39	49	42
— Oakland (A.L.)	2	10	.167	5.96	13	13	2	0	0	77	102	57	51	50	17
1980— Ogden (PCL)	6	9	.400	5.40	20	20	3	0	0	115	135	79	69	77	46
1981— Nashville (Sou.)■.............	8	7	.533	4.42	26	26	7	0	0	169	164	97	83	83	100
1982— New York (A.L.)	7	11	.389	4.37	30	23	2	0	0	150¹/₃	167	77	73	67	71
1983— Toronto (A.L.)■.............	0	3	.000	5.16	16	4	0	0	0	45¹/₃	48	26	26	21	22
— Syracuse (I.L.).................	0	3	.000	5.59	5	4	0	0	1	19¹/₃	20	12	12	13	17
1984— Syracuse (I.L.).................	13	11	.542	4.07	34	28	10	•4	1	*185²/₃	167	•101	84	•100	105
1985— Seattle (A.L.)■.............	1	1	.500	12.00	2	2	0	0	0	6	11	8	8	5	2
— Calgary (PCL).................	0	0	...	4.50	1	1	0	0	0	2	3	1	1	0	0
1986— Seattle (A.L.)	11	•17	.393	4.53	37	33	9	1	1	216¹/₃	243	122	109	86	116
1987— Seattle (A.L.)	12	17	.414	4.65	34	31	8	2	0	207	245	117	107	53	85
1988— Baltimore (A.L.)■.............	1	6	.143	5.43	22	10	2	0	0	71¹/₃	70	45	43	23	29
— Rochester (I.L.)	0	2	.000	4.76	3	3	0	0	0	17	19	10	9	6	7
1989— Los Angeles (N.L.)■.........	8	11	.421	2.53	40	19	0	0	0	152²/₃	130	51	43	33	72
1990— Los Angeles (N.L.)	11	15	.423	3.75	33	33	6	•4	0	211	216	100	88	60	106
1991— Los Angeles (N.L.)	14	10	.583	2.78	34	33	5	1	1	236¹/₃	197	85	73	61	140
1992— Chicago (N.L.)■.............	16	8	.667	2.55	34	34	6	1	0	240	203	80	68	79	123
1993— Chicago (N.L.)	10	15	.400	4.03	32	32	1	1	0	207²/₃	206	100	93	74	111
1994— Chicago (N.L.)	2	10	.167	6.69	15	15	1	0	0	80²/₃	111	65	60	35	57
1995— Orlando (Sou.)	0	2	.000	7.59	2	2	0	0	0	10²/₃	13	9	9	7	5
— Chicago (N.L.)	2	1	.667	2.19	4	4	0	0	0	24²/₃	19	8	6	9	15
— St. Louis (N.L.)■.............	5	6	.455	3.88	17	17	1	0	0	106²/₃	114	48	46	25	46
1996— St. Petersburg (FSL)	1	0	1.000	0.00	1	1	0	0	0	5²/₃	4	0	0	1	4
— Louisville (A.A.).................	1	3	.250	7.04	4	4	1	0	0	23	29	18	18	11	10
— St. Louis (N.L.).................	4	8	.333	5.24	18	18	0	0	0	103	118	63	60	40	55
— Cincinnati (N.L.)■.............	2	3	.400	2.30	5	5	0	0	0	27¹/₃	28	9	7	7	19
1997— Cincinnati (N.L.)	9	12	.429	4.78	31	30	1	0	0	162	165	91	86	49	103

M

Year League	W	L	Pct.	ERA	G	GS	CG	ShO	Sv.	IP	H	R	ER	BB	SO
1998— Minnesota (A.L.)■	4	2	.667	3.49	18	17	0	0	0	98	108	41	38	24	50
— Chicago (N.L.)■................	0	1	.000	7.15	5	5	0	0	0	22²/₃	30	21	18	15	10
1999— Texas (A.L.)■..................	13	10	.565	6.24	34	25	1	0	0	140	184	108	97	48	61
2000— Arizona (N.L.)■	5	5	.500	4.87	60	4	0	0	5	101²/₃	123	55	55	40	56
A.L. totals (10 years)	51	80	.389	4.94	209	161	25	3	2	1023¹/₃	1197	613	562	385	453
N.L. totals (11 years)	88	105	.456	3.77	328	249	21	7	6	1676¹/₃	1660	776	703	527	913
Major League totals (20 years)	139	185	.429	4.22	537	410	46	10	8	2699²/₃	2857	1389	1265	912	1366

DIVISION SERIES RECORD

Year League	W	L	Pct.	ERA	G	GS	CG	ShO	Sv.	IP	H	R	ER	BB	SO
1998— Chicago (N.L.)	0	0	...	0.00	2	0	0	0	0	1¹/₃	0	0	0	0	1

ALL-STAR GAME RECORD

Year League	W	L	Pct.	ERA	GS	CG	ShO	Sv.	IP	H	R	ER	BB	SO
1991— National	0	0	...	0.00	0	0	0	0	1	0	0	0	0	1

MORGAN, SCOTT — OF — ANGELS

PERSONAL: Born July 19, 1973, in Westlake, Calif. ... 6-7/230. ... Bats right, throws right. ... Full name: Scott Alexander Morgan.
HIGH SCHOOL: Lompoc (Calif.).
JUNIOR COLLEGE: Allan Hancock College (Calif.).
COLLEGE: Gonzaga.
TRANSACTIONS/CAREER NOTES: Selected by Milwaukee Brewers organization in 45th round of free-agent draft (June 1, 1992); did not sign. ... Selected by Cleveland Indians organization in seventh round of free-agent draft (June 1, 1995). ... On disabled list (July 11, 1996-remainder of season). ... On Akron disabled list (April 21-30 and June 22-29, 1998). ... Claimed on waivers by Anaheim Angels (April 28, 2000). ... On Edmonton disabled list (August 17-September 7, 2000).
STATISTICAL NOTES: Led Carolina League with .606 slugging percentage in 1997.

						BATTING								FIELDING		
Year Team (League)	Pos.	G	AB	R	H	2B	3B	HR	RBI	Avg.	BB	SO	SB	PO	A	E	Avg.
1995— Watertown (NY-Penn)	OF	66	244	42	64	18	0	2	33	.262	26	63	6	50	3	3	.946
1996— Columbus (S.Atl.)......	OF	87	305	62	95	25	1	22	80	.311	46	70	9	106	6	4	.966
1997— Kinston (Caro.)...........	OF	95	368	*86	116	32	3	23	67	.315	47	87	4	143	7	2	.987
— Akron (East.)............	OF	21	69	11	12	3	0	2	6	.174	8	20	1	37	4	1	.976
1998— Akron (East.).............	OF	119	456	95	134	31	4	25	89	.294	56	124	4	201	4	5	.976
1999— Akron (East.).............	OF-DH	88	344	72	97	26	2	26	70	.282	38	96	6	170	6	6	.967
— Buffalo (I.L.)..........	OF-DH	48	171	32	44	9	0	8	31	.257	18	38	2	101	3	3	.972
2000— Buffalo (I.L.)..............	OF	11	33	5	12	3	0	0	4	.364	7	7	1	14	0	0	1.000
— Edmonton (PCL)■....	OF-1B	90	320	53	79	25	2	9	54	.247	32	74	8	178	7	3	.984

MORRIS, HAL — 1B

PERSONAL: Born April 9, 1965, in Fort Rucker, Ala. ... 6-2/195. ... Bats left, throws left. ... Full name: William Harold Morris III. ... Brother of Bobby Morris, second baseman with four major league organizations (1993-2000).
HIGH SCHOOL: Munster (Ind.).
COLLEGE: Michigan.
TRANSACTIONS/CAREER NOTES: Selected by New York Yankees organization in eighth round of free-agent draft (June 2, 1986). ... On Albany/Colonie disabled list (August 14, 1986-remainder of season). ... Traded by Yankees with P Rodney Imes to Cincinnati Reds for P Tim Leary and OF Van Snider (December 12, 1989). ... On Cincinnati disabled list (April 16-May 17, 1992); included rehabilitation assignment to Nashville (May 14-17). ... On Cincinnati disabled list (August 5-21, 1992). ... On Cincinnati disabled list (March 27-June 7, 1993); included rehabilitation assignment to Indianapolis (June 4-7). ... On suspended list (August 10, 1993). ... On Cincinnati disabled list (June 18-July 13, 1995); included rehabilitation assignment to Indianapolis (July 7-10). ... Granted free agency (November 2, 1995). ... Re-signed by Reds (December 6, 1995). ... On Cincinnati disabled list (July 2-17, 1996); included rehabilitation assignment to Indianapolis (July 16-17). ... On Cincinnati disabled list (July 31-September 10, 1997). ... Granted free agency (October 29, 1997). ... Signed by Kansas City Royals (December 22, 1997). ... On disabled list (May 8-23, 1998). ... Granted free agency (October 23, 1998). ... Signed by Reds (January 14, 1999). ... On disabled list (August 27-September 24, 1999). ... Traded by Reds to Detroit Tigers for cash (July 18, 2000). ... On Detroit disabled list (August 9-September 5, 2000). ... Granted free agency (November 1, 2000).
RECORDS: Shares major league single-inning record for most doubles—2 (August 17, 1996, eighth inning).
STATISTICAL NOTES: Had 29-game hitting streak (August 27-September 29, 1996). ... Career major league grand slams: 1.

						BATTING								FIELDING		
Year Team (League)	Pos.	G	AB	R	H	2B	3B	HR	RBI	Avg.	BB	SO	SB	PO	A	E	Avg.
1986— Oneonta (NY-Penn)	1B	36	127	26	48	9	2	3	30	.378	18	15	1	317	26	3	.991
— Alb./Colonie (East.)	1B	25	79	7	17	5	0	0	4	.215	4	10	0	203	19	2	.991
1987— Alb./Colonie (East.)	1B-OF	135	*530	65	*173	31	4	5	73	.326	36	43	7	1086	79	17	.986
1988— Columbus (I.L.)..........	OF-1B	121	452	41	134	19	4	3	38	.296	36	62	8	543	26	8	.986
— New York (A.L.)..........	OF-DH	15	20	1	2	0	0	0	0	.100	0	9	0	7	0	0	1.000
1989— Columbus (I.L.)..........	1B-OF	111	417	70	136	24	1	17	66	*.326	28	47	5	636	67	9	.987
— New York (A.L.)..........	OF-1B-DH	15	18	2	5	0	0	0	4	.278	1	4	0	12	0	0	1.000
1990— Cincinnati (N.L.)■........	1B-OF	107	309	50	105	22	3	7	36	.340	21	32	9	595	53	4	.994
— Nashville (A.A.)	OF	16	64	8	22	5	0	1	10	.344	5	10	4	23	1	1	.960
1991— Cincinnati (N.L.)	1B-OF	136	478	72	152	33	1	14	59	.318	46	61	10	979	100	9	.992
1992— Cincinnati (N.L.)	1B	115	395	41	107	21	3	6	53	.271	45	53	6	841	86	1	*.999
— Nashville (A.A.)	1B	2	6	1	1	1	0	0	0	.167	2	1	0	13	3	0	1.000
1993— Indianapolis (A.A.)......	1B	3	13	4	6	0	1	1	5	.462	1	2	0	26	3	0	1.000
— Cincinnati (N.L.)	1B	101	379	48	120	18	0	7	49	.317	34	51	2	746	75	5	.994
1994— Cincinnati (N.L.)	1B	112	436	60	146	30	4	10	78	.335	34	62	6	901	80	6	.994
1995— Cincinnati (N.L.)	1B	101	359	53	100	25	2	11	51	.279	29	58	1	757	72	5	.994
— Indianapolis (A.A.)......	1B	2	5	2	2	0	0	0	1	.400	1	0	0	13	2	0	1.000

M

Year	Team (League)	Pos.	G	AB	R	H	2B	3B	HR	RBI	Avg.	BB	SO	SB	PO	A	E	Avg.
									BATTING						FIELDING		
1996—	Cincinnati (N.L.)	1B	142	528	82	165	32	4	16	80	.313	50	76	7	1129	91	8	.993
	— Indianapolis (A.A.)......	1B	1	4	1	2	1	0	1	1	.500	0	1	0	2	0	0	1.000
1997—	Cincinnati (N.L.)	1B	96	333	42	92	20	1	1	33	.276	23	43	3	672	52	7	.990
1998—	Kansas City (A.L.)■ ...	1B-DH-OF	127	472	50	146	27	2	1	40	.309	32	52	1	396	35	4	.991
1999—	Cincinnati (N.L.)■	1B-OF-DH	80	102	10	29	9	0	0	16	.284	10	21	0	110	6	1	.991
2000—	Cincinnati (N.L.)	1B-DH-OF	59	63	9	14	2	1	2	6	.222	12	10	0	50	12	0	1.000
	— Detroit (A.L.)■	1B-OF	40	106	15	33	7	0	1	8	.311	19	16	0	264	23	3	.990
American League totals (4 years)			197	616	68	186	34	2	2	52	.302	52	81	1	679	58	7	.991
National League totals (10 years)			1049	3382	467	1030	212	19	74	461	.305	304	467	44	6780	627	46	.994
Major League totals (13 years)			1246	3998	535	1216	246	21	76	513	.304	356	548	45	7459	685	53	.994

DIVISION SERIES RECORD

Year	Team (League)	Pos.	G	AB	R	H	2B	3B	HR	RBI	Avg.	BB	SO	SB	PO	A	E	Avg.
									BATTING						FIELDING		
1995—	Cincinnati (N.L.)	1B	3	10	5	5	1	0	0	2	.500	3	1	1	22	2	0	1.000

CHAMPIONSHIP SERIES RECORD

Year	Team (League)	Pos.	G	AB	R	H	2B	3B	HR	RBI	Avg.	BB	SO	SB	PO	A	E	Avg.
									BATTING						FIELDING		
1990—	Cincinnati (N.L.)	1B-PH	5	12	3	5	1	0	0	1	.417	1	0	0	20	2	0	1.000
1995—	Cincinnati (N.L.)	1B-PH	4	12	0	2	1	0	0	1	.167	1	1	1	27	3	0	1.000
Championship series totals (2 years)			9	24	3	7	2	0	0	2	.292	2	1	1	47	5	0	1.000

WORLD SERIES RECORD

NOTES: Member of World Series championship team (1990).

Year	Team (League)	Pos.	G	AB	R	H	2B	3B	HR	RBI	Avg.	BB	SO	SB	PO	A	E	Avg.
									BATTING						FIELDING		
1990—	Cincinnati (N.L.)	1B-DH	4	14	0	1	0	0	0	2	.071	1	1	0	18	1	0	1.000

MORRIS, JIM — P — DODGERS

PERSONAL: Born January 19, 1964, in Brownwood, Texas. ... 6-3/215. ... Throws left, bats left. ... Full name: James Samuel Morris Jr.
HIGH SCHOOL: Brownwood (Texas).
JUNIOR COLLEGE: Ranger (Texas) College.
TRANSACTIONS/CAREER NOTES: Selected by Milwaukee Brewers organization in first round of secondary phase of free-agent draft (January 11, 1983). ... On disabled list (August 16-29, 1984). ... On temporary inactive list (April 12-May 13, 1985). ... On disabled list (April 11, 1986-entire season). ... Released by Brewers (June 15, 1987). ... Missed entire 1988 season due to injury. ... Signed by Chicago White Sox organization (September 25, 1988). ... Granted free agency (October 22, 1989). ... Out of organized baseball (1990-99). ... Signed by Tampa Bay Devil Rays organization (June 23, 1999). ... On St. Petersburg disabled list (June 25-July 15, 1999). ... On Durham disabled list (May 15, 2000-remainder of season). ... Released by Devil Rays (November 27, 2000). ... Signed by Los Angeles Dodgers organization (December 14, 2000).

Year	League	W	L	Pct.	ERA	G	GS	CG	ShO	Sv.	IP	H	R	ER	BB	SO
1983—	Paintsville (Appl.)	3	6	.333	5.10	13	13	0	0	0	67	58	50	38	42	75
1984—	Beloit (Midw.)...................	8	9	.471	5.05	24	22	1	0	0	112 1/3	107	80	63	79	109
1985—	Beloit (Midw.)...................	0	0	...	0.00	1	0	0	0	1	3	0	0	0	0	4
	— Stockton (Calif.)	5	6	.455	6.04	19	13	0	0	0	73	85	63	49	57	43
1986—									Did not play.							
1987—	Stockton (Calif.)	1	0	1.000	0.75	4	0	0	0	0	12	6	5	1	12	9
1988—									Did not play.							
1989—	Sarasota (FSL)■................	0	1	.000	10.13	2	2	0	0	0	2 2/3	3	3	3	2	4
1999—	Orlando (Sou.)■	0	1	.000	1.80	3	0	0	0	1	5	6	1	1	1	6
	— Durham (I.L.)	3	1	.750	5.48	18	0	0	0	0	23	21	14	14	19	16
	— Tampa Bay (A.L.)..............	0	0	...	5.79	5	0	0	0	0	4 2/3	3	3	3	2	3
2000—	Durham (I.L.)	0	0	...	9.00	1	0	0	0	0	1	1	1	1	2	1
	— Tampa Bay (A.L.)..............	0	0	...	4.35	16	0	0	0	0	10 1/3	10	9	5	7	10
Major League totals (2 years)		0	0	...	4.80	21	0	0	0	0	15	13	12	8	9	13

MORRIS, MATT — P — CARDINALS

PERSONAL: Born August 9, 1974, in Middletown, N.Y. ... 6-5/210. ... Throws right, bats right. ... Full name: Matthew Christian Morris.
HIGH SCHOOL: Valley Central (Montgomery, N.Y.).
COLLEGE: Seton Hall.
TRANSACTIONS/CAREER NOTES: Selected by Milwaukee Brewers organization in 25th round of free-agent draft (June 1, 1992); did not sign. ... Selected by St. Louis Cardinals organization in first round (12th pick overall) of free-agent draft (June 1, 1995). ... On St. Louis disabled list (March 24-April 11 and April 12-July 10, 1998); included rehabilitation assignments to Arkansas (April 6-11) and Memphis (June 21-July 10). ... On disabled list (March 26, 1999-entire season). ... On St. Louis disabled list (April 2-May 28, 2000); included rehabilitation assignments to Arkansas (May 2-11) and Memphis (May 12-May 28).
HONORS: Named N.L. Rookie Pitcher of the Year by THE SPORTING NEWS (1997).
MISCELLANEOUS: Struck out in only appearance as pinch hitter (1997). ... Appeared in one game as pinch runner (2000).

Year	League	W	L	Pct.	ERA	G	GS	CG	ShO	Sv.	IP	H	R	ER	BB	SO
1995—	New Jersey (NY-Penn)	2	0	1.000	1.64	2	2	0	0	0	11	12	3	2	3	13
	— St. Petersburg (FSL)	3	2	.600	2.38	6	6	1	1	0	34	22	16	9	11	31
1996—	Arkansas (Texas)...............	12	12	.500	3.88	27	27	4	*4	0	167	178	79	72	48	120
	— Louisville (A.A.)................	0	1	.000	3.38	1	1	0	0	0	8	8	3	3	1	9
1997—	St. Louis (N.L.).................	12	9	.571	3.19	33	33	3	0	0	217	208	88	77	69	149
1998—	Arkansas (Texas)...............	0	0	...	0.00	1	0	0	0	0	4	4	0	0	0	2
	— St. Louis (N.L.).................	7	5	.583	2.53	17	17	2	1	0	113 2/3	101	37	32	42	79
	— Memphis (PCL)	1	0	1.000	4.50	4	4	0	0	0	14	16	8	7	4	21

M

Year League	W	L	Pct.	ERA	G	GS	CG	ShO	Sv.	IP	H	R	ER	BB	SO
1999— St. Louis (N.L.)							Did not play.								
2000— Arkansas (Texas)	0	0	...	6.43	2	2	0	0	0	7	8	5	5	4	7
— Memphis (PCL)	1	2	.333	7.98	3	3	0	0	0	14²/₃	20	13	13	6	8
— St. Louis (N.L.)	3	3	.500	3.57	31	0	0	0	4	53	53	22	21	17	34
Major League totals (3 years)	22	17	.564	3.05	81	50	5	1	4	383²/₃	362	147	130	128	262

DIVISION SERIES RECORD

Year League	W	L	Pct.	ERA	G	GS	CG	ShO	Sv.	IP	H	R	ER	BB	SO
2000— St. Louis (N.L.)	0	0	...	0.00	2	0	0	0	0	2	0	0	0	1	0

CHAMPIONSHIP SERIES RECORD

Year League	W	L	Pct.	ERA	G	GS	CG	ShO	Sv.	IP	H	R	ER	BB	SO
2000— St. Louis (N.L.)	0	0	...	4.91	2	0	0	0	0	3²/₃	2	2	2	2	2

MORRIS, WARREN — 2B — PIRATES

PERSONAL: Born January 11, 1974, in Alexandria, La. ... 5-11/179. ... Bats left, throws right. ... Full name: Warren Randall Morris.
HIGH SCHOOL: Bolton (Alexandria, La.).
COLLEGE: Louisiana State.
TRANSACTIONS/CAREER NOTES: Selected by Texas Rangers organization in fifth round of free-agent draft (June 2, 1996). ... Traded by Rangers with P Todd Van Poppel to Pittsburgh Pirates for P Esteban Loaiza (July 17, 1998).
MISCELLANEOUS: Member of 1996 U.S. Olympic baseball team.

Year Team (League)	Pos.	G	AB	R	H	2B	3B	HR	RBI	Avg.	BB	SO	SB	PO	A	E	Avg.
1997— Charlotte (FSL)	2B-3B	128	494	78	151	27	9	12	75	.306	62	100	16	193	247	18	.961
— Oklahoma City (A.A.)	2B	8	32	3	7	1	0	1	3	.219	3	5	0	17	31	0	1.000
1998— Tulsa (Texas)	2B	95	390	59	129	22	5	14	73	.331	43	63	12	179	274	17	.964
— Carolina (Sou.)■	2B	44	151	28	50	8	3	5	30	.331	24	34	5	87	100	7	.964
1999— Pittsburgh (N.L.)	2B	147	511	65	147	20	3	15	73	.288	59	88	3	263	403	14	.979
2000— Pittsburgh (N.L.)	2B	144	528	68	137	31	2	3	43	.259	65	78	7	291	414	15	.979
Major League totals (2 years)		291	1039	133	284	51	5	18	116	.273	124	166	10	554	817	29	.979

MOSS, DAMIAN — P — BRAVES

PERSONAL: Born November 24, 1976, in Darlinghurst, Australia. ... 6-0/187. ... Throws left, bats right. ... Full name: Damian Joseph Moss.
HIGH SCHOOL: Liverpool Boys (Australia).
TRANSACTIONS/CAREER NOTES: Signed as non-drafted free agent by Atlanta Braves organization (July 1, 1993). ... On disabled list (March 27, 1998-entire season). ... On Atlanta disabled list (April 3-June 1, 1999).
STATISTICAL NOTES: Led Appalachian League with 14 hit batsmen in 1994. ... Tied for International League with six errors in 2000.

Year League	W	L	Pct.	ERA	G	GS	CG	ShO	Sv.	IP	H	R	ER	BB	SO
1994— Danville (Appl.)	2	5	.286	3.58	12	12	1	1	0	60¹/₃	30	28	24	55	77
1995— Macon (S.Atl.)	9	10	.474	3.56	27	27	0	0	0	149¹/₃	134	73	59	70	•177
1996— Durham (Caro.)	9	1	*.900	2.25	14	14	0	0	0	84	52	25	21	40	89
— Greenville (Sou.)	2	5	.286	4.97	11	10	0	0	0	58	57	41	32	35	48
1997— Greenville (Sou.)	6	8	.429	5.35	21	19	1	0	0	112²/₃	111	73	67	58	116
1998— Greenville (Sou.)							Did not play.								
1999— Macon (S.Atl.)	0	3	.000	4.32	12	12	0	0	0	41²/₃	33	20	20	15	49
— Greenville (Sou.)	1	3	.250	8.54	7	7	0	0	0	32²/₃	50	33	31	21	22
2000— Richmond (I.L.)	9	6	.600	3.14	29	28	0	0	0	160²/₃	130	67	56	*106	123

MOTA, DANNY — P — TWINS

PERSONAL: Born October 9, 1975, in Santo Domingo, Dominican Republic. ... 6-0/170. ... Throws right, bats right. ... Full name: Daniel Avila Mota.
TRANSACTIONS/CAREER NOTES: Signed as non-drafted free agent by New York Yankees organization (April 15, 1994). ... Traded by Yankees with P Eric Milton, SS Cristian Guzman, OF Brian Buchanan and cash to Minnesota Twins for 2B Chuck Knoblauch (February 5, 1998). ... On Fort Myers disabled list (April 8-27, 1999). ... On New Britain disabled list (June 26, 1999-remainder of season).

Year League	W	L	Pct.	ERA	G	GS	CG	ShO	Sv.	IP	H	R	ER	BB	SO
1994— Dominican Yankees (DSL)	2	3	.400	4.53	13	12	0	0	0	57²/₃	50	39	29	24	51
1995— Gulf Coast Yankees (GCL)	2	3	.400	2.20	14	0	0	0	0	32²/₃	27	9	8	4	35
1996— Oneonta (NY-Penn)	0	1	.000	4.50	10	0	0	0	7	10	10	5	5	2	11
1997— Oneonta (NY-Penn)	1	0	1.000	2.22	27	0	0	0	*17	28¹/₃	21	8	7	16	40
— Greensboro (S.Atl.)	2	0	1.000	1.82	20	0	0	0	1	29²/₃	17	6	6	11	30
1998— Fort Wayne (Midw.)■	4	3	.571	2.25	25	0	0	0	7	32	24	14	8	8	39
— Fort Myers (FSL)	3	5	.375	2.85	19	4	0	0	0	47¹/₃	45	21	15	22	49
1999— Fort Myers (FSL)	1	1	.500	2.41	11	0	0	0	0	18²/₃	19	5	5	5	22
— New Britain (East.)	0	1	.000	3.55	6	0	0	0	0	12²/₃	11	5	5	5	12
2000— Fort Myers (FSL)	2	2	.500	2.05	29	1	0	0	4	48¹/₃	38	20	11	23	52
— New Britain (East.)	3	1	.750	2.86	24	0	0	0	4	28¹/₃	19	13	9	8	40
— Salt Lake (PCL)	0	0	...	1.59	4	0	0	0	0	5²/₃	5	1	1	1	5
— Minnesota (A.L.)	0	0	...	8.44	4	0	0	0	0	5¹/₃	10	5	5	1	3
Major League totals (1 year)	0	0	...	8.44	4	0	0	0	0	5¹/₃	10	5	5	1	3

M

PERSONAL: Born July 25, 1973, in San Pedro de Macoris, Dominican Republic. ... 6-4/205. ... Throws right, bats right. ... Full name: Guillermo Reynoso Mota.

HIGH SCHOOL: Jose Joaquin Perez (San Pedro de Macoris, Dominican Republic).

TRANSACTIONS/CAREER NOTES: Signed as non-drafted free agent by New York Mets organization (September 7, 1990). ... Selected by Montreal Expos organization from Mets organization in Rule 5 minor league draft (December 9, 1996). ... Re-signed by Expos organization (March 20, 1999).

STATISTICAL NOTES: Led Gulf Coast League third basemen with .943 fielding percentage; tied for lead with 40 putouts and 11 double plays in 1993. ... Led Appalachian League third basemen with 44 putouts, 157 assists, 214 total chances, 12 double plays and .939 fielding percentage in 1994. ... Led South Atlantic League shortstops with 615 total chances and 66 double plays in 1995. ... Hit home run in first major league at-bat (June 9, 1999).

MISCELLANEOUS: Played infield (1991-96).

Year League	W	L	Pct.	ERA	G	GS	CG	ShO	Sv.	IP	H	R	ER	BB	SO
1997— Cape Fear (S.Atl.)■	5	10	.333	4.36	25	23	...	...	0	126	135	65	61	33	112
1998— Jupiter (FSL)	3	2	.600	0.66	20	0	0	0	2	41	18	6	3	6	27
— Harrisburg (East.)	2	0	1.000	1.06	12	0	0	0	4	17	10	2	2	2	19
1999— Ottawa (I.L.)	2	0	1.000	1.89	14	0	0	0	5	19	16	6	4	5	17
— Montreal (N.L.)	2	4	.333	2.93	51	0	0	0	0	55 1/3	54	24	18	25	27
2000— Ottawa (I.L.)	4	5	.444	2.29	35	0	0	0	7	63	49	16	16	31	35
— Montreal (N.L.)	1	1	.500	6.00	29	0	0	0	0	30	27	21	20	12	24
Major League totals (2 years)	3	5	.375	4.01	80	0	0	0	0	85 1/3	81	45	38	37	51

RECORD AS POSITION PLAYER

Year Team (League)	Pos.	G	AB	R	H	2B	3B	HR	RBI	Avg.	BB	SO	SB	PO	A	E	Avg.
1991— Dom. Mets (DSL)		32	90	4	22	2	0	0	12	.244	9	19	0	...	...	...	...
1992— Dom. Mets (DSL)		70	228	49	68	10	3	6	40	.298	28	40	10	133	173	24	.927
1993— GC Mets (GCL)	3B-SS	43	169	23	42	7	2	1	22	.249	7	37	1	‡42	95	8	*.945
1994— St. Lucie (FSL)	3B	1	4	1	0	0	0	0	0	.000	0	0	0	1	5	1	.857
— Kingsport (Appl.)	3B-SS	65	245	40	60	10	2	9	37	.245	20	78	5	†55	†175	16	†.935
1995— Columbia (S.Atl.)	SS-1B	123	400	45	97	24	3	4	45	.243	32	127	8	205	373	40	.935
1996— St. Lucie (FSL)	SS-3B	102	304	34	71	10	3	1	21	.234	34	90	8	127	293	21	.952

PERSONAL: Born October 31, 1977, in Glendale, Calif. ... 6-1/170. ... Bats both, throws right. ... Full name: Antonio Nicolas Mota. ... Son of Manny Mota, coach, Los Angeles Dodgers and outfielder with four major league teams (1962-82).

HIGH SCHOOL: Miami Springs (Fla.).

TRANSACTIONS/CAREER NOTES: Selected by Los Angeles Dodgers organization in 17th round of free-agent draft (June 1, 1995). ... On Albuquerque disabled list (April 30-May 10 and May 19-June 7, 2000). ... Released by Dodgers (December 11, 2000). ... Re-signed by Dodgers organization (January 4, 2001).

STATISTICAL NOTES: Led California League outfielders with four double plays in 1997.

Year Team (League)	Pos.	G	AB	R	H	2B	3B	HR	RBI	Avg.	BB	SO	SB	PO	A	E	Avg.
1996— Yakima (N'West)	OF	60	225	29	62	11	3	3	29	.276	13	37	13	59	2	0	1.000
1997— San Bern. (Calif.)	OF	111	420	53	101	14	13	4	49	.240	30	97	11	225	15	4	.984
1998— Vero Beach (FSL)	OF	61	254	45	81	18	5	7	35	.319	18	27	13	118	3	2	.984
— San Antonio (Texas)	OF	59	222	20	54	10	6	2	22	.243	12	36	16	89	5	3	.969
1999— San Antonio (Texas)	OF	98	345	65	112	31	2	15	75	.325	41	56	13	111	8	3	.975
2000— Albuquerque (PCL)	OF	102	372	57	100	11	4	6	47	.269	28	61	8	155	6	3	.982

M

PERSONAL: Born October 15, 1971, in Augusta, Ga. ... 6-3/220. ... Bats right, throws right. ... Full name: Charles Edward Mottola.

HIGH SCHOOL: St. Thomas Aquinas (Fort Lauderdale, Fla.).

COLLEGE: Central Florida.

TRANSACTIONS/CAREER NOTES: Selected by Baltimore Orioles organization in 10th round of free-agent draft (June 5, 1989); did not sign. ... Selected by Cincinnati Reds organization in first round (fifth pick overall) of free-agent draft (June 1, 1992). ... On disabled list (May 11-20, 1994). ... Traded by Reds to Texas Rangers for a player to be named later (April 18, 1998). ... On Oklahoma disabled list (May 18-June 30, 1998). ... Granted free agency (October 15, 1998). ... Signed by Chicago White Sox organization (December 17, 1998). ... Granted free agency (October 15, 1999). ... Signed by Toronto Blue Jays organization (November 17, 1999). ... Traded by Blue Jays to Florida Marlins for player to be named later or cash (January 16, 2001).

HONORS: Named International League Most Valuable Player (2000).

STATISTICAL NOTES: Tied for International League lead with four double plays by outfielder in 1999. ... Led International League with .566 slugging percentage in 2000.

Year Team (League)	Pos.	G	AB	R	H	2B	3B	HR	RBI	Avg.	BB	SO	SB	PO	A	E	Avg.
1992— Billings (Pio.)	OF	57	213	53	61	8	3	12	37	.286	25	43	12	89	9	3	.970
1993— Win.-Salem (Caro.)	OF	137	493	76	138	25	3	21	91	.280	62	109	13	214	*20	*15	.940
1994— Chattanooga (Sou.)	OF	118	402	44	97	19	1	7	41	.241	30	68	9	230	17	1	.996
1995— Chattanooga (Sou.)	OF	51	181	32	53	13	1	10	39	.293	13	32	1	106	6	3	.974
— Indianapolis (A.A.)	OF	69	239	40	62	11	1	8	37	.259	20	50	8	151	11	4	.976
1996— Indianapolis (A.A.)	OF-DH	103	362	45	95	24	3	9	47	.262	21	93	9	176	8	6	.968
— Cincinnati (N.L.)	OF	35	79	10	17	3	0	3	6	.215	6	16	2	42	2	0	1.000
1997— Indianapolis (A.A.)	OF-DH	83	284	33	82	10	6	7	45	.289	16	43	12	136	8	8	.947
— Chattanooga (Sou.)	OF-DH	46	174	35	63	9	3	5	32	.362	16	23	7	74	5	3	.963

Year Team (League)	Pos.	G	AB	R	H	2B	3B	HR	RBI	Avg.	BB	SO	SB	PO	A	E	Avg.
1998—Indianapolis (I.L.)......	OF	5	12	2	5	0	0	1	2	.417	4	0	0	7	2	0	1.000
—Tulsa (Texas)■..........	DH-OF	8	26	9	13	1	0	1	7	.500	10	1	3	5	0	0	1.000
—Oklahoma (PCL)......	OF-DH	74	257	29	68	13	1	2	22	.265	18	49	8	118	5	6	.953
1999—Charlotte (I.L.)■........	OF-DH	140	511	95	164	32	4	20	94	.321	60	83	18	288	•17	6	.981
2000—Syracuse (I.L.)■.......	OF	134	505	85	156	25	3	*33	102	.309	37	99	30	259	8	*10	.964
—Toronto (A.L.)............	OF	3	9	1	2	0	0	0	2	.222	0	4	0	5	0	0	1.000
American League totals (1 year)		3	9	1	2	0	0	0	2	.222	0	4	0	5	0	0	1.000
National League totals (1 year)		35	79	10	17	3	0	3	6	.215	6	16	2	42	2	0	1.000
Major League totals (2 years)		38	88	11	19	3	0	3	8	.216	6	20	2	47	2	0	1.000

MOUTON, JAMES — OF — BREWERS

PERSONAL: Born December 29, 1968, in Denver. ... 5-9/175. ... Bats right, throws right. ... Full name: James Raleigh Mouton. ... Name pronounced MOO-tawn.
HIGH SCHOOL: Burbank (Calif.).
COLLEGE: St. Mary's (Calif.).
TRANSACTIONS/CAREER NOTES: Selected by New York Yankees organization in 42nd round of free-agent draft (June 2, 1987); did not sign. ... Selected by Minnesota Twins organization in eighth round of free-agent draft (June 4, 1990); did not sign. ... Selected by Houston Astros organization in seventh round of free-agent draft (June 3, 1991). ... On Houston disabled list (June 12-30, 1995); included rehabilitation assignment to Tucson (June 27-30). ... Traded by Astros to San Diego Padres for P Sean Bergman (January 14, 1998). ... On San Diego disabled list (May 16-June 1, 1998); included rehabilitation assignment to Las Vegas (May 27-June 1). ... Granted free agency (December 21, 1998). ... Signed by Montreal Expos organization (April 5, 1999). ... Granted free agency (October 15, 1999). ... Signed by Milwaukee Brewers organization (December 13, 1999). ... Granted free agency (October 30, 2000). ... Re-signed by Brewers organization (December 7, 2000).
HONORS: Named Pacific Coast League Most Valuable Player (1993).
STATISTICAL NOTES: Led New York-Pennsylvania League in caught stealing with 18 in 1991. ... Led New York-Pennsylvania League second basemen with 382 total chances in 1991. ... Led Florida State League second basemen with 623 total chances in 1992. ... Led Pacific Coast League with 286 total bases and tied for lead in caught stealing with 18 in 1993. ... Led Pacific Coast League second basemen with 674 total chances and 75 double plays in 1993. ... Career major league grand slams: 1.

Year Team (League)	Pos.	G	AB	R	H	2B	3B	HR	RBI	Avg.	BB	SO	SB	PO	A	E	Avg.
1991—Auburn (NY-Penn)......	2B	76	288	71	76	15	*10	2	40	.264	55	32	*60	*170	184	*28	.927
1992—Osceola (FSL)............	2B	133	507	*110	143	•30	6	11	62	.282	71	78	*51	*288	294	*41	.934
1993—Tucson (PCL)	2B	134	*546	*126	*172	*42	12	16	92	.315	72	82	40	*277	*354	*43	.936
1994—Houston (N.L.)	OF	99	310	43	76	11	0	2	16	.245	27	69	24	163	5	3	.982
—Tucson (PCL)	OF	4	17	2	7	1	0	1	1	.412	2	3	1	7	1	0	1.000
1995—Tucson (PCL)	OF	3	11	1	5	0	0	1	1	.455	0	2	0	1	0	1	.500
—Houston (N.L.)	OF	104	298	42	78	18	2	4	27	.262	25	59	25	136	4	0	1.000
1996—Houston (N.L.)	OF	122	300	40	79	15	1	3	34	.263	38	55	21	158	7	5	.971
—Tucson (PCL)	OF	1	4	1	1	0	0	0	0	.250	1	0	0	2	0	0	1.000
1997—Houston (N.L.)	OF	86	180	24	38	9	1	3	23	.211	18	30	9	86	1	0	1.000
1998—San Diego (N.L.)■.......	OF-DH	55	63	8	12	2	1	0	7	.190	7	11	4	30	1	1	.969
—Las Vegas (PCL)	OF-DH-2B	50	192	38	68	17	3	4	31	.354	17	31	15	57	2	1	.983
1999—Montreal (N.L.)■........	OF-DH	95	122	18	32	5	1	2	13	.262	18	31	6	50	2	1	.981
2000—Milwaukee (N.L.).........	OF	87	159	28	37	7	1	2	17	.233	30	43	13	84	3	1	.989
Major League totals (7 years)		648	1432	203	352	67	7	16	137	.246	163	298	102	707	23	11	.985

MOUTON, LYLE — OF

PERSONAL: Born May 13, 1969, in Lafayette, La. ... 6-4/230. ... Bats right, throws right. ... Full name: Lyle Joseph Mouton. ... Name pronounced MOO-tawn.
HIGH SCHOOL: St. Thomas More (Lafayette, La.).
COLLEGE: Louisiana State.
TRANSACTIONS/CAREER NOTES: Selected by New York Yankees organization in fifth round of free-agent draft (June 3, 1991). ... Traded by Yankees to Chicago White Sox (April 22, 1995), completing deal in which White Sox traded P Jack McDowell to Yankees for P Keith Heberling and a player to be named later (December 14, 1994). ... On Chicago disabled list (May 11-27, 1997); included rehabilitation assignment to Birmingham (May 25-27). ... Contract sold by White Sox to Yakult Swallows of Japan Central League (November 21, 1997). ... Contract purchased by Baltimore Orioles organization (July 2, 1998). ... Traded by Orioles to Milwaukee Brewers for OF Todd Dunn (June 1, 1999). ... On disabled list (June 2-June 16, 2000). ... Released by Brewers (November 27, 2000).

Year Team (League)	Pos.	G	AB	R	H	2B	3B	HR	RBI	Avg.	BB	SO	SB	PO	A	E	Avg.
1991—Oneonta (NY-Penn)	OF	70	272	53	84	11	2	7	41	.309	31	38	15	106	5	5	.957
1992—Prince Will. (Caro.)......	OF	50	189	28	50	14	1	6	34	.265	17	42	4	49	5	4	.931
—Albany (East.)............	OF	64	214	25	46	12	2	2	27	.215	24	55	1	102	1	0	1.000
1993—Albany (East.)............	OF	135	491	74	125	22	3	16	76	.255	50	125	18	189	9	5	.975
1994—Alb./Colonie (East.)	OF-3B	74	274	42	84	23	1	12	42	.307	27	62	7	118	4	2	.984
—Columbus (I.L.)..........	OF	59	204	26	64	14	5	4	32	.314	14	45	5	99	5	1	.990
1995—Nashville (A.A.)■.......	OF-DH	71	267	40	79	17	0	8	41	.296	23	58	10	123	8	3	.978
—Chicago (A.L.)	OF-DH	58	179	23	54	16	0	5	27	.302	19	46	1	93	5	1	.990
1996—Chicago (A.L.)	OF-DH	87	214	25	63	8	1	7	39	.294	22	50	3	64	1	2	.970
1997—Chicago (A.L.)	OF-DH	88	242	26	65	9	0	5	23	.269	14	66	4	126	1	4	.969
—Birmingham (Sou.).....	OF	3	11	1	2	0	0	1	1	.182	1	4	0	5	0	0	1.000
1998—Yakult (Jap. Cen.)■.....	OF	30	97	7	21	8	0	3	12	.216	9	27	0	...	...	...	...
—Rochester (I.L.)■........	OF-DH	37	137	23	44	9	2	7	32	.321	13	31	1	56	1	1	.983
—Baltimore (A.L.)..........	OF	18	39	5	12	2	0	2	7	.308	4	8	0	19	1	0	1.000
1999—Rochester (I.L.)	OF-DH	44	162	25	36	9	1	4	17	.222	13	31	3	63	1	4	.941
—Louisville (I.L.)■	OF-DH-1B	83	305	64	109	34	2	19	77	.357	27	67	19	181	7	2	.989
—Milwaukee (N.L.)........	OF	14	17	2	3	1	0	1	3	.176	2	3	0	1	0	0	1.000
2000—Milwaukee (N.L.)........	OF	42	97	14	27	7	1	2	16	.278	10	29	1	41	4	1	.978
—Indianapolis (I.L.)........	OF	52	197	33	60	23	0	12	51	.305	23	41	4	107	2	1	.991
American League totals (4 years)		251	674	79	194	35	1	19	96	.288	59	170	8	302	8	7	.978
National League totals (2 years)		56	114	16	30	8	1	3	19	.263	12	32	1	42	4	1	.979
Major League totals (6 years)		307	788	95	224	43	2	22	115	.284	71	202	9	344	12	8	.978

M

PERSONAL: Born November 18, 1962, in Sellersville, Pa. ... 6-0/175. ... Throws left, bats left. ... Son-in-law of Digger Phelps, ESPN college basketball analyst, and Notre Dame basketball coach (1971-72 through 1990-91).

HIGH SCHOOL: Souderton (Pa.) Area.

COLLEGE: St. Joseph's (Pa.).

TRANSACTIONS/CAREER NOTES: Selected by Chicago Cubs organization in sixth round of free-agent draft (June 4, 1984). ... Traded by Cubs with OF Rafael Palmeiro and P Drew Hall to Texas Rangers for P Mitch Williams, P Paul Kilgus, P Steve Wilson, IF Curtis Wilkerson, IF Luis Benitez and OF Pablo Delgado (December 5, 1988). ... On Texas disabled list (May 31-September 1, 1989); included rehabilitation assignments to Gulf Coast Rangers (August 5-14) and Tulsa (August 15-24). ... Released by Rangers (November 13, 1990). ... Signed by St. Louis Cardinals organization (January 9, 1991). ... Released by Cardinals (October 14, 1991). ... Signed by Cubs organization (January 8, 1992). ... Released by Cubs (March 30, 1992). ... Signed by Detroit Tigers organization (May 24, 1992). ... Granted free agency (December 8, 1992). ... Signed by Baltimore Orioles organization (December 14, 1992). ... Granted free agency (November 1, 1995). ... Signed by Boston Red Sox (January 2, 1996). ... Traded by Red Sox to Seattle Mariners for OF Darren Bragg (July 30, 1996). ... Granted free agency (October 29, 1996). ... Re-signed by Mariners (November 20, 1996). ... On Seattle disabled list (March 23-April 29, 1997); included rehabilitation assignment to Tacoma (April 24-29). ... On disabled list (April 15-June 2, 2000).

HONORS: Named lefthanded pitcher on The Sporting News A.L. All-Star team (1999).

STATISTICAL NOTES: Led American Association with 16 home runs allowed in 1991. ... Led A.L. with .813 winning percentage in 1996. ... Led A.L. pitchers with 47 assists and nine double plays in 1999.

Year League	W	L	Pct.	ERA	G	GS	CG	ShO	Sv.	IP	H	R	ER	BB	SO
1984—Geneva (NY-Penn)	•9	3	.750	1.89	14	14	5	2	0	*104 2/3	59	27	22	31	*120
1985—Winston-Salem (Caro.)	8	2	.800	2.30	12	12	6	2	0	94	82	36	24	22	94
—Pittsfield (East.)	7	6	.538	3.72	15	15	3	0	0	96 2/3	99	49	40	32	51
1986—Pittsfield (East.)	3	1	.750	0.88	6	6	0	0	0	41	27	10	4	16	42
—Iowa (A.A.)	3	2	.600	2.55	6	6	2	0	0	42 1/3	25	14	12	11	25
—Chicago (N.L.)	7	4	.636	5.05	16	16	1	1	0	87 1/3	107	52	49	42	45
1987—Chicago (N.L.)	12	15	.444	5.10	35	33	1	0	0	201	210	127	*114	97	147
1988—Chicago (N.L.)	9	15	.375	3.48	34	30	3	1	0	202	212	84	78	55	121
1989—Texas (A.L.)■	4	9	.308	4.86	15	15	1	0	0	76	84	51	41	33	44
—Gulf Coast Rangers (GCL)	1	0	1.000	1.64	3	3	0	0	0	11	8	4	2	1	18
—Tulsa (Texas)	1	1	.500	5.11	2	2	1	1	0	12 1/3	16	8	7	3	9
1990—Texas (A.L.)	2	6	.250	4.66	33	10	1	0	0	102 1/3	115	59	53	39	58
1991—St. Louis (N.L.)■	0	5	.000	5.74	8	7	0	0	0	31 1/3	38	21	20	16	20
—Louisville (A.A.)	5	10	.333	3.80	20	20	1	0	0	125 2/3	125	64	53	43	69
1992—Toledo (I.L.)■	10	8	.556	2.86	21	20	5	0	0	138 2/3	128	48	44	37	80
1993—Rochester (I.L.)■	6	0	1.000	1.67	8	8	1	1	0	54	42	13	10	13	41
—Baltimore (A.L.)	12	9	.571	3.43	25	25	3	1	0	152	154	63	58	38	90
1994—Baltimore (A.L.)	5	7	.417	4.77	23	23	0	0	0	149	158	81	79	38	87
1995—Baltimore (A.L.)	8	6	.571	5.21	27	18	0	0	0	115 2/3	117	70	67	30	65
1996—Boston (A.L.)■	7	1	.875	4.50	23	10	0	0	0	90	111	50	45	27	50
—Seattle (A.L.)■	6	2	§.750	3.31	11	11	0	0	0	70 2/3	66	36	26	19	29
1997—Tacoma (PCL)	1	0	1.000	0.00	1	1	0	0	0	5	1	0	0	0	6
—Seattle (A.L.)	17	5	.773	3.86	30	30	2	0	0	188 2/3	187	82	81	43	113
1998—Seattle (A.L.)	15	9	.625	3.53	34	34	4	3	0	234 1/3	234	99	92	42	158
1999—Seattle (A.L.)	14	8	.636	3.87	32	32	4	0	0	228	235	108	98	48	137
2000—Seattle (A.L.)	13	10	.565	5.49	26	26	0	0	0	154	173	103	94	53	98
A.L. totals (10 years)	103	72	.589	4.23	279	234	15	4	0	1560 2/3	1634	802	734	410	929
N.L. totals (4 years)	28	39	.418	4.50	93	86	5	2	0	521 2/3	567	284	261	210	333
Major League totals (14 years)	131	111	.541	4.30	372	320	20	6	0	2082 1/3	2201	1086	995	620	1262

DIVISION SERIES RECORD

Year League	W	L	Pct.	ERA	G	GS	CG	ShO	Sv.	IP	H	R	ER	BB	SO
1997—Seattle (A.L.)	0	1	.000	5.79	1	1	0	0	0	4 2/3	5	3	3	1	2

PERSONAL: Born March 17, 1971, in Maryland Heights, Mo. ... 5-10/180. ... Bats both, throws right. ... Full name: William Richard Mueller. ... Name pronounced MILL-er.

HIGH SCHOOL: DeSmet (Creve Coeur, Mo.).

COLLEGE: Southwest Missouri State.

TRANSACTIONS/CAREER NOTES: Selected by San Francisco Giants organization in 15th round of free-agent draft (June 3, 1993). ... On disabled list (July 1-16, 1997). ... On San Francisco disabled list (April 6-May 17, 1999); included rehabilitation assignment to Fresno (May 11-17). ... Traded by Giants to Chicago Cubs for P Tim Worrell (November 19, 2000).

STATISTICAL NOTES: Led California League with .435 on-base percentage in 1994. ... Led Pacific Coast League third basemen with 25 double plays in 1996. ... Had 17-game hitting streak (April 24-May 14, 1998). ... Had 15-game hitting streak (May 1-19, 2000). ... Led N.L. third basemen with .974 fielding percentage in 2000. ... Career major league grand slams: 2.

							BATTING							FIELDING		
Year Team (League)	Pos.	G	AB	R	H	2B	3B	HR	RBI	Avg.	BB	SO	SB	PO	A	E	Avg.
1993—Everett (N'West)	2B	58	200	31	60	8	2	1	24	.300	42	17	13	86	143	8	.966
1994—San Jose (Calif.)	3B-2B-SS	120	431	79	130	20	•9	5	72	.302	*103	47	4	83	276	29	.925
1995—Shreveport (Texas)	3B-2B	88	330	56	102	16	2	1	39	.309	53	36	6	52	169	5	.978
—Phoenix (PCL)	3B-2B	41	172	23	51	13	6	2	19	.297	19	31	0	26	85	7	.941
1996—Phoenix (PCL)	3-S-2-DH	106	440	73	133	14	6	4	36	.302	44	40	2	92	250	11	.969
—San Francisco (N.L.)	3B-2B	55	200	31	66	15	1	0	19	.330	24	26	0	51	99	6	.962
1997—San Francisco (N.L.)	3B	128	390	51	114	26	3	7	44	.292	48	71	4	85	218	14	.956
1998—San Francisco (N.L.)	3B-2B	145	534	93	157	27	0	9	59	.294	79	83	3	99	287	19	.953
1999—San Francisco (N.L.)	3B-2B	116	414	61	120	24	0	2	36	.290	65	52	4	83	195	12	.959
—Fresno (PCL)	3B	3	12	3	5	0	1	0	6	.417	0	0	0	2	10	3	.800
2000—San Francisco (N.L.)	3B-2B	153	560	97	150	29	4	10	55	.268	52	62	4	100	244	9	†.975
Major League totals (5 years)		597	2098	333	607	121	8	28	213	.289	268	294	15	418	1043	60	.961

DIVISION SERIES RECORD

				BATTING											FIELDING		
Year Team (League)	Pos.	G	AB	R	H	2B	3B	HR	RBI	Avg.	BB	SO	SB	PO	A	E	Avg.
1997— San Francisco (N.L.) ..	3B	3	12	1	3	0	0	1	1	.250	0	0	0	2	9	0	1.000
2000— San Francisco (N.L.) ..	3B	4	20	2	5	2	0	0	0	.250	0	4	0	3	5	0	1.000
Division series totals (2 years)		7	32	3	8	2	0	1	1	.250	0	4	0	5	14	0	1.000

MULDER, MARK   P   ATHLETICS

PERSONAL: Born August 5, 1977, in South Holland, Ill. ... 6-6/200. ... Throws left, bats left. ... Full name: Mark Alan Mulder.
HIGH SCHOOL: Thornwood (South Holland, Ill.).
COLLEGE: Michigan State.
TRANSACTIONS/CAREER NOTES: Selected by Detroit Tigers organization in 55th round of free-agent draft (June 1, 1995); did not sign. ... Selected by Oakland Athletics organization in first round (second pick overall) of free-agent draft (June 2, 1998).

Year League	W	L	Pct.	ERA	G	GS	CG	ShO	Sv.	IP	H	R	ER	BB	SO
1999— Vancouver (PCL)	6	7	.462	4.06	22	22	1	0	0	128²/₃	152	69	58	31	81
2000— Sacramento (PCL)	1	1	.500	5.40	2	2	0	0	0	8¹/₃	15	11	5	4	6
— Oakland (A.L.)	9	10	.474	5.44	27	27	0	0	0	154	191	106	93	69	88
Major League totals (1 year)	9	10	.474	5.44	27	27	0	0	0	154	191	106	93	69	88

MULHOLLAND, TERRY   P   PIRATES

PERSONAL: Born March 9, 1963, in Uniontown, Pa. ... 6-3/220. ... Throws left, bats right. ... Full name: Terence John Mulholland.
HIGH SCHOOL: Laurel Highlands (Uniontown, Pa.).
COLLEGE: Marietta College (Ohio).
TRANSACTIONS/CAREER NOTES: Selected by San Francisco Giants organization in first round (24th pick overall) of free-agent draft (June 4, 1984); pick received as compensation for Detroit Tigers signing free-agent IF Darrell Evans. ... On San Francisco disabled list (August 1, 1988-remainder of season). ... Traded by Giants with P Dennis Cook and 3B Charlie Hayes to Philadelphia Phillies for P Steve Bedrosian and a player to be named later (June 18, 1989); Giants acquired IF Rick Parker to complete deal (August 7, 1989). ... On Philadelphia disabled list (June 12-28, 1990); included rehabilitation assignment to Scranton/Wilkes-Barre (June 23-24). ... Traded by Phillies with a player to be named later to New York Yankees for P Bobby Munoz, 2B Kevin Jordan and P Ryan Karp (February 9, 1994); Yankees acquired P Jeff Patterson to complete deal (November 8, 1994). ... Granted free agency (October 17, 1994). ... Signed by Giants (April 8, 1995). ... On San Francisco disabled list (June 6-July 4, 1995); included rehabilitation assignment to Phoenix (June 23-July 4). ... Granted free agency (November 3, 1995). ... Signed by Phillies organization (February 17, 1996). ... Traded by Phillies to Seattle Mariners for IF Desi Relaford (July 31, 1996). ... Granted free agency (October 28, 1996). ... Signed by Chicago Cubs (December 10, 1996). ... Claimed on waivers by Giants (August 8, 1997). ... Granted free agency (October 27, 1997). ... Signed by Cubs (February 2, 1998). ... Granted free agency (October 28, 1998). ... Re-signed by Cubs (November 6, 1998). ... Traded by Cubs with IF Jose Hernandez to Atlanta Braves for P Micah Bowie, P Ruben Quevado and a player to be named later (July 31, 1999); Cubs acquired P Joey Nation to complete deal (August 24, 1999). ... Granted free agency (October 31, 2000). ... Signed by Pittsburgh Pirates (December 10, 2000).
STATISTICAL NOTES: Pitched 6-0 no-hit victory for Philadelphia against San Francisco (August 15, 1990).
MISCELLANEOUS: Appeared in one game as pinch runner (1991). ... Appeared in one game as pinch runner with San Francisco (1995).

Year League	W	L	Pct.	ERA	G	GS	CG	ShO	Sv.	IP	H	R	ER	BB	SO
1984— Everett (N'West)	1	0	1.000	0.00	3	3	0	0	0	19	10	2	0	4	15
—Fresno (Calif.)	5	2	.714	2.95	9	9	0	0	0	42²/₃	32	17	14	36	39
1985— Shreveport (Texas)	9	8	.529	2.90	26	26	8	*3	0	176²/₃	166	79	57	87	122
1986— Phoenix (PCL)	8	5	.615	4.46	17	17	3	0	0	111	112	60	55	56	77
—San Francisco (N.L.)	1	7	.125	4.94	15	10	0	0	0	54²/₃	51	33	30	35	27
1987— Phoenix (PCL)	7	12	.368	5.07	37	*29	3	1	1	172¹/₃	200	*124	•97	90	94
1988— Phoenix (PCL)	7	3	.700	3.58	19	14	3	2	0	100²/₃	116	45	40	44	57
—San Francisco (N.L.)	2	1	.667	3.72	9	6	2	1	0	46	50	20	19	7	18
1989— San Francisco (N.L.)	0	0	...	4.09	5	1	0	0	0	11	15	5	5	4	6
—Phoenix (PCL)	4	5	.444	2.99	13	10	3	0	0	78¹/₃	67	30	26	26	61
—Philadelphia (N.L.)■	4	7	.364	5.00	20	17	2	1	0	104¹/₃	122	61	58	32	60
1990— Philadelphia (N.L.)	9	10	.474	3.34	33	26	6	1	0	180²/₃	172	78	67	42	75
—Scranton/W.B. (I.L.)	0	1	.000	3.00	1	1	0	0	0	6	9	4	2	2	2
1991— Philadelphia (N.L.)	16	13	.552	3.61	34	34	8	3	0	232	231	100	93	49	142
1992— Philadelphia (N.L.)	13	11	.542	3.81	32	32	*12	2	0	229	227	101	97	46	125
1993— Philadelphia (N.L.)	12	9	.571	3.25	29	28	7	2	0	191	177	80	69	40	116
1994— New York (A.L.)■	6	7	.462	6.49	24	19	2	0	0	120²/₃	150	94	87	37	72
1995— San Francisco (N.L.)■	5	13	.278	5.80	29	24	2	0	0	149	190	112	96	38	65
—Phoenix (PCL)	0	0	...	2.25	1	1	0	0	0	4	4	3	1	1	4
1996— Philadelphia (N.L.)■	8	7	.533	4.66	21	21	3	0	0	133¹/₃	157	74	69	21	52
—Seattle (A.L.)■	5	4	.556	4.67	12	12	0	0	0	69¹/₃	75	38	36	28	34
1997— Chicago (N.L.)■	6	12	.333	4.07	25	25	1	0	0	157	162	79	71	45	74
—San Francisco (N.L.)■	0	1	.000	5.16	15	2	0	0	0	29²/₃	28	21	17	6	25
1998— Chicago (N.L.)■	6	5	.545	2.89	70	6	0	0	3	112	100	49	36	39	72
1999— Chicago (N.L.)	6	6	.500	5.15	26	16	0	0	0	110	137	71	63	32	44
—Atlanta (N.L.)■	4	2	.667	2.98	16	8	0	0	1	60¹/₃	64	24	20	13	39
2000— Atlanta (N.L.)	9	9	.500	5.11	54	20	1	0	1	156²/₃	198	96	89	41	78
A.L. totals (2 years)	11	11	.500	5.83	36	31	2	0	0	190	225	132	123	65	106
N.L. totals (13 years)	101	113	.472	4.14	433	276	44	10	5	1956²/₃	2081	1004	899	490	1018
Major League totals (14 years)	112	124	.475	4.28	469	307	46	10	5	2146²/₃	2306	1136	1022	555	1124

DIVISION SERIES RECORD

Year League	W	L	Pct.	ERA	G	GS	CG	ShO	Sv.	IP	H	R	ER	BB	SO
1998— Chicago (N.L.)	0	1	.000	11.57	2	0	0	0	0	2¹/₃	2	3	3	2	2
1999— Atlanta (N.L.)	0	0	...	27.00	2	0	0	0	0	²/₃	3	2	2	0	0
2000— Atlanta (N.L.)	0	0	...	5.40	3	0	0	0	0	3¹/₃	1	2	2	2	1
Division series totals (3 years)	0	1	.000	9.95	7	0	0	0	0	6¹/₃	6	7	7	4	3

CHAMPIONSHIP SERIES RECORD

Year	League	W	L	Pct.	ERA	G	GS	CG	ShO	Sv.	IP	H	R	ER	BB	SO
1993—	Philadelphia (N.L.)	0	1	.000	7.20	1	1	0	0	0	5	9	5	4	1	2
1999—	Atlanta (N.L.)	0	0	...	0.00	2	0	0	0	0	$2^2/_3$	1	0	0	1	2
Champ. series totals (2 years)		0	1	.000	4.70	3	1	0	0	0	$7^2/_3$	10	5	4	2	4

WORLD SERIES RECORD

Year	League	W	L	Pct.	ERA	G	GS	CG	ShO	Sv.	IP	H	R	ER	BB	SO
1993—	Philadelphia (N.L.)	1	0	1.000	6.75	2	2	0	0	0	$10^2/_3$	14	8	8	3	5
1999—	Atlanta (N.L.)	0	0	...	7.36	2	0	0	0	0	$3^2/_3$	5	3	3	1	3
World Series totals (2 years)		1	0	1.000	6.91	4	2	0	0	0	$14^1/_3$	19	11	11	4	8

ALL-STAR GAME RECORD

Year	League	W	L	Pct.	ERA	GS	CG	ShO	Sv.	IP	H	R	ER	BB	SO
1993—	National	0	0	...	4.50	1	0	0	0	2	1	1	1	2	0

MULLEN, SCOTT   P   ROYALS

PERSONAL: Born January 17, 1975, in San Benito, Texas. ... 6-2/190. ... Throws left, bats right. ... Full name: Kenneth Scott Mullen.
HIGH SCHOOL: Beaufort (S.C.).
COLLEGE: Dallas Baptist.
TRANSACTIONS/CAREER NOTES: Selected by Kansas City Royals organization in seventh round of free-agent draft (June 4, 1996).

Year	League	W	L	Pct.	ERA	G	GS	CG	ShO	Sv.	IP	H	R	ER	BB	SO
1996—	Spokane (N'West)	5	6	.455	3.92	15	15	0	0	0	$80^1/_3$	78	45	35	29	78
1997—	Lansing (Midw.)	5	2	.714	3.70	16	16	0	0	0	$92^1/_3$	90	46	38	31	78
—	Wilmington (Caro.)	4	4	.500	4.55	11	11	0	0	0	$59^1/_3$	64	35	30	26	43
1998—	Wilmington (Caro.)	8	4	.667	2.21	14	14	1	1	0	$85^2/_3$	68	28	21	25	56
—	Wichita (Texas)	8	2	.800	4.11	12	12	0	0	0	70	66	34	32	26	42
1999—	Wichita (Texas)	4	3	.571	4.01	9	9	0	0	0	$49^1/_3$	47	28	22	18	30
—	Omaha (PCL)	6	7	.462	6.26	20	20	0	0	0	$119^1/_3$	150	91	83	53	87
2000—	Wichita (Texas)	3	2	.600	3.19	33	1	0	0	7	$73^1/_3$	65	27	26	26	61
—	Omaha (PCL)	2	1	.667	3.05	16	0	0	0	0	$20^2/_3$	15	10	7	8	21
—	Kansas City (A.L.)	0	0	...	4.35	11	0	0	0	0	$10^1/_3$	10	5	5	3	7
Major League totals (1 year)		0	0	...	4.35	11	0	0	0	0	$10^1/_3$	10	5	5	3	7

MUNOZ, MIKE   P   RANGERS

PERSONAL: Born July 12, 1965, in Baldwin Park, Calif. ... 6-2/205. ... Throws left, bats left. ... Full name: Michael Anthony Munoz.
HIGH SCHOOL: Bishop Amat (La Puente, Calif.).
COLLEGE: Cal Poly Pomona.
TRANSACTIONS/CAREER NOTES: Selected by Los Angeles Dodgers organization in third round of free-agent draft (June 2, 1986). ... Traded by Dodgers to Detroit Tigers for P Mike Wilkins (September 30, 1990). ... Granted free agency (May 12, 1993). ... Signed by Colorado Rockies organization (May 14, 1993). ... On Colorado disabled list (July 27-August 15, 1996); included rehabilitation assignment to Colorado Springs (August 10-15). ... Granted free agency (October 27, 1997). ... Re-signed by Rockies (January 27, 1998). ... Granted free agency (October 26, 1998). ... Signed by Texas Rangers organization (January 12, 1999). ... Granted free agency (November 1, 1999). ... Re-signed by Rangers (December 7, 1999). ... On disabled list (April 26, 2000-remainder of season). ... Granted free agency (November 1, 2000). ... Re-signed by Rangers organization (December 13, 2000).

Year	League	W	L	Pct.	ERA	G	GS	CG	ShO	Sv.	IP	H	R	ER	BB	SO
1986—	Great Falls (Pio.)	4	4	.500	3.21	14	14	2	2	0	$81^1/_3$	85	44	29	38	49
1987—	Bakersfield (Calif.)	8	7	.533	3.74	52	12	2	0	9	118	125	68	49	43	80
1988—	San Antonio (Texas)	7	2	.778	1.00	56	0	0	0	14	$71^2/_3$	63	18	8	24	71
1989—	Albuquerque (PCL)	6	4	.600	3.08	60	0	0	0	6	79	72	32	27	40	81
—	Los Angeles (N.L.)	0	0	...	16.88	3	0	0	0	0	$2^2/_3$	5	5	5	2	3
1990—	Los Angeles (N.L.)	0	1	.000	3.18	8	0	0	0	0	$5^2/_3$	6	2	2	3	2
—	Albuquerque (PCL)	4	1	.800	4.25	49	0	0	0	6	$59^1/_3$	65	33	28	19	40
1991—	Toledo (I.L.)■	2	3	.400	3.83	38	1	0	0	8	54	44	30	23	35	38
—	Detroit (A.L.)	0	0	...	9.64	6	0	0	0	0	$9^1/_3$	14	10	10	5	3
1992—	Detroit (A.L.)	1	2	.333	3.00	65	0	0	0	2	48	44	16	16	25	23
1993—	Detroit (A.L.)	0	1	.000	6.00	8	0	0	0	0	3	4	2	2	6	1
—	Colorado Springs (PCL)■	1	2	.333	1.67	40	0	0	0	3	$37^2/_3$	46	10	7	9	30
—	Colorado (N.L.)	2	1	.667	4.50	21	0	0	0	0	18	21	12	9	9	16
1994—	Colorado (N.L.)	4	2	.667	3.74	57	0	0	0	1	$45^2/_3$	37	22	19	31	32
1995—	Colorado (N.L.)	2	4	.333	7.42	64	0	0	0	2	$43^2/_3$	54	38	36	27	37
1996—	Colorado (N.L.)	2	2	.500	6.65	54	0	0	0	0	$44^2/_3$	55	33	33	16	45
—	Colorado Springs (PCL)	1	1	.500	2.03	10	0	0	0	3	$13^1/_3$	8	3	3	6	13
1997—	Colorado (N.L.)	3	3	.500	4.53	64	0	0	0	2	$45^2/_3$	52	25	23	13	26
1998—	Colorado (N.L.)	2	2	.500	5.66	40	0	0	0	3	$41^1/_3$	53	32	26	16	24
1999—	Texas (A.L.)■	2	1	.667	3.93	56	0	0	0	1	$52^2/_3$	52	24	23	18	27
2000—	Texas (A.L.)	0	1	.000	13.50	7	0	0	0	0	4	11	6	6	3	1
A.L. totals (5 years)		3	5	.375	4.38	142	0	0	0	3	117	125	58	57	57	55
N.L. totals (8 years)		15	15	.500	5.57	311	0	0	0	8	$247^1/_3$	283	169	153	117	185
Major League totals (12 years)		18	20	.474	5.19	453	0	0	0	11	$364^1/_3$	408	227	210	174	240

DIVISION SERIES RECORD

Year	League	W	L	Pct.	ERA	G	GS	CG	ShO	Sv.	IP	H	R	ER	BB	SO
1995—	Colorado (N.L.)	0	1	.000	13.50	4	0	0	0	0	$1^1/_3$	4	2	2	1	1
1999—	Texas (A.L.)							Did not play.								

PERSONAL: Born June 14, 1975, in Flushing, N.Y. ... 6-2/210. ... Throws right, bats right. ... Full name: Peter Daniel Munro.
HIGH SCHOOL: Benjamin Cardozo (Bayside, N.Y.).
JUNIOR COLLEGE: Okaloosa-Walton Community College (Fla.).
TRANSACTIONS/CAREER NOTES: Signed as non-drafted free agent by Boston Red Sox organization (May 25, 1994). ... On Pawtucket disabled list (May 24-June 8, 1998). ... Traded by Red Sox with P Jay Yennaco to Toronto Blue Jays for 1B/DH Mike Stanley (July 30, 1998). ... On Toronto disabled list (June 4-July 3, 2000); included rehabilitation assignments to Dunedin (June 12-July 1) and Syracuse (July 2-3). ... Traded by Blue Jays to Texas Rangers (August 8, 2000); completing deal in which Rangers traded OF Dave Martinez to Blue Jays for a player to be named later (August 4, 2000). ... Granted free agency (December 21, 2000). ... Re-signed by Rangers organization (January 2, 2001).

Year	League	W	L	Pct.	ERA	G	GS	CG	ShO	Sv.	IP	H	R	ER	BB	SO
1995—	Utica (NY-Penn)	5	4	.556	2.60	14	14	0	0	0	90	79	38	26	33	74
1996—	Sarasota (FSL)	11	6	.647	3.60	27	25	2	•2	1	155	153	76	62	62	115
1997—	Trenton (East.)	7	10	.412	4.95	22	22	1	0	0	116 1/3	113	76	64	47	109
1998—	Pawtucket (I.L.)	5	4	.556	4.05	18	17	0	0	0	106 2/3	111	49	48	35	75
	— Syracuse (I.L.)■	2	5	.286	7.46	8	8	0	0	0	44 2/3	58	42	37	23	42
1999—	Toronto (A.L.)	0	2	.000	6.02	31	2	0	0	0	55 1/3	70	38	37	23	38
	— Syracuse (I.L.)	6	1	.857	3.10	18	11	0	0	0	69 2/3	70	29	24	33	68
2000—	Syracuse (I.L.)	4	3	.571	2.48	10	10	2	0	0	61 2/3	52	20	17	25	45
	— Toronto (A.L.)	1	1	.500	5.96	9	3	0	0	0	25 2/3	38	22	17	16	16
	— Dunedin (FSL)	0	1	.000	5.56	3	3	0	0	0	11 1/3	11	7	7	4	12
	— Oklahoma (PCL)■	1	2	.333	4.65	5	5	1	1	0	31	27	17	16	14	15
Major League totals (2 years)		1	3	.250	6.00	40	5	0	0	0	81	108	60	54	39	54

PERSONAL: Born October 3, 1977, in San Diego, Calif. ... 6-3/220. ... Bats left, throws right.
HIGH SCHOOL: Mount Carmel (San Diego).
COLLEGE: Southern California.
TRANSACTIONS/CAREER NOTES: Selected by Atlanta Braves organization in second round of free-agent draft (June 4, 1996); did not sign. ... Selected by Detroit Tigers organization in first round (third pick overall) of free-agent draft (June 2, 1999). ... On Jacksonville disabled list (August 28-September 18, 2000).

							BATTING								FIELDING		
Year	Team (League)	Pos.	G	AB	R	H	2B	3B	HR	RBI	Avg.	BB	SO	SB	PO	A	E	Avg.
1999—	Lakeland (FSL)	DH	2	6	0	2	0	0	0	1	.333	1	1	0	...	...	...	...
	— W. Mich. (Midw.)	1B-C	67	252	42	67	16	1	14	44	.266	37	47	3	319	29	3	.991
2000—	Jacksonville (Sou.)	1B	98	365	52	92	21	4	15	68	.252	39	96	5	640	51	8	.989
	— Detroit (A.L.)	1B	3	5	0	0	0	0	0	1	.000	0	1	0	16	0	1	.941
Major League totals (1 year)			3	5	0	0	0	0	0	1	.000	0	1	0	16	0	1	.941

M

PERSONAL: Born July 30, 1971, in Dallas. ... 5-11/190. ... Bats right, throws right. ... Full name: Calvin Duane Murray.
HIGH SCHOOL: Warren Travis White (Dallas).
COLLEGE: Texas.
TRANSACTIONS/CAREER NOTES: Selected by San Francisco Giants organization in first round (seventh pick overall) of free-agent draft (June 1, 1992).
HONORS: Named Pacific Coast League Most Valuable Player (1999).
STATISTICAL NOTES: Led Pacific Coast League with 297 total bases in 1999. ... Career major league grand slams: 1.
MISCELLANEOUS: Member of 1992 U.S. Olympic Baseball team.

							BATTING								FIELDING		
Year	Team (League)	Pos.	G	AB	R	H	2B	3B	HR	RBI	Avg.	BB	SO	SB	PO	A	E	Avg.
1993—	San Jose (Calif.)	OF	85	345	61	97	24	1	9	42	.281	40	63	42	203	9	2	.991
	— Shreveport (Texas)	OF	37	138	15	26	6	0	0	6	.188	14	29	12	79	2	2	.976
	— Phoenix (PCL)	OF	5	19	4	6	1	1	0	0	.316	2	5	1	13	0	2	.867
1994—	Shreveport (Texas)	OF	480	480	67	111	19	5	2	35	.231	47	81	33	268	5	3	.989
1995—	Phoenix (PCL)	OF	13	50	8	9	1	0	4	10	.180	4	6	2	19	2	0	1.000
	— Shreveport (Texas)	OF	110	441	77	104	17	3	2	29	.236	59	70	26	286	9	2	.993
1996—	Phoenix (PCL)	OF	50	169	32	44	7	0	7	24	.260	25	33	6	89	4	3	.969
	— Phoenix (PCL)	OF	83	311	50	76	16	6	3	28	.244	43	60	12	207	3	2	.991
1997—	Shreveport (Texas)	OF	122	419	83	114	25	3	10	56	.272	66	73	*52	214	9	5	.978
1998—	Fresno (PCL)	OF	33	90	16	21	3	1	3	5	.233	12	18	3	27	1	0	1.000
	— Shreveport (Texas)	OF	88	337	63	104	22	5	8	39	.309	58	45	34	198	3	7	.966
1999—	Fresno (PCL)	OF-DH	130	*548	*122	*183	31	7	23	73	.334	49	88	*42	284	8	6	.980
	— San Francisco (N.L.)	OF	15	19	1	5	2	0	0	5	.263	2	4	1	6	0	0	1.000
2000—	San Francisco (N.L.)	OF	108	194	35	47	12	1	2	22	.242	29	33	9	143	2	3	.980
Major League totals (2 years)			123	213	36	52	14	1	2	27	.244	31	37	10	149	2	3	.981

DIVISION SERIES RECORD

							BATTING								FIELDING		
Year	Team (League)	Pos.	G	AB	R	H	2B	3B	HR	RBI	Avg.	BB	SO	SB	PO	A	E	Avg.
2000—	San Francisco (N.L.)	OF	3	5	0	1	0	0	0	0	.200	0	3	0	3	0	0	1.000

PERSONAL: Born November 21, 1973, in Los Alamitos, Calif. ... 6-1/195. ... Throws right, bats right. ... Full name: Daniel Saffle Murray.
HIGH SCHOOL: Pacifica (Garden Grove, Calif.).
COLLEGE: San Diego State.

TRANSACTIONS/CAREER NOTES: Selected by New York Mets organization in 10th round of free-agent draft (June 1, 1995). ... Traded by Mets to Kansas City Royals for P Glendon Rusch (September 14, 1999).
STATISTICAL NOTES: Led Pacific Coast League pitchers with 17 putouts in 2000.

Year League	W	L	Pct.	ERA	G	GS	CG	ShO	Sv.	IP	H	R	ER	BB	SO
1995— Pittsfield (NY-Penn)...........	0	6	.000	1.97	22	0	0	0	6	32	24	17	7	16	34
1996— St. Lucie (FSL)	7	5	.583	4.25	33	13	0	0	0	101²/₃	114	60	48	53	56
1997— St. Lucie (FSL)	12	10	.545	3.45	30	24	4	•2	0	156¹/₃	150	75	60	55	91
1998— Binghamton (East.)	11	6	.647	3.18	27	27	1	1	0	164¹/₃	153	64	58	54	159
1999— Norfolk (I.L.)	12	10	.545	4.97	29	27	3	1	0	145	149	91	80	70	96
— New York (N.L.).................	0	0	...	13.50	1	0	0	0	0	2	4	3	3	2	1
— Kansas City (A.L.)■...........	0	0	...	6.48	4	0	0	0	0	8¹/₃	9	8	6	4	8
2000— Omaha (PCL).....................	10	9	.526	5.57	27	22	1	1	1	140²/₃	148	99	87	60	102
— Kansas City (A.L.)	0	0	...	4.66	10	0	0	0	0	19¹/₃	20	10	10	10	16
A.L. totals (2 years)	0	0	...	5.20	14	0	0	0	0	27²/₃	29	18	16	14	24
N.L. totals (1 year)........................	0	0	...	13.50	1	0	0	0	0	2	4	3	3	2	1
Major League totals (2 years)	0	0	...	5.76	15	0	0	0	0	29²/₃	33	21	19	16	25

MUSSINA, MIKE   P   YANKEES

PERSONAL: Born December 8, 1968, in Williamsport, Pa. ... 6-2/185. ... Throws right, bats right. ... Full name: Michael Cole Mussina. ... Name pronounced myoo-SEEN-uh.
HIGH SCHOOL: Montoursville (Pa.).
COLLEGE: Stanford.
TRANSACTIONS/CAREER NOTES: Selected by Baltimore Orioles organization in 11th round of free-agent draft (June 2, 1987); did not sign. ... Selected by Orioles organization in first round (20th pick overall) of free-agent draft (June 4, 1990). ... On Rochester disabled list (May 5-12, 1991). ... On Baltimore disabled list (July 22-August 20, 1993); included rehabilitation assignment to Bowie (August 9-20). ... On disabled list (April 17-May 3 and May 15-June 6, 1998). ... Granted free agency (October 27, 2000). ... Signed by New York Yankees (November 30, 2000).
HONORS: Named International League Most Valuable Pitcher (1991). ... Named righthanded pitcher on THE SPORTING NEWS A.L. All-Star team (1995). ... Won A.L. Gold Glove at pitcher (1996-99).
STATISTICAL NOTES: Pitched 8-0 one-hit, complete-game victory against Texas (July 17, 1992). ... Pitched 3-0 one-hit, complete-game victory against Cleveland (May 30, 1997). ... Struck out 15 batters in one game (August 1 and September 24, 2000). ... Pitched 10-0 one-hit, complete-game victory against Minnesota (August 1, 2000).

Year League	W	L	Pct.	ERA	G	GS	CG	ShO	Sv.	IP	H	R	ER	BB	SO
1990— Hagerstown (East.)............	3	0	1.000	1.49	7	7	2	1	0	42¹/₃	34	10	7	7	40
— Rochester (I.L.)	0	0	...	1.35	2	2	0	0	0	13¹/₃	8	2	2	4	15
1991— Rochester (I.L.)	10	4	.714	2.87	19	19	3	1	0	122¹/₃	108	42	39	31	107
— Baltimore (A.L.)	4	5	.444	2.87	12	12	2	0	0	87²/₃	77	31	28	21	52
1992— Baltimore (A.L.).................	18	5	*.783	2.54	32	32	8	4	0	241	212	70	68	48	130
1993— Baltimore (A.L.).................	14	6	.700	4.46	25	25	3	2	0	167²/₃	163	84	83	44	117
— Bowie (East.)...................	1	0	1.000	2.25	2	2	0	0	0	8	5	2	2	1	10
1994— Baltimore (A.L.).................	16	5	.762	3.06	24	24	3	0	0	176¹/₃	163	63	60	42	99
1995— Baltimore (A.L.).................	*19	9	.679	3.29	32	32	7	*4	0	221²/₃	187	86	81	50	158
1996— Baltimore (A.L.).................	19	11	.633	4.81	36	*36	4	1	0	243¹/₃	264	137	130	69	204
1997— Baltimore (A.L.).................	15	8	.652	3.20	33	33	4	1	0	224²/₃	197	87	80	54	218
1998— Baltimore (A.L.).................	13	10	.565	3.49	29	29	4	2	0	206¹/₃	189	85	80	41	175
1999— Baltimore (A.L.).................	18	7	.720	3.50	31	31	4	0	0	203¹/₃	207	88	79	52	172
2000— Baltimore (A.L.).................	11	15	.423	3.79	34	34	6	1	0	*237²/₃	236	105	100	46	210
Major League totals (10 years)	147	81	.645	3.53	288	288	45	15	0	2009²/₃	1895	836	789	467	1535

DIVISION SERIES RECORD

Year League	W	L	Pct.	ERA	G	GS	CG	ShO	Sv.	IP	H	R	ER	BB	SO
1996— Baltimore (A.L.).................	0	0	...	4.50	1	1	0	0	0	6	7	4	3	2	6
1997— Baltimore (A.L.).................	2	0	1.000	1.93	2	2	0	0	0	14	7	3	3	3	16
Division series totals (2 years)	2	0	1.000	2.70	3	3	0	0	0	20	14	7	6	5	22

CHAMPIONSHIP SERIES RECORD

Year League	W	L	Pct.	ERA	G	GS	CG	ShO	Sv.	IP	H	R	ER	BB	SO
1996— Baltimore (A.L.).................	0	1	.000	5.87	1	1	0	0	0	7²/₃	8	5	5	2	6
1997— Baltimore (A.L.).................	0	0	...	0.60	2	2	0	0	0	15	4	1	1	4	25
Champ. series totals (2 years)	0	1	.000	2.38	3	3	0	0	0	22²/₃	12	6	6	6	31

ALL-STAR GAME RECORD

Year League	W	L	Pct.	ERA	GS	CG	ShO	Sv.	IP	H	R	ER	BB	SO
1992— American	0	0	...	0.00	0	0	0	0	1	0	0	0	0	0
1993— American						Did not play.								
1994— American	0	0	...	0.00	0	0	0	0	1	1	0	0	0	1
1997— National						Did not play.								
1999— American	0	0	...	0.00	0	0	0	0	1	1	0	0	1	2
All-Star Game totals (3 years)	0	0	...	0.00	0	0	0	0	3	2	0	0	1	3

MYERS, GREG   C   ORIOLES

PERSONAL: Born April 14, 1966, in Riverside, Calif. ... 6-2/225. ... Bats left, throws right. ... Full name: Gregory Richard Myers.
HIGH SCHOOL: Riverside (Calif.) Polytechnical.
TRANSACTIONS/CAREER NOTES: Selected by Toronto Blue Jays organization in third round of free-agent draft (June 4, 1984). ... On disabled list (June 17, 1988-remainder of season). ... On Toronto disabled list (March 26-June 5, 1989); included rehabilitation assignment to Knoxville (May 17-June 5). ... On Toronto disabled list (May 5-25, 1990); included rehabilitation assignment to Syracuse (May 21-24). ... Traded by Blue Jays with OF Rob Ducey to California Angels for P Mark Eichhorn (July 30, 1992). ... On California disabled list (August 27, 1992-remainder of season). ... On California disabled list (April 24-June 21, 1994); included rehabilitation assignments to Lake Elsinore (May 20-June 6 and

M

June 13-21). ... On disabled list (April 21-May 6, June 1-21 and September 30, 1995-remainder of season). ... Granted free agency (November 3, 1995). ... Signed by Minnesota Twins (December 8, 1995). ... On disabled list (July 14-August 2, 1996). ... On Minnesota disabled list (August 9-24, 1997). ... Traded by Twins to Atlanta Braves for a player to be named later (September 5, 1997); Twins acquired 1B Steve Hacker to complete deal (December 18, 1997). ... Granted free agency (October 28, 1997). ... Signed by San Diego Padres (November 25, 1997). ... On San Diego disabled list (June 4-July 24, 1998); included rehabilitation assignments to Rancho Cucamonga (July 17-19) and Las Vegas (July 21-23). ... On San Diego disabled list (June 29-July 26, 1999); included rehabilitation assignment to Rancho Cucamonga (July 20-26). ... Traded by Padres to Braves for P Doug Dent (July 26, 1999). ... Granted free agency (November 1, 1999). ... Signed by Baltimore Orioles (December 17, 1999). ... On disabled list (April 2-17, 2000).

STATISTICAL NOTES: Led California League catchers with 967 total chances in 1986. ... Led International League catchers with 698 total chances in 1987.

Year Team (League)	Pos.	G	AB	R	H	2B	3B	HR	RBI	Avg.	BB	SO	SB	PO	A	E	Avg.
1984—Medicine Hat (Pio.)	C	38	133	20	42	9	0	2	20	.316	16	6	0	216	24	4	.984
1985—Florence (S.Atl.)	C	134	489	52	109	19	2	5	62	.223	39	54	0	551	61	7	*.989
1986—Ventura (Calif.)	C	124	451	65	133	23	4	20	79	.295	43	46	9	*849	99	19	.980
1987—Syracuse (I.L.)............	C	107	342	35	84	19	1	10	47	.246	22	46	3	*637	50	11	.984
—Toronto (A.L.)............	C	7	9	1	1	0	0	0	0	.111	0	3	0	24	1	0	1.000
1988—Syracuse (I.L.)............	C	34	120	18	34	7	1	7	21	.283	8	24	1	63	9	1	.986
1989—Knoxville (Sou.)..........	C	29	90	11	30	10	0	5	19	.333	3	16	1	130	12	1	.993
—Toronto (A.L.)............	C-DH	17	44	0	5	2	0	0	1	.114	2	9	0	46	6	0	1.000
—Syracuse (I.L.)............	C	24	89	8	24	6	0	1	11	.270	4	9	0	60	7	1	.985
1990—Toronto (A.L.)............	C	87	250	33	59	7	1	5	22	.236	22	33	0	411	30	3	.993
—Syracuse (I.L.)............	C	3	11	0	2	1	0	0	2	.182	1	1	0	14	0	0	1.000
1991—Toronto (A.L.)............	C	107	309	25	81	22	0	8	36	.262	21	45	0	484	37	11	.979
1992—Toronto (A.L.)............	C	22	61	4	14	6	0	1	13	.230	5	5	0	92	13	1	.991
—California (A.L.)■.......	C-DH	8	17	0	4	1	0	0	0	.235	0	6	0	33	3	0	1.000
1993—California (A.L.)	C-DH	108	290	27	74	10	0	7	40	.255	17	47	3	369	44	6	.986
1994—California (A.L.)	C-DH	45	126	10	31	6	0	2	8	.246	10	27	0	194	28	2	.991
—Lake Elsinore (Calif.) ..	C-DH	10	32	4	8	2	0	0	5	.250	2	6	0	31	3	0	1.000
1995—California (A.L.)	C-DH	85	273	35	71	12	2	9	38	.260	17	49	0	341	21	4	.989
1996—Minnesota (A.L.)■	C	97	329	37	94	22	3	6	47	.286	19	52	0	488	27	8	.985
1997—Minnesota (A.L.)	C-DH	62	165	24	44	11	1	5	28	.267	16	29	0	196	11	3	.986
—Atlanta (N.L.)■..........	C	9	9	0	1	0	0	0	1	.111	1	3	0	11	2	0	1.000
1998—San Diego (N.L.)■	C	69	171	19	42	10	0	4	20	.246	17	36	0	276	29	4	.987
—Rancho Cuca. (Calif.) .	C-DH	3	9	1	0	0	0	0	0	.000	2	1	0	8	0	0	1.000
—Las Vegas (PCL)	C	3	9	0	5	0	0	0	1	.556	0	0	0	16	1	0	1.000
1999—San Diego (N.L.)	C	50	128	9	37	4	0	3	15	.289	13	14	0	199	14	3	.986
—Rancho Cuca. (Calif.) .	C-DH	3	3	0	0	0	0	0	0	.000	1	1	0	7	1	0	1.000
—Atlanta (N.L.)■..........	C	34	72	10	16	2	0	2	9	.222	13	16	0	166	12	1	.994
2000—Baltimore (A.L.)■.......	C-DH	43	125	9	28	6	0	3	12	.224	8	29	0	166	14	0	1.000
American League totals (11 years)		688	1998	205	506	105	7	46	245	.253	137	334	3	2844	235	38	.988
National League totals (3 years)		162	380	38	96	16	0	9	45	.253	44	69	0	652	57	8	.989
Major League totals (13 years)		850	2378	243	602	121	7	55	290	.253	181	403	3	3496	292	46	.988

DIVISION SERIES RECORD

Year Team (League)	Pos.	G	AB	R	H	2B	3B	HR	RBI	Avg.	BB	SO	SB	PO	A	E	Avg.
1998—San Diego (N.L.)	C	1	0	0	0	0	0	0	0	...	0	0	0	0	0	0	...
1999—Atlanta (N.L.)										Did not play.							

CHAMPIONSHIP SERIES RECORD

Year Team (League)	Pos.	G	AB	R	H	2B	3B	HR	RBI	Avg.	BB	SO	SB	PO	A	E	Avg.
1991— Toronto (A.L.)										Did not play.							
1998—San Diego (N.L.)	PH	2	1	1	1	0	0	1	2	1.000	1	0	0	...	...	...	...
1999—Atlanta (N.L.).............	C	2	2	0	0	0	0	0	0	.000	1	1	0	8	0	0	1.000
Championship series totals (2 years)		4	3	1	1	0	0	1	2	.333	2	1	0	8	0	0	1.000

WORLD SERIES RECORD

Year Team (League)	Pos.	G	AB	R	H	2B	3B	HR	RBI	Avg.	BB	SO	SB	PO	A	E	Avg.
1998—San Diego (N.L.)	PH-C	2	4	0	0	0	0	0	0	.000	0	2	0	4	1	0	1.000
1999—Atlanta (N.L.).............	PH-C	4	6	0	2	0	0	0	1	.333	1	0	0	9	0	0	1.000
World Series totals (2 years)		6	10	0	2	0	0	0	1	.200	1	2	0	13	1	0	1.000

MYERS, MIKE   P   ROCKIES

PERSONAL: Born June 26, 1969, in Arlington Heights, Ill. ... 6-4/214. ... Throws left, bats left. ... Full name: Michael Stanley Myers.
HIGH SCHOOL: Crystal Lake (Ill.) Central.
COLLEGE: Iowa State.
TRANSACTIONS/CAREER NOTES: Selected by San Francisco Giants organization in fourth round of free-agent draft (June 4, 1990). ... On Clinton disabled list (June 3-September 16, 1991; April 9-June 2 and June 21-July 6, 1992). ... Selected by Florida Marlins from Giants organization in Rule 5 major league draft (December 7, 1992). ... On Edmonton disabled list (April 13-June 7, 1994). ... On Florida disabled list (June 7-August 5, 1994); included rehabilitation assignment to Brevard County (June 23-July 11). ... Traded by Marlins to Detroit Tigers (August 9, 1995), completing deal in which Marlins acquired P Buddy Groom for a player to be named later (August 7, 1995). ... Traded by Tigers with P Rick Greene and SS Santiago Perez to Milwaukee Brewers for P Bryce Florie and a player to be named later (November 20, 1997). ... Traded by Brewers to Colorado Rockies for P Curtis Leskanic (November 17, 1999).
STATISTICAL NOTES: Led Pacific Coast League with 10 hit batsmen in 1993.

Year League	W	L	Pct.	ERA	G	GS	CG	ShO	Sv.	IP	H	R	ER	BB	SO
1990— Everett (N'West)	4	5	.444	3.90	15	14	1	0	0	85 1/3	91	43	37	30	73
1991— Clinton (Midw.)	5	3	.625	2.62	11	11	1	0	0	65 1/3	61	23	19	18	59
1992— San Jose (Calif.)	5	1	.833	2.30	8	8	0	0	0	54 2/3	43	20	14	17	40
— Clinton (Midw.)	1	2	.333	1.19	7	7	0	0	0	37 2/3	28	11	5	8	32
1993— Edmonton (PCL)■	7	14	.333	5.18	27	27	3	0	0	161 2/3	195	109	93	52	112
1994— Edmonton (PCL)	1	5	.167	5.55	12	11	0	0	0	60	78	42	37	21	55
— Brevard County (FSL)	0	0	...	0.79	3	2	0	0	0	11 1/3	7	1	1	4	15
1995— Charlotte (I.L.)	0	5	.000	5.65	37	0	0	0	0	36 2/3	41	25	23	15	24
— Florida (N.L.)	0	0	...	0.00	2	0	0	0	0	2	1	0	0	3	0
— Toledo (I.L.)■	0	0	...	4.32	6	0	0	0	0	8 1/3	6	4	4	3	8
— Detroit (A.L.)	1	0	1.000	9.95	11	0	0	0	0	6 1/3	10	7	7	4	4
1996— Detroit (A.L.)	1	5	.167	5.01	•83	0	0	0	6	64 2/3	70	41	36	34	69
1997— Detroit (A.L.)	0	4	.000	5.70	*88	0	0	0	2	53 2/3	58	36	34	25	50
1998— Milwaukee (N.L.)■	2	2	.500	2.70	70	0	0	0	1	50	44	19	15	22	40
1999— Milwaukee (N.L.)	2	1	.667	5.23	71	0	0	0	0	41 1/3	46	24	24	13	35
2000— Colorado (N.L.)■	0	1	.000	1.99	78	0	0	0	1	45 1/3	24	10	10	24	41
A.L. totals (3 years)	2	9	.182	5.56	182	0	0	0	8	124 2/3	138	84	77	63	123
N.L. totals (4 years)	4	4	.500	3.18	221	0	0	0	2	138 2/3	115	53	49	62	116
Major League totals (6 years)	6	13	.316	4.31	403	0	0	0	10	263 1/3	253	137	126	125	239

MYERS, RODNEY — P — PADRES

PERSONAL: Born June 26, 1969, in Rockford, Ill. ... 6-1/215. ... Throws right, bats right. ... Full name: Rodney Luther Myers.
HIGH SCHOOL: Rockford (Ill.) East.
COLLEGE: Wisconsin.
TRANSACTIONS/CAREER NOTES: Selected by Kansas City Royals organization in 12th round of free-agent draft (June 4, 1990). ... On disabled list (May 17-June 3 and June 21-September 15, 1994; and June 30-July 21, 1995). ... Selected by Chicago Cubs from Royals organization in Rule 5 major league draft (December 4, 1995). ... On Iowa disabled list (June 7-15, 1998). ... Traded by Cubs to San Diego Padres for OF Gary Matthews Jr. (March 23, 2000). ... On San Diego disabled list (March 29-May 5 and May 12, 2000-remainder of season); included rehabilitation assignment to Rancho Cucamonga (April 30-May 5).
MISCELLANEOUS: Doubled in only appearance as pinch hitter (1999).

Year League	W	L	Pct.	ERA	G	GS	CG	ShO	Sv.	IP	H	R	ER	BB	SO
1990— Eugene (N'West)	0	2	.000	1.19	6	4	0	0	0	22 2/3	19	9	3	13	17
1991— Appleton (Midw.)	1	1	.500	2.60	9	4	0	0	0	27 2/3	22	9	8	26	29
1992— Lethbridge (Pio.)	5	•8	.385	4.01	15	15	*5	0	0	*103 1/3	93	57	46	61	76
1993— Rockford (Midw.)	7	3	.700	1.79	12	12	5	2	0	85 1/3	65	22	17	18	65
— Memphis (Sou.)	3	6	.333	5.62	12	12	1	1	0	65 2/3	73	46	41	32	42
1994— Wilmington (Caro.)	1	1	.500	4.82	4	0	0	0	1	9 1/3	9	6	5	1	9
— Memphis (Sou.)	5	1	.833	1.03	42	0	0	0	9	69 2/3	45	20	8	29	53
1995— Omaha (A.A.)	4	5	.444	4.10	38	0	0	0	2	48 1/3	52	26	22	19	38
1996— Chicago (N.L.)■	2	1	.667	4.68	45	0	0	0	0	67 1/3	61	38	35	38	50
1997— Iowa (A.A.)	7	8	.467	4.09	24	23	1	0	0	140 2/3	140	76	64	38	79
— Chicago (N.L.)	0	0	...	6.00	5	1	0	0	0	9	12	6	6	7	6
1998— Iowa (PCL)	7	5	.583	3.91	33	13	2	1	11	101 1/3	84	47	44	45	86
— Chicago (N.L.)	0	0	...	7.00	12	0	0	0	0	18	26	14	14	6	15
1999— Iowa (PCL)	2	4	.333	4.06	20	1	0	0	2	31	29	18	14	11	24
— Chicago (N.L.)	3	1	.750	4.38	46	0	0	0	0	63 2/3	71	34	31	25	41
2000— San Diego (N.L.)■	0	0	...	4.50	3	0	0	0	0	2	2	1	1	0	3
— Rancho Cuca. (Calif.)	0	0	...	0.00	3	2	0	0	0	4	2	0	0	0	4
Major League totals (5 years)	5	2	.714	4.89	111	1	0	0	0	160	172	93	87	76	115

MYETTE, AARON — P — RANGERS

PERSONAL: Born September 26, 1977, in New Westminster, B.C. ... 6-4/195. ... Throws right, bats right. ... Full name: Aaron Kenneth Myette. ... Son of Kenneth Myette, pitcher with Cincinnati Reds organization (1969).
HIGH SCHOOL: Johnston Heights Sectional (Surrey, B.C.).
JUNIOR COLLEGE: Central Arizona College.
TRANSACTIONS/CAREER NOTES: Selected by Chicago White Sox organization in supplemental round ("sandwich pick" between first and second round, 43rd pick overall) of free-agent draft (June 3, 1997); pick received as part of compensation for Florida Marlins signing P Alex Fernandez. ... On Hickory disabled list (April 2-May 2, 1998). ... On Birmingham disabled list (July 25-August 2, 1999). ... On Chicago disabled list (March 25-May 9, 2000). ... Traded by White Sox with P Brian Schmack to Texas Rangers for SS Royce Clayton (December 14, 2000).
STATISTICAL NOTES: Led Southern League with 15 hit batsmen in 1999.

Year League	W	L	Pct.	ERA	G	GS	CG	ShO	Sv.	IP	H	R	ER	BB	SO
1997— Bristol (Appl.)	4	3	.571	3.61	9	8	1	0	0	47 1/3	39	28	19	20	50
— Hickory (S.Atl.)	3	1	.750	1.14	5	5	0	0	0	31 2/3	19	6	4	11	27
1998— Hickory (S.Atl.)	9	4	.692	2.47	17	17	0	0	0	102	84	43	28	30	103
— Winston-Salem (Caro.)	4	2	.667	2.01	6	6	1	1	0	44 2/3	32	14	10	14	54
1999— Birmingham (Sou.)	12	7	.632	3.66	28	•28	0	0	0	164 2/3	138	76	67	77	135
— Chicago (A.L.)	0	2	.000	6.32	4	3	0	0	0	15 2/3	17	11	11	14	11
2000— Birmingham (Sou.)	2	0	1.000	3.52	3	3	0	0	0	15 1/3	11	7	6	8	21
— Charlotte (I.L.)	5	5	.500	4.35	19	18	0	0	0	111 2/3	103	58	54	56	85
— Chicago (A.L.)	0	0	...	0.00	2	0	0	0	0	2 2/3	0	0	0	4	1
Major League totals (2 years)	0	2	.000	5.40	6	3	0	0	0	18 1/3	17	11	11	18	12

M

PERSONAL: Born May 5, 1967, in Fairfield, Conn. ... 6-3/200. ... Throws right, bats left. ... Full name: Charles Harrison Nagy. ... Name pronounced NAG-ee.

HIGH SCHOOL: Roger Ludlowe (Fairfield, Conn.).

COLLEGE: Connecticut.

TRANSACTIONS/CAREER NOTES: Selected by Cleveland Indians organization in first round (17th pick overall) of free-agent draft (June 1, 1988); pick received as part of compensation for San Francisco Giants signing Type A free-agent OF Brett Butler. ... On Cleveland disabled list (May 16-October 1, 1993); included rehabilitation assignment to Canton/Akron (June 10-24). ... On Cleveland disabled list (May 17-September 14 and September 25, 2000-remainder of season); included rehabilitation assignments to Buffalo (June 19-July 12 and September 3-14) and Akron (July 13 and August 28-September 2).

HONORS: Named Carolina League Pitcher of the Year (1989).

STATISTICAL NOTES: Pitched 6-0 one-hit, complete-game victory against Baltimore (August 8, 1992).

MISCELLANEOUS: Member of 1988 U.S. Olympic baseball team. ... Struck out once in two appearances as designated hitter and appeared in one game as pinch runner (1999).

Year League	W	L	Pct.	ERA	G	GS	CG	ShO	Sv.	IP	H	R	ER	BB	SO
1989— Kinston (Caro.)	8	4	.667	1.51	13	13	6	*4	0	95 $^1/_3$	69	22	16	24	99
— Canton/Akron (East.)	4	5	.444	3.35	15	14	2	0	0	94	102	44	35	32	65
1990— Canton/Akron (East.)	13	8	.619	2.52	23	23	•9	0	0	175	132	62	49	39	99
— Cleveland (A.L.)	2	4	.333	5.91	9	8	0	0	0	45 $^2/_3$	58	31	30	21	26
1991— Cleveland (A.L.)	10	15	.400	4.13	33	33	6	1	0	211 $^1/_3$	228	103	97	66	109
1992— Cleveland (A.L.)	17	10	.630	2.96	33	33	10	3	0	252	245	91	83	57	169
1993— Cleveland (A.L.)	2	6	.250	6.29	9	9	1	0	0	48 $^2/_3$	66	38	34	13	30
— Canton/Akron (East.)	0	0	...	1.13	2	2	0	0	0	8	8	1	1	2	4
1994— Cleveland (A.L.)	10	8	.556	3.45	23	23	3	0	0	169 $^1/_3$	175	76	65	48	108
1995— Cleveland (A.L.)	16	6	.727	4.55	29	29	2	1	0	178	194	95	90	61	139
1996— Cleveland (A.L.)	17	5	.773	3.41	32	32	5	0	0	222	217	89	84	61	167
1997— Cleveland (A.L.)	15	11	.577	4.28	34	34	1	1	0	227	253	115	108	77	149
1998— Cleveland (A.L.)	15	10	.600	5.22	33	33	2	0	0	210 $^1/_3$	250	*139	122	66	120
1999— Cleveland (A.L.)	17	11	.607	4.95	33	32	1	0	0	202	238	120	111	59	126
2000— Cleveland (A.L.)	2	7	.222	8.21	11	11	0	0	0	57	71	53	52	21	41
— Buffalo (I.L.)	1	1	.500	4.30	3	3	0	0	0	14 $^2/_3$	12	7	7	4	5
— Akron (East.)	1	0	1.000	1.00	2	2	0	0	0	9	4	1	1	2	10
Major League totals (11 years)	123	93	.569	4.32	279	277	31	6	0	1823 $^1/_3$	1995	950	876	550	1184

DIVISION SERIES RECORD

RECORDS: Holds career record for most earned runs allowed—23; and bases on balls allowed—18. ... Shares A.L. career record for most wins—3.

Year League	W	L	Pct.	ERA	G	GS	CG	ShO	Sv.	IP	H	R	ER	BB	SO
1995— Cleveland (A.L.)	1	0	1.000	1.29	1	1	0	0	0	7	4	1	1	5	6
1996— Cleveland (A.L.)	0	1	.000	7.15	2	2	0	0	0	11 $^1/_3$	15	9	9	5	13
1997— Cleveland (A.L.)	0	1	.000	9.82	1	1	0	0	0	3 $^2/_3$	2	5	4	6	1
1998— Cleveland (A.L.)	1	0	1.000	1.13	1	1	0	0	0	8	4	1	1	0	3
1999— Cleveland (A.L.)	1	0	1.000	7.20	2	2	0	0	0	10	11	9	8	2	6
Division series totals (5 years)	3	2	.600	5.18	7	7	0	0	0	40	36	25	23	18	29

CHAMPIONSHIP SERIES RECORD

RECORDS: Shares A.L. single-game record for most consecutive strikeouts—4 (October 13, 1995).

Year League	W	L	Pct.	ERA	G	GS	CG	ShO	Sv.	IP	H	R	ER	BB	SO
1995— Cleveland (A.L.)	0	0	...	1.13	1	1	0	0	0	8	5	2	1	0	6
1997— Cleveland (A.L.)	0	0	...	2.77	2	2	0	0	0	13	17	4	4	5	5
1998— Cleveland (A.L.)	0	1	.000	3.72	2	2	0	0	0	9 $^2/_3$	13	7	4	1	6
Champ. series totals (3 years)	0	1	.000	2.64	5	5	0	0	0	30 $^2/_3$	35	13	9	6	17

WORLD SERIES RECORD

RECORDS: Shares single-inning record for most consecutive bases on balls allowed—3 (October 21, 1997, third inning).

Year League	W	L	Pct.	ERA	G	GS	CG	ShO	Sv.	IP	H	R	ER	BB	SO
1995— Cleveland (A.L.)	0	0	...	6.43	1	1	0	0	0	7	8	5	5	1	4
1997— Cleveland (A.L.)	0	1	.000	6.43	2	1	0	0	0	7	8	6	5	5	5
World Series totals (2 years)	0	1	.000	6.43	3	2	0	0	0	14	16	11	10	6	9

ALL-STAR GAME RECORD

Year League	W	L	Pct.	ERA	GS	CG	ShO	Sv.	IP	H	R	ER	BB	SO
1992— American	0	0	...	0.00	0	0	0	0	1	0	0	0	0	1
1996— American	0	1	.000	13.50	1	0	0	0	2	4	3	3	0	1
1999— American					Selected, did not play.									
All-Star Game totals (2 years)	0	1	.000	9.00	1	0	0	0	3	4	3	3	0	2

N

PERSONAL: Born November 22, 1974, in Houston. ... 6-4/195. ... Throws right, bats right. ... Full name: Joseph Michael Nathan.

HIGH SCHOOL: Pine Bush (N.Y.).

COLLEGE: New York-Stony Brook.

TRANSACTIONS/CAREER NOTES: Selected by San Francisco Giants organization in sixth round of free-agent draft (June 1, 1995). ... On San Francisco disabled list (May 13-June 6 and July 14-August 19, 2000); included rehabilitation assignments to San Jose (May 26-31), Bakersfield (May 31-June 6) and Fresno (August 2-19).

MISCELLANEOUS: Played shortstop (1995).

Year League	W	L	Pct.	ERA	G	GS	CG	ShO	Sv.	IP	H	R	ER	BB	SO
1996—					Did not play-attended New York-Stony Brook.										
1997—Salem-Kaizer (N'West)	2	1	.667	2.47	18	5	0	0	2	62	53	22	17	26	44
1998—San Jose (Calif.)	8	6	.571	3.32	22	22	0	0	0	122	100	51	45	48	118
—Shreveport (Texas)	1	3	.250	8.80	4	4	0	0	0	15 1/3	20	15	15	9	10
1999—Shreveport (Texas)	0	1	.000	3.12	2	2	0	0	0	8 2/3	5	4	3	7	7
—San Francisco (N.L.)	7	4	.636	4.18	19	14	0	0	1	90 1/3	84	45	42	46	54
—Fresno (PCL)	6	4	.600	4.46	13	13	1	0	0	74 2/3	68	44	37	36	82
2000—San Francisco (N.L.)	5	2	.714	5.21	20	15	0	0	0	93 1/3	89	63	54	63	61
—San Jose (Calif.)	0	1	.000	3.60	1	1	0	0	0	5	4	2	2	1	2
—Bakersfield (Calif.)	1	0	1.000	5.06	1	1	0	0	0	5 1/3	2	3	3	7	6
—Fresno (PCL)	0	2	.000	4.40	3	3	0	0	0	14 1/3	15	8	7	7	9
Major League totals (2 years)	12	6	.667	4.70	39	29	0	0	1	183 2/3	173	108	96	109	115

RECORD AS POSITION PLAYER

						BATTING							FIELDING		
Year Team (League)	Pos.	G	AB	R	H	2B	3B	HR	RBI	Avg.	BB	SO	SB	PO	A	E	Avg.
1995—Bellingham (N'West) ..	SS	56	177	23	41	7	2	3	20	.232	22	48	3	76	150	26	.897

NATION, JOEY — P — CUBS

PERSONAL: Born September 28, 1978, in Oklahoma City. ... 6-2/205. ... Throws left, bats left. ... Full name: Joseph Paul Nation.
HIGH SCHOOL: Putnam City (Oklahoma City).
TRANSACTIONS/CAREER NOTES: Selected by Atlanta Braves organization in second-round of free-agent draft (June 3, 1997). ... Traded by Braves to Chicago Cubs (August 24, 1999), completing deal in which Cubs traded P Terry Mulholland and SS Jose Hernandez to Braves for P Micah Bowie, P Ruben Quevedo and a player to be named later (July 31, 1999).

Year League	W	L	Pct.	ERA	G	GS	CG	ShO	Sv.	IP	H	R	ER	BB	SO
1997—Danville (Appl.)	1	2	.333	2.73	8	8	0	0	0	26 1/3	24	11	8	5	41
1998—Macon (S.Atl.)	6	12	.333	5.03	29	28	1	0	0	143	179	102	80	39	141
1999—Macon (S.Atl.)	1	1	.500	2.96	6	6	0	0	0	27 1/3	27	10	9	9	31
—Myrtle Beach (Caro.)	5	4	.556	4.39	19	17	0	0	0	96 1/3	88	51	47	37	87
—Daytona (FSL)■	2	0	1.000	1.38	2	2	0	0	0	13	8	2	2	2	11
2000—West Tenn (Sou.)	11	10	.524	3.31	27	27	1	1	0	166	137	72	61	65	165
—Chicago (N.L.)	0	2	.000	6.94	2	2	0	0	0	11 2/3	12	9	9	8	8
Major League totals (1 year)	0	2	.000	6.94	2	2	0	0	0	11 2/3	12	9	9	8	8

NAVARRO, JAIME — P — BLUE JAYS

PERSONAL: Born March 27, 1968, in Bayamon, Puerto Rico. ... 6-0/250. ... Throws right, bats right. ... Son of Julio Navarro, pitcher with three major league teams (1962-66 and 1970).
HIGH SCHOOL: Luis Pales Matos (Bayamon, Puerto Rico).
JUNIOR COLLEGE: Miami-Dade Community College-New World Center.
TRANSACTIONS/CAREER NOTES: Selected by Baltimore Orioles organization in second round of free-agent draft (January 14, 1986); did not sign. ... Selected by Orioles organization in secondary phase of free-agent draft (June 2, 1986); did not sign. ... Selected by Milwaukee Brewers organization in third round of free-agent draft (June 2, 1987). ... Granted free agency (April 7, 1995). ... Signed by Chicago Cubs (April 9, 1995). ... Granted free agency (November 1, 1995). ... Re-signed by Cubs (December 8, 1995). ... Granted free agency (November 1, 1996). ... Signed by Chicago White Sox (December 11, 1996). ... Traded by White Sox with P John Snyder to Brewers for P Cal Eldred and SS Jose Valentin (January 12, 2000). ... Released by Brewers (April 30, 2000). ... Signed by Colorado Rockies organization (May 15, 2000). ... Released by Rockies (June 15, 2000). ... Signed by Cleveland Indians (June 16, 2000). ... On Buffalo disabled list (August 20-September 1, 2000). ... Granted free agency (October 2, 2000). ... Signed by Toronto Blue Jays organization (December 13, 2000).
RECORDS: Shares major league record for most errors by pitcher in one inning—3 (August 18, 1996, third inning). ... Shares A.L. single-season record for most sacrifice flies allowed—17 (1993).
STATISTICAL NOTES: Led A.L. with five balks in 1990. ... Tied for A.L. lead with 14 wild pitches in 1997. ... Led A.L. with 18 wild pitches in 1998.

Year League	W	L	Pct.	ERA	G	GS	CG	ShO	Sv.	IP	H	R	ER	BB	SO
1987—Helena (Pio.)	4	3	.571	3.57	13	13	3	0	0	85 2/3	87	37	34	18	95
1988—Stockton (Calif.)	15	5	.750	3.09	26	23	8	2	0	174 2/3	148	70	60	74	151
1989—El Paso (Texas).................	5	2	.714	2.47	11	11	1	0	0	76 2/3	61	29	21	35	78
—Denver (A.A.).....................	1	1	.500	3.60	3	3	1	0	0	20	24	8	8	7	17
—Milwaukee (A.L.)	7	8	.467	3.12	19	17	1	0	0	109 2/3	119	47	38	32	56
1990—Milwaukee (A.L.)	8	7	.533	4.46	32	22	3	0	1	149 1/3	176	83	74	41	75
—Denver (A.A.).....................	2	3	.400	4.20	6	6	1	0	0	40 2/3	41	27	19	14	28
1991—Milwaukee (A.L.)	15	12	.556	3.92	34	34	10	2	0	234	237	117	102	73	114
1992—Milwaukee (A.L.)	17	11	.607	3.33	34	34	5	3	0	246	224	98	91	64	100
1993—Milwaukee (A.L.)	11	12	.478	5.33	35	34	5	1	0	214 1/3	254	135	*127	73	114
1994—Milwaukee (A.L.)	4	9	.308	6.62	29	10	0	0	0	89 2/3	115	71	66	35	65
1995—Chicago (N.L.)■	14	6	.700	3.28	29	29	1	1	0	200 1/3	194	79	73	56	128
1996—Chicago (N.L.)	15	12	.556	3.92	35	35	4	1	0	*236 2/3	244	116	103	72	158
1997—Chicago (A.L.)■	9	14	.391	5.79	33	33	2	0	0	209 2/3	*267	*155	*135	73	142
1998—Chicago (A.L.)	8	•16	.333	6.36	37	27	1	0	1	172 2/3	223	135	122	77	71
1999—Chicago (A.L.)	8	13	.381	6.09	32	27	0	0	0	159 2/3	206	126	108	71	74
2000—Milwaukee (N.L.)■	0	5	.000	12.54	5	5	0	0	0	18 2/3	34	31	26	18	7
—Colorado Springs (PCL)■ ..	3	2	.600	5.30	5	5	0	0	0	35 2/3	48	26	21	6	20
—Buffalo (I.L.)■	1	2	.333	4.44	12	2	0	0	0	26 1/3	36	16	13	10	13
—Cleveland (A.L.).................	0	1	.000	7.98	7	2	0	0	0	14 2/3	20	13	13	5	9
A.L. totals (10 years)	87	103	.458	4.93	292	240	27	6	2	1599 2/3	1841	980	876	544	820
N.L. totals (3 years)	29	23	.558	3.99	69	69	5	2	0	455 2/3	472	226	202	146	293
Major League totals (12 years)	116	126	.479	4.72	361	309	32	8	2	2055 1/3	2313	1206	1078	690	1113

N

PERSONAL: Born September 13, 1968, in Gambrills, Md. ... 6-3/225. ... Throws left, bats left. ... Full name: Dennis Edward Neagle Jr. ... Name pronounced NAY-ghul.

HIGH SCHOOL: Arundel (Gambrills, Md.).

COLLEGE: Minnesota.

TRANSACTIONS/CAREER NOTES: Selected by Minnesota Twins organization in third round of free-agent draft (June 5, 1989). ... On Portland disabled list (April 5-23, 1991). ... On Minnesota disabled list (July 28-August 12, 1991). ... Traded by Twins with OF Midre Cummings to Pittsburgh Pirates for P John Smiley (March 17, 1992). ... Traded by Pirates to Atlanta Braves for 1B Ron Wright and a player to be named later (August 28, 1996); Pirates acquired P Jason Schmidt to complete deal (August 30, 1996). ... Traded by Braves with OF Michael Tucker and P Rob Bell to Cincinnati Reds for 2B Bret Boone and P Mike Remlinger (November 10, 1998). ... On Cincinnati disabled list (March 24-April 21 and May 24-July 29, 1999); included rehabilitation assignment to Indianapolis (April 8-21 and July 23-29). ... Traded by Reds with OF Mike Frank to New York Yankees for 3B Drew Henson, OF Jackson Melian, P Brian Reith and P Ed Yarnall (July 12, 2000). ... Granted free agency (October 31, 2000). ... Signed by Colorado Rockies (December 4, 2000).

HONORS: Named lefthanded pitcher on THE SPORTING NEWS N.L. All-Star team (1997).

STATISTICAL NOTES: Tied for N.L. lead with 16 sacrifice hits in 1996. ... Career major league grand slams: 1.

MISCELLANEOUS: Appeared in one game as pinch runner (1992). ... Appeared in one game as pinch runner (1995). ... Doubled and had a sacrifice hit in three appearances as pinch hitter with Pittsburgh (1996). ... Struck out in only appearance as pinch hitter with Cincinnati (2000).

Year League	W	L	Pct.	ERA	G	GS	CG	ShO	Sv.	IP	H	R	ER	BB	SO
1989—Elizabethton (Appl.)	1	2	.333	4.50	6	3	0	0	1	22	20	11	11	8	32
— Kenosha (Midw.)	2	1	.667	1.65	6	6	1	1	0	43²/₃	25	9	8	16	40
1990—Visalia (Calif.)	8	0	1.000	1.43	10	10	0	0	0	63	39	13	10	16	92
—Orlando (Sou.)	12	3	.800	2.45	17	17	4	1	0	121¹/₃	94	40	33	31	94
1991—Portland (PCL)	9	4	.692	3.27	19	17	1	1	0	104²/₃	101	41	38	32	94
—Minnesota (A.L.)	0	1	.000	4.05	7	3	0	0	0	20	28	9	9	7	14
1992—Pittsburgh (N.L.)■	4	6	.400	4.48	55	6	0	0	2	86¹/₃	81	46	43	43	77
1993—Pittsburgh (N.L.)	3	5	.375	5.31	50	7	0	0	1	81¹/₃	82	49	48	37	73
—Buffalo (A.A.)	0	0	...	0.00	3	0	0	0	0	3¹/₃	3	0	0	2	6
1994—Pittsburgh (N.L.)	9	10	.474	5.12	24	24	2	0	0	137	135	80	78	49	122
1995—Pittsburgh (N.L.)	13	8	.619	3.43	31	•31	5	1	0	•209²/₃	*221	91	80	45	150
1996—Pittsburgh (N.L.)	14	6	.700	3.05	27	27	1	0	0	182²/₃	186	67	62	34	131
—Atlanta (N.L.)■	2	3	.400	5.59	6	6	1	0	0	38²/₃	40	26	24	14	18
1997—Atlanta (N.L.)	*20	5	.800	2.97	34	34	4	4	0	233¹/₃	204	87	77	49	172
1998—Atlanta (N.L.)	16	11	.593	3.55	32	31	5	2	0	210¹/₃	196	91	83	60	165
1999—Indianapolis (I.L.)■	2	0	1.000	4.67	3	3	0	0	0	17¹/₃	11	9	9	2	9
—Cincinnati (N.L.)	9	5	.643	4.27	20	19	0	0	0	111²/₃	95	54	53	40	76
2000—Cincinnati (N.L.)	8	2	.800	3.52	18	18	0	0	0	117²/₃	111	48	46	50	88
—New York (A.L.)■	7	7	.500	5.81	16	15	1	0	0	91¹/₃	99	61	59	31	58
A.L. totals (2 years)	7	8	.467	5.50	23	18	1	0	0	111¹/₃	127	70	68	38	72
N.L. totals (9 years)	98	61	.616	3.80	297	203	18	7	3	1408²/₃	1351	639	594	421	1072
Major League totals (10 years)	105	69	.603	3.92	320	221	19	7	3	1520	1478	709	662	459	1144

DIVISION SERIES RECORD

Year League	W	L	Pct.	ERA	G	GS	CG	ShO	Sv.	IP	H	R	ER	BB	SO
1998— Atlanta (N.L.)							Did not play.								
2000— New York (A.L.)							Did not play.								

CHAMPIONSHIP SERIES RECORD

Year League	W	L	Pct.	ERA	G	GS	CG	ShO	Sv.	IP	H	R	ER	BB	SO
1992— Pittsburgh (N.L.)	0	0	...	27.00	2	0	0	0	0	1²/₃	4	5	5	3	0
1996— Atlanta (N.L.)	0	0	...	2.35	2	1	0	0	0	7²/₃	2	2	2	3	8
1997— Atlanta (N.L.)	1	0	1.000	0.00	2	1	1	1	0	12	5	0	0	1	9
1998— Atlanta (N.L.)	0	0	...	3.52	2	1	0	0	0	7²/₃	8	3	3	2	9
2000— New York (A.L.)	0	2	.000	4.50	2	2	0	0	0	10	6	5	5	7	7
Champ. series totals (5 years)	1	2	.333	3.46	10	5	1	1	0	39	25	15	15	16	33

WORLD SERIES RECORD

NOTES: Member of World Series championship team (2000).

Year League	W	L	Pct.	ERA	G	GS	CG	ShO	Sv.	IP	H	R	ER	BB	SO
1996— Atlanta (N.L.)	0	0	...	3.00	2	1	0	0	0	6	5	3	2	4	3
2000— New York (A.L.)	0	0	...	3.86	1	1	0	0	0	4²/₃	4	2	2	2	3
World Series totals (2 years)	0	0	...	3.38	3	2	0	0	0	10²/₃	9	5	4	6	6

ALL-STAR GAME RECORD

Year League	W	L	Pct.	ERA	GS	CG	ShO	Sv.	IP	H	R	ER	BB	SO
1995— National	0	0	...	0.00	0	0	0	0	1	1	0	0	0	1
1997— National							Did not play.							

PERSONAL: Born November 17, 1966, in Baltimore. ... 6-8/235. ... Throws right, bats right. ... Full name: Jeffrey Allan Nelson. ... Nephew of Cole Nelson, who played in the Washington Senators organization.

HIGH SCHOOL: Catonsville (Md.).

JUNIOR COLLEGE: Catonsville (Md.) Community College.

TRANSACTIONS/CAREER NOTES: Selected by Los Angeles Dodgers organization in 22nd round of free-agent draft (June 4, 1984). ... On Great Falls disabled list (April 10-June 4, 1986). ... Selected by Seattle Mariners organization from Dodgers organization in Rule 5 minor league draft (December 9, 1986). ... On disabled list (July 16, 1989-remainder of season). ... Traded by Mariners with 1B Tino Martinez and P Jim Mecir to New York Yankees for P Sterling Hitchcock and 3B Russ Davis (December 7, 1995). ... On suspended list (September 3-5, 1996). ... On suspended list (May 28-29, 1998). ... On New York disabled list (June 26-September 4, 1998); included rehabilitation assignment to Tampa (August 31-September 4). ... On New York disabled list (May 3-20 and June 3-August 11, 1999); included rehabilitation assignments to Gulf

Coast Yankees (August 2-4 and August 9-10) and Tampa (August 5-8). ... Granted free agency (October 31, 2000). ... Signed by Mariners (December 4, 2000).

MISCELLANEOUS: Appeared in one game as outfielder with no chances for Seattle (1993).

Year	League	W	L	Pct.	ERA	G	GS	CG	ShO	Sv.	IP	H	R	ER	BB	SO
1984—	Great Falls (Pio.)	0	0	...	54.00	1	0	0	0	0	$^2/_3$	3	4	4	3	1
	—Gulf Coast Dodgers (GCL)..	0	0	...	1.35	9	0	0	0	0	$13^1/_3$	6	3	2	6	7
1985—	Gulf Coast Dodgers (GCL)..	0	5	.000	5.51	14	7	0	0	0	$47^1/_3$	72	50	29	32	31
1986—	Great Falls (Pio.)	0	0	...	13.50	3	0	0	0	0	2	5	3	3	3	1
	—Bakersfield (Calif.)	0	7	.000	6.69	24	11	0	0	0	$71^1/_3$	79	83	53	84	37
1987—	Salinas (Calif.)■	3	7	.300	5.74	17	16	1	0	0	80	80	61	51	71	43
1988—	San Bernardino (Calif.)	8	9	.471	5.54	27	27	1	1	0	$149^1/_3$	163	115	92	91	94
1989—	Williamsport (East.)	7	5	.583	3.31	15	15	2	0	0	$92^1/_3$	72	41	34	53	61
1990—	Williamsport (East.)	1	4	.200	6.44	10	10	0	0	0	$43^1/_3$	65	35	31	18	14
	—Peninsula (Caro.)	2	2	.500	3.15	18	7	1	1	6	60	47	21	21	25	49
1991—	Jacksonville (Sou.)	4	0	1.000	1.27	21	0	0	0	12	$28^1/_3$	23	5	4	9	34
	—Calgary (PCL)	3	4	.429	3.90	28	0	0	0	21	$32^1/_3$	39	19	14	15	26
1992—	Calgary (PCL)	1	0	1.000	0.00	2	0	0	0	0	$3^2/_3$	0	0	0	1	0
	—Seattle (A.L.)	1	7	.125	3.44	66	0	0	0	6	81	71	34	31	44	46
1993—	Calgary (PCL)	1	0	1.000	1.17	5	0	0	0	1	$7^2/_3$	6	1	1	2	6
	—Seattle (A.L.)	5	3	.625	4.35	71	0	0	0	1	60	57	30	29	34	61
1994—	Seattle (A.L.)	0	0	...	2.76	28	0	0	0	0	$42^1/_3$	35	18	13	20	44
	—Calgary (PCL)	1	4	.200	2.84	18	0	0	0	8	$25^1/_3$	21	9	8	7	30
1995—	Seattle (A.L.)	7	3	.700	2.17	62	0	0	0	2	$78^2/_3$	58	21	19	27	96
1996—	New York (A.L.)■	4	4	.500	4.36	73	0	0	0	2	$74^1/_3$	75	38	36	36	91
1997—	New York (A.L.)	3	7	.300	2.86	77	0	0	0	2	$78^2/_3$	53	32	25	37	81
1998—	New York (A.L.)	5	3	.625	3.79	45	0	0	0	3	$40^1/_3$	44	18	17	22	35
	—Tampa (FSL)	0	0	...	0.00	2	1	0	0	0	2	1	1	0	1	4
1999—	New York (A.L.)	2	1	.667	4.15	39	0	0	0	1	$30^1/_3$	27	14	14	22	35
	—Gulf Coast Yankees (GCL)..	0	0	...	0.00	2	2	0	0	0	2	1	0	0	1	3
	—Tampa (FSL)	0	0	...	0.00	3	3	0	0	0	3	1	0	0	2	5
2000—	New York (A.L.)	8	4	.667	2.45	73	0	0	0	0	$69^2/_3$	44	24	19	45	71
Major League totals (9 years)		35	32	.522	3.29	534	0	0	0	17	$555^1/_3$	464	229	203	287	560

DIVISION SERIES RECORD

RECORDS: Holds career record for most games by pitcher—16.

Year	League	W	L	Pct.	ERA	G	GS	CG	ShO	Sv.	IP	H	R	ER	BB	SO
1995—	Seattle (A.L.)	0	1	.000	3.18	3	0	0	0	0	$5^2/_3$	7	2	2	3	7
1996—	New York (A.L.)	1	0	1.000	0.00	2	0	0	0	0	$3^2/_3$	2	0	0	3	5
1997—	New York (A.L.)	0	0	...	0.00	4	0	0	0	0	4	4	0	0	2	0
1998—	New York (A.L.)	0	0	...	0.00	2	0	0	0	0	$2^2/_3$	2	0	0	1	2
1999—	New York (A.L.)	0	0	...	0.00	3	0	0	0	0	$1^2/_3$	1	0	0	1	3
2000—	New York (A.L.)	0	0	...	0.00	2	0	0	0	0	2	0	0	0	0	2
Division series totals (6 years)		1	1	.500	0.92	16	0	0	0	0	$19^2/_3$	16	2	2	10	19

CHAMPIONSHIP SERIES RECORD

Year	League	W	L	Pct.	ERA	G	GS	CG	ShO	Sv.	IP	H	R	ER	BB	SO
1995—	Seattle (A.L.)	0	0	...	0.00	2	0	0	0	0	3	3	0	0	5	3
1996—	New York (A.L.)	0	1	.000	11.57	2	0	0	0	0	$2^1/_3$	5	3	3	0	2
1998—	New York (A.L.)	0	1	.000	20.25	3	0	0	0	0	$1^1/_3$	3	3	3	1	3
1999—	New York (A.L.)	0	0	...	0.00	2	0	0	0	0	$^2/_3$	0	0	0	0	0
2000—	New York (A.L.)	0	0	...	9.00	3	0	0	0	0	3	5	3	3	0	6
Champ. series totals (5 years)		0	2	.000	7.84	13	0	0	0	0	$10^1/_3$	16	9	9	6	14

WORLD SERIES RECORD

NOTES: Member of World Series championship team (1996, 1998, 1999 and 2000).

Year	League	W	L	Pct.	ERA	G	GS	CG	ShO	Sv.	IP	H	R	ER	BB	SO
1996—	New York (A.L.)	0	0	...	0.00	3	0	0	0	0	$4^1/_3$	1	0	0	1	5
1998—	New York (A.L.)	0	0	...	0.00	3	0	0	0	0	$2^1/_3$	2	1	0	1	4
1999—	New York (A.L.)	0	0	...	0.00	4	0	0	0	0	$2^2/_3$	2	0	0	1	3
2000—	New York (A.L.)	1	0	1.000	10.13	3	0	0	0	0	$2^2/_3$	5	3	3	1	1
World Series totals (4 years)		1	0	1.000	2.25	13	0	0	0	0	12	10	4	3	4	13

NEN, ROBB   P   GIANTS

N

PERSONAL: Born November 28, 1969, in San Pedro, Calif. ... 6-5/215. ... Throws right, bats right. ... Full name: Robert Allen Nen. ... Son of Dick Nen, first baseman with three major league teams (1963, 1965-68 and 1970).

HIGH SCHOOL: Los Alamitos (Calif.).

TRANSACTIONS/CAREER NOTES: Selected by Texas Rangers organization in 32nd round of free-agent draft (June 2, 1987). ... On Charlotte disabled list (April 6-26 and May 6-24, 1990). ... On disabled list (April 23-June 10, June 28-July 8 and July 11-September 3, 1991; and May 7-September 9, 1992). ... On Texas disabled list (June 12-July 17, 1993); included rehabilitation assignment to Oklahoma City (June 21-July 17). ... Traded by Rangers with P Kurt Miller to Florida Marlins for P Cris Carpenter (July 17, 1993). ... Traded by Marlins to San Francisco Giants for P Mike Villano, P Joe Fontenot and P Mick Pageler (November 18, 1997).

MISCELLANEOUS: Holds Florida Marlins all-time record for most games pitched (269) and most saves (108).

Year	League	W	L	Pct.	ERA	G	GS	CG	ShO	Sv.	IP	H	R	ER	BB	SO
1987—	Gulf Coast Rangers (GCL)..	0	0	...	7.71	2	0	0	0	0	$2^1/_3$	4	2	2	3	4
1988—	Gastonia (S.Atl.)	0	5	.000	7.45	14	10	0	0	0	$48^1/_3$	69	57	40	45	36
	—Butte (Pio.)	4	5	.444	8.75	14	13	0	0	0	$48^1/_3$	65	55	47	45	30
1989—	Gastonia (S.Atl.)	7	4	.636	2.41	24	24	1	1	0	$138^1/_3$	96	47	37	76	146
1990—	Charlotte (FSL)	1	4	.200	3.69	11	11	1	0	0	$53^2/_3$	44	28	22	36	38
	—Tulsa (Texas)	0	5	.000	5.06	7	7	0	0	0	$26^2/_3$	23	20	15	21	21
1991—	Tulsa (Texas)	0	2	.000	5.79	6	6	0	0	0	28	24	21	18	20	23
1992—	Tulsa (Texas)	1	1	.500	2.16	4	4	1	0	0	25	21	7	6	2	20

Year	League	W	L	Pct.	ERA	G	GS	CG	ShO	Sv.	IP	H	R	ER	BB	SO
1993—	Texas (A.L.)	1	1	.500	6.35	9	3	0	0	0	22 2/3	28	17	16	26	12
—	Oklahoma City (A.A.)	0	2	.000	6.67	6	5	0	0	0	28 1/3	45	22	21	18	12
—	Florida (N.L.)■	1	0	1.000	7.02	15	1	0	0	0	33 1/3	35	28	26	20	27
1994—	Florida (N.L.)	5	5	.500	2.95	44	0	0	0	15	58	46	20	19	17	60
1995—	Florida (N.L.)	0	7	.000	3.29	62	0	0	0	23	65 2/3	62	26	24	23	68
1996—	Florida (N.L.)	5	1	.833	1.95	75	0	0	0	35	83	67	21	18	21	92
1997—	Florida (N.L.)	9	3	.750	3.89	73	0	0	0	35	74	72	35	32	40	81
1998—	San Francisco (N.L.)■	7	7	.500	1.52	78	0	0	0	40	88 2/3	59	21	15	25	110
1999—	San Francisco (N.L.)	3	8	.273	3.98	72	0	0	0	37	72 1/3	79	36	32	27	77
2000—	San Francisco (N.L.)	4	3	.571	1.50	68	0	0	0	41	66	37	15	11	19	92
A.L. totals (1 year)		1	1	.500	6.35	9	3	0	0	0	22 2/3	28	17	16	26	12
N.L. totals (8 years)		34	34	.500	2.94	487	1	0	0	226	541	457	202	177	192	607
Major League totals (8 years)		35	35	.500	3.08	496	4	0	0	226	563 2/3	485	219	193	218	619

DIVISION SERIES RECORD

Year	League	W	L	Pct.	ERA	G	GS	CG	ShO	Sv.	IP	H	R	ER	BB	SO
1997—	Florida (N.L.)	1	0	1.000	0.00	2	0	0	0	0	2	1	1	0	2	2
2000—	San Francisco (N.L.)	0	0	...	0.00	2	0	0	0	0	2 1/3	2	0	0	1	3
Division series totals (2 years)		1	0	1.000	0.00	4	0	0	0	0	4 1/3	3	1	0	3	5

CHAMPIONSHIP SERIES RECORD

Year	League	W	L	Pct.	ERA	G	GS	CG	ShO	Sv.	IP	H	R	ER	BB	SO
1997—	Florida (N.L.)	0	0	...	0.00	2	0	0	0	2	2	0	0	0	0	0

WORLD SERIES RECORD

NOTES: Member of World Series championship team (1997).

Year	League	W	L	Pct.	ERA	G	GS	CG	ShO	Sv.	IP	H	R	ER	BB	SO
1997—	Florida (N.L.)	0	0	...	7.71	4	0	0	0	2	4 2/3	8	5	4	2	7

ALL-STAR GAME RECORD

Year	League	W	L	Pct.	ERA	GS	CG	ShO	Sv.	IP	H	R	ER	BB	SO
1998—	National	0	0	...	9.00	0	0	0	0	1	3	3	1	0	0
1999—	National							Selected, did not play—injured.							

NEVIN, PHIL — 3B — PADRES

PERSONAL: Born January 19, 1971, in Fullerton, Calif. ... 6-2/231. ... Bats right, throws right. ... Full name: Phillip Joseph Nevin.
HIGH SCHOOL: El Dorado (Placentia, Calif.).
COLLEGE: Cal State Fullerton.
TRANSACTIONS/CAREER NOTES: Selected by Los Angeles Dodgers organization in third round of free-agent draft (June 5, 1989); did not sign. ... Selected by Houston Astros organization in first round (first pick overall) of free-agent draft (June 1, 1992). ... On Tucson disabled list (July 12-30, 1995). ... Traded by Astros to Detroit Tigers (August 15, 1995), completing deal in which Astros acquired P Mike Henneman for a player to be named later (August 10, 1995). ... On Detroit disabled list (March 21-April 16, 1997); included rehabilitation assignment to Lakeland (April 8-16). ... Traded by Tigers with C Matt Walbeck to Anaheim Angels for P Nick Skuse (November 20, 1997). ... On suspended list (June 12-15, 1998). ... Traded by Angels with P Keith Volkman to San Diego Padres for INF Andy Sheets and OF Gus Kennedy (March 29, 1999). ... On San Diego disabled list (April 1-16, 1999); included rehabilitaion assignment to Las Vegas (April 12-15).
HONORS: Named Golden Spikes Award winner by USA Baseball (1992). ... Named third baseman on THE SPORTING NEWS college All-America team (1992). ... Named Most Outstanding Player of College World Series (1992).
STATISTICAL NOTES: Led Pacific Coast League third basemen with .891 fielding percentage in 1993. ... Led Pacific Coast League in grounding into double plays with 21 in 1994. ... Led Pacific Coast League third basemen with 31 errors and 32 double plays in 1994. ... Led A.L. catchers with 20 passed balls in 1998. ... Career major league grand slams: 1.
MISCELLANEOUS: Member of 1992 U.S. Olympic baseball team.

									BATTING								FIELDING			
Year	Team (League)	Pos.	G	AB	R	H	2B	3B	HR	RBI	Avg.	BB	SO	SB	PO	A	E	Avg.
1993—	Tucson (PCL)	3B-OF	123	448	67	128	21	3	10	93	.286	52	99	8	68	187	29	†.898
1994—	Tucson (PCL)	3B-OF	118	445	67	117	20	1	12	79	.263	55	101	3	73	240	†32	.907
1995—	Tucson (PCL)	3B-DH	62	223	31	65	16	0	7	41	.291	27	39	2	39	128	14	.923
—	Houston (N.L.)	3B	18	60	4	7	1	0	0	1	.117	7	13	1	10	32	3	.933
—	Toledo (I.L.)■	OF-DH	7	23	3	7	2	0	1	3	.304	1	5	0	2	0	0	1.000
—	Detroit (A.L.)	OF-DH	29	96	9	21	3	1	2	12	.219	11	27	0	50	2	2	.963
1996—	Jacksonville (Sou.)	C-DH-3-O-1	98	344	77	101	18	1	24	69	.294	60	83	6	384	76	11	.977
—	Detroit (A.L.)	3B-OF-C-DH	38	120	15	35	5	0	8	19	.292	8	39	1	45	51	5	.950
1997—	Lakeland (FSL)	DH-1B-3B	3	9	3	5	1	0	1	4	.556	3	2	0	9	4	1	.929
—	Toledo (I.L.)••••	1B-DH-3B	5	19	1	3	0	0	1	3	.158	2	9	0	19	4	0	1.000
—	Detroit (A.L.)	O-DH-3-1-C	93	251	32	59	16	1	9	35	.235	25	68	0	94	18	2	.982
1998—	Anaheim (A.L.)■	C-DH-1B	75	237	27	54	8	1	8	27	.228	17	67	0	402	32	5	.989
1999—	Las Vegas (PCL)■	C-1B-3B	3	10	2	2	0	0	2	2	.200	0	2	0	12	4	0	1.000
—	San Diego (N.L.)	3-C-O-1-DH	128	383	52	103	27	0	24	85	.269	51	82	1	276	154	5	.989
2000—	San Diego (N.L.)	3B	143	538	87	163	34	1	31	107	.303	59	121	2	96	242	*26	.929
American League totals (4 years)			235	704	83	169	32	3	27	93	.240	61	201	1	591	103	14	.980
National League totals (3 years)			289	981	143	273	62	1	55	193	.278	117	216	4	382	428	34	.960
Major League totals (6 years)			524	1685	226	442	94	4	82	286	.262	178	417	5	973	531	48	.969

NEWHAN, DAVID — 2B — PHILLIES

PERSONAL: Born September 7, 1973, in Fullerton, Calif. ... 5-10/180. ... Bats left, throws right. ... Full name: David Matthew Newhan.
HIGH SCHOOL: Esperanza (Calif.).
COLLEGE: Pepperdine.

TRANSACTIONS/CAREER NOTES: Selected by Oakland Athletics organization in 17th round of free-agent draft (June 1, 1995). ... Traded by A's with P Don Wengert to San Diego Padres for P Doug Bochtler and SS Jorge Velandia (December 15, 1997). ... On Las Vegas disabled list (June 15-July 6, 2000). ... Traded by Padres to Philadelphia Phillies (August 7, 2000), completing deal in which Phillies traded SS Desi Relaford to Padres for a player to be named (August 4, 2000).

							BATTING								FIELDING			
Year	Team (League)	Pos.	G	AB	R	H	2B	3B	HR	RBI	Avg.	BB	SO	SB	PO	A	E	Avg.
1995— S. Oregon (N'West)....		OF	42	145	25	39	8	1	6	21	.269	29	30	10	50	4	2	.964
1996— Modesto (Calif.)		OF	117	455	96	137	27	3	25	75	.301	62	106	17	128	5	5	.964
— W. Mich. (Midw.)........		OF	25	96	9	21	5	0	3	8	.219	13	26	3	37	3	1	.976
1997— Visalia (Calif.)		2B	67	241	52	67	15	2	7	48	.278	44	58	9	123	157	10	.966
— Huntsville (Sou.)		2B	57	212	40	67	13	2	5	35	.316	28	59	5	96	129	16	.934
1998— Mobile (Sou.)■	2B-3B-SS	121	491	89	128	26	3	12	45	.261	68	110	27	228	314	14	.975
1999— Las Vegas (PCL)		2B-SS	98	374	49	107	25	1	14	49	.286	30	84	22	164	235	20	.952
— San Diego (N.L.)	2B-3B-1B	32	43	7	6	1	0	2	6	.140	1	11	2	28	36	2	.970
2000— Las Vegas (PCL)		2B-OF	66	244	41	62	5	2	5	35	.254	37	61	9	132	140	7	.975
— San Diego (N.L.)	OF-2B-3B	14	20	5	3	1	0	1	2	.150	6	7	0	9	4	0	1.000
— Scranton/W.B. (I.L.)■		2B	25	83	10	21	3	0	3	8	.253	11	15	3	42	71	1	.991
— Philadelphia (N.L.)......		2B	10	17	3	3	0	0	0	0	.176	2	6	0	9	15	0	1.000
Major League totals (2 years)			56	80	15	12	2	0	3	8	.150	9	24	2	46	55	2	.981

NEWMAN, ALAN   P

PERSONAL: Born October 2, 1969, in La Habra, Calif. ... 6-6/240. ... Throws left, bats left. ... Full name: Alan Spencer Newman.
HIGH SCHOOL: La Habra (Calif.).
COLLEGE: Cal State Fullerton.
TRANSACTIONS/CAREER NOTES: Selected by San Diego Padres organization in 26th round of free-agent draft (June 2, 1987); did not sign. ... Selected by Minnesota Twins organization in second round of free-agent draft (June 1, 1988). ... On disabled list (April 16-26 and August 5-September 6, 1992). ... Traded by Twins with IF Tom Houk to Cincinnati Reds for 3B Gary Scott (June 30, 1993). ... Selected by Chicago Cubs organization from Reds organization in Rule 5 minor league draft (December 13, 1993). ... Released by Cubs (April 1, 1994). ... Signed by Alexandria Aces, Texas-Louisiana League (May 10, 1995). ... Contract sold by Alexandria to San Diego Padres organization (September 27, 1994). ... Released by Padres (April 1, 1995). ... Signed by Alexandria (May 1995). ... Contract sold by Alexandria to Chicago White Sox organization (January 14, 1997). ... Granted free agency (October 17, 1997). ... Signed by Padres organization (November 12, 1997). ... Granted free agency (October 15, 1998). ... Signed by Tampa Bay Devil Rays organization (November 19, 1998). ... Released by Devil Rays (December 13, 1999). ... Signed by Cleveland Indians organization (January 26, 2000). ... On Buffalo disabled list (May 28-June 10, 2000). ... Granted free agency (October 2, 2000).
STATISTICAL NOTES: Led Appalachian League with 17 wild pitches in 1988.

Year	League	W	L	Pct.	ERA	G	GS	CG	ShO	Sv.	IP	H	R	ER	BB	SO
1988— Elizabethton (Appl.)...........		2	•8	.200	8.13	13	12	2	0	0	55 1/3	57	62	50	56	51
1989— Kenosha (Midw.)...............		3	9	.250	2.84	18	18	1	0	0	88 2/3	65	41	28	74	82
1990— Kenosha (Midw.)...............		10	4	.714	*1.64	22	22	5	1	0	154	95	41	28	78	158
— Visalia (Calif.)................		3	1	.750	2.23	5	5	0	0	0	36 1/3	29	15	9	22	42
1991— Visalia (Calif.)		6	5	.545	3.51	15	15	0	0	0	92 1/3	86	49	36	49	79
— Orlando (Sou.)		5	4	.556	2.69	11	11	2	0	0	67	53	28	20	30	53
1992— Orlando (Sou.)		4	8	.333	4.15	18	18	2	1	0	102	94	54	47	67	86
1993— Nashville (Sou.)................		1	6	.143	6.03	14	11	1	0	0	65 2/3	75	52	44	40	35
— Indianapolis (A.A.)■........		1	3	.250	8.55	8	3	0	0	0	20	24	23	19	27	15
1994— Alexandria (Tex.-La.)■		9	2	.818	2.83	20	21	6	•3	0	143	127	58	45	76	128
1995— Alexandria (Tex.-La.)		10	8	.556	5.19	23	21	5	2	0	137	141	87	79	74	*129
1996— Alexandria (Tex.-La.)		6	6	.500	4.56	35	11	0	0	2	118 1/3	136	70	60	43	82
1997— Birmingham (Sou.)■		7	3	.700	2.49	44	0	0	0	10	72 1/3	55	34	20	40	64
1998— Las Vegas (PCL)■		3	3	.500	3.30	63	0	0	0	7	76 1/3	58	29	28	50	76
1999— Durham (I.L.)■		10	0	*1.000	2.24	50	0	0	0	0	80 1/3	59	24	20	20	76
— Tampa Bay (A.L.)...............		2	2	.500	6.89	18	0	0	0	0	15 2/3	22	12	12	9	20
2000— Buffalo (I.L.)■...................		7	4	.636	3.39	32	6	0	0	0	71 2/3	71	34	27	22	63
— Cleveland (A.L.).................		0	0	...	20.25	1	0	0	0	0	1 1/3	6	3	3	1	0
Major League totals (2 years)		2	2	.500	7.94	19	0	0	0	0	17	28	15	15	10	20

N

NICHOLSON, KEVIN   SS   PADRES

PERSONAL: Born March 29, 1976, in Vancouver, B.C. ... 5-10/190. ... Bats both, throws right. ... Full name: Kevin R. Nicholson.
HIGH SCHOOL: Queen Elizabeth (Surrey, B.C.).
COLLEGE: Stetson.
TRANSACTIONS/CAREER NOTES: Selected by San Diego Padres organization in first round (27th pick overall) of free-agent draft (June 3, 1997). ... On San Diego disabled list (September 5, 2000-remainder of season).
STATISTICAL NOTES: Led Southern League shortstops with 621 total chances in 1999. ... Tied for Southern League shortstops lead with 75 double plays in 1999.

							BATTING								FIELDING			
Year	Team (League)	Pos.	G	AB	R	H	2B	3B	HR	RBI	Avg.	BB	SO	SB	PO	A	E	Avg.
1997— Ariz. Padres (Ariz.)		SS	7	34	7	9	1	0	2	8	.265	2	5	0	11	25	3	.923
— Rancho Cuca. (Calif.) .		SS	17	65	7	21	5	0	1	9	.323	4	15	2	21	28	6	.891
1998— Mobile (Sou.)		SS	132	488	64	105	27	3	5	52	.215	47	114	9	201	363	*38	.937
1999— Mobile (Sou.)		SS	127	489	84	141	38	3	13	81	.288	46	92	16	187	*402	32	.948
2000— Las Vegas (PCL)		SS-2B	91	326	48	91	26	3	6	44	.279	35	62	4	116	232	20	.946
— San Diego (N.L.)		SS-2B	37	97	7	21	6	1	1	8	.216	4	31	1	39	87	4	.969
Major League totals (1 year)			37	97	7	21	6	1	1	8	.216	4	31	1	39	87	4	.969

PERSONAL: Born May 13, 1966, in Cincinnati. ... 6-1/205. ... Throws right, bats right. ... Full name: Christopher Thomas Nichting. ... Name pronounced NICK-ting.
HIGH SCHOOL: Elder (Cincinnati).
COLLEGE: Northwestern.
TRANSACTIONS/CAREER NOTES: Selected by Los Angeles Dodgers organization in third round of free-agent draft (June 2, 1987). ... On San Antonio disabled list (April 10, 1990-entire season). ... On Yakima disabled list (June 17, 1991-remainder of season). ... On San Antonio disabled list (August 12, 1992-remainder of season). ... On Albuquerque disabled list (April 8-July 2, 1993). ... On Vero Beach disabled list (July 15-26 and July 28, 1993-remainder of season). ... On San Antonio disabled list (April 7-23, 1994). ... Granted free agency (October 15, 1994). ... Signed by Texas Rangers (November 18, 1994). ... On Oklahoma City suspended list (June 8-10, 1995). ... On Texas disabled list (March 22-September 3, 1996); included rehabilitation assignment to Oklahoma City (August 19-September 3). ... Granted free agency (October 15, 1996). ... Signed by Oakland Athletics organization (November 19, 1996). ... Granted free agency (October 15, 1997). ... Signed by Cleveland Indians organization (February 26, 1998). ... Granted free agency (October 15, 1998). ... Signed by New York Yankees organization (December 15, 1998). ... On Columbus disabled list (July 7-15, 1999). ... Granted free agency (October 15, 1999). ... Signed by Cleveland Indians (February 8, 2000). ... Granted free agency (October 18, 2000).

Year—League	W	L	Pct.	ERA	G	GS	CG	ShO	Sv.	IP	H	R	ER	BB	SO
1988—Vero Beach (FSL)	11	4	.733	2.09	21	19	5	1	1	138	90	40	32	51	*151
1989—San Antonio (Texas)	4	*14	.222	5.03	26	26	2	0	0	154	160	96	86	*101	*136
1990—San Antonio (Texas)				Did not play.											
1991—San Antonio (Texas)				Did not play.											
1992—Albuquerque (PCL)	1	3	.250	7.93	10	9	0	0	0	42	64	42	37	23	25
—San Antonio (Texas)	4	5	.444	2.52	13	13	0	0	0	78 2/3	58	25	22	37	81
1993—Vero Beach (FSL)	0	1	.000	4.15	4	4	0	0	0	17 1/3	18	9	8	6	18
1994—San Antonio (Texas)	3	4	.429	1.64	21	8	0	0	1	65 2/3	47	21	12	34	74
—Albuquerque (PCL)	2	2	.500	7.40	10	7	0	0	0	41 1/3	61	39	34	28	25
1995—Oklahoma City (A.A.)■	5	5	.500	2.13	23	7	3	•2	1	67 2/3	58	19	16	19	72
—Texas (A.L.)	0	0	...	7.03	13	0	0	0	0	24 1/3	36	19	19	13	6
1996—Oklahoma City (A.A.)	1	0	1.000	1.00	4	1	0	0	0	9	9	1	1	3	7
1997—Edmonton (PCL)■	7	13	.350	7.76	33	24	3	0	1	131	170	120	*113	46	90
1998—Buffalo (I.L.)■	8	6	.571	4.39	43	5	0	0	1	96 1/3	104	54	47	37	97
1999—Columbus (I.L.)■	8	5	.615	5.29	25	21	2	0	0	127 2/3	135	80	75	47	110
2000—Buffalo (I.L.)■	2	3	.400	4.23	47	3	0	0	26	66	65	31	31	16	60
—Cleveland (A.L.)	0	0	...	7.00	7	0	0	0	0	9	13	7	7	5	7
Major League totals (2 years)	0	0	...	7.02	20	0	0	0	0	33 1/3	49	26	26	18	13

PERSONAL: Born October 2, 1974, in Sonoma, Calif. ... 6-4/210. ... Throws right, bats right. ... Full name: Douglas A. Nickle.
HIGH SCHOOL: Sonoma Valley (Sonoma, Calif.).
COLLEGE: California (degree in political science).
TRANSACTIONS/CAREER NOTES: Selected by Anaheim Angels organization in 13th round of free-agent draft (June 3, 1997). ... Traded by Angels to Philadelphia Phillies (September 10, 1998), completing deal in which Phillies traded OF Gregg Jefferies for a player to be named later (August 26, 1998). ... On Reading disabled list (May 3-26, 2000).

Year—League	W	L	Pct.	ERA	G	GS	CG	ShO	Sv.	IP	H	R	ER	BB	SO
1997—Boise (N'West)	0	1	.000	6.41	17	2	0	0	0	19 2/3	27	17	14	8	22
1998—Cedar Rapids (Midw.)	8	4	.667	3.78	20	7	1	1	0	69	66	30	29	20	59
—Lake Elsinore (Calif.)	3	4	.429	4.48	11	10	1	0	0	66 1/3	68	40	33	25	69
1999—Clearwater (FSL)■	2	4	.333	2.29	*60	0	0	0	28	70 2/3	60	25	18	23	70
2000—Reading (East.)	8	3	.727	2.44	49	0	0	0	16	77 1/3	55	25	21	22	58
—Philadelphia (N.L.)	0	0	...	13.50	4	0	0	0	0	2 2/3	5	4	4	2	0
Major League totals (1 year)	0	0	...	13.50	4	0	0	0	0	2 2/3	5	4	4	2	0

PERSONAL: Born June 16, 1975, in Guacara, Venezuela. ... 6-1/180. ... Bats right, throws right. ... Full name: Jose Miguel Nieves Pinto. ... Brother of Juan Nieves, outfielder, Toronto Blue Jays organization. ... Name pronounced nee-Á-vez.
HIGH SCHOOL: Enrique Delgado Palacios (Carabobo, Venezuela).
TRANSACTIONS/CAREER NOTES: Signed as non-drafted free agent by Milwaukee Brewers organization (June 10, 1992). ... Released by Brewers (October 19, 1993). ... Signed by Chicago Cubs organization (June 30, 1994). ... On disabled list (May 29-June 12, 1997). ... On Chicago disabled list (May 31-June 18, 2000); included rehabilitation assignments to Daytona (June 14-16) and West Tenn (June 16-18).

Year—Team (League)	Pos.	G	AB	R	H	2B	3B	HR	RBI	Avg.	BB	SO	SB	PO	A	E	Avg.
1992—Dom. Brewers (DSL)	IF	8	15	2	5	0	0	1	3	.333	4	4	0	9	13	5	.815
1993—Dom. Brewers (DSL)	IF	54	144	21	29	4	3	2	14	.201	22	25	6	43	78	19	.864
1994—Dom. Cubs (DSL)■	2B	37	137	21	39	6	1	4	24	.285	13	23	5	50	76	9	.933
1995—Williamsport (NY-P)	SS-2B	69	276	46	59	13	1	4	44	.214	21	39	11	85	193	33	.894
1996—Rockford (Midw.)	SS-2B-3B	113	396	55	96	20	4	5	57	.242	33	59	17	156	318	37	.928
1997—Daytona (FSL)	SS-2B	85	331	51	91	20	1	4	42	.275	17	55	16	151	218	27	.932
1998—West Tenn (Sou.)	SS-2B	82	314	42	91	27	5	8	39	.290	18	55	17	130	211	24	.934
—Iowa (PCL)	SS	19	75	7	19	4	0	0	4	.253	2	11	1	35	61	4	.960
—Chicago (N.L.)	SS	2	1	0	0	0	0	0	0	.000	0	0	0	0	0	0	...
1999—Iowa (PCL)	SS-2B	104	392	55	105	25	3	11	59	.268	24	65	11	122	315	19	.958
—Chicago (N.L.)	SS	54	181	16	45	9	1	2	18	.249	8	25	0	67	162	16	.935
2000—Chicago (N.L.)	SS	82	198	17	42	6	3	5	24	.212	11	43	1	46	103	5	.968
—Daytona (FSL)	3B-SS	2	6	2	1	0	0	0	0	.167	1	0	0	2	4	0	1.000
—West Tenn (Sou.)	3B-SS	2	7	2	4	0	0	2	2	.571	0	0	0	4	1	0	1.000
—Iowa (PCL)	3B-SS-2B	7	32	7	9	4	1	1	7	.281	2	5	1	3	15	1	.947
Major League totals (3 years)		138	380	33	87	15	4	7	42	.229	19	68	1	113	265	21	.947

PERSONAL: Born November 25, 1975, in San Cristobal, Dominican Republic. ... 6-0/185. ... Throws right, bats right. ... Full name: Elvin Alexis Nina.
HIGH SCHOOL: Elizabeth (N.J.).
COLLEGE: Oklahoma State.
TRANSACTIONS/CAREER NOTES: Selected by Oakland Athletics organization in 17th round of free-agent draft (June 3, 1997). ... Traded by A's with OF Jeff DaVanon and OF Nathan Haynes to Anaheim Angels for P Omar Olivares and 2B Randy Velarde (July 29, 1999). ... On Erie disabled list (August 24, 1999-remainder of season). ... On Erie disabled list (April 6-24 and June 26-July 20, 2000). ... On Edmonton disabled list (August 17-September 2, 2000).

Year	League	W	L	Pct.	ERA	G	GS	CG	ShO	Sv.	IP	H	R	ER	BB	SO
1997—Southern Oregon (N'West).		1	3	.250	5.23	18	2	0	0	1	31	36	24	18	18	26
1998—Visalia (Calif.)		8	8	.500	4.49	30	21	1	1	0	130 1/3	135	77	65	62	131
—Edmonton (PCL)		0	0	...	0.00	1	0	0	0	0	1/3	1	0	0	2	0
1999—Modesto (Calif.)		5	2	.714	2.09	17	12	0	0	0	73 1/3	59	31	17	41	74
—Midland (Texas)		3	2	.600	4.80	7	4	0	0	0	30	36	21	16	18	18
—Erie (East.)■		3	0	1.000	4.07	4	4	0	0	0	24 1/3	20	12	11	15	19
2000—Erie (East.)		2	4	.333	4.24	12	10	2	0	0	57 1/3	51	31	27	24	30
—Edmonton (PCL)		0	0	...	2.89	3	2	0	0	0	9 1/3	11	6	3	6	3

PERSONAL: Born March 9, 1973, in Suffern, N.Y. ... 6-3/205. ... Throws left, bats left. ... Full name: Christopher John Nitkowski.
HIGH SCHOOL: Don Bosco (N.J.).
COLLEGE: St. John's.
TRANSACTIONS/CAREER NOTES: Selected by Cincinnati Reds organization in first round (ninth pick overall) of free-agent draft (June 2, 1994). ... Traded by Reds with P David Tuttle and a player to be named later to Detroit Tigers for P David Wells (July 31, 1995); Tigers acquired IF Mark Lewis to complete deal (November 16, 1995). ... On Detroit disabled list (August 11-29, 1996). ... Traded by Tigers with C Brad Ausmus, P Jose Lima, P Trever Miller and IF Daryle Ward to Houston Astros for OF Brian Hunter, IF Orlando Miller, P Doug Brocail, P Todd Jones and cash (December 10, 1996). ... Traded by Astros with C Brad Ausmus to Tigers for C Paul Bako, P Dean Crow, P Mark Persails, P Brian Powell and 3B Carlos Villalobos (January 14, 1999). ... On suspended list (May 28-30, 1999).
RECORDS: Shares major league record for most hit batsmen in one inning—3 (August 3, 1998, eighth inning).
STATISTICAL NOTES: Tied for A.L. lead with three balks in 1999.
MISCELLANEOUS: Struck out in only appearance as pinch hitter and appeared in one game as pinch runner (1999).

Year	League	W	L	Pct.	ERA	G	GS	CG	ShO	Sv.	IP	H	R	ER	BB	SO
1994—Chattanooga (Sou.)		6	3	.667	3.50	14	14	0	0	0	74 2/3	61	30	29	40	60
1995—Chattanooga (Sou.)		4	2	.667	2.50	8	8	0	0	0	50 1/3	39	20	14	20	52
—Indianapolis (A.A.)		0	2	.000	5.20	6	6	0	0	0	27 2/3	28	16	16	10	21
—Cincinnati (N.L.)		1	3	.250	6.12	9	7	0	0	0	32 1/3	41	25	22	15	18
—Detroit (A.L.)■		1	4	.200	7.09	11	11	0	0	0	39 1/3	53	32	31	20	13
1996—Toledo (I.L.)		4	6	.400	4.46	19	19	1	0	0	111	104	60	55	53	103
—Detroit (A.L.)		2	3	.400	8.08	11	8	0	0	0	45 2/3	62	44	41	38	36
1997—New Orleans (A.A.)■		8	10	.444	3.98	28	28	1	0	0	174 1/3	183	82	77	56	*141
1998—Houston (N.L.)		3	3	.500	3.77	43	0	0	0	3	59 2/3	49	27	25	23	44
—New Orleans (PCL)		0	1	.000	6.00	5	3	0	0	1	15	22	12	10	7	18
1999—Detroit (A.L.)■		4	5	.444	4.30	68	7	0	0	0	81 2/3	63	44	39	45	66
2000—Detroit (A.L.)		4	9	.308	5.25	67	11	0	0	0	109 2/3	124	79	64	49	81
A.L. totals (4 years)		11	21	.344	5.70	157	37	0	0	0	276 1/3	302	199	175	152	196
N.L. totals (2 years)		4	6	.400	4.60	52	7	0	0	0	92	90	52	47	38	62
Major League totals (5 years)		15	27	.357	5.42	209	44	0	0	3	368 1/3	392	251	222	190	258

PERSONAL: Born April 11, 1974, in Durham, N.C. ... 6-2/200. ... Bats left, throws left. ... Full name: Christopher Trotman Nixon.
HIGH SCHOOL: New Hanover (Wilmington, N.C.).
TRANSACTIONS/CAREER NOTES: Selected by Boston Red Sox organization in first round (seventh pick overall) of free-agent draft (June 3, 1993). ... On disabled list (July 12, 1994-remainder of season). ... On Boston disabled list (June 27-July 25, 2000); included rehabilitation assignment to Gulf Coast Red Sox (July 8-9 and July 20-23).
STATISTICAL NOTES: Tied for Eastern League lead with four double plays by outfielders in 1996. ... Tied for International League lead with 11 errors and three double plays by outfielder in 1998. ... Hit three home runs in one game (July 24, 1999). ... Career major league grand slams: 1.

Year	Team (League)	Pos.	G	AB	R	H	2B	3B	HR	RBI	Avg.	BB	SO	SB	PO	A	E	Avg.
1994—Lynchburg (Caro.)		OF	71	264	33	65	12	0	12	43	.246	44	53	10	143	8	4	.974
1995—Sarasota (FSL)		OF	73	264	43	80	11	4	5	39	.303	45	46	7	140	4	2	.986
—Trenton (East.)		OF	25	94	9	15	3	1	2	8	.160	7	20	2	66	2	0	1.000
1996—Trenton (East.)		OF-DH	123	438	55	110	11	4	11	63	.251	50	65	7	224	*14	5	.979
—Boston (A.L.)		OF	2	4	2	2	1	0	0	0	.500	0	1	1	3	0	0	1.000
1997—Pawtucket (I.L.)		OF	130	475	80	116	18	3	20	61	.244	63	86	11	268	10	4	.986
1998—Pawtucket (I.L.)		OF-DH-1B	135	509	97	158	26	4	23	74	.310	76	81	26	231	11	‡11	.957
—Boston (A.L.)		OF-DH	13	27	3	7	1	0	0	0	.259	1	3	0	16	0	0	1.000
1999—Boston (A.L.)		OF	124	381	67	103	22	5	15	52	.270	53	75	3	209	3	7	.968
2000—Boston (A.L.)		OF-DH	123	427	66	118	27	8	12	60	.276	63	85	8	216	8	2	.991
—GC Red Sox (GCL)		OF	3	10	3	4	0	0	1	5	.400	2	0	0	3	0	0	1.000
Major League totals (4 years)			262	839	138	230	51	13	27	112	.274	117	164	12	444	11	9	.981

DIVISION SERIES RECORD

Year Team (League)	Pos.	G	AB	R	H	2B	3B	HR	RBI	Avg.	BB	SO	SB	PO	A	E	Avg.
							BATTING								FIELDING		
1998— Boston (A.L.).............	OF	2	3	0	1	0	0	0	0	.333	1	0	0	3	0	0	1.000
1999— Boston (A.L.).............	OF	5	14	5	3	3	0	0	6	.214	4	5	0	3	0	0	1.000
Division series totals (2 years)	7	17	5	4	3	0	0	6	.235	5	5	0	6	0	0	1.000

CHAMPIONSHIP SERIES RECORD

Year Team (League)	Pos.	G	AB	R	H	2B	3B	HR	RBI	Avg.	BB	SO	SB	PO	A	E	Avg.
							BATTING								FIELDING		
1999— Boston (A.L.).............	OF	4	14	2	4	2	0	0	0	.286	1	5	0	7	0	0	1.000

NOEL, TODD — P — YANKEES

PERSONAL: Born September 28, 1978, in Abbeville, La. ... 6-4/225. ... Throws right, bats right. ... Full name: Todd Anthony Noel.
HIGH SCHOOL: North Vermillion (Maurice, La.).
TRANSACTIONS/CAREER NOTES: Selected by Chicago Cubs organization in first round (17th pick overall) of free-agent draft (June 4, 1996). ... Traded by Cubs with P Justin Speier and 3B Kevin Orie to Florida Marlins for P Steve Hoff and P Felix Heredia (June 31, 1998). ... Traded by Marlins with P Ed Yarnall and P Mark Johnson to New York Yankees for 3B Mike Lowell (February 1, 1999). ... On Tampa disabled list (April 22-May 1 and July 6-August 26, 1999). ... On Norwich disabled list (April 7-May 22, 2000). ... On Tampa disabled list (June 9-September 7, 2000).

Year League	W	L	Pct.	ERA	G	GS	CG	ShO	Sv.	IP	H	R	ER	BB	SO
1996— Gulf Coast Cubs (GCL).......	0	0	...	6.75	3	0	0	0	0	4	4	4	3	2	4
1997— Arizona Cubs (Ariz.)	5	1	.833	1.98	12	11	0	0	1	59	39	27	13	30	63
1998— Rockford (Midw.)	6	6	.500	4.03	16	16	1	0	0	89 1/3	83	45	40	37	70
— Kane County (Midw.)■.......	2	2	.500	5.30	7	5	0	0	0	37 1/3	45	25	22	17	26
1999— Tampa (FSL)■....................	3	7	.300	4.34	17	17	0	0	0	93 1/3	101	56	45	33	80
2000— Tampa (FSL).....................	0	0	...	10.80	4	4	0	0	0	10	18	13	12	8	11

NOMO, HIDEO — P — RED SOX

PERSONAL: Born August 31, 1968, in Osaka, Japan. ... 6-2/230. ... Throws right, bats right.
HIGH SCHOOL: Seijyo Kogyo (Japan).
TRANSACTIONS/CAREER NOTES: Selected by Kintetsu Buffaloes in first round of 1989 Japanese free-agent draft. ... Signed as free agent by Los Angeles Dodgers organization (February 8, 1995). ... On Albuquerque temporarily inactive list (April 3-27, 1995). ... Traded by Dodgers with P Brad Clontz to New York Mets for P Dave Mlicki and P Greg McMichael (June 4, 1998). ... Released by Mets (March 26, 1999). ... Signed by Chicago Cubs organization (April 2, 1999). ... Released by Cubs (April 23, 1999). ... Signed by Milwaukee Brewers (April 29, 1999). ... Claimed on waivers by Philadelphia Phillies (October 28, 1999). ... Granted free agency (October 29, 1999). ... Signed by Detroit Tigers organization (January 21, 2000). ... On disabled list (July 30-August 18, 2000). ... Released by Tigers (November 2, 2000). ... Signed by Boston Red Sox (December 15, 2000).
HONORS: Named N.L. Rookie Pitcher of the Year by THE SPORTING NEWS (1995). ... Named N.L. Rookie of the Year by Baseball Writers' Association of America (1995).
STATISTICAL NOTES: Struck out 16 batters in one game (June 14, 1995). ... Pitched 3-0 one-hit, complete-game victory against San Francisco (August 5, 1995). ... Led N.L. with 19 wild pitches and five balks in 1995. ... Led N.L. with five balks in 1995 and four in 1997. ... Struck out 17 batters in one game (April 13, 1996). ... Pitched 9-0 no-hit victory against Colorado (September 17, 1996).
MISCELLANEOUS: Member of 1988 Japanese Olympic baseball team. ... Appeared in one game as pinch runner (1999).

Year League	W	L	Pct.	ERA	G	GS	CG	ShO	Sv.	IP	H	R	ER	BB	SO
1990— Kintetsu (Jap. Pac.)............	*18	8	.692	*2.91	29	27	21	2	0	235	167	...	76	*109	*287
1991— Kintetsu (Jap. Pac.)............	*17	11	.607	3.05	31	29	22	*4	1	242 1/3	183	...	82	*128	*287
1992— Kintetsu (Jap. Pac.)............	*18	8	.692	2.66	30	29	17	*5	0	216 2/3	150	...	64	*117	*228
1993— Kintetsu (Jap. Pac.)............	*17	12	.586	3.70	32	32	14	2	0	243 1/3	*201	...	100	*148	*276
1994— Kintetsu (Jap. Pac.)............	8	7	.533	3.63	17	17	6	0	0	114	...	...	46	86	126
1995— Bakersfield (Calif.)■..........	0	1	.000	3.38	1	1	0	0	0	5 1/3	6	2	2	1	6
— Los Angeles (N.L.)	13	6	.684	2.54	28	28	4	•3	0	191 1/3	124	63	54	78	*236
1996— Los Angeles (N.L.)	16	11	.593	3.19	33	33	3	2	0	228 1/3	180	93	81	85	234
1997— Los Angeles (N.L.)	14	12	.538	4.25	33	33	1	0	0	207 1/3	193	104	98	92	233
1998— Los Angeles (N.L.)	2	7	.222	5.05	12	12	2	0	0	67 2/3	57	39	38	38	73
— New York (N.L.)■.............	4	5	.444	4.82	17	16	1	0	0	89 2/3	73	49	48	56	94
1999— Iowa (PCL)■....................	1	1	.500	3.71	3	3	0	0	0	17	12	7	7	12	18
— Huntsville (Sou.)■..........	1	0	1.000	0.00	1	1	0	0	0	7	5	0	0	1	7
— Milwaukee (N.L.).............	12	8	.600	4.54	28	28	0	0	0	176 1/3	173	96	89	78	161
2000— Detroit (A.L.)■	8	12	.400	4.74	32	31	1	0	0	190	191	102	100	89	181
A.L. totals (1 year)	8	12	.400	4.74	32	31	1	0	0	190	191	102	100	89	181
N.L. totals (5 years)	61	49	.555	3.82	151	150	11	5	0	960 2/3	800	444	408	427	1031
Major League totals (6 years)	69	61	.531	3.97	183	181	12	5	0	1150 2/3	991	546	508	516	1212

DIVISION SERIES RECORD

RECORDS: Shares N.L. career record for most earned runs allowed—10.

Year League	W	L	Pct.	ERA	G	GS	CG	ShO	Sv.	IP	H	R	ER	BB	SO
1995— Los Angeles (N.L.)	0	1	.000	9.00	1	1	0	0	0	5	7	5	5	2	6
1996— Los Angeles (N.L.)	0	1	.000	12.27	1	1	0	0	0	3 2/3	5	5	5	5	3
Division series totals (2 years)	0	2	.000	10.38	2	2	0	0	0	8 2/3	12	10	10	7	9

ALL-STAR GAME RECORD

Year League	W	L	Pct.	ERA	GS	CG	ShO	Sv.	IP	H	R	ER	BB	SO
1995— National	0	0	...	0.00	1	0	0	0	2	1	0	0	0	3

N

PERSONAL: Born December 6, 1977, in Austin, Texas. ... 6-3/185. ... Throws left, bats both. ... Full name: Benjamin Owen Norris.
HIGH SCHOOL: Westwood (Austin, Texas).
TRANSACTIONS/CAREER NOTES: Selected by Arizona Diamondbacks organization in 13th round of free-agent draft (June 4, 1996). ... On El Paso disabled list (July 26-September 12, 2000).

Year League	W	L	Pct.	ERA	G	GS	CG	ShO	Sv.	IP	H	R	ER	BB	SO
1996— Ariz. D-backs (Ariz.)	2	2	.500	4.60	8	7	0	0	0	31 1/3	33	21	16	4	37
— Lethbridge (Pio.)	0	0	...	6.35	3	3	0	0	0	11 1/3	14	9	8	5	12
1997— South Bend (Midw.)	1	8	.111	4.03	14	13	0	0	0	60 1/3	69	44	27	31	40
— Lethbridge (Pio.)	7	3	.700	4.86	14	14	0	0	0	83 1/3	93	61	45	23	54
1998— South Bend (Midw.)	1	5	.167	3.32	15	15	0	0	0	89 1/3	98	44	33	27	53
— High Desert (Calif.)	2	2	.500	5.53	9	6	0	0	1	40 2/3	48	27	25	18	17
1999— High Desert (Calif.)	2	2	.500	4.43	8	8	0	0	0	40 2/3	39	27	20	24	45
— El Paso (Texas)	10	6	.625	4.16	20	20	0	0	0	119	132	61	55	53	87

PERSONAL: Born July 6, 1972, in San Leandro, Calif. ... 6-1/205. ... Bats both, throws right. ... Full name: Gregory Blakemoor Norton. ... Son of Jerry Norton, outfielder with Pittsburgh Pirates organization.
HIGH SCHOOL: Bishop O'Dowd (Oakland).
COLLEGE: Oklahoma.
TRANSACTIONS/CAREER NOTES: Selected by San Francisco Giants organization in seventh round of free-agent draft (June 4, 1990); did not sign. ... Selected by Chicago White Sox organization in second round of free-agent draft (June 3, 1993). ... Granted free agency (December 21, 2000). ... Signed by Colorado Rockies (January 5, 2001).
STATISTICAL NOTES: Led Midwest League third basemen with 387 total chances in 1994. ... Led American Association with .534 slugging percentage in 1997. ... Led American Association third basemen with 29 errors in 1997. ... Tied for A.L. third baseman lead with 25 errors in 1999.

Year Team (League)	Pos.	G	AB	R	H	2B	3B	HR	RBI	Avg.	BB	SO	SB	PO	A	E	Avg.
1993— GC White Sox (GCL)	3B	3	9	1	2	0	0	0	2	.222	1	1	0	1	7	0	1.000
— Hickory (S.Atl.)	3B-SS	71	254	36	62	12	2	4	36	.244	41	44	0	57	161	17	.928
1994— South Bend (Midw.)	3B	127	477	73	137	22	2	6	64	.287	62	71	5	92	*265	30	.922
1995— Birmingham (Sou.)	3B	133	469	65	162	23	2	6	60	.345	64	90	19	102	277	25	*.938
1996— Birmingham (Sou.)	SS	76	287	40	81	14	3	8	44	.282	33	55	5	104	214	17	.949
— Nashville (A.A.)	SS-DH-3B	43	164	28	47	14	2	7	26	.287	17	42	2	43	95	13	.914
— Chicago (A.L.)	SS-3B-DH	11	23	4	5	0	0	2	3	.217	4	6	0	8	5	2	.867
1997— Nashville (A.A.)	3-S-2-DH	114	414	82	114	27	1	26	76	.275	57	101	3	83	247	†38	.897
— Chicago (A.L.)	3B-DH	18	34	5	9	2	2	0	1	.265	2	8	0	4	15	3	.864
1998— Chicago (A.L.)	1-3-DH-2	105	299	38	71	17	2	9	36	.237	26	77	3	654	42	6	.991
1999— Chicago (A.L.)	3B-1B-DH	132	436	62	111	26	0	16	50	.255	69	93	4	160	204	‡27	.931
2000— Chicago (A.L.)	3B-1B-DH	71	201	25	49	6	1	6	28	.244	26	47	1	126	66	8	.960
— Charlotte (I.L.)	3B-SS-1B	29	97	18	28	4	0	5	17	.289	24	23	1	55	54	1	.991
Major League totals (5 years)		337	993	134	245	51	5	33	118	.247	127	231	8	952	332	46	.965

BATTING / FIELDING

PERSONAL: Born February 1, 1976, in Texarkana, Texas. ... 6-1/190. ... Throws left, bats right. ... Full name: Phillip Douglas Norton.
HIGH SCHOOL: Pleasant Grove (Texarkana, Texas).
JUNIOR COLLEGE: Texarkana (Texas) College.
TRANSACTIONS/CAREER NOTES: Selected by Chicago Cubs organization in 10th round of free-agent draft (June 4, 1996).
RECORDS: Shares major league record for most home runs allowed in one inning—4 (August 8, 2000, fourth inning).

Year League	W	L	Pct.	ERA	G	GS	CG	ShO	Sv.	IP	H	R	ER	BB	SO
1996— Gulf Coast Cubs (GCL)	0	0	...	0.00	1	0	0	0	0	3	1	0	0	0	6
— Williamsport (NY-Penn)	7	4	.636	2.54	15	13	2	1	0	85	68	33	24	33	77
1997— Rockford (Midw.)	9	3	.750	3.22	18	18	3	0	0	109	92	51	39	44	114
— Daytona (FSL)	3	2	.600	2.34	7	6	3	0	0	42 1/3	40	11	11	12	44
— Orlando (Sou.)	1	0	1.000	2.57	2	1	0	0	0	7	8	2	2	2	7
1998— Daytona (FSL)	4	3	.571	3.27	10	10	0	0	0	66	57	30	24	26	54
— West Tenn (Sou.)	6	6	.500	3.52	19	19	1	1	0	120 1/3	118	60	47	50	119
1999— West Tenn (Sou.)	7	4	.636	2.39	14	13	0	0	0	86 2/3	72	32	23	42	81
— Iowa (PCL)	5	6	.455	6.67	14	14	0	0	0	79 2/3	98	63	59	33	61
2000— Iowa (PCL)	8	*13	.381	4.96	28	26	2	1	0	159 2/3	166	100	88	*104	126
— Chicago (N.L.)	0	1	.000	9.35	2	2	0	0	0	8 2/3	14	10	9	7	6
Major League totals (1 year)	0	1	.000	9.35	2	2	0	0	0	8 2/3	14	10	9	7	6

PERSONAL: Born March 16, 1976, in Santo Domingo, Dominican Republic. ... 5-11/185. ... Bats both, throws right. ... Full name: Abraham Orlando Nunez Adames.
HIGH SCHOOL: Emmanuel (Santo Domingo, Dominican Republic).
TRANSACTIONS/CAREER NOTES: Signed as non-drafted free agent by Toronto Blue Jays organization (May 5, 1994). ... Traded by Blue Jays with P Mike Halperin and C/OF Craig Wilson to Pittsburgh Pirates (December 11, 1996), completing deal in which Blue Jays traded P Jose Silva, P Jose Pett, IF Brandon Cromer and three players to be named later to Pirates for OF/1B Orlando Merced, IF Carlos Garcia, and P Dan Plesac (November 14, 1996).
STATISTICAL NOTES: Tied for New York-Pennsylvania League lead in caught stealing with 14 in 1996. ... Led New York-Pennsylvania League shortstops with .953 fielding percentage 1996.

N

Year	Team (League)	Pos.	G	AB	R	H	2B	3B	HR	RBI	Avg.	BB	SO	SB	PO	A	E	Avg.
															BATTING			FIELDING
1994—	Dom. Blue Jays (DSL)	2B	59	188	31	47	5	0	0	15	.250	42	37	22	155	27	12	.938
1995—	Dom. Blue Jays (DSL)	2B	54	186	49	56	10	3	4	25	.301	30	27	24	80	97	7	.962
1996—	St. Catharines (NY-P)	SS-2B	75	*297	43	83	6	4	3	26	.279	31	43	37	136	239	15	•.962
1997—	Lynchburg (Caro.)■..	SS	78	304	45	79	9	4	3	32	.260	23	47	29	100	219	15	.955
—	Carolina (Sou.)..........	SS	47	198	31	65	6	1	1	14	.328	20	28	10	76	129	11	.949
—	Pittsburgh (N.L.)........	SS-2B	19	40	3	9	2	2	0	6	.225	3	10	1	14	37	0	1.000
1998—	Nashville (PCL)	SS	94	366	50	91	12	3	3	32	.249	39	73	16	155	274	21	.953
—	Lynchburg (Caro.)......	SS-2B	5	18	2	4	1	0	0	2	.222	3	1	1	6	18	1	.960
—	Pittsburgh (N.L.)	SS	24	52	6	10	2	0	1	2	.192	12	14	4	33	60	7	.930
1999—	Pittsburgh (N.L.)	SS-2B	90	259	25	57	8	0	0	17	.220	28	54	9	113	214	14	.959
—	Nashville (PCL)	SS	15	58	12	18	0	0	0	3	.310	5	8	1	23	43	2	.971
2000—	Pittsburgh (N.L.)	SS-2B	40	91	10	20	1	0	1	8	.220	8	14	0	43	65	2	.982
Major League totals (4 years)			173	442	44	96	13	2	2	33	.217	51	92	14	203	376	23	.962

NUNEZ, FRANKLIN — P — PHILLIES

PERSONAL: Born January 18, 1977, in Nagua, Dominican Republic. ... 6-0/175. ... Throws right, bats right.
HIGH SCHOOL: Escuela Cano Abajo (Dominican Republic).
TRANSACTIONS/CAREER NOTES: Signed as non-drafted free agent by Los Angeles Dodgers organization (September 1, 1994). ... Released by Dodgers (January 12, 1996). ... Signed by Philadelphia Phillies organization (June 20, 1998). ... On disabled list (July 13, 1999-remainder of season).

Year	League	W	L	Pct.	ERA	G	GS	CG	ShO	Sv.	IP	H	R	ER	BB	SO
1995—	Dom. Dodgers (DSL)	1	0	1.000	7.36	12	1	0	0	0	22	27	25	18	20	17
1996—	....							Did not play.								
1997—	....							Did not play.								
1998—	Dom. Phillies (DSL)■	0	2	.000	2.18	5	5	1	0	0	33	23	14	8	14	37
—	Martinsville (Appl.).............	2	2	.500	2.49	6	4	0	0	0	25 1/3	23	10	7	8	19
1999—	Piedmont (S.Atl.)...............	4	8	.333	3.39	13	13	1	0	0	77	69	39	29	25	88
2000—	Clearwater (FSL)	10	4	.714	3.62	23	14	1	0	2	112	112	54	45	57	81

NUNEZ, JORGE — 2B/SS — METS

PERSONAL: Born March 1, 1978, in Villa Mella, Dominican Republic. ... 5-10/158. ... Bats right, throws right. ... Full name: Jorge Marte Nunez.
TRANSACTIONS/CAREER NOTES: Signed as non-drafted free agent by Toronto Blue Jays organization (April 17, 1995). ... Traded by Blue Jays with OF Shawn Green to Los Angeles Dodgers for OF Raul Mondesi and P Pedro Borbon (November 8, 1999). ... Granted free agency (December 21, 2000). ... Re-signed by Dodgers organization (January 4, 2001). ... Selected by New York Mets from Dodgers organization in Rule 5 major league draft (December 11, 2000).
STATISTICAL NOTES: Led Pioneer League shortstops with 35 errors in 1998. ... Led Florida State League with 22 caught stealing in 2000. ... Led Florida State League shortstops with 656 total chances in 2000.

Year	Team (League)	Pos.	G	AB	R	H	2B	3B	HR	RBI	Avg.	BB	SO	SB	PO	A	E	Avg.
															BATTING			FIELDING
1995—	Dom. Blue Jays (DSL)	SS	13	15	1	2	0	0	1	4	.133	1	5	0	0	1	0	1.000
1996—	Dom. Blue Jays (DSL)	IF	69	258	51	76	10	2	7	40	.295	19	36	19	69	182	38	.869
1997—	Dom. Blue Jays (DSL)	1B-2B	71	262	46	66	5	5	4	33	.252	29	48	*44	...	...	...	...
1998—	Medicine Hat (Pio.)	SS-2B-3B	74	*317	74	101	9	*11	6	52	.319	28	45	31	121	215	38	.898
—	Hagerstown (S.Atl.)....	3B	4	16	0	4	0	0	0	1	.250	0	1	1	2	3	1	.833
1999—	Hagerstown (S.Atl.)....	2B-SS-3B	133	564	*116	151	28	•11	14	61	.268	40	103	51	247	387	32	.952
2000—	Albuquerque (PCL)■..	SS	1	3	0	0	0	0	0	0	.000	0	0	0	0	0	0	...
—	Vero Beach (FSL)	SS	128	534	86	154	17	8	4	39	.288	38	104	54	*212	386	*58	.912

NUNEZ, VLADIMIR — P — MARLINS

PERSONAL: Born March 15, 1975, in Havana, Cuba. ... 6-4/224. ... Throws right, bats right. ... Full name: Vladimir Nunez Zarabaza.
TRANSACTIONS/CAREER NOTES: Signed as non-drafted free agent by Arizona Diamondbacks organization (February 1, 1996). ... On Tucson disabled list (April 7-24, 1998). ... Traded by Diamondbacks with P Brad Penny and a player to be named later to Florida Marlins for P Matt Mantei (July 9, 1999); Marlins acquired OF Abraham Nunez to complete deal (December 13, 1999).
STATISTICAL NOTES: Led California League with 36 home runs allowed in 1997.

Year	League	W	L	Pct.	ERA	G	GS	CG	ShO	Sv.	IP	H	R	ER	BB	SO
1996—	Visalia (Calif.)	1	6	.143	5.43	12	10	0	0	0	53	64	45	32	17	37
—	Lethbridge (Pio.)	*10	0	*1.000	*2.22	14	13	0	0	0	85	78	25	21	10	*93
1997—	High Desert (Calif.)............	8	5	.615	5.17	28	28	1	1	0	158 1/3	169	102	91	40	142
1998—	Tucson (PCL)	4	4	.500	4.91	31	13	1	0	2	95 1/3	103	58	52	37	78
—	Arizona (N.L.)	0	0	...	10.13	4	0	0	0	0	5 1/3	7	6	6	2	2
1999—	Tucson (PCL)	1	0	1.000	6.75	3	0	0	0	0	2 2/3	5	2	2	0	3
—	Arizona (N.L.)	3	2	.600	2.91	27	0	0	0	1	34	29	15	11	20	28
—	Florida (N.L.)■	4	8	.333	4.58	17	12	0	0	0	74 2/3	66	48	38	34	58
2000—	Florida (N.L.)	0	6	.000	7.90	17	12	0	0	0	68 1/3	88	63	60	34	45
—	Calgary (PCL)	6	7	.462	4.12	15	15	1	0	0	89 2/3	92	43	41	38	95
Major League totals (3 years)		7	16	.304	5.68	65	24	0	0	1	182 1/3	190	132	115	90	133

NUNNALLY, JON — OF

PERSONAL: Born November 9, 1971, in Danville, Va. ... 5-10/190. ... Bats left, throws right. ... Full name: Jonathan Keith Nunnally.
HIGH SCHOOL: Hargrave Military Institute (Chatham, Va.).
JUNIOR COLLEGE: Miami-Dade (South) Community College.

TRANSACTIONS/CAREER NOTES: Selected by Baltimore Orioles organization in 39th round of free-agent draft (June 4, 1990); did not sign. ... Selected by Cleveland Indians organization in third round of free-agent draft (June 1, 1992). ... Selected by Kansas City Royals from Indians organization in Rule 5 major league draft (December 5, 1994). ... Traded by Royals with IF/OF Chris Stynes to Cincinnati Reds for P Hector Carrasco and P Scott Service (July 15, 1997). ... Traded by Reds to Boston Red Sox for P Pat Flury (March 25, 1999). ... Traded by Red Sox to New York Mets for OF Jermaine Allensworth (November 12, 1999). ... Contract sold by Mets to Orix of Japan Pacific League (June 8, 2000).
STATISTICAL NOTES: Tied for American Association lead with eight bases on balls received in 1996. ... Tied for American Association lead with five double plays by outfielder in 1996. ... Career major league grand slams: 1.
MISCELLANEOUS: Hit home run in first major league at-bat (April 29, 1995).

							BATTING								FIELDING		
Year Team (League)	Pos.	G	AB	R	H	2B	3B	HR	RBI	Avg.	BB	SO	SB	PO	A	E	Avg.
1992— Watertown (NY-Penn)	OF	69	246	39	59	10	4	5	43	.240	32	55	12	146	2	8	.949
1993— Columbus (S.Atl.)	2B-OF	125	438	81	110	15	2	15	56	.251	63	108	17	226	202	25	.945
1994— Kinston (Caro.)	OF	132	483	70	129	29	2	22	74	.267	64	125	23	263	*14	9	.969
1995— Kansas City (A.L.)■	OF-DH	119	303	51	74	15	6	14	42	.244	51	86	6	197	5	6	.971
1996— Kansas City (A.L.)	OF-DH	35	90	16	19	5	1	5	17	.211	13	25	0	61	0	2	.968
— Omaha (A.A.)	OF-DH	103	345	76	97	21	4	25	77	.281	47	100	10	182	12	4	.980
1997— Omaha (A.A.)	OF	68	230	35	64	11	1	15	33	.278	39	67	8	173	8	7	.963
— Kansas City (A.L.)	OF	13	29	8	7	0	1	1	4	.241	5	7	0	12	0	0	1.000
— Cincinnati (N.L.)■	OF	65	201	38	64	12	3	13	35	.318	26	51	7	120	3	2	.984
1998— Cincinnati (N.L.)	OF	74	174	29	36	9	0	7	20	.207	34	38	3	126	5	6	.956
— Indianapolis (I.L.)	OF	79	290	53	73	18	2	11	53	.252	47	71	7	146	8	8	.951
1999— Pawtucket (I.L.)■	OF-DH	133	494	90	132	24	3	23	76	.267	85	103	26	271	12	5	.983
— Boston (A.L.)	DH-OF	10	14	4	4	1	0	0	1	.286	0	6	0	0	0	0	...
2000— New York (N.L.)■	OF	48	74	16	14	5	1	2	6	.189	17	26	3	38	4	1	.977
American League totals (4 years)		177	436	79	104	21	8	20	64	.239	69	124	6	270	5	8	.972
National League totals (3 years)		187	449	83	114	26	4	22	61	.254	77	115	13	284	12	9	.970
Major League totals (6 years)		364	885	162	218	47	12	42	125	.246	146	239	19	554	17	17	.971

NUNNARI, TALMADGE　　　　1B/OF　　　　EXPOS

PERSONAL: Born April 9, 1975, in Pensacola, Fla. ... 6-1/200. ... Bats left, throws left. ... Full name: Talmadge Raphael Nunnari.
HIGH SCHOOL: Booker T. Washington (Pensacola, Fla.).
COLLEGE: Jacksonville.
TRANSACTIONS/CAREER NOTES: Selected by Montreal Expos organization in ninth round of free-agent draft (June 3, 1997). ... On Ottawa disabled list (July 31-August 11, 2000).

							BATTING								FIELDING		
Year Team (League)	Pos.	G	AB	R	H	2B	3B	HR	RBI	Avg.	BB	SO	SB	PO	A	E	Avg.
1996— GC Expos (GCL)		54	187	35	47	7	1	0	21	.251	22	25	8	...		26	.000
1997— Vermont (NY-Penn)	1B	62	236	30	75	11	3	4	32	.318	31	37	6	507	35	6	.989
— Cape Fear (S.Atl.)	1B	9	35	8	13	1	1	1	6	.371	1	5	2	73	7	0	1.000
1998— Cape Fear (S.Atl.)	1B-OF	79	299	51	88	18	0	2	51	.294	42	44	4	656	59	7	.990
— Jupiter (FSL)	1B	56	201	18	59	14	0	2	34	.294	30	39	1	491	50	4	.993
1999— Jupiter (FSL)	1B-DH	71	261	41	93	17	1	5	44	.356	27	36	10	391	25	6	.986
— Harrisburg (East.)	1B-OF-DH	63	239	45	79	17	1	6	29	.331	39	46	7	372	21	4	.990
2000— Ottawa (I.L.)	1B-OF	44	135	17	38	12	1	0	12	.281	23	31	0	299	24	3	.991
— Harrisburg (East.)	1B-OF	92	317	46	85	16	2	5	54	.268	48	66	10	718	64	6	.992
— Montreal (N.L.)	1B	18	5	2	1	0	0	0	1	.200	6	2	0	23	2	0	1.000
Major League totals (1 year)		18	5	2	1	0	0	0	1	.200	6	2	0	23	2	0	1.000

O'BRIEN, CHARLIE　　　　C

PERSONAL: Born May 1, 1961, in Tulsa, Okla. ... 6-2/205. ... Bats right, throws right. ... Full name: Charles Hugh O'Brien. ... Brother of John O'Brien, first baseman in St. Louis Cardinals organization (1991-93).
HIGH SCHOOL: Bishop Kelley (Tulsa, Okla.).
JUNIOR COLLEGE: McLennan Community College (Texas).
COLLEGE: Wichita State.
TRANSACTIONS/CAREER NOTES: Selected by Texas Rangers organization in 14th round of free-agent draft (June 6, 1978); did not sign. ... Selected by Seattle Mariners organization in 21st round of free-agent draft (June 8, 1981); did not sign. ... Selected by Oakland Athletics organization in fourth round of free-agent draft (June 7, 1982). ... On disabled list (July 31, 1983-remainder of season). ... On Albany/Colonie disabled list (April 13-May 15, 1984). ... Traded by A's with IF Steve Kiefer, P Mike Fulmer and P Pete Kendrick to Milwaukee Brewers for P Moose Haas (March 30, 1986). ... Traded by Brewers with a player to be named later to New York Mets for two players to be named later (August 30, 1990); Brewers acquired P Julio Machado and P Kevin Brown (September 7, 1990) and Mets acquired P Kevin Carmody (September 11, 1990) to complete deal. ... Granted free agency (October 29, 1993). ... Signed by Atlanta Braves (November 26, 1993). ... Granted free agency (October 30, 1995). ... Signed by Toronto Blue Jays (December 14, 1995). ... Granted free agency (October 27, 1997). ... Signed by Chicago White Sox (December 10, 1997). ... On Chicago disabled list (July 19-30, 1998). ... Traded by White Sox to Anaheim Angels for P Jason Stockstill and P Brian Tokarse (July 30, 1998). ... On Anaheim disabled list (July 30-September 1 and September 18, 1998-remainder of season); included rehabilitation assignment to Midland (August 25-31). ... On disabled list (June 3-July 23, 1999). ... Released by Angels (August 6, 1999). ... Signed by Montreal Expos organization (February 4, 2000). ... On Ottawa disabled list (April 6-May 20, 2000). ... Released by Expos (June 22, 2000).
STATISTICAL NOTES: Career major league grand slams: 1.

							BATTING								FIELDING		
Year Team (League)	Pos.	G	AB	R	H	2B	3B	HR	RBI	Avg.	BB	SO	SB	PO	A	E	Avg.
1982— Medford (N'West)	C	17	60	11	17	3	0	3	14	.283	10	10	0	116	18	4	.971
— Modesto (Calif.)	C	41	140	23	42	6	0	3	32	.300	20	19	7	239	44	5	.983
1983— Alb./Colonie (East.)	C-1B	92	285	50	83	12	1	14	56	.291	52	39	3	478	82	11	.981
1984— Modesto (Calif.)	C	9	32	8	9	2	0	1	5	.281	2	4	1	41	8	0	1.000
— Tacoma (PCL)	C-OF	69	195	33	44	11	0	9	22	.226	28	31	0	260	39	0	1.000

Year Team (League)	Pos.	G	AB	R	H	2B	3B	HR	RBI	Avg.	BB	SO	SB	PO	A	E	Avg.
1985— Huntsville (Sou.)	C	33	115	20	24	5	0	7	16	.209	16	20	0	182	29	5	.977
— Oakland (A.L.)	C	16	11	3	3	1	0	0	1	.273	3	3	0	23	0	1	.958
— Modesto (Calif.)	C	9	27	5	8	4	1	1	2	.296	2	5	0	33	8	1	.976
— Tacoma (PCL)	C	18	57	5	9	4	0	0	7	.158	6	17	0	110	9	3	.975
1986— Vancouver (PCL)■....	C	6	17	1	2	0	0	0	1	.118	4	4	0	22	3	2	.926
— El Paso (Texas).........	C-OF-1B	92	336	72	109	20	3	15	75	.324	50	30	0	437	43	4	.992
1987— Denver (A.A.)	C	80	266	37	75	12	1	8	35	.282	41	33	5	415	53	6	.987
— Milwaukee (A.L.)	C	10	35	2	7	3	1	0	0	.200	4	4	0	78	11	0	1.000
1988— Denver (A.A.)	C	48	153	16	43	5	0	4	25	.281	19	19	1	243	44	3	.990
— Milwaukee (A.L.)	C	40	118	12	26	6	0	2	9	.220	5	16	0	210	20	2	.991
1989— Milwaukee (A.L.)	C	62	188	22	44	10	0	6	35	.234	21	11	0	314	36	5	.986
1990— Milwaukee (A.L.)	C	46	145	11	27	7	2	0	11	.186	11	26	0	217	24	2	.992
— New York (N.L.)■........	C	28	68	6	11	3	0	0	9	.162	10	8	0	191	21	3	.986
1991— New York (N.L.).........	C	69	168	16	31	6	0	2	14	.185	17	25	0	396	37	4	.991
1992— New York (N.L.).........	C	68	156	15	33	12	0	2	13	.212	16	18	0	287	44	7	.979
1993— New York (N.L.).........	C	67	188	15	48	11	0	4	23	.255	14	14	1	325	39	5	.986
1994— Atlanta (N.L.)■.........	C	51	152	24	37	11	0	8	28	.243	15	24	0	308	26	3	.991
1995— Atlanta (N.L.)	C	67	198	18	45	7	0	9	23	.227	29	40	0	446	23	4	.992
1996— Toronto (A.L.)■........	C	109	324	33	77	17	0	13	44	.238	29	68	0	613	37	3	.995
1997— Toronto (A.L.)	C	69	225	22	49	15	1	4	27	.218	22	45	0	543	41	3	.995
1998— Chicago (A.L.)■.......	C	57	164	12	43	9	0	4	18	.262	9	31	0	305	22	4	.988
— Midland (Texas)■.......	C	5	17	1	2	0	0	0	2	.118	2	4	1	33	0	0	1.000
— Anaheim (A.L.)	C	5	11	1	2	0	0	0	0	.182	1	2	0	20	2	0	1.000
1999— Anaheim (A.L.)	C	27	62	3	6	0	0	1	4	.097	1	12	0	140	11	1	.993
2000— Harrisburg (East.)■ ...	C	5	18	3	4	2	0	1	5	.222	2	5	0	8	0	0	1.000
— Montreal (N.L.)	C	9	19	1	4	1	0	1	2	.211	2	7	0	25	2	0	1.000
American League totals (9 years)		441	1283	121	284	68	4	30	149	.221	106	218	0	2463	204	21	.992
National League totals (7 years)		359	949	95	209	51	0	26	112	.220	103	136	1	1978	192	26	.988
Major League totals (15 years)		800	2232	216	493	119	4	56	261	.221	209	354	1	4441	396	47	.990

DIVISION SERIES RECORD

Year Team (League)	Pos.	G	AB	R	H	2B	3B	HR	RBI	Avg.	BB	SO	SB	PO	A	E	Avg.
1995— Atlanta (N.L.)..............	C	2	5	0	1	0	0	0	0	.200	1	1	0	8	1	0	1.000

CHAMPIONSHIP SERIES RECORD

Year Team (League)	Pos.	G	AB	R	H	2B	3B	HR	RBI	Avg.	BB	SO	SB	PO	A	E	Avg.
1995— Atlanta (N.L.)..............	C-PH	2	5	1	2	0	0	1	3	.400	0	1	0	3	1	0	1.000

WORLD SERIES RECORD

NOTES: Member of World Series championship team (1995).

Year Team (League)	Pos.	G	AB	R	H	2B	3B	HR	RBI	Avg.	BB	SO	SB	PO	A	E	Avg.
1995— Atlanta (N.L.)..............	C	2	3	0	0	0	0	0	0	.000	0	0	0	7	2	0	1.000

OCHOA, ALEX   OF   REDS

PERSONAL: Born March 29, 1972, in Miami Lakes, Fla. ... 6-0/195. ... Bats right, throws right.

HIGH SCHOOL: Hialeah (Fla.) Miami Lakes.

TRANSACTIONS/CAREER NOTES: Selected by Baltimore Orioles organization in third round of free-agent draft (June 3, 1991). ... Traded by Orioles with OF Damon Buford to New York Mets for 3B/OF Bobby Bonilla and a player to be named later (July 28, 1995); Orioles acquired P Jimmy Williams to complete deal (August 17, 1995). ... Traded by Mets to Minnesota Twins for OF Rich Becker (December 12, 1997). ... Traded by Twins to Milwaukee Brewers for a player to be named later (December 14, 1998); Twins acquired OF Darrell Nicholas to complete deal (December 15, 1998). ... Traded by Brewers to Cincinnati Reds for OF/1B Mark Sweeney and a player to be named later (January 14, 2000); Brewers acquired P Gene Altman to complete deal (May 15, 2000). ... On Cincinnati disabled list (May 31-June 16, 2000); included rehabilitation assignment to Chattanooga (June 11-16).

STATISTICAL NOTES: Led Carolina League in grounding into double plays with 15 in 1993. ... Led Eastern League with 12 sacrifice flies in 1994. ... Tied for Eastern League lead in double plays by outfielder with five in 1994. ... Led International League outfielders with 249 putouts and 266 total chances in 1995. ... Hit for the cycle (July 3, 1996). ... Tied for International League lead in double plays by outfielder with three in 1996. ... Career major league grand slams: 1.

Year Team (League)	Pos.	G	AB	R	H	2B	3B	HR	RBI	Avg.	BB	SO	SB	PO	A	E	Avg.
1991— GC Orioles (GCL)........	OF	53	179	26	55	8	3	1	30	.307	16	14	11	45	3	2	.960
1992— Kane County (Midw.)..	OF	133	499	65	147	22	7	1	59	.295	58	55	31	225	•17	•12	.953
1993— Frederick (Caro.)	OF	137	532	84	147	29	5	13	90	.276	46	67	34	169	13	11	.943
1994— Bowie (East.)	OF	134	519	77	156	25	2	14	82	.301	49	67	28	237	*22	6	.977
1995— Rochester (I.L.)	OF	91	336	41	92	18	2	8	46	.274	26	50	17	183	9	5	.975
— Norfolk (I.L.)...............	OF-DH	34	123	17	38	6	2	2	15	.309	14	12	7	§66	1	2	.971
— New York (N.L.)..........	OF	11	37	7	11	1	0	0	0	.297	2	10	1	20	1	0	1.000
1996— Norfolk (I.L.)	OF-DH	67	233	45	79	12	4	8	39	.339	32	22	5	110	9	5	.960
— New York (N.L.)..........	OF	82	282	37	83	19	3	4	33	.294	17	30	4	135	8	5	.966
1997— New York (N.L.).........	OF-DH	113	238	31	58	14	1	3	22	.244	18	32	3	104	7	2	.982
1998— Minnesota (A.L.)■......	OF-DH	94	249	35	64	14	2	2	25	.257	10	35	6	117	8	4	.969
1999— Milwaukee (N.L.)■......	OF-DH	119	277	47	83	16	3	8	40	.300	45	43	6	133	5	3	.979
2000— Cincinnati (N.L.)■......	OF	118	244	50	77	21	3	13	58	.316	24	27	8	125	4	3	.977
— Chattanooga (Sou.)	OF	4	16	3	3	2	0	1	2	.188	2	1	1	7	0	0	1.000
American League totals (1 year)		94	249	35	64	14	2	2	25	.257	10	35	6	117	8	4	.969
National League totals (5 years)		443	1078	172	312	71	10	28	153	.289	106	142	22	517	25	13	.977
Major League totals (6 years)		537	1327	207	376	85	12	30	178	.283	116	177	28	634	33	17	.975

PERSONAL: Born January 4, 1977, in Cincinnati. ... 6-2/190. ... Throws left, bats left. ... Full name: Brian Michael O'Connor.
HIGH SCHOOL: Reading (Ohio).
TRANSACTIONS/CAREER NOTES: Selected by Pittsburgh Pirates organization in 11th round of free-agent draft (June 1, 1995).
STATISTICAL NOTES: Led Eastern League with 21 wild pitches in 1999.

Year	League	W	L	Pct.	ERA	G	GS	CG	ShO	Sv.	IP	H	R	ER	BB	SO
1995—	Gulf Coast Pirates (GCL)	2	2	.500	1.88	14	5	0	0	1	43	33	22	9	13	43
1996—	Augusta (S.Atl.)	0	1	.000	3.06	19	0	0	0	1	35 1/3	33	13	12	8	37
	— Erie (NY-Penn)	4	*10	.286	5.85	15	•15	0	0	0	67 2/3	75	*60	44	47	60
1997—	Augusta (S.Atl.)	2	7	.222	4.41	25	14	0	0	0	85 2/3	90	54	42	39	91
	— Lynchburg (Caro.)	2	1	.667	3.46	11	0	0	0	2	13	11	5	5	6	14
1998—	Lynchburg (Caro.)	6	2	.750	2.60	14	14	1	0	0	86 2/3	86	34	25	22	84
	— Carolina (Sou.)	2	4	.333	8.25	14	13	0	0	0	64 1/3	86	65	59	53	41
1999—	Altoona (East.)	7	11	.389	4.70	28	27	1	0	0	153 1/3	152	98	80	*92	106
2000—	Altoona (East.)	12	4	.750	3.76	22	22	4	0	0	129 1/3	120	69	54	61	76
	— Pittsburgh (N.L.)	0	0	...	5.11	6	1	0	0	0	12 1/3	12	11	7	11	7
	— Nashville (PCL)	2	2	.500	6.84	5	5	0	0	0	26 1/3	30	23	20	14	19
Major League totals (1 year)........		0	0	...	5.11	6	1	0	0	0	12 1/3	12	11	7	11	7

PERSONAL: Born November 8, 1968, in San Pedro de Macoris, Dominican Republic. ... 6-0/190. ... Bats both, throws right. ... Full name: Jose Antonio Dono Offerman.
HIGH SCHOOL: Colegio Biblico Cristiano (Dominican Republic).
TRANSACTIONS/CAREER NOTES: Signed as non-drafted free agent by Los Angeles Dodgers organization (July 24, 1986). ... Traded by Dodgers to Kansas City Royals for P Billy Brewer (December 17, 1995). ... On Kansas City disabled list (April 6-29, July 10-22 and August 14-September 6, 1997). ... Granted free agency (October 23, 1998). ... Signed by Boston Red Sox (November 16, 1998). ... On disabled list (May 27-June 10 and July 30-August 16, 2000).
RECORDS: Holds A.L. single-season record for most consecutive games batted safely by switch hitter—27 (1998).
HONORS: Named Minor League Player of the Year by THE SPORTING NEWS (1990). ... Named Pacific Coast League Player of the Year (1990).
STATISTICAL NOTES: Tied for Pioneer League lead in caught stealing with 10 in 1988. ... Tied for Pacific Coast League lead in caught stealing with 18 in 1990. ... Led Pacific Coast League shortstops with 36 errors in 1990. ... Hit home run in first major league at-bat (August 19, 1990). ... Led N.L. with 25 sacrifice hits in 1993. ... Had 27-game hitting streak (July 11-August 7, 1998). ... Career major league grand slams: 1.

Year	Team (League)	Pos.	G	AB	R	H	2B	3B	HR	RBI	Avg.	BB	SO	SB	PO	A	E	Avg.
							BATTING									FIELDING		
1987—	....						Dominican Summer League statistics unavailable.											
1988—	Vero Beach (FSL)	SS	4	14	4	4	2	0	0	2	.286	2	0	0	4	5	5	.643
	— Great Falls (Pio.)	SS	60	251	75	83	11	5	2	28	.331	38	42	*57	82	143	18	*.926
1989—	Bakersfield (Calif.)	SS	62	245	53	75	9	4	2	22	.306	35	48	37	94	179	30	.901
	— San Antonio (Texas)...	SS	68	278	47	80	6	3	2	22	.288	40	39	32	106	168	20	.932
1990—	Albuquerque (PCL).....	SS-2B	117	454	104	148	16	11	0	56	.326	71	81	*60	174	361	†36	.937
	— Los Angeles (N.L.).....	SS	29	58	7	9	0	0	1	7	.155	4	14	1	30	40	4	.946
1991—	Albuquerque (PCL).....	SS	79	289	58	86	8	4	0	29	.298	47	58	32	126	241	17	.956
	— Los Angeles (N.L.).....	SS	52	113	10	22	2	0	0	3	.195	25	32	3	50	121	10	.945
1992—	Los Angeles (N.L.)	SS	149	534	67	139	20	8	1	30	.260	57	98	23	208	398	*42	.935
1993—	Los Angeles (N.L.)	SS	158	590	77	159	21	6	1	62	.269	71	75	30	250	454	*37	.950
1994—	Los Angeles (N.L.)	SS	72	243	27	51	8	4	1	25	.210	38	38	2	123	195	11	.967
	— Albuquerque (PCL).....	SS	56	224	43	74	7	5	1	31	.330	37	48	9	91	196	13	.957
1995—	Los Angeles (N.L.)	SS	119	429	69	123	14	6	4	33	.287	69	67	2	165	312	*35	.932
1996—	Kansas City (A.L.)■.....1B-2B-SS-OF	151	561	85	170	33	8	5	47	.303	74	98	24	920	234	16	.986
1997—	Kansas City (A.L.)	2B-DH	106	424	59	126	23	6	2	39	.297	41	64	9	201	254	9	.981
1998—	Kansas City (A.L.)	2B-DH	158	607	102	191	28	*13	7	66	.315	89	96	45	277	440	19	.974
1999—	Boston (A.L.)■...........	2B-DH-1B	149	586	107	172	37	*11	8	69	.294	96	79	18	285	321	14	.977
2000—	Boston (A.L.)	2B-1B-DH	116	451	73	115	14	3	9	41	.255	70	70	0	403	231	11	.983
American League totals (5 years)			680	2629	426	774	135	41	31	262	.294	370	407	96	2086	1480	69	.981
National League totals (6 years)			579	1967	257	503	65	24	8	160	.256	264	324	61	826	1520	139	.944
Major League totals (11 years)			1259	4596	683	1277	200	65	39	422	.278	634	731	157	2912	3000	208	.966

DIVISION SERIES RECORD

Year	Team (League)	Pos.	G	AB	R	H	2B	3B	HR	RBI	Avg.	BB	SO	SB	PO	A	E	Avg.
							BATTING									FIELDING		
1995—	Los Angeles (N.L.)	PR	1	0	0	0	0	0	0	0	...	0	0	0	...	...	...	...
1999—	Boston (A.L.)..............	2B	5	18	4	7	1	0	1	6	.389	7	0	0	11	9	0	1.000
Division series totals (2 years)			6	18	4	7	1	0	1	6	.389	7	0	0	11	9	0	1.000

CHAMPIONSHIP SERIES RECORD

RECORDS: Shares single-game record for most at-bats (nine-inning game)—6 (October 16, 1999).

Year	Team (League)	Pos.	G	AB	R	H	2B	3B	HR	RBI	Avg.	BB	SO	SB	PO	A	E	Avg.
							BATTING									FIELDING		
1999—	Boston (A.L.)..............	2B	5	24	4	11	0	1	0	2	.458	1	3	1	16	6	2	.917

ALL-STAR GAME RECORD

Year	League	Pos.	AB	R	H	2B	3B	HR	RBI	Avg.	BB	SO	SB	PO	A	E	Avg.
						BATTING									FIELDING		
1995—	National	SS	0	0	0	0	0	0	0	...	0	0	0	0	0	0	...
1999—	American	2B	1	0	0	0	0	0	0	.000	0	0	0	3	0	1	.750
All-Star Game totals (2 years)			1	0	0	0	0	0	0	.000	0	0	0	3	0	1	.750

PERSONAL: Born March 18, 1976, in Kyoto, Japan. ... 6-1/179. ... Throws right, bats right. ... Full name: Tomokazu Ohka.
HIGH SCHOOL: Kyoto Siesio (Kyoto, Japan).
TRANSACTIONS/CAREER NOTES: Contract purchased by Boston Red Sox from Yokohama Bay Stars of Japan Central League (November 20, 1998).
STATISTICAL NOTES: Pitched 2-0 no-hit victory for Pawtucket against Charlotte (June 1, 2000).

Year League	W	L	Pct.	ERA	G	GS	CG	ShO	Sv.	IP	H	R	ER	BB	SO
1994— Yokohama (Jap. Cen.)	1	1	.500	4.18	15	2	0	0	0	28	29	13	13	18	18
1995— Yokohama (Jap. Cen.)	0	0	...	1.93	3	1	0	0	0	9 1/3	3	2	2	13	6
1996— Yokohama (Jap. Cen.)	0	1	.000	9.50	14	1	0	0	0	18	27	19	19	14	11
1997—					Japan minor league statistics unavailable.										
1998— Yokohama (Jap. Cen.)	0	0	...	9.00	2	0	0	0	0	2	2	2	2	2	1
1999— Trenton (East.)■	8	0	1.000	3.00	12	12	0	0	0	72	63	26	24	25	53
— Pawtucket (I.L.)	7	0	1.000	1.58	12	12	1	1	0	68 1/3	60	17	12	11	63
— Boston (A.L.)	1	2	.333	6.23	8	2	0	0	0	13	21	12	9	6	8
2000— Pawtucket (I.L.)	9	6	.600	2.96	19	19	3	•2	0	130 2/3	111	52	43	23	78
— Boston (A.L.)	3	6	.333	3.12	13	12	0	0	0	69 1/3	70	25	24	26	40
Major League totals (2 years)	4	8	.333	3.61	21	14	0	0	0	82 1/3	91	37	33	32	48

PERSONAL: Born August 13, 1977, in Frankfurt, West Germany. ... 6-2/195. ... Throws left, bats left. ... Full name: William McDaniel Ohman.
HIGH SCHOOL: Ponderos (Parker, Colo.).
COLLEGE: Pepperdine.
TRANSACTIONS/CAREER NOTES: Selected by Chicago Cubs organization in eighth round of free-agent draft (June 2, 1998).

Year League	W	L	Pct.	ERA	G	GS	CG	ShO	Sv.	IP	H	R	ER	BB	SO
1998— Williamsport (NY-Penn)	4	4	.500	8.77	10	7	0	0	0	39	39	32	38	13	35
— Rockford (Midw.)	1	1	.500	4.44	4	4	0	0	0	24 1/3	25	13	12	7	21
1999— Daytona (FSL)	4	7	.364	3.46	31	15	2	•2	5	106 2/3	102	59	41	41	97
2000— West Tenn (Sou.)	6	4	.600	1.89	59	0	0	0	3	71 1/3	53	20	15	36	85
— Chicago (N.L.)	1	0	1.000	8.10	6	0	0	0	0	3 1/3	4	3	3	4	2
Major League totals (1 year)	1	0	1.000	8.10	6	0	0	0	0	3 1/3	4	3	3	4	2

PERSONAL: Born December 20, 1974, in Eldorado Culican, Mexico. ... 5-9/170. ... Bats both, throws right. ... Full name: Octavio Augie Ojeda.
HIGH SCHOOL: Pius X (Downey, Calif.).
JUNIOR COLLEGE: Cypress (Calif.) College.
COLLEGE: Tennessee.
TRANSACTIONS/CAREER NOTES: Selected by Baltimore Orioles organization in 13th round of free-agent draft (June 4, 1996). ... Traded by Orioles to Chicago Cubs for P Richard Negrette (December 13, 1999).
STATISTICAL NOTES: Led Eastern League with 25 sacrifice hits in 1999. ... Led Eastern League shortstops with .969 fielding percentage in 1999. ... Led Pacific Coast League shortstops with .976 fielding percentage in 2000.
MISCELLANEOUS: Member of 1996 U.S. Olympic baseball team.

Year Team (League)	Pos.	G	AB	R	H	2B	3B	HR	RBI	Avg.	BB	SO	SB	PO	A	E	Avg.
1997— Bowie (East.)	SS	58	204	33	60	9	1	2	23	.294	31	17	7	84	176	9	.967
— Frederick (Caro.)	SS	34	128	25	44	11	1	1	20	.344	18	18	2	36	108	5	.966
— Rochester (I.L.)	SS	15	47	5	11	3	1	0	6	.234	8	4	1	24	35	5	.922
1998— GC Orioles (GCL)	SS	4	15	6	6	2	0	0	2	.400	3	1	3	9	16	0	1.000
— Bowie (East.)	SS-3B	73	254	36	65	10	2	1	19	.256	36	30	0	95	199	11	.964
1999— Rochester (I.L.)	SS	1	1	0	0	0	0	0	0	.000	0	0	0	0	0	0	...
— Bowie (East.)	SS-3B	134	460	73	123	18	4	10	60	.267	57	47	6	211	379	19	†.969
2000— Iowa (PCL)■	SS-2B	113	396	56	111	23	2	8	43	.280	33	27	16	161	294	11	.976
— Chicago (N.L.)	SS-2B	28	77	10	17	3	1	2	8	.221	10	9	0	30	65	1	.990
Major League totals (1 year)		28	77	10	17	3	1	2	8	.221	10	9	0	30	65	1	.990

PERSONAL: Born August 4, 1969, in Compton, Calif. ... 6-0/200. ... Bats left, throws left. ... Full name: Troy Franklin O'Leary.
HIGH SCHOOL: Cypress (Calif.).
JUNIOR COLLEGE: Chaffey College (Calif.).
TRANSACTIONS/CAREER NOTES: Selected by Milwaukee Brewers organization in 13th round of free-agent draft (June 2, 1987). ... Claimed on waivers by Boston Red Sox (April 14, 1995). ... On Boston disabled list (June 19-July 3, 2000); included rehabilitation assignment to Gulf Coast Red Sox (June 30-July 3).
HONORS: Named Texas League Most Valuable Player (1992).
STATISTICAL NOTES: Led Pioneer League with 144 total bases in 1989. ... Led Texas League with 227 total bases and .399 on-base percentage in 1992. ... Led Texas League outfielders with 242 total chances in 1992. ... Had 15-game hitting streak (July 30-August 14, 1999). ... Career major league grand slams: 2.

Year Team (League)	Pos.	G	AB	R	H	2B	3B	HR	RBI	Avg.	BB	SO	SB	PO	A	E	Avg.
1987— Helena (Pio.)	OF	3	5	0	2	0	0	0	1	.400	0	0	0	0	0	0	...
1988— Helena (Pio.)	OF	67	203	40	70	11	1	0	27	.345	30	32	10	64	4	3	.958
1989— Beloit (Midw.)	OF	42	115	7	21	4	0	0	8	.183	15	20	1	55	1	1	.982
— Helena (Pio.)	OF	•68	263	54	*89	16	3	11	*56	.338	28	43	9	92	6	3	.970
1990— Beloit (Midw.)	OF	118	436	73	130	29	1	6	62	.298	41	90	12	184	14	8	.961
— Stockton (Calif.)	OF	2	6	1	3	1	0	0	0	.500	2	1	0	3	0	1	.750

O

Year	Team (League)	Pos.	G	AB	R	H	2B	3B	HR	RBI	Avg.	BB	SO	SB	PO	A	E	Avg.
1991— Stockton (Calif.)		OF	126	418	63	110	20	4	5	46	.263	73	96	4	163	4	3	.982
1992— El Paso (Texas)..........		OF	*135	*506	*92	*169	27	8	5	79	*.334	59	87	28	*220	11	*11	.955
1993— New Orleans (A.A.)		OF-1B	111	388	65	106	32	1	7	59	.273	43	61	6	189	8	6	.970
—Milwaukee (A.L.)		OF	19	41	3	12	3	0	0	3	.293	5	9	0	32	1	0	1.000
1994— New Orleans (A.A.)		OF-DH-1B	63	225	44	74	18	5	8	43	.329	32	37	10	99	10	2	.982
—Milwaukee (A.L.)		OF-DH	27	66	9	18	1	1	2	7	.273	5	12	1	37	2	0	1.000
1995— Boston (A.L.)■..........		OF-DH	112	399	60	123	31	6	10	49	.308	29	64	5	196	6	5	.976
1996— Boston (A.L.)		OF	149	497	68	129	28	5	15	81	.260	47	80	3	227	8	7	.971
1997— Boston (A.L.)		OF-DH	146	499	65	154	32	4	15	80	.309	39	70	0	267	8	6	.979
1998— Boston (A.L.)		OF	156	611	95	165	36	8	23	83	.270	36	108	2	303	9	3	.990
1999— Boston (A.L.)		OF	157	596	84	167	36	4	28	103	.280	56	91	1	296	9	2	.993
2000— Boston (A.L.)		OF	138	513	68	134	30	4	13	70	.261	44	76	0	243	9	3	.988
—GC Red Sox (GCL)		DH	3	8	3	6	1	0	0	1	.750	3	1	0	...	...	...	...
Major League totals (8 years)			904	3222	452	902	197	32	106	476	.280	261	510	12	1601	52	26	.985

DIVISION SERIES RECORD

RECORDS: Shares single-game record for most home runs—2; grand slams—1; and runs batted in—7 (October 11, 1999). ... Shares single-inning record for most runs batted in—4 (October 11, 1999, third inning).

Year	Team (League)	Pos.	G	AB	R	H	2B	3B	HR	RBI	Avg.	BB	SO	SB	PO	A	E	Avg.
1998— Boston (A.L.)		OF	4	16	0	1	0	0	0	0	.063	1	4	0	8	0	0	1.000
1999— Boston (A.L.)		OF	5	20	4	4	0	0	2	7	.200	2	3	0	7	0	0	1.000
Division series totals (2 years)			9	36	4	5	0	0	2	7	.139	3	7	0	15	0	0	1.000

CHAMPIONSHIP SERIES RECORD

Year	Team (League)	Pos.	G	AB	R	H	2B	3B	HR	RBI	Avg.	BB	SO	SB	PO	A	E	Avg.
1999— Boston (A.L.)			5	20	2	7	3	0	0	1	.350	2	5	0	7	0	0	1.000

OLERUD, JOHN   1B   MARINERS

PERSONAL: Born August 5, 1968, in Seattle. ... 6-5/220. ... Bats left, throws left. ... Full name: John Garrett Olerud. ... Son of John E. Olerud, minor league catcher (1965-70); and cousin of Dale Sveum, infielder with seven major league teams (1986-99). ... Name pronounced OH-luh-rude.
HIGH SCHOOL: Interlake (Bellevue, Wash.).
COLLEGE: Washington State.
TRANSACTIONS/CAREER NOTES: Selected by New York Mets organization in 27th round of free-agent draft (June 2, 1986); did not sign. ... Selected by Toronto Blue Jays organization in third round of free-agent draft (June 5, 1989). ... Traded by Blue Jays with cash to Mets for P Robert Person (December 20, 1996). ... Granted free agency (October 27, 1997). ... Re-signed by Mets (November 24, 1997). ... Granted free agency (October 29, 1999). ... Signed by Seattle Mariners (December 15, 1999).
RECORDS: Shares A.L. single-season records for most intentional bases on balls received—33 (1993); and most intentional bases on balls received by lefthanded hitter—33 (1993). ... Shares N.L. single-season record for most consecutive times reached base safely—15 (September 16 [1], 18 [5], 20 [4], 22 [1], 1998; 6 singles, 1 double, 2 home runs, 6 bases on balls).
HONORS: Won A.L. Gold Glove as first baseman (2000).
STATISTICAL NOTES: Tied for A.L. lead with 10 sacrifice flies in 1991. ... Had 26-game hitting streak (May 26-June 22, 1993). ... Led A.L. with 33 intentional bases on balls received and .473 on-base percentage in 1993. ... Hit for the cycle (September 11, 1997). ... Had 23-game hitting streak (July 19-August 9, 1998). ... Career major league grand slams: 5.

Year	Team (League)	Pos.	G	AB	R	H	2B	3B	HR	RBI	Avg.	BB	SO	SB	PO	A	E	Avg.
1989— Toronto (A.L.)		1B-DH	6	8	2	3	0	0	0	0	.375	0	1	0	19	2	0	1.000
1990— Toronto (A.L.)		DH-1B	111	358	43	95	15	1	14	48	.265	57	75	0	133	10	2	.986
1991— Toronto (A.L.)		1B-DH	139	454	64	116	30	1	17	68	.256	68	84	0	1120	78	5	.996
1992— Toronto (A.L.)		1B-DH	138	458	68	130	28	0	16	66	.284	70	61	1	1057	81	7	.994
1993— Toronto (A.L.)		1B-DH	158	551	109	200	*54	2	24	107	*.363	114	65	0	1160	97	10	.992
1994— Toronto (A.L.)		1B-DH	108	384	47	114	29	2	12	67	.297	61	53	1	824	68	6	.993
1995— Toronto (A.L.)		1B	135	492	72	143	32	0	8	54	.291	84	54	0	1099	89	4	.997
1996— Toronto (A.L.)		1B-DH	125	398	59	109	25	0	18	61	.274	60	37	1	781	56	2	.998
1997— New York (N.L.)■		1B	154	524	90	154	34	1	22	102	.294	85	67	0	1292	120	7	.995
1998— New York (N.L.)		1B	160	557	91	197	36	4	22	93	.354	96	73	2	1258	116	5	.996
1999— New York (N.L.)		1B	•162	581	107	173	39	0	19	96	.298	125	66	3	1344	105	9	.994
2000— Seattle (A.L.)■		1B	159	565	84	161	45	0	14	103	.285	102	96	0	1271	*132	5	*.996
American League totals (9 years)			1079	3668	548	1071	258	6	123	574	.292	616	526	3	7464	613	41	.995
National League totals (3 years)			476	1662	288	524	109	5	63	291	.315	306	206	5	3894	341	21	.995
Major League totals (12 years)			1555	5330	836	1595	367	11	186	865	.299	922	732	8	11358	954	62	.995

DIVISION SERIES RECORD

Year	Team (League)	Pos.	G	AB	R	H	2B	3B	HR	RBI	Avg.	BB	SO	SB	PO	A	E	Avg.
1999— New York (N.L.)		1B	4	16	3	7	0	0	1	6	.438	3	2	0	31	4	0	1.000
2000— Seattle (A.L.)		1B	3	10	2	3	0	0	1	2	.300	2	1	0	25	0	0	1.000
Division series totals (2 years)			7	26	5	10	0	0	2	8	.385	5	3	0	56	4	0	1.000

CHAMPIONSHIP SERIES RECORD

Year	Team (League)	Pos.	G	AB	R	H	2B	3B	HR	RBI	Avg.	BB	SO	SB	PO	A	E	Avg.
1991— Toronto (A.L.)		1B	5	19	1	3	0	0	0	3	.158	3	1	0	40	3	0	1.000
1992— Toronto (A.L.)		1B	6	23	4	8	2	0	1	4	.348	2	5	0	51	1	0	1.000
1993— Toronto (A.L.)		1B	6	23	5	8	1	0	0	3	.348	4	1	0	48	9	1	.983
1999— New York (N.L.)		1B	6	27	4	8	0	0	2	6	.296	2	3	0	59	4	2	.969
2000— Seattle (A.L.)		1B	6	20	3	7	3	0	1	2	.350	2	2	1	45	7	0	1.000
Championship series totals (5 years)			29	112	17	34	6	0	4	18	.304	13	12	1	243	24	3	.989

O

NOTES: Member of World Series championship team (1992 and 1993).

Year Team (League)	Pos.	G	AB	R	H	2B	3B	HR	RBI	Avg.	BB	SO	SB	PO	A	E	Avg.
1992— Toronto (A.L.)...........	1B	4	13	2	4	0	0	0	0	.308	0	4	0	25	3	0	1.000
1993— Toronto (A.L.)...........	1B	5	17	5	4	1	0	1	2	.235	4	1	0	36	0	0	1.000
World Series totals (2 years)		9	30	7	8	1	0	1	2	.267	4	5	0	61	3	0	1.000

ALL-STAR GAME RECORD

Year League	Pos.	AB	R	H	2B	3B	HR	RBI	Avg.	BB	SO	SB	PO	A	E	Avg.
1993— American	1B	2	0	0	0	0	0	0	.000	0	0	0	4	0	0	1.000

OLIVARES, OMAR P ATHLETICS

PERSONAL: Born July 6, 1967, in Mayaguez, Puerto Rico. ... 6-1/205. ... Throws right, bats right. ... Full name: Omar Palqu Olivares. ... Son of Ed Olivares, outfielder with St. Louis Cardinals (1960-61).

HIGH SCHOOL: Hostos (Mayaguez, Puerto Rico).

JUNIOR COLLEGE: Miami Dade College (Fla.).

TRANSACTIONS/CAREER NOTES: Signed as non-drafted free agent by San Diego Padres organization (September 15, 1986). ... Traded by Padres to St. Louis Cardinals for OF Alex Cole and P Steve Peters (February 27, 1990). ... On St. Louis disabled list (May 27-June 13, 1992; and June 4-20, 1993). ... Granted free agency (April 7, 1995). ... Signed by Colorado Rockies (April 9, 1995). ... Claimed on waivers by Philadelphia Phillies (July 11, 1995). ... Granted free agency (October 16, 1995). ... Signed by Detroit Tigers (December 20, 1995). ... On Detroit disabled list (April 16-May 30, 1996); included rehabilitation assignment to Toledo (May 24-30). ... Traded by Tigers with P Felipe Lira to Seattle Mariners for P Scott Sanders, P Dean Crow and 3B Carlos Villalobos (July 18, 1997). ... Granted free agency (October 30, 1997). ... Signed by Anaheim Angels (December 11, 1997). ... Traded by Angels with 2B Randy Velarde to Oakland Athletics for P Elvin Nina, OF Jeff DaVanon and OF Nathan Hayes (July 29, 1999). ... Granted free agency (October 29, 1999). ... Re-signed by A's (January 8, 2000). ... On Oakland disabled list (June 17-August 12, 2000); included rehabilitation assignments to Modesto (July 28-August 7) and Sacramento (August 8-12).

RECORDS: Shares major league single-season record for fewest double plays by pitcher who led league in double plays—4 (1992). ... Shares A.L. single-game record for most hit batsmen (nine innings)—4 (June 13, 1999).

STATISTICAL NOTES: Tied for Texas League lead with 10 hit batsmen in 1989.

MISCELLANEOUS: Appeared in one game as pinch runner and singled and scored in three games as pinch hitter (1992). ... Appeared in one game as pinch runner and made an out in one game as pinch hitter (1993). ... Made an out in only appearance as pinch hitter with St. Louis (1994). ... Appeared in one game as pinch runner with Colorado (1995). ... Hit two-run home run in only appearance as pinch hitter with Philadelphia (1995). ... Appeared in three games as pinch hitter with Detroit (1997). ... Struck out in only appearance as pinch hitter and scored one run in two games as pinch runner (1998).

Year League	W	L	Pct.	ERA	G	GS	CG	ShO	Sv.	IP	H	R	ER	BB	SO
1987— Charleston, S.C. (S.Atl.)	4	14	.222	4.60	31	24	5	0	0	170 1/3	182	107	87	57	86
1988— Charleston, S.C. (S.Atl.)	13	6	.684	2.23	24	24	*10	3	0	185 1/3	166	63	46	43	94
— Riverside (Calif.)................	3	0	1.000	1.16	4	3	1	0	0	23 1/3	18	9	3	9	16
1989— Wichita (Texas)	12	11	.522	3.39	26	26	6	1	0	*185 2/3	175	87	70	61	79
1990— Louisville (A.A.)■..............	10	11	.476	2.82	23	23	5	2	0	159 1/3	127	58	50	59	88
— St. Louis (N.L.)...................	1	1	.500	2.92	9	6	0	0	0	49 1/3	45	17	16	17	20
1991— Louisville (A.A.)...............	1	2	.333	3.47	6	6	0	0	0	36 1/3	39	15	14	16	27
1992— St. Louis (N.L.)...............	9	9	.500	3.84	32	30	1	0	0	197	189	84	84	63	124
1993— St. Louis (N.L.)...............	5	3	.625	4.17	58	9	0	0	1	118 2/3	134	60	55	54	63
1994— Louisville (A.A.)...............	2	1	.667	4.37	9	9	0	0	0	47 1/3	47	24	23	16	38
— St. Louis (N.L.)...................	3	4	.429	5.74	14	12	1	0	1	73 2/3	84	53	47	37	26
1995— Colorado Springs (PCL)■..	0	1	.000	5.40	3	2	0	0	0	11 2/3	14	7	7	2	6
— Colorado (N.L.)	1	3	.250	7.39	11	6	0	0	0	31 2/3	44	28	26	21	15
— Philadelphia (N.L.)■	0	1	.000	5.40	5	0	0	0	0	10	11	6	6	2	7
— Scranton/W.B. (I.L.)	0	3	.000	4.87	7	7	0	0	0	44 1/3	49	25	24	20	28
1996— Detroit (A.L.)■.................	7	11	.389	4.89	25	25	4	0	0	160	169	90	87	75	81
— Toledo (I.L.)....................	1	0	1.000	8.44	1	1	0	0	0	5 1/3	4	5	5	3	5
1997— Detroit (A.L.)..................	5	6	.455	4.70	19	19	3	2	0	115	110	68	60	53	74
— Seattle (A.L.)...................	1	4	.200	5.49	13	12	0	0	0	62 1/3	81	41	38	28	29
1998— Anaheim (A.L.)■...............	9	9	.500	4.03	37	26	1	0	0	183	189	92	82	91	112
1999— Anaheim (A.L.)	8	9	.471	4.05	20	20	3	0	0	131	135	62	59	49	49
— Oakland (A.L.)■.................	7	2	.778	4.34	12	12	1	0	0	74 2/3	82	43	36	32	36
2000— Oakland (A.L.)	4	8	.333	6.75	21	16	1	0	0	108	134	86	81	60	57
— Modesto (Calif.)	0	0	...	1.50	2	2	0	0	0	6	3	1	1	1	3
— Sacramento (PCL)............	0	0	...	0.00	1	1	0	0	0	6	3	1	0	2	3
A.L. totals (5 years)	41	49	.456	4.78	147	130	13	2	0	834	900	482	443	388	438
N.L. totals (5 years)	19	21	.475	4.38	129	63	2	0	2	480 1/3	507	248	234	194	255
Major League totals (10 years)	60	70	.462	4.64	276	193	15	2	2	1314 1/3	1407	730	677	582	693

OLIVER, DARREN P RANGERS

PERSONAL: Born October 6, 1970, in Kansas City, Mo. ... 6-2/198. ... Throws left, bats right. ... Full name: Darren Christopher Oliver. ... Son of Bob Oliver, first baseman/outfielder with five major league teams (1965 and 1969-1975).

HIGH SCHOOL: Rio Linda (Calif.) Senior.

TRANSACTIONS/CAREER NOTES: Selected by Texas Rangers organization in third round of free-agent draft (June 1, 1988). ... On Gulf Coast Rangers disabled list (April 6-August 9, 1990). ... On disabled list (May 1, 1991-remainder of season). ... On Tulsa disabled list (July 1, 1992-remainder of season). ... On disabled list (June 27, 1995-remainder of season). ... On Texas disabled list (June 11-26, 1998); included rehabilitation assignment to Oklahoma City (June 21-26). ... Traded by Rangers with 3B Fernando Tatis and a player to be named later to St. Louis Cardinals for P Todd Stottlemyre and SS Royce Clayton (July 31, 1998); Cardinals acquired OF Mark Little to complete deal (August 9, 1998). ... Granted free agency (October 29, 1999). ... Signed by Rangers (January 27, 2000). ... On Texas disabled list (June 21-July 20 and August 1-September 1, 2000); included rehabilitation assignments to Oklahoma (July 5-20 and August 12-26) and Tulsa (August 27-31).

MISCELLANEOUS: Made an out in only appearance as pinch hitter with St. Louis (1998). ... Had one sacrifice hit and struck out once in five appearances as pinch hitter (1999).

Year League	W	L	Pct.	ERA	G	GS	CG	ShO	Sv.	IP	H	R	ER	BB	SO
1988— Gulf Coast Rangers (GCL)..	5	1	.833	2.15	12	9	0	0	0	54 1/3	39	16	13	18	59
1989— Gastonia (S.Atl.)................	8	7	.533	3.16	24	23	2	1	0	122 1/3	86	54	43	82	108
1990— Gulf Coast Rangers (GCL)..	0	0	...	0.00	3	3	0	0	0	6	1	1	0	1	7
— Gastonia (S.Atl.).................	0	0	...	13.50	1	1	0	0	0	2	1	3	3	4	2
1991— Charlotte (FSL).................	0	1	.000	4.50	2	2	0	0	0	8	6	4	4	3	12
1992— Charlotte (FSL).................	1	0	1.000	0.72	8	2	1	1	2	25	11	2	2	10	33
— Tulsa (Texas)	0	1	.000	3.14	3	3	0	0	0	14 1/3	15	9	5	4	14
1993— Tulsa (Texas)	7	5	.583	1.96	46	0	0	0	6	73 1/3	51	18	16	41	77
— Texas (A.L.)	0	0	...	2.70	2	0	0	0	0	3 1/3	2	1	1	1	4
1994— Texas (A.L.)	4	0	1.000	3.42	43	0	0	0	2	50	40	24	19	35	50
— Oklahoma City (A.A.).........	0	0	...	0.00	6	0	0	0	1	7 1/3	1	0	0	3	6
1995— Texas (A.L.)	4	2	.667	4.22	17	7	0	0	0	49	47	25	23	32	39
1996— Charlotte (FSL)	0	1	.000	3.00	2	1	0	0	0	12	8	4	4	3	9
— Texas (A.L.)	14	6	.700	4.66	30	30	1	1	0	173 2/3	190	97	90	76	112
1997— Texas (A.L.)	13	12	.520	4.20	32	32	3	1	0	201 1/3	213	111	94	82	104
1998— Texas (A.L.)	6	7	.462	6.53	19	19	2	0	0	103 1/3	140	84	75	43	58
— Oklahoma (PCL)................	0	0	...	0.00	1	1	0	0	0	5	2	0	0	1	1
— St. Louis (N.L.)■	4	4	.500	4.26	10	10	0	0	0	57	64	31	27	23	29
1999— St. Louis (N.L.)	9	9	.500	4.26	30	30	2	1	0	196 1/3	197	96	93	74	119
2000— Texas (A.L.)■...................	2	9	.182	7.42	21	21	0	0	0	108	151	95	89	42	49
— Oklahoma (PCL)................	2	1	.667	1.97	7	7	1	1	0	32	22	11	7	14	28
— Tulsa (Texas)	0	1	.000	11.57	1	1	0	0	0	4 2/3	10	7	6	2	5
A.L. totals (7 years)	43	36	.544	5.11	164	109	6	2	2	688 2/3	783	437	391	311	416
N.L. totals (2 years)	13	13	.500	4.26	40	40	2	1	0	253 1/3	261	127	120	97	148
Major League totals (8 years)	56	49	.533	4.88	204	149	8	3	2	942	1044	564	511	408	564

DIVISION SERIES RECORD

Year League	W	L	Pct.	ERA	G	GS	CG	ShO	Sv.	IP	H	R	ER	BB	SO
1996— Texas (A.L.)	0	1	.000	3.38	1	1	0	0	0	8	6	3	3	2	3

OLIVER, JOE   C   YANKEES

PERSONAL: Born July 24, 1965, in Memphis. ... 6-3/220. ... Bats right, throws right. ... Full name: Joseph Melton Oliver.
HIGH SCHOOL: Boone (Orlando).
TRANSACTIONS/CAREER NOTES: Selected by Cincinnati Reds organization in second round of free-agent draft (June 6, 1983); pick received as compensation for New York Yankees signing Type A free-agent P Bob Shirley. ... On disabled list (April 23-May 6, 1986; and April 12, 1994-remainder of season). ... Released by Reds (November 3, 1994). ... Signed by Milwaukee Brewers organization (March 24, 1995). ... On Milwaukee disabled list (July 14-August 15, 1995); included rehabilitation assignment to New Orleans (August 10-15). ... Granted free agency (October 31, 1995). ... Signed by Reds (February 26, 1996). ... Granted free agency (November 18, 1996). ... Re-signed by Reds organization (February 8, 1997). ... Granted free agency (October 30, 1997). ... Signed by Detroit Tigers organization (December 22, 1997). ... Released by Tigers (July 16, 1998). ... Signed by Seattle Mariners (July 24, 1998). ... Granted free agency (October 27, 1998). ... Signed by Tampa Bay Devil Rays organization (February 3, 1999). ... On Durham disabled list (June 13-24, 1999). ... Traded by Devil Rays with C Humberto Cota to Pittsburgh Pirates for OF Jose Guillen and P Jeff Sparks (July 23, 1999). ... Granted free agency (November 5, 1999). ... Signed by Mariners organization (January 19, 2000). ... Granted free agency (November 4, 2000). ... Signed by New York Yankees (November 21, 2000).
STATISTICAL NOTES: Led Pioneer League catchers with .989 fielding percentage, 425 putouts, 38 assists and 468 total chances in 1983. ... Led Midwest League catchers with 855 total chances and 30 passed balls in 1984. ... Led Florida State League catchers with 84 assists and 33 passed balls in 1985. ... Led American Association catchers with 13 errors in 1989. ... Tied for N.L. lead with 16 passed balls in 1990. ... Led N.L. catchers with 925 putouts and 997 total chances in 1992. ... Career major league grand slams: 5.

Year Team (League)	Pos.	G	AB	R	H	2B	3B	HR	RBI	Avg.	BB	SO	SB	PO	A	E	Avg.
1983— Billings (Pio.)	C-1B	56	186	21	40	4	0	4	28	.215	15	47	1	†426	†39	5	†.989
1984— Cedar Rapids (Midw.) ..	C	102	335	34	73	11	0	3	29	.218	17	83	2	*757	85	13	.985
1985— Tampa (FSL).............	C-1B	112	386	38	104	23	2	7	62	.269	32	75	1	615	†94	16	.978
1986— Vermont (East.).........	C	84	282	32	78	18	1	6	41	.277	21	47	2	383	62	14	.969
1987— Vermont (East.).........	C-1B	66	236	31	72	13	2	10	60	.305	17	30	0	247	35	10	.966
1988— Nashville (A.A.)	C	73	220	19	45	7	2	4	24	.205	18	39	0	413	37	7	.985
— Chattanooga (Sou.)....	C	28	105	9	26	6	0	3	12	.248	5	19	0	176	15	0	1.000
1989— Nashville (A.A.)	C-1B	71	233	22	68	13	0	6	31	.292	13	35	0	388	37	†13	.970
— Cincinnati (N.L.)	C	49	151	13	41	8	0	3	23	.272	6	28	0	260	21	4	.986
1990— Cincinnati (N.L.)	C	121	364	34	84	23	0	8	52	.231	37	75	1	686	59	6	*.992
1991— Cincinnati (N.L.)	C	94	269	21	58	11	0	11	41	.216	18	53	0	496	40	11	.980
1992— Cincinnati (N.L.)	C-1B	143	485	42	131	25	1	10	57	.270	35	75	2	†926	64	8	.992
1993— Cincinnati (N.L.)	C-1B-OF	139	482	40	115	28	0	14	75	.239	27	91	0	825	70	7	.992
1994— Cincinnati (N.L.)	C	6	19	1	4	0	0	1	5	.211	2	3	0	48	2	1	.980
1995— Milwaukee (A.L.)■	C-DH-1B	97	337	43	92	20	0	12	51	.273	27	66	2	414	40	8	.983
— New Orleans (A.A.).....	C-DH	4	13	0	1	1	0	0	0	.077	0	3	0	14	7	0	1.000
1996— Cincinnati (N.L.)■......	C-1B-OF	106	289	31	70	12	1	11	46	.242	28	54	2	583	45	5	.992
1997— Indianapolis (A.A.)	C	2	9	1	3	0	0	1	1	.333	0	1	0	21	4	0	1.000
— Cincinnati (N.L.)	C-1B	111	349	28	90	13	0	14	43	.258	25	58	1	681	55	7	.991
1998— Detroit (A.L.)■	C-1B-DH	50	155	8	35	8	0	4	22	.226	7	33	0	261	17	5	.982
— Seattle (A.L.)■..........	C	29	85	12	19	3	0	2	10	.224	10	15	1	174	9	3	.984
1999— Durham (I.L.)■	C-DH-3B	57	219	27	66	18	1	7	43	.301	7	50	1	399	27	7	.984
— Pittsburgh (N.L.)■	C	45	134	10	27	8	0	1	13	.201	10	33	2	285	12	2	.993
2000— Seattle (A.L.)■..........	C-DH-1B	69	200	33	53	13	1	10	35	.265	14	38	2	359	18	2	.995
— Tacoma (PCL)	C	18	61	2	12	2	0	0	8	.197	5	12	0	118	12	1	.992
American League totals (3 years)		245	777	96	199	44	1	28	118	.256	58	152	5	1208	84	18	.986
National League totals (9 years)		814	2542	220	620	128	2	73	355	.244	188	470	8	4790	368	51	.990
Major League totals (12 years)		1059	3319	316	819	172	3	101	473	.247	246	622	13	5998	452	69	.989

DIVISION SERIES RECORD

						BATTING									FIELDING		
Year	Team (League)	Pos.	G	AB	R	H	2B	3B	HR	RBI	Avg.	BB	SO	SB	PO	A	E	Avg.
2000—Seattle (A.L.)		C	3	4	4	4	0	0	1	1	1.000	0	1	0	12	0	0	1.000

CHAMPIONSHIP SERIES RECORD

						BATTING									FIELDING		
Year	Team (League)	Pos.	G	AB	R	H	2B	3B	HR	RBI	Avg.	BB	SO	SB	PO	A	E	Avg.
1990—Cincinnati (N.L.)		C	5	14	1	2	0	0	0	0	.143	0	2	0	27	1	0	1.000
2000—Seattle (A.L.)		C	4	6	0	1	0	0	0	0	.167	1	1	0	22	1	0	1.000
Championship series totals (2 years)			9	20	1	3	0	0	0	0	.150	1	3	0	49	2	0	1.000

WORLD SERIES RECORD

NOTES: Member of World Series championship team (1990).

						BATTING									FIELDING		
Year	Team (League)	Pos.	G	AB	R	H	2B	3B	HR	RBI	Avg.	BB	SO	SB	PO	A	E	Avg.
1990—Cincinnati (N.L.)		C	4	18	2	6	3	0	0	2	.333	0	1	0	27	1	3	.903

OLSON, GREGG   P   DODGERS

PERSONAL: Born October 11, 1966, in Scribner, Neb. ... 6-4/208. ... Throws right, bats right. ... Full name: Gregg William Olson.

HIGH SCHOOL: Northwest (Omaha, Neb.).

COLLEGE: Auburn.

TRANSACTIONS/CAREER NOTES: Selected by Baltimore Orioles organization in first round (fourth pick overall) of free-agent draft (June 1, 1988). ... On disabled list (August 9-September 20, 1993). ... Granted free agency (December 20, 1993). ... Signed by Atlanta Braves (February 8, 1994). ... On Atlanta disabled list (March 26-May 30, 1994); included rehabilitation assignment to Richmond (May 14-30). ... Granted free agency (December 23, 1994). ... Signed by Cleveland Indians organization (March 24, 1995). ... On Buffalo disabled list (April 6-14, 1995). ... Contract sold by Buffalo to Kansas City Royals (July 24, 1995). ... Granted free agency (November 1, 1995). ... Signed by St. Louis Cardinals organization (January 23, 1996). ... Released by Cardinals (March 26, 1996). ... Signed by Cincinnati Reds organization (March 26, 1996). ... Traded by Reds to Detroit Tigers for IF Yuri Sanchez (April 26, 1996). ... Traded by Tigers to Houston Astros for two players to be named later (August 26, 1996); Tigers acquired P Kevin Gallaher and IF Pedro Santana to complete deal (August 27, 1996). ... Granted free agency (October 28, 1996). ... Signed by Minnesota Twins organization (December 20, 1996). ... Released by Twins (May 16, 1997). ... Signed by Royals organization (May 25, 1997). ... Granted free agency (October 28, 1997). ... Signed by Arizona Diamondbacks organization (January 31, 1998). ... On disabled list (June 23-July 8, 1999). ... Granted free agency (October 29, 1999). ... Signed by Los Angeles Dodgers (January 10, 2000). ... On Los Angeles disabled list (April 9-July 28, 2000); included rehabilitation assignment to San Bernardino (May 5-6 and June 30-July 13) and Albuquerque (July 13-27).

HONORS: Named righthanded pitcher on THE SPORTING NEWS college All-America team (1988). ... Named A.L. Rookie of the Year by Baseball Writers' Association of America (1989).

STATISTICAL NOTES: Pitched one inning, combining with starter Bob Milacki (six innings), Mike Flanagan (one inning) and Mark Williamson (one inning) in 2-0 no-hit victory against Oakland (July 13, 1991).

MISCELLANEOUS: Holds Baltimore Orioles all-time record for most saves (160). ... Holds Arizona Diamondbacks all-time records for most games pitched (125) and most saves (44). ... Struck out in only plate appearance (1993).

Year	League	W	L	Pct.	ERA	G	GS	CG	ShO	Sv.	IP	H	R	ER	BB	SO
1988—Hagerstown (Caro.)		1	0	1.000	2.00	8	0	0	0	4	9	5	2	2	2	9
—Charlotte (Sou.)		0	1	.000	5.87	8	0	0	0	1	$15\,^1/_3$	24	13	10	6	22
—Baltimore (A.L.)		1	1	.500	3.27	10	0	0	0	0	11	10	4	4	10	9
1989—Baltimore (A.L.)		5	2	.714	1.69	64	0	0	0	27	85	57	17	16	46	90
1990—Baltimore (A.L.)		6	5	.545	2.42	64	0	0	0	37	$74\,^1/_3$	57	20	20	31	74
1991—Baltimore (A.L.)		4	6	.400	3.18	72	0	0	0	31	$73\,^2/_3$	74	28	26	29	72
1992—Baltimore (A.L.)		1	5	.167	2.05	60	0	0	0	36	$61\,^1/_3$	46	14	14	24	58
1993—Baltimore (A.L.)		0	2	.000	1.60	50	0	0	0	29	45	37	9	8	18	44
1994—Richmond (I.L.)■		0	0	...	1.59	8	2	0	0	2	$11\,^1/_3$	8	3	2	8	13
—Atlanta (N.L.)		0	2	.000	9.20	16	0	0	0	1	$14\,^2/_3$	19	15	15	13	10
1995—Buffalo (A.A.)■		1	0	1.000	2.49	18	0	0	0	13	$21\,^2/_3$	16	6	6	9	25
—Cleveland (A.L.)		0	0	...	13.50	3	0	0	0	0	$2\,^2/_3$	5	4	4	2	0
—Omaha (A.A.)		0	0	...	0.00	1	0	0	0	0	1	0	0	0	1	1
—Kansas City (A.L.)		3	3	.500	3.26	20	0	0	0	3	$30\,^1/_3$	23	11	11	17	21
1996—Indianapolis (A.A.)■		0	0	...	4.26	7	0	0	0	4	$6\,^1/_3$	6	4	3	6	4
—Detroit (A.L.)■		3	0	1.000	5.02	43	0	0	0	8	43	43	25	24	28	29
—Houston (N.L.)■		1	0	1.000	4.82	9	0	0	0	0	$9\,^1/_3$	12	5	5	7	8
1997—Minnesota (A.L.)■		0	0	...	18.36	11	0	0	0	0	$8\,^1/_3$	19	17	17	11	6
—Omaha (A.A.)■		3	1	.750	3.31	9	5	0	0	0	$35\,^1/_3$	30	13	13	10	20
—Kansas City (A.L.)		4	3	.571	3.02	34	0	0	0	1	$41\,^2/_3$	39	18	14	17	28
1998—Arizona (N.L.)		3	4	.429	3.01	64	0	0	0	30	$68\,^2/_3$	56	25	23	25	55
1999—Arizona (N.L.)		9	4	.692	3.71	61	0	0	0	14	$60\,^2/_3$	54	28	25	25	45
2000—Los Angeles (N.L.)■		0	1	.000	5.09	13	0	0	0	0	$17\,^2/_3$	21	11	10	7	15
—San Bernardino (Calif.)		0	0	...	4.05	6	4	0	0	0	$6\,^2/_3$	8	4	3	4	8
—Albuquerque (PCL)		0	0	...	4.50	4	0	0	0	0	4	3	2	2	2	2
A.L. totals (9 years)		27	27	.500	2.99	431	0	0	0	172	$476\,^1/_3$	410	167	158	233	431
N.L. totals (5 years)		13	11	.542	4.11	163	0	0	0	45	171	162	84	78	77	133
Major League totals (13 years)		40	38	.513	3.28	594	0	0	0	217	$647\,^1/_3$	572	251	236	310	564

DIVISION SERIES RECORD

Year	League	W	L	Pct.	ERA	G	GS	CG	ShO	Sv.	IP	H	R	ER	BB	SO
1999—Arizona (N.L.)		0	0	...	0.00	2	0	0	0	0	$^1/_3$	0	1	0	1	0

ALL-STAR GAME RECORD

Year	League	W	L	Pct.	ERA	GS	CG	ShO	Sv.	IP	H	R	ER	BB	SO
1990—American							Did not play.								

PERSONAL: Born February 25, 1963, in Columbus, Ohio. ... 6-4/215. ... Bats left, throws left. ... Full name: Paul Andrew O'Neill. ... Son of Charles O'Neill, minor league pitcher (1945-48).

HIGH SCHOOL: Brookhaven (Columbus, Ohio).

COLLEGE: Otterbein College (Ohio).

TRANSACTIONS/CAREER NOTES: Selected by Cincinnati Reds organization in fourth round of free-agent draft (June 8, 1981). ... On Denver disabled list (May 10-July 16, 1986). ... On Cincinnati disabled list (July 21-September 1, 1989); included rehabilitation assignment to Nashville (August 27-September 1). ... Traded by Reds with 1B Joe DeBerry to New York Yankees for OF Roberto Kelly (November 3, 1992). ... On disabled list (May 7-23, 1995). ... On suspended list (September 6-8, 1996). ... Granted free agency (November 10, 2000). ... Re-signed by Yankees (November 16, 2000).

STATISTICAL NOTES: Led American Association outfielders with 19 assists and eight double plays in 1985. ... Hit three home runs in one game (August 31, 1995). ... Had 17-game hitting streak (May 24-June 10, 1998). ... Tied for A.L. lead in grounding into double plays with 22 in 1998. ... Led A.L. outfielders with six double plays in 1998. ... Career major league grand slams: 4.

Year Team (League)	Pos.	G	AB	R	H	2B	3B	HR	RBI	Avg.	BB	SO	SB	PO	A	E	Avg.
1981— Billings (Pio.)	OF	66	241	37	76	7	2	3	29	.315	21	35	6	87	4	5	.948
1982— Cedar Rapids (Midw.)	OF	116	386	50	105	19	2	8	71	.272	21	79	12	137	7	8	.947
1983— Tampa (FSL)	OF-1B	121	413	62	115	23	7	8	51	.278	56	70	20	218	14	10	.959
— Waterbury (East.)	OF	14	43	6	12	0	0	0	6	.279	6	8	2	26	0	0	1.000
1984— Vermont (East.)	OF	134	475	70	126	31	5	16	76	.265	52	72	29	246	5	7	.973
1985— Denver (A.A.)	OF-1B	*137	*509	63	*155	*32	3	7	74	.305	28	73	5	248	†20	7	.975
— Cincinnati (N.L.)	OF	5	12	1	4	1	0	0	1	.333	0	2	0	3	1	0	1.000
1986— Cincinnati (N.L.)	PH	3	2	0	0	0	0	0	0	.000	1	1	0	...	...	...	...
— Denver (A.A.)	OF	55	193	20	49	9	2	5	27	.254	9	28	1	98	7	4	.963
1987— Cincinnati (N.L.)	OF-1B-P	84	160	24	41	14	1	7	28	.256	18	29	2	90	2	4	.958
— Nashville (A.A.)	OF	11	37	12	11	0	0	3	6	.297	5	5	1	19	1	0	1.000
1988— Cincinnati (N.L.)	OF-1B	145	485	58	122	25	3	16	73	.252	38	65	8	410	13	6	.986
1989— Cincinnati (N.L.)	OF	117	428	49	118	24	2	15	74	.276	46	64	20	223	7	4	.983
— Nashville (A.A.)	OF	4	12	1	4	0	0	0	0	.333	3	1	1	7	1	0	1.000
1990— Cincinnati (N.L.)	OF	145	503	59	136	28	0	16	78	.270	53	103	13	271	12	2	.993
1991— Cincinnati (N.L.)	OF	152	532	71	136	36	0	28	91	.256	73	107	12	301	13	2	.994
1992— Cincinnati (N.L.)	OF	148	496	59	122	19	1	14	66	.246	77	85	6	291	12	1	*.997
1993— New York (A.L.)■	OF-DH	141	498	71	155	34	1	20	75	.311	44	69	2	230	7	2	.992
1994— New York (A.L.)	OF-DH	103	368	68	132	25	1	21	83	*.359	72	56	5	203	7	1	.995
1995— New York (A.L.)	OF-DH	127	460	82	138	30	4	22	96	.300	71	76	1	220	3	3	.987
1996— New York (A.L.)	OF-DH-1B	150	546	89	165	35	1	19	91	.302	102	76	0	293	7	0	•1.000
1997— New York (A.L.)	OF-DH-1B	149	553	89	179	42	0	21	117	.324	75	92	10	293	7	5	.984
1998— New York (A.L.)	OF-DH	152	602	95	191	40	2	24	116	.317	57	103	15	293	11	4	.987
1999— New York (A.L.)	OF	153	597	70	170	39	4	19	110	.285	66	89	11	291	10	8	.974
2000— New York (A.L.)	OF-DH	142	566	79	160	26	0	18	100	.283	51	90	14	293	5	2	.993
American League totals (8 years)		1117	4190	643	1290	271	13	164	788	.308	538	651	58	2116	57	25	.989
National League totals (8 years)		799	2618	321	679	147	7	96	411	.259	306	456	61	1589	60	19	.989
Major League totals (16 years)		1916	6808	964	1969	418	20	260	1199	.289	844	1107	119	3705	117	44	.989

DIVISION SERIES RECORD

Year Team (League)	Pos.	G	AB	R	H	2B	3B	HR	RBI	Avg.	BB	SO	SB	PO	A	E	Avg.
1995— New York (A.L.)	OF-PH	5	18	5	6	0	0	3	6	.333	5	5	0	13	0	0	1.000
1996— New York (A.L.)	OF	4	15	0	2	0	0	0	0	.133	0	2	0	13	0	0	1.000
1997— New York (A.L.)	OF	5	19	5	8	2	0	2	7	.421	3	0	0	9	0	0	1.000
1998— New York (A.L.)	OF	3	11	1	4	2	0	1	1	.364	1	1	0	2	0	0	1.000
1999— New York (A.L.)	OF	2	8	2	2	0	0	0	0	.250	1	1	0	4	0	0	1.000
2000— New York (A.L.)	OF	5	19	4	4	1	0	0	0	.211	2	4	0	8	1	0	1.000
Division series totals (6 years)		24	90	17	26	5	0	6	14	.289	12	13	0	49	1	0	1.000

CHAMPIONSHIP SERIES RECORD

Year Team (League)	Pos.	G	AB	R	H	2B	3B	HR	RBI	Avg.	BB	SO	SB	PO	A	E	Avg.
1990— Cincinnati (N.L.)	OF	5	17	1	8	3	0	1	4	.471	1	1	1	9	2	0	1.000
1996— New York (A.L.)	OF	4	11	1	3	0	0	1	2	.273	3	2	0	9	1	0	1.000
1998— New York (A.L.)	OF	6	25	6	7	2	0	1	3	.280	3	4	2	10	0	0	1.000
1999— New York (A.L.)	OF	5	21	2	6	0	0	0	1	.286	1	5	0	18	0	0	1.000
2000— New York (A.L.)	OF	6	20	0	5	0	0	0	5	.250	1	2	0	8	0	0	1.000
Championship series totals (5 years)		26	94	10	29	5	0	3	15	.309	9	14	3	54	3	0	1.000

WORLD SERIES RECORD

NOTES: Member of World Series championship team (1990, 1996, 1998, 1999 and 2000).

Year Team (League)	Pos.	G	AB	R	H	2B	3B	HR	RBI	Avg.	BB	SO	SB	PO	A	E	Avg.
1990— Cincinnati (N.L.)	OF	4	12	2	1	0	0	0	1	.083	5	2	1	11	0	0	1.000
1996— New York (A.L.)	OF-PH	5	12	1	2	2	0	0	0	.167	3	2	0	12	0	0	1.000
1998— New York (A.L.)	OF	4	19	3	4	1	0	0	0	.211	1	2	0	8	0	1	.889
1999— New York (A.L.)	OF	4	15	0	3	0	0	0	4	.200	2	2	0	8	0	0	1.000
2000— New York (A.L.)	OF	5	19	2	9	2	2	0	2	.474	3	4	0	10	0	0	1.000
World Series totals (5 years)		22	77	8	19	5	2	0	7	.247	14	12	1	49	0	1	.980

ALL-STAR GAME RECORD

Year League	Pos.	AB	R	H	2B	3B	HR	RBI	Avg.	BB	SO	SB	PO	A	E	Avg.
						BATTING							FIELDING			
1991—National	OF	2	0	0	0	0	0	0	.000	0	1	0	0	0	0	...
1994—American	PH	1	0	0	0	0	0	0	.000	0	0	0	...	...	...	...
1995—American	OF	1	0	0	0	0	0	0	.000	0	0	0	0	0	0	...
1997—American	OF	2	0	0	0	0	0	0	.000	0	1	0	1	0	0	1.000
1998—American	OF	2	0	0	0	0	0	0	.000	0	0	0	0	1	0	1.000
All-Star Game totals (5 years)		8	0	0	0	0	0	0	.000	0	2	0	1	1	0	1.000

RECORD AS PITCHER

Year League	W	L	Pct.	ERA	G	GS	CG	ShO	Sv.	IP	H	R	ER	BB	SO
1987—Cincinnati (N.L.)	0	0	...	13.50	1	0	0	0	0	2	2	3	3	4	2

ONTIVEROS, STEVE   P   METS

PERSONAL: Born March 5, 1961, in Tularosa, N.M. ... 6-0/190. ... Throws right, bats right. ... Full name: Steven Ontiveros. ... Name pronounced AHN-tih-VAIR-oss.

HIGH SCHOOL: St. Joseph (South Bend, Ind.).

COLLEGE: Michigan.

TRANSACTIONS/CAREER NOTES: Selected by Oakland Athletics organization in second round of free-agent draft (June 7, 1982). ... On West Haven temporarily inactive list (July 27-August 6, 1982). ... On disabled list (April 16-August 8, 1984). ... On Tacoma disabled list (April 16-28, 1985). ... On disabled list (July 24-September 14, 1986). ... On Oakland disabled list (March 30-April 24, 1987); included rehabilitation assignment to Tacoma (April 21-24). ... On disabled list (June 12-August 2 and August 3, 1988-remainder of season). ... Released by A's (December 21, 1988). ... Signed by Philadelphia Phillies organization (February 16, 1989). ... On Philadelphia disabled list (April 20-June 6, 1989); included rehabilitation assignment to Scranton/Wilkes-Barre (May 14-22). ... On Philadelphia disabled list (June 21, 1989-remainder of season); included rehabilitation assignment to Scranton/Wilkes-Barre (June 28). ... On Philadelphia disabled list (March 30-September 8, 1990); included rehabilitation assignments to Clearwater (August 2-16) and Reading (August 17-19 and August 27-September 2). ... On Philadelphia disabled list (March 29, 1991-entire season); included rehabilitation assignments to Scranton/Wilkes-Barre (April 28-May 15 and August 22-September 2). ... Granted free agency (November 11, 1991). ... Signed by Detroit Tigers organization (February 28, 1992). ... On Toledo disabled list (April 9-16, 1992). ... Released by Tigers (April 16, 1992). ... Signed by Minnesota Twins organization (April 5, 1993). ... Traded by Twins to Seattle Mariners for OF Greg Shockey (August 10, 1993). ... Granted free agency (October 8, 1993). ... Signed by A's (January 31, 1994). ... Granted free agency (October 24, 1994). ... Re-signed by A's (April 11, 1995). ... On disabled list (July 16-August 24, 1995). ... Granted free agency (November 1, 1995). ... Signed by California Angels (January 26, 1996). ... On California disabled list (March 25, 1996-entire season); included rehabilitation assignment to Lake Elsinore (May 31-June 8). ... Granted free agency (October 10, 1996). ... Signed by Anaheim Angels organization (January 20, 1997). ... On disabled list (March 25, 1997-entire season). ... Released by Angels (October 6, 1997). ... Signed by St. Louis Cardinals organization (February 15, 1998). ... Released by Cardinals (April 23, 1998). ... Signed by Baltimore Orioles organization (May 1, 1998). ... Released by Orioles organization (July 25, 1998). ... Signed by Tampa Bay Devil Rays organization (January 20, 1999). ... Released by Devil Rays (March 31, 1999). ... Signed by Milwaukee Brewers organization (May 24, 1999). ... On Louisville disabled list (July 1-24, 1999). ... On voluntary retired list (July 24, 1999-July 7, 2000). ... Signed by Colorado Rockies organiation (July 7, 2000). ... Released by Rockies (September 9, 2000). ... Signed by Boston Red Sox (September 10, 2000). ... Granted free agency (November 1, 2000). ... Signed by New York Mets organization (January 5, 2001).

STATISTICAL NOTES: Pitched 3-0 one-hit, complete-game victory against New York (May 27, 1995).

MISCELLANEOUS: Appeared in one game as pinch runner (1986). ... Appeared in two games as pinch runner (1988).

Year League	W	L	Pct.	ERA	G	GS	CG	ShO	Sv.	IP	H	R	ER	BB	SO
1982—Medford (N'West)	1	0	1.000	0.00	4	0	0	0	0	8	3	0	0	4	9
—West Haven (East.)	2	2	.500	6.33	16	2	0	0	0	27	34	26	19	12	28
1983—Albany/Colonie (East.)	8	4	.667	3.75	32	13	5	0	5	129 2/3	131	62	54	36	91
1984—Madison (Midw.)	3	1	.750	2.05	5	5	2	0	0	30 2/3	23	10	7	6	26
—Tacoma (PCL)	1	1	.500	7.94	2	2	0	0	0	11 1/3	18	11	10	5	6
1985—Tacoma (PCL)	3	0	1.000	2.94	15	0	0	0	2	33 2/3	26	13	11	21	30
—Oakland (A.L.)	1	3	.250	1.93	39	0	0	0	8	74 2/3	45	17	16	19	36
1986—Oakland (A.L.)	2	2	.500	4.71	46	0	0	0	10	72 2/3	72	40	38	25	54
1987—Tacoma (PCL)	0	0	...	3.00	1	1	0	0	0	3	1	1	1	2	1
—Oakland (A.L.)	10	8	.556	4.00	35	22	2	1	1	150 2/3	141	78	67	50	97
1988—Oakland (A.L.)	3	4	.429	4.61	10	10	0	0	0	54 2/3	57	32	28	21	30
1989—Philadelphia (N.L.)■	2	1	.667	3.82	6	5	0	0	0	30 2/3	34	15	13	15	12
—Scranton/W.B. (I.L.)	0	0	...	0.00	1	1	0	0	0	3 1/3	3	0	0	3	0
1990—Clearwater (FSL)	0	0	...	2.35	3	3	0	0	0	7 2/3	4	2	2	3	2
—Reading (East.)	0	2	.000	9.00	2	2	0	0	0	6	7	6	6	2	8
—Philadelphia (N.L.)	0	0	...	2.70	5	0	0	0	0	10	9	3	3	3	6
1991—Scranton/W.B. (I.L.)	2	1	.667	2.90	7	7	0	0	0	31	29	11	10	10	21
1992—							Did not play.								
1993—Portland (PCL)■	7	6	.538	2.87	20	16	2	0	0	103 1/3	90	40	33	20	73
—Seattle (A.L.)■	0	2	.000	1.00	14	0	0	0	0	18	18	3	2	6	13
1994—Oakland (A.L.)■	6	4	.600	*2.65	27	13	2	0	0	115 1/3	93	39	34	26	56
1995—Oakland (A.L.)	9	6	.600	4.37	22	22	2	1	0	129 2/3	144	75	63	38	77
1996—Lake Elsinore (Calif.)	1	1	.500	2.25	2	2	0	0	0	8	12	3	2	0	8
1997—Lake Elsinore (Calif.)	0	1	.000	27.00	1	1	0	0	0	1/3	0	1	1	1	0
1998—Memphis (PCL)■	0	1	.000	8.38	3	3	0	0	0	9 2/3	14	11	9	2	10
—Rochester (I.L.)■	5	1	.833	3.68	16	14	0	0	1	80 2/3	77	35	33	25	64
1999—Louisville (I.L.)■	5	1	.833	4.44	8	8	0	0	0	48 2/3	47	26	24	12	33
2000—Colorado Springs (PCL)■..	4	1	.800	2.91	8	8	0	0	0	43 1/3	36	15	14	10	33
—Boston (A.L.)■	1	1	.500	10.13	3	1	0	0	0	5 1/3	9	6	6	4	1
A.L. totals (8 years)	32	30	.516	3.68	196	68	6	2	19	621	579	290	254	189	364
N.L. totals (2 years)	2	1	.667	3.54	11	5	0	0	0	40 2/3	43	18	16	18	18
Major League totals (10 years)	34	31	.523	3.67	207	73	6	2	19	661 2/3	622	308	270	207	382

ALL-STAR GAME RECORD

Year League	W	L	Pct.	ERA	GS	CG	ShO	Sv.	IP	H	R	ER	BB	SO
1995—American	0	1	.000	13.50	0	0	0	0	2/3	1	1	1	0	1

ORDAZ, LUIS SS ROYALS

PERSONAL: Born August 12, 1975, in Maracaibo, Venezuela. ... 5-11/170. ... Bats right, throws right. ... Full name: Luis Javier Ordaz.
HIGH SCHOOL: Santa Maria Gorette (Maracaibo, Venezuela).
TRANSACTIONS/CAREER NOTES: Signed as non-drafted free agent by Cincinnati Reds organization (January 27, 1993). ... Traded by Reds to St. Louis Cardinals as part of three-team deal in which Reds sent P Mike Remlinger to Kansas City Royals, Cardinals sent OF Andre King to Reds and Royals sent OF Miguel Mejia to Cardinals (December 4, 1995). ... On Memphis disabled list (April 7-16, 1998). ... Traded by Cardinals to Arizona Diamondbacks for OF Dante Powell (December 15, 1999). ... Claimed on waivers by Kansas City Royals (April 5, 2000).
STATISTICAL NOTES: Led Appalachian League shortstops with 277 total chances and 24 errors and tied for lead with 173 assists in 1994. ... Led Texas League in grounding into double plays with 19 in 1997.

										BATTING				FIELDING		
Year	Team (League)	Pos.	G	AB	R	H	2B	3B	HR	RBI	Avg.	BB	SO	SB	PO	A	E	Avg.
1993—Princeton (Appl.)		3B-SS-2B	57	217	28	65	9	7	2	39	.300	7	32	3	58	117	13	.931
1994—Char., W.Va. (SAL)		SS	9	31	3	7	0	0	0	0	.226	1	4	1	16	18	7	.829
—Princeton (Appl.)		SS-2B	60	211	33	52	12	3	0	12	.246	10	27	7	81	‡173	†24	.914
1995—Char., W.Va. (SAL)		SS	112	359	43	83	14	7	2	42	.231	13	47	12	164	290	22	.954
1996—St. Peters. (FSL)■		SS	126	423	46	115	13	3	3	49	.272	30	53	10	228	317	21	.963
1997—Arkansas (Texas)		SS-DH	115	390	44	112	20	6	4	58	.287	22	39	11	149	327	33	.935
—St. Louis (N.L.)		SS	12	22	3	6	1	0	0	1	.273	1	2	3	9	17	1	.963
1998—Memphis (PCL)		SS-2B	59	214	29	62	9	2	6	35	.290	16	20	3	104	174	14	.952
—St. Louis (N.L.)		SS-3B-2B	57	153	9	31	5	0	0	8	.203	12	18	2	70	157	13	.946
1999—St. Louis (N.L.)		SS-2B-3B	10	9	3	1	0	0	0	2	.111	1	2	1	4	8	3	.800
—Memphis (PCL)		SS	107	362	31	103	25	4	1	45	.285	24	40	3	150	346	23	.956
2000—Kansas City (A.L.)■		SS-2B	65	104	17	23	2	0	0	11	.221	5	10	4	64	65	1	.992
American League totals (1 year)			65	104	17	23	2	0	0	11	.221	5	10	4	64	65	1	.992
National League totals (3 years)			79	184	15	38	6	0	0	11	.207	14	22	6	83	182	17	.940
Major League totals (4 years)			144	288	32	61	8	0	0	22	.212	19	32	10	147	247	18	.956

ORDONEZ, MAGGLIO OF WHITE SOX

PERSONAL: Born January 28, 1974, in Caracas, Venezuela. ... 6-0/200. ... Bats right, throws right.
TRANSACTIONS/CAREER NOTES: Signed as non-drafted free agent by Chicago White Sox organization (May 18, 1991). ... On suspended list (May 1-6, 2000).
HONORS: Named American Association Most Valuable Player (1997). ... Named outfielder on THE SPORTING NEWS A.L. All-Star team (2000). ... Named outfielder on THE SPORTING NEWS A.L. Silver Slugger team (2000).
STATISTICAL NOTES: Led American Association with nine sacrifice flies and tied for league lead with 249 total bases in 1997. ... Led A.L. with 15 sacrifice flies in 2000. ... Career major league grand slams: 3.

										BATTING				FIELDING		
Year	Team (League)	Pos.	G	AB	R	H	2B	3B	HR	RBI	Avg.	BB	SO	SB	PO	A	E	Avg.
1992—GC White Sox (GCL)		OF	38	111	17	20	10	2	1	14	.180	13	26	6	26	2	0	1.000
1993—Hickory (S.Atl.)		OF	84	273	32	59	14	4	3	20	.216	26	66	5	131	10	6	.959
1994—Hickory (S.Atl.)		OF	132	490	86	144	24	5	11	69	.294	45	57	16	275	16	6	.980
1995—Prince William (Caro.)		OF	131	487	61	116	24	2	12	65	.238	41	71	11	256	5	6	.978
1996—Birmingham (Sou.)		OF	130	479	66	126	41	0	18	67	.263	39	74	9	231	12	6	.976
1997—Nashville (A.A.)		OF-DH	135	523	65	*172	29	3	14	90	*.329	32	61	14	278	8	5	.983
—Chicago (A.L.)		OF	21	69	12	22	6	0	4	11	.319	2	8	1	43	1	0	1.000
1998—Chicago (A.L.)		OF	145	535	70	151	25	2	14	65	.282	28	53	9	323	10	5	.985
1999—Chicago (A.L.)		OF-DH	157	624	100	188	34	3	30	117	.301	47	64	13	331	12	3	.991
2000—Chicago (A.L.)		OF	153	588	102	185	34	3	32	126	.315	60	64	18	280	12	5	.983
Major League totals (4 years)			476	1816	284	546	99	8	80	319	.301	137	189	41	977	35	13	.987

DIVISION SERIES RECORD

										BATTING				FIELDING		
Year	Team (League)	Pos.	G	AB	R	H	2B	3B	HR	RBI	Avg.	BB	SO	SB	PO	A	E	Avg.
2000—Chicago (A.L.)		OF	3	11	0	2	0	1	0	1	.182	2	2	1	8	1	0	1.000

ALL-STAR GAME RECORD

						BATTING							FIELDING		
Year	League	Pos.	AB	R	H	2B	3B	HR	RBI	Avg.	BB	SO	SB	PO	A	E	Avg.
1999—American		OF	1	0	0	0	0	0	0	.000	0	0	0	0	0	0	...
2000—American		OF	1	0	1	1	0	0	1	1.000	0	0	0	1	0	0	1.000
All-Star Game totals (2 years)			2	0	1	1	0	0	1	.500	0	0	0	1	0	0	1.000

ORDONEZ, REY SS METS

PERSONAL: Born November 11, 1972, in Havana, Cuba. ... 5-9/159. ... Bats right, throws right. ... Full name: Reynaldo Ordonez.
HIGH SCHOOL: Espa (Havana, Cuba).
COLLEGE: Fajardo College (Havana, Cuba).
TRANSACTIONS/CAREER NOTES: Played with St. Paul Saints of Northern League (1993). ... Rights acquired by New York Mets organization in lottery of Cuban defectors (October 29, 1993). ... Signed by Mets organization (February 8, 1994). ... On disabled list (June 2-July 11, 1997; and May 30-2000-remainder of season).
RECORDS: Holds major league career record for most consecutive errorless games by shortstop—100 (June 14-October 4, 1999). ... Holds N.L. career record for most consecutive chances accepted without an error by shorstop—412 (June 13-October 4, 1999). ... Holds N.L. single-season records for highest fielding average by shortstop (150 or more games)—.994 (1999); fewest errors by shortstop (150 or more games—4 (1999); most consecutive errorless games by shortstop—100 (June 14-October 4, 1999); and most consecutive chances accepted without an error by shortstop—412 (June 13-October 4, 1999).
HONORS: Won N.L. Gold Glove at shortstop (1997-99).
STATISTICAL NOTES: Led International League shortstops in total chances with 645 in 1995. ... Led N.L. shortstops with 705 total chances and 102 double plays in 1996. ... Career major league grand slams: 1.

Year	Team (League)	Pos.	G	AB	R	H	2B	3B	HR	RBI	Avg.	BB	SO	SB	PO	A	E	Avg.
											BATTING					FIELDING		
1993—St. Paul (Nor.)		SS-2B	15	60	10	17	4	0	0	7	.283	3	9	3	18	48	2	.971
1994—St. Lucie (FSL)■		SS	79	314	47	97	21	2	2	40	.309	14	28	11	141	291	15	.966
—Binghamton (East.)		SS	48	191	22	50	10	2	1	20	.262	4	18	4	57	139	8	.961
1995—Norfolk (I.L.)		SS	125	439	49	94	21	4	2	50	.214	27	50	11	188	*436	21	.967
1996—New York (N.L.)		SS	151	502	51	129	12	4	1	30	.257	22	53	1	228	450	27	.962
1997—New York (N.L.)		SS	120	356	35	77	5	3	1	33	.216	18	36	11	171	355	9	*.983
1998—New York (N.L.)		SS	153	505	46	124	20	2	1	42	.246	23	60	3	265	401	17	.975
1999—New York (N.L.)		SS	154	520	49	134	24	2	1	60	.258	49	59	8	220	416	4	*.994
2000—New York (N.L.)		SS	45	133	10	25	5	0	0	9	.188	17	16	0	58	108	6	.965
Major League totals (5 years)			623	2016	191	489	66	11	4	174	.243	129	224	23	942	1730	63	.977

DIVISION SERIES RECORD

Year	Team (League)	Pos.	G	AB	R	H	2B	3B	HR	RBI	Avg.	BB	SO	SB	PO	A	E	Avg.
											BATTING					FIELDING		
1999—New York (N.L.)		SS	4	14	1	4	1	0	0	2	.286	0	5	1	7	9	0	1.000

CHAMPIONSHIP SERIES RECORD

Year	Team (League)	Pos.	G	AB	R	H	2B	3B	HR	RBI	Avg.	BB	SO	SB	PO	A	E	Avg.
											BATTING					FIELDING		
1999—New York (N.L.)		SS	6	24	0	1	0	0	0	0	.042	0	2	0	7	24	0	1.000

OROSCO, JESSE　　　　　P

PERSONAL: Born April 21, 1957, in Santa Barbara, Calif. ... 6-2/205. ... Throws left, bats right. ... Full name: Jesse Russell Orosco. ... Name pronounced oh-ROSS-koh.
HIGH SCHOOL: Santa Barbara (Calif.).
JUNIOR COLLEGE: Santa Barbara (Calif.) City College.
TRANSACTIONS/CAREER NOTES: Selected by St. Louis Cardinals organization in seventh round of free-agent draft (January 11, 1977); did not sign. ... Selected by Minnesota Twins organization in second round of free-agent draft (January 10, 1978). ... Traded by Twins to New York Mets (February 7, 1979), completing deal in which Twins traded P Greg Field and a player to be named later to Mets for P Jerry Koosman (December 8, 1978). ... Traded by Mets as part of an eight-player, three-team deal in which Mets sent Orosco to Oakland Athletics (December 11, 1987); A's then traded Orosco, SS Alfredo Griffin and P Jay Howell to Los Angeles Dodgers for P Bob Welch, P Matt Young and P Jack Savage; A's then traded Savage, P Wally Whitehurst and P Kevin Tapani to Mets. ... Granted free agency (November 4, 1988). ... Signed by Cleveland Indians (December 3, 1988). ... Traded by Indians to Milwaukee Brewers for a player to be named later (December 6, 1991); deal settled in cash. ... Granted free agency (November 5, 1992). ... Re-signed by Brewers (December 4, 1992). ... Granted free agency (October 15, 1994). ... Signed by Baltimore Orioles (April 9, 1995). ... Granted free agency (October 27, 1996). ... Re-signed by Orioles (November 15, 1996). ... Traded by Orioles to Mets for P Chuck McElroy (December 10, 1999). ... Traded by Mets to Cardinals for 2B/OF Joe McEwing (March 18, 2000). ... On St. Louis disabled list (April 9-June 9 and June 22, 2000-remainder of season); included rehabilitation assignments to Peoria (May 30-June 5) and Memphis (June 6-9). ... Granted free agency (October 30, 2000).
RECORDS: Holds major league career records for most games pitched—1,096; and most games as relief pitcher—1,092.
MISCELLANEOUS: Appeared in one game as outfielder with one putout (1986). ... Struck out in only plate appearance (1993).

Year	League	W	L	Pct.	ERA	G	GS	CG	ShO	Sv.	IP	H	R	ER	BB	SO
1978—Elizabethton (Appl.)		4	4	.500	1.13	20	0	0	0	6	40	29	7	5	20	48
1979—Tidewater (I.L.)■		4	4	.500	3.89	16	15	1	0	0	81	82	45	35	43	55
—New York (N.L.)		1	2	.333	4.89	18	2	0	0	0	35	33	20	19	22	22
1980—Jackson (Texas)		4	4	.500	3.68	37	1	0	0	3	71	52	36	29	62	85
1981—Tidewater (I.L.)		9	5	.643	3.31	46	10	0	0	8	87	80	39	32	32	81
—New York (N.L.)		0	1	.000	1.59	8	0	0	0	1	17	13	4	3	6	18
1982—New York (N.L.)		4	10	.286	2.72	54	2	0	0	4	109 1/3	92	37	33	40	89
1983—New York (N.L.)		13	7	.650	1.47	62	0	0	0	17	110	76	27	18	38	84
1984—New York (N.L.)		10	6	.625	2.59	60	0	0	0	31	87	58	29	25	34	85
1985—New York (N.L.)		8	6	.571	2.73	54	0	0	0	17	79	66	26	24	34	68
1986—New York (N.L.)		8	6	.571	2.33	58	0	0	0	21	81	64	23	21	35	62
1987—New York (N.L.)		3	9	.250	4.44	58	0	0	0	16	77	78	41	38	31	78
1988—Los Angeles (N.L.)■		3	2	.600	2.72	55	0	0	0	9	53	41	18	16	30	43
1989—Cleveland (A.L.)■		3	4	.429	2.08	69	0	0	0	3	78	54	20	18	26	79
1990—Cleveland (A.L.)		5	4	.556	3.90	55	0	0	0	2	64 2/3	58	35	28	38	55
1991—Cleveland (A.L.)		2	0	1.000	3.74	47	0	0	0	0	45 2/3	52	20	19	15	36
1992—Milwaukee (A.L.)■		3	1	.750	3.23	59	0	0	0	1	39	33	15	14	13	40
1993—Milwaukee (A.L.)		3	5	.375	3.18	57	0	0	0	8	56 2/3	47	25	20	17	67
1994—Milwaukee (A.L.)		3	1	.750	5.08	40	0	0	0	0	39	32	26	22	26	36
1995—Baltimore (A.L.)■		2	4	.333	3.26	*65	0	0	0	3	49 2/3	28	19	18	27	58
1996—Baltimore (A.L.)		3	1	.750	3.40	66	0	0	0	0	55 2/3	42	22	21	28	52
1997—Baltimore (A.L.)		6	3	.667	2.32	71	0	0	0	0	50 1/3	29	13	13	30	46
1998—Baltimore (A.L.)		4	1	.800	3.18	69	0	0	0	7	56 2/3	46	20	20	28	50
1999—Baltimore (A.L.)		0	2	.000	5.34	65	0	0	0	1	32	28	21	19	20	35
2000—St. Louis (N.L.)■		0	0	...	3.86	6	0	0	0	0	2 1/3	3	3	1	3	4
—Peoria (Midw.)		0	0	...	0.00	2	2	0	0	0	1 2/3	0	0	0	0	1
—Memphis (PCL)		0	1	.000	9.00	2	1	0	0	0	1	1	1	1	0	0
A.L. totals (11 years)		34	26	.567	3.36	663	0	0	0	25	567 1/3	449	236	212	268	554
N.L. totals (10 years)		50	49	.505	2.74	433	4	0	0	116	650 2/3	524	228	198	273	553
Major League totals (21 years)		84	75	.528	3.03	1096	4	0	0	141	1218	973	464	410	541	1107

DIVISION SERIES RECORD

Year	League	W	L	Pct.	ERA	G	GS	CG	ShO	Sv.	IP	H	R	ER	BB	SO
1996—Baltimore (A.L.)		0	1	.000	36.00	4	0	0	0	0	1	2	4	4	3	2
1997—Baltimore (A.L.)		0	0	...	0.00	2	0	0	0	0	1 1/3	1	0	0	0	1
Division series totals (2 years)		0	1	.000	15.43	6	0	0	0	0	2 1/3	3	4	4	3	3

CHAMPIONSHIP SERIES RECORD

RECORDS: Holds single-series record for most games won—3 (1986).

Year League	W	L	Pct.	ERA	G	GS	CG	ShO	Sv.	IP	H	R	ER	BB	SO
1986— New York (N.L.).................	3	0	1.000	3.38	4	0	0	0	0	8	5	3	3	2	10
1988— Los Angeles (N.L.)	0	0	...	7.71	4	0	0	0	0	2 1/3	4	2	2	3	0
1996— Baltimore (A.L.).................	0	0	...	4.50	4	0	0	0	0	2	2	1	1	2	2
1997— Baltimore (A.L.).................	0	0	...	0.00	2	0	0	0	0	1 1/3	0	0	0	1	1
Champ. series totals (4 years)	3	0	1.000	3.95	14	0	0	0	0	13 2/3	11	6	6	8	13

WORLD SERIES RECORD

NOTES: Member of World Series championship team (1986 and 1988).

Year League	W	L	Pct.	ERA	G	GS	CG	ShO	Sv.	IP	H	R	ER	BB	SO
1986— New York (N.L.).................	0	0	...	0.00	4	0	0	0	2	5 2/3	2	0	0	0	6
1988— Los Angeles (N.L.)								Did not play.							

ALL-STAR GAME RECORD

Year League	W	L	Pct.	ERA	GS	CG	ShO	Sv.	IP	H	R	ER	BB	SO
1983— National	0	0	...	0.00	0	0	0	0	1/3	0	0	0	0	1
1984— National							Did not play.							

ORTEGA, BILL   OF   CARDINALS

PERSONAL: Born July 24, 1975, in Havana, Cuba. ... 6-4/205. ... Bats right, throws right. ... Full name: William Ortega.
TRANSACTIONS/CAREER NOTES: Signed as non-drafted free agent by St. Louis Cardinals organization (March 11, 1997).
STATISTICAL NOTES: Led Carolina League outfielders with 266 total chances in 1999.

Year Team (League)	Pos.	G	AB	R	H	2B	3B	HR	RBI	Avg.	BB	SO	SB	PO	A	E	Avg.
1997— Prince William (Caro.)	OF	73	249	23	57	14	0	0	15	.229	21	42	1	89	5	7	.931
1998— Peoria (Midw.)............	OF	105	398	57	110	23	2	2	60	.276	39	69	4	74	3	4	.951
1999— Potomac (Caro.)........	OF	110	421	66	129	27	4	9	74	.306	38	69	7	*252	11	3	*.989
— Arkansas (Texas)........	OF	20	69	10	26	9	0	2	10	.377	10	9	0	43	0	0	1.000
2000— Arkansas (Texas)........	OF	86	332	51	108	18	5	12	62	.325	28	42	1	163	8	8	.955

ORTIZ, DAVID   1B   TWINS

PERSONAL: Born November 18, 1975, in Santo Domingo, Dominican Republic. ... 6-4/230. ... Bats left, throws left. ... Full name: David Americo Ortiz.
HIGH SCHOOL: Estudia Espallat (Dominican Republic).
TRANSACTIONS/CAREER NOTES: Signed as non-drafted free agent by Seattle Mariners organization (November 28, 1992). ... Traded by Mariners to Minnesota Twins (September 13, 1996), completing deal in which Twins traded 3B Dave Hollins to Mariners for a player to be named later (August 29, 1996). ... On Minnesota disabled list (May 10-July 9, 1998); included rehabilitation assignment to Salt Lake (June 25-July 9).
STATISTICAL NOTES: Led Arizona League first basemen with 393 total chances in 1994. ... Career major league grand slams: 1.

Year Team (League)	Pos.	G	AB	R	H	2B	3B	HR	RBI	Avg.	BB	SO	SB	PO	A	E	Avg.
1994— Ariz. Mariners (Ariz.) ..	1B	53	167	14	41	10	1	2	20	.246	14	46	1	*372	15	6	.985
1995— Ariz. Mariners (Ariz.) ..	1B	48	184	30	61	18	4	4	37	.332	23	52	2	436	*27	5	*.989
1996— Wis. Rapids (Midw.)...	1B-DH-3B	129	485	89	156	34	2	18	93	.322	52	108	3	1126	80	13	.989
1997— Fort Myers (FSL)■....	1B-DH	61	239	45	79	15	0	13	58	.331	22	53	2	524	44	9	.984
— New Britain (East.)	DH-1B	69	258	40	83	22	2	14	56	.322	21	78	2	268	16	3	.990
— Salt Lake (PCL)	1B-DH	10	42	5	9	1	0	4	10	.214	2	11	0	71	2	0	1.000
— Minnesota (A.L.)	1B-DH	15	49	10	16	3	0	1	6	.327	2	19	0	84	10	1	.989
1998— Minnesota (A.L.)	1B-DH	86	278	47	77	20	0	9	46	.277	39	72	1	503	46	6	.989
— Salt Lake (PCL)	1B-DH	11	37	5	9	3	0	2	6	.243	3	9	0	76	10	3	.966
1999— Salt Lake (PCL)	1B-DH	130	476	85	150	35	3	30	*110	.315	79	105	2	896	77	•20	.980
— Minnesota (A.L.)	DH-1B	10	20	1	0	0	0	0	0	.000	5	12	0	7	0	0	1.000
2000— Minnesota (A.L.)	DH-1B	130	415	59	117	36	1	10	63	.282	57	81	1	210	12	1	.996
Major League totals (4 years)		241	762	117	210	59	1	20	115	.276	103	184	2	804	68	8	.991

ORTIZ, HECTOR   C   ROYALS

PERSONAL: Born October 14, 1969, in Rio Piedras, Puerto Rico. ... 6-0/205. ... Bats right, throws right. ... Full name: Hector Ortiz Jr.
HIGH SCHOOL: Luis Hernaiz Verone (Canovanas, Puerto Rico).
JUNIOR COLLEGE: Ranger (Texas) College.
TRANSACTIONS/CAREER NOTES: Selected by Los Angeles Dodgers organization in 35th round of free-agent draft (June 1, 1988). ... Granted free agency (October 17, 1994). ... Signed by Chicago Cubs organization (January 22, 1995). ... Granted free agency (October 15, 1996). ... Signed by Kansas City Royals organization (January 29, 1997). ... On Omaha disabled list (May 19-June 6, 1998). ... Granted free agency (October 15, 1998). ... Signed by Dodgers organization (January 18, 1999). ... Granted free agency (October 15, 1999). .'. Signed by Royals organization (November 30, 1999).
STATISTICAL NOTES: Led Northwest League catchers with seven double plays and 461 total chances in 1990.

Year Team (League)	Pos.	G	AB	R	H	2B	3B	HR	RBI	Avg.	BB	SO	SB	PO	A	E	Avg.
1988— Salem (N'West)	C-3B	32	77	5	11	1	0	0	4	.143	5	16	0	157	19	7	.962
1989— Vero Beach (FSL)	C	42	85	5	12	0	1	0	4	.141	6	15	0	174	23	6	.970
— Salem (N'West)	C	44	140	13	32	3	1	0	12	.229	4	24	2	268	24	*12	.961
1990— Yakima (N'West)	C	52	173	16	47	3	1	0	12	.272	5	15	1	*392	*62	7	.985
1991— Vero Beach (FSL)	C	42	123	3	28	2	0	0	8	.228	5	8	0	238	28	7	.974

O

Year Team (League)	Pos.	G	AB	R	H	2B	3B	HR	RBI	Avg.	BB	SO	SB	PO	A	E	Avg.
							BATTING								FIELDING		
1992—Bakersfield (Calif.)	C	63	206	19	58	8	1	1	31	.282	21	16	2	428	44	3	.994
—San Antonio (Texas)	C	26	59	1	12	1	0	0	5	.203	11	13	0	140	23	3	.982
1993—San Antonio (Texas)	C-3B	49	131	6	28	5	0	1	6	.214	9	17	0	311	43	8	.978
—Albuquerque (PCL)	C	18	44	0	8	1	1	0	3	.182	0	6	0	78	11	2	.978
1994—Albuquerque (PCL)	C	34	93	7	28	1	1	0	10	.301	3	12	0	144	20	4	.976
—San Antonio (Texas)	C-P	24	75	4	9	0	0	0	4	.120	2	7	0	166	23	2	.990
1995—Orlando (Sou.)■	C	96	299	13	70	12	0	0	18	.234	20	39	0	567	72	6	.991
1996—Orlando (Sou.)	C	78	216	16	47	8	0	0	15	.218	26	23	1	475	32	6	.988
—Iowa (A.A.)	C	27	79	6	19	2	0	0	3	.241	3	16	0	139	9	2	.987
1997—Omaha (A.A.)■	C	21	63	7	12	3	0	0	3	.190	13	15	0	130	6	3	.978
—Wichita (Texas)	C	59	180	20	45	3	0	1	25	.250	21	15	1	340	40	*15	.962
1998—Wichita (Texas)	C	4	13	1	2	0	0	0	0	.154	2	1	0	24	6	1	.968
—Omaha (PCL)	C	63	191	17	43	7	0	0	12	.225	9	26	0	318	30	8	.978
—Kansas City (A.L.)	C-1B	4	4	1	0	0	0	0	0	.000	0	0	0	4	0	0	1.000
1999—San Antonio (Texas)■	C	40	121	10	29	4	0	0	13	.240	10	17	0	238	26	6	.978
—Albuquerque (PCL)	C-1B	55	164	21	50	9	0	6	20	.305	7	27	2	312	32	10	.972
2000—Omaha (PCL)■	C	68	227	30	73	12	0	6	24	.322	22	18	4	291	28	6	.982
—Kansas City (A.L.)	C	26	88	15	34	6	0	0	5	.386	8	8	0	130	18	1	.993
Major League totals (2 years)		30	92	16	34	6	0	0	5	.370	8	8	0	134	18	1	.993

RECORD AS PITCHER

Year League	W	L	Pct.	ERA	G	GS	CG	ShO	Sv.	IP	H	R	ER	BB	SO
1994—San Antonio (Texas)	0	0	...	0.00	1	0	0	0	0	1	0	0	0	1	1

ORTIZ, JOSE — 2B/SS — ATHLETICS

PERSONAL: Born June 13, 1977, in Santo Domingo, Dominican Republic. ... 5-9/177. ... Bats right, throws right. ... Full name: Jose Daniel Ortiz Santos.

TRANSACTIONS/CAREER NOTES: Signed as non-drafted free agent by Oakland Athletics organization (November 8, 1994). ... On disabled list (May 10-June 30, 1998). ... On Vancouver disabled list (June 15-25, 1999).

HONORS: Named Pacific Coast League Most Valuable Player (2000).

STATISTICAL NOTES: Led Arizona League with .530 slugging percentage in 1996. ... Led Arizona League shortstops with 279 total chances and 42 double plays in 1996. ... Led California League shortstops with 53 errors and 80 double plays in 1997.

Year Team (League)	Pos.	G	AB	R	H	2B	3B	HR	RBI	Avg.	BB	SO	SB	PO	A	E	Avg.
							BATTING								FIELDING		
1995—Dom. Athletics (DSL)	SS	61	217	45	65	12	2	9	41	.300	32	22	14	182	38	17	.928
1996—Ariz. Athletics (Ariz.)	SS	52	200	*43	66	12	8	4	25	.330	20	34	16	*93	*165	21	.925
—Modesto (Calif.)	2B	1	4	0	1	0	0	0	0	.250	0	1	0	2	5	0	1.000
1997—Modesto (Calif.)	SS-2B	128	497	92	122	25	7	16	58	.245	60	107	22	186	373	†53	.913
1998—Huntsville (Sou.)	2B-SS-OF	94	354	70	98	24	2	6	55	.277	48	63	22	159	274	27	.941
1999—Vancouver (PCL)	SS-2B	107	377	66	107	29	2	9	45	.284	29	50	13	179	295	28	.944
2000—Sacramento (PCL)	2B-SS-3B	131	*518	107	*182	34	5	24	108	.351	47	64	22	247	347	32	.949
—Oakland (A.L.)	DH-2B	7	11	4	2	0	0	0	1	.182	2	3	0	2	4	1	.857
Major League totals (1 year)		7	11	4	2	0	0	0	1	.182	2	3	0	2	4	1	.857

ORTIZ, RAMON — P — ANGELS

PERSONAL: Born May 23, 1976, in Cotui, Dominican Republic. ... 6-0/175. ... Throws right, bats right. ... Full name: Diogenes Ramon Ortiz.

HIGH SCHOOL: 8th Intermedian (Dominican Republic).

TRANSACTIONS/CAREER NOTES: Signed as non-drafted free agent by California Angels organization (June 20, 1995). ... Angels franchise renamed Anaheim for 1997 season. ... On disabled list (May 9, 1998-remainder of season). ... On Anaheim disabled list (March 20-April 11, 2000); included rehabilitation assignment to Lake Elsinore (April 6).

STATISTICAL NOTES: Pitched 12-0 no-hit victory against Quad City (August 7, 1997).

Year League	W	L	Pct.	ERA	G	GS	CG	ShO	Sv.	IP	H	R	ER	BB	SO
1995—Dom. Angels (DSL)	8	6	.571	2.23	16	15	7	0	0	97	79	44	24	64	100
1996—Arizona Angels (Ariz.)	5	4	.556	2.12	16	8	•2	*2	1	68	55	28	16	27	78
—Boise (N'West)	1	1	.500	3.66	3	3	0	0	0	$19\frac{2}{3}$	21	10	8	6	18
1997—Cedar Rapids (Midw.)	11	10	.524	3.58	27	•27	*8	*4	0	181	156	78	72	53	*225
1998—Midland (Texas)	2	1	.667	5.55	7	7	0	0	0	47	50	31	29	16	53
1999—Erie (East.)	9	4	.692	2.82	15	15	2	2	0	102	88	38	32	40	86
—Edmonton (PCL)	5	3	.625	4.05	9	9	0	0	0	$53\frac{1}{3}$	46	26	24	19	64
—Anaheim (A.L.)	2	3	.400	6.52	9	9	0	0	0	$48\frac{1}{3}$	50	35	35	25	44
2000—Lake Elsinore (Calif.)	1	0	1.000	3.00	1	1	0	0	0	6	8	2	2	2	7
—Anaheim (A.L.)	8	6	.571	5.09	18	18	2	0	0	$111\frac{1}{3}$	96	69	63	55	73
—Edmonton (PCL)	6	6	.500	4.55	15	15	1	0	0	89	74	49	45	37	76
Major League totals (2 years)	10	9	.526	5.52	27	27	2	0	0	$159\frac{2}{3}$	146	104	98	80	117

ORTIZ, RUSS — P — GIANTS

PERSONAL: Born June 5, 1974, in Encino, Calif. ... 6-1/210. ... Throws right, bats right. ... Full name: Russell Reid Ortiz.

HIGH SCHOOL: Montclair Prep (Van Nuys, Calif.).

COLLEGE: Oklahoma.

TRANSACTIONS/CAREER NOTES: Selected by San Francisco Giants organization in fourth round of free-agent draft (June 1, 1995).

RECORDS: Shares N.L. single-inning record for most consecutive home runs allowed—3 (August 10, 1998, fifth inning).

O

Year	League	W	L	Pct.	ERA	G	GS	CG	ShO	Sv.	IP	H	R	ER	BB	SO
1995—Bellingham (N'West)		2	0	1.000	0.52	25	0	0	0	11	34 1/3	19	4	2	13	55
—San Jose (Calif.)		0	1	.000	1.50	5	0	0	0	0	6	4	1	1	2	7
1996—San Jose (Calif.)		0	0	...	0.25	34	0	0	0	23	36 2/3	16	2	1	20	63
—Shreveport (Texas)		1	2	.333	4.05	26	0	0	0	13	26 2/3	22	14	12	21	29
1997—Shreveport (Texas)		2	3	.400	4.13	12	12	0	0	0	56 2/3	52	28	26	37	50
—Phoenix (PCL)		4	3	.571	5.51	14	14	0	0	0	85	96	57	52	34	70
1998—San Francisco (N.L.)		4	4	.500	4.99	22	13	0	0	0	88 1/3	90	51	49	46	75
—Fresno (PCL)		3	1	.750	1.60	10	10	0	0	0	50 2/3	35	10	9	22	59
1999—San Francisco (N.L.)		18	9	.667	3.81	33	33	3	0	0	207 2/3	189	109	88	*125	164
2000—San Francisco (N.L.)		14	12	.538	5.01	33	32	0	0	0	195 2/3	192	117	109	112	167
Major League totals (3 years)		**36**	**25**	**.590**	**4.50**	**88**	**78**	**3**	**0**	**0**	**491 2/3**	**471**	**277**	**246**	**283**	**406**

DIVISION SERIES RECORD

Year	League	W	L	Pct.	ERA	G	GS	CG	ShO	Sv.	IP	H	R	ER	BB	SO
2000—San Francisco (N.L.)		0	0	...	1.69	1	1	0	0	0	5 1/3	2	1	1	4	4

OSIK, KEITH   C   PIRATES

PERSONAL: Born October 22, 1968, in Port Jefferson, N.Y. ... 6-0/192. ... Bats right, throws right. ... Full name: Keith Richard Osik. ... Name pronounced OH-sik.

HIGH SCHOOL: Shoreham (N.Y.)-Wading River.

COLLEGE: Louisiana State.

TRANSACTIONS/CAREER NOTES: Selected by Texas Rangers organization in 47th round of free-agent draft (June 2, 1987); did not sign. ... Selected by Pittsburgh Pirates organization in 24th round of free-agent draft (June 4, 1990). ... On Pittsburgh disabled list (July 16-August 13, 1996); included rehabilitation assignment to Erie (August 10-13). ... On Pittsburgh disabled list (July 21-August 13, 1999); included rehabilitation assignment to Nashville (August 9-13).

								BATTING							FIELDING		
Year	Team (League)	Pos.	AB	R	H	2B	3B	HR	RBI	Avg.	BB	SO	SB	PO	A	E	Avg.
1990—Welland (NY-Penn).....	3-C-1-2-S	29	97	13	27	4	0	1	20	.278	11	12	2	59	29	2	.978
1991—Salem (Caro.)	C-3B-2B	87	300	31	81	12	1	6	35	.270	38	48	2	307	85	12	.970
—Carolina (Sou.)	C-3B	17	43	9	13	3	1	0	5	.302	5	5	0	84	13	2	.980
1992—Carolina (Sou.)	3B-C-2B-P	129	425	41	110	17	1	5	45	.259	52	69	2	222	195	19	.956
1993—Carolina (Sou.)	C-3B-DH	103	371	47	104	21	2	10	47	.280	30	46	0	662	69	6	.992
1994—Buffalo (A.A.)..........	C-O-1-DH-P-2	83	260	27	55	16	0	5	33	.212	28	41	0	403	50	8	.983
1995—Calgary (PCL)	C-1B-OF-P-3B	90	301	40	101	25	1	10	59	.336	21	42	2	458	35	4	.992
1996—Pittsburgh (N.L.)	C-3B-OF	48	140	18	41	14	1	1	14	.293	14	22	1	237	25	6	.978
—Erie (NY-Penn)	C	3	10	1	3	1	0	0	2	.300	1	2	0	19	2	0	1.000
1997—Pittsburgh (N.L.)......	C-2B-1B-3B	49	105	10	27	9	1	0	7	.257	9	21	0	163	14	2	.989
1998—Pittsburgh (N.L.)	C-3B	39	98	8	21	4	0	0	7	.214	13	16	1	152	30	1	.995
1999—Pittsburgh (N.L.)	C-P	66	167	12	31	3	1	2	13	.186	11	30	0	289	22	1	.997
—Nashville (PCL)	C-OF	4	11	0	1	0	0	0	0	.091	0	1	0	24	3	0	1.000
2000—Pittsburgh (N.L.) C-3B-1B-DH-P	46	123	11	36	6	1	4	22	.293	14	11	3	156	23	2	.989
Major League totals (5 years)		248	633	59	156	36	4	7	63	.246	61	100	5	997	114	12	.989

RECORD AS PITCHER

Year	League	W	L	Pct.	ERA	G	GS	CG	ShO	Sv.	IP	H	R	ER	BB	SO
1992—Carolina (Sou.)..................		0	0	...	0.00	2	0	0	0	0	2 2/3	2	0	0	0	3
1994—Buffalo (A.A.)....................		0	1	.000	13.50	1	0	0	0	0	2/3	2	1	1	0	1
1995—Calgary (PCL)		0	0	...	4.50	2	0	0	0	0	2	1	1	1	1	3
1999—Pittsburgh (N.L.)		0	0	...	36.00	1	0	0	0	0	1	2	4	4	2	1
2000—Pittsburgh (N.L.)		0	0	...	45.00	1	0	0	0	0	1	5	5	5	0	1
Major League totals (2 years)		**0**	**0**	**...**	**40.50**	**2**	**0**	**0**	**0**	**0**	**2**	**7**	**9**	**9**	**2**	**2**

OSTING, JIMMY   P   PHILLIES

PERSONAL: Born April 7, 1977, in Louisville, Ky. ... 6-5/180. ... Throws left, bats right. ... Full name: James Michael Osting.

HIGH SCHOOL: Trinity (Louisville, Ky.).

TRANSACTIONS/CAREER NOTES: Selected by Atlanta Braves in fourth round of free-agent draft (June 1, 1995). ... On disabled list (April 2, 1998-entire season). ... Traded by Braves with P Bruce Chen to Philadelphia Phillies for P Andy Ashby (July 12, 2000).

Year	League	W	L	Pct.	ERA	G	GS	CG	ShO	Sv.	IP	H	R	ER	BB	SO
1995—Danville (Appl.).................	2	7	.222	7.15	11	10	0	0	0	39	46	34	31	25	43
1996—Eugene (N'West)	2	1	.667	2.59	5	5	0	0	0	24 1/3	14	11	7	13	35
1997—Macon (S.Atl.)..................	2	3	.400	3.28	15	15	0	0	0	57 2/3	54	28	21	29	62
1998—								Did not play.								
1999—Macon (S.Atl.).................	*14	4	.778	2.88	27	22	0	0	2	147	130	52	47	30	131
2000—Myrtle Beach (Caro.)	2	2	.500	3.13	4	4	0	0	0	23	25	8	8	5	17
—Greenville (Sou.)	2	6	.250	2.65	11	11	0	0	0	71 1/3	67	30	21	29	52
—Richmond (I.L.)	0	2	.000	11.57	3	3	0	0	0	9 1/3	15	12	12	11	2
—Reading (East.)■	4	2	.667	2.38	10	9	1	1	0	56 2/3	53	17	15	26	31

OSUNA, ANTONIO   P   DODGERS

PERSONAL: Born April 12, 1973, in Sinaloa, Mexico. ... 5-11/206. ... Throws right, bats right. ... Full name: Antonio Pedro Osuna.

HIGH SCHOOL: Secundaria Federal (Mexico).

TRANSACTIONS/CAREER NOTES: Signed as non-drafted free agent by Los Angeles Dodgers organization (June 12, 1991). ... On suspended list (April 8-July 17, 1993). ... On San Antonio disabled list (June 8-June 6, 1994). ... On Los Angeles disabled list (May 19-June 16, 1995); included rehabilitation assignment to San Bernardino (June 6-16). ... On disabled list (September 9, 1998-remainder of season). ... On Los Angeles disabled list (March 25-April 16, April 18-May 3 and May 19, 1999-remainder of season); included rehabilitation assignments to San Bernardino (April 10-16, April 25-May 3, July 7-15 and September 1-29). ... On Los Angeles disabled list (March 31-May 5, 2000); included rehabilitation assignment to San Bernardino (April 8-May 5).

O

Year League	W	L	Pct.	ERA	G	GS	CG	ShO	Sv.	IP	H	R	ER	BB	SO
1991— Gulf Coast Dodgers (GCL)..	0	0	...	0.82	8	0	0	0	4	11	8	5	1	0	13
— Yakima (N'West)	0	0	...	3.20	13	0	0	0	5	25 1/3	18	10	9	8	39
1992— Mexico City Tigers (Mex.) ..	13	7	.650	4.05	28	26	3	1	0	166 2/3	181	80	75	74	129
1993— Bakersfield (Calif.).............	0	2	.000	4.91	14	2	0	0	2	18 1/3	19	10	10	5	20
1994— San Antonio (Texas)..........	1	2	.333	0.98	35	0	0	0	19	46	19	6	5	18	53
— Albuquerque (PCL).............	0	0	...	0.00	6	0	0	0	4	6	5	1	0	1	8
1995— Los Angeles (N.L.)	2	4	.333	4.43	39	0	0	0	0	44 2/3	39	22	22	20	46
— San Bernardino (Calif.).......	0	0	...	1.29	5	0	0	0	0	7	3	1	1	5	11
— Albuquerque (PCL).............	0	1	.000	4.42	19	0	0	0	11	18 1/3	15	9	9	9	19
1996— Albuquerque (PCL)	0	0	...	0.00	1	0	0	0	0	1	2	0	0	0	1
— Los Angeles (N.L.)	9	6	.600	3.00	73	0	0	0	4	84	65	33	28	32	85
1997— Albuquerque (PCL)	1	1	.500	1.93	13	0	0	0	6	14	9	3	3	4	26
— Los Angeles (N.L.)	3	4	.429	2.19	48	0	0	0	0	61 2/3	46	15	15	19	68
1998— Los Angeles (N.L.)	7	1	.875	3.06	54	0	0	0	6	64 2/3	50	26	22	32	72
1999— San Bernardino (Calif.).......	0	0	...	2.33	13	4	0	0	0	19 1/3	19	6	5	6	27
— Los Angeles (N.L.)	0	0	...	7.71	5	0	0	0	0	4 2/3	4	5	4	3	5
2000— San Bernardino (Calif.).......	0	2	.000	4.91	3	3	0	0	0	7 1/3	4	4	4	3	11
— Los Angeles (N.L.)	3	6	.333	3.74	46	0	0	0	0	67 1/3	57	30	28	35	70
— Albuquerque (PCL)	0	0	...	0.00	3	1	0	0	0	5 2/3	2	2	0	5	7
Major League totals (6 years)	24	21	.533	3.28	265	0	0	0	10	327	261	131	119	141	346

DIVISION SERIES RECORD

Year League	W	L	Pct.	ERA	G	GS	CG	ShO	Sv.	IP	H	R	ER	BB	SO
1995— Los Angeles (N.L.)	0	1	.000	2.70	3	0	0	0	0	3 1/3	3	1	1	1	3
1996— Los Angeles (N.L.)	0	1	.000	4.50	2	0	0	0	0	2	3	1	1	1	4
Division series totals (2 years)	0	2	.000	3.38	5	0	0	0	0	5 1/3	6	2	2	2	7

OWENS, ERIC — OF — PADRES

PERSONAL: Born February 3, 1971, in Danville, Va. ... 6-0/198. ... Bats right, throws right. ... Full name: Eric Blake Owens.
HIGH SCHOOL: Tunstall (Dry Fork, Va.).
COLLEGE: Ferrum (Va.).
TRANSACTIONS/CAREER NOTES: Selected by Cincinnati Reds organization in fourth round of free-agent draft (June 1, 1992). ... On Indianapolis disabled list (August 20-September 11, 1995). ... Traded by Reds to Florida Marlins for a player to be named later (March 21, 1998); Reds acquired P Jesus Martinez to complete deal (March 26, 1998). ... Contract sold by Marlins to Milwaukee Brewers (March 25, 1998). ... Granted free agency (October 15, 1998). ... Signed by San Diego Padres organization (December 10, 1998).
HONORS: Named American Association Most Valuable Player (1995).
STATISTICAL NOTES: Led Pioneer League shortstops with 28 errors in 1992. ... Tied for American Association lead in errors by second baseman with 17 in 1997. ... Had 18-game hitting streak (June 17-July 6, 1999). ... Led N.L. outfielders with 1.000 fielding percentage in 2000.

							BATTING						FIELDING		
Year Team (League)	Pos.	G	AB	R	H	2B	3B	HR	RBI	Avg.	BB	SO	SB	PO	A	E	Avg.
1992— Billings (Pio.)	SS-3B	67	239	41	72	10	3	3	26	.301	23	22	15	82	164	†29	.895
1993— Win.-Salem (Caro.)	SS	122	487	74	132	25	4	10	63	.271	53	69	21	*215	347	34	.943
1994— Chattanooga (Sou.)	3B-2B	134	523	73	133	17	3	3	36	.254	54	86	38	151	266	40	.912
1995— Indianapolis (A.A.)......	2B	108	427	*86	134	24	•8	12	63	.314	52	61	*33	219	274	*17	.967
— Cincinnati (N.L.)	3B	2	2	0	2	0	0	0	1	1.000	0	0	0	0	0	0	...
1996— Indianapolis (A.A.)......SS-3B-2B-OF		33	128	24	41	8	2	4	14	.320	11	16	6	44	64	6	.947
— Cincinnati (N.L.)	OF-2B-3B	88	205	26	41	6	0	0	9	.200	23	38	16	76	14	2	.978
1997— Cincinnati (N.L.)	OF-2B	27	57	8	15	0	0	0	3	.263	4	11	3	15	0	1	.938
— Indianapolis (A.A.)......	2-S-O-3	104	391	56	112	15	4	11	44	.286	42	55	23	184	241	‡27	.940
1998— Milwaukee (N.L.)■.....	OF	34	40	5	5	2	0	1	4	.125	2	6	0	14	2	1	.941
— Louisville (I.L.)	OF-3B-DH	77	254	48	85	11	4	5	40	.335	34	30	21	85	57	8	.947
1999— San Diego (N.L.)■ OF-1B-3B-2B		149	440	55	117	22	3	9	61	.266	38	50	33	278	12	4	.986
2000— San Diego (N.L.)	OF-2B	145	583	87	171	19	7	6	51	.293	45	63	29	315	6	0	1.000
Major League totals (6 years)		445	1327	181	351	49	10	16	129	.265	112	168	81	698	34	8	.989

OZUNA, PABLO — SS — MARLINS

PERSONAL: Born August 25, 1978, in Santo Domingo, Dominican Republic. ... 6-0/160. ... Bats right, throws right. ... Full name: Pablo Jose Ozuna.
TRANSACTIONS/CAREER NOTES: Signed as non-drafted free agent by St. Louis Cardinals orgnaization (April 8, 1996). ... Traded by Cardinals with P Braden Looper and P Armando Almanza to Florida Marlins for SS Edgar Renteria (December 14, 1998).
HONORS: Named Midwest League Most Valuable Player (1998).
STATISTICAL NOTES: Tied for Appalachian League lead in sacrifice hits with six in 1997. ... Led Midwest League with 26 caught stealing and tied for lead in double plays by a shortstop with 80 in 1998. ... Tied for Midwest League lead with 80 double plays by shortstop in 1998. ... Led Eastern League with 24 caught stealing in 2000.

							BATTING						FIELDING		
Year Team (League)	Pos.	G	AB	R	H	2B	3B	HR	RBI	Avg.	BB	SO	SB	PO	A	E	Avg.
1996— Dom. Cardinals (DSL)	SS	74	295	57	107	12	4	6	60	.363	23	19	19	126	219	32	.915
1997— Johnson City (Appl.) ..	SS	56	232	40	75	13	1	5	24	.323	10	24	23	80	139	25	.898
1998— Peoria (Midw.)............	SS	133	538	*122	*192	27	10	9	62	*.357	29	56	62	195	*395	45	.929
1999— Portland (East.)■	SS	117	502	62	141	25	7	7	46	.281	13	50	31	179	309	28	.946
2000— Portland (East.)	2B	118	464	74	143	25	6	7	59	.308	40	55	35	*242	302	*25	.956
— Florida (N.L.).............	2B	14	24	2	8	1	0	0	0	.333	0	2	1	12	17	1	.967
Major League totals (1 year)		14	24	2	8	1	0	0	0	.333	0	2	1	12	17	1	.967

PADILLA, ROY   P   INDIANS

PERSONAL: Born August 4, 1975, in Panama City, Panama. ... 6-5/227. ... Bats left, throws left. ... Full name: Roy R. Padilla.
HIGH SCHOOL: Melchior College (Panama).
TRANSACTIONS/CAREER NOTES: Signed as non-drafted free agent by Boston Red Sox organization (September 30, 1992). ... Selected by Cleveland Indians from Red Sox organization in Rule 5 minor league draft (December 14, 1998). ... On Kinston disabled list (April 15-23 and April 24-May 19, 2000). ... On Buffalo disabled list (August 31-September 7, 2000).
STATISTICAL NOTES: Led Florida State League outfielders with 347 total chances in 1997.

Year League	W	L	Pct.	ERA	G	GS	CG	ShO	Sv.	IP	H	R	ER	BB	SO
1993—GC Red Sox (GCL)	0	1	.000	2.35	13	1	0	0	0	30$^2/_3$	25	10	8	17	18
1994—GC Red Sox (GCL)	6	1	.857	2.99	15	12	0	0	1	72$^1/_3$	68	39	24	34	52
1995—Michigan (Midw.)	0	1	.000	6.48	4	1	0	0	0	8$^1/_3$	10	9	6	7	7
—Butte (Pio.)	2	7	.222	5.91	15	14	0	0	0	70	80	60	46	54	49
1999—Columbus (S. Atl.)■	2	2	.500	3.02	30	0	0	0	3	59$^2/_3$	53	27	20	27	56
—Kinston (Caro.)	0	0	...	4.15	8	0	0	0	1	13	9	6	6	10	7
2000—Kinston (Caro.)	1	1	.500	4.94	14	0	0	0	0	23$^2/_3$	14	21	13	21	32
—Akron (East.)	0	1	.000	4.24	16	0	0	0	0	23$^1/_3$	20	16	11	25	18

RECORD AS POSITION PLAYER

						BATTING								FIELDING		
Year Team (League)	Pos.	G	AB	R	H	2B	3B	HR	RBI	Avg.	BB	SO	SB	PO	A	E	Avg.
1996—Sarasota (FSL)	OF	8	27	2	8	2	0	0	2	.296	2	3	4	17	0	1	.944
—Michigan (Midw.)	OF	103	386	58	108	20	6	2	40	.280	34	56	21	225	5	8	.966
1997—Sarasota (FSL)	OF-DH	130	463	66	114	16	4	2	38	.246	41	80	24	*327	9	11	.968
1998—Sarasota (FSL)	OF	109	365	46	93	17	3	3	53	.255	28	66	12	232	7	8	.968

PADILLA, VICENTE   P   PHILLIES

PERSONAL: Born September 27, 1977, in Chinandoga, Nicaragua. ... 6-2/200. ... Throws right, bats right. ... Full name: Vicente D. Padilla.
HIGH SCHOOL: Ruben Dario (Nicaragua).
TRANSACTIONS/CAREER NOTES: Signed as non-drafted free agent by Arizona Diamondbacks organization (August 31, 1998). ... Traded by Diamondbacks with OF Travis Lee, P Omar Daal and P Nelson Figueroa to Philadelphia Phillies for P Curt Schilling (July 26, 2000).

Year League	W	L	Pct.	ERA	G	GS	CG	ShO	Sv.	IP	H	R	ER	BB	SO
1999—High Desert (Calif.)	4	1	.800	3.73	9	9	0	0	0	50$^2/_3$	50	27	21	17	55
—Tucson (PCL)	7	4	.636	3.75	18	14	0	0	0	93$^2/_3$	107	47	39	24	58
—Arizona (N.L.)	0	1	.000	16.88	5	0	0	0	0	2$^2/_3$	7	5	5	3	0
2000—Tucson (PCL)	0	0	...	4.42	12	3	0	0	1	18$^1/_3$	22	9	9	8	22
—Arizona (N.L.)	2	1	.667	2.31	27	0	0	0	0	35	32	10	9	10	30
—Philadelphia (N.L.)■	2	6	.250	5.34	28	0	0	0	2	30$^1/_3$	40	23	18	18	21
Major League totals (2 years)	4	8	.333	4.24	60	0	0	0	2	68	79	38	32	31	51

PAINTER, LANCE   P   BLUE JAYS

PERSONAL: Born July 21, 1967, in Bedford, England. ... 6-1/200. ... Throws left, bats left. ... Full name: Lance Telford Painter.
HIGH SCHOOL: Nicolet (Glendale, Wis.).
COLLEGE: Wisconsin.
TRANSACTIONS/CAREER NOTES: Selected by San Diego Padres organization in 25th round of free-agent draft (June 4, 1990). ... Selected by Colorado Rockies in second round (34th pick overall) of expansion draft (November 17, 1992). ... On disabled list (April 17-May 6, 1995). ... On disabled list (August 6, 1996-remainder of season). ... Claimed on waivers by St. Louis Cardinals (December 2, 1996). ... On St. Louis disabled list (April 5-May 12 and May 20-June 20, 1997); included rehabilitation assignment to Louisville (May 1-12). ... On St. Louis disabled list (June 13-29, 1999); included rehabilitation assignment to Arkansas (June 28-29). ... Traded by Cardinals with C Alberto Castillo and P Matt DeWitt to Toronto Blue Jays for P Pat Hentgen and P Paul Spoljaric (November 11, 1999). ... On Toronto disabled list (May 17-June 6, 2000); included rehabilitation assignment to Dunedin (June 4).
STATISTICAL NOTES: Led Texas League with 10 hit batsmen in 1992.
MISCELLANEOUS: Received base on balls in only appearance as pinch hitter with Colorado (1995). ... Struck out twice in two appearances as pinch hitter (1996).

Year League	W	L	Pct.	ERA	G	GS	CG	ShO	Sv.	IP	H	R	ER	BB	SO
1990—Spokane (N'West)	7	3	.700	1.51	23	1	0	0	3	71$^2/_3$	45	18	12	15	104
1991—Waterloo (Midw.)	14	8	.636	2.30	28	28	7	*4	0	200	162	64	51	57	201
1992—Wichita (Texas)	10	5	*.667	3.53	27	•27	1	1	0	163$^1/_3$	138	74	64	55	137
1993—Colorado Springs (PCL)■	9	7	.563	4.30	23	22	•4	1	0	138	165	90	66	44	91
—Colorado (N.L.)	2	2	.500	6.00	10	6	1	0	0	39	52	26	26	9	16
1994—Colorado Springs (PCL)	4	3	.571	4.79	13	13	1	0	0	71$^1/_3$	83	42	38	28	59
—Colorado (N.L.)	4	6	.400	6.11	15	14	0	0	0	73$^2/_3$	91	51	50	26	41
1995—Colorado (N.L.)	3	0	1.000	4.37	33	1	0	0	1	45$^1/_3$	55	23	22	10	36
—Colorado Springs (PCL)	0	3	.000	5.96	11	4	0	0	0	25$^2/_3$	32	20	17	11	12
1996—Colorado (N.L.)	4	2	.667	5.86	34	1	0	0	0	50$^2/_3$	56	37	33	25	48
1997—St. Louis (N.L.)■	1	1	.500	4.76	14	0	0	0	0	17	13	9	9	8	11
—Louisville (A.A.)	1	0	1.000	5.23	18	2	0	0	0	20$^2/_3$	18	14	12	4	22
1998—St. Louis (N.L.)	4	0	1.000	3.99	65	0	0	0	1	47$^1/_3$	42	24	21	28	39
1999—St. Louis (N.L.)	4	5	.444	4.83	56	4	0	0	1	63$^1/_3$	63	37	34	25	56
—Arkansas (Texas)	0	0	...	0.00	1	0	0	0	0	2	1	0	0	0	4
2000—Toronto (A.L.)■	2	0	1.000	4.72	42	2	0	0	0	66$^2/_3$	69	37	35	22	53
—Dunedin (FSL)	0	0	...	0.00	1	1	0	0	0	1	0	0	0	0	0
A.L. totals (1 year)	2	0	1.000	4.72	42	2	0	0	0	66$^2/_3$	69	37	35	22	53
N.L. totals (7 years)	22	16	.579	5.22	227	26	1	0	3	336$^1/_3$	372	207	195	131	247
Major League totals (8 years)	24	16	.600	5.14	269	28	1	0	3	403	441	244	230	153	300

DIVISION SERIES RECORD

NOTES: Struck out in only appearance as pinch hitter (1995).

Year League	W	L	Pct.	ERA	G	GS	CG	ShO	Sv.	IP	H	R	ER	BB	SO
1995—Colorado (N.L.)	0	0	...	5.40	1	1	0	0	0	5	5	3	3	2	4

P

PALACIOS, VICENTE   P

PERSONAL: Born July 19, 1963, in Mataloma, Mexico. ... 6-2/180. ... Throws right, bats right. ... Full name: Vicente Hernandez Diaz Palacios. ... Name pronounced puh-LAH-see-os.

HIGH SCHOOL: Secundaria Tecnica (Soleda Vera Cruz, Mexico).

TRANSACTIONS/CAREER NOTES: Signed as free agent by Aguila of Mexican League (April 23, 1982). ... Contract sold by Aguila to Chicago White Sox organization (July 20, 1984). ... Loaned by White Sox organization to Mexico City Reds of Mexican League (May 28-September 3, 1985). ... Loaned by White Sox to Aguila of Mexican League (April 5-September 1, 1986). ... Released by White Sox (November 10, 1986). ... Signed by Pittsburgh Pirates organization (December 4, 1986). ... Selected by Milwaukee Brewers from Pirates organization in Rule 5 major league draft (December 8, 1986). ... Returned to Pirates (April 3, 1987). ... On disabled list (April 1-June 12 and July 4, 1989-remainder of season). ... On Pittsburgh disabled list (August 8-September 6, 1991); included rehabilitation assignment to Buffalo (August 28-September 6). ... On disabled list (June 19, 1992-remainder of season). ... Released by Pirates (November 18, 1992). ... Signed by San Diego Padres organization (February 1, 1993). ... Released by Padres (March 29, 1993). ... Played in Mexican League (1993). ... Signed as free agent by St. Louis Cardinals organization (December 23, 1993). ... On disabled list (June 22, 1995-remainder of season). ... Released by Cardinals (November 15, 1995). ... Signed by Toronto Blue Jays organization (January 19, 1999). ... Released by Blue Jays (March 21, 1999). ... Signed by New York Mets organization (July 30, 1999). ... Granted free agency (October 15, 1999). ... Signed by Padres organization (November 4, 1999). ... Released by Padres (August 3, 2000). ... Signed by Chicago Cubs organization (August 7, 2000). ... Granted free agency (October 18, 2000).

STATISTICAL NOTES: Led Mexican League with three balks in 1983. ... Tied for Eastern League lead with four balks in 1985. ... Pitched 10-0 one-hit, complete-game victory against Houston (July 19, 1994).

Year League	W	L	Pct.	ERA	G	GS	CG	ShO	Sv.	IP	H	R	ER	BB	SO
1982—Aguila (Mex.)				Did not play.											
1983—Aguila (Mex.)	12	6	.667	2.61	22	22	10	3	0	165⅓	121	53	48	60	125
1984—Aguila (Mex.)	7	8	.467	3.52	24	20	7	1	4	128	117	64	50	79	120
—Glens Falls (East.)■	1	2	.333	2.49	5	5	0	0	0	25⅓	23	12	7	11	10
1985—Glens Falls (East.)	1	1	.500	4.76	8	4	0	0	1	39⅔	44	25	21	29	20
—Mexico City Reds (Mex.)■	7	2	.778	3.87	13	13	4	1	0	74⅓	86	44	32	44	49
1986—Aguila (Mex.)■	5	14	.263	4.41	23	20	11	2	1	138⅔	157	75	68	78	121
1987—Vancouver (PCL)■	13	5	.722	*2.58	27	26	7	*5	0	*185	140	63	53	85	*148
—Pittsburgh (N.L.)	2	1	.667	4.30	6	4	0	0	0	29⅓	27	14	14	9	13
1988—Pittsburgh (N.L.)	1	2	.333	6.66	7	3	0	0	0	24⅓	28	18	18	15	15
—Buffalo (A.A.)	3	0	1.000	1.99	5	5	1	1	0	31⅔	26	7	7	5	23
1989—Buffalo (A.A.)	0	2	.000	7.20	2	2	0	0	0	10	9	8	8	8	8
1990—Buffalo (A.A.)	13	7	.650	3.43	28	28	5	0	0	183⅔	173	77	70	53	137
—Pittsburgh (N.L.)	0	0	...	0.00	7	0	0	0	3	15	4	0	0	2	8
1991—Pittsburgh (N.L.)	6	3	.667	3.75	36	7	1	1	3	81⅔	69	34	34	38	64
—Buffalo (A.A.)	0	0	...	1.42	3	0	0	0	2	6⅓	7	1	1	2	8
1992—Pittsburgh (N.L.)	3	2	.600	4.25	20	8	0	0	0	53	56	25	25	27	33
1993—Yucatan (Mex.)■	4	4	.500	3.94	38	2	0	0	20	59⅓	47	27	26	40	57
1994—St. Louis (N.L.)■	3	8	.273	4.44	31	17	1	1	1	117⅔	104	60	58	43	95
1995—St. Louis (N.L.)	2	3	.400	5.80	20	5	0	0	0	40⅓	48	29	26	19	34
1996—Aguascalientes (Mex.)■	2	1	.333	3.77	11	0	0	0	2	14⅓	13	6	6	4	15
1997—Monterrey (Mex.)	11	4	.733	3.59	23	22	3	0	0	148	143	66	59	51	120
1998—Monterrey (Mex.)	7	2	.778	1.18	61	0	0	0	25	76⅓	61	11	10	21	71
1999—Reynosa (Mex.)■	5	2	.714	0.95	43	0	0	0	10	66	47	8	7	20	68
—Norfolk (I.L.)■	2	1	.667	1.86	7	0	0	0	1	9⅔	9	2	2	4	9
2000—Las Vegas (PCL)■	4	1	.800	3.42	36	0	0	0	7	47⅓	41	20	18	17	40
—San Diego (N.L.)	0	1	.000	6.75	7	0	0	0	0	10⅔	12	10	8	5	8
—Iowa (PCL)■	2	2	.500	5.70	6	5	1	0	0	30	39	20	19	6	23
Major League totals (8 years)	17	20	.459	4.43	134	44	2	2	7	372	348	190	183	158	270

PALMEIRO, ORLANDO   OF   ANGELS

PERSONAL: Born January 19, 1969, in Hoboken, N.J. ... 5-11/175. ... Bats left, throws left. ... Cousin of Rafael Palmeiro, first baseman, Texas Rangers. ... Name pronounced pal-MAIR-oh.

HIGH SCHOOL: Southridge (Miami).

JUNIOR COLLEGE: Miami-Dade (South) Community College.

COLLEGE: Miami (Fla.).

TRANSACTIONS/CAREER NOTES: Selected by California Angels organization in 33rd round of free-agent draft (June 3, 1991). ... On disabled list (September 1-26, 1994). ... Angels franchise renamed Anaheim Angels for 1997 season. ... On disabled list (August 23-September 7, 1997).

STATISTICAL NOTES: Tied for Northwest League lead in double plays by outfielder with two in 1991. ... Led Texas League with 18 sacrifice hits in 1993. ... Led Texas League outfielders with 328 total chances in 1993. ... Led Pacific Coast League in caught stealing with 16 in 1994. ... Led Pacific Coast League with 11 sacrifice hits in 1995.

							BATTING								FIELDING		
Year Team (League)	Pos.	G	AB	R	H	2B	3B	HR	RBI	Avg.	BB	SO	SB	PO	A	E	Avg.
1991—Boise (N'West)	OF	70	277	56	77	11	2	1	24	.278	33	22	8	130	8	2	*.986
1992—Quad City (Midw.)	OF	127	451	83	143	22	4	0	41	*.317	56	41	31	211	9	6	.973
1993—Midland (Texas)	OF	131	*535	85	163	19	5	0	64	.305	42	35	18	*307	12	9	.973
1994—Vancouver (PCL)	OF	117	458	79	150	28	4	1	47	.328	58	46	21	254	6	1	.996
1995—Vancouver (PCL)	OF-DH	107	398	66	122	21	4	0	47	.307	41	34	16	192	4	1	*.995
—California (A.L.)	OF-DH	15	20	3	7	0	0	0	1	.350	1	1	0	7	0	0	1.000
1996—Vancouver (PCL)	OF	62	245	40	75	13	4	0	33	.306	30	19	7	113	4	5	.959
—California (A.L.)	OF-DH	50	87	6	25	6	1	0	6	.287	8	13	0	33	0	0	1.000
1997—Anaheim (A.L.)	OF-DH	74	134	19	29	2	2	0	8	.216	17	11	2	78	1	2	.975
1998—Vancouver (PCL)	OF	43	140	21	42	13	3	1	29	.300	16	10	3	70	4	0	1.000
—Anaheim (A.L.)	OF-DH	75	165	28	53	7	2	0	21	.321	20	11	5	92	0	1	1.000
1999—Anaheim (A.L.)	OF-DH	109	317	46	88	12	1	1	23	.278	39	30	5	154	6	1	.994
2000—Anaheim (A.L.)	OF-DH	108	243	38	73	20	2	0	25	.300	38	20	4	117	6	2	.984
Major League totals (6 years)		431	966	140	275	47	8	1	84	.285	123	86	16	481	13	5	.990

PERSONAL: Born September 24, 1964, in Havana, Cuba. ... 6-0/190. ... Bats left, throws left. ... Full name: Rafael Corrales Palmeiro. ... Cousin of Orlando Palmeiro, outfielder, Anaheim Angels. ... Name pronounced pal-MAIR-oh.

HIGH SCHOOL: Jackson (Miami).

COLLEGE: Mississippi State.

TRANSACTIONS/CAREER NOTES: Selected by New York Mets organization in eighth round of free-agent draft (June 7, 1982); did not sign. ... Selected by Chicago Cubs organization in first round (22nd pick overall) of free-agent draft (June 3, 1985); pick received as compensation for San Diego Padres signing Type A free-agent P Tim Stoddard. ... Traded by Cubs with P Jamie Moyer and P Drew Hall to Texas Rangers for P Mitch Williams, P Paul Kilgus, P Steve Wilson, IF Curtis Wilkerson, IF Luis Benitez and OF Pablo Delgado (December 5, 1988). ... Granted free agency (October 25, 1993). ... Signed by Baltimore Orioles (December 12, 1993). ... Granted free agency (October 23, 1998). ... Signed by Rangers (December 4, 1998).

RECORDS: Shares A.L. career record for most major league ballparks, one or more home runs (since 1900)—27. ... Shares A.L. record for most seasons leading league in assists by first baseman—6.

HONORS: Named outfielder on THE SPORTING NEWS college All-America team (1985). ... Named Eastern League Most Valuable Player (1986). ... Won A.L. Gold Glove at first base (1997-99). ... Named first baseman on THE SPORTING NEWS A.L. All-Star team (1998 and 1999). ... Named first baseman on THE SPORTING NEWS A.L. Silver Slugger team (1998). ... Named Major League Player of the Year by THE SPORTING NEWS (1999). ... Named designated hitter on THE SPORTING NEWS A.L. Silver Slugger team (1999).

STATISTICAL NOTES: Led Eastern League with 225 total bases, 13 sacrifice flies and 13 intentional bases on balls received in 1986. ... Had 20-game hitting streak (July 18-August 11, 1988). ... Led A.L. first basemen in total chances with 1,540 in 1993 and 1,510 in 1996. ... Led A.L. first basemen in double plays with 133 in 1993 and 157 in 1996. ... Led A.L. first basemen with 1,568 total chances in 1998. ... Had 24-game hitting streak (April 23-May 22, 1994). ... Career major league grand slams: 8.

Year	Team (League)	Pos.	G	AB	R	H	2B	3B	HR	RBI	Avg.	BB	SO	SB	PO	A	E	Avg.
1985—	Peoria (Midw.)	OF	73	279	34	83	22	4	5	51	.297	31	34	9	113	7	1	.992
1986—	Pittsfield (East.)	OF	•140	509	66	*156	29	2	12	*95	.306	54	32	15	248	9	3	*.988
—Chicago (N.L.)		OF	22	73	9	18	4	0	3	12	.247	4	6	1	34	2	4	.900
1987—	Iowa (A.A.)	OF-1B	57	214	36	64	14	3	11	41	.299	22	22	4	150	13	2	.988
—Chicago (N.L.)		OF-1B	84	221	32	61	15	1	14	30	.276	20	26	2	176	9	1	.995
1988—	Chicago (N.L.)	OF-1B	152	580	75	178	41	5	8	53	.307	38	34	12	322	11	5	.985
1989—	Texas (A.L.)■	1B-DH	156	559	76	154	23	4	8	64	.275	63	48	4	1167	*119	12	.991
1990—	Texas (A.L.)	1B-DH	154	598	72	*191	35	6	14	89	.319	40	59	3	1215	91	7	.995
1991—	Texas (A.L.)	1B-DH	159	631	115	203	*49	3	26	88	.322	68	72	4	1305	96	*12	.992
1992—	Texas (A.L.)	1B-DH	159	608	84	163	27	4	22	85	.268	72	83	2	1251	*143	7	.995
1993—	Texas (A.L.)	1B	160	597	*124	176	40	2	37	105	.295	73	85	22	*1388	*147	5	.997
1994—	Baltimore (A.L.)■	1B	111	436	82	139	32	0	23	76	.319	54	63	7	959	66	4	.996
1995—	Baltimore (A.L.)	1B	143	554	89	172	30	2	39	104	.310	62	65	3	1181	*119	4	.997
1996—	Baltimore (A.L.)	1B-DH	162	626	110	181	40	2	39	142	.289	95	96	8	*1383	*119	8	.995
1997—	Baltimore (A.L.)	1B-DH	158	614	95	156	24	2	38	110	.254	67	109	5	1305	112	10	.993
1998—	Baltimore (A.L.)	1B-DH	162	619	98	183	36	1	43	121	.296	79	91	11	*1435	*124	9	.994
1999—	Texas (A.L.)■	DH-1B	158	565	96	183	30	1	47	148	.324	97	69	2	261	13	1	.996
2000—	Texas (A.L.)	1B-DH	158	565	102	163	29	3	39	120	.288	103	77	2	820	56	4	.995
American League totals (12 years)			1840	6972	1143	2064	395	30	375	1252	.296	873	917	73	13670	1205	83	.994
National League totals (3 years)			258	874	116	257	60	6	25	95	.294	62	66	15	532	22	10	.982
Major League totals (15 years)			2098	7846	1259	2321	455	36	400	1347	.296	935	983	88	14202	1227	93	.994

DIVISION SERIES RECORD

Year	Team (League)	Pos.	G	AB	R	H	2B	3B	HR	RBI	Avg.	BB	SO	SB	PO	A	E	Avg.
1996—	Baltimore (A.L.)	1B	4	17	4	3	1	0	1	2	.176	1	6	0	35	1	1	.973
1997—	Baltimore (A.L.)	1B	4	12	2	3	2	0	0	0	.250	0	2	0	27	2	0	1.000
1999—	Texas (A.L.)	DH	3	11	0	3	0	0	0	0	.273	1	1	0	...	...	...	...
Division series totals (3 years)			11	40	6	9	3	0	1	2	.225	2	9	0	62	3	1	.985

NOTES: Hit home run in first at-bat (October 9, 1996).

CHAMPIONSHIP SERIES RECORD

Year	Team (League)	Pos.	G	AB	R	H	2B	3B	HR	RBI	Avg.	BB	SO	SB	PO	A	E	Avg.
1996—	Baltimore (A.L.)	1B	5	17	4	4	0	0	2	4	.235	4	4	0	44	3	0	1.000
1997—	Baltimore (A.L.)	1B	6	25	3	7	2	0	1	2	.280	0	10	0	55	2	0	1.000
Championship series totals (2 years)			11	42	7	11	2	0	3	6	.262	4	14	0	99	5	0	1.000

ALL-STAR GAME RECORD

Year	League	Pos.	AB	R	H	2B	3B	HR	RBI	Avg.	BB	SO	SB	PO	A	E	Avg.
1988—	National	PH-OF	0	0	0	0	0	0	0	...	1	0	0	1	0	0	1.000
1991—	American	1B	0	0	0	0	0	0	0	...	1	0	0	2	0	0	1.000
1998—	American	1B	2	1	2	0	0	0	1	1.000	0	0	0	2	0	0	1.000
1999—	American	DH	2	0	1	0	0	0	1	.500	0	0	0	...	...	...	...
All-Star Game totals (4 years)			4	1	3	0	0	0	2	.750	2	0	0	5	0	0	1.000

PALMER, DEAN — 3B — TIGERS

PERSONAL: Born December 27, 1968, in Tallahassee, Fla. ... 6-1/210. ... Bats right, throws right. ... Full name: Dean William Palmer.

HIGH SCHOOL: Florida (Tallahassee, Fla.).

TRANSACTIONS/CAREER NOTES: Selected by Texas Rangers organization in third round of free-agent draft (June 2, 1986). ... On disabled list (July 19, 1988-remainder of season; April 28-May 13, 1994; and June 4-September 22, 1995). ... Traded by Rangers to Kansas City Royals for OF Tom Goodwin (July 25, 1997). ... Granted free agency (October 27, 1997). ... Re-signed by Royals (December 15, 1997). ... Granted free agency (October 23, 1998). ... Signed by Detroit Tigers (November 13, 1998). ... On suspended list (April 28-May 5, 2000).

P

RECORDS: Shares major league single-season record for fewest assists by third baseman (150 or more games)—221 (1996). ... Holds A.L. single-season record for fewest chances accepted by third baseman (150 or more games)—326 (1996). ... Shares A.L. single-season record for fewest double plays by third baseman (150 or more games)—17 (1996).

HONORS: Named third baseman on THE SPORTING NEWS A.L. Silver Slugger team (1998 and 1999). ... Named third baseman on THE SPORTING NEWS A.L. All-Star team (1999).

STATISTICAL NOTES: Led Texas League third basemen with 30 errors in 1989. ... Led A.L. third basemen with 29 errors in 1993. ... Career major league grand slams: 8.

								BATTING								FIELDING		
Year	Team (League)	Pos.	G	AB	R	H	2B	3B	HR	RBI	Avg.	BB	SO	SB	PO	A	E	Avg.
1986—	GC Rangers (GCL)......	3B	50	163	19	34	7	1	0	12	.209	22	34	6	25	75	13	.885
1987—	Gastonia (S.Atl.).........	3B	128	484	51	104	16	0	9	54	.215	36	126	5	58	209	*59	.819
1988—	Charlotte (FSL)..........	3B	74	305	38	81	12	1	4	35	.266	15	69	0	49	144	28	.873
1989—	Tulsa (Texas)	3B-SS	133	498	82	125	32	5	*25	90	.251	41	*152	15	85	213	†31	.906
	— Texas (A.L.)	3B-DH-SS-OF	16	19	0	2	2	0	0	1	.105	0	12	0	3	4	2	.778
1990—	Tulsa (Texas)	3B	7	24	4	7	0	1	3	9	.292	4	10	0	9	6	3	.833
	— Oklahoma City (A.A.) ..	3B-1B	88	316	33	69	17	4	12	39	.218	20	106	1	206	110	21	.938
1991—	Oklahoma City (A.A.)..	3B-OF	60	234	45	70	11	2	*22	59	.299	20	61	4	49	105	11	.933
	— Texas (A.L.)	3B-OF-DH	81	268	38	50	9	2	15	37	.187	32	98	0	69	75	9	.941
1992—	Texas (A.L.)	3B	152	541	74	124	25	0	26	72	.229	62	*154	10	124	254	22	.945
1993—	Texas (A.L.)	3B-SS	148	519	88	127	31	2	33	96	.245	53	154	11	86	258	†29	.922
1994—	Texas (A.L.)	3B	93	342	50	84	14	2	19	59	.246	26	89	3	50	179	*22	.912
1995—	Texas (A.L.)	3B	36	130	40	40	6	0	9	24	.336	21	21	1	19	72	5	.948
1996—	Texas (A.L.)	3B-DH	154	582	98	163	26	2	38	107	.280	59	145	2	105	221	16	.953
1997—	Texas (A.L.)	3B	94	355	47	87	21	0	14	55	.245	26	84	1	72	162	10	.959
	— Kansas City (A.L.)■	3B-DH	49	187	23	52	10	1	9	31	.278	15	50	1	27	82	9	.924
1998—	Kansas City (A.L.)	3B-DH	152	572	84	159	27	2	34	119	.278	48	134	8	69	187	22	.921
1999—	Detroit (A.L.)■	3B-DH	150	560	92	147	25	2	38	100	.263	57	153	3	89	240	19	.945
2000—	Detroit (A.L.)	3B-1B-DH	145	524	73	134	22	2	29	102	.256	66	146	4	188	185	25	.937
	Major League totals (11 years)		1270	4588	697	1169	218	15	264	803	.255	465	1240	44	901	1919	190	.937

DIVISION SERIES RECORD

								BATTING								FIELDING		
Year	Team (League)	Pos.	G	AB	R	H	2B	3B	HR	RBI	Avg.	BB	SO	SB	PO	A	E	Avg.
1996—	Texas (A.L.)	3B	4	19	3	4	1	0	1	2	.211	0	5	0	3	10	1	.929

ALL-STAR GAME RECORD

						BATTING							FIELDING		
Year	League	Pos.	AB	R	H	2B	3B	HR	RBI	Avg.	BB	SO	SB	PO	A	E	Avg.
1998—	American	PH	1	0	0	0	0	0	0	.000	0	0	0	...	...	...

P

PANIAGUA, JOSE   P   MARINERS

PERSONAL: Born August 20, 1973, in San Jose de Ocoa, Dominican Republic. ... 6-2/190. ... Throws right, bats right. ... Full name: Jose Luis Sanchez Paniagua.

HIGH SCHOOL: Liceo Nuestra Senora del Altagracia (Santo Domingo, Dominican Republic).

TRANSACTIONS/CAREER NOTES: Signed as non-drafted free agent by Montreal Expos organization (September 17, 1990). ... On Montreal disabled list (May 25-June 11, 1996). ... On Ottawa disabled list (July 16-August 2, 1996). ... Selected by Tampa Bay Devil Rays in second round (50th pick overall) of expansion draft (November 18, 1997). ... Claimed on waivers by Seattle Mariners (March 26, 1998). ... On suspended list (August 10-16, 1999).

Year	League	W	L	Pct.	ERA	G	GS	CG	ShO	Sv.	IP	H	R	ER	BB	SO
1992—	Dom. Expos (DSL)	3	7	.300	4.15	13	13	3	1	0	$73\frac{2}{3}$	69	50	34	46	60
1993—	Gulf Coast Expos (GCL)	3	0	1.000	0.67	4	4	1	0	0	27	13	2	2	5	25
1994—	West Palm Beach (FSL)	9	9	.500	3.64	26	26	1	0	0	141	131	82	57	54	110
1995—	Harrisburg (East.)...............	7	•12	.368	5.34	25	25	2	1	0	$126\frac{1}{3}$	140	84	75	62	89
1996—	Ottawa (I.L.)	9	5	.643	3.18	15	14	2	1	0	85	72	39	30	23	61
	— Montreal (N.L.).................	2	4	.333	3.53	13	11	0	0	0	51	55	24	20	23	27
	— Harrisburg (East.).............	3	0	1.000	0.00	3	3	0	0	0	18	12	1	0	2	16
1997—	West Palm Beach (FSL)	1	0	1.000	0.00	2	2	0	0	0	10	5	0	0	2	11
	— Ottawa (I.L.)	8	10	.444	4.64	22	22	1	0	0	$137\frac{2}{3}$	164	79	71	44	87
	— Montreal (N.L.).................	1	2	.333	12.00	9	3	0	0	0	18	29	24	24	16	8
1998—	Tacoma (PCL)■	3	1	.750	2.77	44	0	0	0	5	$68\frac{1}{3}$	66	25	21	22	61
	— Seattle (A.L.)...................	2	0	1.000	2.05	18	0	0	0	1	22	15	5	5	5	16
1999—	Seattle (A.L.).....................	6	11	.353	4.06	59	0	0	0	3	$77\frac{2}{3}$	75	37	35	52	74
2000—	Seattle (A.L.).....................	3	0	1.000	3.47	69	0	0	0	5	$80\frac{1}{3}$	68	31	31	38	71
	A.L. totals (3 years)	11	11	.500	3.55	146	0	0	0	9	180	158	73	71	95	161
	N.L. totals (2 years)	3	6	.333	5.74	22	14	0	0	0	69	84	48	44	39	35
	Major League totals (5 years)	14	17	.452	4.16	168	14	0	0	9	249	242	121	115	134	196

DIVISION SERIES RECORD

Year	League	W	L	Pct.	ERA	G	GS	CG	ShO	Sv.	IP	H	R	ER	BB	SO
2000—	Seattle (A.L.)	1	0	1.000	0.00	2	0	0	0	0	$2\frac{1}{3}$	1	0	0	2	3

CHAMPIONSHIP SERIES RECORD

Year	League	W	L	Pct.	ERA	G	GS	CG	ShO	Sv.	IP	H	R	ER	BB	SO
2000—	Seattle (A.L.)	0	1	.000	4.15	5	0	0	0	0	$4\frac{1}{3}$	4	2	1	1	4

P

PAQUETTE, CRAIG   3B/OF   CARDINALS

PERSONAL: Born March 28, 1969, in Long Beach, Calif. ... 6-0/190. ... Bats right, throws right. ... Full name: Craig Howard Paquette.

HIGH SCHOOL: Ranchos Alamitos (Garden Grove, Calif.).

JUNIOR COLLEGE: Golden West College (Calif.).

TRANSACTIONS/CAREER NOTES: Selected by Minnesota Twins organization in 36th round of free-agent draft (June 2, 1987); did not sign. ... Selected by Oakland Athletics organization in eighth round of free-agent draft (June 5, 1989). ... On Modesto disabled list (April 10-May 5, 1991). ... On Huntsville disabled list (June 1-11, 1991). ... On Tacoma disabled list (July 18, 1994-remainder of season). ... Released by A's (March 26, 1996). ... Signed by Kansas City Royals organization (April 3, 1996). ... Granted free agency (October 15, 1997). ... Signed by New York Mets organization (December 23, 1997). ... On New York disabled list (May 7, 1998-remainder of season). ... Granted free agency (October 15, 1998). ... Re-signed by Mets organization (December 18, 1998). ... On Norfolk disabled list (April 22-May 1, 1999). ... Traded by Mets to St. Louis Cardinals for IF/OF Shawon Dunston (July 31, 1999).

STATISTICAL NOTES: Tied for Northwest League lead with 163 total bases in 1989. ... Led Northwest League third basemen with .936 fielding percentage and 12 double plays in 1989. ... Led Southern League third basemen with 349 total chances in 1992. ... Career major league grand slams: 2.

Year	Team (League)	Pos.	G	AB	R	H	2B	3B	HR	RBI	Avg.	BB	SO	SB	PO	A	E	Avg.
1989—	S. Oregon (N'West)	3B-SS-2B	71	277	53	93	*22	3	14	56	.336	30	46	9	61	155	15	†.935
1990—	Modesto (Calif.)	3B	130	495	65	118	23	4	15	59	.238	47	123	8	*88	218	26	*.922
1991—	Huntsville (Sou.)	3B-1B	102	378	50	99	18	1	8	60	.262	28	87	0	51	132	16	.920
1992—	Huntsville (Sou.)	3B	115	450	59	116	25	4	17	71	.258	29	118	13	69	*248	*32	.908
—	Tacoma (PCL)	3B	17	66	10	18	7	0	2	11	.273	2	16	3	14	33	3	.940
1993—	Tacoma (PCL)	3B-SS-2B	50	183	29	49	8	0	8	29	.268	14	54	3	32	116	15	.908
—	Oakland (A.L.)	3B-DH-OF	105	393	35	86	20	4	12	46	.219	14	108	4	82	165	13	.950
1994—	Tacoma (PCL)	3B	65	245	39	70	12	3	17	48	.286	14	48	3	40	166	14	.936
—	Oakland (A.L.)	3B	14	49	0	7	2	0	0	0	.143	0	14	1	14	22	0	1.000
1995—	Oakland (A.L.)	3-O-S-1	105	283	42	64	13	1	13	49	.226	12	88	5	72	92	8	.953
1996—	Omaha (A.A.)■	DH-3B-1B-OF	18	63	9	21	3	0	4	13	.333	8	14	1	24	9	3	.917
—	Kansas City (A.L.)	3-O-1-S-DH	118	429	61	111	15	1	22	67	.259	23	101	5	261	102	14	.963
1997—	Kansas City (A.L.)	3B-OF	77	252	26	58	15	1	8	33	.230	10	57	2	51	130	12	.938
—	Omaha (A.A.)	3B-DH	23	91	9	28	6	0	3	20	.308	6	26	0	12	29	2	.953
1998—	Norfolk (I.L.)■	3B-SS-OF	15	61	11	17	1	1	3	14	.279	1	13	2	9	39	4	.923
—	New York (N.L.)	3B-OF	7	19	3	5	2	0	0	0	.263	0	6	1	5	2	0	1.000
1999—	Norfolk (I.L.)	3B-OF-1B-SS	70	283	40	77	20	3	15	54	.272	10	47	3	168	82	8	.969
—	St. Louis (N.L.)■	OF-3B-2B-1B	48	157	21	45	6	0	10	37	.287	6	38	1	75	42	3	.975
2000—	St. Louis (N.L.)	3B-OF-1B-2B	134	384	47	94	24	2	15	61	.245	27	83	4	216	123	15	.958
American League totals (5 years)			419	1406	164	326	65	7	55	195	.232	59	368	17	480	511	47	.955
National League totals (3 years)			189	560	71	144	32	2	25	98	.257	33	127	6	296	167	18	.963
Major League totals (8 years)			608	1966	235	470	97	9	80	293	.239	92	495	23	776	678	65	.957

DIVISION SERIES RECORD

Year	Team (League)	Pos.	G	AB	R	H	2B	3B	HR	RBI	Avg.	BB	SO	SB	PO	A	E	Avg.
2000—	St. Louis (N.L.)	OF-3B	2	2	0	0	0	0	0	0	.000	0	0	0	2	0	0	1.000

CHAMPIONSHIP SERIES RECORD

Year	Team (League)	Pos.	G	AB	R	H	2B	3B	HR	RBI	Avg.	BB	SO	SB	PO	A	E	Avg.
2000—	St. Louis (N.L.)	3B-OF-PH	4	6	0	1	0	0	0	0	.167	0	2	0	2	1	0	1.000

PARK, CHAN HO — P — DODGERS

PERSONAL: Born June 30, 1973, in Kong Ju City, Korea. ... 6-2/204. ... Throws right, bats right. ... Full name: Chan Ho Park.
HIGH SCHOOL: Kong Ju (Kong Ju City, Korea).
COLLEGE: Hanyang University (Seoul, Korea).
TRANSACTIONS/CAREER NOTES: Signed as non-drafted free agent by Los Angeles Dodgers organization (January 14, 1994). ... On Albuquerque disabled list (July 16-29, 1995). ... On suspended list (June 8-17, 1999).
RECORDS: Shares major league single-season record for most grand slams allowed—4 (1999).

Year	League	W	L	Pct.	ERA	G	GS	CG	ShO	Sv.	IP	H	R	ER	BB	SO
1994—	Los Angeles (N.L.)	0	0	...	11.25	2	0	0	0	0	4	5	5	5	5	6
—	San Antonio (Texas)	5	7	.417	3.55	20	20	0	0	0	101 1/3	91	52	40	57	100
1995—	Albuquerque (PCL)	6	7	.462	4.91	23	22	0	0	0	110	93	64	60	76	101
—	Los Angeles (N.L.)	0	0	...	4.50	2	1	0	0	0	4	2	2	2	2	7
1996—	Los Angeles (N.L.)	5	5	.500	3.64	48	10	0	0	0	108 2/3	82	48	44	71	119
1997—	Los Angeles (N.L.)	14	8	.636	3.38	32	29	2	0	0	192	149	80	72	70	166
1998—	Los Angeles (N.L.)	15	9	.625	3.71	34	34	2	0	0	220 2/3	199	101	91	97	191
1999—	Los Angeles (N.L.)	13	11	.542	5.23	33	33	0	0	0	194 1/3	208	120	113	100	174
2000—	Los Angeles (N.L.)	18	10	.643	3.27	34	34	3	1	0	226	173	92	82	124	217
Major League totals (7 years)		65	43	.602	3.88	185	141	7	1	0	949 2/3	818	448	409	469	880

PARQUE, JIM — P — WHITE SOX

PERSONAL: Born February 8, 1976, in Norwalk, Calif. ... 5-11/165. ... Throws left, bats left. ... Full name: James Vo Parque.
HIGH SCHOOL: Crescenta Valley (Calif.).
COLLEGE: UCLA.
TRANSACTIONS/CAREER NOTES: Selected by Chicago White Sox organization in second round of free-agent draft (June 3, 1997). ... On suspended list (May 7-9, 2000).
STATISTICAL NOTES: Tied for A.L. lead with three balks in 1998. ... Led A.L. with five balks in 2000.
MISCELLANEOUS: Member of 1996 U.S. Olympic baseball team.

P

Year League	W	L	Pct.	ERA	G	GS	CG	ShO	Sv.	IP	H	R	ER	BB	SO
1997—Winston-Salem (Caro.).......	7	2	.778	2.77	11	11	0	0	0	61²/₃	29	19	19	23	76
—Nashville (PCL)	1	0	1.000	4.22	2	2	0	0	0	10²/₃	9	5	5	9	5
1998—Calgary (PCL)	2	3	.400	3.94	8	8	0	0	0	48	49	26	21	25	31
—Chicago (A.L.)	7	5	.583	5.10	21	21	0	0	0	113	135	72	64	49	77
1999—Chicago (A.L.)	9	15	.375	5.13	31	30	1	0	0	173²/₃	210	111	99	79	111
2000—Chicago (A.L.)	13	6	.684	4.28	33	32	0	0	0	187	208	105	89	71	111
Major League totals (3 years)	29	26	.527	4.79	85	83	1	0	0	473²/₃	553	288	252	199	299

DIVISION SERIES RECORD

Year League	W	L	Pct.	ERA	G	GS	CG	ShO	Sv.	IP	H	R	ER	BB	SO
2000—Chicago (A.L.)	0	0	...	4.50	1	1	0	0	0	6	6	3	3	1	2

PARRA, JOSE   P

PERSONAL: Born November 28, 1972, in Jacagua, Dominican Republic. ... 5-11/175. ... Throws right, bats right. ... Full name: Jose Miguel Parra.

HIGH SCHOOL: Liceo Evangelico Jacagua (Dominican Republic).

TRANSACTIONS/CAREER NOTES: Signed as non-drafted free agent by Los Angeles Dodgers organization (December 7, 1989). ... On disabled list (May 15-June 17 and August 13, 1993-remainder of season). ... Traded by Dodgers with 3B/1B Ron Coomer, P Greg Hansell and a player to be named later to Minnesota Twins for P Kevin Tapani and P Mark Guthrie (July 31, 1995); Twins acquired OF Chris Latham to complete deal (October 30, 1995). ... Granted free agency (October 17, 1997). ... Signed by Samsung, Korean League (February 3, 1998). ... Signed by Yomiuri Giants of Japan Central League (January 13, 1999). ... Signed by Pittsbugh Pirates organization (January 14, 2000). ... On Nashville disabled list (June 3-10, 2000). ... Granted free agency (October 2, 2000).

STATISTICAL NOTES: Led Pacific Coast League with 14 wild pitches in 2000.

Year League	W	L	Pct.	ERA	G	GS	CG	ShO	Sv.	IP	H	R	ER	BB	SO
1989—Dom. Dodgers (DSL)	8	1	.889	1.87	13	11	4	3	2	67¹/₃	60	21	14	20	51
1990—Gulf Coast Dodgers (GCL)..	5	3	.625	2.67	10	10	1	0	0	57¹/₃	50	22	17	18	50
1991—Great Falls (Pio.)	4	6	.400	6.16	14	14	1	1	0	64¹/₃	86	58	44	18	55
1992—Bakersfield (Calif.).............	7	8	.467	3.59	24	23	3	0	0	143	151	73	57	47	107
—San Antonio (Texas)	2	0	1.000	6.14	3	3	0	0	0	14²/₃	22	12	10	7	7
1993—San Antonio (Texas)	1	8	.111	3.15	17	17	0	0	0	111¹/₃	103	46	39	12	87
1994—Albuquerque (PCL)............	10	10	.500	4.78	27	27	1	0	0	145	190	92	77	38	90
1995—Albuquerque (PCL)............	3	2	.600	5.13	12	10	1	1	1	52²/₃	62	33	30	17	33
—Los Angeles (N.L.)	0	0	...	4.35	8	0	0	0	0	10¹/₃	10	8	5	6	7
—Minnesota (A.L.)■	1	5	.167	7.59	12	12	0	0	0	61²/₃	83	59	52	22	29
1996—Salt Lake (PCL)	5	3	.625	5.11	23	1	0	0	8	44	51	25	25	13	26
—Minnesota (A.L.)	5	5	.500	6.04	27	5	0	0	0	70	88	48	47	27	50
1997—Salt Lake (PCL)	2	8	.200	6.03	50	4	0	0	8	94	126	73	63	30	61
1998—Samsung (Korean)■..........	7	8	.467	3.67	60	4	0	0	19	95²/₃	79	45	39	40	55
1999—Yomiuri (Jap. Cen.)■	2	3	.400	5.32	12	9	0	0	0	47¹/₃	43	29	28	23	25
2000—Nashville (PCL)■.............	6	5	.545	5.22	23	21	0	0	1	101²/₃	106	66	59	65	68
—Pittsburgh (N.L.)	0	1	.000	6.94	6	2	0	0	0	11²/₃	17	9	9	7	9
A.L. totals (2 years)	6	10	.375	6.77	39	17	0	0	0	131²/₃	171	107	99	49	79
N.L. totals (2 years)	0	1	.000	5.73	14	2	0	0	0	22	27	17	14	13	16
Major League totals (3 years)	6	11	.353	6.62	53	19	0	0	0	153²/₃	198	124	113	62	95

PARRIS, STEVE   P   BLUE JAYS

PERSONAL: Born December 17, 1967, in Joliet, Ill. ... 6-0/195. ... Throws right, bats right. ... Full name: Steven Michael Parris.

HIGH SCHOOL: Joliet (Ill.) West.

COLLEGE: College of St. Francis (Ill.).

TRANSACTIONS/CAREER NOTES: Selected by Philadelphia Phillies organization in fifth round of free-agent draft (June 5, 1989). ... Claimed on waivers by Los Angeles Dodgers (April 19, 1993). ... Claimed on waivers by Seattle Mariners (April 26, 1993). ... On Jacksonville disabled list (May 12-June 23 and July 17-31, 1993). ... Released by Mariners (July 31, 1993). ... Signed by Pittsburgh Pirates organization (June 24, 1994). ... On Pittsburgh disabled list (March 6-July 11 and August 18-September 10, 1996); included rehabilitation assignments to Augusta (June 12-13) and Carolina (June 13-July 11). ... Released by Pirates (March 13, 1997). ... Signed by Cincinnati Reds organization (May 6, 1997). ... Granted free agency (October 15, 1997). ... Re-signed by Reds organization (October 27, 1997). ... On Cincinnati disabled list (July 31-September 1, 1999); included rehabilitation assignment to Indianapolis (August 22-30). ... Traded by Reds to Toronto Blue Jays for P Clayton Andrews and P Leo Estrella (November 22, 2000).

STATISTICAL NOTES: Tied for N.L. lead in double plays by a pitcher with six in 1999.

MISCELLANEOUS: Scored one run in two appearances as pinch runner (2000).

Year League	W	L	Pct.	ERA	G	GS	CG	ShO	Sv.	IP	H	R	ER	BB	SO
1989—Batavia (NY-Penn)	3	5	.375	3.91	13	10	1	0	0	66²/₃	69	38	29	20	46
1990—Batavia (NY-Penn)	7	1	*.875	2.64	14	14	0	0	0	81²/₃	70	34	24	22	50
1991—Clearwater (FSL)	7	5	.583	3.39	43	6	0	0	1	93	101	43	35	25	59
1992—Reading (East.)	5	7	.417	4.64	18	14	0	0	0	85¹/₃	94	55	44	21	60
—Scranton/W.B. (I.L.)	3	3	.500	4.03	11	6	0	0	1	51¹/₃	57	25	23	17	29
1993—Scranton/W.B. (I.L.)	0	0	...	12.71	3	0	0	0	0	5²/₃	9	9	8	3	4
—Jacksonville (Sou.)■............	0	1	.000	5.93	7	1	0	0	0	13²/₃	15	9	9	6	5
1994—Salem (Caro.) ■	3	3	.500	3.63	17	7	0	0	0	57	58	24	23	21	48
1995—Carolina (Sou.)	9	1	.900	2.51	14	14	2	2	0	89²/₃	61	25	25	16	86
—Pittsburgh (N.L.)	6	6	.500	5.38	15	15	1	1	0	82	89	49	49	33	61
1996—Augusta (S.Atl.)	0	0	...	0.00	1	1	0	0	0	5	1	0	0	1	6
—Carolina (Sou.)	2	0	1.000	3.04	5	5	0	0	0	26²/₃	24	11	9	6	22
—Pittsburgh (N.L.)	0	3	.000	7.18	8	4	0	0	0	26¹/₃	35	22	21	11	27
1997—Chattanooga (Sou.)■	6	2	.750	4.13	14	14	0	0	0	80²/₃	78	44	37	29	68
—Indianapolis (A.A.).............	2	3	.400	3.57	5	5	1	0	0	35¹/₃	26	15	14	11	27
1998—Indianapolis (I.L.)	6	1	.857	3.84	13	13	1	1	0	84¹/₃	74	38	36	26	102
—Cincinnati (N.L.)	6	5	.545	3.73	18	16	1	1	0	99	89	44	41	32	77

Year	League	W	L	Pct.	ERA	G	GS	CG	ShO	Sv.	IP	H	R	ER	BB	SO
1999— Indianapolis (I.L.)		0	2	.000	4.04	6	6	0	0	0	35 2/3	39	16	16	9	31
— Cincinnati (N.L.)		11	4	.733	3.50	22	21	2	1	0	128 2/3	124	59	50	52	86
2000— Cincinnati (N.L.)		12	17	.414	4.81	33	33	0	0	0	192 2/3	227	109	103	71	117
Major League totals (5 years)		35	35	.500	4.49	96	89	4	3	0	528 2/3	564	283	264	199	368

PARRISH, JOHN — P — ORIOLES

PERSONAL: Born November 26, 1977, in Lancaster, Pa. ... 5-11/180. ... Throws left, bats left. ... Full name: John Henry Parrish Jr.
HIGH SCHOOL: J.P. McCaskey (Lancaster, Pa.).
TRANSACTIONS/CAREER NOTES: Selected by Baltimore Orioles organization in 25th round of free-agent draft (June 4, 1996).

Year	League	W	L	Pct.	ERA	G	GS	CG	ShO	Sv.	IP	H	R	ER	BB	SO
1996— Gulf Coast Orioles (GCL)		2	0	1.000	1.86	11	0	0	0	2	19 1/3	13	5	4	11	33
— Bluefield (Appl.)		2	1	.667	2.70	8	0	0	0	1	13 1/3	11	6	4	9	18
1997— Delmarva (S.Atl.)		3	3	.500	3.84	23	10	0	0	1	72 2/3	69	39	31	32	76
— Bowie (East.)		1	0	1.000	1.80	1	1	0	0	0	5	3	1	1	2	3
— Frederick (Caro.)		1	3	.250	6.04	5	5	0	0	0	22 1/3	23	18	15	16	17
1998— Frederick (Caro.)		4	4	.500	3.27	16	16	1	0	0	82 2/3	77	39	30	27	81
1999— Delmarva (S.Atl.)		0	1	.000	7.20	4	0	0	0	0	10	9	8	8	6	10
— Frederick (Caro.)		2	2	.500	4.17	6	6	0	0	0	36 2/3	34	17	17	12	44
— Bowie (East.)		0	2	.000	4.04	10	0	0	0	0	55 2/3	49	28	25	43	42
2000— Bowie (East.)		2	0	1.000	1.69	3	3	0	0	0	16	12	3	3	7	16
— Rochester (I.L.)		6	7	.462	4.24	18	18	0	0	0	104	85	54	49	56	87
— Baltimore (A.L.)		2	4	.333	7.18	8	8	0	0	0	36 1/3	40	32	29	35	28
Major League totals (1 year)		2	4	.333	7.18	8	8	0	0	0	36 1/3	40	32	29	35	28

PATTERSON, COREY — OF — CUBS

PERSONAL: Born August 13, 1979, in Atlanta. ... 5-10/180. ... Bats left, throws right. ... Full name: Donald Corey Patterson. ... Son of Don Patterson, defensive back with Detroit Lions (1979) and New York Giants (1980).
HIGH SCHOOL: Harrison (Kennesaw, Ga.).
TRANSACTIONS/CAREER NOTES: Selected by Chicago Cubs organization in first round (third pick overall) of free-agent draft (June 2, 1998). ... On disabled list (May 27-June 11, 1999).
STATISTICAL NOTES: Led Midwest League in slugging percentage with .592 in 1999.

Year	Team (League)	Pos.	G	AB	R	H	2B	3B	HR	RBI	Avg.	BB	SO	SB	PO	A	E	Avg.
							BATTING									FIELDING		
1999— Lansing (Midw.)		OF	112	475	94	152	35	*17	20	79	.320	25	85	33	244	7	9	.965
2000— West Tenn (Sou.)		OF	118	444	73	116	26	5	22	82	.261	45	115	27	296	7	3	.990
— Chicago (N.L.)		OF	11	42	9	7	1	0	2	2	.167	3	14	1	26	0	1	.963
Major League totals (1 year)			11	42	9	7	1	0	2	2	.167	3	14	1	0	0	1	.000

PATTERSON, DANNY — P — TIGERS

PERSONAL: Born February 17, 1971, in San Gabriel, Calif. ... 6-0/225. ... Throws right, bats right. ... Full name: Danny Shane Patterson.
HIGH SCHOOL: San Gabriel (Calif.).
JUNIOR COLLEGE: Cerritos College (Calif.).
TRANSACTIONS/CAREER NOTES: Selected by Texas Rangers organization in 47th round of free-agent draft (June 5, 1989). ... On Texas disabled list (May 22-June 14, 1997); included rehabilitation assignment to Tulsa (June 9-14). ... On Texas disabled list (March 22-April 17, 1998); included rehabilitation assignments to Tulsa (April 7-12) and Oklahoma (April 13-17). ... Traded by Rangers with OF Juan Gonzalez and C Gregg Zaun to Detroit Tigers for P Justin Thompson, P Francisco Cordero, OF Gabe Kapler, C Bill Haselman, 2B Frank Catalanotto and P Alan Webb (November 2, 1999). ... On disabled list (July 22-August 7, 2000).

Year	League	W	L	Pct.	ERA	G	GS	CG	ShO	Sv.	IP	H	R	ER	BB	SO
1990— Butte (Pio.)		0	3	.000	6.35	13	3	0	0	1	28 1/3	36	23	20	14	18
1991— Gulf Coast Rangers (GCL)		5	3	.625	3.24	11	9	0	0	0	50	43	21	18	12	46
1992— Gastonia (S.Atl.)		4	6	.400	3.59	23	21	3	1	0	105 1/3	106	47	42	33	84
1993— Charlotte (FSL)		5	6	.455	2.51	47	0	0	0	7	68	55	22	19	28	41
1994— Tulsa (Texas)		1	4	.200	1.64	30	1	0	0	6	44	35	13	8	17	33
— Charlotte (FSL)		1	0	1.000	4.61	7	0	0	0	0	13 2/3	13	7	7	5	9
1995— Tulsa (Texas)		2	2	.500	6.19	26	0	0	0	5	36 1/3	45	27	25	13	24
— Oklahoma City (A.A.)		1	0	1.000	1.65	14	0	0	0	2	27 1/3	23	8	5	9	9
1996— Oklahoma City (A.A.)		6	2	.750	1.68	44	0	0	0	10	80 1/3	79	22	15	15	53
— Texas (A.L.)		0	0	...	0.00	7	0	0	0	0	8 2/3	10	4	0	3	5
1997— Texas (A.L.)		10	6	.625	3.42	54	0	0	0	1	71	70	29	27	23	69
— Tulsa (Texas)		0	0	...	4.50	2	2	0	0	0	2	5	4	1	0	6
1998— Tulsa (Texas)		0	0	...	4.50	2	1	0	0	0	4	3	2	2	0	4
— Oklahoma (PCL)		0	0	...	4.50	1	0	0	0	0	2	4	1	1	1	2
— Texas (A.L.)		2	5	.286	4.45	56	0	0	0	2	60 2/3	64	31	30	19	33
1999— Texas (A.L.)		2	0	1.000	5.67	53	0	0	0	0	60 1/3	77	38	38	19	43
— Oklahoma (PCL)		1	0	1.000	0.00	2	0	0	0	0	3	1	0	0	1	4
2000— Detroit (A.L.)■		5	1	.833	3.97	58	0	0	0	0	56 2/3	69	26	25	14	29
Major League totals (5 years)		19	12	.613	4.20	228	0	0	0	3	257 1/3	290	128	120	78	179

DIVISION SERIES RECORD

Year	League	W	L	Pct.	ERA	G	GS	CG	ShO	Sv.	IP	H	R	ER	BB	SO
1996— Texas (A.L.)		0	0	...	0.00	1	0	0	0	0	1/3	1	0	0	0	0
1999— Texas (A.L.)		0	0	...	0.00	1	0	0	0	0	1	1	0	0	0	0
Division series totals (2 years)		0	0	...	0.00	2	0	0	0	0	1 1/3	2	0	0	0	0

P

PERSONAL: Born May 19, 1975, in Evanston, Ill. ... 6-1/185. ... Bats right, throws right. ... Full name: Joshua William Paul.
HIGH SCHOOL: Buffalo Grove (Ill.).
COLLEGE: Vanderbilt.
TRANSACTIONS/CAREER NOTES: Selected by Chicago White Sox organization in second round of free-agent draft (June 4, 1996). ... On Birmingham disabled list (April 13-July 13, 1997; and July 9-27, 1999). ... On Charlotte disabled list (July 5-August 3, 2000).
STATISTICAL NOTES: Led Carolina League catchers with 939 total chances in 1998.

							BATTING								FIELDING		
Year Team (League)	Pos.	G	AB	R	H	2B	3B	HR	RBI	Avg.	BB	SO	SB	PO	A	E	Avg.
1996— Hickory (S.Atl.)..........	C	59	226	41	74	16	0	8	37	.327	21	53	13	197	29	2	.991
1997— Birmingham (Sou.).....	C	34	115	18	34	5	0	1	16	.296	12	25	6	221	17	3	.988
— GC White Sox (GCL) ..	C	5	14	3	6	0	1	0	0	.429	1	3	1	21	6	3	.900
1998— Win.-Salem (Caro.)	C	123	444	66	113	20	7	11	63	.255	38	91	20	*818	*118	3	*.997
1999— Birmingham (Sou.).....	C-DH	93	319	47	89	19	3	4	42	.279	29	68	6	526	66	5	*.992
— Chicago (A.L.)...........	C	6	18	2	4	1	0	0	1	.222	0	4	0	40	2	0	1.000
2000— Chicago (A.L.)...........	C-OF	36	71	15	20	3	2	1	8	.282	5	17	1	130	17	4	.974
— Charlotte (I.L.)...........	C-OF	51	168	28	40	5	1	4	19	.238	13	38	6	291	25	2	.994
Major League totals (2 years)		42	89	17	24	4	2	1	9	.270	5	21	1	170	19	4	.979

DIVISION SERIES RECORD

							BATTING								FIELDING		
Year Team (League)	Pos.	G	AB	R	H	2B	3B	HR	RBI	Avg.	BB	SO	SB	PO	A	E	Avg.
2000— Chicago (A.L.)	PR-C	1	0	0	0	0	0	0	0	...	0	0	0	1	0	0	1.000

PERSONAL: Born January 8, 1976, in New Britain, Conn. ... 6-5/230. ... Throws right, bats right. ... Full name: Carl Anthony Pavano.
HIGH SCHOOL: Southington (Conn.).
TRANSACTIONS/CAREER NOTES: Selected by Boston Red Sox organization in 13th round of free-agent draft (June 2, 1994). ... Traded by Red Sox with a player to be named later to Montreal Expos for P Pedro J. Martinez (November 18, 1997); Expos acquired P Tony Armas Jr. to complete deal (December 18, 1997). ... On Montreal disabled list (July 12-September 11, 1999); included rehabilitation assignments to Ottawa (July 29-30 and September 6-7). ... On disabled list (June 25, 2000-remainder of season).
HONORS: Named Eastern League Pitcher of the Year (1996).

Year League	W	L	Pct.	ERA	G	GS	CG	ShO	Sv.	IP	H	R	ER	BB	SO
1994— Gulf Coast Red Sox (GCL)..	4	3	.571	1.84	9	7	0	0	0	44	31	14	9	7	47
1995— Michigan (Midw.)	6	6	.500	3.45	22	22	1	0	0	141	118	63	54	52	138
1996— Trenton (East.)	*16	5	.762	2.63	27	26	•6	2	0	185	154	66	54	47	146
1997— Pawtucket (I.L.)	11	6	.647	3.12	23	23	3	0	0	161 2/3	148	62	56	34	147
1998— Jupiter (FSL)■	0	0	...	6.60	4	4	0	0	0	15	20	11	11	3	14
— Ottawa (I.L.)	1	0	1.000	2.41	3	3	0	0	0	18 2/3	12	5	5	7	14
— Montreal (N.L.)	6	9	.400	4.21	24	23	0	0	0	134 2/3	130	70	63	43	83
1999— Montreal (N.L.)	6	8	.429	5.63	19	18	1	1	0	104	117	66	65	35	70
— Ottawa (I.L.)	0	1	.000	9.00	2	2	0	0	0	5	7	5	5	0	3
2000— Montreal (N.L.)	8	4	.667	3.06	15	15	0	0	0	97	89	40	33	34	64
Major League totals (3 years)	20	21	.488	4.32	58	56	1	1	0	335 2/3	336	176	161	112	217

PERSONAL: Born November 22, 1972, in Zanesville, Ohio. ... 5-10/185. ... Bats right, throws right. ... Full name: Jayson Lee Payton.
HIGH SCHOOL: Zanesville (Ohio).
COLLEGE: Georgia Tech.
TRANSACTIONS/CAREER NOTES: Selected by New York Mets organization in supplemental round ("sandwich pick" between first and second round, 29th pick overall) of free-agent draft (June 2, 1994); pick received as part of compensation for Baltimore Orioles signing Type A free-agent P Sid Fernandez. ... On Norfolk disabled list (April 29-July 3, 1996). ... On disabled list (April 3, 1997-entire season). ... On Norfolk disabled list (May 27-June 15 and June 24-July 20, 1998). ... On New York disabled list (March 21-June 8, 1999); included rehabilitation assignment to St. Lucie (May 30-June 8). ... On Norfolk disabled list (July 10-August 19, 1999).
STATISTICAL NOTES: Career major league grand slams: 1.

							BATTING								FIELDING		
Year Team (League)	Pos.	G	AB	R	H	2B	3B	HR	RBI	Avg.	BB	SO	SB	PO	A	E	Avg.
1994— Pittsfield (NY-Penn)....	OF	58	219	47	80	16	2	3	37	.365	23	18	10	124	8	5	.964
— Binghamton (East.)	OF	8	25	3	7	1	0	0	1	.280	2	3	1	11	0	1	.917
1995— Binghamton (East.)	OF	85	357	59	123	20	3	14	54	.345	29	32	16	230	7	3	.988
— Norfolk (I.L.)	OF	50	196	33	47	11	4	4	30	.240	11	22	11	106	3	2	.982
1996— GC Mets (GCL)..........	DH	3	13	3	5	1	0	1	2	.385	0	1	1	...	...	...	...
— Norfolk (I.L.)	DH-OF	55	153	30	47	6	3	6	26	.307	11	26	10	7	1	0	1.000
— Binghamton (East.)						Did not play.											
— St. Lucie (FSL)..........						Did not play.											
1997—						Did not play.											
1998— Norfolk (I.L.)	OF-1B-DH	82	322	45	84	14	4	8	30	.261	26	50	12	315	20	7	.980
— St. Lucie (FSL)	OF	3	7	0	1	0	0	0	0	.143	3	1	0	8	0	0	1.000
— New York (N.L.)	OF	15	22	2	7	1	0	0	0	.318	1	4	0	6	1	0	1.000
1999— St. Lucie (FSL)	OF	7	26	3	9	1	1	0	3	.346	4	5	0	20	1	1	.955
— Norfolk (I.L.)	OF-DH	38	144	27	56	13	2	8	35	.389	12	13	2	59	3	1	.984
— New York (N.L.)	OF	13	8	1	2	1	0	0	1	.250	0	2	1	3	0	0	1.000
2000— New York (N.L.)	OF	149	488	63	142	23	1	17	62	.291	30	60	5	311	7	6	.981
Major League totals (3 years)		177	518	66	151	25	1	17	63	.292	31	66	6	320	8	6	.982

DIVISION SERIES RECORD

Year	Team (League)	Pos.	G	AB	R	H	2B	3B	HR	RBI	Avg.	BB	SO	SB	PO	A	E	Avg.
2000—	New York (N.L.).........	OF	4	17	1	3	0	0	0	2	.176	0	4	1	10	0	0	1.000

CHAMPIONSHIP SERIES RECORD

Year	Team (League)	Pos.	G	AB	R	H	2B	3B	HR	RBI	Avg.	BB	SO	SB	PO	A	E	Avg.
2000—	New York (N.L.)..........	OF	5	19	1	3	0	0	1	3	.158	2	5	0	10	0	0	1.000

WORLD SERIES RECORD

Year	Team (League)	Pos.	G	AB	R	H	2B	3B	HR	RBI	Avg.	BB	SO	SB	PO	A	E	Avg.
2000—	New York (N.L.)..........	OF	5	21	3	7	0	0	1	3	.333	0	5	0	17	0	2	.895

PENA, ANGEL — C — DODGERS

PERSONAL: Born February 16, 1975, in San Pedro de Macoris, Dominican Republic. ... 5-10/228. ... Bats right, throws right. ... Full name: Angel Maria Pena.
HIGH SCHOOL: Escuela Puerto Rico (San Pedro de Macoris, Dominican Republic).
TRANSACTIONS/CAREER NOTES: Signed as non-drafted free agent by Los Angeles Dodgers organization (July 24, 1992). ... Missed entire 1994 season due to injury. ... On San Bernardino disabled list (July 26-September 17, 1997). ... On Albuquerque disabled list (August 24, 1999-remainder of season). ... On Albuquerque disabled list (April 30-May 19 and May 30-June 9, 2000).
STATISTICAL NOTES: Led California League catchers with 31 passed balls in 1997. ... Led Texas League catchers with 781 putouts, 81 assists, 14 errors and 876 total chances in 1998.

Year	Team (League)	Pos.	G	AB	R	H	2B	3B	HR	RBI	Avg.	BB	SO	SB	PO	A	E	Avg.
1993—	Dom. Dodgers (DSL) .	C	50	168	27	47	3	2	1	24	.280	10	41	6	197	57	15	.944
1994—							Did not play.											
1995—	Great Falls (Pio.)	C	49	138	24	40	11	4	1	15	.290	21	32	2	297	42	7	.980
1996—	Savannah (S.Atl.)	C	36	127	13	26	4	0	6	16	.205	7	37	1	238	39	6	.979
—	Dom. Dodgers (DSL) .	C	23	78	30	37	9	1	8	40	.474	24	12	1	86	11	1	.990
1997—	San Bern. (Calif.)	C	86	322	53	89	22	4	16	64	.276	32	84	3	661	83	10	.987
1998—	San Antonio (Texas)...	C-OF	126	483	81	162	32	2	22	105	.335	48	80	9	†781	†81	†14	.984
—	Los Angeles (N.L.).....	C	6	13	1	3	0	0	0	0	.231	0	6	0	26	2	0	1.000
1999—	Albuquerque (PCL)	C-DH	34	127	15	37	10	1	1	24	.291	10	24	3	200	28	3	.987
—	Los Angeles (N.L.)	C	43	120	14	25	6	0	4	21	.208	12	24	0	233	26	3	.989
2000—	Albuquerque (PCL).....	C-1B-3B	87	315	52	97	12	3	17	61	.308	28	75	3	531	60	7	.988
Major League totals (2 years)			49	133	15	28	6	0	4	21	.211	12	30	0	259	28	3	.990

PENA, ELVIS — 2B/SS — ROCKIES

PERSONAL: Born September 15, 1976, in Santo Domingo, Dominican Republic. ... 5-11/155. ... Bats both, throws right.
TRANSACTIONS/CAREER NOTES: Signed as non-drafted free agent by Colorado Rockies organization (June 22, 1993).
STATISTICAL NOTES: Led Carolina League with 14 sacrifice hits in 1997.

Year	Team (League)	Pos.	G	AB	R	H	2B	3B	HR	RBI	Avg.	BB	SO	SB	PO	A	E	Avg.
1994—	Ariz. Rockies (Ariz.)....	2B-SS	49	171	31	39	5	2	0	9	.228	35	47	20	86	143	21	.916
1995—	Asheville (S.Atl.).........	2B	48	145	27	33	2	0	0	4	.228	28	32	23	86	140	11	.954
—	Portland (N'West)	2B	58	215	29	54	6	3	0	18	.251	26	45	28	92	137	11	.954
1996—	Salem (Caro.).............	2B	102	341	48	76	9	4	0	28	.223	61	70	30	211	245	19	.960
1997—	Salem (Caro.)	2B-SS-3B	93	279	41	62	9	2	1	30	.222	37	53	16	127	199	20	.942
1998—	Asheville (S.Atl.).........	2B	115	428	93	123	24	4	6	48	.287	70	85	41	197	306	29	.945
1999—	Carolina (Sou.)...........	2B-SS	110	356	57	107	24	6	2	31	.301	48	64	21	206	267	13	.973
—	Colo. Springs (PCL) ...	SS-2B	13	43	5	7	1	0	0	1	.163	3	7	4	23	33	7	.889
2000—	Colorado (N.L.)	SS-2B	10	9	1	3	1	0	0	1	.333	1	1	1	1	2	0	1.000
—	Carolina (Sou.)..........	SS-2B	126	477	92	143	16	7	3	37	.300	69	76	*48	205	321	33	.941
Major League totals (1 year)			10	9	1	3	1	0	0	1	.333	1	1	1	1	2	0	1.000

PENA, JESUS — P — RED SOX

PERSONAL: Born March 8, 1975, in Santo Domingo, Dominican Republic. ... 6-0/170. ... Throws left, bats left.
HIGH SCHOOL: Liceo Nocturno (Santo Domingo, Dominican Republic).
TRANSACTIONS/CAREER NOTES: Signed as non-drafted free agent by Pittsburgh Pirates organization (January 19, 1993). ... On suspended list (June 29, 1994-entire season). ... Selected by Chicago White Sox organization from Pirates organization in Rule 5 minor league draft (December 9, 1996). ... Traded by White Sox to Boston Red Sox for a player to be named later (September 20, 2000).

Year	League	W	L	Pct.	ERA	G	GS	CG	ShO	Sv.	IP	H	R	ER	BB	SO
1993—	Dom. Pirates (DSL)............	6	3	.667	2.37	18	10	0	0	2	68 1/3	48	27	18	51	79
1994—	Kingsport (Appl.)...............				Did not play—suspended.											
1995—	Erie (NY-Penn)	0	0	.000	12.66	3	3	0	0	0	10 2/3	18	16	15	7	5
—	Gulf Coast Pirates (GCL)....	0	0	...	2.57	7	6	0	0	0	35	20	11	10	19	36
1996—	Erie (NY-Penn)	2	5	.286	4.79	21	3	0	0	0	35 2/3	32	24	19	24	34
1997—	Hickory (S.Atl.)■...............	5	3	.625	2.22	43	0	0	0	8	65	55	24	16	19	57
1998—	Winston-Salem (Caro.).......	3	4	.429	3.13	23	0	0	0	7	31 2/3	20	11	11	12	37
—	Birmingham (Sou.)...........	0	2	.000	3.86	22	0	0	0	2	23 1/3	20	12	10	10	28
1999—	Birmingham (Sou.)...........	3	2	.600	2.36	40	0	0	0	5	45 2/3	31	12	12	18	49
—	Chicago (A.L.)	0	0	...	5.31	26	0	0	0	0	20 1/3	21	15	12	23	20

P

Year	League	W	L	Pct.	ERA	G	GS	CG	ShO	Sv.	IP	H	R	ER	BB	SO
2000— Charlotte (I.L.)................		0	0	...	3.12	21	0	0	0	4	17 1/3	10	6	6	10	19
— Chicago (A.L.)..................		2	1	.667	5.40	20	0	0	0	1	23 1/3	25	18	14	16	19
— Birmingham (Sou.)............		1	2	.333	3.38	23	0	0	0	10	21 1/3	19	9	8	6	25
— Boston (A.L.)■		0	0	...	3.00	2	0	0	0	0	3	3	1	1	3	1
Major League totals (2 years).......		2	1	.667	5.21	48	0	0	0	1	46 2/3	49	34	27	42	40

PENA, JUAN   P   RED SOX

PERSONAL: Born June 27, 1977, in Santo Domingo, Dominican Republic. ... 6-5/215. ... Throws right, bats right. ... Full name: Juan Francisco Pena.

HIGH SCHOOL: Miami High.

JUNIOR COLLEGE: Miami-Dade (Wolfson) Community College.

TRANSACTIONS/CAREER NOTES: Selected by Boston Red Sox organization in 27th round of free-agent draft (June 1, 1995). ... On disabled list (April 9-24 and June 17-27, 1998). ... On Boston disabled list (May 20-June 6 and June 11-July 22, 1999; included rehabilitation assignments to Pawtucket (May 30-June 6), Gulf Coast Red Sox (July 8-11) and Sarasota (July 12-22). ... On Pawtucket disabled list (July 31-August 9 and August 12, 1999-remainder of season). ... On disabled list (March 29, 2000-entire season).

STATISTICAL NOTES: Pitched 5-0 no-hit victory for Pawtucket against Durham (July 22, 1998).

Year	League	W	L	Pct.	ERA	G	GS	CG	ShO	Sv.	IP	H	R	ER	BB	SO
1995— Gulf Coast Red Sox (GCL)..		3	2	.600	1.95	13	4	2	1	1	55 1/3	41	17	12	6	47
— Sarasota (FSL)		1	1	.500	4.91	2	2	0	0	0	7 1/3	8	4	4	3	5
1996— Michigan (Midw.)		12	10	.545	2.97	26	26	4	0	0	*187 2/3	149	70	62	34	156
1997— Sarasota (FSL)		4	6	.400	2.96	13	13	3	0	0	91 1/3	67	39	30	23	88
— Trenton (East.)		5	6	.455	4.73	16	14	0	0	0	97	98	56	51	31	79
1998— Pawtucket (I.L.)		8	10	.444	4.38	24	23	1	1	0	139 2/3	141	73	68	51	*146
1999— Pawtucket (I.L.)		4	2	.667	4.13	10	10	0	0	0	48	44	28	22	13	61
— Boston (A.L.)....................		2	0	1.000	0.69	2	2	0	0	0	13	9	1	1	3	15
— Gulf Coast Red Sox (GCL)..		0	0	...	0.00	1	1	0	0	0	2	0	0	0	0	4
— Sarasota (FSL)		0	1	.000	7.11	2	2	0	0	0	6 1/3	12	6	5	0	5
2000— Boston (A.L.).....................								Did not play.								
Major League totals (1 year)........		2	0	1.000	0.69	2	2	0	0	0	13	9	1	1	3	15

PENA, WILY   OF   YANKEES

PERSONAL: Born January 23, 1982, in LaGunda Salada, Dominican Republic. ... 6-3/215. ... Bats right, throws right. ... Full name: Wily Modesto Pena.

TRANSACTIONS/CAREER NOTES: Signed by New York Mets organization (1998); contract nullified by Baseball Commissioner's Office. ... Declared a free agent (March 7, 1999). ... Signed by New York Yankees organization (April 1, 1999). ... On New York disabled list (July 13, 2000-remainder of season).

Year	Team (League)	Pos.	G	AB	R	H	2B	3B	HR	RBI	Avg.	BB	SO	SB	PO	A	E	Avg.
															FIELDING			
1999— GC Yankees (GCL)......		OF	45	166	21	41	10	1	7	26	.247	12	54	3	35	1	2	.947
2000— Greensboro (S.Atl.)		OF	67	249	41	51	7	1	10	28	.205	18	91	6	102	6	4	.964
— Staten Island (NY-P) ..		OF	20	73	7	22	1	2	0	10	.301	2	23	2	37	0	0	1.000

PENNY, BRAD   P   MARLINS

PERSONAL: Born May 24, 1978, in Broken Arrow, Okla. ... 6-4/200. ... Throws right, bats right. ... Full name: Bradley Wayne Penny.

HIGH SCHOOL: Broken Arrow (Okla.).

TRANSACTIONS/CAREER NOTES: Selected by Arizona Diamondbacks organization in fifth round of free-agent draft (June 4, 1996). ... On El Paso disabled list (April 20-30, 1999). ... Traded by Diamondbacks with P Vladimir Nunez and a player to be named later to Florida Marlins for P Matt Mantei (July 9, 1999); Marlins acquired OF Abraham Nunez to complete deal (December 13, 1999). ... On Florida disabled list (July 20-September 2, 2000); included rehabilitation assignments to Brevard County (August 5-15) and Calgary (August 16-September 2).

HONORS: Named California League Most Valuable Player and Pitcher of the Year (1998).

MISCELLANEOUS: Flied out in only appearance as pinch hitter (2000).

Year	League	W	L	Pct.	ERA	G	GS	CG	ShO	Sv.	IP	H	R	ER	BB	SO
1996— Ariz. D-backs (Ariz.)		2	2	.500	2.36	11	8	0	0	0	49 2/3	36	18	13	14	52
1997— South Bend (Midw.)		10	5	.667	2.73	25	25	0	0	0	118 2/3	91	44	36	43	116
1998— High Desert (Calif.)...........		*14	5	.737	2.96	28	•28	1	0	0	164	138	65	54	35	*207
1999— El Paso (Texas)............		2	7	.222	4.80	17	17	0	0	0	90	109	56	48	25	100
— Portland (East.)■		1	0	1.000	3.90	6	6	0	0	0	32 1/3	28	15	14	14	35
2000— Florida (N.L.)................		8	7	.533	4.81	23	22	0	0	0	119 2/3	120	70	64	60	80
— Brevard County (FSL)........		0	1	.000	1.13	2	2	0	0	0	8	5	2	1	4	11
— Calgary (PCL)....................		2	0	1.000	1.80	3	3	0	0	0	15	8	8	3	10	16
Major League totals (1 year)........		8	7	.533	4.81	23	22	0	0	0	119 2/3	120	70	64	60	80

PEOPLES, DANNY   OF   INDIANS

PERSONAL: Born January 20, 1975, in Round Rock, Texas. ... 6-1/207. ... Bats right, throws right. ... Full name: Daniel Laurence Peoples.

HIGH SCHOOL: Round Rock (Texas).

COLLEGE: Texas.

TRANSACTIONS/CAREER NOTES: Selected by Cleveland Indians organization in first round (28th pick overall) of free-agent draft (June 4, 1996). ... On disabled list (July 31, 1996-remainder of season). ... On disabled list (April 10-24, June 3-10, June 15-July 31 and August 21, 1998-remainder of season). ... On Buffalo disabled list (April 8-21, 2000).

Year Team (League)	Pos.	G	AB	R	H	2B	3B	HR	RBI	Avg.	BB	SO	SB	PO	A	E	Avg.
1996—Watertown (NY-Penn)	DH	35	117	20	28	7	0	3	26	.239	28	36	3	...	...	...	...
1997—Kinston (Caro.)	OF	121	409	82	102	21	1	*34	84	.249	84	145	8	86	2	4	.957
1998—Akron (East.)	OF	60	222	30	62	19	0	8	32	.279	29	61	1	71	2	2	.973
1999—Akron (East.)	1B-DH	127	494	75	124	23	3	21	78	.251	55	142	2	775	81	14	.984
2000—Buffalo (I.L.)	1B	124	420	68	109	19	2	21	74	.260	63	122	2	945	60	7	.993

PERCIVAL, TROY   P   ANGELS

PERSONAL: Born August 9, 1969, in Fontana, Calif. ... 6-3/236. ... Throws right, bats right. ... Full name: Troy Eugene Percival. ... Name pronounced PER-sih-vol.

HIGH SCHOOL: Moreno Valley (Calif.).

COLLEGE: UC Riverside.

TRANSACTIONS/CAREER NOTES: Selected by California Angels organization in sixth round of free-agent draft (June 5, 1990). ... On Palm Springs disabled list (June 3-July 2, 1992). ... On disabled list (May 28, 1993-remainder of season). ... Angels franchise renamed Anaheim Angels for 1997 season. ... On disabled list (April 7-May 16, 1997); included rehabilitation assignment to Lake Elsinore (May 13-16). ... On Anaheim disabled list (August 5-26, 2000); included rehabilitation assignment to Lake Elsinore (August 22-26).

MISCELLANEOUS: Played catcher (1990). ... Struck out in only appearance as pinch hitter (1996). ... Holds Anaheim Angels franchise all-time record for most saves (171).

Year League	W	L	Pct.	ERA	G	GS	CG	ShO	Sv.	IP	H	R	ER	BB	SO
1991—Boise (N'West)	2	0	1.000	1.41	28	0	0	0	*12	38 1/3	23	7	6	18	63
1992—Palm Springs (Calif.)	1	1	.500	5.06	11	0	0	0	2	10 2/3	6	7	6	8	16
—Midland (Texas)	3	0	1.000	2.37	20	0	0	0	5	19	18	5	5	11	21
1993—Vancouver (PCL)	0	1	.000	6.27	18	0	0	0	4	18 2/3	24	14	13	13	19
1994—Vancouver (PCL)	2	6	.250	4.13	49	0	0	0	15	61	63	31	28	29	73
1995—California (A.L.)	3	2	.600	1.95	62	0	0	0	3	74	37	19	16	26	94
1996—California (A.L.)	0	2	.000	2.31	62	0	0	0	36	74	38	20	19	31	100
1997—Anaheim (A.L.)	5	5	.500	3.46	55	0	0	0	27	52	40	20	20	22	72
—Lake Elsinore (Calif.)	0	0	...	0.00	2	1	0	0	0	2	1	0	0	0	3
1998—Anaheim (A.L.)	2	7	.222	3.64	67	0	0	0	42	66 2/3	45	31	27	37	87
1999—Anaheim (A.L.)	4	6	.400	3.79	60	0	0	0	31	57	38	24	24	22	58
2000—Anaheim (A.L.)	5	5	.500	4.50	54	0	0	0	32	50	42	27	25	30	49
—Lake Elsinore (Calif.)	0	0	...	4.50	2	2	0	0	0	2	1	1	1	1	1
Major League totals (6 years)	19	27	.413	3.16	360	0	0	0	171	373 2/3	240	141	131	168	460

ALL-STAR GAME RECORD

Year League	W	L	Pct.	ERA	GS	CG	ShO	Sv.	IP	H	R	ER	BB	SO
1996—American	0	0	...	0.00	0	0	0	0	1	1	0	0	0	1
1998—American	0	0	...	0.00	0	0	0	0	1	1	0	0	0	2
1999—American							Selected, did not play.							
All-Star Game totals (2 years)	0	0	...	0.00	0	0	0	0	2	2	0	0	0	3

RECORD AS POSITION PLAYER

Year Team (League)	Pos.	G	AB	R	H	2B	3B	HR	RBI	Avg.	BB	SO	SB	PO	A	E	Avg.
1990—Boise (N'West)	C	29	79	12	16	0	0	0	5	.203	19	25	0	215	25	5	.980

PEREZ, CARLOS   P   DODGERS

PERSONAL: Born January 14, 1971, in Nigua, Dominican Republic. ... 6-3/210. ... Throws left, bats left. ... Full name: Carlos Gross Perez. ... Brother of Melido Perez, pitcher with Chicago White Sox (1988-91) and New York Yankees (1992-96); brother of Pascual Perez, pitcher with four major league teams (1980-85 and 1987-92); brother of Vladimir Perez, minor league pitcher (1986-94); brother of Reuben Dario Perez, minor league pitcher (1988-94); and brother of Valerio Perez, minor league pitcher (1983-84).

TRANSACTIONS/CAREER NOTES: Signed as non-drafted free agent by Montreal Expos organization (January 7, 1988). ... On disabled list (April 9-24 and May 18-July 7, 1992). ... On suspended list (July 7-October 22, 1992). ... On disabled list (March 31, 1996-entire season). ... Traded by Expos with SS Mark Grudzielanek and OF Hiram Bocachica to Los Angeles Dodgers for 2B Wilton Guerrero, P Ted Lilly, OF Peter Bergeron and 1B Jonathan Tucker (July 31, 1998). ... On disabled list (September 7, 1999-remainder of season).

MISCELLANEOUS: Struck out in only appearance as pinch hitter (2000). ... Appeared in one game as pinch runner (2000).

Year League	W	L	Pct.	ERA	G	GS	CG	ShO	Sv.	IP	H	R	ER	BB	SO
1989—Dom. Expos (DSL)	3	3	.500	3.07	16	4	0	0	2	44	25	21	15	32	45
1990—Gulf Coast Expos (GCL)	3	1	.750	2.52	13	2	0	0	2	35 2/3	24	14	10	15	38
1991—Sumter (S.Atl.)	2	2	.500	2.44	16	12	0	0	0	73 2/3	57	29	20	32	69
1992—Rockford (Midw.)	0	1	.000	5.79	7	1	0	0	1	9 1/3	12	7	6	5	8
1993—Burlington (Midw.)	1	0	1.000	3.24	12	1	0	0	0	16 2/3	13	6	6	9	21
—San Bernardino (Calif.)	8	7	.533	3.44	20	18	0	0	0	131	120	57	50	44	98
1994—Harrisburg (East.)	7	2	.778	1.94	12	11	2	2	1	79	55	27	17	18	69
—Ottawa (I.L.)	7	5	.583	3.33	17	17	3	0	0	119	130	50	44	41	82
1995—Montreal (N.L.)	10	8	.556	3.69	28	23	2	1	0	141 1/3	142	61	58	28	106
1996—Montreal (N.L.)							Did not play.								
1997—Montreal (N.L.)	12	13	.480	3.88	33	32	8	*5	0	206 2/3	206	109	89	48	110
1998—Montreal (N.L.)	7	10	.412	3.75	23	23	3	0	0	163 1/3	177	79	68	33	82
—Los Angeles (N.L.)■	4	4	.500	3.24	11	11	4	2	0	77 2/3	67	30	28	30	46
1999—Los Angeles (N.L.)	2	10	.167	7.43	17	16	0	0	0	89 2/3	116	77	74	39	40
—Albuquerque (PCL)	3	3	.500	5.92	6	6	2	0	0	38	46	28	25	10	14
2000—Los Angeles (N.L.)	5	8	.385	5.56	30	22	0	0	0	144	192	95	89	33	64
Major League totals (5 years)	40	53	.430	4.44	142	127	17	8	0	822 2/3	900	451	406	211	448

ALL-STAR GAME RECORD

Year League	W	L	Pct.	ERA	GS	CG	ShO	Sv.	IP	H	R	ER	BB	SO
1995—National	0	0	...	0.00	0	0	0	0	1/3	1	0	0	1	0

P

PERSONAL: Born May 4, 1968, in Cuidad Ojeda, Venezuela. ... 6-1/185. ... Bats right, throws right. ... Full name: Eduardo Rafael Perez.
HIGH SCHOOL: Doctor Raul Cuenca (Cuidad Ojeda, Venezuela).
TRANSACTIONS/CAREER NOTES: Signed as non-drafted free agent by Atlanta Braves organization (September 27, 1986). ... On disabled list (August 30-September 14, 1996; and May 5, 2000-remainder of season).
STATISTICAL NOTES: Led South Atlantic League catchers with 13 double plays in 1989. ... Tied for International League lead in errors by catcher with 11 in 1994. ... Led International League catchers with 539 putouts, 69 assists and 615 total chances in 1995. ... Tied for International League lead with seven double plays in 1995.

Year	Team (League)	Pos.	G	AB	R	H	2B	3B	HR	RBI	Avg.	BB	SO	SB	PO	A	E	Avg.
											BATTING				**FIELDING**			
1987—	GC Braves (GCL)	C	31	89	8	18	1	0	1	5	.202	8	14	0	161	31	4	.980
1988—	Burlington (Midw.)	C-1B	64	186	14	43	8	0	4	19	.231	10	33	1	245	42	11	.963
1989—	Sumter (S.Atl.)	C-1B	114	401	39	93	21	0	5	44	.232	44	68	2	760	96	16	.982
1990—	Sumter (S.Atl.)	C-1B	41	123	11	22	7	1	3	17	.179	14	18	0	315	32	3	.991
—	Durham (Caro.)	C-1B	31	93	9	22	1	0	3	10	.237	1	12	0	197	17	3	.986
1991—	Durham (Caro.)	C-1B	92	277	38	75	10	1	9	41	.271	17	33	0	497	55	8	.986
—	Greenville (Sou.)	1B	1	4	0	1	0	0	0	0	.250	0	1	0	9	0	0	1.000
1992—	Greenville (Sou.)	C-1B	91	275	28	63	16	0	6	41	.229	24	41	3	631	64	14	.980
1993—	Greenville (Sou.)	1B-C	28	84	15	28	6	0	6	17	.333	2	8	1	146	19	3	.982
1994—	Richmond (I.L.)	C-1B	113	388	37	101	16	2	9	49	.260	18	47	1	718	80	‡12	.985
1995—	Richmond (I.L.)	C-DH-1B	92	324	31	86	19	0	5	40	.265	12	58	1	†540	†69	7	.989
—	Atlanta (N.L.)	C-1B	7	13	1	4	1	0	1	4	.308	0	2	0	34	2	0	1.000
1996—	Atlanta (N.L.)	C-1B	68	156	19	40	9	1	4	17	.256	8	19	0	281	22	3	.990
1997—	Atlanta (N.L.)	C-1B	73	191	20	41	5	0	6	18	.215	10	35	0	417	24	5	.989
1998—	Atlanta (N.L.)	C-1B-DH	61	149	18	50	12	0	6	32	.336	15	28	1	290	29	2	.994
1999—	Atlanta (N.L.)	C-1B	104	309	30	77	17	0	7	30	.249	17	40	0	620	48	5	.993
2000—	Atlanta (N.L.)	C	7	22	0	4	1	0	0	3	.182	0	2	0	39	2	1	.976
Major League totals (6 years)			320	840	88	216	45	1	24	104	.257	50	126	1	1681	127	16	.991

DIVISION SERIES RECORD

RECORDS: Shares career record for most grand slams—1 (October 3, 1998). ... Shares single-inning record for most runs batted in—4 (October 3, 1998, eighth inning).

Year	Team (League)	Pos.	G	AB	R	H	2B	3B	HR	RBI	Avg.	BB	SO	SB	PO	A	E	Avg.
											BATTING				**FIELDING**			
1995—	Atlanta (N.L.)								Did not play.									
1996—	Atlanta (N.L.)	C	1	3	0	1	0	0	0	0	.333	0	0	0	10	0	0	1.000
1997—	Atlanta (N.L.)	C	1	3	0	0	0	0	0	0	.000	0	1	0	6	0	0	1.000
1998—	Atlanta (N.L.)	C	1	5	1	1	0	0	1	4	.200	0	2	0	6	0	0	1.000
1999—	Atlanta (N.L.)	C	4	16	1	4	0	0	0	3	.250	0	3	0	35	1	0	1.000
Division series totals (4 years)			7	27	2	6	0	0	1	7	.222	0	6	0	57	1	0	1.000

CHAMPIONSHIP SERIES RECORD

NOTES: Named Most Valuable Player (1999).

Year	Team (League)	Pos.	G	AB	R	H	2B	3B	HR	RBI	Avg.	BB	SO	SB	PO	A	E	Avg.
											BATTING				**FIELDING**			
1995—	Atlanta (N.L.)								Did not play.									
1996—	Atlanta (N.L.)	C-1B	4	1	0	0	0	0	0	0	.000	1	0	0	7	0	0	1.000
1997—	Atlanta (N.L.)	C	2	3	0	0	0	0	0	0	.000	0	0	0	14	0	0	1.000
1998—	Atlanta (N.L.)	C	3	4	0	3	0	0	0	0	.750	0	0	0	6	0	0	1.000
1999—	Atlanta (N.L.)	C	6	20	2	10	2	0	2	5	.500	1	3	0	42	2	0	1.000
Championship series totals (4 years)			15	28	2	13	2	0	2	5	.464	2	3	0	69	2	0	1.000

WORLD SERIES RECORD

NOTES: Member of World Series championship team (1995).

Year	Team (League)	Pos.	G	AB	R	H	2B	3B	HR	RBI	Avg.	BB	SO	SB	PO	A	E	Avg.
											BATTING				**FIELDING**			
1995—	Atlanta (N.L.)								Did not play.									
1996—	Atlanta (N.L.)	C	2	1	0	0	0	0	0	0	.000	0	0	0	2	0	0	1.000
1999—	Atlanta (N.L.)	C	3	8	0	1	0	0	0	0	.125	1	3	0	23	2	0	1.000
World Series totals (2 years)			5	9	0	1	0	0	0	0	.111	1	3	0	25	2	0	1.000

PERSONAL: Born September 11, 1969, in Cincinnati. ... 6-4/215. ... Bats right, throws right. ... Full name: Eduardo Antanacio Perez. ... Son of Tony Perez, special assistant to general manager, Florida Marlins; major league infielder with four teams (1964-86) and manager, Cincinnati Reds (1993); and brother of Victor Perez, minor league outfielder/first baseman (1990).
HIGH SCHOOL: Robinson (Santurce, Puerto Rico).
COLLEGE: Florida State.
TRANSACTIONS/CAREER NOTES: Selected by California Angels organization in first round (17th pick overall) of free-agent draft (June 3, 1991). ... On Palm Springs disabled list (May 9-19, 1992). ... On Vancouver disabled list (June 26-July 7, 1994). ... Traded by Angels to Cincinnati Reds for P Will Pennyfeather (April 5, 1996). ... Released by Reds (December 14, 1998). ... Signed by St. Louis Cardinals organization (February 16, 1999). ... Granted free agency (October 15, 1999). ... Re-signed by Cardinals organization (February 3, 2000). ... On St. Louis disabled list (June 25-July 13 and August 13-September 1, 2000); included rehabilitation assignment to Memphis (August 24-September 1). ... Contract sold by Cardinals to Hanshin Tigers of Japan Central League (December 20, 2000).
STATISTICAL NOTES: Career major league grand slams: 2.

P

Year	Team (League)	Pos.	G	AB	R	H	2B	3B	HR	RBI	Avg.	BB	SO	SB	PO	A	E	Avg.
1991— Boise (N'West)	OF-1B	46	160	35	46	13	0	1	22	.288	19	39	12	87	6	3	.969
1992— Palm Springs (Calif.)..	3B-SS-OF	54	204	37	64	8	4	3	35	.314	23	33	14	30	90	16	.882
— Midland (Texas).......	3B-OF-1B	62	235	27	54	8	1	3	23	.230	22	49	19	53	97	13	.920
1993— Vancouver (PCL)	3B-1B-OF	96	363	66	111	23	6	12	70	.306	28	83	21	98	174	23	.922
— California (A.L.)..........	3B-DH	52	180	16	45	6	2	4	30	.250	9	39	5	24	101	5	.962
1994— California (A.L.).........	1B	38	129	10	27	7	0	5	16	.209	12	29	3	305	15	1	.997
— Vancouver (PCL)	3B-DH	61	219	37	65	14	3	7	38	.297	34	53	9	35	116	12	.926
— Arizona Angels (Ariz.).	3B	1	3	0	0	0	0	0	0	.000	1	1	0	0	3	0	1.000
1995— Vancouver (PCL)	3B-DH-1B	69	246	39	80	12	7	6	37	.325	25	34	6	94	90	6	.968
— California (A.L.).........	3B-DH	29	71	9	12	4	1	1	7	.169	12	9	0	16	37	7	.883
1996— Indianapolis (A.A.)■..	3B-1B-DH	122	451	84	132	29	5	21	84	.293	51	69	11	110	215	21	.939
— Cincinnati (N.L.).........	1B-3B	18	36	8	8	0	0	3	5	.222	5	9	0	59	11	0	1.000
1997— Cincinnati (N.L.) 1B-OF-3B-DH		106	297	44	75	18	0	16	52	.253	29	76	5	506	49	2	.996
1998— Cincinnati (N.L.)	1B-3B-OF	84	172	20	41	4	0	4	30	.238	21	45	0	291	47	5	.985
1999— Memphis (PCL)■........	1B-3B-DH	119	416	67	133	31	0	18	82	.320	45	92	7	715	95	9	.989
— St. Louis (N.L.)..........	OF-1B	21	32	6	11	2	0	1	9	.344	7	6	0	29	3	1	.970
2000— Memphis (PCL)	1B-DH	77	277	57	80	12	3	19	66	.289	43	48	10	329	70	8	.980
— St. Louis (N.L.)..........	1B-OF-3B	35	91	9	27	4	0	3	10	.297	5	19	1	167	13	0	1.000
American League totals (3 years)		119	380	35	84	17	3	10	53	.221	33	77	8	345	153	13	.975
National League totals (5 years)		264	628	87	162	28	0	27	106	.258	67	155	6	1052	123	8	.993
Major League totals (8 years)		383	1008	122	246	45	3	37	159	.244	100	232	14	1397	276	21	.988

PEREZ, JOSUE — OF — PHILLIES

PERSONAL: Born August 12, 1977, in Havana, Cuba. ... 6-0/180. ... Bats both, throws right. ... Full name: Josue Perez Perez.
HIGH SCHOOL: Manuel Permuy.
TRANSACTIONS/CAREER NOTES: Signed as non-drafted free agent by Los Angeles Dodgers organization (March 27, 1998). ... Contract voided by Baseball Commissioner's office because Perez had been signed out of Cuba (June 25, 1999). ... Signed by Philadelphia Phillies organization (August 5, 1999).

Year	Team (League)	Pos.	G	AB	R	H	2B	3B	HR	RBI	Avg.	BB	SO	SB	PO	A	E	Avg.
1998— Dom. Dodgers (DSL) .		48	167	56	56	8	7	2	17	.335	39	16	24	...	...	...	...
1999— Vero Beach (FSL)	OF	62	201	24	56	14	1	2	22	.279	21	29	14	120	4	2	.984
— Clearwater (FSL)■.....	OF	23	93	15	23	2	0	0	6	.247	7	17	6	54	0	0	1.000
2000— Clearwater (FSL)	OF	70	279	41	83	9	8	3	32	.297	28	48	18	143	7	1	.993
— Reading (East.)...........	OF	32	96	10	23	5	1	1	8	.240	9	19	2	61	1	1	.984

PEREZ, NEIFI — SS — ROCKIES

PERSONAL: Born June 2, 1975, in Villa Mella, Dominican Republic. ... 6-0/175. ... Bats both, throws right. ... Full name: Neifi Neftali Perez Diaz.
TRANSACTIONS/CAREER NOTES: Signed as non-drafted free agent by Colorado Rockies organization (November 9, 1992).
RECORDS: Holds N.L. single-season record for most at-bats with no intentional bases on balls—690 (1999).
HONORS: Won N.L. Gold Glove as shortstop (2000).
STATISTICAL NOTES: Led California League shortstops with 650 total chances and 86 double plays in 1994. ... Tied for Eastern League lead in double plays by shortstop with 80 in 1995. ... Led Pacific Coast League shortstops with 678 total chances and 91 double plays in 1996. ... Hit for the cycle (July 25, 1998). ... Had 15-game hitting streak (July 27-August 11, 1998). ... Led N.L. with 22 sacrifice hits in 1998. ... Led N.L. shortstops with 272 putouts, 516 assists, 808 total chances and 127 double plays in 1998. ... Led N.L. shortstops with 755 total chances and 124 double plays in 1999. ... Led N.L. shortstops with 829 total chances and 120 double plays in 2000. ... Career major league grand slams: 1.
MISCELLANEOUS: Holds Colorado Rockies all-time record for most triples (41).

Year	Team (League)	Pos.	G	AB	R	H	2B	3B	HR	RBI	Avg.	BB	SO	SB	PO	A	E	Avg.
1993— Bend (N'West)...........	SS-2B	75	296	35	77	11	4	3	32	.260	19	43	19	127	244	25	.937
1994— Central Valley (Calif.)..	SS	•134	506	64	121	16	7	1	35	.239	32	79	9	*223	388	*39	.940
1995— Colo. Springs (PCL) ...	SS	11	36	4	10	4	0	0	2	.278	0	5	1	16	28	3	.936
— New Haven (East.).....	SS	116	427	59	108	28	3	5	43	.253	24	52	5	175	358	18	*.967
1996— Colo. Springs (PCL) ...	SS	133	*570	77	180	28	12	7	72	.316	21	48	16	*244	*409	*25	.963
— Colorado (N.L.).........	SS-2B	17	45	4	7	2	0	0	3	.156	0	8	2	21	28	2	.961
1997— Colo. Springs (PCL) ...	SS	68	303	68	110	24	3	8	46	.363	17	27	8	119	198	8	.975
— Colorado (N.L.)	SS-2B-3B	83	313	46	91	13	10	5	31	.291	21	43	4	185	287	9	.981
1998— Colorado (N.L.)	SS-C	•162	647	80	177	25	9	9	59	.274	38	70	5	†272	†516	20	.975
1999— Colorado (N.L.)	SS	157	*690	108	193	27	•11	12	70	.280	28	54	13	*260	*481	14	.981
2000— Colorado (N.L.)	SS	•162	651	92	187	39	11	10	71	.287	30	63	3	288	523	18	.978
Major League totals (5 years)		581	2346	330	655	106	41	36	234	.279	117	238	27	1026	1835	63	.978

PEREZ, ODALIS — P — BRAVES

PERSONAL: Born June 7, 1978, in Las Matas de Farfan, Dominican Republic. ... 6-0/150. ... Throws left, bats left. ... Full name: Odalis Amadol Perez.
HIGH SCHOOL: Damian Davis Ortiz (Las Matas de Farfan, Dominican Republic).
TRANSACTIONS/CAREER NOTES: Signed as non-drafted free agent by Atlanta Braves organization (July 2, 1994). ... On disabled list (July 23, 1999-remainder of season; April 2, 2000-entire season).

P

Year League	W	L	Pct.	ERA	G	GS	CG	ShO	Sv.	IP	H	R	ER	BB	SO
1995— Gulf Coast Braves (GCL)	3	5	.375	2.22	12	12	1	1	0	65	48	22	16	18	62
1996— Eugene (N'West)	2	1	.667	3.80	10	6	0	0	0	23 2/3	26	16	10	11	38
1997— Macon (S.Atl.)	4	5	.444	1.65	36	0	0	0	5	87 1/3	67	31	16	27	100
1998— Greenville (Sou.)	6	5	.545	4.02	23	21	0	0	.0	132	127	67	59	53	143
— Richmond (I.L.)	1	2	.333	2.96	13	0	0	0	3	24 1/3	26	10	8	7	22
— Atlanta (N.L.)	0	1	.000	4.22	10	0	0	0	0	10 2/3	10	5	5	4	5
1999— Atlanta (N.L.)	4	6	.400	6.00	18	17	0	0	0	93	100	65	62	53	82
2000— Atlanta (N.L.)							Did not play.								
Major League totals (2 years)	4	7	.364	5.82	28	17	0	0	0	103 2/3	110	70	67	57	87

DIVISION SERIES RECORD

Year League	W	L	Pct.	ERA	G	GS	CG	ShO	Sv.	IP	H	R	ER	BB	SO
1998— Atlanta (N.L.)	1	0	1.000	0.00	1	0	0	0	0	2/3	0	0	0	0	1

CHAMPIONSHIP SERIES RECORD

Year League	W	L	Pct.	ERA	G	GS	CG	ShO	Sv.	IP	H	R	ER	BB	SO
1998— Atlanta (N.L.)	0	0	...	54.00	2	0	0	0	0	1/3	5	2	2	3	0

PEREZ, SANTIAGO — SS — PADRES

PERSONAL: Born December 30, 1975, in Santo Domingo, Dominican Republic. ... 6-2/150. ... Bats both, throws right. ... Full name: Santiago Alberto Perez.

HIGH SCHOOL: Liceo Victor Estrella Luz (Santo Domingo, Dominican Republic).

TRANSACTIONS/CAREER NOTES: Signed as non-drafted free agent by Detroit Tigers organization (March 10, 1993). ... Traded by Tigers with P Mike Myers and P Rick Greene to Milwaukee Brewers for P Bryce Florie and a player to be named later (November 20, 1997). ... On Louisville disabled list (August 1-14 and August 19-31, 1999). ... Traded by Brewers with a player to be named later or cash to San Deigo Padres for P Brandon Kolb (December 1, 2000); Padres traded P Wil Cunnane to Brewers for OF Chad Green to complete deal (December 20, 2000).

STATISTICAL NOTES: Led International League shortstops with 29 errors in 1999. ... Led International League shortstops with 27 errors in 2000.

Year Team (League)	Pos.	G	AB	R	H	2B	3B	HR	RBI	Avg.	BB	SO	SB	PO	A	E	Avg.
1993— Dom. Tigers (DSL)	IF-OF	58	171	28	45	6	2	0	17	.263	20	22	17	59	47	16	.869
1994— Dom. Tigers (DSL)	SS	60	227	54	78	7	9	2	47	.344	32	43	20	106	183	39	.881
1995— Fayetteville (S.Atl.)	SS	130	425	54	101	15	1	4	44	.238	30	98	10	176	327	46	.916
1996— Lakeland (FSL)	SS	122	418	33	105	18	2	1	27	.251	16	88	6	192	310	41	.924
1997— Lakeland (FSL)	SS	111	445	66	122	20	12	4	46	.274	20	98	21	148	322	34	.933
1998— El Paso (Texas)■	SS	107	454	73	139	20	*13	11	64	.306	28	70	21	186	310	*36	.932
— Louisville (I.L.)	SS-2B	36	133	18	36	4	3	3	14	.271	6	31	6	67	91	6	.963
1999— Louisville (I.L.)	SS-2B-DH	108	407	57	107	23	8	7	38	.263	31	94	21	150	281	†30	.935
2000— Indianapolis (I.L.)■...	SS-2B	106	408	74	112	26	7	5	34	.275	44	96	31	156	274	27	.941
— Milwaukee (N.L.)	SS	24	52	8	9	2	0	0	2	.173	8	9	4	21	45	6	.917
Major League totals (1 year)		24	52	8	9	2	0	0	2	.173	8	9	4	21	45	6	.917

PEREZ, TIMO — OF — METS

PERSONAL: Born April 8, 1977, in Bani, Dominican Republic. ... 5-9/165. ... Bats left, throws left. ... Full name: Timoniel Perez.

TRANSACTIONS/CAREER NOTES: Played with Hiroshima Toyo Carp of Japan Central League (1996-99). ... Signed as non-drafted free agent by New York Mets organization (March 17, 2000).

Year Team (League)	Pos.	G	AB	R	H	2B	3B	HR	RBI	Avg.	BB	SO	SB	PO	A	E	Avg.
1996— Hiroshima (Jap. Cen.)		31	54	8	15	1	0	1	7	.278	2	7	3	...	...	...	...
1997— Hiroshima (Jap. Cen.)		86	139	17	34	4	2	3	15	.245	10	16	4	...	...	...	...
1998— Hiroshima (Jap. Cen.)		98	230	22	68	8	1	5	35	.296	20	21	2	...	...	...	...
1999— Hiroshima (Jap. Cen.)		12	23	2	4	0	0	0	2	.174	3	3	0	...	...	...	...
2000— St. Lucie (FSL)■	OF	8	31	3	11	4	0	1	8	.355	2	1	3	11	2	0	1.000
— Norfolk (I.L.)	OF	72	291	45	104	17	5	6	37	.357	16	25	13	198	7	5	.976
— New York (N.L.)..........	OF	24	49	11	14	4	1	1	3	.286	3	5	1	30	2	1	.970
Major League totals (1 year)		24	49	11	14	4	1	1	3	.286	3	5	1	30	2	1	.970

DIVISION SERIES RECORD

Year Team (League)	Pos.	G	AB	R	H	2B	3B	HR	RBI	Avg.	BB	SO	SB	PO	A	E	Avg.
2000— New York (N.L.)..........	PH-RF	4	17	2	5	1	0	0	3	.294	0	2	1	10	0	0	1.000

CHAMPIONSHIP SERIES RECORD

Year Team (League)	Pos.	G	AB	R	H	2B	3B	HR	RBI	Avg.	BB	SO	SB	PO	A	E	Avg.
2000— New York (N.L.)..........	OF	5	23	8	7	2	0	0	0	.304	1	3	2	16	2	1	.947

WORLD SERIES RECORD

Year Team (League)	Pos.	G	AB	R	H	2B	3B	HR	RBI	Avg.	BB	SO	SB	PO	A	E	Avg.
2000— New York (N.L.)..........	OF	5	16	1	2	0	0	0	0	.125	1	4	0	8	1	1	.900

P

PEREZ, TOMAS — IF — PHILLIES

PERSONAL: Born December 29, 1973, in Barquisimeto, Venezuela. ... 5-11/177. ... Bats both, throws right. ... Full name: Tomas Orlando Perez.

TRANSACTIONS/CAREER NOTES: Signed as non-drafted free agent by Montreal Expos organization (July 11, 1991). ... Selected by California Angels from Expos organization in Rule 5 major league draft (December 5, 1994). ... Contract sold by Angels to Toronto Blue Jays (December 5, 1994). ... On Toronto disabled list (June 25-July 25, 1997); included rehabilitation assignment to Syracuse (July 12-24). ... Traded by Blue Jays to Angels for IF Dave Hollins and cash (March 30, 1999). ... On Edmonton disabled list (April 21-June 10, 1999). ... Granted free agency (October 15, 1999). ... Signed by Philadelphia Phillies organization (December 15, 1999).

STATISTICAL NOTES: Led Midwest League shortstops with 217 putouts and 65 double plays in 1994. ... Led International League with 14 sacrifice hits in 1997. ... Led International League shortstops with .977 fielding percentage in 1998.

Year	Team (League)	Pos.	G	AB	R	H	2B	3B	HR	RBI	Avg.	BB	SO	SB	PO	A	E	Avg.
1992—	Dom. Expos (DSL)	IF	44	151	35	46	7	0	1	19	.305	27	20	12	112	138	12	.954
1993—	GC Expos (GCL)	SS	52	189	27	46	3	1	2	21	.243	23	25	8	*121	*205	12	*.964
1994—	Burlington (Midw.)	SS-2B	119	465	76	122	22	1	8	47	.262	48	78	8	†221	347	34	.944
1995—	Toronto (A.L.)■.........	SS-2B-3B	41	98	12	24	3	1	1	8	.245	7	18	0	48	77	5	.962
1996—	Syracuse (I.L.)..........	SS-2B	40	123	15	34	10	1	1	13	.276	7	19	8	80	97	7	.962
	Toronto (A.L.)..........	2B-3B-SS	91	295	24	74	13	4	1	19	.251	25	29	1	151	250	15	.964
1997—	Syracuse (I.L.)..........	SS	89	303	32	68	13	0	1	20	.224	37	67	3	158	274	12	.973
	Toronto (A.L.)..........	SS-2B	40	123	9	24	3	2	0	9	.195	11	28	1	58	124	3	.984
1998—	Syracuse (I.L.)..........	SS-2B	116	404	40	102	15	4	3	37	.252	18	67	4	205	437	15	†.977
	Toronto (A.L.)..........	SS-2B	6	9	1	1	0	0	0	0	.111	1	3	0	6	6	0	1.000
1999—	Edmonton (PCL)■	SS-2B	83	296	31	77	17	1	4	40	.260	19	43	2	149	243	11	.973
2000—	Reading (East.)■......	PR	0	0	0	0	0	0	0	0	...	0	0	0	...	...	...	...
	Philadelphia (N.L.)......	SS	45	140	17	31	7	1	1	13	.221	11	30	1	76	89	4	.976
	Scranton/W.B. (I.L.) ...	3B-SS-2B	77	279	44	82	16	2	10	56	.294	16	48	4	72	158	9	.962
American League totals (4 years)			178	525	46	123	19	7	2	36	.234	44	78	2	263	457	23	.969
National League totals (1 year)			45	140	17	31	7	1	1	13	.221	11	30	1	76	89	4	.976
Major League totals (5 years)			223	665	63	154	26	8	3	49	.232	55	108	3	339	546	27	.970

PEREZ, YORKIS — P

PERSONAL: Born September 30, 1967, in Bajos de Haina, Dominican Republic. ... 6-0/213. ... Throws left, bats both. ... Full name: Yorkis Miguel Perez.

TRANSACTIONS/CAREER NOTES: Signed as non-drafted free agent by Minnesota Twins organization (February 23, 1983). ... Traded by Twins with P Neal Heaton, P Al Cardwood and C Jeff Reardon and C Tom Nieto for P Jeff Reardon and C Tom Nieto (February 3, 1987). ... Granted free agency (October 15, 1990). ... Signed by Atlanta Braves organization (February 1, 1991). ... Traded by Braves with P Turk Wendell to Chicago Cubs for P Mike Bielecki and C Damon Berryhill (September 29, 1991). ... Released by Cubs (December 11, 1991). ... Signed by Yomiuri Giants of Japan Central League (1992). ... Released by Yomiuri (August 17, 1992). ... Signed as free agent by Seattle Mariners organization (August 19, 1992). ... Released by Mariners (January 11, 1993). ... Signed by Montreal Expos organization (February 15, 1993). ... Granted free agency (October 15, 1993). ... Signed by Florida Marlins organization (December 15, 1993). ... On Florida disabled list (June 10-30, 1994); included rehabilitation assignment to Portland (June 20-30). ... Traded by Marlins to Braves for P Martin Sanchez (December 13, 1996). ... Claimed on waivers by New York Mets (March 31, 1997). ... On New York disabled list (April 5-June 5, 1997); included rehabilitation assignment to Norfolk (May 15-June 5). ... Granted free agency (October 15, 1997). ... Signed by Philadelphia Phillies organization (January 23, 1998). ... On Scranton/Wilkes-Barre disabled list (April 9-16, 1998). ... On Philadelphia disabled list (May 25-June 17, 1998); included rehabilitation assignments to Reading (June 14) and Scranton/Wilkes-Barre (June 16). ... On disabled list (July 2, 1999-remainder of season). ... Granted free agency (October 8, 1999). ... Signed by Philadelphia Phillies organization (December 17, 1999). ... Traded by Phillies to Houston Astros for P Trever Miller (March 29, 2000). ... Released by Astros (July 22, 2000).

Year	League	W	L	Pct.	ERA	G	GS	CG	ShO	Sv.	IP	H	R	ER	BB	SO
1983—	Elizabethton (Appl.)	0	1	.000	20.25	3	1	0	0	0	4	5	9	9	9	6
1984—	Elizabethton (Appl.)	0	0	...	0.00	1	0	0	0	0	1 1/3	1	0	0	1	1
1985—	Santiago (DSL)	6	8	.429	3.17	21	16	7	2	1	122	104	58	43	63	69
1986—	Kenosha (Midw.)	4	11	.267	5.15	31	18	3	0	0	131	120	81	75	88	144
1987—	West Palm Beach (FSL)■ ..	6	2	.750	2.34	15	15	3	0	0	100	78	36	26	46	111
	Jacksonville (Sou.)	2	7	.222	4.05	12	10	1	1	1	60	61	34	27	30	60
1988—	Jacksonville (Sou.)	8	12	.400	5.82	27	25	2	1	0	130	142	96	84	94	105
1989—	West Palm Beach (FSL)	7	6	.538	2.76	18	12	0	0	1	94 2/3	62	34	29	54	85
	Jacksonville (Sou.)	4	3	.571	3.60	20	0	0	0	0	35	25	16	14	34	50
1990—	Jacksonville (Sou.)	2	2	.500	6.00	28	2	0	0	1	42	36	34	28	34	39
	Indianapolis (A.A.)	1	1	.500	2.31	9	0	0	0	0	11 2/3	8	5	3	6	8
1991—	Richmond (I.L.)	•12	2	•.800	3.79	36	10	0	0	1	107	99	47	45	53	102
	Chicago (N.L.)■..............	1	0	1.000	2.08	3	0	0	0	0	4 1/3	2	1	1	2	3
1992—	Yomiuri (Jap. Cen.)■	0	1	.000	7.11	3	0	0	0	0	6 1/3	8	6	5	3	6
1993—	Harrisburg (East.)■	4	2	.667	3.45	34	0	0	0	3	44 1/3	49	26	17	20	58
	Ottawa (I.L.)	0	1	.000	3.60	20	0	0	0	5	20	14	12	8	7	17
1994—	Florida (N.L.)■..............	3	0	1.000	3.54	44	0	0	0	0	40 2/3	33	18	16	14	41
	Portland (East.)	0	0	...	0.00	2	0	0	0	0	2	1	0	0	0	2
1995—	Florida (N.L.)	2	6	.250	5.21	69	0	0	0	1	46 2/3	35	29	27	28	47
1996—	Florida (N.L.)	3	4	.429	5.29	64	0	0	0	0	47 2/3	51	28	28	31	47
	Charlotte (I.L.)	3	0	1.000	4.22	9	0	0	0	0	10 2/3	6	5	5	3	13
1997—	New York (N.L.)■	0	1	.000	8.31	9	0	0	0	0	8 2/3	15	8	8	4	7
	Norfolk (I.L.)	1	0	1.000	3.48	17	0	0	0	3	20 2/3	22	9	8	7	24
	Binghamton (East.)	2	1	.667	0.66	12	3	0	0	0	27 1/3	15	4	2	12	39
1998—	Scranton/W.B. (I.L.)■	0	0	...	0.00	4	1	0	0	0	4 1/3	2	1	0	1	3
	Philadelphia (N.L.)............	0	2	.000	3.81	57	0	0	0	0	52	40	23	22	25	42
	Reading (East.)	0	0	...	0.00	1	1	0	0	0	1	0	0	0	0	1
1999—	Philadelphia (N.L.)■..........	3	1	.750	3.94	35	0	0	0	0	32	29	15	14	15	26
2000—	Houston (N.L.)■..............	2	1	.667	5.16	33	0	0	0	0	22 2/3	25	18	13	14	21
Major League totals (8 years)		14	15	.483	4.56	314	0	0	0	0	254 2/3	230	140	129	133	234

P

PERISHO, MATT · P · TIGERS

PERSONAL: Born June 8, 1975, in Burlington, Iowa. ... 6-0/205. ... Throws left, bats left. ... Full name: Matthew Alan Perisho.
HIGH SCHOOL: McClintock (Tempe, Ariz.).
TRANSACTIONS/CAREER NOTES: Selected by California Angels organization in third round of free-agent draft (June 3, 1993). ... Angels franchise renamed Anaheim Angels for 1997 season. ... Traded by Angels to Texas Rangers for IF Mike Bell (October 31, 1997). ... On Oklahoma disabled list (June 29-July 25, 1998). ... Traded by Rangers to Detroit Tigers for P Kevin Mobley and P Brandon Villafuerte (December 15, 2000).

Year League	W	L	Pct.	ERA	G	GS	CG	ShO	Sv.	IP	H	R	ER	BB	SO
1993—Arizona Angels (Ariz.)........	7	3	.700	3.66	11	11	1	1	0	64	58	32	26	23	65
1994—Cedar Rapids (Midw.)	12	9	.571	4.33	27	27	0	0	0	147²/₃	165	90	71	88	107
1995—Lake Elsinore (Calif.)	8	9	.471	6.32	24	22	0	0	0	115¹/₃	137	91	81	60	68
1996—Lake Elsinore (Calif.)	7	5	.583	4.20	21	18	1	1	0	128²/₃	131	72	60	58	97
— Midland (Texas).................	3	2	.600	3.21	8	8	0	0	0	53¹/₃	48	22	19	20	50
1997—Midland (Texas).................	5	2	.714	2.96	10	10	3	•1	0	73	60	26	24	26	62
— Anaheim (A.L.)	0	2	.000	6.00	11	8	0	0	0	45	59	34	30	28	35
— Vancouver (PCL)	4	4	.500	5.33	9	9	1	0	0	52¹/₃	68	42	31	29	47
1998—Tulsa (Texas)■..................	0	0	...	6.00	1	1	0	0	0	3	3	2	2	3	1
— Oklahoma (PCL)	8	5	.615	3.89	15	15	1	0	0	90¹/₃	91	41	39	42	60
— Texas (A.L.)	0	2	.000	27.00	2	2	0	0	0	5	15	17	15	8	2
1999—Oklahoma (PCL)................	*15	7	.682	4.61	27	27	2	0	0	156¹/₃	160	86	80	*78	150
— Texas (A.L.)	0	0	...	2.61	4	1	0	0	0	10¹/₃	8	3	3	2	17
2000—Texas (A.L.)	2	7	.222	7.37	34	13	0	0	0	105	136	99	86	67	74
Major League totals (4 years)	**2**	**11**	**.154**	**7.29**	**51**	**24**	**0**	**0**	**0**	**165¹/₃**	**218**	**153**	**134**	**105**	**128**

PERRY, CHAN · OF/1B · INDIANS

PERSONAL: Born September 13, 1972, in Live Oak, Fla. ... 6-2/200. ... Bats right, throws right. ... Full name: Chan Everett Perry. ... Brother of Herbert Perry, third baseman, Chicago White Sox.
HIGH SCHOOL: Lafayette (Mayo, Fla.).
COLLEGE: Florida.
TRANSACTIONS/CAREER NOTES: Selected by Cleveland Indians organization in 44th round of free-agent draft (June 2, 1994). ... On Buffalo disabled list (June 26-July 21, 2000).

Year Team (League)	Pos.	G	AB	R	H	2B	3B	HR	RBI	Avg.	BB	SO	SB	PO	A	E	Avg.
1994—Burlington (Appl.).......	1B-OF	52	185	28	58	16	1	5	32	.314	18	28	6	239	13	5	.981
1995—Columbus (S.Atl.).......	1B-OF	113	411	64	117	30	4	9	50	.285	53	49	7	598	37	2	.997
1996—Kinston (Caro.)...........	1B-OF-3B	96	358	44	104	27	1	10	62	.291	36	33	2	247	25	2	.993
1997—Akron (East.)	1B-OF-3B	119	476	74	150	•34	2	20	96	.315	28	61	3	459	38	3	.994
1998—Buffalo (I.L.)...............	1B-OF	13	49	8	11	4	0	0	3	.224	6	10	1	71	3	2	.974
— Akron (East.)	OF-1B	54	203	36	57	17	2	5	27	.281	23	43	3	66	9	1	.987
1999—Buffalo (I.L.)...............	1B-OF	79	273	44	77	17	0	10	59	.282	19	34	5	433	33	7	.985
— Akron (East.)	1B-OF	37	154	24	43	14	0	7	30	.279	11	27	1	101	16	2	.983
2000—Buffalo (I.L.)...............	OF-1B	92	362	48	107	18	1	10	65	.296	21	55	1	286	17	3	.990
— Cleveland (A.L.).........	OF-1B	13	14	1	1	0	0	0	0	.071	0	5	0	8	0	0	1.000
Major League totals (1 year)		**13**	**14**	**1**	**1**	**0**	**0**	**0**	**0**	**.071**	**0**	**5**	**0**	**8**	**0**	**0**	**1.000**

PERRY, HERBERT · 1B · WHITE SOX

PERSONAL: Born September 15, 1969, in Mayo, Fla. ... 6-2/220. ... Bats right, throws right. ... Full name: Herbert Edward Perry Jr. ... Brother of Chan Perry, outfielder/first baseman, Cleveland Indians organization.
HIGH SCHOOL: Lafayette (Mayo, Fla.).
COLLEGE: Florida.
TRANSACTIONS/CAREER NOTES: Selected by Cleveland Indians organization in second round of free-agent draft (June 3, 1991). ... On disabled list (June 18-July 13, 1991; and July 23, 1993-remainder of season). ... On Buffalo disabled list (June 7-27, 1996). ... On Cleveland disabled list (September 11, 1996-remainder of season; and March 26, 1997-entire season). ... Selected by Tampa Bay Devil Rays in third round (68th pick overall) of expansion draft (November 18, 1997). ... On Tampa Bay disabled list (March 25, 1998-entire season); included rehabilitation assignments to Durham (June 1-7), Gulf Coast Devil Rays (August 17-25) and St. Petersburg (August 27-28). ... On Tampa Bay disabled list (July 22-September 1, 1999); included rehabilitation assignment to Durham (August 25-31). ... Claimed on waivers by Chicago White Sox (April 21, 2000).
STATISTICAL NOTES: Led Eastern League in being hit by pitch with 15 in 1993.

Year Team (League)	Pos.	G	AB	R	H	2B	3B	HR	RBI	Avg.	BB	SO	SB	PO	A	E	Avg.
1991—Watertown (NY-Penn)	DH	14	52	3	11	2	0	0	5	.212	8	7	0	...	...	...	...
1992—Kinston (Caro.)..........	1B-OF-3B	121	449	74	125	16	1	19	77	.278	46	89	12	297	39	5	.985
1993—Canton/Akron (East.)..1B-3B-DH-OF	89	327	52	88	21	1	9	55	.269	37	47	7	378	86	10	.979
1994—Charlotte (I.L.)...........	1-3-DH-O	102	376	67	123	20	4	13	70	.327	41	55	9	747	55	6	.993
— Cleveland (A.L.).........	1B-3B	4	9	1	1	0	0	0	1	.111	3	1	0	25	5	1	.968
1995—Buffalo (A.A.).............	1B-DH	49	180	27	57	14	1	2	17	.317	15	18	1	419	44	3	.994
— Cleveland (A.L.).........	1B-3B	52	162	23	51	13	1	3	23	.315	13	28	1	391	30	0	1.000
1996—Buffalo (A.A.).............1B-3B-DH-OF	40	151	21	51	7	1	5	30	.338	7	19	4	217	24	4	.984
— Cleveland (A.L.).........	1B-3B	7	12	1	1	1	0	0	0	.083	1	2	1	29	2	0	1.000
1997—						Did not play.											
1998—Durham (I.L.)■	1B-DH	5	17	1	5	4	0	0	1	.294	0	2	0	19	2	0	1.000
— GC Devil Rays (GCL)...	DH-3B	8	26	1	3	0	0	0	1	.115	3	5	0	1	8	1	.900
— St. Petersburg (FSL)...	3B	2	8	1	1	0	0	0	0	.125	2	2	0	2	5	1	.875

P

Year	Team (League)	Pos.	G	AB	R	H	2B	3B	HR	RBI	Avg.	BB	SO	SB	PO	A	E	Avg.
											BATTING					FIELDING		
1999—	Durham (I.L.)	DH-1B-3B	27	103	21	32	8	0	5	20	.311	6	21	0	56	12	2	.971
	— Tampa Bay (A.L.) 3B-1B-OF-DH	66	209	29	53	10	1	6	32	.254	16	42	0	113	79	5	.975
2000—	Tampa Bay (A.L.)	3B-1B	7	28	2	6	1	0	0	1	.214	2	7	0	7	10	1	.944
	— Chicago (A.L.)■	3B-DH-1B	109	383	69	118	29	1	12	61	.308	22	68	4	92	200	9	.970
Major League totals (5 years)			245	803	125	230	54	3	21	118	.286	57	148	6	657	326	16	.984

DIVISION SERIES RECORD

Year	Team (League)	Pos.	G	AB	R	H	2B	3B	HR	RBI	Avg.	BB	SO	SB	PO	A	E	Avg.
											BATTING					FIELDING		
1995—	Cleveland (A.L.)	PH	1	1	0	0	0	0	0	0	.000	0	0	0	...	...	...	...
2000—	Chicago (A.L.)	3B	3	9	0	4	1	0	0	1	.444	2	2	0	5	7	0	1.000
Division series totals (2 years)			4	10	0	4	1	0	0	1	.400	2	2	0	5	7	0	1.000

CHAMPIONSHIP SERIES RECORD

Year	Team (League)	Pos.	G	AB	R	H	2B	3B	HR	RBI	Avg.	BB	SO	SB	PO	A	E	Avg.
											BATTING					FIELDING		
1995—	Cleveland (A.L.)	1B	3	8	0	0	0	0	0	0	.000	1	3	0	30	0	0	1.000

WORLD SERIES RECORD

Year	Team (League)	Pos.	G	AB	R	H	2B	3B	HR	RBI	Avg.	BB	SO	SB	PO	A	E	Avg.
											BATTING					FIELDING		
1995—	Cleveland (A.L.)	1B	3	5	0	0	0	0	0	0	.000	0	2	0	13	2	0	1.000

PERSON, ROBERT   P   PHILLIES

PERSONAL: Born October 6, 1969, in St. Louis. ... 6-0/194. ... Throws right, bats right. ... Full name: Robert Alan Person.
HIGH SCHOOL: University City (Mo.).
JUNIOR COLLEGE: Seminole (Okla.) Junior College.
TRANSACTIONS/CAREER NOTES: Selected by Cleveland Indians organization in 25th round of free-agent draft (June 5, 1989). ... Loaned by Indians organization to Bend, independent (June 12-25, 1991). ... Traded by Indians to Chicago White Sox for P Grady Hall (June 27, 1991). ... On disabled list (April 10-May 13, 1992). ... Selected by Florida Marlins in second round (47th pick overall) of expansion draft (November 17, 1992). ... Granted free agency (December 19, 1992). ... Re-signed by Marlins organization (January 8, 1993). ... Traded by Marlins to New York Mets for P Steve Long (March 30, 1994). ... Traded by Mets to Toronto Blue Jays for 1B John Olerud and cash (December 20, 1996). ... On Toronto disabled list (May 8-26 and September 9-28, 1997). ... On Syracuse disabled list (April 19-27, 1998). ... On Toronto disabled list (March 25-April 12, 1999); included rehabilitation assignment to Dunedin (April 9-10). ... Traded by Blue Jays to Philadelphia Phillies for P Paul Spoljaric (May 5, 1999). ... On Philadelphia disabled list (June 19-July 22, 2000); included rehabilitation assignments to Clearwater (July 12-16) and Reading (July 17-22).
MISCELLANEOUS: Appeared in two games as pinch runner with New York (1996).

Year	League	W	L	Pct.	ERA	G	GS	CG	ShO	Sv.	IP	H	R	ER	BB	SO
1989—	Burlington (Appl.)...............	0	1	.000	3.18	10	5	0	0	1	34	23	13	12	17	19
1990—	Watertown (NY-Penn)	1	0	1.000	1.10	5	2	0	0	0	16 1/3	8	2	2	7	19
	— Kinston (Caro.)...............	1	0	1.000	2.70	4	3	0	0	0	16 2/3	17	6	5	9	7
	— Gulf Coast Indians (GCL) ..	0	2	.000	7.36	24	0	0	0	2	7 1/3	10	7	6	4	8
1991—	Kinston (Caro.)...............	3	5	.375	4.67	11	11	0	0	0	52	56	37	27	42	45
	— Bend (N'West)■...............	1	1	.500	3.60	2	2	0	0	0	10	6	6	4	5	6
	— South Bend (Midw.)■	4	3	.571	3.30	13	13	0	0	0	76 1/3	50	35	28	56	66
1992—	Sarasota (FSL)	5	7	.417	3.59	19	18	1	0	0	105 1/3	90	48	42	62	85
1993—	High Desert (Calif.)■	12	10	.545	4.69	28	26	4	0	0	169	184	*115	88	48	107
1994—	Binghamton (East.)■...........	9	6	.600	3.45	31	23	3	2	0	159	124	68	61	68	130
1995—	Binghamton (East.)	5	4	.556	3.11	26	7	1	0	7	66 2/3	46	27	23	25	65
	— Norfolk (I.L.)...............	2	1	.667	4.50	5	4	0	0	0	32	30	17	16	13	33
	— New York (N.L.)...............	1	0	1.000	0.75	3	1	0	0	0	12	5	1	1	2	10
1996—	New York (N.L.)...............	4	5	.444	4.52	27	13	0	0	0	89 2/3	86	50	45	35	76
	— Norfolk (I.L.)...............	5	0	1.000	3.35	8	8	0	0	0	43	33	16	16	21	32
1997—	Toronto (A.L.)■...............	5	10	.333	5.61	23	22	0	0	0	128 1/3	125	86	80	60	99
	— Syracuse (I.L.)...............	1	0	1.000	0.00	1	1	0	0	0	7	4	1	0	2	5
1998—	Toronto (A.L.)...............	3	1	.750	7.04	27	0	0	0	6	38 1/3	45	31	30	22	31
	— Syracuse (I.L.)...............	3	3	.500	2.29	20	6	1	0	0	59	38	17	15	29	55
1999—	Dunedin (FSL)	0	0	...	3.00	1	1	0	0	0	3	4	1	1	1	3
	— Toronto (A.L.)...............	0	2	.000	9.82	11	0	0	0	2	11	9	12	12	15	12
	— Philadelphia (N.L.)■........	10	5	.667	4.27	31	22	0	0	0	137	130	72	65	70	127
2000—	Philadelphia (N.L.)...........	9	7	.563	3.63	28	28	1	1	0	173 1/3	144	73	70	95	164
	— Clearwater (FSL)	0	0	...	6.75	1	1	0	0	0	2 2/3	3	2	2	1	2
	— Reading (East.)...............	1	0	1.000	5.79	1	1	0	0	0	4 2/3	3	3	3	3	7
A.L. totals (3 years)	....	8	13	.381	6.18	61	22	0	0	8	177 2/3	179	129	122	97	142
N.L. totals (4 years)	....	24	17	.585	3.95	89	64	1	1	0	412	365	196	181	202	377
Major League totals (6 years)	....	32	30	.516	4.62	150	86	1	1	8	589 2/3	544	325	303	299	519

RECORD AS POSITION PLAYER

Year	Team (League)	Pos.	G	AB	R	H	2B	3B	HR	RBI	Avg.	BB	SO	SB	PO	A	E	Avg.
											BATTING					FIELDING		
1990—	GC Indians (GCL)	OF	24	46	6	4	0	0	0	3	.087	10	12	1	10	2	0	1.000

PETERS, CHRIS   P   EXPOS

PERSONAL: Born January 28, 1972, in Fort Thomas, Ky. ... 6-1/170. ... Throws left, bats left. ... Full name: Christopher Michael Peters.
HIGH SCHOOL: Peters Township (McMurray, Pa.).
COLLEGE: Indiana.

TRANSACTIONS/CAREER NOTES: Selected by Pittsburgh Pirates organization in 37th round of free-agent draft (June 3, 1993). ... On Pittsburgh disabled list (May 24-August 21, 1999); included rehabilitation assignments to Nashville (June 8-18, June 28-July 16 and July 30-August 21). ... On Pittsburgh disabled list (August 11, 2000-remainder of season); included rehabilitation assignment to Nashville (August 28-September 3). ... Granted free agency (December 21, 2000). ... Signed by Montreal Expos organization (January 10, 2001).

Year League	W	L	Pct.	ERA	G	GS	CG	ShO	Sv.	IP	H	R	ER	BB	SO
1993— Welland (NY-Penn)	1	0	1.000	4.55	16	0	0	0	0	27²/₃	33	16	14	20	25
1994— Augusta (S.Atl.)	4	5	.444	4.30	54	0	0	0	4	60²/₃	51	34	29	33	83
— Salem (Caro.)	1	0	1.000	13.50	3	0	0	0	0	3¹/₃	5	5	5	1	2
1995— Lynchburg (Caro.)	11	5	.688	2.43	24	24	3	*3	0	144²/₃	126	57	39	35	132
— Carolina (Sou.)	2	0	1.000	1.29	2	2	0	0	0	14	9	2	2	2	7
1996— Carolina (Sou.)	7	3	.700	2.64	14	14	0	0	0	92	73	37	27	34	69
— Calgary (PCL)	1	1	.500	0.98	4	4	0	0	0	27²/₃	18	3	3	8	16
— Pittsburgh (N.L.)	2	4	.333	5.63	16	10	0	0	0	64	72	43	40	25	28
1997— Calgary (PCL)	2	4	.333	4.38	14	9	0	0	1	51¹/₃	52	32	25	30	55
— Pittsburgh (N.L.)	2	2	.500	4.58	31	1	0	0	0	37¹/₃	38	23	19	21	17
1998— Pittsburgh (N.L.)	8	10	.444	3.47	39	21	1	0	1	148	142	63	57	55	103
1999— Pittsburgh (N.L.)	5	4	.556	6.59	19	11	0	0	0	71	98	59	52	27	46
— Nashville (PCL)	3	1	.750	2.19	11	9	0	0	1	49¹/₃	54	18	12	15	34
2000— Pittsburgh (N.L.)	0	1	.000	2.86	18	0	0	0	1	28¹/₃	23	9	9	14	16
— Nashville (PCL)	2	4	.333	5.47	11	11	0	0	0	52²/₃	71	38	32	26	32
Major League totals (5 years)	17	21	.447	4.57	123	43	1	0	2	348²/₃	373	197	177	142	210

PETERSON, KYLE P BREWERS

PERSONAL: Born April 9, 1976, in Elkhorn, Neb. ... 6-3/215. ... Throws right, bats left. ... Full name: Kyle J. Peterson.
HIGH SCHOOL: Creighton Prep (Omaha, Neb.).
COLLEGE: Stanford.
TRANSACTIONS/CAREER NOTES: Selected by Milwaukee Brewers organization in first round (13th pick overall) of free-agent draft (June 3, 1997). ... On Milwaukee disabled list (March 28, 2000-entire season); included rehabilitation assignments to Beloit (August 1-12) and Huntsville (August 13-18).

Year League	W	L	Pct.	ERA	G	GS	CG	ShO	Sv.	IP	H	R	ER	BB	SO
1997— Ogden (Pio.)	0	0	...	0.87	3	3	0	0	0	10¹/₃	5	2	1	4	11
1998— Stockton (Calif.)	4	7	.364	3.55	17	17	0	0	0	96¹/₃	99	54	38	33	109
— El Paso (Texas)	3	2	.600	4.40	7	7	1	0	0	43	41	24	21	16	33
— Louisville (I.L.)	1	0	1.000	7.94	1	1	0	0	0	5²/₃	8	5	5	2	4
1999— Louisville (I.L.)	7	6	.538	3.55	18	18	1	1	0	109	90	52	43	42	95
— Milwaukee (N.L.)	4	7	.364	4.56	17	12	0	0	0	77	87	46	39	25	34
2000— Beloit (Midw.)	1	1	.500	1.80	3	3	0	0	0	15	10	4	3	4	17
— Huntsville (Sou.)	0	1	.000	7.71	1	1	0	0	0	4²/₃	6	7	4	4	1
Major League totals (1 year)	4	7	.364	4.56	17	12	0	0	0	77	87	46	39	25	34

PETKOVSEK, MARK P RANGERS

PERSONAL: Born November 18, 1965, in Beaumont, Texas. ... 6-0/198. ... Throws right, bats right. ... Full name: Mark Joseph Petkovsek. ... Name pronounced PET-kie-zeck.
HIGH SCHOOL: Kelly (Beaumont, Texas).
COLLEGE: Texas.
TRANSACTIONS/CAREER NOTES: Selected by Texas Rangers organization in supplemental round ("sandwich pick" between first and second round, 29th pick overall) of free-agent draft (June 2, 1987); pick received as compensation for New York Yankees signing Type A free-agent OF Gary Ward. ... Granted free agency (October 16, 1991). ... Signed by Pittsburgh Pirates organization (January 22, 1992). ... Granted free agency (October 15, 1992). ... Re-signed by Pirates organization (November 9, 1992). ... On Buffalo disabled list (July 4-23, 1993). ... Granted free agency (October 12, 1993). ... Signed by Houston Astros organization (March 4, 1994). ... On disabled list (July 20-August 14, 1994). ... Granted free agency (October 15, 1994). ... Signed by St. Louis Cardinals organization (November 18, 1994). ... On Louisville suspended list (May 12-17, 1995). ... On St. Louis disabled list (March 22-April 19, 1996); included rehabilitation assignments to St. Petersburg (April 5-12) and Louisville (April 12-19). ... On suspended list (September 9-12, 1997). ... Traded by Cardinals to Anaheim Angels for a player to be named later or cash (December 14, 1998); Cardinals acquired C Matt Garrick to complete deal (December 14, 1998). ... On Anaheim disabled list (May 17-June 12, 2000); included rehabilitation assignment to Lake Elsinore (June 7-12). ... Granted free agency (November 1, 2000). ... Signed by Texas Rangers (December 10, 2000).
STATISTICAL NOTES: Pitched 5-0 no-hit victory against Colorado Springs (May 16, 1994).

Year League	W	L	Pct.	ERA	G	GS	CG	ShO	Sv.	IP	H	R	ER	BB	SO
1987— Gulf Coast Rangers (GCL)	0	0	...	3.18	3	1	0	0	0	5²/₃	4	2	2	2	7
— Charlotte (FSL)	3	4	.429	4.02	11	10	0	0	0	56	67	36	25	17	23
1988— Charlotte (FSL)	10	11	.476	2.97	28	28	7	•5	0	175²/₃	156	71	58	42	95
1989— Tulsa (Texas)	8	5	.615	3.47	21	21	1	0	0	140	144	63	54	35	66
— Oklahoma City (A.A.)	0	4	.000	7.34	6	6	0	0	0	30²/₃	39	27	25	18	8
1990— Oklahoma City (A.A.)	7	*14	.333	5.25	28	28	2	1	0	151	*187	*103	88	42	81
1991— Oklahoma City (A.A.)	9	8	.529	4.93	25	24	3	1	0	149²/₃	162	89	82	38	67
— Texas (A.L.)	0	1	.000	14.46	4	1	0	0	0	9¹/₃	21	16	15	4	6
1992— Buffalo (A.A.)■	8	8	.500	3.53	32	22	1	0	1	150¹/₃	150	76	59	44	49
1993— Buffalo (A.A.)	3	4	.429	4.33	14	11	1	0	0	70²/₃	74	38	34	16	27
— Pittsburgh (N.L.)	3	0	1.000	6.96	26	0	0	0	0	32¹/₃	43	25	25	9	14
1994— Tucson (PCL)■	10	7	.588	4.62	25	23	1	1	0	138¹/₃	176	87	71	40	69
1995— Louisville (A.A.)■	4	1	.800	2.32	8	8	2	1	0	54¹/₃	38	16	14	8	30
— St. Louis (N.L.)	6	6	.500	4.00	26	21	1	1	0	137¹/₃	136	71	61	35	71
1996— St. Petersburg (FSL)	0	0	...	4.50	3	0	0	0	0	6	6	3	3	0	5
— Louisville (A.A.)	0	1	.000	9.00	2	1	0	0	0	3	5	4	3	1	4
— St. Louis (N.L.)	11	2	.846	3.55	48	6	0	0	0	88²/₃	83	37	35	35	45
1997— St. Louis (N.L.)	4	7	.364	5.06	55	2	0	0	2	96	109	61	54	31	51
1998— St. Louis (N.L.)	7	4	.636	4.77	48	10	0	0	0	105²/₃	131	63	56	36	55

P

Year	League	W	L	Pct.	ERA	G	GS	CG	ShO	Sv.	IP	H	R	ER	BB	SO
1999—Anaheim (A.L.)■		10	4	.714	3.47	64	0	0	0	1	83	85	37	32	21	43
2000—Anaheim (A.L.)		4	2	.667	4.22	64	1	0	0	2	81	86	39	38	23	31
—Lake Elsinore (Calif.)		0	0	...	3.38	2	0	0	0	0	2 2/3	3	1	1	3	3
A.L. totals (3 years)		14	7	.667	4.41	132	2	0	0	3	173 1/3	192	92	85	48	80
N.L. totals (5 years)		31	19	.620	4.52	203	39	1	1	2	460	502	257	231	146	236
Major League totals (8 years)		45	26	.634	4.49	335	41	1	1	5	633 1/3	694	349	316	194	316

DIVISION SERIES RECORD

Year	League	W	L	Pct.	ERA	G	GS	CG	ShO	Sv.	IP	H	R	ER	BB	SO
1996—St. Louis (N.L.)		0	0	...	0.00	1	0	0	0	0	2	0	0	0	0	1

CHAMPIONSHIP SERIES RECORD

RECORDS: Shares single-series record for most games pitched—6 (1996).

Year	League	W	L	Pct.	ERA	G	GS	CG	ShO	Sv.	IP	H	R	ER	BB	SO
1996—St. Louis (N.L.)		0	1	.000	7.36	6	0	0	0	0	7 1/3	11	6	6	4	7

PETRICK, BEN — C — ROCKIES

PERSONAL: Born April 7, 1977, in Hillsboro, Ore. ... 6-0/205. ... Bats right, throws right. ... Full name: Benjamin Wayne Petrick.

HIGH SCHOOL: Glencoe (Hillsboro, Ore.).

TRANSACTIONS/CAREER NOTES: Selected by Colorado Rockies organization in second round of free-agent draft (June 3, 1995). ... On Carolina disabled list (April 26-May 6, 1999).

STATISTICAL NOTES: Led Pacific Coast League catchers with 14 passed balls in 1999.

							BATTING								FIELDING		
Year	Team (League)	Pos.	G	AB	R	H	2B	3B	HR	RBI	Avg.	BB	SO	SB	PO	A	E	Avg.
1996—Asheville (S.Atl.)		C-DH	122	446	74	105	24	2	14	52	.235	75	98	19	766	95	12	.986
1997—Salem (Caro.)		C-DH	121	412	68	102	23	3	15	56	.248	62	100	30	754	91	10	.988
1998—New Haven (East.)		C-DH-OF	106	349	52	83	21	3	18	50	.238	56	89	7	536	43	5	.991
1999—Carolina (Sou.)		C-DH	20	68	18	21	5	1	4	22	.309	9	15	3	113	10	1	.992
—Colo. Springs (PCL)		C-DH-OF	84	282	56	88	16	5	19	64	.312	44	58	9	411	32	9	.980
—Colorado (N.L.)		C	19	62	13	20	3	0	4	12	.323	10	13	1	100	7	2	.982
2000—Colo. Springs (PCL)		C	63	248	38	78	22	3	9	47	.315	32	40	7	375	39	6	.986
—Colorado (N.L.)		C	52	146	32	47	10	1	3	20	.322	20	33	1	248	19	4	.985
Major League totals (2 years)			71	208	45	67	13	1	7	32	.322	30	46	2	348	26	6	.984

PETTITTE, ANDY — P — YANKEES

PERSONAL: Born June 15, 1972, in Baton Rouge, La. ... 6-5/225. ... Throws left, bats left. ... Full name: Andrew Eugene Pettitte.

HIGH SCHOOL: Deer Park (Texas).

JUNIOR COLLEGE: San Jacinto (North) College (Texas).

TRANSACTIONS/CAREER NOTES: Selected by New York Yankees organization in 22nd round of free-agent draft (June 4, 1990); did not sign. ... Signed as non-drafted free agent by Yankees organization (May 25, 1991). ... On Albany temporarily inactive list (June 5-10, 1994). ... On New York disabled list (March 26-April 17, 1999); included rehabilitation assignment to Tampa (April 12). ... On disabled list (April 13-26, 2000).

HONORS: Named lefthanded pitcher on THE SPORTING NEWS A.L. All-Star team (1996).

Year	League	W	L	Pct.	ERA	G	GS	CG	ShO	Sv.	IP	H	R	ER	BB	SO
1991—Gulf Coast Yankees (GCL)		4	1	.800	0.98	6	6	0	0	0	36 2/3	16	6	4	8	51
—Oneonta (NY-Penn)		2	2	.500	2.18	6	6	1	0	0	33	33	18	8	16	32
1992—Greensboro (S.Atl.)		10	4	.714	2.20	27	27	2	1	0	168	141	53	41	55	130
1993—Prince William (Caro.)		11	9	.550	3.04	26	26	2	1	0	159 2/3	146	68	54	47	129
—Albany (S.Atl.)		1	0	1.000	3.60	1	1	0	0	0	5	5	4	2	2	6
1994—Albany/Colonie (East.)		7	2	.778	2.71	11	11	0	0	0	73	60	32	22	18	50
—Columbus (I.L.)		7	2	.778	2.98	16	16	3	0	0	96 2/3	101	40	32	21	61
1995—Columbus (I.L.)		0	0	...	0.00	2	2	0	0	0	11 2/3	7	0	0	0	8
—New York (A.L.)		12	9	.571	4.17	31	26	3	0	0	175	183	86	81	63	114
1996—New York (A.L.)		*21	8	.724	3.87	35	34	2	0	0	221	229	105	95	72	162
1997—New York (A.L.)		18	7	.720	2.88	35	•35	4	1	0	240 1/3	233	86	77	65	166
1998—New York (A.L.)		16	11	.593	4.24	33	32	5	0	0	216 1/3	226	110	102	87	146
1999—Tampa (FSL)		1	0	1.000	0.00	1	1	0	0	0	5	4	0	0	2	8
—New York (A.L.)		14	11	.560	4.70	31	31	0	0	0	191 2/3	216	105	100	89	121
2000—New York (A.L.)		19	9	.679	4.35	32	32	3	1	0	204 2/3	219	111	99	80	125
Major League totals (6 years)		100	55	.645	3.99	197	190	17	2	0	1249	1306	603	554	456	834

DIVISION SERIES RECORD

RECORDS: Holds career records for most games started—8; innings pitched 50 2/3; runs allowed—26; and earned runs allowed—26. ... Holds A.L. career record for most hits allowed—53.

Year	League	W	L	Pct.	ERA	G	GS	CG	ShO	Sv.	IP	H	R	ER	BB	SO
1995—New York (A.L.)		0	0	...	5.14	1	1	0	0	0	7	9	4	4	3	0
1996—New York (A.L.)		0	0	...	5.68	1	1	0	0	0	6 1/3	4	4	4	6	3
1997—New York (A.L.)		0	2	.000	8.49	2	2	0	0	0	11 2/3	15	11	11	1	5
1998—New York (A.L.)		1	0	1.000	1.29	1	1	0	0	0	7	3	1	1	0	8
1999—New York (A.L.)		1	0	1.000	1.23	1	1	0	0	0	7 1/3	7	1	1	0	5
2000—New York (A.L.)		1	0	1.000	3.97	2	2	0	0	0	11 1/3	15	5	5	3	7
Division series totals (6 years)		3	2	.600	4.62	8	8	0	0	0	50 2/3	53	26	26	13	28

P

CHAMPIONSHIP SERIES RECORD

Year League	W	L	Pct.	ERA	G	GS	CG	ShO	Sv.	IP	H	R	ER	BB	SO
1996— New York (A.L.).................	1	0	1.000	3.60	2	2	0	0	0	15	10	6	6	5	7
1998— New York (A.L.).................	0	1	.000	11.57	1	1	0	0	0	4 2/3	8	6	6	3	1
1999— New York (A.L.).................	1	0	1.000	2.45	1	1	0	0	0	7 1/3	8	2	2	1	5
2000— New York (A.L.).................	1	0	1.000	2.70	1	1	0	0	0	6 2/3	9	2	2	1	2
Champ. series totals (4 years)	3	1	.750	4.28	5	5	0	0	0	33 2/3	35	16	16	10	15

WORLD SERIES RECORD

RECORDS: Shares single-game record for most earned runs allowed—7 (October 20, 1996).

NOTES: Member of World Series championship team (1996, 1998, 1999 and 2000).

Year League	W	L	Pct.	ERA	G	GS	CG	ShO	Sv.	IP	H	R	ER	BB	SO
1996— New York (A.L.).................	1	1	.500	5.91	2	2	0	0	0	10 2/3	11	7	7	4	5
1998— New York (A.L.).................	1	0	1.000	0.00	1	1	0	0	0	7 1/3	5	0	0	3	4
1999— New York (A.L.).................	0	0	...	12.27	1	1	0	0	0	3 2/3	10	5	5	1	1
2000— New York (A.L.).................	0	0	...	1.98	2	2	0	0	0	13 2/3	16	5	3	4	9
World Series totals (4 years)	2	1	.667	3.82	6	6	0	0	0	35 1/3	42	17	15	12	19

ALL-STAR GAME RECORD

Year League	W	L	Pct.	ERA	GS	CG	ShO	Sv.	IP	H	R	ER	BB	SO
1996— American						Did not play.								

PHELPS, JOSH — C — BLUE JAYS

PERSONAL: Born May 12, 1978, in Anchorage, Alaska. ... 6-3/215. ... Bats right, throws right. ... Full name: Joshua Lee Phelps.

HIGH SCHOOL: Lakeland (Rathdrum, Idaho).

TRANSACTIONS/CAREER NOTES: Selected by Toronto Blue Jays organization in 10th round of free-agent draft (June 4, 1996). ... On Tennessee disabled list (April 6-May 1, 2000).

STATISTICAL NOTES: Tied for South Atlantic League with seven double plays by catcher in 1997. ... Led South Atlantic League catchers with 19 errors in 1998. ... Led Florida State League with a .562 slugging percentage in 1999.

							BATTING								FIELDING		
Year Team (League)	Pos.	G	AB	R	H	2B	3B	HR	RBI	Avg.	BB	SO	SB	PO	A	E	Avg.
1996— Medicine Hat (Pio.)	C-OF	59	191	26	46	3	0	5	29	.241	27	65	5	214	24	9	.964
1997— Hagerstown (S.Atl.)....	C	68	233	26	49	9	1	7	24	.210	15	72	3	519	56	21	.965
1998— Hagerstown (S.Atl.)....	C-3B-OF	117	385	48	102	24	1	8	44	.265	40	80	2	688	62	†19	.975
1999— Dunedin (FSL)...........	DH-C	110	406	72	133	27	4	20	88	.328	28	104	6	161	13	1	.994
2000— Tennessee (Sou.)	C	56	184	23	42	9	1	9	28	.228	15	66	1	274	15	5	.983
— Toronto (A.L.)........	C	1	1	0	0	0	0	0	0	.000	0	1	0	1	0	0	1.000
— Dunedin (FSL)...........	C	30	113	26	36	7	0	12	34	.319	12	34	0	98	19	1	.992
Major League totals (1 year)		1	1	0	0	0	0	0	0	.000	0	1	0	1	0	0	1.000

PIATT, ADAM — OF/DH — ATHLETICS

PERSONAL: Born February 8, 1976, in Chicago. ... 6-2/195. ... Bats right, throws right. ... Full name: Adam David Piatt.

HIGH SCHOOL: Bishop Verot (Fort Myers, Fla.).

COLLEGE: Mississippi State.

TRANSACTIONS/CAREER NOTES: Selected by Oakland Athletics organization in eighth round of free-agent draft (June 3, 1997).

HONORS: Named Texas League Most Valuable Player (1999).

STATISTICAL NOTES: Led California League third basemen with 32 errors in 1998. ... Led Texas League with 335 total bases, .451 on-base percentage, .704 slugging percentage and 10 intentional bases on balls received in 1999.

							BATTING								FIELDING		
Year Team (League)	Pos.	G	AB	R	H	2B	3B	HR	RBI	Avg.	BB	SO	SB	PO	A	E	Avg.
1997— S. Oregon (N'West)...	3B-1B	57	216	63	63	9	1	13	35	.292	35	58	19	26	107	21	.864
1998— Modesto (Calif.)	3B-2B	133	500	91	144	•40	3	20	*107	.288	80	99	20	64	200	†32	.892
1999— Midland (Texas)........	3B-SS-DH	129	476	*128	164	48	3	*39	*135	*.345	•93	101	7	91	253	31	.917
— Vancouver (PCL)	3B-SS	6	18	1	4	1	0	0	3	.222	6	2	0	6	16	2	.917
2000— Sacramento (PCL)......	OF-3B-1B	65	254	36	72	15	0	8	42	.283	26	57	3	160	49	9	.959
— Oakland (A.L.) OF-DH-3B-1B		60	157	24	47	5	5	5	23	.299	23	44	0	46	12	2	.967
Major League totals (1 year)		60	157	24	47	5	5	5	23	.299	23	44	0	46	12	2	.967

DIVISION SERIES RECORD

							BATTING								FIELDING		
Year Team (League)	Pos.	G	AB	R	H	2B	3B	HR	RBI	Avg.	BB	SO	SB	PO	A	E	Avg.
2000— Oakland (A.L.)	OF-PR-DH	3	6	2	1	0	0	0	C	.167	0	1	0	5	0	0	1.000

PIAZZA, MIKE — C — METS

PERSONAL: Born September 4, 1968, in Norristown, Pa. ... 6-3/215. ... Bats right, throws right. ... Full name: Michael Joseph Piazza. ... Name pronounced pee-AH-za.

HIGH SCHOOL: Phoenixville (Pa.) Area.

JUNIOR COLLEGE: Miami-Dade (North) Community College.

TRANSACTIONS/CAREER NOTES: Selected by Los Angeles Dodgers organization in 62nd round of free-agent draft (June 1, 1988). ... On disabled list (May 11-June 4, 1995). ... Traded by Dodgers with 3B Todd Zeile to Florida Marlins for OF Gary Sheffield, 3B Bobby Bonilla, C Charlie Johnson, OF Jim Eisenreich and P Manuel Barrios (May 15, 1998). ... Traded by Marlins to New York Mets for OF Preston Wilson, P Ed Yarnall and P Geoff Goetz (May 22, 1998). ... On disabled list (April 10-25, 1999).

P

– 448 –

RECORDS: Shares major league single-season record for most major league ballparks, one or more home runs—18 (2000). ... Shares major league record for most grand slams in two consecutive games—2 (August 9 and 10, 1998). ... Shares major league single-month record for most grand slams—3 (April 1998). ... Holds single-season record for highest batting average by a catcher (100 or more games)—.362 (1997). ... Shares N.L. career record for most major league ballparks, one or more home runs (since 1900)—25.

HONORS: Named N.L. Rookie Player of the Year by THE SPORTING NEWS (1993). ... Named catcher on THE SPORTING NEWS N.L. All-Star team (1993-2000). ... Named catcher on THE SPORTING NEWS N.L. Silver Slugger team (1993-2000). ... Named N.L. Rookie of the Year by Baseball Writers' Association of America (1993).

STATISTICAL NOTES: Led California League with .540 slugging percentage and in grounding into double plays with 19 in 1991. ... Led N.L. catchers with 98 assists and tied for lead with 11 errors in 1993. ... Led N.L. catchers in total chances with 866 in 1995 and 1,055 in 1996. ... Led N.L. catchers in passed balls with 12 in 1995 and 12 in 1996. ... Hit three home runs in one game (June 29, 1996). ... Led N.L. catchers in total chances with 1,135 in 1997. ... Led N.L. catchers with 83 assists in 1998. ... Had 24-game hitting streak (May 25-June 22, 1999). ... Led N.L. in grounding into double plays with 27 in 1999. ... Led N.L. catchers in total chances with 1,011 in 1999. ... Had 21-game hitting streak (June 7-July 3, 2000). ... Career major league grand slams: 12.

Year	Team (League)	Pos.	G	AB	R	H	2B	3B	HR	RBI	Avg.	BB	SO	SB	PO	A	E	Avg.
1989—	Salem (N'West)	C	57	198	22	53	11	0	8	25	.268	13	51	0	230	21	6	.977
1990—	Vero Beach (FSL)	C-1B	88	272	27	68	20	0	6	45	.250	11	68	0	428	38	16	.967
1991—	Bakersfield (Calif.)	C-1B	117	448	71	124	27	2	29	80	.277	47	83	0	723	69	15	.981
1992—	San Antonio (Texas)	C	31	114	18	43	11	0	7	21	.377	13	18	0	189	22	4	.981
	—Albuquerque (PCL)	C-1B	94	358	54	122	22	5	16	69	.341	37	57	1	550	50	9	.985
	—Los Angeles (N.L.)	C	21	69	5	16	3	0	1	7	.232	4	12	0	94	7	1	.990
1993—	Los Angeles (N.L.)	C-1B	149	547	81	174	24	2	35	112	.318	46	86	3	901	†98	‡11	.989
1994—	Los Angeles (N.L.)	C	107	405	64	129	18	0	24	92	.319	33	65	1	640	38	*10	.985
1995—	Los Angeles (N.L.)	C	112	434	82	150	17	0	32	93	.346	39	80	1	*805	52	9	.990
1996—	Los Angeles (N.L.)	C	148	547	87	184	16	0	36	105	.336	81	93	0	*1055	70	9	.992
1997—	Los Angeles (N.L.)	C-DH	152	556	104	201	32	1	40	124	.362	69	77	5	*1045	74	*16	.986
1998—	Los Angeles (N.L.)	C	37	149	20	42	5	0	9	30	.282	11	27	0	277	25	2	.993
	—Florida (N.L.)■	C	5	18	1	5	0	1	0	5	.278	0	0	0	27	3	1	.968
	—New York (N.L.)■	C-DH	109	394	67	137	33	0	23	76	.348	47	53	1	680	†57	8	.989
1999—	New York (N.L.)	C-DH	141	534	100	162	25	0	40	124	.303	51	70	2	*953	47	11	.989
2000—	New York (N.L.)	C-DH	136	482	90	156	26	0	38	113	.324	58	69	4	862	38	3	*.997
Major League totals (9 years)			1117	4135	701	1356	199	4	278	881	.328	439	632	17	7339	509	81	.990

DIVISION SERIES RECORD

Year	Team (League)	Pos.	G	AB	R	H	2B	3B	HR	RBI	Avg.	BB	SO	SB	PO	A	E	Avg.
1995—	Los Angeles (N.L.)	C	3	14	1	3	1	0	1	1	.214	0	2	0	31	0	0	1.000
1996—	Los Angeles (N.L.)	C	3	10	1	3	0	0	0	2	.300	1	2	0	25	4	0	1.000
1999—	New York (N.L.)	C	2	9	0	2	0	0	0	0	.222	0	4	0	13	0	0	1.000
2000—	New York (N.L.)	C	4	14	1	3	1	0	0	0	.214	4	3	0	32	2	0	1.000
Division series totals (4 years)			12	47	3	11	2	0	1	3	.234	5	11	0	101	6	0	1.000

CHAMPIONSHIP SERIES RECORD

Year	Team (League)	Pos.	G	AB	R	H	2B	3B	HR	RBI	Avg.	BB	SO	SB	PO	A	E	Avg.
1999—	New York (N.L.)	C	6	24	1	4	0	0	1	4	.167	1	6	0	44	3	3	.940
2000—	New York (N.L.)	C	5	17	7	7	3	0	2	4	.412	5	0	0	40	1	0	1.000
Championship series totals (2 years)			11	41	8	11	3	0	3	8	.268	6	6	0	84	4	3	.967

WORLD SERIES RECORD

Year	Team (League)	Pos.	G	AB	R	H	2B	3B	HR	RBI	Avg.	BB	SO	SB	PO	A	E	Avg.
2000—	New York (N.L.)	DH-C	5	22	3	6	2	0	2	4	.273	0	4	0	34	1	0	1.000

ALL-STAR GAME RECORD

NOTES: Named Most Valuable Player (1996).

Year	League	Pos.	AB	R	H	2B	3B	HR	RBI	Avg.	BB	SO	SB	PO	A	E	Avg.
1993—	National	C	1	0	0	0	0	0	0	.000	0	1	0	3	0	0	1.000
1994—	National	C	4	0	1	0	0	0	1	.250	0	0	0	6	0	0	1.000
1995—	National	C	3	1	1	0	0	1	1	.333	0	0	0	6	1	0	1.000
1996—	National	C	3	1	2	1	0	1	2	.667	0	1	0	6	1	0	1.000
1997—	National	C	1	0	0	0	0	0	0	.000	1	0	0	2	0	0	1.000
1998—	National	C	3	0	1	0	0	0	0	.333	0	0	0	2	0	0	1.000
1999—	National	C	2	0	1	0	0	0	0	.500	0	1	0	6	0	0	1.000
2000—	National							Selected, did not play—injured.									
All-Star Game totals (7 years)			17	2	6	1	0	2	4	.353	1	3	0	31	2	0	1.000

PICHARDO, HIPOLITO   P   RED SOX

PERSONAL: Born August 22, 1969, in Esperanza, Dominican Republic. ... 6-1/195. ... Throws right, bats right. ... Full name: Hipolito Antonio Pichardo. ... Name pronounced ee-POL-uh-toe puh-CHAR-doh.

HIGH SCHOOL: Liceo Enriguillo (Jicome Esperanza, Dominican Republic).

TRANSACTIONS/CAREER NOTES: Signed as non-drafted free agent by Kansas City Royals organization (December 16, 1987). ... On disabled list (August 14-September 1, 1993; and August 15-September 1, 1995). ... On Kansas City disabled list (July 5-August 25, 1997); included rehabilitation assignment to Omaha (July 25-August 25). ... Granted free agency (October 31, 1997). ... Re-signed by Royals (December 4, 1997). ... On Kansas City disabled list (May 6-23 and August 21, 1998-remainder of season); included rehabilitation assignment to Lansing (August 21). ... On Kansas City disabled list (March 28, 1999-entire season). ... Granted free agency (November 11, 1999). ... Signed by Boston Red Sox organization (February 16, 2000). ... On Pawtucket disabled list (April 6-20, 2000).

STATISTICAL NOTES: Pitched 8-0 one-hit, complete-game victory for Kansas City against Boston (July 21, 1992).

MISCELLANEOUS: Struck out in only appearance as pinch hitter (2000).

Year League	W	L	Pct.	ERA	G	GS	CG	ShO	Sv.	IP	H	R	ER	BB	SO
1988— Gulf Coast Royals (GCL)	0	0	...	13.50	1	0	0	0	0	1 1/3	3	2	2	1	3
1989— Appleton (Midw.)................	5	4	.556	2.97	12	12	2	0	0	75 2/3	58	29	25	18	50
1990— Baseball City (FSL)............	1	6	.143	3.80	11	10	0	0	0	45	47	28	19	25	40
1991— Memphis (Sou.).................	3	11	.214	4.27	34	11	0	0	0	99	116	56	47	38	75
1992— Memphis (Sou.)	0	0	...	0.64	2	2	0	0	0	14	13	2	1	1	10
— Kansas City (A.L.)	9	6	.600	3.95	31	24	1	1	0	143 2/3	148	71	63	49	59
1993— Kansas City (A.L.)	7	8	.467	4.04	30	25	2	0	0	165	183	85	74	53	70
1994— Kansas City (A.L.)	5	3	.625	4.92	45	0	0	0	3	67 2/3	82	42	37	24	36
1995— Kansas City (A.L.)	8	4	.667	4.36	44	0	0	0	1	64	66	34	31	30	43
1996— Kansas City (A.L.)	3	5	.375	5.43	57	0	0	0	3	68	74	41	41	26	43
1997— Kansas City (A.L.)	3	5	.375	4.22	47	0	0	0	11	49	51	24	23	24	34
— Omaha (A.A.)..................	0	0	...	5.79	5	1	0	0	1	4 2/3	5	3	3	3	3
1998— Kansas City (A.L.)	7	8	.467	5.13	27	18	0	0	1	112 1/3	126	73	64	43	55
— Lansing (Midw.)	0	0	...	0.00	1	0	0	0	0	1	0	0	0	0	0
1999— Kansas City (A.L.)							Did not play.								
2000— Pawtucket (I.L.)■.............	0	0	...	0.00	3	0	0	0	0	4 2/3	2	0	0	0	4
— Sarasota (FSL)	1	1	.500	1.38	7	2	0	0	0	13	9	3	2	0	12
— Boston (A.L.)...................	6	3	.667	3.46	38	1	0	0	1	65	63	29	25	26	37
Major League totals (8 years).......	48	42	.533	4.39	319	68	3	1	20	734 2/3	793	399	358	275	377

PICKERING, CALVIN — 1B — ORIOLES

PERSONAL: Born September 29, 1976, in St. Thomas, Virgin Islands. ... 6-5/278. ... Bats left, throws left. ... Full name: Calvin E. Pickering.
HIGH SCHOOL: King (Tampa).
TRANSACTIONS/CAREER NOTES: Selected by Baltimore Orioles organization in 35th round of free-agent draft (June 3, 1995). ... On disabled list (June 20-August 6, 2000).
HONORS: Named Eastern League Most Valuable Player (1998).
STATISTICAL NOTES: Led Appalachian League with 135 totals bases, .675 slugging pecentage and four intentional bases on balls received in 1996. ... Led Eastern League with 276 total bases, .434 on-base percentage, .566 slugging percentage, 16 intentional bases on balls received and grounding into double plays with 20 in 1998. ... Led Eastern League first basemen with 20 errors in 1998.

Year Team (League)	Pos.	G	AB	R	H	2B	3B	HR	RBI	Avg.	BB	SO	SB	PO	A	E	Avg.
1995— GC Orioles (GCL)........	1B-DH	15	60	8	30	10	0	1	22	.500	2	6	0	86	6	3	.968
1996— Bluefield (Appl.)	1B-DH	60	200	45	65	14	1	*18	*66	.325	28	64	8	396	26	9	.979
1997— Delmarva (S.Atl.)........	1B-DH	122	444	88	138	31	1	25	79	.311	53	139	6	940	70	*27	.974
1998— Bowie (East.).............	1B-OF-DH	139	488	93	151	28	2	*31	*114	.309	*98	119	4	1068	60	†22	.981
— Baltimore (A.L.).........	1B-DH	9	21	4	5	0	0	2	3	.238	3	4	1	31	0	1	.969
1999— Rochester (I.L.).........	1B-DH-OF	103	372	63	106	20	0	16	63	.285	60	99	1	822	45	13	.985
— Baltimore (A.L.).........	1B-DH	23	40	4	5	1	0	1	5	.125	11	16	0	46	2	2	.960
2000— Rochester (I.L.)	1B	60	197	20	43	10	0	6	30	.218	36	70	2	497	30	12	.978
Major League totals (2 years)		32	61	8	10	1	0	3	8	.164	14	20	1	77	2	3	.963

PIERRE, JUAN — OF — ROCKIES

PERSONAL: Born August 14, 1977, in Mobile, Ala. ... 6-0/170. ... Bats left, throws left. ... Full name: Juan D'Vaughn Pierre.
HIGH SCHOOL: Alexandria (La.).
COLLEGE: South Alabama.
TRANSACTIONS/CAREER NOTES: Selected by Colorado Rockies organization in 13th round of free-agent draft (June 2, 1998).
STATISTICAL NOTES: Tied for South Atlantic League lead in double plays by outfielder with four in 1999. ... Had 16-game hitting streak (August 8-23, 2000). ... Had 15-game hitting streak (September 6-22, 2000).

Year Team (League)	Pos.	G	AB	R	H	2B	3B	HR	RBI	Avg.	BB	SO	SB	PO	A	E	Avg.
1998— Portland (N'West)	OF	64	264	55	93	9	2	0	30	*.352	19	11	*38	100	5	5	.955
1999— Asheville (S.Atl.)........	OF	*140	*585	93	*187	28	5	1	55	.320	38	37	66	193	13	4	.981
2000— Carolina (Sou.)	OF	107	439	63	143	16	4	0	32	.326	33	26	46	261	2	2	.992
— Colo. Springs (PCL) ...	OF	4	17	3	8	0	1	0	1	.471	0	0	1	11	0	0	1.000
— Colorado (N.L.)	OF	51	200	26	62	2	0	0	20	.310	13	15	7	115	1	3	.975
Major League totals (1 year)		51	200	26	62	2	0	0	20	.310	13	15	7	115	1	3	.975

PIERZYNSKI, A.J. — C — TWINS

PERSONAL: Born December 30, 1976, in Bridgehampton, N.Y. ... 6-3/220. ... Bats left, throws right. ... Full name: Anthony John Pierzynski.
HIGH SCHOOL: Dr. Phillips (Orlando).
TRANSACTIONS/CAREER NOTES: Selected by Minnesota Twins organization in third round of free-agent draft (June 2, 1994). ... On Salt Lake disabled list (August 24, 1999-remainder of season).
STATISTICAL NOTES: Tied for Appalachian League lead in errors by catcher with 12 in 1995. ... Led Appalachian League catchers with 71 assists in 1995. ... Tied for Midwest League lead with 20 errors by catcher in 1996.

Year Team (League)	Pos.	G	AB	R	H	2B	3B	HR	RBI	Avg.	BB	SO	SB	PO	A	E	Avg.
1994— GC Twins (GCL)..........	C-DH	43	152	21	44	8	1	1	19	.289	12	19	0	198	28	8	.966
1995— Fort Wayne (Midw.).....	C	22	84	10	26	5	1	2	14	.310	2	10	0	119	34	10	.939
— Elizabethton (Appl.)	C-1B	56	205	29	68	13	1	7	45	.332	14	23	0	376	†72	†12	.974
1996— Fort Wayne (Midw.).....	C-DH-OF	114	431	48	118	30	3	7	70	.274	22	53	0	658	80	†21	.972
1997— Fort Myers (FSL)	C-DH-1B	118	412	49	115	23	1	9	64	.279	16	59	2	677	78	10	.987

Year	Team (League)	Pos.	G	AB	R	H	2B	3B	HR	RBI	Avg.	BB	SO	SB	PO	A	E	Avg.
1998—	New Britain (East.)	C-DH	59	212	30	63	11	0	3	17	.297	10	25	0	409	37	2	.996
	—Salt Lake (PCL)	C	59	208	29	53	7	2	7	30	.255	9	24	3	366	30	7	.983
	—Minnesota (A.L.)	C	7	10	1	3	0	0	0	1	.300	1	2	0	33	2	0	1.000
1999—	Salt Lake (PCL)	C-DH	67	228	29	59	10	0	1	25	.259	16	29	0	376	45	7	.984
	—Minnesota (A.L.)	C	9	22	3	6	2	0	0	3	.273	1	4	0	35	2	0	1.000
2000—	New Britain (East.)	C	62	228	36	68	17	2	4	34	.298	8	22	0	304	31	6	.982
	—Salt Lake (PCL)	C	41	155	22	52	14	1	4	25	.335	5	22	1	263	20	3	.990
	—Minnesota (A.L.)	C	33	88	12	27	5	1	2	11	.307	5	14	1	160	10	0	1.000
Major League totals (3 years)			49	120	16	36	7	1	2	15	.300	7	20	1	228	10	0	1.000

PINEIRO, JOEL P MARINERS

PERSONAL: Born September 25, 1978, in Rio Pedres, Puerto Rico. ... 6-1/180. ... Throws right, bats right. ... Full name: Joel Alberto Pineiro.
HIGH SCHOOL: Colonial (Orlando).
JUNIOR COLLEGE: Edison Community College (Fla.).
TRANSACTIONS/CAREER NOTES: Selected by Seattle Mariners organization in 12th round of free-agent draft (June 3, 1997).

Year	League	W	L	Pct.	ERA	G	GS	CG	ShO	Sv.	IP	H	R	ER	BB	SO
1997—	Arizona Mariners (Ariz.)	1	0	1.000	0.00	1	0	0	0	0	3	1	0	0	0	4
	—Everett (N'West)	4	2	.667	5.33	18	6	0	0	2	49	54	33	29	18	59
1998—	Wisconsin (Midw.)	8	4	.667	3.19	16	16	1	0	0	96	92	40	34	28	84
	—Lancaster (Calif.)	2	0	1.000	7.80	9	9	1	•1	0	45	58	40	39	22	48
	—Orlando (Sou.)	1	0	1.000	5.40	1	1	0	0	0	5	7	4	3	2	2
1999—	New Haven (East.)	10	15	.400	4.72	28	25	4	0	0	166	190	105	87	52	116
2000—	New Haven (East.)	2	1	.667	4.13	9	9	0	0	0	52 1/3	42	25	24	12	43
	—Tacoma (PCL)	7	1	.875	2.80	10	9	2	2	0	61	53	20	19	22	41
	—Seattle (A.L.)	1	0	1.000	5.59	8	1	0	0	0	19 1/3	25	13	12	13	10
Major League totals (1 year)		1	0	1.000	5.59	8	1	0	0	0	19 1/3	25	13	12	13	10

PLESAC, DAN P BLUE JAYS

PERSONAL: Born February 4, 1962, in Gary, Ind. ... 6-5/217. ... Throws left, bats left. ... Full name: Daniel Thomas Plesac. ... Name pronounced PLEE-sack.
HIGH SCHOOL: Crown Point (Ind.).
COLLEGE: North Carolina State.
TRANSACTIONS/CAREER NOTES: Selected by St. Louis Cardinals organization in second round of free-agent draft (June 3, 1980); did not sign. ... Selected by Milwaukee Brewers organization in first round (26th pick overall) of free-agent draft (June 6, 1983). ... Granted free agency (October 27, 1992). ... Signed by Chicago Cubs (December 8, 1992). ... Granted free agency (October 25, 1994). ... Signed by Pittsburgh Pirates (November 9, 1994). ... Traded by Pirates with OF Orlando Merced and IF Carlos Garcia to Toronto Blue Jays for P Jose Silva, P Jose Pett, IF Brandon Cromer and three players to be named later (November 14, 1996); Pirates acquired P Mike Halperin, IF Abraham Nunez and C/OF Craig Wilson to complete deal (December 11, 1996). ... Traded by Blue Jays to Arizona Diamondbacks for SS Tony Batista and P John Frascatore (June 12, 1999). ... Granted free agency (October 30, 2000). ... Signed by Blue Jays (December 8, 2000).
STATISTICAL NOTES: Led Appalachian League pitchers with three balks in 1983.
MISCELLANEOUS: Holds Milwaukee Brewers all-time records for lowest earned run average (3.21), most games pitched (365) and most saves (133).

Year	League	W	L	Pct.	ERA	G	GS	CG	ShO	Sv.	IP	H	R	ER	BB	SO
1983—	Paintsville (Appl.)	*9	1	.900	3.50	14	•14	2	0	0	82 1/3	76	44	32	57	*85
1984—	Stockton (Calif.)	6	6	.500	3.32	16	16	2	0	0	108 1/3	106	51	40	50	101
	—El Paso (Texas)	2	2	.500	3.46	7	7	0	0	0	39	43	19	15	16	24
1985—	El Paso (Texas)	12	5	.706	4.97	25	24	2	0	0	150 1/3	171	91	83	68	128
1986—	Milwaukee (A.L.)	10	7	.588	2.97	51	0	0	0	14	91	81	34	30	29	75
1987—	Milwaukee (A.L.)	5	6	.455	2.61	57	0	0	0	23	79 1/3	63	30	23	23	89
1988—	Milwaukee (A.L.)	1	2	.333	2.41	50	0	0	0	30	52 1/3	46	14	14	12	52
1989—	Milwaukee (A.L.)	3	4	.429	2.35	52	0	0	0	33	61 1/3	47	16	16	17	52
1990—	Milwaukee (A.L.)	3	7	.300	4.43	66	0	0	0	24	69	67	36	34	31	65
1991—	Milwaukee (A.L.)	2	7	.222	4.29	45	10	0	0	8	92 1/3	92	49	44	39	61
1992—	Milwaukee (A.L.)	5	4	.556	2.96	44	4	0	0	1	79	64	28	26	35	54
1993—	Chicago (N.L.)■	2	1	.667	4.74	57	0	0	0	0	62 2/3	74	37	33	21	47
1994—	Chicago (N.L.)	2	3	.400	4.61	54	0	0	0	0	54 2/3	61	30	28	13	53
1995—	Pittsburgh (N.L.)■	4	4	.500	3.58	58	0	0	0	3	60 1/3	53	26	24	27	57
1996—	Pittsburgh (N.L.)	6	5	.545	4.09	73	0	0	0	11	70 1/3	67	35	32	24	76
1997—	Toronto (A.L.)■	2	4	.333	3.58	73	0	0	0	0	50 1/3	47	22	20	19	61
1998—	Toronto (A.L.)	4	3	.571	3.78	78	0	0	0	4	50	41	23	21	16	55
1999—	Toronto (A.L.)	0	3	.000	8.34	30	0	0	0	0	22 2/3	28	21	21	9	26
	—Arizona (N.L.)■	2	1	.667	3.32	34	0	0	0	1	21 2/3	22	9	8	8	27
2000—	Arizona (N.L.)	5	1	.833	3.15	62	0	0	0	0	40	34	21	14	26	45
A.L. totals (10 years)		35	47	.427	3.46	546	14	0	0	138	647 1/3	576	273	249	230	590
N.L. totals (6 years)		21	15	.583	4.04	338	0	0	0	16	309 2/3	311	158	139	119	305
Major League totals (15 years)		56	62	.475	3.65	884	14	0	0	154	957	887	431	388	349	895

DIVISION SERIES RECORD

Year	League	W	L	Pct.	ERA	G	GS	CG	ShO	Sv.	IP	H	R	ER	BB	SO
1999—	Arizona (N.L.)	0	0	...	54.00	1	0	0	0	0	1/3	3	2	2	0	0

ALL-STAR GAME RECORD

Year	League	W	L	Pct.	ERA	GS	CG	ShO	Sv.	IP	H	R	ER	BB	SO
1987—	American	0	0	...	0.00	0	0	0	0	1	0	0	0	0	1
1988—	American	0	0	...	0.00	0	0	0	0	1/3	0	0	0	0	1
1989—	American	0	0	...	...	0	0	0	0	1	0	0	0	0	0
All-Star Game totals (3 years)		0	0	...	0.00	0	0	0	0	1 1/3	1	0	0	0	2

P

PERSONAL: Born October 10, 1975, in Santo Domingo, Dominican Republic. ... 5-10/168. ... Bats right, throws right. ... Full name: Placido Enrique Polanco. ... Name pronounced plah-SEE-doh Poh-LAHN-co.
HIGH SCHOOL: Santo Clara (Santo Domingo, Dominican Republic).
JUNIOR COLLEGE: Miami-Dade (Wolfson) Community College.
TRANSACTIONS/CAREER NOTES: Selected by St. Louis Cardinals in 19th round of free-agent draft (June 3, 1994). ... On Memphis suspended list (August 28-29, 1999). ... On disabled list (July 1-16, 2000).
STATISTICAL NOTES: Led Florida State League in grounding into double plays with 31 in 1996. ... Tied for Texas League lead in double plays by second baseman with 110 in 1997. ... Career major league grand slams: 1.

							BATTING								FIELDING		
Year Team (League)	Pos.	G	AB	R	H	2B	3B	HR	RBI	Avg.	BB	SO	SB	PO	A	E	Avg.
1994— Ariz. Cardinals (Ariz.) .	SS-2B	32	127	17	27	4	0	1	10	.213	7	15	4	47	89	10	.932
1995— Peoria (Midw.)	SS-2B	103	361	43	96	7	4	2	41	.266	18	30	7	114	285	21	.950
1996— St. Petersburg (FSL) ..	2B	*137	540	65	*157	29	5	0	51	.291	24	34	4	198	*383	4	*.993
1997— Arkansas (Texas)	2B	129	508	71	148	16	3	2	51	.291	29	51	19	240	*425	14	*.979
1998— Memphis (PCL)	2B-SS	70	246	36	69	19	1	1	21	.280	16	15	6	113	193	5	.984
— St. Louis (N.L.)	SS-2B	45	114	10	29	3	2	1	11	.254	5	9	2	72	102	7	.961
1999— St. Louis (N.L.)	2B-3B-SS	88	220	24	61	9	3	1	19	.277	15	24	1	123	150	8	.972
— Memphis (PCL)	2B-SS-3B	29	120	18	33	4	1	0	10	.275	3	11	2	43	84	2	.984
2000— St. Louis (N.L.)	2B-3B-SS-1B	118	323	50	102	12	3	5	39	.316	16	26	4	131	202	3	.991
Major League totals (3 years)		251	657	84	192	24	8	7	69	.292	36	59	7	326	454	18	.977

DIVISION SERIES RECORD

							BATTING								FIELDING		
Year Team (League)	Pos.	G	AB	R	H	2B	3B	HR	RBI	Avg.	BB	SO	SB	PO	A	E	Avg.
2000— St. Louis (N.L.)	3B	3	10	1	3	0	0	0	3	.300	1	0	1	1	5	0	1.000

CHAMPIONSHIP SERIES RECORD

							BATTING								FIELDING		
Year Team (League)	Pos.	G	AB	R	H	2B	3B	HR	RBI	Avg.	BB	SO	SB	PO	A	E	Avg.
2000— St. Louis (N.L.)	3B-PH	4	5	0	1	0	0	0	0	.200	2	1	0	2	4	0	1.000

PERSONAL: Born February 27, 1974, in St. Louis. ... 5-11/185. ... Throws right, bats right. ... Full name: Cliff Anthony Politte. ... Son of Clifford Politte, pitcher in St. Louis Cardinals organization (1959-65). ... Name pronounced po-LEET.
HIGH SCHOOL: Vianney (Kirkwood, Mo.).
JUNIOR COLLEGE: Jefferson College (Mo.).
TRANSACTIONS/CAREER NOTES: Selected by St. Louis Cardinals organization in 54th round of free agent draft (June 1, 1995). ... Traded by Cardinals with OF Ron Gant and P Jeff Brantley to Philadelphia Phillies for P Ricky Bottalico and P Garrett Stephenson (November 19, 1998). ... On Scranton/Wilkes-Barre disabled list (April 30-May 9, 2000).
HONORS: Named Carolina League Pitcher of the Year (1997).

Year League	W	L	Pct.	ERA	G	GS	CG	ShO	Sv.	IP	H	R	ER	BB	SO
1996— Peoria (Midw.)	14	6	.700	2.59	25	25	0	0	0	149²/₃	108	50	43	47	151
1997— Prince William (Caro.)	11	1	*.917	*2.24	19	19	0	0	0	120¹/₃	89	37	30	31	118
— Arkansas (Texas)	4	1	.800	2.15	6	6	0	0	0	37²/₃	35	15	9	9	26
1998— St. Louis (N.L.)	2	3	.400	6.32	8	8	0	0	0	37	45	32	26	18	22
— Memphis (PCL)	1	4	.200	7.64	10	10	0	0	0	50²/₃	71	46	43	24	42
— Arkansas (Texas)	5	3	.625	2.96	10	10	1	1	0	67	56	25	22	16	61
1999— Reading (East.)■	9	8	.529	3.63	37	13	1	0	5	109	112	45	44	33	97
— Philadelphia (N.L.)	1	0	1.000	7.13	13	0	0	0	0	17²/₃	19	14	14	15	15
2000— Scranton/W.B. (I.L.)	8	4	.667	3.12	21	20	1	0	0	112²/₃	94	45	39	41	106
— Philadelphia (N.L.)	4	3	.571	3.66	12	8	0	0	0	59	55	24	24	27	50
Major League totals (3 years)	7	6	.538	5.07	33	16	0	0	0	113²/₃	119	70	64	60	87

PERSONAL: Born October 27, 1964, in Santiago City, Dominican Republic. ... 5-8/150. ... Bats left, throws left. ... Full name: Luis Andrew Polonia. ... Name pronounced po-LONE-yuh.
HIGH SCHOOL: San Francisco (Santiago City, Dominican Republic).
TRANSACTIONS/CAREER NOTES: Signed as non-drafted free agent by Oakland Athletics organization (January 3, 1984). ... Traded by A's with P Greg Cadaret and P Eric Plunk to New York Yankees for OF Rickey Henderson (June 21, 1989). ... Traded by Yankees to California Angels for OF Claudell Washington and P Rich Monteleone (April 28, 1990). ... On suspended list (September 30-October 3, 1992). ... Granted free agency (October 27, 1993). ... Signed by Yankees (December 20, 1993). ... Traded by Yankees to Atlanta Braves for OF Troy Hughes (August 11, 1995). ... Granted free agency (November 2, 1995). ... Signed by Seattle Mariners organization (February 1, 1996). ... Released by Mariners (March 26, 1996). ... Signed by Baltimore Orioles organization (April 19, 1996). ... Released by Orioles (August 12, 1996). ... Signed by Braves (August 17, 1996). ... Granted free agency (November 18, 1996). ... Signed by Tampa Bay Devil Rays organization (March 11, 1997). ... Loaned by Devil Rays to Mexico City Tigers, Mexican League (March 20, 1997-entire season; and April 18, 1998-entire season). ... Granted free agency (October 15, 1998). ... Signed by Detroit Tigers organization (December 18, 1998). ... Granted free agency (November 4, 1999). ... Re-signed by Tigers (November 15, 1999). ... On suspended list (May 19-21, 2000). ... Released by Tigers (July 31, 2000). ... Signed by New York Yankees organization (August 3, 2000). ... Granted free agency (October 30, 2000).
STATISTICAL NOTES: Led Midwest League in caught stealing with 24 in 1984. ... Led Pacific Coast League in caught stealing with 21 in 1986. ... Led A.L. in caught stealing with 23 in 1991 and 21 in 1992 and tied for lead with 24 in 1993. ... Had 16-game hitting streak (May 31-June 21, 1999). ... Career major league grand slams: 1.
MISCELLANEOUS: Batted as switch-hitter (1984-86 and Tacoma, 1987-88).

P

Year — Team (League)	Pos.	G	AB	R	H	2B	3B	HR	RBI	Avg.	BB	SO	SB	PO	A	E	Avg.
1984— Madison (Midw.)........	OF	135	*528	103	*162	21	10	8	64	.307	57	95	55	202	9	10	.955
1985— Huntsville (Sou.)	OF	130	515	82	149	15	*18	2	36	.289	58	53	39	236	13	12	.954
1986— Tacoma (PCL)	OF	134	*549	98	*165	20	4	3	63	.301	52	65	36	*318	8	10	.970
1987— Tacoma (PCL)	OF	14	56	18	18	1	2	0	8	.321	14	6	4	28	1	1	.967
— Oakland (A.L.)	OF-DH	125	435	78	125	16	10	4	49	.287	32	64	29	235	2	5	.979
1988— Tacoma (PCL)	OF	65	254	58	85	13	5	2	27	.335	29	28	31	129	7	7	.951
— Oakland (A.L.)	OF-DH	84	288	51	84	11	4	2	27	.292	21	40	24	155	3	2	.988
1989— Oakland (A.L.)	OF-DH	59	206	31	59	6	4	1	17	.286	9	15	13	126	3	2	.985
— New York (A.L.)■......	OF-DH	66	227	39	71	11	2	2	29	.313	16	29	9	105	6	2	.982
1990— New York (A.L.)	DH	11	22	2	7	0	0	0	3	.318	0	1	1	...	...	...	...
— California (A.L.)■......	OF-DH	109	381	50	128	7	9	2	32	.336	25	42	20	142	3	3	.980
1991— California (A.L.)	OF-DH	150	604	92	179	28	8	2	50	.296	52	74	48	246	9	5	.981
1992— California (A.L.)	OF-DH	149	577	83	165	17	4	0	35	.286	45	64	51	192	8	4	.980
1993— California (A.L.)	OF-DH	152	576	75	156	17	6	1	32	.271	48	53	55	286	12	5	.983
1994— New York (A.L.)■......	OF-DH	95	350	62	109	21	6	1	36	.311	37	36	20	155	9	4	.976
1995— New York (A.L.)	OF	67	238	37	62	9	3	2	15	.261	25	29	10	132	5	0	1.000
— Atlanta (N.L.)■......	OF	28	53	6	14	7	0	0	2	.264	3	9	3	9	0	0	1.000
1996— Rochester (I.L.)■......	OF-DH	13	50	9	12	2	0	0	3	.240	7	8	5	18	0	0	1.000
— Baltimore (A.L.)	OF-DH	58	175	25	42	4	1	2	14	.240	10	20	8	56	1	1	.983
— Atlanta (N.L.)■......	OF	22	31	3	13	0	0	0	2	.419	1	3	1	4	0	1	.800
1997— M.C. Tigers (Mex.)■...	OF	110	408	105	154	29	5	7	59	.377	75	33	48	...	...	...	...
1998— M.C. Tigers (Mex.)		86	357	82	136	15	*14	9	63	.381	52	31	36	...	...	...	...
1999— Toledo (I.L.)■............	OF-DH	42	161	20	52	7	1	3	22	.323	10	28	13	64	2	1	.985
— Detroit (A.L.)	DH-OF	87	333	46	108	21	8	10	32	.324	16	32	17	68	4	1	.986
2000— Detroit (A.L.)	DH-OF	80	267	37	73	10	5	6	25	.273	22	25	8	44	2	0	1.000
— New York (A.L.)■......	OF-DH	37	77	11	22	4	0	1	5	.286	7	7	4	32	0	1	.970
American League totals (12 years)		1329	4756	719	1390	182	70	36	401	.292	365	531	317	1974	67	35	.983
National League totals (2 years)		50	84	9	27	7	0	0	4	.321	4	12	4	13	0	1	.929
Major League totals (12 years)		1379	4840	728	1417	189	70	36	405	.293	369	543	321	1987	67	36	.983

DIVISION SERIES RECORD

Year — Team (League)	Pos.	G	AB	R	H	2B	3B	HR	RBI	Avg.	BB	SO	SB	PO	A	E	Avg.
1995— Atlanta (N.L.)..............	PH	3	3	0	1	0	0	0	2	.333	0	1	1	...	...	...	...
1996— Atlanta (N.L.)..............	PH	2	2	0	0	0	0	0	0	.000	0	1	0	...	...	...	...
2000— New York (A.L.)..........	PH	1	1	0	1	0	0	0	0	1.000	0	0	0	...	...	...	...
Division series totals (3 years)		6	6	0	2	0	0	0	2	.333	0	2	1	...	...	...	...

CHAMPIONSHIP SERIES RECORD

Year — Team (League)	Pos.	G	AB	R	H	2B	3B	HR	RBI	Avg.	BB	SO	SB	PO	A	E	Avg.
1988— Oakland (A.L.)	PR-OF-PH	3	5	0	2	0	0	0	0	.400	1	2	0	2	0	0	1.000
1995— Atlanta (N.L.)..............	OF-PR-PH	3	2	0	1	0	0	0	1	.500	0	0	0	0	0	0	...
1996— Atlanta (N.L.)..............	PH	3	3	0	0	0	0	0	0	.000	0	0	0	0	0	0	...
2000— New York (A.L.)..........										Did not play.							
Championship series totals (3 years)		9	10	0	3	0	0	0	1	.300	1	2	0	2	0	0	1.000

WORLD SERIES RECORD

NOTES: Member of World Series championship team (1995 and 2000).

Year — Team (League)	Pos.	G	AB	R	H	2B	3B	HR	RBI	Avg.	BB	SO	SB	PO	A	E	Avg.
1988— Oakland (A.L.)	PH-OF	3	9	1	1	0	0	0	0	.111	0	2	0	2	0	0	1.000
1995— Atlanta (N.L.)..............	PH-OF	4	14	3	4	1	0	1	4	.286	1	3	1	3	0	0	1.000
1996— Atlanta (N.L.)..............	PH	6	5	0	0	0	0	0	0	.000	1	3	0	...	...	...	...
2000— New York (A.L.)..........	PH	2	2	0	1	0	0	0	0	.500	0	0	0	...	...	...	...
World Series totals (4 years)		15	30	4	6	1	0	1	4	.200	2	8	1	5	0	0	1.000

PONSON, SIDNEY   P   ORIOLES

PERSONAL: Born November 2, 1976, in Noord, Aruba. ... 6-1/225. ... Throws right, bats right. ... Full name: Sidney Alton Ponson.
COLLEGE: Maria (Aruba).
TRANSACTIONS/CAREER NOTES: Signed as non-drafted free agent by Baltimore Orioles organization (August 17, 1993). ... On Bowie disabled list (June 13-July 15, 1997).

Year — League	W	L	Pct.	ERA	G	GS	CG	ShO	Sv.	IP	H	R	ER	BB	SO
1994— Gulf Coast Orioles (GCL)....	4	3	.571	2.96	12	10	1	0	0	73	68	30	24	17	53
1995— Bluefield (Appl.)	6	3	.667	4.17	13	13	0	0	0	77²/₃	79	44	36	16	56
1996— Frederick (Caro.)	7	6	.538	3.45	18	16	3	0	0	107	98	56	41	28	110
1997— Bowie (East.).....................	2	7	.222	5.42	13	13	1	1	0	74²/₃	7	51	45	32	56
— Gulf Coast Orioles (GCL)....	1	0	1.000	0.00	1	1	0	0	0	2	0	0	0	0	1
1998— Rochester (I.L.).................	1	0	1.000	0.00	1	1	0	0	0	5	4	0	0	1	3
— Baltimore (A.L.).................	8	9	.471	5.27	31	20	0	0	1	135	157	82	79	42	85
1999— Baltimore (A.L.).................	12	12	.500	4.71	32	32	6	0	0	210	227	118	110	80	112
2000— Baltimore (A.L.).................	9	13	.409	4.82	32	32	6	1	0	222	223	125	119	83	152
Major League totals (3 years)	29	34	.460	4.89	95	84	12	1	1	567	607	325	308	205	349

P

PERSONAL: Born April 28, 1966, in Rochester, N.Y. ... 6-1/203. ... Throws left, bats left. ... Full name: James Richard Poole.
HIGH SCHOOL: LaSalle (Philadelphia).
COLLEGE: Georgia Tech.
TRANSACTIONS/CAREER NOTES: Selected by Los Angeles Dodgers organization in 34th round of free-agent draft (June 2, 1987); did not sign. ... Selected by Dodgers organization in ninth round of free-agent draft (June 1, 1988). ... Traded by Dodgers with cash to Texas Rangers for P Steve Allen and P David Lynch (December 30, 1990). ... Claimed on waivers by Baltimore Orioles (May 31, 1991). ... On Baltimore disabled list (April 3-June 23, 1992); included rehabilitation assignments to Hagerstown (May 25-June 12) and Rochester (June 12-23). ... Granted free agency (December 23, 1994). ... Signed by Cleveland Indians organization (March 18, 1995). ... Traded by Indians with a player to be named later or cash to San Francisco Giants for 1B/OF Mark Carreon (July 9, 1996). ... Released by Giants (July 15, 1998). ... Signed by Indians organization (July 22, 1998). ... Granted free agency (October 30, 1998). ... Signed by Philadelphia Phillies (December 17, 1998). ... Released by Phillies (August 23, 1999). ... Signed by Indians organization (August 26, 1999). ... Granted free agency (October 4, 1999). ... Signed by Detroit Tigers organization (December 20, 1999). ... Released by Tigers (May 17, 2000). ... Signed by Montreal Expos organization (May 19, 2000). ... Released by Expos (June 7, 2000). ... Signed by Indians organization (June 9, 2000). ... On Buffalo disabled list (July 4-August 1, 2000).

Year	League	W	L	Pct.	ERA	G	GS	CG	ShO	Sv.	IP	H	R	ER	BB	SO
1988—	Vero Beach (FSL)	1	1	.500	3.77	10	0	0	0	0	14 1/3	13	7	6	9	12
1989—	Vero Beach (FSL)	11	4	.733	1.61	*60	0	0	0	19	78 1/3	57	16	14	24	93
—	Bakersfield (Calif.)	0	0	...	0.00	1	0	0	0	0	1 2/3	2	1	0	0	1
1990—	San Antonio (Texas)	6	7	.462	2.40	54	0	0	0	16	63 2/3	55	31	17	27	77
—	Los Angeles (N.L.)	0	0	...	4.22	16	0	0	0	0	10 2/3	7	5	5	8	6
1991—	Oklahoma City (A.A.)■	0	0	...	0.00	10	0	0	0	3	12 1/3	4	0	0	1	14
—	Texas (A.L.)	0	0	...	4.50	5	0	0	0	1	6	10	4	3	3	4
—	Rochester (I.L.)■	3	2	.600	2.79	27	0	0	0	9	29	29	11	9	9	25
—	Baltimore (A.L.)	3	2	.600	2.00	24	0	0	0	0	36	19	10	8	9	34
1992—	Hagerstown (East.)	0	1	.000	2.77	7	3	0	0	0	13	14	4	4	1	4
—	Rochester (I.L.)	1	6	.143	5.31	32	0	0	0	10	42 1/3	40	26	25	18	30
—	Baltimore (A.L.)	0	0	...	0.00	6	0	0	0	0	3 1/3	3	3	0	1	3
1993—	Baltimore (A.L.)	2	1	.667	2.15	55	0	0	0	2	50 1/3	30	18	12	21	29
1994—	Baltimore (A.L.)	1	0	1.000	6.64	38	0	0	0	0	20 1/3	32	15	15	11	18
1995—	Buffalo (A.A.)■	0	0	...	27.00	1	0	0	0	0	2 2/3	7	8	8	2	0
—	Cleveland (A.L.)	3	3	.500	3.75	42	0	0	0	0	50 1/3	40	22	21	17	41
1996—	Cleveland (A.L.)	4	0	1.000	3.04	32	0	0	0	0	26 2/3	29	15	9	14	19
—	San Francisco (N.L.)■	2	1	.667	2.66	35	0	0	0	0	23 2/3	15	7	7	13	19
1997—	San Francisco (N.L.)	3	1	.750	7.11	63	0	0	0	0	49 1/3	73	44	39	25	26
1998—	San Francisco (N.L.)	1	3	.250	5.29	26	0	0	0	0	32 1/3	38	20	19	9	16
—	Buffalo (I.L.)■	1	0	1.000	0.87	13	0	0	0	0	10 1/3	6	3	1	2	16
—	Cleveland (A.L.)	0	0	...	5.14	12	0	0	0	0	7	9	4	4	3	11
1999—	Philadelphia (N.L.)■	1	1	.500	4.33	51	0	0	0	1	35 1/3	48	20	17	15	22
—	Akron (East.)■	0	0	...	0.00	2	0	0	0	0	2 2/3	0	0	0	0	4
—	Cleveland (A.L.)	1	0	1.000	18.00	3	0	0	0	0	1	2	2	2	3	0
2000—	Detroit (A.L.)■	1	0	1.000	7.27	18	0	0	0	0	8 2/3	13	8	7	1	5
—	Montreal (N.L.)■	0	0	...	27.00	5	0	0	0	0	2	8	6	6	3	3
—	Buffalo (I.L.)■	2	2	.500	6.00	10	0	0	0	1	12	16	10	8	6	8
A.L. totals (9 years)		15	6	.714	3.48	235	0	0	0	3	209 2/3	187	101	81	83	164
N.L. totals (6 years)		7	6	.538	5.46	196	0	0	0	1	153 1/3	189	102	93	73	92
Major League totals (11 years)		22	12	.647	4.31	431	0	0	0	4	363	376	203	174	156	256

DIVISION SERIES RECORD

Year	League	W	L	Pct.	ERA	G	GS	CG	ShO	Sv.	IP	H	R	ER	BB	SO
1995—	Cleveland (A.L.)	0	0	...	5.40	1	0	0	0	0	1 2/3	2	1	1	1	2
1998—	Cleveland (A.L.)	0	0	...	0.00	2	0	0	0	0	2	1	0	0	1	2
Division series totals (2 years)		0	0	...	2.45	3	0	0	0	0	3 2/3	3	1	1	2	4

CHAMPIONSHIP SERIES RECORD

Year	League	W	L	Pct.	ERA	G	GS	CG	ShO	Sv.	IP	H	R	ER	BB	SO
1995—	Cleveland (A.L.)	0	0	...	0.00	1	0	0	0	0	1	0	0	0	0	2
1998—	Cleveland (A.L.)	0	0	...	0.00	4	0	0	0	0	1 1/3	0	0	0	1	2
Champ. series totals (2 years)		0	0	...	0.00	5	0	0	0	0	2 1/3	0	0	0	1	4

WORLD SERIES RECORD

Year	League	W	L	Pct.	ERA	G	GS	CG	ShO	Sv.	IP	H	R	ER	BB	SO
1995—	Cleveland (A.L.)	0	1	.000	3.86	2	0	0	0	0	2 1/3	1	1	1	0	1

PERSONAL: Born July 5, 1972, in Newark, N.J. ... 6-2/195. ... Bats right, throws right. ... Full name: Marquis Donnell Porter.
HIGH SCHOOL: Weequahic (Newark, N.J.).
COLLEGE: Iowa.
TRANSACTIONS/CAREER NOTES: Selected by Chicago Cubs organization in 40th round of free-agent draft (June 3, 1993). ... Selected by Oakland A's from Cubs organization in Rule 5 major league draft (December 13, 1999). ... Claimed on waivers by Texas Rangers (October 11, 2000).
STATISTICAL NOTES: Led Midwest League outfielders with seven double plays in 1996. ... Tied for Pacific Coast League lead in caught stealing with 17 in 1999.

							BATTING							FIELDING		
Year	Team (League)	Pos.	G	AB	R	H	2B	3B	HR	RBI	Avg.	BB	SO	SB	PO	A	E	Avg.
1994—	Peoria (Midw.)	OF	66	221	40	60	11	2	6	29	.271	27	59	6	128	3	3	.978
1995—	Daytona (FSL)	OF	113	336	54	73	12	2	3	19	.217	32	104	22	183	10	4	.980
1996—	Daytona (FSL)	OF	20	63	9	11	4	1	0	6	.175	6	24	5	44	3	4	.922
—	Rockford (Midw.)	OF	105	378	83	91	22	3	7	44	.241	72	107	30	172	8	3	.984
1997—	Daytona (FSL)	OF-2B	122	440	87	135	20	6	17	65	.307	61	115	23	237	10	4	.984
—	Orlando (Sou.)	OF	8	31	4	8	1	0	1	3	.258	0	11	0	13	2	1	.938

Year	Team (League)	Pos.	G	AB	R	H	2B	3B	HR	RBI	Avg.	BB	SO	SB	PO	A	E	Avg.
1998—	West Tenn (Sou.)	OF	125	464	91	134	26	*11	10	68	.289	82	117	*50	258	10	3	.989
—	Iowa (PCL)	OF	4	11	2	4	1	0	0	3	.364	4	4	1	6	0	0	1.000
1999—	Iowa (PCL)	OF-DH	111	414	86	121	24	2	27	64	.292	65	121	15	223	5	0	*1.000
—	Chicago (N.L.)	OF	24	26	2	5	1	0	0	0	.192	2	13	0	16	0	1	.941
2000—	Sacramento (PCL)■...	OF	129	481	94	131	21	3	14	64	.272	88	117	39	299	6	3	.990
—	Oakland (A.L.)	OF	17	13	3	2	0	0	1	2	.154	2	5	0	13	0	0	1.000
American League totals (1 year)			17	13	3	2	0	0	1	2	.154	2	5	0	13	0	0	1.000
National League totals (1 year)			24	26	2	5	1	0	0	0	.192	2	13	0	16	0	1	.941
Major League totals (2 years)			41	39	5	7	1	0	1	2	.179	4	18	0	29	0	1	.967

DIVISION SERIES RECORD

Year	Team (League)	Pos.	G	AB	R	H	2B	3B	HR	RBI	Avg.	BB	SO	SB	PO	A	E	Avg.
2000—	Oakland (A.L.)	OF-PR	2	1	0	1	0	0	0	1	1.000	0	0	0	1	0	0	1.000

POSADA, JORGE   C   YANKEES

PERSONAL: Born August 17, 1971, in Santurce, Puerto Rico. ... 6-2/200. ... Bats both, throws right. ... Full name: Jorge Rafael Posada Jr. ... Name pronounced HOR-hay po-SOD-a.

HIGH SCHOOL: Colegio Alejandrino (Puerto Rico).

JUNIOR COLLEGE: Calhoon Community College (Ala.).

TRANSACTIONS/CAREER NOTES: Selected by New York Yankees organization in 24th round of free-agent draft (June 4, 1990). ... On disabled list (July 26-September 4, 1994). ... On Columbus disabled list (May 3-12, 1995).

HONORS: Named catcher on THE SPORTING NEWS A.L. All-Star team (2000). ... Named catcher on THE SPORTING NEWS A.L. Silver Slugger team (2000).

STATISTICAL NOTES: Led New York-Pennsylvania League second basemen with 42 double plays in 1991. ... Led Carolina League with 38 passed balls in 1993. ... Led Carolina League in intentional bases on balls received with four in 1993. ... Tied for International League lead in errors by catcher with 11 in 1994. ... Tied for International League lead in double plays by catcher with seven in 1995. ... Led International League with 14 passed balls in 1995. ... Switch-hit home runs in one game three times (August 23, 1998; July 10, 1999; and April 23, 2000).

Year	Team (League)	Pos.	G	AB	R	H	2B	3B	HR	RBI	Avg.	BB	SO	SB	PO	A	E	Avg.
1991—	Oneonta (NY-Penn)	2B-C	71	217	34	51	5	5	4	33	.235	51	51	6	172	205	21	.947
1992—	Greensboro (S.Atl.)	C-3B	101	339	60	94	22	4	12	58	.277	58	87	11	263	39	11	.965
1993—	Prince William (Caro.)	C-3B	118	410	71	106	27	2	17	61	.259	67	90	17	677	98	15	.981
—	Albany (East.)	C	7	25	3	7	0	0	0	0	.280	2	7	0	39	7	2	.958
1994—	Columbus (I.L.)	C-OF	92	313	46	75	13	3	11	48	.240	32	81	5	425	39	‡11	.977
1995—	Columbus (I.L.)	C-DH	108	368	60	94	32	5	8	51	.255	54	101	4	500	58	4	*.993
—	New York (A.L.)	C	1	0	0	0	0	0	0	0	...	0	0	0	1	0	0	1.000
1996—	Columbus (I.L.)	C-DH-OF	106	354	76	96	22	6	11	62	.271	*79	86	3	598	51	10	.985
—	New York (A.L.)	C-DH	8	14	1	1	0	0	0	1	.071	1	6	0	17	2	0	1.000
1997—	New York (A.L.)	C	60	188	29	47	12	0	6	25	.250	30	33	1	367	23	3	.992
1998—	New York (A.L.)	C-DH-1B	111	358	56	96	23	0	17	63	.268	47	92	0	594	47	4	.994
1999—	New York (A.L.)	C-DH-1B	112	379	50	93	19	2	12	57	.245	53	91	1	709	47	5	.993
2000—	New York (A.L.)	C-1B-DH	151	505	92	145	35	1	28	86	.287	107	151	2	955	64	8	.992
Major League totals (6 years)			443	1444	228	382	89	3	63	231	.265	238	373	4	2643	183	20	.993

DIVISION SERIES RECORD

Year	Team (League)	Pos.	G	AB	R	H	2B	3B	HR	RBI	Avg.	BB	SO	SB	PO	A	E	Avg.
1995—	New York (A.L.)	PR	1	0	1	0	0	0	0	0	...	0	0	0	...	...	...	...
1997—	New York (A.L.)	C-PH	2	2	0	0	0	0	0	0	.000	0	1	0	1	1	0	1.000
1998—	New York (A.L.)	C	1	2	1	0	0	0	0	0	.000	1	2	0	11	1	0	1.000
1999—	New York (A.L.)	C	1	4	0	1	1	0	0	0	.250	0	0	0	5	0	0	1.000
2000—	New York (A.L.)	C	5	17	2	4	2	0	0	1	.235	3	5	0	34	1	0	1.000
Division series totals (5 years)			10	25	4	5	3	0	0	1	.200	4	8	0	51	3	0	1.000

CHAMPIONSHIP SERIES RECORD

Year	Team (League)	Pos.	G	AB	R	H	2B	3B	HR	RBI	Avg.	BB	SO	SB	PO	A	E	Avg.
1998—	New York (A.L.)	C-PH	5	11	1	2	0	0	1	2	.182	4	2	0	35	1	0	1.000
1999—	New York (A.L.)	C	3	10	1	1	0	0	1	2	.100	1	2	0	20	1	1	.955
2000—	New York (A.L.)	C	6	19	2	3	1	0	0	3	.158	5	5	0	51	3	0	1.000
Championship series totals (3 years)			14	40	4	6	1	0	2	7	.150	10	9	0	106	5	1	.991

WORLD SERIES RECORD

NOTES: Member of World Series championship team (1998, 1999 and 2000).

Year	Team (League)	Pos.	G	AB	R	H	2B	3B	HR	RBI	Avg.	BB	SO	SB	PO	A	E	Avg.
1998—	New York (A.L.)	C-PH	4	9	2	3	0	0	1	2	.333	2	2	0	20	0	0	1.000
1999—	New York (A.L.)	C	2	8	0	2	1	0	0	1	.250	0	3	0	17	1	0	1.000
2000—	New York (A.L.)	C	5	18	2	4	1	0	0	1	.222	5	4	0	52	1	0	1.000
World Series totals (3 years)			11	35	4	9	2	0	1	4	.257	7	9	0	89	2	0	1.000

ALL-STAR GAME RECORD

Year	League	Pos.	AB	R	H	2B	3B	HR	RBI	Avg.	BB	SO	SB	PO	A	E	Avg.
2000—	American	C	2	0	0	0	0	0	0	.000	0	1	0	2	0	0	1.000

P

PERSONAL: Born February 11, 1967, in Davenport, Iowa. ... 5-11/190. ... Bats left, throws right. ... Full name: Scott Vernon Pose.
HIGH SCHOOL: Dowling (West Des Moines, Iowa).
COLLEGE: Arkansas.
TRANSACTIONS/CAREER NOTES: Selected by Cincinnati Reds organization in 34th round of free-agent draft (June 5, 1989). ... Selected by Florida Marlins from Reds organization in Rule 5 major league draft (December 7, 1992). ... Granted free agency (March 23, 1994). ... Signed by Milwaukee Brewers organization (April 5, 1994). ... Contract sold by Brewers organization to Los Angeles Dodgers organization (February 9, 1995). ... Released by Dodgers (April 17, 1995). ... Signed by Minnesota Twins organization (June 1, 1995). ... Granted free agency (October 16, 1995). ... Signed by Cleveland Indians organization (December 6, 1995). ... Traded by Indians to Toronto Blue Jays for IF Joe Lis (March 13, 1996). ... Granted free agency (October 15, 1996). ... Signed by New York Yankees organization (November 27, 1996). ... Granted free agency (October 15, 1997). ... Re-signed by Yankees organization (December 18, 1997). ... Granted free agency (October 15, 1998). ... Signed by Kansas City Royals organization (December 17, 1998). ... Granted free agency (October 10, 2000). ... Signed by Houston Astros organization (January 8, 2001).
STATISTICAL NOTES: Tied for Pioneer League lead with three intentional bases on balls received in 1989. ... Led South Atlantic League with eight intentional bases on balls received and .435 on-base percentage in 1990. ... Led Southern League in on-base percentage with .414 and in caught stealing with 27 in 1992. ... Led International League in caught stealing with 16 in 1996. ... Led International League outfielders with .990 fielding percentage in 1996.

Year Team (League)	Pos.	G	AB	R	H	2B	3B	HR	RBI	Avg.	BB	SO	SB	PO	A	E	Avg.
1989—Billings (Pio.)	OF-2B	60	210	52	74	7	2	0	25	.352	*54	31	26	94	19	7	.942
1990—Char., W.Va. (SAL)	OF	135	480	*106	143	13	5	0	46	.298	*114	56	49	210	*17	3	*.987
1991—Chattanooga (Sou.)	OF	117	402	61	110	8	5	1	31	.274	69	50	17	215	9	1	*.996
—Nashville (A.A.)	OF	15	52	7	10	0	0	0	3	.192	2	9	3	23	0	1	.958
1992—Chattanooga (Sou.)	OF	136	•526	*87	*180	22	8	2	45	*.342	63	66	21	216	10	1	*.996
1993—Florida (N.L.)■	OF	15	41	0	8	2	0	0	3	.195	2	4	0	14	0	0	1.000
—Edmonton (PCL)	OF	109	398	61	113	8	6	0	27	.284	42	36	19	192	4	6	.970
1994—New Orleans (A.A.)■	OF-P-2B	124	429	60	121	13	7	0	52	.282	47	52	20	196	9	1	.995
1995—Albuquerque (PCL)■	OF-DH	7	16	5	3	1	0	0	1	.188	2	0	2	2	0	0	1.000
—Salt Lake (PCL)■	OF-DH-P	70	219	46	66	10	1	0	20	.301	31	28	15	92	8	2	.980
1996—Syracuse (I.L.)■	OF-P-1B	113	419	71	114	11	6	0	39	.272	58	71	30	195	9	2	†.990
1997—Columbus (I.L.)■	OF-DH	57	227	50	70	10	7	2	32	.308	32	29	13	113	6	1	.992
—New York (A.L.)	OF-DH	54	87	19	19	2	1	0	5	.218	9	11	3	44	2	0	1.000
1998—Columbus (I.L.)	OF-DH	133	489	78	145	23	10	3	46	.297	53	72	*47	158	11	3	.983
1999—Kansas City (A.L.)■	OF-DH	86	137	27	39	3	0	0	12	.285	21	22	6	29	3	1	.970
2000—Kansas City (A.L.)	OF-DH	47	48	6	9	0	0	0	1	.188	6	13	0	6	0	0	1.000
American League totals (3 years)		187	272	52	67	5	1	0	18	.246	36	46	9	79	5	1	.988
National League totals (1 year)		15	41	0	8	2	0	0	3	.195	2	4	0	14	0	0	1.000
Major League totals (4 years)		202	313	52	75	7	1	0	21	.240	38	50	9	93	5	1	.990

DIVISION SERIES RECORD

Year Team (League)	Pos.	G	AB	R	H	2B	3B	HR	RBI	Avg.	BB	SO	SB	PO	A	E	Avg.
1997—New York (A.L.)	PR	1	0	0	0	0	0	0	0	...	0	0	0	...	...	...	...

RECORD AS PITCHER

Year League	W	L	Pct.	ERA	G	GS	CG	ShO	Sv.	IP	H	R	ER	BB	SO
1994—New Orleans (A.A.)	0	0	...	0.00	2	0	0	0	0	2	3	0	0	2	2
1995—Salt Lake (PCL)	0	0	...	0.00	1	0	0	0	0	1	0	0	0	1	0
1996—Syracuse (I.L.)	0	0	...	13.50	2	0	0	0	0	2	4	3	3	2	3

PERSONAL: Born August 27, 1971, in Evergreen Park, Ill. ... 6-3/208. ... Throws right, bats right. ... Full name: Louis William Pote.
HIGH SCHOOL: De La Salle Institute (Chicago).
JUNIOR COLLEGE: Kishwaukee (Illinois).
TRANSACTIONS/CAREER NOTES: Selected by San Francisco Giants organization in 29th round of free-agent draft (June 4, 1990). ... On Shreveport disabled list (April 8-July 31, 1994). ... Traded by Giants to Montreal Expos for P Luis Aquino (July 24, 1995). ... Released by Expos (March 28, 1996). ... Signed by St. Louis Cardinals organization (August 7, 1997). ... Granted free agency (October 17, 1997). ... Signed by Anaheim Angels organization (December 15, 1997).

Year League	W	L	Pct.	ERA	G	GS	CG	ShO	Sv.	IP	H	R	ER	BB	SO
1991—Arizona Giants (Ariz.)	2	3	.400	2.55	8	8	0	0	0	42 1/3	38	23	12	19	41
—Everett (N'West)	2	0	1.000	2.51	5	4	0	0	0	28 2/3	24	8	8	7	26
1992—Shreveport (Texas)	4	2	.667	0.96	20	3	0	0	0	37 2/3	20	7	4	15	26
—San Jose (Calif.)	0	1	.000	4.66	4	3	0	0	0	9 2/3	11	5	5	7	8
1993—Shreveport (Texas)	8	7	.533	4.07	19	19	0	0	0	108 1/3	111	53	49	45	81
1994—Arizona Giants (Ariz.)	1	0	1.000	0.00	4	4	0	0	0	19 2/3	9	0	0	6	30
—Shreveport (Texas)	2	2	.500	2.83	5	5	0	0	0	28 2/3	31	11	9	7	15
1995—Shreveport (Texas)	2	2	.500	5.33	28	0	0	0	3	50 2/3	63	41	30	26	30
—Harrisburg (East.)■	0	1	.000	5.40	9	4	0	0	0	28 1/3	32	17	17	7	24
1996—Harrisburg (East.)	1	7	.125	5.07	25	18	0	0	1	104 2/3	114	66	59	48	61
1997—Arkansas (Texas)■	0	0	...	1.54	7	3	0	0	0	23 1/3	15	10	4	8	21
1998—Midland (Texas)■	8	10	.444	5.31	32	19	6	1	0	154 1/3	194	110	91	54	117
1999—Edmonton (PCL)	7	9	.438	4.50	24	23	3	0	0	150	171	80	75	41	118
—Anaheim (A.L.)	1	1	.500	2.15	20	0	0	0	0	29 1/3	23	9	7	12	20
2000—Anaheim (A.L.)	1	1	.500	3.40	32	1	0	0	1	50 1/3	52	23	19	17	44
—Edmonton (PCL)	2	1	.667	3.52	24	0	0	0	12	30 2/3	27	14	12	14	28
Major League totals (2 years)	2	2	.500	2.94	52	1	0	0	4	79 2/3	75	32	26	29	64

P

POWELL, BRIAN — P — ASTROS

PERSONAL: Born October 10, 1973, in Bainbridge, Ga. ... 6-2/205. ... Throws right, bats right. ... Full name: William Brian Powell.
HIGH SCHOOL: Bainbridge (Ga.).
COLLEGE: Georgia.
TRANSACTIONS/CAREER NOTES: Selected by Detroit Tigers organization in second round of free-agent draft (June 1, 1995). ... Traded by Tigers with C Paul Bako, P Dean Crow, P Mark Persails and 3B Carlos Villalobos to Houston Astros for C Brad Ausmus and P C.J. Nitkowski (January 14, 1999). ... On disabled list (May 25, 1999-remainder of season). ... On New Orleans disabled list (April 6-22, 2000).

Year League	W	L	Pct.	ERA	G	GS	CG	ShO	Sv.	IP	H	R	ER	BB	SO
1995— Jamestown (NY-Penn)	2	1	.667	3.08	5	5	0	0	0	26 1/3	19	12	9	8	15
— Fayetteville (S.Atl.)	4	0	1.000	1.61	5	5	0	0	0	28	15	5	5	11	37
1996— Lakeland (FSL)	8	13	.381	4.90	29	27	*5	0	0	*174 1/3	*195	106	*95	47	84
1997— Lakeland (FSL)	13	9	.591	2.50	27	27	*8	2	0	*183 1/3	153	70	51	35	122
1998— Jacksonville (Sou.)	10	2	*.833	3.07	14	14	2	1	0	93 2/3	84	37	32	24	51
— Toledo (I.L.)	0	0	...	0.00	1	1	0	0	0	7	5	0	0	0	7
— Detroit (A.L.)	3	8	.273	6.35	18	16	0	0	0	83 2/3	101	67	59	36	46
1999— New Orleans (PCL)■	4	4	.500	6.19	9	9	0	0	0	48	54	39	33	21	36
2000— New Orleans (PCL)	9	4	.692	4.95	18	18	1	0	0	103 2/3	103	63	57	41	57
— Houston (N.L.)	2	1	.667	5.74	9	5	0	0	0	31 1/3	34	21	20	13	14
A.L. totals (1 year)	3	8	.273	6.35	18	16	0	0	0	83 2/3	101	67	59	36	46
N.L. totals (1 year)	2	1	.667	5.74	9	5	0	0	0	31 1/3	34	21	20	13	14
Major League totals (2 years)	5	9	.357	6.18	27	21	0	0	0	115	135	88	79	49	60

POWELL, JAY — P — ASTROS

PERSONAL: Born January 9, 1972, in Meridian, Miss. ... 6-4/225. ... Throws right, bats right. ... Full name: James Willard Powell Jr. ... Brother-in-law of Bud Brown, defensive back with Miami Dolphins (1984-88).
HIGH SCHOOL: West Lauderdale (Collinsville, Miss.).
COLLEGE: Mississippi State.
TRANSACTIONS/CAREER NOTES: Selected by San Diego Padres organization in 11th round of free-agent draft (June 4, 1990); did not sign. ... Selected by Baltimore Orioles organization in first round (19th pick overall) of free-agent draft (June 3, 1993). ... On disabled list (April 7-26, 1994). ... Traded by Orioles to Florida Marlins for IF Bret Barberie (December 6, 1994). ... On Florida disabled list (April 20-May 10, 1996); included rehabilitation assignment to Brevard County (May 8-10). ... Traded by Marlins with C Scott Makarewicz to Houston Astros for C Ramon Castro (July 6, 1998). ... On Houston disabled list (May 17-June 3, June 19-August 6 and August 18, 2000-remainder of season); included rehabilitation assignments to New Orleans (May 30-June 3) and Round Rock (August 3).
MISCELLANEOUS: Struck out in only appearance as pinch hitter with Florida (1996). ... Struck out in only appearance as pinch hitter (2000).

Year League	W	L	Pct.	ERA	G	GS	CG	ShO	Sv.	IP	H	R	ER	BB	SO
1993— Albany (S.Atl.)	0	2	.000	4.55	6	6	0	0	0	27 2/3	29	19	14	13	29
1994— Frederick (Caro.)	7	7	.500	4.96	26	20	0	0	1	123 1/3	132	79	68	54	87
1995— Portland (East.)■	5	4	.556	1.87	50	0	0	0	*24	53	42	12	11	15	53
— Florida (N.L.)	0	0	...	1.08	9	0	0	0	0	8 1/3	7	2	1	6	4
1996— Florida (N.L.)	4	3	.571	4.54	67	0	0	0	2	71 1/3	71	41	36	36	52
— Brevard County (FSL)	0	0	...	0.00	1	1	0	0	0	2	0	0	0	0	4
1997— Florida (N.L.)	7	2	.778	3.28	74	0	0	0	2	79 2/3	71	35	29	30	65
1998— Florida (N.L.)	4	4	.500	4.21	33	0	0	0	3	36 1/3	36	19	17	22	24
— Houston (N.L.)■	3	3	.500	2.38	29	0	0	0	4	34	22	9	9	15	38
1999— Houston (N.L.)	5	4	.556	4.32	67	0	0	0	4	75	82	38	36	40	77
2000— Houston (N.L.)	1	1	.500	5.67	29	0	0	0	0	27	29	18	17	19	16
— New Orleans (PCL)	0	0	...	4.50	2	1	0	0	0	2	2	1	1	2	2
— Round Rock (Texas)	0	0	...	0.00	1	1	0	0	0	2	0	0	0	1	1
Major League totals (6 years)	24	17	.585	3.93	308	0	0	0	15	331 2/3	318	162	145	168	276

DIVISION SERIES RECORD

Year League	W	L	Pct.	ERA	G	GS	CG	ShO	Sv.	IP	H	R	ER	BB	SO
1997— Florida (N.L.)							Did not play.								
1998— Houston (N.L.)	0	0	...	11.57	3	0	0	0	0	2 1/3	2	3	3	3	3
1999— Houston (N.L.)	0	1	.000	6.00	3	0	0	0	0	3	3	2	2	1	3
Division series totals (2 years)	0	1	.000	8.44	6	0	0	0	0	5 1/3	5	5	5	4	6

CHAMPIONSHIP SERIES RECORD

Year League	W	L	Pct.	ERA	G	GS	CG	ShO	Sv.	IP	H	R	ER	BB	SO
1997— Florida (N.L.)	0	0	...	0.00	1	0	0	0	0	2/3	0	0	0	0	1

WORLD SERIES RECORD

NOTES: Member of World Series championship team (1997).

Year League	W	L	Pct.	ERA	G	GS	CG	ShO	Sv.	IP	H	R	ER	BB	SO
1997— Florida (N.L.)	1	0	1.000	7.36	4	0	0	0	0	3 2/3	5	3	3	4	2

POWELL, JEREMY — P — PADRES

PERSONAL: Born June 18, 1976, in La Miranda, Calif. ... 6-5/230. ... Throws right, bats right. ... Full name: Jeremy Robert Powell.
HIGH SCHOOL: Highlands (North Highlands, Calif.).
TRANSACTIONS/CAREER NOTES: Selected by Montreal Expos organization in fourth round of free-agent draft (June 2, 1994). ... Granted free agency (October 18, 2000). ... Signed by San Diego Padres organization (December 15, 2000).

Year League	W	L	Pct.	ERA	G	GS	CG	ShO	Sv.	IP	H	R	ER	BB	SO
1994— Gulf Coast Expos (GCL)	2	2	.500	2.93	9	9	1	0	0	43	37	16	14	14	36
1995— Albany (S.Atl.)	1	0	1.000	1.59	1	1	0	0	0	5 2/3	4	1	1	1	6
— Vermont (NY-Penn)	5	5	.500	4.34	15	•15	0	0	0	87	88	48	42	34	47
1996— Delmarva (S.Atl.)	12	9	.571	3.03	27	27	1	0	0	157 2/3	127	68	53	66	109

P

Year League	W	L	Pct.	ERA	G	GS	CG	ShO	Sv.	IP	H	R	ER	BB	SO
1997—West Palm Beach (FSL)	9	10	.474	3.02	26	26	1	0	0	155	162	75	52	62	121
1998—Harrisburg (East.)...............	9	7	.563	3.01	22	22	1	0	0	131²/₃	115	54	44	37	77
—Montreal (N.L.)..................	1	5	.167	7.92	7	6	0	0	0	25	27	25	22	11	14
1999—Ottawa (I.L.)	3	5	.375	2.97	16	16	0	0	0	91	85	37	30	37	72
—Montreal (N.L.)..................	4	8	.333	4.73	17	17	0	0	0	97	113	60	51	44	44
2000—Montreal (N.L.)..................	0	3	.000	7.96	11	4	0	0	0	26	35	27	23	9	19
—Ottawa (I.L.)	5	13	.278	6.91	25	24	0	0	0	126¹/₃	160	101	•97	55	99
Major League totals (3 years).......	5	16	.238	5.84	35	27	0	0	0	148	175	112	96	64	77

PRATT, TODD   C   METS

PERSONAL: Born February 9, 1967, in Bellevue, Neb. ... 6-3/230. ... Bats right, throws right. ... Full name: Todd Alan Pratt.
HIGH SCHOOL: Hilltop (Chula Vista, Calif.).
TRANSACTIONS/CAREER NOTES: Selected by Boston Red Sox organization in sixth round of free-agent draft (June 3, 1985). ... Selected by Cleveland Indians organization from Red Sox organization in Rule 5 minor league draft (December 7, 1987). ... Returned to Red Sox organization (March 28, 1988). ... Granted free agency (October 15, 1991). ... Signed by Baltimore Orioles organization (November 13, 1991). ... Selected by Philadelphia Phillies from Orioles organization in Rule 5 major league draft (December 9, 1991). ... On Philadelphia disabled list (April 28-May 27, 1993); included rehabilitation assignment to Scranton/Wilkes-Barre (May 23-27). ... Granted free agency (December 23, 1994). ... Signed by Chicago Cubs organization (April 8, 1995). ... Granted free agency (October 16, 1995). ... Signed by Seattle Mariners organization (January 25, 1996). ... Released by Mariners (March 27, 1996). ... Signed by New York Mets organization (December 23, 1996). ... On New York disabled list (May 7-June 23, 1998); included rehabilitation assignments to St. Lucie (June 14-18), Gulf Coast Mets (June 19-21) and Norfolk (June 22-23).
STATISTICAL NOTES: Led South Atlantic League catchers with 660 putouts and nine double plays and tied for lead with 13 errors in 1986. ... Led Eastern League catchers with 11 errors in 1989. ... Career major league grand slams: 1.

							BATTING							FIELDING		
Year Team (League)	Pos.	G	AB	R	H	2B	3B	HR	RBI	Avg.	BB	SO	SB	PO	A	E	Avg.
1985—Elmira (NY-Penn)	C	39	119	7	16	1	1	0	5	.134	10	27	0	254	29	6	.979
1986—Greensboro (S.Atl.)	C-1B	107	348	63	84	16	0	12	56	.241	75	114	0	†826	55	‡15	.983
1987—Winter Haven (FSL)....	C-1B-OF	118	407	57	105	22	0	12	65	.258	70	94	0	672	64	15	.980
1988—New Britain (East.)	C-1B	124	395	41	89	15	2	8	49	.225	41	110	1	540	46	15	.975
1989—New Britain (East.)	C-1B	109	338	30	77	17	1	2	35	.228	44	66	1	435	42	†11	.977
1990—New Britain (East.)	C-1B	70	195	15	45	14	1	2	22	.231	18	56	0	166	15	4	.978
1991—Pawtucket (I.L.)..........	C-1B	68	219	68	64	16	0	11	41	.292	23	42	0	236	21	4	.985
1992—Reading (East.)■	C	41	132	20	44	6	1	6	26	.333	24	28	2	90	6	3	.970
—Scranton/W.B. (I.L.)	C-1B	41	125	20	40	9	1	7	28	.320	30	14	1	152	16	4	.977
—Philadelphia (N.L.)......	C	16	46	6	13	1	0	2	10	.283	4	12	0	65	4	2	.972
1993—Philadelphia (N.L.)......	C	33	87	8	25	6	0	5	13	.287	5	19	0	169	7	2	.989
—Scranton/W.B. (I.L.)	C	3	9	1	2	1	0	0	1	.222	3	1	0	11	0	0	1.000
1994—Philadelphia (N.L.)......	C	28	102	10	20	6	1	2	9	.196	12	29	0	172	8	0	1.000
1995—Iowa (A.A.)■.............	C-1B-DH	23	58	3	19	1	0	0	5	.328	4	17	0	82	8	2	.978
—Chicago (N.L.)...........	C	25	60	3	8	2	0	0	4	.133	6	21	0	149	9	3	.981
1996—						Out of organized baseball.											
1997—Norfolk (I.L.)■..........	C-DH	59	206	42	62	8	3	9	34	.301	26	48	1	317	24	4	.988
—New York (N.L.)........	C	39	106	12	30	6	0	2	19	.283	13	32	0	186	22	2	.990
1998—Norfolk (I.L.) DH-C-OF-1B		35	118	16	42	6	0	7	30	.356	15	19	2	115	8	2	.984
—New York (N.L.)........	C-1B	41	69	9	19	9	1	2	18	.275	2	20	0	78	4	2	.976
—St. Lucie (FSL)	C-1B-OF	5	20	2	9	1	0	1	3	.450	1	5	1	40	6	0	1.000
—GC Mets (GCL)..........	C-OF	2	4	1	1	0	0	0	0	.250	4	1	0	7	0	0	1.000
1999—New York (N.L.)........	C-1B-DH	71	140	18	41	4	0	3	21	.293	15	32	2	263	13	1	.996
2000—New York (N.L.)........	C-DH	80	160	33	44	6	0	8	25	.275	22	31	0	314	24	1	.997
Major League totals (8 years)		333	770	99	200	40	2	24	119	.260	79	196	2	1396	91	13	.991

DIVISION SERIES RECORD

							BATTING							FIELDING		
Year Team (League)	Pos.	G	AB	R	H	2B	3B	HR	RBI	Avg.	BB	SO	SB	PO	A	E	Avg.
1999—New York (N.L.)..........	PH-C	3	8	2	1	0	0	1	1	.125	2	1	0	11	1	0	1.000
2000—New York (N.L.)..........	PH-C	1	1	0	0	0	0	0	0	.000	0	0	0	4	0	0	1.000
Division series totals (2 years)		4	9	2	1	0	0	1	1	.111	2	1	0	15	1	0	1.000

CHAMPIONSHIP SERIES RECORD

							BATTING							FIELDING		
Year Team (League)	Pos.	G	AB	R	H	2B	3B	HR	RBI	Avg.	BB	SO	SB	PO	A	E	Avg.
1993—Philadelphia (N.L.)......	C	1	1	0	0	0	0	0	0	.000	0	1	0	1	0	0	1.000
1999—New York (N.L.)..........	PH-C	4	2	0	1	0	0	0	3	.500	1	1	0	6	0	0	1.000
Championship series totals (2 years)		5	3	0	1	0	0	0	3	.333	1	2	0	7	0	0	1.000

WORLD SERIES RECORD

							BATTING							FIELDING		
Year Team (League)	Pos.	G	AB	R	H	2B	3B	HR	RBI	Avg.	BB	SO	SB	PO	A	E	Avg.
1993—Philadelphia (N.L.)							Did not play.										
2000—New York (N.L.)..........	C	1	2	1	0	0	0	0	0	.000	1	2	0	10	0	0	1.000

PRIDE, CURTIS   OF   EXPOS

PERSONAL: Born December 17, 1968, in Washington, D.C. ... 6-0/200. ... Bats left, throws right. ... Full name: Curtis John Pride.
HIGH SCHOOL: John F. Kennedy (Silver Spring, Md.).
COLLEGE: William & Mary.
TRANSACTIONS/CAREER NOTES: Selected by New York Mets organization in 10th round of free-agent draft (June 2, 1986). ... Granted free agency (October 15, 1992). ... Signed by Montreal Expos organization (December 8, 1992). ... On Ottawa disabled list (April 7-May 13, July

6-15 and August 7-14, 1994). ... Granted free agency (October 16, 1995). ... Signed by Detroit Tigers (March 31, 1996). ... On Detroit disabled list (April 13-May 10, 1996); included rehabilitation assignment to Toledo (April 30-May 10). ... Granted free agency (August 21, 1997). ... Signed by Boston Red Sox organization (August 30, 1997). ... Granted free agency (October 15, 1997). ... Signed by Atlanta Braves organization (February 6, 1998). ... On suspended list (May 27-28, 1998). ... On Atlanta disabled list (June 28-July 14, 1998); included rehabilitation assignment to Richmond (July 13-14). ... Released by Braves (December 1, 1998). ... Signed by Kansas City Royals organization (February 24, 1999). ... Released by Royals (March 4, 1999). ... Signed by Mets organization (January 20, 2000). ... Traded by Mets to Red Sox for a player to be named later (April 26, 2000). ... Released by Red Sox (July 8, 2000). ... Signed by Los Angeles Dodgers organization (July 18, 2000). ... Granted free agency (October 18, 2000). ... Signed by Expos organization (December 21, 2000).

Year	Team (League)	Pos.	G	AB	R	H	2B	3B	HR	RBI	Avg.	BB	SO	SB	PO	A	E	Avg.
1986—	Kingsport (Appl.)	OF	27	46	5	5	0	0	1	4	.109	6	24	5	17	1	0	1.000
1987—	Kingsport (Appl.)	OF	31	104	22	25	4	0	1	9	.240	16	34	14	39	3	5	.894
1988—	Kingsport (Appl.)	OF	70	268	*59	76	13	1	8	27	.284	50	48	23	118	6	5	.961
1989—	Pittsfield (NY-Penn)	OF	55	212	35	55	7	3	6	23	.259	25	47	9	105	3	4	.964
1990—	Columbia (S.Atl.)	OF	53	191	38	51	4	4	6	25	.267	21	45	11	72	4	11	.874
1991—	St. Lucie (FSL)	OF	116	392	57	102	21	7	9	37	.260	43	94	24	199	5	4	.981
1992—	Binghamton (East.)	OF	118	388	54	88	15	3	10	42	.227	47	110	14	214	3	8	.964
1993—	Harrisburg (East.)■	OF	50	180	51	64	6	3	15	39	.356	12	36	21	69	0	2	.972
—	Ottawa (I.L.)	OF	69	262	55	79	11	4	6	22	.302	34	61	29	136	3	2	.986
—	Montreal (N.L.)	OF	10	9	3	4	1	1	1	5	.444	0	3	1	2	0	0	1.000
1994—	W.P. Beach (FSL)	OF	3	8	5	6	1	0	1	3	.750	4	2	2	11	0	0	1.000
—	Ottawa (I.L.)	OF-DH	82	300	56	77	16	4	9	32	.257	39	81	22	164	1	3	.982
1995—	Ottawa (I.L.)	OF-DH	42	154	25	43	8	3	4	24	.279	12	35	8	69	5	2	.974
—	Montreal (N.L.)	OF	48	63	10	11	1	0	0	2	.175	5	16	3	23	0	2	.920
1996—	Detroit (A.L.)■	OF-DH	95	267	52	80	17	5	10	31	.300	31	63	11	89	0	3	.967
—	Toledo (I.L.)	DH-OF	9	26	4	6	1	0	1	2	.231	9	7	4	3	0	0	1.000
1997—	Detroit (A.L.)	OF-DH	79	162	21	34	4	4	2	19	.210	24	45	6	49	0	1	.980
—	Pawtucket (I.L.)■	OF	1	3	0	0	0	0	0	0	.000	0	2	0	2	0	0	1.000
—	Boston (A.L.)	PH	2	2	1	1	0	0	1	1	.500	0	1	0	...	...	...	...
1998—	Atlanta (N.L.)■	OF-DH	70	107	19	27	6	1	3	9	.252	9	29	4	41	0	0	1.000
—	Richmond (I.L.)	OF-DH	21	78	11	19	2	1	2	6	.244	15	17	8	28	1	0	1.000
1999—	Nashua (Atl.)■	DH	14	32	0	2	0	0	0	2	.063	7	11	0	0	0	0	...
2000—	Norfolk (I.L.)	OF	15	31	9	9	2	2	1	4	.290	11	7	3	13	0	1	.929
—	Pawtucket (I.L.)■	OF	48	154	44	47	10	2	9	31	.305	38	31	12	102	0	1	.990
—	Boston (A.L.)	OF-DH	9	20	4	5	1	0	0	0	.250	1	7	0	15	0	0	1.000
—	Albuquerque (PCL)■	OF	38	133	30	39	7	3	6	17	.293	20	37	7	68	2	3	.959
American League totals (3 years)			185	451	78	120	22	9	13	51	.266	56	116	17	153	0	4	.975
National League totals (3 years)			128	179	32	42	8	2	4	16	.235	14	48	8	66	0	2	.971
Major League totals (6 years)			313	630	110	162	30	11	17	67	.257	70	164	25	219	0	6	.973

PRIETO, ARIEL P ATHLETICS

PERSONAL: Born October 22, 1969, in Havana, Cuba. ... 6-2/247. ... Throws right, bats right.
COLLEGE: Fajardo University (Isle of Pines, Cuba).
TRANSACTIONS/CAREER NOTES: Selected by Oakland Athletics organization in first round (fifth pick overall) of free-agent draft (June 1, 1995). ... On disabled list (August 19-September 3, 1995). ... On Oakland disabled list (May 19-July 28, 1996); included rehabilitation assignments to Modesto (July 1-11) and Edmonton (July 11-28). ... On Oakland disabled list (July 13-August 8 and August 23, 1997-remainder of season); included rehabilitation assignment to Edmonton (August 8-17). ... On Edmonton disabled list (July 29-September 10, 1998). ... On disabled list (March 26, 1999-remainder of season). ... On Sacramento disabled list (August 16-24, 2000).
STATISTICAL NOTES: Led Pacific Coast League pitchers with five double plays in 2000.

Year	League	W	L	Pct.	ERA	G	GS	CG	ShO	Sv.	IP	H	R	ER	BB	SO
1995—	Oakland (A.L.)	2	6	.250	4.97	14	9	1	0	0	58	57	35	32	32	37
1996—	Oakland (A.L.)	6	7	.462	4.15	21	21	2	0	0	125 2/3	130	66	58	54	75
—	Modesto (Calif.)	0	0	...	3.00	2	1	0	0	1	9	9	4	3	2	8
—	Edmonton (PCL)	3	0	1.000	0.57	3	3	0	0	0	15 2/3	11	1	1	6	18
1997—	Oakland (A.L.)	6	8	.429	5.04	22	22	0	0	0	125	155	84	70	70	90
—	Edmonton (PCL)	0	0	...	1.50	2	2	0	0	0	6	4	1	1	1	7
1998—	Edmonton (PCL)	5	1	.833	2.56	10	10	1	0	0	52 2/3	47	20	15	12	50
—	Oakland (A.L.)	0	1	.000	11.88	2	2	0	0	0	8 1/3	17	11	11	5	8
1999—	Oakland (A.L.)							Did not play.								
2000—	Sacramento (PCL)	8	4	.667	3.27	20	18	0	0	0	113	110	51	41	31	79
—	Oakland (A.L.)	1	2	.333	5.12	8	6	0	0	0	31 2/3	42	21	18	13	19
Major League totals (5 years)		15	24	.385	4.88	67	60	3	0	0	348 2/3	401	217	189	174	229

PRINCE, TOM C TWINS

PERSONAL: Born August 13, 1964, in Kankakee, Ill. ... 5-11/206. ... Bats right, throws right. ... Full name: Thomas Albert Prince.
HIGH SCHOOL: Bradley-Bourbonnais (Bradley, Ill.).
JUNIOR COLLEGE: Kankakee (Ill.) Community College.
TRANSACTIONS/CAREER NOTES: Selected by Atlanta Braves organization in eighth round of free-agent draft (January 11, 1983); did not sign. ... Selected by Braves organization in secondary phase of free-agent draft (June 6, 1983); did not sign. ... Selected by Pittsburgh Pirates organization in secondary phase of free-agent draft (January 17, 1984). ... On Pittsburgh disabled list (August 13-September 1, 1991); included rehabilitation assignment to Buffalo (August 28-September 1). ... Granted free agency (October 15, 1993). ... Signed by Los Angeles Dodgers organization (November 12, 1993). ... On Albuquerque disabled list (April 30-May 7, 1994). ... Released by Dodgers (December 5, 1994). ... Re-signed by Dodgers organization (January 5, 1995). ... On Los Angeles disabled list (June 4-July 10, 1995); included rehabilitation assignment to Albuquerque (June 26-July 10). ... Granted free agency (October 15, 1995). ... Re-signed by Dodgers organization (November 1, 1995). ... Granted free agency (October 22, 1998). ... Signed by Philadelphia Phillies (December 18, 1998). ... On Philadelphia disabled list (March 23-September 3, 1999); included rehabilitation assignments to Gulf Coast Phillies (July 21-28), Clearwater (July 29-August 9) and Scranton (August 10-29). ... Granted free agency (October 31, 2000). ... Signed by Minnesota Twins organization (December 19, 2000).

STATISTICAL NOTES: Led South Atlantic League catchers with 930 total chances, 10 double plays and 27 passed balls in 1985. ... Led Carolina League catchers with 954 total chances and 15 passed balls in 1986. ... Led Eastern League catchers with 721 total chances and nine double plays in 1987. ... Led American Association catchers with 12 double plays in 1992. ... Led Pacific Coast League catchers with 677 total chances and nine double plays in 1994.

Year	Team (League)	Pos.	G	AB	R	H	2B	3B	HR	RBI	Avg.	BB	SO	SB	PO	A	E	Avg.
1984—	Watertown (NY-P)	C-3B	23	69	6	14	3	0	2	13	.203	9	13	0	155	26	2	.989
—	GC Pirates (GCL)	C-1B	18	48	4	11	0	0	1	6	.229	8	10	1	75	16	4	.958
1985—	Macon (S.Atl.)	C	124	360	60	75	20	1	10	42	.208	96	92	13	*810	*101	*19	.980
1986—	Prince William (Caro.)	C	121	395	59	100	34	1	10	47	.253	50	74	4	*821	•113	20	.979
1987—	Harrisburg (East.)	C	113	365	41	112	23	2	6	54	.307	51	46	6	*622	*88	•11	.985
—	Pittsburgh (N.L.)	C	4	9	1	2	1	0	1	2	.222	0	2	0	14	3	0	1.000
1988—	Buffalo (A.A.)	C	86	304	35	79	16	0	14	42	.260	23	53	3	456	51	*12	.977
—	Pittsburgh (N.L.)	C	29	74	3	13	2	0	0	6	.176	4	15	0	108	8	2	.983
1989—	Buffalo (A.A.)	C	65	183	21	37	8	1	6	33	.202	22	30	2	312	22	5	.985
—	Pittsburgh (N.L.)	C	21	52	1	7	4	0	0	5	.135	6	12	1	85	11	4	.960
1990—	Pittsburgh (N.L.)	C	4	10	1	1	0	0	0	0	.100	1	2	0	16	1	0	1.000
—	Buffalo (A.A.)	C-1B	94	284	38	64	13	0	7	37	.225	39	46	4	461	62	8	.985
1991—	Pittsburgh (N.L.)	C-1B	26	34	4	9	3	0	1	2	.265	7	3	0	53	9	1	.984
—	Buffalo (A.A.)	C	80	221	29	46	8	3	6	32	.208	37	31	3	379	61	5	.989
1992—	Pittsburgh (N.L.)	C-3B	27	44	1	4	2	0	0	5	.091	6	9	1	76	8	2	.977
—	Buffalo (A.A.)	C-OF	75	244	34	64	17	0	9	35	.262	20	35	3	307	50	8	.978
1993—	Pittsburgh (N.L.)	C	66	179	14	35	14	0	2	24	.196	13	38	1	271	31	5	.984
1994—	Albuquerque (PCL)■..	C-DH	103	330	61	94	31	2	20	54	.285	51	67	2	593	*75	9	.987
—	Los Angeles (N.L.)	C	3	6	2	2	0	0	0	1	.333	1	3	0	11	1	0	1.000
1995—	Los Angeles (N.L.)	C	18	40	3	8	2	1	1	4	.200	4	10	0	71	8	1	.988
—	Albuquerque (PCL)	C-DH	61	192	30	61	15	0	7	36	.318	27	41	0	310	34	4	.989
1996—	Albuquerque (PCL).....C-DH-3B-OF		32	95	24	39	5	1	7	22	.411	15	14	0	88	20	1	.991
—	Los Angeles (N.L.)	C	40	64	6	19	6	0	1	11	.297	6	15	0	161	11	1	.994
1997—	Los Angeles (N.L.)	C	47	100	17	22	5	0	3	14	.220	5	15	0	221	25	1	.996
1998—	Los Angeles (N.L.)	C	37	81	7	15	5	1	0	5	.185	7	24	0	175	16	0	1.000
1999—	GC Phillies (GCL)■..	C-DH	7	21	3	5	3	0	0	3	.238	4	0	0	19	6	0	1.000
—	Clearwater (FSL)	C	9	33	5	12	0	0	2	9	.364	3	3	1	47	4	1	.981
—	Scranton/W.B. (I.L.)	C-DH	7	22	2	2	0	0	1	1	.091	3	5	1	31	2	0	1.000
—	Philadelphia (N.L.)	C	4	6	1	1	0	0	0	0	.167	1	1	0	13	1	0	1.000
2000—	Philadelphia (N.L.)	C	46	122	14	29	9	0	2	16	.238	13	31	1	250	20	1	.996
Major League totals (14 years)			372	821	75	167	53	2	11	95	.203	74	180	4	1525	153	18	.989

PRITCHETT, CHRIS — 1B

PERSONAL: Born January 31, 1970, in Merced, Calif. ... 6-4/212. ... Bats left, throws right. ... Full name: Christopher David Pritchett.
HIGH SCHOOL: Central Catholic (Modesto, Calif.).
COLLEGE: UCLA.
TRANSACTIONS/CAREER NOTES: Selected by California Angels organization in second round of free-agent draft (June 3, 1991). ... Angels franchise renamed Anaheim Angels for 1997 season. ... On Anaheim disabled list (March 30-April 16, 1998). ... Granted free agency (October 15, 1999). ... Signed by Philadelphia Phillies organization (November 1, 1999). ... Granted free agency (October 3, 2000).
STATISTICAL NOTES: Tied for Midwest League lead with six intentional bases on balls received in 1992. ... Led Texas League first basemen with 1,075 putouts, 19 errors and 1,182 total chances in 1993. ... Led Texas League with .421 on-base percentage in 1994. ... Led Texas League first basemen with 100 double plays in 1994. ... Tied for Pacific Coast League lead with 11 intentional bases on balls received in 1996. ... Led Pacific Coast League first baseman with 1,107 putouts, 98 assists, 1,211 total chances, .995 fielding percentage and 107 double plays in 1996.

Year	Team (League)	Pos.	G	AB	R	H	2B	3B	HR	RBI	Avg.	BB	SO	SB	PO	A	E	Avg.
1991—	Boise (N'West)	1B	70	255	41	68	10	3	9	50	.267	47	41	1	636	26	5	*.993
1992—	Quad City (Midw.)	1B	128	448	79	130	19	1	13	72	.290	71	88	9	*1059	84	13	*.989
1993—	Midland (Texas)	1B-2B	127	464	61	143	30	6	2	66	.308	61	72	3	†1076	92	†19	.984
1994—	Midland (Texas)	1B-OF-3B	127	460	86	142	25	4	6	91	.309	*92	87	5	1028	94	13	.989
1995—	Vancouver (PCL)	1B-OF	123	434	66	120	27	4	8	53	.276	56	79	2	999	92	12	.989
1996—	Vancouver (PCL)	1B-OF	130	485	78	143	39	1	16	73	.295	71	96	5	†1116	†98	6	†.995
—	California (A.L.)	1B	5	13	1	2	0	0	0	1	.154	0	3	0	29	1	0	1.000
1997—	Vancouver (PCL)	1B-DH-OF	109	383	60	107	30	3	7	47	.279	42	72	5	621	51	7	.990
1998—	Vancouver (PCL)	1B-DH	104	374	42	97	21	1	7	41	.259	37	72	2	739	55	10	.988
—	Anaheim (A.L.)	1B	31	80	12	23	2	1	2	8	.288	4	16	2	190	20	1	.995
1999—	Edmonton (PCL)	1B-DH-OF	96	348	60	97	15	1	12	45	.279	47	70	1	717	64	9	.989
—	Anaheim (A.L.)	1B-DH	20	45	3	7	1	0	1	2	.156	2	9	1	96	8	1	.990
2000—	Scranton/W.B. (I.L.)■	1B	117	391	55	93	18	2	6	60	.238	56	65	5	904	50	4	*.996
—	Philadelphia (N.L.)	1B	5	11	0	1	0	0	0	0	.091	1	3	0	15	4	0	1.000
American League totals (3 years)			56	138	16	32	3	1	3	11	.232	6	28	3	315	29	2	.994
National League totals (1 year)			5	11	0	1	0	0	0	0	.091	1	3	0	15	4	0	1.000
Major League totals (4 years)			61	149	16	33	3	1	3	11	.221	7	31	3	330	33	2	.995

PROKOPEC, LUKE — P — DODGERS

P

PERSONAL: Born February 23, 1978, in Blackwood, South Australia. ... 5-11/166. ... Throws right, bats left. ... Full name: Kenneth Luke Prokopec.
HIGH SCHOOL: Renmark (South Australia).
TRANSACTIONS/CAREER NOTES: Signed as non-drafted free agent by Los Angeles Dodgers organization (August 28, 1994). ... On San Antonio disabled list (April 29-May 12 and July 8-21, 2000).
MISCELLANEOUS: Played outfield (1995-97). ... Appeared in one game as pinch runner (2000).

Year	League	W	L	Pct.	ERA	G	GS	CG	ShO	Sv.	IP	H	R	ER	BB	SO
1997— Savannah (S.Atl.)		3	1	.750	4.07	13	6	0	0	0	42	37	21	19	12	45
1998— San Bernardino (Calif.).......		8	5	.615	2.69	20	20	0	0	0	110 1/3	99	43	33	33	148
— San Antonio (Texas)..........		3	0	1.000	1.38	5	5	0	0	0	26	16	5	4	13	25
1999— San Antonio (Texas)		8	12	.400	5.42	27	27	0	0	0	157 2/3	172	*113	*95	46	128
2000— San Antonio (Texas)		7	3	.700	2.45	22	22	1	0	0	128 2/3	118	40	35	23	124
— Los Angeles (N.L.)		1	1	.500	3.00	5	3	0	0	0	21	19	10	7	9	12
Major League totals (1 year)........		1	1	.500	3.00	5	3	0	0	0	21	19	10	7	9	12

RECORD AS POSITION PLAYER

Year	Team (League)	Pos.	G	AB	R	H	2B	3B	HR	RBI	Avg.	BB	SO	SB	PO	A	E	Avg.
								BATTING								FIELDING		
1995— Great Falls (Pio.)		OF	43	119	16	29	6	2	2	24	.244	8	37	5	30	4	0	1.000
1996— Savannah (S.Atl.)		OF	82	245	34	53	12	1	4	29	.216	27	78	0	59	5	8	.889
1997— Savannah (S.Atl.)		OF	61	164	11	38	7	3	2	20	.232	12	49	3	79	11	2	.978

PUJOLS, ALBERT 3B CARDINALS

PERSONAL: Born January 16, 1980, in Santo Domingo, Dominican Republic. ... 6-3/210. ... Bats right, throws right. ... Full name: Jose Albert Pujols.
HIGH SCHOOL: Fort Osage (Independence, Mo.).
JUNIOR COLLEGE: Maple Woods Community College (Mo.).
TRANSACTIONS/CAREER NOTES: Selected by St. Louis Cardinals organization in 13th round of free-agent draft (June 2, 1999).
HONORS: Named Midwest League Most Valuable Player (2000).

Year	Team (League)	Pos.	G	AB	R	H	2B	3B	HR	RBI	Avg.	BB	SO	SB	PO	A	E	Avg.
								BATTING								FIELDING		
2000— Peoria (Midw.)...........		3B	109	395	62	128	32	6	17	84	.324	38	37	2	92	254	19	.948
— Potomac (Caro.).........		3B	21	81	11	23	8	1	2	10	.284	7	8	1	12	54	3	.957
— Memphis (PCL)		3B-OF	3	14	1	3	1	0	0	2	.214	1	2	1	7	2	0	1.000

PULSIPHER, BILL P. DEVIL RAYS

PERSONAL: Born October 9, 1973, in Fort Benning, Ga. ... 6-3/200. ... Throws left, bats left. ... Full name: William Thomas Pulsipher.
HIGH SCHOOL: Fairfax (Va.).
TRANSACTIONS/CAREER NOTES: Selected by New York Mets organization in second round of free-agent draft (June 3, 1991). ... On disabled list (March 22, 1996-entire season). ... On New York disabled list (March 24-May 3, 1997); included rehabilitation assignment to Norfolk (April 4-May 3). ... On Norfolk disabled list (June 30-July 30, 1997). ... Traded by Mets to Milwaukee Brewers for 3B Mike Kinkade (July 31, 1998). ... On Milwaukee disabled list (April 19-July 3, 1999); included rehabilitation assignment to Louisville (June 1-30). ... Traded by Brewers to Mets for IF Luis Lopez (January 21, 2000). ... On Norfolk disabled list (April 6-14, 2000). ... Traded by Mets to Arizona Diamondbacks for IF/OF Lenny Harris (June 2, 2000). ... On Tucson disabled list (June 22-July 17, 2000). ... Granted free agency (October 14, 2000). ... Signed by Tampa Bay Devil Rays organization (November 2, 2000).
STATISTICAL NOTES: Tied for Eastern League lead with four balks in 1994.
MISCELLANEOUS: Appeared in one game as pinch runner with Mets (1998).

Year	League	W	L	Pct.	ERA	G	GS	CG	ShO	Sv.	IP	H	R	ER	BB	SO
1992— Pittsfield (NY-Penn)...........		6	3	.667	2.84	14	14	0	0	0	95	88	40	30	56	83
1993— Capital City (S.Atl.)		2	3	.400	2.08	6	6	1	0	0	43 1/3	34	17	10	12	29
— St. Lucie (FSL)		7	3	.700	2.24	13	13	3	1	0	96 1/3	63	27	24	39	102
1994— Binghamton (East.)		14	9	.609	3.22	28	28	5	1	0	*201	179	90	72	89	171
1995— Norfolk (I.L.)		6	4	.600	3.14	13	13	•4	2	0	91 2/3	84	36	32	33	63
— New York (N.L.).................		5	7	.417	3.98	17	17	2	0	0	126 2/3	122	58	56	45	81
1996— New York (N.L.).................								Did not play.								
1997— Norfolk (I.L.)		0	5	.000	7.81	8	5	0	0	0	27 2/3	23	29	24	38	18
— St. Lucie (FSL)		1	4	.200	5.89	12	7	0	0	0	36 2/3	29	27	24	35	35
— Binghamton (East.)		0	0	...	1.42	10	0	0	0	0	12 2/3	11	3	2	7	12
— Gulf Coast Mets (GCL)		0	0	...	1.80	2	2	0	0	0	5	3	1	1	1	4
1998— Norfolk (I.L.)		7	5	.583	3.96	14	14	1	0	0	86 1/3	91	50	38	41	58
— New York (N.L.).................		0	0	...	6.91	15	1	0	0	0	14 1/3	23	11	11	5	13
— Milwaukee (N.L.)■.............		3	4	.429	4.66	11	10	0	0	0	58	63	30	30	26	38
1999— Milwaukee (N.L.)...............		5	6	.455	5.98	19	16	0	0	0	87 1/3	100	65	58	36	42
— Louisville (I.L.)		0	2	.000	4.28	6	6	0	0	0	27 1/3	22	14	13	19	21
2000— Norfolk (I.L.)■.................		2	3	.400	6.55	7	5	0	0	0	33	41	28	24	15	25
— New York (N.L.).................		0	2	.000	12.15	2	2	0	0	0	6 2/3	12	9	9	6	7
— Tucson (PCL)■.................		3	8	.273	3.95	13	13	0	0	0	70 2/3	73	39	31	37	51
— Ariz. D-backs (Ariz.)		0	0	...	4.50	3	3	0	0	0	6	8	3	3	0	4
Major League totals (4 years).......		13	19	.406	5.04	64	46	2	0	0	293	320	173	164	118	181

PUNTO, NICK SS PHILLIES

PERSONAL: Born November 8, 1977, in San Diego. ... 5-9/170. ... Bats right, throws right. ... Full name: Nicholas Paul Punto.
HIGH SCHOOL: Trabuco Hills (Mission Vieh Vijo, Calif.).
JUNIOR COLLEGE: Saddleback Community College (Calif.).
TRANSACTIONS/CAREER NOTES: Selected by Minnesota Twins organization in 33rd round of free-agent draft (June 3, 1997); did not sign. ... Selected by Philadelphia Phillies organization in 21st round of free-agent draft (June 2, 1998).
STATISTICAL NOTES: Led New York-Pennsylvania League shortstops with 45 double plays in 1998.

Year	Team (League)	Pos.	G	AB	R	H	2B	3B	HR	RBI	Avg.	BB	SO	SB	PO	A	E	Avg.
								BATTING								FIELDING		
1998— Batavia (NY-Penn)		SS-2B	72	279	51	69	9	4	1	20	.247	42	48	19	107	222	27	.924
1999— Clearwater (FSL)		SS	106	400	65	122	18	6	1	48	.305	67	53	16	168	380	24	.958
2000— Reading (East.)..........		SS	121	456	77	116	15	4	5	47	.254	69	71	33	186	331	20	.963

P

QUANTRILL, PAUL   P   BLUE JAYS

PERSONAL: Born November 3, 1968, in London, Ont. ... 6-1/190. ... Throws right, bats left. ... Full name: Paul John Quantrill. ... Name pronounced KWON-trill.
HIGH SCHOOL: Okemos (Mich.).
COLLEGE: Wisconsin.
TRANSACTIONS/CAREER NOTES: Selected by Los Angeles Dodgers organization in 26th round of free-agent draft (June 2, 1986); did not sign. ... Selected by Boston Red Sox organization in sixth round of free-agent draft (June 5, 1989). ... Traded by Red Sox with OF Billy Hatcher to Philadelphia Phillies for OF Wes Chamberlain and P Mike Sullivan (May 31, 1994). ... Traded by Phillies to Toronto Blue Jays for 3B Howard Battle and P Ricardo Jordan (December 6, 1995). ... On Toronto disabled list (March 27-June 15, 1999); included rehabilitation assignments to Dunedin (June 4-10) and Syracuse (June 11-13).

Year League	W	L	Pct.	ERA	G	GS	CG	ShO	Sv.	IP	H	R	ER	BB	SO
1989—Gulf Coast Red Sox (GCL)..	0	0	...	0.00	2	0	0	0	2	5	2	0	0	0	5
—Elmira (NY-Penn)	5	4	.556	3.43	20	7	•5	0	2	76	90	37	29	12	57
1990—Winter Haven (FSL)	2	5	.286	4.14	7	7	1	0	0	45 2/3	46	24	21	6	14
—New Britain (East.)	7	11	.389	3.53	22	22	1	1	0	132 2/3	148	65	52	23	53
1991—New Britain (East.)	2	1	.667	2.06	5	5	1	0	0	35	32	14	8	8	18
—Pawtucket (I.L.)	10	7	.588	4.45	25	23	•6	2	0	155 2/3	169	81	77	30	75
1992—Pawtucket (I.L.)	6	8	.429	4.46	19	18	4	1	0	119	143	63	59	20	56
—Boston (A.L.)	2	3	.400	2.19	27	0	0	0	1	49 1/3	55	18	12	15	24
1993—Boston (A.L.)	6	12	.333	3.91	49	14	1	1	1	138	151	73	60	44	66
1994—Boston (A.L.)	1	1	.500	3.52	17	0	0	0	0	23	25	10	9	5	15
—Philadelphia (N.L.)■	2	2	.500	6.00	18	1	0	0	1	30	39	21	20	10	13
—Scranton/W.B. (I.L.)	3	3	.500	3.47	8	8	1	1	0	57	55	25	22	6	36
1995—Philadelphia (N.L.)	11	12	.478	4.67	33	29	0	0	0	179 1/3	212	102	93	44	103
1996—Toronto (A.L.)■	5	14	.263	5.43	38	20	0	0	0	134 1/3	172	90	81	51	86
1997—Toronto (A.L.)	6	7	.462	1.94	77	0	0	0	5	88	103	25	19	17	56
1998—Toronto (A.L.)	3	4	.429	2.59	82	0	0	0	7	80	88	26	23	22	59
1999—Dunedin (FSL)	0	1	.000	4.50	5	4	0	0	0	6	5	3	3	1	2
—Syracuse (I.L.)	0	0	...	0.00	2	0	0	0	0	2	1	0	0	0	1
—Toronto (A.L.)	3	2	.600	3.33	41	0	0	0	0	48 2/3	53	19	18	17	28
2000—Toronto (A.L.)	2	5	.286	4.52	68	0	0	0	1	83 2/3	100	45	42	25	47
A.L. totals (8 years)	28	48	.368	3.68	399	34	1	1	15	645	747	306	264	196	381
N.L. totals (2 years)	13	14	.481	4.86	51	30	0	0	1	209 1/3	251	123	113	54	116
Major League totals (9 years)	41	62	.398	3.97	450	64	1	1	16	854 1/3	998	429	377	250	497

QUEVEDO, RUBEN   P   CUBS

PERSONAL: Born January 5, 1979, in Valencia, Venezuela. ... 6-1/230. ... Throws right, bats right. ... Full name: Ruben Eduardo Quevedo Yetez. ... Name pronounced keh-VAY-doh.
HIGH SCHOOL: Don Bosco (Valencia, Venezuela).
TRANSACTIONS/CAREER NOTES: Signed as non-drafted free agent by Atlanta Braves organization (September 6, 1995). ... Traded by Braves with P Micah Bowie and a player to be named later to Chicago Cubs for P Terry Mulholland and SS Jose Hernandez (July 31, 1999); Cubs acquired P Joey Nation to complete deal (August 24, 1999).

Year League	W	L	Pct.	ERA	G	GS	CG	ShO	Sv.	IP	H	R	ER	BB	SO
1996—Gulf Coast Braves (GCL)	2	6	.250	2.17	10	10	0	0	0	58	50	19	14	9	49
1997—Danville (Appl.)	1	5	.167	3.56	13	11	0	0	0	68 1/3	46	37	27	27	78
1998—Macon (S.Atl.)	11	3	.786	3.13	25	15	1	0	0	112	114	50	39	31	117
—Danville (Caro.)	0	2	.000	3.58	6	6	0	0	0	32 2/3	28	22	13	13	35
1999—Richmond (I.L.)	6	5	.545	5.37	21	21	0	0	0	105 2/3	112	65	63	34	98
—Iowa (PCL)■	3	1	.750	3.45	7	7	1	1	0	44 1/3	34	18	17	21	50
2000—Iowa (PCL)	7	2	.778	4.22	13	13	0	0	0	74 2/3	68	37	35	31	77
—Chicago (N.L.)	3	10	.231	7.47	21	15	1	0	0	88	96	81	73	54	65
Major League totals (1 year)	3	10	.231	7.47	21	15	1	0	0	88	96	81	73	54	65

QUINN, MARK   OF   ROYALS

PERSONAL: Born May 21, 1974, in La Miranda, Calif. ... 6-1/195. ... Bats right, throws right. ... Full name: Mark David Quinn.
HIGH SCHOOL: Clements (Sugar Land, Texas).
COLLEGE: Rice.
TRANSACTIONS/CAREER NOTES: Selected by Kansas City Royals organization in 11th round of free-agent draft (June 1, 1995).
RECORDS: Shares major league record for most home runs, first game in major leagues—2 (September 14, 1999, second game).
HONORS: Named A.L. Rookie Player of the Year by THE SPORTING NEWS (2000).
STATISTICAL NOTES: Career major league grand slams: 1.

Year Team (League)	Pos.	G	AB	R	H	2B	3B	HR	RBI	Avg.	BB	SO	SB	PO	A	E	Avg.
1995—Spokane (N'West)	3B	44	162	28	46	12	2	6	36	.284	15	28	0	8	33	8	.837
1996—Lansing (Midw.)	OF	113	437	63	132	23	3	9	71	.302	43	54	14	143	15	7	.958
1997—Wilmington (Caro.)	OF	87	299	51	92	22	3	16	71	.308	42	47	3	75	7	6	.932
—Wichita (Texas)	OF	26	96	26	36	13	0	2	19	.375	15	19	1	35	0	1	.972
1998—Wichita (Texas)	OF	100	372	82	130	26	6	16	84	*.349	43	54	4	157	11	8	.955
1999—Omaha (PCL)	OF-DH	107	428	67	154	27	0	25	84	*.360	28	69	7	216	13	4	.983
—Kansas City (A.L.)	OF-DH	17	60	11	20	4	1	6	18	.333	4	11	1	25	2	1	.964
2000—Kansas City (A.L.)	OF-DH	135	500	76	147	33	2	20	78	.294	35	91	5	158	9	2	.988
—Omaha (PCL)	OF	13	61	8	23	5	0	3	13	.377	0	8	0	23	1	0	1.000
Major League totals (2 years)		152	560	87	167	37	3	26	96	.298	39	102	6	183	11	3	.985

RADINSKY, SCOTT   P   INDIANS

PERSONAL: Born March 3, 1968, in Glendale, Calif. ... 6-3/215. ... Throws left, bats left. ... Full name: Scott David Radinsky.
HIGH SCHOOL: Simi Valley (Calif.).
TRANSACTIONS/CAREER NOTES: Selected by Chicago White Sox organization in third round of free-agent draft (June 2, 1986). ... On Chicago disabled list (March 2, 1994-entire season). ... On Chicago disabled list (July 17-August 15, 1995); included rehabilitation assignment to South Bend (August 1-15). ... Granted free agency (December 21, 1995). ... Signed by Los Angeles Dodgers organization (January 16, 1996). ... On Los Angeles disabled list (March 28-April 12, 1996); included rehabilitation assignment to San Bernardino (April 4-12). ... Granted free agency (October 23, 1998). ... Signed by St. Louis Cardinals (November 23, 1998). ... On disabled list (July 27, 1999-remainder of season; April 2-May 27 and June 2, 2000-remainder of season). ... Granted free agency (October 31, 2000). ... Signed by Cleveland Indians organization (January 20, 2001).

Year League	W	L	Pct.	ERA	G	GS	CG	ShO	Sv.	IP	H	R	ER	BB	SO
1986— GC White Sox (GCL)	1	0	1.000	3.38	7	7	0	0	0	26²/₃	24	20	10	17	18
1987— Peninsula (Caro.)	1	7	.125	5.77	12	8	0	0	0	39	43	30	25	32	37
— GC White Sox (GCL)	3	3	.500	2.31	11	10	0	0	0	58¹/₃	43	23	15	39	41
1988— GC White Sox (GCL)	0	0	...	5.40	5	0	0	0	0	3¹/₃	2	2	2	4	7
1989— South Bend (Midw.)	7	5	.583	1.75	53	0	0	0	31	61²/₃	39	21	12	19	83
1990— Chicago (A.L.)	6	1	.857	4.82	62	0	0	0	4	52¹/₃	47	29	28	36	46
1991— Chicago (A.L.)	5	5	.500	2.02	67	0	0	0	8	71¹/₃	53	18	16	23	49
1992— Chicago (A.L.)	3	7	.300	2.73	68	0	0	0	15	59¹/₃	54	21	18	34	48
1993— Chicago (A.L.)	8	2	.800	4.28	73	0	0	0	4	54²/₃	61	33	26	19	44
1994— Chicago (A.L.)					Did not play.										
1995— Chicago (A.L.)	2	1	.667	5.45	46	0	0	0	1	38	46	23	23	17	14
— South Bend (Midw.)	0	0	...	0.00	6	0	0	0	2	9²/₃	5	0	0	0	11
1996— San Bernardino (Calif.)■..	0	0	...	2.08	3	0	0	0	0	4¹/₃	2	1	1	2	4
— Los Angeles (N.L.)	5	1	.833	2.41	56	0	0	0	1	52¹/₃	52	19	14	17	48
1997— Los Angeles (N.L.)	5	1	.833	2.89	75	0	0	0	3	62¹/₃	54	22	20	21	44
1998— Los Angeles (N.L.)	6	6	.500	2.63	62	0	0	0	13	61²/₃	63	21	18	20	45
1999— St. Louis (N.L.)■	2	1	.667	4.88	43	0	0	0	3	27²/₃	27	16	15	18	17
2000— St. Louis (N.L.)	0	0	...	...	1	0	0	0	0	0	0	0	0	1	0
A.L. totals (5 years)	24	16	.600	3.62	316	0	0	0	32	275²/₃	261	124	111	129	201
N.L. totals (5 years)	18	9	.667	2.96	237	0	0	0	20	204	196	78	67	77	154
Major League totals (10 years).....	42	25	.627	3.34	553	0	0	0	52	479²/₃	457	202	178	206	355

DIVISION SERIES RECORD

Year League	W	L	Pct.	ERA	G	GS	CG	ShO	Sv.	IP	H	R	ER	BB	SO
1996— Los Angeles (N.L.)	0	0	...	0.00	2	0	0	0	0	1¹/₃	0	0	0	1	2

CHAMPIONSHIP SERIES RECORD

Year League	W	L	Pct.	ERA	G	GS	CG	ShO	Sv.	IP	H	R	ER	BB	SO
1993— Chicago (A.L.)	0	0	...	10.80	4	0	0	0	0	1²/₃	3	4	2	1	1

RADKE, BRAD   P   TWINS

PERSONAL: Born October 27, 1972, in Eau Claire, Wis. ... 6-2/188. ... Throws right, bats right. ... Full name: Brad William Radke.
HIGH SCHOOL: Jesuit (Tampa).
TRANSACTIONS/CAREER NOTES: Selected by Minnesota Twins organization in eighth round of free-agent draft (June 3, 1991).
STATISTICAL NOTES: Led A.L. in home runs allowed with 32 in 1995 and 40 in 1996. ... Led A.L. pitchers with 1.000 fielding percentage in 1999.

Year League	W	L	Pct.	ERA	G	GS	CG	ShO	Sv.	IP	H	R	ER	BB	SO
1991— Gulf Coast Twins (GCL)	3	4	.429	3.08	10	9	1	0	1	49²/₃	41	21	17	14	46
1992— Kenosha (Midw.)	10	10	.500	2.93	26	25	4	1	0	165²/₃	149	70	54	47	127
1993— Fort Myers (FSL)	3	5	.375	3.82	14	14	0	0	0	92	85	42	39	21	69
— Nashville (Sou.)	2	6	.250	4.62	13	13	1	0	0	76	81	42	39	16	76
1994— Nashville (Sou.)	12	9	.571	2.66	29	*28	5	1	0	186¹/₃	167	66	55	34	123
1995— Minnesota (A.L.)	11	14	.440	5.32	29	28	2	1	0	181	195	112	107	47	75
1996— Minnesota (A.L.)	11	16	.407	4.46	35	35	3	0	0	232	231	125	115	57	148
1997— Minnesota (A.L.)	20	10	.667	3.87	35	•35	4	1	0	239²/₃	238	114	103	48	174
1998— Minnesota (A.L.)	12	14	.462	4.30	32	32	5	1	0	213²/₃	238	109	102	43	146
1999— Minnesota (A.L.)	12	14	.462	3.75	33	33	4	0	0	218²/₃	239	97	91	44	121
2000— Minnesota (A.L.)	12	*16	.429	4.45	34	34	4	1	0	226²/₃	261	119	112	51	141
Major League totals (6 years)	78	84	.481	4.32	198	197	22	4	0	1311²/₃	1402	676	630	290	805

ALL-STAR GAME RECORD

Year League	W	L	Pct.	ERA	GS	CG	ShO	Sv.	IP	H	R	ER	BB	SO
1998— American	0	0	...	9.00	0	0	0	0	1	2	1	1	1	1

RADMANOVICH, RYAN   OF   PADRES

PERSONAL: Born August 9, 1971, in Calgary, Alta. ... 6-2/200. ... Bats left, throws right. ... Full name: Ryan Ashley Radmanovich.
HIGH SCHOOL: John Diefenbaker (Calgary, Alta.).
JUNIOR COLLEGE: Allan Hancock College (Calif.).
COLLEGE: Pepperdine.
TRANSACTIONS/CAREER NOTES: Selected by Minnesota Twins organization in 14th round of free-agent draft (June 3, 1993). ... On disabled list (April 21-May 12 and May 23-September 15, 1995). ... Claimed on waivers by Seattle Mariners (March 27, 1998). ... Granted free agency (October 15, 1999). ... Signed by San Diego Padres organization (November 4, 1999). ... On Las Vegas disabled list (May 6-15, 2000).
STATISTICAL NOTES: Led Midwest League third basemen with 21 double plays in 1994.
MISCELLANEOUS: Member of 1992 Canadian Olympic baseball team.

Year Team (League)	Pos.	G	AB	R	H	2B	3B	HR	RBI	Avg.	BB	SO	SB	PO	A	E	Avg.
1993—Fort Wayne (Midw.)....	OF	62	204	36	59	7	5	8	38	.289	30	60	8	84	6	3	.968
1994—Fort Myers (FSL)........	3B-OF	26	85	11	16	4	0	2	9	.188	7	19	3	12	47	12	.831
—Fort Wayne (Midw.)....	3B	101	383	64	105	20	6	19	69	.274	45	98	19	75	169	28	.897
1995—Fort Myers (FSL)........	3B	12	41	3	13	2	0	0	5	.317	2	8	0	7	22	7	.806
1996—New Britain (East.).....	OF	125	453	77	127	31	2	25	86	.280	49	122	4	246	3	4	.984
1997—Salt Lake (PCL)..........	OF-DH-3B	133	485	92	128	25	4	28	78	.264	67	*138	11	226	7	9	.963
1998—Tacoma (PCL)■........	OF-DH	110	397	73	119	33	2	15	65	.300	46	83	2	164	4	3	.982
—Seattle (A.L.)...............	OF-1B	25	69	5	15	4	0	2	10	.217	4	25	1	34	2	0	1.000
1999—Tacoma (PCL)	OF-DH-3B	109	420	69	120	24	3	17	80	.286	53	83	10	185	15	4	.980
2000—Las Vegas (PCL)■	OF	120	399	74	109	31	3	11	59	.273	60	84	4	168	3	1	*.994
Major League totals (1 year)		25	69	5	15	4	0	2	10	.217	4	25	1	34	2	0	1.000

R

RAIN, STEVE   P

PERSONAL: Born June 2, 1975, in Los Angeles. ... 6-6/260. ... Throws right, bats right. ... Full name: Steven Nicholas Rain.
HIGH SCHOOL: Walnut (Calif.).
TRANSACTIONS/CAREER NOTES: Selected by Chicago Cubs organization in 11th round of free-agent draft (June 3, 1993). ... On Iowa disabled list (June 24-July 6, 1998). ... Granted free agency (December 21, 2000).

Year League	W	L	Pct.	ERA	G	GS	CG	ShO	Sv.	IP	H	R	ER	BB	SO
1993—Gulf Coast Cubs (GCL)....	1	3	.250	3.89	10	6	0	0	0	37	37	20	16	17	29
1994—Huntington (Appl.)	3	3	.500	2.65	14	10	1	1	0	68	55	26	20	19	55
1995—Rockford (Midw.)	5	2	.714	1.21	53	0	0	0	23	59 1/3	38	12	8	23	66
1996—Orlando (Sou.)	1	0	1.000	2.56	35	0	0	0	10	38 2/3	32	15	11	12	48
—Iowa (A.A.)	2	1	.667	3.12	26	0	0	0	10	26	17	9	9	8	23
1997—Iowa (A.A.)	7	1	.875	5.89	40	0	0	0	1	44 1/3	51	30	29	34	50
—Orlando (Sou.)	1	2	.333	3.07	14	0	0	0	4	14 2/3	16	7	5	8	11
1998—Iowa (PCL)	4	6	.400	6.68	29	14	1	0	0	103 2/3	118	82	77	64	83
1999—West Tenn (Sou.)	3	1	.750	1.59	40	0	0	0	24	45 1/3	32	9	8	16	55
—Chicago (N.L.)..................	0	1	.000	9.20	16	0	0	0	0	14 2/3	28	17	15	7	12
—Iowa (PCL)	0	1	.000	2.00	8	0	0	0	2	9	7	2	2	4	9
2000—Iowa (PCL)	0	2	.000	3.45	28	0	0	0	6	31 1/3	31	14	12	6	34
—Chicago (N.L.)..................	3	4	.429	4.35	37	0	0	0	0	49 2/3	46	25	24	27	54
Major League totals (2 years)	3	5	.375	5.46	53	0	0	0	0	64 1/3	74	42	39	34	66

RAKERS, JASON   P   ROYALS

PERSONAL: Born June 29, 1973, in Pittsburgh. ... 6-2/200. ... Throws right, bats right. ... Full name: Jason Paul Rakers.
HIGH SCHOOL: Shaler Area (Pittsburgh).
COLLEGE: Pittsburgh, then New Mexico State.
TRANSACTIONS/CAREER NOTES: Selected by Cleveland Indians organization in 25th round of free-agent draft (June 1, 1995). ... On disabled list (April 4-June 23, 1996). ... On Buffalo disabled list (July 8-17, 1999). ... On Cleveland disabled list (August 31, 1999-remainder of season). ... Claimed on waivers by Kansas City Royals (November 17, 1999).
STATISTICAL NOTES: Pitched 8-0 no-hit for Kinston victory against Durham (June 4, 1997, first game).

Year League	W	L	Pct.	ERA	G	GS	CG	ShO	Sv.	IP	H	R	ER	BB	SO
1995—Watertown (NY-Penn)	4	3	.571	3.00	14	14	1	•1	0	75	72	27	25	24	73
1996—Columbus (S.Atl.)...............	5	4	.556	3.61	14	14	1	1	0	77 1/3	84	37	31	17	64
1997—Kinston (Caro.)....................	8	5	.615	3.07	17	17	2	2	0	102 2/3	93	41	35	18	105
—Buffalo (A.A.).....................	1	0	1.000	0.00	1	1	0	0	0	7	5	0	0	1	3
—Akron (East.).....................	1	4	.200	4.39	7	7	1	1	0	41	36	21	20	11	31
1998—Akron (East.).....................	3	1	.750	2.59	5	5	0	0	0	31 1/3	35	10	9	7	27
—Cleveland (A.L.)..................	0	0	...	9.00	1	0	0	0	0	1	0	1	1	3	0
—Buffalo (I.L.).....................	8	6	.571	4.57	21	21	1	0	0	126	134	70	64	38	89
1999—Buffalo (I.L.).....................	7	8	.467	4.92	23	20	1	0	0	131 2/3	151	83	72	31	85
—Cleveland (A.L.)..................	0	0	...	4.50	1	0	0	0	0	2	2	1	1	1	0
2000—Omaha (PCL)■.................	3	2	.600	5.52	32	6	0	0	2	75	83	49	46	17	68
—Kansas City (A.L.)	2	0	1.000	9.14	11	0	0	0	0	21 2/3	33	22	22	7	16
Major League totals (3 years)	2	0	1.000	8.76	13	0	0	0	0	24 2/3	35	24	24	11	16

RAMIREZ, ALEX   OF

PERSONAL: Born October 3, 1974, in Caracas, Venezuela. ... 5-11/176. ... Bats right, throws right. ... Full name: Alexander Ramon Ramirez.
TRANSACTIONS/CAREER NOTES: Signed as non-drafted free agent by Cleveland Indians organization (July 1, 1991). ... On Buffalo disabled list (May 21-June 4, 1998). ... Traded by Indians with IF Enrique Wilson to Pittsburgh Pirates for 1B/OF Wil Cordero (July 28, 2000). ... Contract sold by Pirates to Yakult of Japan Central League (November 1, 2000).
STATISTICAL NOTES: Led Appalachian League outfielders with three double plays in 1993.

Year Team (League)	Pos.	G	AB	R	H	2B	3B	HR	RBI	Avg.	BB	SO	SB	PO	A	E	Avg.
1992—Dom. Indians (DSL) ...	OF	69	272	28	79	13	3	8	48	.290	13	34	17	136	9	8	.948
1993—Kinston (Caro.)..........	OF	3	12	0	2	0	0	0	1	.167	0	5	0	3	0	1	.750
—Burlington (Appl.)........	OF	64	252	44	68	14	4	13	58	.270	13	52	13	85	8	7	.930
1994—Columbus (S.Atl.).......	OF	125	458	64	115	23	3	18	57	.251	26	100	7	168	6	9	.951
1995—Bakersfield (Calif.)	OF	98	406	56	131	25	2	10	52	.323	18	76	13	150	9	10	.941
—Canton/Akron (East.)...	OF	33	133	15	33	3	4	1	11	.248	5	24	3	72	5	2	.975
1996—Canton/Akron (East.)..	OF	131	513	79	*169	28	*12	14	85	.329	16	74	18	209	4	5	.977
1997—Buffalo (A.A.)..............	OF-DH	119	416	59	119	19	*8	11	44	.286	24	95	10	167	8	*10	.946

Year	Team (League)	Pos.	G	AB	R	H	2B	3B	HR	RBI	Avg.	BB	SO	SB	PO	A	E	Avg.
1998—	Buffalo (I.L.)...............	OF-DH	121	521	94	156	21	8	34	103	.299	16	101	6	224	7	9	.963
	—Cleveland (A.L.).........	OF	3	8	1	1	0	0	0	0	.125	0	3	0	5	0	1	.833
1999—	Buffalo (I.L.)...............	OF-DH	75	305	50	93	20	2	12	50	.305	17	52	5	167	6	4	.977
	—Cleveland (A.L.).........	OF-DH	48	97	11	29	6	1	3	18	.299	3	26	1	22	1	2	.920
2000—	Cleveland (A.L.).........	OF-DH	41	112	13	32	5	1	5	12	.286	5	17	1	44	1	1	.978
	—Pittsburgh (N.L.)■.....	OF-1B	43	115	13	24	6	1	4	18	.209	7	32	1	55	1	3	.949
American League totals (3 years)			92	217	25	62	11	2	8	30	.286	8	46	2	71	2	4	.948
National League totals (1 year)			43	115	13	24	6	1	4	18	.209	7	32	1	55	1	3	.949
Major League totals (3 years)			135	332	38	86	17	3	12	48	.259	15	78	3	126	3	7	.949

RAMIREZ, ARAMIS — 3B — PIRATES

R

PERSONAL: Born June 25, 1978, in Santo Domingo, Dominican Republic. ... 6-1/219. ... Bats right, throws right. ... Full name: Aramis Nin Ramirez.

TRANSACTIONS/CAREER NOTES: Signed as non-drafted free agent by Pittsburgh Pirates organization (November 7, 1994). ... On suspended list (July 24-29, 1998). ... On Pittsburgh disabled list (August 10-September 4, 1998); included rehabilitation assignment to Nashville (August 27). ... On Pittsburgh disabled list (August 29, 2000-remainder of season).

HONORS: Named Carolina League Most Valuable Player (1997).

STATISTICAL NOTES: Led Carolina League third basemen with 379 total chances in 1997. ... Career major league grand slams: 2.

Year	Team (League)	Pos.	G	AB	R	H	2B	3B	HR	RBI	Avg.	BB	SO	SB	PO	A	E	Avg.
1995—	Dom. Pirates (DSL)....	3B	64	214	41	63	13	0	11	54	.294	42	26	2	65	82	19	.886
1996—	Erie (NY-Penn)	3B	61	223	37	68	14	4	9	42	.305	31	41	0	39	107	17	.896
	—Augusta (S.Atl.)..........	3B	6	20	3	4	1	0	1	2	.200	1	7	0	3	7	2	.833
1997—	Lynchburg (Caro.)	3B-DH	137	482	85	134	24	2	29	*114	.278	80	103	5	75	*265	*39	.897
1998—	Nashville (PCL)	3B-DH-SS	47	168	19	46	10	0	5	18	.274	24	28	0	33	77	8	.932
	—Pittsburgh (N.L.)	3B	72	251	23	59	9	1	6	24	.235	18	72	0	29	114	9	.941
1999—	Nashville (PCL)	3B-DH	131	460	92	151	35	1	21	74	.328	73	56	5	70	250	*42	.884
	—Pittsburgh (N.L.)	3B	18	56	2	10	2	1	0	7	.179	6	9	0	11	29	3	.930
2000—	Pittsburgh (N.L.)	3B	73	254	19	65	15	2	6	35	.256	10	36	0	26	128	14	.917
	—Nashville (PCL)	3B	44	167	28	59	12	2	4	26	.353	11	26	2	34	85	9	.930
Major League totals (3 years)			163	561	44	134	26	4	12	66	.239	34	117	0	66	271	26	.928

RAMIREZ, HECTOR — P

PERSONAL: Born December 15, 1971, in El Seybo, Dominican Republic. ... 6-3/218. ... Throws right, bats right. ... Full name: Hector Bienvenido Ramirez.

HIGH SCHOOL: Liceo Local (El Seybo, Dominican Republic).

TRANSACTIONS/CAREER NOTES: Signed as non-drafted free agent by New York Mets organization (August 22, 1988). ... Traded by Mets to Baltimore Orioles for IF Manny Alexander and IF Scott McLain (March 22, 1997). ... Claimed on waivers by New York Yankees (January 20, 1998). ... Claimed on waivers by Orioles (January 30, 1998). ... Traded by Orioles to Florida Marlins for a player to be named later and cash (February 4, 1998). ... Granted free agency (October 15, 1998). ... Signed by Milwaukee Brewers organization (November 20, 1998). ... Granted free agency (December 21, 1999). ... Signed by Milwaukee Brewers organization (January 26, 2000). ... Released by Brewers (June 2, 2000). ... Signed by Baltimore Orioles organization (June 8, 2000). ... Released by Orioles (August 24, 2000). ... Signed by Houston Astros organization (August 25, 2000). ... Granted free agency (October 18, 2000).

STATISTICAL NOTES: Tied for Florida State League lead with eight balks in 1994.

Year	League	W	L	Pct.	ERA	G	GS	CG	ShO	Sv.	IP	H	R	ER	BB	SO
1989—	Gulf Coast Mets (GCL)	0	5	.000	4.50	15	5	0	0	0	42	35	29	21	24	14
1990—	Gulf Coast Mets (GCL)	3	5	.375	4.26	11	8	1	0	0	50 2/3	54	34	24	21	43
1991—	Kingsport (Appl.)	8	2	.800	2.65	14	13	0	0	0	85	83	39	25	28	64
1992—	Columbia (S.Atl.)	5	4	.556	3.61	17	17	1	0	0	94 2/3	93	50	38	33	53
1993—	Gulf Coast Mets (GCL)	1	0	1.000	0.00	1	1	0	0	0	7	5	1	0	1	6
	—Capital City (S.Atl.)	4	6	.400	5.34	14	14	0	0	0	64	86	51	38	23	42
1994—	St. Lucie (FSL)	11	12	.478	3.43	27	27	•6	1	0	*194	*202	86	74	50	110
1995—	Binghamton (East.)	4	•12	.250	4.60	20	20	2	0	0	123 1/3	127	69	63	48	63
1996—	Binghamton (East.)	1	5	.167	5.14	38	0	0	0	6	56	51	34	32	23	49
	—Norfolk (I.L.)	1	0	1.000	3.38	3	1	0	0	0	10 2/3	13	7	4	3	8
1997—	Rochester (I.L.)	8	7	.533	4.91	39	9	0	0	3	102 2/3	114	65	56	38	50
1998—	Charlotte (I.L.)■	3	3	.500	6.75	55	0	0	0	3	86 2/3	106	68	65	30	50
1999—	Louisville (I.L.)■	3	3	.500	3.80	58	0	0	0	9	94 2/3	91	45	40	33	55
	—Milwaukee (N.L.)	1	2	.333	3.43	15	0	0	0	0	21	19	8	8	11	9
2000—	Indianapolis (I.L.)■	3	0	1.000	3.04	15	0	0	0	0	23 2/3	24	9	8	5	18
	—Milwaukee (N.L.)	0	1	.000	10.00	6	0	0	0	0	9	11	10	10	5	4
	—Rochester (I.L.)■	2	2	.500	7.34	26	0	0	0	1	41 2/3	55	36	34	19	28
	—New Orleans (PCL)■.........	0	0	...	1.80	5	0	0	0	0	5	6	1	1	1	4
Major League totals (2 years)		1	3	.250	5.40	21	0	0	0	0	30	30	18	18	16	13

RAMIREZ, JULIO — OF — WHITE SOX

PERSONAL: Born August 10, 1977, in San Juan de la Maguana, Dominican Republic. ... 5-11/170. ... Bats right, throws right. ... Full name: Julio Caesar Ramirez.

HIGH SCHOOL: Escuela Otilia Pelaez (Santo Domingo, Dominican Republic).

TRANSACTIONS/CAREER NOTES: Signed as non-drafted free agent by Florida Marlins organization (December 6, 1993). ... On Calgary disabled list (April 15-May 2 and July 18-August 14, 2000). ... Traded by Marlins to Chicago White Sox for OF Jeff Abbott (December 10, 2000).

STATISTICAL NOTES: Led Florida State League outfielders with 390 total chances in 1998. ... Led Eastern League outfielders with 351 total chances in 1999.

Year Team (League)	Pos.	G	AB	R	H	2B	3B	HR	RBI	Avg.	BB	SO	SB	PO	A	E	Avg.
1994—Dom. Marlins (DSL)...	OF	67	274	54	75	18	0	7	32	.274	28	41	29	136	11	10	.936
1995—GC Marlins (GCL).......	OF	48	204	35	58	9	4	2	13	.284	13	42	17	109	7	2	.983
1996—Brevard County (FSL).	OF	17	61	11	15	0	1	0	2	.246	4	18	2	12	2	1	.933
— GC Marlins (GCL)......	OF	43	174	35	50	5	4	0	16	.287	15	34	26	95	2	2	.980
1997—Kane County (Midw.)..	OF	99	376	70	96	18	7	14	53	.255	37	122	41	179	8	4	.979
1998—Brevard County (FSL).	OF	135	*559	90	156	20	12	13	58	.279	45	147	71	*365	•17	8	.979
1999—Portland (East.).........	OF	138	*568	87	148	30	10	13	64	.261	39	150	*64	*326	14	•11	.969
— Florida (N.L.)...............	OF	15	21	3	3	1	0	0	2	.143	1	6	0	19	0	1	.950
2000—Calgary (PCL).............	OF	94	350	45	93	18	3	7	52	.266	21	86	20	220	9	*11	.954
Major League totals (1 year)		15	21	3	3	1	0	0	2	.143	1	6	0	19	0	1	.950

R RAMIREZ, MANNY — OF — RED SOX

PERSONAL: Born May 30, 1972, in Santo Domingo, Dominican Republic. ... 6-0/205. ... Bats right, throws right. ... Full name: Manuel Aristides Ramirez.

HIGH SCHOOL: George Washington (New York).

TRANSACTIONS/CAREER NOTES: Selected by Cleveland Indians organization in first round (13th pick overall) of free-agent draft (June 3, 1991). ... On disabled list (July 10, 1992-remainder of season). ... On suspended list (June 8-11, 1999). ... On Cleveland disabled list (May 30-July 13, 2000); included rehabilitation assignments to Akron (June 16-23) and Buffalo (July 6-13). ... Granted free agency (October 27, 2000). ... Signed by Boston Red Sox (December 13, 2000).

RECORDS: Shares major league record for most consecutive home runs—4 (September 15 [3], 16 [1], 1998); most home runs in two consecutive games—5 (September 15 [3], 16 [2], 1998); and most home runs in three consecutive games—6 (September 15 [3], 16 [2], 17 [1], 1998).

HONORS: Named Appalachian League Most Valuable Player (1991). ... Named outfielder on THE SPORTING NEWS A.L. All-Star team (1995 and 1999). ... Named outfielder on THE SPORTING NEWS A.L. Silver Slugger team (1995, 1999 and 2000).

STATISTICAL NOTES: Led Appalachian League with 146 total bases and .679 slugging percentage in 1991. ... Hit three home runs in one game (September 15, 1998 and August 25, 1999). ... Led A.L. with a .663 slugging percentage in 1999 and .697 slugging percentage in 2000. ... Had 20-game hitting streak (August 15-September 5, 2000). ... Career major league grand slams: 13.

Year Team (League)	Pos.	G	AB	R	H	2B	3B	HR	RBI	Avg.	BB	SO	SB	PO	A	E	Avg.
1991—Burlington (Appl.).......	OF	59	215	44	70	11	4	*19	*63	.326	34	41	7	83	2	3	.966
1992—Kinston (Caro.)..........	OF	81	291	52	81	18	4	13	63	.278	45	74	1	128	3	6	.956
1993—Canton/Akron (East.)..	OF	89	344	67	117	32	0	17	79	*.340	45	68	2	142	4	5	.967
—Charlotte (I.L.)............	OF	40	145	38	46	12	0	14	36	.317	27	35	1	70	3	3	.961
—Cleveland (A.L.)...........	DH-OF	22	53	5	9	1	0	2	5	.170	2	8	0	3	0	0	1.000
1994—Cleveland (A.L.).........	OF-DH	91	290	51	78	22	0	17	60	.269	42	72	4	150	7	1	.994
1995—Cleveland (A.L.).........	OF-DH	137	484	85	149	26	1	31	107	.308	75	112	6	220	3	5	.978
1996—Cleveland (A.L.).........	OF-DH	152	550	94	170	45	3	33	112	.309	85	104	8	272	*19	9	.970
1997—Cleveland (A.L.).........	OF-DH	150	561	99	184	40	0	26	88	.328	79	115	2	259	10	7	.975
1998—Cleveland (A.L.).........	OF-DH	150	571	108	168	35	2	45	145	.294	76	121	5	291	10	7	.977
1999—Cleveland (A.L.).........	OF-DH	147	522	131	174	34	3	44	*165	.333	96	131	2	267	7	7	.975
2000—Cleveland (A.L.).........	OF-DH	118	439	92	154	34	2	38	122	.351	86	117	1	134	7	2	.986
—Akron (East.).............	DH	1	2	1	1	0	0	1	2	.500	2	1	0	...	...	...	...
—Buffalo (I.L.).............	DH	5	11	5	5	1	0	3	7	.455	6	1	0	...	...	...	...
Major League totals (8 years)		967	3470	665	1086	237	11	236	804	.313	541	780	28	1596	63	38	.978

DIVISION SERIES RECORD

RECORDS: Shares career record for most extra-base hits—10. ... Shares single-game record for most home runs—2 (October 2, 1998).

Year Team (League)	Pos.	G	AB	R	H	2B	3B	HR	RBI	Avg.	BB	SO	SB	PO	A	E	Avg.
1995—Cleveland (A.L.).........	OF	3	12	1	0	0	0	0	0	.000	1	2	0	3	0	0	1.000
1996—Cleveland (A.L.).........	OF	4	16	4	6	2	0	2	2	.375	1	4	0	8	2	0	1.000
1997—Cleveland (A.L.).........	OF	5	21	2	3	1	0	0	3	.143	0	3	0	3	0	1	.750
1998—Cleveland (A.L.).........	OF	4	14	2	5	2	0	2	3	.357	1	4	0	4	0	0	1.000
1999—Cleveland (A.L.).........	OF	5	18	5	1	1	0	0	1	.056	4	8	0	8	1	0	1.000
Division series totals (5 years)		21	81	14	15	6	0	4	9	.185	7	21	0	26	3	1	.967

CHAMPIONSHIP SERIES RECORD

Year Team (League)	Pos.	G	AB	R	H	2B	3B	HR	RBI	Avg.	BB	SO	SB	PO	A	E	Avg.
1995—Cleveland (A.L.).........	OF	6	21	2	6	0	0	2	2	.286	2	5	0	9	0	0	1.000
1997—Cleveland (A.L.).........	OF	6	21	3	6	1	0	2	3	.286	5	5	0	14	0	1	.933
1998—Cleveland (A.L.).........	OF	6	21	2	7	1	0	2	4	.333	4	9	0	12	0	0	1.000
Championship series totals (3 years)		18	63	7	19	2	0	6	9	.302	11	19	0	35	0	1	.972

WORLD SERIES RECORD

Year Team (League)	Pos.	G	AB	R	H	2B	3B	HR	RBI	Avg.	BB	SO	SB	PO	A	E	Avg.
1995—Cleveland (A.L.).........	OF	6	18	2	4	0	0	1	2	.222	4	5	1	8	0	0	1.000
1997—Cleveland (A.L.).........	OF	7	26	3	4	0	0	2	6	.154	6	5	0	16	1	1	.944
World Series totals (2 years)		13	44	5	8	0	0	3	8	.182	10	10	1	24	1	1	.962

ALL-STAR GAME RECORD

Year League	Pos.	AB	R	H	2B	3B	HR	RBI	Avg.	BB	SO	SB	PO	A	E	Avg.
1995—American.....................	PH-OF	0	0	0	0	0	0	0	...	2	0	0	2	0	0	1.000
1998—American.....................	OF	1	0	0	0	0	0	1	.000	0	0	0	0	0	0	...
1999—American.....................	OF	1	1	0	0	0	0	0	.000	1	1	0	0	0	0	...
2000—American.....................							Selected, did not play—injured.									
All-Star Game totals (3 years)		2	1	0	0	0	0	1	.000	3	1	0	2	0	0	1.000

PERSONAL: Born December 3, 1973, in Vancouver, Wash. ... 6-5/215. ... Throws left, bats left. ... Full name: Robert Arthur Ramsay.
HIGH SCHOOL: Mountain View (Vancouver, Wash.).
COLLEGE: Washington State.
TRANSACTIONS/CAREER NOTES: Selected by Boston Red Sox organization in seventh round of free-agent draft (June 2, 1996). ... Traded by Red Sox to Seattle Mariners for OF Butch Huskey (July 26, 1999). ... On Seattle disabled list (August 14-29, 2000); included rehabilitation assignment to Everett (August 26-29).

Year League	W	L	Pct.	ERA	G	GS	CG	ShO	Sv.	IP	H	R	ER	BB	SO
1996—Gulf Coast Red Sox (GCL)..	0	1	.000	4.91	2	0	0	0	0	3 2/3	5	2	2	3	5
—Sarasota (FSL)	2	2	.500	6.09	12	7	0	0	0	34	42	23	23	27	32
1997—Sarasota (FSL)	9	9	.500	4.78	23	22	1	0	0	135 2/3	134	90	72	63	115
1998—Trenton (East.)	12	6	.667	3.49	27	27	1	1	0	162 2/3	137	67	63	50	166
1999—Pawtucket (I.L.)	6	6	.500	5.35	20	20	0	0	0	114 1/3	114	81	68	36	79
—Seattle (A.L.)■	0	2	.000	6.38	6	3	0	0	0	18 1/3	23	13	13	9	11
—Tacoma (PCL)	4	1	.800	1.08	5	5	0	0	0	33 1/3	20	6	4	14	37
2000—Tacoma (PCL)	0	1	.000	4.50	3	3	0	0	0	16	16	8	8	6	6
—Seattle (A.L.)	1	1	.500	3.40	37	1	0	0	0	50 1/3	43	22	19	40	32
—Everett (N'West)	0	0	...	0.00	1	1	0	0	0	2	2	0	0	0	4
Major League totals (2 years)	1	3	.250	4.19	43	4	0	0	0	68 2/3	66	35	32	49	43

CHAMPIONSHIP SERIES RECORD

Year League	W	L	Pct.	ERA	G	GS	CG	ShO	Sv.	IP	H	R	ER	BB	SO
2000—Seattle (A.L.)	0	0	...	0.00	2	0	0	0	0	1 2/3	2	0	0	0	1

PERSONAL: Born December 18, 1969, in Milwaukee. ... 5-11/190. ... Bats right, throws right. ... Full name: Joseph Gregory Randa.
HIGH SCHOOL: Kettle-Moraine (Wales, Wis.).
JUNIOR COLLEGE: Indian River Community College (Fla.).
COLLEGE: Tennessee.
TRANSACTIONS/CAREER NOTES: Selected by California Angels organization in 30th round of free-agent draft (June 5, 1989); did not sign. ... Selected by Kansas City Royals organization in 11th round of free-agent draft (June 3, 1991). ... On Kansas City disabled list (May 5-27, 1996); included rehabilitation assignment to Omaha (May 23-27). ... Traded by Royals with P Jeff Granger, P Jeff Martin and P Jeff Wallace to Pittsburgh Pirates for SS Jay Bell and 1B Jeff King (December 13, 1996). ... On Pittsburgh disabled list (June 28-July 27, 1997); included rehabilitation assignment to Calgary (July 25-27). ... Selected by Arizona Diamondbacks in third round (57th pick overall) of expansion draft (November 18, 1997). ... Traded by Diamondbacks with P Matt Drews and 3B Gabe Alvarez to Detroit Tigers for 3B Travis Fryman (November 18, 1997). ... Traded by Tigers to New York Mets for P Willie Blair (December 4, 1998). ... Traded by Mets to Royals for OF Juan LeBron (December 10, 1998).
RECORDS: Holds major league single-season record for fewest putouts by third baseman for leader—119 (1999).
HONORS: Named Northwest League Most Valuable Player (1991).
STATISTICAL NOTES: Led Northwest League with 150 total bases and .438 on-base percentage in 1991. ... Led Northwest League third basemen with 182 total chances and 12 double plays in 1991. ... Led Southern League with 10 sacrifice flies in 1993. ... Led American Association third basemen with 433 total chances and 28 double plays in 1994. ... Had 18-game hitting streak (July 1-21, 1999). ... Led A.L. third baseman with 455 total chances and 28 double plays in 1999.

Year Team (League)	Pos.	G	AB	R	H	2B	3B	HR	RBI	Avg.	BB	SO	SB	PO	A	E	Avg.
1991—Eugene (N'West)	3B	72	275	53	*93	20	2	11	59	.338	46	29	6	*57	*111	14	*.923
1992—Appleton (Midw.)	3B	72	266	55	80	13	0	5	43	.301	34	37	6	53	137	12	.941
—Baseball City (FSL)	3B-SS	51	189	22	52	7	0	1	12	.275	12	21	4	43	105	6	.961
1993—Memphis (Sou.)	3B	131	505	74	149	31	5	11	72	.295	39	64	8	*97	309	25	.942
1994—Omaha (A.A.)	3B	127	455	65	125	27	2	10	51	.275	30	49	5	*85	*324	*24	.945
1995—Omaha (A.A.)	3B	64	233	33	64	10	2	8	33	.275	22	33	2	42	96	6	.958
—Kansas City (A.L.)	3B-2B-DH	34	70	6	12	2	0	1	5	.171	6	17	0	15	44	3	.952
1996—Kansas City (A.L.)	3-2-1-DH	110	337	36	102	24	1	6	47	.303	26	47	13	80	160	10	.960
—Omaha (A.A.)	3B	3	9	1	1	0	1	0	0	.111	1	1	0	1	10	0	1.000
1997—Pittsburgh (N.L.)■	3B-2B	126	443	58	134	27	9	7	60	.302	41	64	4	91	288	21	.948
—Calgary (PCL)	3B	3	11	4	4	1	0	1	4	.364	3	4	0	2	7	1	.900
1998—Detroit (A.L.)■	3-2-DH-1	138	460	56	117	21	2	9	50	.254	41	70	8	102	252	7	.981
1999—Kansas City (A.L.)■	3B	156	628	92	197	36	8	16	84	.314	50	80	5	*119	*314	22	.952
2000—Kansas City (A.L.)	3B-DH	158	612	88	186	29	4	15	106	.304	36	66	4	*132	293	19	.957
American League totals (5 years)		596	2107	278	614	112	15	47	292	.291	159	280	32	448	1063	61	.954
National League totals (1 year)		126	443	58	134	27	9	7	60	.302	41	64	4	91	288	21	.948
Major League totals (6 years)		722	2550	336	748	139	24	54	352	.293	200	344	36	539	1351	82	.958

PERSONAL: Born January 19, 1979, in Tampa, Fla. ... 6-0/180. ... Bats both, throws right. ... Full name: Jaisen Jacob Randolph.
HIGH SCHOOL: Hillsborough (Tampa, Fla.).
TRANSACTIONS/CAREER NOTES: Selected by Chicago Cubs organization in fifth round of free-agent draft (June 3, 1997).
STATISTICAL NOTES: Led Arizona League outfielders with four double plays in 1997. ... Led Florida State League in caught stealing with 26 in 1999.

Year Team (League)	Pos.	G	AB	R	H	2B	3B	HR	RBI	Avg.	BB	SO	SB	PO	A	E	Avg.
1997—Arizona Cubs (Ariz.)	OF	53	218	42	58	1	4	0	26	.266	26	45	24	76	•8	3	.966
1998—Rockford (Midw.)	OF	128	491	78	142	18	9	1	33	.289	40	113	32	222	6	6	.974
1999—Daytona (FSL)	OF	130	511	70	139	16	5	2	37	.272	43	86	25	264	14	11	.962
2000—West Tenn (Sou.)	OF	126	490	76	119	15	5	5	31	.243	56	96	46	222	11	7	.971

PERSONAL: Born May 1, 1974, in Okinawa, Japan. ... 6-3/185. ... Throws left, bats left. ... Full name: Stephen LaCharles Randolph.
HIGH SCHOOL: James Bowie (Simms, Texas).
JUNIOR COLLEGE: Galveston (Texas) College.
COLLEGE: Texas.
TRANSACTIONS/CAREER NOTES: Selected by New York Yankees organization in 18th round of free-agent draft (June 1, 1995). ... Selected by Arizona Diamondbacks from Yankees organization in Rule 5 major league draft (December 15, 1997). ... On Tucson disabled list (June 1-July 25, 1999); included rehabilitation assignment to Arizona League Diamondbacks (July 16-25). ... On El Paso disabled list (May 4-September 12, 2000).

Year League	W	L	Pct.	ERA	G	GS	CG	ShO	Sv.	IP	H	R	ER	BB	SO
1995—Tampa (FSL)	4	0	1.000	2.22	8	3	0	0	0	24 1/3	11	7	6	16	34
— Oneonta (NY-Penn)	0	3	.000	7.48	6	6	0	0	0	21 2/3	19	22	18	23	31
1996—Greensboro (S.Atl.)	4	7	.364	3.77	32	17	0	0	0	100 1/3	64	46	42	96	111
1997—Tampa (FSL)	4	7	.364	3.87	34	13	1	0	1	95 1/3	74	55	41	63	108
1998—High Desert (Calif.)■	4	4	.500	3.59	17	17	0	0	0	85 1/3	71	44	34	42	104
— Tucson (PCL)	1	3	.250	3.18	17	1	0	0	0	22 2/3	16	11	8	19	23
1999—El Paso (Texas)	2	2	.500	2.64	8	8	0	0	0	44 1/3	39	14	13	23	38
— Tucson (PCL)	0	7	.000	6.91	11	10	1	0	0	41 2/3	47	37	32	32	26
— Ariz. D-backs (Ariz.)	0	0	...	4.50	2	2	0	0	0	6	5	3	3	2	7

PERSONAL: Born July 13, 1967, in Jennings, La. ... 6-3/215. ... Throws right, bats right. ... Full name: Patrick Leland Rapp.
HIGH SCHOOL: Sulphur (La.).
JUNIOR COLLEGE: Hinds Community College (Miss.).
COLLEGE: Southern Mississippi.
TRANSACTIONS/CAREER NOTES: Selected by San Francisco Giants organization in 15th round of free-agent draft (June 5, 1989). ... Selected by Florida Marlins in first round (10th pick overall) of expansion draft (November 17, 1992). ... Traded by Marlins to Giants for P Brandon Leese and P Bobby Rector (July 18, 1997). ... On San Francisco disabled list (July 20-August 5, 1997). ... Granted free agency (December 21, 1997). ... Signed by Kansas City Royals organization (January 22, 1998). ... Granted free agency (December 21, 1998). ... Signed by Boston Red Sox (January 11, 1999). ... Granted free agency (November 2, 1999). ... Signed by Baltimore Orioles (January 28, 2000). ... Granted free agency (October 31, 2000). ... Signed by Anaheim Angels (December 11, 2000).
STATISTICAL NOTES: Pitched 17-0 one-hit, complete-game victory against Colorado (September 17, 1995).
MISCELLANEOUS: Appeared in one game as pinch runner (1994). ... Holds Florida Marlins all-time records for most wins (37), strikeouts (384) and innings pitched (665.2).

Year League	W	L	Pct.	ERA	G	GS	CG	ShO	Sv.	IP	H	R	ER	BB	SO
1989—Pocatello (Pio.)	4	6	.400	5.30	16	12	1	0	0	73	90	54	43	29	40
1990—Clinton (Midw.)	14	10	.583	2.64	27	26	4	0	0	167 1/3	132	60	49	79	132
1991—San Jose (Calif.)	7	5	.583	2.50	16	15	1	0	0	90	88	41	25	37	73
— Shreveport (Texas)	6	2	.750	2.69	10	10	1	1	0	60 1/3	52	23	18	22	46
1992—Phoenix (PCL)	7	8	.467	3.05	39	12	2	1	3	121	115	54	41	40	79
— San Francisco (N.L.)	0	2	.000	7.20	3	2	0	0	0	10	8	8	8	6	3
1993—Edmonton (PCL)■	8	3	.727	3.43	17	17	•4	1	0	107 2/3	89	45	41	34	93
— Florida (N.L.)	4	6	.400	4.02	16	16	1	0	0	94	101	49	42	39	57
1994—Florida (N.L.)	7	8	.467	3.85	24	23	2	1	0	133 1/3	132	67	57	69	75
1995—Charlotte (I.L.)	0	1	.000	6.00	1	1	0	0	0	6	6	4	4	1	5
— Florida (N.L.)	14	7	.667	3.44	28	28	3	2	0	167 1/3	158	72	64	76	102
1996—Florida (N.L.)	8	•16	.333	5.10	30	29	0	0	0	162 1/3	184	95	92	91	86
— Charlotte (I.L.)	1	1	.500	8.18	2	2	0	0	0	11	18	12	10	4	9
1997—Florida (N.L.)	4	6	.400	4.47	19	19	1	1	0	108 2/3	121	59	54	51	64
— San Francisco (N.L.)■	1	2	.333	6.00	8	6	0	0	0	33	37	24	22	21	28
— Phoenix (PCL)	2	0	1.000	3.60	3	3	0	0	0	15	16	6	6	9	6
1998—Kansas City (A.L.)■	12	13	.480	5.30	32	32	1	1	0	188 1/3	208	117	111	107	132
1999—Boston (A.L.)■	6	7	.462	4.12	37	26	0	0	0	146 1/3	147	78	67	69	90
2000—Baltimore (A.L.)■	9	12	.429	5.90	31	30	0	0	0	174	203	125	114	83	106
A.L. totals (3 years)	27	32	.458	5.17	100	88	1	1	0	508 2/3	558	320	292	259	328
N.L. totals (6 years)	38	47	.447	4.31	128	123	7	4	0	708 2/3	741	374	339	353	415
Major League totals (9 years)	65	79	.451	4.67	228	211	8	5	0	1217 1/3	1299	694	631	612	743

DIVISION SERIES RECORD

Year League	W	L	Pct.	ERA	G	GS	CG	ShO	Sv.	IP	H	R	ER	BB	SO
1999—Boston (A.L.)							Did not play.								

CHAMPIONSHIP SERIES RECORD

Year League	W	L	Pct.	ERA	G	GS	CG	ShO	Sv.	IP	H	R	ER	BB	SO
1999—Boston (A.L.)	0	0	...	0.00	1	0	0	0	0	1	0	0	0	1	0

PERSONAL: Born December 22, 1971, in Syracuse, N.Y. ... 6-4/195. ... Throws right, bats right. ... Full name: Jon Charles Ratliff.
HIGH SCHOOL: Liverpool Central (N.Y.).
COLLEGE: Lemoyne (N.Y.).
TRANSACTIONS/CAREER NOTES: Selected by San Diego Padres organization in 22nd round of free-agent draft (June 4, 1990); did not sign. ... Selected by Chicago Cubs organization in first round (24th pick overall) of free-agent draft (June 3, 1993); pick received as part of compensation for Atlanta Braves signing Type A free-agent P Greg Maddux. ... Selected by Detroit Tigers from Cubs organization in Rule 5 major league draft (December 4, 1995). ... Returned to Cubs (March 13, 1996). ... On disabled list (April 26-May 17, 1996). ... Traded by Cubs to Atlanta Braves for P Ray King (January 20, 1998). ... Granted free agency (October 15, 1999). ... Signed by Oakland Athletics organization (November 3, 1999). ... On Sacramento disabled list (April 14-May 12 and July 5-21, 2000).

Year	League	W	L	Pct.	ERA	G	GS	CG	ShO	Sv.	IP	H	R	ER	BB	SO
1993—	Geneva (NY-Penn)	1	1	.500	3.21	3	3	0	0	0	14	12	8	5	8	7
—	Daytona (FSL)	2	4	.333	3.95	8	8	0	0	0	41	50	29	18	23	15
1994—	Daytona (FSL)	3	2	.600	3.50	8	8	1	0	0	54	64	23	21	5	17
—	Iowa (A.A.)	1	3	.250	5.40	5	4	0	0	0	28 1/3	39	19	17	7	10
—	Orlando (Sou.)	1	9	.100	5.63	12	12	1	0	0	62 1/3	78	44	39	26	19
1995—	Orlando (Sou.)	10	5	.667	3.47	26	25	1	1	0	140	143	67	54	42	94
1996—	Iowa (A.A.)	4	8	.333	5.28	32	13	0	0	1	93 2/3	107	63	55	31	59
1997—	Iowa (A.A.)	1	3	.250	5.57	9	4	0	0	1	32 1/3	30	20	20	7	25
—	Orlando (Sou.)	6	4	.600	4.35	18	15	0	0	0	101 1/3	112	59	49	32	68
1998—	Richmond (I.L.)■	12	13	.480	4.94	29	29	2	0	0	151 1/3	167	90	83	65	143
1999—	Richmond (I.L.)	5	12	.294	4.45	27	27	0	0	0	157 2/3	154	88	78	44	129
2000—	Sacramento (PCL)■	8	4	.667	3.44	20	18	0	0	1	107 1/3	102	48	41	31	72
—	Oakland (A.L.)	0	0	...	0.00	1	0	0	0	0	1	0	0	0	0	0
Major League totals (1 year)		0	0	...	0.00	1	0	0	0	0	1	0	0	0	0	0

REAMES, BRITT — P — EXPOS

PERSONAL: Born August 19, 1973, in Seneca, S.C. ... 5-11/175. ... Throws right, bats right. ... Full name: William Britt Reames.
HIGH SCHOOL: Seneca (S.C.).
COLLEGE: The Citadel.
TRANSACTIONS/CAREER NOTES: Selected by St. Louis Cardinals organization in 17th round of free-agent draft (June 1, 1995). ... On disabled list (April 4, 1997-entire season; and April 10, 1998-entire season). ... On Potomac disabled list (April 23-June 10 and June 14-August 10, 1999). ... On Arkansas disabled list (April 19-29, 2000). ... On Memphis disabled list (July 7-14 and July 20-August 3, 2000). ... Traded by Cardinals with 3B Fernando Tatis to Montreal Expos for P Dustin Hermanson and P Steve Kline (December 14, 2000).
MISCELLANEOUS: Appeared in two games as pinch runner (2000).

Year	League	W	L	Pct.	ERA	G	GS	CG	ShO	Sv.	IP	H	R	ER	BB	SO
1995—	New Jersey (NY-Penn)	2	1	.667	1.52	5	5	0	0	0	29 2/3	19	7	5	12	42
—	Savannah (S.Atl.)	3	5	.375	3.46	10	10	1	0	0	54 2/3	41	23	21	15	63
1996—	Peoria (Midw.)	15	7	.682	*1.90	25	25	2	1	0	161	97	43	34	41	*167
1997—									Did not play.							
1998—									Did not play.							
1999—	Potomac (Caro.)	3	2	.600	3.19	10	8	0	0	0	36 2/3	34	21	13	21	22
2000—	Arkansas (Texas)	2	3	.400	6.13	8	8	0	0	0	39 2/3	46	28	27	18	39
—	Memphis (PCL)	6	2	.750	2.28	13	13	2	1	0	75	55	20	19	20	77
—	St. Louis (N.L.)	2	1	.667	2.88	8	7	0	0	0	40 2/3	30	17	13	23	31
Major League totals (1 year)		2	1	.667	2.88	8	7	0	0	0	40 2/3	30	17	13	23	31

DIVISION SERIES RECORD

Year	League	W	L	Pct.	ERA	G	GS	CG	ShO	Sv.	IP	H	R	ER	BB	SO
2000—	St. Louis (N.L.)	1	0	1.000	0.00	2	0	0	0	0	3 1/3	0	0	0	3	2

CHAMPIONSHIP SERIES RECORD

Year	League	W	L	Pct.	ERA	G	GS	CG	ShO	Sv.	IP	H	R	ER	BB	SO
2000—	St. Louis (N.L.)	0	0	...	1.42	2	0	0	0	0	6 1/3	5	1	1	4	6

REBOULET, JEFF — IF

PERSONAL: Born April 30, 1964, in Dayton, Ohio. ... 6-0/175. ... Bats right, throws right. ... Full name: Jeffrey Allen Reboulet. ... Brother of Jim Reboulet, second baseman in St. Louis Cardinals and Pittsburgh Pirates organizations. ... Name pronounced REB-uh-lay.
HIGH SCHOOL: Alter (Kettering, Ohio).
JUNIOR COLLEGE: Triton Junior College (Illinois).
COLLEGE: Louisiana State.
TRANSACTIONS/CAREER NOTES: Selected by Houston Astros organization in 26th round of free-agent draft (June 3, 1985); did not sign. ... Selected by Minnesota Twins organization in 10th round of free-agent draft (June 2, 1986). ... Granted free agency (October 4, 1996). ... Signed by Baltimore Orioles organization (January 30, 1997). ... Traded by Orioles to Kansas City Royals for a player to be named later (December 12, 1999). ... Granted free agency (October 31, 2000).
STATISTICAL NOTES: Led Southern League shortstops with 602 total chances in 1988. ... Led Pacific Coast League with 17 sacrifice hits in 1991. ... Led Pacific Coast League shortstops with 649 total chances and 99 double plays in 1991.

			BATTING												FIELDING		
Year	Team (League)	Pos.	G	AB	R	H	2B	3B	HR	RBI	Avg.	BB	SO	SB	PO	A	E	Avg.
---	---	---	---	---	---	---	---	---	---	---	---	---	---	---	---	---	---	---
1986—	Visalia (Calif.)	SS	72	254	54	73	13	1	0	29	.287	54	33	14	118	188	20	.939
1987—	Orlando (Sou.)	SS-2B-3B	129	422	52	108	15	1	1	35	.256	58	56	9	220	370	26	.958
1988—	Orlando (Sou.)	SS	125	439	57	112	24	2	4	41	.255	53	55	18	*225	347	30	.950
—	Portland (PCL)	2B-SS	4	12	0	1	0	0	0	1	.083	3	2	0	8	13	1	.955
1989—	Portland (PCL)	SS-2B-3B-OF	26	65	9	16	1	0	0	3	.246	12	11	2	38	62	7	.935
—	Orlando (Sou.)	SS-2B-OF	81	291	43	63	5	1	0	26	.216	49	33	11	129	228	22	.942
1990—	Orlando (Sou.)	2-3-S-O-1	97	287	43	66	12	2	2	28	.230	57	37	10	131	230	12	.968
1991—	Portland (PCL)	SS	134	391	50	97	27	3	3	46	.248	57	52	5	*202	415	*32	.951
1992—	Portland (PCL)	SS	48	161	21	46	11	1	2	21	.286	35	18	3	72	141	7	.968
—	Minnesota (A.L.)	S-3-2-O-DH	73	137	15	26	7	1	1	16	.190	23	26	3	71	163	5	.979
1993—	Minnesota (A.L.)	S-3-2-O-DH	109	240	33	62	8	0	1	15	.258	35	37	5	122	215	6	.983
1994—	Minnesota (A.L.)	S-2-1-3-O-DH	74	189	28	49	11	1	3	23	.259	18	23	0	150	131	7	.976
1995—	Minnesota (A.L.)	S-3-1-2-C	87	176	39	63	11	0	4	23	.292	27	34	1	164	160	4	.988
1996—	Minnesota (A.L.)	S-3-2-1-O-D	107	234	20	52	9	0	0	23	.222	25	34	4	138	114	2	.992
1997—	Baltimore (A.L.)■	2B-SS-3B-OF	99	228	26	54	9	0	4	27	.237	23	44	3	106	163	7	.975
1998—	Baltimore (A.L.)	2B-SS-3B	79	126	20	31	6	0	1	8	.246	19	34	0	51	120	6	.966
1999—	Baltimore (A.L.)	3B-2B-SS	99	154	25	25	4	0	0	4	.162	33	29	1	79	152	2	.991
2000—	Kansas City (A.L.)■	2B-3B-SS-DH	66	182	29	44	7	0	0	14	.242	23	32	3	84	167	9	.965
Major League totals (9 years)			793	1706	235	406	72	2	14	153	.238	226	293	20	965	1385	48	.980

DIVISION SERIES RECORD

				BATTING										FIELDING		
Year Team (League)	Pos.	G	AB	R	H	2B	3B	HR	RBI	Avg.	BB	SO	SB	PO	A	E	Avg.
1997—Baltimore (A.L.).........	2B	2	5	1	1	0	0	1	1	.200	0	2	0	2	3	0	1.000

CHAMPIONSHIP SERIES RECORD

				BATTING										FIELDING		
Year Team (League)	Pos.	G	AB	R	H	2B	3B	HR	RBI	Avg.	BB	SO	SB	PO	A	E	Avg.
1997—Baltimore (A.L.)..........	SS-PR	1	2	1	0	0	0	0	0	.000	0	1	0	0	0	0	...

REDMAN, MARK — P — TWINS

PERSONAL: Born January 5, 1974, in San Diego. ... 6-5/220. ... Throws left, bats left. ... Full name: Mark Allen Redman.
HIGH SCHOOL: Escondido (Calif.).
COLLEGE: The Master's College (Calif.), then Oklahoma.
TRANSACTIONS/CAREER NOTES: Selected by Detroit Tigers organization in 41st round of free-agent draft (June 1, 1992); did not sign. ... Selected by Minnesota Twins organization in first round (13th pick overall) of free-agent draft (June 1, 1995). ... On Salt Lake disabled list (August 1-8, 1998). ... On Minnesota disabled list (July 25-August 10, 1999).

Year League	W	L	Pct.	ERA	G	GS	CG	ShO	Sv.	IP	H	R	ER	BB	SO
1995—Fort Myers (FSL)................	2	1	.667	2.76	8	5	0	0	0	32²/₃	28	13	10	13	26
1996—Fort Myers (FSL)................	3	4	.429	1.85	13	13	0	0	0	82²/₃	63	24	17	34	75
— New Britain (East.)............	7	7	.500	3.81	16	16	3	0	0	106¹/₃	101	51	45	50	96
— Salt Lake (PCL).................	0	0	...	9.00	1	1	0	0	0	4	7	4	4	2	4
1997—Salt Lake (PCL).................	8	*15	.348	6.31	29	28	0	0	1	158¹/₃	204	*123	111	80	125
1998—New Britain (East.)............	4	2	.667	1.52	8	8	0	0	0	47¹/₃	40	11	8	17	51
— Salt Lake (PCL).................	6	7	.462	5.53	19	18	0	0	0	99¹/₃	111	75	61	41	88
1999—Salt Lake (PCL).................	9	9	.500	5.05	24	24	1	0	0	133²/₃	141	87	75	51	114
— Minnesota (A.L.)................	1	0	1.000	8.53	5	1	0	0	0	12²/₃	17	13	12	7	11
2000—Minnesota (A.L.)................	12	9	.571	4.76	32	24	0	0	0	151¹/₃	168	81	80	45	117
Major League totals (2 years).......	13	9	.591	5.05	37	25	0	0	0	164	185	94	92	52	128

REDMAN, TIKE — OF — PIRATES

PERSONAL: Born March 10, 1977, in Tuscaloosa, Ala. ... 5-11/166. ... Bats left, throws left. ... Full name: Julian Jawann Redman.
HIGH SCHOOL: Tuscaloosa (Ala.) Academy.
TRANSACTIONS/CAREER NOTES: Selected by Pittsburgh Pirates organization in fifth round of free-agent draft (June 4, 1996).
STATISTICAL NOTES: Tied Pacific Coast League lead with 18 caught stealing in 2000.

					BATTING									FIELDING		
Year Team (League)	Pos.	G	AB	R	H	2B	3B	HR	RBI	Avg.	BB	SO	SB	PO	A	E	Avg.
1996—GC Pirates (GCL)........	OF	26	104	20	31	4	1	1	16	.298	12	12	15	43	2	1	.978
— Erie (NY-Penn)	OF	43	170	31	50	4	6	2	21	.294	17	30	7	79	1	7	.920
1997—Lynchburg (Caro.)	OF-1B	125	415	55	104	18	5	4	45	.251	45	82	21	227	8	6	.975
1998—Lynchburg (Caro.)	OF	131	525	70	135	26	10	6	46	.257	32	73	36	263	7	8	.971
1999—Altoona (East.)	OF	136	532	84	143	20	*12	3	60	.269	52	52	29	301	12	9	.972
2000—Nashville (PCL)	OF	121	506	62	132	24	11	4	51	.261	32	73	24	251	5	5	.981
— Pittsburgh (N.L.)	OF	9	18	2	6	1	0	1	1	.333	1	7	1	12	1	0	1.000
Major League totals (1 year)		9	18	2	6	1	0	1	1	.333	1	7	1	12	1	0	1.000

REDMOND, MIKE — C — MARLINS

PERSONAL: Born May 5, 1971, in Seattle. ... 6-1/185. ... Bats right, throws right. ... Full name: Michael Patrick Redmond.
HIGH SCHOOL: Gonzaga Prep (Spokane, Wash.).
COLLEGE: Gonzaga.
TRANSACTIONS/CAREER NOTES: Signed as a non-drafted free agent by Florida Marlins organization (August 18, 1992). ... On Florida disabled list (August 24-September 8, 1998).
STATISTICAL NOTES: Led Eastern League catchers with 95 assists in 1995. ... Led Eastern League catchers with 906 total chances in 1996.

					BATTING									FIELDING		
Year Team (League)	Pos.	G	AB	R	H	2B	3B	HR	RBI	Avg.	BB	SO	SB	PO	A	E	Avg.
1993—Kane County (Midw.)..	C	43	100	10	20	2	0	0	10	.200	6	17	2	213	26	1	.996
1994—Kane County (Midw.)..	C	92	306	39	83	10	0	1	24	.271	26	31	3	638	78	6	.992
— Brevard County (FSL).	C	12	42	4	11	4	0	0	2	.262	3	4	0	60	10	0	1.000
1995—Portland (East.)	C-3B	105	333	37	85	11	1	3	39	.255	22	27	2	657	•95	6	.992
1996—Portland (East.)	C	120	394	43	113	22	0	4	44	.287	26	45	3	*814	88	4	*.996
1997—Charlotte (I.L.)...........	C	22	61	8	13	5	1	1	2	.213	1	10	0	119	13	2	.985
— GC Marlins (GCL).......	DH	16	55	7	19	3	0	0	5	.345	9	5	2	...	...	...	...
— Brevard County (FSL).	1B	5	17	2	0	0	0	0	0	.000	2	2	0	8	0	0	1.000
1998—Portland (East.)	C	8	28	7	9	4	0	1	7	.321	2	2	0	53	6	1	.983
— Charlotte (I.L.)...........	C	18	58	4	14	2	0	2	7	.241	0	3	0	101	20	0	1.000
— Florida (N.L.).............	C	37	118	10	39	9	0	2	12	.331	5	16	0	216	25	2	.992
1999—Florida (N.L.).............	C	84	242	22	73	9	0	1	27	.302	26	34	0	444	45	4	.992
2000—Florida (N.L.).............	C	87	210	17	53	8	1	0	15	.252	13	19	0	446	40	2	.996
Major League totals (3 years)		208	570	49	165	26	1	3	54	.289	44	69	0	1106	110	8	.993

PERSONAL: Born November 12, 1962, in Joliet, Ill. ... 6-2/200. ... Bats left, throws right. ... Full name: Jeffrey Scott Reed. ... Brother of Curtis Reed, minor league outfielder (1977-84).

HIGH SCHOOL: West (Joliet, Ill.).

TRANSACTIONS/CAREER NOTES: Selected by Minnesota Twins organization in first round (12th pick overall) of free-agent draft (June 3, 1980). ... Traded by Twins with P Neal Heaton, P Al Cardwood and P Yorkis Perez to Montreal Expos for P Jeff Reardon and C Tom Nieto (February 3, 1987). ... On Montreal disabled list (April 20-May 25, 1987); included rehabilitation assignment to Indianapolis (May 19-25). ... Traded by Expos with OF Herm Winningham and P Randy St. Claire to Cincinnati Reds for OF Tracy Jones and P Pat Pacillo (July 13, 1988). ... On disabled list (July 1-19, 1991). ... On Cincinnati disabled list (April 26-September 1, 1992); included rehabilitation assignment to Nashville (August 17-September 1). ... Granted free agency (October 27, 1992). ... Signed by San Francisco Giants organization (January 15, 1993). ... On San Francisco disabled list (June 30-August 3, 1993); included rehabilitation assignment to San Jose (July 21-22 and July 30-August 3). ... Granted free agency (November 3, 1995). ... Signed by Colorado Rockies (December 18, 1995). ... Granted free agency (October 27, 1997). ... Re-signed by Rockies (November 18, 1997). ... Released by Rockies (July 2, 1999). ... Signed by Chicago Cubs (July 8, 1999). ... Granted free agency (October 31, 2000). ... Re-signed by Cubs organization (January 17, 2001).

RECORDS: Holds modern N.L. single-inning record for most errors by catcher—3 (July 28, 1987, seventh inning).

STATISTICAL NOTES: Led California League catchers with 758 total chances and tied for lead with nine double plays in 1982. ... Led Southern League catchers with 714 total chances and 12 double plays in 1983. ... Led International League catchers with 720 total chances in 1985. ... Career major league grand slams: 2.

							BATTING							FIELDING		
Year Team (League)	Pos.	G	AB	R	H	2B	3B	HR	RBI	Avg.	BB	SO	SB	PO	A	E	Avg.
1980—Elizabethton (Appl.)....	C	65	225	39	64	15	1	1	20	.284	51	23	2	269	*41	9	.972
1981—Wis. Rapids (Midw.)...	C	106	312	63	73	12	1	4	34	.234	86	36	4	547	*93	7	.989
—Orlando (Sou.)	C	3	4	0	1	0	0	0	0	.250	1	0	0	4	1	0	1.000
1982—Visalia (Calif.)	C	125	395	69	130	19	2	5	54	.329	78	32	1	*642	•106	10	.987
1983—Orlando (Sou.)	C	118	379	52	100	16	5	6	45	.264	76	40	2	*618	*88	8	*.989
—Toledo (I.L.)	C	14	41	5	7	1	1	0	3	.171	5	9	0	77	6	1	.988
1984—Minnesota (A.L.)	C	18	21	3	3	3	0	0	1	.143	2	6	0	41	2	1	.977
—Toledo (I.L.)	C	94	301	30	80	16	3	3	35	.266	37	35	1	546	43	5	*.992
1985—Toledo (I.L.)	C	122	404	53	100	15	3	5	36	.248	59	49	1	*627	*81	12	.983
—Minnesota (A.L.)	C	7	10	2	2	0	0	0	0	.200	0	3	0	9	3	0	1.000
1986—Minnesota (A.L.)	C	68	165	13	39	6	1	2	9	.236	16	19	1	332	19	2	.994
—Toledo (I.L.)	C	25	71	10	22	5	3	1	14	.310	17	9	0	108	22	2	.985
1987—Montreal (N.L.)■.......	C	75	207	15	44	11	0	1	21	.213	12	20	0	357	36	12	.970
—Indianapolis (A.A.)......	C	5	17	0	3	0	0	0	0	.176	1	2	0	27	2	0	1.000
1988—Montreal (N.L.)	C	43	123	10	27	3	2	0	9	.220	13	22	1	197	20	1	.995
—Indianapolis (A.A.)......	C	8	22	1	7	3	0	0	1	.318	2	2	0	30	11	0	1.000
—Cincinnati (N.L.)■......	C	49	142	10	33	6	0	1	7	.232	15	19	0	271	18	2	.993
1989—Cincinnati (N.L.)	C	102	287	16	64	11	0	3	23	.223	34	46	0	504	50	7	.988
1990—Cincinnati (N.L.)	C	72	175	12	44	8	1	3	16	.251	24	26	0	358	26	5	.987
1991—Cincinnati (N.L.)	C	91	270	20	72	15	2	3	31	.267	23	38	0	527	29	5	.991
1992—Nashville (A.A.)	C	14	25	1	6	1	0	1	2	.240	2	7	0	47	4	0	1.000
—Cincinnati (N.L.)	C	15	25	2	4	0	0	0	2	.160	1	4	0	29	2	0	1.000
1993—San Fran. (N.L.)■.......	C	66	119	10	31	3	0	6	12	.261	16	22	0	180	14	0	1.000
—San Jose (Calif.)........	C	4	10	2	5	1	0	0	2	.500	1	0	0	19	2	0	1.000
1994—San Francisco (N.L.) ..	C	50	103	11	18	3	0	1	7	.175	11	21	0	138	9	1	.993
1995—San Francisco (N.L.) ..	C	66	113	12	30	2	0	0	9	.265	20	17	0	175	21	1	.995
1996—Colorado (N.L.)■........	C	116	341	34	97	20	1	8	37	.284	43	65	2	546	51	11	.982
1997—Colorado (N.L.)	C	90	256	43	76	10	0	17	47	.297	35	55	2	428	37	6	.987
1998—Colorado (N.L.)	C	113	259	43	75	17	1	9	39	.290	37	57	0	452	27	7	.986
1999—Colorado (N.L.)	C-DH	46	106	11	27	5	0	2	11	.255	17	24	0	160	15	3	.983
—Chicago (N.L.)■........	C-3B	57	150	18	39	11	2	1	17	.260	28	34	1	282	17	4	.987
2000—Chicago (N.L.)	C	90	229	26	49	10	0	4	25	.214	44	68	0	469	19	5	.990
American League totals (3 years)		93	196	18	44	9	1	2	10	.224	18	28	1	382	24	3	.993
National League totals (14 years)		1141	2905	293	730	135	9	59	313	.251	373	538	6	5073	391	70	.987
Major League totals (17 years)		1234	3101	311	774	144	10	61	323	.250	391	566	7	5455	415	73	.988

CHAMPIONSHIP SERIES RECORD

							BATTING							FIELDING		
Year Team (League)	Pos.	G	AB	R	H	2B	3B	HR	RBI	Avg.	BB	SO	SB	PO	A	E	Avg.
1990—Cincinnati (N.L.)	C	4	7	0	0	0	0	0	0	.000	2	0	0	24	1	0	1.000

WORLD SERIES RECORD

NOTES: Member of World Series championship team (1990).

							BATTING							FIELDING		
Year Team (League)	Pos.	G	AB	R	H	2B	3B	HR	RBI	Avg.	BB	SO	SB	PO	A	E	Avg.
1990—Cincinnati (N.L.).........								Did not play.									

PERSONAL: Born August 16, 1965, in Huntington, W.Va. ... 6-1/195. ... Throws right, bats right. ... Full name: Richard Allen Reed.
HIGH SCHOOL: Huntington (W.Va.).
COLLEGE: Marshall.
TRANSACTIONS/CAREER NOTES: Selected by Pittsburgh Pirates organization in 26th round of free-agent draft (June 2, 1986). ... On Buffalo disabled list (May 2-13, 1991). ... Granted free agency (April 3, 1992). ... Signed by Kansas City Royals organization (April 4, 1992). ... Granted free agency (August 5, 1993). ... Signed by Texas Rangers organization (August 11, 1993). ... Claimed on waivers by Cincinnati Reds (May 13, 1994). ... On Indianapolis disabled list (May 29-June 9, 1995). ... Granted free agency (October 16, 1995). ... Signed by New York Mets organization (November 7, 1995). ... On New York Mets disabled list (April 12-May 3 and August 9-September 4, 1999); included rehabilitation assignments to Norfolk (August 27-31) and Binghamton (September 1-4). ... On disabled list (June 30-July 17, 2000). ... Granted free agency (November 8, 2000). ... Re-signed by Mets (December 6, 2000).
HONORS: Named American Association Most Valuable Pitcher (1991).
MISCELLANEOUS: Appeared in one game as outfielder with no chances (1999).

Year League	W	L	Pct.	ERA	G	GS	CG	ShO	Sv.	IP	H	R	ER	BB	SO
1986—GC Pirates (GCL)	0	2	.000	3.75	8	3	0	0	0	24	20	12	10	6	15
—Macon (S.Atl.)	0	0	...	2.84	1	1	0	0	0	6 1/3	5	3	2	2	1
1987—Macon (S.Atl.)	8	4	.667	2.50	46	0	0	0	7	93 2/3	80	38	26	29	92
1988—Salem (Caro.)	6	2	.750	2.74	15	8	4	1	0	72 1/3	56	28	22	17	73
—Harrisburg (East.)	1	0	1.000	1.13	2	2	0	0	0	16	11	2	2	2	17
—Buffalo (A.A.)	5	2	.714	1.64	10	9	3	2	0	77	62	15	14	12	50
—Pittsburgh (N.L.)	1	0	1.000	3.00	2	2	0	0	0	12	10	4	4	2	6
1989—Buffalo (A.A.)	9	8	.529	3.72	20	20	3	0	0	125 2/3	130	58	52	28	75
—Pittsburgh (N.L.)	1	4	.200	5.60	15	7	0	0	0	54 2/3	62	35	34	11	34
1990—Buffalo (A.A.)	7	4	.636	3.46	15	15	2	2	0	91	82	37	35	21	63
—Pittsburgh (N.L.)	2	3	.400	4.36	13	8	1	1	1	53 2/3	62	32	26	12	27
1991—Buffalo (A.A.)	*14	4	*.778	*2.15	25	25	•5	2	0	167 1/3	151	45	40	26	102
—Pittsburgh (N.L.)	0	0	...	10.38	1	1	0	0	0	4 1/3	8	6	5	1	2
1992—Omaha (A.A.)■	5	4	.556	4.35	11	10	3	0	1	62	67	33	30	12	35
—Kansas City (A.L.)	3	7	.300	3.68	19	18	1	1	0	100 1/3	105	47	41	20	49
1993—Omaha (A.A.)	11	4	.733	3.09	19	19	3	*2	0	128 1/3	116	48	44	14	58
—Kansas City (A.L.)	0	0	...	9.82	1	0	0	0	0	3 2/3	6	4	4	1	3
—Oklahoma City (A.A.)■	1	3	.250	4.19	5	5	1	0	0	34 1/3	43	20	16	2	21
—Texas (A.L.)	1	0	1.000	2.25	2	0	0	0	0	4	6	1	1	1	2
1994—Oklahoma City (A.A.)	1	1	.500	3.86	2	2	0	0	0	11 2/3	10	5	5	0	8
—Texas (A.L.)	1	1	.500	5.94	4	3	0	0	0	16 2/3	17	13	11	7	12
—Indianapolis (A.A.)■	9	5	.643	4.68	21	21	3	1	0	140 1/3	162	80	73	19	79
1995—Indianapolis (A.A.)	11	4	.733	3.33	22	21	3	1	0	135	127	60	50	26	92
—Cincinnati (N.L.)	0	0	...	5.82	4	3	0	0	0	17	18	12	11	3	10
1996—Norfolk (I.L.)■	8	10	.444	3.16	28	28	1	0	0	182	164	72	64	33	128
1997—New York (N.L.)	13	9	.591	2.89	33	31	2	0	0	208 1/3	186	76	67	31	113
1998—New York (N.L.)	16	11	.593	3.48	31	31	2	1	0	212 1/3	208	84	82	29	153
1999—New York (N.L.)	11	5	.688	4.58	26	26	1	1	0	149 1/3	163	77	76	47	104
—Norfolk (I.L.)	0	1	.000	27.00	1	1	0	0	0	3	10	9	9	2	2
—Binghamton (East.)	0	0	...	1.80	1	1	0	0	0	5	1	1	1	1	5
2000—New York (N.L.)	11	5	.688	4.11	30	30	0	0	0	184	192	90	84	34	121
A.L. totals (3 years)	5	8	.385	4.11	26	21	1	1	0	124 2/3	134	65	57	29	66
N.L. totals (9 years)	55	37	.598	3.91	155	139	6	3	1	895 2/3	909	416	389	170	570
Major League totals (12 years)	60	45	.571	3.93	181	160	7	4	1	1020 1/3	1043	481	446	199	636

DIVISION SERIES RECORD

Year League	W	L	Pct.	ERA	G	GS	CG	ShO	Sv.	IP	H	R	ER	BB	SO
1999—New York (N.L.)	1	0	1.000	3.00	1	1	0	0	0	6	4	2	2	3	2
2000—New York (N.L.)	0	0	...	3.00	1	1	0	0	0	6	7	2	2	2	6
Division series totals (2 years)	1	0	1.000	3.00	2	2	0	0	0	12	11	4	4	5	8

CHAMPIONSHIP SERIES RECORD

Year League	W	L	Pct.	ERA	G	GS	CG	ShO	Sv.	IP	H	R	ER	BB	SO
1999—New York (N.L.)	0	0	...	2.57	1	1	0	0	0	7	3	2	2	0	5
2000—New York (N.L.)	0	1	.000	10.80	1	1	0	0	0	3 1/3	8	5	4	1	4
Champ. series totals (2 years)	0	1	.000	5.23	2	2	0	0	0	10 1/3	11	7	6	1	9

WORLD SERIES RECORD

Year League	W	L	Pct.	ERA	G	GS	CG	ShO	Sv.	IP	H	R	ER	BB	SO
2000—New York (N.L.)	0	0	...	3.00	1	1	0	0	0	6	6	2	2	1	8

ALL-STAR GAME RECORD

Year League	W	L	Pct.	ERA	GS	CG	ShO	Sv.	IP	H	R	ER	BB	SO
1998—National				Did not play.										

REED, STEVE   P   INDIANS

PERSONAL: Born March 11, 1966, in Los Angeles. ... 6-2/212. ... Throws right, bats right. ... Full name: Steven Vincent Reed.
HIGH SCHOOL: Chatsworth (Calif.).
COLLEGE: Lewis-Clark State College (Idaho).
TRANSACTIONS/CAREER NOTES: Signed as non-drafted free agent by San Francisco Giants organization (June 24, 1988). ... On disabled list (July 17-August 13, 1990). ... Selected by Colorado Rockies in third round (60th pick overall) of expansion draft (November 17, 1992). ... Granted free agency (December 21, 1997). ... Signed by Giants (December 24, 1997). ... Traded by Giants with OF Jacob Cruz to Cleveland Indians for P Jose Mesa, IF Shawon Dunston and P Alvin Morman (July 23, 1998).
MISCELLANEOUS: Holds Colorado Rockies all-time record for lowest earned-run average (3.68).

Year League	W	L	Pct.	ERA	G	GS	CG	ShO	Sv.	IP	H	R	ER	BB	SO
1988—Pocatello (Pio.)	4	1	.800	2.54	31	0	0	0	*13	46	42	20	13	8	49
1989—Clinton (Midw.)	5	3	.625	1.05	60	0	0	0	26	94 2/3	54	16	11	38	104
—San Jose (Calif.)	0	0	...	0.00	2	0	0	0	0	2	0	0	1	3
1990—Shreveport (Texas)	3	1	.750	1.64	45	1	0	0	8	60 1/3	53	20	11	20	59
1991—Shreveport (Texas)	2	0	1.000	0.83	15	0	0	0	7	21 2/3	17	2	2	3	26
—Phoenix (PCL)	2	3	.400	4.31	41	0	0	0	6	56 1/3	62	33	27	12	46
1992—Shreveport (Texas)	1	0	1.000	0.62	27	0	0	0	23	29	18	3	2	0	33
—Phoenix (PCL)	0	1	.000	3.48	29	0	0	0	20	31	27	13	12	10	30
—San Francisco (N.L.)	1	0	1.000	2.30	18	0	0	0	0	15 2/3	13	5	4	3	11
1993—Colorado (N.L.)■	9	5	.643	4.48	64	0	0	0	3	84 1/3	80	47	42	30	51
—Colorado Springs (PCL)	0	0	...	0.00	11	0	0	0	7	12 1/3	8	1	0	3	10
1994—Colorado (N.L.)	3	2	.600	3.94	*61	0	0	0	3	64	79	33	28	26	51
1995—Colorado (N.L.)	5	2	.714	2.14	71	0	0	0	3	84	61	24	20	21	79
1996—Colorado (N.L.)	4	3	.571	3.96	70	0	0	0	0	75	66	38	33	19	51
1997—Colorado (N.L.)	4	6	.400	4.04	63	0	0	0	6	62 1/3	49	28	28	27	43

Year	League	W	L	Pct.	ERA	G	GS	CG	ShO	Sv.	IP	H	R	ER	BB	SO
1998—San Francisco (N.L.)■		2	1	.667	1.48	50	0	0	0	1	54²/₃	30	10	9	19	50
—Cleveland (A.L.)■...............		2	2	.500	6.66	20	0	0	0	0	25²/₃	26	19	19	8	23
1999—Cleveland (A.L.).................		3	2	.600	4.23	63	0	0	0	0	61²/₃	69	33	29	20	44
2000—Cleveland (A.L.).................		2	0	1.000	4.34	57	0	0	0	0	56	58	30	27	21	39
A.L. totals (3 years)		7	4	.636	4.71	140	0	0	0	0	143¹/₃	153	82	75	49	106
N.L. totals (7 years)		28	19	.596	3.35	397	0	0	0	16	440	378	185	164	145	336
Major League totals (9 years)		35	23	.603	3.69	537	0	0	0	16	583¹/₃	531	267	239	194	442

DIVISION SERIES RECORD

Year	League	W	L	Pct.	ERA	G	GS	CG	ShO	Sv.	IP	H	R	ER	BB	SO
1995—Colorado (N.L.)		0	0	...	0.00	3	0	0	0	0	2²/₃	2	0	0	1	3
1998—Cleveland (A.L.).................		1	0	1.000	40.50	2	0	0	0	0	²/₃	1	3	3	1	1
1999—Cleveland (A.L.).................		0	0	...	30.86	2	0	0	0	0	2¹/₃	9	8	8	1	1
Division series totals (3 years)		1	0	1.000	17.47	7	0	0	0	0	5²/₃	12	11	11	3	5

CHAMPIONSHIP SERIES RECORD

Year	League	W	L	Pct.	ERA	G	GS	CG	ShO	Sv.	IP	H	R	ER	BB	SO
1998—Cleveland (A.L.).................		0	0	...	0.00	3	0	0	0	0	1²/₃	0	0	0	1	0

REESE, POKEY 2B REDS

PERSONAL: Born June 10, 1973, in Columbia, S.C. ... 5-11/180. ... Bats right, throws right. ... Full name: Calvin Reese Jr.
HIGH SCHOOL: Lower Richland (Hopkins, S.C.).
TRANSACTIONS/CAREER NOTES: Selected by Cincinnati Reds organization in first round (20th pick overall) of free-agent draft (June 3, 1991). ... On disabled list (June 23-July 25, 1995; September 17, 1996-remainder of season; and July 31, 1998-remainder of season).
RECORDS: Shares N.L. record for most errors by shortstop in opening game of season (nine-inning game) since 1900—4 (March 31, 1998).
HONORS: Won N.L. Gold Glove at second base (1999 and 2000).

							BATTING							FIELDING		
Year	Team (League)	Pos.	G	AB	R	H	2B	3B	HR	RBI	Avg.	BB	SO	SB	PO	A	E	Avg.
1991—Princeton (Appl.)........		SS	62	231	30	55	8	3	3	27	.238	23	44	10	93	146	*31	.885
1992—Char., W.Va. (SAL)......		SS	106	380	50	102	19	3	6	53	.268	24	75	19	181	287	34	.932
1993—Chattanooga (Sou.)		SS	102	345	35	73	17	4	3	37	.212	23	77	8	181	300	25	.951
1994—Chattanooga (Sou.)		SS	134	484	77	130	23	4	12	49	.269	43	75	21	*221	362	38	.939
1995—Indianapolis (A.A.)......		SS	89	343	51	82	21	1	10	46	.239	36	81	8	131	258	27	.935
1996—Indianapolis (A.A.)......		SS-3B	79	280	26	65	16	0	1	23	.232	21	46	5	131	239	22	.944
1997—Cincinnati (N.L.)		SS-2B-3B	128	397	48	87	15	0	4	26	.219	31	82	25	182	284	15	.969
—Indianapolis (A.A.)......		SS-2B	17	72	12	17	2	0	4	11	.236	9	12	4	43	42	3	.966
1998—Cincinnati (N.L.)		3B-SS-2B	59	133	20	34	2	2	1	16	.256	14	28	3	50	78	8	.941
1999—Cincinnati (N.L.)		2B-SS	149	585	85	167	37	5	10	52	.285	35	81	38	340	425	7	.991
2000—Cincinnati (N.L.)		2B	135	518	76	132	20	6	12	46	.255	45	86	29	289	393	14	.980
Major League totals (4 years)			471	1633	229	420	74	13	27	140	.257	125	277	95	861	1180	44	.979

REICHERT, DAN P ROYALS

PERSONAL: Born July 12, 1976, in Monterey, Calif. ... 6-3/175. ... Throws right, bats right. ... Full name: Daniel Robert Reichert.
HIGH SCHOOL: Turlock (Calif.).
COLLEGE: Pacific.
TRANSACTIONS/CAREER NOTES: Selected by Kansas City Royals organization in first round (seventh pick overall) of free-agent draft (June 3, 1997). ... On Kansas City disabled list (August 25, 1999-remainder of season).
STATISTICAL NOTES: Led A.L. in wild pitches with 18 in 2000.

Year	League	W	L	Pct.	ERA	G	GS	CG	ShO	Sv.	IP	H	R	ER	BB	SO
1997—Spokane (N'West)		3	4	.429	2.84	9	9	0	0	0	38	40	25	12	16	39
1998—Wichita (Texas)		1	4	.200	9.75	8	8	0	0	0	36	52	40	39	29	24
—Lansing (Midw.)..................		1	1	.500	3.28	13	6	0	0	0	35²/₃	25	16	13	20	35
—Wilmington (Caro.).............		2	0	1.000	3.21	2	2	0	0	0	14	13	5	5	4	10
—Omaha (PCL).......................		1	1	.500	4.67	3	3	0	0	0	17¹/₃	14	10	9	2	11
1999—Omaha (PCL).....................		9	2	.818	3.71	17	17	1	0	0	111²/₃	92	51	46	50	123
—Kansas City (A.L.)		2	2	.500	9.08	8	8	0	0	0	36²/₃	48	38	37	32	20
2000—Kansas City (A.L.)		8	10	.444	4.70	44	18	1	1	2	153¹/₃	157	92	80	91	94
Major League totals (2 years)		10	12	.455	5.54	52	26	1	1	2	190	205	130	117	123	114

REITH, BRIAN P REDS

PERSONAL: Born February 28, 1978, in Fort Wayne, Ind. ... 6-5/190. ... Throws right, bats right. ... Full name: Brian Eric Reith.
HIGH SCHOOL: Concordia Lutheran (Fort Wayne, Ind.).
TRANSACTIONS/CAREER NOTES: Selected by New York Yankees organization in sixth round of free-agent draft (June 4, 1996). ... Traded by Yankees with 3B Drew Henson, OF Jackson Melian and P Ed Yarnall to Cincinnati Reds for P Denny Neagle and OF Mike Frank (July 12, 2000).

Year	League	W	L	Pct.	ERA	G	GS	CG	ShO	Sv.	IP	H	R	ER	BB	SO
1996—Gulf Coast Yankees (GCL)..		2	3	.400	4.13	10	4	0	0	0	32²/₃	31	16	15	16	21
1997—Gulf Coast Yankees (GCL)..		4	2	.667	2.86	12	11	1	0	0	63	70	28	20	14	40
1998—Greensboro (S.Atl.)		6	7	.462	2.28	20	20	3	1	0	118¹/₃	86	42	30	32	116
1999—Tampa (FSL).......................		9	9	.500	4.70	26	23	0	0	0	139²/₃	174	87	73	35	101
2000—Tampa (FSL).......................		9	4	.692	2.18	18	18	1	1	0	119²/₃	101	39	29	33	100
—Dayton (Midw.)■		2	1	.667	2.88	5	5	0	0	0	34¹/₃	33	12	11	8	30
—Chattanooga (Sou.)		1	3	.250	3.90	5	5	0	0	0	30	31	14	13	11	29

REITSMA, CHRIS — P — REDS

PERSONAL: Born December 31, 1977, in Minneapolis. ... 6-5/214. ... Throws right, bats right. ... Full name: Christopher Michael Reitsma.
HIGH SCHOOL: Calgary (Alta.) Christian.
TRANSACTIONS/CAREER NOTES: Selected by Boston Red Sox organization as "sandwich pick" between first and second round of free-agent draft (June 4, 1996); pick received as compensation for Toronto Blue Jays signing P Erik Hanson. ... On disabled list (June 5-September 8, 1997). ... On disabled list (April 8-May 3, 1999). ... Selected by Tampa Bay Devil Rays from Red Sox organization in Rule 5 major league draft (December 13, 1999). ... Returned to Red Sox (March 28, 2000). ... On Trenton disabled list (July 14-22, 2000). ... Traded by Red Sox with P John Curtice to Cincinnati Reds for OF Dante Bichette (August 31, 2000).

Year	League	W	L	Pct.	ERA	G	GS	CG	ShO	Sv.	IP	H	R	ER	BB	SO
1996—	Gulf Coast Red Sox (GCL)..	3	1	.750	1.35	7	6	0	0	0	26 2/3	24	7	4	1	32
1997—	Michigan (Midw.)	4	1	.800	2.90	9	9	0	0	0	49 2/3	57	23	16	13	41
1998—	Sarasota (FSL)	0	0	...	2.84	8	8	0	0	0	12 2/3	12	6	4	5	9
1999—	Sarasota (FSL)	4	10	.286	5.61	19	19	0	0	0	96 1/3	116	71	60	31	79
2000—	Trenton (East.)	7	2	.778	2.58	14	14	1	0	0	90 2/3	78	28	26	21	58
—	Sarasota (FSL)	3	4	.429	3.66	11	11	0	0	0	64	57	29	26	17	47

REKAR, BRYAN — P — DEVIL RAYS

PERSONAL: Born June 3, 1972, in Oak Lawn, Ill. ... 6-3/220. ... Throws right, bats right. ... Full name: Bryan Robert Rekar. ... Cousin of Pete Bercich, linebacker, Minnesota Vikings; and nephew of Bob Bercich, defensive back with Dallas Cowboys (1960 and 1961).
HIGH SCHOOL: Providence Catholic (New Lenox, Ill.).
COLLEGE: Bradley.
TRANSACTIONS/CAREER NOTES: Selected by Colorado Rockies organization in second round of free-agent draft (June 3, 1993). ... Selected by Tampa Bay Devil Rays in second round (38th pick overall) of expansion draft (November 18, 1997). ... On Tampa Bay disabled list (March 19-July 6, 1998); included rehabilitation assignments to St. Petersburg (May 16-25 and June 25-July 4) and Durham (May 26-June 1 and July 4-6). ... On Tampa Bay disabled list (March 31-April 30, 2000); included rehabilitation assignment to Durham (April 9-30).

Year	League	W	L	Pct.	ERA	G	GS	CG	ShO	Sv.	IP	H	R	ER	BB	SO
1993—	Bend (N'West)	3	5	.375	4.08	13	13	1	0	0	75	81	36	34	18	59
1994—	Central Valley (Calif.)	6	6	.500	3.48	22	19	0	0	0	111 1/3	120	52	43	31	91
1995—	New Haven (East.)	6	3	.667	2.13	12	12	1	1	0	80 1/3	65	28	19	16	80
—	Colorado Springs (PCL)	4	2	.667	1.49	7	7	2	1	0	48 1/3	29	10	8	13	39
—	Colorado (N.L.)	4	6	.400	4.98	15	14	1	0	0	85	95	51	47	24	60
1996—	Colorado Springs (PCL)	8	8	.500	4.46	19	19	0	0	0	123	138	68	61	36	75
—	Colorado (N.L.)	2	4	.333	8.95	14	11	0	0	0	58 1/3	87	61	58	26	25
1997—	Colorado Springs (PCL)	10	9	.526	5.46	28	25	0	0	0	145	169	96	88	39	116
—	Colorado (N.L.)	1	0	1.000	5.79	2	2	0	0	0	9 1/3	11	7	6	6	4
1998—	St. Petersburg (FSL)■	0	0	...	0.69	4	4	0	0	0	13	6	2	1	2	15
—	Durham (I.L.)	0	1	.000	3.27	3	3	0	0	0	11	10	4	4	2	9
—	Tampa Bay (A.L.)	2	8	.200	4.98	16	15	1	0	0	86 2/3	95	56	48	21	55
1999—	Durham (I.L.)	4	1	.800	3.86	6	5	0	0	0	35	29	15	15	8	26
—	Tampa Bay (A.L.)	6	6	.500	5.80	27	12	0	0	0	94 2/3	121	68	61	41	55
2000—	Durham (I.L.)	3	0	1.000	2.05	4	4	0	0	0	22	16	5	5	4	18
—	Tampa Bay (A.L.)	7	10	.412	4.41	30	27	2	0	0	173 1/3	200	92	85	39	95
A.L. totals (3 years)		15	24	.385	4.92	73	54	3	0	0	354 2/3	416	216	194	101	205
N.L. totals (3 years)		7	10	.412	6.54	31	27	1	0	0	152 2/3	193	119	111	56	89
Major League totals (6 years)		22	34	.393	5.41	104	81	4	0	0	507 1/3	609	335	305	157	294

RELAFORD, DESI — SS — METS

PERSONAL: Born September 16, 1973, in Valdosta, Ga. ... 5-9/174. ... Bats both, throws right. ... Full name: Desmond Lamont Relaford.
HIGH SCHOOL: Sandalwood (Jacksonville).
TRANSACTIONS/CAREER NOTES: Selected by Seattle Mariners organization in fourth round of free-agent draft (June 3, 1991). ... Traded by Mariners to Philadelphia Phillies for P Terry Mulholland (July 31, 1996). ... On Philadelphia disabled list (June 17-September 13, 1999); included rehabilitation assignment to Clearwater (September 4-13). ... Traded by Phillies to San Diego Padres for a player to be named later (August 4, 2000); Phillies acquired INF David Newhan to complete deal (August 7, 2000). ... Claimed on waivers by New York Mets (October 12, 2000).
STATISTICAL NOTES: Led California League shortstops with 601 total chances in 1992. ... Led Southern League shortstops with 35 errors in 1993. ... Led International League shortstops with 587 total chances and 81 double plays in 1997. ... Led N.L. shortstops with 31 errors in 2000.

Year	Team (League)	Pos.	G	AB	R	H	2B	3B	HR	RBI	Avg.	BB	SO	SB	PO	A	E	Avg.
1991—	Ariz. Mariners (Ariz.)..	SS-2B	46	163	36	44	7	3	0	18	.270	22	24	17	58	126	24	.885
1992—	Peninsula (Caro.)	SS	130	445	53	96	18	1	3	34	.216	39	88	27	167	*382	*52	.913
1993—	Jacksonville (Sou.)	SS-2B-3B	133	472	49	115	16	4	8	47	.244	50	103	16	157	386	†38	.935
1994—	Jacksonville (Sou.).......	SS	37	143	24	29	7	3	3	11	.203	22	28	10	71	119	4	.979
—	Riverside (Calif.)........	SS	99	374	95	116	27	5	5	59	.310	78	78	27	125	296	36	.921
1995—	Port City (Sou.)	SS-2B-DH	90	352	51	101	11	2	7	27	.287	41	58	25	134	276	31	.930
—	Tacoma (PCL)	2B-SS	30	113	20	27	5	1	2	7	.239	13	24	6	52	93	6	.960
1996—	Tacoma (PCL)	2B-SS-DH	93	317	27	65	12	0	4	32	.205	23	58	10	174	306	20	.960
—	Scranton/W.B. (I.L.)■	SS	21	85	12	20	4	1	1	11	.235	8	19	7	25	65	6	.938
—	Philadelphia (N.L.)	SS-2B	15	40	2	7	2	0	0	1	.175	3	9	1	21	26	2	.959
1997—	Scranton/W.B. (I.L.)	SS	131	517	82	138	34	4	9	53	.267	43	77	29	180	*373	34	.942
—	Philadelphia (N.L.)	SS	15	38	3	7	1	2	0	6	.184	5	6	3	12	31	1	.977
1998—	Philadelphia (N.L.)......	SS	142	494	45	121	25	3	5	41	.245	33	87	9	189	380	24	.960
1999—	Philadelphia (N.L.)......	SS	65	211	31	51	11	2	1	26	.242	19	34	4	97	182	14	.952
—	Clearwater (FSL)	SS	2	7	1	2	0	0	0	1	.286	1	1	0	3	1	1	.800
2000—	Philadelphia (N.L.)......	SS	83	253	29	56	12	3	3	30	.221	48	45	5	116	202	24	.930
—	San Diego (N.L.)■	SS	45	157	26	32	2	0	2	16	.204	27	26	8	73	120	§7	.965
Major League totals (5 years)			365	1193	136	274	53	10	11	120	.230	135	207	30	508	941	72	.953

PERSONAL: Born March 23, 1966, in Middletown, N.Y. ... 6-1/210. ... Throws left, bats left. ... Full name: Michael John Remlinger. ... Name pronounced REM-lynn-jer.
HIGH SCHOOL: Carver (Plymouth, Mass.).
COLLEGE: Dartmouth.
TRANSACTIONS/CAREER NOTES: Selected by San Francisco Giants organization in first round (16th pick overall) of free-agent draft (June 2, 1987). ... On disabled list (April 30, 1988-remainder of season). ... Traded by Giants with OF Kevin Mitchell to Seattle Mariners for P Bill Swift, P Mike Jackson and P Dave Burba (December 11, 1991). ... On Jacksonville disabled list (July 30, 1992-remainder of season). ... Granted free agency (October 15, 1993). ... Signed by New York Mets organization (November 22, 1993). ... Traded by Mets to Cincinnati Reds for OF Cobi Cradle (May 11, 1995). ... Granted free agency (October 6, 1995). ... Re-signed by Reds (October 22, 1995). ... Traded by Reds to Kansas City Royals as part of a three-team deal in which Reds sent SS Luis Ordaz to St. Louis Cardinals for OF Andre King. Royals then sent OF Miguel Mejia to Cardinals to complete deal (December 4, 1995). ... Claimed on waivers by Reds (April 4, 1996). ... Traded by Reds with 2B Bret Boone to Atlanta Braves for P Denny Neagle, OF Michael Tucker and P Rob Bell (November 10, 1998). ... On disabled list (April 3-18, 1999; June 23-July 13, 2000).
RECORDS: Shares major league record for pitching shutout in first major league game (June 15, 1991).
STATISTICAL NOTES: Led American Association with 18 wild pitches in 1996. ... Led N.L. with 12 wild pitches in 1997.
MISCELLANEOUS: Appeared in two games as pinch runner (1997).

Year	League	W	L	Pct.	ERA	G	GS	CG	ShO	Sv.	IP	H	R	ER	BB	SO
1987—	Everett (N'West)	0	0	...	3.60	2	1	0	0	0	5	1	2	2	5	11
	— Clinton (Midw.)	2	1	.667	3.30	6	5	0	0	0	30	21	12	11	14	43
	— Shreveport (Texas)	4	2	.667	2.36	6	6	0	0	0	34 1/3	14	11	9	22	51
1988—	Shreveport (Texas)	1	0	1.000	0.69	3	3	0	0	0	13	7	4	1	4	18
1989—	Shreveport (Texas)	4	6	.400	2.98	16	16	0	0	0	90 2/3	68	43	30	73	92
	— Phoenix (PCL)	1	6	.143	9.21	11	10	0	0	0	43	51	47	44	52	28
1990—	Shreveport (Texas)	9	11	.450	3.90	25	25	2	1	0	147 2/3	149	82	64	72	75
1991—	Phoenix (PCL)	5	5	.500	6.38	19	19	1	1	0	108 2/3	134	86	77	59	68
	— San Francisco (N.L.)	2	1	.667	4.37	8	6	1	1	0	35	36	17	17	20	19
1992—	Calgary (PCL)■	1	7	.125	6.65	21	11	0	0	0	70 1/3	97	65	52	48	24
	— Jacksonville (Sou.)	1	1	.500	3.46	5	5	0	0	0	26	25	15	10	11	21
1993—	Calgary (PCL)	4	3	.571	5.53	19	18	0	0	0	84 2/3	100	57	52	52	51
	— Jacksonville (Sou.)	1	3	.250	6.58	7	7	0	0	0	39 2/3	40	30	29	19	23
1994—	Norfolk (I.L.)■	2	4	.333	3.14	12	9	0	0	0	63	57	29	22	25	45
	— New York (N.L.)	1	5	.167	4.61	10	9	0	0	0	54 2/3	55	30	28	35	33
1995—	New York (N.L.)	0	1	.000	6.35	5	0	0	0	0	5 2/3	7	5	4	2	6
	— Cincinnati (N.L.)■	0	0	...	9.00	2	0	0	0	0	1	2	1	1	3	1
	— Indianapolis (A.A.)	5	3	.625	4.05	41	1	0	0	0	46 2/3	40	24	21	32	58
1996—	Indianapolis (A.A.)	4	3	.571	2.52	28	13	0	0	0	89 1/3	64	29	25	44	97
	— Cincinnati (N.L.)	0	1	.000	5.60	19	4	0	0	0	27 1/3	24	17	17	19	19
1997—	Cincinnati (N.L.)	8	8	.500	4.14	69	12	2	0	2	124	100	61	57	60	145
1998—	Cincinnati (N.L.)	8	15	.348	4.82	35	28	1	1	0	164 1/3	164	96	88	87	144
1999—	Atlanta (N.L.)■	10	1	.909	2.37	73	0	0	0	1	83 2/3	66	24	22	35	81
2000—	Atlanta (N.L.)	5	3	.625	3.47	71	0	0	0	12	72 2/3	55	29	28	37	72
Major League totals (8 years)		**34**	**35**	**.493**	**4.15**	**292**	**59**	**4**	**2**	**15**	**568 1/3**	**509**	**280**	**262**	**298**	**520**

DIVISION SERIES RECORD

Year	League	W	L	Pct.	ERA	G	GS	CG	ShO	Sv.	IP	H	R	ER	BB	SO
1999—	Atlanta (N.L.)	0	0	...	9.82	2	0	0	0	0	3 2/3	4	4	4	3	4
2000—	Atlanta (N.L.)	0	0	...	2.70	3	0	0	0	0	3 1/3	6	1	1	0	3
Division series totals (2 years)		**0**	**0**	...	**6.43**	**5**	**0**	**0**	**0**	**0**	**7**	**10**	**5**	**5**	**3**	**7**

CHAMPIONSHIP SERIES RECORD

Year	League	W	L	Pct.	ERA	G	GS	CG	ShO	Sv.	IP	H	R	ER	BB	SO
1999—	Atlanta (N.L.)	0	1	.000	3.18	5	0	0	0	0	5 2/3	3	2	2	3	4

WORLD SERIES RECORD

Year	League	W	L	Pct.	ERA	G	GS	CG	ShO	Sv.	IP	H	R	ER	BB	SO
1999—	Atlanta (N.L.)	0	1	.000	9.00	2	0	0	0	0	1	1	1	1	1	0

PERSONAL: Born August 7, 1975, in Barranquilla, Colombia. ... 6-1/180. ... Bats right, throws right. ... Full name: Edgar Enrique Renteria. ... Brother of Edinson Renteria, infielder in Houston Astros and Florida Marlins organizations (1985-94).
HIGH SCHOOL: Instituto Los Alpes (Barranquilla, Colombia).
TRANSACTIONS/CAREER NOTES: Signed as non-drafted free agent by Florida Marlins organization (February 14, 1992). ... On Florida disabled list (June 24-July 11, 1996); included rehabilitation assignment to Charlotte (July 3-11). ... On disabled list (August 25-September 9, 1998). ... Traded by Marlins to St. Louis Cardinals for P Braden Looper, P Armando Almanza and SS Pablo Ozuna (December 14, 1998).
HONORS: Named shortstop on The Sporting News N.L. All-Star team (2000). ... Named shortstop on The Sporting News N.L. Silver Slugger team (2000).
STATISTICAL NOTES: Had 22-game hitting streak (July 25-August 16, 1996). ... Led N.L. with 19 sacrifice hits in 1997. ... Led N.L. in caught stealing with 22 in 1998.

Year	Team (League)	Pos.	G	AB	R	H	2B	3B	HR	RBI	Avg.	BB	SO	SB	PO	A	E	Avg.
							BATTING								FIELDING			
1992—	GC Marlins (GCL)	SS	43	163	25	47	8	1	0	9	.288	8	29	10	56	152	*24	.897
1993—	Kane County (Midw.)	SS	116	384	40	78	8	0	1	35	.203	35	94	7	•173	306	34	.934
1994—	Brevard County (FSL)	SS	128	439	46	111	15	1	0	36	.253	35	56	6	167	372	23	.959
1995—	Portland (East.)	SS	135	508	70	147	15	7	7	68	.289	32	85	30	179	379	33	.944
1996—	Charlotte (I.L.)	SS	35	132	17	37	8	0	2	16	.280	9	17	10	48	114	7	.959
	— Florida (N.L.)	SS	106	431	68	133	18	3	5	31	.309	33	68	16	163	344	11	.979
1997—	Florida (N.L.)	SS	154	617	90	171	21	3	4	52	.277	45	108	32	*242	415	17	.975
1998—	Florida (N.L.)	SS	133	517	79	146	18	2	3	31	.282	48	78	41	194	372	20	.966
1999—	St. Louis (N.L.)■	SS	154	585	92	161	36	2	11	63	.275	53	82	37	219	393	26	.959
2000—	St. Louis (N.L.)	SS	150	562	94	156	32	1	16	76	.278	63	77	21	231	379	27	.958
Major League totals (5 years)			**697**	**2712**	**423**	**767**	**125**	**11**	**39**	**253**	**.283**	**242**	**413**	**147**	**1049**	**1903**	**101**	**.967**

R

DIVISION SERIES RECORD

Year Team (League)	Pos.	G	AB	R	H	2B	3B	HR	RBI	Avg.	BB	SO	SB	PO	A	E	Avg.
1997— Florida (N.L.)	SS	3	13	1	2	0	0	0	1	.154	2	4	0	9	11	2	.909
2000— St. Louis (N.L.)..........	SS	3	10	5	2	0	0	0	0	.200	4	1	2	6	4	1	.909
Division series totals (2 years)		6	23	6	4	0	0	0	1	.174	6	5	2	15	15	3	.909

CHAMPIONSHIP SERIES RECORD

RECORDS: Shares N.L. single-game record for most stolen bases—3 (October 12, 2000).

Year Team (League)	Pos.	G	AB	R	H	2B	3B	HR	RBI	Avg.	BB	SO	SB	PO	A	E	Avg.
1997— Florida (N.L.)	SS	6	22	4	5	1	0	0	0	.227	3	6	1	14	15	0	1.000
2000— St. Louis (N.L.)..........	SS	5	20	4	6	1	0	0	4	.300	0	2	3	5	12	0	1.000
Championship series totals (2 years)		11	42	8	11	2	0	0	4	.262	3	8	4	19	27	0	1.000

WORLD SERIES RECORD

RECORDS: Holds record for most strikeouts in one inning—2 (October 23, 1997, sixth inning).
NOTES: Member of World Series championship team (1997).

Year Team (League)	Pos.	G	AB	R	H	2B	3B	HR	RBI	Avg.	BB	SO	SB	PO	A	E	Avg.
1997— Florida (N.L.)	SS	7	31	3	9	2	0	0	3	.290	3	5	0	12	26	1	.974

ALL-STAR GAME RECORD

Year League	Pos.	AB	R	H	2B	3B	HR	RBI	Avg.	BB	SO	SB	PO	A	E	Avg.
1998— National	SS	1	1	0	0	0	0	0	.000	0	0	0	3	0	1.000
2000— National	SS	2	0	0	0	0	0	0	.000	0	0	0	0	2	0	1.000
All-Star Game totals (2 years)		3	1	0	0	0	0	0	.000	0	0	0	0	5	0	1.000

REYES, AL   P   DODGERS

PERSONAL: Born April 10, 1971, in San Cristobal, Dominican Republic. ... 6-1/206. ... Throws right, bats right. ... Full name: Rafael Alberto Reyes.
HIGH SCHOOL: Francisco del Rosario Sanche (Santo Domingo, Dominican Republic).
TRANSACTIONS/CAREER NOTES: Signed as non-drafted free agent by Montreal Expos organization (February 17, 1988). ... On disabled list (May 23, 1991-remainder of season). ... Selected by Milwaukee Brewers from Expos organization in Rule 5 major league draft (December 5, 1994). ... On disabled list (July 19, 1995-remainder of season). ... On New Orleans disabled list (April 4-August 2, 1996). ... On Milwaukee disabled list (July 25-September 8, 1998); included rehabilitation assignment to Louisville (September 1-8). ... Traded by Brewers to Baltimore Orioles (July 21, 1999), completing deal in which Orioles traded P Rocky Coppinger to Brewers for a player to be named later (July 16, 1999). ... Traded by Orioles to Los Angeles Dodgers for P Alan Mills and cash considerations (June 13, 2000).

Year League	W	L	Pct.	ERA	G	GS	CG	ShO	Sv.	IP	H	R	ER	BB	SO
1989— Dom. Expos (DSL)	3	4	.429	2.79	12	10	1	0	0	71	68	36	22	33	49
1990— West Palm Beach (FSL)	5	4	.556	4.74	16	10	0	0	1	57	58	32	30	32	47
1991— Rockford (Midw.)	0	1	.000	5.56	3	3	0	0	0	11 1/3	14	8	7	2	10
1992— Albany (S.Atl.)	0	2	.000	3.95	27	0	0	0	4	27 1/3	24	14	12	13	29
1993— Burlington (Midw.)	7	6	.538	2.68	53	0	0	0	11	74	52	33	22	26	80
1994— Harrisburg (East.)	2	2	.500	3.25	60	0	0	0	*35	69 1/3	68	26	25	13	60
1995— Milwaukee (A.L.)■	1	1	.500	2.43	27	0	0	0	1	33 1/3	19	9	9	18	29
1996— Beloit (Midw.)	1	0	1.000	1.83	13	0	0	0	0	19 2/3	17	7	4	6	22
— Milwaukee (A.L.)	1	0	1.000	7.94	5	0	0	0	0	5 2/3	8	5	5	2	2
1997— Tucson (PCL)	2	4	.333	5.02	38	0	0	0	7	57 1/3	52	39	32	34	70
— Milwaukee (A.L.)	1	2	.333	5.46	19	0	0	0	1	29 2/3	32	19	18	9	28
1998— Milwaukee (N.L.)	5	1	.833	3.95	50	0	0	0	0	57	55	26	25	31	58
— Louisville (I.L.)	0	1	.000	8.31	3	2	0	0	0	4 1/3	5	5	4	2	5
1999— Louisville (I.L.)	0	2	.000	8.38	6	0	0	0	0	9 2/3	12	9	9	7	8
— Milwaukee (N.L.)	2	0	1.000	4.25	26	0	0	0	0	36	27	17	17	25	39
— Baltimore (A.L.)■	2	3	.400	4.85	27	0	0	0	0	29 2/3	23	16	16	16	28
2000— Rochester (I.L.)	0	1	.000	7.71	9	0	0	0	2	11 2/3	13	11	10	9	17
— Baltimore (A.L.)	1	0	1.000	6.92	13	0	0	0	0	13	13	10	10	11	10
— Albuquerque (PCL)■	3	2	.600	3.72	30	0	0	0	8	38 2/3	33	20	16	21	39
— Los Angeles (N.L.)	0	0	...	0.00	6	0	0	0	0	6 2/3	2	0	0	1	8
A.L. totals (5 years)	6	6	.500	4.69	91	0	0	0	2	111 1/3	95	59	58	56	97
N.L. totals (3 years)	7	1	.875	3.79	82	0	0	0	0	99 2/3	84	43	42	57	105
Major League totals (6 years)	13	7	.650	4.27	173	0	0	0	2	211	179	102	100	113	202

REYES, CARLOS   P   PADRES

PERSONAL: Born April 4, 1969, in Miami. ... 6-0/190. ... Throws right, bats both. ... Full name: Carlos Alberto Reyes.
HIGH SCHOOL: Tampa Catholic.
JUNIOR COLLEGE: Brevard Community College (Fla.).
COLLEGE: Florida Southern.
TRANSACTIONS/CAREER NOTES: Signed as non-drafted free agent by Atlanta Braves organization (June 21, 1991). ... Selected by Oakland Athletics from Braves organization in Rule 5 major league draft (December 13, 1993). ... On Oakland disabled list (July 18-August 4, 1994); included rehabilitation assignment to Modesto (July 25-30). ... Granted free agency (December 20, 1996). ... Signed by New York Yankees organization (February 6, 1997). ... Released by Yankees (April 8, 1997). ... Signed by A's (April 10, 1997). ... On Oakland disabled list (August 21-September 12, 1997); included rehabilitation assignment to Edmonton (September 3-12). ... Granted free agency (October 15, 1997). ... Signed by San Diego Padres (November 7, 1997). ... Traded by Padres with P Dario Veras and C Mandy Romero to Boston Red Sox for C Jim Leyritz and OF Ethan Faggett (June 21, 1998). ... Released by Red Sox (December 14, 1998). ... Signed by Padres organization (February 4, 1999). ... Claimed on waivers by Philadelphia Phillies (October 6, 1999). ... On Philadelphia disabled list (March 29-April 13, 2000); included rehabilitation assignment to Reading (April 10-13). ... Released by Phillies (May 11, 2000). ... Signed by Padres organization (May 22, 2000).

Year League	W	L	Pct.	ERA	G	GS	CG	ShO	Sv.	IP	H	R	ER	BB	SO
1991— Gulf Coast Braves (GCL)	3	2	.600	1.77	20	0	0	0	5	45²/₃	44	15	9	9	37
1992— Macon (S.Atl.)	2	3	.400	2.10	23	0	0	0	2	60	57	16	14	11	57
— Durham (Caro.)	2	1	.667	2.43	21	0	0	0	5	40²/₃	31	11	11	10	33
1993— Greenville (Sou.)	8	1	.889	2.06	33	2	0	0	2	70	64	22	16	24	57
— Richmond (I.L.)	1	0	1.000	3.77	18	1	0	0	1	28²/₃	30	12	12	11	30
1994— Oakland (A.L.)■	0	3	.000	4.15	27	9	0	0	1	78	71	38	36	44	57
— Modesto (Calif.)	0	0	...	0.00	3	3	0	0	0	5	2	0	0	0	3
1995— Oakland (A.L.)	4	6	.400	5.09	40	1	0	0	0	69	71	43	39	28	48
1996— Oakland (A.L.)	7	10	.412	4.78	46	10	0	0	0	122¹/₃	134	71	65	61	78
1997— Columbus (I.L.)■	0	0	...	18.00	1	1	0	0	0	2	5	4	4	0	2
— Edmonton (PCL)■	2	0	1.000	3.48	5	4	1	0	0	31	30	14	12	3	23
— Oakland (A.L.)	3	4	.429	5.82	37	6	0	0	0	77¹/₃	101	52	50	25	43
1998— Las Vegas (PCL)■	0	0	...	0.00	1	0	0	0	0	1²/₃	1	0	0	0	2
— San Diego (N.L.)	2	2	.500	3.58	22	0	0	0	1	27²/₃	23	11	11	6	24
— Boston (A.L.)■	1	1	.500	3.52	24	0	0	0	0	38¹/₃	35	15	15	14	23
1999— San Diego (N.L.)■	2	4	.333	3.72	65	0	0	0	1	77¹/₃	76	38	32	24	57
2000— Reading (East.)■	0	0	...	0.00	2	0	0	0	0	3	1	0	0	0	3
— Philadelphia (N.L.)	0	2	.000	5.23	10	0	0	0	0	10¹/₃	10	6	6	5	4
— Las Vegas (PCL)■	0	2	.000	2.86	16	0	0	0	1	28¹/₃	28	13	9	9	24
— San Diego (N.L.)	1	1	.500	6.00	12	0	0	0	1	18	15	12	12	8	13
A.L. totals (5 years)	15	24	.385	4.79	174	26	0	0	1	385	412	219	205	172	249
N.L. totals (3 years)	5	9	.357	4.12	109	0	0	0	3	133¹/₃	124	67	61	43	98
Major League totals (7 years)	20	33	.377	4.62	283	26	0	0	4	518¹/₃	536	286	266	215	347

REYES, DENNYS   P   REDS

PERSONAL: Born April 19, 1977, in Higuera de Zaragoza, Mexico. ... 6-3/246. ... Throws left, bats right.
HIGH SCHOOL: Ignacio Zaragoza (Higuera de Zaragoza, Mexico).
TRANSACTIONS/CAREER NOTES: Signed as non-drafted free agent by Los Angeles Dodgers organization (July 5, 1993). ... Traded by Dodgers with 1B/3B Paul Konerko to Cincinnati Reds for P Jeff Shaw (July 4, 1998).

Year League	W	L	Pct.	ERA	G	GS	CG	ShO	Sv.	IP	H	R	ER	BB	SO
1994— Vero Beach (FSL)	2	4	.333	6.70	9	9	0	0	0	41²/₃	58	37	31	18	25
— Great Falls (Pio.)	7	1	.875	3.78	14	9	0	0	0	66²/₃	71	37	28	25	70
1995— Vero Beach (FSL)	1	0	1.000	1.80	3	2	0	0	0	10	8	2	2	6	9
— M.C. Red Devils (Mex.)■	5	5	.500	6.60	17	15	1	0	0	58¹/₃	76	49	43	41	44
1996— San Bernardino (Calif.)■	11	12	.478	4.17	29	•28	0	0	■	166	166	106	77	77	176
1997— San Antonio (Texas)	8	1	.889	3.02	12	12	1	0	0	80¹/₃	79	33	27	28	66
— Albuquerque (PCL)	6	3	.667	5.65	10	10	1	0	0	57¹/₃	70	40	36	33	45
— Los Angeles (N.L.)	2	3	.400	3.83	14	5	0	0	0	47	51	21	20	18	36
1998— Albuquerque (PCL)	1	4	.200	1.44	7	7	1	1	0	43²/₃	31	13	7	18	58
— Los Angeles (N.L.)	0	4	.000	4.71	11	3	0	0	0	28²/₃	27	17	15	20	33
— Indianapolis (I.L.)■	2	0	1.000	3.00	4	4	0	0	0	24	20	10	8	14	27
— Cincinnati (N.L.)	3	1	.750	4.42	8	7	0	0	0	38²/₃	35	19	19	27	44
1999— Cincinnati (N.L.)	2	2	.500	3.79	65	1	0	0	2	61²/₃	53	30	26	39	72
2000— Cincinnati (N.L.)	2	1	.667	4.53	62	0	0	0	0	43²/₃	43	31	22	29	36
Major League totals (4 years)	9	11	.450	4.18	160	16	0	0	2	219²/₃	209	118	102	133	221

REYNOLDS, SHANE   P   ASTROS

PERSONAL: Born March 26, 1968, in Bastrop, La. ... 6-3/210. ... Throws right, bats right. ... Full name: Richard Shane Reynolds.
HIGH SCHOOL: Ouachita Christian (Monroe, La.).
JUNIOR COLLEGE: Faulkner State Junior College (Ala.).
COLLEGE: Texas.
TRANSACTIONS/CAREER NOTES: Selected by Houston Astros organization in third round of free-agent draft (June 5, 1989). ... On Houston disabled list (June 10-July 14, 1997); included rehabilitation assignment to New Orleans (July 10-14). ... On disabled list (August 2, 2000-remainder of season).
STATISTICAL NOTES: Led N.L. with 17 sacrifice hits in 1999. ... Led N.L. pitchers with a 1.000 fielding percentage in 1999.
MISCELLANEOUS: Appeared in one game as pinch runner (1995).

Year League	W	L	Pct.	ERA	G	GS	CG	ShO	Sv.	IP	H	R	ER	BB	SO
1989— Auburn (NY-Penn)	3	2	.600	2.31	6	6	1	0	0	35	36	16	9	14	23
— Asheville (S.Atl.)	5	3	.625	3.68	8	8	2	1	0	51¹/₃	53	25	21	21	33
1990— Columbus (Sou.)	9	10	.474	4.81	29	27	2	1	0	155¹/₃	•181	104	83	70	92
1991— Jackson (Texas)	8	9	.471	4.47	27	•27	2	0	0	151	165	93	75	62	116
1992— Tucson (PCL)	9	8	.529	3.68	25	22	2	0	1	142	156	73	58	34	106
— Houston (N.L.)	1	3	.250	7.11	8	5	0	0	0	25¹/₃	42	22	20	6	10
1993— Tucson (PCL)	10	6	.625	3.62	25	20	2	0	1	139¹/₃	147	74	56	21	106
— Houston (N.L.)	0	0	...	0.82	5	1	0	0	0	11	11	4	1	6	10
1994— Houston (N.L.)	8	5	.615	3.05	33	14	1	1	0	124	128	46	42	21	110
1995— Houston (N.L.)	10	11	.476	3.47	30	30	3	2	0	189¹/₃	196	87	73	37	175
1996— Houston (N.L.)	16	10	.615	3.65	35	35	4	1	0	239	227	103	97	44	204
1997— Houston (N.L.)	9	10	.474	4.23	30	30	2	0	0	181	189	92	85	47	152
— New Orleans (A.A.)	1	0	1.000	0.00	1	1	0	0	0	5	3	0	0	1	6
1998— Houston (N.L.)	19	8	.704	3.51	35	•35	3	1	0	233¹/₃	257	99	91	53	209
1999— Houston (N.L.)	16	14	.533	3.85	35	•35	4	2	0	231²/₃	250	108	99	37	197
2000— Houston (N.L.)	7	8	.467	5.22	22	22	0	0	0	131	150	86	76	45	93
Major League totals (9 years)	86	69	.555	3.85	233	207	17	7	0	1365²/₃	1450	647	584	296	1160

DIVISION SERIES RECORD

Year — League	W	L	Pct.	ERA	G	GS	CG	ShO	Sv.	IP	H	R	ER	BB	SO
1997— Houston (N.L.)	0	1	.000	3.00	1	1	0	0	0	6	5	2	2	1	5
1998— Houston (N.L.)	0	0	...	2.57	1	1	0	0	0	7	4	2	2	1	5
1999— Houston (N.L.)	1	1	.500	4.09	2	2	0	0	0	11	16	5	5	3	5
Division series totals (3 years)	1	2	.333	3.38	4	4	0	0	0	24	25	9	9	5	15

ALL-STAR GAME RECORD

Year — League	W	L	Pct.	ERA	GS	CG	ShO	Sv.	IP	H	R	ER	BB	SO
2000— National							Did not play.							

REYNOSO, ARMANDO   P   DIAMONDBACKS

PERSONAL: Born May 1, 1966, in San Luis Potosi, Mexico. ... 6-0/204. ... Throws right, bats right. ... Full name: Martin Armando Gutierrez Reynoso. ... Name pronounced ray-NO-so.

HIGH SCHOOL: Escuela Secandaria Mita del Estado (Jalisco, Mexico).

TRANSACTIONS/CAREER NOTES: Signed as free agent by Saltillo of Mexican League (1988). ... Contract sold by Saltillo to Atlanta Braves organization (August 15, 1990). ... Selected by Colorado Rockies in third round (58th pick overall) of expansion draft (November 17, 1992). ... On disabled list (May 21, 1994-remainder of season). ... On Colorado disabled list (April 17-June 18, 1995); included rehabilitation assignments to Colorado Springs (May 9-20 and June 8-14). ... Traded by Rockies to New York Mets for P Jerry Dipoto (November 27, 1996). ... On New York disabled list (March 24-April 15 and July 17, 1997-remainder of season); included rehabilitation assignment to St. Lucie (April 5-15). ... On New York disabled list (March 24-July 24, 1998); included rehabilitation assignments to St. Lucie (June 18-July 3) and Norfolk (July 12-17). ... Granted free agency (October 26, 1998). ... Signed by Arizona Diamondbacks (December 2, 1998). ... Granted free agency (November 1, 2000). ... Re-signed by Diamondbacks (December 6, 2000).

STATISTICAL NOTES: Led International League with six balks in 1991 and five in 1992. ... Tied for International League lead with 10 hit batsmen in 1991.

MISCELLANEOUS: Appeared in one game as pinch runner with Colorado (1993).

Year — League	W	L	Pct.	ERA	G	GS	CG	ShO	Sv.	IP	H	R	ER	BB	SO
1988— Saltillo (Mex.)	11	11	.500	4.30	32	29	10	2	2	180	176	98	86	85	92
1989— Saltillo (Mex.)	13	9	.591	3.48	27	25	7	2	0	160 1/3	155	78	62	64	107
1990— Saltillo (Mex.)	*20	3	.870	2.60	27	•27	12	5	0	200 2/3	174	61	58	73	*170
— Richmond (I.L.)■	3	1	.750	2.25	4	3	0	0	0	24	26	7	6	7	15
1991— Richmond (I.L.)	10	6	.625	*2.61	22	19	3	•3	0	131	117	44	38	39	97
— Atlanta (N.L.)	2	1	.667	6.17	6	5	0	0	0	23 1/3	26	18	16	10	10
1992— Richmond (I.L.)	12	9	.571	2.66	28	27	4	1	0	169 1/3	156	65	50	52	108
— Atlanta (N.L.)	1	0	1.000	4.70	3	1	0	0	1	7 2/3	11	4	4	2	2
1993— Colorado Springs (PCL)■	2	1	.667	3.22	4	4	0	0	0	22 1/3	19	10	8	8	22
— Colorado (N.L.)	12	11	.522	4.00	30	30	4	0	0	189	206	101	84	63	117
1994— Colorado (N.L.)	3	4	.429	4.82	9	9	1	0	0	52 1/3	54	30	28	22	25
1995— Colorado Springs (PCL)	2	1	.667	1.57	5	5	0	0	0	23	14	4	4	6	17
— Colorado (N.L.)	7	7	.500	5.32	20	18	0	0	0	93	116	61	55	36	40
1996— Colorado (N.L.)	8	9	.471	4.96	30	30	0	0	0	168 2/3	195	97	93	49	88
1997— St. Lucie (FSL)■	1	1	.500	2.70	2	2	0	0	0	10	9	3	3	1	6
— New York (N.L.)	6	3	.667	4.53	16	16	1	1	0	91 1/3	95	47	46	29	47
1998— St. Lucie (FSL)	0	1	.000	3.75	4	4	0	0	0	12	14	6	5	1	6
— Norfolk (I.L.)	0	2	.000	10.61	2	2	0	0	0	9 1/3	14	11	11	4	8
— New York (N.L.)	7	3	.700	3.82	11	11	0	0	0	68 1/3	64	31	29	32	40
1999— Arizona (N.L.)■	10	6	.625	4.37	31	27	0	0	0	167	178	90	81	67	79
2000— Arizona (N.L.)	11	12	.478	5.27	31	30	2	0	0	170 2/3	179	102	100	52	89
Major League totals (10 years)	67	56	.545	4.68	187	177	8	1	1	1031 1/3	1124	581	536	362	537

DIVISION SERIES RECORD

Year — League	W	L	Pct.	ERA	G	GS	CG	ShO	Sv.	IP	H	R	ER	BB	SO
1995— Colorado (N.L.)	0	0	...	0.00	1	0	0	0	0	1	2	0	0	0	0
1999— Arizona (N.L.)							Did not play.							

RHODES, ARTHUR   P   MARINERS

PERSONAL: Born October 24, 1969, in Waco, Texas. ... 6-2/205. ... Throws left, bats left. ... Full name: Arthur Lee Rhodes Jr. ... Brother of Ricky Rhodes, pitcher in New York Yankees organization (1988-92).

HIGH SCHOOL: LaVega (Waco, Texas).

TRANSACTIONS/CAREER NOTES: Selected by Baltimore Orioles organization in second round of free-agent draft (June 1, 1988). ... On Hagerstown disabled list (May 13-June 5, 1991). ... On Baltimore disabled list (May 16-August 2, 1993); included rehabilitation assignment to Rochester (July 4-August 2). ... On Baltimore disabled list (May 2-20, 1994); included rehabilitation assignment to Frederick (May 16-20). ... On Baltimore disabled list (August 25, 1995-remainder of season). ... On disabled list (July 14-August 2 and August 6-September 27, 1996). ... On Baltimore disabled list (July 5-August 17, 1998); included rehabilitation assignment to Rochester (August 15-17). ... Granted free agency (November 1, 1999). ... Signed by Seattle Mariners (December 21, 1999).

HONORS: Named Eastern League Pitcher of the Year (1991).

MISCELLANEOUS: Appeared in one game as pinch runner (1997).

Year — League	W	L	Pct.	ERA	G	GS	CG	ShO	Sv.	IP	H	R	ER	BB	SO
1988— Bluefield (Appl.)	3	4	.429	3.31	11	7	0	0	0	35 1/3	29	17	13	15	44
1989— Erie (NY-Penn)	2	1	1.000	1.16	5	5	1	0	0	31	13	7	4	10	45
— Frederick (Caro.)	2	2	.500	5.18	7	6	0	0	0	24 1/3	19	16	14	19	28
1990— Frederick (Caro.)	4	6	.400	2.12	13	13	3	0	0	80 2/3	62	25	19	21	103
— Hagerstown (East.)	3	4	.429	3.73	12	12	0	0	0	72 1/3	62	32	30	39	60
1991— Hagerstown (East.)	7	4	.636	2.70	19	19	2	2	0	106 2/3	73	37	32	47	115
— Baltimore (A.L.)	0	3	.000	8.00	8	8	0	0	0	36	47	35	32	23	23
1992— Rochester (I.L.)	6	6	.500	3.72	17	17	1	0	0	101 2/3	84	48	42	46	115
— Baltimore (A.L.)	7	5	.583	3.63	15	15	2	1	0	94 1/3	87	39	38	38	77

– 478 –

Year	League	W	L	Pct.	ERA	G	GS	CG	ShO	Sv.	IP	H	R	ER	BB	SO
1993—	Baltimore (A.L.)..........	5	6	.455	6.51	17	17	0	0	0	85 2/3	91	62	62	49	49
—	Rochester (I.L.).............	1	1	.500	4.05	6	6	0	0	0	26 2/3	26	12	12	15	33
1994—	Baltimore (A.L.)..........	3	5	.375	5.81	10	10	3	2	0	52 2/3	51	34	34	30	47
—	Frederick (Caro.)	0	0	...	0.00	1	1	0	0	0	5	3	0	0	0	7
—	Rochester (I.L.).............	7	5	.583	2.79	15	15	3	0	0	90 1/3	70	41	28	34	86
1995—	Rochester (I.L.)	2	1	.667	2.70	4	4	1	0	0	30	27	12	9	8	33
—	Baltimore (A.L.)...........	2	5	.286	6.21	19	9	0	0	0	75 1/3	68	53	52	48	77
1996—	Baltimore (A.L.)..........	9	1	.900	4.08	28	2	0	0	1	53	48	28	24	23	62
1997—	Baltimore (A.L.)..........	10	3	.769	3.02	53	0	0	0	1	95 1/3	75	32	32	26	102
1998—	Baltimore (A.L.)..........	4	4	.500	3.51	45	0	0	0	4	77	65	30	30	34	83
—	Rochester (I.L.).............	0	0	...	4.50	1	1	0	0	0	2	3	1	1	1	1
1999—	Baltimore (A.L.)..........	3	4	.429	5.43	43	0	0	0	3	53	43	37	32	45	59
2000—	Seattle (A.L.)	5	8	.385	4.28	72	0	0	0	0	69 1/3	51	34	33	29	77
Major League totals (10 years).....		48	44	.522	4.80	310	61	5	3	9	691 2/3	626	384	369	345	656

DIVISION SERIES RECORD

Year	League	W	L	Pct.	ERA	G	GS	CG	ShO	Sv.	IP	H	R	ER	BB	SO
1996—	Baltimore (A.L.).............	0	0	...	9.00	2	0	0	0	0	1	1	1	1	1	1
1997—	Baltimore (A.L.).............	0	0	...	0.00	1	0	0	0	0	2 1/3	0	0	0	0	4
2000—	Seattle (A.L.)	0	0	...	0.00	3	0	0	0	0	2 2/3	0	0	0	2	2
Division series totals (3 years)		0	0	...	1.50	6	0	0	0	0	6	1	1	1	3	7

CHAMPIONSHIP SERIES RECORD

Year	League	W	L	Pct.	ERA	G	GS	CG	ShO	Sv.	IP	H	R	ER	BB	SO
1996—	Baltimore (A.L.).............	0	0	...	0.00	3	0	0	0	0	2	2	0	0	0	2
1997—	Baltimore (A.L.).............	0	0	...	0.00	2	0	0	0	0	2 1/3	2	0	0	3	2
2000—	Seattle (A.L.)	0	1	.000	31.50	4	0	0	0	0	2	8	7	7	4	5
Champ. series totals (3 years)		0	1	.000	9.95	9	0	0	0	0	6 1/3	12	7	7	7	9

RICHARD, CHRIS — 1B/OF — ORIOLES

PERSONAL: Born June 7, 1974, in San Diego. ... 6-2/185. ... Bats left, throws left. ... Full name: Christopher Robert Richard.
HIGH SCHOOL: University City (San Diego).
JUNIOR COLLEGE: San Diego City College, then San Diego Mesa College.
COLLEGE: Oklahoma State.
TRANSACTIONS/CAREER NOTES: Selected by St. Louis Cardinals organization in 19th round of free-agent draft (June 1, 1995). ... On Arkansas disabled list (April 2-June 16, 1998 and July 31-August 11, 1998). ... On Prince William disabled list (June 28-July 16, 1998). ... Traded by Cardinals with P Mark Nussbeck to Baltimore Orioles for P Mike Timlin and cash (July 29, 2000).
STATISTICAL NOTES: Led Texas League first basemen with 119 double plays in 1999. ... Hit home run in first major league at-bat (July 17, 2000).

							BATTING								FIELDING		
Year	Team (League)	Pos.	G	AB	R	H	2B	3B	HR	RBI	Avg.	BB	SO	SB	PO	A	E	Avg.
1995—	New Jersey (NY-P)	1B	75	284	36	80	14	3	3	43	.282	47	31	6	620	43	11	.984
1996—	St. Petersburg (FSL) ..	1B-OF	129	460	65	130	28	6	14	82	.283	57	50	7	1138	58	7	.994
1997—	Arkansas (Texas)	1B-OF	113	390	62	105	24	3	11	58	.269	60	59	6	924	68	10	.990
1998—	Prince Will. (Caro.).....	DH	8	30	5	8	2	0	0	1	.267	1	5	1	0	0	0	...
—	Arkansas (Texas)........	1B	28	89	7	18	5	1	2	17	.202	9	10	0	202	8	3	.986
1999—	Arkansas (Texas)	1B-OF	133	442	78	130	26	3	29	94	.294	43	75	7	1079	68	13	.989
—	Memphis (PCL)	1B	4	17	3	7	2	0	1	4	.412	1	2	0	34	5	0	1.000
2000—	Memphis (PCL)	OF-1B	95	375	64	104	24	0	16	75	.277	50	70	9	274	15	2	.993
—	St. Louis (N.L.)...........	OF-1B	6	16	1	2	0	0	1	1	.125	2	2	0	10	0	0	1.000
—	Baltimore (A.L.)■.......	1B-DH-OF	56	199	38	55	14	2	13	36	.276	15	38	7	443	18	5	.989
American League totals (1 year)			56	199	38	55	14	2	13	36	.276	15	38	7	443	18	5	.989
National League totals (1 year)			6	16	1	2	0	0	1	1	.125	2	2	0	10	0	0	1.000
Major League totals (1 year)			62	215	39	57	14	2	14	37	.265	17	40	7	453	18	5	.989

RICKETTS, CHAD — P — DODGERS

PERSONAL: Born February 12, 1975, in Waterloo, Ont. ... 6-5/225. ... Throws right, bats right. ... Full name: Robert Chad Ricketts.
HIGH SCHOOL: East Lake (Tarpon Springs, Fla.).
JUNIOR COLLEGE: Polk Community College (Fla.).
TRANSACTIONS/CAREER NOTES: Selected by Chicago Cubs organization in ninth round of free-agent draft (June 1, 1995). ... Traded by Cubs with P Terry Adams and a player to be named later to Los Angeles Dodgers for P Ismael Valdes and 2B Eric Young (December 12, 1999); Dodgers acquired P Brian Stephenson to complete deal (December 16, 1999).

Year	League	W	L	Pct.	ERA	G	GS	CG	ShO	Sv.	IP	H	R	ER	BB	SO
1995—	Gulf Coast Cubs (GCL).......	1	0	1.000	0.00	2	2	0	0	0	9	1	1	0	1	5
—	Williamsport (NY-Penn)	4	5	.444	4.19	12	12	0	0	0	68 2/3	89	46	32	16	37
1996—	Rockford (Midw.)	3	8	.273	5.03	37	9	0	0	4	87 2/3	89	60	49	29	70
1997—	Rockford (Midw.)	4	0	1.000	2.48	16	0	0	0	3	29	19	9	8	11	32
—	Daytona (FSL)	3	1	.750	0.44	20	0	0	0	8	20 1/3	13	4	1	6	18
—	Orlando (Sou.)	0	0	...	18.00	2	0	0	0	2	2	7	4	4	2	3
1998—	Daytona (FSL)	2	1	.667	1.84	47	0	0	0	19	49	41	15	10	11	59
—	West Tenn (Sou.)	0	2	.000	3.52	13	0	0	0	6	15 1/3	19	7	6	4	13
1999—	West Tenn (Sou.)	6	4	.600	3.09	57	0	0	0	8	67	55	25	23	21	80
2000—	Albuquerque■...............	6	2	.750	3.46	54	0	0	0	7	67 2/3	59	35	26	36	75

RIEDLING, JOHN — P — REDS

PERSONAL: Born August 29, 1975, in Fort Lauderdale, Fla. ... 5-11/190. ... Throws right, bats right. ... Full name: John Richard Riedling Jr.
HIGH SCHOOL: Ely (Pompano Beach, Fla.).
TRANSACTIONS/CAREER NOTES: Selected by Cincinnati Reds organization in 22nd round of free-agent draft (June 2, 1994). ... Released by Reds (December 14, 1998). ... Re-signed by Reds organization (January 5, 1999).

Year League	W	L	Pct.	ERA	G	GS	CG	ShO	Sv.	IP	H	R	ER	BB	SO
1994— Billings (Pio.)	4	1	.800	5.48	15	15	0	0	0	44 1/3	62	36	27	28	27
1995— Billings (Pio.)	2	2	.500	7.04	13	7	0	0	1	38 1/3	51	38	30	21	28
1996— Charleston, W.Va. (S.Atl.)	6	10	.375	3.99	26	26	0	0	0	140	135	85	62	66	90
1997— Burlington (Midw.)	4	6	.400	5.26	35	16	0	0	0	102 2/3	101	70	60	47	104
1998— Chattanooga (Sou.)	3	10	.231	5.00	24	20	0	0	0	102 2/3	112	70	57	60	86
1999— Chattanooga (Sou.)	9	5	.643	3.43	40	0	0	0	5	42	41	23	16	20	38
— Indianapolis (I.L.)	1	0	1.000	1.54	24	0	0	0	1	35	19	9	6	18	24
2000— Louisville (I.L.)	6	3	.667	2.52	53	0	0	0	5	75	63	24	21	30	75
— Cincinnati (N.L.)	3	1	.750	2.35	13	0	0	0	1	15 1/3	11	7	4	8	18
Major League totals (1 year)	3	1	.750	2.35	13	0	0	0	1	15 1/3	11	7	4	8	18

RIGBY, BRAD — P — ASTROS

PERSONAL: Born May 14, 1973, in Milwaukee. ... 6-6/215. ... Throws right, bats right. ... Full name: Bradley Kenneth Rigby.
HIGH SCHOOL: Lake Brantley (Altamonte Springs, Fla.).
COLLEGE: Georgia Tech.
TRANSACTIONS/CAREER NOTES: Selected by Oakland Athletics organization in second round of free-agent draft (June 2, 1994). ... On Oakland disabled list (August 8-23, 1997; and March 26-April 10, 1998). ... On Edmonton disabled list (July 4-September 10, 1998). ... Traded by A's with P Blake Stein and P Jeff D'Amico to Kansas City Royals for P Kevin Appier (July 31, 1999). ... Traded by Royals to Montreal Expos for P Miguel Batista (April 25, 2000). ... Granted free agency (October 18, 2000). ... Signed by Houston Astros organization (January 8, 2001).

Year League	W	L	Pct.	ERA	G	GS	CG	ShO	Sv.	IP	H	R	ER	BB	SO
1994— Modesto (Calif.)	2	1	.667	3.80	11	1	0	0	2	23 2/3	20	10	10	10	28
1995— Modesto (Calif.)	11	4	.733	3.84	31	23	0	0	2	154 2/3	135	79	66	48	145
1996— Huntsville (Sou.)	9	12	.429	3.95	26	26	3	0	0	159 1/3	161	89	70	59	127
1997— Edmonton (PCL)	8	4	.667	4.37	15	15	0	0	0	82 1/3	95	49	40	26	49
— Oakland (A.L.)	1	7	.125	4.87	14	14	0	0	0	77 2/3	92	44	42	22	34
1998— Edmonton (PCL)	5	6	.455	5.94	13	13	0	0	0	69 2/3	86	52	46	17	34
1999— Oakland (A.L.)	3	4	.429	4.33	29	0	0	0	0	62 1/3	69	31	30	26	26
— Vancouver (PCL)	0	1	1.000	1.93	1	1	0	0	0	4 2/3	6	3	1	2	6
— Kansas City (A.L.)■	1	2	.333	7.17	20	0	0	0	0	21 1/3	33	20	17	5	10
2000— Kansas City (A.L.)	0	0	...	16.20	4	0	0	0	1	8 1/3	19	16	15	5	3
— Montreal (N.L.)■	0	0	...	5.06	6	0	0	0	1	5 1/3	8	5	3	3	2
— Ottawa (I.L.)	3	10	.231	6.67	24	14	0	0	0	83 2/3	117	77	62	26	51
A.L. totals (3 years)	5	13	.278	5.52	67	14	0	0	1	169 2/3	213	111	104	58	73
N.L. totals (1 year)	0	0	...	5.06	6	0	0	0	1	5 1/3	8	5	3	3	2
Major League totals (3 years)	5	13	.278	5.50	73	14	0	0	2	175	221	116	107	61	75

RIGDON, PAUL — P — BREWERS

PERSONAL: Born November 2, 1975, in Jacksonville. ... 6-5/210. ... Throws right, bats right. ... Full name: Paul David Rigdon.
HIGH SCHOOL: Trinity Christian Academy (Jacksonville, Fla.).
COLLEGE: Florida.
TRANSACTIONS/CAREER NOTES: Selected by Cleveland Indians organization in sixth-round of free-agent draft (June 4, 1996). ... On disabled list (June 17, 1997-entire season). ... Traded by Indians with 1B/OF Richie Sexson, P Kane Davis and a player to be named later to Milwaukee Brewers for P Bob Wickman, P Steve Woodard and P Jason Bere (July 28, 2000); Brewers acquired 2B Marcos Scutaro to complete deal (August 30). ... On disabled list (May 22-June 7, 2000).

Year League	W	L	Pct.	ERA	G	GS	CG	ShO	Sv.	IP	H	R	ER	BB	SO
1996— Watertown (NY-Penn)	2	2	.500	4.08	22	0	0	0	6	39 2/3	41	24	18	10	46
1997—					Did not play.										
1998— Kinston (Caro.)	11	7	.611	4.03	24	24	0	0	0	127 1/3	126	65	57	35	97
1999— Akron (East.)	7	0	1.000	0.90	8	7	0	0	0	50	20	5	5	10	25
— Buffalo (I.L.)	7	4	.636	4.53	19	19	0	0	0	103 1/3	114	60	52	28	60
2000— Buffalo (I.L.)	6	1	.857	3.30	12	12	1	0	0	71	72	27	26	18	41
— Cleveland (A.L.)	1	1	.500	7.64	5	4	0	0	0	17 2/3	21	15	15	9	15
— Milwaukee (N.L.)■	4	4	.500	4.52	12	12	0	0	0	69 2/3	68	37	35	26	48
A.L. totals (1 year)	1	1	.500	7.64	5	4	0	0	0	17 2/3	21	15	15	9	15
N.L. totals (1 year)	4	4	.500	4.52	12	12	0	0	0	69 2/3	68	37	35	26	48
Major League totals (1 year)	5	5	.500	5.15	17	16	0	0	0	87 1/3	89	52	50	35	63

RIGGAN, JERROD — P — METS

PERSONAL: Born May 16, 1974, in Brewster, Wash. ... 6-3/200. ... Throws right, bats right. ... Full name: Jerrod Ashley Riggan.
HIGH SCHOOL: Brewster (Wash.).
COLLEGE: San Diego State.
TRANSACTIONS/CAREER NOTES: Selected by California Angels organization in eighth round of free-agent draft (June 4, 1996). ... Angels franchise renamed Anaheim Angels for 1997 season. ... Released by Angels (April 17, 1998). ... Signed by New York Mets organization (July 9, 1998).

Year League	W	L	Pct.	ERA	G	GS	CG	ShO	Sv.	IP	H	R	ER	BB	SO
1996—Boise (N'West)	3	5	.375	4.63	15	15	•1	0	0	89 1/3	90	62	46	38	80
1997—Cedar Rapids (Midw.)	9	8	.529	4.89	19	19	3	1	0	116	132	70	63	36	65
—Lake Elsinore (Calif.)	2	5	.286	6.07	8	8	0	0	0	43	60	36	29	16	31
1998—Capital City (S.Atl.)■......	4	1	.800	3.70	14	0	0	0	1	41 1/3	38	21	17	14	40
1999—St. Lucie (FSL)	5	5	.500	3.33	44	0	0	0	12	73	69	33	27	24	66
2000—Binghamton (East.)	2	0	1.000	1.11	52	0	0	0	•28	65	43	9	8	18	79
—New York (N.L.)	0	0	...	0.00	1	0	0	0	0	2	3	2	0	0	1
Major League totals (1 year)........	0	0	...	0.00	1	0	0	0	0	2	3	2	0	0	1

RILEY, MATT   P   ORIOLES

R

PERSONAL: Born August 2, 1979, in Antioch, Calif. ... 6-1/201. ... Throws left, bats left. ... Full name: Matthew P. Riley.
HIGH SCHOOL: Linerty Union (Oakley, Calif.).
JUNIOR COLLEGE: Sacramento City College.
TRANSACTIONS/CAREER NOTES: Selected by Baltimore Orioles organization in third round of free-agent draft (June 3, 1997). ... On Bowie disabled list (June 30-July 8, 1999). ... On Rochester disabled list (April 16-May 28, 2000). ... On Baltimore disabled list (September 29, 2000-remainder of season).

Year League	W	L	Pct.	ERA	G	GS	CG	ShO	Sv.	IP	H	R	ER	BB	SO
1998—Delmarva (S.Atl.)...............	5	4	.556	1.19	16	14	0	0	0	83	42	19	11	44	136
1999—Frederick (Caro.)	3	2	.600	2.61	8	8	0	0	0	51 2/3	34	19	15	14	58
—Bowie (East.)...................	10	6	.625	3.22	20	20	3	0	0	125 2/3	113	53	45	42	131
—Baltimore (A.L.)...............	0	0	...	7.36	3	3	0	0	0	11	17	9	9	13	6
2000—Rochester (I.L.)..............	0	2	.000	14.14	2	2	0	0	0	7	15	12	11	4	8
—Bowie (East.)	5	7	.417	6.08	19	14	2	0	1	74	74	56	50	49	66
Major League totals (1 year)........	0	0	...	7.36	3	3	0	0	0	11	17	9	9	13	6

RILEY, MICHAEL   P   GIANTS

PERSONAL: Born January 2, 1975, in Milford, Del. ... 6-1/162. ... Throws left, bats left. ... Full name: Michael Eugene Riley.
HIGH SCHOOL: Seaford (Del.).
COLLEGE: West Virginia.
TRANSACTIONS/CAREER NOTES: Selected by San Francisco Giants organization in 16th round of free-agent draft (June 4, 1996). ... On Fresno disabled list (August 28-September 10, 2000). ... On San Francisco disabled list (September 11, 2000-remainder of season).

Year League	W	L	Pct.	ERA	G	GS	CG	ShO	Sv.	IP	H	R	ER	BB	SO
1996—Bellingham (N'West)	1	3	.250	4.17	17	3	0	0	0	36 2/3	38	26	17	29	38
1997—Bakersfield (Calif.)............	1	2	.333	8.41	8	4	0	0	0	20 1/3	25	20	19	8	17
—Salem-Kaizer (N'West)	•9	2	.818	3.46	15	15	•1	0	0	88 1/3	76	39	34	28	*96
1998—Bakersfield (Calif.)............	6	12	.333	4.50	40	15	2	0	2	128	130	73	64	58	110
1999—Shreveport (Texas)	8	3	.727	2.11	30	13	1	1	1	111	80	35	26	53	107
2000—Fresno (PCL)	6	8	.429	5.91	24	24	0	0	0	128	141	92	84	54	114

RINCON, RICKY   P   INDIANS

PERSONAL: Born April 13, 1970, in Veracruz, Mexico ... 5-10/187. ... Throws left, bats left. ... Full name: Ricardo Rincon Espinoza.
TRANSACTIONS/CAREER NOTES: Signed as non-drafted free agent by Pittsburgh Pirates organization (March 30, 1997). ... On Pittsburgh disabled list (March 22-April 14, 1998); included rehabilitation assignments to Carolina (April 6) and Nashville (April 11-April 14). ... Traded by Pirates to Cleveland Indians for OF Brian Giles (November 18, 1998). ... On Cleveland disabled list (April 12-May 14, 1999); included rehabilitation assignment to Akron (May 11-14). ... On Cleveland disabled list (May 17-August 23, 2000); included rehabilitation assignment to Buffalo (August 20-23).

Year League	W	L	Pct.	ERA	G	GS	CG	ShO	Sv.	IP	H	R	ER	BB	SO
1990—Union Laguna (Mex.)	3	0	1.000	3.78	19	4	0	0	0	47 2/3	53	22	20	32	29
1991—Union Laguna (Mex.)	2	8	.200	6.54	32	9	0	0	1	74 1/3	99	60	54	48	66
1992—Union Laguna (Mex.)	6	5	.545	3.91	49	9	0	0	4	89 2/3	87	45	39	46	91
1993—Torreon (Mex.)■	7	3	.700	3.17	57	4	0	0	8	82 1/3	80	33	29	36	81
1994—M.C. Red Devils (Mex.)■...	2	4	.333	3.21	20	9	0	0	1	53 1/3	57	23	19	20	38
1995—M.C. Red Devils (Mex.)	6	6	.500	5.16	27	11	0	0	3	75	86	45	43	41	41
1996—M.C. Red Devils (Mex.)	5	3	.625	2.97	50	0	0	0	10	78 2/3	58	28	26	27	60
1997—Pittsburgh (N.L.)■	4	8	.333	3.45	62	0	0	0	4	60	51	26	23	24	71
1998—Carolina (Sou.)	0	0	...	6.00	2	0	0	0	0	3	5	2	2	2	1
—Nashville (PCL)	0	0	...	0.00	1	0	0	0	0	1	0	0	0	0	1
—Pittsburgh (N.L.)	0	2	.000	2.91	60	0	0	0	14	65	50	31	21	29	64
1999—Cleveland (A.L.)■	2	3	.400	4.43	59	0	0	0	0	44 2/3	41	22	22	24	30
—Akron (East.)	0	0	...	5.40	2	2	0	0	0	1 2/3	2	1	1	0	2
2000—Cleveland (A.L.)...............	2	0	1.000	2.70	35	0	0	0	0	20	17	7	6	13	20
—Buffalo (I.L.)....................	0	0	...	0.00	2	0	0	0	0	2	1	1	0	0	2
A.L. totals (2 years)	4	3	.571	3.90	94	0	0	0	0	64 2/3	58	29	28	37	50
N.L. totals (2 years)	4	10	.286	3.17	122	0	0	0	18	125	101	57	44	53	135
Major League totals (4 years)	8	13	.381	3.42	216	0	0	0	18	189 2/3	159	86	72	90	185

DIVISION SERIES RECORD

Year League	W	L	Pct.	ERA	G	GS	CG	ShO	Sv.	IP	H	R	ER	BB	SO
1999—Cleveland (A.L.).................	0	0	...	40.50	1	0	0	0	0	2/3	2	3	3	1	1

RIOS, ARMANDO — OF — GIANTS

PERSONAL: Born September 13, 1971, in Santurce, Puerto Rico. ... 5-9/185. ... Bats left, throws left.
HIGH SCHOOL: Villa Fontana (Carolina, Puerto Rico).
COLLEGE: UNC Charlotte, then Louisiana State.
TRANSACTIONS/CAREER NOTES: Signed as non-drafted free agent by San Francisco Giants organization (January 6, 1994). ... On disabled list (May 15-29, 1996). ... On San Francisco disabled list (June 22-September 2, 1999); included rehabilitation assignment to Fresno (July 23-30 and August 12-31).
STATISTICAL NOTES: Career major league grand slams: 1.

Year Team (League)	Pos.	G	AB	R	H	2B	3B	HR	RBI	Avg.	BB	SO	SB	PO	A	E	Avg.
1994— Clinton (Midw.)	OF	119	407	67	120	23	4	8	60	.295	59	69	16	216	17	12	.951
1995— San Jose (Calif.)	OF	128	488	76	143	34	3	8	75	.293	74	75	51	220	16	9	.963
1996— Shreveport (Texas)	OF	92	329	62	93	22	2	12	49	.283	44	42	9	165	*15	7	.963
1997— Shreveport (Texas)	OF-DH	127	461	86	133	30	6	14	79	.289	63	85	17	191	*17	6	.972
1998— Fresno (PCL)	OF-DH-1B	125	445	85	134	23	1	26	103	.301	55	73	17	226	14	7	.972
— San Francisco (N.L.) ..	OF	12	7	3	4	0	0	2	3	.571	3	2	0	5	0	0	1.000
1999— Fresno (PCL)	OF-DH-1B	31	109	24	30	3	0	4	21	.275	11	22	3	28	1	0	1.000
— San Francisco (N.L.) ..	OF	72	150	32	49	9	0	7	29	.327	24	35	7	84	5	2	.978
2000— San Francisco (N.L.) ..	OF-1B	115	233	38	62	15	5	10	50	.266	31	43	3	133	6	6	.959
Major League totals (3 years)		199	390	73	115	24	5	19	82	.295	58	80	10	222	11	8	.967

DIVISION SERIES RECORD

Year Team (League)	Pos.	G	AB	R	H	2B	3B	HR	RBI	Avg.	BB	SO	SB	PO	A	E	Avg.
2000— San Francisco (N.L.) ..	PH	2	2	1	1	0	0	0	0	.500	0	0	0	...	...	0	...

RIPKEN, CAL — 3B — ORIOLES

PERSONAL: Born August 24, 1960, in Havre de Grace, Md. ... 6-4/220. ... Bats right, throws right. ... Full name: Calvin Edwin Ripken Jr. ... Son of Cal Ripken Sr., minor league catcher (1957-62 and 1964), manager with Baltimore Orioles (1987-88) and coach, Orioles (1976-86 and 1989-92); and brother of Bill Ripken, infielder with four major league teams (1987-98).
HIGH SCHOOL: Aberdeen (Md.).
TRANSACTIONS/CAREER NOTES: Selected by Baltimore Orioles organization in second round of free-agent draft (June 6, 1978). ... On disabled list (April 18-May 13 and August 1-September 1, 1999; and June 28-September 1, 2000).
RECORDS: Holds major league career records for most consecutive games played—2,632 (May 30, 1982-September 19, 1998); most years leading league in games played—9; most consecutive years played all club's games—15 (1983-97); most years played all club's games—15 (1983-97); most home runs by shortstop—345; most years leading league in games by shortstop—12; most consecutive games by shortstop—2,216; and most years leading league in double plays by shortstop—8. ... Holds major league single-season records for most at-bats without a triple—646 (1989); highest fielding percentage by shortstop (150 or more games)—.996 (1990); fewest errors by shortstop (150 or more games)—3 (1990). ... Holds A.L. career records for most double plays by shortstop—1,565; most years leading league in putouts by shortstop—6; most consecutive years played 150 or more games—12 (1982-93); and most years with 600 or more at-bats—13. ... Holds A.L. single-season record for most assists by shortstop—583 (1984). ... Shares A.L. career records for most years leading league in assists by shortstop—7; and most years with 150 or more games played—14.
HONORS: Named A.L. Rookie Player of the Year by THE SPORTING NEWS (1982). ... Named A.L. Rookie of the Year by Baseball Writers' Association of America (1982). ... Named Major League Player of the Year by THE SPORTING NEWS (1983 and 1991). ... Named A.L. Player of the Year by THE SPORTING NEWS (1983 and 1991). ... Named shortstop on THE SPORTING NEWS A.L. All-Star team (1983-85, 1989, 1991 and 1993-95). ... Named shortstop on THE SPORTING NEWS A.L. Silver Slugger team (1983-86, 1989, 1991 and 1993-94). ... Named A.L. Most Valuable Player by Baseball Writers' Association of America (1983 and 1991). ... Won A.L. Gold Glove at shortstop (1991-92). ... Named Sportsman of the Year by THE SPORTING NEWS (1995).
STATISTICAL NOTES: Tied for Appalachian League lead in double plays by shortstop with 31 in 1978. ... Led Southern League third basemen with .933 fielding percentage, 119 putouts, 268 assists, 415 total chances and 34 double plays in 1980. ... Tied for Southern League lead with nine sacrifice flies in 1980. ... Led A.L. shortstops with 831 total chances in 1983, 906 in 1984, 815 in 1989, 806 in 1991 and 738 in 1993. ... Led A.L. shortstops with 113 double plays in 1983, 122 in 1984, 123 in 1985, 119 in 1989, 114 in 1991, 119 in 1992, 72 in 1994 and 100 in 1995. ... Hit for the cycle (May 6, 1984). ... Tied for A.L. lead with 15 game-winning RBIs in 1986. ... Tied for A.L. lead with 10 sacrifice flies in 1988. ... Led A.L. with 368 total bases in 1991. ... Hit three home runs in one game (May 28, 1996). ... Led A.L. in grounding into double plays with 28 in 1996. ... Collected six hits in one game (June 13, 1999). ... Career major league grand slams: 8.
MISCELLANEOUS: Holds Baltimore Orioles all-time records for most hits (3,070), runs (1,604), doubles (587), home runs (417) and runs batted in (1,627).

Year Team (League)	Pos.	G	AB	R	H	2B	3B	HR	RBI	Avg.	BB	SO	SB	PO	A	E	Avg.
1978— Bluefield (Appl.)	SS	63	239	27	63	7	1	0	24	.264	24	46	1	*92	204	*33	.900
1979— Miami (FSL)	3B-SS-2B	105	393	51	119	*28	1	5	54	.303	31	64	4	149	260	30	.932
— Charlotte (Sou.)	3B	17	61	6	11	0	1	3	8	.180	3	13	1	13	26	3	.929
1980— Charlotte (Sou.)	3B-SS	•144	522	91	144	28	5	25	78	.276	77	81	4	†151	†341	35	†.934
1981— Rochester (I.L.)	3B-SS	114	437	74	126	31	4	23	75	.288	66	85	0	128	320	21	.955
— Baltimore (A.L.)	SS-3B	23	39	1	5	0	0	0	0	.128	1	8	0	13	30	3	.935
1982— Baltimore (A.L.)	SS-3B	160	598	90	158	32	5	28	93	.264	46	95	3	221	440	19	.972
1983— Baltimore (A.L.)	SS	•162	*663	*121	*211	*47	2	27	102	.318	58	97	0	272	*534	25	.970
1984— Baltimore (A.L.)	SS	•162	641	103	195	37	7	27	86	.304	71	89	2	*297	*583	26	.971
1985— Baltimore (A.L.)	SS	161	642	116	181	32	5	26	110	.282	67	68	2	*286	474	26	.967
1986— Baltimore (A.L.)	SS	162	627	98	177	35	1	25	81	.282	70	60	4	240	*482	13	.982
1987— Baltimore (A.L.)	SS	*162	624	97	157	28	3	27	98	.252	81	77	3	240	*480	20	.973
1988— Baltimore (A.L.)	SS	161	575	87	152	25	1	23	81	.264	102	69	2	*284	480	21	.973
1989— Baltimore (A.L.)	SS	•162	646	80	166	30	0	21	93	.257	57	72	3	*276	*531	8	.990
1990— Baltimore (A.L.)	SS	161	600	78	150	28	4	21	84	.250	82	66	3	242	435	3	*.996
1991— Baltimore (A.L.)	SS	•162	650	99	210	46	5	34	114	.323	53	46	6	*267	*528	11	*.986
1992— Baltimore (A.L.)	SS	*162	637	73	160	29	1	14	72	.251	64	50	4	*287	445	12	.984
1993— Baltimore (A.L.)	SS	*162	*641	87	165	26	3	24	90	.257	65	58	1	226	*495	17	.977

Year	Team (League)	Pos.	G	AB	R	H	2B	3B	HR	RBI	Avg.	BB	SO	SB	PO	A	E	Avg.
								BATTING								FIELDING		
1994— Baltimore (A.L.)..........		SS	112	444	71	140	19	3	13	75	.315	32	41	1	132	321	7	*.985
1995— Baltimore (A.L.)..........		SS	144	550	71	144	33	2	17	88	.262	52	59	0	206	409	7	*.989
1996— Baltimore (A.L.)..........		SS-3B	*163	640	94	178	40	1	26	102	.278	59	78	1	233	483	14	.981
1997— Baltimore (A.L.)..........		3B-SS	•162	615	79	166	30	0	17	84	.270	56	73	1	100	313	22	.949
1998— Baltimore (A.L.)..........		3B	161	601	65	163	27	1	14	61	.271	51	68	0	101	265	8	*.979
1999— Baltimore (A.L.)..........		3B	86	332	51	113	27	0	18	57	.340	13	31	0	36	142	13	.932
2000— Baltimore (A.L.)..........		3B-DH	83	309	43	79	16	0	15	56	.256	23	37	0	56	134	5	.974
Major League totals (20 years)			2873	11074	1604	3070	587	44	417	1627	.277	1103	1242	36	4015	8004	280	.977

DIVISION SERIES RECORD

RECORDS: Holds career record for highest batting average (20 or more at-bats)—.441.

Year	Team (League)	Pos.	G	AB	R	H	2B	3B	HR	RBI	Avg.	BB	SO	SB	PO	A	E	Avg.
								BATTING								FIELDING		
1996— Baltimore (A.L.)..........		SS	4	18	2	8	3	0	0	2	.444	0	3	0	7	15	0	1.000
1997— Baltimore (A.L.)..........		3B	4	16	1	7	2	0	0	1	.438	2	2	0	4	4	0	1.000
Division series totals (2 years)			8	34	3	15	5	0	0	3	.441	2	5	0	11	19	0	1.000

CHAMPIONSHIP SERIES RECORD

Year	Team (League)	Pos.	G	AB	R	H	2B	3B	HR	RBI	Avg.	BB	SO	SB	PO	A	E	Avg.
								BATTING								FIELDING		
1983— Baltimore (A.L.)..........		SS	4	15	5	6	2	0	0	1	.400	2	3	0	7	11	0	1.000
1996— Baltimore (A.L.)..........		SS	5	20	1	5	1	0	0	0	.250	1	4	0	4	14	1	.947
1997— Baltimore (A.L.)..........		3B	6	23	3	8	2	0	1	3	.348	4	6	0	1	14	0	1.000
Championship series totals (3 years)			15	58	9	19	5	0	1	4	.328	7	13	0	12	39	1	.981

WORLD SERIES RECORD

NOTES: Member of World Series championship team (1983).

Year	Team (League)	Pos.	G	AB	R	H	2B	3B	HR	RBI	Avg.	BB	SO	SB	PO	A	E	Avg.
								BATTING								FIELDING		
1983— Baltimore (A.L.)..........		SS	5	18	2	3	0	0	0	1	.167	3	4	0	6	14	0	1.000

ALL-STAR GAME RECORD

RECORDS: Holds major league record for most consecutive games started—16. ... Shares single-game record for most at-bats (nine-inning game)—5 (July 12, 1994).

NOTES: Named Most Valuable Player (1991).

Year	League	Pos.	AB	R	H	2B	3B	HR	RBI	Avg.	BB	SO	SB	PO	A	E	Avg.
							BATTING								FIELDING		
1983— American..................	SS		0	0	0	0	0	0	0	...	1	0	0	1	0	0	1.000
1984— American..................	SS		3	0	0	0	0	0	0	.000	0	0	0	0	0	0	...
1985— American..................	SS		3	0	1	0	0	0	0	.333	0	0	0	2	1	0	1.000
1986— American..................	SS		4	0	0	0	0	0	0	.000	0	0	0	0	1	0	1.000
1987— American..................	SS		2	0	1	0	0	0	0	.500	0	0	0	1	5	0	1.000
1988— American..................	SS		3	0	0	0	0	0	0	.000	1	0	0	1	4	0	1.000
1989— American..................	SS		3	0	1	1	0	0	0	.333	0	0	0	0	0	0	...
1990— American..................	SS		2	0	0	0	0	0	0	.000	0	0	0	1	1	0	1.000
1991— American..................	SS		3	1	2	0	0	1	3	.667	0	0	0	2	1	0	1.000
1992— American..................	SS		3	0	1	0	0	0	1	.333	0	0	0	1	1	0	1.000
1993— American..................	SS		3	0	0	0	0	0	0	.000	0	1	0	1	2	0	1.000
1994— American..................	SS		5	0	1	1	0	0	0	.200	0	2	0	1	2	0	1.000
1995— American..................	SS		3	0	2	0	0	0	0	.667	0	0	0	2	1	0	1.000
1996— American..................	SS		3	0	0	0	0	0	0	.000	0	0	0	1	1	0	1.000
1997— American..................	3B		2	0	1	0	0	0	0	.500	0	0	0	0	4	0	1.000
1998— American..................	3B		4	1	1	1	0	0	2	.250	0	0	0	1	1	0	1.000
1999— American..................	3B		1	1	1	0	0	0	1	1.000	0	0	0	0	0	0	...
2000— American..................								Selected, did not play—injured.										
All-Star Game totals (17 years)			47	3	12	3	0	1	7	.255	2	3	0	14	25	0	1.000

RISKE, DAVE   P   INDIANS

PERSONAL: Born October 23, 1976, in Renton, Wash. ... 6-2/180. ... Throws right, bats right. ... Full name: David R. Riske.
HIGH SCHOOL: Lindbergh (Renton, Wash.).
JUNIOR COLLEGE: Green River (Wash.) Community College.
TRANSACTIONS/CAREER NOTES: Selected by Cleveland Indians organization in 56th round of free-agent draft (June 4, 1996). ... On Cleveland disabled list (March 25-April 28 and May 29-September 4 and September 14, 2000-remainder of season); included rehabilitation assignments to Akron (April 22-26 and August 28-September 4).

Year	League	W	L	Pct.	ERA	G	GS	CG	ShO	Sv.	IP	H	R	ER	BB	SO
1997— Kinston (Caro.)..................		4	4	.500	2.25	39	0	0	0	2	72	58	22	18	33	90
1998— Kinston (Caro.)..................		1	1	.500	2.33	53	0	0	0	*33	54	48	15	14	15	67
— Akron (East.)......................		0	0	...	0.00	2	0	0	0	1	3	1	0	0	1	5
1999— Akron (East.)......................		0	0	...	1.90	23	0	0	0	12	23²/₃	5	6	5	13	33
— Buffalo (I.L.)......................		3	0	1.000	0.65	23	0	0	0	6	27²/₃	14	3	2	7	22
— Cleveland (A.L.).................		1	1	.500	8.36	12	0	0	0	0	14	20	15	13	6	16
2000— Akron (East.)......................		0	0	...	0.00	3	1	0	0	1	4	2	0	0	0	4
— Buffalo (I.L.)......................		0	0	...	3.00	2	0	0	0	0	3	2	1	1	2	2
Major League totals (1 year)........		1	1	.500	8.36	12	0	0	0	0	14	20	15	13	6	16

RITCHIE, TODD   P   PIRATES

PERSONAL: Born November 7, 1971, in Portsmouth, Va. ... 6-3/222. ... Throws right, bats right. ... Full name: Todd Everett Ritchie.
HIGH SCHOOL: Duncanville (Texas).
TRANSACTIONS/CAREER NOTES: Selected by Minnesota Twins organization in first round (12th pick overall) of free-agent draft (June 4, 1990). ... On disabled list (August 19, 1991-remainder of season; June 24-July 9, 1993; and April 28, 1994-remainder of season). ... Released by Twins (October 3, 1998). ... Signed by Pittsburgh Pirates organization (December 22, 1998). ... On Pittsburgh disabled list (August 21-September 6, 1999). ... On disabled list (July 24-August 11, 2000).
MISCELLANEOUS: Grounded out in only appearance as pinch hitter (1999).

Year League	W	L	Pct.	ERA	G	GS	CG	ShO	Sv.	IP	H	R	ER	BB	SO
1990— Elizabethton (Appl.)	5	2	.714	1.94	11	11	1	0	0	65	45	22	14	24	49
1991— Kenosha (Midw.)	7	6	.538	3.55	21	21	0	0	0	116 2/3	113	53	46	50	101
1992— Visalia (Calif.)	11	9	.550	5.06	28	•28	3	1	0	172 2/3	193	113	97	65	129
1993— Nashville (Sou.)	3	2	.600	3.66	12	10	0	0	0	46 2/3	46	21	19	15	41
1994— Nashville (Sou.)	0	2	.000	4.24	4	4	0	0	0	17	24	10	8	7	9
1995— New Britain (East.)	4	9	.308	5.73	24	21	0	0	0	113	135	78	72	54	60
1996— New Britain (East.)	3	7	.300	5.44	29	10	0	0	4	82 2/3	101	55	50	30	53
— Salt Lake (PCL)	0	4	.000	5.47	16	0	0	0	0	24 2/3	27	15	15	11	19
1997— Minnesota (A.L.)	2	3	.400	4.58	42	0	0	0	0	74 2/3	87	41	38	28	44
1998— Minnesota (A.L.)	0	0	...	5.63	15	0	0	0	0	24	30	17	15	9	21
— Salt Lake (PCL)	1	3	.250	4.15	36	0	0	0	4	60 2/3	55	38	28	31	62
1999— Nashville (PCL)■	0	0	...	1.80	1	1	0	0	0	5	6	1	1	1	2
— Pittsburgh (N.L.)	15	9	.625	3.49	28	26	2	0	0	172 2/3	169	79	67	54	107
2000— Pittsburgh (N.L.)	9	8	.529	4.81	31	31	1	1	0	187	208	111	100	51	124
A.L. totals (2 years)	2	3	.400	4.83	57	0	0	0	0	98 2/3	117	58	53	37	65
N.L. totals (2 years)	24	17	.585	4.18	59	57	3	1	0	359 2/3	377	190	167	105	231
Major League totals (4 years)	26	20	.565	4.32	116	57	3	1	0	458 1/3	494	248	220	142	296

RIVAS, LUIS   SS   TWINS

PERSONAL: Born August 30, 1979, in La Guaria, Venezuela. ... 5-11/175. ... Bats right, throws right. ... Full name: Luis Wilfredo Rivas.
HIGH SCHOOL: Riceniado Le Guaria (La Guaria, Venezuela).
TRANSACTIONS/CAREER NOTES: Signed as non-drafted free agent by Minnesota Twins organization (October 9, 1995). ... On New Britain disabled list (July 7-21, 2000).
STATISTICAL NOTES: Led Gulf Coast League shortstops with 40 double plays in 1996. ... Led Midwest League shortstops with 621 total chances and 92 double plays in 1997. ... Led Florida State League shortstops with 632 total chances and 78 double plays in 1998. ... Led Eastern League shortstops with 37 errors in 1999.

Year Team (League)	Pos.	G	AB	R	H	2B	3B	HR	RBI	Avg.	BB	SO	SB	PO	A	E	Avg.
1996— GC Twins (GCL)	SS	53	201	29	52	12	1	1	13	.259	18	37	•35	68	181	21	.922
1997— Fort Wayne (Midw.)	SS	121	419	61	100	20	6	1	30	.239	33	90	28	169	*394	*58	.907
1998— Fort Myers (FSL)	SS	126	463	58	130	21	5	4	51	.281	14	75	34	162	*415	*55	.913
1999— New Britain (East.)	SS-2B	132	527	78	134	30	7	7	49	.254	41	92	31	164	392	†39	.934
2000— New Britain (East.)	2B-SS	82	328	56	82	23	6	3	40	.250	36	41	11	141	226	11	.971
— Salt Lake (PCL)	2B-SS	41	157	33	50	14	1	3	25	.318	13	21	7	70	107	2	.989
— Minnesota (A.L.)	2B-SS	16	58	8	18	4	1	0	6	.310	2	4	2	31	29	1	.984
Major League totals (1 year)		16	58	8	18	4	1	0	6	.310	2	4	2	31	29	1	.984

RIVERA, LUIS   P   ORIOLES

PERSONAL: Born June 21, 1978, in Chihuahua, Mexico. ... 6-3/163. ... Throws right, bats right. ... Full name: Luis Gutierrez Rivera.
HIGH SCHOOL: Sistema Preparatoria Abierta (Telucha, Mexico).
TRANSACTIONS/CAREER NOTES: Signed as non-drafted free agent by Atlanta Braves organization (February 18, 1995). ... On Myrtle Beach disabled list (April 18-May 14, 1999). ... On Richmond disabled list (May 5-June 29, 2000). ... Traded by Braves with OF Trenidad Hubbard and C Fernando Lunar to Baltimore Orioles for OF B.J. Surhoff and P Gabe Molina (July 31, 2000).

Year League	W	L	Pct.	ERA	G	GS	CG	ShO	Sv.	IP	H	R	ER	BB	SO
1996— Gulf Coast Braves (GCL)	1	1	.500	2.59	8	6	0	0	0	24 1/3	18	9	7	7	26
1997— Danville (Appl.)	3	1	.750	2.41	9	9	0	0	0	41	28	15	11	17	57
— Macon (S.Atl.)	2	0	1.000	1.29	4	4	0	0	0	21	13	4	3	7	27
1998— Macon (S.Atl.)	5	5	.500	3.98	20	20	0	0	0	92 2/3	78	53	41	41	118
1999— Myrtle Beach (Caro.)	0	2	.000	3.11	25	13	0	0	0	66 2/3	45	25	23	23	81
2000— Atlanta (N.L.)	1	0	1.000	1.35	5	0	0	0	0	6 2/3	4	1	1	5	5
— Richmond (I.L.)	0	2	.000	8.06	8	7	0	0	0	22 1/3	29	20	20	18	12
— Gulf Coast Braves (GCL)	0	0	...	0.00	3	3	0	0	0	4	2	0	0	1	2
— Rochester (I.L.)■	0	1	.000	3.38	3	3	0	0	0	8	11	5	3	5	4
— Baltimore (A.L.)	0	0	...	0.00	1	0	0	0	0	2/3	1	0	0	1	0
A.L. totals (1 year)	0	0	...	0.00	1	0	0	0	0	2/3	1	0	0	1	0
N.L. totals (1 year)	1	0	1.000	1.35	5	0	0	0	0	6 2/3	4	1	1	5	5
Major League totals (1 year)	1	0	1.000	1.23	6	0	0	0	0	7 1/3	5	1	1	6	5

RIVERA, MARIANO   P   YANKEES

PERSONAL: Born November 29, 1969, in Panama City, Panama. ... 6-2/185. ... Throws right, bats right. ... Cousin of Ruben Rivera, outfielder, San Diego Padres.
TRANSACTIONS/CAREER NOTES: Signed as non-drafted free agent by New York Yankees organization (February 17, 1990). ... On disabled list (April 10-May 19, July 11-28 and August 12-September 8, 1992). ... On Albany/Colonie disabled list (April 9-June 28, 1993). ... On Greensboro disabled list (September 6, 1993-remainder of season). ... On Tampa disabled list (April 23-May 9, 1994). ... On Columbus disabled list (August 4-14, 1994). ... On disabled list (April 6-24, 1998).

HONORS: Named A.L. Fireman of the Year by THE SPORTING NEWS (1997 and 1999).
STATISTICAL NOTES: Pitched seven-inning, 3-0 no-hit victory against Gulf Coast Pirates (August 31, 1990). ... Pitched five-inning, 3-0 no-hit victory for Columbus against Rochester (June 26, 1995).

Year	League	W	L	Pct.	ERA	G	GS	CG	ShO	Sv.	IP	H	R	ER	BB	SO
1990—	Gulf Coast Yankees (GCL)..	5	1	.833	*0.17	22	1	1	1	1	52	17	3	1	7	58
1991—	Greensboro (S.Atl.)	4	9	.308	2.75	29	15	1	0	0	114 2/3	103	48	35	36	123
1992—	Fort Lauderdale (FSL)	5	3	.625	2.28	10	10	3	1	0	59 1/3	40	17	15	5	42
1993—	Greensboro (S.Atl.)	1	0	1.000	2.06	10	10	0	0	0	39 1/3	31	12	9	15	32
	— Gulf Coast Yankees (GCL)..	0	1	.000	2.25	2	2	0	0	0	4	2	1	1	1	6
1994—	Tampa (FSL)	3	0	1.000	2.21	7	7	0	0	0	36 2/3	34	12	9	12	27
	— Albany/Colonie (East.)	3	0	1.000	2.27	9	9	0	0	0	63 1/3	58	20	16	8	39
	— Columbus (I.L.)	4	2	.667	5.81	6	6	1	0	0	31	34	22	20	10	23
1995—	Columbus (I.L.)	2	2	.500	2.10	7	7	1	1	0	30	25	10	7	3	30
	— New York (A.L.)	5	3	.625	5.51	19	10	0	0	0	67	71	43	41	30	51
1996—	New York (A.L.)	8	3	.727	2.09	61	0	0	0	5	107 2/3	73	25	25	34	130
1997—	New York (A.L.)	6	4	.600	1.88	66	0	0	0	43	71 2/3	65	17	15	20	68
1998—	New York (A.L.)	3	0	1.000	1.91	54	0	0	0	36	61 1/3	48	13	13	17	36
1999—	New York (A.L.)	4	3	.571	1.83	66	0	0	0	*45	69	43	15	14	18	52
2000—	New York (A.L.)	7	4	.636	2.85	66	0	0	0	36	75 2/3	58	26	24	25	58
Major League totals (6 years)		33	17	.660	2.63	332	10	0	0	165	452 1/3	358	139	132	144	395

DIVISION SERIES RECORD

RECORDS: Holds career record for most saves—8.

Year	League	W	L	Pct.	ERA	G	GS	CG	ShO	Sv.	IP	H	R	ER	BB	SO
1995—	New York (A.L.)	1	0	1.000	0.00	3	0	0	0	0	5 1/3	3	0	0	1	8
1996—	New York (A.L.)	0	0	...	0.00	2	0	0	0	0	4 2/3	0	0	0	1	1
1997—	New York (A.L.)	0	0	...	4.50	2	0	0	0	1	2	2	1	1	0	1
1998—	New York (A.L.)	0	0	...	0.00	3	0	0	0	2	3 1/3	1	0	0	1	2
1999—	New York (A.L.)	0	0	...	0.00	2	0	0	0	2	3	1	0	0	0	3
2000—	New York (A.L.)	0	0	...	0.00	3	0	0	0	3	5	2	0	0	0	2
Division series totals (6 years)		1	0	1.000	0.39	15	0	0	0	8	23 1/3	9	1	1	3	17

CHAMPIONSHIP SERIES RECORD

Year	League	W	L	Pct.	ERA	G	GS	CG	ShO	Sv.	IP	H	R	ER	BB	SO
1996—	New York (A.L.)	1	0	1.000	0.00	2	0	0	0	0	4	6	0	0	1	5
1998—	New York (A.L.)	0	0	...	0.00	4	0	0	0	1	5 2/3	0	0	0	1	5
1999—	New York (A.L.)	1	0	1.000	0.00	3	0	0	0	2	4 2/3	5	0	0	0	3
2000—	New York (A.L.)	0	0	...	1.93	3	0	0	0	1	4 2/3	4	1	1	0	1
Champ. series totals (4 years)		2	0	1.000	0.47	12	0	0	0	4	19	15	1	1	2	14

WORLD SERIES RECORD

RECORDS: Holds career record for most saves—7.
NOTES: Named Most Valuable Player (1999). ... Member of World Series championship team (1996, 1998, 1999 and 2000).

Year	League	W	L	Pct.	ERA	G	GS	CG	ShO	Sv.	IP	H	R	ER	BB	SO
1996—	New York (A.L.)	0	0	...	1.59	4	0	0	0	0	5 2/3	4	1	1	3	4
1998—	New York (A.L.)	0	0	...	0.00	3	0	0	0	3	4 1/3	5	0	0	0	4
1999—	New York (A.L.)	1	0	1.000	0.00	3	0	0	0	2	4 2/3	3	0	0	1	3
2000—	New York (A.L.)	0	0	...	3.00	4	0	0	0	2	6	4	2	2	1	7
World Series totals (4 years)		1	0	1.000	1.31	14	0	0	0	7	20 2/3	16	3	3	5	18

ALL-STAR GAME RECORD

Year	League	W	L	Pct.	ERA	GS	CG	ShO	Sv.	IP	H	R	ER	BB	SO
1997—	American	0	0	...	0.00	0	0	0	1	1	0	0	0	0	1
1999—	American				Selected, did not play—injured.										
2000—	American	0	0	...	0.00	0	0	0	1	2	2	1	0	0	0
All-Star Game totals (2 years)		0	0	...	0.00	0	0	0	1	2	2	1	0	0	1

RIVERA, RUBEN   OF   PADRES

PERSONAL: Born November 14, 1973, in La Chorrera, Panama ... 6-3/208. ... Bats right, throws right. ... Full name: Ruben Moreno Rivera. ... Cousin of Mariano Rivera, pitcher, New York Yankees.
TRANSACTIONS/CAREER NOTES: Signed as non-drafted free agent by New York Yankees organization (November 21, 1990). ... On New York disabled list (March 27-May 30, 1997). ... Traded by Yankees with P Rafael Medina and $3 million to San Diego Padres for the rights to P Hideki Irabu, 2B Homer Bush, OF Gordon Amerson and a player to be named later (April 22, 1997); Yankees acquired OF Vernon Maxwell to complete deal (June 9, 1997). ... On San Diego disabled list (May 30-August 13, 1997); included rehabilitation assignments to Rancho Cucamonga (May 30-July 22) and Las Vegas (July 23-August 4). ... On San Diego disabled list (April 12-May 5, 2000); included rehabilitation assignment to Las Vegas (May 3-5).
HONORS: Named New York-Pennsylvania League Most Valuable Player (1993). ... Named South Atlantic League Most Valuable Player (1994).
STATISTICAL NOTES: Led New York-Pennsylvania League outfielders with three double plays in 1993. ... Led South Atlantic League with .573 slugging percentage in 1994. ... Career major league grand slams: 2.

							BATTING								FIELDING		
Year	Team (League)	Pos.	G	AB	R	H	2B	3B	HR	RBI	Avg.	BB	SO	SB	PO	A	E	Avg.
1991—	Dom. Yankees (DSL)..		51	170	27	34	3	2	2	16	.200	23	37	14	...	...	...	...
1992—	GC Yankees (GCL)	OF	53	194	37	53	10	3	1	20	.273	42	49	21	67	10	4	.951
1993—	Oneonta (NY-Penn)	OF	55	199	45	55	7	6	13	47	.276	32	66	12	111	9	3	.976
1994—	Greensboro (S.Atl.)	OF	105	400	83	115	24	3	•28	81	.288	47	125	36	217	14	5	.979
	— Tampa (FSL)	OF	34	134	18	35	4	3	5	20	.261	8	38	12	76	6	2	.976
1995—	Norwich (East.)	OF	71	256	49	75	16	8	9	39	.293	37	77	16	176	7	3	.984
	— Columbus (I.L.)	OF	48	174	37	47	8	2	15	35	.270	26	62	8	113	6	3	.975
	— New York (A.L.)	OF	5	1	0	0	0	0	0	0	.000	0	1	0	2	0	0	1.000
1996—	Columbus (I.L.)	OF	101	362	59	85	20	4	10	46	.235	40	96	15	239	6	7	.972
	— New York (A.L.)	OF	46	88	17	25	6	1	2	16	.284	13	26	6	77	2	0	1.000

Year	Team (League)	Pos.	G	AB	R	H	2B	3B	HR	RBI	Avg.	BB	SO	SB	PO	A	E	Avg.
1997—	Rancho Cuca. (Calif.)■	DH	6	23	6	4	1	0	1	3	.174	3	9	1	...	...	...	...
—	Las Vegas (PCL)	DH-1B	12	48	6	12	5	1	1	6	.250	1	20	1	1	0	0	1.000
—	San Diego (N.L.)	OF	17	20	2	5	1	0	0	1	.250	2	9	2	13	0	0	1.000
1998—	Las Vegas (PCL)	OF	30	104	9	15	3	0	3	11	.144	11	42	4	53	2	0	1.000
—	San Diego (N.L.)	OF	95	172	31	36	7	2	6	29	.209	28	52	5	104	3	3	.973
1999—	San Diego (N.L.)	OF	147	411	65	80	16	1	23	48	.195	55	143	18	312	8	8	.976
2000—	San Diego (N.L.)	OF	135	423	62	88	18	6	17	57	.208	44	137	8	303	10	5	.984
—	Las Vegas (PCL)	OF	2	10	1	2	0	0	0	1	.200	0	3	0	1	0	0	1.000
American League totals (2 years)			51	89	17	25	6	1	2	16	.281	13	27	6	79	2	0	1.000
National League totals (4 years)			394	1026	160	209	42	9	46	135	.204	129	341	33	732	21	16	.979
Major League totals (6 years)			445	1115	177	234	48	10	48	151	.210	142	368	39	811	23	16	.981

DIVISION SERIES RECORD

Year	Team (League)	Pos.	G	AB	R	H	2B	3B	HR	RBI	Avg.	BB	SO	SB	PO	A	E	Avg.
1996—	New York (A.L.)	OF-PH	2	1	0	0	0	0	0	0	.000	0	1	0	0	0	0	...
1998—	San Diego (N.L.)	OF	3	6	0	0	0	0	0	0	.000	0	3	0	3	0	0	1.000
Division series totals (2 years)			5	7	0	0	0	0	0	0	.000	0	4	0	3	0	0	1.000

CHAMPIONSHIP SERIES RECORD

Year	Team (League)	Pos.	G	AB	R	H	2B	3B	HR	RBI	Avg.	BB	SO	SB	PO	A	E	Avg.
1996—	New York (A.L.)								Did not play.									
1998—	San Diego (N.L.)	OF-PH	6	13	1	3	2	0	0	0	.231	0	7	1	8	1	0	1.000

WORLD SERIES RECORD

NOTES: Member of World Series championship team (1996); inactive due to injury.

Year	Team (League)	Pos.	G	AB	R	H	2B	3B	HR	RBI	Avg.	BB	SO	SB	PO	A	E	Avg.
1996—	New York (A.L.)								Did not play.									
1998—	San Diego (N.L.)	PH-OF-PR	3	5	1	4	2	0	0	1	.800	0	0	0	3	0	0	1.000

ROBERTS, DAVE   OF   INDIANS

PERSONAL: Born May 31, 1972, in Okinawa, Japan. ... 5-10/175. ... Bats left, throws left. ... Full name: David Ray Roberts.
HIGH SCHOOL: Rancho Buena Vista (Oceanside, Calif.).
COLLEGE: UCLA.
TRANSACTIONS/CAREER NOTES: Selected by Detroit Tigers organization in 28th round of free-agent draft (June 2, 1994). ... Loaned to Oakland Athletics organization (March 30-August 30, 1996). ... Traded by Tigers with P Tim Worrell to Cleveland Indians for OF Geronimo Berroa (June 24, 1998). ... On Akron disabled list (August 10-18, 1998).
STATISTICAL NOTES: Career major league grand slams: 1.

Year	Team (League)	Pos.	G	AB	R	H	2B	3B	HR	RBI	Avg.	BB	SO	SB	PO	A	E	Avg.
1994—	Jamestown (NY-P)	OF	54	178	33	52	7	2	0	12	.292	29	27	12	2	0	0	1.000
1995—	Lakeland (FSL)	OF	92	357	67	108	10	5	3	30	.303	39	43	30	61	3	1	.985
1996—	Visalia (Calif.)■	OF	126	482	*112	131	24	7	5	37	.272	98	105	*65	201	8	5	.977
—	Jacksonville (Sou.)■	OF	3	9	0	2	0	0	0	0	.222	1	0	0	5	0	0	1.000
1997—	Jacksonville (Sou.)	OF	105	415	76	123	24	2	4	41	.296	45	62	23	82	1	4	.954
1998—	Jacksonville (Sou.)	OF	69	279	71	91	14	5	5	42	.326	53	59	21	105	1	0	1.000
—	Akron (East.)■	OF	56	227	49	82	10	5	7	33	.361	35	30	28	124	4	1	.992
—	Buffalo (I.L.)	OF	5	15	2	2	0	0	0	2	.133	0	3	2	12	1	0	1.000
1999—	Buffalo (I.L.)	OF-DH	89	350	65	95	17	*10	0	38	.271	43	52	39	247	4	1	.996
—	Cleveland (A.L.)	OF	41	143	26	34	4	0	2	12	.238	9	16	11	87	0	0	1.000
2000—	Buffalo (I.L.)	OF	120	462	93	135	16	3	13	55	.292	59	68	39	284	8	1	*.997
—	Cleveland (A.L.)	OF	19	10	1	2	0	0	0	0	.200	2	2	1	10	0	0	1.000
Major League totals (2 years)			60	153	27	36	4	0	2	12	.235	11	18	12	97	0	0	1.000

DIVISION SERIES RECORD

Year	Team (League)	Pos.	G	AB	R	H	2B	3B	HR	RBI	Avg.	BB	SO	SB	PO	A	E	Avg.
1999—	Cleveland (A.L.)	PH-OF	2	3	0	0	0	0	0	0	.000	0	2	0	3	0	0	1.000

ROBERTS, GRANT   P   METS

PERSONAL: Born September 13, 1977, in El Cajon, Calif. ... 6-3/205. ... Throws right, bats right. ... Full name: Grant William Roberts.
HIGH SCHOOL: Grossmont (La Mesa, Calif.).
TRANSACTIONS/CAREER NOTES: Selected by New York Mets organization in 11th round of free-agent draft (June 1, 1995).
STATISTICAL NOTES: Tied for International League lead with 12 wild pitches in 2000.

Year	League	W	L	Pct.	ERA	G	GS	CG	ShO	Sv.	IP	H	R	ER	BB	SO
1995—	Gulf Coast Mets (GCL)	2	1	.667	2.15	11	3	0	0	0	29 1/3	19	13	7	14	24
1996—	Kingsport (Appl.)	*9	1	*.900	2.10	13	13	2	*2	0	68 2/3	43	18	16	37	*92
1997—	Capital City (S.Atl.)	11	3	*.786	2.36	22	22	2	1	0	129 2/3	98	37	34	44	122
1998—	St. Lucie (FSL)	4	5	.444	4.23	17	17	0	0	0	72 1/3	72	37	34	37	70
1999—	Binghamton (East.)	7	6	.538	4.87	23	23	0	0	0	131 1/3	135	81	71	49	94
—	Norfolk (I.L.)	2	1	.667	4.50	5	5	0	0	0	28	32	15	14	11	30
2000—	Norfolk (I.L.)	7	8	.467	3.38	25	25	5	0	0	157 1/3	154	67	59	63	115
—	New York (N.L.)	0	0	...	11.57	4	1	0	0	0	7	11	10	9	4	6
Major League totals (1 year)		0	0	...	11.57	4	1	0	0	0	7	11	10	9	4	6

ROCKER, JOHN — P — BRAVES

PERSONAL: Born October 17, 1974, in Statesboro, Ga. ... 6-4/225. ... Throws left, bats right. ... Full name: John Loy Rocker.
HIGH SCHOOL: First Presbyterian Day School (Macon, Ga.).
COLLEGE: Mercer (Ga.).
TRANSACTIONS/CAREER NOTES: Selected by Atlanta Braves organization in 18th round of free-agent draft (June 3, 1993). ... On suspended list (April 3-18, 2000).
STATISTICAL NOTES: Pitched 2-0 no-hit victory against Charleston, S.C. (June 9, 1996). ... Led Southern League in wild pitches with 17 in 1997.

Year League	W	L	Pct.	ERA	G	GS	CG	ShO	Sv.	IP	H	R	ER	BB	SO
1994— Danville (Appl.)	1	5	.167	3.53	12	12	1	0	0	63 2/3	50	36	25	38	72
1995— Eugene (N'West)	1	5	.167	5.16	12	12	0	0	0	59 1/3	45	40	34	36	74
— Macon (S.Atl.)	4	4	.500	4.50	16	16	0	0	0	86	86	50	43	52	61
1996— Macon (S.Atl.)	5	3	.625	3.89	20	19	2	2	0	106 1/3	85	60	46	63	107
— Durham (Caro.)	4	3	.571	3.39	9	9	0	0	0	58 1/3	63	24	22	25	43
1997— Durham (Caro.)	1	1	.500	4.33	11	1	0	0	0	35 1/3	33	21	17	22	39
— Greenville (Sou.)	5	6	.455	4.86	22	18	0	0	0	113	119	69	61	61	96
1998— Richmond (I.L.)	1	1	.500	1.42	9	0	0	0	1	19	13	4	3	10	22
— Atlanta (N.L.)	1	3	.250	2.13	47	0	0	0	2	38	22	10	9	22	42
1999— Atlanta (N.L.)	4	5	.444	2.49	74	0	0	0	38	72 1/3	47	24	20	37	104
2000— Atlanta (N.L.)	1	2	.333	2.89	59	0	0	0	24	53	42	25	17	48	77
— Richmond (I.L.)	0	0	...	3.00	3	0	0	0	1	3	3	1	1	1	6
Major League totals (3 years)	6	10	.375	2.53	180	0	0	0	64	163 1/3	111	59	46	107	223

DIVISION SERIES RECORD

Year League	W	L	Pct.	ERA	G	GS	CG	ShO	Sv.	IP	H	R	ER	BB	SO
1998— Atlanta (N.L.)	0	0	...	0.00	2	0	0	0	0	1 1/3	1	0	0	0	2
1999— Atlanta (N.L.)	1	0	1.000	0.00	2	0	0	0	1	3 1/3	0	0	0	2	5
2000— Atlanta (N.L.)	0	0	...	0.00	1	0	0	0	0	2/3	0	0	0	1	0
Division series totals (3 years)	1	0	1.000	0.00	5	0	0	0	1	5 1/3	1	0	0	3	7

CHAMPIONSHIP SERIES RECORD

RECORDS: Shares single-series record for most games pitched—6 (1998 and 1999).

Year League	W	L	Pct.	ERA	G	GS	CG	ShO	Sv.	IP	H	R	ER	BB	SO
1998— Atlanta (N.L.)	1	0	1.000	0.00	6	0	0	0	0	4 2/3	3	0	0	1	5
1999— Atlanta (N.L.)	0	0	...	0.00	6	0	0	0	2	6 2/3	3	2	0	2	9
Champ. series totals (2 years)	1	0	1.000	0.00	12	0	0	0	2	11 1/3	6	2	0	3	14

WORLD SERIES RECORD

Year League	W	L	Pct.	ERA	G	GS	CG	ShO	Sv.	IP	H	R	ER	BB	SO
1999— Atlanta (N.L.)	0	0	...	0.00	2	0	0	0	0	3	2	0	0	2	4

RODRIGUEZ, ALEX — SS — RANGERS

PERSONAL: Born July 27, 1975, in New York. ... 6-3/195. ... Bats right, throws right. ... Full name: Alexander Emmanuel Rodriguez.
HIGH SCHOOL: Westminster Christian (Miami).
TRANSACTIONS/CAREER NOTES: Selected by Seattle Mariners organization in first round (first pick overall) of free-agent draft (June 3, 1993). ... On Seattle disabled list (April 22-May 7, 1996); included rehabilitation assignment to Tacoma (May 5-7). ... On disabled list (June 12-27, 1997; April 7-May 14, 1999; and July 8-24, 2000). ... Granted free agency (October 30, 2000). ... Signed by Texas Rangers (December 11, 2000).
RECORDS: Hold A.L. single-season record for most home runs by shortstop—42 (1998 and 1999).
HONORS: Named Major League Player of the Year by THE SPORTING NEWS (1996). ... Named shortstop on THE SPORTING NEWS A.L. All-Star team (1996, 1998 and 2000). ... Named shortstop on THE SPORTING NEWS A.L. Silver Slugger team (1996, 1998, 1999 and 2000).
STATISTICAL NOTES: Had 20-game hitting streak (August 16-September 4, 1996). ... Led A.L. with 379 total bases in 1996. ... Hit for the cycle (June 5, 1997). ... Led A.L. shortstops with 731 total chances in 1998. ... Led A.L. in grounding into double plays with 31 in 1999. ... Hit three home runs in one game (April 16, 2000). ... Had 17-game hitting streak (May 5-23, 2000). ... Led A.L. shortstops with 123 double plays in 2000. ... Career major league grand slams: 7.

Year Team (League)	Pos.	G	AB	R	H	2B	3B	HR	RBI	Avg.	BB	SO	SB	PO	A	E	Avg.
1994— Appleton (Midw.)	SS-DH	65	248	49	79	17	6	14	55	.319	24	44	16	86	185	19	.934
— Jacksonville (Sou.)	SS	17	59	7	17	4	1	1	8	.288	10	13	2	17	63	3	.964
— Seattle (A.L.)	SS	17	54	4	11	0	0	0	2	.204	3	20	3	20	45	6	.915
— Calgary (PCL)	SS	32	119	22	37	7	4	6	21	.311	8	25	2	45	104	3	.980
1995— Tacoma (PCL)	SS-DH	54	214	37	77	12	3	15	45	.360	18	44	2	90	157	10	.961
— Seattle (A.L.)	SS-DH	48	142	15	33	6	2	5	19	.232	6	42	4	56	106	8	.953
1996— Seattle (A.L.)	SS	146	601	*141	215	*54	1	36	123	*.358	59	104	15	238	404	15	.977
— Tacoma (PCL)	SS	2	5	0	1	0	0	0	0	.200	2	1	0	1	4	1	.833
1997— Seattle (A.L.)	SS-DH	141	587	100	176	40	3	23	84	.300	41	99	29	209	394	*24	.962
1998— Seattle (A.L.)	SS-DH	161	*686	123	*213	35	5	42	124	.310	45	121	46	268	445	18	.975
1999— Seattle (A.L.)	SS	129	502	110	143	25	0	42	111	.285	56	109	21	213	382	14	.977
2000— Seattle (A.L.)	SS	148	554	134	175	34	2	41	132	.316	100	121	15	243	438	10	.986
Major League totals (7 years)		790	3126	627	966	194	13	189	595	.309	310	616	133	1247	2214	95	.973

DIVISION SERIES RECORD

Year Team (League)	Pos.	G	AB	R	H	2B	3B	HR	RBI	Avg.	BB	SO	SB	PO	A	E	Avg.
1995— Seattle (A.L.)	SS-PR	1	1	1	0	0	0	0	0	.000	0	0	0	0	0	0	...
1997— Seattle (A.L.)	SS	4	16	1	5	1	0	1	1	.313	0	5	0	5	10	0	1.000
2000— Seattle (A.L.)	SS	3	13	0	4	0	0	0	2	.308	0	2	0	8	9	0	1.000
Division series totals (3 years)		8	30	2	9	1	0	1	3	.300	0	7	0	13	19	0	1.000

R

CHAMPIONSHIP SERIES RECORD

RECORDS: Shares A.L. single-game record for most long hits—3 (October 17, 2000).

Year Team (League)	Pos.	G	AB	R	H	2B	3B	HR	RBI	Avg.	BB	SO	SB	PO	A	E	Avg.
1995— Seattle (A.L.)	PH	1	1	0	0	0	0	0	0	.000	0	1	0	...	...	...	...
2000— Seattle (A.L.)	SS	6	22	4	9	2	0	2	5	.409	3	8	1	9	11	0	1.000
Championship series totals (2 years)		7	23	4	9	2	0	2	5	.391	3	9	1	9	11	0	1.000

ALL-STAR GAME RECORD

Year League	Pos.	AB	R	H	2B	3B	HR	RBI	Avg.	BB	SO	SB	PO	A	E	Avg.
1996— American	SS	1	0	0	0	0	0	0	.000	0	0	0	0	0	0	...
1997— American	SS	3	0	1	0	0	0	0	.333	0	2	0	0	1	0	1.000
1998— American	SS	3	2	2	0	0	1	1	.667	0	1	0	1	2	0	1.000
2000— American						Selected, did not play—injured.											
All-Star Game totals (3 years)		7	2	3	0	0	1	1	.429	0	3	0	1	3	0	1.000

RODRIGUEZ, FELIX   P   GIANTS

PERSONAL: Born December 5, 1972, in Monte Cristi, Dominican Republic. ... 6-1/190. ... Throws right, bats right. ... Full name: Felix Antonio Rodriguez.

HIGH SCHOOL: Liceo Bijiador (Monte Cristi, Dominican Republic).

TRANSACTIONS/CAREER NOTES: Signed as non-drafted free agent by Los Angeles Dodgers organization (October 17, 1989). ... On disabled list (August 11, 1992-remainder of season). ... On Albuquerque disabled list (July 5-18, 1995). ... On disabled list (April 20-May 2 and May 12-27, 1996). ... Claimed on waivers by Cincinnati Reds (December 18, 1996). ... Traded by Reds to Arizona Diamondbacks for a player to be named later (November 11, 1997); Reds acquired P Scott Winchester to complete deal (November 18, 1997). ... On Arizona disabled list (June 21-July 30, 1998); included rehabilitation assignments to Arizona League Diamondbacks (July 20-27) and Tucson (July 28-30). ... Traded by Diamondbacks to San Francisco Giants for future considerations (December 8, 1998); Diamondbacks acquired P Troy Brohawn and OF Chris Van Rossum to complete deal (December 21, 1998).

STATISTICAL NOTES: Pitched 11-0 no-hit victory against Sarasota (August 28, 1993).

MISCELLANEOUS: Played catcher (1990-92).

Year League	W	L	Pct.	ERA	G	GS	CG	ShO	Sv.	IP	H	R	ER	BB	SO
1993— Vero Beach (FSL)	8	8	.500	3.75	32	20	2	1	0	132	109	71	55	71	80
1994— San Antonio (Texas)	6	8	.429	4.03	26	26	0	0	0	136 1/3	106	70	61	*88	126
1995— Albuquerque (PCL)	3	2	.600	4.24	14	11	0	0	0	51	52	29	24	26	46
— Los Angeles (N.L.)	1	1	.500	2.53	11	0	0	0	0	10 2/3	11	3	3	5	5
1996— Albuquerque (PCL)	3	9	.250	5.53	27	19	0	0	0	107 1/3	111	70	66	60	65
1997— Indianapolis (A.A.)■	3	3	.500	1.01	23	0	0	0	1	26 2/3	22	10	3	16	26
— Cincinnati (N.L.)	0	0	...	4.30	26	1	0	0	0	46	48	23	22	28	34
1998— Arizona (N.L.)■	0	2	.000	6.14	43	0	0	0	5	44	44	31	30	29	36
— Ariz. D-backs (Ariz.)	0	0	...	4.15	3	2	0	0	0	4 1/3	3	4	2	2	5
— Tucson (PCL)	0	0	...	9.00	1	0	0	0	0	1	1	1	1	2	0
1999— San Francisco (N.L.)■	2	3	.400	3.80	47	0	0	0	0	66 1/3	67	32	28	29	55
2000— San Francisco (N.L.)	4	2	.667	2.64	76	0	0	0	3	81 2/3	65	29	24	42	95
Major League totals (5 years)	7	8	.467	3.87	203	1	0	0	8	248 2/3	235	118	107	133	225

DIVISION SERIES RECORD

Year League	W	L	Pct.	ERA	G	GS	CG	ShO	Sv.	IP	H	R	ER	BB	SO
2000— San Francisco (N.L.)	0	1	.000	6.23	3	0	0	0	0	4 1/3	6	3	3	1	6

RECORD AS POSITION PLAYER

Year Team (League)	Pos.	G	AB	R	H	2B	3B	HR	RBI	Avg.	BB	SO	SB	PO	A	E	Avg.
1990— Dom. Dodgers (DSL)		63	241	23	55	10	0	2	33	.228	15	52	4	...	...	...	...
1991— GC Dodgers (GCL)	C	45	139	15	37	8	1	2	21	.266	6	32	1	161	18	5	.973
1992— Great Falls (Pio.)	C-OF	32	110	20	32	8	0	2	20	.291	1	16	2	221	33	2	.992

RODRIGUEZ, FRANKIE   P   REDS

PERSONAL: Born December 11, 1972, in Brooklyn, N.Y. ... 6-0/210. ... Throws right, bats right. ... Full name: Francisco Rodriguez.

HIGH SCHOOL: Eastern District (Brooklyn, N.Y.).

JUNIOR COLLEGE: Howard College (Texas).

TRANSACTIONS/CAREER NOTES: Selected by Boston Red Sox in second round of free-agent draft (June 4, 1990); pick received as compensation for Atlanta Braves signing of Type B free-agent 1B Nick Esasky. ... Traded by Red Sox with a player to be named later to Minnesota Twins for P Rick Aguilera (July 6, 1995); Twins acquired OF J.J. Johnson to complete deal (October 11, 1995). ... Claimed on waivers by Seattle Mariners (May 26, 1999). ... On suspended list (August 17-25, 1999). ... On Seattle disabled list (July 7-September 1, 2000); included rehabilitation assignment to Tacoma (July 24-September 1). ... Released by Mariners (December 20, 2000). ... Signed by Cincinnati Reds organization (January 16, 2001).

STATISTICAL NOTES: Pitched 2-1 no-hit victory for Salt Lake against Iowa (May 8, 1999; first game).

MISCELLANEOUS: Played shortstop (1991). ... Scored one run in two appearances as pinch hitter (1999).

Year League	W	L	Pct.	ERA	G	GS	CG	ShO	Sv.	IP	H	R	ER	BB	SO
1992— Lynchburg (Caro.)	12	7	.632	3.09	25	25	1	0	0	148 2/3	125	56	51	65	129
1993— New Britain (East.)	7	11	.389	3.74	28	26	•4	1	0	170 2/3	147	79	71	78	151
1994— Pawtucket (I.L.)	8	13	.381	3.92	28	28	*8	1	0	*186	182	95	81	60	*160
1995— Boston (A.L.)	0	2	.000	10.57	9	2	0	0	0	15 1/3	21	19	18	10	14
— Pawtucket (I.L.)	1	1	.500	4.00	13	2	0	0	2	27	19	12	12	8	18
— Minnesota (A.L.)■	5	6	.455	5.38	16	16	0	0	0	90 1/3	93	64	54	47	45
1996— Minnesota (A.L.)	13	14	.481	5.05	38	33	3	0	2	206 2/3	218	129	116	78	110
1997— Minnesota (A.L.)	3	6	.333	4.62	43	15	0	0	0	142 1/3	147	82	73	60	65
1998— Minnesota (A.L.)	4	6	.400	6.56	20	11	0	0	0	70	88	58	51	30	62
— Salt Lake (PCL)	5	7	.417	4.67	16	16	2	1	0	96 1/3	97	53	50	35	79

Year	League	W	L	Pct.	ERA	G	GS	CG	ShO	Sv.	IP	H	R	ER	BB	SO
1999—	Salt Lake (PCL)	3	4	.429	6.70	9	9	1	0	0	43	40	34	32	14	33
—	Seattle (A.L.)■	2	4	.333	5.65	28	5	0	0	3	73⅓	94	47	46	30	47
2000—	Seattle (A.L.)	2	1	.667	6.27	23	0	0	0	0	47⅓	60	33	33	22	19
—	Tacoma (PCL)	2	1	.667	4.84	9	6	0	0	0	35⅓	30	20	19	11	26
Major League totals (6 years)		29	39	.426	5.45	177	82	3	0	5	645⅓	721	432	391	277	362

RECORD AS POSITION PLAYER

							BATTING								FIELDING		
Year	Team (League)	Pos.	G	AB	R	H	2B	3B	HR	RBI	Avg.	BB	SO	SB	PO	A	E	Avg.
1991—	GC Red Sox (GCL)	SS	3	14	3	7	0	1	0	3	.500	0	1	0	9	10	1	.950
—	Elmira (NY-Penn)	SS	67	255	36	69	5	3	6	31	.271	13	38	3	95	209	24	.927

RODRIGUEZ, GUILLERMO   C   GIANTS

R

PERSONAL: Born May 15, 1978, in Barquisimeto, Venezuela. ... 5-11/195. ... Bats right, throws right. ... Full name: Guillermo Segundo Rodriguez.
HIGH SCHOOL: V.E. Formacion Deportiva (Barquisimeto, Venezuela).
TRANSACTIONS/CAREER NOTES: Signed as non-drafted free agent by San Francisco Giants organization (November 17, 1995).
STATISTICAL NOTES: Led California League with 950 total chances, eight double plays and 23 passed balls in 2000.

							BATTING								FIELDING		
Year	Team (League)	Pos.	G	AB	R	H	2B	3B	HR	RBI	Avg.	BB	SO	SB	PO	A	E	Avg.
1996—	Bellingham (N'West) ..	OF	3	4	1	0	0	0	0	0	.000	0	1	0	1	0	0	1.000
1997—	Salem-Kaizer (N.W.) ...	C-1B	11	39	3	9	3	0	0	3	.231	5	12	0	82	10	1	.989
—	San Jose (Calif.)	1B-C	13	27	2	4	3	1	0	2	.148	0	9	0	61	7	0	1.000
1998—	Salem-Kaizer (N.W.) ...	C	1	4	0	1	0	0	0	0	.250	0	1	0	8	0	0	1.000
—	San Jose (Calif.)	C	32	101	16	33	3	0	5	26	.327	13	19	9	1	0	0	1.000
1999—	Bakersfield (Calif.)	C-1B	41	93	10	27	5	0	1	11	.290	3	18	4	159	21	6	.968
—	Salem-Kaizer (N.W.) ...	C	33	114	16	29	5	0	6	34	.254	9	28	1	248	26	5	.982
2000—	Bakersfield (Calif.)	C	118	437	63	105	27	1	10	58	.240	30	101	20	*823	*112	15	.984

RODRIGUEZ, HENRY   OF

PERSONAL: Born November 8, 1967, in Santo Domingo, Dominican Republic. ... 6-2/225. ... Bats left, throws left. ... Full name: Henry Anderson Lorenzo Rodriguez Garcia.
HIGH SCHOOL: Liceo Republica de Paraguay. (Santo Domingo).
TRANSACTIONS/CAREER NOTES: Signed as non-drafted free agent by Los Angeles Dodgers organization (July 14, 1985). ... Traded by Dodgers with IF Jeff Treadway to Montreal Expos for OF Roberto Kelly and P Joey Eischen (May 23, 1995). ... On Montreal disabled list (June 2-September 1, 1995); included rehabilitation assignment to Ottawa (August 7-16). ... On suspended list (August 16-19, 1996). ... Traded by Expos to Chicago Cubs for P Miguel Batista (December 12, 1997). ... On disabled list (August 24-September 8, 1998). ... Granted free agency (October 23, 1998). ... Re-signed by Cubs (December 2, 1998). ... Traded by Cubs to Florida Marlins for 1B/OF Ross Gload and P Dave Noyce (July 31, 2000). ... Granted free agency (November 1, 2000).
HONORS: Named Texas League Most Valuable Player (1990).
STATISTICAL NOTES: Tied for Gulf Coast League lead with seven intentional bases on balls received in 1987. ... Led Texas League with 14 sacrifice flies in 1990. ... Tied for Pacific Coast League lead with 10 sacrifice flies in 1992. ... Had 15-game hitting streak (July 31-August 14, 1999). ... Career major league grand slams: 5.

							BATTING								FIELDING		
Year	Team (League)	Pos.	G	AB	R	H	2B	3B	HR	RBI	Avg.	BB	SO	SB	PO	A	E	Avg.
1987—	GC Dodgers (GCL)	1B-SS	49	148	23	49	7	3	0	15	*.331	16	15	3	309	23	6	.982
1988—	Dom. Dodgers (DSL) .	N	19	21	9	8	2	0	0	10	.381	10	6	4	...	...	...	...
—	Salem (N'West)	1B	72	291	47	84	14	4	2	39	.289	21	42	14	585	*38	7	.989
1989—	Vero Beach (FSL)	1B-OF	126	433	53	123	*33	1	10	73	.284	48	58	7	1072	66	12	.990
—	Bakersfield (Calif.)	1B	3	9	2	2	0	0	1	2	.222	0	3	0	8	0	0	1.000
1990—	San Antonio (Texas) ...	OF	129	495	82	144	22	9	*28	*109	.291	61	66	5	223	5	10	.958
1991—	Albuquerque (PCL).....	OF-1B	121	446	61	121	22	5	10	67	.271	25	62	4	234	12	5	.980
1992—	Albuquerque (PCL).....	1B-OF	94	365	59	111	21	5	14	72	.304	31	57	1	484	41	10	.981
—	Los Angeles (N.L.)	OF-1B	53	146	11	32	7	0	3	14	.219	8	30	0	68	8	3	.962
1993—	Albuquerque (PCL).....	1B-OF	46	179	26	53	13	5	4	30	.296	14	37	1	277	18	5	.983
—	Los Angeles (N.L.)	OF-1B	76	176	20	39	10	0	8	23	.222	11	39	1	127	9	1	.993
1994—	Los Angeles (N.L.)	OF-1B	104	306	33	82	14	2	8	49	.268	17	58	0	198	9	2	.990
1995—	Los Angeles (N.L.)	OF-1B	21	80	6	21	4	1	1	10	.263	5	17	0	37	0	0	1.000
—	Montreal (N.L.)■........	1B-OF	24	58	7	12	0	0	1	5	.207	6	11	0	88	7	1	.990
—	Ottawa (I.L.)	DH	4	15	0	3	1	0	0	2	.200	1	4	0	...	...	...	...
1996—	Montreal (N.L.)	OF-1B	145	532	81	147	42	1	36	103	.276	37	*160	2	528	33	11	.981
1997—	Montreal (N.L.)	OF-1B	132	476	55	116	28	3	26	83	.244	42	149	3	220	6	3	.987
1998—	Chicago (N.L.)■..........	OF-DH	128	415	56	104	21	1	31	85	.251	54	113	1	215	7	1	.996
1999—	Chicago (N.L.)	OF-DH	130	447	72	136	29	0	26	87	.304	56	113	2	222	7	6	.974
2000—	Chicago (N.L.)	OF	76	259	37	65	15	1	18	51	.251	22	76	1	110	5	2	.983
—	Florida (N.L.)■..........	OF	36	108	10	29	6	0	2	10	.269	14	23	0	40	1	0	1.000
Major League totals (9 years)			925	3003	388	783	176	9	160	520	.261	272	789	10	1853	92	30	.985

DIVISION SERIES RECORD

							BATTING								FIELDING		
Year	Team (League)	Pos.	G	AB	R	H	2B	3B	HR	RBI	Avg.	BB	SO	SB	PO	A	E	Avg.
1998—	Chicago (N.L.)	OF-PH	3	7	0	1	0	0	0	0	.143	1	2	0	5	1	0	1.000

ALL-STAR GAME RECORD

						BATTING							FIELDING		
Year	League	Pos.	AB	R	H	2B	3B	HR	RBI	Avg.	BB	SO	SB	PO	A	E	Avg.
1996—	National	PH	1	0	1	0	0	0	1	1.000	0	0	0	...	...	...

PERSONAL: Born November 30, 1971, in Vega Baja, Puerto Rico. ... 5-9/205. ... Bats right, throws right. ... Nickname: Pudge.

HIGH SCHOOL: Lina Padron Rivera (Vega Baja, Puerto Rico).

TRANSACTIONS/CAREER NOTES: Signed as non-drafted free agent by Texas Rangers organization (July 27, 1988). ... On disabled list (June 6-27, 1992; July 25, 2000-remainder of season).

RECORDS: Shares major league single-inning record for most doubles—2 (June 14, 2000, fourth inning). ... Holds A.L. single-season record for most home runs by catcher—35 (1999).

HONORS: Won A.L. Gold Glove at catcher (1992-2000). ... Named catcher on THE SPORTING NEWS A.L. All-Star team (1994-99). ... Named catcher on THE SPORTING NEWS A.L. Silver Slugger team (1994-99). ... Named A.L. Most Valuable Player by Baseball Writers' Association of America (1999).

STATISTICAL NOTES: Led South Atlantic League catchers with 34 double plays in 1989. ... Led Florida State League catchers with 842 total chances in 1990. ... Led A.L. catchers with 941 total chances and 11 double plays in 1996. ... Hit three home runs in one game (September 11, 1997). ... Led A.L. catchers with 942 total chances in 1998. ... Had 20-game hitting streak (May 8-June 1, 1999). ... Led A.L. in grounding into double plays with 31 in 1999. ... Led A.L. catchers with 10 double plays in 2000. ... Career major league grand slams: 2.

MISCELLANEOUS: Holds Texas Rangers all-time record for hits (1,459) and doubles (288).

Year	Team (League)	Pos.	G	AB	R	H	2B	3B	HR	RBI	Avg.	BB	SO	SB	PO	A	E	Avg.
1989—	Gastonia (S.Atl.)	C	112	386	38	92	22	1	7	42	.238	21	58	2	691	*96	11	.986
1990—	Charlotte (FSL)	C	109	408	48	117	17	7	2	55	.287	12	50	1	*727	101	14	.983
1991—	Tulsa (Texas)	C	50	175	16	48	7	2	3	28	.274	6	27	1	210	33	3	.988
—	Texas (A.L.)	C	88	280	24	74	16	0	3	27	.264	5	42	0	517	62	10	.983
1992—	Texas (A.L.)	C-DH	123	420	39	109	16	1	8	37	.260	24	73	0	763	85	*15	.983
1993—	Texas (A.L.)	C-DH	137	473	56	129	28	4	10	66	.273	29	70	8	801	76	8	.991
1994—	Texas (A.L.)	C	99	363	56	108	19	1	16	57	.298	31	42	6	600	44	5	.992
1995—	Texas (A.L.)	C-DH	130	492	56	149	32	2	12	67	.303	16	48	0	707	*67	8	.990
1996—	Texas (A.L.)	C-DH	153	639	116	192	47	3	19	86	.300	38	55	5	*850	*81	•10	.989
1997—	Texas (A.L.)	C-DH	150	597	98	187	34	4	20	77	.313	38	89	7	821	*75	7	.992
1998—	Texas (A.L.)	C-DH	145	579	88	186	40	4	21	91	.321	32	88	9	*864	*72	6	.994
1999—	Texas (A.L.)	C-DH	144	600	116	199	29	1	35	113	.332	24	64	25	850	83	7	.993
2000—	Texas (A.L.)	C-DH	91	363	66	126	27	4	27	83	.347	19	48	5	507	34	2	*.996
Major League totals (10 years)			1260	4806	715	1459	288	24	171	704	.304	256	619	65	7280	679	78	.990

DIVISION SERIES RECORD

Year	Team (League)	Pos.	G	AB	R	H	2B	3B	HR	RBI	Avg.	BB	SO	SB	PO	A	E	Avg.
1996—	Texas (A.L.)	C	4	16	1	6	1	0	0	2	.375	2	3	0	21	3	0	1.000
1998—	Texas (A.L.)	C	3	10	0	1	0	0	0	1	.100	0	5	0	27	3	0	1.000
1999—	Texas (A.L.)	C	3	12	0	3	1	0	0	0	.250	0	2	1	21	0	0	1.000
Division series totals (3 years)			10	38	1	10	2	0	0	3	.263	2	10	1	69	6	0	1.000

ALL-STAR GAME RECORD

RECORDS: Shares single-game record for most at-bats (nine-inning game)—5 (July 12, 1994). ... Shares single-game records for most putouts by catcher—10; and most chances accepted by catcher—11 (1999).

Year	League	Pos.	AB	R	H	2B	3B	HR	RBI	Avg.	BB	SO	SB	PO	A	E	Avg.
1992—	American	C	2	0	0	0	0	0	0	.000	0	1	0	4	0	0	1.000
1993—	American	C	2	1	1	1	0	0	0	.500	0	0	0	3	0	0	1.000
1994—	American	C	5	1	2	0	0	0	0	.400	0	1	0	5	0	0	1.000
1995—	American	C	3	0	0	0	0	0	0	.000	0	1	0	6	1	0	1.000
1996—	American	C	2	0	0	0	0	0	0	.000	0	1	0	6	2	0	1.000
1997—	American	C	2	0	0	0	0	0	0	.000	0	0	0	3	1	0	1.000
1998—	American	C	4	1	3	0	0	0	1	.750	0	0	1	5	0	0	1.000
1999—	American	C	2	0	0	0	0	0	0	.000	0	1	0	10	1	0	1.000
2000—	American	C	3	0	1	0	0	0	0	.333	0	0	0	3	0	0	1.000
All-Star Game totals (9 years)			25	3	7	1	0	0	1	.280	0	5	1	45	5	0	1.000

PERSONAL: Born December 18, 1974, in Santurce, Puerto Rico. ... 6-1/215. ... Throws left, bats left. ... Full name: Jose I. Rodriguez.

COLLEGE: Florida International.

TRANSACTIONS/CAREER NOTES: Selected by St. Louis Cardinals organization in 24th round of free-agent draft (June 4, 1997).

Year	League	W	L	Pct.	ERA	G	GS	CG	ShO	Sv.	IP	H	R	ER	BB	SO
1997—	Johnson City (Appl.)	0	0	...	4.05	4	0	0	0	0	6 2/3	4	3	3	3	8
1998—	Peoria (Midw.)	2	4	.333	4.58	40	40	0	0	0	39 1/3	47	32	20	19	30
1999—	Arkansas (Texas)	1	2	.333	3.25	30	0	0	0	0	36	38	16	13	25	30
—	Peoria (Midw.)	2	3	.400	3.31	15	0	0	0	0	16 1/3	14	7	6	8	15
2000—	Arkansas (Texas)	1	0	1.000	2.45	10	0	0	0	1	11	7	3	3	4	8
—	Memphis (PCL)	4	2	.667	3.80	40	0	0	0	3	47 1/3	48	21	20	19	37
—	St. Louis (N.L.)	0	0	...	0.00	6	0	0	0	0	4	2	2	0	3	2
Major League totals (1 year)		0	0	...	0.00	6	0	0	0	0	4	2	2	0	3	2

PERSONAL: Born March 22, 1973, in Bani, Dominican Republic. ... 6-1/205. ... Throws right, bats right.

TRANSACTIONS/CAREER NOTES: Signed as non-drafted free agent by Chicago White Sox organization (February 2, 1990). ... Selected by Baltimore Orioles organization from White Sox organization in Rule 5 minor league draft (December 5, 1994). ... On Frederick disabled list (April 5-August 11, 1996). ... On Baltimore disabled list (May 26-June 30, 1998); included rehabilitation assignment to Bowie (June 24-30).

... Traded by Orioles with OF Shannon Carter to Toronto Blue Jays for P Juan Guzman (July 31, 1998). ... Claimed on waivers by New York Mets (March 28, 2000). ... Claimed on waivers by Boston Red Sox (March 30, 2000). ... Granted free agency (October 18, 2000). ... Signed by Mets organization (November 17, 2000).

STATISTICAL NOTES: Led Gulf Coast League catchers with 312 total chances in 1992.

MISCELLANEOUS: Played catcher (1990-95).

Year League	W	L	Pct.	ERA	G	GS	CG	ShO	Sv.	IP	H	R	ER	BB	SO
1995— High Desert (Calif.)............	0	0	...	1.80	7	0	0	0	0	10	8	2	2	7	10
1996— Frederick (Caro.)	8	7	.533	2.26	24	17	1	0	2	111 1/3	83	42	28	40	114
— Baltimore (A.L.).................	0	1	.000	4.32	8	1	0	0	0	16 2/3	18	11	8	7	12
— Rochester (I.L.).................	1	0	1.000	1.80	2	2	0	0	0	15	10	3	3	2	6
1997— Rochester (I.L.).................	11	10	.524	3.90	27	27	1	1	0	168 1/3	124	82	73	62	*160
— Baltimore (A.L.).................	2	1	.667	4.91	6	2	0	0	0	22	21	15	12	8	11
1998— Rochester (I.L.).................	1	4	.200	5.47	5	5	0	0	0	24 2/3	24	16	15	10	19
— Baltimore (A.L.).................	1	3	.250	8.05	6	4	0	0	0	19	25	17	17	9	8
— Bowie (East.)..................	0	1	.000	4.50	2	2	0	0	0	4	6	2	2	0	7
— Toronto (A.L.)■..............	1	0	1.000	9.72	7	0	0	0	0	8 1/3	10	9	9	8	3
1999— Syracuse (I.L.).................	10	8	.556	4.54	27	27	1	1	0	162 1/3	161	84	82	53	137
— Toronto (A.L.).................	0	1	.000	13.50	2	0	0	0	0	2	2	3	3	2	2
2000— Pawtucket (I.L.)■..............	0	1	.000	9.49	12	1	0	0	0	24 2/3	38	28	26	9	23
— Trenton (East.)	7	7	.500	4.77	19	19	1	0	0	109 1/3	115	64	58	34	93
Major League totals (4 years)	4	6	.400	6.49	29	7	0	0	0	68	76	55	49	34	36

RECORD AS POSITION PLAYER

Year Team (League)	Pos.	G	AB	R	H	2B	3B	HR	RBI	Avg.	BB	SO	SB	PO	A	E	Avg.
1991— GC White Sox (GCL) ..	C	26	89	4	20	1	0	0	8	.225	2	24	3	153	23	5	.972
1992— GC White Sox (GCL) ..	C	41	122	18	33	8	1	2	13	.270	10	31	1	*257	43	*12	.962
1993— Hickory (S.Atl.)..........	C	82	262	31	54	9	2	4	32	.206	27	70	4	476	45	13	.976
1994— South Bend (Midw.)......	C	18	59	4	13	4	0	0	8	.220	2	14	0	95	19	0	1.000
— Prince William (Caro.)	C	6	19	2	4	1	1	0	1	.211	1	9	0	34	6	0	1.000
1995— Bowie (East.)■..........	C	3	4	0	0	0	0	0	0	.000	2	2	0	13	1	0	1.000
— High Desert (Calif.).....	C	58	144	20	34	7	0	4	12	.236	18	50	5	325	34	8	.978

RODRIGUEZ, RICH · P · METS

PERSONAL: Born March 1, 1963, in Downey, Calif. ... 6-0/205. ... Throws left, bats left. ... Full name: Richard Anthony Rodriguez.
HIGH SCHOOL: Mountain View (El Monte, Calif.).
COLLEGE: Tennessee.
TRANSACTIONS/CAREER NOTES: Selected by Kansas City Royals organization in 17th round of free-agent draft (June 8, 1981); did not sign. ... Selected by New York Mets organization in ninth round of free-agent draft (June 4, 1984). ... Traded by Mets to San Diego Padres for 1B Brad Pounders and 1B Bill Stevenson (January 13, 1989). ... Traded by Padres with 3B Gary Sheffield to Florida Marlins for P Trevor Hoffman, P Jose Martinez and P Andres Berumen (June 24, 1993). ... Released by Marlins (March 29, 1994). ... Signed by St. Louis Cardinals (April 1, 1994). ... On disabled list (April 27, 1995-remainder of season). ... Released by Cardinals (November 20, 1995). ... Signed by Cincinnati Reds organization (January 2, 1996). ... Released by Reds (March 24, 1996). ... Signed by Kansas City Royals organization (April 9, 1996). ... On disabled list (May 18-29, 1996). ... Granted free agency (October 15, 1996). ... Signed by San Francisco Giants organization (November 25, 1996). ... Granted free agency (October 30, 1997). ... Re-signed by Giants (December 7, 1997). ... Granted free agency (October 28, 1999). ... Signed by Mets (February 8, 2000).
MISCELLANEOUS: Appeared in one game as pinch runner (1991). ... Had sacrifice hit in only appearance as pinch hitter (1992).

Year League	W	L	Pct.	ERA	G	GS	CG	ShO	Sv.	IP	H	R	ER	BB	SO
1984— Little Falls (NY-Penn)	2	1	.667	2.80	25	1	0	0	0	35 1/3	28	21	11	36	27
1985— Columbia (S.Atl.)...............	6	3	.667	4.03	49	3	0	0	6	80 1/3	89	41	36	36	71
1986— Lynchburg (Caro.)..............	2	1	.667	3.57	36	0	0	0	3	45 1/3	37	20	18	19	38
— Jackson (Texas)	3	4	.429	9.00	13	5	1	0	0	33	51	35	33	15	15
1987— Lynchburg (Caro.)..............	3	1	.750	2.78	*69	0	0	0	5	68	69	23	21	26	59
1988— Jackson (Texas)	2	7	.222	2.87	47	1	0	0	6	78 1/3	66	35	25	42	68
1989— Wichita (Texas)■..............	8	3	.727	3.63	54	0	0	0	8	74 1/3	74	30	30	37	40
1990— Las Vegas (PCL)	3	4	.429	3.51	27	2	0	0	8	59	50	24	23	22	46
— San Diego (N.L.)	1	1	.500	2.83	32	0	0	0	1	47 2/3	52	17	15	16	22
1991— San Diego (N.L.)	3	1	.750	3.26	64	1	0	0	0	80	66	31	29	44	40
1992— San Diego (N.L.)	6	3	.667	2.37	61	1	0	0	0	91	77	28	24	29	64
1993— San Diego (N.L.)	2	3	.400	3.30	34	0	0	0	2	30	34	15	11	9	22
— Florida (N.L.)■..............	0	1	.000	4.11	36	0	0	0	1	46	39	23	21	24	21
1994— St. Louis (N.L.)■..............	3	5	.375	4.03	56	0	0	0	0	60 1/3	62	30	27	26	43
1995— St. Louis (N.L.)...............	0	0	...	0.00	1	0	0	0	0	1 2/3	0	0	0	0	0
1996— Omaha (A.A.)■..............	2	3	.400	3.99	47	0	0	0	3	70	75	40	31	20	68
1997— San Francisco (N.L.)■..	4	3	.571	3.17	71	0	0	0	1	65 1/3	65	24	23	21	32
1998— San Francisco (N.L.)	4	0	1.000	3.70	68	0	0	0	2	65 2/3	69	28	27	20	44
1999— San Francisco (N.L.)	3	0	1.000	5.24	62	0	0	0	1	56 2/3	60	33	33	28	44
2000— New York (N.L.)■..............	0	1	.000	7.78	32	0	0	0	0	37	59	40	32	15	18
— Norfolk (I.L.)	0	1	.000	3.05	14	3	0	0	1	20 2/3	17	7	7	6	16
Major League totals (10 years)	26	18	.591	3.75	517	2	0	0	7	581 1/3	583	269	242	232	350

DIVISION SERIES RECORD

Year League	W	L	Pct.	ERA	G	GS	CG	ShO	Sv.	IP	H	R	ER	BB	SO
1997— San Francisco (N.L.)	0	0	...	0.00	2	0	0	0	0	1	1	0	0	0	0

RODRIGUEZ, WILFREDO · P · ASTROS

PERSONAL: Born March 20, 1979, in Ciudad Bolivar, Venezuela. ... 6-3/180. ... Throws left, bats left. ... Full name: Wilfredo Jose Rodriguez.
TRANSACTIONS/CAREER NOTES: Signed as non-drafted free agent by Houston Astros organization (July 25, 1995). ... On Round Rock disabled list (April 6-May 10, 2000).
STATISTICAL NOTES: Led Midwest League with nine balks in 1998.

Year	League	W	L	Pct.	ERA	G	GS	CG	ShO	Sv.	IP	H	R	ER	BB	SO
1996—	Dom. Astros (DSL)	1	2	.333	2.97	18	0	0	0	0	33 1/3	28	17	11	21	29
1997—	Gulf Coast Astros (GCL)	•8	2	.800	3.04	12	12	1	1	0	68	54	30	23	32	71
1998—	Quad City (Midw.)	11	5	.688	3.05	28	27	1	0	0	165	122	70	56	62	170
1999—	Kissimmee (FSL)	*15	7	.682	2.88	25	24	0	0	0	153 1/3	108	55	49	62	*148
2000—	Round Rock (Texas)	2	4	.333	5.77	11	11	0	0	0	57 2/3	54	42	37	52	55
—	Kissimmee (FSL)	3	5	.375	4.75	9	9	1	0	0	53	43	29	28	30	52

ROGERS, KENNY — P — RANGERS

PERSONAL: Born November 10, 1964, in Savannah, Ga. ... 6-1/217. ... Throws left, bats left. ... Full name: Kenneth Scott Rogers.
HIGH SCHOOL: Plant City (Fla.).
TRANSACTIONS/CAREER NOTES: Selected by Texas Rangers organization in 39th round of free-agent draft (June 7, 1982). ... On Tulsa disabled list (April 12-30, 1986). ... Granted free agency (October 31, 1995). ... Signed by New York Yankees (December 30, 1995). ... Traded by Yankees with IF Mariano Duncan and P Kevin Henthorne to San Diego Padres for OF Greg Vaughn, P Kerry Taylor and P Chris Clark (July 4, 1997); trade later voided because Vaughn failed physical (July 6). ... Traded by Yankees with cash to Oakland Athletics for a player to be named later (November 7, 1997); Yankees acquired 3B Scott Brosius to complete deal (November 18, 1997). ... Traded by A's to New York Mets for OF Terrance Long and P Leo Vasquez (July 23, 1999). ... Granted free agency (October 29, 1999). ... Signed by Rangers (December 29, 1999).
HONORS: Won A.L. Gold Glove as pitcher (2000).
STATISTICAL NOTES: Tied for A.L. lead with five balks in 1993. ... Pitched 4-0 perfect game against California (July 28, 1994). ... Led A.L. pitchers with 46 assists in 2000. ... Led A.L. pitchers with 66 total chances in 2000. ... Led A.L. pitchers with five double plays in 2000.

Year	League	W	L	Pct.	ERA	G	GS	CG	ShO	Sv.	IP	H	R	ER	BB	SO
1982—	Gulf Coast Rangers (GCL)	0	0	...	0.00	2	0	0	0	0	3	0	0	0	0	4
1983—	Gulf Coast Rangers (GCL)	4	1	.800	2.36	15	6	0	0	1	53 1/3	40	21	14	20	36
1984—	Burlington (Midw.)	4	7	.364	3.98	39	4	1	0	3	92 2/3	87	52	41	33	93
1985—	Daytona Beach (FSL)	0	1	.000	7.20	6	0	0	0	0	10	12	9	8	11	9
—	Burlington (Midw.)	2	5	.286	2.84	33	4	2	1	4	95	67	34	30	62	96
1986—	Tulsa (Texas)	0	3	.000	9.91	10	4	0	0	0	26 1/3	39	30	29	18	23
—	Salem (Caro.)	2	7	.222	6.27	12	12	0	0	0	66	75	54	46	26	46
1987—	Charlotte (FSL)	0	3	.000	4.76	5	3	0	0	0	17	17	13	9	8	14
—	Tulsa (Texas)	1	5	.167	5.35	28	6	0	0	2	69	80	51	41	35	59
1988—	Tulsa (Texas)	4	6	.400	4.00	13	13	2	0	0	83 1/3	73	43	37	34	76
—	Charlotte (FSL)	2	0	1.000	1.27	8	6	0	0	1	35 1/3	22	8	5	11	26
1989—	Texas (A.L.)	3	4	.429	2.93	73	0	0	0	2	73 2/3	60	28	24	42	63
1990—	Texas (A.L.)	10	6	.625	3.13	69	3	0	0	15	97 2/3	93	40	34	42	74
1991—	Texas (A.L.)	10	10	.500	5.42	63	9	0	0	5	109 2/3	121	80	66	61	73
1992—	Texas (A.L.)	3	6	.333	3.09	*81	0	0	0	6	78 2/3	80	32	27	26	70
1993—	Texas (A.L.)	16	10	.615	4.10	35	33	5	0	0	208 1/3	210	108	95	71	140
1994—	Texas (A.L.)	11	8	.579	4.46	24	24	6	2	0	167 1/3	169	93	83	52	120
1995—	Texas (A.L.)	17	7	.708	3.38	31	31	3	1	0	208	192	85	78	76	140
1996—	New York (A.L.)■	12	8	.600	4.68	30	30	2	1	0	179	179	97	93	83	92
1997—	New York (A.L.)	6	7	.462	5.65	31	22	1	0	0	145	161	100	91	62	78
1998—	Oakland (A.L.)■	16	8	.667	3.17	34	34	7	1	0	238 2/3	215	96	84	67	138
1999—	Oakland (A.L.)	5	3	.625	4.30	19	19	3	0	0	119 1/3	135	66	57	41	68
—	New York (N.L.)■	5	1	.833	4.03	12	12	2	1	0	76	71	35	34	28	58
2000—	Texas (A.L.)■	13	13	.500	4.55	34	34	2	0	0	227 1/3	257	126	115	78	127
A.L. totals (12 years)		122	90	.575	4.11	524	239	29	5	28	1852 2/3	1872	953	847	701	1183
N.L. totals (1 year)		5	1	.833	4.03	12	12	2	1	0	76	71	35	34	28	58
Major League totals (12 years)		127	91	.583	4.11	536	251	31	6	28	1928 2/3	1943	988	881	729	1241

DIVISION SERIES RECORD

Year	League	W	L	Pct.	ERA	G	GS	CG	ShO	Sv.	IP	H	R	ER	BB	SO
1996—	New York (A.L.)	0	0	...	9.00	2	1	0	0	0	2	5	2	2	2	1
1999—	New York (N.L.)	0	1	.000	8.31	1	1	0	0	0	4 1/3	5	4	4	2	6
Division series totals (2 years)		0	1	.000	8.53	3	2	0	0	0	6 1/3	10	6	6	4	7

CHAMPIONSHIP SERIES RECORD

Year	League	W	L	Pct.	ERA	G	GS	CG	ShO	Sv.	IP	H	R	ER	BB	SO
1996—	New York (A.L.)	0	0	...	12.00	1	1	0	0	0	3	5	4	4	2	3
1999—	New York (N.L.)	0	2	.000	5.87	3	1	0	0	0	7 2/3	11	5	5	7	2
Champ. series totals (2 years)		0	2	.000	7.59	4	2	0	0	0	10 2/3	16	9	9	9	5

WORLD SERIES RECORD

NOTES: Member of World Series championship team (1996).

Year	League	W	L	Pct.	ERA	G	GS	CG	ShO	Sv.	IP	H	R	ER	BB	SO
1996—	New York (A.L.)	0	0	...	22.50	1	1	0	0	0	2	5	5	5	2	0

ALL-STAR GAME RECORD

Year	League	W	L	Pct.	ERA	GS	CG	ShO	Sv.	IP	H	R	ER	BB	SO
1995—	American	0	0	...	9.00	0	0	0	0	1	1	1	1	0	2

ROLEN, SCOTT — 3B — PHILLIES

PERSONAL: Born April 4, 1975, in Jasper, Ind. ... 6-4/226. ... Bats right, throws right. ... Full name: Scott Bruce Rolen.
HIGH SCHOOL: Jasper (Ind.).
TRANSACTIONS/CAREER NOTES: Selected by Philadelphia Phillies organization in second round of free-agent draft (June 3, 1993). ... On disabled list (May 24-June 8, 2000).
RECORDS: Shares major league single-game record for most strikeouts (nine-inning game)—5 (August 23, 1999).
HONORS: Named N.L. Rookie Player of the Year by THE SPORTING NEWS (1997). ... Named N.L. Rookie of the Year by Baseball Writers' Association of America (1997). ... Won N.L. Gold Glove at third base (1998 and 2000).

STATISTICAL NOTES: Led South Atlantic League third basemen with 457 total chances and 36 double plays in 1994. ... Led N.L. third basemen in total chances with 459 in 1997 and 468 in 1998. ... Career major league grand slams: 2.

Year	Team (League)	Pos.	G	AB	R	H	2B	3B	HR	RBI	Avg.	BB	SO	SB	PO	A	E	Avg.
1993—Martinsville (Appl.).....		3B	25	80	8	25	5	0	0	12	.313	10	15	3	23	57	10	.889
1994—Spartanburg (S.Atl.)...		3B	138	513	83	151	34	5	14	72	.294	55	90	6	96	323	38	.917
1995—Clearwater (FSL)...		3B	66	238	45	69	13	2	10	39	.290	37	46	4	43	135	20	.899
—Reading (East.)..........		3B	20	76	16	22	3	0	3	15	.289	7	14	1	10	47	4	.934
1996—Reading (East.)......		3B	61	230	44	83	22	2	9	42	.361	34	32	8	41	125	9	.949
—Scranton/W.B. (I.L.)...		3B	45	168	23	46	17	0	2	19	.274	28	28	4	32	88	6	.952
—Philadelphia (N.L.).....		3B	37	130	10	33	7	0	4	18	.254	13	27	0	29	54	4	.954
1997—Philadelphia (N.L.)....		3B	156	561	93	159	35	3	21	92	.283	76	138	16	*144	291	24	.948
1998—Philadelphia (N.L.)....		3B	160	601	120	174	45	4	31	110	.290	93	141	14	*135	319	14	.970
1999—Philadelphia (N.L.).....		3B	112	421	74	113	28	1	26	77	.268	67	114	12	111	227	14	.960
2000—Philadelphia (N.L.).....		3B	128	483	88	144	32	6	26	89	.298	51	99	8	89	245	10	.971
Major League totals (5 years)			593	2196	385	623	147	14	108	386	.284	300	519	50	508	1136	66	.961

ROLISON, NATE — 1B — MARLINS

PERSONAL: Born March 27, 1977, in Hattiesburg, Miss. ... 6-6/240. ... Bats left, throws right. ... Full name: Nathan Mardis Rolison.
HIGH SCHOOL: Petal (Miss.).
TRANSACTIONS/CAREER NOTES: Selected by Florida Marlins organization in second round of free-agent draft (June 1, 1995). ... On Calgary disabled list (April 19-May 2, 2000).
STATISTICAL NOTES: Led Midwest League first basemen with 1,254 total chances and 114 double plays in 1996. ... Led Florida State first basemen with 89 double plays in 1997.

Year	Team (League)	Pos.	G	AB	R	H	2B	3B	HR	RBI	Avg.	BB	SO	SB	PO	A	E	Avg.
1995—GC Marlins (GCL).......		1B	37	134	22	37	10	2	1	19	.276	15	34	0	283	20	5	.984
1996—Kane County (Midw.)..		1B	131	474	63	115	28	1	14	75	.243	66	170	3	*1161	•80	13	.990
1997—Brevard County (FSL).		1B	122	473	59	121	22	0	16	65	.256	38	*143	3	1036	69	17	.985
1998—Portland (East.)		1B	131	484	80	134	35	2	16	83	.277	64	150	5	1081	85	13	.989
1999—Portland (East.)		1B-DH	124	438	71	131	20	1	17	69	.299	68	112	0	920	69	13	.987
2000—Calgary (PCL).............		1B	123	443	88	146	37	3	23	88	.330	70	117	3	945	76	•12	.988
—Florida (N.L.)...............		1B	8	13	0	1	0	0	0	2	.077	1	4	0	21	2	0	1.000
Major League totals (1 year)			8	13	0	1	0	0	0	2	.077	1	4	0	21	2	0	1.000

ROLLINS, JIMMY — SS — PHILLIES

PERSONAL: Born November 27, 1978, in Oakland. ... 5-8/154. ... Bats both, throws right. ... Full name: James Calvin Rollins. ... Cousin of Tony Tarasco, outfielder with six major league teams (1988-99).
HIGH SCHOOL: Encinal (Alameda, Calif.).
TRANSACTIONS/CAREER NOTES: Selected by Philadelphia Phillies organization in second round of free-agent draft (June 4, 1996).
STATISTICAL NOTES: Led South Atlantic League shortstops wth 648 total chances in 1997.

Year	Team (League)	Pos.	G	AB	R	H	2B	3B	HR	RBI	Avg.	BB	SO	SB	PO	A	E	Avg.
1996—Martinsville (Appl.).....		SS	49	172	22	41	3	1	1	16	.238	28	20	11	66	126	20	.906
1997—Piedmont (S.Atl.)........		SS	139	560	94	151	22	8	6	59	.270	52	80	46	*201	*421	26	*.960
1998—Clearwater (FSL)		SS	119	495	72	121	18	9	6	35	.244	41	62	23	192	380	29	*.952
1999—Reading (East.)...........		SS	133	532	81	145	21	8	11	56	.273	51	47	24	211	*392	22	.965
—Scranton/W.B. (I.L.) ...		SS	4	13	0	1	1	0	0	0	.077	1	1	1	9	15	1	.960
2000—Scranton/W.B. (I.L.) ...		SS	133	470	67	129	28	•11	12	69	.274	49	55	24	183	*411	26	.958
—Philadelphia (N.L.)......		SS	14	53	5	17	1	1	0	5	.321	2	7	3	23	22	1	.978
Major League totals (1 year)			14	53	5	17	1	1	0	5	.321	2	7	3	23	22	1	.978

ROLLS, DAMIAN — 3B — DEVIL RAYS

PERSONAL: Born September 15, 1977, in Manhattan, Kan. ... 6-2/205. ... Bats right, throws right. ... Full name: Damian Michael Rolls.
HIGH SCHOOL: F.L. Schlagle (Kansas City, Kan.).
TRANSACTIONS/CAREER NOTES: Selected by Los Angeles Dodgers organization in first round (23rd pick overall) of free-agent draft (June 4, 1996). ... Selected by Kansas City Royals from Dodgers organization in Rule 5 major league draft (December 13, 1999). ... Traded by Royals to Tampa Bay Devil Rays for a player to be named later and cash (December 13, 1999). ... On Tampa Bay disabled list (March 25-September 1, 2000); included rehabilitation assignments to St. Petersburg (August 12-18) and Orlando (August 19-September 1).
STATISTICAL NOTES: Led Northwest League third basemen with 215 total chances in 1996. ... Led South Atlantic League third basemen with 388 total chances in 1997.

Year	Team (League)	Pos.	G	AB	R	H	2B	3B	HR	RBI	Avg.	BB	SO	SB	PO	A	E	Avg.
1996—Yakima (N'West)		3B	66	257	31	68	11	1	4	27	.265	7	46	8	*58	*134	•23	.893
1997—Savannah (S.Atl.)		3B	130	475	57	100	17	5	5	47	.211	38	83	11	*111	*246	31	.920
1998—Vero Beach (FSL)		3B	73	266	28	65	9	0	0	30	.244	23	43	13	65	187	13	.951
—San Antonio (Texas)...		3B	50	160	18	35	6	0	1	9	.219	6	28	2	38	124	9	.947
1999—Vero Beach (FSL)		3B-2B	127	474	68	141	26	2	9	54	.297	36	66	24	91	213	25	.924
2000—St. Petersburg (FSL) ..		3B	5	16	2	3	2	0	0	0	.188	2	3	1	2	9	0	1.000
—Orlando (Sou.)		3B	14	51	6	13	5	0	0	3	.255	7	6	1	7	22	3	.906
—Tampa Bay (A.L.)........		DH-3B	4	3	0	1	0	0	0	0	.333	0	1	0	0	0	0	...
Major League totals (1 year)			4	3	0	1	0	0	0	0	.333	0	1	0	0	0	0	...

R

ROMERO, J.C.　　　　　P　　　　　TWINS

PERSONAL: Born June 4, 1976, in Rio Piedras, Puerto Rico. ... 5-11/195. ... Throws left, bats both. ... Full name: Juan C. Romero.
HIGH SCHOOL: Berwing (San Juan, Puerto Rico).
COLLEGE: Mobile.
TRANSACTIONS/CAREER NOTES: Selected by Minnesota Twins organization in 21st round of free-agent draft (June 3, 1997). ... On Minnesota disabled list (March 25-May 10, 2000); included rehabilitation assignment to Fort Myers (May 3-10).

Year	League	W	L	Pct.	ERA	G	GS	CG	ShO	Sv.	IP	H	R	ER	BB	SO
1997—	Elizabethton (Appl.)	3	2	.600	4.88	18	0	0	0	3	24	27	16	13	7	29
—	Fort Myers (FSL)	1	1	.500	4.38	7	1	0	0	0	12 1/3	11	6	6	4	9
1998—	New Britain (East.)	6	3	.667	2.19	51	1	0	0	2	78	48	28	19	43	79
1999—	New Britain (East.)	4	4	.500	3.40	36	1	0	0	7	53	51	25	20	34	53
—	Salt Lake (PCL)	4	1	.800	3.20	15	0	0	0	1	19 2/3	18	11	7	14	20
—	Minnesota (A.L.)	0	0	...	3.72	5	0	0	0	0	9 2/3	13	4	4	0	4
2000—	Fort Myers (FSL)	0	0	...	1.93	2	0	0	0	0	4 2/3	4	1	1	1	3
—	Minnesota (A.L.)	2	7	.222	7.02	12	11	0	0	0	57 2/3	72	51	45	30	50
—	Salt Lake (PCL)	4	2	.667	3.44	17	11	1	0	4	65 1/3	60	40	25	25	38
Major League totals (2 years)		2	7	.222	6.55	17	11	0	0	0	67 1/3	85	55	49	30	54

ROMERO, MANDY　　　　　C　　　　　MARLINS

PERSONAL: Born October 29, 1967, in Miami. ... 5-11/196. ... Bats both, throws right. ... Full name: Armando Romero. ... Brother of Andy Romero, minor league first baseman/outfielder (1977-80).
HIGH SCHOOL: Miami Senior.
JUNIOR COLLEGE: Brevard Community College (Fla.).
TRANSACTIONS/CAREER NOTES: Selected by Pittsburgh Pirates in 19th round of free-agent draft (June 1, 1988). ... On disabled list (April 11-29 and June 20-28, 1991; July 13-August 7, 1992; and June 28-July 8 and August 23, 1993-remainder of season). ... Released by Pirates (May 6, 1994). ... Signed by Kansas City Royals organization (January 30, 1995). ... Granted free agency (October 16, 1995). ... Signed by San Diego Padres organization (November 25, 1995). ... Granted free agency (October 15, 1996). ... Re-signed by Padres (October 27, 1996). ... Traded by Padres with P Carlos Reyes and P Dario Veras to Boston Red Sox for C Jim Leyritz and OF Ethan Faggett (June 21, 1998). ... On Pawtucket disabled list (July 29-August 5, 1998). ... Traded by Red Sox to New York Mets for a player to be named later (July 30, 1999). ... Granted free agency (October 5, 1999). ... Signed by Cleveland Indians organization (December 22, 1999). ... On Buffalo disabled list (August 6-September 6, 2000). ... Granted free agency (October 18, 2000). ... Signed by Florida Marlins organization (November 21, 2000).
STATISTICAL NOTES: Led South Atlantic League catchers with .989 fielding percentage in 1989. ... Led Carolina League with 222 total bases and .483 slugging percentage in 1990. ... Tied for Southern League lead with 14 passed balls in 1991. ... Tied for Southern League lead in errors by catcher with 14 in 1992.

Year	Team (League)	Pos.	G	AB	R	H	2B	3B	HR	RBI	Avg.	BB	SO	SB	PO	A	E	Avg.
								BATTING								**FIELDING**		
1988—	Princeton (Appl.)	C	30	71	7	22	6	0	2	11	.310	13	15	1	143	14	2	.987
1989—	Augusta (S.Atl.)	C-3B	121	388	58	87	26	3	4	55	.224	67	74	8	629	74	9	†.987
1990—	Salem (Caro.)	C	124	460	62	134	31	3	17	*90	.291	55	68	0	565	60	7	.989
1991—	Carolina (Sou.)	C	98	323	29	70	12	0	3	31	.217	45	53	1	552	63	4	*.994
1992—	Carolina (Sou.)	C-3B	80	269	28	58	16	0	3	27	.216	29	39	0	523	43	‡14	.976
1993—	Buffalo (A.A.)	C	42	136	11	31	6	1	2	14	.228	6	12	1	168	13	5	.973
1994—	Buffalo (A.A.)	C	7	23	3	3	0	0	0	1	.130	2	1	0	34	5	0	1.000
1995—	Wichita (Texas)■	DH-C-1B	121	440	73	133	32	1	21	82	.302	69	60	1	159	18	4	.978
1996—	Memphis (Sou.)■	C-DH	88	297	40	80	15	0	10	46	.269	41	52	3	657	52	12	.983
1997—	Mobile (Sou.)	C-DH	61	222	50	71	22	0	13	52	.320	38	31	0	436	33	6	.987
—	Las Vegas (PCL)	C-3B-DH-1B	33	91	19	28	4	1	3	13	.308	11	19	0	145	8	3	.981
—	San Diego (N.L.)	C	21	48	7	10	0	0	2	4	.208	2	18	1	96	8	0	1.000
1998—	Las Vegas (PCL)	C-1B-DH	40	131	25	38	8	0	8	22	.290	20	25	0	307	29	7	.980
—	San Diego (N.L.)	C	6	9	1	0	0	0	0	0	.000	1	3	0	24	2	1	.963
—	Pawtucket (I.L.)■	C-DH	45	139	20	46	5	0	8	27	.331	24	15	0	311	27	3	.991
—	Boston (A.L.)	C-DH	12	13	2	3	1	0	0	1	.231	3	3	0	11	0	0	1.000
1999—	Pawtucket (I.L.)	C	46	143	8	31	7	0	3	22	.217	13	26	0	316	20	2	.994
—	Norfolk (I.L.)■	C-DH	28	97	7	25	6	0	1	9	.258	9	18	0	162	10	3	.983
2000—	Akron (East.)■	C	79	280	55	87	19	2	12	46	.311	43	34	1	484	46	2	*.996
—	Buffalo (I.L.)	C	4	17	1	7	2	0	0	4	.412	0	2	0	26	3	0	1.000
American League totals (1 year)			12	13	2	3	1	0	0	1	.231	3	3	0	11	0	0	1.000
National League totals (2 years)			27	57	8	10	0	0	2	4	.175	3	21	1	120	10	1	.992
Major League totals (2 years)			39	70	10	13	1	0	2	5	.186	6	24	1	131	10	1	.993

ROQUE, RAFAEL　　　　　P　　　　　BREWERS

PERSONAL: Born October 27, 1973, in Cotui, Dominican Republic. ... 6-4/189. ... Throws left, bats left. ... Full name: Rafael Antonio Roque.
TRANSACTIONS/CAREER NOTES: Signed as non-drafted free agent by New York Mets organization (March 15, 1991). ... Granted free agency (October 17, 1997). ... Signed by Milwaukee Brewers organization (October 31, 1997).

Year	League	W	L	Pct.	ERA	G	GS	CG	ShO	Sv.	IP	H	R	ER	BB	SO
1991—	Dom. Mets (DSL)	1	0	1.000	5.40	4	0	0	0	1	5	4	6	3	9	1
1992—	Gulf Coast Mets (GCL)	3	1	.750	2.14	20	0	0	0	8	33 2/3	28	13	8	16	33
1993—	Kingsport (Appl.)	1	3	.250	6.15	14	7	0	0	0	45 1/3	58	44	31	26	36
1994—	St. Lucie (FSL)	0	0	...	0.00	2	0	0	0	0	3	1	0	0	3	2
—	Columbia (S.Atl.)	6	3	.667	2.40	15	15	1	0	0	86 1/3	73	26	23	30	74
1995—	St. Lucie (FSL)	6	9	.400	3.56	24	24	2	1	0	136 2/3	114	65	54	72	81
1996—	Binghamton (East.)	0	4	.000	7.27	13	13	0	0	0	60 2/3	71	57	49	39	46
—	St. Lucie (FSL)	6	4	.600	2.12	14	12	1	0	0	76 1/3	57	22	18	39	59
1997—	Binghamton (East.)	1	1	.500	6.84	16	0	0	0	0	26 1/3	35	26	20	17	23
—	St. Lucie (FSL)	2	10	.167	4.29	17	13	1	0	0	77 2/3	81	42	37	25	54

Year League	W	L	Pct.	ERA	G	GS	CG	ShO	Sv.	IP	H	R	ER	BB	SO
1998— El Paso (Texas)■	5	6	.455	4.40	16	16	1	0	0	94	113	56	46	35	70
— Louisville (I.L.)	5	2	.714	3.62	9	8	0	0	0	49 2/3	42	21	20	19	43
— Milwaukee (N.L.)	4	2	.667	4.88	9	9	0	0	0	48	42	28	26	24	34
1999— Milwaukee (N.L.)	1	6	.143	5.34	43	9	0	0	1	84 1/3	96	52	50	42	66
— Louisville (I.L.)	1	0	1.000	0.00	2	2	0	0	0	10	4	0	0	3	3
2000— Indianapolis (I.L.)	9	4	.692	4.15	25	20	1	1	0	132 1/3	127	66	61	63	111
— Milwaukee (N.L.)	0	0	...	10.13	4	0	0	0	0	5 1/3	7	6	6	7	4
Major League totals (3 years)	5	8	.385	5.36	56	18	0	0	1	137 2/3	145	86	82	73	104

ROSADO, JOSE   P   ROYALS

PERSONAL: Born November 9, 1974, in Jersey City, N.J. ... 6-0/185. ... Throws left, bats left. ... Full name: Jose Antonio Rosado.
HIGH SCHOOL: Jose S. Alegria (Dorado, Puerto Rico).
JUNIOR COLLEGE: Galveston College (Texas).
TRANSACTIONS/CAREER NOTES: Selected by Kansas City Royals organization in 12th round of free-agent draft (June 2, 1994). ... On disabled list (May 1, 2000-remainder of season).
MISCELLANEOUS: Appeared in one game as pinch runner (1997).

Year League	W	L	Pct.	ERA	G	GS	CG	ShO	Sv.	IP	H	R	ER	BB	SO
1994— Gulf Coast Royals (GCL)	6	2	.750	*1.25	14	12	0	0	0	64 2/3	45	14	9	7	56
1995— Wilmington (Caro.)	10	7	.588	3.13	25	25	0	0	0	138	128	53	48	30	117
1996— Wichita (Texas)	2	0	1.000	0.00	2	2	0	0	0	13	10	0	0	1	12
— Omaha (A.A.)	8	3	.727	3.17	15	15	1	0	0	96 2/3	80	38	34	38	82
— Kansas City (A.L.)	8	6	.571	3.21	16	16	2	1	0	106 2/3	101	39	38	26	64
1997— Kansas City (A.L.)	9	12	.429	4.69	33	33	2	0	0	203 1/3	208	117	106	73	129
1998— Kansas City (A.L.)	8	11	.421	4.69	38	25	2	1	1	174 2/3	180	106	91	57	135
1999— Kansas City (A.L.)	10	14	.417	3.85	33	33	5	0	0	208	197	103	89	72	141
2000— Kansas City (A.L.)	2	2	.500	5.86	5	5	0	0	0	27 2/3	29	18	18	9	15
Major League totals (5 years)	37	45	.451	4.27	125	112	11	2	1	720 1/3	715	383	342	237	484

ALL-STAR GAME RECORD

Year League	W	L	Pct.	ERA	GS	CG	ShO	Sv.	IP	H	R	ER	BB	SO
1997— American	1	0	1.000	9.00	0	0	0	0	1	2	1	1	1	1
1999— American	0	0	...	0.00	0	0	0	0	1	1	0	0	0	1
All-Star Game totals (2 years)	1	0	1.000	4.50	0	0	0	0	2	3	1	1	1	2

ROSE, BRIAN   P   ROCKIES

PERSONAL: Born February 13, 1976, in New Bedford, Mass. ... 6-3/215. ... Throws right, bats right. ... Full name: Brian Leonard Rose.
HIGH SCHOOL: Dartmouth (North Dartmouth, Mass.).
TRANSACTIONS/CAREER NOTES: Selected by Boston Red Sox organization in third round of free-agent draft (June 2, 1994). ... On Boston disabled list (May 13, 1998-remainder of season); included rehabilitation assignment to Pawtucket (June 13-July 10). ... Traded by Red Sox with P John Wasdin, P Jeff Taglienti and 2B Jeff Frye to Colorado Rockies for P Rolando Arrojo, P Rick Croushore, 2B Mike Lansing and cash (July 27, 2000).
HONORS: Named International League Most Valuable Pitcher (1997).

Year League	W	L	Pct.	ERA	G	GS	CG	ShO	Sv.	IP	H	R	ER	BB	SO
1995— Michigan (Midw.)	8	5	.615	3.44	21	20	2	0	0	136	127	63	52	31	105
1996— Trenton (East.)	12	7	.632	4.01	27	27	4	2	0	163 2/3	157	82	73	45	115
1997— Pawtucket (I.L.)	*17	5	.773	*3.02	27	26	3	0	0	*190 2/3	188	74	64	46	116
— Boston (A.L.)	0	0	...	12.00	1	1	0	0	0	3	5	4	4	2	3
1998— Boston (A.L.)	1	4	.200	6.93	8	8	0	0	0	37 2/3	43	32	29	14	18
— Pawtucket (I.L.)	0	3	.000	7.64	6	6	0	0	0	17 2/3	24	19	15	4	17
1999— Pawtucket (I.L.)	2	1	.667	2.89	7	7	0	0	0	28	28	10	9	8	30
— Boston (A.L.)	7	6	.538	4.87	22	18	0	0	0	98	112	59	53	29	51
2000— Boston (A.L.)	3	5	.375	6.11	15	12	0	0	0	53	58	37	36	21	24
— Pawtucket (I.L.)	4	1	.800	3.19	5	5	1	0	0	31	28	13	11	13	20
— Colorado (N.L.)■	4	5	.444	5.51	12	12	0	0	0	63 2/3	72	41	39	30	40
A.L. totals (4 years)	11	15	.423	5.73	46	39	0	0	0	191 2/3	218	132	122	66	96
N.L. totals (1 year)	4	5	.444	5.51	12	12	0	0	0	63 2/3	72	41	39	30	40
Major League totals (4 years)	15	20	.429	5.67	58	51	0	0	0	255 1/3	290	173	161	96	136

DIVISION SERIES RECORD

Year League	W	L	Pct.	ERA	G	GS	CG	ShO	Sv.	IP	H	R	ER	BB	SO
1999— Boston (A.L.)							Did not play.								

CHAMPIONSHIP SERIES RECORD

Year League	W	L	Pct.	ERA	G	GS	CG	ShO	Sv.	IP	H	R	ER	BB	SO
1999— Boston (A.L.)							Did not play.								

ROSE, TED   P   EXPOS

PERSONAL: Born August 23, 1973, in Lima, Ohio. ... 6-2/185. ... Throws right, bats left. ... Full name: Teddy Michael Rose.
HIGH SCHOOL: St. Clairsville (Ohio).
COLLEGE: Kent.
TRANSACTIONS/CAREER NOTES: Selected by Cincinnati Reds organization in 14th round of free-agent draft (June 4, 1996). ... On Chattanooga disabled list (April 23-August 11, 1999). ... Selected by Montreal Expos from Reds organization in Rule 5 major league draft (December 11, 2000).

Year	League	W	L	Pct.	ERA	G	GS	CG	ShO	Sv.	IP	H	R	ER	BB	SO
1996—Princeton (Appl.)		3	5	.375	6.22	11	11	1	0	0	59 1/3	70	44	41	21	53
1997—Charleston, W.Va. (S.Atl.)		11	6	.647	2.51	38	13	2	2	4	129 1/3	108	44	36	27	132
1998—Chattanooga (Sou.)		11	10	.524	4.60	29	•29	1	0	0	168 1/3	191	97	86	66	108
1999—Chattanooga (Sou.)		2	0	1.000	4.24	13	0	0	0	2	17	17	8	8	9	23
—Gulf Coast Reds (GCL)		0	0	...	9.00	1	0	0	0	0	2	4	2	2	1	3
2000—Chattanooga (Sou.)		4	2	.667	1.10	31	0	0	0	8	41	24	8	5	9	51
—Louisville (I.L.)		2	2	.500	4.97	23	0	0	0	2	38	36	23	21	13	33

ROSKOS, JOHN — OF/C

PERSONAL: Born November 19, 1974, in Victorville, Calif. ... 5-11/195. ... Bats right, throws right. ... Full name: John Edward Roskos.
HIGH SCHOOL: Cibola (Albuquerque, N.M.).
TRANSACTIONS/CAREER NOTES: Selected by Florida Marlins organization in second round of free-agent draft (June 3, 1993). ... On disabled list (August 9-September 19, 1994). ... On disabled list (August 28-September 7, 1995). ... Granted free agency (December 21, 1997). ... Re-signed by Marlins organization (December 21, 1997). ... Granted free agency (October 5, 1999). ... Signed by San Diego Padres organization (November 22, 1999). ... On Las Vegas disabled list (July 27-August 3, 2000). ... Granted free agency (October 18, 2000).

Year	Team (League)	Pos.	G	AB	R	H	2B	3B	HR	RBI	Avg.	BB	SO	SB	PO	A	E	Avg.
1993—GC Marlins (GCL)	C	11	40	6	7	1	0	1	3	.175	5	11	1	18	2	2	.909
1994—Elmira (NY-Penn)	C	39	136	11	38	7	0	4	23	.279	27	37	0	143	13	4	.975
1995—Kane County (Midw.)	C	114	418	74	124	36	3	12	88	.297	42	86	2	431	47	7	.986
1996—Portland (East.)	1B-C	121	396	53	109	26	3	9	58	.275	67	102	3	719	50	10	.987
1997—Portland (East.)	C-1B	123	451	66	139	31	1	24	84	.308	50	81	4	630	37	8	.988
1998—Charlotte (I.L.)	1B-OF	115	416	54	118	23	1	10	62	.284	43	84	0	647	38	4	.994
—Florida (N.L.)	1B	10	10	1	1	0	0	0	0	.100	0	5	0	1	0	0	1.000
1999—Calgary (PCL)	O-1-DH-C-3	134	506	85	162	*44	2	24	90	.320	52	112	2	374	22	6	.985
—Florida (N.L.)	C	13	12	0	2	0	0	0	1	.167	1	7	0	5	0	0	1.000
2000—Las Vegas (PCL)■	O-1B-C-3B	99	377	75	120	29	0	18	74	.318	53	67	2	268	14	4	.986
—San Diego (N.L.)	OF-1B	14	27	0	1	1	0	0	1	.037	3	7	0	7	1	1	.889
Major League totals (3 years)		37	49	1	4	3	0	0	2	.082	4	19	0	13	1	1	.933

RUETER, KIRK — P — GIANTS

PERSONAL: Born December 1, 1970, in Centralia, Ill. ... 6-2/205. ... Throws left, bats left. ... Full name: Kirk Wesley Rueter. ... Name pronounced REE-ter.
HIGH SCHOOL: Nashville (Ill.) Community.
COLLEGE: Murray State.
TRANSACTIONS/CAREER NOTES: Selected by Montreal Expos organization in 19th round of free-agent draft (June 3, 1991). ... On Montreal disabled list (May 10-26, 1996); included rehabilitation assignment to Ottawa (May 20-24). ... Traded by Expos with P Tim Scott to San Francisco Giants for P Mark Leiter (July 30, 1996).
HONORS: Named N.L. Rookie Pitcher of the Year by THE SPORTING NEWS (1993).
STATISTICAL NOTES: Pitched 1-0 one-hit, complete-game victory for Montreal against San Francisco (August 27, 1995).
MISCELLANEOUS: Caught stealing in only appearance as pinch runner (1998). ... Scored one run in two appearances as pinch runner (2000).

Year	League	W	L	Pct.	ERA	G	GS	CG	ShO	Sv.	IP	H	R	ER	BB	SO
1991—Gulf Coast Expos (GCL)	1	1	.500	0.95	5	4	0	0	0	19	16	5	2	4	19
—Sumter (S.Atl.)	3	1	.750	1.33	8	5	0	0	0	40 2/3	32	8	6	10	27
1992—Rockford (Midw.)	11	9	.550	2.58	26	26	6	•2	0	174 1/3	150	68	50	36	153
1993—Harrisburg (East.)	5	0	1.000	1.36	9	8	1	1	0	59 2/3	47	10	9	7	36
—Ottawa (I.L.)	4	2	.667	2.70	7	7	1	0	0	43 1/3	46	20	13	3	27
—Montreal (N.L.)	8	0	1.000	2.73	14	14	1	0	0	85 2/3	85	33	26	18	31
1994—Montreal (N.L.)	7	3	.700	5.17	20	20	0	0	0	92 1/3	106	60	53	23	50
—Ottawa (I.L.)	0	0	...	4.50	1	1	0	0	0	2	1	1	1	0	1
1995—Montreal (N.L.)	5	3	.625	3.23	9	9	1	1	0	47 1/3	38	17	17	9	28
—Ottawa (I.L.)	9	7	.563	3.06	20	20	3	1	0	120 2/3	120	50	41	25	67
1996—Ottawa (I.L.)	1	2	.333	4.20	3	3	1	0	0	15	21	7	7	3	3
—Montreal (N.L.)	5	6	.455	4.58	16	16	0	0	0	78 2/3	91	44	40	22	30
—San Francisco (N.L.)■	1	2	.333	1.93	4	3	0	0	0	23 1/3	18	6	5	5	16
—Phoenix (PCL)	1	2	.333	3.51	5	5	0	0	0	25 2/3	25	12	10	12	15
1997—San Francisco (N.L.)	13	6	.684	3.45	32	32	0	0	0	190 2/3	194	83	73	51	115
1998—San Francisco (N.L.)	16	9	.640	4.36	33	33	1	0	0	187 2/3	193	100	91	70	102
1999—San Francisco (N.L.)	15	10	.600	5.41	33	33	1	0	0	184 2/3	219	118	111	55	94
2000—San Francisco (N.L.)	11	9	.550	3.96	32	31	0	0	0	184	205	92	81	62	71
Major League totals (8 years)	81	48	.628	4.16	193	191	4	1	0	1074 1/3	1149	553	497	302	537

DIVISION SERIES RECORD

Year	League	W	L	Pct.	ERA	G	GS	CG	ShO	Sv.	IP	H	R	ER	BB	SO
1997—San Francisco (N.L.)	0	0	...	1.29	1	1	0	0	0	7	4	1	1	3	5
2000—San Francisco (N.L.)	0	0	...	0.00	1	0	0	0	0	4 1/3	3	0	0	1	1
Division series totals (2 years)	0	0	...	0.79	2	1	0	0	0	11 1/3	7	1	1	4	6

RUFFIN, JOHNNY — P — DIAMONDBACKS

PERSONAL: Born July 29, 1971, in Butler, Ala. ... 6-3/170. ... Throws right, bats right. ... Full name: Johnny Renando Ruffin.
HIGH SCHOOL: Choctaw County (Butler, Ala.).
TRANSACTIONS/CAREER NOTES: Selected by Chicago White Sox organization in fourth round of free-agent draft (June 1, 1988). ... Traded by White Sox with P Jeff Pierce to Cincinnati Reds for P Tim Belcher (July 31, 1993). ... On Cincinnati disabled list (September 1, 1995-remainder of season). ... Granted free agency (December 20, 1996). ... Signed by Boston Red Sox organization (December 27, 1996). ... Contract

sold by Red Sox to Kintetsu Buffaloes of Japan Pacific League (May 1, 1997). ... Signed by Milwaukee Brewers organization (November 17, 1997). ... Granted free agency (October 15, 1998). ... Signed by Kansas City Royals organization (March 1, 1999). ... Released by Royals (March 27, 1999). ... Signed by Los Angeles Dodgers organization (April 30, 1999). ... Granted free agency (October 15, 1999). ... Signed by Cincinnati Reds organization (January 20, 2000). ... Released by Reds (March 5, 2000). ... Signed by Arizona Diamondbacks organization (April 10, 2000). ... On disabled list (August 14, 2000-remainder of season).

STATISTICAL NOTES: Pitched 6-1 no-hit victory against Charlotte (June 14, 1991, second game).

Year League	W	L	Pct.	ERA	G	GS	CG	ShO	Sv.	IP	H	R	ER	BB	SO
1988— GC White Sox (GCL)	4	2	.667	2.30	13	11	1	0	0	58²/₃	43	27	15	22	31
1989— Utica (NY-Penn)	4	8	.333	3.36	15	15	0	0	0	88¹/₃	67	43	33	46	92
1990— South Bend (Midw.)	7	6	.538	4.17	24	24	0	0	0	123	117	86	57	82	92
1991— Sarasota (FSL)	11	4	.733	3.23	26	26	6	2	0	158²/₃	126	68	57	62	117
1992— Birmingham (Sou.).............	0	7	.000	6.04	10	10	0	0	0	47²/₃	51	48	32	34	44
— Sarasota (FSL)	3	7	.300	5.89	23	8	0	0	0	62²/₃	56	46	41	41	61
1993— Birmingham (Sou.).............	0	4	.000	2.82	11	0	0	0	2	22¹/₃	16	9	7	9	23
— Nashville (A.A.)	3	4	.429	3.30	29	0	0	0	1	60	48	24	22	16	69
— Indianapolis (A.A.)■	1	1	.500	1.35	3	0	0	0	1	6²/₃	3	1	1	2	6
— Cincinnati (N.L.)	2	1	.667	3.58	21	0	0	0	2	37²/₃	36	16	15	11	30
1994— Cincinnati (N.L.)	7	2	.778	3.09	51	0	0	0	1	70	57	26	24	27	44
1995— Cincinnati (N.L.)	0	0	...	1.35	10	0	0	0	0	13¹/₃	4	3	2	11	11
— Indianapolis (A.A.).............	3	1	.750	2.90	36	1	0	0	0	49²/₃	27	19	16	37	58
1996— Cincinnati (N.L.)	1	3	.250	5.49	49	0	0	0	0	62¹/₃	71	42	38	37	69
1997— Pawtucket (I.L.)■	0	1	.000	4.50	6	1	0	0	0	14	5	7	7	16	16
— Kintetsu (Jap. Pac.)■........	0	0	...	5.40	1	1	0	0	0	5	3	3	3	...	...
1998— Louisville (I.L.)■..............	5	3	.625	3.00	35	2	0	0	0	60	40	27	20	48	57
— Norfolk (I.L.)■................	1	0	1.000	2.77	17	3	0	0	0	39	31	15	12	20	40
1999— Oaxaca (Mex.)■	0	1	.000	5.68	5	0	0	0	1	6¹/₃	5	6	4	5	5
— Albuquerque (PCL)■............	1	1	.500	3.17	46	0	0	0	10	54	41	21	19	26	66
2000— Tucson (PCL)■	5	3	.625	2.98	45	0	0	0	20	57¹/₃	48	21	19	25	66
— Arizona (N.L.)■................	0	0	...	9.00	5	0	0	0	0	9	14	9	9	3	5
Major League totals (5 years)	10	6	.625	4.12	136	0	0	0	3	192¹/₃	182	96	88	89	159

RUNYAN, SEAN   P   TIGERS

PERSONAL: Born June 21, 1974, in Fort Smith, Ark. ... 6-3/210. ... Throws left, bats left. ... Full name: Sean David Runyan.
HIGH SCHOOL: Urbandale (Iowa).
TRANSACTIONS/CAREER NOTES: Selected by Houston Astros organization in fifth round of free-agent draft (June 1, 1992). ... Traded by Astros to San Diego Padres for IF Luis Lopez (March 15, 1997). ... Selected by Detroit Tigers from Padres organization in Rule 5 major league draft (December 15, 1997). ... On Detroit disabled list (May 7, 1999-remainder of season); included rehabilitation assignment to Toledo (June 4-July 1). ... On Detroit disabled list (March 28-June 4, 2000); included rehabilitation assignments to Jacksonville (April 6-11 and April 20-23) and Toledo (April 24-June 3). ... Granted free agency (October 18, 2000). ... Re-signed by Tigers organization (October 24, 2000).
RECORDS: Holds major league rookie-season record for most games pitched—88 (1998).

Year League	W	L	Pct.	ERA	G	GS	CG	ShO	Sv.	IP	H	R	ER	BB	SO
1992— Gulf Coast Astros (GCL)......	3	3	.500	3.20	10	10	0	0	0	45	54	19	16	16	30
1993— Gulf Coast Astros (GCL)......	4	3	.571	2.98	12	12	0	0	0	66¹/₃	66	35	22	24	52
1994— Auburn (NY-Penn).............	7	5	.583	3.49	14	14	2	1	0	95¹/₃	90	49	37	19	66
1995— Quad City (Midw.)	4	6	.400	3.66	22	11	0	0	0	76¹/₃	67	37	31	29	65
1996— Quad City (Midw.)	9	4	.692	3.88	29	17	0	0	0	132¹/₃	128	61	57	30	104
1997— Mobile (Sou.)	5	2	.714	2.34	40	1	0	0	1	61²/₃	54	25	16	28	52
1998— Detroit (A.L.)■...............	1	4	.200	3.58	*88	0	0	0	1	50¹/₃	47	23	20	28	39
1999— Detroit (A.L.)..................	0	1	.000	3.38	12	0	0	0	0	10²/₃	9	4	4	3	6
— Toledo (I.L.)....................	0	0	...	3.48	10	0	0	0	0	10¹/₃	7	4	4	6	7
2000— Jacksonville (Sou.)............	0	0	...	21.60	3	0	0	0	0	1²/₃	4	4	4	2	1
— Toledo (I.L.).....................	1	2	.333	5.84	44	0	0	0	1	49¹/₃	58	36	32	35	32
— Detroit (A.L.)	0	0	...	6.00	3	0	0	0	0	3	2	2	2	2	1
Major League totals (3 years)	1	5	.167	3.66	103	0	0	0	1	64	58	29	26	33	46

RUPE, RYAN   P   DEVIL RAYS

PERSONAL: Born March 31, 1975, in Houston. ... 6-5/230. ... Throws right, bats right. ... Full name: Ryan Kittman Rupe.
HIGH SCHOOL: Northbrook (Houston).
COLLEGE: Texas A&M.
TRANSACTIONS/CAREER NOTES: Selected by New York Mets organization in 19th round of free-agent draft (June 3, 1993); did not sign. ... Selected by Kansas City Royals organization in 36th round of free-agent draft (June 4, 1996); did not sign. ... Selected by Tampa Bay Devil Rays organization in sixth round of free-agent draft (June 2, 1998). ... On Durham disabled list (May 9-June 16, 2000). ... On Tampa Bay disabled list (September 11, 2000-remainder of season).

Year League	W	L	Pct.	ERA	G	GS	CG	ShO	Sv.	IP	H	R	ER	BB	SO
1998— Hudson Valley (NY-Penn)...	1	0	1.000	0.68	3	3	0	0	0	13¹/₃	8	1	1	2	18
— Charleston, S.C. (S.Atl.) ...	6	1	.857	2.40	10	10	0	0	0	56¹/₃	33	18	15	9	62
1999— Orlando (Sou.)	2	2	.500	2.73	5	5	0	0	0	26¹/₃	18	13	8	6	22
— Tampa Bay (A.L.)................	8	9	.471	4.55	24	24	0	0	0	142¹/₃	136	81	72	57	97
2000— Tampa Bay (A.L.)............	5	6	.455	6.92	18	18	0	0	0	91	121	75	70	31	61
— Durham (I.L.)	0	1	.000	6.52	5	5	0	0	0	19¹/₃	24	16	14	7	18
Major League totals (2 years)	13	15	.464	5.48	42	42	0	0	0	233¹/₃	257	156	142	88	158

RUSCH, GLENDON   P   METS

PERSONAL: Born November 7, 1974, in Seattle. ... 6-1/200. ... Throws left, bats left. ... Full name: Glendon James Rusch.
HIGH SCHOOL: Shorecrest (Seattle).

TRANSACTIONS/CAREER NOTES: Selected by Kansas City Royals organization in 17th round of free-agent draft (June 3, 1993). ... On Kansas City disabled list (June 16-July 1, 1997); included rehabilitation assignment to Omaha (June 26-July 1). ... On Kansas City disabled list (August 9-September 4, 1998); included rehabilitation assignment to Omaha (August 24-September 4). ... On Omaha disabled list (May 31-July 1, 1999). ... Traded by Royals to New York Mets for P Dan Murray (September 14, 1999).

STATISTICAL NOTES: Pitched 9-0 no-hit victory against Kane County (August 7, 1994).

Year League	W	L	Pct.	ERA	G	GS	CG	ShO	Sv.	IP	H	R	ER	BB	SO
1993— Gulf Coast Royals (GCL)	4	2	.667	1.60	11	10	0	0	0	62	43	14	11	11	48
— Rockford (Midw.)	0	1	.000	3.38	2	2	0	0	0	8	10	6	3	7	8
1994— Rockford (Midw.)	8	5	.615	4.66	28	17	1	1	1	114	111	61	59	34	122
1995— Wilmington (Caro.)...........	*14	6	.700	*1.74	26	26	1	1	0	165²/₃	110	41	32	34	147
1996— Omaha (A.A.)...................	11	9	.550	3.98	28	28	1	0	0	169²/₃	177	88	75	40	117
1997— Kansas City (A.L.)	6	9	.400	5.50	30	27	1	0	0	170¹/₃	206	111	104	52	116
— Omaha (A.A.)...................	0	1	.000	4.50	1	1	0	0	0	6	7	3	3	1	2
1998— Kansas City (A.L.)	6	15	.286	5.88	29	24	1	1	1	154²/₃	191	104	101	50	94
— Omaha (PCL)...................	1	1	.500	7.98	3	3	0	0	0	14²/₃	20	18	13	6	14
1999— Omaha (PCL)...................	4	7	.364	4.42	20	20	1	0	0	114	143	68	56	33	102
— Gulf Coast Royals (GCL)	0	0	...	1.50	2	2	0	0	0	6	3	1	1	3	9
— Kansas City (A.L.)	0	1	.000	15.75	3	0	0	0	0	4	7	7	7	3	4
— New York (N.L.)■..............	0	0	...	0.00	1	0	0	0	0	1	1	0	0	0	0
2000— New York (N.L.).................	11	11	.500	4.01	31	30	2	0	0	190²/₃	196	91	85	44	157
A.L. totals (3 years)	12	25	.324	5.80	62	51	2	1	1	329	404	222	212	105	214
N.L. totals (2 years)	11	11	.500	3.99	32	30	2	0	0	191²/₃	197	91	85	44	157
Major League totals (4 years).......	23	36	.390	5.13	94	81	4	1	1	520²/₃	601	313	297	149	371

DIVISION SERIES RECORD

Year League	W	L	Pct.	ERA	G	GS	CG	ShO	Sv.	IP	H	R	ER	BB	SO
2000— New York (N.L.).................	0	0	...	0.00	1	0	0	0	0	²/₃	0	0	0	0	2

CHAMPIONSHIP SERIES RECORD

Year League	W	L	Pct.	ERA	G	GS	CG	ShO	Sv.	IP	H	R	ER	BB	SO
2000— New York (N.L.).................	1	0	1.000	0.00	2	0	0	0	0	3²/₃	3	0	0	0	3

WORLD SERIES RECORD

Year League	W	L	Pct.	ERA	G	GS	CG	ShO	Sv.	IP	H	R	ER	BB	SO
2000— New York (N.L.).................	0	0	...	2.25	3	0	0	0	0	4	6	1	1	2	2

RYAN, B.J. P ORIOLES

PERSONAL: Born December 28, 1975, in Bossier City, La. ... 6-6/230. ... Throws left, bats left. ... Full name: Robert Victor Ryan Jr.

HIGH SCHOOL: Airline (Bossier City, La.).

COLLEGE: Southwestern Louisiana.

TRANSACTIONS/CAREER NOTES: Selected by Cincinnati Reds organization in 17th round of free-agent draft (June 2, 1998). ... Traded by Reds with P Jacobo Sequea to Baltimore Orioles for P Juan Guzman (July 31, 1999).

Year League	W	L	Pct.	ERA	G	GS	CG	ShO	Sv.	IP	H	R	ER	BB	SO
1998— Billings (Pio.)	2	1	.667	1.93	14	0	0	0	4	18²/₃	15	4	4	5	25
— Charleston, W.Va. (S.Atl.)...	0	0	...	2.08	3	0	0	0	2	4¹/₃	1	1	1	1	5
— Chattanooga (Sou.)	1	0	1.000	2.20	16	0	0	0	4	16¹/₃	13	4	4	6	21
1999— Chattanooga (Sou.)	2	1	.667	2.59	35	0	0	0	6	41²/₃	33	13	12	17	46
— Indianapolis (I.L.)	1	0	1.000	4.00	11	0	0	0	0	9	9	4	4	3	12
— Cincinnati (N.L.)	0	0	...	4.50	1	0	0	0	0	2	4	1	1	1	1
— Rochester (I.L.)■................	0	0	...	2.51	11	0	0	0	1	14¹/₃	8	4	4	4	20
— Baltimore (A.L.).................	1	0	1.000	2.95	13	0	0	0	0	18¹/₃	9	6	6	12	28
2000— Baltimore (A.L.).................	2	3	.400	5.91	42	0	0	0	0	42²/₃	36	29	28	31	41
— Rochester (I.L.).................	0	1	.000	4.74	14	4	0	0	0	24²/₃	23	13	13	9	28
A.L. totals (2 years)	3	3	.500	5.02	55	0	0	0	0	61	45	35	34	43	69
N.L. totals (1 year)	0	0	...	4.50	1	0	0	0	0	2	4	1	1	1	1
Major League totals (2 years).......	3	3	.500	5.00	56	0	0	0	0	63	49	36	35	44	70

RYAN, JASON P

PERSONAL: Born January 23, 1976, in Long Branch, N.J. ... 6-3/195. ... Throws right, bats both. ... Full name: Jason Paul Ryan. ... Son of Tim Ryan, pitcher in Los Angeles Dodgers and Atlanta Braves organizations; brother of Sean Ryan, minor league infielder with Philadelphia Phillies organization (1990-93); and nephew of Ed Madjeski, catcher with three major league teams (1932-34 and 1937).

HIGH SCHOOL: Immaculata (Somerville, N.J.).

TRANSACTIONS/CAREER NOTES: Selected by Chicago Cubs organization in ninth round of free-agent draft (June 2, 1994). ... Traded by Cubs with P Kyle Lohse to Minnesota Twins for P Rick Aguilera and P Scott Downs (May 21, 1999). ... Released by Twins (December 11, 2000).

Year League	W	L	Pct.	ERA	G	GS	CG	ShO	Sv.	IP	H	R	ER	BB	SO
1994— Gulf Coast Cubs (GCL).......	1	2	.333	4.09	7	7	0	0	0	33	32	19	15	4	30
— Huntington (Appl.)	2	0	1.000	0.35	4	4	1	1	0	26	7	1	1	8	32
— Orlando (Sou.)	2	0	1.000	2.45	2	2	0	0	0	11	6	3	3	6	12
1995— Daytona (FSL)	11	5	.688	3.48	26	26	0	0	0	134²/₃	128	61	52	54	98
1996— Orlando (Sou.)	2	5	.286	5.71	7	7	0	0	0	34²/₃	39	30	22	24	25
— Daytona (FSL)	1	8	.111	5.24	17	10	0	0	1	67	72	42	39	33	49
1997— Daytona (FSL)	9	8	.529	4.44	27	27	5	0	0	170¹/₃	168	105	84	55	140
1998— West Tenn (Sou.)	3	•13	.188	4.88	30	25	2	0	0	147²/₃	172	97	80	57	121
1999— West Tenn (Sou.)	5	0	1.000	1.41	8	7	0	0	0	44²/₃	29	12	7	15	53
— New Britain (East.)■...........	2	4	.333	4.80	8	8	0	0	0	50²/₃	48	29	27	24	42
— Salt Lake (PCL)	4	4	.500	5.13	9	9	0	0	0	54¹/₃	57	36	31	24	24
— Minnesota (A.L.)	1	4	.200	4.87	8	8	1	0	0	40²/₃	46	23	22	17	15
2000— Salt Lake (PCL)	9	2	.818	4.38	17	17	2	1	0	96²/₃	94	52	47	31	66
— Minnesota (A.L.)	0	1	.000	7.62	16	1	0	0	0	26	37	24	22	10	19
Major League totals (2 years).......	1	5	.167	5.94	24	9	1	0	0	66²/₃	83	47	44	27	34

PERSONAL: Born June 24, 1973, in Havre, Mont. ... 5-11/190. ... Bats left, throws left. ... Full name: Robert James Ryan.
HIGH SCHOOL: Shadle Park (Spokane, Wash.).
COLLEGE: Washington State.
TRANSACTIONS/CAREER NOTES: Selected by Arizona Diamondbacks organization in 36th round of free-agent draft (June 4, 1996). ... On Tucson disabled list (June 15-July 3, 2000).

Year	Team (League)	Pos.	G	AB	R	H	2B	3B	HR	RBI	Avg.	BB	SO	SB	PO	A	E	Avg.
1996—Lethbridge (Pio.)		OF	59	211	55	64	8	1	4	37	.303	43	33	23	107	3	4	.965
1997—South Bend (Midw.)		OF	121	421	71	132	35	5	8	73	.314	89	58	12	188	11	7	.966
1998—Tucson (PCL)		OF	116	394	71	125	18	2	17	66	.317	63	61	9	224	3	4	.983
1999—Tucson (PCL)		OF-DH	117	414	72	120	30	5	19	88	.290	56	70	4	182	8	6	.969
—Arizona (N.L.)		OF	20	29	4	7	1	0	2	5	.241	1	8	0	7	0	0	1.000
2000—Tucson (PCL)		OF	92	332	56	102	19	1	8	55	.307	45	35	1	156	7	1	.994
—Arizona (N.L.)		OF-DH	27	27	4	8	1	1	0	2	.296	4	7	0	1	0	0	1.000
Major League totals (2 years)			47	56	8	15	2	1	2	7	.268	5	15	0	8	0	0	1.000

R
S

PERSONAL: Born April 11, 1964, in Chicago Heights, Ill. ... 6-1/200. ... Throws right, bats right. ... Full name: Bret William Saberhagen. ... Name pronounced SAY-ber-HAY-gun.
HIGH SCHOOL: Cleveland (Reseda, Calif.).
TRANSACTIONS/CAREER NOTES: Selected by Kansas City Royals organization in 19th round of free-agent draft (June 7, 1982). ... On disabled list (August 10-September 1, 1986; July 16-September 10, 1990; and June 15-July 13, 1991). ... Traded by Royals with IF Bill Pecota to New York Mets for OF Kevin McReynolds, IF Gregg Jefferies and 2B Keith Miller (December 11, 1991). ... On disabled list (May 16-July 18 and August 2-September 7, 1992 and August 3, 1993-remainder of season). ... On suspended list (April 3-8, 1994). ... Traded by Mets with a player to be named later to Colorado Rockies for P Juan Acevedo and P Arnold Gooch (July 31, 1995); Rockies acquired P David Swanson to complete deal (August 4, 1995). ... On disabled list (March 22, 1996-entire season). ... Granted free agency (October 29, 1996). ... Signed by Boston Red Sox organization (December 9, 1996). ... On Boston disabled list (March 31-August 22, 1997); included rehabilitation assignments to Lowell (August 1-7) and Trenton (August 1-12) and Pawtucket (August 12-22). ... Granted free agency (October 31, 1997). ... Re-signed by Red Sox (November 17, 1997). ... On Boston disabled list (May 7-June 1, June 8-23 and August 18-September 10, 1999); included rehabilitation assignment to Trenton (May 27-June 1). ... On Boston disabled list (March 19, 2000-entire season); included rehabilitation assignments to Sarasota (May 15-16), Lowell (July 18-24), Pawtucket (July 25-August 6 and August 19-September 1) and Trenton (August 14-18).
HONORS: Named A.L. Pitcher of the Year by THE SPORTING NEWS (1985 and 1989). ... Named righthanded pitcher on THE SPORTING NEWS A.L. All-Star team (1985 and 1989). ... Named A.L. Cy Young Award winner by Baseball Writers' Association of America (1985 and 1989). ... Named A.L. Comeback Player of the Year by THE SPORTING NEWS (1987 and 1998). ... Won A.L. Gold Glove at pitcher (1989).
STATISTICAL NOTES: Pitched 7-0 no-hit victory against Chicago (August 26, 1991).
MISCELLANEOUS: Appeared in one game as pinch runner (1984). ... Appeared in three games as pinch runner (1989).

Year League	W	L	Pct.	ERA	G	GS	CG	ShO	Sv.	IP	H	R	ER	BB	SO
1983—Fort Myers (FSL)	10	5	.667	2.30	16	16	3	1	0	109 2/3	98	34	28	19	82
—Jacksonville (Sou.)	6	2	.750	2.91	11	11	2	1	0	77 1/3	66	31	25	29	48
1984—Kansas City (A.L.)	10	11	.476	3.48	38	18	2	1	1	157 2/3	138	71	61	36	73
1985—Kansas City (A.L.)	20	6	.769	2.87	32	32	10	1	0	235 1/3	211	79	75	38	158
1986—Kansas City (A.L.)	7	12	.368	4.15	30	25	4	2	0	156	165	77	72	29	112
1987—Kansas City (A.L.)	18	10	.643	3.36	33	33	15	4	0	257	246	99	96	53	163
1988—Kansas City (A.L.)	14	16	.467	3.80	35	35	9	0	0	260 2/3	*271	122	110	59	171
1989—Kansas City (A.L.)	*23	6	.793	*2.16	36	35	*12	4	0	*262 1/3	209	74	63	43	193
1990—Kansas City (A.L.)	5	9	.357	3.27	20	20	5	0	0	135	146	52	49	28	87
1991—Kansas City (A.L.)	13	8	.619	3.07	28	28	7	2	0	196 1/3	165	76	67	45	136
1992—New York (N.L.)■	3	5	.375	3.50	17	15	1	1	0	97 2/3	84	39	38	27	81
1993—New York (N.L.)	7	7	.500	3.29	19	19	4	1	0	139 1/3	131	55	51	17	93
1994—New York (N.L.)	14	4	.778	2.74	24	24	4	0	0	177 1/3	169	58	54	13	143
1995—New York (N.L.)■	5	5	.500	3.35	16	16	3	0	0	110	105	45	41	20	71
—Colorado (N.L.)■	2	1	.667	6.28	9	9	0	0	0	43	60	33	30	13	29
1996—Colorado (N.L.)					Did not play.										
1997—Lowell (NY-Penn)■	0	0	...	0.00	1	1	0	0	0	3	1	0	0	0	2
—Trenton (East.)	0	0	...	0.00	2	2	0	0	0	8	2	0	0	1	9
—Pawtucket (I.L.)	0	1	.000	3.27	2	2	0	0	0	11	11	4	4	1	9
—Boston (A.L.)	0	1	.000	6.58	6	6	0	0	0	26	30	20	19	10	14
1998—Boston (A.L.)	15	8	.652	3.96	31	31	0	0	0	175	181	82	77	29	100
1999—Boston (A.L.)	10	6	.625	2.95	22	22	0	0	0	119	122	43	39	11	81
—Trenton (East.)	1	0	1.000	0.00	1	1	0	0	0	6	2	0	0	0	5
2000—Sarasota (FSL)	0	1	.000	27.00	1	1	0	0	0	1	5	3	3	0	2
—Lowell (NY-Penn)	0	0	...	0.00	1	1	0	0	0	3	1	0	0	0	5
—Pawtucket (I.L.)	0	0	...	5.54	4	4	0	0	0	13	14	8	8	4	9
—Trenton (East.)	0	0	...	6.00	1	1	0	0	0	3	1	2	2	1	3
A.L. totals (11 years)	135	93	.592	3.31	311	285	64	14	1	1980 1/3	1884	795	728	381	1288
N.L. totals (4 years)	31	22	.585	3.39	85	83	12	2	0	567 1/3	549	230	214	90	417
Major League totals (15 years)	166	115	.591	3.33	396	368	76	16	1	2547 2/3	2433	1025	942	471	1705

DIVISION SERIES RECORD

Year League	W	L	Pct.	ERA	G	GS	CG	ShO	Sv.	IP	H	R	ER	BB	SO
1995—Colorado (N.L.)	0	1	.000	11.25	1	1	0	0	0	4	7	6	5	1	3
1998—Boston (A.L.)	0	1	.000	3.86	1	1	0	0	0	7	4	3	3	1	7
1999—Boston (A.L.)	0	1	.000	27.00	2	2	0	0	0	3 2/3	9	11	11	4	2
Division series totals (3 years)	0	3	.000	11.66	4	4	0	0	0	14 2/3	20	20	19	6	12

CHAMPIONSHIP SERIES RECORD

Year League	W	L	Pct.	ERA	G	GS	CG	ShO	Sv.	IP	H	R	ER	BB	SO
1984— Kansas City (A.L.)	0	0	...	2.25	1	1	0	0	0	8	6	3	2	1	5
1985— Kansas City (A.L.)	0	0	...	6.14	2	2	0	0	0	7 1/3	12	5	5	2	6
1999— Boston (A.L.)......................	0	1	.000	1.50	1	1	0	0	0	6	5	3	1	1	5
Champ. series totals (3 years)	0	1	.000	3.38	4	4	0	0	0	21 1/3	23	11	8	4	16

NOTES: Named Most Valuable Player (1985). ... Member of World Series championship team (1985).

WORLD SERIES RECORD

Year League	W	L	Pct.	ERA	G	GS	CG	ShO	Sv.	IP	H	R	ER	BB	SO
1985— Kansas City (A.L.)	2	0	1.000	0.50	2	2	2	1	0	18	11	1	1	1	10

ALL-STAR GAME RECORD

Year League	W	L	Pct.	ERA	GS	CG	ShO	Sv.	IP	H	R	ER	BB	SO
1987— American	0	0	...	0.00	1	0	0	0	3	1	0	0	0	0
1990— American	1	0	1.000	0.00	0	0	0	0	2	0	0	0	0	1
1994— National								Did not play.						
All-Star Game totals (2 years)	1	0	1.000	0.00	1	0	0	0	5	1	0	0	0	1

SADLER, DONNIE   IF   REDS

S

PERSONAL: Born June 17, 1975, in Gohlson, Texas. ... 5-6/175. ... Bats right, throws right. ... Full name: Donnie Lamont Sadler.
HIGH SCHOOL: Valley Mills (Texas).
TRANSACTIONS/CAREER NOTES: Selected by Boston Red Sox organization in 10th round of free-agent draft (June 2, 1994). ... On Pawtucket disabled list (May 4-June 4 and June 23-30, 1998; and June 25-July 18, 1999). ... Traded by Red Sox with OF Michael Coleman to Cincinnati Reds for IF Chris Stynes (November 16, 2000).
STATISTICAL NOTES: Tied for International League lead in errors by second baseman with 12 in 1997. ... Tied for International League lead in caught stealing with 14 in 1997.

							BATTING							FIELDING		
Year Team (League)	Pos.	G	AB	R	H	2B	3B	HR	RBI	Avg.	BB	SO	SB	PO	A	E	Avg.
1994— GC Red Sox (GCL)	SS-3B-2B	53	206	52	56	8	6	1	16	.272	23	27	32	80	151	18	.928
— Fort Myers (GCL)	SS	53	206	52	56	8	6	1	16	.272	23	27	32	...	...	...	...
1995— Michigan (Midw.)	SS	118	438	*103	124	25	8	9	55	.283	79	85	41	168	307	28	.944
1996— Trenton (East.)	SS-OF	115	454	68	121	20	8	6	46	.267	38	75	34	185	237	27	.940
1997— Pawtucket (I.L.)..........	2B-SS-OF	125	481	74	102	18	2	11	36	.212	57	121	20	252	354	‡15	.976
1998— Boston (A.L.)..............	2B-DH-SS	58	124	21	28	4	4	3	15	.226	6	28	4	81	101	5	.973
— Pawtucket (I.L.)	2B-SS	36	131	25	29	5	1	2	10	.221	26	23	11	73	104	4	.978
1999— Boston (A.L.)..............S-2-3-0-DH		49	107	18	30	5	1	0	4	.280	5	20	2	46	52	9	.916
— Pawtucket (I.L.)	SS-DH	43	172	23	50	12	4	1	17	.291	16	36	4	73	96	10	.944
— GC Red Sox (GCL)	SS	4	13	2	5	2	0	0	1	.385	2	1	0	7	12	1	.950
2000— Pawtucket (I.L.)..........	OF-SS-2B	91	313	45	63	6	5	5	23	.201	45	60	10	211	108	7	.979
— Boston (A.L.)..............	S-0-2-3-D	49	99	14	22	5	0	1	10	.222	5	18	3	49	71	3	.976
Major League totals (3 years)		156	330	53	80	14	5	4	29	.242	16	66	9	176	224	17	.959

DIVISION SERIES RECORD

							BATTING							FIELDING		
Year Team (League)	Pos.	G	AB	R	H	2B	3B	HR	RBI	Avg.	BB	SO	SB	PO	A	E	Avg.
1998— Boston (A.L.)..............	2B-PR	3	0	0	0	0	0	0	0	...	0	0	0	1	1	0	1.000
1999— Boston (A.L.)..............PH-3B-PR-DH		2	2	1	1	1	0	0	0	.500	0	1	0	1	1	0	1.000
Division series totals (2 years)		5	2	1	1	1	0	0	0	.500	0	1	0	2	2	0	1.000

CHAMPIONSHIP SERIES RECORD

							BATTING							FIELDING		
Year Team (League)	Pos.	G	AB	R	H	2B	3B	HR	RBI	Avg.	BB	SO	SB	PO	A	E	Avg.
1999— Boston (A.L.)..............	PR-OF-DH	2	0	0	0	0	0	0	0	...	0	0	0	0	0	0	...

SAENZ, OLMEDO   3B/1B   ATHLETICS

PERSONAL: Born October 8, 1970, in Chitre Herrera, Panama. ... 6-0/185. ... Bats right, throws right. ... Full name: Olmedo Sanchez Saenz. ... Name pronounced SIGNS.
TRANSACTIONS/CAREER NOTES: Signed as non-drafted free agent by Chicago White Sox organization (May 11, 1990). ... Granted free agency (October 15, 1997). ... Re-signed by White Sox organization (January 25, 1998). ... Granted free agency (October 15, 1998). ... Signed by Oakland Athletics (November 13, 1998). ... On Oakland disabled list (July 26-August 16, 1999); included rehabilitation assignment to Vancouver (August 13-16). ... On Oakland disabled list (August 1-September 19, 2000); included rehabilitation assignment to Sacramento (August 29-30).
STATISTICAL NOTES: Led American Association third basemen with 395 total chances in 1995. ... Tied for American Association lead in being hit by pitch with 13 in 1996. ... Led American Association third basemen with 363 total chances and 24 double plays in 1996. ... Led Pacific Coast League in being hit by pitch with 22 in 1998.

							BATTING							FIELDING		
Year Team (League)	Pos.	G	AB	R	H	2B	3B	HR	RBI	Avg.	BB	SO	SB	PO	A	E	Avg.
1991— South Bend (Midw.) ...	3B	56	192	23	47	10	1	2	22	.245	21	48	5	29	68	12	.890
— Sarasota (FSL)	3B	5	19	1	2	0	1	0	2	.105	2	0	0	5	11	3	.842
1992— South Bend (Midw.) ...	3B-1B	132	493	66	121	26	4	7	59	.245	36	52	16	113	294	48	.895
1993— South Bend (Midw.) ...	3B	13	50	3	18	4	1	0	7	.360	7	7	1	11	31	4	.913
— Sarasota (FSL)	3B	33	121	13	31	9	4	0	27	.256	9	18	3	15	55	5	.933
— Birmingham (Sou.)......	3B	49	173	30	60	17	2	6	29	.347	20	21	2	38	87	14	.899
1994— Nashville (A.A.)	3B-DH	107	383	48	100	27	2	12	59	.261	30	57	3	76	167	22	.917
— Chicago (A.L.)	3B	5	14	2	2	0	1	0	0	.143	0	5	0	3	5	0	1.000

– 500 –

Year	Team (League)	Pos.	G	AB	R	H	2B	3B	HR	RBI	Avg.	BB	SO	SB	PO	A	E	Avg.
1995—Nashville (A.A.)	3B	111	415	60	126	26	1	13	74	.304	45	60	0	*82	*289	*24	*.939
1996—Nashville (A.A.)	3B-DH	134	476	86	124	29	1	18	63	.261	53	80	4	*97	244	22	.939
1997—GC White Sox (GCL) ..	DH	2	1	0	1	1	0	0	0	1.000	0	0	0	0	0	0	...
1998—Calgary (PCL)............	3B-DH	124	466	89	146	29	0	29	102	.313	45	49	3	75	235	21	.937
1999—Oakland (A.L.).■........	3B-1B-DH	97	255	41	70	18	0	11	41	.275	22	47	1	180	91	8	.971
—Vancouver (PCL)......	3B	2	5	1	3	1	0	0	2	.600	0	0	0	1	0	0	1.000
2000—Oakland (A.L.)...........	DH-3B-1B	76	214	40	67	12	2	9	33	.313	25	40	1	137	33	4	.977
—Sacramento (PCL)......	DH	1	4	1	2	0	0	0	1	.500	0	0	0	...	...	...	...
Major League totals (3 years)		178	483	83	139	30	3	20	74	.288	47	92	2	320	129	12	.974

DIVISION SERIES RECORD

Year	Team (League)	Pos.	G	AB	R	H	2B	3B	HR	RBI	Avg.	BB	SO	SB	PO	A	E	Avg.
2000—Oakland (A.L.)	PH-DH	4	13	1	3	0	0	1	4	.231	0	2	0	...	...	...	...

SALMON, TIM   OF   ANGELS

S

PERSONAL: Born August 24, 1968, in Long Beach, Calif. ... 6-3/231. ... Bats right, throws right. ... Full name: Timothy James Salmon. ... Brother of Mike Salmon, safety with San Francisco 49ers (1997).

HIGH SCHOOL: Greenway (Phoenix).

COLLEGE: Grand Canyon (Ariz.).

TRANSACTIONS/CAREER NOTES: Selected by Atlanta Braves organization in 18th round of free-agent draft (June 2, 1986); did not sign. ... Selected by California Angels organization in third round of free-agent draft (June 5, 1989). ... On disabled list (May 12-23 and May 27-August 7, 1990; and July 18-August 3, 1994). ... Angels franchise renamed Anaheim Angels for 1997 season. ... On disabled list (April 23-May 9, 1998). ... On Anaheim disabled list (May 4-July 17, 1999); included rehabilitation assignment to Lake Elsinore (July 16-17).

RECORDS: Shares major league record for fewest double plays by outfielder (150 or more games)—0 (1996). ... Shares major league single-inning record for most doubles—2 (September 23, 2000, second inning). ... Shares A.L. record for most hits in three consecutive games—13 (May 10 [4], 11 [4] and 13 [5], 1994).

HONORS: Named Minor League Player of the Year by THE SPORTING NEWS (1992). ... Named Pacific Coast League Most Valuable Player (1992). ... Named A.L. Rookie Player of the Year by THE SPORTING NEWS (1993). ... Named A.L. Rookie of the Year by Baseball Writers' Association of America (1993). ... Named outfielder on THE SPORTING NEWS A.L. All-Star team (1995 and 1997). ... Named outfielder on THE SPORTING NEWS Silver Slugger team (1995).

STATISTICAL NOTES: Led Pacific Coast League with 275 total bases, .672 slugging percentage and .469 on-base percentage in 1992. ... Led A.L. outfielders with four double plays in 1994. ... Tied for A.L. lead in double plays by outfielder with five in 1997. ... Had 17-game hitting streak (July 23-August 9, 2000). ... Career major league grand slams: 5.

MISCELLANEOUS: Holds Angels all-time record for home runs (230).

Year	Team (League)	Pos.	G	AB	R	H	2B	3B	HR	RBI	Avg.	BB	SO	SB	PO	A	E	Avg.
1989—Bend (N'West)............	OF	55	196	37	48	6	5	6	31	.245	33	60	2	84	7	4	.958
1990—Palm Springs (Calif.)...	OF	36	118	19	34	6	0	2	21	.288	21	44	11	63	3	1	.985
—Midland (Texas).........	OF	27	97	17	26	3	1	3	16	.268	18	38	1	51	6	3	.950
1991—Midland (Texas).........	OF	131	465	100	114	26	4	23	94	.245	*89	*166	12	265	16	10	.966
1992—Edmonton (PCL)........	OF	118	409	•101	142	38	4	*29	*105	.347	91	103	9	231	14	3	.988
—California (A.L.)..........	OF	23	79	8	14	1	0	2	6	.177	11	23	1	40	1	2	.953
1993—California (A.L.)..........	OF-DH	142	515	93	146	35	1	31	95	.283	82	135	5	335	12	7	.980
1994—California (A.L.)..........	OF	100	373	67	107	18	2	23	70	.287	54	102	1	219	9	8	.966
1995—California (A.L.)..........	OF-DH	143	537	111	177	34	3	34	105	.330	91	111	5	320	7	4	.988
1996—California (A.L.)..........	OF-DH	156	581	90	166	27	4	30	98	.286	93	125	4	299	13	8	.975
1997—Anaheim (A.L.)..........	OF-DH	157	582	95	172	28	1	33	129	.296	95	142	9	352	15	11	.971
1998—Anaheim (A.L.)..........	DH-OF	136	463	84	139	28	1	26	88	.300	90	100	0	46	1	2	.959
1999—Anaheim (A.L.)..........	OF-DH	98	353	60	94	24	2	17	69	.266	63	82	4	204	7	4	.981
—Lake Elsinore (Calif.)..	DH	1	5	0	3	2	0	0	2	.600	0	1	0	...	...	...	...
2000—Anaheim (A.L.)..........	OF-DH	158	568	108	165	36	2	34	97	.290	104	139	0	274	12	6	.979
Major League totals (9 years)		1113	4051	716	1180	231	16	230	757	.291	683	959	29	2089	77	52	.977

SANCHEZ, ALEX   OF   DEVIL RAYS

PERSONAL: Born August 26, 1976, in Havana, Cuba. ... 5-10/180. ... Bats left, throws left. ... Full name: Alexis Sanchez.

JUNIOR COLLEGE: Miami-Dade (Wolfson) Community College.

TRANSACTIONS/CAREER NOTES: Selected by Tampa Bay Devil Rays organization in fifth round of free-agent draft (June 4, 1996).

STATISTICAL NOTES: Led Gulf Coast League with 12 caught stealing in 1996. ... Led South Atlantic League outfielders with 296 total chances in 1997. ... Led South Atlantic League in caught stealing with 40 in 1997. ... Led Florida State League in caught stealing with 33 and sacrifice flies with 12 in 1998. ... Led Southern League in caught stealing with 27 and sacrifice hits with 10 in 1999. ... Led International League in caught stealing with 20 in 2000.

Year	Team (League)	Pos.	G	AB	R	H	2B	3B	HR	RBI	Avg.	BB	SO	SB	PO	A	E	Avg.
1996—GC Devil Rays (GCL) ..	OF	56	227	36	64	7	6	1	22	.282	10	35	20	91	1	3	.968
1997—Char., S.C. (SAL)	OF	131	537	73	155	15	6	0	34	.289	37	72	*92	279	6	•11	.963
1998—St. Petersburg (FSL) ..	OF	128	545	77	*180	17	9	1	50	.330	31	70	66	330	5	•12	.965
1999—Orlando (Sou.)	OF	121	500	68	127	12	4	2	29	.254	26	88	48	314	8	*14	.958
—Durham (I.L.)	OF	3	10	2	2	1	0	0	0	.200	1	0	0	8	0	0	1.000
2000—Durham (I.L.)	OF	107	446	76	130	18	3	2	33	.291	30	66	*52	243	11	6	.977
—Orlando (Sou.)	OF	20	86	12	25	2	1	0	4	.291	1	13	2	34	1	1	.972

SANCHEZ, JESUS P MARLINS

PERSONAL: Born October 11, 1974, in Nizao Bani, Dominican Republic. ... 5-10/155. ... Throws left, bats left. ... Full name: Jesus Paulino Sanchez.
TRANSACTIONS/CAREER NOTES: Signed as non-drafted free agent by New York Mets organization (June 7, 1992). ... On disabled list (April 4-May 28, 1996). ... Traded by Mets with P A.J. Burnett and OF Robert Stratton to Florida Marlins for P Al Leiter and 2B Ralph Milliard (February 6, 1998).
STATISTICAL NOTES: Led Dominican Summer League in home runs allowed with 14 in 1992.
MISCELLANEOUS: Appeared in two games as pinch runner (1998). ... Appeared in one game as pinch runner (1999). ... Scored two runs in 13 appearances as pinch runner (2000).

Year League	W	L	Pct.	ERA	G	GS	CG	ShO	Sv.	IP	H	R	ER	BB	SO
1992— Dom. Mets (DSL)	5	5	.500	4.19	15	15	1	0	0	81 2/3	86	52	38	38	72
1993— Dom. Mets (DSL)	7	3	.700	2.40	16	13	2	•2	0	82 1/3	63	30	22	36	94
1994— Kingsport (Appl.)	7	4	.636	1.96	13	12	•3	0	0	87 1/3	61	27	19	27	71
1995— Capital City (S.Atl.)	9	7	.563	3.13	27	4	0	0	0	169 2/3	154	76	59	58	•177
1996— St. Lucie (FSL)	9	3	.750	1.96	16	16	2	1	0	92	53	22	20	24	81
1997— Binghamton (East.)	*13	10	.565	4.30	26	26	3	0	0	165 1/3	146	87	79	61	*176
1998— Florida (N.L.)■	7	9	.438	4.47	35	29	0	0	0	173	178	98	86	91	137
1999— Florida (N.L.)	5	7	.417	6.01	59	10	0	0	0	76 1/3	84	53	51	60	62
— Calgary (PCL)	0	0	...	5.79	4	1	0	0	1	9 1/3	8	6	6	5	14
2000— Florida (N.L.)	9	12	.429	5.34	32	32	2	2	0	182	197	118	108	76	123
Major League totals (3 years)	21	28	.429	5.11	126	71	2	2	0	431 1/3	459	269	245	227	322

S SANCHEZ, REY SS ROYALS

PERSONAL: Born October 5, 1967, in Rio Piedras, Puerto Rico. ... 5-9/175. ... Bats right, throws right. ... Full name: Rey Francisco Guadalupe Sanchez.
HIGH SCHOOL: Live Oak (Morgan Hill, Calif.).
TRANSACTIONS/CAREER NOTES: Selected by Texas Rangers organization in 13th round of free-agent draft (June 2, 1986). ... Traded by Rangers to Chicago Cubs for IF Bryan House (January 3, 1990). ... On disabled list (April 6, 1990-entire season). ... On Chicago disabled list (May 6-21, 1992); included rehabilitation assignment to Iowa (May 13-21). ... On disabled list (July 24-August 9, 1995). ... On Chicago disabled list (June 5-July 20 and August 11-September 1, 1996); included rehabilitation assignment to Iowa (July 16-20). ... Traded by Cubs to New York Yankees for P Frisco Parotte (August 16, 1997). ... Granted free agency (November 3, 1997). ... Signed by San Francisco Giants (January 22, 1998). ... Granted free agency (November 5, 1998). ... Signed by Kansas City Royals (December 11, 1998). ... Granted free agency (October 29, 1999). ... Re-signed by Royals (December 7, 1999).
STATISTICAL NOTES: Led Gulf Coast League shortstops with .932 fielding percentage in 1986. ... Led American Association shortstops with 104 double plays in 1989. ... Led American Association shortstops with 596 total chances and 81 double plays in 1992.

						BATTING								FIELDING		
Year Team (League)	Pos.	G	AB	R	H	2B	3B	HR	RBI	Avg.	BB	SO	SB	PO	A	E	Avg.
1986— GC Rangers (GCL)	SS-2B	52	169	27	49	3	1	0	23	.290	41	18	10	69	158	15	†.938
1987— Gastonia (S.Atl.)	SS	50	160	19	35	1	2	1	10	.219	22	17	6	88	162	18	.933
— Butte (Pio.)	SS	49	189	36	69	10	6	0	25	.365	21	12	22	84	162	12	.953
1988— Charlotte (FSL)	SS	128	418	60	128	6	5	0	38	.306	35	24	29	226	*415	35	.948
1989— Oklahoma City (A.A.)	SS	134	464	38	104	10	4	1	39	.224	21	50	4	*237	*418	29	*.958
1990— Iowa (A.A.)■							Did not play.										
1991— Iowa (A.A.)	SS	126	417	60	121	16	5	2	46	.290	37	27	13	204	*375	11	*.971
— Chicago (N.L.)	SS-2B	13	23	1	6	0	0	0	2	.261	4	3	0	11	25	0	1.000
1992— Chicago (N.L.)	SS-2B	74	255	24	64	14	3	1	19	.251	10	17	2	148	202	9	.975
— Iowa (A.A.)	SS-2B	20	76	12	26	3	0	0	3	.342	4	1	6	31	77	5	.956
1993— Chicago (N.L.)	SS	105	344	35	97	11	2	0	28	.282	15	22	1	158	316	15	.969
1994— Chicago (N.L.)	2B-SS-3B	96	291	26	83	13	1	0	24	.285	20	29	2	152	278	6	.979
1995— Chicago (N.L.)	2B-SS	114	428	57	119	22	2	3	27	.278	14	48	6	195	351	7	.987
1996— Chicago (N.L.)	SS	95	289	28	61	9	0	1	12	.211	22	42	7	151	307	11	.977
— Iowa (A.A.)	SS	3	12	2	2	0	0	0	1	.167	1	2	2	4	10	1	.933
1997— Chicago (N.L.)	SS-2B-3B	97	205	14	51	9	0	1	12	.249	11	26	4	100	157	6	.977
— New York (A.L.)■	2B-SS	38	138	21	43	12	0	1	15	.312	5	21	0	66	110	4	.978
1998— San Fran. (N.L.)■	SS-2B	109	316	44	90	14	2	2	30	.285	16	47	0	142	261	8	.981
1999— Kansas City (A.L.)■	SS	134	479	66	141	18	6	2	56	.294	22	48	11	242	452	13	.982
2000— Kansas City (A.L.)	SS	143	509	68	139	18	2	1	38	.273	28	55	7	224	446	4	.994
American League totals (3 years)		315	1126	155	323	48	8	4	109	.287	55	124	18	532	1008	21	.987
National League totals (8 years)		703	2151	229	571	92	10	8	154	.265	112	234	22	1057	1897	65	.978
Major League totals (10 years)		1018	3277	384	894	140	18	12	263	.273	167	358	40	1589	2905	86	.981

DIVISION SERIES RECORD

						BATTING								FIELDING		
Year Team (League)	Pos.	G	AB	R	H	2B	3B	HR	RBI	Avg.	BB	SO	SB	PO	A	E	Avg.
1997— New York (A.L.)	2B	5	15	1	3	1	0	0	1	.200	0	2	0	15	14	0	1.000

SANDBERG, JARED 3B DEVIL RAYS

PERSONAL: Born March 2, 1978, in Olympia, Wash. ... 6-3/212. ... Bats right, throws right. ... Full name: Jared Lawrence Sandberg. ... Nephew of Ryne Sandberg, second baseman with Philadelphia Phillies (1981) and Chicago Cubs (1982-94 and 1996-97).
HIGH SCHOOL: Capital (Olympia, Wash.).
TRANSACTIONS/CAREER NOTES: Selected by Tampa Bay Devil Rays organization in 16th round of free-agent draft (June 4, 1996). ... On Orlando disabled list (April 13-25 and May 9-June 30, 2000).
HONORS: Named Appalachian League Player of the Year (1997).

STATISTICAL NOTES: Led Appalachian League with 157 total bases amd five intentional bases on balls received in 1997. ... Led New York-Pennsylvania League with 133 total bases in 1998. ... Led New York-Pennsylvania League third basemen with 234 total chances and 15 double plays in 1998. ... Led Florida State League third basemen with 423 total chances in 1999. ... Tied for Florida State League lead with 25 double plays by third basemen in 1999.

Year	Team (League)	Pos.	G	AB	R	H	2B	3B	HR	RBI	Avg.	BB	SO	SB	PO	A	E	Avg.
1996—	GC Devil Rays (GCL)..	2B	22	77	6	13	2	1	0	7	.169	9	26	1	30	63	3	.969
1997—	St. Petersburg (FSL) ..	2B	2	3	1	1	0	0	0	2	.333	2	2	0	4	5	0	1.000
—	Princeton (Appl.)........	2B-3B	•67	*268	61	81	15	5	17	*68	.302	42	94	12	84	158	13	.949
1998—	Char., S.C. (SAL)........	3B	56	191	31	35	11	0	3	15	.183	27	76	4	43	•94	22	.862
—	Hudson Valley (NY-P).	3B	73	271	49	78	15	2	•12	54	.288	42	76	13	*55	*159	20	.915
1999—	St. Petersburg (FSL) ..	3B	136	504	73	139	24	1	22	96	.276	51	133	8	*102	*284	*37	.913
2000—	Orlando (Sou.)	3B	67	244	30	63	15	1	5	35	.258	33	55	5	45	131	10	.946
—	Durham (I.L.)	3B	3	15	2	6	3	0	2	7	.400	0	6	0	1	13	1	.933

SANDERS, ANTHONY   OF   MARINERS

PERSONAL: Born March 2, 1974, in Tucson, Ariz. ... 6-2/200. ... Bats right, throws right. ... Full name: Anthony Marcus Sanders.
HIGH SCHOOL: Santa Rita (Tucson, Ariz.).
TRANSACTIONS/CAREER NOTES: Selected by Toronto Blue Jays organization in seventh round of free-agent draft (June 1, 1992). ... On Syracuse disabled list (July 22, 1998-remainder of season). ... Claimed on waivers by Seattle Mariners (March 31, 2000). ... On Tacoma disabled list (July 17-28, 2000).

Year	Team (League)	Pos.	G	AB	R	H	2B	3B	HR	RBI	Avg.	BB	SO	SB	PO	A	E	Avg.
1993—	Medicine Hat (Pio.)	OF	63	225	44	59	9	3	4	33	.262	20	49	6	88	8	2	.980
1994—	St. Catharines (NY-P) .	OF	74	258	36	66	17	3	6	45	.256	27	53	8	120	9	3	.977
1995—	Hagerstown (S.Atl.)....	OF	133	512	72	119	28	1	8	48	.232	52	103	26	274	15	3	.990
1996—	Dunedin (FSL)	OF	102	417	75	108	25	0	17	50	.259	34	93	16	209	8	4	.982
—	Knoxville (Sou.)..........	OF	38	133	16	36	8	0	1	18	.271	7	33	1	66	1	3	.957
1997—	Dunedin (FSL)	OF	1	5	0	1	1	0	0	1	.200	1	1	0	1	0	0	1.000
—	Knoxville (Sou.)..........	OF-DH	111	429	68	114	20	4	26	69	.266	44	121	20	224	7	4	.983
1998—	Syracuse (I.L.)............	OF	60	209	23	40	9	2	4	19	.191	20	65	5	145	6	1	.993
—	Knoxville (Sou.)..........	OF	6	25	9	10	2	0	4	9	.400	2	6	0	15	3	0	1.000
1999—	Syracuse (I.L.)............	OF-DH	124	496	71	121	22	5	18	59	.244	46	111	18	279	•17	6	.980
—	Toronto (A.L.)	DH-OF	3	7	1	2	1	0	0	2	.286	0	2	0	1	0	0	1.000
2000—	Tacoma (PCL)■...........	OF	114	428	72	131	21	3	20	80	.306	33	109	9	177	11	3	.984
—	Seattle (A.L.)	OF	1	1	1	1	0	0	0	0	1.000	0	0	0	1	0	0	1.000
Major League totals (2 years)			4	8	2	3	1	0	0	2	.375	0	2	0	2	0	0	1.000

SANDERS, REGGIE   OF   DIAMONDBACKS

PERSONAL: Born December 1, 1967, in Florence, S.C. ... 6-1/185. ... Bats right, throws right. ... Full name: Reginald Laverne Sanders.
HIGH SCHOOL: Wilson (Florence, S.C.).
COLLEGE: Spartanburg (S.C.) Methodist.
TRANSACTIONS/CAREER NOTES: Selected by Cincinnati Reds organization in seventh round of free-agent draft (June 2, 1987). ... On disabled list (July 11-September 15, 1988; and July 15-September 5, 1989). ... On Chattanooga disabled list (June 30-July 26, 1991). ... On Cincinnati disabled list (August 24-September 20, 1991; and May 13-29 and July 17-August 2, 1992). ... On suspended list (June 3-9, 1994). ... On Cincinnati disabled list (April 20-May 22, May 31-June 15 and September 17, 1996-remainder of season); included rehabilitation assignment to Indianapolis (May 17-22). ... On Cincinnati disabled list (April 19-May 6 and May 24-July 23, 1997); included rehabilitation assignments to Chattanooga (May 3-5) and Indianapolis (July 15-22). ... Traded by Reds with SS Damian Jackson and P Josh Harris to San Diego Padres for OF Greg Vaughn and OF/1B Mark Sweeney (February 2, 1999). ... On disabled list (June 3-18, 1999). ... Traded by Padres with 2B Quilvio Veras and 1B Wally Joyner to Atlanta Braves for OF/1B Ryan Klesko, 2B Bret Boone and P Jason Shiell (December 22, 1999). ... On disabled list (April 30-May 23 and July 28-August 15, 2000). ... Granted free agency (October 31, 2000). ... Signed by Arizona Diamondbacks (January 5, 2001).
HONORS: Named Midwest League Most Valuable Player (1990). ... Named outfielder on THE SPORTING NEWS N.L. All-Star team (1995).
STATISTICAL NOTES: Hit three home runs in one game (August 15, 1995).

Year	Team (League)	Pos.	G	AB	R	H	2B	3B	HR	RBI	Avg.	BB	SO	SB	PO	A	E	Avg.
1988—	Billings (Pio.)	SS	17	64	11	15	1	1	0	3	.234	6	4	10	18	33	3	.944
1989—	Greensboro (S.Atl.)	SS	81	315	53	91	18	5	9	53	.289	29	63	21	125	169	42	.875
1990—	Cedar Rapids (Midw.)	OF	127	466	89	133	21	4	17	63	.285	59	97	40	241	10	10	.962
1991—	Chattanooga (Sou.)	OF	86	302	50	95	15	•8	8	49	.315	41	67	15	158	2	3	.982
—	Cincinnati (N.L.)	OF	9	40	6	8	0	0	1	3	.200	0	9	1	22	0	0	1.000
1992—	Cincinnati (N.L.)	OF	116	385	62	104	26	6	12	36	.270	48	98	16	262	11	6	.978
1993—	Cincinnati (N.L.)	OF	138	496	90	136	16	4	20	83	.274	51	118	27	312	3	8	.975
1994—	Cincinnati (N.L.)	OF	107	400	66	105	20	8	17	62	.263	41	*114	21	218	12	6	.975
1995—	Cincinnati (N.L.)	OF	133	484	91	148	36	6	28	99	.306	69	122	36	268	12	5	.982
1996—	Cincinnati (N.L.)	OF	81	287	49	72	17	1	14	33	.251	44	86	24	160	7	2	.988
—	Indianapolis (A.A.)......	OF-DH	4	12	3	5	2	0	0	1	.417	1	4	0	4	1	0	1.000
1997—	Cincinnati (N.L.)	OF	86	312	52	79	19	2	19	56	.253	42	93	13	183	4	5	.974
—	Chattanooga (Sou.)	OF	3	11	3	6	1	1	1	3	.545	1	2	0	11	0	0	1.000
—	Indianapolis (A.A.)......	OF	5	19	1	4	0	0	0	1	.211	1	6	0	6	0	2	.750
1998—	Cincinnati (N.L.)	OF	135	481	83	129	18	6	14	59	.268	51	137	20	263	4	6	.978
1999—	San Diego (N.L.)	OF-DH	133	478	92	136	24	7	26	72	.285	65	108	36	233	4	6	.975
2000—	Atlanta (N.L.)■..........	OF	103	340	43	79	23	1	11	37	.232	32	78	21	155	7	6	.964
Major League totals (10 years)			1041	3703	634	996	199	41	162	540	.269	443	963	215	2076	64	50	.977

DIVISION SERIES RECORD

Year	Team (League)	Pos.	G	AB	R	H	2B	3B	HR	RBI	Avg.	BB	SO	SB	PO	A	E	Avg.
1995— Cincinnati (N.L.)		OF	3	13	3	2	1	0	1	2	.154	1	9	2	7	0	1	.875
2000— Atlanta (N.L.)		OF	3	9	0	0	0	0	0	0	.000	2	5	0	0	0	0	...
Division series totals (2 years)			6	22	3	2	1	0	1	2	.091	3	14	2	7	0	1	.875

CHAMPIONSHIP SERIES RECORD

Year	Team (League)	Pos.	G	AB	R	H	2B	3B	HR	RBI	Avg.	BB	SO	SB	PO	A	E	Avg.
1995— Cincinnati (N.L.)		OF	4	16	0	2	0	0	0	0	.125	2	10	0	7	0	1	.875

ALL-STAR GAME RECORD

Year	League	Pos.	AB	R	H	2B	3B	HR	RBI	Avg.	BB	SO	SB	PO	A	E	Avg.
1995— National	OF	1	0	0	0	0	0	0	.000	0	1	0	0	0	0	...

SANTANA, JOHAN   P   TWINS

PERSONAL: Born March 13, 1979, in Tovar, Venezuela. ... 6-0/195. ... Throws left, bats left. ... Full name: Johan Alexander Santana.
HIGH SCHOOL: Liceo Nucete Sardi (Venezuela).
TRANSACTIONS/CAREER NOTES: Signed as non-drafted free agent by Houston Astros organization (July 2, 1995). ... Selected by Florida Marlins from Astros organization in Rule 5 major league draft (December 13, 1999). ... Traded by Marlins with cash to Minnesota Twins for P Jared Camp (December 13, 1999).
STATISTICAL NOTES: Led New York-Pennsylvania League with 10 hit batsmen in 1998.

Year	League	W	L	Pct.	ERA	G	GS	CG	ShO	Sv.	IP	H	R	ER	BB	SO
1996— Dom. Astros (DSL)		4	3	.571	2.70	23	1	0	0	3	40	26	16	12	22	51
1997— Gulf Coast Astros (GCL)		0	4	.000	7.93	9	5	1	0	0	36 1/3	49	36	32	18	25
— Auburn (NY-Penn)		0	0	...	2.25	1	1	0	0	0	4	1	1	1	6	5
1998— Quad City (Midw.)		0	1	.000	9.45	2	1	0	0	0	6 2/3	14	7	7	3	6
— Auburn (NY-Penn)		7	5	.583	4.36	15	15	1	•1	0	86 2/3	81	52	42	21	88
1999— Michigan (Midw.)		8	8	.500	4.66	27	26	1	0	0	160 1/3	162	94	83	55	150
2000— Minnesota (A.L.)■		2	3	.400	6.49	30	5	0	0	0	86	102	64	62	54	64
Major League totals (1 year)		2	3	.400	6.49	30	5	0	0	0	86	102	64	62	54	64

SANTANA, JULIO   P   METS

PERSONAL: Born January 20, 1974, in San Pedro de Macoris, Dominican Republic ... 6-0/225. ... Throws right, bats right. ... Full name: Julio Franklin Santana. ... Nephew of Rico Carty, outfielder with seven major league teams (1963-79).
HIGH SCHOOL: Divina Providence (Dominican Republic).
TRANSACTIONS/CAREER NOTES: Signed as non-drafted free agent by Texas Rangers organization (February 18, 1990). ... On Texas disabled list (July 15-August 10, 1997). ... Claimed on waivers by Tampa Bay Devil Rays (April 27, 1998). ... On Tampa Bay disabled list (May 3-24, 1999). ... Traded by Devil Rays to Boston Red Sox for a player to be named later and cash (July 21, 1999); Devil Rays acquired P Will Silverthorn to complete deal (July 30, 1999). ... On Boston disabled list (July 22, 1999-remainder of season). ... Granted free agency (December 21, 1999). ... Re-signed by Red Sox organization (February 2, 2000). ... Released by Red Sox (June 15, 2000). ... Signed by Montreal Expos (June 18, 2000). ... Granted free agency (October 10, 2000). ... Signed by San Francisco Giants organization (November 11, 2000). ... Selected by New York Mets from Giants organization in Rule 5 major league draft (December 11, 2000).

Year	League	W	L	Pct.	ERA	G	GS	CG	ShO	Sv.	IP	H	R	ER	BB	SO
1992— San Pedro (DSL)		0	1	.000	3.24	4	1	0	0	0	8 1/3	8	5	3	7	5
1993— Gulf Coast Rangers (GCL)		4	1	.800	1.38	*26	0	0	0	7	39	31	9	6	7	50
1994— Charleston, W.Va. (S.Atl.)		6	7	.462	2.46	16	16	0	0	0	91 1/3	65	38	25	44	103
— Tulsa (Texas)		7	2	.778	2.90	11	11	2	0	0	71 1/3	50	26	23	41	45
1995— Oklahoma City (A.A.)		0	2	.000	39.00	2	2	0	0	0	3	9	14	13	7	6
— Charlotte (FSL)		0	3	.000	3.73	5	5	1	0	0	31 1/3	32	16	13	16	27
— Tulsa (Texas)		6	4	.600	3.23	15	15	3	0	0	103	91	40	37	52	71
1996— Oklahoma City (A.A.)		11	12	.478	4.02	29	29	4	1	0	185 2/3	171	102	83	66	113
1997— Texas (A.L.)		4	6	.400	6.75	30	14	0	0	0	104	141	86	78	49	64
— Oklahoma City (A.A.)		0	0	...	15.00	1	1	0	0	0	3	9	6	5	2	1
1998— Texas (A.L.)		0	0	...	8.44	3	0	0	0	0	5 1/3	7	5	5	4	1
— Tampa Bay (A.L.)■		5	6	.455	4.23	32	19	1	0	0	140 1/3	144	72	66	58	60
1999— Tampa Bay (A.L.)		1	4	.200	7.32	22	5	0	0	0	55 1/3	66	49	45	32	34
2000— Pawtucket (I.L.)■		5	3	.625	4.71	12	12	0	0	0	65	61	34	34	23	55
— Montreal (N.L.)■		1	5	.167	5.67	36	4	0	0	0	66 2/3	69	45	42	33	58
A.L. totals (3 years)		10	16	.385	5.72	87	38	1	0	0	305	358	212	194	143	159
N.L. totals (1 year)		1	5	.167	5.67	36	4	0	0	0	66 2/3	69	45	42	33	58
Major League totals (4 years)		11	21	.344	5.71	123	42	1	0	0	371 2/3	427	257	236	176	217

RECORD AS POSITION PLAYER

Year	Team (League)	Pos.	G	AB	R	H	2B	3B	HR	RBI	Avg.	BB	SO	SB	PO	A	E	Avg.
1990— San Pedro (DSL)			11	34	4	7	0	0	1	3	.206	5	7	0	...	...	...	...
1991— San Pedro (DSL)			55	161	27	42	7	0	2	12	.261	27	37	5	...	...	...	...
1992— San Pedro (DSL)		OF-IF	17	48	7	11	2	0	2	2	.229	11	8	0	50	2	4	.929

SANTANGELO, F.P.   OF/IF   DODGERS

PERSONAL: Born October 24, 1967, in Livonia, Mich. ... 5-10/190. ... Bats both, throws right. ... Full name: Frank Paul Santangelo.
HIGH SCHOOL: Valley (Sacramento).
JUNIOR COLLEGE: Sacramento City College.

COLLEGE: Miami (Fla.).

TRANSACTIONS/CAREER NOTES: Selected by Montreal Expos organization in 20th round of free-agent draft (June 5, 1989). ... On disabled list (April 21-May 2, 1994). ... On Montreal disabled list (July 16-31, 1998); included rehabilitation assignment to Ottawa (July 28-31). ... Granted free agency (December 21, 1998). ... Signed by San Francisco Giants (December 23, 1998). ... Granted free agency (December 21, 1999). ... Signed by Los Angeles Dodgers (January 11, 2000). ... On Los Angeles disabled list (July 17-August 2 and August 23-September 22, 2000); included rehabilitation assignment to San Bernardino (July 24-August 2). ... On suspended list (August 2-8, 2000).

STATISTICAL NOTES: Led Eastern League with 13 sacrifice hits in 1991. ... Switch-hit home runs in one game (June 7, 1997).

Year Team (League)	Pos.	G	AB	R	H	2B	3B	HR	RBI	Avg.	BB	SO	SB	PO	A	E	Avg.
1989— Jamestown (NY-P)	2B	2	6	0	3	1	0	0	0	.500	1	0	1	5	5	2	.833
— W.P. Beach (FSL)	SS-2B-OF	57	173	18	37	4	0	0	14	.214	23	12	3	32	67	8	.925
1990— W.P. Beach (FSL)	S-O-2-3	116	394	63	109	19	2	0	38	.277	51	49	22	151	202	22	.941
1991— Harrisburg (East.)	2-O-S-3	132	462	78	113	12	7	5	42	.245	74	45	21	234	253	16	.968
1992— Indianapolis (A.A.)	O-2-S-3	137	462	83	123	25	0	5	34	.266	62	58	12	291	119	4	.990
1993— Ottawa (I.L.)	O-S-3-2	131	453	86	124	21	2	4	45	.274	59	52	18	246	186	14	.969
1994— Ottawa (I.L.)	O-2-S-3	119	413	62	104	28	1	5	41	.252	59	64	7	235	140	12	.969
1995— Ottawa (I.L.)	3-2-O-S-C	95	267	37	68	15	3	2	25	.255	32	22	7	89	185	10	.965
— Montreal (N.L.)	OF-2B	35	98	11	29	5	1	1	9	.296	12	9	1	47	0	1	.979
1996— Montreal (N.L.)	O-3-2-S	152	393	54	109	20	5	7	56	.277	49	61	5	251	45	6	.980
1997— Montreal (N.L.)	O-3-2-S	130	350	56	87	19	5	5	31	.249	50	73	8	175	56	3	.987
1998— Montreal (N.L.)	OF-2B-3B	122	383	53	82	18	0	4	23	.214	44	72	7	211	77	5	.983
— Ottawa (I.L.)	DH-OF	2	8	1	2	0	0	0	1	.250	0	3	0	2	0	0	1.000
1999— San Fran. (N.L.)	O-2-3-S	113	254	49	66	17	3	3	26	.260	53	54	12	144	25	1	.994
2000— Los Angeles (N.L.)■	OF-2B	81	142	19	28	4	0	1	9	.197	21	33	3	76	15	2	.978
— San Bern. (Calif.)	OF-2B	7	19	2	9	2	1	0	1	.474	2	2	1	10	1	0	1.000
Major League totals (6 years)		633	1620	242	401	83	14	21	154	.248	229	302	36	904	218	18	.984

SANTIAGO, BENITO   C

PERSONAL: Born March 9, 1965, in Ponce, Puerto Rico. ... 6-1/195. ... Bats right, throws right. ... Full name: Benito Rivera Santiago.

HIGH SCHOOL: John F. Kennedy (Ponce, Puerto Rico).

TRANSACTIONS/CAREER NOTES: Signed as non-drafted free agent by San Diego Padres organization (September 1, 1982). ... On disabled list (June 21-July 2, 1985). ... On San Diego disabled list (June 15-August 10, 1990); included rehabilitation assignment to Las Vegas (August 2-9). ... On San Diego disabled list (May 31-July 11, 1992); included rehabilitation assignment to Las Vegas (July 7-11). ... Granted free agency (October 26, 1992). ... Signed by Florida Marlins (December 16, 1992). ... On suspended list (May 5-9, 1994). ... Granted free agency (October 20, 1994). ... Signed by Cincinnati Reds (April 17, 1995). ... On disabled list (May 8-July 4, 1995). ... Granted free agency (October 31, 1995). ... Signed by Philadelphia Phillies (January 30, 1996). ... Granted free agency (November 18, 1996). ... Signed by Toronto Blue Jays (December 9, 1996). ... On disabled list (April 14-29, 1997). ... On Toronto disabled list (March 18-September 3, 1998); included rehabilitation assignments to Dunedin (August 15-26) and Syracuse (August 28-September 3). ... Granted free agency (October 23, 1998). ... Signed by Chicago Cubs (December 10, 1998). ... Granted free agency (October 29, 1999). ... Signed by Reds organization (February 24, 2000). ... Granted free agency (November 3, 2000).

RECORDS: Holds major league rookie-season record for most consecutive games batted safely—34 (August 25-October 2, 1987). ... Shares major league single-season record for fewest passed balls (100 or more games)—0 (1992). ... Shares major league record for most consecutive home runs—4 (September 14 [1] and 15 [3], 1996).

HONORS: Named N.L. Rookie Player of the Year by THE SPORTING NEWS (1987). ... Named catcher on THE SPORTING NEWS N.L. All-Star team (1987, 1989 and 1991). ... Named catcher on THE SPORTING NEWS N.L. Silver Slugger team (1987-88 and 1990-91). ... Named N.L. Rookie of the Year by Baseball Writers' Association of America (1987). ... Won N.L. Gold Glove at catcher (1988-90).

STATISTICAL NOTES: Led Florida State League catchers with 26 passed balls and 12 double plays in 1983. ... Led Texas League catchers with 78 assists and 16 passed balls in 1985. ... Led Pacific Coast League catchers with 655 total chances in 1986. ... Had 34-game hitting streak (August 25-October 2, 1987). ... Led N.L. with 22 passed balls in 1987, 14 in 1989 and 23 in 1993. ... Led N.L. in grounding into double plays with 21 in 1991. ... Tied for N.L. lead in double plays by catcher with 11 in 1988 and 14 in 1991. ... Led N.L. catchers with 100 assists and 14 errors in 1991. ... Led N.L. catchers with .996 fielding percentage in 1995. ... Hit three home runs in one game (September 15, 1996). ... Career major league grand slams: 7.

Year Team (League)	Pos.	G	AB	R	H	2B	3B	HR	RBI	Avg.	BB	SO	SB	PO	A	E	Avg.
1983— Miami (FSL)	C	122	429	34	106	25	3	5	56	.247	11	79	3	471	*69	*21	.963
1984— Reno (Calif.)	C	114	416	64	116	20	6	16	83	.279	36	75	5	692	96	25	.969
1985— Beaumont (Texas)	C-1B-3B	101	372	55	111	16	6	5	52	.298	16	59	12	525	†78	15	.976
1986— Las Vegas (PCL)	C	117	437	55	125	26	3	17	71	.286	17	81	19	*563	71	*21	.968
— San Diego (N.L.)	C	17	62	10	18	2	0	3	6	.290	2	12	0	80	7	5	.946
1987— San Diego (N.L.)	C	146	546	64	164	33	2	18	79	.300	16	112	21	817	80	*22	.976
1988— San Diego (N.L.)	C	139	492	49	122	22	2	10	46	.248	24	82	15	725	*75	*12	.985
1989— San Diego (N.L.)	C	129	462	50	109	16	3	16	62	.236	26	89	11	685	81	*20	.975
1990— San Diego (N.L.)	C	100	344	42	93	8	5	11	53	.270	27	55	5	538	51	12	.980
— Las Vegas (PCL)	C	6	20	5	6	2	0	1	8	.300	3	1	0	25	5	0	1.000
1991— San Diego (N.L.)	C-OF	152	580	60	155	22	3	17	87	.267	23	114	8	830	†100	†14	.985
1992— San Diego (N.L.)	C	106	386	37	97	21	0	10	42	.251	21	52	2	584	53	*12	.982
— Las Vegas (PCL)	C	4	13	3	4	0	0	1	2	.308	1	1	0	13	2	0	1.000
1993— Florida (N.L.)■	C-OF	139	469	49	108	19	6	13	50	.230	37	88	10	740	64	11	.987
1994— Florida (N.L.)	C	101	337	35	92	14	2	11	41	.273	25	57	1	511	*66	5	.991
1995— Cincinnati (N.L.)■	C-1B	81	266	40	76	20	0	11	44	.286	24	48	2	480	35	2	†.996
1996— Philadelphia (N.L.)■	C-1B	136	481	71	127	21	2	30	85	.264	49	104	2	834	67	11	.988
1997— Toronto (A.L.)■	C-DH	97	341	31	83	10	0	13	42	.243	17	80	1	621	40	2	.997
1998— Dunedin (FSL)	DH-C	11	37	4	6	1	0	1	5	.162	3	9	3	19	6	0	1.000
— Syracuse (I.L.)	C-DH	5	22	0	5	2	0	0	2	.227	1	3	0	19	1	0	1.000
— Toronto (A.L.)	C	15	29	3	9	5	0	0	4	.310	1	6	0	45	2	0	1.000
1999— Chicago (N.L.)■	C-1B	109	350	28	87	18	3	7	36	.249	32	71	1	562	43	6	.990
2000— Cincinnati (N.L.)	C	89	252	22	66	11	1	8	45	.262	19	45	2	428	36	3	.994
American League totals (2 years)		112	370	34	92	15	0	13	46	.249	18	86	1	666	42	2	.997
National League totals (13 years)		1444	5027	557	1314	227	29	165	676	.261	325	929	80	7814	758	135	.984
Major League totals (15 years)		1556	5397	591	1406	242	29	178	722	.261	343	1015	81	8480	800	137	.985

NOTES: Hit home run in first at-bat (October 3, 1995).

DIVISION SERIES RECORD

Year	Team (League)	Pos.	G	AB	R	H	2B	3B	HR	RBI	Avg.	BB	SO	SB	PO	A	E	Avg.
							BATTING								**FIELDING**			
1995—	Cincinnati (N.L.)	C	3	9	2	3	0	0	1	3	.333	3	3	0	20	0	0	1.000

CHAMPIONSHIP SERIES RECORD

Year	Team (League)	Pos.	G	AB	R	H	2B	3B	HR	RBI	Avg.	BB	SO	SB	PO	A	E	Avg.
							BATTING								**FIELDING**			
1995—	Cincinnati (N.L.)	C	4	13	0	3	0	0	0	0	.231	2	3	0	23	1	0	1.000

ALL-STAR GAME RECORD

Year	League	Pos.	AB	R	H	2B	3B	HR	RBI	Avg.	BB	SO	SB	PO	A	E	Avg.
							BATTING								**FIELDING**		
1989—	National	C	1	0	0	0	0	0	0	.000	0	1	0	0	0	1	.000
1990—	National							Selected, did not play—injured.										
1991—	National	C	3	0	0	0	0	0	0	.000	0	1	0	4	0	0	1.000
1992—	National	C	1	0	0	0	0	0	0	.000	0	1	0	3	0	0	1.000
All-Star Game totals (3 years)			5	0	0	0	0	0	0	.000	0	3	0	7	0	1	.875

SANTIAGO, JOSE — P — ROYALS

PERSONAL: Born November 5, 1974, in Fajardo, Puerto Rico. ... 6-3/215. ... Throws right, bats right. ... Full name: Jose Rafael Santiago.
HIGH SCHOOL: Carlos Escobar Lopez (Loiza, Puerto Rico).
TRANSACTIONS/CAREER NOTES: Selected by Kansas City Royals organization in 70th round of free agent draft (June 3, 1994). ... On Kansas City disabled list (June 26-July 9, 1997). ... On Kansas City disabled list (June 20-September 13, 1999); included rehabilitation assignments to Gulf Coast Royals (July 3-9), Wichita (July 10-11 and August 30-September 5) and Omaha (July 18-19 and September 6-12).

Year	League	W	L	Pct.	ERA	G	GS	CG	ShO	Sv.	IP	H	R	ER	BB	SO
1994—	Gulf Coast Royals (GCL)	1	0	1.000	2.37	10	1	0	0	2	19	17	7	5	7	10
1995—	Spokane (N'West)	2	4	.333	3.14	22	0	0	0	1	48²/₃	60	26	17	20	32
1996—	Lansing (Midw.)	7	6	.538	3.74	54	0	0	0	19	77	78	34	32	21	55
1997—	Wilmington (Caro.)	1	1	.500	4.91	4	0	0	0	2	3²/₃	3	3	2	1	1
	— Lansing (Midw.)	1	0	1.000	2.08	9	0	0	0	1	13	10	6	3	6	8
	— Kansas City (A.L.)	0	0	...	1.93	4	0	0	0	0	4²/₃	7	2	1	2	1
	— Wichita (Texas)	2	1	.667	4.00	22	0	0	0	3	27	32	13	12	8	12
1998—	Wichita (Texas)	3	4	.429	3.61	52	0	0	0	22	72¹/₃	79	36	29	27	31
	— Kansas City (A.L.)	0	0	...	9.00	2	0	0	0	0	2	4	2	2	0	2
	— Omaha (PCL)	0	0	...	7.04	4	0	0	0	1	7²/₃	10	9	6	5	4
1999—	Kansas City (A.L.)	3	4	.429	3.42	34	0	0	0	2	47¹/₃	46	23	18	14	15
	— Gulf Coast Royals (GCL)	0	0	...	1.80	3	3	0	0	0	5	1	1	1	0	4
	— Wichita (Texas)	0	1	.000	2.00	4	2	0	0	0	9	8	2	2	0	0
	— Omaha (PCL)....................	0	0	...	0.00	1	0	0	0	0	1²/₃	3	0	0	0	0
2000—	Kansas City (A.L.)	8	6	.571	3.91	45	0	0	0	2	69	70	33	30	26	44
	— Omaha (PCL)....................	0	1	.000	3.18	11	0	0	0	4	17	19	7	6	3	14
Major League totals (4 years)		11	10	.524	3.73	85	0	0	0	4	123	127	60	51	42	62

SASAKI, KAZUHIRO — P — MARINERS

PERSONAL: Born February 22, 1968, in Sendai City, Japan. ... 6-4/209. ... Throws right, bats right.
COLLEGE: Tohoku Fukushi University (Sendai City, Japan).
TRANSACTIONS/CAREER NOTES: Signed as non-drafted free agent by Seattle Mariners (December 18, 1999).
RECORDS: Holds A.L. rookie-season record for most saves—37 (2000).
HONORS: Named A.L. Rookie Pitcher of the Year by THE SPORTING NEWS (2000). ... Named A.L. Rookie of the Year by Baseball Writers' Association of America (2000).

Year	League	W	L	Pct.	ERA	G	GS	CG	ShO	Sv.	IP	H	R	ER	BB	SO
1990—	Yokohama (Jap. Cen.)	2	4	.333	5.85	16	...	...	...	2	47²/₃	49	31	31	30	44
1991—	Yokohama (Jap. Cen.)	6	9	.400	2.00	58	...	...	...	17	117	72	33	26	55	137
1992—	Yokohama (Jap. Cen.)	12	6	.667	2.46	53	...	...	...	21	87²/₃	47	32	24	40	135
1993—	Yokohama (Jap. Cen.)	3	6	.333	3.27	38	...	...	...	20	55	35	24	20	23	84
1994—	Yokohama (Jap. Cen.)	3	1	.750	2.15	31	...	...	...	10	46	27	11	11	15	59
1995—	Yokohama (Jap. Cen.)	7	2	.778	1.75	47	...	...	...	32	56²/₃	30	12	11	17	78
1996—	Yokohama (Jap. Cen.)	4	3	.571	2.90	39	...	...	...	25	49²/₃	37	17	16	17	80
1997—	Yokohama (Jap. Cen.)	3	0	1.000	0.90	49	...	...	...	38	60	25	6	6	18	99
1998—	Yokohama (Jap. Cen.)	1	1	.500	0.64	51	...	...	...	45	56	32	7	4	14	78
1999—	Yokohama (Jap. Cen.)	1	1	.500	1.93	23	...	...	...	19	23¹/₃	19	5	5	16	34
2000—	Seattle (A.L.)■	2	5	.286	3.16	63	0	0	0	37	62²/₃	42	25	22	31	78
Major League totals (1 year)		2	5	.286	3.16	63	0	0	0	37	62²/₃	42	25	22	31	78

DIVISION SERIES RECORD

Year	League	W	L	Pct.	ERA	G	GS	CG	ShO	Sv.	IP	H	R	ER	BB	SO
2000—	Seattle (A.L.)	0	0	...	0.00	2	0	0	0	2	2	1	0	0	0	5

CHAMPIONSHIP SERIES RECORD

Year	League	W	L	Pct.	ERA	G	GS	CG	ShO	Sv.	IP	H	R	ER	BB	SO
2000—	Seattle (A.L.)	0	0	...	0.00	2	0	0	0	1	2²/₃	3	0	0	1	3

SASSER, ROB — 3B — EXPOS

PERSONAL: Born March 9, 1975, in Philadelphia. ... 6-3/205. ... Bats right, throws right. ... Full name: Robert Dofell Sasser.
HIGH SCHOOL: Oakland High.

TRANSACTIONS/CAREER NOTES: Selected by Atlanta Braves organization in 10th round of free-agent draft (June 10, 1993). ... Selected by California Angels organization from Braves organization in Rule 5 minor league draft (December 9, 1996). ... Angels franchise renamed Anaheim Angels for 1997 season. ... Traded by Angels to Texas Rangers (October 31, 1997), completing deal in which Rangers traded P Ken Hill to Angels for C Jim Leyritz and a player to be named later (July 29, 1997). ... On Tulsa disabled list (April 6-May 2, 1998). ... Claimed on waivers by Detroit Tigers (April 15, 1999). ... Granted free agency (October 18, 2000). ... Signed by Montreal Expos organization (November 17, 2000).

STATISTICAL NOTES: Led South Atlantic League third basemen with 45 errors in 1996. ... Led Midwest League third basemen with 435 total chances in 1997. ... Led Texas League third basemen with 229 assists and 321 total chances in 1998. ... Tied for Texas League lead in errors by third basemen with 26 in 1998. ... Led Southern League third baseman with 27 double plays in 1999. ... Led International League third basemen with 24 errors in 2000.

Year Team (League)	Pos.	G	AB	R	H	2B	3B	HR	RBI	Avg.	BB	SO	SB	PO	A	E	Avg.
1993— GC Braves (GCL)	3B	33	113	19	27	4	0	0	7	.239	6	25	2	15	61	10	.884
1994— Idaho Falls (Pio.)	3B-SS	58	219	32	50	9	6	2	26	.228	19	58	13	35	122	20	.887
1995— Danville (Appl.)	3B	12	47	8	15	2	1	0	7	.319	4	7	5	7	16	4	.852
— Eugene (N'West)	SS-3B	57	216	40	58	9	1	9	32	.269	23	51	14	77	111	31	.858
1996— Macon (S.Atl.)	3-1-S-2	135	465	64	122	35	3	8	64	.262	65	108	38	247	262	†51	.909
1997— Cedar Rapids (Midw.)	3B-SS	134	497	103	135	26	5	17	77	.272	69	92	37	104	303	28	.936
1998— Tulsa (Texas)■	3B-2B	111	417	57	117	25	2	8	62	.281	60	98	18	68	†233	‡26	.920
— Charlotte (FSL)	3B	4	13	1	4	2	0	0	3	.308	3	5	1	2	9	0	1.000
— Texas (A.L.)	PH	1	1	0	0	0	0	0	0	.000	0	0	0	...	...	...	...
1999— Tulsa (Texas)	OF-DH	5	19	3	5	2	0	0	0	.263	1	2	0	7	0	0	1.000
— Jacksonville (Sou.)■	3B-DH	117	424	60	120	38	1	7	61	.283	57	101	9	82	*276	*35	.911
2000— Toledo (I.L.)	3-1-S-O-2	137	487	77	131	29	1	25	63	.269	52	106	7	214	245	26	.946
Major League totals (1 year)		1	1	0	0	0	0	0	0	.000	0	0	0	0	0	0	...

SATURRIA, LUIS — OF — CARDINALS

PERSONAL: Born July 21, 1976, in San Pedro de Macoris, Dominican Republic. ... 6-2/165. ... Bats right, throws right. ... Full name: Luis Arturo Saturria. ... Name pronounced sah-TUR-E-ah.

TRANSACTIONS/CAREER NOTES: Signed as non-drafted free agent by St. Louis Cardinals organization (March 5, 1994). ... Selected by Toronto Blue Jays from Cardinals organization in Rule 5 major league draft (December 15, 1997). ... Returned to Cardinals (March 20, 1998).

STATISTICAL NOTES: Tied for Carolina League lead with three double plays by outfielder in 1998. ... Led Texas League outfielders with 350 total chances in 2000. ... Tied for Texas League outfielders lead with three double plays in 2000.

Year Team (League)	Pos.	G	AB	R	H	2B	3B	HR	RBI	Avg.	BB	SO	SB	PO	A	E	Avg.
1994— Dom. Cardinals (DSL)	OF	61	227	29	63	2	6	1	23	.278	25	49	16	118	13	8	.942
1995— Dom. Cardinals (DSL)	OF	66	245	48	78	16	7	2	33	.318	34	26	12	126	14	22	.864
1996— Johnson City (Appl.)	OF	57	227	43	58	7	1	5	40	.256	24	61	12	68	5	3	.961
1997— Peoria (Midw.)	OF	122	445	81	122	19	5	11	51	.274	44	95	23	196	*24	9	.961
1998— Prince William (Caro.)	OF	129	462	70	136	25	9	12	73	.294	28	104	26	235	11	*15	.943
1999— Arkansas (Texas)	OF	•139	484	66	118	30	4	16	61	.244	35	134	16	255	13	9	.968
2000— Arkansas (Texas)	OF	129	478	78	131	25	10	20	76	.274	45	124	18	*338	9	3	.991
— St. Louis (N.L.)	OF	12	5	1	0	0	0	0	0	.000	1	3	0	3	0	0	1.000
Major League totals (1 year)		12	5	1	0	0	0	0	0	.000	1	3	0	3	0	0	1.000

SAUERBECK, SCOTT — P — PIRATES

PERSONAL: Born November 9, 1971, in Cincinnati. ... 6-3/197. ... Throws left, bats right. ... Full name: Scott William Sauerbeck.
HIGH SCHOOL: Northwest (Cincinnati).
COLLEGE: Miami of Ohio.
TRANSACTIONS/CAREER NOTES: Selected by New York Mets organization in 23rd round of free-agent draft (June 2, 1994). ... Selected by Pittsburgh Pirates from Mets organization in Rule 5 major league draft (December 14, 1998). ... On Pittsburgh disabled list (June 14-July 3, 2000); included rehabilitation assignment to Nashville (June 29-July 3).

Year League	W	L	Pct.	ERA	G	GS	CG	ShO	Sv.	IP	H	R	ER	BB	SO
1994— Pittsfield (NY-Penn)	3	1	.750	2.05	21	0	0	0	1	48 1/3	39	16	11	19	39
1995— St. Lucie (FSL)	0	1	.000	2.03	20	1	0	0	0	26 2/3	26	10	6	14	25
— Capital City (S.Atl.)	5	4	.556	3.27	19	0	0	0	2	33	28	14	12	14	33
1996— St. Lucie (FSL)	6	6	.500	2.27	17	16	2	2	0	99 1/3	101	37	25	27	62
— Binghamton (East.)	3	3	.500	3.47	8	8	2	0	0	46 2/3	48	24	18	12	30
1997— Binghamton (East.)	8	9	.471	4.93	27	20	2	0	0	131 1/3	144	89	72	50	88
— Norfolk (I.L.)	1	0	1.000	3.60	1	1	0	0	0	5	3	2	2	4	4
1998— Norfolk (I.L.)	7	13	.350	3.93	27	27	2	0	0	160 1/3	178	82	70	69	119
1999— Pittsburgh (N.L.)■	4	1	.800	2.00	65	0	0	0	2	67 2/3	53	19	15	38	55
2000— Pittsburgh (N.L.)	5	4	.556	4.04	75	0	0	0	1	75 2/3	76	36	34	61	83
— Nashville (PCL)	0	0	...	0.00	2	0	0	0	0	2	1	0	0	0	0
Major League totals (2 years)	9	5	.643	3.08	140	0	0	0	3	143 1/3	129	55	49	99	138

SAUVEUR, RICH — P

PERSONAL: Born November 23, 1963, in Arlington, Va. ... 6-4/195. ... Throws left, bats left. ... Full name: Richard Daniel Sauveur. ... Name pronounced SO-vurr.
HIGH SCHOOL: Falls Church (Va.).
JUNIOR COLLEGE: Manatee Junior College (Fla.).
TRANSACTIONS/CAREER NOTES: Selected by Pittsburgh Pirates organization in 11th round of free-agent draft (January 11, 1983); did not sign. ... Selected by Pirates organization in secondary phase of free-agent draft (June 6, 1983). ... On Prince William disabled list (May 25-July 5, 1984). ... On Hawaii disabled list (August 10-September 5, 1986). ... Selected by Montreal Expos organization from Pirates organiza-

S

tion in Rule 5 minor league draft (December 7, 1987). ... On disabled list (May 4, 1989-remainder of season). ... Granted free agency (October 15, 1989). ... Signed by Pirates organization (December 15, 1989). ... Released by Pirates (March 31, 1990). ... Signed by Miami, independent (May 17, 1990). ... Released by Miami (July 11, 1990). ... Signed by Expos organization (July 16, 1990). ... Granted free agency (October 15, 1990). ... Signed by New York Mets organization (January 22, 1991). ... On Tidewater disabled list (August 8-20, 1991). ... Released by Mets (January 23, 1992). ... Signed by Kansas City Royals organization (February 8, 1992). ... Released by Royals organization (March 27, 1993). ... Signed by Minatitlan, Mexican League (1993). ... Signed by Cincinnati Reds organization (August 10, 1993). ... Granted free agency (October 15, 1993). ... Re-signed by Reds organization (November 16, 1993). ... Granted free agency (October 15, 1994). ... Re-signed by Indianapolis (November 15, 1994). ... On disabled list (April 18-26, 1995). ... Granted free agency (October 16, 1995). ... Signed by Nashville, Chicago White Sox organization (January 12, 1996). ... Granted free agency (October 15, 1996). ... Signed by Los Angeles Dodgers organization (December 28, 1996). ... Released by Dodgers (March 28, 1997). ... Signed by Tabasco, Mexican League (1997). ... Contract purchased by Chicago Cubs organization from Tabasco (May 10, 1997). ... Granted free agency (October 17, 1997). ... Signed by Reds organization (March 1, 1998). ... On Indianapolis disabled list (April 10-18, 1998). ... Released by Reds (May 12, 1998). ... Signed by Pittsburgh Pirates organization (May 12, 1998). ... Granted free agency (October 16, 1998). ... Re-signed by Pirates organization (November 11, 1998). ... On Nashville disabled list (April 29-May 7, 1999). ... Granted free agency (October 15, 1999). ... Signed by Oakland Athletics organization (November 23, 1999). ... Granted free agency (October 2, 2000).

STATISTICAL NOTES: Tied for New York-Pennsylvania League lead with four balks in 1983. ... Led Eastern League with four balks in 1984 and tied for lead with four in 1985.

Year	League	W	L	Pct.	ERA	G	GS	CG	ShO	Sv.	IP	H	R	ER	BB	SO
1983—	Watertown (NY-Penn)	7	5	.583	2.31	16	12	1	0	0	93²/₃	80	41	24	31	73
1984—	Prince William (Caro.)	3	3	.500	3.13	10	10	0	0	0	54²/₃	43	22	19	31	54
—	Nashua (East.)	5	3	.625	2.93	10	10	2	2	0	70²/₃	54	27	23	34	48
1985—	Nashua (East.)	9	10	.474	3.55	25	25	4	2	0	157¹/₃	146	73	62	78	85
1986—	Nashua (East.)	3	1	.750	1.18	5	5	2	1	0	38	21	5	5	11	28
—	Hawaii (PCL)	7	6	.538	3.03	14	14	6	1	0	92	73	40	31	45	68
—	Pittsburgh (N.L.)	0	0	...	6.00	3	3	0	0	0	12	17	8	8	6	6
1987—	Harrisburg (East.)	13	6	.684	2.86	30	•27	7	1	0	*195	174	71	62	96	*160
1988—	Jacksonville (Sou.)■	0	2	.000	4.05	8	0	0	0	1	6²/₃	7	5	3	5	8
—	Indianapolis (A.A.)	7	4	.636	2.43	43	3	0	0	10	81¹/₃	60	26	22	28	58
—	Montreal (N.L.)	0	0	...	6.00	4	0	0	0	0	3	3	2	2	2	3
1989—	Indianapolis (A.A.)	0	1	.000	7.45	8	0	0	0	1	9²/₃	10	8	8	6	8
1990—	Miami (FSL)■	0	4	.000	3.32	11	6	1	0	0	40²/₃	41	16	15	17	34
—	Indianapolis (A.A.)■	2	2	.500	1.93	14	7	0	0	0	56	45	14	12	25	24
1991—	Tidewater (I.L.)■	2	2	.500	2.38	42	0	0	0	6	45¹/₃	31	14	12	23	49
—	New York (N.L.)	0	0	...	10.80	6	0	0	0	0	3¹/₃	7	4	4	2	4
1992—	Omaha (A.A.)■	7	6	.538	3.22	34	13	1	0	0	117¹/₃	93	54	42	39	88
—	Kansas City (A.L.)	0	1	.000	4.40	8	0	0	0	0	14¹/₃	15	7	7	8	7
1993—	Minatitlan (Mex.)■	3	3	.500	3.27	7	7	1	0	0	44	40	19	16	23	31
—	Indianapolis (A.A.)■	2	0	1.000	1.82	5	5	0	0	0	34²/₃	41	10	7	7	21
1994—	Indianapolis (A.A.)	3	3	.500	2.82	53	1	0	0	12	67	47	25	21	23	65
1995—	Indianapolis (A.A.)	5	2	.714	2.05	52	0	0	0	15	57	43	17	13	18	47
1996—	Nashville (A.A.)■	4	3	.571	3.70	61	3	0	0	8	73	63	34	30	28	69
—	Chicago (A.L.)	0	0	...	15.00	3	0	0	0	0	3	3	5	5	5	1
1997—	Tabasco (Mex.)■	0	2	.000	3.86	9	0	0	0	3	9	7	5	4	8	7
—	Iowa (A.A.)■	1	3	.250	3.38	39	1	0	0	2	45¹/₃	46	19	17	21	37
1998—	Indianapolis (I.L.)■	0	0	...	3.00	7	0	0	0	1	9	9	8	3	4	6
—	Nashville (PCL)■	1	4	.200	1.81	46	0	0	0	10	44²/₃	34	15	9	17	43
1999—	Nashville (PCL)	5	2	.714	1.95	53	3	0	0	7	64²/₃	62	21	14	16	61
2000—	Sacramento (PCL)■	5	2	.714	4.57	25	11	0	0	1	82²/₃	88	48	42	25	59
—	Oakland (A.L.)	0	0	...	4.35	10	0	0	0	0	10¹/₃	13	5	5	1	7
A.L. totals (3 years)		0	1	.000	5.53	21	0	0	0	0	27²/₃	31	17	17	14	15
N.L. totals (3 years)		0	0	...	6.87	13	3	0	0	0	18¹/₃	27	14	14	10	13
Major League totals (6 years)		0	1	.000	6.07	34	3	0	0	0	46	58	31	31	24	28

SCANLAN, BOB   P   EXPOS

PERSONAL: Born August 9, 1966, in Beverly Hills, Calif. ... 6-7/215. ... Throws right, bats right. ... Full name: Robert Guy Scanlan Jr.
HIGH SCHOOL: Harvard (North Hollywood, Calif.).
TRANSACTIONS/CAREER NOTES: Selected by Philadelphia Phillies organization in 25th round of free-agent draft (June 4, 1984). ... Traded by Phillies with P Chuck McElroy to Chicago Cubs organization for P Mitch Williams (April 7, 1991). ... On suspended list (September 30-October 4, 1992; and September 17-20, 1993). ... Traded by Cubs to Milwaukee Brewers for P Rafael Novoa and OF Mike Carter (December 19, 1993). ... On Milwaukee disabled list (June 12-August 21, 1995); included rehabilitation assignment to New Orleans (August 4-21). ... Released by Brewers (December 18, 1995). ... Signed by Detroit Tigers organization (January 15, 1996). ... Claimed on waivers by Kansas City Royals organization (August 8, 1996). ... Released by Royals (March 26, 1997). ... Signed by San Diego Padres organization (May 29, 1997). ... Granted free agency (October 15, 1997). ... Signed by Houston Astros organization (December 22, 1997). ... Granted free agency (October 15, 1998). ... Re-signed by Astros organization (January 21, 1999). ... Granted free agency (October 15, 1999). ... Signed by Milwaukee Brewers organization (January 14, 2000). ... Granted free agency (October 13, 2000). ... Signed by Montreal Expos organization (December 21, 2000).
STATISTICAL NOTES: Led International League with 17 wild pitches in 1988. ... Tied for Pacific Coast League lead with 12 hit batsmen in 1999.

Year	League	W	L	Pct.	ERA	G	GS	CG	ShO	Sv.	IP	H	R	ER	BB	SO
1984—	Gulf Coast Phillies (GCL)	0	2	.000	6.48	13	6	0	0	0	33¹/₃	43	31	24	30	17
1985—	Spartanburg (S.Atl.)	8	12	.400	4.14	26	25	4	0	0	152¹/₃	160	95	70	53	108
1986—	Clearwater (FSL)	8	12	.400	4.15	24	22	5	0	0	125²/₃	146	73	58	45	51
1987—	Reading (East.)	*15	5	.750	5.10	27	26	3	1	0	164	187	98	93	55	91
1988—	Maine (I.L.)	5	*18	.217	5.59	28	27	4	1	0	161	181	*110	*100	50	79
1989—	Reading (East.)	6	10	.375	5.78	31	17	4	1	0	118¹/₃	124	88	•76	53	64
1990—	Scranton/W.B. (I.L.)	8	1	.889	4.85	23	23	1	0	0	130	128	79	70	59	74
1991—	Iowa (A.A.)■	2	0	1.000	2.95	4	3	0	0	0	18¹/₃	14	8	6	10	15
—	Chicago (N.L.)	7	8	.467	3.89	40	13	0	0	1	111	114	60	48	40	44
1992—	Chicago (N.L.)	3	6	.333	2.89	69	0	0	0	14	87¹/₃	76	32	28	30	42
1993—	Chicago (N.L.)	4	5	.444	4.54	70	0	0	0	0	75¹/₃	79	41	38	28	44
1994—	Milwaukee (A.L.)■	2	6	.250	4.11	30	12	0	0	2	103	117	53	47	28	65
1995—	Milwaukee (A.L.)	4	7	.364	6.59	17	14	0	0	0	83¹/₃	101	66	61	44	29
—	New Orleans (A.A.)	0	1	.000	5.40	3	3	0	0	0	11²/₃	17	7	7	3	5

S

Year	League	W	L	Pct.	ERA	G	GS	CG	ShO	Sv.	IP	H	R	ER	BB	SO
1996—	Lakeland (FSL)■	0	1	.000	5.00	2	2	0	0	0	9	9	6	5	3	4
	—Toledo (I.L.)	1	3	.250	7.50	14	5	0	0	0	36	46	35	30	15	18
	—Detroit (A.L.)	0	0	...	10.64	8	0	0	0	0	11	16	15	13	9	3
	—Omaha (A.A.)■	0	0	...	0.73	12	0	0	0	5	12 1/3	10	2	1	3	9
	—Kansas City (A.L.)	0	1	.000	3.18	9	0	0	0	0	11 1/3	13	4	4	3	3
1997—	Las Vegas (PCL)■	3	1	.750	3.53	36	1	0	0	1	51	51	24	20	17	20
1998—	Houston (N.L.)■	0	1	.000	3.08	27	0	0	0	0	26 1/3	24	12	9	13	9
	—New Orleans (PCL)	5	4	.556	6.46	14	12	1	0	0	61 1/3	90	50	44	24	35
1999—	New Orleans (PCL)	8	*15	.348	5.61	28	•28	2	0	0	163 2/3	*208	116	•102	55	78
2000—	Indianapolis (I.L.)■	2	2	.500	1.79	57	0	0	0	*35	60 1/3	42	16	12	18	23
	—Milwaukee (N.L.)	0	0	...	27.00	2	0	0	0	0	1 2/3	6	6	5	0	1
A.L. totals (3 years)		6	14	.300	5.39	64	26	0	0	2	208 2/3	247	138	125	84	100
N.L. totals (5 years)		14	20	.412	3.82	208	13	0	0	15	301 2/3	299	151	128	111	140
Major League totals (8 years)		20	34	.370	4.46	272	39	0	0	17	510 1/3	546	289	253	195	240

SCHILLING, CURT   P   DIAMONDBACKS

PERSONAL: Born November 14, 1966, in Anchorage, Alaska. ... 6-4/231. ... Throws right, bats right. ... Full name: Curtis Montague Schilling.
HIGH SCHOOL: Shadow Mountain (Phoenix).
JUNIOR COLLEGE: Yavapai College (Ariz.).
TRANSACTIONS/CAREER NOTES: Selected by Boston Red Sox organization in second round of free-agent draft (January 14, 1986). ... Traded by Red Sox with OF Brady Anderson to Baltimore Orioles for P Mike Boddicker (July 29, 1988). ... Traded by Orioles with P Pete Harnisch and OF Steve Finley to Houston Astros for 1B Glenn Davis (January 10, 1991). ... Traded by Astros to Philadelphia Phillies for P Jason Grimsley (April 2, 1992). ... On Philadelphia disabled list (May 17-July 25, 1994); included rehabilitation assignments to Scranton/Wilkes-Barre (July 10-15) and Reading (July 15-20). ... On disabled list (July 19, 1995-remainder of season). ... On Philadelphia disabled list (March 23-May 14, 1996); included rehabilitation assignments to Clearwater (April 23-May 3) and Scranton/Wilkes-Barre (May 3-14). ... On disabled list (August 8-September 3, 1999). ... On Philadelphia disabled list (March 25-April 30, 2000); included rehabilitation assignments to Clearwater (April 6-29) and Scranton/Wilkes-Barre (April 30). ... Traded by Phillies to Arizona Diamondbacks for OF Travis Lee, P Omar Daal, P Vicente Padilla and P Nelson Figueroa (July 26, 2000).
RECORDS: Shares major league single-season record for fewest complete games for leader—8 (1996 and 2000). ... Holds N.L. single-season record for most strikeouts by righthander—319 (1997).
STATISTICAL NOTES: Tied for International League lead with six balks in 1989. ... Pitched 2-1 one-hit, complete-game victory against New York (September 9, 1992). ... Struck out 15 batters in one game (July 21, 1997 and April 5, 1998). ... Struck out 16 batters in one game (September 1, 1997).
MISCELLANEOUS: Struck out once in two appearances as pinch hitter with Philadelphia (1996).

Year	League	W	L	Pct.	ERA	G	GS	CG	ShO	Sv.	IP	H	R	ER	BB	SO
1986—	Elmira (NY-Penn)	7	3	.700	2.59	16	15	2	1	0	93 2/3	92	34	27	30	75
1987—	Greensboro (S.Atl.)	8	*15	.348	3.82	29	28	7	3	0	184	179	96	78	65	*189
1988—	New Britain (East.)	8	5	.615	2.97	21	17	4	1	0	106	91	44	35	40	62
	—Charlotte (Sou.)■	5	2	.714	3.18	7	7	2	1	0	45 1/3	36	19	16	23	32
	—Baltimore (A.L.)	0	3	.000	9.82	4	4	0	0	0	14 2/3	22	19	16	10	4
1989—	Rochester (I.L.)	•13	11	.542	3.21	27	•27	•9	•3	0	*185 1/3	176	76	66	59	109
	—Baltimore (A.L.)	0	1	.000	6.23	5	1	0	0	0	8 2/3	10	6	6	3	6
1990—	Rochester (I.L.)	4	4	.500	3.92	15	14	1	0	0	87 1/3	95	46	38	25	83
	—Baltimore (A.L.)	1	2	.333	2.54	35	0	0	0	3	46	38	13	13	19	32
1991—	Houston (N.L.)■	3	5	.375	3.81	56	0	0	0	8	75 2/3	79	35	32	39	71
	—Tucson (PCL)	0	1	.000	3.42	13	0	0	0	3	23 2/3	16	9	9	12	21
1992—	Philadelphia (N.L.)■	14	11	.560	2.35	42	26	10	4	2	226 1/3	165	67	59	59	147
1993—	Philadelphia (N.L.)	16	7	.696	4.02	34	34	7	2	0	235 1/3	234	114	105	57	186
1994—	Philadelphia (N.L.)	2	8	.200	4.48	13	13	1	0	0	82 1/3	87	42	41	28	58
	—Scranton/W.B. (I.L.)	0	0	...	1.80	2	2	0	0	0	10	6	2	2	5	6
	—Reading (East.)	0	0	...	0.00	1	1	0	0	0	4	6	0	0	1	4
1995—	Philadelphia (N.L.)	7	5	.583	3.57	17	17	1	0	0	116	96	52	46	26	114
1996—	Clearwater (FSL)	2	0	1.000	1.29	2	2	0	0	0	14	9	2	2	1	17
	—Scranton/W.B. (I.L.)	1	0	1.000	1.38	2	2	0	0	0	13	9	2	2	5	10
	—Philadelphia (N.L.)	9	10	.474	3.19	26	26	*8	2	0	183 1/3	149	69	65	50	182
1997—	Philadelphia (N.L.)	17	11	.607	2.97	35	•35	7	2	0	254 1/3	208	96	84	58	*319
1998—	Philadelphia (N.L.)	15	14	.517	3.25	35	•35	*15	2	0	*268 2/3	236	101	97	61	*300
1999—	Philadelphia (N.L.)	15	6	.714	3.54	24	24	8	1	0	180 1/3	159	74	71	44	152
2000—	Clearwaqter (FSL)	1	0	1.000	1.31	4	4	0	0	0	20 2/3	10	3	3	2	23
	—Scranton/W.B. (I.L.)	0	0	...	3.60	1	1	0	0	0	5	9	2	2	1	7
	—Philadelphia (N.L.)	6	6	.500	3.91	16	16	4	1	0	112 2/3	110	49	49	32	96
	—Arizona (N.L.)■	5	6	.455	3.69	13	13	§4	1	0	97 2/3	94	41	40	13	72
A.L. totals (3 years)		1	6	.143	4.54	44	5	0	0	3	69 1/3	70	38	35	32	42
N.L. totals (10 years)		109	89	.551	3.38	311	239	65	15	10	1832 2/3	1617	740	689	467	1697
Major League totals (13 years)		110	95	.537	3.43	355	244	65	15	13	1902	1687	778	724	499	1739

CHAMPIONSHIP SERIES RECORD

RECORDS: Holds single-game records for most consecutive strikeouts—5; and most consecutive strikeouts from start of the game—5 (October 6, 1993).
NOTES: Named N.L. Championship Series Most Valuable Player (1993).

Year	League	W	L	Pct.	ERA	G	GS	CG	ShO	Sv.	IP	H	R	ER	BB	SO
1993—	Philadelphia (N.L.)	0	0	...	1.69	2	2	0	0	0	16	11	4	3	5	19

WORLD SERIES RECORD

Year	League	W	L	Pct.	ERA	G	GS	CG	ShO	Sv.	IP	H	R	ER	BB	SO
1993—	Philadelphia (N.L.)	1	1	.500	3.52	2	2	1	1	0	15 1/3	13	7	6	5	9

ALL-STAR GAME RECORD

Year	League	W	L	Pct.	ERA	GS	CG	ShO	Sv.	IP	H	R	ER	BB	SO
1997—	National	0	0	...	0.00	0	0	0	0	2	2	0	0	0	3
1998—	National				Did not play.										
1999—	National	0	1	.000	9.00	1	0	0	0	2	3	2	2	1	3
All-Star Game totals (2 years)		0	1	.000	4.50	1	0	0	0	4	5	2	2	1	6

PERSONAL: Born January 29, 1973, in Lewiston, Idaho. ... 6-5/213. ... Throws right, bats right. ... Full name: Jason David Schmidt.
HIGH SCHOOL: Kelso (Wash.).
TRANSACTIONS/CAREER NOTES: Selected by Atlanta Braves organization in eighth round of free-agent draft (June 3, 1991). ... On Atlanta disabled list (July 15-August 30, 1996); included rehabilitation assignment to Greenville (August 11-30). ... Traded by Braves to Pittsburgh Pirates (August 30, 1996), completing deal in which Pirates traded P Denny Neagle to Braves for a player to be named later (August 28, 1996). ... On Pittsburgh disabled list (April 15-May 1 and June 10, 2000-remainder of season); included rehabilitation assignment to Gulf Coast Pirates (July 29-August 23).
RECORDS: Shares N.L. single-inning record for most consecutive home runs allowed—3 (August 22, 1999, first inning).
STATISTICAL NOTES: Led N.L. with 15 wild pitches in 1998. ... Tied for N.L. lead with four balks in 1999.
MISCELLANEOUS: Received base on balls in only appearance as pinch hitter with Atlanta (1995).

Year League	W	L	Pct.	ERA	G	GS	CG	ShO	Sv.	IP	H	R	ER	BB	SO
1991—Gulf Coast Braves (GCL)	3	4	.429	2.38	11	11	0	0	0	45 1/3	32	21	12	23	44
1992—Pulaski (Appl.)..................	3	4	.429	4.01	11	11	0	0	0	58 1/3	38	36	26	31	56
— Macon (S.Atl.)	0	3	.000	4.01	7	7	0	0	0	24 2/3	31	18	11	19	33
1993—Durham (Caro.)	7	11	.389	4.94	22	22	0	0	0	116 2/3	128	69	64	47	110
1994—Greenville (Sou.)	8	7	.533	3.65	24	24	1	0	0	140 2/3	135	64	57	54	131
1995—Atlanta (N.L.)..................	2	2	.500	5.76	9	2	0	0	0	25	27	17	16	18	19
—Richmond (I.L.).................	8	6	.571	*2.25	19	19	0	0	0	116	97	40	29	48	95
1996—Atlanta (N.L.)..................	3	4	.429	6.75	13	11	0	0	0	58 2/3	69	48	44	32	48
—Richmond (I.L.).................	3	0	1.000	2.56	7	7	0	0	0	45 2/3	36	17	13	19	41
—Greenville (Sou.)	0	0	...	9.00	1	1	0	0	0	2	4	2	2	0	2
—Pittsburgh (N.L.)■............	2	2	.500	4.06	6	6	1	0	0	37 2/3	39	19	17	21	26
1997—Pittsburgh (N.L.)	10	9	.526	4.60	32	32	2	0	0	187 2/3	193	106	96	76	136
1998—Pittsburgh (N.L.)	11	14	.440	4.07	33	33	0	0	0	214 1/3	228	106	97	71	148
1999—Pittsburgh (N.L.)	13	11	.542	4.19	33	33	2	0	0	212 2/3	219	110	99	85	148
2000—Pittsburgh (N.L.)	2	5	.286	5.40	11	11	0	0	0	63 1/3	71	43	38	41	51
—Gulf Coast Pirates (GCL)	0	0	...	2.25	1	1	0	0	0	4	4	2	1	1	1
Major League totals (6 years)	43	47	.478	4.58	137	128	5	0	0	799 1/3	846	449	407	344	586

PERSONAL: Born November 26, 1976, in Jacksonville. ... 6-1/200. ... Bats left, throws right. ... Full name: Brian Duncan Schneider.
HIGH SCHOOL: Northampton (Pa.).
TRANSACTIONS/CAREER NOTES: Selected by Montreal Expos organization in fifth round of free-agent draft (June 1, 1995).
STATISTICAL NOTES: Led Eastern League catchers with 91 assists in 1999. ... Tied for International League lead with nine sacrifice flies in 2000.

Year Team (League)	Pos.	G	AB	R	H	2B	3B	HR	RBI	Avg.	BB	SO	SB	PO	A	E	Avg.
							BATTING								FIELDING		
1995—GC Expos (GCL)	C	30	97	7	22	3	0	0	4	.227	14	23	2	138	26	3	.982
1996—GC Expos (GCL)	C	52	144	26	44	5	2	0	23	.306	24	15	2	214	26	3	.988
—Delmarva (S.Atl.)........	C	5	9	0	3	0	0	0	1	.333	1	1	0	20	3	0	1.000
1997—Cape Fear (S.Atl.)	C	113	381	46	96	20	1	4	49	.252	53	45	3	724	99	10	.988
1998—Cape Fear (S.Atl.)	C	38	134	33	40	7	2	7	30	.299	16	9	6	261	32	6	.980
—Jupiter (FSL)	C	82	302	32	82	12	1	3	30	.272	22	38	4	483	81	11	.981
1999—Harrisburg (East.).......	C-DH-1B	121	421	48	111	19	1	17	66	.264	32	56	2	622	†92	6	.992
2000—Ottawa (I.L.)............	C-1B	67	238	22	59	22	3	4	31	.248	16	42	1	391	52	8	.982
—Montreal (N.L.)..........	C	45	115	6	27	6	0	0	11	.235	7	24	0	205	19	6	.974
Major League totals (1 year)		45	115	6	27	6	0	0	11	.235	7	24	0	205	19	6	.974

PERSONAL: Born October 2, 1973, in Long Branch, N.J. ... 6-0/186. ... Throws left, bats left. ... Full name: Scott David Schoeneweis.
HIGH SCHOOL: Lenape (Medford, N.J.).
COLLEGE: Duke.
TRANSACTIONS/CAREER NOTES: Selected by California Angels organization in third round of free-agent draft (June 4, 1996). ... Angels franchise renamed Anaheim Angels for 1997 season. ... On Anaheim disabled list (June 17-July 26, 2000); included rehabilitation assignment to Lake Elsinore (July 14-17) and Edmonton (July 18-24).

Year League	W	L	Pct.	ERA	G	GS	CG	ShO	Sv.	IP	H	R	ER	BB	SO
1996— Lake Elsinore (Calif.)	8	3	.727	3.94	14	12	0	0	0	93 2/3	86	47	41	27	83
1997— Midland (Texas)................	7	5	.583	5.96	20	20	3	0	0	113 1/3	145	84	75	39	84
1998— Vancouver (PCL)	11	8	.579	4.50	27	27	2	0	0	180	188	102	90	59	133
1999— Anaheim (A.L.)	1	1	.500	5.49	31	0	0	0	0	39 1/3	47	27	24	14	22
—Edmonton (PCL)	2	4	.333	7.64	9	7	0	0	0	35 1/3	58	35	30	12	29
2000— Anaheim (A.L.)	7	10	.412	5.45	27	27	1	1	0	170	183	112	103	67	78
—Lake Elsinore (Calif.)	0	0	...	1.93	1	1	0	0	0	4 2/3	3	1	1	3	3
—Edmonton (PCL)	0	0	...	0.00	1	1	0	0	0	7	2	1	0	1	6
Major League totals (2 years)	8	11	.421	5.46	58	27	1	1	0	209 1/3	230	139	127	81	100

PERSONAL: Born May 10, 1969, in Austin, Texas. ... 6-5/220. ... Throws left, bats left. ... Full name: Peter Alan Schourek. ... Name pronounced SHUR-ek.
HIGH SCHOOL: George C. Marshall (Falls Church, Va.).

TRANSACTIONS/CAREER NOTES: Selected by New York Mets organization in second round of free-agent draft (June 2, 1987). ... On disabled list (June 17, 1988-entire season). ... Claimed on waivers by Cincinnati Reds (April 7, 1994). ... On disabled list (June 1-22 and July 2, 1996-remainder of season). ... On disabled list (June 14-July 18 and July 31-September 2, 1997). ... Released by Reds (October 10, 1997). ... Signed by Houston Astros organization (January 9, 1998). ... On New Orleans disabled list (April 7-24, 1998). ... Traded by Astros to Boston Red Sox for cash (August 6, 1998). ... Granted free agency (October 23, 1998). ... Signed by Pittsburgh Pirates (December 18, 1998). ... On disabled list (August 17-September 1, 1999). ... Released by Pirates (March 29, 2000). ... Signed by Boston Red Sox (April 2, 2000). ... On Boston disabled list (July 21-September 2 and September 20, 2000-remainder of season); included rehabilitation assignment to Pawtucket (August 22-28) and Sarasota (August 28-September 2). ... Granted free agency (November 1, 2000). ... Re-signed by Red Sox organization (December 7, 2000).

HONORS: Named lefthanded pitcher on The Sporting News N.L. All-Star team (1995).

STATISTICAL NOTES: Pitched 9-0 one-hit, complete-game victory for New York against Montreal (September 10, 1991).

MISCELLANEOUS: Appeared in one game as pinch runner with New York (1992). ... Struck out in only appearance as pinch hitter (1996). ... Appeared in one game as pinch runner (1997). ... Singled in only appearance as pinch hitter (2000).

Year League	W	L	Pct.	ERA	G	GS	CG	ShO	Sv.	IP	H	R	ER	BB	SO
1987—Kingsport (Appl.)	4	5	.444	3.68	12	12	2	0	0	78⅓	70	37	32	34	57
1988—Little Falls (NY-Penn)					Did not play.										
1989—Columbia (S.Atl.)	5	9	.357	2.85	27	19	5	1	1	136	120	66	43	66	131
—St. Lucie (FSL)	0	0	...	2.25	2	1	0	0	0	4	3	1	1	2	4
1990—St. Lucie (FSL)	4	1	.800	0.97	5	5	2	2	0	37	29	4	4	8	28
—Tidewater (I.L.)	1	0	1.000	2.57	2	2	1	1	0	14	9	4	4	5	14
—Jackson (Texas)	11	4	.733	3.04	19	19	1	0	0	124⅓	109	53	42	39	94
1991—Tidewater (I.L.)	1	1	.500	2.52	4	4	0	0	0	25	18	7	7	10	17
—New York (N.L.)	5	4	.556	4.27	35	8	1	1	2	86⅓	82	49	41	43	67
1992—Tidewater (I.L.)	2	5	.286	2.73	8	8	2	1	0	52⅔	46	20	16	23	42
—New York (N.L.)	6	8	.429	3.64	22	21	0	0	0	136	137	60	55	44	60
1993—New York (N.L.)	5	12	.294	5.96	41	18	0	0	0	128⅓	168	90	85	45	72
1994—Cincinnati (N.L.)■	7	2	.778	4.09	22	10	0	0	0	81⅓	90	39	37	29	69
1995—Cincinnati (N.L.)	18	7	.720	3.22	29	29	2	0	0	190⅓	158	72	68	45	160
1996—Cincinnati (N.L.)	4	5	.444	6.01	12	12	0	0	0	67⅓	79	48	45	24	54
1997—Cincinnati (N.L.)	5	8	.385	5.42	18	17	0	0	0	84⅔	78	59	51	38	59
1998—Kissimmee (FSL)■	0	0	...	1.08	2	1	0	0	0	8⅓	8	1	1	4	9
—Houston (N.L.)	7	6	.538	4.50	15	15	0	0	0	80	82	43	40	36	59
—Boston (A.L.)■	1	3	.250	4.30	10	8	0	0	0	44	45	21	21	14	36
1999—Pittsburgh (N.L.)■	4	7	.364	5.34	30	17	0	0	0	113	128	75	67	49	94
2000—Boston (A.L.)■	3	10	.231	5.11	21	21	0	0	0	107⅓	116	67	61	38	63
—Pawtucket (I.L.)	0	0	...	0.00	1	1	0	0	0	3	1	0	0	1	1
—Sarasota (FSL)	0	0	...	2.08	1	1	0	0	0	4⅓	2	1	1	0	5
A.L. totals (2 years)	4	13	.235	4.88	31	29	0	0	0	151⅓	161	88	82	52	99
N.L. totals (9 years)	61	59	.508	4.55	224	147	3	1	2	967⅓	1002	535	489	353	694
Major League totals (10 years)	65	72	.474	4.59	255	176	3	1	2	1118⅔	1163	623	571	405	793

DIVISION SERIES RECORD

Year League	W	L	Pct.	ERA	G	GS	CG	ShO	Sv.	IP	H	R	ER	BB	SO
1995—Cincinnati (N.L.)	1	0	1.000	2.57	1	1	0	0	0	7	5	2	2	3	5
1998—Boston (A.L.)	0	0	...	0.00	1	1	0	0	0	5⅓	2	0	0	4	1
Division series totals (2 years)	1	0	1.000	1.46	2	2	0	0	0	12⅓	7	2	2	7	6

CHAMPIONSHIP SERIES RECORD

Year League	W	L	Pct.	ERA	G	GS	CG	ShO	Sv.	IP	H	R	ER	BB	SO
1995—Cincinnati (N.L.)	0	1	.000	1.26	2	2	0	0	0	14⅓	14	2	2	3	13

SCHRENK, STEVE　　　　P　　　　ATHLETICS

PERSONAL: Born November 20, 1968, in Great Lakes, Ill. ... 6-3/215. ... Throws right, bats right. ... Full name: Steven Wayne Schrenk.

HIGH SCHOOL: North Marion (Aurora, Ore.).

TRANSACTIONS/CAREER NOTES: Selected by Chicago White Sox organization in fourth round of free-agent draft (June 2, 1987). ... On disabled list (April 11-September 3, 1991). ... On Nashville disabled list (April 21, 1995-remainder of season). ... On disabled list (April 4-25 and July 30-September 6, 1996). ... Granted free agency (October 15, 1996). ... Signed by Baltimore Orioles organization (Janaury 14, 1997). ... Granted free agency (October 15, 1997). ... Signed by St. Louis Cardinals organization (November 25, 1997). ... Released by Cardinals (April 3, 1998). ... Signed by Boston Red Sox organization (May 22, 1998). ... Granted free agency (October 15, 1998). ... Signed by Philadelphia Phillies organization (November 5, 1998). ... Granted free agency (October 18, 2000). ... Signed by Oakland Athletics organization (December 5, 2000).

Year League	W	L	Pct.	ERA	G	GS	CG	ShO	Sv.	IP	H	R	ER	BB	SO
1987—GC White Sox (GCL)	1	2	.333	0.95	8	6	1	1	0	28⅓	23	10	3	12	19
1988—South Bend (Midw.)	3	7	.300	5.00	21	18	1	0	0	90	95	63	50	37	58
1989—South Bend (Midw.)	5	2	.714	4.33	16	16	1	1	0	79	71	44	38	44	49
1990—South Bend (Midw.)	7	6	.538	2.95	20	14	2	1	0	103⅔	79	44	34	25	92
1991—GC White Sox (GCL)	1	3	.250	2.92	11	7	0	0	0	37	30	20	12	6	39
1992—Sarasota (FSL)	15	2	.882	2.05	25	22	4	2	1	154	130	48	35	40	113
—Birmingham (Sou.)	1	1	.500	3.65	2	2	0	0	0	12⅓	13	5	5	11	9
1993—Birmingham (Sou.)	5	1	.833	1.17	8	8	2	1	0	61⅔	31	11	8	7	51
—Nashville (A.A.)	6	8	.429	3.90	21	20	0	0	0	122⅓	117	61	53	47	78
1994—Nashville (A.A.)	14	6	.700	3.48	29	28	2	1	0	178⅔	175	82	69	69	134
1995—GC White Sox (GCL)	0	1	.000	0.00	2	2	0	0	0	7	5	2	0	0	6
1996—Nashville (A.A.)	4	10	.286	4.42	16	15	1	0	0	95⅔	93	54	47	29	58
1997—Rochester (I.L.)	4	7	.364	4.66	25	24	1	0	0	125⅔	127	73	65	36	99
1998—Pawtucket (I.L.)■	8	3	.727	2.82	34	0	0	0	1	60⅔	60	27	19	23	45
1999—Scranton/W.B. (I.L.)■	3	1	.750	2.93	32	0	0	0	0	43	38	17	14	21	34
—Philadelphia (N.L.)	1	3	.250	4.29	32	2	0	0	1	50⅓	41	24	24	14	36
2000—Scranton/W.B. (I.L.)	2	1	.667	1.31	26	0	0	0	3	34⅓	18	5	5	5	27
—Philadelphia (N.L.)	2	3	.400	7.33	20	0	0	0	0	23⅓	25	20	19	13	19
Major League totals (2 years)	3	6	.333	5.25	52	2	0	0	1	73⅔	66	44	43	27	55

SEANEZ, RUDY   P

PERSONAL: Born October 20, 1968, in Brawley, Calif. ... 5-11/205. ... Throws right, bats right. ... Full name: Rudy Caballero Seanez. ... Name pronounced see-AHN-yez.
HIGH SCHOOL: Brawley (Calif.) Union.
TRANSACTIONS/CAREER NOTES: Selected by Cleveland Indians organization in fourth round of free-agent draft (June 10, 1986). ... On disabled list (May 4-July 11 and August 9-29, 1987). ... On Cleveland disabled list (April 1-16 and July 30-September 2, 1991); included rehabilitation assignment to Colorado Springs (August 14-September 2). ... Traded by Indians to Los Angeles Dodgers for P Dennis Cook and P Mike Christopher (December 10, 1991). ... On disabled list (March 29, 1992-entire season). ... Traded by Dodgers to Colorado Rockies for 2B Jody Reed (November 17, 1992). ... On Colorado disabled list (April 4-July 16, 1993); included rehabilitation assignments to Central Valley (June 16-July 4) and Colorado Springs (July 4-15). ... Granted free agency (July 16, 1993). ... Signed by San Diego Padres organization (July 22, 1993). ... Released by Padres (November 18, 1993). ... Signed by Dodgers organization (January 12, 1994). ... On Los Angeles disabled list (May 28-June 16, 1995); included rehabilitation assignment to San Bernardino (June 9-16). ... Granted free agency (October 15, 1996). ... Signed by New York Mets organization (January 15, 1997). ... Traded by Mets to Kansas City Royals for future considerations (May 30, 1997). ... Granted free agency (October 15, 1997). ... Signed by Atlanta Braves organization (December 9, 1997). ... On disabled list (August 21, 1999-remainder of season). ... Granted free agency (November 2, 1999). ... Re-signed by Braves (December 12, 1999). ... On Atlanta disabled list (March 23-April 27, 2000 and June 14-remainder of season); included rehabilitation assignment to Greenville (April 22-27). ... Granted free agency (October 30, 2000).
STATISTICAL NOTES: Pitched 4-0 no-hit victory against Pulaski (August 2, 1986).

Year	League	W	L	Pct.	ERA	G	GS	CG	ShO	Sv.	IP	H	R	ER	BB	SO
1986—	Burlington (Appl.)	5	2	.714	3.20	13	12	1	1	0	76	59	37	27	32	56
1987—	Waterloo (Midw.)	0	4	.000	6.75	10	10	0	0	0	34 2/3	35	29	26	23	23
1988—	Waterloo (Midw.)	6	6	.500	4.69	22	22	1	1	0	113 1/3	98	69	59	68	93
1989—	Kinston (Caro.)	8	10	.444	4.14	25	25	1	0	0	113	94	66	52	*111	149
—	Colorado Springs (PCL)	0	0	...	0.00	1	0	0	0	0	1	1	0	0	0	0
—	Cleveland (A.L.)	0	0	...	3.60	5	0	0	0	0	5	1	2	2	4	7
1990—	Canton/Akron (East.)	1	0	1.000	2.16	15	0	0	0	5	16 2/3	9	4	4	12	25
—	Cleveland (A.L.)	2	1	.667	5.60	24	0	0	0	0	27 1/3	22	17	17	25	24
—	Colorado Springs (PCL)	1	4	.200	6.75	12	0	0	0	1	12	15	10	9	10	7
1991—	Colorado Springs (PCL)	0	0	...	7.27	16	0	0	0	0	17 1/3	17	14	14	22	19
—	Canton/Akron (East.)	4	2	.667	2.58	25	0	0	0	7	38 1/3	17	12	11	30	73
—	Cleveland (A.L.)	0	0	...	16.20	5	0	0	0	0	5	10	12	9	7	7
1992—	Los Angeles (N.L.)■							Did not play.								
1993—	Central Valley (Calif.)■	0	2	.000	9.72	5	1	0	0	0	8 1/3	9	9	9	11	7
—	Colorado Springs (PCL)	0	0	...	9.00	3	0	0	0	0	3	3	3	3	1	5
—	Las Vegas (PCL)■	0	1	.000	6.41	14	0	0	0	0	19 2/3	24	15	14	11	14
—	San Diego (N.L.)	0	0	...	13.50	3	0	0	0	0	3 1/3	8	6	5	2	1
1994—	Albuquerque (PCL)■	2	1	.667	5.32	20	0	0	0	9	22	28	14	13	13	26
—	Los Angeles (N.L.)	1	1	.500	2.66	17	0	0	0	0	23 2/3	24	7	7	9	18
1995—	Los Angeles (N.L.)	1	3	.250	6.75	37	0	0	0	3	34 2/3	39	27	26	18	29
—	San Bernardino (Calif.)	2	0	1.000	0.00	4	0	0	0	1	6	2	0	0	3	5
1996—	Albuquerque (PCL)	0	2	.000	6.52	21	0	0	0	6	19 1/3	27	18	14	11	20
1997—	Norfolk (I.L.)■	1	0	1.000	4.05	9	0	0	0	0	13 1/3	12	8	6	11	17
—	Omaha (A.A.)■	2	5	.286	6.51	28	3	0	0	0	47	53	42	34	25	46
1998—	Richmond (I.L.)■	2	0	1.000	1.29	16	0	0	0	7	21	13	9	3	7	33
—	Atlanta (N.L.)	4	1	.800	2.75	34	0	0	0	2	36	25	13	11	16	50
1999—	Atlanta (N.L.)	6	1	.857	3.35	56	0	0	0	3	53 2/3	47	21	20	21	41
2000—	Greenville (Sou.)	0	0	...	0.00	2	1	0	0	0	2	2	0	0	0	3
—	Atlanta (N.L.)	2	4	.333	4.29	23	0	0	0	2	21	15	11	10	9	20
A.L. totals (3 years)		2	1	.667	6.75	34	0	0	0	0	37 1/3	33	31	28	36	38
N.L. totals (6 years)		14	10	.583	4.13	170	0	0	0	10	172 1/3	158	85	79	75	159
Major League totals (9 years)		16	11	.593	4.59	204	0	0	0	10	209 2/3	191	116	107	111	197

DIVISION SERIES RECORD

Year	League	W	L	Pct.	ERA	G	GS	CG	ShO	Sv.	IP	H	R	ER	BB	SO
1998—	Atlanta (N.L.)	0	0	...	0.00	1	0	0	0	0	1	0	0	0	0	0

CHAMPIONSHIP SERIES RECORD

Year	League	W	L	Pct.	ERA	G	GS	CG	ShO	Sv.	IP	H	R	ER	BB	SO
1998—	Atlanta (N.L.)	0	0	...	6.00	4	0	0	0	0	3	2	2	2	1	4

SEELBACH, CHRIS   P   BRAVES

PERSONAL: Born December 18, 1972, in Lufkin, Texas. ... 6-4/180. ... Throws right, bats right. ... Full name: Christopher Don Seelbach.
HIGH SCHOOL: Lufkin (Texas).
TRANSACTIONS/CAREER NOTES: Selected by Atlanta Braves organization in fourth round of free-agent draft (June 3, 1991). ... Traded by Braves to Florida Marlins (September 15, 1995), completing deal in which Braves acquired P Alejandro Pena for a player to be named later (August 31, 1995). ... Granted free agency (October 17, 1997). ... Signed by Seattle Mariners (January 20, 1998). ... Granted free agency (October 15, 1998). ... Signed by Braves organization (November 19, 1998). ... On Richmond disabled list (April 8-May 18, 1999). ... Granted free agency (October 15, 1999). ... Re-signed by Braves organization (October 28, 1999). ... On Richmond disabled list (August 15-31, 2000).
STATISTICAL NOTES: Led International League with 26 home runs allowed in 1996.

Year	League	W	L	Pct.	ERA	G	GS	CG	ShO	Sv.	IP	H	R	ER	BB	SO
1991—	Gulf Coast Braves (GCL)	0	1	.000	4.20	4	4	0	0	0	15	13	7	7	6	19
1992—	Macon (S.Atl.)	9	11	.450	3.20	27	27	1	0	0	157 1/3	134	65	56	68	144
1993—	Durham (Caro.)	9	9	.500	4.93	25	25	0	0	0	131 1/3	133	85	72	74	112
1994—	Greenville (Sou.)	4	6	.400	2.33	15	15	2	0	0	92 2/3	64	26	24	38	79
—	Richmond (I.L.)	3	5	.375	4.84	12	11	0	0	0	61 1/3	68	37	33	36	35
1995—	Richmond (I.L.)	4	6	.400	4.66	14	14	1	0	0	73 1/3	64	39	38	39	65
—	Greenville (Sou.)	6	0	1.000	1.64	9	9	1	1	0	60 1/3	38	15	11	30	65
1996—	Charlotte (I.L.)■	6	*13	.316	7.35	25	25	1	0	0	138 1/3	167	*123	*113	76	98
1997—	Charlotte (I.L.)	5	0	1.000	6.26	16	6	0	0	0	50 1/3	58	36	35	34	50

Year	League	W	L	Pct.	ERA	G	GS	CG	ShO	Sv.	IP	H	R	ER	BB	SO
1998—	Orlando (Sou.)■	8	3	.727	4.03	23	21	0	0	0	116	103	63	52	52	106
—	Tacoma (PCL)	1	0	1.000	6.17	6	0	0	0	0	11 $2/3$	13	9	8	2	10
1999—	Richmond (I.L.)■	6	1	.857	5.15	13	8	1	0	0	57 $2/3$	51	34	33	34	48
—	Greenville (Sou.)	3	2	.600	3.89	8	6	1	0	0	39 $1/3$	31	18	17	19	47
2000—	Richmond (I.L.)	5	9	.357	4.78	29	22	1	1	2	118 $2/3$	118	71	63	55	96
—	Atlanta (N.L.)	0	1	.000	10.80	2	0	0	0	0	1 $2/3$	3	2	2	0	1
Major League totals (1 year)		0	1	.000	10.80	2	0	0	0	0	1 $2/3$	3	2	2	0	1

SEFCIK, KEVIN — OF

PERSONAL: Born February 10, 1971, in Oak Lawn, Ill. ... 5-10/182. ... Bats right, throws right. ... Full name: Kevin John Sefcik.
HIGH SCHOOL: Victor Andrews (Tinley Park, Ill.).
COLLEGE: St. Xavier (Ill.).
TRANSACTIONS/CAREER NOTES: Selected by Philadelphia Phillies organization in 33rd round of free-agent draft (June 3, 1993). ... Granted free agency (November 20, 2000).
STATISTICAL NOTES: Led New York-Pennsylvania League second basemen with 212 assists and 359 total chances in 1993.

								BATTING							FIELDING		
Year	Team (League)	Pos.	G	AB	R	H	2B	3B	HR	RBI	Avg.	BB	SO	SB	PO	A	E	Avg.
1993—	Batavia (NY-Penn)	2B-3B	74	281	49	84	24	4	2	28	.299	27	22	20	136	†216	16	.957
1994—	Clearwater (FSL)	3B-2B	130	516	83	147	29	8	2	46	.285	49	43	30	91	293	21	.948
1995—	Scranton/W.B. (I.L.)	2B	7	26	5	9	6	1	0	6	.346	3	1	0	13	16	0	1.000
—	Reading (East.)	SS-3B-DH	128	508	68	138	18	4	4	46	.272	38	48	14	166	349	18	.966
—	Philadelphia (N.L.)	3B	5	4	1	0	0	0	0	0	.000	0	2	0	0	1	0	1.000
1996—	Philadelphia (N.L.)	SS-3B-2B	44	116	10	33	5	3	0	9	.284	9	16	3	30	83	7	.942
—	Scranton/W.B. (I.L.)	2B-3B	45	180	34	60	7	5	0	19	.333	15	20	11	63	143	10	.954
1997—	Philadelphia (N.L.)	2B-SS-3B	61	119	11	32	3	0	2	6	.269	4	9	1	39	62	4	.962
—	Scranton/W.B. (I.L.)	2B-3B-OF	29	123	19	41	11	2	1	7	.333	9	11	5	51	56	6	.947
1998—	Philadelphia (N.L.)	O-3-DH-2	104	169	27	53	7	2	3	20	.314	25	32	4	89	1	2	.978
1999—	Philadelphia (N.L.)	OF-2B	111	209	28	58	15	3	1	11	.278	29	24	9	93	18	2	.982
2000—	Philadelphia (N.L.)	OF-DH	99	153	15	36	6	2	0	10	.235	13	19	4	74	0	0	1.000
Major League totals (6 years)			424	770	92	212	36	10	6	56	.275	80	102	21	325	165	15	.970

SEGUI, DAVID — 1B/DH — ORIOLES

PERSONAL: Born July 19, 1966, in Kansas City, Kan. ... 6-1/202. ... Bats both, throws left. ... Full name: David Vincent Segui. ... Son of Diego Segui, pitcher with five major league teams (1962-75 and 1977); and brother of Dan Segui, minor league infielder (1987-90). ... Name pronounced seh-GHEE.
HIGH SCHOOL: Bishop Ward (Kansas City, Kan.).
JUNIOR COLLEGE: Kansas City Kansas Community College.
COLLEGE: Louisiana Tech.
TRANSACTIONS/CAREER NOTES: Selected by Baltimore Orioles organization in 18th round of free-agent draft (June 2, 1987). ... On Rochester disabled list (April 19-26, 1991). ... On suspended list (August 16-19, 1993). ... Traded by Orioles to New York Mets for SS Kevin Baez and P Tom Wegmann (March 27, 1994). ... On disabled list (June 20-July 5, 1994). ... Traded by Mets to Montreal Expos for P Reid Cornelius (June 8, 1995). ... On disabled list (July 4-August 16, 1996). ... On disabled list (June 4-21, 1997). ... On suspended list (July 26, 1997). ... Granted free agency (October 28, 1997). ... Signed by Seattle Mariners (December 12, 1997). ... Traded by Mariners to Toronto Blue Jays for P Tom Davey and P Steve Sinclair (July 28, 1999). ... On suspended list (July 30-31, 1999). ... On Toronto disabled list (August 8-September 2, 1999). ... Granted free agency (October 29, 1999). ... Re-signed by Blue Jays (January 18, 2000). ... Traded by Blue Jays with cash to Texas Rangers as part of three-way deal in which Rangers sent 1B Lee Stevens to Montreal Expos and Expos sent 1B Brad Fullmer to Blue Jays (March 16, 2000). ... Traded by Rangers to Cleveland Indians for OF Ricky Ledee (July 28, 2000). ... Granted free agency (October 30, 2000). ... Signed by Orioles (December 21, 2000).
RECORDS: Shares major league career record for highest fielding percentage for first baseman—.996.
STATISTICAL NOTES: Led N.L. first basemen with .996 fielding percentage in 1994. ... Switch-hit home runs in one game (April 1, 1998). ... Led A.L. first basemen with .999 fielding percentage in 1998. ... Had 15-game hitting streak (May 10-29, 1999). ... Career major league grand slams: 6.

								BATTING							FIELDING		
Year	Team (League)	Pos.	G	AB	R	H	2B	3B	HR	RBI	Avg.	BB	SO	SB	PO	A	E	Avg.
1988—	Hagerstown (Caro.)	1B-OF	60	190	35	51	12	4	3	31	.268	22	23	0	342	25	9	.976
1989—	Frederick (Caro.)	1B	83	284	43	90	19	0	10	50	.317	41	32	2	707	47	4	.995
—	Hagerstown (East.)	1B	44	173	22	56	14	1	1	27	.324	16	16	0	381	30	1	.998
1990—	Rochester (I.L.)	1B-OF	86	307	55	103	28	0	2	51	.336	45	28	5	704	62	3	.996
—	Baltimore (A.L.)	1B-DH	40	123	14	30	7	0	2	15	.244	11	15	0	283	26	3	.990
1991—	Rochester (I.L.)	1B-OF	28	96	9	26	2	0	1	10	.271	15	6	1	165	15	0	1.000
—	Baltimore (A.L.)	OF-1B-DH	86	212	15	59	7	0	2	22	.278	12	19	1	264	23	3	.990
1992—	Baltimore (A.L.)	1B-OF	115	189	21	44	9	0	1	17	.233	20	23	1	406	35	1	.998
1993—	Baltimore (A.L.)	1B-DH	146	450	54	123	27	0	10	60	.273	58	53	2	1152	98	5	.996
1994—	New York (N.L.)■	1B-OF	92	336	46	81	17	1	10	43	.241	33	43	0	695	52	5	†.993
1995—	New York (N.L.)	OF-1B	33	73	9	24	3	1	2	11	.329	12	9	1	56	5	0	1.000
—	Montreal (N.L.)■	1B-OF	97	383	59	117	22	3	10	57	.305	28	38	1	840	70	3	.997
1996—	Montreal (N.L.)	1B	115	416	69	119	30	1	11	58	.286	60	54	4	944	90	7	.993
1997—	Montreal (N.L.)	1B	125	459	75	141	22	3	21	68	.307	57	66	1	1035	88	6	.995
1998—	Seattle (A.L.)■	1B-OF	143	522	79	159	36	1	19	84	.305	49	80	3	1045	116	1	†.999
1999—	Seattle (A.L.)	1B	90	345	43	101	22	3	9	39	.293	32	43	1	700	61	3	.996
—	Toronto (A.L.)■	DH-1B	31	95	14	30	5	0	5	13	.316	8	17	0	19	2	1	.955
2000—	Texas (A.L.)■	DH-1B	93	351	52	118	29	1	11	57	.336	34	51	0	295	28	0	1.000
—	Cleveland (A.L.)■	1B-DH-OF	57	223	41	74	13	0	8	46	.332	19	33	0	267	33	0	1.000
American League totals (7 years)			801	2510	333	738	155	5	67	353	.294	243	334	8	4431	422	17	.997
National League totals (4 years)			462	1667	258	482	94	9	54	237	.289	190	210	7	3570	305	21	.995
Major League totals (11 years)			1263	4177	591	1220	249	14	121	590	.292	433	544	15	8001	727	38	.996

PERSONAL: Born January 19, 1975, in Bocas del Toro, Panama. ... 6-5/230. ... Bats both, throws right. ... Full name: Fernando Alfredo Seguignol.
HIGH SCHOOL: Almirante de Bocas del Toro (Bocas del Toro, Panama).
TRANSACTIONS/CAREER NOTES: Signed as non-drafted free agent by New York Yankees organization (January 29, 1993). ... Traded by Yankees with and cash to Montreal Expos for P John Wetteland (April 5, 1995). ... On Harrisburg disabled list (June 24-July 17, 1998). ... On Montreal disabled list (July 11-September 7, 1999); included rehabilitation assignment to Ottawa (August 9-September 7). ... On Ottawa disabled list (May 1-12, 2000).
STATISTICAL NOTES: Led Florida State League with 14 sacrifice flies in 1997. ... Tied for Florida State League lead in assists by first basemen with 91 in 1997.

Year Team (League)	Pos.	G	AB	R	H	2B	3B	HR	RBI	Avg.	BB	SO	SB	PO	A	E	Avg.
1993— GC Yankees (GCL)	OF-1B	45	161	16	35	3	3	2	20	.217	9	37	2	86	8	2	.979
1994— Oneonta (NY-Penn)	OF	73	266	36	77	14	*9	2	32	.289	16	61	4	77	3	4	.952
1995— Albany (S.Atl.)■	OF	121	457	59	95	22	2	12	66	.208	28	141	12	205	7	8	.964
1996— Delmarva (S.Atl.)	OF	118	410	59	98	14	5	8	55	.239	48	126	12	173	4	4	.978
1997— W.P. Beach (FSL)	1B-OF	124	456	70	116	27	5	18	83	.254	30	129	5	967	‡91	15	.986
1998— Harrisburg (East.)	1B-OF	80	281	54	81	13	0	25	69	.288	29	77	6	503	50	9	.984
— Ottawa (I.L.)	OF-1B	32	109	16	28	8	0	6	16	.257	12	43	0	44	2	1	.979
— Montreal (N.L.)	OF-1B	16	42	6	11	4	0	2	3	.262	3	15	0	65	5	0	1.000
1999— Ottawa (I.L.)	1B-DH-OF	87	312	54	89	17	3	23	74	.285	40	96	3	397	40	10	.978
— Montreal (N.L.)	1B-OF	35	105	14	27	9	0	5	10	.257	5	33	0	183	11	2	.990
2000— Ottawa (I.L.)	1B-OF	41	141	20	39	16	0	8	31	.277	13	26	1	213	23	5	.979
— Montreal (N.L.)	OF-1B-DH	76	162	22	45	8	0	10	22	.278	9	46	0	161	12	5	.972
Major League totals (3 years)		127	309	42	83	21	0	17	35	.269	17	94	0	409	28	7	.984

S

PERSONAL: Born June 11, 1970, in Monroeville, Mich. ... 5-9/190. ... Bats left, throws right. ... Full name: William Frank Selby.
HIGH SCHOOL: Horn Lake (Mich.).
JUNIOR COLLEGE: Northwest Mississippi Community College.
COLLEGE: Southern Mississippi.
TRANSACTIONS/CAREER NOTES: Selected by Boston Red Sox organization in 13th round of free-agent draft (June 1, 1992). ... Granted free agency (October 16, 1998). ... Signed by Cleveland Indians organization (February 3, 1999). ... Granted free agency (October 15, 1999). ... Re-signed by Indians organization (December 23, 1999). ... Released by Indians (October 20, 2000).
STATISTICAL NOTES: Led New York-Pennsylvania League with six intentional bases on balls received in 1992.

Year Team (League)	Pos.	G	AB	R	H	2B	3B	HR	RBI	Avg.	BB	SO	SB	PO	A	E	Avg.
1992— Elmira (NY-Penn)	3B-2B	73	275	38	72	16	1	10	41	.262	31	53	4	75	138	16	.930
1993— Lynchburg (Caro.)	3B-1B	113	394	57	99	22	1	7	38	.251	24	66	1	66	99	8	.954
1994— Lynchburg (Caro.)	3B-2B-1B	97	352	58	109	20	2	19	69	.310	28	62	3	96	185	23	.924
— New Britain (East.)	3B	35	107	15	28	5	0	1	18	.262	15	16	0	23	57	6	.930
1995— Trenton (East.)	3B-2B-DH	117	451	64	129	29	2	13	68	.286	46	52	4	119	206	29	.918
1996— Pawtucket (I.L.)	2B-3B-OF	71	260	39	66	14	5	11	47	.254	22	39	0	95	140	16	.936
— Boston (A.L.)	2B-3B-OF	40	95	12	26	4	0	3	6	.274	9	11	1	30	43	4	.948
1997— Yokohama (Jp. Cn.)■	...		171	19	39	4	1	5	17	.228				...	...	...	...
1998— Buffalo (I.L.)■	3B-2B-OF	97	334	45	85	23	0	14	52	.254	38	50	3	45	74	4	.967
— Akron (East.)	OF-3B-2B	20	77	15	30	7	1	3	10	.390	3	11	3	32	10	1	.977
1999— Buffalo (I.L.)	3B-OF-2B	122	447	75	132	32	5	20	85	.295	57	63	4	65	80	5	.967
2000— Buffalo (I.L.)	3B-OF-2B	100	384	69	106	21	6	21	86	.276	48	61	1	108	172	15	.949
— Cleveland (A.L.)	OF-DH-2B-3B	30	46	8	11	1	0	0	4	.239	1	9	0	19	3	0	1.000
Major League totals (2 years)		70	141	20	37	5	0	3	10	.262	10	20	1	19	3	0	1.000

PERSONAL: Born June 25, 1970, in Golden Valley, Minn. ... 6-5/215. ... Throws right, bats right. ... Full name: Aaron Helmer Sele. ... Name pronounced SEE-lee.
HIGH SCHOOL: North Kitsap (Poulsbo, Wash.).
COLLEGE: Washington State.
TRANSACTIONS/CAREER NOTES: Selected by Minnesota Twins organization in 37th round of free-agent draft (June 1, 1988); did not sign. ... Selected by Boston Red Sox organization in first round (23rd pick overall) of free-agent draft (June 3, 1991). ... On Boston disabled list (May 24, 1995-remainder of season); included rehabilitation assignments to Trenton (June 19-22), Sarasota (July 10-21 and August 7-16) and Pawtucket (August 16-23). ... On Boston disabled list (August 14-September 1, 1996); included rehabilitation assignment to Pawtucket (August 26-27). ... Traded by Red Sox with P Mark Brandenburg and C Bill Haselman to Texas Rangers for C Jim Leyritz and OF Damon Buford (November 6, 1997). ... Granted free agency (November 5, 1999). ... Signed by Seattle Mariners (January 10, 2000).
HONORS: Named A.L. Rookie Pitcher of the Year by THE SPORTING NEWS (1993). ... Named International League Most Valuable Pitcher (1993).
STATISTICAL NOTES: Led Carolina League with 14 hit batsmen in 1992. ... Tied for A.L. lead with nine hit batsmen in 1994.

Year League	W	L	Pct.	ERA	G	GS	CG	ShO	Sv.	IP	H	R	ER	BB	SO
1991— Winter Haven (FSL)	3	6	.333	4.96	13	11	4	0	1	69	65	42	38	32	51
1992— Lynchburg (Caro.)	13	5	.722	2.91	20	19	2	1	0	127	104	51	41	46	112
— New Britain (East.)	2	1	.667	6.27	7	6	1	0	0	33	43	29	23	15	29
1993— Pawtucket (I.L.)	8	2	.800	2.19	14	14	2	1	0	94 1/3	74	30	23	23	87
— Boston (A.L.)	7	2	.778	2.74	18	18	0	0	0	111 2/3	100	42	34	48	93
1994— Boston (A.L.)	8	1	.533	3.83	22	22	2	0	0	143 1/3	140	68	61	60	105
1995— Boston (A.L.)	3	1	.750	3.06	6	6	0	0	0	32 1/3	32	14	11	14	21
— Trenton (East.)	0	1	.000	3.38	2	2	0	0	0	8	8	3	3	2	9
— Sarasota (FSL)	0	0	...	0.00	2	2	0	0	0	7	6	0	0	1	8
— Pawtucket (I.L.)	0	0	...	9.00	2	2	0	0	0	5	9	5	5	2	1

Year	League	W	L	Pct.	ERA	G	GS	CG	ShO	Sv.	IP	H	R	ER	BB	SO
1996—Boston (A.L.)		7	11	.389	5.32	29	29	1	0	0	$157\frac{1}{3}$	192	110	93	67	137
—Pawtucket (I.L.)		0	0	...	6.00	1	1	0	0	0	3	3	2	2	1	4
1997—Boston (A.L.)		13	12	.520	5.38	33	33	1	0	0	$177\frac{1}{3}$	196	115	106	80	122
1998—Texas (A.L.)■		19	11	.633	4.23	33	33	3	2	0	$212\frac{2}{3}$	239	116	100	84	167
1999—Texas (A.L.)		18	9	.667	4.79	33	33	2	2	0	205	244	115	109	70	186
2000—Seattle (A.L.)■		17	10	.630	4.51	34	34	2	2	0	$211\frac{2}{3}$	221	110	106	74	137
Major League totals (8 years)		92	63	.594	4.46	208	208	11	6	0	$1251\frac{1}{3}$	1364	690	620	497	968

DIVISION SERIES RECORD

Year	League	W	L	Pct.	ERA	G	GS	CG	ShO	Sv.	IP	H	R	ER	BB	SO
1998—Texas (A.L.)		0	1	.000	6.00	1	1	0	0	0	6	8	4	4	1	4
1999—Texas (A.L.)		0	1	.000	5.40	1	1	0	0	0	5	6	4	3	5	3
2000—Seattle (A.L.)		0	0	...	1.23	1	1	0	0	0	$7\frac{1}{3}$	3	1	1	3	1
Division series totals (3 years)		0	2	.000	3.93	3	3	0	0	0	$18\frac{1}{3}$	17	9	8	9	8

CHAMPIONSHIP SERIES RECORD

Year	League	W	L	Pct.	ERA	G	GS	CG	ShO	Sv.	IP	H	R	ER	BB	SO
2000—Seattle (A.L.)		0	1	.000	6.00	1	1	0	0	0	6	9	4	4	0	4

ALL-STAR GAME RECORD

Year	League	W	L	Pct.	ERA	GS	CG	ShO	Sv.	IP	H	R	ER	BB	SO
1998—American							Did not play.								
2000—American		0	0	...	0.00	0	0	0	0	1	1	0	0	0	0

SERAFINI, DANIEL — P — PIRATES

S

PERSONAL: Born January 25, 1974, in San Francisco. ... 6-1/195. ... Throws left, bats both. ... Full name: Daniel Joseph Serafini.
HIGH SCHOOL: Serra (San Mateo, Calif.).
TRANSACTIONS/CAREER NOTES: Selected by Minnesota Twins organization in first round (26th pick overall) of free-agent draft (June 1, 1992). ... On Salt Lake disabled list (May 11-31, 1996). ... Traded by Twins to Chicago Cubs for cash (March 31, 1999). ... Traded by Cubs to San Diego Padres for OF Brandon Pernell (December 22, 1999). ... Traded by Padres to Pittsburgh Pirates for a player to be named later (June 28, 2000).

Year	League	W	L	Pct.	ERA	G	GS	CG	ShO	Sv.	IP	H	R	ER	BB	SO
1992—Gulf Coast Twins (GCL)		1	0	1.000	3.64	8	6	0	0	0	$29\frac{2}{3}$	27	16	12	15	33
1993—Fort Wayne (Midw.)		10	8	.556	3.65	27	27	1	1	0	$140\frac{2}{3}$	117	72	57	83	147
1994—Fort Myers (FSL)		9	9	.500	4.61	23	23	2	1	0	$136\frac{2}{3}$	149	84	70	57	130
1995—New Britain (East.)		12	9	.571	3.38	27	27	1	1	0	$162\frac{2}{3}$	155	74	61	72	123
—Salt Lake (PCL)		0	0	...	6.75	1	0	0	0	1	4	4	3	3	1	4
1996—Salt Lake (PCL)		7	7	.500	5.58	25	23	1	0	0	$130\frac{2}{3}$	164	84	81	58	109
—Minnesota (A.L.)		0	1	.000	10.38	1	1	0	0	0	$4\frac{1}{3}$	7	5	5	2	1
1997—Salt Lake (PCL)		9	7	.563	4.97	28	24	2	0	0	152	166	87	84	55	118
—Minnesota (A.L.)		2	1	.667	3.42	6	4	1	0	0	$26\frac{1}{3}$	27	11	10	11	15
1998—Salt Lake (PCL)		2	4	.333	3.71	9	8	0	0	0	$53\frac{1}{3}$	56	29	22	21	39
—Minnesota (A.L.)		7	4	.636	6.48	28	9	0	0	0	75	95	58	54	29	46
1999—Chicago (N.L.)■		3	2	.600	6.93	42	4	0	0	1	$62\frac{1}{3}$	86	51	48	32	17
—Iowa (PCL)		0	0	...	2.77	2	2	0	0	0	13	12	6	4	5	11
2000—San Diego (N.L.)■		0	0	...	18.00	3	0	0	0	0	3	9	6	6	2	3
—Las Vegas (PCL)		2	4	.333	6.88	26	4	0	0	0	51	74	44	39	23	45
—Pittsburgh (N.L.)■		2	5	.286	4.91	11	11	0	0	0	$62\frac{1}{3}$	70	35	34	26	32
—Nashville (PCL)		4	3	.571	2.68	7	7	0	0	0	47	39	17	14	18	22
A.L. totals (3 years)		9	6	.600	5.88	35	14	1	0	0	$105\frac{2}{3}$	129	74	69	42	62
N.L. totals (2 years)		5	7	.417	6.20	56	15	0	0	1	$127\frac{2}{3}$	165	92	88	60	52
Major League totals (5 years)		14	13	.519	6.06	91	29	1	0	1	$233\frac{1}{3}$	294	166	157	102	114

SERRANO, WASCAR — P — PADRES

PERSONAL: Born June 2, 1978, in Santo Domingo, Dominican Republic. ... 6-2/178. ... Throws right, bats right. ... Full name: Wascar Radames Serrano.
HIGH SCHOOL: Las Carreres (Dominican Republic).
TRANSACTIONS/CAREER NOTES: Signed as non-drafted free agent by San Diego Padres organization (May 31, 1995). ... On Mobile disabled list (July 30-August 28, 2000).

Year	League	W	L	Pct.	ERA	G	GS	CG	ShO	Sv.	IP	H	R	ER	BB	SO
1995—Dominican Padres (DSL)		3	3	.500	3.11	12	7	0	0	0	$46\frac{1}{3}$	63	24	16	15	23
1996—Dominican Padres (DSL)		3	3	.300	7.88	22	2	0	0	1	$53\frac{2}{3}$	77	58	47	24	44
1997—Idaho Falls (Pio.)		0	1	.000	11.88	2	2	0	0	0	$8\frac{1}{3}$	13	12	11	4	13
—Arizona Padres (Ariz.)		•6	3	.667	3.18	12	11	0	0	1	$70\frac{2}{3}$	60	43	25	22	75
—Clinton (Midw.)		0	1	.000	6.00	1	1	1	0	0	6	6	5	4	2	2
1998—Clinton (Midw.)		9	7	.563	3.22	26	26	0	0	0	$156\frac{2}{3}$	150	74	56	54	143
1999—Rancho Cuca. (Calif.)		9	8	.529	3.33	21	21	1	1	0	$132\frac{1}{3}$	110	58	49	43	129
—Mobile (Sou.)		2	3	.400	5.53	7	7	0	0	0	$42\frac{1}{3}$	48	27	26	17	29
2000—Mobile (Sou.)		9	4	.692	2.80	20	20	1	0	0	$112\frac{1}{3}$	93	42	35	42	112
—Las Vegas (PCL)		0	1	.000	14.18	4	4	0	0	0	$13\frac{1}{3}$	24	23	21	10	19

SERVAIS, SCOTT — C — TIGERS

PERSONAL: Born June 4, 1967, in La Crosse, Wis. ... 6-2/210. ... Bats right, throws right. ... Full name: Scott Daniel Servais. ... Name pronounced SER-viss.
HIGH SCHOOL: Westby (Wis.).
COLLEGE: Creighton.

TRANSACTIONS/CAREER NOTES: Selected by New York Mets organization in second round of free-agent draft (June 3, 1985); did not sign. ... Selected by Houston Astros organization in third round of free-agent draft (June 1, 1988). ... On Tucson disabled list (June 29-July 1, 1991). ... On Houston disabled list (August 4-September 7, 1991). ... Traded by Astros with OF Luis Gonzalez to Chicago Cubs for C Rick Wilkins (June 28, 1995). ... On Chicago disabled list (July 10-August 3, 1995). ... Granted free agency (October 23, 1998). ... Signed by San Francisco Giants (January 17, 1999). ... On San Francisco disabled list (June 17-July 9, 1999); included rehabilitation assignment to Fresno (July 4-9). ... Granted free agency (October 29, 1999). ... Signed by Colorado Rockies organization (December 17, 1999). ... On Colorado disabled list (April 18-May 3 and July 9-August 22, 2000); included rehabilitation assignments to Colorado Springs (April 28-May 3 and July 26-August 16). ... Claimed on waivers by Giants (August 31, 2000). ... Granted free agency (October 31, 2000). ... Signed by Detroit Tigers organization (January 16, 2001).

STATISTICAL NOTES: Tied for Pacific Coast League lead in double plays by catcher with nine in 1990. ... Led N.L. catchers with 12 errors in 1995.

MISCELLANEOUS: Member of 1988 U.S. Olympic baseball team.

Year Team (League)	Pos.	G	AB	R	H	2B	3B	HR	RBI	Avg.	BB	SO	SB	PO	A	E	Avg.
1989— Osceola (FSL)............	C-1B	46	153	16	41	9	0	2	23	.268	16	35	0	168	24	4	.980
— Columbus (Sou.)........	C	63	199	20	47	5	0	1	22	.236	19	42	0	330	45	3	.992
1990— Tucson (PCL)...........	C	89	303	37	66	11	3	5	37	.218	18	61	0	453	63	9	.983
1991— Tucson (PCL)	C	60	219	34	71	12	0	2	27	.324	13	19	0	350	33	6	.985
— Houston (N.L.)	C	16	37	0	6	3	0	0	6	.162	4	8	0	77	4	1	.988
1992— Houston (N.L.)..........	C	77	205	12	49	9	0	0	15	.239	11	25	0	386	27	2	.995
1993— Houston (N.L.)..........	C	85	258	24	63	11	0	11	32	.244	22	45	0	493	40	2	.996
1994— Houston (N.L.)..........	C	78	251	27	49	15	1	9	41	.195	10	44	0	481	29	2	.996
1995— Houston (N.L.)..........	C	28	89	7	20	10	0	1	12	.225	9	15	0	198	17	5	.977
— Chicago (N.L.)■........	C	52	175	31	50	12	0	12	35	.286	23	37	2	328	33	§7	.981
1996— Chicago (N.L.)	C-1B	129	445	42	118	20	0	11	63	.265	30	75	0	798	73	11	.988
1997— Chicago (N.L.)	C-DH-1B	122	385	36	100	21	0	6	45	.260	24	56	0	736	73	8	.990
1998— Chicago (N.L.)	C-1B	113	325	35	72	15	1	7	36	.222	26	51	1	654	48	4	.994
1999— San Fran. (N.L.)■......	C-1B	69	198	21	54	10	0	5	21	.273	13	31	0	363	23	3	.992
— Fresno (PCL)	C	3	11	3	3	1	1	0	2	.273	0	1	0	23	1	0	1.000
2000— Colorado (N.L.)■	C	33	101	6	22	4	0	1	13	.218	7	16	0	204	17	3	.987
— Colo. Springs (PCL) ...	C	20	65	7	19	2	1	3	12	.292	4	8	0	80	8	1	.989
— San Fran. (N.L.)■.......	C	7	8	1	2	0	0	0	0	.250	2	1	0	18	0	0	1.000
Major League totals (10 years)		809	2477	242	605	130	2	63	319	.244	181	404	3	4736	384	48	.991

DIVISION SERIES RECORD

Year Team (League)	Pos.	G	AB	R	H	2B	3B	HR	RBI	Avg.	BB	SO	SB	PO	A	E	Avg.
1998— Chicago (N.L.)...........	C	1	3	0	2	0	0	0	0	.667	0	0	0	6	1	0	1.000
2000— San Fran. (N.L.)■.......								Did not play.									

SERVICE, SCOTT   P   DODGERS

PERSONAL: Born February 26, 1967, in Cincinnati. ... 6-6/240. ... Throws right, bats right. ... Full name: David Scott Service.
HIGH SCHOOL: Aiken (Cincinnati).
TRANSACTIONS/CAREER NOTES: Signed as non-drafted free agent by Philadelphia Phillies organization (August 24, 1985). ... Granted free agency (October 11, 1990). ... Ssigned by Montreal Expos organization (November 15, 1990). ... Contract sold by Expos to Chunichi Dragons of Japan Central League (August 1991). ... Re-signed by Expos organization (January 10, 1992). ... Granted free agency (June 8, 1992). ... Signed by Cincinnati Reds organization (June 9, 1992). ... On Indianapolis disabled list (May 15-22, 1993). ... Claimed on waivers by Colorado Rockies (June 28, 1993). ... Claimed on waivers by Reds (July 7, 1993). ... On Indianapolis disabled list (April 17-24, 1994). ... Released by Reds (November 17, 1994). ... Re-signed by Reds organization (February 24, 1995). ... Traded by Reds with OF Deion Sanders, P John Roper, P Ricky Pickett and IF Dave McCarty to San Francisco Giants for OF Darren Lewis, P Mark Portugal and P Dave Burba (July 21, 1995). ... Released by Giants (March 26, 1996). ... Signed by Reds organization (April 2, 1996). ... Claimed on waivers by Oakland Athletics (March 27, 1997). ... Claimed on waivers by Reds (April 4, 1997). ... Traded by Reds with P Hector Carrasco to Kansas City Royals for OF Jon Nunnally and IF/OF Chris Stynes (July 15, 1997). ... On suspended list (June 15-16, 1998). ... Released by Royals (December 17, 1999). ... Signed by Oakland Athletics (December 30, 1999). ... Granted free agency (October 18, 2000). ... Signed by Los Angeles Dodgers organization (January 4, 2001).
STATISTICAL NOTES: Led American Association with .800 winning percentage in 1992. ... Led American Association with 24 saves in 1997.
MISCELLANEOUS: Made an out in only appearance as pinch hitter with Cincinnati (1993).

Year League	W	L	Pct.	ERA	G	GS	CG	ShO	Sv.	IP	H	R	ER	BB	SO
1986— Spartanburg (S.Atl.)	1	6	.143	5.83	14	9	1	0	0	58²/₃	68	44	38	34	49
— Utica (NY-Penn)	5	4	.556	2.67	10	10	2	0	0	70²/₃	65	30	21	18	43
— Clearwater (FSL)	1	2	.333	3.20	4	4	1	1	0	25¹/₃	20	10	9	15	19
1987— Reading (East.)..................	0	3	.000	7.78	5	4	0	0	0	19²/₃	22	19	17	16	12
— Clearwater (FSL)	13	4	.765	2.48	21	21	5	2	0	137²/₃	127	46	38	32	73
1988— Reading (East.)...................	3	4	.429	2.86	10	9	1	1	0	56²/₃	52	25	18	22	39
— Maine (I.L.)	8	8	.500	3.67	19	18	1	0	0	110¹/₃	109	51	45	31	87
— Philadelphia (N.L.)..............	0	0	...	1.69	5	0	0	0	0	5¹/₃	7	1	1	1	6
1989— Scranton/W.B. (I.L.)	3	1	.750	2.16	23	0	0	0	6	33¹/₃	27	8	8	23	23
— Reading (East.)................	6	6	.500	3.26	23	10	1	1	1	85²/₃	71	36	31	23	82
1990— Scranton/W.B. (I.L.)	5	4	.556	4.76	45	9	0	0	2	96¹/₃	96	56	51	44	94
1991— Indianapolis (A.A.)■	6	7	.462	2.97	18	17	3	1	0	121¹/₃	83	42	40	39	91
— Chunichi (Jap. Cen.)■.......	0	0	...	9.00	1	...	...	...	0	1	...	...	1	0	0
1992— Indianapolis (A.A.)■	2	0	1.000	0.74	13	0	0	0	2	24¹/₃	12	3	2	9	25
— Montreal (N.L.).................	0	0	...	14.14	5	0	0	0	0	7	15	11	11	5	11
— Nashville (A.A.)■	6	2	§.750	2.29	39	2	0	0	4	70²/₃	54	22	18	35	87
1993— Indianapolis (A.A.)	4	2	.667	4.45	21	1	0	0	2	30¹/₃	25	16	15	17	28
— Colorado (N.L.)■■.............	0	0	...	9.64	3	0	0	0	0	4²/₃	8	5	5	1	3
— Cincinnati (N.L.)■.............	2	2	.500	3.70	26	0	0	0	0	41¹/₃	36	19	17	15	40
1994— Indianapolis (A.A.)	5	5	.500	2.31	40	0	0	0	13	58¹/₃	35	16	15	27	67
— Cincinnati (N.L.)	1	2	.333	7.36	6	0	0	0	0	7¹/₃	8	9	6	3	5
1995— Indianapolis (A.A.)	4	1	.800	2.18	36	0	0	0	18	41¹/₃	33	13	10	15	48
— San Francisco (N.L.)■	3	1	.750	3.19	28	0	0	0	0	31	18	11	11	20	30

Year	League	W	L	Pct.	ERA	G	GS	CG	ShO	Sv.	IP	H	R	ER	BB	SO
1996— Indianapolis (A.A.)■		1	4	.200	3.00	35	1	0	0	15	48	34	18	16	10	58
—Cincinnati (N.L.)		1	0	1.000	3.94	34	1	0	0	0	48	51	21	21	18	46
1997—Cincinnati (N.L.)		0	0	...	11.81	4	0	0	0	0	5 1/3	11	7	7	1	3
—Indianapolis (A.A.)		3	2	.600	3.71	33	0	0	0	15	34	30	15	14	12	53
—Omaha (A.A.)■		0	0	...	0.00	16	0	0	0	§9	14 2/3	9	0	0	4	16
—Kansas City (A.L.)		0	3	.000	4.76	12	0	0	0	0	17	17	9	9	5	19
1998—Kansas City (A.L.)		6	4	.600	3.48	73	0	0	0	4	82 2/3	70	35	32	34	95
1999—Kansas City (A.L.)		5	5	.500	6.09	68	0	0	0	8	75 1/3	87	51	51	42	68
2000—Oakland (A.L.)■		1	2	.333	6.38	20	0	0	0	1	36 2/3	45	31	26	19	35
—Sacramento (PCL)		6	2	.750	1.30	33	0	0	0	13	41 2/3	27	8	6	11	50
A.L. totals (4 years)		12	14	.462	5.02	173	0	0	0	13	211 2/3	219	126	118	100	217
N.L. totals (7 years)		7	5	.583	4.74	111	1	0	0	2	150	154	84	79	64	144
Major League totals (10 years)		19	19	.500	4.90	284	1	0	0	15	361 2/3	373	210	197	164	361

SEXSON, RICHIE — 1B — BREWERS

PERSONAL: Born December 29, 1974, in Portland. ... 6-7/225. ... Bats right, throws right. ... Full name: Richmond Lockwood Sexson.

HIGH SCHOOL: Prairie (Brush Prairie, Wash.).

TRANSACTIONS/CAREER NOTES: Selected by Cleveland Indians organization in 24th round of free-agent draft (June 2, 1993). ... Traded by Indians with P Paul Rigdon, P Kane Davis and a player to be named later to Milwaukee Brewers for P Bob Wickman, P Steve Woodard and P Jason Bere (July 28, 2000); Brewers acquired 2B Marcos Scutaro to complete deal (August 30).

STATISTICAL NOTES: Led Carolina League with 251 total bases in 1995. ... Led Carolina League first basemen with 1,226 total chances and 109 double plays in 1995. ... Led American Association first basemen with 1,003 total chances and 105 double plays in 1997. ... Career major league grand slams: 3.

S

							BATTING								FIELDING			
Year	Team (League)	Pos.	G	AB	R	H	2B	3B	HR	RBI	Avg.	BB	SO	SB	PO	A	E	Avg.
1993—Burlington (Appl.)		1B	40	97	11	18	3	0	1	5	.186	18	21	1	309	15	4	.988
1994—Columbus (S.Atl.)		1B	130	488	88	133	25	2	14	77	.273	37	87	7	933	*63	10	*.990
1995—Kinston (Caro.)		1B	131	494	80	*151	*34	0	22	*85	.306	43	115	4	*1135	*79	12	.990
1996—Canton/Akron (East.)..		1B	133	518	85	143	33	3	16	76	.276	39	118	2	892	76	11	.989
1997—Buffalo (A.A.)		1B-DH	115	434	57	113	20	2	*31	88	.260	27	87	5	*922	*77	4	*.996
—Cleveland (A.L.)		1B-DH	5	11	1	3	0	0	0	0	.273	0	2	0	11	1	0	1.000
1998—Buffalo (I.L.)		OF-1B-DH	89	344	58	102	20	1	21	74	.297	50	68	1	270	29	3	.990
—Cleveland (A.L.)		1B-OF-DH	49	174	28	54	14	1	11	35	.310	6	42	1	325	38	6	.984
1999—Cleveland (A.L.)		1B-OF-DH	134	479	72	122	17	7	31	116	.255	34	117	3	583	54	7	.989
2000—Cleveland (A.L.)		OF-1B-DH	91	324	45	83	16	1	16	44	.256	25	96	1	277	28	1	.997
—Milwaukee (N.L.)■		1B	57	213	44	63	14	0	14	47	.296	34	63	1	470	66	5	.991
American League totals (4 years)			279	988	146	262	47	9	58	195	.265	65	257	5	1196	121	14	.989
National League totals (1 year)			57	213	44	63	14	0	14	47	.296	34	63	1	470	66	5	.991
Major League totals (4 years)			336	1201	190	325	61	9	72	242	.271	99	320	6	1666	187	19	.990

DIVISION SERIES RECORD

							BATTING								FIELDING			
Year	Team (League)	Pos.	G	AB	R	H	2B	3B	HR	RBI	Avg.	BB	SO	SB	PO	A	E	Avg.
1998—Cleveland (A.L.)		1B	3	2	0	0	0	0	0	0	.000	2	1	0	12	1	0	1.000
1999—Cleveland (A.L.)		PH-1B-OF	3	6	1	1	0	0	0	1	.167	1	3	0	1	0	0	1.000
Division series totals (2 years)			6	8	1	1	0	0	0	1	.125	3	4	0	13	1	0	1.000

CHAMPIONSHIP SERIES RECORD

							BATTING								FIELDING			
Year	Team (League)	Pos.	G	AB	R	H	2B	3B	HR	RBI	Avg.	BB	SO	SB	PO	A	E	Avg.
1998—Cleveland (A.L.)		1B	3	6	0	0	0	0	0	0	.000	0	3	0	20	3	0	1.000

SEXTON, CHRIS — IF/OF

PERSONAL: Born August 3, 1971, in Cincinnati. ... 5-11/178. ... Bats right, throws right. ... Full name: Christopher Philip Sexton.

HIGH SCHOOL: St. Xavier (Cincinnati).

COLLEGE: Miami of Ohio.

TRANSACTIONS/CAREER NOTES: Selected by Cincinnati Reds organization in 10th round of free-agent draft (June 3, 1993). ... Traded by Reds to Colorado Rockies for P Marcus Moore (April 10, 1995). ... Granted free agency (October 15, 1999). ... Signed by Reds organization (November 3, 1999). ... Granted free agency (October 6, 2000).

STATISTICAL NOTES: Led South Atlantic League with .412 on-base percentage in 1994. ... Led South Atlantic League shortstops with 71 double plays in 1994. ... Led Carolina League with 84 runs and 97 bases on balls received in 1995. ... Led Carolina League shortstops with .966 fielding percentage, 201 putouts, 423 assists, 646 total chances and 73 double plays in 1995.

							BATTING								FIELDING			
Year	Team (League)	Pos.	G	AB	R	H	2B	3B	HR	RBI	Avg.	BB	SO	SB	PO	A	E	Avg.
1993—Billings (Pio.)		SS-3B-2B-OF	72	273	*63	91	14	4	4	46	.333	35	27	13	94	174	23	.921
1994—Char., S.C. (SAL)		SS-OF	133	467	82	140	21	4	5	59	.300	91	67	18	189	326	36	.935
1995—Win.-Salem (Caro.)		SS	4	15	3	6	0	0	1	5	.400	4	0	0	6	17	0	1.000
—Salem (Caro.)■		SS	123	461	§81	123	16	6	4	32	.267	§93	55	14	§195	§406	22	§.965
—New Haven (East.)		SS	1	3	0	0	0	0	0	0	.000	0	0	0	0	3	0	1.000
1996—New Haven (East.)		SS-OF	127	444	50	96	12	2	0	28	.216	71	68	8	190	294	23	.955
1997—Nashville (A.A.)		SS-OF	98	360	65	107	22	4	1	38	.297	62	37	8	178	200	14	.964
—Colo. Springs (PCL)		SS	33	112	18	30	3	1	1	8	.268	16	21	1	57	87	5	.966
1998—Colo. Springs (PCL) ...		S-2-3-O	132	462	88	131	22	6	2	43	.284	72	67	7	219	352	25	.958
1999—Colo. Springs (PCL) ...		S-3-O-2-DH	60	171	23	58	9	0	0	17	.339	28	22	5	82	90	5	.972
—Colorado (N.L.)		OF-2B-SS	35	59	9	14	0	1	1	7	.237	11	10	4	34	26	2	.968
2000—Louisville (I.L.)■		SS-2B-OF	99	389	79	126	19	1	7	50	.324	63	45	8	178	303	10	.980
—Cincinnati (N.L.)		SS-2B-3B	35	100	9	21	4	0	0	10	.210	13	12	4	44	67	3	.974
Major League totals (2 years)			70	159	18	35	4	1	1	17	.220	24	22	8	78	93	5	.972

PERSONAL: Born July 7, 1966, in Washington Courthouse, Ohio. ... 6-2/200. ... Throws right, bats right. ... Full name: Jeffrey Lee Shaw.
HIGH SCHOOL: Washington (Washington Court House, Ohio).
JUNIOR COLLEGE: Cuyahoga Community College-Western Campus (Ohio).
COLLEGE: Rio Grande (Ohio) College.
TRANSACTIONS/CAREER NOTES: Selected by Cleveland Indians organization in first round (first pick overall) of free-agent draft (January 14, 1986). ... Granted free agency (October 16, 1992). ... Signed by Kansas City Royals organization (November 9, 1992). ... Traded by Royals with C Tim Spehr to Montreal Expos for P Mark Gardner and P Doug Piatt (December 9, 1992). ... Granted free agency (February 17, 1995). ... Re-signed by Expos organization (April 9, 1995). ... Traded by Expos to Chicago White Sox for P Jose DeLeon (August 28, 1995). ... Granted free agency (December 21, 1995). ... Signed by Cincinnati Reds (January 2, 1996). ... Traded by Reds to Los Angeles Dodgers for 1B/3B Paul Konerko and P Dennis Reyes (July 4, 1998). ... On disabled list (June 27-July 13, 2000).
HONORS: Named N.L. Fireman of the Year by THE SPORTING NEWS (1997).
STATISTICAL NOTES: Led Eastern League with 14 hit batsmen in 1989. ... Tied for Pacific Coast League lead with 10 hit batsmen in 1992.

Year League	W	L	Pct.	ERA	G	GS	CG	ShO	Sv.	IP	H	R	ER	BB	SO
1986— Batavia (NY-Penn)	8	4	.667	2.44	14	12	3	1	0	88²/₃	79	32	24	35	71
1987— Waterloo (Midw.)	11	11	.500	3.52	28	*28	6	*4	0	184¹/₃	192	89	72	56	117
1988— Williamsport (East.)	5	*19	.208	3.63	27	•27	6	1	0	163²/₃	•173	*94	66	75	61
1989— Canton/Akron (East.)	7	10	.412	3.62	30	22	6	3	0	154¹/₃	134	84	62	67	95
1990— Colorado Springs (PCL)	10	3	.769	4.29	17	16	4	0	0	98²/₃	98	54	47	52	55
— Cleveland (A.L.)	3	4	.429	6.66	12	9	0	0	0	48²/₃	73	38	36	20	25
1991— Colorado Springs (PCL)	6	3	.667	4.64	12	12	1	0	0	75²/₃	77	47	39	25	55
— Cleveland (A.L.)	0	5	.000	3.36	29	1	0	0	1	72¹/₃	72	34	27	27	31
1992— Colorado Springs (PCL)	10	5	.667	4.76	25	24	1	0	0	155	174	88	82	45	84
— Cleveland (A.L.)	0	1	.000	8.22	2	1	0	0	0	7²/₃	7	7	7	4	3
1993— Ottawa (I.L.)■	0	0	...	0.00	2	1	0	0	0	4	5	0	0	2	1
— Montreal (N.L.)	2	7	.222	4.14	55	8	0	0	0	95²/₃	91	47	44	32	50
1994— Montreal (N.L.)	5	2	.714	3.88	46	0	0	0	1	67¹/₃	67	32	29	15	47
1995— Montreal (N.L.)	1	6	.143	4.62	50	0	0	0	3	62¹/₃	58	35	32	26	45
— Chicago (A.L.)■	0	0	...	6.52	9	0	0	0	0	9²/₃	12	7	7	1	6
1996— Cincinnati (N.L.)■	8	6	.571	2.49	78	0	0	0	4	104²/₃	99	34	29	29	69
1997— Cincinnati (N.L.)	4	2	.667	2.38	78	0	0	0	*42	94²/₃	79	26	25	12	74
1998— Cincinnati (N.L.)	2	4	.333	1.81	39	0	0	0	23	49²/₃	40	11	10	12	29
— Los Angeles (N.L.)■	1	4	.200	2.55	34	0	0	0	25	35¹/₃	35	11	10	7	26
1999— Los Angeles (N.L.)	2	4	.333	2.78	64	0	0	0	34	68	64	25	21	15	43
2000— Los Angeles (N.L.)	3	4	.429	4.24	60	0	0	0	27	57¹/₃	61	29	27	16	39
A.L. totals (4 years)	3	10	.231	5.01	52	11	0	0	1	138¹/₃	164	86	77	52	65
N.L. totals (8 years)	28	39	.418	3.22	504	8	0	0	159	635	594	250	227	164	422
Major League totals (11 years)	31	49	.388	3.54	556	19	0	0	160	773¹/₃	758	336	304	216	487

ALL-STAR GAME RECORD

Year League	W	L	Pct.	ERA	GS	CG	ShO	Sv.	IP	H	R	ER	BB	SO
1998— National	0	0	...	9.00	0	0	0	0	1	3	1	1	0	0

PERSONAL: Born November 19, 1971, in Baton Rouge, La. ... 6-2/180. ... Bats right, throws right. ... Full name: Andrew Mark Sheets.
HIGH SCHOOL: St. Amant (La.).
COLLEGE: Tulane, then Louisiana State.
TRANSACTIONS/CAREER NOTES: Selected by Seattle Mariners organization in fourth round of free-agent draft (June 1, 1992). ... Selected by Tampa Bay Devil Rays in first round (24th pick overall) of expansion draft (November 18, 1997). ... Traded by Devil Rays with P Brian Boehringer to San Diego Padres for C John Flaherty (November 18, 1997). ... Traded by Padres with OF Gus Kennedy to Anaheim Angels for C Phil Nevin and P Keith Volkman (March 29, 1999). ... Granted free agency (December 21, 1999). ... Signed by Red Sox organization (January 23, 2000). ... Granted free agency (October 13, 2000). ... Signed by Devil Rays organization (November 15, 2000).
STATISTICAL NOTES: Led Pacific Coast League shortstops with .973 fielding percentage in 1997. ... Career major league grand slams: 1.

Year Team (League)	Pos.	G	AB	R	H	2B	3B	HR	RBI	Avg.	BB	SO	SB	PO	A	E	Avg.
1993— Riverside (Calif.)	SS	52	176	23	34	9	1	1	12	.193	17	51	2	80	159	17	.934
— Appleton (Midw.)	SS-2B-OF	69	259	32	68	10	4	1	25	.263	20	59	7	98	194	11	.964
1994— Riverside (Calif.)	SS	31	100	17	27	5	1	2	10	.270	16	22	6	39	95	14	.905
— Jacksonville (Sou.)	SS	70	232	26	51	12	0	0	17	.220	20	54	3	105	205	17	.948
— Calgary (PCL)	SS	26	93	22	32	8	1	2	16	.344	11	20	1	32	80	2	.982
1995— Tacoma (PCL)	SS	132	437	57	128	29	9	2	47	.293	32	83	8	157	382	27	.952
1996— Tacoma (PCL)	SS-2B-3B	62	232	44	83	16	5	5	33	.358	25	56	6	95	176	14	.951
— Seattle (A.L.)	3B-2B-SS	47	110	18	21	8	0	0	9	.191	10	41	2	40	77	5	.959
1997— Tacoma (PCL)	SS-2B-3B	113	401	57	104	23	0	14	53	.259	46	97	7	174	314	13	.974
— Seattle (A.L.)	3B-SS-2B	32	89	18	22	3	0	4	9	.247	7	34	2	14	62	8	.905
1998— San Diego (N.L.)■	SS-3B-2B-1B	88	194	31	47	5	3	7	29	.242	21	62	7	96	145	9	.964
1999— Anaheim (A.L.)■	SS-3B-2B	87	244	22	48	10	0	3	29	.197	14	59	1	113	182	12	.961
— Edmonton (PCL)	SS-2B	12	45	6	13	1	1	0	4	.289	2	11	0	13	34	1	.979
2000— Pawtucket (I.L.)■	SS-3B-2B-1B	83	281	38	64	9	3	8	36	.228	38	48	4	125	159	9	.969
— Boston (A.L.)	SS-DH-1B	12	21	1	2	0	0	0	1	.095	0	3	0	7	18	0	1.000
American League totals (4 years)		178	464	59	93	21	0	7	48	.200	31	137	5	174	339	25	.954
National League totals (1 year)		88	194	31	47	5	3	7	29	.242	21	62	7	96	145	9	.964
Major League totals (5 years)		266	658	90	140	26	3	14	77	.213	52	199	12	270	484	34	.957

DIVISION SERIES RECORD

Year Team (League)	Pos.	G	AB	R	H	2B	3B	HR	RBI	Avg.	BB	SO	SB	PO	A	E	Avg.
1997— Seattle (A.L.)	3B	2	3	0	1	0	0	0	0	.333	0	2	0	0	0	0	...
1998— San Diego (N.L.)	PR-2B	2	0	0	0	0	0	0	0	...	0	0	0	0	0	0	...
Division series totals (2 years)		4	3	0	1	0	0	0	0	.333	0	2	0	0	0	0	...

Year	Team (League)	Pos.	G	AB	R	H	2B	3B	HR	RBI	Avg.	BB	SO	SB	PO	A	E	Avg.
					BATTING											FIELDING		
1998—San Diego (N.L.)		SS-PH	3	3	0	0	0	0	0	0	.000	0	1	0	0	2	0	1.000

WORLD SERIES RECORD

Year	Team (League)	Pos.	G	AB	R	H	2B	3B	HR	RBI	Avg.	BB	SO	SB	PO	A	E	Avg.
					BATTING											FIELDING		
1998—San Diego (N.L.)		SS	2	2	0	0	0	0	0	0	.000	0	1	0	0	2	0	1.000

SHEFFIELD, GARY   OF   DODGERS

PERSONAL: Born November 18, 1968, in Tampa. ... 5-11/205. ... Bats right, throws right. ... Full name: Gary Antonian Sheffield. ... Nephew of Dwight Gooden, pitcher, New York Yankees.

HIGH SCHOOL: Hillsborough (Tampa).

TRANSACTIONS/CAREER NOTES: Selected by Milwaukee Brewers organization in first round (sixth pick overall) of free-agent draft (June 2, 1986). ... On Milwaukee disabled list (July 14-September 9, 1989). ... On suspended list (August 31-September 3, 1990). ... On disabled list (June 15-July 3 and July 25, 1991-remainder of season). ... Traded by Brewers with P Geoff Kellogg to San Diego Padres for P Ricky Bones, SS Jose Valentin and OF Matt Mieske (March 27, 1992). ... Traded by Padres with P Rich Rodriguez to Florida Marlins for P Trevor Hoffman, P Jose Martinez and P Andres Berumen (June 24, 1993). ... On Florida suspended list (July 9-12, 1993). ... On Florida disabled list (May 10-25 and May 28-June 12, 1994); included rehabilitation assignment to Portland (June 10-12). ... On disabled list (June 11-September 1, 1995; and May 14-29, 1997). ... Traded by Marlins with 3B Bobby Bonilla, C Charles Johnson, OF Jim Eisenreich and P Manuel Barrios to Los Angeles Dodgers for C Mike Piazza and 3B Todd Zeile (May 15, 1998). ... On suspended list (August 4-6, 1998). ... On suspended list (August 23-27, 2000).

RECORDS: Shares major league record for fewest double plays by outfielder (150 or more games)—0 (1996). ... Shares major league single-inning record for most home runs—2 (July 13, 1997, fourth inning).

HONORS: Named Minor League co-Player of the Year by THE SPORTING NEWS (1988). ... Named Major League Player of the Year by THE SPORTING NEWS (1992). ... Named N.L. Comeback Player of the Year by THE SPORTING NEWS (1992). ... Named third baseman on THE SPORTING NEWS N.L. All-Star team (1992). ... Named third baseman on THE SPORTING NEWS N.L. Silver Slugger team (1992). ... Named outfielder on THE SPORTING NEWS N.L. All-Star team (1996). ... Named outfielder on THE SPORTING NEWS N.L. Silver Slugger team (1996).

STATISTICAL NOTES: Led Pioneer League shortstops with 34 double plays in 1986. ... Led California League shortstops with 77 double plays in 1987. ... Led N.L. with 323 total bases in 1992. ... Led N.L. with .465 on-base percentage in 1996. ... Career major league grand slams: 7.

MISCELLANEOUS: Holds Florida Marlins all-time records for most home runs (122) and runs (365).

Year	Team (League)	Pos.	G	AB	R	H	2B	3B	HR	RBI	Avg.	BB	SO	SB	PO	A	E	Avg.
							BATTING									FIELDING		
1986—Helena (Pio.)		SS	57	222	53	81	12	2	15	*71	.365	20	14	14	97	149	24	.911
1987—Stockton (Calif.)		SS	129	469	84	130	23	3	17	*103	.277	81	49	25	235	345	39	.937
1988—El Paso (Texas)...........		SS-3B-OF	77	296	70	93	19	3	19	65	.314	35	41	5	130	206	23	.936
—Denver (A.A.)...............		3B-SS	57	212	42	73	9	5	9	54	.344	21	22	8	54	97	8	.950
—Milwaukee (A.L.)		SS	24	80	12	19	1	0	4	12	.238	7	7	3	39	48	3	.967
1989—Milwaukee (A.L.)		SS-3B-DH	95	368	34	91	18	0	5	32	.247	27	33	10	100	238	16	.955
—Denver (A.A.)...............		SS	7	29	3	4	1	1	0	0	.138	2	0	0	2	6	0	1.000
1990—Milwaukee (A.L.)		3B	125	487	67	143	30	1	10	67	.294	44	41	25	98	254	25	.934
1991—Milwaukee (A.L.)		3B-DH	50	175	25	34	12	2	2	22	.194	19	15	5	29	65	8	.922
1992—San Diego (N.L.)■		3B	146	557	87	184	34	3	33	100	*.330	48	40	5	99	299	16	.961
1993—San Diego (N.L.)		3B	68	258	34	76	12	2	10	36	.295	18	30	5	41	102	15	.905
—Florida (N.L.)■..........		3B	72	236	33	69	8	3	10	37	.292	29	34	12	38	123	19	.894
1994—Florida (N.L.)		OF	87	322	61	89	16	1	27	78	.276	51	50	12	154	7	5	.970
—Portland (East.)		OF	2	7	1	2	1	0	0	0	.286	1	3	0	3	0	0	1.000
1995—Florida (N.L.)		OF	63	213	46	69	8	0	16	46	.324	55	45	19	109	5	7	.942
1996—Florida (N.L.)		OF	161	519	118	163	33	1	42	120	.314	142	66	16	238	8	6	.976
1997—Florida (N.L.)		OF-DH	135	444	86	111	22	1	21	71	.250	121	79	11	226	14	5	.980
1998—Florida (N.L.)		OF	40	136	21	37	11	1	6	28	.272	26	16	4	68	3	1	.986
—Los Angeles (N.L.)■ ..		OF	90	301	52	95	16	1	16	57	.316	69	30	18	149	6	1	.994
1999—Los Angeles (N.L.)		OF-DH	152	549	103	165	20	0	34	101	.301	101	64	11	235	7	7	.972
2000—Los Angeles (N.L.)		OF-DH	141	501	105	163	24	3	43	109	.325	101	71	4	203	5	•10	.954
American League totals (4 years)			294	1110	138	287	61	3	21	133	.259	97	96	43	266	605	52	.944
National League totals (9 years)			1155	4036	746	1221	204	16	258	783	.303	761	525	117	1560	579	92	.959
Major League totals (13 years)			1449	5146	884	1508	265	19	279	916	.293	858	621	160	1826	1184	144	.954

DIVISION SERIES RECORD

Year	Team (League)	Pos.	G	AB	R	H	2B	3B	HR	RBI	Avg.	BB	SO	SB	PO	A	E	Avg.
					BATTING											FIELDING		
1997—Florida (N.L.)		OF	3	9	3	5	1	0	1	1	.556	5	0	1	6	0	0	1.000

CHAMPIONSHIP SERIES RECORD

Year	Team (League)	Pos.	G	AB	R	H	2B	3B	HR	RBI	Avg.	BB	SO	SB	PO	A	E	Avg.
					BATTING											FIELDING		
1997—Florida (N.L.)		OF	6	17	6	4	0	0	1	1	.235	7	3	0	5	2	0	1.000

NOTES: Member of World Series championship team (1997).

WORLD SERIES RECORD

Year	Team (League)	Pos.	G	AB	R	H	2B	3B	HR	RBI	Avg.	BB	SO	SB	PO	A	E	Avg.
					BATTING											FIELDING		
1997—Florida (N.L.)		OF	7	24	4	7	1	0	1	5	.292	8	5	0	16	0	1	.941

ALL-STAR GAME RECORD

Year	League	Pos.	AB	R	H	2B	3B	HR	RBI	Avg.	BB	SO	SB	PO	A	E	Avg.
				BATTING											FIELDING		
1992—National		3B	2	0	0	0	0	0	0	.000	0	0	0	0	0	0	...
1993—National		3B	3	1	2	0	0	1	2	.667	0	0	0	0	2	0	1.000

Year League	Pos.	AB	R	H	2B	3B	BATTING HR	RBI	Avg.	BB	SO	SB	PO	FIELDING A	E	Avg.
1996— National	OF	1	0	0	0	0	0	0	.000	0	0	0	2	0	0	1.000
1998— National	PH	1	0	0	0	0	0	0	.000	0	0	0	0	0	0	...
1999— National	PH-DH	1	0	0	0	0	0	0	.000	0	0	0	0	0	0	...
2000— National	OF	1	1	0	0	0	0	0	.000	1	0	0	1	0	0	1.000
All-Star Game totals (6 years)		9	2	2	0	0	1	2	.222	1	0	0	3	2	0	1.000

SHELDON, SCOTT — IF — RANGERS

PERSONAL: Born November 20, 1968, in Hammond, Ind. ... 6-3/215. ... Bats right, throws right. ... Full name: Scott Patrick Sheldon.
HIGH SCHOOL: Clear Lake (Houston).
COLLEGE: Houston.
TRANSACTIONS/CAREER NOTES: Selected by Oakland Athletics organization in eighth round of free-agent draft (June 3, 1991). ... Granted free agency (October 17, 1997). ... Signed by Texas Rangers organization (November 20, 1997).

Year Team (League)	Pos.	G	AB	R	H	2B	3B	BATTING HR	RBI	Avg.	BB	SO	SB	PO	FIELDING A	E	Avg.
1991— S. Oregon (N'West)	2B-3B-SS-1B	65	229	34	58	10	3	0	24	.253	23	44	9	122	124	14	.946
1992— Madison (Midw.)	SS-1B	74	275	41	76	16	0	6	24	.276	32	78	5	107	217	25	.928
1993— Madison (Midw.)	3B-SS	131	428	67	91	22	1	8	67	.213	49	121	8	90	275	26	.934
1994— Huntsville (Sou.)	3-O-S-2-1	91	268	31	62	10	1	0	28	.231	28	69	7	69	185	11	.958
1995— Huntsville (Sou.)	2B-SS-1B-3B	66	235	25	51	10	2	4	15	.217	23	60	5	203	188	12	.970
— Edmonton (PCL)	3B-SS-1B-2B	45	128	21	33	7	1	4	12	.258	15	15	4	44	89	5	.964
1996— Edmonton (PCL)	S-1-2-3-O	98	350	61	105	27	3	10	60	.300	43	83	5	259	230	14	.972
1997— Edmonton (PCL)	SS-2B	118	422	89	133	39	6	19	77	.315	59	104	5	139	313	11	.976
— Oakland (A.L.)	SS-2B-3B	13	24	2	6	0	0	1	2	.250	1	6	0	16	18	2	.944
1998— Oklahoma (PCL)■	SS-OF	131	493	74	126	31	4	29	96	.256	62	143	2	163	397	24	.959
— Texas (A.L.)	3B-SS-DH-1B	7	16	0	2	0	0	0	1	.125	1	6	0	8	11	1	.950
1999— Oklahoma (PCL)	2-S-1-3-C-O	122	453	94	141	35	3	28	97	.311	56	112	12	254	325	9	.985
— Texas (A.L.)	3B	2	2	0	0	0	0	0	0	.000	0	0	0	2	3	0	1.000
2000— Texas (A.L.)	IF-OF-DH-P	58	124	21	35	11	0	4	19	.282	10	37	0	93	85	5	.973
Major League totals (4 years)		80	166	23	43	11	0	5	22	.259	12	49	0	119	117	8	.967

RECORD AS PITCHER

Year League	W	L	Pct.	ERA	G	GS	CG	ShO	Sv.	IP	H	R	ER	BB	SO
2000— Texas (A.L.)	0	0	...	0.00	1	0	0	0	0	$1/3$	0	0	0	0	1

SHIELDS, SCOT — P — ANGELS

PERSONAL: Born July 22, 1975, in Fort Lauderdale, Fla. ... 6-1/175. ... Throws right, bats right. ... Full name: Robert Scot Shields.
HIGH SCHOOL: Fort Lauderdale (Fla.).
COLLEGE: Lincoln Memorial University (Tenn.).
TRANSACTIONS/CAREER NOTES: Selected by Anaheim Angels organization in 38th round of free-agent draft (June 3, 1997).
STATISTICAL NOTES: Led Pacific Coast League with 14 hit batsmen in 2000.

Year League	W	L	Pct.	ERA	G	GS	CG	ShO	Sv.	IP	H	R	ER	BB	SO
1997— Boise (N'West)	7	2	.778	2.94	30	0	0	0	2	52	45	20	17	24	61
1998— Cedar Rapids (Midw.)	6	5	.545	3.65	58	0	0	0	7	74	62	33	30	29	81
1999— Lake Elsinore (Calif.)	10	3	.769	2.52	24	9	2	1	1	$107 1/3$	91	37	30	39	113
— Erie (East.)	4	4	.500	2.89	10	10	1	1	0	$74 2/3$	57	26	24	26	81
2000— Edmonton (PCL)	7	13	.350	5.41	27	27	4	1	0	163	158	114	98	82	*156

SHUEY, PAUL — P — INDIANS

PERSONAL: Born September 16, 1970, in Lima, Ohio. ... 6-3/215. ... Throws right, bats right. ... Full name: Paul Kenneth Shuey. ... Name pronounced SHOO-ee.
HIGH SCHOOL: Millbrook (Raleigh, N.C.).
COLLEGE: North Carolina.
TRANSACTIONS/CAREER NOTES: Selected by Cleveland Indians organization in first round (second pick overall) of free-agent draft (June 1, 1992). ... On Cleveland disabled list (June 27-July 21, 1994); included rehabilitation assignment to Charlotte (July 5-21). ... On Cleveland disabled list (May 4-22, 1995). ... On Buffalo disabled list (June 2-July 10, 1995). ... On Cleveland disabled list (April 25-May 18, June 19-July 4 and July 11-August 1, 1997); included rehabilitation assignments to Buffalo (May 5-10) and Akron (May 1-18). ... On Cleveland disabled list (April 11-June 15, 1998); included rehabilitation assignments to Akron (April 24) and Buffalo (May 23-June 14). ... On Cleveland disabled list (April 26-May 11, 1999); included rehabilitation assignment to Buffalo (May 9-11). ... On Cleveland disabled list (May 21-June 27, 2000); included rehabilitation assignment to Akron (June 24-27).
RECORDS: Shares major single-inning league record for most strikeouts—4 (May 14, 1994, ninth inning).

Year League	W	L	Pct.	ERA	G	GS	CG	ShO	Sv.	IP	H	R	ER	BB	SO
1992— Columbus (S.Atl.)	5	5	.500	3.35	14	14	0	0	0	78	62	35	29	47	73
1993— Canton/Akron (East.)	4	8	.333	7.30	27	7	0	0	0	$61 2/3$	76	50	50	36	41
— Kinston (Caro.)	1	0	1.000	4.84	15	0	0	0	0	$22 1/3$	29	12	12	8	27
1994— Kinston (Caro.)	1	0	1.000	3.75	13	0	0	0	8	12	10	5	5	3	16
— Cleveland (A.L.)	0	1	.000	8.49	14	0	0	0	5	$11 2/3$	14	11	11	12	16
— Charlotte (I.L.)	2	1	.667	1.93	20	0	0	0	10	$23 1/3$	15	9	5	10	25
1995— Cleveland (A.L.)	0	2	.000	4.26	7	0	0	0	0	$6 1/3$	5	4	3	5	5
— Buffalo (A.A.)	1	2	.333	2.63	25	0	0	0	11	$27 1/3$	21	9	8	7	27
1996— Buffalo (A.A.)	3	2	.600	0.81	19	0	0	0	4	$33 1/3$	14	4	3	9	57
— Cleveland (A.L.)	5	2	.714	2.85	42	0	0	0	4	$53 2/3$	45	19	17	26	44
1997— Cleveland (A.L.)	4	2	.667	6.20	40	0	0	0	2	45	52	31	31	28	41
— Buffalo (A.A.)	0	0	...	3.60	2	0	0	0	0	5	4	2	2	4	6
— Akron (East.)	0	0	...	3.38	3	0	0	0	0	8	10	3	3	0	9

Year League	W	L	Pct.	ERA	G	GS	CG	ShO	Sv.	IP	H	R	ER	BB	SO
1998— Cleveland (A.L.)	5	4	.556	3.00	43	0	0	0	2	51	44	19	17	25	58
— Akron (East.)	0	0	...	54.00	1	0	0	0	0	$^1/_3$	3	2	2	1	0
— Buffalo (I.L.)	0	0	...	2.51	11	0	0	0	2	14 $^1/_3$	11	4	4	6	22
1999— Cleveland (A.L.)	8	5	.615	3.53	72	0	0	0	6	81 $^2/_3$	68	37	32	40	103
— Buffalo (I.L.)	0	0	...	0.00	1	0	0	0	0	1	0	0	0	1	1
2000— Cleveland (A.L.)	4	2	.667	3.39	57	0	0	0	0	63 $^2/_3$	51	25	24	30	69
— Akron (East.)	0	0	...	4.50	2	1	0	0	0	2	1	1	1	1	1
Major League totals (7 years)	26	18	.591	3.88	275	0	0	0	19	313	279	146	135	166	341

DIVISION SERIES RECORD

Year League	W	L	Pct.	ERA	G	GS	CG	ShO	Sv.	IP	H	R	ER	BB	SO
1996— Cleveland (A.L.)	0	0	...	9.00	3	0	0	0	0	2	5	2	2	2	2
1998— Cleveland (A.L.)	0	0	...	0.00	3	0	0	0	0	3	3	0	0	1	4
1999— Cleveland (A.L.)	1	1	.500	11.25	3	0	0	0	0	4	4	5	5	4	5
Division series totals (3 years)	1	1	.500	7.00	9	0	0	0	0	9	12	7	7	7	11

CHAMPIONSHIP SERIES RECORD

Year League	W	L	Pct.	ERA	G	GS	CG	ShO	Sv.	IP	H	R	ER	BB	SO
1998— Cleveland (A.L.)	0	0	...	0.00	5	0	0	0	0	6 $^1/_3$	4	0	0	9	7

SHUMPERT, TERRY — IF/OF — ROCKIES

S

PERSONAL: Born August 16, 1966, in Paducah, Ky. ... 6-0/200. ... Bats right, throws right. ... Full name: Terrance Darnell Shumpert.
HIGH SCHOOL: Paducah (Ky.) Tilghman.
COLLEGE: Kentucky.
TRANSACTIONS/CAREER NOTES: Selected by Kansas City Royals organization in second round of free-agent draft (June 2, 1987). ... On disabled list (July 19-August 13, 1989). ... On Kansas City disabled list (June 3-September 10, 1990); included rehabilitation assignment to Omaha (August 7-25). ... On Kansas City disabled list (August 7-September 7, 1992). ... Traded by Royals to Boston Red Sox for a player to be named later (December 13, 1994). ... Granted free agency (October 6, 1995). ... Signed by Chicago Cubs organization (March 12, 1996). ... On Chicago disabled list (August 19-September 3, 1996). ... Granted free agency (October 15, 1996). ... Signed by San Diego Padres (November 4, 1996). ... On San Diego disabled list (May 27-August 5, 1997). ... Released by Padres (August 5, 1997). ... Signed by Colorado Rockies organization (August 13, 1997). ... Granted free agency (October 15, 1998). ... Re-signed by Rockies organization (December 18, 1998). ... On Colorado disabled list (May 13-23, 1999). ... Granted free agency (October 29, 1999). ... Re-signed by Rockies (January 1, 1999).
STATISTICAL NOTES: Led American Association with 21 sacrifice hits in 1993. ... Career major league grand slams: 1.

							BATTING								FIELDING		
Year Team (League)	Pos.	G	AB	R	H	2B	3B	HR	RBI	Avg.	BB	SO	SB	PO	A	E	Avg.
1987— Eugene (N'West)	2B	48	186	38	54	16	1	4	22	.290	27	41	16	81	107	11	.945
1988— Appleton (Midw.)	2B-OF	114	422	64	102	*37	4	7	38	.242	56	90	36	235	266	20	.962
1989— Omaha (A.A.)	2B	113	355	54	88	29	2	4	22	.248	25	63	23	218	295	*22	.959
1990— Omaha (A.A.)	2B	39	153	24	39	6	4	2	12	.255	14	28	18	72	95	7	.960
— Kansas City (A.L.)	2B-DH	32	91	7	25	6	1	0	8	.275	2	17	3	56	74	3	.977
1991— Kansas City (A.L.)	2B	144	369	45	80	16	4	5	34	.217	30	75	17	249	368	16	.975
1992— Kansas City (A.L.)	2B-DH-SS	36	94	6	14	5	1	1	11	.149	3	17	2	50	77	4	.969
— Omaha (A.A.)	2B-SS	56	210	23	42	12	0	1	14	.200	13	33	3	113	154	9	.967
1993— Omaha (A.A.)	2B	111	413	70	124	29	1	14	59	.300	41	62	*36	190	303	14	.972
— Kansas City (A.L.)	2B	8	10	0	1	0	0	0	0	.100	2	2	1	11	11	0	1.000
1994— Kansas City (A.L.)	2B-3B-DH-SS	64	183	28	44	6	2	8	24	.240	13	39	18	70	129	8	.961
1995— Boston (A.L.)■	2B-3B-SS-DH	21	47	6	11	3	0	0	3	.234	4	13	3	21	35	2	.966
— Pawtucket (I.L.)	3B-2B-DH-OF	37	133	17	36	7	0	2	11	.271	14	27	10	29	69	11	.899
1996— Iowa (A.A.)■	2-3-DH-SS	72	246	45	68	13	4	5	32	.276	24	44	13	119	165	7	.976
— Chicago (N.L.)	3B-2B-SS	27	31	5	7	1	0	2	6	.226	2	11	0	11	9	1	.952
1997— Las Vegas (PCL)■	3B-2B-SS-DH	32	109	18	31	8	1	1	16	.284	9	20	3	37	58	4	.960
— San Diego (N.L.)	2B-OF-3B	13	33	4	9	3	0	1	6	.273	3	4	0	23	17	2	.952
— New Haven (East.)■■	2B	5	17	2	4	0	0	1	1	.235	0	2	0	8	17	0	1.000
— Colo. Springs (PCL)	SS-2B-3B-OF	10	37	8	11	3	0	1	2	.297	2	7	0	8	20	5	.848
1998— Colo. Springs (PCL)	2-0-3-DH-S	97	376	66	115	29	8	12	50	.306	35	59	11	141	133	4	.986
— Colorado (N.L.)	2B	23	26	3	6	1	0	1	2	.231	2	8	0	2	14	0	1.000
1999— Colo. Springs (PCL)	3B-2B-SS-DH	29	79	15	30	8	1	6	17	.380	4	9	3	23	36	5	.922
— Colorado (N.L.)	2B-OF-3B-SS	92	262	58	91	26	3	10	37	.347	31	41	14	129	165	5	.983
2000— Colorado (N.L.)	OF-IF-DH	115	263	52	68	11	7	9	40	.259	28	40	8	109	58	4	.977
American League totals (6 years)		305	794	92	175	36	8	14	80	.220	54	163	44	457	694	33	.972
National League totals (5 years)		270	615	122	181	42	10	23	91	.294	66	104	22	274	263	12	.978
Major League totals (11 years)		575	1409	214	356	78	18	37	171	.253	120	267	66	731	957	45	.974

SIERRA, RUBEN — OF — RANGERS

PERSONAL: Born October 6, 1965, in Rio Piedras, Puerto Rico. ... 6-1/200. ... Bats both, throws right. ... Full name: Ruben Angel Garcia Sierra.
HIGH SCHOOL: Dr. Secario Rosario (Rio Piedras, Puerto Rico).
TRANSACTIONS/CAREER NOTES: Signed as non-drafted free agent by Texas Rangers organization (November 21, 1982). ... Traded by Rangers with P Jeff Russell, P Bobby Witt and cash to Oakland Athletics for OF Jose Canseco (August 31, 1992). ... Granted free agency (October 26, 1992). ... Re-signed by A's (December 21, 1992). ... On Oakland disabled list (July 7-22, 1995). ... Traded by A's with P Jason Beverlin to New York Yankees for OF/DH Danny Tartabull (July 28, 1995). ... Traded by Yankees with P Matt Drews to Detroit Tigers for 1B/DH Cecil Fielder (July 31, 1996). ... Traded by Tigers to Cincinnati Reds for OF Decomba Conner and P Ben Bailey (October 28, 1996). ... Released by Reds (May 9, 1997). ... Signed by Toronto Blue Jays organization (May 11, 1997). ... Released by Blue Jays (June 16, 1997). ... Signed by Chicago White Sox organization (January 9, 1998). ... Released by White Sox (May 29, 1998). ... Signed by New York Mets organization (June 20, 1998). ... Granted free agency (October 16, 1998). ... Signed by Atlantic City, Atlantic League (May 1, 1999). ... Signed by Cleveland Indians organization (December 23, 1999). ... Released by Indians (March 20, 2000). ... Signed by Rangers organization (May 1, 2000). ... Granted free agency (October 30, 2000). ... Re-signed by Rangers organization (December 13, 2000).

HONORS: Named A.L. Player of the Year by The Sporting News (1989). ... Named outfielder on The Sporting News A.L. All-Star team (1989). ... Named outfielder on The Sporting News A.L. Silver Slugger team (1989).

STATISTICAL NOTES: Switch-hit home runs in one game five times (September 13, 1986; August 27, 1988; June 8, 1989; June 7, 1994; and June 22, 1996). ... Led A.L. with 12 sacrifice flies in 1987. ... Led A.L. outfielders with six double plays in 1987. ... Led A.L. with 344 total bases and .543 slugging percentage in 1989. ... Led Pacific Coast League in grounding into double plays with 24 in 2000. ... Career major league grand slams: 3.

MISCELLANEOUS: Holds Texas Rangers all-time record for most triples (43). ... Batted righthanded only (1983).

Year	Team (League)	Pos.	G	AB	R	H	2B	3B	HR	RBI	Avg.	BB	SO	SB	PO	A	E	Avg.
1983—	GC Rangers (GCL)	OF	48	182	26	44	7	3	1	26	.242	16	38	3	67	6	4	.948
1984—	Burlington (Midw.)	OF	•138	482	55	127	33	5	6	75	.263	49	97	13	239	18	*20	.928
1985—	Tulsa (Texas)	OF	*137	*545	63	138	34	*8	13	74	.253	35	111	22	234	12	*15	.943
1986—	Oklahoma City (A.A.)	OF	46	189	31	56	11	2	9	41	.296	15	27	8	114	4	2	.983
	— Texas (A.L.)	OF-DH	113	382	50	101	13	10	16	55	.264	22	65	7	200	7	6	.972
1987—	Texas (A.L.)	OF	158	*643	97	169	35	4	30	109	.263	39	114	16	272	•17	11	.963
1988—	Texas (A.L.)	OF-DH	156	615	77	156	32	2	23	91	.254	44	91	18	310	11	7	.979
1989—	Texas (A.L.)	OF	•162	634	101	194	35	*14	29	*119	.306	43	82	8	313	13	9	.973
1990—	Texas (A.L.)	OF-DH	159	608	70	170	37	2	16	96	.280	49	86	9	283	7	10	.967
1991—	Texas (A.L.)	OF	161	661	110	203	44	5	25	116	.307	56	91	16	305	15	7	.979
1992—	Texas (A.L.)	OF-DH	124	500	66	139	30	6	14	70	.278	31	59	12	224	6	7	.970
	— Oakland (A.L.)■	OF-DH	27	101	17	28	4	1	3	17	.277	14	9	2	59	0	0	1.000
1993—	Oakland (A.L.)	OF-DH	158	630	77	147	23	5	22	101	.233	52	97	25	291	9	7	.977
1994—	Oakland (A.L.)	OF-DH	110	426	71	114	21	1	23	92	.268	23	64	8	155	8	*9	.948
1995—	Oakland (A.L.)	OF-DH	70	264	40	70	17	0	12	42	.265	24	42	4	89	1	4	.957
	— New York (A.L.)■	DH-OF	56	215	33	56	15	0	7	44	.260	22	34	1	18	1	1	.950
1996—	Campeche (Mex.)■	OF	1	1	1	0	0	0	0	0	.000	0	0	0	0	0	0	...
	— New York (A.L.)■	DH-OF	96	360	39	93	17	1	11	52	.258	40	58	1	56	5	1	.984
	— Detroit (A.L.)■	OF-DH	46	158	22	35	9	1	1	20	.222	20	25	3	52	1	5	.914
1997—	Cincinnati (N.L.)■	OF	25	90	6	22	5	1	2	7	.244	6	21	0	34	3	0	1.000
	— Syracuse (I.L.)■	OF	8	32	5	7	2	0	1	5	.219	2	6	0	10	2	1	.923
	— Toronto (A.L.)	OF-DH	14	48	4	10	0	2	1	5	.208	3	13	0	13	0	1	.929
1998—	Chicago (A.L.)■	OF-DH	27	74	7	16	4	1	4	11	.216	3	11	2	19	1	0	1.000
	— Norfolk (I.L.)■	OF-DH	28	108	16	28	5	0	3	19	.259	13	18	3	50	1	0	1.000
1999—	Atlantic City (Atl.)■	DH-OF	112	422	76	124	22	2	28	82	.294	59	63	3	71	1	3	.960
2000—	Oklahoma (PCL)■	DH	20	60	5	14	0	0	1	7	.233	4	9	1	...	...	...	...
	— Oklahoma (PCL)	OF	112	439	70	143	26	3	18	82	.326	55	63	5	141	9	6	.962
American League totals (14 years)			1657	6379	886	1715	336	55	238	1047	.269	489	950	133	2659	102	85	.970
National League totals (1 year)			25	90	6	22	5	1	2	7	.244	6	21	0	34	3	0	1.000
Major League totals (14 years)			1682	6469	892	1737	341	56	240	1054	.269	495	971	133	2693	105	85	.971

DIVISION SERIES RECORD

RECORDS: Shares single-game record for most at-bats—7 (October 4, 1995).

Year	Team (League)	Pos.	G	AB	R	H	2B	3B	HR	RBI	Avg.	BB	SO	SB	PO	A	E	Avg.
1995—	New York (A.L.)	DH	5	23	2	4	2	0	2	5	.174	2	7	0	...	...	...	...

CHAMPIONSHIP SERIES RECORD

Year	Team (League)	Pos.	G	AB	R	H	2B	3B	HR	RBI	Avg.	BB	SO	SB	PO	A	E	Avg.
1992—	Oakland (A.L.)	OF	6	24	4	8	2	1	1	7	.333	2	1	1	12	0	0	1.000

ALL-STAR GAME RECORD

Year	League	Pos.	AB	R	H	2B	3B	HR	RBI	Avg.	BB	SO	SB	PO	A	E	Avg.
1989—	American	OF	3	1	2	0	0	0	1	.667	0	0	0	1	0	0	1.000
1991—	American	OF	2	0	0	0	0	0	0	.000	0	2	0	0	0	0	...
1992—	American	OF	2	2	1	0	0	1	2	.500	0	0	0	1	0	0	1.000
1994—	American	OF	2	0	1	0	0	0	0	.500	0	0	0	1	0	0	1.000
All-Star Game totals (4 years)			9	3	4	0	0	1	3	.444	0	2	0	3	0	0	1.000

SIKORSKI, BRIAN — P — RANGERS

PERSONAL: Born July 27, 1974, in Detroit. ... 6-1/190. ... Throws right, bats right. ... Full name: Brian Patrick Sikorski.

HIGH SCHOOL: Roseville (Mich.).

COLLEGE: Western Michigan.

TRANSACTIONS/CAREER NOTES: Selected by Houston Astros organization in fourth round of free-agent draft (June 1, 1995). ... Claimed on waivers by Texas Rangers (November 9, 1999).

STATISTICAL NOTES: Led Midwest League with 12 balks in 1996. ... Led Pacific Coast League with five balks in 2000.

Year	League	W	L	Pct.	ERA	G	GS	CG	ShO	Sv.	IP	H	R	ER	BB	SO
1995—	Auburn (NY-Penn)	1	2	.333	2.10	23	0	0	0	12	34 1/3	22	8	8	14	35
	— Quad City (Midw.)	1	0	1.000	0.00	2	0	0	0	0	3	1	1	0	0	4
1996—	Quad City (Midw.)	11	8	.579	3.13	26	25	1	0	0	166 2/3	140	79	58	70	150
1997—	Kissimmee (FSL)	8	2	.800	3.06	11	11	0	0	0	67 2/3	64	29	23	16	46
	— Jackson (Texas)	5	5	.500	4.63	17	17	0	0	0	93 1/3	91	55	48	31	74
1998—	Jackson (Texas)	6	4	.600	4.07	15	15	0	0	0	97 1/3	83	50	44	44	80
	— New Orleans (PCL)	5	8	.385	5.79	15	14	1	0	0	84	86	57	54	32	64
1999—	New Orleans (PCL)	7	10	.412	4.95	28	27	2	1	0	158 1/3	169	92	87	58	122
2000—	Oklahoma (PCL)■	10	9	.526	4.04	24	23	5	2	1	140 1/3	131	73	63	60	99
	— Texas (A.L.)	1	3	.250	5.73	10	5	0	0	0	37 2/3	46	31	24	25	32
Major League totals (1 year)		1	3	.250	5.73	10	5	0	0	0	37 2/3	46	31	24	25	32

SILVA, CARLOS   P   PHILLIES

PERSONAL: Born April 23, 1979, in Bolivar, Venezuela. ... 6-4/225. ... Throws right, bats right.
HIGH SCHOOL: U.E. General Ezequiel Zamora Bolivar.
TRANSACTIONS/CAREER NOTES: Signed as non-drafted free agent by Philadelphia Phillies organization (March 22, 1996).

Year League	W	L	Pct.	ERA	G	GS	CG	ShO	Sv.	IP	H	R	ER	BB	SO
1996—Martinsville (Appl.)	0	0	...	4.00	7	1	0	0	0	18	20	11	8	5	16
1997—Martinsville (Appl.)	2	2	.500	5.15	11	11	0	0	0	57²/₃	66	46	33	14	31
1998—Martinsville (Appl.)	1	4	.200	5.05	7	7	1	0	0	41	48	24	23	4	21
—Batavia (NY-Penn)	2	3	.400	6.35	9	7	0	0	0	45¹/₃	61	37	32	9	27
1999—Piedmont (S.Atl.)	11	8	.579	3.12	26	26	3	1	0	164¹/₃	176	79	57	41	99
2000—Clearwater (FSL)	8	13	.381	3.57	26	24	4	0	0	176¹/₃	229	99	70	26	82

SILVA, JOSE   P   PIRATES

PERSONAL: Born December 19, 1973, in Tijuana, Mexico. ... 6-5/235. ... Throws right, bats right. ... Full name: Jose Leonel Silva.
HIGH SCHOOL: Hilltop (Chula Vista, Calif.).
TRANSACTIONS/CAREER NOTES: Selected by Toronto Blue Jays organization in sixth round of free-agent draft (June 3, 1991). ... On disabled list (April 6-August 17, 1995). ... On Knoxville disabled list (April 4-June 5, 1996). ... Traded by Blue Jays with IF Jose Pett, IF Brandon Cromer and three players to be named later to Pittsburgh Pirates for OF Orlando Merced, IF Carlos Garcia and P Dan Plesac (November 14, 1996); Pirates acquired P Mike Halperin, IF Abraham Nunez and C/OF Craig Wilson to complete deal (December 11, 1996). ... On Calgary disabled list (April 29-June 2, 1997). ... On Pittsburgh disabled list (June 17-September 10, 1998); included rehabilitation assignment to Nashville (August 25-September 6). ... On Pittsburgh disabled list (March 26-April 23, 1999); included rehabilitation assignment to Nashville (April 14-23).

Year League	W	L	Pct.	ERA	G	GS	CG	ShO	Sv.	IP	H	R	ER	BB	SO
1992—GC Blue Jays (GCL)	6	4	.600	2.28	12	•12	0	0	0	59¹/₃	42	23	15	18	78
1993—Hagerstown (S.Atl.)	12	5	.706	2.52	24	24	0	0	0	142²/₃	103	50	40	62	161
1994—Dunedin (FSL)	0	2	.000	3.77	8	7	0	0	0	43	41	32	18	24	41
—Knoxville (Sou.)	4	8	.333	4.14	16	16	1	1	0	91¹/₃	89	47	42	31	71
1995—Knoxville (Sou.)	0	0	...	9.00	3	0	0	0	0	2	3	2	2	6	2
1996—Knoxville (Sou.)	2	3	.400	4.91	22	6	0	0	0	44	45	27	24	22	26
—Toronto (A.L.)	0	0	...	13.50	2	0	0	0	0	2	5	3	3	0	0
1997—Calgary (PCL)■	5	1	.833	3.41	17	11	0	0	0	66	74	27	25	22	54
—Pittsburgh (N.L.)	2	1	.667	5.94	11	4	0	0	0	36¹/₃	52	26	24	16	30
1998—Pittsburgh (N.L.)	6	7	.462	4.40	18	18	1	0	0	100¹/₃	104	55	49	30	64
—Nashville (PCL)	0	0	...	4.82	3	3	0	0	0	9¹/₃	10	5	5	4	6
1999—Nashville (PCL)	2	0	1.000	1.50	2	2	0	0	0	12	14	4	2	4	10
—Pittsburgh (N.L.)	2	8	.200	5.73	34	12	0	0	4	97¹/₃	108	70	62	39	77
2000—Pittsburgh (N.L.)	11	9	.550	5.56	51	19	1	0	0	136	178	96	84	50	98
A.L. totals (1 year)	0	0	...	13.50	2	0	0	0	0	2	5	3	3	0	0
N.L. totals (4 years)	21	25	.457	5.33	114	53	2	0	4	370	442	247	219	135	269
Major League totals (5 years)	21	25	.457	5.37	116	53	2	0	4	372	447	250	222	135	269

SIMAS, BILL   P   WHITE SOX

PERSONAL: Born November 28, 1971, in Hanford, Calif. ... 6-3/235. ... Throws right, bats left. ... Full name: William Anthony Simas Jr.
HIGH SCHOOL: St. Joseph (Calif.).
COLLEGE: Fresno (Calif.) City College.
TRANSACTIONS/CAREER NOTES: Selected by California Angels organization in sixth round of free-agent draft (June 1, 1992). ... Traded by Angels with P Andrew Lorraine, P John Snyder and OF McKay Christensen to Chicago White Sox for P Jim Abbott and P Tim Fortugno (July 27, 1995). ... On disabled list (July 23-August 5 and August 17, 1997-remainder of season).

Year League	W	L	Pct.	ERA	G	GS	CG	ShO	Sv.	IP	H	R	ER	BB	SO
1992—Boise (N'West)	6	5	.545	3.95	14	12	0	0	1	70²/₃	82	44	31	29	39
1993—Cedar Rapids (Midw.)	5	8	.385	4.95	35	6	0	0	6	80	93	60	44	36	62
1994—Lake Elsinore (Calif.)	5	2	.714	2.11	37	0	0	0	13	47	44	17	11	10	34
—Midland (Texas)	2	0	1.000	0.59	13	0	0	0	6	15¹/₃	5	1	1	2	12
1995—Vancouver (PCL)	6	3	.667	3.55	30	0	0	0	6	38	44	19	15	14	44
—Nashville (A.A.)■	1	1	.500	3.86	7	0	0	0	0	11²/₃	12	5	5	3	12
—Chicago (A.L.)	1	1	.500	2.57	14	0	0	0	0	14	15	5	4	10	16
1996—Chicago (A.L.)	2	8	.200	4.58	64	0	0	0	2	72²/₃	75	39	37	39	65
1997—Chicago (A.L.)	3	1	.750	4.14	40	0	0	0	1	41¹/₃	46	23	19	24	38
1998—Calgary (PCL)	1	0	1.000	0.00	5	0	0	0	1	9	3	1	0	2	11
—Chicago (A.L.)	4	3	.571	3.57	60	0	0	0	18	70²/₃	54	29	28	22	56
1999—Chicago (A.L.)	6	3	.667	3.75	70	0	0	0	2	72	73	36	30	32	41
2000—Chicago (A.L.)	2	3	.400	3.46	60	0	0	0	0	67²/₃	69	27	26	22	49
Major League totals (6 years)	18	19	.486	3.83	308	0	0	0	23	338¹/₃	332	159	144	149	265

DIVISION SERIES RECORD

Year League	W	L	Pct.	ERA	G	GS	CG	ShO	Sv.	IP	H	R	ER	BB	SO
2000—Chicago (A.L.)	0	0	...	6.75	2	0	0	0	0	1¹/₃	0	1	1	1	2

SIMMONS, BRIAN   OF   BLUE JAYS

PERSONAL: Born September 4, 1973, in Lebanon, Pa. ... 6-2/190. ... Bats both, throws right. ... Full name: Brian Lee Simmons.
HIGH SCHOOL: Peters Township (McMurray, Pa.).
COLLEGE: Michigan.

S

TRANSACTIONS/CAREER NOTES: Selected by Baltimore Orioles organization in 35th round of free-agent draft (June 1, 1992); did not sign. ... Selected by Chicago White Sox organization in second round of free-agent draft (June 1, 1995). ... On South Bend disabled list (April 5-17, 1996). ... On Calgary disabled list (June 22-August 10, 1998); included rehabilitation assignment to Arizona White Sox (August 1-8). ... On Chicago disabled list (March 31-April 29, 1999); included rehabilitation assignment to Charlotte (April 8-27). ... On disabled list (March 30, 2000-remainder of season). ... Traded by White Sox with P Mike Sirotka, P Kevin Beirne and P Mike Williams to Toronto Blue Jays for P David Wells and P Matt DeWitt (January 14, 2001).

STATISTICAL NOTES: Led Southern League outfielders with 334 total chances in 1997. ... Switch-hit home runs in one game (September 26, 1998).

								BATTING						FIELDING			
Year — Team (League)	Pos.	G	AB	R	H	2B	3B	HR	RBI	Avg.	BB	SO	SB	PO	A	E	Avg.
1995— Sarasota (GCL)	OF	5	17	5	3	1	0	1	5	.176	6	1	0	13	1	0	1.000
— Hickory (S.Atl.)	OF	41	163	13	31	6	1	2	11	.190	19	44	4	77	2	1	.988
1996— South Bend (Midw.)	OF-DH	92	356	73	106	29	6	17	58	.298	48	69	14	204	10	7	.968
— Prince William (Caro.)	OF	33	131	17	26	4	3	4	14	.198	9	39	2	70	2	2	.973
1997— Birmingham (Sou.)	OF	138	546	108	143	28	*12	15	72	.262	*88	124	15	*322	7	5	.985
1998— Calgary (PCL)	OF-DH	94	355	72	103	21	4	13	51	.290	41	82	10	197	6	7	.967
— Ariz. White Sox (Ariz.)	OF-DH	5	12	1	2	0	0	0	0	.167	1	1	0	3	0	0	1.000
— Chicago (A.L.)	OF	5	19	4	7	0	0	2	6	.368	0	2	0	13	0	0	1.000
1999— Chicago (A.L.)	OF-DH	54	126	14	29	3	3	4	17	.230	9	30	4	79	2	2	.976
— Charlotte (I.L.)	OF	78	285	53	77	14	0	10	44	.270	37	60	8	171	6	5	.973
2000— Chicago (A.L.)								Did not play.									
Major League totals (2 years)		59	145	18	36	3	3	6	23	.248	9	32	4	92	2	2	.979

SINGLETON, CHRIS — OF — WHITE SOX

PERSONAL: Born August 15, 1972, in Mesa, Ariz. ... 6-2/195. ... Bats left, throws left. ... Full name: Christopher Verdell Singleton.
HIGH SCHOOL: Pinole (Calif.) Valley.
COLLEGE: Nevada.
TRANSACTIONS/CAREER NOTES: Selected by San Francisco Giants organization in second round of free-agent draft (June 3, 1993). ... Traded by Giants with P Alberto Castillo to New York Yankees for 3B Charlie Hayes and cash (November 11, 1997). ... Traded by Yankees to Chicago White Sox for a player to be named later (December 8, 1998); Yankees acquired P Rich Pratt to complete deal (January 10, 1999).
STATISTICAL NOTES: Led Texas League with nine sacrifice flies in 1997. ... Led Texas League outfielders with 271 total chances and tied for league lead with four double plays in 1997. ... Tied for Texas League lead with four intentional bases on balls in 1997. ... Hit for the cycle (July 6, 1999).

								BATTING						FIELDING			
Year — Team (League)	Pos.	G	AB	R	H	2B	3B	HR	RBI	Avg.	BB	SO	SB	PO	A	E	Avg.
1993— Everett (N'West)	OF	58	219	39	58	14	4	3	18	.265	18	46	14	106	6	3	.974
1994— San Jose (Calif.)	OF	113	425	51	106	17	5	2	49	.249	27	62	19	248	10	13	.952
1995— San Jose (Calif.)	OF	94	405	55	112	13	5	2	31	.277	17	49	33	142	6	7	.955
1996— Shreveport (Texas)	OF	129	500	68	149	31	9	5	72	.298	24	58	27	262	10	4	.986
— Phoenix (PCL)	OF	9	32	3	4	0	0	0	0	.125	1	2	0	18	1	0	1.000
1997— Shreveport (Texas)	OF	126	464	85	147	26	10	9	61	.317	22	50	27	*253	11	7	.974
1998— Columbus (I.L.)■	OF	121	413	55	105	17	10	6	45	.254	27	78	9	251	10	7	.974
1999— Chicago (A.L.)■	OF-DH	133	496	72	149	31	6	17	72	.300	22	45	20	376	9	4	.990
2000— Chicago (A.L.)	OF-DH	147	511	83	130	22	5	11	62	.254	35	85	22	373	9	3	.992
Major League totals (2 years)		280	1007	155	279	53	11	28	134	.277	57	130	42	749	18	7	.991

DIVISION SERIES RECORD

								BATTING						FIELDING			
Year — Team (League)	Pos.	G	AB	R	H	2B	3B	HR	RBI	Avg.	BB	SO	SB	PO	A	E	Avg.
2000— Chicago (A.L.)	OF	3	9	1	1	0	1	0	1	.111	0	2	0	3	0	0	1.000

SIROTKA, MIKE — P — BLUE JAYS

PERSONAL: Born May 13, 1971, in Chicago. ... 6-1/200. ... Throws left, bats left. ... Full name: Michael Robert Sirotka.
HIGH SCHOOL: Westfield (Houston).
COLLEGE: Louisiana State.
TRANSACTIONS/CAREER NOTES: Selected by Chicago White Sox organization in 15th round of free-agent draft (June 3, 1993). ... On Hickory disabled list (July 1-28, 1993). ... On South Bend temporarily inactive list (August 27-October 4, 1993). ... Traded by White Sox with P Kevin Beirne, OF Brian Simmons and P Mike Williams to Toronto Blue Jays for P David Wells and P Matt DeWitt (January 14, 2001).
RECORDS: Shares major league single-inning record for most errors by pitcher—3 (April 9, 1999, fifth inning).

Year — League	W	L	Pct.	ERA	G	GS	CG	ShO	Sv.	IP	H	R	ER	BB	SO
1993— GC White Sox (GCL)	0	0	...	0.00	3	0	0	0	0	5	4	1	0	2	8
— South Bend (Midw.)	0	1	.000	6.10	7	1	0	0	0	10 1/3	12	8	7	6	12
1994— South Bend (Midw.)	12	9	.571	3.07	27	27	8	2	0	196 2/3	183	99	67	56	173
1995— Birmingham (Sou.)	7	6	.538	3.20	16	16	1	0	0	101 1/3	95	42	36	22	79
— Chicago (A.L.)	1	2	.333	4.19	6	6	0	0	0	34 1/3	39	16	16	17	19
— Nashville (A.A.)	1	5	.167	2.83	8	8	0	0	0	54	51	21	17	13	34
1996— Nashville (A.A.)	7	5	.583	3.60	15	15	1	1	0	90	90	44	36	24	58
— Chicago (A.L.)	1	2	.333	7.18	15	4	0	0	0	26 1/3	34	27	21	12	11
1997— Nashville (A.A.)	7	5	.583	3.28	19	19	1	0	0	112 1/3	115	49	41	22	92
— Chicago (A.L.)	3	0	1.000	2.25	7	4	0	0	0	32	36	9	8	5	24
1998— Chicago (A.L.)	14	15	.483	5.06	33	33	5	0	0	211 2/3	255	137	119	47	128
1999— Chicago (A.L.)	11	13	.458	4.00	32	32	3	1	0	209	236	108	93	57	125
2000— Chicago (A.L.)	15	10	.600	3.79	32	32	1	0	0	197	203	101	83	69	128
Major League totals (6 years)	45	42	.517	4.31	125	111	9	1	0	710 1/3	803	398	340	207	435

DIVISION SERIES RECORD

Year — League	W	L	Pct.	ERA	G	GS	CG	ShO	Sv.	IP	H	R	ER	BB	SO
2000— Chicago (A.L.)	0	1	.000	4.76	1	1	0	0	0	5 2/3	7	4	3	2	0

SLOCUMB, HEATHCLIFF   P

PERSONAL: Born June 7, 1966, in Jamaica, N.Y. ... 6-3/220. ... Throws right, bats right.
HIGH SCHOOL: John Bowne (Flushing, N.Y.).
TRANSACTIONS/CAREER NOTES: Signed as non-drafted free agent by New York Mets organization (July 10, 1984). ... Selected by Chicago Cubs organization from Mets organization in Rule 5 minor league draft (December 9, 1986). ... Traded by Cubs to Cleveland Indians for SS Jose Hernandez (June 1, 1993). ... Traded by Indians to Philadelphia Phillies for OF Ruben Amaro (November 2, 1993). ... Traded by Phillies with P Larry Wimberly and OF Rick Holifield to Boston Red Sox for P Ken Ryan, OF Lee Tinsley and OF Glenn Murray (January 29, 1996). ... Traded by Red Sox to Seattle Mariners for C Jason Varitek and P Derek Lowe (July 31, 1997). ... Granted free agency (October 23, 1998). ... Signed by Baltimore Orioles (January 15, 1999). ... Released by Orioles (April 30, 1999). ... Signed by St. Louis Cardinals organization (May 15, 1999). ... On St. Louis disabled list (June 23-July 16, 1999). ... Granted free agency (November 10, 1999). ... Re-signed by Cardinals (November 24, 1999). ... Traded by Cardinals with OF Ben Johnson to San Diego Padres for C Carlos Hernandez and IF/OF Nate Tebbs (July 31, 2000). ... Released by Padres (January 12, 2001).
STATISTICAL NOTES: Led Carolina League with 19 wild pitches in 1988.
MISCELLANEOUS: Appeared in one game as pinch runner with St. Louis (2000).

Year League	W	L	Pct.	ERA	G	GS	CG	ShO	Sv.	IP	H	R	ER	BB	SO
1984— Kingsport (Appl.)	0	0	...	0.00	1	0	0	0	0	1/3	0	1	0	1	0
— Little Falls (NY-Penn)	0	0	...	11.00	4	1	0	0	0	9	8	11	11	16	10
1985— Kingsport (Appl.)	3	2	.600	3.78	11	9	1	0	0	52 1/3	47	32	22	31	29
1986— Little Falls (NY-Penn)	3	1	.750	1.65	25	0	0	0	1	43 2/3	24	17	8	36	41
1987— Winston-Salem (Caro.)■	1	2	.333	6.26	9	4	0	0	0	27 1/3	26	25	19	26	27
— Peoria (Midw.)	10	4	.714	2.60	16	16	3	1	0	103 2/3	97	44	30	42	81
1988— Winston-Salem (Caro.)	6	6	.500	4.96	25	19	2	1	1	119 2/3	122	75	66	90	78
1989— Peoria (Midw.)	5	3	.625	1.78	49	0	0	0	22	55 2/3	31	16	11	33	52
1990— Charlotte (Sou.)	3	1	.750	2.15	43	0	0	0	12	50 1/3	50	20	12	32	37
— Iowa (A.A.)	3	2	.600	2.00	20	0	0	0	1	27	16	10	6	18	21
1991— Chicago (N.L.)	2	1	.667	3.45	52	0	0	0	1	62 2/3	53	29	24	30	34
— Iowa (A.A.)	1	0	1.000	4.05	12	0	0	0	1	13 1/3	10	8	6	6	9
1992— Chicago (N.L.)	0	3	.000	6.50	30	0	0	0	1	36	52	27	26	21	27
— Iowa (A.A.)	1	3	.250	2.59	36	1	0	0	7	41 2/3	36	13	12	16	47
1993— Iowa (A.A.)	1	0	1.000	1.50	10	0	0	0	7	12	7	2	2	8	10
— Chicago (N.L.)	1	0	1.000	3.38	10	0	0	0	0	10 2/3	7	5	4	4	4
— Cleveland (A.L.)■	3	1	.750	4.28	20	0	0	0	0	27 1/3	28	14	13	16	18
— Charlotte (I.L.)	3	2	.600	3.56	23	0	0	0	1	30 1/3	25	14	12	11	25
1994— Philadelphia (N.L.)■	5	1	.833	2.86	52	0	0	0	0	72 1/3	75	32	23	28	58
1995— Philadelphia (N.L.)	5	6	.455	2.89	61	0	0	0	32	65 1/3	64	26	21	35	63
1996— Boston (A.L.)■	5	5	.500	3.02	75	0	0	0	31	83 1/3	68	31	28	55	88
1997— Boston (A.L.)	0	5	.000	5.79	49	0	0	0	17	46 2/3	58	32	30	34	36
— Seattle (A.L.)■	0	4	.000	4.13	27	0	0	0	10	28 1/3	26	13	15	15	28
1998— Seattle (A.L.)	2	5	.286	5.32	57	0	0	0	3	67 2/3	72	40	40	44	51
1999— Baltimore (A.L.)■	0	0	...	12.46	10	0	0	0	0	8 2/3	15	12	12	9	12
— Memphis (PCL)■	0	0	...	4.50	2	0	0	0	0	2	3	1	1	0	2
— St. Louis (N.L.)	3	2	.600	2.36	40	0	0	0	2	53 1/3	49	16	14	30	48
2000— St. Louis (N.L.)	2	3	.400	5.44	43	0	0	0	1	49 2/3	50	32	30	24	34
— San Diego (N.L.)■	0	1	.000	3.79	22	0	0	0	0	19	19	11	8	13	12
A.L. totals (5 years)	10	20	.333	4.67	238	0	0	0	61	262	267	142	136	173	233
N.L. totals (7 years)	18	17	.514	3.66	310	0	0	0	37	369	369	178	150	185	280
Major League totals (10 years)	28	37	.431	4.08	548	0	0	0	98	631	636	320	286	358	513

DIVISION SERIES RECORD

Year League	W	L	Pct.	ERA	G	GS	CG	ShO	Sv.	IP	H	R	ER	BB	SO
1997— Seattle (A.L.)	0	0	...	4.50	2	0	0	0	0	2	3	1	1	1	0

ALL-STAR GAME RECORD

Year League	W	L	Pct.	ERA	GS	CG	ShO	Sv.	IP	H	R	ER	BB	SO
1995— National	1	0	1.000	0.00	0	0	0	0	1	1	0	0	0	2

SLUSARSKI, JOE   P

PERSONAL: Born December 19, 1966, in Indianapolis. ... 6-4/195. ... Throws right, bats right. ... Full name: Joseph Andrew Slusarski.
HIGH SCHOOL: Griffin (Springfield, Ill.).
JUNIOR COLLEGE: Lincoln Land Community College (Ill.).
COLLEGE: New Orleans.
TRANSACTIONS/CAREER NOTES: Selected by Seattle Mariners organization in sixth round of free-agent draft (June 2, 1987); did not sign. ... Selected by Oakland Athletics organization in second round of free-agent draft (June 1, 1988). ... On Huntsville disabled list (May 18-25, 1990). ... On Tacoma disabled list (August 2-11, 1992 and July 22-August 11, 1993). ... Released by A's (May 11, 1994). ... Signed by Philadelphia Phillies organization (June 3, 1994). ... Granted free agency (October 15, 1994). ... Signed by Cleveland Indians organization (January 20, 1995). ... Released by Indians (April 24, 1995). ... Signed by Milwaukee Brewers organization (May 19, 1995). ... Granted free agency (October 16, 1995). ... Signed by California Angels organization (February 26, 1996). ... Released by Angels (April 4, 1996). ... Signed by Brewers organization (May 12, 1996). ... Granted free agency (October 15, 1996). ... Signed by Sinon, Taiwan (1997). ... Signed by Houston Astros organization (May 4, 1998). ... Granted free agency (October 16, 1998). ... Re-signed by Astros organization (December 17, 1998). ... On Houston disabled list (July 9-24, 1999). ... Granted free agency (October 20, 1999). ... Re-signed by Astros organization (January 3, 2000). ... Granted free agency (December 21, 2000).
STATISTICAL NOTES: Led California League with 15 home runs allowed in 1989.
MISCELLANEOUS: Member of 1988 U.S. Olympic baseball team.

Year League	W	L	Pct.	ERA	G	GS	CG	ShO	Sv.	IP	H	R	ER	BB	SO
1989— Modesto (Calif.)	•13	10	.565	3.18	27	27	4	1	0	184	155	78	65	50	160
1990— Huntsville (Sou.)	6	8	.429	4.47	17	17	2	0	0	108 2/3	114	65	54	35	75
— Tacoma (PCL)	4	2	.667	3.40	9	9	0	0	0	55 2/3	54	24	21	22	37

Year League	W	L	Pct.	ERA	G	GS	CG	ShO	Sv.	IP	H	R	ER	BB	SO
1991— Oakland (A.L.)	5	7	.417	5.27	20	19	1	0	0	109 1/3	121	69	64	52	60
— Tacoma (PCL)	4	2	.667	2.72	7	7	0	0	0	46 1/3	42	20	14	10	25
1992— Oakland (A.L.)	5	5	.500	5.45	15	14	0	0	0	76	85	52	46	27	38
— Tacoma (PCL)	2	4	.333	3.77	11	10	0	0	0	57 1/3	67	30	24	18	26
1993— Tacoma (PCL)	7	5	.583	4.76	24	21	1	1	0	113 1/3	133	67	60	40	61
— Oakland (A.L.)	0	0	...	5.19	2	1	0	0	0	8 2/3	9	5	5	11	1
1994— Tacoma (PCL)	2	3	.400	6.03	7	7	0	0	0	37 1/3	45	28	25	11	24
— Reading (East.)■	1	2	.333	4.63	5	4	0	0	0	23 1/3	25	15	12	5	17
— Scranton/W.B. (I.L.)	2	3	.400	7.82	10	4	0	0	0	38	50	36	33	10	29
1995— Buffalo (A.A.)■	1	1	.500	6.32	4	2	0	0	0	15 2/3	18	12	11	4	9
— New Orleans (A.A.)■	1	1	.500	1.12	33	0	0	0	11	48 1/3	37	10	6	11	30
— Milwaukee (A.L.)	1	1	.500	5.40	12	0	0	0	0	15	21	11	9	6	6
1996— New Orleans (A.A.)	2	4	.333	4.95	40	0	0	0	1	60	70	38	33	24	36
1997— Sinon (Taiwan)■	2	4	.333	4.18	25	...	...	...	2	71	76	...	...	24	31
1998— Jackson (Texas)■	2	2	.500	6.33	9	2	0	0	0	21 1/3	22	17	15	2	13
— New Orleans (PCL)	1	4	.200	5.11	31	0	0	0	2	49 1/3	53	31	28	9	32
1999— New Orleans (PCL)	1	4	.200	3.64	40	2	0	0	1	64 1/3	71	31	26	13	40
— Houston (N.L.)	0	0	...	0.00	3	0	0	0	0	3 2/3	1	0	0	3	3
2000— New Orleans (PCL)	2	1	.667	2.25	13	0	0	0	0	20	14	9	5	7	21
— Houston (N.L.)	2	7	.222	4.21	54	0	0	0	3	77	80	36	36	22	54
A.L. totals (4 years)	11	13	.458	5.34	49	34	1	0	0	209	236	137	124	96	105
N.L. totals (2 years)	2	7	.222	4.02	57	0	0	0	3	80 2/3	81	36	36	25	57
Major League totals (6 years)	13	20	.394	4.97	106	34	1	0	3	289 2/3	317	173	160	121	162

S

SMART, J.D.   P   EXPOS

PERSONAL: Born November 12, 1973, in San Saba, Texas. ... 6-2/180. ... Throws right, bats right. ... Full name: Jon David Smart.
HIGH SCHOOL: Westlake (Austin, Texas).
COLLEGE: Texas.
TRANSACTIONS/CAREER NOTES: Selected by Montreal Expos organization in fourth round of free-agent draft (June 1, 1995). ... On Ottawa disabled list (August 16, 1999-remainder of season). ... On Ottawa disabled list (April 23-May 30, 2000). ... On Montreal disabled list (May 31, 2000-remainder of season).

Year League	W	L	Pct.	ERA	G	GS	CG	ShO	Sv.	IP	H	R	ER	BB	SO
1995— Gulf Coast Expos (GCL)	2	0	1.000	1.69	2	2	0	0	0	10 2/3	10	2	2	1	6
— Vermont (NY-Penn)	0	1	.000	2.28	5	5	0	0	0	27 2/3	29	9	7	7	21
1996— Delmarva (S.Atl.)	9	8	.529	3.39	25	25	3	2	0	156 2/3	155	75	59	31	109
1997— West Palm Beach (FSL)	5	4	.556	3.26	17	13	1	0	1	102	105	45	37	21	65
— Harrisburg (East.)	6	3	.667	3.69	12	12	0	0	0	70 2/3	75	34	29	24	43
1998— Cape Fear (S.Atl.)	3	0	1.000	2.45	3	1	0	0	0	11	7	3	3	0	12
— Harrisburg (East.)	3	5	.375	2.45	14	11	2	0	1	77	67	23	21	18	47
— Ottawa (I.L.)	2	3	.400	4.89	6	6	0	0	0	35	34	22	19	11	16
1999— Montreal (N.L.)	0	1	.000	5.02	29	0	0	0	0	52	56	30	29	17	21
— Ottawa (I.L.)	0	1	.000	2.61	6	4	0	0	0	20 2/3	22	7	6	6	9
2000— Ottawa (I.L.)	0	1	.000	10.80	4	0	0	0	1	6 2/3	15	8	8	1	3
Major League totals (1 year)	0	1	.000	5.02	29	0	0	0	0	52	56	30	29	17	21

SMITH, BOBBY   IF   DEVIL RAYS

PERSONAL: Born May 10, 1974, in Oakland. ... 6-3/190. ... Bats right, throws right. ... Full name: Robert Eugene Smith.
HIGH SCHOOL: Fremont (Oakland).
TRANSACTIONS/CAREER NOTES: Selected by Atlanta Braves organization in 11th round of free-agent draft (June 1, 1992). ... Selected by Tampa Bay Devil Rays in first round (12th pick overall) of expansion draft (November 18, 1997). ... On disabled list (May 13-28, 1998). ... On Tampa Bay disabled list (July 6-August 19, 2000); included rehabilitation assignment to Durham (August 14-19). ... On suspended list (September 8-9, 2000).
STATISTICAL NOTES: Tied for Carolina League lead in grounding into double plays with 19 in 1994. ... Led Carolina League third basemen with 388 total chances and 27 double plays in 1994.

Year Team (League)	Pos.	G	AB	R	H	2B	3B	HR	RBI	Avg.	BB	SO	SB	PO	A	E	Avg.
							BATTING								FIELDING		
1992— GC Braves (GCL)	3B	57	217	31	51	9	1	3	28	.235	17	55	5	37	115	15	.910
1993— Macon (S.Atl.)	3B	108	384	53	94	16	7	4	38	.245	23	81	12	65	167	30	.885
1994— Durham (Caro.)	3B	127	478	49	127	27	2	12	71	.266	41	112	18	104	253	31	*.920
1995— Greenville (Sou.)	3B	127	444	75	116	27	3	14	58	.261	40	109	12	*120	265	26	.937
1996— Richmond (I.L.)	3B-SS-DH	124	445	49	114	27	0	8	58	.256	32	114	15	116	228	24	.935
1997— Richmond (I.L.)	SS-DH	100	357	47	88	10	2	12	47	.246	44	109	6	161	297	*23	.952
1998— Tampa Bay (A.L.)■	3-DH-S-2	117	370	44	102	15	3	11	55	.276	34	110	5	89	203	13	.957
1999— Tampa Bay (A.L.)	3B-2B	68	199	18	36	4	1	3	19	.181	16	64	4	48	132	11	.942
— Durham (I.L.)	3B-SS	57	225	52	75	15	3	14	47	.333	27	61	13	46	126	10	.945
2000— Durham (I.L.)	2B-SS-3B	66	261	48	76	20	2	17	58	.291	23	61	15	120	184	9	.971
— Tampa Bay (A.L.)	2B-3B	49	175	21	41	8	0	6	26	.234	14	59	2	84	151	8	.967
Major League totals (3 years)		234	744	83	179	27	4	20	100	.241	64	233	11	221	486	32	.957

SMITH, BRIAN   P

PERSONAL: Born July 19, 1972, in Salisbury, N.C. ... 5-11/185. ... Throws right, bats right. ... Full name: Randall Brian Smith.
HIGH SCHOOL: South Rowan (China Grove, N.C.).
COLLEGE: North Carolina-Wilmington.

TRANSACTIONS/CAREER NOTES: Selected by Toronto Blue Jays organization in 27th round of free-agent draft (June 2, 1994). ... Selected by Pittsburgh Pirates from Blue Jays organization in Rule 5 major league draft (December 13, 1999). ... Granted free agency (December 21, 1999). ... Re-signed by Pirates organization (December 21, 1999). ... On Nashville disabled list (April 6-July 13, 2000). ... Granted free agency (October 18, 2000).

Year League	W	L	Pct.	ERA	G	GS	CG	ShO	Sv.	IP	H	R	ER	BB	SO
1994— Medicine Hat (Pio.)	5	4	.556	3.38	20	5	0	0	4	64	58	36	24	20	53
1995— Hagerstown (East.).............	9	1	*.900	0.87	47	0	0	0	21	104	77	18	10	16	101
1996— Knoxville (Sou.)..................	3	5	.375	3.81	54	0	0	0	16	75 2/3	76	42	32	31	58
1997— Syracuse (I.L.)..................	7	11	.389	5.37	31	21	0	0	0	137 1/3	169	89	82	51	73
— Knoxville (Sou.)................	0	0	...	0.00	1	0	0	0	0	1	0	0	0	1	1
1998— Dunedin (FSL)..................	1	0	1.000	3.38	4	0	0	0	2	10 2/3	8	4	4	3	9
— Knoxville (Sou.)................	4	2	.667	4.06	42	0	0	0	7	71	72	39	32	25	50
1999— Knoxville (Sou.)..................	1	2	.333	5.14	29	0	0	0	13	35	42	25	20	6	27
— Syracuse (I.L.)................	7	4	.636	3.50	29	0	0	0	7	46 1/3	45	22	18	24	46
2000— Gulf Coast Pirates (GCL)■ .	0	0	...	0.00	5	2	0	0	0	6	0	0	0	1	5
— Altoona (East.)	3	4	.429	0.99	22	0	0	0	12	27 1/3	14	6	3	8	23
— Pittsburgh (N.L.)	0	0	...	10.38	3	0	0	0	0	4 1/3	6	5	5	2	3
Major League totals (1 year)........	**0**	**0**	...	**10.38**	**3**	**0**	**0**	**0**	**0**	**4 1/3**	**6**	**5**	**5**	**2**	**3**

SMITH, CHUCK   P   MARLINS

PERSONAL: Born October 21, 1969, in Memphis, Tenn. ... 6-1/185. ... Throws right, bats right. ... Full name: Charles Edward Smith.
HIGH SCHOOL: John Adams (Cleveland).
JUNIOR COLLEGE: Central Arizona College.
COLLEGE: Indiana State.
TRANSACTIONS/CAREER NOTES: Signed as non-drafted free agent by Houston Astros organization (June 17, 1991). ... Selected by Chicago White Sox organization from Astros organization in Rule 5 minor league draft (December 6, 1994). ... Granted free agency (October 17, 1997). ... Signed by Sioux Falls, Northern League (May 1998). ... Contract purchased by Colorado Rockies organization from Sioux Falls (December 15, 1998). ... Released by Rockies (April 2, 1999). ... Signed by Texas Rangers organization (April 9, 1999). ... On Oklahoma disabled list (July 22-August 5, 1999). ... Traded by Rangers to Florida Marlins for IF/OF Brant Brown (June 9, 2000).
MISCELLANEOUS: Appeared in two games as pinch runner (2000).

Year League	W	L	Pct.	ERA	G	GS	CG	ShO	Sv.	IP	H	R	ER	BB	SO
1991— Gulf Coast Astros (GCL)	4	3	.571	3.49	15	7	2	0	0	59 1/3	56	36	23	37	64
1992— Asheville (S.Atl.).................	9	9	.500	5.18	28	20	1	0	1	132	120	93	76	78	117
1993— Quad City (Midw.)	7	5	.583	4.64	22	17	2	0	0	110 2/3	109	73	57	52	103
1994— Jackson (Texas)	0	0	...	4.50	2	0	0	0	0	6	6	6	3	5	7
— Osceola (FSL)..................	4	4	.500	3.72	35	2	0	0	0	84 2/3	73	41	35	49	60
1995— South Bend (Midw.)■	10	10	.500	2.69	26	25	4	•2	0	167	128	70	50	61	*145
1996— Prince William (Caro.)	6	6	.500	4.01	20	20	2	1	0	123 1/3	125	65	55	49	99
— Birmingham (Sou.).............	2	1	.667	2.64	7	3	0	0	1	30 2/3	25	11	9	15	30
— Nashville (A.A.)	0	0	...	27.00	1	0	0	0	0	2/3	2	2	2	1	1
1997— Birmingham (Sou.)......	2	2	.500	3.16	25	0	0	0	0	62 2/3	63	35	22	27	57
— Nashville (A.A.)	0	3	.000	8.81	20	1	0	0	0	31 2/3	39	33	31	23	29
1998— Sioux Falls (Nor.)■..........	5	3	.625	2.62	8	8	2	•1	0	55	44	18	16	21	70
1999— Oklahoma (PCL)■..............	5	4	.556	2.96	32	4	2	0	4	85	73	31	28	28	76
2000— Oklahoma (PCL)................	5	3	.625	3.78	11	11	1	0	0	66 2/3	73	31	28	38	73
— Florida (N.L.)■	6	6	.500	3.23	19	19	1	0	0	122 2/3	111	53	44	54	118
Major League totals (1 year)........	**6**	**6**	**.500**	**3.23**	**19**	**19**	**1**	**0**	**0**	**122 2/3**	**111**	**53**	**44**	**54**	**118**

SMITH, DAN   P   INDIANS

PERSONAL: Born September 15, 1975, in Flemington, N.J. ... 6-3/210. ... Throws right, bats right. ... Full name: Daniel Charles Smith Jr.
HIGH SCHOOL: Girard (Kan.).
TRANSACTIONS/CAREER NOTES: Selected by Texas Rangers organization in seventh round of free-agent draft (June 3, 1993). ... On Charlotte disabled list (June 12-July 7, 1995). ... Claimed on waivers by Montreal Expos (December 14, 1998). ... Granted free agency (December 21, 1999). ... Signed by Boston Red Sox organization (June 2, 2000). ... Granted free agency (October 18, 2000). ... Signed by Cleveland Indians organization (November 15, 2000).

Year League	W	L	Pct.	ERA	G	GS	CG	ShO	Sv.	IP	H	R	ER	BB	SO
1993— Gulf Coast Rangers (GCL)..	3	2	.600	2.87	12	10	1	0	0	53 1/3	50	19	17	8	27
1994— Charlotte (FSL).................	0	0	...	0.00	2	0	0	0	0	3 2/3	2	0	0	2	3
— Char., S.C. (SAL).............	7	10	.412	4.92	27	27	4	0	0	157 1/3	171	*111	86	55	86
1995— Gulf Coast Rangers (GCL)..	0	3	.000	4.26	4	3	0	0	0	19	19	9	9	5	12
— Charlotte (FSL).................	5	1	.833	2.95	9	9	1	1	0	58	53	23	19	16	34
1996— Charlotte (FSL).................	3	7	.300	5.07	18	18	1	0	0	87	100	61	49	38	55
1997— Charlotte (FSL).................	8	10	.444	4.43	26	25	2	0	0	160 2/3	169	93	79	66	113
1998— Tulsa (Texas)	13	9	.591	5.81	26	25	1	0	0	153 1/3	162	101	99	58	105
— Oklahoma (PCL)................	0	0	...	6.00	1	1	0	0	0	6	6	4	4	1	3
1999— Ottawa (I.L.)■..................	5	4	.556	3.68	11	11	0	0	0	71	61	31	29	27	59
— Montreal (N.L.).................	4	9	.308	6.02	20	17	0	0	0	89 2/3	104	64	60	39	72
2000— Pawtucket (I.L.)■.............	7	10	.412	4.84	24	21	2	1	0	124 2/3	134	72	67	41	70
— Boston (A.L.).................	0	0	...	8.10	2	0	0	0	0	3 1/3	2	3	3	3	1
A.L. totals (1 year)	**0**	**0**	...	**8.10**	**2**	**0**	**0**	**0**	**0**	**3 1/3**	**2**	**3**	**3**	**3**	**1**
N.L. totals (1 year)	**4**	**9**	**.308**	**6.02**	**20**	**17**	**0**	**0**	**0**	**89 2/3**	**104**	**64**	**60**	**39**	**72**
Major League totals (2 years)	**4**	**9**	**.308**	**6.10**	**22**	**17**	**0**	**0**	**0**	**93**	**106**	**67**	**63**	**42**	**73**

PERSONAL: Born May 7, 1970, in Pasadena, Calif. ... 6-3/225. ... Bats right, throws right. ... Full name: Mark Edward Smith.
HIGH SCHOOL: Arcadia (Calif.).
COLLEGE: Southern California.
TRANSACTIONS/CAREER NOTES: Selected by Baltimore Orioles organization in first round (ninth pick overall) of free-agent draft (June 3, 1991). ... On Baltimore disabled list (July 23, 1996-remainder of season); included rehabilitation assignments to Frederick (August 12-13), Bowie (August 21-23) and Rochester (September 3-13). ... Traded by Orioles to San Diego Padres for C Leroy McKinnis (January 9, 1997). ... Traded by Padres with P Hal Garrett to Pittsburgh Pirates for OF Trey Beamon and OF Angelo Encarnacion (March 29, 1997). ... On Pittsburgh disabled list (May 23-June 14, 1997); included rehabilitation assignment to Carolina (June 12-14). ... On Pittsburgh disabled list (May 4-19, 1998); included rehabilitation assignment to Nashville (May 9-19). ... Granted free agency (September 29, 1998). ... Signed by Florida Marlins organization (December 22, 1999). ... On disabled list (May 11-June 5, 2000). ... Granted free agency (October 5, 2000). ... Signed by Montreal Expos organization (November 17, 2000).

Year	Team (League)	Pos.	G	AB	R	H	2B	3B	HR	RBI	Avg.	BB	SO	SB	PO	A	E	Avg.
											BATTING						FIELDING	
1991—	Frederick (Caro.)	OF	38	148	20	37	5	1	4	29	.250	9	24	1	49	1	1	.980
1992—	Hagerstown (East.)	OF	128	472	51	136	*32	6	4	62	.288	45	55	15	226	9	4	.983
1993—	Rochester (I.L.)	OF-DH	129	485	69	136	27	1	12	68	.280	37	90	4	261	9	7	.975
1994—	Rochester (I.L.)	OF-DH	114	437	69	108	27	1	19	66	.247	35	88	4	207	9	5	.977
—	Baltimore (A.L.)	OF	3	7	0	1	0	0	0	2	.143	0	2	0	8	0	0	1.000
1995—	Rochester (I.L.)	OF-DH	96	364	55	101	25	3	12	66	.277	24	69	7	167	4	7	.961
—	Baltimore (A.L.)	OF	37	104	11	24	5	0	3	15	.231	12	22	3	60	2	0	1.000
1996—	Rochester (I.L.)	OF-DH	39	132	24	46	14	1	8	32	.348	14	22	10	55	1	2	.966
—	Baltimore (A.L.)	OF-DH	27	78	9	19	2	0	4	10	.244	3	20	0	50	0	1	.980
—	Frederick (Caro.)	DH	1	1	0	0	0	0	0	0	.000	0	0	0	0	0	0	...
—	Bowie (East.)	DH	6	22	1	2	0	0	1	2	.091	1	6	0	0	0	0	...
1997—	Calgary (PCL)■	OF-DH	39	137	37	51	14	1	14	42	.372	21	15	2	55	1	1	.982
—	Pittsburgh (N.L.)	OF-1B-DH	71	193	29	55	13	1	9	35	.285	28	36	3	111	9	0	1.000
—	Carolina (Sou.)	OF	3	12	5	5	1	0	3	4	.417	0	1	0	4	0	1	.800
1998—	Pittsburgh (N.L.)	OF-1B-DH	59	128	18	25	6	0	2	13	.195	10	26	7	72	4	1	.987
—	Nashville (PCL)	OF-1B-3B-DH	24	93	18	33	10	1	8	30	.355	11	20	3	83	17	2	.980
2000—	Florida (N.L.)■	OF-DH	104	192	22	47	8	1	5	27	.245	17	54	2	65	4	0	1.000
American League totals (3 years)			67	189	20	44	7	0	7	27	.233	15	44	3	118	2	1	.992
National League totals (3 years)			234	513	69	127	27	2	16	75	.248	55	116	12	248	17	1	.996
Major League totals (6 years)			301	702	89	171	34	2	23	102	.244	70	160	15	366	19	2	.995

PERSONAL: Born May 15, 1967, in Warren, Mich. ... 6-3/220. ... Throws right, bats right. ... Full name: John Andrew Smoltz.
HIGH SCHOOL: Waverly (Lansing, Mich.).
TRANSACTIONS/CAREER NOTES: Selected by Detroit Tigers organization in 22nd round of free-agent draft (June 3, 1985). ... Traded by Tigers to Atlanta Braves for P Doyle Alexander (August 12, 1987). ... On suspended list (June 20-29, 1994). ... Granted free agency (October 31, 1996). ... Re-signed by Braves (November 20, 1996). ... On Atlanta disabled list (March 29-April 15, and May 24-June 20, 1998); included rehabilitation assignments to Greenville (April 2-10 and June 10-14) and Macon (April 10-14 and June 14-16). ... On Atlanta disabled list (May 17-June 1 and July 5-24, 1999); included rehabilitation assignment to Greenville (July 15-18). ... On disabled list (April 2, 2000-entire season).
RECORDS: Shares major league record for most home runs allowed in one inning—4 (June 19, 1994, first inning).
HONORS: Named N.L. Pitcher of the Year by THE SPORTING NEWS (1996). ... Named righthanded pitcher on THE SPORTING NEWS N.L. All-Star team (1996). ... Named N.L. Cy Young Award winner by Baseball Writers' Association of America (1996). ... Named pitcher on THE SPORTING NEWS N.L. Silver Slugger team (1997).
STATISTICAL NOTES: Tied for Florida State League lead with six balks in 1986. ... Led N.L. with 14 wild pitches in 1990, 20 in 1991 and 17 in 1992. ... Struck out 15 batters in one game (May 24, 1992). ... Pitched 3-0 one-hit, complete-game victory against Cincinnati (May 28, 1995).
MISCELLANEOUS: Appeared in three games as pinch runner and struck out in only appearance in pinch hitter (1989). ... Appeared in four games as pinch runner (1990). ... Appeared in two games as pinch runner (1991). ... Struck out in only appearance as pinch hitter (1992). ... Appeared in one game as pinch runner (1997).

Year	League	W	L	Pct.	ERA	G	GS	CG	ShO	Sv.	IP	H	R	ER	BB	SO
1986—	Lakeland (FSL)	7	8	.467	3.56	17	14	2	1	0	96	86	44	38	31	47
1987—	Glens Falls (East.)	4	10	.286	5.68	21	21	0	0	0	130	131	89	82	81	86
—	Richmond (I.L.)■	0	1	.000	6.19	3	3	0	0	0	16	17	11	11	11	5
1988—	Richmond (I.L.)	10	5	.667	2.79	20	20	3	0	0	135 1/3	118	49	42	37	115
—	Atlanta (N.L.)	2	7	.222	5.48	12	12	0	0	0	64	74	40	39	33	37
1989—	Atlanta (N.L.)	12	11	.522	2.94	29	29	5	0	0	208	160	79	68	72	168
1990—	Atlanta (N.L.)	14	11	.560	3.85	34	34	6	2	0	231 1/3	206	109	99	*90	170
1991—	Atlanta (N.L.)	14	13	.519	3.80	36	36	5	0	0	229 2/3	206	101	97	77	148
1992—	Atlanta (N.L.)	15	12	.556	2.85	35	•35	3	3	0	246 2/3	206	90	78	80	*215
1993—	Atlanta (N.L.)	15	11	.577	3.62	35	35	3	1	0	243 2/3	208	104	98	100	208
1994—	Atlanta (N.L.)	6	10	.375	4.14	21	21	1	0	0	134 2/3	120	69	62	48	113
1995—	Atlanta (N.L.)	12	7	.632	3.18	29	29	2	1	0	192 2/3	166	76	68	72	193
1996—	Atlanta (N.L.)	*24	8	*.750	2.94	35	35	6	2	0	*253 2/3	199	93	83	55	*276
1997—	Atlanta (N.L.)	15	12	.556	3.02	35	•35	7	2	0	*256	*234	97	86	63	241
1998—	Greenville (Sou.)	0	1	.000	2.57	3	3	0	0	0	14	11	4	4	3	16
—	Macon (S.Atl.)	0	0	...	3.60	2	2	0	0	0	10	7	4	4	1	4
—	Atlanta (N.L.)	17	3	*.850	2.90	26	26	2	2	0	167 2/3	145	58	54	44	173
1999—	Atlanta (N.L.)	11	8	.579	3.19	29	29	1	1	0	186 1/3	168	70	66	40	156
—	Greenville (Sou.)	0	0	...	4.50	2	1	0	0	0	4	5	2	2	1	7
2000—	Atlanta (N.L.)							Did not play.								
Major League totals (12 years)		157	113	.581	3.35	356	356	47	14	0	2414 1/3	2092	986	898	774	2098

DIVISION SERIES RECORD

RECORDS: Holds N.L. single-game record for most strikeouts—11 (October 3, 1997). ... Holds N.L. career record for most strikeouts—33. ... Shares career record for most wins—4. ... Shares N.L. career record for most earned runs allowed—12.

Year League	W	L	Pct.	ERA	G	GS	CG	ShO	Sv.	IP	H	R	ER	BB	SO
1995— Atlanta (N.L.).....................	0	0	...	7.94	1	1	0	0	0	5 2/3	5	5	5	1	6
1996— Atlanta (N.L.).....................	1	0	1.000	1.00	1	1	0	0	0	9	4	1	1	2	7
1997— Atlanta (N.L.).....................	1	0	1.000	1.00	1	1	1	0	0	9	3	1	1	1	11
1998— Atlanta (N.L.).....................	1	0	1.000	1.17	1	1	0	0	0	7 2/3	5	1	1	0	6
1999— Atlanta (N.L.).....................	1	0	1.000	5.14	1	1	0	0	0	7	6	4	4	3	3
Division series totals (5 years)	4	0	1.000	2.82	5	5	1	0	0	38 1/3	23	12	12	7	33

CHAMPIONSHIP SERIES RECORD

RECORDS: Holds career records for most innings pitched—92 1/3; most strikeouts—88; and most bases on balls allowed—34. ... Shares career records for most games started—13; and hits allowed—81. ... Holds N.L. career records for most wins—6; and home runs allowed—8.

NOTES: Named Most Valuable Player (1992).

Year League	W	L	Pct.	ERA	G	GS	CG	ShO	Sv.	IP	H	R	ER	BB	SO
1991— Atlanta (N.L.).....................	2	0	1.000	1.76	2	2	1	1	0	15 1/3	14	3	3	3	15
1992— Atlanta (N.L.).....................	2	0	1.000	2.66	3	3	0	0	0	20 1/3	14	7	6	10	19
1993— Atlanta (N.L.).....................	0	1	.000	0.00	1	1	0	0	0	6 1/3	8	2	0	5	10
1995— Atlanta (N.L.).....................	0	0	...	2.57	1	1	0	0	0	7	7	2	2	2	2
1996— Atlanta (N.L.).....................	2	0	1.000	1.20	2	2	0	0	0	15	12	2	2	3	12
1997— Atlanta (N.L.).....................	0	1	.000	7.50	1	1	0	0	0	6	5	5	5	5	9
1998— Atlanta (N.L.).....................	0	0	...	3.95	2	2	0	0	0	13 2/3	13	6	6	6	13
1999— Atlanta (N.L.).....................	0	0	...	6.23	3	1	0	0	1	8 2/3	8	6	6	0	8
Champ. series totals (8 years)	6	2	.750	2.92	15	13	1	1	1	92 1/3	81	33	30	34	88

WORLD SERIES RECORD

NOTES: Appeared in one game as pinch runner (1992). ... Member of World Series championship team (1995).

Year League	W	L	Pct.	ERA	G	GS	CG	ShO	Sv.	IP	H	R	ER	BB	SO
1991— Atlanta (N.L.).....................	0	0	...	1.26	2	2	0	0	0	14 1/3	13	2	2	1	11
1992— Atlanta (N.L.).....................	1	0	1.000	2.70	2	2	0	0	0	13 1/3	13	5	4	7	12
1995— Atlanta (N.L.).....................	0	0	...	15.43	1	1	0	0	0	2 1/3	6	4	4	2	4
1996— Atlanta (N.L.).....................	1	1	.500	0.64	2	2	0	0	0	14	6	2	1	8	14
1999— Atlanta (N.L.).....................	0	1	.000	3.86	1	1	0	0	0	7	6	3	3	3	11
World Series totals (5 years)	2	2	.500	2.47	8	8	0	0	0	51	44	16	14	21	52

ALL-STAR GAME RECORD

RECORDS: Shares single-game record for most wild pitches—2 (July 13, 1993). ... Shares single-inning record for most wild pitches—2 (July 13, 1993, sixth inning).

Year League	W	L	Pct.	ERA	GS	CG	ShO	Sv.	IP	H	R	ER	BB	SO
1989— National.............................	0	1	.000	9.00	0	0	0	0	1	2	1	1	0	0
1992— National.............................	0	0	...	0.00	0	0	0	0	1/3	1	0	0	0	0
1993— National.............................	0	0	...	0.00	0	0	0	0	1/3	0	0	0	1	0
1996— National.............................	1	0	1.000	0.00	1	0	0	0	2	2	0	0	1	1
All-Star Game totals (4 years)	1	1	.500	2.45	1	0	0	0	3 2/3	5	1	1	1	1

SNEAD, ESIX   OF   CARDINALS

PERSONAL: Born June 7, 1976, in Fort Myers, Fla. ... 5-10/175. ... Bats both, throws right.
HIGH SCHOOL: Williston (Fla.).
COLLEGE: Central Florida.
TRANSACTIONS/CAREER NOTES: Selected by St. Louis Cardinals organization in 18th round of free-agent draft (June 2, 1998).

									BATTING					FIELDING		
Year Team (League)	Pos.	G	AB	R	H	2B	3B	HR	RBI	Avg.	BB	SO	SB	PO	A	E	Avg.
1998— New Jersey (NY-P)	OF	58	193	38	45	4	4	1	16	.233	33	54	*42	123	1	3	.976
1999— Potomac (Caro.).........	OF	67	249	37	45	8	5	0	14	.181	32	57	45	179	4	2	.989
— Peoria (Midw.)...........	OF	59	181	35	35	7	1	2	18	.193	35	42	29	153	4	4	.975
2000— Potomac (Caro.).........	OF	132	493	82	116	14	3	1	34	.235	72	98	*109	313	10	7	.979

SNEED, JOHN   P   TWINS

PERSONAL: Born June 30, 1976, in Houston. ... 6-6/250. ... Throws right, bats left. ... Full name: John Andrew Sneed.
HIGH SCHOOL: Westfield (Houston).
COLLEGE: Texas A&M.
TRANSACTIONS/CAREER NOTES: Selected by Toronto Blue Jays organization in 22nd round of free-agent draft (June 3, 1997). ... Traded by Blue Jays to Philadelphia Phillies (July 31, 2000), completing deal in which Phillies traded OF Rob Ducey to Blue Jays for a player to be named later (July 26, 2000). ... Claimed on waivers by Blue Jays (October 2, 2000). ... Claimed on waivers by Twins (October 6, 2000).

Year League	W	L	Pct.	ERA	G	GS	CG	ShO	Sv.	IP	H	R	ER	BB	SO
1997— Medicine Hat (Pio.)	6	1	*.857	*1.29	15	10	2	0	0	69 2/3	42	19	10	20	79
1998— Hagerstown (S.Atl.)...........	*16	2	*.889	2.56	27	27	2	1	0	161 2/3	123	59	46	58	210
1999— Dunedin (FSL)...................	11	2	*.846	3.45	21	20	0	0	0	125 1/3	107	53	48	36	143
— Knoxville (Sou.)................	3	1	.750	5.08	6	6	0	0	0	28 1/3	33	17	16	21	28
2000— Tennessee (Sou.)	5	9	.357	4.54	21	21	0	0	0	121	124	81	61	56	100
— Reading (East.)■	1	3	.250	8.77	6	6	0	0	0	25 2/3	31	28	25	19	24

SNOW, J.T. — 1B — GIANTS

PERSONAL: Born February 26, 1968, in Long Beach, Calif. ... 6-2/205. ... Bats left, throws left. ... Full name: Jack Thomas Snow Jr. ... Son of Jack Snow, wide receiver with Los Angeles Rams (1965-75).

HIGH SCHOOL: Los Alamitos (Calif.).

COLLEGE: Arizona.

TRANSACTIONS/CAREER NOTES: Selected by New York Yankees organization in fifth round of free-agent draft (June 5, 1989). ... Traded by Yankees with P Jerry Nielsen and P Russ Springer to California Angels for P Jim Abbott (December 6, 1992). ... Traded by Angels to San Francisco Giants for P Allen Watson and P Fausto Macey (November 27, 1996).

RECORDS: Shares major league career record for highest fielding percentage for first baseman—.996.

HONORS: Named International League Most Valuable Player (1992). ... Won A.L. Gold Glove at first base (1995-96). ... Won N.L. Gold Glove at first base (1997-2000).

STATISTICAL NOTES: Led New York-Pennsylvania League first basemen with 649 total chances in 1989. ... Led Carolina League in grounding into double plays with 20 in 1990. ... Led Carolina League first basemen with 1,298 total chances and 120 double plays in 1990. ... Tied for Eastern League lead with 10 sacrifice flies in 1991. ... Led Eastern League first basemen with 1,200 total chances in 1991. ... Led International League with 11 intentional bases on balls received in 1992. ... Led International League first basemen with .995 fielding percentage, 1,097 putouts, 93 assists, 1,196 total chances and 107 double plays in 1992. ... Switch-hit home runs in one game (June 9, 1996). ... Led N.L. in sacrifice flies with 14 in 2000. ... Career major league grand slams: 7.

MISCELLANEOUS: Batted as switch-hitter (1989-98).

Year Team (League)	Pos.	G	AB	R	H	2B	3B	HR	RBI	Avg.	BB	SO	SB	PO	A	E	Avg.
1989— Oneonta (NY-Penn)	1B	73	274	41	80	18	2	8	51	.292	29	35	4	*590	53	6	*.991
1990— Prince William (Caro.)	1B	*138	520	57	133	25	1	8	72	.256	46	65	2	*1208	*78	12	.991
1991— Alb./Colonie (East.)	1B	132	477	78	133	33	3	13	76	.279	67	78	5	*1102	90	8	*.993
1992— Columbus (I.L.)	1B-OF	135	492	81	154	26	4	15	78	•.313	70	65	3	†1103	†93	8	†.993
— New York (A.L.)..........	1B-DH	7	14	1	2	1	0	0	2	.143	5	5	0	43	2	0	1.000
1993— California (A.L.)■.......	1B	129	419	60	101	18	2	16	57	.241	55	88	3	1010	81	6	.995
— Vancouver (PCL)........	1B	23	94	19	32	9	1	5	24	.340	10	13	0	200	13	2	.991
1994— Vancouver (PCL)	1B-DH	53	189	35	56	13	2	8	43	.296	22	32	1	413	42	1	.998
— California (A.L.).........	1B	61	223	22	49	4	0	8	30	.220	19	48	0	489	37	2	.996
1995— California (A.L.).........	1B	143	544	80	157	22	1	24	102	.289	52	91	2	1161	57	4	.997
1996— California (A.L.).........	1B	155	575	69	148	20	1	17	67	.257	56	96	1	1274	103	10	.993
1997— San Fran. (N.L.)■......	1B	157	531	81	149	36	1	28	104	.281	96	124	6	1308	108	7	.995
1998— San Francisco (N.L.) ..	1B	138	435	65	108	29	1	15	79	.248	58	84	1	1040	94	1	*.999
1999— San Francisco (N.L.) ..	1B	161	570	93	156	25	2	24	98	.274	86	121	0	1221	122	6	.996
2000— San Francisco (N.L.) ..	1B	155	536	82	152	33	2	19	96	.284	66	129	1	1197	91	6	.995
American League totals (5 years)		495	1775	232	457	65	4	65	258	.257	187	328	6	3977	280	22	.995
National League totals (4 years)		611	2072	321	565	123	6	86	377	.273	306	458	8	4766	415	20	.996
Major League totals (9 years)		1106	3847	553	1022	188	10	151	635	.266	493	786	14	8743	695	42	.996

DIVISION SERIES RECORD

Year Team (League)	Pos.	G	AB	R	H	2B	3B	HR	RBI	Avg.	BB	SO	SB	PO	A	E	Avg.
1997— San Francisco (N.L.) ..	1B	3	6	0	1	0	0	0	0	.167	1	1	0	12	0	0	1.000
2000— San Francisco (N.L.) ..	1B-PH	4	10	1	4	0	0	1	3	.400	4	1	0	23	0	0	1.000
Division series totals (2 years)		7	16	1	5	0	0	1	3	.313	5	2	0	35	0	0	1.000

SNYDER, JOHN — P — BREWERS

PERSONAL: Born August 16, 1974, in Southfield, Mich. ... 6-3/200. ... Throws right, bats right. ... Full name: John Michael Snyder.

HIGH SCHOOL: Westlake (Westlake Village, Calif.).

TRANSACTIONS/CAREER NOTES: Selected by California Angels organization in 13th round of free-agent draft (June 1, 1992). ... Traded by Angels with P Andrew Lorraine, P Bill Simas and OF McKay Christensen to Chicago White Sox for P Jim Abbott and P Tim Fortugno (July 27, 1995). ... On Gulf Coast disabled list (July 21, 1996-remainder of season). ... On disabled list (April 3-May 4, 1997). ... Traded by White Sox with P Jaime Navarro to Milwaukee Brewers for P Cal Eldred and SS Jose Valentin (January 12, 2000). ... On Milwaukee disabled list (March 25-May 19, 2000); included rehabilitation assignments to Huntsville (May 5-13) and Indianapolis (May 14-16).

MISCELLANEOUS: Appeared in one game as pinch runner (2000).

Year League	W	L	Pct.	ERA	G	GS	CG	ShO	Sv.	IP	H	R	ER	BB	SO
1992— Arizona Angels (Ariz.)........	2	4	.333	3.27	15	0	0	0	3	44	40	27	16	16	38
1993— Cedar Rapids (Midw.)	5	6	.455	5.91	21	16	1	1	0	99	125	88	65	39	79
1994— Lake Elsinore (Calif.)	10	11	.476	4.47	26	26	2	0	0	159	181	101	79	56	108
1995— Midland (Texas).................	8	9	.471	5.74	21	21	0	0	0	133 1/3	158	93	85	48	81
— Birmingham (Sou.)■	1	0	1.000	6.64	5	4	0	0	0	20 1/3	24	16	15	6	13
1996— Birmingham (Sou.)	3	5	.375	4.83	9	9	0	0	0	54	59	35	29	16	58
— GC White Sox (GCL)	1	0	1.000	1.65	4	4	0	0	0	16 1/3	5	3	3	4	23
1997— Birmingham (Sou.)............	7	8	.467	4.64	20	20	2	1	0	114 1/3	130	76	59	43	90
1998— Calgary (PCL)...................	7	3	.700	4.36	15	15	1	0	0	97	112	49	47	34	63
— Chicago (A.L.)	7	2	.778	4.80	15	14	1	0	0	86 1/3	96	49	46	23	52
1999— Chicago (A.L.)	9	12	.429	6.68	25	25	1	0	0	129 1/3	167	103	96	49	67
— Charlotte (I.L.)	3	0	1.000	4.24	3	3	0	0	0	17	17	9	8	5	9
2000— Huntsville (Sou.)■	1	1	.500	2.19	2	2	0	0	0	12 1/3	6	3	3	5	6
— Indianapolis (I.L.)............	0	1	.000	2.57	1	1	0	0	0	7	6	2	2	0	5
— Milwaukee (N.L.)	3	10	.231	6.17	23	23	0	0	0	127	147	95	87	77	69
A.L. totals (2 years)	16	14	.533	5.93	40	39	2	0	0	215 2/3	263	152	142	72	119
N.L. totals (1 year)	3	10	.231	6.17	23	23	0	0	0	127	147	95	87	77	69
Major League totals (3 years)	19	24	.442	6.01	63	62	2	0	0	342 2/3	410	247	229	149	188

PERSONAL: Born January 3, 1966, in Barquisimeto, Venezuela. ... 5-11/185. ... Bats right, throws right. ... Name pronounced SO-ho.

TRANSACTIONS/CAREER NOTES: Signed as non-drafted free agent by Toronto Blue Jays organization (January 3, 1986). ... Traded by Blue Jays with OF Junior Felix and a player to be named later to California Angels for OF Devon White, P Willie Fraser and a player to be named later (December 2, 1990); Blue Jays acquired P Marcus Moore and Angels acquired C Ken Rivers to complete deal (December 4, 1990). ... Traded by Angels to Blue Jays for 3B Kelly Gruber and cash (December 8, 1992). ... On Toronto disabled list (May 10-30, 1993). ... Granted free agency (October 15, 1993). ... Signed by Seattle Mariners organization (January 10, 1994). ... On Seattle disabled list (June 7-23, 1995); included rehabilitation assignment to Tacoma (June 19-23). ... Claimed on waivers by New York Yankees (August 22, 1996). ... Granted free agency (December 20, 1996). ... Re-signed by Yankees (January 9, 1997). ... On disabled list (August 15, 1997-remainder of season). ... Granted free agency (October 31, 1997). ... Re-signed by Yankees (November 12, 1997). ... On New York disabled list (March 22-April 27, 1998); included rehabilitation assignments to Tampa (April 17-20) and Columbus (April 20-27). ... Granted free agency (November 10, 1999). ... Signed by Pittsburgh Pirates organization (January 19, 2000). ... On Pittsburgh disabled list (July 6-24, 2000). ... Traded by Pirates to Yankees for P Chris Spurling (August 7, 2000). ... Granted free agency (November 7, 2000). ... Re-signed by Yankees (December 7, 2000).

STATISTICAL NOTES: Led International League shortstops with .957 fielding percentage in 1989. ... Led International League with nine sacrifice flies in 1990. ... Led A.L. with 19 sacrifice hits in 1991. ... Career major league grand slams: 1.

Year	Team (League)	Pos.	G	AB	R	H	2B	3B	HR	RBI	Avg.	BB	SO	SB	PO	A	E	Avg.
1986—	....						Dominican Summer League statistics unavailable.											
1987—	Myrtle Beach (S.Atl.)	SS-2B-3B-OF	72	223	23	47	5	4	2	15	.211	17	18	5	104	123	14	.942
1988—	Myrtle Beach (S.Atl.)	SS	135	*536	83	*155	22	5	5	56	.289	35	35	14	191	407	28	.955
1989—	Syracuse (I.L.)	SS-2B	121	482	54	133	20	5	3	54	.276	21	42	9	170	348	23	†.957
1990—	Syracuse (I.L.)	2B-SS	75	297	39	88	12	3	6	25	.296	14	23	10	138	212	10	.972
—	Toronto (A.L.)	2-S-O-3-DH	33	80	14	18	3	0	1	9	.225	5	5	1	34	31	5	.929
1991—	California (A.L.)■	2-S-3-O-DH	113	364	38	94	14	1	3	20	.258	14	26	4	233	335	11	.981
1992—	Edmonton (PCL)	3B-2B-SS	37	145	22	43	9	1	1	24	.297	9	17	4	32	106	4	.972
—	California (A.L.)	2B-3B-SS	106	368	37	100	12	3	7	43	.272	14	24	7	196	293	9	.982
1993—	Toronto (A.L.)■	SS-2B-3B	19	47	5	8	2	0	0	6	.170	4	2	0	24	35	2	.967
—	Syracuse (I.L.)	2-O-DH-3-S-1	43	142	17	31	7	2	1	12	.218	8	12	2	46	60	4	.964
1994—	Calgary (PCL)■	SS-2B-DH	24	102	19	33	9	3	1	18	.324	10	7	5	36	81	2	.983
—	Seattle (A.L.)	2B-SS-DH-3B	63	213	32	59	9	2	6	22	.277	8	25	2	97	186	7	.976
1995—	Seattle (A.L.)	SS-2B-OF	102	339	50	98	18	2	7	39	.289	23	19	4	141	221	9	.976
—	Tacoma (PCL)	2B-DH-SS	4	17	1	3	0	0	1	1	.176	0	2	0	4	9	0	1.000
1996—	Seattle (A.L.)	3B-2B-SS	77	247	20	52	8	1	1	16	.211	10	13	2	97	158	8	.970
—	New York (A.L.)■	2B-SS-3B	18	40	3	11	2	0	0	5	.275	1	4	0	16	37	0	1.000
1997—	New York (A.L.)	2B-SS-3B-1B	77	215	27	66	6	1	2	25	.307	16	14	3	131	153	5	.983
1998—	Tampa (FSL)	SS	3	9	1	2	0	0	0	0	.222	2	0	0	4	8	1	.923
—	Columbus (I.L.)	SS-DH-2B	6	23	1	5	2	0	0	2	.217	1	1	1	9	16	1	.962
—	New York (A.L.)	S-1-2-3-DH	54	147	16	34	3	1	0	14	.231	4	15	1	146	74	3	.987
1999—	New York (A.L.)	3-2-S-1-DH	49	127	20	32	6	0	2	16	.252	4	17	1	65	72	2	.986
2000—	Pittsburgh (N.L.)■	3B-2B	61	176	14	50	11	0	5	20	.284	11	16	1	24	97	5	.960
—	New York (A.L.)■	2B-3B-1B-SS	34	125	19	36	7	1	2	17	.288	6	6	1	64	75	2	.986
American League totals (11 years)			745	2312	281	608	90	12	31	232	.263	109	170	26	1244	1670	63	.979
National League totals (1 year)			61	176	14	50	11	0	5	20	.284	11	16	1	24	97	5	.960
Major League totals (11 years)			806	2488	295	658	101	12	36	252	.264	120	186	27	1268	1767	68	.978

DIVISION SERIES RECORD

RECORDS: Shares single-game record for most at-bats—7 (October 4, 1995).

Year	Team (League)	Pos.	G	AB	R	H	2B	3B	HR	RBI	Avg.	BB	SO	SB	PO	A	E	Avg.
1995—	Seattle (A.L.)	SS	5	20	0	5	0	0	3	.250	0	3	0	9	15	1	.960	
1996—	New York (A.L.)	2B	2	0	0	0	0	0	0	0	...	0	0	0	1	1	0	1.000
1998—	New York (A.L.)						Did not play.											
1999—	New York (A.L.)						Did not play.											
2000—	New York (A.L.)	2B	5	16	2	3	2	0	0	5	.188	2	1	0	9	22	1	.969
Division series totals (3 years)			12	36	2	8	2	0	0	8	.222	2	4	0	19	38	2	.966

CHAMPIONSHIP SERIES RECORD

Year	Team (League)	Pos.	G	AB	R	H	2B	3B	HR	RBI	Avg.	BB	SO	SB	PO	A	E	Avg.
1995—	Seattle (A.L.)	SS	6	20	0	5	2	0	0	1	.250	0	2	0	9	18	1	.964
1996—	New York (A.L.)	2B	3	5	0	1	0	0	0	0	.200	0	1	0	4	4	0	1.000
1998—	New York (A.L.)	1B	1	0	0	0	0	0	0	0	...	0	0	0	1	1	0	1.000
1999—	New York (A.L.)	PH-2B	2	1	0	0	0	0	0	0	.000	0	0	0	1	1	0	1.000
2000—	New York (A.L.)	2B-3B	6	23	1	6	1	0	0	2	.261	2	3	0	10	15	0	1.000
Championship series totals (5 years)			18	49	1	12	3	0	0	3	.245	2	6	0	25	39	1	.985

WORLD SERIES RECORD

NOTES: Member of World Series championship team (1996, 1998, 1999 and 2000).

Year	Team (League)	Pos.	G	AB	R	H	2B	3B	HR	RBI	Avg.	BB	SO	SB	PO	A	E	Avg.
1996—	New York (A.L.)	PH-2B	5	5	0	3	1	0	0	1	.600	0	0	0	5	2	0	1.000
1998—	New York (A.L.)						Did not play.											
1999—	New York (A.L.)	2B	1	0	0	0	0	0	0	0	...	0	0	0	1	1	0	1.000
2000—	New York (A.L.)	3B-2B	4	7	0	2	0	0	0	2	.286	1	0	1	4	1	0	1.000
World Series totals (3 years)			10	12	0	5	1	0	0	3	.417	1	0	1	10	4	0	1.000

S

SORIANO, ALFONSO   SS   YANKEES

PERSONAL: Born January 7, 1978, in San Pedro de Macoris, Dominican Republic. ... 6-1/160. ... Bats right, throws right.
HIGH SCHOOL: Eugenio Maria de Osto (Dominican Republic).
TRANSACTIONS/CAREER NOTES: Signed by Hiroshima Toyo Carp of Japan Central League (November 1994). ... Played in Toyo Carp organization (1995-97). ... Retired from Japan Central League and declared free agent by Major League Baseball (1998). ... Signed by New York Yankees (September 29, 1998). ... On Norwich disabled list (July 15-August 15, 1999).

								BATTING							FIELDING		
Year	Team (League)	Pos.	G	AB	R	H	2B	3B	HR	RBI	Avg.	BB	SO	SB	PO	A	E	Avg.
1995—	....					Japan minor league statistics unavailable.												
1996—	....					Japan minor league statistics unavailable.												
1997—	Hiroshima (Jap. Cen.)	OF	9	17	2	2	0	0	0	0	.118	2	4	0	...	...	...	...
1998—	....					Out of organized baseball.												
1999—	Norwich (East.)■	SS-DH	89	361	57	110	20	3	15	68	.305	32	67	24	160	243	27	.937
	— GC Yankees (GCL)......	SS-DH	5	19	7	5	2	0	1	5	.263	1	3	0	2	11	1	.929
	— Columbus (I.L.).........	SS-3B-2B	20	82	8	15	5	1	2	11	.183	5	18	1	19	44	3	.955
	— New York (A.L.)..........	DH-SS	9	8	2	1	0	0	1	1	.125	0	3	0	0	1	1	.500
2000—	Columbus (I.L.)	SS-2B	111	459	90	133	32	6	12	66	.290	25	85	14	175	245	21	.952
	— New York (A.L.)..........3B-SS-DH-2B	22	50	5	9	3	0	2	3	.180	1	15	2	18	18	7	.837
Major League totals (2 years)			31	58	7	10	3	0	3	4	.172	1	18	2	18	19	8	.822

S

SOSA, JUAN   SS   ROCKIES

PERSONAL: Born August 19, 1975, in San Francisco de Macoris, Dominican Republic. ... 6-1/175. ... Bats right, throws right. ... Full name: Juan Luis Encarnacion Sosa.
HIGH SCHOOL: Renacimento (Dominican Republic).
TRANSACTIONS/CAREER NOTES: Signed as non-drafted free agent by Los Angeles Dodgers organization (July 24, 1993). ... Selected by Colorado Rockies organization from Dodgers organization in Rule 5 minor league draft (December 15, 1997). ... On disabled list (April 6-21, 2000).
STATISTICAL NOTES: Led Carolina League shortstops with 555 total chances in 1998. ... Led Southern League shortstops with 191 putouts and .958 fielding percentage in 1999.

								BATTING							FIELDING		
Year	Team (League)	Pos.	G	AB	R	H	2B	3B	HR	RBI	Avg.	BB	SO	SB	PO	A	E	Avg.
1993—	Dom. Dodgers (DSL) .	IF	63	237	51	66	7	4	0	39	.278	45	52	8	209	28	16	.937
1994—	Dom. Dodgers (DSL) .	2B	59	224	55	65	11	3	6	60	.290	44	27	13	141	168	17	.948
1995—	Vero Beach (FSL)	2B-SS	8	27	2	6	1	1	1	6	.222	0	4	0	10	21	1	.969
	— Yakima (N'West)	2B-3B-SS	61	217	26	51	10	4	3	16	.235	15	39	8	93	174	16	.943
1996—	Savannah (S.Atl.) 2B-SS-3B-OF	112	370	58	94	21	2	7	38	.254	30	64	14	139	261	22	.948
1997—	Vero Beach (FSL)	SS-2B-3B	92	250	32	55	5	2	5	29	.220	14	39	20	130	193	19	.944
1998—	Salem (Caro.)■	SS	133	529	88	147	20	*12	8	47	.278	43	83	*64	*196	328	31	.944
1999—	Carolina (Sou.)	SS-OF	125	490	70	135	22	5	7	42	.276	31	65	38	†202	361	24	†.959
	— Colo. Springs (PCL) ...	OF-SS	6	28	3	11	1	1	1	5	.393	0	1	1	15	8	1	.958
	— Colorado (N.L.)	OF-SS	11	9	3	2	0	0	0	0	.222	2	2	0	6	3	1	.900
2000—	Colo. Springs (PCL) ...	SS-OF	118	449	67	123	25	9	9	69	.274	31	54	23	177	334	25	.953
Major League totals (1 year)			11	9	3	2	0	0	0	0	.222	2	2	0	6	3	1	.900

SOSA, SAMMY   OF   CUBS

PERSONAL: Born November 12, 1968, in San Pedro de Macoris, Dominican Repubic. ... 6-0/220. ... Bats right, throws right. ... Full name: Samuel Sosa Peralta.
TRANSACTIONS/CAREER NOTES: Signed as non-drafted free agent by Texas Rangers organization (July 30, 1985). ... Traded by Rangers with SS Scott Fletcher and P Wilson Alvarez to Chicago White Sox for OF Harold Baines and IF Fred Manrique (July 29, 1989). ... Traded by White Sox with P Ken Patterson to Chicago Cubs for OF George Bell (March 30, 1992). ... On Chicago disabled list (June 13-July 27, and August 7-September 16, 1992); included rehabilitation assignment to Iowa (July 21-27). ... On disabled list (August 21, 1996-remainder of season).
RECORDS: Holds major league single-season records for most home runs by outfielder—66 (1998); and most at-bats without a triple—643 (1998). ... Holds major league single-month record for most home runs—20 (June 1998). ... Shares major league single-season record for most major league ballparks, one or more home runs—18 (1998). ... Shares major league record for most grand slams in two consecutive games—2 (July 27 and 28, 1998). ... Shares major league single-season record for most times hitting two or more home runs in a game—11 (1998). ... Shares major league single-inning record for most home runs—2 (May 16, 1996, seventh inning). ... Holds N.L. records for most seasons with 50 or more home runs—3; and most consecutive seasons with 50 or more home runs—3 (1998-2000).
HONORS: Named outfielder on THE SPORTING NEWS N.L. All-Star team (1995, 1998, 1999 and 2000). ... Named outfielder on THE SPORTING NEWS N.L. Silver Slugger team (1995, 1998, 1999 and 2000). ... Named co-Sportsman of the Year by THE SPORTING NEWS (1998). ... Named Major League Player of the Year by THE SPORTING NEWS (1998). ... Named N.L. Most Valuable Player by Baseball Writers' Association of America (1998).
STATISTICAL NOTES: Led Gulf Coast League with 96 total bases in 1986. ... Tied for South Atlantic League lead in double plays by outfielder with four in 1987. ... Collected six hits in one game (July 2, 1993). ... Tied for N.L. lead in double plays by outfielder with four in 1995. ... Hit three home runs in one game (June 5, 1996 and June 15, 1998). ... Led N.L. with 416 total bases in 1998. ... Had 18-game hitting streak (May 26-June 15, 1999). ... Led N.L. with 397 total bases in 1999. ... Had 15-game hitting streak (July 4-22, 2000). ... Career major league grand slams: 4.

								BATTING							FIELDING		
Year	Team (League)	Pos.	G	AB	R	H	2B	3B	HR	RBI	Avg.	BB	SO	SB	PO	A	E	Avg.
1986—	GC Rangers (GCL)......	OF	61	229	38	63	*19	1	4	28	.275	22	51	11	92	9	•6	.944
1987—	Gastonia (S.Atl.)........	OF	129	519	73	145	27	4	11	59	.279	21	123	22	183	12	17	.920
1988—	Charlotte (FSL)..........	OF	131	507	70	116	13	*12	9	51	.229	35	106	42	227	11	7	.971
1989—	Tulsa (Texas)............	OF	66	273	45	81	15	4	7	31	.297	15	52	16	110	7	4	.967
	— Texas (A.L.)..............	OF-DH	25	84	8	20	3	0	1	3	.238	0	20	0	33	1	2	.944
	— Oklahoma City (A.A.)..	OF	10	39	2	4	2	0	0	3	.103	2	8	4	22	0	2	.917
	— Vancouver (PCL)	OF	13	49	7	18	3	0	1	5	.367	0	20	0	43	1	0	1.000
	— Chicago (A.L.)■	OF	33	99	19	27	5	0	3	10	.273	11	27	7	61	1	2	.969

Year	Team (League)	Pos.	G	AB	R	H	2B	3B	HR	RBI	Avg.	BB	SO	SB	PO	A	E	Avg.
							BATTING									FIELDING		
1990—Chicago (A.L.)	OF	153	532	72	124	26	10	15	70	.233	33	150	32	315	14	*13	.962	
1991—Chicago (A.L.)	OF-DH	116	316	39	64	10	1	10	33	.203	14	98	13	214	6	6	.973	
—Vancouver (PCL)	OF	32	116	19	31	7	2	3	19	.267	17	32	9	95	2	3	.970	
1992—Chicago (N.L.)■	OF	67	262	41	68	7	2	8	25	.260	19	63	15	145	4	6	.961	
—Iowa (A.A.)	OF	5	19	3	6	2	0	0	1	.316	1	2	5	14	0	0	1.000	
1993—Chicago (N.L.)	OF	159	598	92	156	25	5	33	93	.261	38	135	36	344	17	9	.976	
1994—Chicago (N.L.)	OF	105	426	59	128	17	6	25	70	.300	25	92	22	248	5	7	.973	
1995—Chicago (N.L.)	OF	•144	564	89	151	17	3	36	119	.268	58	134	34	320	13	*13	.962	
1996—Chicago (N.L.)	OF	124	498	84	136	21	2	40	100	.273	34	134	18	253	15	10	.964	
1997—Chicago (N.L.)	OF	•162	642	90	161	31	4	36	119	.251	45	*174	22	325	16	8	.977	
1998—Chicago (N.L.)	OF	159	643	*134	198	20	0	66	*158	.308	73	*171	18	334	14	9	.975	
1999—Chicago (N.L.)	OF	•162	625	114	180	24	2	63	141	.288	78	*171	7	399	8	9	.978	
2000—Chicago (N.L.)	OF	156	604	106	193	38	1	*50	138	.320	91	168	7	318	3	•10	.970	
American League totals (3 years)		327	1031	138	235	44	11	29	116	.228	58	295	52	623	22	23	.966	
National League totals (9 years)		1238	4862	809	1371	200	25	357	963	.282	461	1242	179	2686	95	81	.972	
Major League totals (12 years)		1565	5893	947	1606	244	36	386	1079	.273	519	1537	231	3309	117	104	.971	

DIVISION SERIES RECORD

Year	Team (League)	Pos.	G	AB	R	H	2B	3B	HR	RBI	Avg.	BB	SO	SB	PO	A	E	Avg.
							BATTING									FIELDING		
1998—Chicago (N.L.)	OF	3	11	0	2	1	0	0	0	.182	1	4	0	5	0	0	1.000	

ALL-STAR GAME RECORD

NOTES: Named to All-Star team for 1998 game; replaced by Bret Boone due to injury.

Year	League	Pos.	AB	R	H	2B	3B	HR	RBI	Avg.	BB	SO	SB	PO	A	E	Avg.
						BATTING									FIELDING		
1995—National	OF	1	0	0	0	0	0	0	.000	0	0	0	2	0	0	1.000
1998—National						Selected, did not play—injured.											
1999—National	OF	3	0	0	0	0	0	0	.000	0	2	0	1	0	0	1.000
2000—National	OF	3	0	0	0	0	0	0	.000	0	1	0	1	0	0	1.000
All-Star Game totals (3 years)		7	0	0	0	0	0	0	.000	0	3	0	4	0	0	1.000

S

SPARKS, JEFF   P

PERSONAL: Born April 4, 1972, in Houston. ... 6-3/220. ... Throws right, bats right. ... Full name: James Jeffrey Sparks.
HIGH SCHOOL: Waller (Texas).
COLLEGE: St. Mary's (Texas).
TRANSACTIONS/CAREER NOTES: Selected by Cincinnati Reds organization in 24th round of free-agent draft (June 1, 1995). ... Released by Reds (July 25, 1997). ... Signed by Winnipeg, Northern League (August 1997). ... Signed by Colorado Rockies organization (February 18, 1998). ... Released by Rockies (April 4, 1998). ... Signed by Winnipeg (May 1998). ... Signed by Pittsburgh Pirates organization (January 6, 1999). ... Traded by Pirates with OF Jose Guillen to Tampa Bay Devil Rays for C Joe Oliver and C Humberto Cota (July 23, 1999). ... Released by Devil Rays (November 27, 2000).

Year	League	W	L	Pct.	ERA	G	GS	CG	ShO	Sv.	IP	H	R	ER	BB	SO
1995—Princeton (Appl.)	2	0	1.000	3.23	16	2	0	0	2	39	32	19	14	27	49
1996—Charleston, W.Va. (S.Atl.)	2	7	.222	4.74	46	3	0	0	0	89 1/3	79	51	47	46	94
—Chattanooga (Sou.)	0	0	...	4.50	3	0	0	0	0	2	5	1	1	1	2
1997—Burlington (Midw.)	2	5	.286	5.72	22	9	0	0	0	61 1/3	61	49	39	39	72
—Winnipeg (Nor.)■	1	1	.500	4.15	7	0	0	0	0	13	11	8	6	10	20
1998—Winnipeg (Nor.)	2	1	.667	3.12	38	0	0	0	17	49	30	21	17	42	85
1999—Nashville (PCL)■	5	3	.625	3.83	34	0	0	0	0	49 1/3	37	25	21	23	69
—Durham (I.L.)■	3	0	1.000	3.38	18	0	0	0	0	24	16	11	9	14	31
—Tampa Bay (A.L.)	0	0	...	5.40	8	0	0	0	1	10	6	6	6	12	17
2000—Durham (I.L.)	0	1	.000	14.21	9	1	0	0	0	12 2/3	11	21	20	23	17
—Tampa Bay (A.L.)	0	1	.000	3.54	15	0	0	0	0	20 1/3	13	8	8	18	24
—St. Petersburg (FSL)	1	4	.200	3.21	13	1	0	0	3	28	9	13	10	26	33
—Orlando (Sou.)	0	2	.000	6.75	3	3	0	0	0	10 2/3	9	13	8	11	8
Major League totals (2 years)	0	1	.000	4.15	23	0	0	0	1	30 1/3	19	14	14	30	41

SPARKS, STEVE   P   TIGERS

PERSONAL: Born July 2, 1965, in Tulsa, Okla. ... 6-0/180. ... Throws right, bats right. ... Full name: Steven William Sparks.
HIGH SCHOOL: Holland Hall (Tulsa, Okla.).
COLLEGE: Sam Houston State.
TRANSACTIONS/CAREER NOTES: Selected by Milwaukee Brewers organization in fifth round of free-agent draft (June 2, 1987). ... On disabled list (March 24, 1997-entire season). ... Granted free agency (October 15, 1997). ... Signed by Anaheim Angels (February 23, 1998). ... On Cedar Rapids disabled list (April 9-19, 1998). ... Granted free agency (October 15, 1999). ... Signed by Philadelphia Phillies organization (February 1, 2000). ... Released by Phillies (February 28, 2000). ... Signed by Detroit Tigers organization (March 2, 2000).
RECORDS: Shares major league single-inning record for most hit batsmen—3 (May 22, 1999, third inning). ... Shares A.L. single-game record for most hit batsmen (nine innings)—4 (May 22, 1999).
MISCELLANEOUS: Appeared in one game as pinch runner (1999).

Year	League	W	L	Pct.	ERA	G	GS	CG	ShO	Sv.	IP	H	R	ER	BB	SO
1987—Helena (Pio.)	6	3	.667	4.68	10	9	2	0	0	57 2/3	68	44	30	20	47
1988—Beloit (Midw.)	9	13	.409	3.79	25	24	5	1	0	164	162	80	69	51	96
1989—Stockton (Calif.)	•13	5	.722	2.41	23	22	3	2	0	164	125	55	44	53	126
1990—Stockton (Calif.)	10	7	.588	3.69	19	19	5	1	0	129 1/3	136	63	53	31	77
—El Paso (Texas)	1	2	.333	6.53	7	6	1	0	0	30 1/3	43	24	22	15	17
1991—Stockton (Calif.)	9	10	.474	3.06	24	24	•8	2	0	179 2/3	160	70	61	98	139
—El Paso (Texas)	1	2	.333	9.53	4	4	0	0	0	17	30	22	18	9	10

Year League	W	L	Pct.	ERA	G	GS	CG	ShO	Sv.	IP	H	R	ER	BB	SO
1992— El Paso (Texas)	9	8	.529	5.37	28	22	3	0	1	140 2/3	159	99	84	50	79
1993— New Orleans (A.A.)	9	13	.409	3.84	29	•28	*7	1	0	*180 1/3	174	89	77	*80	104
1994— New Orleans (A.A.)	10	12	.455	4.46	28	27	5	1	0	*183 2/3	183	101	91	68	105
1995— Milwaukee (A.L.)	9	11	.450	4.63	33	27	3	0	0	202	210	111	104	86	96
1996— Milwaukee (A.L.)	4	7	.364	6.60	20	13	1	0	0	88 2/3	103	66	65	52	21
— New Orleans (A.A.)	2	6	.250	4.99	11	10	3	2	0	57 2/3	64	43	32	35	27
1997— Milwaukee (A.L.)						Did not play.									
1998— Midland (Texas)■	0	4	.000	7.08	7	7	0	0	0	40 2/3	49	38	32	15	34
— Vancouver (PCL)	0	4	.000	2.89	4	4	2	0	0	28	23	11	9	6	19
— Anaheim (A.L.)	9	4	.692	4.34	22	20	0	0	0	128 2/3	130	66	62	58	90
1999— Anaheim (A.L.)	5	11	.313	5.42	28	26	0	0	0	147 2/3	165	101	89	82	73
2000— Toledo (I.L.)■	5	7	.417	3.77	16	14	1	0	0	90 2/3	86	53	38	41	44
— Detroit (A.L.)	7	5	.583	4.07	20	15	1	1	1	104	108	55	47	29	53
Major League totals (5 years)	34	38	.472	4.92	123	101	5	1	1	671	716	399	367	307	333

PERSONAL: Born March 28, 1975, in Mobile, Ala. ... 6-4/210. ... Throws right, bats right. ... Full name: Stephen Lanier Sparks.
COLLEGE: South Alabama.
TRANSACTIONS/CAREER NOTES: Selected by Pittsburgh Pirates organization in 28th round of free-agent draft (June 2, 1998).

Year League	W	L	Pct.	ERA	G	GS	CG	ShO	Sv.	IP	H	R	ER	BB	SO
1998— Erie (NY-Penn)	2	7	.222	4.43	14	10	0	0	0	63	55	38	31	30	61
— Augusta (S.Atl.)	0	1	.000	6.23	2	2	0	0	0	8 2/3	11	9	6	4	12
1999— Hickory (S.Atl.)	4	6	.400	4.47	25	12	1	0	0	88 2/3	97	60	44	51	72
— Lynchburg (Caro.)	2	3	.400	6.23	5	5	1	0	0	26	36	20	18	15	20
2000— Altoona (East.)	6	7	.462	4.77	23	17	3	2	0	109 1/3	103	66	58	54	66
— Pittsburgh (N.L.)	0	0	...	6.75	3	0	0	0	0	4	4	3	3	5	2
Major League totals (1 year)	0	0	...	6.75	3	0	0	0	0	4	4	3	3	5	2

PERSONAL: Born November 6, 1973, in Walnut Creek, Calif. ... 6-4/205. ... Throws right, bats right. ... Full name: Justin James Speier. ... Son of Chris Speier, infielder with five major league teams (1971-89).
HIGH SCHOOL: Brophy College Prep (Phoenix).
COLLEGE: San Francisco, then Nicholls State.
TRANSACTIONS/CAREER NOTES: Selected by Chicago Cubs organization in 55th round of free-agent draft (June 1, 1995). ... Traded by Cubs with 3B Kevin Orie and P Todd Noel to Florida Marlins for P Felix Heredia and P Steve Hoff (July 31, 1998). ... Traded by Marlins to Atlanta Braves for a player to be named (April 1, 1999); Marlins acquired P Matthew Targac to complete deal (June 11, 1999). ... Claimed on waivers by Cleveland Indians (November 23, 1999).

Year League	W	L	Pct.	ERA	G	GS	CG	ShO	Sv.	IP	H	R	ER	BB	SO
1995— Williamsport (NY-Penn)	2	1	.667	1.49	30	0	0	0	12	36 1/3	27	6	6	4	39
1996— Daytona (FSL)	2	4	.333	3.76	33	0	0	0	13	38 1/3	32	19	16	19	34
— Orlando (Sou.)	4	1	.800	2.05	24	0	0	0	6	26 1/3	23	7	6	5	14
1997— Orlando (Sou.)	6	5	.545	4.48	50	0	0	0	6	78 1/3	77	46	39	23	63
— Iowa (A.A.)	2	0	1.000	0.00	8	0	0	0	1	12 1/3	5	0	0	1	9
1998— Iowa (PCL)	3	3	.500	5.05	45	0	0	0	12	51 2/3	52	31	29	19	49
— Chicago (N.L.)	0	0	...	13.50	1	0	0	0	0	1 1/3	2	2	2	1	2
— Florida (N.L.)■	0	3	.000	8.38	18	0	0	0	0	19 1/3	25	18	18	12	15
1999— Richmond (I.L.)■	2	4	.333	5.62	27	0	0	0	3	41 2/3	51	28	26	22	39
— Atlanta (N.L.)	0	0	...	5.65	19	0	0	0	0	28 2/3	28	18	18	13	22
2000— Buffalo (I.L.)■	0	0	...	4.15	13	0	0	0	9	13	13	6	6	3	12
— Cleveland (A.L.)	5	2	.714	3.29	47	0	0	0	0	68 1/3	57	27	25	28	69
A.L. totals (1 year)	5	2	.714	3.29	47	0	0	0	0	68 1/3	57	27	25	28	69
N.L. totals (2 years)	0	3	.000	6.93	38	0	0	0	0	49 1/3	55	38	38	26	39
Major League totals (3 years)	5	5	.500	4.82	85	0	0	0	0	117 2/3	112	65	63	54	108

PERSONAL: Born May 29, 1975, in Seattle. ... 5-11/185. ... Throws left, bats left. ... Full name: Sean James Spencer.
HIGH SCHOOL: South Kitsap (Port Orchard, Wash.).
COLLEGE: Washington.
TRANSACTIONS/CAREER NOTES: Selected by Seattle Mariners organization in 40th round of free-agent draft (June 4, 1996). ... Traded by Mariners to Montreal Expos for C Chris Widger (August 10, 2000).

Year League	W	L	Pct.	ERA	G	GS	CG	ShO	Sv.	IP	H	R	ER	BB	SO
1997— Lancaster (Calif.)	2	3	.400	1.64	39	0	0	0	18	60 1/3	41	12	11	15	72
1998— Orlando (Sou.)	2	1	.667	2.95	37	0	0	0	*18	42 2/3	33	18	14	18	43
— Tacoma (PCL)	2	0	1.000	4.85	9	0	0	0	1	13	10	7	7	7	16
1999— Tacoma (PCL)	2	1	.667	3.47	44	0	0	0	7	49 1/3	41	21	19	23	53
— Seattle (A.L.)	0	0	...	21.60	2	0	0	0	0	1 2/3	5	4	4	3	2
2000— Tacoma (PCL)	3	2	.600	3.38	42	0	0	0	0	45 1/3	35	21	17	37	46
— Ottawa (I.L.)■	1	1	.500	9.90	10	0	0	0	1	10	15	12	11	6	8
— Montreal (N.L.)	0	0	...	5.40	8	0	0	0	0	6 2/3	7	4	4	3	6
A.L. totals (1 year)	0	0	...	21.60	2	0	0	0	0	1 2/3	5	4	4	3	2
N.L. totals (1 year)	0	0	...	5.40	8	0	0	0	0	6 2/3	7	4	4	3	6
Major League totals (2 years)	0	0	...	8.64	10	0	0	0	0	8 1/3	12	8	8	6	8

PERSONAL: Born February 20, 1972, in Key West, Fla. ... 5-11/210. ... Bats right, throws right. ... Full name: Michael Shane Spencer.
HIGH SCHOOL: Granite Hills (El Cajon, Calif.).
TRANSACTIONS/CAREER NOTES: Selected by New York Yankees organization in 28th round of free-agent draft (June 4, 1990). ... On disabled list (April 10-May 9, 1994). ... On New York disabled list (July 3-27, 1999); included rehabilitation assignment to Columbus (July 21-27). ... On disabled list (July 12, 2000-remainder of season).
RECORDS: Shares major league single-month record for most grand slams—3 (September 1998).
HONORS: Named Florida State League Most Valuable Player (1995).
STATISTICAL NOTES: Led Florida State League with 235 total bases in 1995. ... Career major league grand slams: 3.

Year Team (League)	Pos.	G	AB	R	H	2B	3B	HR	RBI	Avg.	BB	SO	SB	PO	A	E	Avg.
1990—GC Yankees (GCL)	OF	42	147	20	27	4	0	0	7	.184	20	23	11	79	3	3	.965
1991—GC Yankees (GCL)	OF	44	160	25	49	7	0	0	30	.306	14	19	9	64	6	3	.959
—Oneonta (NY-Penn)	OF	18	53	10	13	2	1	0	3	.245	10	9	2	11	0	1	.917
1992—Greensboro (S.Atl.)	OF-P	83	258	43	74	10	2	3	27	.287	33	37	8	135	6	0	1.000
1993—Greensboro (S.Atl.)	OF-P	122	431	89	116	35	2	12	80	.269	52	62	14	138	10	5	.967
1994—Tampa (FSL)	OF	90	334	44	97	22	3	8	53	.290	30	53	5	90	10	4	.962
1995—Tampa (FSL)	OF	•134	500	87	*150	31	3	16	*88	.300	61	60	14	166	6	6	.966
1996—Norwich (East.)	OF-1B-3B	126	450	70	114	19	0	29	89	.253	68	99	4	218	24	3	.988
—Columbus (I.L.)	OF	9	31	7	11	4	0	3	6	.355	5	5	0	25	1	1	.963
1997—Columbus (I.L.)	OF-DH-3B	125	452	78	109	34	4	30	86	.241	71	105	0	189	7	4	.980
1998—New York (A.L.)	OF-DH-1B	27	67	18	25	6	0	10	27	.373	5	12	0	29	2	0	1.000
—Columbus (I.L.)	OF-DH-1B	87	342	66	110	29	1	18	67	.322	41	59	1	225	11	5	.979
1999—New York (A.L.)	OF-DH	71	205	25	48	8	0	8	20	.234	18	51	0	108	5	0	1.000
—Columbus (I.L.)	OF-DH	14	50	17	18	2	0	2	10	.360	9	8	0	23	0	1	.958
2000—New York (A.L.)	OF-DH	73	248	33	70	11	3	9	40	.282	19	45	1	83	3	1	.989
Major League totals (3 years)		171	520	76	143	25	3	27	87	.275	42	108	1	220	10	1	.996

DIVISION SERIES RECORD

Year Team (League)	Pos.	G	AB	R	H	2B	3B	HR	RBI	Avg.	BB	SO	SB	PO	A	E	Avg.
1998—New York (A.L.)	OF	2	6	3	3	0	0	2	4	.500	0	1	0	1	0	0	1.000
1999—New York (A.L.)							Did not play.										

CHAMPIONSHIP SERIES RECORD

Year Team (League)	Pos.	G	AB	R	H	2B	3B	HR	RBI	Avg.	BB	SO	SB	PO	A	E	Avg.
1998—New York (A.L.)	OF	3	10	1	1	0	0	0	0	.100	1	3	0	7	1	0	1.000
1999—New York (A.L.)	OF	3	9	1	1	0	0	0	0	.111	1	6	0	5	0	0	1.000
Championship series totals (2 years)		6	19	2	2	0	0	0	0	.105	2	9	0	12	1	0	1.000

WORLD SERIES RECORD

NOTES: Member of World Series championship team (1998 and 1999).

Year Team (League)	Pos.	G	AB	R	H	2B	3B	HR	RBI	Avg.	BB	SO	SB	PO	A	E	Avg.
1998—New York (A.L.)	OF	1	3	1	1	1	0	0	0	.333	0	2	0	2	1	0	1.000
1999—New York (A.L.)							Did not play.										

RECORD AS PITCHER

Year League	W	L	Pct.	ERA	G	GS	CG	ShO	Sv.	IP	H	R	ER	BB	SO
1992—Greensboro (S.Atl.)	0	0	...	0.00	1	0	0	0	0	1	2	0	0	1	1
1993—Greensboro (S.Atl.)	0	0	...	4.50	2	0	0	0	0	4	5	2	2	2	5

PERSONAL: Born August 7, 1969, in Vancouver, B.C. ... 6-4/223. ... Throws right, bats right. ... Full name: Stanley Roger Spencer.
HIGH SCHOOL: Columbia River (Vancouver, B.C.).
COLLEGE: Stanford.
TRANSACTIONS/CAREER NOTES: Selected by Boston Red Sox organization in 26th round of free-agent draft (June 2, 1987); did not sign. ... Selected by Montreal Expos organization in supplemental round ("sandwich pick" between first and second round, 35th pick overall) of free-agent draft (June 4, 1990); pick received as part of compensation for Los Angeles Dodgers signing Type A free-agent OF Hubie Brooks. ... On disabled list (July 2, 1990-entire season; and July 18, 1991-remainder of season). ... On Harrisburg disabled list (April 9, 1992-entire season). ... Selected by Florida Marlins from Expos organization in Rule 5 major league draft (December 7, 1992). ... On disabled list (April 8-June 24, 1993). ... On Portland disabled list (July 9-16, 1994). ... Granted free agency (October 11, 1995). ... Signed by San Diego Padres organization (February 7, 1997). ... On Rancho Cucamonga disabled list (May 9-22, 1997). ... Granted free agency (October 15, 1997). ... Re-signed by Padres organization (December 29, 1997). ... On Las Vegas disabled list (May 16-June 1, 1998; and May 27-July 5, 1999). ... Granted free agency (October 12, 1999). ... Re-signed by Padres organization (November 22, 1999). ... On San Diego disabled list (June 20, 2000-remainder of season). ... Granted free agency (October 18, 2000). ... Re-signed by Padres organization (January 24, 2001).
HONORS: Named righthanded pitcher on THE SPORTING NEWS college All-America team (1990).
STATISTICAL NOTES: Tied for Eastern League lead with three balks in 1991.
MISCELLANEOUS: Struck out in only appearance as pinch hitter (2000).

Year League	W	L	Pct.	ERA	G	GS	CG	ShO	Sv.	IP	H	R	ER	BB	SO
1990—West Palm Beach (FSL)							Did not play.								
1991—Harrisburg (East.)	6	1	.857	4.40	17	17	1	0	0	92	90	52	45	30	66
1992—Harrisburg (East.)							Did not play.								
1993—High Desert (Calif.)■	4	4	.500	4.09	13	13	0	0	0	61 2/3	67	33	28	18	38
1994—Brevard County (FSL)	1	0	1.000	3.15	6	5	0	0	0	20	20	9	7	6	22
—Portland (East.)	9	4	.692	3.48	20	20	1	0	0	124	113	52	48	30	96

Year League	W	L	Pct.	ERA	G	GS	CG	ShO	Sv.	IP	H	R	ER	BB	SO
1995— Charlotte (I.L.)	1	4	.200	7.84	9	9	0	0	0	41 1/3	61	37	36	24	19
— Portland (East.)	1	4	.200	7.38	8	8	0	0	0	39	57	39	32	19	32
1996—				Out of organized baseball.											
1997— Rancho Cuca. (Calif.)■	3	1	.750	3.35	7	7	0	0	0	40 1/3	37	18	15	5	46
— Las Vegas (PCL)	3	2	.600	3.75	8	8	0	0	0	48	48	23	20	18	47
1998— Las Vegas (PCL)	12	6	.667	3.93	22	22	0	0	0	137 1/3	120	67	60	42	136
— San Diego (N.L.)	1	0	1.000	4.70	6	5	0	0	0	30 2/3	29	16	16	4	31
1999— San Diego (N.L.)	0	7	.000	9.16	9	8	0	0	0	38 1/3	56	44	39	11	36
— Las Vegas (PCL)	5	4	.556	5.47	12	10	0	0	0	54 1/3	69	35	33	15	50
2000— Las Vegas (PCL)	4	0	1.000	1.72	6	6	0	0	0	36 2/3	29	9	7	7	40
— San Diego (N.L.)	2	2	.500	3.26	8	8	0	0	0	49 2/3	44	22	18	19	40
Major League totals (3 years)	3	9	.250	5.54	23	21	0	0	0	118 2/3	129	82	73	34	107

SPIERS, BILL IF ASTROS

PERSONAL: Born June 5, 1966, in Orangeburg, S.C. ... 6-2/190. ... Bats left, throws right. ... Full name: William James Spiers III. ... Name pronounced SPY-ers.

HIGH SCHOOL: Wade Hampton Academy (Orangeburg, S.C.).

COLLEGE: Clemson.

TRANSACTIONS/CAREER NOTES: Selected by Milwaukee Brewers organization in first round (13th pick overall) of free-agent draft (June 2, 1987). ... On Milwaukee disabled list (April 6-May 15, 1990); included rehabilitation assignment to Denver (April 27-May 14). ... On Milwaukee disabled list (April 5-September 2, 1992); included rehabilitation assignments to Beloit (May 6-15 and August 20-September 2). ... Granted free agency (December 20, 1993). ... Re-signed by Brewers (December 21, 1993). ... Claimed on waivers by New York Mets (October 25, 1994). ... On New York disabled list (May 15-June 5 and June 26-July 16, 1995); included rehabilitation assignment to Norfolk (May 22-June 5). ... Granted free agency (November 3, 1995). ... Signed by Houston Astros organization (January 10, 1996). ... Granted free agency (November 14, 1996). ... Re-signed by Astros (December 2, 1996). ... Granted free agency (November 3, 1997). ... Re-signed by Astros (November 25, 1997).

HONORS: Named shortstop on The Sporting News college All-America team (1987).

STATISTICAL NOTES: Career major league grand slams: 3.

Year Team (League)	Pos.	G	AB	R	H	2B	3B	HR	RBI	Avg.	BB	SO	SB	PO	A	E	Avg.
						BATTING									FIELDING		
1987— Helena (Pio.)	SS	6	22	4	9	1	0	0	3	.409	3	3	2	8	6	6	.700
— Beloit (Midw.)	SS	64	258	43	77	10	1	3	26	.298	15	38	11	111	160	20	.931
1988— Stockton (Calif.)	SS	84	353	68	95	17	3	5	52	.269	42	41	27	140	240	19	.952
— El Paso (Texas)	SS	47	168	22	47	5	2	3	21	.280	15	20	4	73	141	13	.943
1989— Milwaukee (A.L.)	S-3-2-DH-1	114	345	44	88	9	3	4	33	.255	21	63	10	164	295	21	.956
— Denver (A.A.)	SS	14	47	9	17	2	1	2	8	.362	5	6	1	32	33	2	.970
1990— Denver (A.A.)	SS	11	38	6	12	0	0	1	7	.316	10	8	1	22	23	2	.957
— Milwaukee (A.L.)	SS	112	363	44	88	15	3	2	36	.242	16	46	11	159	326	12	.976
1991— Milwaukee (A.L.)	SS-DH-OF	133	414	71	117	13	6	8	54	.283	34	55	14	201	345	17	.970
1992— Beloit (Midw.)	SS	16	55	9	13	3	0	0	7	.236	7	7	4	12	28	3	.930
— Milwaukee (A.L.)	SS-2B-DH-3B	12	16	2	5	2	0	0	2	.313	1	4	1	6	6	0	1.000
1993— Milwaukee (A.L.)	2-O-S-DH	113	340	43	81	8	4	2	36	.238	29	51	9	213	231	13	.972
1994— Milwaukee (A.L.)	3-S-DH-O-1	73	214	27	54	10	1	0	17	.252	19	42	7	70	129	8	.961
1995— New York (N.L.)■	3B-2B	63	72	5	15	2	1	0	11	.208	12	15	0	13	30	7	.860
— Norfolk (I.L.)	2B-3B	12	41	4	9	2	0	0	4	.220	8	6	0	23	29	4	.929
1996— Houston (N.L.)■	3-2-S-1-O	122	218	27	55	10	1	6	26	.252	20	34	7	44	108	5	.968
1997— Houston (N.L.)	3-S-1-2	132	291	51	93	27	4	4	48	.320	61	42	10	104	200	18	.944
1998— Houston (N.L.)	3-2-1-S	123	384	66	105	27	4	4	43	.273	45	62	11	101	183	9	.969
1999— Houston (N.L.)	3-O-S-2-1	127	393	56	113	18	5	4	39	.288	47	45	10	110	176	9	.969
2000— Houston (N.L.)	3-S-2-O	124	355	41	107	17	3	3	43	.301	49	38	7	118	196	8	.975
American League totals (6 years)		557	1692	231	433	57	17	16	178	.256	120	261	52	813	1332	71	.968
National League totals (6 years)		691	1713	246	488	101	18	21	210	.285	234	236	45	490	894	56	.961
Major League totals (12 years)		1248	3405	477	921	158	35	37	388	.270	354	497	97	1303	2226	127	.965

DIVISION SERIES RECORD

Year Team (League)	Pos.	G	AB	R	H	2B	3B	HR	RBI	Avg.	BB	SO	SB	PO	A	E	Avg.
						BATTING									FIELDING		
1997— Houston (N.L.)	3B	3	11	1	0	0	0	0	0	.000	1	2	0	1	3	0	1.000
1998— Houston (N.L.)	3B-PH	4	14	2	4	3	0	0	1	.286	1	3	0	1	5	0	1.000
1999— Houston (N.L.)	OF-PH	4	11	0	3	0	0	0	1	.273	0	1	1	3	0	1	.750
Division series totals (3 years)		11	36	3	7	3	0	0	2	.194	2	6	1	5	8	1	.929

SPIEZIO, SCOTT 2B ANGELS

PERSONAL: Born September 21, 1972, in Joliet, Ill. ... 6-2/225. ... Bats both, throws right. ... Full name: Scott Edward Spiezio. ... Son of Ed Spiezio, third baseman with St. Louis Cardinals (1964-68), San Diego Padres (1969-72) and Chicago White Sox (1972).

HIGH SCHOOL: Morris (Ill.).

COLLEGE: Illinois.

TRANSACTIONS/CAREER NOTES: Selected by Oakland Athletics organization in sixth round of free-agent draft (June 3, 1993). ... On Oakland disabled list (June 8-25, 1997); included rehabilitation assignment to Southern Oregon (June 23-25). ... On Oakland disabled list (June 15-July 31, 1998); included rehabilitation assignment to Edmonton (July 26-31). ... Granted free agency (December 21, 1999). ... Signed by Anaheim Angels (January 11, 2000).

STATISTICAL NOTES: Led California League third basemen with .948 fielding percentage in 1994. ... Led Southern League with 14 sacrifice flies in 1995. ... Led Southern League third basemen with 291 assists, 29 errors, 424 total chances and 34 double plays in 1995. ... Led Pacific Coast League third basemen with 91 putouts, 302 assists, 405 total chances and .970 fielding percentage in 1996. ... Led A.L. second basemen with .990 fielding percentage in 1997. ... Had 18-game hitting streak (May 21-June 9, 1998). ... Career major league grand slams: 3.

Year	Team (League)	Pos.	G	AB	R	H	2B	3B	HR	RBI	Avg.	BB	SO	SB	PO	A	E	Avg.
1993—	S. Oregon (N'West)....	3B-1B	31	125	32	41	10	2	3	19	.328	16	18	0	76	40	9	.928
	— Modesto (Calif.)	3B-1B	32	110	12	28	9	1	1	13	.255	23	19	1	42	51	5	.949
1994—	Modesto (Calif.)	3B-1B-SS	127	453	84	127	32	5	14	68	.280	88	72	5	66	281	18	†.951
1995—	Huntsville (Sou.)	3B-1B-2B	141	528	78	149	33	8	13	86	.282	67	78	10	122	†295	†29	.935
1996—	Edmonton (PCL)	3B-1B-DH	*140	523	87	137	30	4	20	91	.262	56	66	6	†174	†304	15	†.970
	— Oakland (A.L.)	3B-DH	9	29	6	9	2	0	2	8	.310	4	4	0	6	5	2	.846
1997—	Oakland (A.L.)	2B-3B	147	538	58	131	28	4	14	65	.243	44	75	9	280	415	7	†.990
	— S. Oregon (N'West)	DH-2B	2	9	1	5	0	0	0	2	.556	2	1	0	3	4	1	.875
1998—	Oakland (A.L.)	2B-DH	114	406	54	105	19	1	9	50	.259	44	56	1	198	316	13	.975
	— Edmonton (PCL)	2B-DH	5	13	3	3	1	0	1	4	.231	3	2	0	5	3	1	.889
1999—	Oakland (A.L.)	2B-3B-1B-DH	89	247	31	60	24	0	8	33	.243	29	36	0	124	163	7	.976
	— Vancouver (PCL)	2B-DH-3B	28	105	27	41	7	1	6	27	.390	15	16	0	50	73	4	.969
2000—	Anaheim (A.L.)■	D-1-3-O-2	123	297	47	72	11	2	17	49	.242	40	56	1	164	21	3	.984
	Major League totals (5 years)		482	1517	196	377	84	7	50	205	.249	161	227	11	772	920	32	.981

SPIVEY, JUNIOR   2B/SS   DIAMONDBACKS

PERSONAL: Born January 28, 1975, in Oklahoma City. ... 6-0/185. ... Bats right, throws right. ... Full name: Ernest Lee Spivey Jr.
HIGH SCHOOL: Douglass (Oklahoma City).
JUNIOR COLLEGE: Cowley County Community College (Kan.).
TRANSACTIONS/CAREER NOTES: Selected by Arizona Diamondbacks organization in 26th round of free-agent draft (June 4, 1996). ... Loaned by Diamondbacks to Tulsa, Texas Rangers organization (July 18-August 29, 1998). ... On El Paso disabled list (April 8-May 15 and July 4-August 19, 1999). ... On Arizona disabled list (August 19, 1999-remainder of season). ... On Tucson disabled list (May 8-June 14, 2000). ... On El Paso disabled list (June 25-August 17, 2000). ... On Arizona disabled list (August 31, 2000-remainder of season).
STATISTICAL NOTES: Led California League second basemen with 653 total chances in 1997. ... Tied for California League lead with 20 errors by second baseman in 1998.

Year	Team (League)	Pos.	G	AB	R	H	2B	3B	HR	RBI	Avg.	BB	SO	SB	PO	A	E	Avg.
1996—	Ariz. D-backs (Ariz.)	2B-SS-3B	20	69	13	23	0	0	0	3	.333	12	16	11	35	61	3	.970
	— Lethbridge (Pio.)	2B-SS	31	107	30	36	3	4	2	25	.336	23	24	8	63	70	10	.930
1997—	High Desert (Calif.)	2B	136	491	88	134	24	6	6	53	.273	69	115	14	226	*394	*33	.949
1998—	High Desert (Calif.)	2B-3B-SS	79	285	64	80	14	5	5	35	.281	64	61	34	147	224	‡20	.949
	— Tulsa (Texas)■	2B	34	119	26	37	10	1	3	16	.311	28	25	8	62	84	3	.980
1999—	El Paso (Texas)■	2B-SS	44	164	40	48	10	4	3	19	.293	36	27	14	115	119	9	.963
2000—	Tucson (PCL)	2B-SS-3B	28	117	21	33	8	4	3	16	.282	11	17	3	63	74	6	.958
	— El Paso (Texas)	2B	6	19	5	8	5	0	1	2	.421	0	5	0	12	11	0	1.000

SPOLJARIC, PAUL   P   DEVIL RAYS

PERSONAL: Born September 24, 1970, in Kelowna, B.C. ... 6-3/210. ... Throws left, bats right. ... Full name: Paul Nikola Spoljaric. ... Name pronounced spole-JAIR-ick.
HIGH SCHOOL: Springvalley Secondary (Kelowna, B.C.).
COLLEGE: Douglas College (B.C.).
TRANSACTIONS/CAREER NOTES: Signed as non-drafted free agent by Toronto Blue Jays organization (August 26, 1989). ... On Toronto disabled list (July 25-August 18, 1996); included rehabilitation assignment to St. Catharines (August 10-18). ... On Toronto disabled list (March 23-April 18, 1997); included rehabilitation assignment to Dunedin (April 4-17). ... Traded by Blue Jays with P Mike Timlin to Seattle Mariners for OF Jose Cruz Jr. (July 31, 1997). ... Traded by Mariners to Philadelphia Phillies for P Mark Leiter (November 9, 1998). ... Traded by Phillies to Blue Jays for P Robert Person (May 5, 1999). ... On suspended list (September 2-5, 1999). ... Traded by Blue Jays with P Pat Hentgen to St. Louis Cardinals for P Lance Painter, C Alberto Castillo and P Matt DeWitt (November 11, 1999). ... Released by Cardinals (March 29, 2000). ... Signed by Kansas City Royals organization (April 3, 2000). ... On Kansas City disabled list (August 11-September 4, 2000); included rehabilitation assignment to Omaha (August 28-September 4). ... Granted free agency (October 10, 2000). ... Signed by Tampa Bay Devil Rays organization (November 9, 2000).
HONORS: Named South Atlantic League Most Outstanding Pitcher (1992).
STATISTICAL NOTES: Tied for A.L. lead with three balks in 1997.

Year	League	W	L	Pct.	ERA	G	GS	CG	ShO	Sv.	IP	H	R	ER	BB	SO
1990—	Medicine Hat (Pio.)	3	7	.300	4.34	15	13	0	0	1	66 1/3	57	43	32	35	62
1991—	St. Catharines (NY-Penn)	0	2	.000	4.82	4	4	0	0	0	18 2/3	21	14	10	9	21
1992—	Myrtle Beach (S.Atl.)	10	8	.556	2.82	26	26	1	0	0	162 2/3	111	68	51	58	161
1993—	Dunedin (FSL)	3	0	1.000	1.38	4	4	0	0	0	26	16	5	4	12	29
	— Knoxville (Sou.)	4	1	.800	2.28	7	7	0	0	0	43 1/3	30	12	11	22	51
	— Syracuse (I.L.)	8	7	.533	5.29	18	18	1	1	0	95 1/3	97	63	56	52	88
1994—	Toronto (A.L.)	0	1	.000	38.57	2	1	0	0	0	2 1/3	5	10	10	9	2
	— Syracuse (I.L.)	1	5	.167	5.70	8	8	0	0	0	47 1/3	47	37	30	28	38
	— Knoxville (Sou.)	6	5	.545	3.62	17	16	0	0	0	102	88	50	41	48	79
1995—	Syracuse (I.L.)	2	10	.167	4.93	43	9	0	0	10	87 2/3	69	51	48	54	108
1996—	Syracuse (I.L.)	3	0	1.000	3.27	17	0	0	0	4	22	20	9	8	6	24
	— Toronto (A.L.)	2	2	.500	3.08	28	0	0	0	1	38	30	17	13	19	38
	— St. Catharines (NY-Penn)	0	0	...	0.00	2	2	0	0	0	5	3	0	0	0	7
1997—	Dunedin (FSL)	0	0	...	1.69	4	3	0	0	0	10 2/3	10	3	2	2	10
	— Toronto (A.L.)	0	3	.000	3.19	37	0	0	0	3	48	37	17	17	21	43
	— Seattle (A.L.)■	0	0	...	4.76	20	0	0	0	0	22 2/3	24	13	12	15	27
1998—	Seattle (A.L.)	4	6	.400	6.48	53	6	0	0	0	83 1/3	85	67	60	55	89
1999—	Philadelphia (N.L.)■	0	3	.000	15.09	5	3	0	0	0	11 1/3	23	24	19	7	10
	— Toronto (A.L.)■	2	2	.500	4.65	37	2	0	0	0	62	62	41	32	32	63
2000—	Omaha (PCL)■	1	2	.333	2.82	43	0	0	0	7	51	44	17	16	19	56
	— Kansas City (A.L.)	0	0	...	6.52	13	0	0	0	0	9 2/3	9	7	7	5	6
	A.L. totals (6 years)	8	14	.364	5.11	190	9	0	0	4	266	252	172	151	156	268
	N.L. totals (1 year)	0	3	.000	15.09	5	3	0	0	0	11 1/3	23	24	19	7	10
	Major League totals (6 years)	8	17	.320	5.52	195	12	0	0	4	277 1/3	275	196	170	163	278

DIVISION SERIES RECORD

Year	League	W	L	Pct.	ERA	G	GS	CG	ShO	Sv.	IP	H	R	ER	BB	SO
1997—	Seattle (A.L.)	0	0	...	0.00	2	0	0	0	0	1 2/3	4	0	0	0	1

PERSONAL: Born June 14, 1967, in Fullerton, Calif. ... 6-7/260. ... Throws right, bats both. ... Full name: Jerry Carl Spradlin.
HIGH SCHOOL: Katella (Anaheim).
COLLEGE: Fullerton (Calif.) College.
TRANSACTIONS/CAREER NOTES: Selected by Cincinnati Reds organization in 19th round of free-agent draft (June 1, 1988). ... Claimed on waivers by Florida Marlins (August 4, 1994). ... Granted free agency (October 16, 1995). ... Signed by Reds orgnization (February 11, 1996). ... On Indianapolis disabled list (May 24-June 1, 1996). ... Released by Reds (October 30, 1996). ... Signed by Philadelphia Phillies (December 9, 1996). ... Traded by Phillies to Cleveland Indians for P Chad Ogea (November 13, 1998). ... Traded by Indians to San Francisco Giants for OF Dan McKinley and a player to be named later (April 23, 1999); Indians acquired P Josh Santos to complete deal (June 27, 1999). ... Traded by Giants to Kansas City Royals for a player to be named later (December 13, 1999); Giants acquired P Ken Ray to complete deal (January 7, 2000). ... Released by Royals (August 30, 2000). ... Signed by Chicago Cubs (September 8, 2000). ... Released by Cubs (November 27, 2000). ... Signed by Indians organization (January 20, 2001).
RECORDS: Shares major league single-inning record for most strikeouts—4 (July 22, 2000, seventh inning).
HONORS: Named Southern League co-Most Valuable Pitcher (1992).

Year League	W	L	Pct.	ERA	G	GS	CG	ShO	Sv.	IP	H	R	ER	BB	SO
1988—Billings (Pio.)	4	1	.800	3.21	17	5	0	0	0	47 2/3	45	25	17	14	23
1989—Greensboro (S.Atl.)	7	2	.778	2.76	42	1	0	0	2	94 2/3	88	35	29	23	56
1990—Cedar Rapids (Midw.)	0	1	.000	3.00	5	0	0	0	0	12	13	8	4	5	6
—Charleston, W.Va. (S.Atl.)	3	4	.429	2.54	43	1	1	0	17	74 1/3	74	23	21	17	39
1991—Chattanooga (Sou.)	7	3	.700	3.09	48	1	0	0	4	96	95	38	33	32	73
1992—Chattanooga (Sou.)	3	3	.500	1.38	59	0	0	0	*34	65 1/3	52	11	10	13	35
—Cedar Rapids (Midw.)	1	0	1.000	7.71	1	0	0	0	0	2 1/3	5	2	2	0	4
1993—Indianapolis (A.A.)	3	2	.600	3.49	34	0	0	0	1	56 2/3	58	24	22	12	46
—Cincinnati (N.L.)	2	1	.667	3.49	37	0	0	0	2	49	44	20	19	9	24
1994—Indianapolis (A.A.)	3	3	.500	3.68	28	5	0	0	3	73 1/3	87	36	30	16	49
—Cincinnati (N.L.)	0	0	...	10.13	6	0	0	0	0	8	12	11	9	2	4
—Edmonton (PCL)■	1	0	1.000	2.53	6	0	0	0	1	10 2/3	12	3	3	4	3
1995—Charlotte (I.L.)	3	3	.500	3.03	41	0	0	0	1	59 1/3	59	26	20	15	38
1996—Indianapolis (A.A.)■	6	8	.429	3.33	49	8	0	0	15	100	94	49	37	23	79
—Cincinnati (N.L.)	0	0	...	0.00	1	0	0	0	0	1/3	0	0	0	0	0
1997—Philadelphia (N.L.)■	4	8	.333	4.74	76	0	0	0	1	81 2/3	86	45	43	27	67
1998—Philadelphia (N.L.)■	4	4	.500	3.53	69	0	0	0	1	81 2/3	63	34	32	20	76
1999—Cleveland (A.L.)■	0	0	...	18.00	4	0	0	0	0	3	6	6	6	3	2
—San Francisco (N.L.)■	3	1	.750	4.19	59	0	0	0	0	58	59	31	27	29	52
2000—Kansas City (A.L.)■	4	4	.500	5.52	50	0	0	0	7	75	81	49	46	27	54
—Chicago (N.L.)■	0	1	.000	8.40	8	1	0	0	0	15	20	15	14	5	13
A.L. totals (2 years)	4	4	.500	6.00	54	0	0	0	7	78	87	55	52	30	56
N.L. totals (7 years)	13	15	.464	4.41	256	1	0	0	0	293 2/3	284	156	144	92	236
Major League totals (7 years)	17	19	.472	4.75	310	1	0	0	11	371 2/3	371	211	196	122	292

PERSONAL: Born July 25, 1967, in Castro Valley, Calif. ... 6-2/205. ... Bats right, throws right. ... Full name: Edward Nelson Sprague Jr. ... Son of Ed Sprague, major league pitcher with four teams (1968-69 and 1971-76); and husband of Kristen Babb, Olympic gold-medal synchronized swimmer (1992).
HIGH SCHOOL: St. Mary's (Stockton, Calif.).
COLLEGE: Stanford.
TRANSACTIONS/CAREER NOTES: Selected by Boston Red Sox organization in 26th round of free-agent draft (June 3, 1985); did not sign. ... Selected by Toronto Blue Jays organization in first round (25th pick overall) of free-agent draft (June 1, 1988). ... On suspended list (August 8-10, 1993). ... On disabled list (September 4-28, 1997). ... Traded by Blue Jays to Oakland Athletics for P Scott Rivette (July 31, 1998). ... Granted free agency (October 27, 1998). ... Signed by Pittsburgh Pirates (December 16, 1998). ... On disabled list (September 20, 1999-remainder of season). ... Granted free agency (October 29, 1999). ... Signed by San Diego Padres organization (February 3, 2000). ... Traded by Padres to Red Sox for P Dennis Tankersly and IF Cesar Saba (June 30, 2000). ... Released by Red Sox (August 23, 2000). ... Re-signed by Padres organization (August 31, 2000). ... Granted free agency (October 31, 2000). ... Re-signed by Padres organization (December 7, 2000).
STATISTICAL NOTES: Led International League third basemen with 31 errors and 364 total chances and tied for lead with 240 assists in 1990. ... Led A.L. in grounding into double plays with 23 in 1993. ... Led A.L. third basemen with 98 putouts in 1994 and 133 in 1995. ... Led A.L. in being hit by pitch with 15 in 1995. ... Led N.L. in being hit by pitch with 17 in 1999. ... Career major league grand slams: 4.
MISCELLANEOUS: Member of 1988 U.S. Olympic baseball team.

Year Team (League)	Pos.	G	AB	R	H	2B	3B	HR	RBI	Avg.	BB	SO	SB	PO	A	E	Avg.
1989—Dunedin (FSL)	3B	52	192	21	42	9	2	7	23	.219	16	40	1	33	86	14	.895
—Syracuse (I.L.)	3B	86	288	23	60	14	1	5	33	.208	18	73	0	51	149	*25	.889
1990—Syracuse (I.L.)	3B-1B-C	142	*519	60	124	23	5	20	75	.239	31	100	4	171	‡246	†35	.923
1991—Syracuse (I.L.)	C-3B	23	88	24	32	8	0	5	25	.364	10	21	2	111	17	6	.955
—Toronto (A.L.)	3B-1B-C-DH	61	160	17	44	7	0	4	20	.275	19	43	0	167	72	14	.945
1992—Syracuse (I.L.)	C-1B-3B	100	369	49	102	18	2	16	50	.276	44	73	0	438	44	12	.976
—Toronto (A.L.)	C-1B-DH-3B	22	47	6	11	2	0	1	7	.234	3	7	0	82	5	1	.989
1993—Toronto (A.L.)	3B	150	546	50	142	31	1	12	73	.260	32	85	1	*127	232	17	.955
1994—Toronto (A.L.)	3B-1B	109	405	38	97	19	1	11	44	.240	23	95	1	†117	147	14	.950
1995—Toronto (A.L.)	3B-1B-DH	144	521	77	127	27	2	18	74	.244	58	96	0	†167	234	17	.959
1996—Toronto (A.L.)	3B-DH	159	591	88	146	35	2	36	101	.247	60	146	0	108	218	15	.956
1997—Toronto (A.L.)	3B-DH	138	504	63	115	29	4	14	48	.228	51	102	0	106	202	18	.945
1998—Toronto (A.L.)	3B	105	382	49	91	20	0	17	51	.238	24	73	0	87	157	20	.924
—Oakland (A.L.)■	3B-1B	27	87	8	13	5	0	3	7	.149	2	17	1	24	37	6	.910
1999—Pittsburgh (N.L.)■	3B	137	490	71	131	27	2	22	81	.267	50	93	3	79	254	*29	.920
2000—San Diego (N.L.)■	1B-3B-OF-2B	73	157	19	41	12	0	10	27	.261	33	40	0	194	21	7	.968
—Rancho Cuca. (Calif.)	2B	2	7	1	2	0	0	1	2	.286	1	0	0	6	0		1.000
—Boston (A.L.)■	3B-1B-DH	33	111	11	24	4	0	2	9	.216	12	18	0	36	54	2	.978
American League totals (9 years)		948	3354	407	810	179	10	118	434	.242	284	682	3	1021	1358	124	.950
National League totals (2 years)		210	647	90	172	39	2	32	108	.266	63	133	3	273	275	36	.938
Major League totals (10 years)		1158	4001	497	982	218	12	150	542	.245	347	815	6	1294	1633	160	.948

Year	Team (League)	Pos.	G	AB	R	H	2B	3B	HR	RBI	Avg.	BB	SO	SB	PO	A	E	Avg.
1991— Toronto (A.L.)						Did not play.												
1992— Toronto (A.L.).............	PH	2	2	0	1	0	0	0	0	.500	0	1	0	...	...	...	...
1993— Toronto (A.L.).............	3B	6	21	0	6	0	1	0	4	.286	2	4	0	5	9	0	1.000
Championship series totals (2 years)		8	23	0	7	0	1	0	4	.304	2	5	0	5	9	0	1.000

WORLD SERIES RECORD

NOTES: Hit home run in first at-bat (October 18, 1992). ... Member of World Series championship team (1992 and 1993).

Year	Team (League)	Pos.	G	AB	R	H	2B	3B	HR	RBI	Avg.	BB	SO	SB	PO	A	E	Avg.
1992— Toronto (A.L.).............	PH-1B	3	2	1	1	0	0	1	2	.500	1	0	0	0	0	0	...
1993— Toronto (A.L.).............	3B-PH-1B	5	15	0	1	0	0	0	2	.067	1	6	0	4	9	2	.867
World Series totals (2 years)		8	17	1	2	0	0	1	4	.118	2	6	0	4	9	2	.867

ALL-STAR GAME RECORD

Year	League	Pos.	AB	R	H	2B	3B	HR	RBI	Avg.	BB	SO	SB	PO	A	E	Avg.
1999— National	3B	1	0	0	0	0	0	0	.000	0	0	0	0	0	0	...

SPRINGER, DENNIS   P

PERSONAL: Born February 12, 1965, in Fresno, Calif. ... 5-10/185. ... Throws right, bats both. ... Full name: Dennis LeRoy Springer.
HIGH SCHOOL: Washington (Fresno, Calif.).
JUNIOR COLLEGE: Kings River Community College (Calif.).
COLLEGE: Fresno State.
TRANSACTIONS/CAREER NOTES: Selected by Los Angeles Dodgers organization in 21st round of free-agent draft (June 2, 1987). ... On San Antonio disabled list (April 19-27, 1992). ... On disabled list (August 24-September 6, 1993). ... Granted free agency (October 15, 1993). ... Signed by Philadelphia Phillies organization (May 19, 1994). ... Granted free agency (December 21, 1995). ... Signed by California Angels organization (January 5, 1996). ... Angels franchise renamed Anaheim Angels for 1997 season. ... Selected by Tampa Bay Devil Rays in first round (26th pick overall) of expansion draft (November 18, 1997). ... Released by Devil Rays (November 3, 1998). ... Signed by Florida Marlins organization (January 29, 1999). ... Granted free agency (October 6, 1999). ... Signed by New York Mets organization (February 4, 2000). ... Granted free agency (October 18, 2000).

Year	League	W	L	Pct.	ERA	G	GS	CG	ShO	Sv.	IP	H	R	ER	BB	SO
1987— Great Falls (Pio.)		4	3	.571	2.88	23	5	1	0	6	65 2/3	70	38	21	16	54
1988— Bakersfield (Calif.)		13	7	.650	3.27	32	20	6	•4	2	154	135	75	56	62	108
1989— San Antonio (Texas).........		6	8	.429	3.15	19	19	4	1	0	140	128	58	49	46	89
—Albuquerque (PCL)............		4	1	.800	4.83	8	7	0	0	0	41	58	28	22	14	18
1990— San Antonio (Texas).........		8	6	.571	3.31	24	24	3	0	0	*163 1/3	147	76	60	73	77
1991— San Antonio (Texas).........		10	10	.500	4.43	30	24	2	0	0	164 2/3	153	96	81	91	*138
1992— San Antonio (Texas).........		6	7	.462	4.35	18	18	4	0	0	122	114	61	59	49	73
—Albuquerque (PCL)............		2	7	.222	5.66	11	11	1	0	0	62	70	45	39	22	36
1993— Albuquerque (PCL)............		3	8	.273	5.99	35	18	0	0	0	130 2/3	173	104	87	39	69
1994— Reading (East.)■		5	8	.385	3.40	24	19	2	0	2	135	125	74	51	44	118
1995— Scranton/W.B. (I.L.)		10	11	.476	4.68	30	23	4	0	0	171	163	*101	89	47	115
—Philadelphia (N.L.)............		0	3	.000	4.84	4	4	0	0	0	22 1/3	21	15	12	9	15
1996— California (A.L.)■............		5	6	.455	5.51	20	15	2	1	0	94 2/3	91	65	58	43	64
—Vancouver (PCL)		10	3	.769	2.72	16	12	6	0	0	109 1/3	89	35	33	36	78
1997— Anaheim (A.L.)		9	9	.500	5.18	32	28	3	1	0	194 2/3	199	118	112	73	75
—Vancouver (PCL)		1	1	.500	3.00	2	2	2	0	0	15	12	6	5	6	7
1998— Tampa Bay (A.L.)■..........		3	11	.214	5.45	29	17	1	0	0	115 2/3	120	77	70	60	46
—Durham (I.L.)		2	3	.400	2.87	5	5	0	0	0	37 2/3	34	13	12	15	23
1999— Florida (N.L.)■................		6	16	.273	4.86	38	29	3	2	1	196 1/3	231	121	106	64	83
2000— Norfolk (I.L.)■		5	5	.500	4.38	25	17	1	1	0	117	120	65	57	35	35
—New York (N.L.)................		0	1	.000	8.74	2	2	0	0	0	11 1/3	20	11	11	5	5
A.L. totals (3 years)		17	26	.395	5.33	81	60	6	2	0	405	410	260	240	176	185
N.L. totals (3 years)		6	20	.231	5.05	44	35	3	2	1	230	272	147	129	78	103
Major League totals (6 years)		23	46	.333	5.23	125	95	9	4	1	635	682	407	369	254	288

SPRINGER, RUSS   P   DIAMONDBACKS

PERSONAL: Born November 7, 1968, in Alexandria, La. ... 6-4/205. ... Throws right, bats right. ... Full name: Russell Paul Springer.
HIGH SCHOOL: Grant (Dry Prong, La.).
COLLEGE: Louisiana State.
TRANSACTIONS/CAREER NOTES: Selected by New York Yankees organization in seventh round of free-agent draft (June 5, 1989). ... Traded by Yankees with 1B J.T. Snow and P Jerry Nielsen to California Angels for P Jim Abbott (December 6, 1992). ... On California disabled list (August 2, 1993-remainder of season). ... Traded by Angels to Philadelphia Phillies (August 15, 1995), completing deal in which Phillies traded OF Dave Gallagher to Angels for 2B Kevin Flora and a player to be named later (August 9, 1995). ... Released by Phillies (December 20, 1996). ... Signed by Houston Astros organization (December 30, 1996). ... On Houston disabled list (June 17-July 10, 1997); included rehabilitation assignment to Jackson (July 8-10). ... Selected by Arizona Diamondbacks in third round (61st pick overall) of expansion draft (November 18, 1997). ... Traded by Diamondbacks to Atlanta Braves for P Alan Embree (June 23, 1998). ... On Atlanta disabled list (August 6-21, 1998). ... On Atlanta disabled list (April 3-May 17, 1999); included rehabilitation assignment to Richmond (April 20-May 16). ... Granted free agency (November 2, 1999). ... Signed by Diamondbacks (December 3, 1999).

Year	League	W	L	Pct.	ERA	G	GS	CG	ShO	Sv.	IP	H	R	ER	BB	SO
1989— Gulf Coast Yankees (GCL)..		3	0	1.000	1.50	6	6	0	0	0	24	14	8	4	10	34
1990— Gulf Coast Yankees (GCL)..		0	2	.000	1.20	4	4	0	0	0	15	10	6	2	4	17
—Greensboro (S.Atl.)		2	3	.400	3.67	10	10	0	0	0	56 1/3	51	33	23	31	51
1991— Fort Lauderdale (FSL)		5	9	.357	3.49	25	25	2	0	0	152 1/3	118	68	59	62	139
—Albany/Colonie (East.)........		1	0	1.000	1.80	2	2	0	0	0	15	9	4	3	6	16

Year League	W	L	Pct.	ERA	G	GS	CG	ShO	Sv.	IP	H	R	ER	BB	SO
1992—Columbus (I.L.)	8	5	.615	2.69	20	20	1	0	0	123 2/3	89	46	37	54	95
—New York (A.L.)	0	0	...	6.19	14	0	0	0	0	16	18	11	11	10	12
1993—Vancouver (PCL)■	5	4	.556	4.27	11	9	1	0	0	59	58	37	28	33	40
—California (A.L.)	1	6	.143	7.20	14	9	1	0	0	60	73	48	48	32	31
1994—Vancouver (PCL)	7	4	.636	3.04	12	12	•4	0	0	83	77	35	28	19	58
—California (A.L.)	2	2	.500	5.52	18	5	0	0	2	45 2/3	53	28	28	14	28
1995—Vancouver (PCL)	2	0	1.000	3.44	6	6	0	0	0	34	24	16	13	23	23
—California (A.L.)	1	2	.333	6.10	19	6	0	0	1	51 2/3	60	37	35	25	38
—Philadelphia (N.L.)■	0	0	...	3.71	14	0	0	0	0	26 2/3	22	11	11	10	32
1996—Philadelphia (N.L.)	3	10	.231	4.66	51	7	0	0	0	96 2/3	106	60	50	38	94
1997—Houston (N.L.)■	3	3	.500	4.23	54	0	0	0	3	55 1/3	48	28	26	27	74
—Jackson (Texas)	0	0	...	9.00	1	0	0	0	0	1	2	1	1	0	2
1998—Arizona (N.L.)■	4	3	.571	4.13	26	0	0	0	0	32 2/3	29	16	15	14	37
—Atlanta (N.L.)■	1	1	.500	4.05	22	0	0	0	0	20	22	10	9	16	19
1999—Richmond (I.L.)	1	0	1.000	1.17	11	0	0	0	2	15 1/3	9	2	2	1	13
—Atlanta (N.L.)	2	1	.667	3.42	49	0	0	0	1	47 1/3	31	20	18	22	49
2000—Arizona (N.L.)■	2	4	.333	5.08	52	0	0	0	0	62	63	36	35	34	59
A.L. totals (4 years)	4	10	.286	6.33	65	20	1	0	3	173 1/3	204	124	122	81	109
N.L. totals (6 years)	15	22	.405	4.33	268	7	0	0	4	340 2/3	321	181	164	161	364
Major League totals (9 years)	19	32	.373	5.01	333	27	1	0	7	514	525	305	286	242	473

DIVISION SERIES RECORD

Year League	W	L	Pct.	ERA	G	GS	CG	ShO	Sv.	IP	H	R	ER	BB	SO
1997—Houston (N.L.)	0	0	...	5.40	2	0	0	0	0	1 2/3	2	1	1	1	3
1998—Atlanta (N.L.)				Did not play.											
1999—Atlanta (N.L.)	0	0	...	0.00	1	0	0	0	0	1	2	0	0	1	1
Division series totals (2 years)	0	0	...	3.38	3	0	0	0	0	2 2/3	4	1	1	2	4

CHAMPIONSHIP SERIES RECORD

Year League	W	L	Pct.	ERA	G	GS	CG	ShO	Sv.	IP	H	R	ER	BB	SO
1998—Atlanta (N.L.)				Did not play.											
1999—Atlanta (N.L.)	1	0	1.000	0.00	2	0	0	0	0	2	0	0	0	1	1

WORLD SERIES RECORD

Year League	W	L	Pct.	ERA	G	GS	CG	ShO	Sv.	IP	H	R	ER	BB	SO
1999—Atlanta (N.L.)	0	0	...	0.00	2	0	0	0	0	2 1/3	1	0	0	0	1

SPURGEON, JAY   P   ORIOLES

PERSONAL: Born July 5, 1976, in West Covina, Calif. ... 6-6/210. ... Throws right, bats right. ... Full name: Jay Aaron Spurgeon.
HIGH SCHOOL: Yosemite (Oakhurst, Calif.).
COLLEGE: Hawaii.
TRANSACTIONS/CAREER NOTES: Selected by Houston Astros organization in 46th round of free-agent draft (June 2, 1994); did not sign. ... Selected by Baltimore Orioles organization eighth round of free-agent draft (June 3, 1997).

Year League	W	L	Pct.	ERA	G	GS	CG	ShO	Sv.	IP	H	R	ER	BB	SO
1997—Bluefield (Appl.)	1	1	.500	3.34	9	7	0	0	0	35	35	13	13	14	32
1998—Delmarva (S.Atl.)	11	3	.786	2.64	27	20	0	0	0	136 1/3	112	49	40	48	103
1999—Frederick (Caro.)	6	9	.400	4.75	26	26	1	0	0	146	176	99	77	53	87
2000—Frederick (Caro.)	8	2	.800	4.12	16	15	1	0	0	91 2/3	75	47	42	31	92
—Bowie (East.)	3	1	.750	1.62	6	6	2	1	0	39	32	10	7	7	27
—Rochester (I.L.)	2	0	1.000	0.66	2	2	0	0	0	13 2/3	5	1	1	9	10
—Baltimore (A.L.)	1	1	.500	6.00	7	4	0	0	0	24	26	16	16	15	11
Major League totals (1 year)	1	1	.500	6.00	7	4	0	0	0	24	26	16	16	15	11

STAIRS, MATT   OF   CUBS

PERSONAL: Born February 27, 1968, in Saint John, N.B. ... 5-9/217. ... Bats left, throws right. ... Full name: Matthew Wade Stairs.
HIGH SCHOOL: Fredericton (N.B.).
TRANSACTIONS/CAREER NOTES: Signed as non-drafted free agent by Montreal Expos organization (January 17, 1989). ... On disabled list (May 16-23, 1991). ... On Ottawa disabled list (May 7-18, 1993). ... Contract sold by Expos to Chunichi Dragons of Japan Central League (June 8, 1993). ... Signed by Expos organization (December 15, 1993). ... Traded by Expos with P Pete Young to Boston Red Sox for cash (February 18, 1994). ... Granted free agency (October 14, 1995). ... Signed by Oakland Athletics organization (December 1, 1995). ... Traded by A's to Chicago Cubs for P Eric Ireland (November 20, 2000).
HONORS: Named Eastern League Most Valuable Player (1991).
STATISTICAL NOTES: Led Eastern League with .509 slugging percentage, 257 total bases and tied for lead with eight intentional bases on balls received in 1991. ... Career major league grand slams: 7.
MISCELLANEOUS: Member of 1988 Canadian Olympic baseball team.

Year Team (League)	Pos.	G	AB	R	H	2B	3B	HR	RBI	Avg.	BB	SO	SB	PO	A	E	Avg.
1989—W.P. Beach (FSL)	3B-SS-2B	36	111	12	21	3	1	1	9	.189	9	18	0	21	66	4	.956
—Jamestown (NY-P)	2B-3B	14	43	8	11	1	0	1	5	.256	3	5	1	15	35	6	.893
—Rockford (Midw.)	3B	44	141	20	40	9	2	2	14	.284	15	29	5	30	62	7	.929
1990—W.P. Beach (FSL)	3B-2B	55	183	30	62	9	3	3	30	.339	41	19	15	40	112	17	.899
—Jacksonville (Sou.)	3B-OF-2B-SS	79	280	26	71	17	0	3	34	.254	22	43	5	76	107	22	.893
1991—Harrisburg (East.)	2B-3B-OF	129	505	87	*168	30	•10	13	78	*.333	66	47	23	193	314	22	.958
1992—Indianapolis (A.A.)	OF	110	401	57	107	23	4	11	56	.267	49	61	11	188	11	3	.985
—Montreal (N.L.)	OF	13	30	2	5	2	0	0	5	.167	7	7	0	14	0	1	.933
1993—Ottawa (I.L.)	OF	34	125	18	35	4	2	3	20	.280	11	15	4	49	4	0	1.000
—Montreal (N.L.)	OF	6	8	1	3	1	0	0	2	.375	0	1	0	1	0	0	1.000
—Chunichi (Jap. Cen.)■		60	132	10	33	6	0	6	23	.250	7	34	1	...	...	...	...

Year	Team (League)	Pos.	G	AB	R	H	2B	3B	HR	RBI	Avg.	BB	SO	SB	PO	A	E	Avg.
							BATTING									FIELDING		
1994—	New Britain (East.)■..	OF-DH-1B	93	317	44	98	25	2	9	61	.309	53	38	10	106	12	3	.975
1995—	Pawtucket (I.L.).........	OF-DH	75	271	40	77	17	0	13	56	.284	29	41	3	79	13	0	1.000
	—Boston (A.L.)............	OF-DH	39	88	8	23	7	1	1	17	.261	4	14	0	19	2	2	.913
1996—	Oakland (A.L.)■........	OF-DH-1B	61	137	21	38	5	1	10	23	.277	19	23	1	65	11	1	.987
	—Edmonton (PCL)	DH-OF-1B	51	180	35	62	16	1	8	41	.344	21	34	0	49	2	3	.944
1997—	Oakland (A.L.)	OF-DH-1B	133	352	62	105	19	0	27	73	.298	50	60	3	142	9	4	.974
1998—	Oakland (A.L.)	DH-OF-1B	149	523	88	154	33	1	26	106	.294	59	93	8	67	11	0	1.000
1999—	Oakland (A.L.)	OF-DH-1B	146	531	94	137	26	3	38	102	.258	89	124	2	247	13	5	.981
2000—	Oakland (A.L.)	OF-DH-1B	143	476	74	108	26	0	21	81	.227	78	122	5	187	5	4	.980
American League totals (6 years)			671	2107	347	565	116	6	123	402	.268	299	436	19	727	51	16	.980
National League totals (2 years)			19	38	3	8	3	0	0	7	.211	7	8	0	15	0	1	.938
Major League totals (8 years)			690	2145	350	573	119	6	123	409	.267	306	444	19	742	51	17	.979

DIVISION SERIES RECORD

Year	Team (League)	Pos.	G	AB	R	H	2B	3B	HR	RBI	Avg.	BB	SO	SB	PO	A	E	Avg.
							BATTING									FIELDING		
1995—	Boston (A.L.).............	PH	1	1	0	0	0	0	0	0	.000	0	1	0	...	...	...	...
2000—	Oakland (A.L.)	OF-PH	3	9	0	1	1	0	0	0	.111	0	1	0	6	0	0	1.000
Division series totals (2 years)			4	10	0	1	1	0	0	0	.100	0	2	0	6	0	0	1.000

STANDRIDGE, JASON   P   DEVIL RAYS

PERSONAL: Born November 9, 1978, in Birmingham, Ala. ... 6-4/217. ... Throws right, bats right. ... Full name: Jason Wayne Standridge.
HIGH SCHOOL: Hewitt-Trussville (Ala.).
TRANSACTIONS/CAREER NOTES: Selected by Tampa Bay Devil Rays organization in first round (31st pick overall) of free-agent draft (June 3, 1997).
HONORS: Named South Atlantic League Most Valuable Pitcher (1999).

Year	League	W	L	Pct.	ERA	G	GS	CG	ShO	Sv.	IP	H	R	ER	BB	SO
1997—	GC Devil Rays (GCL)	0	6	.000	3.59	13	13	0	0	0	57 2/3	56	30	23	13	55
1998—	Prince William (Caro.)	4	4	.500	7.00	12	12	0	0	0	63	82	61	49	28	47
1999—	Charleston, S.C. (S.Atl.)	9	1	.900	*2.02	18	18	3	*3	0	116	80	35	26	31	84
	—St. Petersburg (FSL)	4	4	.500	3.91	8	8	0	0	0	48 1/3	49	21	21	20	26
2000—	St. Petersburg (FSL)	2	4	.333	3.38	10	10	1	0	0	56	45	28	21	31	41
	—Orlando (Sou.)	6	8	.429	3.62	17	17	2	0	0	97	85	46	39	43	55

STANIFER, ROB   P   CUBS

PERSONAL: Born March 10, 1972, in Easley, S.C. ... 6-3/205. ... Throws right, bats right. ... Full name: Robert Wayne Stanifer.
HIGH SCHOOL: Easley (S.C.).
COLLEGE: Anderson (S.C.); degree in sports administration, 1994.
TRANSACTIONS/CAREER NOTES: Selected by Florida Marlins organization in 12th round of free-agent draft (June 2, 1994). ... Traded by Marlins to Boston Red Sox for P Brian Partenheimer (May 31, 1999). ... Released by Red Sox (November 20, 2000). ... Signed by Chicago Cubs organization (December 13, 2000).

Year	League	W	L	Pct.	ERA	G	GS	CG	ShO	Sv.	IP	H	R	ER	BB	SO
1994—	Elmira (NY-Penn)	2	1	.667	2.57	9	8	1	0	0	49	54	17	14	12	38
	—Brevard County (FSL)........	1	2	.333	6.29	5	5	0	0 .	0	24 1/3	32	20	17	10	12
1995—	Brevard County (FSL)........	3	6	.333	4.14	18	13	0	0	0	82 2/3	97	47	38	15	45
1996—	Brevard County (FSL)........	4	2	.667	2.39	22	0	0	0	0	49	54	17	13	9	32
	—Portland (East.)	3	1	.750	1.57	18	0	0	0	2	34 1/3	27	15	6	9	33
1997—	Charlotte (I.L.)....................	4	0	1.000	4.88	22	0	0	0	5	27 2/3	34	16	15	7	25
	—Florida (N.L.).....................	1	2	.333	4.60	36	0	0	0	1	45	43	23	23	16	28
1998—	Charlotte (I.L.)....................	4	2	.667	4.31	21	1	0	0	4	39 2/3	39	20	19	13	29
	—Florida (N.L.).....................	2	4	.333	5.63	38	0	0	0	1	48	54	33	30	22	30
1999—	Calgary (PCL).....................	1	2	.333	12.38	16	0	0	0	0	16	32	23	22	6	15
	—Trenton (East.)■................	0	0	...	0.00	5	0	0	0	1	9	6	0	0	4	11
	—Pawtucket (I.L.).................	3	1	.750	2.04	31	0	0	0	3	39 2/3	34	21	9	15	29
2000—	Pawtucket (I.L.).................	3	4	.429	1.89	41	0	0	0	16	52 1/3	40	13	11	20	42
	—Boston (A.L.)....................	0	0	...	7.62	8	0	0	0	0	13	22	19	11	4	3
A.L. totals (1 year)		0	0	...	7.62	8	0	0	0	0	13	22	19	11	4	3
N.L. totals (2 years)		3	6	.333	5.13	74	0	0	0	2	93	97	56	53	38	58
Major League totals (3 years)		3	6	.333	5.43	82	0	0	0	2	106	119	75	64	42	61

STANLEY, MIKE   DH/1B

PERSONAL: Born June 25, 1963, in Fort Lauderdale, Fla. ... 6-0/205. ... Bats right, throws right. ... Full name: Michael Robert Stanley.
HIGH SCHOOL: St. Thomas Aquinas (Fort Lauderdale, Fla.).
COLLEGE: Florida.
TRANSACTIONS/CAREER NOTES: Selected by Texas Rangers organization in 16th round of free-agent draft (June 3, 1985). ... On disabled list (July 24-August 14, 1988; and August 18-September 2, 1989). ... Granted free agency (November 15, 1990). ... Re-signed by Rangers organization (February 4, 1991). ... Granted free agency (October 14, 1991). ... Signed by New York Yankees (January 21, 1992). ... On disabled list (May 14-29, 1994). ... Granted free agency (November 1, 1995). ... Signed by Boston Red Sox (December 14, 1995). ... Traded by Red Sox with IF Randy Brown to Yankees for P Tony Armas Jr. and a player to be named later (August 13, 1997); Red Sox acquired P Jim Mecir to complete deal (September 29, 1997). ... Granted free agency (October 27, 1997). ... Signed by Toronto Blue Jays (December 8, 1997). ... Traded by Blue Jays to Red Sox for P Peter Munro and P Jay Yennaco (July 30, 1998). ... On disabled list (July 3-23, 2000). ... Released by Red Sox (July 31, 2000). ... Signed by Oakland Athletics (August 4, 2000). ... Granted free agency (October 30, 2000).
HONORS: Named catcher on THE SPORTING NEWS A.L. All-Star team (1993). ... Named catcher on THE SPORTING NEWS A.L. Silver Slugger team (1993).
STATISTICAL NOTES: Hit three home runs in one game (August 10, 1995, first game). ... Led A.L. catchers with 18 passed balls in 1996. ... Career major league grand slams: 8.

S

Year	Team (League)	Pos.	G	AB	R	H	2B	3B	HR	RBI	Avg.	BB	SO	SB	PO	A	E	Avg.
								BATTING								FIELDING		
1985— Salem (Caro.)	1B-C	4	9	2	5	0	0	0	3	.556	1	1	0	19	1	1	.952
— Burlington (Midw.)	C-1B-OF	13	42	8	13	2	0	1	6	.310	6	5	0	45	2	0	1.000
— Tulsa (Texas)	C-1B-OF-2B	46	165	24	51	10	0	3	17	.309	24	18	6	289	18	6	.981
1986— Tulsa (Texas)	C-1B-3B	67	235	41	69	16	2	6	35	.294	34	26	5	379	45	2	.995
— Texas (A.L.)	3B-C-DH-OF	15	30	4	10	3	0	1	1	.333	3	7	1	14	8	1	.957
— Oklahoma City (A.A.)	C-3B-1B	56	202	37	74	13	3	5	49	.366	44	42	1	206	55	9	.967
1987— Oklahoma City (A.A.)	C-1B	46	182	43	61	8	3	13	54	.335	29	36	2	277	32	2	.994
— Texas (A.L.)	C-1B-DH-OF	78	216	34	59	8	1	6	37	.273	31	48	3	389	26	7	.983
1988— Texas (A.L.)	C-DH-1B-3B	94	249	21	57	8	0	3	27	.229	37	62	0	342	17	4	.989
1989— Texas (A.L.)	C-DH-1B-3B	67	122	9	30	3	1	1	11	.246	12	29	1	117	8	3	.977
1990— Texas (A.L.)	C-DH-3B-1B	103	189	21	47	8	1	2	19	.249	30	25	1	261	25	4	.986
1991— Texas (A.L.)	C-1-3-DH-O	95	181	25	45	13	1	3	25	.249	34	44	0	288	20	6	.981
1992— New York (A.L.)■	C-DH-1B	68	173	24	43	7	0	8	27	.249	33	45	0	287	30	6	.981
1993— New York (A.L.)	C-DH	130	423	70	129	17	1	26	84	.305	57	85	1	652	46	3	*.996
1994— New York (A.L.)	C-1B-DH	82	290	54	87	20	0	17	57	.300	39	56	0	442	35	5	.990
1995— New York (A.L.)	C-DH	118	399	63	107	29	1	18	83	.268	57	106	1	651	35	5	.993
1996— Boston (A.L.)■	C-DH	121	397	73	107	20	1	24	69	.270	69	62	2	654	19	•10	.985
1997— Boston (A.L.)	DH-1B-C	97	260	45	78	17	0	13	53	.300	39	50	0	284	21	2	.993
— New York (A.L.)■	DH-1B	28	87	16	25	8	0	3	12	.287	15	22	0	71	3	0	1.000
1998— Toronto (A.L.)■	DH-1B-OF	98	341	49	82	13	0	22	47	.240	56	86	2	172	12	1	.995
— Boston (A.L.)■	DH-1B	47	156	25	45	12	0	7	32	.288	26	43	1	108	6	0	1.000
1999— Boston (A.L.)	1B-DH	136	427	59	120	22	0	19	72	.281	70	94	0	830	60	11	.988
2000— Boston (A.L.)	1B-DH	58	185	22	41	5	0	10	28	.222	30	44	0	264	31	1	.997
— Oakland (A.L.)■	1B-DH	32	97	11	26	7	0	4	18	.268	14	21	0	146	13	2	.988
Major League totals (15 years)		1467	4222	625	1138	220	7	187	702	.270	652	929	13	5972	415	71	.989

DIVISION SERIES RECORD

RECORDS: Shares single-game records for most at-bats (nine-inning game)—6; and hits—5 (October 10, 1999). ... Shares single-inning record for most at-bats—2 (October 10, 1999, second inning).

Year	Team (League)	Pos.	G	AB	R	H	2B	3B	HR	RBI	Avg.	BB	SO	SB	PO	A	E	Avg.
								BATTING								FIELDING		
1995— New York (A.L.)	C	4	16	2	5	0	0	1	3	.313	2	1	0	30	0	1	.968
1997— New York (A.L.)	PH-DH	2	4	1	3	1	0	0	1	.750	0	1	0	...	...	...	...
1998— Boston (A.L.)	DH	4	15	1	4	0	0	0	0	.267	2	5	0	...	...	...	...
1999— Boston (A.L.)	1B	5	20	4	10	2	1	0	2	.500	2	3	0	38	6	0	1.000
2000— Oakland (A.L.)										Did not play.							
Division series totals (4 years)		15	55	8	22	3	1	1	6	.400	6	10	0	68	6	1	.987

CHAMPIONSHIP SERIES RECORD

Year	Team (League)	Pos.	G	AB	R	H	2B	3B	HR	RBI	Avg.	BB	SO	SB	PO	A	E	Avg.
								BATTING								FIELDING		
1999— Boston (A.L.)	1B	5	18	1	4	0	0	0	1	.222	2	4	0	35	2	1	.974

ALL-STAR GAME RECORD

Year	League	Pos.	AB	R	H	2B	3B	HR	RBI	Avg.	BB	SO	SB	PO	A	E	Avg.
							BATTING								FIELDING		
1995— American	C	1	0	0	0	0	0	0	.000	0	0	0	3	0	0	1.000

STANTON, MIKE   P   YANKEES

PERSONAL: Born June 2, 1967, in Houston. ... 6-1/215. ... Throws left, bats left. ... Full name: William Michael Stanton.
HIGH SCHOOL: Midland (Texas).
JUNIOR COLLEGE: Alvin (Texas) Community College.
TRANSACTIONS/CAREER NOTES: Selected by Atlanta Braves organization in 13th round of free-agent draft (June 2, 1987). ... On Atlanta disabled list (April 27, 1990-remainder of season); included rehabilitation assignments to Greenville (May 31-June 5 and August 21-29). ... Granted free agency (December 23, 1994). ... Re-signed by Braves (April 12, 1995). ... Traded by Braves to Boston Red Sox for two players to be named later (July 31, 1995); Red Sox acquired P Matt Murray and Braves acquired OF Marc Lewis and P Mike Jacobs to complete deal (August 31, 1995). ... Traded by Red Sox to Texas Rangers for P Mark Brandenburg and P Kerry Lacy (July 31, 1996). ... Granted free agency (October 27, 1996). ... Signed by New York Yankees (December 11, 1996). ... On suspended list (July 3-10, 1998). ... Granted free agency (November 5, 1999). ... Re-signed by Yankees (November 29, 1999).

Year	League	W	L	Pct.	ERA	G	GS	CG	ShO	Sv.	IP	H	R	ER	BB	SO
1987— Pulaski (Appl.)	4	8	.333	3.24	15	13	3	2	0	83 1/3	64	37	30	42	82
1988— Burlington (Midw.)	11	5	.688	3.62	30	23	1	1	0	154	154	86	62	69	160
— Durham (Caro.)	1	0	1.000	1.46	2	2	1	1	0	12 1/3	14	3	2	5	14
1989— Greenville (Sou.)	4	1	.800	1.58	47	0	0	0	19	51 1/3	32	10	9	31	58
— Richmond (I.L.)	2	0	1.000	0.00	13	0	0	0	8	20	6	0	0	13	20
— Atlanta (N.L.)	0	1	.000	1.50	20	0	0	0	7	24	17	4	4	8	27
1990— Atlanta (N.L.)	0	3	.000	18.00	7	0	0	0	2	7	16	16	14	4	7
— Greenville (Sou.)	0	1	.000	1.59	4	4	0	0	0	5 2/3	7	1	1	3	4
1991— Atlanta (N.L.)	5	5	.500	2.88	74	0	0	0	7	78	62	27	25	21	54
1992— Atlanta (N.L.)	5	4	.556	4.10	65	0	0	0	8	63 2/3	59	32	29	20	44
1993— Atlanta (N.L.)	4	6	.400	4.67	63	0	0	0	27	52	51	35	27	29	43
1994— Atlanta (N.L.)	3	1	.750	3.55	49	0	0	0	3	45 2/3	41	18	18	26	35
1995— Atlanta (N.L.)	1	1	.500	5.59	26	0	0	0	1	19 1/3	31	14	12	6	13
— Boston (A.L.)■	1	0	1.000	3.00	22	0	0	0	0	21	17	9	7	8	10
1996— Boston (A.L.)■	4	3	.571	3.83	59	0	0	0	1	56 1/3	58	24	24	23	46
— Texas (A.L.)■	0	1	.000	3.22	22	0	0	0	0	22 1/3	20	8	8	4	14

Year League	W	L	Pct.	ERA	G	GS	CG	ShO	Sv.	IP	H	R	ER	BB	SO
1997— New York (A.L.)■	6	1	.857	2.57	64	0	0	0	3	66 2/3	50	19	19	34	70
1998— New York (A.L.)	4	1	.800	5.47	67	0	0	0	6	79	71	51	48	26	69
1999— New York (A.L.)	2	2	.500	4.33	73	1	0	0	0	62 1/3	71	30	30	18	59
2000— New York (A.L.)	2	3	.400	4.10	69	0	0	0	0	68	68	32	31	24	75
A.L. totals (6 years)	19	11	.633	4.00	376	1	0	0	10	375 2/3	355	173	167	137	343
N.L. totals (7 years)	18	21	.462	4.01	304	0	0	0	55	289 2/3	277	146	129	114	223
Major League totals (12 years)	37	32	.536	4.00	680	1	0	0	65	665 1/3	632	319	296	251	566

DIVISION SERIES RECORD

Year League	W	L	Pct.	ERA	G	GS	CG	ShO	Sv.	IP	H	R	ER	BB	SO
1995— Boston (A.L.)	0	0	...	0.00	1	0	0	0	0	2 1/3	1	0	0	0	4
1996— Texas (A.L.)	0	1	.000	2.70	3	0	0	0	0	3 1/3	2	2	1	3	3
1997— New York (A.L.)	0	0	...	0.00	3	0	0	0	0	1	1	0	0	1	3
1998— New York (A.L.)							Did not play.								
1999— New York (A.L.)							Did not play.								
2000— New York (A.L.)	1	0	1.000	2.08	3	0	0	0	0	4 1/3	5	1	1	1	3
Division series totals (4 years)	1	1	.500	1.64	10	0	0	0	0	11	9	3	2	5	13

CHAMPIONSHIP SERIES RECORD

Year League	W	L	Pct.	ERA	G	GS	CG	ShO	Sv.	IP	H	R	ER	BB	SO
1991— Atlanta (N.L.)	0	0	...	2.45	3	0	0	0	0	3 2/3	4	1	1	3	3
1992— Atlanta (N.L.)	0	0	...	0.00	5	0	0	0	0	4 1/3	2	1	0	2	5
1993— Atlanta (N.L.)	0	0	...	0.00	1	0	0	0	0	1	1	0	0	1	0
1998— New York (A.L.)	0	0	...	0.00	3	0	0	0	0	3 2/3	2	0	0	2	4
1999— New York (A.L.)	0	0	...	0.00	3	0	0	0	0	1/3	1	0	0	1	0
2000— New York (A.L.)							Did not play.								
Champ. series totals (5 years)	0	0	...	0.69	15	0	0	0	0	13	10	2	1	9	12

WORLD SERIES RECORD

NOTES: Member of World Series championship team (1998, 1999 and 2000).

Year League	W	L	Pct.	ERA	G	GS	CG	ShO	Sv.	IP	H	R	ER	BB	SO
1991— Atlanta (N.L.)	1	0	1.000	0.00	5	0	0	0	0	7 1/3	5	0	0	2	7
1992— Atlanta (N.L.)	0	0	...	0.00	4	0	0	0	1	5	3	0	0	2	1
1998— New York (A.L.)	0	0	...	27.00	1	0	0	0	0	2/3	3	2	2	0	1
1999— New York (A.L.)	0	0	...	0.00	1	0	0	0	0	1/3	0	0	0	0	1
2000— New York (A.L.)	2	0	1.000	0.00	4	0	0	0	0	4 1/3	0	0	0	0	7
World Series totals (5 years)	3	0	1.000	1.02	15	0	0	0	1	17 2/3	11	2	2	4	17

STARK, DENNIS P MARINERS

PERSONAL: Born October 27, 1974, in Hicksville, Ohio. ... 6-2/210. ... Throws right, bats right.
HIGH SCHOOL: Edgerton (Ohio).
COLLEGE: Toledo.
TRANSACTIONS/CAREER NOTES: Selected by Seattle Mariners organization in fourth round of free-agent draft (June 4, 1996). ... On Lancaster disabled list (April 26, 1998-remainder of season); included rehabilitation assignment to Arizona Mariners (July 30-August 11). ... On New Haven disabled list (May 20-August 30, 2000). ... On Seattle disabled list (August 31, 2000-remainder of season).
STATISTICAL NOTES: Tied for Eastern League lead with four double plays in 2000.

Year League	W	L	Pct.	ERA	G	GS	CG	ShO	Sv.	IP	H	R	ER	BB	SO
1996— Everett (N'West)	1	3	.250	4.45	12	4	0	0	0	30 1/3	25	19	15	17	49
1997— Wisconsin (Midw.)	6	3	.667	1.97	16	15	1	0	0	91 1/3	52	27	20	33	105
— Lancaster (East.)	1	1	.500	3.24	3	3	0	0	0	16 2/3	13	7	6	10	17
1998— Lancaster (Calif.)	1	2	.333	4.29	5	5	0	0	0	21	18	12	10	17	21
— Arizona Mariners (Ariz.)	0	0	...	2.16	3	1	0	0	0	8 1/3	9	2	2	2	13
1999— New Haven (East.)	9	11	.450	4.40	26	26	2	1	0	147 1/3	151	82	72	62	103
— Seattle (A.L.)	0	0	...	9.95	5	0	0	0	0	6 1/3	10	8	7	4	4
2000— New Haven (East.)	4	3	.571	2.19	8	8	1	0	0	49 1/3	31	13	12	17	42
Major League totals (1 year)	0	0	...	9.95	5	0	0	0	0	6 1/3	10	8	7	4	4

STECHSCHULTE, GENE P CARDINALS

PERSONAL: Born August 12, 1973, in Lima, Ohio. ... 6-5/210. ... Throws right, bats right. ... Full name: Gene Urban Stechschulte.
HIGH SCHOOL: Kalida (Ohio).
COLLEGE: Ashland (Ohio).
TRANSACTIONS/CAREER NOTES: Signed as non-drafted free agent by St. Louis Cardinals organization (June 13, 1996). ... On Arkansas disabled list (July 31-September 1, 1999).
STATISTICAL NOTES: Led Midwest League pitchers with 51 games finished in 1998.

Year League	W	L	Pct.	ERA	G	GS	CG	ShO	Sv.	IP	H	R	ER	BB	SO
1996— New Jersey (NY-Penn)	1	2	.333	3.27	20	1	0	0	0	33	41	17	12	16	27
1997— New Jersey (NY-Penn)	1	1	.500	3.22	30	0	0	0	1	36 1/3	45	16	13	16	28
1998— Peoria (Midw.)	4	8	.333	2.59	57	0	0	0	*33	66	58	26	19	21	70
1999— Arkansas (Texas)	2	6	.250	3.40	39	0	0	0	19	42 1/3	41	26	16	20	41
— Memphis (PCL)	0	0	...	7.71	2	0	0	0	0	2 1/3	2	2	2	5	2
2000— Memphis (PCL)	4	1	.800	2.45	41	0	0	0	26	47 2/3	38	13	13	18	37
— St. Louis (N.L.)	1	0	1.000	6.31	20	0	0	0	0	25 2/3	24	22	18	17	12
— Arkansas (Texas)	0	0	...	0.00	2	0	0	0	0	2	0	0	0	0	3
Major League totals (1 year)	1	0	1.000	6.31	20	0	0	0	0	25 2/3	24	22	18	17	12

S

STEFANSKI, MIKE   C   CARDINALS

PERSONAL: Born September 12, 1969, in Flint, Mich. ... 6-2/218. ... Bats right, throws right. ... Full name: Michael Joseph Stefanski.
HIGH SCHOOL: Redford (Mich.) Union.
COLLEGE: Detroit.
TRANSACTIONS/CAREER NOTES: Selected by Milwaukee Brewers organization in 40th round of free-agent draft (June 3, 1991). ... On disabled list (April 13-29, 1993; April 8-23 and July 6-21, 1994). ... Traded by Brewers to St. Louis Cardinals for C Marc Ronan (October 19, 1995). ... Granted free agency (October 15, 1997). ... Re-signed by Cardinals organization (November 10, 1997). ... Granted free agency (October 16, 1998). ... Re-signed by Cardinals organization (November 8, 1998). ... On Memphis disabled list (August 2-11, 1999). ... Granted free agency (October 15, 1999). ... Signed by Cincinnati Reds organization (November 15, 1999). ... On Louisville disabled list (April 6-May 20 and June 5-July 8, 2000). ... Granted free agency (October 18, 2000). ... Signed by Cardinals organization (November 15, 2000).
STATISTICAL NOTES: Led Arizona League catchers with 364 putouts and .988 fielding percentage in 1991.

							BATTING								FIELDING		
Year	Team (League)	Pos.	G	AB	R	H	2B	3B	HR	RBI	Avg.	BB	SO	SB	PO	A	E	Avg.
1991— Ariz. Brewers (Ariz.) ...		C-1B	56	206	43	75	5	5	0	43	*.364	22	21	3	†386	40	6	†.986
1992— Beloit (Midw.)............		C-1B-OF	116	385	66	105	12	0	4	45	.273	55	81	9	724	95	13	.984
1993— Stockton (Calif.)		C-3B-1B	97	345	58	111	22	2	10	57	.322	49	45	6	471	92	14	.976
1994— El Paso (Texas)..........		C-DH-OF	95	312	59	82	7	6	8	56	.263	32	80	4	456	81	5	.991
1995— New Orleans (A.A.).....		C-3-D-1-O	78	228	30	56	10	2	2	24	.246	14	28	2	364	37	2	.995
— El Paso (Texas)...........		3B	6	27	5	11	3	0	1	6	.407	0	3	1	2	14	3	.842
1996— Louisville (A.A.)■........		C-OF-P-1B	53	126	11	26	7	1	2	9	.206	11	11	1	243	21	6	.978
1997— Louisville (A.A.)...........		C-1B-DH-P	1	197	26	60	10	0	6	22	.305	12	20	0	318	43	8	.978
— Arkansas (Texas)........		C	1	4	1	1	0	1	0	0	.250	0	0	0	4	1	0	1.000
1998— Memphis (PCL)..........		C-1B-DH-3B	95	298	34	79	19	1	6	44	.265	23	42	1	645	56	5	.993
1999— Memphis (PCL)..........		C-DH-1B	64	201	27	60	12	0	4	22	.299	17	28	3	412	26	9	.980
2000— Louisville (I.L.)■........		C-1B	32	96	12	22	7	0	2	10	.229	4	17	0	153	17	0	1.000

RECORD AS PITCHER

Year	League	W	L	Pct.	ERA	G	GS	CG	ShO	Sv.	IP	H	R	ER	BB	SO
1997— Louisville (A.A.).................		0	0	...	9.00	1	0	0	0	0	1	3	1	1	0	1

STEIN, BLAKE   P   ROYALS

PERSONAL: Born August 3, 1973, in McComb, Miss. ... 6-7/240. ... Throws right, bats right. ... Full name: William Blake Stein.
HIGH SCHOOL: Covington (La.).
COLLEGE: Spring Hill College (Ala.).
TRANSACTIONS/CAREER NOTES: Selected by St. Louis Cardinals organization in sixth round of free-agent draft (June 2, 1994). ... Traded by Cardinals with P T.J. Mathews and P Eric Ludwick to Oakland Athletics for 1B Mark McGwire (July 31, 1997). ... Traded by A's with P Jeff D'Amico and P Brad Rigby to Kansas City Royals for P Kevin Appier (July 31, 1999). ... On Kansas City disabled list (March 24-July 5, 2000); included rehabilitation assignments to Wilmington (June 7-18), Wichita (June 21-22) and Omaha (June 23-July 5).
RECORDS: Shares major league single-inning record for most strikeouts—4 (July 27, 1998, fourth inning).

Year	League	W	L	Pct.	ERA	G	GS	CG	ShO	Sv.	IP	H	R	ER	BB	SO
1994— Johnson City (Appl.)		4	1	.800	2.87	13	13	1	0	0	59²/₃	44	21	19	24	69
1995— Peoria (Midw.)................		10	6	.625	3.80	27	•27	1	0	0	139²/₃	122	69	59	61	133
1996— St. Petersburg (FSL)		•16	5	.762	*2.15	28	27	2	1	1	172	122	48	41	54	*159
1997— Arkansas (Texas)...............		8	7	.533	4.24	22	22	1	0	0	133²/₃	128	67	63	49	114
— Huntsville (Sou.)■........		3	2	.600	5.71	7	7	0	0	0	34²/₃	36	24	22	20	25
1998— Edmonton (PCL)............		3	1	.750	3.47	5	4	0	0	0	23¹/₃	22	13	9	11	31
— Oakland (A.L.)..............		5	9	.357	6.37	24	20	1	1	0	117¹/₃	117	92	83	71	89
1999— Vancouver (PCL)............		4	2	.667	4.10	19	19	0	0	0	109²/₃	94	54	50	43	111
— Oakland (A.L.)		0	0	...	16.88	1	1	0	0	0	2²/₃	6	5	5	6	4
— Kansas City (A.L.)■........		1	2	.333	4.09	12	11	0	0	0	70¹/₃	59	33	32	41	43
2000— Wilmington (Caro.)........		0	0	...	6.75	2	2	0	0	0	5¹/₃	6	4	4	2	12
— Wichita (Texas)		1	0	1.000	6.23	2	2	0	0	0	8²/₃	10	6	6	1	12
— Omaha (PCL)...................		2	0	1.000	0.73	2	2	0	0	0	12¹/₃	9	1	1	2	14
— Kansas City (A.L.)		8	5	.615	4.68	17	17	1	0	0	107²/₃	98	57	56	57	78
Major League totals (3 years).......		14	16	.467	5.32	54	49	2	1	0	298	280	187	176	175	214

STENSON, DERNELL   1B/OF   RED SOX

PERSONAL: Born June 17, 1978, in La Grange, Ga. ... 6-1/230. ... Bats left, throws left. ... Full name: Dernell Renauld Stenson.
HIGH SCHOOL: La Grange (Ga.).
TRANSACTIONS/CAREER NOTES: Selected by Boston Red Sox organization in third round of free-agent draft (June 2, 1996). ... On Pawtucket disabled list (June 24-July 15, 1999). ... On disabled list (April 17-May 10 and June 1-18, 2000).

							BATTING								FIELDING		
Year	Team (League)	Pos.	G	AB	R	H	2B	3B	HR	RBI	Avg.	BB	SO	SB	PO	A	E	Avg.
1996— GC Red Sox (GCL)		OF	32	97	16	21	3	1	2	15	.216	16	26	4	30	2	0	1.000
1997— Michigan (Midw.)		OF	131	471	79	137	35	2	15	80	.291	72	105	6	145	11	14	.918
1998— Trenton (East.)...........		OF	138	505	90	130	21	1	24	71	.257	84	135	5	218	*15	6	.975
1999— Pawtucket (I.L.)..........		1B-DH	121	440	64	119	28	2	18	82	.270	55	119	2	919	56	*34	.966
— GC Red Sox (GCL)		DH-1B	6	23	2	5	0	0	2	7	.217	3	5	0	16	2	1	.947
2000— Pawtucket (I.L.).........		1B-OF	98	380	59	102	14	0	23	71	.268	45	99	0	559	41	12	.980

STEPHENSON, GARRETT   P   CARDINALS

PERSONAL: Born January 2, 1972, in Takoma Park, Md. ... 6-5/208. ... Throws right, bats right. ... Full name: Garrett Charles Stephenson.
HIGH SCHOOL: Boonsboro (Md.).

S

JUNIOR COLLEGE: Ricks College (Idaho).
COLLEGE: Idaho State.
TRANSACTIONS/CAREER NOTES: Selected by Baltimore Orioles organization in 18th round of free-agent draft (June 1, 1992). ... Traded by Orioles with P Calvin Maduro to Philadelphia Phillies (September 4, 1996), completing deal in which Phillies traded 3B Todd Zeile and OF Pete Incaviglia to Orioles for two players to be named later (August 29, 1996). ... On Philadelphia disabled list (June 5-22 and August 18-September 2, 1997). ... On Scranton/Wilkes-Barre disabled list (July 8-August 3, 1998). ... Traded by Phillies with P Ricky Bottalico to St. Louis Cardinals for OF Ron Gant, P Jeff Brantley and P Cliff Politte (November 19, 1998). ... On Memphis disabled list (April 8-June 13, 1999).
STATISTICAL NOTES: Led Eastern League with 23 home runs allowed and 18 hit batsmen in 1995.

Year	League	W	L	Pct.	ERA	G	GS	CG	ShO	Sv.	IP	H	R	ER	BB	SO
1992—	Bluefield (Appl.)	3	1	.750	4.73	12	3	0	0	0	32 1/3	35	22	17	7	30
1993—	Albany (S.Atl.)	16	7	.696	2.84	30	24	3	•2	1	171 1/3	142	65	54	44	147
1994—	Frederick (Caro.)	7	5	.583	4.02	18	17	1	0	0	107 1/3	91	62	48	36	133
	Bowie (East.)	3	2	.600	5.15	7	7	1	1	0	36 2/3	47	22	21	11	32
1995—	Bowie (East.)	7	10	.412	3.64	29	*29	1	0	0	175 1/3	154	87	71	47	139
1996—	Rochester (I.L.)	7	6	.538	4.81	23	21	3	1	0	121 2/3	123	66	65	44	86
	Baltimore (A.L.)	0	1	.000	12.79	3	0	0	0	0	6 1/3	13	9	9	3	3
1997—	Scranton/W.B. (I.L.)■	3	1	.750	5.90	7	3	0	0	0	29	27	19	19	12	27
	Philadelphia (N.L.)	8	6	.571	3.15	20	18	2	0	0	117	104	45	41	38	81
1998—	Philadelphia (N.L.)	0	2	.000	9.00	6	6	0	0	0	23	31	24	23	19	17
	Scranton/W.B. (I.L.)	1	8	.111	5.25	13	11	2	0	0	73 2/3	81	49	43	16	48
1999—	Memphis (PCL)■	1	1	.500	3.16	4	4	0	0	0	25 2/3	22	9	9	7	19
	Arkansas (Texas)	0	0	...	3.38	1	1	0	0	0	5 1/3	8	3	2	1	2
	St. Louis (N.L.)	6	3	.667	4.22	18	12	0	0	0	85 1/3	90	43	40	29	59
2000—	St. Louis (N.L.)	16	9	.640	4.49	32	31	3	2	0	200 1/3	209	105	100	63	123
A.L. totals (1 year)		0	1	.000	12.79	3	0	0	0	0	6 1/3	13	9	9	3	3
N.L. totals (4 years)		30	20	.600	4.31	76	67	5	2	0	425 2/3	434	217	204	149	280
Major League totals (5 years)		30	21	.588	4.44	79	67	5	2	0	432	447	226	213	152	283

DIVISION SERIES RECORD

Year	League	W	L	Pct.	ERA	G	GS	CG	ShO	Sv.	IP	H	R	ER	BB	SO
2000—	St. Louis (N.L.)	0	0	...	2.45	1	1	0	0	0	3 2/3	3	1	1	2	2

STEVENS, DAVE · P

PERSONAL: Born March 4, 1970, in Fullerton, Calif. ... 6-3/215. ... Throws right, bats right. ... Full name: David James Stevens.
HIGH SCHOOL: La Habra (Calif.).
COLLEGE: Fullerton (Calif.) College.
TRANSACTIONS/CAREER NOTES: Selected by Chicago Cubs organization in 20th round of free-agent draft (June 5, 1989). ... On disabled list (June 17-July 4, 1991). ... On Iowa disabled list (April 8-May 20, 1993). ... Traded by Cubs with C Matt Walbeck to Minnesota Twins for P Willie Banks (November 24, 1993). ... On disabled list (May 30-June 21 and July 21-August 9, 1996). ... Claimed on waivers by Cubs (July 31, 1997). ... Released by Cubs (December 3, 1998). ... Signed by Cleveland Indians organization (January 26, 1999). ... Released by Indians (June 21, 1999). ... Signed by Seattle Mariners organization (July 1, 1999). ... Released by Mariners (July 30, 1999). ... Signed by Pittsburgh Pirates organization (February 9, 2000). ... Released by Pirates (April 1, 2000). ... Signed by Atlanta Braves organization (April 12, 2000). ... Granted free agency (October 13, 2000).
MISCELLANEOUS: Appeared in one game as pinch runner with Chicago (1998).

Year	League	W	L	Pct.	ERA	G	GS	CG	ShO	Sv.	IP	H	R	ER	BB	SO
1990—	Huntington (Appl.)	2	4	.333	4.61	13	11	0	0	0	56 2/3	48	44	29	47	55
1991—	Geneva (NY-Penn)	2	3	.400	2.85	9	9	1	0	0	47 1/3	49	20	15	14	44
1992—	Charlotte (Sou.)	9	13	.409	3.91	26	26	2	0	0	149 2/3	147	79	65	53	89
1993—	Iowa (A.A.)	4	0	1.000	4.19	24	0	0	0	4	34 1/3	24	16	16	14	29
	Orlando (Sou.)	6	1	.857	4.22	11	11	1	1	0	70 1/3	69	36	33	35	49
1994—	Salt Lake (PCL)■	6	2	.750	1.67	23	0	0	0	3	43	41	13	8	16	30
	Minnesota (A.L.)	5	2	.714	6.80	24	0	0	0	0	45	55	35	34	23	24
1995—	Minnesota (A.L.)	5	4	.556	5.07	56	0	0	0	10	65 2/3	74	40	37	32	47
1996—	Minnesota (A.L.)	3	3	.500	4.66	49	0	0	0	11	58	58	31	30	25	29
1997—	Salt Lake (PCL)	9	3	.750	4.30	16	14	1	0	0	90	93	52	43	31	71
	Minnesota (A.L.)	1	3	.250	9.00	6	6	0	0	0	23	41	23	23	17	16
	Iowa (A.A.)■	1	1	.500	4.70	6	0	0	0	1	7 2/3	8	4	4	5	8
	Chicago (N.L.)	0	2	.000	9.64	10	0	0	0	0	9 1/3	13	11	10	9	13
1998—	Iowa (PCL)	4	1	.800	3.08	26	0	0	0	2	49 2/3	41	19	17	16	39
	Chicago (N.L.)	1	2	.333	4.74	31	0	0	0	0	38	42	20	20	17	31
1999—	Buffalo (I.L.)■	1	0	1.000	1.52	20	0	0	0	12	23 2/3	12	4	4	14	28
	Cleveland (A.L.)	0	0	...	10.00	5	0	0	0	0	9	10	10	10	8	6
	Tacoma (PCL)■	1	1	.500	12.60	7	0	0	0	0	10	14	14	14	6	8
2000—	Richmond (I.L.)■	1	9	.100	5.00	51	0	0	0	7	72	73	44	40	31	50
	Atlanta (N.L.)	0	0	...	12.00	2	0	0	0	0	3	5	4	4	1	4
A.L. totals (5 years)		14	12	.538	6.01	140	6	0	0	21	200 2/3	238	139	134	105	122
N.L. totals (3 years)		1	4	.200	6.08	43	0	0	0	0	50 1/3	60	35	34	27	48
Major League totals (7 years)		15	16	.484	6.02	183	6	0	0	21	251	298	174	168	132	170

STEVENS, LEE · 1B · EXPOS

PERSONAL: Born July 10, 1967, in Kansas City, Mo. ... 6-4/235. ... Bats left, throws left. ... Full name: DeWain Lee Stevens.
HIGH SCHOOL: Lawrence (Kan.).
TRANSACTIONS/CAREER NOTES: Selected by California Angels organization in first round (22nd pick overall) of free-agent draft (June 2, 1986). ... Traded by Angels to Montreal Expos for P Jeff Tuss (January 15, 1993); Tuss announced his retirement and Angels acquired P Keith Morrison to complete deal (January 21, 1993). ... Released by Expos (March 30, 1993). ... Signed by Toronto Blue Jays organization (April 8, 1993). ... Granted free agency (October 15, 1993). ... Signed by Angels organization (October 25, 1993). ... Contract sold by Angels to Kintetsu of Japan Pacific League (November 16, 1993). ... Signed by Texas Rangers organization (April 3, 1996). ... On Texas disabled list (August 4-

September 1, 1996); included rehabilitation assignment to Oklahoma City (August 13-September 1, 1996). ... On Texas disabled list (August 8-September 1, 1998); included rehabilitation assignment to Oklahoma (August 25-September 1). ... Traded by Rangers to Expos as part of three-way deal in which Expos sent 1B Brad Fullmer to Toronto Blue Jays and Blue Jays sent 1B/DH David Segui and cash to Rangers (March 16, 2000).

HONORS: Named American Association Most Valuable Player (1996).

STATISTICAL NOTES: Led California League first basemen with .986 fielding percentage, 1,028 putouts and 66 assists in 1987. ... Led Texas League outfielders with 12 errors in 1988. ... Tied for Pacific Coast League lead with 11 intentional bases on balls received in 1990. ... Led American Association with 277 total bases, .643 slugging percentage and .404 on-base percentage in 1996. ... Tied for American Association lead with eight intentional bases on balls received in 1996. ... Hit three home runs in one game (April 13, 1998). ... Career major league grand slams: 2.

									BATTING						FIELDING		
Year Team (League)	Pos.	G	AB	R	H	2B	3B	HR	RBI	Avg.	BB	SO	SB	PO	A	E	Avg.
1986—Salem (N'West).........	OF-1B	72	267	45	75	18	2	6	47	.281	45	49	13	231	18	5	.980
1987—Palm Springs (Calif.)..	1B-OF	140	532	82	130	29	2	19	97	.244	61	117	1	†1031	†68	18	†.984
1988—Midland (Texas).........	OF-1B	116	414	79	123	26	2	23	76	.297	58	108	0	217	16	†14	.943
1989—Edmonton (PCL)	1B-OF	127	446	72	110	29	9	14	74	.247	61	115	5	635	40	7	.990
1990—Edmonton (PCL)	OF-1B	90	338	57	99	31	2	16	66	.293	55	83	1	284	10	6	.980
—California (A.L.).........	1B	67	248	28	53	10	0	7	32	.214	22	75	1	597	36	4	.994
1991—Edmonton (PCL)	OF-1B	123	481	75	151	29	3	19	96	.314	37	79	3	519	33	7	.987
—California (A.L.).........	OF-1B	18	58	8	17	7	0	0	9	.293	6	12	1	100	6	1	.991
1992—California (A.L.).........	1B-DH	106	312	25	69	19	0	7	37	.221	29	64	1	764	49	4	.995
1993—Syracuse (I.L.)■.........	1B-OF	116	401	61	106	30	1	14	66	.264	39	85	2	201	12	3	.986
1994—Kintetsu (Jap. Pac.)■.	OF	93	302	44	87	21	0	20	66	.288	28	100	0	...	...	...	...
1995—Kintetsu (Jap. Pac.)....	OF	129	476	54	117	29	1	23	70	.246	46	129	0	...	...	...	...
1996—Okla. City (A.A.)■......	DH-1B-OF	117	431	84	140	*37	2	*32	94	.325	58	90	3	348	24	3	.992
—Texas (A.L.).............	1B-OF	27	78	6	18	2	3	3	12	.231	6	22	0	157	14	1	.994
1997—Texas (A.L.).............	1B-DH-OF	137	426	58	128	24	2	21	74	.300	23	83	1	486	33	3	.994
1998—Texas (A.L.).............	DH-1B-OF	120	344	52	91	17	4	20	59	.265	31	93	0	220	15	1	.996
—Oklahoma (PCL).......	DH-1B	3	12	2	4	0	0	1	1	.333	0	2	0	12	1	0	1.000
1999—Texas (A.L.).............	1B-DH	146	517	76	146	31	1	24	81	.282	52	132	2	1228	60	8	.994
2000—Montreal (N.L.)■.......	1B	123	449	60	119	27	2	22	75	.265	48	105	0	1072	85	11	.991
American League totals (7 years)		621	1983	253	522	110	10	82	304	.263	169	481	6	3552	213	22	.994
National League totals (1 year)		123	449	60	119	27	2	22	75	.265	48	105	0	1072	85	11	.991
Major League totals (8 years)		744	2432	313	641	137	12	104	379	.264	217	586	6	4624	298	33	.993

DIVISION SERIES RECORD

									BATTING						FIELDING		
Year Team (League)	Pos.	G	AB	R	H	2B	3B	HR	RBI	Avg.	BB	SO	SB	PO	A	E	Avg.
1998—Texas (A.L.).............	DH	1	3	0	0	0	0	0	0	.000	0	1	0	...	...	...	...
1999—Texas (A.L.).............	1B	3	9	0	1	1	0	0	0	.111	1	2	0	25	2	0	1.000
Division series totals (2 years)		4	12	0	1	1	0	0	0	.083	1	3	0	25	2	0	1.000

STEWART, SHANNON   OF   BLUE JAYS

PERSONAL: Born February 25, 1974, in Cincinnati. ... 6-1/205. ... Bats right, throws right. ... Full name: Shannon Harold Stewart.

HIGH SCHOOL: Southridge Senior (Miami).

TRANSACTIONS/CAREER NOTES: Selected by Toronto Blue Jays organization in first round (19th pick overall) of free-agent draft (June 1, 1992); pick received as part of compensation for Los Angeles Dodgers signing Type A free-agent P Tom Candiotti. ... On disabled list (June 13, 1994-remainder of season). ... On Syracuse disabled list (May 13-31, 1996). ... On Toronto disabled list (May 1-14, 2000); included rehabilitation assignment to Dunedin (May 12-14).

RECORDS: Shares major league single-game record for most doubles—4 (July 18, 2000).

STATISTICAL NOTES: Led International League outfielders with 286 total chances in 1996. ... Had 16-game hitting streak (June 15-30, 1999). ... Had 26-game hitting streak (August 1-29, 1999). ... Tied for A.L. lead in caught stealing with 14 in 1999.

									BATTING						FIELDING		
Year Team (League)	Pos.	G	AB	R	H	2B	3B	HR	RBI	Avg.	BB	SO	SB	PO	A	E	Avg.
1992—GC Blue Jays (GCL)....	OF	50	172	44	40	1	0	1	11	.233	24	27	*32	81	1	1	.988
1993—St. Catharines (NY-P)..	OF	75	*301	•53	84	15	2	3	29	.279	33	43	25	81	0	0	1.000
1994—Hagerstown (S.Atl.)....	OF	56	225	39	73	10	5	4	25	.324	23	39	15	92	4	1	.990
1995—Knoxville (Sou.)..........	OF-DH	138	498	89	143	24	6	5	55	.287	*89	61	42	283	6	6	.980
—Toronto (A.L.).............	OF	12	38	2	8	0	0	0	1	.211	5	5	2	20	1	1	.955
1996—Syracuse (I.L.)..........	OF	112	420	77	125	26	8	6	42	.298	54	61	*35	*274	7	5	.983
—Toronto (A.L.).............	OF	7	17	2	3	1	0	0	2	.176	1	4	1	4	0	1	.800
1997—Toronto (A.L.).............	OF-DH	44	168	25	48	13	7	0	22	.286	19	24	10	97	1	2	.980
—Syracuse (I.L.)..........	OF	58	208	41	72	13	1	5	24	.346	36	26	9	115	1	2	.983
1998—Toronto (A.L.).............	OF	144	516	90	144	29	3	12	55	.279	67	77	51	295	4	6	.980
1999—Toronto (A.L.).............	OF-DH	145	608	102	185	28	2	11	67	.304	59	83	37	257	4	5	.981
2000—Toronto (A.L.).............	OF	136	583	107	186	43	5	21	69	.319	37	90	20	298	5	2	.993
—Dunedin (FSL)...........	OF	1	3	2	3	1	0	0	1	1.000	2	0	0	0	0	0	...
Major League totals (6 years)		488	1930	328	574	114	17	44	216	.297	188	272	121	971	15	17	.983

STINNETT, KELLY   C   REDS

PERSONAL: Born February 4, 1970, in Lawton, Okla. ... 5-11/225. ... Bats right, throws right. ... Full name: Kelly Lee Stinnett. ... Name pronounced stih-NET.

HIGH SCHOOL: Lawton (Okla.).

JUNIOR COLLEGE: Seminole (Okla.) Junior College.

TRANSACTIONS/CAREER NOTES: Selected by Cleveland Indians organization in 11th round of free-agent draft (June 5, 1989). ... Selected by New York Mets from Indians organization in Rule 5 major league draft (December 13, 1993). ... Traded by Mets to Milwaukee Brewers for P Cory Lidle (January 17, 1996). ... On Milwaukee disabled list (July 27-September 2, 1997). ... Selected by Arizona Diamondbacks in third round (65th pick overall) of expansion draft (November 18, 1997). ... Granted free agency (December 21, 2000). ... Signed by Cincinnati Reds (January 9, 2001).

STATISTICAL NOTES: Led New York-Pennsylvania League catchers with 18 errors in 1990. ... Led South Atlantic League catchers with 27 errors in 1991. ... Tied for American Association lead in being hit by pitch with 13 in 1996. ... Led American Association catchers with 10 errors and tied for lead with nine double plays in 1996.

											BATTING					FIELDING		
Year	Team (League)	Pos.	G	AB	R	H	2B	3B	HR	RBI	Avg.	BB	SO	SB	PO	A	E	Avg.
1990—	Watertown (NY-Penn)	C-1B	60	192	29	46	10	2	2	21	.240	40	43	3	348	48	†18	.957
1991—	Columbus (S.Atl.)	C-1B	102	384	49	101	15	1	14	74	.263	26	70	4	685	100	†28	.966
1992—	Canton/Akron (East.)	C	91	296	37	84	10	0	6	32	.284	16	43	7	560	57	*13	.979
1993—	Charlotte (I.L.)	C	98	288	42	79	10	3	6	33	.274	17	52	0	495	48	8	.985
1994—	New York (N.L.)■	C	47	150	20	38	6	2	2	14	.253	11	28	2	211	20	5	.979
1995—	New York (N.L.)	C	77	196	23	43	8	1	4	18	.234	29	65	2	380	22	7	.983
1996—	Milwaukee (A.L.)■	C-DH	14	26	1	2	0	0	0	0	.077	2	11	0	46	2	2	.960
	New Orleans (A.A.)	C-DH-3B	95	334	63	96	21	1	27	70	.287	31	83	3	485	52	†11	.980
1997—	Tucson (PCL)	C-DH-1B	64	209	50	67	15	3	10	43	.321	42	46	1	256	34	2	.993
	Milwaukee (A.L.)	C-DH	30	36	2	9	4	0	0	3	.250	3	9	0	81	5	1	.989
1998—	Arizona (N.L.)■	C-DH	92	274	35	71	14	1	11	34	.259	35	74	0	458	37	8	.984
1999—	Arizona (N.L.)	C	88	284	36	66	13	0	14	38	.232	24	83	2	549	37	6	.990
2000—	Arizona (N.L.)	C	76	240	22	52	7	0	8	33	.217	19	56	0	539	40	6	.990
American League totals (2 years)			44	62	3	11	4	0	0	3	.177	5	20	0	127	7	3	.978
National League totals (5 years)			380	1144	136	270	48	4	39	137	.236	118	306	6	2137	156	32	.986
Major League totals (7 years)			424	1206	139	281	52	4	39	140	.233	123	326	6	2264	163	35	.986

DIVISION SERIES RECORD

											BATTING					FIELDING		
Year	Team (League)	Pos.	G	AB	R	H	2B	3B	HR	RBI	Avg.	BB	SO	SB	PO	A	E	Avg.
1999—	Arizona (N.L.)	C	4	14	1	2	1	0	0	0	.143	1	4	0	29	2	0	1.000

S

STOCKER, KEVIN   SS

PERSONAL: Born February 13, 1970, in Spokane, Wash. ... 6-1/180. ... Bats both, throws right. ... Full name: Kevin Douglas Stocker.
HIGH SCHOOL: Central Valley (Veradale, Wash.).
COLLEGE: Washington.
TRANSACTIONS/CAREER NOTES: Selected by Philadelphia Phillies organization in second round of free-agent draft (June 3, 1991). ... On Philadelphia disabled list (April 28-June 1, 1994); included rehabilitation assignment to Scranton/Wilkes-Barre (May 28-June 1). ... Traded by Phillies to Tampa Bay Devil Rays for OF Bob Abreu (November 18, 1997). ... On disabled list (August 30, 1998-remainder of season). ... On Tampa Bay disabled list (July 22, 1999-remainder of season); included rehabilitation assignment to St. Petersburg (August 25-31). ... Released by Devil Rays (May 25, 2000). ... Signed by Anaheim Angels (May 30, 2000). ... On Anaheim disabled list (June 24-July 7, 2000). ... Granted free agency (October 31, 2000).

											BATTING					FIELDING		
Year	Team (League)	Pos.	G	AB	R	H	2B	3B	HR	RBI	Avg.	BB	SO	SB	PO	A	E	Avg.
1991—	Spartanburg (S.Atl.)	SS	70	250	26	55	11	1	0	20	.220	31	37	15	83	176	18	.935
1992—	Clearwater (FSL)	SS	63	244	43	69	13	4	1	33	.283	27	31	15	102	220	16	.951
	Reading (East.)	SS	62	240	31	60	9	2	1	13	.250	22	30	17	100	172	14	.951
1993—	Scranton/W.B. (I.L.)	SS-DH	83	313	54	73	14	1	3	17	.233	29	56	17	122	248	15	.961
	Philadelphia (N.L.)	SS	70	259	46	84	12	3	2	31	.324	30	43	5	118	202	14	.958
1994—	Philadelphia (N.L.)	SS	82	271	38	74	11	2	2	28	.273	44	41	2	118	253	16	.959
	Scranton/W.B. (I.L.)	SS	4	13	1	4	1	0	0	2	.308	1	0	0	5	11	0	1.000
1995—	Philadelphia (N.L.)	SS	125	412	42	90	14	3	1	32	.218	43	75	6	147	383	17	.969
1996—	Philadelphia (N.L.)	SS	119	394	46	100	22	6	5	41	.254	43	89	6	165	352	13	.975
	Scranton/W.B. (I.L.)	SS	12	44	5	10	3	0	2	6	.227	0	4	1	17	39	1	.982
1997—	Philadelphia (N.L.)	SS	149	504	51	134	23	5	4	40	.266	51	91	11	190	376	11	.981
1998—	Tampa Bay (A.L.)■	SS	112	336	37	70	11	3	6	25	.208	27	80	5	186	335	11	.979
1999—	Tampa Bay (A.L.)■	SS	79	254	39	76	11	2	1	27	.299	24	41	9	137	216	16	.957
	St. Petersburg (FSL)	SS	3	11	2	1	0	0	0	0	.091	1	2	0	5	10	0	1.000
2000—	Tampa Bay (A.L.)	SS	40	114	20	30	7	1	2	8	.263	19	27	1	43	111	11	.933
	Anaheim (A.L.)■	SS	70	229	21	45	13	3	0	16	.197	32	54	0	98	216	7	.978
American League totals (3 years)			301	933	117	221	42	9	9	76	.237	102	202	15	464	872	45	.967
National League totals (5 years)			545	1840	223	482	82	19	14	172	.262	211	339	30	738	1566	71	.970
Major League totals (8 years)			846	2773	340	703	124	28	23	248	.254	313	541	45	1202	2438	116	.969

CHAMPIONSHIP SERIES RECORD

											BATTING					FIELDING		
Year	Team (League)	Pos.	G	AB	R	H	2B	3B	HR	RBI	Avg.	BB	SO	SB	PO	A	E	Avg.
1993—	Philadelphia (N.L.)	SS	6	22	0	4	1	0	0	1	.182	2	5	0	10	13	1	.958

WORLD SERIES RECORD

											BATTING					FIELDING		
Year	Team (League)	Pos.	G	AB	R	H	2B	3B	HR	RBI	Avg.	BB	SO	SB	PO	A	E	Avg.
1993—	Philadelphia (N.L.)	SS	6	19	1	4	1	0	0	1	.211	5	5	0	8	13	0	1.000

STOTTLEMYRE, TODD   P   DIAMONDBACKS

PERSONAL: Born May 20, 1965, in Yakima, Wash. ... 6-3/215. ... Throws right, bats left. ... Full name: Todd Vernon Stottlemyre. ... Son of Mel Stottlemyre Sr., pitching coach, New York Yankees; pitcher with New York Yankees (1964-74) and pitching coach for New York Mets (1984-93); and brother of Mel Stottlemyre Jr., pitcher with Kansas City Royals (1990).
HIGH SCHOOL: A.C. Davis (Yakima, Wash.).
JUNIOR COLLEGE: Yakima (Wash.) Valley College.
COLLEGE: UNLV.

TRANSACTIONS/CAREER NOTES: Selected by New York Yankees organization in fifth round of free-agent draft (June 6, 1983); did not sign. ... Selected by St. Louis Cardinals organization in secondary phase of free-agent draft (January 9, 1985); did not sign. ... Selected by Toronto Blue Jays organization in secondary phase of free-agent draft (June 3, 1985). ... On disabled list (June 20-July 13, 1992). ... On suspended list (September 23-28, 1992). ... On disabled list (May 23-June 13, 1993). ... Granted free agency (October 18, 1994). ... Signed by Oakland Athletics (April 11, 1995). ... Traded by A's to St. Louis Cardinals for P Bret Wagner, P Jay Witasick and P Carl Dale (January 9, 1996). ... Traded by Cardinals with SS Royce Clayton to Texas Rangers for P Darren Oliver, 3B Fernando Tatis and a player to be named later (July 31, 1998); Cardinals acquired OF Mark Little to complete deal (August 9, 1998). ... Granted free agency (October 22, 1998). ... Signed by Arizona Diamondbacks (December 2, 1998). ... On Arizona disabled list (May 18-August 19, 1999); included rehabilitation assignment to Arizona League Diamondbacks (August 3-15). ... On Arizona disabled list (May 30-June 15 and June 26-September 1, 2000); included rehabilitation assignment to Arizona League Diamondbacks (August 23-September 1).

STATISTICAL NOTES: Pitched 9-0 one-hit, complete-game victory against Chicago (August 26, 1992). ... Struck out 15 batters in one game (June 16, 1995).

MISCELLANEOUS: Struck out in only appearance as pinch hitter (1997).

Year	League	W	L	Pct.	ERA	G	GS	CG	ShO	Sv.	IP	H	R	ER	BB	SO
1986—	Ventura County (Calif.)	9	4	.692	2.43	17	17	2	0	0	103²/₃	76	39	28	36	104
—	Knoxville (Sou.)	8	7	.533	4.18	18	18	1	0	0	99	93	56	46	49	81
1987—	Syracuse (I.L.)	11	•13	.458	4.44	34	*34	1	0	0	186²/₃	189	•103	*92	*87	143
1988—	Toronto (A.L.)	4	8	.333	5.69	28	16	0	0	0	98	109	70	62	46	67
—	Syracuse (I.L.)	5	0	1.000	2.05	7	7	1	0	0	48¹/₃	36	12	11	8	51
1989—	Toronto (A.L.)	7	7	.500	3.88	27	18	0	0	0	127²/₃	137	56	55	44	63
—	Syracuse (I.L.)	3	2	.600	3.23	10	9	2	0	0	55²/₃	46	23	20	15	45
1990—	Toronto (A.L.)	13	17	.433	4.34	33	33	4	0	0	203	214	101	98	69	115
1991—	Toronto (A.L.)	15	8	.652	3.78	34	34	1	0	0	219	194	97	92	75	116
1992—	Toronto (A.L.)	12	11	.522	4.50	28	27	6	2	0	174	175	99	87	63	98
1993—	Toronto (A.L.)	11	12	.478	4.84	30	28	1	1	0	176²/₃	204	107	95	69	98
1994—	Toronto (A.L.)	7	7	.500	4.22	26	19	3	1	1	140²/₃	149	67	66	48	105
1995—	Oakland (A.L.)■	14	7	.667	4.55	31	31	2	0	0	209²/₃	228	117	106	80	205
1996—	St. Louis (N.L.)■	14	11	.560	3.87	34	33	5	2	0	223¹/₃	191	100	96	93	194
1997—	St. Louis (N.L.)	12	9	.571	3.88	28	28	0	0	0	181	155	86	78	65	160
1998—	St. Louis (N.L.)	9	9	.500	3.51	23	23	3	0	0	161¹/₃	146	74	63	51	147
—	Texas (A.L.)■	5	4	.556	4.33	10	10	0	0	0	60¹/₃	68	33	29	30	57
1999—	Arizona (N.L.)■	6	3	.667	4.09	17	17	0	0	0	101¹/₃	106	51	46	40	74
—	Ariz. D-backs (Ariz.)	2	0	1.000	0.53	3	3	1	0	0	17	11	1	1	1	25
2000—	Arizona (N.L.)	9	6	.600	4.91	18	18	0	0	0	95¹/₃	98	55	52	36	76
—	Ariz. D-backs (Ariz.)	1	1	.500	3.60	2	2	0	0	0	10	10	4	4	1	10
A.L. totals (9 years)		88	81	.521	4.41	247	216	17	4	1	1409	1478	747	690	524	924
N.L. totals (5 years)		50	38	.568	3.95	120	119	8	2	0	762¹/₃	696	366	335	285	651
Major League totals (13 years)		138	119	.537	4.25	367	335	25	6	1	2171¹/₃	2174	1113	1025	809	1575

DIVISION SERIES RECORD

Year	League	W	L	Pct.	ERA	G	GS	CG	ShO	Sv.	IP	H	R	ER	BB	SO
1996—	St. Louis (N.L.)	1	0	1.000	1.35	1	1	0	0	0	6²/₃	5	1	1	2	7
1998—	Texas (A.L.)	0	1	.000	2.25	1	1	1	0	0	8	6	2	2	4	8
1999—	Arizona (N.L.)	1	0	1.000	1.35	1	1	0	0	0	6²/₃	4	1	1	5	6
Division series totals (3 years)		2	1	.667	1.69	3	3	1	0	0	21¹/₃	15	4	4	11	21

CHAMPIONSHIP SERIES RECORD

RECORDS: Shares single-series record for most earned runs allowed—11 (1996). ... Shares single-game record for most earned runs allowed—7 (October 14, 1996). ... Shares record for most hits allowed in one inning—6 (October 14, 1996, first inning).

Year	League	W	L	Pct.	ERA	G	GS	CG	ShO	Sv.	IP	H	R	ER	BB	SO
1989—	Toronto (A.L.)	0	1	.000	7.20	1	1	0	0	0	5	7	4	4	2	3
1991—	Toronto (A.L.)	0	1	.000	9.82	1	1	0	0	0	3²/₃	7	4	4	1	3
1992—	Toronto (A.L.)	0	0	...	2.45	1	0	0	0	0	3²/₃	3	1	1	0	1
1993—	Toronto (A.L.)	0	1	.000	7.50	1	1	0	0	0	6	6	5	5	4	4
1996—	St. Louis (N.L.)	1	1	.500	12.38	3	2	0	0	0	8	15	11	11	3	11
Champ. series totals (5 years)		1	4	.200	8.54	7	5	0	0	0	26¹/₃	38	25	25	10	22

WORLD SERIES RECORD

RECORDS: Shares records for most bases on balls allowed in one inning—4 (October 20, 1993, first inning); and most consecutive bases on balls allowed in one inning—3 (October 20, 1993, first inning).

NOTES: Member of World Series championship team (1992 and 1993).

Year	League	W	L	Pct.	ERA	G	GS	CG	ShO	Sv.	IP	H	R	ER	BB	SO
1992—	Toronto (A.L.)	0	0	...	0.00	4	0	0	0	0	3²/₃	4	0	0	0	4
1993—	Toronto (A.L.)	0	0	...	27.00	1	1	0	0	0	2	3	6	6	4	1
World Series totals (2 years)		0	0	...	9.53	5	1	0	0	0	5²/₃	7	6	6	4	5

STRICKLAND, SCOTT   P   EXPOS

PERSONAL: Born April 26, 1976, in Houston. ... 5-11/180. ... Throws right, bats right. ... Full name: Scott Michael Strickland.
HIGH SCHOOL: Klein Oak (Spring, Texas).
COLLEGE: New Mexico.
TRANSACTIONS/CAREER NOTES: Selected by Montreal Expos organization in 10th round of free-agent draft (June 3, 1997). ... On Montreal disabled list (May 3-July 3, 2000); included rehabilitation assignment to Ottawa (June 25-July 1).

Year	League	W	L	Pct.	ERA	G	GS	CG	ShO	Sv.	IP	H	R	ER	BB	SO
1997—	Cape Fear (S.Atl.)	0	1	.000	6.35	3	1	0	0	1	5²/₃	8	7	4	1	8
—	Vermont (NY-Penn)	5	2	.714	3.82	15	9	1	0	0	61¹/₃	56	27	26	20	69
1998—	Cape Fear (S.Atl.)	0	3	.000	4.46	15	2	0	0	4	36¹/₃	36	19	18	12	53
—	Jupiter (FSL)	4	3	.571	3.39	22	11	0	0	2	69	64	28	26	20	51
1999—	Jupiter (FSL)	1	1	.500	3.51	12	1	0	0	2	25²/₃	21	11	10	4	33
—	Harrisburg (East.)	1	1	.500	2.48	14	1	0	0	3	29	25	8	8	10	36
—	Ottawa (I.L.)	3	0	1.000	1.63	19	0	0	0	5	27²/₃	23	5	5	11	34
—	Montreal (N.L.)	0	1	.000	4.50	17	0	0	0	0	18	15	10	9	11	23
2000—	Montreal (N.L.)	4	3	.571	3.00	49	0	0	0	9	48	38	18	16	16	48
—	Ottawa (I.L.)	0	0	...	0.00	3	0	0	0	0	4	1	0	0	0	4
Major League totals (2 years)		4	4	.500	3.41	66	0	0	0	9	66	53	28	25	27	71

STRONG, JOE P MARLINS

PERSONAL: Born September 9, 1962, in Fairfield, Calif. ... 6-0/200. ... Throws right, bats right. ... Full name: Joseph Benjamin Strong.
HIGH SCHOOL: St. Patrick's (Vallejo, Calif.).
JUNIOR COLLEGE: Contra Costa College (Calif.).
COLLEGE: UC Riverside.
TRANSACTIONS/CAREER NOTES: Selected by Oakland Athletics organization in 15th round of free-agent draft (June 4, 1984). ... Released by A's (January 7, 1987). ... Signed by Reno, California League (April 7, 1988). ... Released by Reno (January 1, 1990). ... Pitched in Taiwan 1990-92). ... Signed by San Diego Padres organization (February 12, 1993). ... Released by Padres (September 2, 1993). ... Signed by San Bernardino, California League (April 6, 1994). ... Granted free agency (October 17, 1994). ... Signed by Chicago Cubs organization (January 24, 1995). ... Released by Cubs (April 2, 1995). ... Signed by Surrey, Western League (May 1995). ... Signed by Hyundai, Korean League 1998). ... Signed by Tampa Bay Devil Rays organization (February 23, 1999). ... On Durham disabled list (April 27-May 7, 1999). ... Loaned by Devil Rays to Mexico City Tigres, Mexican League (July 5-September 20, 1999). ... Granted free agency (October 15, 1999). ... Signed by Florida Marlins organization (February 1, 2000). ... On Calgary disabled list (April 12-24, 2000). ... Granted free agency (October 18, 2000). ... Re-signed by Marlins organization (November 3, 2000).

Year	League	W	L	Pct.	ERA	G	GS	CG	ShO	Sv.	IP	H	R	ER	BB	SO
1984—	Medford (N'West)	5	6	.455	3.88	20	9	3	0	2	72	64	33	31	36	66
1985—	Modesto (Calif.)	7	7	.500	5.06	42	11	2	0	6	110 1/3	103	79	62	60	82
1986—	Modesto (Calif.)	2	2	.500	3.42	36	0	0	0	11	52 2/3	43	23	20	28	39
1987—									Did not play.							
1988—	Reno (Calif.)■	4	13	.235	4.79	31	24	2	0	0	161 2/3	168	114	86	96	107
1989—	Reno (Calif.)	8	1	.889	3.58	53	0	0	0	18	73	62	35	29	22	79
1990—	Taipei (Taiwan)■	18	7	.720	3.58	...	...	...	...	...	73	...	...	...	...	...
1991—	Taipei (Taiwan)	15	7	.682	3.58	...	...	...	...	...	73	...	...	...	...	...
1992—	Taipei (Taiwan)	12	10	.545	3.58	...	...	...	...	...	73	...	...	...	...	...
1993—	Las Vegas (PCL)■	1	3	.250	5.67	21	0	0	0	0	27	37	23	17	10	18
	Rancho Cuca. (Calif.)	1	0	1.000	2.70	7	0	0	0	1	10	10	3	3	2	13
	Wichita (Texas)	1	0	1.000	6.75	4	3	0	0	0	14 2/3	13	13	11	11	13
1994—	San Bernardino (Calif.)■	2	3	.400	6.71	12	11	0	0	0	53 2/3	60	46	40	27	43
1995—	Surrey (West.)■	8	9	.471	2.75	20	19	9	...	0	131	120	55	40	48	129
1996—									Did not play.							
1997—									Did not play.							
1998—	Hyundai (Korean)■	6	5	.545	6.21	53	0	0	0	27	58	64	...		29	54
1999—	Durham (I.L.)■	0	1	.000	7.98	6	1	0	0	1	14 2/3	20	13	13	8	12
	Orlando (Sou.)	1	4	.200	5.68	11	7	2	0	0	38	40	24	24	18	34
	M.C. Tigres (Mex.)■	1	1	.500	4.72	11	0	0	0	2	13 1/3	17	9	7	10	10
2000—	Calgary (PCL)■	2	1	.667	4.03	29	1	0	0	9	44 2/3	44	21	20	20	33
	Florida (N.L.)	1	1	.500	7.32	18	0	0	0	1	19 2/3	26	16	16	12	18
Major League totals (1 year)		1	1	.500	7.32	18	0	0	0	1	19 2/3	26	16	16	12	18

STULL, EVERETT P • BREWERS

PERSONAL: Born August 24, 1971, in Fort Riley, Ga. ... 6-3/200. ... Throws right, bats right. ... Full name: Everett James Stull.
HIGH SCHOOL: Redan (Stone Mountain, Ga.).
COLLEGE: Tennessee State.
TRANSACTIONS/CAREER NOTES: Selected by Montreal Expos organization in third round of free-agent draft (June 1, 1992). ... Traded by Expos to Baltimore Orioles (October 31, 1997), completing deal in which Orioles traded P Mike Johnson to Expos for a player to be named later (July 31, 1997). ... On Baltimore disabled list (March 19-July 27, 1998); included rehabilitation assignment to Rochester (June 13-July 27). ... Granted free agency (October 15, 1998). ... Signed by Atlanta Braves organization (January 20, 1999). ... Granated free agency (March 20, 2000). ... Signed by Milwaukee Brewers organization (March 30, 2000).
STATISTICAL NOTES: Led New York-Pennsylvania League with 18 wild pitches in 1992.

Year	League	W	L	Pct.	ERA	G	GS	CG	ShO	Sv.	IP	H	R	ER	BB	SO
1992—	Jamestown (NY-Penn)	3	5	.375	5.40	14	14	0	0	0	63 1/3	52	49	38	*61	64
1993—	Burlington (Midw.)	4	9	.308	3.83	15	15	0	0	0	82 1/3	68	44	35	59	85
1994—	West Palm Beach (FSL)	10	10	.500	3.31	27	26	3	1	0	147	116	60	54	78	165
1995—	Harrisburg (East.)	3	•12	.200	5.54	24	24	0	0	0	126 2/3	114	88	78	79	132
1996—	Harrisburg (East.)	6	3	.667	3.15	14	14	0	0	0	80	64	31	28	52	81
	Ottawa (I.L.)	2	6	.250	6.33	13	13	1	0	0	69 2/3	87	57	49	39	69
1997—	Ottawa (I.L.)	8	10	.444	5.82	27	27	1	0	0	159 1/3	166	110	*103	86	130
	Montreal (N.L.)	0	1	.000	16.20	3	0	0	0	0	3 1/3	7	7	6	4	2
1998—	Rochester (I.L.)■	1	4	.200	8.86	21	7	0	0	0	42 2/3	49	44	42	45	39
1999—	Richmond (I.L.)■	8	8	.500	4.47	30	22	0	0	0	139	124	75	69	73	126
	Atlanta (N.L.)	0	0	...	13.50	1	0	0	0	0	2/3	2	3	1	2	0
2000—	Indianapolis (I.L.)■	7	5	.583	2.95	16	16	1	1	0	103 2/3	95	41	34	43	74
	Milwaukee (N.L.)	2	3	.400	5.82	20	4	0	0	0	43 1/3	41	30	28	30	33
Major League totals (3 years)		2	4	.333	6.65	24	4	0	0	0	47 1/3	50	40	35	36	35

STURTZE, TANYON P DEVIL RAYS

PERSONAL: Born October 12, 1970, in Worcester, Mass. ... 6-5/205. ... Throws right, bats right. ... Full name: Tanyon James Sturtze. ... Name pronounced STURTS.
HIGH SCHOOL: St. Peter-Marian (Worcester, Mass.).
JUNIOR COLLEGE: Quinsigamond Community College (Mass.).
TRANSACTIONS/CAREER NOTES: Selected by Oakland Athletics organization in 23rd round of free-agent draft (June 4, 1990). ... On Huntsville disabled list (April 7-16, 1994). ... Selected by Chicago Cubs from A's organization in Rule 5 major league draft (December 5, 1994). ... Granted free agency (October 15, 1996). ... Signed by Texas Rangers (November 20, 1996). ... Released by Rangers (March 6, 1998). ... Re-signed by Rangers organization (March 11, 1998). ... Granted free agency (October 15, 1998). ... Signed by Florida Marlins organization (November 23, 1998). ... Signed by Chicago White Sox organization (November 23, 1998). ... On suspended list (May 1-3, 2000). ... Traded by White Sox to Tampa Bay Devil Rays for 2B/SS Tony Graffanino (May 31, 2000). ... On Tampa Bay disabled list (August 27, 2000-remainder of season).
STATISTICAL NOTES: Pitched 5-0 no-hit victory against Chattanooga (June 13, 1993).

Year	League	W	L	Pct.	ERA	G	GS	CG	ShO	Sv.	IP	H	R	ER	BB	SO
1990— Arizona Athletics (Ariz.)......		2	5	.286	5.44	12	10	0	0	0	48	55	41	29	27	30
1991— Madison (Midw.)................		10	5	.667	3.09	27	27	0	0	0	163	136	77	56	58	88
1992— Modesto (Calif.)...............		7	11	.389	3.75	25	25	1	0	0	151	143	72	63	78	126
1993— Huntsville (Sou.)		5	12	.294	4.78	28	•28	1	1	0	165 2/3	169	102	*88	85	112
1994— Huntsville (Sou.)		6	3	.667	3.22	17	17	1	0	0	103 1/3	100	40	37	39	63
— Tacoma (PCL)		4	5	.444	4.04	11	9	0	0	0	64 2/3	73	36	29	34	28
1995— Chicago (N.L.)■.............		0	0	...	9.00	2	0	0	0	0	2	2	2	2	1	0
— Iowa (A.A.).....................		4	7	.364	6.80	23	17	1	1	0	86	108	66	65	42	48
1996— Iowa (A.A.)		6	4	.600	4.85	51	1	0	0	4	72 1/3	80	42	39	33	51
— Chicago (N.L.)		1	0	1.000	9.00	6	0	0	0	0	11	16	11	11	5	7
1997— Oklahoma City (A.A.)■......		8	6	.571	5.10	25	19	1	0	0	114 2/3	133	76	65	47	79
— Texas (A.L.)		1	1	.500	8.27	9	5	0	0	0	32 2/3	45	30	30	18	18
1998— Gulf Coast Rangers (GCL)..		0	1	.000	7.71	3	3	0	0	0	7	12	7	6	4	10
— Charlotte (FSL).................		0	1	.000	6.00	1	0	0	0	0	3	2	3	2	1	3
— Tulsa (Texas)		1	0	1.000	5.40	1	0	0	0	0	1 2/3	2	1	1	2	3
— Oklahoma (PCL)		3	1	.750	3.34	13	3	0	0	0	35	33	13	13	18	31
1999— Charlotte (I.L.)■.............		9	4	.692	4.05	33	14	2	1	3	104 1/3	83	53	47	41	107
— Chicago (A.L.)		0	0	...	0.00	1	1	0	0	0	6	4	0	0	2	2
2000— Chicago (A.L.)		1	2	.333	12.06	10	1	0	0	0	15 2/3	25	23	21	15	6
— Tampa Bay (A.L.)■...........		4	0	1.000	2.56	19	5	0	0	0	52 2/3	47	16	15	14	38
A.L. totals (3 years)		6	3	.667	5.55	39	12	0	0	0	107	121	69	66	49	64
N.L. totals (2 years)		1	0	1.000	9.00	8	0	0	0	0	13	18	13	13	6	7
Major League totals (5 years)		7	3	.700	5.93	47	12	0	0	0	120	139	82	79	55	71

S

STYNES, CHRIS   IF   RED SOX

PERSONAL: Born January 19, 1973, in Queens, N.Y. ... 5-10/185. ... Bats right, throws right. ... Full name: Christopher Desmond Stynes.
HIGH SCHOOL: Boca Raton (Fla.).
TRANSACTIONS/CAREER NOTES: Selected by Toronto Blue Jays in third round of free-agent draft (June 3, 1991). ... Traded by Blue Jays with P David Sinnes and IF Tony Medrano to Kansas City Royals for P David Cone (April 6, 1995). ... Traded by Royals with OF Jon Nunnally to Cincinnati Reds for P Hector Carrasco and P Scott Service (July 15, 1997). ... Traded by Reds to Boston Red Sox for OF Michael Coleman and IF Donnie Sadler (November 16, 2000).
STATISTICAL NOTES: Tied for Florida State League lead in double plays by third basemen with 22 in 1993. ... Led Southern League with 237 total bases in 1994.

								BATTING							FIELDING		
Year	Team (League)	Pos.	G	AB	R	H	2B	3B	HR	RBI	Avg.	BB	SO	SB	PO	A	E	Avg.
1991— GC Blue Jays (GCL)....		3B	57	219	29	67	15	1	4	39	.306	9	39	10	42	*138	8	*.957
1992— Myrtle Beach (S.Atl.)..		3B	127	489	67	139	36	0	7	46	.284	16	43	28	86	208	26	.919
1993— Dunedin (FSL)		3B	123	496	72	151	28	5	7	48	.304	25	40	19	83	234	21	*.938
1994— Knoxville (Sou.).........		2B	136	*545	79	*173	32	4	8	79	.317	23	36	28	247	•366	20	.968
1995— Omaha (A.A.)■		2B-3B	83	306	51	84	12	5	9	42	.275	27	24	4	144	204	13	.964
— Kansas City (A.L.)		2B-DH	22	35	7	6	1	0	0	2	.171	4	3	0	21	35	1	.982
1996— Omaha (A.A.)...........OF-3B-2B-DH			72	284	50	101	22	2	10	40	.356	18	17	7	98	77	9	.951
— Kansas City (A.L.) OF-2B-DH-3B			36	92	8	27	6	0	0	6	.293	2	5	5	38	8	3	.939
1997— Omaha (A.A.)...........2B-OF-DH-3B			82	332	53	88	18	1	8	44	.265	19	25	3	101	80	10	.948
— Indianapolis (A.A.)■ ..		2B	21	86	14	31	8	0	1	17	.360	2	5	4	47	61	2	.982
— Cincinnati (N.L.)		OF-2B-3B	49	198	31	69	7	1	6	28	.348	11	13	11	87	33	2	.984
1998— Cincinnati (N.L.)		O-3-2-S	123	347	52	88	10	1	6	27	.254	32	36	15	148	54	2	.990
1999— Cincinnati (N.L.)		2B-3B-OF	73	113	18	27	1	0	2	14	.239	12	13	5	50	71	6	.953
2000— Cincinnati (N.L.)		3B-2B-OF	119	380	71	127	24	1	12	40	.334	32	54	5	83	145	7	.970
American League totals (2 years)			58	127	15	33	7	0	0	8	.260	6	8	5	59	43	4	.962
National League totals (4 years)			364	1038	172	311	42	3	26	109	.300	87	116	36	368	303	17	.975
Major League totals (6 years)			422	1165	187	344	49	3	26	117	.295	93	124	41	427	346	21	.974

SULLIVAN, SCOTT   P   REDS

PERSONAL: Born March 13, 1971, in Carrollton, Ala. ... 6-3/210. ... Throws right, bats right. ... Full name: William Scott Sullivan.
HIGH SCHOOL: Pickens Academy (Carrollton, Ala.).
COLLEGE: Auburn.
TRANSACTIONS/CAREER NOTES: Selected by Cincinnati Reds organization in second round of free-agent draft (June 3, 1993). ... On Indianapolis disabled list (August 21, 1995-remainder of season).
MISCELLANEOUS: Appeared in one game as pinch runner (2000).

Year	League	W	L	Pct.	ERA	G	GS	CG	ShO	Sv.	IP	H	R	ER	BB	SO
1993— Billings (Pio.)		5	0	1.000	1.67	18	7	2	2	3	54	33	13	10	25	79
1994— Chattanooga (Sou.)		11	7	.611	3.41	34	13	2	0	7	121 1/3	101	60	46	40	111
1995— Indianapolis (A.A.).............		4	3	.571	3.53	44	0	0	0	1	58 2/3	51	31	23	24	54
— Cincinnati (N.L.)		0	0	...	4.91	3	0	0	0	0	3 2/3	4	2	2	2	2
1996— Indianapolis (A.A.).............		5	2	.714	2.73	53	3	0	0	1	108 2/3	95	38	33	37	77
— Cincinnati (N.L.)		0	0	...	2.25	7	0	0	0	0	8	7	2	2	5	3
1997— Cincinnati (N.L.)		5	3	.625	3.24	59	0	0	0	1	97 1/3	79	36	35	30	96
— Indianapolis (A.A.)............		3	1	.750	1.30	19	0	0	0	2	27 2/3	16	4	4	4	23
1998— Cincinnati (N.L.)		5	5	.500	5.21	67	0	0	0	1	102	98	62	59	36	86
1999— Cincinnati (N.L.)		5	4	.556	3.01	79	0	0	0	3	113 2/3	88	41	38	47	78
2000— Cincinnati (N.L.)		3	6	.333	3.47	79	0	0	0	3	106 1/3	87	44	41	38	96
Major League totals (6 years)		18	18	.500	3.70	294	0	0	0	8	431	363	187	177	158	361

SUPPAN, JEFF   P   ROYALS

PERSONAL: Born January 2, 1975, in Oklahoma City. ... 6-2/210. ... Throws right, bats right. ... Full name: Jeffrey Scot Suppan.

HIGH SCHOOL: Crespi (Encino, Calif.).

TRANSACTIONS/CAREER NOTES: Selected by Boston Red Sox organization in second round of free-agent draft (June 3, 1993). ... On Trenton disabled list (April 9-29, 1995). ... On Boston disabled list (August 25, 1996-remainder of season). ... Selected by Arizona Diamondbacks in first round (third pick overall) of expansion draft (November 18, 1997). ... Contract purchased by Kansas City Royals from Diamondbacks (September 3, 1998).

STATISTICAL NOTES: Led A.L. with 36 home runs allowed in 2000.

Year	League	W	L	Pct.	ERA	G	GS	CG	ShO	Sv.	IP	H	R	ER	BB	SO
1993—	Gulf Coast Red Sox (GCL)..	4	3	.571	2.18	10	9	2	1	0	57²/₃	52	20	14	16	64
1994—	Sarasota (FSL)	•13	7	.650	3.26	27	27	4	2	0	174	153	74	63	50	*173
1995—	Trenton (East.)	6	2	.750	2.36	15	15	1	1	0	99	86	35	26	26	88
—	Boston (A.L.)......................	1	2	.333	5.96	8	3	0	0	0	22²/₃	29	15	15	5	19
—	Pawtucket (I.L.).................	2	3	.400	5.32	7	7	0	0	0	45²/₃	50	29	27	9	32
1996—	Boston (A.L.)......................	1	1	.500	7.54	8	4	0	0	0	22²/₃	29	19	19	13	13
—	Pawtucket (I.L.).................	10	6	.625	3.22	22	22	7	1	0	145¹/₃	130	66	52	25	142
1997—	Pawtucket (I.L.).................	5	1	.833	3.71	9	9	2	1	0	60²/₃	51	26	25	15	40
—	Boston (A.L.)......................	7	3	.700	5.69	23	22	0	0	0	112¹/₃	140	75	71	36	67
1998—	Arizona (N.L.)■..................	1	7	.125	6.68	13	13	1	0	0	66	82	55	49	21	39
—	Tucson (PCL)	4	3	.571	3.63	13	12	0	0	0	67	75	29	27	17	62
—	Kansas City (A.L.)■	0	0	...	0.71	4	1	0	0	0	12²/₃	9	1	1	1	12
1999—	Kansas City (A.L.)	10	12	.455	4.53	32	32	4	1	0	208²/₃	222	113	105	62	103
2000—	Kansas City (A.L.)	10	9	.526	4.94	35	33	3	1	0	217	240	121	119	84	128
A.L. totals (6 years)		29	27	.518	4.98	110	95	7	2	0	596	669	344	330	201	342
N.L. totals (1 year)		1	7	.125	6.68	13	13	1	0	0	66	82	55	49	21	39
Major League totals (6 years)		30	34	.469	5.15	123	108	8	2	0	662	751	399	379	222	381

SURHOFF, B.J.   OF   BRAVES

PERSONAL: Born August 4, 1964, in Bronx, N.Y. ... 6-1/200. ... Bats left, throws right. ... Full name: William James Surhoff. ... Son of Dick Surhoff, forward with New York Knicks and Milwaukee Hawks of National Basketball Association (1952-53 and 1953-54); and brother of Rich Surhoff, pitcher with Philadelphia Phillies and Texas Rangers (1985).

HIGH SCHOOL: Rye (N.Y.).

COLLEGE: North Carolina.

TRANSACTIONS/CAREER NOTES: Selected by New York Yankees organization in fifth round of free-agent draft (June 7, 1982); did not sign. ... Selected by Milwaukee Brewers organization in first round (first pick overall) of free-agent draft (June 3, 1985). ... On suspended list (August 23-25, 1990). ... On Milwaukee disabled list (March 25-April 16, April 20-May 23 and July 7, 1994-remainder of season); included rehabilitation assignments to El Paso (April 12-16) and New Orleans (May 17-23). ... Granted free agency (October 20, 1994). ... Re-signed by Brewers organization (April 7, 1995). ... Granted free agency (November 6, 1995). ... Signed by Baltimore Orioles (December 20, 1995). ... On disabled list (May 18-June 2, 1996). ... Granted free agency (October 26, 1998). ... Re-signed by Orioles (December 7, 1998). ... Traded by Orioles with P Gabe Molina to Atlanta Braves for OF Trenidad Hubbard, C Fernando Lunar and P Luis Rivera (July 31, 2000).

RECORDS: Shares major league single-inning record for most doubles—2 (September 14, 1999, fifth inning).

HONORS: Named College Player of the Year by THE SPORTING NEWS (1985). ... Named catcher on THE SPORTING NEWS college All-America team (1985).

STATISTICAL NOTES: Tied for Pacific Coast League lead in double plays by catcher with 10 in 1986. ... Led A.L. catchers with 68 assists in 1991. ... Had 15-game hitting streak (May 9-25, 1999). ... Had 21-game hitting streak (May 29-June 20, 1999). ... Led A.L. outfielders with 1.000 fielding percentage in 1999. ... Had 21-game hitting streak (June 5-28, 2000). ... Career major league grand slams: 5.

MISCELLANEOUS: Member of 1984 U.S. Olympic baseball team.

								BATTING							FIELDING		
Year	Team (League)	Pos.	G	AB	R	H	2B	3B	HR	RBI	Avg.	BB	SO	SB	PO	A	E	Avg.
1985—	Beloit (Midw.)............	C	76	289	39	96	13	4	7	58	.332	22	35	10	475	44	3	.994
1986—	Vancouver (PCL)	C	116	458	71	141	19	3	5	59	.308	29	30	21	539	70	7	*.989
1987—	Milwaukee (A.L.)	C-3-DH-1	115	395	50	118	22	3	7	68	.299	36	30	11	648	56	11	.985
1988—	Milwaukee (A.L.)	C-3-1-S-O	139	493	47	121	21	0	5	38	.245	31	49	21	550	94	8	.988
1989—	Milwaukee (A.L.)	C-DH-3B	126	436	42	108	17	4	5	55	.248	25	29	14	530	58	10	.983
1990—	Milwaukee (A.L.)	C-3B	135	474	55	131	21	4	6	59	.276	41	37	18	619	62	12	.983
1991—	Milwaukee (A.L.) C-DH-3-O-2		143	505	57	146	19	4	5	68	.289	26	33	5	665	†71	4	.995
1992—	Milwaukee (A.L.) C-1-DH-O-3		139	480	63	121	19	1	4	62	.252	46	41	14	699	74	6	.992
1993—	Milwaukee (A.L.)	3-O-1-C-DH	148	552	66	151	38	3	7	79	.274	36	47	12	175	220	18	.956
1994—	El Paso (Texas)...........	OF	3	12	2	3	1	0	0	0	.250	0	2	0	3	0	0	1.000
—	Milwaukee (A.L.) 3-C-1-O-DH		40	134	20	35	11	2	5	22	.261	16	14	0	121	29	4	.974
—	New Orleans (A.A.).....	3B-OF-C-1B	5	19	3	6	2	0	0	1	.316	1	2	0	21	3	0	1.000
1995—	Milwaukee (A.L.)	O-1-C-DH	117	415	72	133	26	3	13	73	.320	37	43	7	530	44	5	.991
1996—	Baltimore (A.L.)■........	3-O-DH-1	143	537	74	157	27	6	21	82	.292	47	79	0	137	178	15	.955
1997—	Baltimore (A.L.)..........	O-DH-1-3	147	528	80	150	30	4	18	88	.284	49	60	1	268	16	2	.993
1998—	Baltimore (A.L.)..........	OF-1B	162	573	79	160	34	1	22	92	.279	49	81	9	256	12	3	.989
1999—	Baltimore (A.L.)..........	OF-DH-3B	*162	*673	104	207	38	1	28	107	.308	43	78	5	283	21	0	†1.000
2000—	Baltimore (A.L.)..........	OF-DH	103	411	56	120	27	0	13	57	.292	29	46	7	226	5	3	.987
—	Atlanta (N.L.)■..........	OF	44	128	13	37	9	2	1	11	.289	12	12	3	50	1	0	1.000
American League totals (14 years)			1819	6606	865	1858	350	36	159	950	.281	511	667	124	5707	940	101	.985
National League totals (1 year)			44	128	13	37	9	2	1	11	.289	12	12	3	50	1	0	1.000
Major League totals (14 years)			1863	6734	878	1895	359	38	160	961	.281	523	679	127	5757	941	101	.985

DIVISION SERIES RECORD

RECORDS: Shares single-game record for most home runs—2 (October 1, 1996).

								BATTING							FIELDING		
Year	Team (League)	Pos.	G	AB	R	H	2B	3B	HR	RBI	Avg.	BB	SO	SB	PO	A	E	Avg.
1996—	Baltimore (A.L.)..........	OF-PH	4	13	3	5	0	0	3	5	.385	0	1	0	6	0	0	1.000
1997—	Baltimore (A.L.)..........	OF-PH	3	11	0	3	1	0	0	2	.273	0	2	0	1	1	0	1.000
2000—	Atlanta (N.L.)............	PH	2	2	0	1	0	0	0	0	.500	0	0	0	...	...	...	...
Division series totals (3 years)			9	26	3	9	1	0	3	7	.346	0	3	0	7	1	0	1.000

Year	Team (League)	Pos.	G	AB	R	H	2B	3B	HR	RBI	Avg.	BB	SO	SB	PO	A	E	Avg.
1996—	Baltimore (A.L.)..........	OF-PH	5	15	0	4	0	0	0	2	.267	1	2	0	11	1	0	1.000
1997—	Baltimore (A.L.)..........	OF-1B	6	25	1	5	2	0	0	1	.200	2	2	0	13	0	0	1.000
Championship series totals (2 years)			11	40	1	9	2	0	0	3	.225	3	4	0	24	1	0	1.000

ALL-STAR GAME RECORD

Year	League	Pos.	AB	R	H	2B	3B	HR	RBI	Avg.	BB	SO	SB	PO	A	E	Avg.
1999—	American	OF	2	0	0	0	0	0	0	.000	0	0	0	0	0	0	...

SUTTON, LARRY — 1B/OF — CARDINALS

PERSONAL: Born May 14, 1970, in West Covina, Calif. ... 6-0/185. ... Bats left, throws left. ... Full name: Larry James Sutton.
HIGH SCHOOL: Mater Dei (Santa Ana, Calif.).
COLLEGE: Illinois.
TRANSACTIONS/CAREER NOTES: Selected by Kansas City organization in 21st round of free-agent draft (June 1, 1992). ... On Kansas City disabled list (June 6-July 27, 1999); included rehabilitation assignments to Gulf Coast Royals (July 5-15) and Omaha (July 16-25). ... Granted free agency (October 18, 1999). ... Signed by St. Louis Cardinals organization (December 8, 1999).
HONORS: Named Northwest League Most Valuable Player (1992). ... Named Carolina League Most Valuable Player (1994).
STATISTICAL NOTES: Led Northwest League with 142 total bases in 1992. ... Led Midwest League first basemen with 92 double plays in 1993. ... Led Carolina League with .542 slugging percentage, 10 intentional bases on balls received and nine sacrifice flies in 1994. ... Led Texas League first basemen with .989 fielding percentage in 1996. ... Career major league grand slams: 1.

Year	Team (League)	Pos.	G	AB	R	H	2B	3B	HR	RBI	Avg.	BB	SO	SB	PO	A	E	Avg.
1992—	Eugene (N'West)	1B	70	238	45	74	17	3	*15	*58	.311	48	33	3	517	29	14	.975
	— Appleton (Midw.)........	DH	1	2	1	0	0	0	0	0	.000	2	1	0	...	...	...	...
1993—	Rockford (Midw.)	1B	113	361	67	97	24	1	7	50	.269	*95	65	3	911	76	11	.989
1994—	Wilmington (Caro.).....	1B	129	480	91	147	33	1	26	94	.306	*81	71	2	1086	71	12	*.990
1995—	Wichita (Texas)	1B	53	197	31	53	11	1	5	32	.269	26	33	1	452	25	7	.986
1996—	Wichita (Texas)	1B-OF-DH	125	463	84	137	22	2	22	84	.296	77	66	4	1105	76	13	*.989
1997—	Omaha (A.A.).............	1B-DH	106	380	61	114	27	1	19	72	.300	61	57	0	839	54	5	.994
	— Kansas City (A.L.)	1B-DH-OF	27	69	9	20	2	0	2	8	.290	5	12	0	92	8	0	1.000
1998—	Kansas City (A.L.)	OF-1B-DH	111	310	29	76	14	2	5	42	.245	29	46	3	179	7	2	.989
1999—	Kansas City (A.L.)	1B-DH-OF	43	102	14	23	6	0	2	15	.225	13	17	1	215	13	3	.987
	— GC Royals (GCL)	1B-DH-OF	9	31	7	8	2	0	1	6	.258	7	6	0	43	0	1	.977
	— Omaha (PCL).............	1B-OF	39	148	28	41	8	1	3	12	.277	27	24	4	247	21	4	.985
2000—	Memphis (PCL)■.......	1B	95	347	61	89	21	2	12	70	.256	67	56	4	771	84	8	.991
	— St. Louis (N.L.).......	1B-OF	23	25	5	8	0	0	1	6	.320	5	7	0	31	2	0	1.000
American League totals (3 years)			181	481	52	119	22	2	9	65	.247	47	75	4	486	28	5	.990
National League totals (1 year)			23	25	5	8	0	0	1	6	.320	5	7	0	31	2	0	1.000
Major League totals (4 years)			204	506	57	127	22	2	10	71	.251	52	82	4	517	30	5	.991

SUZUKI, MAC — P — ROYALS

PERSONAL: Born May 31, 1975, in Kobe, Japan. ... 6-3/205. ... Throws right, bats right. ... Full name: Makoto Suzuki.
HIGH SCHOOL: Takigawa Daini (Kobe, Japan).
TRANSACTIONS/CAREER NOTES: Played with Salinas, independent (August 30, 1992). ... Signed by San Bernardino, independent (April 9, 1993). ... Contract purchased by Seattle Mariners organization from San Bernardino (September 5, 1993). ... On disabled list (April 19-June 15 and July 10, 1994-remainder of season). ... On Riverside temporarily inactive list (April 22-August 3, 1995). ... On Riverside disabled list (August 3-18, 1995). ... On Port City disabled list (May 8-17, 1996). ... Traded by Mariners with a player to be named later to New York Mets for P Allen Watson and cash (June 18, 1999); Mets acquired P Justin Dunning to complete deal (September 14, 1999). ... Claimed on waivers by Kansas City Royals (June 22, 1999).

Year	League	W	L	Pct.	ERA	G	GS	CG	ShO	Sv.	IP	H	R	ER	BB	SO
1992—	Salinas (Calif.)....................	0	0	...	0.00	1	0	0	0	0	1	0	0	0	0	1
1993—	San Bernardino (Calif.)■....	4	4	.500	3.68	48	1	0	0	12	80²/₃	59	37	33	56	87
1994—	Jacksonville (Sou.).............	1	0	1.000	2.84	8	0	0	0	1	12²/₃	15	4	4	6	10
1995—	Riverside (Calif.)................	0	1	.000	4.70	6	0	0	0	0	7²/₃	10	4	4	6	6
	— Arizona Mariners (Ariz.)	1	0	1.000	6.75	4	3	0	0	0	4	5	4	3	0	3
1996—	Tacoma (PCL)	0	3	.000	7.25	13	2	0	0	0	22¹/₃	31	19	18	12	14
	— Port City (Sou.)	3	6	.333	4.72	16	16	0	0	0	74¹/₃	69	41	39	32	66
	— Seattle (A.L.)	0	0	...	20.25	1	0	0	0	0	1¹/₃	2	3	3	2	1
1997—	Tacoma (PCL)	4	9	.308	5.94	32	10	0	0	0	83¹/₃	79	60	55	64	63
1998—	Tacoma (PCL)	9	10	.474	4.37	28	21	2	1	0	131²/₃	130	70	64	70	117
	— Seattle (A.L.)	1	2	.333	7.18	6	5	0	0	0	26¹/₃	34	23	21	15	19
1999—	Seattle (A.L.)	0	2	.000	9.43	16	4	0	0	0	42	47	47	44	34	32
	— Kansas City (A.L.)■	2	3	.400	5.16	22	9	0	0	0	68	77	45	39	30	36
2000—	Kansas City (A.L.)	8	10	.444	4.34	32	29	1	1	0	188²/₃	195	100	91	94	135
Major League totals (4 years).......		11	17	.393	5.46	77	47	1	1	0	326¹/₃	355	218	198	175	223

SWEENEY, MARK — OF/1B — BREWERS

PERSONAL: Born October 26, 1969, in Framingham, Mass. ... 6-1/215. ... Bats left, throws left. ... Full name: Mark Patrick Sweeney.
HIGH SCHOOL: Holliston (Mass.).
COLLEGE: Maine.

TRANSACTIONS/CAREER NOTES: Selected by Los Angeles Dodgers organization in 39th round of free-agent draft (June 4, 1990); did not sign. ... Selected by California Angels organization in ninth round of free-agent draft (June 3, 1991). ... Traded by Angels organization with a player to be named later to St. Louis Cardinals for P John Habyan (July 8, 1995); Cardinals acquired IF Rod Correia to complete deal (January 31, 1996). ... Traded by Cardinals with P Danny Jackson and P Rich Batchelor to San Diego Padres for P Fernando Valenzuela, 3B Scott Livingstone and OF Phil Plantier (June 13, 1997). ... Traded by Padres with OF Greg Vaughn to Cincinnati Reds for OF Reggie Sanders, SS Damian Jackson and P Josh Harris (February 2, 1999). ... Traded by Reds with a player to be named later to Milwaukee Brewers for OF Alex Ochoa (January 14, 2000); Brewers acquired P Gene Altman to complete deal (May 15, 2000). ... On Milwaukee disabled list (March 31-May 7 and July 18-August 14, 2000); included rehabilitation assignments to Indianapolis (July 21-26 and August 3-14). ... Granted free agency (October 5, 2000). ... Re-signed by Brewers organization (January 3, 2000).

							BATTING							FIELDING		
Year	Team (League)	Pos.	G	AB	R	H	2B	3B	HR	RBI	Avg.	BB	SO	SB	PO	A	E	Avg.
1991—Boise (N'West)	OF	70	234	45	66	10	3	4	34	.282	*51	42	9	81	2	4	.954
1992—Quad City (Midw.)	OF	120	424	65	115	20	5	14	76	.271	47	85	15	205	5	4	.981
1993—Palm Springs (Calif.)..	OF-1B-DH	66	245	41	87	18	3	3	47	.355	42	29	9	145	2	7	.955
—Midland (Texas).........	OF	51	188	41	67	13	2	9	32	.356	27	22	1	85	3	1	.989
1994—Vancouver (PCL)	DH-1B-OF	103	344	59	98	12	3	8	49	.285	59	50	3	330	12	2	.994
—Midland (Texas).........	OF-1B-DH	14	50	13	15	3	0	3	18	.300	10	10	1	66	5	2	.973
1995—Vancouver (PCL)	OF-DH-1B	69	226	48	78	14	2	7	59	.345	43	33	3	102	2	2	.981
—Louisville (A.A.)■.......	1B	22	76	15	28	8	0	2	22	.368	14	8	2	176	19	2	.990
—St. Louis (N.L.)...........	1B-OF	37	77	5	21	2	0	2	13	.273	10	15	1	153	11	2	.988
1996—St. Louis (N.L.)..........	OF-1B	98	170	32	45	9	0	3	22	.265	33	29	3	126	3	3	.977
1997—St. Louis (N.L.)..........	OF-1B	44	61	5	13	3	0	0	4	.213	9	14	0	31	1	0	1.000
—San Diego (N.L.)■......	OF-1B	71	103	11	33	4	0	2	19	.320	11	18	2	41	3	2	.957
1998—San Diego (N.L.)	OF-1B-DH	122	192	17	45	8	3	2	15	.234	26	37	1	165	5	1	.994
1999—Cincinnati (N.L.)■.....	1B-OF	37	31	6	11	3	0	2	7	.355	4	9	0	3	0	0	1.000
—Indianapolis (I.L.).......	OF-DH-1B	86	311	66	100	17	1	12	51	.322	59	40	3	257	9	5	.982
2000—Indianapolis (I.L.)■.....	1B-OF	18	55	13	28	8	0	2	14	.509	10	8	0	18	3	0	1.000
—Milwaukee (N.L.)	DH-OF-1B	71	73	9	16	6	0	1	6	.219	12	18	0	11	0	0	1.000
Major League totals (6 years)		480	707	85	184	35	3	12	86	.260	105	140	7	530	23	8	.986

DIVISION SERIES RECORD

							BATTING							FIELDING		
Year	Team (League)	Pos.	G	AB	R	H	2B	3B	HR	RBI	Avg.	BB	SO	SB	PO	A	E	Avg.
1996—St. Louis (N.L.)..........	PH	1	1	0	1	0	0	0	0	1.000	0	0	0	...	...	...	...
1998—San Diego (N.L.)	PH	2	1	0	0	0	0	0	0	.000	1	0	0	...	...	...	...
Division series totals (2 years)		3	2	0	1	0	0	0	0	.500	1	0	0	...	...	...	...

CHAMPIONSHIP SERIES RECORD

							BATTING							FIELDING		
Year	Team (League)	Pos.	G	AB	R	H	2B	3B	HR	RBI	Avg.	BB	SO	SB	PO	A	E	Avg.
1996—St. Louis (N.L.)..........	PH-OF	5	4	1	0	0	0	0	0	.000	0	2	0	2	0	0	1.000
1998—San Diego (N.L.)	PH	3	2	1	0	0	0	0	0	.000	1	1	0	...	...	...	...
Championship series totals (2 years)		8	6	2	0	0	0	0	0	.000	1	3	0	2	0	0	1.000

WORLD SERIES RECORD

							BATTING							FIELDING		
Year	Team (League)	Pos.	G	AB	R	H	2B	3B	HR	RBI	Avg.	BB	SO	SB	PO	A	E	Avg.
1998—San Diego (N.L.)	PH	3	3	0	2	0	0	0	1	.667	0	0	0	...	...	...	...

SWEENEY, MIKE — 1B — ROYALS

PERSONAL: Born July 22, 1973, in Orange, Calif. ... 6-3/225. ... Bats right, throws right. ... Full name: Michael John Sweeney.
HIGH SCHOOL: Ontario (Calif.).
TRANSACTIONS/CAREER NOTES: Selected by Kansas City Royals organization in 10th round of free-agent draft (June 3, 1991). ... On disabled list (May 24-July 5, 1994).
RECORDS: Shares A.L. single-season record for most consecutive games with one or more runs batted in—13 (June 23-July 4, 1999).
STATISTICAL NOTES: Led Carolina League with .548 slugging percentage in 1995. ... Tied for A.L. lead in double plays by catcher with 13 in 1997. ... Had 16-game hitting streak (June 22-July 7, 1999). ... Had 25-game hitting streak (July 18-August 13, 1999). ... Had 16-game hitting streak (August 13-30, 2000). ... Tied for A.L. lead in being hit by pitch with 15 in 2000. ... Career major league grand slams: 1.

							BATTING							FIELDING		
Year	Team (League)	Pos.	G	AB	R	H	2B	3B	HR	RBI	Avg.	BB	SO	SB	PO	A	E	Avg.
1991—GC Royals (GCL)........	C-1B	38	102	8	22	3	0	1	11	.216	11	9	1	124	16	4	.972
1992—Eugene (N'West)	C	59	199	17	44	12	1	4	28	.221	13	54	3	367	42	14	.967
1993—Eugene (N'West)	C	53	175	32	42	10	2	6	29	.240	30	41	1	364	46	7	.983
1994—Rockford (Midw.)	C	86	276	47	83	20	3	10	52	.301	55	43	0	453	54	6	.988
1995—Wilmington (Caro.)......	C-DH-3B	99	332	61	103	23	1	18	53	*.310	60	39	6	575	45	7	.989
—Kansas City (A.L.)	C	4	4	1	1	0	0	0	0	.250	0	0	0	7	0	1	.875
1996—Wichita (Texas)	DH-C	66	235	45	75	18	1	14	51	.319	32	29	3	201	13	1	.995
—Omaha (A.A.).............	C-DH	25	101	14	26	9	0	3	16	.257	6	13	0	167	8	0	1.000
—Kansas City (A.L.)	C-DH	50	165	23	46	10	0	4	24	.279	18	21	1	158	7	1	.994
1997—Kansas City (A.L.)	C-DH	84	240	30	58	8	0	7	31	.242	17	33	3	425	31	3	.993
—Omaha (A.A.).............	C-DH	40	144	22	34	8	1	10	29	.236	18	20	0	229	15	1	.996
1998—Kansas City (A.L.)	C	92	282	32	73	18	0	8	35	.259	24	38	2	517	33	•9	.984
1999—Kansas City (A.L.)	1B-DH-C	150	575	101	185	44	2	22	102	.322	54	48	6	588	43	12	.981
2000—American (A.L.)	PH	1	1	0	0	0	0	0	0	.000	0	0	0	...	...	...	...
—Kansas City (A.L.)	1B-DH	159	618	105	206	30	0	29	144	.333	71	67	8	960	88	9	.991
Major League totals (6 years)		540	1885	292	569	110	2	70	336	.302	184	207	20	2655	202	35	.988

PERSONAL: Born January 2, 1965, in Fort Worth, Texas. ... 6-3/230. ... Throws left, bats left. ... Full name: Forest Gregory Swindell.

HIGH SCHOOL: Sharpstown (Houston).

COLLEGE: Texas.

TRANSACTIONS/CAREER NOTES: Selected by Cleveland Indians organization in first round (second pick overall) of free-agent draft (June 2, 1986). ... On disabled list (June 30, 1987-remainder of season; and July 26-August 30, 1989). ... Traded by Indians to Cincinnati Reds for P Jack Armstrong, P Scott Scudder and P Joe Turek (November 15, 1991). ... On disabled list (August 23-September 7, 1992). ... Granted free agency (October 26, 1992). ... Signed by Houston Astros (December 4, 1992). ... On disabled list (July 6-26, 1993). ... On Houston disabled list (April 20-May 22, 1996). ... Released by Astros (June 3, 1996). ... Signed by Indians (June 15, 1996). ... On Cleveland disabled list (July 4-21, 1996). ... Granted free agency (October 3, 1996). ... Signed by Minnesota Twins organization (December 18, 1996). ... Traded by Twins with 1B Orlando Merced to Boston Red Sox for P Matt Kinney, P Joe Thomas and P John Barnes (July 31, 1998). ... Granted free agency (October 27, 1998). ... Signed by Arizona Diamondbacks (November 13, 1998). ... On disabled list (June 13-28, 1999).

HONORS: Named lefthanded pitcher on THE SPORTING NEWS college All-America team (1985-86).

STATISTICAL NOTES: Struck out 15 batters in one game (May 10, 1987).

MISCELLANEOUS: Struck out in only appearance as pinch hitter (1995).

Year League	W	L	Pct.	ERA	G	GS	CG	ShO	Sv.	IP	H	R	ER	BB	SO
1986— Waterloo (Midw.)	2	1	.667	1.00	3	3	0	0	0	18	12	2	2	3	25
— Cleveland (A.L.)	5	2	.714	4.23	9	9	1	0	0	61²/₃	57	35	29	15	46
1987— Cleveland (A.L.)	3	8	.273	5.10	16	15	4	1	0	102¹/₃	112	62	58	37	97
1988— Cleveland (A.L.)	18	14	.563	3.20	33	33	12	4	0	242	234	97	86	45	180
1989— Cleveland (A.L.)	13	6	.684	3.37	28	28	5	2	0	184¹/₃	170	71	69	51	129
1990— Cleveland (A.L.)	12	9	.571	4.40	34	34	3	0	0	214²/₃	245	110	105	47	135
1991— Cleveland (A.L.)	9	16	.360	3.48	33	33	7	0	0	238	241	112	92	31	169
1992— Cincinnati (N.L.)■	12	8	.600	2.70	31	30	5	3	0	213²/₃	210	72	64	41	138
1993— Houston (N.L.)■	12	13	.480	4.16	31	30	1	1	0	190¹/₃	215	98	88	40	124
1994— Houston (N.L.)	8	9	.471	4.37	24	24	1	0	0	148¹/₃	175	80	72	26	74
1995— Houston (N.L.)	10	9	.526	4.47	33	26	1	1	0	153	180	86	76	39	96
1996— Houston (N.L.)	0	3	.000	7.83	8	4	0	0	0	23	35	25	20	11	15
— Cleveland (A.L.)■	1	1	.500	6.59	13	2	0	0	0	28²/₃	31	21	21	8	21
1997— Minnesota (A.L.)■	7	4	.636	3.58	65	1	0	0	1	115²/₃	102	46	46	25	75
1998— Boston (A.L.)■	2	3	.400	3.38	29	0	0	0	0	24	25	13	9	13	18
1999— Arizona (N.L.)■	4	0	1.000	2.51	63	0	0	0	1	64²/₃	54	19	18	21	51
2000— Arizona (N.L.)	2	6	.250	3.20	64	0	0	0	1	76	71	29	27	20	64
A.L. totals (9 years)	70	63	.526	3.83	260	155	32	7	1	1211¹/₃	1217	567	515	272	870
N.L. totals (7 years)	48	48	.500	3.78	254	114	8	5	2	869	940	409	365	198	562
Major League totals (15 years)	118	111	.515	3.81	514	269	40	12	3	2080¹/₃	2157	976	880	470	1432

DIVISION SERIES RECORD

Year League	W	L	Pct.	ERA	G	GS	CG	ShO	Sv.	IP	H	R	ER	BB	SO
1998— Boston (A.L.)	0	0	...	0.00	1	0	0	0	0	1¹/₃	0	0	0	1	1
1999— Arizona (N.L.)	0	0	...	0.00	3	0	0	0	0	3¹/₃	1	0	0	3	1
Division series totals (2 years)	0	0	...	0.00	4	0	0	0	0	4²/₃	1	0	0	4	2

ALL-STAR GAME RECORD

Year League	W	L	Pct.	ERA	GS	CG	ShO	Sv.	IP	H	R	ER	BB	SO
1989— American	0	0	...	0.00	0	0	0	0	1²/₃	2	0	0	0	3

PERSONAL: Born August 19, 1970, in Fullerton, Calif. ... 6-1/202. ... Throws right, bats right. ... Full name: Jeffery Eugene Tam.

HIGH SCHOOL: Eau Gaille (Melbourne, Fla.).

COLLEGE: Florida State.

TRANSACTIONS/CAREER NOTES: Signed as a non-drafted free agent by New York Mets organization (June 27, 1993). ... On New York disabled list (March 21-May 16, 1999); included rehabilitation assignment to St. Lucie (May 2-16). ... Claimed on waivers by Cleveland Indians (June 18, 1999). ... On Buffalo disabled list (July 23-August 1, 1999). ... Claimed on waivers by Mets (August 11, 1999). ... Granted free agency (October 15, 1999). ... Signed by Oakland Athletics organization (November 23, 1999).

Year League	W	L	Pct.	ERA	G	GS	CG	ShO	Sv.	IP	H	R	ER	BB	SO
1993— Pittsfield (NY-Penn)	3	3	.500	3.35	21	1	0	0	0	40¹/₃	50	21	15	7	31
1994— Columbia (S.Atl.)	1	1	.500	1.29	26	0	0	0	18	28	23	14	4	6	22
— St. Lucie (FSL)	0	0	...	0.00	24	0	0	0	16	26²/₃	13	0	0	6	15
— Binghamton (East.)	0	0	...	8.10	4	0	0	0	0	6²/₃	9	6	6	5	7
1995— Binghamton (East.)	0	2	.000	4.50	14	0	0	0	3	18	20	11	9	4	9
— Gulf Coast Mets (GCL)	0	0	...	3.00	2	1	0	0	0	3	2	1	1	1	2
1996— Binghamton (East.)	6	2	.750	2.44	49	0	0	0	2	62²/₃	51	19	17	16	48
1997— Norfolk (I.L.)	7	5	.583	4.67	40	11	0	0	6	111²/₃	137	72	58	14	67
1998— Norfolk (I.L.)	3	3	.500	1.83	45	0	0	0	11	64	42	14	13	6	54
— New York (N.L.)	1	1	.500	6.28	15	0	0	0	0	14¹/₃	13	10	10	4	8
1999— St. Lucie (FSL)	0	0	...	3.38	2	0	0	0	0	2²/₃	4	1	1	0	3
— Norfolk (I.L.)	0	1	.000	3.10	16	0	0	0	3	20¹/₃	24	7	7	3	10
— Buffalo (I.L.)■	2	2	.500	2.08	16	0	0	0	0	26	23	9	6	8	13
— Cleveland (A.L.)	0	0	...	81.00	1	0	0	0	0	¹/₃	2	3	3	1	0
— New York (N.L.)■	0	0	...	3.18	9	0	0	0	0	11¹/₃	6	4	4	3	8
2000— Oakland (A.L.)■	3	3	.500	2.63	72	0	0	0	3	85²/₃	86	30	25	23	46
A.L. totals (2 years)	3	3	.500	2.93	73	0	0	0	3	86	88	33	28	24	46
N.L. totals (2 years)	1	1	.500	4.91	24	0	0	0	0	25²/₃	19	14	14	7	16
Major League totals (3 years)	4	4	.500	3.39	97	0	0	0	3	111²/₃	107	47	42	31	62

DIVISION SERIES RECORD

Year League	W	L	Pct.	ERA	G	GS	CG	ShO	Sv.	IP	H	R	ER	BB	SO
2000— Oakland (A.L.)	0	0	...	0.00	3	0	0	0	0	2	3	1	0	1	1

PERSONAL: Born February 18, 1964, in Des Moines, Iowa. ... 6-1/190. ... Throws right, bats right. ... Full name: Kevin Ray Tapani. ... Name pronounced TAP-ah-nee.

HIGH SCHOOL: Escanaba (Mich.).

COLLEGE: Central Michigan (degree in finance, 1987).

TRANSACTIONS/CAREER NOTES: Selected by Chicago Cubs organization in ninth round of free-agent draft (June 3, 1985); did not sign. ... Selected by Oakland Athletics organization in second round of free-agent draft (June 2, 1986). ... Traded by A's as part of an eight-player, three-team deal in which New York Mets traded P Jesse Orosco to A's (December 11, 1987); A's traded Orosco, SS Alfredo Griffin and P Jay Howell to Los Angeles Dodgers for P Bob Welch, P Matt Young and P Jack Savage. A's then traded Savage, P Wally Whitehurst and Tapani to Mets. ... Traded by Mets with P Tim Drummond to Minnesota Twins (August 1, 1989), as partial completion of deal in which Twins traded P Frank Viola to Mets for P Rick Aguilera, P David West and three players to be named later (July 31, 1989); Twins acquired P Jack Savage to complete deal (October 16, 1989). ... On disabled list (August 17-September 10, 1990). ... Traded by Twins with P Mark Guthrie to Los Angeles Dodgers for 1B/3B Ron Coomer, P Greg Hansell, P Jose Parra and a player to be named later (July 31, 1995); Twins acquired OF Chris Latham to complete deal (October 30, 1995). ... Granted free agency (December 21, 1995). ... Signed by Chicago White Sox (February 3, 1996). ... Granted free agency (October 29, 1996). ... Signed by Cubs (December 16, 1996). ... On Chicago disabled list (March 27-July 23, 1997); included rehabilitation assignments to Rockford (June 25-26 and July 12-13), Orlando (July 1-7), Daytona (July 7-8) and Iowa (July 18-19). ... On disabled list (April 13-May 1 and August 26-September 25, 1999). ... On disabled list (September 18, 2000-remainder of season).

STATISTICAL NOTES: Pitched 5-0 one-hit, complete-game victory for Chicago against Cincinnati (September 16, 1997). ... Career major league grand slams: 1.

Year League	W	L	Pct.	ERA	G	GS	CG	ShO	Sv.	IP	H	R	ER	BB	SO
1986— Medford (N'West)	1	0	1.000	0.00	2	2	0	0	0	8 1/3	6	3	0	3	9
— Modesto (Calif.)	6	1	.857	2.48	11	11	1	0	0	69	74	26	19	22	44
— Huntsville (Sou.)	1	0	1.000	6.00	1	1	0	0	0	6	8	4	4	1	2
— Tacoma (PCL)	0	1	.000	15.43	1	1	0	0	0	2 1/3	5	6	4	1	1
1987— Modesto (Calif.)	10	7	.588	3.76	24	24	6	1	0	148 1/3	122	74	62	60	121
1988— St. Lucie (FSL)■	1	0	1.000	1.42	3	3	0	0	0	19	17	5	3	4	11
— Jackson (Texas)	5	1	.833	2.74	24	5	0	0	3	62 1/3	46	23	19	19	35
1989— Tidewater (I.L.)	7	5	.583	3.47	17	17	2	1	0	109	113	49	42	25	63
— New York (N.L.)	0	0	...	3.68	3	0	0	0	0	7 1/3	5	3	3	4	2
— Portland (PCL)■	4	2	.667	2.20	6	6	1	0	0	41	38	15	10	12	30
— Minnesota (A.L.)	2	2	.500	3.86	5	5	0	0	0	32 2/3	34	15	14	8	21
1990— Minnesota (A.L.)	12	8	.600	4.07	28	28	1	1	0	159 1/3	164	75	72	29	101
1991— Minnesota (A.L.)	16	9	.640	2.99	34	34	4	1	0	244	225	84	81	40	135
1992— Minnesota (A.L.)	16	11	.593	3.97	34	34	4	1	0	220	226	103	97	48	138
1993— Minnesota (A.L.)	12	15	.444	4.43	36	35	3	1	0	225 2/3	243	123	111	57	150
1994— Minnesota (A.L.)	11	7	.611	4.62	24	24	4	1	0	156	181	86	80	39	91
1995— Minnesota (A.L.)	6	11	.353	4.92	20	20	3	1	0	133 2/3	155	79	73	34	88
— Los Angeles (N.L.)■	4	2	.667	5.05	13	11	0	0	0	57	72	37	32	14	43
1996— Chicago (A.L.)■	13	10	.565	4.59	34	34	1	0	0	225 1/3	236	123	115	76	150
1997— Rockford (Midw.)	1	0	1.000	0.82	2	2	0	0	0	11	5	1	1	0	7
— Orlando (Sou.)	0	0	...	4.50	1	1	0	0	0	4	3	2	2	2	2
— Daytona (FSL)	0	0	...	3.86	1	1	0	0	0	4 2/3	5	2	2	2	4
— Iowa (A.A.)	0	1	.000	4.00	1	1	1	0	0	9	5	4	4	1	4
— Chicago (N.L.)	9	3	.750	3.39	13	13	1	1	0	85	77	33	32	23	55
1998— Chicago (N.L.)	19	9	.679	4.85	35	34	2	2	0	219	244	120	118	62	136
1999— Chicago (N.L.)	6	12	.333	4.83	23	23	1	0	0	136	151	81	73	73	73
2000— Chicago (N.L.)	8	12	.400	5.01	30	30	2	0	0	195 2/3	208	113	109	47	150
A.L. totals (8 years)	88	73	.547	4.14	215	214	20	6	0	1396 2/3	1464	688	643	331	874
N.L. totals (6 years)	46	38	.548	4.72	117	111	6	3	0	700	757	387	367	183	459
Major League totals (12 years)	134	111	.547	4.34	332	325	26	9	0	2096 2/3	2221	1075	1010	514	1333

DIVISION SERIES RECORD

Year League	W	L	Pct.	ERA	G	GS	CG	ShO	Sv.	IP	H	R	ER	BB	SO
1995— Los Angeles (N.L.)	0	0	...	81.00	2	0	0	0	0	1/3	0	3	3	4	1
1998— Chicago (N.L.)	0	0	...	1.00	1	1	0	0	0	9	5	1	1	3	6
Division series totals (2 years)	0	0	...	3.86	3	1	0	0	0	9 1/3	5	4	4	7	7

CHAMPIONSHIP SERIES RECORD

Year League	W	L	Pct.	ERA	G	GS	CG	ShO	Sv.	IP	H	R	ER	BB	SO
1991— Minnesota (A.L.)	0	1	.000	7.84	2	2	0	0	0	10 1/3	16	9	9	3	9

WORLD SERIES RECORD

NOTES: Member of World Series championship team (1991).

Year League	W	L	Pct.	ERA	G	GS	CG	ShO	Sv.	IP	H	R	ER	BB	SO
1991— Minnesota (A.L.)	1	1	.500	4.50	2	2	0	0	0	12	13	6	6	2	7

PERSONAL: Born January 1, 1975, in San Pedro de Macoris, Dominican Republic. ... 5-10/180. ... Bats right, throws right. ... Full name: Fernando Tatis Jr. ... Name pronounced ta-TEES.

TRANSACTIONS/CAREER NOTES: Signed as non-drafted free agent by Texas Rangers organization (August 25, 1992). ... Traded by Rangers with P Darren Oliver and a player to be named later to St. Louis Cardinals for P Todd Stottlemyre and SS Royce Clayton (July 31, 1998); Cardinals acquired OF Mark Little to complete deal (August 9, 1998). ... On St. Louis disabled list (April 30-June 30, 2000); included rehabilitation assignment to Memphis (June 26-30). ... Traded by Cardinals with P Britt Reames to Montreal Expos for P Dustin Hermanson and P Steve Kline (December 14, 2000).

RECORDS: Holds major league single-inning records for most grand slams—2; and most runs batted in—8 (April 23, 1999, third inning). ... Shares major league single-game record for most grand slams—2 (April 23, 1999). ... Shares major league single-inning record for most home runs—2 (April 23, 1999, third inning).

STATISTICAL NOTES: Tied for Gulf Coast League lead in intentional bases on balls received with four in 1994. ... Led Gulf Coast League third basemen with 165 assists and 227 total chances in 1994. ... Tied for Texas League lead with four intentional bases on balls in 1997. ... Career major league grand slams: 5.

Year	Team (League)	Pos.	G	AB	R	H	2B	3B	HR	RBI	Avg.	BB	SO	SB	PO	A	E	Avg.
1993—	Dom. Rangers (DSL)..	IF	59	198	22	54	5	1	4	34	.273	27	12	7	135	37	11	.940
1994—	GC Rangers (GCL)......	3B-2B	•60	212	34	70	10	2	6	32	.330	25	33	21	47	†168	17	.927
1995—	Charlotte (Sou.).........		131	499	74	•151	*43	4	15	84	.303	45	94	22	...	...	...	...
1996—	Charlotte (FSL)..........	3B	85	325	46	93	25	0	12	53	.286	30	48	9	53	148	24	.893
—	Oklahoma City (A.A.)..	3B	2	4	0	2	1	0	0	0	.500	0	1	0	0	1	0	1.000
1997—	Tulsa (Texas)	3B-DH	102	382	73	120	26	1	24	61	.314	46	72	17	53	193	21	.921
—	Texas (A.L.)	3B	60	223	29	57	9	0	8	29	.256	14	42	3	45	90	7	.951
1998—	Texas (A.L.)	3B	95	330	41	89	17	2	3	32	.270	12	66	6	74	184	15	.945
—	St. Louis (N.L.)■	3B-SS	55	202	28	58	16	2	8	26	.287	24	57	7	36	123	12	.930
1999—	St. Louis (N.L.)...........	3B	149	537	104	160	31	2	34	107	.298	82	128	21	101	267	16	.958
2000—	St. Louis (N.L.).....	3B-DH-1B	96	324	59	82	21	1	18	64	.253	57	94	2	42	129	8	.955
—	Memphis (PCL)	3B	3	9	0	0	0	0	0	0	.000	1	3	0	3	2	0	1.000
American League totals (2 years)			155	553	70	146	26	2	11	61	.264	26	108	9	119	274	22	.947
National League totals (3 years)			300	1063	191	300	68	5	60	197	.282	163	279	30	179	519	36	.951
Major League totals (4 years)			455	1616	261	446	94	7	71	258	.276	189	387	39	298	793	58	.950

DIVISION SERIES RECORD

Year	Team (League)	Pos.	G	AB	R	H	2B	3B	HR	RBI	Avg.	BB	SO	SB	PO	A	E	Avg.
2000—	St. Louis (N.L.)...........								Did not play.									

CHAMPIONSHIP SERIES RECORD

Year	Team (League)	Pos.	G	AB	R	H	2B	3B	HR	RBI	Avg.	BB	SO	SB	PO	A	E	Avg.
2000—	St. Louis (N.L.)...........	PH-3B	5	13	1	3	2	0	0	2	.231	1	5	0	3	5	2	.800

TAUBENSEE, EDDIE — C — INDIANS

PERSONAL: Born October 31, 1968, in Beeville, Texas. ... 6-3/230. ... Bats left, throws right. ... Full name: Edward Kenneth Taubensee. ... Name pronounced TAW-ben-see.

HIGH SCHOOL: Lake Howell (Casselberry, Fla.).

TRANSACTIONS/CAREER NOTES: Selected by Cincinnati Reds organization in sixth round of free-agent draft (June 2, 1986). ... Selected by Oakland Athletics from Reds organization in Rule 5 major league draft (December 3, 1990). ... Claimed on waivers by Cleveland Indians (April 4, 1991). ... Traded by Indians with P Willie Blair to Houston Astros for OF Kenny Lofton and IF Dave Rohde (December 10, 1991). ... Traded by Astros to Reds for P Ross Powell and P Marty Lister (April 19, 1994). ... On disabled list (August 1, 2000-remainder of season). ... Traded by Reds to Indians for P Jim Brower and P Robert Pugmire (November 16, 2000).

STATISTICAL NOTES: Led Pioneer League with 19 passed balls in 1987. ... Tied for South Atlantic League lead in double plays by catcher with seven in 1988. ... Had 16-game hitting streak (May 22-June 13, 1999). ... Career major league grand slams: 1.

Year	Team (League)	Pos.	G	AB	R	H	2B	3B	HR	RBI	Avg.	BB	SO	SB	PO	A	E	Avg.
1986—	GC Reds (GCL)...........	C-1B	35	107	8	21	3	0	1	11	.196	11	33	0	208	27	8	.967
1987—	Billings (Pio.)	C	55	162	24	43	7	0	5	28	.265	25	47	2	344	29	6	.984
1988—	Greensboro (S.Atl.)	C	103	330	36	85	16	1	10	41	.258	44	93	8	640	70	15	.979
—	Chattanooga (Sou.)	C	5	12	2	2	0	0	1	1	.167	3	4	0	17	5	1	.957
1989—	Cedar Rapids (Midw.) ..	C	59	196	25	39	5	0	8	22	.199	25	55	4	400	9	1	.998
—	Chattanooga (Sou.)	C	45	127	11	24	2	0	3	13	.189	11	28	0	213	31	6	.976
1990—	Cedar Rapids (Midw.) ..	C	122	417	57	108	21	1	16	62	.259	51	98	11	795	94	16	.982
1991—	Cleveland (A.L.)■........	C	26	66	5	16	2	1	0	8	.242	5	16	0	89	6	2	.979
—	Colo. Springs (PCL) ...	C	91	287	53	89	23	3	13	39	.310	31	61	0	412	47	12	.975
1992—	Houston (N.L.)■	C	104	297	23	66	15	0	5	28	.222	31	78	2	557	66	5	.992
—	Tucson (PCL)	C	20	74	13	25	8	1	1	10	.338	8	17	0	127	10	4	.972
1993—	Houston (N.L.)	C	94	288	26	72	11	1	9	42	.250	21	44	1	551	41	5	.992
1994—	Houston (N.L.)	C	5	10	0	1	0	0	0	0	.100	0	3	0	19	2	0	1.000
—	Cincinnati (N.L.)■........	C	61	177	29	52	8	2	8	21	.294	15	28	2	362	17	4	.990
1995—	Cincinnati (N.L.)	C-1B	80	218	32	62	14	2	9	44	.284	22	52	2	338	22	6	.984
1996—	Cincinnati (N.L.)	C	108	327	46	95	20	0	12	48	.291	26	64	3	538	42	11	.931
1997—	Cincinnati (N.L.) C-OF-1B-DH		108	254	26	68	18	0	10	34	.268	22	66	0	408	26	5	.989
1998—	Cincinnati (N.L.)	C	130	431	61	120	27	0	11	72	.278	52	93	1	776	44	10	.988
1999—	Cincinnati (N.L.)	C	126	424	58	132	22	2	21	87	.311	30	67	0	733	48	9	.989
2000—	Cincinnati (N.L.)	C	81	266	29	71	12	0	6	24	.267	21	44	0	420	26	5	.989
American League totals (1 year)			26	66	5	16	2	1	0	8	.242	5	16	0	89	6	2	.979
National League totals (9 years)			897	2692	330	739	147	7	91	400	.275	240	539	11	4702	334	60	.988
Major League totals (10 years)			923	2758	335	755	149	8	91	408	.274	245	555	11	4791	340	62	.988

CHAMPIONSHIP SERIES RECORD

Year	Team (League)	Pos.	G	AB	R	H	2B	3B	HR	RBI	Avg.	BB	SO	SB	PO	A	E	Avg.
1995—	Cincinnati (N.L.)	PH-C	2	2	0	1	0	0	0	0	.500	0	0	0	0	0	0	...

TAVAREZ, JULIAN — P — CUBS

PERSONAL: Born May 22, 1973, in Santiago, Dominican Republic. ... 6-2/190. ... Throws right, bats left.

HIGH SCHOOL: Santiago (Dominican Republic) Public School.

TRANSACTIONS/CAREER NOTES: Signed as non-drafted free agent by Cleveland Indians organization (March 16, 1990). ... On Cleveland suspended list (June 18-21, 1996). ... Traded by Indians with IF Jeff Kent, IF Jose Vizcaino and a player to be named later to San Francisco Giants for 3B Matt Williams and a player to be named later (November 13, 1996); Indians traded P Joe Roa to Giants for OF Trenidad Hubbard to complete deal (December 16, 1996). ... On San Francisco disabled list (July 13-August 7, 1998); included rehabilitation assignment to Fresno (August 5-7). ... On suspended list (September 14-16, 1998). ... On San Francisco disabled list (May 1-June 1, 1999); included rehabilitation assignment to Fresno (May 25-June 1). ... Claimed on waivers by Colorado Rockies (November 21, 1999). ... Granted free agency (October 31, 2000). ... Signed by Chicago Cubs (November 16, 2000).

HONORS: Named A.L. Rookie Pitcher of the Year by THE SPORTING NEWS (1995).

STATISTICAL NOTES: Led Appalachian League with 10 hit batsmen in 1993.

Year League	W	L	Pct.	ERA	G	GS	CG	ShO	Sv.	IP	H	R	ER	BB	SO
1990— Dom. Indians (DSL)	5	5	.500	3.29	14	12	3	0	0	82	85	53	30	48	33
1991— Dom. Indians (DSL)	8	2	.800	2.67	19	18	1	0	0	121 1/3	95	41	36	28	75
1992— Burlington (Appl.).............	6	3	.667	2.68	14	*14	2	•2	0	87 1/3	86	41	26	12	69
1993— Kinston (Caro.)..................	11	5	.688	2.42	18	18	2	0	0	119	102	48	32	28	107
— Canton/Akron (East.).......	2	1	.667	0.95	3	2	1	1	0	19	14	2	2	1	11
— Cleveland (A.L.)...............	2	2	.500	6.57	8	7	0	0	0	37	53	29	27	13	19
1994— Charlotte (I.L.)...................	•15	6	.714	3.48	26	26	2	2	0	176	167	79	68	43	102
— Cleveland (A.L.)...............	0	1	.000	21.60	1	1	0	0	0	1 2/3	6	8	4	1	0
1995— Cleveland (A.L.).................	10	2	.833	2.44	57	0	0	0	0	85	76	36	23	21	68
1996— Cleveland (A.L.).................	4	7	.364	5.36	51	4	0	0	0	80 2/3	101	49	48	22	46
— Buffalo (A.A.)...................	1	0	1.000	1.29	2	2	0	0	0	14	10	2	2	3	10
1997— San Francisco (N.L.)■	6	4	.600	3.87	*89	0	0	0	0	88 1/3	91	43	38	34	38
1998— San Francisco (N.L.)	5	3	.625	3.80	60	0	0	0	1	85 1/3	96	41	36	36	52
— Fresno (PCL)	0	0	...	19.29	1	0	0	0	0	2 1/3	6	5	5	0	1
1999— San Francisco (N.L.)	2	0	1.000	5.93	47	0	0	0	0	54 2/3	65	38	36	25	33
— Fresno (PCL)	0	0	...	2.25	4	1	0	0	0	8	3	2	2	3	9
— San Jose (Calif.)............	0	0	...	0.00	1	1	0	0	0	4	1	0	0	1	3
2000— Colorado (N.L.)■.............	11	5	.688	4.43	51	12	1	0	1	120	124	68	59	53	62
A.L. totals (4 years)	16	12	.571	4.49	117	12	0	0	0	204 1/3	236	122	102	57	133
N.L. totals (4 years)	24	12	.667	4.37	247	12	1	0	2	348 1/3	376	190	169	148	185
Major League totals (8 years)	40	24	.625	4.41	364	24	1	0	2	552 2/3	612	312	271	205	318

DIVISION SERIES RECORD

Year League	W	L	Pct.	ERA	G	GS	CG	ShO	Sv.	IP	H	R	ER	BB	SO
1995— Cleveland (A.L.)	0	0	...	6.75	3	0	0	0	0	2 2/3	5	2	2	0	3
1996— Cleveland (A.L.)	0	0	...	0.00	2	0	0	0	0	1 1/3	1	0	0	2	1
1997— San Francisco (N.L.)	0	1	.000	4.50	3	0	0	0	0	4	4	2	2	2	0
Division series totals (3 years)	0	1	.000	4.50	8	0	0	0	0	8	10	4	4	4	4

CHAMPIONSHIP SERIES RECORD

Year League	W	L	Pct.	ERA	G	GS	CG	ShO	Sv.	IP	H	R	ER	BB	SO
1995— Cleveland (A.L.)..........	0	1	.000	2.70	4	0	0	0	0	3 1/3	3	1	1	1	2

WORLD SERIES RECORD

Year League	W	L	Pct.	ERA	G	GS	CG	ShO	Sv.	IP	H	R	ER	BB	SO
1995— Cleveland (A.L.).................	0	0	...	0.00	5	0	0	0	0	4 1/3	3	0	0	2	1

TAYLOR, BILL   P

PERSONAL: Born October 16, 1961, in Monticello, Fla. ... 6-8/235. ... Throws right, bats right. ... Full name: William Howell Taylor.

HIGH SCHOOL: Central (Thomasville, Ga.).

COLLEGE: Abraham Baldwin Agricultural College (Ga.).

TRANSACTIONS/CAREER NOTES: Selected by Texas Rangers organization in second round of free-agent draft (January 8, 1980). ... Loaned by Rangers organization to Wausau, Seattle Mariners organization (April 5-June 23, 1982). ... Granted free agency (October 22, 1988). ... Signed by San Diego Padres organization (March 30, 1989). ... Granted free agency (October 22, 1989). ... Signed by Atlanta Braves organization (August 16, 1990). ... Selected by Toronto Blue Jays from Braves organization in Rule 5 major league draft (December 7, 1992). ... Returned to Braves organization (April 3, 1993). ... Granted free agency (October 15, 1993). ... Signed by Oakland Athletics organization (December 13, 1993). ... On disabled list (July 27, 1994-remainder of season; April 12, 1995-entire season; and August 15-September 13, 1996). ... Traded by A's to New York Mets for P Jason Isringhausen and P Greg McMichael (July 31, 1999). ... Granted free agency (December 21, 1999). ... Signed by Colorado Rockies (February 4, 2000). ... Released by Rockies (March 23, 2000). ... Signed by Tampa Bay Devil Rays organization (March 31, 2000). ... Granted free agency (October 10, 2000).

Year League	W	L	Pct.	ERA	G	GS	CG	ShO	Sv.	IP	H	R	ER	BB	SO
1980— Asheville (S.Atl.)................	0	2	.000	10.93	6	2	0	0	0	14	24	24	17	9	12
— Gulf Coast Rangers (GCL)..	0	0	...	2.31	14	2	0	0	0	35	36	14	9	16	22
1981— Asheville (S.Atl.)................	1	7	.125	4.64	14	12	1	0	0	64	76	43	33	35	44
— Gulf Coast Rangers (GCL)..	4	2	.667	2.72	12	11	0	0	0	53	42	23	16	29	35
1982— Wausau (Midw.)■.............	2	5	.286	5.03	19	1	0	0	2	39 1/3	36	27	22	27	34
— Burlington (Midw.)■..........	5	4	.556	3.72	18	8	2	0	1	72 2/3	64	37	30	36	61
1983— Salem (Caro.)..................	1	1	.500	6.26	7	7	1	0	0	41 2/3	30	34	29	42	42
— Tulsa (Texas)	5	8	.385	6.87	21	12	0	0	0	76	86	65	58	51	75
1984— Tulsa (Texas)	5	3	.625	3.83	42	2	0	0	7	80	65	38	34	51	80
1985— Tulsa (Texas)	3	9	.250	3.47	20	17	2	0	0	103 2/3	84	55	40	48	87
1986— Tulsa (Texas)	3	7	.300	3.95	11	11	2	1	0	68 1/3	65	40	30	37	64
— Oklahoma City (A.A.)........	5	5	.500	4.60	16	16	1	0	0	101 2/3	94	56	52	57	68
1987— Oklahoma City (A.A.)........	*12	9	.571	5.61	28	•28	0	0	0	168 1/3	198	122	105	91	100
1988— Oklahoma City (A.A.)........	4	8	.333	5.49	20	12	1	1	1	82	98	55	50	35	42
1989— Las Vegas (PCL)■	7	4	.636	5.13	47	0	0	0	1	79	93	48	45	27	71
1990— Durham (Caro.)■.............	0	0	...	3.24	5	0	0	0	0	8 1/3	8	3	3	1	10
— Richmond (I.L.)	0	0	...	0.00	2	0	0	0	0	2 1/3	4	0	0	0	0
1991— Greenville (Sou.)	6	2	.750	1.51	•59	0	0	0	22	77 1/3	49	16	13	15	65
1992— Richmond (I.L.)	2	3	.400	2.28	47	0	0	0	12	79	72	27	20	27	82
1993— Richmond (I.L.)	2	4	.333	1.98	59	0	0	0	*26	68 1/3	56	19	15	26	81
1994— Oakland (A.L.)■	1	3	.250	3.50	41	0	0	0	1	46 1/3	38	24	18	18	48
1995— Oakland (A.L.)							Did not play.								
1996— Edmonton (PCL)	0	0	...	0.79	7	0	0	0	4	11 1/3	10	1	1	3	13
— Oakland (A.L.)	6	3	.667	4.33	55	0	0	0	17	60 1/3	52	30	29	25	67
1997— Oakland (A.L.)	3	4	.429	3.82	72	0	0	0	23	73	70	32	31	36	66

Year League	W	L	Pct.	ERA	G	GS	CG	ShO	Sv.	IP	H	R	ER	BB	SO
1998—Oakland (A.L.)	4	9	.308	3.58	70	0	0	0	33	73	71	37	29	22	58
1999—Oakland (A.L.)	1	5	.167	3.98	43	0	0	0	26	43	48	23	19	14	38
—New York (N.L.)■	0	1	.000	8.10	18	0	0	0	0	13 1/3	20	12	12	9	14
2000—Durham (I.L.)■	4	0	1.000	4.17	42	0	0	0	26	45 1/3	47	22	21	17	47
—Tampa Bay (A.L.)	1	3	.250	8.56	17	0	0	0	0	13 2/3	13	13	13	9	13
A.L. totals (6 years)	16	27	.372	4.04	298	0	0	0	100	309 1/3	292	159	139	124	290
N.L. totals (1 year)	0	1	.000	8.10	18	0	0	0	0	13 1/3	20	12	12	9	14
Major League totals (6 years)	16	28	.364	4.21	316	0	0	0	100	322 2/3	312	171	151	133	304

DIVISION SERIES RECORD

Year League	W	L	Pct.	ERA	G	GS	CG	ShO	Sv.	IP	H	R	ER	BB	SO
1999—New York (N.L.)								Did not play.							

CHAMPIONSHIP SERIES RECORD

Year League	W	L	Pct.	ERA	G	GS	CG	ShO	Sv.	IP	H	R	ER	BB	SO
1999—New York (N.L.)								Did not play.							

TAYLOR, REGGIE — OF — PHILLIES

PERSONAL: Born January 12, 1977, in Newberry, S.C. ... 6-1/178. ... Bats left, throws right. ... Full name: Reginald Tremain Taylor.
HIGH SCHOOL: Newberry (S.C.).
TRANSACTIONS/CAREER NOTES: Selected by Philadelphia Phillies organization in first round (14th pick overall) of free-agent draft (June 1, 1995). ... On disabled list (July 23, 1998-remainder of season). ... On Scranton/Wilkes-Barre disabled list (April 6-May 26, 2000).
STATISTICAL NOTES: Led South Atlantic League outfielders with 308 total chances in 1996. ... Led Florida State League outfielders with 354 total chances in 1997. ... Led Eastern League in caught stealing with 22 in 1999.

Year Team (League)	Pos.	G	AB	R	H	2B	3B	HR	RBI	Avg.	BB	SO	SB	PO	A	E	Avg.
1995—Martinsville (Appl.)	OF	64	239	36	53	4	6	2	32	.222	23	58	18	116	9	8	.940
1996—Piedmont (S.Atl.)	OF	128	499	68	131	20	6	0	31	.263	29	136	36	287	9	*12	.961
1997—Clearwater (FSL)	OF	134	545	73	133	18	6	12	47	.244	30	130	40	324	*19	11	.969
1998—Reading (East.)	OF	79	337	49	92	14	6	5	22	.273	12	73	22	164	6	10	.944
1999—Reading (East.)	OF	127	526	75	140	17	10	15	61	.266	18	79	38	295	9	9	.971
2000—Scranton/W.B. (I.L.)	OF	98	422	60	116	10	8	15	43	.275	21	87	23	241	9	5	.980
—Philadelphia (N.L.)	OF	9	11	1	1	0	0	0	0	.091	0	8	1	3	0	1	.750
Major League totals (1 year)		9	11	1	1	0	0	0	0	.091	0	8	1	3	0	1	.750

TEJADA, MIGUEL — SS — ATHLETICS

PERSONAL: Born May 25, 1976, in Bani, Dominican Republic. ... 5-9/188. ... Bats right, throws right. ... Full name: Miguel Odalis Tejada.
TRANSACTIONS/CAREER NOTES: Signed as non-drafted free agent by Oakland Athletics organization (July 17, 1993). ... On suspended list (July 4-7, 1996). ... On disabled list (July 20-August 10, 1996). ... On Oakland disabled list (March 22-May 20, 1998); included rehabilitation assignments to Edmonton (May 11-12) and Huntsville (May 12-20).
STATISTICAL NOTES: Led California League shortstops with 44 errors in 1996. ... Led Southern League shortstops with 688 total chances and 97 double plays in 1997. ... Hit three home runs in one game (June 11, 1999). ... Led A.L. shortstops with 755 total chances in 2000. ... Career major league grand slams: 2.

Year Team (League)	Pos.	G	AB	R	H	2B	3B	HR	RBI	Avg.	BB	SO	SB	PO	A	E	Avg.
1993—																	
					Dominican Summer League statistics unavailable.												
1994—Dom. Athletics (DSL)	2B	74	218	51	64	9	1	18	62	.294	37	36	13	76	126	16	.927
1995—S. Oregon (N'West)	SS	74	269	45	66	15	5	8	44	.245	41	54	19	*129	*214	26	.930
1996—Modesto (Calif.)	SS-DH-3B	114	458	97	128	12	5	20	72	.279	51	93	27	194	358	†45	.925
1997—Huntsville (Sou.)	SS	128	502	85	138	20	3	22	97	.275	50	99	15	*229	*423	*36	.948
—Oakland (A.L.)	SS	26	99	10	20	3	2	2	10	.202	2	22	2	54	69	4	.969
1998—Edmonton (PCL)	SS	1	3	0	0	0	0	0	0	.000	1	1	0	0	5	0	1.000
—Huntsville (Sou.)	SS-DH	15	52	9	17	6	0	2	7	.327	4	8	1	18	41	5	.922
—Oakland (A.L.)	SS	105	365	53	85	20	1	11	45	.233	28	86	5	173	327	26	.951
1999—Oakland (A.L.)	SS	159	593	93	149	33	4	21	84	.251	57	94	8	*292	471	21	.973
2000—Oakland (A.L.)	SS	160	607	105	167	32	1	30	115	.275	66	102	6	233	*501	21	.972
Major League totals (4 years)		450	1664	261	421	88	8	64	254	.253	153	304	21	752	1368	72	.967

DIVISION SERIES RECORD

Year Team (League)	Pos.	G	AB	R	H	2B	3B	HR	RBI	Avg.	BB	SO	SB	PO	A	E	Avg.
2000—Oakland (A.L.)	SS	5	20	5	7	2	0	0	1	.350	2	2	1	8	14	0	1.000

TEJERA, MICHAEL — P — MARLINS

PERSONAL: Born October 18, 1976, in Havana, Cuba. ... 5-9/175. ... Throws left, bats left.
HIGH SCHOOL: Southwest (Miami).
TRANSACTIONS/CAREER NOTES: Selected by Florida Marlins organization in sixth round of free-agent draft (June 1, 1995). ... On disabled list (April 2, 2000-entire season).
HONORS: Named Eastern League Pitcher of the Year (1999).

Year League	W	L	Pct.	ERA	G	GS	CG	ShO	Sv.	IP	H	R	ER	BB	SO
1995—Gulf Coast Marlins (GCL)	3	1	.750	2.65	11	3	0	0	2	34	28	13	10	16	28
1996—Gulf Coast Marlins (GCL)	1	0	1.000	3.60	2	0	0	0	0	5	6	2	2	0	2
1997—Utica (NY-Penn)	3	3	.500	3.76	12	12	0	0	0	69 1/3	65	36	29	11	67

Year League	W	L	Pct.	ERA	G	GS	CG	ShO	Sv.	IP	H	R	ER	BB	SO
1998— Kane County (Midw.)..........	6	1	.857	2.77	10	10	0	0	0	55 1/3	44	20	17	13	47
— Portland (East.).................	9	5	.643	4.11	18	18	2	2	0	107 1/3	113	55	49	36	97
1999— Portland (East.).................	13	4	.765	2.62	25	25	0	0	0	154 2/3	137	55	45	45	152
— Calgary (PCL)...................	0	2	.000	12.00	2	2	0	0	0	9	19	14	12	4	5
— Florida (N.L.).....................	0	0	...	11.37	3	1	0	0	0	6 1/3	10	8	8	5	7
2000— Florida (N.L.).....................							Did not play.								
Major League totals (1 year)........	0	0	...	11.37	3	1	0	0	0	6 1/3	10	8	8	5	7

TELEMACO, AMAURY   P   PHILLIES

PERSONAL: Born January 19, 1974, in Higuey, Dominican Republic. ... 6-3/222. ... Throws right, bats right. ... Full name: Amaury Regalado Telemaco. ... Name pronounced AH-mer-ee tel-ah-MAH-ko.

HIGH SCHOOL: Cristo Rey (La Romana, Dominican Republic).

TRANSACTIONS/CAREER NOTES: Signed as non-drafted free agent by Chicago Cubs organization (May 23, 1991). ... On temporarily inactive list (August 17, 1993-remainder of season). ... On Orlando disabled list (August 23-September 8, 1994). ... On Chicago disabled list (August 20-September 4, 1996); included rehabilitation assignment to Iowa (September 2-4). ... Claimed on waivers by Arizona Diamondbacks (May 15, 1998). ... On Arizona disabled list (March 26-May 8, 1999); included rehabilitation assignment to Tucson (April 8-May 7). ... Claimed on waivers by Philadelphia Phillies (June 8, 1999). ... On Scranton/Wilkes-Barre disabled list (July 19-August 5, 2000).

Year League	W	L	Pct.	ERA	G	GS	CG	ShO	Sv.	IP	H	R	ER	BB	SO
1991— Puerta Plata (DSL)	3	3	.500	3.55	15	13	0	0	0	66	81	43	26	32	43
1992— Huntington (Appl.)	3	5	.375	4.01	12	12	2	0	0	76 1/3	71	45	34	17	*93
— Peoria (Midw.).................	0	1	.000	7.94	2	1	0	0	0	5 2/3	9	5	5	5	5
1993— Peoria (Midw.).................	8	11	.421	3.45	23	23	3	0	0	143 2/3	129	69	55	54	133
1994— Daytona (FSL).................	7	3	.700	3.40	11	11	2	0	0	76 2/3	62	35	29	23	59
— Orlando (Sou.).................	3	5	.375	3.45	12	12	2	0	0	62 2/3	56	29	24	20	49
1995— Orlando (Sou.).................	8	8	.500	3.29	22	22	3	1	0	147 2/3	112	60	54	42	151
1996— Iowa (A.A.).....................	3	1	.750	3.06	8	8	1	0	0	50	38	19	17	18	42
— Chicago (N.L.).................	5	7	.417	5.46	25	17	0	0	0	97 1/3	108	67	59	31	64
1997— Iowa (A.A.).....................	5	9	.357	4.51	18	18	3	•2	0	113 2/3	121	70	57	38	75
— Chicago (N.L.).................	0	3	.000	6.16	10	5	0	0	0	38	47	26	26	11	29
— Orlando (Sou.).................	1	0	1.000	2.25	1	1	0	0	0	8	9	2	2	2	6
1998— Chicago (N.L.).................	1	1	.500	3.90	14	0	0	0	0	27 2/3	23	12	12	13	18
— Arizona (N.L.)■..............	6	9	.400	3.94	27	18	0	0	0	121	127	63	53	33	60
1999— Tucson (PCL)	0	3	.000	5.09	13	12	0	0	0	17 2/3	21	11	10	6	17
— Arizona (N.L.).................	1	0	1.000	7.50	5	0	0	0	0	6	7	5	5	6	2
— Philadelphia (N.L.)■	3	0	1.000	5.55	44	0	0	0	0	47	45	29	29	20	41
2000— Philadelphia (N.L.)...........	1	3	.250	6.66	13	2	0	0	0	24 1/3	25	22	18	14	22
— Scranton/W.B. (I.L.)	8	3	.727	3.87	21	21	0	0	0	123 1/3	115	60	53	42	88
Major League totals (5 years)	17	23	.425	5.03	138	42	0	0	0	361 1/3	382	224	202	128	236

TELFORD, ANTHONY   P   EXPOS

PERSONAL: Born March 6, 1966, in San Jose, Calif. ... 6-0/195. ... Throws right, bats right. ... Full name: Anthony Charles Telford.

HIGH SCHOOL: Silver Creek (Calif.).

COLLEGE: San Jose State.

TRANSACTIONS/CAREER NOTES: Selected by Baltimore Orioles organization in third round of free-agent draft (June 2, 1987). ... On disabled list (April 20, 1988-remainder of season). ... On Frederick disabled list (April 7-18, 1989). ... On Erie disabled list (June 16-30, 1989). ... Granted free agency (October 15, 1993). ... Signed by Atlanta Braves organization (November 23, 1993). ... Granted free agency (October 15, 1994). ... Signed by Oakland Athletics organization (January 20, 1995). ... Released by A's (May 16, 1995). ... Signed by Cleveland Indians organization (June 15, 1995). ... Granted free agency (October 16, 1995). ... Signed by Montreal Expos organization (February 22, 1996). ... Granted free agency (October 15, 1996). ... Re-signed by Montreal Expos organization (December 18, 1996). ... On disabled list (May 19-June 3, 2000).

Year League	W	L	Pct.	ERA	G	GS	CG	ShO	Sv.	IP	H	R	ER	BB	SO
1987— Newark (NY-Penn)............	1	0	1.000	1.02	6	2	0	0	0	17 2/3	16	2	2	3	27
— Hagerstown (Caro.)........	1	0	1.000	1.59	2	2	0	0	0	11 1/3	9	2	2	5	10
— Rochester (I.L.)................	0	0	...	0.00	1	0	0	0	0	2	0	0	0	3	3
1988— Hagerstown (Caro.)........	1	0	1.000	0.00	1	1	0	0	0	7	3	0	0	0	10
1989— Frederick (Caro.)	2	1	.667	4.21	9	5	0	0	1	25 2/3	25	15	12	12	19
1990— Frederick (Caro.)	4	2	.667	1.68	8	8	1	0	0	53 2/3	35	15	10	11	49
— Hagerstown (East.)........	10	2	.833	1.97	14	13	3	1	0	96	80	26	21	25	73
— Baltimore (A.L.)................	3	3	.500	4.95	8	8	0	0	0	36 1/3	43	22	20	19	20
1991— Rochester (I.L.)................	•12	9	.571	3.95	27	25	3	0	0	157 1/3	166	82	69	48	115
— Baltimore (A.L.)................	0	0	...	4.05	9	1	0	0	0	26 2/3	27	12	12	6	24
1992— Rochester (I.L.)................	12	7	.632	4.18	27	26	3	0	0	*181	*183	89	84	64	129
1993— Rochester (I.L.)................	7	7	.500	4.27	38	6	0	0	2	90 2/3	98	51	43	33	66
— Baltimore (A.L.)................	0	0	...	9.82	3	0	0	0	0	7 1/3	11	8	8	1	6
1994— Richmond (I.L.)■............	10	6	.625	4.23	38	20	3	1	0	142 2/3	148	82	67	41	111
1995— Edmonton (PCL)■	3	2	.600	7.18	8	6	0	0	0	36 1/3	47	32	29	16	17
— Canton/Akron (East.)■.......	2	0	1.000	0.82	2	2	0	0	0	11	6	2	1	4	4
— Buffalo (A.A.).................	4	1	.800	3.46	16	2	0	0	0	39	35	15	15	10	24
1996— Ottawa (I.L.)■..................	7	2	.778	4.11	30	15	1	1	0	118 1/3	128	62	54	34	69
1997— Montreal (N.L.)...............	4	6	.400	3.24	65	0	0	0	1	89	77	34	32	33	61
1998— Montreal (N.L.)...............	3	6	.333	3.86	77	0	0	0	1	91	85	45	39	36	59
1999— Montreal (N.L.)...............	5	4	.556	3.94	79	0	0	0	2	96	112	52	42	38	69
2000— Montreal (N.L.)...............	5	4	.556	3.79	64	0	0	0	3	78 1/3	76	38	33	23	68
A.L. totals (3 years)	3	3	.500	5.12	20	9	0	0	0	70 1/3	81	42	40	26	50
N.L. totals (4 years)	17	20	.459	3.71	285	0	0	0	7	354 1/3	350	169	146	130	257
Major League totals (7 years)	20	23	.465	3.94	305	9	0	0	7	424 2/3	431	211	186	156	307

TESSMER, JAY   P   ROCKIES

PERSONAL: Born December 26, 1971, in Meadville, Pa. ... 6-3/188. ... Throws right, bats right. ... Full name: Jay Weldon Tessmer.
HIGH SCHOOL: Cochranton (Pa.).
COLLEGE: Miami (Fla.).
TRANSACTIONS/CAREER NOTES: Selected by New York Yankees organization in 19th round of free-agent draft (June 1, 1995). ... Traded by Yankees with SS Seth Taylor to Colorado Rockies for P David Lee (January 3, 2001).
HONORS: Name Florida State League Most Valuable Player (1996).

Year League	W	L	Pct.	ERA	G	GS	CG	ShO	Sv.	IP	H	R	ER	BB	SO
1995—Oneonta (NY-Penn)	2	0	1.000	0.95	34	0	0	0	20	38	27	8	4	12	52
1996—Tampa (FSL)	12	4	.750	1.48	*68	0	0	0	*35	97 1/3	68	18	16	19	104
1997—Norwich (East.)	3	6	.333	5.31	55	0	0	0	17	62 2/3	78	41	37	24	51
1998—Norwich (East.)	3	4	.429	1.09	45	0	0	0	29	49 2/3	50	8	6	13	57
—Columbus (I.L.)	1	1	.500	0.49	12	0	0	0	5	18 1/3	8	2	1	1	14
—New York (A.L.)	1	0	1.000	3.12	7	0	0	0	0	8 2/3	4	3	3	4	6
1999—Columbus (I.L.)	3	3	.500	3.34	51	0	0	0	*28	56 2/3	52	22	21	12	42
—New York (A.L.)	0	0	...	14.85	6	0	0	0	0	6 2/3	16	11	11	4	3
2000—Columbus (I.L.)	4	8	.333	3.80	*60	0	0	0	34	66 1/3	73	36	28	19	40
—New York (A.L.)	0	0	...	6.75	7	0	0	0	0	6 2/3	9	6	5	1	5
Major League totals (3 years)	1	0	1.000	7.77	20	0	0	0	0	22	29	20	19	9	14

TEUT, NATHAN   P   CUBS

PERSONAL: Born March 11, 1976, in Newton, Iowa. ... 6-7/215. ... Throws left, bats right. ... Full name: Nathan Mark Teut. ... Name pronounced TOIT.
HIGH SCHOOL: Paton-Churdan (Churdan, Iowa).
COLLEGE: Iowa State.
TRANSACTIONS/CAREER NOTES: Selected by Chicago Cubs organization in fourth round of free-agent draft (June 3, 1997).

Year League	W	L	Pct.	ERA	G	GS	CG	ShO	Sv.	IP	H	R	ER	BB	SO
1997—Williamsport (NY-Penn)	3	4	.429	2.57	9	9	0	0	0	49	55	23	14	6	37
—Rockford (Midw.)	0	1	.000	10.13	2	2	0	0	0	10 2/3	18	12	12	2	6
1998—Rockford (Midw.)	8	5	.615	3.31	16	16	1	0	0	103 1/3	99	49	38	23	67
—Daytona (FSL)	5	3	.625	5.48	11	11	1	0	0	65 2/3	88	48	40	19	54
1999—Daytona (FSL)	5	12	.294	6.38	26	26	1	0	0	132 2/3	180	113	94	41	91
2000—West Tenn (Sou.)	11	6	.647	3.06	27	21	1	1	0	138 1/3	133	53	47	44	106

THOMAS, EVAN   P   PHILLIES

PERSONAL: Born June 14, 1974, in Miami. ... 5-10/170. ... Throws right, bats right. ... Full name: Evan William Thomas.
HIGH SCHOOL: Miramar (Fla.).
JUNIOR COLLEGE: Miami-Dade (North) Community College.
COLLEGE: Florida International.
TRANSACTIONS/CAREER NOTES: Selected by Philadelphia Phillies organization in 10th round of free-agent draft (June 4, 1996).

Year League	W	L	Pct.	ERA	G	GS	CG	ShO	Sv.	IP	H	R	ER	BB	SO
1996—Batavia (NY-Penn)	10	2	.833	2.78	13	13	0	0	0	81	60	29	25	23	75
1997—Clearwater (FSL)	5	5	.500	2.44	13	12	2	0	0	84 2/3	68	30	23	23	89
—Reading (East.)	3	6	.333	4.12	15	15	0	0	0	83	98	51	38	32	83
1998—Reading (East.)	8	5	.615	3.35	24	24	3	*3	0	158 1/3	180	66	59	44	134
—Scranton/W.B. (I.L.)	0	1	.000	8.00	2	2	0	0	0	9	9	8	8	6	5
1999—Reading (East.)	9	5	.643	3.25	36	15	1	0	3	127 1/3	123	53	46	50	127
2000—Scranton/W.B. (I.L.)	13	10	.565	3.53	29	27	3	2	0	171	163	70	67	50	127

THOMAS, FRANK   DH/1B   WHITE SOX

PERSONAL: Born May 27, 1968, in Columbus, Ga. ... 6-5/270. ... Bats right, throws right. ... Full name: Frank Edward Thomas.
HIGH SCHOOL: Columbus (Ga.).
COLLEGE: Auburn.
TRANSACTIONS/CAREER NOTES: Selected by Chicago White Sox organization in first round (seventh pick overall) of free-agent draft (June 5, 1989). ... On disabled list (July 11-30, 1996; and June 7-22, 1997).
RECORDS: Shares major league single-inning record for most doubles—2 (September 3, 2000, first inning). ... Shares A.L. single-season record for most intentional bases on balls received by righthanded batter—29 (1995).
HONORS: Named first baseman on THE SPORTING NEWS college All-America team (1989). ... Named designated hitter on THE SPORTING NEWS A.L. All-Star team (1991). ... Named designated hitter on THE SPORTING NEWS A.L. Silver Slugger team (1991 and 2000). ... Named Major League Player of the Year by THE SPORTING NEWS (1993). ... Named first baseman on THE SPORTING NEWS A.L. All-Star team (1993-94). ... Named first baseman on THE SPORTING NEWS A.L. Silver Slugger team (1993-94). ... Named A.L. Most Valuable Player by Baseball Writers' Association of America (1993-94). ... Named A.L. Comeback Player of the Year by THE SPORTING NEWS (2000).
STATISTICAL NOTES: Led Southern League with .581 slugging percentage and .487 on-base percentage in 1990. ... Led A.L. with .453 on-base percentage in 1991, .439 in 1992, .487 in 1994 and .456 in 1997. ... Led A.L. first basemen with 1,533 total chances in 1992. ... Led A.L. with .729 slugging percentage in 1994. ... Led A.L. with 12 sacrifice flies in 1995. ... Led A.L. with 29 intentional bases on balls received in 1995 and 26 in 1996. ... Hit three home runs in one game (September 15, 1996). ... Had 21-game hitting streak (May 24-June 15, 1999). ... Career major league grand slams: 7.
MISCELLANEOUS: Holds Chicago White Sox all-time record for most home runs (344) and runs batted in (1,183).

Year	Team (League)	Pos.	G	AB	R	H	2B	3B	HR	RBI	Avg.	BB	SO	SB	PO	A	E	Avg.
							BATTING								FIELDING			
1989—	GC White Sox (GCL) ..	1B	17	52	8	19	5	0	1	11	.365	10	24	4	130	8	2	.986
	—Sarasota (FSL)	1B	55	188	27	52	9	1	4	30	.277	31	33	0	420	31	7	.985
1990—	Birmingham (Sou.).....	1B	109	353	85	114	27	5	18	71	.323	*112	74	7	954	77	14	.987
	—Chicago (A.L.)	1B-DH	60	191	39	63	11	3	7	31	.330	44	54	0	428	26	5	.989
1991—	Chicago (A.L.)	DH-1B	158	559	104	178	31	2	32	109	.318	*138	112	1	459	27	2	.996
1992—	Chicago (A.L.)	1B-DH	160	573	108	185	•46	2	24	115	.323	•122	88	6	*1428	92	13	.992
1993—	Chicago (A.L.)	1B-DH	153	549	106	174	36	0	41	128	.317	112	54	4	1222	83	15	.989
1994—	Chicago (A.L.)	1B-DH	113	399	*106	141	34	1	38	101	.353	*109	61	2	735	45	7	.991
1995—	Chicago (A.L.)	1B-DH	•145	493	102	152	27	0	40	111	.308	*136	74	3	738	34	7	.991
1996—	Chicago (A.L.)	1B	141	527	110	184	26	0	40	134	.349	109	70	1	1098	85	9	.992
1997—	Chicago (A.L.)	1B-DH	146	530	110	184	35	0	35	125	*.347	109	69	1	739	49	11	.986
1998—	Chicago (A.L.)	DH-1B	160	585	109	155	35	2	29	109	.265	110	93	7	116	6	2	.984
1999—	Chicago (A.L.)	DH-1B	135	486	74	148	36	0	15	77	.305	87	66	3	385	18	4	.990
2000—	Chicago (A.L.)	DH-1B	159	582	115	191	44	0	43	143	.328	112	94	1	267	15	1	.996
Major League totals (11 years)			1530	5474	1083	1755	361	10	344	1183	.321	1188	835	29	7615	480	76	.991

DIVISION SERIES RECORD

Year	Team (League)	Pos.	G	AB	R	H	2B	3B	HR	RBI	Avg.	BB	SO	SB	PO	A	E	Avg.
							BATTING								FIELDING			
2000—	Chicago (A.L.)	DH-1B	3	9	0	0	0	0	0	0	.000	4	0	0	8	0	0	1.000

CHAMPIONSHIP SERIES RECORD

RECORDS: Holds single-series record for most bases on balls received—10 (1993). ... Shares single-game record for most bases on balls received—4 (October 5, 1993).

Year	Team (League)	Pos.	G	AB	R	H	2B	3B	HR	RBI	Avg.	BB	SO	SB	PO	A	E	Avg.
							BATTING								FIELDING			
1993—	Chicago (A.L.)	1B-DH	6	17	2	6	0	0	1	3	.353	10	5	0	24	3	0	1.000

ALL-STAR GAME RECORD

Year	League	Pos.	AB	R	H	2B	3B	HR	RBI	Avg.	BB	SO	SB	PO	A	E	Avg.
						BATTING								FIELDING			
1993—	American	PH-DH	1	0	1	0	0	0	0	1.000	0	0	0	...	...	...	...
1994—	American	1B	2	1	2	0	0	0	1	1.000	1	0	0	6	0	0	1.000
1995—	American	1B	2	1	1	0	0	1	2	.500	0	0	0	5	1	0	1.000
1996—	American..................						Selected, did not play—injured.										
1997—	American..................						Selected, did not play—injured.										
All-Star Game totals (3 years)			5	2	4	0	0	1	3	.800	1	0	0	11	1	0	1.000

THOME, JIM — 1B — INDIANS

PERSONAL: Born August 27, 1970, in Peoria, Ill. ... 6-4/240. ... Bats left, throws right. ... Full name: James Howard Thome. ... Name pronounced TOE-me.
HIGH SCHOOL: Limestone (Bartonville, Ill.).
JUNIOR COLLEGE: Illinois Central College.
TRANSACTIONS/CAREER NOTES: Selected by Cleveland Indians organization in 13th round of free-agent draft (June 5, 1989). ... On Cleveland disabled list (March 28-May 18, 1992); included rehabilitation assignment to Canton/Akron (May 9-18). ... On Cleveland disabled list (May 20-June 15, 1992); included rehabilitation assignment to Canton/Akron (June 1-15). ... On disabled list (August 8-September 16, 1998).
RECORDS: Shares major league single-game record for most strikeouts (nine-inning game)—5 (April 9, 2000).
HONORS: Named International League Most Valuable Player (1993). ... Named third baseman on THE SPORTING NEWS A.L. All-Star team (1995 and 1996). ... Named third baseman on THE SPORTING NEWS A.L. Silver Slugger team (1996).
STATISTICAL NOTES: Led International League with .441 on-base percentage in 1993. ... Hit three home runs in one game (July 22, 1994). ... Had 16-game hitting streak (May 25-June 10, 1998). ... Career major league grand slams: 5.

Year	Team (League)	Pos.	G	AB	R	H	2B	3B	HR	RBI	Avg.	BB	SO	SB	PO	A	E	Avg.
							BATTING								FIELDING			
1989—	GC Indians (GCL)	SS-3B	55	186	22	44	5	3	0	22	.237	21	33	6	65	144	21	.909
1990—	Burlington (Appl.).......	3B	34	118	31	44	7	1	12	34	.373	27	18	6	28	79	11	.907
	—Kinston (Caro.).........	3B	33	117	19	36	4	1	4	16	.308	24	26	4	10	66	8	.905
1991—	Canton/Akron (East.)..	3B	84	294	47	99	20	2	5	45	.337	44	58	8	41	167	17	.924
	—Colo. Springs (PCL) ...	3B	41	151	20	43	7	3	2	28	.285	12	29	0	28	84	6	.949
	—Cleveland (A.L.).........	3B	27	98	7	25	4	2	1	9	.255	5	16	1	12	60	8	.900
1992—	Colo. Springs (PCL)	3B	12	48	11	15	4	1	2	14	.313	6	16	0	9	20	8	.784
	—Cleveland (A.L.).........	3B	40	117	8	24	3	1	2	12	.205	10	34	2	21	61	11	.882
	—Canton/Akron (East.)..	3B	30	107	16	36	9	2	1	14	.336	24	30	0	11	35	4	.920
1993—	Charlotte (I.L.)...........	3B-DH	115	410	85	136	21	4	25	*102	*.332	76	94	1	67	226	15	.951
	—Cleveland (A.L.).........	3B	47	154	28	41	11	0	7	22	.266	29	36	2	29	86	6	.950
1994—	Cleveland (A.L.).........	3B	98	321	58	86	20	1	20	52	.268	46	84	3	62	173	15	.940
1995—	Cleveland (A.L.).........	3B-DH	137	452	92	142	29	3	25	73	.314	97	113	4	75	214	16	.948
1996—	Cleveland (A.L.).........	3B-DH	151	505	122	157	28	5	38	116	.311	123	141	2	86	262	17	.953
1997—	Cleveland (A.L.).........	1B	147	496	104	142	25	0	40	102	.286	*120	146	1	1233	95	10	.993
1998—	Cleveland (A.L.).........	1B-DH	123	440	89	129	34	2	30	85	.293	89	141	1	998	85	10	.991
1999—	Cleveland (A.L.).........	1B-DH	146	494	101	137	27	2	33	108	.277	*127	*171	0	930	83	6	.994
2000—	Cleveland (A.L.).........	1B-DH	158	557	106	150	33	1	37	106	.269	118	171	1	834	91	5	.995
Major League totals (10 years)			1074	3634	715	1033	214	17	233	685	.284	764	1053	17	4280	1210	104	.981

DIVISION SERIES RECORD

RECORDS: Holds career records for most home runs—7; and most strikeouts—26. ... Shares single-game records for most home runs—2 (October 11, 1999); and most grand slams—1 (October 7, 1999). ... Shares single-inning record for most runs batted in—4 (October 7, 1999, fourth inning).

Year	Team (League)	Pos.	G	AB	R	H	2B	3B	HR	RBI	Avg.	BB	SO	SB	PO	A	E	Avg.
1995—Cleveland (A.L.)..........		3B	3	13	1	2	0	0	1	3	.154	1	6	0	6	6	0	1.000
1996—Cleveland (A.L.)..........		3B	4	10	1	3	0	0	0	0	.300	1	5	0	1	1	0	1.000
1997—Cleveland (A.L.)..........		1B	4	15	1	3	0	0	0	1	.200	0	5	0	44	3	0	1.000
1998—Cleveland (A.L.)..........		1B-DH	4	15	2	2	0	0	2	2	.133	3	5	0	26	1	0	1.000
1999—Cleveland (A.L.)..........		1B	5	17	7	6	0	0	4	10	.353	4	5	0	29	7	0	1.000
Division series totals (5 years)			20	70	12	16	0	0	7	16	.229	9	26	0	106	18	0	1.000

CHAMPIONSHIP SERIES RECORD

RECORDS: Shares single-game record for most grand slams—1 (October 13, 1998). ... Shares single-inning record for most runs batted in—4 (October 13, 1998, fifth inning). ... Shares A.L. single series record for most home runs—4 (1998).

Year	Team (League)	Pos.	G	AB	R	H	2B	3B	HR	RBI	Avg.	BB	SO	SB	PO	A	E	Avg.
1995—Cleveland (A.L.)..........		3B	5	15	2	4	0	0	2	5	.267	2	3	0	1	5	1	.857
1997—Cleveland (A.L.)..........		1B-PH	6	14	3	1	0	0	0	0	.071	5	4	0	35	2	0	1.000
1998—Cleveland (A.L.)..........		DH-1B	6	23	4	7	0	0	4	8	.304	1	8	0	45	4	0	1.000
Championship series totals (3 years)			17	52	9	12	0	0	6	13	.231	8	15	0	81	11	1	.989

WORLD SERIES RECORD

Year	Team (League)	Pos.	G	AB	R	H	2B	3B	HR	RBI	Avg.	BB	SO	SB	PO	A	E	Avg.
1995—Cleveland (A.L.)..........		3B-PH	6	19	1	4	1	0	1	2	.211	2	5	0	3	5	1	.889
1997—Cleveland (A.L.)..........		1B	7	28	8	8	0	1	2	4	.286	5	7	0	57	5	1	.984
World Series totals (2 years)			13	47	9	12	1	1	3	6	.255	7	12	0	60	10	2	.972

ALL-STAR GAME RECORD

Year	League	Pos.	AB	R	H	2B	3B	HR	RBI	Avg.	BB	SO	SB	PO	A	E	Avg.
1997—American		PH-DH	1	0	0	0	0	0	0	.000	0	0	0	...	...	...	...
1998—American		1B	2	1	0	0	0	0	0	.000	2	1	0	4	0	0	1.000
1999—American		1B	2	1	1	0	0	0	1	.500	1	0	0	4	0	0	1.000
All-Star Game totals (3 years)			5	2	1	0	0	0	1	.200	3	1	0	8	0	0	1.000

T

THOMPSON, ANDY   OF   BLUE JAYS

PERSONAL: Born October 8, 1975, in Oconomowoc, Wis. ... 6-3/215. ... Bats right, throws right. ... Full name: Andrew John Thompson.
HIGH SCHOOL: Sun Prairie (Wis.).
TRANSACTIONS/CAREER NOTES: Selected by Toronto Blue Jays organization in 23rd round of free-agent draft (June 2, 1994).

Year	Team (League)	Pos.	G	AB	R	H	2B	3B	HR	RBI	Avg.	BB	SO	SB	PO	A	E	Avg.
1995—Hagerstown (S.Atl.)....		3B	124	461	48	110	19	2	6	57	.239	29	108	2	86	200	*43	.869
1996—Dunedin (FSL)..........		3B	129	425	64	120	26	5	11	50	.282	60	108	16	75	259	*47	.877
1997—Knoxville (Sou.)..........		3B	124	448	75	128	25	3	15	71	.286	63	76	0	72	202	31	.898
1998—Knoxville (Sou.)..........		OF-3B	125	481	74	137	33	2	14	88	.285	54	69	8	138	75	26	.891
1999—Knoxville (Sou.)..........		OF	67	254	56	62	16	3	15	53	.244	34	55	7	108	3	4	.965
—Syracuse (I.L.)...........		OF	62	229	42	67	17	2	16	42	.293	21	45	5	89	4	0	1.000
2000—Syracuse (I.L.)...........		OF	121	426	59	105	27	2	22	65	.246	50	95	9	205	*17	7	.969
—Toronto (A.L.)...........		OF	2	6	2	1	0	0	0	1	.167	3	2	0	2	0	0	1.000
Major League totals (1 year)			2	6	2	1	0	0	0	1	.167	3	2	0	2	0	0	1.000

THOMPSON, JUSTIN   P   RANGERS

PERSONAL: Born March 8, 1973, in San Antonio. ... 6-4/215. ... Throws left, bats left. ... Full name: Justin Willard Thompson.
HIGH SCHOOL: Klein Oak (Spring, Texas).
TRANSACTIONS/CAREER NOTES: Selected by Detroit Tigers organization in supplemental round ("sandwich pick" between first and second round, 32nd pick overall) of free-agent draft (June 3, 1991); pick received as part of compensation for Minnesota Twins signing Type A free-agent P Jack Morris. ... On disabled list (April 8, 1994-entire season). ... On Detroit disabled list (June 3-August 17, 1996); included rehabilitation assignments to Fayetteville (July 19-23), Visalia (July 23-26) and Toledo (July 26-August 11). ... On disabled list (July 6-21, 1997). ... On disabled list (August 16, 1999-remainder of season). ... Traded by Tigers with P Francisco Cordero, OF Gabe Kapler, C Bill Haselman, 2B Frank Catalanotto and P Alan Webb to Texas Rangers for OF Juan Gonzalez, P Danny Patterson and C Gregg Zaun (November 2, 1999). ... On Texas disabled list (April 1, 2000-entire season); included rehabilitation assignments to Charlotte (April 15-20), Tulsa (April 21-25) and Oklahoma (April 26-May 1).

Year	League	W	L	Pct.	ERA	G	GS	CG	ShO	Sv.	IP	H	R	ER	BB	SO
1991—Bristol (Appl.).................		2	5	.286	3.60	10	10	0	0	0	50	45	29	20	24	60
1992—Fayetteville (S.Atl.)		4	4	.500	2.18	20	19	0	0	0	95	79	32	23	40	88
1993—Lakeland (FSL)		4	4	.500	3.56	11	11	0	0	0	55 2/3	65	25	22	16	46
—London (East.)		3	6	.333	4.09	14	14	1	0	0	83 2/3	96	51	38	37	72
1994—Trenton (East.)								Did not play.								
1995—Lakeland (FSL)		2	1	.667	4.88	6	6	0	0	0	24	30	13	13	8	20
—Jacksonville (Sou.)		6	7	.462	3.73	18	18	3	0	0	123	110	55	51	38	98
1996—Toledo (I.L.)		6	3	.667	3.42	13	13	3	1	0	84 1/3	74	36	32	26	69
—Detroit (A.L.)		1	6	.143	4.58	11	11	0	0	0	59	62	35	30	31	44
—Fayetteville (S.Atl.)		0	0	...	3.00	1	1	0	0	0	3	1	1	1	0	5
—Visalia (Calif.)		0	0	...	0.00	1	1	0	0	0	3	2	0	0	2	7
1997—Detroit (A.L.)		15	11	.577	3.02	32	32	4	0	0	223 1/3	188	82	75	66	151
1998—Detroit (A.L.)		11	15	.423	4.05	34	34	5	0	0	222	227	114	100	79	149
1999—Detroit (A.L.)		9	11	.450	5.11	24	24	0	0	0	142 2/3	152	85	81	59	83

Year	League	W	L	Pct.	ERA	G	GS	CG	ShO	Sv.	IP	H	R	ER	BB	SO
2000—Charlotte (FSL)■	0	0	...	2.08	1	1	0	0	0	4 1/3	3	1	1	3	2
—Tulsa (Texas)	1	0	1.000	4.76	1	1	0	0	0	5 2/3	8	3	3	1	4
—Oklahoma (PCL)	0	0	...	11.12	1	1	0	0	0	5 2/3	10	8	7	4	4
Major League totals (4 years)	36	43	.456	3.98	101	101	9	0	0	647	629	316	286	235	427

ALL-STAR GAME RECORD

Year	League	W	L	Pct.	ERA	GS	CG	ShO	Sv.	IP	H	R	ER	BB	SO
1997—American	0	0	...	0.00	0	0	0	0	1	0	0	0	0	1

THOMPSON, MARK — P

PERSONAL: Born April 7, 1971, in Russellville, Ky. ... 6-2/212. ... Throws right, bats right. ... Full name: Mark Radford Thompson.

HIGH SCHOOL: Logan County (Russellville, Ky.).

COLLEGE: Kentucky.

TRANSACTIONS/CAREER NOTES: Selected by Colorado Rockies organization in second round of free-agent draft (June 1, 1992). ... On Colorado Springs disabled list (June 30-September 7, 1993; August 9-18 and August 27-September 5, 1994). ... On Colorado disabled list (May 8, 1997-remainder of season); included rehabilitation assignments to Asheville (June 29-July 15) and Colorado Springs (July 15-July 20). ... On Colorado disabled list (May 7, 1998-remainder of season); included rehabilitation assignments to Arizona League Rockies (August 14), Salem (August 19-29) and Colorado Springs (September 3). ... Granted free agency (October 20, 1998). ... Signed by Cincinnati Reds organization (December 15, 1998). ... On Indianapolis disabled list (May 7-June 15, 1999). ... Released by Reds (July 17, 1999). ... Signed by St. Louis Cardinals organization (July 18, 1999). ... On St. Louis disabled list (April 13-May 16 and August 28, 2000-remainder of season); included rehabilitation assignment to Arkansas (May 8-16). ... On Memphis disabled list (August 3-15, 2000). ... Granted free agency (October 19, 2000).

RECORDS: Shares N.L. single-inning record for most consecutive home runs allowed—3 (June 30, 1996, third inning).

Year	League	W	L	Pct.	ERA	G	GS	CG	ShO	Sv.	IP	H	R	ER	BB	SO
1992—Bend (N'West)	8	4	.667	1.95	16	•16	*4	0	0	*106 1/3	81	32	23	31	*102
1993—Central Valley (Calif.)	3	2	.600	2.20	11	11	0	0	0	69 2/3	46	19	17	18	72
—Colorado Springs (PCL)	3	0	1.000	2.70	4	4	2	0	0	33 1/3	31	13	10	11	22
1994—Colorado Springs (PCL)	8	9	.471	4.49	23	23	•4	1	0	140 1/3	169	83	70	57	82
—Colorado (N.L.)	1	1	.500	9.00	2	2	0	0	0	9	16	9	9	8	5
1995—Colorado (N.L.)	2	3	.400	6.53	21	5	0	0	0	51	73	42	37	22	30
—Colorado Springs (PCL)	5	3	.625	6.10	11	10	0	0	0	62	73	43	42	25	38
1996—Colorado (N.L.)	9	11	.450	5.30	34	28	3	1	0	169 2/3	189	109	100	74	99
1997—Colorado (N.L.)	3	3	.500	7.89	6	6	0	0	0	29 2/3	40	27	26	13	9
—Asheville (S.Atl.)	0	2	.000	2.70	4	4	0	0	0	13 1/3	11	5	4	5	9
—Colorado Springs (PCL)	0	0	...	12.00	1	1	0	0	0	3	6	4	4	1	1
1998—Colorado (N.L.)	1	2	.333	7.71	6	6	0	0	0	23 1/3	36	22	20	12	14
—Arizona Rockies (Ariz.)	0	0	...	0.00	1	1	0	0	0	3	1	0	0	0	2
—Salem (Caro.)	0	0	...	3.95	3	3	0	0	0	13 2/3	17	7	6	3	10
—Colorado Springs (PCL)	0	1	.000	18.90	1	1	0	0	0	3 1/3	10	7	7	1	1
1999—Indianapolis (I.L.)■	2	6	.250	5.13	11	10	0	0	0	54 1/3	50	31	31	29	28
—Memphis (PCL)■	4	2	.667	2.94	9	8	0	0	0	52	50	22	17	20	27
—St. Louis (N.L.)	1	3	.250	2.76	5	5	0	0	0	29 1/3	26	12	9	17	22
2000—Arkansas (Texas)	0	0	...	4.91	1	1	0	0	0	3 2/3	6	2	2	0	3
—St. Louis (N.L.)	1	1	.500	5.04	20	0	0	0	0	25	24	21	14	15	19
—Memphis (PCL)	2	0	1.000	2.03	6	5	0	0	0	31	31	9	7	5	15
Major League totals (7 years)	18	24	.429	5.74	94	52	3	1	0	337	404	242	215	161	198

DIVISION SERIES RECORD

Year	League	W	L	Pct.	ERA	G	GS	CG	ShO	Sv.	IP	H	R	ER	BB	SO
1995—Colorado (N.L.)	0	0	...	0.00	1	0	0	0	1	1	0	0	0	0	0

THOMPSON, RYAN — OF — BLUE JAYS

PERSONAL: Born November 4, 1967, in Chestertown, Md. ... 6-3/215. ... Bats right, throws right. ... Full name: Ryan Orlando Thompson.

HIGH SCHOOL: Kent County (Rock Hall, Md.).

TRANSACTIONS/CAREER NOTES: Selected by Toronto Blue Jays organization in 13th round of free-agent draft (June 2, 1987). ... On disabled list (May 29-June 7, 1991). ... On Syracuse disabled list (May 4-11 and July 20-27, 1992). ... Traded by Blue Jays to New York Mets (September 1, 1992), completing deal in which Mets traded P David Cone to Blue Jays for IF Jeff Kent and a player to be named later (August 27, 1992). ... On New York disabled list (April 18-May 30 and July 18-August 18, 1995); included rehabilitation assignments to Norfolk (May 13-30) and Binghamton (August 16-18). ... Traded by Mets with P Reid Cornelius to Cleveland Indians for P Mark Clark (March 30, 1996). ... Granted free agency (December 20, 1996). ... Signed by Kansas City Royals organization (January 16, 1997). ... Released by Royals (March 26, 1997). ... Signed by Indians organization (April 21, 1997). ... Traded by Indians to Toronto Blue Jays for IF Jeff Manto (June 6, 1997). ... Granted free agency (October 15, 1997). ... Signed to play for Fukuoka Dalei Hawks of Japan Pacific League (1998). ... Signed by Houston Astros organization (January 21, 1999). ... On New Orleans disabled list (August 5-13, 1999). ... Granted free agency (October 20, 1999). ... Signed by New York Yankees organization (December 15, 1999). ... Signed by Yankees (April 2, 2000). ... Re-signed by Yankees organization (May 1, 2000). ... Released by Yankees (November 15, 2000). ... Signed by Blue Jays organization (December 13, 2000).

STATISTICAL NOTES: Led American Association outfielders with 334 total chances in 1996. ... Career major league grand slams: 1.

					BATTING								FIELDING		
Year	Team (League)	Pos.	G	AB	R	H	2B	3B	HR	RBI	Avg.	BB	SO	SB	PO	A	E	Avg.
1987—Medicine Hat (Pio.)	OF	40	110	13	27	3	1	1	9	.245	6	34	1	56	2	4	.935
1988—St. Catharines (NY-P.)	OF	23	57	13	10	4	0	0	2	.175	24	21	2	29	1	4	.882
—Dunedin (FSL)	OF	17	29	2	4	0	0	1	2	.138	2	12	0	11	0	0	1.000
1989—St. Catharines (NY-P.)	OF	74	278	39	76	14	1	6	36	.273	16	60	9	111	•11	5	.961
1990—Dunedin (FSL)	OF	117	438	56	101	15	5	6	37	.231	20	100	18	237	7	7	.972
1991—Knoxville (Sou.)	OF	114	403	48	97	14	3	8	40	.241	26	88	17	222	5	4	.983
1992—Syracuse (I.L.)■	OF	112	429	74	121	20	7	14	46	.282	43	114	10	270	8	4	.986
—New York (N.L.)■	OF	30	108	15	24	7	1	3	10	.222	8	24	2	77	2	1	.988

Year Team (League)	Pos.	G	AB	R	H	2B	3B	HR	RBI	Avg.	BB	SO	SB	PO	A	E	Avg.
1993— New York (N.L.).........	OF	80	288	34	72	19	2	11	26	.250	19	81	2	228	4	3	.987
— Norfolk (I.L.)	OF	60	224	39	58	11	2	12	34	.259	24	81	6	138	4	4	.973
1994— New York (N.L.).........	OF	98	334	29	75	14	1	18	59	.225	28	94	1	274	5	3	.989
1995— Norfolk (I.L.)	OF-DH	15	53	7	18	3	0	2	11	.340	4	15	4	15	2	0	1.000
— New York (N.L.).........	OF	75	267	39	67	13	0	7	31	.251	19	77	3	193	4	3	.985
— Binghamton (East.)	OF	2	8	2	4	0	0	1	4	.500	1	2	0	2	0	0	1.000
1996— Buffalo (A.A.)■	OF-DH	•138	*540	79	140	26	4	21	83	.259	21	119	12	*317	8	*9	.973
— Cleveland (A.L.)..........	OF	8	22	2	7	0	0	1	5	.318	1	6	0	5	0	0	1.000
1997— Buffalo (A.A.)............	OF-DH	24	66	10	16	0	0	1	6	.242	5	16	2	20	1	1	.955
— Syracuse (I.L.)■	OF-DH	83	330	37	95	23	1	16	58	.288	21	59	4	117	4	1	.992
1998— Fukuoka (Jap. Pac.)■..		26	107	10	29	7	0	2	16	.271	12	32	1	...	...	...	...
1999— New Orleans (PCL)■..	OF-DH	112	404	60	125	23	2	16	58	.309	37	78	4	209	12	8	.965
— Houston (N.L.)	OF	12	20	2	4	1	0	1	5	.200	2	7	0	3	1	1	.800
2000— Columbus (I.L.)■......	OF	86	326	45	93	23	3	23	75	.285	27	72	10	155	10	2	.988
— New York (A.L.).........	OF	33	50	12	13	3	0	3	14	.260	5	12	0	33	0	0	1.000
American League totals (2 years)		41	72	14	20	3	0	4	19	.278	6	18	0	38	0	0	1.000
National League totals (5 years)		295	1017	119	242	54	4	40	131	.238	76	283	8	775	16	11	.986
Major League totals (7 years)		336	1089	133	262	57	4	44	150	.241	82	301	8	813	16	11	.987

THOMPSON, TRAVIS　　　　P　　　　ROCKIES

PERSONAL: Born January 10, 1975, in Milwaukee. ... 6-3/189. ... Throws right, bats right. ... Full name: Travis Michael Thompson.
HIGH SCHOOL: Pulaski (Milwaukee).
JUNIOR COLLEGE: Madison (Wis.) Area Technical.
TRANSACTIONS/CAREER NOTES: Selected by Colorado Rockies organization in 12th round of free-agent draft (June 4, 1996).

Year League	W	L	Pct.	ERA	G	GS	CG	ShO	Sv.	IP	H	R	ER	BB	SO
1996— Arizona Rockies (Ariz.).......	4	1	.800	3.30	9	3	0	0	0	30	34	12	11	5	25
— Portland (N'West)	0	2	.000	5.94	9	0	0	0	0	16²/₃	21	11	11	6	8
1997— Portland (N'West)	5	5	.500	4.50	18	11	0	0	0	74	88	51	37	16	51
1998— Asheville (S.Atl.)................	6	7	.462	3.24	26	24	0	0	0	147¹/₃	155	71	53	36	113
1999— Salem (Caro.)...................	3	3	.500	1.74	56	0	0	0	*27	62	54	19	12	24	53
2000— Carolina (Sou.)	3	7	.300	6.33	50	0	0	0	17	58¹/₃	70	44	41	30	43

THOMSON, JOHN　　　　P　　　　ROCKIES

PERSONAL: Born October 1, 1973, in Vicksburg, Miss. ... 6-3/187. ... Throws right, bats right. ... Full name: John Carl Thomson.
HIGH SCHOOL: Sulphur (La.).
JUNIOR COLLEGE: Blinn College (Texas).
COLLEGE: McNeese State.
TRANSACTIONS/CAREER NOTES: Selected by Colorado Rockies organization in seventh round of free-agent draft (June 3, 1993). ... On Colorado disabled list (June 16-July 26, 1998); included rehabilitation assignment to Asheville (July 16-22). ... On Colorado Springs disabled list (May 19-July 19, 1999); included rehabilitation assignment to Salem (July 17-19). ... On Colorado disabled list (March 23, 2000-remainder of season); included rehabilitation assignments to Arizona League Rockies (August 16-September 1) and Portland (September 2-4).
STATISTICAL NOTES: Tied for Arizona League lead with 14 wild pitches in 1993.

Year League	W	L	Pct.	ERA	G	GS	CG	ShO	Sv.	IP	H	R	ER	BB	SO
1993— Arizona Rockies (Ariz.).......	3	5	.375	4.62	11	11	0	0	0	50²/₃	43	40	26	31	36
1994— Asheville (S.Atl.)................	6	6	.500	2.85	19	15	1	1	0	88¹/₃	70	34	28	33	79
— Central Valley (Calif.)..........	3	1	.750	3.28	9	8	0	0	0	49¹/₃	43	20	18	18	41
1995— New Haven (East.)..............	7	8	.467	4.18	26	24	0	0	0	131¹/₃	132	69	61	56	82
1996— New Haven (East.)..............	9	4	.692	2.86	16	16	1	0	0	97²/₃	82	35	31	27	86
— Colorado Springs (PCL)	4	7	.364	5.04	11	11	0	0	0	69²/₃	76	45	39	26	62
1997— Colorado Springs (PCL)	4	2	.667	3.43	7	7	0	0	0	42	36	18	16	14	49
— Colorado (N.L.)	7	9	.438	4.71	27	27	2	1	0	166¹/₃	193	94	87	51	106
1998— Colorado (N.L.)	8	11	.421	4.81	26	26	2	0	0	161	174	86	86	49	106
— Asheville (S.Atl.)................	1	0	1.000	0.00	2	2	0	0	0	9	5	1	0	1	12
1999— Colorado (N.L.)	1	10	.091	8.04	14	13	1	0	0	62²/₃	85	62	56	36	34
— Colorado Springs (PCL)	0	2	.000	9.45	5	5	1	0	0	20	36	25	21	8	19
— Salem (Caro.)	0	1	.000	9.00	1	1	0	0	0	2	4	2	2	2	4
2000— Arizona Rockies (Ariz.).......	0	1	.000	13.50	3	3	0	0	0	5¹/₃	8	8	8	4	7
— Portland (N'West)	0	0	...	2.25	1	1	0	0	0	4	4	1	1	1	3
Major League totals (3 years).......	16	30	.348	5.28	67	66	5	1	0	390	452	242	229	136	246

THURMAN, MIKE　　　　P　　　　EXPOS

PERSONAL: Born July 22, 1973, in Corvallis, Ore. ... 6-5/210. ... Throws right, bats right. ... Full name: Michael Richard Thurman.
HIGH SCHOOL: Philomath (Ore.).
COLLEGE: Oregon State.
TRANSACTIONS/CAREER NOTES: Selected by Montreal Expos organization in supplemental round ("sandwich pick" between first and second round, 31st pick overall) of free-agent draft (June 2, 1994); pick received as compensation for Cleveland Indians signing Type A free-agent P Dennis Martinez. ... On Harrisburg disabled list (June 17-July 5, 1997). ... On Montreal disabled list (March 23-May 12 and May 25-July 21, 2000); included rehabilitation assignments to Jupiter (April 21-May 7) and Ottawa (May 8-9, June 29-July 10 and July 17-19) and Harrisburg (July 11-16).

Year League	W	L	Pct.	ERA	G	GS	CG	ShO	Sv.	IP	H	R	ER	BB	SO
1994— Vermont (NY-Penn)	0	1	.000	5.40	2	2	0	0	0	$6^2/_3$	6	4	4	2	3
1995— Albany (S.Atl.)	3	8	.273	5.47	22	22	2	0	0	$110^1/_3$	133	79	67	32	77
1996— West Palm Beach (FSL)	6	8	.429	3.33	19	19	0	0	0	$113^2/_3$	122	53	42	23	68
— Harrisburg (East.)	3	1	.750	5.11	4	4	1	0	0	$24^2/_3$	25	14	14	5	14
1997— Harrisburg (East.)	9	6	.600	3.81	20	20	1	0	0	$115^2/_3$	102	54	49	30	85
— Ottawa (I.L.)	1	3	.250	5.49	4	4	0	0	0	$19^2/_3$	17	13	12	9	15
— Montreal (N.L.)	1	0	1.000	5.40	5	2	0	0	0	$11^2/_3$	8	9	7	4	8
1998— Ottawa (I.L.)	7	7	.500	3.41	19	19	0	0	0	$105^2/_3$	107	50	40	49	76
— Montreal (N.L.)	4	5	.444	4.70	14	13	0	0	0	67	60	38	35	26	32
1999— Montreal (N.L.)	7	11	.389	4.05	29	27	0	0	0	$146^2/_3$	140	84	66	52	85
2000— Jupiter (FSL)	1	1	.500	2.08	3	3	0	0	0	13	14	3	3	0	6
— Ottawa (I.L.)	0	3	.000	7.71	4	4	0	0	0	$16^1/_3$	23	14	14	9	8
— Montreal (N.L.)	4	9	.308	6.42	17	17	0	0	0	$88^1/_3$	112	69	63	46	52
— Harrisburg (East.)	0	0	...	4.15	1	0	0	0	0	$4^1/_3$	4	2	2	3	1
Major League totals (4 years)	16	25	.390	4.91	65	59	0	0	0	$313^2/_3$	320	200	171	128	177

TIMLIN, MIKE   P   CARDINALS

PERSONAL: Born March 10, 1966, in Midland, Texas. ... 6-4/210. ... Throws right, bats right. ... Full name: Michael August Timlin.
HIGH SCHOOL: Midland (Texas).
COLLEGE: Southwestern University (Texas).
TRANSACTIONS/CAREER NOTES: Selected by Toronto Blue Jays organization in fifth round of free-agent draft (June 2, 1987). ... On disabled list (April 4-May 2, 1989 and August 2-17, 1991). ... On Toronto disabled list (March 27-June 12, 1992); included rehabilitation assignments to Dunedin (April 11-15 and May 24-June 5) and Syracuse (June 5-12). ... On disabled list (May 25-June 9, 1994). ... On Toronto disabled list (June 22-August 18, 1995); included rehabilitation assignment to Syracuse (July 31-August 18). ... Traded by Blue Jays with P Paul Spoljaric to Seattle Mariners for OF Jose Cruz Jr. (July 31, 1997). ... Granted free agency (October 22, 1998). ... Signed by Baltimore Orioles (November 16, 1998). ... On Baltimore disabled list (April 2-17, 2000). ... Traded by Orioles with cash to St. Louis Cardinals for 1B Chris Richard and P Mark Nussbeck (July 29, 2000).
STATISTICAL NOTES: Led South Atlantic League with 19 hit batsmen in 1988.

Year League	W	L	Pct.	ERA	G	GS	CG	ShO	Sv.	IP	H	R	ER	BB	SO
1987— Medicine Hat (Pio.)	4	8	.333	5.14	13	12	2	0	0	$75^1/_3$	79	50	43	26	66
1988— Myrtle Beach (S.Atl.)	10	6	.625	2.86	35	22	0	0	0	151	119	68	48	77	106
1989— Dunedin (FSL)	5	8	.385	3.25	33	7	1	0	7	$88^2/_3$	90	44	32	36	64
1990— Dunedin (FSL)	7	2	.778	1.43	42	0	0	0	22	$50^1/_3$	36	11	8	16	46
— Knoxville (Sou.)	1	2	.333	1.73	17	0	0	0	8	26	20	6	5	7	21
1991— Toronto (A.L.)	11	6	.647	3.16	63	3	0	0	3	$108^1/_3$	94	43	38	50	85
1992— Dunedin (FSL)	0	0	...	0.90	6	1	0	0	1	10	9	2	1	2	7
— Syracuse (I.L.)	0	1	.000	8.74	7	1	0	0	3	$11^1/_3$	15	11	11	5	7
— Toronto (A.L.)	0	2	.000	4.12	26	0	0	0	1	$43^2/_3$	45	23	20	20	35
1993— Toronto (A.L.)	4	2	.667	4.69	54	0	0	0	1	$55^2/_3$	63	32	29	27	49
— Dunedin (FSL)	0	0	...	1.00	4	0	0	0	1	9	4	1	1	0	8
1994— Toronto (A.L.)	0	1	.000	5.18	34	0	0	0	2	40	41	25	23	20	38
1995— Toronto (A.L.)	4	3	.571	2.14	31	0	0	0	5	42	38	13	10	17	36
— Syracuse (I.L.)	1	1	.500	1.04	8	0	0	0	0	$17^1/_3$	13	6	2	4	13
1996— Toronto (A.L.)	1	6	.143	3.65	59	0	0	0	31	$56^2/_3$	47	25	23	18	52
1997— Toronto (A.L.)	3	2	.600	2.87	38	0	0	0	9	47	41	17	15	15	36
— Seattle (A.L.)■	3	2	.600	3.86	26	0	0	0	1	$25^2/_3$	28	13	11	5	9
1998— Seattle (A.L.)	3	3	.500	2.95	70	0	0	0	19	$79^1/_3$	78	26	26	16	60
1999— Baltimore (A.L.)■	3	9	.250	3.57	62	0	0	0	27	63	51	30	25	23	50
2000— Baltimore (A.L.)	2	3	.400	4.89	37	0	0	0	11	35	37	22	19	15	26
— St. Louis (N.L.)■	3	1	.750	3.34	25	0	0	0	1	$29^2/_3$	30	11	11	20	26
A.L. totals (10 years)	34	39	.466	3.61	500	3	0	0	110	$596^1/_3$	563	269	239	226	476
N.L. totals (1 year)	3	1	.750	3.34	25	0	0	0	1	$29^2/_3$	30	11	11	20	26
Major League totals (10 years)	37	40	.481	3.59	525	3	0	0	111	626	593	280	250	246	502

DIVISION SERIES RECORD

Year League	W	L	Pct.	ERA	G	GS	CG	ShO	Sv.	IP	H	R	ER	BB	SO
1997— Seattle (A.L.)	0	0	...	54.00	1	0	0	0	0	$^2/_3$	3	4	4	1	1
2000— St. Louis (N.L.)	0	0	...	10.80	2	0	0	0	0	$1^2/_3$	5	2	2	1	2
Division series totals (2 years)	0	0	...	23.14	3	0	0	0	0	$2^1/_3$	8	6	6	2	3

CHAMPIONSHIP SERIES RECORD

Year League	W	L	Pct.	ERA	G	GS	CG	ShO	Sv.	IP	H	R	ER	BB	SO
1991— Toronto (A.L.)	0	1	.000	3.18	4	0	0	0	0	$5^2/_3$	5	4	2	2	5
1992— Toronto (A.L.)	0	0	...	6.75	2	0	0	0	0	$1^1/_3$	4	1	1	0	1
1993— Toronto (A.L.)	0	0	...	3.86	1	0	0	0	0	$2^1/_3$	3	1	1	0	2
2000— St. Louis (N.L.)	0	1	.000	0.00	3	0	0	0	0	$3^1/_3$	1	3	0	2	0
Champ. series totals (4 years)	0	2	.000	2.84	10	0	0	0	0	$12^2/_3$	13	9	4	4	8

WORLD SERIES RECORD

NOTES: Member of World Series championship team (1992 and 1993).

Year League	W	L	Pct.	ERA	G	GS	CG	ShO	Sv.	IP	H	R	ER	BB	SO
1992— Toronto (A.L.)	0	0	...	0.00	2	0	0	0	1	$1^1/_3$	0	0	0	0	0
1993— Toronto (A.L.)	0	0	...	0.00	2	0	0	0	0	$2^1/_3$	2	0	0	0	4
World Series totals (2 years)	0	0	...	0.00	4	0	0	0	1	$3^2/_3$	2	0	0	0	4

TIMMONS, OZZIE — OF

PERSONAL: Born September 18, 1970, in Tampa. ... 6-2/220. ... Bats right, throws right. ... Full name: Osborne Llewellyn Timmons.
HIGH SCHOOL: Brandon (Fla.).
COLLEGE: Tampa.
TRANSACTIONS/CAREER NOTES: Selected by Chicago White Sox organization in 44th round of free-agent draft (June 1, 1988); did not sign. ... Selected by Chicago Cubs organization in fifth round of free-agent draft (June 3, 1991). ... On disabled list (August 9, 1993-remainder of season). ... Traded by Cubs with P Jayson Peterson to Cincinnati Reds for P Curt Lyons (March 31, 1997). ... Granted free agency (October 15, 1998). ... Signed by Seattle Mariners organization (March 12, 1999). ... Granted free agency (October 11, 1999). ... Signed by Tampa Bay Devil Rays organization (October 29, 1999). ... Released by Devil Rays (November 27, 2000).

								BATTING						FIELDING		
Year	Team (League)	Pos.	G	AB	R	H	2B	3B	HR	RBI	Avg.	BB	SO	SB	PO	A	E	Avg.
1991—	Geneva (NY-Penn)	OF	73	294	35	65	10	1	•12	47	.221	18	39	4	118	3	4	.968
1992—	Win.-Salem (Caro.)	OF	86	305	64	86	18	0	18	56	.282	58	46	11	90	7	1	.990
	—Charlotte (Sou.)	OF	36	122	13	26	7	0	3	13	.213	12	26	2	41	3	1	.978
1993—	Orlando (Sou.)	OF	107	359	65	102	22	2	18	58	.284	62	80	5	169	14	6	.968
1994—	Iowa (A.A.)	OF-DH	126	440	63	116	30	2	22	66	.264	36	93	0	228	14	6	.976
1995—	Chicago (N.L.)	OF	77	171	30	45	10	1	8	28	.263	13	32	3	63	1	2	.970
1996—	Chicago (N.L.)	OF	65	140	18	28	4	0	7	16	.200	15	30	1	65	1	1	.985
	—Iowa (A.A.)	OF-DH	59	213	32	53	7	0	17	40	.249	28	42	1	98	1	3	.971
1997—	Cincinnati (N.L.)■	OF	6	9	1	3	1	0	0	0	.333	0	1	0	0	0	1	.000
	—Indianapolis (A.A.)	OF-DH	125	407	46	103	14	1	14	55	.253	60	100	1	172	3	3	.983
1998—	Indianapolis (I.L.)	OF-DH-3B	117	327	46	86	21	3	12	36	.263	29	65	2	134	5	2	.986
1999—	Tacoma (PCL)■	OF-DH	82	297	56	81	22	0	21	66	.273	53	81	0	106	3	3	.973
	—Seattle (A.L.)	OF-DH-1B	26	44	4	5	2	0	1	3	.114	4	12	0	13	0	0	1.000
2000—	Durham (I.L.)■	OF-1B	137	506	*100	152	32	1	29	*104	.300	73	105	5	156	11	3	.982
	—Tampa Bay (A.L.)	OF-DH	12	41	9	14	3	0	4	13	.341	1	7	0	8	0	0	1.000
	American League totals (2 years)		38	85	13	19	5	0	5	16	.224	5	19	0	21	0	0	1.000
	National League totals (3 years)		148	320	49	76	15	1	15	44	.238	28	63	4	128	2	4	.970
	Major League totals (5 years)		186	405	62	95	20	1	20	60	.235	33	82	4	149	2	4	.974

TOCA, JORGE — 1B — METS

PERSONAL: Born January 7, 1975, in Villaclara, Cuba. ... 6-3/220. ... Bats right, throws right. ... Full name: Jorge Luis Toca.
TRANSACTIONS/CAREER NOTES: Signed as non-drafted free agent by New York Mets organization (September 7, 1998).
MISCELLANEOUS: Member of Cuban National Team (1994-95).

								BATTING						FIELDING		
Year	Team (League)	Pos.	G	AB	R	H	2B	3B	HR	RBI	Avg.	BB	SO	SB	PO	A	E	Avg.
1999—	Binghamton (East.)	OF-1B-DH-3B	75	279	60	86	15	1	20	67	.308	32	43	5	251	22	5	.982
	—Norfolk (I.L.)	1B-DH-OF	49	176	25	59	12	1	5	29	.335	6	23	0	351	42	5	.987
	—New York (N.L.)	1B	4	3	0	1	0	0	0	0	.333	0	2	0	2	0	0	1.000
2000—	Norfolk (I.L.)	1B-OF	120	453	58	123	25	3	11	70	.272	17	72	9	665	46	12	.983
	—Binghamton (East.)	1B	3	11	1	1	1	0	0	0	.091	0	0	0	13	3	0	1.000
	—New York (N.L.)	1B-OF	8	7	1	3	1	0	0	4	.429	0	1	0	9	0	0	1.000
	Major League totals (2 years)		12	10	1	4	1	0	0	4	.400	0	3	0	11	0	0	1.000

TOLAR, KEVIN — P — TIGERS

PERSONAL: Born January 28, 1971, in Panama City, Fla. ... 6-3/225. ... Throws left, bats right. ... Full name: Kevin Anthony Tolar.
HIGH SCHOOL: A. Crawford Mosley (Panama City, Fla.).
TRANSACTIONS/CAREER NOTES: Selected by Chicago White Sox organization in ninth round of free-agent draft (June 5, 1989). ... Released by White Sox (April 4, 1994). ... Signed by Pittsburgh Pirates organization (March 28, 1995). ... Granted free agency (October 15, 1996). ... Signed by Chicago Cubs organization (November 30, 1996). ... Released by Cubs (March 28, 1997). ... Signed by New York Mets organization (April 16, 1997). ... Granted free agency (December 27, 1997). ... Signed by Pirates organization (December 27, 1997). ... Traded by Pirates organization to Cincinnati Reds for future considerations (July 31, 1998). ... Granted free agency (October 15, 1999). ... Signed by Detroit Tigers organization (December 17, 1999). ... On Toledo disabled list (June 20-July 3, 2000).

Year	League	W	L	Pct.	ERA	G	GS	CG	ShO	Sv.	IP	H	R	ER	BB	SO
1989—	GC White Sox (GCL)	6	2	.750	1.65	13	12	1	0	0	60	29	16	11	*54	58
1990—	Utica (NY-Penn)	4	6	.400	3.29	15	15	1	0	0	90 1/3	80	44	33	61	69
1991—	South Bend (Midw.)	8	5	.615	2.83	30	19	0	0	1	114 2/3	87	54	36	85	87
1992—	Salinas (Calif.)	1	8	.111	6.07	14	8	3	0	0	53 1/3	55	43	36	46	24
	—South Bend (Midw.)	6	5	.545	2.88	18	10	0	0	0	81 1/3	59	34	26	41	81
1993—	Sarasota (FSL)	2	6	.250	5.35	23	11	0	0	1	77 1/3	75	55	46	51	60
1994—						Did not play.										
1995—	Lynchburg (Caro.)	2	0	1.000	2.79	18	0	0	0	0	19 1/3	13	7	6	6	19
	—Carolina (Sou.)	1	0	1.000	3.65	12	0	0	0	0	12 1/3	16	5	5	7	9
1996—	Canton/Akron (East.)	1	3	.250	2.62	50	0	0	0	1	44 2/3	42	19	13	26	39
1997—	Binghamton (East.)	1	1	.500	5.12	22	0	0	0	0	31 2/3	38	20	18	22	26
	—St. Lucie (Fla.)	0	0	...	2.03	9	0	0	0	0	13 1/3	9	3	3	6	8
1998—	Carolina (Sou.)	1	2	.333	2.22	42	0	0	0	1	48 2/3	35	12	12	33	48
	—Nashville (PCL)	0	0	...	6.00	1	0	0	0	0	3	2	2	2	4	1
	—Indianapolis (I.L.)	0	1	.000	10.43	19	0	0	0	0	14 2/3	21	18	17	17	19
1999—	Chattanooga (Sou.)	4	4	.500	4.97	47	1	0	0	1	54 1/3	61	32	30	45	60
	—Indianapolis (I.L.)	1	0	1.000	2.08	8	1	0	0	0	13	8	4	3	7	18
2000—	Jacksonville (Sou.)■	2	0	1.000	0.52	9	0	0	0	0	17 1/3	7	3	1	8	19
	—Toledo (I.L.)	4	2	.667	3.30	33	0	0	0	2	46 1/3	37	23	17	26	42
	—Detroit (A.L.)	0	0	...	3.00	5	0	0	0	0	3	1	1	1	1	3
	Major League totals (1 year)	0	0	...	3.00	5	0	0	0	0	3	1	1	1	1	3

TOLLBERG, BRIAN   P   PADRES

PERSONAL: Born September 16, 1972, in Tampa. ... 6-3/195. ... Throws right, bats right. ... Full name: Brian Patrick Tollberg.
HIGH SCHOOL: Manatee (Bradenton, Fla.).
COLLEGE: North Florida.
TRANSACTIONS/CAREER NOTES: Signed by Chillicothe, Frontier League (1994). ... Signed as non-drafted free agent by Milwaukee Brewers organization (January 31, 1995). ... Traded by Brewers to San Diego Padres for 3B Antonio Fernandez (March 13, 1997). ... On Las Vegas disabled list (May 6, 1999-remainder of season).

Year League	W	L	Pct.	ERA	G	GS	CG	ShO	Sv.	IP	H	R	ER	BB	SO
1994— Chillicothe (Fron.)...............	7	4	.636	2.85	13	13	4	0	0	94 2/3	90	34	30	27	69
1995— Beloit (Midw.)■................	13	4	.765	3.41	22	22	1	1	0	132	119	59	50	27	110
1996— El Paso (Texas).................	7	5	.583	4.90	26	26	0	0	0	154 1/3	183	90	84	23	109
1997— Mobile (Sou.)■	6	3	.667	3.72	31	13	1	0	0	123 1/3	123	60	51	24	108
1998— Mobile (Sou.)...................	3	2	.600	2.41	6	6	1	0	0	41	31	11	11	4	45
— Las Vegas (PCL)	6	6	.500	6.38	33	15	1	0	3	110	138	85	78	27	109
1999— Las Vegas (PCL)	1	2	.333	4.50	5	5	0	0	0	29 2/3	34	17	16	6	23
— Arizona Padres (Ariz.)	0	0	...	4.50	2	2	0	0	0	4	4	2	2	0	6
2000— Las Vegas (PCL)	6	0	1.000	2.83	13	13	0	0	0	76 1/3	72	28	24	11	60
— San Diego (N.L.)	4	5	.444	3.58	19	19	1	0	0	118	126	58	47	35	76
Major League totals (1 year)........	4	5	.444	3.58	19	19	1	0	0	118	126	58	47	35	76

TOMKO, BRETT   P   MARINERS

PERSONAL: Born April 7, 1973, in San Diego. ... 6-4/215. ... Throws right, bats right. ... Full name: Brett Daniel Tomko.
HIGH SCHOOL: El Dorado (Placentia, Calif.).
JUNIOR COLLEGE: Mt. San Antonio College (Calif.).
COLLEGE: Florida Southern.
TRANSACTIONS/CAREER NOTES: Selected by Cincinnati Reds organization in second round of free-agent draft (June 1, 1995). ... Traded by Reds with OF Mike Cameron, IF Antonio Perez and P Jake Meyer to Seattle Mariners for OF Ken Griffey Jr. (February 10, 2000). ... On disabled list (June 7-24, 2000).
RECORDS: Shares N.L. single-inning record for most consecutive home runs allowed—3 (April 28, 1999, first inning).
MISCELLANEOUS: Appeared in two games as pinch runner (1997). ... Appeared in one game as pinch runner and struck out in only appearance as pinch hitter (1998).

Year League	W	L	Pct.	ERA	G	GS	CG	ShO	Sv.	IP	H	R	ER	BB	SO
1995— Charleston, W.Va. (S.Atl.)...	4	2	.667	1.84	9	7	0	0	0	49	41	12	10	9	46
1996— Chattanooga (Sou.)	11	7	.611	3.88	27	27	0	0	0	157 2/3	131	73	68	54	164
1997— Indianapolis (A.A.).............	6	3	.667	2.95	10	10	0	0	0	61	53	21	20	9	60
— Cincinnati (N.L.)	11	7	.611	3.43	22	19	0	0	0	126	106	50	48	47	95
1998— Cincinnati (N.L.)	13	12	.520	4.44	34	34	1	0	0	210 2/3	198	111	104	64	162
1999— Cincinnati (N.L.)	5	7	.417	4.92	33	26	1	0	0	172	175	103	94	60	132
— Indianapolis (I.L.)	2	0	1.000	4.97	2	2	0	0	0	12 2/3	15	7	7	1	9
2000— Tacoma (PCL)■	1	0	1.000	2.84	2	2	0	0	0	12 2/3	13	4	4	5	8
— Seattle (A.L.)	7	5	.583	4.68	32	8	0	0	1	92 1/3	92	53	48	40	59
A.L. totals (1 year)	7	5	.583	4.68	32	8	0	0	1	92 1/3	92	53	48	40	59
N.L. totals (3 years)	29	26	.527	4.35	89	79	2	0	0	508 2/3	479	264	246	171	389
Major League totals (4 years).......	36	31	.537	4.40	121	87	2	0	1	601	571	317	294	211	448

DIVISION SERIES RECORD

Year League	W	L	Pct.	ERA	G	GS	CG	ShO	Sv.	IP	H	R	ER	BB	SO
2000— Seattle (A.L.)	0	0	...	0.00	1	0	0	0	0	2 2/3	1	0	0	1	0

CHAMPIONSHIP SERIES RECORD

Year League	W	L	Pct.	ERA	G	GS	CG	ShO	Sv.	IP	H	R	ER	BB	SO
2000— Seattle (A.L.)	0	0	...	7.20	2	0	0	0	0	5	3	4	4	4	4

TORREALBA, YORVIT   C   GIANTS

PERSONAL: Born July 19, 1978, in Caracas, Venezuela. ... 5-11/190. ... Bats right, throws right. ... Full name: Yorvit Adolfo Torrealba.
HIGH SCHOOL: Vincente Emilio Sojo (Venezuela).
COLLEGE: Alberto Sequin Vera (Venezuela).
TRANSACTIONS/CAREER NOTES: Signed as non-drafted free agent by San Francisco Giants organization (September 14, 1994).
STATISTICAL NOTES: Led California League catchers with 10 double plays in 1997.

Year Team (League)	Pos.	G	AB	R	H	2B	3B	HR	RBI	Avg.	BB	SO	SB	PO	A	E	Avg.
1995— Bellingham (N'West) ..	C	26	71	2	11	3	0	0	8	.155	2	14	0	152	26	5	.973
1996— San Jose (Calif.)	C	2	5	0	0	0	0	0	0	.000	1	1	0	16	1	0	1.000
— Burlington (Midw.)	C	1	4	0	0	0	0	0	0	.000	0	1	0	7	1	0	1.000
— Bellingham (N'West) ..	C	48	150	23	40	4	0	1	10	.267	9	27	4	290	33	2	.994
1997— Bakersfield (Calif.)......	C	119	446	52	122	15	3	4	40	.274	31	58	4	779	*119	6	.993
1998— Shreveport (Texas).....	C	59	196	18	46	7	0	0	13	.235	18	30	0	397	70	2	.996
— San Jose (Calif.)........	C	21	70	10	20	2	0	0	10	.286	1	6	2	171	16	2	.989
— Fresno (PCL).............	C	4	11	1	2	1	0	0	1	.182	1	4	0	22	0	0	1.000
1999— Shreveport (Texas)	C-DH	65	217	25	53	10	1	4	19	.244	9	34	0	299	43	2	.994
— Fresno (PCL).............	C	17	63	9	16	2	0	2	10	.254	4	11	0	155	12	2	.988
— San Jose (Calif.)........	C	19	73	10	23	3	0	2	14	.315	6	15	0	176	16	5	.975
2000— Shreveport (Texas)	C	108	398	50	114	21	1	4	32	.286	34	55	2	719	86	8	.990

PERSONAL: Born October 31, 1970, in Oxnard, Calif. ... 6-4/205. ... Throws right, bats right. ... Full name: Stephen Christopher Trachsel. ... Name pronounced TRACK-sul.
HIGH SCHOOL: Troy (Fullerton, Calif.).
JUNIOR COLLEGE: Fullerton (Calif.) College.
COLLEGE: Long Beach State.
TRANSACTIONS/CAREER NOTES: Selected by Chicago Cubs organization in eighth round of free-agent draft (June 3, 1991). ... On Chicago disabled list (July 20-August 4, 1994). ... Granted free agency (October 28, 1999). ... Signed by Tampa Bay Devil Rays (January 28, 2000). ... Traded by Devil Rays with P Mark Guthrie to Toronto Blue Jays for 2B Brent Abernathy and a player to be named later (July 31, 2000). ... Granted free agency (October 31, 2000). ... Signed by New York Mets (December 11, 2000).
HONORS: Named N.L. Rookie Pitcher of the Year by THE SPORTING NEWS (1994).
STATISTICAL NOTES: Pitched 4-2 no-hit victory for Winston-Salem against Peninsula (July 12, 1991, second game). ... Pitched 6-0 one-hit, complete-game victory against Houston (May 13, 1996). ... Led N.L. with 32 home runs allowed in 1997. ... Led A.L. pitchers with a 1.000 fielding percentage in 2000.

Year League	W	L	Pct.	ERA	G	GS	CG	ShO	Sv.	IP	H	R	ER	BB	SO
1991— Geneva (NY-Penn)	1	0	1.000	1.26	2	2	0	0	0	14 $\frac{1}{3}$	10	2	2	6	7
— Winston-Salem (Caro.)	4	4	.500	3.67	12	12	1	0	0	73 $\frac{2}{3}$	70	38	30	19	69
1992— Charlotte (Sou.)	•13	8	.619	3.06	29	•29	5	2	0	*191	180	76	65	35	135
1993— Iowa (A.A.)	13	6	.684	3.96	27	26	1	1	0	170 $\frac{2}{3}$	170	78	75	45	135
— Chicago (N.L.)	0	2	.000	4.58	3	3	0	0	0	19 $\frac{2}{3}$	16	10	10	3	14
1994— Chicago (N.L.)	9	7	.563	3.21	22	22	1	0	0	146	133	57	52	54	108
— Iowa (A.A.)	0	2	.000	10.00	2	2	0	0	0	9	11	10	10	7	8
1995— Chicago (N.L.)	7	13	.350	5.15	30	29	2	0	0	160 $\frac{2}{3}$	174	104	92	76	117
1996— Orlando (Sou.)	0	1	.000	2.77	2	2	0	0	0	13	11	6	4	0	12
— Chicago (N.L.)	13	9	.591	3.03	31	31	3	2	0	205	181	82	69	62	132
1997— Chicago (N.L.)	8	12	.400	4.51	34	34	0	0	0	201 $\frac{1}{3}$	225	110	101	69	160
1998— Chicago (N.L.)	15	8	.652	4.46	33	33	1	0	0	208	204	107	103	84	149
1999— Chicago (N.L.)	8	*18	.308	5.56	34	34	4	0	0	205 $\frac{2}{3}$	226	133	127	64	149
2000— Tampa Bay (A.L.)■	6	10	.375	4.58	23	23	3	1	0	137 $\frac{2}{3}$	160	76	70	49	78
— Toronto (A.L.)■	2	5	.286	5.29	11	11	0	0	0	63	72	40	37	25	32
A.L. totals (1 year)	8	15	.348	4.80	34	34	3	1	0	200 $\frac{2}{3}$	232	116	107	74	110
N.L. totals (7 years)	60	69	.465	4.35	187	186	11	2	0	1146 $\frac{1}{3}$	1159	603	554	412	829
Major League totals (8 years)	68	84	.447	4.42	221	220	14	3	0	1347	1391	719	661	486	939

ALL-STAR GAME RECORD

Year League	W	L	Pct.	ERA	GS	CG	ShO	Sv.	IP	H	R	ER	BB	SO
1996— National	0	0	...	0.00	0	0	0	0	1	0	0	0	0	3

PERSONAL: Born December 11, 1973, in Bowling Green, Ohio. ... 6-3/220. ... Bats left, throws left. ... Full name: Andrew Michael Tracy.
HIGH SCHOOL: Bowling Green (Ohio).
COLLEGE: Bowling Green State.
TRANSACTIONS/CAREER NOTES: Selected by Montreal Expos organization in 16th round of free-agent draft (June 4, 1996). ... On disabled list (July 31-August 7, 1999).
HONORS: Named Eastern League Most Valuable Player (1999).
STATISTICAL NOTES: Led Eastern League with 276 total bases in 1999. ... Career major league grand slams: 1.

Year Team (League)	Pos.	G	AB	R	H	2B	3B	HR	RBI	Avg.	BB	SO	SB	PO	A	E	Avg.
1996— Vermont (NY-Penn)	1B-3B	57	175	26	47	11	4	4	24	.269	32	37	1	426	33	6	.987
1997— Cape Fear (S.Atl.)	1B	59	210	31	63	9	2	8	43	.300	21	47	6	483	37	8	.985
1998— Jupiter (FSL)	1B-3B	71	251	37	67	16	1	11	53	.267	39	69	6	638	51	5	.993
— Harrisburg (East.)	1B-OF	62	211	33	48	12	3	10	33	.227	24	62	1	481	36	6	.989
1999— Harrisburg (East.)	3B-1B-OF	134	493	96	135	26	2	37	*128	.274	70	139	6	227	200	25	.945
2000— Ottawa (I.L.)	1B-3B	55	195	28	60	18	0	10	36	.308	34	63	2	367	56	6	.986
— Montreal (N.L.)	3B-1B	83	192	29	50	8	1	11	32	.260	22	61	1	187	46	6	.975
Major League totals (1 year)		83	192	29	50	8	1	11	32	.260	22	61	1	187	46	6	.975

PERSONAL: Born November 6, 1971, in Knoxville, Tenn. ... 6-2/220. ... Bats right, throws right. ... Full name: Thomas Bubba Trammell.
HIGH SCHOOL: Knoxville (Tenn.) Central.
JUNIOR COLLEGE: Cleveland (Tenn.) State Community College.
COLLEGE: Tennessee.
TRANSACTIONS/CAREER NOTES: Selected by Detroit Tigers organization in 11th round of free-agent draft (June 2, 1994). ... Selected by Tampa Bay Devil Rays in first round (22nd pick overall) of expansion draft (November 18, 1997). ... On Durham disabled list (May 17-25, 1999). ... Traded by Devil Rays with P Rick White to New York Mets for OF Jason Tyner and P Paul Wilson (July 28, 2000). ... Traded by Mets to San Diego Padres for P Donne Wall (December 11, 2000).

Year Team (League)	Pos.	G	AB	R	H	2B	3B	HR	RBI	Avg.	BB	SO	SB	PO	A	E	Avg.
1994— Jamestown (NY-P)	OF	65	235	37	70	18	6	5	41	.298	23	32	9	77	3	5	.941
1995— Lakeland (FSL)	OF	122	454	61	129	32	6	16	72	.284	48	80	13	176	7	5	.973
1996— Jacksonville (Sou.)	OF	83	311	63	102	23	2	27	75	.328	32	61	3	100	6	5	.955
— Toledo (I.L.)	OF	51	180	32	53	14	1	6	24	.294	22	44	5	72	5	1	.987
1997— Detroit (A.L.)	OF-DH	44	123	14	28	5	0	4	13	.228	15	35	3	52	1	0	1.000
— Toledo (I.L.)	OF-DH	90	319	56	80	15	1	28	75	.251	38	91	2	103	3	3	.972
1998— Tampa Bay (A.L.)■	OF-DH	59	199	28	57	18	1	12	35	.286	16	45	0	50	3	0	1.000
— Durham (I.L.)	OF	57	217	46	63	12	0	16	48	.290	38	42	6	110	5	2	.983

Year	Team (League)	Pos.	G	AB	R	H	2B	3B	HR	RBI	Avg.	BB	SO	SB	PO	A	E	Avg.
							BATTING								FIELDING			
1999— Durham (I.L.)	OF-DH-3B	47	186	25	50	12	0	7	31	.269	15	36	0	65	8	3	.961
— Tampa Bay (A.L.).......	OF-DH	82	283	49	82	19	0	14	39	.290	43	37	0	142	2	1	.993
2000— Tampa Bay (A.L.).......	OF-DH	66	189	19	52	11	2	7	33	.275	21	30	3	66	2	0	1.000
— New York (N.L.)■	OF	36	56	9	13	2	0	3	12	.232	8	19	1	25	1	1	.963
American League totals (4 years)		251	794	110	219	53	3	37	120	.276	95	147	6	310	8	1	.997
National League totals (1 year)		36	56	9	13	2	0	3	12	.232	8	19	1	25	1	1	.963
Major League totals (4 years)		287	850	119	232	55	3	40	132	.273	103	166	7	335	9	2	.994

DIVISION SERIES RECORD

Year	Team (League)	Pos.	G	AB	R	H	2B	3B	HR	RBI	Avg.	BB	SO	SB	PO	A	E	Avg.
							BATTING								FIELDING			
2000— New York (N.L.)..........									Did not play.								

CHAMPIONSHIP SERIES RECORD

Year	Team (League)	Pos.	G	AB	R	H	2B	3B	HR	RBI	Avg.	BB	SO	SB	PO	A	E	Avg.
							BATTING								FIELDING			
2000— New York (N.L.)..........	PH	3	3	0	0	0	0	0	0	.000	0	2	0	...	...	...	...

WORLD SERIES RECORD

Year	Team (League)	Pos.	G	AB	R	H	2B	3B	HR	RBI	Avg.	BB	SO	SB	PO	A	E	Avg.
							BATTING								FIELDING			
2000— New York (N.L.)..........	PH-OF	4	5	1	2	0	0	0	3	.400	1	1	0	3	0	1	.750

TROMBLEY, MIKE   P   ORIOLES

PERSONAL: Born April 14, 1967, in Springfield, Mass. ... 6-2/204. ... Throws right, bats right. ... Full name: Michael Scott Trombley.
HIGH SCHOOL: Minnechaug Regional (Wilbraham, Mass.).
COLLEGE: Duke.
TRANSACTIONS/CAREER NOTES: Selected by Minnesota Twins organization in 14th round of free-agent draft (June 5, 1989). ... Granted free agency (October 29, 1999). ... Signed by Baltimore Orioles (November 18, 1999).
STATISTICAL NOTES: Pitched 3-0 no-hit victory against Knoxville (August 8, 1991). ... Led Pacific Coast League with 18 home runs allowed in 1992.

Year	League	W	L	Pct.	ERA	G	GS	CG	ShO	Sv.	IP	H	R	ER	BB	SO
1989— Kenosha (Midw.)		5	1	.833	3.12	12	3	0	0	2	49	45	23	17	13	41
— Visalia (Calif.)		2	2	.500	2.14	6	6	2	1	0	42	31	12	10	11	36
1990— Visalia (Calif.)		14	6	.700	3.43	27	25	3	1	0	176	163	79	67	50	164
1991— Orlando (Sou.)		12	7	.632	2.54	27	27	7	2	0	*191	153	65	54	57	*175
1992— Portland (PCL)		10	8	.556	3.65	25	25	2	0	0	165	149	70	67	58	*138
— Minnesota (A.L.)		3	2	.600	3.30	10	7	0	0	0	46 1/3	43	20	17	17	38
1993— Minnesota (A.L.)		6	6	.500	4.88	44	10	0	0	2	114 1/3	131	72	62	41	85
1994— Minnesota (A.L.)		2	0	1.000	6.33	24	0	0	0	0	48 1/3	56	36	34	18	32
— Salt Lake (PCL)		4	4	.500	5.04	11	10	0	0	0	60 2/3	75	37	34	20	63
1995— Salt Lake (PCL)		5	3	.625	3.62	12	12	0	0	0	69 2/3	71	32	28	26	59
— Minnesota (A.L.)		4	8	.333	5.62	20	18	0	0	0	97 2/3	107	68	61	42	68
1996— Salt Lake (PCL)		2	2	.500	2.45	24	0	0	0	10	36 2/3	24	12	10	10	38
— Minnesota (A.L.)		5	1	.833	3.01	43	0	0	0	6	68 2/3	61	24	23	25	57
1997— Minnesota (A.L.)		2	3	.400	4.37	67	0	0	0	1	82 1/3	77	43	40	31	74
1998— Minnesota (A.L.)		6	5	.545	3.63	77	1	0	0	1	96 2/3	90	41	39	41	89
1999— Minnesota (A.L.)		2	8	.200	4.33	75	0	0	0	24	87 1/3	93	42	42	28	82
2000— Baltimore (A.L.)■..............		4	5	.444	4.13	75	0	0	0	4	72	67	34	33	38	72
Major League totals (9 years)		34	38	.472	4.43	435	36	0	0	38	713 2/3	725	380	351	281	597

TRUBY, CHRIS   3B   ASTROS

PERSONAL: Born December 9, 1973, in Palm Springs, Calif. ... 6-2/190. ... Bats right, throws right. ... Full name: Christopher John Truby.
HIGH SCHOOL: Damien (Hawaii).
TRANSACTIONS/CAREER NOTES: Signed as non-drafted free agent by Houston Astros organization (August 25, 1992). ... On disabled list (April 26-May 11, 1999).
STATISTICAL NOTES: Led Gulf Coast League third basemen with 21 errors in 1993. ... Led New York-Pennsylvania League with 114 total bases and eight sacrifice flies in 1994. ... Led Midwest League third basemen with 279 assists and 26 double plays in 1995. ... Led Texas League with 12 sacrifice flies in 1999. ... Led Texas League third basemen with 93 putouts, 35 double plays and a .950 fielding percentage in 1999. ... Career major league grand slams: 1.

Year	Team (League)	Pos.	G	AB	R	H	2B	3B	HR	RBI	Avg.	BB	SO	SB	PO	A	E	Avg.
							BATTING								FIELDING			
1993— GC Astros (GCL)	3B-SS	57	215	30	49	10	2	1	24	.228	22	30	16	42	158	†26	.885
— Osceola (FSL)............	3B	3	13	0	0	0	0	0	0	.000	0	2	0	3	9	2	.857
1994— Quad City (Midw.)......	3B-1B	36	111	12	24	4	1	2	19	.216	3	29	1	54	29	6	.933
— Auburn (NY-Penn)......	3B	73	282	*56	*91	17	6	7	*61	.323	23	48	20	48	153	•27	.882
1995— Quad City (Midw.)......	3B-OF	118	400	68	93	23	4	9	64	.233	41	66	27	73	†279	38	.903
1996— Quad City (Midw.)......	1B-3B	109	362	45	91	15	3	8	37	.251	28	74	6	545	128	17	.975
1997— Quad City (Midw.)......	3B	68	268	34	75	14	1	7	46	.280	22	32	13	39	149	15	.926
— Kissimmee (FSL).......3B-1B-SS-2B		57	199	23	49	11	0	2	29	.246	8	40	8	52	122	16	.916
1998— Kissimmee (FSL).........	3B	52	212	36	66	16	1	14	48	.311	19	30	6	45	130	9	.951
— Jackson (Texas)	3B-1B	80	308	46	89	20	5	16	63	.289	20	50	8	94	161	15	.944
— New Orleans (PCL).....	3B	5	17	6	7	1	1	1	1	.412	1	3	1	4	7	1	.917
1999— Jackson (Texas)	3B-SS	124	465	78	131	21	3	28	87	.282	36	88	20	†95	275	20	†.949
2000— Houston (N.L.)	3B	78	258	28	67	15	4	11	59	.260	10	56	2	51	125	14	.926
— New Orleans (PCL).....	3B	64	268	31	76	11	3	2	30	.284	17	32	6	46	151	12	.943
Major League totals (1 year)		78	258	28	67	15	4	11	59	.260	10	56	2	51	125	14	.926

TUCKER, MICHAEL — OF — REDS

PERSONAL: Born June 25, 1971, in South Boston, Va. ... 6-2/185. ... Bats left, throws right. ... Full name: Michael Anthony Tucker.
HIGH SCHOOL: Bluestone (Skipwith, Va.).
COLLEGE: Longwood (Va.).
TRANSACTIONS/CAREER NOTES: Selected by Kansas City Royals organization in first round (10th pick overall) of free-agent draft (June 1, 1992). ... On Kansas City disabled list (June 4-21 and August 28, 1996-remainder of season); included rehabilitation assignment to Wichita (June 15-21). ... Traded by Royals with IF Keith Lockhart to Atlanta Braves for OF Jermaine Dye and P Jamie Walker (March 27, 1997). ... Traded by Braves with P Denny Neagle and P Rob Bell to Cincinnati Reds for 2B Bret Boone and P Mike Remlinger (November 10, 1998).

Year Team (League)	Pos.	G	AB	R	H	2B	3B	HR	RBI	Avg.	BB	SO	SB	PO	A	E	Avg.
1993—Wilmington (Caro.)	2B	61	239	42	73	14	2	6	44	.305	34	49	12	120	157	10	.965
—Memphis (Sou.)	2B	72	244	38	68	7	4	9	35	.279	42	51	12	153	176	13	.962
1994—Omaha (A.A.)	OF	132	485	75	134	16	7	21	77	.276	69	111	11	196	11	•7	.967
1995—Kansas City (A.L.)	OF-DH	62	177	23	46	10	0	4	17	.260	18	51	2	67	3	1	.986
—Omaha (A.A.)	OF	71	275	37	84	18	4	4	28	.305	24	39	11	133	11	2	.986
1996—Kansas City (A.L.)	OF-1B-DH	108	339	55	88	18	4	12	53	.260	40	69	10	235	8	2	.992
—Wichita (Texas)	OF-1B	6	20	4	9	1	3	0	7	.450	5	4	0	17	1	0	1.000
1997—Atlanta (N.L.)■	OF	138	499	80	141	25	7	14	56	.283	44	116	12	237	6	5	.980
1998—Atlanta (N.L.)	OF	130	414	54	101	27	3	13	46	.244	49	112	8	194	5	1	.995
1999—Cincinnati (N.L.)■	OF	133	296	55	75	8	5	11	44	.253	37	81	11	182	8	2	.990
2000—Cincinnati (N.L.)	OF-2B	148	270	55	72	13	4	15	36	.267	44	64	13	153	5	5	.969
American League totals (2 years)		170	516	78	134	28	4	16	70	.260	58	120	12	302	11	3	.991
National League totals (4 years)		549	1479	244	389	73	19	53	182	.263	174	373	44	766	24	13	.984
Major League totals (6 years)		719	1995	322	523	101	23	69	252	.262	232	493	56	1068	35	16	.986

DIVISION SERIES RECORD

Year Team (League)	Pos.	G	AB	R	H	2B	3B	HR	RBI	Avg.	BB	SO	SB	PO	A	E	Avg.
1997—Atlanta (N.L.)	OF	2	6	0	1	0	0	0	1	.167	0	1	0	3	0	0	1.000
1998—Atlanta (N.L.)	OF	3	8	1	2	0	0	1	2	.250	3	0	1	6	0	0	1.000
Division series totals (2 years)		5	14	1	3	0	0	1	3	.214	3	1	1	9	0	0	1.000

CHAMPIONSHIP SERIES RECORD

Year Team (League)	Pos.	G	AB	R	H	2B	3B	HR	RBI	Avg.	BB	SO	SB	PO	A	E	Avg.
1997—Atlanta (N.L.)	OF-PH	5	10	1	1	0	0	1	1	.100	3	4	0	5	1	0	1.000
1998—Atlanta (N.L.)	OF-PH	6	13	1	5	1	0	1	5	.385	2	5	0	7	0	0	1.000
Championship series totals (2 years)		11	23	2	6	1	0	2	6	.261	5	9	0	12	1	0	1.000

TUCKER, T.J. — P — EXPOS

PERSONAL: Born August 20, 1978, in Clearwater, Fla. ... 6-3/245. ... Throws right, bats right. ... Full name: Thomas John Tucker.
HIGH SCHOOL: River Ridge (New Port Richey, Fla.).
TRANSACTIONS/CAREER NOTES: Selected by Montreal Expos organization in supplemental round ("sandwich pick" between first and second round, 47th pick overall) of free-agent draft (June 3, 1997); pick received as compensation for Chicago Cubs signing P Mel Rojas. ... On Harrisburg disabled list (April 6-23, 2000). ... On Montreal disabled list (June 10, 2000-remainder of season).

Year League	W	L	Pct.	ERA	G	GS	CG	ShO	Sv.	IP	H	R	ER	BB	SO
1997—Gulf Coast Expos (GCL)	1	0	1.000	1.93	3	2	0	0	0	4 2/3	5	1	1	1	11
1998—Gulf Coast Expos (GCL)	1	0	1.000	0.75	7	7	0	0	0	36	23	5	3	5	40
—Vermont (NY-Penn)	3	1	.750	2.18	6	6	0	0	0	33	24	9	8	15	34
—Jupiter (FSL)	1	1	.500	1.00	2	1	0	0	0	9	5	1	1	0	10
1999—Jupiter (FSL)	5	1	.833	1.23	7	7	0	0	0	44	24	7	6	16	35
—Harrisburg (East.)	8	5	.615	4.10	19	19	1	1	0	116 1/3	110	55	53	38	85
2000—Harrisburg (East.)	2	1	.667	3.60	8	8	0	0	0	45	33	19	18	17	24
—Montreal (N.L.)	0	1	.000	11.57	2	2	0	0	0	7	11	9	9	3	2
Major League totals (1 year)	0	1	.000	11.57	2	2	0	0	0	7	11	9	9	3	2

TURNBOW, DERRICK — P — ANGELS

PERSONAL: Born January 25, 1978, in Union City, Tenn. ... 6-3/180. ... Throws right, bats right. ... Full name: Thomas Derrick Turnbow.
HIGH SCHOOL: Franklin (Tenn.).
TRANSACTIONS/CAREER NOTES: Selected by Philadelphia Phillies organization in fifth round of free-agent draft (June 3, 1997). ... Selected by Anaheim Angels from Phillies organization in Rule 5 major league draft (December 13, 1999).

Year League	W	L	Pct.	ERA	G	GS	CG	ShO	Sv.	IP	H	R	ER	BB	SO
1997—Martinsville (Appl.)	1	3	.250	7.40	7	7	0	0	0	24 1/3	34	29	20	16	7
1998—Martinsville (Appl.)	2	6	.250	5.01	13	13	1	0	0	70	66	44	39	26	45
1999—Piedmont (S.Atl.)	12	8	.600	3.35	26	26	•4	1	0	161	130	67	60	53	149
2000—Anaheim (A.L.)■	0	0	...	4.74	24	1	0	0	0	38	36	21	20	36	25
Major League totals (1 year)	0	0	...	4.74	24	1	0	0	0	38	36	21	20	36	25

TURNER, CHRIS — C — PHILLIES

PERSONAL: Born March 23, 1969, in Bowling Green, Ky. ... 6-3/200. ... Bats right, throws right. ... Full name: Christopher Wan Turner.
HIGH SCHOOL: Warren Central (Bowling Green, Ky.).
COLLEGE: Western Kentucky.

TRANSACTIONS/CAREER NOTES: Selected by California Angels organization in seventh round of free-agent draft (June 3, 1991). ... Angels franchise renamed Anaheim Angels for 1997 season. ... On Anaheim disabled list (March 31-July 4, 1997); included rehabilitation assignment to Lake Elsinore (July 2-4). ... Granted free agency (October 10, 1997). ... Signed by Minnesota Twins organization (December 5, 1997). ... On Salt Lake suspended list (April 7-17, 1998). ... Released by Twins (April 20, 1998). ... Signed by Kansas City Royals organization (April 20, 1998). ... Granted free agency (October 15, 1998). ... Signed by Cleveland Indians organization (January 5, 1999). ... Granted free agency (October 4, 1999). ... Signed by New York Yankees organization (December 17, 1999). ... Released by Yankees (November 21, 2000). ... Signed by Philadelphia Phillies organization (January 4, 2001).
STATISTICAL NOTES: Led Northwest League catchers with .997 fielding percentage in 1991. ... Led Pacific Coast League with 17 passed balls in 1993.

										BATTING					FIELDING		
Year	Team (League)	Pos.	G	AB	R	H	2B	3B	HR	RBI	Avg.	BB	SO	SB	PO	A	E	Avg.
1991—	Boise (N'West)	C-OF	52	163	26	37	5	0	2	29	.227	32	32	10	360	39	2	†.995
1992—	Quad City (Midw.)	C-1B	109	330	66	83	18	1	9	53	.252	85	65	8	727	98	9	.989
1993—	Vancouver (PCL)	C-1B-DH	90	283	50	78	12	1	4	57	.276	49	44	6	524	56	6	.990
	— California (A.L.)	C	25	75	9	21	5	0	1	13	.280	9	16	1	116	14	1	.992
1994—	California (A.L.)	C	58	149	23	36	7	1	1	12	.242	10	29	3	268	29	1	.997
	— Vancouver (PCL)	DH-C	3	10	1	2	1	0	0	1	.200	0	2	0	10	1	1	.917
1995—	Vancouver (PCL) C-3-DH-1-O		80	282	44	75	20	2	3	48	.266	34	54	3	345	49	6	.985
	— California (A.L.)	C	5	10	0	1	0	0	0	1	.100	0	3	0	17	2	0	1.000
1996—	Vancouver (PCL) C-DH-O-3-1		113	390	51	100	19	1	2	47	.256	61	85	1	396	57	8	.983
	— California (A.L.)	C-OF	4	3	1	1	0	0	0	1	.333	1	0	0	3	2	0	1.000
1997—	Lake Elsinore (Calif.) ..	C	3	12	0	1	0	1	0	1	.083	0	3	0	25	1	1	.963
	— Vancouver (PCL) 1B-C-DH-OF		37	135	26	50	10	0	4	22	.370	14	22	0	291	15	5	.984
	— Anaheim (A.L.) C-1B-DH-OF		13	23	4	6	1	1	1	2	.261	5	8	0	34	2	0	1.000
1998—	Kansas City (A.L.)■....	C	4	9	0	0	0	0	0	0	.000	0	4	0	16	0	0	1.000
	— Omaha (PCL) C-DH-OF-3B		66	196	31	60	14	1	1	16	.306	38	36	6	328	19	3	.991
1999—	Buffalo (I.L.)■............	C-1B	69	231	36	63	9	0	9	33	.273	34	45	2	424	43	6	.987
	— Cleveland (A.L.)	C	12	21	3	4	0	0	0	0	.190	1	8	1	50	3	2	.964
2000—	Columbus (I.L.)■........	OF-C-1B	14	44	6	12	3	0	2	3	.273	3	11	0	58	3	1	.984
	— New York (A.L.)	C-1B	37	89	9	21	3	0	1	7	.236	10	21	0	172	5	0	1.000
Major League totals (8 years)			158	379	49	90	16	2	4	36	.237	36	89	5	676	57	4	.995

TYNER, JASON   OF   DEVIL RAYS

PERSONAL: Born April 23, 1977, in Beaumont, Texas. ... 6-1/170. ... Bats left, throws left. ... Full name: Jason Renyt Tyner.
HIGH SCHOOL: Westbrook (Beaumont, Texas).
COLLEGE: Texas A&M.
TRANSACTIONS/CAREER NOTES: Selected by New York Mets organization in first round (21st pick overall) of free-agent draft (June 2, 1998). ... Traded by Mets with P Paul Wilson to Tampa Bay Devil Rays for P Rick White and OF Bubba Trammell (July 28, 2000).

										BATTING					FIELDING		
Year	Team (League)	Pos.	G	AB	R	H	2B	3B	HR	RBI	Avg.	BB	SO	SB	PO	A	E	Avg.
1998—	St. Lucie (FSL)	OF	50	201	30	61	2	3	0	16	.303	17	20	15	80	0	2	.976
1999—	Binghamton (East.)	OF	129	518	91	162	19	5	0	33	.313	62	46	49	255	11	2	.993
	— Norfolk (I.L.)	OF	3	8	0	0	0	0	0	0	.000	0	5	0	4	0	0	1.000
2000—	Norfolk (I.L.)■	OF	84	327	54	105	5	2	0	28	.321	30	32	33	188	5	1	.995
	— New York (N.L.)	OF	13	41	3	8	2	0	0	5	.195	1	4	1	22	1	2	.920
	— Tampa Bay (A.L.)■....	OF-DH	37	83	6	20	2	0	0	8	.241	4	12	6	51	4	0	1.000
American League totals (1 year)			37	83	6	20	2	0	0	8	.241	4	12	6	51	4	0	1.000
National League totals (1 year)			13	41	3	8	2	0	0	5	.195	1	4	1	22	1	2	.920
Major League totals (1 year)			50	124	9	28	4	0	0	13	.226	5	16	7	73	5	2	.975

UNROE, TIM   1B/3B

PERSONAL: Born October 7, 1970, in Round Lake, Ill. ... 6-3/220. ... Bats right, throws right. ... Full name: Timothy Brian Unroe.
HIGH SCHOOL: Round Lake (Ill.).
JUNIOR COLLEGE: College of Lake County (Ill.).
COLLEGE: Lewis University (Ill.).
TRANSACTIONS/CAREER NOTES: Selected by Milwaukee Brewers organization in 28th round of free-agent draft (June 1, 1992). ... Released by Brewers (September 2, 1997). ... Signed by Chicago Cubs organization (January 7, 1998). ... On West Tenn disabled list (June 26-July 15, 1998). ... Released by Cubs (July 15, 1998). ... Signed by Anaheim Angels organization (October 27, 1998). ... Released by Angels (July 22, 1999). ... Signed by Kansas City Royals organization (September 2, 1999). ... Granted free agency (October 15, 1999). ... Signed by Atlanta Braves organization (January 10, 2000). ... Granted free agency (October 17, 2000).
HONORS: Named Texas League Player of the Year (1994).
STATISTICAL NOTES: Led Pioneer League third basemen with 62 putouts, 155 assists, 16 double plays and 236 total chances in 1992. ... Led California League third basemen with .936 fielding percentage, 78 putouts, 244 assists and 344 total chances in 1993. ... Led Texas League with 242 total bases and nine sacrifice flies in 1994. ... Career major league grand slams: 1.

										BATTING					FIELDING		
Year	Team (League)	Pos.	G	AB	R	H	2B	3B	HR	RBI	Avg.	BB	SO	SB	PO	A	E	Avg.
1992—	Helena (Pio.)	3B-1B	74	266	61	74	13	2	*16	58	.278	47	91	3	†70	†155	20	.918
1993—	Stockton (Calif.)	3B-OF	108	382	57	96	21	6	12	63	.251	36	96	9	†81	†244	23	†.934
1994—	El Paso (Texas)..........	3B-1B-OF	126	474	*97	*147	36	7	15	*103	.310	42	107	14	383	203	19	.969
1995—	New Orleans (A.A.).....	3-1-DH-O	102	371	43	97	21	2	6	45	.261	18	94	4	373	160	12	.978
	— Milwaukee (A.L.)	1B	2	4	0	1	0	0	0	0	.250	0	0	0	11	0	0	1.000
1996—	New Orleans (A.A.).....3-1-S-DH-O		109	404	72	109	26	4	25	67	.270	36	121	8	175	231	25	.942
	— Milwaukee (A.L.)	1-3-DH-O	14	16	5	3	0	0	0	0	.188	4	5	0	41	10	1	.981
1997—	Tucson (PCL) 3-0-2-DH-S		63	234	45	68	17	1	9	46	.291	9	62	3	65	92	7	.957
	— Milwaukee (A.L.) 1B-3B-OF-2B		32	16	3	4	1	0	2	5	.250	2	9	2	59	9	2	.971
1998—	Iowa (PCL)■ 3B-1B-OF-2B		39	104	9	18	5	0	1	9	.173	10	30	1	37	53	1	.989
	— West Tenn (Sou.)	3B-2B	16	54	6	13	6	0	0	9	.241	8	20	0	17	32	7	.875

Year	Team (League)	Pos.	G	AB	R	H	2B	3B	HR	RBI	Avg.	BB	SO	SB	PO	A	E	Avg.
1999—	Anaheim (A.L.)■	OF-DH-3B-2B	27	54	5	13	2	0	1	6	.241	4	16	0	14	3	0	1.000
—Edmonton (PCL)		OF-3B	10	44	10	17	5	1	5	18	.386	5	9	0	17	4	1	.955
—Omaha (PCL)■		DH-OF	5	22	4	5	0	0	1	2	.227	0	5	0	3	0	0	1.000
2000—	Richmond (I.L.)■	OF-1B-2B-3B	121	418	59	116	28	2	24	87	.278	27	114	2	426	61	7	.986
—Atlanta (N.L.)		1B-OF	4	5	0	0	0	0	0	0	.000	1	2	0	12	2	0	1.000
American League totals (4 years)			75	90	13	21	3	0	3	11	.233	10	30	2	125	22	3	.980
National League totals (1 year)			4	5	0	0	0	0	0	0	.000	1	2	0	12	2	0	1.000
Major League totals (5 years)			79	95	13	21	3	0	3	11	.221	11	32	2	137	24	3	.982

URBINA, UGUETH — P — EXPOS

PERSONAL: Born February 15, 1974, in Caracas, Venezuela. ... 6-0/205. ... Throws right, bats right. ... Full name: Ugueth Urtain Urbina. ... Name pronounced OOO-get.

HIGH SCHOOL: Liceo Peres Bonalde de Miranda (Miranda, Venezuela).

TRANSACTIONS/CAREER NOTES: Signed as non-drafted free agent by Montreal Expos organization (July 2, 1990). ... On disabled list (April 8-17, 1994). ... On temporarily inactive list (May 9-June 6, 1994). ... On Ottawa disabled list (August 10-September 14, 1995). ... On disabled list (May 9, 2000-remainder of season).

HONORS: Named N.L. Fireman of the Year by THE SPORTING NEWS (1999).

Year	League	W	L	Pct.	ERA	G	GS	CG	ShO	Sv.	IP	H	R	ER	BB	SO
1991—	Gulf Coast Expos (GCL)	3	3	.500	2.29	10	10	3	•1	0	63	58	24	16	10	51
1992—	Albany (S.Atl.)	7	•13	.350	3.22	24	24	5	2	0	142 1/3	111	68	51	54	100
1993—	Burlington (Midw.)	2	3	.400	4.50	10	8	0	0	0	46	41	31	23	22	30
—Harrisburg (East.)		4	5	.444	3.99	11	11	3	1	0	70	66	32	31	32	45
1994—	Harrisburg (East.)	9	3	.750	3.28	21	21	0	0	0	120 2/3	95	49	44	43	86
1995—	West Palm Beach (FSL)	1	0	1.000	0.00	2	2	0	0	0	9	4	0	0	1	11
—Ottawa (I.L.)		6	2	.750	3.04	13	11	2	1	0	68	46	26	23	26	55
—Montreal (N.L.)		2	2	.500	6.17	7	4	0	0	0	23 1/3	26	17	16	14	15
1996—	West Palm Beach (FSL)	1	1	.500	1.29	3	3	0	0	0	14	13	3	2	3	21
—Ottawa (I.L.)		2	0	1.000	2.66	5	5	0	0	0	23 2/3	17	9	7	6	28
—Montreal (N.L.)		10	5	.667	3.71	33	17	0	0	0	114	102	54	47	44	108
1997—	Montreal (N.L.)	5	8	.385	3.78	63	0	0	0	27	64 1/3	52	29	27	29	84
1998—	Montreal (N.L.)	6	3	.667	1.30	64	0	0	0	34	69 1/3	37	11	10	33	94
1999—	Montreal (N.L.)	6	6	.500	3.69	71	0	0	0	*41	75 2/3	59	35	31	36	100
2000—	Montreal (N.L.)	0	1	.000	4.05	13	0	0	0	8	13 1/3	11	6	6	5	22
Major League totals (6 years)		29	25	.537	3.42	251	21	0	0	110	360	287	152	137	161	423

ALL-STAR GAME RECORD

Year	League	W	L	Pct.	ERA	GS	CG	ShO	Sv.	IP	H	R	ER	BB	SO
1998—	National	0	1	.000	27.00	0	0	0	0	1	3	3	3	1	2

VALDES, ISMAEL — P — ANGELS

PERSONAL: Born August 21, 1973, in Victoria, Mexico. ... 6-4/225. ... Throws right, bats right.

HIGH SCHOOL: Mexico (Ciudad Victoria).

TRANSACTIONS/CAREER NOTES: Signed as non-drafted free agent by Los Angeles Dodgers (June 14, 1991). ... Loaned by Dodgers organization to Mexico City Tigers of Mexican League (April 21-June 26, 1992; and March 17-August 19, 1993). ... On disabled list (July 6-28, 1997). ... On Los Angeles disabled list (July 26-September 1, 1998); included rehabilitation assignments to Vero Beach (August 22) and San Bernardino (August 27). ... Traded by Dodgers with 2B Eric Young to Chicago Cubs for P Terry Adams, P Chad Ricketts and a player to be named later (December 12, 1999); Dodgers acquired P Brian Stephenson to complete deal (December 16, 1999). ... On Chicago disabled list (March 20-May 4, 2000); included rehabilitation assignment to Daytona (April 29-May 1). ... Traded by Cubs to Dodgers for P Jamie Arnold, OF Jorge Piedra and cash (July 26, 2000). ... On suspended list (September 12-18, 2000). ... Granted free agency (October 30, 2000). ... Signed by Anaheim Angels (January 4, 2001).

STATISTICAL NOTES: Led N.L. with five balks in 1996. ... Pitched 2-0 one-hit, complete-game victory against Pittsburgh (June 27, 1998).

MISCELLANEOUS: Had sacrifice hit in only appearance as pinch hitter (2000).

Year	League	W	L	Pct.	ERA	G	GS	CG	ShO	Sv.	IP	H	R	ER	BB	SO
1991—	Gulf Coast Dodgers (GCL)	2	2	.500	2.32	10	10	0	0	0	50 1/3	44	15	13	13	44
1992—	M.C. Tigers (Mex.)■	0	0	...	19.64	5	0	0	0	0	3 2/3	15	9	8	1	2
—La Vega (DSL)■		3	0	1.000	1.42	6	0	0	0	0	38	27	9	6	17	34
1993—	M.C. Tigers (Mex.)■	16	7	.696	3.94	26	25	11	1	0	173 2/3	192	87	76	55	113
—San Antonio (Texas)■		1	0	1.000	1.38	3	2	0	0	0	13	12	2	2	0	11
1994—	San Antonio (Texas)	2	3	.400	3.38	8	8	0	0	0	53 1/3	54	22	20	9	55
—Albuquerque (PCL)		4	1	.800	3.40	8	8	0	0	0	45	44	21	17	13	39
—Los Angeles (N.L.)		3	1	.750	3.18	21	1	0	0	0	28 1/3	21	10	10	10	28
1995—	Los Angeles (N.L.)	13	11	.542	3.05	33	27	6	2	1	197 2/3	168	76	67	51	150
1996—	Los Angeles (N.L.)	15	7	.682	3.32	33	33	0	0	0	225	219	94	83	54	173
1997—	Los Angeles (N.L.)	10	11	.476	2.65	30	30	0	0	0	196 2/3	171	68	58	47	140
1998—	Los Angeles (N.L.)	11	10	.524	3.98	27	27	2	2	0	174	171	82	77	66	122
—Vero Beach (FSL)		0	0	...	0.00	1	1	0	0	0	3	2	0	0	1	3
—San Bernardino (Calif.)		1	0	1.000	2.84	1	1	0	0	0	6 1/3	7	2	2	1	4
1999—	Los Angeles (N.L.)	9	14	.391	3.98	32	32	2	1	0	203 1/3	213	97	90	58	143
2000—	Daytona (FSL)■	1	0	1.000	1.80	1	1	0	0	0	5	3	2	1	3	5
—Chicago (N.L.)		2	4	.333	5.37	12	12	0	0	0	67	71	40	40	27	45
—Los Angeles (N.L.)■		0	3	.000	6.07	9	8	0	0	0	40	53	29	27	13	29
Major League totals (7 years)		63	61	.508	3.59	197	170	10	5	1	1132	1087	496	452	326	830

DIVISION SERIES RECORD

Year	League	W	L	Pct.	ERA	G	GS	CG	ShO	Sv.	IP	H	R	ER	BB	SO
1995—	Los Angeles (N.L.)	0	0	...	0.00	1	1	0	0	0	7	3	2	0	1	6
1996—	Los Angeles (N.L.)	0	1	.000	4.26	1	1	0	0	0	6 1/3	5	3	3	0	5
Division series totals (2 years)		0	1	.000	2.03	2	2	0	0	0	13 1/3	8	5	3	1	11

VALDES, MARC   P

PERSONAL: Born December 20, 1971, in Dayton, Ohio. ... 6-0/185. ... Throws right, bats right. ... Full name: Marc Christopher Valdes.
HIGH SCHOOL: Jesuit (Tampa).
COLLEGE: Florida.
TRANSACTIONS/CAREER NOTES: Selected by Cincinnati Reds organization in 20th round of free-agent draft (June 4, 1990); did not sign. ... Selected by Florida Marlins organization in first round (27th pick overall) of free-agent draft (June 3, 1993). ... Claimed on waivers by Montreal Expos (December 12, 1996). ... On disabled list (May 27-June 11 and June 23, 1998-remainder of season). ... Granted free agency (December 21, 1998). ... Signed by Tampa Bay Devil Rays organization (January 20, 1999). ... On Durham disabled list (April 8-June 18, 1999). ... Granted free agency (October 15, 1999). ... Re-signed by Devil Rays organization (January 14, 2000). ... Traded by Devil Rays to Houston Astros for 3B Russ Johnson (May 27, 2000). ... Granted free agency (December 21, 2000).

Year League	W	L	Pct.	ERA	G	GS	CG	ShO	Sv.	IP	H	R	ER	BB	SO
1993—Elmira (NY-Penn)	0	2	.000	5.59	3	3	0	0	0	9 2/3	8	9	6	7	15
1994—Kane County (Midw.)	7	4	.636	2.95	11	11	2	0	0	76 1/3	62	30	25	21	68
—Portland (East.)	8	4	.667	2.55	15	15	0	0	0	99	77	31	28	39	70
1995—Charlotte (I.L.)	9	•13	.409	4.86	27	27	3	2	0	170 1/3	189	98	•92	59	104
—Florida (N.L.)	0	0	...	14.14	3	3	0	0	0	7	17	13	11	9	2
1996—Charlotte (I.L.)	2	4	.333	5.12	8	8	1	0	0	51	66	32	29	15	24
—Portland (East.)	6	2	.750	2.66	10	10	1	0	0	64 1/3	60	25	19	12	49
—Florida (N.L.)	1	3	.250	4.81	11	8	0	0	0	48 2/3	63	32	26	23	13
1997—Montreal (N.L.)■	4	4	.500	3.13	48	7	0	0	2	95	84	36	33	39	54
1998—Montreal (N.L.)	1	3	.250	7.43	20	4	0	0	0	36 1/3	41	34	30	21	28
1999—Durham (I.L.)■	1	2	.333	5.18	9	9	0	0	0	40	39	25	23	12	23
—Orlando (Sou.)	0	1	.000	5.87	2	2	0	0	0	7 2/3	7	5	5	2	5
2000—Durham (I.L.)	5	2	.714	4.15	9	9	0	0	0	47 2/3	52	25	22	17	25
—Houston (N.L.)■	5	5	.500	5.08	53	0	0	0	2	56 2/3	69	41	32	25	35
Major League totals (5 years)	11	15	.423	4.88	135	22	0	0	4	243 2/3	274	156	132	117	132

VALDES, PEDRO   OF/1B

PERSONAL: Born June 29, 1973, in Fajardo, Peurto Rico. ... 6-1/190. ... Bats left, throws left. ... Full name: Pedro Jose Valdes Manzo.
HIGH SCHOOL: Carlos Escobar Lopez (Loiza, Puerto Rico).
TRANSACTIONS/CAREER NOTES: Selected by Chicago Cubs organization in 12th round of free-agent draft (June 4, 1990). ... On Iowa disabled list (August 4-11, 1996). ... On Iowa disabled list (April 19-May 4, 1998). ... On Chicago disabled list (July 6-September 1, 1998); included rehabilitation assignment to Iowa (August 14-September 1). ... Released by Cubs (December 8, 1998). ... Signed by Boston Red Sox organization (January 12, 1999). ... Released by Red Sox (April 5, 1999). ... Signed by Texas Rangers (April 18, 1999). ... Granted free agency (October 15, 1999). ... Re-signed by Rangers organization (January 18, 2000). ... Contract sold by Rangers to Fukuoka of Japan Pacific League (November 1, 2000).
STATISTICAL NOTES: Led Southern League outfielders with six double plays in 1995.

Year Team (League)	Pos.	G	AB	R	H	2B	3B	HR	RBI	Avg.	BB	SO	SB	PO	A	E	Avg.
1991—Huntington (Appl.)	OF	49	152	17	44	11	1	0	16	.289	17	30	5	66	4	6	.921
1992—Peoria (Midw.)	OF	33	112	8	26	7	0	0	20	.232	7	32	0	32	1	1	.971
—Geneva (NY-Penn)	OF-1B	66	254	27	69	10	0	5	24	.272	3	33	4	210	18	9	.962
1993—Peoria (Midw.)	OF-1B	65	234	33	74	11	1	7	36	.316	10	40	2	51	2	1	.981
—Daytona (FSL)	OF-1B	60	230	27	66	16	1	8	49	.287	9	30	3	176	7	3	.984
1994—Orlando (Sou.)	OF	116	365	39	103	14	4	1	37	.282	20	45	2	177	12	7	.964
1995—Orlando (Sou.)	OF-DH	114	426	57	128	28	3	7	68	.300	37	77	3	172	11	4	.979
1996—Iowa (A.A.)	OF-DH	103	397	61	117	23	0	15	60	.295	31	57	2	183	7	5	.974
—Chicago (N.L.)	OF	9	8	2	1	1	0	0	1	.125	1	5	0	1	0	0	1.000
1997—Iowa (A.A.)	OF-DH	125	464	65	132	30	1	14	60	.284	48	67	9	256	13	3	.989
1998—Iowa (PCL)	OF-DH	65	229	49	72	12	0	17	40	.314	27	38	2	106	3	4	.965
—Chicago (N.L.)	OF	14	23	1	5	1	1	0	2	.217	1	3	0	10	0	0	1.000
1999—Tulsa (Texas)■	DH-1B-OF	11	34	3	12	4	0	1	4	.353	8	6	0	36	0	1	.973
—Oklahoma (PCL)	DH-OF-1B	110	394	72	129	27	1	21	72	.327	52	60	1	158	8	1	.994
2000—Oklahoma (PCL)	OF	92	352	64	117	30	2	16	78	.332	45	41	2	153	4	2	.987
—Texas (A.L.)	OF-DH	30	54	4	15	5	0	1	5	.278	6	7	0	17	0	0	1.000
American League totals (1 year)		30	54	4	15	5	0	1	5	.278	6	7	0	17	0	0	1.000
National League totals (2 years)		23	31	3	6	2	1	0	3	.194	2	8	0	11	0	0	1.000
Major League totals (3 years)		53	85	7	21	7	1	1	8	.247	8	15	0	28	0	0	1.000

V

VALDEZ, MARIO   1B/OF   ATHLETICS

PERSONAL: Born November 19, 1974, in Obregon, Mexico ... 6-1/210. ... Bats left, throws right. ... Full name: Mario A. Valdez.
HIGH SCHOOL: Miami Senior.
JUNIOR COLLEGE: Miami-Dade (North) Community College.
TRANSACTIONS/CAREER NOTES: Selected by Chicago White Sox organization in 48th round of free-agent draft (June 3, 1993). ... On Charlotte disabled list (June 18-26 and July 25-August 1, 1999). ... Claimed on waivers by Minnesota Twins (September 29, 1999). ... Traded by Twins to Oakland Athletics for C Danny Ardoin (July 31, 2000). ... On Sacramento disabled list (July 31-August 7, 2000). ... On Oakland disabled list (September 8, 2000-remainder of season).
STATISTICAL NOTES: Led Pacific Coast League first basemen with 14 errors in 1998.

Year Team (League)	Pos.	G	AB	R	H	2B	3B	HR	RBI	Avg.	BB	SO	SB	PO	A	E	Avg.
1994—GC White Sox (GCL)	1B-OF	53	157	20	37	11	2	2	25	.236	30	28	0	351	28	8	.979
1995—Hickory (S.Atl.)	1B	130	441	65	120	30	5	11	56	.272	67	107	9	1040	67	12	.989
1996—South Bend (Midw.)	1B	61	202	46	76	19	0	10	43	.376	36	42	2	438	41	8	.984
—Birmingham (Sou.)	1B-OF	50	168	22	46	10	2	3	28	.274	32	34	0	284	26	2	.994

Year	Team (League)	Pos.	G	AB	R	H	2B	3B	HR	RBI	Avg.	BB	SO	SB	PO	A	E	Avg.
1997— Nashville (A.A.)	1B-DH	81	282	44	79	20	1	15	61	.280	43	77	1	616	44	6	.991
— Chicago (A.L.)	1B-DH-3B	54	115	11	28	7	0	1	13	.243	17	39	1	256	12	0	1.000
1998— Calgary (PCL)	1B-DH-OF	123	448	86	148	32	0	20	81	.330	60	102	1	1003	75	†15	.986
1999— Charlotte (I.L.)	1B-OF-DH	121	402	78	110	17	2	26	76	.274	76	91	1	762	54	7	.991
2000— Salt Lake (PCL)■	1B-OF-3B	88	317	76	116	24	1	18	85	.366	57	46	1	353	34	5	.987
— Sacramento (PCL)■....	1B	17	61	11	14	3	0	2	11	.230	9	13	0	122	6	0	1.000
— Visalia (Calif.)	1B	1	2	0	1	0	0	0	0	.500	1	1	0	5	1	0	1.000
— Oakland (A.L.)	1B	5	12	0	0	0	0	0	0	.000	0	3	0	26	2	0	1.000
Major League totals (2 years)		59	127	11	28	7	0	1	13	.220	17	42	1	282	14	0	1.000

VALENT, ERIC — OF — PHILLIES

PERSONAL: Born April 4, 1977, in La Mirada, Calif. ... 6-0/190. ... Bats left, throws left. ... Full name: Eric Christian Valent.
HIGH SCHOOL: Canyon (Anaheim, Calif.).
COLLEGE: UCLA.
TRANSACTIONS/CAREER NOTES: Selected by Detroit Tigers organization in 26th round of free-agent draft (June 1, 1995); did not sign. ... Selected by Philadelphia Phillies organization in supplemental round ("sandwich pick" between first and second round, 42nd pick overall) of free-agent draft (June 2, 1998); pick received for failure to sign 1997 first-round pick J.D. Drew.

Year	Team (League)	Pos.	G	AB	R	H	2B	3B	HR	RBI	Avg.	BB	SO	SB	PO	A	E	Avg.
1998— Piedmont (S.Atl.)........	OF	22	89	24	38	12	0	8	28	.427	14	19	0	38	2	2	.952
— Clearwater (FSL)	OF	34	125	24	33	8	1	5	25	.264	16	29	1	57	6	0	1.000
1999— Clearwater (FSL)	OF	134	520	91	150	31	9	20	*106	.288	58	110	5	265	17	9	.969
2000— Reading (East.)..........	OF	128	469	81	121	22	5	22	90	.258	70	89	2	233	16	4	.984

VALENTIN, JAVIER — C — TWINS

PERSONAL: Born September 19, 1975, in Manati, Puerto Rico. ... 5-10/192. ... Bats both, throws right. ... Full name: Jose Javier Valentin. ... Brother of Jose Valentin, shortstop, Chicago White Sox. ... Name pronounced VAL-un-TEEN.
HIGH SCHOOL: Fernando Callejo (Manati, Puerto Rico).
TRANSACTIONS/CAREER NOTES: Selected by Minnesota Twins organization in third round of free-agent draft (June 3, 1993). ... On disabled list (May 25-July 5 and September 4-20, 2000).
STATISTICAL NOTES: Led Appalachian League catchers with 48 assists and 348 total chances in 1993. ... Led Midwest League catchers with 730 putouts, 108 assists, 861 total chances, 23 errors and 11 double plays in 1995.

Year	Team (League)	Pos.	G	AB	R	H	2B	3B	HR	RBI	Avg.	BB	SO	SB	PO	A	E	Avg.
1993— GC Twins (GCL)..........	C-DH-3B	32	103	18	27	6	1	1	19	.262	14	19	0	120	23	5	.966
— Elizabethton (Appl.)...	C	9	24	3	5	1	0	0	3	.208	4	2	0	81	3	2	.977
1994— Elizabethton (Appl.)...	C-3B	54	210	23	44	5	0	9	27	.210	15	44	0	288	†50	12	.966
1995— Fort Wayne (Midw.)...	C-3B	112	383	59	124	26	5	19	65	.324	47	75	0	†736	†122	†23	.974
1996— Fort Myers (FSL)........	C-DH-3B	87	338	34	89	26	1	7	54	.263	32	65	1	360	71	4	.991
— New Britain (East.)	C-3B-DH	48	165	22	39	8	0	3	14	.236	16	35	0	188	36	5	.978
1997— New Britain (East.)	C-DH-3B	102	370	41	90	17	0	8	50	.243	30	61	2	516	65	6	.990
— Minnesota (A.L.)	C	4	7	1	2	0	0	0	0	.286	0	3	0	11	2	0	1.000
1998— Minnesota (A.L.)	C-DH	55	162	11	32	7	1	3	18	.198	11	30	0	281	17	5	.983
1999— Minnesota (A.L.)	C	78	218	22	54	12	1	5	28	.248	22	39	0	387	27	1	.998
2000— Salt Lake (PCL)	C	39	140	25	50	16	2	7	35	.357	9	27	1	155	11	1	.994
Major League totals (3 years)		137	387	34	88	19	2	8	46	.227	33	72	0	679	46	6	.992

VALENTIN, JOHN — 3B — RED SOX

PERSONAL: Born February 18, 1967, in Mineola, N.Y. ... 6-0/185. ... Bats right, throws right. ... Full name: John William Valentin.
HIGH SCHOOL: St. Anthony (Jersey City, N.J.).
COLLEGE: Seton Hall.
TRANSACTIONS/CAREER NOTES: Selected by Boston Red Sox organization in fifth round of free-agent draft (June 1, 1988). ... On Boston disabled list (April 1-20, 1993); included rehabilitation assignment to Pawtucket (April 16-20). ... On Boston disabled list (May 4-June 6, 1994); included rehabilitation assignment to Pawtucket (May 31-June 6). ... On disabled list (August 3-18, 1996; June 26-July 11 and August 31-September 23, 1999; April 6-May 19 and May 31, 2000-remainder of season).
HONORS: Named shortstop on THE SPORTING NEWS A.L. Silver Slugger team (1995).
STATISTICAL NOTES: Led New York-Pennsylvania League shortstops with .949 fielding percentage in 1988. ... Hit three home runs in one game (June 2, 1995). ... Led A.L. shortstops with 659 total chances in 1995. ... Hit for the cycle (June 6, 1996). ... Led A.L. third basemen with 121 putouts in 1998. ... Career major league grand slams: 4.
MISCELLANEOUS: Turned unassisted triple play while playing shortstop (July 8, 1994, sixth inning); 10th player ever to accomplish feat.

Year	Team (League)	Pos.	G	AB	R	H	2B	3B	HR	RBI	Avg.	BB	SO	SB	PO	A	E	Avg.
1988— Elmira (NY-Penn)	SS-3B	60	207	18	45	5	1	2	16	.217	36	35	5	96	175	14	†.951
1989— Winter Haven (FSL)....	SS-3B	55	215	27	58	13	1	3	18	.270	13	29	4	99	177	12	.958
— Lynchburg (Caro.)	SS	75	264	47	65	7	2	8	34	.246	41	40	5	105	220	16	.953
1990— New Britain (East.)	SS	94	312	20	68	18	1	2	31	.218	25	46	1	139	266	21	.951
1991— New Britain (East.)	SS	23	81	8	16	3	0	0	5	.198	9	14	1	50	65	3	.951
— Pawtucket (I.L.)..........	SS	100	329	52	87	22	4	9	49	.264	60	42	0	184	300	25	.951
1992— Pawtucket (I.L.)..........	SS	97	331	47	86	18	1	9	29	.260	48	50	1	148	*358	20	.962
— Boston (A.L.)..............	SS	58	185	21	51	13	0	5	25	.276	20	17	1	79	182	10	.963
1993— Pawtucket (I.L.)..........	SS	2	9	3	3	0	0	1	1	.333	0	1	0	8	9	0	1.000
— Boston (A.L.)..............	SS	144	468	50	130	40	3	11	66	.278	49	77	3	238	432	20	.971

Year—Team (League)	Pos.	G	AB	R	H	2B	3B	HR	RBI	Avg.	BB	SO	SB	PO	A	E	Avg.
						BATTING									FIELDING		
1994— Boston (A.L.)..............	SS-DH	84	301	53	95	26	2	9	49	.316	42	38	3	134	242	8	.979
— Pawtucket (I.L.)..........	SS	5	18	2	6	0	0	1	2	.333	3	4	0	7	16	3	.885
1995— Boston (A.L.)..............	SS	135	520	108	155	37	2	27	102	.298	81	67	20	227	*414	•18	.973
1996— Boston (A.L.)..............	SS-3B-DH	131	527	84	156	29	3	13	59	.296	63	59	9	202	357	17	.970
1997— Boston (A.L.)..............	2B-3B	143	575	95	176	*47	5	18	77	.306	58	66	7	239	380	22	.966
1998— Boston (A.L.)..............	3B-2B	153	588	113	145	44	1	23	73	.247	77	82	4	†121	292	15	.965
1999— Boston (A.L.)..............	3B-DH	113	449	58	114	27	1	12	70	.254	40	68	0	84	208	14	.954
2000— Boston (A.L.)..............	3B	10	35	6	9	1	0	2	2	.257	2	5	0	6	9	0	1.000
Major League totals (9 years)		971	3648	588	1031	264	17	120	523	.283	432	479	47	1330	2516	124	.969

DIVISION SERIES RECORD

RECORDS: Shares single-game records for most home runs—2; and most runs batted in—7 (October 10, 1999).

Year—Team (League)	Pos.	G	AB	R	H	2B	3B	HR	RBI	Avg.	BB	SO	SB	PO	A	E	Avg.
						BATTING									FIELDING		
1995— Boston (A.L.)..............	SS	3	12	1	3	1	0	1	2	.250	3	1	0	5	5	1	.909
1998— Boston (A.L.)..............	3B	4	15	5	7	1	0	0	0	.467	3	1	0	5	10	0	1.000
1999— Boston (A.L.)..............	3B	5	22	6	7	2	0	3	12	.318	0	4	0	5	11	2	.889
Division series totals (3 years)		12	49	12	17	4	0	4	14	.347	6	6	0	15	26	3	.932

CHAMPIONSHIP SERIES RECORD

RECORDS: Shares single-game record for most at-bats (nine-inning game)—6 (October 16, 1999).

Year—Team (League)	Pos.	G	AB	R	H	2B	3B	HR	RBI	Avg.	BB	SO	SB	PO	A	E	Avg.
						BATTING									FIELDING		
1999— Boston (A.L.)..............	3B	5	23	3	8	2	0	1	5	.348	2	4	0	4	7	0	1.000

VALENTIN, JOSE — SS — WHITE SOX

PERSONAL: Born October 12, 1969, in Manati, Puerto Rico. ... 5-10/173. ... Bats left, throws right. ... Full name: Jose Antonio Valentin. ... Brother of Javier Valentin, catcher, Minnesota Twins.
HIGH SCHOOL: Fernando Callejo (Manati, Puerto Rico).
TRANSACTIONS/CAREER NOTES: Signed as non-drafted free agent by San Diego Padres organization (October 12, 1986). ... On disabled list (April 16-May 1 and May 18-July 11, 1990). ... Traded by Padres with P Ricky Bones and OF Matt Mieske to Milwaukee Brewers for 3B Gary Sheffield and P Geoff Kellogg (March 27, 1992). ... On Milwaukee disabled list (April 14-May 5, 1997); included rehabilitation assignment to Beloit (May 3-5). ... On Milwaukee disabled list (April 13-June 16, 1999); included rehabilitation assignment to Louisville (June 9-16). ... Traded by Brewers with P Cal Eldred to Chicago White Sox for P Jaime Navarro and P John Snyder (January 12, 2000). ... Granted free agency (October 30, 2000). ... Re-signed by White Sox (November 22, 2000).
STATISTICAL NOTES: Led Texas League shortstops with 658 total chances in 1991. ... Led American Association shortstops with 639 total chances and 70 double plays in 1992. ... Led American Association shortstops with 211 putouts and 80 double plays in 1993. ... Led A.L. shortstops with 20 errors in 1994. ... Hit three home runs in one game (April 3, 1998). ... Hit for the cycle (April 27, 2000). ... Switch-hit home runs twice (September 30, 2000). ... Led A.L. shortstops with 36 errors in 2000. ... Career major league grand slams: 5.

Year—Team (League)	Pos.	G	AB	R	H	2B	3B	HR	RBI	Avg.	BB	SO	SB	PO	A	E	Avg.
						BATTING									FIELDING		
1987— Spokane (N'West)	SS	70	244	52	61	8	2	2	24	.250	35	38	8	101	175	26	.914
1988— Char., S.C. (SAL)	SS	133	444	56	103	20	1	6	44	.232	45	83	11	204	412	60	.911
1989— Riverside (Calif.).........	SS	114	381	40	74	10	5	10	41	.194	37	93	8	*227	333	*46	.924
—Wichita (Texas)	SS-3B	18	49	8	12	1	0	2	5	.245	5	12	1	26	45	8	.899
1990— Wichita (Texas)	SS	11	36	4	10	2	0	0	2	.278	5	7	2	14	33	2	.959
1991— Wichita (Texas)	SS	129	447	73	112	22	5	17	68	.251	55	115	8	176	*442	40	.939
1992— Denver (A.A.)■	SS	*139	492	78	118	19	11	3	45	.240	53	99	9	*187	*414	*38	.941
—Milwaukee (A.L.)	SS-2B	4	3	1	0	0	0	0	1	1.000	0	0	0	1	1	1	.667
1993— New Orleans (A.A.)......	SS-1B	122	389	56	96	22	5	9	53	.247	47	87	9	†212	351	29	.951
—Milwaukee (A.L.)	SS	19	53	10	13	1	2	1	7	.245	7	16	1	20	51	6	.922
1994— Milwaukee (A.L.) SS-2B-DH-3B	97	285	47	68	19	0	11	46	.239	38	75	12	151	336	†20	.961
1995— Milwaukee (A.L.)	SS-DH-3B	112	338	62	74	23	3	11	49	.219	37	83	16	164	335	15	.971
1996— Milwaukee (A.L.)	SS	154	552	90	143	33	7	24	95	.259	66	145	17	243	460	*37	.950
1997— Milwaukee (A.L.)	SS-DH	136	494	58	125	23	1	17	58	.253	39	109	19	208	383	20	.967
—Beloit (Midw.)............	SS	2	6	3	3	1	0	0	1	.500	2	1	0	1	8	0	1.000
1998— Milwaukee (N.L.)	SS-DH	151	428	65	96	24	0	16	49	.224	63	105	10	173	370	21	.963
1999— Milwaukee (N.L.)	SS	89	256	45	58	9	5	10	38	.227	48	52	3	113	214	22	.937
—Louisville (I.L.)	SS	6	20	6	5	0	0	3	3	.250	4	3	0	7	17	0	1.000
2000— Chicago (A.L.)■.........	SS-OF	144	568	107	155	37	6	25	92	.273	59	106	19	233	456	†36	.950
American League totals (7 years)		666	2293	375	578	136	19	89	348	.252	246	534	84	1020	2022	155	.958
National League totals (2 years)		240	684	110	154	33	5	26	87	.225	111	157	13	286	584	43	.953
Major League totals (9 years)		906	2977	485	732	169	24	115	435	.246	357	691	97	1306	2606	178	.956

DIVISION SERIES RECORD

Year—Team (League)	Pos.	G	AB	R	H	2B	3B	HR	RBI	Avg.	BB	SO	SB	PO	A	E	Avg.
						BATTING									FIELDING		
2000— Chicago (A.L.)	SS	3	10	2	3	2	0	0	1	.300	2	2	3	10	17	1	.964

VALERA, YOHANNY — C — DEVIL RAYS

PERSONAL: Born August 17, 1976, in Santo Domingo, Dominican Republic. ... 6-1/205. ... Bats right, throws right.
TRANSACTIONS/CAREER NOTES: Signed as non-drafted free agent by New York Mets organization (May 28, 1993). ... Granted free agency (October 15, 1999). ... Signed by Montreal Expos organization (November 17, 1999). ... Granted free agency (October 18, 2000). ... Signed by Tampa Bay Devils Rays organization (November 15, 2000).
STATISTICAL NOTES: Tied for Appalachian League lead in double plays by catcher with four in 1995. ... Led South Atlantic League catchers with 989 total chances in 1996.

V

Year Team (League)	Pos.	G	AB	R	H	2B	3B	HR	RBI	Avg.	BB	SO	SB	PO	A	E	Avg.
1993— Dom. Mets (DSL)	C	35	89	15	22	3	0	4	18	.247	12	17	2	144	27	6	.966
1994— Dom. Mets (DSL)	C	39	124	16	31	4	0	3	16	.250	11	17	1	209	29	5	.979
1995— Kingsport (Appl.)	C	56	204	30	60	13	0	3	36	.294	11	33	2	409	58	5	.989
1996— Capital City (S.Atl.)	C	108	372	38	19	18	0	6	38	.051	17	78	2	*857	*123	9	*.991
1997— Capital City (S.Atl.)	C	94	293	32	56	14	0	8	33	.191	21	101	2	651	107	10	.987
1998— St. Lucie (FSL)	C	91	298	37	61	21	1	14	42	.205	21	92	1	506	54	4	.993
1999— Binghamton (East.)	C-1B	57	204	33	59	14	3	9	39	.289	17	57	2	367	47	14	.967
— Norfolk (I.L.)	C	23	65	3	10	2	0	1	6	.154	4	16	0	138	14	4	.974
2000— Harrisburg (East.)■	C-1B	92	281	28	66	8	3	3	34	.235	24	56	1	443	59	7	.986
— Ottawa (I.L.)	C	21	68	6	10	1	0	2	10	.147	4	19	0	113	11	4	.969
— Montreal (N.L.)	C	7	10	1	0	0	0	0	1	.000	1	5	0	24	2	0	1.000
Major League totals (1 year)		7	10	1	0	0	0	0	1	.000	1	5	0	24	2	0	1.000

VAN POPPEL, TODD   P   CUBS

PERSONAL: Born December 9, 1971, in Hinsdale, Ill. ... 6-5/210. ... Throws right, bats right. ... Full name: Todd Matthew Van Poppel.
HIGH SCHOOL: St. Martin (Arlington, Texas).
TRANSACTIONS/CAREER NOTES: Selected by Oakland Athletics organization in first round (14th pick overall) of free-agent draft (June 4, 1990); pick received as part of compensation for Milwaukee Brewers signing Type A free-agent DH Dave Parker. ... On disabled list (May 28-September 11, 1992). ... Claimed on waivers by Detroit Tigers (August 6, 1996). ... Claimed on waivers by California Angels (November 12, 1996). ... Released by Angels (March 26, 1997). ... Signed by Kansas City Royals organization (April 17, 1997). ... Released by Royals (June 6, 1997). ... Signed by Texas Rangers organization (June 20, 1997). ... Traded by Rangers with 2B Warren Morris to Pittsburgh Pirates for P Esteban Loaiza (July 17, 1998). ... Granted free agency (October 15, 1998). ... Re-signed by Pirates (January 18, 1999). ... Granted free agency (October 15, 1999). ... Signed by Chicago Cubs organization (November 22, 1999).

Year League	W	L	Pct.	ERA	G	GS	CG	ShO	Sv.	IP	H	R	ER	BB	SO
1990— Southern Oregon (N'West)	1	1	.500	1.13	5	5	0	0	0	24	10	5	3	9	32
— Madison (Midw.)	2	1	.667	3.95	3	3	0	0	0	13 2/3	8	11	6	10	17
1991— Huntsville (Sou.)	6	*13	.316	3.47	24	24	1	1	0	132 1/3	118	69	51	90	115
— Oakland (A.L.)	0	0	...	9.64	1	1	0	0	0	4 2/3	7	5	5	2	6
1992— Tacoma (PCL)	4	2	.667	3.97	9	9	0	0	0	45 1/3	44	22	20	35	29
1993— Tacoma (PCL)	4	8	.333	5.83	16	16	0	0	0	78 2/3	67	53	51	54	71
— Oakland (A.L.)	6	6	.500	5.04	16	16	0	0	0	84	76	50	47	62	47
1994— Oakland (A.L.)	7	10	.412	6.09	23	23	0	0	0	116 2/3	108	80	79	•89	83
1995— Oakland (A.L.)	4	8	.333	4.88	36	14	1	0	0	138 1/3	125	77	75	56	122
1996— Oakland (A.L.)	1	5	.167	7.71	28	6	0	0	1	63	86	56	54	33	37
— Detroit (A.L.)■	2	4	.333	11.39	9	9	1	1	0	36 1/3	53	51	46	29	16
1997— Omaha (A.A.)■	1	5	.167	8.03	11	6	0	0	0	37	50	36	33	24	27
— Charlotte (FSL)■	0	4	.000	4.04	6	6	2	0	0	35 2/3	36	19	16	10	33
— Tulsa (Texas)■	3	3	.500	5.06	7	7	0	0	0	42 2/3	53	27	24	15	26
1998— Tulsa (Texas)■	0	0	...	4.50	1	1	0	0	0	4	2	2	2	4	2
— Oklahoma (PCL)	5	5	.500	3.72	15	13	2	0	0	87	88	44	36	25	69
— Texas (A.L.)	1	2	.333	8.84	4	4	0	0	0	19 1/3	26	20	19	10	10
— Pittsburgh (N.L.)■	1	2	.333	5.36	18	7	0	0	0	47	53	32	28	18	32
1999— Nashville (PCL)	10	6	.625	4.95	27	27	2	0	0	163 2/3	173	95	90	62	*157
2000— Iowa (PCL)■	3	4	.429	3.10	10	6	0	0	0	40 2/3	37	18	14	10	52
— Chicago (N.L.)	4	5	.444	3.75	51	2	0	0	2	86	80	38	36	48	77
A.L. totals (6 years)	21	35	.375	6.33	117	73	2	1	1	462 1/3	481	339	325	281	321
N.L. totals (2 years)	5	7	.417	4.32	69	9	0	0	2	133 1/3	133	70	64	66	109
Major League totals (7 years)	26	42	.382	5.88	186	82	2	1	3	595 2/3	614	409	389	347	430

VANDER WAL, JOHN   OF/IF   PIRATES

PERSONAL: Born April 29, 1966, in Grand Rapids, Mich. ... 6-2/197. ... Bats left, throws left. ... Full name: John Henry Vander Wal.
HIGH SCHOOL: Hudsonville (Mich.).
COLLEGE: Western Michigan.
TRANSACTIONS/CAREER NOTES: Selected by Houston Astros organization in eighth round of free-agent draft (June 4, 1984); did not sign. ... Selected by Montreal Expos organization in third round of free-agent draft (June 2, 1987). ... Contract purchased by Rockies with OF Ronnie Hall from Expos (March 31, 1994). ... Traded by Rockies to San Diego Padres for a player to be named later (August 31, 1998). ... Granted free agency (October 26, 1998). ... Re-signed by Padres (November 13, 1998). ... Traded by Padres with P Geraldo Padua and P James Sak to Pittsburgh Pirates for OF Al Martin and cash (February 23, 2000).
RECORDS: Holds major league single-season record for most hits by pinch hitter—28 (1995).
STATISTICAL NOTES: Had 16-game hitting streak (August 29-September 16, 2000). ... Career major league grand slams: 2.

Year Team (League)	Pos.	G	AB	R	H	2B	3B	HR	RBI	Avg.	BB	SO	SB	PO	A	E	Avg.
1987— Jamestown (NY-P)	OF	18	69	24	33	12	3	3	15	.478	3	14	3	20	0	0	1.000
— W.P. Beach (FSL)	OF	50	189	29	54	11	2	2	22	.286	30	25	8	103	1	3	.972
1988— W.P. Beach (FSL)	OF	62	231	50	64	15	2	10	33	.277	32	40	11	109	3	1	.991
— Jacksonville (Sou.)	OF	58	208	22	54	14	0	3	14	.260	17	49	3	99	0	0	1.000
1989— Jacksonville (Sou.)	OF	71	217	30	55	9	2	6	24	.253	22	51	2	72	3	1	.987
1990— Indianapolis (A.A.)	OF	51	135	16	40	6	0	2	14	.296	13	28	0	48	4	2	.963
— Jacksonville (Sou.)	OF	77	277	45	84	25	3	8	40	.303	39	46	6	106	4	1	.991
1991— Indianapolis (A.A.)	OF	133	478	84	140	36	8	15	71	.293	79	118	8	197	7	1	*.995
— Montreal (N.L.)	OF	21	61	4	13	4	1	1	8	.213	1	18	0	29	0	0	1.000
1992— Montreal (N.L.)	OF-1B	105	213	21	51	8	2	4	20	.239	24	36	3	122	6	2	.985
1993— Montreal (N.L.)	1B-OF	106	215	34	50	7	4	5	30	.233	27	30	6	271	14	4	.986
1994— Colorado (N.L.)■	1B-OF	91	110	12	27	3	1	5	15	.245	16	31	2	106	3	0	1.000
1995— Colorado (N.L.)	1B-OF	105	101	15	35	8	1	5	21	.347	16	23	1	51	4	2	.965

Year	Team (League)	Pos.	G	AB	R	H	2B	3B	HR	RBI	Avg.	BB	SO	SB	PO	A	E	Avg.
1996—Colorado (N.L.)	OF-1B	104	151	20	38	6	2	5	31	.252	19	38	2	72	2	1	.987	
1997—Colorado (N.L.)	OF-1B-DH	76	92	7	16	2	0	1	11	.174	10	33	1	38	0	1	.974	
—Colo. Springs (PCL)	1B	25	103	29	42	12	1	3	19	.408	11	28	1	158	10	4	.977	
1998—Colorado (N.L.)	OF-DH-1B	89	104	18	30	10	1	5	20	.288	16	29	0	29	3	0	1.000	
—San Diego (N.L.)■	OF-1B	20	25	3	6	3	0	0	0	.240	6	5	0	21	2	0	1.000	
1999—San Diego (N.L.)	OF-1B	132	246	26	67	18	0	6	41	.272	37	59	2	227	10	1	.996	
2000—Pittsburgh (N.L.)■	OF-1B-DH	134	384	74	115	29	0	24	94	.299	72	92	11	385	12	6	.985	
Major League totals (10 years)		983	1702	234	448	98	12	61	291	.263	244	394	28	1351	56	17	.988	

DIVISION SERIES RECORD

RECORDS: Holds career record for most games by pinch-hitter—7. ... Shares career record for most triples—1.

Year	Team (League)	Pos.	G	AB	R	H	2B	3B	HR	RBI	Avg.	BB	SO	SB	PO	A	E	Avg.
1995—Colorado (N.L.)	PH	4	4	0	0	0	0	0	0	.000	0	2	0	...	...	...	...	
1998—San Diego (N.L.)	PH	3	3	1	1	0	1	0	2	.333	0	1	0	...	...	...	...	
Division series totals (2 years)		7	7	1	1	0	1	0	2	.143	0	3	0	...	...	...	...	

CHAMPIONSHIP SERIES RECORD

Year	Team (League)	Pos.	G	AB	R	H	2B	3B	HR	RBI	Avg.	BB	SO	SB	PO	A	E	Avg.
1998—San Diego (N.L.)	OF-PH	3	7	1	3	0	0	1	2	.429	0	2	0	5	1	0	1.000	

WORLD SERIES RECORD

Year	Team (League)	Pos.	G	AB	R	H	2B	3B	HR	RBI	Avg.	BB	SO	SB	PO	A	E	Avg.
1998—San Diego (N.L.)	OF-PH	4	5	0	2	1	0	0	0	.400	0	2	0	1	0	0	1.000	

VARGAS, MARTIN — P — INDIANS

PERSONAL: Born February 22, 1978, in San Pedro de Macoris, Dominican Republic. ... 6-0/155. ... Throws right, bats right.
TRANSACTIONS/CAREER NOTES: Signed as non-drafted free agent by Cleveland Indians organization (July 5, 1995).

Year	League	W	L	Pct.	ERA	G	GS	CG	ShO	Sv.	IP	H	R	ER	BB	SO
1997—Dom. Indians (DSL)	3	5	.375	2.45	14	14	0	0	0	$69^2/_3$	52	33	19	39	43
1998—Burlington (Appl.)	3	7	.300	4.76	13	13	1	0	0	$73^2/_3$	78	49	39	35	64
—Columbus (S.Atl.)	1	4	.200	10.01	7	7	0	0	0	$29^2/_3$	42	36	33	24	25
1999—Columbus (S.Atl.)	6	3	.667	4.95	15	12	0	0	0	$67^1/_3$	80	46	37	20	51
—Kinston (Caro.)	6	1	.857	2.76	20	0	0	0	2	$42^1/_3$	31	16	13	20	44
2000—Akron (East.)	10	8	.556	5.42	53	0	0	0	7	$81^1/_3$	96	52	49	30	58

RECORD AS POSITION PLAYER

Year	Team (League)	Pos.	G	AB	R	H	2B	3B	HR	RBI	Avg.	BB	SO	SB	PO	A	E	Avg.
1996—Dom. Indians (DSL)	OF	39	103	7	23	6	1	0	12	.223	12	25	1	197	12	12	.947	

VARITEK, JASON — C — RED SOX

PERSONAL: Born April 11, 1972, in Rochester, Minn. ... 6-2/220. ... Bats both, throws right. ... Full name: Jason A. Varitek.
HIGH SCHOOL: Lake Brantley (Longwood, Fla.).
COLLEGE: Georgia Tech.
TRANSACTIONS/CAREER NOTES: Selected by Minnesota Twins organization first round (21st pick overall) of free-agent draft (June 3, 1993); did not sign. ... Selected by Seattle Mariners organization in first round (14th pick overall) of free-agent draft (June 2, 1994). ... Traded by Mariners with P Derek Lowe to Boston Red Sox for P Heathcliff Slocumb (July 31, 1997).
STATISTICAL NOTES: Tied for Southern League lead in double plays by catcher with 10 in 1996. ... Led Southern League catchers with .993 fielding percentage and tied for lead with 10 double plays in 1996. ... Led A.L. catchers with 1,049 total chances and 25 passed balls in 1999. ... Led A.L. catchers with 14 passed balls in 2000.

Year	Team (League)	Pos.	G	AB	R	H	2B	3B	HR	RBI	Avg.	BB	SO	SB	PO	A	E	Avg.
1995—Port City (Sou.)	C	104	352	42	79	14	3	10	44	.224	61	126	0	589	59	8	.988	
1996—Port City (Sou.)	C-DH-3B-OF	134	503	63	132	34	1	12	67	.262	66	93	1	663	79	5	*.993	
1997—Tacoma (PCL)	C-DH	87	307	54	78	13	0	15	48	.254	34	71	0	613	49	3	*.995	
—Pawtucket (I.L.)■	C	20	66	6	13	5	0	1	5	.197	8	12	0	123	10	1	.993	
—Boston (A.L.)	C	1	1	0	1	0	0	0	0	1.000	0	0	0	1	0	0	1.000	
1998—Boston (A.L.)	C-DH	86	221	31	56	13	0	7	33	.253	17	45	2	367	32	5	.988	
1999—Boston (A.L.)	C-DH	144	483	70	130	39	2	20	76	.269	46	85	1	*972	66	*11	.990	
2000—Boston (A.L.)	C-DH	139	448	55	111	31	1	10	65	.248	60	84	1	867	46	7	.992	
Major League totals (4 years)		370	1153	156	298	83	3	37	174	.258	123	214	4	2207	144	23	.990	

DIVISION SERIES RECORD

RECORDS: Holds single-game record for most runs scored—5 (October 10, 1999). ... Shares career and single-series record for most consecutive hits—5 (October 9-10, 1999).

Year	Team (League)	Pos.	G	AB	R	H	2B	3B	HR	RBI	Avg.	BB	SO	SB	PO	A	E	Avg.
1998—Boston (A.L.)	C	1	4	0	1	0	0	0	1	.250	0	1	0	5	0	0	1.000	
1999—Boston (A.L.)	C	5	21	7	5	3	0	1	3	.238	0	4	0	40	0	0	1.000	
Division series totals (2 years)		6	25	7	6	3	0	1	4	.240	0	5	0	45	0	0	1.000	

CHAMPIONSHIP SERIES RECORD

Year	Team (League)	Pos.	G	AB	R	H	2B	3B	HR	RBI	Avg.	BB	SO	SB	PO	A	E	Avg.
1999—Boston (A.L.)	C	5	20	1	4	1	1	1	1	.200	1	4	0	44	1	1	.978	

V

VAUGHN, GREG — OF/DH — DEVIL RAYS

PERSONAL: Born July 3, 1965, in Sacramento. ... 6-0/202. ... Bats right, throws right. ... Full name: Gregory Lamont Vaughn. ... Cousin of Mo Vaughn, first baseman, Anaheim Angels; and cousin of Jerry Royster, infielder with five major league teams (1973-88).
HIGH SCHOOL: John F. Kennedy (Sacramento).
JUNIOR COLLEGE: Sacramento City College.
COLLEGE: Miami (Fla.).
TRANSACTIONS/CAREER NOTES: Selected by St. Louis Cardinals organization in fifth round of free-agent draft (January 17, 1984); did not sign. ... Selected by Milwaukee Brewers organization in secondary phase of free-agent draft (June 4, 1984); did not sign. ... Selected by Pittsburgh Pirates organization in secondary phase of free-agent draft (January 9, 1985); did not sign. ... Selected by California Angels organization in secondary phase of free-agent draft (June 3, 1985); did not sign. ... Selected by Brewers organization in secondary phase of free-agent draft (June 2, 1986). ... On disabled list (May 26-June 10, 1990). ... On Milwaukee disabled list (April 8-27, 1994); included rehabilitation assignment to Beloit (April 25-27). ... Traded by Brewers with a player to be named later to San Diego Padres for P Bryce Florie, P Ron Villone and OF Marc Newfield (July 31, 1996); Padres acquired OF Gerald Parent to complete deal (September 16, 1996). ... Granted free agency (October 28, 1996). ... Re-signed by Padres (December 19, 1996). ... Traded by Padres with P Kerry Taylor and P Chris Clark to New York Yankees for P Kenny Rogers, IF Mariano Duncan and P Kevin Henthorne (July 4, 1997); trade later voided because Vaughn failed physical (July 6, 1997). ... Traded by Padres with OF/1B Mark Sweeney to Cincinnati Reds for OF Reggie Sanders, SS Damian Jackson and P Josh Harris (February 2, 1999). ... Granted free agency (October 28, 1999). ... Signed by Tampa Bay Devil Rays (December 13, 1999). ... On disabled list (June 18-July 7, 2000).
HONORS: Named Midwest League co-Most Valuable Player (1987). ... Named American Association Most Valuable Player (1989). ... Named N.L. Comeback Player of the Year by THE SPORTING NEWS (1998). ... Named outfielder on THE SPORTING NEWS N.L. All-Star team (1998). ... Named outfielder on THE SPORTING NEWS N.L. Silver Slugger team (1998).
STATISTICAL NOTES: Led Midwest League with 292 total bases in 1987. ... Led Texas League with 279 total bases in 1988. ... Led American Association with .548 slugging percentage in 1989. ... Hit three home runs in one game (September 7, 1999). ... Career major league grand slams: 4.

Year Team (League)	Pos.	G	AB	R	H	2B	3B	HR	RBI	Avg.	BB	SO	SB	PO	A	E	Avg.
1986—Helena (Pio.)	OF	66	258	64	75	13	2	16	54	.291	30	69	23	99	5	3	.972
1987—Beloit (Midw.)	OF	139	492	*120	150	31	6	*33	105	.305	102	115	36	247	11	10	.963
1988—El Paso (Texas)	OF	131	505	*104	152	*39	2	*28	*105	.301	63	120	22	216	12	7	.970
1989—Denver (A.A.)	OF	110	387	74	107	17	5	*26	*92	.276	62	94	20	140	4	3	.980
—Milwaukee (A.L.)	OF-DH	38	113	18	30	3	0	5	23	.265	13	23	4	32	1	2	.943
1990—Milwaukee (A.L.)	OF-DH	120	382	51	84	26	2	17	61	.220	33	91	7	195	8	7	.967
1991—Milwaukee (A.L.)	OF-DH	145	542	81	132	24	5	27	98	.244	62	125	2	315	5	2	.994
1992—Milwaukee (A.L.)	OF-DH	141	501	77	114	18	2	23	78	.228	60	123	15	288	6	3	.990
1993—Milwaukee (A.L.)	OF-DH	154	569	97	152	28	2	30	97	.267	89	118	10	214	1	3	.986
1994—Milwaukee (A.L.)	OF-DH	95	370	59	94	24	1	19	55	.254	51	93	9	162	5	3	.982
—Beloit (Midw.)	DH	2	6	1	1	0	0	0	0	.167	4	1	0	...	...	...	...
1995—Milwaukee (A.L.)	DH	108	392	67	88	19	1	17	59	.224	55	89	10	...	...	...	...
1996—Milwaukee (A.L.)	OF-DH	102	375	78	105	16	0	31	95	.280	58	99	5	192	5	4	.980
—San Diego (N.L.)■	OF	43	141	20	29	3	1	10	22	.206	24	31	4	74	2	2	.974
1997—San Diego (N.L.)	OF-DH	120	361	60	78	10	0	18	57	.216	56	110	7	153	7	1	.994
1998—San Diego (N.L.)	OF-DH	158	573	112	156	28	4	50	119	.272	79	121	11	270	5	2	.993
1999—Cincinnati (N.L.)■	OF-DH	153	550	104	135	20	2	45	118	.245	85	137	15	264	8	4	.986
2000—Tampa Bay (A.L.)■	OF-DH	127	461	83	117	27	1	28	74	.254	80	128	8	145	6	1	.993
American League totals (9 years)		1030	3705	611	916	185	14	197	640	.247	501	889	70	1543	37	25	.984
National League totals (4 years)		474	1625	296	398	61	7	123	316	.245	244	399	37	761	22	9	.989
Major League totals (12 years)		1504	5330	907	1314	246	21	320	956	.247	745	1288	107	2304	59	34	.984

DIVISION SERIES RECORD

Year Team (League)	Pos.	G	AB	R	H	2B	3B	HR	RBI	Avg.	BB	SO	SB	PO	A	E	Avg.
1996—San Diego (N.L.)	PH	3	3	0	0	0	0	0	0	.000	0	1	0	...	...	...	...
1998—San Diego (N.L.)	OF	4	15	2	5	1	0	1	1	.333	0	4	0	2	0	0	1.000
Division series totals (2 years)		7	18	2	5	1	0	1	1	.278	0	5	0	2	0	0	1.000

CHAMPIONSHIP SERIES RECORD

Year Team (League)	Pos.	G	AB	R	H	2B	3B	HR	RBI	Avg.	BB	SO	SB	PO	A	E	Avg.
1998—San Diego (N.L.)	OF-PH	3	8	1	2	0	0	0	0	.250	1	1	0	2	0	0	1.000

WORLD SERIES RECORD

Year Team (League)	Pos.	G	AB	R	H	2B	3B	HR	RBI	Avg.	BB	SO	SB	PO	A	E	Avg.
1998—San Diego (N.L.)	OF-DH	4	15	3	2	0	0	2	4	.133	1	2	0	4	0	1	.800

ALL-STAR GAME RECORD

Year League	Pos.	AB	R	H	2B	3B	HR	RBI	Avg.	BB	SO	SB	PO	A	E	Avg.
1993— American	OF	1	1	1	0	0	0	0	1.000	0	0	0	0	0	0	
1996— American				Selected, did not play.												
1998— National	OF	1	0	1	0	0	0	2	1.000	0	0	0	0	0	0	
All-Star Game totals (2 years)		2	1	2	0	0	0	2	1.000	0	0	0	0	0	0	

V

VAUGHN, MO — 1B — ANGELS

PERSONAL: Born December 15, 1967, in Norwalk, Conn. ... 6-1/268. ... Bats left, throws right. ... Full name: Maurice Samuel Vaughn. ... Cousin of Greg Vaughn, outfielder/designated hitter, Tampa Bay Devil Rays.
HIGH SCHOOL: Trinity Pawling Prep (Pawling, N.Y.).
COLLEGE: Seton Hall.

TRANSACTIONS/CAREER NOTES: Selected by Boston Red Sox organization in first round (23rd pick overall) of free-agent draft (June 9, 1989). ... On disabled list (June 17-July 10, 1997). ... Granted free agency (October 23, 1998). ... Signed by Anaheim Angels (December 11, 1998). ... On disabled list (April 7-22, 1999).
RECORDS: Holds major league single-season record for most strikeouts by lefthander—181 (2000). ... Shares A.L. record for most seasons leading league in errors by first baseman—5.
HONORS: Named first baseman on THE SPORTING NEWS A.L. All-Star team (1995). ... Named first baseman on THE SPORTING NEWS A.L. Silver Slugger team (1995). ... Named A.L. Most Valuable Player by Baseball Writers' Association of America (1995).
STATISTICAL NOTES: Led A.L. with 20 intentional bases on balls received in 1994. ... Led A.L. first basemen with 103 double plays in 1994. ... Led A.L. first basemen with 1,368 total chances and 128 double plays in 1995. ... Hit three home runs in one game (September 24, 1996 and May 30, 1997). ... Had 16-game hitting streak (September 13-27, 1998). ... Career major league grand slams: 10.

Year	Team (League)	Pos.	G	AB	R	H	2B	3B	HR	RBI	Avg.	BB	SO	SB	PO	A	E	Avg.
1989—	New Britain (East.)	1B	73	245	28	68	15	0	8	38	.278	25	47	1	541	45	•10	.983
1990—	Pawtucket (I.L.)	1B	108	386	62	114	26	1	22	72	.295	44	87	3	828	60	11	.988
1991—	Pawtucket (I.L.)	1B	69	234	35	64	10	0	14	50	.274	60	44	2	432	24	3	.993
	— Boston (A.L.)	1B-DH	74	219	21	57	12	0	4	32	.260	26	43	2	378	26	6	.985
1992—	Boston (A.L.)	1B-DH	113	355	42	83	16	2	13	57	.234	47	67	3	741	57	*15	.982
	— Pawtucket (I.L.)	1B	39	149	15	42	6	0	6	28	.282	18	35	1	368	15	8	.980
1993—	Boston (A.L.)	1B-DH	152	539	86	160	34	1	29	101	.297	79	130	4	1110	70	*16	.987
1994—	Boston (A.L.)	1B-DH	111	394	65	122	25	1	26	82	.310	57	112	4	880	57	•10	.989
1995—	Boston (A.L.)	1B-DH	140	550	98	165	28	3	39	•126	.300	68	*150	11	*1262	95	11	.992
1996—	Boston (A.L.)	1B-DH	161	635	118	207	29	1	44	143	.326	95	154	2	1207	74	*15	.988
1997—	Boston (A.L.)	1B-DH	141	527	91	166	24	0	35	96	.315	86	154	2	1088	75	*14	.988
1998—	Boston (A.L.)	1B-DH	154	609	107	205	31	2	40	115	.337	61	144	0	1176	90	12	.991
1999—	Anaheim (A.L.)■	1B-DH	139	524	63	147	20	0	33	108	.281	54	127	0	584	35	3	.995
2000—	Anaheim (A.L.)	1B-DH-OF	161	614	93	167	31	0	36	117	.272	79	*181	2	1257	69	14	.990
Major League totals (10 years)			1346	4966	784	1479	250	10	299	977	.298	652	1262	30	9683	648	116	.989

DIVISION SERIES RECORD

RECORDS: Shares single-game records for most home runs—2 (September 29, 1998); and most runs batted in—7 (September 29, 1998).
NOTES: Shares postseason single-game record for most runs batted in—7 (September 29, 1998).

Year	Team (League)	Pos.	G	AB	R	H	2B	3B	HR	RBI	Avg.	BB	SO	SB	PO	A	E	Avg.
1995—	Boston (A.L.)	1B	3	14	0	0	0	0	0	0	.000	1	7	0	27	2	0	1.000
1998—	Boston (A.L.)	1B	4	17	3	7	2	0	2	7	.412	1	5	0	30	4	0	1.000
Division series totals (2 years)			7	31	3	7	2	0	2	7	.226	2	12	0	57	6	0	1.000

ALL-STAR GAME RECORD

NOTES: Named to A.L. All-Star team for 1998 game; replaced by Rafael Palmeiro due to injury.

Year	League	Pos.	AB	R	H	2B	3B	HR	RBI	Avg.	BB	SO	SB	PO	A	E	Avg.
1995—	American	1B	2	0	0	0	0	0	0	.000	0	2	0	4	0	0	1.000
1998—	American							Selected, did not play—injured.									

VAZQUEZ, JAVIER   P   EXPOS

PERSONAL: Born July 25, 1976, in Ponce, Puerto Rico. ... 6-2/195. ... Throws right, bats right. ... Full name: Javier Carlos Vazquez.
HIGH SCHOOL: Colegio de Ponce (Ponce, Puerto Rico).
TRANSACTIONS/CAREER NOTES: Selected by Montreal Expos organization in fifth round of free-agent draft (June 2, 1994). ... On suspended list (July 23-27, 1998).
STATISTICAL NOTES: Pitched 3-0 one-hit, complete-game victory against Los Angeles (September 14, 1999).

Year	League	W	L	Pct.	ERA	G	GS	CG	ShO	Sv.	IP	H	R	ER	BB	SO
1994—	Gulf Coast Expos (GCL)	5	2	.714	2.53	15	11	1	1	0	67²/₃	37	25	19	15	56
1995—	Albany (S.Atl.)	6	6	.500	5.08	21	21	1	0	0	102²/₃	109	67	58	47	87
1996—	Delmarva (S.Atl.)	14	3	*.824	2.68	27	27	1	0	0	164¹/₃	138	64	49	57	173
1997—	Harrisburg (East.)	4	0	1.000	1.07	6	6	1	0	0	42	15	5	5	12	47
	— West Palm Beach (FSL)	6	3	.667	2.16	19	19	1	0	0	112²/₃	98	40	27	28	100
1998—	Montreal (N.L.)	5	15	.250	6.06	33	32	0	0	0	172¹/₃	196	121	116	68	139
1999—	Montreal (N.L.)	9	8	.529	5.00	26	26	3	1	0	154²/₃	154	98	86	52	113
	— Ottawa (I.L.)	4	2	.667	4.85	7	7	0	0	0	42²/₃	45	24	23	16	46
2000—	Montreal (N.L.)	11	9	.550	4.05	33	33	2	1	0	217²/₃	247	104	98	61	196
Major League totals (3 years)		25	32	.439	4.96	92	91	5	2	0	544²/₃	597	323	300	181	448

V

VELANDIA, JORGE   IF

PERSONAL: Born January 12, 1975, in Caracas, Venezuela. ... 5-9/185. ... Bats right, throws right. ... Full name: Jorge Macias Velandia.
TRANSACTIONS/CAREER NOTES: Signed as non-drafted free agent by Detroit Tigers organization (January 15, 1992). ... Traded by Tigers with 3B Scott Livingstone to San Diego Padres for P Gene Harris (May 11, 1994). ... Traded by Padres with P Doug Bochtler to Oakland Athletics for P Don Wengert and IF David Newhan (November 26, 1997). ... On disabled list (August 7, 1999-remainder of season). ... Traded by A's to New York Mets for OF Nelson Cruz (August 30, 2000). ... Granted free agency (December 21, 2000).
STATISTICAL NOTES: Led Pacific Coast League shortstop with 648 total chances and 93 double plays in 1998.

Year	Team (League)	Pos.	G	AB	R	H	2B	3B	HR	RBI	Avg.	BB	SO	SB	PO	A	E	Avg.
1992—	Bristol (Appl.)	SS-2B	45	119	20	24	6	1	0	9	.202	15	16	3	54	88	12	.922
1993—	Niagara Falls (NY-P)	SS	72	212	30	41	11	0	1	22	.193	19	48	22	82	186	24	.918
	— Fayetteville (S.Atl.)	SS-2B-3B	37	106	15	17	4	0	0	11	.160	13	21	5	47	94	9	.940
1994—	Lakeland (FSL)	SS-2B-3B	22	60	8	14	4	0	0	3	.233	6	14	0	40	56	4	.960
	— Springfield (Midw.)■	SS-2B	98	290	42	71	14	0	4	36	.245	21	46	5	118	303	26	.942

Year	Team (League)	Pos.	G	AB	R	H	2B	3B	HR	RBI	Avg.	BB	SO	SB	PO	A	E	Avg.
1995—	Memphis (Sou.)	SS	63	186	23	38	10	2	4	17	.204	14	37	0	88	152	12	.952
—	Las Vegas (PCL)	SS	66	206	25	54	12	3	0	25	.262	13	37	0	97	190	*31	.903
1996—	Memphis (Sou.)	SS	122	392	42	94	19	0	9	48	.240	31	65	3	173	368	33	.943
1997—	Las Vegas (PCL)	SS	114	405	46	110	15	2	3	35	.272	29	62	13	170	*347	21	.961
—	San Diego (N.L.)	SS-2B-3B	14	29	0	3	2	0	0	0	.103	1	7	0	11	23	3	.919
1998—	Oakland (A.L.)■	SS-2B	8	4	0	1	0	0	0	0	.250	0	1	0	4	10	1	.933
—	Edmonton (PCL)	SS-DH	128	488	64	140	35	1	6	57	.287	37	52	8	203	*428	17	.974
1999—	Oakland (A.L.)	2B-SS-3B-DH	63	48	4	9	1	0	0	2	.188	2	13	2	46	79	3	.977
2000—	Oakland (A.L.)	2B-SS	18	24	1	3	1	0	0	2	.125	0	6	0	17	24	0	1.000
—	Sacramento (PCL)	SS	83	302	56	84	20	1	9	57	.278	34	52	4	127	262	11	.973
—	Norfolk (I.L.)■	2B	4	10	0	1	0	0	0	0	.100	1	1	1	7	10	0	1.000
—	New York (N.L.)	2B-SS-3B	15	7	1	0	0	0	0	0	.000	2	2	0	8	5	1	.929
American League totals (3 years)			89	76	5	13	2	0	0	4	.171	2	20	2	67	113	4	.978
National League totals (2 years)			29	36	1	3	2	0	0	0	.083	3	9	0	19	28	4	.922
Major League totals (4 years)			118	112	6	16	4	0	0	4	.143	5	29	2	86	141	8	.966

VELARDE, RANDY   2B   RANGERS

PERSONAL: Born November 24, 1962, in Midland, Texas. ... 6-0/200. ... Bats right, throws right. ... Full name: Randy Lee Velarde. ... Name pronounced vel-ARE-dee.

HIGH SCHOOL: Robert E. Lee (Midland, Texas).

COLLEGE: Lubbock (Texas) Christian College.

TRANSACTIONS/CAREER NOTES: Selected by Chicago White Sox organization in 19th round of free-agent draft (June 3, 1985). ... Traded by White Sox with P Pete Filson to New York Yankees for P Scott Nielsen and IF Mike Soper (January 5, 1987). ... On New York disabled list (August 9-29, 1989). ... On New York disabled list (June 6-July 30, 1993); included rehabilitation assignment to Albany/Colonie (July 24-30). ... Granted free agency (December 23, 1994). ... Re-signed by Yankees organization (April 12, 1995). ... Granted free agency (November 2, 1995). ... Signed by California Angels (November 21, 1995). ... Angels franchise renamed Anaheim Angels for 1997 season. ... On disabled list (March 23-September 1 and September 2, 1997-remainder of season). ... On Anaheim disabled list (March 19-May 13 and May 16-August 3, 1998); included rehabilitation assignments to Lake Elsinore (May 7-13) and Vancouver (July 29-August 3). ... Granted free agency (October 23, 1998). ... Re-signed by Angels (December 7, 1998). ... Traded by Angels with P Omar Olivares to Oakland Athletics for P Elvin Nina, OF Jeff DaVanon and OF Nathan Hayes (July 29, 1999). ... On Oakland disabled list (April 2-May 8, 2000); included rehabilitation assignments to Midland (April 28-May 2) and Sacramento (May 3-8). ... Traded by A's to Texas Rangers for P Ryan Cullen and P Aaron Harang (November 17, 2000).

STATISTICAL NOTES: Led Midwest League shortstops with 52 errors in 1986. ... Had 21-game hitting streak (June 9-July 4, 1996). ... Led A.L. second baseman with 805 total chances in 1999. ... Career major league grand slams: 1.

Year	Team (League)	Pos.	G	AB	R	H	2B	3B	HR	RBI	Avg.	BB	SO	SB	PO	A	E	Avg.
1985—	Niagara Falls (NY-P)	OF-SS-2B-3B	67	218	28	48	7	3	1	16	.220	35	72	8	124	117	15	.941
1986—	Appleton (Midw.)	SS-3B-OF	124	417	55	105	31	4	11	50	.252	58	96	13	205	300	†54	.903
—	Buffalo (A.A.)	SS	9	20	2	4	1	0	0	2	.200	2	4	1	9	28	3	.925
1987—	Alb./Colonie (East.)■	SS-OF	71	263	40	83	20	2	7	32	.316	25	47	8	128	254	17	.957
—	Columbus (I.L.)	SS	49	185	21	59	10	6	5	33	.319	15	36	8	100	164	16	.943
—	New York (A.L.)	SS	8	22	1	4	0	0	0	1	.182	0	6	0	8	20	2	.933
1988—	Columbus (I.L.)	SS-2B-3B	78	293	39	79	23	4	5	37	.270	25	71	7	123	271	25	.940
—	New York (A.L.)	2B-SS-3B	48	115	18	20	6	0	5	12	.174	8	24	1	72	98	8	.955
1989—	Columbus (I.L.)	SS-3B	103	387	59	103	26	3	11	53	.266	38	105	3	150	295	22	.953
—	New York (A.L.)	3B-SS	33	100	12	34	4	2	2	11	.340	7	14	0	26	61	4	.956
1990—	New York (A.L.)	3-S-O-2-DH	95	229	21	48	6	2	5	19	.210	20	53	0	70	159	12	.950
1991—	New York (A.L.)	3B-SS-OF	80	184	19	45	11	1	1	15	.245	18	43	3	64	148	15	.934
1992—	New York (A.L.)	S-3-0-2	121	412	57	112	24	1	7	46	.272	38	78	7	179	257	15	.967
1993—	New York (A.L.)	OF-SS-3B-DH	85	226	28	68	13	2	7	24	.301	18	39	2	102	92	9	.956
—	Alb./Colonie (East.)	SS-OF-DH	5	17	2	4	0	0	1	2	.235	2	2	0	6	12	2	.900
1994—	New York (A.L.)	SS-3B-OF-2B	77	280	47	78	16	1	9	34	.279	22	61	4	92	188	19	.936
1995—	New York (A.L.)	2-S-O-3	111	367	60	102	19	1	7	46	.278	55	64	5	168	258	10	.977
1996—	California (A.L.)■	2B-3B-SS	136	530	82	151	27	3	14	54	.285	70	118	7	255	306	16	.972
1997—	Anaheim (A.L.)	PR	1	0	0	0	0	0	0	0	...	0	0	0	...	...	...	...
1998—	Lake Elsinore (Calif.)	2B	5	20	6	11	2	1	1	7	.550	2	0	1	10	18	1	.966
—	Anaheim (A.L.)	2B	51	188	29	49	13	1	4	26	.261	34	42	7	88	132	4	.982
—	Vancouver (PCL)	2B-DH	4	16	0	4	2	0	0	2	.250	1	4	1	3	7	0	1.000
1999—	Anaheim (A.L.)	2B	95	376	57	115	15	4	9	48	.306	43	56	13	191	§307	7	.986
—	Oakland (A.L.)■	2B	61	255	48	85	10	3	7	28	.333	27	42	11	107	§186	7	.977
2000—	Midland (Texas)	2B	5	16	4	2	0	0	1	1	.125	4	4	0	7	9	1	.941
—	Sacramento (PCL)	2B	3	11	3	5	0	0	0	2	.455	4	2	2	6	11	0	1.000
—	Oakland (A.L.)	2B	122	485	82	135	23	0	12	41	.278	54	95	9	243	399	12	.982
Major League totals (14 years)			1124	3769	561	1046	187	21	89	405	.278	414	735	69	1665	2611	140	.968

DIVISION SERIES RECORD

Year	Team (League)	Pos.	G	AB	R	H	2B	3B	HR	RBI	Avg.	BB	SO	SB	PO	A	E	Avg.
1995—	New York (A.L.)	2B-3B-OF	5	17	3	3	0	0	0	1	.176	6	4	0	15	11	1	.963
2000—	Oakland (A.L.)	2B	5	20	2	5	1	0	0	3	.250	2	3	1	9	14	2	.920
Division series totals (2 years)			10	37	5	8	1	0	0	4	.216	8	7	1	24	25	3	.942

VENAFRO, MIKE   P   RANGERS

PERSONAL: Born August 2, 1973, in Takoma Park, Md. ... 5-10/180. ... Throws left, bats left. ... Full name: Michael Robert Venafro.

HIGH SCHOOL: Paul VI (Fairfax, Va.).

COLLEGE: James Madison.

TRANSACTIONS/CAREER NOTES: Selected by Texas Rangers organization in 29th round of free-agent draft (June 1, 1995).

V

Year	League	W	L	Pct.	ERA	G	GS	CG	ShO	Sv.	IP	H	R	ER	BB	SO
1995—	Hudson Valley (NY-Penn)...	9	1	.900	2.13	32	0	0	0	2	50²/₃	37	13	12	21	32
1996—	Charleston, S.C. (S.Atl.)	1	3	.250	3.51	50	0	0	0	19	59	57	27	23	21	62
1997—	Charlotte (FSL)	4	2	.667	3.43	35	0	0	0	10	44²/₃	51	17	17	21	35
—	Tulsa (Texas)	0	1	1.000	3.45	11	0	0	0	1	15²/₃	13	12	6	12	13
1998—	Tulsa (Texas)	3	4	.429	3.10	46	0	0	0	14	52¹/₃	42	21	18	26	45
—	Oklahoma City (PCL)..........	0	0	...	6.35	13	0	0	0	0	17	19	12	12	10	15
1999—	Oklahoma (PCL)..................	0	0	...	5.40	6	0	0	0	1	11²/₃	16	7	7	0	7
—	Texas (A.L.)	3	2	.600	3.29	65	0	0	0	0	68¹/₃	63	29	25	22	37
2000—	Texas (A.L.)	3	1	.750	3.83	77	0	0	0	1	56¹/₃	64	27	24	21	32
Major League totals (2 years).......		6	3	.667	3.54	142	0	0	0	1	124²/₃	127	56	49	43	69

DIVISION SERIES RECORD

Year	League	W	L	Pct.	ERA	G	GS	CG	ShO	Sv.	IP	H	R	ER	BB	SO
1999—	Texas (A.L.)	0	0	...	0.00	2	0	0	0	0	1	2	2	0	1	0

VENTURA, ROBIN   3B   METS

PERSONAL: Born July 14, 1967, in Santa Maria, Calif. ... 6-1/198. ... Bats left, throws right. ... Full name: Robin Mark Ventura.

HIGH SCHOOL: Righetti (Santa Maria, Calif.).

COLLEGE: Oklahoma State.

TRANSACTIONS/CAREER NOTES: Selected by Chicago White Sox organization in first round (10th pick overall) of free-agent draft (June 1, 1988). ... On suspended list (August 23-25, 1993). ... On disabled list (March 31-July 24, 1997); included rehabilitation assignments to Nashville (July 13-17) and Birmingham (July 18-22). ... Granted free agency (October 23, 1998). ... Signed by New York Mets (December 1, 1998). ... On disabled list (July 14-29, 2000).

RECORDS: Holds A.L. single-season record for fewest chances accepted by third baseman for leader—372 (1996). ... Shares major league single-season record for highest fielding average by third baseman (150 or more games)—.980 (1999). ... Shares major league single-game record for most grand slams—2 (September 4, 1995).

HONORS: Named College Player of the Year by THE SPORTING NEWS (1987-88). ... Named third baseman on THE SPORTING NEWS college All-America team (1987-88). ... Named Golden Spikes Award winner by USA Baseball (1988). ... Won A.L. Gold Glove at third base (1991-93, 1996 and 1998). ... Won N.L. Gold Glove at third base (1999).

STATISTICAL NOTES: Led Southern League with 12 intentional bases on balls received in 1989. ... Led Southern League third basemen with .930 fielding percentage and tied for lead with 21 double plays in 1989. ... Led A.L. third basemen with 18 errors in 1991. ... Led A.L. third basemen in putouts with 134 in 1991, 141 in 1992 and 133 in 1996. ... Led A.L. third basemen in total chances with 536 in 1992, 404 in 1993 and 382 in 1996. ... Led A.L. third basemen with 372 assists and tied for lead in double plays with 29 in 1992. ... Led A.L. third basemen in double plays with 22 in 1994 and 34 in 1996 and tied for lead with 29 in 1992. ... Led A.L. with 15 intentional bases on balls in 1998. ... Led A.L. third basemen with 447 total chances and 38 double plays in 1998. ... Led N.L. third basemen with 320 assists, 452 total chances and .980 fielding percentage in 1999. ... Career major league grand slams: 14.

MISCELLANEOUS: Member of 1988 U.S. Olympic baseball team.

							BATTING							FIELDING		
Year	Team (League)	Pos.	G	AB	R	H	2B	3B	HR	RBI	Avg.	BB	SO	SB	PO	A	E	Avg.
1989—	Birmingham (Sou.).....	3B-1B-2B	129	454	75	126	25	2	3	67	.278	93	51	9	108	249	27	†.930
—	Chicago (A.L.)	3B	16	45	5	8	3	0	0	7	.178	8	6	0	17	33	2	.962
1990—	Chicago (A.L.)	3B-1B	150	493	48	123	17	1	5	54	.249	55	53	1	116	268	25	.939
1991—	Chicago (A.L.)	3B-1B	157	606	92	172	25	1	23	100	.284	80	67	2	†225	291	†18	.966
1992—	Chicago (A.L.)	3B-1B	157	592	85	167	38	1	16	93	.282	93	71	2	†141	†375	23	.957
1993—	Chicago (A.L.)	3B-1B	157	554	85	145	27	1	22	94	.262	105	82	1	119	278	14	.966
1994—	Chicago (A.L.)	3B-1B-SS	109	401	57	113	15	1	18	78	.282	61	69	3	89	180	20	.931
1995—	Chicago (A.L.)	3B-1B-DH	135	492	79	145	22	0	26	93	.295	75	98	4	201	216	19	.956
1996—	Chicago (A.L.)	3B-1B	158	586	96	168	31	2	34	105	.287	78	81	1	†189	247	11	.975
1997—	Nashville (A.A.)	3B-DH	5	15	3	6	1	0	2	5	.400	2	1	0	1	12	0	1.000
—	Birmingham (Sou.).....	3B	4	17	3	5	1	0	1	2	.294	1	1	0	2	3	2	.714
—	Chicago (A.L.)	3B	54	183	27	48	10	1	6	26	.262	34	21	0	53	99	7	.956
1998—	Chicago (A.L.)	3B	161	590	84	155	31	4	21	91	.263	79	111	1	102	*330	15	.966
1999—	New York (N.L.)■	3B-1B	161	588	88	177	38	0	32	120	.301	74	109	1	124	†320	9	†.980
2000—	New York (N.L.)	3B-1B	141	469	61	109	23	1	24	84	.232	75	91	3	96	261	17	.955
American League totals (10 years)			1254	4542	658	1244	219	12	171	741	.274	668	659	15	1252	2317	154	.959
National League totals (2 years)			302	1057	149	286	61	1	56	204	.271	149	200	4	220	581	26	.969
Major League totals (12 years)			1556	5599	807	1530	280	13	227	945	.273	817	859	19	1472	2898	180	.960

DIVISION SERIES RECORD

							BATTING							FIELDING		
Year	Team (League)	Pos.	G	AB	R	H	2B	3B	HR	RBI	Avg.	BB	SO	SB	PO	A	E	Avg.
1999—	New York (N.L.)........	3B	4	14	1	3	2	0	0	1	.214	4	2	0	3	8	0	1.000
2000—	New York (N.L.)..........	3B-1B	4	14	1	2	0	0	1	2	.143	4	1	0	7	6	0	1.000
Division series totals (2 years)			8	28	2	5	2	0	1	3	.179	8	3	0	10	14	0	1.000

CHAMPIONSHIP SERIES RECORD

							BATTING							FIELDING		
Year	Team (League)	Pos.	G	AB	R	H	2B	3B	HR	RBI	Avg.	BB	SO	SB	PO	A	E	Avg.
1993—	Chicago (A.L.)..........	3B-1B	6	20	2	4	0	0	1	5	.200	6	6	0	9	6	1	.938
1999—	New York (N.L.).........	3B	6	25	2	3	1	0	0	1	.120	2	5	0	5	16	0	1.000
2000—	New York (N.L.).........	3B	5	14	4	3	1	0	0	5	.214	6	0	0	2	13	1	.938
Championship series totals (3 years)			17	59	8	10	2	0	1	11	.169	14	11	0	16	35	2	.962

WORLD SERIES RECORD

							BATTING							FIELDING		
Year	Team (League)	Pos.	G	AB	R	H	2B	3B	HR	RBI	Avg.	BB	SO	SB	PO	A	E	Avg.
2000—	New York (N.L.)..........	3B	5	20	1	3	1	0	1	1	.150	1	5	0	1	8	0	1.000

ALL-STAR GAME RECORD

						BATTING							FIELDING		
Year	League	Pos.	AB	R	H	2B	3B	HR	RBI	Avg.	BB	SO	SB	PO	A	E	Avg.
1992—	American	3B	2	1	2	1	0	0	1	1.000	0	0	0	1	1	0	1.000

V

VERAS, QUILVIO — 2B — BRAVES

PERSONAL: Born April 3, 1971, in Santo Domingo, Dominican Republic. ... 5-10/183. ... Bats both, throws right. ... Full name: Quilvio Alberto Perez Veras.

HIGH SCHOOL: Victor E. Liz (Santo Domingo, Dominican Republic).

TRANSACTIONS/CAREER NOTES: Signed as non-drafted free agent by New York Mets organization (November 22, 1989). ... On suspended list (July 31-August 2, 1994). ... On disabled list (August 7-15, 1994). ... Traded by Mets to Florida Marlins for OF Carl Everett (November 29, 1994). ... On Florida disabled list (May 10-June 21, 1996); included rehabilitation assignment to Charlotte (June 13-21). ... Traded by Marlins to San Diego Padres for P Dustin Hermanson (November 21, 1996). ... On disabled list (August 8-23). ... Traded by Padres with 1B Wally Joyner and OF Reggie Sanders to Atlanta Braves for OF/1B Ryan Klesko, 2B Bret Boone and P Jason Shiell (December 22, 1999). ... On disabled list (July 16, 2000-remainder of season).

STATISTICAL NOTES: Tied for Appalachian League lead in double plays by second baseman with 30 in 1991. ... Led Appalachian League second basemen with 282 total chances in 1991. ... Led South Atlantic League in on-base percentage with .441 and in caught stealing with 35 in 1992. ... Led Eastern League in on-base percentage with .430 and in caught stealing with 19 in 1993. ... Led Eastern League second basemen with 669 total chances in 1993. ... Led International League in caught stealing with 18 in 1994. ... Led International League second basemen with 589 total chances and 84 double plays in 1994. ... Led N.L. in caught stealing with 21 in 1995. ... Career major league grand slams: 1.

Year Team (League)	Pos.	G	AB	R	H	2B	3B	HR	RBI	Avg.	BB	SO	SB	PO	A	E	Avg.
1990— GC Mets (GCL)	2B	30	98	26	29	3	3	1	5	.296	19	16	16	45	76	3	.976
— Kingsport (Appl.)	2B	24	94	21	36	6	0	1	14	.383	13	14	9	55	79	8	.944
1991— Kingsport (Appl.)	2B	64	226	*54	76	11	4	1	16	.336	36	28	38	*113	*161	8	.972
— Pittsfield (NY-Penn)	2B-SS	5	15	3	4	0	1	0	2	.267	5	1	2	16	16	1	.970
1992— Columbia (S.Atl.)	2B	117	414	97	132	24	10	2	40	*.319	84	52	*66	208	313	20	.963
1993— Binghamton (East.)	2B	128	444	87	136	19	7	2	51	.306	*91	62	52	*274	*372	23	.966
1994— Norfolk (I.L.)	2B-DH	123	457	71	114	22	4	0	43	.249	59	56	40	*267	*308	*14	.976
1995— Florida (N.L.)■	2B-OF	124	440	86	115	20	7	5	32	.261	80	68	*56	299	315	9	.986
1996— Florida (N.L.)	2B	73	253	40	64	8	1	4	14	.253	51	42	8	174	191	5	.986
— Charlotte (I.L.)	2B-DH	28	104	22	34	5	2	2	8	.327	13	14	8	44	66	3	.973
1997— San Diego (N.L.)■	2B	145	539	74	143	23	1	3	45	.265	72	84	33	276	407	11	.984
1998— San Diego (N.L.)	2B	138	517	79	138	24	2	6	45	.267	84	78	24	258	405	9	.987
1999— San Diego (N.L.)	2B	132	475	95	133	25	2	6	41	.280	65	88	30	271	334	12	.981
2000— Atlanta (N.L.)■	2B	84	298	56	92	15	0	5	37	.309	51	50	25	146	223	6	.984
Major League totals (6 years)		696	2522	430	685	115	13	29	214	.272	403	410	176	1424	1875	52	.984

DIVISION SERIES RECORD

Year Team (League)	Pos.	G	AB	R	H	2B	3B	HR	RBI	Avg.	BB	SO	SB	PO	A	E	Avg.
1998— San Diego (N.L.)	2B	4	15	1	2	0	0	0	0	.133	1	6	0	8	12	0	1.000

CHAMPIONSHIP SERIES RECORD

Year Team (League)	Pos.	G	AB	R	H	2B	3B	HR	RBI	Avg.	BB	SO	SB	PO	A	E	Avg.
1998— San Diego (N.L.)	2B	6	24	2	6	1	0	0	2	.250	5	7	0	7	13	0	1.000

WORLD SERIES RECORD

Year Team (League)	Pos.	G	AB	R	H	2B	3B	HR	RBI	Avg.	BB	SO	SB	PO	A	E	Avg.
1998— San Diego (N.L.)	2B	4	15	3	3	2	0	0	1	.200	3	4	0	9	16	0	1.000

VERAS, WILTON — 3B — RED SOX

PERSONAL: Born January 19, 1978, in Monte Cristi, Dominican Republic. ... 6-2/198. ... Bats right, throws right. ... Full name: Wilton Andres Veras.

HIGH SCHOOL: Monte Cristi (Dominican Republic).

TRANSACTIONS/CAREER NOTES: Signed as non-drafted free agent by Boston Red Sox organization (February 9, 1995).

STATISTICAL NOTES: Led New York-Pennsylvania League in grounding into double plays with nine in 1996. ... Led Midwest League third basemen with 29 double plays in 1997. ... Led Midwest League in grounding into double plays with 19 in 1997. ... Led Eastern League third basemen with 377 total chances in 1998. ... Led Eastern League in grounding into double plays with 23 in 1999. ... Led Eastern League third basemen with 27 double plays in 1999.

Year Team (League)	Pos.	G	AB	R	H	2B	3B	HR	RBI	Avg.	BB	SO	SB	PO	A	E	Avg.
1995— GC Red Sox (GCL)	1B-3B	31	91	7	24	1	0	0	5	.264	7	9	1	80	2	1	.988
1996— Lowell (NY-Penn)	3B	67	250	22	60	15	0	0	19	.240	13	29	2	*57	106	12	.931
1997— Michigan (Midw.)	3B	131	489	51	141	21	3	8	68	.288	31	51	3	99	220	19	*.944
1998— Trenton (East.)	3B	126	470	70	137	27	4	16	67	.291	15	66	5	*100	*259	18	*.952
1999— Trenton (East.)	3B-DH	116	474	65	133	23	2	11	75	.281	23	55	7	83	*245	19	.945
— Boston (A.L.)	3B	36	119	14	34	5	1	2	13	.286	5	14	0	23	56	6	.929
2000— Pawtucket (I.L.)	3B	60	218	18	46	9	0	3	25	.211	12	18	0	45	98	4	.973
— Boston (A.L.)	3B	49	164	21	40	7	1	0	14	.244	7	20	0	33	94	13	.907
Major League totals (2 years)		85	283	35	74	12	2	2	27	.261	12	34	0	56	150	19	.916

DIVISION SERIES RECORD

Year Team (League)	Pos.	G	AB	R	H	2B	3B	HR	RBI	Avg.	BB	SO	SB	PO	A	E	Avg.
1999— Boston (A.L.)							Did not play.										

CHAMPIONSHIP SERIES RECORD

Year Team (League)	Pos.	G	AB	R	H	2B	3B	HR	RBI	Avg.	BB	SO	SB	PO	A	E	Avg.
1999— Boston (A.L.)							Did not play.										

VERES, DAVE   P   CARDINALS

PERSONAL: Born October 19, 1966, in Montgomery, Ala. ... 6-2/220. ... Throws right, bats right. ... Full name: David Scott Veres. ... Name pronounced VEERZ.
HIGH SCHOOL: Gresham (Ore.).
JUNIOR COLLEGE: Mount Hood Community College (Ore.).
TRANSACTIONS/CAREER NOTES: Selected by Oakland Athletics organization in fourth round of free-agent draft (January 14, 1986). ... Traded by A's to Los Angeles Dodgers for P Kevin Campbell (January 15, 1991). ... Loaned by Dodgers organization to Mexico City Tigers of Mexican League (April 3-May 15, 1992). ... Released by Dodgers (May 15, 1992). ... Signed by Houston Astros organization (May 28, 1992). ... Traded by Astros with C Raul Chavez to Montreal Expos for 3B Sean Berry (December 20, 1995). ... On disabled list (August 21-September 17, 1997). ... Traded by Expos with a player to be named later to Colorado Rockies for OF Terry Jones and a player to be named later (December 10, 1997). ... Traded by Rockies with P Darryl Kile and P Luther Hackman to St. Louis Cardinals for P Jose Jimenez, P Manny Aybar, P Rick Croushore and SS Brent Butler (November 16, 1999).
STATISTICAL NOTES: Tied for California League lead with 29 wild pitches in 1987. ... Led Southern League with 16 wild pitches in 1989.
MISCELLANEOUS: Made an out in only appearance as pinch hitter (1998).

Year League	W	L	Pct.	ERA	G	GS	CG	ShO	Sv.	IP	H	R	ER	BB	SO
1986— Medford (N'West)	5	2	.714	3.26	15	•15	0	0	0	77 1/3	58	38	28	57	60
1987— Modesto (Calif.)	8	9	.471	4.79	26	26	2	0	0	148 1/3	124	90	79	108	124
1988— Modesto (Calif.)	4	11	.267	3.31	19	19	3	0	0	125	100	61	46	78	91
— Huntsville (Sou.)	3	4	.429	4.15	8	8	0	0	0	39	50	20	18	15	17
1989— Huntsville (Sou.)	8	11	.421	4.86	29	28	2	1	0	159 1/3	160	93	86	83	105
1990— Tacoma (PCL)	11	8	.579	4.69	32	23	2	0	1	151 2/3	136	90	79	88	88
1991— Albuquerque (PCL)■	7	6	.538	4.47	57	3	0	0	5	100 2/3	89	52	50	52	81
1992— M.C. Tigers (Mex.)■	1	5	.167	8.10	14	1	0	0	1	23 1/3	29	21	21	12	12
— Tucson (PCL)■	2	3	.400	5.30	29	1	0	0	0	52 2/3	60	36	31	17	46
1993— Tucson (PCL)	6	10	.375	4.90	43	15	1	0	5	130 1/3	156	88	71	32	122
1994— Tucson (PCL)	1	1	.500	1.88	16	0	0	0	1	24	17	8	5	10	19
— Houston (N.L.)	3	3	.500	2.41	32	0	0	0	1	41	39	13	11	7	28
1995— Houston (N.L.)	5	1	.833	2.26	72	0	0	0	1	103 1/3	89	29	26	30	94
1996— Montreal (N.L.)■	6	3	.667	4.17	68	0	0	0	4	77 2/3	85	39	36	32	81
1997— Montreal (N.L.)	2	3	.400	3.48	53	0	0	0	1	62	68	28	24	27	47
1998— Colorado (N.L.)■	3	1	.750	2.83	63	0	0	0	8	76 1/3	67	26	24	27	74
1999— Colorado (N.L.)	4	8	.333	5.14	73	0	0	0	31	77	88	46	44	37	71
2000— St. Louis (N.L.)■	3	5	.375	2.85	71	0	0	0	29	75 2/3	65	26	24	25	67
Major League totals (7 years)	26	24	.520	3.32	432	0	0	0	75	513	501	207	189	185	462

DIVISION SERIES RECORD

Year League	W	L	Pct.	ERA	G	GS	CG	ShO	Sv.	IP	H	R	ER	BB	SO
2000— St. Louis (N.L.)	0	0	...	0.00	2	0	0	0	1	2	1	1	0	0	4

CHAMPIONSHIP SERIES RECORD

Year League	W	L	Pct.	ERA	G	GS	CG	ShO	Sv.	IP	H	R	ER	BB	SO
2000— St. Louis (N.L.)	0	0	...	0.00	3	0	0	0	0	2 1/3	2	0	0	0	3

VIDRO, JOSE   2B   EXPOS

PERSONAL: Born August 27, 1974, in Mayaguez, Puerto Rico. ... 5-11/190. ... Bats both, throws right. ... Full name: Jose Angel Cetty Vidro.
HIGH SCHOOL: Blanco Morales (Sabana Grande, Puerto Rico).
TRANSACTIONS/CAREER NOTES: Selected by Montreal Expos organization in sixth round of free agent draft (June 1, 1992). ... On disabled list (June 1-15 and July 26, 1993-remainder of season).
RECORDS: Shares N.L. single-season record for fewest putouts by second baseman (150 or more games)—260 (2000). ... Shares major league single-season record for most doubles by switch-hitter—51 (2000).
STATISTICAL NOTES: Switch-hit home runs in one game (July 3, 2000). ... Career major league grand slams: 1.

Year Team (League)	Pos.	G	AB	R	H	2B	3B	HR	RBI	Avg.	BB	SO	SB	PO	A	E	Avg.
1992— GC Expos (GCL)	2B	54	200	29	66	6	2	4	31	.330	16	31	10	114	107	4	*.982
1993— Burlington (Midw.)	2B	76	287	39	69	19	0	2	34	.240	28	54	3	107	153	7	.974
1994— W.P. Beach (FSL)	2B	125	465	57	124	30	2	4	49	.267	51	56	8	204	328	20	.964
1995— W.P. Beach (FSL)	IF	44	163	20	53	15	2	3	24	.325	8	21	0	101	110	4	.981
— Harrisburg (East.)	IF	64	246	33	64	16	2	4	38	.260	20	37	7	97	162	9	.966
1996— Harrisburg (East.)	IF	126	452	57	117	25	3	18	82	.259	29	71	3	135	271	15	.964
1997— Ottawa (I.L.)	3B-2B-DH	73	279	40	90	17	0	13	47	.323	22	40	2	70	161	8	.967
— Montreal (N.L.)	3B-DH-2B	67	169	19	42	12	1	2	17	.249	11	20	1	25	59	4	.955
1998— Montreal (N.L.)	2B-3B	83	205	24	45	12	0	0	18	.220	27	33	2	81	126	6	.972
— Ottawa (I.L.)	2B-3B-DH	63	235	35	68	14	2	2	32	.289	24	25	5	91	124	6	.973
1999— Montreal (N.L.)	2-1-0-3	140	494	67	150	45	2	12	59	.304	29	51	0	270	296	11	.981
2000— Montreal (N.L.)	2B	153	606	101	200	51	2	24	97	.330	49	69	5	260	*442	10	.986
Major League totals (4 years)		443	1474	211	437	120	5	38	191	.296	116	173	8	636	923	31	.981

ALL-STAR GAME RECORD

Year League	Pos.	AB	R	H	2B	3B	HR	RBI	Avg.	BB	SO	SB	PO	A	E	Avg.
2000— National	PH-2B	1	0	0	0	0	0	0	.000	0	0	0	0	0	1	.000

VILLAFUERTE, BRANDON   P   RANGERS

PERSONAL: Born December 17, 1975, in Hilo, Hawaii. ... 5-11/165. ... Throws right, bats right. ... Full name: Brandon Paul Villafuerte.
HIGH SCHOOL: Live Oak (Morgan Hill, Calif.).
JUNIOR COLLEGE: West Valley College (Calif.).

TRANSACTIONS/CAREER NOTES: Selected by New York Mets organization 66th round of free-agent draft (June 2, 1994). ... Traded by Mets with a player to be named later to Florida Marlins for OF Robert Stratton (March 20,1998); Marlins acquired 2B Cesar Crespo to complete deal (September 14, 1998). ... Traded by Marlins to Detroit Tigers for P Mike Drumright (July 31, 1999). ... Traded by Tigers with P Kevin Mobley to Texas Rangers for P Matt Perisho (December 15, 2000).

STATISTICAL NOTES: Tied for International League lead with 12 wild pitches in 2000.

Year League	W	L	Pct.	ERA	G	GS	CG	ShO	Sv.	IP	H	R	ER	BB	SO
1995— Little Falls (NY-Penn)	5	1	.833	5.63	20	0	0	0	0	32	28	21	20	26	42
1996— Pittsfield (NY-Penn)...........	8	3	.727	3.02	18	7	1	0	1	62 2/3	53	21	21	27	59
1997— Capital City (S.Atl.)	3	1	.750	2.38	47	3	0	0	7	75 2/3	58	23	20	33	88
1998— Brevard County (FSL)■......	1	0	1.000	0.93	3	0	0	0	0	9 2/3	7	3	1	1	6
— Portland (East.)	0	2	.000	4.97	30	0	0	0	1	54 1/3	68	35	30	33	52
— Charlotte (I.L.)...................	1	0	1.000	6.35	10	0	0	0	0	11 1/3	15	8	8	8	9
1999— Portland (East.)	6	8	.429	3.50	22	12	0	0	0	100 1/3	97	45	39	40	85
— Jacksonville (Sou.)■.............	0	2	.000	1.88	15	0	0	0	5	24	17	6	5	12	20
2000— Toledo (I.L.)......................	4	9	.308	6.67	46	6	0	0	4	87 2/3	112	70	65	49	85
— Detroit (A.L.)	0	0	...	10.38	3	0	0	0	0	4 1/3	4	5	5	4	1
Major League totals (1 year)........	0	0	...	10.38	3	0	0	0	0	4 1/3	4	5	5	4	1

VILLEGAS, ISMAEL   P   BRAVES

PERSONAL: Born August 12, 1976, in Rio Piedras, Puerto Rico. ... 6-1/188. ... Throws right, bats right.
HIGH SCHOOL: Magarita Janer Palacios (Guaynabo, Puerto Rico).
TRANSACTIONS/CAREER NOTES: Selected by Chicago Cubs organization in fifth round of free-agent draft (June 1, 1995). ... Traded by Cubs to Atlanta Braves for C Tyler Houston (July 27, 1996).

Year League	W	L	Pct.	ERA	G	GS	CG	ShO	Sv.	IP	H	R	ER	BB	SO
1995— Gulf Coast Cubs (GCL)	3	2	.600	2.40	11	10	0	0	0	41 1/3	33	17	11	11	26
1996— Rockford (Midw.)	2	5	.286	5.13	10	10	1	0	0	47 1/3	63	40	27	25	30
— Williamsport (NY-Penn)	0	0	...	2.57	2	2	0	0	0	7	7	3	2	4	5
— Danville (Appl.)■	0	0	...	3.00	1	0	0	0	0	3	2	1	1	1	4
— Macon (S.Atl.)	3	7	.300	5.00	12	12	2	1	0	72	80	46	40	19	60
1997— Durham (Caro.)	2	5	.286	5.07	30	1	0	0	1	55	60	33	31	32	44
1998— Greenville (Sou.)	7	6	.538	5.28	40	17	1	0	3	124 1/3	134	78	73	71	120
1999— Richmond (I.L.)	6	7	.462	4.40	44	2	0	0	1	92	93	51	45	39	61
2000— Richmond (I.L.)	0	5	.000	4.81	41	0	0	0	3	63 2/3	66	38	34	31	51
— Atlanta (N.L.)	0	0	...	13.50	1	0	0	0	0	2 2/3	4	4	4	2	2
— Greenville (Sou.)	2	1	.667	4.50	8	0	0	0	1	16	20	12	8	7	16
Major League totals (1 year)........	0	0	...	13.50	1	0	0	0	0	2 2/3	4	4	4	2	2

VILLONE, RON   P   ROCKIES

PERSONAL: Born January 16, 1970, in Englewood, N.J. ... 6-3/237. ... Throws left, bats left. ... Full name: Ronald Thomas Villone Jr.
HIGH SCHOOL: South Bergenfield (Bergenfield, N.J.).
COLLEGE: Massachusetts.
TRANSACTIONS/CAREER NOTES: Selected by Seattle Mariners in first round (14th pick overall) of free-agent draft (June 1, 1992). ... On disabled list (April 19-26, 1994). ... Traded by Mariners with OF Marc Newfield to San Diego Padres for P Andy Benes and a player to be named later (July 31, 1995); Mariners acquired P Greg Keagle to complete deal (September 16, 1995). ... Traded by Padres with P Bryce Florie and OF Marc Newfield to Milwaukee Brewers for OF Greg Vaughn and a player to be named later (July 31, 1996); Padres acquired OF Gerald Parent to complete deal (September 16, 1996). ... Traded by Brewers with P Ben McDonald and P Mike Fetters to Cleveland Indians for OF Marquis Grissom and P Jeff Juden (December 8, 1997). ... On Cleveland disabled list (August 15-September 1, 1998); included rehabilitation assignment to Buffalo (August 22-September 1). ... Released by Indians (April 2, 1999). ... Signed by Cincinnati Reds organization (April 5, 1999). ... Traded by Reds to Colorado Rockies for two players to be named later (November 8, 2000); Reds acquired P Jeff Taglienti and P Justin Carter to complete deal (December 20, 2000).
STATISTICAL NOTES: Tied for N.L. lead in errors by a pitcher with six in 1999. ... Struck out 15 batters in one game (September 29, 2000).
MISCELLANEOUS: Member of 1992 U.S. Olympic baseball team.

Year League	W	L	Pct.	ERA	G	GS	CG	ShO	Sv.	IP	H	R	ER	BB	SO
1993— Riverside (Calif.).................	7	4	.636	4.21	16	16	0	0	0	83 1/3	74	47	39	62	82
— Jacksonville (Sou.).............	3	4	.429	4.38	11	11	0	0	0	63 2/3	49	34	31	41	66
1994— Jacksonville (Sou.).............	6	7	.462	3.86	41	5	0	0	8	79 1/3	56	37	34	68	94
1995— Seattle (A.L.)	0	2	.000	7.91	19	0	0	0	0	19 1/3	20	19	17	23	26
— Tacoma (PCL)	1	0	1.000	0.61	22	0	0	0	13	29 2/3	9	6	2	19	43
— San Diego (N.L.)■	2	1	.667	4.21	19	0	0	0	1	25 2/3	24	12	12	11	23
1996— Las Vegas (PCL)	2	1	.667	1.64	23	0	0	0	3	22	13	5	4	9	29
— San Diego (N.L.)	1	1	.500	2.95	21	0	0	0	0	18 1/3	17	6	6	7	19
— Milwaukee (A.L.)■	0	0	...	3.28	23	0	0	0	2	24 2/3	14	9	9	18	19
1997— Milwaukee (A.L.)	1	0	1.000	3.42	50	0	0	0	0	52 2/3	54	23	20	36	40
1998— Buffalo (I.L.)■	2	2	.500	2.01	23	0	0	0	7	22 1/3	20	11	5	11	28
— Cleveland (A.L.).................	0	0	...	6.00	25	0	0	0	0	27	30	18	18	22	15
1999— Indianapolis (I.L.)■............	2	0	1.000	1.42	18	0	0	0	1	19	9	3	3	13	23
— Cincinnati (N.L.)	9	7	.563	4.23	29	22	0	0	2	142 2/3	114	70	67	73	97
2000— Cincinnati (N.L.)	10	10	.500	5.43	35	23	2	0	0	141	154	95	85	78	115
A.L. totals (4 years)	1	2	.333	4.66	117	0	0	0	2	123 2/3	118	69	64	99	100
N.L. totals (4 years)	22	19	.537	4.67	104	45	2	0	3	327 2/3	309	183	170	169	230
Major League totals (6 years)	23	21	.523	4.67	221	45	2	0	5	451 1/3	427	252	234	268	330

VINA, FERNANDO   2B   CARDINALS

PERSONAL: Born April 16, 1969, in Sacramento. ... 5-9/174. ... Bats left, throws right. ... Name pronounced VEEN-ya.
HIGH SCHOOL: Valley (Sacramento).

JUNIOR COLLEGE: Cosumnes River College (Calif.), then Sacramento City College.
COLLEGE: Arizona State.
TRANSACTIONS/CAREER NOTES: Selected by New York Yankees organization in 51st round of free-agent draft (June 1, 1988); did not sign. ... Selected by New York Mets organization in ninth round of free-agent draft (June 4, 1990). ... Selected by Seattle Mariners from Mets organization in Rule 5 major league draft (December 7, 1992). ... Returned to Mets organization (June 15, 1993). ... On New York disabled list (May 22-June 6, 1994). ... On Norfolk disabled list (August 30-September 6, 1994). ... Traded by Mets to Milwaukee Brewers (December 22, 1994), completing deal in which Brewers traded P Doug Henry for two players to be named later (November 30, 1994); Brewers acquired C Javier Gonzalez as partial completion of deal (December 6, 1994). ... On Milwaukee disabled list (April 20-July 17, 1997); included rehabilitation assignments to Stockton (July 9-11) and Tucson (July 12-17). ... On suspended list (May 11-13 and May 25-27, 1999). ... On Milwaukee disabled list (May 10-25 and June 4, 1999-remainder of season); included rehabilitation assignment to Beloit (August 6-8). ... Traded by Brewers to St. Louis Cardinals for P Juan Acevedo and two players to be named later (December 20, 1999); Brewers acquired P Matt Parker and C Eliezer Alfonzo to complete deal (June 13, 2000). ... On disabled list (June 20-July 4, 2000).
STATISTICAL NOTES: Tied for South Atlantic League lead in caught stealing with 22 in 1991. ... Led South Atlantic League second basemen with 600 total chances and 61 double plays in 1991. ... Led Florida State League second basemen with 85 double plays in 1992. ... Led N.L. in being hit by pitch with 12 in 1994. ... Led A.L. second basemen with 116 double plays in 1996. ... Led N.L. second basemen with 884 total chances and 135 double plays in 1998. ... Had 17-game hitting streak (August 8-25, 2000). ... Led N.L. in being hit by pitch with 28 in 2000. ... Career major league grand slams: 1.

							BATTING							FIELDING		
Year Team (League)	Pos.	G	AB	R	H	2B	3B	HR	RBI	Avg.	BB	SO	SB	PO	A	E	Avg.
1991— Columbia (S.Atl.)	2B	129	498	77	135	23	6	6	50	.271	46	27	42	194	*385	21	*.965
1992— St. Lucie (FSL)	2B	111	421	61	124	15	5	1	42	.295	32	26	36	219	*360	17	.971
— Tidewater (I.L.)	2B	11	30	3	6	0	0	0	2	.200	0	2	0	16	28	1	.978
1993— Seattle (A.L.)■	2B-SS-DH	24	45	5	10	2	0	0	2	.222	4	3	6	28	40	0	1.000
— Norfolk (I.L.)■	SS-2B-DH-OF	73	287	24	66	6	4	4	27	.230	7	17	16	146	232	14	.964
1994— New York (N.L.)	2B-3B-SS-OF	79	124	20	31	6	0	0	6	.250	12	11	3	46	59	4	.963
— Norfolk (I.L.)	SS-2B	6	17	2	3	0	0	0	1	.176	1	1	1	9	11	1	.952
1995— Milwaukee (A.L.)■	2B-SS-3B	113	288	46	74	7	7	3	29	.257	22	28	6	194	245	8	.982
1996— Milwaukee (A.L.)	2B	140	554	94	157	19	10	7	46	.283	38	35	16	*333	417	*16	.979
1997— Milwaukee (A.L.)	2B-DH	79	324	37	89	12	2	4	28	.275	12	23	8	149	227	7	.982
— Stockton (Calif.)	2B	3	9	2	4	0	1	0	3	.444	0	0	0	2	7	0	1.000
— Tucson (PCL)	2B	6	19	3	9	3	0	1	5	.474	3	1	0	8	16	2	.923
1998— Milwaukee (N.L.)	2B	159	637	101	198	39	7	7	45	.311	54	46	22	404	468	12	.986
1999— Milwaukee (N.L.)	2B	37	154	17	41	7	0	1	16	.266	14	6	5	84	104	1	.995
— Beloit (Midw.)	DH-2B	2	10	1	2	1	0	0	0	.200	0	2	0	0	2	2	.500
2000— St. Louis (N.L.)■	2B	123	487	81	146	24	6	4	31	.300	36	36	10	261	325	7	*.988
American League totals (4 years)		356	1211	182	330	40	19	14	105	.273	76	89	36	704	924	31	.981
National League totals (4 years)		398	1402	219	416	76	13	12	98	.297	116	99	40	795	956	24	.986
Major League totals (8 years)		754	2613	401	746	116	32	26	203	.285	192	188	76	1499	1880	55	.984

DIVISION SERIES RECORD

							BATTING							FIELDING		
Year Team (League)	Pos.	G	AB	R	H	2B	3B	HR	RBI	Avg.	BB	SO	SB	PO	A	E	Avg.
2000— St. Louis (N.L.)	2B	3	13	3	4	0	0	1	3	.308	1	1	0	7	13	0	1.000

CHAMPIONSHIP SERIES RECORD

							BATTING							FIELDING		
Year Team (League)	Pos.	G	AB	R	H	2B	3B	HR	RBI	Avg.	BB	SO	SB	PO	A	E	Avg.
2000— St. Louis (N.L.)	2B	5	23	3	6	1	0	0	1	.261	1	4	0	14	10	1	.960

ALL-STAR GAME RECORD

						BATTING							FIELDING		
Year League	Pos.	AB	R	H	2B	3B	HR	RBI	Avg.	BB	SO	SB	PO	A	E	Avg.
1998— National	2B	1	0	1	0	0	0	0	1.000	1	0	0	1	1	1	.667

VITIELLO, JOE   1B/OF

V

PERSONAL: Born April 11, 1970, in Cambridge, Mass. ... 6-3/230. ... Bats right, throws right. ... Full name: Joseph David Vitiello. ... Name pronounced VIT-ee-ELL-oh.
HIGH SCHOOL: Stoneham (Mass.).
COLLEGE: Alabama.
TRANSACTIONS/CAREER NOTES: Selected by New York Yankees organization in 31st round of free-agent draft (June 1, 1988); did not sign. ... Selected by Kansas City Royals organization in first round (seventh pick overall) of free-agent draft (June 3, 1991). ... On disabled list (April 12-23, 1992; June 2-11, 1993; and May 23-June 16, 1994). ... On disabled list (June 17-July 28 and August 13, 1997-remainder of season); included rehabilitation assignment to Omaha (July 15-28). ... On Kansas City disabled list (April 8-May 18, 1998); included rehabilitation assignment to Omaha (April 21-May 9). ... On Omaha disabled list (August 4-12, 1998). ... Granted free agency (October 15, 1998). ... Re-signed by Royals organization (December 17, 1998). ... Granted free agency (October 8, 1999). ... Signed by San Diego Padres organization (November 22, 1999). ... Granted free agency (October 18, 2000).
STATISTICAL NOTES: Led American Association with .440 on-base percentage in 1994.

							BATTING							FIELDING		
Year Team (League)	Pos.	G	AB	R	H	2B	3B	HR	RBI	Avg.	BB	SO	SB	PO	A	E	Avg.
1991— Eugene (N'West)	OF-1B	19	64	16	21	2	0	6	21	.328	11	18	1	49	4	1	.981
— Memphis (Sou.)	OF-1B	36	128	15	28	4	1	0	18	.219	23	36	0	77	4	1	.988
1992— Baseball City (FSL)	1B	115	400	52	113	16	1	8	65	.283	46	101	0	879	44	13	.986
1993— Memphis (Sou.)	1B	117	413	62	119	25	2	15	66	.288	57	95	2	830	53	•17	.981
1994— Omaha (A.A.)	1B-DH	98	352	46	121	28	3	10	61	*.344	56	63	3	605	46	8	.988
1995— Kansas City (A.L.)	DH-1B	53	130	13	33	4	0	7	21	.254	8	25	0	51	3	1	.982
— Omaha (A.A.)	DH-1B-OF	59	229	33	64	14	2	12	42	.279	12	50	0	225	21	4	.984
1996— Kansas City (A.L.)	DH-1B-OF	85	257	29	62	15	1	8	40	.241	38	69	2	40	5	0	1.000
— Omaha (A.A.)	1B	36	132	26	37	7	0	9	31	.280	16	32	1	281	20	3	.990
1997— Kansas City (A.L.)	OF-DH-1B	51	130	11	31	6	0	5	18	.238	14	37	0	56	0	1	.982
— Omaha (A.A.)	DH-OF	13	42	5	9	1	0	3	9	.214	5	16	0	1	0	0	1.000

Year	Team (League)	Pos.	G	AB	R	H	2B	3B	HR	RBI	Avg.	BB	SO	SB	PO	A	E	Avg.
									BATTING							**FIELDING**		
1998—Kansas City (A.L.)	DH	3	7	0	1	0	0	0	0	.143	1	2	0	...	...	...	...
—Omaha (PCL)	1B-DH-3B	103	376	44	107	20	2	18	71	.285	39	68	0	738	56	8	.990
1999—Omaha (PCL)	DH-1B	122	447	70	142	33	0	28	98	.318	66	84	3	289	21	6	.981
—Kansas City (A.L.)	1B-DH	13	41	4	6	1	0	1	4	.146	2	9	0	65	7	0	1.000
2000—Las Vegas (PCL)■	1B	77	274	43	96	31	0	11	46	.350	27	59	2	492	46	5	.991
—San Diego (N.L.)	1B-OF	39	52	7	13	3	0	2	8	.250	10	9	0	78	7	3	.966
American League totals (5 years)		205	565	57	133	26	1	21	83	.235	63	142	2	212	15	2	.991
National League totals (1 year)		39	52	7	13	3	0	2	8	.250	10	9	0	78	7	3	.966
Major League totals (6 years)		244	617	64	146	29	1	23	91	.237	73	151	2	290	22	5	.984

VIZCAINO, JOSE   IF   ASTROS

PERSONAL: Born March 26, 1968, in San Cristobal, Dominican Republic. ... 6-1/180. ... Bats both, throws right. ... Full name: Jose Luis Pimental Vizcaino. ... Name pronounced VIS-ky-EE-no.

HIGH SCHOOL: Americo Tolentino (Palenque de San Cristobal, Dominican Republic).

TRANSACTIONS/CAREER NOTES: Signed as non-drafted free agent by Los Angeles Dodgers organization (February 18, 1986). ... Traded by Dodgers to Chicago Cubs for IF Greg Smith (December 14, 1990). ... On disabled list (April 20-May 6 and August 26-September 16, 1992). ... Traded by Cubs to New York Mets for P Anthony Young and P Ottis Smith (March 30, 1994). ... Traded by Mets with IF Jeff Kent to Cleveland Indians for 2B Carlos Baerga and IF Alvaro Espinoza (July 29, 1996). ... Traded by Indians with IF Jeff Kent, P Julian Tavarez and a player to be named later to San Francisco Giants for 3B Matt Williams and a player to be named later (November 13, 1996); Indians traded P Joe Roa to Giants for OF Trenidad Hubbard to complete deal (December 16, 1996). ... Granted free agency (October 29, 1997). ... Signed by Dodgers (December 8, 1997). ... On disabled list (June 22-September 9, 1998; and May 19-June 4, 1999). ... Traded by Dodgers to New York Yankees for IF/DH Jim Leyritz (June 20, 2000). ... Granted free agency (November 1, 2000). ... Signed by Houston Astros (November 20, 2000).

STATISTICAL NOTES: Led Gulf Coast League shortstops with 23 double plays in 1987. ... Led Pacific Coast League shortstops with 611 total chances and 82 double plays in 1989. ... Tied for N.L. lead in fielding percentage by shortstop with .984 and assists by shortstop with 411 in 1995.

Year	Team (League)	Pos.	G	AB	R	H	2B	3B	HR	RBI	Avg.	BB	SO	SB	PO	A	E	Avg.
									BATTING							**FIELDING**		
1987—GC Dodgers (GCL)	SS-1B	49	150	26	38	5	1	0	12	.253	22	24	8	73	107	13	.933
1988—Bakersfield (Calif.)	SS	122	433	77	126	11	4	0	38	.291	50	54	13	185	340	30	.946
1989—Albuquerque (PCL).....	SS	129	434	60	123	10	4	1	44	.283	33	41	16	*191	*390	*30	.951
—Los Angeles (N.L.)	SS	7	10	2	2	0	0	0	0	.200	0	1	0	6	9	2	.882
1990—Albuquerque (PCL).....	2B-SS	81	276	46	77	10	2	2	38	.279	30	33	13	141	229	14	.964
—Los Angeles (N.L.)	SS-2B	37	51	3	14	1	1	0	2	.275	4	8	1	23	27	2	.962
1991—Chicago (N.L.)■	3B-SS-2B	93	145	7	38	5	0	0	10	.262	5	18	2	49	118	7	.960
1992—Chicago (N.L.)	SS-3B-2B	86	285	25	64	10	4	1	17	.225	14	35	3	93	195	9	.970
1993—Chicago (N.L.)	SS-3B-2B	151	551	74	158	19	4	4	54	.287	46	71	12	217	410	17	.974
1994—New York (N.L.)■	SS	103	410	47	105	13	3	3	33	.256	33	62	1	136	291	13	.970
1995—New York (N.L.)	SS-2B	135	509	66	146	21	5	3	56	.287	35	76	8	189	‡411	10	‡.984
1996—New York (N.L.).........	2B	96	363	47	110	12	6	1	32	.303	28	58	9	179	259	6	.986
—Cleveland (A.L.)■.........	2B-SS-DH	48	179	23	51	5	2	0	13	.285	7	24	6	82	135	4	.982
1997—San Fran. (N.L.)■......	SS-2B	151	568	77	151	19	7	5	50	.266	48	87	8	206	450	16	.976
1998—Los Angeles (N.L.)■ ..	SS	67	237	30	62	9	0	3	29	.262	17	35	7	89	172	4	.985
1999—Los Angeles (N.L.)	SS-2B	94	266	27	67	9	0	1	29	.252	20	23	2	98	192	7	.976
2000—Los Angeles (N.L.) ...	S-3-2-D-1	40	93	9	19	2	1	0	4	.204	10	15	1	24	63	2	.978
—New York (A.L.)■ ...2B-3B-DH-SS		73	174	23	48	8	1	0	10	.276	12	28	5	88	127	2	.991
American League totals (2 years)		121	353	46	99	13	3	0	23	.280	19	52	11	170	262	6	.986
National League totals (12 years)		1060	3488	414	936	120	31	21	316	.268	260	489	54	1309	2597	95	.976
Major League totals (12 years)		1181	3841	460	1035	133	34	21	339	.269	279	541	65	1479	2859	101	.977

DIVISION SERIES RECORD

Year	Team (League)	Pos.	G	AB	R	H	2B	3B	HR	RBI	Avg.	BB	SO	SB	PO	A	E	Avg.
									BATTING							**FIELDING**		
1996—Cleveland (A.L.)..........	2B	3	12	1	4	2	0	0	1	.333	1	1	0	4	3	1	.875
1997—San Francisco (N.L.) ..	SS	3	11	1	2	1	0	0	0	.182	0	5	0	3	10	0	1.000
2000—New York (A.L.)..........	PR-2B	1	0	1	0	0	0	0	0	...	0	0	0	0	1	0	1.000
Division series totals (3 years)		7	23	3	6	3	0	0	1	.261	1	6	0	7	14	1	.955

CHAMPIONSHIP SERIES RECORD

Year	Team (League)	Pos.	G	AB	R	H	2B	3B	HR	RBI	Avg.	BB	SO	SB	PO	A	E	Avg.
									BATTING							**FIELDING**		
2000—New York (A.L.)..........	PR-2B	4	2	3	2	1	0	0	2	1.000	0	0	2	0	2	0	1.000

WORLD SERIES RECORD

NOTES: Member of World Series championship team (2000).

Year	Team (League)	Pos.	G	AB	R	H	2B	3B	HR	RBI	Avg.	BB	SO	SB	PO	A	E	Avg.
									BATTING							**FIELDING**		
2000—New York (A.L.)..........	2B	4	17	0	4	0	0	0	1	.235	0	5	0	9	6	0	1.000

VIZCAINO, LUIS   P   ATHLETICS

PERSONAL: Born June 1, 1977, in Bani, Dominican Republic. ... 5-11/169. ... Throws right, bats right. ... Full name: Luis Viczaino Arias.

TRANSACTIONS/CAREER NOTES: Signed as non-drafted free agent by Oakland Athletics organization (December 9, 1994).

Year	League	W	L	Pct.	ERA	G	GS	CG	ShO	Sv.	IP	H	R	ER	BB	SO
1995—Dominican Athletics (DSL).	10	2	.833	2.27	16	15	5	1	0	*115	93	41	29	29	89
1996—Arizona Athletics (Ariz.)......	6	3	.667	4.07	15	10	0	0	1	59²/₃	58	36	27	24	52
1997—Southern Oregon (N'West).	1	6	.143	7.93	22	5	0	0	0	47²/₃	62	51	42	27	42
—Modesto (Calif.)	0	3	.000	13.19	7	0	0	0	0	14¹/₃	24	24	21	13	15
1998—Modesto (Calif.)	6	3	.667	2.74	23	16	0	0	0	102	72	39	31	43	108
—Huntsville (Sou.)	3	2	.600	4.66	7	7	0	0	0	38²/₃	43	27	20	22	26

Year League	W	L	Pct.	ERA	G	GS	CG	ShO	Sv.	IP	H	R	ER	BB	SO
1999— Midland (Texas)	8	7	.533	5.85	25	19	0	0	0	104 2/3	120	74	68	48	88
— Vancouver (PCL)	0	1	.000	1.38	7	0	0	0	0	13	13	4	2	6	7
— Oakland (A.L.)	0	0	...	5.40	1	0	0	0	0	3 1/3	3	2	2	3	2
2000— Oakland (A.L.)	0	1	.000	7.45	12	0	0	0	0	19 1/3	25	17	16	11	18
— Sacramento (PCL)	6	2	.750	5.03	33	2	0	0	5	48 1/3	48	27	27	21	41
Major League totals (2 years)	0	1	.000	7.15	13	0	0	0	0	22 2/3	28	19	18	14	20

VIZQUEL, OMAR — SS — INDIANS

PERSONAL: Born April 24, 1967, in Caracas, Venezuela. ... 5-9/185. ... Bats both, throws right. ... Full name: Omar Enrique Vizquel. ... Name pronounced vis-KEL.

HIGH SCHOOL: Francisco Espejo (Caracas, Venezuela).

TRANSACTIONS/CAREER NOTES: Signed as non-drafted free agent by Seattle Mariners organization (April 1, 1984). ... On Seattle disabled list (April 7-May 13, 1990); included rehabilitation assignments to Calgary (May 3-7) and San Bernardino (May 8-12). ... On Seattle disabled list (April 13-May 11, 1992); included rehabilitation assignment to Calgary (May 5-11). ... Traded by Mariners to Cleveland Indians for SS Felix Fermin, 1B Reggie Jefferson and cash (December 20, 1993). ... On Cleveland disabled list (April 23-June 13, 1994); included rehabilitation assignment to Charlotte (June 6-13). ... On suspended list (September 17-18, 1998).

RECORDS: Shares major league career record for highest fielding percentage by shortstop (1,000 or more games)—.982; fewest errors by shortstop (150 or more games)—3 (2000); and most consecutive errorless games by shortstop—95 (September 26, 1999 through July 21, 2000).

HONORS: Won A.L. Gold Glove at shortstop (1993-2000).

STATISTICAL NOTES: Led Midwest League shortstops with .969 fielding percentage in 1986. ... Tied for A.L. lead in double plays by shortstop with 108 in 1993. ... Led A.L. with 16 sacrifice hits in 1997 and with 17 in 1999. ... Career major league grand slams: 4.

MISCELLANEOUS: Batted righthanded only (1984-88).

Year Team (League)	Pos.	G	AB	R	H	2B	3B	HR	RBI	Avg.	BB	SO	SB	PO	A	E	Avg.
1984— Butte (Pio.)	SS-2B	15	45	7	14	2	0	0	4	.311	3	8	2	13	29	5	.894
1985— Bellingham (N'West)	SS-2B	50	187	24	42	9	0	5	17	.225	12	27	4	85	175	19	.932
1986— Wausau (Midw.)	SS-2B	105	352	60	75	13	2	4	28	.213	64	56	19	153	328	16	†.968
1987— Salinas (Calif.)	SS-2B	114	407	61	107	12	8	0	38	.263	57	55	25	81	295	25	.938
1988— Vermont (East.)	SS	103	374	54	95	18	2	2	35	.254	42	44	30	173	268	19	*.959
— Calgary (PCL)	SS	33	107	10	24	2	3	1	12	.224	5	14	2	43	92	6	.957
1989— Calgary (PCL)	SS	7	28	3	6	2	0	0	3	.214	3	4	0	15	14	0	1.000
— Seattle (A.L.)	SS	143	387	45	85	7	3	1	20	.220	28	40	1	208	388	18	.971
1990— Calgary (PCL)	SS	48	150	18	35	6	2	0	8	.233	13	10	4	70	142	6	.972
— San Bern. (Calif.)	SS	6	28	5	7	0	0	0	3	.250	3	1	1	11	21	3	.914
— Seattle (A.L.)	SS	81	255	19	63	3	2	2	18	.247	18	22	4	103	239	7	.980
1991— Seattle (A.L.)	SS-2B	142	426	42	98	16	4	1	41	.230	45	37	7	224	422	13	.980
1992— Seattle (A.L.)	SS	136	483	49	142	20	4	0	21	.294	32	38	15	223	403	7	*.989
— Calgary (PCL)	SS	6	22	0	6	1	0	0	2	.273	1	3	0	14	21	1	.972
1993— Seattle (A.L.)	SS-DH	158	560	68	143	14	2	2	31	.255	50	71	12	245	475	15	.980
1994— Cleveland (A.L.)■	SS	69	286	39	78	10	1	1	33	.273	23	23	13	113	204	6	.981
— Charlotte (I.L.)	SS	7	26	3	7	1	0	0	1	.269	2	1	1	11	18	1	.967
1995— Cleveland (A.L.)	SS	136	542	87	144	28	0	6	56	.266	59	59	29	210	405	9	.986
1996— Cleveland (A.L.)	SS	151	542	98	161	36	1	9	64	.297	56	42	35	226	447	20	.971
1997— Cleveland (A.L.)	SS	153	565	89	158	23	6	5	49	.280	57	58	43	245	428	10	.985
1998— Cleveland (A.L.)	SS	151	576	86	166	30	6	2	50	.288	62	64	37	*273	442	5	*.993
1999— Cleveland (A.L.)	SS-OF	144	574	112	191	36	4	5	66	.333	65	50	42	221	396	15	.976
2000— Cleveland (A.L.)	SS	156	613	101	176	27	3	7	66	.287	87	72	22	231	414	3	*.995
Major League totals (12 years)		1620	5809	835	1605	250	36	41	515	.276	582	576	260	2522	4663	128	.982

DIVISION SERIES RECORD

RECORDS: Shares career records for most stolen bases—9.

Year Team (League)	Pos.	G	AB	R	H	2B	3B	HR	RBI	Avg.	BB	SO	SB	PO	A	E	Avg.
1995— Cleveland (A.L.)	SS	3	12	2	2	1	0	0	4	.167	2	2	1	4	11	0	1.000
1996— Cleveland (A.L.)	SS	4	14	4	6	1	0	0	2	.429	3	4	4	6	10	0	1.000
1997— Cleveland (A.L.)	SS	5	18	3	9	0	0	0	1	.500	2	1	4	12	14	0	1.000
1998— Cleveland (A.L.)	SS	4	15	1	1	0	0	0	0	.067	1	0	0	4	16	0	1.000
1999— Cleveland (A.L.)	SS	5	21	3	5	1	1	0	3	.238	2	3	0	7	9	0	1.000
Division series totals (5 years)		21	80	13	23	3	1	0	10	.288	10	10	9	33	60	0	1.000

CHAMPIONSHIP SERIES RECORD

Year Team (League)	Pos.	G	AB	R	H	2B	3B	HR	RBI	Avg.	BB	SO	SB	PO	A	E	Avg.
1995— Cleveland (A.L.)	SS	6	23	2	2	1	0	0	2	.087	5	2	3	9	21	0	1.000
1997— Cleveland (A.L.)	SS	6	25	1	1	0	0	0	0	.040	2	10	0	16	15	0	1.000
1998— Cleveland (A.L.)	SS	6	25	2	11	0	1	0	0	.440	1	3	4	11	26	1	.974
Championship series totals (3 years)		18	73	5	14	1	1	0	2	.192	8	15	7	36	62	1	.990

WORLD SERIES RECORD

RECORDS: Shares single-inning record for most stolen bases—2 (October 26, 1997).

Year Team (League)	Pos.	G	AB	R	H	2B	3B	HR	RBI	Avg.	BB	SO	SB	PO	A	E	Avg.
1995— Cleveland (A.L.)	SS	6	23	3	4	0	1	0	1	.174	3	5	1	12	22	0	1.000
1997— Cleveland (A.L.)	SS	7	30	5	7	2	0	0	1	.233	3	5	5	12	17	0	1.000
World Series totals (2 years)		13	53	8	11	2	1	0	2	.208	6	10	6	24	39	0	1.000

ALL-STAR GAME RECORD

Year League	Pos.	AB	R	H	2B	3B	HR	RBI	Avg.	BB	SO	SB	PO	A	E	Avg.
1998— American	SS	2	0	1	0	0	0	0	.500	0	0	0	1	1	0	1.000
1999— American	SS	1	0	0	0	0	0	0	.000	0	0	0	1	4	0	1.000
All-Star Game totals (2 years)		3	0	1	0	0	0	0	.333	0	0	0	2	5	0	1.000

V

PERSONAL: Born July 22, 1977, in Charlotte. ... 6-3/195. ... Throws right, bats right. ... Full name: Ryan Andrew Vogelsong.
HIGH SCHOOL: Octorara Area (Atglen, Pa.).
COLLEGE: Kutztown (Pa.).
TRANSACTIONS/CAREER NOTES: Selected by San Francisco Giants organization in fifth round of free agent draft (June 2, 1998).
STATISTICAL NOTES: Led Texas League with 13 hit batsmen and four balks in 2000.

Year League	W	L	Pct.	ERA	G	GS	CG	ShO	Sv.	IP	H	R	ER	BB	SO
1998— Salem-Kaizer (N'West)	6	1	.857	1.77	10	10	0	0	0	56	37	15	11	16	66
— San Jose (Calif.)................	0	0	...	7.58	4	4	0	0	0	19	23	16	16	4	26
1999— San Jose (Calif.)................	4	4	.500	2.45	13	13	0	0	0	69²/₃	37	26	19	27	86
— Shreveport (Texas)............	0	2	.000	7.31	6	6	0	0	0	28¹/₃	40	25	23	15	23
2000— Shreveport (Texas)............	6	10	.375	4.23	27	27	1	0	0	155¹/₃	153	82	73	69	*147
— San Francisco (N.L.)	0	0	...	0.00	4	0	0	0	0	6	4	0	0	2	6
Major League totals (1 year)........	0	0	...	0.00	4	0	0	0	0	6	4	0	0	2	6

PERSONAL: Born September 28, 1961, in Tucson, Ariz. ... 6-1/210. ... Throws left, bats left. ... Full name: Edward John Vosberg. ... Nephew of Don Vosberg, defensive end with New York Giants (1941).
HIGH SCHOOL: Salpointe (Tucson, Ariz.).
COLLEGE: Arizona.
TRANSACTIONS/CAREER NOTES: Selected by St. Louis Cardinals organization in third round of free-agent draft (June 5, 1979); did not sign. ... Selected by Toronto Blue Jays organization in 11th round of free-agent draft (June 7, 1982); did not sign. ... Selected by San Diego Padres organization in third round of free-agent draft (June 6, 1983). ... Traded by Padres to Houston Astros for C Dan Walters (December 13, 1988). ... Traded by Astros to Los Angeles Dodgers (August 1, 1989), completing deal in which Dodgers traded OF Javier Ortiz to Astros for a player to be named later (July 22, 1989). ... Granted free agency (October 15, 1989). ... Signed by San Francisco Giants organization (March 13, 1990). ... Granted free agency (October 15, 1990). ... Signed by California Angels organization (December 4, 1990). ... Released by Angels (May 11, 1991). ... Signed by Seattle Mariners organization (May 20, 1991). ... Released by Mariners (July 10, 1991). ... Pitched in Italy (1992). ... Signed by Chicago Cubs organization (March 17, 1993). ... Granted free agency (October 15, 1993). ... Signed by Oakland Athletics organization (December 3, 1993). ... Granted free agency (October 15, 1994). ... Re-signed by A's organization (November 11, 1994). ... Selected by Los Angeles Dodgers from A's organization in Rule 5 major league draft (December 5, 1994). ... Granted free agency (April 24, 1995). ... Signed by Texas Rangers organization (April 26, 1995). ... Traded by Rangers to Florida Marlins for P Rick Helling (August 12, 1997). ... Traded by Marlins to Padres for P Chris Clark (November 20, 1997). ... On disabled list (March 25, 1998-entire season). ... On San Diego disabled list (March 30-April 24, 1999); included rehabilitation assignment to Las Vegas (April 8-24). ... Released by Padres (June 5, 1999). ... Signed by Arizona Diamondbacks organization (June 10, 1999). ... Granted free agency (October 15, 1999). ... Signed by Colorado Rockies organization (November 17, 1999). ... Traded by Rockies to Philadelphia Phillies for a player to be named later (June 28, 2000). ... Granted free agency (October 12, 2000). ... Re-signed by Phillies organization (December 20, 2000).
STATISTICAL NOTES: Led Pacific Coast League with 11 balks in 1987.

Year League	W	L	Pct.	ERA	G	GS	CG	ShO	Sv.	IP	H	R	ER	BB	SO
1983— Reno (Calif.).....................	6	6	.500	3.87	15	15	3	0	0	97²/₃	111	61	42	39	70
— Beaumont (Texas)	1	0	1.000	0.00	1	1	1	1	0	7	2	0	0	2	1
1984— Beaumont (Texas)	13	•11	.542	3.43	27	•27	5	2	0	183²/₃	196	87	70	74	100
1985— Beaumont (Texas)	9	11	.450	3.91	27	•27	2	1	0	175	178	92	76	69	124
1986— Las Vegas (PCL)	7	8	.467	4.72	25	24	2	1	0	129²/₃	136	80	68	64	93
— San Diego (N.L.)	0	1	.000	6.59	5	3	0	0	0	13²/₃	17	11	10	9	8
1987— Las Vegas (PCL)	9	8	.529	3.92	34	24	3	0	0	167²/₃	154	88	73	97	99
1988— Las Vegas (PCL)	11	7	.611	4.15	45	11	1	0	2	128	137	67	59	56	75
1989— Tucson (PCL)■	4	7	.364	6.78	23	14	0	0	1	87²/₃	122	70	66	49	68
— Albuquerque (PCL)■.........	2	1	.667	2.70	12	0	0	0	0	20	17	8	6	5	18
1990— Phoenix (PCL)■	1	3	.250	2.65	24	0	0	0	3	34	36	14	10	16	28
— San Francisco (N.L.)	1	1	.500	5.55	18	0	0	0	0	24¹/₃	21	16	15	12	12
1991— Edmonton (PCL)■.............	0	1	.000	6.28	12	0	0	0	0	14¹/₃	19	10	10	5	14
— Calgary (PCL)■	0	2	.000	7.23	16	0	0	0	2	23²/₃	38	26	19	12	15
1992—							Italian statistics unavailable.								
1993— Iowa (A.A.)■....................	5	1	.833	3.57	52	0	0	0	3	63	67	32	25	22	64
1994— Tacoma (PCL)■	4	2	.667	3.35	26	1	0	0	3	53²/₃	39	21	20	19	54
— Oakland (A.L.)	0	2	.000	3.95	16	0	0	0	0	13²/₃	16	7	6	5	12
1995— Oklahoma City (A.A.)■.......	1	0	1.000	0.00	1	0	0	0	0	1²/₃	1	0	0	1	2
— Texas (A.L.)	5	5	.500	3.00	44	0	0	0	4	36	32	15	12	16	33
1996— Texas (A.L.)	1	1	.500	3.27	52	0	0	0	8	44	51	17	16	21	32
1997— Texas (A.L.)	1	2	.333	4.61	42	0	0	0	1	41	44	23	21	15	29
— Florida (N.L.)■	1	1	.500	3.75	17	0	0	0	1	12	15	7	5	6	8
1998— San Diego (N.L.)■							Did not play.								
1999— Las Vegas (PCL)	0	0	...	1.08	8	0	0	0	1	8¹/₃	3	1	1	4	12
— San Diego (N.L.)	0	0	...	9.72	15	0	0	0	0	8¹/₃	16	11	9	3	6
— Tucson (PCL)■	1	0	1.000	0.78	26	0	0	0	7	34²/₃	26	5	3	8	30
— Arizona (N.L.)	0	1	.000	3.38	4	0	0	0	0	2²/₃	6	1	1	0	2
2000— Colorado Springs (PCL)■...	1	2	.333	6.86	29	3	0	0	2	42	59	41	32	20	37
— Scranton/W.B. (I.L.)■	0	0	...	0.00	1	0	0	0	0	2	0	0	0	0	0
— Philadelphia (N.L.)............	1	1	.500	4.13	31	0	0	0	0	24	21	11	11	18	23
A.L. totals (4 years)	7	10	.412	3.68	154	0	0	0	12	134²/₃	143	62	55	57	109
N.L. totals (5 years)	3	5	.375	5.40	90	3	0	0	1	85	96	57	51	48	59
Major League totals (8 years)........	10	15	.400	4.34	244	3	0	0	13	219²/₃	239	119	106	105	168

DIVISION SERIES RECORD

Year League	W	L	Pct.	ERA	G	GS	CG	ShO	Sv.	IP	H	R	ER	BB	SO
1996— Texas (A.L.)	0	0	...	...	1	0	0	0	0	1	0	0	0	0	0

CHAMPIONSHIP SERIES RECORD

Year League	W	L	Pct.	ERA	G	GS	CG	ShO	Sv.	IP	H	R	ER	BB	SO
1997— Florida (N.L.)	0	0	...	0.00	2	0	0	0	0	2²/₃	2	0	0	1	3

WORLD SERIES RECORD

NOTES: Member of World Series championship team (1997).

Year League	W	L	Pct.	ERA	G	GS	CG	ShO	Sv.	IP	H	R	ER	BB	SO
1997— Florida (N.L.)	0	0	...	6.00	2	0	0	0	0	3	3	2	2	3	2

WAGNER, BILLY   P   ASTROS

PERSONAL: Born July 25, 1971, in Tannersville, Va. ... 5-11/180. ... Throws left, bats left. ... Full name: William Edward Wagner.
HIGH SCHOOL: Tazewell (Va.).
COLLEGE: Ferrum (Va.).
TRANSACTIONS/CAREER NOTES: Selected by Houston Astros organization in first round (12th pick overall) of free-agent draft (June 3, 1993). ... On Houston disabled list (August 23-September 7, 1996). ... On Houston disabled list (July 16-August 7, 1998); included rehabilitation assignment to Jackson (August 1-7). ... On disabled list (June 21, 2000-remainder of season).

Year League	W	L	Pct.	ERA	G	GS	CG	ShO	Sv.	IP	H	R	ER	BB	SO
1993— Auburn (NY-Penn)	1	3	.250	4.08	7	7	0	0	0	28 2/3	25	19	13	25	31
1994— Quad City (Midw.)	8	9	.471	3.29	26	26	2	0	0	153	99	71	56	*91	*204
1995— Jackson (Texas)	2	2	.500	2.57	12	12	0	0	0	70	49	25	20	36	77
— Tucson (PCL)	5	3	.625	3.18	13	13	0	0	0	76 1/3	70	28	27	32	80
— Houston (N.L.)	0	0	...	0.00	1	0	0	0	0	1/3	0	0	0	0	0
1996— Tucson (PCL)	6	2	.750	3.28	12	12	1	1	0	74	62	32	27	33	86
— Houston (N.L.)	2	2	.500	2.44	37	0	0	0	9	51 2/3	28	16	14	30	67
1997— Houston (N.L.)	7	8	.467	2.85	62	0	0	0	23	66 1/3	49	23	21	30	106
1998— Houston (N.L.)	4	3	.571	2.70	58	0	0	0	30	60	46	19	18	25	97
— Jackson (Texas)	0	0	...	0.00	3	1	0	0	0	3	1	0	0	0	7
1999— Houston (N.L.)	4	1	.800	1.57	66	0	0	0	39	74 2/3	35	14	13	23	124
2000— Houston (N.L.)	2	4	.333	6.18	28	0	0	0	6	27 2/3	28	19	19	18	28
Major League totals (6 years)	19	18	.514	2.73	252	0	0	0	107	280 2/3	186	91	85	126	422

DIVISION SERIES RECORD

Year League	W	L	Pct.	ERA	G	GS	CG	ShO	Sv.	IP	H	R	ER	BB	SO
1997— Houston (N.L.)	0	0	...	18.00	1	0	0	0	0	1	3	2	2	0	2
1998— Houston (N.L.)	1	0	1.000	18.00	1	0	0	0	0	1	4	2	2	0	1
1999— Houston (N.L.)	0	0	...	0.00	1	0	0	0	0	1	0	0	0	0	1
Division series totals (3 years)	1	0	1.000	12.00	3	0	0	0	0	3	7	4	4	0	4

ALL-STAR GAME RECORD

Year League	W	L	Pct.	ERA	GS	CG	ShO	Sv.	IP	H	R	ER	BB	SO
1999— National	0	0	...	0.00	0	0	0	0	2/3	0	0	0	0	2

WAINHOUSE, DAVE   P   CUBS

PERSONAL: Born November 7, 1967, in Toronto. ... 6-2/196. ... Throws right, bats left. ... Full name: David Paul Wainhouse.
HIGH SCHOOL: Mercer Island (Wash.).
COLLEGE: Washington State.
TRANSACTIONS/CAREER NOTES: Selected by Montreal Expos organization in first round (19th pick overall) of free-agent draft (June 1, 1988). ... On Harrisburg disabled list (April 25-May 3, 1991). ... On disabled list (August 13-September 8, 1992). ... Traded by Expos with P Kevin Foster to Seattle Mariners for IF Frank Bolick and a player to be named later (November 20, 1992); Expos acquired C Miah Bradbury to complete deal (December 8, 1992). ... On Calgary disabled list (April 23-August 3, 1993). ... Released by Mariners (March 29, 1994). ... Signed by Toronto Blue Jays organization (December 20, 1994). ... Released by Blue Jays (June 5, 1995). ... Signed by Florida Marlins organization (June 8, 1995). ... Granted free agency (October 16, 1995). ... Signed by Pittsburgh Pirates organization (January 28, 1996). ... Granted free agency (October 15, 1997). ... Signed by Colorado Rockies organization (November 14, 1997). ... Granted free agency (October 12, 1999). ... Signed by St. Louis Cardinals organization (January 19, 2000). ... On St. Louis disabled list (April 28-July 26, 2000); included rehabilitation assignment to Memphis (June 26-July 25). ... Granted free agency (October 3, 2000). ... Signed by Chicago Cubs organization (December 13, 2000).
MISCELLANEOUS: Member of 1988 Canadian Olympic baseball team.

Year League	W	L	Pct.	ERA	G	GS	CG	ShO	Sv.	IP	H	R	ER	BB	SO
1989— West Palm Beach (FSL)	1	5	.167	4.07	13	13	0	0	0	66 1/3	75	35	30	19	26
1990— West Palm Beach (FSL)	6	3	.667	2.11	12	12	2	1	0	76 2/3	68	28	18	34	58
— Jacksonville (Sou.)	7	7	.500	4.33	17	16	2	0	0	95 2/3	97	59	46	47	59
1991— Harrisburg (East.)	2	2	.500	2.60	33	0	0	0	11	52	49	17	15	17	46
— Indianapolis (A.A.)	2	0	1.000	4.08	14	0	0	0	1	28 2/3	28	14	13	15	13
— Montreal (N.L.)	0	1	.000	6.75	2	0	0	0	0	2 2/3	2	2	2	4	1
1992— Indianapolis (A.A.)	5	4	.556	4.11	44	0	0	0	21	46	48	22	21	24	37
1993— Seattle (A.L.)■	0	0	...	27.00	3	0	0	0	0	2 1/3	7	7	7	5	2
— Calgary (PCL)	0	1	.000	4.02	13	0	0	0	5	15 2/3	10	7	7	7	7
1994—						Out of organized baseball.									
1995— Syracuse (I.L.)■	3	2	.600	3.70	26	0	0	0	5	24 1/3	29	13	10	11	18
— Portland (East.)■	2	1	.667	7.20	17	0	0	0	0	25	39	22	20	8	16
— Charlotte (I.L.)	0	0	...	9.82	4	0	0	0	0	3 2/3	6	6	4	4	2
1996— Carolina (Sou.)■	5	3	.625	3.16	45	0	0	0	25	51 1/3	43	22	18	31	34
— Pittsburgh (N.L.)	1	0	1.000	5.70	17	0	0	0	0	23 2/3	22	16	15	10	16
1997— Pittsburgh (N.L.)	0	1	.000	8.04	25	0	0	0	0	28	34	28	25	17	21
— Calgary (PCL)	2	0	1.000	5.92	25	0	0	0	1	38	46	25	25	13	24
1998— Colorado Springs (PCL)■	2	3	.400	3.60	38	0	0	0	4	50	47	25	20	23	44
— Colorado (N.L.)	1	0	1.000	4.91	10	0	0	0	0	11	15	6	6	5	3
1999— Colorado Springs (PCL)	1	3	.250	3.19	38	0	0	0	*22	42 1/3	42	19	15	7	42
— Colorado (N.L.)	0	0	...	6.91	19	0	0	0	0	28 2/3	37	22	22	16	18
2000— St. Louis (N.L.)■	0	1	.000	9.35	9	0	0	0	0	8 2/3	13	10	9	4	5
— Memphis (PCL)	4	4	.500	6.28	20	6	0	0	0	43	55	32	30	20	20
A.L. totals (1 year)	0	0	...	27.00	3	0	0	0	0	2 1/3	7	7	7	5	2
N.L. totals (6 years)	2	3	.400	6.93	82	0	0	0	0	102 2/3	123	84	79	56	64
Major League totals (7 years)	2	3	.400	7.37	85	0	0	0	0	105	130	91	86	61	66

W

WAKEFIELD, TIM   P   RED SOX

PERSONAL: Born August 2, 1966, in Melbourne, Fla. ... 6-2/210. ... Throws right, bats right. ... Full name: Timothy Stephen Wakefield.
HIGH SCHOOL: Eau Gallie (Melbourne, Fla.).
COLLEGE: Florida Tech.
TRANSACTIONS/CAREER NOTES: Selected by Pittsburgh Pirates organization in eighth round of free-agent draft (June 1, 1988). ... Released by Pirates (April 20, 1995). ... Signed by Boston Red Sox organization (April 26, 1995). ... On disabled list (April 15-May 6, 1997). ... Granted free agency (November 1, 2000). ... Re-signed by Red Sox (December 7, 2000).
RECORDS: Shares major league single-inning record for most strikeouts—4 (August 10, 1999, ninth inning).
HONORS: Named N.L. Rookie Pitcher of the Year by THE SPORTING NEWS (1992). ... Named A.L. Comeback Player of the Year by THE SPORTING NEWS (1995).
STATISTICAL NOTES: Led Carolina League with 24 home runs allowed in 1990. ... Led American Association with 27 home runs allowed and 23 hit batsmen in 1994. ... Led A.L. with 16 hit batsmen in 1997.
MISCELLANEOUS: Appeared in one game as pinch runner with Pittsburgh (1992). ... Had a sacrifice hit in only appearance as pinch hitter (1998). ... Had a sacrifice hit in only appearance as pinch hitter (2000).

Year League	W	L	Pct.	ERA	G	GS	CG	ShO	Sv.	IP	H	R	ER	BB	SO
1989— Welland (NY-Penn)	1	1	.500	3.40	36	1	0	0	2	39 2/3	30	17	15	21	42
1990— Salem (Caro.)	10	•14	.417	4.73	28	•28	2	0	0	*190 1/3	*187	109	*100	*85	127
1991— Carolina (Sou.)	15	8	.652	2.90	26	25	•8	1	0	183	155	68	59	51	120
— Buffalo (A.A.)	0	1	.000	11.57	1	1	0	0	0	4 2/3	8	6	6	1	4
1992— Buffalo (A.A.)	10	3	.769	3.06	20	20	*6	1	0	135 1/3	122	52	46	51	71
— Pittsburgh (N.L.)	8	1	.889	2.15	13	13	4	1	0	92	76	26	22	35	51
1993— Pittsburgh (N.L.)	6	11	.353	5.61	24	20	3	2	0	128 1/3	145	83	80	75	59
— Carolina (Sou.)	3	5	.375	6.99	9	9	1	0	0	56 2/3	68	48	44	22	36
1994— Buffalo (A.A.)	5	*15	.250	5.84	30	•29	4	1	0	175 2/3	*197	*127	*114	*98	83
1995— Pawtucket (I.L.)■	2	1	.667	2.52	4	4	0	0	0	25	23	10	7	9	14
— Boston (A.L.)	16	8	.667	2.95	27	27	6	1	0	195 1/3	163	76	64	68	119
1996— Boston (A.L.)	14	13	.519	5.14	32	32	6	0	0	211 2/3	238	*151	121	90	140
1997— Boston (A.L.)	12	•15	.444	4.25	35	29	4	2	0	201 1/3	193	109	95	87	151
1998— Boston (A.L.)	17	8	.680	4.58	36	33	2	0	0	216	211	123	110	79	146
1999— Boston (A.L.)	6	11	.353	5.08	49	17	0	0	15	140	146	93	79	72	104
2000— Boston (A.L.)	6	10	.375	5.48	51	17	0	0	0	159 1/3	170	107	97	65	102
A.L. totals (6 years)	71	65	.522	4.53	230	155	18	3	15	1123 2/3	1121	659	566	461	762
N.L. totals (2 years)	14	12	.538	4.17	37	33	7	3	0	220 1/3	221	109	102	110	110
Major League totals (8 years)	85	77	.525	4.47	267	188	25	6	15	1344	1342	768	668	571	872

DIVISION SERIES RECORD

Year League	W	L	Pct.	ERA	G	GS	CG	ShO	Sv.	IP	H	R	ER	BB	SO
1995— Boston (A.L.)	0	1	.000	11.81	1	1	0	0	0	5 1/3	5	7	7	5	4
1998— Boston (A.L.)	0	1	.000	33.75	1	1	0	0	0	1 1/3	3	5	5	2	1
1999— Boston (A.L.)	0	0	...	13.50	2	0	0	0	0	2	3	3	3	4	4
Division series totals (3 years)	0	2	.000	15.58	4	2	0	0	0	8 2/3	11	15	15	11	9

CHAMPIONSHIP SERIES RECORD

RECORDS: Shares single-series record for most complete games—2 (1992). ... Shares N.L. career record for most complete games—2.

Year League	W	L	Pct.	ERA	G	GS	CG	ShO	Sv.	IP	H	R	ER	BB	SO
1992— Pittsburgh (N.L.)	2	0	1.000	3.00	2	2	2	0	0	18	14	6	6	5	7
1999— Boston (A.L.)							Did not play.								

RECORD AS POSITION PLAYER

			BATTING								FIELDING			
Year Team (League)	Pos.	G	AB	R	H	2B	3B	HR	RBI	Avg.	BB	SO	SB	PO	A	E	Avg.
1988— Watertown (NY-Penn)	1B	54	159	24	30	6	2	3	20	.189	25	57	3	377	25	8	.980
1989— Augusta (S.Atl.)	3B-1B	11	34	5	8	2	1	0	5	.235	1	14	1	27	6	3	.917
— Welland (NY-Penn)	3B-2B-1B	36	63	7	13	4	0	1	3	.206	3	21	1	26	31	8	.877

WAKELAND, CHRIS   OF   TIGERS

PERSONAL: Born June 15, 1974, in Huntington Beach, Calif. ... 6-0/185. ... Bats left, throws left. ... Full name: Christopher Robert Wakeland.
HIGH SCHOOL: St. Helens (Ore.).
COLLEGE: Oregon State.
TRANSACTIONS/CAREER NOTES: Selected by Detroit Tigers organization in 15th round of free-agent draft (June 4, 1996). ... On Jacksonville disabled list (June 6-August 26, 1999).

			BATTING								FIELDING			
Year Team (League)	Pos.	G	AB	R	H	2B	3B	HR	RBI	Avg.	BB	SO	SB	PO	A	E	Avg.
1996— Jamestown (NY-P)	OF	70	220	38	68	14	5	10	49	.309	43	83	8	79	9	2	.978
1997— W. Mich. (Midw.)	OF	111	414	64	118	38	2	7	75	.285	43	120	20	169	7	5	.972
1998— Lakeland (FSL)	OF	131	487	82	147	26	5	18	89	.302	66	111	19	194	•17	9	.959
1999— Jacksonville (Sou.)	OF	55	212	42	68	16	3	13	36	.321	35	53	6	97	4	6	.944
— GC Tigers (GCL)	OF	4	14	2	1	0	0	0	1	.071	0	4	0	6	0	0	1.000
— Lakeland (FSL)	OF	4	17	3	7	1	0	0	7	.412	0	0	1	4	0	0	1.000
2000— Toledo (I.L.)	OF	141	492	65	133	25	2	28	76	.270	60	*148	4	217	10	8	.966

WALBECK, MATT   C

PERSONAL: Born October 2, 1969, in Sacramento. ... 5-11/188. ... Bats both, throws right. ... Full name: Matthew Lovick Walbeck.
HIGH SCHOOL: Sacramento High.

W

TRANSACTIONS/CAREER NOTES: Selected by Chicago Cubs organization in eighth round of free-agent draft (June 2, 1987). ... On Winston-Salem disabled list (April 12-July 11, 1990). ... On Charleston, W.Va. disabled list (September 5, 1992-remainder of season). ... Traded by Cubs with P Dave Stevens to Minnesota Twins for P Willie Banks (November 24, 1993). ... On Minnesota disabled list (March 31-June 17, 1996); included rehabilitation assignments to Fort Myers (May 31-June 11) and New Britain (June 12-17). ... Traded by Twins to Detroit Tigers for P Brent Stentz (December 11, 1996). ... On Detroit disabled list (April 19-July 9, 1997); included rehabilitation assignments to Lakeland (June 12-15) and Toledo (June 16-July 9). ... Traded by Tigers with 3B Phil Nevin to Anaheim Angels for P Nick Skuse (November 20, 1997). ... On disabled list (August 17-September 1, 2000). ... Granted free agency (November 1, 2000).
STATISTICAL NOTES: Tied for Carolina League lead with 10 sacrifice flies in 1991. ... Led American Association catchers with 561 total chances and tied for lead with nine double plays in 1993. ... Career major league grand slams: 2.

MISCELLANEOUS: Batted righthanded only (1987-89).

Year	Team (League)	Pos.	G	AB	R	H	2B	3B	HR	RBI	Avg.	BB	SO	SB	PO	A	E	Avg.
							BATTING									FIELDING		
1987—Wytheville (Appl.)		C	51	169	24	53	9	3	1	28	.314	22	39	0	293	22	1	*.997
1988—Char., W.Va. (S.Atl.)		C	104	312	28	68	9	0	2	24	.218	30	44	7	549	68	14	.978
1989—Peoria (Midw.)		C	94	341	38	86	19	0	4	47	.252	20	47	5	605	72	11	.984
1990—Peoria (Midw.)		C	25	66	2	15	1	0	0	5	.227	5	7	1	137	16	2	.987
1991—Win.-Salem (Caro.)		C	91	260	25	70	11	0	3	41	.269	20	23	3	473	64	12	.978
1992—Charlotte (Sou.)		C-1B	105	385	48	116	22	1	7	42	.301	33	56	0	552	80	10	.984
1993—Chicago (N.L.)		C	11	30	2	6	2	0	1	6	.200	1	6	0	49	2	0	1.000
— Iowa (A.A.)		C	87	331	31	93	18	2	6	43	.281	18	47	1	496	*64	1	*.998
1994—Minnesota (A.L.)■		C-DH	97	338	31	69	12	0	5	35	.204	17	37	1	496	45	4	.993
1995—Minnesota (A.L.)		C	115	393	40	101	18	1	1	44	.257	25	71	3	604	35	6	.991
1996—Fort Myers (FSL)		C-DH	9	33	4	9	1	1	0	9	.273	4	2	0	46	6	0	1.000
— New Britain (East.)		DH-C	7	24	1	5	0	0	0	0	.208	1	1	0	11	2	0	1.000
— Minnesota (A.L.)		C	63	215	25	48	10	0	2	24	.223	9	34	3	326	19	2	.994
1997—Detroit (A.L.)■		C	47	137	18	38	3	0	3	10	.277	12	19	3	240	15	3	.988
— Lakeland (FSL)		C-DH	4	10	4	5	1	0	0	3	.500	4	1	0	14	0	1	.933
— Toledo (I.L.)		C-DH	17	59	6	18	2	1	1	8	.305	4	15	0	55	9	3	.955
1998—Anaheim (A.L.)■		C-DH	108	338	41	87	15	2	6	46	.257	30	68	1	682	46	7	.990
1999—Anaheim (A.L.)		C-DH	107	288	26	69	8	1	3	22	.240	26	46	2	407	46	5	.989
2000—Anaheim (A.L.)		C-1B-DH	47	146	17	29	5	0	6	12	.199	7	22	0	201	16	2	.991
American League totals (7 years)			584	1855	198	441	71	4	26	193	.238	126	297	13	2956	222	29	.991
National League totals (1 year)			11	30	2	6	2	0	1	6	.200	1	6	0	49	2	0	1.000
Major League totals (8 years)			595	1885	200	447	73	4	27	199	.237	127	303	13	3005	224	29	.991

WALKER, KEVIN　　　　P　　　　PADRES

PERSONAL: Born September 20, 1976, in Irvin, Texas. ... 6-4/190. ... Throws left, bats left. ... Full name: Kevin Michael Walker.
HIGH SCHOOL: Grand Prairie (Texas).
TRANSACTIONS/CAREER NOTES: Selected by San Diego Padres organization in sixth round of free-agent draft (June 1, 1995). ... On Mobile disabled list (April 8-24, 1999). ... On Rancho Cucamonga disabled list (June 19-July 30, 1999).

Year	League	W	L	Pct.	ERA	G	GS	CG	ShO	Sv.	IP	H	R	ER	BB	SO
1995—Arizona Padres (Ariz.)		5	5	.500	3.01	13	12	0	0	0	71 2/3	74	34	24	12	69
1996—Idaho Falls (Pio.)		1	0	1.000	3.00	1	1	0	0	0	6	4	3	2	2	4
— Clinton (Midw.)		4	6	.400	4.74	13	13	0	0	0	76	80	46	40	33	43
1997—Clinton (Midw.)		6	10	.375	4.88	19	19	3	1	0	110 2/3	133	80	60	37	80
1998—Clinton (Midw.)		2	0	1.000	1.23	2	2	0	0	0	14 2/3	11	2	2	7	10
— Rancho Cuca. (Calif.)		11	7	.611	4.15	22	22	0	0	0	121 1/3	122	62	56	48	94
1999—Rancho Cuca. (Calif.)		1	1	.500	3.46	27	1	0	0	4	39	35	19	15	19	35
2000—Mobile (Sou.)		0	1	.000	2.25	4	0	0	0	0	4	1	1	1	1	6
— San Diego (N.L.)		7	1	.875	4.18	70	0	0	0	0	66 2/3	49	35	31	38	56
Major League totals (1 year)		7	1	.875	4.18	70	0	0	0	0	66 2/3	49	35	31	38	56

WALKER, LARRY　　　　OF　　　　ROCKIES

PERSONAL: Born December 1, 1966, in Maple Ridge, B.C. ... 6-3/237. ... Bats left, throws right. ... Full name: Larry Kenneth Robert Walker.
HIGH SCHOOL: Maple Ridge (B.C.) Senior Secondary School.
TRANSACTIONS/CAREER NOTES: Signed as non-drafted free agent by Montreal Expos organization (November 14, 1984). ... On disabled list (April 4, 1988-entire season; June 28-July 13, 1991; and May 26-June 10, 1993). ... On suspended list (June 24-28, 1994). ... Granted free agency (October 24, 1994). ... Signed by Colorado Rockies (April 8, 1995). ... On Colorado disabled list (June 10-August 15, 1996); included rehabilitation assignments to Salem (August 6-9) and Colorado Springs (August 9-15). ... On disabled list (June 18-July 3, 1998; March 29-April 14, 1999; May 11-June 9 and August 20, 2000-remainder of season).

RECORDS: Shares major league record for most extra-base hits in two consecutive games (May 21-22, 1996; 2 doubles, 3 triples and 1 home run). ... Holds N.L. single-season records for most consecutive long hits—6 (May 21-22, 1996; 2 doubles, 3 triples and 1 home run); and highest slugging average by a lefthander (100 or more games)—.720 (1997).
HONORS: Named outfielder on THE SPORTING NEWS N.L. All-Star team (1992, 1997 and 1999). ... Won N.L. Gold Glove as outfielder (1992-93 and 1997-99). ... Named outfielder on THE SPORTING NEWS N.L. Silver Slugger team (1992, 1997 and 1999). ... Named N.L. Most Valuable Player by Baseball Writers' Association of America (1997).
STATISTICAL NOTES: Hit three home runs in one game (April 5, 1997 and April 28, 1999). ... Led N.L. with 409 total bases in 1997. ... Led N.L. with .452 on-base percentage in 1997. ... Led N.L. in slugging percentage with .720 in 1997. ... Led N.L. outfielders in double plays with four in 1997 and tied for lead with four in 2000. ... Had 20-game hitting streak (May 4-25, 1998). ... Had 21-game hitting streak (April 25-May 21, 1999). ... Had 18-game hitting streak (June 14-July 3, 1999). ... Led N.L. with a .710 slugging percentage and a .458 on-base percentage in 1999. ... Career major league grand slams: 4.
MISCELLANEOUS: Holds Colorado Rockies all-time record for highest career batting average (.339).

Year	Team (League)	Pos.	G	AB	R	H	2B	3B	HR	RBI	Avg.	BB	SO	SB	PO	A	E	Avg.
1985—Utica (NY-Penn)	1B-3B	62	215	24	48	8	2	2	26	.223	18	57	12	354	62	8	.981	
1986—Burlington (Midw.)	OF-3B	95	332	67	96	12	6	29	74	.289	46	112	16	106	51	10	.940	
—W.P. Beach (FSL)	OF	38	113	20	32	7	5	4	16	.283	26	32	2	44	5	0	1.000	
1987—Jacksonville (Sou.)	OF	128	474	91	136	25	7	26	83	.287	67	120	24	263	9	9	.968	
1988—Montreal (N.L.)					Did not play.													
1989—Indianapolis (A.A.)	OF	114	385	68	104	18	2	12	59	.270	50	87	36	241	*18	*11	.959	
—Montreal (N.L.)	OF	20	47	4	8	0	0	0	4	.170	5	13	1	19	2	0	1.000	
1990—Montreal (N.L.)	OF	133	419	59	101	18	3	19	51	.241	49	112	21	249	12	4	.985	
1991—Montreal (N.L.)	OF-1B	137	487	59	141	30	2	16	64	.290	42	102	14	536	36	6	.990	
1992—Montreal (N.L.)	OF	143	528	85	159	31	4	23	93	.301	41	97	18	269	16	2	.993	
1993—Montreal (N.L.)	OF-1B	138	490	85	130	24	5	22	86	.265	80	76	29	316	16	6	.982	
1994—Montreal (N.L.)	OF-1B	103	395	76	127	44	2	19	86	.322	47	74	15	423	29	9	.980	
1995—Colorado (N.L.)■	OF	131	494	96	151	31	5	36	101	.306	49	72	16	225	13	3	.988	
1996—Colorado (N.L.)	OF	83	272	58	75	18	4	18	58	.276	20	58	18	153	4	1	.994	
—Salem (Caro.)	DH	2	8	3	4	3	0	1	1	.500	0	1	0	...	...	...	...	
—Colo. Springs (PCL)	OF	3	11	2	4	0	0	2	8	.364	1	4	0	6	2	0	1.000	
1997—Colorado (N.L.)	OF-1B-DH	153	568	143	208	46	4	*49	130	.366	78	90	33	254	14	2	.993	
1998—Colorado (N.L.)	O-DH-2-3	130	454	113	165	46	3	23	67	*.363	64	61	14	236	8	4	.984	
1999—Colorado (N.L.)	OF-DH	127	438	108	166	26	4	37	115	*.379	57	52	11	204	13	4	.982	
2000—Colorado (N.L.)	OF-DH	87	314	64	97	21	7	9	51	.309	46	40	5	161	11	1	.994	
Major League totals (12 years)			1385	4906	950	1528	335	43	271	906	.311	578	847	195	3045	174	42	.987

DIVISION SERIES RECORD

Year	Team (League)	Pos.	G	AB	R	H	2B	3B	HR	RBI	Avg.	BB	SO	SB	PO	A	E	Avg.
1995—Colorado (N.L.)	OF	4	14	3	3	0	0	1	3	.214	3	4	1	3	0	0	1.000	

ALL-STAR GAME RECORD

Year	League	Pos.	AB	R	H	2B	3B	HR	RBI	Avg.	BB	SO	SB	PO	A	E	Avg.
1992—National	PH	1	0	1	0	0	0	0	1.000	0	0	0	...	...	...	...
1997—National	OF	1	0	0	0	0	0	0	.000	1	0	0	0	0	0	...
1998—National	OF	1	1	0	0	0	0	0	.000	1	0	0	2	0	0	1.000
1999—National	OF	2	0	0	0	0	0	0	.000	0	1	0	1	0	0	1.000
All-Star Game totals (4 years)		5	1	1	0	0	0	0	.200	2	1	0	3	0	0	1.000

WALKER, PETE — P — ROCKIES

PERSONAL: Born April 8, 1969, in Beverly, Mass. ... 6-2/195. ... Throws right, bats right. ... Full name: Peter Brian Walker.
HIGH SCHOOL: East Lyme (Conn.).
COLLEGE: Connecticut.
TRANSACTIONS/CAREER NOTES: Selected by New York Mets organization in seventh round of free-agent draft (June 4, 1990). ... On disabled list (June 6-18, 1992; and April 25-May 9, 1993). ... On Norfolk disabled list (April 7-May 16, 1994). ... On Norfolk suspended list (August 5-6, 1994). ... Traded by Mets with P Luis Arroyo to San Diego Padres for 1B Roberto Petagine and P Scott Adair (March 17, 1996). ... On Las Vegas disabled list (May 4-July 11, 1996). ... Granted free agency (October 15, 1996). ... Signed by Boston Red Sox organization (June 30, 1997). ... Granted free agency (October 17, 1997). ... Re-signed by Red Sox organization (January 14, 1998). ... On Pawtucket disabled list (June 11-22 and June 26-September 8, 1998). ... Granted free agency (October 16, 1998). ... Signed by Colorado Rockies organization (February 8, 1999). ... On Colorado Springs disabled list (July 16-August 6, 1999). ... Granted free agency (October 15, 1999). ... Re-signed by Rockies organization (November 17, 1999).

Year	League	W	L	Pct.	ERA	G	GS	CG	ShO	Sv.	IP	H	R	ER	BB	SO
1990—Pittsfield (NY-Penn)	5	7	.417	4.16	16	13	1	0	0	80	74	43	37	46	73
1991—St. Lucie (FSL)	10	12	.455	3.21	26	25	1	0	0	151 1/3	145	77	54	52	95
1992—Binghamton (East.)	7	12	.368	4.12	24	23	4	0	0	139 2/3	159	77	64	46	72
1993—Binghamton (East.)	4	9	.308	3.44	45	10	0	0	19	99 1/3	89	45	38	46	89
1994—St. Lucie (FSL)	0	0	...	2.25	3	0	0	0	0	4	3	2	1	1	5
—Norfolk (I.L.)	2	4	.333	3.97	37	0	0	0	3	47 2/3	48	22	21	24	42
1995—Norfolk (I.L.)	5	2	.714	3.91	34	1	0	0	8	48 1/3	51	24	21	16	39
—New York (N.L.)	1	0	1.000	4.58	13	0	0	0	0	17 2/3	24	9	9	5	5
1996—Las Vegas (PCL)■	5	1	.833	6.83	26	0	0	0	0	27 2/3	37	22	21	14	23
—Arizona Padres (Ariz.)	0	1	.000	2.25	2	2	0	0	0	4	4	1	1	0	5
—San Diego (N.L.)	0	0	...	0.00	1	0	0	0	0	2/3	0	0	0	3	1
1997—Pawtucket (I.L.)■	0	0	...	5.40	7	0	0	0	0	11 2/3	14	8	7	7	8
—Gulf Coast Red Sox (GCL)	0	0	...	0.96	4	3	0	0	0	9 1/3	5	1	1	1	14
—Trenton (East.)	0	0	...	4.05	8	0	0	0	3	13 1/3	14	6	6	7	13
1998—Pawtucket (I.L.)	1	4	.200	5.94	22	0	0	0	0	33 1/3	34	26	22	17	19
1999—Colorado Springs (PCL)■	8	4	.667	4.48	48	0	0	0	5	62 1/3	64	37	31	28	57
2000—Colorado Springs (PCL)	7	3	.700	3.07	58	0	0	0	5	73 1/3	64	29	25	30	61
—Colorado (N.L.)	0	0	...	17.36	3	0	0	0	0	4 2/3	10	9	9	4	2
Major League totals (3 years)	1	0	1.000	7.04	17	0	0	0	0	23	34	18	18	12	8

WALKER, TODD — 2B — ROCKIES

PERSONAL: Born May 25, 1973, in Bakersfield, Calif. ... 6-0/181. ... Bats left, throws right. ... Full name: Todd Arthur Walker.
HIGH SCHOOL: Airline (Bossier City, La.).
COLLEGE: Louisiana State.
TRANSACTIONS/CAREER NOTES: Selected by Texas Rangers organization in 51st round of free-agent draft (June 3, 1991); did not sign. ... Selected by Minnesota Twins organization in first round (eighth pick overall) of free-agent draft (June 2, 1994). ... Traded by Twins with OF/1B Butch Huskey to Colorado Rockies for 2B Todd Sears and cash considerations (July 16, 2000).

STATISTICAL NOTES: Led Pacific Coast League with 330 total bases and .599 slugging percentage and tied for lead in intentional bases on balls received with 11 in 1996.

									BATTING							FIELDING		
Year	Team (League)	Pos.	G	AB	R	H	2B	3B	HR	RBI	Avg.	BB	SO	SB	PO	A	E	Avg.
1994— Fort Myers (FSL)		2B	46	171	29	52	5	2	10	34	.304	32	15	6	98	112	9	.959
1995— New Britain (East.)		2B-3B	137	513	83	149	27	3	21	85	.290	63	101	23	215	355	27	.955
1996— Salt Lake (PCL)		3B-2B-DH	135	551	94	*187	*41	9	*28	*111	.339	57	91	13	129	276	19	.955
— Minnesota (A.L.)		3B-2B-DH	25	82	8	21	6	0	0	6	.256	4	13	2	16	39	2	.965
1997— Minnesota (A.L.)		3B-2B-DH	52	156	15	37	7	1	3	16	.237	11	30	7	35	86	4	.968
— Salt Lake (PCL)		3B-DH	83	322	69	111	20	1	11	53	.345	46	49	5	44	174	*24	.901
1998— Minnesota (A.L.)		2B-DH	143	528	85	167	41	3	12	62	.316	47	65	19	219	363	13	.978
1999— Minnesota (A.L.)		2B-DH	143	531	62	148	37	4	6	46	.279	52	83	18	168	270	7	.984
2000— Minnesota (A.L.)		2B-DH	23	77	14	18	1	0	2	8	.234	7	10	3	34	36	4	.946
— Salt Lake (PCL)		2B	63	249	51	81	14	1	2	37	.325	32	32	8	114	180	11	.964
— Colorado (N.L.)■		2B	57	171	28	54	10	4	7	36	.316	20	19	4	81	118	5	.975
American League totals (5 years)			386	1374	184	391	92	8	23	138	.285	121	201	49	472	794	30	.977
National League totals (1 year)			57	171	28	54	10	4	7	36	.316	20	19	4	81	118	5	.975
Major League totals (5 years)			443	1545	212	445	102	12	30	174	.288	141	220	53	553	912	35	.977

WALL, DONNE — P — METS

PERSONAL: Born July 11, 1967, in Potosi, Mo. ... 6-1/205. ... Throws right, bats right. ... Full name: Donnell Lee Wall. ... Name pronounced DON-ee.
HIGH SCHOOL: Festus (Mo.).
JUNIOR COLLEGE: Jefferson College (Mo.), then St. Louis Community College at Meramec.
COLLEGE: Southwestern Louisiana.
TRANSACTIONS/CAREER NOTES: Selected by Houston Astros organization in 18th round of free-agent draft (June 5, 1989). ... On disabled list (May 27-June 16, 1994). ... Claimed on waivers by Cincinnati Reds (October 7, 1997). ... Traded by Reds with C Paul Bako to Detroit Tigers for OF Melvin Nieves (November 11, 1997). ... Traded by Tigers with P Dan Miceli and 3B Ryan Balfe to San Diego Padres for P Tim Worrell and OF Trey Beamon (November 19, 1997). ... On San Diego disabled list (June 1-July 1, 2000); included rehabilitation assignment to Las Vegas (June 28-July 1). ... Traded by Padres to New York Mets for OF Bubba Trammell (December 11, 2000).
STATISTICAL NOTES: Led South Atlantic League with 18 home runs allowed in 1990.

Year	League	W	L	Pct.	ERA	G	GS	CG	ShO	Sv.	IP	H	R	ER	BB	SO
1989— Auburn (NY-Penn)		7	0	*1.000	1.79	12	8	3	1	1	65 1/3	45	17	13	12	69
1990— Asheville (S.Atl.)		6	8	.429	5.18	28	22	1	0	1	132	149	87	76	47	111
1991— Burlington (Midw.)		7	5	.583	2.03	16	16	3	1	0	106 2/3	73	30	24	21	102
— Osceola (FSL)		6	3	.667	2.09	12	12	4	2	0	77 1/3	55	22	18	11	62
1992— Osceola (FSL)		3	1	.750	2.63	7	7	0	0	0	41	37	13	12	8	30
— Jackson (Texas)		9	6	.600	3.54	18	18	2	0	0	114 1/3	114	51	45	26	99
1993— Tucson (PCL)		6	4	.600	3.83	25	22	0	0	0	131 2/3	147	73	56	25	89
1994— Tucson (PCL)		11	8	.579	4.43	26	24	2	2	0	148 1/3	171	87	73	35	84
1995— Tucson (PCL)		*17	6	.739	*3.30	28	•28	0	0	0	*177 1/3	190	72	65	32	*119
— Houston (N.L.)		3	1	.750	5.55	6	5	0	0	0	24 1/3	33	19	15	5	16
1996— Tucson (PCL)		3	3	.500	4.13	8	8	0	0	0	52 1/3	67	30	24	6	36
— Houston (N.L.)		9	8	.529	4.56	26	23	2	1	0	150	170	84	76	34	99
1997— New Orleans (A.A.)		8	7	.533	3.85	17	17	1	0	0	110	109	49	47	24	84
— Houston (N.L.)		2	5	.286	6.26	8	8	0	0	0	41 2/3	53	31	29	16	25
1998— Las Vegas (PCL)■		2	0	1.000	4.80	3	3	0	0	0	15	11	8	8	8	12
— San Diego (N.L.)		5	4	.556	2.43	46	1	0	0	1	70 1/3	50	20	19	32	56
1999— San Diego (N.L.)		7	4	.636	3.07	55	0	0	0	0	70 1/3	58	31	24	23	53
2000— San Diego (N.L.)		5	2	.714	3.35	44	0	0	0	1	53 2/3	36	20	20	21	29
— Las Vegas (PCL)		0	0	...	0.00	2	0	0	0	0	2	3	0	0	2	1
Major League totals (6 years)		31	24	.564	4.01	185	37	2	1	2	410 1/3	400	205	183	131	278

DIVISION SERIES RECORD

Year	League	W	L	Pct.	ERA	G	GS	CG	ShO	Sv.	IP	H	R	ER	BB	SO
1998— San Diego (N.L.)		0	0	...	9.00	1	0	0	0	0	1	2	1	1	0	2

CHAMPIONSHIP SERIES RECORD

Year	League	W	L	Pct.	ERA	G	GS	CG	ShO	Sv.	IP	H	R	ER	BB	SO
1998— San Diego (N.L.)		0	0	...	3.00	3	0	0	0	1	3	3	2	1	4	4

WORLD SERIES RECORD

Year	League	W	L	Pct.	ERA	G	GS	CG	ShO	Sv.	IP	H	R	ER	BB	SO
1998— San Diego (N.L.)		0	1	.000	6.75	2	0	0	0	0	2 2/3	3	2	2	3	1

WALLACE, JEFF — P — DEVIL RAYS

W

PERSONAL: Born April 12, 1976, in Wheeling, W.Va. ... 6-2/238. ... Throws left, bats left. ... Full name: Jeffrey Allen Wallace.
HIGH SCHOOL: Minerva (Ohio).
TRANSACTIONS/CAREER NOTES: Selected by Kansas City Royals organization in 25th round of free-agent draft (June 1, 1995). ... Traded by Royals with P Jeff Granger, P Jeff Martin and 3B Joe Randa to Pittsburgh Pirates for SS Jay Bell and 1B Jeff King (December 13, 1996). ... On disabled list (March 22, 1998-entire season). ... On Pittsburgh disabled list (July 3-August 19, 1999); included rehabilitation assignment to Nashville (July 20-August 18). ... Claimed on waivers by Cincinnati Reds (December 1, 2000). ... Granted free agency (December 21, 2000). ... Signed by Tampa Bay Devil Rays organization (January 10, 2001).

Year	League	W	L	Pct.	ERA	G	GS	CG	ShO	Sv.	IP	H	R	ER	BB	SO
1995—	Sarasota Royals (GCL)	5	3	.625	1.22	12	7	0	0	1	44 1/3	28	20	6	15	51
1996—	Lansing (Midw.)	4	9	.308	5.30	30	21	0	0	0	122 1/3	140	79	72	66	84
1997—	Lynchburg (Caro.)■	5	0	1.000	1.65	9	0	0	0	1	16 1/3	9	3	3	10	13
—	Carolina (Sou.)	4	8	.333	5.40	38	0	0	0	3	43 1/3	43	37	26	36	39
—	Pittsburgh (N.L.)	0	0	...	0.75	11	0	0	0	0	12	8	2	1	8	14
1998—	Pittsburgh (N.L.)							Did not play.								
1999—	Nashville (PCL)	2	2	.500	8.79	15	0	0	0	3	14 1/3	18	15	14	8	14
—	Pittsburgh (N.L.)	1	0	1.000	3.69	41	0	0	0	0	39	26	17	16	38	41
2000—	Nashville (PCL)	0	0	...	0.64	13	0	0	0	1	14	11	1	1	6	12
—	Pittsburgh (N.L.)	2	0	1.000	7.07	38	0	0	0	0	35 2/3	42	32	28	34	27
Major League totals (3 years)		3	0	1.000	4.67	90	0	0	0	0	86 2/3	76	51	45	80	82

WARD, BRYAN   P   RED SOX

PERSONAL: Born January 25, 1972, in Bristol, Pa. ... 6-2/205. ... Throws left, bats left. ... Full name: Bryan Matthew Ward.
HIGH SCHOOL: Rancoccas Valley Regional (Mount Holly, N.J.).
JUNIOR COLLEGE: County College of Morris (N.J.).
COLLEGE: South Carolina-Aiken.
TRANSACTIONS/CAREER NOTES: Selected by Florida Marlins organization in 20th round of free-agent draft (June 3, 1993). ... On Portland disabled list (April 23-May 1, 1997). ... Claimed on waivers by Chicago White Sox (October 14, 1997). ... Granted free agency (October 4, 1999). ... Signed by Philadelphia Phillies organization (November 2, 1999). ... Released by Phillies (August 12, 2000). ... Signed by Anaheim Angels organization (August 16, 2000). ... Granted free agency (October 6, 2000). ... Signed by Boston Red Sox organization (January 5, 2001).

Year	League	W	L	Pct.	ERA	G	GS	CG	ShO	Sv.	IP	H	R	ER	BB	SO
1993—	Elmira (NY-Penn)	2	5	.286	4.99	14	11	0	0	0	61 1/3	82	41	34	26	63
1994—	Kane County (Midw.)	3	4	.429	3.40	47	0	0	0	11	55 2/3	46	27	21	21	62
1995—	Brevard County (FSL)	5	1	.833	2.88	11	11	0	0	0	72	68	27	23	17	65
—	Portland (East.)	7	3	.700	4.50	20	11	1	1	2	72	70	42	36	31	71
1996—	Portland (East.)	9	9	.500	4.91	28	25	2	0	0	146 2/3	170	97	80	32	124
1997—	Portland (East.)	6	3	.667	3.91	12	12	0	0	0	76	71	39	33	19	69
—	Charlotte (I.L.)	2	9	.182	6.93	15	14	2	0	0	75 1/3	102	62	58	30	48
1998—	Birmingham (Sou.)■	2	3	.400	2.36	29	0	0	0	12	42	33	19	11	25	40
—	Chicago (A.L.)	1	2	.333	3.33	28	0	0	0	1	27	30	13	10	7	17
1999—	Chicago (A.L.)	0	1	.000	7.55	40	0	0	0	0	39 1/3	63	36	33	11	35
—	Charlotte (I.L.)	2	0	1.000	3.52	14	0	0	0	1	15 1/3	15	7	6	3	15
2000—	Philadelphia (N.L.)■	0	0	...	2.33	20	0	0	0	0	19 1/3	14	5	5	8	11
—	Scranton/W.B. (I.L.)	3	2	.600	2.30	22	0	0	0	6	27 1/3	23	11	7	8	17
—	Edmonton (PCL)■	0	0	...	4.26	6	0	0	0	1	6 1/3	12	4	3	1	3
—	Anaheim (A.L.)	0	0	...	5.63	7	0	0	0	0	8	8	6	5	2	3
A.L. totals (3 years)		1	3	.250	5.81	75	0	0	0	1	74 1/3	101	55	48	20	55
N.L. totals (1 year)		0	0	...	2.33	20	0	0	0	0	19 1/3	14	5	5	8	11
Major League totals (3 years)		1	3	.250	5.09	95	0	0	0	1	93 2/3	115	60	53	28	66

WARD, DARYLE   OF/1B   ASTROS

PERSONAL: Born June 27, 1975, in Lynwood, Calif. ... 6-2/230. ... Bats left, throws left. ... Full name: Daryle Lamar Ward. ... Son of Gary Ward, outfielder with four major league teams (1979-90); and hitting coach, Charlotte Knights of International League.
HIGH SCHOOL: Brethren Christian (Riverside, Calif.).
JUNIOR COLLEGE: Rancho Santiago College (Calif.).
TRANSACTIONS/CAREER NOTES: Selected by Detroit Tigers organization in 15th round of free-agent draft (June 2, 1994). ... Traded by Tigers with C Brad Ausmus, P Jose Lima, P C.J. Nitkowski and P Trever Miller to Houston Astros for OF Brian Hunter, IF Orlando Miller, P Doug Brocail, P Todd Jones and cash (December 10, 1996).
STATISTICAL NOTES: Tied for Texas League lead with four intentional bases on balls in 1997.

								BATTING							FIELDING		
Year	Team (League)	Pos.	G	AB	R	H	2B	3B	HR	RBI	Avg.	BB	SO	SB	PO	A	E	Avg.
1994—	Bristol (Appl.)	1B	48	161	17	43	6	0	5	30	.267	19	33	5	308	23	11	.968
1995—	Fayetteville (S.Atl.)	1B	137	524	75	149	32	0	14	106	.284	46	111	1	1009	77	14	.987
1996—	Lakeland (FSL)	1B-DH	128	464	65	135	29	4	10	68	.291	57	77	1	1058	103	8	.993
—	Toledo (I.L.)	1B	6	23	1	4	0	0	0	1	.174	0	3	0	42	5	1	.979
1997—	Jackson (Texas)■	1B-DH	114	422	72	139	25	0	19	90	.329	46	68	4	951	76	12	.988
—	New Orleans (A.A.)	1B-DH	14	48	4	18	1	0	2	8	.375	7	7	0	75	6	2	.976
1998—	New Orleans (PCL)	OF-1B-DH	116	463	78	141	31	1	23	96	.305	41	78	2	482	48	13	.976
—	Houston (N.L.)	PH	4	3	1	1	0	0	0	0	.333	1	2	0	...	...	...	...
1999—	New Orleans (PCL)	1B-OF	61	241	56	85	15	1	28	65	.353	23	43	1	528	35	5	.991
—	Houston (N.L.)	OF-1B-DH	64	150	11	41	6	0	8	30	.273	9	31	0	69	3	2	.973
2000—	Houston (N.L.)	OF-1B-DH	119	264	36	68	10	2	20	47	.258	15	61	0	125	4	1	.992
Major League totals (3 years)			187	417	48	110	16	2	28	77	.264	25	94	0	194	7	3	.985

DIVISION SERIES RECORD

								BATTING							FIELDING		
Year	Team (League)	Pos.	G	AB	R	H	2B	3B	HR	RBI	Avg.	BB	SO	SB	PO	A	E	Avg.
1999—	Houston (N.L.)	OF-PH	3	7	1	1	0	0	1	1	.143	0	2	0	3	0	1	.750

WARD, TURNER   OF   PHILLIES

PERSONAL: Born April 11, 1965, in Orlando. ... 6-2/204. ... Bats both, throws right. ... Full name: Turner Max Ward.
HIGH SCHOOL: Satsuma (Ala.).
JUNIOR COLLEGE: Faulkner State Community College (Ala.).

COLLEGE: South Alabama.

TRANSACTIONS/CAREER NOTES: Selected by New York Yankees organization in 18th round of free-agent draft (June 2, 1986). ... Traded by Yankees with C Joel Skinner to Cleveland Indians for OF Mel Hall (March 19, 1989). ... On Gulf Coast Indians disabled list (April 7-July 24, 1989). ... Traded by Indians with P Tom Candiotti to Toronto Blue Jays for P Denis Boucher, OF Glenallen Hill, OF Mark Whiten and a player to be named later (June 27, 1991); Indians acquired cash to complete deal (October 15, 1991). ... On Toronto disabled list (August 2-September 1, 1993); included rehabilitation assignment to Knoxville (August 21-September 1). ... Claimed on waivers by Milwaukee Brewers (November 24, 1993). ... On Milwaukee disabled list (June 7-22, July 2-19 and July 24, 1995-remainder of season); included rehabilitation assignments to Beloit (July 17-19) and New Orleans (August 10-17 and August 31-September 5). ... On Milwaukee disabled list (May 25-September 1, 1996). ... Released by Brewers (November 1, 1996). ... Signed by Pittsburgh Pirates organization (April 22, 1997). ... On disabled list (August 5-20, 1998). ... On Pittsburgh disabled list (June 9-August 11, 1999); included rehabilitation assignments to Altoona (June 23-24) and Nashville (June 25-August 1 and August 2-9). ... Released by Pirates (August 11, 1999). ... Signed by Arizona Diamondbacks organization (August 18, 1999). ... On Arizona disabled list (August 31-September 15, 1999). ... Granted free agency (November 1, 1999). ... Re-signed by Diamondbacks organization (February 19, 2000). ... On Tucson disabled list (June 21-September 1, 2000). ... Released by Diamondbacks (October 5, 2000). ... Signed by Philadelphia Phillies organization (December 20, 2000).

STATISTICAL NOTES: Led Pacific Coast League outfielders with 292 putouts and 308 total chances in 1990.

Year	Team (League)	Pos.	G	AB	R	H	2B	3B	HR	RBI	Avg.	BB	SO	SB	PO	A	E	Avg.
1986—	Oneonta (NY-Penn)	OF-1B-3B	63	221	42	62	4	1	1	19	.281	31	39	6	97	6	5	.954
1987—	Fort Lauderdale (FSL)	OF-3B	130	493	83	145	15	2	7	55	.294	64	83	25	332	11	8	.977
1988—	Columbus (I.L.)	OF	134	490	55	123	24	1	7	50	.251	48	100	28	223	5	1	*.996
1989—	GC Indians (GCL)■	DH	4	15	2	3	0	0	0	1	.200	2	2	1	...	...	...	...
	— Canton/Akron (East.) ..	OF	30	93	19	28	5	1	0	3	.301	15	16	1	2	0	0	1.000
1990—	Colo. Springs (PCL) ...	OF-2B	133	495	89	148	24	9	6	65	.299	72	70	22	†292	7	9	.971
	— Cleveland (A.L.)	OF-DH	14	46	10	16	2	1	1	10	.348	3	8	3	20	2	1	.957
1991—	Cleveland (A.L.)	OF	40	100	11	23	7	0	0	5	.230	10	16	0	65	1	0	1.000
	— Colo. Springs (PCL) ...	OF	14	51	5	10	1	1	1	3	.196	6	9	2	30	0	1	.968
	— Toronto (A.L.)■	OF	8	13	1	4	0	0	0	2	.308	1	2	0	5	0	0	1.000
	— Syracuse (I.L.)	OF	59	218	40	72	11	3	7	32	.330	47	22	9	136	5	0	1.000
1992—	Toronto (A.L.)	OF	18	29	7	10	3	0	1	3	.345	4	4	0	18	1	0	1.000
	— Syracuse (I.L.)	OF	81	280	41	67	10	2	10	29	.239	44	43	7	143	3	5	.967
1993—	Toronto (A.L.)	OF-1B	72	167	20	32	4	2	4	28	.192	23	26	3	97	2	1	.990
	— Knoxville (Sou.)	OF	7	23	6	6	2	0	0	2	.261	7	3	3	20	0	0	1.000
1994—	Milwaukee (A.L.)■	OF-3B	102	367	55	85	15	2	9	45	.232	52	68	6	260	9	4	.985
1995—	Milwaukee (A.L.)	OF-DH	44	129	19	34	3	1	4	16	.264	14	21	6	81	5	1	.989
	— Beloit (Midw.)	OF	2	5	0	0	0	0	0	0	.000	3	1	0	1	0	0	1.000
	— New Orleans (A.A.)	OF-DH	11	33	3	8	1	1	1	3	.242	4	10	0	9	0	1	.900
1996—	Milwaukee (A.L.)	OF-DH	43	67	7	12	2	1	2	10	.179	13	17	3	54	1	0	1.000
	— New Orleans (A.A.)	DH	9	23	4	8	1	0	1	1	.348	7	4	0	...	...	...	...
1997—	Calgary (PCL)■	OF-DH-1B	59	209	44	71	18	3	9	44	.340	24	26	7	87	6	3	.969
	— Pittsburgh (N.L.)	OF	71	167	33	59	16	1	7	33	.353	18	17	4	71	2	0	1.000
1998—	Pittsburgh (N.L.)	OF-DH	123	282	33	74	13	3	9	46	.262	27	40	5	163	7	3	.983
1999—	Pittsburgh (N.L.)	OF	49	91	2	19	2	0	0	8	.209	13	9	2	41	1	2	.955
	— Altoona (East.)	DH	1	3	1	0	0	0	0	0	.000	2	2	0	0	0	0	...
	— Nashville (PCL)	OF-DH	35	89	15	26	3	1	2	17	.292	16	14	3	17	1	2	.900
	— Tucson (PCL)■	OF	12	40	9	15	2	0	2	8	.375	7	4	4	18	1	2	.905
	— Arizona (N.L.)	OF	10	23	6	8	1	0	2	7	.348	2	6	0	11	0	0	1.000
2000—	Tucson (PCL)	OF	32	82	24	31	10	1	4	16	.378	17	7	0	30	1	0	1.000
	— Arizona (N.L.)	OF	15	52	5	9	4	0	0	4	.173	5	7	1	35	0	0	1.000
American League totals (7 years)			341	918	130	216	36	7	21	119	.235	120	162	21	600	21	7	.989
National League totals (4 years)			268	615	79	169	36	4	18	98	.275	65	79	12	321	10	5	.985
Major League totals (11 years)			609	1533	209	385	72	11	39	217	.251	185	241	33	921	31	12	.988

DIVISION SERIES RECORD

Year	Team (League)	Pos.	G	AB	R	H	2B	3B	HR	RBI	Avg.	BB	SO	SB	PO	A	E	Avg.
1999—	Arizona (N.L.)	PH	3	2	2	1	0	0	1	3	.500	1	0	0	...	...	...	...

WASDIN, JOHN   P   ROCKIES

PERSONAL: Born August 5, 1972, in Fort Belvoir, Va. ... 6-2/195. ... Throws right, bats right. ... Full name: John Truman Wasdin.

HIGH SCHOOL: Amos P. Godby (Tallahassee, Fla.).

COLLEGE: Florida State.

TRANSACTIONS/CAREER NOTES: Selected by New York Yankees organization in 41st round of free-agent draft (June 4, 1990); did not sign. ... Selected by Oakland Athletics organization in first round (25th pick overall) of free-agent draft (June 3, 1993). ... Traded by A's with cash to Boston Red Sox for OF Jose Canseco (January 27, 1997). ... On Boston disabled list (July 18-August 5, 1999); included rehabilitation assignment to Gulf Coast Red Sox (July 30-31). ... Traded by Red Sox with P Brian Rose, P Jeff Taglienti and 2B Jeff Frye to Colorado Rockies for P Rolando Arrojo, P Rick Croushore, 2B Mike Lansing and cash (July 27, 2000). ... On suspended list (September 8-10, 2000).

STATISTICAL NOTES: Led Pacific Coast League with 26 home runs allowed in 1995.

Year	League	W	L	Pct.	ERA	G	GS	CG	ShO	Sv.	IP	H	R	ER	BB	SO
1993—	Arizona Athletics (Ariz.)	0	0	...	3.00	1	1	0	0	0	3	3	1	1	0	1
	— Madison (Midw.)	2	3	.400	1.86	9	9	0	0	0	48 1/3	32	11	10	9	40
	— Modesto (Calif.)	0	3	.000	3.86	3	3	0	0	0	16 1/3	17	9	7	4	11
1994—	Modesto (Calif.)	3	1	.750	1.69	6	4	0	0	0	26 2/3	17	6	5	5	30
	— Huntsville (Sou.)	12	3	.800	3.43	21	21	0	0	0	141 2/3	126	61	54	29	108
1995—	Edmonton (PCL)	12	8	.600	5.52	29	•28	2	1	0	174 1/3	193	117	107	38	111
	— Oakland (A.L.)	1	1	.500	4.67	5	2	0	0	0	17 1/3	14	9	9	3	6
1996—	Edmonton (PCL)	2	1	.667	4.14	9	9	0	0	0	50	52	23	23	17	30
	— Oakland (A.L.)	8	7	.533	5.96	25	21	1	0	0	131 1/3	145	96	87	50	75
1997—	Boston (A.L.)■	4	6	.400	4.40	53	7	0	0	0	124 2/3	121	68	61	38	84
1998—	Boston (A.L.)	6	4	.600	5.25	47	8	0	0	0	96	111	57	56	27	59
	— Pawtucket (I.L.)	1	0	1.000	3.00	4	2	0	0	0	12	11	6	4	5	10

Year League	W	L	Pct.	ERA	G	GS	CG	ShO	Sv.	IP	H	R	ER	BB	SO
1999— Pawtucket (I.L.)	1	1	.500	2.12	5	5	0	0	0	29 2/3	19	9	7	7	28
— Boston (A.L.)	8	3	.727	4.12	45	0	0	0	2	74 1/3	66	38	34	18	57
— Gulf Coast Red Sox (GCL)	0	0	...	0.00	1	1	0	0	0	2	1	0	0	0	4
2000— Boston (A.L.)	1	3	.250	5.04	25	1	0	0	1	44 2/3	48	25	25	15	36
— Pawtucket (I.L.)	1	0	1.000	2.25	5	3	0	0	1	16	7	4	4	2	11
— Colorado (N.L.)■	0	3	.000	5.80	14	3	1	0	0	35 2/3	42	23	23	9	35
A.L. totals (6 years)	28	24	.538	5.01	200	39	1	0	3	488 1/3	505	293	272	151	317
N.L. totals (1 year)	0	3	.000	5.80	14	3	1	0	0	35 2/3	42	23	23	9	35
Major League totals (6 years)	28	27	.509	5.07	214	42	2	0	3	524	547	316	295	160	352

DIVISION SERIES RECORD

Year League	W	L	Pct.	ERA	G	GS	CG	ShO	Sv.	IP	H	R	ER	BB	SO
1998— Boston (A.L.)	0	0	...	10.80	1	0	0	0	0	1 2/3	2	2	2	1	2
1999— Boston (A.L.)	0	0	...	27.00	2	0	0	0	0	1 2/3	2	5	5	4	1
Division series totals (2 years)	0	0	...	18.90	3	0	0	0	0	3 1/3	4	7	7	5	3

CHAMPIONSHIP SERIES RECORD

Year League	W	L	Pct.	ERA	G	GS	CG	ShO	Sv.	IP	H	R	ER	BB	SO
1999— Boston (A.L.)				Did not play.											

WASHBURN, JARROD P ANGELS

PERSONAL: Born August 13, 1974, in La Crosse, Wis. ... 6-1/198. ... Throws left, bats left. ... Full name: Jarrod Michael Washburn.
HIGH SCHOOL: Webster (Wis.).
COLLEGE: Wisconsin-Oshkosh.
TRANSACTIONS/CAREER NOTES: Selected by California Angels organization in second round of free-agent draft (June 1, 1995). ... Angels franchise renamed Anaheim Angels for 1997 season. ... On Edmonton disabled list (April 26-June 17, 1999). ... On Anaheim disabled list (March 25-April 9, July 22-August 7 and August 8, 2000-remainder of season); included rehabilitation assignment to Lake Elsinore (April 7).

Year League	W	L	Pct.	ERA	G	GS	CG	ShO	Sv.	IP	H	R	ER	BB	SO
1995— Cedar Rapids (Midw.)	0	1	.000	3.44	3	3	0	0	0	18 1/3	17	7	7	7	20
— Boise (N'West)	3	2	.600	3.33	8	8	0	0	0	46	35	17	17	14	54
1996— Lake Elsinore (Calif.)	6	3	.667	3.30	14	14	3	0	0	92 2/3	79	38	34	33	93
— Midland (Texas)	5	6	.455	4.40	13	13	1	0	0	88	77	44	43	25	58
— Vancouver (PCL)	0	2	.000	10.80	2	2	0	0	0	8 1/3	12	16	10	...	12
1997— Midland (Texas)	15	•12	.556	4.80	29	*29	29	•1	0	*189 1/3	*211	*115	*101	65	*146
— Vancouver (PCL)	0	0	...	3.60	1	1	0	0	0	5	4	2	2	2	6
1998— Vancouver (PCL)	4	5	.444	4.32	14	14	2	0	0	91 2/3	91	44	44	43	66
— Anaheim (A.L.)	6	3	.667	4.62	15	11	0	0	0	74	70	40	38	27	48
— Midland (Texas)	0	1	.000	6.23	1	1	0	0	0	8 2/3	13	8	6	2	8
1999— Edmonton (PCL)	1	5	.167	4.73	11	11	1	0	0	59	50	31	31	17	55
— Anaheim (A.L.)	4	5	.444	5.25	16	10	0	0	0	61 2/3	61	36	36	26	39
2000— Lake Elsinore (Calif.)	0	0	...	6.00	1	1	0	0	0	3	3	2	2	2	7
— Edmonton (PCL)	3	0	1.000	3.52	5	5	0	0	0	30 2/3	35	13	12	13	20
— Anaheim (A.L.)	7	2	.778	3.74	14	14	0	0	0	84 1/3	64	38	35	37	49
Major League totals (3 years)	17	10	.630	4.46	45	35	0	0	0	220	195	114	109	90	136

WASZGIS, B.J. C MARLINS

PERSONAL: Born August 24, 1970, in Omaha, Neb. ... 6-2/215. ... Bats right, throws right. ... Full name: Robert Michael Waszgis Jr. ... Name pronounced WAZ-gis.
HIGH SCHOOL: South (Omaha, Neb.).
JUNIOR COLLEGE: Fort Scott Community College (Kan.).
COLLEGE: McNeese State.
TRANSACTIONS/CAREER NOTES: Selected by Philadelphia Phillies organization in 21st round of free agent draft (June 4, 1990); did not sign. ... Selected by Baltimore Orioles organization in 10th round of free-agent draft (June 3, 1991). ... Claimed on waivers by Boston Red Sox (September 25, 1997). ... On disabled list (July 29-August 12, 1998). ... Granted free agency (October 16, 1998). ... Signed by New York Yankees organization (March 1, 1999). ... Granted free agency (October 15, 1999). ... Signed by Texas Rangers organization (December 20, 1999). ... Granted free agency (October 14, 2000). ... Signed by Florida Marlins organization (November 2, 2000).
STATISTICAL NOTES: Led Carolina League catchers with 78 assists and 21 passed balls in 1994. ... Led Eastern League catchers with 782 putouts, 16 errors, 23 passed balls and 887 total chances in 1995.

Year Team (League)	Pos.	G	AB	R	H	2B	3B	HR	RBI	Avg.	BB	SO	SB	PO	A	E	Avg.
1991— Bluefield (Appl.)	C	12	35	8	8	1	0	3	8	.229	5	11	3	71	11	1	.988
1992— Kane County (Midw.)	C-1B	111	340	39	73	18	1	11	47	.215	54	94	3	517	71	14	.977
1993— Albany (S.Atl.)	C	86	300	45	92	25	3	8	52	.307	27	55	4	369	49	8	.981
— Frederick (Caro.)	C	31	109	12	27	4	0	3	9	.248	9	30	1	159	23	2	.989
1994— Frederick (Caro.)	C-1B	122	426	76	120	16	3	21	*100	.282	65	94	6	688	†84	16	.980
1995— Bowie (East.)	C-1B	130	438	53	111	22	0	10	50	.253	70	91	2	†783	89	†16	.982
1996— Rochester (I.L.)	C-DH-1B	96	304	37	81	16	0	11	48	.266	41	87	2	511	53	6	.989
1997— Rochester (I.L.)	C-DH-1B	100	315	61	82	15	1	13	48	.260	56	78	1	561	39	12	.980
1998— Pawtucket (I.L.)■	C-1B	66	208	31	42	9	0	9	41	.202	26	52	2	400	34	7	.984
1999— Columbus (I.L.)■	C-1B-DH	63	191	36	53	12	0	6	31	.277	27	55	4	417	27	10	.978
2000— Oklahoma (PCL)■	C-1B	77	259	45	68	11	3	13	62	.263	55	68	2	483	47	11	.980
— Texas (A.L.)	C-1B	24	45	6	10	1	0	0	4	.222	4	10	0	70	2	0	1.000
Major League totals (1 year)		24	45	6	10	1	0	0	4	.222	4	10	0	70	2	0	1.000

PERSONAL: Born November 18, 1970, in New York. ... 6-1/224. ... Throws left, bats left. ... Full name: Allen Kenneth Watson.

HIGH SCHOOL: Christ the King (Queens, N.Y.).

COLLEGE: New York State Institute of Technology.

TRANSACTIONS/CAREER NOTES: Selected by St. Louis Cardinals organization in first round (21st pick overall) of free-agent draft (June 3, 1991); pick received as part of compensation for Toronto Blue Jays signing Type A free-agent P Ken Dayley. ... On Savannah disabled list (August 19, 1991-remainder of season). ... On suspended list (June 25-July 3, 1994). ... On St. Louis disabled list (June 7-July 8, 1995); included rehabilitation assignments to Arkansas (June 21-26) and Louisville (June 26-July 8). ... Traded by Cardinals with P Rich DeLucia and P Doug Creek to San Francisco Giants for SS Royce Clayton and a player to be named later (December 14, 1995); Cardinals acquired 2B Chris Wimmer to complete deal (January 16, 1996). ... On San Francisco disabled list (July 2-25, 1996); included rehabilitation assignment to San Jose (July 15-25). ... Traded by Giants with P Fausto Macey to Anaheim Angels for 1B J.T. Snow (November 27, 1996). ... On Anaheim disabled list (May 24-July 13, 1998); included rehabilitation assignments to Midland (June 16), Lake Elsinore (June 21) and Vancouver (June 26). ... Granted free agency (December 21, 1998). ... Signed by New York Mets (January 19, 1999). ... Traded by Mets with cash to Seattle Mariners for P Mac Suzuki and a player to be named later (June 18, 1999); Mets acquired P Justin Dunning to complete deal (September 14, 1999). ... Released by Mariners (June 28, 1999). ... Signed by New York Yankees organization (July 3, 1999). ... Granted free agency (November 5, 1999). ... Re-signed by Yankees (December 7, 1999). ... On New York disabled list (April 24-May 26, June 29-August 4 and August 11, 2000-remainder of season); included rehabilitation assignments to Columbus (May 14-25), Tampa (July 31-August 2) and Gulf Coast Yankees (August 3).

STATISTICAL NOTES: Led A.L. with 37 home runs allowed in 1997.

MISCELLANEOUS: Singled in three games as pinch hitter with San Francisco (1996).

Year League	W	L	Pct.	ERA	G	GS	CG	ShO	Sv.	IP	H	R	ER	BB	SO
1991— Hamilton (NY-Penn)	1	1	.500	2.52	8	8	0	0	0	39 1/3	22	15	11	17	46
— Savannah (S.Atl.)	1	1	.500	3.95	3	3	0	0	0	13 2/3	16	7	6	8	12
1992— St. Petersburg (FSL)	5	4	.556	1.91	14	14	2	0	0	89 2/3	81	31	19	18	80
— Arkansas (Texas)	8	5	.615	2.15	14	14	3	1	0	96 1/3	77	24	23	23	93
— Louisville (A.A.)	1	0	1.000	1.46	2	2	0	0	0	12 1/3	8	4	2	5	9
1993— Arkansas (Texas)	5	4	.556	2.91	17	17	2	0	0	120 2/3	101	46	39	31	86
— St. Louis (N.L.)	6	7	.462	4.60	16	15	0	0	0	86	90	53	44	28	49
1994— St. Louis (N.L.)	6	5	.545	5.52	22	22	0	0	0	115 2/3	130	73	71	53	74
1995— St. Louis (N.L.)	7	9	.438	4.96	21	19	0	0	0	114 1/3	126	68	63	41	49
— Louisville (A.A.)	2	2	.500	2.63	4	4	1	1	0	24	20	10	7	6	19
— Arkansas (Texas)	1	0	1.000	0.00	1	1	0	0	0	5	4	1	0	0	7
1996— San Francisco (N.L.)■	8	12	.400	4.61	29	29	2	0	0	185 2/3	189	105	95	69	128
— San Jose (Calif.)	0	0	...	1.42	2	2	0	0	0	6 1/3	7	1	1	0	12
1997— Anaheim (A.L.)■	12	12	.500	4.93	35	34	0	0	0	199	220	121	109	73	141
1998— Anaheim (A.L.)	6	7	.462	6.04	28	14	1	0	0	92 1/3	122	67	62	34	64
— Midland (Texas)	0	0	...	2.25	1	1	0	0	0	4	6	2	1	1	3
— Lake Elsinore (Calif.)	1	0	1.000	0.00	1	1	0	0	0	5	3	0	0	1	6
— Vancouver (PCL)	0	1	.000	4.50	1	1	0	0	0	6	6	3	3	2	8
1999— New York (N.L.)■	2	2	.500	4.08	14	4	0	0	1	39 2/3	36	18	18	22	32
— Seattle (A.L.)■	0	1	.000	12.00	3	0	0	0	0	3	6	9	4	3	2
— Columbus (I.L.)■	0	0	...	6.14	2	2	0	0	0	7 1/3	7	5	5	2	5
— New York (A.L.)	4	0	1.000	2.10	21	0	0	0	0	34 1/3	30	8	8	10	30
2000— New York (A.L.)	0	0	...	10.23	17	0	0	0	0	22	30	25	25	18	20
— Columbus (I.L.)	0	1	.000	1.35	5	1	0	0	0	6 2/3	3	2	1	2	4
— Tampa (FSL)	0	0	...	0.00	1	1	0	0	0	2	0	0	0	1	1
— Gulf Coast Yankees (GCL)	0	0	...	0.00	1	1	0	0	0	1	1	0	0	0	2
A.L. totals (4 years)	22	20	.524	5.34	104	48	1	0	0	350 2/3	408	230	208	138	257
N.L. totals (5 years)	29	35	.453	4.84	102	89	2	0	1	541 1/3	571	317	291	213	332
Major League totals (8 years)	51	55	.481	5.03	206	137	3	0	1	892	979	547	499	351	589

DIVISION SERIES RECORD

Year League	W	L	Pct.	ERA	G	GS	CG	ShO	Sv.	IP	H	R	ER	BB	SO
1999— New York (A.L.)							Did not play.								

CHAMPIONSHIP SERIES RECORD

Year League	W	L	Pct.	ERA	G	GS	CG	ShO	Sv.	IP	H	R	ER	BB	SO
1999— New York (A.L.)	0	0	...	0.00	3	0	0	0	0	1	2	0	0	2	1

WORLD SERIES RECORD

NOTES: Member of World Series championship team (1999).

Year League	W	L	Pct.	ERA	G	GS	CG	ShO	Sv.	IP	H	R	ER	BB	SO
1999— New York (A.L.)							Did not play.								

WATSON, MARK   P   MARINERS

W

PERSONAL: Born January 23, 1974, in Atlanta. ... 6-4/215. ... Throws left, bats right. ... Full name: Mark Bradford Watson.

HIGH SCHOOL: Marist (Atlanta).

COLLEGE: Clemson, then Georgia.

TRANSACTIONS/CAREER NOTES: Signed as non-drafted free agent by Milwaukee Brewers organization (June 16, 1996). ... Traded by Brewers to Cleveland Indians for P Ben McDonald (March 11, 1998); traded arranged as compensation for McDonald, who was injured and had been acquired by Indians (December 8, 1997). ... Claimed on waivers by Seattle Mariners (June 23, 2000). ... On Tacoma disabled list (August 27-September 21, 2000).

Year League	W	L	Pct.	ERA	G	GS	CG	ShO	Sv.	IP	H	R	ER	BB	SO
1996— Helena (Pio.)	5	2	.714	4.77	13	13	0	0	0	60 1/3	59	43	32	28	68
1997— Beloit (Midw.)	0	3	.000	6.68	8	7	0	0	0	32 1/3	40	33	24	20	33
— Ogden (Pio.)	4	3	.571	4.15	10	10	1	0	0	47 2/3	44	26	22	19	49
1998— Columbus (S.Atl.)■	3	4	.429	4.05	31	12	1	0	0	97 2/3	95	53	44	32	77
— Kinston (Caro.)	0	1	.000	0.00	1	1	0	0	0	6 1/3	3	4	0	2	8
1999— Kinston (Caro.)	6	0	1.000	1.04	11	4	0	0	0	43 1/3	28	7	5	10	40
— Akron (East.)	9	8	.529	4.34	19	17	0	0	0	110	143	64	53	38	57
2000— Buffalo (I.L.)	1	2	.333	4.43	16	0	0	0	1	20 1/3	18	11	10	12	16
— Cleveland (A.L.)	0	1	.000	8.53	6	0	0	0	0	6 1/3	12	7	6	2	4
— Tacoma (PCL)■	2	1	.667	3.96	16	0	0	0	0	25	30	16	11	6	17
Major League totals (1 year)	0	1	.000	8.53	6	0	0	0	0	6 1/3	12	7	6	2	4

WEATHERS, DAVE   P   BREWERS

PERSONAL: Born September 25, 1969, in Lawrenceburg, Tenn. ... 6-3/230. ... Throws right, bats right. ... Full name: John David Weathers.
HIGH SCHOOL: Loretto (Tenn.).
JUNIOR COLLEGE: Motlow State Community College (Tenn.).
TRANSACTIONS/CAREER NOTES: Selected by Toronto Blue Jays organization in third round of free-agent draft (June 1, 1988). ... On Syracuse disabled list (May 11-July 31, 1992). ... Selected by Florida Marlins in second round (29th pick overall) of expansion draft (November 17, 1992). ... On Florida disabled list (June 26-July 13, 1995); included rehabilitation assignments to Brevard County (July 4-10) and Charlotte (July 11-13). ... Traded by Marlins to New York Yankees for P Mark Hutton (July 31, 1996). ... Traded by Yankees to Cleveland Indians for OF Chad Curtis (June 9, 1997). ... Claimed on waivers by Cincinnati Reds (December 20, 1997). ... Claimed on waivers by Milwaukee Brewers (June 24, 1998). ... Granted free agency (October 29, 1999). ... Re-signed by Brewers (December 2, 1999). ... On disabled list (August 2-22, 2000).
MISCELLANEOUS: Appeared in two games as pinch runner (1994). ... Appeared in one game as pinch runner with Florida (1996). ... Struck out in only appearance as pinch hitter (1999).

Year League	W	L	Pct.	ERA	G	GS	CG	ShO	Sv.	IP	H	R	ER	BB	SO
1988—St. Catharines (NY-Penn)	4	4	.500	3.02	15	12	0	0	0	62²/₃	58	30	21	26	36
1989—Myrtle Beach (S.Atl.)	11	•13	.458	3.86	31	*31	2	0	0	172²/₃	163	99	74	86	111
1990—Dunedin (FSL)	10	7	.588	3.70	27	•27	2	0	0	158	158	82	65	59	96
1991—Knoxville (Sou.)	10	7	.588	2.45	24	22	5	2	0	139¹/₃	121	51	38	49	114
— Toronto (A.L.)	1	0	1.000	4.91	15	0	0	0	0	14²/₃	15	9	8	17	13
1992—Syracuse (I.L.)	1	4	.200	4.66	12	10	0	0	0	48¹/₃	48	29	25	21	30
— Toronto (A.L.)	0	0	...	8.10	2	0	0	0	0	3¹/₃	5	3	3	2	3
1993—Edmonton (PCL)■	11	4	•.733	3.83	22	22	3	1	0	141	150	77	60	47	117
— Florida (N.L.)	2	3	.400	5.12	14	6	0	0	0	45²/₃	57	26	26	13	34
1994—Florida (N.L.)	8	12	.400	5.27	24	24	0	0	0	135	166	87	79	59	72
1995—Florida (N.L.)	4	5	.444	5.98	28	15	0	0	0	90¹/₃	104	68	60	52	60
— Brevard County (FSL)	0	0	...	0.00	1	1	0	0	0	4	4	0	0	1	3
— Charlotte (I.L.)	0	1	.000	9.00	1	1	0	0	0	5	10	5	5	5	0
1996—Florida (N.L.)	2	2	.500	4.54	31	8	0	0	0	71¹/₃	85	41	36	28	40
— Charlotte (I.L.)	0	0	...	7.71	1	1	0	0	0	2¹/₃	5	2	2	3	0
— New York (A.L.)■■	0	2	.000	9.35	11	4	0	0	0	17¹/₃	23	19	18	14	13
— Columbus (I.L.)	0	2	.000	5.40	3	3	0	0	0	16²/₃	20	13	10	5	7
1997—New York (A.L.)	0	1	.000	10.00	10	0	0	0	0	9	15	10	10	7	4
— Columbus (I.L.)	2	2	.500	3.19	5	5	1	0	0	36²/₃	35	18	13	7	35
— Buffalo (A.A.)■	4	3	.571	3.15	11	11	2	1	0	68²/₃	71	37	24	17	51
— Cleveland (A.L.)	1	2	.333	7.56	9	1	0	0	0	16²/₃	23	14	14	8	14
1998—Cincinnati (N.L.)■	2	4	.333	6.21	16	9	0	0	0	62¹/₃	86	47	43	27	51
— Milwaukee (N.L.)■	4	1	.800	3.21	28	0	0	0	0	47²/₃	44	22	17	14	43
1999—Milwaukee (N.L.)	7	4	.636	4.65	63	0	0	0	2	93	102	49	48	38	74
2000—Milwaukee (N.L.)	3	5	.375	3.07	69	0	0	0	1	76¹/₃	73	29	26	32	50
A.L. totals (4 years)	2	5	.286	7.82	47	5	0	0	0	61	81	55	53	48	47
N.L. totals (7 years)	32	36	.471	4.85	273	62	0	0	3	621²/₃	717	369	335	263	424
Major League totals (10 years)	34	41	.453	5.12	320	67	0	0	3	682²/₃	798	424	388	311	471

DIVISION SERIES RECORD

Year League	W	L	Pct.	ERA	G	GS	CG	ShO	Sv.	IP	H	R	ER	BB	SO
1996—New York (A.L.)	1	0	1.000	0.00	2	0	0	0	0	5	1	0	0	0	5

CHAMPIONSHIP SERIES RECORD

Year League	W	L	Pct.	ERA	G	GS	CG	ShO	Sv.	IP	H	R	ER	BB	SO
1996—New York (A.L.)	1	0	1.000	0.00	2	0	0	0	0	3	3	0	0	0	0

WORLD SERIES RECORD

NOTES: Member of World Series championship team (1996).

Year League	W	L	Pct.	ERA	G	GS	CG	ShO	Sv.	IP	H	R	ER	BB	SO
1996—New York (A.L.)	0	0	...	3.00	3	0	0	0	0	3	2	1	1	4	3

WEAVER, ERIC   P

PERSONAL: Born August 4, 1973, in Springfield, Ill. ... 6-5/230. ... Throws right, bats right. ... Full name: James Eric Weaver.
HIGH SCHOOL: Illiopolis (Ill.).
TRANSACTIONS/CAREER NOTES: Signed as non-drafted free agent by Los Angeles Dodgers organization (July 22, 1991). ... On disabled list (May 1-August 31, 1994). ... Traded by Dodgers to Seattle Mariners for P Scott Proutty (October 12, 1998). ... On Seattle disabled list (May 15, 1999-remainder of season); included rehabilitation assignment to Tacoma (July 23-August 13 and August 26-September 7). ... Granted free agency (October 8, 1999). ... Signed by Anaheim Angels organization (January 26, 2000). ... Granted free agency (October 5, 2000).
STATISTICAL NOTES: Pitched 2-1 no-hit victory against Fort Lauderdale (July 17, 1992, first game).

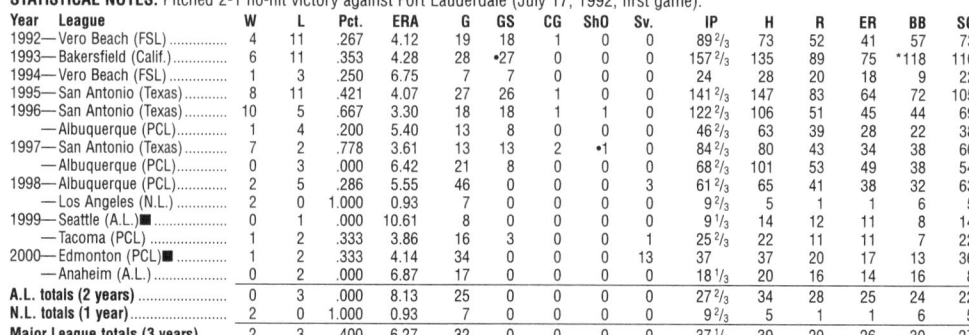

Year League	W	L	Pct.	ERA	G	GS	CG	ShO	Sv.	IP	H	R	ER	BB	SO
1992—Vero Beach (FSL)	4	11	.267	4.12	19	18	1	0	0	89²/₃	73	52	41	57	73
1993—Bakersfield (Calif.)	6	11	.353	4.28	28	•27	0	0	0	157²/₃	135	89	75	*118	110
1994—Vero Beach (FSL)	1	3	.250	6.75	7	7	0	0	0	24	28	20	18	9	22
1995—San Antonio (Texas)	8	11	.421	4.07	27	26	1	0	0	141²/₃	147	83	64	72	105
1996—San Antonio (Texas)	10	5	.667	3.30	18	18	1	1	0	122²/₃	106	51	45	44	69
— Albuquerque (PCL)	1	4	.200	5.40	13	8	0	0	0	46²/₃	63	39	28	22	38
1997—San Antonio (Texas)	7	2	.778	3.61	13	13	2	•1	0	84²/₃	80	43	34	38	60
— Albuquerque (PCL)	0	3	.000	6.42	21	8	0	0	0	68²/₃	101	53	49	38	54
1998—Albuquerque (PCL)	2	5	.286	5.55	46	0	0	0	3	61²/₃	65	44	38	32	63
— Los Angeles (N.L.)	2	0	1.000	0.93	7	0	0	0	0	9²/₃	5	1	1	6	5
1999—Seattle (A.L.)■	0	1	.000	10.61	8	0	0	0	0	9¹/₃	14	12	11	8	14
— Tacoma (PCL)	1	2	.333	4.20	16	3	0	0	1	25²/₃	22	11	11	7	22
2000—Edmonton (PCL)■	1	2	.333	4.14	34	0	0	0	13	37	37	20	17	13	36
— Anaheim (A.L.)	0	2	.000	6.87	17	0	0	0	0	18¹/₃	20	16	14	16	8
A.L. totals (2 years)	0	3	.000	8.13	25	0	0	0	0	27²/₃	34	28	25	24	22
N.L. totals (1 year)	2	0	1.000	0.93	7	0	0	0	0	9²/₃	5	1	1	6	5
Major League totals (3 years)	2	3	.400	6.27	32	0	0	0	0	37¹/₃	39	29	26	30	27

W

WEAVER, JEFF — P — TIGERS

PERSONAL: Born August 22, 1976, in Northridge, Calif. ... 6-5/210. ... Throws right, bats right. ... Full name: Jeffery Charles Weaver. ... Cousin of Jed Weaver, tight end, Miami Dolphins.
HIGH SCHOOL: Simi Valley (Calif.).
COLLEGE: Fresno State.
TRANSACTIONS/CAREER NOTES: Selected by Chicago White Sox organziation in second-round of free-agent draft (June 3, 1997); did not sign. ... Selected by Detroit Tigers organization in first round (14th pick overall) of free-agent draft (June 2, 1998).
STATISTICAL NOTES: Led A.L. pitchers with 17 hit batsmen in 1999 and 15 in 2000.
MISCELLANEOUS: Member of 1996 U.S. Olympic baseball team. ... Appeared in one game as pinch runner (1999).

Year League	W	L	Pct.	ERA	G	GS	CG	ShO	Sv.	IP	H	R	ER	BB	SO
1998—Jamestown (NY-Penn)	1	0	1.000	1.50	3	3	0	0	0	12	6	4	2	1	12
—West Michigan (Midw.)	1	0	1.000	1.38	2	2	0	0	0	13	8	3	2	0	21
1999—Jacksonville (Sou.)	0	0	...	3.00	1	1	0	0	0	6	5	2	2	0	6
—Detroit (A.L.)	9	12	.429	5.55	30	29	0	0	0	163 2/3	176	104	101	56	114
2000—Toledo (I.L.)	0	1	.000	3.38	1	1	0	0	0	5 1/3	5	2	2	1	10
—Detroit (A.L.)	11	15	.423	4.32	31	30	2	0	0	200	205	102	96	52	136
Major League totals (2 years)	20	27	.426	4.88	61	59	2	0	0	363 2/3	381	206	197	108	250

WEBER, BEN — P — ANGELS

PERSONAL: Born November 17, 1969, in Port Arthur, Texas. ... 6-4/180. ... Throws right, bats right. ... Full name: Benjamin Edward Weber.
HIGH SCHOOL: Port Neches-Groves (Port Neches, Texas).
COLLEGE: Houston.
TRANSACTIONS/CAREER NOTES: Selected by Toronto Blue Jays organization in 20th round of free-agent draft (June 3, 1991). ... Released by Blue Jays (March 24, 1996). ... Signed by Salinas, Western League (May 1996). ... Signed by Taipei, Taiwan League (1997). ... Signed by San Francisco Giants organization (October 30, 1998). ... Claimed on waivers by Anaheim Angels (August 30, 2000).

Year League	W	L	Pct.	ERA	G	GS	CG	ShO	Sv.	IP	H	R	ER	BB	SO
1991—St. Catharines (NY-Penn)	6	3	.667	3.24	16	14	1	0	0	97 1/3	•105	43	35	24	60
1992—Myrtle Beach (S.Atl.)	4	7	.364	1.64	41	1	0	0	6	98 2/3	83	27	18	29	65
1993—Dunedin (FSL)	8	3	.727	2.92	55	0	0	0	12	83 1/3	87	36	27	25	45
1994—Dunedin (FSL)	3	2	.600	2.73	18	0	0	0	3	26 1/3	25	8	8	5	19
—Knoxville (Sou.)	4	3	.571	3.76	25	10	0	0	0	95 2/3	103	49	40	16	55
1995—Syracuse (I.L.)	4	5	.444	5.40	25	15	0	0	1	91 2/3	111	62	55	27	38
—Knoxville (Sou.)	4	1	.800	3.91	12	1	0	0	0	25 1/3	26	12	11	6	16
1996—Salinas (West.)■	•12	6	.667	3.47	22	22	0	...	0	148	138	68	57	42	102
1997—Taipei (Taiwan)■	7	3	.700	5.18	40	...	...	...	5	99	85	...	...	33	78
1998—Taipei (Taiwan)	12	7	.632	3.56	56	...	...	...	7	144	150	...	...	52	122
1999—Fresno (PCL)■	2	4	.333	3.34	51	0	0	0	8	86 1/3	78	34	32	28	67
2000—San Francisco (N.L.)	0	1	.000	14.63	9	0	0	0	0	8	16	13	13	4	6
—Fresno (PCL)	4	8	.333	2.42	38	3	0	0	7	78	72	31	21	20	66
—Erie (East.)■	0	1	.000	16.20	2	0	0	0	0	1 2/3	3	5	3	2	2
—Anaheim (A.L.)	1	0	1.000	1.84	10	0	0	0	0	14 2/3	12	6	3	2	8
A.L. totals (1 year)	1	0	1.000	1.84	10	0	0	0	0	14 2/3	12	6	3	2	8
N.L. totals (1 year)	0	1	.000	14.63	9	0	0	0	0	8	16	13	13	4	6
Major League totals (1 year)	1	1	.500	6.35	19	0	0	0	0	22 2/3	28	19	16	6	14

WEBSTER, LENNY — C

PERSONAL: Born February 10, 1965, in New Orleans. ... 5-9/200. ... Bats right, throws right. ... Full name: Leonard Irell Webster.
HIGH SCHOOL: Lutcher (La.).
COLLEGE: Grambling State.
TRANSACTIONS/CAREER NOTES: Selected by Minnesota Twins organization in 16th round of free-agent draft (June 7, 1982); did not sign. ... Selected by Twins organization in 21st round of free-agent draft (June 3, 1985). ... Traded by Twins to Montreal Expos for a player to be named later (March 14, 1994). ... Granted free agency (December 23, 1994). ... Signed by Philadelphia Phillies organization (April 7, 1995). ... Claimed on waivers by Expos (March 29, 1996). ... Granted free agency (October 16, 1996). ... Signed by Baltimore Orioles organization (December 18, 1996). ... Granted free agency (October 30, 1997). ... Re-signed by Orioles (November 24, 1997). ... On Baltimore disabled list (May 13-July 16, 1999); included rehabilitation assignment to Rochester (June 22-July 8). ... Released by Orioles (July 21, 1999). ... Signed by Boston Red Sox (July 28, 1999). ... Released by Red Sox (August 20, 1999). ... Signed by Montreal Expos organization (January 13, 2000). ... On disabled list (June 7-22 and August 17-September 1, 2000). ... Granted free agency (October 31, 2000).
HONORS: Named Midwest League Most Valuable Player (1988).

Year Team (League)	Pos.	G	AB	R	H	2B	3B	HR	RBI	Avg.	BB	SO	SB	PO	A	E	Avg.
1986—Kenosha (Midw.)	C	22	65	2	10	2	0	0	8	.154	10	12	0	87	9	0	1.000
—Elizabethton (Appl.)	C	48	152	29	35	4	0	3	14	.230	22	21	1	88	11	3	.971
1987—Kenosha (Midw.)	C	52	140	17	35	7	0	3	17	.250	17	20	2	228	29	5	.981
1988—Kenosha (Midw.)	C	129	465	82	134	23	2	11	87	.288	71	47	3	606	96	14	.980
1989—Visalia (Calif.)	C	63	231	36	62	7	0	5	39	.268	27	27	2	352	57	4	.990
—Orlando (Sou.)	C	59	191	29	45	7	0	2	17	.236	44	20	2	293	46	4	.988
—Minnesota (A.L.)	C	14	20	3	6	2	0	0	1	.300	3	2	0	32	0	1	1.000
1990—Orlando (Sou.)	C	126	455	69	119	31	0	8	71	.262	68	57	0	629	70	9	.987
—Minnesota (A.L.)	C	2	6	1	2	1	0	0	0	.333	1	1	0	9	0	1	1.000
1991—Portland (PCL)	C	87	325	43	82	18	0	7	34	.252	24	32	1	477	65	6	*.989
—Minnesota (A.L.)	C	18	34	7	10	1	0	3	8	.294	6	10	0	61	10	1	.986
1992—Minnesota (A.L.)	C-DH	53	118	10	33	10	1	1	13	.280	9	11	0	190	11	1	.995
1993—Minnesota (A.L.)	C-DH	49	106	14	21	2	0	1	8	.198	11	8	1	177	13	0	1.000
1994—Montreal (N.L.)■	C	57	143	13	39	10	0	5	23	.273	16	24	0	237	19	1	.996

Year	Team (League)	Pos.	G	AB	R	H	2B	3B	HR	RBI	Avg.	BB	SO	SB	PO	A	E	Avg.
1995— Philadelphia (N.L.)■ ..	C	49	150	18	40	9	0	4	14	.267	16	27	0	274	18	3	.990
1996— Montreal (N.L.)■.......	C	78	174	18	40	10	0	2	17	.230	25	21	0	390	25	1	.998
1997— Baltimore (A.L.)■......	C-DH	98	259	29	66	8	1	7	37	.255	22	46	0	532	36	3	.995
1998— Baltimore (A.L.).......	C-DH	108	309	37	88	16	0	10	46	.285	15	38	0	528	39	4	.993
1999— Baltimore (A.L.).........	C-DH	16	36	1	6	1	0	0	3	.167	8	5	0	67	6	1	.986
— Rochester (I.L.).........	C-DH	13	43	8	13	5	0	3	9	.302	4	8	0	49	4	0	1.000
— Boston (A.L.)■.........	C	6	14	0	0	0	0	0	1	.000	2	2	0	25	3	0	1.000
2000— Montreal (N.L.)■.......	C	39	81	6	17	3	0	0	5	.210	6	14	0	126	9	0	1.000
American League totals (8 years)		364	902	102	232	41	2	22	117	.257	77	123	1	1621	118	10	.994
National League totals (4 years)		223	548	55	136	32	0	11	59	.248	63	86	0	1027	71	5	.995
Major League totals (12 years)		587	1450	157	368	73	2	33	176	.254	140	209	1	2648	189	15	.995

DIVISION SERIES RECORD

Year	Team (League)	Pos.	G	AB	R	H	2B	3B	HR	RBI	Avg.	BB	SO	SB	PO	A	E	Avg.
1997— Baltimore (A.L.).........	C	3	6	1	1	0	0	0	1	.167	1	0	0	20	0	0	1.000

CHAMPIONSHIP SERIES RECORD

Year	Team (League)	Pos.	G	AB	R	H	2B	3B	HR	RBI	Avg.	BB	SO	SB	PO	A	E	Avg.
1997— Baltimore (A.L.)..........	C-PH	4	9	0	2	0	0	0	0	.222	0	1	0	14	0	2	.875

WEHNER, JOHN — OF/3B — PIRATES

PERSONAL: Born June 29, 1967, in Pittsburgh. ... 6-3/206. ... Bats right, throws right. ... Full name: John Paul Wehner. ... Name pronounced WAY-ner.

HIGH SCHOOL: Carrick (Pittsburgh).

COLLEGE: Indiana.

TRANSACTIONS/CAREER NOTES: Selected by Pittsburgh Pirates organization in seventh round of free-agent draft (June 1, 1988). ... On Pittsburgh disabled list (August 29-October 7, 1991; and July 20, 1994-remainder of season). ... Claimed on waivers by Los Angeles Dodgers (October 15, 1996). ... Released by Dodgers (March 17, 1997). ... Signed by Florida Marlins organization (March 21, 1997). ... On Florida disabled list (June 26-September 1, 1997). ... Released by Marlins (November 20, 1997). ... Re-signed by Marlins organization (March 4, 1998). ... Granted free agency (September 29, 1998). ... Signed by Pittsburgh Pirates organization (June 9, 1999). ... Granted free agency (October 12, 1999). ... Re-signed by Pirates organization (January 18, 2000). ... On Nashville disabled list (April 6-13, 2000). ... Granted free agency (October 11, 2000). ... Re-signed by Pirates organization (January 9, 2001).

STATISTICAL NOTES: Led New York-Pennsylvania League third basemen with 219 total chances and 14 double plays in 1988. ... Led Carolina League third basemen with 403 total chances and tied for lead with 24 double plays in 1989. ... Led Eastern League third basemen with 476 total chances and 40 double plays in 1990. ... Led Pacific Coast League second basemen with .984 fielding percentage in 2000.

Year	Team (League)	Pos.	G	AB	R	H	2B	3B	HR	RBI	Avg.	BB	SO	SB	PO	A	E	Avg.
1988— Watertown (NY-P)	3B	70	265	41	73	6	0	3	31	.275	21	39	18	*65	137	17	.922
1989— Salem (Caro.)............	3B	*137	*515	69	*155	32	6	14	73	.301	42	81	21	*89	*278	36	.911
1990— Harrisburg (East.).......	3B	•138	*511	71	147	27	1	4	62	.288	40	51	24	*109	*317	*50	.895
1991— Carolina (Sou.)...........	3B-1B	61	234	30	62	5	1	3	21	.265	24	32	17	182	134	10	.969
— Buffalo (A.A.).............	3B	31	112	18	34	9	2	1	15	.304	14	12	6	30	69	8	.925
— Pittsburgh (N.L.)........	3B	37	106	15	36	7	0	0	7	.340	7	17	3	23	65	6	.936
1992— Buffalo (A.A.)............	2B-1B-3B	60	223	37	60	13	2	7	27	.269	29	30	10	226	122	7	.980
— Pittsburgh (N.L.)........	3B-1B-2B	55	123	11	22	6	0	0	4	.179	12	22	3	96	64	4	.976
1993— Pittsburgh (N.L.)........	OF-3B-2B	29	35	3	5	0	0	0	0	.143	6	10	0	17	8	0	1.000
— Buffalo (A.A.).............	3B-2B-OF	89	330	61	83	22	2	7	34	.252	40	53	17	133	256	17	.958
1994— Buffalo (A.A.).............	OF-3B-2B	88	330	52	100	19	3	4	44	.303	32	36	21	131	113	11	.957
— Pittsburgh (N.L.)........	3B	2	4	1	1	1	0	0	3	.250	0	1	0	0	2	0	1.000
1995— Calgary (PCL)............	3B-2B-OF	40	158	30	52	12	2	4	24	.329	12	16	8	36	98	12	.918
— Pittsburgh (N.L.)....OF-3B-C-SS		52	107	13	33	0	3	0	5	.308	10	17	3	35	29	0	1.000
1996— Pittsburgh (N.L.).....OF-3B-2B-C		86	139	19	36	9	1	2	13	.259	8	22	1	60	43	2	.981
1997— Charlotte (I.L.)■.........3B-OF-1B-2B		31	93	16	26	5	0	3	11	.280	6	18	3	32	33	2	.970
— Florida (N.L.).............	OF-3B	44	36	8	10	2	0	0	2	.278	2	5	1	14	3	0	1.000
1998— Charlotte (I.L.).........	OF-DH-P	30	83	12	27	1	0	3	15	.325	4	16	5	29	3	2	.941
— Florida (N.L.).............	3B	53	88	10	20	2	0	0	5	.227	7	12	1	27	12	0	1.000
1999— Altoona (East.)■	3B-OF	4	12	2	2	0	0	0	2	.167	0	0	1	2	5	1	.875
— Nashville (PCL)........	SS-OF-2B	17	58	14	25	3	0	8	15	.431	3	6	0	22	37	3	.952
— Pittsburgh (N.L.)....OF-3B-SS-2B		39	65	6	12	2	0	1	4	.185	7	12	1	28	4	1	.970
2000— Nashville (PCL).....2B-3B-1B-OF		121	427	57	109	23	0	16	63	.255	56	65	14	264	303	12	.979
— Pittsburgh (N.L.)........	3B-OF	21	50	10	15	3	0	1	9	.300	4	6	0	14	22	1	.973
Major League totals (10 years)		418	753	96	190	32	4	4	52	.252	63	124	13	314	252	14	.976

DIVISION SERIES RECORD

Year	Team (League)	Pos.	G	AB	R	H	2B	3B	HR	RBI	Avg.	BB	SO	SB	PO	A	E	Avg.
1997— Florida (N.L.)..............	PR-OF	1	0	0	0	0	0	0	0	...	0	0	0	0	0	0	...

CHAMPIONSHIP SERIES RECORD

Year	Team (League)	Pos.	G	AB	R	H	2B	3B	HR	RBI	Avg.	BB	SO	SB	PO	A	E	Avg.
1992— Pittsburgh (N.L.)	PH	2	2	0	0	0	0	0	0	.000	0	2	0	...	...	...	...

RECORD AS PITCHER

Year	League	W	L	Pct.	ERA	G	GS	CG	ShO	Sv.	IP	H	R	ER	BB	SO
1998— Charlotte (I.L.).................	0	0	...	0.00	1	0	0	0	0	1	0	0	0	1	0

W

PERSONAL: Born November 28, 1963, in Tuxedo, N.Y. ... 6-0/188. ... Bats both, throws right. ... Full name: Walter William Weiss Jr.
HIGH SCHOOL: Suffern (N.Y.).
COLLEGE: North Carolina.
TRANSACTIONS/CAREER NOTES: Selected by Baltimore Orioles organization in 10th round of free-agent draft (June 7, 1982); did not sign. ... Selected by Oakland Athletics organization in first round (11th pick overall) of free-agent draft (June 3, 1985). ... On Oakland disabled list (May 18-July 31, 1989); included rehabilitation assignments to Tacoma (July 18-25) and Modesto (July 26-31). ... On disabled list (August 23-September 7, 1990; April 15-30 and June 7, 1991-remainder of season). ... On Oakland disabled list (March 30-June 3, 1992); included rehabilitation assignment to Tacoma (May 26-June 3). ... Traded by A's to Florida Marlins for C Eric Helfand and a player to be named later (November 17, 1992); A's acquired P Scott Baker to complete deal (November 20, 1992). ... Granted free agency (October 25, 1993). ... Signed by Colorado Rockies (January 7, 1994). ... Granted free agency (November 3, 1995). ... Re-signed by Rockies (December 6, 1995). ... On disabled list (July 22-August 8, 1997). ... Granted free agency (October 27, 1997). ... Signed by Atlanta Braves (November 17, 1997). ... On disabled list (June 7-July 1, 1999). ... On disabled list (May 5-21, 2000). ... Granted free agency (October 30, 2000).
HONORS: Named A.L. Rookie Player of the Year by The Sporting News (1988). ... Named A.L. Rookie of the Year by Baseball Writers' Association of America (1988).
STATISTICAL NOTES: Led N.L. shortstops with 99 double plays in 1995. ... Career major league grand slams: 1.

Year Team (League)	Pos.	G	AB	R	H	2B	3B	HR	RBI	Avg.	BB	SO	SB	PO	A	E	Avg.
1985— Pocatello (Pio.)...........	SS	40	158	19	49	9	3	0	21	.310	12	18	6	51	126	11	.941
— Modesto (Calif.)	SS	30	122	17	24	4	1	0	7	.197	12	20	3	36	97	7	.950
1986— Madison (Midw.)	SS	84	322	50	97	15	5	2	54	.301	33	66	12	143	251	20	.952
— Huntsville (Sou.)	SS	46	160	19	40	2	1	0	13	.250	11	39	5	72	142	11	.951
1987— Huntsville (Sou.)	SS	91	337	43	96	16	2	1	32	.285	47	67	23	152	259	17	.960
— Oakland (A.L.)	SS-DH	16	26	3	12	4	0	0	1	.462	2	2	1	8	30	1	.974
— Tacoma (PCL)	SS	46	179	35	47	4	3	0	17	.263	28	31	8	76	140	11	.952
1988— Oakland (A.L.)	SS	147	452	44	113	17	3	3	39	.250	35	56	4	254	431	15	.979
1989— Oakland (A.L.)	SS	84	236	30	55	11	0	3	21	.233	21	39	6	106	195	15	.953
— Tacoma (PCL)	SS	2	9	1	1	1	0	0	1	.111	0	0	0	3	3	1	.750
— Modesto (Calif.)	SS	5	8	1	3	0	0	0	1	.375	4	1	0	6	9	0	1.000
1990— Oakland (A.L.)	SS	138	445	50	118	17	1	2	35	.265	46	53	9	194	373	12	.979
1991— Oakland (A.L.)	SS	40	133	15	30	6	1	0	13	.226	12	14	6	64	99	5	.970
1992— Tacoma (PCL)	SS	4	13	2	3	1	0	0	3	.231	2	1	0	8	14	1	.957
— Oakland (A.L.)	SS	103	316	36	67	5	2	0	21	.212	43	39	6	144	270	19	.956
1993— Florida (N.L.)■.........	SS	158	500	50	133	14	2	1	39	.266	79	73	7	229	406	15	.977
1994— Colorado (N.L.)■.......	SS	110	423	58	106	11	4	1	32	.251	56	58	12	157	318	13	.973
1995— Colorado (N.L.)	SS	137	427	65	111	17	3	1	25	.260	98	57	15	201	406	16	.974
1996— Colorado (N.L.)	SS	155	517	89	146	20	2	8	48	.282	80	78	10	220	450	*30	.957
1997— Colorado (N.L.)	SS	121	393	52	106	23	5	4	38	.270	66	56	5	191	372	10	.983
1998— Atlanta (N.L.)■.........	SS	96	347	64	97	18	2	0	27	.280	59	53	7	97	257	12	.967
1999— Atlanta (N.L.)	SS	110	279	38	63	13	4	2	29	.226	35	48	7	108	203	12	.963
2000— Atlanta (N.L.)	SS	80	192	29	50	6	2	0	18	.260	26	32	1	83	197	15	.949
American League totals (6 years)		528	1608	178	395	60	7	8	130	.246	159	203	32	770	1398	67	.970
National League totals (8 years)		967	3078	445	812	122	24	17	256	.264	499	455	64	1286	2609	123	.969
Major League totals (14 years)		1495	4686	623	1207	182	31	25	386	.258	658	658	96	2056	4007	190	.970

DIVISION SERIES RECORD

Year Team (League)	Pos.	G	AB	R	H	2B	3B	HR	RBI	Avg.	BB	SO	SB	PO	A	E	Avg.
1995— Colorado (N.L.)	SS	4	12	1	2	0	0	0	0	.167	3	3	1	6	12	0	1.000
1998— Atlanta (N.L.).............	SS	3	13	2	2	0	0	0	0	.154	1	3	0	6	3	0	1.000
1999— Atlanta (N.L.).............	SS-PH	3	6	1	1	0	0	0	0	.167	0	2	0	0	5	0	1.000
2000— Atlanta (N.L.).............	SS	1	3	0	2	1	0	0	2	.667	0	0	0	2	1	0	1.000
Division series totals (4 years)		11	34	4	7	1	0	0	2	.206	4	8	1	14	21	0	1.000

CHAMPIONSHIP SERIES RECORD

Year Team (League)	Pos.	G	AB	R	H	2B	3B	HR	RBI	Avg.	BB	SO	SB	PO	A	E	Avg.
1988— Oakland (A.L.)	SS	4	15	2	5	2	0	0	2	.333	0	4	0	7	10	0	1.000
1989— Oakland (A.L.)	SS-PR	4	9	2	1	1	0	0	0	.111	1	1	1	5	9	0	1.000
1990— Oakland (A.L.)	SS	2	7	2	0	0	0	0	0	.000	2	2	0	2	7	1	.900
1992— Oakland (A.L.)	SS	3	6	1	1	0	0	0	0	.167	2	1	2	5	6	0	1.000
1998— Atlanta (N.L.)	SS	4	15	0	3	0	0	0	1	.200	2	5	1	4	11	0	1.000
1999— Atlanta (N.L.)	SS	6	21	2	6	2	0	0	1	.286	2	4	2	9	14	1	.958
Championship series totals (6 years)		23	73	9	16	5	0	0	4	.219	9	17	6	32	57	2	.978

WORLD SERIES RECORD

NOTES: Member of World Series championship team (1989).

Year Team (League)	Pos.	G	AB	R	H	2B	3B	HR	RBI	Avg.	BB	SO	SB	PO	A	E	Avg.
1988— Oakland (A.L.)	SS	5	16	1	1	0	0	0	0	.063	0	1	0	5	11	1	.941
1989— Oakland (A.L.)	SS	4	15	3	2	0	0	1	1	.133	2	2	0	7	8	0	1.000
1999— Atlanta (N.L.)	SS	3	9	1	2	0	0	0	0	.222	0	1	0	6	5	0	1.000
World Series totals (3 years)		12	40	5	5	0	0	1	1	.125	2	4	0	18	24	1	.977

ALL-STAR GAME RECORD

Year League	Pos.	AB	R	H	2B	3B	HR	RBI	Avg.	BB	SO	SB	PO	A	E	Avg.
1998— National	SS	3	1	2	0	0	0	1	.667	0	0	0	2	2	0	1.000

W

PERSONAL: Born November 1, 1966, in Yakima, Wash. ... 6-0/200. ... Throws right, bats right. ... Full name: Robert Lee Wells.
HIGH SCHOOL: Eisenhower (Yakima, Wash.).
JUNIOR COLLEGE: Spokane Falls Community College (Wash.).
TRANSACTIONS/CAREER NOTES: Signed as non-drafted free agent by Philadelphia Phillies organization (August 18, 1988). ... On Reading disabled list (July 21, 1991-remainder of season). ... On Scranton/Wilkes-Barre disabled list (April 9-28, 1992). ... On Reading disabled list (June 9, 1992-remainder of season and April 8-June 13, 1993). ... Claimed on waivers by Seattle Mariners (June 30, 1994). ... On Seattle disabled list (April 16-May 19, 1998); included rehabilitation assignment to Wisconsin (May 12-19). ... Released by Mariners (November 19, 1998). ... Signed by Minnesota Twins organization (January 27, 1999).

Year League	W	L	Pct.	ERA	G	GS	CG	ShO	Sv.	IP	H	R	ER	BB	SO
1989— Martinsville (Appl.)	0	0	...	4.50	4	0	0	0	0	6	8	5	3	2	3
1990— Spartanburg (S.Atl.)	5	8	.385	2.87	20	19	2	0	0	113	94	47	36	40	73
— Clearwater (FSL)	0	2	.000	4.91	6	1	0	0	1	14²/₃	17	9	8	6	11
1991— Clearwater (FSL)	7	2	.778	3.11	24	9	1	0	0	75¹/₃	63	27	26	19	66
— Reading (East.)	1	0	1.000	3.60	1	1	0	0	0	5	4	2	2	1	3
1992— Clearwater (FSL)	1	0	1.000	3.86	9	0	0	0	5	9¹/₃	10	4	4	3	9
— Reading (East.)	0	1	.000	1.17	3	3	0	0	0	15¹/₃	12	2	2	5	11
1993— Clearwater (FSL)	1	0	1.000	0.98	12	1	0	0	2	27²/₃	23	5	3	6	24
— Scranton/W.B. (I.L.)	1	1	.500	2.79	11	0	0	0	0	19¹/₃	19	7	6	5	8
1994— Reading (East.)	1	3	.250	2.79	14	0	0	0	4	19¹/₃	18	6	6	3	19
— Philadelphia (N.L.)	1	0	1.000	1.80	6	0	0	0	0	5	4	1	1	3	3
— Scranton/W.B. (I.L.)	0	2	.000	2.45	11	0	0	0	0	14²/₃	18	6	4	6	13
— Calgary (PCL)■	3	2	.600	6.54	6	6	0	0	0	31²/₃	43	27	23	9	17
— Seattle (A.L.)	1	0	1.000	2.25	1	0	0	0	0	4	4	1	1	1	3
1995— Seattle (A.L.)	4	3	.571	5.75	30	4	0	0	0	76²/₃	88	51	49	39	38
1996— Seattle (A.L.)	12	7	.632	5.30	36	16	1	1	0	130²/₃	141	78	77	46	94
1997— Seattle (A.L.)	2	0	1.000	5.75	46	1	0	0	2	67¹/₃	88	49	43	18	51
1998— Seattle (A.L.)	2	2	.500	6.10	30	0	0	0	0	51²/₃	54	38	35	16	29
— Wisconsin (Midw.)	0	1	.000	3.00	1	1	0	0	0	3	4	2	1	0	2
1999— Minnesota (A.L.)■	8	3	.727	3.81	•76	0	0	0	1	87¹/₃	79	41	37	28	44
2000— Minnesota (A.L.)	0	7	.000	3.65	76	0	0	0	10	86¹/₃	80	39	35	15	76
A.L. totals (7 years)	29	22	.569	4.95	295	21	1	1	13	504	534	297	277	163	335
N.L. totals (1 year)	1	0	1.000	1.80	6	0	0	0	0	5	4	1	1	3	3
Major League totals (7 years)	30	22	.577	4.92	301	21	1	1	13	509	538	298	278	166	338

DIVISION SERIES RECORD

Year League	W	L	Pct.	ERA	G	GS	CG	ShO	Sv.	IP	H	R	ER	BB	SO
1995— Seattle (A.L.)	0	0	...	9.00	1	0	0	0	0	1	2	1	1	0	0
1997— Seattle (A.L.)	0	0	...	0.00	1	0	0	0	0	1¹/₃	1	0	0	0	1
Division series totals (2 years)	0	0	...	3.86	2	0	0	0	0	2¹/₃	3	1	1	1	1

CHAMPIONSHIP SERIES RECORD

Year League	W	L	Pct.	ERA	G	GS	CG	ShO	Sv.	IP	H	R	ER	BB	SO
1995— Seattle (A.L.)	0	0	...	3.00	1	0	0	0	0	3	2	1	1	2	2

PERSONAL: Born May 20, 1963, in Torrance, Calif. ... 6-4/235. ... Throws left, bats left. ... Full name: David Lee Wells.
HIGH SCHOOL: Point Loma (San Diego).
TRANSACTIONS/CAREER NOTES: Selected by Toronto Blue Jays organization in second round of free-agent draft (June 7, 1982). ... On Knoxville disabled list (June 28, 1984-remainder of season). ... On disabled list (April 10, 1985-entire season). ... On Knoxville disabled list (July 7-August 20, 1986). ... Released by Blue Jays (March 30, 1993). ... Signed by Detroit Tigers (April 3, 1993). ... On disabled list (August 1-20, 1993). ... Granted free agency (October 28, 1993). ... Re-signed by Tigers (December 13, 1993). ... On Detroit disabled list (April 19-June 6, 1994); included rehabilitation assignment to Lakeland (May 27-June 6). ... Traded by Tigers to Cincinnati Reds for P C.J. Nitkowski, P David Tuttle and a player to be named later (July 31, 1995); Tigers acquired IF Mark Lewis to complete deal (November 16, 1995). ... Traded by Reds to Baltimore Orioles for OF Curtis Goodwin and OF Trovin Valdez (December 26, 1995). ... Granted free agency (October 29, 1996). ... Signed by New York Yankees (December 24, 1996). ... Traded by Yankees with P Graeme Lloyd and 2B Homer Bush to Blue Jays for P Roger Clemens (February 18, 1999). ... Traded by Blue Jays with P Matt DeWitt to Chicago White Sox for P Mike Sirotka, P Kevin Beirne, OF Brian Simmons and P Mike Williams (January 14, 2001).
RECORDS: Holds A.L. single-season records for most consecutive batsmen retired—38 (May 12 [last 10], 17 [all 27] and 23 [first], 1998); fewest innings pitched by leader—231²/₃ (1999); and fewest complete games for leader—7 (1999).
HONORS: Named lefthanded pitcher on THE SPORTING NEWS A.L. All-Star team (1998 and 2000).
STATISTICAL NOTES: Struck out 16 batters in one game (July 30, 1997). ... Pitched 4-0 perfect game against Minnesota (May 17, 1998).

Year League	W	L	Pct.	ERA	G	GS	CG	ShO	Sv.	IP	H	R	ER	BB	SO
1982— Medicine Hat (Pio.)	4	3	.571	5.18	12	12	1	0	0	64¹/₃	71	42	37	32	53
1983— Kinston (Caro.)	6	5	.545	3.73	25	25	5	0	0	157	141	81	65	71	115
1984— Kinston (Caro.)	1	6	.143	4.71	7	7	0	0	0	42	51	29	22	19	44
— Knoxville (Sou.)	3	2	.600	2.59	8	8	3	1	0	59	58	22	17	17	34
1985— Syracuse (I.L.)							Did not play.								
1986— Florence (S.Atl.)	0	0	...	3.55	4	1	0	0	0	12²/₃	7	6	5	9	14
— Ventura (Calif.)	2	1	.667	1.89	5	2	0	0	0	19	13	5	4	4	26
— Knoxville (Sou.)	1	3	.250	4.05	10	7	1	0	0	40	42	24	18	18	32
— Syracuse (I.L.)	0	1	.000	9.82	3	0	0	0	0	3²/₃	6	4	4	1	2
1987— Syracuse (I.L.)	4	6	.400	3.87	43	12	0	0	6	109¹/₃	102	49	47	32	106
— Toronto (A.L.)	4	3	.571	3.99	18	2	0	0	1	29¹/₃	37	14	13	12	32
1988— Toronto (A.L.)	3	5	.375	4.62	41	0	0	0	4	64¹/₃	65	36	33	31	56
— Syracuse (I.L.)	0	0	...	0.00	6	0	0	0	3	5²/₃	7	1	0	2	8
1989— Toronto (A.L.)	7	4	.636	2.40	54	0	0	0	2	86¹/₃	66	25	23	28	78
1990— Toronto (A.L.)	11	6	.647	3.14	43	25	0	0	3	189	165	72	66	45	115
1991— Toronto (A.L.)	15	10	.600	3.72	40	28	2	0	1	198¹/₃	188	88	82	49	106

Year League	W	L	Pct.	ERA	G	GS	CG	ShO	Sv.	IP	H	R	ER	BB	SO
1992— Toronto (A.L.)..................	7	9	.438	5.40	41	14	0	0	2	120	138	84	72	36	62
1993— Detroit (A.L.)■.............	11	9	.550	4.19	32	30	0	0	0	187	183	93	87	42	139
1994— Lakeland (FSL).............	0	0	...	0.00	2	2	0	0	0	6	5	1	0	0	3
— Detroit (A.L.)..................	5	7	.417	3.96	16	16	5	1	0	111 1/3	113	54	49	24	71
1995— Detroit (A.L.)..............	10	3	.769	3.04	18	18	3	0	0	130 1/3	120	54	44	37	83
— Cincinnati (N.L.)■.............	6	5	.545	3.59	11	11	3	0	0	72 2/3	74	34	29	16	50
1996— Baltimore (A.L.)■..........	11	14	.440	5.14	34	34	3	0	0	224 1/3	247	132	128	51	130
1997— New York (A.L.)■..........	16	10	.615	4.21	32	32	5	2	0	218	239	109	102	45	156
1998— New York (A.L.)..............	18	4	*.818	3.49	30	30	8	*5	0	214 1/3	195	86	83	29	163
1999— Toronto (A.L.)■..............	17	10	.630	4.82	34	34	*7	1	0	*231 2/3	*246	132	124	62	169
2000— Toronto (A.L.)................	•20	8	.714	4.11	35	•35	*9	1	0	229 2/3	*266	115	105	31	166
A.L. totals (14 years)	155	102	.603	4.07	468	298	42	10	13	2234	2268	1094	1011	522	1526
N.L. totals (1 year)	6	5	.545	3.59	11	11	3	0	0	72 2/3	74	34	29	16	50
Major League totals (14 years)	161	107	.601	4.06	479	309	45	10	13	2306 2/3	2342	1128	1040	538	1576

DIVISION SERIES RECORD

RECORDS: Shares career record for most wins—4. ... Shares A.L. career record for most wins—3.

Year League	W	L	Pct.	ERA	G	GS	CG	ShO	Sv.	IP	H	R	ER	BB	SO
1995— Cincinnati (N.L.)	1	0	1.000	0.00	1	1	0	0	0	6 1/3	6	1	0	1	8
1996— Baltimore (A.L.)................	1	0	1.000	4.61	2	2	0	0	0	13 2/3	15	7	7	5	6
1997— New York (A.L.)..............	1	0	1.000	1.00	1	1	1	0	0	9	5	1	1	0	1
1998— New York (A.L.)..............	1	0	1.000	0.00	1	1	0	0	0	8	5	0	0	1	9
Division series totals (4 years)	4	0	1.000	1.95	5	5	1	0	0	37	31	9	8	7	24

CHAMPIONSHIP SERIES RECORD

NOTES: Named A.L. Championship Series Most Valuable Player (1998).

Year League	W	L	Pct.	ERA	G	GS	CG	ShO	Sv.	IP	H	R	ER	BB	SO
1989— Toronto (A.L.)................	0	0	...	0.00	1	0	0	0	0	1	0	1	0	2	1
1991— Toronto (A.L.)................	0	0	...	2.35	4	0	0	0	0	7 2/3	6	2	2	2	9
1992— Toronto (A.L.)................								Did not play.							
1995— Cincinnati (N.L.).............	0	1	.000	4.50	1	1	0	0	0	6	8	3	3	2	3
1996— Baltimore (A.L.).............	1	0	1.000	4.05	1	1	0	0	0	6 2/3	8	3	3	3	6
1998— New York (A.L.).............	2	0	1.000	2.87	2	2	0	0	0	15 2/3	12	5	5	2	18
Champ. series totals (5 years)	3	1	.750	3.16	9	4	0	0	0	37	34	14	13	11	37

WORLD SERIES RECORD

NOTES: Member of World Series championship team (1992 and 1998).

Year League	W	L	Pct.	ERA	G	GS	CG	ShO	Sv.	IP	H	R	ER	BB	SO
1992— Toronto (A.L.)................	0	0	...	0.00	4	0	0	0	0	4 1/3	1	0	0	2	3
1998— New York (A.L.)................	1	0	1.000	6.43	1	1	0	0	0	7	7	5	5	2	4
World Series totals (2 years)	1	0	1.000	3.97	5	1	0	0	0	11 1/3	8	5	5	4	7

ALL-STAR GAME RECORD

Year League	W	L	Pct.	ERA	GS	CG	ShO	Sv.	IP	H	R	ER	BB	SO
1995— American	0	0	...	0.00	0	0	0	0	1/3	0	0	0	0	1
1998— American	0	0	...	0.00	1	0	0	0	2	0	0	0	1	1
2000— American	0	0	...	0.00	1	0	0	0	2	2	0	0	0	2
All-Star Game totals (3 years)	0	0	...	0.00	2	0	0	0	4 1/3	2	0	0	1	4

WELLS, KIP   P   WHITE SOX

PERSONAL: Born April 21, 1977, in Houston. ... 6-3/196. ... Throws right, bats right. ... Full name: Robert Kip Wells.
HIGH SCHOOL: Elkins (Fort Bend, Texas).
COLLEGE: Baylor.
TRANSACTIONS/CAREER NOTES: Selected by Milwaukee Brewers organization in 58th round of free-agent draft (June 1, 1995); did not sign. ... Selected by Chicago White Sox organization in first round (16th pick overall) of free-agent draft (June 2, 1998).

Year League	W	L	Pct.	ERA	G	GS	CG	ShO	Sv.	IP	H	R	ER	BB	SO
1999— Winston-Salem (Caro.).......	5	6	.455	3.57	14	14	0	0	0	85 2/3	78	39	34	34	95
— Birmingham (Sou.).............	8	2	.800	2.94	11	11	0	0	0	70 1/3	49	24	23	31	44
— Chicago (A.L.)....................	4	1	.800	4.04	7	7	0	0	0	35 2/3	33	17	16	15	29
2000— Chicago (A.L.)................	6	9	.400	6.02	20	20	0	0	0	98 2/3	126	76	66	58	71
— Charlotte (I.L.)................	5	3	.625	5.37	12	12	2	1	0	62	67	38	37	27	38
Major League totals (2 years)	10	10	.500	5.49	27	27	0	0	0	134 1/3	159	93	82	73	100

WELLS, VERNON   OF   BLUE JAYS

PERSONAL: Born December 8, 1978, in Shreveport, La. ... 6-1/210. ... Bats right, throws right. ... Full name: Vernon Wells III.
HIGH SCHOOL: Bowie (Arlington, Texas).
TRANSACTIONS/CAREER NOTES: Selected by Toronto Blue Jays organization in first round (fifth pick overall) of free-agent draft (June 3, 1997).
HONORS: Named Florida State League Most Valuable Player (1999).

Year Team (League)	Pos.	G	AB	R	H	2B	3B	HR	RBI	Avg.	BB	SO	SB	PO	A	E	Avg.
							BATTING								FIELDING		
1997— St. Catharines (NY-P).	OF	66	264	52	81	20	1	10	31	.307	30	44	8	135	6	7	.953
1998— Hagerstown (S.Atl.)....	OF	134	509	86	145	35	2	11	65	.285	49	84	13	243	6	5	.980
1999— Dunedin (FSL).............	OF-DH	70	265	43	91	16	2	11	43	.343	26	34	13	130	3	1	.993
— Knoxville (Sou.)..........	OF	26	106	18	36	6	2	3	17	.340	12	15	6	56	4	0	1.000
— Syracuse (I.L.)...........	OF	33	129	20	40	8	1	4	21	.310	10	22	5	79	2	2	.976
— Toronto (A.L.).............	OF	25	88	8	23	5	0	1	8	.261	4	18	1	50	4	0	1.000
2000— Syracuse (I.L.)...........	OF	127	493	76	120	31	7	16	66	.243	48	88	23	293	8	3	.990
— Toronto (A.L.).............	OF	3	2	0	0	0	0	0	0	.000	0	0	0	2	0	0	1.000
Major League totals (2 years)		28	90	8	23	5	0	1	8	.256	4	18	1	52	4	0	1.000

W

PERSONAL: Born May 19, 1967, in Pittsfield, Mass. ... 6-2/205. ... Throws right, bats left. ... Full name: Steven John Wendell.
HIGH SCHOOL: Wahconah Regional (Dalton, Mass.).
COLLEGE: Quinnipiac College (Conn.).
TRANSACTIONS/CAREER NOTES: Selected by Atlanta Braves organization in fifth round of free-agent draft (June 1, 1988). ... Traded by Braves with P Yorkis Perez to Chicago Cubs for P Mike Bielecki and C Damon Berryhill (September 29, 1991). ... On disabled list (May 4, 1992-remainder of season). ... On Chicago disabled list (April 16-May 27, 1995); included rehabilitation assignments to Daytona (May 5-15) and Orlando (May 15-27). ... Traded by Cubs with OF Brian McRae and P Mel Rojas to New York Mets for OF Lance Johnson and two players to be named later (August 8, 1997); Cubs acquired P Mark Clark (August 11, 1997) and IF Manny Alexander (August 14, 1997) to complete deal. ... Granted free agency (November 3, 2000). ... Re-signed by Mets (December 1, 2000).

Year — League	W	L	Pct.	ERA	G	GS	CG	ShO	Sv.	IP	H	R	ER	BB	SO
1988— Pulaski (Appl.)	3	•8	.273	3.83	14	14	*6	1	0	*101	85	50	43	30	87
1989— Burlington (Midw.)	9	11	.450	2.21	22	22	•9	*5	0	159	127	63	39	41	153
— Greenville (Sou.)	0	0	...	9.82	1	1	0	0	0	3 2/3	7	5	4	1	3
— Durham (Caro.)	2	0	1.000	1.13	3	3	1	0	0	24	13	4	3	6	27
1990— Durham (Caro.)	1	3	.250	1.86	6	5	1	0	0	38 2/3	24	10	8	15	26
— Greenville (Sou.)	4	9	.308	5.74	36	13	1	1	2	91	105	70	58	48	85
1991— Greenville (Sou.)	11	3	*.786	2.56	25	20	1	1	0	147 2/3	130	47	42	51	122
— Richmond (I.L.)	0	2	.000	3.43	3	3	1	0	0	21	20	9	8	16	18
1992— Iowa (A.A.)■	2	0	1.000	1.44	4	4	0	0	0	25	17	7	4	15	12
1993— Iowa (A.A.)	10	8	.556	4.60	25	25	3	0	0	148 2/3	148	88	76	47	110
— Chicago (N.L.)	1	2	.333	4.37	7	4	0	0	0	22 2/3	24	13	11	8	15
1994— Iowa (A.A.)	11	6	.647	2.95	23	23	6	•3	0	168	141	58	55	28	118
— Chicago (N.L.)	0	1	.000	11.93	6	2	0	0	0	14 1/3	22	20	19	10	9
1995— Daytona (FSL)	0	0	...	1.17	4	2	0	0	0	7 2/3	5	2	1	1	8
— Orlando (Sou.)	1	0	1.000	3.86	5	0	0	0	1	7	6	3	3	4	7
— Chicago (N.L.)	3	1	.750	4.92	43	0	0	0	0	60 1/3	71	35	33	24	50
1996— Chicago (N.L.)	4	5	.444	2.84	70	0	0	0	18	79 1/3	58	26	25	44	75
1997— Chicago (N.L.)	3	5	.375	4.20	52	0	0	0	4	60	53	32	28	39	54
— New York (N.L.)■	0	0	...	4.96	13	0	0	0	0	16 1/3	15	10	9	14	10
1998— New York (N.L.)	5	1	.833	2.93	66	0	0	0	4	76 2/3	62	25	25	33	58
1999— New York (N.L.)	5	4	.556	3.05	80	0	0	0	3	85 2/3	80	31	29	37	77
2000— New York (N.L.)	8	6	.571	3.59	77	0	0	0	1	82 2/3	60	36	33	41	73
Major League totals (8 years)	29	25	.537	3.83	414	6	0	0	31	498	445	228	212	250	421

DIVISION SERIES RECORD

Year — League	W	L	Pct.	ERA	G	GS	CG	ShO	Sv.	IP	H	R	ER	BB	SO
1999— New York (N.L.)	1	0	1.000	0.00	2	0	0	0	0	2	0	0	0	2	0
2000— New York (N.L.)	0	0	...	0.00	2	0	0	0	0	2	0	0	0	1	5
Division series totals (2 years)	1	0	1.000	0.00	4	0	0	0	0	4	0	0	0	3	5

CHAMPIONSHIP SERIES RECORD

Year — League	W	L	Pct.	ERA	G	GS	CG	ShO	Sv.	IP	H	R	ER	BB	SO
1999— New York (N.L.)	1	0	1.000	4.76	5	0	0	0	0	5 2/3	2	3	3	4	5
2000— New York (N.L.)	1	0	1.000	0.00	2	0	0	0	0	1 1/3	1	0	0	1	2
Champ. series totals (2 years)	2	0	1.000	3.86	7	0	0	0	0	7	3	3	3	5	7

WORLD SERIES RECORD

Year — League	W	L	Pct.	ERA	G	GS	CG	ShO	Sv.	IP	H	R	ER	BB	SO
2000— New York (N.L.)	0	1	.000	5.40	2	0	0	0	0	1 2/3	3	1	1	2	2

PERSONAL: Born November 6, 1969, in Sioux City, Iowa. ... 6-3/205. ... Throws right, bats right. ... Full name: Donald Paul Wengert. ... Brother of Bill Wengert, pitcher with Los Angeles Dodgers, San Diego Padres and Boston Red Sox organizations (1988-95).
HIGH SCHOOL: Heelan Catholic (Sioux City, Iowa).
COLLEGE: Iowa State.
TRANSACTIONS/CAREER NOTES: Selected by Cincinnati Reds organization in 60th round of free-agent draft (June 1, 1988); did not sign. ... Selected by Oakland Athletics organization in fourth round of free-agent draft (June 1, 1992). ... On Oakland disabled list (July 30-August 18, 1995); included rehabilitation assignment to Edmonton (August 7-18). ... On disabled list (July 24-August 8, 1996). ... Traded by A's with IF David Newhan to San Diego Padres for P Doug Bochtler and IF Jorge Velandia (November 26, 1997). ... Traded by Padres to Chicago Cubs for P Ben VanRyn (May 5, 1998). ... Granted free agency (November 25, 1998). ... Signed by Kansas City Royals organization (December 21, 1998). ... Released by Royals (July 15, 1999). ... Signed by New York Yankees organization (July 27, 1999). ... Released by Yankees (August 27, 1999). ... Signed by Atlanta Braves organization (August 30, 1999). ... Granted free agency (October 15, 1999). ... Signed by Houston Astros organization (January 5, 2000). ... Released by Astros (March 14, 2000). ... Signed by Braves organization (March 30, 2000). ... Granted free agency (October 2, 2000).
MISCELLANEOUS: Appeared in two games as pinch runner and had a sacrifice hit in only appearance as pinch hitter with Chicago (1998).

Year — League	W	L	Pct.	ERA	G	GS	CG	ShO	Sv.	IP	H	R	ER	BB	SO
1992— Southern Oregon (N'West.)	2	0	1.000	1.46	6	5	1	0	0	37	32	6	6	7	29
— Madison (Midw.)	3	4	.429	3.38	7	7	0	0	0	40	42	20	15	17	29
1993— Madison (Midw.)	6	5	.545	3.32	13	13	2	0	0	78 2/3	79	30	29	18	46
— Modesto (Calif.)	3	6	.333	4.73	12	12	0	0	0	70 1/3	75	42	37	29	43
1994— Modesto (Calif.)	4	1	.800	2.95	10	7	0	0	2	42 2/3	40	15	14	11	52
— Huntsville (Sou.)	6	4	.600	3.26	17	17	1	0	0	99 1/3	86	43	36	33	92
1995— Oakland (A.L.)	1	1	.500	3.34	19	0	0	0	0	29 2/3	30	14	11	12	16
— Edmonton (PCL)	1	1	.500	7.38	16	6	0	0	1	39	55	32	32	16	20
1996— Oakland (A.L.)	7	11	.389	5.58	36	25	1	1	0	161 1/3	200	102	100	60	75
1997— Oakland (A.L.)	5	11	.313	6.04	49	12	1	0	2	134	177	96	90	41	68

Year League	W	L	Pct.	ERA	G	GS	CG	ShO	Sv.	IP	H	R	ER	BB	SO
1998— San Diego (N.L.)■	0	0	...	5.93	10	0	0	0	1	13 2/3	21	9	9	5	5
—Chicago (N.L.)■	1	5	.167	5.07	21	6	0	0	0	49 2/3	55	29	28	23	41
—Iowa (PCL)	3	1	.750	4.58	9	9	1	0	0	53	58	30	27	14	48
1999— Kansas City (A.L.)■	0	1	.000	9.25	11	1	0	0	0	24 1/3	41	26	25	5	10
—Omaha (PCL)	4	0	1.000	4.17	16	2	0	0	0	41	41	20	19	9	24
—Columbus (I.L.)■	0	1	.000	7.63	6	2	0	0	0	15 1/3	25	13	13	3	5
—Richmond (I.L.)■	0	0	...	4.50	1	1	0	0	0	6	7	3	3	0	3
2000— Richmond (I.L.)	4	7	.364	4.23	29	12	1	0	0	110 2/3	117	55	52	22	83
—Atlanta (N.L.)	0	1	.000	7.20	10	0	0	0	0	10	12	9	8	5	7
A.L. totals (4 years)	13	24	.351	5.82	115	38	2	1	2	349 1/3	448	238	226	118	169
N.L. totals (2 years)	1	6	.143	5.52	41	6	0	0	1	73 1/3	88	47	45	33	53
Major League totals (6 years)	14	30	.318	5.77	156	44	2	1	3	422 2/3	536	285	271	151	222

WESTBROOK, JAKE   P   INDIANS

PERSONAL: Born September 29, 1977, in Athens, Ga. ... 6-3/185. ... Throws right, bats right. ... Full name: Jacob Cauthen Westbrook.
HIGH SCHOOL: Madison County (Danielsville, Ga.).
TRANSACTIONS/CAREER NOTES: Selected by Colorado Rockies organization in first round (21st pick overall) of free-agent draft (June 4, 1996). ... Traded by Rockies with P John Nicholson and OF Mark Hamlin to Montreal Expos for 2B Mike Lansing (December 16, 1997). ... Traded by Expos with two players to be named later to New York Yankees for P Hideki Irabu (December 22, 1999); Yankees acquired P Ted Lilly (March 17, 2000) and P Christian Parker (March 22, 2000) to complete deal. ... On Columbus disabled list (July 5-23, 2000). ... Traded by Yankees with P Zach Day to Cleveland Indians (July 25, 2000), completing deal in which Indians traded OF Dave Justice to Yankees for OF Ricky Ledee and two players to be named later (June 29, 2000). ... On Buffalo disabled list (July 25-September 1, 2000). ... On Cleveland disabled list (September 1, 2000-remainder of season).
STATISTICAL NOTES: Led Eastern League pitchers with 19 putouts, 40 assists, 61 total chances and six double plays in 1999.

Year League	W	L	Pct.	ERA	G	GS	CG	ShO	Sv.	IP	H	R	ER	BB	SO
1996— Arizona Rockies (Ariz.)	4	2	.667	2.87	11	11	0	0	0	62 2/3	66	33	20	14	57
—Portland (N'West)	1	1	.500	2.55	4	4	0	0	0	24 2/3	22	8	7	5	19
1997— Asheville (S.Atl.)	*14	11	.560	4.82	28	27	3	2	0	170	176	93	91	55	92
1998— Jupiter (FSL)■	11	6	.647	3.26	27	27	2	0	0	171	169	70	62	60	79
1999— Harrisburg (East.)	11	5	.688	3.92	27	27	2	2	0	174 2/3	180	88	76	63	90
2000— Columbus (I.L.)■	5	7	.417	4.65	16	15	2	0	0	89	94	53	46	38	61
—New York (A.L.)	0	2	.000	13.50	3	2	0	0	0	6 2/3	15	10	10	4	1
Major League totals (1 year)	0	2	.000	13.50	3	2	0	0	0	6 2/3	15	10	10	4	1

WETTELAND, JOHN   P

PERSONAL: Born August 21, 1966, in San Mateo, Calif. ... 6-2/215. ... Throws right, bats right. ... Full name: John Karl Wetteland.
HIGH SCHOOL: Cardinal Newman (Santa Rosa, Calif.).
COLLEGE: College of San Mateo (Calif.).
TRANSACTIONS/CAREER NOTES: Selected by New York Mets organization in 12th round of free-agent draft (June 4, 1984); did not sign. ... Selected by Los Angeles Dodgers organization in secondary phase of free-agent draft (January 9, 1985). ... Selected by Detroit Tigers from Dodgers organization in Rule 5 major league draft (December 7, 1987). ... Returned to Dodgers organization (March 29, 1988). ... On Albuquerque disabled list (May 1-8 and June 3-29, 1991). ... Traded by Dodgers with P Tim Belcher to Cincinnati Reds for OF Eric Davis and P Kip Gross (November 25, 1991). ... Traded by Reds with P Bill Risley to Montreal Expos for OF Dave Martinez, P Scott Ruskin and SS Willie Greene (December 11, 1991). ... On Montreal disabled list (March 23-April 23, 1993); included rehabilitation assignment to West Palm Beach (April 18-23). ... On disabled list (April 18-May 4, 1994). ... Traded by Expos to New York Yankees for OF Fernando Seguignol and cash (April 5, 1995). ... On disabled list (August 13-September 6, 1996). ... Granted free agency (November 5, 1996). ... Signed by Texas Rangers (December 17, 1996). ... Granted free agency (November 1, 2000).
HONORS: Named A.L. Fireman of the Year by THE SPORTING NEWS (1996).
STATISTICAL NOTES: Tied for Florida State League lead with 11 home runs allowed and 17 wild pitches in 1987. ... Led Texas League with 22 wild pitches in 1988.
MISCELLANEOUS: Holds Texas Rangers all-time record for saves (140).

Year League	W	L	Pct.	ERA	G	GS	CG	ShO	Sv.	IP	H	R	ER	BB	SO
1985— Great Falls (Pio.)	1	1	.500	3.92	11	2	0	0	0	20 2/3	17	10	9	15	23
1986— Bakersfield (Calif.)	0	7	.000	5.78	15	12	4	0	0	67	71	50	43	46	38
—Great Falls (Pio.)	4	3	.571	5.45	12	12	1	0	0	69 1/3	70	51	42	40	59
1987— Vero Beach (FSL)	12	7	.632	3.13	27	27	7	2	0	175 2/3	150	81	61	92	144
1988— San Antonio (Texas)	10	8	.556	3.88	25	25	3	1	0	162 1/3	141	74	70	•77	140
1989— Albuquerque (PCL)	5	3	.625	3.65	10	10	1	0	0	69	61	28	28	20	73
—Los Angeles (N.L.)	5	8	.385	3.77	31	12	0	0	1	102 2/3	81	46	43	34	96
1990— Los Angeles (N.L.)	2	4	.333	4.81	22	5	0	0	0	43	44	28	23	17	36
—Albuquerque (PCL)	2	2	.500	5.59	8	5	1	0	0	29	27	19	18	13	26
1991— Albuquerque (PCL)	4	3	.571	2.79	41	4	0	0	20	61 1/3	48	22	19	26	55
—Los Angeles (N.L.)	1	0	1.000	0.00	6	0	0	0	0	9	5	2	0	3	9
1992— Montreal (N.L.)■	4	4	.500	2.92	67	0	0	0	37	83 1/3	64	27	27	36	99
1993— West Palm Beach (FSL)	0	0	...	0.00	2	2	0	0	0	3	0	0	0	0	6
—Montreal (N.L.)	9	3	.750	1.37	70	0	0	0	43	85 1/3	58	17	13	28	113
1994— Montreal (N.L.)	4	6	.400	2.83	52	0	0	0	25	63 2/3	46	22	20	21	68
1995— New York (A.L.)■	1	5	.167	2.93	60	0	0	0	31	61 1/3	40	22	20	14	66
1996— New York (A.L.)	2	3	.400	2.83	62	0	0	0	*43	63 2/3	54	23	20	21	69
1997— Texas (A.L.)■	7	2	.778	1.94	61	0	0	0	31	65	43	18	14	21	63
1998— Texas (A.L.)	3	1	.750	2.03	63	0	0	0	42	62	47	17	14	14	72
1999— Texas (A.L.)	4	4	.500	3.68	62	0	0	0	43	66	67	30	27	19	60
2000— Texas (A.L.)	6	5	.545	4.20	62	0	0	0	34	60	67	35	28	24	53
A.L. totals (6 years)	23	20	.535	2.93	370	0	0	0	224	378	318	145	123	113	383
N.L. totals (6 years)	25	25	.500	2.93	248	17	0	0	106	387	298	142	126	139	421
Major League totals (12 years)	48	45	.516	2.93	618	17	0	0	330	765	616	287	249	252	804

W

DIVISION SERIES RECORD

Year	League	W	L	Pct.	ERA	G	GS	CG	ShO	Sv.	IP	H	R	ER	BB	SO
1995— New York (A.L.)................		0	1	.000	14.54	3	0	0	0	0	4 1/3	8	7	7	2	5
1996— New York (A.L.)................		0	0	...	0.00	3	0	0	0	2	4	2	0	0	5	4
1998— Texas (A.L.)...................		0	0	...	0.00	1	0	0	0	0	1	0	0	0	1	1
1999— Texas (A.L.)...................		0	0	...	0.00	1	0	0	0	0	1	0	0	0	0	1
Division series totals (4 years)		**0**	**1**	**.000**	**6.10**	**8**	**0**	**0**	**0**	**2**	**10 1/3**	**10**	**7**	**7**	**8**	**11**

CHAMPIONSHIP SERIES RECORD

Year	League	W	L	Pct.	ERA	G	GS	CG	ShO	Sv.	IP	H	R	ER	BB	SO
1996— New York (A.L.)................		0	0	...	4.50	4	0	0	0	1	4	2	2	2	1	5

WORLD SERIES RECORD

RECORDS: Holds single-series record for most saves—4 (1996).
NOTES: Named Most Valuable Player (1996). ... Member of World Series championship team (1996).

Year	League	W	L	Pct.	ERA	G	GS	CG	ShO	Sv.	IP	H	R	ER	BB	SO
1996— New York (A.L.)................		0	0	...	2.08	5	0	0	0	4	4 1/3	4	1	1	1	6

ALL-STAR GAME RECORD

Year	League	W	L	Pct.	ERA	GS	CG	ShO	Sv.	IP	H	R	ER	BB	SO
1996— American..........................							Did not play.								
1998— American..........................		0	0	...	0.00	0	0	0	0	1	0	0	0	0	1
1999— American..........................		0	0	...	0.00	0	0	0	1	1	1	0	0	0	1
All-Star Game totals (2 years)		**0**	**0**	**...**	**0.00**	**0**	**0**	**0**	**1**	**2**	**1**	**0**	**0**	**0**	**2**

WHEELER, DAN   P   DEVIL RAYS

PERSONAL: Born December 10, 1977, in Providence, R.I. ... 6-3/222. ... Throws right, bats right. ... Full name: Daniel Michael Wheeler.
HIGH SCHOOL: Pilgrim (Warwick, R.I.).
JUNIOR COLLEGE: Central Arizona College.
TRANSACTIONS/CAREER NOTES: Selected by Tampa Bay Devil Rays organization in 34th round of free-agent draft (June 4, 1996).
STATISTICAL NOTES: Led International League with 35 home runs allowed in 2000.

Year	League	W	L	Pct.	ERA	G	GS	CG	ShO	Sv.	IP	H	R	ER	BB	SO
1997— Hudson Valley (NY-Penn)...		6	7	.462	3.00	15	15	0	0	0	84	75	38	28	17	81
1998— Charleston, S.C. (S.Atl.)		12	14	.462	4.43	29	29	3	1	0	181	206	96	89	29	136
1999— Orlando (Sou.)..................		3	0	1.000	3.26	9	9	0	0	0	58	56	27	21	8	53
— Durham (I.L.)...................		7	5	.583	4.92	14	14	2	1	0	82 1/3	103	59	45	25	58
— Tampa Bay (A.L.).............		0	4	.000	5.87	6	6	0	0	0	30 2/3	35	20	20	13	32
2000— Tampa Bay (A.L.)...............		1	1	.500	5.48	11	2	0	0	0	23	29	14	14	11	17
— Durham (I.L.)...................		5	11	.313	5.63	26	26	0	0	0	150 1/3	183	109	94	42	91
Major League totals (2 years).......		**1**	**5**	**.167**	**5.70**	**17**	**8**	**0**	**0**	**0**	**53 2/3**	**64**	**34**	**34**	**24**	**49**

WHISENANT, MATT   P   DODGERS

PERSONAL: Born June 8, 1971, in Los Angeles. ... 6-3/215. ... Throws left, bats right. ... Full name: Matthew Michael Whisenant.
HIGH SCHOOL: La Canada (Calif.).
JUNIOR COLLEGE: Glendale (Ariz.) Community College.
TRANSACTIONS/CAREER NOTES: Selected by Philadelphia Phillies organization in 18th round of free-agent draft (June 5, 1989). ... Traded by Phillies with P Joel Adamson to Florida Marlins for P Danny Jackson (November 17, 1992). ... On disabled list (July 13, 1993-remainder of season). ... On Florida disabled list (March 28-July 4, 1997); included rehabilitation assignments to Brevard County (April 18-21) and Charlotte (May 5-July 4). ... Traded by Marlins to Kansas City Royals for C Matt Treanor (July 29, 1997). ... Released by Royals (August 14, 1999). ... Signed by San Diego Padres (August 20, 1999). ... On Las Vegas disabled list (July 27-August 11, 2000). ... Granted free agency (October 3, 2000). ... Signed by Los Angeles Dodgers organization (December 14, 2000).
STATISTICAL NOTES: Led International League with 30 wild pitches in 1996.
MISCELLANEOUS: Appeared in one game as pinch runner with Kansas City (1997).

Year	League	W	L	Pct.	ERA	G	GS	CG	ShO	Sv.	IP	H	R	ER	BB	SO
1990— Princeton (Appl.)...............		0	0	...	11.40	9	2	0	0	0	15	16	27	19	20	25
1991— Batavia (NY-Penn)		2	1	.667	2.45	11	10	0	0	0	47 2/3	31	19	13	42	55
1992— Spartanburg (S.Atl.)		11	7	.611	3.23	27	27	2	0	0	150 2/3	117	69	54	85	151
1993— Kane County (Midw.)∎......		2	6	.250	4.69	15	15	0	0	0	71	68	45	37	56	74
1994— Brevard County (FSL)........		6	9	.400	3.38	28	26	5	1	0	160	125	71	60	82	103
1995— Portland (East.)................		10	6	.625	3.50	23	22	2	0	0	128 2/3	106	57	50	65	107
— Portland (East.)................		10	6	.625	3.50	23	22	2	0	0	128 2/3	103	57	50	65	107
1996— Charlotte (I.L.)..................		8	10	.444	6.92	28	22	1	0	0	121	149	107	93	101	97
1997— Brevard County (FSL)........		0	0	...	8.10	2	1	0	0	0	3 1/3	3	3	3	3	4
— Charlotte (I.L.).................		2	1	.667	7.20	16	0	0	0	0	15	16	12	12	12	19
— Florida (N.L.)...................		0	0	...	16.88	4	0	0	0	0	2 2/3	4	6	5	6	4
— Kansas City (A.L.)∎..........		1	0	1.000	2.84	24	0	0	0	0	19	15	7	6	12	16
1998— Kansas City (A.L.)		2	1	.667	4.90	70	0	0	0	2	60 2/3	61	37	33	33	45
1999— Kansas City (A.L.)		4	4	.500	6.35	48	0	0	0	1	39 2/3	40	28	28	26	27
— San Diego (N.L.)∎		0	1	.000	3.68	19	0	0	0	0	14 2/3	10	6	6	10	10
2000— San Diego (N.L.)		2	2	.500	3.80	24	0	0	0	0	21 1/3	16	12	9	17	12
— Las Vegas (PCL)		0	3	.000	5.31	33	0	0	0	0	39	49	26	23	26	24
A.L. totals (3 years)		**7**	**5**	**.583**	**5.05**	**142**	**0**	**0**	**0**	**3**	**119 1/3**	**116**	**72**	**67**	**71**	**88**
N.L. totals (3 years)		**2**	**3**	**.400**	**4.66**	**47**	**0**	**0**	**0**	**0**	**38 2/3**	**30**	**24**	**20**	**33**	**26**
Major League totals (4 years)		**9**	**8**	**.529**	**4.96**	**189**	**0**	**0**	**0**	**3**	**158**	**146**	**96**	**87**	**104**	**114**

W

PERSONAL: Born December 29, 1962, in Kingston, Jamaica. ... 6-2/190. ... Bats both, throws right. ... Full name: Devon Markes White.

HIGH SCHOOL: Park West (New York).

TRANSACTIONS/CAREER NOTES: Selected by California Angels organization in sixth round of free-agent draft (June 8, 1981). ... On suspended list (June 11-12 and July 19, 1982-remainder of season). ... On Edmonton disabled list (May 12-22, 1986). ... On disabled list (May 7-June 10, 1988). ... Traded by Angels with P Willie Fraser and a player to be named later to Toronto Blue Jays for OF Junior Felix, IF Luis Sojo and a player to be named later (December 2, 1990); Blue Jays acquired P Marcus Moore and Angels acquired C Ken Rivers to complete deal (December 4, 1990). ... Granted free agency (November 1, 1995). ... Signed by Florida Marlins (November 21, 1995). ... On disabled list (April 25-May 30 and June 8-July 28, 1997). ... Traded by Marlins to Arizona Diamondbacks for P Jesus Martinez (November 18, 1997). ... Granted free agency (October 23, 1998). ... Signed by Los Angeles Dodgers (November 9, 1998). ... On Los Angeles disabled list (May 3-July 23, 2000); included rehabilitation assignment to San Bernardino (July 20-22).

RECORDS: Shares major league record for most stolen bases in one inning—3 (September 9, 1989, sixth inning).

HONORS: Won A.L. Gold Glove as outfielder (1988-89 and 1991-95).

STATISTICAL NOTES: Led Midwest League outfielders with 286 total chances in 1983. ... Led California League outfielders with 351 total chances in 1984. ... Led Pacific Coast League outfielders with 339 total chances in 1986. ... Switch-hit home runs in one game three times (June 23, 1987; June 29, 1990; and June 1, 1992). ... Led A.L. outfielders with 449 total chances in 1987, 448 in 1991 and 458 in 1992. ... Career major league grand slams: 8.

							BATTING							FIELDING		
Year — Team (League)	Pos.	G	AB	R	H	2B	3B	HR	RBI	Avg.	BB	SO	SB	PO	A	E	Avg.
1981— Idaho Falls (Pio.)	OF-3B-1B	30	106	10	19	2	0	0	10	.179	12	34	4	33	10	3	.935
1982— Danville (Midw.)	OF	57	186	21	40	6	1	1	11	.215	11	41	11	89	3	8	.920
1983— Peoria (Midw.)	OF	117	430	69	109	17	6	13	66	.253	36	124	32	267	8	11	.962
—Nashua (East.)	OF	17	70	11	18	7	2	0	2	.257	7	22	5	37	0	3	.925
1984— Redwood (Calif.)	OF	138	520	101	147	25	5	7	55	.283	56	118	36	*322	16	13	.963
1985— Midland (Texas)	OF	70	260	52	77	10	4	4	35	.296	35	46	38	176	10	4	.979
—Edmonton (PCL)	OF	66	277	53	70	16	5	4	39	.253	24	77	21	205	6	2	.991
—California (A.L.)	OF	21	7	7	1	0	0	0	0	.143	1	3	1	10	1	0	1.000
1986— Edmonton (PCL)	OF	112	461	84	134	25	10	14	60	.291	31	90	*42	317	•16	6	.982
—California (A.L.)	OF	29	51	8	12	1	1	1	3	.235	6	8	6	49	0	2	.961
1987— California (A.L.)	OF	159	639	103	168	33	5	24	87	.263	39	135	32	*424	16	9	.980
1988— California (A.L.)	OF	122	455	76	118	22	2	11	51	.259	23	84	17	364	7	9	.976
1989— California (A.L.)	OF-DH	156	636	86	156	18	13	12	56	.245	31	129	44	430	10	5	.989
1990— California (A.L.)	OF	125	443	57	96	17	3	11	44	.217	44	116	21	302	11	9	.972
—Edmonton (PCL)	OF	14	55	9	20	4	4	0	6	.364	7	12	4	31	1	3	.914
1991— Toronto (A.L.)■	OF	156	642	110	181	40	10	17	60	.282	55	135	33	*439	8	1	*.998
1992— Toronto (A.L.)	OF-DH	153	641	98	159	26	7	17	60	.248	47	133	37	*443	6	7	.985
1993— Toronto (A.L.)	OF	146	598	116	163	42	6	15	52	.273	57	127	34	399	6	3	.993
1994— Toronto (A.L.)	OF	100	403	67	109	24	6	13	49	.270	21	80	11	268	3	6	.978
1995— Toronto (A.L.)	OF	101	427	61	121	23	5	10	53	.283	29	97	11	261	7	3	.989
1996— Florida (N.L.)■	OF	146	552	77	151	37	6	17	84	.274	38	99	22	296	5	4	.987
1997— Florida (N.L.)	OF	74	265	37	65	13	1	6	34	.245	32	65	13	152	4	2	.987
1998— Arizona (N.L.)■	OF	146	563	84	157	32	1	22	85	.279	42	102	22	371	3	5	.987
1999— Los Angeles (N.L.)■	OF-DH	134	474	60	127	20	2	14	68	.268	39	88	19	273	3	4	.986
2000— Los Angeles (N.L.)	OF	47	158	26	42	5	1	4	13	.266	9	30	3	68	2	2	.972
—San Bern. (Calif.)	OF	2	5	2	2	1	0	0	1	.400	1	1	0	3	0	0	1.000
American League totals (11 years)		1268	4942	789	1284	246	58	131	515	.260	353	1047	249	3389	77	54	.985
National League totals (5 years)		547	2012	284	542	107	11	63	284	.269	160	384	79	1160	17	17	.986
Major League totals (16 years)		1815	6954	1073	1826	353	69	194	799	.263	513	1431	328	4549	94	71	.985

DIVISION SERIES RECORD

							BATTING							FIELDING		
Year — Team (League)	Pos.	G	AB	R	H	2B	3B	HR	RBI	Avg.	BB	SO	SB	PO	A	E	Avg.
1997— Florida (N.L.)	OF	3	11	1	2	0	0	1	4	.182	2	3	0	3	0	0	1.000

CHAMPIONSHIP SERIES RECORD

RECORDS: Holds A.L. career record for highest batting average (50 or more at-bats)—.392. ... Holds single-series record for most times caught stealing—4 (1992). ... Shares A.L. single-series record for most hits—12 (1993). ... Shares A.L. single-game record for most at-bats—6 (October 11, 1992, 11 innings).

							BATTING							FIELDING		
Year — Team (League)	Pos.	G	AB	R	H	2B	3B	HR	RBI	Avg.	BB	SO	SB	PO	A	E	Avg.
1986— California (A.L.)	OF-PR	4	2	2	1	0	0	0	0	.500	0	1	0	3	0	0	1.000
1991— Toronto (A.L.)	OF	5	22	5	8	1	0	0	0	.364	2	3	3	16	0	0	1.000
1992— Toronto (A.L.)	OF	6	23	2	8	2	0	0	2	.348	5	6	0	16	0	1	.941
1993— Toronto (A.L.)	OF	6	27	3	12	1	1	1	2	.444	1	5	0	15	0	0	1.000
1997— Florida (N.L.)	OF	6	21	4	4	1	0	0	1	.190	2	7	1	16	0	0	1.000
Championship series totals (5 years)		27	95	16	33	5	1	1	5	.347	10	22	4	66	0	1	.985

WORLD SERIES RECORD

RECORDS: Shares record for most consecutive strikeouts in one series—5 (October 21 [1] and 22 [4], 1997).

NOTES: Member of World Series championship team (1992, 1993 and 1997).

							BATTING							FIELDING		
Year — Team (League)	Pos.	G	AB	R	H	2B	3B	HR	RBI	Avg.	BB	SO	SB	PO	A	E	Avg.
1992— Toronto (A.L.)	OF	6	26	2	6	1	0	0	2	.231	0	6	1	22	0	0	1.000
1993— Toronto (A.L.)	OF	6	24	8	7	3	2	1	7	.292	4	7	1	16	0	0	1.000
1997— Florida (N.L.)	OF	7	33	0	8	3	1	0	2	.242	3	10	1	16	0	0	1.000
World Series totals (3 years)		19	83	10	21	7	3	1	11	.253	7	23	3	54	0	0	1.000

ALL-STAR GAME RECORD

						BATTING							FIELDING		
Year — League	Pos.	AB	R	H	2B	3B	HR	RBI	Avg.	BB	SO	SB	PO	A	E	Avg.
1989— American	OF	1	0	0	0	0	0	0	.000	0	0	0	0	0	0	...
1993— American	OF	2	1	1	1	0	0	1	.500	0	0	0	1	0	0	1.000
1998— National	OF	3	1	3	0	1	0	0	1.000	0	0	0	0	0	0	...
All-Star Game totals (3 years)		6	2	4	1	1	0	1	.667	0	0	0	1	0	0	1.000

W

WHITE, GABE   P   ROCKIES

PERSONAL: Born November 20, 1971, in Sebring, Fla. ... 6-2/200. ... Throws left, bats left. ... Full name: Gabriel Allen White.
HIGH SCHOOL: Sebring (Fla.).
TRANSACTIONS/CAREER NOTES: Selected by Montreal Expos organization in supplemental round ("sandwich pick" between first and second round, 28th pick overall) of free-agent draft (June 4, 1990); pick received as part of compensation for California Angels signing Type A free-agent P Mark Langston. ... On Harrisburg disabled list (July 2-27, 1993). ... On Ottawa disabled list (April 7-May 6, 1994). ... Traded by Expos to Cincinnati Reds for 2B Jhonny Carvajal (December 15, 1995). ... On disabled list (September 17, 1996-remainder of season). ... Traded by Reds to Colorado Rockies for P Manny Aybar (April 7, 2000).
RECORDS: Shares N.L. record for most consecutive home runs allowed in one inning—3 (July 7, 1995, second inning).

Year League	W	L	Pct.	ERA	G	GS	CG	ShO	Sv.	IP	H	R	ER	BB	SO
1990— Gulf Coast Expos (GCL)	4	2	.667	3.14	11	11	1	0	0	57 1/3	50	21	20	12	41
1991— Sumter (S.Atl.)	6	9	.400	3.26	24	24	5	0	0	149	127	73	54	53	140
1992— Rockford (Midw.)	14	8	.636	2.84	27	27	7	0	0	187	148	73	59	61	*176
1993— Harrisburg (East.).............	7	2	.778	2.16	16	16	2	1	0	100	80	30	24	28	80
— Ottawa (I.L.)	2	1	.667	3.12	6	6	1	1	0	40 1/3	38	15	14	6	28
1994— West Palm Beach (FSL)	1	0	1.000	1.50	1	1	0	0	0	6	2	2	1	1	4
— Ottawa (I.L.)	8	3	.727	5.05	14	14	0	0	0	73	77	49	41	28	63
— Montreal (N.L.)..................	1	1	.500	6.08	7	5	0	0	1	23 2/3	24	16	16	11	17
1995— Ottawa (I.L.)	2	3	.400	3.90	12	12	0	0	0	62 1/3	58	31	27	17	37
— Montreal (N.L.)..................	1	2	.333	7.01	19	1	0	0	0	25 2/3	26	21	20	9	25
1996— Indianapolis (A.A.)■	6	3	.667	2.77	11	11	0	0	0	68 1/3	69	25	21	9	51
1997— Indianapolis (A.A.)	7	4	.636	2.82	20	19	0	0	0	118	119	46	37	18	62
— Cincinnati (N.L.)	2	2	.500	4.39	12	6	0	0	1	41	39	20	20	8	25
1998— Cincinnati (N.L.)	5	5	.500	4.01	69	3	0	0	9	98 2/3	86	46	44	27	83
1999— Cincinnati (N.L.)	1	2	.333	4.43	50	0	0	0	0	61	68	31	30	14	61
2000— Cincinnati (N.L.)	0	0	...	18.00	1	0	0	0	0	1	2	2	2	1	2
— Colorado (N.L.)■	11	2	.846	2.17	67	0	0	0	5	83	62	21	20	14	82
Major League totals (6 years).......	21	14	.600	4.10	225	15	0	0	16	334	307	157	152	84	295

WHITE, RICK   P   METS

PERSONAL: Born December 23, 1968, in Springfield, Ohio. ... 6-4/230. ... Throws right, bats right. ... Full name: Richard Allen White.
HIGH SCHOOL: Kenton Ridge (Springfield, Ohio).
JUNIOR COLLEGE: Paducah (Ky.) Community College.
TRANSACTIONS/CAREER NOTES: Selected by Pittsburgh Pirates organization in 15th round of free-agent draft (June 4, 1990). ... On Carolina disabled list (May 15-July 6, 1993). ... On Buffalo disabled list (August 28-September 4, 1993). ... On Pittsburgh disabled list (April 14-May 17, 1995); included rehabilitation assignment to Gulf Coast Pirates (April 26-May 17). ... Granted free agency (December 21, 1995). ... Re-signed by Pirates organization (December 21, 1995). ... On Calgary disabled list (April 4-August 7, 1996). ... On Carolina disabled list (August 7-23, 1996). ... Granted free agency (October 15, 1996). ... Signed by Tampa Bay Devil Rays organization (February 4, 1997). ... Loaned by Devil Rays to Orlando, Chicago Cubs organization (April 3-September 11, 1997). ... Traded by Devil Rays with OF Bubba Trammell to New York Mets for OF Jason Tyner and P Paul Wilson (July 28, 2000).
MISCELLANEOUS: Struck out and grounded out in two appearances as pinch hitter with New York (2000).

Year League	W	L	Pct.	ERA	G	GS	CG	ShO	Sv.	IP	H	R	ER	BB	SO
1990— Gulf Coast Pirates (GCL)	3	1	.750	0.76	7	6	0	0	0	35 2/3	26	11	3	4	27
— Welland (NY-Penn)............	1	4	.200	3.26	9	5	1	0	0	38 2/3	39	19	14	14	43
1991— Augusta (S.Atl.).................	4	4	.500	3.00	34	0	0	0	6	63	68	26	21	18	52
— Salem (Caro.)	2	3	.400	4.66	13	5	1	0	1	46 1/3	41	27	24	9	36
1992— Salem (Caro.)	7	9	.438	3.80	18	18	•5	0	0	120 2/3	116	58	51	24	70
— Carolina (Sou.)	1	7	.125	4.21	10	10	1	0	0	57 2/3	59	32	27	18	45
1993— Carolina (Sou.)	4	3	.571	3.50	12	12	1	0	0	69 1/3	59	29	27	12	52
— Buffalo (A.A.)	0	3	.000	3.54	7	3	0	0	0	28	25	13	11	8	16
1994— Pittsburgh (N.L.)	4	5	.444	3.82	43	5	0	0	6	75 1/3	79	35	32	17	38
1995— Pittsburgh (N.L.)	2	3	.400	4.75	15	9	0	0	0	55	66	33	29	18	29
— Calgary (PCL)	6	4	.600	4.20	14	11	1	0	0	79 1/3	97	40	37	10	56
1996— Carolina (Sou.)	0	1	.000	11.37	2	1	0	0	0	6 1/3	9	8	8	1	7
— Gulf Coast Pirates (GCL)	0	0	...	2.25	3	3	0	0	0	12	8	4	3	3	3
1997— Orlando (Sou.)■	5	7	.417	4.71	39	8	0	0	12	86	93	55	45	22	65
1998— Durham (I.L.)■	4	2	.667	4.22	9	9	1	0	0	53 1/3	63	29	25	11	31
— Tampa Bay (A.L.)...............	2	6	.250	3.80	38	3	0	0	0	68 2/3	66	32	29	23	39
1999— Tampa Bay (A.L.)..............	5	3	.625	4.08	63	1	0	0	0	108	132	56	49	38	81
2000— Tampa Bay (A.L.)..............	3	6	.333	3.41	44	0	0	0	2	71 1/3	57	30	27	26	47
— New York (N.L.)■	2	3	.400	3.81	22	0	0	0	1	28 1/3	26	14	12	12	20
A.L. totals (3 years)	10	15	.400	3.81	145	4	0	0	2	248	255	118	105	87	167
N.L. totals (3 years)	8	11	.421	4.14	80	14	0	0	7	158 2/3	171	82	73	47	87
Major League totals (5 years).......	18	26	.409	3.94	225	18	0	0	9	406 2/3	426	200	178	134	254

DIVISION SERIES RECORD

Year League	W	L	Pct.	ERA	G	GS	CG	ShO	Sv.	IP	H	R	ER	BB	SO
2000— New York (N.L.).................	1	0	1.000	0.00	2	0	0	0	0	2 2/3	6	0	0	2	4

CHAMPIONSHIP SERIES RECORD

Year League	W	L	Pct.	ERA	G	GS	CG	ShO	Sv.	IP	H	R	ER	BB	SO
2000— New York (N.L.).................	0	0	...	9.00	1	0	0	0	0	3	5	3	3	1	1

WORLD SERIES RECORD

Year League	W	L	Pct.	ERA	G	GS	CG	ShO	Sv.	IP	H	R	ER	BB	SO
2000— New York (N.L.).................	0	0	...	6.75	1	0	0	0	0	1 1/3	1	1	1	1	1

W

PERSONAL: Born February 23, 1972, in Milledgeville, Ga. ... 6-0/210. ... Bats right, throws right. ... Full name: Rondell Bernard White.
HIGH SCHOOL: Jones County (Gray, Ga.).
TRANSACTIONS/CAREER NOTES: Selected by Montreal Expos organization in first round (24th pick overall) of free-agent draft (June 4, 1990); pick received as part of compensation for California Angels signing Type A free-agent P Mark Langston. ... On Montreal disabled list (April 28-July 16, 1996); included rehabilitation assignments to West Palm Beach (July 5-10), Gulf Coast Expos (July 5-10) and Harrisburg (July 10-16). ... On disabled list (July 21, 1998-remainder of season; and June 14-29 and July 2-17, 1999). ... On Montreal disabled list (July 8-31, 2000). ... Traded by Expos to Chicago Cubs for P Scott Downs (July 31, 2000). ... On Chicago disabled list (August 1-6 and August 27, 2000-remainder of season).
STATISTICAL NOTES: Led Gulf Coast League with 96 total bases in 1990. ... Hit for the cycle (June 11, 1995, 13 innings). ... Collected six hits in one game (June 11, 1995). ... Led N.L. outfielders in total chances with 385 in 1997. ... Career major league grand slams: 2.

Year Team (League)	Pos.	G	AB	R	H	2B	3B	HR	RBI	Avg.	BB	SO	SB	PO	A	E	Avg.
1990— GC Expos (GCL)	OF	57	221	33	66	7	4	5	34	.299	17	33	10	71	1	2	.973
1991— Sumter (S.Atl.)	OF	123	465	80	122	23	6	13	68	.262	57	109	50	215	6	3	*.987
1992— W.P. Beach (FSL)........	OF	111	450	80	142	10	*12	4	41	.316	46	78	42	187	2	3	.984
— Harrisburg (East.).......	OF	21	89	22	27	7	1	2	7	.303	6	14	6	29	1	2	.938
1993— Harrisburg (East.).......	OF	90	372	72	122	16	10	12	52	.328	22	72	21	179	4	1	.995
— Ottawa (I.L.)..............	OF-DH	37	150	28	57	8	2	7	32	.380	12	20	10	79	0	1	.988
— Montreal (N.L.)..........	OF	23	73	9	19	3	1	2	15	.260	7	16	1	33	0	0	1.000
1994— Montreal (N.L.)..........	OF	40	97	16	27	10	1	2	13	.278	9	18	1	34	1	2	.946
— Ottawa (I.L.)..............	OF	42	169	23	46	7	0	7	18	.272	15	17	9	91	4	2	.979
1995— Montreal (N.L.)..........	OF	130	474	87	140	33	4	13	57	.295	41	87	25	270	5	4	.986
1996— Montreal (N.L.)..........	OF	88	334	35	98	19	4	6	41	.293	22	53	14	185	5	2	.990
— W.P. Beach (FSL)........	DH-OF	3	10	0	2	1	0	0	2	.200	0	4	0	2	0	0	1.000
— GC Expos (GCL)	OF	3	12	3	3	0	0	2	4	.250	0	1	1	4	0	0	1.000
— Harrisburg (East.).......	OF	5	20	5	7	1	0	3	6	.350	1	1	1	12	0	0	1.000
1997— Montreal (N.L.)..........	OF	151	592	84	160	29	5	28	82	.270	31	111	16	*376	6	3	*.992
1998— Montreal (N.L.)..........	OF-DH	97	357	54	107	21	2	17	58	.300	30	57	16	261	7	1	.996
1999— Montreal (N.L.)..........	OF	138	539	83	168	26	6	22	64	.312	32	85	10	286	7	11	.964
2000— Montreal (N.L.)..........	OF	75	290	52	89	24	0	11	54	.307	28	67	5	158	4	1	.994
— Chicago (N.L.)■........	OF	19	67	7	22	2	0	2	7	.328	5	12	0	41	0	0	1.000
Major League totals (8 years)		761	2823	427	830	167	23	103	391	.294	205	506	88	1644	35	24	.986

PERSONAL: Born November 25, 1966, in Pensacola, Fla. ... 6-3/235. ... Bats both, throws right. ... Full name: Mark Anthony Whiten.
HIGH SCHOOL: Pensacola (Fla.).
JUNIOR COLLEGE: Pensacola (Fla.) Junior College.
TRANSACTIONS/CAREER NOTES: Selected by Toronto Blue Jays organization in fifth round of free-agent draft (January 14, 1986). ... On Toronto suspended list (May 23-25, 1991). ... Traded by Blue Jays with P Denis Boucher, OF Glenallen Hill and a player to be named later to Cleveland Indians for P Tom Candiotti and OF Turner Ward (June 27, 1991); Indians acquired cash to complete deal (October 15, 1991). ... Traded by Indians to St. Louis Cardinals for P Mark Clark and SS Juan Andujar (March 31, 1993). ... On St. Louis disabled list (April 18-May 5, 1994); included rehabilitation assignment to Louisville (May 2-5). ... Traded by Cardinals with P Rheal Cormier to Boston Red Sox for 3B Scott Cooper, P Cory Bailey and a player to be named later (April 8, 1995). ... On Boston disabled list (May 22-June 9, 1995); included rehabilitation assignment to Pawtucket (June 2-9). ... Traded by Red Sox to Philadelphia Phillies for 1B Dave Hollins (July 24, 1995). ... Released by Phillies (June 17, 1996). ... Signed by Atlanta Braves (June 24, 1996). ... Traded by Braves to Seattle Mariners for P Roger Blanco (August 14, 1996). ... Granted free agency (December 7, 1996). ... Signed by New York Yankees (January 9, 1997). ... Released by Yankees (August 15, 1997). ... Signed by Indians (May 6, 1998). ... Granted free agency (October 30, 1998). ... Re-signed by Indians (December 8, 1998). ... On Cleveland disabled list (March 30-June 23, 1999); included rehabilitation assignment to Buffalo (June 2-21). ... On Buffalo disabled list (August 2-9 and August 13-20, 1999). ... Granted free agency (October 15, 1999). ... Re-signed by Indians organization (February 18, 2000). ... On Buffalo disabled list (June 21-July 2, 2000). ... Granted free agency (October 18, 2000).
RECORDS: Shares major league single-game records for most home runs—4 (September 7, 1993, second game); and most runs batted in—12 (September 7, 1993, second game). ... Shares major league record for most runs batted in during doubleheader—13 (September 7, 1993). ... Shares N.L. record for most runs batted in during two consecutive games—13 (September 7, 1993, first and second games).
STATISTICAL NOTES: Tied for Pioneer League lead in being hit by pitch with six in 1986. ... Led South Atlantic League outfielders with 322 total chances and tied for lead with four double plays in 1987. ... Led South Atlantic League in being hit by pitch with 16 and tied for lead in intentional bases on balls received with 10 in 1987. ... Led Southern League in being hit by pitch with 11 in 1989. ... Hit four home runs in one game (September 7, 1993, second game). ... Switch-hit home runs in one game (September 14, 1993). ... Career major league grand slams: 4.
MISCELLANEOUS: Batted righthanded only (1988-89).

Year Team (League)	Pos.	G	AB	R	H	2B	3B	HR	RBI	Avg.	BB	SO	SB	PO	A	E	Avg.
1986— Medicine Hat (Pio.)	OF	•70	270	53	81	16	3	10	44	.300	29	56	22	111	9	*10	.923
1987— Myrtle Beach (S.Atl.)..	OF	*139	494	90	125	22	5	15	64	.253	76	149	49	*292	*18	12	.963
1988— Dunedin (FSL)...........	OF	99	385	61	97	8	5	7	37	.252	41	69	17	200	*21	9	.961
— Knoxville (Sou.).........	OF	28	108	20	28	3	1	2	9	.259	12	20	6	62	3	4	.942
1989— Knoxville (Sou.).........	OF	129	423	75	109	13	6	12	47	.258	60	114	11	223	17	8	.968
1990— Syracuse (I.L.)..........	OF	104	390	65	113	19	4	14	48	.290	37	72	14	158	14	6	.966
— Toronto (A.L.)............	OF-DH	33	88	12	24	1	1	2	7	.273	7	14	2	60	3	0	1.000
1991— Toronto (A.L.)............	OF	46	149	12	33	4	3	2	19	.221	11	35	0	90	2	0	1.000
— Cleveland (A.L.)■.......	OF-DH	70	258	34	66	14	4	7	26	.256	19	50	4	166	11	7	.962
1992— Cleveland (A.L.)........	OF-DH	148	508	73	129	19	4	9	43	.254	72	102	16	321	14	7	.980
1993— St. Louis (N.L.)■........	OF	152	562	81	142	13	4	25	99	.253	58	110	15	329	9	10	.971
1994— St. Louis (N.L.)..........	OF	92	334	57	98	18	2	14	53	.293	37	75	10	234	9	9	.964
— Louisville (A.A.)..........	OF	3	10	2	3	1	0	1	3	.300	1	1	0	3	0	0	1.000

W

Year	Team (League)	Pos.	G	AB	R	H	2B	3B	HR	RBI	Avg.	BB	SO	SB	PO	A	E	Avg.
1995—	Boston (A.L.)■...........	OF-DH	32	108	13	20	3	0	1	10	.185	8	23	1	52	4	0	1.000
—	Pawtucket (I.L.)..........	OF-DH	28	102	19	29	3	1	4	13	.284	19	30	4	43	4	3	.940
—	Philadelphia (N.L.)■ ..	OF	60	212	38	57	10	1	11	37	.269	31	63	7	105	4	4	.965
1996—	Philadelphia (N.L.)......	OF	60	182	33	43	8	0	7	21	.236	33	62	13	97	6	6	.945
—	Atlanta (N.L.)..............	OF	36	90	12	23	5	1	3	17	.256	16	25	2	41	1	3	.933
—	Seattle (A.L.)■	OF	40	140	31	42	7	0	12	33	.300	21	40	2	90	4	3	.969
1997—	New York (A.L.)■.......	OF	69	215	34	57	11	0	5	24	.265	30	47	4	102	2	5	.954
1998—	Cleveland (A.L.)■.......	OF-DH-P	88	226	31	64	14	0	6	29	.283	29	60	2	124	7	4	.970
1999—	Buffalo (I.L.)...............	OF-DH	48	175	32	49	10	0	6	19	.280	22	38	3	88	4	1	.989
—	Cleveland (A.L.)..........	OF	8	25	2	4	1	0	1	4	.160	3	4	0	11	1	0	1.000
2000—	Buffalo (I.L.)...............	OF	98	355	59	98	27	1	10	39	.276	33	72	5	139	9	7	.955
—	Cleveland (A.L.)..........	OF	6	7	2	2	1	0	0	1	.286	3	2	0	3	0	0	1.000
American League totals (9 years)			540	1724	244	441	75	12	45	196	.256	203	377	31	1019	48	26	.976
National League totals (4 years)			400	1380	221	363	54	8	60	227	.263	175	335	47	806	29	32	.963
Major League totals (11 years)			940	3104	465	804	129	20	105	423	.259	378	712	78	1825	77	58	.970

DIVISION SERIES RECORD

Year	Team (League)	Pos.	G	AB	R	H	2B	3B	HR	RBI	Avg.	BB	SO	SB	PO	A	E	Avg.
1998—	Cleveland (A.L.)								Did not play.									

CHAMPIONSHIP SERIES RECORD

Year	Team (League)	Pos.	G	AB	R	H	2B	3B	HR	RBI	Avg.	BB	SO	SB	PO	A	E	Avg.
1998—	Cleveland (A.L.).........	OF	2	7	2	2	1	0	1	1	.286	1	3	0	3	0	0	1.000

RECORD AS PITCHER

Year	League	W	L	Pct.	ERA	G	GS	CG	ShO	Sv.	IP	H	R	ER	BB	SO
1998—	Cleveland (A.L.).................	0	0	...	9.00	1	0	0	0	0	1	1	1	1	2	3

WHITESIDE, MATT — P — BRAVES

PERSONAL: Born August 8, 1967, in Charleston, Mo. ... 6-0/200. ... Throws right, bats right. ... Full name: Matthew Christopher Whiteside.
HIGH SCHOOL: Charleston (Mo.).
COLLEGE: Arkansas State.
TRANSACTIONS/CAREER NOTES: Selected by Texas Rangers organization in 25th round of free-agent draft (June 4, 1990). ... On disabled list (May 9-25, 1995). ... Granted free agency (October 30, 1996). ... Re-signed by Rangers (November 22, 1996). ... Released by Rangers (March 23, 1998). ... Signed by Philadelphia Phillies (March 27, 1998). ... Granted free agency (October 15, 1998). ... Signed by San Diego Padres organization (November 23, 1998). ... Granted free agency (October 8, 1999). ... Re-signed by Padres (October 25, 1999). ... On Las Vegas disabled list (April 21-28, 2000). ... Granted free agency (October 2, 2000). ... Signed by Atlanta Braves organization (January 18, 2001).
STATISTICAL NOTES: Tied for American Association lead with three balks in 1996.

Year	League	W	L	Pct.	ERA	G	GS	CG	ShO	Sv.	IP	H	R	ER	BB	SO
1990—	Butte (Pio.)......................	4	4	.500	3.45	18	5	0	0	2	57 1/3	57	33	22	25	45
1991—	Gastonia (S.Atl.).................	3	1	.750	2.15	48	0	0	0	29	62 2/3	44	19	15	21	71
1992—	Tulsa (Texas)	0	1	.000	2.41	33	0	0	0	21	33 2/3	31	9	9	3	30
—	Oklahoma City (A.A.)...........	1	0	1.000	0.79	12	0	0	0	8	11 1/3	7	1	1	3	13
—	Texas (A.L.).......................	1	1	.500	1.93	20	0	0	0	4	28	26	8	6	11	13
1993—	Texas (A.L.).......................	2	1	.667	4.32	60	0	0	0	1	73	78	37	35	23	39
—	Oklahoma City (A.A.)...........	2	1	.667	5.56	8	0	0	0	1	11 1/3	17	7	7	8	10
1994—	Texas (A.L.).......................	2	2	.500	5.02	47	0	0	0	1	61	68	40	34	28	37
1995—	Texas (A.L.).......................	5	4	.556	4.08	40	0	0	0	3	53	48	24	24	19	46
1996—	Texas (A.L.).......................	0	1	.000	6.68	14	0	0	0	0	32 1/3	43	24	24	11	15
—	Oklahoma City (A.A.)...........	9	6	.600	3.45	36	7	0	0	0	94	95	41	36	24	52
1997—	Oklahoma City (A.A.)...........	1	1	.500	3.54	10	1	0	0	1	28	30	14	11	13	11
—	Texas (A.L.).......................	4	1	.800	5.08	42	1	0	0	0	72 2/3	85	45	41	26	44
1998—	Philadelphia (N.L.)■	1	1	.500	8.50	10	0	0	0	0	18	27	18	17	5	14
—	Scranton/W.B. (I.L.)	1	4	.200	6.48	30	1	0	0	5	33 1/3	47	24	24	7	21
1999—	Las Vegas (PCL)■	9	5	.643	5.12	47	3	1	1	7	89 2/3	99	59	51	29	88
—	San Diego (N.L.)	1	0	1.000	13.91	10	0	0	0	0	11	19	17	17	5	9
2000—	San Diego (N.L.)	2	3	.400	4.14	28	0	0	0	0	37	32	21	17	17	27
—	Las Vegas (PCL)	2	5	.286	5.28	23	1	0	0	0	30 2/3	34	21	18	15	31
A.L. totals (6 years)		14	10	.583	4.61	223	1	0	0	9	320	348	178	164	118	194
N.L. totals (3 years)		4	4	.500	6.95	48	0	0	0	0	66	78	56	51	27	50
Major League totals (9 years)		18	14	.563	5.01	271	1	0	0	9	386	426	234	215	145	244

WICKMAN, BOB — P — INDIANS

PERSONAL: Born February 6, 1969, in Green Bay, Wis. ... 6-1/234. ... Throws right, bats right. ... Full name: Robert Joe Wickman.
HIGH SCHOOL: Oconto Falls (Wis.).
COLLEGE: Wisconsin-Whitewater.
TRANSACTIONS/CAREER NOTES: Selected by Chicago White Sox organization in second round of free-agent draft (June 4, 1990). ... Traded by White Sox with P Melido Perez and P Domingo Jean to New York Yankees for 2B Steve Sax and cash (January 10, 1992). ... Traded by Yankees with OF Gerald Williams to Milwaukee Brewers for P Graeme Lloyd and OF Pat Listach (August 23, 1996). ... Traded by Brewers with P Steve Woodard and P Jason Bere to Cleveland Indians for 1B/OF Richie Sexson, P Paul Rigdon, P Kane Davis and a player to be named later (July 28, 2000); Brewers acquired 2B Marcos Scutaro to complete deal (August 30).

Year	League	W	L	Pct.	ERA	G	GS	CG	ShO	Sv.	IP	H	R	ER	BB	SO
1990— GC White Sox (GCL)		2	0	1.000	2.45	2	2	0	0	0	11	7	4	3	1	15
— Sarasota (FSL)		0	1	.000	1.98	2	2	0	0	0	13 2/3	17	7	3	4	8
— South Bend (Midw.)		7	2	.778	1.38	9	9	3	0	0	65 1/3	50	16	10	16	50
1991— Sarasota (FSL)		5	1	.833	2.05	7	7	1	1	0	44	43	16	10	11	32
— Birmingham (Sou.)..........		6	10	.375	3.56	20	20	4	1	0	131 1/3	127	68	52	50	81
1992— Columbus (I.L.)■.............		12	5	.706	2.92	23	23	2	1	0	157	131	61	51	55	108
— New York (A.L.)................		6	1	.857	4.11	8	8	0	0	0	50 1/3	51	25	23	20	21
1993— New York (A.L.)................		14	4	.778	4.63	41	19	1	1	4	140	156	82	72	69	70
1994— New York (A.L.)................		5	4	.556	3.09	*53	0	0	0	6	70	54	26	24	27	56
1995— New York (A.L.)................		2	4	.333	4.05	63	1	0	0	1	80	77	38	36	33	51
1996— New York (A.L.)................		4	1	.800	4.67	58	0	0	0	0	79	94	41	41	34	61
— Milwaukee (A.L.)■...........		3	0	1.000	3.24	12	0	0	0	0	16 2/3	12	9	6	10	14
1997— Milwaukee (A.L.)		7	6	.538	2.73	74	0	0	0	1	95 2/3	89	32	29	41	78
1998— Milwaukee (N.L.)		6	9	.400	3.72	72	0	0	0	25	82 1/3	79	38	34	39	71
1999— Milwaukee (N.L.)		3	8	.273	3.39	71	0	0	0	37	74 1/3	75	31	28	38	60
2000— Milwaukee (N.L.)		2	2	.500	2.93	43	0	0	0	16	46	37	18	15	20	44
— Cleveland (A.L.)■...........		1	3	.250	3.38	26	0	0	0	14	26 2/3	27	12	10	12	11
A.L. totals (7 years)		42	23	.646	3.88	335	28	1	1	26	558 1/3	560	265	241	246	362
N.L. totals (3 years)		11	19	.367	3.42	186	0	0	0	78	202 2/3	191	87	77	97	175
Major League totals (9 years)......		53	42	.558	3.76	521	28	1	1	104	761	751	352	318	343	537

DIVISION SERIES RECORD

Year	League	W	L	Pct.	ERA	G	GS	CG	ShO	Sv.	IP	H	R	ER	BB	SO
1995— New York (A.L.)................		0	0	...	0.00	3	0	0	0	0	3	5	0	0	0	3

ALL-STAR GAME RECORD

Year	League	W	L	Pct.	ERA	GS	CG	ShO	Sv.	IP	H	R	ER	BB	SO
2000— National		0	0	...	0.00	0	0	0	0	1	0	0	0	0	1

WIDGER, CHRIS   C   MARINERS

PERSONAL: Born May 21, 1971, in Wilmington, Del. ... 6-2/215. ... Bats right, throws right. ... Full name: Christopher Jon Widger. ... Nephew of Mike Widger, linebacker with Montreal Alouettes and Ottawa Rough Riders of Canadian Football League (1970-78).
HIGH SCHOOL: Pennsville (N.J.).
COLLEGE: George Mason.
TRANSACTIONS/CAREER NOTES: Selected by Seattle Mariners organization in third round of free-agent draft (June 1, 1992). ... On disabled list (June 6-16, 1993). ... Traded by Mariners with P Trey Moore and P Matt Wagner to Montreal Expos for P Jeff Fassero and P Alex Pacheco (October 29, 1996). ... On Montreal disabled list (May 25-June 9, 2000). ... Traded by Expos to Mariners for two players to be named later (August 8, 2000); Expos acquired OF Terrmel Sledge (September 28) and Sean Spencer (August 10) to complete deal.
STATISTICAL NOTES: Led N.L. catchers with 14 passed balls and tied for lead with 12 double plays in 1998. ... Career major league grand slams: 1.

							BATTING								FIELDING		
Year	Team (League)	Pos.	G	AB	R	H	2B	3B	HR	RBI	Avg.	BB	SO	SB	PO	A	E	Avg.
1992— Bellingham (N'West) ..		C	51	166	28	43	7	2	5	30	.259	22	36	8	266	39	4	*.987
1993— Riverside (Calif.)........		C-OF	97	360	44	95	28	2	9	58	.264	19	64	5	472	63	14	.974
1994— Jacksonville (Sou.).....		C-OF-1B	116	388	58	101	15	3	16	59	.260	39	69	8	564	73	13	.980
1995— Tacoma (PCL)		C-DH-OF	50	174	29	48	11	1	9	21	.276	9	29	0	189	22	4	.981
— Seattle (A.L.)		C-OF-DH	23	45	2	9	0	0	1	2	.200	3	11	0	64	1	0	1.000
1996— Tacoma (PCL)		C-DH	97	352	42	107	20	2	13	48	.304	27	62	7	622	41	8	.988
— Seattle (A.L.)		C	8	11	1	2	0	0	0	0	.182	0	5	0	18	1	2	.905
1997— Montreal (N.L.)■........		C	91	278	30	65	20	3	7	37	.234	22	59	2	516	40	11	.981
1998— Montreal (N.L.)..........		C	125	417	36	97	18	1	15	53	.233	29	85	6	752	64	14	.983
1999— Montreal (N.L.)..........		C	124	383	42	101	24	1	14	56	.264	28	86	1	662	54	6	.992
2000— Montreal (N.L.)..........		C	86	281	31	67	17	2	12	34	.238	29	61	1	503	38	8	.985
— Seattle (A.L.)■ C-DH-1B-OF			10	11	1	1	0	0	1	1	.091	1	2	0	20	0	0	1.000
American League totals (3 years)			41	67	4	12	0	0	2	3	.179	4	18	0	102	2	2	.981
National League totals (4 years)			426	1359	139	330	79	7	48	180	.243	108	291	10	2433	196	39	.985
Major League totals (6 years)			467	1426	143	342	79	7	50	183	.240	112	309	10	2535	198	41	.985

DIVISION SERIES RECORD

							BATTING								FIELDING		
Year	Team (League)	Pos.	G	AB	R	H	2B	3B	HR	RBI	Avg.	BB	SO	SB	PO	A	E	Avg.
1995— Seattle (A.L.)		C	2	3	0	0	0	0	0	0	.000	0	3	0	14	0	0	1.000
2000— Seattle (A.L.)										Did not play.								

CHAMPIONSHIP SERIES RECORD

							BATTING								FIELDING		
Year	Team (League)	Pos.	G	AB	R	H	2B	3B	HR	RBI	Avg.	BB	SO	SB	PO	A	E	Avg.
1995— Seattle (A.L.)		C	3	1	0	0	0	0	0	0	.000	0	1	0	7	0	0	1.000
2000— Seattle (A.L.)										Did not play.								

W

WILKINS, MARC   P   PIRATES

PERSONAL: Born October 21, 1970, in Mansfield, Ohio. ... 5-11/212. ... Throws right, bats right. ... Full name: Marc Allen Wilkins.
HIGH SCHOOL: Ontario (Ohio).
COLLEGE: Toledo.
TRANSACTIONS/CAREER NOTES: Selected by Pittsburgh Pirates organization in 47th round of free-agent draft (June 1, 1992). ... On Pittsburgh disabled list (April 26-May 11 and May 23, 1998-remainder of season); included rehabilitation assignments to Carolina (May 8-10) and Nashville (August 7-September 6). ... On Pittsburgh disabled list (March 26-May 1, 1999); included rehabilitation assignments to Altoona (April 16-25) and Nashville (April 26-May 1). ... Claimed on waivers by Oakland Athletics (October 13, 2000). ... Released by Athletics (December 15, 2000). ... Re-signed by Pirates organization (January 12, 2001).
STATISTICAL NOTES: Led Carolina League with 22 hit batsmen in 1994.

Year	League	W	L	Pct.	ERA	G	GS	CG	ShO	Sv.	IP	H	R	ER	BB	SO
1992— Welland (NY-Penn)		4	2	.667	7.29	28	1	0	0	1	42	49	36	34	24	42
1993— Augusta (S.Atl.)		5	6	.455	4.21	48	5	0	0	1	77	83	52	36	31	73
1994— Salem (Caro.)		8	5	.615	3.70	28	•28	0	0	0	151	155	84	62	45	90
1995— Carolina (Sou.)		5	3	.625	3.99	37	12	0	0	0	99 1/3	91	47	44	44	80
1996— Carolina (Sou.)		2	3	.400	4.01	11	3	0	0	0	24 2/3	19	12	11	11	19
— Pittsburgh (N.L.)		4	3	.571	3.84	47	2	0	0	1	75	75	36	32	36	62
1997— Pittsburgh (N.L.)		9	5	.643	3.69	70	0	0	0	2	75 2/3	65	33	31	33	47
1998— Pittsburgh (N.L.)		0	0	...	3.52	16	0	0	0	0	15 1/3	13	6	6	9	17
— Carolina (Sou.)		0	0	...	4.50	2	0	0	0	0	2	1	1	1	0	4
— Nashville (PCL)		1	0	1.000	10.38	5	0	0	0	0	4 1/3	3	5	5	3	4
1999— Altoona (East.)		0	1	.000	1.50	4	0	0	0	0	6	4	2	1	4	5
— Nashville (PCL)		1	1	.500	0.79	8	0	0	0	3	11 1/3	9	3	1	3	8
— Pittsburgh (N.L.)		2	3	.400	4.24	46	0	0	0	0	51	49	28	24	26	44
2000— Pittsburgh (N.L.)		4	2	.667	5.07	52	0	0	0	0	60 1/3	54	34	34	43	37
— Nashville (PCL)		2	3	.400	4.97	17	4	0	0	3	38	34	23	21	24	33
Major League totals (5 years)		19	13	.594	4.12	231	2	0	0	3	277 1/3	256	137	127	147	207

WILKINS, RICK C PADRES

PERSONAL: Born June 4, 1967, in Jacksonville. ... 6-2/215. ... Bats left, throws right. ... Full name: Richard David Wilkins.
HIGH SCHOOL: The Bolles School (Jacksonville).
JUNIOR COLLEGE: Florida Community College-Jacksonville.
COLLEGE: Furman.
TRANSACTIONS/CAREER NOTES: Selected by Chicago Cubs organization in 23rd round of free-agent draft (June 2, 1986). ... On Chicago disabled list (June 2-28, 1995). ... Traded by Cubs to Houston Astros for OF Luis Gonzalez and C Scott Servais (June 28, 1995). ... On Houston disabled list (July 2-September 5, 1995); included rehabilitation assignments to Jackson (August 28-September 1) and Tucson (September 1-5). ... Traded by Astros with cash to San Francisco Giants for C Kirt Manwaring (July 27, 1996). ... Released by Giants (August 1, 1997). ... Signed by Seattle Mariners organization (August 15, 1997). ... On Seattle disabled list (August 15-September 1, 1997); included rehabilitation assignment to Tacoma (August 15-September 1). ... Granted free agency (October 16, 1997). ... Re-signed by Mariners (December 15, 1997). ... Traded by Mariners to New York Mets for P Lindsay Gulin (May 12, 1998). ... On Norfolk disabled list (July 20-August 30, 1998). ... Granted free agency (October 15, 1998). ... Signed by Los Angeles Dodgers organization (March 6, 1999). ... Granted free agency (October 4, 1999). ... Signed by St. Louis Cardinals organization (February 3, 2000). ... Granted free agency (October 31, 2000). ... Signed by San Diego Padres organization (January 29, 2001).
STATISTICAL NOTES: Led Appalachian League with eight intentional bases on balls received in 1987. ... Led Appalachian League catchers with .989 fielding percentage, 483 putouts and 540 total chances and tied for lead with six double plays in 1987. ... Led Midwest League catchers with 984 total chances in 1988. ... Led Carolina League catchers with 860 total chances and tied for lead with eight double plays in 1989. ... Led Southern League catchers with 857 total chances, 11 double plays and 15 passed balls in 1990. ... Tied for N.L. lead with 10 sacrifice flies in 1996. ... Career major league grand slams: 2.

							BATTING								FIELDING		
Year	Team (League)	Pos.	G	AB	R	H	2B	3B	HR	RBI	Avg.	BB	SO	SB	PO	A	E	Avg.
1987— Geneva (NY-Penn)		C-1B	75	243	35	61	8	2	8	43	.251	58	40	7	†503	51	7	†.988
1988— Peoria (Midw.)		C	137	490	54	119	30	1	8	63	.243	67	110	4	*864	*101	*19	.981
1989— Win.-Salem (Caro.)		C	132	445	61	111	24	1	12	54	.249	50	87	6	*764	*78	*18	.979
1990— Charlotte (Sou.)		C	127	449	48	102	18	1	17	71	.227	43	95	4	*740	*103	14	.984
1991— Iowa (A.A.)		C-OF	38	107	12	29	3	1	5	14	.271	11	17	1	204	24	3	.987
— Chicago (N.L.)		C	86	203	21	45	9	0	6	22	.222	19	56	3	373	42	3	.993
1992— Chicago (N.L.)		C	83	244	20	66	9	1	8	22	.270	28	53	0	408	47	3	.993
— Iowa (A.A.)		C	47	155	20	43	11	2	5	28	.277	19	42	0	177	18	2	.990
1993— Chicago (N.L.)		C	136	446	78	135	23	1	30	73	.303	50	99	2	717	89	3	.996
1994— Chicago (N.L.)		C-1B	100	313	44	71	25	2	7	39	.227	40	86	4	550	51	4	.993
1995— Chicago (N.L.)		C-1B	50	162	24	31	2	0	6	14	.191	36	51	0	294	31	4	.988
— Houston (N.L.)■		C	15	40	6	10	1	0	1	5	.250	10	10	0	87	4	0	1.000
— Jackson (Texas)		C	4	11	0	0	0	0	0	0	.000	3	2	0	23	1	0	1.000
— Tucson (PCL)		C	4	12	0	4	0	0	0	4	.333	2	0	0	27	4	0	1.000
1996— Houston (N.L.)		C	84	254	34	54	8	2	6	23	.213	46	81	0	550	39	6	.990
— San Fran. (N.L.)■		C-1B	52	157	19	46	10	0	8	36	.293	21	40	0	240	34	2	.993
1997— San Francisco (N.L.) ..		C	66	190	18	37	5	0	6	23	.195	17	65	0	326	37	5	.986
— Tacoma (PCL)■		C-DH-1B	17	68	16	23	8	0	1	14	.338	8	12	0	82	4	1	.989
— Seattle (A.L.)		C-DH	5	12	2	3	1	0	1	4	.250	1	2	0	9	1	0	1.000
1998— Seattle (A.L.)		C-1B-DH	19	41	5	8	1	1	1	4	.195	4	14	0	70	4	0	1.000
— New York (N.L.)■		C	5	15	3	2	0	0	0	1	.133	2	2	0	21	1	1	.957
— Norfolk (I.L.)		C-DH-1B	45	158	17	41	13	1	1	20	.259	14	37	1	231	15	3	.988
1999— Los Angeles (N.L.)■		C	3	4	0	0	0	0	0	0	.000	0	2	0	1	0	0	1.000
— Albuquerque (PCL)		C-1B-DH	92	300	39	76	8	1	8	33	.253	29	87	1	546	49	9	.985
2000— Memphis (PCL)■		C-1B	63	187	23	43	6	1	4	25	.230	27	57	0	344	42	4	.990
— St. Louis (N.L.)		C	4	11	3	3	0	0	0	1	.273	2	2	0	28	3	0	1.000
American League totals (2 years)			24	53	7	11	2	1	2	8	.208	5	16	0	79	5	0	1.000
National League totals (10 years)			684	2039	270	500	92	6	78	259	.245	271	547	9	3595	378	31	.992
Major League totals (10 years)			708	2092	277	511	94	7	80	267	.244	276	563	9	3674	383	31	.992

DIVISION SERIES RECORD

							BATTING								FIELDING		
Year	Team (League)	Pos.	G	AB	R	H	2B	3B	HR	RBI	Avg.	BB	SO	SB	PO	A	E	Avg.
1997— Seattle (A.L.)		C-PH	1	1	0	0	0	0	0	0	.000	1	0	0	2	0	0	1.000
2000— St. Louis (N.L.)									Did not play.									

CHAMPIONSHIP SERIES RECORD

							BATTING								FIELDING		
Year	Team (League)	Pos.	G	AB	R	H	2B	3B	HR	RBI	Avg.	BB	SO	SB	PO	A	E	Avg.
2000— St. Louis (N.L.)		PH	2	2	0	0	0	0	0	0	.000	0	0	0	...	...	...	...

W

PERSONAL: Born September 13, 1968, in San Juan, Puerto Rico. ... 6-2/205. ... Bats both, throws right. ... Full name: Bernabe Figueroa Williams.

HIGH SCHOOL: Escuela Libre de Musica (San Juan, Puerto Rico).

COLLEGE: Puerto Rico.

TRANSACTIONS/CAREER NOTES: Signed as non-drafted free agent by New York Yankees organization (September 13, 1985). ... On disabled list (July 15, 1988-remainder of season; and May 13-June 7, 1993). ... On disabled list (May 11-May 26, 1996; June 16-July 2 and July 15-August 1, 1997). ... On New York disabled list (June 11-July 18, 1998); included rehabilitation assignments to Tampa (July 6-7) and Norwich (July 14-16). ... Granted free agency (October 26, 1998). ... Re-signed by Yankees (November 25, 1998).

RECORDS: Shares major league single-game record for most strikeouts (nine-inning game)—5 (August 21, 1991). ... Shares major league single-inning record for most doubles—2 (June 22, 1994, seventh inning). ... Shares modern major league record for most long hits in one inning—2 (June 22, 1994, seventh inning).

HONORS: Won A.L. Gold Glove as outfielder (1997-2000). ... Named outfielder on THE SPORTING NEWS A.L. All-Star team (2000).

STATISTICAL NOTES: Led Gulf Coast League outfielders with 123 total chances in 1986. ... Tied for Gulf Coast League lead in caught stealing with 12 in 1986. ... Led Eastern League in caught stealing with 18 in 1990. ... Led Eastern League outfielders with 307 total chances and tied for lead with four double plays in 1990. ... Had 21-game hitting streak (August 1-23, 1993). ... Switch-hit home runs in one game six times (June 6, 1994; September 12, 1996; September 4, 1998; May 4, 1999; and April 23 and May 17, 2000). ... Led A.L. outfielders with 441 total chances in 1995. ... Had 16-game hitting streak (July 31-August 14, 1998). ... Had 17-game hitting streak (June 8-July 6, 1999). ... Tied for A.L. lead with 17 intentional bases on balls received in 1999. ... Had 17-game hitting streak (June 19-July 7, 2000). ... Career major league grand slams: 9.

MISCELLANEOUS: Batted righthanded only (1986-88).

							BATTING								FIELDING		
Year	Team (League)	Pos.	G	AB	R	H	2B	3B	HR	RBI	Avg.	BB	SO	SB	PO	A	E	Avg.
1986— GC Yankees (GCL)	OF	61	230	*45	62	5	3	2	25	.270	39	40	33	*117	3	3	.976
1987— Fort Lauderdale (FSL)	OF	25	71	11	11	3	0	0	4	.155	18	22	9	49	1	0	1.000
— Oneonta (NY-Penn)	OF	25	93	13	32	4	0	0	15	.344	10	14	9	40	0	2	.952
1988— Prince Will. (Caro.)	OF	92	337	72	113	16	7	7	45	*.335	65	65	29	186	8	5	.975
1989— Columbus (I.L.)	OF	50	162	21	35	8	1	2	16	.216	25	38	11	112	2	1	.991
— Alb./Colonie (East.)	OF	91	314	63	79	11	8	11	42	.252	60	72	26	180	5	5	.974
1990— Alb./Colonie (East.)	OF	134	466	*91	131	28	5	8	54	.281	*98	97	*39	*288	15	4	.987
1991— Columbus (I.L.)	OF	78	306	52	90	14	6	8	37	.294	38	43	9	164	2	1	.994
— New York (A.L.)	OF	85	320	43	76	19	4	3	34	.238	48	57	10	230	3	5	.979
1992— New York (A.L.)	OF	62	261	39	73	14	2	5	26	.280	29	36	7	187	5	1	.995
— Columbus (I.L.)	OF	95	363	68	111	23	•9	8	50	.306	52	61	20	205	2	2	.990
1993— New York (A.L.)	OF	139	567	67	152	31	4	12	68	.268	53	106	9	366	5	4	.989
1994— New York (A.L.)	OF	108	408	80	118	29	1	12	57	.289	61	54	16	277	7	3	.990
1995— New York (A.L.)	OF	144	563	93	173	29	9	18	82	.307	75	98	8	*432	1	•8	.982
1996— New York (A.L.)	OF-DH	143	551	108	168	26	7	29	102	.305	82	72	17	334	10	5	.986
1997— New York (A.L.)	OF	129	509	107	167	35	6	21	100	.328	73	80	15	270	2	2	.993
1998— New York (A.L.)	OF-DH	128	499	101	169	30	5	26	97	*.339	74	81	15	298	4	3	.990
— Tampa (FSL)	OF	1	2	0	1	1	0	0	0	.500	1	0	0	2	0	0	1.000
— Norwich (East.)	OF	3	11	6	6	2	0	2	5	.545	2	1	0	5	0	0	1.000
1999— New York (A.L.)	OF-DH	158	591	116	202	28	6	25	115	.342	100	95	9	381	9	5	.987
2000— New York (A.L.)	OF-DH	141	537	108	165	37	6	30	121	.307	71	84	13	353	2	0	*1.000
Major League totals (10 years)		1237	4806	862	1463	278	50	181	802	.304	666	763	119	3128	48	36	.989

DIVISION SERIES RECORD

RECORDS: Holds career records for most runs batted in—18; total bases—52; and extra-base hits—13. ... Shares career record for most games—25. ... Holds A.L. career record for most bases on balls—16. ... Shares single-game record for most home runs—2 (October 6, 1995 and October 5, 1996).

							BATTING								FIELDING		
Year	Team (League)	Pos.	G	AB	R	H	2B	3B	HR	RBI	Avg.	BB	SO	SB	PO	A	E	Avg.
1995— New York (A.L.)	OF	5	21	8	9	2	0	2	5	.429	7	3	1	13	0	0	1.000
1996— New York (A.L.)	OF	4	15	5	7	0	0	3	5	.467	2	1	1	10	0	0	1.000
1997— New York (A.L.)	OF	5	17	3	2	1	0	0	1	.118	4	3	0	7	0	0	1.000
1998— New York (A.L.)	OF	3	11	0	0	0	0	0	0	.000	1	4	0	8	0	0	1.000
1999— New York (A.L.)	OF	3	11	2	4	1	0	1	6	.364	1	2	0	15	0	0	1.000
2000— New York (A.L.)	OF	5	20	3	5	3	0	0	1	.250	1	4	0	10	0	0	1.000
Division series totals (6 years)		25	95	21	27	7	0	6	18	.284	16	17	2	63	0	0	1.000

CHAMPIONSHIP SERIES RECORD

NOTES: Named Most Valuable Player (1996).

							BATTING								FIELDING		
Year	Team (League)	Pos.	G	AB	R	H	2B	3B	HR	RBI	Avg.	BB	SO	SB	PO	A	E	Avg.
1996— New York (A.L.)	OF	5	19	6	9	3	0	2	6	.474	6	4	1	20	0	0	1.000
1998— New York (A.L.)	OF	6	21	4	8	1	0	0	5	.381	7	4	1	14	0	0	1.000
1999— New York (A.L.)	OF	5	20	3	5	1	0	1	2	.250	2	5	1	13	1	0	1.000
2000— New York (A.L.)	OF	6	23	5	10	1	0	1	3	.435	2	3	1	14	0	0	1.000
Championship series totals (4 years)		22	83	18	32	6	0	4	16	.386	17	16	4	61	1	0	1.000

WORLD SERIES RECORD

NOTES: Member of World Series championship team (1996, 1998, 1999 and 2000).

							BATTING								FIELDING		
Year	Team (League)	Pos.	G	AB	R	H	2B	3B	HR	RBI	Avg.	BB	SO	SB	PO	A	E	Avg.
1996— New York (A.L.)	OF	6	24	3	4	0	0	1	4	.167	4	6	1	15	0	0	1.000
1998— New York (A.L.)	OF	4	16	2	1	0	0	1	3	.063	3	5	0	6	0	0	1.000
1999— New York (A.L.)	OF	4	13	2	3	0	0	0	0	.231	4	2	1	2	0	0	1.000
2000— New York (A.L.)	OF	5	18	2	2	0	0	1	1	.111	5	5	0	10	0	0	1.000
World Series totals (4 years)		19	71	9	10	0	0	3	8	.141	16	18	2	33	0	0	1.000

W

NOTES: Named to All-Star team for 1998 game; replaced by Manny Ramirez due to injury.

Year League	Pos.	AB	R	H	2B	3B	HR	RBI	Avg.	BB	SO	SB	PO	A	E	Avg.
1997— American	OF	0	1	0	0	0	0	0	...	1	0	1	1	0	0	1.000
1998— American							Selected, did not play—injured.									
1999— American	OF	1	0	0	0	0	0	0	.000	0	1	0	0	0	0	...
2000— American	OF	3	0	0	0	0	0	0	.000	0	0	0	0	0	...	...
All-Star Game totals (3 years)		4	1	0	0	0	0	0	.000	1	1	1	1	0	0	1.000

WILLIAMS, BRIAN P RED SOX

PERSONAL: Born February 15, 1969, in Lancaster, S.C. ... 6-3/230. ... Throws right, bats right. ... Full name: Brian O'Neal Williams.
HIGH SCHOOL: Lewisville (Fort Lawn, S.C.).
COLLEGE: South Carolina.
TRANSACTIONS/CAREER NOTES: Selected by Pittsburgh Pirates organization in third round of free-agent draft (June 2, 1987); did not sign. ... Selected by Houston Astros organization in supplemental round ("sandwich pick" between first and second round, 31st pick overall) of free-agent draft (June 4, 1990); pick received as part of compensation for San Francisco Giants signing Type A free-agent OF Kevin Bass. ... On Tucson disabled list (May 25-June 1, 1992). ... On Houston disabled list (August 5-20, 1993); included rehabilitation assignment to Tucson (August 15-20). ... On Houston disabled list (August 1-September 19, 1994). ... Traded by Astros with 3B Ken Caminiti, OF Steve Finley, SS Andujar Cedeno, 1B Robert Petagine and a player to be named later to San Diego Padres for OF Phil Plantier, OF Derek Bell, P Pedro Martinez, P Doug Brocail, IF Craig Shipley and SS Ricky Gutierrez (December 28, 1994); Padres acquired P Sean Fesh to complete deal (May 1, 1995). ... Granted free agency (December 21, 1995). ... Signed by Detroit Tigers (January 10, 1996). ... Released by Tigers (November 20, 1996). ... Signed by Baltimore Orioles organization (January 21, 1997). ... Released by Orioles (December 11, 1997). ... Signed by Astros organization (January 21, 1999). ... Granted free agency (October 28, 1999). ... Signed by Chicago Cubs (January 7, 2000). ... Released by Cubs (May 30, 2000). ... Signed by Cleveland Indians organization (June 5, 2000). ... Granted free agency (October 5, 2000). ... Signed by Boston Red Sox organization (January 4, 2001).
MISCELLANEOUS: Appeared in four games as pinch runner with Houston (1992).

Year League	W	L	Pct.	ERA	G	GS	CG	ShO	Sv.	IP	H	R	ER	BB	SO
1990— Auburn (NY-Penn)	0	0	...	4.05	3	3	0	0	0	6²/₃	6	5	3	6	7
1991— Osceola (FSL)................	6	4	.600	2.91	15	15	0	0	0	89²/₃	72	41	29	40	67
— Jackson (Texas)	2	1	.667	4.20	3	3	0	0	0	15	17	8	7	7	15
— Tucson (PCL)	0	1	.000	4.93	7	7	0	0	0	38¹/₃	39	25	21	22	29
— Houston (N.L.)	0	1	.000	3.75	2	2	0	0	0	12	11	5	5	4	4
1992— Tucson (PCL)	6	1	.857	4.50	12	12	0	0	0	70	78	37	35	26	58
— Houston (N.L.)	7	6	.538	3.92	16	16	0	0	0	96¹/₃	92	44	42	42	54
1993— Houston (N.L.)	4	4	.500	4.83	42	5	0	0	3	82	76	48	44	38	56
— Tucson (PCL)	1	0	1.000	0.00	2	0	0	0	0	3	1	0	0	0	3
1994— Houston (N.L.)	6	5	.545	5.74	20	13	0	0	0	78¹/₃	112	64	50	41	49
— Tucson (PCL)	2	0	1.000	2.21	3	3	0	0	0	20¹/₃	22	6	5	9	17
1995— San Diego (N.L.)■	3	10	.231	6.00	44	6	0	0	0	72	79	54	48	38	75
1996— Detroit (A.L.)■	3	10	.231	6.77	40	17	2	1	2	121	145	107	91	85	72
— Toledo (I.L.)	1	2	.333	5.49	3	3	1	0	0	19²/₃	22	13	12	9	21
1997— Rochester (I.L.)■	4	3	.571	3.89	22	9	0	0	8	69¹/₃	68	33	30	23	78
— Baltimore (A.L.)	0	0	...	3.00	13	0	0	0	0	24	20	8	8	18	14
1999— Houston (N.L.)	2	1	.667	4.41	50	0	0	0	0	67¹/₃	69	35	33	35	53
2000— Chicago (N.L.)■	1	1	.500	9.62	22	0	0	0	1	24¹/₃	28	27	26	23	14
— Buffalo (I.L.)■	4	3	.571	2.57	18	0	0	0	3	21	23	7	6	11	21
— Cleveland (A.L.).................	0	0	...	4.00	7	0	0	0	0	18	23	9	8	8	6
A.L. totals (3 years)	3	10	.231	5.91	60	17	2	1	2	163	188	124	107	111	92
N.L. totals (7 years)	23	28	.451	5.16	196	42	0	0	4	432¹/₃	467	277	248	221	305
Major League totals (9 years)	26	38	.406	5.37	256	59	2	1	6	595¹/₃	655	401	355	332	397

WILLIAMS, GEORGE C

PERSONAL: Born April 22, 1969, in La Crosse, Wis. ... 5-10/215. ... Bats both, throws right. ... Full name: George Erik Williams.
HIGH SCHOOL: La Crosse (Wis.) Central.
JUNIOR COLLEGE: Mira Costa Junior College (Oceanside, Calif,).
COLLEGE: Texas-Pan American.
TRANSACTIONS/CAREER NOTES: Selected by Oakland Athletics organization in 24th round of free-agent draft (June 3, 1991). ... On disabled list (April 7-June 23, 1994). ... On Oakland disabled list (April 14-May 5 and July 20-August 21, 1997); included rehabilitation assignments to Modesto (April 29-May 5 and August 13-21) and Edmonton (August 10-12). ... On Oakland disabled list (March 22, 1998-entire season); included rehabilitation assignment to Arizona League Athletics (August 20). ... Granted free agency (November 26, 1998). ... Signed by Minnesota Twins organization (December 21, 1998). ... Traded by Twins to Houston Astros for C Josh Dimmick (August 3, 1999). ... Granted free agency (October 15, 1999). ... Signed by San Diego Padres organization (November 22, 1999). ... Granted free agency (October 18, 2000).
STATISTICAL NOTES: Tied for Midwest League lead with six intentional bases on balls received in 1992. ... Career major league grand slams: 2.

Year Team (League)	Pos.	G	AB	R	H	2B	3B	HR	RBI	Avg.	BB	SO	SB	PO	A	E	Avg.
1991— S. Oregon (N'West)	C-3B	55	174	24	41	10	0	2	24	.236	38	36	9	126	44	6	.966
1992— Madison (Midw.)	C-OF	115	349	56	106	18	2	5	42	.304	76	53	9	455	57	18	.966
1993— Huntsville (Sou.)	C-OF-3B	124	434	80	128	26	2	14	77	.295	67	66	6	430	63	11	.978
1994— W. Mich. (Midw.)	DH-C	63	221	40	67	20	1	8	48	.303	44	47	6	21	3	0	1.000
1995— Edmonton (PCL)	C-DH-OF	81	290	53	90	20	0	13	55	.310	50	52	0	310	44	7	.981
— Oakland (A.L.)	C-DH	29	79	13	23	5	1	3	14	.291	11	21	0	58	7	3	.956
1996— Oakland (A.L.)	C-DH	56	132	17	20	5	0	3	10	.152	28	32	0	154	12	3	.982
— Edmonton (PCL)	C-DH-OF	14	57	10	23	5	0	5	18	.404	6	11	0	76	0	0	1.000
1997— Oakland (A.L.)	C-DH	76	201	30	58	9	1	3	22	.289	35	46	0	337	27	6	.984
— Modesto (Calif.)	C-DH	13	44	8	14	4	0	1	6	.318	7	14	0	53	9	0	1.000
— Edmonton (PCL)	C-DH	3	7	0	0	0	0	0	0	.000	1	1	0	8	1	0	1.000

W

Year Team (League)	Pos.	G	AB	R	H	2B	3B	HR	RBI	Avg.	BB	SO	SB	PO	A	E	Avg.
1998— Ariz. Athletics (Ariz.)..	DH	1	2	0	1	0	0	0	0	.500	1	0	0	...	...	...	...
1999— Salt Lake (PCL)■.......	C-DH-OF	74	228	38	69	16	1	6	31	.303	42	51	0	332	16	4	.989
— New Orleans (PCL)■..	C-1B-DH	29	100	18	24	5	0	3	14	.240	13	19	1	183	17	4	.980
2000— Las Vegas (PCL)■..	C-1B-3B	63	176	27	42	8	2	8	35	.239	36	44	0	306	26	10	.971
— San Diego (N.L.)	C	11	16	2	3	0	0	1	2	.188	0	4	0	16	2	0	1.000
American League totals (3 years)		161	412	60	101	19	2	9	46	.245	74	99	0	549	46	12	.980
National League totals (1 year)		11	16	2	3	0	0	1	2	.188	0	4	0	16	2	0	1.000
Major League totals (4 years)		172	428	62	104	19	2	10	48	.243	74	103	0	565	48	12	.981

WILLIAMS, GERALD — OF — DEVIL RAYS

PERSONAL: Born August 10, 1966, in New Orleans. ... 6-2/187. ... Bats right, throws right. ... Full name: Gerald Floyd Williams.
HIGH SCHOOL: East St. John (Reserve, La.).
COLLEGE: Grambling State.
TRANSACTIONS/CAREER NOTES: Selected by New York Yankees organization in 14th round of free-agent draft (June 2, 1987). ... Traded by Yankees with P Bob Wickman to Milwaukee Brewers for P Graeme Lloyd and OF Pat Listach (August 23, 1996). ... Traded by Brewers to Atlanta Braves for P Chad Fox (December 11, 1997). ... Granted free agency (November 3, 1999). ... Signed by Tampa Bay Devil Rays (December 19, 1999). ... On suspended list (September 22-25, 2000).
STATISTICAL NOTES: Led Carolina League outfielders with 307 total chances in 1989. ... Led International League outfielders with 354 total chances in 1992. ... Tied for International League lead in double plays by outfielder with five in 1992. ... Collected six hits in one game (May 1, 1996). ... Had 15-game hitting streak (July 23-August 13, 1999). ... Career major league grand slams: 3.

Year Team (League)	Pos.	G	AB	R	H	2B	3B	HR	RBI	Avg.	BB	SO	SB	PO	A	E	Avg.
1987— Oneonta (NY-Penn)	OF	29	115	26	42	6	2	2	29	.365	16	18	6	68	3	3	.959
1988— Prince Will. (Caro.).....	OF	54	159	20	29	3	0	2	18	.182	15	47	6	71	2	3	.961
— Fort Laud. (FSL)........	OF	63	212	21	40	7	2	2	17	.189	16	56	4	163	2	6	.965
1989— Prince Will. (Caro.).....	OF	134	454	63	104	19	6	13	69	.229	51	120	15	*292	7	8	.974
1990— Fort Laud. (FSL)........	OF	50	204	25	59	4	5	7	43	.289	16	52	19	115	1	3	.975
— Alb./Colonie (East.)	OF	96	324	54	81	17	2	13	58	.250	35	74	18	210	6	7	.969
1991— Alb./Colonie (East.)	OF	45	175	28	50	15	0	5	32	.286	18	26	18	109	4	3	.974
— Columbus (I.L.)..........	OF	61	198	20	51	8	3	2	27	.258	16	39	9	124	1	3	.977
1992— Columbus (I.L.)..........	OF	*142	547	92	*156	31	6	16	86	.285	38	98	36	*332	*14	8	.977
— New York (A.L.)..........	OF	15	27	7	8	2	0	3	6	.296	0	3	2	20	1	2	.913
1993— Columbus (I.L.)..........	OF	87	336	53	95	19	6	8	38	.283	20	66	29	191	6	3	.985
— New York (A.L.)..........	OF-DH	42	67	11	10	2	3	0	6	.149	1	14	2	41	2	2	.956
1994— New York (A.L.)..........	OF-DH	57	86	19	25	8	0	4	13	.291	4	17	1	43	2	2	.957
1995— New York (A.L.)..........	OF-DH	100	182	33	45	18	2	6	28	.247	22	34	4	138	6	1	.993
1996— New York (A.L.)■........	OF	26	92	6	19	4	0	0	4	.207	4	18	3	75	3	1	.987
1997— Milwaukee (A.L.)........	OF-DH	155	566	73	143	32	2	10	41	.253	19	90	23	357	11	3	.992
1998— Atlanta (N.L.)■..........	OF	129	266	46	81	19	2	10	44	.305	17	48	11	158	2	5	.970
1999— Atlanta (N.L.)...........	OF	143	422	76	116	24	1	17	68	.275	33	67	19	188	9	3	.985
2000— Tampa Bay (A.L.)■.....	OF-DH	146	632	87	173	30	2	21	89	.274	34	103	12	349	6	6	.983
American League totals (7 years)		640	1885	273	486	111	13	49	217	.258	99	318	54	1155	32	20	.983
National League totals (2 years)		272	688	122	197	43	3	27	112	.286	50	115	30	346	11	8	.978
Major League totals (9 years)		912	2573	395	683	154	16	76	329	.265	149	433	84	1501	43	28	.982

DIVISION SERIES RECORD

Year Team (League)	Pos.	G	AB	R	H	2B	3B	HR	RBI	Avg.	BB	SO	SB	PO	A	E	Avg.
1995— New York (A.L.)..........	OF-PR	5	5	1	0	0	0	0	0	.000	2	3	0	7	1	0	1.000
1998— Atlanta (N.L.)............	OF	2	2	1	1	0	0	0	1	.500	0	1	0	2	0	0	1.000
1999— Atlanta (N.L.)............	OF	4	18	2	7	1	0	0	3	.389	0	3	1	4	0	0	1.000
Division series totals (3 years)		11	25	4	8	1	0	0	4	.320	2	7	1	13	1	0	1.000

CHAMPIONSHIP SERIES RECORD

RECORDS: Shares single-game record for most strikeouts—4 (October 10, 1998).

Year Team (League)	Pos.	G	AB	R	H	2B	3B	HR	RBI	Avg.	BB	SO	SB	PO	A	E	Avg.
1998— Atlanta (N.L.)■..........	PH-OF	5	13	0	2	0	0	0	0	.154	1	6	1	3	0	0	1.000
1999— Atlanta (N.L.)............	OF	6	28	4	5	2	0	1	1	.179	2	2	3	12	0	1	.923
Championship series totals (2 years)		11	41	4	7	2	0	1	1	.171	3	8	4	15	0	1	.938

WORLD SERIES RECORD

Year Team (League)	Pos.	G	AB	R	H	2B	3B	HR	RBI	Avg.	BB	SO	SB	PO	A	E	Avg.
1999— Atlanta (N.L.)............	OF	4	17	2	3	0	1	0	0	.176	0	4	0	6	0	0	1.000

W

WILLIAMS, JEFF — P — DODGERS

PERSONAL: Born June 6, 1972, in Canberra, Australia. ... 6-0/185. ... Throws left, bats right. ... Full name: Jeffrey F. Williams.
COLLEGE: Hawker (Canberra, Australia), then Southeastern Louisiana.
TRANSACTIONS/CAREER NOTES: Signed as non-drafted free agent by Los Angeles Dodgers organization (July 3, 1996). ... On Los Angeles disabled list (April 20-June 27, 2000).

Year League	W	L	Pct.	ERA	G	GS	CG	ShO	Sv.	IP	H	R	ER	BB	SO
1997— San Bernardino (Calif.)	10	4	.714	3.10	18	18	0	0	0	116	101	52	40	34	72
— San Antonio (Texas)	2	1	.667	5.81	5	5	0	0	0	26 1/3	30	17	17	7	14
1998— San Antonio (Texas)	3	0	1.000	2.59	7	7	0	0	0	41 2/3	43	19	12	13	35
— Albuquerque (PCL)	8	8	.500	4.98	21	21	0	0	0	121	160	87	67	49	93
1999— Albuquerque (PCL)	9	7	.563	5.01	42	14	1	1	4	125 2/3	151	77	70	47	86
— Los Angeles (N.L.)	2	0	1.000	4.08	5	3	0	0	0	17 2/3	12	10	8	9	7
2000— Albuquerque (PCL)	4	3	.571	4.26	12	12	0	0	0	63 1/3	64	33	30	28	38
— Los Angeles (N.L.)	0	0	...	15.88	7	0	0	0	0	5 2/3	12	11	10	8	3
Major League totals (2 years)	2	0	1.000	6.94	12	3	0	0	0	23 1/3	24	21	18	17	10

WILLIAMS, MATT   3B   DIAMONDBACKS

PERSONAL: Born November 28, 1965, in Bishop, Calif. ... 6-2/214. ... Bats right, throws right. ... Full name: Matthew Derrick Williams. ... Grandson of Bartholomew (Bart) Griffith, outfielder/first baseman with Brooklyn Dodgers and Washington Senators (1922-24).
HIGH SCHOOL: Carson (Nev.).
COLLEGE: UNLV.
TRANSACTIONS/CAREER NOTES: Selected by New York Mets organization in 27th round of free-agent draft (June 6, 1983); did not sign. ... Selected by San Francisco Giants organization in first round (third pick overall) of free-agent draft (June 2, 1986). ... On disabled list (June 28-July 14, 1993). ... On San Francisco disabled list (June 4-August 19, 1995); included rehabilitation assignments to San Jose (July 24-25 and August 13-19). ... On disabled list (August 5, 1996-remainder of season). ... Traded by Giants with a player to be named later to Cleveland Indians for IF Jeff Kent, IF Jose Vizcaino, P Julian Tavarez and a player to be named later (November 13, 1996); Giants traded OF Trinidad Hubbard to Indians for P Joe Roa to complete deal (December 16, 1996). ... Traded by Indians to Arizona Diamondbacks for 3B Travis Fryman, P Tom Martin and cash (December 1, 1997). ... On Arizona disabled list (July 18-August 3, 1998); included rehabilitation assignment to Tucson (July 31-August 3). ... On Arizona disabled list (March 29-May 23 and June 25-July 13, 2000); included rehabilitation assignments to El Paso (May 16-23) and High Desert (July 8-10).
RECORDS: Shares major league record for most home runs in two consecutive games—5 (April 25 [3] and 26 [2], 1997).
HONORS: Named shortstop on The Sporting News college All-America team (1986). ... Named third baseman on The Sporting News N.L. All-Star team (1990 and 1993-94). ... Named third baseman on The Sporting News N.L. Silver Slugger team (1990 and 1993-94). ... Won N.L. Gold Glove at third base (1991 and 1993-94). ... Named third baseman on The Sporting News A.L. All-Star team (1997). ... Won A.L. Gold Glove at third base (1997). ... Named third baseman on The Sporting News A.L. Silver Slugger team (1997).
STATISTICAL NOTES: Led N.L. third basemen with 33 double plays in 1990 and 1992 and 34 in 1993. ... Tied for N.L. lead in total chances by third baseman with 465 in 1990. ... Led N.L. third basemen with 131 putouts in 1991. ... Led N.L. third basemen with 326 total chances in 1994. ... Hit three home runs in one game (April 25, 1997). ... Had 24-game hitting streak (August 13-September 8, 1997). ... Had 19-game hitting streak (May 26-June 18, 1997). ... Career major league grand slams: 10.
MISCELLANEOUS: Holds Arizona Diamondbacks all-time records for runs batted in (260).

							BATTING							FIELDING		
Year Team (League)	Pos.	G	AB	R	H	2B	3B	HR	RBI	Avg.	BB	SO	SB	PO	A	E	Avg.
1986— Everett (N'West)	SS	4	17	3	4	0	1	1	10	.235	1	4	0	5	10	2	.882
— Clinton (Midw.)	SS	68	250	32	60	14	3	7	29	.240	23	62	3	89	150	10	.960
1987— Phoenix (PCL)	3B-2B-SS	56	211	36	61	15	2	6	37	.289	19	53	6	53	136	14	.931
— San Francisco (N.L.)	SS-3B	84	245	28	46	9	2	8	21	.188	16	68	4	110	234	9	.975
1988— Phoenix (PCL)	3B-SS-2B-OF	82	306	45	83	19	1	12	51	.271	13	56	6	56	173	13	.946
— San Francisco (N.L.)	3B-SS	52	156	17	32	6	1	8	19	.205	8	41	0	48	108	7	.957
1989— San Francisco (N.L.)	3B-SS	84	292	31	59	18	1	18	50	.202	14	72	1	90	168	10	.963
— Phoenix (PCL)	3B-SS-OF	76	284	61	91	20	2	26	61	.320	32	51	9	57	197	11	.958
1990— San Francisco (N.L.)	3B	159	617	87	171	27	2	33	*122	.277	33	138	7	*140	306	19	.959
1991— San Francisco (N.L.)	3B-SS	157	589	72	158	24	5	34	98	.268	33	128	5	†134	295	16	.964
1992— San Francisco (N.L.)	3B	146	529	58	120	13	5	20	66	.227	39	109	7	105	289	*23	.945
1993— San Francisco (N.L.)	3B	145	579	105	170	33	4	38	110	.294	27	80	1	117	266	12	.970
1994— San Francisco (N.L.)	3B	112	445	74	119	16	3	*43	96	.267	33	87	1	79	*235	12	.963
1995— San Francisco (N.L.)	3B	76	283	53	95	17	1	23	65	.336	30	58	2	49	178	10	.958
— San Jose (Calif.)	3B	4	11	2	2	0	0	1	2	.182	0	3	0	4	0	0	1.000
1996— San Francisco (N.L.)	3B-1B-SS	105	404	69	122	16	1	22	85	.302	39	91	1	164	191	14	.962
1997— Cleveland (A.L.)■	3B	151	596	86	157	32	3	32	105	.263	34	108	12	89	301	12	.970
1998— Arizona (N.L.)■	3B	135	510	72	136	26	1	20	71	.267	43	102	5	99	282	11	.972
— Tucson (PCL)	3B	2	5	0	1	0	0	0	0	.200	0	0	0	0	1	0	1.000
1999— Arizona (N.L.)	3B	154	627	98	190	37	2	35	142	.303	41	93	2	123	299	10	.977
2000— El Paso (Texas)	3B	5	13	3	6	2	0	0	1	.462	2	1	0	2	4	0	1.000
— Arizona (N.L.)	3B-DH	96	371	43	102	18	2	12	47	.275	20	51	1	68	172	9	.964
— High Desert (Calif.)	3B	2	8	1	3	0	0	1	1	.375	0	1	0	1	1	0	1.000
American League totals (1 year)		151	596	86	157	32	3	32	105	.263	34	108	12	89	301	12	.970
National League totals (13 years)		1505	5647	807	1520	260	30	314	992	.269	376	1118	37	1326	3023	162	.964
Major League totals (14 years)		1656	6243	893	1677	292	33	346	1097	.269	410	1226	49	1415	3324	174	.965

DIVISION SERIES RECORD

							BATTING							FIELDING		
Year Team (League)	Pos.	G	AB	R	H	2B	3B	HR	RBI	Avg.	BB	SO	SB	PO	A	E	Avg.
1997— Cleveland (A.L.)	3B	5	17	4	4	1	0	1	3	.235	3	5	0	2	10	0	1.000
1999— Arizona (N.L.)	3B	4	16	3	6	1	0	0	0	.375	0	1	0	3	9	0	1.000
Division series totals (2 years)		9	33	7	10	2	0	1	3	.303	3	4	0	5	19	0	1.000

CHAMPIONSHIP SERIES RECORD

RECORDS: Holds N.L. single-series record for most runs batted in—9 (1989).

							BATTING							FIELDING		
Year Team (League)	Pos.	G	AB	R	H	2B	3B	HR	RBI	Avg.	BB	SO	SB	PO	A	E	Avg.
1987— San Francisco (N.L.)								Did not play.									
1989— San Francisco (N.L.)	3B-SS	5	20	2	6	1	0	2	9	.300	0	2	0	5	12	0	1.000
1997— Cleveland (A.L.)	3B	6	23	1	5	1	0	0	2	.217	3	7	1	6	18	2	.923
Championship series totals (2 years)		11	43	3	11	2	0	2	11	.256	3	9	1	11	30	2	.953

WORLD SERIES RECORD

Year Team (League)	Pos.	G	AB	R	H	2B	3B	HR	RBI	Avg.	BB	SO	SB	PO	A	E	Avg.
						BATTING								FIELDING			
1989— San Francisco (N.L.) ..	SS-3B	4	16	1	2	0	0	1	1	.125	0	6	0	4	12	0	1.000
1997— Cleveland (A.L.).........	3B	7	26	8	10	1	0	1	3	.385	7	6	0	5	9	0	1.000
World Series totals (2 years)		11	42	9	12	1	0	2	4	.286	7	12	0	9	21	0	1.000

ALL-STAR GAME RECORD

NOTES: Named to N.L. All-Star team for 1996 game; replaced by Ken Caminiti due to injury.

Year League	Pos.	AB	R	H	2B	3B	HR	RBI	Avg.	BB	SO	SB	PO	A	E	Avg.
				BATTING									FIELDING			
1990— National	PH	1	0	0	0	0	0	0	.000	0	1	0	...	...	...	...
1994— National	3B	3	0	0	0	0	0	0	.000	0	2	0	0	1	1	.500
1995— National							Selected, did not play—injured.										
1996— National							Selected, did not play—injured.										
1999— National	3B	3	0	1	0	0	0	0	.333	0	1	0	1	0	1	.500
All-Star Game totals (3 years)		7	0	1	0	0	0	0	.143	0	4	0	1	1	2	.500

WILLIAMS, MATT   P

PERSONAL: Born April 12, 1971, in Virginia Beach, Va. ... 6-0/190. ... Throws left, bats both. ... Full name: Matthew Taylor Williams.
HIGH SCHOOL: Floyd Kellam (Virginia Beach, Va.).
COLLEGE: Virginia Commonwealth.
TRANSACTIONS/CAREER NOTES: Selected by Cleveland Indians organization in fourth round of free-agent draft (June 1, 1992). ... Loaned to High Desert (July 21-August 15, 1994). ... Loaned to Bakersfield (April 5-May 13, 1995). ... Traded by Indians to Houston Astros for C Scooter Tucker (May 15, 1995). ... Released by Astros (March 28, 1996). ... Signed by Pittsburgh Pirates organization (April 20, 1996). ... Granted free agency (October 15, 1996). ... Signed by Tampa Bay Devil Rays organization (December 18, 1996). ... Selected by New York Yankees from Devil Rays organization in Rule 5 major league draft (December 15, 1997). ... Selected by Milwaukee Brewers from Yankees organization in Rule 5 major league draft (December 13, 1999). ... Returned to Yankees organization (May 3, 2000). ... On Columbus disabled list (May 17-June 28, 2000). ... Granted free agency (October 18, 2000).

Year League	W	L	Pct.	ERA	G	GS	CG	ShO	Sv.	IP	H	R	ER	BB	SO
1992— Watertown (NY-Penn)	1	0	1.000	1.65	6	6	0	0	0	32 2/3	22	15	6	9	29
1993— Kinston (Caro.)..................	12	•12	.500	3.17	27	27	2	1	0	153 1/3	125	65	54	*100	134
1994— Kinston (Caro.)..................	4	6	.400	6.09	15	15	1	0	0	81 1/3	86	63	55	33	67
—Canton/Akron (East.)	0	3	.000	7.61	5	4	0	0	1	23 2/3	30	22	20	14	9
—High Desert (Calif.)■........	1	4	.200	13.00	5	5	0	0	0	18	33	29	26	13	10
1995— Bakersfield (Calif.)■.........	2	0	1.000	2.36	7	7	0	0	0	34 1/3	34	9	9	14	30
—Kissimmee (FSL)■.............	4	6	.400	4.63	19	18	2	0	0	101	115	60	52	44	71
1996— Lynchburg (Caro.)■..........	0	0	...	5.23	23	0	0	0	0	41 1/3	40	27	24	28	45
1997— St. Petersburg (FSL)■......	9	5	.643	2.97	43	0	0	0	1	63 2/3	57	26	21	24	50
1998— Norwich (East.)■.............	8	11	.421	4.60	31	28	2	0	0	160 1/3	186	93	82	66	112
1999— Norwich (East.)	1	1	.500	2.40	22	0	0	0	0	30	22	9	8	18	44
—Columbus (I.L.)	0	2	.000	3.86	13	1	0	0	0	21	15	9	9	11	22
2000— Milwaukee (N.L.)■............	0	0	...	7.00	11	0	0	0	0	9	7	7	7	13	7
—Columbus (I.L.)■..............	4	2	.667	5.25	27	0	0	0	2	36	37	24	21	16	35
Major League totals (1 year)........	0	0	...	7.00	11	0	0	0	0	9	7	7	7	13	7

WILLIAMS, MIKE   P   PIRATES

PERSONAL: Born July 29, 1968, in Radford, Va. ... 6-2/204. ... Throws right, bats right. ... Full name: Michael Darren Williams.
HIGH SCHOOL: Giles (Pearisburg, Va.).
COLLEGE: Virginia Tech.
TRANSACTIONS/CAREER NOTES: Selected by Philadelphia Phillies organization in 14th round of free-agent draft (June 4, 1990). ... On suspended list (September 26, 1996-remainder of season). ... Granted free agency (December 20, 1996). ... Signed by Boston Red Sox organization (February 15, 1997). ... Released by Red Sox (March 14, 1997). ... Signed by Kansas City Royals organization (April 30, 1997). ... On suspended list (May 16-18, 1997). ... Granted free agency (October 15, 1997). ... Signed by Pittsburgh Pirates organization (December 18, 1997). ... On disabled list (June 24-July 9, 1999).
STATISTICAL NOTES: Led N.L. with 16 wild pitches in 1996.
MISCELLANEOUS: Appeared in one game as pinch runner (1996).

Year League	W	L	Pct.	ERA	G	GS	CG	ShO	Sv.	IP	H	R	ER	BB	SO
1990— Batavia (NY-Penn)	2	3	.400	2.30	27	0	0	0	11	47	39	17	12	13	42
1991— Clearwater (FSL)	7	3	.700	1.74	14	14	2	1	0	93 1/3	65	23	18	14	76
—Reading (East.)...................	7	5	.583	3.69	16	15	2	1	0	102 1/3	93	44	42	36	51
1992— Reading (East.)..................	1	2	.333	5.17	3	3	0	0	0	15 2/3	17	10	9	7	12
—Scranton/W.B. (I.L.)	9	1	*.900	2.43	16	16	3	1	0	92 2/3	84	26	25	30	59
—Philadelphia (N.L.).............	1	1	.500	5.34	5	5	1	0	0	28 2/3	29	20	17	7	5
1993— Scranton/W.B. (I.L.)	9	2	*.818	2.87	14	13	1	1	0	97 1/3	93	34	31	16	53
—Philadelphia (N.L.).............	1	3	.250	5.29	17	4	0	0	0	51	50	32	30	22	33
1994— Philadelphia (N.L.).............	2	4	.333	5.01	12	8	0	0	0	50 1/3	61	31	28	20	29
—Scranton/W.B. (I.L.)	2	7	.222	5.79	14	14	1	0	0	84	91	55	54	36	53
1995— Philadelphia (N.L.).............	3	3	.500	3.29	33	8	0	0	0	87 2/3	78	37	32	29	57
—Scranton/W.B. (I.L.)	0	1	.000	4.66	3	3	1	0	0	9 2/3	8	5	5	2	8
1996— Philadelphia (N.L.).............	6	14	.300	5.44	32	29	0	0	0	167	188	107	101	67	103
1997— Omaha (A.A.)■	3	6	.333	4.22	20	11	1	0	5	79	71	41	37	38	68
—Kansas City (A.L.)	0	2	.000	6.43	10	0	0	0	1	14	20	11	10	8	10
1998— Pittsburgh (N.L.)■............	4	2	.667	1.94	37	0	0	0	0	51	39	12	11	16	59
—Nashville (PCL)	0	2	.000	5.59	16	4	0	0	1	37	36	25	23	14	34
1999— Pittsburgh (N.L.)	3	4	.429	5.09	58	0	0	0	23	58 1/3	63	36	33	37	76
2000— Pittsburgh (N.L.)	3	4	.429	3.50	72	0	0	0	24	72	56	34	28	40	71
A.L. totals (1 year)	0	2	.000	6.43	10	0	0	0	1	14	20	11	10	8	10
N.L. totals (8 years)	23	35	.397	4.45	266	55	1	0	47	566	564	309	280	238	433
Major League totals (9 years)	23	37	.383	4.50	276	55	1	0	48	580	584	320	290	246	443

W

PERSONAL: Born August 19, 1966, in Houston. ... 6-0/195. ... Throws right, bats right. ... Full name: Gregory Scott Williams.
HIGH SCHOOL: Cypress-Fairbanks (Houston).
COLLEGE: Houston.
TRANSACTIONS/CAREER NOTES: Selected by Toronto Blue Jays organization in 28th round of free-agent draft (June 1, 1988). ... On disabled list (April 9-May 17, 1992). ... On Toronto disabled list (July 17, 1995-remainder of season); included rehabilitation assignment to Syracuse (August 15-25). ... On Toronto disabled list (March 22-May 31 and June 11-July 26, 1996); included rehabilitation assignments to Dunedin (May 2-10), Syracuse (May 10-28 and July 13-20) and St. Catharines (July 20-26). ... Traded by Blue Jays with P Carlos Almanzar and OF Peter Tucci to San Diego Padres for P Joey Hamilton (December 13, 1998). ... On San Diego disabled list (May 2-July 2, 2000); included rehabilitation assignment to Rancho Cucamonga (June 22-27) and Las Vegas (June 28).
MISCELLANEOUS: Appeared in one game as pinch runner (1999). ... Scored three runs in four appearances as pinch runner (2000). ... Struck out twice in two appearances as pinch hitter (2000).

Year League	W	L	Pct.	ERA	G	GS	CG	ShO	Sv.	IP	H	R	ER	BB	SO
1988— St. Catharines (NY-Penn) ...	8	2	.800	1.54	12	12	2	0	0	76	48	22	13	21	58
— Knoxville (Sou.).................	2	2	.500	3.81	6	4	0	0	0	28 1/3	27	13	12	12	25
1989— Dunedin (FSL)..................	3	5	.375	2.32	20	9	0	0	3	81 1/3	63	26	21	27	60
— Knoxville (Sou.).................	3	5	.375	3.55	14	12	2	•2	1	71	61	32	28	33	51
1990— Knoxville (Sou.)...............	7	9	.438	3.14	42	12	0	0	5	126	111	55	44	39	74
— Syracuse (I.L.)...................	0	1	.000	10.00	3	0	0	0	0	9	15	10	10	4	8
1991— Knoxville (Sou.)...............	3	2	.600	3.59	18	1	0	0	3	42 2/3	42	18	17	14	37
— Syracuse (I.L.)...................	3	4	.429	4.12	31	0	0	0	6	54 2/3	52	27	25	27	37
1992— Syracuse (I.L.)...............	6	8	.429	3.13	25	16	1	0	1	120 2/3	115	46	42	41	81
1993— Syracuse (I.L.)...............	1	1	.500	2.20	12	0	0	0	3	16 1/3	15	5	4	5	16
— Toronto (A.L.)..................	3	1	.750	4.38	30	0	0	0	0	37	40	18	18	22	24
— Dunedin (FSL)..................	0	0	...	0.00	2	0	0	0	0	4	0	0	0	2	2
1994— Toronto (A.L.)..............	1	3	.250	3.64	38	0	0	0	0	59 1/3	44	24	24	33	56
— Syracuse (I.L.).................	0	0	...	0.00	1	0	0	0	1	1 2/3	0	0	0	0	1
1995— Toronto (A.L.)..............	1	2	.333	3.69	23	3	0	0	0	53 2/3	44	23	22	28	41
— Syracuse (I.L.).................	0	0	...	3.52	5	1	0	0	1	7 2/3	5	3	3	5	13
1996— Dunedin (FSL)................	0	2	.000	8.22	2	2	0	0	0	7 2/3	9	7	7	2	11
— Syracuse (I.L.).................	3	1	.750	1.41	7	7	1	1	0	32	22	5	5	7	33
— Toronto (A.L.)..................	4	5	.444	4.73	12	10	1	0	0	59	64	33	31	21	43
— St. Catharines (NY-Penn) ...	0	0	...	3.68	2	2	0	0	0	7 1/3	7	3	3	4	12
1997— Toronto (A.L.)..............	9	14	.391	4.35	31	31	0	0	0	194 2/3	201	98	94	66	124
1998— Toronto (A.L.)..............	10	9	.526	4.46	32	32	1	1	0	209 2/3	196	112	104	81	151
1999— San Diego (N.L.)■.............	12	12	.500	4.41	33	33	0	0	0	208 1/3	213	106	102	73	137
2000— San Diego (N.L.)	10	8	.556	3.75	23	23	4	0	0	168	152	74	70	54	111
— Rancho Cuca. (Calif.)	0	0	...	0.00	1	1	0	0	0	5	3	0	0	0	10
— Las Vegas (PCL)	0	0	...	1.50	1	1	0	0	0	6	7	2	1	0	5
A.L. totals (6 years)	28	34	.452	4.30	166	76	2	1	0	613 1/3	589	308	293	251	439
N.L. totals (2 years)	22	20	.524	4.11	56	56	4	0	0	376 1/3	365	180	172	127	248
Major League totals (8 years)	50	54	.481	4.23	222	132	6	1	0	989 2/3	954	488	465	378	687

PERSONAL: Born February 17, 1976, in Fort Polk, La. ... 6-0/185. ... Throws right, bats right. ... Full name: Scott Ryan Williamson.
HIGH SCHOOL: Friendswood (Texas).
COLLEGE: Tulane, then Oklahoma State.
TRANSACTIONS/CAREER NOTES: Selected by Cincinnati Reds organization in ninth round of free-agent draft (June 3, 1997). ... On disabled list (August 24-September 8, 2000).
RECORDS: Shares N.L. single-game record for most consecutive strikeouts by relief pitcher—6 (May 27, 1999).
HONORS: Named N.L. Rookie Pitcher of the Year by THE SPORTING NEWS (1999). ... Named N.L. Rookie of the Year by Baseball Writers' Association of America (1999).
STATISTICAL NOTES: Tied for Pioneer League lead in shutouts with one and in wild pitches with 12 in 1997.

Year League	W	L	Pct.	ERA	G	GS	CG	ShO	Sv.	IP	H	R	ER	BB	SO
1997— Billings (Pio.)	•8	2	.800	1.78	13	13	2	•1	0	86	66	25	17	23	*101
1998— Chattanooga (Sou.)	4	5	.444	3.78	18	18	0	0	0	100	85	49	42	46	105
— Indianapolis (I.L.)..............	0	0	...	3.48	5	5	0	0	0	20 2/3	20	9	8	9	17
1999— Cincinnati (N.L.)	12	7	.632	2.41	62	0	0	0	19	93 1/3	54	29	25	43	107
2000— Cincinnati (N.L.)	5	8	.385	3.29	48	10	0	0	6	112	92	45	41	75	136
Major League totals (2 years)	17	15	.531	2.89	110	10	0	0	25	205 1/3	146	74	66	118	243

ALL-STAR GAME RECORD

Year League	W	L	Pct.	ERA	GS	CG	ShO	Sv.	IP	H	R	ER	BB	SO
1999— National							Selected—did not play.							

PERSONAL: Born September 3, 1970, in Chicago. ... 6-0/185. ... Bats right, throws right. ... Full name: Craig Franklin Wilson.
HIGH SCHOOL: Leyden (Franklin Park, Ill.).
COLLEGE: Kansas State.
TRANSACTIONS/CAREER NOTES: Selected by San Francisco Giants in 13th round of free-agent draft (June 3, 1991); did not sign. ... Selected by Chicago White Sox in 13th round of free-agent draft (June 1, 1992). ... On Chicago disabled list (June 3-July 13, 2000); included rehabilitation assignment to Charlotte (June 23-July 13). ... Released by White Sox (November 7, 2000).

W

Year	Team (League)	Pos.	G	AB	R	H	2B	3B	HR	RBI	Avg.	BB	SO	SB	PO	A	E	Avg.
1993— South Bend (Midw.) ...		SS	132	455	56	118	27	2	5	59	.259	49	50	4	166	388	21	.963
1994— Prince William (Caro.)		SS	131	496	70	131	36	4	4	66	.264	58	44	1	187	388	11	.981
1995— Birmingham (Sou.).....		SS	132	471	56	136	19	1	4	46	.289	43	44	2	193	389	34	.945
1996— Nashville (A.A.)		SS	44	123	13	22	4	1	1	6	.179	10	5	0	43	97	10	.933
— Birmingham (Sou.).....		SS	58	202	36	57	9	0	3	26	.282	40	28	1	67	148	19	.919
1997— Nashville (A.A.)		SS	137	453	71	123	20	2	6	42	.272	48	31	4	189	398	20	.967
1998— Calgary (PCL)............	2-S-3-1-O	120	432	67	132	21	1	14	69	.306	37	41	4	279	248	9	.983
— Chicago (A.L.)	SS-2B-3B	13	47	14	22	5	0	3	10	.468	3	6	1	20	27	0	1.000
1999— Chicago (A.L.)	3-S-2-DH-1	98	252	28	60	8	1	4	26	.238	23	22	1	86	155	7	.972
2000— Chicago (A.L.)	3B-SS-2B	28	73	12	19	3	0	0	4	.260	5	11	1	31	61	3	.968
— Charlotte (I.L.)...........	3B-SS	62	230	43	85	14	2	3	34	.370	32	26	0	48	128	8	.957
Major League totals (3 years)			139	372	54	101	16	1	7	40	.272	31	39	3	137	243	10	.974

WILSON, DAN   C   MARINERS

PERSONAL: Born March 25, 1969, in Arlington Heights, Ill. ... 6-3/202. ... Bats right, throws right. ... Full name: Daniel Allen Wilson.
HIGH SCHOOL: Barrington (Ill.).
COLLEGE: Minnesota.
TRANSACTIONS/CAREER NOTES: Selected by New York Mets organization in 26th round of free-agent draft (June 2, 1987); did not sign. ... Selected by Cincinnati Reds organization in first round (seventh pick overall) of free-agent draft (June 4, 1990). ... Traded by Reds with P Bobby Ayala to Seattle Mariners for P Erik Hanson and 2B Bret Boone (November 2, 1993). ... On disabled list (July 21-September 1, 1998). ... On Seattle disabled list (June 15-July 14, 2000); included rehabilitation assignment to Everett (July 12-13) and Tacoma (July 14).
RECORDS: Shares major league single-game record for most putouts by catcher (nine-inning game)—20 (August 8, 1997); most putouts by catcher (extra-inning game)—21 (March 31, 1996, 12 innings); and most chances accepted by catcher (nine-inning game) since 1900—20 (August 8, 1997). ... Shares A.L. single-game record for most putouts by catcher (extra-inning game)—21 (March 31, 1996, 12 innings).
STATISTICAL NOTES: Led American Association catchers with 810 total chances in 1992. ... Led A.L. catchers with 952 total chances in 1995 and 1,129 in 1997. ... Hit three home runs in one game (April 11, 1996). ... Tied for A.L. lead in double plays by catcher with 13 in 1997. ... Career major league grand slams: 2.

Year	Team (League)	Pos.	G	AB	R	H	2B	3B	HR	RBI	Avg.	BB	SO	SB	PO	A	E	Avg.
1990— Char., W.Va. (S.Atl.)....	C	32	113	16	28	9	1	2	17	.248	13	17	0	190	24	1	.995
1991— Char., W.Va. (S.Atl.)....	C	52	197	25	62	11	1	3	29	.315	25	21	1	355	41	3	.992
— Chattanooga (Sou.)	C	81	292	32	75	19	2	2	38	.257	21	39	2	486	49	4	.993
1992— Nashville (A.A.)	C	106	366	27	92	16	1	4	34	.251	31	58	1	*733	*69	*8	.990
— Cincinnati (N.L.)	C	12	25	2	9	1	0	0	3	.360	3	8	0	42	4	0	1.000
1993— Cincinnati (N.L.)	C	36	76	6	17	3	0	0	8	.224	9	16	0	146	9	1	.994
— Indianapolis (A.A.)........	C	51	191	18	50	11	1	1	17	.262	19	31	1	314	24	2	.994
1994— Seattle (A.L.)■..........	C	91	282	24	61	14	2	3	27	.216	10	57	1	602	45	*9	.986
1995— Seattle (A.L.)	C	119	399	40	111	22	3	9	51	.278	33	63	2	*895	52	5	.995
1996— Seattle (A.L.)	C	138	491	51	140	24	0	18	83	.285	32	88	1	834	58	4	.996
1997— Seattle (A.L.)	C	146	508	66	137	31	1	15	74	.270	39	72	7	*1051	72	6	.995
1998— Seattle (A.L.)	C	96	325	39	82	17	1	9	44	.252	24	56	2	677	35	4	.994
1999— Seattle (A.L.)	C-1B	123	414	46	110	23	2	7	38	.266	29	83	5	753	48	4	.995
2000— Seattle (A.L.)	C-1B-3B	90	268	31	63	12	0	5	27	.235	22	51	1	485	30	5	.990
— Everett (N'West)...........	C	1	2	2	1	0	0	1	1	.500	1	0	0	3	1	0	1.000
— Tacoma (PCL)	DH	1	4	0	1	1	0	0	0	.250	0	1	0	0	0	0	...
American League totals (7 years)		803	2687	297	704	143	9	66	344	.262	189	470	19	5297	340	37	.993
National League totals (2 years)		48	101	8	26	4	0	0	11	.257	12	24	0	188	13	1	.995
Major League totals (9 years)		851	2788	305	730	147	9	66	355	.262	201	494	19	5485	353	38	.994

DIVISION SERIES RECORD

Year	Team (League)	Pos.	G	AB	R	H	2B	3B	HR	RBI	Avg.	BB	SO	SB	PO	A	E	Avg.
1995— Seattle (A.L.)	C	5	17	0	2	0	0	0	1	.118	2	6	0	34	1	0	1.000
1997— Seattle (A.L.)	C	4	13	0	0	0	0	0	0	.000	0	9	0	29	1	0	1.000
2000— Seattle (A.L.)	C	2	3	0	0	0	0	0	1	.000	1	2	0	5	0	1	.833
Division series totals (3 years)		11	33	0	2	0	0	0	2	.061	3	17	0	68	2	1	.986

CHAMPIONSHIP SERIES RECORD

Year	Team (League)	Pos.	G	AB	R	H	2B	3B	HR	RBI	Avg.	BB	SO	SB	PO	A	E	Avg.
1995— Seattle (A.L.)	C	6	16	0	0	0	0	0	0	.000	0	4	0	35	3	1	.974
2000— Seattle (A.L.)	C	4	11	0	1	0	0	0	0	.091	1	5	0	20	4	1	.960
Championship series totals (2 years)		10	27	0	1	0	0	0	0	.037	1	9	0	55	7	2	.969

ALL-STAR GAME RECORD

Year	League	Pos.	AB	R	H	2B	3B	HR	RBI	Avg.	BB	SO	SB	PO	A	E	Avg.
1996— American	PH	1	0	0	0	0	0	0	.000	0	0	0	...	...	...	...

W

WILSON, ENRIQUE   IF   PIRATES

PERSONAL: Born July 27, 1975, in Santo Domingo, Dominican Republic. ... 5-11/160. ... Bats both, throws right. ... Full name: Enrique Martes Wilson.
HIGH SCHOOL: Liceo Ramon Amelio Jiminez (Santo Domingo, Dominican Republic).
TRANSACTIONS/CAREER NOTES: Signed as non-drafted free agent by Minnesota Twins organization (April 15, 1992). ... Traded by Twins to Cleveland Indians (February 21, 1994), completing deal in which Twins acquired P Shawn Bryant for a player to be named later (February 21, 1994). ... On Cleveland disabled list (April 4-June 15, 1998); included rehabilitation assignment to Buffalo (June 2-15). ... On Cleveland disabled list (July 14-July 28, 2000). ... Traded by Indians with OF Alex Ramirez to Pittsburgh Pirates for 1B/OF Wil Cordero (July 28, 2000). ... On Pittsburgh disabled list (July 29-August 1, 2000); included rehabilitation assignment to Nashville (July 31-August 1).
STATISTICAL NOTES: Led South Atlantic League shortstops with 625 total chances and 66 double plays in 1994. ... Led Carolina League with 10 sacrifice flies in 1995. ... Led Eastern League shortstops with 74 double plays in 1996. ... Career major league grand slams: 1.

Year Team (League)	Pos.	G	AB	R	H	2B	3B	HR	RBI	Avg.	BB	SO	SB	PO	A	E	Avg.
1992— GC Twins (GCL).........	SS	13	44	12	15	1	0	0	8	.341	4	4	3	9	26	4	.897
1993— Elizabethton (Appl.).....	SS-3B	58	197	42	57	8	4	13	50	.289	14	18	5	50	139	19	.909
1994— Columbus (S.Atl.)■....	SS	133	512	82	143	28	12	10	72	.279	44	34	21	*185	*407	33	.947
1995— Kinston (Caro.)............	SS-2B	117	464	55	124	24	•7	6	52	.267	25	38	18	181	375	21	.964
1996— Canton/Akron (East.)..	SS-2B	117	484	70	147	17	5	5	50	.304	31	46	23	179	344	28	.949
— Buffalo (A.A.).............	3B-SS	3	8	1	4	1	0	0	0	.500	1	1	0	1	2	1	.750
1997— Buffalo (A.A.)..........	SS-2B-3B	118	451	78	138	20	3	11	39	.306	42	41	9	218	332	20	.965
— Cleveland (A.L.)........	SS-2B	5	15	2	5	0	0	0	1	.333	0	2	0	7	13	1	.952
1998— Cleveland (A.L.).........	2B-SS-3B	32	90	13	29	6	0	2	12	.322	4	8	2	43	76	2	.983
— Buffalo (I.L.)...............	2B-SS	56	221	40	62	13	0	4	23	.281	19	21	8	108	141	6	.976
1999— Cleveland (A.L.)........	3-S-2-DH	113	332	41	87	22	1	2	24	.262	25	41	5	77	163	8	.968
2000— Cleveland (A.L.)..........3B-DH-2B-SS		40	117	16	38	9	0	2	12	.325	7	11	2	20	44	1	.985
— Nashville (PCL)■......	2B	2	7	0	2	0	0	0	1	.286	0	0	0	4	4	1	.889
— Pittsburgh (N.L.)......	3B-2B-SS	40	122	11	32	6	1	3	15	.262	11	13	0	24	73	6	.942
American League totals (4 years)		190	554	72	159	37	1	6	49	.287	36	62	9	147	296	12	.974
National League totals (1 year)		40	122	11	32	6	1	3	15	.262	11	13	0	24	73	6	.942
Major League totals (4 years)		230	676	83	191	43	2	9	64	.283	47	75	9	171	369	18	.968

DIVISION SERIES RECORD

Year Team (League)	Pos.	G	AB	R	H	2B	3B	HR	RBI	Avg.	BB	SO	SB	PO	A	E	Avg.
1998— Cleveland (A.L.).........	2B	1	2	0	0	0	0	0	0	.000	0	0	0	2	2	0	1.000
1999— Cleveland (A.L.).........	2B-PH	3	2	0	0	0	0	0	0	.000	0	0	0	3	0	0	1.000
Division series totals (2 years)		4	4	0	0	0	0	0	0	.000	0	0	0	5	2	0	1.000

CHAMPIONSHIP SERIES RECORD

Year Team (League)	Pos.	G	AB	R	H	2B	3B	HR	RBI	Avg.	BB	SO	SB	PO	A	E	Avg.
1998— Cleveland (A.L.).........	PR-2B	5	14	2	3	0	0	0	1	.214	1	3	0	5	19	1	.960

WILSON, KRIS   P   ROYALS

PERSONAL: Born August 6, 1976, in Washington, D.C. ... 6-4/225. ... Throws right, bats right. ... Full name: Kristopher Kyle Wilson.
HIGH SCHOOL: Tarpon Springs (Fla.).
COLLEGE: Georgia Tech.
TRANSACTIONS/CAREER NOTES: Selected by Kansas City Royals organization in ninth round of free-agent draft (June 3, 1997).

Year League	W	L	Pct.	ERA	G	GS	CG	ShO	Sv.	IP	H	R	ER	BB	SO
1997— Spokane (N'West)	5	3	.625	4.52	15	15	0	0	0	73²/₃	101	50	37	21	72
1998— Wilmington (Caro.)............	0	3	.000	3.75	10	2	0	0	1	24	19	10	10	6	20
— Lansing (Midw.)	10	5	.667	3.53	18	18	1	0	0	117¹/₃	119	50	46	15	74
1999— Wilmington (Caro.)............	8	1	.889	1.13	14	4	0	0	0	48	25	7	6	11	45
— Omaha (PCL)....................	0	1	.000	8.44	1	1	0	0	0	5¹/₃	8	5	5	0	3
— Wichita (Texas)	5	7	.417	5.45	23	10	0	0	0	74¹/₃	91	51	45	14	45
2000— Kansas City (A.L.)	0	1	.000	4.19	20	0	0	0	0	34¹/₃	38	16	16	11	17
— Wichita (Texas)	7	3	.700	3.51	21	15	1	0	0	102²/₃	99	52	40	21	69
Major League totals (1 year)........	0	1	.000	4.19	20	0	0	0	0	34¹/₃	38	16	16	11	17

WILSON, PAUL   P   DEVIL RAYS

PERSONAL: Born March 28, 1973, in Orlando. ... 6-5/235. ... Throws right, bats right. ... Full name: Paul Anthony Wilson.
HIGH SCHOOL: William R. Boone (Orlando).
COLLEGE: Florida State.
TRANSACTIONS/CAREER NOTES: Selected by New York Mets organization in first round (first pick overall) of free-agent draft (June 2, 1994). ... On New York disabled list (June 5-July 15, 1996); included rehabilitation assignments to St. Lucie (June 28-July 10) and Binghamton (July 10-15). ... On New York disabled list (March 27, 1997-entire season); included rehabilitation assignments to Gulf Coast Mets (August 2-23) and St. Lucie (August 28-September 8). ... On New York disabled list (March 13-August 4, 1998); included rehabilitation assignment to St. Lucie (July 9-August 1). ... On Norfolk disabled list (April 8, 1999-entire season). ... Traded by Mets with OF Jason Tyner to Tampa Bay Devil Rays for OF Bubba Trammell and P Rick White (July 28, 2000).
STATISTICAL NOTES: Named Eastern League Pitcher of the Year (1995).

Year League	W	L	Pct.	ERA	G	GS	CG	ShO	Sv.	IP	H	R	ER	BB	SO
1994— Gulf Coast Mets (GCL)	0	2	.000	3.00	3	3	0	0	0	12	8	4	4	4	13
— St. Lucie (FSL)..................	0	5	.000	5.06	8	8	0	0	0	37¹/₃	32	23	21	17	37
1995— Binghamton (East.)	6	3	.667	*2.17	16	16	4	1	0	120¹/₃	89	34	29	24	127
— Norfolk (I.L.)	5	3	.625	2.85	10	10	*4	2	0	66¹/₃	59	25	21	20	67
1996— New York (N.L.).................	5	12	.294	5.38	26	26	1	0	0	149	157	102	89	71	109
— St. Lucie (FSL)..................	0	1	.000	3.38	2	2	0	0	0	8	6	5	3	4	5
— Binghamton (East.)	0	1	.000	7.20	1	1	0	0	0	5	6	4	4	5	5
1997— Gulf Coast Mets (GCL)	1	0	1.000	1.45	4	3	0	0	1	18²/₃	14	7	3	4	18
— St. Lucie (FSL)..................	0	0	...	2.57	1	1	0	0	0	7	6	2	2	0	6
1998— St. Lucie (FSL).................	0	1	.000	6.38	5	5	0	0	0	18¹/₃	23	13	13	4	16
— Norfolk (I.L.)	4	1	.800	4.42	7	7	0	0	0	38²/₃	42	19	19	9	30
1999— Norfolk (I.L.)						Did not play.									
2000— St. Lucie (FSL)	2	0	1.000	1.40	5	5	0	0	0	25²/₃	22	9	4	4	19
— Norfolk (I.L.)	5	5	.500	4.23	15	13	0	0	0	83	85	40	39	25	56
— Tampa Bay (A.L.)■............	1	4	.200	3.35	11	7	0	0	0	51	38	20	19	16	40
A.L. totals (1 year)	1	4	.200	3.35	11	7	0	0	0	51	38	20	19	16	40
N.L. totals (1 year)	5	12	.294	5.38	26	26	1	0	0	149	157	102	89	71	109
Major League totals (2 years)	6	16	.273	4.86	37	33	1	0	0	200	195	122	108	87	149

W

WILSON, PRESTON — OF — MARLINS

PERSONAL: Born July 19, 1974, in Bamberg, S.C. ... 6-2/193. ... Bats right, throws right. ... Full name: Preston James Richard Wilson. ... Son of Mookie Wilson, first base/outfield coach, New York Mets; and outfielder with Mets (1980-89) and Toronto Blue Jays (1989-91).
HIGH SCHOOL: Bamberg Erhardt (Bamberg, S.C.).
TRANSACTIONS/CAREER NOTES: Selected by New York Mets organization in first round (ninth pick overall) of free-agent draft (June 1, 1992). ... On disabled list (April 4-29, May 21-July 13 and July 29-September 8, 1996). ... On Norfolk disabled list (April 20-May 2, 1998). ... Traded by Mets with P Ed Yarnall and P Geoff Goetz to Florida Marlins for C Mike Piazza (May 22, 1998).
HONORS: Named N.L. Rookie Player of the Year by THE SPORTING NEWS (1999).
STATISTICAL NOTES: Led Appalachian League third basemen with 197 total chances in 1993. ... Career major league grand slams: 2.

Year	Team (League)	Pos.	G	AB	R	H	2B	3B	HR	RBI	Avg.	BB	SO	SB	PO	A	E	Avg.
1993—	Kingsport (Appl.)........	3B	66	259	44	60	10	0	*16	48	.232	24	75	6	*45	*127	*25	.873
—	Pittsfield (NY-Penn)....	3B	8	29	6	16	5	1	1	12	.552	2	7	1	5	9	6	.700
1994—	Capital City (S.Atl.).....	3B	131	474	55	108	17	4	14	58	.228	20	135	10	78	281	47	.884
1995—	Capital City (S.Atl.).....	OF	111	442	70	119	26	5	20	61	.269	19	114	20	189	10	8	.961
1996—	St. Lucie (FSL)	OF	23	85	6	15	3	0	1	7	.176	8	21	1	39	4	2	.956
1997—	St. Lucie (FSL)	OF-DH	63	245	32	60	12	1	11	48	.245	8	66	3	104	5	3	.973
—	Binghamton (East.)	OF-DH-3B	70	259	37	74	12	1	19	47	.286	21	71	7	116	3	6	.952
1998—	Norfolk (I.L.).............	OF	18	73	9	18	5	1	1	9	.247	2	22	1	44	2	2	.958
—	New York (N.L.)..........	OF	8	20	3	6	2	0	0	2	.300	2	8	1	10	0	1	.909
—	Charlotte (I.L.)■........	OF-DH	94	356	71	99	25	3	25	77	.278	34	121	14	180	8	4	.979
—	Florida (N.L.).............	OF	14	31	4	2	0	0	1	1	.065	4	13	0	13	0	0	1.000
1999—	Florida (N.L.).............	OF	149	482	67	135	21	4	26	71	.280	46	156	11	320	10	9	.973
2000—	Florida (N.L.).............	OF	161	605	94	160	35	3	31	121	.264	55	*187	36	387	9	5	.988
Major League totals (3 years)			332	1138	168	303	58	7	58	195	.266	107	364	48	730	19	15	.980

WILSON, VANCE — C — METS

PERSONAL: Born March 17, 1973, in Mesa, Ariz. ... 5-11/190. ... Bats right, throws right. ... Full name: Vance Allen Wilson.
HIGH SCHOOL: Red Mountain (Mesa, Ariz.).
JUNIOR COLLEGE: Mesa (Ariz.) Community College.
TRANSACTIONS/CAREER NOTES: Selected by New York Mets organization in 44th round of free-agent draft (June 3, 1993). ... On Norfolk disabled list (May 2-July 18, 1998). ... On New York disabled list (September 8, 1998-remainder of season). ... On Norfolk disabled list (May 13-August 28, 1999). ... On New York disabled list (August 28, 1999-remainder of season).
STATISTICAL NOTES: Led International League with 706 total chances, 10 double plays and 14 passed balls in 2000.

Year	Team (League)	Pos.	G	AB	R	H	2B	3B	HR	RBI	Avg.	BB	SO	SB	PO	A	E	Avg.
1994—	Pittsfield (NY-Penn)....	C	44	166	22	51	12	0	2	20	.307	5	27	4	190	25	5	.977
1995—	Columbia (S.Atl.)........	C	91	324	34	81	11	0	6	32	.250	19	45	4	605	99	*14	.981
1996—	St. Lucie (FSL)	C	93	311	29	76	14	2	6	44	.244	31	41	2	502	87	8	.987
1997—	Binghamton (East.)	C	92	322	46	89	17	0	15	40	.276	20	46	2	604	69	11	.984
1998—	Norfolk (I.L.)	C	46	154	18	40	3	0	4	16	.260	9	29	0	348	29	4	.990
—	GC Mets (GCL)	C	10	28	5	10	5	0	2	9	.357	0	0	0	35	9	2	.957
—	St. Lucie (FSL)	C	4	16	0	1	0	0	0	0	.063	0	5	0	19	3	0	1.000
1999—	Norfolk (I.L.)	C	15	53	10	14	3	0	3	5	.264	4	8	1	95	11	1	.991
—	New York (N.L.)..........	C	1	0	0	0	0	0	0	0	...	0	0	0	0	0	0	...
2000—	Norfolk (I.L.)	C	111	400	47	104	23	1	16	62	.260	24	65	11	*637	*66	3	.996
—	New York (N.L.).........	C	4	4	0	0	0	0	0	0	.000	0	2	0	14	0	0	1.000
Major League totals (2 years)			5	4	0	0	0	0	0	0	.000	0	2	0	14	0	0	1.000

WINCHESTER, SCOTT — P — REDS

PERSONAL: Born April 20, 1973, in Midland, Mich. ... 6-2/210. ... Throws right, bats right. ... Full name: Scott Joseph Winchester.
HIGH SCHOOL: H.H. Dow (Midland, Mich.).
COLLEGE: Clemson.
TRANSACTIONS/CAREER NOTES: Selected by Cleveland Indians organization in 14th round of free-agent draft (June 1, 1995). ... Traded by Indians with P Jim Crowell, P Danny Graves and IF Damian Jackson to Cincinnati Reds for P John Smiley and IF Jeff Branson (July 31, 1997). ... Selected by Arizona Diamondbacks in second round (33rd pick overall) of expansion draft (November 18, 1997). ... Traded by Diamondbacks to Reds (November 18, 1997), completing deal in which Reds traded P Felix Rodriguez to Diamondbacks for a player to be named later (November 11, 1997). ... On Indianapolis disabled list (August 18-September 8, 1998). ... On Cincinnati disabled list (March 24, 1999-entire season); included rehabilitation assignment to Rockford (August 8-September 6).

W

Year	League	W	L	Pct.	ERA	G	GS	CG	ShO	Sv.	IP	H	R	ER	BB	SO
1995—	Watertown (NY-Penn)	3	1	.750	2.83	23	0	0	0	11	28²/₃	24	10	9	6	27
1996—	Columbus (S.Atl.).............	7	3	.700	3.23	52	0	0	0	26	61¹/₃	50	27	22	16	60
—	Columbus (S.Atl.).............	7	3	.700	3.23	52	0	0	0	26	61¹/₃	50	27	22	16	60
1997—	Kinston (Caro.)..................	2	1	.667	1.47	34	0	0	0	29	36²/₃	21	6	6	11	45
—	Akron (East.)	0	0	...	3.86	6	0	0	0	1	7	8	3	3	2	8
—	Chattanooga (Sou.)■........	2	1	.667	1.69	9	0	0	0	3	10²/₃	9	4	2	3	3
—	Indianapolis (A.A.).............	0	0	...	0.00	4	0	0	0	0	5²/₃	2	0	0	2	2
—	Cincinnati (N.L.)..............	0	0	...	6.00	5	0	0	0	0	6	9	5	4	2	3
1998—	Indianapolis (I.L.).............	3	2	.600	6.67	6	5	0	0	0	29²/₃	39	23	22	8	12
—	Cincinnati (N.L.).............	3	6	.333	5.81	16	16	1	0	0	79	101	56	51	27	40
1999—	Rockford (Midw.)	1	1	.500	2.79	6	6	0	0	0	19¹/₃	19	7	6	3	11
2000—	Louisville (I.L.)	1	2	.333	4.08	43	0	0	0	3	57¹/₃	67	29	26	15	33
—	Cincinnati (N.L.)	0	0	...	3.68	5	0	0	0	0	7¹/₃	10	4	3	2	3
Major League totals (3 years)		3	6	.333	5.65	26	16	1	0	0	92¹/₃	120	65	58	31	46

WINN, RANDY — OF — DEVIL RAYS

PERSONAL: Born June 9, 1974, in Los Angeles. ... 6-2/193. ... Bats both, throws right. ... Full name: Dwight Randolph Winn.
HIGH SCHOOL: San Ramon Valley (Danville, Calif.).
COLLEGE: Santa Clara.
TRANSACTIONS/CAREER NOTES: Selected by Florida Marlins organization in third round of free-agent draft (June 1, 1995). ... On disabled list (August 22-September 11, 1995). ... Selected by Tampa Bay Devil Rays in third round (58th pick overall) of expansion draft (November 18, 1997).
STATISTICAL NOTES: Led Eastern League in caught stealing with 20 in 1997. ... Career major league grand slams: 1.
MISCELLANEOUS: Holds Tampa Bay Devil Rays record for most triples (13).

Year	Team (League)	Pos.	G	AB	R	H	2B	3B	HR	RBI	Avg.	BB	SO	SB	PO	A	E	Avg.
1995—	Elmira (NY-Penn)	OF	51	213	38	67	7	4	0	22	.315	15	31	19	103	1	5	.954
1996—	Kane County (Midw.)..	OF	130	514	90	139	16	3	0	35	.270	47	115	30	260	2	8	.970
1997—	Brevard County (FSL).	OF	36	143	26	45	8	2	0	15	.315	16	28	16	95	0	0	1.000
—	Portland (East.)	OF	96	384	66	112	15	6	8	36	.292	42	92	35	182	6	4	.979
1998—	Durham (I.L.)■	OF	29	123	25	35	5	2	1	16	.285	15	24	10	55	1	2	.966
—	Tampa Bay (A.L.)	OF-DH	109	338	51	94	9	9	1	17	.278	29	69	26	192	7	4	.980
1999—	Tampa Bay (A.L.)	OF	79	303	44	81	16	4	2	24	.267	17	63	9	180	4	1	.995
—	Durham (I.L.)	OF	46	207	38	73	20	3	3	30	.353	16	27	9	113	2	4	.966
2000—	Durham (I.L.)	OF	79	303	67	100	24	5	7	40	.330	48	53	18	158	10	7	.960
—	Tampa Bay (A.L.)	OF-DH	51	159	28	40	5	0	1	16	.252	26	25	6	92	4	1	.990
Major League totals (3 years)			239	800	123	215	30	13	4	57	.269	72	157	41	464	15	6	.988

WISE, DeWAYNE — OF — BLUE JAYS

PERSONAL: Born February 24, 1978, in Columbia, S.C. ... 6-1/180. ... Bats left, throws left. ... Full name: Larry DeWayne Wise.
HIGH SCHOOL: Chapin (S.C.).
TRANSACTIONS/CAREER NOTES: Selected by Cincinnati Reds organization in fifth round of free-agent draft (June 3, 1997). ... Selected by Toronto Blue Jays from Reds organization in Rule 5 major league draft (December 13, 1999). ... On Toronto disabled list (June 6-September 1, 2000); included rehabilitation assignment to Tennessee (August 11-30).
STATISTICAL NOTES: Led Pioneer League outfielders with 140 total chances in 1997. ... Led Midwest League with nine sacrifice flies in 1998. ... Led Midwest League with 14 sacrifice flies in 1999.

Year	Team (League)	Pos.	G	AB	R	H	2B	3B	HR	RBI	Avg.	BB	SO	SB	PO	A	E	Avg.
1997—	Billings (Pio.)	OF	62	268	53	84	13	*9	7	41	.313	9	47	18	•118	9	*13	.907
1998—	Burlington (Midw.)	OF	127	496	61	111	15	9	2	44	.224	41	111	27	233	8	7	.972
1999—	Rockford (Midw.)	OF	131	502	70	127	20	13	11	81	.253	42	81	35	294	16	8	.975
2000—	Toronto (A.L.)■	OF-DH	28	22	3	3	0	0	0	0	.136	1	5	1	20	0	0	1.000
—	Tennessee (Sou.)	OF	15	56	10	14	5	2	2	8	.333	7	13	3	29	1	4	.882
Major League totals (1 year)			28	22	3	3	0	0	0	0	.136	1	5	1	20	0	0	1.000

WISE, MATT — P — ANGELS

PERSONAL: Born November 18, 1975, in Montclair, Calif. ... 6-4/190. ... Throws right, bats right. ... Full name: Matthew John Wise.
HIGH SCHOOL: Bonita (Calif.).
COLLEGE: Pepperdine, then Cal State Fullerton.
TRANSACTIONS/CAREER NOTES: Selected by Anaheim Angels organization in sixth round of free-agent draft (June 3, 1997). ... On disabled list (July 9, 1999-remainder of season).

Year	League	W	L	Pct.	ERA	G	GS	CG	ShO	Sv.	IP	H	R	ER	BB	SO
1997—	Boise (N'West)	•9	1	*.900	3.25	15	15	0	0	0	83	82	37	30	34	86
1998—	Midland (Texas)	9	10	.474	5.42	27	27	3	•1	0	167 2/3	195	114	101	48	131
1999—	Erie (East.)	8	5	.615	3.77	16	16	3	0	0	98	102	48	41	24	72
2000—	Edmonton (PCL)	9	6	.600	3.69	19	19	2	1	0	124 1/3	122	54	51	26	82
—	Anaheim (A.L.)	3	3	.500	5.54	8	6	0	0	0	37 1/3	40	23	23	13	20
Major League totals (1 year)		3	3	.500	5.54	8	6	0	0	0	37 1/3	40	23	23	13	20

WITASICK, JAY — P — PADRES

PERSONAL: Born August 28, 1972, in Baltimore. ... 6-4/235. ... Throws right, bats right. ... Full name: Gerald Alphonse Witasick Jr.
HIGH SCHOOL: C. Milton Wright (Bel Air, Md.).
JUNIOR COLLEGE: Brevard Community College (Fla.).
COLLEGE: Maryland-Baltimore County.
TRANSACTIONS/CAREER NOTES: Selected by St. Louis Cardinals organization in second round of free-agent draft (June 3, 1993). ... On disabled list (July 17, 1995-remainder of season). ... Traded by Cardinals with OF Allen Battle, P Bret Wagner and P Carl Dale to Oakland Athletics for P Todd Stottlemyre (January 9, 1996). ... On Oakland disabled list (March 31-June 14, 1997); included rehabilitation assignment to Modesto (June 11-14). ... Traded by A's to Kansas City Royals for a player to be named later and cash (March 30, 1999); A's acquired P Scott Chiasson to complete deal (June 10, 1999). ... Traded by Royals to San Diego Padres for P Brian Meadows (July 31, 2000).

Year	League	W	L	Pct.	ERA	G	GS	CG	ShO	Sv.	IP	H	R	ER	BB	SO
1993—	Johnson City (Appl.)	4	3	.571	4.12	12	12	0	0	0	67 2/3	65	42	31	19	74
—	Savannah (S.Atl.)	1	0	1.000	4.50	1	1	0	0	0	6	7	3	3	2	6
1994—	Madison (Midw.)	10	4	.714	2.32	18	18	2	0	0	112 1/3	74	36	29	42	141

W

Year	League	W	L	Pct.	ERA	G	GS	CG	ShO	Sv.	IP	H	R	ER	BB	SO
1995— St. Petersburg (FSL)		7	7	.500	2.74	18	18	1	1	0	105	80	39	32	36	109
— Arkansas (Texas)		2	4	.333	6.88	7	7	0	0	0	34	46	29	26	16	26
1996— Huntsville (Sou.)■		0	3	.000	2.30	25	6	0	0	4	66²/₃	47	21	17	26	63
— Oakland (A.L.)		1	1	.500	6.23	12	0	0	0	0	13	12	9	9	5	12
— Edmonton (PCL)		0	0	...	4.15	6	0	0	0	2	8²/₃	9	4	4	6	9
1997— Modesto (Calif.)		0	1	.000	4.15	9	2	0	0	1	17¹/₃	16	9	8	5	29
— Edmonton (PCL)		3	2	.600	4.28	13	1	0	0	0	27¹/₃	25	13	13	15	17
— Oakland (A.L.)		0	0	...	5.73	8	0	0	0	0	11	14	7	7	6	8
1998— Edmonton (PCL)		11	7	.611	3.87	27	26	2	1	0	149	126	74	64	49	155
— Oakland (A.L.)		1	3	.250	6.33	7	3	0	0	0	27	36	24	19	15	29
1999— Kansas City (A.L.)■		9	12	.429	5.57	32	28	1	1	0	158¹/₃	191	108	98	83	102
2000— Kansas City (A.L.)		3	8	.273	5.94	22	14	2	0	0	89¹/₃	109	65	59	38	67
— San Diego (N.L.)■		3	2	.600	5.64	11	11	0	0	0	60²/₃	69	42	38	35	54
A.L. totals (5 years)		14	24	.368	5.79	81	45	3	1	0	298²/₃	362	213	192	147	218
N.L. totals (1 year)		3	2	.600	5.64	11	11	0	0	0	60²/₃	69	42	38	35	54
Major League totals (5 years)		17	26	.395	5.76	92	56	3	1	0	359¹/₃	431	255	230	182	272

WITT, BOBBY   P

PERSONAL: Born May 11, 1964, in Arlington, Va. ... 6-2/215. ... Throws right, bats right. ... Full name: Robert Andrew Witt.
HIGH SCHOOL: Canton (Mass.).
COLLEGE: Oklahoma.
TRANSACTIONS/CAREER NOTES: Selected by Cincinnati Reds organization in seventh round of free-agent draft (June 7, 1982); did not sign. ... Selected by Texas Rangers organization in first round (third pick overall) of free-agent draft (June 3, 1985). ... On Texas disabled list (May 21-June 20, 1987); included rehabilitation assignments to Oklahoma City (June 7-12) and Tulsa (June 13). ... On Texas disabled list (May 27-July 31, 1991); included rehabilitation assignment to Oklahoma City (July 22-29). ... Traded by Rangers with OF Ruben Sierra, P Jeff Russell and cash to Oakland Athletics for OF Jose Canseco (August 31, 1992). ... Granted free agency (October 26, 1994). ... Signed by Florida Marlins (April 9, 1995). ... Traded by Marlins to Rangers for two players to be named later (August 8, 1995); Marlins acquired P Wilson Heredia (August 11, 1995) and OF Scott Podsednik (October 2, 1995) to complete deal. ... Granted free agency (November 3, 1995). ... Re-signed by Rangers (December 24, 1995). ... Granted free agency (October 27, 1997). ... Re-signed by Rangers (January 19, 1998). ... Traded by Rangers to St. Louis Cardinals for a player to be named later or cash (June 23, 1998). ... Granted free agency (October 29, 1998). ... Signed by Tampa Bay Devil Rays organization (January 20, 1999). ... Granted free agency (November 5, 1999). ... Signed by Cleveland Indians organization (January 19, 2000). ... Released by Indians (May 18, 2000).
RECORDS: Shares major league record for most strikeouts in one inning—4 (August 2, 1987, second inning).
HONORS: Named righthanded pitcher on THE SPORTING NEWS college All-America team (1985).
STATISTICAL NOTES: Led A.L. with 22 wild pitches in 1986 and tied for lead with 16 in 1988. ... Pitched 4-0 one-hit, complete-game victory against Kansas City (June 23, 1994).
MISCELLANEOUS: Member of 1984 U.S. Olympic baseball team. ... Struck out in only appearance as pinch hitter with Texas (1987). ... Appeared in two games as pinch runner (1990). ... Appeared in one game as pinch runner (1994). ... Appeared in two games as pinch runner with Florida (1995). ... Made an out in only appearance as pinch hitter with Texas (1998). ... Shares Tampa Bay Devil Rays all-time record for most shutouts (2).

Year	League	W	L	Pct.	ERA	G	GS	CG	ShO	Sv.	IP	H	R	ER	BB	SO
1985— Tulsa (Texas)		0	6	.000	6.43	11	8	0	0	0	35	26	26	25	44	39
1986— Texas (A.L.)		11	9	.550	5.48	31	31	0	0	0	157²/₃	130	104	96	*143	174
1987— Texas (A.L.)		8	10	.444	4.91	26	25	1	0	0	143	114	82	78	*140	160
— Oklahoma City (A.A.)		1	0	1.000	9.00	1	1	0	0	0	5	5	5	5	3	2
— Tulsa (Texas)		0	1	.000	5.40	1	1	0	0	0	5	5	9	3	6	2
1988— Texas (A.L.)		8	10	.444	3.92	22	22	13	2	0	174¹/₃	134	83	76	101	148
— Oklahoma City (A.A.)		4	6	.400	4.34	11	11	3	0	0	76²/₃	69	42	37	47	70
1989— Texas (A.L.)		12	13	.480	5.14	31	31	5	1	0	194¹/₃	182	123	•111	*114	166
1990— Texas (A.L.)		17	10	.630	3.36	33	32	7	1	0	222	197	98	83	110	221
1991— Texas (A.L.)		3	7	.300	6.09	17	16	1	1	0	88²/₃	84	66	60	74	82
— Oklahoma City (A.A.)		1	1	.500	1.13	2	2	0	0	0	8	3	1	1	8	12
1992— Texas (A.L.)		9	13	.409	4.46	25	25	0	0	0	161¹/₃	152	87	80	95	100
— Oakland (A.L.)■		1	1	.500	3.41	6	6	0	0	0	31²/₃	31	12	12	19	25
1993— Oakland (A.L.)		14	13	.519	4.21	35	33	5	1	0	220	226	112	103	91	131
1994— Oakland (A.L.)		8	10	.444	5.04	24	24	5	3	0	135²/₃	151	88	76	70	111
1995— Florida (N.L.)■		2	7	.222	3.90	19	19	1	0	0	110²/₃	104	52	48	47	95
— Texas (A.L.)■		3	4	.429	4.55	10	10	1	0	0	61¹/₃	81	35	31	21	46
1996— Texas (A.L.)		16	12	.571	5.41	33	32	2	0	0	199²/₃	235	129	120	96	157
1997— Texas (A.L.)		12	12	.500	4.82	34	32	3	0	0	209	245	118	112	74	121
1998— Texas (A.L.)		5	4	.556	7.66	14	13	0	0	0	69¹/₃	95	62	59	33	30
— St. Louis (N.L.)■		2	5	.286	4.94	17	5	0	0	0	47¹/₃	55	32	26	20	28
1999— Tampa Bay (A.L.)■		7	15	.318	5.84	32	32	3	2	0	180¹/₃	213	130	117	96	123
2000— Cleveland (A.L.)■		0	1	.000	7.63	7	2	0	0	0	15¹/₃	28	13	13	6	6
A.L. totals (15 years)		134	144	.482	4.88	380	366	46	11	0	2263²/₃	2298	1342	1227	1283	1801
N.L. totals (2 years)		4	12	.250	4.22	36	24	1	0	0	158	159	84	74	67	123
Major League totals (15 years)		138	156	.469	4.84	416	390	47	11	0	2421²/₃	2457	1426	1301	1350	1924

DIVISION SERIES RECORD

Year	League	W	L	Pct.	ERA	G	GS	CG	ShO	Sv.	IP	H	R	ER	BB	SO
1996— Texas (A.L.)		0	0	...	8.10	1	1	0	0	0	3¹/₃	4	3	3	2	3

CHAMPIONSHIP SERIES RECORD

Year	League	W	L	Pct.	ERA	G	GS	CG	ShO	Sv.	IP	H	R	ER	BB	SO
1992— Oakland (A.L.)		0	0	...	18.00	1	0	0	0	0	1	2	2	2	1	1

W

PERSONAL: Born January 23, 1970, in Holyoke, Mass. ... 6-4/207. ... Throws right, bats right. ... Full name: Mark Edward Wohlers.
HIGH SCHOOL: Holyoke (Mass.).
TRANSACTIONS/CAREER NOTES: Selected by Atlanta Braves organization in eighth round of free-agent draft (June 1, 1988). ... On Atlanta disabled list (May 3-24 and August 21, 1998-remainder of season); included rehabilitation assignments to Greenville (May 23) and Richmond (August 25-September 8). ... Traded by Braves with cash to Cincinnati Reds for P John Hudek (April 16, 1999). ... On Cincinnati disabled list (April 17, 1999-remainder of season); included rehabilitation assignments to Indianapolis (May 2-3), Rockford (June 17-21) and Chattanooga (June 22-July 1). ... Granted free agency (November 5, 1999). ... Re-signed by Reds organization (January 28, 2000). ... On Louisville disabled list (April 6-May 29, 2000). ... Granted free agency (October 31, 2000). ... Re-signed by Reds (December 15, 2000).
RECORDS: Shares major league single-inning record for most strikeouts—4 (June 7, 1995, ninth inning).
HONORS: Named Southern League Outstanding Pitcher (1991).
STATISTICAL NOTES: Pitched two innings, combining with starter Kent Mercker (six innings) and Alejandro Pena (one inning) in 1-0 no-hit victory for Atlanta against San Diego (September 11, 1991). ... Led International League with 17 wild pitches in 1998.

Year League	W	L	Pct.	ERA	G	GS	CG	ShO	Sv.	IP	H	R	ER	BB	SO
1988— Pulaski (Appl.)	5	3	.625	3.32	13	9	1	0	0	59 2/3	47	37	22	50	49
1989— Sumter (S.Atl.)	2	7	.222	6.49	14	14	0	0	0	68	74	55	49	59	51
— Pulaski (Appl.)	1	1	.500	5.48	14	8	0	0	0	46	48	36	28	28	50
1990— Greenville (Sou.)	0	1	.000	4.02	14	0	0	0	6	15 2/3	14	7	7	14	20
— Sumter (S.Atl.)	5	4	.556	1.88	37	2	0	0	5	52 2/3	27	13	11	20	85
1991— Greenville (Sou.)	0	0	...	0.57	28	0	0	0	21	31 1/3	9	4	2	13	44
— Richmond (I.L.)	1	0	1.000	1.03	23	0	0	0	11	26 1/3	23	4	3	12	22
— Atlanta (N.L.)	3	1	.750	3.20	17	0	0	0	2	19 2/3	17	7	7	13	13
1992— Richmond (I.L.)	0	2	.000	3.93	27	2	0	0	9	34 1/3	32	16	15	17	33
— Atlanta (N.L.)	1	2	.333	2.55	32	0	0	0	4	35 1/3	28	11	10	14	17
1993— Richmond (I.L.)	1	3	.250	1.84	25	0	0	0	4	29 1/3	21	7	6	11	39
— Atlanta (N.L.)	6	2	.750	4.50	46	0	0	0	0	48	37	25	24	22	45
1994— Atlanta (N.L.)	7	2	.778	4.59	51	0	0	0	1	51	51	35	26	33	58
1995— Atlanta (N.L.)	7	3	.700	2.09	65	0	0	0	25	64 2/3	51	16	15	24	90
1996— Atlanta (N.L.)	2	4	.333	3.03	77	0	0	0	39	77 1/3	71	30	26	21	100
1997— Atlanta (N.L.)	5	7	.417	3.50	71	0	0	0	33	69 1/3	57	29	27	38	92
1998— Atlanta (N.L.)	0	1	.000	10.18	27	0	0	0	8	20 1/3	18	23	23	33	22
— Greenville (Sou.)	0	0	...	0.00	1	1	0	0	0	1	1	1	0	1	1
— Richmond (I.L.)	0	3	.000	20.43	16	0	0	0	0	12 1/3	21	28	28	36	16
1999— Atlanta (N.L.)	0	0	...	27.00	2	0	0	0	0	2/3	1	2	2	6	0
— Indianapolis (I.L.)■	0	0	...	108.00	1	0	0	0	0	1/3	1	4	4	5	1
— Rockford (Midw.)	0	0	...	4.50	2	0	0	0	0	2	1	1	1	2	4
— Chattanooga (Sou.)	0	0	...	16.20	2	0	0	0	0	1 2/3	1	3	3	3	3
2000— Dayton (Midw.)	0	0	...	3.00	3	3	0	0	0	3	1	1	1	1	7
— Louisville (I.L.)	1	2	.333	6.10	17	2	0	0	0	20 2/3	30	21	14	9	16
— Cincinnati (N.L.)	1	2	.333	4.50	20	0	0	0	0	28	19	14	14	17	20
Major League totals (10 years)	32	24	.571	3.78	408	0	0	0	112	414 1/3	350	192	174	221	457

DIVISION SERIES RECORD

RECORDS: Holds N.L. career record for most saves—5.

Year League	W	L	Pct.	ERA	G	GS	CG	ShO	Sv.	IP	H	R	ER	BB	SO
1995— Atlanta (N.L.)	0	1	.000	6.75	3	0	0	0	2	2 2/3	6	2	2	2	4
1996— Atlanta (N.L.)	0	0	...	0.00	3	0	0	0	3	3 1/3	1	0	0	0	4
1997— Atlanta (N.L.)	0	0	...	0.00	1	0	0	0	0	1	1	0	0	0	1
Division series totals (3 years)	0	1	.000	2.57	7	0	0	0	5	7	8	2	2	2	9

CHAMPIONSHIP SERIES RECORD

RECORDS: Holds N.L. career records for most games pitched—18; and most games as relief pitcher—18.

Year League	W	L	Pct.	ERA	G	GS	CG	ShO	Sv.	IP	H	R	ER	BB	SO
1991— Atlanta (N.L.)	0	0	...	0.00	3	0	0	0	0	1 2/3	3	0	0	1	1
1992— Atlanta (N.L.)	0	0	...	0.00	3	0	0	0	0	3	2	0	0	1	2
1993— Atlanta (N.L.)	0	1	.000	3.38	4	0	0	0	0	5 1/3	2	2	2	3	10
1995— Atlanta (N.L.)	1	0	1.000	1.80	4	0	0	0	0	5	2	1	1	0	8
1996— Atlanta (N.L.)	0	0	...	0.00	3	0	0	0	2	3	0	0	0	0	4
1997— Atlanta (N.L.)	0	0	...	0.00	1	0	0	0	0	1	0	0	0	1	1
Champ. series totals (6 years)	1	1	.500	1.42	18	0	0	0	2	19	9	3	3	6	26

WORLD SERIES RECORD

NOTES: Member of World Series championship team (1995).

Year League	W	L	Pct.	ERA	G	GS	CG	ShO	Sv.	IP	H	R	ER	BB	SO
1991— Atlanta (N.L.)	0	0	...	0.00	3	0	0	0	0	1 2/3	2	0	0	2	1
1992— Atlanta (N.L.)	0	0	...	0.00	2	0	0	0	0	2/3	0	0	0	1	0
1995— Atlanta (N.L.)	0	0	...	1.80	4	0	0	0	0	5	4	1	1	3	3
1996— Atlanta (N.L.)	0	0	...	6.23	4	0	0	0	0	4 1/3	7	3	3	3	4
World Series totals (4 years)	0	0	...	3.09	13	0	0	0	0	11 2/3	13	4	4	9	8

ALL-STAR GAME RECORD

Year League	W	L	Pct.	ERA	GS	CG	ShO	Sv.	IP	H	R	ER	BB	SO
1996— National	0	0	...	0.00	0	0	0	0	2/3	1	0	0	0	0

WOLF, RANDY   P   PHILLIES

PERSONAL: Born August 22, 1976, in Canoga Park, Calif. ... 6-0/194. ... Throws left, bats left. ... Full name: Randall C. Wolf.
HIGH SCHOOL: El Camino Real (Los Angeles).
COLLEGE: Pepperdine.

W

TRANSACTIONS/CAREER NOTES: Selected by Los Angeles Dodgers organization in 25th round of free-agent draft (June 2, 1994); did not sign. ... Selected by Philadelphia Phillies organization in second round of free-agent draft (June 3, 1997).

Year League	W	L	Pct.	ERA	G	GS	CG	ShO	Sv.	IP	H	R	ER	BB	SO
1997—Batavia (NY-Penn)	4	0	1.000	1.58	7	7	0	0	0	40	29	8	7	8	53
1998—Reading (East.)	2	0	1.000	1.44	4	4	0	0	0	25	15	4	4	4	33
—Scranton/W.B. (I.L.)	9	7	.563	4.62	24	23	1	0	0	148	167	88	76	48	118
1999—Scranton/W.B. (I.L.)	4	5	.444	3.61	12	12	0	0	0	77 1/3	73	36	31	29	72
—Philadelphia (N.L.)	6	9	.400	5.55	22	21	0	0	0	121 2/3	126	78	75	67	116
2000—Philadelphia (N.L.)	11	9	.550	4.36	32	32	1	0	0	206 1/3	210	107	100	83	160
Major League totals (2 years)	17	18	.486	4.80	54	53	1	0	0	328	336	185	175	150	276

WOMACK, TONY   SS/OF   DIAMONDBACKS

PERSONAL: Born September 25, 1969, in Danville, Va. ... 5-9/159. ... Bats left, throws right. ... Full name: Anthony Darrell Womack.
HIGH SCHOOL: Gretna (Va.).
COLLEGE: Guilford (N.C.); then UNC Greensboro (did not play).
TRANSACTIONS/CAREER NOTES: Selected by Pittsburgh Pirates organization in seventh round of free-agent draft (June 3, 1991). ... On disabled list (April 17-26 and August 28, 1992-remainder of season). ... Traded by Pirates to Arizona Diamondbacks for OF Paul Weichard and a player to be named later (February 26, 1999); Pirates acquired P Jason Boyd to complete deal (August 25, 1999). ... On Arizona disabled list (March 26-April 12, 1999); included rehabilitation assignments to Tucson (April 8-12).
STATISTICAL NOTES: Tied for American Association lead with 12 sacrifice hits in 1994. ... Led Pacific Coast League with 14 sacrifice hits in 1996. ... Led N.L. second basemen with 20 errors in 1997. ... Had 16-game hitting streak (July 3-22, 1998). ... Had 24-game hitting streak (May 2-29, 2000). ... Career major league grand slams: 1.
MISCELLANEOUS: Holds Arizona Diamondbacks all-time record for most stolen bases (117) and triples (24).

					BATTING									FIELDING		
Year Team (League)	Pos.	G	AB	R	H	2B	3B	HR	RBI	Avg.	BB	SO	SB	PO	A	E	Avg.
1991—Welland (NY-Penn)	SS-2B	45	166	30	46	3	0	1	8	.277	17	39	26	78	109	16	.921
1992—Augusta (S.Atl.)	SS-2B	102	380	62	93	8	3	0	18	.245	41	59	50	186	291	40	.923
1993—Salem (Caro.)	SS	72	304	41	91	11	3	2	18	.299	13	34	28	130	223	28	.927
—Carolina (Sou.)	SS	60	247	41	75	7	2	0	23	.304	17	34	21	102	169	11	.961
—Pittsburgh (N.L.)	SS	15	24	5	2	0	0	0	0	.083	3	3	2	11	22	1	.971
1994—Buffalo (A.A.)	SS-2B	106	421	40	93	9	2	0	18	.221	19	76	41	211	283	22	.957
—Pittsburgh (N.L.)	2B-SS	5	12	4	4	0	0	0	1	.333	2	3	0	3	6	2	.818
1995—Calgary (PCL)	2B-SS	30	107	12	30	3	1	0	6	.280	12	11	7	37	94	5	.963
—Carolina (Sou.)	SS-2B	82	332	52	85	9	4	1	19	.256	19	36	27	126	241	18	.953
1996—Calgary (PCL)	S-2-O-DH	131	506	75	151	19	11	1	47	.298	31	79	37	258	335	24	.961
—Pittsburgh (N.L.)	OF-2B	17	30	11	10	3	1	0	7	.333	6	1	2	11	8	2	.905
1997—Pittsburgh (N.L.)	2B-SS	155	641	85	178	26	9	6	50	.278	43	109	*60	335	430	†20	.975
1998—Pittsburgh (N.L.)	2B-OF-SS	159	655	85	185	26	7	3	45	.282	38	94	*58	309	451	17	.978
1999—Tucson (PCL)■	OF	4	16	1	4	1	0	1	3	.250	2	3	0	8	1	0	1.000
—Arizona (N.L.)	OF-2B-SS	144	614	111	170	25	10	4	41	.277	52	68	*72	293	85	5	.987
2000—Arizona (N.L.)	SS-OF	146	617	95	167	21	*14	7	57	.271	30	74	45	218	365	18	.970
Major League totals (7 years)		641	2593	396	716	101	41	20	201	.276	174	352	239	1180	1367	65	.975

DIVISION SERIES RECORD

					BATTING									FIELDING		
Year Team (League)	Pos.	G	AB	R	H	2B	3B	HR	RBI	Avg.	BB	SO	SB	PO	A	E	Avg.
1999—Arizona (N.L.)	OF-SS	4	18	2	2	0	1	0	0	.111	0	6	0	5	5	2	.833

ALL-STAR GAME RECORD

			BATTING									FIELDING		
Year League	Pos.	AB	R	H	2B	3B	HR	RBI	Avg.	BB	SO	SB	PO	A	E	Avg.
1997—National	2B	1	0	0	0	0	0	0	.000	0	0	0	1	0	0	1.000

WOOD, KERRY   P   CUBS

PERSONAL: Born June 16, 1977, in Irving, Texas. ... 6-5/230. ... Throws right, bats right. ... Full name: Kerry Lee Wood.
HIGH SCHOOL: Grand Prairie (Texas).
TRANSACTIONS/CAREER NOTES: Selected by Chicago Cubs organization in first round (fourth pick overall) of free-agent draft (June 1, 1995). ... On disabled list (May 24-June 19, 1996). ... On disabled list (March 31, 1999-entire season). ... On Chicago disabled list (March 25-May 2 and July 30-August 22, 2000); included rehabilitation assignments to Daytona (April 13-23) and Iowa (April 23-April 28). ... On suspended list (September 8-11, 2000).
RECORDS: Shares major league single-game record for most strikeouts (nine-inning game)—20 (May 6, 1998). ... Holds N.L. record for most strikeouts in consecutive games—33 (May 6 [20] and 11 [13], 1998).
HONORS: Named N.L. Rookie Pitcher of the Year by THE SPORTING NEWS (1998). ... Named N.L. Rookie of the Year by Baseball Writers' Association of America (1998).
STATISTICAL NOTES: Led Florida State League with 14 hit batsmen and seven balks in 1996. ... Pitched 2-0 one-hit, complete-game victory against Houston (May 6, 1998). ... Struck out 20 batters in one game (May 6, 1998). ... Struck out 16 batters in one game (August 26, 1998).
MISCELLANEOUS: Struck out and had sacrifice hit in two appearances as pinch hitter (2000).

W

Year League	W	L	Pct.	ERA	G	GS	CG	ShO	Sv.	IP	H	R	ER	BB	SO
1995—Fort Myers (FSL)	0	0	...	0.00	1	1	0	0	0	3	0	0	0	1	2
—Williamsport (NY-Penn)	0	0	...	10.38	2	2	0	0	0	4 1/3	5	8	5	5	5
1996—Daytona (FSL)	10	2	•.833	2.91	22	22	0	0	0	114 1/3	72	51	37	70	136
1997—Orlando (Sou.)	6	7	.462	4.50	19	19	0	0	0	94	58	49	47	79	106
—Iowa (A.A.)	4	2	.667	4.68	10	10	0	0	0	57 2/3	35	35	30	52	80
1998—Iowa (PCL)	1	0	1.000	0.00	1	1	0	0	0	5	1	0	0	2	11
—Chicago (N.L.)	13	6	.684	3.40	26	26	1	1	0	166 2/3	117	69	63	85	233

Year	League	W	L	Pct.	ERA	G	GS	CG	ShO	Sv.	IP	H	R	ER	BB	SO
1999— Chicago (N.L.)								Did not play.								
2000— Daytona (FSL)		2	0	1.000	1.50	2	2	0	0	0	12	3	2	2	5	17
— Iowa (PCL)		0	0	...	2.57	1	1	0	0	0	7	4	2	2	4	7
— Chicago (N.L.)		8	7	.533	4.80	23	23	1	0	0	137	112	77	73	87	132
Major League totals (2 years)		21	13	.618	4.03	49	49	2	1	0	303 2/3	229	146	136	172	365

DIVISION SERIES RECORD

Year	League	W	L	Pct.	ERA	G	GS	CG	ShO	Sv.	IP	H	R	ER	BB	SO
1998— Chicago (N.L.)		0	1	.000	1.80	1	1	0	0	0	5	3	1	1	4	5

WOODARD, STEVE   P   INDIANS

PERSONAL: Born May 15, 1975, in Hartselle, Ala. ... 6-4/217. ... Throws right, bats left. ... Full name: Steve Larry Woodard Jr.
HIGH SCHOOL: Hartselle (Ala.).
TRANSACTIONS/CAREER NOTES: Selected by Milwaukee Brewers organization in fifth round of free-agent draft (June 2, 1994). ... On disabled list (August 14-September 11, 1999). ... Traded by Brewers with P Bob Wickman and P Jason Bere to Cleveland Indians for 1B/OF Richie Sexson, P Paul Rigdon, P Kane Davis and a player to be named later (July 28, 2000); Brewers acquired 2B Marcos Scutaro to complete deal (August 30).
RECORDS: Shares A.L. record for most strikeouts in first major league game—12 (July 28, 1997).
HONORS: Named Texas League Pitcher of the Year (1997).

Year	League	W	L	Pct.	ERA	G	GS	CG	ShO	Sv.	IP	H	R	ER	BB	SO
1994— Stockton (Calif.)		8	0	1.000	2.40	15	12	2	0	0	82 2/3	68	29	22	13	85
— Arizona Brewers (Ariz.)		•8	0	1.000	2.40	15	12	2	0	0	82 2/3	68	29	22	13	85
1995— Beloit (Midw.)		7	4	.636	4.54	21	21	0	0	0	115	113	68	58	31	94
1996— Stockton (Calif.)		12	9	.571	4.02	28	•28	0	0	0	*181 1/3	201	89	81	33	142
1997— El Paso (Texas)		14	3	.824	3.17	19	19	*6	•1	0	136 1/3	136	56	48	25	97
— Tucson (PCL)		1	0	1.000	0.00	1	1	0	0	0	7	3	0	0	1	6
— Milwaukee (A.L.)		3	3	.500	5.15	7	7	0	0	0	36 2/3	39	25	21	6	32
1998— Milwaukee (N.L.)		10	12	.455	4.18	34	26	0	0	0	165 2/3	170	83	77	33	135
1999— Milwaukee (N.L.)		11	8	.579	4.52	31	29	2	0	0	185	219	101	93	36	119
2000— Milwaukee (N.L.)		1	7	.125	5.96	27	11	1	0	0	93 2/3	125	70	62	33	65
— Cleveland (A.L.)■		3	3	.500	5.67	13	11	0	0	0	54	57	35	34	11	35
A.L. totals (2 years)		6	6	.500	5.46	20	18	0	0	0	90 2/3	96	60	55	17	67
N.L. totals (3 years)		22	27	.449	4.70	92	66	3	0	0	444 1/3	514	254	232	102	319
Major League totals (4 years)		28	33	.459	4.83	112	84	3	0	0	535	610	314	287	119	386

WOODWARD, CHRIS   IF   BLUE JAYS

PERSONAL: Born June 27, 1976, in Covina, Calif. ... 6-0/173. ... Bats right, throws right. ... Full name: Christopher Michael Woodward.
HIGH SCHOOL: Northview (Covina, Calif.).
JUNIOR COLLEGE: Mount Sacramento (Walnut, Calif.).
TRANSACTIONS/CAREER NOTES: Selected by Toronto Blue Jays organization in 54th round of free-agent draft (June 2, 1994). ... On Syracuse disabled list (May 2-17 and May 21-June 6, 1999).
STATISTICAL NOTES: Led Pioneer League shortstops with 338 total chances in 1995.

							BATTING							FIELDING		
Year	Team (League)	Pos.	G	AB	R	H	2B	3B	HR	RBI	Avg.	BB	SO	SB	PO	A	E	Avg.
1995— Medicine Hat (Pio.)		SS	72	241	44	56	8	0	3	21	.232	33	41	9	*106	*202	*30	.911
1996— Hagerstown (S.Atl.)		SS	123	424	41	95	24	2	1	48	.224	43	70	11	*214	366	30	.951
1997— Dunedin (FSL)		SS	91	314	38	92	13	4	1	38	.293	52	52	4	145	267	12	.972
1998— Knoxville (Sou.)		SS	73	253	36	62	12	0	3	27	.245	26	47	3	145	220	11	.971
— Syracuse (I.L.)		SS	25	85	9	17	6	0	2	6	.200	7	20	1	29	69	4	.961
1999— Syracuse (I.L.)		SS-2B	75	281	46	82	20	3	1	20	.292	38	49	4	114	200	11	.966
— Toronto (A.L.)		SS-3B	14	26	1	6	1	0	0	2	.231	2	6	0	8	26	2	.944
2000— Toronto (A.L.)	SS-3B-1B-2B	37	104	16	19	7	0	3	14	.183	10	28	1	42	88	5	.963
— Syracuse (I.L.)		2B-3B-SS	37	143	23	46	13	2	5	25	.322	11	30	2	48	110	2	.988
Major League totals (2 years)			51	130	17	25	8	0	3	16	.192	12	34	1	50	114	7	.959

W

WORRELL, TIM   P   GIANTS

PERSONAL: Born July 5, 1967, in Pasadena, Calif. ... 6-4/231. ... Throws right, bats right. ... Full name: Timothy Howard Worrell. ... Brother of Todd Worrell, pitcher with St. Louis Cardinals (1985-92) and Los Angeles Dodgers (1993-97).
HIGH SCHOOL: Maranatha (Sierra Madre, Calif.).
COLLEGE: Biola (Calif.).
TRANSACTIONS/CAREER NOTES: Selected by San Diego Padres organization in 20th round of free-agent draft (June 5, 1989). ... On disabled list (April 19, 1994-remainder of season). ... On San Diego disabled list (April 24-September 1, 1995); included rehabilitation assignments to Rancho Cucamonga (May 3-17 and August 1-10) and Las Vegas (May 17-June 1 and August 10-30). ... Traded by Padres with P Trey Beamon to Detroit Tigers for P Dan Miceli, P Donne Wall and 3B Ryan Balfe (November 19, 1997). ... Traded by Tigers with OF David Roberts to Cleveland Indians for OF Geronimo Berroa (June 24, 1998). ... Traded by Indians to Oakland Athletics for a player to be named later (July 12, 1998); Indians acquired SS Adam Robinson to complete deal (July 27, 1998). ... On Oakland disabled list (July 20-August 8, 1999); included rehabilitation assignment to Modesto (August 5-8). ... Granted free agency (October 29, 1999). ... Signed by Baltimore Orioles organization (February 4, 2000). ... Released by Orioles (May 1, 2000). ... Signed by Chicago Cubs organization (May 8, 2000). ... Traded by Cubs to San Francisco Giants for 3B Bill Mueller (November 19, 2000).
STATISTICAL NOTES: Pitched 2-0 no-hit victory for Las Vegas against Phoenix (September 5, 1992).

Year League	W	L	Pct.	ERA	G	GS	CG	ShO	Sv.	IP	H	R	ER	BB	SO
1989—							Did not play.								
1990— Charleston, S.C. (S.Atl.)	5	8	.385	4.64	20	19	3	0	0	110 2/3	120	65	57	28	68
1991— Waterloo (Midw.)	8	4	.667	3.34	14	14	3	2	0	86 1/3	70	36	32	33	83
— High Desert (Calif.)............	5	2	.714	4.24	11	11	2	0	0	63 2/3	65	32	30	33	70
1992— Wichita (Texas)	8	6	.571	2.86	19	19	1	1	0	125 2/3	115	46	40	32	109
— Las Vegas (PCL)	4	2	.667	4.26	10	10	1	1	0	63 1/3	61	32	30	19	32
1993— Las Vegas (PCL)	5	6	.455	5.48	15	14	2	0	0	87	102	61	53	26	89
— San Diego (N.L.)	2	7	.222	4.92	21	16	0	0	0	100 2/3	104	63	55	43	52
1994— San Diego (N.L.)	0	1	.000	3.68	3	3	0	0	0	14 2/3	9	7	6	5	14
1995— Rancho Cuca. (Calif.)	0	2	.000	5.16	9	3	0	0	1	22 2/3	25	17	13	6	17
— Las Vegas (PCL)	0	2	.000	6.00	10	3	0	0	0	24	27	21	16	17	18
— San Diego (N.L.)	1	0	1.000	4.72	9	0	0	0	0	13 1/3	16	7	7	6	13
1996— San Diego (N.L.)	9	7	.563	3.05	50	11	0	0	1	121	109	45	41	39	99
1997— San Diego (N.L.)	4	8	.333	5.16	60	10	0	0	3	106 1/3	116	67	61	50	81
1998— Detroit (A.L.)■..............	2	6	.250	5.98	15	9	0	0	0	61 2/3	66	42	41	19	47
— Cleveland (A.L.)■..............	0	0	...	5.06	3	0	0	0	0	5 1/3	6	3	3	2	2
— Oakland (A.L.)■..............	0	1	.000	4.00	25	0	0	0	0	36	34	17	16	8	33
1999— Oakland (A.L.)	2	2	.500	4.15	53	0	0	0	0	69 1/3	69	38	32	34	62
— Modesto (Calif.)	0	0	...	0.00	1	1	0	0	0	2	0	0	0	0	5
2000— Baltimore (A.L.)■..............	2	2	.500	7.36	5	0	0	0	0	7 1/3	12	6	6	5	5
— Iowa (PCL)■..............	2	0	1.000	5.06	6	0	0	0	0	10 2/3	9	6	6	5	7
— Chicago (N.L.)	3	4	.429	2.47	54	0	0	0	3	62	60	20	17	24	52
A.L. totals (3 years)	6	11	.353	4.91	101	9	0	0	0	179 2/3	187	106	98	68	149
N.L. totals (6 years)	19	27	.413	4.03	197	40	0	0	7	418	414	209	187	167	311
Major League totals (8 years)	25	38	.397	4.29	298	49	0	0	7	597 2/3	601	315	285	235	460

DIVISION SERIES RECORD

Year League	W	L	Pct.	ERA	G	GS	CG	ShO	Sv.	IP	H	R	ER	BB	SO
1996— San Diego (N.L.)	0	0	...	2.45	2	0	0	0	0	3 2/3	4	1	1	1	2

WRIGHT, JAMEY   P   BREWERS

PERSONAL: Born December 24, 1974, in Oklahoma City. ... 6-5/221. ... Throws right, bats right. ... Full name: Jamey Alan Wright.
HIGH SCHOOL: Westmoore (Moore, Okla.).
TRANSACTIONS/CAREER NOTES: Selected by Colorado Rockies organization in first round (28th pick overall) of free-agent draft (June 3, 1993). ... On Colorado disabled list (May 15-June 8, 1997); included rehabilitation assignment to Salem (June 1-8). ... Traded by Rockies with C Henry Blanco to Milwaukee Brewers as part of three-way deal in which Rockies received 3B Jeff Cirillo, P Scott Karl and cash from Brewers, Oakland Athletics received P Justin Miller and cash from Rockies and Brewers received P Jimmy Haynes to Athletics (December 13, 1999). ... On Milwaukee disabled list (March 28-May 23, 2000); included rehabilitation assignment to Huntsville (May 6-13) and Indianapolis (14-May 20).
STATISTICAL NOTES: Led N.L. pitchers with 18 hit batsmen in 2000.

Year League	W	L	Pct.	ERA	G	GS	CG	ShO	Sv.	IP	H	R	ER	BB	SO
1993— Arizona Rockies (Ariz.).......	1	3	.250	4.00	8	8	8	0	0	36	35	19	16	9	26
1994— Asheville (S.Atl.)..............	7	•14	.333	5.97	28	27	2	0	0	143 1/3	*188	107	*95	59	103
1995— Salem (Caro.)	10	8	.556	2.47	26	26	2	1	0	*171	160	74	47	72	95
— New Haven (East.)..............	0	1	.000	9.00	1	1	1	0	0	3	6	6	3	3	0
1996— New Haven (East.)..............	5	1	.833	0.81	7	7	1	1	0	44 2/3	27	7	4	12	54
— Colorado Springs (PCL)	4	2	.667	2.72	9	9	0	0	0	59 2/3	53	20	18	22	40
— Colorado (N.L.)..............	4	4	.500	4.93	16	15	0	0	0	91 1/3	105	60	50	41	45
1997— Colorado (N.L.)..............	8	12	.400	6.25	26	26	1	0	0	149 2/3	198	113	104	71	59
— Salem (Caro.)	0	1	.000	9.00	1	1	0	0	0	1	1	1	1	1	1
— Colorado Springs (PCL)	1	0	1.000	1.64	2	2	0	0	0	11	9	3	2	5	11
1998— Colorado (N.L.)..............	9	14	.391	5.67	34	34	1	0	0	206 1/3	235	143	130	95	86
1999— Colorado (N.L.)..............	4	3	.571	4.87	16	16	0	0	0	94 1/3	110	52	51	54	49
— Colorado Springs (PCL)	5	7	.417	6.46	17	16	2	0	0	100 1/3	133	87	72	38	75
2000— Huntsville (Sou.)■..............	2	0	1.000	0.00	2	2	0	0	0	12 1/3	7	0	0	5	10
— Indianapolis (I.L.)..............	0	0	...	1.80	1	1	0	0	0	5	8	5	1	3	7
— Milwaukee (N.L.)	7	9	.438	4.10	26	25	0	0	0	164 2/3	157	81	75	88	96
Major League totals (5 years)	32	42	.432	5.22	118	116	2	0	0	706 1/3	805	449	410	349	335

WRIGHT, JARET   P   INDIANS

W

PERSONAL: Born December 29, 1975, in Anaheim, Calif. ... 6-2/230. ... Throws right, bats right. ... Full name: Jaret Samuel Wright. ... Son of Clyde Wright, pitcher with California Angels (1966-73), Milwaukee Brewers (1974) and Texas Rangers (1975).
HIGH SCHOOL: Katella (Anaheim, Calif.).
TRANSACTIONS/CAREER NOTES: Selected by Cleveland Indians organization in first round (10th pick overall) of free-agent draft (June 2, 1994). ... On disabled list (June 19-September 23, 1996). ... On suspended list (May 10-16, 1999). ... On disabled list (July 9-August 3 and August 9-September 10, 1999); included rehabilitation assignments to Buffalo (September 2) and Akron (September 6). ... On Cleveland disabled list (May 12-27 and June 3, 2000-remainder of season); included rehabilitation assignments to Buffalo (July 29-August 2) and Akron (August 3-10).

Year League	W	L	Pct.	ERA	G	GS	CG	ShO	Sv.	IP	H	R	ER	BB	SO
1994— Burlington (Appl.)..............	0	1	.000	5.40	4	4	0	0	0	13 1/3	13	10	8	9	16
1995— Columbus (S.Atl.)..............	5	6	.455	3.00	24	24	0	0	0	129	93	55	43	79	113
1996— Kinston (Caro.)..............	7	4	.636	2.50	19	19	0	0	0	101	65	32	28	55	109
1997— Cleveland (A.L.)..............	8	3	.727	4.38	16	16	0	0	0	90 1/3	81	45	44	35	63
— Buffalo (A.A.)..............	4	1	.800	1.80	7	7	1	1	0	45	30	16	9	19	47
— Akron (East.)	3	3	.500	3.67	8	8	1	0	0	54	43	26	22	23	59
1998— Cleveland (A.L.).................	12	10	.545	4.72	32	32	1	1	0	192 2/3	207	109	101	87	140

Year	League	W	L	Pct.	ERA	G	GS	CG	ShO	Sv.	IP	H	R	ER	BB	SO
1999— Cleveland (A.L.)		8	10	.444	6.06	26	26	0	0	0	133 2/3	144	99	90	77	91
— Buffalo (I.L.)		0	0	...	0.00	1	1	0	0	0	3	0	0	0	0	4
— Akron (East.)		1	0	1.000	0.00	1	1	0	0	0	5	3	0	0	1	6
2000— Cleveland (A.L.)		3	4	.429	4.70	9	9	1	1	0	51 2/3	44	27	27	28	36
— Buffalo (I.L.)		0	0	...	0.00	1	1	0	0	0	2	0	0	0	1	1
— Akron (East.)		0	0	...	3.38	2	2	0	0	0	8	4	3	3	3	5
Major League totals (4 years)		31	27	.534	5.03	83	83	2	2	0	468 1/3	476	280	262	227	330

DIVISION SERIES RECORD

Year	League	W	L	Pct.	ERA	G	GS	CG	ShO	Sv.	IP	H	R	ER	BB	SO
1997— Cleveland (A.L.)		2	0	1.000	3.97	2	2	0	0	0	11 1/3	11	6	5	7	10
1998— Cleveland (A.L.)		0	1	.000	12.46	1	1	0	0	0	4 1/3	7	6	6	2	6
1999— Cleveland (A.L.)		0	1	.000	22.50	1	0	0	0	0	2	4	5	5	1	1
Division series totals (3 years)		2	2	.500	8.15	4	3	0	0	0	17 2/3	22	17	16	10	17

CHAMPIONSHIP SERIES RECORD

RECORDS: Shares single-game record for most home runs allowed—3 (October 12, 1997).

Year	League	W	L	Pct.	ERA	G	GS	CG	ShO	Sv.	IP	H	R	ER	BB	SO
1997— Cleveland (A.L.)		0	0	...	15.00	1	1	0	0	0	3	6	5	5	2	3
1998— Cleveland (A.L.)		0	1	.000	8.10	2	1	0	0	0	6 2/3	7	6	6	8	4
Champ. series totals (2 years)		0	1	.000	10.24	3	2	0	0	0	9 2/3	13	11	11	10	7

WORLD SERIES RECORD

Year	League	W	L	Pct.	ERA	G	GS	CG	ShO	Sv.	IP	H	R	ER	BB	SO
1997— Cleveland (A.L.)		1	0	1.000	2.92	2	2	0	0	0	12 1/3	7	4	4	10	12

WUNSCH, KELLY   P   WHITE SOX

PERSONAL: Born July 12, 1972, in Houston. ... 6-5/190. ... Throws left, bats left. ... Full name: Kelly Douglas Wunsch.
HIGH SCHOOL: Bellaire (Texas).
COLLEGE: Texas A&M.
TRANSACTIONS/CAREER NOTES: Selected by Atlanta Braves organization in 54th round of free-agent draft (June 4, 1990); did not sign. ... Selected by Milwaukee Brewers organization in first round (26th pick overall) of free-agent draft (June 3, 1993); pick received as compensation for Toronto Blue Jays signing Type-A free agent Paul Molitor. ... On El Paso disabled list (April 4-May 13, 1996; and April 8-May 7, 1998) ... On Stockton disabled list (June 19-September 10, 1996). ... On Louisville disabled list (July 10-17, 1999). ... Granted free agency (October 15, 1999). ... Signed by Chicago White Sox organization (November 15, 1999).

Year	League	W	L	Pct.	ERA	G	GS	CG	ShO	Sv.	IP	H	R	ER	BB	SO
1993— Beloit (Midw.)		1	5	.167	4.83	12	12	0	0	0	63 1/3	58	39	34	39	61
1994— Beloit (Midw.)		3	10	.231	6.16	17	17	0	0	0	83 1/3	88	69	57	47	77
— Helena (Pio.)		4	2	.667	5.12	9	9	1	0	0	51	52	39	29	30	57
1995— Beloit (Midw.)		4	7	.364	4.20	14	14	3	1	0	85 2/3	90	47	40	37	66
— Stockton (Calif.)		5	6	.455	5.33	14	13	1	1	0	74 1/3	89	51	44	39	62
1996—							Did not play.									
1997— Stockton (Calif.)		7	9	.438	3.46	24	22	2	2	0	143	141	65	55	62	98
1998— El Paso (Texas)		5	6	.455	5.95	17	17	1	1	0	101 1/3	127	81	67	31	70
— Louisville (I.L.)		3	1	.750	3.83	9	8	0	0	0	51 2/3	53	23	22	15	36
1999— Huntsville (Sou.)		4	1	.800	1.95	22	3	0	0	1	50 2/3	40	13	11	23	35
— Louisville (I.L.)		2	1	.667	4.75	16	2	0	0	0	41 2/3	52	23	22	14	20
2000— Chicago (A.L.)■		6	3	.667	2.93	*83	0	0	0	1	61 1/3	50	22	20	29	51
Major League totals (1 year)		6	3	.667	2.93	83	0	0	0	1	61 1/3	50	22	20	29	51

DIVISION SERIES RECORD

Year	League	W	L	Pct.	ERA	G	GS	CG	ShO	Sv.	IP	H	R	ER	BB	SO
2000— Chicago (A.L.)		0	1	.000	0.00	3	0	0	0	0	2/3	2	1	0	0	0

YAN, ESTEBAN   P   DEVIL RAYS

PERSONAL: Born June 22, 1974, in Campina Del Seibo, Dominican Republic. ... 6-4/230. ... Throws right, bats right. ... Full name: Esteban Luis Yan.
HIGH SCHOOL: Escuela Hicayagua (Dominican Republic).
TRANSACTIONS/CAREER NOTES: Signed as non-drafted free agent by Atlanta Braves organization (November 21, 1990). ... Traded by Braves with OF Roberto Kelly and OF Tony Tarasco to Montreal Expos for OF Marquis Grissom (April 6, 1995). ... Contract sold by Expos to Baltimore Orioles organization (April 6, 1996). ... Selected by Tampa Bay Devil Rays in first round (18th pick overall) of expansion draft (November 18, 1997). ... On Tampa Bay disabled list (June 17-July 15, 1999); included rehabilitation assignment to St. Petersburg (July 10-15).
STATISTICAL NOTES: Led South Atlantic League with six balks in 1994. ... Hit home run in first major league at-bat (June 4, 2000).

Year	League	W	L	Pct.	ERA	G	GS	CG	ShO	Sv.	IP	H	R	ER	BB	SO
1991— San Pedro (DSL)		4	1	.800	3.63	18	11	0	0	0	72	61	36	29	26	34
1992— San Pedro (DSL)		12	3	.800	1.32	16	16	7	4	0	115 2/3	85	37	17	23	86
1993— Danville (Appl.)		4	7	.364	3.03	14	14	0	0	0	71 1/3	73	46	24	24	50
1994— Macon (S.Atl.)		11	12	.478	3.27	28	•28	4	•3	0	170 2/3	155	85	62	34	121
1995— West Palm Beach (FSL)■		6	8	.429	3.07	24	21	1	0	1	137 2/3	139	63	47	33	89
1996— Bowie (East.)■		0	2	.000	5.63	9	1	0	0	0	16	18	12	10	8	15
— Rochester (I.L.)		5	4	.556	4.27	22	10	0	0	1	71 2/3	75	37	34	18	61
— Baltimore (A.L.)		3	0	...	5.79	4	0	0	0	0	9 1/3	13	7	6	3	7
1997— Rochester (I.L.)		11	5	.688	3.10	34	12	0	0	2	119	107	54	41	37	131
— Baltimore (A.L.)		0	1	.000	15.83	3	2	0	0	0	9 2/3	20	18	17	7	4
1998— Tampa Bay (A.L.)■		5	4	.556	3.86	64	0	0	0	1	88 2/3	78	41	38	41	77
1999— Tampa Bay (A.L.)		3	4	.429	5.90	50	1	0	0	0	61	77	41	40	32	46
— St. Petersburg (FSL)		0	0	...	0.00	2	2	0	0	0	4	3	1	0	1	0
2000— Tampa Bay (A.L.)		7	8	.467	6.21	43	20	0	0	0	137 2/3	158	98	95	42	111
Major League totals (5 years)		15	17	.469	5.76	164	23	0	0	1	306 1/3	346	205	196	125	245

W
Y

YARNALL, ED   P   REDS

PERSONAL: Born December 4, 1975, in Lima, Pa. ... 6-3/234. ... Throws left, bats left. ... Full name: Harvey Edward Yarnall.
HIGH SCHOOL: St. Thomas Aquinas (Fort Lauderdale, Fla.).
COLLEGE: Louisiana State.
TRANSACTIONS/CAREER NOTES: Selected by New York Mets organization in third round of free-agent draft (June 4, 1996). ... Traded by Mets with OF Preston Wilson and P Geoff Goetz to Florida Marlins for C Mike Piazza (May 22, 1998). ... Traded by Marlins with P Mark Johnson and P Todd Noel to New York Yankees for 3B Mike Lowell (February 1, 1999). ... On Columbus disabled list (May 6-June 17, 2000). ... Traded by Yankees with 3B Drew Henson, OF Jackson Melian and P Brian Reith to Cincinnati Reds for P Denny Neagle and OF Mike Frank (July 12, 2000).
HONORS: Named International League Most Valuable Pitcher (1999).

Year	League	W	L	Pct.	ERA	G	GS	CG	ShO	Sv.	IP	H	R	ER	BB	SO
1997—	St. Lucie (FSL)	5	8	.385	2.48	18	18	2	0	0	105 1/3	93	33	29	30	114
	— Norfolk (I.L.)	0	1	.000	14.40	1	1	0	0	0	5	11	8	8	7	2
	— Binghamton (East.)	3	2	.600	3.06	5	5	0	0	0	32 1/3	20	11	11	11	32
1998—	Binghamton (East.)	7	0	1.000	0.39	7	7	0	0	0	46 2/3	20	5	2	17	52
	— Portland (East.)■	2	0	1.000	2.93	2	2	0	0	0	15 1/3	9	5	5	4	15
	— Charlotte (I.L.)	4	5	.444	6.20	15	13	2	0	0	69 2/3	79	60	48	39	47
1999—	Columbus (I.L.)■	13	4	.765	•3.47	23	23	1	1	0	145 1/3	136	61	56	57	146
	— New York (A.L.)	1	0	1.000	3.71	5	2	0	0	0	17	17	8	7	10	13
2000—	New York (A.L.)	0	0	...	15.00	2	1	0	0	0	3	5	5	5	3	1
	— Columbus (I.L.)■	2	1	.667	4.56	10	10	1	0	0	49 1/3	43	27	25	26	34
	— Louisville (I.L.)	3	4	.429	3.86	11	11	0	0	0	67 2/3	72	32	29	34	59
Major League totals (2 years)		1	0	1.000	5.40	7	3	0	0	0	20	22	13	12	13	14

YENNACO, JAY   P   CUBS

PERSONAL: Born November 17, 1975, in Lawrence, Mass. ... 6-2/225. ... Throws right, bats right. ... Full name: Jay Robert Yennaco. ... Name pronounced yih-NOK-koh.
HIGH SCHOOL: Pinkerton Academy (Derry, N.H.).
TRANSACTIONS/CAREER NOTES: Selected by Boston Red Sox organization in third round of free-agent draft (June 1, 1995). ... Traded by Red Sox with P Peter Munro to Toronto Blue Jays for 1B Mike Stanley (July 30, 1998). ... Traded by Blue Jays to Chicago Cubs (December 21, 1999), completing deal in which Blue Jays obtained OF Scott Sollmann from Cubs (December 14, 1999).
STATISTICAL NOTES: Tied for Midwest League lead in wild pitches with 20 in 1996.

Year	League	W	L	Pct.	ERA	G	GS	CG	ShO	Sv.	IP	H	R	ER	BB	SO
1996—	Michigan (Midw.)	10	10	.500	4.61	28	28	4	•1	0	169 2/3	195	112	87	68	117
1997—	Sarasota (FSL)	4	0	1.000	2.23	7	7	2	1	0	44 1/3	30	12	11	19	41
	— Trenton (East.)	5	11	.313	6.33	21	21	0	0	0	122 1/3	146	89	86	54	73
1998—	Trenton (East.)	3	3	.500	4.86	9	9	0	0	0	53 2/3	50	30	29	19	23
	— Pawtucket (I.L.)	3	2	.600	5.82	11	11	1	0	0	60 1/3	77	43	39	16	34
	— Syracuse (I.L.)■	0	3	.000	5.35	7	6	1	0	0	38 2/3	55	27	23	10	27
1999—	Syracuse (I.L.)	2	6	.250	6.86	15	15	0	0	0	80	107	68	61	42	45
	— Dunedin (FSL)	2	0	1.000	0.82	3	2	0	0	0	11	10	2	1	0	11
	— Knoxville (Sou.)	3	4	.429	6.60	8	6	1	0	0	43 2/3	52	34	32	17	30
2000—	West Tenn (Sou.)■	5	4	.556	2.67	60	0	0	0	10	70 2/3	53	25	21	31	79

YOSHII, MASATO   P   ROCKIES

PERSONAL: Born April 20, 1965, in Osaka, Japan. ... 6-2/210. ... Throws right, bats right.
HIGH SCHOOL: Minoshima (Japan).
TRANSACTIONS/CAREER NOTES: Played for Kintetsu Buffaloes of Japan Pacific League (1985-94). ... Played for Yakult Swallows of Japan Central League (1995-97). ... Signed as non-drafted free agent by New York Mets (January 13, 1998). ... Traded by Mets to Colorado Rockies for P Bobby M. Jones and P Larial Gonzalez (January 14, 2000).

Year	League	W	L	Pct.	ERA	G	GS	CG	ShO	Sv.	IP	H	R	ER	BB	SO
1985—	Kintetsu (Jap. Pac.)	0	1	.000	21.00	2	...	...	...	0	3	...		7	3	1
1986—	Kintetsu (Jap. Pac.)	0	0	...	23.14	2	...	...	...	0	2 1/3	...		6	2	2
1987—	Kintetsu (Jap. Pac.)	2	1	.667	4.75	13	...	...	...	0	36	...		19	12	23
1988—	Kintetsu (Jap. Pac.)	10	2	.833	2.69	50	...	...	...	24	80 1/3	...		24	44	44
1989—	Kintetsu (Jap. Pac.)	5	5	.500	2.99	47	...	...	...	20	84 1/3	...		28	37	44
1990—	Kintetsu (Jap. Pac.)	8	9	.471	3.39	45	...	...	...	15	74 1/3	...		28	30	55
1991—	Kintetsu (Jap. Pac.)	2	1	.667	3.42	21	...	...	...	2	26 1/3	...		10	6	13
1992—	Kintetsu (Jap. Pac.)	1	0	1.000	2.31	9	...	...	...	0	11 2/3	...		3	2	4
1993—	Kintetsu (Jap. Pac.)	5	5	.500	2.67	22	...	...	...	0	104 2/3	...		31	25	66
1994—	Kintetsu (Jap. Pac.)	7	7	.500	5.47	21	...	...	...	0	97	...		59	37	42
1995—	Yakult (Jap. Cen.)■	10	7	.588	3.12	25	...	...	...	0	147 1/3	...		51	39	91
1996—	Yakult (Jap. Cen.)	10	7	.588	3.24	25	9	...	...	0	180 1/3	...		65	47	145
1997—	Yakult (Jap. Cen.)	13	6	.684	2.99	28	26	6	2	0	174 1/3	149	61	58	48	104
1998—	New York (N.L.)■	6	8	.429	3.93	29	29	1	0	0	171 2/3	166	79	75	53	117
1999—	New York (N.L.)	12	8	.600	4.40	31	29	1	0	0	174	168	86	85	58	105
2000—	Colorado (N.L.)■	6	15	.286	5.86	29	29	0	0	0	167 1/3	201	112	109	53	88
Major League totals (3 years)		24	31	.436	4.72	89	87	2	0	0	513	535	277	269	164	310

DIVISION SERIES RECORD

Year	League	W	L	Pct.	ERA	G	GS	CG	ShO	Sv.	IP	H	R	ER	BB	SO
1999—	New York (N.L.)	0	0	...	6.75	1	1	0	0	0	5 1/3	6	4	4	0	3

CHAMPIONSHIP SERIES RECORD

Year	League	W	L	Pct.	ERA	G	GS	CG	ShO	Sv.	IP	H	R	ER	BB	SO
1999—	New York (N.L.)	0	1	.000	4.70	2	2	0	0	0	7 2/3	9	4	4	3	4

Y

PERSONAL: Born November 3, 1971, in Smyrna, Texas. ... 6-4/210. ... Throws left, bats right. ... Full name: Daniel Bracey Young Jr.
HIGH SCHOOL: Cannon County (Woodbury, Tenn.).
JUNIOR COLLEGE: Aquinas College (Tenn.).
TRANSACTIONS/CAREER NOTES: Selected by Houston Astros organization in 83rd round of free-agent draft (June 4, 1990). ... Released by Astros (April 1, 1994). ... Signed by Pittsburgh Pirates organization (April 3, 1994). ... Selected by Chicago Cubs organization from Pirates organization in Rule 5 minor league draft (December 15, 1997). ... On disabled list (April 8-May 6 and May 13-22, 1999). ... On Iowa disabled list (July 7-September 5, 2000). ... Granted free agency (October 18, 2000).

Year League	W	L	Pct.	ERA	G	GS	CG	ShO	Sv.	IP	H	R	ER	BB	SO
1991— Gulf Coast Astros (GCL).....	1	4	.200	7.99	13	7	0	0	0	32 2/3	32	33	29	39	41
1992— Asheville (S.Atl.)................	3	10	.231	4.28	20	20	0	0	0	94 2/3	106	65	45	70	64
1993— Asheville (S.Atl.)................	5	14	.263	6.12	32	24	2	1	0	142 2/3	174	*114	*97	95	101
1994— Augusta (S.Atl.)■............	2	5	.286	3.38	21	9	0	0	0	66 2/3	58	32	25	33	73
— Salem (Caro.).....................	2	0	1.000	7.71	10	0	0	0	0	18 2/3	32	17	16	9	12
1995— Lynchburg (Caro.).............	2	4	.333	7.40	24	2	0	0	0	41 1/3	52	37	34	27	34
— Augusta (S.Atl.).................	1	0	1.000	2.51	6	2	0	0	0	14 1/3	9	6	4	16	11
1996— Augusta (S.Atl.)................	0	4	.000	5.88	22	1	0	0	2	33 2/3	36	33	22	29	36
1997— Lynchburg (Caro.).............	0	0	...	5.92	15	0	0	0	0	24 1/3	27	17	16	14	22
— Augusta (S.Atl.).................	0	2	.000	9.82	3	2	0	0	0	7 1/3	16	15	8	2	5
1998— Daytona (FSL)■.............	1	1	.500	5.19	7	0	0	0	0	8 2/3	9	5	5	8	6
— West Tenn (Sou.)	0	2	.000	3.67	23	1	0	0	0	27	22	13	11	15	20
— Iowa (PCL)	0	0	...	0.00	2	0	0	0	0	2	1	0	0	1	1
1999— West Tenn (Sou.)	3	5	.375	3.28	27	8	0	0	0	60 1/3	48	25	22	38	67
2000— Chicago (N.L.)..................	0	1	.000	21.00	4	0	0	0	0	3	5	7	7	6	0
— Iowa (PCL)	2	1	.667	5.59	27	0	0	0	1	37	36	27	23	22	30
Major League totals (1 year)........	**0**	**1**	**.000**	**21.00**	**4**	**0**	**0**	**0**	**0**	**3**	**5**	**7**	**7**	**6**	**0**

PERSONAL: Born October 11, 1973, in Vicksburg, Miss. ... 6-2/235. ... Bats both, throws right. ... Full name: Dmitri Dell Young.
HIGH SCHOOL: Rio Mesa (Oxnard, Calif.).
TRANSACTIONS/CAREER NOTES: Selected by St. Louis Cardinals organization in first round (fourth pick overall) of free-agent draft (June 3, 1991). ... On disabled list (June 2-9, 1994). ... On Arkansas suspended list (August 1-11 and August 17-27, 1995). ... On Louisville disabled list (July 14-24, 1996). ... On St. Louis disabled list (May 11-29, 1997); included rehabilitation assignment to Louisville (May 25-29). ... Traded by Cardinals to Cincinnati Reds for P Jeff Brantley (November 10, 1997). ... Selected by Tampa Bay Devil Rays in first round (16th pick overall) of expansion draft (November 18, 1997). ... Traded by Devil Rays to Reds (November 18, 1997), completing deal in which Reds traded OF Mike Kelly to Devil Rays for a player to be named later (November 11, 1997).
STATISTICAL NOTES: Led Texas League with 14 intentional bases on balls received in 1994. ... Led Texas League first basemen with 15 errors in 1994. ... Tied for American Association lead with eight bases on balls received in 1996. ... Led American Association first basemen with 1,182 total chances and 102 double plays in 1996. ... Had 18-game hitting streak (April 20-May 13, 2000). ... Career major league grand slams: 1.

Year Team (League)	Pos.	G	AB	R	H	2B	3B	HR	RBI	Avg.	BB	SO	SB	PO	A	E	Avg.
1991— Johnson City (Appl.) ..	3B	37	129	22	33	10	0	2	22	.256	21	28	2	19	49	5	.932
1992— Springfield (Midw.)	3B	135	493	74	153	*36	6	14	72	.310	51	94	14	66	239	42	.879
1993— St. Petersburg (FSL) ..	3B-1B	69	270	31	85	13	3	5	43	.315	24	28	3	260	90	10	.972
— Arkansas (Texas)........	1B-3B	45	166	13	41	11	2	3	21	.247	9	29	4	348	29	7	.982
1994— Arkansas (Texas)........	OF-1B	125	453	53	123	33	2	8	54	.272	36	60	0	485	44	†16	.971
1995— Arkansas (Texas)........	OF-1B	97	367	54	107	18	6	10	62	.292	30	46	2	116	5	9	.931
— Louisville (A.A.).........	OF	2	7	3	2	0	0	0	0	.286	1	1	0	3	0	1	.750
1996— Louisville (A.A.).........	1B	122	459	*90	153	31	8	15	64	*.333	34	67	16	*1091	83	8	.993
— St. Louis (N.L.)..........	1B	16	29	3	7	0	0	0	2	.241	4	5	0	39	1	1	.976
1997— St. Louis (N.L.)..........	1B-OF-DH	110	333	38	86	14	3	5	34	.258	38	63	6	641	47	13	.981
— Louisville (A.A.).........	OF-1B	24	84	10	23	7	0	4	14	.274	13	15	1	64	2	1	.985
1998— Cincinnati (N.L.)■	OF-1B	144	536	81	166	48	1	14	83	.310	47	94	2	458	25	12	.976
1999— Cincinnati (N.L.)	OF-1B-DH	127	373	63	112	30	2	14	56	.300	30	71	3	216	5	4	.982
2000— Cincinnati (N.L.)	OF-1B-DH	152	548	68	166	37	6	18	88	.303	36	80	0	401	20	8	.981
Major League totals (5 years)		**549**	**1819**	**253**	**537**	**129**	**12**	**51**	**263**	**.295**	**155**	**313**	**11**	**1755**	**98**	**38**	**.980**

DIVISION SERIES RECORD

Year Team (League)	Pos.	G	AB	R	H	2B	3B	HR	RBI	Avg.	BB	SO	SB	PO	A	E	Avg.
1996— St. Louis (N.L.)								Did not play.									

CHAMPIONSHIP SERIES RECORD

Year Team (League)	Pos.	G	AB	R	H	2B	3B	HR	RBI	Avg.	BB	SO	SB	PO	A	E	Avg.
1996— St. Louis (N.L.)...........	PH-1B	4	7	1	2	0	1	0	2	.286	0	2	0	11	1	0	1.000

Y

PERSONAL: Born May 18, 1967, in New Brunswick, N.J. ... 5-8/175. ... Bats right, throws right. ... Full name: Eric Orlando Young.
HIGH SCHOOL: New Brunswick (N.J.).
COLLEGE: Rutgers.
TRANSACTIONS/CAREER NOTES: Selected by Los Angeles Dodgers organization in 43rd round of free-agent draft (June 5, 1989). ... Selected by Colorado Rockies organization in first round (11th pick overall) of expansion draft (November 17, 1992). ... On Colorado disabled list (March 22-April 22, 1996); included rehabilitation assignments to New Haven (April 5-10), Salem (April 10-13) and Colorado Springs (April

13-22). ... Traded by Rockies to Dodgers for P Pedro Astacio (August 19, 1997). ... On disabled list (July 13-31, 1998). ... On Los Angeles disabled list (July 24-August 13, 1999); included rehabilitation assignment to San Bernardino (August 8-13). ... Traded by Dodgers with P Ismael Valdes to Chicago Cubs for P Terry Adams, P Chad Ricketts and a player to be named later (December 12, 1999); Dodgers acquired P Brian Stephenson to complete deal (December 16, 1999).

RECORDS: Shares major league record for most stolen bases in one inning—3 (June 30, 1996, third inning).

HONORS: Named second baseman on THE SPORTING NEWS N.L. All-Star team (1996). ... Named second baseman on THE SPORTING NEWS N.L. Silver Slugger team (1996).

STATISTICAL NOTES: Led Florida State League second basemen with 24 errors in 1990. ... Led Texas League in caught stealing with 26 in 1991. ... Led Texas League second basemen with .974 fielding percentage in 1991. ... Tied for N.L. lead in errors by second baseman with 11 in 1995. ... Hit three home runs in one game (May 10, 1996). ... Led N.L. in caught stealing with 19 in 1996. ... Led N.L. second basemen with 109 double plays in 1996 and 111 in 1997. ... Led N.L. in caught stealing with 22 in 1999.

MISCELLANEOUS: Holds Colorado Rockies all-time record for most stolen bases (180).

							BATTING								FIELDING		
Year Team (League)	Pos.	G	AB	R	H	2B	3B	HR	RBI	Avg.	BB	SO	SB	PO	A	E	Avg.
1989—GC Dodgers (GCL)	2B	56	197	53	65	11	5	2	22	.330	33	16	*41	104	128	*15	.939
1990—Vero Beach (FSL)	2B-OF	127	460	*101	132	23	7	2	50	.287	69	35	*76	156	218	†25	.937
1991—San Antonio (Texas)...	2B-OF	127	461	82	129	17	4	3	35	.280	67	36	*70	206	282	13	†.974
—Albuquerque (PCL)......	2B	1	5	0	2	0	0	0	0	.400	0	0	1	2	1	0	1.000
1992—Albuquerque (PCL).....	2B	94	350	61	118	16	5	3	49	.337	33	18	28	210	287	•20	.961
—Los Angeles (N.L.)	2B	49	132	9	34	1	0	1	11	.258	8	9	6	85	114	9	.957
1993—Colorado (N.L.)■.....	2B-OF	144	490	82	132	16	8	3	42	.269	63	41	42	254	230	18	.964
1994—Colorado (N.L.)	OF-2B	90	228	37	62	13	1	7	30	.272	38	17	18	97	4	2	.981
1995—Colorado (N.L.)	2B-OF	120	366	68	116	21	•9	6	36	.317	49	29	35	180	230	11	.974
1996—New Haven (East.).....	2B	3	15	0	1	0	0	0	0	.067	0	3	0	9	5	0	1.000
—Salem (Caro.)............	2B	3	10	2	3	3	0	0	0	.300	3	1	2	8	6	2	.875
—Colo. Springs (PCL) ...	2B	7	23	4	6	1	1	0	3	.261	5	1	0	15	18	3	.917
—Colorado (N.L.)	2B	141	568	113	184	23	4	8	74	.324	47	31	*53	340	431	12	.985
1997—Colorado (N.L.)	2B	118	468	78	132	29	6	6	45	.282	57	37	32	258	414	15	.978
—Los Angeles (N.L.)■..	2B	37	154	28	42	4	2	2	16	.273	14	17	13	60	79	3	.979
1998—Los Angeles (N.L.)	2B-DH	117	452	78	129	24	1	8	43	.285	45	32	42	225	304	13	.976
1999—Los Angeles (N.L.)	2B	119	456	73	128	24	2	2	41	.281	63	26	51	216	321	9	.984
—San Bern. (Calif.)	2B	3	12	0	3	0	0	0	0	.250	0	2	0	3	7	2	.833
2000—Chicago (N.L.)■.........	2B	153	607	98	180	40	2	6	47	.297	63	39	54	313	400	15	.979
Major League totals (9 years)		1088	3921	664	1139	195	35	49	385	.290	447	278	346	2028	2527	107	.977

DIVISION SERIES RECORD

							BATTING								FIELDING		
Year Team (League)	Pos.	G	AB	R	H	2B	3B	HR	RBI	Avg.	BB	SO	SB	PO	A	E	Avg.
1995—Colorado (N.L.)	2B	4	16	3	7	1	0	1	2	.438	2	2	1	8	13	3	.875

ALL-STAR GAME RECORD

						BATTING								FIELDING		
Year League	Pos.	AB	R	H	2B	3B	HR	RBI	Avg.	BB	SO	SB	PO	A	E	Avg.
1996—National	PR-2B	1	0	0	0	0	0	0	.000	0	0	0	2	1	0	1.000

YOUNG, ERNIE OF PADRES

PERSONAL: Born July 8, 1969, in Chicago. ... 6-1/234. ... Bats right, throws right. ... Full name: Ernest Wesley Young.

HIGH SCHOOL: Mendel Catholic (Chicago).

COLLEGE: Lewis (Ill.).

TRANSACTIONS/CAREER NOTES: Selected by Oakland Athletics organization in 10th round of free-agent draft (June 4, 1990). ... On disabled list (July 11, 1992-remainder of season). ... Traded by A's to Kansas City Royals for cash (March 17, 1998). ... On Kansas City disabled list (May 22-June 15, 1998); included rehabilitation assignment to Omaha (June 5-15). ... Granted free agency (October 15, 1998). ... Signed by Arizona Diamondbacks organization (December 17, 1998). ... Released by Diamondbacks (November 22, 1999). ... Signed by St. Louis Cardinals organization (January 19, 2000). ... Granted free agency (October 18, 2000). ... Signed by San Diego Padres organization (November 20, 2000).

STATISTICAL NOTES: Led California League with .635 slugging percentage in 1993.

							BATTING								FIELDING		
Year Team (League)	Pos.	G	AB	R	H	2B	3B	HR	RBI	Avg.	BB	SO	SB	PO	A	E	Avg.
1990—S. Oregon (N'West)....	OF	50	168	34	47	6	2	6	23	.280	29	53	4	62	5	2	.971
1991—Madison (Midw.)........	OF	114	362	75	92	19	2	15	71	.254	58	115	20	204	9	7	.968
1992—Modesto (Calif.)	OF	74	253	55	63	12	4	11	33	.249	47	74	11	126	11	6	.958
1993—Modesto (Calif.)	OF	85	301	83	92	18	6	23	71	.306	72	92	23	178	8	3	.984
—Huntsville (Sou.)	OF-DH	45	120	26	25	5	0	5	15	.208	24	36	8	97	8	4	.963
1994—Huntsville (Sou.)	OF-DH	72	257	45	89	19	4	14	55	.346	37	45	5	98	13	2	.982
—Oakland (A.L.)	OF-DH	11	30	2	2	1	0	0	3	.067	1	8	0	22	1	1	.958
—Tacoma (PCL)	OF-DH	29	102	19	29	4	0	6	16	.284	13	27	0	53	2	2	.965
1995—Edmonton (PCL)	OF-DH	95	347	70	96	21	4	15	72	.277	49	73	2	194	7	6	.971
—Oakland (A.L.)	OF	26	50	9	10	3	0	2	5	.200	8	12	0	35	0	2	.946
1996—Oakland (A.L.)	OF	141	462	72	112	19	4	19	64	.242	52	118	7	353	8	1	.997
1997—Oakland (A.L.)	OF	71	175	22	39	7	0	5	15	.223	19	57	1	135	4	4	.972
—Edmonton (PCL)	OF	54	195	39	63	10	0	9	45	.323	37	46	5	100	5	1	.991
1998—Kansas City (A.L.)■ ...	OF	25	53	2	10	3	0	1	3	.189	2	9	2	43	2	0	1.000
—Omaha (PCL).............	OF-DH	79	297	58	97	13	1	22	55	.327	29	68	6	174	10	2	.989
1999—Arizona (N.L.)■.........	OF	6	11	1	2	0	0	0	0	.182	3	2	0	10	1	0	1.000
—Tucson (PCL)	OF-DH	126	453	78	133	25	1	30	95	.294	57	129	4	142	11	2	.987
2000—Memphis (PCL)■.......	OF	124	453	76	119	16	0	35	98	.263	66	117	11	184	13	2	.990
American League totals (5 years)		274	770	107	173	33	4	27	90	.225	82	204	10	588	15	8	.987
National League totals (1 year)		6	11	1	2	0	0	0	0	.182	3	2	0	10	1	0	1.000
Major League totals (6 years)		280	781	108	175	33	4	27	90	.224	85	206	10	598	16	8	.987

YOUNG, KEVIN — 1B — PIRATES

PERSONAL: Born June 16, 1969, in Alpena, Mich. ... 6-3/222. ... Bats right, throws right. ... Full name: Kevin Stacey Young.
HIGH SCHOOL: Washington (Kansas City, Kan.).
JUNIOR COLLEGE: Kansas City Kansas Community College.
COLLEGE: Southern Mississippi.
TRANSACTIONS/CAREER NOTES: Selected by Pittsburgh Pirates organization in seventh round of free-agent draft (June 4, 1990). ... On Pittsburgh disabled list (July 24-August 8, 1995). ... Released by Pirates (March 26, 1996). ... Signed by Kansas City Royals organization (April 1, 1996). ... Released by Royals (December 5, 1996). ... Signed by Pirates (March 31, 1997). ... On suspended list (September 28-30, 2000).
STATISTICAL NOTES: Tied for Southern League lead in errors by third baseman with 26 in 1991. ... Tied for American Association lead in being hit by pitch with 11 in 1992. ... Led American Association third basemen with 300 assists, 32 errors, 436 total chances and 41 double plays in 1992. ... Led N.L. first basemen with .998 fielding percentage in 1993. ... Had 15-game hitting streak (April 23-May 8, 1999). ... Led N.L. first basemen with 1,533 total chances in 1999. ... Career major league grand slams: 2.

| | | | | | | | | BATTING | | | | | | | | FIELDING | | |
Year	Team (League)	Pos.	G	AB	R	H	2B	3B	HR	RBI	Avg.	BB	SO	SB	PO	A	E	Avg.
1990—	Welland (NY-Penn).....	SS	72	238	46	58	16	2	5	30	.244	31	36	10	*79	118	26	.883
1991—	Salem (Caro.).............	3B	56	201	38	63	12	4	6	28	.313	20	34	3	54	93	12	.925
	—Carolina (Sou.)...........	3B-1B	75	263	36	90	19	6	3	33	.342	15	38	9	157	116	‡28	.907
	—Buffalo (A.A.)..............	3B-1B	4	9	1	2	1	0	0	2	.222	0	0	1	6	6	2	.857
1992—	Buffalo (A.A.)...........	3B-1B	137	490	*91	154	29	6	8	65	.314	67	67	18	129	†313	†32	.932
	—Pittsburgh (N.L.)........	3B-1B	10	7	2	4	0	0	0	4	.571	2	0	1	3	1	1	.800
1993—	Pittsburgh (N.L.).......	1B-3B	141	449	38	106	24	3	6	47	.236	36	82	2	1122	112	3	†.998
1994—	Pittsburgh (N.L.).......	1B-3B-OF	59	122	15	25	7	2	1	11	.205	8	34	0	179	45	3	.987
	—Buffalo (A.A.).............	3B-1B	60	228	26	63	14	5	5	27	.276	15	45	6	59	162	4	.982
1995—	Calgary (PCL)...........	3B-1B-DH	45	163	24	58	23	1	8	34	.356	15	21	6	144	85	12	.950
	—Pittsburgh (N.L.)........	3B-1B	56	181	13	42	9	0	6	22	.232	8	53	1	58	110	12	.933
1996—	Omaha (A.A.)■	1B-3B-DH	50	186	29	57	11	1	13	46	.306	12	41	3	280	45	5	.985
	—Kansas City (A.L.)...	1B-3B-DH	55	132	20	32	6	0	8	23	.242	11	32	3	199	19	1	.995
1997—	Pittsburgh (N.L.)■	1B-3B-OF	97	333	59	100	18	3	18	74	.300	16	89	11	644	66	5	.993
1998—	Pittsburgh (N.L.)	1B	159	592	88	160	40	2	27	108	.270	44	127	15	*1334	80	8	.994
1999—	Pittsburgh (N.L.)	1B	156	584	103	174	41	6	26	106	.298	75	124	22	*1413	97	*23	.985
2000—	Pittsburgh (N.L.)	1B-DH	132	496	77	128	27	0	20	88	.258	32	96	8	1109	59	*17	.986
American League totals (1 year)			55	132	20	32	6	0	8	23	.242	11	32	3	199	19	1	.995
National League totals (8 years)			810	2764	395	739	166	16	104	460	.267	221	605	60	5862	570	72	.989
Major League totals (9 years)			865	2896	415	771	172	16	112	483	.266	232	637	63	6061	589	73	.989

YOUNG, MIKE — 2B/SS — RANGERS

PERSONAL: Born October 19, 1976, in Covina, Calif. ... 6-0/185. ... Bats right, throws right. ... Full name: Michael B. Young.
HIGH SCHOOL: Bishop Amat (La Puente, Calif.).
COLLEGE: UC Santa Barbara.
TRANSACTIONS/CAREER NOTES: Selected by Toronto Blue Jays organization in fifth round of free-agent draft (June 3, 1997). ... Traded by Blue Jays with P Darwin Cubillan to Texas Rangers for P Esteban Loaiza (July 19, 2000).
STATISTICAL NOTES: Led South Atlantic League second basemen with .978 fielding percentage in 1998.

| | | | | | | | | BATTING | | | | | | | | FIELDING | | |
Year	Team (League)	Pos.	G	AB	R	H	2B	3B	HR	RBI	Avg.	BB	SO	SB	PO	A	E	Avg.
1997—	St. Catharines (NY-P).	SS-2B	74	276	49	85	18	3	9	48	.308	33	59	9	115	199	18	.946
1998—	Hagerstown (S.Atl.)....	2B-SS-OF	*140	522	86	147	33	5	16	87	.282	55	96	16	216	341	13	†.977
1999—	Dunedin (FSL)...........	2B-SS	129	495	86	155	•36	3	5	83	.313	61	78	30	163	375	22	.961
2000—	Tennessee (Sou.)	2B-SS	91	345	51	95	24	5	6	47	.275	36	72	16	187	250	16	.965
	—Tulsa (Texas)■..........	SS	43	188	30	60	13	5	1	32	.319	17	28	9	67	125	7	.965
	—Texas (A.L.)...............	2B	1	0	0	0	0	0	0	0	...	0	1	0	0	0	0	...
Major League totals (1 year)			1	0	0	0	0	0	0	0	...	0	1	0	0	0	0	...

YOUNG, TIM — P — RED SOX

PERSONAL: Born October 15, 1973, in Gulfport, Miss. ... 5-9/170. ... Throws left, bats left. ... Full name: Timothy R. Young.
HIGH SCHOOL: Liberty County (Bristol, Fla.).
JUNIOR COLLEGE: Chipola Junior College (Fla.).
COLLEGE: Alabama.
TRANSACTIONS/CAREER NOTES: Selected by Montreal Expos organization in 19th round of free-agent draft (June 4, 1996). ... Granted free agency (December 21, 1998). ... Signed by Boston Red Sox organization (February 3, 1999). ... On Pawtucket disabled list (April 8-June 5, 1999).

Year	League	W	L	Pct.	ERA	G	GS	CG	ShO	Sv.	IP	H	R	ER	BB	SO
1996—	Vermont (NY-Penn)...........	1	0	1.000	0.31	27	0	0	0	18	29 1/3	14	1	1	4	46
1997—	Cape Fear (S.Atl.).............	1	1	.500	1.50	45	0	0	0	18	54	33	12	9	15	66
	—West Palm Beach (FSL)	0	0	...	0.57	11	0	0	0	5	15 2/3	8	1	1	4	13
	—Harrisburg (East.)...........	0	0	...	0.00	1	0	0	0	0	2	1	0	0	0	3
1998—	Harrisburg (East.)..............	3	3	.500	3.79	26	0	0	0	3	35 2/3	28	17	15	10	52
	—Ottawa (I.L.)...................	1	1	.500	2.03	20	0	0	0	2	26 2/3	26	14	6	12	34
	—Montreal (N.L.)...............	0	0	...	6.00	10	0	0	0	0	6	6	4	4	4	7
1999—	Trenton (East.)■	4	4	.500	4.37	31	0	0	0	2	45 1/3	38	26	22	26	52
2000—	Pawtucket (I.L.).................	1	1	.500	2.40	32	0	0	0	6	41 1/3	35	13	11	12	43
	—Boston (A.L.)..................	0	0	...	6.43	8	0	0	0	0	7	7	5	5	2	6
A.L. totals (1 year)......................		0	0	...	6.43	8	0	0	0	0	7	7	5	5	2	6
N.L. totals (1 year)......................		0	0	...	6.00	10	0	0	0	0	6	6	4	4	4	7
Major League totals (2 years).......		0	0	...	6.23	18	0	0	0	0	13	13	9	9	6	13

Y

Z

PERSONAL: Born April 14, 1971, in Glendale, Calif. ... 5-10/190. ... Bats both, throws right. ... Full name: Gregory Owen Zaun. ... Nephew of Rick Dempsey, manager, Norfolk Tides and catcher with six major league teams (1969-92).

HIGH SCHOOL: St. Francis (La Canada, Calif.).

TRANSACTIONS/CAREER NOTES: Selected by Baltimore Orioles organization in 17th round of free-agent draft (June 5, 1989). ... On Bowie disabled list (June 17-July 15, 1993). ... Traded by Orioles to Florida Marlins (August 23, 1996), completing deal in which Marlins traded P Terry Mathews to Orioles for a player to be named later (August 21, 1996). ... Traded by Marlins to Texas Rangers for a player to be named later or cash (November 23, 1998); Marlins received cash to complete deal (April 15, 1999). ... Traded by Rangers with OF Juan Gonzalez and P Danny Patterson to Detroit Tigers for P Justin Thompson, P Francisco Cordero, OF Gabe Kapler, C Bill Haselman, 2B Frank Catalanotto and P Alan Webb (November 2, 1999). ... Traded by Tigers to Kansas City Royals for a player to be named later or cash (March 7, 2000). ... On Kansas City disabled list (April 15-May 29, 2000); included rehabilitation assignment to Omaha (May 16-29).

STATISTICAL NOTES: Led Appalachian League catchers with 460 putouts and 501 total chances in 1990. ... Led Midwest League catchers with 796 total chances in 1991. ... Led Carolina League catchers with 746 putouts, 91 assists, 18 errors, 855 total chances and 10 double plays in 1992. ... Led International League catchers with 841 total chances and 11 double plays in 1994. ... Tied for N.L. lead with 12 double plays by catcher in 1998.

							BATTING							FIELDING			
Year	Team (League)	Pos.	G	AB	R	H	2B	3B	HR	RBI	Avg.	BB	SO	SB	PO	A	E	Avg.
1990—	Wausau (Midw.)	C	37	100	3	13	0	1	1	7	.130	7	17	0	270	26	3	.990
—	Bluefield (Appl.)	C-3B-SS-P	61	184	29	55	5	2	2	21	.299	23	15	5	†462	34	10	.980
1991—	Kane County (Midw.)	C	113	409	67	112	17	5	4	51	.274	50	41	4	*697	83	16	.980
1992—	Frederick (Caro.)	C-2B	108	383	54	96	18	6	6	52	.251	42	45	3	†746	†91	†18	.979
1993—	Bowie (East.)	C-DH-2-3-P	79	258	25	79	10	0	3	38	.306	27	26	4	423	51	10	.979
—	Rochester (I.L.)	C	21	78	10	20	4	2	1	11	.256	6	11	0	141	18	4	.975
1994—	Rochester (I.L.)	C	123	388	61	92	16	4	7	43	.237	56	72	4	*750	82	9	*.989
1995—	Rochester (I.L.)	C-DH	42	140	26	41	13	1	6	18	.293	14	21	0	243	18	3	.989
—	Baltimore (A.L.)	C	40	104	18	27	5	0	3	14	.260	16	14	1	216	13	3	.987
1996—	Baltimore (A.L.)	C	50	108	16	25	8	1	1	13	.231	11	15	0	215	10	3	.987
—	Rochester (I.L.)	C-DH	14	47	11	15	2	0	0	4	.319	11	6	0	52	3	2	.965
—	Florida (N.L.)■	C	10	31	4	9	1	0	1	2	.290	3	5	1	60	6	0	1.000
1997—	Florida (N.L.)	C-1B	58	143	21	43	10	2	2	20	.301	26	18	1	329	25	8	.978
1998—	Florida (N.L.)	C-2B	106	298	19	56	12	2	5	29	.188	35	52	5	531	49	8	.986
1999—	Texas (A.L.)■	C-DH	43	93	12	23	2	1	1	12	.247	10	7	1	165	15	3	.984
2000—	Kansas City (A.L.)■	C-1B-2B	83	234	36	64	11	0	7	33	.274	43	34	7	377	31	5	.988
—	Omaha (PCL)	C	9	25	7	7	3	0	0	3	.280	4	3	1	44	3	0	1.000
American League totals (4 years)			216	539	82	139	26	2	12	72	.258	80	70	9	973	69	14	.987
National League totals (3 years)			174	472	44	108	23	4	8	51	.229	64	75	7	920	80	16	.984
Major League totals (6 years)			390	1011	126	247	49	6	20	123	.244	144	145	16	1893	149	30	.986

DIVISION SERIES RECORD

							BATTING							FIELDING			
Year	Team (League)	Pos.	G	AB	R	H	2B	3B	HR	RBI	Avg.	BB	SO	SB	PO	A	E	Avg.
1997—	Florida (N.L.)							Did not play.										

CHAMPIONSHIP SERIES RECORD

							BATTING							FIELDING			
Year	Team (League)	Pos.	G	AB	R	H	2B	3B	HR	RBI	Avg.	BB	SO	SB	PO	A	E	Avg.
1997—	Florida (N.L.)	C	1	0	0	0	0	0	0	0	...	0	0	0	2	0	0	1.000

WORLD SERIES RECORD

NOTES: Member of World Series championship team (1997).

							BATTING							FIELDING			
Year	Team (League)	Pos.	G	AB	R	H	2B	3B	HR	RBI	Avg.	BB	SO	SB	PO	A	E	Avg.
1997—	Florida (N.L.)	PH-C-PR	2	2	0	0	0	0	0	0	.000	0	0	0	3	0	0	1.000

RECORD AS PITCHER

Year	League	W	L	Pct.	ERA	G	GS	CG	ShO	Sv.	IP	H	R	ER	BB	SO
1990—	Bluefield (Appl.)	0	0	...	0.00	1	0	0	0	0	1	1	0	0	1	1
1993—	Bowie (East.)	0	0	...	0.00	1	0	0	0	0	2 1/3	1	0	0	0	0

PERSONAL: Born September 9, 1965, in Van Nuys, Calif. ... 6-1/200. ... Bats right, throws right. ... Full name: Todd Edward Zeile. ... Husband of Julianne McNamara, Olympic gold-medal gymnast (1984). ... Name pronounced ZEEL.

HIGH SCHOOL: Hart (Newhall, Calif.).

COLLEGE: UCLA.

TRANSACTIONS/CAREER NOTES: Selected by Kansas City Royals organization in 30th round of free-agent draft (June 6, 1983); did not sign. ... Selected by St. Louis Cardinals organization in supplemental round ("sandwich pick" between second and third round 55th pick overall) of free-agent draft (June 2, 1986); pick received as compensation for New York Yankees signing Type C free-agent IF Ivan DeJesus. ... On St. Louis disabled list (April 23-May 9, 1995); included rehabilitation assignment to Louisville (May 6-9). ... Traded by Cardinals with cash to Chicago Cubs for P Mike Morgan, 3B/OF Paul Torres and C Francisco Morales (June 16, 1995). ... Granted free agency (December 21, 1995). ... Signed by Philadelphia Phillies (December 22, 1995). ... Traded by Phillies with OF Pete Incaviglia to Baltimore Orioles for two players to be named later (August 29, 1996); Phillies acquired P Calvin Maduro and P Garrett Stephenson to complete deal (September 4, 1996). ... Granted free agency (October 27, 1996). ... Signed by Los Angeles Dodgers (December 8, 1996). ... Traded by Dodgers with C Mike Piazza to Florida Marlins for OF Gary Sheffield, 3B Bobby Bonilla, C Charles Johnson, OF Jim Eisenreich and P Manuel Barrios (May 15, 1998). ... Traded by Marlins to Texas Rangers for 3B Jose Santo and P Dan DeYoung (July 31, 1998). ... Granted free agency (October 28, 1999). ... Signed by New York Mets (December 11, 1999).

RECORDS: Holds N.L. single-season record for fewest putouts by third baseman (150 or more games)—83 (1993). ... Shares A.L. single-game record for most errors by first baseman—4 (August 7, 1996).

HONORS: Named Midwest League co-Most Valuable Player (1987).

STATISTICAL NOTES: Led New York-Pennsylvania League with six sacrifice flies in 1986. ... Tied for New York-Pennsylvania League lead in double plays by catcher with seven in 1986. ... Led Texas League catchers with 687 putouts and 761 total chances in 1988. ... Led American Association catchers with .992 fielding percentage and 17 passed balls in 1989. ... Had 17-game hitting streak (June 21-July 10, 1999). ... Tied for A.L. third baseman lead with 25 errors in 1999. ... Career major league grand slams: 9.

Year Team (League)	Pos.	G	AB	R	H	2B	3B	HR	RBI	Avg.	BB	SO	SB	PO	A	E	Avg.
1986—Erie (NY-Penn)	C	70	248	40	64	14	1	14	*63	.258	37	52	5	407	*66	8	.983
1987—Springfield (Midw.)	C-3B	130	487	94	142	24	4	25	*106	.292	70	85	1	867	79	14	.985
1988—Arkansas (Texas).......	C-OF-1B	129	430	95	117	33	2	19	75	.272	83	64	6	†697	66	10	.987
1989—Louisville (A.A.).........	C-3B-1B	118	453	71	131	26	3	19	85	.289	45	78	0	583	71	6	†.991
—St. Louis (N.L.).........	C	28	82	7	21	3	1	1	8	.256	9	14	0	125	10	4	.971
1990—St. Louis (N.L.)..........C-3B-1B-1B-OF		144	495	62	121	25	3	15	57	.244	67	77	2	648	106	15	.980
1991—St. Louis (N.L.).........	3B	155	565	76	158	36	3	11	81	.280	62	94	17	124	290	*25	.943
1992—St. Louis (N.L.).........	3B	126	439	51	113	18	4	7	48	.257	68	70	7	81	235	13	.960
—Louisville (A.A.).........	3B	21	74	11	23	4	1	5	13	.311	9	13	0	15	41	5	.918
1993—St. Louis (N.L.).........	3B	157	571	82	158	36	1	17	103	.277	70	76	5	83	310	33	.923
1994—St. Louis (N.L.).........	3B	113	415	62	111	25	1	19	75	.267	52	56	1	66	224	12	.960
1995—Louisville (A.A.).........	1B	2	8	0	1	0	0	0	0	.125	0	2	0	11	1	1	.923
—St. Louis (N.L.).........	1B	34	127	16	37	6	0	5	22	.291	18	23	1	310	30	7	.980
—Chicago (N.L.)■.........	3B-OF-1B	79	299	34	68	16	0	9	30	.227	16	53	0	52	134	12	.939
1996—Philadelphia (N.L.)■ ..	3B-1B	134	500	61	134	24	0	20	80	.268	67	88	1	295	195	14	.972
—Baltimore (A.L.)■.........	3B	29	117	17	28	8	0	5	19	.239	15	16	0	24	56	3	.964
1997—Los Angeles (N.L.)■..	3B	160	575	89	154	17	0	31	90	.268	85	112	8	105	248	*26	.931
1998—Los Angeles (N.L.)	3B-1B	40	158	22	40	6	1	7	27	.253	10	24	1	27	53	6	.930
—Florida (N.L.)■..........	3B	66	234	37	68	12	1	6	39	.291	31	34	2	43	122	5	.971
—Texas (A.L.)■...........	3B	52	180	26	47	14	1	6	28	.261	28	32	1	38	91	12	.915
1999—Texas (A.L.)	3B-DH-1B	156	587	80	172	41	1	24	98	.293	56	94	1	105	294	±25	.941
2000—New York (N.L.)■	1B	153	544	67	146	36	3	22	79	.268	74	85	3	1205	95	10	.992
American League totals (3 years)		237	884	123	247	63	2	35	145	.279	99	142	2	167	441	40	.938
National League totals (11 years)		1389	5004	666	1329	260	18	170	739	.266	629	806	48	3164	2052	182	.966
Major League totals (12 years)		1626	5888	789	1576	323	20	205	884	.268	728	948	50	3331	2493	222	.963

DIVISION SERIES RECORD

Year Team (League)	Pos.	G	AB	R	H	2B	3B	HR	RBI	Avg.	BB	SO	SB	PO	A	E	Avg.
1996—Baltimore (A.L.).........	3B	4	19	2	5	1	0	0	0	.263	2	5	0	4	9	2	.867
1998—Texas (A.L.)	3B	3	9	0	3	0	0	0	0	.333	0	2	0	0	4	0	1.000
1999—Texas (A.L.)	3B	3	10	0	1	0	0	0	0	.100	2	1	0	1	4	2	.714
2000—New York (N.L.).........	1B	4	14	0	1	1	0	0	0	.071	4	3	0	30	4	0	1.000
Division series totals (4 years)		14	52	2	10	2	0	0	0	.192	8	11	0	35	21	4	.933

CHAMPIONSHIP SERIES RECORD

Year Team (League)	Pos.	G	AB	R	H	2B	3B	HR	RBI	Avg.	BB	SO	SB	PO	A	E	Avg.
1996—Baltimore (A.L.).........	3B	5	22	3	8	0	0	3	.364	5	2	1	3	7	1	.909	
2000—New York (N.L.).........	1B	5	19	1	7	3	0	1	8	.368	2	4	0	38	1	0	1.000
Championship series totals (2 years)		10	41	4	15	3	0	1	11	.366	7	6	1	41	8	1	.980

WORLD SERIES RECORD

Year Team (League)	Pos.	G	AB	R	H	2B	3B	HR	RBI	Avg.	BB	SO	SB	PO	A	E	Avg.
2000—New York (N.L.).........	1B	5	20	1	8	2	0	0	1	.400	1	5	0	39	2	0	1.000

ZIMMERMAN, JEFF   P   RANGERS

PERSONAL: Born August 9, 1972, in Kelowna, B.C. ... 6-1/200. ... Throws right, bats right. ... Full name: Jeffery Ross Zimmerman.
HIGH SCHOOL: John G. Diefenbaker (Vancouver).
COLLEGE: Texas Christian, then Simon Fraser (B.C.).
TRANSACTIONS/CAREER NOTES: Signed by Winnipeg, Northern League (May 1997). ... Signed as non-drafted free agent by Texas Rangers organization (January 6, 1998).

Year League	W	L	Pct.	ERA	G	GS	CG	ShO	Sv.	IP	H	R	ER	BB	SO
1997—Winnipeg (Nor.).................	9	2	.818	2.82	18	16	3	0	0	118	94	49	37	35	140
1998—Charlotte (FSL)■...............	2	1	.667	1.26	10	0	0	0	0	14 1/3	10	2	2	1	14
—Tulsa (Texas)	3	1	.750	1.29	41	0	0	0	9	63	38	16	9	20	67
1999—Oklahoma (PCL)	1	0	1.000	0.00	2	0	0	0	1	3 2/3	0	0	0	0	2
—Texas (A.L.)	9	3	.750	2.36	65	0	0	0	3	87 2/3	50	24	23	23	67
2000—Texas (A.L.)	4	5	.444	5.30	65	0	0	0	1	69 2/3	80	45	41	34	74
Major League totals (2 years)	13	8	.619	3.66	130	0	0	0	4	157 1/3	130	69	64	57	141

DIVISION SERIES RECORD

Year League	W	L	Pct.	ERA	G	GS	CG	ShO	Sv.	IP	H	R	ER	BB	SO
1999—Texas (A.L.)......................	0	0	...	0.00	1	0	0	0	0	1	1	0	0	0	1

ALL-STAR GAME RECORD

Year League	W	L	Pct.	ERA	GS	CG	ShO	Sv.	IP	H	R	ER	BB	SO
1999—American	0	0	...	0.00	0	0	0	0	1	0	0	0	2	0

ZIMMERMAN, JORDAN   P   MARINERS

PERSONAL: Born April 28, 1975, in Kelowna, B.C. ... 6-0/200. ... Throws left, bats right. ... Full name: Jordan William Zimmerman.
HIGH SCHOOL: Brenham (Texas).
JUNIOR COLLEGE: Blinn College (Texas).

TRANSACTIONS/CAREER NOTES: Selected by Seattle Mariners organization in 32nd round of free-agent draft (June 2, 1994). ... On disabled list (July 7, 1995-remainder of season). ... On disabled list (June 18, 1996-remainder of season). ... On Lancaster disabled list (April 2-August 12, 1998). ... On Seattle disabled list (July 5-August 8, 1999); included rehabilitation assignment to Tacoma (July 18-23) and Everett (July 24-August 8). ... On Tacoma disabled list (April 6-22, May 3-10 and May 12-July 25, 2000).

Year	League	W	L	Pct.	ERA	G	GS	CG	ShO	Sv.	IP	H	R	ER	BB	SO
1995—	....							Did not play.								
1996—	....							Did not play.								
1997—	Everett (N'West)	2	3	.400	4.15	11	9	0	0	0	39	37	27	18	23	54
	— Wisconsin (Midw.)	0	1	.000	5.82	3	3	0	0	0	17	18	11	11	10	18
1998—	Arizona Mariners (Ariz.)	0	1	.000	3.00	5	3	0	0	0	12	14	6	4	7	11
	— Lancaster (Calif.)	0	1	.000	4.86	3	3	0	0	0	16 $^2/_3$	21	9	9	8	8
1999—	New Haven (East.)	1	4	.200	1.08	22	0	0	0	2	33 $^1/_3$	26	8	4	19	33
	— Seattle (A.L.)	0	0	...	7.88	12	0	0	0	0	8	14	8	7	4	3
	— Tacoma (PCL)	0	0	...	5.14	9	0	0	0	0	7	13	4	4	4	4
	— Everett (N'West)	0	0	...	27.00	1	0	0	0	0	$^2/_3$	3	2	2	0	1
2000—	Arizona Mariners (Ariz.)	0	0	...	0.00	10	10	0	0	0	12	7	3	0	3	14
	— Tacoma (PCL)	0	1	.000	6.65	15	0	0	0	0	23	27	20	17	11	23
	— Lancaster (Calif.)	0	0	...	0.00	3	0	0	0	0	3 $^1/_3$	0	0	0	2	2
Major League totals (1 year)........		0	0	...	7.88	12	0	0	0	0	8	14	8	7	4	3

ZITO, BARRY P ATHLETICS

PERSONAL: Born May 13, 1978, in Las Vegas, Nev. ... 6-4/205. ... Throws left, bats left. ... Full name: Barry William Zito.
HIGH SCHOOL: University (San Diego).
JUNIOR COLLEGE: Pierce Junior College (Calif.).
COLLEGE: UC Santa Barbara, then Southern California.
TRANSACTIONS/CAREER NOTES: Selected by Texas Rangers organization in third round of free-agent draft (June 2, 1998); did not sign. ... Selected by Oakland Athletics organization in first round (ninth pick overall) of free-agent draft (June 2, 1999).

Year	League	W	L	Pct.	ERA	G	GS	CG	ShO	Sv.	IP	H	R	ER	BB	SO
1999—	Visalia (Calif.)	3	0	1.000	2.45	8	8	0	0	0	40 $^1/_3$	21	13	11	22	62
	— Midland (Texas)................	2	1	.667	4.91	4	4	0	0	0	22	22	15	12	11	29
	— Vancouver (PCL)	1	0	1.000	1.50	1	1	0	0	0	6	5	1	1	2	6
2000—	Sacramento (PCL).............	8	5	.615	3.19	18	18	0	0	0	101 $^2/_3$	88	44	36	45	91
	— Oakland (A.L.)	7	4	.636	2.72	14	14	1	1	0	92 $^2/_3$	64	30	28	45	78
Major League totals (1 year)........		7	4	.636	2.72	14	14	1	1	0	92 $^2/_3$	64	30	28	45	78

DIVISION SERIES RECORD

Year	League	W	L	Pct.	ERA	G	GS	CG	ShO	Sv.	IP	H	R	ER	BB	SO
2000—	Oakland (A.L.)	1	0	1.000	1.59	1	1	0	0	0	5 $^2/_3$	7	1	1	2	5

ZOSKY, EDDIE SS

PERSONAL: Born February 10, 1968, in Whittier, Calif. ... 6-0/180. ... Bats right, throws right. ... Full name: Edward James Zosky. ... Name pronounced ZAH-skee.
HIGH SCHOOL: St. Paul (Sante Fe Springs, Calif.).
COLLEGE: Fresno State.
TRANSACTIONS/CAREER NOTES: Selected by New York Mets organization in fifth round of free-agent draft (June 2, 1986); did not sign. ... Selected by Toronto Blue Jays organization in first round (19th pick overall) of free-agent draft (June 5, 1989). ... On Toronto disabled list (March 26-August 11, 1993); included rehabilitation assignments to Hagerstown (July 26-August 2) and Syracuse (August 2-11). ... On disabled list (June 29-August 10, 1994). ... Traded by Blue Jays to Florida Marlins for a player to be named later (November 18, 1994); Blue Jays acquired P Scott Pace to complete deal (December 14, 1994). ... Granted free agency (October 16, 1995). ... Signed by Baltimore Orioles organization (January 24, 1996). ... On Rochester disabled list (July 24-August 19, 1996). ... Granted free agency (October 15, 1996). ... Signed by San Francisco Giants organization (November 25, 1996). ... Granted free agency (October 15, 1997). ... Signed by Milwaukee Brewers organization (December 17, 1997). ... On Louisville disabled list (June 13-20 and July 2-9, 1998). ... Granted free agency (October 15, 1998). ... Re-signed by Brewers organization (December 11, 1998). ... Granted free agency (October 7, 1999). ... Signed by Pittsburgh Pirates organization (January 18, 2000). ... On Nashville disabled list (July 9-August 23, 2000). ... Traded by Pirates to Houston Astros for a player to be named later (August 23, 2000). ... Granted free agency (October 11, 2000).
HONORS: Named shortstop on THE SPORTING NEWS college All-America team (1989).
STATISTICAL NOTES: Led Southern League shortstops with 80 double plays in 1990. ... Led International League shortstops with 616 total chances and 88 double plays in 1991.

								BATTING						FIELDING		
Year	Team (League)	Pos.	G	AB	R	H	2B	3B	HR	RBI	Avg.	BB	SO	SB	PO	A	E	Avg.
1989—	Knoxville (Sou.)..........	SS	56	208	21	46	5	3	2	14	.221	10	32	1	94	135	8	.966
1990—	Knoxville (Sou.)..........	SS	115	450	53	122	20	7	3	45	.271	26	72	3	*196	295	31	*.941
1991—	Syracuse (I.L.)...........	SS	119	511	69	135	18	4	6	39	.264	35	82	9	*221	*371	24	*.961
	— Toronto (A.L.)...........	SS	18	27	2	4	1	1	0	2	.148	0	8	0	12	26	0	1.000
1992—	Syracuse (I.L.)...........	SS	96	342	31	79	11	6	4	38	.231	19	53	3	123	249	27	.932
	— Toronto (A.L.)...........	SS	8	7	1	2	0	1	0	1	.286	0	2	0	2	10	1	.923
1993—	Hagerstown (S.Atl.).....	SS	5	20	2	2	0	0	0	1	.100	2	1	0	10	15	0	1.000
	— Syracuse (I.L.)...........	SS	28	93	9	20	5	0	0	8	.215	1	20	0	48	71	5	.960
1994—	Syracuse (I.L.)...........	2B-SS-3B	85	284	41	75	15	3	7	37	.264	9	46	3	120	212	15	.957
1995—	Florida (N.L.)■..........	SS-2B	6	5	0	1	0	0	0	0	.200	0	0	0	1	2	1	.750
	— Charlotte (I.L.).........	SS-2B-3B	92	312	27	77	15	2	3	42	.247	7	48	2	161	279	15	.967
1996—	Rochester (I.L.)■.......	SS-2B-3B	95	340	42	87	22	4	3	34	.256	21	40	5	159	257	21	.952
	— GC Orioles (GCL)	SS	1	3	1	1	1	0	0	0	.333	1	0	0	3	2	0	1.000
1997—	Phoenix (PCL)	3B-SS-2B	86	241	38	67	10	4	9	45	.278	16	38	3	93	161	11	.958
1998—	Louisville (I.L.)■........	S-3-2-P-O	90	257	36	63	12	1	8	35	.245	15	47	1	99	211	14	.957
1999—	Louisville (I.L.)..........	SS	116	415	60	122	22	3	12	47	.294	23	68	5	141	278	19	.957
	— Milwaukee (N.L.).......	3B-2B	8	7	1	1	0	0	0	0	.143	1	2	0	1	4	0	1.000

Year Team (League)	Pos.	G	AB	R	H	2B	3B	HR	RBI	Avg.	BB	SO	SB	PO	A	E	Avg.
2000—Nashville (PCL)■	SS-2B	53	131	14	29	5	2	2	16	.221	6	24	0	73	118	6	.970
—GC Pirates (GCL)........	SS	8	30	7	10	6	0	0	3	.333	3	1	1	17	25	2	.955
—New Orleans (PCL)■..	2B-SS-3B	11	33	3	9	0	0	0	3	.273	4	8	0	21	21	1	.977
—Houston (N.L.)	PH	4	4	0	0	0	0	0	0	.000	0	1	0	0	0	0	...
American League totals (2 years)		26	34	3	6	1	2	0	3	.176	0	10	0	14	36	1	.980
National League totals (3 years)		18	16	1	2	0	0	0	0	.125	1	3	0	2	6	1	.889
Major League totals (5 years)		44	50	4	8	1	2	0	3	.160	1	13	0	16	42	2	.967

RECORD AS PITCHER

Year League	W	L	Pct.	ERA	G	GS	CG	ShO	Sv.	IP	H	R	ER	BB	SO
1998—Louisville (I.L.)	0	0	...	0.00	1	0	0	0	0	$1/3$	1	0	0	0	1

ZULETA, JULIO   1B   CUBS

PERSONAL: Born March 28, 1975, in Panama City, Panama. ... 6-6/230. ... Bats right, throws right. ... Full name: Julio Ernesto Zuleta.
HIGH SCHOOL: Don Bosco Institute (Panama City, Panama).
COLLEGE: Panama Technological University.
TRANSACTIONS/CAREER NOTES: Signed as non-drafted free agent by Chicago Cubs organization (September 15, 1992).
STATISTICAL NOTES: Led Southern League in being hit by pitch with 20 in 1999. ... Tied Pacific Coast League lead first basemen with 12 errors in 2000.

Year Team (League)	Pos.	G	AB	R	H	2B	3B	HR	RBI	Avg.	BB	SO	SB	PO	A	E	Avg.
1993—GC Cubs (GCL)..........	C-OF	17	53	3	13	0	1	0	6	.245	3	12	0	20	2	3	.880
1994—Huntington (Appl.)	C	6	15	0	1	0	0	0	2	.067	4	4	0	22	7	2	.935
—GC Cubs (GCL)..........	C	30	100	11	31	1	0	0	8	.310	8	18	5	176	19	2	.990
1995—Williamsport (NY-P) ...	C	30	75	9	13	3	1	0	6	.173	11	12	0	131	12	5	.966
1996—Williamsport (NY-P) ...	1B	62	221	35	57	12	2	1	29	.258	19	36	7	338	25	4	.989
1997—Rockford (Midw.)	1B	119	430	59	124	30	5	6	77	.288	35	88	5	828	62	14	.985
1998—Daytona (FSL)	1B	94	366	69	126	25	1	16	86	.344	35	59	6	643	58	13	.982
—West Tenn (Sou.)	1B	40	139	18	41	9	0	2	20	.295	10	30	0	203	18	2	.991
1999—West Tenn (Sou.)	1B	133	482	75	142	37	4	21	97	.295	35	122	4	897	63	9	.991
2000—Chicago (N.L.)	1B-OF	30	68	13	20	8	0	3	12	.294	2	19	0	83	8	3	.968
—Iowa (PCL)	1B-OF-3B	107	392	76	122	25	1	26	94	.311	31	77	5	680	51	13	.983
Major League totals (1 year)		30	68	13	20	8	0	3	12	.294	2	19	0	83	8	3	.968

ALOU, FELIPE | EXPOS

PERSONAL: Born May 12, 1935, in Haina, Dominican Republic. ... 6-1/195. ... Batted right, threw right. ... Full name: Felipe Rojas Alou. ... Father of Moises Alou, outfielder, Houston Astros; brother of Jesus Alou, major league outfielder with four teams (1965-75 and 1978-79); brother of Matty Alou, major league outfielder with six teams (1960-74); and uncle of Mel Rojas, pitcher with five major league teams 1990-99).

COLLEGE: Santo Domingo (Dominican Republic).

TRANSACTIONS/CAREER NOTES: Signed as free agent by New York Giants organization (November 14, 1955). ... Giants franchise moved from New York to San Francisco (1958). ... Traded by Giants with P Billy Hoeft, C Ed Bailey and a player to be named later to Milwaukee Braves for P Bob Hendley, P Bob Shaw and C Del Crandall (December 3, 1963); Braves acquired IF Ernie Bowman to complete deal (January 4, 1964). ... Braves franchise moved from Milwaukee to Atlanta (1966). ... Traded by Braves to Oakland Athletics for P Jim Nash (December 3, 1969). ... Traded by A's to New York Yankees for P Rob Gardner and P Ron Klimkowski (April 9, 1971). ... Contract sold by Yankees to Montreal Expos (September 5, 1973). ... Contract sold by Expos to Milwaukee Brewers (December , 1973). ... Released by Brewers (April 29, 1974).

HONORS: Named first baseman on THE SPORTING NEWS N.L. All-Star team (1966).

STATISTICAL NOTES: Led N.L. with 355 total bases in 1966. ... Career major league grand slams: 2.

							BATTING								FIELDING		
Year Team (League)	Pos.	G	AB	R	H	2B	3B	HR	RBI	Avg.	BB	SO	SB	PO	A	E	Avg.
1956— Lake Charles (Evan.) ..	OF	5	9	1	2	0	0	0	1	.222	...	...	0	6	1	0	1.000
—Cocoa (FSL)	OF-3B	119	445	111	169	15	6	21	99	*.380	68	40	*48	199	60	23	.918
1957— Minneapolis (A.A.)......	OF	24	57	7	12	2	0	0	3	.211	5	8	1	32	1	1	.971
—Springfield (East.)	OF-3B	106	359	45	110	14	3	12	71	.306	27	29	18	215	26	9	.964
1958— Phoenix (PCL)	OF	55	216	61	69	16	2	13	42	.319	17	24	10	150	3	3	.981
—San Francisco (N.L.) ..	OF	75	182	21	46	9	2	4	16	.253	19	34	4	126	2	2	.985
1959— San Francisco (N.L.) ..	OF	95	247	38	68	13	2	10	33	.275	17	38	5	111	2	3	.974
1960— San Francisco (N.L.) ..	OF	106	322	48	85	17	3	8	44	.264	16	42	10	156	5	7	.958
1961— San Francisco (N.L.) ..	OF	132	415	59	120	19	0	18	52	.289	26	41	11	196	10	2	.990
1962— San Francisco (N.L.) ..	OF	154	561	96	177	30	3	25	98	.316	33	66	10	262	7	8	.971
1963— San Francisco (N.L.) ..	OF	157	565	75	159	31	9	20	82	.281	27	87	11	279	9	4	.986
1964— Milwaukee (N.L.)■......	OF-1B	121	415	60	105	26	3	9	51	.253	30	41	5	329	12	5	.986
1965— Milwaukee (N.L.)........	O-1-3-S	143	555	80	165	29	2	23	78	.297	31	63	8	626	43	6	.991
1966— Atlanta (N.L.).............	1-O-3-S	154	*666	*122	*218	32	6	31	74	.327	24	51	5	935	64	13	.987
1967— Atlanta (N.L.).............	1B-OF	140	574	76	157	26	3	15	43	.274	32	50	6	864	34	9	.990
1968— Atlanta (N.L.).............	OF	160	*662	72	•210	37	5	11	57	.317	48	56	12	379	8	8	.980
1969— Atlanta (N.L.).............	OF	123	476	54	134	13	1	5	32	.282	23	23	4	260	4	3	.989
1970— Oakland (A.L.)■.........	OF-1B	154	575	70	156	25	3	8	55	.271	32	31	10	290	11	7	.977
1971— Oakland (A.L.).........	OF	2	8	0	2	1	0	0	0	.250	0	1	0	7	0	0	1.000
—New York (A.L.)■......	OF-1B	131	461	52	133	20	6	8	69	.289	32	24	5	506	23	4	.992
1972— New York (A.L.).........	1B-OF	120	324	33	90	18	1	6	37	.278	22	27	1	669	54	7	.990
1973— New York (A.L.).........	1B-OF	93	280	25	66	12	0	4	27	.236	9	25	0	512	31	7	.987
—Montreal (N.L.)■.......	OF-1B	19	48	4	10	1	0	1	4	.208	2	4	0	30	3	0	1.000
1974— Milwaukee (A.L.)■......	OF	3	3	0	0	0	0	0	0	.000	0	2	0	0	0	1	.000
American League totals (5 years)		503	1651	180	447	76	10	26	188	.271	95	110	16	1984	119	26	.988
National League totals (13 years)		1579	5688	805	1654	283	39	180	664	.291	328	596	91	4553	203	70	.985
Major league totals (17 years)		2082	7339	985	2101	359	49	206	852	.286	423	706	107	6537	322	96	.986

CHAMPIONSHIP SERIES RECORD

						BATTING								FIELDING		
Year Team (League)	Pos.	G	AB	R	H	2B	3B	HR	RBI	Avg.	BB	SO	SB	PO	A	E	Avg.
1969— Atlanta (N.L.)..............	PH	1	1	0	0	0	0	0	0	.000	0	0	0	...	...	...	...

WORLD SERIES RECORD

						BATTING								FIELDING		
Year Team (League)	Pos.	G	AB	R	H	2B	3B	HR	RBI	Avg.	BB	SO	SB	PO	A	E	Avg.
1962— San Francisco (N.L.) ..	OF	7	26	2	7	1	1	0	1	.269	1	4	0	8	0	1	.889

ALL-STAR GAME RECORD

					BATTING								FIELDING		
Year League	Pos.	AB	R	H	2B	3B	HR	RBI	Avg.	BB	SO	SB	PO	A	E	Avg.
1962— National	OF	0	0	0	0	0	0	1	...	0	0	0	0	0	0	...
1966— National								Did not play.								
1968— National	OF	0	0	0	0	0	0	0	...	0	0	0	0	0	0	...
All-Star Game totals (2 years)		0	0	0	0	0	0	1		0	0	0	0	0	0	

RECORD AS MANAGER

BACKGROUND: Spring training instructor, Montreal Expos (1976). ... Coach, Expos (1979-80, 1984 and October 8, 1991-May 22, 1992).

HONORS: Named Florida State League Manager of the Year (1990). ... Named N.L. Manager of the Year by THE SPORTING NEWS (1994). ... Named N.L. Manager of the Year by Baseball Writers' Association of America (1994).

	REGULAR SEASON				Playoff		Champ. Series		World Series		All-Star Game	
Year Team (League)	W	L	Pct.	Pos.	W	L	W	L	W	L	W	L
1977— West Palm Beach (Florida State)	77	55	.583	1st (S)	1	2	—	—	—	—	—	—
1978— Memphis (Southern)...............................	71	73	.493	2nd (W)	—	—	—	—	—	—	—	—
1981— Denver (American Association)	76	60	.559	2nd (W)	4	0	—	—	—	—	—	—
1982— Wichita (American Association)...............	70	67	.511	2nd (W)	—	—	—	—	—	—	—	—
1983— Wichita (American Association)...............	65	71	.478	3rd (W)	—	—	—	—	—	—	—	—
1985— Indianapolis (American Association)	61	81	.430	4th (E)	—	—	—	—	—	—	—	—
1986— West Palm Beach (Florida State)	80	55	.593	1st (S)	3	3	—	—	—	—	—	—

| | | REGULAR SEASON | | | | POSTSEASON | | | | | | | |
Year Team (League)	W	L	Pct.	Pos.	Playoff W	L	Champ. Series W	L	World Series W	L	All-Star Game W	L
1987— West Palm Beach (Florida State)	75	63	.543	2nd (S)	—	—	—	—	—	—	—	—
1988— West Palm Beach (Florida State)	41	27	.603	2nd (E)	—	—	—	—	—	—	—	—
— (Second half)	30	36	.455	3rd (E)	2	2	—	—	—	—	—	—
1989— West Palm Beach (Florida State)	39	31	.557	T2nd (E)	—	—	—	—	—	—	—	—
— (Second half)	35	33	.515	2nd (E)	—	—	—	—	—	—	—	—
1990— West Palm Beach (Florida State)	49	19	.721	1st (E)	—	—	—	—	—	—	—	—
— (Second half)	43	21	.672	1st (E)	3	3	—	—	—	—	—	—
1991— West Palm Beach (Florida State)	33	31	.516	4th (E)	—	—	—	—	—	—	—	—
— (Second half)	39	28	.582	2nd (E)	6	1	—	—	—	—	—	—
1992— Montreal (N.L.)	70	55	.560	2nd (E)	—	—	—	—	—	—	—	—
1993— Montreal (N.L.)	94	68	.580	2nd (E)	—	—	—	—	—	—	—	—
1994— Montreal (N.L.)	74	40	.649		—	—	—	—	—	—	—	—
1995— Montreal (N.L.)	66	78	.458	5th (E)	—	—	—	—	—	—	1	0
1996— Montreal (N.L.)	88	74	.543	2nd (E)	—	—	—	—	—	—	—	—
1997— Montreal (N.L.)	78	84	.481	4th (E)	—	—	—	—	—	—	—	—
1998— Montreal (N.L.)	65	97	.401	4th (E)	—	—	—	—	—	—	—	—
1999— Montreal (N.L.)	68	94	.420	4th (E)	—	—	—	—	—	—	—	—
2000— Montreal (N.L.)	67	95	.414	4th (E)	—	—	—	—	—	—	—	—
Major league totals (9 years)	670	685	.495		—	—	—	—	—	—	1	0

NOTES:
1977—Lost to St. Petersburg in semifinals.
1978—Memphis tied one game.
1981—Defeated Omaha in league championship.
1986—Defeated Winter Haven, two games to none, in semifinals; lost to St. Petersburg, three games to one, in league championship.
1988—Defeated Vero Beach, two games to none, in first round; lost to Osceola, two games to none, in semifinals.
1990—Defeated Lakeland, two games to one, in semifinals; lost to Vero Beach, two games to one, in league championship.
1991—Defeated Vero Beach, two games to one, in first round; defeated Lakeland, two games to none, in semifinals; defeated Clearwater, two games to none, in league championship.
1992—Replaced Montreal manager Tom Runnells with club in fourth place and record of 17-20 (May 22).
1994—Montreal was in first place in N.L. East at time of season-ending strike (August 12).

BAKER, DUSTY — GIANTS

PERSONAL: Born June 15, 1949, in Riverside, Calif. ... 6-2/200. ... Batted right, threw right. ... Full name: Johnnie B. Baker Jr.
HIGH SCHOOL: Del Campo (Fair Oaks, Calif.).
COLLEGE: American River College (Calif.).
TRANSACTIONS/CAREER NOTES: Selected by Atlanta Braves organization in 26th round of free-agent draft (June 6, 1967). ... On West Palm Beach restricted list (April 5-June 13, 1968). ... On Atlanta military list (January 24-April 3, 1969 and June 17-July 3, 1972). ... Traded by Braves with 1B/3B Ed Goodson to Los Angeles Dodgers for OF Jimmy Wynn, 2B Lee Lacy, 1B/OF Tom Paciorek and IF Jerry Royster (November 17, 1975). ... Released on waivers by Dodgers (February 10, 1984); San Francisco Giants claim rejected (February 16, 1984). ... Granted free agency (February 21, 1984). ... Signed by Giants (April 1, 1984). ... On restricted list (April 2-11, 1984). ... Traded by Giants to Oakland Athletics for P Ed Puikunas and C Dan Winters (March 24, 1985). ... Granted free agency (November 10, 1986).
RECORDS: Shares major league records for most plate appearances, most at-bats and most times faced pitcher as batsman in one inning—3 (September 20, 1972, second inning); and most stolen bases in one inning—3 (June 27, 1984, third inning).
HONORS: Named outfielder on THE SPORTING NEWS N.L. All-Star team (1980). ... Named outfielder on THE SPORTING NEWS N.L. Silver Slugger team (1980-81). ... Won N.L. Gold Glove as outfielder (1981).
STATISTICAL NOTES: Led N.L. outfielders with 407 total chances in 1973. ... Career major league grand slams: 4.

Year Team (League)	Pos.	G	AB	R	H	2B	3B	HR	RBI	Avg.	BB	SO	SB	PO	A	E	Avg.
1967— Austin (Texas)	OF	9	39	6	9	1	0	0	1	.231	2	7	0	17	0	1	.944
1968— W.Palm Beach (FSL) ..	OF	6	21	2	4	0	0	0	2	.190	1	4	0	6	2	0	1.000
— Greenwood (W. Car.)..	OF	52	199	45	68	11	3	6	39	.342	23	39	6	82	1	3	.965
— Atlanta (N.L.)	OF	6	5	0	2	0	0	0	0	.400	0	1	0	0	0	0	...
1969— Shreveport (Texas)	OF	73	265	40	68	5	1	9	31	.257	36	41	2	135	10	3	.980
— Richmond (Int'l)	OF-3B	25	89	7	22	4	0	0	8	.247	11	22	3	40	9	4	.925
— Atlanta (N.L.)	OF	3	7	0	0	0	0	0	0	.000	0	3	0	2	0	0	1.000
1970— Richmond (I.L.)	OF	118	461	97	150	29	3	11	51	.325	53	45	10	236	10	7	.972
— Atlanta (N.L.)	OF	13	24	3	7	0	0	4	4	.292	2	4	0	11	1	3	.800
1971— Richmond (I.L.)	OF-3B	80	341	62	106	23	2	11	41	.311	25	37	10	136	13	4	.974
— Atlanta (N.L.)	OF	29	62	2	14	2	0	0	4	.226	1	14	0	29	1	0	1.000
1972— Atlanta (N.L.)	OF	127	446	62	143	27	2	17	76	.321	45	68	4	344	8	4	.989
1973— Atlanta (N.L.)	OF	159	604	101	174	29	4	21	99	.288	67	72	24	*390	11	7	.983
1974— Atlanta (N.L.)	OF	149	574	80	147	35	0	20	69	.256	71	87	18	359	10	7	.981
1975— Atlanta (N.L.)	OF	142	494	63	129	18	2	19	72	.261	67	57	12	287	10	3	.990
1976— Los Angeles (N.L.)▪■..	OF	112	384	36	93	13	0	4	39	.242	31	54	2	254	3	1	.996
1977— Los Angeles (N.L.)	OF	153	533	86	155	26	1	30	86	.291	58	89	2	227	8	3	.987
1978— Los Angeles (N.L.)	OF	149	522	62	137	24	1	11	66	.262	47	66	12	250	13	4	.985
1979— Los Angeles (N.L.)	OF	151	554	86	152	29	1	23	88	.274	56	70	11	289	14	3	.990
1980— Los Angeles (N.L.)	OF	153	579	80	170	26	4	29	97	.294	43	66	12	308	5	3	.991
1981— Los Angeles (N.L.)	OF	103	400	48	128	17	3	9	49	.320	29	43	10	181	8	2	.990
1982— Los Angeles (N.L.)	OF	147	570	80	171	19	1	23	88	.300	56	62	17	226	7	6	.975
1983— Los Angeles (N.L.)	OF	149	531	71	138	25	1	15	73	.260	72	59	7	249	4	5	.981
1984— San Fran. (N.L.)■▪......	OF	100	243	31	71	7	2	3	32	.292	40	27	4	112	1	3	.974
1985— Oakland (A.L.)■..........	1B-OF-DH	111	343	48	92	15	1	14	52	.268	50	47	2	465	29	5	.990
1986— Oakland (A.L.)	OF-DH-1B	83	242	25	58	8	0	4	19	.240	27	37	0	90	4	0	1.000
American League totals (2 years)		194	585	73	150	23	1	18	71	.256	77	84	2	555	33	5	.992
National League totals (17 years)		1845	6532	891	1831	297	22	224	942	.280	685	842	135	3518	103	54	.985
Major league totals (19 years)		2039	7117	964	1981	320	23	242	1013	.278	762	926	137	4073	136	59	.986

MAJOR LEAGUE MANAGERS

DIVISION SERIES RECORD

Year Team (League)	Pos.	G	AB	R	H	2B	3B	HR	RBI	Avg.	BB	SO	SB	PO	A	E	Avg.
						BATTING									FIELDING		
1981— Los Angeles (N.L.)	OF	5	18	2	3	1	0	0	1	.167	2	0	0	12	0	0	1.000

CHAMPIONSHIP SERIES RECORD

RECORDS: Shares single-game record for most grand slams—1 (October 5, 1977). ... Shares single-inning record for most runs batted in—4 (October 5, 1977, fourth inning). ... Shares N.L. single-game record for most hits—4 (October 7, 1978).

NOTES: Named N.L. Championship Series Most Valuable Player (1977).

Year Team (League)	Pos.	G	AB	R	H	2B	3B	HR	RBI	Avg.	BB	SO	SB	PO	A	E	Avg.
						BATTING									FIELDING		
1977— Los Angeles (N.L.)	OF	4	14	4	5	1	0	2	8	.357	2	3	0	3	0	0	1.000
1978— Los Angeles (N.L.)	OF	4	15	1	7	2	0	0	1	.467	3	0	0	5	0	0	1.000
1981— Los Angeles (N.L.)	OF	5	19	3	6	1	0	0	3	.316	1	0	0	10	0	1	.909
1983— Los Angeles (N.L.)	OF	4	14	4	5	1	0	1	1	.357	2	0	0	9	0	0	1.000
Championship series totals (4 years)		17	62	12	23	5	0	3	13	.371	8	3	0	27	0	1	.964

WORLD SERIES RECORD

NOTES: Member of World Series championship team (1981).

Year Team (League)	Pos.	G	AB	R	H	2B	3B	HR	RBI	Avg.	BB	SO	SB	PO	A	E	Avg.
						BATTING									FIELDING		
1977— Los Angeles (N.L.)	OF	6	24	4	7	0	0	1	5	.292	0	2	0	11	0	1	.917
1978— Los Angeles (N.L.)	OF	6	21	2	5	0	0	1	1	.238	1	3	0	12	0	0	1.000
1981— Los Angeles (N.L.)	OF	6	24	3	4	0	0	0	1	.167	1	6	0	13	0	0	1.000
World Series totals (3 years)		18	69	9	16	0	0	2	7	.232	2	11	0	36	0	1	.973

ALL-STAR GAME RECORD

Year League	Pos.	AB	R	H	2B	3B	HR	RBI	Avg.	BB	SO	SB	PO	A	E	Avg.
						BATTING								FIELDING		
1981— National	OF	2	0	1	0	0	0	0	.500	0	0	0	2	0	0	1.000
1982— National	OF	2	0	0	0	0	0	0	.000	0	0	0	0	0	0	...
All-Star Game totals (2 years)		4	0	1	0	0	0	0	.250	0	0	0	2	0	0	1.000

RECORD AS MANAGER

BACKGROUND: Coach, San Francisco Giants (1988-92). ... Manager, Scottsdale Scorpions, Arizona Fall League (1992, record: 20-22, second place/Northern Division).

HONORS: Named N.L. Manager of the Year by Baseball Writers' Association of America (1993 and 2000). ... Coach, N.L. All-Star team (1994 and 1997). ... Named N.L. Manager of the Year by THE SPORTING NEWS (1997 and 2000).

Year Team (League)	REGULAR SEASON				POSTSEASON							
					Playoff		Champ. Series		World Series		All-Star Game	
	W	L	Pct.	Pos.	W	L	W	L	W	L	W	L
1993— San Francisco (N.L.)	103	59	.636	2nd (W)	—	—	—	—	—	—	—	—
1994— San Francisco (N.L.)	55	60	.478		—	—	—	—	—	—	—	—
1995— San Francisco (N.L.)	67	77	.465	4th (W)	—	—	—	—	—	—	—	—
1996— San Francisco (N.L.)	68	94	.420	4th (W)	—	—	—	—	—	—	—	—
1997— San Francisco (N.L.)	90	72	.556	1st (W)	0	3	—	—	—	—	—	—
1998— San Francisco (N.L.)	89	74	.546	2nd (W)	—	—	—	—	—	—	—	—
1999— San Francisco (N.L.)	86	76	.531	2nd (W)	—	—	—	—	—	—	—	—
2000— San Francisco (N.L.)	97	65	.599	1st (W)	1	3	—	—	—	—	—	—
Major league totals (8 years)	655	577	.532		1	6	—	—	—	—	—	—

NOTES:

1994—San Francisco was in second place in N.L. West at time of season-ending strike (August 12).

1997—Lost to Florida in N.L. divisional playoff.

2000—Lost to New York Mets in N.L. divisional playoff.

BAYLOR, DON   CUBS

PERSONAL: Born June 28, 1949, in Austin, Texas. ... 6-1/220. ... Batted right, threw right. ... Full name: Donald Edward Baylor. ... Cousin of Pat Ballage, safety with Indianapolis Colts (1986-87).

HIGH SCHOOL: Stephen F. Austin (Austin, Texas).

JUNIOR COLLEGE: Miami-Dade Junior College and Blinn College (Texas).

TRANSACTIONS/CAREER NOTES: Selected by Baltimore Orioles organization in second round of free-agent draft (June 6, 1967). ... Traded by Orioles with P Mike Torrez and P Paul Mitchell to Oakland Athletics for OF Reggie Jackson, P Ken Holtzman and P Bill Van Bommel (April 2, 1976). ... Granted free agency (November 1, 1976). ... Signed by California Angels (November 16, 1976). ... On disabled list (May 11-June 26, 1980). ... Granted free agency (November 10, 1982). ... Signed by New York Yankees (December 1, 1982). ... Traded by Yankees to Boston Red Sox for DH Mike Easler (March 28, 1986). ... Traded by Red Sox to Minnesota Twins for a player to be named later (August 31, 1987); Red Sox acquired P Enrique Rios to complete deal (December 18, 1987). ... Released by Twins (December 21, 1987). ... Signed by A's (February 9, 1988). ... Granted free agency (November 4, 1988).

RECORDS: Holds major league career record for most times hit by pitch—267. ... Shares major league records for most consecutive home runs in two consecutive games—4 (July 1 [1] and 2 [3], 1975, bases on balls included); and most long hits in opening game of season—4 (2 doubles, 1 triple, 1 home run, April 6, 1973). ... Shares major league record for most times caught stealing in one inning—2 (June 15, 1974, ninth inning). ... Shares modern major league single-game record for most at-bats (nine-inning game)—7 (August 25, 1979). ... Holds N.L. single-season record for most times hit by pitch—35 (1986).

MAJOR LEAGUE MANAGERS

HONORS: Named Appalachian League Player of the Year (1967). ... Named Minor League Player of the Year by THE SPORTING NEWS (1970). ... Named A.L. Player of the Year by THE SPORTING NEWS (1979). ... Named A.L. Most Valuable Player by Baseball Writers' Association of America (1979). ... Named designated hitter on THE SPORTING NEWS A.L. All-Star team (1979, 1985-86). ... Named designated hitter on THE SPORTING NEWS A.L. Silver Slugger team (1983 and 1985-86).

STATISTICAL NOTES: Led Appalachian League with 135 total bases and tied for lead in caught stealing with 6 in 1967. ... Led Texas League in being hit by pitch with 13 in 1969. ... Led International League with 296 total bases in 1970. ... Led International League in being hit by pitch with 19 in 1970 and 16 in 1971. ... Led A.L. in being hit by pitch with 13 in 1973, 20 in 1976, 18 in 1978, 23 in 1984, 24 in 1985, 35 in 1986, 28 in 1987 and tied for lead with 13 in 1975. ... Hit three home runs in one game (July 2, 1975). ... Led A.L. with 12 sacrifice flies in 1978. ... Led A.L. with 21 game-winning RBIs in 1982. ... Career major league grand slams: 12.

Year Team (League)	Pos.	G	AB	R	H	2B	3B	HR	RBI	Avg.	BB	SO	SB	PO	A	E	Avg.
1967— Bluefield (Appal.)........	OF	•67	246	50	*85	10	*8	8	47	*.346	35	52	*26	106	5	5	.957
1968— Stockton (California) ..	OF	68	244	52	90	6	3	7	40	.369	35	45	14	135	3	7	.952
— Elmira (East.).........	OF	6	24	4	8	1	1	1	3	.333	3	4	1	10	1	0	1.000
— Rochester (I.L.)..........	OF	15	46	4	10	2	0	0	4	.217	3	17	1	29	1	4	.882
1969— Miami (FSL).........	OF	17	56	13	21	5	4	3	24	.375	7	8	3	30	2	3	.914
— Dall./Ft. Worth (Tex.)..	OF	109	406	71	122	17	•10	11	57	.300	48	77	19	241	7	*13	.950
1970— Rochester (I.L.).........	OF	•140	508	*127	166	*34	*15	22	107	.327	76	99	26	286	5	7	.977
— Baltimore (A.L.).........	OF	8	17	4	4	0	0	0	4	.235	2	3	1	15	0	0	1.000
1971— Rochester (I.L.).........	OF	136	492	104	154	•31	10	20	95	.313	79	73	25	210	4	9	.960
— Baltimore (A.L.).........	OF	1	2	0	0	0	0	0	1	.000	2	1	0	4	0	0	1.000
1972— Baltimore (A.L.).........	OF-1B	102	320	33	81	13	3	11	38	.253	29	50	24	206	4	5	.977
1973— Baltimore (A.L.).........	OF-1B-DH	118	405	64	116	20	4	11	51	.286	35	48	32	228	10	6	.975
1974— Baltimore (A.L.).........	OF-1B	137	489	66	133	22	1	10	59	.272	43	56	29	260	2	5	.981
1975— Baltimore (A.L.).........	OF-DH-1B	145	524	79	148	21	6	25	76	.282	53	64	32	286	8	5	.983
1976— Oakland (A.L.)■........	OF-1B-DH	157	595	85	147	25	1	15	68	.247	58	72	52	781	45	12	.986
1977— California (A.L.)■......	OF-DH-1B	154	561	87	141	27	0	25	75	.251	62	76	26	280	16	7	.977
1978— California (A.L.).........	DH-OF	158	591	103	151	26	0	34	99	.255	56	71	22	194	9	6	.971
1979— California (A.L.)■......	OF-DH-1B	•162	628	*120	186	33	3	36	*139	.296	71	51	22	203	3	5	.976
1980— California (A.L.).........	OF-DH	90	340	39	85	12	2	5	51	.250	24	32	6	119	4	4	.969
1981— California (A.L.).........	DH-1B-OF	103	377	52	90	18	1	17	66	.239	42	51	3	38	3	0	1.000
1982— California (A.L.).........	DH	157	608	80	160	24	1	24	93	.263	57	69	10	...	...	...	...
1983— New York (A.L.)■......	DH-OF-1B	144	534	82	162	33	3	21	85	.303	40	53	17	23	2	1	.962
1984— New York (A.L.).........	DH-OF	134	493	84	129	29	1	27	89	.262	38	68	1	8	0	1	.889
1985— New York (A.L.).........	DH	142	477	70	110	24	1	23	91	.231	52	90	0	...	...	...	...
1986— Boston (A.L.)■..........	DH-1B-OF	160	585	93	139	23	1	31	94	.238	62	111	3	71	4	1	.987
1987— Boston (A.L.).........	DH	108	339	64	81	8	0	16	57	.239	40	47	5	...	...	...	...
— Minnesota (A.L.)■.....	DH	20	49	3	14	1	0	0	6	.286	5	12	0	...	...	...	...
1988— Oakland (A.L.)■........	DH	92	264	28	58	7	0	7	34	.220	34	44	0	...	...	...	...
Major league totals (19 years)		2292	8198	1236	2135	366	28	338	1276	.260	805	1069	285	2716	110	58	.980

CHAMPIONSHIP SERIES RECORD

RECORDS: Holds career record for most clubs played with—5. ... Holds single-series record for most runs batted in—10 (1982). ... Shares single-game records for most times reached base safely—5 (October 8, 1986); and most grand slams—1 (October 9, 1982). ... Shares record for most runs batted in in one inning—4 (October 9, 1982, eighth inning). ... Holds A.L. record for most consecutive games with one or more hits—12 (1982 [last three games], 1986-87). ... Shares A.L. single-game record for most runs batted in—5 (October 5, 1982).

Year Team (League)	Pos.	G	AB	R	H	2B	3B	HR	RBI	Avg.	BB	SO	SB	PO	A	E	Avg.
1973— Baltimore (A.L.).........	OF-PH	4	11	3	3	0	0	0	1	.273	3	5	0	7	0	0	1.000
1974— Baltimore (A.L.).........	OF-DH	4	15	0	4	0	0	0	0	.267	0	2	0	9	0	0	1.000
1979— California (A.L.).........	DH-OF	4	16	2	3	0	0	1	2	.188	1	2	0	4	0	0	1.000
1982— California (A.L.).........	DH	5	17	2	5	1	1	1	10	.294	2	0	0	...	...	...	...
1986— Boston (A.L.).........	DH	7	26	6	9	3	0	1	3	.346	4	5	0	...	...	...	...
1987— Minnesota (A.L.)	PH-DH	2	5	0	2	0	0	0	1	.400	0	0	0	...	...	...	...
1988— Oakland (A.L.)	DH	2	6	0	0	0	0	0	0	.000	1	2	0	...	...	...	...
Championship series totals (7 years)		28	96	13	26	4	1	3	17	.271	11	16	0	20	0	0	1.000

WORLD SERIES RECORD

RECORDS: Shares record for most at-bats in one inning—2 (October 17, 1987, fourth inning).

NOTES: Member of World Series championship team (1987).

Year Team (League)	Pos.	G	AB	R	H	2B	3B	HR	RBI	Avg.	BB	SO	SB	PO	A	E	Avg.
1986— Boston (A.L.)..............	DH-PH	4	11	1	2	1	0	0	1	.182	1	3	0	...	...	...	...
1987— Minnesota (A.L.)	DH-PH	5	13	3	5	0	0	1	3	.385	1	1	0	...	...	...	...
1988— Oakland (A.L.)	PH	1	1	0	0	0	0	0	0	.000	0	1	0	...	...	...	...
World Series totals (3 years)		10	25	4	7	1	0	1	4	.280	2	5	0	...	...	...	...

ALL-STAR GAME RECORD

Year League	Pos.	AB	R	H	2B	3B	HR	RBI	Avg.	BB	SO	SB	PO	A	E	Avg.
1979— American	OF	4	2	2	1	0	0	1	.500	0	0	0	1	0	0	1.000

RECORD AS MANAGER

BACKGROUND: Special assistant to general manager, Milwaukee Brewers (September 5-December 4, 1989). ... Coach, Brewers (December 4, 1989-91). ... Coach, St. Louis Cardinals (1992) ... Coach, Atlanta Braves (1999).

HONORS: Coach, N.L. All-Star team (1994). ... Named N.L. Manager of the Year by THE SPORTING NEWS (1995). ... Named N.L. Manager of the Year by Baseball Writers' Association of America (1995).

| Year | Team (League) | REGULAR SEASON | | | | POSTSEASON | | | | | | All-Star Game | |
| | | W | L | Pct. | Pos. | Playoff | | Champ. Series | | World Series | | | |
						W	L	W	L	W	L	W	L
1993—	Colorado (N.L.)	67	95	.414	6th (W)	—	—	—	—	—	—	—	—
1994—	Colorado (N.L.)	53	64	.453		—	—	—	—	—	—	—	—
1995—	Colorado (N.L.)	77	67	.535	2nd (W)	1	3	—	—	—	—	—	—
1996—	Colorado (N.L.)	83	79	.512	3rd (W)	—	—	—	—	—	—	—	—
1997—	Colorado (N.L.)	83	79	.512	3rd (W)	—	—	—	—	—	—	—	—
1998—	Colorado (N.L.)	77	85	.475	4th (W)	—	—	—	—	—	—	—	—
2000—	Chicago (N.L.)	65	97	.401	6th (C)	—	—	—	—	—	—	—	—
Major league totals (7 years)		**505**	**566**	**.472**		**1**	**3**	**—**	**—**	**—**	**—**	**—**	**—**

NOTES:

1994—Colorado was in third place in N.L. West at time of season-ending strike (August 12).

1995—Lost to Atlanta in N.L. divisional playoff.

BELL, BUDDY — ROCKIES

PERSONAL: Born August 27, 1951, in Pittsburgh. ... 6-3/200. ... Batted right, threw right. ... Full name: David Gus Bell. ... Father of David Bell, infielder, Seattle Mariners; father of Mike Bell, minor league infielder (1993-2000); and son of Gus Bell, major league outfielder with four teams (1950-64).

HIGH SCHOOL: Moeller (Cincinnati).

COLLEGE: Xavier, then Miami of Ohio.

TRANSACTIONS/CAREER NOTES: Selected by Cleveland Indians organization in 16th round of free-agent draft (June 5, 1969). ... On disabled list (May 27-June 17 and August 8-September 1, 1974). ... Traded by Indians to Texas Rangers for 3B Toby Harrah (December 8, 1978). ... On disabled list (June 9-24, 1980). ... Traded by Rangers to Cincinnati Reds for OF Duane Walker and a player to be named later (July 19, 1985); Rangers acquired P Jeff Russell to complete deal (July 23, 1985). ... On Cincinnati disabled list (March 26-April 10 and April 14-May 11, 1988). ... Traded by Reds to Houston Astros for a player to be named later (June 19, 1988); Reds acquired P Carl Grovom to complete deal (October 20, 1988). ... On Houston disabled list (August 4-19, 1988). ... Released by Astros (December 21, 1988). ... Signed by Rangers (January 9, 1989). ... On disabled list (April 8-28, 1989). ... Announced retirement (June 24, 1989).

HONORS: Won A.L. Gold Glove at third base (1979-84). ... Named third baseman on THE SPORTING NEWS A.L. All-Star team (1981 and 1984). ... Named third baseman on THE SPORTING NEWS A.L. Silver Slugger team (1984).

STATISTICAL NOTES: Led Gulf Coast League second basemen with 26 double plays in 1969. ... Led A.L. third basemen with 144 putouts and 44 double plays in 1973. ... Led A.L. third basemen with 495 total chances in 1978, 361 in 1981, 540 in 1982 and 523 in 1983. ... Tied for A.L. lead in double plays by third basemen with 30 in 1978. ... Had 21-game hitting streak (June 24-July 17, 1980). ... Led A.L. third basemen with 364 assists in 1979 and 281 in 1981. ... Led A.L. third basemen with .981 fielding percentage in 1980 and .976 in 1982. ... Led A.L. with 10 sacrifice flies in 1981. ... Career major league grand slams: 8.

Year	Team (League)	Pos.	G	AB	R	H	2B	3B	HR	RBI	Avg.	BB	SO	SB	PO	A	E	Avg.
1969—	Sarasota (GCL)	2B	51	170	18	39	4	•3	3	24	.229	17	15	3	119	108	7	*.970
1970—	Sumter (SAL)	3B-2B-SS	121	442	81	117	19	3	12	75	.265	44	43	9	116	189	27	.919
1971—	Wichita (A.A.)	3-2-S-O	129	470	65	136	23	1	11	59	.289	42	51	7	*139	203	16	.955
1972—	Cleveland (A.L.)	OF-3B	132	466	49	119	21	1	9	36	.255	34	29	5	284	23	3	.990
1973—	Cleveland (A.L.)	3B-OF	156	631	86	169	23	7	14	59	.268	49	47	7	†146	363	22	.959
1974—	Cleveland (A.L.)	3B	116	423	51	111	15	1	7	46	.262	35	29	1	112	274	15	.963
1975—	Cleveland (A.L.)	3B	153	553	66	150	20	4	10	59	.271	51	72	6	*146	330	25	.950
1976—	Cleveland (A.L.)	3B-1B	159	604	75	170	26	2	7	60	.281	44	49	3	109	331	20	.957
1977—	Cleveland (A.L.)	3B-OF	129	479	64	140	23	4	11	64	.292	45	63	1	134	253	16	.960
1978—	Cleveland (A.L.)	3B	142	556	71	157	27	8	6	62	.282	39	43	1	125	*355	15	.970
1979—	Texas (A.L.)■	3B-SS	•162	*670	89	200	42	3	18	101	.299	30	45	3	147	†429	17	.971
1980—	Texas (A.L.)	3B-SS	129	490	76	161	24	4	17	83	.329	40	39	3	125	282	8	†.981
1981—	Texas (A.L.)	3B-SS	97	360	44	106	16	1	10	64	.294	42	30	1	67	†284	14	.962
1982—	Texas (A.L.)	3B-SS	148	537	62	159	27	2	13	67	.296	70	50	5	*131	397	13	†.976
1983—	Texas (A.L.)	3B	156	618	75	171	35	3	14	66	.277	50	48	3	123	*383	17	.967
1984—	Texas (A.L.)	3B	148	553	88	174	36	5	11	83	.315	63	54	2	129	323	•20	.958
1985—	Texas (A.L.)	3B	84	313	33	74	13	3	4	32	.236	33	21	3	70	192	16	.942
	—Cincinnati (N.L.)■	3B	67	247	28	54	15	2	6	36	.219	34	27	0	54	105	9	.946
1986—	Cincinnati (N.L.)	3B-2B	155	568	89	158	29	3	20	75	.278	73	49	2	105	291	10	.975
1987—	Cincinnati (N.L.)	3B	143	522	74	148	19	2	17	70	.284	71	39	4	93	241	7	*.979
1988—	Cincinnati (N.L.)	3B-1B	21	54	3	10	0	0	0	3	.185	7	3	0	14	26	2	.952
	—Houston (N.L.)■	3B-1B	74	269	24	68	10	1	7	37	.253	19	29	1	74	114	13	.935
1989—	Texas (A.L.)■	3B-1B	34	82	4	15	4	0	0	3	.183	7	10	0	10	13	0	1.000
American League totals (15 years)			1945	7335	933	2076	352	48	151	885	.283	632	629	48	1858	4232	221	.965
National League totals (4 years)			460	1660	218	438	73	8	50	221	.264	204	147	7	340	777	41	.965
Major league totals (18 years)			2405	8995	1151	2514	425	56	201	1106	.279	836	776	55	2198	5009	262	.965

ALL-STAR GAME RECORD

Year	League	Pos.	AB	R	H	2B	3B	HR	RBI	Avg.	BB	SO	SB	PO	A	E	Avg.
1973—	American	PH	1	0	1	0	1	0	0	1.000	0	0	0	...	...	...	...
1980—	American	3B	2	0	0	0	0	0	0	.000	0	1	0	0	2	0	1.000
1981—	American	3B	1	0	0	0	0	0	1	.000	0	0	0	1	2	0	1.000
1982—	American	PH-3B	3	0	0	0	0	0	0	.000	0	2	0	0	1	1	.500
1984—	American	3B	1	0	0	0	0	0	0	.000	0	0	0	0	1	0	1.000
All-Star Game totals (5 years)			8	0	1	0	1	0	1	.125	0	3	0	1	6	1	.875

MAJOR LEAGUE MANAGERS

RECORD AS MANAGER

BACKGROUND: Minor league hitting instructor, Cleveland Indians organization (1990). ... Director of minor league instruction, Chicago White Sox organization (1991-93). ... Coach, Indians (1994-95). ... Minor league field coordinator, Cincinnati Reds (September 23, 1998-August 4, 1999). ... Director of player development, Reds (August 5, 1999-remainder of season).

					Playoff		Champ. Series		World Series		All-Star Game	
		REGULAR SEASON			POSTSEASON							
Year Team (League)	W	L	Pct.	Pos.	W	L	W	L	W	L	W	L
1996— Detroit (A.L.)	53	109	.327	5th (E)	—	—	—	—	—	—	—	—
1997— Detroit (A.L.)	79	83	.488	3rd (E)	—	—	—	—	—	—	—	—
1998— Detroit (A.L.)	52	85	.379		—	—	—	—	—	—	—	—
2000— Colorado (N.L.)	82	80	.506	4th (W)	—	—	—	—	—	—	—	—
Major league totals (4 years)	266	357	.427		—	—	—	—	—	—	—	—

NOTES:
1998—Replaced as Detroit manager on interim basis by Larry Parrish with club in fifth place (September 1).

BOCHY, BRUCE — PADRES

PERSONAL: Born April 16, 1955, in Landes de Boussac, France. ... 6-4/225. ... Batted right, threw right. ... Full name: Bruce Douglas Bochy. ... Brother of Joe Bochy, catcher in Minnesota Twins organization (1969-72). ... Name pronounced BO-chee.
HIGH SCHOOL: Melbourne (Fla.).
JUNIOR COLLEGE: Brevard Community College (Fla.).
COLLEGE: Florida State.
TRANSACTIONS/CAREER NOTES: Selected by Chicago White Sox organization in eighth round of free-agent draft (January 9, 1975); did not sign. ... Selected by Houston Astros organization in secondary phase of free-agent draft (June 4, 1975). ... Traded by Astros to New York Mets organization for two players to be named later (February 11, 1981); Astros acquired IF Randy Rodgers and C Stan Hough to complete deal (April 3, 1981). ... Released by Mets (January 21, 1983). ... Signed by San Diego Padres organization (February 23, 1983). ... On disabled list (April 13-May 6, 1987). ... Granted free agency (November 9, 1987).
STATISTICAL NOTES: Tied for Florida State League lead with 12 passed balls in 1977.

							BATTING								FIELDING		
Year Team (League)	Pos.	G	AB	R	H	2B	3B	HR	RBI	Avg.	BB	SO	SB	PO	A	E	Avg.
1975— Covington (Appal.)	C	37	145	31	49	9	0	4	34	.338	11	18	0	231	36	4	.985
1976— Columbus (Sou.)	C	69	230	9	53	6	0	0	16	.230	14	30	0	266	45	6	.981
—Dubuque (Midwest)	C-1B	30	103	9	25	4	0	1	8	.243	12	11	1	165	25	5	.974
1977— Cocoa (FSL)	C	128	430	40	109	18	2	3	35	.253	35	50	0	*492	67	12	.979
1978— Columbus (Sou.)	C	79	261	25	70	10	2	7	34	.268	13	30	0	419	49	7	.985
—Houston (N.L.)	C	54	154	8	41	8	0	3	15	.266	11	35	0	268	35	8	.974
1979— Houston (N.L.)	C	56	129	11	28	4	0	1	6	.217	17	25	0	198	29	7	.970
1980— Houston (N.L.)	C-1B	22	22	0	4	1	0	0	0	.182	0	0	0	19	1	0	1.000
1981— Tidewater (I.L.)■	C	85	269	23	61	11	2	8	38	.227	22	47	0	253	35	3	.990
1982— Tidewater (I.L.)	C	81	251	32	57	11	0	15	52	.227	19	47	2	427	57	5	.990
—New York (N.L.)	C-1B	17	49	4	15	4	0	2	8	.306	4	6	0	92	8	4	.962
1983— Las Vegas (PCL)■	C	42	145	28	44	8	1	11	33	.303	15	25	3	157	21	3	.983
—San Diego (N.L.)	C	23	42	2	9	1	1	0	3	.214	0	9	0	51	5	0	1.000
1984— Las Vegas (PCL)	C	34	121	18	32	7	0	7	22	.264	17	13	0	189	17	2	.990
—San Diego (N.L.)	C	37	92	10	21	5	1	4	15	.228	3	21	0	147	12	2	.988
1985— San Diego (N.L.)	C	48	112	16	30	2	0	6	13	.268	6	30	0	148	11	2	.988
1986— San Diego (N.L.)	C	63	127	16	32	9	0	8	22	.252	14	23	1	202	22	2	.991
1987— San Diego (N.L.)	C	38	75	8	12	3	0	2	11	.160	11	21	0	95	7	4	.962
1988— Las Vegas (PCL)	C	53	147	17	34	5	0	5	13	.231	17	28	0	207	19	3	.987
Major league totals (9 years)		358	802	75	192	37	2	26	93	.239	66	170	1	1220	130	29	.979

CHAMPIONSHIP SERIES RECORD

							BATTING								FIELDING		
Year Team (League)	Pos.	G	AB	R	H	2B	3B	HR	RBI	Avg.	BB	SO	SB	PO	A	E	Avg.
1980— Houston (N.L.)	C	1	1	0	0	0	0	0	0	.000	0	0	0	5	1	0	1.000

WORLD SERIES RECORD

							BATTING								FIELDING		
Year Team (League)	Pos.	G	AB	R	H	2B	3B	HR	RBI	Avg.	BB	SO	SB	PO	A	E	Avg.
1984— San Diego (N.L.)	PH	1	1	0	1	0	0	0	0	1.000	0	0	0	...	...	...	

RECORD AS MANAGER

BACKGROUND: Player/coach, Las Vegas, San Diego Padres organization (1988). ... Coach, Padres (1993-94).
HONORS: Named N.L. Manager of the Year by THE SPORTING NEWS (1996 and 1998). ... Named N.L. Manager of the Year by Baseball Writers' Association of America (1996).

					Playoff		Champ. Series		World Series		All-Star Game	
		REGULAR SEASON			POSTSEASON							
Year Team (League)	W	L	Pct.	Pos.	W	L	W	L	W	L	W	L
1989— Spokane (Northwest)	41	34	.547	1st (N)	2	1	—	—	—	—	—	—
1990— Riverside (California)	35	36	.493	4th (S)	—	—	—	—	—	—	—	—
—(Second half)	29	42	.408	5th (S)	—	—	—	—	—	—	—	—
1991— High Desert (California)	31	37	.456	3rd (S)	—	—	—	—	—	—	—	—
—(Second half)	42	26	.618	1st (S)	6	2	—	—	—	—	—	—
1992— Wichita (Texas)	39	29	.574	1st (W)	—	—	—	—	—	—	—	—
—(Second half)	31	37	.456	4th (W)	6	1	—	—	—	—	—	—
1995— San Diego (N.L.)	70	74	.486	3rd (W)	—	—	—	—	—	—	—	—

| | | REGULAR SEASON | | | | POSTSEASON | | | | | | |
| | | | | | | Playoff | | Champ. Series | | World Series | | All-Star Game | |
Year	Team (League)	W	L	Pct.	Pos.	W	L	W	L	W	L	W	L
1996— San Diego (N.L.)		91	71	.562	1st (W)	0	3	—	—	—	—	—	—
1997— San Diego (N.L.)		76	86	.469	4th (W)	—	—	—	—	—	—	—	—
1998— San Diego (N.L.)		98	64	.605	1st (W)	3	1	4	2	0	4	—	—
1999— San Diego (N.L.)		74	88	.457	4th (W)	—	—	—	—	—	—	—	—
2000— San Diego (N.L.)		76	86	.469	5th (W)	—	—	—	—	—	—	—	—
Major league totals (6 years)		**485**	**469**	**.508**		**3**	**4**	**4**	**2**	**0**	**4**	**—**	**—**

NOTES:
1989—Defeated Southern Oregon in league championship.
1991—Defeated Bakersfield, three games to none, in semifinals; defeated Stockton, three games to two, in league championship.
1992—Defeated El Paso, two games to one, in semifinals; defeated Shreveport, four games to none, in league championship.
1996—Lost to St. Louis in N.L. divisional playoff.
1998—Defeated Houston in N.L. divisional playoff; defeated Atlanta in N.L. Championship Series; lost to New York Yankees in World Series.

BOLES, JOHN   MARLINS

PERSONAL: Born August 19, 1948, in Chicago. ... 5-10/165. ... Full name: John Boles Jr.
COLLEGE: Lewis University (degree in sociology), then St. Xavier College.

RECORD AS MANAGER

BACKGROUND: Head coach, St. Xavier College (1973-79). ... Head coach, University of Louisville (1980-81). ... Director of player development, Kansas City Royals (July 26, 1986-1989). ... Minor league coordinator, Montreal Expos (1990). ... Director of player development, Expos (1991). ... Director of player development, Florida Marlins (November 1, 1991-July 28, 1995). ... Vice president of player development, Marlins (July 28, 1995-present).
HONORS: Named Gulf Coast League Manager of the Year (1982).

| | | REGULAR SEASON | | | | POSTSEASON | | | | | | |
| | | | | | | Playoff | | Champ. Series | | World Series | | All-Star Game | |
Year	Team (League)	W	L	Pct.	Pos.	W	L	W	L	W	L	W	L
1981— Gulf Coast White Sox (GCL)		41	23	.641	2nd	—	—	—	—	—	—	—	—
1982— Gulf Coast White Sox (GCL)		40	23	.635	2nd	—	—	—	—	—	—	—	—
1983— Appleton (Midwest)		87	50	.635	1st (N)	5	2	—	—	—	—	—	—
1984— Glens Falls (Eastern)		75	63	.543	2nd	1	3	—	—	—	—	—	—
1985— Buffalo (American Association)		66	76	.465	3rd (E)	—	—	—	—	—	—	—	—
1986— Omaha (American Association)		40	36	.526		—	—	—	—	—	—	—	—
1996— Florida (N.L.)		40	35	.540	3rd (E)	—	—	—	—	—	—	—	—
1999— Florida (N.L.)		64	98	.395	5th (E)	—	—	—	—	—	—	—	—
2000— Florida (N.L.)		79	82	.491	3rd (E)	—	—	—	—	—	—	—	—
Major league totals (3 years)		**183**	**215**	**.460**		**—**	**—**	**—**	**—**	**—**	**—**	**—**	**—**

NOTES:
1983—Defeated Waterloo, two games to one, in league semifinals; defeated Springfield, three games to one, to win league championship.
1984—Glens Falls tied one game; lost to Waterbury in league semifinals.
1986—Replaced as Omaha manager by Frank Funk (June 25).
1996—Replaced Florida manager Rene Lachemann with club in fourth place and record of 40-47 (July 8).

BOONE, BOB   REDS

PERSONAL: Born November 19, 1947, in San Diego. ... 6-2/207. ... Batted right, threw right. ... Full name: Robert Raymond Boone. ... Son of Ray Boone, major league infielder with six teams (1948-60); brother of Rodney Boone, minor league catcher/outfielder (1972-75); father of Bret Boone, second baseman, Seattle Mariners; and father of Aaron Boone, third baseman, Cincinnati Reds.
HIGH SCHOOL: Crawford (San Diego).
COLLEGE: Stanford.
TRANSACTIONS/CAREER NOTES: Selected by Philadelphia Phillies organization in 20th round of free-agent draft (June 5, 1969). ... On military list (May 26, 1970-remainder of season). ... On disabled list (April 10-June 4, 1971). ... Contract sold by Phillies to California Angels (December 6, 1981). ... Granted free agency (November 12, 1986). ... Re-signed by Angels (May 1, 1987). ... Granted free agency (October 24, 1988). ... Signed by Kansas City Royals (November 30, 1988). ... On disabled list (May 17-July 20, 1990). ... Granted free agency (November 5, 1990). ... Signed by Oakland Athletics organization (May 31, 1993). ... Released by A's (June 1, 1993).
RECORDS: Holds major league career record for most years by catcher (100 or more games)—15.
HONORS: Named catcher on THE SPORTING NEWS N.L. All-Star team (1976). ... Won N.L. Gold Glove at catcher (1978-79). ... Won A.L. Gold Glove at catcher (1982 and 1986-1989).
STATISTICAL NOTES: Tied for Carolina League lead in double plays by third baseman with 18 in 1969. ... Led Northwest League catchers with 18 passed balls and 13 double plays in 1972. ... Led N.L. catchers with 924 total chances in 1974. ... Led N.L. catchers with .991 fielding percentage in 1978. ... Led A.L. catchers with 745 total chances in 1982 and 823 in 1989. ... Led A.L. catchers with 12 double plays in 1983, 15 in 1985 and 16 in 1986. ... Career major league grand slams: 2.

| | | | | | | BATTING | | | | | | | | | FIELDING | | | |
Year	Team (League)	Pos.	G	AB	R	H	2B	3B	HR	RBI	Avg.	BB	SO	SB	PO	A	E	Avg.
1969— Ral./Dur. (Caro.)		3B	80	300	45	90	13	1	5	46	.300	19	24	0	71	160	20	.920
1970— Reading (East.)		3B	20	80	12	23	2	0	2	10	.288	7	9	0	28	38	7	.904
1971— Reading (East.)		3B-C-SS	92	328	41	87	14	3	4	37	.265	28	28	1	206	138	17	.953
1972— Eugene (N'West)		C	138	513	77	158	32	4	17	67	.308	45	35	2	*699	*77	*24	.970
— Philadelphia (N.L.)		C	16	51	4	14	1	0	1	4	.275	5	7	1	66	7	5	.936
1973— Philadelphia (N.L.)		C	145	521	42	136	20	2	10	61	.261	41	36	3	868	*89	10	.990
1974— Philadelphia (N.L.)		C	146	488	41	118	24	3	3	52	.242	35	29	3	*825	77	*22	.976
1975— Philadelphia (N.L.)		C-3B	97	289	28	71	14	2	2	20	.246	32	14	1	459	48	5	.990

| | | | | REGULAR SEASON | | | | | | | POSTSEASON | | | | | | | | |
| | | | | | | | | | | Playoff | | Champ. Series | | | World Series | | | All-Star Game | |
Year Team (League)			W	L	Pct.		Pos.			W	L	W	L		W	L		W	L
1976— Philadelphia (N.L.)......	C-1B	121	361	40	98	18	2	4	54	.271	45	44	2	587	39	6	.991
1977— Philadelphia (N.L.)......	C-3B	132	440	55	125	26	4	11	66	.284	42	54	5	654	83	8	.989
1978— Philadelphia (N.L.)......	C-1B-OF	132	435	48	123	18	4	12	62	.283	46	37	2	650	55	8	†.989
1979— Philadelphia (N.L.)......	C-3B	119	398	38	114	21	3	9	58	.286	49	33	1	527	66	8	.987
1980— Philadelphia (N.L.)......	C	141	480	34	110	23	1	9	55	.229	48	41	3	741	88	*18	.979
1981— Philadelphia (N.L.)......	C	76	227	19	48	7	0	4	24	.211	22	16	2	365	32	6	.985
1982— California (A.L.)■......	C	143	472	42	121	17	0	7	58	.256	39	34	0	*650	*87	8	.989
1983— California (A.L.)..........	C	142	468	46	120	18	0	9	52	.256	24	42	4	606	*83	*14	.980
1984— California (A.L.)..........	C	139	450	33	91	16	1	3	32	.202	25	45	3	640	*71	12	.984
1985— California (A.L.)..........	C	150	460	37	114	17	0	5	55	.248	37	35	1	670	71	10	.987
1986— California (A.L.)..........	C	144	442	48	98	12	2	7	49	.222	43	30	1	812	*84	11	.988
1987— Palm Springs (Calif.)..	C	3	9	0	1	1	0	0	0	.111	1	0	0	17	4	1	.955
— California (A.L.)..........	C-DH	128	389	42	94	18	0	3	33	.242	35	36	0	684	56	*13	.983
1988— California (A.L.)..........	C	122	352	38	104	17	0	5	39	.295	29	26	2	506	*66	8	.986
1989— Kansas City (A.L.)■ ...	C	131	405	33	111	13	2	1	43	.274	49	37	3	*752	64	7	.991
1990— Kansas City (A.L.)	C	40	117	11	28	3	0	0	9	.239	17	12	1	243	19	4	.985
American League totals (9 years)		1139	3555	330	881	131	5	40	370	.248	298	297	15	5583	601	87	.986
National League totals (10 years)		1125	3690	349	957	172	21	65	456	.259	365	311	23	5742	584	96	.985
Major League totals (19 years)		2264	7245	679	1838	303	26	105	826	.254	663	608	38	11325	1185	183	.986

DIVISION SERIES RECORD

| | | | | | | BATTING | | | | | | | | FIELDING | | | |
Year Team (League)	Pos.	G	AB	R	H	2B	3B	HR	RBI	Avg.	BB	SO	SB	PO	A	E	Avg.
1981— Philadelphia (N.L.)......	C	3	5	0	0	0	0	0	0	.000	0	0	0	10	2	0	1.000

CHAMPIONSHIP SERIES RECORD

RECORDS: Holds career record for most sacrifice hits—5. ... Shares single-series records for most consecutive hits—5; most singles—9 (1986); and most sacrifice hits—2 (1982). ... Shares A.L. career record for most consecutive hits—5.

| | | | | | | BATTING | | | | | | | | FIELDING | | | |
Year Team (League)	Pos.	G	AB	R	H	2B	3B	HR	RBI	Avg.	BB	SO	SB	PO	A	E	Avg.
1976— Philadelphia (N.L.)......	C	3	7	0	2	0	0	0	1	.286	1	0	0	8	2	0	1.000
1977— Philadelphia (N.L.)......	C	4	10	1	4	0	0	0	0	.400	0	0	0	18	2	0	1.000
1978— Philadelphia (N.L.)......	C	3	11	0	2	0	0	0	0	.182	0	1	0	16	2	1	.947
1980— Philadelphia (N.L.)......	C	5	18	1	4	0	0	0	2	.222	1	2	0	22	3	0	1.000
1982— California (A.L.)..........	C	5	16	3	4	0	0	1	4	.250	0	2	0	30	3	0	1.000
1986— California (A.L.)..........	C	7	22	4	10	0	0	1	2	.455	1	3	0	33	3	0	1.000
Championship series totals (6 years)		27	84	9	26	0	0	2	9	.310	3	8	0	127	15	1	.993

WORLD SERIES RECORD

NOTES: Member of World Series championship team (1980).

| | | | | | | BATTING | | | | | | | | FIELDING | | | |
Year Team (League)	Pos.	G	AB	R	H	2B	3B	HR	RBI	Avg.	BB	SO	SB	PO	A	E	Avg.
1980— Philadelphia (N.L.)......	C	6	17	3	7	2	0	0	4	.412	4	0	0	49	3	0	1.000

ALL-STAR GAME RECORD

| | | | | | BATTING | | | | | | | | FIELDING | | | |
Year League	Pos.	AB	R	H	2B	3B	HR	RBI	Avg.	BB	SO	SB	PO	A	E	Avg.
1976— National	C	2	0	0	0	0	0	0	.000	0	0	0	5	0	0	1.000
1978— National	C	1	1	1	0	0	0	2	1.000	0	0	0	3	1	0	1.000
1979— National	C	2	1	1	0	0	0	0	.500	0	0	0	0	0	0	...
1983— American	C	0	0	0	0	0	0	0	...	0	0	0	1	0	0	1.000
All-Star Game totals (4 years)		5	2	2	0	0	0	2	.400	0	0	0	9	1	0	1.000

RECORD AS MANAGER

BACKGROUND: Coach, Cincinnati Reds (1994). ... Special assistant to general manager, Reds (1998-2000).

| | | REGULAR SEASON | | | | POSTSEASON | | | | | | | |
| | | | | | | Playoff | | Champ. Series | | World Series | | All-Star Game | |
Year Team (League)	W	L	Pct.	Pos.		W	L	W	L	W	L	W	L
1992— Tacoma (PCL)	26	45	.366	5th (N)		—	—	—	—	—	—	—	—
— (Second half)	30	42	.417	5th (N)									
1993— Tacoma (PCL)	30	42	.417	5th (N)		—	—	—	—	—	—	—	—
— (Second half)	37	35	.514	3rd (N)									
1995— Kansas City (A.L.)	70	74	.486	2nd (C)		—	—	—	—	—	—	—	—
1996— Kansas City (A.L.)	75	86	.466	5th (C)		—	—	—	—	—	—	—	—
1997— Kansas City (A.L.)	36	46	.439	—		—	—	—	—	—	—	—	—
Major League Totals (3 years)	181	206	.468			—	—	—	—	—	—	—	—

NOTES:
1997—Replaced as Kansas City manager by Tony Muser, with club in fourth place (July 9).

BOWA, LARRY   PHILLIES

PERSONAL: Born December 6, 1945, in Sacramento. ... 5-10/155. ... Batted both, threw right. ... Full name: Lawrence Robert Bowa.
HIGH SCHOOL: McClathy (Sacramento).
JUNIOR COLLEGE: Sacramento City College.
TRANSACTIONS/CAREER NOTES: Signed as non-drafted free agent by Philadelphia Phillies organization (October 12, 1965). ... On military list (March 7-July 18, 1967). ... On disabled list (July 26-September 1, 1973). ... On disabled list (May 27-June 23, 1975). ... On disabled list (May 25-June 9, 1979). ... Traded with 2B Ryne Sandberg to Chicago Cubs for SS Ivan DeJesus (January 27, 1982). ... Released by Cubs (August 13, 1985). ... Signed by New York Mets (August 20, 1985). ... Granted free agency (November 12, 1985).

STATISTICAL NOTES: Led National League in sacrifice hits with 18 in 1972. ... Led National League shortstops in total chances with 843 in 1971. ... Tied for National League lead in double plays by shortstops with 97 in 1971. ... Led Pacific Coast League in stolen bases with 48 in 1969. ... Led Pacific Coast League shortstops in putouts with 468 in 1969. ... Led Eastern League shortstops in double plays with 77 in 1968. ... Named shortstop on THE SPORTING NEWS National League All-Star Team (1975 and 1978). ... Named shortstop on THE SPORTING NEWS National League All-Star fielding team (1972 and 1978).

								BATTING							FIELDING		
Year	Team (League)	Pos.	G	AB	R	H	2B	3B	HR	RBI	Avg.	BB	SO	SB	PO	A	E	Avg.
1966— Spartanburg (W.Car.) .		SS	97	429	70	134	14	4	2	36	.312	...	...	...	138	284	12	.972
— San Diego (PCL)		SS	5	19	0	6	0	1	0	1	.316	...	...	...	13	20	2	.943
1967— Bakersfield (Calif.)......		SS-2B	7	32	4	6	2	0	0	3	.188	...	...	...	15	12	1	.964
— Reading (East.)..........		SS	22	89	11	25	4	0	0	9	.281	...	...	...	35	79	9	.927
1968— Reading (East.)..........		SS	133	480	47	116	14	2	3	36	.242	...	...	...	192	•395	24	.961
1969— Eugene (PCL)..........		SS-2B	135	568	80	163	11	6	1	26	.287	...	...	...	*215	469	18	.974
1970— Philadelphia (N.L.)......		SS-2B	145	547	50	137	17	6	0	34	.250	21	48	24	202	418	13	.979
1971— Philadelphia (N.L.)......		SS	159	650	74	162	18	5	0	25	.249	36	61	28	272	*560	11	*.987
1972— Philadelphia (N.L.)......		SS	152	579	67	145	11	*13	1	31	.250	31	32	17	212	494	9	*.987
1973— Philadelphia (N.L.)......		SS	122	446	42	94	11	3	0	23	.211	24	31	10	191	361	12	.979
1974— Philadelphia (N.L.)......		SS	162	669	97	184	19	10	1	36	.275	23	52	39	256	462	12	*.984
1975— Philadelphia (N.L.)......		SS	156	624	71	155	15	9	0	49	.248	32	31	30	227	403	25	.962
1976— Philadelphia (N.L.)......		SS	156	624	17	155	15	9	0	49	.248	32	31	30	180	492	17	.975
1977— Philadelphia (N.L.)......		SS	154	624	93	175	19	3	4	41	.280	32	32	32	222	518	13	.983
1978— Philadelphia (N.L.)......		SS	156	654	78	192	31	5	3	43	.294	24	40	27	224	502	10	*.986
1979— Philadelphia (N.L.)......		SS	147	539	74	130	17	11	0	31	.241	61	32	20	229	448	6	*.991
1980— Philadelphia (N.L.)......		SS	147	540	57	144	16	4	2	39	.267	24	28	21	225	449	17	.975
1981— Philadelphia (N.L.)......		SS	103	360	34	102	14	3	0	31	.283	26	17	16	117	309	11	.975
1982— Chicago (N.L.)■......		SS	142	499	50	123	15	7	0	29	.246	39	38	8	210	396	17	.973
1983— Chicago (N.L.)		SS	147	499	73	133	20	5	2	43	.267	35	30	7	230	464	11	*.984
1984— Chicago (N.L.)		SS	133	391	33	87	14	2	0	17	.223	28	24	10	217	378	16	.974
1985— Chicago (N.L.)		SS-2B	72	195	13	48	6	4	0	13	.246	11	20	5	91	197	9	.970
— New York (N.L.)■		SS-2B	14	19	2	2	1	0	0	2	.105	2	2	0	9	6	2	.882
Major League totals (16 years)			2267	8459	925	2168	259	99	13	536	.256	481	549	324	3314	6857	211	.980

DIVISION SERIES RECORD

								BATTING							FIELDING		
Year	Team (League)	Pos.	G	AB	R	H	2B	3B	HR	RBI	Avg.	BB	SO	SB	PO	A	E	Avg.
1981— Philadelphia (N.L.)......		SS	5	17	0	3	1	0	0	1	.176	...	...	...	12	9	1	.955

CHAMPIONSHIP SERIES RECORD

								BATTING							FIELDING		
Year	Team (League)	Pos.	G	AB	R	H	2B	3B	HR	RBI	Avg.	BB	SO	SB	PO	A	E	Avg.
1976— Philadelphia (N.L.)......		SS	3	8	1	1	1	0	0	1	.125	3	0	0	2	11	0	1.000
1977— Philadelphia (N.L.)......		SS	4	17	2	2	0	0	0	1	.118	0	1	0	0	17	0	1.000
1978— Philadelphia (N.L.)......		SS	4	18	2	6	0	0	0	0	.333	1	2	0	5	16	0	1.000
1980— Philadelphia (N.L.)......		SS	5	19	2	6	0	0	0	0	.316	3	3	1	4	11	1	.938
1984— Chicago (N.L.)		SS	5	15	1	3	1	0	0	1	.200	1	0	0	8	15	0	1.000
Championship series totals (5 years)			21	77	8	18	2	0	0	3	.234	8	6	1	19	70	1	.989

WORLD SERIES RECORD

								BATTING							FIELDING		
Year	Team (League)	Pos.	G	AB	R	H	2B	3B	HR	RBI	Avg.	BB	SO	SB	PO	A	E	Avg.
1980— Philadelphia (N.L.)......		SS	6	24	3	9	1	0	0	2	.375	0	0	3	5	18	0	1.000

ALL-STAR GAME RECORD

						BATTING							FIELDING		
Year	League	Pos.	AB	R	H	2B	3B	HR	RBI	Avg.	BB	SO	SB	PO	A	E	Avg.
1974— National		SS	2	0	0	0	0	0	0	.000	0	0	0	2	0	0	1.000
1975— National		SS	0	1	0	0	0	0	0	...	0	0	0	2	0	0	1.000
1976— National		SS	1	0	0	0	0	0	0	.000	0	0	0	2	1	0	1.000
1978— National		SS	3	1	2	0	0	0	0	.667	0	0	0	2	4	0	1.000
1979— National		SS	2	0	0	0	0	0	0	.000	0	0	0	1	3	0	1.000
All-Star Game totals (5 years)			8	2	2	0	0	0	0	.250	0	0	1	9	8	0	1.000

RECORD AS MANAGER

BACKGROUND: Coach, Phillies (May 11, 1989-96). ... Coach, Anaheim Angels (1997-99). ... Coach, Seattle Mariners (2000).

		REGULAR SEASON				POSTSEASON						
						Playoff		Champ. Series		World Series		All-Star Game
Year	Team (League)	W	L	Pct.	Pos.	W	L	W	L	W	L	W	L
1986— Las Vegas (PCL)		36	44	.450	3rd (S)	6	4	—	—	—	—	—	—
— (Second half)		44	28	.611	1st (S)								
1987— San Diego (N.L.)		65	97	.401	6th (W)	—	—	—	—	—	—	—	—
1988— San Diego (N.L.)		16	30	.348	—	—	—	—	—	—	—	—	—
Major League Totals (2 years)		81	127	.389		0	0	0	0	0	0	0	0

NOTES:
1986—Defeated Phoenix, three games to two, in league semifinals; defeated Vancouver, three games to two, to win league championship.
1988—Replaced as Padres manager by Jack McKeon, with club in fifth place (May 28).

BRENLY, BOB — DIAMONDBACKS

PERSONAL: Born February 25, 1954, in Coshocton, Ohio. ... 6-2/205. ... Batted right, threw right. ... Full name: Robert Earl Brenly.
COLLEGE: Ohio University.
TRANSACTIONS/CAREER NOTES: Signed as a free agent by San Francisco Giants organization (June 21, 1976). ... On disabled list (March 25-May 13, 1982). ... Released by Giants (December 21, 1988). ... Signed by Toronto Blue Jays (January 18, 1989). ... Released by Blue Jays (July 14, 1989). ... Signed by Giants organization (August 2, 1989). ... Granted free agency (November 13, 1989).

STATISTICAL NOTES: Led National League catchers in assists with 83 in 1987. ... Led National League catchers in fielding percentage with .995 in 1986. ... Led California League third baseman in double plays with 30 in 1978. ... Led Midwest League third baseman in double plays with 21 in 1977.

Year— Team (League)	Pos.	G	AB	R	H	2B	3B	HR	RBI	Avg.	BB	SO	SB	PO	A	E	Avg.
1976— Great Falls (Pio.)	3B	25	86	16	27	5	1	1	17	.314	12	9	1	10	16	2	.929
— Fresno (Calif.)	3B	17	60	16	22	3	1	1	9	.367	12	17	1	2	6	1	.889
1977— Cedar Rapids (Midw.)	3B-OF	136	499	85	135	16	1	22	73	.271	90	108	6	90	*263	•31	.919
1978— Fresno (Calif.)	3B	135	489	102	139	34	5	17	89	.284	81	90	12	*118	247	27	.931
1979— Fresno (Calif.)	3B	56	212	49	65	11	2	9	37	.307	28	31	6	39	133	17	.910
— Shreveport (Texas)	C-3B-OF-1B	64	193	33	57	8	1	9	30	.295	19	38	0	199	55	7	.973
1980— Shreveport (Texas)	3B	2	10	2	3	0	0	1	3	.300	0	3	1	1	2	0	1.000
— Phoenix (PCL)	3B-C-SS-OF	84	287	34	74	9	6	7	45	.258	24	51	2	183	110	20	.936
1981— Phoenix (PCL)	C-OF-3B	76	257	42	75	11	3	7	41	.292	29	37	2	177	41	9	.960
— San Francisco (N.L.)	C-3B-OF	19	45	5	15	2	1	1	4	.333	6	4	0	52	6	4	.935
1982— San Francisco (N.L.)	C-3B	65	180	26	51	4	1	4	15	.283	18	26	6	265	32	12	.961
1983— San Francisco (N.L.)	C-1B-OF	104	281	36	63	12	2	7	34	.224	37	48	10	465	73	9	.984
1984— San Francisco (N.L.)	C-1B-OF	145	506	74	147	28	0	20	80	.291	48	52	6	807	76	13	.985
1985— San Francisco (N.L.)	C-3B-1B	133	440	41	97	16	1	19	56	.220	57	62	1	719	85	17	.979
1986— San Francisco (N.L.)	C-3B-1B	149	472	60	116	26	0	16	62	.246	74	97	10	688	118	16	.981
1987— San Francisco (N.L.)	C-1B-3B	123	375	55	100	19	1	18	51	.267	47	85	10	685	86	9	.988
1988— San Francisco (N.L.)	C	73	206	13	39	7	0	5	22	.189	20	40	1	334	27	6	.984
1989— Toronto (A.L.)■	C-1B	48	88	9	15	3	1	1	6	.170	10	17	0	61	5	1	.985
— Phoenix (PCL)■	C-3B-1B	27	98	11	25	3	0	2	11	.255	8	12	3	78	16	4	.959
— San Francisco (N.L.)	C	12	22	2	4	2	0	0	3	.182	1	7	1	31	5	0	1.000
American League totals (1 year)		48	88	9	15	3	1	1	6	.170	10	17	0	61	5	1	.985
National League totals (9 years)		823	2527	312	632	116	6	90	327	.250	308	421	45	4046	508	86	.981
Major League totals (9 years)		871	2615	321	647	119	7	91	333	.247	318	438	45	4107	513	87	.982

CHAMPIONSHIP SERIES RECORD

Year— Team (League)	Pos.	G	AB	R	H	2B	3B	HR	RBI	Avg.	BB	SO	SB	PO	A	E	Avg.
1987— San Francisco (N.L.)	C-PH	6	17	3	4	1	0	1	2	.235	3	7	0	28	2	0	1.000

ALL-STAR GAME RECORD

Year— League	Pos.	AB	R	H	2B	3B	HR	RBI	Avg.	BB	SO	SB	PO	A	E	Avg.
1984— National	PH	1	0	0	0	0	0	0	.000	0	1	0	...	...	...	...

RECORD AS MANAGER

BACKGROUND: Broadcaster (1989-2000).

COX, BOBBY — BRAVES

PERSONAL: Born May 21, 1941, in Tulsa, Okla. ... 6-0/185. ... Batted right, threw right. ... Full name: Robert Joe Cox.
HIGH SCHOOL: Selma (Calif.).
JUNIOR COLLEGE: Reedley Junior College (Calif.).
TRANSACTIONS/CAREER NOTES: Signed by Los Angeles Dodgers organization (1959). ... Selected by Chicago Cubs organization from Dodgers organization in Rule 5 minor league draft (November 30, 1964). ... Acquired by Atlanta Braves organization (1966). ... On Austin disabled list (May 8-18 and May 30-June 9, 1966). ... On disabled list (May 1-June 12, 1967). ... Traded by Braves to New York Yankees for C Bob Tillman and P Dale Roberts (December 7, 1967); Roberts later was transferred to Richmond. ... On disabled list (May 28-June 18, 1970). ... Released by Yankees (September 22, 1970). ... Signed by Yankees organization (July 17, 1971). ... Released as player by Fort Lauderdale (August 28, 1971).
STATISTICAL NOTES: Led Alabama-Florida League shortstops with 71 double plays in 1961. ... Led Pacific Coast League third basemen with .954 fielding percentage in 1965.

Year— Team (League)	Pos.	G	AB	R	H	2B	3B	HR	RBI	Avg.	BB	SO	SB	PO	A	E	Avg.
1960— Reno (California)	2B	125	440	99	112	20	5	13	75	.255	95	129	28	282	*385	*39	.945
1961— Salem (Northwest)	2B	14	44	3	9	2	0	0	2	.205	0	14	0	25	25	2	.962
— Panama City (Al.-Fla.)	2B	92	335	66	102	27	4	17	73	.304	48	72	17	220	247	8	*.983
1962— Salem (Northwest)	3B-2B	*141	514	83	143	26	7	16	82	.278	63	119	7	174	296	28	.944
1963— Albuquerque (Texas)	3B	17	53	5	15	2	0	2	5	.283	3	12	1	8	27	1	.972
— Great Falls (Pio.)	3B	109	407	103	137	*31	4	19	85	.337	73	84	7	82	211	21	*.933
1964— Albuquerque (Texas)	2B	138	523	98	152	29	13	16	91	.291	52	84	8	*322	*415	*28	.963
1965— Salt Lake (PCL)■	3B-2B	136	473	58	125	32	1	12	55	.264	35	96	1	133	337	22	†.955
1966— Tacoma (PCL)	3B-2B	10	34	2	4	1	0	0	4	.118	6	9	0	23	15	0	1.000
— Austin (Texas)■	2B-3B	92	339	35	77	11	1	7	30	.227	25	55	7	140	216	12	.967
1967— Richmond (I.L.)	3B-1B	99	350	52	104	17	4	14	51	.297	34	73	3	84	136	8	.965
1968— New York (A.L.)■	3B	135	437	33	100	15	1	7	41	.229	41	85	3	98	279	17	.957
1969— New York (A.L.)	3B	85	191	17	41	7	1	2	17	.215	34	41	0	50	147	11	.947
1970— Syracuse (I.L.)	3B-SS-2B	90	251	34	55	15	0	9	30	.219	49	40	0	86	163	13	.950
1971— Fort Laud. (FSL)	2B-P	4	9	1	1	0	0	0	0	.111	1	0	0	4	5	0	1.000
Major league totals (2 years)		220	628	50	141	22	2	9	58	.225	75	126	3	148	426	28	.953

RECORD AS PITCHER

Year— Team (League)	W	L	Pct.	ERA	G	GS	CG	ShO	Sv.	IP	H	R	ER	BB	SO
1971— Fort Lauderdale (FSL)	0	1	.000	5.40	3	0	0	0	0	10	15	9	6	5	4

RECORD AS MANAGER

BACKGROUND: Minor league instructor, New York Yankees (October 28, 1970-March 24, 1971). ... Player/manager, Fort Lauderdale, Yankees organization (1971). ... Coach, Yankees (1977).

HONORS: Named Major League Manager of the Year by THE SPORTING NEWS (1985). ... Named A.L. Manager of the Year by Baseball Writers' Association of America (1985). ... Named N.L. Manager of the Year by THE SPORTING NEWS (1991, 1993 and 1999). ... Named N.L. Manager of the Year by the Baseball Writers' Association of America (1991).

		REGULAR SEASON				POSTSEASON							
						Playoff		Champ. Series		World Series		All-Star Game	
Year	Team (League)	W	L	Pct.	Pos.	W	L	W	L	W	L	W	L
1971— Fort Lauderdale (Florida State)		71	70	.504	4th (E)	—	—	—	—	—	—	—	—
1972— West Haven (East.)		84	56	.600	1st (A)	3	0	—	—	—	—	—	—
1973— Syracuse (International)		76	70	.521	3rd (A)	—	—	—	—	—	—	—	—
1974— Syracuse (International)		74	70	.514	2nd (N)	—	—	—	—	—	—	—	—
1975— Syracuse (International)		72	64	.529	3rd	—	—	—	—	—	—	—	—
1976— Syracuse (International)		82	57	.590	2nd	6	1	—	—	—	—	—	—
1978— Atlanta (N.L.)		69	93	.426	6th (W)	—	—	—	—	—	—	—	—
1979— Atlanta (N.L.)		66	94	.413	6th (W)	—	—	—	—	—	—	—	—
1980— Atlanta (N.L.)		81	80	.503	4th (W)	—	—	—	—	—	—	—	—
1981— Atlanta (N.L.)		25	29	.463	4th (W)	—	—	—	—	—	—	—	—
— (Second half)		25	27	.481	5th (W)	—	—	—	—	—	—	—	—
1982— Toronto (A.L.)		78	84	.481	T6th (E)	—	—	—	—	—	—	—	—
1983— Toronto (A.L.)		89	73	.549	4th (E)	—	—	—	—	—	—	—	—
1984— Toronto (A.L.)		89	73	.549	2nd (E)	—	—	—	—	—	—	—	—
1985— Toronto (A.L.)		99	62	.615	1st (E)	—	—	3	4	—	—	—	—
1990— Atlanta (N.L.)		40	57	.412	6th (W)	—	—	—	—	—	—	—	—
1991— Atlanta (N.L.)		94	68	.580	1st (W)	—	—	4	3	3	4	—	—
1992— Atlanta (N.L.)		98	64	.605	1st (W)	—	—	4	3	2	4	0	1
1993— Atlanta (N.L.)		104	58	.642	1st (W)	—	—	2	4	—	—	0	1
1994— Atlanta (N.L.)		68	46	.596		—	—	—	—	—	—	—	—
1995— Atlanta (N.L.)		90	54	.625	1st (E)	3	1	4	0	4	2	—	—
1996— Atlanta (N.L.)		96	66	.593	1st (E)	3	0	4	3	2	4	1	0
1997— Atlanta (N.L.)		101	61	.623	1st (E)	3	0	2	4	—	—	0	1
1998— Atlanta (N.L.)		106	56	.654	1st (E)	3	0	2	4	—	—	—	—
1999— Atlanta (N.L.)		103	59	.636	1st (E)	3	0	4	2	0	4	—	—
2000— Atlanta (N.L.)		95	67	.586	1st (E)	0	3	—	—	—	—	0	1
American League totals (4 years)		355	292	.549		—	—	3	4	—	—	—	—
National League totals (15 years)		1261	979	.563		15	4	26	23	11	18	1	4
Major league totals (19 years)		1616	1271	.560		15	4	29	27	11	18	1	4

NOTES:
1972—Defeated Three Rivers in playoff.
1976—Defeated Memphis, three games to none, in playoffs; defeated Richmond, three games to one, in league championship.
1985—Lost to Kansas City in A.L. Championship Series.
1990—Replaced Atlanta manager Russ Nixon with club in sixth place and record of 25-40 (June 22).
1991—Defeated Pittsburgh in N.L. Championship Series; lost to Minnesota in World Series.
1992—Defeated Pittsburgh in N.L. Championship Series; lost to Toronto in World Series.
1993—Lost to Philadelphia in N.L. Championship Series.
1994—Atlanta was in second place in N.L. East at time of season-ending strike (August 12).
1995—Defeated Colorado in N.L. divisional playoff; defeated Cincinnati in N.L. Championship Series; defeated Cleveland in World Series.
1996—Defeated Los Angeles in N.L. divisional playoff; defeated St. Louis in N.L. Championship Series; lost to New York Yankees in World Series.
1997—Defeated Houston in N.L. divisional playoff; lost to Florida in N.L. Championship Series.
1998—Defeated Chicago Cubs in N.L. divisional playoff; lost to San Diego in N.L. Championship Series.
1999—Defeated Houston in N.L. divisional playoff; defeated New York Mets in N.L. Championship Series; lost to New York Yankees in World Series.
2000—Lost to St. Louis in N.L. divisional playoff.

DIERKER, LARRY   ASTROS

PERSONAL: Born September 22, 1946, in Hollywood, Calif. ... 6-4/205. ... Threw right, batted right. ... Full name: Lawrence Edward Dierker. ... Brother of Richard Dierker, pitcher in Baltimore Orioles organization (1972-75). ... Name pronounced DUR-ker.

COLLEGE: UC Santa Barbara, then Houston.

TRANSACTIONS/CAREER NOTES: Signed as free agent by Houston Astros organization (1964). ... Served in military (June 25, 1967-remainder of season). ... On disabled list (March 21-May 22 and June 16-July 12, 1973). ... Traded by Astros with IF Jerry DaVanon to St. Louis Cardinals for C/OF Joe Ferguson and OF Bobby Detherage (November 23, 1976). ... On disabled list (March 23-May 19 and July 23, 1977-remainder of season). ... Released by Cardinals (March 28, 1978).

STATISTICAL NOTES: Led N.L. with 20 wild pitches in 1968. ... Pitched 6-0 no-hit victory against Montreal (July 9, 1976).

MISCELLANEOUS: Holds Houston Astros franchise all-time records for most innings pitched (2,296) and shutouts (25). ... Television and radio color analyst, Astros (1979-1996).

Year	Team (League)	W	L	Pct.	ERA	G	GS	CG	ShO	Sv.	IP	H	R	ER	BB	SO
1964— Cocoa (Cocoa Rookie)		2	3	.400	3.23	9	9	0			39	21	19	14	18	61
— Houston (N.L.)		0	1	.000	2.00	3	1	0	0	0	9	7	4	2	3	5
1965— Houston (N.L.)		7	8	.467	3.49	26	19	1	0	0	147	135	69	57	37	109
1966— Houston (N.L.)		10	8	.556	3.18	29	28	8	2	0	187	173	73	66	45	108
1967— Houston (N.L.)		6	5	.545	3.36	15	15	4	0	0	99	95	44	37	25	68
1968— Houston (N.L.)		12	15	.444	3.31	32	32	10	1	0	234	206	95	86	89	161
1969— Houston (N.L.)		20	13	.606	2.33	39	37	20	4	0	305	240	97	79	72	232
1970— Houston (N.L.)		16	12	.571	3.87	37	36	17	2	1	270	263	124	116	82	191
1971— Houston (N.L.)		12	6	.667	2.72	24	23	6	2	0	159	150	50	48	33	91
1972— Houston (N.L.)		15	8	.652	3.39	31	31	12	5	0	215	209	87	81	51	115
1973— Houston (N.L.)		1	1	.500	4.33	14	3	0	0	0	27	27	14	13	13	18
1974— Houston (N.L.)		11	10	.524	2.89	33	33	7	3	0	224	189	76	72	82	150

MAJOR LEAGUE MANAGERS

Year Team (League)	W	L	Pct.	ERA	G	GS	CG	ShO	Sv.	IP	H	R	ER	BB	SO
1975— Houston (N.L.)	14	16	.467	4.00	34	34	14	2	0	232	225	109	103	91	127
1976— Houston (N.L.)	13	14	.481	3.69	28	28	7	4	0	188	171	85	77	72	112
1977— St. Louis (N.L.)■	2	6	.250	4.62	11	9	0	0	0	39	40	21	20	16	6
Major league totals (14 years)	139	123	.531	3.30	356	329	106	25	1	2335	2130	948	857	711	1493

ALL-STAR GAME RECORD

Year League	W	L	Pct.	ERA	GS	CG	ShO	Sv.	IP	H	R	ER	BB	SO
1969— National	0	0	...	0.00	0	0	0	0	1/3	1	0	0	0	0
1971— National							Selected, did not play—injured.							

RECORD AS MANAGER

HONORS: Named N.L. Manager of the Year by Baseball Writers' Association of America (1998).

	REGULAR SEASON				Playoff		Champ. Series		World Series		All-Star Game	
Year Team (League)	W	L	Pct.	Pos.	W	L	W	L	W	L	W	L
1997— Houston (N.L.)	84	78	.519	1st (C)	0	3	—	—	—	—	—	—
1998— Houston (N.L.)	102	60	.630	1st (C)	1	3	—	—	—	—	—	—
1999— Houston (N.L.)	97	65	.599	1st (C)	1	3	—	—	—	—	—	—
2000— Houston (N.L.)	72	90	.444	4th (C)	—	—	—	—	—	—	—	—
Major league totals (4 years)	355	293	.548		2	9						

NOTES:
1997—Lost to Atlanta in N.L. divisional playoff.
1998—Lost to San Diego in N.L. divisional playoff.
1999—Lost to Atlanta in N.L. divisional playoff.

GARNER, PHIL — TIGERS

PERSONAL: Born April 30, 1949, in Jefferson City, Tenn. ... 5-10/177. ... Batted right, threw right. ... Full name: Philip Mason Garner.
HIGH SCHOOL: Beardon (Knoxville, Tenn.).
COLLEGE: Tennessee (degree in general business, 1973).
TRANSACTIONS/CAREER NOTES: Selected by Montreal Expos organization in eighth round of free-agent draft (June 4, 1970); did not sign. ... Selected by Oakland Athletics organization in secondary phase of free-agent draft (January 13, 1971). ... Traded by A's with IF Tommy Helms and P Chris Batton to Pittsburgh Pirates for P Doc Medich, P Dave Giusti, P Rick Langford, OF Mitchell Page and OF Tony Armas (March 15, 1977). ... On Pittsburgh disabled list (April 2-23, 1981). ... Traded by Pirates to Houston Astros for 2B Johnny Ray and two players to be named later (August 31, 1981); Pirates organization acquired OF Kevin Houston and P Randy Niemann to complete deal (September 9, 1981). ... Granted free agency (November 12, 1986). ... Re-signed by Astros (January 6, 1987). ... Traded by Astros to Los Angeles Dodgers for a player to be named later (June 19, 1987); Astros organization acquired P Jeff Edwards to complete deal (June 26, 1987). ... Granted free agency (November 9, 1987). ... Signed by San Francisco Giants (January 28, 1988). ... On San Francisco disabled list (April 13-September 2, 1988); included rehabilitation assignment to Phoenix (August 5-24). ... Granted free agency (November 3, 1988).
RECORDS: Shares major league record for most grand slams in two consecutive games—2 (September 14-15, 1978).
STATISTICAL NOTES: Led Pacific Coast League third basemen with 104 putouts, 261 assists, 35 errors, 400 total chances and 23 double plays in 1973. ... Led A.L. second basemen with 26 errors in 1975. ... Led A.L. second basemen with 865 total chances in 1976. ... Led N.L. second basemen with 499 assists, 21 errors, 869 total chances and 116 double plays in 1980. ... Career major league grand slams: 3.

							BATTING							FIELDING			
Year Team (League)	Pos.	G	AB	R	H	2B	3B	HR	RBI	Avg.	BB	SO	SB	PO	A	E	Avg.
1971— Burlington (Midw.)	3B	116	439	73	122	22	4	11	70	.278	49	73	8	*122	203	29	.918
1972— Birmingham (Sou.)	3B	71	264	45	74	10	6	12	40	.280	27	43	3	74	116	13	.936
— Iowa (A.A.)	3B	70	247	33	60	18	4	9	22	.243	30	73	7	50	140	10	.950
1973— Tucson (PCL)	3B-2B	138	516	87	149	23	12	14	73	.289	72	90	3	†107	†270	†35	.915
— Oakland (A.L.)	3B	9	5	0	0	0	0	0	0	.000	0	3	0	2	3	0	1.000
1974— Tucson (PCL)	3B-SS	96	388	78	128	29	10	11	51	.330	53	58	8	92	182	15	.948
— Oakland (A.L.)	3B-SS-2B	30	28	4	5	1	0	0	1	.179	1	5	1	11	24	1	.972
1975— Oakland (A.L.)	2B-SS	•160	488	46	120	21	5	6	54	.246	30	65	4	355	427	†26	.968
1976— Oakland (A.L.)	2B	159	555	54	145	29	12	8	74	.261	36	71	35	378	*465	22	.975
1977— Pittsburgh (N.L.)■■	3B-2B-SS	153	585	99	152	35	10	17	77	.260	55	65	32	223	351	17	.971
1978— Pittsburgh (N.L.)	3B-2B-SS	154	528	66	138	25	9	10	66	.261	66	71	27	258	389	28	.959
1979— Pittsburgh (N.L.)	3B-2B-SS	150	549	76	161	32	8	11	59	.293	55	74	17	234	396	22	.966
1980— Pittsburgh (N.L.)	2B-SS	151	548	62	142	27	6	5	58	.259	46	53	32	349	†500	†21	.976
1981— Pittsburgh (N.L.)	2B	56	181	22	46	6	2	1	20	.254	21	21	4	121	148	9	.968
— Houston (N.L.)■	2B	31	113	13	27	3	1	0	6	.239	15	11	6	62	102	3	.982
1982— Houston (N.L.)	2B-3B	155	588	65	161	33	8	13	83	.274	40	92	24	285	464	17	.978
1983— Houston (N.L.)	3B	154	567	76	135	24	2	14	79	.238	63	84	18	100	311	24	.945
1984— Houston (N.L.)	3B-2B	128	374	60	104	17	6	4	45	.278	43	63	3	136	251	12	.970
1985— Houston (N.L.)	3B-2B	135	463	65	124	23	10	6	51	.268	34	72	4	101	229	21	.940
1986— Houston (N.L.)	3B-2B	107	313	43	83	14	3	9	41	.265	30	45	12	66	152	23	.905
1987— Houston (N.L.)	SS-2B	43	112	15	25	5	0	3	15	.223	8	20	1	28	55	2	.976
— Los Angeles (N.L.)■	3B-2B-SS	70	126	14	24	4	0	2	8	.190	20	24	5	37	89	11	.920
1988— San Fran. (N.L.)■	3B	15	13	0	2	0	0	0	1	.154	1	3	0	0	0	0	
— Phoenix (PCL)	2B-3B	17	45	5	12	2	1	1	5	.267	4	4	0	12	22	0	1.000
American League totals (4 years)		358	1076	104	270	51	17	14	129	.251	67	144	40	746	919	49	.971
National League totals (12 years)		1502	5060	676	1324	248	65	95	609	.262	497	698	185	2000	3437	210	.963
Major league totals (16 years)		1860	6136	780	1594	299	82	109	738	.260	564	842	225	2746	4356	259	.965

DIVISION SERIES RECORD

							BATTING							FIELDING			
Year Team (League)	Pos.	G	AB	R	H	2B	3B	HR	RBI	Avg.	BB	SO	SB	PO	A	E	Avg.
1981— Houston (N.L.)	2B	5	18	1	2	0	0	0	0	.111	3	3	0	6	8	1	.933

CHAMPIONSHIP SERIES RECORD

							BATTING							FIELDING		
Year	Team (League)	Pos.	G	AB	R	H	2B	3B	HR	RBI	Avg.	BB	SO	SB	PO	A	E	Avg.
1975—Oakland (A.L.)	2B	3	5	0	0	0	0	0	0	.000	0	1	0	7	4	1	.917
1979—Pittsburgh (N.L.)	2B-SS	3	12	4	5	0	1	1	1	.417	1	0	0	8	9	0	1.000
1986—Houston (N.L.)	3B	3	9	1	2	1	0	0	2	.222	1	2	0	1	9	0	1.000
Championship series totals (3 years)		9	26	5	7	1	1	1	3	.269	2	3	0	16	22	1	.974

WORLD SERIES RECORD

RECORDS: Shares single-series record for collecting one or more hits in each game (1979).

NOTES: Member of World Series championship team (1979).

							BATTING							FIELDING		
Year	Team (League)	Pos.	G	AB	R	H	2B	3B	HR	RBI	Avg.	BB	SO	SB	PO	A	E	Avg.
1979—Pittsburgh (N.L.)	2B	7	24	4	12	4	0	0	5	.500	3	1	0	21	23	2	.957

ALL-STAR GAME RECORD

					BATTING							FIELDING		
Year	League	Pos.	AB	R	H	2B	3B	HR	RBI	Avg.	BB	SO	SB	PO	A	E	Avg.
1976—American	2B	1	0	0	0	0	0	0	.000	0	1	0	1	1	0	1.000
1980—National	2B	2	1	1	0	0	0	0	.500	1	1	1	1	3	0	1.000
1981—National	2B	0	0	0	0	0	0	0	...	0	0	0	0	0	0	...
All-Star Game totals (3 years)		3	1	1	0	0	0	0	.333	1	2	1	2	4	0	1.000

BACKGROUND: Coach, Houston Astros (1989-91).

RECORD AS MANAGER

	REGULAR SEASON				POSTSEASON							
					Playoff		Champ. Series		World Series		All-Star Game	
Year	Team (League)	W	L	Pct.	Pos.	W	L	W	L	W	L	W	L
1992—Milwaukee (A.L.)	92	70	.568	2nd (E)	—	—	—	—	—	—	—	—
1993—Milwaukee (A.L.)	69	93	.426	7th (E)	—	—	—	—	—	—	—	—
1994—Milwaukee (A.L.)	53	62	.461		—	—	—	—	—	—	—	—
1995—Milwaukee (A.L.)	65	79	.451	4th (C)	—	—	—	—	—	—	—	—
1996—Milwaukee (A.L.)	80	82	.494	3rd (C)	—	—	—	—	—	—	—	—
1997—Milwaukee (A.L.)	78	83	.484	3rd (C)	—	—	—	—	—	—	—	—
1998—Milwaukee (A.L.)	74	88	.457	5th (C)	—	—	—	—	—	—	—	—
1999—Milwaukee (N.L.)	52	60	.464		—	—	—	—	—	—	—	—
2000—Detroit (A.L.)	79	83	.488	3rd (C)	—	—	—	—	—	—	—	—
American League totals (7 years)	516	552	.483		—	—	—	—	—	—	—	—
National League totals (2 year)	126	148	.460		—	—	—	—	—	—	—	—
Major league totals (9 years)	642	700	.478		—	—	—	—	—	—	—	—

NOTES:
1993—On suspended list (September 24-27).
1994—Milwaukee was in fifth place in A.L. Central at time of season-ending strike (August 12).
1995—On suspended list (July 27-31).
1999—Replaced as manager on interim basis by Joe Lefebvre, with team in fifth place (August 11).

HARGROVE, MIKE   ORIOLES

PERSONAL: Born October 26, 1949, in Perryton, Texas. ... 6-0/195. ... Batted left, threw left. ... Full name: Dudley Michael Hargrove.

HIGH SCHOOL: Perryton (Texas).

COLLEGE: Northwestern State, Okla. (degree in physical education and social sciences).

TRANSACTIONS/CAREER NOTES: Selected by Texas Rangers organization in 25th round of free-agent draft (June 6, 1972). ... Traded by Rangers with 3B Kurt Bevacqua and C Bill Fahey to San Diego Padres for OF Oscar Gamble, C Dave Roberts and cash (October 25, 1978). ... Traded by Padres to Cleveland Indians for OF Paul Dade (June 14, 1979). ... Granted free agency (November 12, 1985).

HONORS: Named Western Carolinas League Player of the Year (1973). ... Named A.L. Rookie Player of the Year by THE SPORTING NEWS (1974). ... Named A.L. Rookie of the Year by Baseball Writers' Association of America (1974).

STATISTICAL NOTES: Led New York-Pennsylvania League first basemen with 58 double plays in 1972. ... Led Western Carolinas League with 247 total bases in 1973. ... Led Western Carolinas League first basemen with 118 double plays in 1973. ... Had 23-game hitting streak (April 16-May 15, 1980). ... Led A.L. first basemen with 1,489 total chances in 1980. ... Led A.L. with .432 on-base percentage in 1981. ... Career major league grand slams: 1.

							BATTING							FIELDING		
Year	Team (League)	Pos.	G	AB	R	H	2B	3B	HR	RBI	Avg.	BB	SO	SB	PO	A	E	Avg.
1972—Geneva (NY-Penn)	1B	•70	243	38	65	8	0	4	37	.267	52	44	3	*537	•40	10	*.983
1973—Gastonia (W. Car.)	1B	•130	456	88	*160	*35	8	12	82	*.351	68	47	10	*1121	•77	14	*.988
1974—Texas (A.L.)	1B-DH-OF	131	415	57	134	18	6	4	66	.323	49	42	0	638	72	9	.987
1975—Texas (A.L.)	OF-1B-DH	145	519	82	157	22	2	11	62	.303	79	66	4	513	45	13	.977
1976—Texas (A.L.)	1B	151	541	80	155	30	1	7	58	.287	*97	64	2	1222	110	*21	.984
1977—Texas (A.L.)	1B	153	525	98	160	28	4	18	69	.305	103	59	2	1393	100	11	.993
1978—Texas (A.L.)	1B-DH	146	494	63	124	24	1	7	40	.251	*107	47	2	1221	*116	*17	.987
1979—San Diego (N.L.)■	1B	52	125	15	24	5	0	0	8	.192	25	15	0	323	17	5	.986
—Cleveland (A.L.)■..........	OF-1B-DH	100	338	60	110	21	4	10	56	.325	63	40	2	356	16	2	.995
1980—Cleveland (A.L.)	1B	160	589	86	179	22	2	11	85	.304	111	36	4	*1391	87	11	.993
1981—Cleveland (A.L.)	1B-DH	94	322	43	102	21	0	2	49	.317	60	16	5	766	76	•9	.989
1982—Cleveland (A.L.)	1B-DH	160	591	67	160	26	1	4	65	.271	101	58	2	1293	*123	5	.996
1983—Cleveland (A.L.)	1B-DH	134	469	57	134	21	4	3	57	.286	78	40	0	1098	115	7	.994
1984—Cleveland (A.L.)	1B	133	352	44	94	14	2	2	44	.267	53	38	0	790	83	8	.991
1985—Cleveland (A.L.)	1B-DH-OF	107	284	31	81	14	1	1	27	.285	39	29	1	599	66	6	.991
American League totals (12 years)		1614	5439	768	1590	261	28	80	678	.292	940	535	24	11280	1010	118	.990
National League totals (1 year)		52	125	15	24	5	0	0	8	.192	25	15	0	323	17	5	.986
Major league totals (12 years)		1666	5564	783	1614	266	28	80	686	.290	965	550	24	11603	1027	123	.990

ALL-STAR GAME RECORD

Year League	Pos.	AB	R	H	2B	3B	HR	RBI	Avg.	BB	SO	SB	PO	A	E	Avg.
						BATTING								FIELDING		
1975— American	PH	1	0	0	0	0	0	0	.000	0	0	0	...	...	...	...

RECORD AS MANAGER

BACKGROUND: Minor league coach, Cleveland Indians organization (1986). ... Coach, Indians (1990-July 6, 1991).

HONORS: Named Carolina League Manager of the Year (1987). ... Named Pacific Coast League Manager of the Year (1989). ... Named A.L. Manager of the Year by THE SPORTING NEWS (1995).

Year Team (League)	W	L	Pct.	Pos.	Playoff W	Playoff L	Champ. Series W	Champ. Series L	World Series W	World Series L	All-Star Game W	All-Star Game L
					REGULAR SEASON			POSTSEASON				
1987— Kinston (Carolina)	33	37	.471	T3rd (S)	—	—	—	—	—	—	—	—
— (Second half)	42	28	.600	1st (S)	3	3	—	—	—	—	—	—
1988— Williamsport (East.)	66	73	.475	6th	—	—	—	—	—	—	—	—
1989— Colorado Springs (Pacific Coast).............	44	26	.629	1st (S)	—	—	—	—	—	—	—	—
— (Second half)	34	38	.472	3rd (S)	2	3	—	—	—	—	—	—
1991— Cleveland (A.L.)	32	53	.376	7th (E)	—	—	—	—	—	—	—	—
1992— Cleveland (A.L.)	76	86	.469	T4th (E)	—	—	—	—	—	—	—	—
1993— Cleveland (A.L.)	76	86	.469	6th (E)	—	—	—	—	—	—	—	—
1994— Cleveland (A.L.)	66	47	.584		—	—	—	—	—	—	—	—
1995— Cleveland (A.L.)	100	44	.694	1st (C)	3	0	4	2	2	4	—	—
1996— Cleveland (A.L.)	99	62	.615	1st (C)	1	3	—	—	—	—	0	1
1997— Cleveland (A.L.)	86	75	.534	1st (C)	3	2	4	2	3	4	—	—
1998— Cleveland (A.L.)	89	73	.549	1st (C)	3	1	2	4	—	—	1	0
1999— Cleveland (A.L.)	97	65	.599	1st (C)	2	3	—	—	—	—	—	—
2000— Baltimore (A.L.)	74	88	.457	4th (E)	—	—	—	—	—	—	—	—
Major league totals (10 years)	**795**	**679**	**.539**		**11**	**9**	**10**	**8**	**5**	**8**	**1**	**1**

NOTES:
1987—Defeated Winston-Salem, two games to none, in playoffs; lost to Salem, three games to one, in league championship.
1989—Lost to Albuquerque in playoffs.
1991—Replaced Cleveland manager John McNamara with club in seventh place and record of 25-52 (July 6).
1994—Cleveland was in second place in A.L. Central at time of season-ending strike (August 12).
1995—Defeated Boston in A.L. divisional playoff; defeated Seattle in A.L. Championship Series; lost to Atlanta in World Series.
1996—Lost to Baltimore in A.L. divisional playoff.
1997—Defeated New York in A.L. divisional playoff; defeated Baltimore in A.L. Championship Series; lost to Florida in World Series.
1998—Defeated Boston in A.L. divisional playoff; lost to New York Yankees in A.L. Championship Series.
1999—Lost to Boston in A.L. divisional playoff.

HOWE, ART   ATHLETICS

PERSONAL: Born December 15, 1946, in Pittsburgh. ... 6-1/185. ... Batted right, threw right. ... Full name: Arthur Henry Howe Jr.

HIGH SCHOOL: Shaler (Glenshaw, Pa.).

COLLEGE: Wyoming (bachelor of science degree in business administration, 1969).

TRANSACTIONS/CAREER NOTES: Signed as free agent by Pittsburgh Pirates organization (June, 1971). ... On disabled list (August 17-September 2, 1972 and April 13-May 6, 1973). ... Traded by Pirates to Houston Astros (January 6, 1976), completing deal in which Astros traded 2B Tommy Helms to Pirates for a player to be named later (December 12, 1975). ... On disabled list (May 12-June 19, 1982 and March 27, 1983-entire season). ... Granted free agency (November 7, 1983). ... Signed by St. Louis Cardinals (March 21, 1984). ... Released by Cardinals (April 22, 1985).

STATISTICAL NOTES: Tied for Carolina League lead in putouts by third baseman with 95 in 1971. ... Led International League third basemen with 22 errors and 24 double plays in 1972. ... Had 23-game hitting streak (May 1-24, 1981). ... Career major league grand slams: 1.

Year Team (League)	Pos.	G	AB	R	H	2B	3B	HR	RBI	Avg.	BB	SO	SB	PO	A	E	Avg.
								BATTING							FIELDING		
1971— Salem (Carolina)	3B-SS	114	382	77	133	27	7	12	79	*.348	82	74	11	‡110	221	21	.940
1972— Char., W.Va. (I.L.).......	3B-2B-SS	109	365	68	99	21	3	14	53	.271	63	69	8	105	248	†24	.936
1973— Char., W.Va. (I.L.).......	3B-2B-SS	119	372	50	85	20	1	8	44	.228	54	70	6	141	229	21	.946
1974— Char., W.Va. (I.L.).......	3B	60	207	26	70	17	4	8	36	.338	31	27	4	35	90	9	.933
— Pittsburgh (N.L.)........	3B-SS	29	74	10	18	4	1	1	5	.243	9	13	0	11	49	4	.938
1975— Char., W.Va. (I.L.).......	3B-2B	11	42	4	15	1	3	0	3	.357	2	4	0	15	23	1	.974
— Pittsburgh (N.L.)........	3B-SS	63	146	13	25	9	0	1	10	.171	15	15	1	19	89	7	.939
1976— Memphis (I.L.)■.......	3B-1B	74	259	50	92	21	3	12	59	.355	34	31	1	93	120	14	.938
— Houston (N.L.)	3B-2B	21	29	0	4	1	0	0	0	.138	6	6	0	17	16	1	.971
1977— Houston (N.L.)	2B-3B-SS	125	413	44	109	23	7	8	58	.264	41	60	0	213	333	8	.986
1978— Houston (N.L.)	2B-3B-1B	119	420	46	123	33	3	7	55	.293	34	41	2	240	302	13	.977
1979— Houston (N.L.)	2B-3B-1B	118	355	32	88	15	2	6	33	.248	36	37	3	188	261	7	.985
1980— Houston (N.L.)	1-3-2-S	110	321	34	91	12	5	10	46	.283	34	29	1	598	86	10	.986
1981— Houston (N.L.)	3B-1B	103	361	43	107	22	4	3	46	.296	41	23	1	67	206	9	.968
1982— Houston (N.L.)	3B-1B	110	365	29	87	15	1	5	38	.238	41	45	2	344	174	7	.987
1983—						Did not play.											
1984— St. Louis (N.L.)■.......	3-1-2-S	89	139	17	30	5	0	2	12	.216	18	18	0	71	80	3	.981
1985— St. Louis (N.L.)..........	1B-3B	4	3	0	0	0	0	0	0	.000	0	0	0	5	1	0	1.000
Major league totals (11 years)		**891**	**2626**	**268**	**682**	**139**	**23**	**43**	**293**	**.260**	**275**	**287**	**10**	**1773**	**1597**	**69**	**.980**

DIVISION SERIES RECORD

Year Team (League)	Pos.	G	AB	R	H	2B	3B	HR	RBI	Avg.	BB	SO	SB	PO	A	E	Avg.
								BATTING							FIELDING		
1981— Houston (N.L.)	3B	5	17	1	4	0	0	1	1	.235	2	1	0	6	9	0	1.000

CHAMPIONSHIP SERIES RECORD

						BATTING								FIELDING		
Year Team (League)	Pos.	G	AB	R	H	2B	3B	HR	RBI	Avg.	BB	SO	SB	PO	A	E	Avg.
1974— Pittsburgh (N.L.)	PH	1	1	0	0	0	0	0	0	.000	0	0	0	...	...	...	...
1980— Houston (N.L.)	1B-PH	5	15	0	3	1	1	0	2	.200	2	2	0	29	3	0	1.000
Championship series totals (2 years)		6	16	0	3	1	1	0	2	.188	2	2	0	29	3	0	1.000

RECORD AS MANAGER

BACKGROUND: Coach, Texas Rangers (May 21, 1985-88). ... Scout, Los Angeles Dodgers organization (1994). ... Coach, Colorado Rockies (1995).

	REGULAR SEASON					POSTSEASON						
					Playoff		Champ. Series		World Series		All-Star Game	
Year Team (League)	W	L	Pct.	Pos.	W	L	W	L	W	L	W	L
1989— Houston (N.L.)	86	76	.531	3rd (W)	—	—	—	—	—	—	—	—
1990— Houston (N.L.)	75	87	.463	T4th (W)	—	—	—	—	—	—	—	—
1991— Houston (N.L.)	65	97	.401	6th (W)	—	—	—	—	—	—	—	—
1992— Houston (N.L.)	81	81	.500	4th (W)	—	—	—	—	—	—	—	—
1993— Houston (N.L.)	85	77	.525	3rd (W)	—	—	—	—	—	—	—	—
1996— Oakland (A.L.)	78	84	.481	3rd (W)	—	—	—	—	—	—	—	—
1997— Oakland (A.L.)	65	97	.401	4th (W)	—	—	—	—	—	—	—	—
1998— Oakland (A.L.)	74	88	.457	4th (W)	—	—	—	—	—	—	—	—
1999— Oakland (A.L.)	87	75	.537	2nd (W)	—	—	—	—	—	—	—	—
2000— Oakland (A.L.)	91	70	.565	1st (W)	2	3	—	—	—	—	—	—
National League totals (5 years)	392	418	.484		—	—	—	—	—	—	—	—
American League totals (5 years)	395	414	.488		2	3	—	—	—	—	—	—
Major league totals (10 years)	787	832	.486		2	3	—	—	—	—	—	—

NOTES:
2000—Lost to New York Yankees in A.L. divisional playoff.

KELLY, TOM   TWINS

PERSONAL: Born August 15, 1950, in Graceville, Minn. ... 5-11/185. ... Batted left, threw left. ... Full name: Jay Thomas Kelly.
HIGH SCHOOL: St. Mary's (South Amboy, N.J.).
JUNIOR COLLEGE: Mesa (Ariz.) Community College.
COLLEGE: Monmouth College (N.J.).
TRANSACTIONS/CAREER NOTES: Selected by Seattle Pilots organization in eighth round of free-agent draft (June 7, 1968). ... Seattle franchise moved to Milwaukee and renamed Brewers (1970). ... On temporarily inactive list (April 16-20, April 25-30 and August 21, 1970-remainder of season). ... On military list (August 27, 1970-February 3, 1971). ... Released by Brewers organization (April 6, 1971). ... Signed by Charlotte, Minnesota Twins organization (April 28, 1971). ... Loaned by Twins organization to Rochester, Baltimore Orioles organization (April 5-September 22, 1976). ... On temporarily inactive list (April 15-19, 1977). ... On disabled list (July 25-August 4, 1977). ... Released by Toledo (December 18, 1978). ... Re-signed by Visalia, Twins organization (January 2, 1979). ... Released by Twins organization (December 2, 1980).
STATISTICAL NOTES: Led Pacific Coast League outfielders with six double plays in 1972.

						BATTING								FIELDING		
Year Team (League)	Pos.	G	AB	R	H	2B	3B	HR	RBI	Avg.	BB	SO	SB	PO	A	E	Avg.
1968— Newark (NY-Penn)......	OF	65	218	50	69	11	4	2	10	.317	43	31	*16	*144	*9	3	.981
1969— Clinton (Midwest).......	OF	100	269	47	60	10	2	6	35	.223	82	31	10	158	15	4	.977
1970— Jacksonville (Sou.)......	OF-1B	93	266	33	64	10	1	8	38	.241	41	37	2	204	19	4	.982
1971— Charlotte (Sou.)■...	1B-OF	100	303	50	89	17	0	6	41	.294	59	52	2	508	38	9	.984
1972— Tacoma (PCL)	OF-1B	132	407	76	114	19	2	10	52	.280	70	95	4	282	19	10	.968
1973— Tacoma (PCL)	OF-1B	114	337	67	87	10	2	17	49	.258	89	64	4	200	20	6	.973
1974— Tacoma (PCL)	OF-1B	115	357	68	110	16	0	18	69	.308	78	41	4	514	41	3	.995
1975— Tacoma (PCL)	OF-1B	62	202	38	51	5	0	9	29	.252	47	36	6	185	12	6	.970
— Minnesota (A.L.) ...	1B-DH-OF	49	127	11	23	5	0	1	11	.181	15	22	0	360	28	6	.985
1976— Rochester (I.L.)■...	OF-1B	127	405	71	117	19	3	18	70	.289	85	71	2	323	28	4	.989
1977— Tacoma (PCL)■	1B-OF-P	113	363	80	99	12	1	12	64	.273	78	61	11	251	15	6	.978
1978— Toledo (I.L.)	1B-OF	119	325	47	74	13	0	10	49	.228	*91	61	2	556	46	5	.992
1979— Visalia (California)■...	1B-P	2	0	0	0	0	0	0	0	...	1	0	0	3	4	0	1.000
Major league totals (1 year)		49	127	11	23	5	0	1	11	.181	15	22	0	360	28	6	.985

RECORD AS PITCHER

Year Team (League)	W	L	Pct.	ERA	G	GS	CG	ShO	Sv.	IP	H	R	ER	BB	SO
1977— Tacoma (PCL)	0	0	...	6.00	1	0	0	0	0	3	2	2	2	3	0
1979— Visalia (California)	1	0	1.000	2.25	1	1	0	0	0	8	5	3	2	7	2
1980— Visalia (California)	0	0	...	0.69	2	1	0	0	0	13	12	1	1	6	2

RECORD AS MANAGER

BACKGROUND: Player/manager, Tacoma, Minnesota Twins organization (June 1977-remainder of season). ... Player/coach, Toledo, Twins organization (1978). ... Coach, Twins (1983-September 11, 1986).
HONORS: Named California League Manager of the Year (1979). ... Named California League co-Manager of the Year (1980). ... Named Southern League Manager of the Year (1981). ... Named A.L. Manager of the Year by THE SPORTING NEWS (1991). ... Named A.L. Manager of the Year by Baseball Writers' Association of America (1991).

	REGULAR SEASON					POSTSEASON						
					Playoff		Champ. Series		World Series		All-Star Game	
Year Team (League)	W	L	Pct.	Pos.	W	L	W	L	W	L	W	L
1977— Tacoma (Pacific Coast)	28	26	.519	3rd (W)	—	—	—	—	—	—	—	—
1979— Visalia (California).................................	44	26	.629	1st (S)	—	—	—	—	—	—	—	—
— (Second half)	42	28	.600	2nd (S)	1	2	—	—	—	—	—	—

| | | REGULAR SEASON | | | | POSTSEASON | | | | | | | |
| | | | | | | Playoff | | Champ. Series | | World Series | | All-Star Game | |
Year Team (League)	W	L	Pct.	Pos.	W	L	W	L	W	L	W	L
1980— Visalia (California)	27	43	.386	4th (S)	—	—	—	—	—	—	—	—
— (Second half)	44	26	.629	1st (S)	2	4	—	—	—	—	—	—
1981— Orlando (Southern)	42	27	.609	1st (E)	—	—	—	—	—	—	—	—
— (Second half)	37	36	.507	3rd (E)	6	2	—	—	—	—	—	—
1982— Orlando (Southern)	31	38	.449	5th (E)	—	—	—	—	—	—	—	—
— (Second half)	43	32	.573	2nd (E)	—	—	—	—	—	—	—	—
1986— Minnesota (A.L.)	12	11	.522	6th (W)	—	—	—	—	—	—	—	—
1987— Minnesota (A.L.)	85	77	.525	1st (W)	—	—	4	1	4	3	—	—
1988— Minnesota (A.L.)	91	71	.562	2nd (W)	—	—	—	—	—	—	1	0
1989— Minnesota (A.L.)	80	82	.494	5th (W)	—	—	—	—	—	—	—	—
1990— Minnesota (A.L.)	74	88	.457	7th (W)	—	—	—	—	—	—	—	—
1991— Minnesota (A.L.)	95	67	.586	1st (W)	—	—	4	1	4	3	—	—
1992— Minnesota (A.L.)	90	72	.556	2nd (W)	—	—	—	—	—	—	1	0
1993— Minnesota (A.L.)	71	91	.438	T5th (W)	—	—	—	—	—	—	—	—
1994— Minnesota (A.L.)	53	60	.469		—	—	—	—	—	—	—	—
1995— Minnesota (A.L.)	56	88	.389	5th (C)	—	—	—	—	—	—	—	—
1996— Minnesota (A.L.)	78	84	.481	4th (C)	—	—	—	—	—	—	—	—
1997— Minnesota (A.L.)	68	94	.420	4th (C)	—	—	—	—	—	—	—	—
1998— Minnesota (A.L.)	70	92	.432	4th (C)	—	—	—	—	—	—	—	—
1999— Minnesota (A.L.)	63	97	.394	5th (C)	—	—	—	—	—	—	—	—
2000— Minnesota (A.L.)	69	93	.426	5th (C)	—	—	—	—	—	—	—	—
Major league totals (15 years)	1055	1167	.475		—	—	8	2	8	6	2	0

NOTES:
1977—Replaced Tacoma manager Del Wilber with record of 40-49 and became player/manager (June).
1979—Lost to San Jose in semifinals.
1980—Defeated Fresno, two games to one, in semifinals; lost to Stockton, three games to none, in league championship.
1981—Defeated Savannah, three games to one, in semifinals; defeated Nashville, three games to one, in league championship.
1986—Replaced Minnesota manager Ray Miller with club in seventh place and record of 59-80 (September 12).
1987—Defeated Detroit in A.L. Championship Series; defeated St. Louis in World Series.
1991—Defeated Toronto in A.L. Championship Series; defeated Atlanta in World Series.
1994—Minnesota was in fourth place in A.L. Central at time of season-ending strike (August 12).

La RUSSA, TONY — CARDINALS

PERSONAL: Born October 4, 1944, in Tampa. ... 6-0/185. ... Batted right, threw right. ... Full name: Anthony La Russa Jr.

HIGH SCHOOL: Jefferson (Tampa).

COLLEGE: University of Tampa, then South Florida (degree in industrial management), then Florida State (law degree, 1980).

TRANSACTIONS/CAREER NOTES: Signed by Kansas City Athletics organization (June 6, 1962). ... On disabled list (May 9-September 8, 1964; June 3-July 15, 1965; and April 12-May 6 and July 3-September 5, 1967). ... A's franchise moved from Kansas City to Oakland (October 1967). ... Contract sold by A's to Atlanta Braves (August 14, 1971). ... Traded by Braves to Chicago Cubs for P Tom Phoebus (October 20, 1972). ... Contract sold by Cubs to Pittsburgh Pirates organization (March 23, 1974). ... Released by Pirates (April 4, 1975). ... Signed by Chicago White Sox organization (April 7, 1975). ... On disabled list (August 8-18, 1976). ... Contract sold by White Sox to St. Louis Cardinals organization (December 13, 1976). ... Released by Cardinals (September 29, 1977).

STATISTICAL NOTES: Led International League in being hit by pitch with 11 in 1972.

| | | | | | | | BATTING | | | | | | | | | | FIELDING | | |
Year Team (League)	Pos.	G	AB	R	H	2B	3B	HR	RBI	Avg.	BB	SO	SB	PO	A	E	Avg.
1962— Daytona Beach (FSL)	SS	64	225	37	58	7	0	1	32	.258	42	47	11	135	173	38	.890
— Binghamton (East.)	SS-2B	12	43	3	8	0	0	0	4	.186	5	9	2	20	27	8	.855
1963— Kansas City (A.L.)	SS-2B	34	44	4	11	1	1	0	1	.250	7	12	0	29	25	2	.964
1964— Lewiston (N'west)	2B-SS	90	329	50	77	22	1	1	25	.234	53	56	10	188	218	18	.958
1965— Birmingham (Sou.)	2B	75	259	24	50	11	2	1	18	.193	26	37	5	202	161	21	.945
1966— Modesto (California)	2B	81	316	67	92	20	1	7	54	.291	44	37	18	201	212	20	.954
— Mobile (Southern)	2B	51	170	20	50	9	4	4	26	.294	23	24	4	117	133	10	.962
1967— Birmingham (Sou.)	2B	41	139	12	32	6	1	5	22	.230	10	11	3	88	120	5	.977
1968— Oakland (A.L.)	PH	5	3	0	1	0	0	0	0	.333	0	0	0	...	...	...	...
— Vancouver (PCL)	2B	122	455	55	109	16	8	5	29	.240	52	58	14	249	321	14	*.976
1969— Iowa (A.A.)	2B	67	235	37	72	11	1	4	27	.306	0	1	5	177	222	15	.964
— Oakland (A.L.)	PH	8	8	0	0	0	0	0	0	.000	42	30	0	...	...	...	...
1970— Iowa (A.A.)	2B	22	88	13	22	5	0	2	5	.250	9	14	0	52	59	3	.974
— Oakland (A.L.)	2B	52	106	6	21	4	1	0	6	.198	15	19	0	67	89	5	.969
1971— Iowa (A.A.)	2-3-S-O	28	107	21	31	5	1	2	11	.290	10	11	0	70	85	2	.987
— Oakland (A.L.)	2B-SS-3B	23	8	3	0	0	0	0	0	.000	0	4	0	8	7	2	.882
— Atlanta (N.L.)■	2B	9	7	1	2	0	0	0	0	.286	1	1	0	8	6	1	.933
1972— Richmond (I.L.)	2B	122	389	68	120	13	2	10	42	.308	72	41	0	305	289	20	.967
1973— Wichita (A.A.)■	2B-1B-3B	106	392	82	123	16	0	5	75	.314	60	46	10	423	213	26	.961
— Chicago (N.L.)	PR	1	0	1	0	0	0	0	0	...	0	0	0	...	...	...	...
1974— Char., W.Va. (I.L.)■	2B	139	457	50	119	17	1	8	35	.260	51	50	4	262	*378	17	.974
1975— Denver (A.A.)■	3-O-S-2	118	354	87	99	23	2	7	46	.280	70	46	13	95	91	10	.949
1976— Iowa (A.A.)	3-2-S-1-O-P	107	332	53	86	11	0	4	34	.259	40	43	10	132	160	22	.930
1977— New Orleans (A.A.)■	2B-3B	50	128	17	24	2	2	3	6	.188	20	21	0	66	87	7	.956
American League totals (5 years)		122	169	13	33	5	2	0	7	.195	64	65	0	104	121	9	.962
National League totals (2 years)		10	7	2	2	0	0	0	0	.286	1	1	0	8	6	1	.933
Major league totals (6 years)		132	176	15	35	5	2	0	7	.199	65	66	0	112	127	10	.960

RECORD AS PITCHER

Year	Team (League)	W	L	Pct.	ERA	G	GS	CG	ShO	Sv.	IP	H	R	ER	BB	SO
1976— Iowa (A.A.)		0	0	...	3.00	3	0	0	0	0	3	3	1	1	0	0

RECORD AS MANAGER

BACKGROUND: Coach, St. Louis Cardinals organization (June 20-September 29, 1977). ... Coach, Chicago White Sox (July 3, 1978-remainder of season).

RECORDS: Shares major league single-season record for most clubs managed—2 (1986).

HONORS: Named Major League Manager of the Year by THE SPORTING NEWS (1983). ... Named A.L. Manager of the Year by Baseball Writers' Association of America (1983, 1988 and 1992). ... Named A.L. Manager of the Year by THE SPORTING NEWS (1988 and 1992).

		REGULAR SEASON				Playoff		Champ. Series		World Series		All-Star Game	
Year	Team (League)	W	L	Pct.	Pos.	W	L	W	L	W	L	W	L
1978— Knoxville (Southern)		49	21	.700	1st (W)	—	—	—	—	—	—	—	—
— (Second half)		4	4	.500		—	—	—	—	—	—	—	—
1979— Iowa (American Association)		54	52	.509		—	—	—	—	—	—	—	—
— Chicago (A.L.)		27	27	.500	5th (W)	—	—	—	—	—	—	—	—
1980— Chicago (A.L.)		70	90	.438	5th (W)	—	—	—	—	—	—	—	—
1981— Chicago (A.L.)		31	22	.585	3rd (W)	—	—	—	—	—	—	—	—
— (Second half)		23	30	.434	6th (W)	—	—	—	—	—	—	—	—
1982— Chicago (A.L.)		87	75	.537	3rd (W)	—	—	—	—	—	—	—	—
1983— Chicago (A.L.)		99	63	.611	1st (W)	—	—	1	3	—	—	—	—
1984— Chicago (A.L.)		74	88	.457	T5th (W)	—	—	—	—	—	—	—	—
1985— Chicago (A.L.)		85	77	.525	3rd (W)	—	—	—	—	—	—	—	—
1986— Chicago (A.L.)		26	38	.406		—	—	—	—	—	—	—	—
— Oakland (A.L.)		45	34	.570	T3rd (W)	—	—	—	—	—	—	—	—
1987— Oakland (A.L.)		81	81	.500	3rd (W)	—	—	—	—	—	—	—	—
1988— Oakland (A.L.)		104	58	.642	1st (W)	—	—	4	0	1	4	—	—
1989— Oakland (A.L.)		99	63	.611	1st (W)	—	—	4	1	4	0	1	0
1990— Oakland (A.L.)		103	59	.636	1st (W)	—	—	4	0	0	4	1	0
1991— Oakland (A.L.)		84	78	.519	4th (W)	—	—	—	—	—	—	1	0
1992— Oakland (A.L.)		96	66	.593	1st (W)	—	—	2	4	—	—	—	—
1993— Oakland (A.L.)		68	94	.420	7th (W)	—	—	—	—	—	—	—	—
1994— Oakland (A.L.)		51	63	.447		—	—	—	—	—	—	—	—
1995— Oakland (A.L.)		67	77	.465	4th (W)	—	—	—	—	—	—	—	—
1996— St. Louis (N.L.)		88	74	.543	1st (C)	3	0	3	4	—	—	—	—
1997— St. Louis (N.L.)		73	89	.451	4th (C)	—	—	—	—	—	—	—	—
1998— St. Louis (N.L.)		83	79	.512	3rd (C)	—	—	—	—	—	—	—	—
1999— St. Louis (N.L.)		75	86	.466	4th (C)	—	—	—	—	—	—	—	—
2000— St. Louis (N.L.)		95	67	.586	1st (C)	3	0	1	4	—	—	—	—
American League totals (17 years)		1320	1183	.527		—	—	15	8	5	8	3	0
National League totals (5 years)		414	395	.512		6	0	4	8	—	—	—	—
Major League totals (22 years)		1734	1578	.524		6	0	22	20	5	8	3	0

NOTES:

1978—Became Chicago White Sox coach and replaced as Knoxville manager by Joe Jones, with club in third place (July 3).

1979—Replaced as Iowa manager by Joe Sparks, with club in second place (August 3); replaced Chicago manager Don Kessinger with club in fifth place and record of 46-60 (August 3).

1983—Lost to Baltimore in A.L. Championship Series.

1986—Replaced as White Sox manager by interim manager Doug Rader, with club in sixth place (June 20); replaced Oakland manager Jackie Moore (record of 29-44) and interim manager Jeff Newman (record of 2-8) with club in seventh place and record of 31-52 (July 7).

1988—Defeated Boston in A.L. Championship Series; lost to Los Angeles in World Series.

1989—Defeated Toronto in A.L. Championship Series; defeated San Francisco in World Series.

1990—Defeated Boston in A.L. Championship Series; lost to Cincinnati in World Series.

1992—Lost to Toronto in A.L. Championship Series.

1993—On suspended list (October 1-remainder of season).

1994—Oakland was in second place in A.L. West at time of season-ending strike (August 12).

1996—Defeated San Diego in N.L. divisional playoff; lost to Atlanta in N.L. Championship Series.

2000—Defeated Atlanta in N.L. divisional playoff; lost to New York Mets in N.L. Championship Series.

LOPES, DAVEY   BREWERS

PERSONAL: Born May 3, 1945, in East Providence, R.I. ... 5-9/170. ... Batted right, threw right. ... Full name: David Earl Lopes.

HIGH SCHOOL: LaSalle Academy (Providence, R.I.).

COLLEGE: Iowa Weslyan, then Washburn (Kan.), degree in education, 1969.

TRANSACTIONS/CAREER NOTES: Selected by San Francisco Giants organization in 28th round of free agent draft (June 6, 1967); did not sign. ... Selected by Los Angeles Dodgers organization in secondary phase of free-agent draft (January 27, 1968). ... On restricted list (April 11-June 13, 1968). ... On military list (July 22, 1969-April 8, 1970). ... On temporary inactive list (June 9-30, 1970). ... On temporary inactive list (April 26-29 and June 8-July 2, 1971). ... On temporary inactive list (June 16-30 and August 28-September 1, 1972). ... On disabled list (March 31-May 3, 1976). ... On disabled list (August 18-September 2,1981). ... Traded by Dodgers to Oakland Athletics for 2B Lance Hudson (February 8, 1982). ... On disabled list (July 7-August 8, 1984). ... Traded by Athletics to Chicago Cubs (August 31, 1984) as partial completion of deal in which Cubs traded P Chuck Rainey and a player to be named later to Athletics for a player to be named later (July 15, 1984); Athletics acquired OF Damon Farmar to complete deal (March 18, 1985). ... Traded by Cubs to Houston Astros for P Frank DiPino (July 21, 1986). ... Granted free agency (November 12, 1986). ... Re~signed by Astros (December 19, 1986). ... On disabled list (April 12-June 19, 1987); included rehabilitation assignment to Tucson (June 9-13, 1987). ... Released by Astros (November 12, 1987).

RECORDS: Shares major league single-inning record for most errors by a second baseman—3 (June 2, 1973, first inning). ... Shares N.L. single-game record for most double plays by a second baseman—5 (May 18, 1975).

HONORS: Named second baseman on THE SPORTING NEWS National League All-Star Team (1978 and 1979). ... Named second baseman on THE SPORTING NEWS National League All-Star fielding team (1978).

STATISTICAL NOTES: Led Pacific Coast League second basemen in errors with 18 in 1972. ... Tied for Pacific Coast League lead in errors by outfielders with 10 in 1970. ... Hit three home runs in one game (August 20, 1974).

Year	Team (League)	Pos.	G	AB	R	H	2B	3B	HR	RBI	Avg.	BB	SO	SB	PO	A	E	Avg.
1968—	Daytona Beach (FSL)..	OF	82	271	39	67	6	6	5	33	.247	24	74	26	109	7	4	.967
1969—	Daytona Beach (FSL)......	OF	72	264	53	74	7	4	9	33	.280	49	42	32	138	16	7	.957
1970—	Spokane (PCL)..........	OF-2B	100	343	48	90	15	4	6	35	.262	37	65	11	202	19	12	.948
1971—	Spokane (PCL)......	OF-2B	94	353	78	108	9	9	6	36	.306	44	65	37	157	103	11	.959
1972—	Albuquerque (PCL).....	2B-OF-SS	104	397	94	126	18	6	11	53	.317	59	64	*48	213	270	21	.958
—	Los Angeles (N.L.)	2B	11	42	6	9	4	0	0	1	.214	7	6	4	27	27	2	.964
1973—	Los Angeles (N.L.)	2-0-S-3	142	535	77	147	13	5	6	37	.275	62	77	36	323	380	11	.985
1974—	Los Angeles (N.L.)	2B	145	530	95	141	26	3	10	35	.266	66	71	59	309	360	*24	.965
1975—	Los Angeles (N.L.)	2B-OF-SS	155	618	108	162	24	6	8	41	.262	91	93	*77	360	386	16	.979
1976—	Los Angeles (N.L.)	2B-OF	117	427	72	103	17	7	4	20	.241	56	49	*63	254	268	19	.965
1977—	Los Angeles (N.L.)	2B	134	502	85	142	19	5	11	53	.283	73	69	47	287	380	14	.979
1978—	Los Angeles (N.L.)	2B-OF	151	587	93	163	25	4	17	58	.278	71	70	45	340	424	*20	.974
1979—	Los Angeles (N.L.)	2B	153	582	109	154	20	6	28	73	.265	97	88	44	341	*384	14	.981
1980—	Los Angeles (N.L.)	2B	141	553	79	139	15	3	10	49	.251	58	71	23	304	416	15	.980
1981—	Los Angeles (N.L.)	2B	58	214	35	44	2	0	5	17	.206	22	35	20	129	161	2	.993
1982—	Oakland (A.L.)■.........	2B-OF	138	450	58	109	19	3	11	42	.242	40	51	28	295	338	15	.977
1983—	Oakland (A.L.)	2B-OF-3B	147	494	64	137	13	4	17	67	.277	51	61	22	267	287	9	.984
1984—	Oakland (A.L.)	OF-2B	72	230	32	59	11	1	9	36	.257	31	36	12	99	47	6	.961
—	Chicago (N.L.)■..........	OF-2B	16	17	5	4	1	0	0	0	.235	6	5	3	6	2	0	1.000
1985—	Chicago (N.L.)	OF-3B-2B	99	275	52	78	11	0	11	44	.284	46	37	47	115	6	1	.992
1986—	Chicago (N.L.)	3B-OF	59	157	38	47	8	2	6	22	.299	31	16	17	51	54	8	.929
—	Houston (N.L.)■	OF-3B	37	98	11	23	2	1	1	13	.235	12	9	8	45	11	0	1.000.
1987—	Houston (N.L.)	OF	47	43	4	10	2	0	1	6	.233	13	8	2	6	0	1	.857
—	Tucson (PCL)	DH	4	14	2	9	3	0	0	3	.643				...	...	...	.000
National League totals (14 years)			1465	5180	869	1366	189	42	118	469	.264	711	704	495	2897	3259	147	.977
American League totals (3 years)			347	1174	154	305	43	8	37	145	.260	122	148	62	661	672	30	.978
Major league totals (16 years)			1812	6354	1023	1671	232	50	155	614	.263	833	852	557	3358	3931	177	.977

DIVISION SERIES RECORD

Year	Team (League)	Pos.	G	AB	R	H	2B	3B	HR	RBI	Avg.	BB	SO	SB	PO	A	E	Avg.
1981—	Los Angeles (N.L.)	2B	5	20	1	4	1	0	0	0	.200	3	7	1	7	12	0	1.000

CHAMPIONSHIP SERIES RECORD

RECORDS: Holds N.L. career record for most stolen bases—9. ... Shares career record for most consecutive games, one or more runs batted in—4. ... Shares N.L. career record for most clubs total Series—3.

Year	Team (League)	Pos.	G	AB	R	H	2B	3B	HR	RBI	Avg.	BB	SO	SB	PO	A	E	Avg.
1974—	Los Angeles (N.L.)	2B	4	15	4	4	0	1	0	3	.267	3	5	1	9	18	1	.964
1977—	Los Angeles (N.L.)	2B	4	17	2	4	0	0	0	3	.235	2	0	0	9	10	1	.950
1978—	Los Angeles (N.L.)	2B	4	18	3	7	1	1	2	5	.389	0	1	1	10	10	2	.909
1981—	Los Angeles (N.L.)	2B	5	18	0	5	0	0	0	0	.278	1	3	5	13	13	0	1.000
1984—	Chicago (N.L.)	OF-PH	2	1	0	0	0	0	0	0	.000	0	0	0	0	0	0	.000
1986—	Houston (N.L.)	PH	3	2	1	0	0	0	0	0	.000	0	0	0	...	...	...	...
Championship series totals (6 years)			22	71	10	20	1	2	2	11	.282	9	5	9	41	51	4	.958

WORLD SERIES RECORD

RECORDS: Shares World Series records for most stolen bases, inning—2 (October 15, 1974, first inning); most putouts by second baseman, game—8 (October 16, 1974); most chances accepted by second baseman, game—13 (October 16, 1974); most putouts by second baseman, inning—3 (October 16, 1974, sixth inning and October 21, 1981, fourth inning); most times home run as leadoff batter, start of game—1 (October 17, 1978); most errors by second baseman, game—3 (October 25, 1981); most errors by second baseman, inning—2 (October 25, 1981, fourth inning).

Year	Team (League)	Pos.	G	AB	R	H	2B	3B	HR	RBI	Avg.	BB	SO	SB	PO	A	E	Avg.
1974—	Los Angeles (N.L.)	2B	5	18	2	2	0	0	0	0	.111	3	4	2	19	9	0	1.000
1977—	Los Angeles (N.L.)	2B	6	24	3	4	0	1	1	2	.167	4	3	2	12	22	0	1.000
1978—	Los Angeles (N.L.)	2B	6	26	7	8	0	0	3	7	.308	2	1	3	10	19	1	.967
1981—	Los Angeles (N.L.)	2B	6	22	6	5	1	0	0	2	.227	4	3	4	26	14	6	.870
World Series totals (4 years)			23	90	18	19	1	1	3	11	.211	13	11	11	67	64	7	.949

ALL.STAR GAME RECORD

Year	Team (League)	Pos.	AB	R	H	2B	3B	HR	RBI	Avg.	BB	SO	SB	PO	A	E	Avg.
1978—	National	PH-2B	1	0	1	0	0	0	1	1.000	0	0	0	0	1	0	1.000
1979—	National	2B	3	0	1	0	0	0	0	.333	0	1	0	4	1	0	1.000
1980—	National	2B	1	0	0	0	0	0	0	.000	0	0	0	0	2	0	1.000
1981—	National	2B	0	0	0	0	0	0	0	.000	1	0	0	1	0	0	1.000
All-Star Game totals (4 years)			5	0	2	0	0	0	1	.400	1	1	0	5	7	0	1.000

RECORD AS MANAGER

BACKGROUND: Coach, Texas Rangers (1988-91). ... Coach, Baltimore Orioles (1992-94). ... Coach, San Diego Padres (1995-99).

		REGULAR SEASON				POSTSEASON						
						Playoff		Champ. Series		World Series		All-Star Game
Year	Team (League)	W	L	Pct.	Pos.	W	L	W	L	W	L	W L
2000—	Milwaukee (N.L.)	73	89	.451	3rd (C)	—	—	—	—	—	—	— —

PERSONAL: Born January 4, 1944, in North Fork, W.Va. ... 6-3/200. ... Batted left, threw right. ... Full name: Charles Fuqua Manuel.
HIGH SCHOOL: Parry McCluer (Buena Vista, Va.).
HONORS: Named Most Valuable Player of Japan Pacific League (1979).
STATISTICAL NOTES: Led Midwest League in total bases with 205 in 1967. ... Led Southern League in total bases with 230 and in sacrifice hits with 10 in 1968.

							BATTING								FIELDING		
Year Team (League)	Pos.	G	AB	R	H	2B	3B	HR	RBI	Avg.	BB	SO	SB	PO	A	E	Avg.
1963— Wytheville (Appal.)	OF	58	173	32	62	9	2	7	45	.358	25	21	7	58	6	3	.955
1964— Orlando (FSL)	OF	114	373	43	99	21	7	4	37	.265	43	47	3	155	*15	5	.966
1965— Wilson (Carolina)	OF	61	167	16	34	6	1	0	19	.204	19	27	2	68	5	0	1.000
1966— Orlando (FSL)............	OF	61	187	14	42	6	1	1	21	.225	21	26	4	...	...	...	...
— Wilson (Carolina)	OF	118	347	39	80	13	5	6	47	.231	43	53	7	140	13	5	.968
1967— Wisconsin (Midw.)	OF	111	399	*76	125	29	3	15	•70	*.313	56	74	4	178	18	4	.980
1968— Charlotte (Sou.)........	OF	138	505	59	143	26	11	13	79	.283	43	89	6	202	8	5	.977
1969— Minnesota (A.L.)	OF	83	64	14	34	6	0	2	24	.207	28	33	1	57	2	2	.967
1970— Evansville (A.A.).......	OF-1B	21	70	13	23	5	0	6	26	.329	6	5	0	43	6	4	.925
— Minnesota (A.L.)	OF	56	64	4	12	0	0	1	7	.188	6	17	1	7	0	0	1.000
1971— Portland (PCL)	OF-1B	63	191	47	71	8	5	19	46	.372	31	29	0	112	2	7	.942
— Minnesota (A.L.)	OF	18	16	1	2	1	0	0	1	.125	1	8	0	0	0	0	.000
1972— Minnesota (A.L.)	OF	63	122	6	25	5	0	1	8	.205	4	16	0	39	4	1	.977
1973— Tacoma (PCL)	OF	105	343	47	94	18	3	16	68	.274	42	58	0	...	...	...	...
1974— Albuquerque (PCL)■.	OF	129	432	82	142	23	2	30	102	.329	80	68	3	...	...	...	...
— Los Angeles (N.L.)	PH	4	3	0	1	0	0	0	1	.333	1	0	0	...	...	...	...
1975— Albuquerque (PCL).....	OF	81	243	40	79	17	1	16	64	.325	39	32	0	...	...	...	...
— Los Angeles (N.L.)	PH	15	15	0	2	0	0	0	2	.133	0	3	0	...	...	...	...
1976— Yakult (Jap. Cen.)■....	OF	84	263	...	64	...	...	11	32	.243	...	...	...	...	...	...	...
1977— Yakult (Jap. Cen.).......	OF	114	358	70	113	8	0	42	97	.316	...	...	3	...	...	...	...
1978— Yakult (Jap. Cen.)	OF	127	468	85	146	12	2	39	103	.312	...	...	1	...	...	...	...
1979— Kintetsu (Jp. Pac.)■ ..	OF	97	333	69	108	18	0	*37	94	.324	...	...	0	...	...	...	...
1980— Kintetsu (Jap. Pac.)....	OF	118	459	88	149	16	0	*48	*129	.325	...	...	0	...	...	...	...
1981— Yakult (Jap. Cen.)■....	OF	81	246	...	64	...	...	12	36	.260	...	...	...	...	...	...	...
American League totals (4 years)		220	366	25	73	12	0	4	40	.199	39	74	1	...	...	...	...
National League totals (2 years)		19	18	0	3	0	0	0	3	.167	1	3	0	...	...	...	...
Major league totals (6 years)		239	384	25	76	12	0	4	43	.198	40	77	1	...	...	...	...

CHAMPIONSHIP SERIES RECORD

							BATTING								FIELDING		
Year Team (League)	Pos.	G	AB	R	H	2B	3B	HR	RBI	Avg.	BB	SO	SB	PO	A	E	Avg.
1969— Minnesota (A.L.)	PH	1	0	0	0	0	0	0	0	.000	0	0	0	0	0	0	.000
1970— Minnesota (A.L.)	PH	1	1	0	0	0	0	0	0	.000	0	0	0	0	0	0	.000
Championship series totals (2 years)		2	1	0	0	0	0	0	0	.000	0	0	0	0	0	0	.000

RECORD AS MANAGER

BACKGROUND: Scout, MInnesota Twins (1982). ... Hitting instructor, Cleveland Indians (1988-89 and 1994-99).
HONORS: Named International League Manager of the Year (1993).

	REGULAR SEASON				POSTSEASON						
					Playoff		Champ. Series		World Series		All-Star Game
Year Team (League)	W	L	Pct.	Pos.	W	L	W	L	W	L	W	L
1983— Wisconsin (Midwest)	71	67	.518	2nd (N)	—	—	—	—	—	—	—	—
1984— Orlando (Southern)	34	35	.493	3rd (E)	—	—	—	—	—	—	—	—
— (Second half)	45	30	.600	2nd (E)	0	1	—	—	—	—	—	—
1985— Orlando (Southern)	29	35	.453	5th (E)	—	—	—	—	—	—	—	—
— (Second half)	43	36	.544	2nd (E)	—	—	—	—	—	—	—	—
1986— Toledo (International)	62	77	.446	6th	—	—	—	—	—	—	—	—
1987— Portland (PCL)	20	49	.290	5th (N)	—	—	—	—	—	—	—	—
— (Second half)	25	47	.347	5th (N)	—	—	—	—	—	—	—	—
1990— Colorado Springs (PCL)........................	37	34	.521	2nd (S)	—	—	—	—	—	—	—	—
— (Second half)	39	33	.541	3rd (S)	—	—	—	—	—	—	—	—
1991— Colorado Springs (PCL)........................	30	41	.422	5th (S)	—	—	—	—	—	—	—	—
— (Second half)	42	26	.617	1st (S)	1	3	—	—	—	—	—	—
1992— Colorado Springs (PCL)........................	36	33	.521	2nd (S)	—	—	—	—	—	—	—	—
— (Second half)	48	24	.666	1st (S)	6	2	—	—	—	—	—	—
1993— Charlotte (International)........................	86	55	.610	1st (W)	6	4	—	—	—	—	—	—
2000— Cleveland (A.L.)	90	72	.556	2nd (C)	—	—	—	—	—	—	—	—

NOTES:
1984—Lost to Charlotte in one game playoff.
1991—Lost to Tucson in playoffs.
1992—Defeated Las Vegas, three games to two, in playoff; defeated Vancouver, three games to none, in championship playoff.
1993—Defeated Richmond, three games to one, in playoff; defeated Rochester, three games to two, in championship playoff.

PERSONAL: Born December 23, 1953, in Hahira, Ga. ... 5-11/180. ... Batted right, threw right.
HIGH SCHOOL: Cordova (Rancho Cordova, Calif.).
TRANSACTIONS/CAREER NOTES: Selected by Detroit Tigers organization in first round (20th pick overall) of free-agent draft (June 6, 1972). ... On disabled list (August 18-September 1, 1978). ... Traded by Tigers to Montreal Expos for C Duffy Dyer (March 14, 1980). ... On disabled list (May 2-July 31, and August 15-September 1, 1981). ... Traded by Expos to San Diego Padres for P Kim Seaman (May 22, 1982). ... Traded

MAJOR LEAGUE MANAGERS

by Padres to Expos for a player to be named later (June 8, 1982); Padres acquired P Mike Griffin to complete deal (August 30, 1982). ... Traded by Expos to Chicago Cubs for C Butch Benton (February 4, 1983). ... Granted free agency following 1983 season. ... Signed by Chicago White Sox organization (April 8, 1984). ... Granted free agency following 1985 season. ... Signed by Expos organization for 1986 season. ... On disabled list (June 23-July 17 and July 25-August 4, 1986).

STATISTICAL NOTES: Led Appalachian League shortstops with 303 total chances and 29 double plays in 1972. ... Led American Association second basemen with 688 total chances and 81 double plays in 1974. ... Led American Association second basemen with 758 total chances and 108 double plays in 1975. ... Led American Association second basemen with 234 putouts, 363 assists and 611 total chances in 1979. ... Led American Association shortstops with 612 total chances in 1980.

Year	Team (League)	Pos.	G	AB	R	H	2B	3B	HR	RBI	Avg.	BB	SO	SB	PO	A	E	Avg.
1972—	Bristol (Appal.)...........	SS	67	233	31	56	8	8	4	29	.240	19	61	11	*112	*176	15	*.950
1973—	Lakeland (FSL)...........	SS	117	433	66	109	17	4	2	28	.252	52	98	20	167	349	29	.947
—	Toledo (I.L.)..............	SS	27	72	8	20	0	0	0	2	.278	3	16	2	44	90	4	.971
1974—	Evansville (A.A.)........	2B	127	384	44	81	5	5	1	24	.211	35	74	3	*315	356	17	.975
1975—	Evansville (A.A.)........	2B	*137	501	63	115	10	4	4	43	.230	44	101	5	*348	*394	16	.979
—	Detroit (A.L.)..............	2B	6	18	0	1	0	0	0	0	.056	0	4	0	11	23	2	.944
1976—	Detroit (A.L.)..............	2B-SS	54	43	4	6	1	0	0	2	.140	3	9	1	40	64	8	.929
—	Evansville (A.A.)........	2B	11	44	6	8	1	0	1	3	.182	2	9	0	25	29	1	.982
1977—	Evansville (A.A.)........	2B-SS	110	375	52	102	19	7	1	38	.272	45	55	12	198	304	17	.967
1978—	Evansville (A.A.)........	2B-SS	114	430	65	113	18	5	7	50	.263	50	83	8	264	321	20	.967
1979—	Evansville (A.A.)........	2B-SS	130	460	71	116	26	3	9	75	.252	67	67	8	†265	†434	22	.969
1980—	Denver (A.A.)■..........	SS	128	491	105	136	23	2	3	61	.277	81	62	11	*333	*357	22	.964
—	Montreal (N.L.)..........	SS	7	6	0	0	0	0	0	0	.000	0	2	0	5	11	1	.941
1981—	Montreal (N.L.)..........	2B-SS	27	55	10	11	5	0	3	10	.200	6	11	0	37	41	1	.987
1982—	Wichita (A.A.)■..........	S-3-2-O	71	263	31	67	22	0	3	37	.255	15	34	2	99	152	11	.958
—	San Diego (N.L.).......	2B-3B-SS	2	5	0	1	0	1	0	1	.200	1	0	0	1	1	0	1.000
—	Hawaii (PCL).............	SS	26	92	8	18	3	1	0	7	.196	11	12	2	41	73	1	.991
1983—	Iowa (A.A.)■.............	2-0-S-3	85	279	37	74	14	3	3	33	.265	22	46	6	129	143	9	.968
1984—	Denver (A.A.)■.........	SS-2B-OF	109	335	43	98	14	3	4	40	.293	37	32	7	184	262	18	.961
1985—	....								Did not play.									
1986—	Indianapolis (A.A.)■..	3B-2B	22	41	4	16	2	0	1	9	.390	2	5	0	5	7	1	.923
	American League totals (2 years)		60	61	4	7	1	0	0	2	.115	3	13	1	51	87	10	.932
	National League totals (3 years)		36	66	10	12	5	1	3	11	.182	7	13	0	43	53	2	.980
	Major league totals (5 years)		96	127	14	19	6	1	3	13	.150	10	26	1	94	140	12	.951

DIVISION SERIES RECORD

Year	Team (League)	Pos.	G	AB	R	H	2B	3B	HR	RBI	Avg.	BB	SO	SB	PO	A	E	Avg.
1981—	Montreal (N.L.)...........	2B	5	14	0	1	0	0	0	0	.071	2	5	0	13	19	3	.914

CHAMPIONSHIP SERIES RECORD

Year	Team (League)	Pos.	G	AB	R	H	2B	3B	HR	RBI	Avg.	BB	SO	SB	PO	A	E	Avg.
1981—	Montreal (N.L.)...........	PR	1	1	0	0	0	0	0	0	.000	0	0	0	...	...	...	...

RECORD AS MANAGER

BACKGROUND: Scout, Chicago White Sox (1985). ... Player/coach, Indianapolis, American Association (1986). ... Roving infield instructor, Montreal Expos organization (1987). ... Minor league field coordinator, Expos (1988-89). ... Coach, Expos (June 3, 1991-1996). ... Coach, Florida Marlins (1997).

HONORS: Named Southern League co-Manager of the Year (1990). ... Named A.L. Manager of the Year by THE SPORTING NEWS (2000). ... Named A.L. Manager of the Year by Baseball Writers' Association of America (2000).

		REGULAR SEASON				POSTSEASON								
								Champ.		World		All-Star	
						Playoff		Series		Series		Game	
Year	Team (League)	W	L	Pct.	Pos.	W	L	W	L	W	L	W	L
1990—	Jacksonville (Southern)	38	33	.535	2nd (E)	—	—	—	—	—	—	—	—
—	(Second half)..	46	27	.630	1st (E)	1	3	—	—	—	—	—	—
1991—	Indianapolis (A.A.).................................	28	22	.560		—	—	—	—	—	—	—	—
1998—	Chicago (A.L.).......................................	80	82	.494	2nd (C)	—	—	—	—	—	—	—	—
1999—	Chicago (A.L.).......................................	75	86	.466	2nd (C)	—	—	—	—	—	—	—	—
2000—	Chicago (A.L)..	95	67	.586	1st (C)	0	3	—	—	—	—	—	—
	Major league totals (3 years)	250	235	.515		0	3	—	—	—	—	—	—

NOTES:
1990—Lost to Orlando in playoffs.
1991—Replaced as Indianapolis manager by Pat Kelly (June 2).
2000—Lost to Seattle in A.L. divisional playoff.

MARTINEZ, BUCK   BLUE JAYS

PERSONAL: Born November 7, 1948, in Redding, Calif. ... 5-11/200. ... Batted right, threw right. ... Full name: John Albert Martinez.
JUNIOR COLLEGE: Sacramento City College.
COLLEGE: Sacramento State.
TRANSACTIONS/CAREER NOTES: Selected by Philadelphia Phillies organization in seventh round of free-agent draft (January 28, 1967); did not sign. ... Drafted by Houston Astros organization (December 2, 1968). ... Traded by Astros with IF Mickey Sinnerud and C Tommie Smith to Kansas City Royals for C John Jones (December 16, 1968). ... On restricted list (April 7-June 17, 1969). ... On military list (April 2-August 10, 1970). ... On disabled list (July 9-August 25, 1972). ... On disabled list (May 20-June 5, 1976). ... Traded by Royals with P Mark Littell to

St. Louis Cardinals for P Al Hrabosky (December 8, 1977). ... Traded by Cardinals to Milwaukee Brewers for P George Frazier (December 8, 1977). ... Traded by Brewers to Toronto Blue Jays for OF Gil Kubski (May 10, 1981). ... Granted free agency (November 13, 1981). ... Re-signed by Blue Jays (December 6, 1981). ... On disabled list (July 10, 1985-remainder of season). ... Granted free agency (November 12, 1986).

Year	Team (League)	Pos.	G	AB	R	H	2B	3B	HR	RBI	Avg.	BB	SO	SB	PO	A	E	Avg.
								BATTING								FIELDING		
1967—	Eugene (N'West)	C-OF-3B	77	269	53	96	16	4	2	46	.357	25	33	4	294	•48	8	.977
1968—	Spartanburg (W.Car.)	C	8	28	6	11	4	0	0	11	.393	4	1	0	51	2	0	1.000
	—Tidewater (Caro.)	C	36	110	10	31	12	1	1	14	.282	7	12	0	272	16	1	.997
1969—	Kansas City (A.L.)	C-OF	72	205	14	47	6	1	4	23	.229	8	25	0	292	26	9	.972
1970—	Kansas City (A.L.)	C	6	9	1	1	0	0	0	0	.111	2	1	0	20	3	1	.958
1971—	Omaha (A.A.)	C	75	269	34	77	23	1	5	39	.286	35	40	0	502	37	8	.985
	—Kansas City (A.L.)	C	22	46	3	7	2	0	0	1	.152	5	9	0	84	6	3	.968
1972—	Omaha (A.A.)	C	67	195	23	34	9	0	4	12	.174	35	34	0	493	47	6	.989
1973—	Omaha (A.A.)	C-1B	82	254	24	69	13	0	5	38	.272	29	22	0	522	47	3	.995
	—Kansas City (A.L.)	C	14	32	2	8	1	0	1	6	.250	4	5	0	52	4	2	.966
1974—	Kansas City (A.L.)	C	107	107	10	23	3	1	1	8	.215	14	19	0	151	16	4	.977
1975—	Kansas City (A.L.)	C	80	226	15	51	9	2	3	23	.226	21	28	1	361	39	8	.980
1976—	Kansas City (A.L.)	C	95	267	24	61	13	3	5	34	.228	16	45	0	420	40	4	.991
1977—	Kansas City (A.L.)	C	29	80	3	18	4	0	1	9	.225	3	12	0	133	8	1	.993
1978—	Milwaukee (A.L.)■	C	89	256	26	56	10	1	1	20	.219	14	42	1	327	32	8	.978
1979—	Milwaukee (A.L.)	C-P	69	196	17	53	8	0	4	26	.270	8	25	0	198	39	8	.967
1980—	Milwaukee (A.L.)	C	76	219	16	49	9	0	3	17	.224	12	33	1	293	33	5	.985
1981—	Toronto (A.L.)■	C	45	128	13	29	8	1	4	21	.227	11	16	1	192	22	2	.991
1982—	Toronto (A.L.)	C	96	260	26	63	17	0	10	37	.242	24	34	1	382	35	5	.988
1983—	Toronto (A.L.)	C	88	221	27	56	14	0	10	33	.253	29	39	0	331	25	4	.989
1984—	Toronto (A.L.)	C	102	232	24	51	13	1	5	37	.220	29	49	0	360	34	2	.995
1985—	Toronto (A.L.)	C	42	99	11	16	3	0	4	14	.162	10	12	0	155	16	2	.988
1986—	Toronto (A.L.)	C	81	160	13	29	8	0	2	12	.181	20	25	0	289	19	2	.994
Major League totals (17 years)			1113	2743	245	618	128	10	58	321	.225	230	419	5	4040	397	70	.984

CHAMPIONSHIP SERIES RECORD

Year	Team (League)	Pos.	G	AB	R	H	2B	3B	HR	RBI	Avg.	BB	SO	SB	PO	A	E	Avg.
								BATTING								FIELDING		
1976—	Kansas City (A.L.)	C	5	15	0	5	0	0	0	4	.333	1	3	0	15	4	0	1.000

RECORD AS PITCHER

Year	Team (League)	W	L	Pct.	ERA	G	GS	CG	ShO	Sv.	IP	H	R	ER	BB	SO
1979—	Milwaukee (A.L.)	0	0	.000	9.00	1	0	0	0	0	1	1	1	1	1	0

McCLENDON, LLOYD — PIRATES

PERSONAL: Born January 11, 1959, in Gary, Ind. ... 6-0/208. ... Batted right, threw right. ... Full name: Lloyd Glenn McClendon.
HIGH SCHOOL: Roosevelt (Gary, Ind.).
COLLEGE: Valparaiso.
TRANSACTIONS/CAREER NOTES: Selected by New York Mets organization in eighth round of free-agent draft (June 3, 1980). ... On disabled list (April 4-27, 1982). ... Traded by Mets with P Charlie Puleo and OF Jason Felice to Cincinnati Reds for P Tom Seaver (December 16, 1982). ... Traded by Reds to Chicago Cubs for OF Rolando Roomes (December 9, 1988). ... Traded by Cubs to Pittsburgh Pirates for a player to be named later (September 7, 1990); Cubs acquired P Mike Pomeranz to complete deal (September 28, 1990). ... Granted free agency (October 25, 1994). ... Signed by Cleveland Indians organization (May 5, 1995). ... Granted free agency (October 16, 1995).
STATISTICAL NOTES: Career major league grand slams: 2.

Year	Team (League)	Pos.	G	AB	R	H	2B	3B	HR	RBI	Avg.	BB	SO	SB	PO	A	E	Avg.
								BATTING								FIELDING		
1980—	Kingsport (Appl.)	C	14	46	7	15	2	0	1	9	.326	5	7	0	19	5	3	.889
	—Little Falls (NY-Penn)	C	40	117	25	32	9	1	3	20	.274	32	20	2	203	20	7	.970
1981—	Lynchburg (Caro.)	C-3B	103	363	55	91	12	6	7	57	.251	60	68	3	437	74	17	.968
1982—	Lynchburg (Caro.)	C-3B	108	384	61	105	25	1	18	78	.273	55	65	4	492	87	15	.975
1983—	Waterbury (East.)■	C-3B-1B	123	434	58	114	19	2	15	57	.263	42	64	4	466	99	8	.986
1984—	Vermont (East.)	C-1B-3B-OF	60	202	36	56	16	0	7	27	.277	28	28	2	174	24	3	.985
	—Wichita (A.A.)	3B-1B-C	48	152	28	45	13	1	6	28	.296	21	33	2	143	45	4	.979
1985—	Denver (A.A.)	1B-3B-C-OF	114	379	57	105	18	5	16	79	.277	51	56	4	470	104	17	.971
1986—	Denver (A.A.)	1B-OF-C-3B	132	433	75	112	30	1	*24	88	.259	70	75	2	656	45	11	.985
1987—	Cincinnati (N.L.)	C-1B-3B-OF	45	72	8	15	5	0	2	13	.208	4	15	1	80	5	2	.977
	—Nashville (A.A.)	1B-C	26	84	11	24	6	0	3	14	.286	17	15	1	72	3	1	.987
1988—	Cincinnati (N.L.)	C-OF-1B-3B	72	137	9	30	4	0	3	14	.219	15	22	4	197	13	4	.981
	—Nashville (A.A.)	OF-C	2	7	0	1	0	0	0	0	.143	1	1	0	12	2	0	1.000
1989—	Iowa (A.A.)■	1B-OF-C	34	109	18	35	10	0	4	13	.321	21	19	4	115	6	6	.953
	—Chicago (N.L.)	OF-1B-3B-C	92	259	47	74	12	1	12	40	.286	37	31	6	310	18	6	.982
1990—	Chicago (N.L.)	1B-OF	49	107	5	17	3	0	1	10	.159	14	21	1	120	9	1	.992
	—Iowa (A.A.)	1B-3B-OF-C	25	91	14	26	2	0	2	10	.286	8	19	3	125	12	2	.986
	—Pittsburgh (N.L.)■	OF	4	3	1	1	0	0	1	2	.333	0	1	0	0	0	0	...
1992—	Pittsburgh (N.L.)	OF-1B	84	190	26	48	8	1	3	20	.253	28	24	1	136	9	3	.980
1993—	Pittsburgh (N.L.)	OF-1B	88	181	21	40	11	1	2	19	.221	23	17	0	98	5	3	.972
1994—	Pittsburgh (N.L.)	OF-1B	51	92	9	22	4	0	4	12	.239	4	11	0	46	2	1	.980
1995—	Buffalo (A.A.)■	OF-DH-3B	37	108	19	30	6	0	5	19	.278	20	20	0	32	1	2	.943
Major League totals (7 years)			485	1041	126	247	47	3	28	130	.237	125	142	13	987	61	20	.981

CHAMPIONSHIP SERIES RECORD

RECORDS: Shares records for most hits in one inning—2 (October 13, 1992, second inning); and most singles in one inning—2 (October 13, 1992, second inning).

MAJOR LEAGUE MANAGERS

Year Team (League)	Pos.	G	AB	R	H	2B	3B	HR	RBI	Avg.	BB	SO	SB	PO	A	E	Avg.
1989— Chicago (N.L.)............	PH-C-OF	3	3	0	2	0	0	0	0	.667	1	0	0	3	0	0	1.000
1991— Pittsburgh (N.L.).......	PH-1B	3	2	0	0	0	0	0	0	.000	1	0	0	0	0	0	...
1992— Pittsburgh (N.L.)	OF-PH	5	11	4	8	2	0	1	4	.727	4	1	0	10	0	0	1.000
Championship series totals (3 years)		11	16	4	10	2	0	1	4	.625	6	1	0	13	0	0	1.000

RECORD AS MANAGER

BACKGROUND: Coach, Pittsburgh Pirates (1996-2000).

MUSER, TONY   ROYALS

PERSONAL: Born August 1, 1947, in Los Angeles. ... 6-2/190. ... Batted left, threw left. ... Full name: Anthony Joseph Muser.
HIGH SCHOOL: Lakewood (Calif.).
JUNIOR COLLEGE: San Diego Mesa.
TRANSACTIONS/CAREER NOTES: Signed as non-drafted free agent by Boston Red Sox organization (1967). ... On military list (beginning of 1968 season-July 15, 1968). ... Traded by Red Sox with P Vicente Romo to Chicago White Sox for P Danny Murphy and C Duane Josephson (March 30, 1971). ... Traded by White Sox to Baltimore Orioles for P Jesse Jefferson (June 15, 1975). ... Released by Orioles (February 21, 1978). ... Signed by Milwaukee Brewers organization (March 20, 1978). ... Released by Brewers (February 12, 1979). ... Played in Japan (1979).

Year Team (League)	Pos.	G	AB	R	H	2B	3B	HR	RBI	Avg.	BB	SO	SB	PO	A	E	Avg.
1967— Waterloo (Midw.)	1B	68	251	40	71	15	1	6	42	.283	38	42	3	674	28	11	.985
1968— Greenv. (W. Car.)........	1B-OF	33	114	13	31	7	0	2	12	.272	18	17	1	223	23	2	.992
— Win.-Salem (Car.).......	OF-1B	7	21	1	8	0	0	0	2	.381	1	3	1	13	1	0	1.000
1969— Louisville (I.L.)	1B	120	457	57	129	14	4	7	62	.282	43	53	7	1029	63	15	.986
— Boston (A.L.).............	1B	2	9	0	1	0	0	0	1	.111	1	1	0	17	3	0	1.000
1970— Louisville (I.L.)	1B	114	462	66	130	25	7	5	45	.281	38	49	1	1013	45	9	*.992
1971— Indianapolis (A.A.)■ ..	1B	85	310	36	91	10	3	3	31	.294	35	27	0	720	42	6	.992
— Chicago (A.L.)	1B	11	16	2	5	0	1	0	0	.313	1	1	0	23	3	1	.963
1972— Tucson (PCL)	1B	83	318	41	86	17	0	3	40	.270	29	28	3	680	49	12	.984
— Chicago (A.L.)	1B-OF	44	61	6	17	2	2	1	9	.279	2	6	1	135	7	2	.986
1973— Chicago (A.L.)	1B-OF	109	309	38	88	14	3	4	30	.285	33	36	8	681	38	6	.992
1974— Chicago (A.L.)	1B	103	206	16	60	5	1	1	18	.291	6	22	1	419	13	1	.998
1975— Chicago (A.L.)	1B	43	111	11	27	3	0	0	6	.243	7	8	2	263	22	2	.993
— Baltimore (A.L.)■.......	1B	80	82	11	26	3	0	0	11	.317	8	9	0	213	15	1	.996
1976— Baltimore (A.L.)	1B-OF	136	326	25	74	7	1	1	30	.227	21	34	1	693	63	7	.991
1977— Baltimore (A.L.)..........	1B-OF	120	118	14	27	6	0	0	7	.229	13	16	1	232	20	3	.988
1978— Spokane (PCL)■.......	1B-OF	78	283	48	83	13	0	6	38	.293	33	25	2	572	50	4	.994
— Milwaukee (A.L.)	1B	15	30	0	4	1	1	0	5	.133	3	5	0	79	5	1	.988
1979— Seibu (Jp. Pac.)■	...	65	168	...	33	...	...	2	10	.196	...	...	...	...	...	...	...
Major league totals (9 years)		663	1268	123	329	41	9	7	117	.259	95	138	14	2755	189	24	.992

RECORD AS MANAGER

BACKGROUND: Coach, Milwaukee Brewers (1985-89). ... Scout, Brewers (1990). ... Coach, Chicago Cubs (1993-July 8, 1997).

Year Team (League)	W	L	Pct.	Pos.	Playoff W	Playoff L	Champ. Series W	Champ. Series L	World Series W	World Series L	All-Star Game W	All-Star Game L
1980— Stockton (California)................................	49	21	.700	1st (N)	—	—	—	—	—	—	—	—
— (Second half)	41	30	.577	1st (N)	3	0	—	—	—	—	—	—
1981— El Paso (Texas)	37	31	.544	2nd (W)	—	—	—	—	—	—	—	—
— (Second half)	28	38	.424	4th (W)	—	—	—	—	—	—	—	—
1982— El Paso (Texas)	42	23	.646	1st (W)	—	—	—	—	—	—	—	—
— (Second half)	34	37	.479	2nd (W)	2	3	—	—	—	—	—	—
1983— El Paso (Texas)	35	33	.515	2nd (W)	—	—	—	—	—	—	—	—
— Vancouver(Pacific Coast)	29	41	.414	4th (N)	—	—	—	—	—	—	—	—
1984— Vancouver (Pacific Coast)	32	40	.444	3rd (N)	—	—	—	—	—	—	—	—
— (Second half)	39	31	.557	3rd (N)	—	—	—	—	—	—	—	—
1991— Denver (American Association)	79	65	.549	1st (W)	7	3	—	—	—	—	—	—
1992— Denver (American Association)	73	71	.507	2nd (W)	—	—	—	—	—	—	—	—
1997— Kansas City (A.L.)	31	48	.392	4th (C)	—	—	—	—	—	—	—	—
1998— Kansas City (A.L.)	72	89	.447	3rd (C)	—	—	—	—	—	—	—	—
1999— Kansas City (A.L.)	64	97	.398	4th (C)	—	—	—	—	—	—	—	—
2000— Kansas City (A.L.)	77	85	.475	4th (C)	—	—	—	—	—	—	—	—
Major league totals (4 years)	244	319	.433		—	—	—	—	—	—	—	—

NOTES:
1980—Defeated Visalia in league championship.
1982—Defeated Midland, two games to one, in playoffs; lost to Tulsa, three games to none, in league championship.
1983—Replaced Vancouver manager Dick Phillips (June 22).
1991—Defeated Buffalo, three games to two, in league championship; defeated Columbus (International League), four games to one, in Class AAA Alliance championship.
1997—Replaced Kansas City manager Bob Boone with club in fourth place and record of 36-46 (July 9).
1998—On suspended list (June 9-17).

PERSONAL: Born January 21, 1946, in Sylva, N.C. ... 5-11/185. ... Batted left, threw right. ... Full name: Johnny Lane Oates.

HIGH SCHOOL: Prince George (Va.).

COLLEGE: Virginia Tech (bachelor of science degree in health and physical education).

TRANSACTIONS/CAREER NOTES: Selected by Chicago White Sox organization in second round of free-agent draft (June 1966); did not sign. ... Selected by Baltimore Orioles organization in secondary phase of free-agent draft (January 28, 1967). ... On military list (April 21-August 22, 1970). ... Traded by Orioles with P Pat Dobson, P Roric Harrison and 2B Dave Johnson to Atlanta Braves for C Earl Williams and IF Taylor Duncan (November 30, 1972). ... On disabled list (July 17-September 2, 1973). ... Traded by Braves with 1B Dick Allen to Philadelphia Phillies for C Jim Essian, OF Barry Bonnell and cash (May 7, 1975). ... On disabled list (April 14-June 1, 1976). ... Traded by Phillies with P Quency Hill to Los Angeles Dodgers for IF Ted Sizemore (December 20, 1976). ... Released by Dodgers (March 27, 1980). ... Signed by New York Yankees (April 4, 1980). ... Granted free agency (November 13, 1980). ... Re-signed by Yankees organization (January 23, 1981). ... On Columbus disabled list (August 3-25, 1981). ... Released by Yankees organization (October 27, 1981).

STATISTICAL NOTES: Led International League catchers with 727 total chances in 1971. ... Led N.L. with 15 passed balls in 1974. ... Tied for N.L. lead in double plays by catcher with 10 in 1975.

							BATTING							FIELDING		
Year Team (League)	Pos.	G	AB	R	H	2B	3B	HR	RBI	Avg.	BB	SO	SB	PO	A	E	Avg.
1967— Bluefield (Appal.)	C	5	12	5	5	1	0	1	4	.417	2	0	0	23	5	0	1.000
— Miami (FSL)	C-OF	48	156	22	45	5	2	3	19	.288	24	13	2	271	37	8	.975
1968— Miami (FSL)	C-OF	70	194	24	51	9	3	0	23	.263	33	14	2	384	42	3	.993
1969— Dall./Ft. Worth (Tex.)	C	66	191	24	55	12	2	1	18	.288	20	9	0	253	42	4	.987
1970— Rochester (I.L.)	C	9	16	1	6	1	0	0	4	.375	4	2	0	24	2	0	1.000
— Baltimore (A.L.)	C	5	18	2	5	0	1	0	2	.278	2	0	0	30	1	2	.939
1971— Rochester (I.L.)	C	114	346	49	96	16	3	7	44	.277	49	31	10	*648	*73	6	.992
1972— Baltimore (A.L.)	C	85	253	20	66	12	1	4	21	.261	28	31	5	391	31	2	*.995
1973— Atlanta (N.L.)■	C	93	322	27	80	6	0	4	27	.248	22	31	1	409	57	9	.981
1974— Atlanta (N.L.)	C	100	291	22	65	10	0	1	21	.223	23	24	2	434	55	4	.992
1975— Atlanta (N.L.)	C	8	18	0	4	1	0	0	0	.222	1	4	0	21	1	0	1.000
— Philadelphia (N.L.)■	C	90	269	28	77	14	0	1	25	.286	33	29	1	429	44	5	.990
1976— Philadelphia (N.L.)	C	37	99	10	25	2	0	0	8	.253	8	12	0	155	15	1	.994
1977— Los Angeles (N.L.)■	C	60	156	18	42	4	0	3	11	.269	11	11	1	258	37	4	.987
1978— Los Angeles (N.L.)	C	40	75	5	23	1	0	0	6	.307	5	3	0	77	10	4	.956
1979— Los Angeles (N.L.)	C	26	46	4	6	2	0	0	2	.130	4	1	0	64	13	2	.975
1980— New York (A.L.)■	C	39	64	6	12	3	0	1	3	.188	2	3	1	99	10	1	.991
1981— New York (A.L.)	C	10	26	4	5	1	0	0	0	.192	2	0	0	49	3	2	.963
American League totals (4 years)		139	361	32	88	16	2	5	26	.244	34	34	6	569	45	7	.989
National League totals (7 years)		454	1276	114	322	40	0	9	100	.252	107	115	5	1847	232	29	.986
Major league totals (11 years)		593	1637	146	410	56	2	14	126	.250	141	149	11	2416	277	36	.987

CHAMPIONSHIP SERIES RECORD

							BATTING							FIELDING		
Year Team (League)	Pos.	G	AB	R	H	2B	3B	HR	RBI	Avg.	BB	SO	SB	PO	A	E	Avg.
1976— Philadelphia (N.L.)	C	1	1	0	0	0	0	0	0	.000	0	0	0	1	0	0	1.000

WORLD SERIES RECORD

							BATTING							FIELDING		
Year Team (League)	Pos.	G	AB	R	H	2B	3B	HR	RBI	Avg.	BB	SO	SB	PO	A	E	Avg.
1977— Los Angeles (N.L.)	C	1	1	0	0	0	0	0	0	.000	0	0	0	1	0	0	1.000
1978— Los Angeles (N.L.)	C	1	1	0	1	0	0	0	0	1.000	1	0	0	3	1	0	1.000
World Series totals (2 years)		2	2	0	1	0	0	0	0	.500	1	0	0	4	1	0	1.000

RECORD AS MANAGER

BACKGROUND: Coach, Columbus, New York Yankees organization (July 30, 1981-remainder of season). ... Coach, Chicago Cubs (1984-87). ... Coach, Baltimore Orioles (1989-May 23, 1991).

HONORS: Named International League Manager of the Year (1988). ... Coach, A.L. All-Star team (1993, 1995 and 1997). ... Named A.L. Manager of the Year by THE SPORTING NEWS (1993 and 1996). ... Named co-A.L. Manager of the Year by Baseball Writers' Association of America (1996).

		REGULAR SEASON			POSTSEASON							
					Playoff		Champ. Series		World Series		All-Star Game	
Year Team (League)	W	L	Pct.	Pos.	W	L	W	L	W	L	W	L
1982— Nashville (Southern)	32	38	.457	4th (W)	—	—	—	—	—	—	—	—
— (Second half)	45	29	.608	1st (W)	6	2	—	—	—	—	—	—
1983— Columbus (International)	83	57	.593	1st	2	3	—	—	—	—	—	—
1988— Rochester (International)	77	64	.546	1st (W)	5	5	—	—	—	—	—	—
1991— Baltimore (A.L.)	54	71	.432	6th (E)	—	—	—	—	—	—	—	—
1992— Baltimore (A.L.)	89	73	.549	3rd (E)	—	—	—	—	—	—	—	—
1993— Baltimore (A.L.)	85	77	.525	T3rd (E)	—	—	—	—	—	—	—	—
1994— Baltimore (A.L.)	63	49	.563		—	—	—	—	—	—	—	—
1995— Texas (A.L.)	74	70	.514	3rd (W)	—	—	—	—	—	—	—	—
1996— Texas (A.L.)	90	72	.556	1st (W)	1	3	—	—	—	—	—	—
1997— Texas (A.L.)	77	85	.475	3rd (W)	—	—	—	—	—	—	—	—
1998— Texas (A.L.)	88	74	.543	1st (W)	0	3	—	—	—	—	—	—
1999— Texas (A.L.)	95	67	.586	1st (W)	0	3	—	—	—	—	—	—
2000— Texas (A.L.)	71	91	.438	4th (W)	—	—	—	—	—	—	—	—
Major league totals (10 years)	786	729	.519		1	9						

MAJOR LEAGUE MANAGERS

PINIELLA, LOU   MARINERS

PERSONAL: Born August 28, 1943, in Tampa. ... 6-2/199. ... Batted right, threw right. ... Full name: Louis Victor Piniella. ... Cousin of Dave Magadan, third baseman/first baseman, San Diego Padres. ... Name pronounced pin-ELL-uh.
HIGH SCHOOL: Jesuit (Tampa).
COLLEGE: Tampa.
TRANSACTIONS/CAREER NOTES: Signed as free agent by Cleveland Indians organization (June 9, 1962). ... Selected by Washington Senators organization from Jacksonville, Indians organization, in Rule 5 major league draft (November 26, 1962). ... On military list (March 9-July 20, 1964). ... Traded by Senators to Baltimore Orioles (August 4, 1964), completing deal in which Orioles traded P Lester (Buster) Narum to Senators for cash and a player to be named later (March 31, 1964). ... On suspended list (June 27-29, 1965). ... Traded by Orioles to Indians for C Camilo Carreon (March 10, 1966). ... On temporarily inactive list (May 19-22, 1967). ... On disabled list (May 22-June 6, 1968). ... On temporarily inactive list (June 6-25, 1968). ... Selected by Seattle Pilots in expansion draft (October 15, 1968). ... Traded by Pilots to Kansas City Royals for OF Steve Whitaker and P John Gelnar (April 1, 1969). ... On military list (August 7-22, 1969). ... On disabled list (May 5-June 8, 1971). ... Traded by Royals with P Ken Wright to New York Yankees for P Lindy McDaniel (December 7, 1973). ... On disabled list (June 17-July 6, 1975; August 23-September 7, 1981; and March 30-April 22, 1983). ... Placed on voluntarily retired list (June 17, 1984).
RECORDS: Shares major league record for most assists by outfielder in one inning—2 (May 27, 1974, third inning).
HONORS: Named A.L. Rookie of the Year by Baseball Writers' Association of America (1969).
STATISTICAL NOTES: Led A.L. in grounding into double plays with 25 in 1972. ... Career major league grand slams: 1.

							BATTING							FIELDING		
Year Team (League)	Pos.	G	AB	R	H	2B	3B	HR	RBI	Avg.	BB	SO	SB	PO	A	E	Avg.
1962— Selma (Ala.-Fla.)	OF	70	278	40	75	10	5	8	44	.270	10	57	4	94	6	9	.917
1963— Peninsula (Caro.)■	OF	143	548	71	170	29	4	16	77	.310	34	70	8	271	*23	8	.974
1964— Aberdeen (North.)	OF	20	74	8	20	8	3	0	12	.270	6	9	1	37	1	1	.974
— Baltimore (A.L.)■	PH	4	1	0	0	0	0	0	0	.000	0	0	0	...	...	...	...
1965— Elmira (East.)	OF	126	490	64	122	29	6	11	64	.249	22	57	5	176	5	7	.963
1966— Portland (PCL)■	OF	133	457	47	132	22	3	7	52	.289	20	52	6	177	11	11	.945
1967— Portland (PCL)	OF	113	396	46	122	20	1	8	56	.308	23	47	2	199	7	6	.972
1968— Portland (PCL)	OF	88	331	49	105	15	3	13	62	.317	19	31	0	167	6	7	.961
— Cleveland (A.L.)	OF	6	5	1	0	0	0	0	1	1.000	0	0	1	1	0	0	1.000
1969— Kansas City (A.L.)■	OF	135	493	43	139	21	6	11	68	.282	33	56	2	278	13	7	.977
1970— Kansas City (A.L.)	OF-1B	144	542	54	163	24	5	11	88	.301	35	42	3	250	6	4	.985
1971— Kansas City (A.L.)	OF	126	448	43	125	21	5	3	51	.279	21	43	5	201	6	3	.986
1972— Kansas City (A.L.)	OF	151	574	65	179	*33	4	11	72	.312	34	59	7	275	8	7	.976
1973— Kansas City (A.L.)	OF	144	513	53	128	28	1	9	69	.250	30	65	5	196	9	3	.986
1974— New York (A.L.)■	OF-DH-1B	140	518	71	158	26	0	9	70	.305	32	58	1	270	16	3	.990
1975— New York (A.L.)	OF-DH	74	199	7	39	4	1	0	22	.196	16	22	0	65	5	1	.986
1976— New York (A.L.)	OF-DH	100	327	36	92	16	6	3	38	.281	18	34	0	199	10	4	.981
1977— New York (A.L.)	OF-DH-1B	103	339	47	112	19	3	12	45	.330	20	31	2	86	3	2	.978
1978— New York (A.L.)	OF-DH	130	472	67	148	34	5	6	69	.314	34	36	3	213	4	7	.969
1979— New York (A.L.)	OF-DH	130	461	49	137	22	2	11	69	.297	17	31	3	204	13	4	.982
1980— New York (A.L.)	OF-DH	116	321	39	92	18	0	2	27	.287	29	20	0	157	8	5	.971
1981— New York (A.L.)	OF-DH	60	159	16	44	9	0	5	18	.277	13	9	0	69	2	1	.986
1982— New York (A.L.)	DH-OF	102	261	33	80	17	1	6	37	.307	18	18	0	68	2	0	1.000
1983— New York (A.L.)	OF-DH	53	148	19	43	9	1	2	16	.291	11	12	1	67	4	3	.959
1984— New York (A.L.)	OF-DH	29	86	8	26	4	1	1	6	.302	7	5	0	40	3	0	1.000
Major league totals (18 years)		1747	5867	651	1705	305	41	102	766	.291	368	541	33	2639	112	54	.981

DIVISION SERIES RECORD

							BATTING							FIELDING		
Year Team (League)	Pos.	G	AB	R	H	2B	3B	HR	RBI	Avg.	BB	SO	SB	PO	A	E	Avg.
1981— New York (A.L.)	DH-PH	4	10	1	2	1	0	1	3	.200	0	0	0	...	...	...	...

CHAMPIONSHIP SERIES RECORD

							BATTING							FIELDING		
Year Team (League)	Pos.	G	AB	R	H	2B	3B	HR	RBI	Avg.	BB	SO	SB	PO	A	E	Avg.
1976— New York (A.L.)	DH-PH	4	11	1	3	1	0	0	0	.273	0	1	0	...	...	...	...
1977— New York (A.L.)	OF-DH	5	21	1	7	3	0	0	2	.333	0	1	0	9	1	0	1.000
1978— New York (A.L.)	OF	4	17	2	4	0	0	0	0	.235	0	3	0	13	0	0	1.000
1980— New York (A.L.)	OF	2	5	1	1	0	0	1	1	.200	2	1	0	5	0	0	1.000
1981— New York (A.L.)	PH-DH-OF	3	5	2	3	0	0	1	3	.600	0	0	0	0	0		
Championship series totals (5 years)		18	59	7	18	4	0	2	6	.305	2	6	0	27	1	0	1.000

WORLD SERIES RECORD

RECORDS: Shares single-series record for collecting one or more hits in each game (1978).
NOTES: Member of World Series championship team (1977-1978).

							BATTING							FIELDING		
Year Team (League)	Pos.	G	AB	R	H	2B	3B	HR	RBI	Avg.	BB	SO	SB	PO	A	E	Avg.
1976— New York (A.L.)	DH-OF-PH	4	9	1	3	1	0	0	0	.333	0	0	0	1	0	0	1.000
1977— New York (A.L.)	OF	6	22	1	6	0	0	0	3	.273	0	3	0	16	1	1	.944
1978— New York (A.L.)	OF	6	25	3	7	0	0	0	4	.280	0	1	1	14	1	0	1.000
1981— New York (A.L.)	OF-PH	6	16	2	7	1	0	0	3	.438	0	1	1	7	0	0	1.000
World Series totals (4 years)		22	72	7	23	2	0	0	10	.319	0	4	2	38	2	1	.976

MAJOR LEAGUE MANAGERS

ALL-STAR GAME RECORD

Year	League	Pos.	AB	R	H	2B	3B	HR	RBI	Avg.	BB	SO	SB	PO	A	E	Avg.
								BATTING								FIELDING	
1972— American		PH	1	0	0	0	0	0	0	.000	0	0	0	...	...	...	...

RECORD AS MANAGER

BACKGROUND: Coach, New York Yankees (June 25, 1984-85). ... Vice-president/general manager, Yankees (beginning of 1988 season-June 22, 1988). ... Special adviser, Yankees (1989).

HONORS: Named A.L. Manager of the Year by Baseball Writers' Association of America (1995).

	REGULAR SEASON				POSTSEASON							
					Playoff		Champ. Series		World Series		All-Star Game	
Year	Team (League)	W	L	Pct.	Pos.	W	L	W	L	W	L	W	L
1986— New York (A.L.)		90	72	.556	2nd (E)	—	—	—	—	—	—	—	—
1987— New York (A.L.)		89	73	.549	4th (E)	—	—	—	—	—	—	—	—
1988— New York (A.L.)		45	48	.484	5th (E)	—	—	—	—	—	—	—	—
1990— Cincinnati (N.L.)		91	71	.562	1st (W)	—	—	4	2	4	0	—	—
1991— Cincinnati (N.L.)		74	88	.457	5th (W)	—	—	—	—	—	—	0	1
1992— Cincinnati (N.L.)		90	72	.556	2nd (W)	—	—	—	—	—	—	—	—
1993— Seattle (A.L.)		82	80	.506	4th (W)	—	—	—	—	—	—	—	—
1994— Seattle (A.L.)		49	63	.438		—	—	—	—	—	—	—	—
1995— Seattle (A.L.)		79	66	.545	1st (W)	3	2	2	4	—	—	—	—
1996— Seattle (A.L.)		85	76	.528	2nd (W)	—	—	—	—	—	—	—	—
1997— Seattle (A.L.)		90	72	.556	1st (W)	1	3	—	—	—	—	—	—
1998— Seattle (A.L.)		76	85	.472	3rd (W)	—	—	—	—	—	—	—	—
1999— Seattle (A.L.)		79	83	.488	3rd (W)	—	—	—	—	—	—	—	—
2000— Seattle (A.L.)		91	71	.562	2nd (W)	3	0	2	4	—	—	—	—
American League totals (11 years)		**855**	**789**	**.520**		**7**	**5**	**4**	**8**	**—**	**—**	**—**	**—**
National League totals (3 years)		**255**	**231**	**.525**		**—**	**—**	**4**	**2**	**4**	**0**	**0**	**1**
Major league totals (14 years)		**1110**	**1020**	**.521**		**7**	**5**	**10**	**14**	**4**	**0**	**0**	**1**

NOTES:
1988—Replaced New York manager Billy Martin, with club in second place and record of 40-28 (June 23).
1990—Defeated Pittsburgh in N.L. Championship Series; defeated Oakland in World Series.
1994—Seattle was in third place in A.L. West at time of season-ending strike (August 12).
1995—Defeated New York in A.L. divisional playoff; lost to Cleveland in A.L. Championship Series.
1997—Lost to Baltimore in A.L. divisional playoff.
2000—Defeated Chicago White Sox in A.L. divisional playoff; lost to New York Yankees in A.L. Championship Series.

ROTHSCHILD, LARRY — DEVIL RAYS

PERSONAL: Born March 12, 1954, in Chicago. ... 6-2/185. ... Threw right, batted right. ... Full name: Lawrence Lee Rothschild.
HIGH SCHOOL: Homewood-Flossmoor (Flossmoor, Ill.).
COLLEGE: Bradley, then Florida State.
TRANSACTIONS/CAREER NOTES: Signed as non-drafted free agent by Cincinnati Reds organization (June 10, 1975). ... Loaned to San Diego Padres organization (May 11, 1978). ... Returned to Reds organization (July 18, 1978). ... Selected by Detroit Tigers from Reds organization in major league draft (December 8, 1980). ... Sold to Las Vegas, Pacific Coast League (February 25, 1983). ... On disabled list (April 10-May 4, 1983). ... Sold to Denver, American Association (December 18, 1983). ... Sold to Iowa, American Association (October 15, 1984).

Year	Team (League)	W	L	Pct.	ERA	G	GS	CG	ShO	Sv.	IP	H	R	ER	BB	SO
1975— Billings (Pioneer)		0	2	.000	7.88	6	0	0	0	1	8	14	11	7	7	12
— Eugene (Northwest)		3	0	1.000	2.73	21	0	0	0	•6	33	17	11	10	21	36
1976— Three Rivers (East.)		11	3	*.786	2.05	30	12	10	5	5	123	96	33	28	29	75
1977— Indianapolis (A.A.)		4	4	.500	4.21	29	14	2	1	1	92	93	51	43	34	43
1978— Nashville (Southern)		0	0	...	4.50	5	0	0	0	1	12	14	7	6	4	9
— Amarillo (Texas)■		5	5	.500	4.17	12	12	5	1	0	82	83	42	38	21	57
— Indianapolis (A.A.)■		4	0	1.000	2.20	8	6	2	0	0	45	31	15	11	19	38
1979— Indianapolis (A.A.)		1	6	.143	5.27	33	10	0	0	6	82	85	52	48	56	68
1980— Indianapolis (A.A.)		8	7	.533	4.22	33	14	1	0	1	113	111	60	53	44	74
1981— Evansville (A.A.)■		8	5	.615	3.27	56	0	0	0	15	77	62	32	28	29	81
— Detroit (A.L.)		0	0	...	1.50	5	0	0	0	0	6	4	1	1	6	1
1982— Evansville (A.A.)		6	4	.600	3.65	45	0	0	0	10	69	73	34	28	30	45
— Detroit (A.L.)		0	0	...	13.50	2	0	0	0	0	2⅔	4	4	4	2	0
1983— Las Vegas (PCL)■		9	2	.818	5.09	38	0	0	0	2	74⅓	88	43	42	34	39
1984— Denver (Am. Assoc.)■		6	3	.667	4.02	31	9	1	1	2	109⅓	109	58	49	51	71
1985— Iowa (Am. Assoc.)■		1	5	.167	5.32	40	3	0	0	0	89⅔	101	58	53	34	58
Major league totals (2 years)		**0**	**0**	**...**	**5.19**	**7**	**0**	**0**	**0**	**0**	**8⅔**	**8**	**5**	**5**	**8**	**1**

RECORD AS MANAGER

BACKGROUND: Coach, Cincinnati Reds organization (1986-89). ... Coach, Reds (1990-May 24, 1993). ... Coach, Atlanta Braves organization (1994). ... Coach, Florida Marlins (1995-97).

	REGULAR SEASON				POSTSEASON							
					Playoff		Champ. Series		World Series		All-Star Game	
Year	Team (League)	W	L	Pct.	Pos.	W	L	W	L	W	L	W	L
1998— Tampa Bay (A.L.)		63	99	.389	5th (E)	—	—	—	—	—	—	—	—
1999— Tampa Bay (A.L.)		69	93	.426	5th (E)	—	—	—	—	—	—	—	—
2000— Tampa Bay (A.L.)		69	92	.429	5th (E)	—	—	—	—	—	—	—	—
Major League totals (3 years)		**201**	**284**	**.414**		**—**	**—**	**—**	**—**	**—**	**—**	**—**	**—**

MAJOR LEAGUE MANAGERS

PERSONAL: Born November 27, 1958, in Upper Darby, Pa. ... 6-2/220. ... Batted left, threw right. ... Full name: Michael Lorri Scioscia. ... Name pronounced SO-sha.

HIGH SCHOOL: Springfield (Pa.).

COLLEGE: Penn State.

TRANSACTIONS/CAREER NOTES: Selected by Los Angeles Dodgers organization in first round (19th pick overall) of free-agent draft (June 8, 1976). ... On disabled list (May 19-August 4, 1978; April 10-20, 1980; May 15, 1983-remainder of season; May 6-21, 1984; June 10-July 15, 1986; June 1-16, 1987; and July 5-20, 1991). ... Granted free agency (November 4, 1992). ... Signed by San Diego Padres (February 11, 1993). ... On San Diego disabled list (March 29, 1993-entire season). ... Released by Padres (October 15, 1993). ... Signed by Texas Rangers organization (December 14, 1993). ... Placed on voluntary retired list (August 2, 1994).

HONORS: Named catcher on THE SPORTING NEWS N.L. All-Star team (1990).

STATISTICAL NOTES: Led Midwest League catchers with 20 errors and 12 double plays in 1977. ... Led Pacific Coast League catchers with 19 double plays and 22 passed balls in 1979. ... Tied for Pacific Coast League lead in being hit by pitch with seven in 1979. ... Led N.L. with 11 passed balls in 1981 and 14 in 1992. ... Led N.L. catchers with 1,016 total chances in 1987, 915 in 1989 and 910 in 1990.

							BATTING								FIELDING		
Year — Team (League)	Pos.	G	AB	R	H	2B	3B	HR	RBI	Avg.	BB	SO	SB	PO	A	E	Avg.
1976— Bellingham (N.W.)	C	46	151	25	42	6	0	7	26	.278	36	22	2	202	35	14	.944
1977— Clinton (Midw.)	C-1B	121	364	58	92	20	1	7	44	.253	79	25	9	764	95	†22	.975
1978— San Antonio (Texas)	C	58	204	29	61	16	0	2	34	.299	31	20	3	214	17	4	.983
1979— Albuquerque (PCL)	C	143	461	80	155	34	0	3	68	.336	73	33	5	*690	*86	*15	.981
1980— Albuquerque (PCL)	C	52	160	33	53	11	1	3	33	.331	36	13	3	207	19	5	.978
— Los Angeles (N.L.)	C	54	134	8	34	5	1	1	8	.254	12	9	1	226	26	2	.992
1981— Los Angeles (N.L.)	C	93	290	27	80	10	0	2	29	.276	36	18	0	493	48	7	.987
1982— Los Angeles (N.L.)	C	129	365	31	80	11	1	5	38	.219	44	31	2	631	57	10	.986
1983— Los Angeles (N.L.)	C	12	35	3	11	3	0	1	7	.314	5	2	0	55	4	0	1.000
1984— Los Angeles (N.L.)	C	114	341	29	93	18	0	5	38	.273	52	26	2	701	64	12	.985
1985— Los Angeles (N.L.)	C	141	429	47	127	26	3	7	53	.296	77	21	3	818	66	•13	.986
1986— Los Angeles (N.L.)	C	122	374	36	94	18	1	5	26	.251	62	23	3	756	64	15	.982
1987— Los Angeles (N.L.)	C	142	461	44	122	26	1	6	38	.265	55	23	7	*925	80	11	.989
1988— Los Angeles (N.L.)	C	130	408	29	105	18	0	3	35	.257	38	31	0	748	63	7	.991
1989— Los Angeles (N.L.)	C	133	408	40	102	16	0	10	44	.250	52	29	0	*822	*82	11	.988
1990— Los Angeles (N.L.)	C	135	435	46	115	25	0	12	66	.264	55	31	4	*842	58	10	.989
1991— Los Angeles (N.L.)	C	119	345	39	91	16	2	8	40	.264	47	32	4	677	51	7	.990
1992— Los Angeles (N.L.)	C	117	348	19	77	6	3	3	24	.221	32	31	3	641	*74	9	.988
1993— San Diego (N.L.)							Did not play.										
1994— Charlotte (FSL)■	C	1	2	0	1	0	0	0	0	.500	0	0	0	3	1	0	1.000
Major League totals (13 years)		1441	4373	398	1131	198	12	68	446	.259	567	307	29	8335	737	114	.988

DIVISION SERIES RECORD

							BATTING								FIELDING		
Year — Team (League)	Pos.	G	AB	R	H	2B	3B	HR	RBI	Avg.	BB	SO	SB	PO	A	E	Avg.
1981— Los Angeles (N.L.)	C	4	13	0	2	0	0	0	1	.154	1	2	0	21	3	0	1.000

CHAMPIONSHIP SERIES RECORD

							BATTING								FIELDING		
Year — Team (League)	Pos.	G	AB	R	H	2B	3B	HR	RBI	Avg.	BB	SO	SB	PO	A	E	Avg.
1981— Los Angeles (N.L.)	C	5	15	1	2	0	0	1	1	.133	2	1	0	27	1	0	1.000
1985— Los Angeles (N.L.)	C	6	16	2	4	0	0	0	1	.250	4	0	0	31	4	1	.972
1988— Los Angeles (N.L.)	C	7	22	3	8	1	0	1	2	.364	1	2	0	37	4	0	1.000
Championship series totals (3 years)		18	53	6	14	1	0	2	4	.264	7	3	0	95	9	1	.990

WORLD SERIES RECORD

NOTES: Member of World Series championship teams (1981 and 1988).

							BATTING								FIELDING		
Year — Team (League)	Pos.	G	AB	R	H	2B	3B	HR	RBI	Avg.	BB	SO	SB	PO	A	E	Avg.
1981— Los Angeles (N.L.)	C-PH	3	4	1	1	0	0	0	0	.250	1	0	0	7	1	0	1.000
1988— Los Angeles (N.L.)	C	4	14	0	3	0	0	0	1	.214	0	2	0	28	0	1	.966
World Series totals (2 years)		7	18	1	4	0	0	0	1	.222	1	2	0	35	1	1	.973

ALL-STAR GAME RECORD

						BATTING								FIELDING		
Year — League	Pos.	AB	R	H	2B	3B	HR	RBI	Avg.	BB	SO	SB	PO	A	E	Avg.
1989— National	C	1	0	0	0	0	0	0	.000	0	0	0	3	0	0	1.000
1990— National	C	2	0	0	0	0	0	0	.000	0	1	0	6	0	0	1.000
All-Star Game totals (2 years)		3	0	0	0	0	0	0	.000	0	1	0	9	0	0	1.000

RECORD AS MANAGER

BACKGROUND: Minor league catching coordinator, Dodgers organization (1995-96). ... Bench coach, Dodgers (1997-98). ... Manager, Peoria Javelinas, Dodgers organization (1997).

	REGULAR SEASON				POSTSEASON							
					Playoff		Champ. Series		World Series		All-Star Game	
Year — Team (League)	W	L	Pct.	Pos.	W	L	W	L	W	L	W	L
1999— Albuquerque (PCL)	65	74	.468	3rd	—	—	—	—	—	—	—	—
2000— Anaheim (A.L.)	82	80	.506	3rd (W)	—	—	—	—	—	—	—	—

PERSONAL: Born July 18, 1940, in Brooklyn, N.Y. ... 6-1/210. ... Batted right, threw right. ... Full name: Joseph Paul Torre. ... Brother of Frank Torre, first baseman with Milwaukee Braves (1956-60) and Philadelphia Phillies (1962-63). ... Name pronounced TORE-ee.

HIGH SCHOOL: St. Francis Prep (Brooklyn, N.Y.).

TRANSACTIONS/CAREER NOTES: Signed by Milwaukee Braves organization (August 24, 1959). ... On military list (September 30, 1962-March 26, 1963). ... Braves franchise moved from Milwaukee to Atlanta (1966). ... On disabled list (April 18-May 9, 1968). ... Traded by Braves to St. Louis Cardinals for 1B Orlando Cepeda (March 17, 1969). ... Traded by Cardinals to New York Mets for P Tommy Moore and P Ray Sadecki (October 13, 1974). ... Released as player by Mets (June 18, 1977).

RECORDS: Shares major league single-game record for most times grounded into double play—4 (July 21, 1975).

HONORS: Named catcher on THE SPORTING NEWS N.L. All-Star team (1964-66). ... Won N.L. Gold Glove at catcher (1965). ... Named Major League Player of the Year by THE SPORTING NEWS (1971). ... Named N.L. Player of the Year by THE SPORTING NEWS (1971). ... Named third baseman on THE SPORTING NEWS N.L. All-Star team (1971). ... Named N.L. Most Valuable Player by Baseball Writers' Association of America (1971).

STATISTICAL NOTES: Led N.L. catchers with .995 fielding percentage in 1964 and .996 in 1968. ... Led N.L. in grounding into double plays with 26 in 1964, 22 in 1965, 22 in 1967 and 21 in 1968. ... Led N.L. catchers with 12 double plays in 1967. ... Led N.L. with 352 total bases in 1971. ... Hit for the cycle (June 27, 1973). ... Led N.L. first basemen with 102 assists and 144 double plays in 1974. ... Career major league grand slams: 3.

						BATTING								FIELDING		
Year Team (League)	Pos.	G	AB	R	H	2B	3B	HR	RBI	Avg.	BB	SO	SB	PO	A	E	Avg.
1960— Eau Claire (North.)	C	117	369	63	127	23	3	16	74	*.344	70	45	7	636	64	9	.987
— Milwaukee (N.L.)........	PH	2	2	0	1	0	0	0	0	.500	0	1	0	...	...	...	...
1961— Louisville (A.A.).........	C	27	111	18	38	8	2	3	24	.342	6	9	0	185	14	2	.990
— Milwaukee (N.L.)........	C	113	406	40	113	21	4	10	42	.278	28	60	3	494	50	10	.982
1962— Milwaukee (N.L.)........	C	80	220	23	62	8	1	5	26	.282	24	24	1	325	39	5	.986
1963— Milwaukee (N.L.)........	C-1B-OF	142	501	57	147	19	4	14	71	.293	42	79	1	919	76	6	.994
1964— Milwaukee (N.L.)........	C-1B	154	601	87	193	36	5	20	109	.321	36	67	4	1081	94	7	†.994
1965— Milwaukee (N.L.)........	C-1B	148	523	68	152	21	1	27	80	.291	61	79	0	1022	73	8	.993
1966— Atlanta (N.L.)..............	C-1B	148	546	83	172	20	3	36	101	.315	60	61	0	874	87	12	.988
1967— Atlanta (N.L.)..............	C-1B	135	477	67	132	18	1	20	68	.277	75	49	2	785	81	8	.991
1968— Atlanta (N.L.)..............	C-1B	115	424	45	115	11	2	10	55	.271	34	72	1	733	48	2	†.997
1969— St. Louis (N.L.)■........	1B-C	159	602	72	174	29	6	18	101	.289	66	85	0	1360	91	7	.995
1970— St. Louis (N.L.)...........	C-3B-1B	•161	624	89	203	27	9	21	100	.325	70	91	2	651	162	13	.984
1971— St. Louis (N.L.)..........	3B	161	634	97	*230	34	8	24	*137	*.363	63	70	4	*136	271	•21	.951
1972— St. Louis (N.L.)..........	3B-1B	149	544	71	157	26	6	11	81	.289	54	74	3	336	198	15	.973
1973— St. Louis (N.L.)..........	1B-3B	141	519	67	149	17	2	13	69	.287	65	78	2	881	128	12	.988
1974— St. Louis (N.L.)..........	1B-3B	147	529	59	149	28	1	11	70	.282	69	68	1	1173	†121	14	.989
1975— New York (N.L.)■.......	3B-1B	114	361	33	89	16	3	6	35	.247	35	55	0	172	157	15	.956
1976— New York (N.L.).........	1B-3B	114	310	36	95	10	3	5	31	.306	21	35	1	593	52	7	.989
1977— New York (N.L.).........	1B-3B	26	51	2	9	3	0	1	9	.176	2	10	0	83	3	1	.989
Major league totals (18 years)		2209	7874	996	2342	344	59	252	1185	.297	805	1058	25	11618	1731	163	.988

ALL-STAR GAME RECORD

					BATTING								FIELDING		
Year League	Pos.	AB	R	H	2B	3B	HR	RBI	Avg.	BB	SO	SB	PO	A	E	Avg.
1963— National......................							Did not play.									
1964— National......................	C	2	0	0	0	0	0	0	.000	0	0	0	5	0	0	1.000
1965— National......................	C	4	1	1	0	0	1	2	.250	0	0	0	5	1	0	1.000
1966— National......................	C	3	0	0	0	0	0	0	.000	0	1	0	5	0	0	1.000
1967— National......................	C	2	0	0	0	0	0	0	.000	0	0	0	4	1	0	1.000
1970— National......................	PH	1	0	0	0	0	0	0	.000	0	0	0	...	...	...	...
1971— National......................	3B	3	0	0	0	0	0	0	.000	0	1	0	1	0	0	1.000
1972— National......................	3B	3	0	0	0	0	0	0	.000	0	1	0	1	2	0	1.000
1973— National......................	1B-3B	3	0	0	0	0	0	0	.000	0	0	0	5	0	0	1.000
All-Star Game totals (8 years)		21	1	1	0	0	1	2	.048	0	3	0	26	4	0	1.000

RECORD AS MANAGER

BACKGROUND: Player/manager, New York Mets (May 31-June 18, 1977).

HONORS: Named Sportsman of the Year by THE SPORTING NEWS (1996). ... Named CO-A.L. Manager of the Year by Baseball Writers' Association of America (1996). ... Named A.L. Manager of the Year by The Sporting News (1998). ... Named A.L. Manager of the Year by Baseball Writers' Association of America (1998).

					POSTSEASON						
	REGULAR SEASON				Playoff		Champ. Series		World Series		All-Star Game
Year Team (League)	W	L	Pct.	Pos.	W	L	W	L	W	L	W L
1977— New York (N.L.)	49	68	.419	6th (E)	—	—	—	—	—	—	— —
1978— New York (N.L.)	66	96	.407	6th (E)	—	—	—	—	—	—	— —
1979— New York (N.L.)	63	99	.389	6th (E)	—	—	—	—	—	—	— —
1980— New York (N.L.)	67	95	.414	5th (E)	—	—	—	—	—	—	— —
1981— New York (N.L.)	17	34	.333	5th (E)	—	—	—	—	—	—	— —
— (Second half)	24	28	.462	4th (E)	—	—	—	—	—	—	— —
1982— Atlanta (N.L.)	89	73	.549	1st (W)	—	—	0	3	—	—	— —
1983— Atlanta (N.L.)	88	74	.543	2nd (W)	—	—	—	—	—	—	— —
1984— Atlanta (N.L.)	80	82	.494	T2nd (W)	—	—	—	—	—	—	— —
1990— St. Louis (N.L.)	24	34	.414	6th (E)	—	—	—	—	—	—	— —
1991— St. Louis (N.L.)	84	78	.519	2nd (E)	—	—	—	—	—	—	— —
1992— St. Louis (N.L.)	83	79	.512	3rd (E)	—	—	—	—	—	—	— —
1993— St. Louis (N.L.)	87	75	.537	3rd (E)	—	—	—	—	—	—	— —
1994— St. Louis (N.L.)	53	61	.465		—	—	—	—	—	—	— —
1995— St. Louis (N.L.)	20	27	.426	4th (C)	—	—	—	—	—	—	— —
1996— New York (A.L.)	92	70	.568	1st (E)	3	1	4	1	4	2	— —
1997— New York (A.L.)	96	66	.593	2nd (E)	2	3	—	—	—	—	1 0

Year Team (League)	REGULAR SEASON				POSTSEASON							
					Playoff		Champ. Series		World Series		All-Star Game	
	W	L	Pct.	Pos.	W	L	W	L	W	L	W	L
1998— New York (A.L.)	114	48	.704	1st (E)	3	0	4	2	4	0	—	—
1999— New York (A.L.)	98	64	.605	1st (E)	3	0	4	1	4	0	—	—
2000— New York (A.L.)	87	74	.540	1st (E)	3	2	4	2	4	1	1	0
American League totals (5 years)	487	322	.602		14	6	16	6	16	3	2	0
National League totals (14 years)	894	1003	.471		—	—	0	3	—	—	—	—
Major league totals (19 years)	1381	1325	.510		14	6	16	9	16	3	2	0

NOTES:
1977—Replaced New York manager Joe Frazier with club in sixth place and record of 15-30 (May 31); served as player/manager (May 31-June 18, when released as player).
1982—Lost to St. Louis in N.L. Championship Series.
1990—Replaced St. Louis manager Whitey Herzog (33-47) and interim manager Red Schoendienst (13-11) with club in sixth place and record of 46-58 (August 1).
1994—St. Louis was tied for third place in N.L. Central at time of season-ending strike (August 12).
1995—Replaced as Cardinals manager by interim manager Mike Jorgensen, with club in fourth place (June 16).
1996—Defeated Texas in A.L. divisional playoff; defeated Baltimore in A.L. Championship Series; defeated Atlanta in World Series.
1997—Lost to Cleveland in A.L. divisional playoff.
1998—Defeated Texas in A.L. divisional playoff; defeated Cleveland in A.L. Championship Series; defeated San Diego in World Series.
1999—Defeated Texas in A.L. divisional playoff; defeated Boston in A.L. Championship Series; defeated Atlanta in World Series.
2000—Defeated Oakland in A.L. divisional playoff; defeated Seattle in A.L. Championship Series; defeated New York Mets in World Series.

TRACY, JIM   DODGERS

PERSONAL: Born December 31, 1955, in Hamilton, Ohio. ... 6-3/205. ... Batted left, threw right. ... Full name: James Edwin Tracy.
HIGH SCHOOL: Badin (Hamilton, Ohio).
COLLEGE: Marietta College (Ohio).
TRANSACTIONS/CAREER NOTES: Selected by Chicago Cubs organization in fourth round of free-agent draft (January 11, 1977). ... Traded by Cubs to Houston Astros for OF Gary Woods (December 9, 1981).

Year Team (League)	Pos.	G	AB	R	H	2B	3B	HR	RBI	Avg.	BB	SO	SB	PO	A	E	Avg.
							BATTING							FIELDING			
1977— Pom. Beach (FSL)	1B-OF	93	261	27	59	13	2	4	34	.226	41	66	1	147	6	4	.975
1978— Pom. Beach (FSL)	1B-OF	78	225	42	55	7	5	6	43	.244	58	34	2	329	27	4	.989
— Midland (Texas)	OF-1B	54	189	34	49	9	2	8	29	.259	20	50	2	174	10	2	.989
1979— Midland (Texas)	1B	86	301	75	107	16	1	15	67	*.355	63	41	7	799	31	6	.993
— Wichita (A.A.)	1B-OF	44	150	26	41	9	1	4	18	.273	21	36	0	364	20	11	.972
1980— Wichita (A.A.)	OF-1B-3B	112	406	66	130	17	6	16	63	.320	67	68	4	428	33	5	.989
— Chicago (N.L.)	OF-1B	42	122	12	31	3	3	3	9	.254	13	37	2	44	0	2	.957
1981— Midland (Texas)	OF-1B	22	73	8	20	3	0	2	7	.274	13	22	0	73	2	0	1.000
— Chicago (N.L.)	OF	45	63	6	15	2	1	0	5	.238	12	14	1	16	0	0	1.000
1982— Tucson (PCL)	OF-1B	133	481	85	153	35	3	12	100	.318	81	83	5	294	14	4	.987
1983— Taiyo (Jap. Cen.)		125	469	61	142	29	2	19	66	.303	32	74	3	...	...	...	...
1984— Taiyo (Jap. Cen.)		3	9	1	2	0	0	1	5	.222	2	1	0	...	...	...	...
— Tucson (PCL)	OF-1B	52	156	22	38	12	3	1	21	.244	31	39	2	67	0	2	.971
Major League totals (2 years)		87	185	18	46	5	4	3	14	.249	25	51	3	60	0	2	.968

RECORD AS MANAGER

BACKGROUND: Coach, Montreal Expos (1995-98). ... Coach, Los Angeles Dodgers (1999 and 2000).
HONORS: Named Minor League Manager of the Year by The Sporting News (1993).

Year Team (League)	REGULAR SEASON				POSTSEASON							
					Playoff		Champ. Series		World Series		All-Star Game	
	W	L	Pct.	Pos.	W	L	W	L	W	L	W	L
1987— Peoria	71	69	.507	2nd(S)	—	—	—	—	—	—	—	—
1988— Peoria	29	40	.420	6th(S)	—	—	—	—	—	—	—	—
— (Second half)	41	30	.577	3rd(S)	—	—	—	—	—	—	—	—
1989— Chattanooga	33	38	.465	4th(S)	—	—	—	—	—	—	—	—
— (Second half)	25	43	.368	5th(S)	—	—	—	—	—	—	—	—
1990— Chattanooga	35	36	.493	4th(S)	—	—	—	—	—	—	—	—
— (Second half)	31	42	.425	4th(S)	—	—	—	—	—	—	—	—
1991— Chattanooga	35	32	.522	2nd(S)	—	—	—	—	—	—	—	—
— (Second half)	38	39	.494	3rd(S)	—	—	—	—	—	—	—	—
1992—Harrisburg	94	44	.681	1st	—	—	—	—	—	—	—	—
1993—Ottawa	70	72	.493	3rd(E)	—	—	—	—	—	—	—	—

NOTES:
1992—Defeated Albany, three games to one in playoff; defeated Canton-Akron, three games to two in championship playoff.

VALENTINE, BOBBY   METS

PERSONAL: Born May 13, 1950, in Stamford, Conn. ... 5-10/185. ... Batted right, threw right. ... Full name: Robert John Valentine. ... Son-in-law of Ralph Branca, pitcher with Brooklyn Dodgers (1944-53 and 1956), Detroit Tigers (1953-54), New York Yankees (1955).
HIGH SCHOOL: Rippowan (Stamford, Conn.).
COLLEGE: Arizona State, then Southern California.

TRANSACTIONS/CAREER NOTES: Selected by Los Angeles Dodgers organization in first round (fifth pick overall) of free-agent draft (June 7, 1968). ... Traded by Dodgers with IF Billy Grabarkewitz, OF Frank Robinson, P Bill Singer and P Mike Strahler to California Angels for P Andy Messersmith and 3B Ken McMullen (November 28, 1972). ... On disabled list (May 17, 1973-remainder of season and May 29-June 13, 1974). ... Loaned by Angels to Charleston, Pittsburgh Pirates organization (April 4-June 20, 1975). ... Traded by Angels with a player to be named later to San Diego Padres for P Gary Ross (September 17, 1975); Padres acquired IF Rudy Meoli to complete deal (November 4, 1975). ... Traded by Padres with P Paul Siebert to New York Mets for IF/OF Dave Kingman (June 15, 1977). ... Released by Mets (March 26, 1979). ... Signed by Seattle Mariners (April 10, 1979). ... Granted free agency (November 1, 1979).
HONORS: Named Pacific Coast League Player of the Year (1970).
STATISTICAL NOTES: Led Pioneer League outfielders with 107 putouts and tied for lead with eight assists in 1968. ... Led Pacific Coast League shortstops with 38 errors in 1969. ... Led Pacific Coast League with 324 total bases, with 10 sacrifice flies and in double plays by shortstop with 106 in 1970. ... Led Pacific Coast League shortstops with 217 putouts and 54 errors in 1970.

									BATTING						FIELDING		
Year	Team (League)	Pos.	G	AB	R	H	2B	3B	HR	RBI	Avg.	BB	SO	SB	PO	A	E	Avg.
1968— Ogden (Pioneer)........	OF-SS	62	224	*62	63	14	4	6	26	.281	39	27	*20	†111	‡10	6	.953
1969— Spokane (PCL)..........	SS-OF	111	402	61	104	19	5	3	35	.259	32	57	34	166	254	†38	.917
— Los Angeles (N.L.)	PR	5	0	3	0	0	0	0	0	...	0	0	0	...	...	...	...
1970— Spokane (PCL)..........	SS-2B	•146	*621	*122	*211	*39	*16	14	80	*.340	47	51	29	†217	474	†54	.928
1971— Spokane (PCL)..........	SS	7	30	7	10	2	0	1	2	.333	3	6	3	13	18	3	.912
— Los Angeles (N.L.)	S-3-2-O	101	281	32	70	10	2	1	25	.249	15	20	5	123	176	16	.949
1972— Los Angeles (N.L.)	2-3-O-S	119	391	42	107	11	2	3	32	.274	27	33	5	178	245	23	.948
1973— California (A.L.)■	SS-OF	32	126	12	38	5	2	1	13	.302	5	9	6	63	75	6	.958
1974— California (A.L.)	O-S-3-DH	117	371	39	97	10	3	3	39	.261	25	25	8	160	116	17	.942
1975— Char., W.Va. (I.L.)■	3B	56	175	27	41	4	0	1	17	.234	30	16	8	44	74	6	.952
— Salt Lake (PCL)■	1-0-3-2	46	147	29	45	6	1	0	17	.306	31	15	13	92	14	3	.972
— California (A.L.)	DH-1-3-O	26	57	5	16	2	0	0	5	.281	4	3	0	27	1	2	.933
— San Diego (N.L.)■	OF	7	15	1	2	0	0	1	1	.133	4	0	1	4	0	0	1.000
1976— Hawaii (PCL)	1-0-3-S	120	395	67	120	23	2	13	89	.304	47	32	9	578	47	4	.994
— San Diego (N.L.)■	OF-1B	15	49	3	18	4	0	0	4	.367	6	2	0	55	6	0	1.000
1977— San Diego (N.L.)	...	44	67	5	12	3	0	1	10	.179	7	10	0	...	...	...	...
— New York (N.L.)■		42	83	8	11	1	0	1	3	.133	6	9	0	...	...	...	...
1978— New York (N.L.)..........	2B-3B	69	160	17	43	7	0	1	18	.269	19	18	1	78	109	6	.969
1979— Seattle (A.L.)■ S-O-2-3-C-DH		62	98	9	27	6	0	0	7	.276	22	5	1	32	38	2	.972
American League totals (4 years)		237	652	65	178	23	5	4	64	.273	56	42	15	282	230	27	.950
National League totals (7 years)		488	1196	124	286	40	4	10	106	.239	97	111	12	...	...	...	...
Major league totals (10 years)		725	1848	189	464	63	9	14	170	.251	153	153	27	...	...	...	...

RECORD AS MANAGER

BACKGROUND: Scout and minor league instructor, San Diego Padres (1981). ... Minor league instructor, New York Mets (1982). ... Coach, Mets (1983-May 15, 1985). ... Coach, Cincinnati Reds (1993).

		REGULAR SEASON				POSTSEASON							
						Playoff		Champ. Series		World Series		All-Star Game	
Year	Team (League)	W	L	Pct.	Pos.	W	L	W	L	W	L	W	L
1985— Texas (A.L.)..............		53	76	.411	7th (W)	—	—	—	—	—	—	—	—
1986— Texas (A.L.)..............		87	75	.537	2nd (W)	—	—	—	—	—	—	—	—
1987— Texas (A.L.)..............		75	87	.463	T6th (W)	—	—	—	—	—	—	—	—
1988— Texas (A.L.)..............		70	91	.435	6th (W)	—	—	—	—	—	—	—	—
1989— Texas (A.L.)..............		83	79	.512	4th (W)	—	—	—	—	—	—	—	—
1990— Texas (A.L.)..............		83	79	.512	3rd (W)	—	—	—	—	—	—	—	—
1991— Texas (A.L.)..............		85	77	.525	3rd (W)	—	—	—	—	—	—	—	—
1992— Texas (A.L.)..............		45	41	.523		—	—	—	—	—	—	—	—
1994— Norfolk (I.L.)		67	75	.472	4th (W)								
1995— Chiba Lotte (Jp. Cen.)		69	58	.543	2nd (P)								
1996— Norfolk (I.L.)		76	57	.571									
— New York (N.L.)		12	19	.387	4th (E)								
1997— New York (N.L.)		88	74	.543	3rd (E)	—	—	—	—	—	—	—	—
1998— New York (N.L.)		88	74	.543	2nd (E)	—	—	—	—	—	—	—	—
1999— New York (N.L.)		97	66	.595	2nd (E)	3	1	2	4				
2000— New York (N.L.)		94	68	.580	2nd (E)	3	1	4	1	1	4		
American League totals (8 years)		581	605	.490		—	—	—	—	—	—	—	—
National League totals (5 years)		379	301	.557		6	2	6	5	1	4	—	—
Major league totals (13 years)		960	906	.515		6	2	6	5	1	4	—	—

NOTES:
1985—Replaced Texas manager Doug Rader with club in seventh place and record of 9-23 (May 16).
1992—Replaced as Texas manager by Toby Harrah with club in third place (July 9).
1995—Chiba Lotte tied three games.
1996—Replaced New York manager Dallas Green with club in fourth place and record of 59-72 (August 26).
1999—Defeated Arizona in N.L. divisional playoff; lost to Atlanta in N.L. Championship Series.
2000—Defeated San Francisco in N.L. divisional playoff;

WILLIAMS, JIMY — RED SOX

PERSONAL: Born October 4, 1943, in Santa Maria, Calif. ... 5-11/170. ... Batted right, threw right. ... Full name: James Francis Williams.
COLLEGE: Fresno State College (bachelor of science degree in agribusiness).
TRANSACTIONS/CAREER NOTES: Selected by St. Louis Cardinals organization from Toronto, Boston Red Sox organization (November 29, 1965). ... In military service (July 24, 1966-remainder of season). ... Traded by Cardinals with C Pat Corrales to Cincinnati Reds for C John Edwards (February 8, 1968). ... Selected by Montreal Expos in expansion draft (October 14, 1968). ... On disabled list (May 13-30 and June 24-September 2, 1969). ... On suspended list (June 7-16, 1971). ... Sold to New York Mets organization (June 16, 1971). ... On temporary inactive list (August 12-16, 1971). ... On disabled list (May 15-July 17 and July 29-August 20, 1975).

Year	Team (League)	Pos.	G	AB	R	H	2B	3B	HR	RBI	Avg.	BB	SO	SB	PO	A	E	Avg.
							BATTING									FIELDING		
1965—	Waterloo (Midw.)	SS	115	435	64	125	19	3	2	31	.287	41	74	10	173	*312	26	*.949
1966—	St. Louis (N.L.)...........	SS-2B	13	11	1	3	0	0	0	1	.273	1	5	0	2	5	0	1.000
1967—	Arkansas (Texas)........	SS	28	101	8	21	1	1	0	8	.208	9	14	0	49	80	2	.985
	— Tulsa (PCL)	SS	61	164	18	37	2	0	1	21	.226	18	33	4	87	156	26	.903
	— St. Louis (N.L.)..........	SS	1	2	0	0	0	0	0	0	.000	0	1	0	6	1	0	1.000
1968—	Indianapolis (PCL)■..	SS-2B	120	403	38	91	19	5	2	34	.226	20	59	5	198	323	27	.951
1969—	Vancouver (PCL)■.....	3B-OF-SS	35	66	7	17	1	1	0	9	.258	4	8	1	17	23	2	.952
1970—	Winnipeg (I.L.)	SS-2B-3B	109	361	49	83	15	0	3	18	.230	34	48	5	178	244	30	.934
1971—	Winn.-Tide. (I.L.)■....	SS-3B-2B	105	327	40	84	7	4	5	31	.257	38	46	7	120	219	22	.939
1972—	....							Did not play.										
1973—	....							Did not play.										
1974—	....							Did not play.										
1975—	El Paso (Texas)..........	DH	6	17	3	2	0	0	0	2	.118	2	2	0	...	...	...	...
Major league totals (2 years)			14	13	1	3	0	0	0	1	.231	0	0	0	8	6	0	1.000

RECORD AS MANAGER

BACKGROUND: Coach, Toronto Blue Jays (1980-85). ... Minor league instructor, Atlanta Braves (October 4, 1989-June 25, 1990). ... Coach, Braves (1990-96).

HONORS: Named Pacific Coast League Manager of the Year (1976 and 1979). ... Named A.L. Manager of the Year by THE SPORTING NEWS (1999). ... Named A.L. Manager of the Year by Baseball Writers' Association of America (1999).

Year	Team (League)	W	L	Pct.	Pos.	Playoff W	Playoff L	Champ. Series W	Champ. Series L	World Series W	World Series L	All-Star Game W	All-Star Game L
		REGULAR SEASON				POSTSEASON							
1974—	Quad Cities (Midwest)	33	26	.559	1st (S)	—	—	—	—	—	—	—	—
	(Second half)	32	32	.500	3rd (S)	1	2	—	—	—	—	—	—
1975—	El Paso (Texas)	62	71	.466	3rd (W)	—	—	—	—	—	—	—	—
1976—	Salt Lake City (Pacific Coast)...................	90	54	.625	1st (E)	2	3	—	—	—	—	—	—
1977—	Salt Lake City (Pacific Coast)...................	74	65	.532	2nd (E)	—	—	—	—	—	—	—	—
1978—	Springfield (American Association)	70	66	.515	3rd (E)	—	—	—	—	—	—	—	—
1979—	Salt Lake City (Pacific Coast)...................	34	40	.447	4th (S)	—	—	—	—	—	—	—	—
	(Second half)	46	28	.622	1st (S)	5	0	—	—	—	—	—	—
1986—	Toronto (A.L.)	86	76	.531	4th (E)	—	—	—	—	—	—	—	—
1987—	Toronto (A.L.)	96	66	.593	2nd (E)	—	—	—	—	—	—	—	—
1988—	Toronto (A.L.)	87	75	.537	T3rd (E)	—	—	—	—	—	—	—	—
1989—	Toronto (A.L.)	12	24	.333		—	—	—	—	—	—	—	—
1997—	Boston (A.L.)	78	84	.481	4th (E)	—	—	—	—	—	—	—	—
1998—	Boston (A.L.)	92	70	.568	2nd (E)	1	3	—	—	—	—	—	—
1999—	Boston (A.L.)	94	68	.580	2nd (E)	3	2	1	4	—	—	—	—
2000—	Boston (A.L.)	85	77	.525	2nd (E)	—	—	—	—	—	—	—	—
Major league totals (8 years)		630	540	.539		4	5	1	4	—	—	—	—

NOTES:
1974—Lost to Danville in playoffs.
1976—Lost to Hawaii in championship playoff.
1979—Defeated Albuquerque, two games to none, in playoff; defeated Hawaii, three games to none, in championship playoff.
1989—Replaced as Toronto manager by Cito Gaston, with club tied for sixth place (May 15).
1998—Lost to Cleveland in A.L. divisional playoff.
1999—Defeated Cleveland in A.L. divisional playoff; lost to New York Yankees in A.L. Championship Series.

THE CLASS OF 2001

PUCKETT, KIRBY   OF

PERSONAL: Born March 14, 1961, in Chicago. ... 5-9/223. ... Bats right, throws right.
HIGH SCHOOL: Calumet (Chicago).
JUNIOR COLLEGE: Triton College (Ill.).
COLLEGE: Bradley.
TRANSACTIONS/CAREER NOTES: Selected by Minnesota Twins organization in first round (third pick overall) of free-agent draft (January 12, 1982). ... Granted free agency (October 28, 1992). ... Re-signed by Twins (December 4, 1992). ... On disabled list (March 28-July 12, 1996). ... Announced retirement (July 12, 1996).
RECORDS: Shares major league single-season record for most at-bats with no sacrifice flies—680 (1986). ... Shares major league record for most consecutive years leading league in hits—3 (1987-89). ... Shares major league single-game records for most doubles—4 (May 13, 1989); and most doubles in two consecutive leagues—6 (May 13 [4] and 14 [2], 1989). ... Shares modern major league record for most hits in first game in majors (nine innings)—4 (May 8, 1984). ... Holds A.L. record for most hits in two consecutive nine-inning games—10 (August 29 [4] and 30 [6], 1987). ... Shares A.L. career record for most seasons with 400 or more putouts by outfielder—5.
HONORS: Named California League Player of the Year (1983). ... Named outfielder on THE SPORTING NEWS A.L. All-Star team (1986-89, 1992 and 1994). ... Named outfielder on THE SPORTING NEWS A.L. Silver Slugger team (1986-89, 1992 and 1994). ... Won A.L. Gold Glove as out-fielder (1986-89 and 1991-92).
STATISTICAL NOTES: Led Appalachian League with 135 total bases in 1982. ... Led California League outfielders with five double plays in 1983. ... Led A.L. outfielders with 492 total chances in 1985, 465 in 1988 and 455 in 1989. ... Hit for the cycle (August 1, 1986). ... Collected six hits in one game (August 30, 1987 and May 23, 1991). ... Led A.L. with 358 total bases in 1988 and 313 in 1992. ... Led A.L. in grounding into double plays with 27 in 1991. ... Career major league grand slams: 7.
MISCELLANEOUS: Holds Minnesota Twins all-time records for most runs (1,071), hits (2,304) and doubles (414). ... Named Minnesota Twins executive vice president of baseball (November 16, 1996).

Year Team (League)	Pos.	G	AB	R	H	2B	3B	HR	RBI	Avg.	BB	SO	SB	PO	A	E	Avg.
1982— Elizabethton (Appl.)....	OF	65	*275	*65	*105	15	3	3	35	*.382	25	27	•43	133	*11	5	.966
1983— Visalia (Calif.).............	OF	138	*548	105	172	29	7	9	97	.314	46	62	48	253	*22	5	.982
1984— Toledo (I.L.)................	OF	21	80	9	21	2	0	1	5	.263	4	14	8	35	1	3	.923
— Minnesota (A.L.)	OF	128	557	63	165	12	5	0	31	.296	16	69	14	438	*16	3	.993
1985— Minnesota (A.L.)	OF	161	*691	80	199	29	13	4	74	.288	41	87	21	*465	19	8	.984
1986— Minnesota (A.L.)	OF	161	680	119	223	37	6	31	96	.328	34	99	20	429	8	6	.986
1987— Minnesota (A.L.)	OF-DH	157	624	96	•207	32	5	28	99	.332	32	91	12	341	8	5	.986
1988— Minnesota (A.L.)	OF	158	*657	109	*234	42	5	24	121	.356	23	83	6	*450	12	3	.994
1989— Minnesota (A.L.)	OF-DH	159	635	75	*215	45	4	9	85	*.339	41	59	11	*438	13	4	.991
1990— Minnesota (A.L.) O-DH-2-3-S	146	551	82	164	40	3	12	80	.298	57	73	5	354	9	4	.989
1991— Minnesota (A.L.)	OF	152	611	92	195	29	6	15	89	.319	31	78	11	373	13	6	.985
1992— Minnesota (A.L.) O-DH-3-2-S	160	639	104	*210	38	4	19	110	.329	44	97	17	394	9	3	.993
1993— Minnesota (A.L.)	OF-DH	156	622	89	184	39	3	22	89	.296	47	93	8	312	13	2	.994
1994— Minnesota (A.L.)	OF-DH	108	439	79	139	32	3	20	*112	.317	28	47	6	204	*13	3	.986
1995— Minnesota (A.L.) O-DH-2-3-S	137	538	83	169	39	0	23	99	.314	56	89	3	195	10	4	.981
Major League totals (12 years)		1783	7244	1071	2304	414	57	207	1085	.318	450	965	134	4393	143	51	.989

CHAMPIONSHIP SERIES RECORD

RECORDS: Shares A.L. single-game record for most at-bats—6 (October 12, 1987).
NOTES: Named Most Valuable Player (1991).

Year Team (League)	Pos.	G	AB	R	H	2B	3B	HR	RBI	Avg.	BB	SO	SB	PO	A	E	Avg.
1987— Minnesota (A.L.)	OF	5	24	3	5	1	0	1	3	.208	0	5	1	7	0	0	1.000
1991— Minnesota (A.L.)	OF	5	21	4	9	1	0	2	6	.429	1	4	0	13	1	0	1.000
Championship series totals (2 years)		10	45	7	14	2	0	3	9	.311	1	9	1	20	1	0	1.000

WORLD SERIES RECORD

RECORDS: Shares record for most at-bats in one inning—2 (October 18, 1987, fourth inning). ... Shares single-game record for most runs—4 (October 24, 1987).
NOTES: Member of World Series championship teams (1987 and 1991).

Year Team (League)	Pos.	G	AB	R	H	2B	3B	HR	RBI	Avg.	BB	SO	SB	PO	A	E	Avg.
1987— Minnesota (A.L.)	OF	7	28	5	10	1	1	0	3	.357	2	1	1	15	1	1	.941
1991— Minnesota (A.L.)	OF	7	24	4	6	0	1	2	4	.250	5	7	1	16	1	0	1.000
World Series totals (2 years)		14	52	9	16	1	2	2	7	.308	7	8	2	31	2	1	.971

ALL-STAR GAME RECORD

NOTES: Named Most Valuable Player (1993).

Year League	Pos.	AB	R	H	2B	3B	HR	RBI	Avg.	BB	SO	SB	PO	A	E	Avg.
1986— American	OF	3	0	1	0	0	0	0	.333	1	0	1	5	0	0	1.000
1987— American	PH-OF	4	0	0	0	0	0	0	.000	0	3	0	1	0	0	1.000
1988— American	OF	1	0	0	0	0	0	0	.000	0	0	0	1	0	0	1.000
1989— American	OF	3	1	1	0	0	0	0	.333	0	0	0	0	0	0	...
1990— American	PH-OF	1	0	1	0	0	0	0	1.000	0	0	0	1	0	0	1.000
1991— American	OF	1	0	0	0	0	0	0	.000	0	0	0	0	0	0	...
1992— American	OF	3	1	1	0	0	0	0	.333	0	1	0	2	0	0	1.000
1993— American	OF	3	1	2	1	0	1	2	.667	0	0	0	1	0	0	1.000
1994— American	OF	3	0	1	0	0	0	1	.333	0	0	0	1	0	0	1.000
1995— American	OF	2	0	0	0	0	0	0	.000	0	1	0	2	0	0	1.000
All-Star Game totals (10 years)		24	3	7	1	0	1	3	.292	1	5	1	14	0	0	1.000

PERSONAL: Born October 3, 1951, in St. Paul, Minn. ... 6-6/245. ... Bats right, throws right. ... Full name: David Mark Winfield.

HIGH SCHOOL: St. Paul (Minn.) Central.

COLLEGE: Minnesota.

TRANSACTIONS/CAREER NOTES: Selected by Baltimore Orioles organization in 40th round of free-agent draft (June 5, 1969); did not sign. ... Selected by San Diego Padres organization in first round (fourth pick overall) of free-agent draft (June 5, 1973). ... Granted free agency (October 22, 1980). ... Signed by New York Yankees (December 15, 1980). ... On disabled list (May 20-June 4, 1982; April 16-May 1, 1984; and March 19, 1989-entire season). ... Traded by Yankees to California Angels for P Mike Witt (May 11, 1990). ... Granted free agency (October 30, 1991). ... Signed by Toronto Blue Jays (December 19, 1991). ... Granted free agency (November 2, 1992). ... Signed by Minnesota Twins (December 17, 1992). ... On disabled list (July 7-23, 1994). ... Traded by Twins to Cleveland Indians for a player to be named later (August 31, 1994). ... Granted free agency (October 17, 1994). ... Re-signed by Indians (April 5, 1995). ... On disabled list (June 11-July 17 and August 12-September 1, 1995). ... Granted free agency (November 6, 1995).

HONORS: Named outfielder on THE SPORTING NEWS college All-America team (1973). ... Named Most Outstanding Player of College World Series (1973). ... Named outfielder on THE SPORTING NEWS N.L. All-Star team (1979). ... Won N.L. Gold Glove as outfielder (1979-80). ... Named outfielder on THE SPORTING NEWS A.L. Silver Slugger team (1981-85). ... Named outfielder on THE SPORTING NEWS A.L. All-Star team (1982-84). ... Won A.L. Gold Glove as outfielder (1982-85 and 1987). ... Named A.L. Comeback Player of the Year by THE SPORTING NEWS (1990). ... Named designated hitter on THE SPORTING NEWS A.L. All-Star team (1992). ... Named designated hitter on THE SPORTING NEWS A.L. Silver Slugger team (1992).

STATISTICAL NOTES: Led N.L. with 333 total bases and 24 intentional bases on balls received in 1979. ... Had 20-game hitting streak (August 17-September 8, 1984). ... Hit three home runs in one game (April 13, 1991). ... Hit for the cycle (June 24, 1991). ... Career major league grand slams: 11.

MISCELLANEOUS: Selected by Atlanta Hawks in fifth round (79th pick overall) of 1973 NBA draft. ... Selected by Utah Stars in sixth round (58th pick overall) of 1973 ABA draft. ... Selected by Minnesota Vikings in 17th round (429th pick overall) of 1973 NFL draft.

Year Team (League)	Pos.	G	AB	R	H	2B	3B	HR	RBI	Avg.	BB	SO	SB	PO	A	E	Avg.
1973— San Diego (N.L.)	OF-1B	56	141	9	39	4	1	3	12	.277	12	19	0	65	1	3	.957
1974— San Diego (N.L.)	OF	145	498	57	132	18	4	20	75	.265	40	96	9	276	11	•12	.960
1975— San Diego (N.L.)	OF	143	509	74	136	20	2	15	76	.267	69	82	23	302	9	9	.972
1976— San Diego (N.L.)	OF	137	492	81	139	26	4	13	69	.283	65	78	26	304	*15	6	.982
1977— San Diego (N.L.)	OF	157	615	104	169	29	7	25	92	.275	58	75	16	368	15	11	.972
1978— San Diego (N.L.)	OF-1B	158	587	88	181	30	5	24	97	.308	55	81	21	328	8	7	.980
1979— San Diego (N.L.)	OF	159	597	97	184	27	10	34	*118	.308	85	71	15	344	14	5	.986
1980— San Diego (N.L.)	OF	162	558	89	154	25	6	20	87	.276	79	83	23	273	20	4	.987
1981— New York (A.L.)■	OF-DH	105	388	52	114	25	1	13	68	.294	43	41	11	196	1	3	.985
1982— New York (A.L.)	OF-DH	140	539	84	151	24	8	37	106	.280	45	64	5	279	*17	8	.974
1983— New York (A.L.)	OF	152	598	99	169	26	8	32	116	.283	58	77	15	313	5	7	.978
1984— New York (A.L.)	OF	141	567	106	193	34	4	19	100	.340	53	71	6	306	3	2	.994
1985— New York (A.L.)	OF-DH	155	633	105	174	34	6	26	114	.275	52	96	19	316	13	3	.991
1986— New York (A.L.)	OF-DH-3B	154	565	90	148	31	5	24	104	.262	77	106	6	292	9	5	.984
1987— New York (A.L.)	OF-DH	156	575	83	158	22	1	27	97	.275	76	96	5	253	6	3	.989
1988— New York (A.L.)	OF-DH	149	559	96	180	37	2	25	107	.322	69	88	9	276	3	3	.989
1989— New York (A.L.)						Did not play.											
1990— New York (A.L.)	OF-DH	20	61	7	13	3	0	2	6	.213	4	13	0	12	0	0	1.000
— California (A.L.)■	OF-DH	112	414	63	114	18	2	19	72	.275	48	68	0	165	7	2	.989
1991— California (A.L.)	OF-DH	150	568	75	149	27	4	28	86	.262	56	109	7	198	7	2	.990
1992— Toronto (A.L.)	DH-OF	156	583	92	169	33	3	26	108	.290	82	89	2	52	1	0	1.000
1993— Minnesota (A.L.)■	DH-OF-1B	143	547	72	148	27	2	21	76	.271	45	106	2	91	3	0	1.000
1994— Minnesota (A.L.)	DH-OF	77	294	35	74	15	3	10	43	.252	31	51	2	3	0	0	1.000
1995— Cleveland (A.L.)■	DH	46	115	11	22	5	0	2	4	.191	14	26	1	0	0	0	...
American League totals (14 years)		1856	7006	1070	1976	361	49	311	1207	.282	753	1101	90	2752	75	38	.987
National League totals (8 years)		1117	3997	599	1134	179	39	154	626	.284	463	585	133	2260	93	57	.976
Major League totals (22 years)		2973	11003	1669	3110	540	88	465	1833	.283	1216	1686	223	5012	168	95	.982

DIVISION SERIES RECORD

Year Team (League)	Pos.	G	AB	R	H	2B	3B	HR	RBI	Avg.	BB	SO	SB	PO	A	E	Avg.
1981— New York (A.L.)	OF	5	20	2	7	3	0	0	0	.350	1	5	0	10	1	0	1.000

CHAMPIONSHIP SERIES RECORD

RECORDS: Shares A.L. single-game record for most at-bats—6 (October 11, 1992, 11 innings).

Year Team (League)	Pos.	G	AB	R	H	2B	3B	HR	RBI	Avg.	BB	SO	SB	PO	A	E	Avg.
1981— New York (A.L.)	OF	3	13	2	2	1	0	0	2	.154	2	2	1	6	0	0	1.000
1992— Toronto (A.L.)	DH	6	24	7	6	1	0	2	3	.250	4	2	0	...	...	...	...
Championship series totals (2 years)		9	37	9	8	2	0	2	5	.216	6	4	1	6	0	0	1.000

WORLD SERIES RECORD

NOTES: Member of World Series championship team (1992).

Year Team (League)	Pos.	G	AB	R	H	2B	3B	HR	RBI	Avg.	BB	SO	SB	PO	A	E	Avg.
1981— New York (A.L.)	OF	6	22	0	1	0	0	0	1	.045	5	4	1	13	1	0	1.000
1992— Toronto (A.L.)	OF-DH	6	22	0	5	1	0	0	3	.227	2	3	0	7	0	0	1.000
World Series totals (2 years)		12	44	0	6	1	0	0	4	.136	7	7	1	20	1	0	1.000

ALL-STAR GAME RECORD

RECORDS: Holds career record for most doubles—7. ... Shares record for most consecutive games with one or more hits—7. ... Shares single-game record for most at-bats in nine-inning game—5 (July 17, 1979).

Year	League	Pos.	AB	R	H	2B	3B	HR	RBI	Avg.	BB	SO	SB	PO	A	E	Avg.
1977— National		OF	2	0	2	1	0	0	2	1.000	0	0	0	1	0	0	1.000
1978— National		OF	2	1	1	0	0	0	0	.500	0	0	0	1	0	0	1.000
1979— National		OF	5	1	1	1	0	0	1	.200	0	1	0	3	0	0	1.000
1980— National		OF	2	0	0	0	0	0	1	.000	0	0	0	2	0	0	1.000
1981— American		OF	4	0	0	0	0	0	0	.000	1	0	0	0	1	0	1.000
1982— American		OF	2	0	1	0	0	0	0	.500	0	0	0	0	0	0	...
1983— American		OF	3	2	3	1	0	0	1	1.000	0	0	0	3	0	0	1.000
1984— American		OF	4	0	1	1	0	0	0	.250	0	0	0	2	1	0	1.000
1985— American		OF	3	0	1	0	0	0	0	.333	0	0	1	0	0	0	...
1986— American		OF	1	1	1	1	0	0	0	1.000	0	0	0	0	0	0	...
1987— American		OF	5	0	1	1	0	0	0	.200	1	0	0	2	0	0	1.000
1988— American		OF	3	1	1	1	0	0	0	.333	0	0	0	1	0	0	1.000
All-Star Game totals (12 years)			36	6	13	7	0	0	5	.361	2	1	1	15	2	0	1.000

2000 STATISTICAL LEADERS

AMERICAN LEAGUE

BATTING LEADERS

Batting average
.372 Nomar Garciaparra, Bos.
.355 Darin Erstad, Ana.
.351 Manny Ramirez, Cle.
.344 Carlos Delgado, Tor.
.339 Derek Jeter, N.Y.

Games
162 Jose Cruz, Tor.
162 Carlos Delgado, Tor.
161 Mo Vaughn, Ana.
160 Miguel Tejada, Oak.
159 Garret Anderson, Ana.
159 Johnny Damon, K.C.
159 Troy Glaus, Ana.
159 John Olerud, Sea.
159 Mike Sweeney, K.C.
159 Frank Thomas, Chi.

At-bats
676 Darin Erstad, Ana.
655 Johnny Damon, K.C.
647 Garret Anderson, Ana.
632 Gerald Williams, T.B.
631 Cristian Guzman, Min.

Runs scored
136 Johnny Damon, K.C.
134 Alex Rodriguez, Sea.
121 Darin Erstad, Ana.
121 Ray Durham, Chi.
120 Troy Glaus, Ana.
119 Derek Jeter, N.Y.

Hits
240 Darin Erstad, Ana.
214 Johnny Damon, K.C.
206 Mike Sweeney, K.C.
201 Derek Jeter, N.Y.
197 Nomar Garciaparra, Bos.

RBIs
145 Edgar Martinez, Sea.
144 Mike Sweeney, K.C.
143 Frank Thomas, Chi.
137 Carlos Delgado, Tor.
137 Jason Giambi, Oak.
132 Alex Rodriguez, Sea.

Total bases
378 Carlos Delgado, Tor.
366 Darin Erstad, Ana.
364 Frank Thomas, Chi.
340 Troy Glaus, Ana.
337 Jermaine Dye, K.C.

Doubles
57 Carlos Delgado, Tor.
51 Nomar Garciaparra, Bos.
46 Deivi Cruz, Det.
45 John Olerud, Sea.
44 Frank Thomas, Chi.

44 Bobby Higginson, Det.
44 Matt Lawton, Min.

Triples
20 Cristian Guzman, Min.
11 Adam Kennedy, Ana.
10 Johnny Damon, K.C.
9 Ray Durham, Chi.
8 Trot Nixon, Bos.
8 Luis Alicea, Tex.

Home runs
47 Troy Glaus, Ana.
43 Jason Giambi, Oak.
43 Frank Thomas, Chi.
41 Alex Rodriguez, Sea.
41 Tony Batista, Tor.
41 Carlos Delgado, Tor.
41 David Justice, Cle.-N.Y.
39 Rafael Palmeiro, Tex.
38 Manny Ramirez, Cle.
37 Jim Thome, Cle.
37 Edgar Martinez, Sea.

Walks
137 Jason Giambi, Oak.
123 Carlos Delgado, Tor.
118 Jim Thome, Cle.
112 Troy Glaus, Ana.
112 Frank Thomas, Chi.
107 Jorge Posada, N.Y.

On-base percentage
.476 Jason Giambi, Oak.
.470 Carlos Delgado, Tor.
.457 Manny Ramirez, Cle.
.436 Frank Thomas, Chi.
.434 Nomar Garciaparra, Bos.

Slugging percentage
.697 Manny Ramirez, Cle.
.664 Carlos Delgado, Tor.
.647 Jason Giambi, Oak.
.625 Frank Thomas, Chi.
.606 Alex Rodriguez, Sea.

Stolen bases
46 Johnny Damon, K.C.
39 Roberto Alomar, Cle.
37 Delino DeShields, Bal.
31 Rickey Henderson, Sea.
30 Kenny Lofton, Cle.
30 Mark McLemore, Sea.

Caught stealing
14 Mark McLemore, Sea.
13 Ray Durham, Chi.
12 Gerald Williams, T.B.
11 Troy Glaus, Ana.
10 Delino DeShields, Bal.
10 Cristian Guzman, Min.
10 Omar Vizquel, Cle.

Sacrifice hits
16 Alex Gonzalez, Tor.
13 Carlos Febles, K.C.
13 Jose Valentin, Chi.
12 Chris Singleton, Chi.
12 Royce Clayton, Tex.
12 Felix Martinez, T.B.
11 Mark McLemore, Sea.
11 Roberto Alomar, Cle.
11 Rey Sanchez, K.C.
11 Dan Wilson, Sea.

Sacrifice flies
15 Magglio Ordonez, Chi.
13 Mike Sweeney, K.C.
12 Johnny Damon, K.C.
11 Paul O'Neill, N.Y.
11 Alex Rodriguez, Sea.
10 John Olerud, Sea.
10 Joe Randa, K.C.
10 Dean Palmer, Det.
10 Travis Fryman, Cle.

Strikeouts
181 Mo Vaughn, Ana.
171 Jim Thome, Cle.
163 Troy Glaus, Ana.
151 Jorge Posada, N.Y.
146 Dean Palmer, Det.

Intentional walks
20 Nomar Garciaparra, Bos.
18 Carlos Delgado, Tor.
18 Frank Thomas, Chi.
17 Rafael Palmeiro, Tex.
11 Mo Vaughn, Ana.
11 John Olerud, Sea.
11 Bernie Williams, N.Y.
11 Albert Belle, Bal.
10 Jorge Posada, N.Y.
10 Fred McGriff, T.B.

PITCHING LEADERS

Earned-run average
1.74 Pedro Martinez, Bos.
3.70 Roger Clemens, N.Y.
3.79 Mike Mussina, Bal.
3.79 Mike Sirotka, Chi.
3.88 Bartolo Colon, Cle.
4.11 David Wells, Tor.

Wins
20 Tim Hudson, Oak.
20 David Wells, Tor.
19 Andy Pettitte, N.Y.
18 Pedro Martinez, Bos.
17 Aaron Sele, Sea.
16 Dave Burba, Cle.
16 Chuck Finley, Cle.
16 Rick Helling, Tex.

Losses
16 Brad Radke, Min.
15 Kelvim Escobar, Tor.

15 Joe Mays, Min.
15 Mike Mussina, Bal.
15 Steve Trachsel, T.B.-Tor.
15 Jeff Weaver, Det.
14 David Cone, N.Y.
13 Rick Helling, Tex.
13 Orlando Hernandez, N.Y.
13 Esteban Loaiza, Tex.-Tor.
13 Albie Lopez, T.B.
13 Sidney Ponson, Bal.
13 Kenny Rogers, Tex.

Games
83 Kelly Wunsch, Chi.
77 Mike Venafro, Tex.
76 Bob Wells, Min.
75 Mike Trombley, Bal.
74 Derek Lowe, Bos.

Games started
35 Rick Helling, Tex.
35 David Wells, Tor.
34 Chuck Finley, Cle.
34 Mike Mussina, Bal.
34 Brad Radke, Min.
34 Kenny Rogers, Tex.
34 Aaron Sele, Sea.
34 Steve Trachsel, T.B.-Tor.
33 Eric Milton, Min.
33 Jeff Suppan, K.C.

Games finished
64 Derek Lowe, Bos.
62 Billy Koch, Tor.
61 Mariano Rivera, N.Y.
60 Todd Jones, Det.
58 Keith Foulke, Chi.
58 Roberto Hernandez, T.B.
58 Kazuhiro Sasaki, Sea.

Complete games
9 David Wells, Tor.
7 Pedro Martinez, Bos.
6 Mike Mussina, Bal.
6 Sidney Ponson, Bal.
4 Albie Lopez, T.B.
4 Brad Radke, Min.
3 Kelvim Escobar, Tor.
3 Chuck Finley, Cle.
3 Orlando Hernandez, N.Y.
3 Andy Pettitte, N.Y.
3 Jeff Suppan, K.C.
3 Steve Trachsel, T.B.-Tor.

Innings pitched
237.2 Mike Mussina, Bal.
229.2 David Wells, Tor.
227.1 Kenny Rogers, Tex.
226.2 Brad Radke, Min.
222.0 Sidney Ponson, Bal.

Shutouts
4 Pedro Martinez, Bos.
2 Tim Hudson, Oak.

2   Aaron Sele, Sea.
1   26 pitchers tied

Hits allowed
266   David Wells, Tor.
261   Brad Radke, Min.
257   Kenny Rogers, Tex.
240   Jeff Suppan, K.C.
236   Mike Mussina, Bal.

Home runs allowed
36   Jeff Suppan, K.C.
35   Eric Milton, Min.
34   James Baldwin, Chi.
34   Orlando Hernandez, N.Y.
31   Hideo Nomo, Det.
31   Tim Wakefield, Bos.
30   Chris Carpenter, Tor.
30   Sidney Ponson, Bal.

Runs allowed
130   Chris Carpenter, Tor.

126   Kenny Rogers, Tex.
125   Sidney Ponson, Bal.
125   Pat Rapp, Bal.
124   David Cone, N.Y.
123   Eric Milton, Min.

Earned runs allowed
122   Chris Carpenter, Tor.
119   David Cone, N.Y.
119   Sidney Ponson, Bal.
119   Jeff Suppan, K.C.
115   Kenny Rogers, Tex.
114   Pat Rapp, Bal.
112   Brad Radke, Min.

Batting average yielded
.167   Pedro Martinez, Bos.
.227   Tim Hudson, Oak.
.233   Bartolo Colon, Cle.
.236   Roger Clemens, N.Y.
.243   Paul Abbott, Sea.

Walks
102   Kevin Appier, Oak.
101   Chuck Finley, Cle.
99   Rick Helling, Tex.
98   Bartolo Colon, Cle.
94   Mac Suzuki, K.C.

Strikeouts
284   Pedro Martinez, Bos.
212   Bartolo Colon, Cle.
210   Mike Mussina, Bal.
189   Chuck Finley, Cle.
188   Roger Clemens, N.Y.

Hit batsmen
15   Jeff Weaver, Det.
14   Pedro Martinez, Bos.
13   Esteban Loaiza, Tex.-Tor.
11   Jim Parque, Chi.
11   Kenny Rogers, Tex.
11   Esteban Yan, T.B.
10   Roger Clemens, N.Y.

Wild pitches
18   Dan Reichert, K.C.
16   Jason Grimsley, N.Y.
16   Hideo Nomo, Det.
14   Hector Carrasco, Min.-Bos.
11   David Cone, N.Y.
11   Joe Mays, Min.
11   Mac Suzuki, K.C.
9   Chuck Finley, Cle.
9   Mark Guthrie, T.B.-Tor.
9   David Wells, Tor.

Saves
42   Todd Jones, Det.
42   Derek Lowe, Bos.
37   Kazuhiro Sasaki, Sea.
36   Mariano Rivera, N.Y.
34   Keith Foulke, Chi.
34   John Wetteland, Tex.
33   Jason Isringhausen, Oak.
33   Billy Koch, Tor.

NATIONAL LEAGUE

BATTING LEADERS

Batting average
.372   Todd Helton, Col.
.355   Moises Alou, Hou.
.345   Vladimir Guerrero, Mon.
.335   Jeffrey Hammonds, Col.
.334   Luis Castillo, Fla.
.334   Jeff Kent, S.F.

Games
162   Luis Gonzalez, Ari.
162   Shawn Green, L.A.
162   Neifi Perez, Col.
161   Jeromy Burnitz, Mil.
161   Andruw Jones, Atl.
161   Preston Wilson, Fla.
160   Todd Helton, Col.
159   Jeff Bagwell, Hou.
159   Jeff Kent, S.F.
158   Derrek Lee, Fla.

At-bats
656   Andruw Jones, Atl.
651   Neifi Perez, Col.
637   Doug Glanville, Phi.
618   Luis Gonzalez, Ari.
617   Mark Grudzielanek, L.A.
617   Tony Womack, Ari.

Runs scored
152   Jeff Bagwell, Hou.
138   Todd Helton, Col.
129   Barry Bonds, S.F.
129   Jim Edmonds, St.L.
122   Andruw Jones, Atl.
118   Richard Hidalgo, Hou.
118   Chipper Jones, Atl.

Hits
216   Todd Helton, Col.
200   Jose Vidro, Mon.
199   Andruw Jones, Atl.

197   Vladimir Guerrero, Mon.
196   Jeff Kent, S.F.

RBIs
147   Todd Helton, Col.
138   Sammy Sosa, Chi.
132   Jeff Bagwell, Hou.
125   Jeff Kent, S.F.
123   Vladimir Guerrero, Mon.
123   Brian Giles, Pit.

Total bases
405   Todd Helton, Col.
383   Sammy Sosa, Chi.
379   Vladimir Guerrero, Mon.
363   Jeff Bagwell, Hou.
355   Richard Hidalgo, Hou.
355   Andruw Jones, Atl.

Doubles
59   Todd Helton, Col.
53   Jeff Cirillo, Col.
51   Jose Vidro, Mon.
47   Luis Gonzalez, Ari.
44   Shawn Green, L.A.

Triples
14   Tony Womack, Ari.
11   Neifi Perez, Col.
11   Vladimir Guerrero, Mon.
10   Bobby Abreu, Phi.
9   Ron Belliard, Mil.
9   Tom Goodwin, Col.-L.A.
7   Jeff Kent, S.F.
7   Brian S. Giles, Pit.
7   Peter Bergeron, Mon.
7   Larry Walker, Col.
7   Danny Bautista, Fla.-Ari.
7   Eric Owens, S.D.
7   Terry Shumpert, Col.

Home runs
50   Sammy Sosa, Chi.

49   Barry Bonds, S.F.
47   Jeff Bagwell, Hou.
44   Vladimir Guerrero, Mon.
44   Richard Hidalgo, Hou.
43   Gary Sheffield, L.A.

Walks
117   Barry Bonds, S.F.
114   Brian S. Giles, Pit.
107   Jeff Bagwell, Hou.
103   Todd Helton, Col.
103   Jim Edmonds, St.L.
101   Gary Sheffield, L.A.

On-base percentage
.463   Todd Helton, Col.
.440   Barry Bonds, S.F.
.438   Gary Sheffield, L.A.
.432   Brian S. Giles, Pit.
.425   Edgardo Alfonzo, N.Y.

Slugging percentage
.698   Todd Helton, Col.
.688   Barry Bonds, S.F.
.664   Vladimir Guerrero, Mon.
.643   Gary Sheffield, L.A.
.636   Richard Hidalgo, Hou.

Stolen bases
62   Luis Castillo, Fla.
55   Tom Goodwin, Col.-L.A.
54   Eric Young, Chi.
45   Tony Womack, Ari.
40   Rafael Furcal, Atl.

Caught stealing
22   Luis Castillo, Fla.
14   Rafael Furcal, Atl.
14   Preston Wilson, Fla.
14   Eric Owens, S.D.
13   Edgar Renteria, St.L.
13   Peter Bergeron, Mon.
12   Quilvio Veras, Atl.

12   Jason Kendall, Pit.
11   Tony Womack, Ari.
11   Roger Cedeno, Hou.
11   Jay Payton, N.Y.

Sacrifice hits
16   Ricky Gutierrez, Chi.
14   Peter Bergeron, Mon.
14   Tom Glavine, Atl.
14   Kevin Brown, L.A.
14   Kevin Millwood, Atl.
14   Rick Reed, N.Y.
13   Javier Vazquez, Mon.
13   Garrett Stephenson, St.L.
12   Doug Glanville, Phi.
12   Masato Yoshii, Col.

Sacrifice flies
14   J.T. Snow, S.F.
12   Luis Gonzalez, Ari.
12   Jeff Cirillo, Col.
12   Eric Karros, L.A.
11   Neifi Perez, Col.
11   Mike Lowell, Fla.
10   Chipper Jones, Atl.
10   Todd Helton, Col.
9   Edgar Renteria, St.L.
9   Steve Finley, Ari.
9   Jeff Kent, S.F.
9   Richard Hidalgo, Hou.
9   Jeromy Burnitz, Mil.
9   Cliff Floyd, Fla.
9   Moises Alou, Hou.

Strikeouts
187   Preston Wilson, Fla.
168   Sammy Sosa, Chi.
167   Jim Edmonds, St.L.
148   Ray Lankford, St.L.
139   Pat Burrell, Phi.

Intentional walks
23   Vladimir Guerrero, Mon.

STATISTICAL LEADERS

22	Barry Bonds, S.F.
22	Todd Helton, Col.
19	Sammy Sosa, Chi.
17	Ken Griffey, Cin.
13	Brian S. Giles, Pit.
13	Brent Mayne, Col.

PITCHING LEADERS
Earned-run average
2.58	Kevin Brown, L.A.
2.64	Randy Johnson, Ari.
2.66	Jeff C. D'Amico, Mil.
3.00	Greg Maddux, Atl.
3.14	Mike Hampton, N.Y.

Wins
21	Tom Glavine, Atl.
20	Darryl Kile, St.L
19	Randy Johnson, Ari.
19	Greg Maddux, Atl.
18	Chan Ho Park, L.A.
17	Scott Elarton, Hou.
17	Livan Hernandez, S.F.

Losses
19	Omar Daal, Ari.-Phi.
17	Matt Clement, S.D.
17	Steve Parris, Cin.
16	Chris Holt, Hou.
16	Jose Lima, Hou.
15	Masato Yoshii, Col.
14	Dustin Hermanson, Mon.

Games
83	Steve Kline, Mon.
79	Scott Sullivan, Cin.
78	Mike Myers, Col.
77	Turk Wendell, N.Y.
76	Armando Benitez, N.Y.
76	Felix Rodriguez, S.F.

Games started
35	Tom Glavine, Atl.
35	Randy Johnson, Ari.
35	Jon Lieber, Chi.
35	Greg Maddux, Atl.
35	Kevin Millwood, Atl.
34	Matt Clement, S.D.
34	Darryl Kile, St.L
34	Chan Ho Park, L.A.
33	Kevin Brown, L.A.
33	Ryan Dempster, Fla.
33	Mike Hampton, N.Y.
33	Jimmy Haynes, Mil.
33	Pat Hentgen, St.L
33	Livan Hernandez, S.F.
33	Jose Lima, Hou.
33	Steve Parris, Cin.
33	Javier Vazquez, Mon.

Games finished
68	Armando Benitez, N.Y.
63	Robb Nen, S.F.
63	Mike Williams, Pit.
62	Antonio Alfonseca, Fla.
61	Dave Veres, St.L
59	Trevor Hoffman, S.D.

Complete games
8	Randy Johnson, Ari.
8	Curt Schilling, Phi.-Ari.
6	Jon Lieber, Chi.
6	Greg Maddux, Atl.
5	Kevin Brown, L.A.
5	Livan Hernandez, S.F.
5	Darryl Kile, St.L
4	Shawn Estes, S.F.
4	Tom Glavine, Atl.
4	Woody Williams, S.D.

Innings pitched
251.0	Jon Lieber, Chi.
249.1	Greg Maddux, Atl.
248.2	Randy Johnson, Ari.
241.0	Tom Glavine, Atl.
240.0	Livan Hernandez, S.F.

Shutouts
3	Randy Johnson, Ari.

3	Greg Maddux, Atl.
2	Shawn Estes, S.F.
2	Tom Glavine, Atl.
2	Livan Hernandez, S.F.
2	Jesus Sanchez, Fla.
2	Curt Schilling, Phi.-Ari.
2	Garrett Stephenson, St.L
1	20 pitchers tied

Hits allowed
254	Livan Hernandez, S.F.
251	Jose Lima, Hou.
248	Jon Lieber, Chi.
247	Chris Holt, Hou.
247	Javier Vazquez, Mon.
228	Jimmy Haynes, Mil.

Home runs allowed
48	Jose Lima, Hou.
38	Brian Anderson, Ari.
36	Jon Lieber, Chi.
35	Kevin Tapani, Chi.
33	Darryl Kile, St.L

Runs allowed
152	Jose Lima, Hou.
131	Matt Clement, S.D.
131	Chris Holt, Hou.
130	Jon Lieber, Chi.
128	Omar Daal, Ari.-Phi.
128	Jimmy Haynes, Mil.
128	Dustin Hermanson, Mon.
124	Andy Ashby, Phi.-Atl.

Earned runs allowed
145	Jose Lima, Hou.
123	Chris Holt, Hou.
123	Jon Lieber, Chi.
118	Jimmy Haynes, Mil.
117	Matt Clement, S.D.
115	Pedro Astacio, Col.

Batting average yielded
.213	Kevin Brown, L.A.
.214	Chan Ho Park, L.A.

.219	Rick Ankiel, St.L
.224	Randy Johnson, Ari.
.228	Al Leiter, N.Y.

Walks
125	Matt Clement, S.D.
124	Chan Ho Park, L.A.
112	Russ Ortiz, S.F.
108	Shawn Estes, S.F.
100	Jimmy Haynes, Mil.

Strikeouts
347	Randy Johnson, Ari.
217	Chan Ho Park, L.A.
216	Kevin Brown, L.A.
209	Ryan Dempster, Fla.
200	Al Leiter, N.Y.

Hit batsmen
18	Jamey Wright, Mil.
16	Matt Clement, S.D.
15	Pedro Astacio, Col.
13	Darryl Kile, St.L
12	Rolando Arrojo, Col.
12	Darren Dreifort, L.A.
12	Chan Ho Park, L.A.

Wild pitches
23	Matt Clement, S.D.
21	Scott Williamson, Cin.
17	Darren Dreifort, L.A.
13	Chan Ho Park, L.A.
12	Rick Ankiel, St.L

Saves
45	Antonio Alfonseca, Fla.
43	Trevor Hoffman, S.D.
41	Armando Benitez, N.Y.
41	Robb Nen, S.F.
30	Danny Graves, Cin.
29	Rick Aguilera, Chi.
29	Dave Veres, St.L